Pediatric
Otolaryngology

V O L U M E   2

Pediatric Otolaryngology

VOLUME 2

Fourth Edition

Charles D. Bluestone, MD
Eberly Professor of Pediatric Otolaryngology
University of Pittsburgh School of Medicine
Director, Department of Pediatric Otolaryngology
Children's Hospital of Pittsburgh
Pittsburgh, Pennsylvania

Sylvan E. Stool, MD
Professor of Pediatrics and Otolaryngology
University of Colorado School of Medicine
Attending Physician
The Children's Hospital of Denver
Denver, Colorado

Cuneyt M. Alper, MD
Associate Professor of Otolaryngology
University of Pittsburgh School of Medicine
Department of Pediatric Otolaryngology
Children's Hospital of Pittsburgh
Pittsburgh, Pennsylvania

Ellis M. Arjmand, MD, PhD
Assistant Professor of Otolaryngology
University of Pittsburgh School of Medicine
Department of Pediatric Otolaryngology
Children's Hospital of Pittsburgh
Pittsburgh, Pennsylvania

Margaretha L. Casselbrant, MD, PhD
Professor of Otolaryngology
University of Pittsburgh School of Medicine
Director of Clinical Research and Education
Department of Pediatric Otolaryngology
Children's Hospital of Pittsburgh
Pittsburgh, Pennsylvania

Joseph E. Dohar, MD
Associate Professor of Otolaryngology
University of Pittsburgh School of Medicine
Department of Pediatric Otolaryngology
Children's Hospital of Pittsburgh
Pittsburgh, Pennsylvania

Robert F. Yellon, MD
Assistant Professor of Otolaryngology
University of Pittsburgh School of Medicine
Co-director and Director of Clinical Services
Department of Pediatric Otolaryngology
Children's Hospital of Pittsburgh
Pittsburgh, Pennsylvania

SAUNDERS
An Imprint of Elsevier Science
Philadelphia   London   New York   St. Louis   Sydney   Toronto

SAUNDERS
An Imprint of Elsevier Science

The Curtis Center
Independence Square West
Philadelphia, Pennsylvania 19106

Volume 1: Part no. 9997619838
Volume 2: Part no. 9997619846
PEDIATRIC OTOLARYNGOLOGY   Two-Volume Set: ISBN 0–7216–9197–8

Notice

Surgery/Otolaryngology is an ever-changing field. Standard safety precautions must be followed, but as new research and clinical experience broaden our knowledge, changes in treatment and drug therapy may become necessary or appropriate. Readers are advised to check the most current product information provided by the manfacturer of each drug to be administered to verify the recommended dose, the method and duration of administration, and the contraindications. It is the responsibility of the treating physician, relying on experience and knowledge of the patient, to determine dosages and the best treatment for each individual patient. Neither the Publisher nor the editor assumes any liability for any injury and/or damage to persons or property arising from this publication.

The Publisher

Library of Congress Cataloging-in-Publication Data

Pediatric otolaryngology / [edited by] Charles D. Bluestone . . . [et al.].—4th ed.
  p.   ;   cm.
   Includes bibliographical references and index.
   ISBN 0–7216–9197–8
  1. Pediatric otolaryngology.   I. Bluestone, Charles D.
   [DNLM: 1. Otorhinolaryngologic Diseases—Infant—Child. WV 140 P37087 2002]
   RF47.C4 P38 2002
618.92′09751—dc21

                                                                2001049400

Acquisitions Editor: Stephanie Donley
Developmental Editor: Melissa Dudlick
Project Manager: Jennifer Ehlers
Book Designer: Gene Harris

PI/MVY

Printed in the United States of America.

Last digit is the print number: 9   8   7   6   5   4   3   2   1

*We dedicate this book
to our families, teachers, colleagues, house staff, and students,
but especially to our young patients and their families,
whom we hope will benefit from the information
contained in these volumes.*

Contributors

Gregory C. Allen, M.D.
Assistant Professor, Department of Otolaryngology—
Head and Neck Surgery, University of Colorado Health
Sciences Center; Attending Physician, Department of
Pediatric Otolaryngology, The Children's Hospital,
Denver, Colorado
Evolution of Pediatric Otolaryngology

Cuneyt M. Alper, M.D.
Associate Professor of Otolaryngology, University of
Pittsburgh School of Medicine; Staff Otolaryngologist,
Children's Hospital of Pittsburgh, Department of
Pediatric Otolaryngology, Pittsburgh, Pennsylvania
Inflammatory Disease of the Mouth and Pharynx
Burns and Acquired Strictures of the Esophagus
Methods of Examination

Jack B. Anon, M.D.
Clinical Professor, University of Pittsburgh, Pittsburgh,
Pennsylvania
Embryology and Anatomy of the Paranasal Sinuses

Ellis M. Arjmand, M.D., Ph.D.
Assistant Professor of Otolaryngology, University of
Pittsburgh School of Medicine; Attending
Otolaryngologist, Children's Hospital of Pittsburgh,
Pittsburgh, Pennsylvania
Congenital Inner Ear Anomalies

Yasser Armanazi, D.M.D.
Associate Professor of Pediatric Dentistry, Case Western
Reserve University, Cleveland, Ohio
Dental and Gingival Disorders

L'Tanya J. Bailey, D.D.S., M.S.
Department of Orthodontics, University of North
Carolina School of Dentistry, Chapel Hill, North Carolina
Orthodontic Problems in Children

Roberto L. Barretto, M.D.
Fellow in Pediatric Otolaryngology, Children's Memorial
Hospital, Feinberg School of Medicine at Northwestern
University, Chicago, Illinois
Injuries of the Mouth, Pharynx, and Esophagus

Paul W. Bauer, M.D.
Assistant Professor, Department of Otolaryngology–Head
and Neck Surgery, Children's Medical Center of Dallas,
University of Texas Southwestern Medical Center, Dallas,
Texas
Neck Masses

Nancy M. Bauman, M.D.
Associate Professor, University of Iowa College of
Medicine; University of Iowa Hospitals, Iowa City, Iowa
Diseases of the Labyrinthine Capsule

Walter M. Belenky
Chief, Department of Pediatric Otolaryngology,
Children's Hospital of Michigan, Detroit, Michigan
Nasal Obstruction and Rhinorrhea

Erica C. Bennett, M.D.
Assistant Professor of Clinical Otolaryngology–Head and
Neck Surgery, University of Southern California Keck
School of Medicine; Attending Physician, Division of
Otolaryngology, Children's Hospital of Los Angeles, Los
Angeles, California
Congenital Malformations of the Trachea and Bronchi
Thyroid

Fred H. Bess, Ph.D.
Professor and Chair, Vanderbilt University School of
Medicine, Nashville, Tennesee
Amplification Selection for Children with Hearing Impairment

F. Owen Black, M.D.
Chief, Good Samaritan Hospital and Medical Center,
Portland, Oregon
Tinnitus in Children

Charles D. Bluestone, M.D.
Eberly Professor of Pediatric Otolaryngology, University
of Pittsburgh School of Medicine; Director, Department
of Pediatric Otolaryngology, Children's Hospital of
Pittsburgh, Pittsburgh, Pennsylvania
Methods of Examination: Clinical Examination
Otitis Media and Eustachian Tube Dysfunction
Intratemporal Complications and Sequelae of Otitis Media
Intracranial Complications of Otitis Media and Mastoiditis

William E. Bolger, M.D., F.A.C.S.
Associate Professor, Department of Otorhinolaryngology/
Head and Neck Surgery, University of Pennsylvania
School of Medicine; Chief, Division of Rhinology,
Department of Otorhinolaryngology/Head and Neck
Surgery, University of Pennsylvania Health System,
Philadelphia, Pennsylvania
Imaging of the Paranasal Sinuses in Pediatric Patients with
   Special Considerations for Endoscopic Sinus Surgery

J. Arturo Bonilla, M.D.
Pediatric Ear, Nose, and Throat Department, Institute of
South Texas, San Antonio, Texas
Surgical Management of Microtia and Congenital Aural Atresia

Jerry Bouquot, D.D.S., M.S.
Director of Research, The Maxillofacial Center for
Diagnostics and Research, Morgantown, West Virginia
Dental and Gingival Disorders

Charles M. Bower, M.D.
Associate Professor, Department of Otolaryngology,
Arkansas Children's Hospital, Little Rock, Arkansas
Diseases of the Salivary Glands

Amy C. Brenski, M.D.
Assistant Professor, University of Texas, Southwestern
Medical School; Medical Staff, Children's Medical Center
of Dallas, Dallas, Texas
Congenital Inner Ear Anomalies

Patrick E. Brookhouser, M.D., F.A.C.S.
Department of Otolaryngology, Boystown National
Research Hospital, Omaha, Nebraska
Diseases of the Inner Ear and Sensorineural Hearing Loss

Thomas C. Calcaterra, M.D.
Professor, Head and Neck Surgery, UCLA School of
Medicine, Los Angeles, California
Orbital Swellings

Thomas F. Campbell, Ph.D.
Director of Department of Audiology and
Communication Disorders, University of Pittsburgh
School of Medicine, Pittsburgh, Pennsylvania
Disorders of Language, Phonology, Fluency, and Voice:
   Indicators for Referral

Joseph A. Carcillo, M.D.
Associate Director, Pediatric Intensive Care Unit,
Children's Hospital of Pittsburgh, Pittsburgh,
Pennsylvania
Intensive Care Management of Infection-Related Acute Upper
   Airway Obstruction in Children

Stephen P. Cass, M.D., M.P.H.
Associate Professor, Department of Otolaryngology,
University of Colorado, Denver, Colorado
Tumors of the Ear and Temporal Bone

Maragaretha L. Casselbrant, M.D., Ph.D.
Professor of Otolaryngology, University of Pittsburgh;
Director, Clinical Research and Education, Children's
Hospital, Pittsburgh, Pennsylvania
Vestibular Evaluation
Balance Disorders
Methods of Examination

Kenny H. Chan, M.D.
Professor, Department of Otolaryngology–Head and
Neck Surgery, University of Colorado Health Sciences
Center; Chair, Department of Pediatric Otolaryngology,
The Children's Hospital, Denver, Colorado
Pediatric Otolaryngology: A Psychosocial Perspective

Kay Chang, M.D.
Menlo Park, California
Idiopathic Conditions of the Mouth and Pharynx

Jack L. Cluckman, M.D.
Professor and Chairman, University of Cincinnati College
of Medicine, Cincinnati, Ohio
Inflammatory Disease of the Mouth and Pharynx

Paul G. Comber, M.D., Ph.D.
Assistant Professor of Pediatrics, Albany Medical College;
Assistant Professor, Children's Hospital at Albany Medical
Center, Pediatric Pulmonary, Albany, New York
Infections of the Lower Respiratory Tract

George H. Conner, M.D.
Professor Emeritus of Surgery, Division of
Otolaryngology, Pennsylvania State University School of
Medicine, Hershey, Pennsylvania
Idiopathic Conditions of the Mouth and Pharynx

Cheryl S. Cotter, M.D.
Pediatric Otolaryngologist, Arnold Palmer Hospital for
Children and Women, Orlando, Florida
Obstructive Sleep Disorders

Robin T. Cotton, M.D.
Professor, Otolaryngology–Head and Neck Surgery,
University of Cincinnati Medical Center; Director,
Pediatric Otolaryngology, Cincinnati Children's Hospital
Medical Center, Cincinnati, Ohio
Gastroesophageal Reflux Disease
Stridor and Airway Obstruction
Management and Prevention of Subglottic Stenosis in Infants
   and Children
Velopharyngeal Insufficiency

Wade Cressman, M.D.
Clinical Assistant Professor, Department of
Otolaryngology, Head and Neck Surgery, University of
South Florida, Tampa, Florida; All Children's Hospital,
St. Petersburg, Florida
Nasal Physiology

William S. Crysdale, M.D.
Professor, University of Toronto; Senior Staff,
Department of Otolaryngology, Hospital for Sick
Children, Toronto, Ontario, Canada
The Management of Drooling

Marvin C. Culbertson, Jr., M.D.
Retired Clinical Professor, Department of Otolaryngology,
University of Texas Southwestern Medical Center, Dallas,
Texas
Epistaxis

Michael J. Cunningham, M.D.
Associate Professor, Department of Otology and
Laryngology, Harvard Medical School; Surgeon,
Department of Otolaryngology, Massachusetts Eye and
Ear Infirmary, Boston, Massachusetts
Malignant Tumors of the Head and Neck

Hugh Curtin, M.D.
Professor of Radiology, Harvard Medical School;
Professor of Radiology, The Massachusetts Eye & Ear
Infirmary, Boston, Massachusetts
Methods of Examination: Radiologic Aspects

David H. Darrow, M.D., D.D.S.
Associate Professor of Otolaryngology–Head and Neck
Surgery and Pediatrics, Eastern Virginia Medical School;
Attending Physician, Otolaryngology–Head and Neck
Surgery and Pediatrics, Children's Hospital of the King's
Daughters, Norfolk, Virginia
Foreign Bodies of the Larynx, Trachea, and Bronchi

Albert R. De Chicchis, Ph.D.
Associate Professor, Department of Communication
Science and Disorders, University of Georgia School of
Medicine, Athens, Georgia
Amplification Selection for Children with Hearing Impairment

Douglas D. Dedo, M.D.
Assistant Clinical Professor of Otolaryngology–Head and
Neck Surgery, University of Miami Medical School,
Miami, Florida
Neurogenic Diseases of the Larynx

Herbert H. Dedo, M.D.
Professor of Otolaryngology–Head and Neck Surgery,
University of California Medical School–Berkeley,
California
Neurogenic Diseases of the Larynx

Craig S. Derkay, M.D.
Professor, Otolaryngology and Pediatrics, Eastern Virginia
Medical School; Director, Pediatric Otolaryngology,
Children's Hospital of the King's Daughters, ENT
Department, Norfolk, Virginia
Physiology of the Mouth, Pharynx, and Esophagus
Dysphagia

**Joseph E. Dohar, M.D., M.S., F.A.A.P.,
F.A.C.S.**
Associate Professor of Otolaryngology, University of
Pittsburgh School of Medicine, University of Pittsburgh,
Pittsburgh, Pennsylvania
Otorrhea

Jay N. Dolitsky, M.D.
Assistant Professor of Otolaryngology, New York Medical
College, Valhalla, New York; Director of Pediatric
Otolaryngology, The New York Eye and Ear Infirmary,
New York, New York
Otalgia

Christine A. Dollaghan, Ph.D.
Professor of Communication Science and Disorders,
University of Pittsburgh, Pittsburgh, Pennsylvania
Disorders of Language, Phonology, Fluency, and Voice in
  Children: Indicators for Referral

Terry L. Donat, M.D.
Clinical Assistant Professor, Loyola University, Stritch
School of Medicine, Maywood, Illinois
Injuries of the Mouth, Pharynx, and Esophagus

John D. Durrant, Ph.D.
Professor of Communication Science and Disorders;
Otolaryngology; Rehabilitation Science, and Technology,
University of Pittsburgh, Pittsburgh, Pennsylvania
Physical and Physiologic Bases of Hearing

Robin A. Dyleski, M.D.
Department of Otolaryngology, Arkansas Children's
Hospital, Little Rock, Arkansas
Diseases of the Salivary Glands

Hamdy El-Hakim, F.R.C.S. Ed
Fellow, Hospital For Sick Children, Toronto, Ontario;
Senior Specialist Registrar, Aberdeen Royal Infirmary,
Aberdeen, Scotland
Hoarseness

Jose N. Fayad, M.D.
Injuries of the Ear and Temporal Bone

Jonathan D. Finder, M.D.
Assistant Professor of Pediatrics, University of Pittsburgh;
Pediatric Pulmonologist, Children's Hospital of
Pittsburgh, Pittsburgh, Pennsylvania
Noninfectious Disorders of the Lower Respiratory Tract

Philip Fireman, M.D.
Professor of Pediatrics and Medicine, University of
Pittsburgh School of Medicine; Children's Hospital,
Pittsburgh, Pennsylvania
Allergic Rhinitis

Jacob Friedberg, M.D.
Professor, University of Toronto; Otolaryngologist-in-
Chief, Hospital for Sick Children, Toronto, Ontario
Hoarseness

Joseph M. Furman, M.D., Ph.D.
Professor, Departments of Otolaryngology, Neurology,
and Bioengineering, University of Pittsburgh, Pittsburgh,
Pennsylvania
Vestibular Evaluation
Balance Disorders

Mark E. Gerber, M.D.
Assistant Professor, Northwestern University Medical
School; Division of Pediatric Otolaryngology, Childrens
Memorial Hospital, Chicago, Illinois
Congenital Laryngeal Anomalies

Chantal M. Giguère, M.D.
Pediatric Otolaryngology Fellow, University of Iowa
College of Medicine; Pediatric Otolaryngology Fellow,
University of Iowa Hospitals, Iowa City, Iowa
Diseases of the Labyrinthine Capsule

Edward Goldson, M.D.
Professor, Department of Pediatrics, The University of
Colorado Health Sciences Center; Staff Pediatrician, The
Children's Hospital, Denver, Colorado
Pediatric Otolaryngology: A Psychosocial Perspective

Nira A. Goldstein, M.D.
Assistant Professor of Otolaryngology, State University of
New York Downstate Medical Center; Attending
Physician, University Hospital of Brooklyn, Long Island
College Hospital, Kings County Hospital Center,
Brooklyn, New York
Embryology and Anatomy of the Mouth, Pharynx, and
  Esophagus

Carlos Gonzales, M.D.
Pediatric Otolaryngologist, Cirugia de Cabeza y Cuello en
Ninos, Santurce, Puerto Rico
Tumors of the Mouth and Pharynx

Christopher B. Gordon, M.D.
Principles and Methods of Management

Steven D. Gray, M.D.
Professor, Otolaryngology–Head and Neck Surgery,
University of Utah, Salt Lake City, Utah
Congenital Malformations of the Mouth and Pharynx
Voice

Kenneth M. Grundfast, M.D.
Department of Otolaryngology, Boston Medical Center,
Roxbury, Massachusetts
Hearing Loss

Joseph Haddad, Jr., M.D.
Associate Professor of Clinical Otolaryngology–Head and
Neck Surgery and Vice Chairman of Otolaryngology/Head
and Neck Surgery, Columbia University College of
Physicians and Surgeons, New York, New York
Methods of Examination

Steven D. Handler, M.D.
Professor, Department of Otorhinolaryngology–Head and
Neck Surgery, University of Pennsylvania School of
Medicine; Associate Director, Division of Otolaryngology,
The Children's Hospital of Philadelphia, Philadelphia,
Pennsylvania
Methods of Examination

Christopher J. Hartnick, M.D.
Department of Otolaryngology, Massachusetts Eye and
Ear Infirmary, Harvard Medical School, Boston,
Massachusetts
Stridor and Airway Obstruction

Michael S. Haupert, D.O.
Department of Pediatric Otolaryngology, Children's
Hospital of Michigan, Detroit, Michigan
Nasal Obstruction and Rhinorrhea

Gerald B. Healy, M.D.
Professor of Otology and Laryngology, Harvard Medical
School; Otolaryngologist-in-Chief, Childrens Hospital,
Boston, Massachusetts
Methods of Examination

Arthur S. Hengerer, M.D.
University of Rochester Medical Center; Professor and
Chair, Division of Otolaryngology, and Acting Chair,
Department of Surgery, Strong Memorial Hospital,
Rochester, New York
Congenital Malformations of the Nose and Paranasal Sinuses
Complications of Nasal and Sinus Infections

Angel W. Hernandez, M.D.
Staff Child Neurologist/Epileptologist, Cook Children's Medical Center, Department of Neurology, Fort Worth, Texas
Neurologic Disorders of the Mouth, Pharynx, and Esophagus

Keiko Hirose, M.D.
Cleveland Clinic Foundation, Cleveland, Ohio
Embryology and Developmental Anatomy of the Ear

Barry E. Hirsch, M.D.
Professor, Department of Otolaryngology, University of Pittsburgh, Pittsburgh, Pennsylvania
Diseases of the External Ear

Lauren D. Holinger, M.D.
Professor of Otolaryngology, Department of Otolaryngology–Head and Neck Surgery, Northwestern University; Head, Division of Pediatric Otolaryngology, Children's Memorial Hospital, Chicago, Illinois
Congenital Laryngeal Anomalies
Congenital Malformations of the Trachea and Bronchi
Foreign Bodies of the Larynx, Trachea, and Bronchi

Andrew J. Hotaling, M.D.
Professor, Department of Otolaryngology–Head and Neck Surgery and Pediatrics, Loyola University Medical Center, Maywood, Illinois
Functional Abnormalities of the Esophagus
Cough

Patricia A. Hughes, D.O.
Albany Medical College, Albany Medical School; Associate Professor of Pediatrics, Section of Pediatric Infectious Disease, Childrens Hospital at Albany Medical College, Albany, New York
Infections of the Lower Respiratory Tract

Dennis J. Hurwitz, M.D.
Clinical Professor of Surgery, University of Pittsburgh School of Medicine, Pittsburgh, Pennsylvania
Principles and Methods of Management
Pediatric Plastic Surgery of the Head and Neck

Barbara Hymer, D.D.S.
Program Director, The Children's Hospital; Clinical Instructor, University of Colorado School of Dentistry, Denver, Colorado
Postnatal Craniofacial Growth and Development

Glenn Isaacson, M.D.
Professor and Chairman, Department of Otolaryngology–Head and Neck Surgery, Temple University School of Medicine; Chief, Pediatric Otolaryngology, Temple University Children's Medical Center, Philadelphia, Pennsylvania
Developmental Anatomy and Physiology of the Larynx, Trachea, and Esophagus

Bruce W. Jafek, M.D.
Professor, Department of Otolaryngology, University of Colorado School of Medicine, Denver, Colorado
Injuries of the Neck

Ivo P. Janecka, M.D.
Professor of Surgery, Harvard Medical School; Director of Skull Base International, Children's Hospital, Boston, Massachusetts
Pediatric Skull Base Surgery

D. Richard Kang, M.D.
Assistant Clinical Professor of Surgery, Uniformed Services University of Health Services; Director, Hearing Center, Childrens Hospital of San Diego, San Diego, California
Tumors of the Larynx, Trachea, and Bronchi

Siloo B. Kapadia, M.D.
Director of Surgical Pathology, Milton S. Hershey Medical Center, Hershey, Pennsylvania
Pediatric Skull Base Surgery

David E. Karas, M.D.
University of Medicine and Dentistry of New Jersey, Newark, New Jersey
Otolaryngologic Manifestations of HIV Infection in Children

Collin S. Karmody, M.D.
New England Medical Center, Boston, Massachusetts
Developmental Anomalies of the Neck

Sandeep Kathju, M.D., Ph.D.
Attending Surgeon, Allegheny General Hospital, Pittsburgh, Pennsylvania
Pediatric Plastic Surgery of the Head and Neck

Ken Kazahaya, M.D.
Assistant Professor, Department of Otorhinolaryngology/Head and Neck Surgery, University of Pennsylvania, School of Medicine; Attending Surgeon, Division of Pediatric Otolaryngology, Children's Hospital of Philadelphia, Philadelphia, Pennsylvania
Imaging of the Paranasal Sinuses in Pediatric Patients with Special Considerations for Endoscopic Sinus Surgery

Peggy E. Kelly, M.D.
Department of Pediatric Otolaryngology, Children's Hospital, Denver, Colorado
Injuries of the Neck

Margaret A. Kenna, M.D.
Associate Professor of Otology and Laryngology, Harvard Medical School; Associate in Otolaryngology, Children's Hospital–Boston, Boston, Massachusetts
Embryology and Developmental Anatomy of the Ear
Sore Throat in Children: Diagnosis and Management

Karen Iler Kirk, Ph.D.
Associate Professor, Department of Otolaryngology,
Indiana University School of Medicine, Indianapolis,
Indiana
Cochlear Implants in Children

Jerome O. Klein, M.D.
Professor of Pediatrics, Boston University School of
Medicine, Boston, Massachusetts
Methods of Examination: Clinical Examination
Otitis Media and Eustachian Tube Dysfunction
Intratemporal Complications and Sequelae of Otitis Media
Intracranial Complications of Otitis Media and Mastoiditis

Darrell Alexander Klotz, M.D.
Chief Resident, Division of Otolaryngology, University of
Rochester School of Medicine; Strong Memorial Hospital,
Rochester, New York
Complications of Nasal and Sinus Infections

Martha L. Lepow, M.D.
Albany Medical College, Albany Medical School;
Professor of Pediatrics, Head, Section of Infectious
Disease, Children's Hospital at Albany Medical College,
Albany, New York
Infections of the Lower Respiratory Tract

David J. Lilly, Ph.D.
Director of Audiology, Good Samaritan Hospital and
Medical Center, Portland, Oregon
Tinnitus in Children

Frank Lucente, M.D.
Professor, SUNY HSCB; Chairman, Long Island College
Hospital, Brooklyn, New York
Facial Pain and Headache

Rodney P. Lusk, M.D.
Division Director, Pediatric Otolaryngology, St. Louis
Children's Hospital; Professor, Washington University, St.
Louis, Missouri
Surgical Management of Chronic Rhinosinusitis
Neck Masses

John Maddalozzo, M.D.
Assistant Professor, Northwestern University Medical
School; Attending Physician, Children's Memorial
Hospital, Chicago, Illinois
Thyroid

Bruce R. Maddern, M.D., F.A.C.S., F.A.A.P.
Courtesy Assistant Professor of Pediatrics, University of
Florida; Chief of Surgery and Otolaryngology, Wolfson
Childrens Hospital, Jacksonville, Florida
Obstructive Sleep Disorders

David N. Madgy, D.O.
Associate Chief, Department of Pediatric Otolaryngology,
Children's Hospital of Michigan, Detroit, Michigan
Nasal Obstruction and Rhinorrhea

Anthony E. Magit, M.D.
Associate Clinical Professor of Pediatrics and Surgery,
University of California, San Diego School of Medicine;
Vice Chairman, Department of Otolaryngology, Children's
Hospital and Health Center, San Diego, California
Tumors of the Nose, Paranasal Sinuses, and Nasopharynx

Robert H. Maisel, M.D.
Professor, Department of OTO-HNS, University of
Minnesota School of Medicine; Chief, Department of
OTO-HNS, Hennepin County Medical Center,
Minneapolis, Minnesota
Injuries of the Mouth, Pharynx, and Esophagus

Scott C. Manning, M.D.
Professor, Department of Otolaryngology, University of
Washington; Chief, Pediatric Otolaryngology, Children's
Hospital and Regional Medical Center, Seattle,
Washington
Epistaxis
Foreign Bodies of the Pharynx and Esophagus

Charles Margozian, M.D.
Associate Professor of Anesthesia, Harvard Medical
School, Boston, Massachusetts
Pediatric Skull Base Surgery

Brian S. Martin, D.M.D.
Clinical Associate Professor, University of Pittsburgh
School of Dental Medicine, Pittsburgh, Pennsylvania
Dental and Gingival Disorders

Mark Marunick, D.D.S., M.S.
Associate Professor and Director of Maxillofacial
Prosthetics, Wayne State University School of Medicine,
Detroit, Michigan
Injuries of the Mouth, Pharynx, and Esophagus

Robert H. Mathog, M.D.
Professor and Chairman, Department of OTO-HNS,
Wayne State University School of Medicine, Detroit,
Michigan
Injuries of the Mouth, Pharynx, and Esophagus

Mark May, M.D.
Clinical Professor, University of Pittsburgh, Pittsburgh,
Pennsylvania
Facial Paralysis in Children

William F. McGuirt, Jr., M.D.
Associate Professor, Department of Otolaryngology, Wake
Forest University Medical Center, Winston Salem, North
Carolina
Injuries of the Ear and Temporal Bone

Arlen D. Meyers, M.D., M.B.A.
Professor, Department of Otolaryngology, University of
Colorado School of Medicine, Denver, Colorado
Aspiration

Makoto Miura, M.D., D. Med. Sc.
Director, Department of Otolaryngology, Toyooka
Hospital, Toyooka City, Japan
Congenital Anomalies of the External and Middle Ears

Richard T. Miyamoto, M.D.
Arilla Spence DeVault Professor and Chairman, Indiana
University Medical School, Department of
Otolaryngology, Riley Hospital, Indianapolis, Indiana
Cochlear Implants in Children

Stephen E. Morrow, M.D.
Fellow, University of North Carolina, Chapel Hill, North
Carolina
Congenital Malformations of the Esophagus

George T. Moynihan, M.D.
Resident, Loyola University Medical Center, Maywood,
Illinois
Cough

Harlan R. Muntz, M.D.
Professor Otolaryngology–Head and Neck Surgery,
University of Utah; Pediatric Otolaryngology, Primary
Children's Medical Center, Salt Lake City, Utah
Congenital Malformations of the Mouth and Pharynx

Don K. Nakayama, M.D.
Chief, Department of Pediatric Surgery, University of
North Carolina, Chapel Hill, North Carolina
Congenital Malformations of the Esophagus

M. M. Nazif, D.D.S., M.D.S.
Director, Dental Services and Dental Residency Program,
Department of Pediatric Dentistry, Children's Hospital of
Pittsburgh, Pittsburgh, Pennsylvania
Dental and Gingival Disorders

Robert Niclerio, M.D.
Chairman, Division of Otolaryngology, Head and Neck
Surgery, University of Chicago, Chicago, Illinois
Nasal Physiology

Robert J. Nozza, Ph.D.
Professor, Department of Otolaryngology—Head and
Neck Surgery, Temple University School of Medicine;
Director of Audiology, Temple University Hospital and
Temple University Children's Medical Center,
Philadelphia, Pennsylvania
The Assessment of Hearing and Middle-Ear Function in
  Children

Michael J. Painter, M.D.
Professor of Neurology and Pediatrics, University of
Pittsburgh School of Medicine; Chief of Division of Child
Neurology, Children's Hospital of Pittsburgh, Pittsburgh,
Pennsylvania
Neurologic Disorders of the Mouth, Pharynx, and Esophagus

Jack L. Paradise, M.D.
Professor of Pediatrics, Family Medicine and Clinical
Epidemiology, and Otolaryngology, University of
Pittsburgh School of Medicine; Pediatrician, Children's
Hospital of Pittsburgh, Pittsburgh, Pennsylvania
Primary Care of Infants and Children with Cleft Palate
Tonsillectomy and Adenoidectomy

Saroj K. Parida, M.D., M.R.C.P.
Assistant Professor, University of Pittsburgh Medical
School, Pittsburgh, Pennsylvania
Respiratory Disorders of the Newborn

Sanjay R. Parikh, M.D.
Instructor in Otolaryngology, Albert Einstein College of
Medicine; Director, Pediatric Otolaryngology, Montefiore
Children's Hospital, Bronx, New York
Sore Throat in Children: Diagnosis and Management

Simon C. Parisier, M.D.
Clinical Professor, Cornell University Medical College,
New York, New York
Injuries of the Ear and Temporal Bone

Susan E. Pearson, M.D.
Children's National Medical Center, Washington, D.C.
Injuries to the Lower Respiratory Tract

Joseph F.A. Petrone, D.D.S., M.S.D.
Assistant Professor and Director, Advanced Education
Program in Orthodontia and Dentofacial Orthopedics,
University of Pittsburgh School of Dental Medicine,
Pittsburgh, Pennsylvania
Postnatal Craniofacial Growth and Development

Robert L. Pincus, M.D.
Associate Professor Otolaryngology, New York Medical
College; Director, New York Otolaryngology Group, New
York, New York
Facial Pain and Headache

Randall L. Plant, M.D.
Assistant Professor, Department of Otolaryngology–Head
and Neck Surgery, Eastern Virginia Medical School,
Norfolk, Virginia
Physiology of the Mouth, Pharynx, and Esophagus
Dysphagia

Avrum N. Pollock, M.D.
Assistant Professor of Radiology, University of Pittsburgh
School of Medicine; Assistant Professor of Radiology,
Children's Hospital of Pittsburgh, Pittsburgh,
Pennsylvania
Methods of Examination: Radiologic Aspects

J. Christopher Post, M.D., Ph.D.
Professor Otolaryngology, MCP Hahnemann School of Medicine, Philadelphia; Director, Pediatric Otolaryngology, and Medical Director, Center for Genomic Sciences, Allegheny General Hospital, Pittsburgh, Pennsylvania
Phylogenetic Aspects and Embryology
Molecular Biology in Pediatric Otolaryngology

William P. Potsic, M.D.
Professor, Department of Otorhinolaryngology–Head and Neck Surgery, University of Pennsylvania School of Medicine; Director, Division of Otolaryngology, The Children's Hospital of Philadelphia, Philadelphia, Pennsylvania
Methods of Examination

Seth M. Pransky, M.D.
Assistant Professor, Division of Otolaryngology, University of California–San Diego; Director, Pediatric Otolaryngology, Children's Specialists, San Diego Children's Hospital, San Diego, California
Tumors of the Larynx, Trachea, and Bronchi

Sheila R. Pratt, Ph.D.
Assistant Professor of Communication Science and Disorders, University of Pittsburgh, Pittsburgh, Pennsylvania
Behavioral Intervention and Education of Children with Hearing Loss

Reza Rahbar, D.M.D., M.D.
Assistant Professor of Otology and Laryngology, Harvard Medical School; Childrens Hospital, Boston, Massachusetts
Methods of Examination

Don S. Respler, M.D.
Clinical Assistant Professor, University of Medicine and Dentistry of New Jersey, Hackensack, New Jersey
Otolaryngologic Manifestations of HIV Infection in Children

James S. Reilly, M.D.
Chairman, Department of Surgery, Alfred L. Dupont Hospital for Children, Wilmington, Delaware
Perilymphatic Fistulas in Infants and Children

Mark A. Richardson, M.D., M.B.A.
Professor and Chair of Otolaryngology/Head and Neck Surgery, Oregon Health and Science University, Portland, Oregon
The Neck: Embryology and Anatomy

Todd A. Ricketts, Ph.D.
Assistant Professor, Vanderbilt University; Director, Dan Maddox Hearing Aid Research Laboratory, Vanderbilt Bill Wilkerson Center, Nashville, Tennessee
Amplification Selection for Children with Hearing Impairment

Keith H. Riding, M.D.
Clinical Professor, B.C. Children's Hospital, Vancouver, British Columbia, Canada
Burns and Acquired Strictures of the Esophagus

Frank L. Rimell, M.D.
Assistant Professor, University of Minnesota Medical School; Director, Pediatric Otolaryngology, University of Minnesota, Minneapolis, Minnesota
Injuries to the Lower Respiratory Tract

Michael Rontal, M.D.
Clinical Professor, University of Michigan, Ann Arbor, Michigan; Attending Staff, WM Beaumont Hospital, Royal Oak, Michigan
Embryology and Anatomy of the Paranasal Sinuses

Richard M. Rosenfeld, M.D., M.P.H.
Professor of Clinical Otolaryngology, SUNY Downstate Medical Center; Director of Pediatric Otolaryngology, Long Island College Hospital and University, Hospital of Brooklyn, Brooklyn, New York
Cervical Adenopathy

Michael J. Rutter, F.R.A.C.S.
Assistant Professor, Department of Pediatric Otolaryngology, Children's Hospital Medical Center, Cincinnati, Ohio
Management and Prevention of Subglottic Stenosis in Infants and Children

Isamu Sando, M.D., D.Med.Sc.
Emeritus Professor, Department of Otolaryngology, University of Pittsburgh, Pittsburgh, Pennsylvania
Congenital Anomalies of the External and Middle Ears

Barry M. Schaitkin, M.D.
Associate Professor of Otolaryngology, University of Pittsburgh; Director, Facial Paralysis Center, UPMC Shadyside, Pittsburgh, Pennsylvania
Facial Paralysis in Children

Rachel Schreiber, M.D.
Fellow, University of Pittsburgh Medical Center, Pittsburgh, Pennsylvania
Allergic Rhinitis

Daniel M. Schwartz, Ph.D.
President, Neurophysiology Associates, Merion Station, Pennsylvania
Amplification Selection for Children with Hearing Impairment

Nancy Sculerati, M.D.
Associate Professor, New York University Medical Center, New York, New York
Foreign Bodies of the Nose

Andrew M. Shapiro, M.D.
Clinical Assistant Professor of Surgery, Penn State
University College of Medicine, Hershey, Pennsylvania
Facial Paralysis in Children
Injuries of the Nose, Facial Bones, and Paranasal Sinuses

Nina L. Shapiro, M.D.
Assistant Professor, Pediatric Otolaryngology, UCLA
School of Medicine, Los Angeles, California
Orbital Swellings

James Sidman, M.D.
Clinical Associate Professor of Otolaryngology, University
of Minnesota Medical School; Chief Otolaryngology,
Children's Hospital, Minneapolis, Minnesota
Injuries to the Lower Respiratory Tract

Kathleen C. Y. Sie, M.D.
Associate Professor, Children's Hospital and Regional
Medical Center, Seattle, Washington
The Neck: Embryology and Anatomy

Laura N. Sinai, M.D.
Pediatrician, Erdenheim Pediatrics, Philadelphia,
Pennsylvania
Oropharyngeal Manifestations of Systemic Disease

Nicole F. Siparsky, M.D.
Washington Hospital Center, Washington, DC
Hearing Loss

Marshall E. Smith, M.D.
Department of Surgery, Division of Otolaryngology,
University of Utah School of Medicine, Salt Lake City,
Utah
Voice

Richard J.H. Smith, M.D.
Professor, University of Iowa College of Medicine;
Professor and Vice Chairman, University of Iowa
Hospitals and Clinics, Iowa City, Iowa
Diseases of the Labyrinthine Capsule

Sylvan E. Stool, M.D.
Professor of Pediatrics and Otolaryngology, University of
Colorado School of Medicine; Attending Physician, The
Childrens Hospital of Denver, Denver, Colorado
Phylogenetic Aspects and Embryology
Postnatal Craniofacial Growth and Development
Evolution of Pediatric Otolaryngology
Foreign Bodies of the Pharynx and Esophagus

R. Casey Strahan, M.D.
Resident, University of Colorado School of Medicine,
Denver, Colorado
Aspiration

Anne Marie Tharpe, Ph.D.
Amplification Selection for Children with Hearing Impairment

Scott W. Thompson, M.D.
Adjunct Assistant Professor, Department of
Communication Sciences and Disorders, School of Public
Health, University of South Carolina; Physician, Midland
Ear, Nose, and Throat Clinic, Columbia, South Carolina
Congenital Anomalies of the External and Middle Ears

Lawrence W.C. Tom, M.D.
Associate Professor, Department of Otorhinolaryngology–
Head and Neck Surgery, University of Pennsylvania
School of Medicine; Associate Surgeon, Division of
Otolaryngology, The Children's Hospital of Philadelphia,
Philadelphia, Pennsylvania
Methods of Examination

Sharon M. Tomaski, M.D.
Pediatric Otolaryngologist, Children's Ear, Head and
Neck Associates, Denver, Colorado
Embryology and Anatomy of the Mouth, Pharynx, and
 Esophagus

Richard B. Towbin, M.D.
Professor of Radiology, University of Pennsylvania;
Professor of Radiology, Children's Hospital of
Philadelphia, Philadelphia, Pennsylvania
Methods of Examination: Radiologic Aspects

Carol-Ann Trotman, B.D.S., M.A., M.S.
University of North Carolina, Chapel Hill, North Carolina
Orthodontic Problems in Children

**Anne Chun-Hui Tsai, M.D., M.Sc., F.A.A.P.,
F.A.C.M.G.**
Assistant Professor, University of Colorado Health
Science Center; Attending Physician and Clinical
Geneticist, The Children's Hospital, Denver, Colorado
Phylogenetic Aspects and Embryology
Genetics, Syndromology, and Craniofacial Anomalies

Atul M. Vaidya, M.D.
Physician, Department of Otolaryngology, Loyola
University Medical Center, Maywood, Illinois
Functional Abnormalities of the Esophagus

Stephanie E. Vallee
Senior Genetic Counselor, University of Colorado Health
Sciences Center, Denver, Colorado
Genetics, Syndromology, and Craniofacial Anomalies

Ryan L. Van De Graaff, M.D.
Resident, University of Colorado Health Sciences Center,
Denver, Colorado
Tumors of the Ear and Temporal Bone

Katherine W.L. Vig, B.D.S., M.S., D.Orth.
Professor and Chair of Orthodontic Department, Section
of Orthonticis, College of Dentistry, Ohio State Health
Sciences Center; Section Chief of Orthodontic Services,
Childrens Hospital, Columbus, Ohio
Postnatal Craniofacial Growth and Development

Ellen R. Wald, M.D.
Professor of Pediatrics and Otolaryngology, University of
Pittsburgh School of Medicine; Chief, Division of Allergy,
Immunology, and Infections Diseases, Children's Hospital
of Pittsburgh, Pittsburgh, Pennsylvania
Rhinitis and Acute and Chronic Sinusitis

Donald W. Warren, D.D.S., M.A., Ph.D.
Kenen Professor and Director, University of North
Carolina Craniofacial Center, Chapel Hill, North Carolina
Orthodontic Problems in Children

Peter C. Weber, M.D., M.B.A.
Professor and Program Director, Cleveland Clinic,
Cleveland, Ohio
Perilymphatic Fistulas in Infants and Children

Richard O. Wein, M.D.
Physician, Otolaryngology–Head and Neck Surgery,
University of Rochester Medical Center, Rochester, New
York
Congenital Malformations of the Nose and Paranasal Sinuses

Jay A. Werkhaven, M.D.
Associate Professor, Department of Otolaryngology,
Vanderbilt University Medical Center, Nashville,
Tennessee
Laser Surgery

Ralph F. Wetmore, M.D.
Surgeon, Department of Otolaryngology, Children's
Hospital of Philadelphia, Philadelphia, Pennsylvania
Tracheotomy

Susan L. Whitney, Ph.D.
Assistant Professor in Physical Therapy and
Otolaryngology, University of Pittsburgh; Director of
Outpatient Vestibular Physical Therapy, Centers for
Rehabilitation Services, Pittsburgh, Pennsylvania
Vestibular Evaluation

Kenneth R. Whittemore, Jr., M.D.
Resident in Otology and Laryngology, Harvard Medical
School; Resident in Otolaryngology, Massachusetts Eye
and Ear Infirmary, Boston, Massachusetts
Malignant Tumors of the Head and Neck

J. Paul Willging, M.D.
Associate Professor Otolaryngology–Head and Neck
Surgery, University of Cincinnati Medical Center and
Children's Hospital Medical Center, Cincinnati, Ohio
Velopharyngeal Insufficiency

Robert E. Wood, Ph.D., M.D.
Professor of Pediatrics and Otolaryngology, Department
of Pulmonary Medicine, Children's Hospital Medical
Center, Cincinnati, Ohio
Physiology of the Larynx, Airways, and Lungs

J. Scott Yaruss, Ph.D.
Assistant Professor, Communication Science and
Disorders; Clinical Research Consultant, Children's
Hospital of Pittsburgh, Pittsburgh, Pennsylvania
Disorders of Language, Phonology, Fluency, and Voice in
    Children: Indicators for Referral

Robert F. Yellon, M.D.
Assistant Professor of Otolaryngology, University of
Pittsburgh School of Medicine; Co-Director Director of
Clinical Services, Children's Hospital of Pittsburgh,
Pittsburgh, Pennsylvania
Gastroesophageal Reflux Disease
Surgical Management of Microtia and Congenital Aural Atresia
Head and Neck Space Infections
Management and Prevention of Subgottic Stenosis in Infants
    and Children
Head and Neck Space Infections

S. James Zinreich, M.D.
Johns Hopkins University, Baltimore, Maryland
Embryology and Anatomy of the Paranasal Sinuses

Preface

We are delighted to edit and contribute to this fourth edition of *Pediatric Otolaryngology*. There have been dramatic advances in almost all aspects of ear, nose, and throat diseases and disorders in infants and children since publication of the first edition in 1983, and we are pleased that the subsequent editions of this text have kept pace during the same period; the scope of the text also includes diseases and disorders of the tracheobronchial tree and esophagus. Not only have there been improvements in the nonsurgical and surgical management of patients, but we have seen a relative explosion in our knowledge base of these conditions. Over this time, chapters such as those devoted to molecular biology, genetics, otolaryngic manifestations of HIV infections, cochlear implants, skull base surgery, imaging of the paranasal sinuses, and gastroesophageal reflux have been added. Not only does the current edition include completely updated chapters and approximately 20% new authors, but we have added new chapters on thyroid disease, surgical correction of external and middle ear anomalies, and balance disorders. We have also included a section on the history of pediatric otolaryngology. As in previous editions, we critiqued all the chapters in the third edition, which aided in updating, revising, and adding new chapters. As in the past three editions, we have continued to include several chapters early in each section that present the differential diagnoses of the common presenting signs and symptoms, so that the reader can then turn to a more comprehensive review of the condition in the appropriate chapter; cross-referencing is used extensively to facilitate this process. We have made no attempt to include detailed chapters on pediatric diseases, such as diabetes and asthma, that may affect children with ear, nose, and throat diseases, because these topics are adequately addressed in current textbooks of pediatrics.

The text is written for all health care professionals who provide health care for infants and children, which includes, but is not limited to, otolaryngologists, pediatricians, family physicians, allergists, speech pathologists, audiologists, house staff, and students. It is not intended for only the pediatric otolaryngologist, who primarily concentrates on special problems or special children, or both, in special institutions, but for all others who encounter children with these problems.

We are pleased and thankful for the hard work and critical evaluation our new co-editors, Drs. Alper, Arjmand, Casselbrant, Dohar, and Yellon, have provided for this fourth edition. As editors, we hope that the health care of infants and children will be improved by those professionals who use this book as a reference in this new century.

Charles D. Bluestone, MD
Sylvan E. Stool, MD

Acknowledgments

The editors wish to acknowledge the distinguished and dedicated authors who contributed chapters to these volumes, without whom there would not be a fourth edition. We also want to acknowledge Deborah Hepple for her dedication and commitment to the coordination and collation of the manuscripts and for her kind but persistent reminders to our authors to adhere to our production schedule. Thanks also goes to Maria B. Bluestone in Pittsburgh, who provided expert and invaluable editorial aid for several of the chapters, to our capable editors at Saunders in Philadelphia, Stephanie Donley and Melissa Dudlick, and to our designer, Gene Harris. As in the past three volumes, Jon Coulter provided valuable photographic support for this edition.

In any effort as time-consuming as this, the authors' families and colleagues must provide support—and ours have made this task easier by their understanding and encouragement.

Contents

VOLUME 2

SECTION III

The Nose, Paranasal Sinuses, Face, and Orbit

33

Embryology and Anatomy of the Paranasal Sinuses

Michael Rontal, M.D., Jack B. Anon, M.D., and S. James Zinreich, M.D.

The embryologic approach to paranasal sinus anatomy provides an understanding of the intricacies of both the immature and adult nasal lateral wall that cannot be achieved by gross dissection alone. The unique structure of any individual specimen is the result of intertwined growth patterns of the various sinus tracts. Thus, iteration of general cell tract growth tendencies can be extremely helpful in understanding the process by which a sinus specimen achieves its ultimate configuration.

Any area of pneumatization can be traced to its source: As a sinus tract develops, its point of origin remains as a permanent record. No matter how long, tortuous, or intertwined the ultimate cellular growth, the sinus tract will always open through its original ostium and meatus.

As the sinuses develop, these growing cell tracts compete for space. The factors that determine which cells will fill out the nasal walls include the date of origin, growth rate, direction of growth, and deflections from other tracts. No two lateral nasal walls are identical, even within the same individual.

At birth, the nose and its structures are not completely developed. Rather, paranasal sinus development is a process that is not finished until puberty. The exact dates of completion vary. In this chapter, we present the usual pattern of development of these nasal parts, including the time when the process commonly occurs or is completed. In this way, the tremendous structural variability seen within and between individuals may be understood.

Earliest Fetal Development[15, 16]

The earliest indications of the nasal apparatus are seen at about 3 to 4 weeks of fetal life, when a thickening of the epithelium begins to develop on the lateral side of the head, just above the oral stoma and ventral to the orbit. The space across the rostral end of the embryo is simultaneously both the nasofrontal process and the floor of the anterior cranial fossa.

The nasal placode, a thickened area of surface ectoderm, is identified at approximately 4.5 weeks (Fig. 33–1). During the fifth week, the nasal placode sinks into the underlying mesenchyme, which is thus stimulated to hypertrophy, producing the medial and lateral nasal processes (Fig. 33–2). The simultaneous sinking and mesenchymal enlargement produce the primary nasal pit on each side of the embryonic head, ventral (or anterior) to the orbit and the maxillary process of the first branchial arch. Enlargement of the maxillary process effects a repositioning of the orbit from directly lateral to forward facing. This reorientation acts to navigate the two nasal pits toward the midline until they fuse (Fig. 33–3). The early external nose has a "boxy" shape, and the entrance of the nasal pits (nostrils) opens directly forward. The two medial nasal processes form the primary nasal septum, the middle part of the upper lip, and the premaxilla.

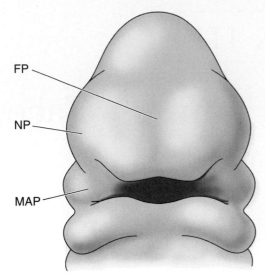

FIGURE 33–1. Fetus at 4.5 weeks. FP, frontonasal process; NP, nasal placode (fetal); MAP, maxillary process.

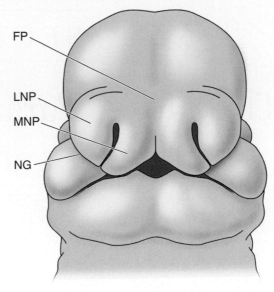

FIGURE 33–2. Fetus at 5 weeks. FP, frontonasal process; LNP, lateral nasal prominence; MNP, medial nasal prominence; NG, nasolacrimal groove (fetal).

Primary Fetal Nasal Cavity

The primary nasal cavity or pit, created by the formation of the medial and lateral nasal processes, is relatively shallow. Fusion of the medial processes into the nasal septum forms a close relationship to the cranial base. The maxillary processes extend to the midline and fuse with the enlarged caudal end of the medial nasal processes (the process of His), thus forming the premaxilla. Eventually, the lateral nasal process also fuses with the maxillary process, thus closing the floor of the nasal pit. The dorsal depth of the nasal pit is defined by the nasobuccal membrane that separates the pit from the oral cavity. At about 38 days of fetal life, this membrane thins and dissipates to allow continuity between the oral cavity and the primary nasal cavity.

Secondary Fetal Nasal Cavity

In the sixth fetal week (42 to 48 days), as the primary nasal pit is maturing, the medial aspect of the maxillary process produces projections called the palatal shelves (Fig. 33–4). At first, these are separated by the tongue (Fig. 33–5), but when the tongue descends, the shelves assume a horizontal position. In the next 9 weeks (complete by 15 weeks), the palatal shelves grow to meet at the midline, posterior or dorsal to the premaxilla region, producing the palate. At first, there is a gap between the completed palate and the premaxilla, which ultimately forms the incisive foramen (Fig. 33–6). This gap gradually closes until it reaches its normal configuration at about 6 prenatal months. Posteriorly, the palate usually closes by 15 weeks. As the palate closes, the nasal cavity is separated from the oral cavity.

During the fusion process of the palate, the nasal septum enlarges posteriorly (dorsally) and caudally, creating the partition between the two sides of the nasal cavity and joining with the palatal shelves to complete the cavity formation.

Lateral Fetal Nasal Wall

At 38 to 40 days, the maxilloturbinal appears as a swelling on the anterior aspect of the lateral nasal wall, just above the palatal shelf. This swelling is the progenitor of the inferior turbinate. Separate structures, the ethmoturbinals, appear at 40 to 43 days at the junction of the nasal septum and the nasal roof. By differential growth, these structures attain a position on the lateral nasal wall. The space between the maxilloturbinal and ethmoturbinals will become the middle meatus; the portion of the ethmoturbinal above the middle meatus produces the middle, superior, and supreme turbinates.

Furrows and ridges that form on the ethmoturbinal generate the superior and supreme turbinates and meatuses. The superior turbinate is first seen at 48 days, and the first supreme turbinate at 95 to 105 days. Further supreme turbinate development occurs after the seventh month, but these further supreme turbinates are usually resorbed during puberty, and the adult configuration is in place by the age of 12 years.

At approximately 60 days, the nasoturbinal appears. This embryologic remnant from lower forms represents the future agger nasi. It is found anterior and slightly cephalic to the structures of the ethmoturbinal. At 65 days, the uncinate process is identifiable on the posterior, medial surface of the agger nasi.

The turbinates have a distinct posterior-inferior to anterior-superior orientation and lie parallel to one another. A bend in the middle meatus and turbinate creates recognizable ascending and descending portions. This is less evident in the superior meatus and is not apparent at all in the supreme meatuses.

Earliest Meatal Differentiation

Between 40 and 60 days, a thickening develops within the anterior middle meatus at the junction of the ascending

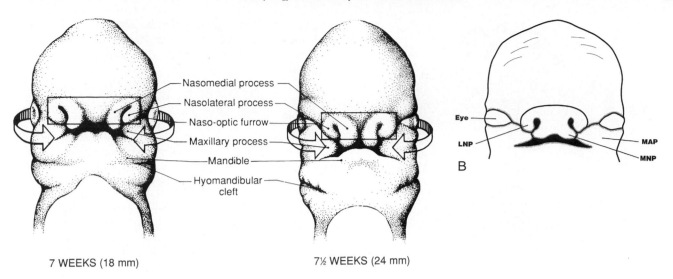

7 WEEKS (18 mm)   7½ WEEKS (24 mm)

- Nasomedial process
- Nasolateral process
- Naso-optic furrow
- Maxillary process
- Mandible
- Hyomandibular cleft

B Eye LNP MAP MNP

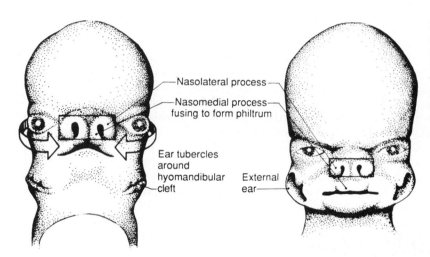

A   8 WEEKS (32 mm)   9 WEEKS (40 mm)

- Nasolateral process
- Nasomedial process fusing to form philtrum
- Ear tubercles around hyomandibular cleft
- External ear

FIGURE 33–3. *A,* Reorientation of the orbit from directly lateral to forward-facing causes the two nasal pits to navigate toward the midline until they fuse (7 to 9 weeks). *B,* Fetus at 7 weeks. LNP, lateral nasal prominence; MAP, maxillary process; MNP, medial nasal prominence.

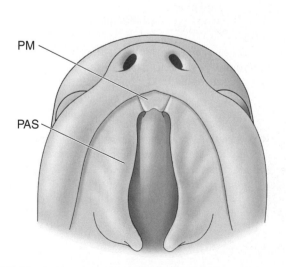

PM
PAS

FIGURE 33–4. Fetus at 6.5 weeks (ventral aspect). PM, premaxilla; PAS, palatine shelf (fetal).

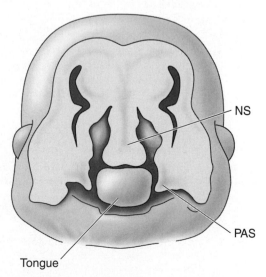

NS
PAS
Tongue

FIGURE 33–5. Fetus at 6.5 weeks (coronal section). NS, nasal septum; PAS, palatine shelf (fetal).

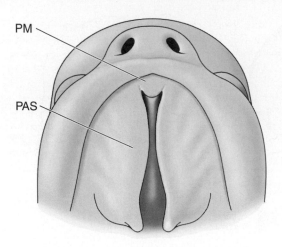

FIGURE 33-6. Fetus at 7.5 weeks (ventral aspect). PM, premaxilla; PS, palatine shelf.

reminiscent of that of the middle meatus. At 110 days, the anterior end of the superior meatus develops a superior and an inferior arm (like the infundibulum) and a crista (like the bulla).

Lamellae

The middle, superior, and supreme turbinates; the ethmoid bulla; and the uncinate are attached to the lamina papyracea. They are the primary and secondary lamellae of the lateral nasal wall. These lamellae are constant throughout development, although lateral wall differentiation may distort them through the process of pneumatization. The lateral wall is partitioned by the lamella, which organizes the cellular development into compartments. The most constant lamella is that of the middle turbinate, the basal lamella. It represents the critical dividing line between the anterior and posterior ethmoid cells.

Nasolacrimal Duct

On the facial surface, the nasolacrimal duct is another early development. At the medial end of the maxillary process, an epithelial thickening forms that descends into the underlying mesoderm. This occurs at about 35 days. This buried epithelial cord extends from the orbit to the maxilloturbinate process. The epithelial cord becomes hollow, and an epithelium-lined tube is left connecting the orbit and the anterior-inferior nasal cavity (inferior nasal meatus). This is the nasolacrimal duct. The lateral nasal process does not participate in this development.

and descending parts. This thickened area grows laterally and stimulates the surrounding mesenchyme and appears to "sink" into the lateral nasal wall. The furrow thus formed is the infundibulum, and the ridge anterior to it on the nasoturbinal is the uncinate. By 65 or 70 days, a pouch (the future maxillary sinus) deepens into the floor of the infundibulum. At approximately 105 days, frontal recess cells develop medial to the uncinate, between it and the anterior attachment of the middle turbinate. Posterior to the infundibular furrow is the ethmoid bulla, although it is not easily identifiable until 120 days. The superior meatus (on the posterior or dorsal side of the middle turbinate) differentiates in a truncated fashion

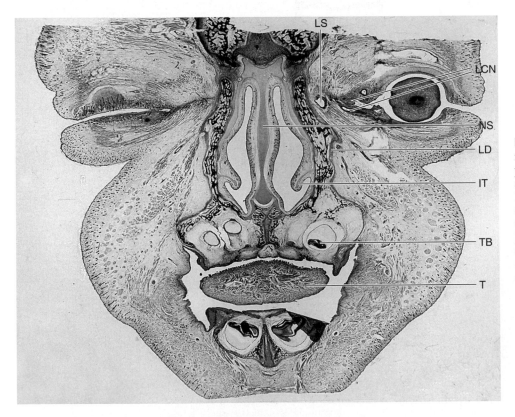

FIGURE 33-7. The following coronal sections are from a 21-week prenatal specimen. LS, lacrimal sac; LCN, lacrimal canaliculus; NS, nasal septum; LD, lacrimal duct; IT, inferior turbinate; TB, tooth bud; T, tongue. (From Anon J, Rontal M, Zinreich SJ. Anatomy and Embryology of the Paranasal Sinuses. New York, Thieme Medical Publishers, 1995.)

Later Ethmoid Development

By the end of the first 4 prenatal months, all of the principal elements of the midfacial nasal structures have been established, and the origins of all eventual structures can be identified. After these early steps, nasal development is an ongoing process that continues through the first 16 to 18 years of life. Development is particularly variable in the first 5 years of postnatal life.

While no specific time can be given for maturation of a particular structure, generalizations are possible. Of importance are the ethmoid sinuses, which tend to mature earlier than others. The following chronicle of ethmoid development represents a process that occurs over a number of years.

Anterior Ethmoid Cellular Formation

The ethmoids are divided into anterior and posterior groups by the basal lamellae of the middle turbinate. This relationship is particularly important given that each cell tract clears itself to empty through its site of origin. The anterior cells open into the middle meatus, and the posterior cells open into the superior or supreme meatuses. Regardless of the extent to which these cells develop, the functional relationship to their point of origin remains.

Frontal Recess Cells (Figs. 33–7 to 33–10)

The fetal frontal recess is a group of cells that develops distinct from the cells of the infundibulum. Found lateral to the anterior attachment of the middle turbinate and medial to the uncinate process, these cells expand to occupy the space anterior and lateral to the middle turbinate (see Fig. 33–9). The group usually consists of three furrows and four ridges. In the majority of cases, the most posterior of these furrows grows most extensively and becomes the frontal sinus. In 60% of specimens, the fetal frontal recess is the origin of the adult frontal sinus.[5] Thus, this form of the frontal sinus opens medial to the uncinate and into the middle meatus. The other frontal recess furrows expand and may grow anteroinferiorly into the agger nasi and uncinate process. These latter cells are particularly prominent when the frontal sinus does not originate from the fetal frontal recess.

Anterior Infundibular Cells

From the cephalic and anterior aspect of the infundibulum, cells expand as anterior infundibular cells, appearing as two furrows and three ridges near the roof of the ethmoid. The most anterior furrow may expand toward the frontal region and become the frontal sinus. This is the origin of the frontal sinus in approximately one third of specimens. These frontal sinuses open into the ethmoid infundibulum, lateral to the uncinate process, and closely relate to the ostium of the maxillary sinus. When the frontal sinus originates with the fetal frontal recess, an anterior infundibular cell that would otherwise have been the frontal sinus may grow into the floor of this sinus as a frontal bulla. Further development of these anterior ethmoid cells can pneumatize the agger nasi, the lacrimal bone, and the uncinate, and may enter the middle turbinate as a concha bullosa. Nondevelopment of the anterior infundibular cells often leads to a thick block along the medial orbital wall.

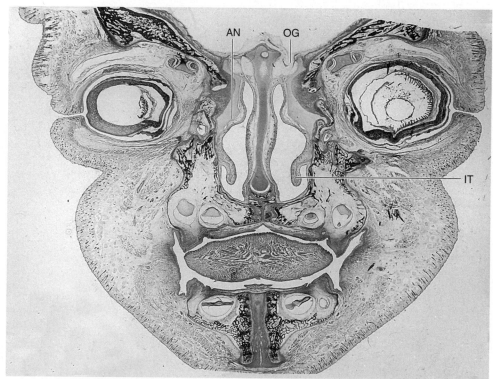

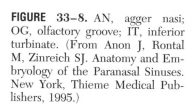

FIGURE 33–8. AN, agger nasi; OG, olfactory groove; IT, inferior turbinate. (From Anon J, Rontal M, Zinreich SJ. Anatomy and Embryology of the Paranasal Sinuses. New York, Thieme Medical Publishers, 1995.)

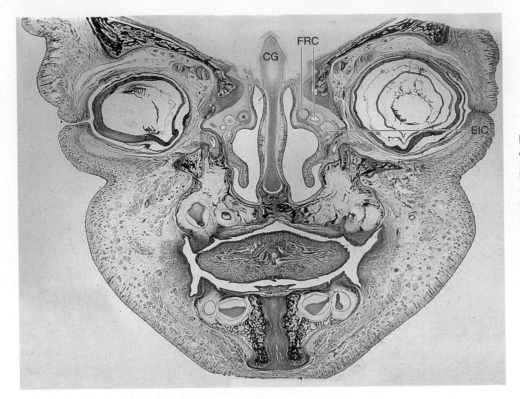

FIGURE 33–9. Frontal recess cells expand to occupy the space anterior and lateral to the middle turbinate. CG, crista galli; FRC, frontal recess cell; EIC, ethmoid infundibular cell. (From Anon J, Rontal M, Zinreich SJ. Anatomy and Embryology of the Paranasal Sinuses. New York, Thieme Medical Publishers, 1995.)

Suprabullar Cells and the Lateralis Sinus

Superior to the bulla, the infundibulum expands into three to four furrows. The ethmoid bulla is almost always pneumatized by one of these furrows (Fig. 33–11). The ethmoid bulla cell has a site of origin, and thus an exit for clearance, on its superior surface. Suprabullar development may also expand anteriorly, posteriorly, and laterally. This is the major source of the supraorbital cells, one of the sources of the frontal sinus, and also the source of a concha bullosa.

In many cases, the ethmoid bulla may be small enough

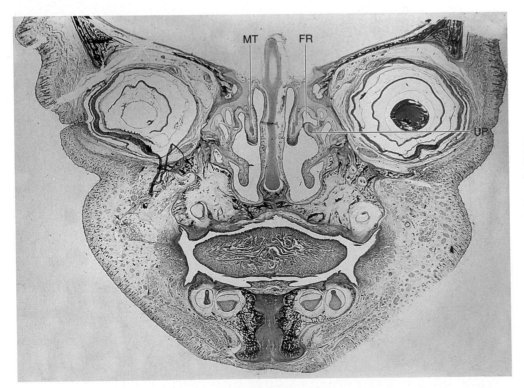

FIGURE 33–10. MT, middle turbinate; FR, fetal frontal recess; UP, uncinate process. (From Anon J, Rontal M, Zinreich SJ. Anatomy and Embryology of the Paranasal Sinuses. New York, Thieme Medical Publishers, 1995.)

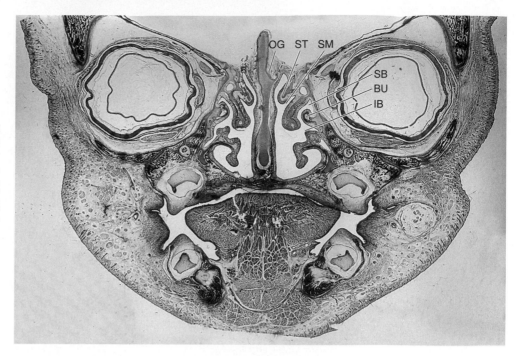

FIGURE 33–11. OG, olfactory groove; ST, superior turbinate; SM, superior meatus; SB, suprabullar cell; BU, ethmoid bulla; IB, infrabullar recess. (From Anon J, Rontal M, Zinreich SJ. Anatomy and Embryology of the Paranasal Sinuses. New York, Thieme Medical Publishers, 1995.)

that a space remains between it and the lamella of the middle turbinate (see Fig. 33–11). In such an instance, there is a continuous space from the infundibulum, over the superior aspect of the bulla, and around its posterior aspect to open inferiorly into the middle meatus. This is the sinus lateralis. Consequently, the lateral sinus forms as a result of ethmoid bulla development and is not actually an independent pneumatization of the lateral wall. If the ethmoid bulla fuses with the basal lamella of the middle turbinate, the sinus lateralis is divided, which creates a suprabullar space and a posterior space. This is called the posterior sinus lateralis.

Infrabullar Cells

Expansion of the infundibulum inferior to the bulla produces the inconstant infrabullar space, which occasionally pneumatizes the bulla (see Fig. 33–11). The infrabullar area can also invade the space between the ethmoids and the maxillary sinus, the ethmomaxillary plate, to form a cell that is found in the posterior, medial-superior aspect of the maxilla. This is the ethmomaxillary cell, or Haller cell, which opens into the middle meatal area. The infrabullar space, however, is not the most common source of the Haller cell. (See Posterior Ethmoid Formation.)

Uncinate Process (see Figs. 33–8 and 33–10 to 33–12)

The uncinate process follows the shape of the infundibulum and is thus curved like a scimitar or boomerang. The uncinate is attached to the agger nasi and extends posterosuperiorly to the inferior turbinate and may or may not attach to the inferior turbinate. The uncinate process forms part of the medial wall of the maxillary sinus.

Posterior Ethmoid Formation (Fig. 33–13)

The anterior end of the superior meatus may be divided into an inferior and a superior arm. When an inferior arm is present, two tracts of cells may be seen. One group may expand anteriorly into the lamellae of the middle turbinate as a common origin of the concha bullosa.

The other group of cells from this area can expand laterally, into the space between the lateral ethmoid wall and the maxilla and the ascending or orbital process of the palate. This group of cells is a more common origin of the Haller cell. It is also the means by which the palate is sometimes seen to be pneumatized.

The posterior ethmoid cells originate from the superior and supreme meatuses. The posterior ethmoids are fewer in number and much larger than the anterior group of ethmoid cells. Posterior ethmoid cells may expand superiorly and laterally over the orbit as supraorbital cells. The extent of their development can be tremendous, reaching as far anteriorly as the vertical portion of the frontal bone and posteriorly into the sphenoid bone.

The relationship between ethmoid and sphenoid cells is responsible for important variations. One such variation is the Onödi cell. This cell is actually a posterior ethmoid air cell that has an intimate relation to the optic nerve. The Onödi cell may envelop the optic nerve. The posterior ethmoid cells may also expand into what would otherwise be expected to be sphenoid. Conversely, the sphenoid may expand anteriorly into posterior ethmoid space.

Chondrification and Ossification of the Nasal Capsule[3, 17, 22]

The cartilaginous nasal capsule can be viewed as the primary skeletal support of the upper face. Pneumatization

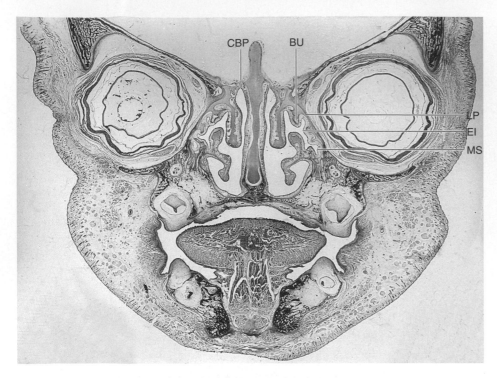

FIGURE 33–12. CBP, cribriform plate, perforated portion; BU, ethmoid bulla; LP, lamina papyracea; EI, ethmoid infundibulum; MS, maxillary sinus. (From Anon J, Rontal M, Zinreich SJ. Anatomy and Embryology of the Paranasal Sinuses. New York, Thieme Medical Publishers, 1995.)

of the lateral nasal wall is confined to the nasal capsule. The left and right capsule fuse as the nasal septum. As the fetal nose matures, the cartilaginous nasal capsule will subsequently give rise to the cartilaginous nasal septum, lower and upper lateral cartilages, and portions of the ethmoid bone.

Chondrification of the nasal region is a late process relative to other parts of the chondrocranium. The mesenchymal cells that will become the chondrocytes may have migrated into the area from the crest of the closing neural tube, as neural crest cells.

These neural crest cells lay down chondroitin that so-

lidifies the areas in and around the developing nasal cavities. The process begins at approximately 3.5 months of prenatal life, in the region of the sphenoid near the skull base. Two weeks later, the lateral nasal wall begins to form cartilage. Each of the turbinates has a separate center for cartilage formation, and all ultimately fuse with the cartilage of the lateral wall. By the fifth prenatal month, the nasal cartilaginous capsule is complete. The fibrovascular tissue at its periphery is the perichondrium that sustains the internal cells. Cartilaginous growth is limited by the ability of the nutrients to diffuse to the chondrocytes.

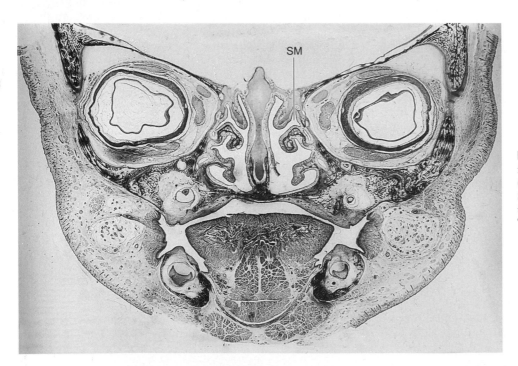

FIGURE 33–13. Posterior ethmoid formation. SM, superior meatus. (From Anon J, Rontal M, Zinreich SJ. Anatomy and Embryology of the Paranasal Sinuses. New York, Thieme Medical Publishers, 1995.)

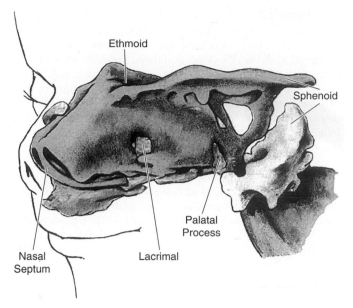

FIGURE 33–14. The cartilaginous nasal capsule 4 months prenatally.

Figure 33–14 shows the cartilaginous nasal capsule. All of the coronal fetal sections show the staining properties as the cartilaginous matrix is laid down in stages, and the lacunae of cells other than the mesenchyme are also seen.

Even before the cartilaginous process is completed, ossification centers are identifiable. At first, there is an almost spontaneous appearance of vascular elements at the periphery of cartilage. The cells associated with these vessels become osteocytes, absorbing cartilage and laying down layers of calcified matrix. Thus, the process of endochondral ossification proceeds as cartilage is resorbed and replaced by bone. Now, however, each cell (osteocyte) is connected to a vessel.

Ossification is first seen in the lateral aspect of the ethmoid, along the orbit. The process spreads into the roof of the ethmoid and into the turbinates during the seventh and eighth fetal months. The inferior turbinate may have a separate center. The process of ossification is incomplete at birth and continues well into the early years of life. Ossification of the cribriform plate is not complete until 3 years of age, and in terms of the entire nasal structure, parts of the septum never ossify.

The endochondral bony nasal capsule does not ossify before invasion by the cell tracts of the paranasal sinuses. Rather, these structures are initiated and set in cartilage, and then the process of ossification begins. Some early structures, such as the turbinates, ossify early, and their origins on the lateral ethmoid or medial orbital wall (the lamellae) are set early. Other formations, like parts of the sphenoid bone or the relations of the ethmoid and maxilla, occur only after the intervening suture lines fuse and are absorbed.

Another type of bone formation also occurs. This is the compact bone or membranous bone seen on the maxilla, on the nasal septum, and around the neurovascular structures. The perichondrium lays down sheets of bone on top of cartilage. Otherwise, this bone is no different from the endochondral type. Again, the pattern follows that structures are established first and ossified or encased in bone later.

The Nasal Septum[6]

The septum begins as the result of fusion of the nasofrontal process and the two medial nasal processes into a primary nasal septum. Secondary growth from this and the cranial floor toward the forming palate creates the secondary septum that persists into later life. Fusion of this septum with the palate defines the nasal chamber and establishes the right and left sides.

Early in fetal development, in the seventh or eighth week, pits and then an actual epithelial organ may be seen on either side of the septum. This nasovomer organ degenerates before birth, although residual pits can occasionally be seen in later life. No function is known for this structure in humans; in other life forms, it may have a chemical sensory function.

The fetal septum has a quadrilateral portion projecting forward with a sphenoidal projection extending to the sphenoid bone, a vomer, and a perpendicular portion that extends to the roof of the ethmoid. The sphenoid strip and the nasovomer portions are absorbed early. Membranous bone encases the vomer and perpendicular cartilaginous plates, and usually, although not always, the cartilage is eventually absorbed. In most cases, the perpendicular plate becomes ossified by age 3 years, at which point the perforated portion of the cribriform finally ossifies as well. Only the quadrangular plate of cartilage remains through life.

The Inferior Turbinate and Inferior Meatus

The inferior turbinate derives from the maxilloturbinal.

Until approximately 6 years of age, the inferior meatus is essentially nonfunctioning. It functions as the drainage outlet of the nasolacrimal duct, but no air can pass through it. As the maxillary sinus enlarges, growth in this area occurs, and by puberty the inferior meatus represents a significant space. Much if not most vertical facial growth is coincident with inferior meatal vertical growth.

The External Nose

Appearance of the external nose is attributable to fusion of the medial and lateral nasal processes. It has a squared form until it thins and elongates in puberty. The cartilaginous capsule includes the external nose, the alar cartilages, and the nasal bones. The nasal bones ossify as membranous bones. The alar cartilages do not ossify and in fact continue to grow throughout life. The lateral nasal process has no cartilage and is a fibrofatty structure. The nostrils open ventral or forward and attain an inferior orientation with puberty.

Time Line

In terms of development of the nose, birth is an artificial milestone in its progress. The child's nasal development is unpredictable through the first 5 to 6 years of life. In early childhood, for example, the ethmoid lateral wall may have small cell tracts with thick, amorphous material between, or there may be well-developed cellular definition. After this early period, definitive cellular areas are easily visualized. By the age of 12 or 14 years, the paranasal sinuses are essentially like those of the adult, and the remainder of puberty allows their final maturation.

Maxillary Sinus[2, 4, 12, 18, 20]

The maxillary sinus, also referred to as the antrum, is the largest and most constant of all the sinuses. It is present within the maxillary bone of the skull, which in turn forms the anterior cheek from the orbital floor to the upper alveolus. In addition, the maxillary bone makes up a large part of the palate and portions of the lateral nasal wall. The maxillary bone articulates with the frontal bone, the zygomatic bone, the alveolar bone, and the palatine bone.

Shortly before the lateral nasal wall of the developing fetus forms the maxillary sinus, there is an increase in the vasculature near the floor of the ethmoid infundibulum (Fig. 33–15). This is thought to represent some type of

local tissue effect that induces the initial outpouching of the maxillary sinus (Vidic B, personal communication). Evagination of the floor of the middle meatus can be observed at 60 to 70 days' gestation. Initially, there is an outgrowth of the middle meatus in the horizontal plane of the cartilaginous nasal capsule. This, however, is not the maxillary sinus. Rather, the maxillary sinus is said to begin when growth actually progresses in the *vertical* plane. The site of origin of the maxillary sinus persists as the primary maxillary sinus ostium. Maxillary sinus growth is confined to within the nasal capsule.

The developing maxillary sinus is largest in its anterior and posterior dimensions and smallest in the vertical, medial, and lateral dimensions. This growth differential is due to the small maxillary bone as well as to the presence of tooth buds and the orbit located superiorly within the maxilla, all of which impede pneumatization. Schaeffer measured the anterior-posterior dimensions of the developing maxillary sinus in fetuses and recorded 2 mm at 100 to 105 days' gestation, 2.5 mm at 120 days' gestation, 5 mm at 210 days' gestation, and 7 mm at term.[16]

The position of the maxillary sinus relative to the teeth, infraorbital nerve, orbit, and floor of the nose is important to understand. The fetal alveolus lies close to

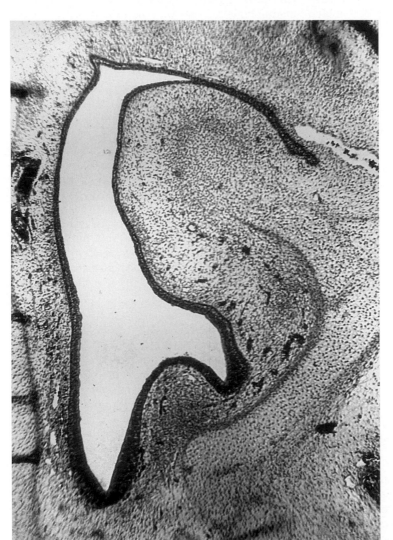

FIGURE 33–15. Increased vasculature near the floor of the ethmoid infundibulum. (Courtesy of Professor B. Vidic.)

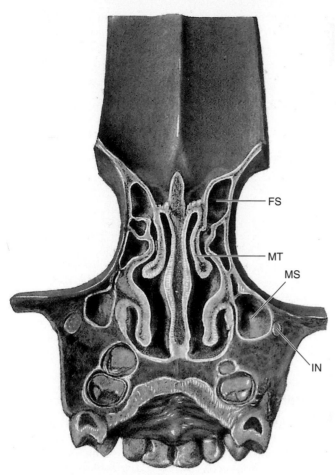

FIGURE 33–16. The maxillary sinus extends laterally to the plane of the infraorbital canal in a 2-year-old child. FS, frontal sinus; MT, middle turbinate; MS, maxillary sinus; IN, infraorbital nerve. (From Davis W. Development and Anatomy of the Nasal Accessory Sinuses in Man. Philadelphia, WB Saunders, 1914.)

the infraorbital rim. This relationship is maintained until the maxillary sinus expands. At about 1.5 to 2 years of age, the maxillary sinus has extended laterally to the plane of the infraorbital canal (Fig. 33–16). By 3 years of age, the sinus has pneumatized beyond the lateral aspect of this canal (Fig. 33–17), and it penetrates the malar process by 8 to 9 years of age.

At birth, the maxillary sinus is also positioned well above the floor of the nose. Onödi[14] documented the size of the maxillary sinus in a number of pediatric specimens. In the newborn to age 12 months group, the size of the sinus ranged from 5 to 19 mm in length, 3 to 9 mm in height, and 2.5 to 8 mm in width. In the 18- to 24-month age group, the length was 10 to 12 mm, height 8 to 9 mm, and width 3 to 7 mm. At 42 months, the sinus was 26 mm in length, 13 mm in height, and 12 mm in width; at 90 months, the sinus measured 38 mm in length, 23 mm in height, and 20 mm in width. Davis[5] also measured the progression of growth of the maxillary sinus in the postnatal period (Table 33–1) and demonstrated growth of approximately 2 mm/year vertically and laterally and 3 mm/year anteriorly and posteriorly during

the first 8 years after birth. The shape of the sinus in these early years has been described as oval, triangular, oblong, square, and irregular.

Relationships of the Maxillary Sinus

In late childhood, the maxillary sinus attains the shape of a tetrahedron. The base of this tetrahedron is the lateral wall of the nose; the zygomatic process is at the apex; and the anterior wall, posterior wall, floor, and roof compose the four walls.

Anterior Wall

The infraorbital foramen exits from this anterior wall centrally. The somewhat flattened, thin concavity of the canine fossa is also identified along the anterior face of the sinus.

Posterior Wall and Lateral Nasal Wall

The posterior wall and lateral wall of the maxillary sinus tend to blend together, blurring their distinct identities. The lateral wall separates the sinus from the infratemporal fossa. The superior aspect of the posterior wall is thin and divides the sinus from the pterygopalatine fossa and inferior orbital fissure.

Inferior Wall (Floor)

The floor of the sinus is formed by the alveolar process of the maxillary bone. The relationship to the underlying dentition is variable, depending on the age of the individual and the degree of pneumatization of the maxilla. In general, the sinus floor lies approximately 4 mm above the nasal floor in infancy, parallel to the floor by age 8 to 9 years, and 4 to 5 mm inferior to the nasal floor in adulthood. The sinus usually lies above the second premolar and the first and second molars. The incisors and premaxilla are not related to the maxillary sinus.

Superior Wall (Roof)

The floor of the orbit is also the roof of the maxillary sinus. The infraorbital nerve and vessels course across this roof through the bony infraorbital canal.

Medial Wall

The medial wall of the maxillary sinus forms part of the lateral nasal wall. The primary maxillary sinus ostium lies within the confines of the ethmoid infundibulum and varies in size and shape. Accessory maxillary sinus ostia are found within the membranous fontanelles of the medial wall of the sinus. These ostia are rarely found in fetal specimens or in infants and are thus thought to be developmental phenomena most likely associated with an infectious process. The nasolacrimal duct courses toward the inferior meatus. It is enveloped by expansion of the maxillary sinus and may therefore form a significant projection along the medial sinus wall.

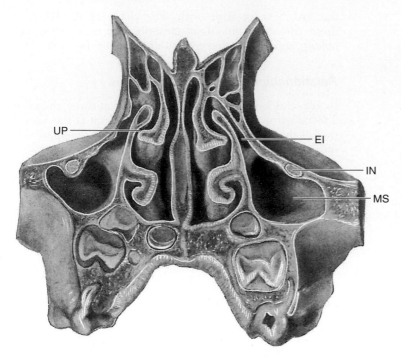

FIGURE 33–17. Pneumatized sinus beyond the lateral aspect of the infraorbital canal in a 4-year-old child. UP, uncinate process; EI, ethmoid infundibulum; IN, infraorbital nerve; MS, maxillary sinus.

Sinus Interior

The interior of the maxillary sinus may be hallmarked by complete as well as incomplete septa. These may be bony or membranous, and they may course in a vertical, oblique, or horizontal fashion.

Variations

The maxillary sinus may range from total absence to extreme hyperpneumatization. Total absence of the sinus is rare. Various degrees of hypoplasia of the maxillary sinus may be seen in 10% of studies. Often, there are associated abnormalities of the uncinate process because of the embryologic co-development of this structure and the maxillary sinus. Lack of development of the maxillary sinus may also be associated with other anomalies, such as choanal atresia, cleft palate, and mandibulofacial dysostosis.

TABLE 33–1. Average Sizes of the Maxillary Sinus

Age	Superior-Inferior	Medial-Lateral	Anterior-Posterior
8 days–1 yr	5.5 mm	4.7 mm	13.4 mm
3–4 yr	11.2 mm	9.3 mm	22.1 mm
5–6 yr	12.5 mm	13.6 mm	26.6 mm
8–9 yr	21.7 mm	17.9 mm	29.9 mm
9–10 yr	18.5 mm	17.8 mm	30.0 mm
12–13 yr	18.3 mm	15.0 mm	25.0 mm
15–16 yr	32.6 mm	26.4 mm	39.1 mm
25 yr	28.4 mm	21.0 mm	32.7 mm

Modified from Davis W. Accessory Sinuses in Man. Philadelphia, WB Saunders, 1914.

Frontal Sinus[13]

The frontal sinus will eventually become a pyramid-shaped air space situated between the anterior and posterior tables of the ascending portion of the frontal bone. The frontal bone consists of a horizontal plate and a vertical plate and forms most of the orbital roof, forehead, and supraorbital rim. The frontal sinuses are actually ethmoid air cells that have extended anteriorly and superiorly into the frontal bone. This type of invasive pneumatization leads to the great variability in size and shape of these sinuses. Embryologically, by approximately 100 days' gestation, the fetal frontal recess or the middle meatus begins to extend anteriorly and superiorly into the region of the fetal frontal recess. The fetal frontal recess at this point contains thickened regions of cartilage that are relatively level with the lateral nasal wall. By term, however, this region exhibits complex folds and furrows as well as developing ethmoid air cells. Examination of the 6-month-old infant reveals air cells within the *horizontal* portion of the frontal bone. At approximately 2 years of age, pneumatization progresses into the vertical segment of the frontal bone, and at this point the true frontal sinus is defined (see Fig. 33–16).

The actual route of development of the frontal sinus is varied. Schaeffer described these potential routes: (1) an extension of the entire fetal frontal recess; (2) an extension of anterior ethmoid cells present within the furrows or pits of the fetal frontal recess; (3) an air cell originating from the anterior aspect of the ethmoid infundibulum; (4) a suprabullar air cell; (5) a continuation of the ethmoid infundibulum; and (6) a combination of any of these that may produce more than one frontal sinus on the examined side.[17]

Onödi measured the dimensions of the frontal sinuses in a group of pediatric specimens.[14] At 2 years of age, the

TABLE 33–2. Average Sizes of the Frontal Sinus

Age	Superior-Inferior	Medial-Lateral	Anterior-Posterior
1–2 yr	4.2 mm	2.7 mm	4.0 mm
3–4 yr	5.8 mm	3.4 mm	5.7 mm
5–6 yr	7.3 mm	4.7 mm	6.5 mm
8–9 yr	11.8 mm	10.2 mm	10.8 mm
9–10 yr	9.0 mm	7.2 mm	7.7 mm
12–13 yr	19.0 mm	18.0 mm	13.8 mm
15–16 yr	29.0 mm	28.8 mm	12.0 mm
25 yr	21.5 mm	18.3 mm	13.8 mm

Modified from Davis W. Accessory Sinuses in Man. Philadelphia, WB Saunders, 1914.

sinus was 4.5 to 9 mm in height, 4 to 5.5 mm in length, and 3 to 4 mm in width. At 4 years of age, the height was 6.5 mm, the length 6 mm, and the width 5 mm. At 7.5 years of age, Onödi measured a height of 14 to 17 mm, a length of 4 to 11 mm, and a width of 7 to 9 mm. Davis also studied the developing frontal sinus and documented these measurements, as shown in Table 33–2.[5]

Relationships of the Frontal Sinus

Anterior Wall

The anterior wall of the frontal sinus is the thickest of all the walls and forms the contour of the brow and the forehead. The metopic suture is the midline suture between the two frontal bones. This suture usually disappears by age 2 years but may persist until age 9 years or may even be permanently present. The presence of this suture precludes the extension of the frontal sinus across the midline.

Posterior Wall

The posterior wall is hard compact bone that forms the anterior wall of the cranial cavity.

Inferior Wall (Floor)

The floor forms portions of the orbital roof, nose, and border of the anterior ethmoid sinuses. The floor of the sinus is relatively thin, and dehiscences may occur. The primary frontal sinus ostium is located in the medial, posterior aspect of the anterior floor. This primary ostium is conically shaped and leads to a more narrow opening inferiorly, the frontal recess. The frontal recess is the communication between the frontal sinus and the anterior ethmoid sinuses. A frontal bulla cell—a separate cell originating from the ethmoid bulla, agger nasi, anterior ethmoids, or uncinate process and not opening directly into the frontal sinus—may also be seen bulging into the floor of the frontal sinus in up to 20% of specimens.

Sinus Interior

The frontal sinuses are divided by the intersinus septum. This is a thin partition of bone that may have bony dehis-

cences. The most inferior aspect of this septum tends to lie in the midline, but progression more superiorly may demonstrate wide shifts from the midline position. This may be so extreme that the septum actually lies over the contralateral sinus.

Variations

The frontal sinus ranges from total absence to aeration of the entire frontal bone with extensions into the greater and lesser wings of the sphenoid, the parietal bone, the temporal bone, and even the maxilla. Extreme sinus development has been associated with osteogenesis imperfecta tarda, Turner syndrome, Klinefelter syndrome, and acromegaly. Small sinuses have been associated with diseases such as Apert syndrome, Down syndrome, Treacher Collins syndrome, and pituitary dwarfism.

Unilateral absence of the sinus occurs in approximately 5% of the population. Total absence occurs in approximately 4%.

Supraorbital air cells—found in approximately 20% of skulls—invade the horizontal plate of the frontal bone. They are usually identified within the medial quarter to third of the orbital roof; however, they may extend as far posteriorly as the optic foramen.[9]

Sphenoid Sinus[11, 21, 22]

The sphenoid sinuses are present within the "bat"-shaped sphenoid bone. This bone has a central body with four associated processes: the lesser wings, the greater wings, and the medial and lateral pterygoids.

The embryologic development of the sphenoid sinuses is unique. These are the only sinuses that do not arise as outpouchings from the lateral nasal wall. Rather, the sphenoid sinuses originate from within the posterior aspect of the cartilaginous nasal capsule of the embryonic nose.

Development of the sphenoid sinus primordium (the actual sphenoid sinus does not exist until the sphenoid bone is invaded and pneumatized) can be identified between 3 and 4 months' gestation (Fig. 33–18). This presphenoid sinus is seen as a small recess within the posterior end of the cartilaginous nasal capsule. Embryologic sections of the sphenoid sinus primordium also reveal a surrounding cartilage ovoid wall. The cartilage plates in this wall contain two ossification centers called the ossicles of Bertin (also referred to as the sphenoid conchae).

Even after birth, the sphenoid sinus primordial capsule grows slowly inferiorly and posteriorly, ossifying during the course of this growth. At about 3 to 4 years of age, the primordium will invade the presphenoid, and pneumatization of the sphenoid bone will occur. The origin of the sphenoid sinus from the posterior nasal cavity is always identified by the sinus ostium.

The sphenoid bone itself derives from two pairs of bony nuclei: the anterior pair is the presphenoid, which will make up part of the sphenoethmoidal recess, and the posterior pair is the basisphenoid.

If the sphenoid sinus primordium fuses with the sphenoid bone, pneumatization by this route will not be seen.

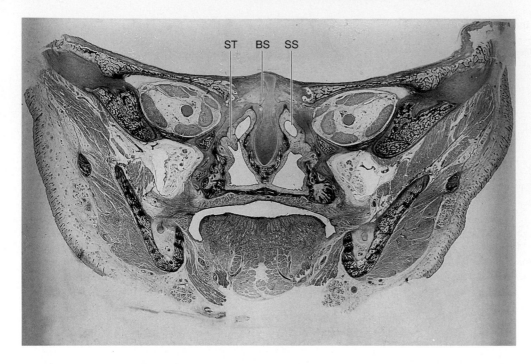

FIGURE 33–18. Development of the sphenoid sinus primordium. ST, superior turbinate; BS, basisphenoid; SS, presphenoid sinus.

Thus, the sphenoid sinus may be undeveloped, or the posterior ethmoids may invade the bone instead.

Sphenoid sinuses are of three types, each of which is descriptive of the degree of pneumatization of the sphenoid in relation to the sella turcica. These types are (1) conchal—the most rudimentary and uncommon type, usually seen in preteen years (Fig. 33–19); (2) presellar—the sphenoid is pneumatized up to the vertical plane of the sella turcica; and (3) sellar—the most com-mon type, with pneumatization beyond the floor of the sella turcica, completely exposing the sella.

Onödi[14] measured the sphenoid sinus in a 3.5-year-old and found a variable height of 4.5 to 6 mm, length of 3.5 to 5 mm, and width of 7 mm. In the 6-year-old, the length was approximately 6.5 mm, height measured 10 mm, and width was 12 mm. Davis[5] also tabulated the average sizes of the growing sphenoid sinus (Table 33–3). In general, the sphenoid sinus grows at a rate of 1.4 mm/year and reaches adult size at 12 to 15 years of age.

Relationships of the Sphenoid Sinus[7, 8]

Anterior Wall

The anterior wall of the sinus is also the posterior boundary of the sphenoethmoidal recess. The primary sinus ostium is located in the midportion of the anterior wall approximately 5 mm lateral to the posterior aspect of the nasal septum.

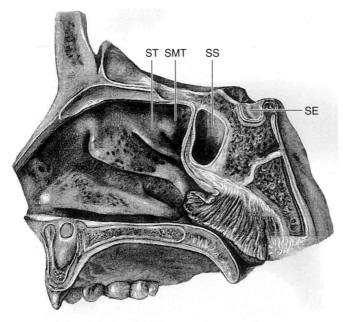

FIGURE 33–19. Sagittal section of 6-year-old. ST, superior turbinate; SMT, supreme turbinate; SS, sphenoid sinus; SE, sella turcica. (From Davis W. Development and Anatomy of the Nasal Accessory Sinuses in Man. Philadelphia, WB Saunders, 1914.)

TABLE 33–3. Average Sizes of the Sphenoid Sinus

Age	Superior-Inferior	Medial-Lateral	Anterior-Posterior
8 days–1 yr	2.9 mm	2.0 mm	1.6 mm
3–4 yr	5.3 mm	3.8 mm	3.0 mm
5–6 yr	7.2 mm	5.1 mm	4.9 mm
8–9 yr	14.4 mm	11.7 mm	11.7 mm
9–10 yr	10.0 mm	11.9 mm	7.6 mm
12–13 yr	9.0 mm	10.0 mm	10.5 mm
15–16 yr	22.8 mm	21.4 mm	22.0 mm
25 yr	18.8 mm	17.5 mm	20.3 mm

Modified from Davis W. Accessory Sinuses in Man. Philadelphia, WB Saunders, 1914.

Posterior Wall

This wall separates the sphenoid sinus from the pons.

Superior Wall (Roof)

The roof of the sinus may be thin and even exhibit areas of dehiscence. The roots of the lesser wings of the sphenoid bone, the optic canal, and the sella turcica are related to this region.

Inferior Wall (Floor)

The floor may demonstrate a bulge due to the pterygoid canal.

Lateral Wall

The lateral wall is often thrown into relief by the impressions of the internal carotid artery (within the cavernous sinus) and the optic canal. The carotid was found by Kennedy and colleagues to be clinically dehiscent in 22% of dissected cadavers.[10] The optic canal lies more superiorly and may be dehiscent in 4% of cases. Other structures within the cavernous sinus may leave ridges on this lateral wall.

Sinus Interior

The intersinus septum is the medial boundary of the sphenoid sinus. This septum may be midline, S-shaped, or C-shaped. Various accessory septa may also subdivide the sinus. These septa may insert onto the carotid artery or the optic nerve.

Variations

Variations of the size and shape of the sphenoid sinuses are the norm rather than the exception. Pneumatization of the greater and lesser wings, anterior clinoid process, occipital bone, rostrum, and pterygoids may be observed. Total absence of both sphenoid sinuses occurs in about 1% of cases.

REFERENCES

1. Anon J, Rontal M, Zinreich SJ. Anatomy and Embryology of the Paranasal Sinuses. New York, Thieme Medical Publishers, 1995.
2. Bolger W, Woodruff W, Morehead J, Parsons D. Maxillary sinus hypoplasia classification and description of associated uncinate process hypoplasia. Otolaryngol Head Neck Surg 103:759, 1990.
3. Burdi AR, Lawton TJ, Grosslight J. Prenatal pattern emergence in early human facial development. Cleft Palate J 25:8, 1988.
4. Cullen R, Vidic B. The dimensions and shape of the human maxillary sinus in the perinatal period. Acta Anat 83:411, 1972.
5. Davis W. Development and Anatomy of the Nasal Accessory Sinuses in Man. Philadelphia, WB Saunders, 1914.
6. Fairbanks D. Embryology and anatomy. In Bluestone CD, Stool SE (eds). Pediatric Otolaryngology. Philadelphia, WB Saunders, 1990, pp 605–631.
7. Fujii K, Chambers SM, Rhoton AL. Neurovascular relationships of the sphenoid sinus: a microsurgical study. J Neurosurg 50:31, 1979.
8. Hammer G, Radberg C. Sphenoidal sinus: anatomical and roentgenologic study with reference to transphenoidal hypophysectomy. Acta Radiol 56:401, 1961.
9. Jovanovic S. Supernumerary frontal sinuses on the roof of the orbit; their clinical significance. Acta Anat 45:133, 1961.
10. Kennedy DW, Zinreich SJ, Hassab MH. The internal carotid artery as it relates to endonasal sphenoidectomy. Am J Rhinol 4:7, 1990.
11. Lang J. Clinical Anatomy of the Nose, Nasal Cavity and Paranasal Sinuses. New York, Thieme Medical Publishers, 1989.
12. Libersa C, Laude M, Christians L. Etude sur le developpement du sinus maxillaire chez l'enfant. Arch Fr Pediatr 20:488, 1963.
13. Nikolic V. On the relationship between the ethmoid labyrinth, the frontal sinus and the bullous protrusions in the frontal sinus. Rad Med Fak Zagreb 11:141, 1963; cited in Salinger S. The paranasal sinuses. Summary of listings in the Index Medicus for 1964. Laryngoscope 75:1761, 1965.
14. Onödi A. Accessory Sinuses of the Nose in Children. New York, William Wood, 1911.
15. Peter K. Vergleichende Anatomie und Entwicklungsgeschichte der Nase und Ihr Nebenhohlen. In Denker A, Kahler O (eds). Handbuch der Hals-Nasen-Ohren-Heilkunde, Bd 1. Berlin, Springer, 1925.
16. Schaeffer JP. The sinus maxillaris and its relations in the embryo, child and adult man. Am J Anat 10:313, 1910.
17. Schaeffer JP. The Nose, Paranasal Sinuses, Nasolacrimal Passageways and Olfactory Organ in Man. Philadelphia, Blakiston's, 1920.
18. Simon E. Anatomy of the opening of the maxillary sinus. Arch Otol 29:640, 1939.
19. Van Alyea O. Nasal Sinuses, an Anatomic and Clinical Consideration. Baltimore, Williams & Wilkins, 1942.
20. Van Alyea O. The ostium maxillare: anatomic study of its surgical accessibility. Arch Otorhinolaryngol 24:553, 1936.
21. Vidic B. The postnatal development of the sphenoidal sinus and its spread into the dorsum sellae and posterior clinoid processes. Am J Roentgenol Radium Ther Nucl Med 104:177, 1968.
22. Zuckerkandl E. Normale und Pathologische Anatomie der Nasenhohle und Ihrer Pneumatischen Anhänge. Vienna, Wilhelm Braumuller, 1893.

34

Nasal Physiology

Wade R. Cressman, M.D., and Robert M. Naclerio, M.D.

The nose is the major portal of air exchange between the internal and external environment. The nose performs the vital functions of air-conditioning inspired air toward a temperature of 37°C and 100% relative humidity, providing local defense measures including immunologic functions, and filtering inhaled particulate matter and gases. Understanding normal physiology provides the basis for recognizing abnormalities.

Physiologic Anatomy

External Nose

The external nose is a pyramidal structure, situated in the midface, with its base on the facial skeleton and its apex projecting anteriorly. The paired nasal bones form the external nose superiorly and two sets of paired cartilage inferiorly. The upper lateral cartilages provide the shape of the middle third of the nose and support for the underlying nasal valve. The paired lower lateral (alar) cartilages are U-shaped and consist of a medial and a lateral crus. The medial crus forms the columella, and the lateral crus defines the shape of the nasal alae. Together, these crura maintain the patency of the underlying nasal vestibule (Fig. 34–1). Internally, the nasal pyramid is supported by the nasal septum.[43]

Nasal growth varies between the sexes. In girls, nasal growth reaches 84% of adult size by age 12 years; in boys, 87% of growth is attained by age 15 years.[25]

Malformations of the external nasal structure occur, and these can adversely affect nasal airflow. Complete or partial nasal agenesis, clefts, and facial dysostosis can occur and are typically seen in combination with a cleft lip.[101] The cleft lip-nose deformity is characterized by the triad of nasal tip deformity, dorsal displacement of the nasal dome, and buckling of the alar cartilages.[73]

Small muscle groups overlying the bony and cartilaginous structure contribute to the function of the external nose. The nasalis muscle extends laterally from the alae and functions to depress the nares. The anterior and posterior dilator naris, the depressor septinasi, and the levator labii superioris alaeque nasi all function to dilate the nostrils and thus decrease nasal resistance.[91] During periods of increased nasal breathing, such as during exercise, an increase in the activity of the dilating muscles occurs and aids in increasing the nasal airway patency.[38] These muscles are innervated by cranial nerve VII (facial nerve). Facial paralysis may thus lead to inspiratory collapse of the naris on the affected side and, hence, increased nasal resistance on that side.

Vestibule

The first part of the respiratory tract to contact the external environment is the vestibule. Unlike the remaining nasal cavity, the vestibule is lined with stratified squamous epithelium. The epithelium of the nasal vestibule changes into pseudostratified columnar epithelium. The vibrissae, thick hairs without piloerector muscles, function to filter out large particulate matter.[27] The anterior nasal glands, located near the junction of the squamous and respiratory epithelium, secrete serous mucus. Forced inspiration, as in sniffing, atomizes these secretions.[17] The vestibule also contains thermoreceptors that are not found in the portion of the nasal cavity lined by respiratory epithelium. On stimulation, this may lead to changes in nasal airway resistance.[76] Inspiring warm air leads to a decrease in nasal resistance, whereas inspiring cold air leads to the opposite effect.[46, 122] The vestibule is the most important area for sensing nasal airflow.[31, 32]

Nasal Valve and Airflow

The nasal valve, lying just posterior to the nasal vestibule, causes approximately half of the total resistance to inspired airflow from ambient air to the pulmonary alveoli[110] (Fig. 34–2). This valve is bounded laterally by the caudal end of the upper lateral cartilage, medially by the septum, and inferiorly by the lower rim of the piriform aperture.[138] The septum in this region contains erectile bodies and capacitance vessels, commonly known as swell bodies, that are rarely appreciated and that contribute functionally to the area of the valve.[33] The cross-sectional area of the nasal valve is 40 mm², whereas this area increases to 150 mm² in the nasal cavity.[34] The cross-sectional area of the nasal valve can be increased by contraction of the dilator naris muscle, thus leading to increased airflow.[91] Clinically, this is manifested as nasal flaring, as seen in periods of respiratory exertion. External

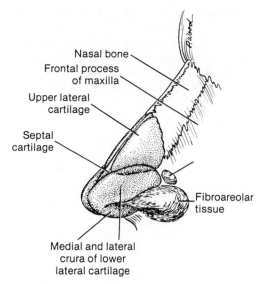

FIGURE 34–1. Lateral view of the nasal skeleton. (Adapted from Graney DO. Anatomy. In Cummings CW, Frederickson JM, Harker LA, et al [eds]. Otolaryngology—Head and Neck Surgery. St Louis, Mosby, 1986, pp 513–526.)

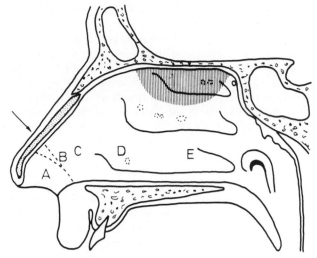

FIGURE 34–2. Lateral wall of nose, with hatched region representing olfactory area. Arrow points to area of nasal valve. Letters give epithelial type at specific locations: *A*, skin in nostril; *B*, squamous epithelium without microvilli; *C*, transitional epithelium with short microvilli; *D*, pseudostratified columnar epithelium with few ciliated cells; *E*, pseudostratified columnar epithelium with many ciliated cells. (From Proctor DF, Andersen IB [eds]. The Nose—Upper Airway Physiology and the Atmospheric Environment. Amsterdam, Elsevier Biomedical Press, 1982.)

nasal dilators, such as adhesive elastic strips placed externally over the nasal valve area, significantly increase the cross-sectional area of the nasal valve.[60, 103] Nasal dilators reduce obstructive episodes, as documented by sleep study in young infants.[124] Alar retraction halves nasal resistance.[34] Rhythmic increases in the tone of the dilator naris muscle occur just before the onset of inspiration, preceding diaphragmatic activation.[134] The nasal valve directs inspired air upward past the middle turbinate, where the inspiratory velocity of air approaches 18 m/second (gale force). Posteriorly, the airflow assumes a horizontal course through the main part of the nasal cavity, where the flow slows to 2 to 3 m/second[34, 136] (Fig. 34–3). The normal nose is capable of sustaining 20 to 30 L of airflow per minute; if larger volumes are required, oral breathing must supplement nasal breathing.

The nasal valve may act as a respiratory brake during expiration to allow adequate time for gas exchange at the alveoli.[65] Minor abnormalities in the area of the nasal valve, such as an anterior deviation of the nasal septum or mucosal edema, can lead to obstruction, whereas only major abnormalities located more posterior can lead to nasal airway compromise.[36] Laminar airflow occurs at the nasal valve, but this flow pattern is not maintained as air passes into the nasal cavity. If laminar flow were maintained in the nasal cavity, effective heat and water exchange between the nasal mucosa and the inspired air would occur less efficiently, because the central air column would not be modified during its passage through the nasal cavity.[35]

After inspired air passes through the nasal valve, the fast laminar flow is lost, and slower turbulent flow occurs. This slow turbulent flow allows inspired air to be in maximal contact with the warmer nasal mucosa, and, thus, ambient air is warmed to 34°C by the time it reaches the nasopharynx, with the greatest increase in temperature occurring in the nasal valve area.[80] This same mechanism

humidifies inspired air so that the relative humidity approaches 100% in the nasopharynx. The now cooler, dryer nasal mucosa reclaims the heat and moisture lost with inspiration during the low-flow portion of expiration in the nasal cavity.

During sleep, nasal airflow has a stimulant effect on breathing; ventilation is increased during nose breathing, compared with mouth breathing.[94] Nasal obstruction may predispose to the development of sleep apnea.[95, 150] Negative pressure applied to the nose of normal individuals will induce sleep apnea.[83]

Nasal resistance decreases with the intensity of exer-

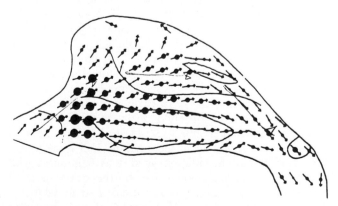

FIGURE 34–3. Schematic illustration of linear velocity and direction of inspired air. Direction is depicted by arrows and velocity by size of dots. (From Proctor DF, Andersen IB [eds]. The Nose—Upper Airway Physiology and the Atmospheric Environment. Amsterdam, Elsevier Biomedical Press, 1982.)

cise.[37, 41, 56, 111] This reaction is probably mediated by sympathetic vasoconstriction.

Alterations of the nasal valve during septorhinoplasty, such as partial resection of the upper lateral cartilages or low lateral osteotomies beginning at the lower lateral portion of the piriform aperture, can weaken or narrow the nasal valve and lead to nasal obstruction. Trimming of the inferior turbinates alters the dynamics of airflow, affecting the distribution of air to the olfactory region and the pattern of airflow through the nasal cavity.[131]

The nasal airway, although physically distinct from the lower airway, should not be separated from the latter conceptually, because changes in the nose affect the lower airway. Many similarities between the two exist, such as the epithelial lining and the immune response. Clinically, this is evident in children with reactive airway disease whose condition is exacerbated by rhinosinusitis. Total nasal obstruction leads to increased pulmonary resistance.[149]

In a healthy adult, total nasal airway resistance remains relatively constant, but the airflow of each nasal cavity varies in a reciprocal fashion (i.e., as the flow in one nasal cavity increases, the flow in the other decreases). This alteration in airflow, known as the nasal cycle, reflects changes in the vascular engorgement of the turbinates. The individual is unaware of this cycling, because the total nasal airway resistance remains constant. The pacemaker for the nasal cycle is located in the hypothalamus.[98] Young children, less than seven years old, do not have a consistent cyclic alteration and may have periods of bilateral nasal congestion, leading to an increase in total nasal airway resistance. This may lead to mouth breathing in the absence of other forms of nasal congestion, such as allergic rhinitis or adenoid hypertrophy. The lack of cycling may be secondary to an incompletely developed sympathetic nervous system.[142]

The adult pattern of nasal cycling begins to emerge between the ages of 7 and 10 years.[97] In adults, nasal cycling is believed to be controlled by the sympathetic nervous system, through fibers of the deep petrosal nerve that join fibers of the greater superficial petrosal nerve (pre-synaptic parasympathetic fibers) to be distributed through branches of the sphenopalatine ganglion; this cycling is eliminated by cervical sympathetic blockade.[57, 114, 147] Topical nasal decongestants lead to increased nasal patency by increasing the vasoconstrictor tone, thus lessening the congestion phase of the cycle.[54] The complaint of alternating nasal obstruction with an acute upper respiratory tract infection shows how the nasal cycle persists during illness.[49]

The dimensions of the nasal cavity are positively correlated with the age of the child. From birth to 2 months of age, the median length is 29.44 mm (range, 21.3 to 40.4 mm), and this median increases to 31.5 mm (range, 25.3 to 36.9 mm) in children aged 4 to 6 months. The anterior bony aperture, which can be the cause of nasal obstruction in neonates, has a normal median width of 13.24 mm (range, 8.8 to 17.2 mm).[39] If a 5 Fr. (OD 1.76 mm) cannot be passed through the anterior aperture, surgical intervention may be needed.[70]

Nasal airflow and cross-sectional area increase and nasal resistance decreases with age to 16 years, leveling off by age 20. Body size and gender affect nasal airflow rates; i.e., airflow rates are higher in boys and in individuals with a greater body mass index.[86] These studies emphasize the need to evaluate children in comparison to age-matched controls and not to adult norms.

Nasal Septum

The nasal septum divides the nasal cavity into two separate compartments, increasing the total mucosal surface area. It consists of an anterior cartilaginous portion, which provides support for the nasal tip, and a posterior bony portion formed by the perpendicular plate of the ethmoid and the vomer.

Structural deviations of the septum affect nasal airway resistance. Small anterior deviations at the level of the nasal valve can lead to significant nasal airway obstruction, whereas large deviations in the posterior portion of the nasal cavity may have no effect on airflow resistance.[36] Also, weakening or collapse of the septal cartilage that results from a septal abscess, surgical intervention, or Wegener granulomatosis leads to loss of nasal tip and nasal valve, thus compromising nasal airflow.[58]

There is concern that surgical correction of nasal septal abnormalities during childhood may have an adverse effect on midfacial growth by affecting the growth of septal cartilage and, hence, lead to long-term nasal functional and cosmetic abnormalities.[74] Studies on human cadavers ranging in age from birth to 62 years show that the septal cartilage completes growth by age 2, whereas bony growth of the perpendicular plate continues to the age of 36 years.[143] Nasal septal cartilage does not appear to be a primary growth center postnatally.[85] Growth centers have not been identified in either septal cartilage or perpendicular plate, as was previously thought, and therefore it is believed that even at a younger age conservative septal surgery is appropriate. Animal studies have shown that complete removal of the septum affects growth; however, clinical series in which resection was limited to the abnormal portion of the septum failed to demonstrate midfacial growth abnormalities.[85, 123, 133, 144] Conservative septal surgery for nasal airway obstruction may prevent the associated developmental abnormalities in children who are chronic mouth breathers, such as long, narrow, and retrognathic facies.

Turbinates

The turbinates are three, occasionally four, scroll-like projections from the lateral nasal wall (Fig. 34–4). The lower two, referred to as the inferior and middle turbinates, are functionally the most significant. Each turbinate consists of a bony frame with overlying respiratory epithelium. Like the nasal septum, these aid in increasing the mucosal surface area of the nasal cavity to approximately 100 to 200 cm^2.[136] Trimming of the anterior portion of the inferior turbinate can lead to a decrease in the total nasal resistance to airflow[146] by enlarging the nasal valve, but this should be considered only after potential causes for its enlargement have been investigated.

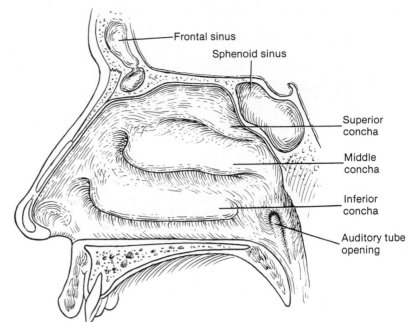

FIGURE 34–4. View of the lateral wall of the nasal cavity. (Adapted from Graney DO. Anatomy. In Cummings CW, Frederickson JM, Harker LA, et al [eds]. Otolaryngology—Head and Neck Surgery. St Louis, Mosby, 1986, pp 513–526.)

Histology

The nasal lining has a mucosal epithelial layer with an underlying submucosal layer. The mucosa consists of pseudostratified columnar epithelium containing goblet cells; ciliated and nonciliated columnar cells with microvilli; and, occasionally, intraepithelial mast cells, eosinophils, and lymphocytes[72] (Fig. 34–5). The cilia, which form 5 μm projections, are composed of a shaft covered by a cell membrane. The shaft, or axoneme, consists of microtubules arranged as nine peripheral doublets surrounding two central singlets. Nexin links connect adjacent pairs of doublets, and each doublet is connected to the central tubules by spokes. Each doublet has two dynein arms that contain ATPase, which provides the energy of motion.[116] The epithelial goblet cells produce secretions that contribute to the mucous blanket.[140] The epithelial cells provide a protective barrier, and they produce inflammatory substances and the secretory portion of immunoglobulin IgA.[87, 100]

The submucosa is separated from the epithelial layer by a basement membrane and contains nerves, blood vessels, and nasal glands. The submucosal nasal glands produce the greatest proportion of nasal secretions. The three major types of nasal glands are anterior serous glands, seromucous glands, and Bowman glands. The anterior nasal glands, located near the nasal vestibule, may aid in moisturizing the nasal mucosa as the inspired air spreads these thin secretions. The seromucous glands account for the largest proportion of nasal secretions. These glands are located throughout the nasal cavity, but the greatest concentration resides in the anterior nasal cavity. Depending on the cell type, these glands secrete either a serous or a mucous secretion. Bowman glands are serous glands in the olfactory region that aid in smell. Inflammatory mediators such as histamine, bradykinin, prostaglandins and cytokines lead to the pathophysiologic response caused by chemical or physical damage or antigen challenge. These mediators lead to nasal symptoms by: 1)

direct action on blood vessels and submucosal glands leading to increased glandular secretions, vasodilation, and increased vascular permeability; 2) sensorineural stimulation (maxillary and ophthalmic divisions of the fifth cranial nerve) leading to glandular secretions and nasal symptoms such as sneezing, itching, pain, and pressure;

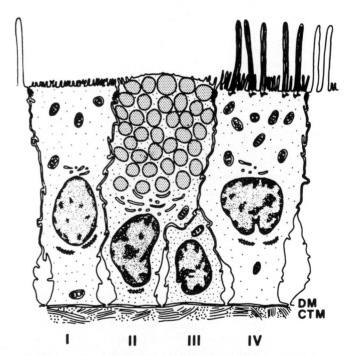

FIGURE 34–5. Transmission electron micrograph of different cell types in pseudostratified columnar epithelium. I, Nonciliated columnar cell with microvilli. II, Goblet cell with numerous mucous granules at its apical surface. III, Basal cell. IV, Ciliated columnar cell. DM, Basement membrane; CTM, connective tissue membrane. (From Proctor DF, Andersen IB [eds]. The Nose—Upper Airway Physiology and the Atmospheric Environment. Amsterdam, Elsevier Biomedical Press, 1982.)

and 3) central nervous system effects leading to head-ache, fatigue, and mood changes.[51] The submucosa does not contain lymphoid aggregates.[22]

Mucociliary Clearance

Mucociliary transport is the mechanism by which the nasal cavity clears itself of secretions and debris. The two major components of this system are the mucous blanket and the ciliated epithelial cells.

A 10- to 15-μm–deep mucous blanket, composed of secretions from goblet cells and submucosal glands and fluid transported across the epithelium, covers the entire nasal cavity.[148] This mucous layer consists of a sol phase, which is the watery periciliary layer, and a gel phase, which is the portion closest to air.

The nose is an excellent filter. Particles larger than 3 μm are filtered mostly in the nasal valve region, whereas particles between 3 and 0.5 μm are filtered by the nasal mucosa and are transported to the nasopharynx by ciliary flow. Filtration of the smaller particles and gases is low, and these pass into the lower respiratory tract. Therefore, surgical alterations to the nasal valve and turbinates may adversely affect the filtering ability of the nose.[125] In addition to its filtering ability, the mucous blanket serves important protective functions. It is the first line of defense against bacterial and viral infection. Submucosally produced IgA is the major immunoglobulin in nasal secretions, and it can prevent pathogens from adhering to the nasal mucosa and thus prevent their entry.[13] The mucous blanket also provides water for humidification.

Estimates of daily mucus production range from 0.1 to 0.3 mg/kg per day.[132] Most of the mucus is produced by the submucosal glands, in which serous glands outnumber mucous glands 8 to 1.[140] Mucin, a large glycoprotein, is produced by the submucosal glands. It consists of a polypeptide backbone with oligosaccharide side chains.[16, 117] Water binds to these side chains to form a matrix that lubricates and protects the mucosal surfaces. Other components of mucus include IgA, IgG, IgE, histamine, albumin, bacteria, lactoferrin, lysozyme, ions, and cellular debris.[11, 12, 26, 55, 71, 88, 102, 115, 145]

The mucous blanket moves posteriorly toward the nasopharynx, except in the region anterior to the inferior turbinate, where transport is anterior. Cilia can transport radiolabeled particles an average of 6 mm/minute, with a range of 1 to 20 mm/minute; thus, this transport can clear inhaled particles from the nasal cavity in 10 to 20 minutes.[4] There is no difference in transport time between adults and newborns.[8] Mucociliary transport times are enhanced with hypertonic saline irrigations and decreased in the presence of chronic sinusitis.[105, 120, 137] Sniffing, sneezing, and nose blowing aid in clearance of secretions.[69] Iodide-containing compounds and guaifenesin may decrease the viscosity of the mucus and, theoretically, lead to more effective clearance of secretions; anticholinergic agents increase the viscosity, thereby decreasing clearance.[21, 30, 45]

Cilia beat in a fixed direction that is determined by the orientation of the basal feet of the cilia. All cilia have

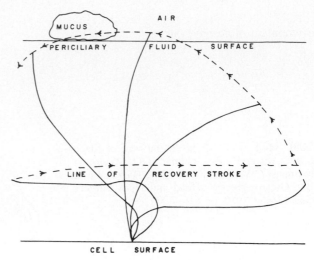

FIGURE 34–6. Motion of cilium during rapid forward beat and slower recovery phase. During forward beat, tip of cilium is at full extension and reaches out of periciliary fluid to contact mucus or gel layer. During recovery stroke, cilium is bent and returns to its starting position in periciliary layer (sol). This results in movement of mucus in only one direction. (From Proctor DF, Andersen IB [eds]. The Nose—Upper Airway Physiology and the Atmospheric Environment. Amsterdam, Elsevier Biomedical Press, 1982.)

a similar orientation.[132] There is a two-stroke pattern to their beat: an effector stroke, in which the cilia straighten, contact the gel phase, and move the mucus; and a recovery stroke, in which the cilia bend and move in the watery sol phase (Fig. 34–6). How ciliary movement is coordinated and synchronized is unknown. The ciliary beat frequency is approximately 1000 beats/minute.[116] It does not vary with age or location.[23, 77] The ciliary beat frequency does not decrease in chronic sinusitis; however, this condition can lead to a decrease in the number of ciliated cells and to ultrastructural changes in the cilia, such as compound cilia, peripheral and central microtubular abnormalities, and ciliary disorganization.[75, 77, 104] Endothelins, which are vasoactive peptides, may increase the ciliary beat frequency. Their exact role in normal and diseased states has not been fully elucidated.[2] The nasal decongestant phenylephrine has a ciliostimulatory effect, whereas benzalkonium chloride, a common preservative in nasal sprays, promotes ciliostasis and reduces mucociliary transport.[15, 109] Temperatures lower than 32°C or higher than 40°C lead to decreased ciliary beating.[59]

Clinically, in disorders of mucociliary transport, pooled secretions are present along the floor of the nasal cavity. In immotile cilia syndrome, there is a defect in the ciliary structure that prevents movement.[1] Common cold viruses can lead to impaired mucociliary transport for up to 2 weeks after inoculation by decreasing the number of ciliated cells.[106, 119] In chronic sinusitis, clearance of nasal secretions may be prolonged because of an increase in the viscosity of the secretions.[121] In cystic fibrosis, abnormal mucus is produced. At the epithelial cell surface, sodium and chloride ion transport is altered, leading to production of thick, tenacious mucus. In all of these disorders, stasis of secretions occurs and can lead to the development of chronic rhinosinusitis.

Mucociliary clearance functions in a wide range of environmental conditions. The nose transforms inspired air to nearly 100% relative humidity by the time it reaches the nasopharynx. Despite loss of both heat and water during inspiration, the two components are partially recovered during expiration, and the mucociliary clearance is not affected.[3]

Nasal Vasculature and Lymphatics

Both the internal and external carotid circulations contribute to the arterial supply of the nasal cavity[27] (Fig. 34–7). The anterior and posterior ethmoidal arteries, branches of the ophthalmic artery, enter the nose after passing through the orbit and the lamina papyracea. The sphenopalatine artery, a terminal branch of the external carotid artery, enters the nose through the posterior lateral inferior wall. These vessels anastomose with branches of the facial artery in the septal part of the vestibule.[42] This area is the most common site of epistaxis.[89] The veins of the nasal cavity run adjacent to the arteries and drain into the pterygoid and ophthalmic venous plexi, with some of the venous drainage subsequently passing intracranially into the cavernous sinus. This is a potential route for spread of infection.[27]

The arteries supplying the subepithelial and glandular zones arise from the perichondrial and periosteal arteries. They ascend toward the surface, giving branches to the cavernous plexi before forming a subepithelial network of fenestrated capillaries.[28] The fenestrations face the respiratory surface and are believed to be the major source of fluid for humidification.[28]

Alteration in blood flow into the cavernous sinusoids of the inferior turbinate, middle turbinate, and septum regulates nasal airflow.[27] The tone of the vessels in the arteriovenous anastomosis and venous drainage regulate the amount of blood in this valveless plexus. Changes in the size of the cavernous sinusoids also occur with recumbency,[112] with elevated levels of inspired carbon dioxide,[92] and with changes in inspired temperature.[46, 62] Vascular engorgement within the sinusoids appears clinically as nasal congestion.

Pharmacologic studies suggest the presence of alpha, beta, cholinergic, histamine, and hormone receptors on blood vessels. Alpha-adrenergic agents cause vasoconstriction in both the arteries and the cavernous plexus.[66, 93] Alpha$_2$-adrenergics constrict both, whereas alpha$_1$-adrenergics primarily affect the cavernous plexus. Phentolamine, an alpha-adrenergic antagonist, blocks alpha-induced vasoconstriction.[48] Nasal administration of beta-agonists causes vasodilatation and some increase in watery secretions.[66] Parasympathomimetics, such as methacholine, induce watery secretions and vasodilatations.[50] Ipratropium, an anticholinergic, completely blocks the watery secretions induced by methacholine, but not the vasodilatation.[20] Vasomotor rhinitis, a type of noninfectious, nonallergic rhinitis, produces nasal airway obstruction and profuse rhinorrhea. The cause of this is unknown. Histamine, administered topically, causes vasodilatation, an increase in vascular permeability, an increase in glandular secretion, and sneezing or a tickling sensation.[14] Premedication with histamine receptor type I (H$_1$) antagonists blocks the symptoms associated with histamine stimulation, with the exception of nasal congestion, which appears to be partially blocked by the addition of a histamine receptor type II (H$_2$) antagonist.[126] The nasal vasculature appears to be four times more sensitive to circulating epinephrine than is the heart.[90] Changes in the levels of circulating hormones during pregnancy can cause rhinitis, which clears post partum.[99] Sexual excitement,[139] hypothyroidism,[111] and emotional stress[67] also affect the nasal vasculature. The physiologic role of adrenergic and cholinergic agents in the normal control of nasal secretions is not certain.

Lymphatic vessels from the nasal vestibule and preturbinate area drain toward the external nose and then drain along the facial vessels to the submandibular lymph node

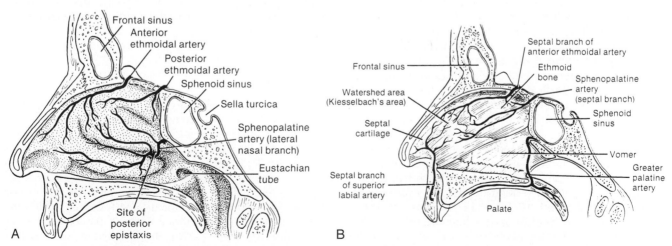

FIGURE 34–7. Blood supply to nasal septum (A) and lateral nasal wall (B). Kiesselbach area, site of most anterior epistaxis as well as most posterior epistaxis, is shown in respective diagrams. (Adapted from Graney DO. Anatomy. In Cummings CW, Frederickson JM, Harker LA, et al [eds]. Otolaryngology—Head and Neck Surgery. St Louis, Mosby, 1986, pp 513–526.)

group, whereas lymphatic vessels of the nasal fossae drain toward the nasopharynx. Two main collecting trunks, one high in the nasal vault and the other located inferiorly, drain toward and around the eustachian tube orifice and into the first-echelon nodal group, the lateral retropharyngeal lymph nodes.[118] These nodes lie along the bodies of the vertebrae and thus cannot be palpated. This pattern of flow explains the rare observation of palpable lymphadenopathy with rhinosinusitis. Lymphatic vessels from the maxillary sinus not only drain through the natural ostia, but in 57% of cases there is also transmural drainage to the nasal lymphatic vessels through bony gaps.[68]

Nervous System

Neuronal control plays a major role in the local regulation of airflow, blood flow, and glandular secretion. Reflexes originating within the nose have distal effects, e.g., sneezing. After irritation of a sensory receptor (to date, only mechanical and pain receptors have been identified in the nasal mucosa[29]), the sneeze propagates one or more spasmodic inspirations. The glottis and velopharyngeal apertures close, allowing an increase in lower-airway pressure. These structures suddenly open, allowing a blast of air to escape through the nose and mouth, in an attempt to clear the nasal passage.[24] This reflex occurs with viral infection,[64] irritants,[7] exposure to allergens,[102] and, in some individuals, exposure to bright light.[52] The last exemplifies afferent sensory innervation of the nasal cavity.

Neuronal stimulation originating within the nose can affect function elsewhere. Mucosal irritation can initiate the submersion reflex, which is marked by apnea, glottic closure, bradycardia, and vasoconstriction,[7, 10, 44] in an attempt to protect the heart and brain by redistributing blood flow to these vital organs.[40] Cooling of the skin causes nasal vasoconstriction, whereas warming of the skin causes an increase in nasal temperature.[46] The increase in temperature is blocked by lidocaine and appears to be secondary to a loss of sympathetic tone.

A nasopulmonary reflex has been hypothesized as explanation of a relationship between events occurring in the upper and lower airways. Sercer[128] suggested the existence of such a reflex after he observed that blowing air into one nostril induced expansion of the ipsilateral thorax. In another study,[79] bronchoconstriction occurred in individuals who had silica dust blown into their nose; and, in one subject who had previously undergone a unilateral trigeminal nerve resection, bronchoconstriction occurred only when dust was blown through the neurologically intact side.[78] The nasopulmonary reflex is also postulated to be responsible for the hypoxia and hypercapnia seen with posterior nasal packing. Allergic inflammation, whether by allergen provocation or seasonal exposure, increases bronchial reactivity. Some investigators, however, have been unable to confirm nasopulmonary reflex.[127, 130]

Fibers of the parasympathetic and sympathetic nervous systems enter the nose through the sphenopalatine foramina. The parasympathetic fibers originate in the superior salivary nucleus of the midbrain and then travel with the fibers of the seventh cranial nerve. At the geniculate ganglion in the temporal bone, these fibers separate to form the greater superficial petrosal nerve. These fibers traverse the floor of the anterior cranial fossa and the pterygomaxillary space and synapse in the sphenopalatine ganglion. From this point, parasympathetic fibers are distributed to mucosal and submucosal appendages by branches from the sphenopalatine ganglion.[18, 47] Stimulation of the parasympathetic nerves induces primarily glandular secretions and some vasodilatation, effects that occur after nasal challenge with cholinergic agents.[20] Sympathetic fibers originate in the hypothalamus. These fibers synapse in the superior cervical ganglion and then travel with the carotid plexus until they join the parasympathetic fibers from the seventh cranial nerve to form, in the pterygoid canal, the vidian nerve.[19] The sympathetic fibers, in contrast to the parasympathetic, do not synapse in the sphenopalatine ganglion. Stimulation of the sympathetic system causes vasoconstriction, with a concomitant decrease in nasal airway resistance.[6] Exercise stimulates the sympathetic system, causing an increase in nasal airflow, which can be blocked by an anesthetic injection into the superior cervical ganglion.[113] Reserpine, an antihypertensive agent that blocks sympathetic innervation, induces nasal congestion.[114]

In addition to the classic cholinergic and adrenergic innervation, the nerve supply to the nose consists of a nonadrenergic, noncholinergic (NANC) system. NANC nerves, which were first described in the gastrointestinal tract, have subsequently been found in the upper respiratory system.[9] The neurotransmitters of the NANC system may be neuropeptides, such as vasoactive intestinal polypeptide (VIP), substance P, neurokinins, or calcitonin-gene-related peptide. The arteries, sinusoids, veins, and arteriovenous anastomoses have been shown to have different patterns of neuropeptide staining. Furthermore, the vessels of rhinitic subjects have a richer innervation than do those of nonrhinitic subjects.[53] An increase in VIP immunoreactive nerves has been reported in the nasal mucosa of patients with vasomotor rhinitis.[84, 141] A decrease in neuropeptide release in response to nasal provocation with capsaicin occurs in patients with nasal polyps.[63] Although the pathophysiologic role of this system is unclear, a further understanding may lead to therapeutic advances.

Olfaction

The roof of the nasal cavity and the area extending inferiorly for 8 to 10 mm along the septum and lateral nasal wall is the olfactory area (see Fig. 32–2). Sniffing brings inspired air into this part of the nasal cavity. The olfactory epithelium contains bipolar neurons from the first cranial (olfactory) nerve.[72] Like the nasal mucosa, the olfactory epithelium is covered by a layer of mucus containing IgA and IgM lactoferrin, and lysozyme, which may aid in preventing intracranial entry of pathogens through the cribriform plate.[96] Also, the ophthalmic and maxillary divisions of the fifth cranial nerve participate in olfaction by mediating a "common chemical sense." This system has little ability for odor identification, but may provide the afferent limb for a generalized nasal response, such as hypersecretion, sneezing, and mucosal edema.[129]

Little is known of the mechanisms of odor differentiation and recognition. Odorant-binding proteins have been identified that act as specific receptors for odorant molecules.[108] These binding proteins help transport the lipophilic odorant molecules through the hydrophilic mucus to the olfactory epithelium, and they may aid in odorant transport to the olfactory receptors that is faster than by simple diffusion.[107] The first step in olfactory processing occurs when the odorant molecules contact the cilia of the receptor cells, whose axons pass through the cribriform plate and into the central nervous system to synapse in the olfactory bulb. From there, projections travel to the piriform cortex, anterior olfactory nucleus, amygdala, entorhinal cortex, hippocampus, hypothalamus, and thalamus.[82]

Although olfaction is better developed in low mammals, humans use the sense of smell to perceive taste, warn of impending hazards, and enhance social interactions. Olfactory learning may begin in newborns within the first 48 hours of life.[135] Congenital nasal obstruction such as found in choanal atresia might prevent early sensory exposures that may be needed for normal central olfactory development.[61]

Olfactory disturbances may arise from inflammatory causes such as rhinosinusitis, viral illness or allergic rhinitis. Although the altered airflow found in these conditions may lead to the olfactory deficits, the olfactory mucosa can mount an inflammatory reaction that may lead to impaired olfaction.[81] Trauma such as foreign bodies, nasal or skull base surgery, or closed head injury; congenital or developmental causes such as adenoidal hypertrophy or Kallman or Turner syndrome; metabolic disorders such as vitamin A or thiamin deficiency; or neoplasm of the nasal or cranial cavity also may lead to olfactory disturbances.

REFERENCES

1. Afzelius B. The immotile cilia syndrome and other ciliary diseases. Int Rev Exp Pathol 19:1, 1979.
2. Amble FR, Lindberg SOH, McCaffrey TV, et al. Mucociliary function and endothelins 1, 2 and 3. Otolaryngol Head Neck Surg 109:634, 1993.
3. Anderson I, Lundqvist G, Jensen PL, et al. Human response after 78 hours' exposure to dry air. Arch Environ Health 29:319, 1974.
4. Anderson I, Lundqvist G, Jensen PL, et al. Human response to controlled levels of sulfur dioxide. Arch Environ Health 28:31, 1974.
5. Anderson I, Lundqvist G, Proctor DF. Human nasal mucosal function under four controlled humidities. Am Rev Respir Dis 119:619, 1979.
6. Angaard A, Denset O. Adrenergic innervation of the nasal mucosa in the cat. Acta Otolaryngol (Stockh) 78:232, 1974.
7. Angell-Jumes JE, Daly M de B. Nasal reflexes. Proc R Soc Med 62:1287, 1969.
8. Armengot M, Basterra J. Nasal mucociliary function in the normal newborn. Int J Pediatr Otolaryngol 22:109, 1991.
9. Barnes PJ. Neuropeptides in the lung: localization, function and pathophysiological implications. J Allergy Clin Immunol 79:285, 1987.
10. Barrow CS, Alarie Y, Stock MF. Sensory irritation and incapacitation evoked by thermal decomposition products of polymers and comparisons with known sensory irritants. Arch Environ Health 33:79, 1978.
11. Bascom R, Wachs M, Naclerio RM, et al. Basophil influx occurs after nasal antigen challenge: effects of topical corticosteroid pretreatment. J Allergy Clin Immunol 81:580, 1988.
12. Baumgarten CR, Togias AG, Naclerio RM, et al. Influx of kininogens into nasal secretions following antigen challenge of allergic individuals. J Clin Invest 76:191, 1985.
13. Bellanti JA, Artenstein MS, Beuscher EL. Characterization of virus-neutralizing antibodies in human serum and nasal secretions. J Immunol 94:344, 1965.
14. Bentley AJ, Jackson RT. Changes in the patency of the upper nasal passage induced by histamine and antihistamine. Laryngoscope 80:1859, 1970.
15. Bernstein IL. Is the use of benzalkonium chloride as a preservative for nasal formulations a safety concern? A cautionary note based on compromised mucociliary transport. J Allergy Clin Immunol 105:39, 2000.
16. Boat TF, Cheng PW, Iyer RN, et al. Human respiratory tract secretions. Mucous glycoproteins of nonpurulent tracheobronchial secretions and sputum of patients with bronchitis and cystic fibrosis. Arch Biochem Biophys 177:95, 1976.
17. Bojsen-Moller F. Glandulae nasales anteriores in the human nose. Ann Otol Rhinol Laryngol 74:363, 1965.
18. Boles R. Neuronanatomy for the otolaryngologist. In Paparella M, Shumrick D (eds). Otolaryngology. Philadelphia, WB Saunders, 1970, pp 148–151.
19. Boles R. Neuronanatomy for the otolaryngologist. In Paparella M, Shumrick D (eds). Otolaryngology. Philadelphia, WB Saunders, 1980, pp 166–170.
20. Borum P. Nasal methacholine challenge. A test for the measurement of nasal reactivity. J Allergy Clin Immunol 63:253, 1979.
21. Boyd EM. Respiratory tract fluid and expectorants. Pharmacol Rev 6:521, 1964.
22. Brandtzaeg P. Immune function of human nasal mucosa and tonsils in health and disease. In Bienenstock J (ed). Immunology of the Lung and Upper Respiratory Tract. New York, McGraw-Hill, 1984.
23. Braverman I, Wright ED, Wang CG, et al. Human nasal ciliary-beat frequency in normal chronic sinusitis subjects. J Otolaryngol 27:145, 1998.
24. Brubaker A. The physiology of sneezing. JAMA 73:585, 1919.
25. Buck DL, Brown CM. A longitudinal study of nose growth from ages 6 to 18. Ann Plast Surg 18:310, 1987.
26. Butler WT, Rossen RP, Waldmann TA. Mechanism of appearance of immunoglobulin A in nasal secretions in man. J Clin Invest 46:1883, 1967.
27. Cauna N. Blood and nerve supply of the nasal lining. In Proctor DF, Anderson IB (eds). The Nose. Amsterdam, Elsevier Biomedical Press, 1982, pp 45–70.
28. Cauna N, Hinderer KH. Fine structure of blood vessels of the human nasal respiratory mucosa. Ann Otol Rhinol Laryngol 78:865, 1969.
29. Cauna N, Hinderer KH, Wentges RT. Sensory receptor organs of the human nasal respiratory mucosa. Am J Anat 124:187, 1969.
30. Chodosh S. Objective sputum changes associated with glyceryl guaiacolate in chronic bronchial diseases. Bull Physiopathol Respir 9:452, 1973.
31. Clarke RW, Jones AS. Nasal airflow receptors: the relative importance of temperature and tactile stimulation. Clin Otolaryngol 17:388, 1992.
32. Clarke RW, Jones AS, Charters P, et al. The role of mucosal receptors in the nasal sensation of airflow. Clin Otolaryngol 17:383, 1991.
33. Cole P. Biophysics of nasal airflow: A review. Am J Rhinol 14:245–249, 2000.
34. Cole P. Nasal and oral airflow resistors. Arch Otolaryngol Head Neck Surg 118:790, 1992.
35. Cole P. Upper respiratory airflow. In Proctor DF, Anderson I (eds). The Nose-Upper Airway Physiology and the Atmospheric Environment. New York, Elsevier Science Publishing, 1982, pp 163–189.
36. Cole P, Chaban R, Naito K, et al. The obstructive nasal septum. Arch Otolaryngol Head Neck Surg 114:410, 1988.
37. Cole P, Forsyth R, Haight JSJ. Effects of cold air and exercise on nasal patency. Ann Otol Rhinol Laryngol 92:116, 1983.
38. Connel DC, Fregosi RF. Influence of nasal airflow and resistance

on nasal dilator muscle activities during exercise. J Appl Physiol 74:2529, 1993.

39. Contencin P, Gumpert L, Sleiman J, et al. Nasal fossae dimensions in the neonate and young infant. Arch Otolaryngol Head Neck Surg 125:777, 1999.
40. Craig AB. Underwater swimming and loss of consciousness. JAMA 176:255, 1961.
41. Dallimore NS, Eccles R. Changes in human nasal resistance associated with exercise, hyperventilation and rebreathing. Acta Otolaryngol (Stockh) 84:416, 1977.
42. Dawes JDK, Pritchard M. Studies of the vascular arrangement of the nose. J Anat 87:311, 1953.
43. Dion MC, Jafek BW, Tobin CJ. The anatomy of the nose: external support. Arch Otolaryngol 104:145, 1978.
44. Dixon WE, Brodie TG. Contributions to the physiology of the lungs. J Physiol 29:97, 1903.
45. Dolovich J, Kennedy L, Vickerson F, et al. Control of the hypersecretion of vasomotor rhinitis by topical ipratropium bromide. J Allergy Clin Immunol 80:274, 1987.
46. Drettner B. Vascular reactions of the human nasal mucosa on exposure to cold. Acta Otolaryngol Suppl (Stockh) 166:1, 1961.
47. Eccles R. Neurological and pharmacological considerations. In Proctor DF, Anderson IB (eds). The Nose. Amsterdam, Elsevier Biomedical Press, 1982, pp 191–214.
48. Eccles R, MacClean AG. Relaxation of smooth muscle following contraction elicited by sympathetic nerve stimulation in vivo. Br J Pharmacol 61:551, 1977.
49. Eccles R, Reilly M, Eccles KS. Changes in the amplitude of the nasal cycle associated with symptoms of acute upper respiratory infection. Acta Otolaryngol 116:77, 1996.
50. Eccles R, Wilson H. The parasympathetic secretory nerves of the nose of the cat. J Physiol 230:213, 1983.
51. Eccles R. Pathophysiology of nasal symptoms. Am J Rhinol 14:335, 2000.
52. Evertt HC. Sneezing in response to light. Neurology 14:483, 1964.
53. Figueroa JM, Mansilla E, Suburo AM. Innervation of nasal turbinate blood vessels in rhinitic and nonrhinitic children. Am J Respir Crit Care Med 157:1959–1966, 1998.
54. Flanagan P, Eccles R. Physiological versus pharmacological decongestion of the nose in healthy human subjects. Acta Otolaryngol 118:110, 1998.
55. Fleming A. On a remarkable bacteriolytic element found in tissues and secretions. Proc R Soc Lond Biol 93:306, 1922.
56. Forsyth RD, Cole P, Shepard RJ. Exercise and nasal patency. J Appl Physiol 55:860, 1983.
57. Fowlefer EP. Unilateral vasomotor rhinitis due to interference with cervical sympathetic system. Arch Otolaryngol 37:710, 1943.
58. Gray L. Deviated nasal septum. III. Its influence on the physiology and disease of the nose and ears. J Laryngol 81:953, 1967.
59. Green A, Smallman LA, Logan AC, et al. The effect of temperature on nasal ciliary beat frequency. Clin Otolaryngol 20:178, 1995.
60. Griffin JW, Hunter G, Ferguson D, et al. Physiologic effects of an external nasal dilator. Laryngoscope 107:1235, 1997.
61. Gross-Isseroff R, Ophir D, Marshak G, et al. Olfactory function following late repair of choanal atresia. Laryngoscope 99:1165, 1989.
62. Gsic B, Krajina Z, Lakic L, et al. Damage of the respiratory mucous membrane of rats exposed to cold. Acta Otolaryngol (Stockh) 57:342, 1964.
63. Gungor A, Baroody FM, Naclerio RM, et al. Decreased neuropeptide release may play a role in the pathogenesis of nasal polyps. Otolaryngol Head Neck Surg 121:585, 1999.
64. Gwaltney JM Jr. The common cold. In Mandell GL, Douglas RG Jr, Bennett JE (eds). Principles and Practice of Infectious Disease. New York, John Wiley, 1979, pp 429–434.
65. Hairfield WM, Warren DW, Hinton VA, et al. Inspiratory and expiratory effects on nasal breathing. Cleft Palate J 24:183, 1987.
66. Hall LJ, Jackson RT. Effects of alpha and beta adrenergic agonists on nasal blood flow. Ann Otol Rhinol Laryngol 77:1120, 1986.
67. Holmes TH, Goddell H, Wolf S, et al. The Nose: An Experimental Study of Reactions within the Nose in Human Subjects During Varying Life Experiences. Springfield, IL, Charles C Thomas, 1950.
68. Hosemann W, Kühnel TH, Burchard AK, et al. Histochemical detection of lymphatic drainage pathways in the middle nasal meatus. Rhinology 36:50, 1998.
69. Hounam RF. The removal of particles from the nasopharyngeal (NP) compartment of the respiratory tract by nose blowing and swabbing. Health Phys 28:743, 1975.
70. Hui Y, Friedberg J, Crysdale WS. Congenital nasal pyriform aperture stenosis as a presenting feature of holoprosencephaly. Int J Pediatr Otorhinolaryngol 31:263, 1995.
71. Ishizaka K, Newcomb RM. Presence of IgE in nasal washes and sputum from asthmatic patients. J Allergy 46:197, 1970.
72. Jafek BW. Ultrastructure of the human nasal mucosa. Laryngoscope 93:1576, 1983.
73. Jaffe BF. Classification and management of anomalies of the nose. Otolaryngol Clin North Am 14:989, 1981.
74. Jennes ML, Waterbury C. Corrective nasal surgery in children: long term results. Arch Otolaryngol 79:145, 1964.
75. Joki S, Toskala E, Saano V, et al. Correlation between ciliary beat frequency and the structure of ciliated epithelia in pathologic human nasal mucosa. Laryngoscope 108:426, 1998.
76. Jones AS, Wight RG, Durham LH. The distribution of thermoreceptors within the nasal cavity. Clin Otolaryngol 14:235, 1989.
77. Jorissen M, Willems T, Van der Schueren B. Nasal ciliary beat frequency is age independent. Laryngoscope 108:1042, 1998.
78. Kaufman J, Chen JC, Wright GW. The effect of trigeminal resection on reflex bronchoconstriction after nasal and nasopharyngeal irritation in man. Am Rev Respir Dis 101:768, 1970.
79. Kaufman J, Wright GW. The effect of nasal and nasopharyngeal irritation on airway resistance in man. Am Rev Respir Dis 100:626, 1969.
80. Keck T, Leiacker R, Riechelmann H, et al. Temperature profile in the nasal cavity. Laryngoscope 110:651, 2000.
81. Keru RC. Chronic sinusitis and anosmia: pathologic changes in the olfactory mucosa. Laryngoscope 110:1071, 2000.
82. Kimmelman CP. Clinical review of olfaction. Am J Otolaryngol 14:227, 1993.
83. King ED, O'Donnell CP, Smith PL, et al. A model of obstructive sleep apnea in normal humans. Am J Respir Crit Care Med 161:1979, 2000.
84. Kurrian SS, Blank MA, Sheppard MN, et al. Vasoactive intestinal peptide (VIP) in vasomotor rhinitis. IRCS Med Sci 11:425, 1983.
85. Kvinusland S. The relationship between the cartilaginous nasal septum and maxillary growth during human fetal life. Cleft Palate J 7:523, 1970.
86. Laine-Alava MT, Minkkinen UK. Variation of nasal respiratory pattern with age during growth and development. Laryngoscope 107:386, 1997.
87. Leikauf GD, Veki IF, Nadel JA. Bradykinin stimulates chloride secretion and prostaglandin E_2 release by canine tracheal epithelium. Am J Physiol 248:F48, 1985.
88. Lorin MI, Gaerlan PF, Mandel ID. Quantitative composition of nasal secretions in normal subjects. J Lab Clin Med 80:275, 1972.
89. Maceri DR. Nasal trauma. In Cummings CW, Fredrickson JM, Harker LA, et al (eds). Otolaryngology-Head and Neck Surgery. St Louis, CV Mosby, 1986, pp 611–624.
90. Malcolmson KG. The vasomotor activities of the nasal mucous membrane. J Laryngol Otol 73:73, 1959.
91. Mann DG, Sasaki CT, Suzuki M, et al. Dilator naris muscle. Arch Otolaryngol 86:362, 1977.
92. McCaffrey TV, Kern EB. Response of nasal airway resistance to hypercapnia and hypoxia in man. Ann Otol Rhinol Laryngol 88:247, 1979.
93. McLaurin JW, Shipman WF, Rosedale R Jr. Oral decongestants. Laryngoscope 71:54, 1961.
94. McNichols WT, Coffey M, Boyle T. Effects of nasal airflow on breathing during sleep in normal humans. Am Rev Respir Dis 147:620, 1993.
95. McNichols WT, Tarlo S, Cole P, et al. Obstructive apneas during sleep in patients with seasonal allergic rhinitis. Am Rev Respir Dis 126:625, 1982.
96. Mellert TK, Getchell ML, Sparks L, et al. Characterization of the immune barrier in human olfactory mucosa. Otolaryngol Head Neck Surg 106:181, 1992.
97. Mennella JA, Beauchamp GK. Developmental changes in nasal airflow patterns. Acta Otolaryngol (Stockh) 112:1025, 1992.

98. Mirza N, Kroger H, Doty RL. Influence of age on the nasal cycle. Laryngoscope 107:62, 1997.

99. Mohun M. Incidence of vasomotor rhinitis during pregnancy. Arch Otolaryngol 37:699, 1943.

100. Mostov KE, Blobel G. A transmembrane precursor of secretory component. The receptor for transcellular transport of polymeric immunoglobulins. J Biol Chem 257:11816, 1982.

101. Myer CM, Cotton RT. Nasal obstruction in the pediatric patient. Pediatrics 72:766, 1983.

102. Naclerio RM, Meier HL, Kagey-Sobotka A, et al. Mediator release after airway challenge with antigen. Am Rev Respir Dis 128:597, 1983.

103. Ng BA, Mamikoglu B, Ahmed MS, et al. The effect of external nasal dilators as measured by acoustic rhinometry. Ear Nose Throat J 77:840, 1998.

104. Nuutinen J, Rauch-Toskala E, Saano V, et al. Ciliary beating frequency in chronic sinusitis. Arch Otolaryngol Head Neck Surg 119:645, 1993.

105. Passali D, Ferri R, Becchini G. Alterations of nasal mucociliary transport in patients with hypertrophy of the anterior turbinates, deviations of the nasal septum and chronic sinusitis. Eur Arch Otorhinolaryngol 256:335, 1999.

106. Pederson M, Sakakura Y, Winther B, et al. Nasal mucociliary transport, number of ciliated cells and beating patterns in naturally occurring colds. Eur J Respir Dis Suppl 128:355, 1983.

107. Pevsner J, Reed RR, Feinstein PG, et al. Molecular cloning of odorant binding protein: member of a ligand carrying family. Science 241:336, 1988.

108. Pevsner J, Trifiletti RR, Strittmatter SM, et al. Isolation and characterization of an olfactory receptor protein for odorant pyrazines. Proc Natl Acad Sci USA 82:3050, 1985.

109. Phillips PP, McCaffrey TV, Keru EB. The in vivo and in vitro effect of phenylephrine on nasal ciliary beat frequency and mucociliary transport. Otolaryngol Head Neck Surg 103:558, 1990.

110. Proctor DF, Adams GK. Physiology and pharmacology of nasal function and mucus secretion. Pharmacol Ther 2B:492, 1976.

111. Proetz AW. Further observations of effects of thyroid insufficiency on the nasal mucosa. Laryngoscope 60:627, 1950.

112. Rao SS, Potdar A. Nasal airflow with body in various positions. J Appl Physiol 28:162, 1970.

113. Richerson HB, Seebohm PM. Nasal airway response to exercise. J Allergy 41:269, 1968.

114. Rooker DN, Jackson RT. The effects of certain drugs, cervical sympathetic stimulation, and section on nasal patency. Ann Otol Rhinol Laryngol 78:403, 1967.

115. Rossen RD, Schade AL, Butler WT, et al. The proteins in nasal secretions: a longitudinal study of the IgA, IgG, albumin, siderophilin, and total protein concentrations in nasal washes from adult male volunteers. J Clin Invest 45:768, 1966.

116. Rossmann CM, Lee R, Forrest JB, et al. Nasal ciliary ultrastructure and function in patients with primary ciliary dyskinesia compared with that in normal subjects and in subjects with various respiratory diseases. Am Rev Respir Dis 129:161, 1984.

117. Roussel P, Degand P, Lamblin G, et al. Biochemical definition of human tracheobronchial mucus. Lung 154:241, 1978.

118. Rouviere H. Anatomy of the Human Lymphatic System. A Compendium. Ann Arbor, MI, Edward Brothers, 1938.

119. Sakakura Y. Changes of mucociliary function during colds. Eur J Respir Dis Suppl 128:348, 1983.

120. Sakakura Y, Majima Y, Harada T. Nasal mucociliary transport of chronic sinusitis in children. Arch Otolaryngol Head Neck Surg 118:1234, 1992.

121. Sakakura Y, Ukai K, Majima Y, et al. Nasal mucociliary clearance under various conditions. Acta Otolaryngol (Stockh) 96:167, 1983.

122. Salman SD, Proctor DF, Swift DL, et al. Nasal resistance: description of a method and effect of temperature and humidity changes. Ann Otol Rhinol Laryngol 80:736, 1971.

123. Sarnat BG, Wexler MR. The snout after resection of nasal septum in adult rabbits. Arch Otolaryngol 86:463, 1967.

124. Scharf MB, Berkowitz DV, McDannold MD, et al. Effects of an external nasal dilator on sleep and breathing patterns in newborn infants with and without congestion. J Pediatr 129:804, 1996.

125. Schwab JA, Zenkel M. Filtration of particles in the human nose. Laryngoscope 108:120, 1998.

126. Secher C, Kirkegaard J, Borum P, et al. Significance of H_1 and H_2 receptors in the human nose. Rationale for topical use of combined antihistamine preparations. J Allergy Clin Immunol 70:211, 1982.

127. Sedee GA. Relation between the functions of nose and lung on the same side of the body. Int Rhinol 7:7, 1969.

128. Sercer A. Investigations sur l'influence reflectorie de la cavité nasale sur le poumon de la meme cote. Acta Otolaryngol (Stockh) 14:82, 1930.

129. Silver NL, Finger TE. The trigeminal system. In Getchell TV, Bartolshuck LM, Doty RL, et al (eds). Smell and Taste in Health and Disease. New York, Raven Press, 1991, pp 97–108.

130. Silverstein EB, Lewis JT, Quenelle DJ. Study of the physiologic relationship of lower and upper airways with xenon-133. Ann Otol Rhinol Laryngol 89:62, 1980.

131. Simmen D, Scherrer JL, Moe K, et al. A dynamic and direct visualization model for the study of nasal airflow. Arch Otolaryngol Head Neck Surg 125:1015, 1999.

132. Sleigh MA. The nature and action of respiratory tract cilia. In Brain JD, Proctor DF, Reid LM (eds). Respiratory Defense Mechanisms. New York, Marcel Dekker, 1977, pp 247–288.

133. Stenstrom SJ, Thilander BL. Effects of nasal septal cartilage resections on young guinea pigs. Plast Reconstr Surg 45:160, 1970.

134. Strohl KP, Hensley MJ, Hallet M, et al. Activation of the upper airway muscle before onset of inspiration in normal humans. J Appl Physiol 49:638, 1980.

135. Sullivan RM, Taborsky-Barba S, Mendoza R, et al. Olfactory classical conditioning in neonates. Pediatr 87:511, 1991.

136. Swift DL, Proctor DF. Access of air to the respiratory tract. In Brain DJ, Proctor DF, Reid LM (eds). Respiratory Defense Mechanisms. New York, Marcel Dekker, 1977, pp 63–93.

137. Talbot AR, Herr TM, Parsons DS. Mucociliary clearance and buffered hypertonic saline solution. Laryngoscope 107:500, 1997.

138. Tarabichi M, Fanous N. Finite element analysis of airflow in the nasal valve. Arch Otolaryngol Head Neck Surg 119:638, 1993.

139. Taylor M. The origin and function of nasal mucus. Laryngoscope 84:612, 1974.

140. Tos M. Goblet cells and glands in the nose and paranasal sinuses. In Proctor DF, Anderson IB (eds). The Nose. Amsterdam, Elsevier Biomedical Press, 1982, pp 99–144.

141. Uddman R, Sundler F. Vasoactive intestinal peptide nerves in human upper respiratory tract. ORL J Otorhinolaryngol Relat Spec 41:221, 1979.

142. van Cauwenberge PB, Deleye L. Nasal cycle in children. Arch Otolaryngol Head Neck Surg 110:108, 1984.

143. Van Loosen J, Van Zanten GA, Howard CV, et al. Growth characteristics of the human nasal septum. Rhinology 34:78, 1996.

144. Walker PJ, Crysdale WS, Farkas LG. External septorhinoplasty in children: outcome and effect on growth of septal excision and reimplantation. Arch Otolaryngol 119:984, 1993.

145. Watson ED, Hoffman NJ, Simmens RW, Rosebury T. Aerobic and anaerobic bacterial counts of nasal washings: presence of organisms resembling Corynebacterium acnes. J Bacteriol 83:144, 1962.

146. Wight RG, Jones AS, Clegg RT. A comparison of anterior and radical trimming of the inferior nasal turbinates and the effects on nasal resistance to airflow. Clin Otolaryngol 13:223, 1988.

147. Wilson H, Yates MS. Bilateral nasal vascular responses to unilateral sympathetic stimulation. Acta Otolaryngol (Stockh) 85:105, 1978.

148. Wilson WR, Allansmith MR. Rapid, atraumatic method for obtaining nasal mucus samples. Ann Otol Rhinol Laryngol 85:391, 1976.

149. Wyllie JW, Kern EB, O'Brien PC, et al. Alteration of pulmonary function associated with artificial nasal obstruction. Surg Forum Mayo Clin 27:535, 1976.

150. Zwilich AN, Pickett CK, Hanson FN, et al. Disturbed sleep and prolonged apnea during nasal obstruction in normal man. Am Rev Respir Dis 124:158, 1981.

35

Methods of Examination

Reza Rahbar, D.M.D., M.D., and Gerald B. Healy, M.D.

A careful history and a complete physical examination are essential in evaluation of any disease process. History is compiled by combining information from the patient, parent, caregivers, referring physician, and all other appropriate sources. Examination of the child requires a careful and gentle approach, with parental participation. All examinations should be performed with the child in a secure and comfortable position, possibly sitting in a parent's lap.

The purpose of this chapter is to provide information and a framework for evaluation of the face, nose, sinuses, and nasopharynx in the pediatric population.

Clinical Examination

The Face

Any lesion in the region of the face should prompt questions regarding its duration, change in size, the presence or absence of pain, any evidence of infection, and history of trauma. The presence of facial swelling should lead to careful examination of the face, salivary glands, oral cavity, teeth, pharynx, and nasopharynx. Disease processes in the deep facial and neck areas may present as distortion of the parapharyngeal structures and medial displacement of the tonsils. The presence of trismus may indicate pathologic conditions involving the pterygoid muscles. Facial asymmetry secondary to seventh cranial nerve dysfunction requires a search into the patient's neurologic and otologic history.

Evaluation of facial masses often requires a search for systemic disease. Any nodular mass, especially if associated with drainage, should prompt a suspicion of tuberculosis or atypical mycobacterial infection. Skin testing as well as serologic evaluation may be necessary. The examiner should be aware of any draining sinuses, because this can indicate congenital defects. A sinus occurring on the dorsum of the nose may indicate a dermoid cyst. Sinus tracts in the parotid and preauricular area or in the lateral neck along the sternocleidomastoid muscle may indicate first or second branchial cleft anomalies. Any rapidly changing mass deserves immediate attention because of the possibility of neoplasm. Status of vision and the presence or absence of diplopia must be ascertained when the orbital region is involved. The punctum of the lacri-

mal sac should be inspected for the presence of debris or purulence in this region. A complete ophthalmologic examination is essential when there is periorbital swelling and/or pain.

The salivary glands are examined with gentle palpation to determine their size and relationships to the underlying structures. Place a gloved finger into the oral cavity adjacent to the gland in question and the first and second fingers of the opposite hand on the outside to perform a bimanual palpation. This allows for evaluation of the presence or absence of a mass, as well as tenderness and mobility. External massage of the glands always should be undertaken to determine flow from the salivary ducts. The appearance and consistency of the secretion should be noted.

The Nose

Evaluation of the nose must be done in a systematic and organized manner. The external nose should be inspected for visible deformities, such as skin lesions, fistulas, swelling, and deviations. The bony and cartilaginous framework must be carefully examined for their relationships to each other and the rest of the face. A history of nasal trauma should lead the clinician to search for point tenderness, dislocation, or mobility of the bony fragments. The nasal bones should be palpated carefully, and the junction of the nasal bones with the upper lateral cartilages, as well as the junction of the cartilages with each other, should be noted. The presence of a supratip crease should be noted, which may indicate the "nasal salute" of allergy.[8]

The internal examination of the nose begins with careful inspection of the vestibular region. Illumination must be adequate and can be provided by a head mirror, a headlight, an otoscope, or a flashlight. Gentle upward rotation of the tip of the nose by the thumb of the examiner gives access to the vestibular region, anterior septum, and inferior turbinate (Fig. 35–1). The vestibular region should be inspected for patency of the air passage and evidence of any lesion. This is particularly important in the newborn infant, in whom a narrow nasal vestibule may be responsible for respiratory distress.

Examination of the septum is an essential part of the nasal examination. Dislocation of the caudal septum may

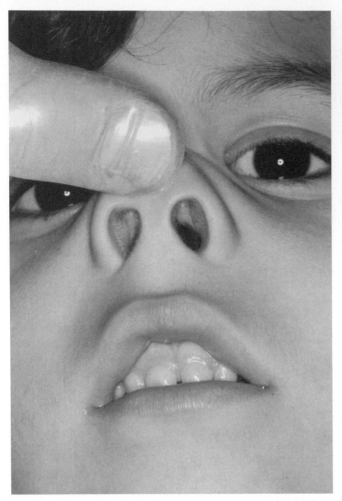

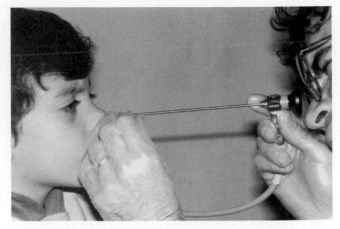

FIGURE 35–2. Nasal endoscopy performed in the awake child.

Rhinoscopy may be performed in the cooperative child after adequate vasoconstriction and topical anesthesia using a rigid nasal telescope or a flexible fiberoptic nasopharyngoscope (Fig. 35–2). Examination of the septum and turbinates is important, noting their size, color, and shape. The middle turbinate region should be observed for the presence of a discharge. The maxillary and anterior ethmoids open into the middle meatus, while the posterior ethmoid and the sphenoid sinus drain into the superior meatus. The frontal sinus drains into the frontal recess, medial to the uncinate process. Clear, watery dis-

FIGURE 35–1. Elevation of the nasal tip by the examiner for inspection of the vestibule and septum. This maneuver avoids the need for nasal speculum.

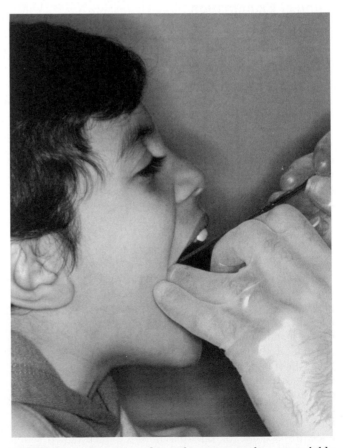

cause nasal obstruction. This is frequently missed due to insertion of instruments such as nasal speculum or nasal head of the otoscope. In case of trauma, a small cotton swab may be used to palpate the septum to evaluate for evidence of septal hematoma or abscess. Patients with a severe nasal septal deviation present with compensatory hypertrophy of the turbinate facing the concavity of the deviation. The anterior nasal septum has a rich vascular supply and is frequently the cause of epistaxis in the pediatric patient. If crusts are present, a bayonet forceps may be used to gently remove them for the proper examination of the internal nose.

Neonates usually have slightly more edematous and moist nasal mucosa than older children. Overall, the nasal mucosa is pink and moist; while pale, cyanotic, and excessively moist mucosa may signal allergy or another pathologic condition.[13] In the presence of swollen nasal mucosa, aerosol such as a .025% or .05% solution of oxymetazoline hydrochloride should be used to obtain adequate vasoconstriction. If topical anesthesia is also required, a mixture of .05% oxymetazoline hydrochloride and 1% lidocaine solution is effective and has a greater safety margin than topical cocaine solution.[9]

FIGURE 35–3. Posterior indirect rhinoscopy in the young child.

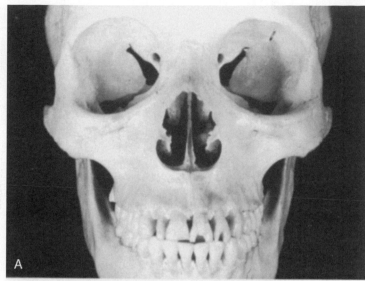

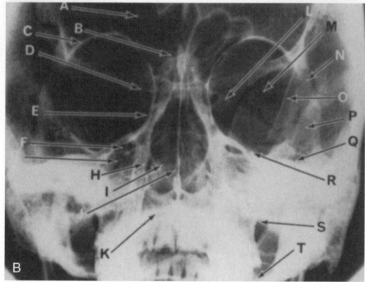

FIGURE 35–4. *A,* Photograph of a dried skull in the Caldwell projection. *B,* Caldwell view: A, frontal sinus; B, crista galli; C, superior orbital margin; D, optic foramen; E, ethmoid sinus; F, foramen rotundum; G, maxillary sinus; H, piriform aperture; I, nasal cavity; J, nasal septum; K, floor of the nose; L, lesser wing of the sphenoid bone; M, greater wing of the sphenoid bone; N, zygomatic-frontal suture; O, temporal line; P, zygomatic bone; Q, petrous ridge of the temporal bone; R, infraorbital foramen; S, lateral wall of the maxillary sinus; T, floor of the posterior cranial fossa. (From Yanagisawa E, Smith HM. Radiographic anatomy of the paranasal sinuses. IV. Caldwell view. Arch Otolaryngol 87:311–322, 1968. Copyright 1968, American Medical Association.)

charge may be associated with vasomotor rhinitis. Any purulent secretion in these areas should be cultured for the presence of pathogenic bacteria.[10] Unilateral nasal discharge may signal the presence of a foreign body, and further evaluation under general anesthesia may be required.

Any evidence of nasal polyps or polypoid changes in the nasal mucosa in the pediatric population may indicate an allergic condition or possibly cystic fibrosis. Further work-up for allergies or a sweat test should be individualized. Mass lesions, such as gliomas and encephaloceles, can be mistaken for nasal polyps in the young child. Radiographic evaluation with computed tomography (CT) scan or magnetic resonance imaging (MRI) is of utmost importance prior to obtaining a biopsy of such lesions.

Any patient with a history of head trauma or recurrent meningitis is at risk for a cerebrospinal leak. A high-resolution coronal CT scan used in combination with intrathecal metrizamide may help to identify a defect in the ethmoid roof, cribriform plate, or sphenoid sinus. Fluorescein dye tests or radioisotope studies (technetium pertechnetate) have also been recommended. Nasal secre-

tions may be tested for B-2-transferrin and glucose content (glucose oxidase-peroxidase test strip or laboratory analysis).

The Sinuses

The development and pneumatization of the sinuses are variable. The maxillary and ethmoid sinuses are present at birth. The sphenoid sinus begins to pneumatize at approximately 3 years of age, and completes its pneumatization by adolescence. The frontal sinus begins its development at the age of 2 to 3 years. It has a unilateral presentation in 11% of children, and never develops in 4% of the population.

The diagnosis of sinus disease requires an adequate history, proper examination, and radiographic evaluation and cultures when indicated. Symptoms of acute sinusitis in the child may be nonspecific. Persistent nasal discharge with daytime or nighttime cough, low-grade fever, periorbital swelling, nasal obstruction, and facial pain or headache may be the presenting manifestations.

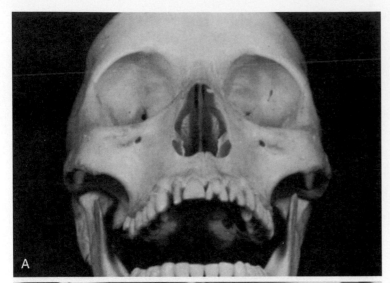

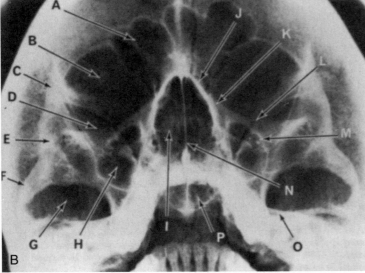

FIGURE 35–5. *A,* Dried skull in Waters projection. *B,* Waters view: A, frontal sinus; B, orbit; C, zygomatic-frontal suture; D, inferior orbital rim; E, zygoma; F, zygomatic arch; G, infratemporal fossa; H, maxillary sinus; I, nasal cavity; J, nasal bone; K, frontal process of the maxilla; L, superior orbital fissure; M, infraorbital foramen; N, nasal septum; O, petrous ridge of the temporal bone; P, sphenoid sinus. (From Merrell RA Jr, Yanagisawa E. Radiographic anatomy of the paranasal sinuses. I. Waters view. Arch Otolaryngol 87:184–195, 1968. Copyright 1968, American Medical Association.)

The examination of the sinuses should start with inspection and palpation of the facial-sinus region. The frontal sinuses, supraorbital regions, medial orbital area (ethmoid sinuses), and midface-cheek area (maxillary sinuses) should be carefully examined. The ascending process of the maxilla and canine fossa must be inspected. The gloved index finger is placed in the gingivobuccal sulcus, and gentle pressure is applied over the anterior and lateral walls of the maxillary sinus. The general status of the teeth and occlusion should be evaluated. Any tenderness and its location should be noted. Transillumination of the sinuses has not been a reliable examination. The examiner cannot distinguish among secretion, pus, tumor, or a hypoplastic-contracted sinus when there is a decrease or lack of transillumination.

Further examination of the nasal cavity and paranasal sinuses requires a complete nasal endoscopy (anterior and posterior rhinoscopy). This examination can be done in a cooperative awake patient with adequate local anesthesia,

or under general anesthesia. Great care must be taken to avoid traumatizing the nasal-septal mucosa.

The Nasopharynx

The nasopharynx is a cuboidal space; bounded superiorly by the rostrum of the sphenoid bone, laterally by the eustachian tube orifice, anteriorly by the choana, posteriorly by the clivus, and inferiorly by the superior aspect of the oropharynx. The nasopharynx should be examined for any mass lesion, which in children commonly represents adenoid tissue. The adenoid is located in the posterosuperior aspect of the nasopharynx and often undergoes hypertrophy in childhood. The possible presence of lesions such as angiofibroma and neoplasms of other types must be kept in mind. The nasopharynx may be examined by the direct or indirect method. Indirect mirror examination requires a cooperative patient and significant skill. The smaller mirrors (no. 10–12) may be used to examine

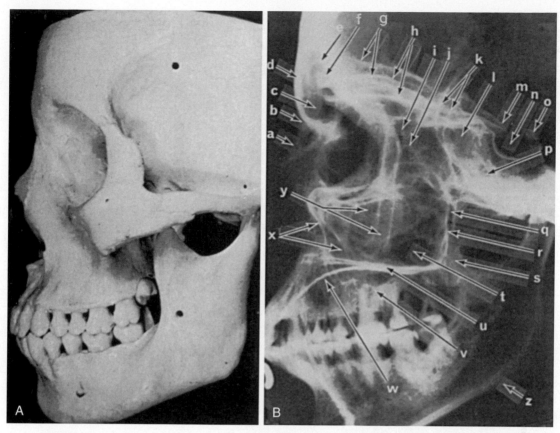

FIGURE 35–6. *A*, Dried skull on lateral projection. *B*, Lateral view showing: a, nasal bone; b, nasofrontal suture; c, frontal sinus; d, anterior wall of the frontal sinus; e, posterior wall of the frontal sinus; f, supraorbital margin; g, cerebral surface orbital plate; h, orbital surface of the orbital plate; i, cribriform plate; j, anterior ethmoid air cells; k, anterior wall of the middle cranial fossa (greater wing of the sphenoid bone); l, posterior ethmoid cells; m, anterior clinoid process; n, sella turcica; o, posterior clinoid process; p, sphenoid sinus; q, pterygomaxillary fissure; r, posterior wall of the maxillary sinus; s, pterygoid plates; t, maxillary sinus; u, floor of the nose; v, floor of the maxillary sinus; w, roof of the mouth; x, anterior wall of the maxillary sinus; y, zygomatic process of the maxilla; z, mandible. (From Yanagisawa E, Smith HW, Thaler S. Radiographic anatomy of the paranasal sinuses. II. Lateral view. Arch Otolaryngol 87:196–209, 1968. Copyright 1968, American Medical Association.)

the nasopharynx after gentle depression of the tongue (Fig. 35–3).

Anterior and Posterior Rhinoscopy

Nasal endoscopy should be performed in a systematic fashion. A flexible nasopharyngoscope or a rigid nasal telescope (0- or 30-degree) may also be used in the cooperative child after administration of a topical anesthetic. First, the scope should be passed along the floor of the nose to evaluate the nasal passage, septum, choana, nasopharynx, Rosenmüller's recess, and the size of the adenoid. The orifice of the nasolacrimal duct can be identified in the inferior nasal meatus also. The scope then should be passed by the upper edge of the choana toward the sphenoethmoidal recess. The sphenoid ostium may be seen in some children. The middle turbinate should be medialized to identify the uncinate process, ethmoidal bulla, hiatus semilunaris, maxillary ostium, and frontal re-

cess. If the patient is unable to tolerate these methods of rhinoscopy, then examination under general anesthesia is required.

Conventional Roentgenography

A complete nasal examination requires a thorough evaluation of the external and internal nasal cavity. This examination is far more valuable than the roentgenograms of the nasal bone; however, radiographic evaluation of the nose (lateral or dental view) may be helpful in cases of nasal trauma or suspected nasal foreign body.

The standard plain film of the face and paranasal sinuses has been used in the evaluation of sinusitis and facial trauma for many years. The four traditional views (Caldwell, Waters, lateral, and submentovertical) are helpful for diagnosis of acute sinusitis in the maxillary, frontal, and sphenoid sinuses, where total opacification or an air-fluid level can be identified. However, these con-

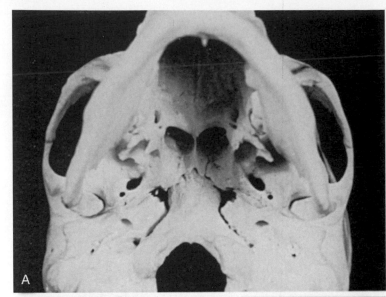

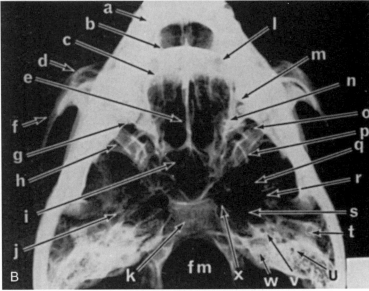

FIGURE 35–7. *A,* Dried skull in submentovertical projection. *B,* Submentovertical view: a, mandible; b, anterior wall of the frontal bone; c, posterior wall of the frontal bone; d, zygoma; e, nasal septum; f, zygomatic arch; g, lateral wall of the antrum; h, lateral wall of the orbit; i, sphenoid sinus; j, eustachian tube; k, clivus; l, lacrimal canal; m, maxillary sinus; n, greater palatine foramen; o, inferior orbital fissure; p, pterygoid plates; q, foramen ovale; r, foramen spinosum; s, carotid canal; t, external auditory canal; u, stylomastoid foramen; v, cochlea; w, internal auditory canal; x, foramen lacerum; fm, foramen magnum. (From Yanagisawa E, Smith HW, Merrell RA, Jr. Radiographic anatomy of the paranasal sinuses. III. Submentovertical view. Arch Otolaryngol 87:299–310, 1968. Copyright 1968, American Medical Association.)

ventional sinus films are not the most sensitive or specific imaging studies for evaluation of: (1) the anterior ethmoid sinuses, (2) chronic or recurrent sinusitis, (3) sinonasal mucosal disease, and (4) the ostiomeatal complex.

The Caldwell, or occipitofrontal, view best delineates the ethmoid and frontal sinuses. The temporal bones and base of the skull are projected onto the maxillary antrum, thereby concealing it and making this an undesirable view for evaluating the maxillary sinuses (Fig. 35–4). The Waters, or occipitomental, view best delineates the maxillary sinus and the orbital floor. It is an important view in the assessment of facial trauma (Fig. 35–5). The lateral view gives good visualization of the anterior and posterior ethmoid cells, as well as of the frontal and sphenoid sinuses. It also shows the thickness of the antral walls and the relationship of the antral floor to the teeth (Fig. 35–6). This view can be used conveniently to evaluate the naso-

pharynx for a mass lesion. A submentovertical view estimates the extent of the posterior ethmoid and sphenoid sinuses and gives an excellent panoramic view of the base of the skull (Fig. 35–7).

Sialography

Sialography may be used to evaluate calculi, obstructive disease, inflammatory lesions, and penetrating trauma of both the parotid and submandibular glands (Fig. 35–8). It is most useful for assessment of the diseases of the ductal system and glandular pattern. The most important contraindications to sialography are iodine allergy and acute sialadenitis.[12] Bilateral studies may be advisable to detect subclinical disease. The diseased side is studied first, and the radiographs of the contralateral side may serve as the baseline.

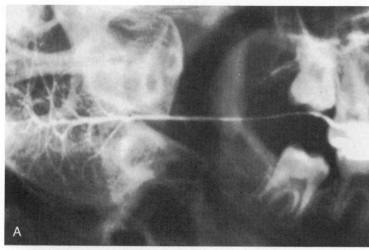

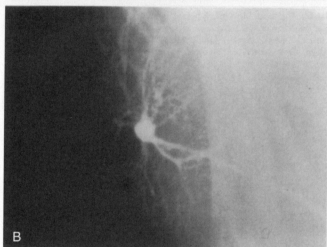

FIGURE 35–8. Normal parotid sialogram. *A*, Lateral view. *B*, Anteroposterior view.

Computed Tomography

CT is the gold standard in the radiographic evaluation of the paranasal sinuses. It nicely demonstrates the bone anatomy, soft tissue and mucosal changes associated with sinusitis, choanal atresia-stenosis, tumors of the sinonasal region, facial trauma, and orbital cellulitis-subperiosteal abscess (Fig. 35–9). CT of the sinuses may be obtained in the individual two-dimensional sections (coronal, axial), or with the spiral technique (Fig. 35–10). The coronal sections are constructed at a right angle, and axial sections are constructed parallel to the orbito-meatal angle. CT images in the coronal plane are important not only diagnostically but also as a critical guide to the surgeon performing an endoscopic sinus procedure.[4] Axial images are helpful to assess the extension of sinus infection or tumor into the orbit, nasopharynx, skull base, and cranial cavity. In the spiral technique images are acquired continuously via a bone or soft tissue algorithm. This allows for the entire examination to be completed in a few seconds; however, the images are less detailed compared to the two-dimensional (coronal, axial) images.

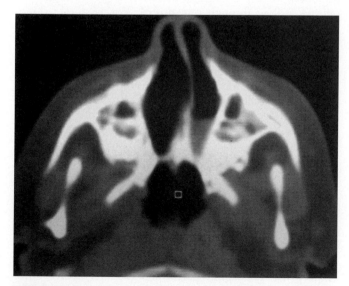

FIGURE 35–9. CT scan of choanal atresia (axial section) demonstrating bony atresia. (Courtesy of Patrick Barnes, M.D., Department of Radiology, Children's Hospital, Boston.)

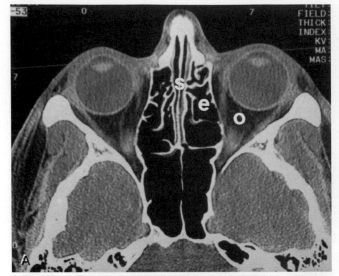

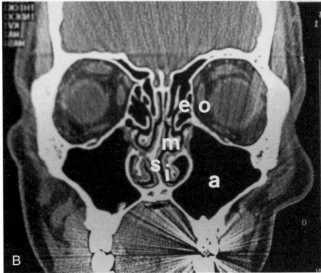

FIGURE 35–10. Computed tomographic (CT) scan of normal paranasal sinuses. *A,* Axial section. *B,* Coronal section: a, maxillary antrum; e, ethmoid sinus; i, inferior turbinate; m, middle turbinate; o, orbit; s, septum.

Magnetic Resonance Imaging

Magnetic resonance imaging is extremely helpful in evaluating sinonasal soft tissue changes and tumors, differentiating fluid from soft tissue density, and extension of diseases into the orbit or intracranial cavity.[5, 11] Encephalocele, glioma, juvenile nasopharyngeal angiofibroma, and salivary gland masses are frequently best delineated by magnetic resonance imaging scan (Fig. 35–11). In addition, it can provide useful information regarding blood supply to vascular tumors. Its ability to provide images without the use of ionizing radiation is also advantageous compared to CT scan. However, magnetic resonance imaging has a limited role in the evaluation of uncomplicated sinus disease due to the poor resolution of bony landmarks.

Ultrasonography and Angiography

Ultrasonography may be used to detect fluid in the frontal and maxillary sinuses with wide variation in its sensitivity and specificity. Gianoli and colleagues evaluated the use of B-mode ultrasonography in evaluation of paranasal-sinus disease.[1] Angiography is the method of choice for preoperative evaluation and embolization of vascular lesions such as juvenile nasopharyngeal angiofibroma and other vascular tumors.

Objective Tests of Nasal Breathing Function

Evaluation of the nasal airway is based on the subjective symptoms of the patient, endoscopic and radiographic evaluation of the nasal cavity, and objective assessment of the nasal aerodynamic function. Many conditions such as septal deformity, mucosal hypertrophy, polyps, and tumors can alter nasal airflow. Various objective tests such as rhinomanometry and acoustic rhinometry have been used to assess the nasal respiratory function.

Rhinomanometry

Rhinomanometry is the oldest and most widely used technique to assess the nasal breathing function. The most important function of rhinomanometry is to provide objective data regarding air pressure and rate of airflow through the nose during nasal breathing;[6] therefore, the clinical application of rhinomanometry requires measurement of transnasal flow and pressure. Nasal airflow is measured with a pneumotachograph at the nares using a body plethysmograph or a face mask. The measurement of transnasal pressure can be made at the nares (anterior rhinomanometry) or mouth (posterior rhinomanometry). For anterior rhinomanometry, one nostril needs to be occluded, which creates a nonphysiologic condition requiring airflow through one nostril. For posterior rhinomanometry, the pressure transducer catheter is placed in the mouth, which can measure the nasopharyngeal pressure and bilateral nasal resistance. The difference between nasopharyngeal and atmospheric pressure is the driving pressure for the nasal airflow. Causes of nasal obstruction could be divided into mucosal hypertrophy (allergy, congestion) or anatomic obstruction (structural, mass affect). By determining nasal resistance before and after maximum nasal decongestion, one can determine the importance of each component.[6] Although rhinomanometry gives an objective measure of nasal resistance, it cannot provide any information on the site or cause of the nasal obstruction.[6, 7]

Acoustic Rhinometry

Hilberg and colleagues performed the first acoustic rhinometry to evaluate nasal cavity geometry in 1989.[2] This technique is based on the fact that changes in the cross-sectional area of the nose will alter the acoustic impedance. When an acoustic pulse is presented into the nasal

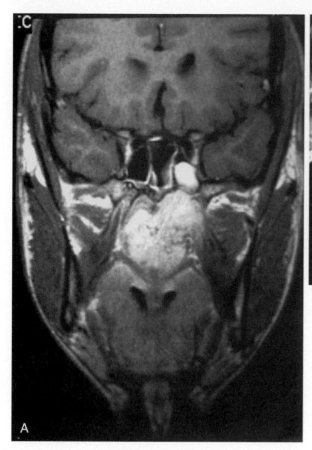

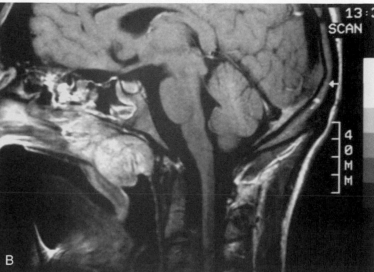

FIGURE 35–11. Magnetic resonance image of juvenile nasopharyngeal angiofibroma, T_1-weighted images. *A*, Coronal section. *B*, Sagittal section. (Courtesy of Patrick Barnes, M.D., Department of Radiology, Children's Hospital, Boston.)

airway, the changes of intensity, phase, and time delay of the reflected sound energy are altered based on the location and degree of the nasal airway obstruction.[3]

This technique is noninvasive, accurate, and reproducible. A nosepiece is placed on the patient's nose without distortion of the anterior nasal structures. An acoustic pulse travels through the nosepiece, and the reflected sound is detected via a microphone and converted to digital data outlining the cross-sectional area of each side of the nose. Nasal cavity volumes can be estimated by combining the measured cross-sectional area.[6]

Acoustic rhinometry is helpful in assessing changes in the nasal cavity geometry following procedures such as septoplasty, nasal reconstruction, and medical treatment for nasal obstruction due to polyps and/or allergies. The most important advantage of acoustic rhinometry is the ability to measure the degree and location of the nasal airway obstruction. However, unlike rhinomanometry, it does not provide any information on the affect of the narrowed nasal passage on the nasal airflow. Therefore, for the proper evaluation of nasal airway function both rhinomanometry and acoustic rhinometry are essential.

Conclusion

The proper evaluation and diagnosis of the diseases of the face, nose, and paranasal sinuses require the physician to be skilled in the methods of examination, diagnostic procedures, interpretation of data, and differential diagnosis.

SELECTED REFERENCES

Crockett DM, Healy GB, McGill TJ, et al. Computed tomography in evaluation of choanal atresia in infants and children. Laryngoscope 97:174, 1987.
An excellent review of the use of CT scans for evaluation of position and thickness of the atresia plate in choanal atresia/stenosis.
Gordon A, McCaffery TV, Kern EB. Rhinomanometry for preoperative and postoperative assessment of nasal obstruction. Otolaryngol Head Neck Surg 101:20, 1989.
An excellent review of the use of rhinomanometry for assessment of nasal obstruction.
McCaffrey TV, Remingtom WJ. Nasal function and evaluation. In Baily BJ (ed). Head and Neck Surgery-otolaryngology. Philadelphia, Lippincott-Raven, 1998.
An excellent review of the techniques for the evaluation of nasal airway.
Stammberger H. Functional Endoscopic Sinus Surgery, the Messerklinger Technique. Philadelphia, Mosby/Decker, 1991.
An excellent presentation of the technique of nasal endoscopy and endoscopic sinus surgery.
Zinreich SJ. Imaging of the nasal cavity and paranasal sinuses. Curr Opin Radiol 4:112, 1992.
An excellent review of radiographic findings of the paranasal sinuses.

REFERENCES

1. Gianoli GJ, Mann WJ, Miller RH. B-mode ultrasonography of the paranasal sinuses compared with CT findings. Otolaryngol Head Neck Surg 107:713, 1992.

2. Hilberg O, Jackson AC, Swift DL, Pedersen OF. Acoustic rhinometry: evaluation of nasal cavity geometry by acoustic reflection. J App Physiol 66:259, 1989.

3. Jackson AC, Butler JP, Millet EJ, et al. Airway geometry by analysis of acoustic pulse response measurements. J Appl Physiol 43:523, 1977.

4. Lesserson JA, Kieserman SP, Finn DG. The radiographic incidence of chronic sinus disease in the pediatric population. Laryngoscope 104:159, 1994.

5. Lloyd GAS, Lund VJ, Phelps PD, et al. Magnetic resonance imaging in the evaluation of nose and paranasal sinus disease. Br J Radiol 60:948, 1987.

6. McCaffrey TV, Remingtom WJ. Nasal function and evaluation. In Baily BJ (ed). Head and Neck. Surgery-Otolaryngology, 2nd ed. New York, Lippincott-Raven, 1998, pp 333–348.

7. Pallanch JF, McCaffrey TV, Kern EB. Normal nasal resistance. Otolaryngol Head Neck Surg 93:778, 1985.

8. Renfro BL. Pediatric otolaryngic allergy. Otolaryngol Clin North Am 25:181, 1992.

9. Riegle EV, Gunter JB, Lusk RP, et al. Comparison of vasoconstrictors for functional endoscopic sinus surgery in children. Laryngoscope 102:820, 1992.

10. Savolainen S, Ylikoski J, Jousimes-Somer H. Predictive value of nasal bacterial culture for etiological agents in acute maxillary sinusitis. Rhinology 25:49, 1987.

11. Teresi L, Lufkin R, Hanafee W. Low cost MRI of the paranasal sinuses. Comp Med Imag Graphics 12:165, 1988.

12. Weber AL. Imaging of the salivary glands. Curr Opin Radiol 4:117, 1992.

13. Zavras AI, White GE, Rich A, Jackson AC. Acoustic rhinometry in the evaluation of children with nasal or oral respiration. J Clin Pediatr Dent 18:203, 1994.

36

Imaging of the Paranasal Sinuses in Pediatric Patients with Special Considerations for Endoscopic Sinus Surgery

Ken Kazahaya, M.D., and William E. Bolger, M.D., F.A.C.S.

The diagnosis of sinusitis in the pediatric patient presents a special challenge to the clinician. Clinical history is heavily relied upon; however, the symptoms of sinusitis, such as mucopurulent rhinorrhea, postnasal drip with cough, nasal congestion, facial pain, headache, malaise, and behavioral change, are shared by several common pathologic processes. Upper respiratory tract infection with viral rhinitis, bacterial rhinitis, and allergic rhinitis, for example, all have symptoms similar to sinusitis. Accurate clinical information from the parents and the referring physician is invaluable and provides the cornerstone in the evaluation of the pediatric sinusitis patient; however, it has certain limitations.

The physical examination is also limited in the evaluation of pediatric patients. Young children often do not cooperate with anterior rhinoscopy and rarely tolerate formal nasal endoscopy. Visualization of the anterior nasal cavity can be provided by use of familiar instruments such as the otoscope. The development of pediatric-sized flexible scopes has enabled safe visualization within the nasal cavity of children. Palpation or percussion of the sinus is often unrevealing, and transillumination has a low degree of predictability for infection because of incomplete pneumatization in the growing sinus.

Plain films (conventional radiographs) have been used for many years as adjuncts in diagnosing sinonasal disease in both the pediatric and adult populations. In the pediatric population, however, this is rapidly being replaced by cross-sectional imaging techniques such as computed tomography (CT) or magnetic resonance imaging (MRI). These modalities represent valuable advances to conventional radiographs and provide markedly improved sensitivity and specificity. Regardless of which modality is used to image the sinuses, the obtained images should still be evaluated in conjunction with the historical and clinical findings. Frequently, patients who are imaged for unrelated reasons have scans that demonstrate soft tissue changes or abnormalities in the paranasal sinuses and yet they have no symptoms. Imaging should not be regarded as the standard for diagnosis.

When endoscopic sinus surgery or aggressive craniofacial surgery for previously unresectable sinonasal neoplasms are planned, these imaging techniques provide precise anatomic detail of the sinonasal cavity and optimal imaging of tumor boundaries. This chapter discusses the role of conventional sinus radiographs, CT, and MRI in pediatric patients with paranasal sinus disease. Special attention is given to imaging in pediatric patients with chronic sinusitis for which endoscopic sinus surgery is being considered.

Paranasal Sinus Embryology, Development, and Anatomic Findings

Before discussing the different radiographic imaging techniques, we briefly discuss the embryology and development of the paranasal sinuses. Effective evaluation of paranasal sinus imaging requires familiarity with the normal findings, growth patterns, and typical abnormalities.

Human sinonasal development is heralded by the appearance of a series of ridges or folds on the lateral nasal wall at approximately the eighth week in utero.[1] Six to seven folds emerge initially; however, through regression and fusion, three to four ridges ultimately persist (Fig. 36–1). Ridges that persist throughout fetal development and into later life are referred to as *ethmoturbinals*. The first ethmoturbinal is rudimentary; its ascending portion forms the agger nasi, while its descending portion forms the uncinate process. The second remaining ethmoturbinal forms the middle turbinate, the third forms the superior turbinate, and the fourth and fifth remaining ethmoturbinals fuse to form the supreme turbinate. These structures are ethmoid in origin. The ethmoturbinals form bony structures that traverse the ethmoid area to attach to the lateral nasal wall, lamina papyracea of the orbit, and skull base.

The nomenclature regarding ethmoid embryology is subject to interpretation. For example, some experts consider the initial second lateral nasal wall fold to be the anlage of the ethmoid bulla, while others propose that the primordial ethmoid bulla arises as a "secondary" lat-

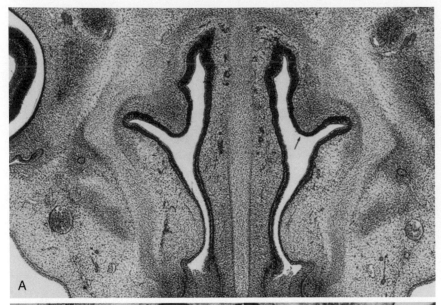

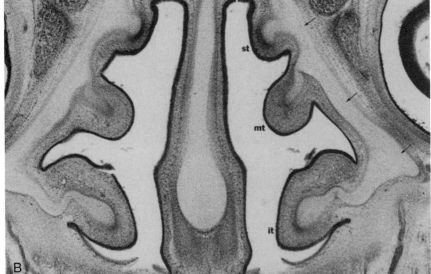

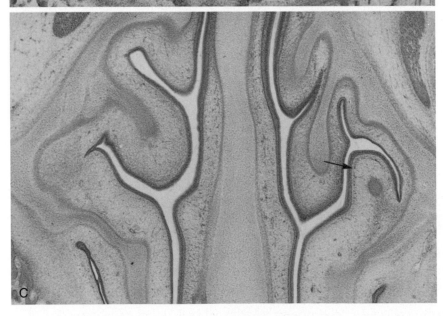

FIGURE 36-1. Human sinonasal development. *A,* Coronal section of human embryo at approximately 56 days' development. The primordial middle turbinate *(arrow)* and inferior turbinate can be seen emerging from the lateral nasal wall. *B,* Coronal section of human fetus at approximately 60 days' development. The primordial superior turbinate (st), middle turbinate (mt), and inferior turbinate (it) can be seen developing directly from the cartilagenous capsule *(arrows).* *C,* Coronal section of human fetus at approximately 63 days' development. The primordial uncinate process can be seen as an evagination from the lateral wall with early ossification *(arrow).* Lateral to the primordial uncinate a corresponding invagination forms the primordial infundibulum.

TABLE 36-1. Postnatal Paranasal Sinus Development

	Newborn			1-4 yr old			4-8 yr old		
	Length (mm)	Height (mm)	Width (mm)	Length (mm)	Height (mm)	Width (mm)	Length (mm)	Height (mm)	Width (mm)
Ethmoid	10	2.5	2	15.5	12	8	21	12.5	11
Maxillary	10	4	3	26	15	15	36	24	21
Frontal	—	—	—	6	7.5	5.5	8	15.5	9
Sphenoid	—	—	—	5	4	7	12.5	9	10

Adapted from Wolf G, Anderhuber W, Kuhn F. Development of the paranasal sinuses in children: implications for paranasal sinus surgery. Ann Otol Rhinol Laryngol 102:705, 1993.

eral nasal wall evagination arising between the first and second remaining ethmoturbinals.[1, 2]

Furrows form between the ethmoturbinals and ultimately establish the primordial nasal meatus and recesses. The first furrow is located between the first and second ethmoturbinals. Its descending aspect forms the ethmoidal infundibulum, hiatus semilunaris, and middle meatus, while its ascending aspect can contribute to the formation of the frontal recess. The primordial maxillary sinus develops from the inferior aspect of the ethmoidal infundibulum.[3-5] The second furrow forms the superior meatus, and the third furrow forms the supreme meatus. Some authors refer to these furrows as "primary" furrows and maintain that "secondary" furrows develop later.[1, 6]

Frontal sinus and frontal recess development is complex and varies greatly among humans. When considering the precise origin of the frontal sinus, the basic developmental theme of lateral evaginations and invaginations is widely accepted; however, subtle differences in the interpretation of events and nomenclature are evident between authors. The frontal sinus has been cited as potentially arising from a direct extension of the frontal recess, from one or more anterior ethmoid cells, or, occasionally, from the anterior superior aspect of the ethmoid infundibulum.[7, 8] Stammberger considers the frontal recess to develop from a superior continuation of the ascending aspect of the groove between the first and second ethmoturbinals and that the frontal sinus originates from the anterior pneumatization of the frontal recess into the frontal bone.[1] Schaeffer proposed that a series of one to four folds and furrows arise within the ventral and caudal aspects of the middle meatus from which the frontal recess forms. At birth, the frontal sinus is not developed. The sinus begins to pneumatize during the first 4 years. From ages 4 to 8 years, frontal pneumatization expands

superiorly, laterally, and medially into the frontal bone. The frontal sinus continues to expand through early adolescence and the teenage years, during which time it attains its full adult size.[6]

Development of the sphenoid sinus deserves special attention. During the third month of fetal development, the nasal mucosa invaginates into the posterior portion of the cartilaginous nasal capsule. The invagination expands to form a pouchlike cavity referred to as the *cartilaginous cupolar* recess of the nasal cavity.[9] The wall surrounding this cartilage is ossified in the later months of fetal development and the complex is referred to as the *ossiculum Bertini*. In the second and third year, the intervening cartilage is resorbed, the ossiculum Bertini becomes attached to the body of the sphenoid, and the cavity definitely becomes sphenoid. Pneumatization progresses posteriorly, laterally, and inferiorly, reaching the nerve of the pterygoid canal in approximately the sixth or seventh year. With continued development, the anterior clinoids and pterygoid process can become pneumatized. Sinus pneumatization is completed between the 9th and 12th year in most humans.[10, 11]

Certainly, all is not known about the complex mechanisms involved in sinus development. However, a basic grasp of sinonasal embryology facilitates understanding of the complex and variable adult paranasal sinus anatomy encountered in surgical patients. A brief overview of postnatal development of the paranasal sinuses is outlined in Table 36-1. Figure 36-2 shows examples of some of the developmental changes revealed in CT images between newborns and adolescent paranasal sinuses.

Several anatomic variants of the paranasal sinuses may be encountered in the evaluation of paranasal sinus CT scans (Table 36-2). Several authors implicate anatomic variations as potential factors that can impair sinus venti-

TABLE 36-2. Anatomic Abnormalities in Patients with Chronic Sinusitis

	Children		Adults	
	April et al [53] N = 124	van der Veken et al [54] N = 196	Bolger et al [17] N = 166	Kennedy and Zinreich [55] N = 230
Concha bullosa	9%	8%	17.4%	36%
Paradoxical middle turbinate	7%	—	27.1%	15%
Haller cells	18%	3%	45.9%	10%
Septal deformity	13%	46%	18.8%	21%
Hypoplastic/atelectatic maxillary sinus	3%	—	3%	—

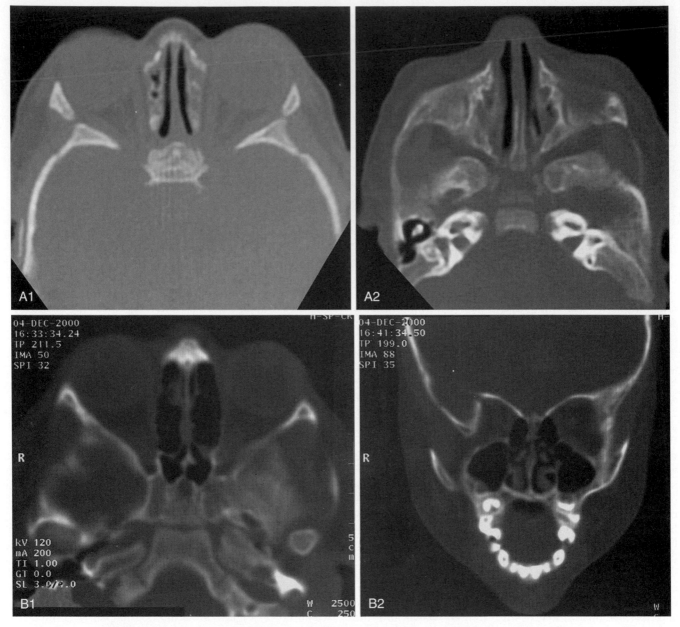

FIGURE 36–2. CT scan of patients through a progression of ages showing the gradual expansion and development of the paranasal sinuses. *A1, A2,* Newborn: Few poorly developed ethmoid air cells exist. The maxillary sinuses are shallow sacs at this stage. Frontal and sphenoid sinuses are absent. *B1, B2,* 4 years old: Ethmoid sinuses expanding in all directions. Maxillary sinus is enlarging inferiorly and laterally, extending laterally to the region of the infraorbital canal. Sphenoid and frontal sinuses are in early stages of development, several millimeters in size.

lation and mucociliary clearance, and hence predispose patients to sinusitis.[12–14] Anatomic variations that have been implicated as possible factors in sinusitis include concha bullosa, Haller cells, paradoxically bent middle turbinates, septal deviations, and uncinate process abnormalities. In support of this premise, the frequency of the concha bullosa has been cited to be higher in patients with chronic or recurrent sinusitis.[15, 16] Some clinicians refer to these variations as anomalies or even abnormalities.

However, caution should be exercised when implicating anatomic variations as a major etiologic factor in sinusitis. Studies have demonstrated that anatomic variations are present in a significant number of patients without sinus disease.[17, 18] Although it is important to identify anatomic variations when evaluating CT scans for chronic sinusitis, it is also important not to label generically these structures as "pathologic." Rather, the pathogenic role of each anatomic variation identified should be evaluated on a patient-by-patient basis.

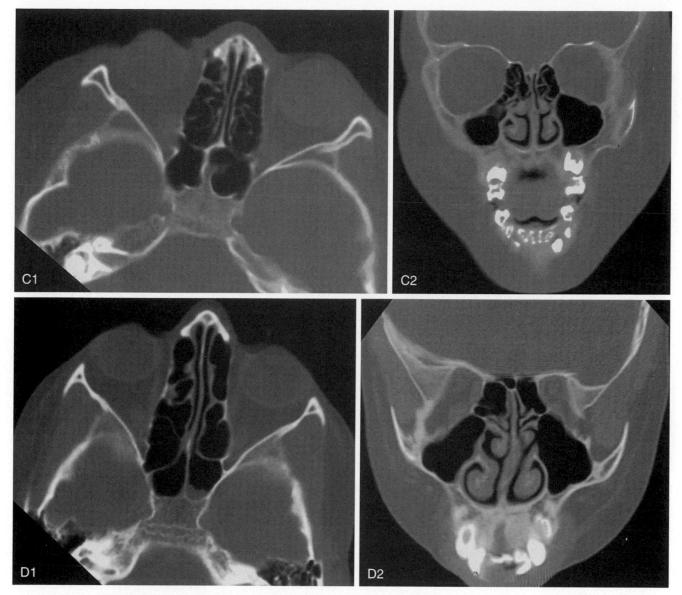

FIGURE 36–2 *Continued.* *C1, C2,* 8 years old: A slowing in the growth of all of the paranasal sinuses is noted, but they continue to expand in all directions. *D1, D2,* 12 years old: The ethmoid and maxillary sinuses are essentially adult sized. Sphenoid pneumatization nears completion, and the frontal sinuses are clinically significant in size. By 18 years of age all of the sinuses have usually completed their growth.

One particular anatomic variation that must be considered in pediatric patients is that of maxillary sinus hypoplasia. In this disorder, patients customarily are seen by the otolaryngologist after having undergone several conventional sinus radiographic studies that have demonstrated unilateral opacification of a maxillary sinus. The primary care physician usually has administered several courses of antibiotics in an effort to treat this "sinusitis," but the sinus has not cleared. CT scan may reveal that the sinus is hypoplastic rather than infected (Fig. 36–3).

Significant maxillary sinus hypoplasia occurs in approximately 3% of patients and has several classic features that are important for the otolaryngologist to be aware of in case surgery is required. The sinus is hypoplastic, the medial wall of the sinus is positioned more laterally than

normal, the infundibulum is obscured or atelectatic, and the uncinate process is hypoplastic, thinned, and lies laterally against the lamina papyracea. If these features are not appreciated by the surgeon, orbital penetration can easily occur when performing infundibulotomy.[19, 20]

Conventional Sinus Radiographs

Conventional sinus radiographic techniques have been employed for many years in the evaluation of pediatric patients with sinusitis. The standard plain film evaluation of the paranasal sinuses in the pediatric population includes the Water, Caldwell, and lateral views. The Towne and submental vertex views, which may be occasionally

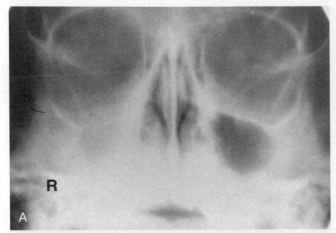

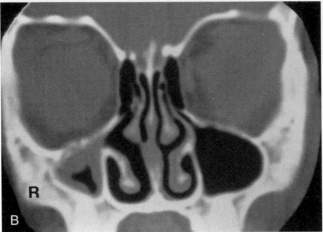

FIGURE 36–3. *A*, An adolescent patient referred from Pediatrics following several courses of antibiotics for a maxillary sinusitis that "would not clear." (From Bolger WE, Kennedy DW. Persistent sinusitis or sinusitis hypoplasia/atelectasis? J Respir Dis 13:1449, 1992.) *B*, CT scan of the same patient reveals a hypoplastic maxillary sinus, an atelectatic infundibulum, and a hypoplastic uncinate process that is laterally deviated against the orbit.

obtained, have a low diagnostic yield in children.[21] Plain films are helpful in establishing the diagnosis of acute sinusitis in adults and adolescents, primarily in the maxillary, frontal, and sphenoid sinuses where the more dominant finding of an air-fluid level or total opacification can be identified. However, they are of limited value because there is no reproducible visualization of the anterior ethmoid sinuses and they provide poor anatomic detail of such areas as the ostiomeatal complex and middle meatus.[22]

Conventional sinus radiographs have several limitations. Overlapping structures make detection of isolated mucosal thickening difficult. In the younger patient, incomplete pneumatization of a sinus can easily be confused with total opacification, mucosal thickening, and even air-fluid levels. Additionally, plain film radiography can be technically demanding to conduct in children. Children may become anxious and distressed, making proper positioning of the head difficult. If patient cooperation is poor, multiple exposures and restraints may be

required to obtain an adequate examination. Poor quality examinations can overestimate the presence and severity of sinusitis or require repeat examination, thus increasing radiation exposure.

The value of conventional radiographs in identifying the extent and location of sinus disease in chronic and recurrent sinusitis in children has been challenged. Multiple studies have compared CT with plain film radiographs and have shown poor correlation between the modalities. In a prospective study of 70 infants and children seen for evaluation of recurrent sinusitis who were symptomatically well on antibiotic therapy, the findings on conventional films and CT, obtained on the same day, did not correlate in nearly 74% on patients. Specifically, 46% of patients with normal conventional studies had abnormalities detected on CT scan, whereas 34% of patients had abnormalities on conventional studies but normal CT scans.[21] Similar findings were noted in a retrospective analysis of 150 pediatric patients evaluated for chronic or recurrent sinusitis with both CT and plain sinus films. CT evaluation was found to be "abnormal" in 18 of 45 (40%) patients with normal plain films. All 18 patients eventually underwent surgery. CT evaluation was "normal" in 38 of 105 (36%) patients with "abnormal" plain films. Importantly, surgery was avoided in these cases where disease was nonexistent. The investigators concluded that plain films were neither specific nor sensitive enough for the diagnosis of chronic sinusitis in children.[23] Based on the data from these studies, plain films are not recommended in determining the need for, or to guide, endoscopic sinus surgery in children.[21]

Computed Tomography

CT has become a significant modality in the diagnostic armamentarium for evaluating paranasal sinus diseases. CT imaging can safely demonstrate bony anatomy, soft tissue, and sinus contents in detail at a relatively low cost and with acceptable radiation exposure, as long as it is used prudently. With the increasing interest in and popularity of endoscopic sinus surgery, thin-section coronal imaging has become a widely adopted technique for imaging the paranasal sinuses. Whereas conventional CT examination is typically well tolerated by adults and older children, infants and toddlers often require sedation to limit patient movement during the examination.

Sedation techniques for pediatric CT examination may vary slightly between institutions. In our institution for children younger than 18 months or weighing less than 12 kg, chloral hydrate is widely used in a dose of 60 to 100 mg/kg (maximum 120 mg/kg or 2 g) administered orally or rectally 1 hour before the examination. The child rests in a dimly lit room adjacent to the CT suite, in the arms of his or her parent, to maximize the effects of the sedative. For children older than 18 months, more than 12 kg, or resistant to chloral hydrate, Nembutal (Pentothal) may be given parenterally (by mouth [PO]) (4 mg/kg), intramuscularly (5 mg/kg), or intravenously (IV) (2 to 4 mg/kg). Nembutal is typically supplemented with morphine or midazolam. IV morphine (0.1 to 0.2 mg/kg, maximum dose—10 mg) is used with the more difficult patients or the ones who have failed sedation in the past. Midazolam may be given PO or IV for other children, especially if the study is short. The onset of IV midazolam effects is immediate, whereas the onset of IV morphine and PO midazolam effects can take 15 to 20 minutes. After achieving adequate sedation, the child is gently secured to the CT cradle with straps. A shielded parent or technologist stands nearby in case the child awakens during the scan and tries to move from the table. All patients receiving sedation are monitored by qualified personnel and patients receiving parenteral sedation are placed on supplemental O_2 and a pulse oximeter. Following sedation, children are observed either in the radiology department or other appropriate recovery setting, such as the "same day" surgery unit, until they show signs of awakening.

Several recommendations regarding CT scanning technique of the paranasal sinus have been published.[13, 24–26] Customarily, the patient lies prone with head extended, but if the patient is unable to maintain the prone position, supine positioning with the head hyperextended over the edge of the CT table is used. The gantry angle is perpendicular to the hard palate. Direct coronal images are obtained from the posterior margin of the sphenoid sinuses to the anterior margin of the posterior ethmoid sinuses using 5-mm contiguous slices, while 3-mm contiguous slices are used from the anterior margin of the posterior ethmoid sinuses to the anterior margin of the frontal sinuses. Scan parameters are kVp 120 and mAs 200 (100 mA × 2 seconds), with bone algorithm (maximum edge enhancement). Images are printed using an intermediate window width of 2000 to 2500 HU and a window center of 100 to 300 HU. Direct axial imaging is performed from the maxillary teeth through the frontal sinuses parallel to the hard palate with 3- to 5-mm contiguous slices. Erosion of the posterior table of the frontal sinus, sphenoethmoidal bony plate, pterygomaxillary fissure, and pterygomaxillary plates are best evaluated on axial scans. Axial slice thickness may be modified to address clinical situations that arise in evaluating sinusitis or neoplasia, such as a need for detailed evaluation of the skull base. Contrast is generally not given for preoperative evaluation of the paranasal sinuses unless preliminary evaluation of a noncontrast examination reveals complicated sinusitis or neoplasia.

The coronal plane is recommended when evaluating chronic or recurrent sinusitis because it is the plane that best displays the anterior ethmoid-ostiomeatal unit and it is the plane that most closely correlates with the endoscopist's view.[13, 27] (Fig. 36–4).

"Limited" CT techniques have been proposed to reduce cost and radiation exposure.[28–30] These techniques are particularly attractive for pediatric patients. However, caution must be exercised so as not to extend the applications of these techniques to clinical situations for which they were not designed. Kronemer[31] reported "limited" CT evaluations missing 20% to 30% of findings found on full CT scans. Another study reported only 70% of "limited" CT examinations adequately demonstrated the ostiomeatal complex.[32]

Gross et al[29] proposed a four-slice examination for follow-up assessment after medical treatment of sinusitis.

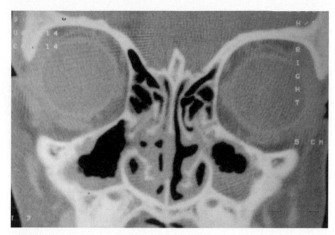

FIGURE 36–4. Coronal CT of a 7-year-old boy with chronic/recurrent sinusitis that has been refractory to multiple courses of oral antibiotics. CT clearly demonstrates the anterior ethmoid-ostiomeatal complex region. Mucosal thickening is evident even after maximal and appropriate medical treatment.

Radiation exposure is reduced from 53.6 mJ (3.35 mJ per slice × 16 slices per examination assuming 3 rad per slice and 112 cm^3 slice volume) to 13.4 mJ, which they felt compared more favorably with 1.7 mJ for a conventional three-view radiographic study. They proposed a "limited" four-slice CT scan as an alternative to conventional radiography in the follow-up assessment of acute or recurrent sinusitis, because it provided superior anatomic definition and accurately identified disease. This technique is not, however, recommended in evaluating chronic sinusitis or for preoperative planning.

Babbel et al[30] proposed a "limited" pre-endoscopic CT scan for both the evaluation of chronic sinusitis and the preoperative planning. The scan is limited in that scan settings have varied, decreasing energy to limit radiation exposure to the patient without compromising image quality. Anteriorly, 3-mm sections are recommended, while 5-mm slices are obtained posteriorly, using a kVp 120 and mAs 200 (100 mA × 2 second scan time). The bone imaging algorithm or maximum edge enhancement program is used and the image is displayed at intermediate window width (2000 to 2500 HU) and window center (100 to 300). A pre-endoscopy type scan is particularly attractive for pediatric patients for several reasons. This scan obtains detailed data that allows diagnosis before endoscopy.

Current recommendations suggest that history and nasal endoscopy be performed before ordering a CT scan.[33] In evaluating pediatric patients, endoscopy is often not tolerated; therefore, this valuable detailed diagnostic information is not available for formulating diagnosis. The practitioner must rely largely on history, which can be difficult, because many rhinologic processes have symptoms similar to sinusitis. A pre-endoscopic CT scan, which is used in adults to gain detailed information regarding the ostiomeatal unit and which gains information similar to the information obtained in endoscopy, would be useful in children when endoscopy is not possible. This scan is especially attractive because the parameters used are designed to reduce radiation exposure. The American College of Radiology Appropriateness Criteria recommends no imaging for suspected uncomplicated rhinosinusitis.[21, 31] Zeifer[22] recommends two particular situations when CT imaging of the paranasal sinuses is indicated: (1) when the diagnosis of sinusitis is unclear based on the history obtained and on the physical examination or (2) for the evaluation of a patient who has recurrent acute or persistent chronic sinusitis that is refractory to medical management. In the latter case, the scan should be performed after full medical therapy has been instituted.

The otolaryngologist is cautioned, however, from simply ordering or approving a limited sinus CT. The term *limited* clearly may have different meanings among radiologists; therefore, the specifics of the scan program should be delineated and understood by the otolaryngologist and radiologist before scanning to avoid the need for repeat studies due to miscommunication.

Although coronal plane imaging is recommended for chronic or recurrent sinusitis, scanning in the axial plane is very useful in certain situations. The axial plane gives superior imaging of the anterior and posterior wall of the frontal sinus and the relationship between the most posterior ethmoid cell and the sphenoid sinus.

Varying the scan parameters can be helpful at times. The "soft tissue" technique allows better demonstration of microcalcifications such as those associated with fungal sinusitis. When the clinical presentation or the initial radiographic study suggests an intracranial complication of sinusitis, limited scan protocols are not recommended; rather, a full sinonasal protocol to include axial and coronal images, bone and soft tissue windowing, and intravenous contrast enhancement is indicated. Additionally, MRI may be considered.

The issue of radiation exposure with CT is particularly important for children who have recalcitrant forms of chronic sinusitis (e.g., cystic fibrosis, sinobronchial syndrome, acetylsalicylic acid/asthma/polyposis triad) and who will undergo repeated CT scans over their lifetimes. Tissue such as the gonads, bone marrow, and lens are said to be more "radiosensitive" or susceptible to the adverse effects of radiation. The lens is of major concern in sinus CT because it is in the scan field and cannot be shielded. The "critical dose" of radiation resulting in cataract formation is estimated at 200 to 400 rad for single exposure and approximately 1000 rad for long-term exposure; the lens is more sensitive in children.[34] In CT scanning, the lens is exposed only on those cuts that pass directly or tangentially through it. One CT cut is estimated to confer approximately 0.4 rad. Because two to three cuts go through the lens, a dose of 1.2 rad would be anticipated per study. Many CT scans, far more than anticipated from even the most complicated clinical course, would need to be performed to induce early cataract formation. In contrast, a three-view conventional sinus radiograph would confer 0.4 to 0.6 rad.[34] In a separate study, Sillers et al[35] reported on radiation exposures to the eyes with respect to different imaging modalities. Plain films delivered, on average, only 0.00085 Gy, thin axial and coronal CT delivered 0.0427 Gy and 0.0434 Gy, respectively, and limited CT delivered 0.0278 Gy. The conventional CT scan

had the highest radiation exposure of 0.0741 Gy, which is still less than 4% of that associated with cataract formation.

Interpretation of paranasal sinus CT scans is important in the evaluation of pediatric patient for sinusitis and warrants discussion. Three major concepts must be kept in mind when evaluating and interpreting scans. First, mucosal abnormalities should be identified; second, anatomic variations or abnormalities that could predispose the patient to poor sinus ventilation and subsequent sinusitis are identified; and third, the borders of the sinuses are examined to ensure that disease has not left the confines of the paranasal sinuses and all areas imaged outside of the sinus are examined for pathology (Fig. 36–5).

When evaluating mucosal abnormalities, several factors should be considered. The use of medical therapy before scanning is an important factor. If soft tissue density is present on CT scan upon completion of or shortly following repeated courses of maximal medical therapy, persistent sinus inflammation may be present and surgical therapy may be indicated. The CT scan may be normal in patients with recurrent sinusitis who are "between episodes" and are symptomatically well at the time of scanning. In these patients, it is important to search for anatomic abnormalities that could impair sinus ventilation and drainage. A formal diagnostic nasal endoscopy or repeat coronal CT scan performed during a sinusitis flare-up may be helpful in objectively establishing the diagnosis of sinusitis and identifying which of the eight paranasal sinuses is involved.

Caution should be exercised when using the term *disease* to refer generically to areas of "opacification" on CT scan of the paranasal sinuses. A descriptive phrase such as *opacification with soft tissue density*, modified when indicated by the terms *homogenous* or *heterogenous*, is more accurate than the term *disease*, which may confer diagnosis of sinusitis. If the radiographic features are sug-

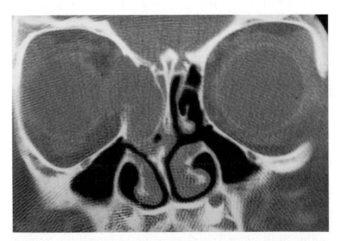

FIGURE 36–5. Coronal CT of an 8-year-old boy with a mucocele of the ethmoid sinus. CT demonstrates that the lamina papyracea has been eroded by the mucocele. The importance of examining the bony limits of the sinuses by CT prior to surgery is highlighted. Interestingly, the patient had previously undergone bilateral endoscopic ethmoidectomy at another institution at age 4 years. Although he had done well for 3½ years following surgery, progressive eye discomfort for six months led to his presentation and successful revision surgery at our institution.

gestive of or consistent with specific pathologic processes, this can and should be noted in addition to the descriptive analysis. Cysts, inflamed mucosa, postoperative changes (e.g., scar or edema), mucus, purulence, and certain tumors can all have a similar appearance on CT scan.

Although interpretation of the CT scan is important, the clinician must correlate the extent and location of radiographic findings with the patient's symptoms. The mere presence of soft tissue density within the paranasal sinuses on CT scan does not indicate sinus disease that requires surgical management. The need to correlate CT findings with patient symptoms is highlighted by reports of a high prevalence of incidental mucosal abnormalities found on sinus CT scans in asymptomatic patients who do not have a history of sinus complaints.[18, 36, 37] In contrast, Gwaltney[38] reported abnormal CT findings in 27 of 31 patients with recent onset of viral upper respiratory symptoms and complete resolution of findings within 2 weeks without antibiotic therapy.

The use of ionic contrast-enhanced CT scans can assist in the assessment of infectious and neoplastic processes. Particularly, in cases of acute orbital or intracranial infectious processes, abscesses can be distinguished from cellulitis, phlegmon, or muscle thickening. An unenhanced CT is more accurate in assessing a patient for acute fungal paranasal sinus disease, being better able to depict concretions and dried secretions.[39]

If surgery is recommended, it is helpful to re-examine the CT scan just shortly before the procedure, directing greater attention to the subtleties of the patient's anatomy rather than to disease identification. The skull base should be examined with special attention given to the medial and anterior region. Keros[40] has described three types of skull bases from an investigation of 100 cadaveric specimens. In type I, the olfactory sulcus is 1 to 3 mm deep and there is a significant portion of frontal bone that backs the ethmoid roof, making the roof thick and the sinus less hazardous to operate in. In type II, the olfactory sulcus is 3 to 7 mm deep. In type III, the olfactory sulcus is 7 to 16 mm deep and a significant portion of the ethmoid roof is not backed by thick frontal bone, making this the most hazardous sinus to operate in. Extreme caution must be taken when operating along the skull base in such a patient, especially medially, in the region of the lateral lamellae of the cribriform plate. In an anatomic study using microscopic techniques, the thickness of the ethmoid roof diminished 10-fold when surgeons worked medially rather than centrally.[41] The authors reported that, clinically, this is the most common site for cerebrospinal fluid leak to occur during the surgery.

Just before beginning the operation, it is also helpful for the otolaryngologist to become refamiliarized with the relationship of the uncinate to the lamina papyracea. The angle of the uncinate with the lateral nasal wall is reported to be greater in children, placing the uncinate closer to the lamina papyracea.[42] It is important to appreciate this on CT scan before surgery so that the depth of the uncinate incision can be limited during infundibulotomy to avoid orbital penetration.

The height of the ethmoid sinuses is an additional important anatomic relationship that should be appreci-ated on CT scan before surgery. If the posterior ethmoid height is small and the posterior ethmoids are not particularly well pneumatized, then the surgeon can highlight the need to stay inferior and medial when dissecting posteriorly to avoid penetration through the skull base.

Spiral Computed Tomography

Recently, there have been significant advances in CT technology, in particular with spiral, or helical, scanners. The spiral, or helical, techniques have advantages over conventional CT techniques. First, the spiral CT scanners acquire information significantly faster, thereby reducing the time a patient is in the scanner. Second, there is less radiation exposure compared with standard CT. Also, the data acquired during an axial scan can be reformatted into coronal and sagittal plane images without having to perform additional scan passes or without awkward positioning of the head and neck.[43] Spiral CT imaging of the paranasal sinus have been touted to be performed in less than 5 minutes, which patients tolerate well.[44] However, at our institution, we have recently upgraded to spiral technology which boasts scan times of 0.25 second per slice (0.5 mm). At this speed, a complete scan of the paranasal sinuses can be performed in less than a minute. With the scan being this short, patient tolerance of the scan may be such that minimal or no sedation may be required in most patients. Furthermore, the image information is sufficient for the coronal reconstructions to have the same resolution as that from direct coronal CT image acquisition, thus alleviating the need for a second scan and awkward head positioning. Significantly more information is gained without expense in time or radiation exposure for the child. Finally, the reported average radiation dose is predicted to be 0.031 Gy, which is approximately that of a limited CT scan and less than half of the dose from a conventional CT scan.

Magnetic Resonance Imaging

MRI of the paranasal sinuses has several distinct advantages and disadvantages when compared with CT scanning. Its ability to provide multiplanar images without the use of ionizing radiation is particularly attractive for the pediatric population. MRI is superior to CT in resolving soft tissue structures and is extremely valuable in the evaluation of sinonasal masses and complicated sinusitis with extension into the orbits or intracranial cavity. MRI can help assess the degree of invasion of aggressive fungal sinusitis or aid in delineating fluid from tissue in patients with mucopyoceles or cystic fibrosis. Additionally, magnetic resonance angiography can provide noninvasive evaluation of major vascular structures. However, the role of MRI in evaluation of patients with chronic uncomplicated sinusitis is limited because it still lacks the high spatial and contrast resolution needed to image the lateral nasal wall, particularly the bone, cartilage, and mucosa of the nasal cavity.[45] This poor resolution is unable to provide the endoscopic surgeon with adequate perception of the bony landmarks of the sinonasal cavity. Because of the sensitivity of MRI in detecting soft tissue, mucosal abnormalities of the paranasal sinuses that are unrelated to the patient's presenting problem are frequently detected and may not represent disease.[46, 47] Other limitations of MRI include long scan times, which necessitate sedation in young children and infants, limited access to the patient while he or she is within the bore of the magnet, and cost. Furthermore, there are potential complicating factors with ferrometallic fragments and objects—traumatic, accidental, or iatrogenic—in a patient undergoing an MRI scan.

MRI examination of the paranasal sinuses can be performed in a standard head coil using spin echo techniques. Surface coils may be placed over the anterior surface of the face for greater resolution of the ostiomeatal complex and frontoethmoid sinuses; however, the sphenoid sinus may be poorly visualized because of the loss of signal. Other pulse sequences such as fast spin echo and fat suppression techniques may be of added benefit in further delineating a disease process, and gadolinium contrast enhancement is valuable in complicated sinusitis and sinonasal masses.[26]

Similar to the problems with correlating CT scans with the clinical findings, MRI scans also reveal abnormalities in 13% to 63% of asymptomatic patients.[46, 48, 49] In contrast, MRI abnormalities have been noted up to 7 weeks after resolution of sinus symptoms.[50] Leopold[51] also noted persistence of bacterial sinusitis soft tissue changes even 8 weeks after treatment.

MRI evaluations are useful in assessing the extent of soft tissue disease within or around the paranasal sinuses, such as orbital and intracranial extensions. Particularly, MRI scans are more sensitive in evaluating meningeal extension of disease.[31] MRI has become the examination of choice in evaluating patients with inflammatory complications of paranasal sinus disease.[52]

Future Directions

The diagnosis and treatment of sinonasal diseases continues to evolve. Improvement in endoscopic surgical procedures has placed a demand on imaging techniques to evaluate the extent and location of disease in the sinonasal cavity and to provide clear precise anatomic detail before treatment.

Imaging systems capable of displaying the complex and variable anatomy of the sinonasal cavity in three dimensions using reconstruction of digitized CT data continue to advance. There continue to be issues of limited image resolution and accuracy and of slow software processing speed. Several image processing/access devices are currently being marketed for use in image-assisted surgery. These systems use sensors and digitized CT data to display axial, coronal, and sagittal images in real time. They have been useful in surgical training and surgical planning, and, at times, in assisting the surgeon in actual surgical procedures. Further technical developments may allow this technique to be applied to MRI data as well and may provide the surgeon with both bony and soft tissue detail simultaneously in real time. Continued advances in imaging techniques will probably be contingent on future development of computer systems capable of

processing the large amounts of data derived from the new generation of high-resolution, high-speed CT and MRI scanners.

Recent MRI investigations have also involved hyperpolarized noble gases that have paramagnetic properties that allow them to be imaged. Helium or xenon gases can be hyperpolarized by excitation, such as by laser, to become paramagnetic and, therefore, capable of being imaged. Images of lung and proximal airway images have been obtained using these gases. By using dynamic imaging, these gases may be used to reveal the pattern of air-gas exchange in normal and diseased paranasal sinuses.[44]

REFERENCES

1. Stammberger H. Functional endoscopic sinus surgery: the Messerklinger technique. Philadelphia, BC Decker, 1991.
2. Libersa C, Laude M, Libersa JC. The pneumatization of the accessory cavities of the nasal fossae during growth. Anat Clin 2:265, 1981.
3. Davis WB. Nasal Accessory Sinus in Man. Philadelphia, WB Saunders, 1914.
4. Hall GW. Embryology and abnormal anatomy of the maxillary sinus. Northwest Medicine 68:1010, 1969.
5. Schaeffer JP. The sinus maxillaris and its relations in the embryo, child and adult man. Am J Anat 10:313, 1912.
6. Schaeffer JP. The genesis, development and adult anatomy of the nasofrontal duct region in man. Am J Anat 20:125, 1916.
7. Hanson NL. Embryological development of the nasal accessory sinuses. Ill Med J 60:386, 1931.
8. Van Alyea OE. Ethmoid labyrinth: anatomic study, with consideration of the clinical significance of its structural characteristics. Arch Otolaryngol 29:881, 1939.
9. Vidic B. The postnatal development of the sphenoidal sinus and its spread into the dorsum sellae and posterior clinoid processes. Am J Rhinol 104:177, 1968.
10. Szolar D, Preidler K, Ranner G, et al. Magnetic resonance assessment of age-related development of the sphenoid sinus. Br J Radiol 67:431, 1999.
11. Van Alyea OE. Sphenoid sinus: anatomic study, with consideration of the clinical significance of the structural characteristics of the sphenoid sinus. Arch Otolaryngol 34:225, 1941.
12. Kennedy DW, Zinreich SJ, Rosenbaum AE, et al. Functional endoscopic sinus surgery: theory and diagnostic evaluation. Arch Otolaryngol 111:576, 1985.
13. Zinreich SJ, Kennedy DW, Rosenbaum AE, et al. Paranasal sinuses: CT imaging requirements for endoscopic surgery. Radiology 163:769, 1987.
14. Stammberger H, Wolf G. Headaches and sinus disease: the endoscopic approach. Ann Otol Rhinol Laryngol 97:(Suppl 134), 1988.
15. Clark ST, Babin RW, Salazar J. The incidence of concha bullosa and its relationship to chronic sinonasal disease. Am J Rhinology 3:11, 1989.
16. Zinreich SJ, Mattox DE, Kennedy DW, et al. Concha bullosa: CT evaluation. J Comput Assist Tomogr 12:778, 1988.
17. Bolger WE, Butzin C, Parsons DS. CT analysis of bony and mucosal abnormalities for endoscopic sinus surgery. Laryngoscope 101:56, 1991.
18. Calhoun K, Waggenspack GA, Simpson CB, et al. CT evaluation of paranasal sinuses in symptomatic and asymptomatic populations. Otolaryngol Head Neck Surg 104:480, 1991.
19. Bolger WE, Woodruff WW, Morehead J, Parsons DS. Maxillary sinus hypoplasia: classification and description of associated uncinate hypoplasia. Otolaryngol Head Neck Surg 103:759, 1990.
20. Furin MJ, Zinreich SJ, Kennedy DW. The atelectatic maxillary sinus. Am J Rhinol 5:79, 1991.
21. McAlister WH, Lusk R, Muntz HR. Comparison of plain radiographs and coronal CT scans in infants and children with recurrent sinusitis. Am J Roentgenol 153:1259, 1989.

22. Zeifer B. Pediatric sinonasal imaging: normal anatomy and inflammatory disease. Neuroimaging Clin N Am 10(1):137, 2000.
23. Lazar RH, Younis RT, Parvey LS. Comparison of plain radiographs, coronal CT, and intraoperative findings in children with chronic sinusitis. Otolaryngol Head Neck Surg 107:29, 1992.
24. Chow JM, Mafee MF. Radiologic assessment preoperative to endoscopic sinus surgery. Otolaryngol Clin North Am 22:691, 1989.
25. Babbel RW, Harnsberger HR, Sonkens J, et al. Recurring patterns of inflammatory sinonasal disease demonstrated on screening sinus CT. Am J Neuroradiol 13:903, 1992.
26. Yousem DM. Imaging of sinonasal inflammatory disease. Radiology 188:303, 1993.
27. Zinreich SJ. Imaging of chronic sinusitis in adults: X-ray, computed tomography, and magnetic resonance imaging. J Allergy Clin Immunol 90:445, 1992.
28. White PS, Robinson JM, Doyle T, et al. The CT mini-series: an alternative to standard paranasal sinus radiology. Aust N Z J Surg 60:25, 1990.
29. Gross GW, McGeady SJ, Kerut T, et al. Limited-slice CT in the evaluation of paranasal sinus disease in children. AJR Am J Roentgenol 156:367, 1991.
30. Babbel R, Harnsberger HR, Nelson B, et al. Optimization of techniques in screening CT of the sinuses. Am J Neuroradiol 157:1093, 1991.
31. Kronemer KA, McAlister WH. Sinusitis and its imaging in the pediatric population. Pediatr Radiol 27:837 1997.
32. Wippold FJ, Levitt RG, Evens RG, et al. Limited coronal CT: an alternative screening examination for sinonasal inflammatory disease. Allergy Proc 16:165, 1995.
33. Kennedy DW. First-line management of sinusitis: a national problem? Overview. Otolaryngol Head Neck Surg 103:847, 1990.
34. Kopp W, Stammberger H. Radiology. In Stammberger H, ed. Functional Endoscopic Sinus Surgery, 1st ed. Philadelphia, BC Decker, 1991, pp 102–103.
35. Sillers MJ, Kuhn FA, Vickery CL. Radiation exposures in paranasal sinus imaging. Otolaryngol Head Neck Surg 112:248, 1995.
36. Maclennan AC, McGarry GW. Diagnosis and management of chronic sinusitis. BMJ 310:529, 1995.
37. Diament MJ, Senac MO, Gilsanz V, et al. Prevalence of incidental paranasal sinuses opacification in pediatric patients: a CT study. J Comput Assist Tomogr 11:426, 1987.
38. Gwaltney JM Jr, Phillips CD, Miller RD, et al. Computed tomographic study of the common cold. N Engl J Med 330:35, 1994.
39. Soom PM. Imaging of paranasal sinus fungal disease. Otolaryngol Clin North Am 26:983, 1993.
40. Keros P. Uber die praktische beteudung der Niveau-Unterschiede der lamina cribrosa des ethmoids. In Naumann HH. Head & Neck Surgery, vol. 1 (Face and Facial Skull). Philadelphia, WB Saunders, 1980, pp 392.
41. Kainz J, Stammberger H. The roof of the anterior ethmoid: a place of least resistance in the skull base. Am J Rhinol 3:191, 1989.
42. Ummat S, Riding M, Kirkpatrick D. Development of the ostiomeatal unit in childhood: a radiological study. J Otolaryngol 21:307, 1992.
43. Goldstein JH, Phillips CD. Current indications and techniques in evaluating inflammatory disease and neoplasia of the sinonasal cavities. Curr Probl Diagn Radiol 27(2):41, 1998.
44. Phillips CD. Current status and new developments in techniques for imaging the nose and sinuses. Otolaryngol Clin North Am 30(3):371, 1997.
45. Zinreich JS. Imaging of the nasal cavity and paranasal sinuses. Curr Opin Radiol 4:112, 1992.
46. Moser EG, Panush D, Rubin JS, et al. Incidental paranasal sinus abnormalities on MRI of the brain. Clin Radiol 43:252, 1991.
47. Rak KM, Newell JD, Yakes WF, et al. Paranasal sinuses on MR images of the brain: significance of mucosal thickening. AJR Am J Roentgenol 156:381, 1991.
48. Cooke LD, Hadley DM. MRI of the paranasal sinuses: incidental abnormalities and their relationship to symptoms. J Laryngol Otol 105:278, 1991.
49. Lesserson JA, Kieserman SP, Finn DG. The radiographic incidence of chronic sinus disease in the pediatric population. Laryngoscope 104:159, 1994.
50. McCaffrey TV. Rhinologic diagnosis and treatment. New York, Thieme, 1997.
51. Leopold DA, Stafford CT, Sod EW, et al. Clinical course of acute sinusitis documented by sequential MRI scanning. Am J Rhinol 8:19, 1992.
52. Mafee MF. Modern imaging of the paranasal sinuses and the role of limited sinus computerized tomography; considerations of time, cost and radiation. Ear Nose Throat J 73(8):532, 1994.
53. April MH, Zinreich SJ, Baroody FM, et al. Coronal CT scan abnormalities in children with chronic sinusitis. Laryngoscope 103:985, 1993.
54. van der Veken PJV, Clement PAR, Buisseret T, et al. CT-Scan study of the incidence of sinus involvement and nasal anatomic variation in 196 children. Rhinology 28:177, 1990.
55. Kennedy DW, Zinreich SJ: The functional endoscopic approach to inflammatory disease: current perspectives and technique modifications. Am J Rhinol 2:89, 1998.

37

Nasal Obstruction and Rhinorrhea

Walter M. Belenky, M.D., David N. Madgy, D.O., and Michael S. Haupert, D.O.

Historical Perspective

The importance of nasal obstruction and rhinorrhea in nasal function and disease was well known and the concern of many physicians in ancient times. Among the earliest writings on this subject, the Hindu Arthava-Veda Sanhita (1500 to 800 BC[137]) listed causes of nasal discharge. Although Hippocrates[50] described nasal discharge in his humoral theory in 415 BC, and this problem was again mentioned by Celsus (c. 30 AD[19]), Galen[37] was the first to postulate on the etiology of rhinorrhea around 160 AD. He suggested that nasal discharge contained waste products from the brain that had been filtered by the pituitary and entered the nose by the cribriform and ethmoid plates. This theory was accepted for 1500 years until Schneider in 1600 AD pronounced that nasal discharge is a product of the membrane lining of the nose.[113]

General Considerations

The obstructed or draining nose is the most common complaint that the otolaryngologist faces in evaluating nasal problems in all patients, including children. The nose acts as the "guardian of the lower respiratory tract" and the "initiator of the immune response to inhaled antigens and pathogens."[129] Nasal obstruction and rhinorrhea may appear as both symptoms and signs, reflecting the anatomic and physiologic importance of the nose in both health and disease. Frequently occurring together, they may vary sufficiently in their characteristics to aid observant clinicians in their diagnosis. The presence of one without the other may be equally significant.

The clinician must recognize the symptoms and signs of nasal obstruction and rhinorrhea and, by means of a thorough history and a complete physical examination, assess the entire patient, particularly the internal and external nose and related structures, to determine whether the condition is of local or systemic, pathologic or physiologic origin.

Nasal obstruction and rhinorrhea manifest in a variety of ways, often in combination. The onset of symptoms may be acute, as in the common cold, or chronic, as in a child suffering from the stuffy, runny nose of perennial allergic rhinitis or chronic rhinosinusitis. These complaints may be the symptoms of a life-threatening disease, such as bilateral choanal atresia, or they may be due simply to the bothersome but normal physiologic changes that occur in the nose during puberty. The symptoms of nasal obstruction and rhinorrhea that may prompt parents to bring a child to the physician for treatment are often accompanied by the non-nasal symptoms of a dry, coated tongue, bad breath, snoring, mouth breathing, "postnasal drip," and chronic cough. Symptoms may also be part of the symptom complex of obstructive sleep apnea.

Nasal Physiology

Vasomotor Reaction

The vasomotor reaction is the primary response of the nasal mucosa to a variety of stimuli and is an etiologic factor in many cases of nasal obstruction and rhinorrhea. The ratio of acetylcholine production to acetylcholine enzymatic destruction is important for determining the intensity and duration of the vasomotor reaction. Numerous factors influence this ratio, but primary control is exerted by the hypothalamus by means of direct stimulation via the autonomic system to release acetylcholine, and indirect control is established via the hypothalamic-pituitary axis and estrogen release, which inhibits acetylcholinesterase function. As is well documented,[21, 123, 126, 127, 129] the control of nasal respiration regulates the oxygen intake of the lungs and thus influences cellular respiration throughout the body. This control is neuroendocrine in nature, originating in the hypothalamus in response to afferent stimuli from body receptors monitoring the internal and external environments of the body.

Control is effected via chemical mediators working directly at cell surface nerve endings or indirectly via hormonal activity. The primary target site effecting control of nasal respiration is the nasal mucosa, which is in a dynamic state, changing constantly under normal and abnormal conditions in response to internal and external stimuli. This complex, integrated neuroendocrine pathway uses the autonomic nervous system efferent nerves and hormonal mediators of the pituitary axis to produce a primary functional response of the nasal mucosa, known as the vasomotor reaction.

The vasomotor reaction is the end result of these multiple interactions and is characterized by increased nasal mucosal surface area, increased nasal obstruction, and increased nasal secretions.[127, 129] The reaction is chemically initiated at the end organ by vasodilating agents; the most important and powerful dilating agent in normal and disease states is acetylcholine, which is produced at parasympathetic nerve endings, delivered to nasal mucosa and submucosal appendages by the vidian nerve after synapse in sphenopalatine ganglion. Its action, in turn, is regulated by acetylcholinesterase activity at the nerve endings.

Nasal obstruction is produced by the vasomotor reaction and in many diseases is controlled by the autonomic nervous system, which acts on the erectile tissue of the nasal lining.

Evaluation of Nasal Obstruction

The clinician must first determine whether nasal obstruction is unilateral or bilateral, complete or partial, intermittent or constant, congenital or acquired, acute or chronic, and of sudden or gradual onset. Physical examination of the nose may determine the anatomic site of obstruction. Cottle[25] described five areas of the nose where abnormalities may occur; this description is still useful for documenting pathologic areas: (1) the vestibular area; (2) the "liminal valve" area, or the relationship of the caudal end of the upper lateral cartilage to the nasal septum, the os internum, the narrowest portion of the nasal passage; (3) the attic, or area of the septum under the bony vault; (4) the anterior turbinates; and (5) the posterior turbinates and choanae. For completeness, a sixth area, the nasopharynx, might be added (see Chap. 34).

From the standpoint of obstruction, certain areas appear to be more important during nasal inspiration and have been described by Bridger and others[12, 13] as nasal valves. These include the liminal valve, which is considered by many to be the most important part during inspiration,[12, 134, 135] the erectile tissue of the nasal turbinates (turbinate valve), and the nasal septum (septal valve). Fanous[31] states that the nasal valve consists of a circular obstruction formed inferiorly by the piriform crest, superiorly by the limen nasi, and medially by the corresponding strip of nasal septum. Internal displacement of any of these components affects the nasal airway. Structures immediately anterior (alar cartilage) or posterior (anterior tip of the inferior turbinate) can influence this area and nasal resistance. Haight and Cole[45] concluded that "the main airflow resistance of the whole respiratory tract is confined to a short nasal segment of a few millimeters which is situated in close proximity with the junction of the compliant cartilaginous vestibule with the rigid bony cavity of the nose." In their studies of the "flow limiting segment," the greater portion of the resistance was situated at the level of the anterior end of the inferior turbinate, and resistance could vary as much as fourfold by the adjusted state of this structure.

However, some conclusions with regard to the pediatric nasal airway must be adjusted in comparison with those regarding the adult. The nasal airway is obviously smaller in newborns than in adults. The resistance to airflow is approximately four times that in adults, and the variability in resistance is much greater.[63]

Nasal Endoscopy

Direct evaluation of nasal and nasopharyngeal anatomy and the causes of obstruction has been enhanced by the development of both rigid and fiberoptic nasoscopes and nasopharyngoscopes. The simplicity of use of these instruments even in children, along with the ability to evaluate both static and dynamic states, is a significant advance and has resulted in these instruments becoming a basic part of the nasal and nasopharyngeal examination of children.

Endoscopy of the area has progressed with the continuing development of sinus endoscopy equipment and techniques.[58] The use of rhinoscopic assessment by Stammberger[122] and others has shown the rhinogenic origin of sinusitis as well as the physiologic changes involved in many other conditions, and has become a standard of care.

Physiology of Nasal Airflow

To aid clinicians and researchers in measuring the degree of obstruction objectively and quantifying nasal functions, rhinomanometry procedures have been developed to measure the air pressure gradient and the rate of airflow through the nasal channel during respiration. These procedures have helped substantiate clinical findings of nasal obstruction; for example, significant airway obstruction may occur with minimal anatomic abnormality in areas 1 and 2, whereas larger deformities in areas 3, 4, and 5 may cause minimal obstructive symptoms.[12, 13]

Furthermore, such data have highlighted the importance of the streamlined airflow in the nose with reduction of eddy currents and resistance. However, studies suggest that airflow through the nose is predominantly nonlaminar; instead, flow through the nose is termed transitional, with a mixture of laminar and turbulent characteristics.[42] Disturbed flow enhances contact between air and mucous membrane, ensuring warming, moistening, and cleansing. Anterior active and passive rhinomanometry[133] and posterior rhinomanometry,[23, 131] along with "head-out" body plethysmography,[85] have been used to enable more complete understanding and measurement of nasal resistance. Parker et al[98] have used active posterior rhinomanometry with computer-assisted head-out plethysmography to obtain results of nasal resistance in children that were highly reproducible. They correlated resistance to the degree of mucosal swelling, adenoid enlargement, and other nasal pathology.[97] However, because of difficulties in performing the various procedures (especially in young children), variability in the nasal airway (e.g., the congestion of erectile tissue), and disturbance of the nasal airway by the instrumentation, the research and clinical value of such studies, although improved, must still be critically interpreted as to its importance in pediatric otolaryngology (see Chap. 34).

Pedersen et al[102] suggest that acoustic rhinometry may be a simple, noninvasive method of assessing nasal airway geometry and adequacy in newborns and young children.

Imaging

In the past, the clinical impression of nasal obstruction could be confirmed by lateral radiographs of the nose and nasopharynx. Such radiographs, if taken with the mouth closed, were especially useful in showing the obstruction of the airway by hypertrophic adenoids. However, interpretation could be misleading and vary according to the position of the soft palate on the radiograph. Contrast-enhanced nasograms also helped demonstrate choanal atresia.

Since the mid-1980s, computed tomography (CT) has become the first objective method of obtaining true cross-sectional imaging of the nose, the nasopharynx, and allied structures. It is still the best mechanism for visualization of the bony dimensions and abnormalities of the area. Slovis et al[118] were the first to show its value in the diagnosis and classification of choanal atresia. Within the past 2 decades, CT has superseded plain film tomography as the preferred method of imaging the nose, nasopharynx, and allied structures. Axial, coronal, and even sagittal views may be helpful in determining the extent of both normal anatomy and congenital or acquired pathology.

Although CT is still the modality of choice for imaging bony anatomy, magnetic resonance imaging (MRI) has emerged as an extremely valuable tool for delineating the anatomy of and characterizing soft tissue lesions.[74] MRI can provide imaging in all three planes without the use of ionizing radiation. Various imaging sequences can be used with MRI to enhance detection of lesions, and the use of gadolinium (diethylenetriaminepentaacetic acid, DPTA)as a contrast agent has improved lesion conspicuity and delineation of even the smallest inflammatory lesion.

Magnetic resonance angiography (MRA), arterial MRA, and venous MRA are replacing much of conventional angiography. However, diagnostic catheter angiography of vascular nasal, nasopharyngeal, and sinus lesions can still provide useful information concerning arterial supply that can aid in presurgical planning, and, with the development of microcatheters, it is now possible to safely perform subselective embolization of feeding arteries in order to facilitate hemostasis at surgery.

Evaluation of Rhinorrhea

As with nasal obstruction, rhinorrhea must first be evaluated by the clinician as to extent, frequency, duration, time and nature of onset, and quantity. By classic definition, rhinorrhea is the "free discharge of a thin nasal mucus."[27]

Mucus Physiology

The increased nasal secretions of the vasomotor reaction are largely composed of mucus from the nasal mucosa. Nasal mucus is the basic ingredient of nasal discharge and consists of 2.3% to 3% nonsulfated and sulfated mucoproteins and mucopolysaccharides, 1% to 2% inorganic salts, and 96% water.[129] It is produced by nasal mucosa from goblet cells, stromal mucosa, serous glands, and duct cells. Transudation can quickly occur via the semipermeable basement membrane and from the capillary loops that pierce the membrane, thus bringing fluid and debris directly onto the surface epithelium and contributing to mucus formation.[128] This fluid may be seen as the sudden, diffuse, watery discharge occurring in several diseases.

Excessive mucus formation or increased viscosity in response to internal and external stimuli may lead to stasis and poor drainage from the nose. Such stasis frequently leads to secondary infections, chronic changes in the nasal mucosa, or both. The normal nasal secretion rate is 0.1 to 0.3 mL/kg per day.

The significance of the mucus and increased nasal secretions that are a part of the vasomotor reaction and that accompany nasal disease lies in the relationship of the specific physiochemical qualities of mucus to nasal function. Along with the erectile nature of the nasal mucosa, nasal mucus provides temperature regulation of the internal environment and inspired air, humidification of inspired air, and vasorespiration control. The peculiar adhesiveness and surface electric activity of nasal mucosa, the result of sulfated mucins, combines with the vibrissae to keep particulate matter from the lower airway. Mucus acts as a primary defense mechanism upon exposure to foreign substances. It contains immunoglobulins, such as IgA, and, when challenged by active infection, can also contain concentrations of IgG and IgM.

For further information, refer to works by Taylor,[127–129] who has written historically significant reviews of nasal physiology.

Normal Physiologic State

At times, infants and children complain of nasal obstruction and rhinorrhea but exhibit no signs of local or systemic disease. In these cases, obstruction and rhinorrhea may represent a normal physiologic nasal function or may be symptoms of a pathologic condition. The frequency of such complaints increases as the child approaches adolescence, and this fact must be taken into consideration when making a differential diagnosis (see Chap. 34).

Table 37–1 lists a number of normal physiologic states in which increased rhinorrhea and nasal obstruction may occur.

TABLE 37–1. Normal Physiologic Causes of Increased Nasal Obstruction and Rhinorrhea

Nasal cycle
Paradoxic nasal obstruction
Nasopulmonary reflex
Puberty
Menses
Psychosomatic factors
External environmental stimuli

The Nasal Cycle

The nasal cycle is a rhythmic, alternating side-to-side congestion and decongestion of the cavernous tissue of the nasal turbinates. Although it occurs in 80% of the population, it is usually unnoticed because the total nasal resistance remains constant. Occasionally, the cycle increases in intensity and produces signs of obstruction without any significant increase in nasal secretions.[129]

As mentioned, there is a greater variability in nasal air resistance exhibited by young neonates and infants,[63] which suggests an immaturity of the vasomotor reaction in their nasal mucosa. This is further shown by the apparent lack of an established nasal cycle in these children.[133] In neonates and infants, instead of the usual adult alternation of nasal air resistance from side to side, the total nasal airway resistance varies, with changes occurring simultaneously in both sides of the nose.

Paradoxic Nasal Obstruction

Older children and adolescents with long-standing, severe unilateral obstruction (e.g., that due to a septal deformity) often complain of intermittent obstruction of the patent nasal airway. In these individuals, the patent side has functioned as the entire nasal airway, and complaints are elicited only when factors such as the nasal cycle intermittently obstruct the patent side.[3]

Nasopulmonary Reflex

Older children with a common cold often complain of breathlessness out of proportion to the degree of nasal obstruction observed by the examiner. This is probably the result of reduced vital capacity secondary to stimulation of a nasopulmonary reflex by increased nasal obstruction.[127] Similarly, hypothalamus-mediated nasopulmonary reflexes account for a common complaint of dependent nasal obstruction in the recumbent position; compression of the dependent lung elicits an ipsilateral nasal obstruction.[115] Ogura et al[87-91, 93] have studied the nasopulmonary reflexes and documented a relationship between nasal and pulmonary resistance. They found that increased nasal resistance produces increased pulmonary resistance and decreased pulmonary compliance with probable decreased alveolar ventilation. This may result in aberration of blood gases, acid-base imbalance, and tissue hypoxemia, which may account for the generalized symptoms of fatigue, restlessness, and irritability seen in children with severe upper airway obstruction.[94, 95] In contrast, in newborns, Lacourt and Polgar[63] found that there are reciprocal changes in nasal and pulmonary resistance: "Changes observed in nasal resistance were in opposite direction to pulmonary resistance changes resulting in stabilization of total air resistance."

Puberty and Menses

Adolescent females, and even males, occasionally complain of intermittent nasal obstruction and rhinorrhea during the pubescent period, resulting from increases in the level of estrogen and, in part, testosterone, which increase the normal vasomotor reaction by decreasing the activity of acetylcholinesterase. Similarly, periodic complaints occur in postpubescent females regarding menstruation[83, 99, 127, 129] and in adolescent pregnancy.

Psychosomatic Factors

Teenagers especially may present with symptoms of intense vasomotor reactions related to emotional states such as anxiety, stress, fatigue, and anger. These are mediated through reflexes centered in the hypothalamus. These symptoms may be accompanied by unilateral migraine headaches, which are mediated by similar reflexes.[54, 127, 129]

External Environmental Stimuli

Numerous complaints of obstruction and rhinorrhea are nothing more than an expression of the nasal vasomotor reaction to external stimuli and reflect the normal function of the nasal mucosa as an interface between the body's internal and external environments. Thus, such symptoms may be dependent on the composition of gases and particulate matter (e.g., dust, fur, smog) or on the temperature and water content of the inspired air. The watery discharge one experiences when going outside during the winter or upon completion of a spicy meal is an example of this type of vasomotor reaction.[127] Chronic symptoms may occur from primary or secondary tobacco smoke exposure.

Nasal Obstruction and Rhinorrhea in Disease

The significance of nasal obstruction and rhinorrhea in nasal disease that may occur in the pediatric patient cannot be stressed too greatly. As discussed, both may be manifestations of the basic vasomotor reaction to abnormal internal or external stimuli. However, obstruction may occur with little contribution from the vasomotor reaction but rather from a single mass blockage of the nasal airway, as seen in choanal atresia (see Chap. 42).

Similarly, rhinorrhea may lack the usual mucous component and instead may be distinctly pathologic in nature, as when it is composed of cerebrospinal fluid (CSF).

Nasal obstruction and rhinorrhea vary in nature according to their etiology. Table 37–2 classifies obstruction and rhinorrhea according to their pathogenesis.

Unique to newborn and infant airways is the impact of nasal obstruction on the physiologic status of the child. It has been well established that many newborns and infants up to several months of age are obligatory nasal breathers and depend almost entirely on this mode of respiration. This relationship is dependent on the degree of neurologic development of the particular newborn, in that some well-developed children can make significant adaptations. Bilateral complete obstruction usually produces a significant respiratory distress state with intermittent cyanosis, apnea, failure to thrive, and, in some cases, life-threatening situations. Even unilateral obstruction may produce some respiratory distress or at least a significant

TABLE 37–2. Nasal Obstruction and Rhinorrhea in Disease

Congenital
Total nasal agenesis
Proboscis lateralis
Congenital occlusion of anterior nares
Posterior choanal atresia
Choanal stenosis
Mandibulofacial dysostoses
    Treacher Collins syndrome
    Crouzon disease
Coronal craniosynostosis
Cleft palate
Congenital cysts of nasal cavity
    Dermoid
    Nasoalveolar
    Dentigerous
    Mucous cysts of floor of nose
    Jacobson organ cysts
Meningoencephalocele
Encephalocele
Pharyngeal bursa (Tornwaldt)
Hamartomas
Craniopharyngiomas
Chordomas
Teratoid tumors
Epignathus
    Possible third branchial cleft cyst[34] (presenting in Rosenmüller fossa)
Congenital squamous cell carcinoma of nasopharynx
Inflammatory
Infectious
Bacterial
    Secondary invaders
        Haemophilus influenzae
        Streptococcus pneumoniae
        Other streptococci
        Staphylococcus
        Branhamella catarrhalis
    Primary agent
        Diphtheria
        Pertussis
        Tuberculosis
        Rhinoscleroma
        Leprosy
        Chlamydia
Viral
    Primary agent
        Acute viral rhinonasopharyngitis
        Rhinovirus
        Adenovirus
        Coxsackieviruses A and B
        Myxoviruses
            Influenza
            Parainfluenza
            Respiratory syncytial virus
    Prodromal stage of virus disease
        Mumps
        Poliomyelitis
        Measles (rubella, rubeola)
        Roseola infantum
        Erythema infectiosum
        Infectious mononucleosis
        Hepatitis
Acquired immunodeficiency syndrome
Spirochetal
    Congenital "snuffles"
    Acquired snuffles

Protozoan
    Leishmaniasis
Fungal
    Moniliasis
    Mucormycosis (immunocompromised children)
    Aspergillosis (immunocompromised children)
Parasitic
Allergic
Acute: Type I (anaphylactic, reagin dependent)
Chronic: nasal polyposis
Toxic
External stimuli
    Inhalants (e.g., urban pollutants)
    Ingested (hormones, iodides, bromides, aspirin)
    Topically applied (nose drops, cocaine) (rhinitis medicamentosa)
Nasopharyngeal
Adenoid hyperplasia
Nasopharyngeal or gastroesophageal reflux
Traumatic
External Deformity
In utero
Neonatal
Acquired in childhood
Internal Deformity
Neonatal
Septal hematoma acquired in childhood
Septal abscess acquired in childhood
Foreign Bodies
Rhinolith
Cerebrospinal Fluid Rhinorrhea
Traumatic
Spontaneous
Neoplastic
Ectodermal origin
Mesodermal origin
Neurogenic origin
    Olfactory neuroblastoma
Odontogenic origin
Idiopathic origin
    Juvenile angiofibroma
    Nasopharyngeal carcinoma
Metabolic
Cystic fibrosis
Calcium abnormalities
Thyroid disease
    Hypothyroidism
    Hyperthyroidism
Diabetes mellitus
Immunodeficiency disease
Idiopathic
Ciliary dyskinesia (Kartagener syndrome, congenital and acquired immotile cilia syndrome)
Atrophic rhinitis
Chronic catarrhal rhinitis
Granulomatosis and vasculitis diseases
    Lupus erythematosus
    Rheumatoid arthritis
    Psoriatic arthritis
    Scleroderma
    Sarcoidosis
    Wegener granulomatosis
    Midline lethal granuloma
    Churg-Strauss syndrome
    Pemphigoid: cicatricial or benign mucoid

feeding problem.[77] A number of factors have been postulated as the cause of such obligation, including (1) "a high cephalic position of cervical viscera with close opposition of the soft palate to the tongue and epiglottis"[124, 129]; (2) the safety provided by the rigid nasal airway in one who spends most of the time recumbent and sleeping; (3) an aid to suckling; and (4) "nature's way" of ensuring maximal exposure of nasal and nasopharyngeal lymphoid tissue to inspired pathogens and allergens, thus promoting the early development of the immune response.[79, 129]

The degree and duration of obligatory nasal breathing is variable. Indeed, some newborns, although distressed by bilateral nasal obstruction, quickly adapt to oral respiration, whereas others become oral breathers only after a number of months.

In general, as mentioned, nasal resistance is higher in children than in adults, and pediatric nasal resistance is much more variable.[63] Unilateral nasal obstruction in a sleeping child often elicits periodic major body movements, seemingly attempts to decrease the airway obstruction.[47, 77] Nasal obstruction in obligatory nasal breathers, such as infants, along with delays in body movement may lead to sufficient hypoxia to produce apnea during rapid eye movement sleep.[43, 129]

Significant nasal obstruction, especially of some chronicity in older developing children, may lead to chronic mouth breathing, abnormal tongue posturing, and resultant dental arch changes with concomitant craniofacial changes.[79] The resultant long-face syndrome (adenoid facies) manifests with vertical excess in the lower third of the facial height, lip incompetence, a narrow maxillary arch with high palate, and a steep mandibular plane angle.[62] Many authors believe there is no conclusive evidence that nasal obstruction alters facial growth and development.[44, 62, 75] Others,[70, 106, 110, 120] in their studies and writings, report at least a closer correlation, if not a direct cause-and-effect relationship, albeit acknowledging that other factors may be present.

The effect of nasal or nasopharyngeal obstruction in children with obstructive sleep apnea syndrome has been studied extensively. It has been well accepted that either site of obstruction, depending on severity, may lead, via hypoxia, alveolar hypoventilation, and pulmonary hypertension, to cor pulmonale.[68] The whole spectrum of obstructive sleep apnea syndrome, with snoring, enuresis, hypersomnia, decreased mental and physical performance, and daytime hypersomnolence, can occur with nasal obstruction, nasopharyngeal obstruction, or both.[65, 66] However, it is still difficult to obtain a correlation between sleep apnea and measured parameters of nasopharyngeal shape or volume of adenoids and dimensions of the nasopharynx.[65] More recent rhinomanometry, intraoperative, and nasopharyngeal dimension studies continue to address this relationship.[14, 98]

Congenital

In view of the varied and complicated plications and involutions that tissues involved in the formation of the face and nose undergo, it is remarkable how infrequently congenital abnormalities of the nose occur. Such abnormalities are most probably due to a combination of exogenous teratogenic factors and inherited gene patterns. In some cases in which nasal development is limited, the cause of the symptoms of obstruction is obvious. Total nose agenesis, although rare, has been reported.[136] Similarly, proboscis lateralis is a rare congenital anomaly.[7, 136] Congenital occlusion of the anterior nares seldom occurs, but, when it does, it may be unilateral or bilateral and complete or

partial, and nasal obstruction may vary accordingly.[136] Rhinorrhea plays a limited role in the complaints that result from these rare anomalies (see Chap. 42).

Congenital nasal piriform aperture stenosis, isolated or in combination with other abnormalities, was first described in 1988[30a] as a slightly more common congenital nasal anomaly. Anterior rhinoscopy reveals a narrow nasal inlet 3 mm or less in width. Axial CT scan confirms the diagnosis.

The almost total dependency of neonates and infants on nasal respiration is highlighted by the acuteness and severity of the symptoms of nasal obstruction in these children with congenital nasal anomalies, especially as seen in choanal atresia, which is the most common. The incidence of congenital choanal atresia ranges from 1 in 5000 births to 1 in 8000 births.[130] It may be unilateral or bilateral, complete or incomplete, and bony or membranous. Unilateral presentation is more common (2:1) and is often diagnosed later in life. Bony atresia is documented more commonly than the membranous form,[117] although often there is a combination of both types in a patient. The high incidence of associated anomalies, up to 72% in some series, has been characterized by the acronym CHARGE, derived from the first letters of the six major categories of associated anomalies occurring in patients with coloboma or choanal atresia: *c*oloboma, *h*eart disease, *a*tresia choanae, *r*etarded development of the central nervous system, *g*enital hypoplasia, and *e*ar anomalies or deafness.[96] The term CHARGE is used when malformations are present in at least four of the six categories.[26] However, in addition to the CHARGE association, studies have indicated multiple motor anomalies in 26% of cases, and a single additional anomaly in 16%.[82]

Newborns with bilateral complete choanal atresia present in acute respiratory distress, as might be expected with complete nasal obstruction in an obligatory nasal breather. The severity and duration of the unattended distress may vary according to the adaptability of the neonate in acquiring oral respiration, which again is related to the degree of neurologic development and maturity. Unilateral choanal atresia may not be recognized until later in life when symptoms of unilateral nasal obstruction and persistent unilateral rhinorrhea are investigated. During infancy, when occlusion of the normal side by acquired disease produces symptoms, the diagnosis may be sought at an earlier age.

The diagnosis is confirmed and evaluation of atresia is best completed by use of axial CT in a plane paralleling the posterior hard palate.[118] This advance led to documentation of the importance of the vomer bone width, the degree of medial pterygoid bowing, and the resultant dimension of the lateral wall of the nasal cavity to the vomer. Also occasionally documented is the presence of nasal obstruction due to choanal stenosis in some neonates. Evaluation of possible gastroesophageal or nasopharyngeal reflux with radiographic studies is important.[6, 24] The vasomotor reaction of even the normal neonatal nose in response to the intermittent or constant stimulus of gastric acid in gastroesophageal reflux or of milk and formula in nasopharyngeal regurgitation can lead to significant nasal obstruction and mimic choanal atresia or exacerbate symptoms in patients with choanal stenosis.

Equally, excessive nasal suctioning in these neonates can lead to acquired stenosis or cicatricial atresia.

Neonates with fetal alcohol syndrome present with nasal obstruction and rhinorrhea secondary to upper airway anomalies, including nasal hypoplasia, choanal stenosis, and contracted nasopharyngeal vault.[132] Midface growth deficiencies have been shown to be a common feature of fetal alcohol syndrome, with maxillary hypoplasia occurring in 64% of infants in a series by Jones and Smith.[55]

Congenital nasal deformity and obstruction may occur as part of the various mandibulofacial dysostoses (e.g., Treacher Collins syndrome and Crouzon disease) secondary to intrauterine disturbance in the development of the first and second branchial arches. There may be associated hypoplasia of the external nose or nasal obstruction secondary to malar, maxillary, and palatal hypoplasia. Coronal craniosynostosis, accompanied by a brachycephalic skull with shortened anteroposterior dimensions, may result in midface contracture and subsequent nasal and nasopharyngeal airway obstruction. Cleft palate deformities also alter the structure of the nasal cavity, because they are accompanied by nasoseptal deformities.[71]

Congenital cysts may occur in the nasal cavity and, depending on their size and location, may manifest with degrees of nasal obstruction. These may be dermoid cysts, nasoalveolar (incisive canal) cysts, nasolacrimal duct cysts, or dentigerous and mucous cysts of the floor of the nose and Jacobson organ. Nasal discharge may be present from a draining sinus tract and may consist of epithelial debris and ectodermal gland secretions.[36, 107] Nasal obstruction in the neonatal period may occur secondary to congenital cerebral herniation into the nose in the form of a meningocele (meninges alone), meningoencephalocele (meninges and a portion of the brain), or encephalocele (brain tissue without meninges) or glioma (glial tissue with no persistent brain connection). Rhinorrhea may be present as a vasomotor response to altered airflow with a purulent component from secondary bacterial infection; however, in herniations with central connections, clear, watery CSF rhinorrhea may occur spontaneously.[36, 107]

Primary congenital neoplasms may occur symptomatically according to size and location, including angiomas, angiofibromas, hemangiopericytomas, and teratomas.

Neonates with nasopharyngeal lesions may present at birth with obstruction, minimal rhinorrhea, mucopurulent crusting, and postnasal discharge secondary to mucostasis. The pharyngeal bursa (Tornwaldt bursa) in the midline of the nasopharynx may be patulous at birth, although this is rarely noted, but later may become cystic, inflamed, and symptomatic.[28, 107] Other uncommon lesions of the nasopharynx include hamartomas, craniopharyngiomas, chordomas, congenital squamous cell carcinomas,[20] and teratoid tumors (embryomas and epignathus). Frazer[34] and others have even postulated that a third branchial cleft cyst could manifest in the fossa of Rosenmüller.[28]

Inflammatory Nasal Disease

By far, the most common nasal disease in children is that due to inflammatory responses of the nasal mucosa to infectious, allergic, or toxic agents. Obstruction and rhinorrhea occur in response to the nasal vasomotor reaction, which is initiated as a specific defense mechanism to dilute the offending agents and to bring specific antibodies, immunoglobulins, and bacteriolytic enzymes (lysozyme) into action. Because most offending agents are airborne, the nasal vasomotor reaction is the first line of body defense. Typically, the reaction works to increase the nasal surface area and increase nasal secretions, which results in increased obstruction; the total effect represents the prodromal symptoms of many common illnesses in children (see Chaps. 43 and 49). The obstruction produced enhances retention of the offending agents in the nose and allows for appropriate sensitization and antibody response from cells in the nasal mucosa.

In acute inflammation, vascular dilatation, along with arteriolar constriction, occurs, accompanied by exudation of protein-rich fluid and the migration of polymorphonuclear leukocytes and monocytes into the inflamed tissues.[129] IgA, the major immunoglobulin in nasal secretions, is synthesized by plasma cells in the mucosa and nasal lymphoid tissues.[86] It is produced locally to a variety of bacterial antigens. It is virus neutralizing and may be active in promoting phagocytosis and intracellular destruction of organisms by macrophages. After acute inflammation, there may be a variable onset of mucosal damage to the epithelial and basal membranes and underlying structures that may be quite extensive, especially in patients with recurrent infection. Mucosal appearance on examination is variable and noncharacteristic, being pale and swollen or red and swollen.

With recurrent episodes of nasal infection, along with abnormal mucociliary transport due to decreased ciliated cells or ultrastructural deficiencies, there may be increased goblet cell or submucosal glands, altered periciliary fluid due to increased tissue fluid leak, and increased purulent secretions due to microabscesses.[104] These changes may take up to 3 to 4 weeks to heal after resolution of the inflammatory process. Chronic inflammation may occur with prolongation of the symptoms of rhinorrhea and infection.

Bacterial infection in the nose is most commonly a secondary infection, often a result of prolongation of the vasomotor reaction with obstruction and mucostasis. With the continuity of nasal and sinus mucosa, acute and chronic rhinosinusitis may subsequently develop for similar reasons. Rhinorrhea becomes more purulent, reflecting the increased inflammatory exudate. Obstruction persists from the swollen turbinates and mucosa. Offending organisms include *Haemophilus influenzae*, *Streptococcus pneumoniae*, other streptococcal species, *Staphylococcus*, and frequently *Moraxella catarrhalis*.[35, 69, 108, 129, 136] With continued sinus ostium obstruction and reduced sinus cavity oxygen saturation, anaerobic organisms proliferate and become a feature of both acute and chronic sinusitis. Appropriate historical information, combined with careful nasal examination for evidence of purulence, is usually sufficient to confirm the diagnosis. Sphenoid sinusitis may manifest with such subtle signs.[69] Bacterial culture of nasal, nasopharyngeal, and pharyngeal secretions may not be indicative of the true sinus pathogen.[35, 108]

Retrospective and prospective studies have reiterated the potential contributory role of gastroesophageal or nasopharyngeal reflux in the development of pediatric chronic rhinosinusitis. Bothwell et al[10a] demonstrated retrospectively an 89% improvement in sinonasal symptoms after treatment of reflux disease. The prospective study by Phipps et al[104a] revealed a higher than expected prevalence of gastroesophageal reflux in patients with pediatric chronic rhinosinusitis as well as a 79% improvement after treatment of their reflux. Pediatric patients with chronic rhinosinusitis may benefit from an evaluation for gastroesophageal reflux before endoscopic sinus surgery.

Reactive airway disease (asthma) unresponsive to control and treatment may be aggravated by recurrent acute or chronic rhinosinusitis in children.[35] Otolaryngologists are now aware that chronic rhinosinusitis or recurrent otitis media often precedes the development of opportunistic infections in children affected with acquired immunodeficiency syndrome[22] and other forms of immunoincompetence.

Special mention must be made of diphtheritic rhinitis, which, although uncommon, is a grave disease that may be fatal if untreated. Caused by *Corynebacterium diphtheriae,* acute nasal diphtheria may manifest with a foul, possibly bilateral nasal discharge that often excoriates the upper lip and nostrils. Chronic nasal diphtheria also occurs and is often called membranous rhinitis. A thin, glairy discharge is frequently seen. Nasal obstruction is found in both diseases. The classic pale-yellow or whitish membranous exudate of diphtheria may be seen covering the mucous membranes of the nose, and the nasal discharge may contain shreds of membranes along with blood.[136]

Other specific bacterial infections producing nasal symptoms in children include pertussis, tuberculosis, rhinoscleroma, and leprosy. The first stage of pertussis is called the catarrhal phase, with symptoms similar to those of the common cold.[67, 136]

In tuberculosis of the skin (lupus vulgaris), involvement of the nasal vestibule and subcutaneous structures of the nose, including cartilage, may be present. This is usually endogenic, with bacilli of *Mycobacterium tuberculosis* produced via the blood, although the organisms may be introduced externally. Obstruction and mucopurulent secretions may characterize the disease in the nose.[67] Primary tuberculosis of the nose is rare but may occur as a result of direct contamination by bacilli in the air or from fingers and instruments or via blood and lymphatic routes. The primary granulomas formed by reaction to the bacilli may ulcerate and obstruct the nose. The symptoms of primary tuberculosis of the nose are related to the degree of nasal ulceration present. When ulceration occurs, the resultant rhinorrhea is usually mucopurulent and tinged with blood.[67]

A more common granulomatous lesion found in the nose, usually on the septum, is a pyogenic granuloma, resulting from a localized inflammatory response to irritation or trauma with secondary bacterial infection.

Other causes of chronic granulomatous disease of the nose include rhinoscleroma and leprosy. However, the obstruction that occurs as a result of these illnesses is usually the first sign of the disease, with mucopurulent and serosanguineous discharge developing later as a result of tissue necrosis.[67]

Chlamydia infection in newborns and infants may be acquired during passage through the birth canal of infected mothers. If the mother is untreated, conjunctivitis will develop in 20% to 50% of the newborns, and pneumonia will develop in 10% to 20%.[119] *Chlamydia trachomatis* is best classified as a bacterium, although it is an obligate intracellular parasite, with nasopharyngeal involvement developing in approximately one fifth of contaminated infants. However, some infected newborns present with obstructions, rhinorrhea, and a fiery red nasal mucosa with positive cell culture for *C. trachomatis*.[46]

Viruses may be present but remain inactive in the nasal cavities of children. Under the proper circumstances, such as cooling of the limbs, a decrease in nasal temperature may occur, which may activate the virus and produce symptoms of infection. Viruses manifest extracellularly, stimulating a vasomotor reaction, and may take part in antigen-antibody reactions.[129] Acute viral rhinitis or rhinonasal pharyngitis, "the common cold," is the most common cause of nasal obstruction and rhinorrhea in children. This self-limiting disease is caused by a number of different viruses, including rhinovirus (the common cold), adenovirus, myxoviruses (including influenza, parainfluenza, and respiratory syncytial virus [RSV]), and coxsackievirus A and B. RSV has been recognized as the most important cause of severe respiratory tract disease in infants and preschool children.[51] It is especially prevalent in infants younger than 2 months of age, although newborns may have a high concentration of antibodies to RSV from their mother.[60, 129] The nasal obstruction resulting from infection by RSV may cause problems in these obligatory nasal breathers. Frequent reinfections can occur, especially in certain closed environments, for example, hospitals and day care centers.

Nasal obstruction and rhinorrhea may appear in the prodromal periods of a variety of other childhood viral illnesses, including mumps, poliomyelitis, measles (both rubella and rubeola), roseola infantum, erythema infectiosum, infectious mononucleosis, and hepatitis.[84]

Spirochetal disease, although rare, may also occur in the nasal cavity of children with treponemal diseases, particularly *Treponema pallidum,* which causes syphilis. Syphilis may be congenital or acquired. The nasal symptoms of congenital syphilis may appear in two stages. Symptoms of the early stage develop between the second week to third month of life and resemble those of acute viral rhinitis. There is a thin, watery discharge that becomes mucopurulent. Marked nasal obstruction develops, with characteristic noisy breathing, termed "snuffles." The later stage of congenital syphilis occurs in children aged 3 years or older and is marked by gummatous involvement of the nose, with persistent obstruction and purulent, sanguineous discharge. In acquired syphilis, the primary stage seldom involves the nose. The secondary stage manifests with acute rhinitis. Tertiary-stage symptoms are secondary to tissue destruction and may include nasoseptal perforations, cartilage collapse, and subsequent saddle nose deformity resulting from gummatous involvement.[67, 76, 136] Other treponemes causing bejel, yaws, and pinta are nonvenereal in nature and rarely involve the nasal cavities. In tropical environments, leishmaniasis from the protozoa *Leishmania tropica* may produce symptoms similar to those of syphilis.[67]

Fungal infection of the nose and paranasal sinuses was once considered rare in children, usually occurring secondary to injury of the nasal mucosa,[67] but more recently the presence of fungal infection must be suspected in the debilitated, immunodeficient, or immunosuppressed child presenting with even the most subtle symptoms of nasal obstruction and rhinorrhea.[64] Mucormycosis and aspergillosis are the most common causes of invasive fungal rhinosinusitis, and diagnosis must be established by biopsy, fungal stains, fungal cultures, or all three. Diabetic patients are more prone to development of invasive mucormycosis infections, while candidal infections are not uncommon in patients with acquired immunodeficiency syndrome. Early diagnosis and treatment are paramount to offset this often fatal complication in the immunocompromised patient. Surgical debridement along with systemic antifungal agents are required to treat invasive fungal rhinosinusitis.

Allergic fungal rhinosinusitis (AFRS) is reportedly the most common form of fungal rhinosinusitis, although its incidence in the pediatric population is unknown. In patients with AFRS, an allergic or hypersensitivity reaction develops to a fungus, with the most common being *Bipolaris, Curvularia,* and *Alternaria.* Polyps frequently develop as a result of the chronic inflammation. Diagnosis of AFRS is made if hyphae are seen in eosinophilic allergic mucin, which is often laminated with necrotic inflammatory cells and Charcot-Leyden crystals, and the patient exhibits fungal atopy. Fungal stains and cultures may contribute further to the diagnosis of AFRS. Management requires surgical removal of all fungus-containing mucin and debris as well as systemic perioperative steroids. The role of systemic and topical antifungal agents is still being evaluated, with results thus far being mixed. Immunotherapy may play a role in decreasing recurrences, but further investigation is needed.

In children, parasitic diseases cause nasal reactions similar to those seen when an organic foreign body is present in the nose. Parasites that may infect the nose include leeches and maggots.

Allergic rhinitis is another common cause of obstruction and rhinorrhea in the pediatric patient. It is characterized by a Gell and Coombs type I anaphylactic IgE-mediated reaction.[38] When sensitized tissue mast cells with allergen-specific IgE attached come into contact with the inciting allergen, a process known as degranulation occurs. This process involves the dissolution of the cell with liberation of its granules, which releases both preformed and newly formed mediators (histamine, leukotrienes, thromboxanes, and prostaglandins) and triggers the acute phase of the allergic reaction.[52] This, in turn, produces vasodilatation, increased capillary permeability, and an intense vasomotor reaction.[121, 129]

Clinically, the result of such an intensive vasomotor response is nasal obstruction and a profuse watery rhinorrhea, often associated with sneezing and nasal pruritus. Mucostasis can occur, with resultant secondary bacterial infection. The symptoms usually occur chronically with a specific periodicity.

With chronic inflammation of the mucous membrane of the nose and paranasal sinuses, manifested by hypersecretion and hyperplasia, nasal and sinus polyps can form. They represent a focal exaggeration of hyperplastic rhinosinusitis in which stromal binding of the intracellular fluid results in the formation of tissue polyps. The obstruction increases, and both water and mucoid secretions are more abundant.[121] Nasal polyps can occur not only with allergy, especially in aspirin-intolerant and intrinsic-asthma patients (Sumpter triad), but also in Young syndrome, cystic fibrosis, and Kartagener and ciliary motility dyskinesis syndromes, along with those conditions secondary to chronic infection and mucostasis.[116] Their underlying etiology can, in part, be differentiated histologically. Chemical mediators that can be found in nasal polyps include histamine, serotonin, leukotriene, eosinophil chemotactic factor of anaphylaxis, norepinephrine, kinin, esterase, and possibly prostaglandin D_2.[116]

Nasopharyngeal adenoid hyperplasia is another common cause of nasal obstruction in children. As part of Waldeyer ring, the adenoids occupy a key position in the development of the immune process. Adenoids are minimal in size at birth and increase in size, usually from 1 to 2 years of age, after immunity has been established. They may recede at puberty,[53, 129] although some evidence suggests a more frequent persistence of size into adulthood than was previously thought. Perhaps this decrease in size of adenoid tissue is just the increased size of the nasopharyngeal airway relative to the actual adenoid tissue present. In the nasopharynx, they are in constant contact with inspired air and are continually bathed by nasal mucus cleared from the posterior choanae by the nasal ciliary mechanism. Thus, they are continually exposed to antigens (bacterial, viral, or allergens) inhaled by the individual, and may serve as a potential reservoir of pathogens. They react by forming their own complement of antibodies to these antigens, and it has been postulated that "they modify the microorganisms encountered and release them or their toxins into the reticuloendothelial system of the body as an antigen stimulus for exciting active immunization."[129] This activity may account for the increase in size of adenoidal tissue with increasing antigen stimulation, often seen in allergic patients, and may explain the occurrence of adenoid hypertrophy. Nasal obstruction and chronic purulent rhinorrhea may result from such hypertrophy.

The severest form of nasal obstruction may occur in the presence of marked hypertrophy of adenoid tissue with or without tonsil enlargement. As mentioned previously, increased nasal airway resistance may lead to increased pulmonary resistance and alveolar hypoventilation, which is mediated by nasopulmonary reflexes. The result may be hypoxia, causing secondary pulmonary vasoconstriction with increased pulmonary vascular resistance. Eventually, prolongation of these symptoms may lead to cor pulmonale.[68, 73]

In newborns and young infants (especially those with central nervous system immaturity), nasal obstruction and rhinorrhea along with recurrent respiratory disorders, oropharyngeal dysphagia, chronic regurgitation, and hematemesis may be secondary to the irritative and inflammatory response of the nasal and nasopharyngeal mucosa, and an indicator of nasopharyngeal regurgitation or gastroesophageal reflux. As mentioned earlier, formula or gastric content in the nasopharynx produces a vasomotor reaction to these chronic irritative stimuli. This reaction is enhanced when the infant receives a bottle in the crib or is placed in the supine position immediately after feeding.[48]

A similar pathogenesis of rhinorrhea and obstruction may be seen in children with oropharyngeal dysphagia, with resultant nasal regurgitation secondary to cerebral disease, peripheral neuropathies, cleft deformities and velopharyngeal insufficiency, inherited or degenerative muscular disorders, cricopharyngeal dysfunctions, and local factors such as tumors of the oropharynx or hypopharynx. Nasopharyngeal reflux due to delayed opening of the cricopharyngeal sphincter in children with familial dysautonomia is a typical example.

A toxic nasal inflammatory response may occur in children in response to stimulation by a variety of external substances, both inhaled and ingested. Inhaled substances may act as chemical irritants and react with the nasal mucosa to cause defensive vasomotor responses. Such responses may be difficult to distinguish from those occurring as part of type I–mediated allergic reactions.[129]

Children may inhale 10,000 to 15,000 L of air per day, much of which is polluted. The urban pollutants may include oxides of nitrogen, carbon monoxide, ozone, aldehydes, ketones, chlorine, sulfur dioxide, ammonia, and hydrocarbons. This exposure from industrial discharge, automotive exhaust, and tobacco smoke may lead to increased nasal discharge as a result of the vasomotor reaction.[127, 129]

Locally applied prescribed and over-the-counter preparations, including sympathomimetic agents, may produce a quick nasal toxic reaction owing to the rebound phenomenon of rhinitis medicamentosa. Although such a phenomenon is less commonly seen in children than in adults, it may account for the persistent obstruction and rhinorrhea following a cold. Currently, adolescents are seen with nasal problems resulting from cocaine, "crack," glue sniffing, and other chemical inhalants. The local vasoconstriction with subsequent reactive hyperemia that occurs when cocaine is snuffed may produce mucoid rhinorrhea. Prolonged use of the drug results in tissue necrosis, septal perforation, and the mucoid drainage may become purulent.[9, 78]

Ingested substances that may produce rhinorrhea and symptoms of nasal obstruction include hormones, iodides, and bromides. Aspirin sensitivity may be the cause of intermittent, profuse watery rhinorrhea and nasal obstruction in adolescents, especially those with polyp formation. Such sensitivity may be the result of the inability of some individuals to counteract the effects of prostaglandin release or inhibition.[121]

Traumatic Disease

The necessity to diagnose traumatic nasal disease in children early has been emphasized in recent years owing to recognition of the importance of nasal respiration and the nasopulmonary reflex on lung physiology and to the realization of the influence of abnormal nasal functions on subsequent facial, dental arch, and palatal growth, as previously mentioned. Conservative management of abnormal nasal function or deformities of the nose is still advocated, but treatment should not be delayed if "marked disturbance in function or distortion exists that also interferes with growth and facial development."[32]

Nasal obstruction is the primary symptom of external and internal nasal trauma. The severity of the effects of such obstruction depends on the extent and location of the injury and the age of the child. Obstruction may be evident and total or more subtle and intermittent, depending on such factors as "paradoxical nasal obstruction" and the nasal cycle (see Chap. 47).

Alteration of the normal streamlined flow of air through the nose may lead to turbulence and eddies in airflow and a resultant vasomotor reaction. Mucosal injury and mucostasis may lead to bacterial invasion, which could cause a mucopurulent nasal discharge. This may be further aggravated by mucociliary damage. Atrophic mucosa may be the end result, with further accentuation of rhinorrhea and obstructive symptoms. With increased turbulence and stasis of air in the nose, particulate matter and allergens accumulate in the mucosa, causing more intense vasomotor, allergic, and inflammatory reactions. This pathogenesis has led to the treatment maxim of restoring the normal streamlining of nasal respirations in order to improve alveolar ventilation and to avoid interference with nasal mucosal function, especially in children.

Nasal obstruction from traumatic deformities may occur at any age but may not be symptomatic in young infants or neonates unless it is severe enough to cause respiratory distress in the obligatory nasal breather. Such obstruction may be obvious in cases of severe external trauma but more occult in younger patients with only septal trauma. Nasal trauma can be classified according to its time of origin. The recent advent of frequent ultrasonic examinations in the prenatal and perinatal periods has shown that nasal abnormalities may occur in utero as a result of fetal head presentation. Nasal trauma may also occur at birth during vaginal deliveries, with or without forceps. Some septal deformities may be evident on careful examination in as many as 70% of newborns; these result from intrauterine or birth trauma.[49, 61]

Additional nasal trauma may occur at any time from birth onward in childhood, but it is often subtle. Such subtle injuries may affect the main growth center of the nose, the septovomerine angle, and may be asymptomatic until adolescence, when the deformity is accentuated by nasal growth. The symptoms at that time depend on the age of the child and the degree and location of the deformity.

In the acute traumatic period, intermittent bleeding and the development of nasal obstruction suggest the development of a septal hematoma. This occurs more commonly in children than in adults because children have a thicker and more elastic mucoperichondrium.[105] Trauma disrupts septal vessels but not the mucoperichondrium, with subsequent development of a septal hematoma. Subsequent throbbing pain and elevated temperature may indicate a septal abscess that, if untreated, may lead to septal perforation with resultant airway turbulence and subsequent increased obstruction and rhinorrhea.

Internal trauma may be the result of the introduction of foreign materials into the nasal cavity, causing an intensive vasomotor reaction, rhinorrhea, and obstruction. Such trauma is characteristically seen in children 3 years of age or younger, who frequently stuff foreign objects into their nostrils. Less often, foreign material enters the nose through the posterior choanae as a result of regurgitation[67] (see Chap. 46).

The symptoms of a foreign body in the nose depend on the nature of the foreign material, its size, the number of objects, the length of time present, and the location. Unilateral purulent, fetid nasal drainage in a child is highly suggestive of a foreign body. Symptoms of a foreign body reaction may be delayed but are earlier in onset when the foreign body is organic. Long-standing symptoms of obstruction may indicate that calcareous deposits have formed about the foreign body and that a rhinolith has developed[67] (see Chap. 46).

In traumatic nasal disease, special attention must be paid to determining the presence or absence of rhinorrhea or CSF. CSF rhinorrhea is most commonly seen after skull trauma, although it may occur spontaneously, either with or without increased intracranial pressure. It may also be a manifestation of CSF otorrhea occurring in the nasal cavity via the eustachian tube. Spontaneous CSF rhinorrhea has been seen with a variety of intracranial lesions, especially intrasellar tumors, but it may also be present in young infants as a result of congenital bone dehiscences.[11, 29, 57, 81]

The presence of CSF rhinorrhea is first suggested by the history and the gross nature of the nasal discharge. A clear, salty, often unilateral drainage from the nose, especially after a head injury, is highly suggestive of CSF rhinorrhea. When such fluid flows profusely from the nose and when the discharge increases in quantity with changes in head position, during a Valsalva maneuver, and with jugular compression, the possibility that the rhinorrhea is CSF is significant. A rapid method of analyzing such nasal drainage is to test it with glucose oxidase–impregnated test sticks. However, because these sticks react to as little as 10 mg/100 mL of glucose, they may give a false-positive reaction because of the presence of lacrimal secretions or the products of an allergic reaction or infectious rhinosinusitis in the nasal secretions. A negative test result is highly significant in ruling out CSF rhinorrhea, whereas a strongly positive reaction to nasal secretions shows the presence of 50 mg/100 mL or more of glucose, indicating the probability of CSF in the nasal discharge.[57] If sufficient fluid can be collected, biochemical analysis for protein, glucose, and electrolytes confirms the diagnosis of CSF rhinorrhea. The laboratory confirmation of beta-2 transferrin in such fluid is even more specific for CSF. Demonstration of the transdural fistula can be made by means of either nuclear cisternography with or without nasal packing or magnetic resonance cisternography. The success of both methods depends on active leakage at the time of the examination. A CT method provides superior bony anatomic delineation and can frequently identify an exact site of bony dehiscence.

Neoplastic Disease

Primary neoplasms of the nasal cavity are rare, accounting for only 0.3% of tumors of the body.[4] When they do occur, they may be of ectodermal, mesodermal, neurogenic, or odontogenic origin.[10] More commonly, neoplasms arise primarily in paranasal sinus and with growth extend into the nasal cavity. Any tumor that occurs in adults may also arise in children, but a few tumors are more commonly seen in and indeed tend to be specific to the pediatric patient (see Chap. 48).

Nasal obstruction and rhinorrhea are the two most common symptoms of nasal tumors. They are related to the increasing size of the neoplastic mass and the effect of the tumor on the nasal mucosa. Symptoms arise early in neoplasms primary to the nasal cavity but are delayed in tumors of the nasopharynx and sinuses until nasal cavity invasion occurs.[10]

Rhinorrhea may occur as a typical vasomotor reaction to nasal airway invasion. Such nasal discharge may become purulent with stasis and secondary infection or sanguineous with tissue necrosis, and eventually may contain CSF as a result of extension of the pathologic lesion into the cranial cavity. The triad of symptoms including nasal obstruction, rhinorrhea, and epistaxis is common in neoplasms. Nasal polyposis may also arise as a secondary sign of nasal neoplasm.

Juvenile nasopharyngeal angiofibromas are specific to the adolescent male, with symptoms usually arising between 7 and 17 years of age, at an average age of 14. The symptoms are progressive: partial unilateral obstruction followed by progressive obstruction of the involved side and then partial obstruction on the opposite side. Epistaxis attacks occur with increasing frequency, along with pathologic symptoms in adjacent structures.[100, 101]

The nose may be the first site of symptoms of nasopharyngeal carcinoma, with 21% of patients with this condition presenting with symptoms of rhinorrhea, obstruction, or loss of smell. Epstein-Barr virus serologic testing may help guide the diagnosis and suggest the prognosis of certain types of nasopharyngeal carcinomas.

Olfactory neuroblastoma is another uncommon neoplasm, but one that may occur in the pediatric patient. Originating primarily in the area of the olfactory mucosa, it may not produce signs of obstruction until it has grown to considerable size. Epistaxis resulting from tissue destruction is the usual presenting sign.[18, 92, 112] In children, neoplasms of the hematopoietic system rarely occur in the nasal cavity, but, when they do, they are usually secondary to metastatic invasion from leukemic disease.[111]

Metabolic Disease in the Nasal Cavity

Nasal symptoms of obstruction and rhinorrhea may be important in the early diagnosis of cystic fibrosis or mucoviscidosis. In the latter, an inherited systemic disease in which the alimentary and respiratory tracts are involved, abnormally viscid mucus is produced. Histologically, the nasal submucosal glands are hyperplastic and appear to be dilated with eosinophilic staining material. Nasal mucous secretions exhibit marked adhesiveness and a changed water-binding capacity and permeability related to an increased calcium concentration.[39] The viscid, tenacious mucus and nasal obstruction characteristic of mucoviscidosis lead to stasis and secondary infection by *Staphylococcus aureus, Pseudomonas, Streptococcus viridans, H. influenzae,* or *M. catarrhalis.* Nasal polyps frequently occur in association with mucoviscidosis and secondary infections.[5]

The nasal obstruction of mucoviscidosis is produced by (1) the thick, tenacious mucus, (2) the chronic, thickened nasal mucosa, and (3) nasal polyps. Chronic sinusitis may aggravate the situation: as many as 90% of children with cystic fibrosis show evidence of severe opacification of the sinuses on radiographic examination.[5, 39] The result is that a child presenting with thick, foul-smelling, purulent, bilateral nasal secretions; chronic nasal obstruction; nasal polyps; and a broad nasal bridge must be considered to have mucoviscidosis until proven otherwise.

In other metabolic diseases, obstruction and rhinorrhea are produced as a result of modification of the normal vasomotor reaction. The effects of endogenous hormones on nasal mucosa are discussed earlier. Exogenous hormones may have a similar effect on the vasomotor reaction.[114]

Calcium and magnesium potentiate the action of acetylcholinesterase in nasal mucosa, and the former modifies the permeability of the basement membrane. Deficiencies of these elements may intensify the vasomotor reaction, while exogenous calcium has been used to alleviate symptoms of vasomotor rhinitis.[127, 129] In hypothyroid states, low levels of ionic calcium are seen and can modify the vasomotor reaction. In hyperthyroidism, thyroxine, through its influence on lung dynamics, may hypothalamically influence the nasal mucosa and produce symptoms of vasomotor rhinitis.[78, 129]

Disorders of carbohydrate metabolism often lead to chronic nasal infection in children. This may be the result of impairment of the system by which carbohydrate metabolism releases antibodies from cells in the nasal mucosa.[78, 129]

In immunodeficiency diseases, there is a general increased incidence of infections, but with isolated IgA deficiency, these infections are confined mostly to the upper respiratory tract. In response to pathogens, a more intensive and prolonged vasomotor reaction is seen, because the lack of IgA allows the invasion of the nasal mucosa by the pathogens.[129]

Idiopathic Nasal Disease

A number of idiopathic systemic diseases, although uncommon in childhood, may exhibit nasal symptoms and signs on presentation. Mucopurulent or serosanguineous rhinorrhea, obstruction, crusting, and epistaxis are characteristic nasal signs of a number of entities of granulomatosis and vasculitis. Nasal septal perforation is a well-known diagnostic criterion of systemic lupus erythematosus[109] and is also commonly seen in conditions such as Wegener granulomatosis. Similar lesions have been described in patients with rheumatoid arthritis, psoriatic arthritis, and scleroderma. Sarcoid noncaseating granulomas may manifest as tiny, 1-mm, yellow nodules on the nasal mucosa surrounded by hyperemic boggy mucosa. Although these lesions are often self-limiting, they may lead to fibrosis, synechiae, and atrophic rhinitis.[41]

More destructive granulomatosis- and vasculitis-type lesions of the nasal cavity and sinuses can be found with Wegener granulomatosis, polymorphic reticulosis, midline lethal granuloma, and Churg-Strauss syndrome. Their clinical and morphologic appearances are similar to each other and to certain fungal diseases such as those caused by *Sporothrix schenckii* and *Coccidioides,* thus highlighting the importance of biopsy, culture, special staining, and overall organ system evaluation to differentiate the diseases that these entities involve.[33, 80]

Cicatricial pemphigoid or benign mucous pemphigoid, a chronic blistering disease of mucosal epithelium, may manifest with nasal lesions.[103]

Among primary nasal diseases of unknown cause, several may be noted in the pediatric patient who presents with characteristic symptoms of obstruction and rhinorrhea. The first is a rapidly evolving syndrome of mucociliary dysfunction or ciliary immotility. Although much of this syndrome is known to occur on an inherited or acquired basis, the rapid assimilation of new knowledge and new case reports prevent the proper classification of this entity. In 1933, Kartagener[56] reported a triad of sinusitis, situs inversus, and bronchiectasis. In 1976, Afzelius[2] identified the cause of the defect as of genetic origin, producing immotile cilia and spermatozoa. Acquired defects of ciliary motility were also discovered; these lesions are currently properly classified as ciliary dyskinesias, either primary or secondary.

Primary ciliary dyskinesia is an inherited disorder such as Kartagener syndrome with axonemal defects, including defective dynein arms, absence of radial spokes, microtubular transposition, and disorientation of the central pair of microtubules. Some of these anomalies may occur in other disorders of the respiratory epithelium, indeed even in normal, healthy subjects.

In secondary ciliary dyskinesia, the noninherited type, these ultrastructural abnormalities are variable and even less specific.[17] Studies needed to determine the nature of the ciliary motility include biopsy with transmission electron microscopy, phase contrast microscopy, and technetium-99m mucociliary clearance testing. When children present with chronic rhinorrhea and obstruction accompanied by chronic bronchitis, sinusitis, otitis media, and nasal polyposis, consideration must be given to the possibility of ciliary dyskinesia (immotile cilia syndrome) and Kartagener syndrome if situs inversus is also present.

Atrophic rhinitis (ozena, rhinitis fetida, rhinitis crustosa) is a chronic nasal disease with onset in childhood that features progressive atrophy in nasal mucosa and underlying bone. The presenting symptoms are obstruction of the nasal airway resulting from enlargement of the nasal cavity and disturbance of normal streamlined airflow. Characteristically, the nasal mucosa is foul-smelling and covered by green crusts,, although there is minimal purulent discharge. The secretions are normally composed of exfoliated nasal mucosal cells. Vitamin, iron, endocrine, and nutritional deficiencies have been implicated, and the disease is most commonly seen in underdeveloped countries.[125] The principal organisms responsi-

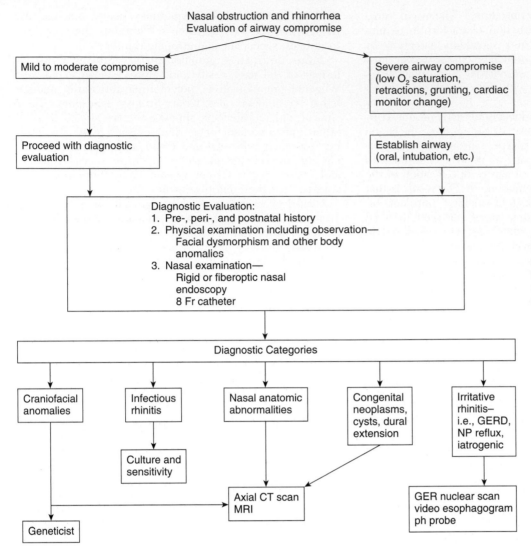

FIGURE 37–1. Evaluation of nasal obstruction and rhinorrhea in the neonate (algorithm). GER, gastroesophageal reflux; NP, nasopharyngeal.

ble for the purulence of the secretions are *Klebsiella ozaenae*, a form of *C. diphtheriae*, and the *Perez-Hofer* bacillus.[40, 136] The isolation of *K. ozaenae* from the nasal cavity is considered a sine qua non for a diagnosis of atrophic rhinitis.[30]

Algorithm for Evaluation of Nasal Obstruction and Rhinorrhea in the Neonate

As previously stated, the presence of nasal obstruction or rhinorrhea in neonates may be indicative of life-threatening disease or a transient and self-resolving process. The increasing frequency of consultation with the otolaryngologist in neonatal units suggests the need for an algorithm (Fig. 37–1) to approach this common symptomatology rationally.

When examining the neonatal patient with obstruction and rhinorrhea, it is helpful to first determine the severity of symptoms. Most patients with symptoms of pathologic significance exhibit stertor, grunting, and snorting respirations, which are exacerbated by feeding. The degree of airway compromise, as exhibited by retractions, cyanosis,

and significant cardiac or oxygen saturation monitor changes, should indicate the severity. Control of the airway is paramount and must be obtained before diagnostic evaluation. This may be achieved by a variety of methods. In the neonate whose airway is severely compromised, airway control and initial evaluation of the nose and nasopharynx may be accomplished in an operating room setting. The otolaryngologist may choose to establish airway control first and then proceed with the evaluation at a later date. This evaluation may include a variety of different laboratory and radiographic studies. In neonates with moderate or mild symptoms, the initial evaluation and airway management can often be performed in the neonatal unit.

Initial evaluation must start with a complete history and physical examination. Observation of facial dysmorphism, use of anterior rhinoscopy with an otoscope, rigid nasal endoscopy, and fiberoptic nasopharyngoscopy may establish an initial diagnosis. The passage of a number 8 French catheter through both nasal cavities may easily be performed at the bedside. A lateral radiograph of the nasopharynx may also be obtained to offer some help in the diagnosis. Once this is accomplished, it is important to place the possible etiology in one or more of five categories: (1) craniofacial anomalies, (2) infectious rhinitis, (3) internal nasal anatomic abnormalities, (4) congenital neoplasms, cysts, and dural extensions, and (5) irritative rhinitis secondary to gastroesophageal or nasopharyngeal reflux.

Craniofacial anomalies such as Crouzon and Pfeiffer syndromes may be self-evident but at times more subtle. Evaluation may eventually be aided by CT and by involvement of the craniofacial team and a geneticist. The facial appearance of the child's parents is also helpful.

Infectious rhinitis may be evident during nasal endoscopy by the appearance of the nasal mucosa. Diagnosis may be aided by cultures, serum titers, and specific laboratory tests.[8, 16] Chlamydia, RSV, and congenital syphilis ("snuffles") must be ruled out.

Congenital internal nasal anatomic obstructions may include piriform aperture stenosis, midnasal stenosis, choanal stenosis, and choanal atresia. Acquired nasal stenosis from instrumentation trauma may occur very early in the neonatal period. Traumatic septal deformities may occur most commonly with difficult or forceps deliveries. Anterior rhinoscopy and rigid or fiberoptic nasopharyngoscopy may well identify the pathology. CT of the nasal cavity often confirms the diagnosis.

Mass lesions of the nasal cavity and nasopharynx or associated facial structures may also be identified initially by nasal endoscopy and confirmed by CT or MRI. These lesions fall into the categories of neoplasms, congenital cysts, dural extensions, or congenital adenoid hypertrophy.

Some neonates exhibit nasal obstruction or rhinorrhea with evidence of mucosal swelling and erythema on nasal endoscopy. Although infectious disease must be ruled out, one must consider the possibility of gastroesophageal reflux with nasopharyngeal regurgitation or primary nasal regurgitation of oral feedings.[24]

One must be careful of diagnostic evaluations because nasal instrumentation in the neonate may easily produce its own trauma or compound preexisting pathology. Colleagues in neonatology units and their nursing staff should be cautioned to minimize nasal examination until appropriate consultation is obtained.

REFERENCES

1. Abedi S, Sismanis A, Choi K, et al. Twenty-five years experience in treating cerebro-rhino-orbital mucormycosis. Laryngoscope 94:1060, 1984.
2. Afzelius BA. A human syndrome caused by immotile cilia. Science 193:317, 1976.
3. Arbour PL, Kern EB. Paradoxical nasal obstruction. Can J Otolaryngol 4:333, 1975.
4. Axtell LM, Cutter SJ, Meyers MH. End results in cancer. Report no. 4. Washington, DC, US Department of Health, Education, and Welfare, Public Health Service, NIH 85–88, 1972.
5. Baker DC, Smith JT. Nasal symptoms of mucoviscidosis. Otolaryngol Clin North Am 3:257, 1970.
6. Beste DJ, Conley SF, Brown CW. Gastroesophageal reflux complicating choanal atresia repair. Int J Pediatr Otorhinolaryngol 29:51, 1994.
7. Biber JJ. Proboscis lateralis: rare malformation of nose; its genesis and treatment. J Laryngol Otol 63:734, 1949.
8. Bickmore JT, Marshall ML. Cytology in nasal secretions: further diagnostic help. Laryngoscope 86:516, 1976.
9. Blue JA. Over-medication of nasal mucosa. Mod Med 37:90, 1969.
10. Bortnick E. Neoplasms of the nasal cavity. Otolaryngol Clin North Am 6:801, 1973.
10a. Bothwell MR, Parsons DS, Talbot A, et al. Outcome of reflux therapy on pediatric chronic sinusitis. Otolaryngol Head Neck Surg 121:255, 1999.
11. Briant TDR, Snell D. Diagnosis of cerebrospinal fluid rhinorrhea and the rhinology approach to its repair. Laryngoscope 7:1390, 1967.
12. Bridger GP. Physiology of the nasal valve. Arch Otolaryngol 92:543, 1970.
13. Bridger GP, Proctor DF. Maximum nasal inspiratory flow and nasal resistance. Ann Otol Rhinol Laryngol 79:481, 1970.
14. Brodsky L, Adler E, Stanevich JF. Nose and oropharyngeal dimensions in children with obstructive sleep apnea. Int J Pediatr Otorhinolaryngol 17:1, 1989.
15. Bryan MP, Bryan WTK. Cytologic and cytochemical aspects of ciliated epithelium in differentiation of nasal inflammatory diseases. Acta Cytol 13:515, 1969.
16. Bryan WTK, Bryan MP. Cytologic diagnosis in otolaryngology. Trans Am Acad Ophthalmol Otolaryngol 63:597, 1959.
17. Burgersdijk FJ, DeGroot JC, Graamans K, et al. Testing ciliary activity in patients with chronic and recurrent infections of the upper airways: experiences in 68 cases. Laryngoscope 96:1029, 1986.
18. Cantrell RW, Ghorayeb BY, Fitz-Hugh GS. Esthesioneuroblastoma: diagnosis and treatment. Ann Otol Rhinol Laryngol 86:760, 1977.
19. Celsus AC. De Medicina [trans] Spencer WG.
20. Chang C, Berrios JA, Strong DD, et al. Squamous cell proliferative lesions of the nasopharynx: a distinct clinicopathologic entity. Pediatr Pathol 1:362, 1983.
21. Chladek V, Pihrt J, Engler V. Vasomotor reactions in nasal mucosa in adolescents. Cesk Hyg 17:241, 1972.
22. Church JA. Human immunodeficiency virus (HIV) infections at Children's Hospital of Los Angeles: recurrent otitis media or chronic sinusitis as the presenting process in pediatric AIDS. Immunol Allergy Pract 9:25, 1987.
23. Cole P, Forsythe R, Haight JSJ. Effects of cold air and exercise on nasal patency. Ann Otol Rhinol Laryngol 92:196, 1983.
24. Contencin P, Narcy P. Nasopharyngeal pH monitoring in infants and children with chronic rhinopharyngitis. Int J Pediatr Otorhinolaryngol 22:249, 1991.
25. Cottle MH. Rhino-manometry: an aid in physical diagnosis. Int Rhinol 6:7, 1968.
26. Dobrowski JM, Grundfast KM, Rosenbaum KN, et al. Otorhinolaryngic manifestations of CHARGE association. Otolaryngol Head Neck Surg 93:798, 1985.
27. Dorland's Illustrated Medical Dictionary, 29th ed. Philadelphia, WB Saunders, 2000.
28. Dorrance GM. The so-called bursa pharyngea in man. Arch Otolaryngol 13:187, 1931.
29. Duckert LG, Mathog RH. Diagnosis in persistent cerebrospinal fluid fistulas. Laryngoscope 87:18, 1977.
30. Dudley JP. Atrophic rhinitis: antibiotic treatment. Am J Otolaryngol 8:387, 1987.
30a. Ey EH, Han RB, Juon WK. Bony inlet stenosis as a cause of nasal airway obstruction. Radiology 168:477, 1988.
31. Fanous N. Anterior turbinectomy. Arch Otolaryngol Head Neck Surg 112:850, 1986.
32. Farrior RT, Connolly ME. Septorhinoplasty in children. Otolaryngol Clin North Am 3:545, 1970.
33. Fauci AS, Haynes BF, Katz P, et al. Wegener's granulomatosis: prospective clinical and therapeutic experience with 85 patients in 21 years. Ann Intern Med 98:76, 1983.
34. Frazer JE. A Manual of Embryology, 2nd ed. London, Bailliere, Tindall & Cox, 1940.
35. Friedman R, Ackerman M, Wald E, et al. Asthma and bacterial sinusitis in children. J Allergy Clin Immunol 74:185, 1984.
36. Furstenberg AC. A Clinical and Pathological Study of Tumors and

Cysts of the Nose, Pharynx, Mouth and Neck of Teratological Origin. Ann Arbor, Mich, Edward Brothers, 1936.

37. Galen C. On the Natural Faculties [trans]. Brock AJ. London, W Heinemann, 1916.

38. Gell PGH, Coombs RRA. Clinical Aspects of Immunology, 2nd ed. Philadelphia, FA Davis, 1968.

39. Gharib R, Allen RP, Joos HA, et al. Paranasal sinuses in cystic fibrosis. Am J Dis Child 108:499, 1964.

40. Goodman WS, DeSouza FM. Atrophic rhinitis. Otolaryngol Clin North Am 6:773, 1973.

41. Gordon WW, Cohn AM, Greenberg SD, et al. Nasal sarcoidosis. Arch Otolaryngol 102:11, 1976.

42. Gragmans K. The significance of nasal resistance under normal and pathological conditions. Acta Otolaryngol (Stockh) 33:495, 1979.

43. Grundfast KM, Quarisco JL, Thomsen JR, Koch B. Airway compromise from nasal obstruction in neonates and infants. Int J Pediatr Otorhinolaryngol 19:241, 1990.

44. Gwynn-Evans E, Ballard CF. Discussion on the mouth-breather. Proc R Soc Med 51:279, 1959.

45. Haight JSJ, Cole P. The site and function of the nasal valve. Laryngoscope 93:49, 1983.

46. Hammerschlag MR. Chlamydia trachomatis. Birth Defects 21:93, 1985.

47. Heimer D, Scharf SM, Lieberman A, et al. Sleep apnea syndrome treated by repair of deviated nasal septum. Chest 84:184, 1983.

48. Hellemans J, Pelemans W, Vantrappen G. Pharyngoesophageal swelling disorders and the pharyngoesophageal sphincter. Med Clin North Am 65:1149, 1981.

49. Hinderer KH. Nasal problems in children. Pediatr Ann 52:499, 1976.

50. Hippocrates. The Aphorisms [trans] Jones WHS, Withington ET. London, W Heinemann, 1922.

51. Hoekstra RE, Herrman EC Jr, O'Connell EJ. Virus infections in children. Am J Dis Child 12:14, 1970.

52. Holgate ST, Church MK. Activation mechanisms of mast cells and basophils. Allergy C4, 1993.

53. Hollender AR. The lymphoid tissue of the nasopharynx. Laryngoscope 69:529, 1959.

54. Holmes TH, Goodell H, Wolf S, et al. The Nose: An Experimental Study of the Reactions within the Nose in Human Subjects during Varying Life Experiences. Springfield, Ill, Charles C Thomas, 1950.

55. Jones KL, Smith DW. The fetal alcohol syndrome. Teratology 12:1, 1975.

56. Kartagener M. Zur Pathogenese die Bronchiecktarien bei Situs viscerum inversus. Beitr Klin Tuherk 83:489, 1933.

57. Kaufman HH. Non-traumatic cerebrospinal fluid rhinorrhea. Arch Neurol 21:59, 1909.

58. Kennedy DW, Zinreich SJ, Rosenbaum AE, et al. Functional endoscopic sinus surgery. Arch Otolaryngol 111:576, 1985.

59. Kern EB. Rhinomanometry. Otolaryngol Clin North Am 6:863, 1973.

60. Kim HW, Bellanti JA, Arrobio JO, et al. Respiratory syncytial virus neutralizing activity in nasal secretions following natural infection. Proc Soc Exp Biol Med 131:658, 1969.

61. Kirchner JA. Traumatic nasal deformity in the newborn. Arch Otolaryngol 62:139, 1955.

62. Klein JC. Nasal respiratory functional and craniofacial growth. Arch Otolaryngol Head Neck Surg 112:843, 1986.

63. Lacourt G, Polgar G. Interaction between nasal and pulmonary resistance in newborn infants. J Appl Physiol 30:870, 1971.

64. Landoy Z, Rotstein C, Shedd D. Aspergillosis of the nose and paranasal sinuses in neutropenic patients at an oncology center. Head Neck Surg 8:83, 1985.

65. Laurikainen E, Erkinjuntii M, Alihanka J, et al. Radiological parameters of the bony nasopharynx and the adenotonsillar size compared with sleep apnea episodes in children. J Pediatr Otorhinolaryngol 12:303, 1987.

66. Lavie P, Fischel N, Zomer J, et al. The effects of partial and complete mechanical occlusion of the nasal passages on sleep structure and breathing in sleep. Acta Otolaryngol (Stockh) 95:161, 1983.

67. Lederer FL. Diseases of the Ear, Nose and Throat, 6th ed. Philadelphia, FA Davis, 1952.

68. Levy AM, Tabakin BS, Hanson JS. Hypertrophied adenoids causing pulmonary hypertension and severe congestive heart failure. N Engl J Med 277:506, 1967.

69. Lew D, Southwick FS, Montgomery WW, et al. Sphenoid sinusitis. A review of 30 cases. N Engl J Med 309:1149, 1983.

70. Linder-Aronson S. Effects of adenoidectomy on the dentition and facial skeleton over a period of 5 years. In Cook JT (ed). Transactions of the Third International Orthodontic Congress. St Louis, CV Mosby, 1975, pp 85–100.

71. Longacre JJ. Craniofacial Anomalies: Pathogenesis and Repair. Philadelphia, JB Lippincott, 1968.

72. Lorin MI, Pureza FG, Irwin DM, et al. Composition of nasal secretions with cystic fibrosis. J Lab Clin Med 88:114, 1976.

73. Luke MJ, Mehrizi A, Folger GM Jr, et al. Chronic nasal obstruction as a cause of cardiomegaly, cor pulmonale and pulmonary edema. Pediatrics 37:76, 1966.

74. Lusk RP, Lee PC. Magnetic resonance imaging of congenital midline nasal masses. Otolaryngol Head Neck Surg 95:303, 1986.

75. Martin R, Vig PS, Warren DW. Nasal resistance and vertical dentofacial features [abstract]. Int Am Dent Res 1981.

76. Martinez SA, Mouney DF. Treponemal infections of the head and neck. Otolaryngol Clin North Am 15:613, 1982.

77. Masing H, Horbasch G. The influence of the nose on the sleeping habits of infants. Int Rhinol 7:41, 1969.

78. May M, West JW. The stuffy nose. Otolaryngol Clin North Am 6:655, 1973.

79. McCaffrey RV. Nasal physiology in children. Rhinology 24:7, 1986.

80. McDonald TJ, DeRemee RA. Wegener's granulomatosis. Laryngoscope 93:220, 1983.

81. Montgomery WW. Cerebrospinal fluid rhinorrhea. Otolaryngol Clin North Am 6:757, 1973.

82. Morgan DW, Bailey CM. Current management of choanal atresia. Int J Pediatr Otorhinolaryngol 19:1, 1990.

83. Mortimer H, Wright RP, Bachman C, et al. Effect of estrogenic hormones on nasal mucosa of monkeys. Proc Soc Exp Biol Med 34:535, 1936.

84. Nelson WE. Textbook of Pediatrics, 10th ed. Philadelphia, WB Saunders, 1975.

85. Niinimaa V, Cole P, Mintz S, et al. A head-out body plethysmograph. J Appl Physiol 47:1336, 1979.

86. Ogra PL, Karzon DT. The role of immunoglobulins in the mechanism of mucosal immunity to virus infection. Pediatr Clin North Am 17:385, 1970.

87. Ogura JH, Dammkuehler R, Nelson JR. Nasal obstruction and the mechanics of breathing. Arch Otolaryngol 83:135, 1966.

88. Ogura JH, Harvey JE. Nasopulmonary mechanics—experimental evidence of the influence of the upper airway upon the lower. Acta Otolaryngol (Stockh) 71:123, 1971.

89. Ogura JH, Nelson JR. Nasal surgery: physiologic considerations of nasal obstruction. Arch Otolaryngol 88:288, 1968.

90. Ogura JH, Nelson JR, Dammkuehler R, et al. Experimental observations on the relationships between upper airway obstruction and pulmonary function. Ann Otol Rhinol Laryngol 73:381, 1964.

91. Ogura JH, Nelson JR, Suemitsu M, et al. Relationship between pulmonary resistance and changes in arterial blood gas tensions in dogs with nasal obstruction and partial laryngeal obstruction. Ann Otol Rhinol Laryngol 82:668, 1973.

92. Ogura JH, Schenck NL. Unusual nasal tumors. Otolaryngol Clin North Am 6:813, 1973.

93. Ogura JH, Unno T, Nelson JR. Baseline values in pulmonary mechanics for physiologic surgery of the nose: preliminary report. Ann Otol Rhinol Laryngol 77:367, 1968.

94. Ohnishi T, Ogura JH. Partitioning of pulmonary resistance in the dog. Laryngoscope 79:1847, 1969.

95. Ohnishi T, Ogura JH, Nelson JR. Effects of nasal obstruction upon the mechanics of the lung in the dog. Laryngoscope 82:712, 1972.

96. Pagon RA, Graham JM Jr, Zonana J, Yong SL. Coloboma, congenital heart disease, and choanal atresia with multiple anomalies: CHARGE association. J Pediatr 99:223, 1981.

97. Parker AJ, Maw AR, Powell JE. Rhinomanometry in the selection for adenoidectomy and its relation to preoperative radiology. Int J Pediatr Otorhinolaryngol 17:155, 1989.

98. Parker LP, Crysdale WS, Cole P, Woodside D. Rhinomanometry in children. Int J Pediatr Otorhinolaryngol 17:127, 1989.

99. Parkes AS, Zuckerman S. Menstrual cycle of primates. II: Some

effects of oestrin on baboons and macaques. J Anthropol 65:272, 1931.

100. Patterson CN. Juvenile nasopharyngeal angiofibroma. Arch Otolaryngol 81:270, 1965.

101. Patterson CN. Juvenile nasopharyngeal angiofibroma. Otolaryngol Clin North Am 6:839, 1973.

102. Pedersen OF, Berkowitz R, Yomigawa M, et al. Nasal cavity dimensions in the newborn measured by acoustic reflections. Laryngoscope 104:1023, 1994.

103. Person JR, Rogers RS III. Bullous and cicatricial pemphigoid. Clinical, histopathologic, and immunopathologic correlations. Mayo Clin Proc 52:54, 1977.

104. Petruson B, Hansson H. Nasal mucosal changes in children with frequent infections. Arch Otolaryngol Head Neck Surg 113:1294, 1987.

104a. Phipps CD, Wood WE, Gibson WS, Cochran WJ. Gastroesophageal reflux contributing to chronic sinus disease in children. Arch Otolaryngol Head Neck Surg 126:831, 2000.

105. Pirsig W. Historical notes and actual observations on the nasal septal abscess especially in children. Int J Pediatr Otorhinolaryngol 8:43, 1984.

106. Principato JJ, Kerrigan JP, Wolf P. Pediatric nasal resistance and lower anterior vertical face height. Otolaryngol Head Neck Surg 95:226, 1986.

107. Proctor B, Proctor C. Congenital lesions of the head and neck. Otolaryngol Clin North Am 3:221, 1979.

108. Rachelefsky GS, Katz RM, Sheldon SC. Chronic sinus disease with associated reactive airway disease in children. Pediatrics 73:526, 1984.

109. Reiter D, Myers AR. Asymptomatic nasal septal perforations in systemic lupus erythematosus. Ann Otol Rhinol Laryngol 89:78, 1980.

110. Richter HJ. Obstruction of the pediatric upper airway. Ear Nose Throat J 66:40, 1987.

111. Sanford DM, Becker GD. Acute leukemia presenting as nasal obstruction. Arch Otolaryngol 85:102, 1967.

112. Schenck NL, Ogura JH. Esthesioneuroblastoma: an enigma in diagnosis, a dilemma in treatment. Arch Otolaryngol 96:322, 1972.

113. Schneider. De Catarrhis Libri, vol. I (cited by Schaeffer, 1932).

114. Schreiber U. Vasomotor rhinitis with hormonal contraception. HNO 21:180, 1973.

115. Sercer A. Researches on the reflex influence of each lung from its corresponding nasal cavity. Acta Otolaryngol (Stockh) 14:99, 1930.

116. Settipane GA. Nasal polyps: epidemiology, pathology, immunology and treatment. Am J Rhinol 1:119, 1987.

117. Skolnik EM, Kotler R, Hanna WA. Choanal atresia. Otolaryngol Clin North Am 6:83, 1973.

118. Slovis TL, Renfro B, Watts FB, et al. Choanal atresia: precise CT evaluation. Radiology 155:345, 1985.

119. Smith JR, Taylor-Robinson D. Infection due to *Chlamydia trachomatis* in pregnancy and the newborn. Baillieres Clin Obstet Gynaecol 7:237, 1993.

120. Solow B, Greve E. Craniocervical angulation and nasal respiratory resistance. In McNamara JA Jr (ed). Nasal Respiratory Function and Craniofacial Growth Symposium, Monograph 9, Craniofacial Growth Series. Ann Arbor, University of Michigan, Center for Human Growth and Development, 1979, pp 87–119.

121. Stahl RH. Allergic disorders of the nose and paranasal sinuses. Otolaryngol Clin North Am 7:703, 1974.

122. Stammberger H. Endoscopic endonasal surgery—concepts in treatment of recurring rhinosinusitis. Part I. Anatomic and pathophysiologic considerations. Otolaryngol Head Neck Surg 94:143, 1986.

123. Stoksted P. The physiologic cycle of the nose under normal and pathologic conditions. Acta Otolaryngol (Stockh) 42:175, 1952.

124. Swift PG, Emery JL. Clinical observations on response to nasal occlusion in infancy. Arch Dis Child 48:947, 1973.

125. Taylor M. Catarrhal rhinitis in children. Proc R Soc Med 54:1961, 1961.

126. Taylor M. An experimental study of the influence of the endocrine system on nasal respiratory mucosa. J Laryngol Otol 75:972, 1961.

127. Taylor M. The nasal vasomotor reaction. Otolaryngol Clin North Am 6:645, 1973.

128. Taylor M. The origin and function of nasal mucus. Laryngoscope 84:61, 1974.

129. Taylor M. Physiology of the nose, paranasal sinuses and nasopharynx. In English GM (ed). Otolaryngology, vol. II. Hagerstown, Md, Harper & Row, 1979.

130. Theogaraj SD, Hoehn JG, Hagan KF. Practical management of congenital choanal atresia. Plast Reconstr Surg 72:634, 1983.

131. Timms DJ. The effect of rapid maxillary expansion on nasal airway resistance. Br J Orthod 13:221, 1986.

132. Usowicz AG, Golabi M, Curry C. Upper airway obstruction with fetal alcohol syndrome. Am J Dis Child 140:1039, 1986.

133. Van Cauwenberge PB, Deleye L. Nasal cycle in children. Arch Otolaryngol 110:108, 1984.

134. Von Dishoeck HAE. Inspiratory nasal resistance. Arch Otolaryngol 30:31, 1942.

135. Von Dishoeck HAE. The part of the valve and the turbinate in total nasal resistance. Int Rhinol 3:19, 1965.

136. Wilson TG. Diseases of the Ear, Nose and Throat in Children, 2nd ed. London, W Heinemann, 1962.

137. Wise TA. Arthava Veda Sanhita. In Commentary on the Hindu System of Medicine. Calcutta, 1898.

38

Epistaxis

Scott C. Manning, M.D., and Marvin C. Culbertson, Jr., M.D.

The respiratory system is widely discussed in the writings of ancient philosophers and medical practitioners; only the poorly understood vascular system receives more attention from these early writers. Pre-Hippocrates references to rhinologic subjects include such topics as the removal of foreign bodies from the respiratory passages, the pain of inflammatory diseases, and the inconvenience of catarrhs. The *Corpus Hippocraticum* frequently mentions epistaxis specifically.[28]

Although epistaxis may occur at any age, it is relatively uncommon in children younger than 2 years and reaches a peak frequency between the ages of 3 and 8 years.[20] Most episodes of epistaxis are never brought to the attention of physicians.[8] When parents do bring in their children for evaluation of recurrent nosebleeds, it is because they perceive the child to have a significant medical problem. Although most childhood epistaxis is self-limiting, physicians should treat the problem seriously and be aware of the level of potential parental anxiety.

Anatomy

The nose receives terminal branches from both the internal and external carotid artery systems (Figs. 38–1 and 38–2). The internal carotid artery supplies blood to the nose through the anterior and posterior ethmoidal arteries, which arise in the posterior orbit from the ophthalmic artery. The anterior ethmoidal artery supplies the lateral wall of the nose, the nasal septum, and the nasal tip; the posterior ethmoidal artery supplies the posterior lateral wall of the nose, including the superior turbinate and the superior aspect of the septum. The sphenopalatine or the terminal branch of the internal maxillary artery is the major terminal artery of the external carotid system that supplies the nose. The major branch enters the nose through the sphenopalatine foramen and supplies the posterior septum and the posterior inferior and middle turbinates. The lower midseptum is supplied by the descending palatine artery, also from the internal maxillary artery. The anterior tip of the septum is supplied by the superior labial branch of the facial artery. Several arteries from both the internal and external carotid systems coalesce in the anterior septum in the Little area or Kiesselbach plexus. Because of an exuberant vascular supply underneath the thin mucosa in the most anterior portion of the nose that is exposed to both dry air and trauma, it is no surprise that this area accounts for more than 90% of pediatric epistaxis.

Etiology

Inflammation

Upper respiratory infections are commonly associated with anterior epistaxis in young children (Table 38–1). Increased vascularity of the nasal mucosa and crusting of the anterior septum and tips of the inferior turbinates can lead to blood vessel injury and bleeding. Childhood exanthems, such as rubella and varicella, may also be associated with nosebleeds[13] (Fig. 38–3).

Inhalant allergies can predispose to epistaxis because of increased vascularity of nasal mucosa and nasal trauma from sneezing and nose rubbing due to facial pruritus. Allergists are probably more aware than are otolaryngologists that inhalant allergies are associated with pediatric epistaxis. Murray and Milner[31] examined a group of 557 children referred to an allergy clinic and found a positive correlation between recurrent nosebleeds and positive skin tests. In addition, epistaxis was significantly correlated with dog ownership. Both upper respiratory infections and inhalant allergy can predispose to sinusitis, which also increases nasal mucosal vascularity and enhances the probability of nosebleeds. Epistaxis may be secondary to foreign bodies with surrounding infected granulation tissue; these are usually associated with a history of foul-smelling unilateral rhinorrhea.

Rare inflammatory conditions that may cause nosebleeds include tuberculosis, glanders, leprosy, and fungal infection.[21] Parasites of the nasal cavity are rarely seen in the United States but may be a common cause of epistaxis in some parts of the world, such as southeast Asia.[3]

Dry Air

The nasal cavity is remarkably designed to condition inspired air to 100% relative humidity and a temperature of 37°C by the time it reaches the posterior nasopharynx. Dry air, especially in winter months, is strongly associated with increased occurrence of epistaxis. In one study of patients hospitalized for epistaxis, there was a doubling in

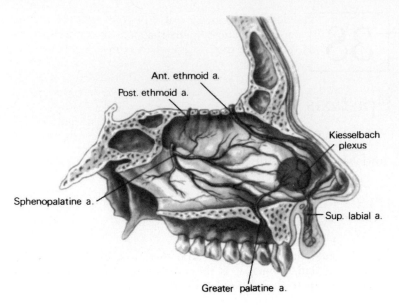

FIGURE 38–1. Arteries that supply the nasal septum.

frequency between the coldest winter month and the warmest summer month.[33] Central air conditioning or heating and indoor and outdoor air pollution also contribute to an increased frequency of nosebleeds. Although uncommon in children, the overuse of topical vasoconstrictive drugs, such as oxymetazoline, can increase the chances for epistaxis.

Trauma

Trauma from nose rubbing or nose picking is commonly associated with other predisposing factors, such as allergic rhinitis. Epistaxis after severe facial trauma is usually due to septal injury.[14, 38] Massive epistaxis after head injury should suggest internal carotid pseudoaneurysm.[7, 35] Barotrauma, such as occurs with diving or with airplane descent during upper respiratory infection or allergy, can contribute to epistaxis. Septal perforations from previous injury or chemical or drug exposure can also lead to chronic nosebleeds.

With the rise of endoscopic sinus surgery in the pediatric age group, postoperative nosebleeds are more common. Nose bleeding after nasal surgery occurs within the first 24 hours and usually resolves with conservative measures. Unremitting epistaxis after surgery warrants a second anesthetic agent for endoscopic nasal visualization with direct cautery or nasal packing.

Other (Rare) Causes

Hereditary hemorrhagic telangiectasia is an autosomal dominant familial disease with a frequency of 1 to 2 : 100,000 population. More than 90% of patients eventually present with recurring epistaxis, with a mean age of onset of 12 years. The epistaxis progressively worsens with age, and adult patients may have a mean of up to 18 episodes per

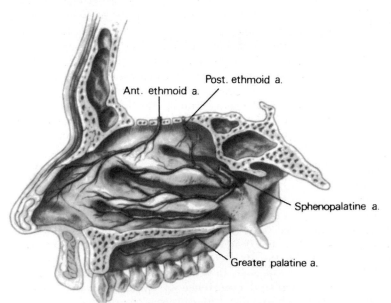

FIGURE 38–2. Arterial supply of the lateral wall of the nasal cavity.

TABLE 38–1. Etiology of Epistaxis in Children

Common Causes

Inflammation
  Upper respiratory tract infections
  Virus
  Bacteria
  Allergic rhinitis
  Childhood exanthems
  Vestibulitis (furunculosis)
  Nonallergic rhinitis with eosinophilia
  Foreign body
Trauma
  Dry air
  Outdoor and indoor air pollution
  Patient induced (nose picking)
  Facial fracture or blunt trauma
  Sudden barometric pressure changes

Uncommon Causes

Anatomic
  Severe septal deviation
  Postsurgical adhesions or atrophic rhinitis
Hematologic
  Platelet abnormalities
    Primary (idiopathic thrombocytopenic purpura)
    Acquired (aspirin, leukemia)
  Coagulation defects
    Primary (von Willebrand, hemophilia)
    Acquired (warfarin, liver disease)
Neoplasms
  Benign
    Nasopharyngeal angiofibroma
    Pyogenic granuloma
    Papillomas
  Malignant
    Rhabdomyosarcoma
    Lymphoma
Vascular abnormalities
  Hereditary hemorrhagic telangiectasia
  Internal carotid pseudoaneurysm
  Hemangioma
Trauma
  Nasogastric or nasotracheal tube placement
  Postsurgical
  Chemical and caustic agents

month.[1] Although adult patients may have other evidence of mucocutaneous telangiectasias or a history of gastrointestinal bleeds or pulmonary or intracranial arteriovenous malformations, children may present initially with only recurrent epistaxis; the clinician must have a high index of suspicion to make the diagnosis.

Tumors can rarely cause epistaxis in children.[18] In newborns and infants, meningoceles and encephaloceles may present initially as nasal bleeding.[5] Likewise, papillomas, polyps, and malignant tumors may be the cause of recurrent nosebleeds. Epistaxis is the most frequent presenting symptom in patients with juvenile angiofibroma. Typically, angiofibroma patients are boys, usually in their teens, who may also have a history of progressive nasal airway obstruction. The diagnosis of angiofibroma is usually confirmed by computed tomography scanning or magnetic resonance imaging that shows a vascular enhancing nasopharyngeal mass with involvement and widening of the pterygomaxillary fissure.[19] Intranasal biopsy of suspected tumors should be avoided in the office because of the risk of massive bleeding.[10]

Rhabdomyosarcoma may also present with severe episodic epistaxis. Patients with rhabdomyosarcoma that involves the nasal cavity or nasopharynx may also have signs of eustachian tube dysfunction, such as an ipsilateral middle-ear effusion, and they can also have deep facial pain and other cranioneuropathies, such as a sixth nerve palsy.

Hypertension is a possible contributing factor to epistaxis and should be considered in any patient with a history of renal disease or in patients receiving systemic corticosteroid therapy. Primary hypertension as a cause of epistaxis is rare in children.

Nosebleeds may result from primary or acquired coagulopathies.[12, 22] Most coagulopathies can be determined from a careful history, with attention paid to factors such as a family history for hemophilia or von Willebrand's disease, the recent use of platelet-inhibiting drugs such as aspirin, or a previous history of unusual bleeding or bruising.[23] Lymphoreticular malignant disease can predispose to epistaxis when the platelet count drops below 20,000 mm³, but nosebleeds are rarely the first symptom of leukemia.

Idiopathic thrombocytopenic purpura often presents as epistaxis in the pediatric age group. In one study of more

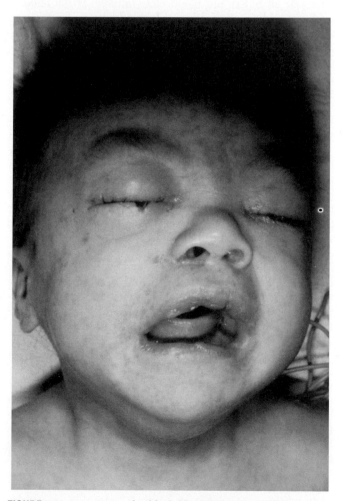

FIGURE 38–3. A 9-month-old child with severe measles coryza. The patient had a diffuse bloody oozing from an excoriated anterior nasal septum, which was treated with topical antibiotic ointment.

than 300 children diagnosed with idiopathic thrombocytopenic purpura during a 10-year period, 17% of patients had episodes of major hemorrhages, often nosebleeds.[26] Most patients responded to medical treatment with corticosteroids, intravenous immunoglobulin, or both. The otolaryngologist should keep in mind that idiopathic thrombocytopenic purpura may present with epistaxis. Every patient with epistaxis should undergo a complete physical examination to check for clinical evidence of platelet dysfunction such as easy bruising.

Management

Management of a child with nosebleeds begins with an appropriate attitude of concern toward the child and the child's family. A quick assessment of the patient's general condition (the degree of blood loss) and a careful history from the parents or child with regard to previously discussed etiologic factors help reassure all parties and focus the management plan.[41]

Perhaps the most overlooked aspect of the management of epistaxis in general practice is an adequate physical examination. The child should be asked, if possible, to blow out all blood and blood clots initially. If the child is unable to blow, then all blood should be carefully suctioned. A topical vasoactive solution, such as 0.025% oxymetazoline, can then be sprayed or dripped into each nasal cavity. This may be combined with an anesthetic agent such as 4% lidocaine. The anterior nasal cavity is then inspected with use of an adequate light source. A traditional otolaryngologic head mirror and nasal speculum may be used. An otoscope is also excellent for obtaining a magnified view of the anterior nasal cavity and is usually well tolerated by children. Attention should first be focused on the anterior nasal septum, because this is the source of the majority of pediatric nosebleeds. Active bleeding vessels can be identified and may be treated, at this point, with either local pressure by gently pinching the nasal ala against the bleeding point on the anterior septum for 5 minutes or the use of silver nitrate or electrocautery. In the majority of cases, by the time the patient reaches the office, the bleeding has ceased. The most common finding, in that case, is small crusts, ulcerations, or prominent blood vessels along the anterior septum. Studies have shown that in the absence of active bleeding, the application of antibiotic ointment to these areas is as effective as chemical cautery.[32, 39]

In a cooperative child, careful examination of the nasal cavity, with use of the otomicroscope (low power) and a small suction device, can help isolate a bleeding point otherwise inaccessible to view. Bleeding from the ostium of the maxillary antrum, a vessel hidden by the inferior turbinate, or one high in the vault can be better identified and treated in this manner. In an uncooperative child, examination with a microscope may require general anesthesia.

When an anterior bleeding point is identified in a child with a history of recurrent epistaxis, attention should be paid to possible predisposing factors with an aim toward deriving a strategy for future prevention (Table 38–2). Allergic rhinitis can be suspected on the basis of a history

TABLE 38–2. Management of Epistaxis in Children

Anterior Epistaxis

General measures
  Humidify (nasal saline lavage)
  Steroid or antibiotic ointment or cream to anterior septum
  Discourage nose rubbing and picking
  Topical or systemic antibiotic treatment for sinusitis
Allergic rhinitis
  Mild corticosteroid ointment to anterior septum
  Cromolyn sodium nasal spray
  Corticosteroid nasal spray as indicated
  Immunotherapy as indicated
Active bleeding
  Blow out or suction all blood clots
  Vasoconstrictive spray or drops, such as oxymetazoline (may be combined with anesthetic, such as 4% lidocaine)
  Anterior pressure (nose pinching) for 5 minutes
Continued bleeding
  Visualize bleeding points
  Chemical cautery or electrocautery
  Absorbable or gauze packing as indicated
  Nasal tampon or balloon pack as indicated
  Evaluate for systemic coagulopathy as indicated

Posterior (or Superior) Epistaxis

Diagnosis known (leukemia, postnasal intubation)
  Suction, vasoconstriction (may require restraint or anesthesia)
  Packing (absorbable, gauze, balloon)
  Correction of known systemic factors (low platelets)
  For uncontrolled or recurrent bleeding: angiography and selective embolization
  For continued bleeding: surgery
  Transnasal endoscopy and direct cautery
  Ethmoidal or internal maxillary artery ligation
Diagnosis unknown
  Suction, vasoconstriction
  Visualize nasal cavities, nasopharynx, oropharynx (and sinuses)
    Flexible or rigid endoscopy (may require anesthesia)
    Computed tomography scanning or magnetic resonance imaging for suspected tumor or sinus disease
  Evaluation for possible systemic disorders
  Packing, embolization, surgery, medical therapy as indicated by diagnosis

of seasonal symptoms of congestion, cough, and facial pruritus. Physical findings are clues, such as bluish, boggy, pitted turbinate mucosa; clear rhinorrhea; "allergic shiners"; and a crease above the nasal tip from continuous nose rubbing. Allergy management, including age-appropriate testing and immunotherapy, may be beneficial. Topical application of mild corticosteroid-containing ointments or creams to the anterior septum, especially at bedtime, can help reduce vascular inflammation and break a cycle of allergy-mediated epistaxis. Newer topical nasal steroids (some approved by the U.S. Food and Drug Administration for patients as young as 4 years) may be a benefit for patients with allergic rhinitis. Patients should be instructed in the correct use of all nasal sprays. Sprays should be directed superior laterally as though aiming behind the orbit or behind the ear. This allows for better dispersion to the critical areas in the sinus outflow tracts and helps to reduce trauma from the spray to the anterior septum. Topical nasal steroids can create more mucosal irritation for patients who live in very dry climates. Where relative humidity is under 40%, nasal steroid sprays should be used very selectively and then only in conjunction with nasal saline humidification.

For patients with suspected rhinitis and sinusitis, an antibiotic topical preparation may be of use. Mupirocin ointment or cream is a non–petroleum-base product that was developed for the problem of nasal carrier state of medical personnel with methicillin-resistant *Staphylococcus aureus*. The ointments or creams are water miscible and can be picked up via the nasal ciliary action. Mupirocin can be combined with nasal saline by placing 5 g of mupirocin in 45 mL of buffered nasal saline. The mupirocin disperses in solution better when the solution is warmed. The patients are instructed to use one or two squirts per nostril once or twice a day. Mupirocin has been approved by the Food and Drug Administration for patients older than 12 years with topical impetigo, infected eczema, or folliculitis caused by *S. aureus*. Mupirocin is not effective against *Enterobacteriaceae, Pseudomonas aeruginosa*, or fungi. Safety and efficacy have not been demonstrated for patients younger than 12 years.

For patients with recurrent anterior bleeding, nasal saline is an efficient way to humidify the nose. In addition, it may help by mechanically removing dust, molds, pollens, dander, and air pollution. Premade pH-balanced solutions warmed to body temperature can be used in virtually all children, if an effort is made to emphasize to the parents the importance of daily preventive treatment. If sinusitis is suspected on the basis of purulent secretions in the middle meati or because of a crusted, excoriated head of the middle turbinate mucosa, appropriate antibiotic therapy is also indicated.

In patients with a history of recurrent epistaxis despite appropriate preventive measures, a hematologic evaluation is warranted. A complete blood cell count can be used to check platelet numbers and partially rule out a diagnosis of lymphoreticular malignant disease. The prothrombin and partial thromboplastin times may shed light on primary or acquired coagulopathies such as von Willebrand disease. Bleeding times may be used as an evaluation of platelet function, but a history of easy bruising and/or petechiae is probably more sensitive. Remember that a normal prothrombin and partial thromboplastin time and/or bleeding time does not rule out von Willebrand disease. More sophisticated tests such a total factor VIII and von Willebrand antigen assay should be performed when von Willebrand disease is suspected because of clinical findings and family history.

Rarely, when anterior epistaxis cannot be controlled with anterior pressure or direct cautery, consideration can be made for anterior nasal packing. Gauze has the advantage of providing a tight pack, but disadvantages include discomfort, the need for subsequent removal, and the possibility of creating further mucosal injury. Biodegradable oxidized cellulose (Oxycel) or gelatin sponge (Gelfoam) may be used for anterior packing and, if used alone, need not be removed later.[16] Toxic shock syndrome has been reported with the use of both anterior and posterior nasal packing; for this reason, packing material should be impregnated with antibiotic ointment, patients should be administered antibiotics while nasal packs are in place, and the packs should be allowed to remain for as short a time as is practical.

Special care must be taken by the clinician in the approach to children with epistaxis in the intensive care unit setting. These patients often have anemia and quantitative or qualitative platelet abnormalities, and they frequently have diffuse mucosal oozing. In addition, they are subject to repeated nasal trauma by the placement of nasogastric and nasotracheal tubes. The approach to these patients should begin with the removal (if possible) of any indwelling nasal tubes, followed by careful inspection and suctioning of the nasal cavity with the use of a portable light source, nasal speculum or scope, and soft suction catheter. Vasoconstriction and local anesthesia can be obtained by placing cotton pledgets soaked in oxymetazoline and 4% lidocaine solutions intranasally for a few minutes. This measure, along with elevation of the head of the bed and 5 minutes of pressure applied by squeezing the anterior nose, will control a large percentage of nosebleeds.

When anterior packs are required, oxidized cellulose or microfibrillar collagen preparations are preferred to gauze because they promote coagulation and do not further irritate already traumatized mucosal surfaces. The clinician should keep in mind that nasal packs can themselves result in severe morbidity and should be avoided when possible, especially in very ill patients. In nonintubated patients, bilateral or unilateral nasal packs can cause an iatrogenic sleep apnea syndrome that can lead to hypoxia and possibly death. Mechanisms might include the nasopulmonary reflex (although not definitively demonstrated in humans) or simply obstructed sleep apnea from loss of the nasal airway. Immunocompromised patients are especially at risk for infectious complications of nasal packing, including sinusitis due to blocked sinus ostia, bacteremia and sepsis, and even toxic shock syndrome.[17] Mechanical complications of nasal packs include injury to the columella or septum from ischemic necrosis and aspiration of a loose pack, possibly causing asphyxiation.[11]

Superior and Posterior Epistaxis

If good visualization of the anterior nasal cavity fails to document a bleeding site, further diagnostic evaluation is indicated. In a stable patient, the flexible fiberoptic nasopharyngoscope is an excellent way to obtain visualization of the entire upper aerodigestive tract. This can be used without sedation in the clinic setting but requires restraint for young patients. Superior and posterior bleeding sites, foreign bodies, tumors, sinusitis, and other diagnoses can easily be made in a matter of minutes. In older cooperative patients, a rigid endoscope can afford better light and optics. Isolated posterior epistaxis usually results from a branch of the sphenopalatine artery just posterior to the tip of the inferior or middle turbinate or along the posterior septum. This is a relatively rare occurrence in the pediatric population. Direct endoscopic visualization and cautery with an insulated nasal cautery under general anesthesia can be an excellent means of managing this problem.[25, 34]

Posterior packing can be accomplished with gauze or urinary catheter balloons.[4] Premade nasal tampons and nasal balloons (e.g., Gottschalk nasostat or Xomed-Treace epistat) (Fig. 38–4) may be used for anterior or posterior packing. Patients with posterior nasal packs should be admitted for airway observation for the reasons mentioned previously.

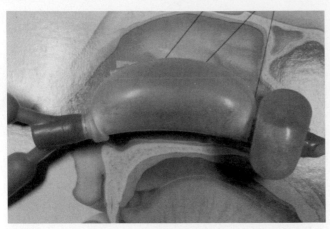

FIGURE 38-4. Picture of an inflated anterior and posterior nasal balloon superimposed on a photograph of the nasal cavity and nasopharynx. After placement of the balloon catheter, the posterior balloon is inflated, anterior traction is applied until the balloon is against the posterior choanal opening, and then the anterior balloon is inflated with saline to achieve cessation of bleeding.

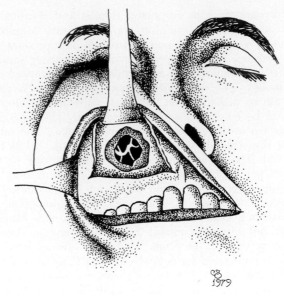

FIGURE 38-5. View of the internal maxillary artery through a fenestra of the posterior wall of the antrum by a Caldwell-Luc approach.

Arterial embolization has been reported by some for severe epistaxis refractory to other therapeutic measures.[27] It has the advantages of avoiding open surgical procedures, delineating the exact bleeding site, and demonstrating aberrant arterial supply to the nose. Disadvantages include the risk of an embolic phenomenon in the internal carotid system; but for experienced angiographers, the technique is highly successful.[15, 30, 37, 42]

For patients with hereditary hemorrhagic telangiectasia, the argon laser combined with septal dermoplasty procedures has been effective in helping to control epistaxis.[33] The argon laser can also be used for excision of other vascular intranasal lesions, such as pyogenic granulomas.

Hereditary hemorrhagic telangiectasia accounts for a large percentage of intractable recurrences in published series of epistaxis management.[40] Lund and Howard[24] described a treatment algorithm based on a series of 15 adult patients aged 15 to 85 years. Epistaxis is usually the predominant bleeding problem for patients with hereditary hemorrhagic telangiectasia, and severe epistaxis usually has its onset before the age of 30. Half of their adult patients had a history of excessive epistaxis in childhood. Recurrent septal cautery had often led to septal perforations in their cohort. Approximately 40% of the patients had received blood transfusions at some point. For patients with mild or moderate disease, the authors recommended sequential argon laser therapy with or without septodermoplasty or hormonal therapy with an estrogen derivative. The authors concluded that severe recurrent epistaxis could be successfully managed only by surgical closure of one or both nostrils (a modified Young's procedure).

Arterial ligation for recurrent epistaxis in children is rarely indicated[6] (Fig. 38-5). For posterior and superior bleeding, ligation of the anterior and posterior ethmoidal arteries is used. For bleeding that arises from the posterior portion of the nose, ligation of the terminal branches of the internal maxillary artery is performed.[2, 29, 36]

Newer reports of arterial ligation for refractory epistaxis in adults emphasize endoscopic approaches to the terminal branches of the internal maxillary artery at the sphenopalatine foramen. Wormald et al[43] described an endoscopic submucosal clipping of the sphenopalatine branches at the sphenopalatine foramen. El-Guindy,[9] in contrast, described a midline transseptal approach to the face of the sphenoid for sphenopalatine artery ligation. Obviously, endoscopic or transseptal approaches for posterior epistaxis control would be much more difficult in children than in adults, owing to children's smaller anatomy.

Conclusion

Epistaxis is a common pediatric problem, and most cases arise from the anterior septum. Identification and treatment of the bleeding source along the anterior septum and preventive measures, such as appropriate allergy control and humidification, result in the successful management of most patients. Severe recurrent epistaxis should warrant further investigation for hematologic disorder, tumor, or other rare conditions.

SELECTED REFERENCES

Stair TO. Epistaxis. In Current Practice of Emergency Medicine, 2nd ed. Philadelphia, BC Decker, 1991, p 217.
    Focus on effective treatment for active bleeding in an emergency setting.
Wurman LH. Epistaxis. In Gates GA, ed. Current Therapy in Otolaryngology Head and Neck Surgery, 5th ed. St Louis, CV Mosby, 1994, p 354.
    Concise overview of current treatment options for anterior and posterior epistaxis.

REFERENCES

1. Aassar OS, Friedman CM, White RI Jr. The natural history of epistaxis in hereditary hemorrhagic telangiectasis. Laryngoscope 101:977, 1991.
2. Adams DM. Transantral internal maxillary artery ligation in prolonged or severe posterior epistaxis. J La State Med Soc 125:389, 1973.
3. Alavi K. Epistaxis and hemoptysis due to *Hirudo medicinalis* (medical leech). Arch Otolaryngol 90:178, 1969.
4. Bell M, Hawke M, Jahn A. New device for the management of postnasal epistaxis: balloon tamponade. Arch Otolaryngol 99:373, 1974.
5. Blumfeld R, Skolnik EM. Intranasal encephaloceles. Arch Otolaryngol 85:527, 1965.
6. Chandler JR, Serrins A. Transantral ligation of the internal maxillary artery for epistaxis. Laryngoscope 75:1151, 1965.
7. Coleman CC Jr. Diagnosis and treatment of congenital arteriovenous fistulas of the head and neck. Am J Surg 126:557, 1973.
8. El Bitar H. The etiology and management of epistaxis: a review of 300 cases. Practitioner 207:800, 1971.
9. El-Guindy A. Endoscopic trans-septal sphenopalatine artery ligation for intractable posterior epistaxis. Ann Otorhinol 107:1033, 1998.
10. English GM, Hemenway WG, Cundy RL. Surgical treatment of invasive angiofibroma. Arch Otolaryngol 96:312, 1972.
11. Fairbanks DF. Complications of nasal packing. Otolaryngol Head Neck Surg 94:412, 1986.
12. Falter MS, Kaufman MF. Congenital factor VII deficiency. J Pediatr 79:298, 1971.
13. Goldstein A. Postvaricella bleeding presenting as epistaxis. Arch Otolaryngol 92:173, 1970.
14. Goode RL, Spooner TR. Management of nasal fractures in children: a review of current practices. Clin Pediatr 119:526, 1972.
15. Hicks JN, Vitek G. Transarterial embolization to control posterior epistaxis. Laryngoscope 199:1027, 1989.
16. Huggins S. Control of hemorrhage in otorhinolaryngologic surgery with oxidized regenerated cellulose. EENT Mo 48:420, 1969.
17. Hull HF, Mann JM, Sands DJ, et al. Toxic shock syndrome related to nasal packing. Arch Otolaryngol 109:627, 1993.
18. Iwamura S, Sugiura S, Nomura Y. Schwannoma of the nasal cavity. Arch Otolaryngol 96:176, 1972.
19. Jafek B, Nahum A, Butler R, et al. Surgical treatment of juvenile nasopharyngeal angiofibroma. Laryngoscope 83:707, 1973.
20. Juselius H. Epistaxis: a clinical study of 1,734 patients. J Laryngol Otol 88:317, 1974.
21. Kahn AA, Khaleque KA, Huda MN. Rhinosporidiosis of the nose. J Laryngol Otol 83:461, 1969.
22. Koltai PJ. Nose bleeds in the hematologically and immunologically compromised child. Laryngoscope 94:114, 1984.
23. Leslie J, Ingram GI. The diagnosis of long-standing bleeding disorders. Semin Hematol 8:140, 1971.
24. Lund VJ, Howard DJ. A treatment algorithm for the management of epistaxis in hereditary hemorrhagic telangiectasis. Am J Rhinol 13:319,1999.
25. Marcus MJ. Nasal endoscope control of epistaxis preliminary report. Otolaryngol Head Neck Surg 102:273, 1990.
26. Medeiros D, Buchanan JR. Major hemorrhage in children with idiopathic thrombocytopenic purpura: immediate response to therapy long-term outcome. J Pediatr 133:313, 1998.
27. Merland JJ, Melki JP, Chiras J, et al. Place of embolization in the treatment of severe epistaxis. Laryngoscope 90:1694, 1980.
28. Mettler CC. History of Medicine. Philadelphia, Blakiston, 1947.
29. Montgomery WW, Lofgren RH, Chasin WD. Analysis of pterygopalatine space surgery. Laryngoscope 80:1179, 1970.
30. Moreau S, DeRugby MG, Babin E, et al. Supraselective embolization in intractable epistaxis: review of 45 cases. Laryngoscope 108:887, 1998.
31. Murray AB, Milner RA. Allergic rhinitis and recurrent epistaxis in children. Ann Allergy Asthma Immunol 74:30, 1995.
32. Murthy P, Nilssen EL, Rao S, McClymont LG. A randomized clinical trial of antiseptic nasal carrier cream and silver nitrate cautery in the treatment of recurrent anterior epistaxis. Clin Otolaryngol 24:228, 1999.
33. Nunez DA, McClymont LG, Evans RA. Epistaxis: a study of the relationship with weather. Clin Otolaryngol 15:49, 1990.
34. O'Leary-Stickney K, Makielski K, Weymuller EA. Rigid endoscopy for the control of epistaxis. Arch Otolaryngol Head Neck Surg 118:966, 1992.
35. Pathak PN. Epistaxis due to ruptured aneurysm of the internal carotid artery. J Laryngol Otol 86:395, 1972.
36. Pearson BW, MacKenzie RG, Goodman WS. The anatomical basis of transantral ligation of the maxillary artery in severe epistaxis. Laryngoscope 79:969, 1969.
37. Remonda L, Schroth G, Caversuccio M, et al. Endovascular treatment of acute and subacute hemorrhage in the head and neck. Arch Otolaryngol Head Neck Surg 126:1255, 2000.
38. Rowe NL. Fractures of the facial skeleton in children. J Oral Surg 26:505, 1968.
39. Ruddy J, Proops DW, Pearman K, Ruddy H. Management of epistaxis in children. Int J Pediatr Otorhinolaryngol 21:139, 1991.
40. Siegel MB, Keane WM, Atkins JP, Rosen MR. Control of epistaxis in patients with hereditary hemorrhagic telangiectasia. Otolaryngol Head Neck Surg 105:675, 1991.
41. Stool SE, Kemper B. Nose, pharynx, and paranasal sinuses. In Kelley V, ed. Brenneman's Practice of Pediatrics, Vol 4. New York, Harper & Row, 1973.
42. Welsh CW, Welsh JJ, Scogna JE, Gregor FA. Role of angiography in the management of refractory epistaxis. Ann Otol Rhinol Laryngol 99:69, 1990.
43. Wormald PJ, Weed TH, van Hasselt CA. Endoscopic ligation of the sphenopalatine artery for refractory posterior epistaxis. Am J Rhinol 14:216, 2000.

39

Facial Pain and Headache

Robert L. Pincus, M.D., and Frank E. Lucente, M.D.

Headache is common in children and adolescents. It is often an incidental finding with systemic illness or fever but can be an important symptom of grave central nervous system disease. By age 7 years, 40% of children will have had one or more headaches. By age 15 years, 75% will have had at least one headache. Twenty percent of 15-year-old adolescents have frequent headaches; one fourth of these headaches are migrainous.[2] Guidetti and Gali followed children with headaches for over 8 years. They found a remission rate of 34% and improvement in 45%. In 15% the headaches were unchanged, and in 6% they worsened over time.[8]

Complaints of facial pain and headache in the child are often difficult to assess if one cannot obtain an accurate history or establish the precise location of the pain. Many of these pains disappear quickly and do not require evaluation by a physician. However, patients with persistent or recurrent symptoms should have complete head and neck examinations. Such evaluation may require a multidisciplinary approach by the otolaryngologist, pediatrician, neurologist, ophthalmologist, dentist, psychiatrist, and social worker. It is the responsibility of the otolaryngologist to explore the potential etiologic role of otolaryngologic structures in facial pain and headache.

Pain in the head may result from stimulation, traction, or pressure on any of the pain-sensitive structures of the head, which include the trigeminal, glossopharyngeal, vagal, and upper cervical nerves; the large arteries at the base of the brain and their major branches; the dura mater at the base of the skull; the cranial sinuses and afferent veins; the arteries of the dura mater; and some extracranial structures, such as the scalp, arteries, and muscles.[5]

Headache may be a recognizable symptom in children 3 years of age and older. The infant or younger child may have irritability or unusual behavior rather than complaints of headache on experiencing the pathologic processes described in this chapter.[11]

Although most pains in the head and neck region result from a pathologic process at or close to the area indicated by the patient, the physician might consider the phenomenon of referred pain when no abnormalities are found in this area. A common example of referred pain is the otalgia produced by inflammatory, infectious, and neoplastic lesions of the pharynx. The external ear and middle ear receive sensory innervation from the fifth, seventh, ninth, and tenth cranial nerves and from the second and third cervical nerves. An irritative process anywhere along the distribution of any of these nerves can cause a referred otalgia.

A thorough history often provides the diagnosis for the pain. It should include questions about severity, duration, location, character, circumstances of onset, exacerbating or remitting factors, repetition, frequency, and associated symptoms in the head and neck region and elsewhere (Table 39–1). In taking the history, the physician should also attempt to become more familiar with the child as a social being by inquiring about the child's family, social, and educational settings. It is often helpful to talk with the child in the absence of the parents, particularly when psychological factors appear to cause, exacerbate, or modify the headache symptoms. The patient should have a complete head and neck examination, including skull, facial bones, eyes, ears, temporomandibular joint, nose, nasopharynx, oral cavity, teeth, oropharynx, larynx, cervical muscles, and associated soft tissues. In palpating the head and neck region, one should begin in asymptomatic areas and move slowly toward symptomatic or tender areas to avoid frightening or hurting the child any more than necessary. Percussion of the teeth, sinuses, and mastoids should also be included. Cervical muscles should be palpated for spasm. One should listen for bruits over the temples and orbits. A thorough neurologic examination should also be performed with particular attention to the cranial nerves.

The performance of ancillary laboratory tests and radiography is guided by the clinical impression obtained from the history and physical examination. There are few, if any, mandatory screening tests, and indiscriminate ordering of tests should be avoided. Neuroradiologic testing is recommended in children with symptoms suggestive of a brain mass. These symptoms include increasing severity of headache, associated neurologic disturbances, focal symptoms or change in personality or school performance, or weight loss.[17] In their absence, neuroimaging studies in children have a low yield.[3]

This chapter presents a differential diagnosis for headache and facial pain (Tables 39–2 to 39–4) and considers a few of the more common causes or conditions associated with these complaints. (More extensive discussion is found in related chapters.)

TABLE 39–1. Sample Questions in the Headache Interview

Age of onset?	Triggering events?
Events surrounding onset?	Stress
Duration of significant headaches?	School
Prodrome?	Family
General malaise	Illness
Visual aura	Exertion
Other	Fatigue
Characteristics of attack?	Food intake
Frequency	Medications
Localization	Behavior between attacks?
Duration	Normal?
Type of pain	Irritable?
Time of day	Clumsy?
Severity of attacks?	Personality change?
Does it require interruption of	Recent changes in patient
normal activity?	Weight loss?
Associated autonomic symptoms?	Disturbed sleep pattern?
Pallor	School performance?
Nausea and vomiting	Appetite?
Abdominal pain	Family history?
Associated neurologic deficits?	Migraine
Type	Tension headache
Temporal relation to headache	Epilepsy
Duration	Psychiatric disorders
Does localization of neurologic	Neurologic disease
deficit correspond to that of	Medications?
headache?	Analgesics
Postictal state?	Birth control pills
What makes it better?	Other
What makes it worse?	Motion sickness?

Modified from Shinnar S, D'Souza BJ. The diagnosis and management of headaches in childhood. Pediatr Clin North Am 29:79, 1981.

TABLE 39–2. Etiologic Classification of Headache

Environmental	**Toxic-Metabolic**
Heat	"Pseudotumor"
Humidity	Steroids
Noxious fumes	Tetracycline
Noise	Vitamin A
Infectious	Other drugs
Extracranial	Sulfa
Teeth	Indomethacin
Sinus	Heavy metals
Pharynx	Lead
Ear	Arsenic
Septicemia	Mercury
Viral exanthems	Hypoglycemia
Musculoskeletal	Metabolic acidosis
Intracranial	Hypoxia
Meningitis	Anemia
Encephalitis	Carbon monoxide poisoning
Brain abscess	Hypercapnia
Vascular	Porphyria
Migraine	**Congenital**
Hypertension	Arnold-Chiari syndrome
Aneurysm	**Cervical**
Vascular malformation	**Neuralgic**
Horton syndrome (histamine	Herpetic
cephalgia)	Postherpetic
Traumatic	Idiopathic
Neoplastic	**Psychological**
Extracranial	Depression
Intracranial	School phobia syndrome
Epileptic	Conversion symptom
Psychomotor	Prolonged postconcussive syndrome
Postictal	
Ocular	
Allergic	

Modified from Meloff KL. Headache in pediatric practice. Headache 13:125, 1973.

Muscle Contraction Headache (Tension Headache)

The muscle contractive headache is probably the most common headache in childhood. It is usually bilateral, steady, nonpulsatile, and less intense than a migraine. The pain tends to present in the occipital region or as a band around the head. Because it probably results from prolonged contraction of muscles of the head and neck, it generally occurs later in the day and after periods of physical or emotional stress or intense intellectual activity. Although less common in children than in adults, it is sometimes seen in hard-working students. The failure of the pain to be intensified by coughing, straining at stool, or placing the head in a dependent position distinguishes this type of headache from those due to intracranial causes. It must also be differentiated from depression, school phobia syndrome, and a conversion syndrome.[7]

On examination, one may find restriction and pain with movement of the neck and tenderness over the occipital nerves. Tenderness in the upper border of the trapezius and intrinsic cervical muscles is also found.

Management varies with the underlying cause. Oral analgesics and local treatment with heat may help, but elimination of the underlying physical or psychological strain is most important. As with other headaches in children, complete and repeated explanation and reassurance are most important.

Migraine Headache

Migraine headaches commonly begin during adolescence, but this syndrome may occasionally be seen in younger children. Although uncommon before the age of 4 years,

TABLE 39–3. Anatomic-Etiologic Classification of Facial Pain

Forehead	**Nasal**
Frontal sinus	Nasal bones
Ocular	Ethmoid sinus
Periorbital	Intranasal
Ocular	**Jaw**
Ethmoid sinus	Mandibular teeth
Preauricular	Periodontal structures
Temporomandibular joint	Submandibular gland
External-ear canal	**Temporal**
Parotid gland	Temporomandibular joint
Periauricular	External-ear canal
Middle ear	Tension
External ear (pinna)	
Midfacial (cheek)	
Maxillary sinus	
Maxillary teeth	
Periodontal structures	
Intranasal	
Parotid gland	

TABLE 39–4. Clinical Summary of Facial Pain and Headache

Disease or Disorder	Location	Character	Usual Frequency	Accompanying Symptoms	Usual Time of Day	General Therapy	Duration
Sinusitis	Frontal Midfacial Periorbital	Dull	Inconsistent	Nasal congestion Nasal drainage	Morning Evening	Decongestant Antibiotic	More than 1 day
Migraine Classic Common	Unilateral Frontotemporal Periorbital	Severe Throbbing	Weekly or monthly	Nausea Vomiting Scotomas	Any time	Ergotamine Tranquilizer Anticonvulsant	Classic: less than 8 hours Common: hours to days
Psychogenic (tension)	Frontal Occipital Bandlike	Inconsistent	Daily	Nervousness Anxiety Withdrawn behavior	During or after stress	Analgesic Tranquilizer	Variable
Brain tumor	Frontal Parietal Occipital	Dull	Daily	Ataxia Behavior change Visual disturbance	Morning Evening	Relief of intracranial pressure	More than 1 day
Ocular disorders	Ocular Frontal	Dull	Daily	Squint Refractive errors	Afternoon Evening	Visual correction	Several hours
Convulsive equivalent	Frontal Temporal	Dull	Daily or weekly	Vomiting Staring episodes Hyperactivity	Any time	Anticonvulsant	Minutes to hours
Meningitis Encephalitis	Frontal Occipital	Dull	Constant	Fever Nuchal rigidity Convulsions	Any time	Antibiotics	Constant

From Jabbour JT, Duenas DA, Gilmartin RC Jr, et al. Pediatric Neurology Handbook. Flushing, NY, Medical Examination Publishing, 1976. Modified and reprinted by permission of Elsevier Science Publishing Company, Inc. Copyright © 1976 by Medical Examination Publishing Company, Inc.

migraine has been reported in infants younger than 1 year.[23]

Some adolescents may experience classic migraine headaches similar to those found in adults, with prodromal anorexia and scotomas, severe unilateral pulsatile headache lasting 4 to 8 hours, followed by diffuse head pain, photophobia, abdominal discomfort, nausea, vomiting, and postictal lethargy. However, younger children more frequently have common (atypical) migraines, which lack the prodromal signs and may last hours to days. For this reason, the diagnosis may be elusive until symptoms have been present for several months. A family history of migraine or convulsive disorders is obtained in 70% to 80% of cases.[16]

Occasionally the child will present with only paroxysmal vomiting, hemiparesis, diplopia, or ataxia. Headache may appear later in the clinical course. The attacks usually last 2 to 3 hours but may last up to 48 hours. They are often followed by a period of sleep and tend to recur at irregular intervals.

There is an equal sex frequency in young children, but in adolescents and adults, migraine occurs more frequently in females. Although emotional stress may precipitate a migraine episode, it should not be considered a psychiatric disorder. There can be significant vestibulocochlear derangements in children with migraine. Forty-five percent have a history of motion sickness, seven times the frequency of other groups.[1] Vestibular symptoms and phonophobia are major symptoms during the majority of migraine attacks.[10] Migraine without aura is about twice as common as migraine with aura in children.[15] The pathogenesis of migraine is thought to involve initial cerebral vasoconstriction followed by rapid vasodilatation.

Patients and their families should be informed of the benign but frequently lifelong prognosis. If precipitating factors can be identified, they should be eliminated. Mild attacks may be relieved with salicylates, nonsteroidal anti-inflammatory drugs, or codeine taken at the onset. Subcutaneous sumatriptan has been shown to be effective in children.[12] Ergot preparations used in treating adult migraines may produce more intense and prolonged effects, possibly resulting in cerebral ischemia. Minor tranquilizers may interrupt the headache if given for a period of several months. The child should be reassured that there is no neoplastic or psychological cause for the headaches. When frequent attacks are present, prophylaxis with agents that inhibit vasoactive substances is indicated, such as antihistamines, nonsteroidal anti-inflammatory drugs, tricyclic antidepressants, and beta-adrenergic blockers. It is important, even in children, to at least discuss the issue of rebound headache, in an attempt to avoid its future development.[22]

Opthalmoplegic migraine is a rare variant of this clinical picture, in which partial or complete third nerve palsy appears 6 to 24 hours after the onset of the headache. Although the ophthalmoplegia generally subsides within a few days, repeated episodes may leave the patient with some residual paralysis.

In basilar artery migraines, symptoms of brain stem dysfunction predominate. Symptoms last for a few minutes and include bilateral visual changes, ataxia, vertigo, dysarthria, paresthesias, and alteration in consciousness.

Chronic Daily Headache

Chronic daily headache (CDH) has recently been described in children as well as in adults. Chronic daily headache is found in 0.5% to 0.9% of children. CDH is defined as a patient having 5 or more days with headache during each week. The pain is usually bifrontal, rather than involving the whole head. Children with CDH rarely have serious associated pathologic findings.[22]

Convulsive Equivalent

Headaches may be associated with a paroxysmal cerebral dysrhythmia or psychomotor seizure. They usually have an acute onset during the day or night and last several minutes to several hours. They are characteristically dull and are located in the frontotemporal region. Pallor, abdominal discomfort, nausea, and vomiting follow onset of the headache. The pain may disappear after a brief period of sleep, and the child then usually feels well. Anticonvulsant medications, such as phenytoin or barbiturates, usually produce a dramatic response.

Traction Headache (Brain Mass Headache)

Traction on intracranial pain-sensitive structures caused by brain tumor, hematoma, aneurysm, or abscess will result in a traction headache. Brain tumors usually produce a steady, aching headache that may be more severe in the early morning. It rarely has the pulsatile pattern of the vascular headache. Brain tumor headache tends to be more severe when the child is lying down and may awaken the child from sleep.[6] Rossi and Vassella[18] found nocturnal headache or headache on arising that was associated with emesis or progressive neurologic symptoms in 65 of 67 children with headaches from brain tumor.

Vascular Malformation Headache

Vascular malformation is an uncommon cause of headache, which usually lasts several days and may be accompanied by seizures or periods of decreased levels of consciousness. Scotomas may also be present, but they are concomitant rather than antecedent as with migraine. The headache reaches its maximal intensity more quickly than the migraine headache, usually within seconds. In determining the etiology of the headache, it is important to look for coincident neurologic abnormalities that may persist long after the headache has disappeared. This type of headache is also associated with seizures and with cerebral hemorrhage.[4]

Hypertension Headache

Hypertension is rarely seen in childhood and is consequently a rare cause of headaches among children. The headaches tend to resemble the hypertension headaches experienced by adults and the brain mass headache. They occur more commonly in the morning and fluctuate rapidly in intensity during the day, sometimes in relationship to the amount or intensity of physical activity. Among the disorders that may be associated with hypertensive headaches are acute and chronic renal disease, neuroblastoma, pheochromocytoma, and adrenal adenomas. Diagnosis is usually simple if the blood pressure is monitored. Therapy involves analgesics and correction of the hypertension.

Neuralgias

The severe pain of trigeminal or glossopharyngeal neuralgia that is seen in adults is extremely rare in children.

Nasal and Paranasal Sinus Disease

The common viral upper respiratory tract infection is a frequent cause of headache, which may be diffuse or limited to the midfacial region. The pain is usually a dull ache that is exacerbated by placing the head in a dependent position. Associated symptoms and signs, including sneezing, nasal congestion, serous drainage, sore throat, malaise, cough, mild fever, and boggy nasal mucous membranes, usually confirm the diagnosis. Recovery is usually spontaneous within 4 to 5 days if there are no bacterial complications (Chap. 43).

If the nasal drainage becomes cloudy and the nasal mucous membranes become markedly inflamed, purulent rhinitis should be suspected. It is usually caused by hemolytic *Staphylococcus aureus*, *Haemophilus influenzae*, *Moraxella catarrhalis*, or *Streptococcus pneumoniae*. When nasal drainage is persistently unilateral, the presence of a foreign body must be excluded (Chap. 46).

Inflammation, infection, or tumors in the paranasal sinuses produce localized or diffuse facial pain more commonly than headache. Pain from the maxillary sinus is experienced in the midface, cheek, or maxillary teeth. Ethmoid pain is felt between the eyes, and frontal pain is felt in the supraorbital region. Pain from the sphenoid sinus is poorly localized, occasionally being described as coming from deep within the head or at the cranial vertex. The frontal and sphenoid sinuses develop slowly and are usually not of clinical significance until adolescence.[21]

Inflammation of the paranasal sinus probably causes far fewer headaches and facial pains than is commonly thought by patients. The sinus ostia, turbinates, and septum are more pain-sensitive than the sinus mucosa itself, and before ascribing midfacial pain to the sinuses, the physician should find corroborative clinical evidence, such as purulent or watery nasal drainage, marked erythema of the nasal mucosa, or tenderness to percussion over the sinuses. Imaging of the sinuses will be helpful in evaluating puzzling patients or in determining therapy. Some think that septal deformation may cause referred pain and chronic headache by exerting pressure on the lateral nasal wall.[19]

Sinus disease in the child can be considerably more serious than in the adult owing to the incomplete development in children of the bony walls of the sinuses. The thinness of the lamina papyracea allows rapid extension of ethmoid infection into the orbit with production of orbital cellulitis or orbital abscess. Localized osteomyelitis may appear with spread of infection from any sinus into contiguous bone. Extension of infection through the posterior wall of the frontal sinus, roof of the ethmoid sinus, or any wall of the sphenoid sinus may lead to intracranial complications, such as epidural abscess, meningitis, or brain abscess. Persistent or severe headache in the child with clinical evidence of sinusitis mandates a thorough examination of areas adjacent to the sinuses.

Ocular Headache

When the patient complaining of headache or facial pain is examined, it is important to consider ocular causes, to examine the eyes, and to obtain an ophthalmologic consultation when indicated. Extensive discussion of ocular causes of pain in this region is not given here. However, several important disorders are mentioned.

Refractive errors and eye imbalance only rarely cause headache. They usually cause a dull periorbital or frontal pain and can be clearly related to prolonged eye strain.

Acute glaucoma, which is rare in children, is characterized by sudden, severe pain in the eye and the supraorbital region. The pain is accompanied by blurring of vision, increased intraocular pressure, dilated pupil, and a cloudy cornea. The glaucoma occurring in infancy has an insidious onset and may be associated with tearing, photophobia, blurred vision, and less severe pain. Glaucoma occurring in childhood is usually asymptomatic. If symptoms are present, they consist of dull periorbital pain, which may only be noticed at night.

Acute iritis (anterior uveitis) is usually associated with photophobia, blurring, and extreme pain radiating from the eye to the forehead and temporal region. The eye is red (circumcorneal flush) and the pupil is small. Iritis in the child with juvenile rheumatoid arthritis may have an insidious onset and is essentially painless (Chap. 40).

Acute retrobulbar neuritis may be associated with unilateral pain deep in the orbit. The pain occurs before blurring and is increased by rapid eye movement. The patient may complain of sudden loss of central vision. This disorder may be seen in teenagers but is uncommon in the young child.

Another rare childhood disorder is herpes zoster ophthalmicus, which begins with severe pain in the region of distribution of the ophthalmic division of the trigeminal nerve. Several days later, vesicles appear on the forehead and eyelids. Pain may persist after the acute infectious stage has passed.

Among the other ocular disorders to be considered with pain around the eyes are foreign bodies and inflammation of the lid or cornea (chronic blepharitis, conjunctivitis, corneal abrasions, or allergic reactions).

Otologic Pain

Inflammatory, infectious, and neoplastic diseases in the external, middle, and inner ears may produce pain that the child may interpret or describe as headache or, rarely, facial pain. The numerous otologic causes for headache and facial pain are considered in Chapters 14, 24, 27, 31, and 32. However, it is appropriate to reemphasize the need for complete otologic and audiometric evaluation of any child with headache, even without associated otologic symptoms (Chap. 14).

Dermatologic Infections

Infections of the skin of the head and neck may produce pain. The areas involved can be overlooked in a cursory examination because they are often hidden. Among the bacterial infections that occur in children are facial cellulitis, nasal vestibulitis, and furunculosis of the external ear canal.

Dental Disease

Inflammation or infection of the teeth or their supporting structures may cause the child to complain of localized, diffuse pain. Inspection, palpation, and percussion of the teeth should be performed carefully and supplemented with radiographic examination when indicated. The condition of the gingivae should also be noted. Among the dental diseases that may present with headache or facial pain are caries, periapical abscess, periodontal disease, eruption of deciduous or permanent teeth, loss of deciduous teeth, dental impaction, infected dental cyst, and aphthous or herpetic stomatitis (Chap. 58).

Temporomandibular Joint Disease

Pain from masticatory dysfunctions involving the temporomandibular joint is usually a dull ache experienced in the preauricular region. It is sometimes more diffuse and may be described by the patient as an earache. The pain is usually steady and is exacerbated by chewing or vigorous jaw motion. It may be seen in conjunction with any generalized or localized disease of synovial joints, such as rheumatoid arthritis. Temporomandibular joint dysfunction may also be seen in children with malocclusion and in children undergoing orthodontia.[13]

Head Trauma

The elicitation of a history of cranial or maxillofacial trauma from the child or parent may be difficult. However, the presence of contusions, ecchymoses, abrasions, or bone tenderness may support the clinical suspicions. Thorough head and neck examination may disclose signs of trauma in regions less visible than the face and the skull. Inconsistencies in the histories given by the child and parents may be noted. Radiographic evaluation should be performed if any trauma is suspected.

Systemic Diseases

Headaches occur in association with fever, hypoxemia, hypercapnia, poisoning, systemic viral or bacterial infections, and postictal states. Headache may often accompany streptococcal pharyngitis in particular. Chronic headache may be part of Lyme disease. Distention of cerebral and pial vessels is the postulated mechanism for the pain. Headaches associated with systemic infections are often accompanied by fever, nausea, and vomiting.

Psychogenic Headaches

It is impossible to detail the psychological significance with which the head, face, and neck are invested. However, the role of psychological factors in the production, modification, and communication of painful sensations in this region cannot be overemphasized. Children learn early that "headache" is a common somatic complaint used by adults to describe a discomfort that may have no relation to physical problems in or around the head. They may use the same phrases, "I have a headache" or "My head hurts," to describe their own experience of that same discomfort experienced by adults or to provide an excuse for their unwillingness to perform a certain act (for instance, going to school, visiting a neighbor, or doing household chores).

They may seek the secondary gain of increased attention that is usually given the sick child, or they may use this somatic complaint as a tool to manipulate parents, teachers, or other associates. It is hoped that careful questioning about both the circumstances of the pain and coincident factors will help identify those patients in whom psychological factors must be explored.

When the history is obtained from a parent, the physician should also be aware of the possibility that the parent is projecting his or her own concerns onto the patient, misstating the history or interpreting it prematurely, or seeking attention for his or her own problems. Inconsistencies in the history or the failure to find physical evidence for an abnormality (evidence of a physical abnormality) may suggest this situation.

However, just as one should not make psychogenic headache a diagnosis by exclusion, so also should one be careful not to eliminate physical causes before a thorough evaluation has been made. In ascribing pain in the head or face to a psychological cause, one should be certain of both the absence of demonstrable organic disease and the presence of detectable emotional disturbance.

SELECTED REFERENCES

Dalessio D, Silberstein, S (eds). Wolff's Headache and Other Head Pain, 6th ed. New York, Oxford University Press, 1993.

This classic text provides a tremendous amount of clinical and experimental material relevant to the many causes of headache. Although headaches in infants and children are not discussed apart from adult disorders, the coverage of each condition includes pertinent aspects of the pediatric problems.

Lucente F, Cooper B (eds). Management of Facial, Head and Neck Pain. Philadelphia, WB Saunders, 1989.

This multidisciplinary text discusses the etiology and management of many types of facial and head and neck pain. Among the subjects covered are functional anatomy, pharmacodynamics, paranasal sinuses, masticatory pain, occlusal disorders, neck pain, pain syndromes, and general examination of the patient.

REFERENCES

1. Barabas G, Matthews WS, Ferrari M. Childhood migraine and motion sickness. Pediatrics 72:188, 1983.
2. Bille B. Migraine in school children. Acta Paediatr Scand 51(Suppl 136):1, 1962.
3. Chu ML, Shinnar S. Headaches in children younger than 7 years of age. Arch Neurol 49:79, 1992.
4. Dalessio D, Silberstein S (eds). Wolff's Headache and Other Pain, 6th ed. New York, Oxford University Press, 1993.
5. Diamond S, Dalessio DJ. The Practicing Physician's Approach to Headache. Baltimore, Williams & Wilkins, 1982.
6. Dyken PR. Headaches in children. Arch Fam Pract 11:106, 1975.
7. Gascon GC. Chronic and recurrent headaches in children and adolescents. Pediatr Clin North Am 31:1027, 1984.
8. Guidetti V, Galli F. Evolution of headache in childhood and adolescence: an 8 year follow up. Cephalgia 18:449, 1988.
9. Jabbour JT, Duenas DA, Gilmartin RC Jr, et al. Pediatric Neurology Handbook. Flushing, NY, Medical Examination Publishing, 1976.
10. Kayan A, Hood JD. Neuro-otologic manifestations of migraine. Brain 107:1123, 1984.
11. Lagos JC. Differential Diagnosis in Pediatric Neurology. Boston, Little, Brown, 1971.
12. Linder SL. Subcutaneous sumatriptan in the clinical setting. The first 50 consecutive patients with acute migraine in a pediatric neurology practice. Headache 36:419, 1996.
13. Lucente F, Cooper B (eds). Management of Facial, Head and Neck Pain. Philadelphia, WB Saunders, 1989.
14. Meloff KL. Headache in pediatric practice. Headache 13:125, 1973.
15. Mortimer MJ, Kay J, Jaron A, et al. Epidemiology of headache and childhood migraine in an urban general practice using Ad Hoc, Vahlquist and IHS criteria. Dev Med Child Neurol 34:109, 1992.
16. Prensky AL, Sommer D. Prognosis and treatment of migraine in children. Neurology 29:506, 1979.
17. Rossi LN. Headache in childhood. Childs Nerv Syst 5:129, 1989.
18. Rossi LN, Vassella F. Headache in children with brain tumors. Childs Nerv Syst 5:307, 1989.
19. Schoensted-Madsen U, Stoksted P, Christensen PH, Koch-Henrichsen N. Chronic headache related to nasal obstruction. J Laryngol Otol 100:165, 1986.
20. Shinnar S, D'Souza BJ. The diagnosis and management of headaches in childhood. Pediatr Clin North Am 29:79, 1981.
21. Strome M. Rhino-sinusitis and midfacial pain in adolescents. Practitioner 217:914, 1976.
22. Winner P. Headache: what's new? Curr Opin Neurol 12(3):269, 1999.
23. Woody RC, Blaw ME. Ophthalmoplegic migraine in infancy. Clin Pediatr 25:82, 1986.

40

Orbital Swellings

Nina L. Shapiro, M.D., and Thomas C. Calcaterra, M.D.

The child with an orbital swelling often represents a diagnostic challenge that may require the expertise of several medical specialists. The otolaryngologist is frequently consulted because many cases of orbital swelling are caused by extracranial disease processes that occur adjacent to the orbit. It is important for the otolaryngologist to be familiar with the spectrum of diseases that may cause orbital swelling, the basic methods of orbital examination, and the diagnostic studies applicable to the orbit.

The orbit is a pyramid-shaped space, open anteriorly, but otherwise surrounded by thin bone. Any expansive disease, either within the orbit or from an adjacent site, may cause protrusion of the globe, a condition termed exophthalmos or proptosis. Accordingly, diseases that can cause exophthalmos may be classified into two major groups: (1) intraorbital, lesions arising within the orbital space, and (2) extraorbital, lesions involving the orbit by direct extension from adjacent structures or by metastasis from distant sites. The latter group can be subdivided into categories of intracranial and extracranial lesions. This latter group of extraorbital lesions, the extracranial lesions, are of major interest to the otolaryngologist because they frequently arise within the nose, paranasal sinuses, nasopharynx, or temporal fossa (Table 40–1).

History

A comprehensive history is important to an evaluation of unilateral exophthalmos. The mode of onset and progression of the exophthalmos, the status of vision, and the presence of pain should be established. The patient should be questioned about previous sinus infections, allergies, nasal discharge, and facial numbness. Slow progression of proptosis suggests a benign tumor or cyst, whereas rapidly developing proptosis implies the presence of infection or malignant tumor. Early loss of vision points to a lesion within the muscle cone involving the optic nerve, such as a glioma. Severe pain is generally suggestive of an acute infection or hemorrhage.

Physical Examination

Direction of Displacement

The direction of displacement often indicates the site of the lesion (Fig. 40–1). Tumors within the muscle cone,

such as an optic nerve glioma, may cause pure axial displacement. Acute inflammation or chronic mucopyocele arising from the frontal or ethmoid sinuses displaces the eye downward, laterally, or in both directions (Fig. 40–2). Displacement of the eye medially often denotes tumors of the lacrimal gland or the temporal fossa. Lesions arising in the maxillary sinus may push the globe upward.

Vertical displacement can be assessed by holding a ruler across both lateral canthi and determining the relationship of the pupils to this straight line. Horizontal displacement is determined by comparing the distance from a mark on the center of the bridge of the nose to each limbus.[15]

External Examination

Examination of the anterior aspect of the globe and eyelids should be performed. While the child is quiet and the radial or carotid pulse is being monitored, any synchronous pulsation of the globe indicates loss of the bony partition between the frontal or temporal lobe and the orbital contents, allowing intracranial pulsations to be transmitted to the eye. Synchronous pulsations may also be observed with a carotid-cavernous sinus fistula. Auscultation over the closed eyelid or temporal region may reveal a bruit suggestive of an arteriovenous vascular malformation. Increased proptosis that becomes apparent while the child is crying suggests an orbital varix, particularly if there is concomitant dilatation of the conjunctival veins. A palpable impulse that occurs when the child coughs suggests an encephalocele.

Chemosis, cellulitis, and fluctuation of the eyelids are signals of an inflammatory process, usually transmitted from the paranasal sinuses. Transillumination of the eyelid may disclose an underlying cyst. Although not as common in children as in adults, lid retraction, lid lag on upward gaze, lid restriction on elevation of the globe, and injection of the blood vessels over the lateral rectus muscle all imply the presence of endocrine exophthalmos.

Severe proptosis may prevent the lids from closing and thereby allow the cornea to dry.[10] The earliest sign of corneal exposure is the loss of normal corneal brightness. Moreover, persistent exposure can lead to ulceration, infection, and permanent scarring.

TABLE 40–1. Diseases Causing Orbital Swellings: Anatomic Classification

> **Intraorbital Lesions**
> Hyperthyroidism
> Pseudotumor
> Histiocytic lesion
> Epidermoid, dermoid, and teratoma
> Optic nerve glioma
> Rhabdomyosarcoma
> Retinoblastoma
> Melanoma
> Lacrimal gland tumors
> Dacryocystitis
> Dacryocystocele
> Hemangioma
> Lymphatic malformation
> Arterial malformations
> Arteriovenous malformations
> Metastatic tumors
> Malignant neoplasms
> **Extraorbital Extracranial Lesions**
> Acute inflammation of any paranasal sinus
> Mucocele of any paranasal sinus
> Fibrous dysplasia
> Osteoma
> Craniosynostosis
> Nasopharyngeal angiofibroma
> Nasopharyngeal cancer
> Osteitis
> Retrograde thrombophlebitis
> **Extraorbital Intracranial Lesions**
> Meningocele and encephalocele
> Meningoencephalocele
> Cavernous sinus thrombosis
> Cavernous sinus fistula
> Anterior cranial fossa tumors
> Middle cranial fossa tumors

Palpation

Palpation of the orbital contents may yield important information, particularly regarding anteriorly located lesions such as mucoceles and lacrimal gland tumors. Ballottement of each globe should be performed to compare orbital resilience in each eye. Inflammatory lesions and tumors tend to feel resistant, whereas less resistance is noted with hemangiomas and endocrine exophthalmos (Fig. 40–3). Fullness in the temporal fossa suggests lateral extension of the disease process, and irregularities of the orbital rim may represent bony destruction.

Ophthalmologic Examination

A complete ophthalmologic evaluation is mandatory. Decreased visual acuity is not characteristic of most intraorbital expansive processes unless the degree of proptosis is great or there is direct pressure on the optic nerve. A tumor directly behind the globe may indent the posterior wall of the retina in such a way as to induce a refractive error. A visual field defect suggests involvement of the optic chiasm. Funduscopic examination may show the presence of retinal striae or scleral flattening, which usually indicates a discrete intraorbital tumor. Papilledema and optic atrophy generally imply direct involvement of the optic nerve by tumor pressure or infiltration.[37]

Limitation of ocular movement may reflect either direct mechanical infringement of the muscles or globe or involvement of the third, fourth, or sixth cranial nerves as they pass through the cavernous sinus or superior orbital fissure. The nature of this limitation of motion may be resolved by the forced duction test: after topical or general anesthesia, the limbus is grasped with conjunctival

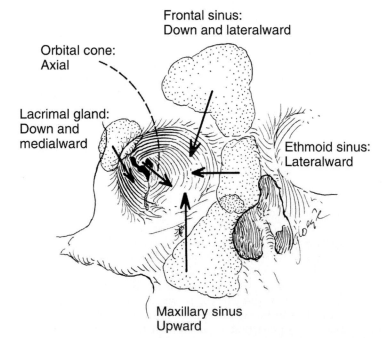

FIGURE 40–1. *Arrows* depict the direction of displacement typically encountered by a disease process within each paranasal sinus.

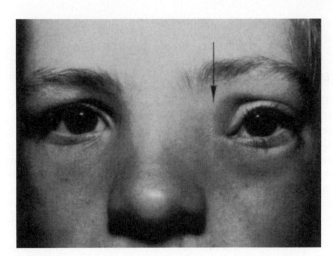

FIGURE 40–2. *Arrow* indicates fullness in the canthal region caused by an ethmoid mucocele, which displaces the left eye in a lateral direction.

forceps. If the eye can be moved fully in the direction of limited motion, paralysis is the likeliest cause of the abnormal ocular movement, whereas if movement is restricted, mechanical infringement by tumor or inflammation probably is present.

Exophthalmometry

Exophthalmos may be established either by an absolute measurement that relates the distance of the corneal apex to a reference point on the skull or by a relative measurement that compares the position of one cornea with that of the other.[10] Proptosis can be discerned easily by visualizing the eyes from above (over the forehead) or from below (over the malar eminences). Absolute measurements can be obtained with various instruments, the most common of which is the Hertle exophthalmometer, which uses the lateral orbital rim as a bony reference and pro-

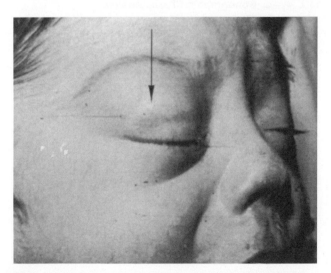

FIGURE 40–3. Infant with orbital and upper lid hemangioma (*arrow*). On palpation the hemangioma produced minimal resistance.

jects a lateral view of the cornea on a millimeter scale. Testing variability may range between 1 and 2 mm, depending on the consistent location of the instrument on the edge of the orbital rim, facial asymmetry, and thickness of the subcutaneous tissue over the bone. This instrument is especially useful in detecting smaller degrees of proptosis and for making objective measurements in serial examinations.

Proptosis is considered to be present when one globe is displaced 2 mm farther forward than the other. This difference is usually accompanied by a widened palpebral fissure. However, a misleading appearance of proptosis may be present in patients with unilateral enophthalmos, lid retraction, or unilateral myopia.

Otolaryngologic Examination

Specific attention must be directed toward the nose, paranasal sinuses, nasopharynx, and neck. Inflammatory mucosal changes, purulent exudate, and polyps in the nose or nasopharynx all indicate possible sinusitis and mucopyocele. Palpation and direct pressure over the sinuses may indicate inflammation or an underlying neoplasm.

The ears should be checked for a serous effusion; it is well known that neoplasia and inflammation of the nasopharynx can impair function of the eustachian tube. The neck should be palpated carefully for the presence of enlarged lymph nodes that may harbor metastatic cells from a primary tumor in the region of the eye. An enlarged thyroid gland suggests hyperthyroidism and thus an endocrine basis for the exophthalmos.

An evaluation of cranial nerve function should be completed, particularly of the first and fifth cranial nerves. Lesions near the cribriform plate or sphenoid ridge may compromise olfaction. The first and second divisions of the fifth cranial nerve course behind, above, and below the orbital cavity, and adjacent lesions may cause deficient sensation over the forehead, cornea, or cheek.

Diagnostic Studies

Basic laboratory studies should include a complete blood cell count to ascertain possible evidence of inflammation or blood dyscrasia, as well as a chest radiograph to rule out granulomatous or metastatic disease. Other studies may include thyroid hormone assays to determine thyroid function, tests of the serum alkaline phosphatase level to determine possible bone disease, and bone marrow aspiration if blood dyscrasia is a possibility.

Computed Tomography and Magnetic Resonance Imaging

The advent of computed tomography (CT) and magnetic resonance imaging (MRI) has considerably improved the diagnosis of orbital lesions, and these are now the most important diagnostic radiologic tests employed.[12, 33, 67] The attainment of orbital detail in CT is aided by the relatively large differences in the x-ray absorption rates of fat, bone, and orbital soft tissue structures.[69] This modality

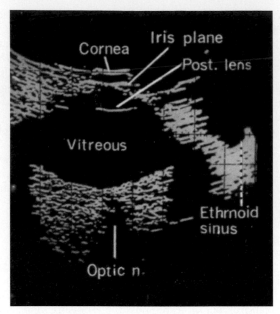

FIGURE 40–4. B scan obtained through the midportion of the orbit. The most echo-dense anatomy appears opaque.

provides cross-sectional imaging in the axial and coronal planes, and software allows reconstruction of accurate three-dimensional images. MRI provides the additional capability of direct sagittal imaging and is particularly well suited for imaging the intracanalicular and intracranial portions of the optic nerve. When undergoing CT or MRI, children usually require sedation or, less frequently, general anesthesia.[8]

The chief value of these types of scans is their reliability in localizing intraorbital lesions. Optic nerves and extraocular muscles can be visualized readily with CT or MRI, and any associated lesions can be outlined. CT provides the most useful information concerning bone anatomy, particularly in cases of orbital trauma and osseous dysplasia. Soft tissue resolution is often maximal on MRI. In regions of high fat content, such as the orbit, anatomic details are not optimally appreciated on conventional MR images. High-intensity lesions may be concealed by the high signal intensity of adjacent fat on short TR/ET (repetition time/echo time) spin echo images. In addition, fat may obscure anatomic details by means of chemical shift artifact. Techniques that combine contrast enhancement using the intravenous paramagnetic agent gadopentetate dimeglumine with various fat-suppression techniques allow more precise delineation of orbital abnormality.[63] This contrast-enhanced fat-suppression method is most advantageous in identifying the extent of disease, dural enhancement, and perineural tumor spread.[7] MRI findings also allow distinction of low-flow vascular lesions (hemangiomas and venous and lymphatic malformations) from high-flow lesions (arteriovenous malformations).[6] More precise characterization of vascular orbital lesions is possible using MR angiography.[2] Another advantage of CT and MRI is the concomitant assessment of other anatomic sites, such as the ethmoid and sphenoid sinuses, nasopharynx, cranial cavity, and skull walls, thereby pro-

viding information about the origin and extent of the disease (see Chap. 36).[21]

Ultrasonography

The orbital contents may also be scanned by the reflection of ultrasonic echoes.[27, 33] These tracings can be recorded on an oscilloscope as a linear display recording the amplitude and time relationship of the echo to the original pulse (A scan) or the storage of the echo pattern to produce a composite picture (B scan) (Fig. 40–4). The A-scan images provide the most precise information concerning the quantitative reflectivity of orbital lesions, which is the most important criterion in distinguishing various orbital lesions (Table 40–2). B-scan imaging provides two-dimensional acoustic sections of the orbit, which may be photographed. Information is obtained regarding the location, size, and margins of the lesion. Infiltrating lesions can often be distinguished from well-circumscribed lesions by this technique. Lesions that contain large blood vessels and fast-flowing blood can be characterized using color-flow Doppler techniques.[51] This painless and noninvasive imaging modality avoids radiation exposure and may be an ideal method for follow-up of lesions treated by observation, radiation, or chemotherapy.

Other Radiographic Studies

To provide a preliminary survey for more specific radiologic studies, routine films of the orbits and paranasal sinuses include posteroanterior, Waters, lateral, basal, and optic foramina views. While occasionally such films can be diagnostic, these examinations have largely been replaced by cross-sectional imaging modalities. Bone scintigraphy is sometimes helpful to demonstrate osseous involvement by infection, metastatic disease, or bone

TABLE 40–2. Sonographic Characteristics of Orbital Swellings

Extremely Low Reflectivity Lesions
  Cysts
  Mucocele
  Varix
Low Reflectivity Lesions
  Orbital cellulitis and abscess
  Optic nerve glioma
  Lymphoma
  Rhabdomyosarcoma
  Pseudotumor
  Neurilemoma
  Capillary hemangioma
  Juvenile angiofibroma
Medium Reflectivity Lesions
  Dermoid
  Meningioma
High Reflectivity Lesions
  Lymphatic malformation
  Cavernous hemangioma
  Lacrimal gland tumor
  Metastatic carcinoma
  Foreign body

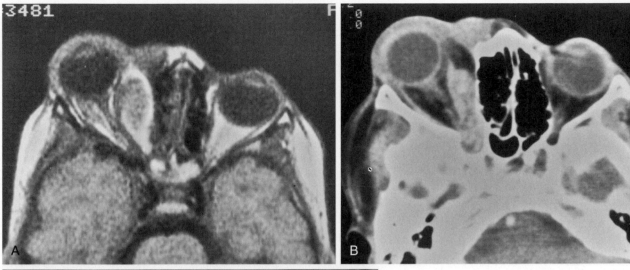

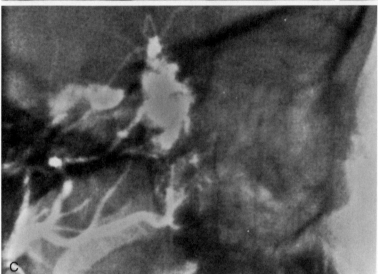

FIGURE 40–5. Right orbital arteriovenous malformation (AVM) in an 11-year-old girl demonstrated by noninvasive and invasive imaging techniques. *A*, Magnetic resonance imaging (MRI) shows a "salt-and-pepper" pattern produced by low-signal-intensity flow voids within a high-signal-intensity background. *B*, Axial computed tomography (CT) demonstrates strong intravenous contrast enhancement. *C*, AVM is demonstrated on an arteriogram of the internal maxillary artery.

infarction. Angiography is occasionally used for the characterization of suspected orbital vascular abnormalities or vascular neoplasms. Because these vascular characteristics can often be defined using noninvasive MRI, contrast-enhanced CT, or Doppler ultrasonography, angiography is often reserved for the management of cases that require a multidisciplinary approach that includes therapeutic embolization (Fig. 40–5).[25, 52]

Fine-Needle Aspiration Biopsy

The diagnosis of pediatric orbital tumors and pseudotumors is usually made after comprehensive clinical and radiographic examination using CT, MRI, or ultrasonography. When the diagnosis remains unclear after evaluation using noninvasive methods, fine-needle aspiration biopsy may be helpful in establishing a pretreatment diagnosis. In children, aspiration cytologic examination is obtained with the patient under general anesthesia using a 22- or 25-gauge needle. Imaging-guided techniques using CT, MRI, or ultrasonography are useful in some instances. The sensitivity of fine-needle aspiration biopsy was 91%,

with a specificity of 100% and overall accuracy of 95% in 81 procedures carried out in 77 pediatric patients with orbital abnormality.[49] Potential complications include tumor seeding in the needle tract and orbital hematoma.

Clinical Features of Orbital Swellings

The origin of proptosis in children can arbitrarily be categorized as being developmental, inflammatory-metabolic, vascular, or neoplastic. This chapter provides an overview of these diseases as they affect the orbit in the child. Many of these diseases are discussed in other chapters inasmuch as the orbit can be involved with disease in contiguous structures.

Congenital Anomalies

Various developmental anomalies of the bony orbit produce exophthalmos simply by insufficient orbital volume, which causes the soft tissue of the eye to protrude. These include several types of craniosynostosis. The most com-

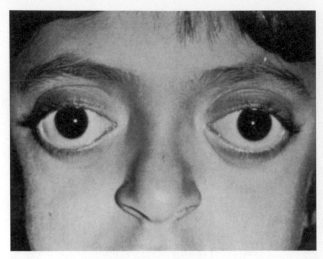

FIGURE 40-6. Child with Crouzon syndrome exhibiting bilateral proptosis resulting from hypoplasia of the maxillae.

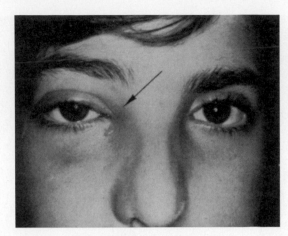

FIGURE 40-7. *Arrow* points to orbital cellulitis and proptosis caused by acute ethmoiditis.

mon syndromes of craniosynostosis that produce proptosis are Crouzon syndrome (craniofacial dysostosis) (Fig. 40-6) and Apert syndrome (acrocephalosyndactyly). Proptosis occurs because of foreshortening of the orbital floors and hypoplasia of the maxillae, which results in relative orbital shallowness. Less common craniosynostosis syndromes that can be associated with proptosis include Pfeiffer disease, Lowry syndrome, Hermann-Opitz syndrome, Sakati-Nyhan-Tisdale syndrome, and the kleeblattschädel anomaly. Severe cases result in complications related to exposure of the cornea and conjunctiva and may require early surgical intervention.[23]

Developmental defects in the orbital roof may allow a herniation of intracranial contents into the orbit. These are termed a meningocele, encephalocele, or hydroencephalocele, depending on what tissues are encompassed in the herniated sac.[37] These soft, compressible masses may transilluminate or pulsate. They also may expand with compression of the jugular veins (Furstenberg test). CT and MRI usually play an important role in establishing the intracranial continuity of orbital encephaloceles.[34]

Dermoid cysts, epidermoid cysts, and teratomas may occur in the orbit. Dermoids, the most common cystic lesion of the orbit,[28] are composed of elements from all three germinal layers and may contain adnexal structures, such as hair follicles, sweat glands, or sebaceous glands. Orbital dermoids constitute 5% of all orbital masses and appear most frequently in the upper outer quadrant of the orbit. Superficial lesions typically present during infancy as an asymptomatic mass lesion, while deep lesions can present with proptosis or globe displacement later in life, from early childhood to the fourth decade. Deep lesions can present with sudden proptosis after spontaneous rupture of a dermoid cyst.[56] Epidermoids consist entirely of ectodermal tissue and are lined by keratinizing epithelium without adnexal components. Orbital teratomas, consisting of all three germ layers, are rare. There is a female-to-male ratio of 2:1, and they typically present at birth as a variegated orbital mass that produces extreme proptosis. The incidence of malignancy within teratomas ranges from 11% to 22% when all sites are considered.

However, the majority of malignant teratomas are gonadal, while malignant behavior within the orbit is rare.[38, 66]

Inflammatory and Metabolic Diseases

Acute inflammatory disease of the orbit in children is likely to result from infection in the paranasal sinuses. Orbital infection is the most common complication of sinusitis.[30] Approximately two thirds of acute orbital infections occur secondary to sinusitis, and 85% of such infections occur in the pediatric population.[44] In children younger than age 10 years, the most common source is acute ethmoiditis (Fig. 40-7). In adolescents, the frontal sinus may be the original site of the infection because, at that stage, the sinus has reached nearly full development. Maxillary sinusitis less commonly produces orbital cellulitis. A more insidious inflammatory swelling may develop with mucocele erosion from any of the adjacent sinuses. On occasion, orbital inflammation arises from infections of the face or nose that extend to the orbit by retrograde thrombophlebitis.

Chandler[13] divided the progression of sinonasal orbital infections into five stages (Table 40-3). The first stage is periorbital inflammatory edema, which is confined anterior to the orbital septum and presents with cellulitis of the eyelids without visual loss or ophthalmoplegia. Extension through the orbital septum (the second stage) is classified as orbital cellulitis, which presents with pain, proptosis, and chemosis. With orbital cellulitis, there may be some degree of ophthalmoplegia related to edema of the extraocular muscles, and there may be a mild decrease in visual acuity related to corneal edema. The

TABLE 40-3. Stages of Orbital Infections

Stage	Characteristics
I	Preseptal inflammatory edema
II	Orbital cellulitis
III	Subperiosteal abscess
IV	Orbital abscess
V	Cavernous sinus thrombosis

third stage of orbital infection involves formation of a subperiosteal abscess between the orbital periosteum and bony wall of the orbit. In addition to those symptoms seen with orbital cellulitis, the globe is displaced in an inferolateral direction by a subperiosteal abscess. The fourth stage of orbital infection is the formation of an orbital abscess within the intraconal soft tissue of the orbit. Severe proptosis, chemosis, ophthalmoplegia, and visual loss are usually present. Retrograde thrombophlebitis of the valveless ophthalmic veins can lead to cavernous sinus thrombosis (the fifth stage), which produces unilateral severe orbital pain, ptosis, proptosis, chemosis, and ophthalmoplegia that rapidly become bilateral.[58] The advent of modern radiographic diagnostic modalities and advances in medical therapies and surgical and anesthetic techniques has greatly facilitated the management of orbital complications of sinusitis.[3, 17, 24, 54] However, even in the post-antibiotic era, the mortality rate of cavernous sinus thrombosis is 30%.[42]

Lacrimal sac infections can occur in children if the nasolacrimal duct is obstructed, causing an inflammatory swelling in the medial quadrant of the orbit. Nasolacrimal duct obstruction may lead to recurrent dacryocystitis, requiring antibiotic therapy and nasolacrimal duct probe and irrigation.[11] Dacryocystoceles, secondary to both proximal and distal nasolacrimal duct obstruction, present as a medial canthal mass. Chronic nasolacrimal duct obstruction with a dacryocystocele may require definitive surgical intervention, such as external or endoscopic dacryocystorhinostomy.[16, 35, 62] Lacrimal gland involvement may accompany mumps in children, and the inflammatory swelling is usually confined to the upper temporal portion of the orbit.

Several specific organisms may be responsible for chronic infection of the orbit. For example, tuberculosis may involve the orbital bone in the form of periostitis; mycotic infection, such as mucormycosis and aspergillosis, may affect the orbit in the juvenile diabetic patient as well as in those undergoing intensive chemotherapy for blood dyscrasias.

Orbital pseudotumor is an idiopathic, noninfectious, nonneoplastic cause of inflammation of the pediatric orbit.[48, 61] Clinical features include the abrupt onset of orbital pain, associated with proptosis, lid swelling and erythema, chemosis, ophthalmoplegia, and visual decrease. Half the patients may be affected bilaterally, and systemic constitutional complaints are common. Radiographic studies, including CT and MRI,[65] and laboratory investigations help to distinguish pseudotumor from other infectious, metabolic, and neoplastic processes. While tissue biopsy is seldom required to confirm the diagnosis, histopathologic examination demonstrates lymphocytic inflammation, frequently associated with fibrosis and eosinophilia. A clinical trial of steroids produces striking resolution of symptoms within 48 hours.

In the pediatric population, Graves ophthalmopathy is rarely seen. When affecting children, symptoms of Graves disease are similar to those seen in adults, although there is less tendency for children to have severe exophthalmos.[31] In general, the degree of proptosis, which results from accumulation of glycosaminoglycans within the perimysial and retro-ocular connective tissues, does not corre-

late strongly with the degree of hyperthyroidism. Acute optic nerve compression is treated effectively with systemic corticosteroids or radiation therapy, while those cases associated with severe proptosis are best managed by orbital decompressive surgery.[5, 42]

Vascular Abnormalities

Cavernous hemangiomas and capillary hemangiomas are the most commonly seen vascular lesions of the orbit (Fig. 40–8).[29, 55] Cavernous hemangiomas occur most frequently as well-encapsulated, intraconal, retro-ocular masses. Although frequently congenital, this tumor may not grow noticeably until well after birth. Patients typically are seen in the second to fourth decades of life with slowly progressive proptosis, extraocular motility difficulties, and impaired visual acuity.[12, 20]

In contrast, capillary hemangiomas are invasive, unencapsulated lesions that typically develop within the first few weeks of life. Superficial lesions present with skin discoloration, while deeper lesions can present with rapidly progressive proptosis, simulating intraorbital malignancies. Associated hemangiomas of the face, neck, and larynx may occur (Fig. 40–9). Capillary hemangiomas usually grow until 2 or 3 years of age, after which they spontaneously involute. While most capillary hemangiomas may be treated expectantly, rare lesions may require treatment with steroids, surgery, or laser photocoagulation for amblyopia, coagulopathy secondary to platelet trapping, or local skin breakdown with infection and necrosis.[9, 14, 59]

Lymphatic malformations are rare tumors of the orbit, constituting between 3% and 8% of orbital tumors. Lymphatic malformations confined to the conjunctiva are more common than those involving the lids or orbit. While lesions with a superficial component typically present during infancy or early childhood, deep lesions may present later in life, after sudden enlargement secondary to spontaneous hemorrhage or infection. Radiographically, lymphatic malformations appear as poorly defined, multilobulated, heterogeneous lesions that fre-

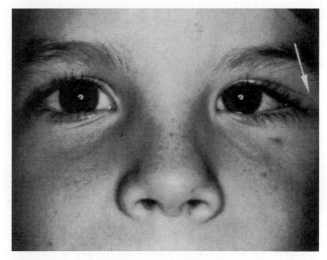

FIGURE 40–8. Child with a cavernous hemangioma occupying the lateral aspect of the left orbit (*arrow*).

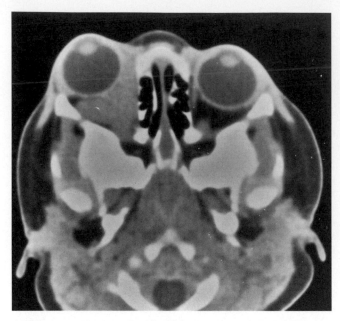

FIGURE 40–9. Six-month-old child presenting with right proptosis and a visible hemangioma on the forehead. CT shows a poorly marginated, infiltrating right orbital mass, consistent with capillary hemangioma.

quently cross anatomic boundaries (Fig. 40–10).[27, 32] Other orbital vascular lesions include orbital varices, which are observed more frequently in older children. Aneurysms of the ophthalmic artery and carotid cavernous sinus fistulas that produce pulsatile proptosis, arteriovenous malformations, angiosarcomas, and hemangiopericytomas are rare in children.[29]

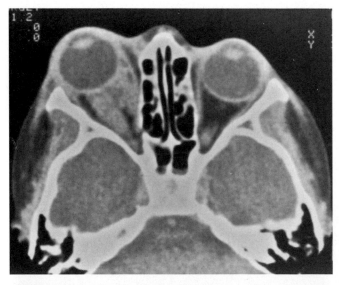

FIGURE 40–10. Axial CT demonstrates a right retro-ocular lymphangioma causing proptosis in an 11-year-old child. Radiographically, the lesion has ill-defined borders and is difficult to distinguish from the optic nerve and extraocular muscles.

Neoplasms

Orbital neoplasms may be primary within the orbit, caused by direct extension from neighboring structures, or metastatic from a distant primary malignancy.[4] The most common primary orbital neoplasms in children are rhabdomyosarcoma, optic nerve glioma, and retinoblastoma. Other primary tumors include histiocytic tumors, fibro-osseous tumors, plexiform neurofibromas, melanoma, meningioma, and lacrimal gland tumors. Metastatic lesions include neuroblastoma, leukemia, Ewing sarcoma, medulloblastoma, and Wilms tumor.

Rhabdomyosarcoma is the most common childhood primary orbital malignancy. It presents with rapidly progressing unilateral proptosis during the first decade of life, with an average age of presentation of 7 years (Fig. 40–11). Other symptoms may include ptosis, eyelid or conjunctival edema, ophthalmoplegia, nasal obstruction, or epistaxis. The most common sites of presentation are the superonasal quadrant of the orbit and a central location behind the globe.[64] After histologic diagnosis has been established, treatment consists of high-dose radiation therapy and systemic chemotherapy. Orbit exenteration is reserved for recurrent or persistent disease.[41] While the globe is spared in more than 90% of cases, visual impairment related to radiation-induced cataract formation is common. The prognosis for localized orbital rhabdomyosarcoma is favorable compared with other head and neck sites, with a 93% 3-year actuarial survival rate reported by the Intergroup Rhabdomyosarcoma Study Committee.[68]

Optic nerve glioma is the most common primary neoplasm of the optic nerve. Ninety percent of cases present within the first 2 decades of life, with a median age of 7 years at presentation. Approximately 30% of children with glioma prove to have von Recklinghausen disease. Presenting signs depend principally on tumor location. One fourth of optic gliomas are confined to the optic nerve and present as an orbital mass, with slowly progressive proptosis and visual loss. The remaining three fourths

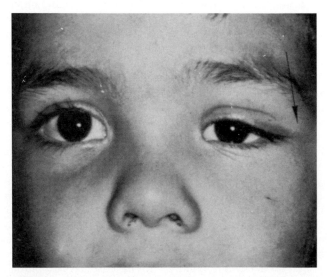

FIGURE 40–11. Child with a rhabdomyosarcoma involving the left lateral orbital space and temporal fossa (arrow).

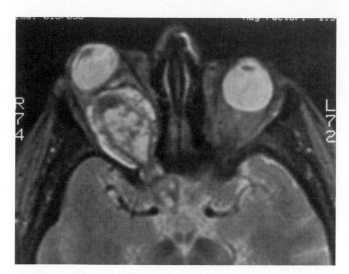

FIGURE 40-12. Axial MRI demonstrates a right optic nerve glioma extending posteriorly to the optic chiasm.

present with optic chiasm involvement, with visual impairment as the primary symptom. CT and MRI demonstrate fusiform enlargement of the optic nerve (Fig. 40-12).[19] These low-grade astrocytomas have unpredictable clinical behavior, with growth rates that vary from slow to rapid.[1] As the clinical course is indolent in many cases, management of unilateral optic nerve gliomas consists of close clinical and radiographic observation, with surgical resection reserved for cases with severe proptosis, blindness, or radiographic evidence of extension toward the optic chiasm. Surgery is of little benefit for tumors involving the optic chiasm or optic tracts, while the roles of radiation therapy and chemotherapy remain undefined.[18] Invasion of the hypothalamus or third ventricle portends poor long-term prognosis, with an ultimate mortality rate of 50%.

Retinoblastoma, which is the most common intraocular malignancy of childhood, may present with leukokoria or proptosis.[22] Ninety percent of cases are diagnosed before the age of 5 years, and 30% have bilateral involvement. Virtually all bilateral cases and 15% of unilateral cases express an inherited form of disease, with a characteristic deletion seen in the q14 band of chromosome 13. Intraocular calcifications in a child seen on CT scan are almost pathognomonic of retinoblastoma[40] (Fig. 40-13). Treatment options, which include enucleation, external beam radiation, cryotherapy, photocoagulation, radioactive implants, and chemotherapy, are determined by the extent of disease. Patients with the inherited form of retinoblastoma are at significantly increased risk to develop secondary malignancies, with osteogenic sarcoma being the most common second tumor. Genetic counseling is indicated for all affected families.[26]

Langerhans cell histiocytosis and histiocytosis X are terms used to describe the three prototypic syndromes of eosinophilic granuloma, Hand-Schüller-Christian disease, and Letterer-Siwe disease. The overall incidence of orbital involvement in these syndromes is approximately 20%. Orbital involvement is usually seen in the chronic form of disease and typically presents with proptosis associated with a lytic lesion of the orbital wall. Rarely, patients with the acute, disseminated form of disease have infiltration of intraocular structures, especially the uveal tract. Treatment is determined by the extent of disease. In patients with isolated eosinophilic granuloma of the orbit, biopsy and curettage may be curative. However, more extensive lesions with marked proptosis or optic nerve compression may require a course of systemic steroids or low-dose radiation therapy. Systemic chemotherapy is generally used to treat patients with disseminated Langerhans cell histiocytosis.[46]

Two additional histiocytic lesions that may involve the pediatric orbit are sinus histiocytosis with massive lymphadenopathy and juvenile xanthogranuloma.[57] The former syndrome is an idiopathic condition in which lymph nodes and sometimes extranodal soft tissues are infiltrated by histiocytes that contain phagocytosed lymphocytes and erythrocytes. The average age of onset is 8 years, and orbital involvement occurs in 10% of cases. Affected patients have cervical lymphadenopathy and bilateral proptosis that may be associated with a palpable mass in the superior portion of the orbits. Juvenile xanthogranuloma usually presents with multiple cutaneous papules in infants but occasionally may produce an orbital mass. These patients have unilateral or bilateral proptosis during the first few weeks of life, and children with orbital involvement usually do not have the typical skin lesions. Diagnosis is often established by biopsy demonstrating the characteristic Touton giant cells, which peripherally have a vacuolated cytoplasm and contain several nuclei arranged in a circular pattern around a central area of eosinophilia. The optimal management for sinus histiocytosis with massive lymphadenopathy and juvenile xanthogranuloma has

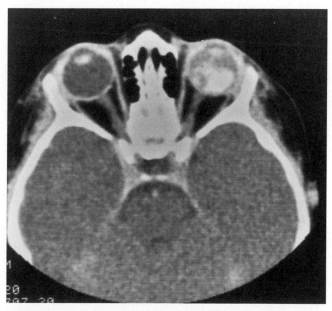

FIGURE 40-13. Axial CT shows a calcified left orbital retinoblastoma in a 4-year-old child. Intraocular calcifications are almost pathognomonic of retinoblastoma in this age group.

not been established, but both may respond to steroid therapy.

Fibrous dysplasia may involve the orbital bone and may decrease orbital volume, thus producing exophthalmos. Proptosis develops in 35% of patients with craniofacial fibrous dysplasia, and visual loss secondary to globe displacement or optic nerve compression is the most common neurologic complication of this disease. Symptoms most often develop during the first 2 decades of life, and the disease may become quiescent after puberty in 60% to 80% of cases. Diminishing visual acuity is an indication for surgical intervention in children with orbital fibrous dysplasia. Some authors advocate aggressive excision with immediate craniofacial reconstruction,[45] while others recommend conservative bone remodeling by curettage.[50] Other fibro-osseous tumors that can involve the pediatric orbit include ossifying fibromas, osteomas, and giant cell lesions.[59]

Secondary invasion of tumors from the paranasal sinuses and nasopharynx is much less frequent in children than in adults. Extension of nasopharyngeal angiofibroma to the orbit is well known in boys. Exophthalmos is the most common sign of orbital involvement, being present in 14% of patients with nasopharyngeal angiofibroma.[60] Sarcomas of the sinuses and adjacent structures involving the orbit are more common than squamous cell carcinomas in children.

The most common metastatic tumor found in the eye is neuroblastoma from the adrenal gland, which usually occurs in children younger than 5 years of age.[37] Orbital metastases from neuroblastoma occur in 30% to 50% of cases, typically being diagnosed 3 months after the primary tumor, and metastases are commonly bilateral.[53] Hematopoietic malignancies that may involve the orbit are leukemia and lymphoma. Leukemia, which is the most common pediatric malignancy, demonstrates ocular findings in 90% of cases. Orbital infiltration by leukemia, which may produce proptosis in severe cases, occurs in approximately 10% of cases. The orbital mass found in myeloid leukemia is termed *chloroma* or *granulocytic sarcoma*, while the analogous orbital tumor seen in lymphoid leukemia is called *lymphosarcoma* or *lymphoblastoma*. Orbital infiltration by acute myelocytic leukemia or acute lymphocytic leukemia carries a poor prognosis.[36]

Surgical exploration of the orbit may be required to provide precise histologic identification of a neoplasm, when the diagnosis remains unclear after clinical, radiographic, and fine-needle aspiration evaluation. The surgical approach is mainly related to the location of the tumor.[43]

SELECTED REFERENCES

Calcaterra TC, Trapp TK. Unilateral proptosis. Otolaryngol Clin North Am 21:53, 1988.
   This article emphasizes those diseases that are otolaryngologic in origin but may present initially as unilateral exophthalmos. The steps in the diagnostic work-up are summarized.
Crawford JS. Diseases of the orbit. In Crawford JS, Morin JD, eds. The Eye in Childhood. New York, Grune & Stratton, 1983.
   This chapter provides a comprehensive review of diseases that may cause proptosis in children. The Hospital for Sick Children experience with 585 cases serves as the source for the review.
Castillo M, Mukherji SK, Wagle NS. Imaging of the pediatric orbit. Neuroimaging Clin N Am 10(1):95, 2000.
   This article reviews multiple ocular abnormalities in children, emphasizing the crucial role of imaging techniques in evaluation and management of the pediatric orbit. It combines excellent clinical descriptions with CT and MRI images.

REFERENCES

1. Alvord EC, Lofton S. Gliomas of the optic nerve or chiasm: outcome by patient's age, tumor site, and treatment. J Neurosurg 68: 85, 1988.
2. Applegate GR, Talagala SL, Applegate LJ. MR angiography of the head and neck: value of two-dimensional phase-contrast projection technique. AJR Am J Roentgenol 159:369, 1992.
3. Arjmand EM, Lusk RP, Muntz HR. Pediatric sinusitis and subperiosteal orbital abscess formation: diagnosis and treatment. Otolaryngol Head Neck Surg 109:886, 1993.
4. Augsburger JJ. Ocular tumors in children. Pediatr Clin North Am 30:1071, 1983.
5. Bahn RS, Bartley GB, Gorman CA. Emergency treatment of Graves' ophthalmopathy. Baillieres Clin Endocrinol Metab 6:95, 1992.
6. Baker LL, Dillon WP, Hieshima GB, et al. Hemangiomas and vascular malformations of the head and neck: MR characterization. AJNR Am J Neuroradiol 14:307, 1993.
7. Barakos JA, Dillon WP, Chew WM. Orbit, skull base, and pharynx: contrast-enhanced fat suppression MR imaging. Radiology 179:191, 1991.
8. Bozzao L, Fantossi LM, Rosa M. Childhood orbital pathology: investigation by computed tomography. J Neurosurg Sci 26:25, 1982.
9. Burstein FD, Simms C, Cohen SR, et al. Intralesional laser therapy of extensive hemangiomas in 100 consecutive patients. Ann Plast Surg 44(2):188, 2000.
10. Calcaterra TC, Trapp TK. Unilateral proptosis. Otolaryngol Clin North Am 21:53, 1988.
11. Campolattaro BN, Lueder GT, Tychsen L. Spectrum of pediatric dacryocystitis: medical and surgical management of 54 cases. J Pediatr Ophthalmol Strabismus 34(3):143, 1997.
12. Castillo M, Mukherji SK, Wagle NS. Imaging of the pediatric orbit. Neuroimaging Clin N Am 10(1):95, 2000.
13. Chandler JR, Langenbrunner DJ, Steven ER. The pathogenesis of orbital complications in acute sinusitis. Laryngoscope 80:1414, 1970.
14. Clymer MA, Fortune DS, Reinisch L, et al. Interstitial Nd:YAG photocoagulation for vascular malformations and hemangiomas in childhood. Arch Otolaryngol Head Neck Surg 124(4):431, 1998.
15. Crawford JS. Diseases of the orbit. In Crawford JS, Morin JD, eds. The Eye in Childhood. New York, Grune & Stratton, 1983.
16. Cunningham MJ, Woog JJ. Endonasal endoscopic dacryocystorhinostomy in children. Arch Otolaryngol Head Neck Surg 124:328, 1998.
17. Dudin A, Othman A. Acute periorbital swelling: evaluation and management protocol. Pediatr Emerg Care 12(1):16, 1996.
18. Dunn DW, Purvin V. Optic pathway gliomas in neurofibromatosis. Dev Med Child Neurol 32:820, 1990.
19. Dutton JJ. Optic nerve gliomas and meningiomas. Neurol Clin 9: 163, 1991.
20. Dyer J, Atkinson L. Cavernous haemangioma of the orbit. Aust N Z J Surg 55:269, 1985.
21. Forbes GS, Earnest F, Waller RR. Computed tomography of orbital tumors, including late generation scanning techniques. Radiology 142:387, 1982.
22. Foster BS, Mukai S. Intraocular retinoblastoma presenting as ocular and orbital inflammation. Int Ophthalmol Clin 36(1):153, 1996.
23. Fries PD, Katowitz JA. Congenital craniofacial anomalies of ophthalmic importance. Surv Ophthalmol 35:87, 1990.
24. Froehlich P, Pransky SM, Fontaine P, et al. Minimal endoscopic approach to subperiosteal orbital abscesses. Arch Otolaryngol Head Neck Surg 123(3):280, 1997.
25. Goldberg RA, Garcia GH, Duckwiler GR. Combined embolization

and surgical treatment of arteriovenous malformation of the orbit. Am J Ophthalmol 116:17, 1993.

26. Grabowski EF, Abramson DH. Intraocular and extraocular retinoblastoma. Hematol Oncol Clin North Am 1:721, 1987.
27. Graeb DA, Rootman J, Robertson WD, et al. Orbital lymphangiomas: clinical, radiologic, and pathologic characteristics. Radiology 175:417, 1990.
28. Gunlap I, Gunduz K. Cystic lesions of the orbit. Int Ophthalmol Clin 20(5):273, 1996.
29. Gunlap I, Gunduz K. Vascular tumors of the orbit. Doc Ophthalmol 89(4):337, 1995.
30. Gurucharri MJ, Lazar RH, Younis RT. Current management and treatment of complications of sinusitis in children. Ear Nose Throat J 70:107, 1991.
31. Hayles AB, Kennedy RLJ, Beahrs OH, Woolner LB. Exophthalmic goiter in children. J Clin Endocrinol Metab 19:138, 1959.
32. Hemmer KM, Marsh JL, Milder B. Orbital lymphangioma. Plast Reconstr Surg 82:340, 1988.
33. Hopper KD, Sherman JL, Boal DK, Eggli KD. CT and MR imaging of the pediatric orbit. Radiographics 12:485, 1992.
34. Hughes GB, Sharpino G, Hunt W, Tucker HM. Management of the congenital midline nasal mass: a review. Head Neck Surg 2:222, 1980.
35. Hulka GF, Kulwin DR, Weeks SM, Cotton RT. Congenital lacrimal sac mucoceles with intranasal extension. Otolaryngol Head Neck Surg 113(5):651, 1995.
36. Kincaid MC, Green R. Ocular and orbital involvement in leukemia. Surv Ophthalmol 27:211, 1983.
37. Kroll AJ, Casten VG. Diseases of the orbit. In Liebman G, Gillis P, eds. The Pediatrician's Ophthalmology. St Louis, CV Mosby, 1966.
38. Levin ML, Leone CR, Kincaid MC. Congenital orbital teratomas. Am J Ophthalmol 102:476, 1986.
39. Levine RA. Orbital ultrasonography. Radiol Clin North Am 25:447, 1987.
40. Mafee MF, Goldberg MF, Greenwald MJ, et al. Retinoblastoma and simulating lesions: role of CT and MR imaging. Radiol Clin North Am 25:667, 1987.
41. Mannor GE, Rose GE, Plowman PN, et al. Multidisciplinary management of refractory orbital rhabdomyosarcoma. Ophthalmol 104(7):1198, 1997.
42. Metson R, Dallow RL, Shore JW. Endoscopic orbital decompression. Laryngoscope 104(8):950, 1994.
43. Migliavacca F, Furnari M, Moise A, Della Grottague B. The surgical approach to intraorbital tumors in children. J Neurosurg Sci 26:29, 1982.
44. Moloney JR, Badham NJ, McRae A. The acute orbit: preseptal (periorbital) cellulitis, subperiosteal abscess, and orbital cellulitis due to sinusitis. J Laryngol Otol 12(Suppl):1, 1987.
45. Moore AT, Bunck JR, Munro IR. Fibrous dysplasia of the orbit in childhood. Clinical features and management. Ophthalmology 92:12, 1985.
46. Moore AT, Pritchard J, Taylor DSI. Histiocytosis X: an ophthalmological review. Br J Ophthalmol 69:7, 1985.
47. Motolese E, Esposti P, Bardelli AM, Frezzotti R. Echographic study

of exophthalmos and neoformative endocular pathology in childhood, V. Neurosurg Sci 26:17, 1982.
48. Mottow-Lippa L, Jakobiec FA, Smith M. Idiopathic inflammatory orbital pseudotumor in childhood II: results of diagnostic tests and biopsies. Ophthalmology 88:565, 1981.
49. O'Hara BJ, Ehya H, Shields JA, et al. Fine needle aspiration biopsy in pediatric ophthalmic tumors and pseudotumors. Acta Cytol (Baltimore) 37:125, 1993.
50. Osguthorpe JD, Gudeman SK. Orbital complications of fibrous dysplasia. Otolaryngol Head Neck Surg 97:403, 1987.
51. Ramji FG, Slovis TL, Baker JD. Orbital sonography in children. Pediatr Radiol 26(4):245, 1996.
52. Rootman J, Kao SCS, Graeb DA. Multidisciplinary approaches to complicated vascular lesions of the orbit. Ophthalmology 99:1440, 1992.
53. Rowe S, Siegel S, Benedict W. Ophthalmologic manifestations of genitourinary diseases. Urology 39:523, 1992.
54. Sajjadian A, Chundru U, Isaacson G. Prospective application of a protocol for selective nonsurgical management of suspected orbital subperiosteal abscesses in children. Ann Otol Rhinol Laryngol 108:459, 1999.
55. Savoiardo M, Strada L, Passerini A. Cavernous hemangiomas of the orbit: value of CT, angiography, and phlebography. AJNR Am J Neuroradiol 4:741, 1983.
56. Sherman RP, Rootman J, Lapointe JS. Orbital dermoids: clinical presentation and management. Br J Ophthalmol 68:642, 1984.
57. Shields JA, Shields CL. Clinical spectrum of histiocytic tumors of the orbit. Trans Pa Acad Ophthalmol Otolaryngol 42:931, 1990.
58. Southwick FS, Richardson EP, Swartz MN. Septic thrombosis of the dural venous sinuses. Medicine 65:82, 1986.
59. Stefanyszyn MA, Handler SD, Wright JE. Pediatric orbital tumors. Otolaryngol Clin North Am 21:103, 1988.
60. Stern RM, Beauchamp GR, Berlin AJ. Ocular findings in juvenile nasopharyngeal angiofibroma. Ophthalmic Surg 17:560, 1986.
61. Stevens JL, Rychwalski PJ, Baker RS, Kielar RS. Pseudotumor of the orbit in early childhood. Am Assoc Pediatr Ophthalmol Strabis 2(2):120, 1998.
62. Szubin L, Papageorge A, Sacks E. Endonasal laser-assisted dacryocystorhinostomy. Am J Rhinol 13(5):371, 1999.
63. Tien RD, Chu PK, Hesselink JR, Szumowski J. Intra- and paraorbital lesions: value of fat-suppression MR imaging with paramagnetic contrast enhancement. AJNR Am J Neuroradiol 12:245, 1991.
64. Vade A, Armstrong MB. Orbital rhabdomyosarcoma in childhood. Radiol Clin North Am 25:701, 1987.
65. Weber AL, Jakobiec FA, Sabates NR. Pseudotumor of the orbit. Neuroimaging Clin N Am 6(1):73, 1996.
66. Weiss AH, Greenwald MJ, Margo CE, Myers W. Primary and secondary orbital teratomas. J Pediatr Ophthalmol Strabismus 26:44, 1989.
67. Wells RG, Sty JR, Gonnering RS. Imaging of the pediatric eye and orbit. Radiographics 9:1023, 1989.
68. Wharam M, Beltangady M, Hays D, et al. Localized orbital rhabdomyosarcoma: an interim report of the Intergroup Rhabdomyosarcoma Study Committee. Ophthalmology 94:251, 1987.
69. Wright JE, Lloyd GA, Ambrose J. Computerized axial tomography in the detection of orbital space-occupying lesions. Am J Ophthalmol 80:78, 1975.

41

Pediatric Plastic Surgery of the Head and Neck

Dennis J. Hurwitz, M.D. and Sandeep Kathju, M.D., Ph.D.

Pediatric plastic and reconstructive surgery of the head and neck encompasses a variety of procedures performed by different specialists. In our practice, congenital deformities dominate, requiring an understanding of clinical genetics, embryology, and growth and development. The surgeon must enjoy managing children along with their parents, often over the children's entire growing years. For more complex problems, a working relationship with a team of specialists is required. Although the techniques in themselves are challenging and interesting and are the focus of this chapter, the fullest enjoyment is in the cooperative and successful interaction of patient, family, and professionals.

As an extension of this philosophy, a basic knowledge of pediatric plastic and reconstructive surgery enhances communication and cooperation among specialists and promotes a better understanding of the challenges that both pediatric plastic surgeons and pediatric otolaryngologists face in their practices. Because a large variety of problems are encountered in pediatric plastic and reconstructive surgery, only those with which we are most experienced are addressed in this chapter.

Cleft Lip and Palate

Frequency of Clefts

Of the craniofacial deformities of the head and neck, cleft lip and palate is the most common. The frequency of clefting varies among races and nations. According to the statistics based on birth records, the highest occurrence was recorded in North American Indians and in the Japanese population (1 in 350). The lowest occurrence (1 in 1500) was noted in Africans and African-Americans. There is a relatively high frequency of clefting in the populations of Scandinavia and the middle European countries. For example, in Denmark and Finland, the rate is 1 in 550; in Poland, 1 in 575; and in the former republic of Czechoslovakia, 1 in 665. In Pennsylvania, the frequency of clefts is approximately 1 in 800 (Dr. Mary Marazita, personal communication, 1999). Only a few countries have a reliable registry of birth defects, so these statistics should be revealed with caution.

According to many studies of cleft lip and palate, males are more often affected than are females. The different types of common facial clefts vary in frequency. Oldfield and Tate[103] reported the following rates of occurrence for the different cleft types: cleft lip only, 22.9%; cleft palate only, 34.6%; and cleft lip, alveolus, and palate, 42.5%. Bardach[12] reported slightly different rates: cleft lip only, 19.8%; cleft palate only, 30.6%; and cleft lip, alveolus, and palate, 49.5%. In Bardach's study, it was also found that most unilateral clefts occur on the left side (1:2.3). Furthermore, there are more unilateral clefts than bilateral clefts (1:2.9).

Types of Clefts

There are a large variety of cleft forms and associated maxillofacial and nasal deformities (Fig. 41–1). Many systems have been introduced to categorize the various cleft types. Some classifications are based on embryologic development, whereas others focus on morphologic changes. In order to comprehensively examine outcomes of team cleft care, the Craniofacial Outcomes Registry committee (COR) of the American Cleft Palate Association (ACPA) has simplified the LAHSHAL anatomic classification system for its 20 or so reporting pilot teams. The surgeon must fill out a two-page form that identifies the anatomic site and extent of clefting, as well as accompanying anomalies and syndromes. LAHSHAL is an acronym for Lip, Alveolus, Hard palate, Soft palate, Hard palate, Alveolus, and Lip extending from left to right. Within the box below the letter, the surgeon writes a "C" for complete, "I" for incomplete, or "X" for not present. An asterisk by the "C" indicates a microform or submucous cleft. Hence, a left incomplete cleft lip with complete cleft of the palate is indicated by: L-I, A-C, H-C, S-C, H-X, A-X, and L-X.

Each cleft is analyzed for the magnitude of deformity and congenital hypoplasia. The most severe deformities are found in complete unilateral or bilateral clefts. These cleft types disrupt the skeletal and soft tissue continuity in the midfacial region. Congenital dysmorphogenesis and hypoplasia of the soft tissue and bony structures create an anatomic disarray and functional imbalance, which distorts facial growth. The palatal cleft also affects dentition, occlusion, speech production, and eustachian tube function. The wide communication between the oral and the nasal cavities contributes to acute and chronic upper res-

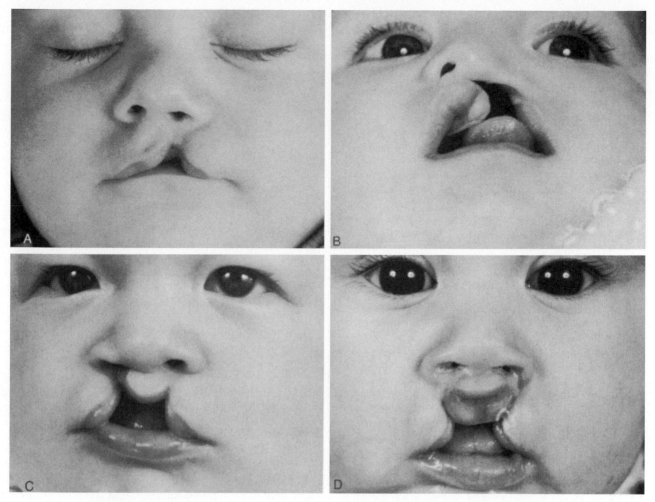

FIGURE 41–1. *A,* Unilateral incomplete cleft. *B,* Unilateral complete cleft lip, alveolus, and palate. Note severe nasal deformity. *C,* Bilateral cleft of the lip, alveolus, and palate, complete on the right side and incomplete on the left side. *D,* Bilateral cleft lip, alveolus, and palate with protruding premaxilla.

piratory tract infections. The complete bilateral cleft with a protruding premaxilla and small prolabium presents the most difficult treatment problem because of the severity of the initial deformity and the resulting morphologic and functional changes.

Cleft severity affects treatment planning and anticipating outcomes.[13] The cleft side has decreased bone, nasal cartilage and lip musculature with shortening of the lip along the edges of the cleft. Complicating the situation is malposition of the maxillary segments, which may result in outward rotation of the premaxilla and collapsed or excessive distance of the lesser element to the greater. The greater the maxillary segment malposition, the worse the nasal deformity.

Despite the recognition of the profound influence of the presenting disorder on surgical technique and outcome, there is no accepted method of rating cleft severity. Dental models and facial moulages have been obtained and analyzed by two- and three-dimensional techniques. Computer-assisted analysis of frontal and submental photographic views is a promising practical means of evaluating treatment of unilateral clefts.[64]

Multidisciplinary Management

Many specialists are needed for coordinated, successful management of cleft lip and palate because it is a multifaceted problem. The goal of multidisciplinary management for cleft lip and palate is to ensure an aesthetic result, satisfactory facial growth, and adequate speech and hearing before the child reaches school age. Orthodontic treatment, bone grafting, and correction of secondary nasal deformities, including septoplasty, and correction of nasal valve collapse continue throughout the school years. Significant jaw size discrepancy remains a common problem, requiring orthognathic intervention toward the completion of facial growth.

Team Approach

Treatment of cleft lip and palate requires a multidisciplinary approach owing to the variety and interdependence of impairments caused by this craniofacial deformity. Though difficult to prove, it is intuitive that an experienced team of dedicated specialists should manage care.

In the opinion of the authors, independent surgical treatment augmented with ad hoc specialists without protocols or peer review is an inferior arrangement that leads to confused parents and unnecessary deformity and dysfunction.

The cornerstones of the multidisciplinary team are the plastic surgeon, the speech pathologist, and the orthodontist. Typically, the director is the speech pathologist or dentist who completely devotes himself or herself to the field and who has gained the interpersonal skills and respect to deal effectively and fairly with a myriad of issues.

Traditionally, surgeons trained in plastic surgery and committed to the care of children direct the medical care and perform the primary operations on the cleft deformity. Secondary lip, nasal, and palatal corrections are also done by the plastic surgeon. Advanced maxillofacial and craniofacial training qualifies them for those types of procedures. Pediatric otolaryngologists treat all ear diseases and nasal airway problems commonly associated with the cleft deformity. Added training and competence in cleft surgery may qualify these specialists for primary surgery. Oral maxillofacial surgeons are frequently involved in treatment related to the dentition and the jaws. Cooperation of this team of specialists serves the basic needs of the patient and instills parental confidence. The cleft palate team should also include pediatricians or nurse practitioners, geneticists, pedodontists, prosthodontists, psychologists, psychiatrists, social workers, and audiologists, who frequently work together. A team approach augments each individual's expertise and forms a broad base for research.

The team of specialists is most effective when all members are within one institution and can communicate often. Full-team planning sessions follow each clinic to review the progress and plan treatment of the patients. These meetings provide a forum for exchange of viewpoints and experiences. Close contact among team members, especially between the surgeon and the orthodontist or between the surgeon and the speech pathologist, has been effective in achieving highly satisfactory results in all phases of treatment. A common example is the functional analysis and therapeutic decision for oronasal fistulas. Cooperation among specialists is also necessary for critically evaluating short- and long-term results and for determining directions for improved treatment strategies.

Mutual respect among specialists allows a critical analysis of outcomes, an essential component for peer review. This may be the best support for the perceived increased cost of cleft team evaluations by third-party payers. The Craniofacial Outcomes Registry of the American Cleft Palate Association is testing examination sheets in about 20 pilot clinics, with quantified observations to document the results of cleft repair. The teamwork not only is important in developing treatment strategies, but also is invaluable in conducting clinical research.

We believe that longitudinal treatment of cleft patients outside an established and functioning cleft palate team is inefficient and unlikely to provide the most advanced care. Unfortunately, with decreased reimbursements for procedures, refusals for preauthorization of treatment and team care by health maintenance organizations, and loss of state and federal subsidies, the financial situation for even established teams is precarious. Increasingly, teams are seeking additional institutional and philanthropic support to run operations.

Treatment Procedures

There are differences in the philosophies of cleft management and in the timings of particular treatment procedures. To exemplify this, a summary of treatment procedures and their timing, as used at the University of Iowa Cleft Palate Center, is presented in Table 41–1. There are significant differences in the approach of the cleft palate–craniofacial team at the University of Pittsburgh.

We initiate presurgical orthopedics within the first week of life for complete unilateral and bilateral clefts. Elastic straps are positioned across the cheeks and the lips to approximate the displaced dental arch. To guide the arches into position and avoid collapse of the lesser segment maxilla under the greater, a custom palatal plate is fashioned. To make this appliance, an impression is made of the maxillary arch with alginate-filled infant trays. The plaster model serves as a template for the acrylic palatal plate that has an alveolar arch gutter that allows inward rotation of the greater segment to meet the lesser one. Hence, this modified McNeil-Burstin technique of external strapping and guiding of acrylic palatal plates improves the relative position of the maxillary segments.[142] Parents appreciate the improved facility with feeding, and surgeons find the lip and primary nasal correction easier.

Within 6 weeks, the alveolus is improved, and at 3 months of age, the lip and nose are repaired with modified Millard[85] rotation-advancement technique and the McComb[82] nasal tip-plasty. First, a bilateral myringotomy with tube insertion is done to drain middle-ear effusions. In the Millard-type repair, the cleft edge side of the philtrum is rotated caudally with a columellar base–to-vermilion sweeping incision to position a horizontal cupid's bow. The lesser segment lip skin is fashioned into a large triangular flap to close the rotation gap and construct the lip along a simulated philtral column. If the rotation is inadequate, we add a small triangular flap at the vermilion border. A triangular lip extension of the cleft-sided shortened hemicolumella is advanced cephalad into the columella. The cleft-edge, obliquely oriented orbicularis muscle is dissected free and oriented transversely with a secure horizontal mattress suture overlap of the lateral muscle over the central. On closure of the lip, the displaced nasal ala is drawn medially, which often causes distortion of the nostril rim. To correct this problem and to elevate the depressed nasal dome and rim, a nasal tip-plasty through the alar base and columellar incisions is performed. Wide dissection frees the cleft-sided alar cartilage from the opposite one and the nasal skin. Positioning and shaping of the ala is achieved through a transnasal 4–0 nylon suspension stitch through a slice of red rubber catheter, which is removed 2 weeks later. We have frequently noticed a residual medial crus inferior displacement, which now prompts direct suturing of the alar cruri across the dome through a rim incision exposure.

TABLE 41–1. Summary of Treatment Procedures*

	Timing	Technique
Surgical Procedures		
Unilateral cleft lip repair	3 months of age	Modification of triangular flap technique
Bilateral cleft lip repair	Two-stage: first at 3 months; second at 4.5 months of age	Modification of triangular flap technique or straight-line closure
Palate repair	12–18 months of age	Two-flap palatoplasty
Primary correction for nasal deformity	3 months (at the time of primary lip repair)	Construction of floor of the nose; repositioning of alar base (limited correction)
Correction for secondary nasal deformity	8–12 years of age	Bardach technique, external approach
Septoplasty	14 years and older	
Correction for secondary lip deformity	Before 5 years of age	Various techniques
Pharyngeal flap	4–6 years of age	Superiorly based pharyngeal flap technique (Hogan modification)
Alveolar bone grafting	4–6 years of age	
Premaxillary recession	4–6 years of age	Bilateral alveolar bone grafting with closure of oronasal and nasolabial fistules
Orthognathic surgery	14 years and older	Mandibular or maxillary osteotomy
Speech Pathology Procedures		
Initial parent counseling of parents about expected speech/language development and about relationship among cleft palate, surgery, and speech production and importance of verbal stimulation	2–3 months of age	
Follow-up examination and counseling of parents	6-month intervals until normal speech/language is developed	
Velopharyngeal function evaluation during speech	Beginning at age 3 years; then at 6-month intervals until adequate velopharyngeal function is established, with examination in later years if indications of developing velopharyngeal disorder	
Language therapy, if needed	Preschool years, if available	
Speech therapy, if needed; continued language therapy, if indicated	Early primary school years	
Definitive diagnosis of velopharyngeal function during speech; referral for secondary surgery if needed	4–7 years of age	
Determine whether audiologic evaluation is needed and make appropriate referrals	Birth to 6 years of age	
During follow-up evaluation, determine extent to which dental-occlusal status influences speech production	Beginning at age 3 years and at yearly intervals until dental-occlusal status is not influencing speech production	
Orthodontic Procedures		
Presurgical orthopedic treatment	Not performed	
Maxillary expansion	3–5 years of age	
Mixed dentition treatment	6–9 years of age	Correction of molar relationships; alignment of maxillary teeth; serial extraction when indicated
Final orthodontic correction	10 years of age and older	Possible appliances or combination of orthodontic treatment and surgery
Otolaryngologic Procedures		
Myringotomy and ventilating tubes	When indicated	
Adenoidectomy before pharyngeal flap surgery	When there is significant adenoid hypertrophy	
Modification of the lateral port size after pharyngeal flap surgery		Enlargement of ports using lasers Teflon injection to narrow port size Disconnection of pharyngeal flap from posterior pharyngeal wall
Nasal-septal reconstruction	When there is nasal airway obstruction: performed between 14 and 16 years of age	
Inferior turbinate surgery	• Partial turbinectomy in severe cases at 7–8 years of age • Submucous resection in severe cases at 7–8 years of age	
Cryotherapy for the nasal mucosa	For mucosal disease; performed at 14–16 years of age	
Cleft septorhinoplasty	For airway obstruction; performed at 14–16 years of age	

* Procedures used at The University of Iowa Cleft Palate Center for management of cleft patients.

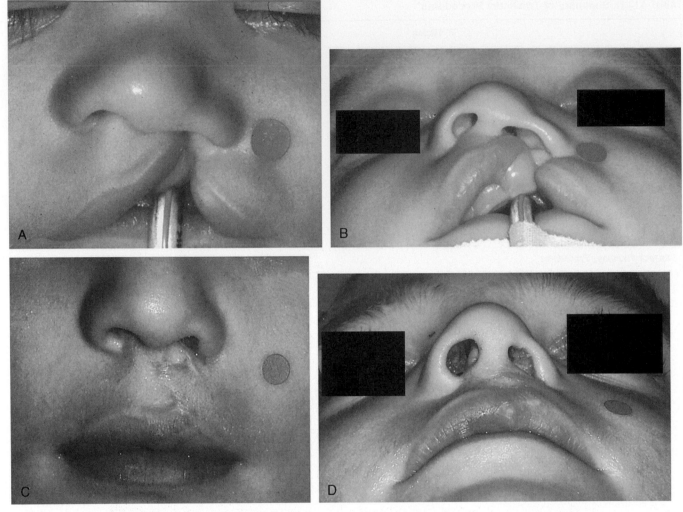

FIGURE 41–2. *A,* Right complete cleft lip with nasal deformity is seen under general anesthesia. *B,* With the drooping cleft-sided alar rim retracted, the markings for the modified Millard and McComb repairs are drawn. *C,* The immediate postoperative result. *D,* The unrevised repair is seen 8 years later.

Sampling of results in a prospective study at the University of Pittsburgh indicated improved early appearance of the unilateral cleft lip and nose with presurgical orthopedics. Bilateral lip clefts are usually closed in one operation.[88, 89] Lip adhesions are used for unilateral or bilateral clefts when presurgical orthopedics has failed. A lip adhesion is a straight-line closure of the cleft, using broad cleft edge flaps with no attempt at lengthening the shortened lip or violating critical lip landmarks. With no cheek tissue undermining, the repair exerts as much force against the prominent segment as possible. Some months after the adhesion has provided the desired effect, it is cut away for definitive lip and nasal repair. We endeavor to complete the lip repair before 1 year of age to take advantage of the usually excellent healing of infancy (Fig. 41–2).

The cleft palate is repaired at 1 year, well before the development of speech. Flaps of hard palate and vomer mucoperiosteum, nasal and oral mucosa, and cleft muscle are mobilized and advanced to close the cleft and lengthen the palate toward the pharynx. No attempt is made to close the cleft alveolus or the bony gap of the hard palate. The alveolar cleft will be closed before the eruption of the canine tooth with an iliac crest bone graft and local mucoperiosteal flaps. At the time of palate repair, persistent middle-ear disease is treated with revision of the myringotomy with tube replacement.

Since the 1970s, we have evolved from the two-stage palatal repair of the hard palate and (6 months later) the soft palate to the single-stage double-opposing Z-plasty (Furlow) technique.[51] When the cleft of the palate is wide, a four-flap palatoplasty with levator muscle retroposition is performed. The Furlow palate repair has become popular because the technique effectively lengthens the soft palate and transposes the cleft muscles to the posterior portion of the palate without exposing hard palate bone. After incising the cleft edge, obliquely oriented incisions, at 60 degrees, are made on the left oral surface from the posterior border of the hard palate to the hamulus of the pterygoid plate and from the base of the uvula to the right hamulus. The posteriorly based left oral side flap includes the cleft muscle. The anteriorly based right side flap, extending from the hard palate, does not. Conversely, the anteriorly based left side nasal mucosal flap has no muscle, whereas the right side nasal flap includes the cleft muscle. The closure positions oral and nasal mucosal flaps between the two muscle-bearing flaps and the posterior border of the hard palate.

Because the Z-plasty closure lengthens the palate by advancing triangular flaps across the midline, wide clefts cannot be closed without additional flaps. Instead, the four-flap palatoplasty with levator muscle reposition, popularized by Bardach, is used.[13] Mucoperiosteal flaps encompassing the entire hard and soft hemipalates are raised. The cleft side nasal mucoperiosteal flap is raised to the lateral nasal wall, and an opposing superiorly based vomer septal flap is elevated, which is turned down and sutured to the nasal floor mucoperiosteal flap.

Evaluation. Most cleft palate centers use different evaluation forms to monitor and document changes after the various treatment procedures. It would be highly beneficial if a standard method of evaluation could be adopted to facilitate comparative studies of management techniques and results. Outcomes measurement should include the appearance of the lip and nose, traditionally revealed by anthropometry[49] or subjective assessment of facial photographs.[33]

Computer-assisted analysis of calibrated, standardized photographs is being investigated at the University of Pittsburgh.[64] The number and extent of revisions are significant.[118] The number and size of palatal fistulas are noted.[77] Speech is assessed, especially for velopharyngeal insufficiency.[82] The greatest efforts have been in the evaluation of facial growth, with lateral cephalometric x-ray analysis being the predominant form.

The University of Iowa Cleft Palate Center and the Dallas Center for Craniofacial Deformities carried out comparative studies that used the same evaluation forms and procedures. The results of these studies indicated a need for further comparative clinical research to critically evaluate current treatment techniques and to explore ways of improving management for cleft patients. More well-designed investigations and statistical data are needed to justify or negate various treatment techniques. Many clinical methods are based on personal experience, with no scientific justification. Cleft lip and palate is a multifaceted problem and must be approached from the viewpoints of many specialists. Because prevention of clefts does not appear possible in the near future, perfection of current treatment techniques remains a primary goal of cleft palate teams.[89, 130]

Planning. There are a variety of cleft forms; therefore, planning of specific treatment procedures depends on a detailed analysis of the deformity. In cleft lip, only the extent of the cleft and the degree of the deformity are determining factors for the choice of surgical procedure. For cleft lip and alveolus with an intact palate, there may be severe nasal deformity and displacement of the maxillary segments. Primary repair of the alveolus is appropriate.

Cases of wide clefts of the lip and palate with severe nasal and alveolar displacement require more than just surgical treatment. We believe, but have not yet proved, that surgery, particularly that involving the nose, should be preceded by lip strapping and specially fitted palatal plates.[140] Aggressive repositioning of the prominent premaxilla in bilateral clefts by lip adhesions or insertion of the Latham[75] prosthesis is indicated. This controversial approach involves pin insertion of custom-fitted, jack screw expandable acrylic palatal plates. A double pin inserts just behind the prominent premaxilla. As the half turns of the jack screw distract the arches 1 mm each day, chain link elastics are reapplied to exert a steady posterior pull on the premaxilla. This reliable positioning device, which facilitates lip and nasal repair, may ultimately inhibit midfacial growth.

It is difficult to anticipate final results in a particular patient because this birth defect must be evaluated in light of the dynamics of the growth and development of the maxillofacial structures. A general management strategy (as presented in Table 41–1) should be adopted. However, evaluation subsequent to each treatment phase is needed before the next treatment steps are undertaken. Various surgical techniques may be used successfully for treatment of similar cleft deformities.

Psychosocial Aspects of Cleft Lip and Palate

The first cleft team encounter may be on learning the ultrasound prenatal diagnosis of a fetal facial cleft. Although this is diagnostic, the full extent of the cleft is rarely appreciated. The treatment protocol and rationale are anticipated, with emphasis on the timing of interventions and parental interactions. The confidence and reassurance displayed by the medical team's representative reduces parental anxiety.

The birth of an infant with a cleft is shocking and disappointing. The reaction of the family varies from anxiety, guilt, depression, resentment, and rejection to acceptance and enthusiastic support. Experience with hundreds of families treated and observed by the authors has indicated that disintegration of the family seldom occurs. More typically, first the mother and then the father and immediate family adopt positive and protective attitudes toward the newborn. It is extremely helpful when, during the first days after the birth of a baby with a cleft, the parents are informed of effective feeding techniques. Then, they better accept the notion that surgery will also be successful. Our nurse practitioner travels to the hospital to accomplish this purpose. Although it is probably a psychologic boost to the parents, we have resisted neonatal lip repair, because that advantage is outweighed by several months of effective presurgical orthopedics, decreased anesthetic risk at an operation at 3 months of age, and improved primary nasal corrections with no increase in lip scarring owing to the brief wait.

On being contacted by a professional from a cleft palate team, the family is assured that the baby will develop and grow well with the indicated treatment during the school-age years. Booklets, schematic drawings, and photographs of similar deformities before and after treatment have a tremendous impact on family and friends because they demonstrate treatment success. The American Cleft Palate/Craniofacial Association and our University of Pittsburgh Cleft Palate/Craniofacial Center have informative Web sites that do not excessively raise family expectations. The stigma of a cleft is reduced. It has been observed that children with clefts treated in the same manner as their siblings and peers usually develop healthy attitudes and a positive self-image. As the child grows, the plastic surgeon has to carefully weigh recommendations for corrective lip and nasal surgery against imparting critical undermining aesthetic judgments. One of the purposes of the annual examination is to anticipate and suggest the need for future corrective surgery in a manner that is nonthreatening and nonjudgmental, so that the child ultimately requests the appropriate change for himself or herself without external pressure. When enough time is taken and parental cooperation is enlisted, it is rare that a teenager needs to be coerced into lip or nasal revision surgery.

Ear Deformities

Congenital Ear Deformity

Congenital auricular deformities in children come in a variety of presentations, ranging from an overly prominent ear to its near absence—microtia. These deformities are sometimes associated with complex severe facial deformity, such as hemifacial microsomia. Or, more often, the deformity is isolated but is nevertheless the cause of peer torment and psychologic problems. Even a minimal deformity is readily apparent, especially in boys with short hair. Parents are sensitive to this and are eager for the defect to be corrected as soon as possible. Some deformities may be corrected successfully before the child goes to school; others may require multistage reconstructive procedures. A multitude of reconstructive procedures have been developed to correct these congenital as well as post-traumatic deformities.

The psychologic impact of an existing deformity in any given child should not be underestimated because behavioral problems may well develop. This point must be emphasized because treatment of some ear deformities (e.g., prominent ear, cup ear) is considered by third-party insurers to be cosmetic surgery. In the authors' opinion, the decision of whether a deformity is purely cosmetic should be made on an individual basis, depending on the extent of the deformity, the psychologic impact of the existing deformity, and how it influences the child's emotional stability.

Prominent Ear Deformity

The most common congenital auricular deformity is the so-called prominent ear. The prominent ear deformity results from an inadequate fold of the antihelix and/or an enlarged concha and/or malpositioned concha. The helix is the encircling roll extending from the superior auricular root at the cheek to the earlobe. The outer upper plane is called the scapha, which ends at the antihelical fold,

which continues with an anterior crus and posterior crus surrounding the fossa triangularis below the superior root. In a right-angle stair-step manner, the antihelical fold descends to the concha, which is a hemi–bowl-shaped cavity, partially septated by the superior root and funneling to the external auditory canal. The canal is shadowed by the overhanging tragus, which is opposed by the antitragus, caused by a cartilaginous prominence superior to the lobe.

Normal protrusion of the ear, measured by the distance between the rim of the helix and the mastoid plane, ranges from 15 to 20 mm. Prominence of the ear may also be measured by the angle between the dorsal surface of the upper helical rim and the mastoid plane; an angle of 20 to 30 degrees is considered within normal limits. When the angle is greater than 40 degrees or the distance between the helical rim and mastoid plane is greater than 20 mm, the ear is classified as prominent. The degree of prominence can vary; the most severe prominent ear can appear perpendicular to the mastoid plane with an angle of up to 90 degrees.[50]

A number of reports have documented successful nonoperative correction of prominent ear deformity (as well as constricted ear and cryptotia) by early splinting of the auricle. The malleability of neonatal cartilage under the influence of high maternal estrogen is believed to allow reshaping of the deformed auricle by application of pressure alone. This is most commonly done with a mold of dental compound. By 2 weeks of age, with declining estrogen, the firmer cartilage tends to retain the premolded shape. The major risk of the technique is skin necrosis from excess pressure at prominent points.[23, 81] Although promising, this technique is not widely adopted. Some surgeons find results inadequate. Many patients are not referred for treatment early enough.

In planning surgery, it is necessary to measure and account for size and prominence of asymmetry. The technique most appropriate to the deformity is chosen (i.e., the most common deformity arising from an obtuse scaphoconchal angle is treated differently from that caused by a malformation of the concha).[122]

Most techniques to create a proper antihelical fold are variations on placement of sutures to create the fold and cartilage weakening to avoid recurrence. The suture technique, popularized by Mustarde,[92] is rarely used as an isolated technique. Typically, an incision is made on the posterior aspect of the auricle, and mattress sutures are placed through and through the cartilage framework to bend an antihelix appropriately. Drawbacks to a suture-only technique include exposure and extrusion of suture as well as partial recurrence. Weakening of the cartilage framework through rasping, scoring, or full-thickness incision to create an antihelix is a more recent development. This, too, has been used as a stand-alone technique but works best with the suture technique. Usually, the lateral surface of the framework is manipulated to allow antihelical folding. Full-thickness incision may lead to sharp antihelical edges and is rarely necessary in children. It may prove necessary in the stiffer cartilage of an adult.[31, 84, 124, 135]

When an enlarged concha contributes to excessive protrusion, an excision of conchal cartilage may be necessary

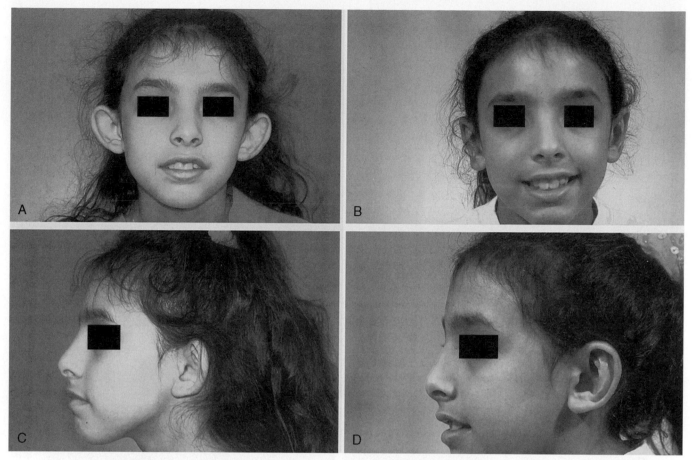

FIGURE 41–3. *A,* The frontal view of prominent ears demonstrates asymmetrically obtuse scaphoconchal angles. *B,* The frontal view shows symmetric correction of the deformity with proper angulation and relative visibility of the helical rims. The lateral view shows the improved position of the helical rim with a smooth antihelical rim.

to correct the deformity. To avoid wrinkling with very large cartilage removal, skin from the lateral (anterior) surface of the auricle is excised as well. Reduction of conchal cartilage, in contrast to through-and-through cartilaginous incisions in the antihelical area, does not leave sharp edges when well approximated by suture.

Conchal setback is a means of addressing the malpositioned, malrotated concha that is not necessarily enlarged. In this technique, postauricular fat and muscle overlying the mastoid bone are excised, creating a depression into which the concha can be comfortably inset. In this manner, the entire pinna can be rotated into the correct position.[51]

Surgeons performing otoplasty must take care that repositioning the concha does not occlude the cartilaginous portion of the ear canal, causing possible stenosis of the external auditory canal. Other possible unsatisfactory outcomes are recurrence of protrusion, contour irregularities, disparity in the height of the helices between ears, antihelical fold that is more prominent than the helix, sharp edge to the antihelical fold, and incorrect angulation of the pinna to the scalp. Otoplasty does not appear to adversely affect subsequent ear growth. Otoplasty by means of limited incisions with the aid of an endoscope

has been reported.[56] The appearance of a young adult before otoplasty (Fig. 41–3*A, C*) and 1 year postoperatively (Fig. 41–3*B, D*) is illustrated.

Constricted Ear Deformity

Sometimes referred to as cup ear or lop ear, constricted ear deformities vary considerably. These deformities may occur in combination with protrusion or outward angulation of the ear. In most cases, the constricted ear deformity affects the upper and middle portions of the pinna, whereas the lobule is positioned normally. The constricted ear is usually smaller than normal side. Hooding of the upper portion of the pinna may be so severe that it covers the entire concha and external auditory meatus. The concha itself may be abnormally large and malpositioned. Constricted ears are typically deficient in skin, cartilage, or both.[30, 72, 133] They are classified into three groups.

Group I deformities often demonstrate prominence (protrusion) of the upper pole and the semblance of a lid of extra skin and cartilage superiorly; the vertical height of the ear is deficient. These deformities are often cor-

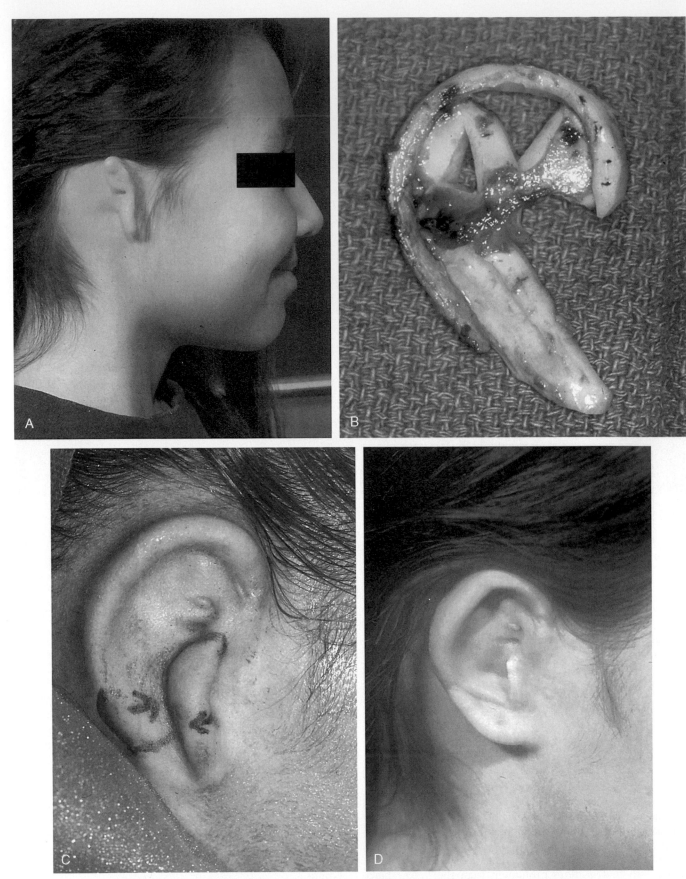

FIGURE 41–4. *A,* Typical microtic remnant is present in an 8-year-old Asian child. *B,* The rib cartilage framework is fabricated at the time the thin mastoid skin is elevated. *C,* At this second stage, the cartilage graft has healed in proper place and the earlobe is rotated into position. *D,* Skin graft elevation has been performed, and result is seen 2 years later.

rectable by excision of the skin and cartilage composing the lid, allowing the remaining constricted framework to attain a fuller height despite the reduction in tissue. A suture to approximate the scapha to the mastoid through an incision on the posterior surface of the auricle may also prove necessary.

Group II deformities, with a more significant skin and cartilage deficiency, are very difficult to correct, usually requiring cartilage grafts (e.g., from ipsilateral or contralateral concha) to support an increased auricular height. These deformities may require degloving of the constricted superior portion of the auricle to allow full release by the use of "banner flaps." The banner flap is an inferiorly based postauricular skin flap that is turned 90 degrees to fill an opening in the ear created by an oblique incision to open the constricted auricle. An alternative method of reconstruction employs a more inferior release with a conchal chondrocutaneous flap to supply cartilage for the increase in auricular height.

Group III deformities are the most severe and have such limited cartilage and skin that they are best treated as an atypical microtia, requiring nearly total auricular rebuilding with costal cartilage grafts.

Cryptotia

Also known as pocket ear, cryptotia is rare in the U.S. population but is more common in Asian populations, occurring with a reported frequency of up to 1 in 500 births. The chief features of this deformity are a buried superior pole of the auricle (beneath scalp skin) with accompanying scaphal underdevelopment and a sharply formed antihelix.

It may appear on initial examination that simple elevation of the buried portion of the pinna would correct this deformity; however, any contemplated repair must allow for sufficient skin to cover the newly created posterior auricular surface as well as re-establish a postauricular crease. This is usually accomplished by means of local rotation or advancement flaps; occasionally, a free skin graft is required.[63, 136]

Stahl ear, sometimes colloquially called Spock's ear, is not a cryptotia but rather an uncommon deformity that features a crus that projects almost at a right angle from the antihelix toward the helical rim. Treatment consists of degloving of the malformed segments, followed by reshaping of the cartilage to bring the wayward crus into proper alignment.[102, 130, 138]

Microtia

The microtic ear represents the most severe form of congenital auricular anomaly, occurring in 1 in 8000 live births. Microtia may exist as an isolated finding or in combination with other skeletal deformities, most notably hemicraniofacial microsomia. Microtic ears are often associated with an absent external auditory meatus and canal. They may contain sinus tracts that must be completely removed in surgery. The reconstruction of the microtic ear remains a formidable surgical task, requiring multiple stages, often ending with less than ideal results.

Microtic ears can be divided into two broad categories described by Brent: classic and atypical.[19, 20] The classic form demonstrates a rudimentary pinna that is nothing more than a longitudinal skinfold, sometimes containing misshapen traces of cartilage. This skinfold, however, provides the tissue from which a lobule can be fashioned—hence the alternative term *lobular microtia* applied by Nagata to this deformity. The atypical form contains a better-developed (though still malformed) cartilage vestige that comprises portions of the concha, crura, and/or tragus; this form is therefore called conchal microtia in the Nagata terminology.[95]

Microtia may occur as an ear deformity accompanied by normal growth and development of the craniofacial complex, or it may be a component of hemifacial or bilateral microsomia. In cases of microsomia, changes in the pinna are accompanied by hypoplasia of the mandible, maxilla, malar, and temporal bones; soft tissue; and muscles of mastication. Treatment of microsomia combined with microtia includes extensive bone grafting and/or distraction osteogenesis to create facial symmetry before any attempt at ear reconstruction. Severe deformities are Goldenhar syndrome, with hemifacial microsomia, epibulbar dermoids, and vertebral dysplasias. Soft tissue augmentation with grafts and free flaps is completed before ear reconstruction. Partial facial nerve paralysis is not uncommon in children with unilateral microsomia, usually involving the mandibular branch and soft palatal elevators. Full-blown expression of Möbius syndrome with panfacial and lateral rectus muscle palsy does accompany microtia.

Treatment of microtia, when not associated with craniofacial microsomia, can usually be initiated at about the time the child reaches school age. By age 6 to 7 years, the auricle has reached seven eighths its adult size; thus, a contralateral unaffected auricle is a fairly good template for an adult-size ear. Reconstruction of the microtic ear typically requires use of rib cartilage; the rib cartilage donor site is rarely substantial enough until 6 to 7 years of age.

The microtic ear has no external auditory canal, and the middle ear bones are poorly developed and abnormally fused. A computed tomography (CT) scan clarifies the disturbed anatomy. Under such conditions, a canal and tympanoplasty cannot create normal hearing. Also, tympanoplasty is troubled by chronic sinus drainage. Construction of external canals in bilateral microtia improves hearing.

In cases of unilateral microtia with a normal-hearing contralateral ear, most surgeons hesitate to recommend canaloplasty or middle ear surgery on the affected side. However, as the advantages of binaural hearing have become increasing recognized and the canaloplasty results have improved, the procedure has become more common in experienced hands. If, however, both plastic and otologic surgery are to be undertaken on the same side in a patient, the plastic operation should precede the otologic, after the ideal location of the proposed external auditory canal is established. Incisions and scarring from a primary otologic procedure might render plastic reconstruction untenable or dictate that a reconstructed auricle should

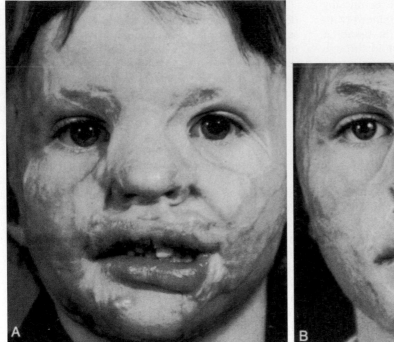
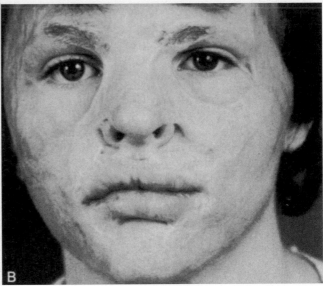

FIGURE 41–5. *A*, Extensive burn to the entire face. Note severe scarring in periorbital area causing eversion of the lower lip. Multiple hypertrophic scars over the entire face. *B*, Nine years later, after several operations using local transposition flaps and free skin grafting.

occupy an unnatural position. In contrast, if the auricular reconstruction is accomplished first, it is usually still possible to gain access to the mastoid and temporal bone without sacrificing the reconstruction.

Although it may be possible to reconstruct some atypical microtia with auricular donor cartilage only (harvested from the contralateral ear), the majority of microtic ears require a bulk of cartilage that is readily obtained from only one donor site: the rib—specifically, the synchondrosis of the sixth, seventh, and eighth ribs. In reconstructing a left ear, the rib cartilage is usually harvested from the right side (to take advantage of more favorable natural curvature). Little long-term morbidity is associated with this donor site, although there is pain in the chest some time.

Repair of classic microtia involves multiple procedures (Fig. 41–4). Using the contralateral ear as a template, the sixth-and-seventh-rib conjoined segments are first fashioned as a baseplate, into which the details of the antihelix and crura can be carved with a septal gouge. Onto this baseplate the separate eighth rib is affixed with sutures as a helix. The entire framework is then placed into a pocket over the mastoid, covered only by a thin flap of skin and subcutaneous tissue. This completes the first stage; at a second stage, the rudimentary skinfold is transposed inferiorly to attach to the reconstructed framework as a new lobule. The whole ear at this point remains continuous to the lateral skull. The third stage, therefore, involves lifting the newly created auricle off the skull, with local flap advancement and skin grafting to provide posterior coverage and to create a postauricular sulcus. The fourth stage addresses creation of a tragus, often

with conchal cartilage from the opposite ear, and deepening of the concha.[21]

This is the classic repair described by Brent; Nagata has reported a related method with several important differences. The Nagata framework includes a carved tragus at the first stage and marries the initial two stages; that is, the lobule transposition is performed simultaneously with framework fashioning and placement. To achieve good projection of the ear, Nagata interposes a wedge of cartilage between the framework and the skull, covering the construct posteriorly with a temporoparietal fascial flap (TPFF) and a split-thickness skin graft.[94]

Complications of microtia repair include hematoma, infection, and skin-pocket necrosis with extrusion of the implanted framework. This last problem can sometimes be rescued by coverage with a TPFF and skin graft. Unfortunately, this often leads to blunting of the auricular contours so painstakingly carved into the framework.[22, 95]

Homologous preserved cartilage has been used to create the framework in microtia repair but suffers from excessive resorption. Preformed Silastic and hydroxyapatite implants have also been used in microtia repair; experience suggests that these artificial substrates have too high an extrusion rate unless primarily covered with TPFF, in which case the cosmetic result may well be compromised. A preformed porous polyethylene framework, covered by a temporoparietal fascial flap and skin graft, is an option with promising early results in more than 100 patients.[113a] One final option for rehabilitation of the microtic ear is use of a total prosthesis affixed to the lateral scalp through a bone-anchored implant.[141] This method affords an outstanding shape but an off-color result. Children are more likely to accept a fair autogenous reconstruction than a well-crafted artificial part; they have difficulty attending to the cleaning and upkeep.[133a]

Post-traumatic Ear Deformities

With its somewhat exposed position, the auricle is frequently lacerated, contused, and/or avulsed. These can present a thorny problem to the surgeon, who is charged with restoration of a delicate three-dimensional shape. The techniques appropriate to reconstruction of any defect depend on the size and location of the defect, as well as the availability and condition of the avulsed tissue and the status of the periauricular soft tissues of the scalp.

If a large fragment of completely avulsed pinna is available, the possibility of microvascular reattachment of the severed fragment is considered. It is sometimes possible to re-establish circulation to the injured segment by microvascular anastomosis to the postauricular vessels.[98, 133] Often, arterial flow can be established but no suitable venous drainage is found; in such cases, the use of medicinal leeches to provide venous outflow can salvage the situation. A successful microvascular replantation can allow a superb cosmetic result and eliminate the need for secondary procedures. Primary reattachment of a major full-thickness ear avulsion without establishment of a blood supply is not recommended. Substantial necrosis and loss of the entire piece will occur.

If no vessels are available, a severed fragment may be "banked" for later use by de-epithelialization and burial of the cartilage in a pocket in the scalp subjacent to its position in the auricle. At the second stage, the cartilage is elevated with a soft tissue cuff, and a skin graft is applied for final cover. Large fragments of cartilage can be deformed, however, by the contractile forces of healing and scar within the pocket, sometimes resulting in a suboptimal aesthetic appearance.[84]

An excellent technique for salvaging detached auricular fragments was described by Baudet in 1972; it is most applicable for defects of the upper two thirds of the pinna. In this technique, the skin is removed from the medial surface of the auricular fragment, and skin is also removed from the lateral mastoid surface, allowing the fragment to be inset in an appropriate position on a well-vascularized bed. Before inset, small fenestrations are made in the cartilage of the fragment to allow vascular ingrowth from the mastoid bed. A second stage sees elevation of the fragment and re-creation of a sulcus with skin grafting to the medial surface of the fragment. Auricular fragments typically retain good definition by this approach.[16]

Finally, wrapping a severed cartilage fragment with a temporoparietal fascial flap and skin graft is another means of addressing injury, but it suffers from the same drawback seen in the use of this technique in microtia—that is, significant muting of the auricular contours.[67]

When traumatic injury has resulted in complete loss of the pinna, with no portion available for reconstruction, it will likely prove necessary to approach the defect as a microtia, using costal cartilage to fashion the whole of a new auricular framework. Scars and skin loss are usually a problem, necessitating coverage with a temporoparietal

fascial graft and skin graft. In these situations and in instances of low hairline or prior failed cartilage reconstruction, a Branemark osteointegrated implant (Nobel Biocare USA Inc, Yorba Linda, Ca) is strongly considered.[133a] If only a partial defect of the pinna exists, cartilage grafting and local flaps are a good option.

A host of local flaps have been described to provide full-thickness resurfacing of various auricular defects. Pedicled tubed skin from the postauricular region is commonly used to reconstruct defects of helix alone.[39] Superior marginal defects may alternatively be reconstructed with a sliding chondrocutaneous flap described by Antia and Buch.[10] A postauricular chondrocutaneous island flap has been described to address defects in the concha and external auditory canal. Upper-third defects can be reconstructed with a pedicled conchal bowl flap. Middle- and lower-third defects often require cartilage grafts in conjunction with local soft tissue flaps.[37, 101, 109] We have also used the platysma cutaneous flap.

Facial Burn Injuries

Thermal injuries in the head and neck are, unfortunately, relatively common in children. More than 30% of all burns occur in children younger than 10 years; more than 50% of patients admitted to burn centers suffer from facial burns as part of their injury.[2, 40] Management and rehabilitation of facial burn injuries present a highly challenging problem to the reconstructive surgeon, especially in children, whose ongoing growth and development may complicate the already-unpredictable process of wound healing the surgeon must confront.

Burns are usually classified according to their depth of penetration. In first-degree burns, there is painful erythema; only the epidermis is injured. Healing is without superficial scar formation, although there may be permanent altered pigmentation. In second-degree burns, the thermal injury has penetrated into and damaged part of the dermis. These injuries typically display erythema, blistering, swelling, and possibly a weeping transudate. Second-degree burns are usually painful owing to damaged or exposed nerve endings. Third-degree burns are the most severe skin injury; these involve complete destruction of the dermis and penetration into the soft tissues (or even bone) underneath. Third-degree burns often have a characteristic dry black eschar. They are less painful owing to deadened nerve endings within the wound. First- and second-degree burns are described as partial thickness and third-degree burns are described as full-thickness.

Healing of second- and third-degree burns results in scarring, which may be hypertrophic and lead to scar contractures with significant attendant functional impairment. Facial burn scar contractures can lead to corneal ulceration from eyelid ectropion, drooling from lower lip eversion, difficulties with articulation, and ingestion of food from microstomia, for example.[63] Untreated scar contractures can lead to skeletal deformities as the child grows, such as a recessed maxilla or mandible with accompanying malocclusion.[121] Of course, even without functional sequelae, the scarring in and of itself may be horribly disfiguring and cause significant distress to the child and parents.

Timing of Intervention

The acute management of facial burn injuries varies from center to center. Some surgeons prefer to wait until eschar separates naturally before resurfacing a wound, feeling this allows them to best identify those areas that will heal without intervention and minimizes the blood loss that can occur with early escharectomy. However, this approach may risk development of hypertrophic scarring and keloids, which is more prevalent when wounds of several weeks' duration are left without stable cover and have developed underlying granulation tissue.

Others prefer early tangential excision of facial eschar (e.g., within 2 weeks of injury) followed by prompt autografting. A growing body of evidence suggests that such early intervention ultimately provides better long-term results—that is, less hypertrophic scarring and fewer secondary procedures.[3, 8, 14, 35, 42] The principle of early excision and grafting is already accepted and widely applied in the management of nonfacial burns.

If further definitive reconstruction is required, unless there is some compelling impairment of function, it is usually advisable to delay surgery for 1 year. This waiting period allows scar maturation. During the intervening period, multiple nonsurgical therapeutic options are available that should be used to limit the extent of scar deformity. Pressure masks, though poorly tolerated, retard hypertrophic scars. Where these already exist, the mask can help soften and flatten the scars. Silicone gel sheets, applied to the skin without pressure, have helped in minimizing hypertrophic scars. Moulages are now available that combine these two treatments.[17] Hypertrophic scars and keloids may also be treated with steroid injections or with massage using vitamin E cream. Scar quality and hyperpigmentation may be helped by cosmetic skin conditioning programs of glycolic acid, Retin-A, hydroquinone, and steroids.[108] Tunable dye lasers decrease scar color and symptoms. Exercises may help limit scar contractures of the neck that restrict head movement or of the mouth that constrict its opening.

The varieties of heavily marketed scar treatment topical agents have raised expectations of parents and children. Although rarely as effective as advertised, a treatment protocol including some of these products is expected.

However, when functional impairment develops such as exposure keratitis from lid ectropion or tethering of the chin to the neck preventing mouth closure, surgical release of the contracture and resurfacing is indicated. The child and family should be warned that scarring and contracture may well recur and that multiple reconstructive procedures may prove necessary, with no assurance that the ultimate appearance will be wholly satisfactory.

Reconstructive Techniques

Deformities resulting from severe burn injuries to the head and neck must be individually evaluated to determine the advisability and feasibility of reconstruction and the choice of surgical technique (Fig. 41–5). In contemplating reconstruction, the surgeon must consider the optimal appearance of entire facial aesthetic subunits, not just isolated scar bands. Similarly, the reconstruction must not create a secondary deformity that might prove more bothersome than the original. The reconstructive tissue must approximate native undamaged tissue in color and texture as closely as possible. The surgeon has a variety of techniques at her or his disposal, including split- and full-thickness skin grafts, Z-plasties and local flaps, regional and microvascular free flaps, tissue expansion, or any combination thereof[2] (Fig. 41–6).

The mainstay of facial burn reconstruction in children remains free split- and full-thickness skin grafting. These skin grafts can be harvested from a variety of potentially hidden donor sites, including groin crease, suprapubic area, and buttock crease. Supraclavicular skin grafts offer an excellent color and texture match for facial resurfacing. One popular site for partial-thickness graft harvest is the scalp, although in up to 17% of patients, there can be some accompanying hair transfer with the harvested graft.[79, 121]

Scalp burns in children often result in large areas of alopecia; in no area of head and neck reconstruction has tissue expansion had greater impact than in scalp reconstruction.[78] Although tissue expansion does not create new hair follicles, it does allow redistribution of existing hair follicles over a greater area; interfollicular distance can be increased twofold without noticeable thinning of the hair. If only 10% to 15% of hair-bearing skin is replaced with scar, successful reconstruction can usually be accomplished in a single procedure by simple excision with a concomitant rotation-advancement flap of adjacent scalp tissue. Defects of up to 50% loss of hair-bearing scalp can often be reconstructed with tissue expansion; however, defects greater than 50% loss are poor candidates for reconstruction with scalp expansion alone. In these patients, attention should be given to forming an adequate anterior hairline and preparing the scalp geometry for receiving a hairpiece. Referral to an expert in cosmetic microhair grafting for hairline restoration and grafting through scars should be considered a finishing touch.

In planning tissue expansion, several principles should be applied. For every centimeter above the scalp the expander rises, the leading edge of the created flap can be advanced the same distance when the prosthesis is removed. It is wise to overexpand beyond the expected tissue requirement by 20%, anticipating some recoil of the expanded tissues once the inset is undertaken. Tissue expanders are silicone elastomer bags of various sizes and shapes that are positioned under the galea through short incisions. They are connected by silicone tubing to remote fill-domes, allowing infusion of saline every 7 to 10 days. These domes are buried subcutaneously or may be left external. Because crescent-shaped expanders minimize the lateral dog ears (fullness), they have been found particularly useful in scalp reconstruction. Multiple expanders may be placed simultaneously should the defect require it. Scalp expansion should be delayed until a child

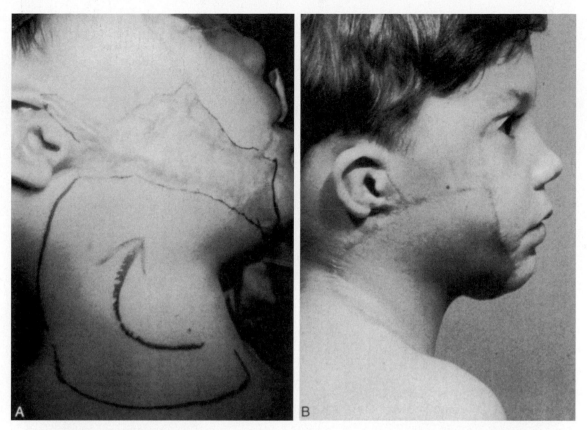

FIGURE 41–6. *A,* Large contracted scar on the cheek after burn. Design of rotation-advancement flap to close the defect after total excision of the existing scar. *B,* Several months later.

is older than 2 years owing to the easy deformability of the skull in an infant.

Tissue expansion techniques seem simple but are attended by a fairly high complication rate, up to 30% in some series. These include implant rupture, implant exposure, infection, and flap embarrassment. If implant exposure or rupture occurs near the end of the planned expansion, however, it may still be possible to use that expanded tissue in the reconstruction as intended. Tissue expansion can also be used at sites remote from a deformity to increase the amount of skin available at a donor site for use as a skin graft.[78]

The forehead is a distinct aesthetic unit; reconstruction of the burned forehead, if undertaken, typically involves use of a sheet of split-thickness skin graft or, if sufficient undamaged forehead is available, tissue expansion of the undamaged component[2] (Fig. 41–7).

Eyebrow alopecia is frequently encountered in patients with head and neck burns. Reconstruction of eyebrow alopecia usually follows one of two paths: use of a vascularized hair-bearing island pedicle flap based on the superficial temporal artery or free composite hair-bearing grafts. If composite grafts are used, best results have been obtained using multiple grafts of no more than 5 mm wide, with a planned second-stage procedure to excise any intervening scar.[112]

Scar contracture and ectropion of the eyelids remain a critical problem in facial burn injuries, often requiring early release with skin grafting. Tight contractures over the face, forehead, and neck can also transmit forces to the eyelids, contributing to the problem. Ectropion occurs more commonly in the lower lid than in the upper lid. Lower lid ectropion release requires an incision extending beyond the medial and lateral canthi, with resurfacing of the defect accomplished most often by full-thickness skin grafts; postauricular skin is frequently used as the source. Upper lid ectropion release requires a similar wide incision, but a thick split-thickness skin graft may be used here because the upper lid is more mobile. Coexisting upper and lower lid ectropions should be released in separate operative sessions to guard against the possibility of troublesome overcorrection. Local flaps (such as Mustarde cheek advancement or paramedian forehead flaps) are rarely available for eyelid reconstruction because of the extent of the thermal injury. If present, they are not commonly used because of excessive bulk.[3, 14]

Reconstruction of the burned nose is a complex problem that depends largely on the depth of injury. In reconstructive planning, the three elements of the nasal architecture (lining, framework, and skin cover) must all be considered, but the precise reconstruction varies greatly depending on the defect. Additionally, the nose itself is composed of aesthetic subunits that must be evaluated in any planned reconstruction. One common defect is loss of the alar margins; these can often be refashioned adequately by turn-down flaps of adjacent skin or scar tissue to provide lining, followed by skin grafting over the nasal alae or whole nasal tip. Alternatively, composite auricular grafts can be used to address alar marginal de-

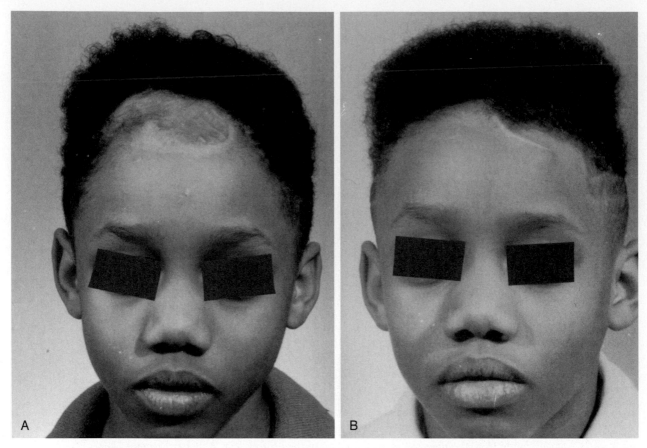

FIGURE 41–7. *A,* This 10-year-old boy has post-traumatic right frontal hairline alopecia several years after a burn with a hot iron. *B,* One year after restoration of the hairline with a scalp flap created by 8 weeks of tissue expansion.

fects. Total nasal resurfacing can be accomplished by means of a (possibly pre-expanded) forehead flap, if available, or tubed pedicled flaps from the supraclavicular areas may be used. The thin, pliable radial forearm free flap has also emerged as an option for total nasal reconstruction.[2]

The cheek is also a distinct aesthetic facial subunit; cheek reconstruction usually involves large sheet grafts of split-thickness skin or advancement of tissue expanded neck/cheek skin. Some surgeons warn against advancing expanded neck skin past the mandibular border, however, citing a too-high incidence of subsequent secondary deformity such as lip distortion or even lower lid ectropion.[95] Fewer such problems were encountered with caudal advancement of expanded cheek skin for lower face reconstruction. The upper lip, also a facial aesthetic subunit, is usually reconstructed with a sheet of split-thickness graft. Auricular composite grafts have recreated the philtrum. Similarly, full aesthetic subunit split-thickness skin grafts are most commonly used to redress deformities of the lower lip–chin complex.[2]

The neck is a frequent site of restrictive scar contracture and can pose a difficult problem. Release of the contracture may require wide excision with a resulting large raw surface area. Free skin grafts, regional flaps, and free flaps with microvascular anastomoses have all been used to resurface these defects. If skin grafts are used, the patient's neck must be kept in extension for a prolonged period of time to avoid recurrence of the contracture; this is done with individually prepared cervical collars and prescribed exercises. Free flaps are less prone to contracture, but owing to their bulk they tend to obliterate the cervicomental angle, with a less satisfactory aesthetic result.[2, 74]

Increasingly, microvascular free flaps are used for large-area burn resurfacing in the head and neck, including "supercharged," "super-thin" flaps and even large fasciocutaneous flaps with multiple free pedicles for full facial resurfacing.[9, 66, 76]

Electric Burns

Electric burns in young children usually occur from contact between the child's mouth and the "female" end of an extension cord, often resulting in severe injury to the lips at the oral commissure and the anterior tongue. More than 90% of such oral commissure burns occur in children younger than 4 years.[32] Immediately after the injury, the full extent of tissue necrosis, even during examination in the operating room, is unclear; consequently, until demarcation is obvious, surgical débridement or attempted reconstruction is delayed.

Three strategies have been advocated for the manage-

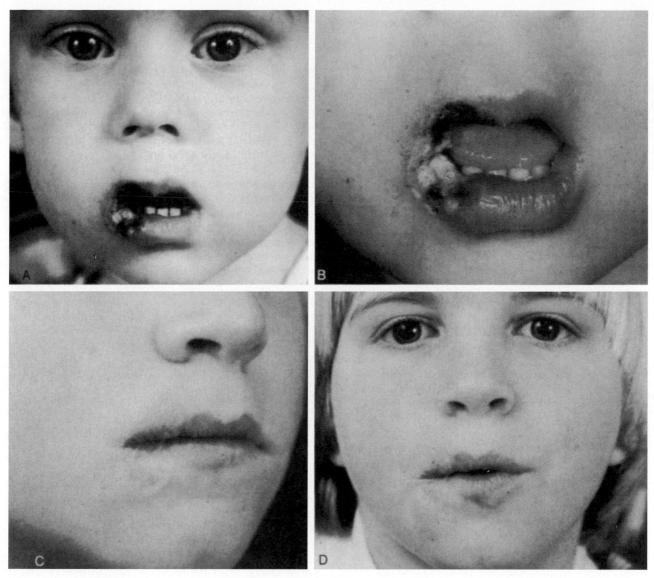

FIGURE 41–8. *A* and *B,* Electric burn of the commissure. *C* and *D,* Six years after commissuroplasty.

ment of these injuries. Use of prosthodontic splints in the treatment of electric cord commissure burns has been widely employed since the early 1980s. Special acrylic and Silastic intraoral appliances are attached to the maxillary dentition with a soft, hooklike extension that wraps around the injured labial commissures to prevent scar contracture between the upper and lower lips. Obviating operative intervention, the splint needs to be worn for about 6 months. These devices require continuous family and patient compliance for treatment success.[29, 120]

Others advocate relatively early surgical débridement of devitalized tissue and eschar as soon as it can be reliably distinguished from surrounding normal tissue. They believe this reduces bleeding and minimizes scarring from the injury before a more definitive reconstructive procedure can be attempted.[105]

A third strategy advocates conservative management initially, with only antibiotic ointment applied to the wound to help prevent infection. Wound healing and scar contracture are allowed to proceed; massage therapy with vitamin E or Kenalog cream may also be applied to the maturing scar. At 6 to 12 months post injury, a planned definitive reconstruction is undertaken[26] (Fig. 41–8).

Oral commissuroplasty in this setting typically relies on local mucosal and/or skin flaps. Buccal and labial mucosal flaps are popular choices, with flaps from remaining lip vermilion another possibility. Tongue flaps have also been used, with good results.[36]

Hypertrophic Scars and Keloids

Excessive scarring subsequent to injury or surgery is not uncommon in children. Hypertrophic scars and keloids are postulated to be different clinical manifestations of the same underlying disorder; that is, abnormal collagen metabolism resulting in excessive collagen deposition. Although histologically similar in many ways, hypertrophic scars and keloids can be differentiated by their clinical characteristics and behavior.

Hypertrophic scars usually present themselves shortly (weeks or months) after their inciting trauma. They typically undergo an initial phase of expansion but usually subside with time. Their size is commensurate with the magnitude of the injury that provoked them, and they remain within the borders of the injured tissue field. Mechanical factors (such as motion or tension across a suture line or scar band) are thought to be exacerbating factors in the development of hypertrophic scars, whereas hormonal influences are not felt to be important in the etiology of hypertrophic scars. Treatment of hypertrophic scars (e.g., by surgical revision) usually results in lasting improvement.[41, 99]

In contrast, keloids may not develop for months after an injury or trauma, but once present they only rarely subside naturally. Keloids often grow far out of proportion to the inciting injury and far beyond the boundaries of the initial wound (e.g., massive lobular keloids after ear piercing). Mechanical factors are not thought to be important in keloid etiology, but hormonal factors have been implicated in keloid development. Keloids may well occur, for example, with the onset of puberty or may enlarge during pregnancy or subside after menopause. Earlobe, neck, shoulder, and presternal skin has a high predilection for keloid formation. Surgical treatment of keloidal scars, as opposed to hypertrophic scars, is often confounded by recurrence.[70, 126]

Keloids and hypertrophic scars are more common in children and adolescents than in adults; they rarely occur in elderly patients. Keloids are much more common with darker skin pigmentation; the incidence of keloids in the African-American and Hispanic populations has been reported to be as high as 4.5% to 16%.[115]

Treatment of keloids and hypertrophic scars usually involves surgery but may require adjunctive measures as well. These include application of local pressure, silicon sheeting, pre- and postoperative corticosteroid injection, topical retinoids,[108] and radiation. In dealing with keloids, some surgeons advocate intralesional excision of tissue to debulk the lesion while leaving in place a thin rim of keloidal tissue, hoping in this manner to avoid stimulating anew the processes that led to keloid formation in the first place.

The utility of pressure and silicon in attempting to prevent the development of hypertrophic scars and keloids has already been mentioned; these treatments are also helpful in ameliorating existing hypertrophic scars. Pressure earrings are a useful adjunct after excision of earlobe keloids. The principal adjunctive treatment, however, remains use of preoperative and postoperative glucocorticoid injections (e.g., with Kenalog) into the keloidal bed to forestall recurrence of the keloid.[55, 61] Preoperative injections often lead to palpable softening of a keloid, suggesting excision may meet with a favorable result. Postoperative low-dose radiation has been employed to treat recalcitrant keloids with marked success; the maximum dose administered is 1000 cGy[38] (Fig. 41–9). However, many physicians are reluctant to subject children to even this small quantity of radiation for fear of engendering secondary malignancies in the treatment of a benign lesion.

Vascular Lesions of the Head and Neck

Vascular lesions of the head and neck in children vary in origin, presentation, and development. Our inadequate understanding of the etiology, pathogenesis, and multiplicity of forms of vascular tumors is reflected in the many descriptive classifications. Bringing order out of chaos, Mulliken advanced a useful biologically based system that separates vascular lesions into two major categories: hemangiomas and vascular malformations.[88] In hemangiomas, the cycling of endothelial cells is felt to be aberrant, resulting in initial rapid endothelial proliferation followed by involution. Vascular malformations are felt to have mature endothelium with normal endothelial cell turnover. On histologic examination, hemangiomas can be differentiated by elevated mast cells and increased mitotic activity.[90, 91]

Hemangioma

Hemangioma is the most common tumor of infancy and childhood, occurring in up to 12% of children. Hemangiomas occur in females three times as commonly as in males; most are solitary, and 60% are located on the face. Hemangiomas can be subclassified as superficial, deep, or mixed. Superficial hemangiomas have a bright, strawberry-red color, whereas deeper hemangiomas, covered by skin, appear blue.[24, 44, 87]

Most hemangiomas are not noted at birth, or they may be anticipated by a so-called herald patch. Of the hemangiomas that develop after birth, 90% are visible by age 4 to 8 weeks. Any lesion arising after age 3 months is unlikely to be hemangioma.

The natural history of hemangioma is one of rapid initial enlargement followed by slow involution. The proliferative phase can continue for up to 1 to 2 years, during which time even initially small lesions can become huge, with substantial attendant deformity and functional impairment. The involutional phase is slower and may be spotty, with other portions of the hemangioma actually proliferating. Ultimately, the entire mass fades, with 50% of hemangiomas virtually disappeared by 5 years and 90% by 9 years. Normal skin is reportedly restored with hemangioma involution in up to 50% of patients, but up to one fourth are left with permanent skin changes, including scarring, atrophy, telangiectasias, and fibrofatty residual tissue[24] (Fig. 41–10).

Complications occur in 20% of hemangiomas. Ulceration, with or without secondary infection, occurs in up to 10% of lesions. Bleeding from hemangiomas is not a major problem; when it does occur, it is typically controlled with direct pressure.[24, 46] Giant enlarging hemangiomas can lead to major functional sequelae from compression or obstruction of vital structures, including airway obstruction and difficulties with speech and swallowing. Periorbital hemangiomas in particular can have a high complication rate, resulting in amblyopia (60%), stra-

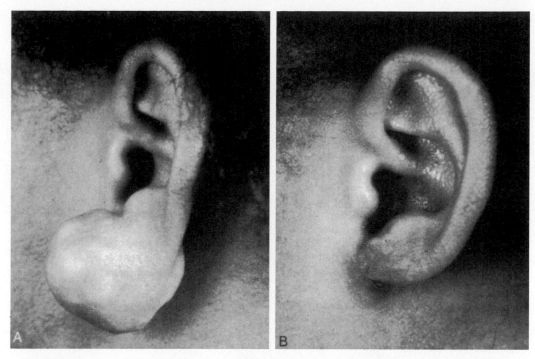

FIGURE 41–9. A, Large keloid of the earlobe after ear piercing. B, One year after excision of the keloid combined with pre- and postsurgical irradiation.

bismus (34%), anisometropia (46%), astigmatism, ptosis, proptosis, and optic nerve atrophy.[59, 114, 125] Giant hemangiomas demand high-volume blood flow; rarely, this can lead to high-output congestive heart failure. Initial treatment is medical, but surgery may be needed if there is no improvement. Giant hemangiomas may also cause bleeding diathesis by platelet trapping within the lesion, (Kasabach-Merritt syndrome); platelet replacement and direct attack on the lesion are indicated.[24]

Treatment of hemangiomas is controversial. Some surgeons advocate early excision; others prefer to wait for maximum involution before addressing any residual deformity. The advisability of early surgery for hemangioma depends on multiple factors, including lesion size, proximity of vital structures, likelihood of total resection, and secondary deformities that might be created. Resection of deforming nasal tip hemangioma is championed (Fig. 41–11). Surgical excision itself may be deforming and, if incomplete, may not prevent progression or recurrence of the lesion. Obviously, in the presence of major functional sequelae, some intervention is mandated.

Multiple nonsurgical options are available in the treatment of hemangiomas. Systemic steroids can be used to reverse a rapidly enlarging lesion; unfortunately, rebound growth often occurs when the drugs are stopped, and long-term steroid use presents its own risks and complications.[87] Steroids can be repeatedly administered through intralesional injection with good effect.[46, 140] Laser therapy, both as an adjunct to surgery and as a stand-alone option, has had promising results. Multiple studies point to the efficacy of intralesional therapy with potassium titanyl phosphate (KTP) or neodymium:yttrium-aluminum-garnet (Nd:YAG) lasers in the management of he-

mangiomas.[4–6, 28] Early laser therapy with the tunable pulsed-dye laser may prevent progression of small lesions. Interferon alfa-2a, an angiogenesis inhibitor, has been used to treat refractory hemangiomas with some success but has significant side effects, including fever, neutropenia, headache, and skin necrosis.[48] Angiography followed by embolization is usually reserved for the larger hemangioma with bleeding diathesis.[25]

Vascular Malformations

Vascular malformations are far less common than hemangiomas. Although they may not be discovered for many years, it is assumed that they are present at birth but do not manifest until they are subjected to minor trauma. When vascular malformations enlarge, there is steady progression and no spontaneous involution. Mulliken classifies malformations as capillary, venous, arterial, lymphatic, or mixed.[44]

The most common vascular malformation is the port-wine stain, a capillary or capillary-venous malformation. Port-wine stains are present in 0.3% to 1% of infants. They occur equally in males and females, most commonly on the face and often as unilateral patches along the distribution of the trigeminal nerve. They begin as macular pink to purple lesions but characteristically become hypertrophic and nodular with progression, with an increased risk for hemorrhage. Port-wine stains in the ophthalmic and maxillary trigeminal distributions are associated with development of glaucoma and retinal detachment; ophthalmologic evaluation is essential.[54, 129]

Color-sensitive lasers reduce the hue intensity of port-

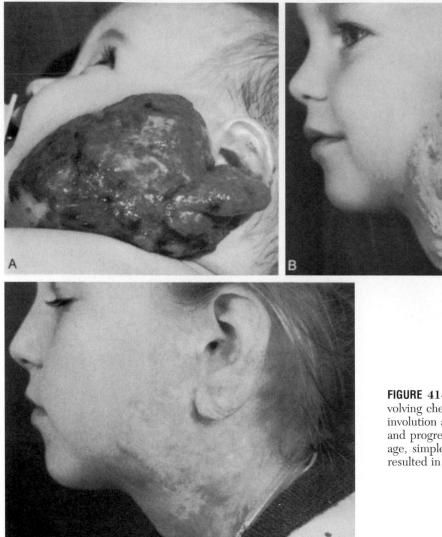
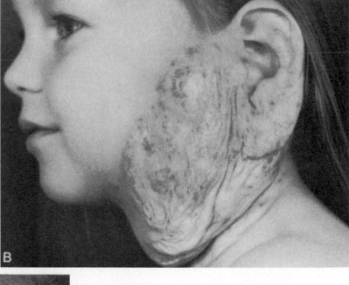

FIGURE 41–10. *A,* Large cavernous hemangioma involving cheek, ear, and neck. *B,* Signs of spontaneous involution appeared at the end of the first year of life and progressed until 3 years of age. *C,* At 4 years of age, simple reduction of redundant and scarred skin resulted in good appearance.

wine stains by selectively cooking the relatively static hemoglobin, which then coagulates the ectatic vessels. Argon lasers were initially used but have fallen out of favor owing to hypertrophic scarring and permanent depigmentation resulting from biphasic wave spectrum that damages both hemoglobin and melanin. More recently, the flashlamp pulsed-dye laser with a more selective hemoglobin wavelength has emerged as the treatment of choice. It is safe for use in infants as young as 2 weeks and poses little risk of depigmentation or scarring. Multiple treatments are usually necessary, and the lesion may become darker as the vessels recannulate with time. A 50% recurrence rate has been reported at 3 to 4 years after completion of initial therapy.[1, 7, 11, 104] Surgical excision of port-wine stains with skin graft reconstruction remains an uncommon option.

Venous malformations are low-flow lesions that can be deeply invasive and are usually progressive. They present as a bluish patch or mass and may become quite bulky. They may also develop thrombi or phleboliths, causing

pain or some functional compromise. Treatment of venous malformations depends on their size, location, and presentation. Surgical excision is one option, but complete removal is difficult to achieve. Lesions of the lips are commonly excised along with a labial reduction. Intralesional KTP laser therapy has been effective and safe for reduction of large cheek malformations. Percutaneous sclerotherapy with intralesional alcohol employing radiographic control has been used alone and in conjunction with surgery. Embolization under fluoroscopy has a few champions. These treatments are followed by considerable swelling, which may require hospitalization.[24, 43, 44]

Arteriovenous malformations (AVMs) are high-flow masses characterized by direct arterial-to-venous communications. Many of these lesions are intracranial, but they can present anywhere and at any age. Localized warmth, thrill, or bruit of a vascular mass suggests an AVM on physical examination. AVMs cause pain, disfigurement, ulceration, bleeding, or throbbing pulsations. Direct trauma or hormonal change (e.g., puberty, pregnancy) accelerates

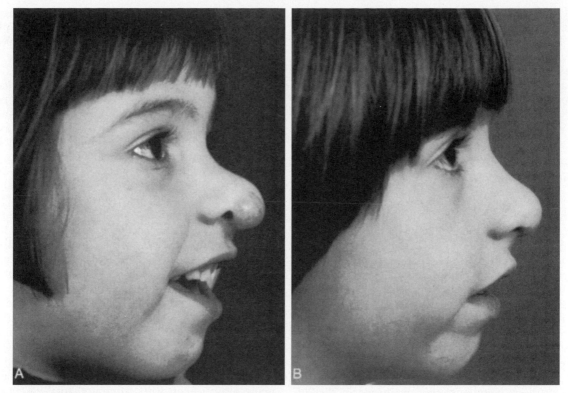

FIGURE 41–11. *A,* Profile view of large cavernous hemangioma of the nasal tip. *B,* One year postoperatively.

AVM enlargement, which may become unresectable over a matter of months. The precise mechanism for enlargement is unknown but relates to the impact of chronic aberrant blood flow through congenitally deformed vessels. Often, seemingly adequate resections are followed by recurrent and more troublesome disease. Arteriovenous malformations are typically aggressive and can become life threatening. Large AVMs may cause high-output cardiac failure.

Management of AVMs depends on location and extent of lesion. A team approach with a radiologist and a reconstructive surgeon is advised. By virtue of the deformity and frequent recurrence, the tendency is to avoid radical resection, adding surgical disfigurement and dysfunction. Angiography identifies feeding and draining vessels. Ligation of these vessels temporarily reduces life-threatening bleeding but is a temporizing measure only. In the long run, the ischemia within the lesion recruits collateral vessels and reactivates the AVM. Embolization alone is of benefit only if the patient cannot withstand surgery. Radiation, conversely, may be helpful in long-term palliation of unresectable AVMs, but it is of no benefit in management of acute complications from AVM.[44, 56]

Surgical resection of the AVM remains the mainstay of treatment, although it is frequently a daunting task in the head and neck. To minimize bleeding, surgery is preceded by embolization 24 to 48 hours earlier.[66] The surgeon should work closely with the interventional radiologist to avoid thrombosis of major vessels to nearby axial pattern flaps that may be used for reconstruction.[25, 64]

Well-vascularized flaps, preferably from a distance (free flaps), have been shown to retard recurrence.[66, 134]

Syndromes Associated with Vascular Lesions

Many syndromes include hemangiomas and vascular malformations as one of their components. One of the most common is Sturge-Weber syndrome, in which a port-wine stain typically appears in the distribution of the trigeminal nerve, although it may also occur on the scalp, neck, trunk, or extremities. Other findings may include ipsilateral leptomeningeal vascular malformations with or without calcifications. Seizures may occur in children, and electroencephalography may demonstrate spiked wave patterns suggestive of epilepsy. Glaucoma develops in up to 45% of those with ophthalmic and maxillary trigeminal involvement.[45, 46]

Klippel-Trenaunay syndrome includes congenital varicose veins, and capillary-venous-lymphatic malformations with hypertrophic skeletal changes. Limb hypertrophy is usually minor.[71] Parkes-Weber syndrome presents a similar constellation of features, but the vascular malformations are arteriovenous, and limb elongation can be substantial.[108]

Vascular malformation in association with dyschondroplasia composes Maffucci syndrome. Involved bones are usually shortened and deformed. Multiple neoplasms, including chondrosarcoma, angiosarcoma, and glioma, have been described in this syndrome. Multiple cutaneous venous malformations with associated gastrointestinal venous lesions compose blue rubber nevus syndrome; the nevi often bleed and can lead to chronic anemia.[46]

Facial port-wine stains associated with macroglossia and macrosomia are present in Beckwith-Wiedemann syndrome. Large facial hemangiomas have been associated with posterior fossa anomalies, including Dandy-Walker syndrome. Rapidly enlarging head circumference or macrocephaly may point to this diagnosis.

Lymphatic Malformations

Lymphatic malformations, also known as lymphangiomas or cystic hygromas, can present a difficult problem. These lesions occur equally in males and females and are seen in all populations; like other vascular malformations, they do not spontaneously regress and variably progress. Some 60% of lymphatic malformations are apparent at birth, with 90% declaring themselves before age 2 years. If a coexisting venous component is present, it is more properly described as lymphaticovenous malformation; older parlance refers to such lesions as lymphohemangiomas. Lymphatic malformations are subdivided into three categories based on their histopathology: simple lymphangioma, composed of thin-walled, capillary-size lymphatic channels; cavernous lymphangioma, composed of dilated lymphatic spaces; and cystic hygroma, composed of cysts that may range from millimeters to several centimeters in size.[15, 104]

Lymphatic malformations most commonly present in the submandibular and parotid regions but often involve the structures of the oral cavity and pharynx as well. Enlargement of the affected side with asymmetry is a common presenting feature. Skin overlying lymphatic malformation usually has normal color and warmth; the mass itself may fluctuate, and its borders are usually not discrete and are difficult to definitively palpate. The lymphangioma may have a large venous component, lending a bluish tone. Spontaneous bleeding causes painful

enlargement. Conservative management is favored, perhaps with the use of a moderate dose of prednisone. Enlargement and pain in a lymphangioma may also be caused by infection, which may need specific antibiotic and steroid therapy.

Mucosal changes such as clear and hemorrhagic blebs in the oral cavity or pharynx suggest the diagnosis (Fig. 41–12). Lymphangiomas are often in intimate association with vital structures in the head and neck. Airway compromise should always be considered with all head and neck hemangiomas and vascular malformations. Indirect and probably direct laryngoscopy is indicated in any lesion encroaching on the airway—certainly if there is stridor or other suggestive breathing limitations. Magnetic resonance imaging (MRI) and CT scans define the extent of the lesion and the tracheal deviation and or narrowing. Tracheostomy needs to be considered, especially if direct intervention is planned. Macroglossia requiring conservative midline tongue reduction is indicated for debilitating conditions. Hypertrophy of the mandible owing to direct involvement or macroglossia may also demand surgery.

These lesions diffusely infiltrate surrounding tissue, making complete resection impossible. Many surgeons avoid sacrificing vital structures, preferring a known subtotal resection rather than infliction of a debilitating iatrogenic injury. Even with attempted total resection, recurrence is common. Patients with expansive lymphatic malformations may undergo multiple resections for appearance or function reasons. Upper respiratory tract infections and minor trauma lead to significant swelling of the tongue, pharynx, and neck, necessitating aggressive use of antibiotics and prednisone. For the multitude of reasons noted, these patients require the surgeon's attention throughout their growing years.

Nonresection options for treatment of lymphatic malformations include sclerotherapy. Intralesional sclerotherapy of lymphangiomas has historically been accomplished with alcohol. Another treatment modality that has met with some success is debulking of lymphatic malformation

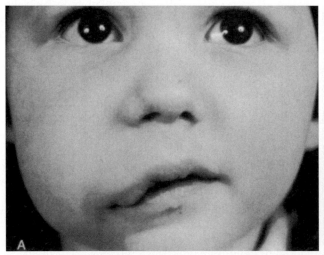
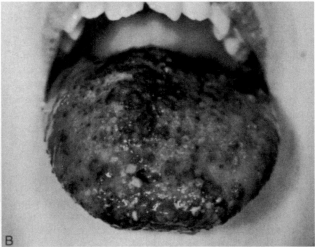

FIGURE 41–12. Lymphangioma of the right cheek (A) and tongue (B).

by suction followed by introduction of fibrin sealant into the residual lesion.[27]

Melanocytic Nevi and Melanoma

Pigmented lesions of childhood that are not of vascular origin are usually nevi. Nevi are composed of cells that are related to melanocytes, likely sharing with them a neuroectodermal origin. Nevi vary significantly in their presentation and history but can be divided into two broad categories: congenital and acquired.

Congenital nevi are visible at birth. These lesions are found in only 1% of newborns.[65, 133] Nevi that appear somewhat later in life, however, sometimes have the same histologic features as congenital nevi, suggesting that they may have been present at birth but lacking pigment and have come to attention only when stimulated to pigment. Congenital nevi are frequently larger and deeper than acquired nevi. The majority of congenital nevi (more than 90%) are still smaller than 4 cm; these are considered "nongiant." Only a small percentage represent true giant congenital melanocytic nevi—that is, larger than 10 cm.[78]

Giant congenital melanocytic nevi are usually deeply pigmented but may have areas of variegation in the lesion. They are often surrounded by smaller satellite lesions and bear hair. They pose a substantial health risk to the patient in that they undergo malignant degeneration into melanoma in up to 12% of cases. As in adults, a change in appearance or growth of the lesion may herald the development of malignancy.[34, 116] Eighty percent of melanomas arising from giant congenital nevi do so by age 7 years, and 50% develop by age 2 years.[47] Thus, there is some urgency to treat giant congenital nevi despite the risk of secondary deformity from surgery. Surgery for giant congenital nevi usually entails serial full-thickness excision, requiring multiple procedures. Giant congenital melanocytic nevi may be associated with other conditions such as von Recklinghausen disease, spina bifida, and leptomeningeal involvement with hydrocephalus.[34]

The relationship of nongiant congenital nevi to melanoma is less clear. Even here, some studies estimate the lifetime risk of developing melanoma in these lesions to be as high as 1 in 20. This has prompted some surgeons to recommend excision in adolescence or earlier if lesions are in areas that are difficult to follow.

Acquired nevi can be divided into three classifications. Junctional nevi, as the name implies, are proliferations of nevus cells at the epidermal-dermal junction. Dermal nevi are contained entirely within the dermis. Compound nevi have features of both—that is, nests of cells that are both junctional and extending into dermis. The incidence of acquired nevi increases with childhood and sharply rises with adolescence. In Caucasians it has been estimated that the average adult has 15 to 40 acquired nevi.[98, 107] These bear close observation because melanoma has been reported to occur in association with pre-existing nevi in up to 70% of cases.[71, 111]

The nevus of Ota is a dermal nevus, bluish in appearance, that occurs in the distribution of the trigeminal nerve; it may be confused with port-wine stain and may involve the conjunctiva. The risk of malignant degeneration is small.[136] The Spitz nevus is a hypervascular dermal nevus that has a more reddish appearance. Histologically, it may closely resemble melanoma and may go through a period of growth after its initial presentation. Excision with narrow margins is the recommended treatment.[113]

Basic Principles of Flap Reconstruction

Defects requiring flap reconstruction in the head and neck are not as common in children as in adults, but the surgeon must nonetheless be aware of the various reconstructive options. Flaps can be divided into three broad categories: local, regional, or "free" flaps from distant sites. In the first two, the flap retains an uninterrupted blood supply; in the last, the flap donor vessels are actually divided and, with microvascular technique, anastomosed to suitable recipient vessels near the defect. Of these types, local flaps are particularly important in pediatric head and neck reconstruction, although increasingly free flaps are being used even in the pediatric population.

Local flaps in the head and neck are typically cutaneous or fasciocutaneous flaps; they fall into one of three groupings. Random pattern flaps do not contain any specific vessel as their blood supply, relying instead on circulation through the subdermal plexus. Examples of random pattern flaps are flaps used in Z-plasty, rhomboid flaps, and bilobed flaps. Axial pattern flaps, in contrast, incorporate a specific artery that supplies the entire flap territory. Examples in the head and neck include paramedian forehead flaps (based on the supratrochlear vessel) and skin flaps based on the superficial temporal artery. The temporoparietal fascial flap and temporalis muscle flap are examples of non–skin-bearing axial pattern flaps also commonly used in the head and neck, although many would consider these regional rather than local flaps. Flaps can also be mixed in their blood supply, being supplied axially in one portion but with only random supply in another portion of the flap. The deltopectoral flap, proximally based on internal mammary perforating vessels but with a random distal segment, is a classic example; this, too, is considered a regional rather than a local flap.

In determining which flap option is best to reconstruct a given defect, multiple factors must be taken into consideration. These include the size, depth, shape, and location of the defect itself; the origin of the defect and the time elapsed from its creation; the health of the surrounding tissue; and the general health of the patient. Care must be taken not to create a secondary deformity more bothersome than the original when choosing a flap. Reconstruction of defects in the area of the eyelids and lips is particularly sensitive to distortion from poor choice of flap design. Donor site morbidity and scarring are other considerations, and other factors (such as need to wear glasses or hearing aids) may also come into play. It may be that the best cosmetic and functional outcome is

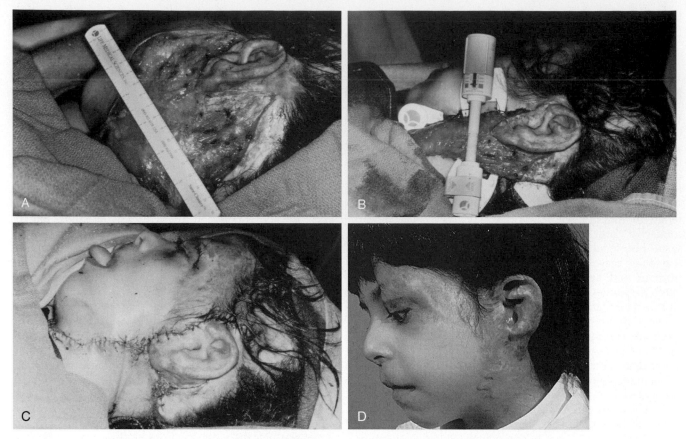

FIGURE 41–13. *A,* 12-cm defect is created after excision of an unsightly involuted hemangioma that extends across the cheek, mandibular border, and upper neck. *B,* The Sure-Closure device has partially closed the wound after 45 minutes of intermittently closing the jaws. *C,* The wound is completely approximated with sutures. *D,* The healing was uneventful as shown by the result 6 months later.

afforded by the least extensive procedure, but this is not always the case.

Flap design of random pattern skin flaps must also account for a number of other concerns. The viability of any random pattern skin flap anywhere on the body depends on the length-width ratio of the flap. Acceptable length-width ratios vary by anatomic site. In the thigh, for example, flap length-width ratio must not exceed 1.5:1. The head and neck area, however, is blessed with a much richer vascular network and can accommodate flaps that have 3:1 or even 4:1 length-width ratios.

The ability to move tissue successfully in a local flap must also be ensured by careful flap design and falls into one of three general categories. Local flaps may be advancement flaps, where a linear vector of displacement of flap tissue results in coverage of the defect (Fig. 41–13). A V-Y advancement flap is one such commonly used flap. Alternatively, they may be rotation flaps, where movement of tissue around a fixed pivot point covers a defect. Rotation flaps are most useful on broad, flat surfaces such as the forehead, temporal area, and cheek. Often, local flaps have both rotational and advancement components, a so-called rotation-advancement flap. Finally, local flaps may be transposition flaps, where a rotational movement over intervening tissue transposes flap tissue into the defect; the classic example is Z-plasty, which essentially con-

sists of mirrored transposition flaps. Optimal flap design avoids tension and kinking of the flap in its inset position.

One stratagem that can be used to enhance flap survival is delay of the desired flap. In this maneuver, a portion of the blood supply to a planned flap territory is severed at a first-stage procedure, leaving intact that portion of the blood supply that ultimately perfuses the elevated and inset flap. This allows increased circulation to develop through the planned flap pedicle and possibly other metabolic adaptations in the flap as well. At a second stage, usually 1 to 2 weeks later, the whole flap is raised and transferred to the defect site. In cutaneous local flaps, delay can be accomplished by incisions around the planned flap territory or by partial elevation of the flap terminus before it is returned to its bed. In myocutaneous or other composite flaps with multiple named feeding vessels, flap delay can be accomplished by division of some of these vessels, leaving the flap territory supplied principally by the vessel on which the flap is to be based. As previously described, tissue expansion augments like tissue for coverage of large wounds[143] (Fig. 41–14).

Regional pedicled flaps are commonly used in head and neck reconstruction in adults; they are much less commonly used in children but may nonetheless offer a useful option. Regional flaps with particular applicability to the head and neck include the pectoralis major flap,

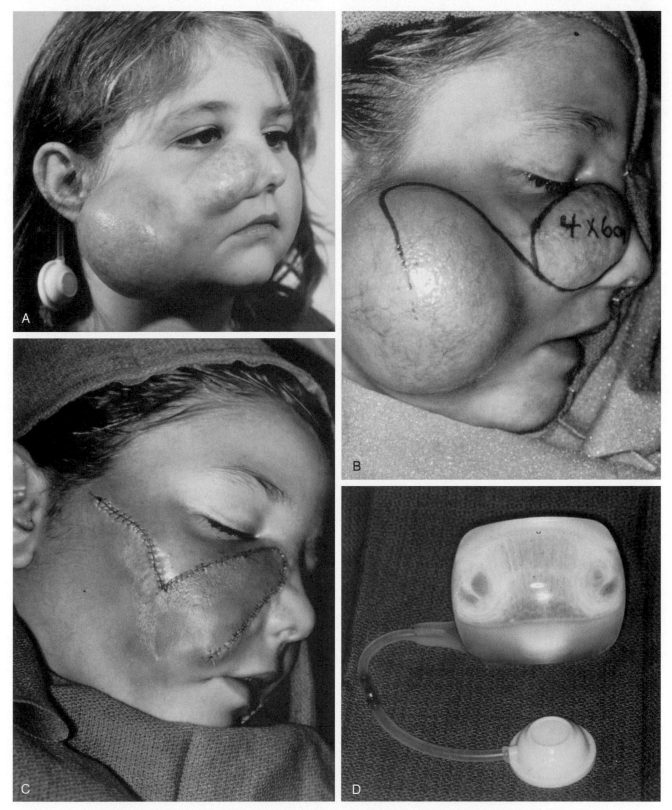

FIGURE 41–14. *A*, There is a 4 × 6 cm, involuted but raised hemangioma between the right lower eyelid and upper lip; 120 ml of saline inflates a right cheek tissue expander. Note the exposed fill dome below the ear. *B*, A single back-cut through the center of the flap is used to rotate a secondary flap into the resection defect. *C*, The sutured wounds. *D*, The filled tissue expander used in this case.

the latissimus dorsi flap, the trapezius flap, the cervicodel-topectoral flap, and the aforementioned temporalis and temporoparietal fascial flaps.

A number of reports have documented an increasing use of free tissue transfer in pediatric head and neck reconstruction. Free flaps in small children are inherently more difficult technically, simply because of the smaller size of the vasculature to be operated, but they have been used successfully to address both soft tissue and bony defects. Iliac crest, fibula, and scapula flaps have been used to rebuild mandible and maxilla in children. Radial forearm, latissimus, and rectus abdominis have been used to rehabilitate facial deformities resulting from trauma, oncologic resection, and burn injury. Deformities pursuant to hemifacial microsomia and Romberg hemifacial atrophy have also been corrected with free flaps.[53, 60, 119]

Aesthetic Considerations in Children and Adolescents

The aesthetic function of the face is to present a normal, socially acceptable appearance. Therefore, congenital and acquired facial deformities present challenging problems for children and young adults. Defects in the head and neck area may range in severity from small, almost undetectable scars to complicated anomalies, post-traumatic or postsurgical tissue loss, functional impairment, and contracted scarring. Psychologic distress develops initially in response to injury or deformity. Surgeons should be alert to psychologic setback and inquire about symptoms indicative of post-traumatic stress syndrome, such as flashbacks, poor sleep, depression, and poor school performance.[117]

Ideally, the plastic surgeon and his or her office staff should be able to respond to the expectations and demands of the cosmetic surgery patient. We have presented the more common disorders and have not provided a comprehensive review of the many afflictions of the head and neck area and their possible reconstructive correction. Common primarily aesthetic issues are discussed subsequently.

The extent of treatment of nasal deformities in children is debatable. Typical nasal deformities include septal deviation, turbinate hypertrophy, and abnormalities of the bony or cartilaginous skeleton (e.g., long nose, short nose, saddle nose, bulbous nasal tip, hanging columella). These deformities may become apparent even in young children; however, complete correction of them is rarely undertaken in childhood for fear of interfering with subsequent facial growth and development.

The septum has long been regarded as the center of midfacial growth, and surgeons have been hesitant to manipulate it, fearing disruption of the normal growth process. Studies in animals and humans offer conflicting evidence on this point, but surgery is often delayed until age 14 years or later to allow nasal development to proceed to near-adult features before intervention. If septoplasty for airway reasons is undertaken at a younger age, the cartilage is often minced and replaced between the septal leaves rather than excised as a submucous resection. There is little evidence that corrective septoplasty without removal of large segments of the septum adversely affects nasal growth, and there is no evidence that early tip rhinoplasty or complete rhinoplasty influences growth. Some studies in cleft lip and palate patients, admittedly a skewed population, have suggested that corrective rhinoplasty at age 7 to 8 years, involving only the cartilaginous skeleton, does not appear to interfere with growth of the midfacial complex. Excision of external nasal lesions such as hemangioma or of intranasal lesions by rhinoplasty approach also does not definitively impede facial growth.

Rhinoplasty for cosmetic purposes only is becoming increasingly popular, especially in the teenage years. Before embarking on this course, it is incumbent on the surgeon to thoroughly assess the motivations of the patient and parents to be sure that the (almost adult) patient is in fact truly desirous of surgery and understands the risks involved. Both patient and family should understand the limitations of what surgery can achieve and understand, too, that cosmetic surgery may not be a panacea for the social troubles that so commonly affect teenagers. Even so, in teenagers as well as in adults, a cosmetic procedure may improve self-esteem and self-image and may be of significant advantage to the properly selected patient.

Eyelid surgery in children often provides a more pleasing aesthetic appearance but usually has a functional component as well. Any interruption of normal binocular visual stimulation in children can lead to decreased vision, a circumstance termed *amblyopia*. Amblyopia occurs in 1% to 2% of the U.S. population and is surprisingly easy to induce in the infant. Eyelid lesions, malformations, and malposition can all lead to the development of amblyopia by visual obstruction. Ptosis of the eyelid is probably the most important eyelid malposition seen by pediatric plastic and head and neck surgeons.

Congenital blepharoptosis is usually unilateral and involves varying degrees of levator palpebrae superioris dysfunction. It may be associated with superior rectus paresis or third-nerve paresis. Children with blepharoptosis may adopt a compensatory chin-up head posture, which can lead to neck problems and a "supercilious" appearance. Repair of the ptotic lid is dependent on the degree of ptosis and levator dysfunction. Procedures progress from advancement of the levator aponeurosis to actual muscle advancement to use of the frontalis muscle to resuspend the eyelid.[18]

An extremely controversial area of pediatric plastic surgery is surgery for aesthetic reasons on children with Down syndrome. These children typically have a characteristic facies, features of which include a large and protuberant tongue, a flat nasal bridge with epicanthal folds, a flat facial profile, a receding chin, and a thick neck. Langdon Down, in his original description, remarked that these children more resembled each other than their immediate relatives.

Surgery for Down syndrome facies attempts to "normalize" the appearance of these children so that they might be more easily accepted into their communities. Tongue reduction is undertaken by wedge resection of the anterior oral tongue. The flat nasal bridge is addressed by dorsal augmentation; cheek and chin implants have also been used to address midface and chin weakness. Canthoplasty is sometimes performed.[102, 139]

The ethical propriety of aesthetic surgery on these children is hotly debated; it has been described as mutilating surgery, similar to female genital mutilation.[69] On the other hand, multiple studies have reported parent satisfaction with these procedures and increased peer acceptance of children who do not display the typical facial features of Down syndrome. Conversely, it has been suggested that normalization of facial appearance in low-ability Down syndrome patients may actually lead to overestimation of their capacities, with corresponding lack of support and unrealistic expectations. The ultimate effect of plastic surgery on Down syndrome children remains unclear and is a very personal choice for parents caring for these special children.

Pediatric plastic surgery of the head and neck, for aesthetic and functional reasons, continues to evolve and to bring promise to the children and parents whose lives it touches. Young children are aware of being different and are sensitive to this, especially if teased by their peers. Fostering a healthy self-image is one of the main goals physicians, parents, family, and school personnel should promote. Consideration of any surgical intervention should acknowledge these concerns and, as much as possible, address the potential psychologic issues involved.

SELECTED READINGS

Bardach J, Salyer KE. Surgical Techniques in Cleft Lip and Palate. St. Louis, Mosby–Year Book, 1991.
> An up-to-date, well-illustrated, and well-written atlas with adequate photographic results. In an informal manner, the authors express both agreement and disagreement with each other's techniques. An indispensable reference for the busy cleft surgeon.

Brent B. Reconstruction of the auricle. In McCarthy J (ed). Plastic Surgery, vol 3. Philadelphia, WB Saunders, 1990, pp 2094–2152.
> A recognized authority's longtime experience in the management of a variety of auricular deformities. Well illustrated.

Cohen IK, Peacock EE. Keloids and hypertrophic scars. In McCarthy J (ed). Plastic Surgery, vol 1. Philadelphia, WB Saunders, 1990, pp 732–747.
> These masters present a succinct compendium of experimental and clinical knowledge on the treatment of scars, including their own major contributions.

Feldman J. Reconstruction of the burned face in children. In Serafin D, Georgiade N (eds). Pediatric Plastic Surgery, vol 1. St. Louis, CV Mosby, 1984, pp 552–632.
> A classic description of the best effect in secondary large skin graft rehabilitation in the burn-deformed child.

Hardesty RA. Advances in management of cleft lip and palate. Clin Plast Surg 20:4, 1993.
> A broad array of important topics written thoughtfully by authorities active in their assigned topic.

Mathes SJ, Nahai F. Reconstructive Surgery: Principles, Anatomy, and Technique. New York, Churchill Livingstone, 1997.
> An excellent text covering both general flap physiology and the anatomic and technical details of many flaps essential to head and neck reconstruction.

Mulliken JB, Young AE. Vascular Birthmarks, Hemangiomas and Malformations. Philadelphia, WB Saunders, 1988.
> A teaching text on the most understandable and accepted classification and treatment concepts for hemangioma and vascular malformations.

REFERENCES

1. Abramowicz M. Laser treatment of cutaneous vascular lesions. Drug Ther Bull 33:104, 1991.
2. Achauer BM. Reconstructing the burned face. Clin Plast Surg 19: 623, 1992.
3. Achauer B, Adair SR. Acute and reconstructive management of the burned eyelid. Clin Plast Surg 27:87, 2000.
4. Achauer BM, Celikoz B, Vander Kam VM. Intralesional bare fiber laser treatment of hemangioma of infancy. Plast Reconstr Surg 105:1212, 1998.
5. Achauer BM, Chang CJ, Vander Kam VM. Management of hemangioma of infancy: review of 245 patients. Plast Reconstr Surg 99:1301, 1997.
6. Achauer BM, Chang CJ, Vander Kam VM, Boyko A. Intralesional photocoagulation of periorbital hemangiomas. Plast Reconstr Surg 103:11, 1999.
7. Achauer BM, Vander Kam VM, Padilla JF 3rd. Clinical experience with the tunable pulsed-dye laser (585 nm) in the treatment of capillary vascular malformations. Plast Reconstr Surg 92:1233, 1993.
8. Almaguer E, Dillon BT, Parry SW. Facial resurfacing at Shriners Burn Institute: a 16-year experience in young burned patients. J Trauma 25:1081, 1985.
9. Angrigiani C, Grilli D. Total face reconstruction with one free flap. Plast Reconstr Surg 99:1566, 1997.
10. Antia NH, Buch VI. Chondrocutaneous advancement flap for the marginal defect of the ear. Plast Reconstr Surg 39:472, 1967.
11. Ashinoff R, Geronemus RG. Flashlamp-pumped pulsed-dye laser for port-wine stains in infancy: earlier versus later treatment. J Am Acad Dermatol 24:467, 1991.
12. Bardach J. Rozszczepy Wargi Gornej i Podniebienia. Warszawa, Panstwowy Zaklad Wydawn, 1967.
13. Bardach J, Salyer KE. Surgical Techniques in Cleft Lip and Palate. Chicago, Year Book, 1987.
14. Barrow RE, Jeschke MG, Herndon DN. Early release of third-degree eyelid burns prevents eye injury. Plast Reconstr Surg 105: 860, 2000.
15. Batsakis JG. Tumors of the Head and Neck: Clinical and Pathological Considerations, 2nd ed. Baltimore, Williams & Wilkins, 1979.
16. Baudet J, Tramond P, Goumain A. [A new technique for the reimplantation of a completely severed auricle.] Ann Chir Plast 17: 67, 1972.
17. Bradford BA, Breault LG, Schneid T, Englemeier RL. Silicone thermoplastic sheeting for treatment of facial scars: an improved technique. J Prosthodont 8:138, 1999.
18. Brady KM, Patrinely JR, Soparkar CNS. Surgery of the eyelids. Clin Plast Surg 25:579, 1998.
19. Brent B. The correction of microtia with autogenous cartilage grafts: I. The classic deformity. Plast Reconstr Surg 66:1, 1980.
20. Brent B. The correction of microtia with autogenous cartilage grafts: II. Atypical and complex deformities. Plast Reconstr Surg 66:13, 1980.
21. Brent B. Auricular repair with autogenous rib cartilage grafts: two decades of experience with 600 cases. Plast Reconstr Surg 90:355, 1992.
22. Brent B, Byrd HS. Secondary ear reconsruction with cartilage grafts covered by axial, random, and free flaps of temporoparietal fascia. Plast Reconstr Surg 72:141, 1983.
23. Brown FE, Colen LB, Addante RR, Graham JM. Correction of congenital auricular deformities by splinting in the neonatal period. Pediatrics 78:406, 1986.
24. Brown TJ, Friedman J, Levy ML. The diagnosis and treatment of common birthmarks. Clin Plast Surg 25:509, 1998.
25. Burrows PE, Lasjaunias PL, Ter Brugge KG, Flodmark O. Urgent

and emergent embolization of lesions of the head and neck: indications and results. Pediatrics 80:386, 1987.

26. Canady JW, Thompson SA, Bardach J. Oral commissure burns in children. Plast Reconstr Surg 97:738, 1996.

27. Castanon M, Margarit J, Carrasco R, et al. Long-term follow-up of nineteen cystic lymphangiomas treated with fibrin sealant. J Pediatr Surg 34:1276, 1999.

28. Clymer MA, Fortune DS, Reinisch L, et al. Interstitial Nd:YAG photocoagulation for vascular malformations and hemangiomas in childhood. Arch Otolaryngol Head Neck Surg 124:431, 1998.

29. Colcleigh RG, Ryan JE. Splinting electrical burns of the mouth in children. Plast Reconstr Surg 48:239, 1976.

30. Cosman B. The constricted ear. Clin Plast Surg 5:389, 1978.

31. Couette-Laberge L, Guay N, Bortoluzzi P, Belleville C. Otoplasty: anterior scoring technique and results in 500 cases. Plast Reconstr Surg 105:504, 2000.

32. Crikelair GF, Dhaliwal AS. The cause and prevention of electrical burns of the mouth in children. Plast Reconstr Surg 58:206, 1976.

33. Cussons PD, Murison MSC, Fernandez AEL, Pigott RW. A panel based assessment of early versus no nasal correction of the cleft lip-nose. Br J Plast Surg 46:7, 1993.

34. DeDavid M, Orlow SJ, Provost N, et al. A study of large congenital melanocytic nevi and associated malignant melanomas: review of cases in the New York University Registry and the world literature. J Am Acad Dermatol 36:409, 1997.

35. Deitch EA, Wheelahan TM, Rose MP, et al. Hypertrophic burn scars: analysis of variables. J Trauma 23:895, 1983.

36. Donelan MB. Reconstruction of electrical burns of the oral commissure with a ventral tongue flap. Plast Reconstr Surg 95:1155, 1995.

37. Donelan MB. Conchal transposition flap for postburn ear deformities. Plast Reconstr Surg 83:641, 1989.

38. Doornbos JF, Stoffel TJ, Hass AC, et al. The role of kilovoltage irradiation in the treatment of keloids. Int J Radiat Oncol Biol Phys 18:833, 1990.

39. Dujon DG, Bowditch M. The thin tube pedicle: a valuable technique in auricular reconstruction after trauma. Br J Plast Surg 48: 35, 1995.

40. Duran V, Teplica D, Gottlieb LJ. Childhood burn injury. Chicago Med 95:14, 1992.

41. English RS, Shenefelt PD. Keloids and hypertrophic scars. Dermatol Surg 25:631, 1999.

42. Engrav LH, Heimbach DM, Walkinshaw MD, Marvin JA. Excision of burns of the face. Plast Reconstr Surg 77:744, 1986.

43. Enjolras O, Ciabrini D, Mazoyer E, et al. Extensive pure venous malformations in the upper or lower limb: a review of 27 cases. J Am Acad Dermatol 36:219, 1997.

44. Enjolras O, Mulliken JB. The current management of vascular birthmarks. Pediatr Dermatol 10:311, 1993.

45. Enjolras O, Riche M, Merland JJ. Facial port-wine stains and Sturge-Weber syndrome. Pediatrics 76:48, 1985.

46. Esterly NB. Cutaneous hemangiomas, vascular stains and malformations, and associated syndromes. Curr Probl Pediatr 26:3, 1996.

47. Everett MA. The management of congenital pigmented nevi. J Okla State Med Assoc 84:213, 1991.

48. Ezekowitz RAB, Mulliken JB, Folkman J. Interferon alfa-2a therapy for life-threatening hemangiomas of infancy. N Engl J Med 326:1456, 1992.

49. Farkas LG. Anthropometry of the Head and Face in Medicine. New York, Elsevier, 1981.

50. Farkas LG. Growth of normal and reconstructed auricles. In Tanzer RC, Edgerton MT (eds). Symposium on Reconstruction of the Auricle, vol 10. St. Louis, CV Mosby, 1974.

51. Furlow L. Cleft palate repair by double reversing Z-plasty. Plast Reconstr Surg 78:5, 1986.

52. Furnas DW. Correction of prominent ears by conchal-mastoid sutures. Plast Reconstr Surg 42:189, 1968.

53. Genden EM, Buchbinder D, Chaplin JM, et al. Reconstruction of the pediatric maxilla and mandible. Arch Otolaryngol Head Neck Surg 126:293, 2000.

54. Geronemus RG, Ashinoff R. The medical necessity of evaluation and treatment of port-wine stains. J Dermatol Surg Oncol 17:76, 1991.

55. Golladay ES. Treatment of keloids by single intraoperative perilesional injection of repository steroid. South Med J 81:736, 1988.

56. Gomes AS, Busuttil RW, Baker JD, et al. Congenital arteriovenous malformations: the role of transcatheter arterial embolization. Arch Surg 118:817, 1983.

57. Graham KE, Gault DT. Endoscopic assisted otoplasty: a preliminary report. Br J Plast Surg 50:47, 1997.

58. Greinwald JH Jr, Burke DK, Sato Y, et al. Treatment of lymphangiomas in children: an update of Picibanil (OK-432) sclerotherapy. Otolaryngol Head Neck Surg 121:381, 1999.

59. Haik BG, Jakobiec FA, Ellsworth RM, et al. Capillary hemangioma of the lids and orbit: an analysis of the clinical features and therapeutic results in 101 cases. Ophthalmology 83:760, 1979.

60. Hemmer KM, Marsh JL, Clement RW. Pediatric facial free flaps. J Reconstr Microsurg 3:221, 1987.

61. Hendricks WM. Complications of ear piercing—treatment and prevention. Cutis 48:386, 1991.

62. Hirose T, Tomono T, Matsuo K, et al. Cryptotia: our classification and treatment. Br J Plast Surg 38:352, 1985.

63. Housinger TA, Hills J, Warden GD. Management of pediatric facial burns. J Burn Care Rehabil 15:408, 1994.

64. Hurwitz DJ, Ashby ER, Llull R, et al. Computer-assisted anthropometry for outcome assessment of cleft lip. Plast Reconstr Surg 103:1608, 1999.

65. Hurwitz DJ, Kerber CW. Hemodynamic considerations in the treatment of arteriovenous malformations of the face and scalp. Plast Reconstr Surg 67:421, 1981.

66. Hyakosoku H, Gao JH. The "super-thin" flap. Br J Plast Surg 47: 457, 1994.

67. Jacobs AH, Walton RG. The incidence of birthmarks in the neonate. Pediatrics 58:218, 1976.

68. Jenkins AM, Finukan T. Primary nonmicrosurgical reconstruction following ear avulsion using the temporoparietal fascial island flap. Plast Reconstr Surg 83:148, 1989.

69. Jones RB. Parental consent to cosmetic facial surgery in Down's syndrome. J Med Ethics 2:101, 2000.

70. Kelly AP. Keloids. Dermatol Clin 6:413, 1988.

71. Kirkwood JM, Tonkonow B, Nordlund JJ, et al. Melanoma: a multidisciplinary overview of current concepts and management. Conn Med 44:21, 1980.

72. Kislov R. Surgical correction of the cupped ear. Plast Reconstr Surg 48:121, 1971.

73. Klippel M, Trenaunay P. Nevus variquex osteo-hypertrophique. Arch Gen Med 3:641, 1900.

74. Kuran I, Turan T, Sadikoglu B, Ozcan H. Treatment of a neck burn contracture with a super-thin occipito-cervico-dorsal flap: a case report. Burns 25:88, 1999.

75. Latham RA, Kusy RP, Georgiade NG. Cleft Palate J 13:252, 1976.

76. Li Y, Li S, Xu J. Application of the free parascapular flap in children. Chung Hua Cheng Hsing Shao Shang Wai Ko Tsa Chih 14:290, 1998.

77. Lindsay WK. The end results of cleft palate surgery and management. In Goldwyn R (ed). Long-Term Results in Plastic and Reconstructive Surgery. Boston, Little, Brown, 1980, p 62.

78. MacLennan SE, Corcoran JF, Neale HW. Tissue expansion in head and neck burn reconstruction. Clin Plast Surg 27:121, 2000.

79. MacLennan SE, Kitzmiller WJ, Mertens D, et al. Scalp autografts and hair transfer to the face in the burned child. Plast Reconstr Surg 102:1865, 1998.

80. Mark GJ, Mihm MC, Liteplo MG, et al. Congenital nevi of the small and garment type. Hum Pathol 4:395, 1973.

81. Matsuo K, Hirose T, Timono T, et al. Nonsurgical correction of congenital auricular deformities in the early neonate: a preliminary report. Plast Reconstr Surg 73:38, 1984.

82. McComb H. Primary correction of unilateral cleft lip nasal deformity: a 10-year review. Plast Reconstr Surg 75:791, 1985.

83. McWilliams BJ, Morris HL, Shelton RL. Cleft Palate Speech. Philadelphia, BC Decker, 1984, p 18.

84. Messner AH, Crysdale WS. Otoplasty. Clinical protocol and long-term results. Arch Otolaryngol Head Neck Surg 122:773, 1996.

85. Millard DR. Cleft Craft: The Evolution of Its Surgery. The Unilateral Deformity, vol 1. Boston, Little, Brown, 1976.

86. Mladick RA, Horton CE, Adamson JE, et al. The pocket principle: a new technique for the reattachment of a severed ear part. Plast Reconstr Surg 48:219, 1971.

87. Morelli JG. Hemangiomas and vascular malformations. Pediatr Ann 25:91, 1996.

88. Mulliken JB. Bilateral cleft lip and nasal deformity: evolution of a surgical concept. Cleft Palate Craniofac J 29:540, 1992.

89. Mulliken JB. Repair of bilateral complete cleft lip and nasal deformity: state of the art. Cleft Palate Craniofac J 37:342, 2000.

90. Mulliken JB, Glowacki J. Hemangiomas and vascular malformations in infants and children: a classification based on endothelial characteristics. Plast Reconstr Surg 92:412, 1982.

91. Mulliken JB, Young AE. Vascular Birthmarks, Hemangiomas and Malformations. Philadelphia, WB Saunders, 1988.

92. Mustarde JC. The treatment of prominent ears by buried mattress sutures—a ten years' survey. Plast Reconstr Surg 39:382, 1967.

93. Nagata S. A new method of total reconstruction of the auricle for microtia. Plast Reconstr Surg 92:187, 1993.

94. Nagata S. Modification of the stages in total reconstruction of the auricle: parts I, II, III, IV. Plast Reconstr Surg 93:221, 1994.

95. Nagata S. Secondary reconstruction for unfavorable microtia results utilizing temporoparietal and innominate fascia flaps. Plast Reconstr Surg 94:254, 1994.

96. Nath RK, Kraemer BA, Azizzadeh A. Complete ear replantation without venous anastomosis. Microsurgery 18:282, 1998.

97. Neale HW, Kurtzman LC, Goh KBC, et al. Tissue expanders in the lower face and anterior neck in pediatric burn patients: limitations and pitfalls. Plast Reconstr Surg 91:624, 1993.

98. Nicholls E. Development and elimination of pigmented moles, and the anatomical distribution of primary malignant melanoma. Cancer 32:191, 1973.

99. Niessen FB, Spauwen PH, Schalkwijk J, Kon M. On the nature of hypertrophic scars and keloids: a review. Plast Reconstr Surg 104:1435, 1999.

100. Noguchi M, Matsuo K, Imai Y, Furuta S. Simple surgical correction of Stahl's ear. Br J Plast Surg 47:570, 1994.

101. Ohsumi N, Iida N. Ear reconstruction with chondrocutaneous postauricular island flap. Plast Reconstr Surg 96:718, 1995.

102. Olbrisch RR. Plastic and aesthetic surgery on children with Down's syndrome. Aesth Plast Surg 9:241, 1985.

103. Oldfield MC, Tate GT. Cleft lip and palate. Br J Plast Surg 17:1, 1964.

104. Orten SS, Waner M, Flock S, et al. Port-wine stains: an assessment of 5 years of treatment. Arch Otolaryngol Head Neck Surg 122:1174, 1996.

105. Ortiz-Monasterio F, Factor R. Early definitive treatment of electrical burns of the mouth. Plast Reconstr Surg 65:169, 1980.

106. Orvidas LJ, Kasperbauer JL. Pediatric lymphangiomas of the head and neck. Ann Otol Rhinol Laryngol 109:411, 2000.

107. Pack GT, Lenson N, Gerber DM. Regional distribution of moles and melanomas. Arch Surg 65:862, 1952.

108. Panabiere-Castaings MH. Retinoic acid in the treatment of keloids. J Dermatol Surg Oncol 14:1275, 1988.

109. Park C, Chung S. A single-stage two-flap method for reconstruction of partial auricular defect. Plast Reconstr Surg 102:1175, 1998.

110. Parkes-Weber F. Hemangiectatic hypertrophy of limbs—congenital phlebarteriectasis and so-called congenital varicose veins. Br J Child Dis 15:13, 1918.

111. Paul E. Growth dynamics of malignant melanoma. A photodocumentary investigation. Arch Dermatol 116:182, 1980.

112. Pensler JM, Dillon B, Parry SW. Reconstruction of the eyebrow in the pediatric burn patient. Plast Reconstr Surg 76:434, 1985.

113. Peters MS, Goellner JR. Spitz naevi and malignant melanomas of childhood and adolescence. Histopathology 10:1289, 1986.

113a. Reinisch J. Microtia reconstruction using a polyethylene implant: an eight year experience. Presented at the 78th annual meeting of the Maerivan Association of Plastic Surgeons, Colorado Springs, Colo, May 5, 1999.

114. Robb RM. Refractive errors associated with hemangiomas of the eyelids and orbit in infancy. Am J Ophthalmol 83:52, 1977.

115. Rockwell WB, Cohen IK, Ehrlich HP. Keloids and hypertrophic scars. A comprehensive review. Plast Reconstr Surg 84:827, 1989.

116. Ruiz-Maldonado R, Tamayo L, Laterza AM, et al. Giant pigmented nevi: clinical, histopathologic, and therapeutic considerations. J Pediatr 120:906, 1992.

117. Rusch MD, Grunert BK, Sanger JR, et al. Psychological adjustment in children after traumatic disfiguring injuries: a 12-month follow-up. Plast Reconstr Surg 106:1451, 2000.

118. Schendel SA. Unilateral cleft lip repair: state of the art. Cleft Palate Craniofac J 37:335, 2000.

119. Serletti JM, Schingo VA Jr, Deuber MA, et al. Free tissue transfer in pediatric patients. Ann Plast Surg 36:561, 1996.

120. Silverglade D, Rubey RL. Nonsurgical management of burns to the lips and commissures. Clin Plast Surg 13:87, 1986.

121. Silverman HJ, Zuker RM, Morris S. Scalp as a donor site for grafts to facial and neck burns in children. Can J Surg 35:312, 1992.

122. Spira M. Otoplasty: what I do now—a 30-year retrospective. Plast Reconstr Surg 104:834, 1999.

123. Staley M, Richard R, Billmire D, Warden G. Head/face/neck burns: therapist considerations for the pediatric patient. J Burn Care Rehabil 18:164, 1997.

125. Stenstrom SJ, Heftner J. The Stenstrom otoplasty. Clin Plast Surg 5:465, 1978.

126. Stigmar G, Crawford JS, Ward CM, et al. Ophthalmologic sequelae of infantile hemangiomas of the eyelids and orbit. Am J Ophthalmol 85:806, 1978.

127. Strucker FJ, Shaw GY. An approach to management of keloids. Arch Otolaryngol Head Neck Surg 118:63, 1992.

128. Sugino H, Tsuzuki K, Bandoh Y, Tange I. Surgical correction of Stahl's ear using the cartilage turnover and rotation method. Plast Reconstr Surg 83:160, 1989.

129. Tallman BT, Tan OT, Morelli JG, et al. Location of port-wine stains and the likelihood of ophthalmic and/or central nervous system complications. Pediatrics 87:323, 1991.

130. Tanaka Y, Tajima S. Completely successful replantation of an amputated ear by microvascular anastomosis. Plast Reconstr Surg 84:665, 1989.

131. Tann KK, Pigott RW. A morbidity review of children with complete unilateral cleft lip-nose at 10 ± 1 years of age. Br J Plast Surg 46:1, 1993.

132. Tanzer RC. The constricted (cup and lop) ear. Plast Reconstr Surg 55:406, 1975.

133. Tark C. Arteriovenous malformations of face and scalp, histologic change after free flap transfer. Plast Reconstr Surg 106:87, 2000.

133a. Thorne CH, Brecht LE, Bradley JP, et al. Auricular reconstruction: indications for autogenous and prosthetic techniques. Plast Reconstr Surg 107:1241, 2001.

134. Tsujiguchi Y, Tajima S, Tanaka Y, Hira M. A new method of correction of Stahl's ear. Ann Plast Surg 28:373, 1992.

135. Vuyk HD. Cartilage-sparing otoplasty: a review with long-term results. J Laryngol Otol 111:424, 1997.

136. Walton R. Pigmented nevi. Pediatr Clin North Am 18:897, 1971.

137. Walton RG, Jacobs AH, Cox AJ. Pigmented lesions in newborn infants. Br J Dermatol 95:389, 1976.

138. Washio H. Cryptotia: pathology and repair. Plast Reconstr Surg 52:648, 1973.

139. Wexler MR, Peled IJ, Rand Y, et al. Rehabilitation of the face in patients with Down's syndrome. Plast Reconstr Surg 77:383, 1986.

140. Williams EF 3rd, Stanislaw P, Dupree M, et al. Hemangiomas in infants and children. An algorithm for intervention. Arch Facial Plast Surg 2:103, 2000.

141. Wilkes GH, Wolfaardt JF. Osseointegrated alloplastic versus autogenous ear reconstruction: criteria for treatment selection. Plast Reconstr Surg 93:967, 1994.

142. Winters J, Hurwitz DJ. Presurgical orthopedics in the management of unilateral cleft lip and palate. Special topic. Plast Reconstruct Surg 95:735, 1995.

143. Zide B, Karp N. Maximizing gain from rectangular tissue expanders. Plast Reconstr Surg 90:500, 1992.

42

Congenital Malformations of the Nose and Paranasal Sinuses

Arthur S. Hengerer, M.D., and Richard O. Wein, M.D.

Normal Embryonic Development

In order to better understand the congenital malformations of the nose and paranasal sinuses, a brief review of normal embryonic development is helpful.

Normal nasal development begins with the neural crest cells migrating from their origin in the dorsal neural folds (Fig. 42–1), proceeding laterally around the eye, and traversing the frontonasal process (Fig. 42–2). This change occurs during the fourth to twelfth weeks of embryonic life. During this time, neural crest cells migrate beneath the epithelium, through a meshwork of hyaluronic acid, and attach to collagen filaments within the facial processes. These pluripotential cells undergo rapid proliferation and differentiation into a matrix of mesenchymal tissue that forms muscle, cartilage, and early bone, thus creating the human facial configuration. During this process facial prominences develop surrounding an ectodermal invagination. This depression, the stomodeum, is surrounded by the frontonasal prominence superiorly, the maxillary prominences laterally, and the mandibular prominences inferiorly. Two small thickenings within the substance of the frontonasal process, representing the nasal placodes, begin to burrow and form nasal pits. Subdivisions of the frontonasal prominence, the lateral and medial nasal swellings, interact with the developing maxillary processes in creating multiple paramedian structures (nasal aperture, nasolacrimal ducts, and upper lip). Eruption of nasal pits into the choana, fusion of the palatal shelves, and growth of nasal septum and soft palate coincide with the development of the lateral nasal wall and primitive sinus anatomy. These changes occur rapidly and require unbelievable accuracy in mesenchymal migration if normal nasal and paranasal growth is to occur. A disruption in the sequence of this development will lead to many of the malformations discussed in this chapter (Fig. 42–3).

Encephaloceles and Nasal Gliomas

Nasal gliomas and encephaloceles are rare lesions of neurogenic origin. They are commonly grouped with dermoids in the differential diagnosis of congenital midline nasal masses (CMNMs). CMNMs occur once in every 20,000 to 40,000 live births.[1] Nasal gliomas lack a direct central nervous system (CNS) attachment, whereas encephaloceles maintain a cerebrospinal fluid (CSF) communication to the subarachnoid space. However, approximately 15% to 20% of gliomas demonstrate a fibrous stalk connecting to the subarachnoid space.

Nasal gliomas are locally aggressive lesions noted at birth or in early childhood. The name itself is misleading and is not to be confused with the malignant form of brain tumor. These benign lesions enlarge and present as either intranasal or extranasal masses. The most common presentation is extranasal (60%), followed by intranasal (30%) and combined lesions (10%). They are not familial but have a gender predilection for males over females of 3:1. In 1986, a review of the literature demonstrated 232 reported cases.[2]

Encephaloceles occur at a rate ranging from 1 in 3000[3] to 1 in 12,500[4] live births. However, this incidence does not reflect the number of children stillborn or lost to premature pregnancy and as a result represents an underestimate. Approximately 40% of infants with encephaloceles have other associated abnormalities. There is no reported familial association or sex predilection; however, a geographic and racial distribution for subgroups of lesions is noted. In North America and Europe, occipital encephaloceles represent three quarters of lesions diagnosed, whereas in Southeast Asia sincipital encephaloceles are nine times more common than occipital.[5] Encephaloceles are divided into occipital, sincipital, and basal types. Sincipital encephaloceles present around the nasal dorsum, orbits, and forehead and are associated with an external mass. Basal encephaloceles are less common and appear in the nasal cavity, nasopharynx, or posterior aspect of the orbits. Encephaloceles may also be subdivided with respect to contents. Meningoceles contain only meninges, encephalomeningoceles contain brain and meninges, and an encephalomeningocystoceles, in addition to brain and meninges, include part of the ventricular system.

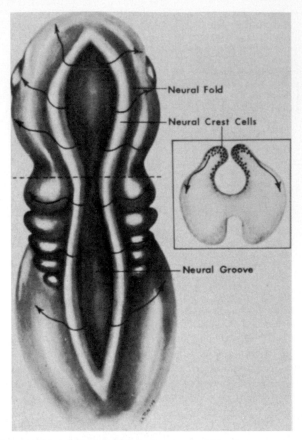

FIGURE 42–1. Dorsal view of a 3½-week-old embryo, representing neural fold. *Inset:* Cross-section locating neural crest cells within folds. (Courtesy of Hengerer AS, Oas R. Congenital Anomalies of the Nose: Their Embryology, Diagnosis, and Management. Washington, DC, The American Academy of Otolaryngology, Head and Neck Surgery Foundation, 1987, p 12.)

Embryology

Most believe encephaloceles and gliomas arise from the same embryonic defect: faulty closure of the foramen caecum at approximately the third week of fetal development, when the anterior neuropore closes. Pertinent spaces in the development of this region include the fonticulus nasofrontalis and the prenasal space. The fonticulus nasofrontalis represents the space between the developing nasal base and frontal bone. This site eventually fuses with the foramen caecum, creating a separation between intracranial and extracranial structures. Incomplete closure of this site results in a potential extranasal/nasofrontal path for herniation. Within the prenasal space, between the developing nasal bone and septal cartilage below the foramen caecum and extending to the nasal tip, lies a projection of prolapsed dura in close proximity to nasal skin (Fig. 42–4). As the foramen caecum closes, the diverticulum of dura detaches from the overlying ectoderm by an ingrowth of mesoderm. If there is an incomplete separation of the epithelial elements, brain tissue remains attached. This prevents mesodermal tissue, which will form the bony-cartilaginous skeleton of the midface, from migrating between them. Thus, an intrana-

sal bony defect is created through which the brain tissue can herniate (Fig. 42–5). If either the fonticulus nasofrontalis or foramen caecum should undergo closure and leave the rest of neural tissue extracranial, the postulated setting for a nasal glioma is established. Evidence that a portion of gliomas retain a fibrous stalk to the CNS lends support to a common developmental process.

Diagnosis

Extranasal gliomas usually appear near the root of the nose as smooth, firm, noncompressible lesions that do not transilluminate. The overlying skin may be discolored or telangiectatic (Fig. 42–6).

Intranasal gliomas are less common and appear as reddish, firm, noncompressible polypoid lesions in the nasal cavity. Intranasal gliomas tend to arise from the lateral nasal wall and allow passage of a probe medial to their base. Large gliomas may cause nasal obstruction, septal distortion, and hypertelorism. The fibrous stalk, seen in a minority of lesions, is more common with intranasal gliomas and displays a superior extent at the border of the cribriform plate.

Sincipital and basal encephaloceles appear as soft, bluish, compressible lesions that may transilluminate and pulsate. They may exhibit a positive Furstenburg sign (expansion of the mass with compression of the jugular veins) as opposed to other congenital midline nasal

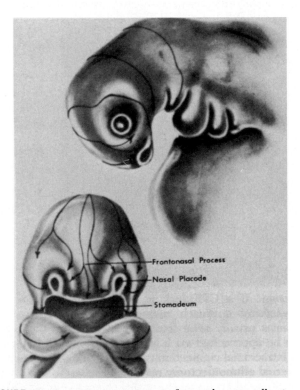

FIGURE 42–2. Migration patterns of neural crest cells. Arrows indicate routes followed by these cells to reach facial processes. (Courtesy of Hengerer AS, Oas R. Congenital Anomalies of the Nose: Their Embryology, Diagnosis, and Management. Washington, DC, The American Academy of Otolaryngology, Head and Neck Surgery Foundation, 1987, p 15.)

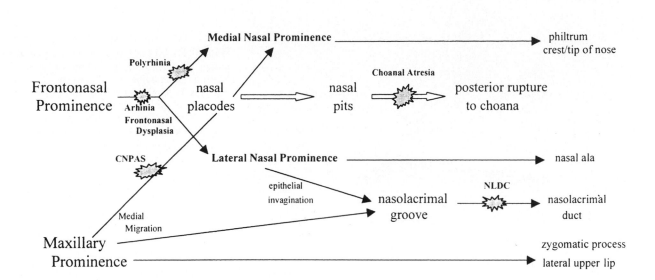

(CNPAS = congenital nasal pyriform aperture stenosis, NLDC = nasolacrimal duct cyst,
✶ = site of developmental insult)

FIGURE 42–3. Flow chart of embryologic midfacial/nasal development.

masses. Sincipital encephaloceles typically present as an extranasal mass (except nasoethmoidal) and may be accompanied by telecanthus and epiphora. Sincipital (also known as frontoethmoidal) encephaloceles must be differentiated from gliomas, congenital dermoid cysts of the nose, obstruction of the lacrimal sac apparatus, epidermal inclusion cysts, and other benign neoplasias of the nasofrontal areas.

Basal encephaloceles present as intranasal masses that arise from the midline and resist medial passage of a probe. They may be confused with polyps or nasal glioma on examination and require an imaging study to rule out intracranial communication prior to biopsy. A history of prior episodes of meningitis or presentation of CSF leak are not uncommon for these lesions.

Congenital dermoid cysts, with an associated sinus, are differentiated by the accompanying pit, which usually contains hair. The pit may be located anywhere between the glabella and the columella of the nose.

Epidermal inclusion cysts are not usually seen until

FIGURE 42–4. Anatomy of the base of the anterior cranial fossa and prenasal space during embryologic development. (Courtesy of Hengerer AS, Oas R. Congenital Anomalies of the Nose: Their Embryology, Diagnosis, and Management. Washington, DC, The American Academy of Otolaryngology, Head and Neck Surgery Foundation, 1987, p 45.)

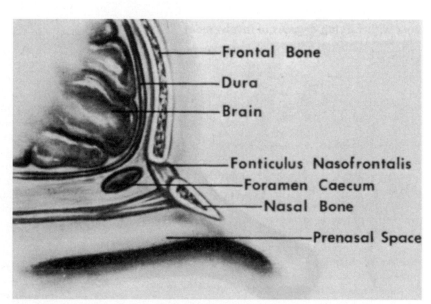

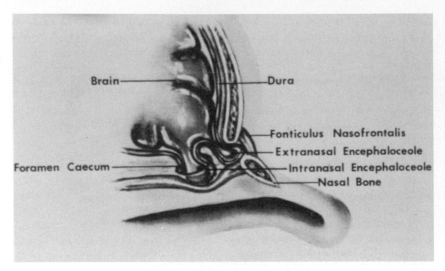

FIGURE 42–5. Pathways taken by neural elements that lead to formation of internal or external encephaloceles. (Courtesy of Hengerer AS, Oas R. Congenital Anomalies of the Nose: Their Embryology, Diagnosis, and Management. Washington, DC, The American Academy of Otolaryngology, Head and Neck Surgery Foundation, 1987, p 56.)

after puberty, whereas meningoencephaloceles are congenital defects.

Sincipital Encephaloceles

The bony defect in sincipital encephaloceles occurs between the frontal and ethmoid bones anterior to the crista galli, corresponding to the site of the foramen caecum. The limits of this space are the nasal, ethmoidal, frontal, and orbital bones. In the majority of patients, the defect is in the midline at the glabella. The size of the mass can vary from a slight elevation to an enormous mass larger than the infant's head. Typically, the larger the mass, the greater the degree of hypertelorism.

The osseous defect is constant; however, the location through which the herniated tissue emerges varies. In 1972, Suwanwela and Suwanwela[6] constructed the commonly used classification for sincipital encephaloceles: (1) nasofrontal, (2) nasoethmoidal, and (3) naso-orbital. Nasofrontal and nasoethmoidal (40% each) types are more common than naso-orbital (20%). Nasofrontal encephaloceles protrude through the site of the former fonticulus nasofrontalis. The defect for nasoethmoidal lesions lies between the nasal bone and cartilage, typically lower

along the nasal dorsum than nasofrontal types, with a superior border of the frontal process of the maxilla. Naso-orbital encephaloceles tend to emerge in the medial orbital wall.

In a review of 120 encephaloceles, Boonvisut et al proposed an additional classification for sincipital lesions. Defects were classified as type IA, IB, IIA, and IIB. Type I lesions demonstrated a single external opening from its bony boundaries, whereas type II lesions demonstrated multiple openings. Type A masses remained in proximity to adjacent bones, whereas type B masses demonstrated diffuse spread. In the study 88% of lesions were type I, of which 71% were also type A (type IA) indicating that most lesions demonstrated limited spread associated with a single opening.[7]

Brown and Sheridan-Pereira, in a review of 34 encephaloceles, noted a survival advantage for infants with anterior (sincipital and basal) defects as opposed to posterior (occipital) lesions. For children with anterior defects, only 17% had hydrocephalus, while only 25% had an identifiable brain abnormality. Those infants without brain abnormality or facial clefting were noted to have good outcomes. They also noted that the presence of a defect within the brain did not portend to a worse outcome, unless the defect was massive.[4] In contrast with the findings of Brown and Sheridan-Pereira, Hoving and Vermeij-Keers noted intracranial abnormalities in 22 of 30 patients with frontoethmoidal encephaloceles, of which 13 patients demonstrated hydrocephalus.[8]

Macfarlane et al performed a 15-year review of 114 cases of encephalocele in an attempt to define whether hypertelorism, associated with anterior defects, required simultaneous reconstruction or could be managed by simply allowing the facial skeleton to remodel after resection. Of these cases, 10% of the defects were sincipital, 4% were considered basal, and the remaining (71% occipital, 10% parietal) were posterior-based lesions. Of the anterior defects, 64% of patients demonstrated the diagnosis externally at birth and 73% were noted to have hypertelorism. All patients underwent transcranial repair at the average age of 2. No deaths occurred. Developmental outcome was normal in 59%, mild mental/physical disability was noted in 18%, and severe impairment was noted

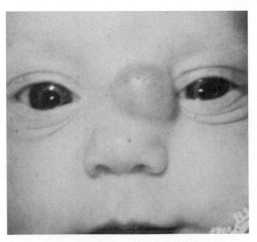

FIGURE 42–6. Nasal glioma.

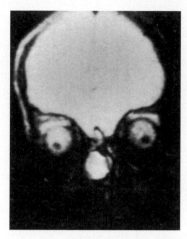

FIGURE 42–7. Magnetic resonance imaging (MRI) showing nasal glioma.

in 23% of patients. Patients with primary and secondary mild hypertelorism were noted to experience regression if the encephalocele was repaired prior to 2 to 3 years of age. As a result, Macfarlane et al advocate early treatment of anterior defects with mild hypertelorism to allow the facial skeleton to remodel with growth.[5] However, other authors propose one-stage reconstruction with orbital translocation[9] or medial orbital wall transposition to best address this issue.[5]

Basal Encephaloceles

Basal encephaloceles, considered the "hidden form," protrude through a defect in the cribriform plate or body of the sphenoid and appear as internal masses. Four types may occur: transethmoidal, sphenoethmoidal, transsphenoidal, and spheno-orbital. Gerhardt et al[10] also included sphenomaxillary as a fifth type in their classification of basal lesions; however, it is commonly excluded in most reports of such lesions. The transethmoidal type is the most common and appears as an anterior intranasal mass, along the cribriform plate, that does not involve the sella turcica. The sphenoethmoidal type also appears as a unilateral intranasal mass that may cause hypertelorism and broadening of the bony nasal vault. Transsphenoidal encephaloceles extend inferiorly from a defect in the floor of the sella turcica and as a result may include the pituitary gland and hypothalamus. Spheno-orbital lesions extend through the superior orbital fissure and result in exophthalmos.[11]

Patients with basal masses present more commonly with nasal-related symptoms such as mouth breathing, nasal obstruction, snoring, and nasal discharge. If the masses are large, they may present with an associated cleft palate.

Assessment

A complete head and neck examination accompanied by nasal endoscopy should prompt the need for additional assessment. A computed tomographic (CT) scan, in conjunction with magnetic resonance imaging (MRI), is the radiographic study of choice (Figs. 42–7 and 42–8). CT scan allows delineation of the bony anatomy and provides the ability to measure intraorbital distance.[5] MRI demonstrates the contents of the encephalocele sac, provides T_1-weighted images, and allows for assessment of associated brain anomalies. T_2-weighted images can help distinguish between bacterial versus fungal infection and inflammatory versus neoplastic processes.[12]

Treatment

Gliomas can be managed by transcranial, extracranial, and endoscopic approaches. Preoperative imaging should guide the selection of technique. An external glioma requires complete excision through an elliptic or Y incision over the nasal dorsum or external rhinoplasty approach. If a CSF leak is encountered, a bifrontal craniotomy ap-

FIGURE 42–8. *A,* Coronal MRI reveals an encephalocele extending into the left nasal cavity. *B,* Sagittal MRI reveals brain herniating into the nasal cavity. (Courtesy of Dr. Rodney Lusk, St. Louis, MO.)

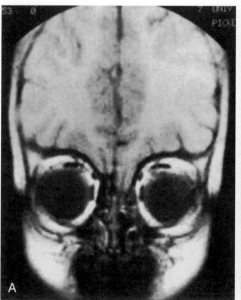
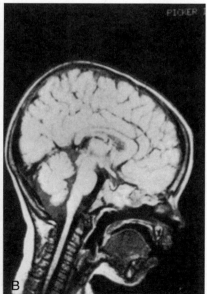

proach may be required. Intranasal gliomas usually arise from the lateral nasal wall and can be approached through a lateral rhinotomy incision. If an intracranial connection is found, a craniotomy or an external ethmoidectomy may be necessary.

Recent reports of experiences with endoscopic management of CSF leaks by Mattox and Kennedy[13] and Lanza et al[14] suggest that intranasal gliomas, regardless of intracranial communication, may be effectively managed by this technique. Mucoperiosteal grafts from a septal donor site or musculofascial graft (from temporalis muscle) with fibrin glue are used in the repair of the leak.[13, 14] With the advent of imaging guidance systems and powered instrumentation assisting the endoscopic surgery, the detail capable in such repairs would appear desirable compared with external approaches for intranasal gliomas.

Encephaloceles may also be repaired by transcranial, extracranial, and endoscopic techniques and require a CSF-leakproof closure of the dural defect. Those patients noted to have hydrocephalus on preoperative imaging may require shunt placement prior to surgery. Early surgical intervention to alleviate the increased risk of meningitis and minimize the cosmetic deformity is often a consideration. However, some studies advocate delay of repair to optimize a patient's general condition prior to intervention.[5] A frontal craniotomy allows accurate identification of the intracranial stalk as well as excellent visualization of the dural defects. Repair of defects may be performed with pericranial grafts or temporalis patches followed by transnasal snaring of the nasal component.[5] An extracranial repair can also be performed simultaneously or deferred to a later date. Small sincipital lesions may be amenable to extracranial repair alone. Surgical

routes for extracranial excision include lateral rhinotomy, osteoplastic flap, or sagittal approach over the root of the nose. Articles describing endoscopic management of intranasal encephaloceles demonstrate promising results, but only small numbers are yet to be reported.[13–15] The technique involves removal of overlying mucosa with bipolar cauterization to shrink the overall size of the mass. All attachments to intranasal tissues are divided to allow for retraction of any remaining stalk followed by grafting with bone, cartilage, myofascia, mucoperiosteal flaps, and fibrin glue.[14, 15] Success rate for endoscopic repair of CSF leak for Lanza et al was 94.4% in 36 patients, 12 of which presented with an encephalocele.[14]

Dermoid Cysts of the Nose

Dermoid cysts, much like gliomas and encephaloceles, are considered within the differential of congenital midline nasal masses and represent the most common entity in this grouping (Fig. 42–9). Unlike teratomas, which contain all three embryonal germ layers, congenital dermoid cysts contain only ectodermal and mesodermal embryonic elements. Mesodermal elements, which include hair follicles, adnexal sweat glands, and sebaceous glands found in the wall of the dermoid cyst, differentiate it from simple epidermoid cysts. Nasal dermoids account for approximately 10% of head and neck dermoids and 1% to 2% of all dermoids.[16] Nasal dermoid cysts are benign lesions, with a slight male predominance,[17] usually occurring in a random fashion, although a familial tendency has been reported. Associated congenital anomalies vary in frequency from 5.3% to 41% and include hydrocephalus, aural atresia, and cardiac and cerebral anomalies.[17]

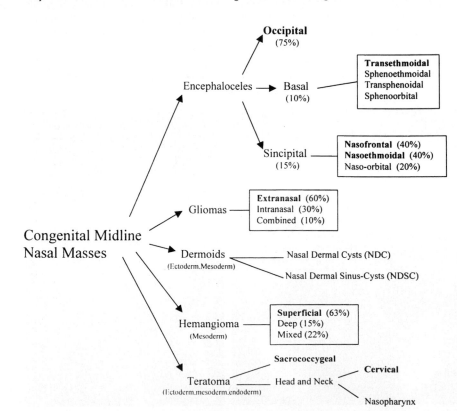

FIGURE 42–9. Flow chart demonstrating congenital midline nasal mass differential diagnosis.

Embryology

Multiple theories exist that explain nasal dermoid development. Sessions divided these theories into cranial and cutaneous developmental errors.[18] Luongo[19] developed the prenasal space theory in an effort to explain the origin of nasal dermoids. As mentioned previously when discussing encephalocele and glioma development, the prenasal space extends from the dura at the base of the skull along the nasal midline to the nasal tip. During embryonic development, this dura develops in close approximation with the skin of the nose. Normally, however, the dura separates from the nasal skin and retracts through the foramen caecum, losing its connection with the skin. If faulty separation or obliteration of the prenasal space occurs, a dermal sinus or cyst may persist anywhere from the foramen caecum to the nasal tip (Fig. 42–10).

Failure of the fonticulus nasofrontalis or foramen caecum to close allows dermal elements to invaginate through the frontonasal suture line area or between the developing nasal bones and cartilage.

Sites of Involvement

Nasal dermoids usually present along the nasal dorsum (Fig. 42–11) typically with a single pit with extruding hair. However, cystic remnants, with or without associated infected fistulas, may present in the forehead, gla-

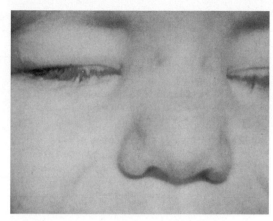

FIGURE 42–11. Nasal dermoid on the dorsum with a single fistula on each side.

bella, nasal tip, or columella or along the nose to the sphenoid sinus with varying degrees of involvement.

Diagnosis

Nasal dermoids can present as an external mass, an intranasal mass, a dermoid sinus without a cyst, a dermoid cyst without a fistula, or a widened nasal base from an extracranial-intracranial mass. In 1982, in an effort to develop a common terminology, Sessions suggested the use of nasal dermal cyst to describe lesions without a sinus tract and nasal dermal sinus cyst (NDSC) to describe those with a sinus tract.[18] Clinically, the dermoid lesion is firm, noncompressible, nonpulsatile, and occasionally lobulated (Table 42–1). Rates of intracranial spread with dural contact range from 4% to 45%.[17] CT scan findings of a wide bifid septum and crista galli and enlarged foramen caecum are suggestive of intracranial spread and warrant appropriate surgical planning.

In an effort to avoid an unnecessary intracranial approach, with the associated 5% risk of postoperative epilepsy, MRI is suggested to correlate findings when the CT scan is suspicious for intracranial spread[17] (Fig. 42–12). However, the ossification process of the lamina perpendicularis (of the ethmoid) and crista galli, occurring between 1 and 5 years of age, can mislead the interpretation of MRI and CT in diagnosing intracranial spread of NDSC.[20]

Dermoids may very rarely present with associated complications of meningitis, cavernous sinus thrombosis, subdural abscess, or periorbital cellulitis. Nasal dermoid cysts must be differentiated from sebaceous cysts, which are also attached to the skin but which are usually not seen before puberty. Nasal dermoid cysts may be differentiated from meningoceles by the fact that meningoceles characteristically transilluminate, whereas dermoids and gliomas do not.

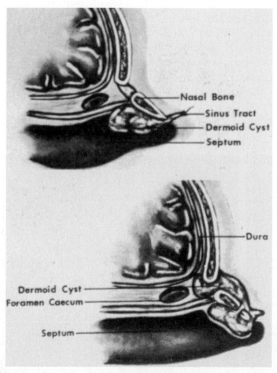

FIGURE 42–10. *Top,* Location of dermoid cyst extending deep to the nasal bones. *Bottom,* Other pathways possible for dermoid cyst and sinus tract development. (Courtesy of Hengerer AS, Oas R. Congenital Anomalies of the Nose: Their Embryology, Diagnosis, and Management. Washington, DC, The American Academy of Otolaryngology, Head and Neck Surgery Foundation, 1987, p 46.)

Treatment

Successful management of dermoid lesions requires complete excision to prevent recurrence. A small, superficial cyst can easily be removed through an incision over the

TABLE 42-1. Differential Diagnosis of Congenital Midline Nasal Masses

	Encephalocele	Glioma	Dermoid
Age	Infants, children	Infants, children	Usually children, rarely adults
Location of mass	Intranasal and extranasal	Intranasal and extranasal	Intranasal and extranasal
Appearance	Soft, bluish, compressible	Reddish blue, solid, noncompressible	Solid, dimple with hair follicle
Pulsation	Yes	No	No
Transillumination	Yes	No	No
CSF leak	Yes	Rarely	Rarely
Furstenburg sign	Present	Absent	Absent
Cranial defect	Yes	Rarely	Rarely
Previous history	Meningitis	Rarely meningitis	Local infection

CSF, cerebrospinal fluid.

nasal dorsum. When a sinus is present, it should be excised with an elliptic incision.

If complete removal of an NDSC is not achieved, progressive expansion, infection, and fistula formation will occur. Surgical treatment must include the excision of cystic structures extending through and beneath the nasal bones into the septum or along the superior nasal septum posteriorly toward the pituitary. Surgery for removal of nasal dermoid cysts is usually dependent on the rate of growth potentially leading to nasal framework complications. Patients may be followed, and if an accelerated rate of growth with nasal destruction is noted, then surgery may be required more urgently. If the growth is slow with no nasal framework complications, surgery can be delayed until just prior to the child's entry to school. However, others advocate early intervention, regardless of growth rate, because of the potential for infectious complications.[17] The surgeon should consider reconstructive options for the area of excision prior to surgery.

In a review of 36 patients with nasal dermoid sinus cysts, Denoyelle et al[17] performed three separate approaches: external rhinoplasty with medial crura section, direct median approach, and paracanthal approach. A 2-year recurrence rate of 5.5% was achieved. They advo-

cated the external rhinoplasty approach as the technique of choice as several other authors have concluded.[21, 22] It provides capacity for wide exposure, adequate control of osteotomies, and ability to follow a tract to the level of skull base with a satisfactory aesthetic result.[17, 22] Growth disturbance, as a result of the approach, is considered minor.[21] Costal cartilage grafts have been used to correct the postexcision dorsal deformity with desirable results.[21] Children undergoing verticomedian approaches can experience widening of the resultant scar in over 50% of cases.[17]

Bifrontal craniotomy, in selected cases, has been proposed for its ability to provide adequate incisional camouflage, wide exposure, control of osteotomies, and adequate exposure of the cribriform plate. It also provides the ability to simultaneously harvest split calvarial bone graft for use in nasal reconstruction.[23] In lesions with intracranial spread noted preoperatively, naso-orbital osteotomy with rhinotomy following anterior craniotomy provides a means for en bloc resection.[22]

In cases in which the operating surgeon is uncertain about the superior margin of dissection, frozen section biopsy of the stalk has been described. If the frozen section is negative for residual epithelial elements, the

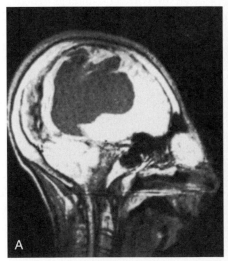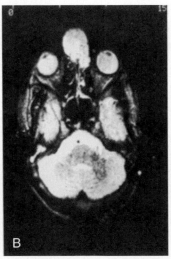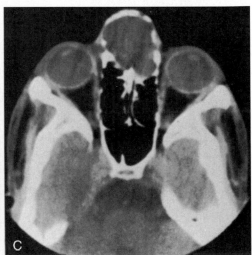

FIGURE 42-12. *A,* Sagittal MRI showing a large glabellar mass found to be a nasal dermoid at the time of surgery. *B,* Axial MRI of the same mass. *C,* Computed tomographic scan of the nasal dermoid. (Courtesy of Dr. Rodney Lusk, St. Louis, MO.)

TABLE 42–2. Severe Degrees of Holoprosencephaly (Arrhinencephaly)

Type of Facies*	Facial Features	Cranium and Brain
Cyclopia	Single eye or partially divided eye in single orbit; arrhinia with proboscis	Microcephaly; alobar holoprosencephaly
Ethmocephaly	Extreme orbital hypotelorism but separate orbits; arrhinia with proboscis	Microcephaly; alobar holoprosencephaly
Cebocephaly	Orbital hypotelorism, proboscis-like nose but no median cleft of lip	Microcephaly; usually has alobar holoprosencephaly
With median cleft lip	Orbital hypotelorism, flat nose	Microcephaly and sometimes trigonocephaly; usually has alobar holoprosencephaly
With median philtrum-premaxilla anlage	Orbital hypotelorism, bilateral cleft of lip with median process representing philtrum-premaxilla anlage	Microcephaly and sometimes trigonocephaly; semilobar or lobar holoprosencephaly

* This table presents five facies diagnostic of holoprosencephaly. Although transitional cases do occur, the facies of each category are remarkably similar from patient to patient.

procedure is completed. If residual elements are noted, the conversion to a combined intracranial/extracranial approach would be required.[24]

Complete Agenesis of the Nose

The absence of the external and internal nasal anatomy is an uncommon malformation. Referred to as arhinia, nasal aplasia, and complete nasal agenesis, a limited number of case reports of individual cases exist within the literature. Associations with arhinia and trisomy 13[25] (with lumbosacral and thoracic malformations and sphenoid irregularities) and trisomy 21[26] (cervical/thoracic/lumbosacral malformations) have been reported. Gifford and MacCollum[27] reported their experience with two cases of arhinia and their repair. The two infants adapted well after birth to oral breathing and feeding; however, this is not uniformly the case with other reports. They described the feeding style of these children as canine-like and expressed concern of the psychological impact of this habit. Establishment of a nasal airway was deferred until age 5 or 6 years. Their technique involves initially elevating the soft palate mucosa and drilling through the hard palate and widening this primitive nasal cavity with a

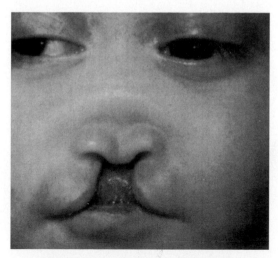

FIGURE 42–13. Central facial hypoplasia.

Kerrison punch, followed by closure of the soft palate and placement of skin graft lined Silastic stents. The high-arched palate facilitated performance of the technique; however, several maxillary incisors required removal for access.[27] This technique provided an adequate airway and had the ability to support an external nasal prosthesis. Nasal reconstruction can be considered when facial growth has completed.

When arhinia is found in presentation with holoprosencephaly (cyclopia and ethmocephaly), long-term survival is considered unrealistic. Nasal aplasia has been noted to present with bilateral bony choanal atresia, hypoplastic maxilla, orbital hypotelorism, microphthalmos, and coloboma of the iris.[28] Shubach and Sanchez have reported a case with associated meningocele and submucous cleft.[29] Latrenta et al reported a patient with frontonasal encephalocele and bifid thumb.[30] Given these potential associated findings, preoperative evaluation with MRI and CT scan to rule out associated malformations is warranted. Postbirth feeding and airway issues are addressed in a fashion similar to those patients with bilateral choanal atresia. Issues with feeding may necessitate placement of a gastrostomy tube prior to repair. It should be recognized that despite the presence of the anomaly, these patients may possess normal intelligence. Finally, true of most craniofacial malformations, care from a multidisciplinary craniofacial team provides these patients the best chance at successful repair.

Median Facial Clefting and Malformations

Ocular hypertelorism, abnormal increased distance between the orbits, not to be confused with telecanthus, increased distance between inner canthi, is a typical finding seen with midline facial and nasal malformations. In 1967, DeMyer categorized multiple abnormal facial features associated with ocular hypertelorism in describing median cleft face syndrome. The hallmarks of this disorder are (1) ocular hypertelorism; (2) broad nasal root; (3) lack of formation of the nasal tip; (4) widow's peak scalp bone anomaly; (5) anterior cranium bifidum occultum; (6) median clefting of the nose, lip, and palate (Fig. 42–13); and (7) unilateral orbital clefting or notching of the nasal ala.[31] DeMyer and colleagues believed that an association between hypertelorism, cephalic anomalies, and the probability of mental deficiency existed in these patients. They noted that the severity of hypertelorism and number of extracephalic anomalies present correlated with a child's likelihood of being mentally deficient. If, on the other hand, the degree of hypertelorism was mild and there were no extracephalic anomalies, the chance that normal or nearly normal CNS formation had occurred was favorable.[31]

Sedano et al[32] modified the DeMyer classification by dividing median facial clefting and lateral notching of the ala nasi into separate categories. Sedano called this nongenetic, congenital disorder frontonasal dysplasia. The groupings ranged from A to D, each including ocular hypertelorism, broad nasal root, and cranium bifidum occultam, and varying with respect to median nasal groove (type A), midline facial groove/true cleft (type B), and notching of ala nasi (type C). Type D represents a combination of types B and C. The two methods of classification, although different, tend to be used interchangeably within the literature.

To further understand median facial anomalies, Tessier[34] proposed a classification based on specific axes (0–14) along the face and cranium. Since the orbit is common to the face and cranium, it conveniently serves to divide the cranial clefts (9–14) from the facial clefts (0–8).[34] The patient with median facial cleft syndrome (or frontonasal dysplasia) would be considered 0/14 per Tessier grading.

Distinct from these descriptions is that of "tissue-deficient" median cerebrofacial dysmorphogenesis. In attempting to describe cases of median facial anomalies with cerebral malformations, DeMyer and associates[33] proposed the term holoprosencephaly for the types of brain morphology witnessed (Table 42–2). Holoprosencephaly is a failure of the embryonic forebrain to cleave sagittally and transversely into cerebral hemispheres, transversely into a diencephalon, and horizontally into olfactory and optic bulbs. Three types of holoprosencephaly exist: lobar, semilobar, and alobar. Five types of facial malformation were matched with these specific brain morphologies (see Table 42–2). Of note, alobar holoprosencephaly, the severest form, in which there is no separation of the cerebral hemispheres and a common single ventricle, is rarely associated with life beyond 1 year of age. Thus, surgical reconstruction of the first three types (cyclopia, ethmocephaly, and cebocephaly) is not considered.[33] The first gene identified as causing holoprosencephaly in humans is the Sonic Hedgehog (SHH) gene.[35] Testing for the SHH gene allows identification of familial forms and evaluation of malformations considered microforms of the disorder.

Embryologically, these defects are formed by a marked reduction in the number of migrating neural crest cells, causing multiple defects in the facial mesenchyme and forebrain derivatives.

Median Nasal Cleft

The severity of malformation in a median nasal cleft deformity is extremely variable, ranging from a simple me-

dian scar at the cephalic end of the nasal dorsum to a completely split nose, forming separate halves and creating independent medial walls. Also known as bifid nose and internasal dysplasia, the anomaly is frequently associated with a median cleft lip.[36] The airway is usually adequate despite the cosmetic appearance. Before surgical reconstruction of these defects, which requires a multidisciplinary approach in severe cases, it is important to rule out a possible dermoid cyst or encephalocele within the nasal-septal area.

Lateral Nasal Clefts

Lateral nasal clefts are rare anomalies involving defects in the nasal alae or lateral nasal wall area. The etiology of lateral nasal clefts involves a mix-up in mesenchymal flow between the medial and the lateral nasal processes. Involvement of the clefts ranges from scarlike lines in the alae to triangle-like defects in the alae that may extend to the inner canthal fold, affecting the nasal lacrimal duct system.

Proboscis Lateralis

Proboscis lateralis is an unusual deformity in which the medial and lateral nasal processes, as well as the globular process, are absent. This causes the maxillary prominence of the affected side to fuse with the opposite nasal and globular processes, forming a tubular structure composed of skin and soft tissue that is attached at the inner canthus. There may be coexistent maldevelopment of the nasal cavity varying from a normal to complete agenesis of the nasal cavity and the paranasal sinuses on the affected side (Fig. 42–14).

The embryology of this lesion is uncertain. The most commonly accepted theory is that imperfect mesodermal proliferation occurs in the frontonasal and maxillary processes after formation of the olfactory pits. Epidermal breakdown then takes place, leaving the lateral nasal process sequestered as a tube arising in the frontonasal re-

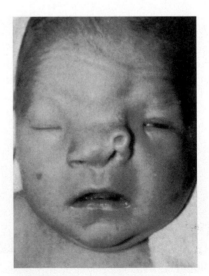

FIGURE 42–14. Proboscis lateralis.

gion. Also, as a result of the epidermal breakdown, no nasolacrimal duct is produced.[37]

When these defects are reconstructed, as much of the soft tissue as is needed may be taken from the tube; the remainder is sacrificed. The skeletal deficiency may be corrected with bone and cartilage grafting.

Polyrhinia (Double Nose)

This defect is an exceedingly rare anomaly associated with pseudohypertelorism. It is hypothesized that the usual development of the frontonasal process is altered. The formation of the two lateral processes of the nose develops as usual. However, the medial nasal processes and septal elements are duplicated, thus forming double noses. Surgical correction involves a transnasal approach to correct the associated choanal atresia, followed by removal of both medial portions of both noses and anastomosis of both lateral halves in the midline.[49]

Cleft Lip with Nasal Deformity

Children with cleft lip and palate usually have a coexisting nasal deformity. With unilateral clefts, the nasal ala on the side of the cleft is laterally based, giving the appearance of a flat, flaring nostril. The dome is retrodisplaced, the columella foreshortened, and an alar-columellar web is present. The caudal septum is displaced to the noncleft side with variable severity. The maxilla on the cleft side is frequently hypoplastic. The nasal tip may also have a bifid appearance.

The most severe defects are those associated with a bilateral complete cleft. Individuals with such deformity frequently have short columellas, 1 to 2 mm in length, and a flattened nasal tip. They may also have bilateral maxillary hypoplasia with relative prognathism.

Children with clefts can have severe nasal septal deformities, which may lead to airway issues. In some instances a conservative septal approach may be required. The surgeon should be aware that the improvement in the nasal airway may have a deleterious effect on speech, leaving the individual with a velopharyngeal incompetence.

Treatment options include primary and secondary rhinoplasty. Primary rhinoplasty, at the time of lip repair, offers improved long-term results with excellent symmetry. This option remains the technique of choice for many surgeons. The possibility for future revision remains viable in these patients and may be required, depending upon the functional and cosmetic results of primary repair. Both open and closed techniques have been described; however, a preference for open technique, given the relative size of the patient's nasal anatomy, has been noted.

Secondary rhinoplasty can be divided into two types: definitive and intermediate. Intermediate rhinoplasty requires two stages of repair. The first stage, at 4 to 6 years of age, is done to provide cosmetic improvement prior to the start of the school years. The second stage, performed at 8 to 12 years of age, comes after orthodontic correction when an optimal skeletal framework is avail-

able. Definitive rhinoplasty is delayed until skeletal growth is completed and is thus performed at 16 to 18 years of age. Madorsky and Wang,[38] in their review of the topic, point out two major concepts of repair: (1) addressing the insufficiency of vestibular skin through advancement of a chondrocutaneous flap and (2) aggressive approach to the alar-columellar web. Use of columellar struts and shield grafts can also provide greater resultant stability and improved cosmetic results. The number of technical approaches to repair is plentiful and as such should allow the surgeon to tailor the technique to the patient's specific problem.

In the children in whom the degree of unilateral maxillary hypoplasia is severe, an implant under the ala of an alloplastic material or costal cartilage can be used to correct this defect.

Choanal Atresia

The first description of choanal atresia came in 1755 by Johann Roederer in describing a newborn with posterior nasochoanal obstruction. The frequency of choanal atresia quoted within the literature varies. Multiple resources note the incidence to be between 1 in 5000 to 7000 live births. Harris et al, reviewing the relationship of the CHARGE association in 444 infants with choanal atresia, examined data from the registries of Central-East France, Sweden, and California. The average incidence for the three regions was 1 in 12,200 with a range of 1 in 8,849 to 1 in 18,500 births.[40] In this review of greater than 5 million births, the female-to-male ratio was noted to be equivalent with no evidence of side predilection.[40] The frequency of unilateral versus bilateral atresia, commonly felt to be 2:1, may be biased by the delayed detection of unilateral cases and potential inclusion of choanal stenoses within statistics. Many large reviews currently demonstrate a 1:1 ratio.[39–41]

The original classification of choanal atresia described by J.S. Fraser in 1910, of bony (90%) versus membranous (10%), has also changed. In a study performed by Brown et al, the CT scans of 63 patients with choanal atresia were reviewed. Their findings noted an incidence of pure bony atresia of 29% versus that of a mixed bony-membranous atresia in 71% of patients. No patients demonstrating a purely membranous atresia were identified.[42] Associated major congenital anomalies have been reported to occur in 47% of patients with choanal atresia.[40]

Syndromes associated with choanal atresia include Apert syndrome, Digeorge sequence, trisomy 18, Treacher Collins syndrome, camptomelic dysplasia, and CHARGE association.[43] The CHARGE association, a nonrandom association of malformations, was first described by Hall in 1979.[44] The acronym—standing for coloboma, heart defects, atresia of choanae, retarded growth or development of the CNS, genitourinary anomalies, and ear anomalies or deafness—was coined by Pagon et al in 1981.[45] The diagnosis of the syndrome requires patients to demonstrate three or more of the cardinal malformations, excluding growth/mental retardation. Choanal atresia has been shown to be present in 7% to 56% of patients felt to have the CHARGE association.[40, 46] Those patients with the diagnosis of CHARGE association have a relatively high frequency of anatomic airway anomalies with resultant respiratory compromise. This finding was noted regardless of choanal patency.[47] The need for tracheostomy is seen in 14% to 30% of patients.[46, 47] CHARGE association patients with choanal atresia have also been noted to demonstrate a higher rate of surgical failure with repair of their atresia and as a result require special attention in treatment planning.[48]

Embryology

Several theories have been proposed to explain the etiology of choanal atresia. These theories include persistence of the buccopharyngeal membrane from the foregut, persistence of the nasobuccal membrane, and the abnormal persistence of mesoderm with the formation of adhesions within the choana. In addition, a fourth theory by Hengerer and Oas[49] proposes misdirection of mesodermal flow secondary to local factors. As discussed earlier, neural crest cells migrate through a meshwork of hyaluronic acid and collagen filaments to reach a preordained position in the nasofrontal prominence. This site, the ectodermal invaginations known as nasal placodes, presents at the third week of fetal development. The ventral portion of the forebrain provides the inductive influence over this

development. If the flow of the neural crest cells is altered with regard to their position or total numbers, the burrowing of the nasal pits may not create the same rotation from the ventrodorsal to the cephalocaudal plane. Thus, the thinning that allows breakthrough at the nasobuccal membrane is altered, resulting in choanal atresia (Fig. 42–15). With normal growth the rupture of the nasobuccal membrane to the stomodeum occurs at the sixth week of development. The palatine shelves, which appear at the sixth week, begin to fuse in the midline at the seventh week to create the secondary palate. The inferior descent of the nasal septum results in fusion with the palate at the ninth week, further defining the region of the choana. By the twelfth week, the posterior growth of the soft palate has separated the nasopharynx from the oral cavity.

Abnormal development of these additional events results in anatomic variations typically associated with choanal atresia. These variations include medial displacement of the lateral nasal walls, an accentuated arch of the hard palate, and a shortened nasopharyngeal vault. These findings would seem to suggest that the development of choanal atresia is not an isolated event but rather a generalized process. The final boundaries of the atresia plate include the vomer medially, the medial pterygoid lamina laterally, the body of sphenoid superiorly, and the secondary palate inferiorly.[50]

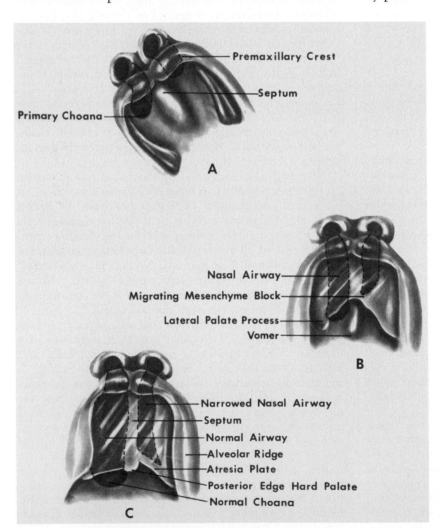

FIGURE 42–15. *A*, Unopened primary choana. *B*, Partial closure of palatal processes with a mesenchyme block migrating posteriorly. *C*, Atresia plate at the posterior choana. Note the tangential plane across the choana.

Diagnosis

The initial presentations of unilateral versus bilateral choanal atresia tend to be markedly different. Bilateral choanal atresia in the newborn presents with the immediate onset of respiratory distress. Paradoxical cyanosis, the relief of airway obstruction with crying and with return of cyanosis with rest, may be noted. Intervention via insertion of an oral airway is often required. This situation occurs because neonates are initially obligate nasal breathers. The relationship of the neonatal tongue to the palate perpetuates this obstruction. The use of a McGovern nipple (a nipple modified with enlarged perforations at the tip) or oral airway acts as a means of breaking this seal and may provide an alternative temporary airway. Mouth breathing, a learned response, occurs approximately 4 to 6 weeks after birth. A child with choanal stenosis may present as a failure-to-thrive infant secondary to an inability to maintain an adequate airway during feeding yet not demonstrate the airway distress classic for bilateral choanal atresia.

Unilateral atresia rarely causes acute respiratory distress and may remain initially undiagnosed. The most common presentation is that of a unilateral nasal obstruction with accompanying mucoid rhinorrhea. Misdiagnosis as chronic pediatric sinusitis may occur.

Many methods to assess for the presence of choanal atresia exist. If a 6 French catheter placed in the nasal cavity fails to pass into the oropharynx, choanal atresia should be suspected. Care should taken when performing this technique to prevent accidental epistaxis that could complicate assessment and potentially the airway stability. A simple bedside test to assess for nasal patency employs a compressed bulb syringe placed in the nasal airway of question. If it remains compressed, the choana is sealed. Examination of the nasal cavity with a flexible nasopharyngoscope is diagnostic and allows visualization of the atresia plate. However, axial CT scan remains the study of choice to delineate the type of atresia and aid with operative planning (transpalatal versus transnasal approach). Adequate preparation of the patient before scanning by aspirating secretions and use of decongestant drops helps ensure the best quality radiographic result (Fig. 42–16). Significant observations that can be made at this time, beyond the type of atresia plate, are the width of the vomer and degree of lateral nasal wall impingement, creating an "hourglass" deformity. Slovis et al defined this space between the two as the choanal air space and noted that its approximate size from birth to age 2 was 7 mm.[51]

Choanal stenosis is defined as choanal narrowing to less than 6 mm (by CT scan), inability to pass a 6 French catheter transnasally more than 32 mm, and endoscopic verification of the suspected diagnosis. It differs from choanal atresia in that surgical treatment is often not required.[52]

In patients with bilateral bony atresias, CT scanning has helped demonstrate that one side is typically narrower than the other. Coniglio et al noted the importance of CT in assessment of CHARGE association patients given their predilection for midline craniofacial malformations.[48] Development of the ipsilateral maxillary sinus has

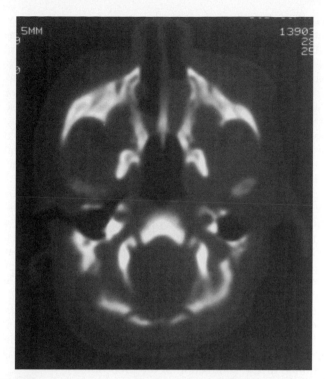

FIGURE 42–16. Axial view CT scan showing bilateral choanal atresia.

been shown to be independent of the presence of choanal atresia. As a result, these patients are not predisposed anatomically to the development of sinusitis.[53]

Treatment

The timing and technique of surgical correction of choanal atresia are dependent upon a patient's clinical presentation and type of atresia. Bilateral cases require initial intervention to address the need for airway assistance prior to surgical planning. Upon stabilizing the airway, via an oropharyngeal airway, nutritional supplementation by nasogastric tube feedings should be initiated. Cases in which an infant requires tracheostomy secondary to aerodigestive tract or cardiac malformations as seen with the CHARGE association, allow for delay in definitive repair. Timing is dependent upon an infant's ability to adapt to oral breathing and acquire adequate nutrition during the first weeks of life. Some surgeons have advocated that a "rule of tens" to guide the timing of intervention, meaning that the child must reach at least 10 weeks of age, 10 lb in weight, and 10 g of hemoglobin.

Today three basic technical approaches to the repair of bilateral and unilateral atresia are used: transpalatal, transseptal, and transnasal. The first technique, developed by Emmert in 1853, was transnasal blind puncture through the atretic plate. Complications of CSF leaks, midbrain trauma, and Gradenigo syndrome make this approach one of historical significance only.

The transpalatal approach was traditionally favored for repair of bony and bilateral atresia, as it provided excellent access for direct visualization. Described drawbacks include increased operative time, blood loss, risk of oronasal fistula, and the incidence of crossbite and midface retrusion. Malocclusion has been noted to occur in up to 50% of patients. Freng attributed this finding to resection of the midpalatal suture line prior to completion of palatal growth.[54] The transpalatal approach allows for preservation of mucosal flaps, effective removal of the posterior septum, and drill access to the lateral nasal wall. These attributes make this technique a desirable option for revision cases. Placement of nasal stents for an extended period is expected. Prisig, in his review of 300 patients on the topic of treatment options, recommended against performing the transpalatal approach before 6 years of age.[55]

The transseptal approach has been considered primarily for use with unilateral atresias in older children. The removal of a portion of posterior nasal septum, creating a window between the two nasal cavities, has the potential of providing a simple and rapid solution for selected patients. If repair is carried further posteriorly, this approach will provide a single central choana rather than individual nasal ports capable of stenosis. Muntz describes a mucosa-sparing technique similar to a Cottle septal approach with the option of sublabial incision, which utilizes endoscopic visualization. Removal of bony septum is performed with bone forceps or drill, and stenting is required at the completion of the procedure.[56]

The transnasal approach has experienced a revolution paralleling the development of endoscopic equipment and techniques. Once considered the repair reserved for "membranous" atresias, endoscopic repair has evolved into the technique of choice for all types of atresia plates.

Stankiewicz is credited with the first series report of endoscopic repair of choanal atresia. His review of four patients, with ages ranging from 5 months to 2.5 years, demonstrated patency in three of the patients after at least 6 months of follow-up. After nasal preparation, a 2.5- to 4-mm rigid endoscope is used in combination with tympanoplasty and pediatric sinus instruments. A bilateral vertical mucosal incision in the posterior bony septum is made with a round knife, and flaps are raised. An inferomedial perforation within the atresia plate is then created that is amenable to serial dilation. Entrance into the nasopharynx is verified after puncture through the atresia plate by visualizing a cotton pledget placed within the nasopharynx at the start of the case. The bony margins of the atresia plate are then evacuated with otologic drill or angled forceps, and the posterior septum is addressed with backbiting forceps until 5 mm of posterior bony septum is resected. Mucosal flaps are replaced and stents are inserted. Stents remain in place for up to 3 weeks.[57] Alternative techniques include the use of microdebriders.

Use of CO_2 and Nd-YAG lasers has been described with transnasal approach. CO_2 laser appears to offer benefit in the treatment of postoperative granulation tissue or scarring. Limitations include access, particularly with patients with septal deviation and arched palates, and inability to address bone without increasing the risk of surrounding soft tissue injury.

A survey conducted by Park et al, in March 1999, of technique preference for the treatment of choanal atresia revealed the current technique of choice for most was an endoscopic approach followed by transpalatal repair, 85% to 60%, respectively. The average length of stenting was 5.8 weeks, during which 93% used a modified endotracheal tube. The survey showed that 87% of respondents place patients on postoperative antibiotics.[58] The senior author of this chapter has used only endoscopic repair in the past 25 cases with 100% success and only 1 revision required.

Nasal Obstruction Without Choanal Atresia

Nasal obstruction without choanal atresia (NOWCA) is a recently described condition that typically presents 3 to 6 weeks after birth, and produces symptoms that may mimic those of choanal atresia. A functional nasal obstruction secondary to adenoid hypertrophy, choanal stenosis, medial impingement of the lateral nasal wall, and edematous mucosal changes, alone or in combination, may occur. Of significant difference to choanal atresia is that NOWCA is generally considered a nonoperative obstruction that should resolve with facial growth. Contencin et al demonstrated that growth at anterior and posterior limits of the nasal cavity (piriform aperture and choana) occurs more rapidly than the middle nasal fossa width. These results suggest that topical treatment with nasal saline and steroids in these infants may be less successful than the results of simple growth over time.[59]

Congenital Nasal Piriform Aperture Stenosis

Congenital nasal piriform aperture stenosis (CNPAS) was first described by Brown et al in 1989, in a review of six patients presenting with symptoms of poor nasal airway, problematic feeding, apneic episodes/retractions relieved with crying, and inability to pass a flexible laryngoscope through the nasal cavity.[60] CNPAS can be considered similar to a bilateral choanal atresia or stenosis of the anterior nasal cavity. Explanation for the finding requires a brief review of the embryology of the region. The migration of the maxillary prominence toward the medial nasal prominence, as the lateral process remains superior to this development, results in the lateral aspect of the piriform aperture. A displacement of the maxillary prominence medially results in CNPAS (Fig. 42–17). The etiology of this finding remains unclear. Brown et al postulate that an overgrowth of ossification in this area is responsible for the anomaly.[60]

Physical examination reveals a narrow anterior nasal airway (1 to 2 mm) secondary to medial protrusion of a lateral bony shelf at the aperture. CT scan provides verification of the diagnosis. Patients may also present with a maxillary "megaincisor." Arlis and Ward noted that the presence of a megaincisor was also common in holoprosencephaly and suggested that CNPAS potentially represented an autosomal-dominant microform of the disorder. Their conclusions were that patients with megaincisor eruption should be considered candidates for chromosomal analysis and CT evaluation of the CNS for malfor-

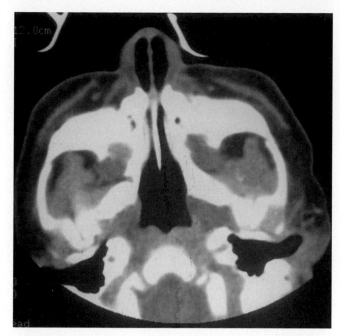

FIGURE 42–17. CT scan of patient with congenital nasal piriform aperture stenosis.

mations and should undergo assessment of their hypopituitary-pituitary-thyroid axis.[61] Beregzaszi et al noted endocrine abnormalities associated with the absence of the anterior pituitary in two patients with CNPAS.[62] Initial treatment in these patients is similar to bilateral choanal atresia with use of an oral airway. Frequent small feedings or gavage feedings may be required. Failure to thrive and inability to obtain adequate nutrition would be indications for surgery. Patients with mild symptoms may be followed expectantly.

Surgical approach is typically sublabial. Dissection with exposure and removal of the lateral bony limits is the goal of intervention. Careful dissection and preservation of the nasolacrimal ducts should also be performed. Inferior dissection should be limited because of potential injury to tooth buds. Upon completion, if a 3.5-mm endotracheal tube can be passed through the nasal inlet, the repair is considered adequate. Stents are typically left in place for 2 to 4 weeks.[60]

Deviated Nasal Septum

In a review of 4090 newborns, the incidence of anterior nasal septal dislocation was noted to be 0.93%.[63] Prolonged labor, intrauterine pressure, misapplication of forceps, and primipara have been noted as contributing factors. The decision to treat is based upon the degree of septal deflection, external deformity, and severity of nasal obstruction. Mild deviation should correct spontaneously within months. A severe dislocation may predispose to the development of secondary deformity. The treatment of septal subluxation involves simple closed reduction with the goal of restoring the septum to the vomerine groove. The procedure is ideally performed within 2 to 3

days of initial diagnosis. Residual deformity to the external nose may take 1 to 2 weeks to resolve.[63]

REFERENCES

1. Hughes GB, Sharpino G, Hunt W, Tucker H. Management of the congenital midline nasal mass: a review. Head Neck Surg 2:222, 1980.
2. Younas M, Coode PE. Nasal glioma and encephalocele: two separate entities. J Neurosurg 64:516, 1986.
3. Kennedy EM, Gruber DP, Billmire DA, Crone KR. Transpalatal approach for the extracranial surgical repair of transsphenoidal cephaloceles in children. J Neurosurg 87:677, 1997.
4. Brown MS, Sheridan-Pereira M. Outlook for the child with a cephalocele. Pediatrics 90:914, 1992.
5. Macfarlane R, Rutka JT, Armstrong D, et al. Encephaloceles of the anterior cranial fossa. Pediatr Neurosurg 23:148, 1995.
6. Suwanwela C, Suwanwela N. A morphological classification of sincipital encephalomeningoceles. J Neurosurg 36:201, 1972.
7. Boonvisut S, Ladpli S, Sujatanond M, et al. Morphologic study of 120 skull base defects in frontoethmoidal encephalomeningoceles. Plast Reconstr Surg 101:1784, 1998.
8. Hoving EW, Vermeij-Keers C. Frontoethmoidal encephaloceles, a study of their pathogenesis. Pediatr Neurosurg 27:246, 1997.
9. Tessier P, Guiot G, Rougerie J, et al. Osteotomies cranio-naso-orbito-faciales, hypertelorisme. Ann Chir Plast 12:103, 1967.
10. Gerhardt HJ, Muhler G, Szdzuy D, et al. Zur Therapieproblematik bei sphenoethmoidalen meningozelen. Zentralbl Neurochir 40:85, 1979.
11. Som PM, Bergeron RT. Head and Neck Imaging, 2nd ed. St. Louis, Mosby–Yearbook, 1991, pp 39-48.
12. Zinreich SJ, Borders JC, Eisele DW, et al. The utility of magnetic resonance imaging in the diagnosis of intranasal meningoencephaloceles. Arch Otolaryngol Head Neck Surg 118:1253, 1992.
13. Mattox DE, Kennedy DW. Endoscopic management of cerebrospinal fluid leaks and cephaloceles. Laryngoscope 100:857, 1990.
14. Lanza DC, O'Brien DA, Kennedy DW. Endoscopic repair of cerebrospinal fluid fistulae and encephaloceles. Laryngoscope 106:1119, 1996.
15. Van Den Abbeele T, Elmaleh M, Herman P, et al. Transnasal endoscopic repair of congenital defects of the skull base in children. Arch Otolaryngol Head Neck Surg 125:580, 1999.
16. Skolnick EM, Campbell JM, Meyers RM. Dermoid cysts of the nose. Laryngoscope 81:1632, 1971.
17. Denoyelle F, Ducroz V, Roger G, Garabedian EN. Nasal dermoid sinus cysts in children. Laryngoscope 107:795, 1997.
18. Sessions RB. Nasal dermal sinuses—new concepts and explanations. Laryngoscope 92:suppl 29,1, 1982.
19. Luongo RA. Dermoid cyst of the nasal dorsum. Arch Otolaryngol 17:755, 1933.
20. Barkovich J, Vandermarck P, Edwards M, Cogen PH. Congenital nasal masses: CT and MRI imaging features in 16 cases. AJNR Am J Neuroradiol 12:105, 1991.
21. Mankarious LA, Smith RJH. External rhinoplasty approach for extirpation and immediate reconstruction of congenital midline nasal dermoids. Ann Otol Rhinol Laryngol 107:786, 1998.
22. Rohrich RJ, Lowe JB, Schwartz MR. The role of open rhinoplasty in the management of nasal dermoid cysts. Plast Reconstruct Surg 104:1459, 1999.
23. Cauchois R, Laccourreye O, Bremond D, et al. Nasal dermoid sinus cyst. Ann Otol Rhinol Laryngol 103:615, 1994.
24. Bartlett SP, Lin KY, Grossman R, Katowitz J. The surgical management of orbitofacial dermoids in the pediatric patient. Plast Reconstruct Surg 91:1208, 1993.
25. Kjaer I, Kelling JW, Hansen FB. Patterns of malformations in the axial skeleton in human trisomy 13 fetuses. Am J Med Genet 70:421, 1997.
26. Kelling JW, Hansen BF, Kjaer I. Pattern of malformations in the axial skeleton in human trisomy 21 fetuses. Am J Med Genet 68:466, 1997.
27. Gifford GH, MacCollum DW. Congenital malformations. In Fergu-

son CF, Kendig EL (eds). Pediatric Otolaryngology. Philadelphia, WB Saunders, 1972.
28. Wang MK. Congenital anomalies of the nose. In Converse JM, McCarthy JG (eds). Reconstructive Plastic Surgery, Vol. 2, 2nd ed. Philadelphia, WB Saunders, 1977, pp 1181-1183.
29. Shubach I, Sanchez C. Nasal aplasia associated with meningocele and submucous cleft palate. ENT J 64:259, 1985.
30. LaTrenta GS, Choi HW, Ward RF, et al. Complete nasal agenesis with bilateral microphthalmia and unilateral duplication of the thumb. Plast Reconstruct Surg 95:1101, 1995.
31. DeMyer W. The median cleft face syndrome. Neurology 17:961, 1967.
32. Sedano HO, Cohen MM, Jirasek JJ, Gorlin RJ. Frontonasal dysplasia. J Pediatr 76:906, 1970.
33. DeMyer W, Zeman W, Palmer CG. Familial alobar holoprosencephaly with median cleft lip and palate. Neurology 13:913, 1963.
34. Tessier P. Anatomic classification of facial, craniofacial and laterofacial clefts. J Maxillofac Surg 4:69, 1976.
35. Ming JE, Muenke M. Holoprosencephaly: from Hower to Hedgehog. Clin Genet 53:155, 1998.
36. Van der Meulen JC, Mazzola R, Vermey-Keers C, et al. A morphogenetic classification of craniofacial malformations. Plast Reconstruct Surg 71:560, 1983.
37. Binns JH. Congenital tubular nostril (proboscis lateralis). Br J Plast Surg 22:265, 1969.
38. Madorsky SJ, Wang TD. Unilateral cleft rhinoplasty. Otolaryngol Clin North Am 32:669, 1999.
39. Benjamin B. Evaluation of choanal atresia. Ann Otol Rhinol Laryngol 94:429, 1985.
40. Harris J, Robert E, Kallen B. Epidemiology of choanal atresia with special reference to the CHARGE association. Pediatrics 99:363, 1997.
41. Leclerc JE, Fearon B. Choanal atresia and associated anomalies. Int J Pediatr Otorhinolaryngol 13:265, 1987.
42. Brown OE, Pownell P, Manning SC. Choanal atresia: a new anatomic classification and clinical management applications. Laryngoscope 106:97, 1996.
43. Telfik TL, Der Kaloustian VM. Congenital Anomalies of the Ear, Nose, and Throat. New York, Oxford University Press, 1997, pp 218-219.
44. Hall BD. Choanal atresia and associated multiple anomalies. J Pediatr 95:395, 1979.
45. Pagon RA, Graham JM, Zonana J, Yong SL. Coloboma, congenital heart disease and choanal atresia with multiple anomalies: CHARGE association. J Pediatr 99:223, 1981.
46. Morgan D, Bailey M, Phelps P, et al. Ear-Nose-Throat abnormalities in the CHARGE association. Arch Otolaryngol Head Neck Surg 119:49, 1993.

47. Roger G, Morisseau-Durand MP, Van den Abbeele T, et al. The CHARGE association: the role of tracheotomy. Arch Otolaryngol Head Neck Surg 125:33, 1999.
48. Coniglio JU, Manzione JV, Hengerer AS. Anatomic findings and management of choanal atresia and the CHARGE association. Ann Otol Rhinol Laryngol 97:448, 1988.
49. Hengerer AS. Congenital Anomalies of the Nose: Their Embryology, Diagnosis and Management. Washington, DC, The American Academy of Otolaryngology, Head and Neck Surgery Foundation, 1987.
50. Hengerer AS, Strome M. Choanal atresia: a new embryologic theory and its influence on surgical management. Laryngoscope 92:913, 1982.
51. Slovis TL, Renfro B, Watts FB, et al. Choanal atresia: precise CT evaluation. Pediatr Radiol 155:345, 1985.
52. Derkay CS, Grundfast KM. Airway compromise from nasal obstruction in neonates and infants. Int J Pediatr Otorhinolaryngol 155:345, 1990.
53. Behar PM, Todd NW. Paranasal sinus development and choanal atresia. Arch Otolaryngol Head Neck Surg 126:155, 2000.
54. Freng A. Surgical treatment of congenital choanal atresia. Ann Otol Rhinol Laryngol 87:346, 1978.
55. Prisig W. Surgery of choanal atresia in infants and children: historical notes and updated review. Int J Pediatr Otorhinolaryngol 11:153, 1986.
56. Muntz HR. Choanal atresia. In Gates GA (ed). Current Therapy in Otolaryngology. Head and Neck Surgery, 6th ed. St. Louis, Mosby–Yearbook, 1998, pp 389-391.
57. Stankiewicz JA. The endoscopic repair of choanal atresia. Otolaryngol Head Neck Surg 103:931, 1990.
58. Park AH, Brockenbrough J, Stankiewicz J. Endoscopic versus traditional approaches to choanal atresia. Otolaryngol Clin North Am 33: 77, 2000.
59. Contencin P, Gumpert L, Sleiman J, et al. Nasal fossae dimensions in the neonate and young infant: a computed tomographic scan study. Arch Otolaryngol Head Neck Surg 125:777, 1999.
60. Brown OE, Myer CM, Manning SC. Congenital nasal pyriform aperture stenosis. Laryngoscope 99:86, 1989.
61. Arlis H, Ward RF. Congenital nasal pyriform aperture stenosis: isolated abnormality vs developmental field defect. Arch Otolaryngol Head Neck Surg 118:989, 1992.
62. Beregzaszi M, Leger L, Garet C, et al. Nasal pyriform aperture stenosis and absence of the anterior pituitary gland: report of two cases. J Pediatr 128:858, 1996.
63. Podoshin L, Gertner R, Fradis M, Berger A. Incidence and treatment of deviation of nasal septum in newborns. ENT J 70:485, 1991.
64. Jazbi B. Subluxation of the nasal septum in the newborn: etiology, diagnosis, and treatment. Otolaryngol Clin North Am 10:125, 1977.

43

Rhinitis and Acute and Chronic Sinusitis

Ellen R. Wald, M.D.

Rhinitis

Infection of the upper respiratory tract is the single most common organic disease seen by the primary care practitioner. It is usually characterized by nasal discharge and nasal congestion, with variable components of cough, conjunctivitis, sore throat, and constitutional symptoms. When rhinitis is self-limited, it is almost certainly infectious in origin. When it is persistent or seasonal, allergic problems must be considered (see Chap. 49).

Viral Rhinitis

Infectious rhinitis is caused by viruses or bacteria; infection with viruses is many times more common than that with bacteria. The common cold is a syndrome caused by more than several hundred antigenically different viruses that may intermittently colonize and infect the upper respiratory tract. The viruses can be divided into four groups: (1) the myxovirus and paramyxovirus groups (containing influenza, parainfluenza, and respiratory syncytial viruses), (2) the adenovirus group (containing 35 different human serotypes), (3) the picornavirus group (containing enteroviruses and more than 100 different rhinoviruses), and (4) the coronavirus group.[44] The specific cause of a cold can be identified in 60% to 70% of cases by using sensitive culture techniques. Rhinoviruses account for 30% to 40% of infections; coronaviruses for at least 10%; and respiratory syncytial viruses (RSVs), influenzaviruses, parainfluenza viruses, and adenoviruses together for about 10% to 15%. Many of the remaining as yet unidentified cases are probably caused by coronaviruses that elude current methods of virus isolation.[44]

Epidemiology

It is common experience, as several epidemiologic studies show, that colds are much more frequent in children than in adults. The range of reported frequencies for upper respiratory infections (URIs) in young children is between six and 21 per year.[5] The incidence of infection in children varies with age, number of siblings, and day care arrangements. Most adults experience two or three colds per year; however, this may increase during the years of parenting young children or when occupational exposure provides contact with a large number of youngsters. The respiratory viruses show definite seasonal trends, with least activity seen in the summer months, except for parainfluenza, which typically causes summer croup. The rhinovirus is found most frequently during fall and spring, whereas the coronaviruses, influenzaviruses, and RSVs are most prevalent in the winter.

The seemingly endless susceptibility of humans to viral infections of the upper respiratory tract is a consequence of (1) incomplete immunity after infection with certain agents (e.g., RSV), (2) multiple viral serotypes in other groups of viruses to which immunity does develop after infection (e.g., adenovirus, rhinovirus, coronavirus), and (3) antigenic shift and drift for influenzaviruses and possibly coronaviruses as well.

Transmission of respiratory viruses from person to person occurs by means of respiratory secretions that are contaminated with virus.[104] The potential routes for spread are inhalation of small airborne particles, inhalation of large airborne particles (when the transmitter and susceptible individual are physically close), and hand contact with contaminated environmental articles or other hands.[21] Although all routes contribute to the spread of infection, the last category seems to be the most important. The susceptible individual can acquire hand colonization with infective virus from contaminated inanimate objects or other hands. Once the susceptible person's hands are colonized, the virus is easily inoculated onto mucosal surfaces through hand-to-eye or hand-to-nose contact.[42, 49] Spread of virus is difficult to control, as virus can be shed for a day or two before the onset of symptoms and (rarely) by an individual who never develops symptoms.

Pathogenesis

The usual method for inducing experimental rhinovirus infection has been instillation of small amounts of virus suspension into each nasal passage, with the volunteer in a supine position. Studies have shown that other effective inoculation sites are the conjunctival sac and the posterior nasopharyngeal wall at the level of the eustachian tube orifices.[116] Infection may first be established in the nasopharynx and then spread secondarily to the nasal turbinates, but recovery of virus from within the nasal cavity may be spotty. Also, the nasal epithelium has appeared normal during symptomatic infections with rhinovirus and coronavirus in several studies.[116, 117] In view of the spottiness of infection and the frequent lack of detectable morphologic change in the nasal mucosa, some authors have speculated that symptoms may result from the release of chemical mediators that activate the inflammatory cascade.[43, 104] Two potent mediators, lysylbradykinin and bradykinin, have been found in the nasal secretions of volunteers with rhinovirus colds.[76]

In contrast to the absence of morphologic changes in the nasal mucosa of patients infected with rhinoviruses, dramatic but focal cytopathic effects may be seen in the nasal mucosa of children naturally infected with influenzavirus. Similarly, dysmorphology of ciliary microtubules of nasal epithelial cells has been observed with adenovirus, influenzavirus, parainfluenza virus, and RSV infections.[14] In these instances the viral infection appears to induce direct cellular injury that may lead to impaired mucociliary transport.

Clinical Features

The clinical features of the common cold are variable and include nasal congestion, nasal discharge (of any quality: serous, mucoid, or purulent), sneezing, cough, conjunctival inflammation, and sore throat with or without the constitutional symptoms of fever, malaise, and myalgias. Appetite and sleep patterns may be disturbed. On physical examination the nasal and pharyngeal mucosae appear erythematous, and lymphoid hyperplasia may be seen in the posterior pharynx. There may be tonsillar and adenoidal hypertrophy; the cervical lymph nodes may be modestly enlarged and slightly tender. Irritative skin manifestations often become apparent around the alar nasi and the upper lip. During the course of a cold, there may be secondary bacterial infection of the middle ears (evidenced by an opaque, immobile tympanic membrane) or paranasal sinuses (evidenced by high fever, purulent nasal discharge, and ill appearance). The duration of most colds is 5 to 7 days; although patients may not be completely asymptomatic by day 10, they are almost always improving.

Diagnosis

In clinical practice, it is rarely necessary to know the precise cause of the common cold. However, virus may be isolated from the nasopharynx (by direct swabbing) or from the nasal cavity (with nasal washes) by conventional tissue culture techniques. These cultures are expensive, and the results are not usually available for 4 to 7 days. Rapid diagnostic techniques such as enzyme immunoassay, fluorescent antibody methods, and polymerase chain reaction have been developed for detecting RSV, parainfluenza virus, and influenzavirus. Although precise etiologic information is not essential for the practitioner, community surveillance cultures may provide useful epidemiologic information, e.g., signaling the onset of influenza season.

Treatment

Specific antiviral chemotherapy for RSV (ribavirin aerosol) is primarily intended to treat the lower respiratory component of this infection. Antiviral treatment of influenza can be accomplished with amantadine, rimantadine, zanamivir, and oseltamivir. Amantadine (5 mg/kg per day for children between 1 and 9 years of age, not to exceed 150 mg/kg per day; 5 mg/kg/day for children over 10 years of age, not to exceed 200 mg/day) is approved for children, and zanamivir (inhaled twice a day for 5 days with a special breath-activated inhaler) is approved for persons at least 12 years of age. Oseltamivir is approved for children 1 year and older. Rimantadine and oseltamivir are not approved for children. Neither amantadine nor rimantadine is effective against influenza B. The new antiviral agents, zanamivir and oseltamivir, are inhibitors of neuraminidase and have activity against both influenza A and B. Recent studies have shown effective use of zanamivir in children as young as 5 years and oseltamivir in children as young as 1 year. In general, antiviral therapy is most effective when started as soon as possible after the onset of symptoms. It is continued for 2 to 5 days or for 24 to 48 hours after the patient becomes asymptomatic.

Apart from specific antiviral therapy, treatment of the common cold is largely symptomatic. Normal saline nose drops may be useful to liquefy nasal mucus, thereby reducing forceful nose blowing. Nasal irrigation with normal saline may also be soothing when used with a Water Pik in the older child or adult. Systemic and topical decongestants are used to decrease nasal secretions and mucosal edema, thereby decreasing nasal resistance and increasing airway patency.

Topical decongestants (sympathomimetic amines), although not tested in clinical trials, usually decrease nasal congestion and provide symptomatic relief. However, if they are used for more than 3 days, rebound congestion (rhinitis medicamentosa) may result. Patients should be cautioned against protracted use.

Antihistamines or antihistamine-decongestant combinations are also available as common cold remedies. All five classes of antihistamines act by competitively blocking the histamine receptor site and may relieve such symptoms as sneezing, nasal itchiness, and watery rhinorrhea. Antihistamines are more likely to be effective for treatment of allergic rhinitis; they have a very modest effect on sneezing and rhinorrhea in adults.[105] Placebo-controlled studies have indicated that over-the-counter antihistamine-decongestant cold medications are no more effective than placebo in children younger than 5 years of age with a cold.[20]

Other symptomatic remedies include acetaminophen (for fever or myalgias), increased fluid intake (to keep secretions liquefied and mucous membranes comfortable), and bed rest, if possible, for comfort.

Prevention

Major efforts to control the common cold have focused on prevention of transmission. Intranasally applied alpha$_2$

interferon has been evaluated for its prophylactic and therapeutic efficacy. Although twice daily use of interferon is effective in the prophylaxis of natural rhinovirus infections, daily use for more than 2 weeks results in the development of nasal stuffiness, dryness, and blood-tinged mucus in 40% of adults. Accordingly, some investigators have assessed the efficacy of interferon for short-term use in the family setting. It has been found to result in about 40% fewer episodes of rhinovirus-associated illness.[28, 51] The major limitation to the use of alpha$_2$ interferon is its lack of effectiveness against parainfluenza viruses, influenzavirus A, and community coronaviruses, thereby considerably reducing its impact on "all" respiratory illnesses.

Another preventive strategy for rhinovirus infection has been intranasal administration of a monoclonal antibody directed at the cellular receptor site to which the rhinovirus attaches (intercellular adhesion molecule-1, or ICAM-1). Although there are numerous rhinoviruses, 88 of 100 clinical isolates attach to one of two cellular receptor sites in tissue culture.[103]

The best way to prevent influenza in high-risk populations is to vaccinate annually. There is current interest in determining whether there is a cost benefit to the universal immunization of all children against influenza.

Bacterial Rhinitis

Group A Streptococcal Infection

The most common clinical expression of infection with *Streptococcus pyogenes* is pharyngitis, often accompanied by fever and tender anterior cervical lymph nodes, in children 5 to 15 years of age. However, persistent rhinitis in infants or children under 3 years of age suggests the possibility of streptococcal infection, or streptococcosis.[82] Streptococcal infection in this age group often fails to localize to the throat and instead causes a clinical picture of a protracted cold with low-grade fever. Occasionally an older child (over 5 years of age) with streptococcal infection and superimposed sinusitis may present with persistent nasal discharge and cough.[107]

If streptococcal infection is proved by culture of the nasopharynx or throat, treatment with penicillin for 10 days is appropriate. Phenoxymethylpenicillin dosages of 250 mg two or three times daily for those under 60 lb, and 500 mg two or three times daily for those over 60 lb, are recommended. In patients who are allergic to penicillin, erythromycin, 40 mg/kg per day in three to four divided doses, is a suitable substitute.

In both infants and older children, paranasal sinusitis should be considered as a cause of persistent nasal discharge (see next section on Sinusitis). Purulent rhinorrhea may also be indicative of an intranasal foreign body, especially when fetor oris is prominent or when the discharge is unilateral, bloody, or both.

Whether bacteria other than group A streptococci can cause purulent rhinitis has not been adequately evaluated. Staphylococcal species, *Haemophilus influenzae*, *Moraxella catarrhalis*, and *Streptococcus pneumoniae* may be normal nasal or nasopharyngeal flora. Therefore, the recovery of these bacteria from superficial cultures of the nose or throat of a child with a cold is not easily interpretable.

Antimicrobial preparations are not recommended for uncomplicated URIs.[29] However, data show that antibiotic prophylaxis (daily or during the course of a cold) may be effective in preventing symptomatic episodes of acute otitis media in children who are prone to otitis.[15]

Pertussis

Early in the catarrhal phase of pertussis, nasal symptoms are prominent (congestion and discharge), and the clinical syndrome is indistinguishable from those of other causes of URI. Only when cough becomes a prominent part of the clinical picture and specific cultures or other diagnostic techniques indicate the presence of *Bordetella pertussis* can the clinician retrospectively implicate pertussis as the cause of the early coryza.

Diphtheria

The most characteristic clinical expression of infection with *Corynebacterium diphtheriae* is a membranous pharyngitis. In some cases, there may be nasal involvement— either occurrence of an actual membrane or nasal secretions that are bloody.

The onset of nasal diphtheria is indistinguishable from that of the common cold. In the early stages the nasal discharge is serous; later, it becomes serosanguineous and occasionally mucopurulent, thereby potentially obscuring the white membrane on the nasal septum. The copious nasal discharge, which is highly contagious, leads to excoriation of the anterior nares and upper lip. Diphtheria toxin is poorly absorbed nasally; consequently, the patient lacks constitutional symptoms, including fever.[61]

Chlamydia trachomatis

A syndrome of afebrile pneumonitis affecting infants aged 3 to 16 weeks was described in 1977.[6] The clinical picture, which is characterized by protracted cough (for more than 7 days), tachypnea, and absence of fever, may be caused by *Chlamydia trachomatis*, *Ureaplasma urealyticum*, *Pneumocystis carinii*, or cytomegalovirus.[96] In each case the protracted cough may be preceded by prominent nasal symptoms: congestion, discharge, and sneezing. Again, these "colds" can only belatedly be recognized to be caused by specific microbiologic agents.

Syphilis

Congenital syphilis is characterized by the triad of rash, "snuffles," and pseudoparalysis. Usually the infant is well at birth but develops a persistent nasal discharge. At first the nasal discharge is watery, then mucoid and intermittently bloody by the end of the first or second week of life. The nasal discharge is irritating to the nares and the upper lip and leads to excoriation and scarring. Involvement of the upper airway may lead to laryngitis with a hoarse or aphonic cry.[89] Other findings may include hepatosplenomegaly, generalized lymphadenopathy, hematologic abnormalities, and central nervous system involvement. The diagnosis of syphilis should be confirmed by serologic tests. Positive results should be obtained with the fluorescent treponemal antibody test and the nontreponemal tests, including the Venereal Disease Research Laboratories (VDRL) test, the rapid plasma reagin (RPR) test, and the standard test for syphilis (STS). Symptomatic infants should be treated for 10 to 14 days with either (1) aqueous crystalline penicillin G, administered intravenously every 12 hours during the first week of life and every 8 hours thereafter, or (2) aqueous procaine penicillin, administered intramuscularly once daily.

Sinusitis

When considering a diagnosis of acute bacterial sinusitis in a child or an adult, the major problem is to distinguish, on the one hand, simple URI or allergic inflammation from, on the other hand, secondary bacterial infection of the paranasal sinuses. The former categories of URI and allergy may prompt consideration of symptomatic treatment, whereas patients with acute bacterial sinusitis will benefit from specific antimicrobial therapy. Both URI and allergic inflammation are recognized risk factors for acute bacterial sinusitis, with URI the most common.

Epidemiology

It was once estimated that 0.5% of URIs were complicated by acute sinusitis.[24] However, more recent data suggest that approximately 5% to 10% of URIs in early childhood are complicated by acute sinusitis.[1, 106, 108] Because adults average two or three colds per year and children average six to eight, sinusitis is a very common problem in clinical practice.[41]

Embryology and Anatomy

All the paranasal sinuses develop as outpouchings of the nasal chamber, with varying extensions into their respective bony vaults. Along the lateral wall of the nasal chamber are three shelflike structures: the inferior, middle, and superior turbinates. Beneath each turbinate is the corresponding meatus. The frontal, maxillary, and anterior ethmoid sinuses open into the middle meatus; the sphenoid and the posterior ethmoid cells open high in the nasal vault into the superior meatus.

The maxillary sinus develops early in the second trimester of fetal life as a lateral outpouching in the posterior aspect of the middle meatus. At birth it is a slitlike structure, with its long axis parallel to the attachment of the inferior turbinate and its floor barely below that. The sinus cavity grows in width and height. Ultimately, at full size, the lateral border of the maxillary sinus reaches the lateral orbital rim. The position of the floor of the sinus is determined by the eruption of the teeth. Infrequently, one can find septa in the maxillary sinus, resulting in separate compartments rather than a single large cavity.[55] The volume of the fully developed maxillary sinus is approximately 12 to 15 mL.

Of special note is the position of the maxillary ostium in relation to the body of the sinus. The location of this outflow tract, high on the medial wall of the maxillary sinus, impedes gravitational drainage of secretions; ciliary activity is required to move secretions from the body of the maxillary sinus through the ostium to the nose. From there, secretions are carried into the nasopharynx to be either expectorated or swallowed.

The ethmoid sinus develops in the fourth month of gestation. It is not a single large cavity but a grouping of individual cells, 3 to 15 in number, each with its own opening, or ostium. Aeration of the ethmoid cells is variable, leading to a honeycombed radiographic appearance. The cells are small anteriorly and large in the posterior group. The walls of the ethmoid labyrinth are thin, especially in the lateral aspect bordering on the orbit. The lateral wall of the ethmoid sinus is referred to as the lamina papyracea, or paper wall. Purulent infection may spread by direct extension from the ethmoid sinus through natural dehiscences in the bone to involve the orbit.[87]

The variability of frontal sinus development is well known. In adults, 80% have bilateral but often asymmetric frontal sinuses, 1% to 4% have agenesis of the frontal sinuses, and the remainder have unilateral hypoplasia. The position of the frontal sinus is supraorbital after age 4 years but is not distinguishable radiographically from the ethmoid sinus until 6 to 8 years of age. After that, it progresses for another 8 to 10 years before reaching full adult size. Depending on the particular cell in the frontal recess or anterior ethmoid sinus, which develops into the frontal sinus, the conduit between sinus and nasal cavity will be either a short and wide ostium or a long and narrow nasofrontal duct.

Although the sphenoid sinus occupies a strategic position in the base of the skull, its slow growth and relative isolation preserve it from frequent infection. Isolated involvement of the sphenoid sinuses is uncommon, but they may be involved as part of a pansinusitis. For further reading see Chapter 31.

Pathophysiology and Pathogenesis

Three key elements are important in the normal physiology of the paranasal sinuses: the patency of the ostia, the function of the ciliary apparatus, and (integral to the latter) the quality of secretions.[85] Retention of secretions in the paranasal sinuses is due to one or more of the following: obstruction of the ostia, reduction in the number of cilia, impaired function of the cilia, and overproduction or change in the viscosity of secretions.

Sinus Ostia

The ostia of the paranasal sinuses are the key to pathologic involvement in the sinus area. The ostia of the maxillary sinuses are small, tubular structures with a diameter of 2.5 mm (cross-sectional area approximately 5 mm) and a length of 6 mm.[31] The diameter of the ostium of each of the individual ethmoid air cells that drain independently into the middle meatus is even smaller, 1 to 2 mm; the anterior ostia are smaller than the posterior.[83] The narrow caliber of these individual ostia sets the stage for obstruction to occur easily and often.

The factors predisposing to ostial obstruction can be divided into those that cause mucosal swelling and those due to mechanical obstruction.[83] The various factors that may cause mucosal swelling, consequent either to systemic illness or to local insults, are listed in Table 43–1, as well as the conditions that predispose to mechanical obstruction of the sinus ostia. Although many conditions may lead to ostial closure, viral URI and allergic inflammation are by far the most frequent and most important causes of ostial obstruction. In acute rhinitis a completely patent ostium is present only 20% of the time.[31]

When complete obstruction of the sinus ostium occurs, there is a transient increase in intrasinal pressure followed by the development of a negative intrasinal pressure.[2] When the ostium opens again, the negative pressure within the sinus relative to atmospheric pressure facilitates the introduction of bacteria into the sinus cavity. Alternatively, sneezing, sniffing, and nose blowing with altered intranasal pressure may facilitate the entry of bacteria and secretions from a heavily colonized posterior nasal chamber into the sinus cavity.[48] The mucosa of the paranasal sinus continues to secrete actively even after obstruction occurs. Clearance of secretions is impossible when the ostium is totally obstructed. If the ostium is patent but reduced in size, removal of secretions will be delayed.

Gas exchange within the sinus cavity is also impaired if the ostium is obstructed. The rapidity and efficiency of gas exchange depend on two factors: (1) ostial patency and (2) nasal breathing.[31] As nasal breathing decreases, which is probable when there is nasal congestion and secondary obstruction, gas exchange in the sinus decreases. A decreased partial pressure of oxygen within the sinus cavity is a local factor that favors the multiplication of certain bacterial species.

The mucociliary apparatus is fairly hardy with regard to alterations in its oxygen supply. Function will not be impaired unless both the oxygen concentration within the sinus cavity and that supplied by the circulation are compromised.[31] While the former is common, on the basis of reduced patency of the sinus ostia, the latter probably occurs only when intrasinal pressure is high enough to impair mucosal blood flow.

Mucociliary Apparatus

Disorders of the mucociliary apparatus in conjunction with reduced patency of the sinus ostia are major pathophysiologic events in acute sinusitis. In the posterior two thirds of the nasal cavity and within the sinuses, the epithelium is pseudostratified columnar, in which most of the cells are ciliated.

The normal motility of the cilia and the adhesive properties of the mucous layer usually protect respiratory epithelium from bacterial invasion. However, certain respiratory viruses may have a direct cytotoxic effect on the cilia. The alteration of cilia number, morphology, and function may facilitate secondary bacterial invasion of the nose and the paranasal sinuses. For further reading, see Chapter 32.

Sinus Secretions

Cilia can beat only in a fluid medium. There appears to be a double layer of mucus in the airways: the gel layer (superficial viscid fluid) and the sol layer (underlying serous fluid). The gel layer acts to trap particulate matter such as bacteria and other debris. The tips of the cilia touch the gel layer during forward movement and thereby move the particulate matter along. However, the bodies of the cilia move through the sol layer, a fluid thin enough to allow the cilia to beat.

Alterations in the mucus, as in cystic fibrosis or asthma, may impair ciliary activity. One can easily imagine that the presence of purulent material in the acutely infected sinus may also impair ciliary movement and further compound the effects of ostial closure. Interestingly, there are conflicting reports regarding the reduction of ciliary activity in chronic purulent sinusitis.[77, 85]

Clinical Presentation

Commonly recognized symptoms of sinusitis in adults and adolescents are facial pain, headache, and fever. However, children with acute sinusitis frequently have complaints that are less specific. During the course of apparent viral URIs, two common clinical developments should alert the clinician to the possibility of bacterial infection of the paranasal sinuses (Table 43–2).

The first and most common clinical situation in which sinusitis should be suspected is when the signs and symptoms of a cold are persistent. Nasal discharge and daytime cough that continue beyond 10 days and are not improving are the principal complaints. The course of most uncomplicated viral URIs is 5 to 7 days. Although the patient may not be asymptomatic by the tenth day, almost always their symptoms have peaked in severity and they have begun to improve. Accordingly, the persistence of respiratory symptoms beyond 10 days, without evi-

TABLE 43–1. Factors Predisposing to Sinus Ostial Obstruction

Mucosal Swelling	Mechanical Obstruction
Systemic disorder	Choanal atresia
Viral URI	Deviated septum
Allergic inflammation	Nasal polyps
Cystic fibrosis	Foreign body
Immune disorders	Tumor
Immotile cilia	
Local insult	
Facial trauma	
Swimming, diving	
Rhinitis medicamentosa	

URI, upper respiratory infection.

TABLE 43–2. Common Clinical Presentation of Acute Sinusitis

"Persistent" Respiratory Symptoms
Nasal discharge of any quality and/or daytime cough for 10–30 days without clinical improvement
Low-grade or no fever
Eye swelling
Fetid breath (children younger than 5 years)
"Severe" Respiratory Symptoms
High fever (>39°C)
Purulent nasal discharge with or without eye swelling or headache

dence of improvement, suggests that the patient may be experiencing a secondary bacterial infection of the paranasal sinuses. The nasal discharge may be of any quality (thin or thick; clear, mucoid, or purulent) and the cough (which may be dry or wet) is usually present in the daytime, although it is often noted to be worse at night. Cough occurring only at night is a common residual symptom of a URI. When it is the only residual symptom, it is usually nonspecific and does not suggest a sinus infection. On the other hand, the persistence of daytime cough is frequently the symptom that brings a child to medical attention. Such a child may not appear ill, and if fever is present, it is usually low grade. Fetid breath is often reported by parents of preschoolers. Facial pain is absent, although intermittent, painless, morning periorbital swelling may have been noted by parents. In this case, it is not the severity of the clinical symptoms but their persistence that calls for attention.

The second and less common presentation is a cold that seems more severe than usual: the fever is high (greater than 39.0°C), the nasal discharge is purulent and copious, and there may be associated periorbital swelling and facial pain. This swelling may involve the upper or lower lid; it is gradual in onset and most obvious in the early morning shortly after awakening. The swelling may decrease and actually disappear during the day, only to reappear once again the following day. A less common complaint is headache (a feeling of fullness or a dull ache either behind or above the eyes), most often reported in children over 5 years of age. Occasionally there may be dental pain, either from infection originating in the teeth or referred from the sinus infection.

Chronic sinusitis should be suspected in children with very protracted respiratory symptoms: nasal discharge, nasal obstruction, or cough that has lasted for more than 30 days. Although the nasal discharge is most often purulent, it may be thin and clear. Occasionally nasal discharge is minimal or absent, and cough and throat clearing are more prominent due to discharge from the posterior ethmoids. Once again, the cough should be present during the daytime, although it is usually reported to be worse at night. When nasal obstruction due to nasal congestion is pronounced, sore throat is frequently present upon awakening secondary to mouth breathing. In addition, the patient may complain of facial pain, headache, or malaise. The appetite may be poor, sleep is frequently impaired, and school performance may suffer. However, unless these less specific complaints are accompanied by respira-

tory symptoms, they should not be attributed to sinus infection. Fever is less prominent and found less frequently than in acute sinusitis.

Diagnosis

Physical Examination

On physical examination the patient with acute bacterial sinusitis may have mucopurulent discharge in the nose or posterior pharynx. The nasal mucosa is erythematous and the throat may show moderate injection. The cervical lymph nodes are usually not significantly enlarged or tender. None of these characteristics differentiates rhinitis from acute bacterial sinusitis. Occasionally there is either tenderness, as the examiner palpates over or percusses the paranasal sinuses, or appreciable periorbital edema— soft and nontender swelling of the upper and lower eyelid, discoloration of the overlying skin, or both. Malodorous breath (in the absence of pharyngitis, poor dental hygiene, or a nasal foreign body) may suggest bacterial sinusitis.

Transillumination may be helpful in diagnosing inflammation of the maxillary or frontal sinuses in adolescents and adults (Fig. 43–1). The patient and the examiner must be in a darkened room. To transilluminate the maxillary sinus, the light source, shielded from the observer, is placed over the midpoint of the inferior orbital rim. The transmission of light through the hard palate is then assessed with the patient's mouth open.[115] Light passing through the alveolar ridges should be excluded in judging light transmission. An alternative method is to place a light source in the patient's mouth and have the patient close his or her lips tightly against the transilluminator; the observer then judges the amount of light transmitted through the maxillary sinuses.[115] Transillumination of the frontal sinus is accomplished by placing a high-intensity light source beneath the medial border of the supraorbi-

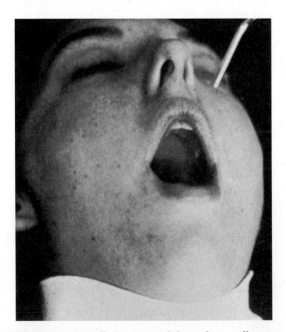

FIGURE 43–1. Transillumination of the right maxillary sinus.

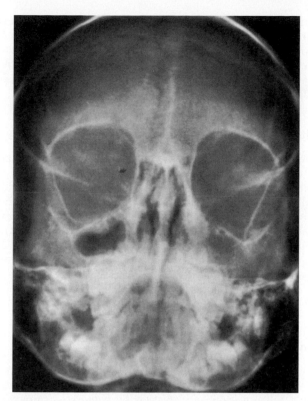

FIGURE 43–2. Radiograph showing complete opacification of the left maxillary sinus and mucosal thickening of the roof of the right maxillary sinus.

tal ridge and evaluating the symmetry of the blush bilaterally. Transillumination is useful in adolescents and adults if light transmission is either normal or absent. "Reduced" transmission or "dull" transillumination are assessments that correlate poorly with clinical disease.[32] The increased thickness of both the soft tissue and the bony vault in children under 10 years of age limits the clinical usefulness of transillumination in the younger age group.[80, 107]

In most children under 10 years of age, the physical examination is generally not very helpful for making a specific diagnosis of acute bacterial sinusitis. On the other hand, if the mucopurulent material can be removed from the nose and the nasal mucosa is treated with topical vasoconstrictors, pus may be seen coming from the middle meatus. The latter observation and periorbital swelling or facial tenderness (when present) are probably the most specific findings in acute bacterial sinusitis.

The signs of chronic sinusitis are not specific. They include mucopurulent nasal discharge, hypertrophied nasal turbinates, and (occasionally) intranasal polyps. The last are seen principally in association with allergy or cystic fibrosis. Some authors have noted that in children with chronic sinusitis, widening of the nasal bridge develops, producing a pseudohypertelorism.

Radiography

Radiography has traditionally been used to confirm the presence or absence of sinus disease. Standard radio-

graphic projections include anteroposterior, lateral, and occipitomental (Waters) views. The anteroposterior view is best for evaluation of the ethmoid sinuses and the lateral view for the frontal and sphenoid sinuses. The occipitomental view, taken after tilting the chin upward 45 degrees to the horizontal, permits evaluation of the maxillary sinuses.

Although much has been written about the frequency of abnormal sinus radiographs in "normal" children, these studies have been flawed either by inattention to the presence of symptoms and signs of respiratory inflammation or by failure to classify abnormal radiographic findings into major (significant) and minor (insignificant) categories.[68, 92] A report in 1984 showed that abnormal maxillary sinus radiographs are infrequent in children beyond their first birthday who are without recent symptoms and signs of respiratory tract inflammation.[59]

The radiographic finding most diagnostic of bacterial sinusitis is an air-fluid level in, or complete opacification of, the sinus cavities. However, an air-fluid level is an uncommon radiographic finding in children younger than 5 years of age with acute bacterial sinusitis. In the absence of an air-fluid level or complete opacification of the sinuses, it may be useful to measure the degree of mucosal swelling (Fig. 43–2). If the width of the sinus mucous membrane is at least 5 mm in adults or 4 mm in children, it is probable that the sinus contains pus or will yield a positive bacterial culture.[50, 109] When clinical signs and symptoms suggesting acute sinusitis are accompanied by abnormal maxillary sinus radiographic findings, bacteria will be present in a sinus aspirate 70% to 75% of the time.[109]

The need for plain radiographs as a confirmatory test of acute sinusitis in children suspected of having acute sinusitis is controversial.[22, 70] Some practitioners may elect to perform sinus radiographs with the expectation or suspicion that the study may be normal. A completely normal plain radiograph is powerful evidence that bacterial sinusitis is not the cause of the clinical syndrome.[59] The American College of Radiology has taken the position that the diagnosis of acute uncomplicated sinusitis should be made on clinical grounds alone.[71] They support this position by noting that plain radiographs of paranasal sinusitis are technically difficult to perform particularly in very young children. Correct positioning may be difficult to achieve, and therefore the radiographic images may both over- and underestimate the presence of abnormalities within the paranasal sinuses.[62, 69] The College would reserve the use of images for situations in which the patient does not recover or worsens during the course of appropriate antimicrobial therapy. A recent set of guidelines generated by the Sinus and Allergy Health partnership (representing numerous constituencies) also do not recommend plain film radiographs, computed tomography (CT), or magnetic resonance imaging (MRI) to diagnose uncomplicated cases of acute bacterial sinusitis.[94] The Subcommittee on Management of Sinusitis and Committee on Quality Improvement of the American Academy of Pediatrics stated that "imaging studies are not necessary to confirm a diagnosis of clinical sinusitis in children less than 6 years of age." However, they did not recommend for or against images in older children, leaving open the possibility that images may be necessary in this age group.

Several studies have examined the frequency of incidental paranasal sinus abnormalities on CT scans in children.[23, 38, 60] In a study by Glasier et al, almost 100% of young children who were undergoing CT examination for reasons other than sinus disease and who had an upper respiratory infection in the previous 2 weeks demonstrated soft tissue changes in their sinuses.[38] A study by Gwaltney illustrated that abnormalities of the paranasal sinuses on CT scan are extremely common in young adults with acute (<72 hours) uncomplicated upper respiratory infection.[45] This study and others serve to underscore that when abnormalities of the mucosa are present on images, they indicate the presence of inflammation but do not disclose whether the inflammatory process is caused by viral infection, bacterial infection, allergy, or chemical irritation (e.g., chlorine exposure in a swimmer).

Unquestionably, CT scans are superior to plain radiographs for delineation of sinus abnormalities; however, they are not necessary in children with uncomplicated acute bacterial sinusitis. On the other hand, for cases of sinusitis that are complicated by intracranial or intraorbital suppuration, CT and MRI are helpful procedures. Appropriate coronal and axial scans permit simultaneous evaluation of the central nervous system, orbit, and paranasal sinuses (Fig. 43–3). For patients with allergy to contrast material or those with a vascular occlusion complicating sinusitis, MRI is best.

In patients with recurrent or persistent sinusitis, there may be a concern that either a congenital bony defect or a traumatic skeletal deformity is the underlying problem. For these patients, CT imaging procedures are ideal for evaluation of skeletal structures of the paranasal sinuses (Fig. 43–4).

Ultrasonography

Several reports have evaluated ultrasonography as an aid in diagnosing maxillary sinusitis.[66, 86, 91] Its advantages as compared with radiography are the use of nonionizing radiation and supposedly better ability to discriminate between mucosal thickening and retained secretions. In several studies performed in children, ultrasound examination yielded falsely normal or indeterminate patterns.[84] At present, there is insufficient experience to permit an assessment of the value of ultrasonography for the diagnosis of sinusitis in children; its use is therefore not recommended.

Sinus Aspiration

A diagnosis of acute bacterial sinusitis is probably best proved by a biopsy of the sinus mucosa that demonstrates acute inflammation and invasion by bacteria. In practice, confirmation of the diagnosis is more often accomplished by culturing an aspirate of sinus secretions. Nonetheless,

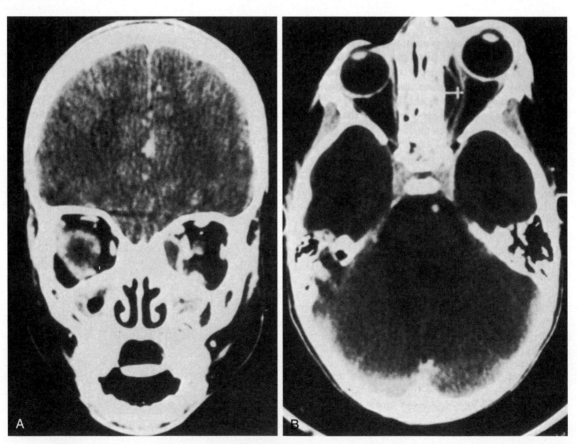

FIGURE 43–3. Coronal (A) and axial (B) computed tomographic (CT) scans of the orbit, sinuses, and brain showing a subperiosteal abscess of the right orbit.

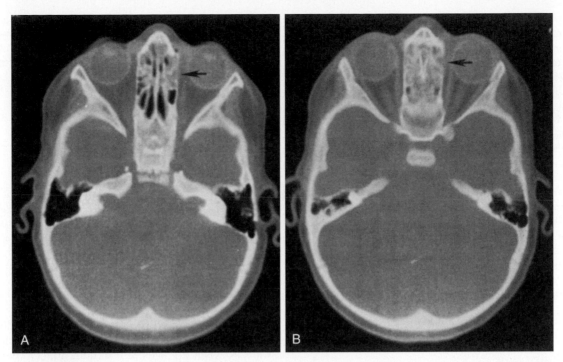

FIGURE 43–4. *A* and *B*, Axial CT scans in a child with recurrent acute sinusitis and periorbital swelling demonstrating a bony defect in the left ethmoid bone.

when simultaneous mucosal biopsies and sinus aspirates are submitted for bacterial cultures, biopsies more often yield positive results.

Although it is by no means a routine procedure, aspiration of the maxillary sinus (the most accessible of the sinuses) can be accomplished easily in an outpatient setting with minimal discomfort to the patient. Puncture is best performed by the transnasal route, with the needle directed beneath the inferior turbinate through the lateral nasal wall (Fig. 43–5). This route for aspiration is preferred in order to avoid injury to the natural ostium and permanent dentition. If the patient is unusually apprehensive or too young to cooperate, a short-acting narcotic agent can be used for sedation, or the procedure may be performed in the operating room with the patient under general anesthesia.

Careful sterilization of the puncture site is essential to prevent contamination by nasal flora. A 4% cocaine solution applied intranasally will achieve mucosal anesthesia and antisepsis. Lidocaine should be injected into the submucosa at the site of the actual puncture. Secretions obtained by aspiration should be submitted for Gram stain and quantitative aerobic and anaerobic cultures. Bacterial isolates should be tested for their sensitivity to various antibiotics. A high bacterial colony count assures that the culture results reflect actual sinus infection rather than contamination; counts of greater than 10^4 colony-forming units/mL give a high degree of confirmation of in situ infection. Alternatively, a Gram stain preparation of sinus secretions may be helpful, as bacteria that are present in a low colony count (likely to be contaminants) are usually not seen on a smear.

Indications for sinus aspiration in patients with suspected sinusitis include clinical unresponsiveness to conventional therapy, sinus disease in an immunosuppressed patient, severe symptoms such as headache and facial pain, and life-threatening complications such as intraorbital or intracranial suppuration at the time of clinical presentation.

Microbiology

A knowledge of the bacteriology of secretions obtained directly from the maxillary sinus by needle aspiration (with careful avoidance of contamination from mucosal

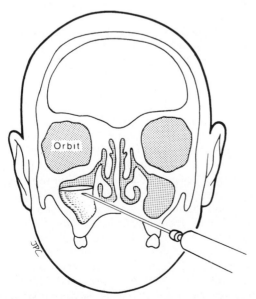

FIGURE 43–5. Preferred method of sinus aspiration.

surfaces) provides essential information for planning of antimicrobial therapy.

Whether there is a "normal" flora of the paranasal sinuses is an area of controversy.[8, 112, 113] Many investigators believe that the paranasal sinuses are, under normal conditions, sterile.[46, 114] It will be difficult to resolve this controversy, because the violation of normal sinus cavities can rarely be justified.

The role of anaerobic bacteria as pathogens in sinusitis has been examined infrequently but with adequate attention to anaerobic transport and culture techniques.[10, 111] Poor drainage of the inflamed sinus results in a lower pH and a lower partial pressure of oxygen, thereby providing an excellent environment for the growth of anaerobic bacteria. However, the in vitro growth of anaerobic bacteria may be impaired in sinus secretions obtained by irrigation, since this procedure increases oxygen pressure and dilutes bacterial titers. Finally, few studies have looked for viral agents as a cause of sinus infection, despite evidence that viruses alone may produce acute sinus disease.

Sinus Aspirates

Two elegant studies performed in adults in which careful attention was given to bacteriologic technique show nontypable *H. influenzae* and *S. pneumoniae* to be the most commonly found pathogens, accounting for approximately 74% of all bacterial strains recovered.[32, 50] Anaerobic bacteria accounted for 9% of isolates. Other bacteria implicated include *M. catarrhalis*, *S. pyogenes* (group A streptococcus), and alpha-hemolytic streptococcus. Mixed infection with heavy growth of two bacterial species was occasionally found, although most cultures grew only a single organism. Viruses were recovered from 12 of the 103 positive specimens; there were seven isolates of rhinovirus, three of influenza A, and two of parainfluenza virus. Five of these specimens also had significant growth of bacteria.

A study performed in 50 children with acute maxillary sinusitis showed the bacteriology of sinus secretions to be similar to that found in adults.[110] The predominant organisms include *S. pneumoniae*, *M. catarrhalis*, and nontypable *H. influenzae*. Both *H. influenzae* and *M. catarrhalis* may produce beta lactamase and consequently may be resistant to amoxicillin. Of interest, only a single anaerobic isolate, a *Peptostreptococcus*, was recovered from sinus secretions during this study. *Staphylococcus aureus* was not isolated from a maxillary sinus aspirate in this series. Several viruses, including adenovirus and parainfluenza virus, were also recovered.[108] Summary figures for the incidence of various bacteria in children with acute, subacute, and recurrent acute bacterial sinusitis are shown in Table 43–3.

Available microbiologic data from children with chronic sinusitis are limited and confusing because of variable definitions of chronic sinusitis, failure to obtain specimens aseptically, lack of quantitation of results, and concurrent use of antibiotics. Brook examined 40 patients alleged to have chronic sinusitis (symptoms longer than 3

TABLE 43–3. Bacteriology of Acute Sinusitis

Bacterial Species	Incidence (%)
Streptococcus pneumoniae	25–30
Moraxella catarrhalis	15–20
Haemophilus influenzae	15–20
Streptococcus pyogenes	2–5
Anaerobes	2–5
Sterile	20–35

weeks); anaerobes were isolated from 92% of patients.[9] The most common were anaerobic gram-positive cocci (staphylococci and streptococci), *Bacteroides* species, and fusobacteria. Aerobes, including staphylococci, streptococci, and *Haemophilus* species, were isolated from 38% of patients. Although the author concluded that anaerobes are an important group of microbes causing chronic sinusitis, the significance of these isolates in the absence of quantitation is uncertain.

Muntz and Lusk reported the bacterial flora of the ethmoid bullae in children with chronic sinusitis who were between the ages of 9 months and 17 years.[74] Specimens were obtained from the mucosa of the anterior ethmoid cell in patients undergoing endoscopic ethmoidectomy. All had received at least two courses of an appropriate antimicrobial agent and were treated until the day before surgery. Although nasal decongestion was achieved with topical application of cocaine, an effective antiseptic, contamination of the mucosa of the ethmoid bullae by nasal flora may not have been completely avoidable. Furthermore, no quantitation of the bacterial isolates was performed, and the antibiotics may have eradicated or prevented growth of other bacterial flora. Coagulase-negative staphylococci, often considered a contaminant of the nasal vault, were recovered from 44% of patients. The other common bacterial species recovered were alpha-hemolytic streptococci and *Staphylococcus aureus*, followed by *S. pneumoniae*, *H. influenzae*, and *M. catarrhalis*. Anaerobic organisms were grown from 6% of specimens.

Data from pediatric patients with chronic sinusitis were included in the discussion of subacute sinusitis by Tinkleman and Silk.[102] "Chronic" sinusitis was defined by symptoms that lasted more than 30 days. The predominant bacterial isolates were *H. influenzae*, *S. pneumoniae*, and *M. catarrhalis* in high density. Otten and Grote studied children with chronic sinusitis (purulent nasal discharge for more than 3 months).[79] Sinus aspiration without nasal preparation or quantitation of results yielded *S. pneumoniae* and *H. influenzae* in the majority of patients. Finally, Orobello et al studied children undergoing endoscopic surgery after at least 12 weeks of persistent symptoms and failure of medical management.[78] Many patients had underlying medical problems such as asthma and immunologic compromise. Although some bacterial species were recovered from 89% of sinuses, these were often polymicrobial, in very low density, and susceptible to the antimicrobial that was being administered. The predominance of *Staphylococcus epidermidis*, alpha-hemolytic streptococci, and other normal respiratory flora indicates, as the authors suggested, that most isolates probably represented contamination.

In patients with acute exacerbations of chronic sinusitis (intermittent episodes characterized by purulent nasal discharge) the usual microorganisms associated with acute sinusitis (i.e., *S. pneumoniae*, *M. catarrhalis*, and *H. influenzae*) are causative.[79, 102] In patients with chronic persistent sinusitis (nasal congestion or rhinorrhea or cough, alone or in combination), the role of bacterial agents is less clear.[74, 78] Most organisms have been recovered in low density, after inadequate sterilization of the contiguous mucosa, and frequently from patients receiving antibiotics to which these organisms are susceptible. The persistence of symptoms despite multiple courses of appropriate antimicrobial agents is counter to the notion that bacterial infection is a significant component of chronic sinusitis. All these observations support the hypothesis that bacterial infection has a minor role, if any, in chronic sinusitis in many patients.

Surface Cultures

It would be desirable to culture the nose, throat, and nasopharynx in patients with acute sinusitis if the predominant flora isolated from these surface cultures were predictive of the bacterial species recovered from the sinus secretions. It is unfortunate that the results of surface cultures have no predictive value; accordingly, nose, throat, and nasopharyngeal cultures cannot be recommended as guides to the bacteriology of and therapy for acute or chronic sinusitis.[109] It is important to note that approximately 20% of pediatric patients with acute sinusitis have pharyngeal infection with group A streptococci.[107] In these patients the mucositis caused by group A streptococci results in obstruction of the sinus ostia and a "secondary" bacterial infection of the paranasal sinuses.

Treatment

Treatment of acute maxillary sinusitis in the preantibiotic era consisted of topical decongestants and analgesics. In severe cases, sinus aspiration was performed. The current availability of numerous antimicrobial agents to which the bacteria recovered from sinus secretions are susceptible prompts consideration of antimicrobial drugs as standard treatment of acute sinusitis. The objectives of antimicrobial therapy for acute sinus infection are achievement of a rapid clinical cure, sterilization of the sinus secretions, prevention of suppurative orbital and intracranial complications, and prevention of chronic sinus disease.

Conflicting reports have appeared regarding the efficacy of antimicrobial drugs in the treatment of acute sinus infection in children and adults as judged by radiographic resolution and findings at subsequent irrigation procedures. An array of antimicrobial agents and varying dosage schedules make comparisons between different studies difficult and discrepancies hard to explain. However, several points emerge:

1. Appropriate antimicrobial agents eradicate suscepti-

ble microorganisms in sinus secretions, whereas inappropriate agents fail to do so.[46, 47, 110]
2. To accomplish sterilization of the sinus secretions, a level of antimicrobial agent exceeding the minimum inhibitory concentration for the infecting microorganism must be present in the sinus secretions.
3. In some instances in which adequate antimicrobial levels within sinus secretions are reported, sterilization of secretions is still not accomplished. This points to the importance of local defense mechanisms (e.g., ciliary activity and phagocytosis) that may be impaired in the altered environment within purulent sinus secretions (decreased partial pressure of oxygen, increased carbon dioxide pressure, and decreased pH). Accordingly, irrigation and drainage of sinus secretions may be required in some patients.
4. There does appear to be a decreased frequency of serious suppurative orbital and intracranial complications of paranasal sinus disease after the use of systemic antimicrobial agents.

Antimicrobial Agents

Acute Bacterial Sinusitis. Medical therapy with an antimicrobial agent is recommended for children diagnosed as having acute bacterial sinusitis. The challenge regarding the selection of appropriate antimicrobial agents for patients with acute bacterial sinusitis relates to the prevalence of bacterial pathogens that are resistant to amoxicillin. Resistance is found among beta-lactamase–producing *H. influenzae* and *M. catarrhalis*. Isolates of *S. pneumoniae* may also be resistant to penicillin and cephalosporins. The mechanism of resistance for *S. pneumoniae* is an alteration of penicillin-binding proteins. There is substantial geographic variability in the susceptibility of all these bacterial species to antimicrobial agents.

Currently, approximately 50% of *H. influenzae* and 100% of *M. catarrhalis* are likely to be beta-lactamase positive nationwide.[25, 26] *S. pneumoniae* is likely to be resistant to penicillin in 15% to 38% (average, 25%) of children; approximately 50% of bacterial species are highly resistant to penicillin and the remaining half are intermediate in resistance.[13, 27, 30, 94] Table 43–4 shows the calculation for the likelihood that a child with acute bacterial sinusitis will harbor a resistant pathogen and not respond to treatment with amoxicillin.

Clinicians must consider the following: the prevalence with which each bacterial species causes acute bacterial sinusitis, the prevalence of resistance among each bacterial species, and the rate of spontaneous improvement. Extrapolating from data derived from patients with acute otitis media, 15% of children with acute bacterial sinusitis caused by *S. pneumoniae* will recover spontaneously, about 50% of the children with acute bacterial sinusitis caused by *H. influenzae* will recover spontaneously (even when untreated), and one half to three quarters of the children infected with *M. catarrhalis* will also recover spontanously.[53] Furthermore, only *S. pneumoniae* that are highly resistant to penicillin will not respond to conven-

TABLE 43–4. Response to Treatment with Standard Doses of Amoxicillin* for Children with Acute Bacterial Sinusitis

Bacterial Species	Prevalence	Spontaneous Cure Rate	Prevalence of Resistance	Failure or Amoxicillin (%)
Streptococcus pneumoniae	30%	15%	25%	3°
Haemophilus influenzae	20%	50%	50%	5
Moraxella catarrhalis	20%	50–75%	100%	5–10

° Consider that 50% of resistant strains are highly resistant to penicillin, and only highly resistant isolates will fail to respond to standard doses of amoxicillin (45 mg/kg per day).

tional doses of amoxicillin. Accordingly, in the absence of any risk factors, approximately 80% of children with acute bacterial sinusitis will respond to treatment with amoxicillin. Risk factors for the presence of bacterial species that are even more likely to be resistant to amoxicillin include (1) attendance at day care, (2) recent receipt (<30 days) of antimicrobial treatment, and (3) age less than 2 years.[7, 64]

The desire to continue to use amoxicillin as first-line therapy in patients suspected of having acute bacterial sinusitis relates to its general effectiveness, safety and tolerability, low cost, and narrow spectrum. For patients with uncomplicated acute bacterial sinusitis that is mild to moderate in degree of severity, who do not attend day care, and who have not recently been treated with an antimicrobial drug, amoxicillin is recommended at either a usual dose of 45 mg/kg per day in two divided doses or a high dose of 90 mg/kg per day in two divided doses (Table 43–5). If the patient is allergic to amoxicillin, either cefdinir, cefuroxime, or cefpodoxime can be used (especially if the allergic reaction was not a type 1 hypersensitivity reaction). In cases of very serious allergic reactions, azithromycin or clarithromycin may be used in an effort to select an antimicrobial agent of an entirely different class. Alternative therapy in the penicillin-allergic patient who is known to be infected with a penicillin-resistant *S. pneumoniae* is clindamycin at 30 to 40 mg/kg per day in three divided doses.

If patients do not improve while receiving the usual dose of amoxicillin (45 mg/kg per day), have recently been treated with an antimicrobial agent, have an illness that is moderate or more severe, or attend day care,

TABLE 43–5. Antimicrobial Agents and Dosage Schedules for the Treatment of Sinusitis in Children

Antimicrobial	Dosage
Amoxicillin	45–90 mg/kg/day in 2 divided doses
Amoxicillin/potassium clavulanate	45/10 mg/kg/day in 2 divided doses
Amoxicillin/potassium clavulanate (high dose)	45/10 mg/kg/day in 2 divided doses plus amoxicillin at 45 mg/kg/day in 2 divided doses
Cefdinir	14 mg/kg/day in 1 or 2 daily doses
Cefuroxime axetil	30 mg/kg/day in 2 divided doses
Cefprozil	30 mg/kg/day in 2 divided doses
Cefpodoxime proxetil	10 mg/kg/day in 2 divided doses
Azithromycin	10 mg/kg/day on day 1; 5 mg/kg/day on days 2–5 in a single daily dose
Clarithromycin	15 mg/kg/day in 2 divided doses

therapy should be initiated with high-dose amoxicillin-clavulanate (80 to 90 mg/kg per day of amoxicillin component, with 6.4 mg/kg per day of clavulanate in two divided doses). This dose of amoxicillin will create a concentration of antimicrobial agent in the sinus cavity that will exceed the minimum inhibitory concentration (MIC) of all *S. pneumoniae* that are intermediate in resistance to penicillin, and some, but not all, that are highly resistant *S. pneumoniae*. There is sufficient potassium clavulanate to inhibit all beta-lactamase–producing *H. influenzae* and *M. catarrhalis*. Alternative therapies include cefdinir, cefuroxime, and cefpodoxime[37, 101] (See Table 43–5). Ceftriaxone (at 50 mg/kg per day), given intravenously or intramuscularly, can be used in children with vomiting that precludes administration of oral antibiotics. When the child has improved an oral antibiotic is then substituted to complete 10 days of therapy.

While trimethoprim-sulfamethoxazole and erythromycin-sulfisoxazole have traditionally been useful in the past as first- and second-line therapy for patients with acute bacterial sinusitis, recent pneumococcal surveillance studies indicate that resistance to these two combination agents is substantial.[27, 54] Therefore, when patients fail to improve while receiving amoxicillin, neither trimethoprim-sulfamethoxazole nor erythromycin-sulfisoxazole are good choices for antimicrobial therapy. For patients who do not improve on a second-line treatment or are acutely ill, it is appropriate to consult an otolaryngologist for consideration of maxillary sinus aspiration to obtain a sample of sinus secretions for culture and sensitivity so that therapy can be adjusted precisely.

The majority of patients with acute bacterial sinusitis who are treated with an appropriate antimicrobial agent respond promptly with a reduction in the nasal discharge and improvement in cough.[46, 114] Fever resolves if present initially. If patients have not shown substantial improvement after 72 hours of antibiotic therapy, either the diagnosis of sinusitis is incorrect or the antimicrobial therapy is ineffective.

Duration of therapy for patients with acute bacterial sinusitis has not received systematic study. Often empiric recommendations are made for 10, 14, 21, or 28 days of therapy. An alternative suggestion has been made that antibiotic therapy be continued until the patient becomes free of symptoms and then for an additional 7 days.[114] This strategy, which individualizes treatment for each patient, avoids prolonged courses of antibiotics in patients who are asymptomatic and thereby unlikely to be compliant.

One additional potential concern in selecting an antimicrobial regimen for patients who have sinusitis is infection with anaerobes. However, these organisms are uncommon isolates in children who have acute and subacute sinus infection. They should be considered in youngsters who either have very protracted symptoms or require surgical intervention. The gram-positive anaerobic streptococci and staphylococci are generally susceptible to penicillin and therefore do not present a problem. Virtually all the therapeutic regimens discussed will be satisfactory. The gram-negative *Bacteroides* species that produce beta-lactamase should respond well to amoxicillin potassium clavulanate.

Patients with acute sinusitis may require hospitalization because of systemic toxicity or inability to take oral antimicrobial agents. These patients may be given cefotaxime 200 mg/kg per day intravenously in four divided doses. Vancomycin at 60 mg/kg per day in four divided doses may be added in patients who appear very toxic. This approach may be necessary because the concentration of cefotaxime within the sinus cavity may not exceed the MIC of the infecting *S. pneumoniae* if it is highly resistant.

There are virtually no data available regarding the duration of antimicrobial therapy for patients with chronic sinusitis. Many clinicians recommend a minimum course of 3 to 4 weeks. In patients who are refractory to oral antimicrobial therapy, intravenous antibiotic therapy, based on results of cultures obtained by aspiration of the maxillary sinus, may be an alternative.[12]

Recurrent Acute Sinusitis. It is not uncommon for some children to have recurrent episodes of acute sinusitis. A definition of recurrent acute sinusitis that may be useful is similar to the one used to characterize recurrent acute otitis media, i.e., three episodes in 6 months or four episodes in a year. Most commonly, frequent viral URIs, often facilitated by day care arrangements, predispose to such recurrent episodes of acute sinusitis. However, it is appropriate when caring for a child with recurrent acute sinusitis to consider the factors listed in Table 43–1 that may predispose to ostial obstruction. A careful physical examination will eliminate the mechanical factors that might be etiologic or the presence of an apical tooth abscess. Further evaluation might include a search for upper respiratory allergy; a sweat test for cystic fibrosis; quantitative immunoglobulins, including immunoglobulin G subclasses (and assessment of responsiveness to polysaccharide antigens); and ciliary function tests. If none of these predisposing conditions is present, prophylactic antimicrobial therapy may be helpful. Although this strategy has not been systematically evaluated, extrapolation from experience with recurrent acute otitis media suggests that this therapy may prevent simple URIs from becoming complicated by bacterial sinusitis. Appropriate antimicrobials might include amoxicillin (20 mg/kg per day given at bedtime) or sulfisoxazole (75 mg/kg per day given in two divided doses) as the two principal agents previously assessed for efficacy in recurrent otitis media. Enthusiasm for this strategy is tempered by concerns regarding the encouragement of bacterial resistance. Accordingly, prophylaxis should only be considered in carefully selected children whose infections have been thoroughly documented.

Adjuvant Therapies

Adjuvant therapies, used to supplement the effect of antimicrobial therapy, have received relatively little systematic investigation.[118] Available agents include saline nasal irrigation (hypertonic or normal saline), antihistamines, decongestants (topical or systemic), mucolytic agents, and topical intranasal steroids.

There are no data presently to recommend the use of H1 antihistamines in children with acute bacterial sinusitis. There is a single prospective study in which children with presumed acute bacterial sinusitis were randomized to receive either decongestant-antihistamine or placebo in addition to amoxicillin. The active treatment group received topical oxymetazoline and oral decongestant-antihistamine syrup (brompheniramine and phenylpropanolamine). No difference in clinical or radiographic resolution was noted between groups.[72]

There has been a single study of intranasal steroids as an adjunct to antibiotics in children with presumed acute bacterial sinusitis. Intranasal budesonide spray had a very modest effect on symptoms only during the second week of therapy.[3] A multicenter, double-blind, randomized, parallel trial evaluating flunisolide spray as an adjunct to oral antibiotic therapy was reported in patients at least 14 years of age.[73] The benefit of flunisolide was marginal and of little clinical importance. There is little reason to expect a substantial benefit from intranasal steroids in patients with acute bacterial sinusitis when antibiotics work effectively in the first 3 to 4 days of treatment.

No clinical trials of mucolytics have been reported in children or adults with acute bacterial sinusitis.[95] Neither saline nose drops nor nasal spray have been studied in patients with acute bacterial sinusitis. However, by preventing crust formation and liquefying secretions, thereby keeping the ostia unobstructed, mucociliary clearance is facilitated. In addition, saline may also act as a mild vasoconstrictor of nasal blood flow.[95] A method for performing a nasal saline flush was reported by Schwartz[90] and may be helpful for parents of children with upper respiratory tract infections. In addition, parents should be informed that "nose blowing" is a risk factor for the development of acute bacterial sinusitis. They should caution their youngsters not to blow their noses but rather to dab or wipe away secretions.[48]

Irrigation and Drainage

Irrigation and drainage of the infected sinus may result in dramatic relief from pain for patients with acute bacterial sinusitis. In addition, with relief of pressure in the sinus, oxygenation and blood flow improve, thus restoring compromised defense mechanisms. Local immunoglobulin and complement levels increase, and proteolytic enzymes decrease in sinus secretions after irrigation procedures. Drainage procedures are usually reserved for those who fail to respond to medical therapy with antimicrobial agents or who have a suppurative intraorbital or intracra-

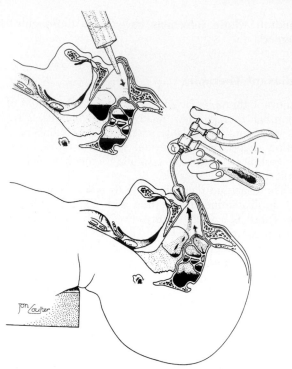

FIGURE 43–6. Sinus irrigation by the Proetz procedure. *Top,* The nose is first partially filled with normal saline. *Bottom,* The saline is then removed by suction through one nostril while the other nostril is occluded. The purpose of the procedure is to irrigate sinuses with partially patent ostia.

nial complication. If an episode of acute or chronic sinusitis cannot be treated effectively by medical therapy alone, drainage of the sinus cavity may be required. Several techniques are available.

The Proetz displacement method is the simplest of these techniques and can be used when obstruction of the sinus ostium is incomplete (Fig. 43–6). The nose and nasopharynx are filled with saline while the patient is supine and the head hyperextended. Suction of the nostrils removes the irrigating solution and nasal secretions. As the irrigation is repeated, the sinus ostia are cleaned and drainage of the sinuses is accomplished. A decongestant such as 0.25% phenylephrine in saline may be used as the irrigating solution. When the obstruction of the sinus ostium is complete, aspiration of the maxillary sinus may be performed as described earlier.

Surgical Therapy

Surgical therapy in children with chronic sinusitis focused initially on creating a nasoantral window, or fistula, in the maxillary sinus to facilitate gravitational drainage. These fistulas proved to be relatively ineffective, however, in part because the cilia that line the maxillary sinus still transport secretions toward the natural meatus. A retrospective review of the efficacy of nasoantral windows in children showed improvement in only 27% of patients at the 6-month follow-up.[74]

Functional endoscopic sinus surgery was introduced to the pediatric population in the late 1980s. The technique in children was modeled after work done by Stammber-

ger[97, 98] in Austria and Kennedy et al[57, 58] in the United States. The surgical technique is designed to alleviate the root cause of chronic sinusitis, a functional and occasionally mechanical obstruction of the outflow tract of the maxillary, ethmoid, and frontal sinuses. The operative technique focuses on the diseased ethmoidal osteomeatal complex, alleviating obstruction and reestablishing ventilation and drainage of the maxillary and frontal sinuses, without manipulation of the larger sinuses. Functional endoscopic sinus surgery has almost completely replaced the creation of nasal antral windows in children with chronic sinusitis.[74]

When functional endoscopic sinus surgery is performed, proper decongestion (vasoconstriction) of the nasal mucosa is essential for adequate visualization and hemostasis. Removal of the uncinate process, the ethmoid bulla, and a variable number of anterior ethmoidal cells is the first step. The maxillary sinus ostium is enlarged and the frontal recess (receiving drainage from the frontal sinus) is examined; diseased tissue is removed from the latter. The net effect is to widen the outflow tract of ethmoid, maxillary, and frontal sinuses. The patient is maintained on an oral antimicrobial regimen. In some centers, nasal steroids, saline solution, and decongestants are used routinely. Complications of the surgery include cerebrospinal fluid leak, temporary or permanent blindness, hemorrhage, and synechiae.[99] There is also a theoretical concern that endoscopic sinus surgery may lead to alteration of growth of the facial bones.

Four retrospective studies of children undergoing functional endoscopic sinus surgery have been reported to date.[40, 63, 65, 81] Many patients had prolonged difficulties; approximately 20% to 30% of those with extensive mucosal disease did not benefit from surgical intervention. Failures often occurred in children with underlying immunodeficiencies, cystic fibrosis, and dysmotile cilia syndrome. Associated problems of asthma and allergy were almost universal. Unfortunately, there was no way to assess the adequacy of the presurgical medical therapy presumed to be "maximal medical therapy." Had each child with underlying allergy received appropriate topical and systemic therapy, including bronchodilators? In those children receiving intranasal corticosteroid therapy, was the delivery system adequate to reach most of the nasal mucosa? The nagging question is whether the surgery was necessary. Furthermore, the effectiveness of this therapy has not been evaluated in any randomized clinical trials; accordingly, recommendations for the surgical management of children with chronic sinusitis are difficult to formulate.[16] The indications for and success of functional endoscopic sinus surgery in children require further study; in the meantime, judicious use of endoscopic surgery in children under 5 years of age is strongly advised.[17]

Odontogenic Sinusitis

The floor of the maxillary sinus is formed by the alveolar process of the maxillary bone. After birth, as the alveolar process and the sinus develop, the roots of the teeth and the sinus come into close proximity, at times separated only by paper-thin bone or sinus mucosa. Because of this proximity, periapical abscesses or periodontitis of the upper teeth may extend into the sinus cavity and cause maxillary sinusitis.[18] Perforation may occur from minor trauma to the area, dental instrumentation, or extraction or displacement of a chronically inflamed tooth. Congenital bony defects or dental cysts may provide a direct channel to the sinus, thus eliminating the need to traverse bone. If perforation of the sinus mucosa is not recognized, the tract may become epithelialized, and an oroantral fistula may form.

The incidence of odontogenic sinusitis in children is unknown but is probably significant, particularly in adolescents. In adults, 10% to 15% of all cases of maxillary sinusitis are thought to be of dental origin.

Symptoms are similar to those of primary sinusitis. A fetid odor may be prominent because the infection is often caused by anaerobic organisms. If an oroantral fistula is present, the patient may complain that pus is dripping into the mouth; fluids and air may pass from the oral cavity into the sinus and nose. Treatment consists of drainage of the dental abscess and operative closure of the oroantral fistula, if present, coupled with antimicrobial therapy[11] (see Chap. 56).

Allergy and Sinusitis

Individuals with atopic disease, either allergic rhinitis or asthma, have an increased frequency of sinusitis. The nasal and sinus mucosa of these patients is hypersecretory. Histologically, there is mucosal hyperplasia and infiltration with plasma cells and eosinophils. Secondary to this immune mediated hyperplastic sinusitis, ostial obstruction followed by bacterial infection is common. This may result in acute exacerbations of respiratory symptoms (particularly cough and rhinorrhea) or in difficulty in controlling symptoms (nasal congestion and wheezing) with usual therapy.

Maxillary sinus aspirates obtained from asthmatic children with exacerbations of asthma despite bronchodilator therapy show bacterial isolates similar to those obtained from nonasthmatic children with acute sinusitis.[36] Clinical symptoms and pulmonary function improve after antibiotic therapy. The antimicrobial agents chosen to treat an infectious episode in the atopic individual are not different from those selected to treat the nonallergic child with sinusitis, except that therapy may need to be continued beyond 14 days (see Chap. 47).

Fungal Sinusitis

Fungal sinusitis can take several different clinical forms and may occur in compromised or otherwise healthy individuals.[33] The compromised subgroup may include immunosuppressed, debilitated, or otherwise impaired patients who have malignancies or diabetes or who are receiving cytotoxic drugs. Depending on the particular fungus involved and the site of infection, this may be a life-threatening event.

In contrast, previously healthy patients may be infected with fungi and do rather well. The most common example is sinusitis caused by Aspergillus species. Patients with this infection usually present with unilateral infection of the maxillary sinus after very long-standing sinus symptoms that are not responsive to the usual antibiotic therapy.[100] A similar disease process may be caused by Alternaria, Petriellidium, Paecilomyces, or Bipolaris, all common soil organisms.[11, 34, 88, 93] Chronic disease and local invasion are the hallmarks of infection. Rarely, death results from local extension of the infectious process into the central nervous system.

Another form of chronic sinus infection is an allergic sinusitis caused by aspergilli and other fungi.[52] This manifestation of infection is similar to allergic bronchopulmonary aspergillosis. Patients usually have asthma or other evidence of atopy. Their sinus symptoms are very protracted, and characteristically more than one sinus is involved. The distinguishing feature, on histologic analysis of the sinus secretions, is degenerated eosinophils, Charcot-Leyden crystals, and an occasional fungal form on a pale amorphous background of mucin.[56] It is speculated that treatment with steroids is helpful, but this has not been carefully studied in children.[75]

A similar picture of allergy-like fungal sinusitis has also been reported to be due to Myriodontium keratinophilum.[67] The patient presented with chronic sinusitis, recurrent nasal polyps, and finally proptosis. The last was due to progressive local invasion of the roof of the orbit and the ethmoid air cells. Treatment was accomplished with amphotericin and drainage. Other cases of allergic fungal sinusitis have been reported to be due to Bipolaris,[39] Dreschlera,[35] and Curvularia and Alternaria.[4] These cases from the 1990s suggest that allergic fungal sinusitis may frequently be caused by bacteria other than Aspergillus species.[52]

In cases of long-standing sinus symptoms, fungal infection must be suspected. Appropriate specimens of sinus secretions and mucosal biopsies are required for definitive diagnosis. Surgical debridement is virtually always necessary for treatment and is sometimes sufficient, particularly in previously healthy persons. On the other hand, in patients with underlying diseases, systemic antifungal agents, usually amphotericin or one of the azoles, are the recommended adjuncts to aggressive local surgical débridement.

SELECTED REFERENCES

Clement PAR, Bluestone DC, Gordts F, et al. Management of rhinosinusitis in children: Consensus Meeting, Brussels, Belgium, September 13, 1996. Arch Otolaryngol Head Neck Surg 124:31, 1998.

Kronemer KA, McAlister WH. Sinusitis and its imaging in the pediatric population. Pediatr Radiol 27:837, 1997.

Sinus and Allergy Health Partnership. Antimicrobial Treatment Guidelines for Acute Bacterial Rhinosinusitis. Otolaryngol Head Neck Surg 123:S1, 2000.

Recommendations for diagnosis and treatment of acute bacterial rhinosinusitis with special emphasis on the appropriate use of antibiotics.

Sinusitis Guidelines. American Academy of Pediatrics: Pediatrics 108: 798, 2001.

Recommendations for health care providers regarding diagnoses, evaluation, and treatment of children with uncomplicated acute, subacute, and recurrent acute bacterial sinusitis in children ages 1 to 21 years.

Wald ER. Chronic sinusitis in children. J Pediatr 127:339, 1995.

A comprehensive review of the literature on chronic sinusitis in children.

REFERENCES

1. Aitken M, Taylor JA. Prevalence of clinical sinusitis in young children followed up by primary care practitioners. Arch Pediatr Adolesc Med 152:244, 1998.
2. Aust R, Drettner B, Falck B. Studies of the effect of peroral phenylpropanolamine on the functional size of the human maxillary ostium. Acta Otolaryngol (Stockh) 88:455, 1979.
3. Barlan IB, Erkan E, Booker M, et al. Intranasal budesonide spray as an adjunct to oral antibiotic therapy for acute sinusitis in children. Ann Allergy Asthma Immunol 78:598, 1997.
4. Bartynski JM, McCaffrey TV, Frigas E. Allergic fungal sinusitis secondary to dermatiaceous fungi—*Curvularia lunata* and *Alternaria*. Otolaryngol Head Neck Surg 103:32, 1990.
5. Beem MO. Acute respiratory illness in nursery school children: a longitudinal study of the occurrence of illness and respiratory viruses. Am J Epidemiol 90:30, 1969.
6. Beem MO, Saxon EM. Respiratory tract colonization and a distinctive pneumonia syndrome in infants infected with *Chlamydia trachomatis*. N Engl J Med 296:306, 1977.
7. Block SL, Harrison CJ, Hedrick JA, et al. Penicillin-resistant *Streptococcus pneumoniae* in acute otitis media: risk factors, susceptibility patterns and antimicrobial management. Pediatr Infect Dis J 16:79, 1997.
8. Brook I. Aerobic and anaerobic bacterial flora of normal maxillary sinuses. Laryngoscope 91:372, 1981.
9. Brook I. Bacteriologic features of chronic sinusitis in children. JAMA 246:967, 1984.
10. Brook I, Yocum P, Shah K. Aerobic and anaerobic bacteriology of concurrent chronic otitis media with effusion and chronic sinusitis in children. Arch Otolaryngol Head Neck Surg 126:174, 2000.
11. Bryan CS, Disalvo AF, Kaufman L, et al. *Petriellidium boydii* infection of the sphenoid sinus. Am J Clin Pathol 74:846, 1980.
12. Buchman CA, Yellon RF, Bluestone DC. Alternative to endoscopic sinus surgery in the management of pediatric chronic rhinosinusitis refractory to oral antimicrobial therapy. Otolaryngol Head Neck Surg 120:219, 1999.
13. Centers for Disease Control and Prevention. Geographic variation in penicillin resistance in Streptococcus pneumoniae-selected sites, United States, 1997. MMWR Morb Mortal Wkly Rep 48:656, 2000.
14. Carson JL, Collier AM, Hu SS. Acquired ciliary defects in nasal epithelium of children with acute viral upper respiratory infections. N Engl J Med 312:463, 1985.
15. Casselbrant ML, Kaleida PH, Rockette HE, et al. Efficacy of antimicrobial prophylaxis and of tympanostomy tube insertion for prevention of recurrent acute otitis media: results of a randomized clinical trial. Pediatr Infect Dis J 11:278, 1992.
16. Chan KH, Winslow CP, Levin MJ, et al: Clinical practice guidelines for the management of chronic sinusitis in children. Otolaryngol Head Neck Surg 120:328, 1999.
17. Chan KH, Winslow DP, Abzug MJ. Persistent rhinosinusitis in children after endoscopic sinus surgery. Otolaryngol Head Neck Surg 121:577, 1999.
18. Chow A, Roser S, Brady F. Orofacial odontogenic infections. Ann Intern Med 88:392, 1978.
19. Clement PAR, Bluestone CD, Gordts F, et al. Management of rhinosinusitis in children: Consensus Meeting, Brussels, Belgium, September 13, 1996. Arch Otolaryngol Head Neck Surg 124:31, 1998.
20. Conrad CJ, Taylor JA, Almquist JR, et al. Is an antihistamine-decongestant combination effective in temporarily relieving symptoms of the common cold in preschool children. J Pediatr 130:463, 1997.
21. Couch RB. The common cold: control? J Infect Dis 150:167, 1984.
22. Diament MJ. The diagnosis of sinusitis in infants and children: xray, computed tomography, and magnetic resonance imaging. J Allergy Clin Immunol 90:442, 1992.
23. Diament MJ, Senac MO, Gilsanz V, et al. Prevalence of incidental paranasal sinus opacification in pediatric patients: a CT study. J Comput Assist Tomogr 11:426, 1987.
24. Dingle JH, Badjer DF, Jordan WS Jr (eds). Patterns of illness. In Illness in the Home. Cleveland, Western Reserve University, 1964, p 347.
25. Doern GV, Brueggemann AB, Pierce G, et al. Antibiotic resistance among clinical isolates of *Haemophilus influenzae* in the United States in 1994 and 1995 and detection of beta-lactamase-positive strains resistant to amoxicillin-clavulanate: Results of a national multicenter surveillance study. Antimicrob Ag Chemother 41:292, 1997.
26. Doern GV, Jones RN, Pfaller MA, Kugler K. *Haemophilus influenzae* and *Moraxella catarrhalis* from patients with community-acquired respiratory tract infections: antimicrobial susceptibility patterns from the SENTRY antimicrobial Surveillance Program (United States and Canada, 1997). Antimicrob Ag Chemother 43:385, 1999.
27. Doern GV, Pfaller MA, Kugler K, et al. Prevalence of antimicrobial resistance among respiratory tract isolates of *Streptococcus pneumoniae* in North America: 1997 results from the SENTRY antimicrobial surveillance program. Clin Infect Dis 27:764, 1998.
28. Douglas RM, Moore BW, Miles HB, et al. Prophylactic efficacy of intranasal alpha$_2$ interferon against rhinovirus infections in the family setting. N Engl J Med 315:65, 1986.
29. Dowell SF, Marcy SM, Phillips WR, et al. Principles of judicious use of antimicrobial agents for pediatric upper respiratory infections. Pediatrics 101:163, 1998.
30. Dowell SF, Butler JC, Giebink GS, et al. Acute otitis media: management and surveillance in an era of pneumococcal resistance—a report from the Drug-resistant Streptococcus pneumoniae Therapeutic Working Group. Pediatr Infect Dis J 18:1, 1999.
31. Drettner B. Pathophysiology of paranasal sinuses with clinical implications. Clin Otolaryngol 5:272, 1980.
32. Evans RD Jr, Sydnor JB, Moore WEC, et al. Sinusitis of the maxillary antrum. N Engl J Med 293:735, 1975.
33. Ferguson BJ. Definitions of fungal rhinosinusitis. Otolaryngol Clin North Am 33:227, 2000.
34. Frenkel L, Kuhls TL, Nitta K, et al. Recurrent *Bipolaris* sinusitis following surgical and antifungal therapy. Pediatr Infect Dis J 6:1130, 1987.
35. Friedman GC, Hartwick RW, Ro JY, et al. Allergic fungal sinusitis. Report of three cases associated with dermatiaceous fungi. Am J Clin Pathol 96:368, 1991.
36. Friedman R, Ackerman M, Wald E, et al. Asthma and bacterial sinusitis in children. J Allergy Immunol 74:185, 1984.
37. Gehanno P, Depondt J, Barry B, et al. Comparison of cefpodoxime proxetil with cefaclor in the treatment of sinusitis. J Antimicrobial Chemother 26 (Suppl E):87, 1990.
38. Glasier CM, Ascher DP, Williams KD. Incidental paranasal sinus abnormalities on CT of children: clinical correlation. AJNR Am J Neuroradiol 7:861, 1986.
39. Gourley DS, Whisman BA, Jorgenson NL, et al. Allergic *Bipolaris* sinusitis: clinical and immunopathologic characteristics. J Allergy Clin Immunol 85:583, 1990.
40. Gross CW, Gurucharri MJ, Lazar RH, Long TE. Functional endoscopic sinus surgery (FESS) in the pediatric age group. Laryngoscope 99:272, 1989.
41. Gwaltney JM Jr, Sydnor A Jr, Sande MA. Etiology and antimicrobial treatment of acute sinusitis. Ann Otol Rhinol Laryngol 90:68, 1981.
42. Gwaltney JM Jr, Hendley JO. Transmission of experimental rhinovirus infection by contaminated surfaces. Am J Epidemiol 116:828, 1982.
43. Gwaltney JM Jr, Hendley JO, Mygind N. Symposium on rhinovirus pathogenesis: summary. Acta Otolaryngol (Stockh) 413:43, 1984.
44. Gwaltney JM Jr. Virology and immunology of the common cold. Rhinology 23:265, 1985.
45. Gwaltney JM Jr, Phillips CD, Miller RD, et al. Computed tomographic study of the common cold. N Engl J Med 330:25, 1994.
46. Gwaltney JM Jr. Acute community-acquired sinusitis. Clin Infect Dis 23:1209, 1996.
47. Gwaltney JM Jr. Acute community-acquired bacterial sinusitis: To treat or not to treat. Can Respir J 6(Suppl A):46A, 1999.
48. Gwaltney JM Jr, Hendley JO, Phillips CD, et al. Nose blowing

propels nasal fluid into the paranasal sinuses. Clin Infect Dis 30: 387, 2000.

49. Hall CB, Douglas RG Jr. Modes of transmission of respiratory syncytial virus. J Pediatr 99:100, 1981.

50. Hamory BH, Sande MA, Sydnor A Jr, et al. Etiology and antimicrobial therapy of acute maxillary sinusitis. J Infect Dis 39:197, 1979.

51. Hayden FG, Albrecht JK, Kaiser DL, et al. Prevention of natural colds by contact prophylaxis with intranasal alpha$_2$ interferon. N Engl J Med 314:71, 1986.

52. Houser SM, Corey JP. Allergic fungal sinusitis: pathophysiology, epidemiology and diagnosis. Otolaryngol Clin North Am 33:399, 2000.

53. Howie VM, Ploussard JH. The in vivo sensitivity test: Bacteriology of middle ear exudate during antimicrobial therapy in otitis media. Pediatrics 44:940, 1969.

54. Jacobs, MR, Bajaksouzian S, Zilles A, et al. Susceptibilities of Streptococcus pneumoniae and Haemophilus influenzae to 10 oral antimicrobial agents based on pharmacodynamic parameters: 1997 U.S. Surveillance study. Antimicrob Ag Chemother 43:1901, 1999.

55. Karmody CS, Carter B, Vincent ME. Developmental anomalies of the maxillary sinus. Trans Am Acad Ophthalmol Otolaryngol 84: 723, 1977.

56. Katzenstein A, Sale SR, Greenberger PA. Pathologic findings in allergic Aspergillus sinusitis. Am J Surg Pathol 7:439, 1983.

57. Kennedy DW, Zinreich SJ, Rosenbaum AE, Johns ME. Functional endoscopic sinus surgery: theory and diagnostic evaluation. Arch Otolaryngol Head Neck Surg 111:577, 1985.

58. Kennedy DW, Zinreich SJ, Shaalan H, et al. Endoscopic middle meatal antrostomy: theory, technique and patency. Laryngoscope 97 (Suppl 43):1, 1987.

59. Kovatch AL, Wald ER, Ledesma Medina J, et al. Maxillary sinus radiographs in children with nonrespiratory complaints. Pediatrics 73:306, 1984.

60. Kronemer KA, McAlister WH. Sinusitis and its imaging in the pediatric population. Pediatr Radiol 27:873, 1997.

61. Krugman S, Katz SL, Gershon AA, et al. Infectious Diseases of Children, 8th ed. St. Louis, CV Mosby, 1985.

62. Lazar RH, Younis RT, Parvey LS. Comparison of plain radiographs, coronal CT, and interoperative findings in children with chronic sinusitis. Otolaryngol Head Neck Surg 107:29, 1992.

63. Lazar RH, Younis RT, Long TE. Functional endoscopic sinus surgery in adults and children. Laryngoscope 103:1, 1993.

64. Levine OS, Parley M, Harrison LH, et al. Risk factors for invasive pneumococcal disease in children: a population-based case-control study in North America. Pediatrics 103:28, 1999.

65. Lusk RP, Muntz HR. Endoscopic sinus surgery in children with chronic sinusitis: a pilot study. Laryngoscope 100:654, 1990.

66. Mann W. Diagnostic ultrasonography in paranasal sinus diseases: a 5 year review. ORL J Otorhinolaryngol Relat Spec 41:168, 1979.

67. Maran AGD, Kwong K, Mine LJR, et al. Frontal sinusitis caused by Myriodontium keratinophilum. Br Med J 290:207, 1985.

68. Maresh M, Washburn AH. Paranasal sinuses from birth to late adolescence. II. Clinical and roentgenographic evidence of infection. Am J Dis Child 60:841, 1940.

69. McAlister WH, Lusk R, Muntz HR. Comparison of plain radiographs and coronal CT scans in infants and children: a clinical correlation. AJR Am J Roentgenol 153:1259, 1989.

70. McAlister WH, Kronemer K. Imaging of sinusitis in children. Pediatr Infect Dis J 18:1019, 1999.

71. McAlister WH, Parker BR, Kushner DC, et al. ACR task force on appropriateness of criteria for imaging and treatment decisions. Expert panel on pediatric imaging for possible acute or chronic sinusitis. American College of Radiology: www.acr.org/appropriateness criteria/sinusitis in the pediatric population.

72. McCormick DP, John SD, Swischuk LE, Uchida T. A double-blind, placebo-controlled trial of decongestant-antihistamine for the treatment of sinusitis in children. Clin Pediatr 35:457, 1996.

73. Meltzer EO, Orgel HA, Backhaus JW, et al. Intranasal flunisolide spray as an adjunct to oral antibiotic therapy for sinusitis. J Allergy Clin Immunol 92:812, 1993.

74. Muntz HR, Lusk RP. Nasal antral windows in children: a retrospective study. Laryngoscope 100:643, 1990.

75. Muntz HR. Allergic fungal sinusitis in children. Otolaryngol Clin North Am 29:185, 1996.

76. Naclerio R, Gwaltney J, Hendley O, et al. Preliminary observations in rhinovirus-induced colds. In Myers EN (ed). New Dimensions in Otorhinolaryngology. Head and Neck Surgery, Vol I. New York, Elsevier, 1985, p 341.

77. Ohashi Y, Nakai Y. Functional and morphological pathology of chronic sinusitis mucous membrane. Acta Otolaryngol (Stockh) 397:11, 1983.

78. Orobello PW Jr, Park RI, Belcher LJ, et al. Microbiology of chronic sinusitis in children. Arch Otolaryngol Head Neck Surg 117:980, 1991.

79. Otten FWA, Grote JJ. Treatment of chronic maxillary sinusitis in children. Int J Pediatr Otorhinolaryngol 15:269, 1988.

80. Otten FWA, Grote JJ. The diagnostic value of transillumination for maxillary sinusitis in children. Int J Otolaryngol 18:9, 1989.

81. Parsons DS, Phillips SE. Functional endoscopic sinus surgery in children: a retrospective analysis of results. Laryngoscope 103:899, 1993.

82. Powers GF, Boivert PD. Age as a factor in streptococcosis. J Pediatr 25:481, 1944.

83. Rachelefsky GS, Katz RM, Siegel SC. Diseases of the paranasal sinuses in children. Curr Probl Pediatr 12:1, 1982.

84. Reilly JS, Hotaling AJ, Chiponis D, et al. Use of ultrasound in detection of sinus disease in children. Int J Pediatr Otorhinolaryngol 17:225, 1989.

85. Reimer A, von Mecklenburg C, Tormalm NG. The mucociliary activity of the upper respiratory tract. III: A functional and morphological study of human and animal material with special reference to maxillary sinus disease. Acta Otolaryngol (Stockh) 355:3, 1978.

86. Revonta M. A-mode ultrasound of maxillary sinusitis in children. Lancet 1:320, 1979.

87. Ritter FN. The Paranasal Sinuses: Anatomy and Surgical Technique. St Louis, CV Mosby, 1973.

88. Rowley SD, Strom CG. Paecilomyces fungus infection of the maxillary sinus. Laryngoscope 92:332, 1982.

89. Sanchez P. Congenital syphilis. Adv Pediatr Infect Dis 7:161, 1992.

90. Schwartz RH. The nasal saline flush procedure. Pediatr Infect Dis J 16:725, 1997.

91. Shapiro GG, Furukawa CT, Person WE, et al. Blinded comparison of maxillary sinus radiography and ultrasound for diagnosis of sinusitis. J Allergy Clin Immunol 77:59, 1986.

92. Shopfner CE, Rossi JO. Roentgen evaluation of the paranasal sinuses in children. AJR Am J Roentgenol 118:176, 1973.

93. Shugar MA, Montgomery WW, Hyslop NE. Alternaria sinusitis. Ann Otol 90:251, 1981.

94. Sinus and Allergy Health Partnership. Antimicrobial treatment guidelines for acute bacterial rhinosinusitis. Otolaryng 123:S1, 2000.

95. Spector SL and the Joint Task Force on Practice Parameters for Allergy and Immunology. Parameters for the diagnosis and management of sinusitis. J Allergy Clin Immunol 102:S107, 1998.

96. Stagno S, Brasfield DM, Brown MB, et al. Infant pneumonitis associated with cytomegalovirus, Chlamydia, Pneumocystis, and Ureaplasma: a prospective study. Pediatrics 68:322, 1981.

97. Stammberger H. Endoscopic endonasal surgery: concepts in the treatment of recurring rhinosinusitis. I. Anatomic and pathophysiologic considerations. Otolaryngol Head Neck Surg 94:143, 1986.

98. Stammberger H. Endoscopic endonasal surgery: concepts in the treatment of recurring rhinosinusitis II. Surgical technique. Otolaryngol Head Neck Surg 94:147, 1986.

99. Stankiewicz JA. Complications of endoscopic intranasal ethmoidectomy. Laryngoscope 97:1270, 1987.

100. Stevens MH. Aspergillosis of the frontal sinus. Arch Otolaryngol 104:153, 1978.

101. Sydnor A Jr, Gwaltney JM Jr, Cocchetto DM, Scheld WM. Comparative evaluation of cefuroxime axetil and cefaclor for therapy of acute bacterial maxillary sinusitis. Arch Otolaryngol Head Neck Surg 115:1430, 1989.

102. Tinkleman DG, Silk HJ. Clinical and bacteriologic features of chronic sinusitis in children. Am J Dis Child 143:938, 1989.

103. Tomassini JE, Colonno RJ. Isolation of a receptor protein involved in attachment of human rhinoviruses. J Virol 58:290, 1986.

104. Turner RB, Hendley JO, Gwaltney JM Jr. Shedding of infected ciliated epithelial cells in rhinovirus colds. J Infect Dis 145:846, 1982.

105. Turner RB, Sperber SJ, Sorrentino JV, et al. Effectiveness of clemastine fumarate for treatment of rhinorrhea and sneezing associated with the common cold. Clin Infect Dis 25:824, 1997.

106. Ueda D, Yoto Y. The ten-day mark as a practical diagnostic approach for acute paranasal sinusitis in children. Pediatr Infect Dis J 15:576, 1996.

107. Wald ER, Chiponis D, Ledesma Medina J. Comparative effectiveness of amoxicillin and amoxicillin-clavulanate potassium in acute paranasal sinus infections in children: a double-blind, placebo-controlled trial. Pediatrics 77:795, 1986.

108. Wald ER, Guerra N, Byers C. Upper respiratory tract infections in young children: duration of and frequency of complications. Pediatrics 87:129, 1991.

109. Wald ER, Milmoe GJ, Bowen A, et al. Acute maxillary sinusitis in children. N Engl J Med 304:749, 1981.

110. Wald ER, Reilly JS, Casselbrant M, et al. Treatment of acute maxillary sinusitis in children: a comparative study of amoxicillin and cefaclor. J Pediatr 104:297, 1984.

111. Wald ER. The microbiology of chronic sinusitis in children. A review. Acta Oto-Rhino-Laryngol Belg 51:51, 1997.

112. Wald ER. Chronic sinusitis in children. J Pediatr 127:339, 1995.

113. Wald ER. Microbiology of acute and chronic sinusitis in children and adults. Am J Med Sci 316:13, 1998.

114. Wald ER. Sinusitis. Pediatr Ann 27:811, 1998.

115. Williams JW Jr, Simel DL. Does their patient have sinusitis? Diagnosing acute sinusitis by history and physical examination. JAMA 270:1242, 1993.

116. Winther B, Gwaltney JM Jr, Mygind N, et al. Sites of rhinovirus recovery after point inoculation of the upper airway. JAMA 256:1763, 1986.

117. Winther B, Gwaltney JM Jr, Mygind N, Hendley O. Viral-induced rhinitis. Am J Rhinol 12:17, 1998.

118. Zeiger RS. Prospects for ancillary treatment of sinusitis in the 1990s. J Allergy Clin Immunol 90:478, 1992.

44

Surgical Management of Chronic Rhinosinusitis

Rodney Lusk, M.D.

The literature evaluating the surgical management of pediatric chronic rhinosinusitis is starting to become clearer. Accumulating evidence indicates that adenoidectomy and endoscopic sinus surgery are efficacious in treating patients with chronic rhinosinusitis. The indications, however, have to be well defined, and endoscopic surgery should be a last resort. The following procedures have been historically advocated for the surgical management of chronic rhinosinusitis.

Tonsillectomy and Adenoidectomy

Early investigators noted an association between the tonsils, adenoids, and sinuses.[34, 52] Merck[29] noted that the larger the adenoid pad, the greater the incidence of maxillary opacification on plain films. The early literature supported tonsillectomy and adenoidectomy as a treatment for recurrent and chronic rhinosinusitis, but the indications and diagnosis were not well defined for either. Numerous authors have noted that tonsillectomy and adenoidectomy did not uniformly correct all cases of rhinosinusitis.[1, 4, 13, 16, 33, 47, 50] Paul[33] observed that chronic rhinorrhea was as effectively treated with antibiotics as with tonsillectomy and adenoidectomy. Large adenoid pads (Fig. 44–1) that cause nasal airway obstruction and stasis of secretions may mimic the symptoms of chronic rhinosinusitis and be associated with the disease. When the adenoid pad is removed, these symptoms often resolve, but it remains unclear whether affected children really had chronic rhinosinusitis.[49] The data of Rosenfeld[37] and Parsons and Phillips[32] indicate that adenoidectomy failed to clear 14 of 14 children with rhinosinusitis documented by computed tomography (CT). Gross et al[8] reported that previous tonsillectomy and adenoidectomy had failed in 57% of all patients undergoing endoscopic surgery. I concur with Gross,[9] who thinks that a patent nasopharynx is essential for normal nasal physiology but that not all cases of rhinosinusitis are cleared by adenoidectomy.

One cannot be emphatic about the positive or negative effects of adenoidectomy in treating pediatric chronic rhinosinusitis. At this stage, the surgeon must exercise judgment regarding adenoidectomy. It would seem prudent, however, to remove a large obstructive adenoid pad as an initial mode of therapy and see whether the symptoms resolve. If symptoms persist, a more thorough investigation for chronic rhinosinusitis is indicated. I think that if rhinosinusitis is significant, adenoidectomy can be performed concurrently with endoscopic sinus surgery; however, if the adenoid pad is enlarged, it is prudent to perform the adenoidectomy first. It is not clear whether adenoid size is the only criterion for removal.

Antral Lavage

Antral lavage has been described as both a diagnostic test and a therapeutic modality for recurrent and chronic rhinosinusitis. In younger children, performing this procedure through the inferior meatus may not be feasible because the floor of the maxillary sinus is not adequately developed. Also, the procedure cannot be performed in most children without a general anesthetic. Antral lavage may be used as a diagnostic maneuver to assess the contents of the maxillary sinus. The anterior wall of the maxillary sinus is thick, and the teeth buds increase the risk with the canine fossa approach for antral lavage. Rarely is one antral lavage successful; several authors have recommended multiple therapeutic lavages.[5, 26, 46, 47] Because of the smallness of the sinus in pediatric patients, the need for general anesthesia, and the need for multiple irrigations, antral lavage is not considered feasible in children. Many authors think that antral lavage is of value as a diagnostic test.

Nasal Antral Windows (Inferior Meatal Antrostomy)

The inferior meatal antrostomy has been advocated for treating chronic rhinosinusitis. Lund[21] found that in 45% of adults and the majority of children, inferior meatal antrostomies were closed at the time of reevaluation. Prospectively, she found that the size of the antrostomy needed to be at least 1 cm × 0.5 cm to maintain patency. The high closure rate in pediatric patients is likely secondary to the inability of the surgeon to make the ostium large enough. In smaller patients, this would require removing much of the medial wall of the maxillary sinus.

Another reason the inferior meatal antrostomy does not function is that the cilia continue to carry secretions

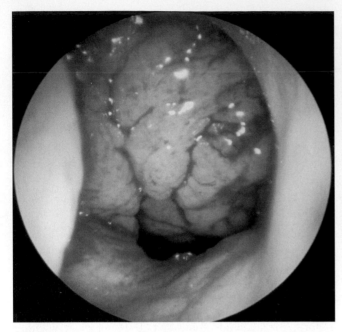

FIGURE 44–1. Patient with a large adenoid pad that likely warrants surgical excision before adenoidectomy is undertaken.

to the obstructed natural ostium, resulting in stasis of secretions.

Muntz and Lusk[31] retrospectively evaluated 35 children who had undergone bilateral inferior meatal antrostomy: symptoms were not controlled in 60% of the patients at 1 month and in 73% at 6 months. The authors therefore elected to abandon this procedure as a primary surgical modality for treating chronic rhinosinusitis in children.

Inferior meatal antrostomy may continue to have a place in patients with ciliary dyskinesia, but this has not been definitively assessed.

The secretions pool in the inferior portion of the maxillary sinus and gravity may play a role in draining the sinuses.

Middle Meatal Antrostomy

An alternative method of ventilating the maxillary sinus is to open the natural ostium through the middle meatus. As noted earlier, there is evidence of accumulation of secretions at the ostium of the maxillary sinus. This suggests that an obstructed ostium is the source of the problem and that enlarging it may be therapeutic.

Early in this century, middle meatal antrostomy was routinely performed in adult patients. Proetz,[35] however, thought that the natural ostium carried the nerves and vascular supply to the maxillary sinus and should therefore not be violated. Hilding[12] performed experiments in nine rabbits and concluded that the chance of infection was highest when the ostium to the maxillary sinus was violated. Although he cautioned clinicians not to extrapolate this idea to humans, it subsequently became heresy to perform a middle meatal maxillary antrostomy.

In the late 1940s, Wilkerson[51] rekindled interest in middle meatal antrostomy, and since then it has once again gained wide acceptance. In 1987, Kennedy et al[17]

evaluated 117 adult patients and found that middle meatal antrostomies were difficult to perform in 17% of patients. The ostium was readily identified in the rest of the cases, and 98% remained widely patent 4 to 32 months later.

Identifying the natural ostium in children is frequently difficult. The uncinate process must almost always be removed. If the ostium can be seen without removal of the uncinate process, the hole is likely an accessory ostium and not the "natural" ostium.

The necessity of a maxillary antrostomy "enlargement of the ostium" in chronic maxillary rhinosinusitis remains controversial.[39] Data are too few to allow a definitive recommendation.

Endoscopic Sinus Surgery

The Hopkins rod lens telescope is the most recent significant advance in instrumentation for rhinosinusitis. These telescopes were used initially for diagnostic work. Over time, the scopes were used to assist in sinus operations. Endoscopic surgery was originally explored in adult patients, and over time smaller instruments were developed to allow procedures in children. As techniques have become more refined and sparing of mucosa, the smaller instruments developed for children have become more common in adult surgery. Development of microdebriders or shavers and sharp through-biting instruments, which preserve mucosa, represent the most recent advances in instrumentation.[16, 22, 41] These instruments have proved invaluable in preserving mucosa of the ethmoid cavity.

In children, endoscopic surgery has some distinct theoretical advantages. Messerklinger[30] described the principles to be used for endoscopic sinus surgery, and the procedure was popularized by Kennedy et al[6, 17, 18] and Stammberger.[40, 44, 45] Preservation of normal structures and mucosa is most important, particularly in the pediatric population (because of the narrowness of the sinus cavity and the fact that structures are still developing). Most chronic rhinosinusitis in children is located in the anterior ethmoid and maxillary sinuses (Table 44–1). It therefore appears appropriate to remove the anterior disease by approaching the anterior ethmoids and maxillary sinuses directly through the middle meatus via the techniques recommended by Messerklinger,[30] Stamberger,[40, 42, 43] and Kennedy et al.[15, 16]

The diagnosis of acute sinusitis does not require radiologic confirmation, but surgical intervention should not be performed without first obtaining a CT scan. This scan is performed to rule out anatomic lesions, which increase the risks of endoscopic surgery, and to confirm the pres-

TABLE 44–1. Chronic Sinusitis in Children

Total with disease in maxillary and ethmoid sinuses	34 (30.09%)
Total with both sinuses clear	45 (39.82%)
Total with ethmoid sinus clear/maxillary diseased	20 (17.70%)
Total with ethmoid sinus diseased/maxillary clear	14 (12.39%)
Total	113 (100.00%)

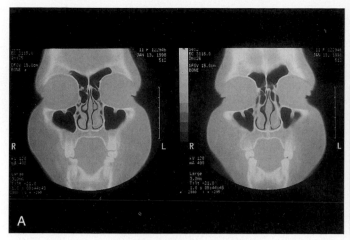 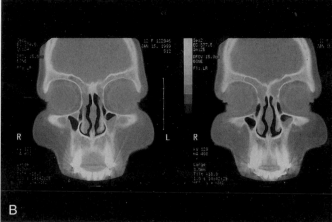

FIGURE 44–2. *A,* Patient with minimal disease prior to surgery. *B,* Significant postoperative frontal sinusitis. Initial surgery was performed by another surgeon.

ence of disease. CT cannot assess the chronicity of an infection, but if the patient has been on prolonged courses of antibiotics (4 to 6 weeks) and the disease is persistent on CT, the infection can be assumed to be chronic. An appropriate work-up for systemic disease and trial of medical management should be instituted prior to considering surgery.

With our current state of knowledge, appropriate medical modalities continue to include several courses of long-term (4 to 6 weeks) broad-spectrum antibiotics and probably topical nasal steroid sprays before surgery is considered. Amoxicillin remains the preferred first course of antibiotics for acute sinusitis largely because of the high spontaneous cure rates (70% to 80%).[14] Alternative antibiotics for patients who are allergic to penicillins include cefdinir, cefuroxime, cefpodoxime, azithromycin, clarithromycin, and clindamycin. If the symptoms recur within a few days, amoxicillin-clavulanate acid (Augmentin) is the appropriate treatment for β-lactamase–producing *Haemophilus influenzae* and *Moraxella catarrhalis* and intermediate-resistant *Streptococcus pneumoniae*. Recently evolved pneumococcal resistance has rendered trimethoprim-sulfamethoxazole and erythromycin-sulfisoxazole no more effective than amoxicillin, and therefore these agents are not recommended as second-line drugs.

Symptoms should have persisted for at least several months; I would be hesitant to perform endoscopic sinus surgery in a child with symptoms of less than 6 months' duration unless other factors were involved. CT should always show evidence of sinusitis, and CT should be performed at the end of a prolonged course of antibiotics. It is important to realize that evidence of disease is not an absolute indication for endoscopic sinus surgery. In fact, harm can be inflicted with inappropriate surgical intervention (Fig. 44–2). At our center, we frequently elect to observe mild disease noted on CT if the patient is asymptomatic. It is important to instruct the parents, *before* the CT scan is obtained, that a small amount of disease does not mean that surgery is indicated. It is also important to note that a single CT scan implies nothing about the chronicity of infections.

In children it is important to assess for the presence of systemic disease. *All patients being considered for endoscopic sinus surgery should undergo allergy evaluation.* The exact relationship between allergies and rhinosinusitis requires further definition. If the symptoms are mild and the amount of disease documented on CT is mild, it may be prudent to first treat the allergies and then assess the severity of symptoms associated with rhinosinusitis. It is important to understand the allergic status of all patients because it is our impression that highly allergic patients are less likely to respond favorably to surgical intervention. This is important when counseling parents about realistic expectations.

Systemic disease should always be considered in patients with rhinosinusitis, otitis media, and pneumonia or bronchitis. Screening tests should be ordered to rule out immune deficiency and in children with severe disease. Cystic fibrosis should be ruled out with a sweat test and genetic counseling. Patients with a history of cough, recurrent pneumonia, or bronchitis should undergo chest radiography to rule out situs inversus, which would raise suspicion of Kartagener syndrome. If ciliary dyskinesia is suspected, tracheal cilia probably represent the best culture site.

Screening immunoglobulins (IgG, IgM, IgA, and possibly IgE) should be obtained in all patients being considered for surgery. In assessing the efficacy of the immune system, it may also be advisable to obtain vaccine titers for HiB, tetanus, pneumococcus, or a combination thereof. In fact, the pediatrician or pediatric allergist usually obtains these titers. The need for obtaining IgG subclasses remains debatable as 10% of the population is abnormal[7] yet asymptomatic. If an underlying immune deficiency is identified, endoscopic sinus surgery should still be considered because symptomatic improvement is often possible.[24] Complete weaning from antibiotics is unlikely in patients with an underlying immune deficiency[24]—a fact to remember during discussions of surgical expectations with parents.

If the patient has rhinosinusitis and pulmonary disease, a sweat test to rule out cystic fibrosis becomes particularly important. The patient must be thoroughly evaluated prior to surgical intervention. The indications for endo-

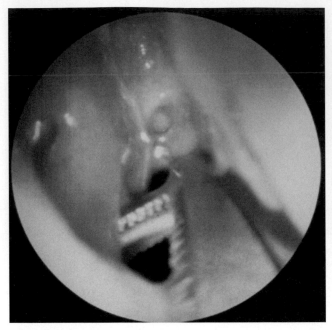

FIGURE 44–3. Back-biter being used to remove the uncinate process of a hypoplastic maxillary sinus.

scopic ethmoidectomy and maxillary antrostomy will and need to undergo further refinement. Currently accepted indications include (1) complete nasal obstruction in cystic fibrosis, (2) antrochoanal polyp, (3) intracranial complications, (4) mucoceles and mucopyoceles, (5) orbital abscess, (6) traumatic injury in the optic canal, (7) dacryocystorhinitis due to sinusitis and resistant to appropriate medical treatment, (8) fungal sinusitis, (9) some meningoencephaloceles, and (10) some neoplasms. Possible indications include chronic rhinosinusitis that persists despite optimal medical management, which includes broad-spectrum oral antibiotics for 2 to 6 weeks, and after exclusion of systemic disease.[3]

The technique of pediatric endoscopic sinus surgery, which is described in detail in other texts,[25] is beyond the scope of this chapter. A few comments regarding technique are appropriate, however.

In children, a general anesthetic is always required. I have found 0.05% oxymetazoline to be a better vasoconstrictor than cocaine or phenylephrine.[36] After approximately 5 minutes, the nose is examined with the telescope. Transoral sphenopalatine blocks with 0.5 mL of 1% lidocaine with 1:100,000 epinephrine are now routinely used with better vasoconstriction and no complications to date. Usually, an obstructive adenoid pad has already been removed as part of an initial surgical intervention.

The pediatric nasal cavity is best examined with a 2.7-mm zero-degree telescope. The zero-degree telescope is used to prevent distortion of the image and to allow the nose to be examined with as little trauma as possible. The best way to examine the middle meatus of children is to slightly displace the middle turbinate medially with a Freer elevator and insert the telescope into the middle meatus. It cannot be overemphasized that this requires gentle technique to avoid medialization or trauma to the

middle turbinate. Examination of the sphenoid recess in children is difficult without first performing an ethmoidectomy. Some surgeons recommend that the 4.0-mm telescope be used in almost all children,[8] but the author thinks that the 2.7-mm telescope should be used more frequently to decrease trauma to the tissues. With practice, the view is not restrictive and the light is adequate.

The uncinate process is identified initially with a zero-degree telescope and a seeker. The best way to remove the inferior portion of the uncinate process is with a back-biter and a seeker. A "window" is cut into the uncinate process with a back-biter. The window should lead up to its anterior-most articulation. The uncinate is then removed inferiorly with a seeker and the mucosal edge is removed with a mechanical shaver or debrider. There is no other way to efficiently remove this mucosa. The uncinate can be removed with a sickle knife as well, but the back-biter is safer. If the patient has hypoplastic maxillary sinuses, the safest way to remove the uncinate is with the back-biter (Fig. 44–3). The superior uncinate process is left intact or removed with the mechanical debrider or a J curette. It is important not to extend the dissection into the root or insertion of the middle turbinate. When all the uncinate process is removed, the middle meatus is maximally opened, and the chance of trauma to the lateral surface of the middle turbinate is minimized. In other words, increased working space in the middle meatus is obtained laterally, not medially, through the complete or partial excision of the uncinate process. The procedure is often started with a 2.7-mm telescope; once the uncinate process is removed, the 4.0-mm telescope can be used.

The ostium of the maxillary sinus is easiest to identify with a seeker and a 30-degree telescope after the uncinate process has been removed (Fig. 44–4). If the ostium

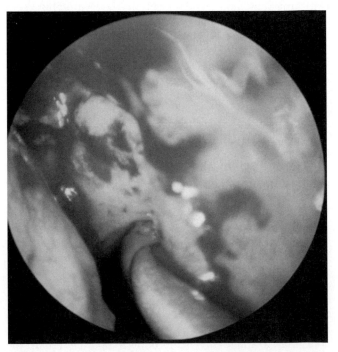

FIGURE 44–4. Ostium of the maxillary sinus being identified with the seeker.

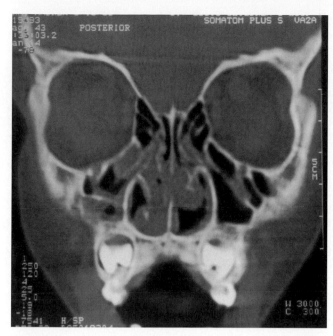

FIGURE 44–5. CT scan of right diseased infraorbital cell and left nondiseased infraorbital cell.

is small or obstructed with edematous mucosa, it remains my practice to open the ostium into the posterior fontanel. However, I do not attempt to create a large ostium, which was my practice in the past. If the ostium can be visualized, I leave it unaltered. If the sinus is filled with purulent secretion, this is the appropriate time for culture. If infraorbital cells are present, they should be removed at the time of antrostomy (Fig. 44–5). Not all these cells require removal, but they may be a reason the ostium fails to remain patent (Fig. 44–6).

Once the maxillary antrostomy has been performed, the ethmoid bulla is entered in a controlled manner. It may be entered with a J curette, cup forceps, or the newer through-biting forceps. I prefer the sharp through-biting forceps as they preserve the mucosa along the lamina papyracea. Anaerobic, aerobic, and fungal cultures are frequently taken at this time. As the medial wall of the ethmoid bulla is removed, care is taken not to traumatize the mucosa on the lateral border of the middle turbinate as this decreases the chance of scarring in the middle meatus. The lateral border of the middle turbinate is followed to the basal lamina, which defines the posterior extent of dissection in an anterior ethmoidectomy. The mucosa over the basal lamella can be kept intact if an anterior ethmoidectomy is all that is necessary.

Once the ethmoid bulla is removed, a 30-degree telescope is used to identify the lamina papyracea (Fig. 44–7). If sharp mucosa-sparing techniques have been used, the mucosa over the lamina papyracea will be preserved and there will be less scar tissue formed during healing. As a general rule, the frontal recess is not dissected unless disease is extensive. I try not to dissect above the root or insertion of the middle turbinate and make every attempt not to strip mucosa from the recess. The appropriate management of the developing frontal recess and frontal sinus remains unclear. It would seem prudent to be very conservative in the frontal recess until more is known about its development. Scarring in this area can cause life-long morbidity.

If there is disease in the posterior ethmoid cells, the basal lamella is penetrated at this time. The posterior cells are larger than the anterior cells, and the roof of the ethmoid is easier to identify posteriorly. The cells are best entered inferiorly, and the forceps are directed along

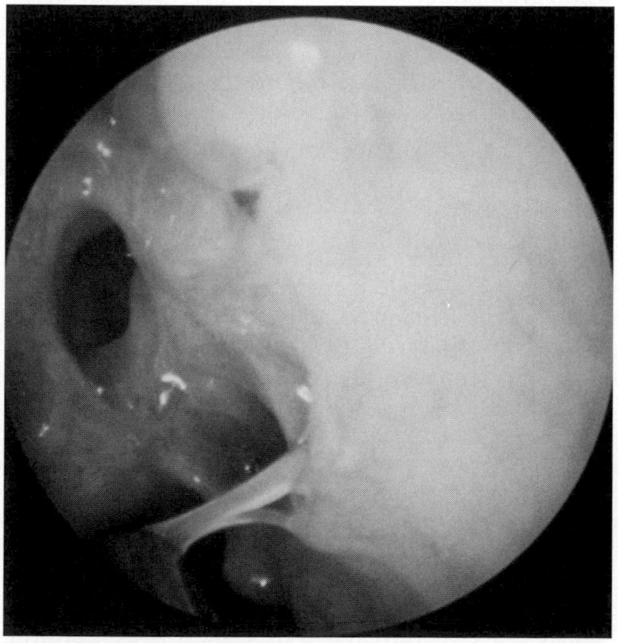

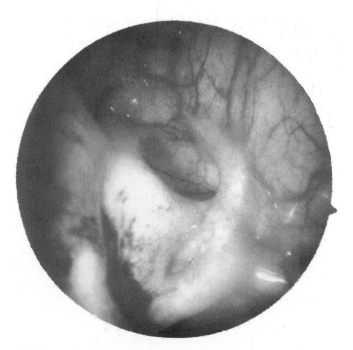

FIGURE 44–6. Failed maxillary antrostomy due to scarring and edematous mucosa anteriorly.

FIGURE 44–7. View of the lamina papyracea, which is still covered with mucosa.

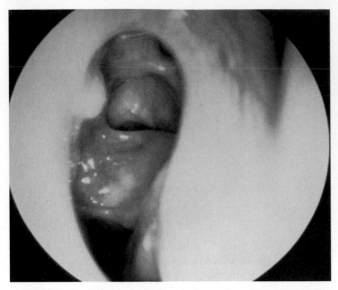

FIGURE 44–8. View of a patent postoperative middle meatus.

the lateral roof toward the thicker frontal bone. The sharp through-biting forceps are extremely helpful in this region as they can preserve mucosa in the posterior ethmoid. As the dissection is carried posteriorly, care should be taken to dissect along the superior medial wall of the posterior ethmoid or sphenoid sinus. This minimizes the risk of damaging the optic nerve.

The sphenoid sinus is not as frequently diseased in children as in adults and therefore is not as frequently opened. In children, the sphenoid must be entered through the ethmoid cells because there is not enough room to enlarge the sphenoid ostium through the sphenoid recess. The sphenoid ostium may be entered through several mechanisms. The first is to follow a line from the root of the inferior turbinate, along the lower one third of the middle and superior turbinate. This usually takes the surgeon to the natural ostium in both children and adults. The middle turbinate usually has to be infractured slightly, for which a 2.7-mm telescope is used. The ostium can also be identified from within the ethmoid cavity through the superior meatus. The inferior half of the superior turbinate may also be transected to allow visualization of the natural ostium of the sphenoid sinus. The sinus can then be enlarged inferiorly with minimal risk of trauma to the surrounding structures.

The usual postoperative care for sinus endoscopy patients must be modified for the pediatric age group. Postoperatively, most children resist manipulation of the nose. I currently stent the ethmoid cavity with rolled MeriGel (Xomed Medtronics, Jacksonville, FL), and I no longer use Gelfilm (Upjohn, Kalamazoo, MI), which is removed at 2 weeks under a second general anesthetic. There is no concrete evidence that either stenting material is superior. The MeriGel has dissolved by 2 weeks, and the second general anesthetic is not necessary. Indeed, there is some evidence that stenting is not necessary at all.[48] During the postoperative phase, the patient remains on full-dose antibiotics. These methods yield very limited scarring (Fig. 44–8). Several groups have reported that endoscopic ethmoidectomy can be performed safely in

children.[8, 10, 20, 23, 28, 32, 38] Gross et al[8] reported 3 to 13 months of follow-up data on 57 children 3 to 13 months old for an overall success rate of 92%, with 64% of patients improved and 28% resolved (or cured).

A meta-analysis by Hebert and Bent[11] showed that most studies reported a success rate of 77% to 100%. These authors showed a positive outcome of 88.7% in 882 children. The failures may be secondary to systemic disease such as immunodeficiencies, cystic fibrosis, or ciliary dyskinesia.

The goal of endoscopic sinus surgery is to create a wider opening into the middle meatus to improve drainage. The most frequent procedure performed, constituting one third of cases, is a bilateral anterior ethmoidectomy and maxillary antrostomy; the next most frequent procedure is a total ethmoidectomy and maxillary antrostomy. Overall, the degree of improvement is remarkably consistent, in the 80% range.[8, 20, 23, 32]

There is little information about the incidence and effectiveness of the revision surgery in children. Lazar et al[19] reported an overall success rate of 78% in their revision surgery patients, but only a small percentage of these patients were children. My overall revision rate is currently 9.5%. I have prospectively collected data on symptoms in 22 of 45 patients.

I demonstrated significant reduction ($p < .002$) in rhinorrhea, nasal obstruction, irritability, day cough, and night cough. There was a trend toward resolution of headaches ($p = .27$), but it was not significant. When the parents were asked to subjectively rate their child's symptoms on a 1 (worst ever) to 10 (normal) scale, 14 were improved, 2 unchanged, and 7 worse according to their last visit. This was a significant improvement ($p = .02$). By physicians' review, 60% of the 45 revision ethmoidectomies yielded significant improvement or resolution. I now have 10-year postoperative data that show statistical improvement in the symptoms of sinusitis and well-being, according to parental assessment, when surgically treated patients are compared with patients who did not undergo surgery. When the individual symptoms are compared at 10 years out, the trend is toward improvement, but this trend is not statistically significant.

Facial Growth

There has been a long-standing concern that endoscopic sinus surgery in a child can cause facial growth abnormalities. Some growth abnormalities have been noted in piglet models[2, 27] but not in children. I elected to evaluate this potential problem in a retrospective age-matched cohort 10-year outcome study in children. Sixty-seven of 131 children meeting exclusion and inclusion criteria participated. There were 46 boys and 21 girls, and the mean age was 3.1 years at presentation and 13.2 years at followup. The study groups consisted of 46 children who underwent endoscopic sinus surgery before age 5 and 21 age-matched children who did not undergo endoscopic surgery.

Quantitative anthropometric analysis was performed using standard measurements and criteria as well as qualitative facial analysis performed by a facial plastic expert

10 years after surgery. Quantitative anthropometric measurements obtained showed *no* statistical significance or trend toward a difference between the surgical and nonsurgical groups. Qualitative analysis of facial proportions also showed no statistically significant difference between groups.

It can now be stated that there is no evidence that facial growth alteration will be clinically significant 10 years after endoscopic sinus surgery in children. These results should aid physicians when discussing risks of endoscopic surgery with parents.

Conclusions

Much work needs to be done on the natural history and the etiology of pediatric chronic rhinosinusitis in children. Rhinosinusitis is undoubtedly multifactorial and therefore difficult to treat. With children's immature immune systems and developing anatomy, a conservative approach is warranted because, with maturation, the situation may well improve. As we understand more about the pathophysiology of rhinosinusitis, we will be able to adopt better medical intervention and appropriately identify children requiring surgical intervention.

REFERENCES

1. Carmack JW. Sinusitis in children. Ann Otol Rhinol Laryngol 40:515, 1931.
2. Carpenter KM, Graham SM, Smith RJ. Facial skeletal growth after endoscopic sinus surgery in the piglet model. Am J Rhinol 11:211, 1997.
3. Clement PA, Bluestone CD, Gordts F, et al. Management of rhinosinusitis in children. Int J Pediatr Otorhinolaryngol 49(Suppl 1):S95, 1999.
4. Cleminson FJ. Nasal sinusitis in children. J Laryngol Otol 36:505, 1921.
5. Crooks J, Signy AG. Accessory nasal sinusitis in childhood. Arch Dis Child 11:281, 1936.
6. Friedman M, Josephson JS, Kennedy DW, et al. Difficult decisions in endoscopic sinus surgery. Otolaryngol Clin North Am 22:777, 1989.
7. Geha RS. IgG antibody response to polysaccharides in children with recurrent infections. Monogr Allergy 23:97, 1988.
8. Gross CW, Gurucharri MJ, Lazar RH, Long TE. Functional endonasal sinus surgery (FESS) in the pediatric age group. Laryngoscope 99:272, 1989.
9. Gross CW. The diagnosis and management of sinusitis in children. Surgical management: an otolaryngologist's perspective. Pediatr Infect Dis 4(Suppl):S67, 1985.
10. Haltom JR, Cannon CR. Functional endoscopic sinus surgery in children. J Miss State Med Assoc 34:1, 1993.
11. Hebert RL, Bent JP. Meta-analysis of outcomes of pediatric functional endoscopic sinus surgery. Laryngoscope 108:796, 1998.
12. Hilding AC. Experimental sinus surgery: effects of operative windows on normal sinuses. Ann Otol Rhinol Laryngol 50:379, 1941.
13. Hoshaw TC, Nickman NJ. Sinusitis and otitis in children. Arch Otolaryngol 100:194, 1974.
14. Howie VM, Owen MJ. Bacteriologic and clinical efficacy of cefixime compared with amoxicillin in acute otitis media. Pediatr Infect Dis J 6:989, 1987.
15. Kennedy DW, Senior BA. Endoscopic sinus surgery. A review. Otolaryngol Clin North Am 30:313, 1997.
16. Kennedy DW, Zinreich SJ, Rosenbaum AE, Johns ME. Functional endoscopic sinus surgery. Theory and diagnostic evaluation. Arch Otolaryngol 111:576, 1985.
17. Kennedy DW, Zinreich SJ, Shaalan H, et al. Endoscopic middle meatal antrostomy: theory, technique, and patency. Laryngoscope 97:1, 1987.
18. Kennedy DW. Serious misconceptions regarding functional endoscopic sinus surgery [letter]. Laryngoscope 96:1170, 1986.
19. Lazar RH, Younis RT, Long TE, Gross CW. Revision functional endonasal sinus surgery. Ear Nose Throat J 71:131, 1992.
20. Lazar RH, Younis RT, Long TE. Functional endonasal sinus surgery in adults and children. Laryngoscope 103:1, 1993.
21. Lund VJ. The results of inferior and middle meatal antrostomy under endoscopic control. The results of inferior and middle meatal antrostomy under endoscopic control [review]. Acta Otorhinolaryngol Belg 47:65, 1993.
22. Lusk RP, Lazar RH, Muntz HR. The diagnosis and treatment of recurrent and chronic sinusitis in children [review]. Pediatr Clin North Am 36:1411, 1989.
23. Lusk RP, Muntz HR. Endoscopic sinus surgery in children with chronic sinusitis—a pilot study. Laryngoscope 100:654, 1990.
24. Lusk RP, Polmar SH, Muntz HR. Endoscopic ethmoidectomy and maxillary antrostomy in immunodeficient patients. Arch Otolaryngol Head Neck Surg 117:60, 1991.
25. Lusk RP. Surgical management of chronic sinusitis. In Lusk RP (ed). Pediatric Sinusitis. New York, Raven Press, 1992, pp 77–126.
26. Maes JJ, Clement PA. The usefulness of irrigation of the maxillary sinus in children with maxillary sinusitis on the basis of the Water's X-ray. Rhinology 25:259, 1987.
27. Mair EA, Bolger WE, Breisch EA. Sinus and facial growth after pediatric endoscopic sinus surgery. Arch Otolaryngol Head Neck Surg 121:547, 1995.
28. Manning SC, Wasserman RL, Silver R, Phillips DL. Results of endoscopic sinus surgery in pediatric patients with chronic sinusitis and asthma [see comments]. Arch Otolaryngol Head Neck Surg 120:1142, 1994.
29. Merck W. Relationship between adenoidal enlargement and maxillary sinusitis. HNO 6:198, 1974.
30. Messerklinger W. Endoscopy of the Nose. Baltimore, Urban & Schwarzenberg, 1978.
31. Muntz HR, Lusk RP. Nasal antral windows in children: a retrospective study. Laryngoscope 100:643, 1990.
32. Parsons DS, Phillips SE. Functional endoscopic surgery in children: a retrospective analysis of results. Laryngoscope 103:899, 1993.
33. Paul D. Sinus infection and adenotonsillitis in pediatric patients. Laryngoscope 91:997, 1981.
34. Preston HG. Maxillary sinusitis in children, its relation to coryza, tonsillectomy and adenoidectomy. Va Med Mon 82:229, 1955.
35. Proetz AW. Essays on the Applied Physiology of the Nose. St Louis, Annals, 1941.
36. Riegle EV, Gunter JB, Lusk RP, et al. Comparison of vasoconstrictors for functional endoscopic sinus surgery in children. Laryngoscope 102:820, 1992.
37. Rosenfeld RM. Pilot study of outcomes in pediatric rhinosinusitis. Arch Otolaryngol Head Neck Surg 121:729, 1995.
38. Rosenfeld RM. Pilot Study of Outcomes in Pediatric Rhinosinusitis. 1993 [unpublished].
39. Setliff RC. The small-hole technique in endoscopic sinus surgery. Otolaryngol Clin North Am 30:341, 1997.
40. Stammberger H, Posawetz W. Functional endoscopic sinus surgery. Concept, indications and results of the Messerklinger technique. Eur Arch Otorhinolaryngol 247:63, 1990.
41. Stammberger H. [Personal endoscopic operative technic for the lateral nasal wall—an endoscopic surgery concept in the treatment of inflammatory diseases of the paranasal sinuses]. Laryngol Rhinol Otol (Stuttg) 64:559, 1985.
42. Stammberger H. Endoscopic endonasal surgery—concepts in treatment of recurring rhinosinusitis. Part II. Surgical technique. Otolaryngol Head Neck Surg 94:147, 1986.
43. Stammberger H. Endoscopic endonasal surgery—concepts in treatment of recurring rhinosinusitis. Part I. Anatomic and pathophysiologic considerations. Otolaryngol Head Neck Surg 94:143, 1986.
44. Stammberger H. Functional Endoscopic Sinus Surgery. Philadelphia, BC Decker, 1991.
45. Stammberger H. Nasal and paranasal sinus endoscopy. A diagnostic and surgical approach to recurrent sinusitis. Endoscopy 18:213, 1986.
46. St. Clair T, Negus VE. Diseases of the Nose and Throat. London, 1937.

47. Stevenson RS. The treatment of subacute maxillary sinusitis especially in children. Proc R Soc Med 40:854, 1947.

48. Tom LW, Palasti S, Potsic WP, et al. The effects of gelatin film stents in the middle meatus. Am J Rhinol 11:229, 1997.

49. Vandenberg SJ, Heatley DG. Efficacy of adenoidectomy in relieving symptoms of chronic sinusitis in children. Arch Otolaryngol Head Neck Surg 123:675, 1997.

50. Walker FM. Tonsillectomy and adenoidectomy: unsatisfactory results due to chronic maxillary sinusitis. Br Med J 2:908, 1947.

51. Wilkerson WW. Antral window in the middle meatus. Arch Ophthalmol 49:463, 1949.

52. Wilson TG. Surgical anatomy of ENT in the newborn. J Laryngol Otol 69:229, 1955.

45

Complications of Nasal and Sinus Infections

Arthur S. Hengerer, M.D., F.A.C.S., and Darrell A. Klotz, M.D.

The treatment of complications of nasal and paranasal sinus infections remains an important portion of the practice of modern pediatric medicine. Although the total number of these complications has been dramatically reduced with the advent of antibiotics, the morbidity and mortality risks of such complications have remained relatively constant, a situation that is likely a reflection of the proximity of such vital structures as the eye and cranial contents. Despite the early and judicious use of antibiotic therapy, complications still occur and may become more common given current concerns regarding the increased occurrences of antibiotic resistance. The contemporary practitioner may not be as well versed as older colleagues in the early recognition of, and therapy for, these problems (see Chaps. 43 and 44).

The proper diagnosis can be made only if the physician knows the presenting characteristics of these complications and maintains a high index of suspicion. This chapter provides an overview of such nasal and paranasal sinus infection complications so the reader will be more attuned to their accurate diagnosis and treatment (Table 45–1).

Nasal Infection Complications

The child's nasal mucosa contains fragile, pseudostratified, ciliated, columnar epithelium that is frequently disturbed and susceptible to complications of infection. Several known specific nasal diseases can affect the child. Furthermore, the child's nose is a prominent structure of facial anatomy exposed to frequent blunt trauma.

Synechiae

Physiologic function of the normal nasal mucosa with its cyclic swelling allows opposing surfaces within the nasal cavity to contact one another. If inflammatory, traumatic, or iatrogenic causes result in a raw surface of granulating tissue, then a fibroblastic matrix may be laid down along these opposing surfaces. Consequently, bands of scar tissue, so-called synechiae, are then formed, stretching between any two anatomic structures within the nasal vault.

Once these bands of scar tissue form, the complications of mechanical blockage occur, with altered air currents and interference with the proper physiologic flow of the "mucus blanket." This may cause chronic rhinorrhea and a change in the viscosity and amount of postnasal drainage. Posterior pharyngeal irritation and eustachian tube inflammation may result. Moreover, metaplastic changes in the nasal mucosa can occur with concomitant crusting, ulceration, and bleeding in the area anterior to the synechiae formation. Synechiae in the lateral aspects of the nose, between the turbinates and the floor of the nose or septum, may alter normal sinus drainage from the semilunar hiatus or from surgically created nasoantral windows. This occurrence may prevent normal drainage of the sinuses (mucociliary system) and result in an obstruction of the sinuses, leading to recurrent sinusitis. This may be an iatrogenic result from sinus surgery or septoplasty in some cases.

Lysis of the synechial bands is usually corrective, as long as the raw surfaces are allowed to heal unopposed. This is best accomplished by the use of Teflon or Silastic sheets placed within the nasal vault between the lateral wall of the nose and the nasal septum. These sheets are sutured through-and-through to the nasal septum to allow them to stay in position for a 10- to 14-day period.

Septal Hematoma and Abscess

Septal hematoma or abscess from nasal trauma, post-septoplasty, or recurrent nasal/paranasal sinus infection is a feared complication because of the significant cosmetic and functional sequelae. Saddle-nose deformity, nasal airway obstruction, nasal septal perforation, and extension of infection into paranasal or even intracranial structures are problems that have occurred as complications of septal hematoma and abscesses. When the hematoma develops, the septal mucosa is erythematous and swollen, often touching the turbinates or lateral nasal wall. The swelling is doughy in consistency and may be tender. Depending on whether there is a communication within the cartilaginous septum, the hematoma or abscess cavity may be either unilateral or bilateral, which can be determined by direct visual examination and palpation. If only unilateral involvement exists, permanent complications are less likely because there is persistent nourishment to the cartilage through the opposite nasal mucoperichondrium (see Chap. 47).

Once recognized, a septal hematoma or abscess must

TABLE 45–1. Complications of Nasal and Sinus Infections

Local
  Synechiae
  Polyps
  Osteomyelitis
  Septal hematomas
  Septal abscesses
  Mucoceles
  Pyoceles
Orbital
  Cellulitis
  Abscesses
Intracranial
  Meningitis
  Brain abscesses
    Epidural
    Subdural
  Cavernous sinus thrombosis
Systemic
  Lower respiratory diseases
  Chronic bronchitis
  Bronchiectasis

be treated by incision and drainage with wide opening of the tissue planes. In most children, general anesthesia is used. The cavity should be packed lightly with ¼-inch iodoform gauze and the patient should receive intravenous antibiotic therapy. High-dose penicillin is the initial drug of choice unless culture reports of the abscess drainage indicate the presence of resistant organisms. When incision and drainage and antibiotic treatment is not given early enough or when results are ineffective, significant complications can develop.

The interruption of the septal cartilage blood supply by the hematoma or abscess may result in eventual cartilage necrosis and resorption. An anterior septal perforation of varying size often develops in this necrotic area and usually persists. The margins of these perforations often contain exposed cartilage edges and areas of granulation tissue, which maintain a superficial infection of saprophytic organisms. This, plus the dryness caused by the irregular air currents passing through the perforation, causes mucosal crusting and the subjective sensation of nasal obstruction. These crusts need to be removed frequently, a process often accompanied by bleeding, which, at times, may be significant. The child's annoyance with such crusting often leads to habitual nose picking, with enlargement of the perforation. Depending on the size of the perforation, a whistling sound may also be created by nose breathing, which is aggravating to both the child and the parent. Repairs of such perforations by the use of various mucosal flaps or connective tissue grafts are satisfactory, but decrease in success the larger the perforation becomes.

Further septal cartilage necrosis can cause collapse of all septal support, with concomitant airway obstruction. Such collapse alters the shape of the nasal vault, specifically in the internal nasal valve area between the septum and the upper lateral cartilage, which is considered important to the patient's awareness of nasal airflow. Similarly, the cartilage collapse also creates the cosmetic de-

formity known as *saddle-nose deformity*. This external collapse may appear immediately if the cartilage loss is severe, or it may develop gradually with increasing age as a result of the loss or as a result of the alteration in the growth centers with maturity. Conservative repair of such a functional and cosmetic deformity need not wait until the child reaches maturity but should be instituted 6 to 12 months after the active disease process has been controlled.

A more serious complication of septal cartilage infection is intracranial extension. Not only can direct extension of infection occur easily as a result of the close proximity of the nose to the base of the skull, but also because the angular veins between the nose and the midportion of the face are without intraluminal valves. Hematogenous extension of infection through these pathways may allow early development of septicemia and involvement of the cavernous sinus, meninges, frontal lobe, and bony cranium. These complications are discussed later.

Paranasal Sinus Infection Complications

When children suffering from generalized metabolic or inherited defects (e.g., diabetes, cystic fibrosis, and aplastic anemias) are excluded, chronic sinus infections are relatively rare in children younger than 16 years. In adults, however, acute and chronic infections occur without associated systemic disease. Complications of acute sinus infections seem to occur more frequently in children than among the general adult population. These complications can be divided into three categories: (1) those with local spread, (2) those with intracranial involvement, and (3) those with systemic symptoms.

The complications that do ensue from acute and chronic sinus disease in children are linked directly to the anatomic relationship of the paranasal sinuses to other structures of the head, neck, and chest. Most commonly involved are the orbit, cranium, cranial vault, and chest. The local, direct extension of disease-causing complications is the result of several distinct factors attributable to the facial structures of children. These influencing tendencies are the thinner bony septa of the sinus walls, larger vascular foramina, more porous bones, and open suture lines. In younger children, the lack of development of a frontal sinus limits development of some intracranial complications in this younger group. Finally, any febrile child younger than 3 months of age should undergo assessment according to the Rochester Criteria for febrile infants.[25]

Orbital Complications

Rhinosinusitis is the predominant cause of orbital infections in children, and subperiosteal abscess is the most common complication of sinusitis (15%).[1, 34, 37, 42] Ocular complications of sinusitis, however, are relatively rare because of the high success rate (75%) of conservative therapy with antibiotics.[37] Early diagnosis and treatment of simple orbital cellulitis can prevent progression to abscess formation, intraconal involvement with visual loss,[36] and life-threatening spread to the intracranial space.

Otolaryngologists are most frequently consulted for orbital cellulitis when associated with sinusitis. Lid edema and erythema represent an inflammatory reaction, which may be the result of many causes, only one of which is rhinosinusitis. One should maintain a working familiarity with other etiologies of orbital cellulitis as listed in Table 45–2.[47] This is particularly pertinent in the pediatric population in which an accurate history is often difficult to obtain and because children often lack some of the classic signs and symptoms of sinusitis such as rhinorrhea, nasal congestion, and cough.[18, 48]

Many classifications of the progression of orbital cellulitis exist, making discussions among otolaryngologists, radiologists, ophthalmologists, and pediatricians at times confusing and frustrating. Using precise terms, emphasis should be placed on the accurate description of the character and extent of disease involving the orbital structures. Less emphasis should be given to fitting a particular classification system to the clinical and radiographic findings. Not all professionals may be readily familiar with the classification chosen. Specific questions to address include the following: (1) What is the extent of post-septal involvement? (2) Is there an organized, drainable abscess or merely a phlegmon/cellulitic process? (3) Is there visual loss or significant diplopia? Understanding the importance of these questions and continually revisiting them allow the physician to logically and safely map out a management plan for the patient. Attempts to classify the step-by-step development of the spread of orbital infection have been suggested by many authors.[6, 32, 37, 42, 47] The classification system in Table 45–3 is an amalgam of others' classifications but most closely resembles that put forth by Pereira.[37]

The paper-thin bony plates separating the ethmoid and maxillary sinuses from the orbit allow infection to easily spread from one to the other, particularly in the pediatric age group.[2] With ethmoid sinusitis, the thickened, inflamed mucosa obstructs natural drainage into the nose. Direct (contiguous) and hematogenous spread of infection from the ethmoid labyrinth into the orbit first produces periorbital inflammation (edema and erythema of the eyelids, especially in the upper medial quadrants). Similarly, spread of infection from isolated maxillary sinusitis may cause only lower lid edema and erythema. There should not be any visual deficits, diplopia, or gaze limitation, and the child should not appear toxic. Treatment at this early

TABLE 45–2. Differential Diagnosis of Orbital Cellulitis

Trauma/skin disruption
Insect bites
Allergies
Hordeolum
Meibomian gland abscess
Blepharitis
Conjunctivitis
Dacryocystitis
Tumors (inflammatory or malignant)

TABLE 45–3. Classification of Orbital Involvement

Preseptal
 Isolated upper and/or lower lid edema and erythema
 Lid erythema/edema with chemosis
 Lid edema and chemosis with mild gaze limitation/diplopia
Postseptal
 Extraconal
  Subperiosteal abscess
  Effacement of periorbital fat, rectus muscle edema
  Proptosis
  Decreased EOM, diplopia, mild visual loss
  Lateral globe displacement
 Intraconal
  Orbital abscess or phlegmon
  Visual loss (severe)
  Proptosis
  Ophthalmoplegia
Cavernous sinus thrombosis
 Proptosis
 Fixed globe
 Severe visual loss
 Bilateral ocular signs
 Meningitis

Modified from Pereira KD, Mitchell RB, Younis RT, Lazar RH. Management of medial subperiosteal abscess of the orbit in children—a 5 year experience. Int J Pediatr Otorhinolaryngol 38:247–254, 1997.

stage consists of oral antibiotics, nasal decongestants, and close (daily) follow-up on an outpatient basis with the pediatrician or otolaryngologist, with a low threshold for admission to the hospital for intravenous antibiotics for a worsening or unchanged examination after 48 hours of oral antibiotics.

Unless appropriately treated at this very early stage with resultant response to antibiotics, the inflammation can rapidly progress to a periorbital cellulitis (Fig. 45–1). Fever occurs, tenderness and edema of the lids increase markedly, and the globe itself may show some forward protrusion. Some chemosis of the conjunctiva may be seen. Patients may complain of diplopia resulting from mild limitation of gaze from the chemosis and lid edema, but acuity on straight gaze is typically normal. Hospitalization and intravenous antibiotic therapy, along with topical nasal decongestants, often abort any further progression of disease.

We find that ophthalmology consultation, if not already obtained, can aid in management at this stage. When the patient starts to complain of diplopia and when decreasing extraocular movement is evident on basic eye examination, a more stringent serial assessment of visual acuity free of interobserver discrepancy is prudent and can help in planning when to move to the next stage of treatment.

If the eye examination results worsen or do not significantly improve after 48 hours of intravenous antibiotics, investigation must commence to rule out progression to a subperiosteal or intraorbital abscess. The most difficult differentiation is between orbital cellulitis (see Fig. 45–1) and a subperiosteal abscess (Fig. 45–2) (Table 45–4).[21] The significance of making this distinction is that orbital cellulitis usually responds to medical therapy, whereas a subperiosteal abscess may require surgical drainage. If surgical drainage is deferred, dire consequences, includ-

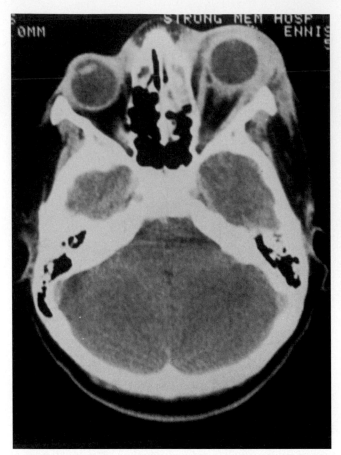

FIGURE 45–1. Computed tomographic (CT) axial view of ethmoid sinusitis and right periorbital cellulitis with proptosis.

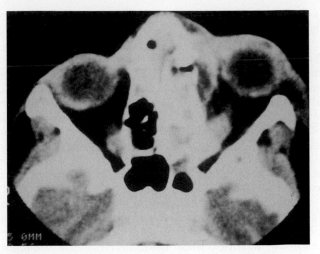

FIGURE 45–2. CT scan axial view showing right ethmoid sinusitis with an organized subperiosteal abscess demonstrating classic central hypolucency/ring enhancement and lateral displacement of the medial rectus muscle.

ing possible permanent vision loss, can ensue. In many cases, the computed tomography (CT) results may not be clear, signifying an early-forming abscess from a present phlegmon/cellulitic process (Fig. 45–3). Figure 45–4A is a schematic diagram that summarizes the routes of spread of infection to a subperiosteal abscess.

Historically, CT evidence of a subperiosteal abscess has indicated the need for surgical management to most otolaryngologists. However, we have successfully treated many cases of early abscess or transitioning phlegmon in children with intravenous antibiotics alone. The case is

followed up closely with serial eye examinations by an ophthalmologist and, if there is no improvement within 48 hours, we then proceed to surgical exploration and drainage. In following such a strategy, the time-dependent pharmacokinetics of antibiotic therapy must be considered. The CT scan may not correlate with the clinical course and the finding of abscess expansion during the early initiation of antibiotic therapy may not predict the clinical outcome.[22, 24, 39] Others have reported similar success with selective conservative treatment of subperiosteal abscess in children.[20, 39, 40] Our trend has been to give every child with a subperiosteal abscess the opportunity to improve on intravenous antibiotics before operative drainage. We have not encountered an increased morbidity or mortality rate with this practice.

Proper use of terminology and a thorough understanding of eye anatomy at this stage become critical. The terms *preseptal, post-septal, extraconal,* and *intraconal* are often found in the literature. The orbital septum forms a curtain over the orbit anteriorly. It begins as an extension of the periosteum of the inferior and superior orbital rim and extends as a thin membrane to the respective lids. This separates the superficial lids from the deeper struc-

TABLE 45–4. Accuracy of Diagnostic Modalities in Determining Treatment of Orbital Complications

Classification	Agreement	False-Negative	False-Positive	Accuracy (%)
Clinical				
Periorbital cellulitis with chemosis	10	0	0	100
Orbital cellulitis	13	11	0	54
Subperiosteal abscess	2	0	2	50
Orbital abscess	1	0	0	100
Total: 39	26	11	2	67
CT Scan				
Periorbital cellulitis with chemosis	9	0	0	100
Orbital cellulitis	9	5	0	65
Subperiosteal abscess	6	0	0	100
Orbital abscess	2	0	0	100
Total: 31	26	5	0	84

Data from Gutowski M, Mulbury PE, Hengerer AS. The use of CT scanning in the management of orbital cellulitis. Int J Pediatr Otorhinolaryngol 15:117, 1988.

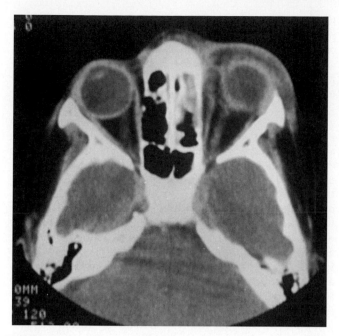

FIGURE 45-3. CT scan axial view of ethmoiditis with a right subperiosteal phlegmon/early abscess.

tures (extraocular muscles, periorbital fat, globe, ophthalmic vessels, and optic nerve) and defines preseptal from post-septal infection. Extension deep (posterior) to this "curtain" is termed post-septal. Therefore, a subperiosteal abscess, although still contained by periosteum, lies posterior to this anterior barrier and is considered *post-septal*. The term *intraconal* is reserved for infectious processes within the cone of extraocular muscles and portends impending visual loss. *Extraconal* involvement implies a *post-septal* infection with involvement of the periorbita (effacement of fat planes) or extraocular muscle edema without extension into the "cone" of extraocular muscles. Table 45-3 lists the stages of orbital involvement. We find that an accurate description of the patient's examination and CT findings, along with this working classification modified from Pereira, makes most sense.[37]

Pus under pressure eventually leads to expansion into the post-septal space of the orbit and development of the most common ocular complication of rhinosinusitis—a subperiosteal abscess. Findings consistent with a subperiosteal abscess include lateral displacement of periosteum with an enhancing mass adjacent to the lamina papyracea (see Fig. 45-2). Whereas early preseptal inflammation may not warrant a CT scan, lack of clinical improvement

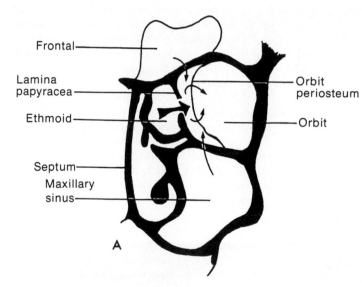

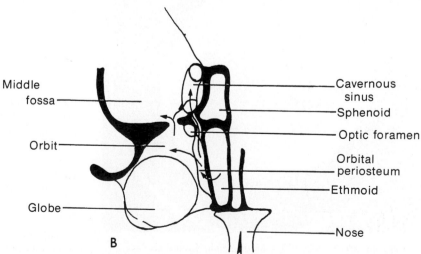

FIGURE 45-4. *A*, Spread of infection from sinuses to the orbit. *B*, Spread of infection directly via the sinus to the orbit and by veins or the lymphatics to the cavernous sinus.

within 48 hours or obvious progression of the infection, such as significant proptosis, limitation of eye movements, or vision change, necessitates immediate CT scan. Furthermore, we believe that imaging is needed for any infectious process beyond mild lid erythema and edema. Waiting to obtain a CT scan for only those cases in which surgical therapy is planned may not be prudent. The physical examination in children is not always reliable and the consequences of delayed diagnosis of a post-septal process can have grave consequences.[47] The CT scan should be done with intravenous contrast and include coronal views of all the sinuses with fine cuts through the orbits. Limited axial cuts of the brain to rule out a frontal abscess (Fig. 45–5) add little extra cost or time to the procedure. Magnetic resonance imaging (MRI) provides better detail of the orbital soft tissues, but is more expensive and often requires sedation because of its lengthy scan time.

There are advantages and disadvantages to both CT and MRI. Because of the low-density fat in the orbit, orbital cellulitis is usually seen easily with CT. MRI, with its high-intensity fat on T_1-weighted images, is competitive with CT for the evaluation of orbital cellulitis but usually more expensive.[51] While CT is superior for identifying defects of the bony walls of the ethmoid sinus by inflammation, it is not useful in the evaluation of the orbital apex. Because of the lack of signal intensity from bone at the orbital apex, inflammation in the orbital region with extension into the cavernous sinus is better evaluated with MRI. Although MRI is recommended by some as a superior imaging modality for the orbital subperiosteal space, a high-resolution CT scan is the initial choice of radiologic evaluation because it offers good differentiation of tissue planes in most cases, a quick scan time, and low expense.[8, 12] MRI is typically reserved for assessment of continued progressive neurologic changes resulting from intracranial complications such as meningitis, brain abscesses, or cavernous sinus thrombosis. If there is no evidence of improvement during a 48-hour period at any time during therapy, repeat imaging is indicated because resistant organisms can develop, the abscess can reaccumulate, the initial procedure may have been inadequate, or an intracranial complication may be evolving.

If such radiologic innovations are not available to the clinician, the progressive symptoms that suggest formation of a purulent abscess (see Fig. 45–4) are increasing edema and lid erythema with the inability to close the eye completely, marked orbital chemosis, proptosis of the eye (either straight forward or in the down-and-out position depending on the site of abscess), further diminution of extraocular motion, and loss of visual acuity. These findings should be followed up closely by a consulting ophthalmologist. Although diagnostic imaging can greatly aid one's decision-making process, the decision to institute further therapy, i.e., surgery, should be primarily a clinical one. Whatever the set of diagnostic circumstances—purely radiologic, purely clinical, or a combination of both—once the diagnosis of subperiosteal abscess is suspected, surgical drainage should be considered immediately because permanent loss of vision can occur rapidly.[29]

The traditional method of draining a periorbital abscess is through an external ethmoidectomy skin incision, midway between the inner canthus of the eye and the midnasal dorsum. The procedure is performed with the patient under general anesthesia with the use of a local anesthetic (Xylocaine) (0.5%); epinephrine (1:200,000) is infiltrated into the skin for its vasoconstrictor effect. A layer dissection should be carried out down to and through the periosteum to preclude inadvertent cutting of the angular vein and concomitant heavy bleeding. The elevation of the periosteum over the nasal projection of the maxillary bone and off the lamina papyracea of the medial wall of the orbit may expose the ethmoid sinus through a necrotic bony defect. Any subperiosteal abscess is rapidly drained.

For an intraorbital (intraconal) abscess, the periorbita must be incised and the abscess drained. This can be safely and adequately done using an 18-gauge needle rather than a more aggressive incision and drainage. However, drainage of an intraorbital abscess is probably best performed in the presence of an ophthalmologist. Not finding a suspected medial subperiosteal abscess upon exposure of the lamina may indicate a more phlegmatic and cellulitic process or location of the abscess elsewhere, i.e., more medial and lateral, and closer examination using CT intraoperatively is needed to find the abscess pocket. In addition to the abscess drainage, a partial ethmoidectomy should be performed to remove diseased tissue, although without attempting a complete and meticulous dissection of all mucosa.

After the abscess is drained, the wound is closed in layers with one small drain from the incision line (sterile rubber band) and another placed intranasally through the middle meatus into the cleaned ethmoid sinus. In some cases, irrigating catheters (red rubber catheters) may be left in place for postoperative wound saline or antibiotic irrigation. If the maxillary sinus is the source of the orbital complication, drainage should be done through ei-

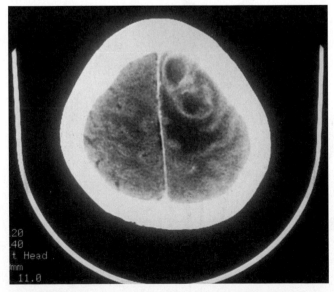

FIGURE 45–5. Axial CT scan of a right frontal abscess.

ther the inferior meatus or the anterior maxillary bony wall with a spinal needle.

The endoscopic ethmoidectomy is another approach used to manage a subperiosteal orbital abscess and is becoming the approach of choice for initial management because of its excellent cosmetic results. This procedure is indicated by the same criteria as for an external ethmoidectomy except in cases of frontal or lateral subperiosteal abscesses that have resulted from frontal or supraorbital ethmoid disease. The procedure must be performed by a physician experienced in pediatric sinus endoscopy. Frequent packing with gauze soaked with a vasoconstrictive agent, frequent cleaning of the endoscope to ensure good visualization, and patience on the operator's part are required to successfully perform this approach. A cut along the inferior aspect of the lamina papyracea is made with a Freer elevator or sickle knife. The lamina is gently, completely elevated, exposing the full length of the abscess pocket but carefully avoiding the lacrimal sac and orbital apex areas. Emphasis should be placed on adequate superior decompression of the lamina. The periorbita should not be incised unless there is an obvious intraconal abscess; the periorbita acts as a natural barrier to further spread of infection and releasing the periorbita may lead to postoperative enophthalmos. Postoperative evaluation and debridement of the cavity are performed using general anesthesia as usual for the young pediatric age group in 2 to 3 weeks. Two disadvantages are associated with this approach: (1) poor visualization caused by bleeding from acutely inflamed sinus mucosa and (2) working with the smaller anatomy of the pediatric nose.

Despite the anatomic challenges, many researchers have reported success with this endoscopic approach. Pereira reported excellent results in 24 patients with medial subperiosteal abscess. Pus was encountered in 88% of the patients, none required another operation, and there were no complications. Ocular signs resolved within 72 hours and patients were discharged home on oral antibiotics in a mean of 52 hours after the procedure.[37] Mann et al[30] used an endoscopic technique in 6 of 20 operative failures and cited inadequate removal of the lamina or a more superior-lateral location of the abscess as the primary reasons for initial failure. They advocated use of silastic drain placement for the cases of missed or reaccumulated superior-lateral abscesses. The drain is placed endonasally and removed several days later in the office, if tolerated, or under general anesthesia. Other researchers have also reported good results with the endoscopic approach.[10, 31, 35]

Despite the availability of nasal endoscopes in otolaryngology and the frequent overzealous desire to use new technology, one should not compromise the safety or adequacy of the operation for the sake of saving a patient a typically excellent-healing scar that is well disguised in an anatomic concavity and natural facial shadow. External ethmoidectomy remains the choice for cases in which orbital signs fail to resolve completely after an endoscopic approach or if the endoscopic approach fails to yield adequate visualization of the ethmoid walls.[31] Once the drainage has been accomplished by either external or endonasal surgical technique and adequate antibiotic ther-

apy is continued, resolution of the fever and associated symptoms is usually dramatic.

If the orbital periosteum does not act as a sufficient barrier to infection, the subperiosteal abscess may extend to involve extraconal and intraconal structures. Effacement of the periorbita or appearance of "dirty fat" on the CT scan and an edematous medial rectus muscle are signs of this extension. One must also be aware of evidence of an intraorbital abscess of cellulitic process (intraconal spread). These complications typically require the assistance of an ophthalmologist intraoperatively.

Facial pain and headache result from the orbital complications and their further progression to intracranial areas. From the onset of sinus infection, all patients note some degree of discomfort. Initially, it is the sense of congestion and pressure within the nasal region that can create the associated complaint of facial pressure and temporal region headache. As the step-by-step progression of the infection occurs, there is a shifting in location and intensity of pain. Once the orbital structures become involved, a severe, deep-seated pain behind the eyes develops, and aggravation of this pain occurs with attempted eye movement. If only the orbit is involved, the pain remains unilateral and is associated with headache, which may be localized or diffuse. The headache is caused by the pus under pressure as well as by the localized vascular changes. With cavernous sinus involvement, the pain becomes more deeply placed in the center of the head. The headache becomes severe as the sinus thrombosis and the venous pressure increase throughout the intracranial vessels. Clinically, the patient's response to this worsening pain is likely to be altered by the obtunded state that frequently accompanies the condition. If the patient is severely toxic, he or she may not be aware of headache or facial pain.

Intracranial Complications

Intracranial spread of infection from the frontal, ethmoid, or sphenoid sinuses can produce further complications, such as meningeal irritation and infection, brain abscess, and peridural abscess. Intracranial complications occur in approximately 2% to 4% of those admitted to the hospital with the diagnosis of sinusitis.[5, 19, 27] Spread of infection may be facilitated by the presence of congenital dehiscence or by contiguous spread from adjacent sinuses, along neural foramina or via valveless communicating veins of the diploic space, or by way of the angular and ethmoidal veins of the orbit. Chronic sinusitis is the most common predisposing factor for the development of intracranial complications, and the frontal sinus is the most frequently involved sinus. Many of these children have pansinusitis that is often due to mixed flora on culture.[33] The vascularity of the diploic system increases in adolescence, which may contribute to spread.[9] Outcomes for intracranial complications have improved in the postantibiotic era, but still carry a 10% to 20% mortality rate.[5]

As previously mentioned, one of the most important benefits of the early CT scan in evaluating sinus complications is the ability to also detect early central nervous system complications. These include epidural abscess, cerebritis, and a brain abscess in the "silent" areas of the frontal lobes where even mass lesions can exist without overt clinical signs and symptoms. However, clinical experience and interpretation are still required to determine which of these studies and treatments are indicated and when. Intracranial complications from sinogenic sources with their associated problems of increased intracranial pressure, seizures, and neurologic compromise are best managed by a multidisciplinary team composed of a pediatrician, a neurologist or a neurosurgeon, and an otolaryngologist.

The early and widespread use of antibiotics has caused osteomyelitis of the frontal or maxillary bones to become a rare occurrence, but it may still be seen in neglected patients or, more commonly, in undertreated cases. In today's era of modern medicine, undertreatment may be secondary to antibiotic resistance and poor antibiotic choice rather than a foreshortened treatment period. In infants and children, it is the spongy bone over the anterior wall of the maxilla that is usually infected, producing erythema, edema, and marked tenderness with swelling. Since the frontal sinus does not begin developing until the age of 6 years or older, complications of bony spread of sinus infection over the frontal area only occurs in the older age group. The signs are similar in that swelling over the sinus, particularly with periosteal edema, is present. This often produces a doughy feeling to the skin over the affected area (Pott's puffy tumor). Similarly, cases of osteomyelitis are prone to epidural abscess formation on the intracranial aspect of the frontal bone.

The patient should be given intravenous antibiotics and the periosteum over the affected area should be opened to evacuate any collection of pus with insertion of drains. When surgery is performed, removal of only the obviously unhealthy and irreversibly diseased bone should be performed. Long-term postoperative intravenous antibiotic therapy of 2 to 3 weeks' duration,[3] as mentioned previously, followed by another 3 weeks of oral medication allows resorption and regeneration of infected bone such that the surgeon can be somewhat conservative in management.[45] The best possible surgical approach is through a noninfected area; thus, a coronal incision and elevation of a scalp flap are ideal procedures for frontal sinus work. However, a buccal incision is made for the maxilla, despite the obviously contaminated field. This has not seemed to be a deterrent to rapid healing.

Meningeal inflammation resulting from the spread of infection from the nasal regions into the cranial vault causes pain in the head and neck region, lethargy, fever, and nuchal rigidity. Unlike in adults, sinogenic sources as the cause of pediatric meningitis are rare, accounting for less than 1% of cases.[18, 19] The pain in these patients is most often a global, intense headache caused by diffuse involvement of the meninges. The pain increases when the head is lowered to a dependent position or when coughing, crying, or straining increases the venous pressure. The same pathologic changes in the meninges are responsible for the pain created by head movement, especially neck flexion done to demonstrate the rigidity. This pain occurs because of the stretching of the in-flamed meninges and nerve roots and is known as the Brudzinski sign.

If meningitis is suspected, a spinal tap for examination of cerebrospinal fluid must be done, and the patient must be hospitalized for administration of high doses of intravenous antibiotics.[4] The response to this therapy is usually satisfactory once the offending organism has been identified and adequately treated. Anticonvulsant therapy is considered necessary and should be started prophylactically to guard against associated seizures of intracranial complications. The occurrence of seizures may approach an 80% frequency.[49] Corticosteroid therapy has been used for intracranial complications of sinusitis. However, experimental work has shown little effect of steroid therapy on the early and late mortality rates, the frequency of abscess formation, or the intensity of the inflammatory response.[43] The use of corticosteroid therapy is still debated, but most clinicians reserve steroids to minimize complications in patients with proven intracranial edema.[9]

Intracerebral abscess is the most common intracranial complication of sinusitis; concomitantly, sinusitis is the most frequent source of cerebral abscess.[9, 19] Intracerebral and peridural abscesses tend to produce a somewhat more chronic and quiet symptom complex, which causes their diagnosis to be made relatively late in their course. This is especially true when the lesion is in the frontal lobe (see Fig. 45–5), where clinical findings are minimal. Classic symptoms of a cerebral abscess include fever, altered mental status, headache, nausea, and vomiting. As mentioned previously, nasal symptoms may be absent or subtle in the pediatric population. Abscesses typically cause a localized cerebritis that manifests as headache initially and then may be quiescent with regard to symptoms for a period of time before progressing to the severe headaches and lethargy that are characteristic of abscess expansion.[28] Seizures and a focal neurologic examination are late findings and portend a poor prognosis. In anyone complaining of deep headaches, difficulty concentrating, and general lethargy who also has an unresolved sinus problem, the clinician's responsibility is to rule out an intracranial problem.[4] In these patients, the CT scan is an invaluable diagnostic tool, allowing a noninvasive technique to be used for intracranial diagnostic purposes. Neurosurgical consultation is obtained immediately in cases of brain abscess. Broad-spectrum antibiotics are used until coverage can be narrowed, such as is done in treatment of other intracranial complications. Cultures obtained at this point often fail to identify an organism but common offenders are anaerobes, Streptococcus species, and Staphylococcus species. Often, sinus surgery is planned in combination with craniotomy for removal of residual intrasinus disease, or it may be done at a later time, but this delay in surgery is rare in children.

Unstopped infection and retrograde venous thrombophlebitis via the nasal and angular veins that surround the ethmoid labyrinth and orbital structures can ultimately spread to cause cavernous sinus thrombosis (see Fig. 45–4B).[38] The sphenoid sinus is one of the first sinuses to develop as an extension of the posterior ethmoids by age 2 years. Involvement of the sphenoid heightens awareness of possible intracranial complications due to its close proximity to the cavernous sinus and cranial vault. This devastating complication is diagnosed mainly by its *bilateral* orbital involvement, including signs of lid edema, erythema, and progressive severe chemosis. In addition, paresis of the extraocular muscles innervated by the oculomotor, abducens, or trochlear nerve may be present, which eventually leads to a complete ophthalmoplegia. In addition, loss of the corneal reflex and anesthesia of the first division of cranial nerve V can be present. The body temperature is usually high from the marked toxic effect and septic emboli, which cause the "picket fence" fever spikes. All these signs and symptoms, however, have been previously mentioned for other, less ominous stages of orbital involvement; therefore, one must have a high index of suspicion and be looking for the earliest evidence of bilateral involvement. MRI is the imaging mode of choice for verifying the clinical diagnosis. Cerebrospinal fluid cultures are typically negative.

Broad-spectrum antibiotic therapy with infectious disease consultation and organ system support are the mainstays of treatment. Adjunctive therapies of anticoagulants (heparin and urokinase) and corticosteroids have been used as treatment in these children. Heparin apparently prevents further propagation of the thrombus but does not lyse an organized clot, whereas urokinase by directed catheter instillation may be effective in clot dissolution and recanalization. Whereas most clinicians favor use of heparin,[11, 14] urokinase remains investigational.[7] However, anticoagulants and corticosteroid therapy remain controversial treatments of cavernous sinus thrombosis and should be individualized to each patient and the respective local medical environment.[46]

Antibiotic Therapy

The most common virulent pathogens in complicated rhinosinusitis are *Streptococcus pneumoniae* and *Streptococcus pyogenes*, *Haemophilus influenzae*, *Moraxella catarrhalis*, penicillinase-producing *Staphylococcus aureus*, and anaerobes such as *Bacteroides*. These account for 90% of the organisms found in complicated rhinosinusitis.[16] *H. influenzae* infection has been on the decline since development of the Hib vaccine, but at least 30% to 40% of *Haemophilus* species are beta-lactamase producers. Eighty-five percent to 100% of *M. catarrhalis* organisms produce beta-lactamase. Approximately 30% of *S. pneumoniae* organisms are resistant as well.[16, 44] These rates all have regional variances, which are highest in the Southwest.[44]

At one time, the combined antibiotics of choice were ampicillin or chloramphenicol and nafcillin.[23, 50] This antimicrobial therapy is no longer used because of the side effects of chloramphenicol, such as aplastic anemia. Nafcillin plus metronidazole covers *Staphylococcus* species and anaerobes with fewer side effects. Vancomycin is substituted for methicillin-resistant *Staphylococcus aureus* (MRSA). Cephalosporins offer better gram-negative coverage with fewer side effects as well. Cefuroxime, a second-generation cephalosporin, and metronidazole are also a good combination for most intracranial and ocular complications of sinus disease. Yet another option includes

ceftazidime with ticarcillin-clavulanate. For pencillin allergies, cefazolin or vancomycin instead of nafcillin and clindamycin with ceftriaxone are additional good choices. The third-generation cephalosporins, such as ceftriaxone, cefotaxime, and cefepime, penetrate the blood-brain barrier well and have good gram-negative coverage but lack better gram-positive and anaerobic activity.[28] For early treatment of complications, i.e., early periorbital cellulitis, one should choose high-dose amoxicillin-clavulanate (80 to 90 mg/kg per day) or combination therapy of amoxicillin or clindamycin with a third-generation cephalosporin as recommended by the Sinus and Allergy Health Partnership for moderate sinus disease.[44]

Regardless of the specific antimicrobials used, therapy should initially provide broad-spectrum coverage against gram-positive, gram-negative, and most anaerobic organisms, including the *Bacteroides* species, and have excellent cerebrospinal fluid penetration in cases of suspected intracranial extension. Once the infection is under control and clear clinical improvement is evident, switching to oral amoxicillin-clavulanate or levofloxacin is appropriate if culture and sensitivity data indicate.[28] The authors have successfully treated many cases of orbital cellulitis or even early abscess with ampicillin-clavulanate monotherapy. Coverage is broadened after 48 hours if no improvement is seen. An infectious disease specialist consultation may be helpful in atypical or in rapidly advancing cases.

Polyps and Mucoceles

Nasal polyps in the prepubescent child are unusual and rarely result from chronic sinus disease. It is more probable that they would arise from a metabolic or immunologic problem, especially cystic fibrosis. For this reason, all children with nasal polyps should undergo testing for immunoglobulin levels and sweat chloride levels. The treatment can then be directed to the basic underlying systemic problem.

Nasal polyps resulting from allergic and inflammatory causes are seen in the older pediatric age group about as frequently as in adults. This non-neoplastic polyp tissue consists of thickened, edematous mucosal stroma, infiltrated with both eosinophils and polymorphonuclear leukocytes. Most often, the polyps project from the ethmoid sinuses via the middle meatus but they may also be found in the superior meatus, where they extend from both the posterior ethmoid air cells and the sphenoid sinus. The primary treatment of these polyps consists of antibiotic therapy and decongestants, with surgical excision reserved only for those obstructive polyps that have become recalcitrant to this treatment. The smaller, non-obstructive polyps are usually not removed unless chronic sinus infection continues behind them. In many cases, the combination of a course of antibiotics and allergic desensitization results in their complete resorption. If surgery becomes necessary, a simple endoscopic polypectomy with limited opening of the sinuses is the procedure of choice. Recurrence of these lesions without resolution of the underlying medical problem, as seen in cystic fibrosis, is common. In this age group, any major intrasinus surgery should be avoided because the effect of major sinus surgery on growth of the facial skeleton is not yet fully known.

The antrochoanal polyp is a clinical entity distinct from other polyps. This polyp is almost always unilateral and tends to cause posterior choanal obstruction. It is a pedunculated mass, with a small stalk extending from one of the maxillary sinus ostia through the nose into the posterior choana. The site of attachment of the stalk is in the sinus itself, most frequently on the lateral wall. These lesions do not respond to decongestants or antibiotic therapy and, therefore, must be removed surgically in every instance. Removal of only that mucosa around the site of the stalk is indicated by endoscopic or Caldwell-Luc approaches. The polyp itself may then be removed through the nose or mouth. The important step is to remove the entire stalk; otherwise, recurrence is frequent, especially if a simple avulsion technique is used.

Chronic sinus disease can, on occasion, produce complete obstruction of the ostia or ducts of the major paranasal sinuses. When this occurs, the mucous lining of the sinus continues to produce secretions, only there is no effective egress available, and a mucocele is formed. Over a period of years, the sinus walls may flatten and bow to accommodate the steadily increasing pressure created by the trapped mucus. When this process occurs from an obstructed nasofrontal duct, there is a downward bulging of the orbital roof, producing an upper inner canthal swelling of the orbit with downward and outward deviation of the eye. On the other hand, mucoceles of the ethmoid and sphenoid sinuses are difficult to diagnose without radiographic evaluation because of the paucity of physical findings except for headache and a feeling of frontal pressure or impaired ocular muscle function. Therefore, diagnosis must be by CT or MRI scan. Plain radiographs have limited utility in sinus imaging.[26] Since mucoceles or their infected equivalent, pyoceles, take years rather than months to develop to any significant size, it is unusual to see these problems in the pediatric age group. However, if they are discovered, treatment must be by surgical intervention. A frontal sinus mucocele can be handled by use of an osteoplastic frontal sinusotomy with fat obliteration of the sinus and its nasofrontal duct. Ethmoid and sphenoid mucoceles can be treated with endoscopic techniques if visualization is adequate but may best be treated by the external ethmoidectomy approach and drainage. Individualization of technique and approach is necessary.

Lower Respiratory Tract Diseases

The spread of infection between the upper and the lower respiratory tracts has been the subject of controversy and conjecture for many years.[15] In children with chronic nasal and paranasal sinus infection, there seems to be an increased frequency of cough and recurrent pneumonitis greater than what would be expected on a purely incidental basis. This is most often seen in the asthmatic child or the child with Kartagener syndrome in whom the immunologic and hereditary dysfunctions are readily apparent. However, there are many other children without any

known metabolic or immunologic deficit who exhibit similar symptoms of malaise, low-grade fevers, chronic sinus mucosal disease, and recurrent tracheobronchitis or pneumonitis. It is in reference to these children that the term *sinobronchial syndrome* has been used.

The pathways of infection in this syndrome are probably twofold: (1) by direct extension along the mucosa from the sinuses, via the pharynx with some laryngeal aspiration leading to intratracheal and bronchial disease, and (2) by lymphatic spread from the sinuses via the mediastinum to the tracheobronchial tree. Studies have been done by several investigators to promote each concept.[41] In the first instance, the mucosal spread could logically be seen to promote a chronic cough and recurrent tracheobronchial infection. On the other hand, it seems apparent that the repeated bouts of interstitial pneumonitis might be more readily explained when attributed to spread along known lymphatic pathways from the sinuses, through the mediastinum, and to the lungs themselves. The rare retropharyngeal or deep neck abscess seen without evidence of Waldeyer ring infection may also be attributed to such spread.

Having discovered this systemic connection when children have recurrent pulmonary disease, the physician should search for associated chronic sinus infection by direct nasal examination and sinus CT scans. If the sinobronchial syndrome is diagnosed, fairly aggressive antibiotic therapy and nasal decongestant therapy should be instituted. Culture specimens should be obtained in the middle meatus, even if no specific purulence is noted, to give some guidance regarding the proper antibiotic agent. Most commonly, either penicillin or one of its derivatives is the drug of choice in controlling the usual gram-positive infections. The maxillary sinuses seem to become secondarily infected. If good resolution of intrasinus disease does not occur after 3 weeks of therapy, an antral irrigation should be done, and repeated culture specimens should be obtained. This is classically performed by a puncture with a sharp, curved trocar or spinal needle through the inferior meatus. In older children, the authors have preferred to perform irrigation by direct puncture through the anterior sinus wall with the patient under local anesthesia. It is hoped that this will resolve the sinusitis and eventually permit resolution of the pulmonary complications.

REFERENCES

1. Arjmand EM, Lusk RP, Muntz HR. Pediatric sinusitis and subperiosteal orbital abscess formation. Diagnosis and treatment. Otolaryngol Head Neck Surg 109:886, 1993.
2. Bernstein L. Pediatric sinus problems. Otolaryngol Clin North Am 4:127, 1971.
3. Blumenfeld RJ, Skolnik EM. Intracranial complications of sinus disease. Trans Am Acad Ophthalmol Otolaryngol 70:899, 1966.
4. Brook I, Kriedman EM. Intracranial complications of sinusitis in children. Ann Otol Rhinol Laryngol 91:41, 1982.
5. Broberg T, Murr A, Fischbein N. Devastating complications of acute pediatric bacterial sinusitis. Otolaryngol Head Neck Surg 120:575, 1999.
6. Chandler JR, Langenbrunner DJ, Stevens ER. The pathogenesis of orbital complications in acute sinusitis. Laryngoscope 80:1414, 1970.

7. Chow K, Gobin YP, Saver J, et al. Endovascular treatment of dural sinus thrombosis with rheolytic thrombectomy and intra-arterial thrombolysis. Stroke 31:1420, 2000.

8. Clary RA, Cunningham MJ, Eavey RD. Orbital complications of acute sinusitis: comparison of computed tomography scan and surgical findings. Ann Otol Rhinol Laryngol 101:599, 1992.

9. Clayman GL, Adams GL, Paugh DR, et al. Intracranial complications of paranasal sinusitis: a combined institutional review. Laryngoscope 101:234, 1991.

10. Deutsch E, Eilon A, Hevron I, et al. Functional endoscopic sinus surgery of orbital subperiosteal abscess in children. Int J Pediatr Otorhinolaryngol 34:181, 1996.

11. deVeber G, Chan A, Monagle P, et al. Anticoagulation therapy in pediatric patients with sinovenous thrombosis: a cohort study. Arch Neurol 55:1533, 1998.

12. Dobben GD, Philip B, Mafee MF, et al. Orbital subperiosteal menatoma, cholesterol granuloma, and infection. Evaluation with MR imaging and CT. Radiol Clin North Am 36:1185, 1998.

13. Donahue SP, Khary JM, Kowalski RD. Common ocular infections. A prescribers guide. Drugs 52:526, 1996.

14. Einhaupl KM, Villringer A, Meister W, et al. Heparin treatment in sinus venous thrombosis. Lancet 338:597, 1991.

15. Farrell JT. The connection of bronchiectasis and sinusitis. JAMA 106:92, 1936.

16. Feigin RD, Cherry JD. Textbook of Pediatric Infectious Disease. Philadelphia, WB Saunders, 1998, pp 183–192, 786–807.

17. Gallagher RM, Gross CW, Phillips CD. Suppurative intracranial complications of sinusitis. Laryngoscope 108:1635, 1998.

18. Giannoni CM, Stewart MG, Alford EL. Intracranial complications of sinusitis. Laryngoscope 107:863, 1997.

19. Giannoni C, Sulek M, Friedman EM. Intracranial complications of sinusitis: a pediatric series. Am J Rhinol 12:173, 1998.

20. Greenberg MF, Pollard ZF. Medical treatment of pediatric subperiosteal orbital abscess secondary to sinusitis. J Am Assoc Pediatr Ophthalmol Strabismus 2:351, 1998.

21. Gutowski M, Mulbury PE, Hengerer AS. The use of CT scanning in the management of orbital cellulitis. Int J Pediatr Otol 15:117, 1988.

22. Handler LC, Davey IC, Hill JC, Lauryssen C. The acute orbit: differentiation of orbital cellulitis from subperiosteal abscess by computerized tomography. Neuroradiology 33:15, 1991.

23. Haynes RE, Cramblett HG. Acute ethmoiditis: its relationship to orbital cellulitis. Am J Dis Child 114:261, 1967.

24. Harris GJ. Subperiosteal abscess of the orbit. Age as a factor in the bacteriology and response to treatment. Ophthalmology 101:585, 1994.

25. Jaskiewicz JA, McCarthy CA, Richardson AC, et al. Febrile infants at low risk for serious bacterial infection—an appraisal of the Rochester criteria and implications for management. Pediatrics 94:390, 1994.

26. Kronemer KA, McAlister WH. Sinusitis and its imaging in the pediatric population. Pediatr Radiol 27:837, 1997.

27. Lerner DN, Choi SS, Zalzal GH, Johnson DL. Intracranial complications of sinusitis in childhood. Ann Otol Rhinol Laryngol 104:288, 1995.

28. Mandell GL, Bennett JE, Dolin R. Principles and Practice of Infectious Disease, 5th ed. New York, Churchill Livingstone, 2000.

29. Maniglia AJ, Kronberg FG, Culbertson W. Visual loss associated with orbital and sinus disease. Laryngoscope 94:1050, 1984.

30. Mann W, Amedee RG, Maurer J. Orbital complications of pediatric sinusitis: treatment of periorbital abscess. Am J Rhinol 11:149, 1997.

31. Manning SC. Endoscopic management of medial subperiosteal orbital abscess. Arch Otolaryngol Head Neck Surg 119:789, 1993.

32. Mortimore S, Wormald PJ. The Groote Shuur Hospital classification of the orbital complications of sinusitis. J Laryngol Otol 111:719, 1997.

33. Odabasi AO, Akgul A. Cavernous sinus thrombosis: a rare complication of sinusitis. Int J Pediatr Otorhinolaryngol 39:77, 1997.

34. Osguthorpe JD, Hochman M. Inflammatory sinus diseases affecting the orbit. Otolaryngol Clin North Am 26:657, 1993.

35. Page EL, Wiatrak BJ. Endoscopic vs external drainage of orbital subperiosteal abscess. Arch Otolaryngol Head Neck Surg 122:737, 1996.

36. Patt BS, Manning SC. Blindness resulting from orbital complications of sinusitis. Otolaryngol Head Neck Surg 104:793, 1991.

37. Pereira KD, Mitchell RB, Younis RT, Lazar RH. Management of medial subperiosteal abscess of the orbit in children—a 5 year experience. Int J Pediatr Otorhinolaryngol 38:247, 1997.

38. Price DD, Hameroff SB, Richards RD. Cavernous sinus thrombosis and orbital cellulitis. South Med J 64:1243, 1971.

39. Rubin SE, Rubin LG, Zito J, et al. Medical management of orbital subperiosteal abscess in children. J Am Assoc Pediatr Ophthalmol Strabismus 26:21, 1989.

40. Sajjadian A, Chundru U, Issacson G. Prospective application of a protocol for selective nonsurgical management of suspected orbital subperiosteal abscesses in children. Ann Otol Rhinol Laryngol 108:459, 1999.

41. Sasaki CT, Kirchner JA. A lymphatic pathway from the sinuses to the mediastinum. Arch Otolaryngol 85:432, 1967.

42. Schramm VV, Carter HD, Kennerdell JS. Evaluation of orbital cellulitis and results of treatment. Laryngoscope 92:732, 1982.

43. Schroeder KA, McKeever PE, Schaberg DR. Effect of dexamethasone on experimental brain abscess. J Neurosurg 66:264, 1987.

44. Sinus and Allergy Health Partnership. Antimicrobial treatment guidelines for acute bacterial rhinosinusitis. Otolaryngol Head Neck Surg 123:S28, 2000.

45. Small M, Dale BA. Intracranial suppuration 1968–1982. A 15 year review. Clin Otolaryngol 9:315, 1984.

46. Sofferman RA. Cavernous sinus thrombophlebitis secondary to sphenoid sinusitis. Laryngoscope 93:797, 1991.

47. Uzcategui N, Warman R, Smith A, Howard CW. Clinical practice guidelines for the management of orbital cellulitis. J Am Assoc Pediatr Ophthalmol Strabismus 35:73, 1998.

48. Wald ER. Rhinitis and acute and chronic sinusitis. In Bluestone CD, et al (eds). Pediatric Otolaryngology, 3rd ed. Philadelphia, WB Saunders, 1996, p 848.

49. Wald ER, Parg D, Milmoe GJ, et al. Sinusitis and its complications in the pediatric patient. Pediatr Clin North Am 28:777, 1981.

50. Watters EC, Waller PH, Hiles DA, et al. Acute orbital cellulitis. Arch Ophthalmol 94:785, 1976.

51. Yousem DM. Imaging of sinonasal inflammatory disease. Radiology 188:303, 1993.

46

Foreign Bodies of the Nose

Nancy Sculerati, M.D.

One of the most basic differences between children and adults is in their behavior. Placing an object into the nasal cavity, and losing it there, is a time-honored mishap of early childhood. Children often tolerate the subsequent discomfort caused by an impacted or superinfected object without complaint once it is placed. Even when confronted with the indisputable evidence of the retrieved foreign body, children usually appear to have forgotten the initial event.

Chevalier Jackson,[7] the master endoscopist who wrote the treatise on the management of foreign bodies in 1936, defined a foreign body as "a substance not normally connected with its surroundings. It may be endogenous—originating within the body, or exogenous—having entered from without."

The two basic routes of entry of exogenous foreign bodies into the nose are anterior, through the nares, and posterior, through the posterior choanae. The former route is clearly the more common, although vomiting or forceful coughing of an ingested or aspirated foreign body accounts for the occasional nasal foreign body lodged from behind.

A child with a witnessed history or in whom there is a strong suspicion of foreign body ingestion, in particular a coin or some other radiopaque object, therefore requires radiographic examination of the nose and nasopharynx if chest and abdominal films fail to demonstrate the object.

Endogenous foreign bodies of the nose include inspissated secretions and bony sequestra, ordinarily the result of chronic inflammation and infection. They may be the sequelae of an exogenous foreign body that has been absorbed or disintegrated. These endogenous foreign bodies are rare and include mineralized concretions termed *rhinoliths*.

Exogenous nasal foreign bodies have included an extensive list of artifacts, both animate and inanimate. Common objects placed by children include beads, toy parts, paper wads, and food.[1] Shapiro[12] reported a retrospective review of 29 patients requiring admission to the Montreal Children's Hospital for removal of nasal foreign bodies under general anesthesia over a 7-year period. The children's ages ranged from 1.5 to 17 years. In one child, the foreign body (a stone) was swallowed and passed into the stomach, and planned nasal examination under anesthesia was cancelled. In four of the remaining children, no for-

eign body was found on examination under anesthesia. Foreign bodies found in the remaining 24 are listed in Table 46–1; three of these children had bilateral foreign objects.

Presentation and Sequelae

Foreign bodies of the nose, unlike those of the pediatric external ear canal, are rarely noted on examination unless they are suspected. They may be seen after rhinoscopy performed because an adult witnessed the child putting something in the nose, because of a child's report that he or she or another child has placed something, or (most commonly) because of persistent rhinitis of unknown cause.

The mucosal lining of the nose is a dynamic surface that requires uninterrupted mucociliary flow patterns to remain free of crusting and inflammation. The presence of any foreign body for more than a brief period is likely to interrupt normal mucociliary clearance sufficiently to cause sequelae of inflammation and infection. Some foreign bodies are not inert and can cause irritation or even caustic burns. Examples include seeds and beans, which swell when moistened by nasal secretions and become increasingly impacted over time, and materials such as foam rubber, which can become increasingly irritating with oxidation and breakdown of the material.

Plastic and other relatively inert materials may be tolerated for long intervals, during which gradual formation of exuberant granulation tissue obscures the foreign body and sometimes causes pressure erosion of surrounding bone, mimicking a tumor.[15]

Button batteries easily fit into a child's nose and rapidly cause severe chemical burns. There are multiple reports of subsequent septal perforations and eventual saddle-nose deformities due to impacted batteries in the nose. The site of maximal damage has been shown to correspond with the negative pole of the battery in one series.[16] A button battery is a painful foreign body and the child is usually in marked distress, although the specific cause is not immediately obvious if there is already enough reaction to cause edema and secretions that obscure visualization of the battery.

Objects placed in the anterior nares may primarily cause obstruction of airflow, if of sufficient size to fill the

TABLE 46–1. Foreign Bodies of the Nose Removed with the Patient Under General Anesthesia at the Montreal Children's Hospital (1970–1977)

Type of Object	Cases, *n*
Plastic objects	5
Buttons	4
Sponges	4 (2 bilateral)
Metal objects	2
Food	2
Paper clip	1
Magnet	1 (bilateral)
Eraser	1
Nut	1
Pit	1
Leather	1
Seed	1

vestibule, or delayed mucosal edema with subsequent crusting, rhinorrhea, and obstruction. A small object often lodges between the septum and the turbinates or between the middle turbinate and the uncinate (Fig. 46–1). Sinusitis may either be a consequence of direct obstruction of the natural ostium by a foreign body, or, most commonly, may be secondary to obstructive mucosal edema from rhinitis induced by the foreign body. Lymphoid tissue hypertrophies in response to infection and inflammation, and a long-standing nasal foreign object producing purulent posterior nasal rhinorrhea may contribute to adenoidal inflammation and enlargement. Epistaxis may also occur as a result of mucosal inflammation.

Although nasal foreign bodies are classically described as causing unilateral purulent rhinorrhea, bilateral symptoms are sometimes present, perhaps because of secondary adenoiditis (Figs. 46–2 and 46–3). Treatment with systemic antibiotics can temporarily reverse the secondary inflammation and produce resolution of symptoms, but obviously inflammatory symptoms will recur unless the

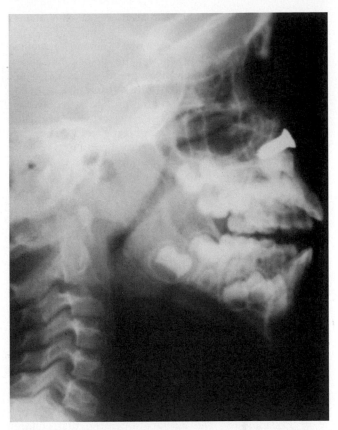

FIGURE 46–2. Radiopaque foreign body (a right-sided metal screw) evident in a 5-year-old girl on lateral radiography. This film was obtained after the child underwent a 10-day course of amoxicillin–clavulanic acid for chronic bilateral rhinorrhea. The symptoms, most consistent with adenoiditis, cleared completely with antibiotic therapy but would surely have recurred without identification and removal of the screw. (Courtesy of the Children's Hospital of Pittsburgh, Pittsburgh, PA.)

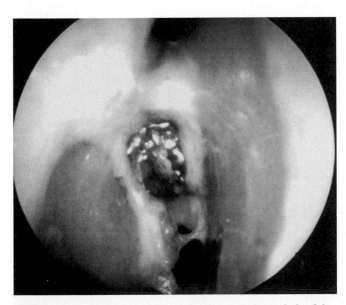

FIGURE 46–1. Endoscopic view of a foreign object lodged between the inferior turbinate and the septum. (Courtesy of Dr. Rodney Lusk, St. Louis Children's Hospital, St. Louis, MO.)

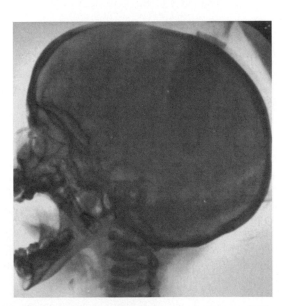

FIGURE 46–3. Lateral neck radiograph showing a radiopaque hairclip in the nasopharynx of a 2-year-old child. The posterior midline position was probably responsible for the presenting symptom of bilateral rhinorrhea.

foreign body is removed. Generally, once the foreign body is removed, secondary inflammation and infection will permanently resolve after a short course of medical treatment directed at the bacterial rhinitis and sinusitis.

Halitosis has occasionally been described as an isolated presenting symptom of a nasal foreign body.

Otitis media is another potential infectious sequela of a nasal foreign body, caused by the posterior nasal inflammation and secretions either refluxing into or causing functional obstruction of the eustachian tube. The otitis media is usually unilateral, on the same side as the nasal foreign body.

Complications and Other Associated Problems

The major complication of a nasal foreign body is aspiration, which is always a potential risk during removal unless the airway is secured. An unknown proportion of foreign bodies removed from the pediatric larynx, trachea, bronchi, and esophagus began as a nasal foreign body before the child reached the attention of a physician.

Although a foreign body itself may not contain lead or any particularly harmful material, a correlation between high blood lead levels and the presence of aural, nasal, or gastrointestinal foreign bodies was shown in a controlled study conducted by Wiley et al[17] at the Children's Hospital of Philadelphia. The authors suggested that children with foreign objects who reside in geographic areas with high endemic rates of lead poisoning should have blood lead levels determined.

It is a general principle of the management of foreign bodies that the identification of one object does not rule out the presence of others. Children who have placed one foreign body in the nose are likely to have placed others elsewhere, and the otolaryngologist is wise to carefully examine both sides of the nose and both ear canals.

Management: Methods of Removal

Successful removal of a nasal foreign body in a child requires visualization and appropriate instrumentation. Fortunately, this is ordinarily a simple procedure. Most foreign objects are removed by pediatricians, emergency room personnel, or even parents with nothing more than a light and a pair of tweezers, a cerumen curette, or a cotton-tipped applicator. However, visualization of a longstanding foreign body with surrounding inflammation and granulation tissue can be extremely difficult, requiring excellent optics and the ability to manipulate the tissues around the object. The individuals most at risk for placement of foreign bodies—younger children and children or adults with mental retardation or a psychiatric disturbance—are usually particularly unwilling to submit to careful intranasal manipulation.

Children who have already failed their own or a parent's attempt at removal of a foreign object in the ear or nose are more likely to fail additional attempts by emergency department personnel and require otolaryngologic referral, according to a survey of 212 consecutive cases of

pediatric aural and nasal foreign bodies presenting to an urban emergency care facility.[1]

Decongestion of the nose is helpful in reducing mucosal swelling and increasing exposure. Anterior rhinoscopy can be performed with magnification using the otoscope even in young children, who rarely tolerate the use of a nasal speculum. Aspiration with a Frazier tip suction tube just at the anterior nares, with care to avoid touching the nasal skin or mucosa, often aids visualization during the office examination.

It is best to have a right-angled hook, a flexible cerumen curette, and alligator forceps laid out and immediately available. It is important to be able to place the instrument alongside or behind the object for successful removal (Fig. 46–4). Pushing the object posteriorly increases the difficulty of removal and increases the risk of displacement out of the nose and aspiration.

The first attempt at removing a foreign body in an awake child is the least difficult, as most children become alarmed with this initial manipulation. It is wise to have the child in a comfortable but restrained position, securely sitting in the parent's lap or at the side of the parent. Restraint is ordinarily required and may be accomplished by having the child sit in the parent's lap with his or her back against the parent's chest. The parent's legs are crossed over the child's legs, and one of the parent's arms extends across both of the child's arms. The parent's other hand may cup the child's forehead to securely rest the back of the head against the parent's chest. Alternatively, an assistant can hold the child's head against the parent's chest, and the parent may have both arms free to cross over the child's body.

Although a head-mirror can be helpful in freeing the otolaryngologist's hands, it is often helpful to have at least an initial look with the otoscope. The head-mirror can be frightening and may provoke attempts at escape rather than cooperation.

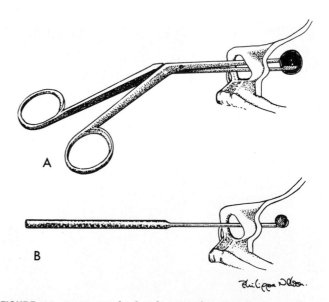

FIGURE 46–4. Removal of a foreign object requires avoidance of posterior displacement. *A,* Object grasped with a Hartmann forceps. *B,* Wire loop placed behind the object before withdrawal.

Passage of the flexible nasopharyngoscope can help visualize a foreign body or rule out its presence. Whenever there are secretions or nasal edema, however, failure to visualize a foreign body does not necessarily preclude its presence.

Although removal of nasal foreign bodies in a papoosed and sedated child can be accomplished safely, an upright position decreases the chance of aspiration of either a dislodged object that moves posteriorly or blood resulting from trauma to surrounding tissue.

For foreign bodies that are not amenable to a careful attempt at removal in the office, the author prefers that they be removed with the child under a brief general anesthetic with the airway secured by an endotracheal tube, rather than have the procedure performed in a sedated child whose airway is unprotected. Examination under anesthesia in the operating room is also indicated when the presence of a foreign body is strongly suspected but none is visualized during the office examination.

Visualization can be accomplished either with the operating microscope, using a 200 or 250 mm objective, or with rigid telescopes. Sizes 5 and 7 Frazier tip suction tubes are more useful than larger sizes. If a suspected foreign body is not seen, the nasopharynx should be examined. Although this may be accomplished with a 120-degree rigid telescope, a better view is usually obtained with transnasal soft red rubber catheters brought out of the mouth and clamped to retract the soft palate, and with mirror visualization of the nasopharynx with a laryngeal or dental mirror. This maneuver may also deliver a nasal foreign object into the nasopharynx.

Unusual Foreign Bodies: Insects and Animate Objects, Iatrogenic Foreign Bodies

Many unusual foreign bodies of the nose have been reported, including insects, parasites, and various iatrogenically placed instruments.

Ascaris lumbricoides, a nematode, or roundworm, is a common helminthic parasite of humans. The distribution of ascariasis is worldwide but is most common in regions with crowding and poor sanitation. Several endemic regions exist in the United States. Human infestation occurs from ingestion of mature eggs in fecally contaminated food or drink. Larvae hatch in the intestine and then penetrate blood or lymph vessels through the intestinal wall. Some larvae reach the portal circulation and are carried to the liver, while others pass through the thoracic duct. By either route, they reach the lungs, where they perforate the alveoli. After increasing massively in size, the larvae migrate up the respiratory passages to the epiglottis and then down the esophagus.[6] The nematodes sometimes lodge in the nose when regurgitated. Mature worms may be up to 10 inches in length.

Maggots have also been described in the nose but are rarely encountered in children in the United States. Such infestations of insects or insect larvae generally require a combination of necrotic material in the nose and neglect.

Iatrogenic foreign bodies are not rare. They include teeth, pieces of hardware from dental manipulation, and remnants of packing from nasal and sinus surgery. The presenting symptoms are usually related to the sequelae of infection and inflammation, and the true diagnosis may be made more obscure by a history of dental or sinus infection preceding the presence of the foreign body.

Conditions Mimicking Nasal Foreign Bodies

Rhinosporidium seeberi infestation is a fungal infection found mainly in India and Sri Lanka. Nasal polyps are formed and contain the spores in all stages of development. The masses appear as slender, filiform, or narrow leaflike processes of a dull pink or reddish tint, with the surface studded with many minute, pale spots owing to the presence of the sporangia in the tissue.[13] The growths are very friable and bleed easily when touched.

Aspergillus infections of the nose cause sneezing, rhinorrhea, headache, and the discharge of pieces of tough, greenish membrane, which may coexist with polyps and granulation tissue.[13]

Nasal infections may be invasive or noninvasive. *Aspergillus* infection seems endemic to the southern regions of the United States. Invasive *Aspergillus* rhinitis and sinusitis are more common in immunocompromised patients.

Wegener granulomatosis generally occurs in adults rather than in children but has been reported in the pediatric age group. Although nasal symptoms are usually bilateral, they may be unilateral. Typically, there is crusting along the septum and nasal obstruction. Deep biopsy shows vasculitis.

Rhinoliths

Rhinoliths are formed from intranasal foreign bodies that become encrusted with mineral salts, usually calcium and magnesium. They are uncommon but not rare, several hundred having been reported in the world's medical literature. Most are thought to arise from exogenous for-

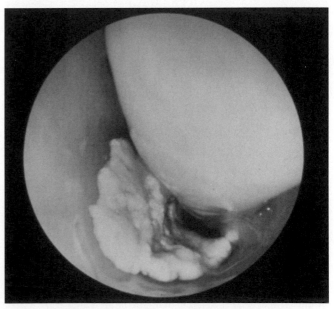

FIGURE 46–5. Telescopic view of an intranasal rhinolith. (Courtesy of Dr. Michael Hawke, Toronto, Ontario, Canada.)

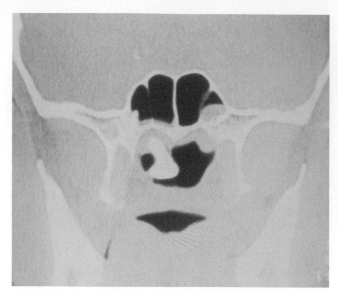

FIGURE 46–6. Coronal computed tomographic scan showing an intranasal rhinolith. (Courtesy of Dr. Michael Hawke, Toronto, Ontario, Canada.)

eign bodies. Although the theoretical possibility of an endogenous foreign body such as a blood clot or dried purulent debris serving as the nucleus of a rhinolith has been hypothesized, most authors doubt this origin. In many cases, the rhinolith can be broken apart and the remains of a foreign body recovered. Adults have had rhinoliths removed and small toys recovered as the nidus of the "stone" that were likely placed years previously during childhood.[14]

The appropriate treatment of a rhinolith is removal. If it is too large to be removed in one piece, it can be broken intranasally and removed in small pieces. Removal of the rhinolith may require displacing it posteriorly and recovering it from the nasopharynx. Occasionally, lateral rhinotomy has been required for removal of a massive rhinolith.

Rhinoliths may be noted on nasal examination with flexible fiberoptic instruments or rigid telescopes (Fig. 46–5). Radiographic examination, including both plain films and computed tomography, may be helpful in establishing the diagnosis (Figs. 46–6 and 46–7).

Conclusion

Foreign bodies may be the cause of nasal obstruction and rhinorrhea in children. Identification and removal require both appropriate suspicion on the part of the otolaryngologist and adequate instrumentation, including the means of careful intranasal examination. Although most foreign objects are easily removed from the nose in an office setting, long-standing objects surrounded by mucosal edema and granulation tissue, and foreign objects that have resisted multiple attempts at removal, are best managed under general anesthesia in an operating room setting. Some advice from Dr. Sylvan E. Stool[15] most appropriately concludes this chapter: "Any attempt at removal of a foreign object which does not succeed will make a bad situation worse. The child is usually apprehensive and the parents are aggravated. The physician, therefore, should be wary of falling into the trap of trying to do a removal without adequate instruments or good control of the patient."

SELECTED REFERENCES

Jackson C. Diseases of the Air and Food Passages of Foreign Body Origin. Philadelphia, WB Saunders, 1936.

This book contains classic descriptions of the presentation and methods of removal of foreign bodies in children. It is written by the otolaryngologist who provided the foundation for recognition and endoscopic retrieval of foreign bodies.

Stoney P, Bringham B, Okuda I, Hawke M. Diagnosis of rhinoliths with rigid endoscopy. J Otolaryngol 20:408, 1991.

This article summarizes the literature on the rhinolith and contains case reports that illustrate the presentation and removal of these concretions.

Tong MC, Van Hasselt CA, Woo JK. The hazards of button batteries in the nose. J Otolaryngol 21:458, 1992.

This article discusses the nasal foreign body that probably presents the greatest danger to children.

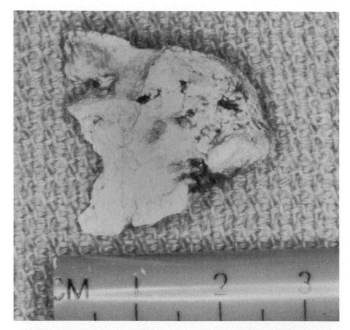

FIGURE 46–7. The intranasal rhinolith imaged in Figure 46–6, after removal. (Courtesy of Dr. Michael Hawke, Toronto, Ontario, Canada.)

REFERENCES

1. Baker MD. Foreign bodies of the ears and nose in childhood. Pediatr Emerg Care 3:67, 1987.
2. Bennet JD. An unexpected cause of halitosis. J R Army Med Corps 134:151, 1988.
3. Bicknell PG. Rhinolith perforating the hard palate. J Laryngol Otol 84:1161, 1970.
4. Capo JM, Lucente FE. Alkaline battery foreign bodies of the ear and nose. Arch Otolaryngol Head Neck Surg 112:562, 1986.

5. Fosarelli P, Feigelman S, Pearson E, Calimano-Diaz A. An unusual intranasal foreign body. Pediatr Emerg Care 4:117, 1988.

6. Hunter GW, Swartzwelder JC, Clyde DF. Tropical Medicine, 5th ed. Philadelphia, WB Saunders, 1976.

7. Jackson C. Diseases of the Air and Food Passages of Foreign Body Origin. Philadelphia, WB Saunders, 1936.

8. Katz HP, Katz JR, Bernstein M, et al. Unusual presentation of nasal foreign bodies in children. JAMA 241:1496, 1979.

9. Kavanaugh KT, Litovitz T. Miniature battery foreign bodies in auditory and nasal cavities. JAMA 255:1470, 1986.

10. Kost KM, Shapiro RS. Button battery ingestion: a case report and review of the literature. J Otolaryngol 16:252, 1987.

11. Nazif M. A rubber dam clamp in the nasal cavity: report of a case. J Am Dent Assoc 82:1099, 1971.

12. Shapiro RS. Foreign bodies of the nose. In Bluestone CD, Stool SE (eds). Pediatric Otolaryngology, Vol II, 2nd ed. Philadelphia, WB Saunders, 1990, pp 752–759.

13. Smith AB. Epistaxis, foreign bodies, and parasites. In Stewart JP (ed). Logan Turner's Diseases of the Nose, Throat, and Ear, 7th ed. Bristol, England, John Wright, 1968, pp 60–62.

14. Stoney P, Bringham B, Okuda I, Hawke M. Diagnosis of rhinoliths with rigid endoscopy. J Otolaryngol 20:408, 1991.

15. Stool SE, McConnel CS Jr. Foreign bodies in pediatric otolaryngology: some diagnostic and therapeutic pointers. Clin Pediatr (Phila) 12:113, 1973.

16. Tong MC, Van Hasselt CA, Woo JK. The hazards of button batteries in the nose. J Otolaryngol 21:458, 1992.

17. Wiley JF 2d, Henretig FM, Selbst SM. Blood lead levels in children with foreign bodies. Pediatrics 89:593, 1992.

47

Injuries of the Nose, Facial Bones, and Paranasal Sinuses

Andrew M. Shapiro, M.D.

The management of maxillofacial trauma has undergone a remarkable evolution in recent years, fueled by advances in modern understanding of bone and soft tissue healing, improved techniques of surgical exposure derived from craniofacial surgery,[37] and availability of new materials and technology applied to rigid internal fixation. While the general management principles in adults and children are similar, characteristic anatomic and physiologic features of childhood require judicious use of these resources. In addition to the aesthetic and functional considerations that determine the optimal approach to therapy in adults, ongoing developmental changes in the growing face must be considered. This chapter is an overview of the management of pediatric facial injuries, with an emphasis on how this care differs from that of the adult.

Incidence

Fractures of the facial skeleton occur rarely in children. In Rowe's series[35] of 1500 facial fractures, less than 5% occurred in children younger than 12 years, and less than 1% occurred in children younger than 6 years. It has been argued that the incidences reported in older studies have been underestimated, because fractures in children tend to be minimally displaced and would not be detected by physical examination and plain radiography alone. In addition, epidemiologic data derived from hospital admissions would fail to account for the large proportion of nasal and alveolar injuries evaluated and treated exclusively in the emergency department.[17] A later series by Gussack and colleagues[16] reported that 14.5% of maxillofacial injuries occurred in children, which may represent a more accurate estimation of the true incidence. These authors emphasized the use of computed tomography (CT) to enhance the diagnosis of fractures in the pediatric patient.

Epidemiology

The interaction of environmental, anatomic, and physiologic factors accounts for the relatively low frequency of maxillofacial injuries in children. Young children exist in a relatively protected environment and are less likely than adults to be injured as a result of alcohol-related vehicular accidents, violent altercations, or "high-impact" team sports. Approximately 50% of facial fractures in children result from incidents involving motor vehicles[17, 26, 34] (Fig. 47–1). The legislated use of car seats and seat belts for children has been beneficial in reducing the number of fatalities involving motor vehicles and has resulted in more children with maxillofacial trauma requiring therapy.[33] A large proportion of toddlers are injured outside the vehicle as pedestrians rather than as passengers. Falls account for a relatively large proportion of injuries in young children, especially when they are learning to walk or ride bicycles.[36] The increasing number of random, violent events in urban society has led to a notable increase in the number of children injured by firearms.[26] Facial fractures resulting from recreational all-terrain vehicles are becoming more common.[9] Finally, the face is a common focus of injury in cases of child abuse, although fractures are less common than soft tissue injuries.[21] The potential of abuse should always be considered when the degree of injury is out of proportion with the proposed mechanism, or when unexplained bruises or other injuries are noted on physical examination.

As the child matures, the gradual evolution in life style is reflected in the increased frequency of maxillofacial injury; by 10 to 12 years of age, children increasingly manifest the characteristics of adult facial trauma. Facial fractures shift from a nearly equal sex distribution in toddlers and young children to a 2:1 male predominance by early school age.[26] In addition, the pattern of injury changes as the facial skeleton matures.

Distribution

The nose is the most commonly reported site of fracture in the face, followed by the mandible (Fig. 47–2). However, it is likely that dental and alveolar injuries of the mandible and maxilla occur more commonly, but they are not appreciated in the typical reviews of hospital records. The distribution of injuries depends on the age and status of skeletal growth (see later discussion). Midfacial fractures, including the zygoma, maxilla, and nasoethmoid

Motor Vehicle Related

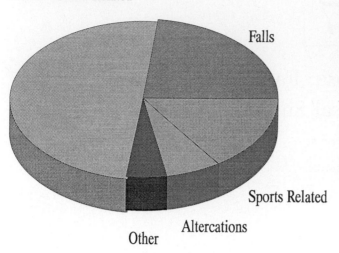

FIGURE 47-1. Etiology of facial fractures in children.

region, are uncommon in children younger than 10 years; fractures of the frontal area are most frequent in children younger than 6 years.[17, 26, 34]

Unique Features of the Pediatric Facial Skeleton

Anatomy

The distinctive characteristics of the craniofacial region in children influence the incidence, pattern, and treatment of facial fractures. A number of anatomic features have been identified as playing a particularly significant role.

Increased Cranial/Facial Ratio. The ratio of the cranium to the face has been estimated to be 8:1 at birth, 4:1 at 5 years of age, and 2.5:1 in the adult[22] (Fig. 47-3). The relatively large cranial vault of the young child, in conjunction with the prominent frontal region, tends to shield the face from injury at the expense of the cranium.

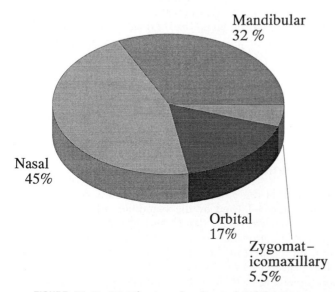

FIGURE 47-2. Distribution of pediatric facial fractures.

FIGURE 47-3. Growth and development of the facial skeleton. The mandible, midface, and nasoethmoid region become increasingly prominent in both projection and vertical height. In contrast, the vulnerable frontal area of the infant slopes posteriorly and accounts for a smaller proportion of the overall facial area. (From Enlow DH. The Human Face. New York, Harper & Row, 1968. Courtesy of William L. Brudon.)

In particular, the lack of projection of the nose, midface, and zygoma results in a low frequency of injuries to these areas in children younger than 10 years; these features also account for the large number of intracranial injuries seen in pediatric trauma patients.

Thick Adipose Layer. The thick layer of subcutaneous fat, particularly in the buccal region, tends to protect the facial bones from impact.

Incomplete Paranasal Sinus Pneumatization. The structure of the facial skeleton in adults can be characterized as a series of strong vertical and horizontal buttresses interposed by thin, eggshell-like bone. This structure tends to distribute an applied force in a fairly predictable way, allowing recognition of specific injury patterns, such as zygomatic complex and Le Fort fractures. On the contrary, the absence of significant sinus development in young children results in a solid block of bone and cartilage, rather than a buttressed structure (Fig. 47-4). This provides increased stability and reduces the likelihood of fracturing the bones of the midface. However, when mid-

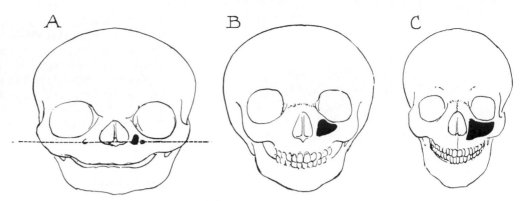

FIGURE 47–4. The skull at birth (A), at 4 years old (B), and in the adult (C) drawn in the same vertical dimension to demonstrate the relative increase in size of the maxillary sinus. (From Converse JM. Surgical Treatment of Facial Injuries. Baltimore, Williams & Wilkins, 1974, p 389. Copyright Williams & Wilkins, 1974.)

facial fractures do occur, they commonly indicate a severe injury, which may extend unpredictably across the midline or superiorly to involve the cranium.[28] The characteristic fracture patterns in adults become more common as maxillary sinus development proceeds beyond the age of 5 or 6 years.

Deciduous Dentition. The presence of multiple tooth buds within the developing mandible and maxilla results in an interlocking "jigsaw puzzle" configuration, making these areas more difficult to fracture and displace (Fig. 47–5). However, the conical shape of the deciduous teeth adds a degree of difficulty and instability to routine arch bar and wire techniques for closed reduction. Furthermore, when the permanent teeth begin to erupt, occlusal patterns may be confusing, which may make reduction and external fixation difficult.

Increased Elasticity. The facial bones of children compared with those of adults demonstrate a higher ratio of cancellous to cortical bone, which provides increased flexibility. Cartilage accounts for a larger proportion of the facial skeleton. In the age group younger than 2 or 3 years, elasticity is further enhanced by reduced mineralization of the bone. As a result, fractures in children tend to be greenstick, and comminution is less likely to occur.

Physiology

An appreciation of the unique physiology of the growing facial skeleton is essential for determining the necessity, timing, and nature of surgical intervention. The factors that must be considered include the following.

Increased Osteogenic Potential. Children have an impressive ability to heal fractures rapidly. Facial fractures in adults can routinely be reduced even at 7 to 10 days after the injury; attempts at reduction at this interval in children usually reveal fractures that are already significantly "knit" and may require osteotomies for mobilization. Surgical repair should optimally be undertaken within 3 to 5 days or as soon as other injuries allow. The decision to proceed in the presence of other significant trauma must be carefully weighed in conjunction with other members of the pediatric trauma team. Nonetheless, the long-term functional and cosmetic significance of inadequately repaired facial injuries must not be underestimated.

Facial Growth. A unique characteristic of the pediatric craniofacial skeleton is the ongoing process of change in size and configuration. This summary is included to emphasize the relationship between growth and the management of craniofacial trauma.

As characterized by Enlow,[12] growth occurs through two interrelated mechanisms (Fig. 47–6). *Displacement* refers to the change in the position of an individual bone in relation to the overall facial structure. For example, the maxilla migrates inferiorly and anteriorly as the face grows (see Fig. 47–3). *Remodeling* refers to the alteration in the shape of the individual bones and is closely related to the process of displacement. Remodeling can be demonstrated conveniently in the changing structure of the mandible; the vertical height increases as the ramus extends posterosuperiorly (see Fig. 47–6). Both of these mechanisms occur through the selective deposition and resorption of bone on the appropriate surfaces of the facial skeleton.

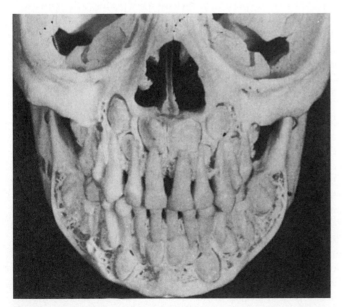

FIGURE 47–5. The unerupted dentition of the infant provides strength to the midface and reduces the likelihood of displacement. (From Enlow DH. Facial Growth. Philadelphia, WB Saunders, 1990, p 24.)

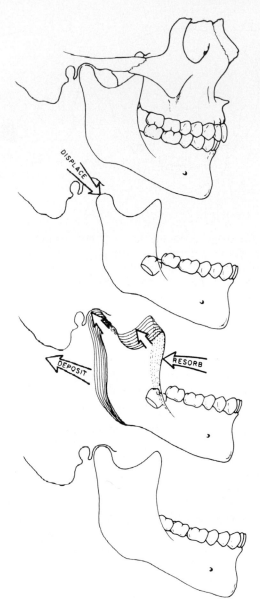

FIGURE 47–6. The two major components of facial growth are closely related. Tension applied to the facial bones from the forces of the overlying soft tissue results in displacement. Remodeling occurs simultaneously in an effort to maintain relationships with the surrounding bones. (From Enlow DH. Facial Growth. Philadelphia, WB Saunders, 1990, p 32.)

The driving force behind facial growth is poorly understood and has been the subject of considerable debate. Traditionally, the concept of "growth centers" has been used to describe particular areas of autonomous osteoblastic activity that drive the bones toward their ultimate position and form. Perhaps the best described of these is the junction of the vomer and quadrangular cartilage in the nasal septum. Injury to this area was thought to lead to diminished midfacial growth and has resulted in the restrained approach toward nasal surgery in children.[2] Other proposed growth centers include the mandibular condyle and the various suture lines of the craniofacial region. Although these areas almost certainly play a role in the postnatal growth and development of the adult face, the "functional matrix" concept provides an attractive, unifying approach to the underlying forces of facial growth.[29] In summary, this theory proposes that growth occurs as a response to the tensions placed on the skeleton by the functional demands of the overlying soft tissues. In the growing child, the expanding intracranial cavity and increasing needs for mastication and deglutition would induce displacement and remodeling.

Evaluation

The need for a complete, systematic evaluation of the child with maxillofacial trauma cannot be overemphasized. Studies have demonstrated that nearly three fourths of pediatric facial trauma patients had associated injuries.[26] The first priority in the care of the traumatized patient is the assessment and maintenance of an adequate airway. The oral cavity should be suctioned to remove clots, loose teeth, and foreign material. A suture or towel clip may be used to extract the tongue in an anterior position. Because displaced midfacial fractures are rare in small children, an impacted maxilla is an unusual cause of a compromised airway. If an artificial airway is required, endotracheal intubation is generally the best option. Tracheotomy may be necessary in laryngeal fractures or when prolonged intubation is anticipated as a result of central nervous system, abdominal, or thoracic trauma. Tracheotomy is ideally accomplished with the airway intubated. Bleeding from head and neck sites should be controlled by direct pressure, avoiding clamps and ligatures, which may inadvertently injure facial nerve branches. Severe bleeding from facial fractures in children is rare.

Once airway control has been established and the patient is hemodynamically stabilized, attention should be turned toward the central nervous system. Cervical spine injuries are surprisingly rare in the pediatric population, occurring in less than 1% in some series.[16, 17] In contrast, associated intracranial injuries are present in approximately 40% to 50% of children with facial fractures and are seen most commonly in children younger than 6 years old.[26] Other common sites of injury include extremities and less commonly the abdomen or chest.

The evaluation of the head and neck should be performed in a thorough, systematic fashion. A history obtained from the pediatric patient is usually incomplete, so the reports of eyewitnesses are essential. The child is commonly apprehensive, and the examiner must be patient and understanding, carefully explaining each step before proceeding. Physical examination can be challenging given the generous subcutaneous fat, extensive edema, and minimal displacement typical of pediatric fractures (Fig. 47–7). The face should be inspected for swelling, ecchymosis, abrasions, or asymmetry. Periorbital ecchymosis ("raccoon eyes") may indicate the presence of an anterior skull base fracture. Palpation of the frontal area, orbital rims, nasal dorsum, alveoli, and mandible should be performed. All lacerations should be gently explored to determine depth and presence of an underlying fracture (Fig. 47–8). The status of facial motor and sensory function and parotid duct integrity should be as-

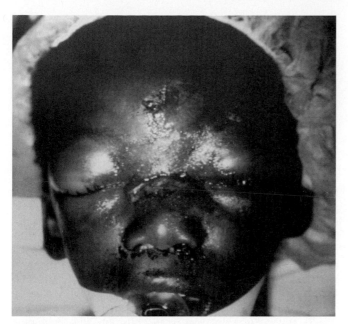

FIGURE 47–7. Marked edema of the midface after blunt trauma. Note telecanthus and flattening of the nasal dorsum resulting from nasoethmoid fracture.

sessed. The ear canals and tympanic membrane should be examined for evidence of disruption, which may suggest condylar or temporal bone fractures. Ecchymosis of the mastoid area (Battle sign) may indicate a fracture of the skull base. Occlusion should be assessed, although mixed dentition can make interpretation challenging. Extraocular movements should be elicited and a visual examination performed in all patients. Injury to periorbital structures indicates the need for ophthalmologic consultation. Sedation is almost never required for physical examination but may be necessary (assuming the absence of a closed head injury) for radiologic studies and for repair of soft tissue trauma.

Radiographic studies play an essential role in the management of pediatric fractures. Although plain nasal films may not be required for the evaluation or treatment of nasal fractures, they are often obtained for medicolegal purposes. On the other hand, all other significant injuries of the facial skeleton must be assessed radiologically. Plain films of the midface in children are difficult to interpret because of the diminished contrast provided by poorly pneumatized sinuses. Thin-cut axial and coronal CT scans demonstrate fractures and displacement that are often not detected on physical examination. The information derived from these studies allows the surgeon to plan the optimal approach to the injuries while avoiding unnecessary exploration. The use of three-dimensional imaging for maxillofacial trauma is well established; at present, the most useful role appears to be in the evaluation of patients requiring reconstruction of secondary defects resulting from trauma, rather than the primary repair. Evaluation of the mandible may be aided by plain films and panoramic imaging, which may detect fractures missed by CT because of the plane of section.

Management

Antibiotics

The use of prophylactic antibiotics for head and neck surgery remains a controversial issue. Antimicrobial agents are commonly used for complex maxillofacial injuries. Chole and Yee[6] demonstrated the benefit of perioperative cefazolin in a prospective study of patients undergoing surgical repair of mandibular fractures. The role of antimicrobial therapy for other injuries is unclear. It appears prudent to use prophylaxis in cases of fractures exposed through skin or mucosa, of through-and-through lacerations, and of crush injuries, or when cartilage is exposed. Tetanus toxoid should be administered to unimmunized patients, to patients who have not received immunization in more than 5 years, and to patients with massive open injuries.

Soft Tissue Injuries

Facial lacerations and abrasions are extremely common in children and often accompany facial fractures. Burst lacerations often result from blunt impacts such as falls and

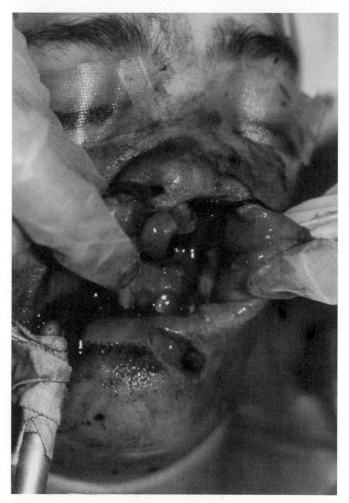

FIGURE 47–8. Careful exploration of all fractures is essential, as in this patient with an underlying diagonal fracture of the maxilla.

may be deceptively extensive. Photodocumentation is an important adjunct. Before vigorous exploration or cleansing of the wound, it is frequently helpful to obtain a degree of anesthesia. TAC, a combination of tetracaine, adrenaline, and cocaine, is an effective topical anesthetic agent and, at the very least, minimizes the pain associated with the administration of locally injectable anesthetic agents.[5] Caution should be maintained when using TAC on mucosal wounds, because seizures have been reported after systemic absorption in this setting.[8] Alternatively, bupivacaine, mepivacaine, or prilocaine combined with a vasoconstrictor provides an effective topical anesthetic. A variety of sedative adjuncts are available—for small lacerations, intranasal midazolam provides a fairly predictable sedative effect without requiring a cooperative "sip" or intravenous access. The wound should be copiously irrigated to remove debris; it is much more difficult to deal with the "traumatic tattoo" resulting from inadequate cleansing after primary repair (Fig. 47–9). Pneumatic devices used to infuse intravenous solutions with a small-caliber intravenous catheter are ideal for irrigation, allowing the rapid, forceful delivery of a large quantity of

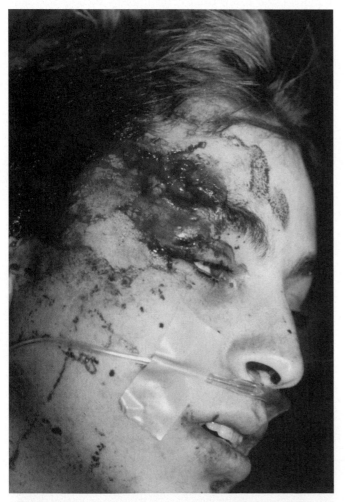

FIGURE 47–9. Soft tissue injury after vehicular trauma demonstrating some of the challenges associated with these injuries: burst lacerations with contusion and loss of surrounding tissues, disruption of aesthetic landmarks (eyebrow), and extensive contamination of the wound with debris.

saline. Pulsed irrigation systems used for debridement of orthopedic injuries have a role in larger injuries. Povidone-iodine antiseptic agents reduce the rate of infection at the margin of the wound but are generally not recommended for introduction into the exposed soft tissues.[30] Wounds of the cheek should be explored for injured branches of the facial nerve or parotid duct. Conservative debridement of necrotic tissue is required, but the impressive blood supply to the facial soft tissues often allows the preservation of marginal tissue.

Hypertrophic scars tend to develop in children. Reducing tension on the wound edges is essential to maximize the cosmetic result of wound closure. Undermining in a plane just deep to the subcutaneous fat is effective and often obviates the need for local flaps. Landmarks such as the vermilion border of the lip, or the margin of the eyebrow, should be approximated initially in an effort to prevent a noticeable break in contour in these areas. The wound should be closed in layers, minimizing dead space that may ultimately result in scar depression. A rapidly absorbing 6-0 gut skin suture covered with Steri-Strips is ideally suited for skin closure in children, who heal rapidly and may be uncooperative when suture removal is attempted. In clean lacerations, the skin layer can also be approximated in a sutureless fashion with cyanoacrylate polymer adhesive. Sutureless closure is quicker, is associated with greater patient satisfaction, obviates suture removal, and results in cosmesis comparable to suture closure.

Penetrating Maxillofacial Trauma

Penetrating craniofacial injuries in children are rare, accounting for only 1% to 2% of pediatric trauma. Both stab wounds and projectiles can produce severe injuries. The initial management of penetrating trauma parallels that of blunt injuries—the first priority is to secure the "ABCs." The stability of the cervical spine must be assured. The recommended management is based on the location of the injury, using an anatomic "zone" classification system similar to that in adults[15, 24]:

Zone 1: Hairline to supraorbital rims. CT of brain and arteriography may be necessary. Neurosurgical consultation for debridement of devitalized bone and brain is essential. Arteriography is often required.

Zone 2: Supraorbital rim to upper lip: CT of face and neck, if necessary. Incidence of ocular injuries is high.

Zone 3: Lower lip to hyoid. This zone blends into the neck, and management is based on the treatment of penetrating cervical trauma. Stable patients can be evaluated by flexible laryngoscopy and contrast imaging of the esophagus. Surgical exploration and rigid endoscopy is mandated for active bleeding or expanding hematoma, subcutaneous emphysema, dysphagia, neurologic injury, or airway compromise.

Facial Fractures in Children

Maxillomandibular Fixation

In adults, occlusion is often the foundation from which the craniofacial skeleton can be reconstructed following injury. The evolving status of a child's dentition can make establishment of occlusion difficult, and special techniques may be necessary to establish maxillomandibular fixation (MMF). For this purpose, the status of dental maturation can be broadly divided into three categories:

1. Primary dentition: birth to 5 years of age. The conical shape of the teeth renders circumdental wiring unstable and more difficult to apply. Erich arch bars or Ivy loops can be used, although cautiously. Acrylic splints (occlusal or lingual) or cast cap splints may be used in patients with limited dental eruption.
2. Mixed dentition: 6 to 11 years of age. The most difficult time to determine proper occlusion. Splints or circumnasal or circumzygomatic wires may be required.
3. Permanent dentition: 12 to 16 years of age. Standard arch bars or wires can be used.

Rigid Internal Fixation

Since the early 1980s, rigid internal fixation (RIF) has become the dominant method of repairing maxillofacial injuries in adults, essentially replacing external fixation or nonrigid wire internal fixation. Broad exposure is obtained through aesthetically acceptable incisions in the gingivolabial sulcus, lateral brow, coronal scalp, and conjunctiva. The use of plates and screws facilitates accurate three-dimensional reduction; furthermore, improved stability of the reduced fragments facilitates rapid healing and diminishes the likelihood of infection. These techniques have dramatically enhanced the ability of the craniofacial surgeon to restore preinjury form and rapid return of function. Complications associated with RIF in adults are generally restricted to local concerns such as palpability, temperature sensitivity, and infection.

The approaches and instrumentation for RIF in adults have been adapted to the pediatric population for surgical reconstruction in craniofacial dysostoses and trauma. However, the impact of these techniques on the growing craniofacial skeleton has remained one of the more controversial issues in reconstructive surgery. One concern is the theoretical effect of rigid fixation on the forces that promote normal growth. If one accepts the "functional matrix" concept, then both the periosteal dissection required for exposure and reduction of fractured segments as well as the "stress shielding" resulting from rigid fixation would disrupt the usual forces that drive growth. Presumably, the earlier this disruption occurs, the greater the impact. For instance, early repair of cleft palate is associated with more significant restriction of maxillary and palatal growth than late repair.[2] In a number of experiments using a rabbit model,[20, 23, 33, 38] elevation of soft tissue, excision of cranial sutures (presumably analogous to trauma), and rigid fixation each results in restrictive growth disturbances and varying degrees of compensatory changes in the remaining cranium. Yaremchuk and colleagues,[40] using a Rhesus monkey model, demonstrated a trend toward progressively greater disturbances in craniofacial growth with increasing numbers of plates and screws.

A second concern arises from clinical experience with RIF in children, primarily from patients with dysostoses. Fixation hardware (including wire) placed on the outer cortex may "migrate" internally, in some cases transgressing the dura.[14] This phenomenon presumably results from the differential resorption and deposition mechanism that results in cranial enlargement. In addition to concerns of central nervous system injury, the presence of hardware makes further surgery more difficult. Isolation of the plate on an island of bone has also been described. A final concern is the potential long-term sensitizing or carcinogenic impact of the alloys used to manufacture the plates and screws on the surrounding tissues.

A number of options have been proposed to circumvent the adverse effects of RIF in children. Persing and associates[32] demonstrated that a "window of opportunity" exists within which removal of fixation hardware results in normalization of growth. Removal of fixation hardware at a defined interval is routine at some centers, but the need for a second procedure involving further soft tissue dissection raises concerns. The promise of a practical *resorbable* fixation system is gradually becoming a reality. The ideal material must provide stability during healing but complete resorption once the fragments are stable, minimal inflammatory reaction, and ease of use in the operating suite. Currently, polymers of polylactic acid, polyglycolic acid, and Polydioxan are used to manufacture fixation systems for clinical use. The most promising is a combination of polylactic acid and polyglycolic acid (LactoSorb, Biomet, Warsaw, Ind.), which, when heated, is rendered malleable enough to be practical.[13] Because the strength of these materials is inferior to titanium plates, resorbable devices have a higher profile than the microplating systems popular for pediatric use. However, resorption eventually reconciles this problem. The screws tend to be relatively fragile; as an alternative, the plates may be glued to the fractured segments. In a pig model, this technique was as effective as metal plates and screws.[1] It is possible that, for minimally displaced fractures, glue alone may provide stability. New materials with enhanced absorption characteristics are being developed.

Despite the potential disadvantages, the use of metallic alloy plates and screws has markedly advanced the management of craniofacial trauma in children. In both animal models and clinical experience following bony injury, the observable differences in appearance between subjects treated with rigid fixation and more traditional techniques were fairly minimal. Despite plate migration, no reports of central nervous system complications resulting from the use of hardware have been published. In a series involving 121 procedures in 96 children undergoing craniofacial rigid fixation, only 8% required removal. Only one patient had a plate removed for presumed growth disturbance.[4]

At present, the primary question is *when* to use these techniques rather than *if* these techniques should be used. The accumulated literature does not provide sufficient evidence to devise an exact template for managing all of the potential fractures in all age groups. The unique anatomic and physiologic characteristics of the growing maxillofacial skeleton must be appreciated when contemplating the management of injuries. Therapy should be individualized on the basis of severity and age. In young children, fractures are much less likely to be significantly displaced; in contrast, greenstick fractures are extremely common. Displaced fractures may be treated with closed reduction techniques without internal stabilization because of the "lock and key" configuration of the unerupted dentition. McCoy and colleagues,[25] reporting in 1966 on their experience with facial fractures, reported excellent long-term results using "pre-RIF" techniques. When open reduction is required, soft tissue and periosteal elevation should be minimized as much as possible while allowing accurate alignment of fractured segments. The use of fixation hardware should be judicious, using wire when possible or short segments of plates.

Nasal Fractures

The nose is the most common site of fracture in children. The nasal pyramid is variably cartilaginous during childhood, and the midline suture is unfused, which makes greenstick fractures common. The typical pattern of pediatric nasal fractures is a "splaying" of the nasal bones over the frontal process of the maxilla rather than the C-shaped deformities commonly seen in adults (Figs. 47–10

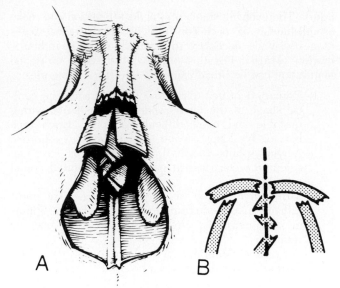

FIGURE 47–11. Characteristic "open book" pattern of pediatric nasal fractures. *A,* Frontal view. *B,* Axial view. (Illustration by Elizabeth Roselius, © 1987. Reprinted with permission from Foster & Sherman. Surgery of Facial Bone Fractures. New York, Churchill Livingstone, 1987, p 29.)

and 47–11). As noted previously, radiography plays a minor role in the diagnosis of these injuries.

Greenstick nasal fractures may go unrecognized in the presence of extensive edema and the absence of crepitus. Examination should focus on the degree of cosmetic and functional impairment caused by the injury. Intranasal examination for septal hematoma is essential; if it is discovered, immediate drainage should be performed with a quilting suture or packing placed to prevent recurrence. A high index of suspicion for cerebrospinal fluid rhinorrhea should be maintained.

Most nasal fractures in children require no therapy, because displacement is usually insignificant. Closed reduction under general anesthesia is usually adequate for displaced nasal fractures. Reduction of greenstick fractures may not be satisfying, because they rarely "snap" into place like their adult counterparts. The possibility that a definitive septorhinoplasty may be necessary in the future should be anticipated and discussed with the family before attempts at reduction are made. In patients with septal fractures resulting in loss of support for the nasal dorsum, a conservative septorhinoplasty with restoration of the septum is a reasonable alternative. Surgery of the nasal tip should be avoided until after puberty, if possible, to optimize the ultimate balance between the nasal tip and the adult face.

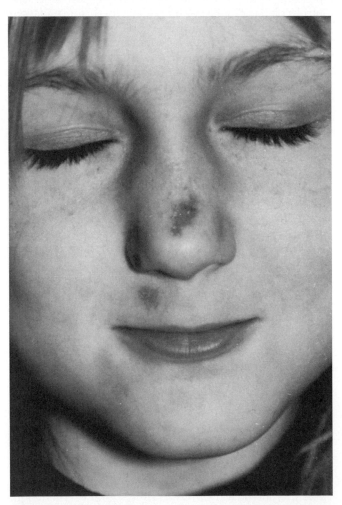

FIGURE 47–10. Typical appearance of nasal fracture 1 week after injury. Note widening and flattening of the dorsum.

Mandibular Fractures

The mandible is the second most frequent site of pediatric facial fractures. The frequency tends to increase with age as the mandible assumes a more prominent anterior location. The majority of fractures occur at the mandibular condyle, followed by the angle and parasymphyseal region. Diagnosis is generally established by history and physical examination, which reveals point tenderness, asymmetry on opening or closing, paresthesia of the inferior alveolar nerve, and malocclusion. Ecchymosis may be seen on the floor of the mouth. Trismus and swelling over the temporomandibular joint and within the ear canal are common with condylar fractures.

Condylar fractures in young children often result from a fall onto the mentum and may be associated with a chin laceration. Whereas adults typically fracture at the condylar neck, children younger than 3 years commonly suffer crush injuries of the spongy bone at the head of the condyle. These injuries can potentially result in marked retardation of mandibular growth and in ankylosis (Fig. 47–12).

Many reports have documented the impact of mandibular fractures on facial growth, with varying conclusions. Marked remodeling can take place following condylar fractures in young children; however, injuries in children younger than 3 years may also produce marked deformity.[21, 35] In contrast, a recent review suggested that injuries in children between 4 and 11 years of age were most likely to require orthognathic surgery. The majority of injuries, if treated properly and managed with orthodon-

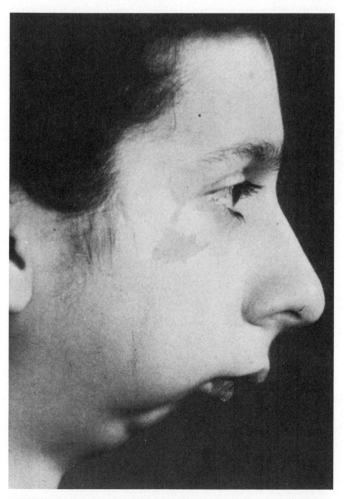

FIGURE 47–12. Example of mandibular hypoplasia and bilateral temporomandibular joint ankylosis after a fall on the chin at 4 years of age. (From Converse JM. Surgical Treatment of Facial Injuries. Baltimore, Williams & Wilkins, 1974, p 374. Copyright Williams & Wilkins, 1974.)

tics when necessary, produce no long-term developmental sequelae.[10]

Dental injuries represent the most common form of mandibular trauma, although patients are less likely to present to an emergency room. Consultation with a dentist or oral surgeon experienced in the care of children is prudent. Compression injuries may lead to necrosis and delayed eruption, as well as loss of secondary teeth. Fractures that expose the pulp constitute dental emergencies. Avulsed teeth can be transported in milk or saline if possible, rather than tap water. Replantation of deciduous teeth should be accomplished within an hour for best results, but is not required for the eruption of the corresponding secondary tooth. Segmental alveolar injuries are managed with replacement and fixation using arch bars or splints.

Condylar fractures can be distinguished into three types:

1. *Intracapsular*, often "crush" injuries of the spongy bone at the condylar head
2. *High*, across the coronoid notch
3. *Low*, in the upper ramus

If occlusion can be obtained and deviation upon opening is absent, unilateral or bilateral condylar injuries in young children can be managed with a soft diet, analgesics, and range-of-motion exercises. These exercises should include gradual repetitions of opening, closing, lateral movement, and projection. In older children, or in younger children if spontaneous occlusion is not possible, a short period of MMF followed by training elastics is recommended. Enhanced healing potential allows a corresponding reduction in the duration of MMF. In young children, 1 to 3 weeks is sufficient, followed by range-of-motion exercises, training elastics, or both. The time spent in MMF increases proportionally with age. In most cases, even a displaced condylar head can be managed with conservative therapy, because remodeling and resorption occur. Absolute indications for open reduction have been described by Zide[41]:

1. Displacement of condylar head into middle cranial fossa
2. Inability to establish occlusion by closed reduction
3. Lateral extracapsular displacement of fractured condyle, producing cosmetic deformity
4. A foreign body in association with the condylar head

Fractures involving the tooth-bearing segments of the mandible, such as body, symphysis, and parasymphyseal regions, are managed differently depending on the age of the patient. Again, minimally displaced fractures in younger children are generally managed conservatively. Splints or arch bars may be used for fixation, based on the state of dentition. In older children, or if reduction cannot be maintained, RIF is required. Applying fixation only on the inferior mandibular margin and using monocortical plates and screws when possible can protect unerupted teeth.[39] Teeth within the fracture line should be preserved whenever possible.

Injuries to the ramus are usually treated with closed techniques and MMF in young children. After the eruption of secondary teeth, conventional MMF and RIF are used, as in adults. Rigid fixation, which may provide a margin of airway safety, can eliminate the need for MMF in patients with seizure disorders or profound mental retardation.

Maxillary Fractures

Maxillary fractures are rare in children younger than 10 years of age. The most common findings are malocclusion and marked edema. Commonly, these injuries involve greenstick fractures of the alveolus or a sagittal split of the palate in the presence of an unfused midpalatal suture. More severe fractures may extend bilaterally or superiorly to involve the frontal region.[28] Approximately 40% of children with maxillary fractures have a central nervous system injury, and 14% have cerebrospinal fluid leak.[16, 35]

The goal of therapy in maxillary fractures is restoration of occlusion, midfacial projection, and height. Most commonly, fractures in young children are minimally displaced and do not require reduction. Injuries of the maxillary alveolus or palate may be treated with intermaxillary fixation for 2 weeks. Open reduction with internal fixation in the young patient is treacherous because of the multiple tooth buds in the maxilla. When necessary, monocort-

ical microplates are generally sufficient to restore anatomic continuity while minimizing the risk of injury to unerupted teeth. As sinus development proceeds, the frequency of these injuries increases and assumes the patterns seen in adults. Management with conventional techniques of internal fixation should be pursued.

Zygomatic Fractures

Following the same trends as other midfacial fractures, these injuries are rare in young children and become more common as the zygomas assume a prominent location. Indicators of displaced zygomatic fractures include depressed contour of the cheek, inferior displacement of the lateral canthus, subconjunctival hemorrhage, and step deformity in fractures with significant displacement. Greenstick injuries involving the zygomatic arch are most common; when displacement does occur, closed reduction is difficult. Reduction through a temporal (Gillies) or gingival sulcus approach allows restoration of contour and generally satisfactory results without the need for internal fixation (Fig. 47–13). Displaced zygomatic complex fractures should be treated with open reduction and internal fixation; the need for two- or three-point fixation depends on the individual case (Fig. 47–14). Onlay bone grafts to restore contour have not been extensively evaluated in

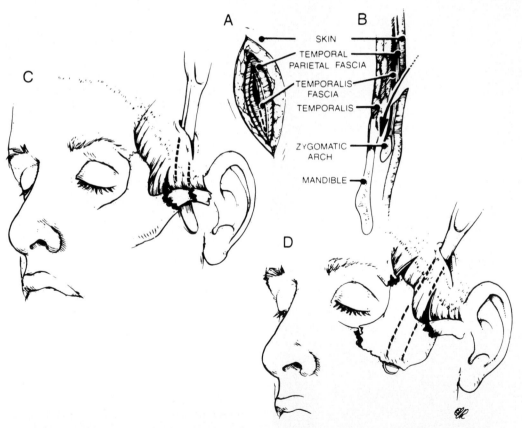

FIGURE 47–13. Temporal approach for reduction of zygomatic fractures. A and B, Incision. C and D, The elevator should be inserted deep to the temporalis fascia and placed underneath the zygoma. In children, this type of reduction alone may be adequate treatment. (Illustration by Elizabeth Roselius, © 1987. Reprinted with permission from Foster & Sherman. Surgery of Facial Bone Fractures. New York, Churchill Livingstone, 1987, p 136.)

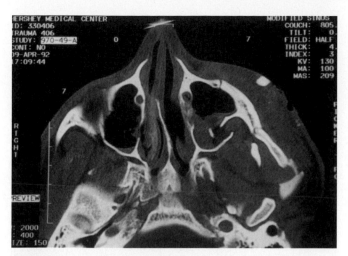

FIGURE 47–14. Computed tomographic scan demonstrating left zygomatic complex fracture with disruption of the zygomatic arch, zygomaticomaxillary suture, and posterior wall of the maxillary sinus.

children, and their use should probably be delayed until facial development is complete.

Orbital Fractures

Fractures involving the orbital rim and floor do not commonly appear until significant pneumatization of the maxillary sinus is present. The symptoms of orbital fractures include diplopia and pain. Physical findings consist of upward gaze restriction, subconjunctival hemorrhage, and anesthesia in the distribution of the infraorbital nerve. Enophthalmos indicates a significant increase in orbital volume or loss of orbital contents into the maxillary sinus secondary to disruption of the orbital floor. Ophthalmologic evaluation should be obtained with any significant injury to the orbit or globe.

Treatment of orbital fractures is necessary when enophthalmos or entrapment is present. An additional surgical indication includes CT demonstration of significant displacement of the orbital rim or floor, especially with demonstration of orbital contents in the maxillary sinus. Although these injuries may be observed for the development of sequelae, the results of late surgical repair do not appear to equal those obtained when treatment is delivered early. Exposure of the orbit through a subciliary or transconjunctival approach with lateral cantholysis provides cosmetically acceptable results[37] (Fig. 47–15). If the orbital floor is comminuted but not significantly displaced, it can be reconstituted with absorbable cellulose film (Gelfilm). Greater degrees of displacement can be repaired with autogenous bone or cartilage grafts. There are no long-term data on the use of permanent alloplastic implants in pediatric reconstruction.

Nasoethmoid Fractures

A posteriorly directed force delivered to the nasal dorsum can collapse the nasal bones and ethmoid cells into the

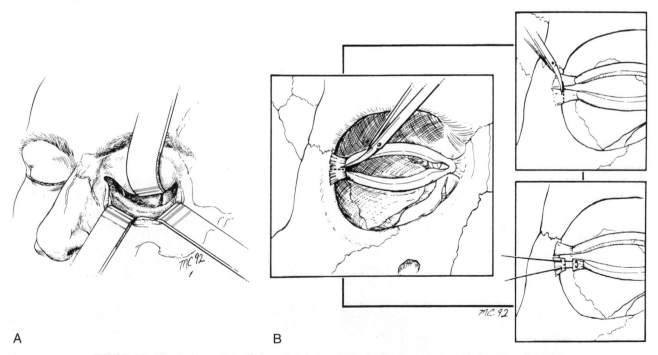

A   B

FIGURE 47–15. *A,* Exposure of the orbital rim through the transconjunctival approach. *B,* To maximize exposure, a lateral cantholysis and inferior canthotomy may be beneficial. Tagging the lateral canthus facilitates careful reapproximation at the termination of the procedure. (From Shumrick KA, Kersten R, Kulwin D, et al. Extended access and internal approaches for the management of facial trauma. Arch Otolaryngol Head Neck Surg 118:1105, 1992. Copyright 1992, American Medical Association.)

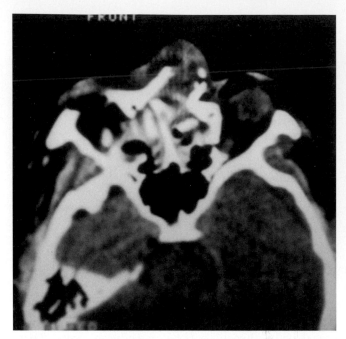

FIGURE 47–16. Nasoethmoid complex fracture with bilateral displacement of the medial canthus–bearing bone.

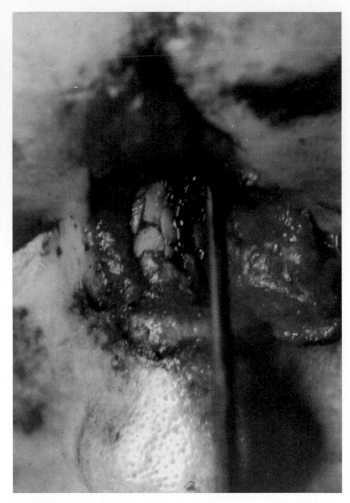

FIGURE 47–18. Repair of a comminuted nasoethmoid fracture through the overlying laceration.

interorbital space (Fig. 47–16). The nasoethmoid region is barely developed before 2 years of age and does not achieve prominence until the age of 5 or 6 years; consequently, these injuries are rarely seen in young children. Physical findings consist of loss of nasal projection, depression of the nasal root, telecanthus, and subconjunctival hemorrhage (Fig. 47–17). The definitive finding is mobility of the medial canthus–bearing bone on bimanual palpation.[31] Reconstruction of the nasoethmoid region is perhaps the most challenging area of facial trauma surgery. The complex bone–soft tissue relationships of the medial canthus must be reestablished correctly or rounding and asymmetry are readily apparent. Knowledge of the anatomy and function of the nasolacrimal apparatus is essential. The use of craniofacial exposure and rigid fixation has dramatically improved the results of repair, and fractures of this area must be treated aggressively regardless of age. Exposure can be obtained through conveniently located lacerations (Fig. 47–18); in

practice, a coronal approach is often used because of coincidental cranial injuries (Fig. 47–19). Treatment consists of anatomic reduction of bone fragments and reestablishment of intercanthal distance. When the medial can-

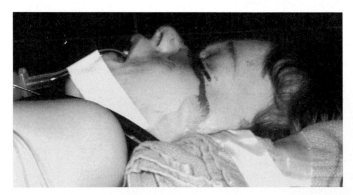

FIGURE 47–17. Loss of nasal projection due to nasoethmoid fracture.

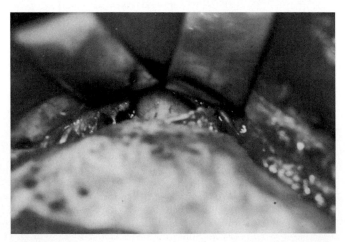

FIGURE 47–19. Exposure of the medial canthus and nasal root through the coronal approach.

thal tendon is attached to a large fragment, plates can be used to reconstitute the anatomic relationships. Greater degrees of comminution require transnasal wires.[7] Nasal projection must be reestablished by careful approximation of fractured segments of cantilevered bone grafts (Fig. 47–20).

Fractures of the Frontal Region

Fractures of the frontal region are most common in children younger than 6 years of age. The frontal sinus does not begin significant development until approximately 5 years of age; before this time, fractures tend to be greenstick and do not comminute. Without the sinus to absorb the impact, the fracture lines often extend to the vertex of the skull or across the orbital roof (Fig. 47–21). With displacement, a bicoronal approach with direct repair of the fracture and associated dural injuries is usually performed in conjunction with a neurosurgeon. Inferiorly displaced orbital roof fractures may result in an encephalocele if they are left untreated. An intracranial approach with primary bone grafting of the orbital roof is effective in preventing this complication.[27] Fractures involving the immature frontal sinus should be repaired with an effort toward reestablishing the nasofrontal ducts and maintaining sinus function. The results of frontal sinus obliteration in children are unknown.

Conclusion

The optimal management of facial fractures in children requires a mastery of the available technology and the insight to know when the technology should be applied. In addition to the considerations of aesthetics and function that guide treatment in adult reconstructive surgery, an understanding of facial growth and development is essential. Closed reduction should be used whenever possible. The results of rigid fixation should be critically assessed in light of the satisfactory results of conservative therapy that have prevailed until the recent past. When required, short segments of microplates generally provide

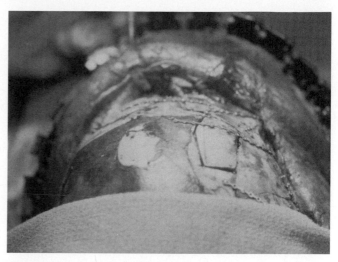

FIGURE 47–21. Extension of frontal fractures to the vertex of a skull repaired with microplates.

sufficient rigidity while minimizing potential growth disturbances.

SELECTED REFERENCES

Enlow DH. Facial Growth. Philadelphia, WB Saunders, 1990.
> *This text should be familiar to all physicians involved in the management of maxillofacial injuries in children; it provides an in-depth discussion of the mechanisms and characteristics of facial growth and development.*

Kaban L. Diagnosis and treatment of fractures of the facial bones in children: 1943–1993. J Oral Maxillofac Surg 51:722, 1993.
> *An interesting review of the evolution of the management of facial trauma in children in the past 60 years, with an up-to-date summary on the current modes of treatment.*

Moss ML, Salentijn L. The primary role of functional matrices in facial growth. Am J Orthod 55:567, 1969.
> *A knowledge of the influence of functional matrices helps in planning the overall approach to the management of facial fractures.*

Shumrick K, Kersten R, Kulwin D, et al. Extended access and internal approaches for the management of facial trauma. Arch Otolaryngol Head Neck Surg 118:1105, 1992.
> *This article provides the state-of-the-art approach to wide but aesthetically satisfactory exposure for repair of complex maxillofacial trauma.*

REFERENCES

1. Ahn DK, Sims CD, Randolph MA, et al. Craniofacial skeletal fixation using biodegradable plates and cyanoacrylate glue. Plast Reconstr Surg, 99:1508, 1997.
2. Bardach J, Kelly KM, Jakobsen JR. Simultaneous cleft lip and palate repair: an experimental study. Plast Reconstr Surg 82:31, 1988.
3. Bernstein L. Early submucous resection of nasal septal cartilage. Arch Otolaryngol 97:278, 1973.
4. Berryhill WE, Rimell FL, Ness J, et al. Fate of rigid fixation in pediatric craniofacial surgery. Otolaryngol Head Neck Surg 121:269, 1999.
5. Bonadio WA, Wagner V. Efficacy of TAC topical anesthetic for the repair of pediatric lacerations. Am J Dis Child 142:203, 1988.

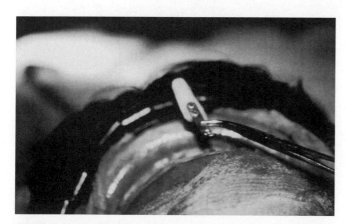

FIGURE 47–20. Placement of cantilevered bone graft through the coronal approach to restore nasal projection.

6. Chole R, Yee J. Antibiotic prophylaxis for facial fractures: a prospective randomized clinical trial. Arch Otolaryngol Head Neck Surg 113:1055, 1987.

7. Crocket DM, Funk GF. Management of complicated fractures involving the orbits and nasoethmoid complex in young children. Otolaryngol Clin North Am 24:119, 1991.

8. Daya MR, Burton BT, Sckleiss MR, et al. Recurrent seizures following mucosal application of TAC. Ann Emerg Med 17:147, 1988.

9. Demas PN, Braun TW. Pediatric facial injuries associated with all terrain vehicles. J Oral Maxillofac Surg 50:1280, 1993.

10. Demianczuk A, Verchere C, Phillips J. The effect of facial growth on pediatric mandibular fractures. J Craniofac Surg 10:323, 1999.

11. Dufresene CR, Manson PN. Pediatric facial trauma. In McCarthy JG, ed. Plastic Surgery. Philadelphia, WB Saunders, 1977, p 599.

12. Enlow DH. Facial Growth. Philadelphia, WB Saunders, 1990.

13. Eppley BL, Prevel CD, Sadove AM, Sarver D. Resorbable bone fixation; its potential role in cranio-maxillofacial trauma. J Craniomaxillofac Trauma 2:56, 1996.

14. Fearon JA, Munro IR, Bruce DA. Observations on the use of rigid fixation for craniofacial deformities in infants and young children. Plast Reconstr Surg 95:634, 1995.

15. Gant TD, Epstein LI. Low-velocity gunshot wounds to the maxillofacial complex. J Trauma 19:674, 1979.

16. Gussack G, Luteman A, Rodgers K, et al. Pediatric maxillofacial trauma: unique features in diagnosis and treatment. Laryngoscope 97:925, 1987.

17. Kaban L. Diagnosis and treatment of fractures of the facial bones in children: 1943–1993. J Oral Maxillofac Surg 51:722, 1993.

18. Kaban LB, Mulliken JB, Murray JE. Facial fractures in children: an analysis of 122 fractures in 109 patients. Plast Reconstr Surg 59:15, 1977.

19. Kellman R, Huckins S, King J, et al. Bioresorbable screws for facial bone reconstruction: a pilot study in rabbits. Laryngoscope 104:556, 1994.

20. Laurenzo JF, Canady JW, Zimmerman M, Smith RJ. Craniofacial growth in rabbits; effects of midfacial surgical trauma and rigid plate fixation. Arch Otolaryngol Head Neck Surg 121:56, 1995.

21. Lund K. Mandibular growth and remodeling processes after condylar fracture: a longitudinal roentgen cephalometric study. Acta Odontol Scand Suppl 32:3, 1974.

22. Maisel H. Postnatal growth and anatomy of the face. In Mathog RH (ed). Maxillofacial Trauma. Baltimore, Williams & Wilkins, 1984, pp 21–38.

23. Marschall M, Chidyllo S, Figueroa A, Cohen M. Long term effects of rigid fixation on the growing craniomaxillofacial skeleton. Craniofac Surg 2:63, 1991.

24. Martin WS, Gussac GS. Pediatric penetrating head and neck trauma. Laryngoscope 100:1288, 1990.

25. McCoy FJ, Chandler RA, Crow ML. Facial fractures in children. Plast Reconstr Surg 37:209, 1966.

26. McGraw B, Cole R. Pediatric maxillofacial trauma: age related variations in injury. Arch Otolaryngol Head Neck Surg 116:41, 1990.

27. Messinger A, Radkowski M, Greenwald M, Pensler J. Orbital roof fractures in the pediatric population. Plast Reconstr Surg 84:213, 1989.

28. Moore MH, David DJ, Cooter RD. Oblique facial fractures in children. J Craniofac Surg 1:4, 1990.

29. Moss ML, Salentijn L. The primary role of functional matrices in facial growth. Am J Orthod 55:567, 1969.

30. Oberg MS, Lindsey D. Do not put hydrogen peroxide or povidone iodine into wounds. Am J Dis Child 14:27, 1987.

31. Paskert JP, Manson PN. The bimanual examination for assessing instability in naso-ethmoidorbital injuries. Plast Reconstr Surg 83:165, 1989.

32. Persing JA, Babler NJ, Nagorsky MJ, et al. Skull expansion in experimental synostosis. Plast Reconstr Surg 78:594, 1986.

33. Polley JW, Figuero A, Hung KF, et al. Effect of rigid microfixation on the craniomaxillofacial skeleton. J Craniofac Surg 6:132, 1995.

34. Posnick J, Wells M, Pron G. Pediatric facial fractures: evolving patterns of treatment. J Oral Maxillofac Surg 51:836, 1993.

35. Rowe NL. Fractures of the jaws in children. J Oral Surg 27:497, 1969.

36. Shinya K, Tairo T, Sawada M, Isshiki N. Facial injuries from falling: age dependent characteristics. Ann Plast Surg 30:417, 1993.

37. Shumrick K, Kersten R, Kulwin D, et al. Extended access and internal approaches for the management of facial trauma. Arch Otolaryngol Head Neck Surg 118:1105, 1992.

38. Wong L, Richtsmeier J, Manson P. Craniofacial growth following rigid fixation: suture excision miniplating and microplating. J Craniofacial Surg 4:234, 1993.

39. Worthington P, Champy M. Monocortical miniplate osteosynthesis. Otolaryngol Clin North Am 20:607, 1987.

40. Yaremchuk M, Fiala T, Barker I, Ragland R. The effects of rigid fixation on craniofacial growth of rhesus monkeys. Plast Reconstr Surg 93:1, 1994.

41. Zide MF, Kent JN. Indications for open reduction of mandibular condyle fractures. J Oral Maxillofac Surg 41:89, 1983.

48

Tumors of the Nose, Paranasal Sinuses, and Nasopharynx

Anthony E. Magit, M.D.

Advances in imaging techniques and surgical instrumentation continue to change the treatment and diagnosis of tumors of the nose, paranasal sinuses, and nasopharynx. Current imaging modalities allow better definition of tumor extent and diagnosis of tumor type. Endoscopic procedures have become commonplace for the surgical management of lesions previously requiring open surgical approaches.

Molecular biology has expanded the understanding of the pathogenesis of various tumors, including the relationship of tumors to systemic disease. Genetic and hormonal influences on the presence and growth of tumors have been uncovered through clinical and basic science research.

Presenting Symptoms and Signs

Nasal obstruction, occasional epistaxis, and nasal discharge are the usual presenting symptoms of nasal tumors in children. An intranasal foreign body should be suspected in cases of unilateral nasal obstruction and foul discharge. The acute onset of bilateral nasal obstruction and rhinorrhea accompanied by systemic symptoms such as malaise, cough, and fever suggests an infectious process that is usually self-limited. Nasal obstruction and rhinorrhea associated with allergic symptoms may manifest exclusively in the fall or spring or be present throughout the year. Rhinonasal tumors should be considered in children with persistent nasal obstruction, nasal discharge, and epistaxis despite treatment for presumed infectious or allergic disease.

Clinical Signs

The presence of the tumor may be evident on external or endoscopic examination. Inspection of the child's face may reveal expansion of the nasal dorsum consistent with a congenital midline tumor. Widening of the intercanthal distance may be associated with ethmoid disease. Proptosis or strabismus is often associated with periorbital disease affecting the ethmoid, maxillary, or frontal sinus. Epiphora is caused by obstruction of the lacrimal duct in the lateral nasal wall. Other clinical signs of potentially serious rhinonasal disease include reduced visual acuity; hypoesthesia of the cheek; trismus; and swelling of the nose, cheek, or periorbita. Intranasal examination may reveal an obstructing mass. In young children, rhinoscopy with a flexible nasopharyngoscope can usually be performed in the office. In older children, the nasopharynx may be examined with a mirror placed transorally in the oropharynx. The nose and nasopharynx may be examined directly with a flexible nasopharyngoscope or rigid nasal endoscope. Oral cavity findings may include ulceration and distortion of the palate and gingival buccal sulcus or an oroantral fistula when a maxillary sinus tumor is present. Regional and distal lymph nodes, including those along the liver and spleen, should be examined, given that lymphoma is the most prevalent malignant tumor of the nose, nasopharynx, and paranasal sinuses in the pediatric age group.

Nasal Tumors

Benign Nasal Tumors

The majority of nasal tumors in children are benign, with congenital midline nasal masses being present in 1 in every 20,000 to 40,000 live births. Congenital midline masses, in order of decreasing frequency, are dermoids, hemangiomas, nasal gliomas, and encephaloceles. Dermoids, gliomas, and encephaloceles which are discussed in Chapter 42, Congenital Malformations of the Nose and the Paranasal Sinuses, by Hengerer and Wein. Nasal polyps and squamous papillomas are the most common acquired benign nasal masses. Malignant nasal tumors are rare in children.

Hemangiomas

Hemangiomas are the most common tumors of infancy, with the head and neck region most commonly involved. Ten to 12 percent of full-term white infants present with a hemangioma by 1 year of age. Hemangiomas can be classified according to the depth of tissue invasion or by histologic features. According to depth of invasion, superficial hemangiomas extend into the superficial dermis, with deep hemangiomas extending into the lower dermis or subcutaneous tissue. Histologically, hemangiomas are composed of thin-walled vessels lined by a single layer of epithelial cells, with intervascular spaces connected by little stroma. The two histologic classes are capillary and cavernous, with capillary lesions composed of many small vessels and cavernous hemangiomas consisting of cystic spaces. Both types of hemangiomas have consistent histologic features throughout the depth of invasion.

Intranasal hemangiomas present with unilateral nasal obstruction and epistaxis. Physical examination will often reveal a dull blue-red mass. Radiographically, the magnetic resonance imaging (MRI) signal for a hemangioma is a T_1-weighted intensity of intermediate value being isodense with normal nasal mucosa and an increased T_2-weighted image.[16] These MRI characteristics overlap with other nasal masses, including pyogenic granulomas and hemangiopericytomas. Septal hemangiomas usually manifest as a polypoid or sessile mass located on the anterior nasal septum. External nasal hemangiomas tend to be bulbous and adherent to underlying soft tissue (Fig. 48–1).

The natural history of hemangiomas consists of rapid growth in the first year of life with spontaneous resolution by 5 years of age. Close observation is the mainstay of therapy unless the lesion persists or complications develop. Special consideration may be given to early surgical treatment of hemangiomas involving the nose because of aplasia of nasal cartilages undergoing development.[41, 54] Hemangiomas involving the nasal tip tend to regress slowly, and the changes of the underlying fibrofatty tissue may remain after the hemangioma involutes. Complications of hemangiomas include Kasabach-Merritt syndrome (consumptive coagulopathy), visual axis obstruction, high-output heart failure, skin breakdown with scarring, and airway obstruction.

Treatment of hemangiomas involves medical or surgical therapy. Systemic or intralesional steroids are the mainstay of medical therapy. Superficial lesions have been successfully treated with neodymium:yttrium-aluminum-garnet (Nd:YAG) or tunable dye laser. Radiation therapy, cryotherapy, and injection of sclerosing agents have been used with some success in deep lesions. Surgical excision, sometimes combined with preoperative arterial embolization, is used for refractory lesions.

Nasal Polyps

Nasal polyps are semitransparent, wet-appearing herniations of respiratory mucosa often detected in the nasal cavity on physical examination. Polyps can be multiple, with origins in the maxillary, ethmoid, sphenoid, or frontal sinuses. Polypoid changes of the middle turbinate can be confused with a discrete polyp on rhinoscopy. Computerized axial tomography (CAT) scan is the preferred method of radiographic imaging for patients with known or suspected nasal and/or sinus polyps. Both axial and coronal views should be obtained, and intravenous contrast is not required for routine cases. CAT scan findings include bony trabecular deossification, widening of the infundibulum, and "truncation of the bony middle turbinate," noted as an absence of the bulbous aspect of the middle turbinate in patients without a history of middle turbinate resection.[36]

The etiology of nasal polyps is unclear, with histologic characteristics often including mucous glands and eosinophils. Patients requiring surgery for nasal polyps tend to have asthma or cystic fibrosis as coexisting conditions.[52] Heredity may play a factor in nasal polyps, with one study showing a statistically significant relationship between patients with nasal polyps and a family history of polyps compared with a control group matched for personal history of atopy and allergy skin tests.[26] Chromosome aberrations have been detected in some nasal polyps associated with histologic characteristics of frequent atypical stromal cells, with detection of vimentin and smooth muscle actin.[55]

Antrochoanal polyps represent one subset of polyps, usually originating in the maxillary sinus with extension through an expanded middle meatus into the nasal cavity, choana, and nasopharynx (Fig. 48–2). Antrochoanal polyps are the most common benign nasal and sinus tumor in children and account for approximately 4% to 6% of all polyps in the general population, with a higher prevalence in the pediatric population. These polyps are dumbbell shaped and occasionally contain pseudosarcomatous changes.[10] The CAT scan findings with antrochoanal polyps typically include a widened middle meatus with opacification of the obstructed sinus. Antrochoanal polyps

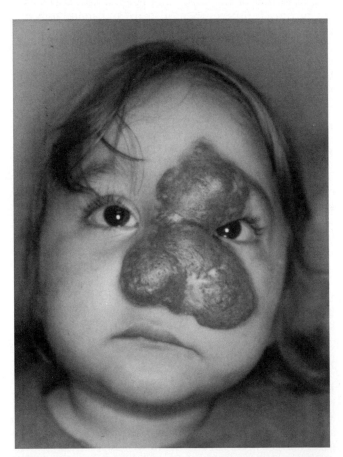

FIGURE 48–1. Large cavernous hemangioma of the midface. (Courtesy of Dr. Marek Dobke.)

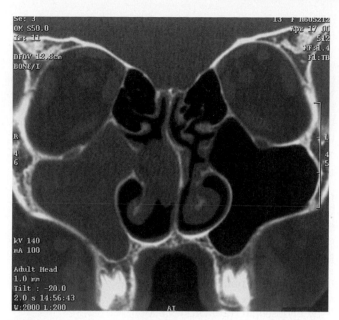

FIGURE 48–2. Antrochoanal polyp expanding the right middle meatus with extension into the nasal cavity.

can also originate from the sphenoid sinus, anterior or posterior ethmoid sinus, and middle turbinate. In cases where the choanal polyp has an origin other than the maxillary sinus, the diagnosis of inverted papilloma should be considered.

The appearance of nasal and sinus polyps in a child younger than 12 years of age should raise the possibility of cystic fibrosis (CF). A sweat chloride test is usually a sufficient test for cystic fibrosis, although genetic testing for cystic fibrosis in now available. Patients with CF requiring surgery for nasal polyposis appear to have different clinical and genotypic characteristics than those CF patients not requiring surgery. In a review of 20,198 patients in a CF database, patients requiring surgery for nasal polyps had different clinical characteristics than those not requiring surgery, including better pulmonary function tests, better nutritional status, and a higher rate of *Pseudomonas aeruginosa* infection.[34] Additionally, surgical patients had a higher prevalence of two genotypes, delta-F508/delta-F508 and delta-F508/G551D. Postoperative antibiotic irrigation in patients with CF has an important role in reducing the degree of polyp recurrence.

Endoscopic sinus surgery has become the standard surgical therapy for nasal and sinus polyps, with external procedures reserved for a small percentage of extensive or recurrent cases.[17] Antrochoanal polyps have an unacceptably high recurrence rate after surgery if the primary sinus disease is not adequately addressed and the polyp is not completely removed.[3, 37] Transcanine sinuscopy is an important adjunct to endoscopic sinus surgery and obviates the need for an open procedure in the majority of cases.

Nasal Papillomas

Papillomas of the nasal vestibule are common lesions seen in pediatric practice. Most vestibular papillomas

manifest as exophytic, 1- to 3-mm, cauliflower-like, pedunculated growths arising medially from the septum or laterally from the mucosa of the vestibule or nasal alae. Evidence of spread from the nose to the external auditory canal subsequent to concurrent nasal and ear surgery supports an infectious etiology. Human papillomavirus (HPV)-11 has been implicated as the infectious agent because HPV-11 DNA has been found to be associated with inverted papillomas.[61] Successful treatment consists of total surgical excision by use of a cold knife, carbon dioxide laser, electrocautery, or cryotherapy. Applications of podophyllin directly to the papilloma have been successful; however, podophyllin has been reported to be toxic.[4, 8, 14] The contact-tip Nd:YAG laser is effective in eradicating papillomas with less power and plume formation than in the noncontact mode.[58]

Frequent follow-up is mandatory for vestibular papillomas because of their tendency to recur. Other types of nasal papillomas include fungiform and cylindric cell papillomas. Fungiform papillomas are confined to the nasal septum and are exophytic, with a wide base. Surgical excision is the treatment or choice. Cylindric cell papillomas arise from the lateral wall of the nasal vestibule and appear as irregular, red, papillary growths. Surgical excision is also the treatment of choice. Their proclivity for recurrence is similar to that of inverted papillomas, and close follow-up is necessary.

Inverted papillomas are the most difficult type of nasal papilloma to cure. Intranasal inverted papillomas typically manifest as unilateral, red, polypoid masses attached to the lateral nasal wall, the middle turbinate, or, less commonly, the septum and nasal vestibule. Histologically, inverted papillomas are podophytic growths of multilayered squamous epithelia involving stroma of the surrounding tissue. The basement membrane is intact, and histologic evidence of malignant change is absent. Seemingly adequate surgical procedures have resulted in recurrence rates of 25% to 75%.[50, 62] Associated squamous cell carcinoma arising in the same area of the papilloma is present in 10% to 15% of inverted papillomas with less than 2% of papillomas showing malignant transformation. Malignant disease usually appears in adults.

Inverted papillomas can be imaged with computed tomographic (CT) scans and MRI. CT scans provide excellent bone detail and are beneficial in assessing invasion into the maxillary or ethmoid sinuses. Inverted papillomas have more T_2-weighted MRI signal intensity than malignant tumors in the nasal cavity.

Surgical therapy for inverted papillomas requires adequate surgical exposure because of the clinical aggressiveness of these tumors. The lateral rhinotomy approach with medial maxillectomy has been the standard of care for tumor exposure and examination of the maxillary sinus for assessing local extension (Fig. 48–3). With the increasing experience with functional endoscopic sinus surgery, endoscopic intranasal surgery has been associated with acceptable recurrence rates when the extent of disease can be adequately visualized.[59] The tumor is completely debulked endoscopically, and the underlying bone is burred with a diamond drill to eliminate deep-reaching infiltration. Patients require close postsurgical follow-up for recurrent or persistent disease.

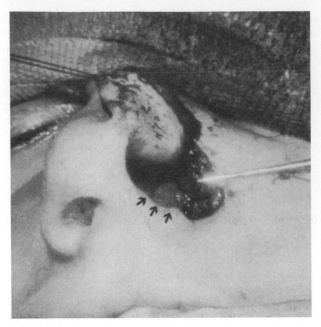

FIGURE 48–3. Lateral rhinotomy approach for resection of inverted papilloma.

Pyogenic Granulomas and Rhinoliths

Pyogenic granulomas are friable, red, soft, sessile, broad-based vascular lesions usually seen on the anterior septum.[48] They can be described as granulation tissue similar to that found in any healing wound, but more exuberant and confined to a localized area. Most occur in the oral cavity; less than 10% occur in the nose. On histologic examination, they are composed of fibroblasts and capillaries. They often arise from insignificant trauma or are associated with retained foreign bodies. Curettage of the lesion, removal of the underlying foreign body, or elimination of stimuli irritating the nasal mucosa usually leads to resolution of the lesion.

Rhinoliths are calcareous encrustations that develop as a result of a neglected or undiagnosed intranasal foreign body.[44] They may invade into the maxillary sinus or perforate the palate. Successful treatment consists of removal of the rhinolith and curettage of the surrounding granulation tissue.

Nasolacrimal Mucoceles

Congenital nasolacrimal mucoceles can result in nasal obstruction requiring surgical intervention.[29] On physical examination, mucoceles appear as cystic lesions attached to the lateral nasal wall. Characteristic CT findings include a medial canthal cystic mass, a dilated ipsilateral nasolacrimal duct, and an intranasal cystic mass.[42] In a series of 21 children with congenital dacryocystocele and intranasal extension, 14 had respiratory distress and were successfully managed with endoscopic marsupialization with resolution of obstruction.[30] Other treatment modalities include nasolacrimal duct probing, probing with silicone tube placement, and probing combined with intranasal marsupialization.

Congenital dacryocystoceles may manifest initially without an intranasal component. In a report of 22 patients with 30 dacryocystoceles, a concurrent intranasal mucocele was found in 23 (77%) of dacryocystoceles with respiratory distress arising in 5 (71%) of 7 patients with bilateral intranasal mucoceles and in 2 (22%) of 9 patients with unilateral mucoceles.[40]

Concha Bullosa

Concha bullosa refers to a pneumatized middle turbinate. On physical examination, an enlarged or obstructing middle turbinate can be mistaken for an intranasal polyp, especially when the overlying mucosa has a polypoid appearance.[66] A concha bullosa can be misdiagnosed as an intranasal mass. The diagnosis of a concha bullosa can only be made radiographically, usually with a CT scan (Fig. 48–4). Treatment of a symptomatic concha bullosa is by endoscopic turbinate reduction.

Other Tumors

Various other benign nasal tumors have been reported, including pleomorphic adenoma of the inferior turbinate, congenital monomorphic adenoma of the nasal septum, lipoma, benign fibrous histiocytoma, and benign osteoblastoma of the nasal bones.[1, 47, 56]

Hemangiopericytomas are tumors of mesenchymal origin that can manifest as congenital or acquired nasal or paranasal sinus lesions. A case has been presented of a congenital hemangiopericytoma with extension to the skull base being resected on the day of birth using an Nd:YAG-KTP laser with no evidence of disease at nine-month follow-up.[25]

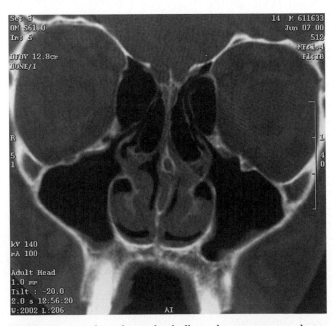

FIGURE 48–4. Bilateral concha bullosa shown on coronal view of nose and paranasal sinuses.

Chondroid hamartoma has been reported as a rare cause of nasal obstruction in a newborn.[33] This lesion can extend beyond the nasal cavity, and preoperative evaluation includes appropriate radiographic imaging to assess local invasion into bone and vessels. Rhinosporidiosis associated with nasal polyps can be diagnosed preoperatively with scrape cytology for *Rhinosporidium seeberi* as the mature spores rupture on or within the mucosa of polyps.[31]

Childhood Malignant Tumors

Malignant tumors of the head and neck are rare in children. Fewer than 2% of 2835 head and neck lesions either excised or examined by biopsy at Buffalo Children's Hospital were malignant neoplasms.[49] Almost half (43%) of the patients had Hodgkin disease. The remaining 57% of lesions were distributed throughout the head and neck.

Malignant Nasal Tumors

Malignant tumors of the nose are rare in the pediatric patient. In most series, the most common malignant nasal tumor in children is rhabdomyosarcoma of the embryonal and aveolar cell types. These lesions can be congenital and grow rapidly during the first year of life. A friable, ulcerating mass is usually present. Facial swelling and cranial nerve palsies are unfavorable signs indicating regional spread with destruction of contiguous structures. Therapy consists of wide local excision if possible and multiple-drug chemotherapy. Radiotherapy may be beneficial, although later deformities and asymmetric facial growth can develop.

The diagnosis of a nasal malignancy requires an open biopsy. Tumor extent is determined with CT scans and MRI. MRI is a superior imaging technique because it provides high contrast resolution of soft tissue tumors and multiplanar imaging. CT is useful to evaluate bone invasion.

Intranasal Carcinomas

Carcinomas of the nose may be mistaken for nasal polyps, septal abscesses, or septal hematomas. Diagnostic principles are similar to those for rhabdomyosarcoma, with undifferentiated carcinoma having a poorer prognosis. Worse outcomes are associated with cranial nerve, orbit, and intracranial involvement.

Lymphomas and Leukemia

Sinonasal lymphomas are relatively rare in Western countries, with a larger prevalence in Asian populations. In Asian populations, sinonasal lymphomas are second only to gastrointestinal lymphomas as the most common type of extranodal lymphomas. Sinonasal lymphomas are separated into B-cell, T-cell and natural killer (NK) cell phenotypes. NK/T lymphomas have the worst prognosis.[11]

Several cases of children with nasopharyngeal and intranasal non-Hodgkin lymphoma of the large cell types and the lymphoblastic types have been reported.[65] In contrast, a series of 208 children with non-Hodgkin lymphoma contained 20 (9.6%) with primary nasal-paranasal oropharyngeal lymphoma, with the majority of tumors being B-cell lymphomas of the diffuse undifferentiated type or small-cell noncleaved types.[64] Nine of these patients (45%) had neck swelling as an initial symptom. Extranodal non-Hodgkin lymphoma arising from the nasal cavity has a poor prognosis, in contrast to Hodgkin lymphoma arising from the Waldeyer ring. In obtaining tumor for biopsy, the specimen should be sent to the laboratory wrapped in a wet saline gauze to allow immunohistochemical studies, B-cell and T-cell studies, cell cultures, and light and electron microscopy to completely characterize the tumor. Staging procedures consist of CT of the head, chest, and abdomen; technetium Tc 99m and gallium Ga 67m scintiscans; bone marrow aspirates and biopsy specimens; and a lumbar puncture. Therapy usually consists of intensive chemotherapy in addition to local or extended-field radiation of bulky disease. Radiation is usually kept below 20 cGy to lessen local morbidity. Survival is good if bone marrow is not involved. Aggressive treatment can result in cure rates of 75%.

One study of 58 patients, including children, compared the characteristics of lymphomas involving the nose and paranasal sinuses.[12] This study demonstrated that lymphomas involving the sinuses without nasal involvement were predominantly diffuse large cell lymphoma as compared to nasal lesions without sinus involvement being predominantly of the natural killer cell type. Studies of Asian and South American populations report that the predominant type of tumor in this population is the natural killer type, with a high proportion of patients testing positive for Epstein-Barr virus (EBV).[51, 57] In comparison, patients with nasal B-cell lymphomas rarely have evidence of EBV infection. B-cell lymphomas represent a greater proportion of lymphomas in the Western population.

Natural killer cell type lymphomas located in the nasal cavity have an aggressive, angioinvasive growth pattern often leading to bony erosion and necrosis. These lesions have previously been included in the less specific category of lethal midline granuloma.

Leukemic lesions are extremely rare as nasal masses. One report described a pediatric patient with acute myeloid leukemia whose presenting sign was a solitary leukemic nodule on the tip of the nose.[6]

Surgical Approaches to Nasal Tumors

The mainstay of intranasal exposure is the lateral rhinotomy incision. The incision begins inferiorly at the base of the ala nasi and can be extended superiorly in the nasoalar groove to explore the ethmoid and cribriform areas. By including the nasal bones in the skin flap and by retracting the orbital contents laterally, complete exposure of the roof of the nasal vault, the ethmoid sinuses, and the sphenoid is possible. In addition, disease in the roof of the nose can be dealt with under direct visualization. Full-thickness en bloc resections of the cribriform plate, ethmoid sinus, and sphenoid can be accomplished in conjunction with a frontal craniotomy, with the osteotomies being made from above as the tumor margins are visualized simultaneously from below. Posterior septal and nasopharyngeal lesions can be approached by a palate-splitting incision.

Complications of lateral rhinotomy include transient blepharitis, lid edema, and transient diplopia. Epiphora and transient dacryocystitis are relatively common. Cosmetic deformities consisting of nasal collapse saddle deformity, columellar collapse, alar retraction, and unacceptable scars developed in 15 (10%) of 148 patients in one series.[5] Postoperative nasal crusting is inevitable and usually resolves within 6 months as re-epithelization of denuded areas occurs.

Sinus Tumors

Benign Sinus Tumors

Antrochoanal Polyps

Antrochoanal polyps are the most common benign sinus tumor in children and have been previously discussed in this chapter.

Mucoceles

Mucous retention cysts arise from inflammation or hyperplasia of sinus mucosa in conjunction with blockage of microscopic secretory ducts. The term *mucocele* generally refers to a greatly enlarged retention cyst within a paranasal sinus. The cyst may cause bone erosion or expansion (Fig. 48–5). Maxillary sinus mucous retention cysts have no relationship to the age of the patient, with prevalence in the general population estimated between 2.7% and 9.6%.[43] Many cysts resolve spontaneously. Most mucous retention cysts are not symptomatic until they become large enough to obstruct the sinus ostia.

Mucous retention cysts and mucoceles may manifest with purulent nasal discharge, facial pain, and dental anomalies (e.g., nonvital posterior maxillary teeth, periodontal abscesses, or postextraction sinus fistulae). Plain sinus radiographs reveal a dome-shaped or egg-shaped, variably sized mass with well-defined margins that are usually more radiopaque than the margin of the normal sinus cavities. The decision to intervene surgically may be difficult because symptoms may be due to other causes (e.g., migraine variants, facial vascular pain, and dental disease), and the sinus retention cyst or mucocele may be an unrelated radiographic finding. If the retention cyst or mucocele is obstructing the sinus ostia, surgical removal is justified. Removal of a maxillary sinus cyst through an intranasal endoscopic approach may be used in older children; otherwise, a keyhole sublabial antrostomy, with care taken to avoid the tooth buds, is commonly used. The cyst should be uncapped, if not totally removed, and a nasoantral window created for continued drainage. Mucoceles of the ethmoid and sphenoid sinuses are rare and have been drained by an external approach in conjunction with an operating microscope. Endoscopic treatment of frontal, ethmoid, and sphenoid mucoceles has been reported.[32] The mucocele is marsupialized, and the functional operative approach preserves the ability to visualize the surgical area with a CT scan.

Odontogenic Tumors and Dentigerous Cysts

These tumors were common in some reviews of maxillary tumors.[46] This frequency probably reflects the contributions of oral surgeons. The adenomatoid odontogenic tumor (adenoameloblastoma) is probably a hamartoma or overgrowth of odontogenic tissue. It is common in girls aged 10 to 20 years and is usually found in the maxillary

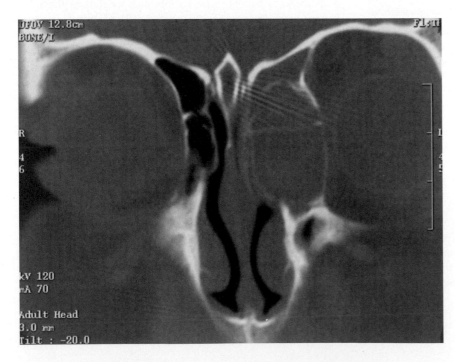

FIGURE 48–5. Mucocele of the left ethmoid sinus in patient with allergic fungal sinusitis.

incisor-cuspid area in association with an impacted tooth. Simple enucleation of the tumor with free margins is usually sufficient treatment.

The dentigerous cyst derives from a developing enamel organ and surrounds the crown of an unerupted tooth. Marsupialization or careful enucleation with the tooth of origin is the treatment of choice.[38]

Fibro-osseous Lesions

Fibro-osseous lesions of the maxilla and midface constitute a group of histologically benign but clinically aggressive lesions that often require surgical treatment. In a classic description of benign tumors of the mandible and maxilla, Dehner reported 15 cases of fibro-osseous lesions.[15] They were divided into three categories: fibrous dysplasia, ossifying fibroma, and cementifying fibroma. *Cementifying* denotes a lesion of the mandible or maxilla containing cementum outside the periodontal membrane with fibro-osseous lesions of the paranasal sinus regions usually lacking cementum. A classification scheme for fibro-osseous lesions of the nose and paranasal sinuses consists of three designations: fibrous dysplasia, ossifying fibroma (sometimes referred to as cementifying fibroma), and psammomatous active ossifying fibroma. An accurate diagnosis of a fibro-osseous lesion is made from a combination of clinical findings, radiographic characteristics, and histologic features.

Fibrous dysplasia describes an idiopathic bone disease in which weak fibrous and osseous tissue replaces medullary bone. Histologically, the fibrous and osseous components can be nondescript, with irregularly shaped trabeculae of bone arising from fibrous stroma to form odd geometric "C" and "S" shapes, referred to as "Chinese characters." Under polarized light the bone appears woven rather the lamellar. This disease can be monostotic, involving a single site, or polyostotic, involving multiple sites. Polyostotic disease carries a poorer prognosis and may be part of the Albright-McCune-Sternberg syndrome, with multiple café au lait spots on the back, precocious puberty, and multiple radiolucent defects in the bones of the lower extremities. Craniofacial and jaw involvement is present in approximately 50% of patients with polyostotic disease and up to 25% of patients with monostotic disease. Clinical presentations include bony deformity, functional impairment, pain, and pathologic fractures with the most common presenting symptoms of craniofacial fibrous dysplasia being painless swelling and facial deformity. The majority of patients diagnosed with fibrous dysplasia are under 30 years of age.

The stage of disease and the amount of bony matter within the lesion influence radiographic characteristics of fibrous dysplasia. Plain radiographs have a "ground glass" appearance. Computerized tomography (CT scan) demonstrates expansion of bone with a heterogeneous pattern of CT densities with a thin, intact cortex. Significant periosteal reaction is not seen in these benign lesions. Magnetic resonance imaging (MRI) has an intermediate T_1-weighted signal and a heterogeneous, hypointense signal on T_2-weighted images.

The clinical course of fibrous dysplasia includes stabilization of disease at puberty. Therapy should be delayed until after puberty if possible. Treatment of fibrous dysplasia consists of conservative surgical excision in cases with functional impairment, progression of deformity, pain, associated fractures, or concerns about a concurrent malignancy. Recurrence rates are low, and death secondary to extension into vital structures is rare.

Ossifying fibromas of the midface are generally asymptomatic, unassociated with pain or swelling, and often diagnosed incidentally by radiographic imaging. The histologic appearance is that of randomly distributed lamellar (mature) bone with spicules rimmed by osteoblasts with fibrous stroma. Radiographic characteristics are related to the stage of disease and the relative percentage of mineralized material. The lesions are well circumscribed and expansile, with smooth contours and a thick rim of bone. In the early stages of development, the fibroma may be a solitary cystic or solid soft tissue mass with minimal calcification. As the lesion matures, it becomes radiopaque. On MRI, ossifying fibromas have a heterogeneous, intermediate signal on T_1-weighted images with a hypointense signal on T_2-weighted images. Although fibrous dysplasia and ossifying fibromas may have similar histologic appearances, ossifying fibromas tend to be better defined radiologically and well circumscribed histologically from normal bone.[19]

The treatment of choice for an ossifying fibroma is surgical excision. Total removal is relatively easy for well-circumscribed lesions. Following complete removal, the prognosis is excellent, and recurrence rates are low.

A third fibro-osseous lesion with an overall younger age distribution than fibrous dysplasia or ossifying fibroma is the psammomatous active ossifying fibroma or aggressive psammomatous ossifying fibroma. The majority of patients affected by this disease are in the first or second decade of life. Clinical manifestations when located in the ethmoid or frontal sinus regions include facial swelling, nasal obstruction, pain, sinusitis, headache, and proptosis. Histologically, these lesions are distinguished from ossifying fibromas by the presence of round to oval calcified concretions with concentric laminations termed psammomatous concretions. The psammomatous fibroma can be locally aggressive, with extension into vital structures. Radiographically, CT scans will demonstrate a lytic or mixed lytic osseous or soft tissue mass. The mass may vary from being well demarcated to being invasive with bone erosion. MRI characteristics include areas of hyperintensity simulating cysts or soft tissue with fluid levels on T_2-weighted images.

Management of a psammomatous active ossifying fibroma can be difficult because of its aggressive nature and potential for involvement of vital structures. Although not always possible, the treatment of choice is complete surgical removal. Following complete surgical excision, the prognosis is good; however, the tumor may recur.

Desmoid Fibromatosis

Desmoid fibromatosis characterizes a group of lesions that histologically lie between benign fibrous lesions and fibrosarcoma.[24] These lesions are nonmetastasizing, well differentiated, and unencapsulated, with a tendency for local invasion and recurrence with the potential for being life-threatening because of local invasion into vital structures. The maxillary sinuses are the most commonly involved of the paranasal sinuses. The most common manifestations include swelling or a mass with pain or tenderness. Desmoid fibromatoses involving the head and neck tend to be more aggressive than extra-abdominal desmoid fibromatoses. In children, more than one third of tumors involve the head and neck. Histologically, the lesions tend to have infiltrative growth into adjacent soft tissue. The tumors usually consist of interlacing fascicles of relatively uniform spindle-shaped fibroblasts. Radiographically, there can be erosion of adjacent bone.

The preferred treatment for desmoid fibromatosis is complete surgical removal. When amenable to complete surgical removal, tumors involving the sinonasal tract have low recurrence rates. Recurrences are best managed surgically if technically possible without risking injury to vital structures. Radiation therapy or chemotherapy is reserved for primary or recurrent tumors that are not candidates for complete surgical removal.

Giant Cell Granuloma and Giant Cell Tumor (Osteoclastoma)

Dehner reported 15 giant cell granulomas in a 1973 review of benign tumors of the mandible and maxilla in children.[15] This number represented approximately one third (15 of 46) of all the benign tumors in this series. In 1979, Schramm reported a lesser incidence (11%) among tumors of the mandible and maxilla.[46] Dehner originally described painless swelling in the upper or lower jaws as the most frequent initial sign. Facial asymmetry and palpable maxillary and palatal masses were described as well as the typical "cherubic facies" in one child. Large, well-circumscribed osteolytic lesions are seen radiographically, with a fine rim of calcification at the margin of the tumors. On histologic examination, these lesions are characterized by multinucleated giant cells, stroma formed from elongated spindle-shaped cells, and erythrocytes located prominently in the stroma.

Handler and colleagues, in a case report of a giant cell tumor of the ethmoid sinuses, make a fine distinction between a giant cell tumor (osteoclastoma) and the previously reported reparative giant cell granuloma, although clinically these lesions act the same.[27] They grow slowly and destroy bone locally. They have a tendency to recur after simple curettage or incomplete excision. Effective treatment involves complete surgical removal, along with a margin of normal tissue. The differential diagnosis includes fibro-osseous lesions, such as fibrous dysplasia and ossifying fibroma. In addition, the "brown tumor" of hyperparathyroidism is similar radiographically and may be clinically differentiated by elevated serum calcium levels.

Myxofibromas, Vascular Malformations, and Hemangiomas of the Sinuses

Myxofibromas and hemangiomas can occur in the paranasal sinuses. Hemangiomas are especially troublesome be-cause they intermittently hemorrhage and destroy bone by local invasion. Depending on the size of a vascular malformation, a significant percentage of the cardiac output may be shunted through these lesions if there are numerous arteriovenous fistulae in this tumor or if the internal carotid system is feeding the tumor. Vascular involvement can be assessed with magnetic resonance angiography or standard arteriography. Multiple surgical excisions as well as partial maxillectomy coupled with vascular embolization may be required for ablation of this tumor.

Malignant Sinus Tumors

The most frequent primary malignant neoplasms of the paranasal sinuses are undifferentiated carcinoma and rhabdomyosarcoma. Other reports of tumors include adenocarcinomas, fibrosarcomas, and lymphomas. In addition, in children, secondary malignant neoplasms may develop in irradiated fields, as demonstrated in one child in whom an osteogenic sarcoma of the maxilla developed in a field postoperatively irradiated for a retinoblastoma that required enucleation.[51]

Tumors of the sinuses usually manifest as facial swellings that are erythematous, tender, and infected. These lesions can be confused clinically with acute sinusitis, although the bone destruction is immediately evident on radiographic studies. CT scans and MRI are necessary to determine the extent of the tumor. Limitations of CT imaging include the inability to always determine whether tumor has invaded or just approached the periorbita. There may also be difficulty in differentiating tumor from soft tissue edema and assessing the extent of tumor infiltration into obstructed sinuses because of similar characteristics of soft tissue attenuation and retained secretions. MRI more accurately delineates tumor from surrounding soft tissue, inflammatory tissue, and retained secretions. Carcinomas are highly cellular, with little free water, and have a homogeneous MRI appearance with low to intermediate signal intensity on T_1- and T_2-weighted images. The enhancement of tumor with gadolinium diethylenetriaminepentaacetic acid (Gd-DTPA) is less than the enhancement of mucosa in most cases.

For maxillary sinus disease, a radical maxillectomy may yield deep margins that are free of tumor. A transfrontal ethmoidectomy and craniofacial resection can be employed for malignant ethmoid sinus disease if the tumor involved is primarily anterior. Resection of posterior ethmoid and sphenoid sinus neoplasms is complicated by the proximity of the optic chiasm and the cavernous sinus. Patients with paranasal sinus malignancies currently do best with combined tumor excision for intended cure when surgically possible. When the tumor is considered unresectable, surgical drainage of the affected sinuses and debulking of the tumor by curettage may be benefical for pain relief and control of infection.

Nasopharyngeal Tumors

Juvenile Nasopharyngeal Angiofibromas

Nasopharyngeal angiofibromas are the most common type of benign nasopharyngeal tumor, accounting for 0.5% of all head and neck tumors.[18] They have a frequency of 1 in 5000 to 1 in 60,000 otolaryngology patients, with the highest reported occurrences in India and Egypt. Nasopharyngeal angiofibromas occur mostly in prepubescent boys. Affected patients present with nasal obstruction and recurrent epistaxis. As the symptoms progress, rhinolalia, deformity of the soft and hard palate, and swelling of the cheek may become evident. The tumor appears as a red, smooth, mucosa-covered compressible mass (Fig. 48–6). Depending on the superior extension of the tumor, orbital proptosis may be present. Cheek or zygomatic swelling is indicative of tumor spread in the infratemporal fossa. CT scanning is excellent for bone detail. In comparison with CT scanning, MRI provides multiplanar imaging, improved definition at the cribriform plate and cavernous sinus, superior differentiation of tumor from inflamed mucosa and fluid in the sinuses, and avoidance of diagnostic radiation in patients who require serial follow-up. Several staging systems have emerged to characterize this tumor; one has combined clinical and radiographic findings. Biopsy is rarely necessary to establish the diagnosis and should be avoided because of the risk of hemorrhage.

Hormonal regulation of nasopharyngeal angiofibromas was suggested by Schiff with the report of two cases treated with androgens and two with estrogens that responded with marked reduction in size.[45] Estrogen, progesterone, and androgen receptors have been identified with varying frequencies in juvenile angiofibromas.[7, 35] The testosterone receptor blocker flutamide reduced stage I and II tumors by an average of 44%.[23] The promise of hormonal therapy is tempered by subsequent reports of the absence of expression of androgen and estrogen receptors in six primary and two recurrent angiofibromas.[22] In these same specimens, nuclear androgen receptor immunoreactivity was weak in a minority of endothelial and stromal cells. Because of the variable evidence of hormonal regulation of juvenile angiofibromas, hormonal therapy is not routinely used. In addition to the variable response to hormonal therapy, its limitations include delay in carrying out definitive removal, undesirable feminizing side effects, and risk of cardiovascular complications.

The preferred method of treatment is complete surgical removal of the tumor. Preoperative embolization with Gelfoam or polyvinyl alcohol foam has reduced intraoperative blood loss. Gelfoam is resorbed in approximately 2 weeks; the alcohol foam is more permanent. Complications of embolization include accidental embolization of the brain and ophthalmic artery, facial nerve palsy, and necrosis of skin and soft tissue. These complications of preoperative embolization should be considered when removal of a small, pedunculated angiofibroma is planned.

The tumor location and effectiveness of embolization should guide the surgical approach to resection of the tumor. Reports of various surgical approaches include endoscopic transnasal, transpalatal, medial maxillectomy, facial translocation, and infratemporal fossa approaches, with and without craniotomy.[20] Endoscopic removal may be appropriate for tumors confined to the nasopharynx, nasal cavity, and paranasal sinuses. Extension into the medial infratemporal fossa or medial cavernous sinus requires a medial maxillectomy. Infratemporal or transfacial approaches are indicated with cavernous sinus or middle cranial fossa involvement, or with extensive involvement of the infratemporal fossa. Tumors extending intracranially should be managed in conjunction with a neurosurgical team. Complete excision of the tumor involving the cavernous sinus may not be possible or prudent despite advances in craniofacial surgery.

A study of sympathetic innervation of tissue from the angiofibromatous tumor parenchyma and tumor border demonstrated no sympathetic innervation in parenchyma and scant noradrenergic fibers in tumor border. Uninvolved nasal mucosa from these patients were filled with noradrenergic innervation. The findings of this study support the importance of maintaining a surgical plane outside of the tumor to reduce surgical blood loss.[60]

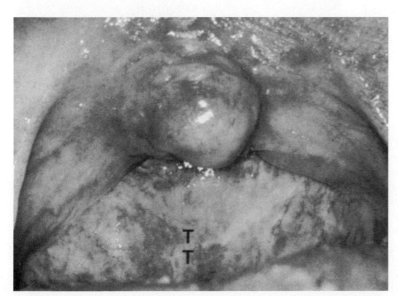

FIGURE 48–6. Large nasopharyngeal angiofibroma hanging down below the soft palate. ("T" indicates the tumor.)

When an external surgical approach is required, the surgical approach should be through an extended lateral rhinotomy, with extension intraorally, over the gingivobuccal sulcus, and behind the maxillary tuberosity. The palate has to be split to give access to the vault of the nasopharynx. An approach to the infratemporal fossa includes the aforementioned incisions, with the addition of a total parotidectomy and retraction of the facial nerve superiorly. At this point, the holes of a minicompression plate may be drilled on the ascending ramus of the mandible, 2 cm inferior to the condylar head. The mandibulotomy is then performed. This approach gives wide exposure to tumors filling the infratemporal fossa. The tumor may then be mobilized from both its lateral and medial aspects. Since the holes for the mandibular plate had been drilled before the mandibulotomy, installation of the plate is easier, and the difficulties of trying to drill an unstable condylar segment are eliminated. In addition, the need for postoperative intermaxillary fixation is obviated.

Recurrence of tumor is probably due to the multilobular nature of the tumor and its ability to invade adjacent sinuses and suture lines. One major risk factor for recurrence is involvement of the cranial base. Recurrent tumors may not be amenable to surgical resection, and angiofibromas with known tumor left at the time of primary resection respond variably to radiation therapy with a range of 3500 to 5200 cGy. Large tumors, residual disease, and intracranial disease require close follow-up. One strategy for follow-up consists of serial MRI scans starting 2 months after resection and twice yearly through adolescence. Cummings and associates reported a series of 55 patients treated with radiation therapy in which 42 had primary radiation therapy.[13] Tumor control was achieved in 44 (80%) of patients. It may take up to 1 year for the effects of radiation therapy to become evident.

Control rates approach 100% for lesions without intracranial extension. Radiation for patients with early lesions is a viable option when operative morbidity might be higher on the basis of medical or religious grounds.

Spontaneous regression of an untreated angiofibroma for a period of 12 years has been reported.[63] Malignant transformation has been documented in six cases of nasal angiofibroma, five having been treated with radiation therapy.[39]

Thornwaldt Cyst

The majority of Thornwaldt cysts manifest in the second or third decade as midline nasopharyngeal masses. Thornwaldt cysts are the result of the primitive notochord remaining connected to the nasopharynx with the development of a bursa or pouch. A cyst can develop from this pouch secondary to occlusion of the bursa from inflammation. On endoscopic examination, these cysts appear as smooth, submucosal masses usually 1 to 2 cm in diameter and located superior to the adenoid pad. One series reported that Thornwaldt cysts were found in 1.9% of routine MRI studies of the brain. These lesions had a high signal intensity on T_1- and T_2-weighted images.[30] Treat-

ment of symptomatic Thornwaldt cysts consists of either resection to periosteum or wide marsupialization.

Other Benign Nasopharyngeal Tumors

Benign nasopharyngeal tumors also include teratomas, nasopharyngeal dermoid tumors ("hairy polyps"), base of skull encephaloceles, fibrous dysplasia, hemangiomas, gliomas, chondromas, ectopic brain tissue, and hamartomas. These tumors are usually covered with mucosa and have a broad, sessile base.[9] Dermoid tumors are the most primitive form of teratoma, being derived only from ectoderm and mesoderm. These lesions usually manifest near the time of birth and often with significant airway obstruction (Fig. 48–7). Heterotopic brain tissue has been found in the nasopharynx. Of 17 reported cases of heterotopic brain tissue in the nasopharynx, 6 had brain tissue located in a cleft palate.[53]

Patients with human immunodeficiency virus (HIV) disease may present with a nasopharyngeal mass due to nasopharyngeal lymphatic tissue hypertrophy.[2] Once the diagnosis of lymphatic tissue hypertrophy is established, curettage of the tissue may be indicated for relief of intractable nasal obstruction.

Malignant Nasopharyngeal Tumors

Malignant neoplasms in the nasopharynx account for only 1% of all malignant tumors in childhood. In Stanievich and coworkers'[49] series of nasopharyngeal tumors, rhabdomyosarcoma and carcinoma occurred with equal frequency in this area. Fewer than 20% of affected children survive 5 years; most die of distant metastases and sepsis. Patients with lymphoma fared better with 50% survival. Fearson and associates reported a series of 25 children

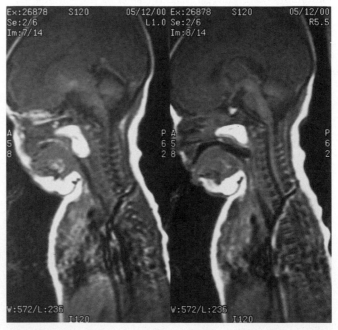

FIGURE 48–7. MRI of a newborn with a nasopharyngeal dermoid ("hairy polyp"). Child presented at delivery with airway distress secondary to nasal obstruction.

with malignant nasopharyngeal tumors (eight rhabdomyosarcomas, eight lymphoepitheliomas, three lymphomas, two lymphosarcomas, and four less common tumor types).[21]

Nasopharyngeal malignant neoplasms often manifest with a firm posterior triangle node, unilateral eustachian tube dysfunction, and nasal obstruction. Horner syndrome, torticollis, and cranial nerve palsy are late signs indicative of regional invasion. An infectious etiology for nasopharyngeal carcinoma is suggested by the finding of Epstein-Barr virus DNA in the cytoplasm of the neoplastic epithelial cells in 9 of 11 tumors examined.[28] There is an increased risk of malignant transformation associated with immunodeficiency states such as common variable hypogammaglobulinemia, ataxia-telangiectasia, Wiskott-Aldrich syndrome, combined immunodeficiency, HIV infection, and bone marrow transplantation. Radiation therapy and chemotherapy are instituted once immunologic and microscopic examinations of the tumor are completed and the disease has been staged. Surgery plays little role in the treatment of rapidly growing, aggressive, undifferentiated tumor. A transcranial approach may be successful for tumors involving multiple sinuses with erosion through the floor of the anterior cranial fossa when transfascial approaches do not provide adequate surgical exposure.

General Principles

The pediatric patient with a tumor of the nose, paranasal sinuses, or nasopharynx poses a significant challenge for the physician and the entire health care team. A high index of suspicion is needed if the patient is to benefit from a timely and appropriate diagnosis. Thorough familiarity with the anatomy, embryology, and clinical presentation of tumors in this region is mandatory for physicians entrusted with the care of children. Appropriate imaging services are mandatory for an accurate assessment of tumor characteristics and resectability. Management of malignant tumors requires the abilities of a multidisciplinary team including a pediatric head and neck surgeon, pediatric oncologist, radiotherapist, diagnostic radiologist, and pathologist. In addition, the abilities of a neurosurgeon and possibly a plastic and reconstructive surgeon are required for large tumors and tumors with intracranial extension.

In recognition of the often poor prognosis of pediatric nasal and sinus malignancies, physicians and nurses should be familiar with the newer techniques of pain management. There is now awareness of the tendency to undertreat pain in pediatric patients. Pharmacologic agents include intravenous meperidine, morphine, and newer synthetic narcotics. When appropriate, these agents may be administered by a patient-controlled intravenous infusion pump. Small incremental doses are given until the patient obtains adequate pain relief. A variety of pharmacologic agents are available to counteract undesirable narcotic side effects, such as pruritis, vomiting, urinary retention, and respiratory depression. Mood elevators are used to treat depression caused by chronic illness and pain. Long-acting narcotics, such as metha-

done, have been used to establish base line levels of analgesia, and pulsed shorter-acting narcotics are used to control exacerbations of pain. Fear of drug dependency should not be an issue when treating pain in children with terminal malignant disease.

Neurosurgical approaches to controlling pain in the head and neck may be useful. These methods include transcutaneous electric nerve stimulation, stereotactic trigeminal thermocoagulation, and trigeminal sensory tractotomy (an intracranial procedure). Newer procedures include deep brain electrode implantation into pain centers and the installation of an infusion pump directly into the ventricular system for pulsed or continuous administration of opiates.

SELECTED REFERENCES

Fagan JJ, Snyderman CH, Carrau RL, et al. Nasopharyngeal angiofibromas: selecting a surgical approach. Head Neck Surg 19:391, 1997.
  A good discussion of decisions involving management of nasopharyngeal angiofibromas.
Kingdom TT, Lee KC, FitzSimmons SC, et al. Clinical characteristics and genotype analysis of patients with cystic fibrosis and nasal polyposis requiring surgery. Arch Otolaryngol Head Neck Surg 122:1209, 1996.
  An interesting presentation of specific features of patients with cystic fibrosis related to nasal and sinus disease.

REFERENCES

1. Baraka ME, Sadek SAA, Salem MH. Pleomorphic adenoma of the inferior turbinate. J Laryngol Otol 98:925, 1984.
2. Barzan L, Carbone A, Tirelli U, et al. Nasopharyngeal lymphatic tissue in patients infected with human immunodeficiency virus. Arch Otolaryngol Head Neck Surg 116:928, 1990.
3. Basak S, Karaman CA, Akdilli A, et al. Surgical approaches to antrochoanal polyps in children. Int J Pediatr Otorhinolaryngol 46: 197, 1998.
4. Bennett RG, Grist WJ. Nasal papilloma successful treatment with podophyllin. South Med J 78:224, 1985.
5. Bernard RG, Lawson W, Biller HF, et al. Complications following rhinotomy: review of 148 patients. Ann Otol Rhinol Laryngol 98: 684, 1989.
6. Brama I, Goldfarb A, Shalev O, et al. Tumour of the nose as a presenting feature of leukemia. J Laryngol Otol 96:83, 1982.
7. Brentani MM, Ossamu B, Oshima CTF, et al. Multiple steroid receptors in nasopharyngeal angiofibroma. Laryngoscope 99:398, 1989.
8. Cassidy DE, Drewry J, Fanning JP. Podophyllum toxicity: a report of a fatal case and a review of the literature. J Toxicol Clin Toxicol 19:35, 1982.
9. Chakravarti A, Vishwakarma SK, Arara VK, et al. Dermoid (hairy polyp) of the nasopharynx. Indian J Pediatr 65:473, 1998.
10. Chen JM, Schlors MD, Azouz ME. Antro-choanal polyp: a 10-year retrospective study in the pediatric population with a review of the literature. J Otolaryngol 18:168, 1989.
11. Cheung MM, Chan JK, Lau WH, et al. Primary non-Hodgkin's lymphoma of the nose and nasopharynx: clinical features, tumor immunophenotype, and treatment outcome in 113 patients. J Clin Oncol 16:70, 1998.
12. Cuadra-Garcia K, Proulx GM, Wu CL. Sinonasal lymphoma: a clinicopathologic analysis of 58 cases from the Massachusetts Hospital. Am J Surg Pathol 23:1356, 1999.
13. Cummings BJ, Blend R, Keane T, et al. Primary radiation therapy

for juvenile nasopharyngeal angiofibroma. Laryngoscope 94:1500, 1984.

14. Dedo HD, Jackler RK. Laryngeal papilloma: results of treatment with the CO$_2$ laser and podophyllum. Ann Otol Rhinol Laryngol 91: 425, 1982.

15. Dehner LP. Tumors of the mandible and maxilla in children. I. Clinicopathologic study of 46 histologically benign lesions. Cancer 31:364, 1973.

16. Dillon WP, Som PM, Roseneau W. Hemangioma of the nasal vault: MR and CT features. Radiology 180:761, 1991.

17. Duplechain JK, White JA, Miller RH. Pediatric sinusitis: the role of endoscopic sinus surgery in cystic fibrosis and other forms of sinonasal disease. Arch Otolaryngol Head Neck Surg 117:422, 1991.

18. Duval AJ, Moreano AE. Juvenile nasopharyngeal angiofibroma: diagnosis and treatment. Head Neck Surg 97:534, 1987.

19. Engelbrecht V, Preis S, Hassler W, et al. CT and MRI of congenital sinonasal ossifying fibroma. Neuroradiology 41:526, 1999.

20. Fagan JJ, Snyderman CH, Carrau RL, et al. Nasopharyngeal angiofibromas: selecting a surgical approach. Head Neck 19:391, 1997.

21. Fearson B, Forte V, Brama K. Malignant nasopharyngeal tumors in children. Laryngoscope 100:470, 1991.

22. Gatalica Z. Immunohistochemical analysis of steroid hormone receptors in nasopharyngeal angiofibroma. Cancer Lett 127:89, 1998.

23. Gates GA, Rice DH, Koopman CF, et al. Flutamide-induced regression of angiofibroma. Laryngoscope 102:641, 1992.

24. Gnepp DR, Henley J, Weiss S, et al. Desmoid fibromatosis of the sinonasal tract and nasopharynx. Cancer 78:2572, 1996.

25. Gotte K, Hormann K, Schmoll J, et al. Congenital nasal hemangiopericytoma: intrauterine, intraoperative, and histologic findings. Ann Otol Rhinol Laryngol 108:589, 1999.

26. Greisner WA, Settipane GA. Hereditary factor for nasal polyps. Allergy Asthma Proc 17:283, 1996.

27. Handler SD, Savino PJ, Peyster RG, et al. Giant cell tumor of the ethmoid sinus: an unusual cause of proptosis in a child. Otolaryngol Head Neck Surg 90:513, 1982.

28. Hawkins EP, Krishir JP, Smith BE, et al. Nasopharyngeal carcinoma in children; a retrospective review and demonstration of Epstein-Barr viral genomes in tumor cell cytoplasm: a report of the pediatric oncology group. Hum Pathol 21:805, 1990.

29. Hepler KM, Woodson BE, Kearns DB. Respiratory distress in the neonate. Sequela of a congenital dacryocystocele. Arch Otolaryngol Head Neck Surg 121:1423, 1995.

30. Ikushima I, Korogi Y, Makita O. MR imaging of Tornwaldt's cysts. AJR Am J Roentgenol 172:1661, 1999.

31. Kamal MM, Luley AS, Mundhada SG, et al. Rhinosporodiosis. Diagnosis by scrape cytology. Acta Cytol 39:931, 1995.

32. Kennedy DW, Josephson JS, Zinteich SJ, et al. Endoscopic sinus surgery for mucoceles: a viable alternative. Laryngoscope 99:885, 1989.

33. Kim DW, Low W, Billman G, et al. Chondroid hamartoma presenting as a neonatal nasal mass. Int J Pediatr Otorhinolaryngol 47:253, 1999.

34. Kingdom TT, Lee KC, FitzSimmons SC, et al. Clinical characteristics and genotype analysis of patients with cystic fibrosis and nasal polyposis requiring surgery. Arch Otolaryngol Head Neck Surg 122: 1209, 1996.

35. Kumagami H. Testosterone and extradiol in juvenile nasopharyngeal angiofibroma. Acta Otolaryngol (Stockh) 111:569, 1991.

36. Liang EY, Lam WW, Woo JK, et al. Another CT sign of sinonasal polyposis: truncation of the bony middle turbinate. Eur Radiol 6: 553, 1996.

37. Lopatin A, Bykova V, Piishunov G. Choanal polyps: one clinical entity, one surgical approach? Rhinology 35:79, 1997.

38. McClatchey K. Odontogenic lesions: tumors and cysts. In: Batsakis JG, ed. Tumors of the Head and Neck. Baltimore, Williams & Wilkins, 1981, pp 531–561.

39. Makek MS, Andrews JC, Fisch U. Malignant transformation of a nasopharyngeal angiofibroma. Laryngoscope 99:1088, 1989.

40. Paysse EA, Coats DK, Bernstein JM, et al. Management and com-

plications of congenital dacryocele with concurrent intranasal mucocele. J AAPOS 4:46, 2000.

41. Pitanguy I, Machado BH, Radwanski HN, et al. Surgical treatment of hemangiomas of the nose. Ann Plast Surg 36:586, 1996.

42. Rand PK, Ball WS, Kulwin DR. Congenital nasolacrimal nucoceles: CT evaluation. Radiology 173:691, 1989.

43. Rhodus NC. The prevalence and clinical significance of maxillary sinus mucous retention cysts in a general clinical population. Ear Nose Throat J 69:82, 1990.

44. Royal SA, Gardner RE. Rhinolithiasis: an unusual pediatric nasal mass. Pediatr Radiol 28:54, 1998.

45. Schiff M. Juvenile nasopharyngeal angiofibroma: a theory of pathogenesis. Laryngoscope 69:981, 1959.

46. Schramm VL. Inflammatory and neoplastic masses of the nose and paranasal sinus in children. Laryngoscope 89:1887, 1979.

47. Shrier DA, Want AR, Patel U, et al. Benign fibrous histiocytoma of the nasal cavity in a newborn: MR and CT findings. Am J Neuroradiol 19:1166, 1998.

48. Simo R, Carpentier J, Rejali D, et al. Pediatric pyogenic granuloma presenting as a unilateral nasal polyp. Rhinology 36:136, 1998.

49. Stanievich JF, Hafeza B, Brodsky L, et al. The incidence of head and neck tumors in the pediatric age group: a 10-year experience at Buffalo Children's Hospital and Roswell Park Memorial Institute. Proceedings of the Second International Congress of Head and Neck Oncology, Arlington, Va, 1987.

50. Stanley RJ, Kelly JA, Matta II, et al. Inverted papilloma in a 10-year old boy. Arch Otolaryngol 110:813, 1984.

51. Suzumiya J, Ohshima K, Takeshita M, et al. Nasal lymphomas in Japan: a high prevalence of Epstein-Barr virus type A and deletion within the latent membrane protein gene. Leuk Lymphoma 35:567, 1999.

52. Triglia JM, Nicollas R. Nasal and sinus polyposis in children. Laryngoscope 107:963, 1997.

53. Uemura T, Yoshikawa A, Onizuka T. Heterotopic brain tissue associated with cleft palate. Cleft Palate Craniofac J 36:248, 1999.

54. Van der Meulen JC, Gilbert M, Roddi R. Early excision of nasal hemangiomas. Plast Reconstr 94:465, 1994.

55. Vanni R, Marras S, Ravarino A, et al. Chromosome changes in nonneoplastic tissue. Numerical and structural abnormalities in nasal polyps with atypical stromal cells. Cancer Genet Cytogenet 88:158, 1996.

56. Vaze P, Aterman K, Hutton C, et al. Monomorphic adenoma of the nasal septum in a newborn. J Laryngol Otol 97:251, 1983.

57. Vidal RW, Devaney K, Ferlito A, et al. Sinonasal malignant lymphomas: a distinct clinicopathological category. Ann Otol Rhinol Laryngol 108:411, 1999.

58. Waguespack RW. Contact-tip Nd:YAG laser applications: squamous nasal papillomatosis. South Med J 84:660, 1991.

59. Waitz G, Wigand ME. Results of endoscopic sinus surgery for the treatment of inverted papillomas. Laryngoscope 102:917, 1992.

60. Wang HW, Su WY, Wang JY. Noradrenergic innervation of juvenile nasopharyngeal angiofibroma. Eur Arch Otorhinolaryngol 251:123, 1994.

61. Weber RS, Shiltoe EJ, Robbins KT, et al. Prevalence of human papillomavirus in inverted nasal papillomas. Arch Otolaryngol Head Neck Surg 114:23, 1988.

62. Weissler MD, Montgomery WW, Montgomery SK, et al. Inverted papilloma. Ann Otol Rhinol 95:215, 1986.

63. Weprin LS, Siemers PT. Spontaneous regression of juvenile nasopharyngeal angiofibroma. Arch Otolaryngol Head Neck Surg 117: 796, 1991.

64. Wollner N, Mandell L, Filippa D, et al. Primary nasal-paranasal oropharyngeal lymphoma in the pediatric age group. Cancer 65: 1438, 1990.

65. Yamanaka N, Harabuchi Y, Sambe S, et al. Non-Hodgkin's lymphoma of Waldeyer's ring and nasal cavity. Clinical and immunologic aspects. Cancer 56:768, 1985.

66. Yellin SA, Weiss MH, O'Malley B, et al. Massive concha bullosa masquerading as an intranasal tumor. Ann Otol Rhinol Laryngol 103:658, 1994.

49

Allergic Rhinitis

Philip Fireman, M.D., and Rachel Schreiber, M.D.

Allergic rhinitis is the most common of all the allergic disorders, estimated to affect over 40 million people in the United States.[18] Allergic rhinitis is also the most common chronic illness affecting children. Because it is not a fatal disease and its symptoms may not be incapacitating, allergic rhinitis may at times be slighted or ignored by the surgical and medical community. As is the case in adults, allergic rhinitis in children is responsible for more debilitation and interference with daily life than the patients, their parents, or their physicians appreciate or recognize. Symptoms often go unnoticed or inadequately treated because a child is typically unable to verbalize or communicate their impact. This unintentional benign neglect leaves children vulnerable not only to the discomfort and disability of allergic rhinitis itself but also to associated illnesses, such as asthma and sinusitis. Thus, this frequent illness causes significant morbidity, which results in the expenditure of several billions of dollars in health care and the loss of millions of workdays and schooldays.[18]

Allergic rhinitis has a familial tendency and is induced by exposure to antigenic environmental factors, called *allergens*, with resultant sneezing, nasal pruritus, watery rhinorrhea, nasal mucosal edema, and subsequent nasal obstruction. Allergic conjunctivitis occurs in at least 50% of patients with allergic rhinitis and is often diagnosed as allergic rhino-conjunctivitis. The symptoms can be intermittent or persistent; when symptoms recur annually during certain months, the syndrome is called *seasonal allergic rhinitis*. Typically, seasonal allergic rhinitis does not develop until after the patient has been sensitized by two or more pollen seasons. It is frequently called *hay fever* or a *summer cold*. These descriptive terms are misleading and should be discarded because fever is not a symptom associated with allergic rhinitis, and neither hay nor the common cold virus is incriminated in the etiology of this syndrome.

Definitions

Although syndromes identical to what we now classify as allergic rhinitis have been described for centuries, the concept of an immunologic pathogenesis dates to the beginning of the 20th century. At first, allergy diagnosis and therapy developed empirically because the criteria for documentation of allergic disease and allergen-antibody interaction were difficult to quantify and were mostly subjective. Recent decades have seen many advances in the elucidation of immunologic phenomena and have enabled the clinician to better understand allergic diseases. These discoveries have had considerable impact on clinical practice; they have provided a scientific basis for many of the diagnostic and therapeutic procedures that developed without well-controlled documentation of efficacy in the past century.

It is necessary to define the terms used by the allergist because the manner in which the words *immunology*, *immunity*, *allergy*, *hypersensitivity*, and *atopy* are used (and at times abused) indicates confusion over their meaning. Medical dictionaries define *immunology* as the study of an antigen-antibody interaction that induces immunity and implies a beneficial protective response induced by the specific antigen. This concept of protective immunity is appropriate for understanding the patient's response to infectious diseases because the body develops serum antibodies and sensitized lymphocytes to control the infectious agents upon re-exposure; however, this limited definition of immunity is inappropriate to describe the host response to noninfectious environmental factors such as pollens, animal products, and drugs. As used in this chapter, *immunology* means the study of antigens, antibodies, and their interaction, whether beneficial or not.

The term *allergy* was introduced by a pediatrician, Clemens von Pirquet, in 1906 to designate the host's altered reactivity to an antigen (allergen) that develops after previous experience with the same material; the end result could be helpful or harmful to the host.[76] This all-inclusive immunologic concept of allergy has been popularized by Coombs and Gell[15] and may have merit in permitting an organized and systematic approach to understanding the pathogenesis of immune mechanisms. Nevertheless, the terms *allergy* and *allergic* as commonly used in clinical practice indicate an adverse reaction, and allergic rhinitis is best defined as that adverse pathophysiologic response of the nose and adjacent organs that results from the interaction of antigen (allergen) with antibody in a host sensitized by previous exposure to that allergen. Most patients with allergic rhinitis experience symptoms within minutes after allergen exposure (the *early-phase response*); in about 50% of patients, this is followed several hours later by a recurrence of symptoms (the *late-phase response*).[65] This immunologic definition of allergic rhinitis is accepted by most clinical allergists and otolaryngologists; however, non-immune processes such as cigarette smoking or other irritants can be additional contributory factors in the clinical expression of allergic diseases.

Hypersensitivity indicates a heightened or exaggerated immune response that develops after more than one exposure to an allergen. Hypersensitivity in this chapter is considered to be synonymous with allergy. The terms *atopy* and *atopic* are also frequently used by allergists, having been introduced by Coca and Cooke in 1923 to classify those allergic diseases, such as allergic rhinitis, asthma, and infantile eczema (atopic dermatitis), that showed a familial predilection and implied genetic predisposition.[9] Other allergic diseases, such as contact dermatitis (poison ivy) and serum sickness, have no familial tendency and are called *nonatopic*. It was also recognized that serum from atopic persons contained a factor identified as a reagin or skin-sensitizing antibody. This serum factor can passively sensitize the skin of a nonsensitive person, and after that site undergoes intradermal challenge with specific allergen, a wheal and flare reaction develops within 20 minutes. This passive transfer test, also known as the Prausnitz-Küstner test, had been described only several years earlier and yielded the first documentation of the specific serum and tissue antibody important in the pathogenesis of allergic diseases.[56] As discussed later, more than 90% of these reaginic antibodies are of the IgE immunoglobulin class.[82] Although some allergists and clinical immunologists, including these authors, frequently use the term *atopic* to identify these allergic patients and their families, the term *atopy* has never gained universal acceptance.

Classically, allergic rhinitis has been subdivided into two classifications: *seasonal*, related to outdoor pollens and molds, and *perennial*, caused by indoor allergens such as dust mites, animal dander, and cockroaches. These terms are not entirely accurate, however: pollens and molds may be perennial, and symptoms of perennial allergy may not be present year-round. Additionally, because of the priming effect of the nasal mucosa, very low levels of allergen (which may not occur during the allergen season) can cause persistent inflammation. In 2001, a collaborative group convened by the World Health Organization released a report suggesting that the terms *intermittent* and *persistent* are more accurate and encompassing.[2] This clinical classification of allergic rhinitis is outlined in Table 49–1.

Epidemiology

Allergic rhinitis was relatively uncommon prior to the industrial revolution at the turn of the 20th century, whereas it is much more common now. Data from many sources and countries support these observations. In addition, diagnostic recognition of the illness has improved remarkably in the past century. Swedish army recruits showed a prevalence of seasonal allergic rhinitis of 4.4%

TABLE 49–1. Clinical Classification of Allergic Rhinitis

Duration

Intermittent (seasonal): Symptoms present
• Less than 4 days per week, *or*
• Less than 4 to 6 weeks per year
Persistent (perennial): Symptoms present
• More than 4 days per week, *and*
• More than 6 weeks

Severity

Mild: Symptoms do not affect lifestyle
Moderate-severe: Symptoms affect lifestyle
• Sleep disturbance
• Impair leisure or sport activities
• Impair school or work

in 1971, increasing to 8.4% in 1981.[7] Broder and colleagues,[4] in a 1970 questionnaire study of a well-defined population in Tecumseh, Michigan, found that the incidence of allergic rhinitis increased during childhood from less than 1% during infancy, to 4% to 5% from ages 5 to 9 years, to 9% during adolescence, to 15% to 16% after adolescence. Although seasonal allergic rhinitis is infrequent in very young children, persistent allergic rhinitis has been recognized in infancy and even in neonates.[26] In a more recent prospective study of children followed from birth in a Tucson, Arizona HMO, allergic rhinitis was diagnosed in 40% of children by age 6 years and confirmed by allergy skin testing in 40% of those children whose families agreed to skin testing.[81] Whereas seasonal allergic rhinitis in the Tecumseh study was shown to be almost twice as common as perennial allergic rhinitis, the more recent Tucson study showed the reverse. In Britain, a community-based questionnaire survey of adolescents and adults showed a prevalence of 16% allergic rhinitis with 8% perennial, 6% combination of both seasonal and perennial, and 2% seasonal.[64] The incidence of allergic rhinitis remains constant in young adults but gradually declines during middle and old age.

For reasons that are not clear, more male than female children, in a ratio of 2:1, are affected with allergic rhinitis before adolescence, whereas females are slightly more often affected with nasal allergy after adolescence. The prevalence of allergic rhinitis may vary both within and among countries. For example, allergic rhinitis is significantly more frequently diagnosed in metropolitan areas than in rural areas. In addition, allergic rhinitis is more common in industrialized developed countries than in developing countries. As discussed in greater detail later in this chapter, allergic rhinitis is a familial, genetically influenced illness. However, migration studies suggest that environmental factors may be more important. In children born to immigrants in a new country, both prevalence and natural history of rhinitis resemble those of native children. In the United States, no differences were found in self-reported allergic rhinitis between white and nonwhite adults.[74]

The basis for the increased prevalence of allergy in recent years has not been established, but some studies suggest that modern lifestyle, fewer infections, and environment are important. Studies of Swiss children have shown that symptoms of allergic rhinitis were reduced and that allergen-specific immunoglobulin E (IgE) antibodies were lower in the offspring of farmers than in other children in the same rural areas.[3] Another concept, the so-called *hygiene hypothesis*, proposes that the decline of childhood infections or lack of exposure to infectious agents or their products (i.e., endotoxin) during the first few months or years of life are responsible for the increase in allergic disease. In children born into families with several older siblings, the risk of allergic sensitization at school age is reduced compared with children with no siblings.[72] Studies show that preadolescent children who attended day care during infancy have less allergic disease than children who did not attend day care.[71] These observations may well be compatible with the immunopathogenetic aspects of allergic disease discussed later in this chapter.

Etiology

The development of allergic rhinitis requires two conditions: the atopic familial predisposition to develop allergy and the environmental exposure of the sensitized patient to the allergen. Patients are not born with allergies but can develop symptoms spontaneously through repeated exposure to allergens in their environment. Therefore, an understanding of the environmental factors that provoke allergy are essential for diagnosing and treating allergic diseases.

Inhalants are the principal allergens responsible for allergic rhinitis and may be present outdoors and indoors. These microscopic airborne particles include the pollens from weeds, grasses, and trees; fungi (mold) spores; animal products; and environmental dusts, either house or occupational.[68] Intermittent (seasonal) allergic rhinitis is primarily induced by pollens from the germination of nonflowering vegetation. In temperate climates, the most important pollens are tree pollens in the spring, grass pollens in the late spring and early summer, and weeds, especially ragweed in the late summer and early fall. Since geographic areas vary from one another, clinicians must become familiar with the pollination patterns in their region. Flowering vegetation, such as roses and fruit blossoms, rarely causes allergic rhinitis because their pollens are too heavy to be airborne and their germination is facilitated by the action of bees and other insects. However, these flower pollens cannot be ignored as potential allergens in florists, gardeners, and flower fanciers or hobbyists.

In warm subtropic or tropic climates, mold spores may be airborne year round. In climates in which snow and freezing occur in the winter months, airborne mold spores are present intermittently during the spring, summer, and fall and decrease after a significant frost. In patients with persistent (perennial) allergic rhinitis, mold spores may be a significant inhalant allergen indoors along with house dust. The principal allergen in household dust can vary, but the major portion is due to the house dust mite *Dermatophagoides*.[77] Several species of house dust mite have been identified, with varying geographic distribution. The specific house mite allergens have been identified in its cuticle and feces. Animal epi-

dermal danders, as well as salivary proteins, urinary proteins, feces, and feathers (especially from pets such as cats, dogs, and birds), are potential inhalant allergens. Most allergens, including the pollens, have been only partially chemically characterized, and each consists of multiple antigenic determinants.

Food allergens cannot be ignored, especially in young children, but these allergens are less important in the etiology of allergic rhinitis than inhalants.[30] Foods are especially important allergens in infancy, probably because the digestive and immune process of the gut are immature, which increases sensitization to ingested substances. Food allergy can appear at any age but most commonly occurs in early life. Gastrointestinal complaints are the most common symptoms, but food allergy can produce upper respiratory complaints of allergic rhinitis as well as asthma, urticaria, angioedema, eczema, and even anaphylaxis. Sensitivity to food frequently decreases as the child becomes older but can be life-long, especially allergic reactions to nuts, fish, and shellfish.

Patients may be sensitive to one or multiple allergens. Although it is clear that exposure to an allergen is necessary for the development of sensitivity and symptoms, it is not known why allergic patients, sometimes even twins with similar exposures, become sensitive to certain allergens but not to others. The threshold of reactivity to each allergen varies greatly from one patient to another; certain individuals react to small allergenic challenges, whereas others tolerate a large allergen dose before experiencing symptoms. In addition to allergens, other nonallergenic factors can provoke nasal symptoms that resemble nasal allergy, except there are no specific IgE antibodies to these nonallergenic substances. These factors include cigarette smoke, aerosolized cosmetics, industrial fumes, and changes in temperature, humidity, and barometric pressure.[6] Psychological and social stresses and anxiety can also contribute to or exacerbate nasal symptoms.[80] The importance of these additional contributory factors varies greatly from patient to patient and should not be neglected in management.

Even though it is not possible to predict with certainty the potentially atopic patient, the familial autosomal nature of allergic rhinitis has been recognized for years, and a positive family history of atopy has been noted in 50% to 75% of cases of allergic rhinitis.[10] Elevated serum levels of IgE are frequently associated with allergic diseases, and a recessive genetic influence has been suggested.[40] Most investigators think that several genetic loci are involved in the expression of allergic disease and that inheritance is multifactorial. A variety of population-based studies using positional cloning techniques and genetic mapping have identified candidate genes or loci that may be involved in allergy. One candidate loci for allergy is on chromosome 5q, near the site of the gene cluster encoding IL-3, IL-4, IL-5, IL-9, IL-13, and the IL-4 receptor.[39] Another candidate locus is on chromosome 11q13, which is the location of the gene encoding the high-affinity IgE receptor.[14] Animal studies have shown that synthesis of specific antibodies to well-characterized antigens is controlled in part by immune response genes, which are linked to the major tissue histocompatibility locus (HLA). Levine and coworkers suggested that ragweed allergic rhinitis and immune responses to purified ragweed antigen E were linked to a particular HLA haplotype in successive generations of allergic families.[36] Marsh and colleagues reported a significant correlation between haplotype HLA-7 and increased IgE antibodies to a low–molecular-weight purified ragweed antigen (Ra5) in a group of patients with allergic rhinitis who were sensitive to this small portion of the ragweed allergen.[38] Similar studies of other purified allergens are indicated in cases of allergic rhinitis because the responses to the more complex allergens, such as those used in clinical practice, may or may not be controlled by similar or different genetic influences.

Immunopathology

Allergic rhinitis, along with allergic asthma and allergic urticaria, are described immunologically as immediate hypersensitivity syndromes and are mediated in large part by IgE antibodies.[28] Allergic (atopic) persons produce high levels of IgE antibodies in response to particular allergens, whereas nonallergic persons generally synthesize other Ig isotypes, such as IgM and IgG antibodies, and minimal IgE antibodies to the specific allergen. Regulation of IgE synthesis depends on the propensity of an individual to mount a response of specific T-helper 2 (T_H2) lymphocytes to an allergen. This propensity is influenced by a variety of factors, including familial genes, the nature of the allergen, and the history of prior allergen exposure. Thus, the allergic patient inherits the risk, but environmental factors (including exposure) determine the nature and extent of the allergic rhinitis.

Upon the first exposure to an antigen, a person with a genetic predisposition to mounting an allergic response becomes sensitized to that antigen. During this exposure, the cells responsible for initiating the inflammatory response are recruited to the site of exposure. At subsequent exposures to the same antigen, these cells are considered to be *primed:* they can rapidly respond to antigen through immediate release of factors that cause inflammatory changes. In the case of allergic rhinitis, there can be a dual temporal reaction with an immediate or early-phase response clinically manifested by nasal itching, sneezing, rhinorrhea, and congestion. In addition, 50% of patients with allergic rhinitis experience a late-phase response characterized mainly by congestion. On a cellular level, this represents the long-term consequences of cellular upregulation that began in the early phase.[54]

The cellular interactions of allergic rhinitis begin with antigen uptake and processing via the antigen-presenting cell. Antigen-presenting cells are identified as macrophages and dendritic cells in the nasal mucosa and submucosa, and they display processed peptides in the form of major histocompatibility complex class II–associated peptides. Naive T lymphocytes, also called T_H0 *cells*, migrate toward antigen-presenting cells and their processed antigen and are stimulated by recognition of the peptide/major histocompatibility complex on the antigen-presenting cell. Upon antigen recognition, the T_H0 cell becomes activated and clonally expands. The progeny of antigen-stimulated T_H0 cells differentiate into effector cells that produce different sets of cytokines and perform different functions. These subsets include two populations, T-helper 1 (T_H1) and T-helper 2 (T_H2) cells.[1a] The T_H1 cells are involved in the production of interferon-γ and tumor necrosis factor β, and the T_H2 cells have the capacity to produce IL-4, IL-5, IL-6, IL-9, IL-10, IL-13, and granulocyte-macrophage colony-stimulating factor (GM-CSF). IgE production is facilitated by IL-4, IL-1, IL-6, and IL-13; eosinophil production by IL-4 and IL-5; and mast cells and basophils by IL-4, IL-9, and IL-10. As the allergic response continues, mast cells, B cells, natural killer cells, eosinophils, and epithelial cells may also release T_H2 cytokines. Thus, the T_H2 cell and its cytokines are critical to and responsible for creating and sustaining the conditions in which both acute and chronic allergic reactions occur (Fig. 49–1).

The T_H2 lymphocytes in conjunction with the cytokine IL-4 facilitate the switch of IgM to IgE antibodies by the allergen-stimulated B-lymphocytes. These B-lymphocytes then mature into IgE-producing plasma cells. The IgE antibodies are synthesized after allergen challenge in large part by plasma cells located in lymphoid tissues adjacent to mucosal membranes of the respiratory or gastrointestinal tissue. The IgE antibodies passively sensitize the cell membranes of regional tissue mast cells and circulating blood basophils at unique high-affinity receptor sites for the Fc portion of the IgE antibody.[11] During this sensitization phase, no deleterious host reaction may be apparent.

Upon subsequent allergen challenge, the allergen combines with its specific IgE antibody at the cell membrane of the sensitized tissue mast cell and blood basophil. When allergen cross-links the bound IgE, this triggers mast cell degranulation.[5] The degranulation begins a cascade that is characterized by two phases: (1) an immediate or early reaction that occurs within 60 minutes and (2) a late-phase reaction that peaks in 3 to 6 hours but may be present for 8 to 24 hours (Figure 49–2).

The combination of allergen and IgE antibody results in a sequence of calcium- and energy-dependent enzyme reactions, with alteration of the mast cell or basophil membrane, which initiates a process of mediator release, synthesis, and transcription. Those factors that are released immediately include the preformed mast cell inflammatory mediators, such as histamine and tryptase. Newly generated lipid mediators, such as leukotriene C4 and prostaglandin D_2, are synthesized from the phospholipid constituents of the mast cell membrane via arachidonic acid metabolism. In addition, cytokines, including IL-4 and IL-13, are transcribed.[5] The interaction of antigen (allergen) and antibody (IgE) at the mast cell membrane also promotes the synthesis of additional mediators, including platelet-activating factor, bradykinin, and IL-4 and IL-5 as well as tumor necrosis factor and GM-CSF. The expression of the early- and late-phase allergic reactions is diagrammed in Figure 49–2. The mediators shown in this figure cause the increased vascular permeability, increased local edema, and increased eosinophil-laden secretions that occur in allergic rhinitis. The early phase of the allergic reaction occurs within minutes after exposure to the allergens. In contrast, patients who manifest the late-phase IgE allergic reaction show prolonged

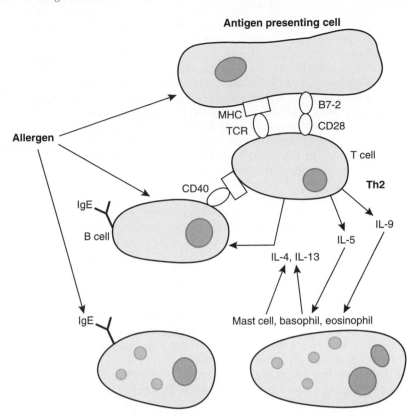

Antigen presenting cell

FIGURE 49–1. The T_H2 cell recognizes allergen bound to the antigen presenting cell (APC), and will produce various cytokines as diagrammed. IL-4 and IL-13 promote B cell switching to produce IgE. IL-5 promotes eosinophil production and survival. IL-9 acts on the eosinophil to increase IL-5 expression. Mast cells, basophils, and eosinophils produce type 2 cytokines that amplify the allergic inflammatory response. Once IgE is cross-linked on basophils and mast cells, histamine is released, eosinophils are degranulated, and lipid mediators are produced, thus increasing allergic inflammation. Adapted from Robinson DS. Th-2 cytokines in allergic disease. Br Med Bull 56(4):956–968, 2000.

tissue inflammation. The total allergic inflammation can resolve within hours but may persist for days, weeks, or months, depending on the extent and duration of allergen exposure.

Histamine promptly released from mast cells as well as from basophils appears to be a major chemical mediator in nasal allergy. The mechanism by which histamine produces tissue edema is based on its ability to produce vasodilatation and to increase capillary permeability.[59] Intranasal challenge with histamine produces immediate pruritus, sneezing, rhinorrhea, and congestion but without eosinophilia. Increased levels of histamine can be found in nasal secretions during both the immediate and late-phase nasal reactions.[45, 46] Histamine stimulates both H_1 and H_2 receptors in the nose, although the H_2 effect in the nose is probably minimal. The increased vascular permeability generated by histamine indirectly leads to the production of kinins, including bradykinin, which require

kallikrein for their formation. Serine esterases, which include tryptase, are elevated in nasal washings during early- and late-phase allergic reactions. The leukotrienes, formerly designated *slow-reacting substance of anaphylaxis*, are potent mediators. Leukotrienes LTC_4, LTD_4, and LTE_4 are found in nasal secretions after both allergen and cold air challenges. All have been found to increase vascular permeability and mucus secretion. LTB_4 has also been found to increase leukocyte adhesion molecule expression and to act as a neutrophil and eosinophil chemoattractant.[54] Prostaglandin D_2 is the only currently studied mediator found to be elevated during the immediate nasal reaction but not during the late phase.[46] Since this prostaglandin is produced by mast cells and not basophils, it has been suggested that mast cells are involved primarily in the early allergic reaction whereas basophils contribute to the late reaction.

The hallmark of allergic pathology is the presence of

TABLE 49–2. Mediators Released During Intranasal Allergen Challenges

Mediator	Challenge	Immediate Reaction	Late-Phase Reaction	Tissue Effects
Histamine (H_1)	Allergen; cold, dry air	+	+	Vasodilatation, plasma protein leakage; mucus hypersecretion; itching and sneezing
Leukotrienes C_4, D_4, E_4, B_4 (SRS-A)	Allergen; cold, dry air	+	?	Mucus hypersecretion; vasodilatation; neutrophil chemotaxis
PGD_2	Allergen; cold, dry air	+	−	Basophil medical release; vasodilatation; neutrophil chemotaxis
Serine esterases (kallikreins)	Allergen; cold, dry air	+	+	Produce kinins; vasodilatation
Kinins	Allergen	+	+	Vasodilatation

PGD_2, prostaglandin D_2; SRS-A, slow-reacting substance of anaphylaxis.

eosinophils in the patient's tissues or secretions. However, the function of the eosinophil that is attracted to nasal tissue has yet to be completely defined. A regulatory or modulatory role for the eosinophil has been suggested because the enzymes histaminase and arylsulfatase, which effectively inactivate histamine and leukotrienes, respectively, are more abundant in eosinophils than in other leukocytes.[32] In addition, phospholipase, which inactivates platelet-activating factor released from mast cells, is located primarily in the eosinophil. Products of eosinophils, major basic protein, and eosinophil cationic protein may participate in the inflammation of the late-phase reaction that accompanies the allergic reaction.[23] The mediators of inflammation, including histamine, leukotriene, and prostaglandins (Table 49–2), have been demonstrated in nasal secretions after specific allergen intranasal provocative challenge in patients with allergic rhinitis.[45, 46] These mediators can directly affect the vascular bed of the nose, and the edema and congestion of the nasal tissues can disturb the balance of autonomic nervous control of nasal functions. Since allergic disease causes an overreaction to cholinergic stimuli, it may be that vascular dilatation and hypersecretion are aggravated by the disturbance and resultant imbalance of autonomic control.

The participation of neurohumors and vasoactive peptides, including factors such as substance P and vasoactive intestinal peptide, has been suggested, but their role needs definition. Histamine appears to bind to H_1 receptors on type C neurons, and depolarization of these neurons causes release of substance P and neurokinin A. Substance P has been shown to increase vascular permeability and eosinophil influx when repeatedly applied to the nasal mucosa in allergic patients.[54]

The immunologic effectors of the immediate hypersensitivity allergic reaction have been shown to be IgE antibodies in most situations. However, it should be emphasized that it is the mediators, such as histamine, leukotrienes, prostaglandins, and eosinophil chemotactic factor of anaphylaxis, that are responsible for the pathophysiology of the immediate hypersensitivity reaction.

Histologic examination of the nasal mucosa after allergen challenge demonstrates distended goblet cells in the presence of enlarged, congested mucous glands, as well as impaired ciliary beating and some epithelial exfoliation. The tissues are infiltrated with eosinophils and T-lymphocytes with a paucity of neutrophils. The intracellular spaces are enlarged, and the basement membrane is thickened. Mast cells are present in both the nasal epithelium and the lamina propria and account for more than 80% of the metachromatic cells (mast cells and basophils) in nasal biopsies, with degranulated mast cells significantly increased 20 minutes after a provocative allergen challenge. Heterogeneity of mast cells has been proposed, with mucosal mast cells in the epithelium and connective tissue mast cells in the lamina propria. Basophils are the predominant metachromatic cell type found in nasal secretion and may be increased during the late phase reactions.[50, 51] Connell[12] found increased numbers of mast cells in nonspecific and vasomotor rhinitis without any evidence of allergy. It appears that the number of mast cells cannot be used in discriminating the pathologic

features of different types of rhinitis. The ground substance surrounding the cells and blood vessels changes during allergic rhinitis from its normal semisolid state to a relatively fluid state.[57] This change may account for the often boggy appearance of the nasal mucosa in allergic rhinitis.

Pathophysiology

Allergic rhinitis adversely affects nasal function, which, besides its role as an airway, includes filtration of particulate matter from inspired air, humidification of air, olfaction, and phonation. The measurement of nasal airflow, i.e., *rhinomanometry,* is being widely used in clinical investigation of allergic rhinitis but has not yet been widely accepted or standardized for routine clinical practice. There are two approaches to the measurement of pressure and flow relationships to assess nasal airway resistance: anterior and posterior rhinomanometry. Anterior rhinomanometry requires minimal patient cooperation but is compromised by the normal nasal cycling phenomenon, in which airflow is predominant on one side of the nose for 2 to 3 hours and then alternates to the contralateral side. This requires measurement of nasal resistance on both sides of the nose, or total nasal airway resistance. Alternatively, posterior rhinomanometry monitors posterior pharyngeal pressure via an oral tube as nasal airflow is being monitored, but 10% of adults cannot perform this test. This method requires a storage oscilloscope because it is necessary to establish that an artifact-free pressure-flow curve has been achieved before nasal resistance can be measured. Computer-assisted rhinomanometry has made this test fast and accurate when used in conjunction with specific allergen intranasal provocation and has provided measurements of obstruction in allergic rhinitis.[69] Computer-assisted rhinomanometry will probably become more widely used in clinical practice. Another tool, acoustic rhinomanometry, has also been applied to study nasal pathophysiology, but it is not yet clinically practical.

It has been shown that posture can affect airway resistance since the supine position was found to increase nasal resistance in allergic rhinitis threefold over that experienced in a sitting position.[60] Exercise and increased activity can also temporarily reverse the nasal obstruction in allergic rhinitis.[58] These effects may contribute to the patient's interpretation of increased symptoms when in bed, resulting potentially not only from allergenic contents of the mattress or pillows in the bedroom such as dust mites but also from the change in posture and activity.

After an intranasal challenge with a specific allergen, the patient with allergic rhinitis not only develops symptoms of allergic rhinitis associated with increased mediators of inflammation in nasal washings and increased nasal resistance as measured by rhinomanometry[46] but also manifests eustachian-tube dysfunction.[22] The allergen-provoked functional eustachian-tube obstruction as detected by tympanometry using the nine-step procedure swallow test or, more recently, sonotubometry depended on allergen dose, being inversely related to serum IgE antibody titer and partially preventable with antihistamines.[19] During allergic rhinitis provoked by seasonal natural pollen exposure, eustachian-tube obstruction develops in 70% of patients and correlates with the quantity of atmospheric pollen counts.[70] Intranasal challenge with histamine provoked eustachian-tube obstruction in patients with allergic rhinitis but not in normal subjects, whereas the degree of nasal obstruction as assessed by rhinomanometry was similar in both groups.[66] Since eustachian-tube obstruction is considered a risk factor for the development of otitis media with effusion, allergic rhinitis–induced eustachian-tube obstruction may also be a risk factor. Intranasal allergen challenge in either humans or laboratory animals has not provoked otitis media in allergic subjects.[20] Allergic rhinitis is also considered a risk factor for the expression of bronchial obstruction, i.e., asthma. Histamine or allergen bronchial challenge provoked bronchial obstruction and increased forced expiratory volume during pulmonary function tests in 30% of patients with allergic rhinitis who had no prior history of asthma.[73] The possibility that allergic rhinitis contributes to the pathogenesis of sinusitis has also been suggested but lacks documentation.

Using airway resistance studies and quantitative pollen challenges, Connell[13] showed that a larger dose of allergen was required to increase resistance in the nasal mucosa that had remained unchallenged than was required to obtain the same effect after a week of daily exposures. He also demonstrated, in patients sensitized to several pollens, that repeated challenges with one allergen conditioned the nasal mucosa to react to a lower dose of the second allergen than would have been needed if the allergen were given singly. This priming phenomenon could well account for the persistence of symptoms experienced in many patients toward the end of the pollen season in spite of decreased allergen exposure. It is also thought that this priming effect favors an increase in responsiveness to nonspecific stimuli, such as changes in humidity and temperature. It has been suggested that patients with allergic rhinitis have a defect in the nasal mucous membrane that permits inhaled allergen macromolecules easier access to the immune recognition system. Salvaggio and colleagues[62] found atopic subjects to have increased permeability to specific allergens instilled in the nose, but other more recent studies were unable to detect any differences in permeability between atopic and nonatopic subjects.[34]

Symptoms and Signs

Initial symptoms in intermittent (seasonal) allergic rhinitis progress from frequent sneezing and nasal pruritus to rhinorrhea and finally to nasal obstruction. Patients with persistent (perennial) allergic rhinitis have more nasal stuffiness and obstruction than just sneezing and pruritus. These symptoms vary considerably from season to season and differ markedly at various times of night and day. Patients complain of early morning and late evening symptoms, and sleep can frequently be interrupted because of nasal obstruction. Patients report not only nasal pruritus but also itching of the eyes, throat, and ears. Many children constantly rub their nose with a hand or arm in an effort to relieve the nasal itch and perhaps to improve the nasal obstruction. Other children may press the palm of the hand upward against their nose in an *allergic salute*. Constant rubbing of the nose often leads to a transverse nasal crease, a horizontal groove across the lower third of the nose.

The patient with nasal obstruction is a constant mouth breather, and snoring is a prominent nighttime symptom. It has been suggested that constant mouth breathing may contribute to the development of orofacial dental abnormalities requiring orthodontic procedures, but this has not been established definitively. Seasonal allergic rhinitis is frequently accompanied by allergic conjunctivitis with lacrimation, bilateral ocular pruritus, bilateral watery ocular secretions, and photophobia. Symptoms of allergic conjunctivitis are the presenting complaints in almost 50% of patients in whom allergic rhinitis is diagnosed.[1b] Symptoms involving the adjacent sinuses may also be evident, especially maxillary discomfort or headaches, when the symptoms of nasal obstruction are severe. In patients with eustachian-tube dysfunction, allergic rhinitis may contribute to the development of otitis media with effusion. Patients may complain of a feeling of fullness or a popping sound in their ears. A hearing loss in a child with chronic or perennial allergic rhinitis should raise the suspicion of a conductive hearing deficit associated with otitis media with effusion. Loss of sense of smell and taste may also be described. Patients may also complain of generalized malaise, irritability, and fatigue; these symptoms are often difficult to differentiate from the side effects of the frequently used over-the-counter antihistamine therapy. Patients with seasonal pollinosis describe a gradual increase in the severity of symptoms as the season progresses, especially on dry, windy days. At times, patients relate a history of continuation of the symptoms beyond the pollen season, and many clinicians think that repeated exposure to allergens increases the reactivity of the nasal mucosa so that ordinarily innocuous doses of allergens and environmental factors can produce symptoms.

The pattern of the patient's symptoms frequently distinguishes those with intermittent (seasonal) from those with persistent (perennial) allergic rhinitis, especially in temperate climates with obvious seasonal climatic changes. In the warmer subtropical climates, the seasonal pollen pattern may not be obvious since the grass pollen season extends over many months and mold spores can remain in the air throughout the year. In much of the United States, trees pollinate in the spring, primarily in March and April; grasses in late spring and summer, especially May, June, and July; and ragweed during the last two weeks of August until the first frost. The arid southwestern United States was traditionally pollen-free, but the advent of irrigation and increased vegetation has changed that environment. Ragweed tends to grow at the edges of cultivated fields and along highways and may cause increased symptoms during automobile trips. Although airborne pollens spread for miles, increased concentrations of pollens are noted in areas of high plant density, and patients frequently complain of more symptoms in areas of high pollen density. If there is direct contact with a substantial quantity of pollen, patients may have prominent symptoms, including angioedema (especially of the eyes and throat) and sometimes urticaria.

As mentioned earlier, ingested foods occasionally cause allergic rhinitis in young children. It behooves the clinician to take a careful environmental history and survey in all patients who complain of intermittent or year-round symptoms that do not fit the usual seasonal pattern previously outlined. In general, patients with year-round symptoms are much more of a diagnostic challenge than those with only intermittent seasonal complaints. The almost continuous exposure to house or industrial factors may induce perennial symptoms because congestion of the mucosal tissues may not have the opportunity to subside or return to normal during the few hours free of allergen exposure. It is also in these patients that the nonallergenic environmental factors (including changes in barometric pressure, temperature, and humidity and aerosolized irritants such as cigarette smoke, automobile fumes, industrial pollutants, and aerosolized cosmetics and drugs) tend to contribute to the symptoms.

With development of the allergic reaction, clear nasal secretions are evident and the nasal mucous membranes become edematous without much erythema. The mucosa appears boggy and blue-gray. With continued exposure to the allergen, the turbinates appear to be congested and swollen and obstruct the nasal airway. If nasal obstruction is present, it may be necessary to shrink the mucosa with a vasoconstrictor to document the absence of nasal polyps. Polyps may complicate allergic rhinitis but are relatively uncommon in allergic rhinitis, occurring in less than 0.5% of patients.[8] Conjunctival edema and hyperemia are frequent findings in patients with associated conjunctivitis. Patients with allergic rhinitis involving significant nasal obstruction and venous congestion, particularly children, may also demonstrate edema and darkening of the tissues beneath the eyes. These so-called *allergic shiners* are not pathognomonic for allergic rhinitis; they also occur in patients with recurrent nasal congestion and venous stasis of any other cause. The conjunctiva may also demonstrate a lymphoid follicular pattern with a cobblestone appearance. Pallor of the palatine and pharyngeal tissues is also evident, and small follicular lymphoid hyperplasia is occasionally noted on the posterior pharyngeal surface without regional cervical lymphadenopathy or tonsillar hypertrophy. Purulent secretions are seen only in the presence of secondary or concomitant infections (see Chapters 41 and 42).

Laboratory Studies

The nasal secretions of patients with allergic rhinitis usually contain increased numbers of eosinophils. Eosinophilia may not be present in patients remotely exposed to specific allergens or when there is a superimposed infection. Steroids can significantly reduce eosinophilia, but antihistamine therapy has no appreciable effect on nasal eosinophils. The usefulness of nasal eosinophilia largely depends on the technique used to obtain the specimens and prepare the slides for examination. It is difficult to quantify nasal eosinophilia accurately; more than 3% eosinophils on a stained smear of expelled nasal secretions is considered an increase. Analysis of the nasal cytologic picture obtained by gently pressing down on the mucosal surface of the inferior turbinate with a flexible plastic nasal probe can be helpful in the differential diagnosis of selected cases of recurrent rhinitis.[41] Increased mucosal basophils or mast cells, or both, are found in varying proportions in allergic rhinitis, nonallergic eosinophilic rhinitis, and primary nasal mastocytosis. Infection is usually evidenced by a predominance of polymorphonuclear leukocytes on the nasal smear. Although several methods of measuring nasal airway resistance by rhinomanometry or inspiratory peak flow meters have been developed in recent years, the diagnostic usefulness of quantifying this parameter in children is yet to be established and documented.

Laboratory confirmation of specific IgE antibody synthesis to specific allergens aids the management of allergic rhinitis. These laboratory tests should be considered in all patients in whom there is no clear-cut seasonal pattern and to help confirm clinical impressions documenting specific IgE antibodies by in vivo skin testing or in vitro serum immunoassay. Testing also reinforces the importance of environmental control by identification of specific allergens. Skin testing with the suspected allergens is mandatory in all patients before initiation of immunotherapy desensitization with allergy extracts because the intensity of the local wheal and flare skin reaction is used as a guide in determining the initial dose of allergen. Clinicians should be selective in the use of allergens for skin or serum allergy testing and should employ only *common* allergens of potential clinical importance in their patients. The most useful allergens in the study of allergic rhinitis are the pollens, molds, house dust mites, and epidermal animal danders. Allergens selected for skin or serum testing should be considered on the basis of potential exposure and prevalence in the patient's home or work environment.

There is no need to test for allergy to foods in patients with clear-cut seasonal allergic rhinitis; food testing should be reserved for patients whose conditions are diagnostic challenges, with intermittent or perennial symptoms. The major problem with skin testing, especially for food allergens, has been the lack of potency, stability, and purity of the allergen solutions. It is well known that great care must be used in interpreting the results of food skin testing because there should be concordance between the production of clinical symptoms upon ingestion of the food and positive skin reaction to the food.

If allergy testing is indicated, antihistamine drugs should be withheld for 72 hours before skin tests are performed to avoid false-negative results. Prick skin testing may be more reliable than intradermal skin testing; the specifics of skin testing are outlined in standard allergy textbooks.[47] As mentioned earlier, the in vitro serum immunoassays (radioallergosorbent test [RAST], fluorescent antibody test [FAST], enzyme-linked immunosorbent assay [ELISA]) for assessing the presence of serum IgE antibodies to various allergens have been employed as a diagnostic aid in allergic rhinitis. For certain allergens,

TABLE 49–3. Comparison of Skin Testing vs. Serum Immunoassay in Allergic Diagnosis

Skin Test	Serum Immunoassay
Less expensive	No patient risk
Greater sensitivity	Patient convenience
Wide allergen selection	Not influenced by drugs
Results available immediately	Results are quantitative
Will detect non–IgE-mediated allergic reactions	Preferable to skin testing in certain patients: Patients with dermographism Patients with widespread dermatitis Uncooperative children

such testing has proved as reliable as a skin test, but the cost has been the major disadvantage. In addition, skin testing is 10% to 20% more sensitive than the serum IgE antibody immunoassays. Table 49–3 compares the usefulness of allergy skin testing with that of serum IgE antibody testing.

On occasion, a nasal provocation test is useful to assess a patient who has had negative results on skin testing and who is suspected of reacting to a particular allergen because of the observations that IgE antibodies may be present in nasal secretions but not evident by skin testing or the presence of serum IgE antibodies.[25] Provocation testing is performed by introducing the allergen into the nostril after its suspension or dilution in saline. A positive reaction is manifested by local pruritus, sneezing, and watery rhinorrhea and edema. It is always necessary to place a diluent control in the opposite nostril for comparison. The sublingual challenge with allergen is not a useful diagnostic tool for allergic rhinitis. The in vitro cytotoxic leukocyte test with foods and other allergens is not useful as a laboratory test in controlled studies and is not recommended.[37]

Differential Diagnosis

Children who present to the clinician with rhinorrhea and nasal obstruction may have symptoms not only of allergy but also of infections, foreign bodies, structural changes, drug reactions, or neoplasms. Allergic rhinitis can be associated with or preceded by a history of atopic dermatitis or allergic asthma, or both. Nasal infections are usually characterized by burning and redness of the nasal mucosa and a purulent discharge. Without a doubt, the common cold virus is the most frequent cause of upper-respiratory infection. At its outset, a viral upper-respiratory infection, with its clear watery rhinorrhea and sneezing, resembles allergic rhinitis. Redness of the nasal mucosa is characteristic of an upper-respiratory infection and distinguishes it from allergic rhinitis. After several days, the purulent nature of the nasal discharge clearly identifies the presence of infection; in a confusing clinical situation, demonstration of the predominance of neutrophils on a smear of nasal secretions confirms that impression. One must realize that nasal infections can be superimposed on allergic rhinitis.

Nasal obstruction and rhinorrhea, usually purulent, can also occur with foreign objects in the nares. However, the symptoms are usually unilateral, and this differentiates the presence of foreign objects from allergic or infectious rhinitis. Nasal obstruction can also occur because of nasal polyps, which may not be associated with allergic disease but can be associated with cystic fibrosis or, rarely, aspirin therapy. Polyps can usually be demonstrated by inspection and the use of a vasoconstrictor to reduce the local edema that may obscure the nasal polyps. Another cause of unilateral nasal obstruction may be deviation of the nasal septum or a neoplasm; both conditions are detectable on visual examination of the nasal airway. Drugs administered systemically can mimic allergic rhinitis. Reserpine treatment of hypertension can produce nasal congestion, and a similar syndrome can be associated with the use of methantheline in the treatment of gastrointestinal disease and ulcers. The cessation of symptoms on withdrawal of the drug establishes this diagnosis. The most common drug rhinopathy is rhinitis medicamentosa after topical administration of vasoconstrictors for more than 5 days. The mucosa becomes pale and edematous, similar to the situation in allergic rhinitis. It is important to question patients carefully to diagnose this condition because some patients consider the use of decongestant nose drops or nasal sprays insignificant in their medical history. Frequently, the seasonal allergic rhinitis or the upper-respiratory infection for which the topical vasoconstrictor was initially applied has subsided by the time it is recognized that topical therapy is perpetuating the problem. Another cause of nasal congestion is pregnancy, which may be considered in appropriate adolescent patients.

The aforementioned conditions can usually be differentiated from allergic rhinitis, but the separation of allergic from nonallergic perennial rhinitis is often complicated (Table 49–4). Nonallergic rhinitis may occur during childhood but is more common in adults. It simulates the persistent (perennial) type of allergic rhinitis, but no immunologic cause can be implicated. In nonallergic rhinitis, the edematous mucous membranes are often pale. Eosinophilia is present occasionally, but the usual methods of detecting a specific allergen and its mediating antibodies cannot suggest a specific cause. When eosinophilia is present, the syndrome is diagnosed as nonallergic rhinitis with eosinophilia (or *NARES*). Vasomotor rhinitis is a nonallergic form of persistent nasal disease also manifested by watery rhinorrhea and nasal obstruction. This is a vague category of chronic or intermittent nasal disease that usually occurs in older children and adults and that does not lend itself to a specific definition. The patient complains of nasal overresponsiveness to minimal changes in air temperature, obnoxious odors, and often changes in position of the head. Eosinophils are not found in nasal secretions, and mast cells and basophils are not detected in the nasal mucosa or submucosa. These patients seem to be unusually aware of their symptoms, and their complaints are disproportionate to the magnitude of the symptoms. It is important to differentiate these patients with nonspecific, nonallergic rhinitis and vasomotor rhinitis from those with allergic disease because of their different responses to therapy. Immunotherapy is not to be used in these diseases, and drug therapy with antihista-

TABLE 49–4. Comparison of Allergic and Nonallergic Rhinitis

	Allergic	Nonallergic	
		NARES	*Vasomotor*
Usual onset	Child	Child	Adult
Family history of allergy	Usual	Coincidental	Coincidental
Collateral allergy	Common	Unusual	Unusual
Symptoms			
Sneezing	Frequent	Occasional	Occasional
Itching	Common	Unusual	Unusual
Rhinorrhea	Profuse	Profuse	Profuse
Congestion	Moderate	Moderate to marked	Moderate to marked
Physical examination			
Edema	Moderate to marked	Moderate	Moderate
Secretions	Watery	Watery	Mucoid to watery
Nasal eosinophilia	Common	Common	Occasional
Allergic evaluation			
Skin tests	Positive	Coincidental	Coincidental
IgE antibodies	Positive	Coincidental	Coincidental
Therapeutic response			
Antihistamines	Good	Fair	Poor to fair
Decongestants	Fair	Fair	Poor to fair
Corticosteroids	Good	Good	Poor to fair
Cromolyn	Fair	Unknown	Poor
Immunotherapy	Good	None	None

NARES, nonallergic rhinitis with eosinophilia.

mine decongestants controls the symptoms inconsistently. As expected, there are no historical or in vivo or in vitro tests to document allergic disease in these patients, and eosinophilia is not as common a laboratory feature with this problem.

Therapy

General Considerations

Successful therapy for allergic rhinitis involves three primary considerations: (1) environmental control by identification and avoidance of the specific allergens and other contributory factors, (2) pharmacologic management, and (3) immunotherapy (desensitization) to alter the patient's immune response to the allergen. An algorithm for the therapy of allergic rhinitis is presented in Table 49–5. Successful management includes identifying the specific precipitants and initiation of appropriate environmental control measures (discussed later). At the same time, the patient's history should be evaluated and, according to symptoms, the condition should be categorized as intermittent (seasonal) or persistent (perennial). The condition should be further defined as mild, moderate, or severe according to symptoms and response to pharmacotherapy. Mild symptoms can be controlled with over-the-counter medications, while the symptoms of moderate rhinitis require daily treatment with prescription therapy. Severe intermittent or persistent symptoms are those that severely affect everyday activities, especially adverse effects on school and work performance, difficulty with sleep, and failure of previous medications to control symptoms. Patients with moderate to severe symptoms not palliated with environmental control and prescription medications require in-depth evaluation through referral to an allergy specialist. Additional therapy may include consideration of

allergen injection immunotherapy. Although rhinomanometric measurements of nasal air flow have been used in clinical and laboratory research, they have not been clinically validated to help the physician in better defining these categories of mild, moderate, and severe rhinitis.

Environmental Control

Complete avoidance of allergens is the best therapy for allergic disease: without exposure, the allergic reaction will not take place. Once the specific allergens responsible for the symptoms are identified, the patient should try to reduce exposure to these allergens. Elimination of exposure to animal dander by disposal of a feather pillow or removal of a pet from the house, or elimination of a food allergen from the diet, may completely or partially relieve symptoms. Avoidance of more ubiquitous allergens, such as pollens, dusts, and molds, may be more difficult. Patients sensitive to grass pollens should avoid increased exposure through gardening and grass cutting during the grass pollen season. During the ragweed pollen seasons, ragweed-sensitive patients should postpone camping trips and picnics in the countryside until another time of the year. Pollen rubbed into the nose and eyes can produce severe local edema, a point particularly important to remember in dealing with children, who often play outdoors in close contact with pollinating plants. Patients should avoid direct contact with pollinating plants. Measures to control house dust mites, especially in the bedroom, can be effective. Such steps include providing rubberized or plastic airtight enclosures for pillows, mattresses, and box springs; the use of synthetic bedding fabrics; and removing stuffed toys, stuffed furniture, heavy drapery, and dust catchers (such as bookshelves) from the bedroom.

TABLE 49–5. Stepwise Algorithm for Management of Allergic Rhinitis

Intermittent (Seasonal)		Persistent (Perennial)	
Mild	*Moderate-Severe*	*Mild*	*Moderate-Severe*
Environmental control *plus* Antihistamine (PRN) ± decongestant *or* Nasal corticosteroid *or* Nasal cromolyn	Environmental control *plus* Antihistamine ± decongestant *plus* Nasal corticosteroid *plus* Specialist referral *consider* Allergen immunotherapy	Environmental control *plus* Antihistamine ± decongestant *or* Nasal corticosteroid *consider* Specialist referral	Environmental control *plus* Antihistamine ± decongestant *plus* Nasal corticosteroid *plus* Specialist referral *consider* Allergen immunotherapy

Environmental control measures should also include removal of hair carpet underpads and, if feasible, sealing of the forced-air heating ducts and vents in the bedroom. Thorough weekly cleaning and vacuuming of the bedding and rugs in the bedroom effectively reduces the concentration of house dust mite allergens. Washing bedding in hot water (130°F or greater) kills the house dust mite. HEPA filters placed in central forced-air heating or cooling systems are the most effective means of removing allergens from room air. Single-room HEPA filter units are less efficient. Electrostatic precipitrons can be installed in central forced-air heating and cooling systems; precipitrons can substantially reduce not only house dust but also pollens and other airborne particles. Single-room air conditioners, which recirculate the air, can also effectively reduce pollen in the bedroom. Because single-room electrostatic precipitron units are less effective and may generate irritating ozone, they are not recommended. Mold-sensitive patients should be advised against raking leaves since the outdoor molds, especially *Alternaria* and *Cladosporium*, thrive on dead leaves and cut vegetation. Damp basements and wallpaper, as well as glass-enclosed shower stalls, are often sources of molds in the home, and removal of the source of moisture eliminates mold proliferation. If the moisture cannot be eliminated, mold retardants can be incorporated into the house paints or used in washing the walls. Molds in damp basements can be reduced by aerosolized paraformaldehyde or other antifungal agents. It is unfortunate that many patients lack the motivation to carry out adequate avoidance procedures that would control symptoms.

Pharmacologic Management

If patients cannot or do not want to avoid the allergens responsible for their symptoms, medications often provide relief. However, not all patients improve or respond to the same medicines for several reasons. Medications shown to be clinically useful in the therapy of allergic rhinitis differ in their mechanisms. These differences translate into differences in the patient's symptom improvement. Table 49–6 lists the various categories of medications used in the therapy of nasal allergy and compares their benefit in relieving the various symptoms of allergic rhinitis. Whereas one patient may respond to one family of medications, another may respond in part or not at all. For example, oral antihistamines are effective for the relief of sneezing, pruritus, and rhinorrhea but not for nasal congestion. If the patient with allergic rhinitis has nasal congestion in addition to the nasal itch and sneezing, the antihistamine provides only partial relief because it is not a decongestant. It would be appropriate to use combination therapy of an antihistamine with a decongestant or to use an intranasal corticosteroid. Allergic eye symptoms should not be ignored and often require combinations of therapy. Intranasal medications usually do little to relieve ocular allergy. Systemic (oral) antihistamine therapy and topical eye drops are needed for management of allergic conjunctivitis.

As outlined in the algorithm (see Table 49–5), mild intermittent symptoms can be controlled with antihistamines on an as-needed basis or with over-the-counter intranasal cromolyn, along with environmental control. If

TABLE 49–6. Comparison of Medications in Relieving Allergic Rhinitis Symptoms

Symptom	Oral Antihistamine	Intranasal Antihistamine	Oral or Nasal Decongestant	Nasal Steroid	Intranasal Anticholinergic	Intranasal Cromolyn	Allergen Immunotherapy
Sneezing	+	+	−	+	−	−	+
Itching	+	+	−	+	−	−	+
Rhinorrhea	+	+	+	+	+	+	+
Congestion	−	+	+	+	−	−	+
Conjunctivitis	+	−	−	−	−	−	+
Vasomotor rhinitis	−	−	+	+	+	−	−
Infectious rhinitis	−	−	+	−	+	−	−

symptoms are moderate to severe and persistent, the use of intranasal steroids along with a second-generation antihistamine is recommended.[2] Patients who do not respond adequately to environment control and pharmacotherapy should be referred to a specialist for allergy testing and considered for allergen immunotherapy. Severe persistent allergic rhinitis frequently is controlled with the combination of intranasal steroids and a second-generation antihistamine with decongestant. Recent studies suggest that montelukast may aid the management of allergic rhinitis, but this drug has not yet been approved by the FDA for this indication.[42] Occasionally, treatment with a short burst of oral corticosteroids may be required to control symptoms. Most clinicians do not recommend intranasal injection of corticosteroids or intramuscular steroid depot injection. Each category of medication will be discussed in greater detail.

Antihistamines

Antihistamines block the H_1 receptor and function by competing with histamine for H_1 receptors on cells. Antihistamines are often used as the first-line medication for treating mild allergic rhinitis and are currently the most prescribed treatment for allergic rhinitis. Most clinicians categorize them as first- and second-generation products. The first-generation antihistamines are lipophilic, cross the blood–brain barrier, and cause sedation. They have a shorter duration of action and have anticholinergic effects but are as effective as the second-generation antihistamines. First-generation agents are available in oral formulations, and lower doses are available without a prescription. First-generation antihistamines include diphenhydramine (Benadryl), azatadine (Optimine), clemastine (Tavist), chlorpheniramine (Chlor-Trimeton), brompheniramine (Dimetane), and hydroxyzine (Atarax, Vistaril). Many of these medications are available in combination with a decongestant or analgesic, or both. Antihistamines taken early in the morning and at bedtime may provide good symptomatic control of pruritus, sneezing, and rhinorrhea but do not relieve congestion or stuffiness. Additional doses may be taken at intervals of 4 to 6 hours. The effectiveness of classic antihistamines is frequently diminished by their side effects, which include drowsiness and anticholinergic effects. Patients should be warned against driving an automobile or operating machinery after taking first-generation antihistamines.

Second-generation antihistamines are preferred by most allergists because they are generally less sedating and do not interfere with school or work performance compared with the first-generation antihistamines. These newer agents are lipophobic, have a larger molecular size, possess an electrostatic charge, and do not readily enter the central nervous system. They have longer duration of action, lack the anticholinergic side effect profile of first-generation drugs, and are well tolerated by the elderly. Products currently approved by the U.S. Food and Drug Administration (FDA) include loratadine (Claritin); desloratadine (Clarinex), the metabolite of loratadine; cetirizine (Zyrtec), the metabolite of hydroxyzine; and fexofenadine (Allegra), the metabolite of terfenadine. Sedation is

similar to placebo (5%) in studies of loratadine, desloratadine, and fexofenadine. Cetirizine's sedation is greater and affects approximately 10% to 15% of patients. Each of these second-generation antihistamines is efficacious compared with placebo in double-blind, placebo-controlled studies. Data have also shown similar benefit from intranasal spray formulations of antihistamines Azelastine (Astelin) and levocabastine (Livostin).[35] However, 10% to 15% of patients complained that these intranasal antihistamines caused sedation. Astemizole (Hismanal) and terfenadine (Seldane) were the first second-generation antihistamines introduced and have been removed from the U.S. market because of drug–drug interactions and their association with torsades de pointes.

Antihistamine effectiveness is enhanced if taken prophylactically or at the onset of symptoms. Contrary to popular belief, tachyphylaxis does not develop and insufficient benefit is usually related to noncompliance. There are currently no double-blind, placebo-controlled, head-to-head trials that compare the clinical efficacy of the four available second-generation oral antihistamines. Several studies have compared two of the second-generation antihistamines with placebo and have described slight differences. These products and their dosages are outlined in Table 49–7.

Intranasal Corticosteroids

Intranasal (topical) corticosteroids (INCSs) are highly effective in the treatments of allergic rhinitis. It has been shown that each of the intranasal steroids is effective in reducing the nasal symptoms of itching, sneezing, rhinorrhea, and obstruction compared with placebo.[18] INCS can affect both the early-phase and late-phase allergic responses after experimental challenge with allergen. Prolonged treatment may inhibit allergen-induced late responses that are associated with the recruitment and activation of T-lymphocytes, T_H2 cytokine secretion, and eosinophilia.[21] Intranasal steroids have been shown to reduce the number of eosinophils and basophils in nasal lavages and decrease the number of activated lymphocytes and chemical mediators.[55] Use of INCSs as first-line therapy has been hampered by the misconception that they are unsafe or that they take a long time to take effect. Newer agents have higher lipid solubility, increased potency, a better safety profile, better efficacy, and a quicker onset of action. Examples of newer agents with these features include beclomethasone dipropionate (Vancenase, Beconase), budesonide (Rhinocort), flunisolide (Nasalide, Nasarel), fluticasone propionate (Flonase), mometasone furoate (Nasonex), and triamcinolone (Nasacort). Table 49–8 lists these intranasal steroids and their dosages. A 3- to 5-day course of a topical decongestant such as oxymetazoline may be used when starting INCS therapy in patients with severe allergic rhinitis to optimize INCS delivery to the nasal mucosa.

Studies comparing INCS with placebo showed decreased histamine levels in the nasal lavages of those treated with the steroids. In perennial rhinitis (allergic or nonallergic), fluticasone propionate was associated with significant improvements in nasal symptom scores, use of

TABLE 49–7. Formulations and Dosages of Selected First-Generation (Classic) H₁ Antagonists

H₁-Receptor Antagonist	Formulation	Recommended Dose
First-Generation		
Chlorpheniramine (Chlor-Trimeton)	Tablets: 4 mg, 8 mg, 12 mg Syrup: 2 mg/5 mL	Adult: 8–12 mg bid Child: 0–0.35 mg/kg/24 hr
Hydroxyzine	Capsules: 25 mg, 50 mg Syrup: 10 mg/5 mL	Adult: 25–50 mg bid Child: 2 mg/kg/24 hr
Diphenhydramine (Benadryl)	Capsules: 25 mg, 50 mg Elixir: 12.5 mg/5 mL Syrup: 6.25 mg/5 mL Parenteral solution: 50 mg/mL	Adult: 25–50 mg tid Child: 5 mg/kg/24 hr
Second-Generation		
Cetirizine (Zyrtec)	Tablets: 10 mg Syrup: 5 mg/5 mL	Adult: 10 mg/day Child: 2–6 yo: 2.5–5 mg/day >6 yo: 5–10 mg/day
Fexofenadine (Allegra)	Tablets: 30 mg, 60 mg, 180 mg	Adult: 60 mg bid or 180 mg/day Child: 6–11 yo: 30 mg bid >12 yo: 60 mg bid or 180 mg/day
Loratadine (Claritin)	Tablets: 10 mg Tablets: 10 mg (sublingual) Syrup: 1 mg/1 mL	Adult: 10 mg/day Child: >3 yo, <30 kg: 5 mg/day >3 yo, >30 kg: 10 mg/day
Desloratadine (Clarinex)	Tablets: 5 mg	Adult: 5 mg/day Child: ≥12 yo: 5 mg/day

rescue medications, and number of symptom-free days. This drug was similar in efficacy to beclomethasone dipropionate in both patient and physician assessments of changes in nasal symptoms.[75] At the end of a 3-month treatment period, both mometasone furoate (200 μg/day) and fluticasone propionate (200 μg/day) were reported to be equally effective by a patient diary in physician-rated total nasal symptom scores and number of symptom-free days.[49, 75] Both topical agents have been found to be effective in adults, adolescents, and children.[49, 75]

Concerns about the systemic side effects of steroids in children have led to numerous growth studies using intranasal steroids. In a year-long study of prepubertal children 6 to 9 years old with perennial allergic rhinitis treated with beclomethasone dipropionate, the overall growth rate was significantly slower (by 1 cm) than in the placebo-treated group. The difference in growth rate was evident as early as 1 month into treatment. No significant intragroup difference was found in the hypothalamic-pituitary-adrenal axis assessment.[67]

A similar 1-year study of 3- to 9-year-old prepubertal patients with perennial allergic rhinitis assessed treatment

TABLE 49–8. Formulations and Dosages of Intranasal Corticosteroids

Generic Name	Brand Name	Formulation	Pediatric Dose	Adult Dose
Beclomethasone dipropionate, monohydrate	Beconase AQ	Spray 42 μg	6–12 yo 1 spray bid°	>12 yo 1–2 sprays bid°
	Vancenase AQ	84 μg	>6 yo 1–2 sprays qd	1–2 sprays qd
Beclomethasone dipropionate	Beconase	Inhalation aerosol 42 μg	6–12 yo 1 spray bid	>12 yo 1 spray bid–qid
Budesonide	Rhinocort AQ	Spray 32 μg	>6 yo 1 spray qd	1–4 sprays qd
Budesonide	Rhinocort	Inhaler 50 μg	>6 yo 1 spray qd	2 sprays bid
Flunisolide	Nasarel	Solution 0.025%	6–14 yo 2 sprays bid	>14 yo 2 sprays bid
Fluticasone propionate	Flonase	Spray 50 μg	>4 yo 1 spray qd	1–2 sprays qd
Mometasone furoate, monohydrate	Nasonex	Spray 50 μg	3–11 yo 1 spray qd	>12 yo 2 sprays qd
Triamcinolone acetonide	Nasacort	Spray or inhaler 55 μg	6–12 yo 1 spray qd	>12 yo 2 sprays qd
	Tri-Nasal	50 μg	>12 yo 2 sprays qd	2 sprays qd

° In each nostril for all intranasal corticosteroids listed.

with mometasone furoate aqueous nasal spray (MFNS). After 1 year, no suppression of growth was detected in subjects treated with MFNS, and mean standing heights were actually higher in the MFNS group than in the placebo group at all time points.[63] Treatment with mometasone (25 μg, 100 μg, 200 μg) or placebo once daily in children 6 to 11 years old showed no significant differences among the three MFNS groups. However, as treatment continued past day 8, symptoms in children treated with 100 or 200 μg of MFNS once daily continued to improve. No differences in symptoms were noted between daily doses of 100 and 200 μg.[63]

Local adverse events associated with INCSs include rare nasal-septal perforation, usually related to improper administration (directing the spray toward the septum instead of to the lateral area of the nasal cavity). More common complaints are dissatisfaction with smell and taste and a drip sensation.

Decongestants

Decongestants contain sympathomimetic agents that activate α-adrenergic receptors and cause vasoconstriction, thus reducing nasal congestion (see Table 49–6). Available oral formulations include pseudoephedrine and phenylephrine. Citing a recent report on the risk of hemorrhagic stroke in patients receiving phenylpropanolamine, the FDA removed this drug from the market. The effective dose for pseudoephedrine is 15 mg/kg four times a day in children 2 to 6 years; 30 mg four times a day in children 6 to 12 years old; and 60 mg four times a day, or 120 mg in extended-release form twice a day, in patients older than 12 years. Unfortunately, some patients experience side effects with pseudoephedrine, including nervousness, irritability, tachycardia, palpitations, headache, and insomnia. These drugs should be used with caution as they may cause urinary retention and increased blood pressure in older patients and may cause prostate hypertrophy in men. Prolonged use of oral decongestants may lead to withdrawal symptoms of headache and fatigue when the drug is discontinued. Decongestants have limited action on the other symptoms of rhinitis, including rhinorrhea, sneezing, and itching. Combinations of antihistamines and decongestants provide patient convenience and additional relief of the symptoms of allergic rhinitis. Pseudoephedrine combined with fexofenadine (Allegra D) and loratadine (Claritin D) are examples of these products.

Mast Cell Stabilizers

Intranasal cromolyn sodium is a nonsteroid mast cell stabilizer that is available without a prescription. Although the mechanism of action remains uncertain, it has antiinflammatory properties and clearly blocks the early- and late-phase responses in a laboratory setting. This drug has been shown clinically to relieve sneezing, rhinorrhea, nasal congestion, and pruritus. In head-to-head clinical trials, however, intranasal corticosteroids are more effective than cromolyn.[79] Cromolyn has an excellent safety profile and may be used immediately prior to an anticipated exposure and should be administered four times a day. Intranasal cromolyn is considered first-line treatment for the pregnant patient with allergic rhinitis.

Leukotriene Receptor Antagonists

Several studies have identified clear increments in leukotriene levels in nasal lavage fluid in association with the immediate nasal response to allergen.[17] Nasal insufflation provocation studies show that both LTC_4 and LTD_4 induce an increase in nasal airway resistance as measured by rhinometry.[33] Two leukotriene receptor antagonists (montelukast and zafirlukast) are currently available in the United States for the therapy of asthma. Both selectively block the receptor that mediates the function of the various leukotrienes. In a multicenter, parallel-group, placebo-controlled 2-week trial of adult patients with spring pollen allergic rhinitis, Meltzer and associates showed that concomitant montelukast and loratadine provided effective treatment for seasonal allergic rhinitis symptoms and associated eye symptoms, with a safety profile similar to that of placebo. However, montelukast alone or loratadine alone did not provide significant improvement.[42] This study suggests that antileukotriene drugs are not likely to have a major role as a sole therapy in rhinitis. Nevertheless, some practitioners are using leukotriene modifiers either individually or combined with antihistamines to manage allergic rhinitis.

Oral Corticosteroids

A short burst (3 to 5 days) of oral steroids may be appropriate for some patients with severe symptoms or to gain control of symptoms during acute exacerbations. Long-term daily treatment with oral steroids is contraindicated; instead, maintenance control of symptoms with intranasal steroids is recommended. The intranasal steroids should be started at the same time as the short steroid burst.

Immunotherapy

If symptomatic drug therapy and avoidance cannot adequately control symptoms or inadvertently provoke significant side effects, immunotherapy (hyposensitization) with allergen solutions should be considered. Before proceeding with immunotherapy, the physician should institute a comprehensive investigation of the causative factors, and the patient's history of symptoms should be closely correlated with the presence of specific IgE antibodies, determined either by skin test results or by an in vitro immunoassay. Positive results of skin or blood tests that do not confirm the clinical presentation are considered to be false-positive reactions and are not used as criteria for immunotherapy. The use and abuse of these false-positive test results contribute to unnecessary and unsuccessful immunotherapy. In several double-blind studies, immunotherapy with solutions of pollen have proved effective in reducing the symptoms of allergic rhinitis.[61] Studies of the clinical efficacy of nonpollen immunotherapy with house dust, molds, and animal dander allergens in peren-

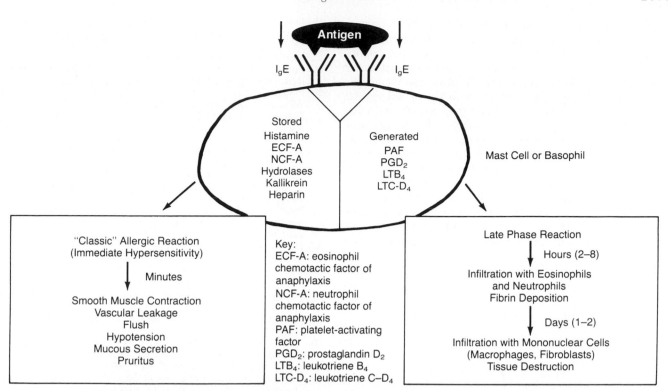

FIGURE 49–2. Mechanism of antigen-IgE reaction and indirect mediator release from mast cell or basophil in patients with allergic rhinitis. Note that both an early-phase (classic) and a late-phase reaction follow the antigen-IgE reaction. (From Skoner DP, Stillwagon PK, Friedman R, et al. Pediatric allergy and immunology. In: Zitelli BJ, Davis HW, eds. Atlas of Pediatric Physical Diagnosis. New York, Gower Medical Publishing, 1987, p 4.2.)

nial allergic rhinitis show that this therapy is effective, but these studies are not as conclusive as those reported for seasonal allergy.[47] There is no place for immunotherapy with allergens that can be removed or avoided; this is especially true for food allergens. The use of animal dander for immunotherapy should be limited to those individuals who cannot or do not avoid exposure to animal products. Even though it is not known precisely how immunotherapy promotes clinical improvement in allergic rhinitis, studies have shown a dose relationship of allergens administered, a decrease in specific IgE antibodies, an increase in IgG blocking antibodies, a decrease in TH_2 lymphocyte responses as well as IL-4, an increase in suppressor T-lymphocytes, and a reduction in the release of leukocyte histamine in vitro.[53] With a ragweed dose-response intranasal provocation challenge test, there was less histamine, prostaglandin D_2, and serine esterase in nasal washes obtained from ragweed-allergic patients after 2 years of immunotherapy than in placebo-treated ragweed-allergic patients.[16] After the decision is made to initiate immunotherapy, the clinician should carefully select the allergens to be employed. The clinical history should be correlated with skin test results, and the magnitude of the local skin reaction should be a guide to the appropriate does of allergen to initiate injection therapy. We do not agree with the suggestion that immunotherapy be initiated on the sole basis of the results of an in vitro serum immunoassay. Not only does this hypothesis lack adequate documentation and clinical confirmation, but it

also contributes to remote provision of clinical care by nonphysician health care providers who do not see or examine the patient. End-point titration skin testing has also been recommmended as a guide for initiation of immunotherapy, but this adds significantly to the cost of skin testing and also requires better documentation and confirmation before widespread acceptance.

The clinician begins with relatively weak subcutaneous injections of aqueous- or alum-precipitated solutions of allergens. These are gradually increased in volume and concentration to the maximally tolerated dose as indicated by a moderate local reaction. It is imperative that the clinician not induce systemic symptoms that provoke exacerbation of allergic rhinitis. After the maximally tolerated dose is reached, allergy injection therapy may be given on a perennial or year-round basis, during which the time interval between injections is increased from weekly to bimonthly to monthly. Another mode of immunotherapy consists of preseasonal weekly injections for several months before the season. Most patients with multiple seasonal sensitivities can more conveniently and practically be treated with a perennial schedule of injections every 4 weeks.

Immunotherapy may be expected to provided significant clinical improvement in 80% to 90% of patients with pollen-induced allergic rhinitis. If improvement is not obtained after a 2-year trial of immunotherapy, the patient should be re-evaluated and discontinuation of immunotherapy considered. Duration of immunotherapy injections in patients who achieve clinical benefits is dependent on their overall clinical response. When there is clinical improvement, patients should be given the opportunity to see whether this is sustained after discontinuing immunotherapy. They should also be given the chance to stop immunotherapy after about 5 years of injections. Many children with allergic rhinitis tend to improve with time but are not "growing out" of the allergy, because improvement is not related to physical growth but to an as-yet undefined cause. It has been shown that immunotherapy in children for seasonal allergic rhinitis may reduce their likelihood of developing pollen-induced asthma.[43] In general, patients with seasonal allergic rhinitis are more responsive to immunotherapy than those with the perennial variety. The factors responsible for clinical improvement are multiple. Certain patients experience exacerbations of symptoms after a spontaneous or induced remission for several seasons, and immunotherapy can be reinstituted without complication. Overall, the prognosis of allergic rhinitis, with or without therapy, is better than that for nonallergic and vasomotor rhinitis.

REFERENCES

1a. Abbas AK, Lichtman AH, Pober JS. Cellular and Molecular Immunology, 4th ed. Philadelphia, WB Saunders, 2000.
1b. Bielory L, Friedlaender MH. Allergic conjunctivitis. Immunol Allergy Clin North Am 17:19, 1997.
2. Bousquet J. Allergic rhinitis and its impact on asthma. J Allergy Clin Immunol 108:S147, 2001.
3. Braun-Fahrlander C, Gassner M, Grize L, et al. Prevalence of hay fever and allergic sensitization in farmer's children and their peers living in the same rural community. SCARPOL team. Swiss study on childhood allergy and respiratory symptoms with respect to air pollution. Clin Exp Allergy 29:28, 1999.
4. Broder I, Higgins MW, Mathews KP, et al. Epidemiology of asthma and allergic rhinitis in a total community, Tecumseh, Michigan. III. Second survey of community. J Allergy Clin Immunol 53:127, 1974.
5. Broide DH. Molecular and cellular mechanisms of allergic disease. J Allergy Clin Immunol 108(suppl):S65, 2001.
6. Brown EB, Ipsen J. Changes in severity of symptoms of asthma and allergic rhinitis due to air pollutants. J Allergy 41:254, 1968.
7. Burney PG, Luczynska C, Chinn S, et al. The European community respiratory health survey. Eur Respir J 7:954, 1994.
8. Caplin I, Haynes JT, Spohn J. Are nasal polyps an allergic phenomenon? Ann Allergy 29:631, 1971.
9. Coca AF, Cooke RA. On the classification of the phenomena of hypersensitiveness. J Immunol 8:163, 1923.
10. Cohen C. Genetic aspects of allergy. Med Clin North Am 58:25, 1974.
11. Coleman JW, Godfrey RC. The number and affinity of IgE receptors on dispersed human lung mast cells. Immunology 44:859, 1981.
12. Connell JT. Nasal mastocytosis. J Allergy 43:182, 1969.
13. Connell JT. Quantitative intranasal pollen challenges. III. Priming effect in allergic rhinitis. J Allergy 43:33, 1969.
14. Cookson WO, Sharp PA, Faux JA, et al. Linkage between immunoglobulin E responses underlying asthma and rhinitis and chromosome 11q. Lancet 1:1292, 1989.
15. Coombs RRA, Gell PGH. The classification of allergic reactions underlying disease. In Gell PGH, Coombs RRA, Lachman PH (eds). Clinical Aspects of Immunology, 3rd ed. Oxford, Blackwell, 1975, p 761.
16. Creticos PS, Marsh DG, Proud D, et al. Responses to ragweed pollen nasal challenge before and after immunotherapy. J Allergy Clin Immunol 84:197, 1989.
17. Creticos PS, Peters SP, Adkinson NF Jr, et al. Peptide leukotriene release after antigen challenge in patients sensitive to ragweed. N Engl J Med 310:1626, 1994.
18. Dykewicz MS, Fineman S, Skoner DP, et al. Diagnosis and management of rhinitis: complete guidelines of the joint task force on practice parameters in allergy, asthma, and immunology. Ann Allergy Asthma Immunol 81:478, 1998.
19. Fireman P. Eustachian tube obstruction and allergy: a role in otitis media with effusion. J Allergy Clin Immunol 76:137, 1985.
20. Fireman P. New concepts of the pathogenesis of otitis media with effusion. Immunol Allergy Clin North Am 7:133, 1987.
21. Fokkens W, Godthelp T, Holm A, et al. Allergic rhinitis and inflammation: the effect of nasal corticosteroid therapy. Allergy 52(suppl):29, 1997.
22. Friedman RA, Doyle WJ, Casselbrant ML, et al. Immunologic-mediated eustachian tube obstruction: a double-blind crossover study. J Allergy Clin Immunol 71:442, 1983.
23. Frigas E, Gleich GJ. The eosinophil and the pathophysiology of allergy. J Allergy Clin Immunol 77:527, 1986.
24. Handelman NI, Friday GA, Schwartz HJ, et al. Cromolyn sodium nasal solution in the prophylactic treatment of pollen-induced seasonal allergic rhinitis. J Allergy Clin Immunol 59:237, 1977.
25. Huggins KG, Brostoff J. Local production of specific IgE antibodies in allergic rhinitis patients with negative skin tests. Lancet 2:148, 1975.
26. Ingall M, Glaser J, Meltzer RS, et al. Allergic rhinitis in early infancy: review of the literature and report of a case in a newborn. Pediatrics 35:108, 1965.
27. Ishizaka K. Cellular events in the IgE antibody response. Adv Immunol 23:1, 1976.
28. Ishizaka K, Ishizaka T, Hornbrook MM. Physicochemical properties of reaginic antibody. V. Correlation of reaginic activity with IgE globulin antibody. J Immunol 97:840, 1966.
29. Johnstone DE. Study of the role of antigen dosage in the treatment of pollinosis and pollen asthma. Am J Dis Child 94:1, 1957.
30. Johnstone DE. Food allergy in children under two years of age. Pediatr Clin North Am 16:211, 1969.
31. Kaliner MA, Wasserman SI, Austen KF. Immunologic release of mediators from human nasal polyps. N Engl J Med 289:277, 1973.
32. Kita H, Adolphson CR, Gleich GJ. Biology of eosinophils. In Middleton E (ed). Allergy: Principles and Practice, 5th ed, vol 1. St Louis, Mosby, 1998, pp 242–261.
33. Knapp HR, Murray JJ. Leukotrienes as mediators of nasal inflammation. Adv Prostaglandin Thromboxane Leukot Res 22:279, 1994.
34. Konton-Karakitsos K, Salvaggio JE, Mathews KP. Comparative nasal absorption of allergens in atopic and nonatopic subjects. J Allergy Clin Immunol 55:241, 1975.
35. LaForce C, Dockhorn RJ, Prenner BM, et al. Safety and efficacy of azelastine nasal spray (Astelin NS) for seasonal allergic rhinitis. Ann Allergy Asthma Immunol 76:181, 1996.
36. Levine BB, Stember RH, Fotino M. Ragweed hayfever, genetic control and linkage to HLA haplotypes. Science 178:1201, 1972.
37. Lieberman P, Crawford L, Bjelland J, et al. Controlled study of the cytotoxic food test. J Allergy Clin Immunol 53:89, 1974.
38. Marsh DG, Bias WB, Hsu SH. Association of the HLA7 crossreacting group with a specific reaginic antibody response in allergic man. Science 179:691, 1973.
39. Marsh DG, Neely JD, Breazeale DR, et al. Linkage analysis of IL-4 and other chromosome 5q markers and total serum immunoglobulin E concentrations. Science 264:1152, 1994.
40. Marsh DG, Bias WB, Ishizaka K. Genetic control of basal immunoglobulin E level and its effect on specific reaginic sensitivity. Proc Natl Acad Sci U S A 71:3588, 1974.
41. Meltzer EO, Zeiger RS, Schatz M, et al. Chronic rhinitis in infants and children. Pediatr Clin North Am 30:847, 1983.
42. Meltzer EO, Malmstrom K, Lu S, et al. Concomitant montelukast and loratadine as treatment for seasonal allergic rhinitis: a randomized, placebo controlled clinical trial. J Allergy Clin Immunol 105:917, 2000.
43. Miller DL, Hirvonen T, Gitlin D. Synthesis of IgE by the human conceptus. J Allergy Clin Immunol 52:182, 1973.
44. Mygind N. Local effect of intranasal beclomethasone aerosol in hayfever. Br Med J 4:464, 1973.
45. Naclerio RM, Meier HL, Kagey-Sobotka A, et al. Mediator release after nasal antigen challenge with allergen. Am Rev Respir Dis 128:597, 1983.
46. Naclerio RM, Proud D, Togias AG, et al. Inflammatory mediators in late antigen-induced rhinitis. N Engl J Med 313:65, 1985.

47. Norman PS. Specific therapy in allergy. Pro (with reservations). Med Clin North Am 58:111, 1974.
48. Norman PS. In vivo methods of study of allergy: skin and mucosal tests, techniques and interpretation. In Middleton E, Reed CE, Ellis EF (eds). Allergy: Principles and Practice, vol I. St Louis, CV Mosby, 1978, p 256.
49. Onrust SV, Lamb HM. Mometasone furoate. A review of its intranasal use in allergic rhinitis. Drugs 56:725, 1998.
50. Otsuka H, Denburg J, Dolovich J, et al. Heterogeneity of the metachromatic cells in the human nose. Significance of mucosal mast cells. J Allergy Clin Immunol 76:695, 1985.
51. Otsuka H, Dolovich J, Befus AD, et al. Basophilic cell progenitors, nasal metachromatic cells, and peripheral blood basophils in ragweed-allergic patients. J Allergy Clin Immunol 78:365, 1986.
52. Paton WDM. Receptors for histamine. In Schacter M (ed). Histamine and Antihistamines, vol I, International Encyclopedia of Pharmacology and Therapeutics. Oxford, Pergamon Press, 1973.
53. Patterson R, Lieberman P, Irons JS, et al. Immunotherapy. In Middleton E, Reed CE, Ellis EF (eds). Allergy: Principles and Practice, vol II. St Louis, CV Mosby, 1978, p 877.
54. Pearlman DS. Pathophysiology of the inflammatory response. J Allergy Clin Immunol 104(suppl):S132, 1999.
55. Pipkorn U, Proud D, Lichtenstein LM, et al. Inhibition of mediator release in allergic rhinitis by pretreatment with topical glucocorticoids. N Engl J Med 316:1506, 1987.
56. Prausnitz C, Küstner H. Studies uber überemphfindlichkeit. Centralbl Baktinol Abt Orig 86:160, 1921.
57. Rappaport BF, Sampter M, Catchpole HR, et al. The mucoproteins of the nasal mucosa of allergic patients before and after treatment with corticotropin. J Allergy 24:35, 1953.
58. Richerson HB, Seebohn PM. Nasal airway response to exercise. J Allergy 41:269, 1968.
59. Riley JF, West GB. The presence of histamine in mast cells. J Physiol (Lond) 120:528, 1953.
60. Rundcrantz A. Postural variations of nasal patency. Acta Otolaryngol (Stockh) 68:1, 1969.
61. Sadan N, Rhyne MB, Mellitis ED, et al. Immunotherapy of pollinosis in children. N Engl J Med 280:623, 1969.
62. Salvaggio JE, Cavanaugh JJA, Lowell FC, et al. A comparison of immunologic responses of normal and atopic individuals to intranasally administered antigen. J Allergy 35:62, 1964.
63. Schenkel EJ, Skoner DP, Bronsky EF, et al. Absence of growth retardation in children with perennial allergic rhinitis after one year treatment with mometasone furoate aqueous nasal spray. Pediatrics 105:E22, 2000.
64. Sibbald B, Strachan D. Epidemiology of rhinitis. In Busse W, Holgate S (eds). Asthma and Rhinitis. London, Blackwell Scientific, 1995, pp 32–43.
65. Skoner DP. Allergic rhinitis: definition, epidemiology, pathophysiology, detection, and diagnosis. J Allergy Clin Immunol 108(suppl):S2, 2001.
66. Skoner DP, Doyle WP, Fireman P. Eustachian tube obstruction (ETO) after histamine nasal provocation: with double-blind dose regimen study. J Allergy Clin Immunol 79:27, 1987.
67. Skoner DP, Rachelefsky GS, Meltaer EO, et al. Detection of growth suppression during treatment with intranasal beclomethasone dipropionate. Pediatrics 105:415, 2000.
68. Solomon WR, Mathews KP. Aerobiology and inhalant allergens. In Middleton E, Reed CE, Ellis EF (eds). Allergy: Principles and Practice, vol II. St Louis, CV Mosby, 1978, p 899.
69. Stillwagon PK, Doyle WJ, Fireman P. Effect of an antihistamine/decongestant on nasal and eustachian tube function following intranasal pollen challenge. Ann Allergy 58:442, 1987.
70. Stillwagon PK, Skoner DP, Chamovitz A, et al. Eustachian tube function and allergic rhinitis during pollen season [abstract]. J Allergy Clin Immunol 75:197, 1985.
71. Strachan D. Hay fever, hygiene, and household size. Br Med J 299:1259, 1989.
72. Strachan DP: Epidemiology of hay fever: towards a community diagnosis. Clin Exp Allergy 25:296–303, 1995.
73. Townley RG, Dennis M, Itkin IH. Comparative action of methacholine, histamine, and pollen antigens in subjects with hay fever and patients with bronchial asthma. J Allergy 36:121, 1965.
74. Turkeltaub PC, Gergen PJ. Prevalence of upper and lower respiratory conditions in the US population by social and environmental factors: data from the second National Health and Nutrition Examination Survey, 1976–1980 (NHANES II). Ann Allergy 67:147, 1991.
75. Wiseman LR, Benfield P. Intranasal fluticasone propionate. A reappraisal of its pharmacology and clinical efficacy in the treatment of rhinitis. Drug 53:885, 1997.
76. von Pirquet C. Allergie. Munch Med Wochenschr 53:1457, 1906.
77. Voorhorst R, Spieksma FTM, Varekamp H, et al. The house dust mite (Dermatophagoides pteronyssinus) and the allergens it produces identify with the house dust allergen. J Allergy 39:325, 1967.
78. Wasserman SI, Goetzl EJ, Austen KF. Inactivation of human SRSA by intact human eosinophils and by eosinophil arylsulfatase. J Allergy Clin Immunol 55:72, 1975.
79. Welsh PW, Stricker WE, Chu CP, et al. Efficacy of beclomethasone nasal solution, flunisolide, and cromolyn in relieving symptoms of ragweed allergy. Mayo Clin Proc 62:125, 1987.
80. Wolf S, Holmes TH, Treuting T, et al. An experimental approach to psychosomatic phenomenon in rhinitis and asthma. J Allergy 21:1, 1950.
81. Wright AI, Holberg CJ, Martinez FD, et al. Epidemiology of physician-diagnosed allergic rhinitis in childhood. Pediatrics 94:895, 1994.
82. Yuninger JW, Gleich G. Impact and discovery of IgE in practice of allergy. Pediatr Clin North Am 22:3, 1975.

The Mouth, Pharynx, and Esophagus

50

Embryology and Anatomy of the Mouth, Pharynx, and Esophagus

Nira A. Goldstein, M.D., and Sharon M. Tomaski, M.D.

The complex process of cephalogenesis begins shortly after conception and continues throughout gestation. With the expansion of perinatology and the advent of fetal surgery, the pediatric clinician must possess a solid embryologic expertise to enhance the diagnosis and treatment of congenital anomalies. This chapter focuses on applied embryology of the mouth, pharynx, and esophagus. Special emphasis is placed on newborn and pediatric anatomy of these regions. Major congenital anomalies are highlighted and pediatric diagnostic imaging findings are discussed. Current developments in fetal craniofacial surgery are presented.

Recent advances in molecular biology have enhanced the understanding of embryogenesis. During the current renaissance in developmental anatomy, scientists continue to demonstrate that the traditional view of embryonic development, with emphasis on qualitative structure and relation, is grossly inadequate to explain the dynamic nature of morphogenesis. In recent years, animal studies have demonstrated that genetic and environmental factors play a role in craniofacial development. In addition, determinants of normal facial structure appear to be coded within DNA and are based on a timed expression of position, structural genes, and regulatory genes.[47, 88] A highly conserved cluster of homeotic genes known as *HOX* genes, along with more recently evolved genes, known as *EUX* and *PAX* genes, are believed to control temporal and spatial patterning in the head and neck region.[49, 70–72, 88, 91] These determinants require complex cell-matrix and cell-cell interactions, including cell proliferation and migration, programmed cell death, induction,

differentiation, fusion, and diffusion among cells of many lineages.[71, 72, 88, 91] Finally, several morphogens, including fibronectin, hyaluronidase, and numerous growth factors, are believed to contribute to growth, differentiation, and spatial patterning in the craniofacial region.[2, 10, 11, 15, 16, 23, 24, 76, 84, 87, 91, 92, 102] Interestingly, given morphogens may have different functions in different phases of development in a given cell type.[88] A proposed schema of embryogenesis is shown in Figure 50–1. The embryonic period, i.e., gestational weeks 4 to 8, is the key time for organogenesis. Craniofacial malformations arise from the misregulation of normally coordinated tissue patterning, cell fate determination, and differentiation of specific cell types.[73, 91] Various head and neck structures arise from the three primitive germ cell layers: endoderm, mesoderm, and ectoderm. The craniofacial derivatives for each layer are summarized in Table 50–1.

Mouth

Roof of the Mouth

The embryogenesis of the palate can be divided into two distinct phases: formation of the primary palate followed by formation of the secondary palate.

Primary Palate

The primary palate is the embryonic structure that separates the oral and nasal cavities anteriorly. Eventually, it forms portions of the upper lip, premaxilla (maxillary al-

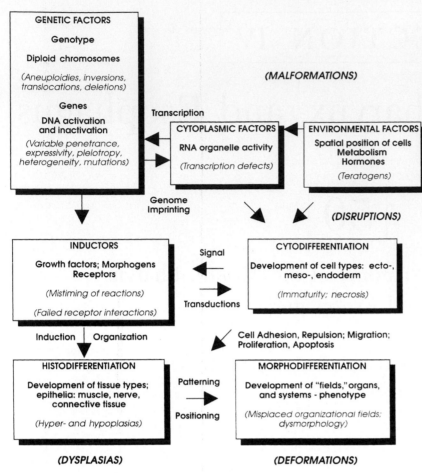

FIGURE 50–1. Schema of embryogenesis. (From Sperber GH. Craniofacial Embryology, 4th ed. Oxford, Butterworth-Heinemann, 1993.)

TABLE 50–1. Craniofacial Derivatives of the Three Primitive Germ Layers

Germ Layer	Derivatives	Function
Ectoderm	Central nervous system Peripheral nervous system Sensory epithelium of ear, nose, eye Skin and appendages Enamel of teeth	Gives rise to organs and structures that maintain contact with outside world.
Mesoderm		Gives rise to mesenchyme for formation of head region.
Para-axial plate mesoderm	Walls and floor of brain case Voluntary craniofacial muscles Dermis and connective tissue in dorsal head region	
Lateral plate mesoderm	Arytenoid and cricoid cartilages Laryngeal connective tissue	
Neural crest	Midfacial and pharyngeal arch skeletal structures, connective tissue, neural tissue, and glandular stroma	
Endoderm	Foregut Thyroid gland Parathyroid gland Eustachian tube Tympanic cavity	Gives rise to epithelial lining of gastrointestinal and respiratory tract.

Adapted from Sadler TW. Langman's Medical Embryology, 6th ed. Baltimore, Williams & Wilkins, 1990.

FIGURE 50–2. Human embryo at 3.5 weeks' gestation. *A,* Lateral view. *B,* Anterior view. The stomodeum is initially closed off by the buccopharyngeal membrane, which ruptures at 3.5 weeks. (Adapted from an original painting by Frank H. Netter, MD, from Clinical Symposia, copyright CIBA Pharmaceutical Co, Division of CIBA-Geigy Corp.)

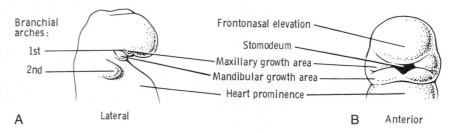

veolar processes), and hard palate anterior to the incisive foramen. In the human embryo, primary palate formation occurs between weeks 4 and 7 and is largely completed before secondary palate formation.

The face develops as a result of these five facial prominences as they envelop the primitive mouth (stomodeum) (Fig. 50–2). Emergence of these facial processes early in the fourth week coincides with the onset of palatal development. The facial prominences include unpaired frontonasal prominences, along with paired maxillary and mandibular prominences. During week 4, the unpaired frontonasal prominence forms and enlarges as a result of neural crest cell migration and proliferation. This becomes the midface region. The paired maxillary and mandibular prominences arise from the first pharyngeal arch and likewise enlarge because of neural crest cell migration and proliferation. A set of epithelial-mesenchymal interactions is believed to be essential for proper outgrowth and pattern formation of these facial primordia.[102] In addition, endogenous retinoids are postulated to act as signaling substances in facial primordia pattern formation.[102]

Nasal placodes, which are ectodermal thickenings on the lateral aspect of the frontonasal prominence, appear as a result of induction by the olfactory nerves. On day 33 (4.7 weeks), this area around the future nose is induced to elevate and undergo differential cell growth. In this way, the medial and lateral nasal prominences appear by day 35 (5 weeks). The nasal placodes then invaginate and form the nasal pits (Fig. 50–3). During days 42 to 49 (weeks 6 and 7), the maxillary prominences enlarge and grow medially, forcing the medial nasal prominences toward the midline. On day 48 (week 7), the medial nasal prominences merge with each other in the midline. This midline fusion forms the tip of the nose, the central portion of the upper lip, and the median tuberculum and philtrum of the upper lip. At a deeper level, the premaxilla (median part of the maxillary bone and its four incisor teeth) and the primary palate (triangular primary palate) are formed. Concurrently, the medial nasal prominence merges with the maxillary prominence to form the lateral

portion of the upper lip and the maxilla. Thus, this fusion of the medial nasal and maxillary prominences results in separation of the nasal pits (primitive nose) from the stomodeum (primitive mouth). These fusions also provide upper jaw and lip continuity.

Superior to this, the primitive nares are formed via programmed cell death between the medial and lateral nasal prominences. Rupture of the oronasal membrane on day 44 (week 6.3) results in the opening of a respiratory passage from the nostril (posterior nares) through the primary choana to the pharynx.[23] Laterally, on either side, the lateral nasal prominence fuses with the maxillary prominence to form the nasal ala. During the fusion of the lateral nasal and maxillary prominences, an epithelial cord becomes buried within this mesenchyme and results in formation of the nasolacrimal duct. The duct becomes patent as a result of programmed cell death. It is important to note that the lateral nasal prominences do not contribute to upper lip formation.

An ectodermal ingrowth along the edge of the upper jaw is called the *labiodental lamina.* The center of this epithelial band disintegrates, leaving a cavity that forms the vestibule of the mouth and lies between the lips and teeth. In the midline, the cavity is incomplete, forming the frenulum. The shelves created are called the *anterior labiodental lamina* and the *posterior dental lamina.* The former becomes the upper lip; the latter becomes the alveolar process. Figure 50–4 shows the anatomy of the structures derived from the primary palate.

Current primary palate morphogenetic research focuses on exactly how these prominences unite. Investigators agree that on about day 37 (week 5.2), the facial prominences responsible for primary palate development make initial contact by means of an epithelial seam, known as the *nasal fin.* On day 41 (week 5.9), a portion of the nasal fin gets replaced by mesenchyme. There are two popular theories regarding the mechanism of this replacement. In the *fusion* theory, it is postulated that an epithelial seam forms and the epithelial cells quickly degenerate or transform into mesenchyme.[23, 33] In the *merging* theory, it is believed that mesenchymal growth and

FIGURE 50–3. Human embryo at 5 weeks. *A,* Lateral view. *B,* Anterior view. Note the formation of the medial and lateral prominences around the nasal pit. (Adapted from Clinical Symposia, copyright CIBA Pharmaceutical Co, Division of CIBA-Geigy Corp.)

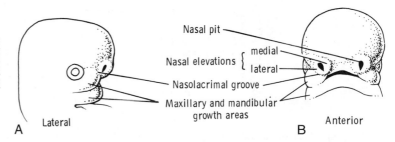

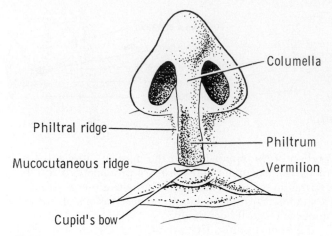

FIGURE 50–4. Anatomy of the structures derived from the primary palate. (Adapted from Clinical Symposia, copyright CIBA Pharmaceutical Co, Division of CIBA-Geigy Corp.)

proliferation deep to the epithelial layer squeezes the epithelium out of the way.[75]

In a 1992 study of human embryos with partial cleft palates, excessive epithelial tissue and a reduction of mesenchymal tissue were noted in the region of the epithelial seam.[23]

Secondary Palate

Secondary palate formation, which occurs between weeks 6.5 and 10, can be broken down into three stages: growth, shelf elevation, and fusion. Genesis of the secondary palate commences after completion of primary palate development. The secondary palate is the portion of the palate posterior to the incisive foramen. It forms as a result of fusion of the two paired outgrowths of the maxillary prominences. These outgrowths, known as bilateral palatal shelves, emerge from the medial aspect of the paired maxillary processes. Initially, the palatal shelves grow vertically down the sides of the tongue (Fig. 50–5). The reason for this initial vertical growth is as yet unknown. In week 7, these shelves elevate quickly to occupy a horizontal position above the dorsum of the tongue

(Fig. 50–6). Shelf elevation is a rapid event, occurring over minutes to hours[11, 30, 32] and is thought to be mainly driven by accumulation of hyaluronic acid.[11, 30, 32, 76] Thus, an intrinsic "shelf-elevating" force is noted. This glycosaminoglycan is synthesized by the palatal mesenchyme cells and is known to bind numerous water molecules. The accumulation and subsequent hydration of the hyaluronic acid is thought to be the mechanism of this palatal shelf elevation, since, as it draws water into the extracellular matrix, it changes the size and orientation of the palatal shelves.[10] Transforming growth factor (TGF)-beta and epidermal growth factor have been shown to stimulate production of the hyaluronic acid.[24, 25, 84] Next, a midline epithelial seam is formed as the medial edge epithelia of the two palatal shelves fuse (Fig. 50–7). This epithelial seam then rapidly degenerates by programmed cell death, and some of the epithelial seam cells migrate deeper into the mesenchyme.[32] During this programmed epithelial cell seam death, the epithelia on the nasal aspect of the palate differentiate into pseudostratified ciliated columnar cells. At the same time, epithelial cells on the oral aspect of the palate differentiate into stratified squamous nonkeratinizing cells.[32] Epithelial differentiation is believed to be specified by the underlying mesenchyme as a result of extracellular matrix as well as local growth factors. Collagen, tenascin, epidermal growth factor, TGF-alpha and -beta, platelet-derived growth factor, and fibroblast growth factor contribute to the process.[24, 32, 84, 92] Posteriorly, the palatal shelves fuse with each other, while anteriorly they fuse with the triangular primary palate, and superiorly with the nasal septum. The area where the three palatal components fuse together is delineated by the incisive papilla, which overlies the incisive foramen. Palatal ossification (hard palate) commences in week 8, and at 10.5 weeks the midpalatal suture is seen. By about week 10, formation of the palate is complete.[90]

Myogenic mesenchymal tissue of the first, second, and fourth branchial arches migrates into the soft palate region and differentiates into palatal and faucial musculature (Table 50–2). The tensor veli palatini develops first at day 40, the palatopharyngeus at day 45, and the levator veli palatini at day 66. The palatoglossus is first seen during the 9th week, and the uvular muscle appears dur-

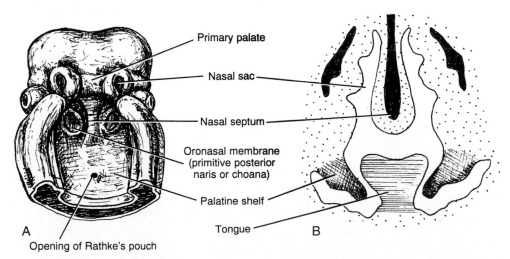

FIGURE 50–5. Roof of the oral cavity in a 6.5-week embryo. *A,* Ventral view. *B,* Frontal section. Note that the palatal shelves are in a vertical position on either side of the tongue. (Adapted from Sadler TW. Langman's Medical Embryology, 6th ed. Baltimore, Williams & Wilkins, 1990, pp 317, 318.)

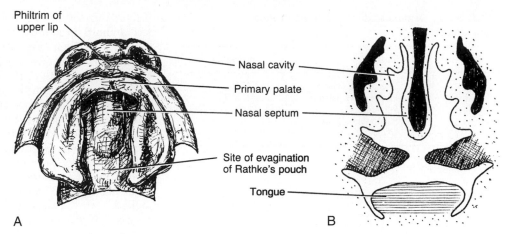

FIGURE 50–6. Roof of the oral cavity in a 7.5-week embryo. *A,* Ventral view. *B,* Frontal section. Note that the palatal shelves have moved into a horizontal position. (Adapted from Sadler TW. Langman's Medical Embryology, 6th ed. Baltimore, Williams & Wilkins, 1990, pp 317, 318.)

ing week 11. After its development from the tongue musculature during week 11, the palatoglossus attaches to the soft palate.

Palatal Anomalies

Cleft lip is due to failure of fusion between the medial nasal prominence and the maxillary prominence or lateral nasal prominence, or both. The typical cleft lip is due to fusion failure between the medial nasal process and maxillary prominences. Failure of formation of the frontonasal prominence results in a rare midline cleft lip. There are many theories regarding the pathogenesis of cleft lip. Some investigators posit that a delay in the neural crest cell migration destined to form the facial prominences results in lack of critical mass of these cells.[48, 71, 72] A second hypothesis suggests that reduced proliferation occurs after formation of normal amounts of neural crest mesenchyme.[31] The third theory is that there may be interference with growth of frontonasal process mesenchyme in late stages of development.[23] A final theory maintains that postclosure opening occurs as a result of vascular hemorrhage.[90]

Cleft palate, including the lesser anomalies of submucous cleft palate and bifid uvula, can result from aberrance of any step in palatal development. Defects in palatal shelf growth, delayed or failed shelf elevation, defective shelf fusion, failure of medial epithelial seam

cell death, postfusion rupture, and failure of mesenchymal consolidation and differentiation are postulated mechanisms of cleft palate (see Chap. 57)[31, 32]

The cause of cleft lip and palate is classically thought to be multifactorial. Cleft lip, with or without cleft palate, is believed to be distinct from cleft palate alone.[34] Current research suggests that nonsyndromic clefting may be the result of certain major genes in a subpopulation of individuals and families. Genetic investigations suggest that the TGF-alpha locus on the short arm of human chromosome 2 at band p13 or the retinoic acid receptor gene may play a role in some cases of cleft lip or palate.[2, 15, 16] While environmental agents have been hypothesized to play a role in cleft lip and palate, isolated clefting has not been proved to be a result of any single toxic prenatal exposure.[47]

A number of superficial cysts may appear on the newborn palate secondary to entrapment of epithelial rests during fusion. These include (1) Epstein pearls, which are located along the median raphe of the hard palate and junction of the hard and soft palate; (2) Bohn nodules, small mucosal gland retention cysts on the buccal and lingual aspects of the alveolar ridges; and (3) dental lamina cysts on the crests of the alveolar ridges. These usually regress by the third month of postnatal life.[90] Overgrowth of midpalatal bone in utero results in torus palatinus, which may enlarge in adulthood and cause denture problems.[99] A more complete discussion of lip and

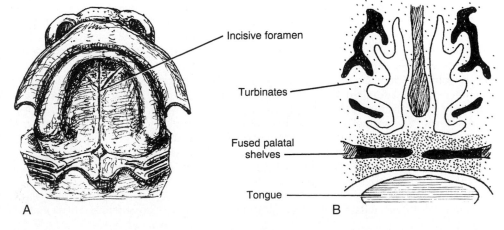

FIGURE 50–7. Roof of the oral cavity in a 8.5-week embryo. *A,* Ventral view. *B,* Frontal section. Note the incisive foramen between the primary and secondary palates. (Adapted from Sadler TW. Langman's Medical Embryology, 6th ed. Baltimore, Williams & Wilkins, 1990, pp 317, 318.)

TABLE 50–2. Origins and Innervations of Palatal Musculature

Arch	Muscle	Innervation
First	Tensor veli palatini	CN V
Second	Levator veli palatini	CN VII
Fourth	Palatoglossus	Pharyngeal plexus
	Palatopharyngeus	
	Uvular	

CN, cranial nerve.

palatal pathologic conditions is found elsewhere in the text.

Newborn Anatomy

Intimate knowledge of lip and palatal anatomy is essential, especially in regard to surgical reapproximation after congenital or traumatic deformity.

The upper lip (see Fig. 50–4) contains the orbicularis oris muscle, which originates from the second branchial arch and is thereby innervated by the facial nerve. In the medial line of the lip, this muscle joins its mirror image. It passes around the mouth without any fascial covering and is in contact anteriorly with the skin and posteriorly with the mucous membrane. Anatomically and functionally, the orbicularis oris has an internal and an external circle of fibers. The internal portion passes between both corners of the mouth and is a true mouth constrictor. The external portion enables mouth opening and allows diminutive expressions of the upper and lower lips. Sensation is supplied by the inferior orbital nerve, a branch of the maxillary division of the trigeminal nerve. The blood supply is from the paired superior labial arteries arising from the facial arteries, which lie beneath the mucous membrane. While there are numerous mucous and sweat glands in the lip, the vermilion zone is devoid of glands and hair follicles. The vermilion, which is red because of the highly vascular connective tissue papillae lying beneath the surface and an increased translucency of the epithelial layers, is lined with nonkeratinizing squamous epithelium. The junction between the skin and the vermilion is known as the *mucocutaneous ridge*. This thick white line must be carefully approximated if it has been interrupted. The arch of the mucocutaneous ridge is broken by the slight concavity of the "Cupid's bow." Extending from this region to the columella is a vertical depression known as the philtrum. The philtrum originates during primary palatal formation from the fused medial nasal processes. The distinctly protruding cristae philtri (philtral ridges), which arose from the maxillary prominences, sit lateral to the philtrum. The minor projection of the vermilion below Cupid's bow is the tubercle. At term, the normal mouth width (intercommissural distance) is 2.6 to 2.7 cm.[50, 65] The normal philtrum length has been reported to be 0.76 cm in Indians[50] and 1.07 in Israeli newborns.[65] The lower lip is almost identical anatomically, with the exception of the Cupid's bow and philtral regions.

A normal infant palate has three portions: the hard palate, the soft palate, and the uvula. A term newborn has a short, broad hard palate measuring approximately 2.3 cm by 2.2 cm (Fig. 50–8).[18, 19, 90] The bony portion is a symmetric structure whose division is based on the embryonic origin of the primary and secondary palate. Thus, structures anterior to the incisive foramen are considered the primary palate; these include the premaxilla, the alveolus, and the lip. In the neonate, a tiny, conical soft tissue projection known as the incisive papilla overlies the incisive foramen. Secondary palate structures include the paired maxillary prominences, palatine bones, and pterygoid plates. Compared with the deeply arched V-shaped adult palate, the U-shaped neonatal palate is only slightly arched.[18, 19, 90] Palatal depth increases as tooth eruption occurs.[47, 90] Palatal and alveolar lining consists of a nonciliated squamous epithelium. The numerous transverse folds noted in the mucosa of the infant palate are thought to aid in securing the nipple during feeding and eventually involute once the suckling period ceases.[18, 90] Most postnatal growth of the lower facial skeleton is secondary to lateral expansion of the hard palate and maxillary sinus development. Until age 7 years, the palate grows laterally by appositional growth, and in late childhood it is more long than wide.[90] Posterior appositional growth continues through adolescence, and complete fusion of the midpalatal suture occurs at approximately 30 years of age.[51] From infancy through adolescence, the nasal surface of the palate resorbs and the oral surface enlarges as a result of continuous bone remodeling of the palate. This produces a lowering of the palate and increased nasal capacity.[90]

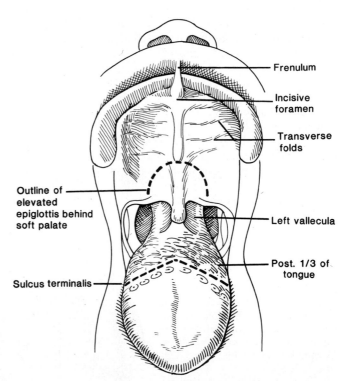

FIGURE 50–8. Newborn U-shaped palate and tongue. Note the high position of epiglottis and that the entire tongue is in the oral cavity. (Adapted from an original painting by Frank H. Netter, M.D., from Clinical Symposia, copyright CIBA Pharmaceutical Co, Division of CIBA-Geigy Corp.)

Six muscles attach to the palate: levator veli palatini, constrictor pharyngis superior, uvular, palatopharyngeus, palatoglossus, and tensor veli palatini. The three muscles believed to contribute the most to velopharyngeal competence are the uvular, the levator veli palatini, and the constrictor pharyngis superior. The palatopharyngeus and superior constrictor muscles are responsible for medial displacement of the pharyngeal wall, whereas the palatopharyngeus and palatoglossus effect downward displacement of the palate. The palatoglossus muscle attaches to the lateral border of the posterior tongue and forms the anterior tonsillar pillar. The palatopharyngeus muscle attaches to the superior cornus of the thyroid cartilage and forms the posterior tonsillar pillar. The tendon of the tensor veli palatini hooks around the hamulus of the pterygoid plates bilaterally, and the aponeurosis of this muscle inserts along the posterior border of the hard palate. The action of this muscle is to improve ventilation and drainage of the eustachian tube.

The hard palate's blood supply is from the anterior palatine artery and is transmitted through the greater palatine foramen via the internal maxillary artery. The soft palate is supplied by the descending branch of the palatine artery from the internal maxillary artery, the ascending palatine branch of the ascending pharyngeal artery (off the external carotid artery), and feeder vessels from the tonsillar branch of the dorsal lingual artery. Palatal sensation is derived from the maxillary division of the trigeminal nerve via the greater and lesser palatine nerves, as well as the nasopalatine nerves as they emerge from the incisive foramina.

The high position of the epiglottis allows direct contact with the soft palate and formation of a seal, permitting the infant to eat and breathe at the same time, as depicted in Figure 50–8. Lacerations or other injuries to the palate and oral cavity are very rare in infants; if they are seen in the absence of a history of trauma, the possibility of child abuse should be considered.[61]

Floor of Mouth

Tongue

The tongue has a dual source of origin: the anterior two thirds is of ectodermal origin (primitive mouth) and the posterior one third is of endodermal origin (foregut). The epithelium of the lips, gum, and tooth enamel is ectodermal and derived from the walls of the stomodeum.

Before the rupture of the buccopharyngeal membrane in the human embryo at 3.5 weeks, the stomodeum (primitive mouth) does not communicate with the foregut (primitive pharynx) (Fig. 50–9). Morphogenesis begins during week 4 when, from the first branchial arch, two paired lateral lingual swellings and the central tuberculum impar appear on the floor of the oral cavity and pharynx (Fig. 50–10). These lingual swellings subsequently overgrow the tuberculum impar and fuse together, creating the anterior two thirds of the tongue body. The point of fusion is a poorly vascularized median raphe. The sensory innervation of this part of the tongue is the trigeminal nerve, the nerve of the first arch. The chorda tympani branch of the facial nerve provides taste (special sensory) to the anterior portion of the tongue. At the same time, the mesoderm of the second, the third, and a portion of the fourth pharyngeal arches contributes a second median swelling known as the hypobranchial eminence, or copula. This ultimately becomes the posterior third, or root, of the tongue. The nerves of the third and fourth arches, the glossopharyngeal and vagus nerves, respectively, supply this part of the tongue. The V-shaped groove called the sulcus terminalis separates the anterior two thirds and posterior one third of the tongue.

The foramen caecum is a blind depression in the midline at the apex of the V-shaped line formed by the circumvallate papillae (Fig. 50–11). The sulcus terminalis extends across the entire base of the tongue along the line of these papillae. These structures lie in between the second and third branchial arch derivatives. The sulcus is where the original buccopharyngeal membrane was in the floor of the mouth before its rupture at 3.5 weeks, and the palatoglossal fold is the remnant of where the buccopharyngeal membrane once stood. Posterior to these structures, the epithelium is derived from the primitive foregut. The thyroid gland originates from the foramen caecum and migrates inferiorly; this is why thyroid tissue can be found anywhere along its descent path in the neck. After merging of the two lingual swellings, the tongue is a fold of mucous membrane and becomes a sac. During week 7, the sac becomes filled with mesoderm that is derived from the first four occipital somites. The intrinsic tongue musculature with its own hypoglossal

FIGURE 50–9. Sagittal section of an embryo at 3 weeks' gestation just before rupture of the buccopharyngeal membrane. (Adapted from Sadler TW. Langman's Medical Embryology, 6th ed. Baltimore, Williams & Wilkins, 1990, p 180.)

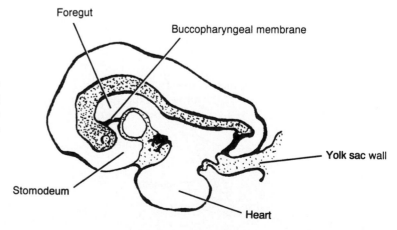

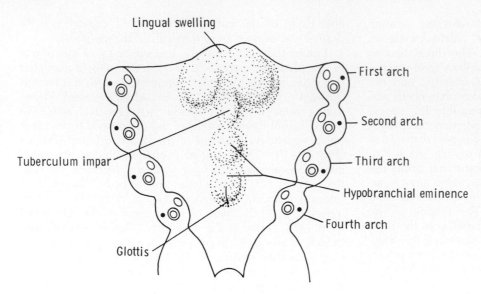

FIGURE 50–10. Superior view of the tongue at 5 weeks' gestation. (Adapted from an original painting by Frank H. Netter, M.D., from Clinical Symposia, copyright CIBA Pharmaceutical Co, Division of CIBA-Geigy Corp.)

nerve supply is thus formed. The circumvallate papillae develop over weeks 8 to 20, and the filiform and fungiform papillae are first seen at week 11. Other parts of the floor of the mouth—the gingiva, gums, and lower lip— are ectodermal derivatives of the first (mandibular) arch. Fusion of the paired mandibular prominences results in the lower lip and lower jaw. The commissures of the mouth are a result of lateral merging of the maxillary and mandibular prominences.

Salivary Glands

The major salivary glands are ectodermal derivatives, originating in the floor of the mouth as epithelial buds between approximately the sixth and the eighth week of fetal life. All three of these glands arise from the first pharyngeal pouch. Morphogenesis of the parotid gland occurs first (5.5 weeks), followed by the submandibular

gland (6 weeks) and sublingual gland (8 weeks). In general, they grow as a branching system of solid ducts ending in acini. Secondarily, by the sixth fetal month, the ducts become hollow and the acini are partially differentiated. Although differentiation of the acini is not completed until after birth, saliva is secreted by the fetus.[3]

The detailed morphogenesis of the human submandibular gland has recently been delineated.[27, 52, 64] The medial paralingual groove constitutes the anlage of the submandibular gland; it first appears at week 6. Its anterior three quarters gives rise to the Wharton duct and its posterior quarter gives rise to the submandibular gland proper.[64] The sublingual process of the submandibular gland originates from a lateral ectodermal bud of the anlage of the submandibular gland, in the posterior quarter of the medial paralingual groove. The submandibular anlage appears at the anterior end of the medial paralingual groove during the eighth week. At the end of the

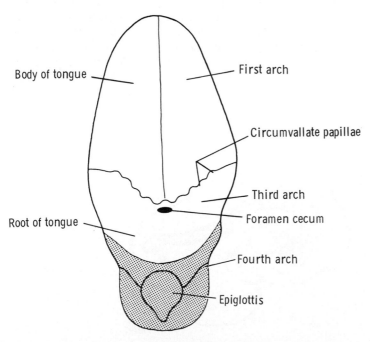

FIGURE 50–11. Human tongue depicting the different origin of the anterior two thirds and the posterior one third. (Adapted from an original painting by Frank H. Netter, M.D., from Clinical Symposia, copyright CIBA Pharmaceutical Co, Division of CIBA-Geigy Corp.)

embryonic period (week 8), the submandibular capsule begins to form. The Wharton duct becomes patent via programmed cell death, and the sublingual salivary papillae begin to form at its anterior end. The pedicle of the major sublingual salivary gland appears in the small groove formed in the external face of the sublingual salivary papilla, as a structure completely independent of the Wharton duct. During the early fetal period (weeks 9 and 10), the submandibular gland branches into lobules and grows to reach the posterior margin of the mylohyoid muscle. The muscle subsequently delimits the submandibular gland and its sublingual process. The last of the intraglandular secretory ductules of the submandibular gland becomes patent during week 11 of fetal development. The ductules drain into the Wharton duct, and during weeks 12 and 13 the adventitial layer of the Wharton duct becomes evident.[64] The body of the gland begins to appear compressed between the base of the mandible and the external face of the mylohyoid muscle, and pre- and retrosaccular extracapsular lymph node primordia make their first appearance. The myoepithelial cells develop during the 15th and 16th weeks.[52] By 16 weeks, intercalated and striated ducts are seen. By 20 weeks, convoluted tubule cells appear, and a transitory secretory activity is noted until 28 weeks of development. The definitive form of the submandibular gland is determined subsequently by the developing mandible. During the 12th to 28th weeks, secretory materials appear in the epithelial cells of both the ducts and the primitive acini and in their lumina. These cells are exclusively serous. Differentiation and growth of the submandibular gland proceeds gradually until 28 weeks, after which time the rate of growth decreases. The gland continues to grow after birth, with the formation of mucous acini.[27]

Development of the labial salivary glands occurs in four stages.[68] Stage I (weeks 9 to 10) is characterized by a localized, rounded thickening of the stomodeal epiblast into the mesenchyme of the mucosal side of the lower lip. During stage II (weeks 11 to 12), the epiblastic thickening assumes the form of a single cord. In stage III (week 13), the single cord branches to form the future secretory lobes. Stage IV, during the 18th week, corresponds to the process of duct formation (see Chapter 65).

Anomalies

Although abnormal tongue size is often associated with abnormal mandibular size, this is not always the case.[85] The major types of tongue anomalies are listed in Table 50-3. A variety of congenital syndromes are caused by malformations of the mouth, tongue, and mandible and are detailed in Chapter 56.

Newborn Anatomy

At birth, the entire tongue sits in the oral cavity (see Fig. 50-8). The tongue attaches to the hyoid bone and to the floor of the mouth and is covered with a stratified squamous mucous membrane that is continuous with the floor of the mouth. A fold of mucous membrane forms the frenulum, an attachment to the floor of the mouth. The

TABLE 50-3. Tongue Malformations

Aglossia
Microglossia
Hemiatrophy
Hemihypertrophy
Macroglossia
Long tongue
Accessory tongue
Ankyloglossia
Cleft or bifid tongue
Median glossitis rhomboid
Lingual thyroid
Nonclassified syndrome

From Emmanouil-Nikoloussi EN, Kerameos-Foroglou C. Developmental malformations of human tongue and associated syndromes [review]. Bull Group Int Rech Sch Stomatol Odontol 35:5, 1992.

tongue is composed of intrinsic and extrinsic groups of musculature. The body of the tongue is formed by the intrinsic muscles—superior and inferior longitudinal, vertical, and transverse, which are derived from the four occipital somites. The extrinsic muscles of the tongue include the genioglossus, hyoglossus, styloglossus, palatoglossus, and geniohyoid. All are paired and all are innervated by the 12th cranial nerve, except the palatoglossus, which is innervated by the pharyngeal plexus. Of the extrinsic muscles, the bilateral genioglossi are of considerable importance, as they alone are capable of protruding the tongue. Bilateral loss of genioglossus function, e.g., during deep general anesthesia or as a consequence of a central neurologic lesion, results in the tongue falling against the posterior wall, with the attendant risk of upper airway obstruction and suffocation. Thus, the normally functioning genioglossi can be considered as "safety muscles" that aid in the patency of the upper airway. It is now known that the genioglossus muscles are innervated with each inspiration and that this important muscle activity can become defunct in certain patients with sleep apnea syndrome.[83] In children with Down syndrome and sleep apnea, the tongue muscle has a higher percentage of type II (fast-twitch) muscle fibers as well as muscle hypertrophy of both type I (slow-twitch) and type II (fast-twitch) muscle fibers. On electron microscopic examination, some tongues in patients with Down syndrome are noted to have degenerative changes in the neuromuscular junction. These findings suggest that in this population of Down syndrome patients, tongue muscle strength may be increased but fatigue resistance is reduced.[100]

Reported dimensions of the newborn tongue are 4 cm long, 2.5 cm wide, and 1.0 cm thick.[18, 85] The anterior two thirds and posterior one third of the tongue are divided by the sulcus terminalis, which is quite prominent in the neonate (see Fig. 50-8). At the apex of the sulcus terminalis lies the foramen caecum, a structure equally well demarcated in the infant tongue. All taste buds are present at birth, but infants have a preference for sweet.[59] Taste sensation is believed to be located in specialized receptor cells in the lingual epithelium. The output of these cells is transferred to higher centers through nerve fibers in the seventh and ninth nerves. The output travels via the tractus solitarius to the thalamus and higher cerebral centers. The level of taste development in infants is unclear.[66] As the larynx descends over the first 5 years of life, the posterior third of the tongue eventually lies in the oropharynx where it becomes the anterior wall. The tongue doubles in thickness, width, and length between birth and adolescence.[85] No sex differences in tongue size have been reported.[85]

The general topography of submandibular and sublingual glands is similar in adults and children, except that the deep portion of the submandibular gland is usually continuous with the sublingual gland in infants, while these are separate in adults.[18] The newborn parotid gland is rounder than its adult counterpart and sits wedged in between the masseter muscle and the auricle. By adolescence, the parotid gland grows over the surface of the Stensen duct, which pierces the buccinator to enter the oral cavity. At birth, the parotid gland weighs 1.8 g, the submandibular gland weighs 0.84 g, and the sublingual gland weighs 0.42 g.[18] Each gland triples in weight over the first 6 months of life and increases in weight by five times by age 2 years, at which age the typical adult histologic appearance is seen. The cells of the parotid gland are all serous, whereas those of the submandibular and sublingual glands are a combination of serous and mucous cells. Salivary secretion, which occurs constantly and spontaneously, is augmented by reflex stimulation. Parasympathetic and sympathetic nerve fibers supply the glands and surrounding vasculature to regulate secretion. Secretion of saliva is assisted by the myoepithelial cells. The composition of the saliva varies according to the proportion secreted by each gland and according to the nature of the stimulus. Heterotopic salivary tissue is found in many locations throughout the head and neck. Age-induced variations and reactive changes include oncocyte proliferation, fatty infiltration, squamous and mucous metaplasia, hypertrophy, atrophy, and regeneration.[62]

Pharynx

Embryology

The pharynx develops from the cephalic end of the foregut, the pharyngeal arches, and the pharyngeal pouches.

Development of Pharynx Before Rupture of Buccopharyngeal Membrane

Over the course of the first 3 weeks of gestation, the embryo first exists as a flattened bilayer of cells in between the amniotic sac dorsally and the yolk sac ventrally. At the beginning of the third week, the process of gastrulation occurs whereby the germ disk becomes trilaminar. At this point, the upper ectodermal layer is continuous with the amnion wall and the lower endodermal layer is continuous with the yolk sac wall. The middle mesodermal layer fills the space between the upper ectodermal and lower endodermal germ layers. Only two parts of the embryonic disk remain, the prochordal plate and the cloacal membrane. The prochordal plate is the site of the future buccopharyngeal (oropharyngeal) membrane; the cloacal membrane is the site of the future anus. The embryo grows rapidly and triples in size. At the beginning of the fourth week, longitudinal and transverse folding

occurs, and the embryo takes on a C shape, as shown in Figure 50–9. The head fold and tail folds are thereby delineated. In the head-fold region, the developing brain grows beyond the buccopharyngeal membrane and overhangs the primitive heart. This folding in the head region incorporates part of the yolk sac into the embryo, and this becomes the primitive foregut, which lies between the brain and the heart. The primitive foregut is thus derived from the yolk sac. Initially, it ends blindly at the buccopharyngeal membrane. This membrane ruptures at 3.5 weeks, and the primitive mouth (stomodeum) then communicates with the foregut (see Fig. 50–9). The upper part of the foregut will develop into the pharynx. A portion of the primitive foregut in conjunction with the branchial apparatus is responsible for development of the pharynx.

Development of Pharyngeal Apparatus

As in the face, pharyngeal morphogenesis depends on formation and modification of the pharyngeal (branchial) apparatus. This apparatus, which consists of pharyngeal arches, grooves, and pouches, is first seen at 3.5 weeks as a series of elevations with deeps grooves in between them on each lateral surface of the embryo in the future head and neck region (Fig. 50–12). The pharyngeal arches are a series of epithelium-covered mesenchymal bars that arch around the lateral and ventral aspects of the primitive oral cavity and pharyngeal portion of the foregut. Each arch consists of a mesenchymal core that is derived from primitive streak mesoderm and neural crest ectomesenchyme and is covered with two epithelial sheets: an internal sheet of pharyngeal endoderm and an external sheet of surface ectoderm. The arches are delineated from one another externally by ectodermal pharyngeal (branchial) grooves and internally by endodermal pharyngeal (branchial) pouches. The arches develop in a cranial to caudal sequence. Initially, the first (mandibular) arch appears on each side of the pharynx in week 3 as a straight bar of tissue located caudal to the ectoderm-lined primitive oral cavity. The cranial limb of this arch is the maxillary prominence, which contributes to the upper jaw, and the caudal limb of the arch is the mandibular prominence, which contributes to the lower jaw. The mandibular prominence is separated from the second pharyngeal arch by the ectoderm-lined first pharyngeal (branchial) groove; the second arch is separated from the third arch by the second pharyngeal (branchial) groove. Six pairs of pharyngeal arches develop in mammalian embryos, but the fifth pair is rudimentary. The fourth, fifth, and six arches have indistinct boundaries and are difficult to distinguish from one another externally.

Each pharyngeal arch contains a core of mesenchymal tissue lined by epithelium of endodermal origin and covered by surface ectoderm (see Fig. 50–10). The mesenchymal core is derived from two populations of cells: (1) para-axial and lateral plate mesoderm and (2) neural crest cells. The para-axial and lateral plate mesoderm gives rise to muscles of mastication and facial expression. The neural crest cells migrate from the neuroectoderm of the fore-, mid-, and hindbrain to give rise to the skeletal and

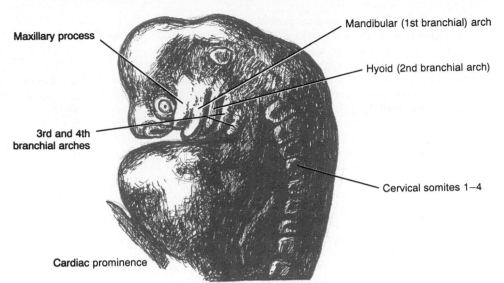

FIGURE 50–12. Lateral view of an embryo at 5 to 6 weeks' gestation. Note the pharyngeal arches embracing the foregut anteriorly and laterally. The first two arches appear in the third week. (Adapted from Sadler TW. Langman's Medical Embryology, 6th ed. Baltimore, Williams & Wilkins, 1990, p 299.)

Labels on figure: Maxillary process; Mandibular (1st branchial) arch; Hyoid (2nd branchial arch); 3rd and 4th branchial arches; Cervical somites 1–4; Cardiac prominence

connective tissues of the face. Each arch also has a vascular and neural (cranial nerve) component. The outer surface of each arch consists of ectoderm and the inner surface of endoderm.

Simultaneously, during the fourth week, the pharyngeal (branchial) pouches appear as a series of bilateral evaginations of the walls of the primitive pharynx. They likewise develop in a craniocaudal sequence. The first set of pharyngeal pouches elongate and fuse with the dorsal wings of the second pouch from which the tubotympanic recess and subsequent middle-ear cavity arises. The eustachian (auditory) tube develops from the proximal part of the first pouch and maintains its connection with the pharynx. The palatine tonsils and tonsillar fossa develop from the second pouch. Derivatives of the third pouch include the inferior parathyroids and the connective tissue of the thymus. The superior parathyroids derive from the fourth pouch and the ultimobranchial body from the sixth pouch.

Corresponding to the paired pouch invaginations are the paired ectodermal invaginations, which are the pharyngeal (branchial) clefts. These clefts normally involute, and in human adults the only significant derivative is the external auditory meatus, which derives from the first pharyngeal (branchial) groove. A transient structure known as the cervical sinus is formed as clefts two to four are obliterated. If any of this sinus persists, a cervical cyst, fistula, or sinus may result. The derivatives of the branchial arches and pouches are listed in Table 50–4.

The nasopharynx arises from the developing nose anterior to the eustachian tube and from the primitive pharynx posterior to it. Pharyngeal pouches in contact with the primitive foregut induce changes within the surrounding neural crest mesoderm, and differentiation occurs. The constrictor musculature as well as the palatopharyngeus and palatoglossus derive from the fourth branchial arch. These approximate with the tonsillar fossa, which forms from the second pharyngeal pouch. Glands in the neck and the recesses and folds of the pharyngeal wall subsequently derive from the third to fifth pouches. The

TABLE 50–4. Derivatives of the Pharyngeal (Branchial) Arches and Pouches

Branchial Arch	Pouch	Muscles	Cartilage	Cranial Nerve
First, mandibular	Auditory tube Middle ear activity	Mastication Mylohyoid Anterior digastric Tensors veli palatini and tympani	Meckel Incus Malleus	V
Second, hyoid	Tonsillar fossa	Facial expression Posterior digastric Stylohyoid Stapedius Levator palatini	Reichert Stapes Styloid process Part of hyoid	VII
Third	Inferior parathyroids Connective tissue of thymus	Stylopharyngeus	Body of hyoid	IX
Fourth	Superior parathyroids	Constrictors Palatopharyngeus Palatoglossus Cricothyroid	Thyroid	X
Fifth and sixth	Ultimobranchial body	Laryngeal muscles	Cricoid Arytenoid	X

From Kleuber KM. Craniofacial morphogenesis. Ear Nose Throat J 71:473, 1992.

final remnants of these pharyngeal pouches are the lateral glossoepiglottic fold from the third pouch, the aryepiglottic fold from the fourth, and the laryngeal ventricles from the sixth. The nasopharynx develops a ciliated respiratory epithelial lining anterior to the eustachian tube, while the rest of the pharynx becomes lined with stratified squamous epithelium.

Morphogenesis of the face and head depends to a large extent on central nervous system development. Noden[72] has performed heterotopic transplants on each of the mesodermal and neural crest cell populations in the head and neck in chick embryos. He took presumptive first arch neural crest cells and transplanted them in place of second and third arch neural crest cells. He discovered that the neural crest structures that developed were morphologically inappropriate for the location to which he transplanted them. Furthermore, the integument that developed over the transplant-derived crest populations was altered. This landmark work indicates that some neural crest precursors contain spatial information while still in association with the central nervous system (neural plate) or developing sensory epithelia (otic, optic, or nasal epithelia). These key experiments imply that changes in formation or delineation of rostrocaudal compartments within the vertebrate neural plate will have profound sequelae in the musculoskeletal assembly of the pharyngeal arches.

Anomalies

Most congenital malformations of the pharynx occur as the pharyngeal apparatus undergoes transformation into adult structures. These anomalies may appear in the neonate if incomplete obliteration of the embryonic spaces occurs. They are discussed in detail in Chapter 98.

Newborn Anatomy

The neonatal pharynx measures a mere 4 cm in total length, about one third the size of the adult pharynx. The pharynx enlarges, and at 6 years of age it reaches adult dimensions.[26] A partially tubular structure, it is a common passage for the alimentary and respiratory systems. It lies anterior to the vertebral column. The pharyngeal wall is composed of six muscle pairs: three pairs of constrictor muscles that course transversely and three pairs of muscles that course longitudinally down the pharynx. The latter are the salpingopharyngeus, stylopharyngeus, and palatopharyngeus. All of these muscles are innervated by the cranial portion of the spinal accessory nerve except the stylopharyngeus, whose nerve supply derives from the glossopharyngeal nerve. The pharyngeal tube extends from the base of the skull to the lower border of the cricoid cartilage, and anteriorly it connects the oral cavity to the esophagus and the posterior nasal cavity (choanae) to the larynx. The pharynx additionally communicates with the middle-ear cleft via the eustachian tube. The anatomy of the pharynx is generally considered to have three parts: nasopharynx, oropharynx, and hypopharynx (Fig. 50–13). The salient comparative pediatric anatomy

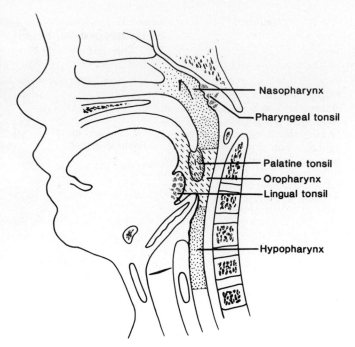

FIGURE 50–13. Relationships of the nasopharynx, oropharynx, and hypopharynx with Waldeyer ring of lymphoid tissue in a 5-year-old child.

of each of these parts is presented in the following sections.

Nasopharynx

At birth, the nasal portion of the pharynx is a narrow, 2.0-cm tube. Initially, it curves inferiorly and very gradually to meet the oropharyngeal portion of the pharynx. By age 5 years, these two portions of the pharynx join at an oblique angle (see Fig. 50–13), and by puberty a right angle is noted at this junction. This region is anatomically considered a part of the pharynx, but functionally it serves as part of the respiratory system (see Chapter 34).

The important anatomic relationships in the pediatric nasopharynx involve the structures surrounding the eustachian tube. The boundaries of the nasopharynx are as follows: anteriorly, the free edge of the soft palate; posteriorly, the posterior pharyngeal wall; and laterally, the palatopharyngeal arches. The sphenoid and upper clivus support the roof of the nasopharnyx, while the lower clivus and upper cervical vertebrae support the posterior wall. Closure of the nasopharynx during speech is accomplished through the combined function of the superior constrictor, palatopharyngeal, salpingopharyngeal, and levator palatini muscles. The tensor veli palatini aids in closure during swallowing. The adenoids (pharyngeal tonsil) are located on the roof of the nasopharynx. The eustachian tubes lie on the lateral aspect of the nasopharynx.

As the lateral wall of the nasopharynx forms posteroinferiorly by the superior constrictor muscle and anteriorly by the pharyngobasilar fascia, the fascia becomes pierced just above the superior border of the muscle by the eustachian tube and the levator palatini muscle. A slitlike recess is thereby formed between the eustachian tube and the constrictor muscle; this is the fossa of Rosenmüller, or the pharyngeal recess. The triangular eustachian tube opening in the nasopharynx has a prominent posterior-superior margin known as the *torus tubarius*. Innervation to the eustachian tube is from the pharyngeal branch of the maxillary nerve and the tympanic plexus of the middle ear. The arterial blood supply to the eustachian tube derives from the ascending pharyngeal branch of the external carotid artery, from the artery of the pterygoid canal and middle meningeal artery, and from the internal maxillary artery. The levator veli palatini muscle descends onto the soft palate anterior to the torus, forming a fold of mucosa known as the salpingopalatine fold. In newborns, the eustachian tube is 1.7 cm long (half the length of the adult eustachian tube), and the orifice is at the level of the hard palate. As the palate grows and descends through puberty, the eustachian tube eventually opens 10 mm above the hard palate.[38] In infants and children, the relatively small size of the nasopharynx and the relatively large size of the peritubal lymphatic tissue adenoids can cause nasal and eustachian tube obstruction.

Oropharynx

The oropharynx is the posterior continuation of the oral cavity beyond the palatine arches of the tonsillar pillars (see Fig. 50–13). The anterior palatine arch is formed by the palatoglossus muscle, and the posterior palatine arch by the palatopharyngeus muscle. Between these two arches, and on either side of the passageway between the mouth and the oropharynx, lie the palatine tonsils. The oropharynx extends superiorly to the line of contact between the soft palate and the posterior pharyngeal wall, and inferiorly to the tip of the epiglottis.

The anatomy of the oropharyngeal region in newborns differs from that in adults. The most striking features of the oropharynx are the base of the tongue and the vallecula. The base of the tongue, which at birth is in the oral cavity, descends with the larynx between the first and fourth years of life. After this descent, the tongue base becomes the anterior wall of the oropharynx; the lingual tonsil is found on this part of the tongue. Between the tongue and the epiglottis lies a median mucosal fold, known as the *glossoepiglottic fold*. Laterally, two mucosal folds extend from the junction of the tongue and the lateral pharyngeal wall to the epiglottis; these are the pharyngoepiglottic folds. The epiglottic vallecula is between the pharyngoepiglottic folds. The roof of the oropharynx is formed by the tip of the soft palate.

In neonates, the tongue is farther forward and the larynx higher than in adults. This allows the newborn epiglottis to actually contact the soft palate to establish a nasal airway for respiration during sucking.[82] Milk flows along the dorsum of the tongue and laterally around the epiglottis to enter the pharynx without spilling into the elevated larynx.[18] In the past, it was assumed that newborns and infants are obligatory nasal breathers for several months. However, investigators have demonstrated that newborns generally have the capacity to switch from nasal breathing as needed.[78] Thus, neonates are now described as "preferential" nasal breathers.

Histologically, the oropharynx and hypopharynx are lined with stratified squamous epithelium supported with a dense network of elastic fibers. The lamina propria contains connective tissue and is penetrated by stratified squamous papillae. It contains numerous seromucinous glands and many polymorphonuclear cells, lymphocytes, and plasma cells. Sensation to the oropharyngeal mucosa, including the dorsal third of the tongue, tonsillar pillars, and adjacent soft palate, is supplied by the glossopharyngeal nerve. The superior laryngeal branch of the vagus nerve also supplies the mucosa of the base of the tongue and the epiglottis.

Hypopharynx

The hypopharynx, the lowest part of the pharynx, extends from the tip of the epiglottis superiorly to the level of the cricopharyngeus inferiorly (see Fig. 50–13). These locations correspond with the level of the hyoid bone superiorly and the cricoid cartilage inferiorly. The posterior and lateral walls are supported by the middle and inferior constrictor muscles. The lateral walls extend anteriorly within the shieldlike thyroid cartilage as the piriform sinuses. The anterior wall consists of the laryngeal structures, the cuneiform, corniculate, and arytenoid cartilages; the aryepiglottic folds; the posterior lamina of the cricoid cartilage; and the laryngeal inlet. At the inferior extent of the pharynx, the oblique fibers of the inferior constrictor end and the horizontal fibers of the cricopharyngeal muscle begin. The cricopharyngeal muscle has no median raphe, as the constrictors do. It is in a state of tonic contraction, thereby functioning as a pharyngoesophageal sphincter. It prevents reflux of gastric contents during straining and keeps air from being swallowed during breathing. It relaxes during deglutition to allow the food bolus to pass into the esophagus below. Killian dehiscence is an area of weakness in the pharyngeal wall between the inferior constrictor above and the cricopharyngeus below. It is a common site of pharyngeal diverticula. The mucosa of the hypopharynx just superior to the cricopharyngeus is thin, making it vulnerable to injury and perforation from foreign bodies and during instrumentation.

Lymphoid Tissue

Embryology

A ring of lymphoid tissue called the *Waldeyer ring* encircles the primitive respiratory and alimentary tracts during the fifth month of gestation. The ring is composed of three large masses of tonsillar tissue: lingual, pharyngeal (adenoid), and faucial (palatine) tonsils (see Fig. 50–13). Morphogenesis of these lymphoid structures is a result of interaction among epithelial, mesenchymal, and lymphoid cell populations.[37] Tonsillar crypt formation occurs when the endodermal epithelial cells form a wedge of epithelial cells in surrounding mesoderm.[67] Programmed cell death occurs centrally, and lumen (crypt) is formed. During the fourth fetal month, epithelial crypts grow down into the epithelial connective tissue and are infiltrated by lymphoid cells. In the fifth month, the first primary follicles are seen. By the seventh month, the fully formed pharyngeal (adenoid) tissue is seen. The palatine tonsils are first seen in the third month and are derived from the ventral portion of the second pharyngeal pouch.[48, 97] During the fourth month, 10 solid epithelial (endodermal) buds entwine within the mesenchyme around the pharyngeal wall, and canalization occurs via programmed cell death.[37] By the third trimester, organized lymph follicles are noted. Growth continues after birth, and the supratonsillar fossa is seen as a persistent depression at the superior pole of the tonsil. This depression is believed to be the only remnant of the second pouch.[37] The tubal tonsils are thought to derive from the first pharyngeal pouch, and the lingual tonsils are noted to develop in association with the posterior two thirds of the tongue.[37] Crypts of the lingual tonsils do not appear until after birth.

Anatomy

The German anatomist Heinrich von Waldeyer is noted for his anatomic description of the lymphoid tissue in the posterior nasopharynx and oropharynx. As mentioned previously, the Waldeyer ring is composed of three large masses of tonsillar tissue: the lingual, pharyngeal (adenoid), and faucial (palatine) tonsils. These are unique in that they contain only efferent and no afferent lymphatic circulation; thus, lymph is not filtered through the tonsillar nodules. Smaller aggregates of lymphoid tissue in this area, the tubal (eustachian) tonsils, lateral pharyngeal bands, pharyngeal granulations, and lymphoid tissue within the laryngeal ventricle, are also part of the ring.

The pharyngeal tonsil (adenoid) tissue, located in the roof of the nasopharynx, increases rapidly in size during the first 6 to 7 years of life and generally atrophies by adolescence.[40] In infants and young children, it may be hypertrophied and fill the nasopharynx, with subsequent nasal airway and eustachian tube obstruction and hyponasal speech.[36] The pharyngeal tonsil consists of a solitary lobulated mass of tissue as compared with the paired palatine tonsils. Invagination of surface epithelium produces crypts that may be prominent. The epithelium covering the adenoid is the respiratory epithelium that lines the nasopharynx, but squamous metaplasia may occur. Adenoid epithelial lining is loosely attached and permits passage of cells and antigens. The pharyngeal plexus is the adenoidal nerve supply. The blood supply is from the ascending palatine branch of the facial artery, ascending pharyngeal artery, pharyngeal branch of the internal maxillary artery, and ascending cervical branch of the thyrocervical trunk. Venous drainage courses to the pharyngeal plexus, to the pterygoid plexus, and ultimately into the internal jugular and facial veins. Efferent lymphatic drainage flows from the retropharyngeal lymph nodes to the upper deep cervical lymph nodes, especially the posterior triangle nodes.[37]

The two oval palatine tonsils can be found in the tonsillar fossa in between the anterior (palatoglossal) and posterior (palatopharyngeal) tonsillar pillars. At birth, the palatine tonsils are approximately 5 mm in anteroposterior diameter and 3.5 mm in vertical diameter and weigh about 0.75 g.[18] During childhood, the palatine tonsils descend within their fossae, as their vertical diameter grows faster than their anteroposterior diameter. In contrast to other oronasal lymphoid tissues, the palatine tonsils are covered with a pharyngobasilar capsule fascia. The capsule is separated from the underlying musculature by loose connective tissue. Pus can collect here and cause a peritonsillar abscess. The glossopharyngeal nerve and styloid process descend almost vertically on the lateral surface of this musculature. Innervation of these tonsils is via the pterygopalatine (sphenopalatine) ganglion through the lesser palatine nerves and from the glossopharyngeal nerve. Pediatric patients often complain of ear pain after tonsillectomy. This is referred pain via the glossopharyngeal nerve, which also supplies the middle-ear cavity, including the medial wall of the tympanic membrane. The blood supply to these tonsils includes the facial artery (tonsillar branch and ascending palatine branch), ascending pharyngeal artery, dorsal lingual branch of the lingual artery, and internal maxillary artery (descending palatine artery, greater palatine artery). An important anatomic relationship to note surgically is that the internal carotid artery is approximately 2.5 cm posterolateral to the tonsil.[37] The tonsil drains into the tonsillar veins and subsequently into the external palatine, pharyngeal, and facial veins. Another important surgical note is that the palatine veins are the most common cause of postoperative tonsillectomy bleeding. The palatine tonsils contain 10 to 20 crypts, which penetrate the surface to reach various depths and may penetrate the entire tonsil to reach the fibrous capsule. The epithelial covering of the palatine tonsils is stratified squamous epithelium, which invaginates into the crypts and blends with the mesenchymal structures. Growth of the palatine tonsils continues postnatally, and the palatine tonsil is active until age 15 years.[37, 89] After puberty, the tonsillar tissue tends to involute, and more fibrosis appears (see Chapter 61).

The lingual tonsils, at the base of the tongue, develop later than the other oronasal tonsils and persist well into adult life. These tonsils are lined by stratified squamous epithelium. The blood supply is the same as that to the base of the tongue. Innervation is via the glossopharyngeal nerve, and lymphatic drainage is to the deep cervical lymph nodes.

The tonsils are active in the synthesis of humoral immunoglobulins such as IgG, IgM, and IgA. They also produce lymphocytes in a complete sequence of lymphopoiesis and are related immunologically to the gut-associated lymphoid system in humans. The tonsils are the first lymphoid aggregates to encounter pathogens that enter the host via the upper respiratory and gastrointestinal tracts, and thus are believed to play a role in host immunity to pathogens.[93]

Imaging Pearls

Prenatal

Before the 1970s, fetoscopy was the sole method of assessing facial anomalies, but prenatal ultrasonographic detection of craniofacial anomalies is now common.[94] Ultrasonography is reported to provide accurate diagnosis of cleft lip and palate between 15 and 20 weeks of gestation.[6, 60, 81] Color Doppler ultrasonographic examination has now been used as a prenatal diagnostic tool for cleft palate.[4]

Newborn

Lateral soft tissue radiographs of the neck are useful to visualize the roof of the nasopharynx and landmarks of the oropharynx. The soft palate, adenoids, tonsils, uvula, base of the tongue, and lingual tonsils can be seen. The eustachian tube is seen on the submentovertex views. Lymphoid tissue is not visible radiographically in a term baby.[26] Normal adenoid tissue becomes visible on radiographic examination within 3 to 6 months after birth.[86] Adenoid pad thickness in pediatric patients is extremely variable and may obscure the plain radiographic diagnosis of a nasopharyngeal tumor. Xeroradiography enhances subtle differences in tissue density and can be helpful in diagnosing upper airway foreign bodies.[86] To prevent a false-positive reading of excessive retropharyngeal soft tissue on a soft tissue lateral neck radiograph, the child's head should be extended and the radiograph taken during inspiration. Thyroid scintigraphy can be used in neonatal and pediatric patients to evaluate neonatal hypothyroidism, hyperthyroidism, and ectopic thyroid tissue or thyroid nodules.[86]

Esophagus

Embryology

Development of the esophagus begins on day 21, when the esophagus and laryngotracheal tubes emerge from a common ventral diverticulum in the primitive foregut. A partition known as the *tracheoesophageal septum* arises from the lateral walls of the foregut. This septum appears first at the carina and subsequently extends cranially. Partitioning is completed by the sixth week (Fig. 50–14). The cephalad portion of this septum is fixed at the level of C1 throughout gestation.[98] During this time, primary ciliated epithelium appears and proliferates, almost obliterating the esophageal lumen. Simultaneous lengthening of the esophageal and tracheal tubes occurs. Over weeks 6 and 7, vacuolization of the lumen occurs via programmed cell death, and the lumen is reformed. By week 8, the fetal esophagus is a hollow lined tube containing primitive muscle and nerve precursors.[35, 43]

During the sixth week, the circular esophageal muscle layer develops from mesenchyme, and in the ninth week the longitudinal muscle layer appears. Muscularis mucosa is detected in the 10th week. From the eighth to 16th weeks, esophageal muscle and its innervation mature. While all muscle is initially smooth muscle, the upper third of the esophagus develops into striated muscle. By the fifth gestational month, the normal adult muscle arrangement and ratios are present. By week 20, ganglion nerve cells of Meissner plexus are noted in the submucosa, while ganglion nerve cells of Auerbach plexus are found between the longitudinal and circular muscle layers. These plexuses arise from neural crest cells that have migrated to the area.

During development, the esophageal lining tissue transforms from stratified columnar to ciliated columnar to stratified squamous epithelium. Over weeks 4 and 5, stratified columnar epithelium lines the esophageal tube and vigorously multiplies. Ciliated cells appear first during week 8, proliferate, and then gradually decrease in number by week 14.[80] By week 10, one layer of simple columnar epithelium lines the proximal and distal esophagus. By the fifth month of gestation, most of the ciliated epithelium is replaced by stratified squamous epithelium. Replacement begins in the midesophagus and then continues cranially and caudally. Submucosal glands arise from the squamous epithelium. At birth, persistent ciliated cells may remain in the proximal esophagus, which is the last area to be covered by squamous epithelium.

Esophageal Anomalies

The key time for embryologic defects is between the third and eighth weeks of development. The most common anomalies of the esophagus are esophageal atresias and tracheoesophageal fistulas. Less common are webs and strictures. These anomalies derive from either abnormal partitioning of the foregut into the trachea and esophagus or recannulation errors.[9, 17, 45, 46, 98] Major congenital malformations are listed in Table 50–5. See Chapter 67 for a detailed description of congenital esophageal malformations.

Anatomy

Anatomically, the esophagus begins at the distal pharynx and extends to the cardia of the stomach. In term infants,

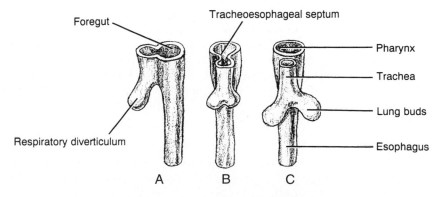

FIGURE 50–14. Partitioning of the primitive foregut. *A,* End of the third week (lateral view). *B* and *C,* During the fourth week (ventral view). (From Sadler TW. Langman's Medical Embryology, 6th ed. Baltimore, Williams & Wilkins, 1990, p 239.)

TABLE 50–5. Esophageal Anomalies

Anomaly	Origin of Defect	Age at Diagnosis	Sex Affected	Relative Frequency
Esophageal atresia, esophageal stenosis, tracheo-esophageal fistula	21–34 days	Birth	Equal	Common
Laryngotracheoesophageal cleft	3rd–5th week	Birth	Equal	Rare
Esophageal webs/rings	3rd–5th week	Variable	Equal	Rare
True duplication	7th week	Variable	?	Very rare
Enterogenous cysts	End of 3rd week	Variable	Female	Rare
Diverticula	5th–9th month	Variable	Male	Uncommon
Heterotopic mucosa	5th–9th month	Variable	Equal	Common
Congenital short esophagus	7th week	Variable	Male	Rare
Achalasia	Late 6th week	Infancy	Equal	Uncommon
Chalasia	Late 6th week	Infancy	Equal	Very common

Adapted from Skandalakis JE, Gray SW, Richetts R. The esophagus. In Skandalakis JE, Gray SW (eds). Embryology for Surgeons, 2nd ed. Baltimore, Williams & Wilkins, 1994, p 69.

the esophageal conduit measures 7 to 14 cm from the upper esophageal sphincter to the lower esophageal sphincter.[101] This conduit doubles in length by age 3 years, after which time longitudinal growth occurs at 0.65 cm annually until puberty, when the adult length of 25 cm is achieved.[18, 101] The neonatal esophageal diameter is 5 to 6 mm.[18, 101]

For descriptive purposes, the esophagus is divided into four thoracic segments: cervical, upper, middle, and lower.[22] Although mobile in its midportion, the esophagus is fixed by the cricoid/cricopharyngeal muscle superiorly and the phrenoesophageal ligament inferiorly.[101] Four innate constriction sites are described: at the cricoid origin, the aortic arch, the left mainstem bronchus, and the diaphragmatic hiatus.

Several important topographic relationships are seen. In the upper cervical esophagus, the trachea sits anteriorly, the recurrent laryngeal nerves just laterally in the tracheoesophageal grooves, and the carotid sheath more laterally. Posterior to the esophagus is the retropharyngeal space and cervical spine. The esophagus bends to the left as it exits the neck, and at this point the left thyroid lobe overlies it. Because of this leftward deviation, the preferred surgical approach to the cervical esophagus is from the left.

In the upper thoracic portion, the esophagus returns to the middle and continues posteriorly to the trachea down to the bifurcation. In the midthoracic segment, the aortic arch, left mainstem bronchus, and left atrium are intimately associated. Esophageal vessels course longitudinally and posteriorly. Both vagi contribute to plexuses on the anterior and posterior wall. At the lower thoracic segment, the esophagus traverses the diaphragm via the esophageal hiatus, whose position is anterior to the aortic hiatus and left posterolateral to the foramen of the inferior vena cava. In adults, the gastroesophageal junction on the left forms a sharp angle, known as the angle of His (incisura). This oblique angle is nearly nonexistent in infants and predisposes neonates to reflux.[39] The petite terminal abdominal esophagus measures less than 1 cm in infants.[53]

Histologically, four layers define the esophageal wall: mucosa, submucosa, muscularis propria, and adventitia

(Fig. 50–15). The tripartite mucosa, lined with nonkeratinizing stratified squamous epithelium, lies in longitudinal folds down to the gastroesophageal junction. The lamina propria is the middle mucosal layer, where loose areolar connective tissue is found interspersed with vessels and mucus-secreting glands. Longitudinally oriented smooth muscle bundles make up the muscularis mucosae. Beneath the mucosa, the submucosa embodies loose areolar tissue, lymph glands, and salivary glands, which are more abundant in the upper and lower segments. An outer longitudinal and inner circular muscle layer make up the muscularis propria. The muscular composition of the esophagus is threefold: purely striated fibers in the upper third, purely smooth fibers in the lower third, and mixed fibers in the middle third. Nervous system contributions include paravertebral sympathetic chains, the vagi, and Meissner and Auerbach plexuses.[22, 101] An external fibrous coat, the tunica adventitia, contains both neural and vascular structures along with a compendium of elastic connective tissue fibers that play a role in distention and deglutination. Serosa is detected only on short segments of the thoracic and intra-abdominal esophagus.[22] The lack of serosa makes perforation during instrumentation more likely. For lymphatic drainage, the cervical esophagus drains into the internal jugular, upper tracheal, and deep cervical lymph nodes. The thoracic esophagus drains into several mediastinal node groups, and the abdominal portion drains into the left gastric nodal chain.[101] A lush network of longitudinally oriented submucosal lymphatics allows extensive intra- and submucosal spread of disease long before an obstructive luminal tumor appears later in life.[22] A richly anastomotic arterial network diminishes the likelihood of esophageal infarction. Three major sources of blood supply are noted. The upper third is supplied by the inferior thyroid arteries as they branch off the thyrocervical trunk. Branches off the thoracic aorta, right and left bronchial arteries, and aortic esophageal arteries supply the middle third. The lower third is supplied by the esophageal branches of the left gastric artery, which are tributaries of the celiac trunk. Both caval and portal venous tributaries drain the esophagus. In the upper two thirds, the venous drainage mirrors the arterial supply. Here, the inferior thyroidal vein and azy-

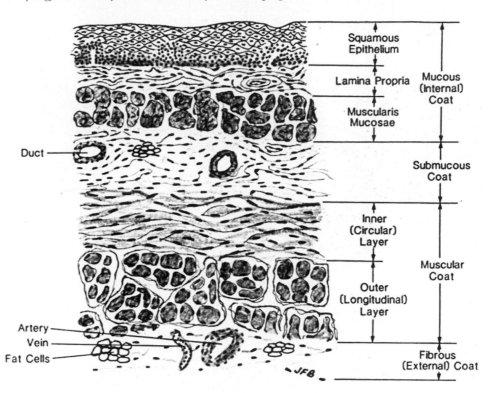

FIGURE 50-15. Histologic cross-section through the wall of the esophagus. (From Beshof JF, Sullivan P. Anatomy and physiology. Ear Nose Throat J 63:15, 1984.)

gous system eventually empty into the superior vena cava. The lower third empties not only into the systemic system via the azygous and left inferior phrenic veins, but also into the portal system via the left gastric and splenic veins. The cavoportal system communicates via submucosal veins. Dilatation of these veins is the basis for esophageal varices in later life.

Imaging Pearls

Prenatal

Esophageal atresia is suspected on prenatal ultrasonograms in the presence of polyhydramnios. This can be seen as early as 24 weeks' gestation. However, prenatal diagnosis is made in only about one third of cases.[42, 77]

Neonatal

Radiographically, the infant esophagus can be localized between C4 (upper esophageal sphincter) and T9 (lower esophageal sphincter), compared with C6 (upper esophageal sphincter) to T11 (lower esophageal sphincter) in adults.[53] The normal sites of narrowing due to the aorta, left mainstem bronchus, and left atrium are less prominent in children on barium esophagograms.[26] The action of the cricopharyngeal "pinchcock" is more pronounced in neonates and appears on cervical radiographs as a transverse indentation at the level of C4.[53] Although 80% of ingested foreign bodies pass through the pediatric gastrointestinal tract, the most common site of foreign body impaction is just below the cricopharyngeus at the level of the thoracic inlet.[69] Air is often visualized in the pediatric esophagus, but excessive or persistent esophageal air may signal a tracheoesophageal anomaly or respiratory disease.[26]

Fetal Craniofacial Surgery: A New Horizon

Postnatal repair and rehabilitation in children with cleft lip or palate, or both, requires a multidisciplinary team of specialists and is costly, time consuming, and stressful for all involved. With the improvements in prenatal ultrasonographic diagnosis, a group of pioneer surgeons and scientists are investigating intrauterine repair of cleft lip and palate (Fig. 50-16). Preliminary studies in animals have demonstrated that repair of epidermal wounds in midgestation results in healing without scar formation.[29, 55, 56, 96] Conversely, repairs in animals in the third trimester have resulted in scar tissue formation.[12] Animals with cleft lips and cleft palates repaired in utero have demonstrated normal maxillary growth postnatally.[5, 13, 63] Both open and endoscopic techniques have demonstrated promising results in laboratory animals.[29, 55] The theoretical advantages of craniofacial fetal surgery are restoration of normal lip form without scarring, with subsequent normal midface growth and development, and prevention of the secondary nasal deformities associated with cleft lip.[20, 74] In addition, psychological, financial, and social benefits must be considered. Currently, the risks to the mother and fetus are great, and human fetal surgery is reserved for life-threatening anomalies such as congenital diaphragmatic hernia.[41, 57] In time, human fetal craniofacial surgery may become a reality.

Ongoing experiments can serve as models for wound healing.[1] On a molecular level, the fetal wounds heal in an extracellular matrix that is much richer in hyaluronic

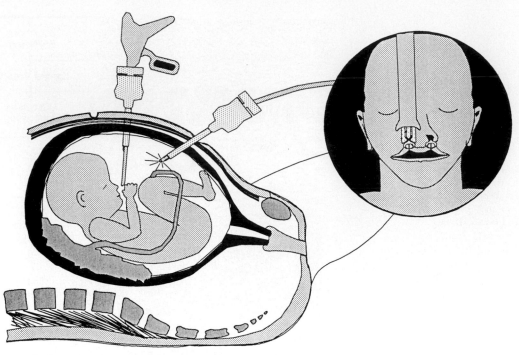

FIGURE 50–16. Future cleft lip repairs in fetuses may employ small endoscopes and delicate instruments to effect cleft edge approximation. Percutaneous endoscopic fetal surgery (PEFS) may reduce the risks of fetal surgery to approach those of amniocentesis. Ideally, the procedure would confer minimal disruption to the mother or the fetus in its protected intrauterine environment. (From Oberg KC, Kirsch WM, Hardesty KA. Prospectives in cleft lip and palate repair. Clin Plast Surg 20:820, 1993.)

acid than are adult wounds. This morphogen facilitates cell mobility and proliferation.[54] A decrease in TGF-alpha expression is seen at the fetal wound site. In adults, a high concentration of TGF-alpha is seen during wound healing, and this enhances scar formation.[14] At the very least, continued study of fetal wound-healing mechanisms may revolutionize treatment of scars in the future.

Acknowledgments

Special thanks to Dr. B. Vidic, Professor of Anatomy at Georgetown University School of Medicine in Washington, D.C., and to Slobodan Vukicevic, M.D., Ph.D., Visiting Scientist and Developmental Anatomist at the National Institutes of Health, for their advice in the planning of this chapter. Accolades to Mr. Steven W. Utter, freelance artist, for his excellent pencil and ink Netter adaptations.

SELECTED REFERENCES

Crelin ES. Functional Anatomy of the Newborn. New Haven, Yale University Press, 1973.

Dr. Crelin's text provides the most complete review of newborn anatomy available. His observations are based on evaluation of newborn infants and on cadaver dissections in neonates.

Crelin ES. Development of the upper respiratory tract. Clin Symp 28:3, 1976.

An excellent monograph with concise explanations of traditional embryology of the head and neck as well as some functional newborn anatomy. There are exquisite color embryologic diagrams by the late Dr. Frank Netter.

Noden DM. Vertebrate craniofacial development: the relation between ontogenetic process and morphological outcome. Brain Behav Evol 38:190, 1991.

This enlightening update on craniofacial morphogenesis, which emphasizes neural crest cells and their derivatives, is presented by Dr. Noden, a noted developmental anatomist and Professor at Cornell University College of Veterinary Medicine.

Ober KC, Kirsch WM, Hardesty RA. Prospectives in cleft lip and palate repair. Clin Plast Surg 20:815, 1993.

An excellent review on the state of the art in fetal craniofacial surgery.

Skandalakis JE, Gray SW. Embryology for Surgeons, 2nd ed. Baltimore, Williams & Wilkins, 1994.

This text is considered a "masterpiece and classic contribution" by Dr. Robert E. Gross, one of the fathers of pediatric surgery. Its goal is to detail the embryogenesis and surgical approaches to congenital defects. Chapters 2 (Pharynx), 3 (Esophagus), and 13 (Trachea and Lungs) are relevant to the pediatric otolaryngologist and worthy of review.

Sperber GH. Craniofacial Embryology, 4th ed. Boston, Butterworth Scientific, 1989.

Dr. Sperber, a professor of anatomy and oral biology, augments this compact craniofacial embryology text with marvelous line diagrams, clinical photographs, and scanning electron micrographs.

Sperber GH, Machin GA. The enigma of cephalogenesis. Cleft Palate Craniofac J 31:91, 1994.

This overview of molecular biologic aspects of head and neck embryology is a "must read" for clinicians interested in developmental anatomy.

Sulik KK, Schoenwolf GC. Highlights of craniofacial morphogenesis in mammalian embryos as revealed by scanning electron microscopy. Scan Electron Microsc (Part IV):1735, 1985.

A magnificent collection of scanning electron micrographs delineating mouse craniofacial development.

REFERENCES

1. Adzick NS, Longaker MT. Scarless fetal healing: therapeutic implications. Ann Surg 215:3, 1992.
2. Ardinger HH, Buetow KH, Bell GI, et al. Association of genetic variation of the transforming growth factor alpha gene with cleft lip and palate. Am J Hum Genet 45:348, 1989.
3. Arey LB. On development, morphology and interpretation of a system of cryptanalogues in the pharyngeal tonsil. Am J Anat 80:203, 1947.
4. Aubry MC. Prenatal diagnosis of cleft palate: contributions of color Doppler ultrasound. Ultrasound Obstet Gynecol 2:221, 1992.
5. Beck GJ, Bruce RA, Fonseca RJ. The effect of a neonatal surgery on postnatal palatal growth in sheep. J Oral Maxillofac Surg 46:217, 1988.
6. Bernacerraf BR, Mulliken JB. Fetal cleft lip and palate: sonographic diagnosis and postnatal outcome. Plast Reconstr Surg 92:1045, 1993.
7. Bershof JF, Sullivan P. Anatomy and physiology. Ear Nose Throat J 63:10, 1986.
8. Bordley JE, Brookhauser PE, Tucker GT. Ear, Nose and Throat Disorders in Children. New York, Raven Press, 1986.
9. Botha GS. Organogenesis and growth of the gastroesophageal region in man. Anat Rec 133:219, 1959.
10. Brinkley LL, Bookstein FL. Cell distribution during mouse secondary palatal closure: II. Mesenchymal cells. J Embryol Exp Morphol 96:111, 1986.
11. Brinkley LL, Morris-Winman J. Computer assisted analysis of hyaluronate distribution during morphogenesis of mouse secondary palate. Development 100:629, 1987.
12. Canady JW, Landas SK, Morris H, et al. In utero cleft palate repair in the ovine model. Cleft Palate Craniofac J 31:37, 1994.
13. Canady JW, Thompson SA, Colburn A. Craniofacial growth after iatrogenic cleft palate repair in a fetal ovine model. Cleft Palate Craniofac J 34:69, 1997.
14. Chang J, Longaker MT, Lorenz HP, et al. Fetal and adult sheep fibroblast TGF-B1 gene expression in vitro: effects of hypoxia and gestational age. Surg Forum 44:720, 1993.
15. Chenevix-Trench G, Jones K, Green AC, et al. Further evidence for an association between genetic variation in transforming growth factor alpha and cleft lip and palate. Am J Hum Genet 48:1012, 1991.
16. Chenevix-Trench G, Jones K, Green AC, et al. Cleft lip with or without cleft palate: associations with transforming growth factor alpha and retinoic acid receptor loci. Am J Hum Genet 51:1377, 1992.
17. Chittmittrapap S, Spitz L, Kiely EM, et al. Oesophageal atresia and associated anomalies. Arch Dis Child 64:364, 1989.
18. Crelin ES. Functional Anatomy of the Newborn. New Haven, Yale University Press, 1973.
19. Crelin ES. Development of the upper respiratory tract. Clin Symp 28:3, 1976.
20. Dado DV, Kernahan DA, Gianopoulos JG. Intrauterine repair of cleft lip: what's involved. Plast Reconstr Surg 85:461, 1990.
21. Davies J, Ducker L. Embryology and anatomy of the head, neck, face, palate, nose, and paranasal sinuses. In Paparella MM, Shumrick DA, Gluckman JL, Meyerhoff WL (eds). Otolaryngology, Vol I, 3rd ed. Philadelphia, WB Saunders, 1991, pp 59–106.
22. DeNardi FG, Riddell RH. The normal esophagus. Am J Surg Pathol 15:296, 1991.
23. Diewert VM, Wang KY. Recent advances in primary palate and midface morphogenesis research. Crit Rev Oral Biol Med 4:111, 1992.
24. Dixon MJ, Ferguson MW. The effects of epidermal growth factor, transforming growth factors alpha and beta and platelet derived growth factor on murine palatal shelves in organ culture. Arch Oral Biol 37:395, 1992.
25. Dixon MJ, Garner J, Ferguson MW. Immunolocalization of epidermal growth factor (EGF), EGF receptor and transforming growth factor alpha (TGF alpha) during murine palatogenesis in vivo and in vitro. Anat Embryol (Berl) 184:83, 1991.
26. Durie PR. Pharynx and esophagus. In Stringer DA (ed). Pediatric Gastrointestinal Imaging. Philadelphia, BC Decker, 1989, pp 83–126.
27. El-Mohandes EA, Botros KG, Bondok AA. Prenatal development of the human submandibular gland. Acta Anat (Basel) 130:213, 1987.
28. Emmanouil-Nikoloussi EN, Kerameos-Foroglou C. Developmental malformations of human tongue and associated syndromes (review). Bull Group Int Rech Sci Stomatol Odontol 35:5, 1992.
29. Estes JM, Whitby DJ, Lorenz P, et al. Endoscopic creation and repair of fetal cleft lip. Plast Reconstr Surg 90:743, 1992.
30. Ferguson MW. Palatal shelf elevation in the Wistar rat fetus. J Anat 125:555, 1978.
31. Ferguson MW. Palate development: mechanisms and malformations. Ir J Med Sci 156:309, 1987.
32. Ferguson MW. Palate development. Development 103(Suppl):41, 1988.
33. Fitchett JE, Hay ED. Medial edge epithelium transforms to mesenchyme after embryonic palatal shelves fuse. Dev Biol 131:455, 1989.
34. Fraser FC. The genetics of cleft lip and cleft palate. Am J Hum Genet 22:336, 1970.
35. Gemonov VV, Kolesnikov LL. Development of oesophageal tissue structures in human embryogenesis. Anat Anz 171:13, 1990.
36. Gerwat J. The structure and function of the nasopharyngeal lymphoid tissue with special reference to the aetiology of secretory otitis. J Laryngol Otol 89:169, 1975.
37. Goeringer GC, Vidic B. The embryogenesis and anatomy of Waldeyer's ring. Otolaryngol Clin North Am 20:207, 1987.
38. Graves GO, Edwards LF. The eustachian tube: a review of its descriptive, microscopic, topographic and clinical anatomy. Arch Otolaryngol 39:359, 1944.
39. Gryboski JD, Thayer SR, Spiro HM. Esophageal motility in infants and children. Pediatrics 31:382, 1961.
40. Handelman CS, Osborne G. Growth of the nasopharynx and adenoid development from one to eighteen years. Angle Orthod 46:243, 1976.
41. Harrison MR, Adzick NS, Longaker MT, et al. Successful repair in utero of a fetal diaphragmatic hernia after removal of herniated viscera from the left thorax. N Engl J Med 322:1582, 1990.
42. Hertzberg BS. Sonography of the fetal gastrointestinal tract: anatomic variants, diagnostic pitfalls, and abnormalities. AJR 162:1175, 1994.
43. Hitchcock RJ, Pemble MJ, Bishop AE, et al. Quantitative study of the development and maturation of human oesophageal innervation. J Anat 180:175, 1992.
44. Hollinshead WH. Anatomy for Surgeons, Vol I, 2nd ed. New York, Harper & Row, 1968.
45. Johns BA. Developmental changes in the esophageal epithelium in man. J Anat 86:431, 1952.
46. Johnson FP. The development of the mucous membranes of the esophagus, stomach and intestine in the human embryo. Am J Anat 10:521, 1910.
47. Jones MC. Facial clefting: etiology and developmental pathogenesis. Clin Plast Surg 20:599, 1993.
48. Kleuber KM. Craniofacial morphogenesis. Ear Nose Throat J 71:472, 1992.
49. Krumlauf R. Hox genes and pattern formation in the branchial region. Trends Genet 9:106, 1993.
50. Kulkarni ML, Rajendran NK. Values for mouth and ear measurements in newborns. Indian Pediatr 29:357, 1992.
51. Latham RA. The development, structure and growth pattern of the human midpalatal suture. J Anat 108:31, 1971.
52. Lee SK, Hwang JO, Chi JG, et al. Prenatal development of myoepithelial cell of human submandibular gland observed by immunohistochemistry of smooth muscle actin and rhodamine-phalloidin fluorescence. Pathol Res Pract 189:332, 1993.
53. Lierse W. The physiology and pathology of the esophagus. Eur J Pediatr Surg 2:323, 1992.
54. Longaker MT, Chiu ES, Adzick NS, et al. Studies in fetal wound healing: a prolonged presence of hyaluronic acid characterizes fetal wound fluid. Ann Surg 213:292, 1991.

55. Longaker MT, Stern M, Lorenz HP, et al. A model for fetal cleft lip repair in lambs. Plast Surg 90:750, 1992.

56. Longaker MT, Whitby DJ, Adzick NJ, et al. Studies in fetal wound healing: VI. Second and early third trimester fetal wounds demonstrate rapid collagen deposition without scar formation. J Pediatr Surg 25:63, 1990.

57. Longaker MT, Whitby DJ, Adzick NJ, et al. Fetal surgery for cleft lip: a plea for caution. Plast Reconstr Surg 88:1087, 1991.

58. Longaker MT, Whitby DJ, Ferguson MW, et al. Studies in fetal wound healing: III. Early deposition of fibronectin distinguishes fetal from adult wound healing. J Pediatr Surg 24:799, 1989.

59. Maller O, Turner RE. Taste in acceptance of sugars in human infants. J Comp Physiol Psychol 84:496, 1973.

60. Manchester DK, Pretorius DH, Avery C, et al. Accuracy of ultrasound diagnoses in pregnancies complicated by suspected fetal anomalies. Prenat Diagn 8:109, 1988.

61. Manning SC, Casselbrant M, Lammers D. Otolaryngologic manifestations of child abuse. Int J Pediatr Otorhinolaryngol 20:7, 1990.

62. Martinez-Madrigal F, Michaeu C. Histology of the major salivary glands. Am J Surg Pathol 13:879, 1989.

63. Mehrara BJ, Longaker MT. New developments in craniofacial surgery research. Cleft Palate Craniofac J 36:377, 1999.

64. Merida-Velasco JA, Sanchez-Montesinos I, Espin-Ferra J, et al. Development of the human submandibular gland. J Dent Res 72:1227, 1993.

65. Merlob P, Sivan Y, Reisner SH. Anthropometric measurements of the newborn infant (27 to 41 gestational weeks). Birth Defects 20:1, 1984.

66. Milla PJ. Feeding, tasting and sucking. In Walker WA, Durie PR, Hamilton JR, et al (eds). Pediatric Gastrointestinal Disease. Philadelphia, BC Decker, 1991, pp 217–235.

67. Minear WL, Arey LB, Milton JT. Prenatal and postnatal development and form of crypts of human palatine tonsils. Arch Otolaryngol 25:487, 1937.

68. Muller M, Jasmin JR, Monteil RA, et al. Embryology and secretory activity of labial salivary glands. J Biol Buccale 19:39, 1991.

69. Nandi P, Ong GB. Foreign body in the oesophagus: review of 2394 cases. Br J Surg 65:5, 1978.

70. Noden DM. Craniofacial development: new views on old problems. Anat Rec 209:1, 1984.

71. Noden DM. Interactions and fates of avian craniofacial mesenchyme. Development 103:121, 1988.

72. Noden DM. Vertebral craniofacial development: the relation between ontogenetic process and morphological outcome. Brain Behav Evol 38:190, 1991.

73. Nuckolls GH, Shum L, Slavkin HC. Progress toward understanding craniofacial malformations. Cleft Palate Craniofac J 36:12, 1999.

74. Oberg KC, Kirsch WM, Hardesty RA. Prospectives in cleft lip and palate surgery. Clin Plast Surg 20:815, 1993.

75. Patten BM. The normal development of the facial region. In Pruzansky S (ed). Congenital Anomalies of the Face and Associated Structures. Springfield, IL, Charles C Thomas, 1961, pp 11–45.

76. Pratt RM, Goggins JF, Wilk AL, et al. Acid mucopolysaccharide synthesis in the secondary palate of the developing rat at the time of rotation and fusion. Dev Biol 32:230, 1973.

77. Pretorius DH, Drose JA, Dennis MA, et al. Tracheoesophageal fistula in utero: twenty-two cases. J Ultrasound Med 6:509, 1987.

78. Rodenstein DO, Perlmutter N, Stanescu DC. Infants are not obligatory nasal breathers. Am Rev Respir Dis 131:343, 1985.

79. Sadler TW. Langman's Medical Embryology, 6th ed. Baltimore, Williams & Wilkins, 1990.

80. Sakai N, Suenaga T, Tanaka K. Electron microscopic study on the esophageal mucosa in human fetuses. Auras Nasus Larynx 16:177, 1989.

81. Saltzman DH, Benacerraf BR, Frigoletto FD. Diagnosis and management of fetal facial clefts. Am J Obstet Gynecol 155:377, 1986.

82. Sasaki CT, Levine PA, Laitman JT, et al. Postnatal descent of the epiglottis in man: a preliminary report. Arch Otolaryngol 103:169, 1977.

83. Saurland EK, Harper EM. The human tongue during sleep: electromyographic activity of the genioglossus muscle. Exp Neurol 51:160, 1976.

84. Sharpe PM, Foreman DM, Carette MJ, et al. The effects of transforming growth factor beta-1 on protein production by mouse embryonic palate mesenchymal cells in the presence or absence of serum. Arch Oral Biol 37:39, 1992.

85. Siebert JR. A morphometric study of normal and abnormal fetal and childhood tongue size. Arch Oral Biol 30:433, 1985.

86. Silverman FN, Slovis T. Neck and upper airway. In Silverman FN, Kuhn JP (eds). Caffrey's Pediatric X-Ray Diagnosis, Vol l, 9th ed. St Louis, CV Mosby, 1993, pp 355–377.

87. Skandalakis JE, Gray SW. Embryology for Surgeons, 2nd ed. Baltimore, Williams & Wilkins, 1994.

88. Slavkin HC. Regulatory issues during early craniofacial development: a summary. Cleft Palate J 27:101, 1990.

89. Slipka J. The development and involution of tonsils. Adv Otorhinolaryngol 47:1, 1992.

90. Sperber GH. Craniofacial Embryology, 4th ed. Boston, Butterworth Scientific, 1989.

91. Sperber GH, Machin GA. The enigma of cephalogenesis. Cleft Palate Craniofac J 31:91, 1994.

92. Sporn MB, Roberts AB, Wakefield LM, et al. Some recent advances in the chemistry and biology of transforming growth factor beta. J Cell Biol 105:1039, 1987.

93. Sprinkle PM, Veltri RW. Microbiology of the head and neck. In English GM (ed). Otolaryngology, Vol 5. New York, Harper & Row, 1988.

94. Straus RP, Davis JU. Prenatal detection and fetal surgery of clefts and craniofacial abnormalities in humans: social and ethical issues. Cleft Palate J 27:176, 1990.

95. Suarez FR. The clinical anatomy of the tonsillar (Waldeyer's) ring. Ear Nose Throat J 59:447, 1980.

96. Sullivan WG. In utero cleft lip repair in the mouse without an incision. Plast Reconstr Surg 84:723, 1989.

97. Sulik KK, Schoenwolf GC. Highlights of craniofacial morphogenesis in mammalian embryos as revealed by scanning electron microscopy. Scan Electron Microsc (Part IV):1735, 1985.

98. Sutliff KS, Hutchins GM. Septation of the respiratory and digestive tracts in human embryos: crucial role of the tracheoesophageal sulcus. Anat Rec 238:237, 1994.

99. Vidic B. The structure of the palatum osseum and its toral overgrowths. Acta Anat 71:94, 1968.

100. Von Lunteren E. Muscles of the pharynx: structural and contractile properties. Ear Nose Throat J 72:27, 1993.

101. Weaver LT. Anatomy and embryology. In Walker WA, Durie PR, Hamilton JR, et al (eds). Pediatric Gastrointestinal Disease, Vol I. Philadelphia, BC Decker, 1991, pp 195–216.

102. Wedden SE, Ralphs JR, Tickle C. Pattern formation in the facial primordia. Development 103(Suppl):31, 1988.

51

Physiology of the Mouth, Pharynx, and Esophagus

Randall L. Plant, M.D., and Craig S. Derkay, M.D.

The mouth, pharynx, and esophagus provide the structural and dynamic components for respiration, speech, and swallowing. This chapter describes the functional anatomy and physiology for this region, with emphasis directed toward those structures involved in swallowing.

Functions of the Anatomic Units

Respiration

The oral cavity plays a passive role in most respiratory efforts. In the newborn, the tongue occupies most of this space, making nasal respiration necessary for the first 2 to 3 weeks of life. At this stage of development, the larynx is positioned high in the neck, allowing the epiglottis to sit behind the inferior aspect of the uvula (Fig. 51–1). This accounts for the infant's ability to sleep and breathe effortlessly and to suckle and breathe simultaneously.

After infancy, the oral cavity may act as a passive conduit in respiration. This occurs during mouth breathing associated with heavy exercise and with chronic obstructive problems of the nose and nasopharynx. In this role, the hyoglossal and intrinsic tongue muscles depress the dorsum of the tongue while the tensor and levator muscles of the palate contract to open the pharyngeal isthmus. The latter action results in closing of the nasopharyngeal port and compounds the mouth breathing problem.

The genioglossus muscle maintains an important role from the outset in drawing the tongue base forward and keeping the hypopharynx open during respiration. This is particularly important during sleep. Lack of proper positioning or inadequate tensing of this muscle, such as in patients with retrognathia or neuromuscular dysfunction, contributes to the development of obstructive sleep apnea.

The anterior tonsillar pillars and pharynx play another role relative to respiration. In any voluntary swallowing activity, except for suckling, there is a signal from these sites to inhibit the respiratory center and to stop respiration. Cranial nerves V, IX, and X conduct the afferent limb of this reflex.

Speech

The lungs and the larynx function respectively as the power supply and sound source for voiced speech production. The pharynx and the oral cavity modulate, articulate, and add character to sound to make it intelligible. During the first 9 months of life, when crying and cooing are the primary forms of communication, this system is used only as a noisemaker. After this stage and when voluntary control over tongue movement is gained, the first attempts at modulation of the basic sounds occur. Simple approximation of the tongue to the hard palate in a repetitive fashion yields the first "da da" sound. The "ma ma" sound comes with repetitive opening and closing of the mouth alone.

Imitation of environmental sounds results in a cascade of new attempts at speech. This occurs with the development of more sophisticated relationships between lip closure, tongue movement, and soft palate closure. Further refinements in speech occur as a result of respiratory control, modulation of the sound at the vocal cord level, and overall sound character imparted by the effects of the nasopharyngeal and nasal cavities.

Salivation

Salivation results from autonomic stimulation of the major salivary glands: the parotid, submandibular, and sublingual glands. The many minor salivary glands lining the oral cavity and the pharynx also contribute to this process. Stimulation of these glands comes from a combination of psychic and physical factors. The physical factors include the presence of food in the oral cavity, as well as the presence of tastes and smells.

Parasympathetic stimulation to the glandular units comes from the salivatory nuclei. The inferior salivatory nuclei send impulses via the otic ganglion to the parotid glands, and the superior salivatory nuclei act similarly via the submandibular ganglia to the sublingual and submandibular glands. The superior cervical sympathetic ganglia provide innervation by way of the nerves that accompany the external carotid system.[6]

Saliva is important for normal function in the oral

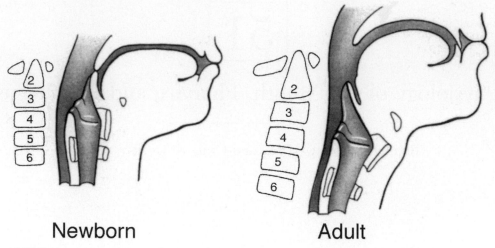

Newborn   Adult

FIGURE 51-1. Cross-sectional view of the upper aerodigestive tract in the infant and the adult. The cervical vertebrae are numbered. (From Myer CM, Cotton RT, Shott SR. The Pediatric Airway, An Interdisciplinary Approach. Philadelphia, JB Lippincott, 1995.)

cavity, pharynx, and esophagus. Mucin acts as a lubricant for tongue, palate, and food movement.[10] The digestive process begins when salivary amylase is mixed with food during chewing. This enzyme converts starch to maltose, which is less complex. Saliva also contains many antibacterial and bacteriostatic substances such as immunoglobulin A lysozyme, lactoferrin, and lactoperoxidase.

During baseline (nonstimulated) conditions, the submandibular gland produces approximately 70% and the parotid gland produces approximately 25% of the daily saliva flow.[4] When stimulated, parotid flow increases to match that of the submandibular gland. Proper tongue and cheek movement is necessary to distribute saliva both during swallowing and between meals. Mouth breathing, mandibular displacement, and neuromuscular dysfunctions affecting the muscles of the tongue and mastication can disrupt movement of saliva and produce drooling or aspiration.

Taste

The end organs for taste appreciation, the taste buds, are found primarily in the tongue, but they have also been found in the cheeks, palate, and pharynx. Afferent fibers from the anterior two thirds of the tongue are in the chorda tympani nerves; those from the posterior one third of the tongue follow the glossopharyngeal nerves. The maxillary and the mandibular divisions of the trigeminal nerve may be important in newborns, because they relate to the extralingual taste buds in the oral cavity and the pharynx. All taste fibers project to the solitary nuclei and tracts, and from there to the thalamic and cortical projections (see Central Nervous System Control).

Taste appreciation is a dynamic process in infants and children.[11] Preferences for sweets occur in early infancy. When sucrose is added to an infant's formula, the "pause and burst" pattern of suckling changes to a low-frequency high-amplitude pattern of suckling without pauses. Bitter tastes produce a negative response in infants, and the response to salty tastes varies. In neonates, bitter tastes

either are not liked or produce no response. Adult patterns for salt appreciation may be present as early as age 2 years. The volatile aspects of foods, such as the taste and the smell of cherry flavoring, may be appreciated by infants (thus the preference or disdain for certain flavored medications), but they are not fully appreciated until age 5 years.

Swallowing

The swallowing process is usually divided into four phases: oral preparatory, oral transport, pharyngeal, and esophageal.

During the *oral preparatory phase*, the food is tasted, chewed, mixed with saliva, and formed into a bolus in preparation for movement into the pharynx and the esophagus. The major muscles of mastication are the masseter, temporalis, and the lateral and medial pterygoids. Coordinated contraction of the tongue and buccal musculature moves the food within the oral cavity for effective chewing. Proper salivary function is crucial to moisten dry food so that it can achieve the proper consistency and to begin the digestive process. The oral preparatory phase is concluded with the food positioned on top of the anterior tongue.

Cranial nerves V, VII, and IX are largely responsible for motor supply to the muscles used in the oral preparatory phase. The oral cavity is lined by a variety of different types of sensory cells that provide feedback during the swallow. Mechanoreceptive cells account for the largest number of cells and for the greatest area of coverage. These cells are concentrated most heavily at the tip of the tongue and along the midline of the palate. Peristaltic tongue movements are produced when the sensory cells on the palate are stimulated with pressure.[2]

The oral cavity also is innervated by thermoreceptive and chemoreceptive cells. The spatial distribution of the thermoreceptive cells is highest along regions of the palate and tongue that come in contact with each other during swallowing. Chemoreceptive cells are distributed most densely along the tongue. The specific role of these receptors in swallowing is not well known.[13]

During the *oral transport phase,* the soft palate rises to contact the posterior pharyngeal wall and the tongue elevates to contact the anterior hard palate. The remainder of the tongue then thrusts upward, pushing the food bolus back into the oropharynx. Simultaneous contraction of the lips and buccinator muscles prevents trapping of food in the buccal sulcus.

As the food bolus travels past the tonsillar pillars, sensory receptors help trigger the *pharyngeal phase* of swallowing. The pharyngeal phase begins with a "leading complex" that comes primarily from the genioglossus muscle, with contributions from the mylohyoid, stylohyoid, geniohyoid, and hyoglossus muscles. These muscles raise the hyoid bone and pull it anteriorly. This positions the larynx beneath the base of the tongue and facilitates closure of the epiglottis.[3]

The leading complex is the first part of a time-locked sequence of muscular contraction. Early in the phase, the velopharynx closes via contraction of the palatopharyngeal and the levator veli palatini muscles. Respiration ceases and the pharyngeal constrictors produce a peristaltic narrowing of the hypopharynx.[14]

The upper esophageal sphincter (UES) prevents air from prematurely entering the esophagus during swallowing and limits reflux of gastric contents between swallows. The cricopharyngeal muscle plays a crucial role in the UES, but its exact functional relationship to surrounding muscles still is not completely understood. The full width of the cricopharyngeus muscle is less than the width of the high-pressure region of the UES identified using manometric studies, so it alone cannot comprise the full sphincter.[5, 9]

Relaxation of the cricopharyngeus muscle begins shortly after the beginning of the pharyngeal phase. The cricopharyngeus muscle and the remainder of the UES remain relaxed as the peristaltic wave from the constrictors passes the bolus into the proximal esophagus.

Sphincter opening and closure occur during the time of maximum laryngeal elevation. The pressure drop occurs simultaneously with the maximum anterior-superior displacement of the hyoid bone. This suggests that the generation of negative pressure and the opening of the UES are at least facilitated by a traction force produced by the displacement of the hyoid. Pressure from the bolus itself contributes, but is not essential, to the opening of the UES.

The act of swallowing is complex and may be disrupted by lack of function, or dysfunction, of any neuromuscular component between or within the phases of deglutition. Aspiration occurs when the food bolus, or saliva alone, enters the hypopharynx at a moment when the larynx has not been drawn superiorly and anteriorly into its protected position or when the cricopharyngeal muscle fails to relax to allow passage into the esophagus.

The *esophageal phase* is entirely under the influence of the autonomic nervous system via the vagus nerve and the cervical and thoracic sympathetic ganglia. This phase begins when the bolus passes through the relaxed cricopharyngeal muscle and enters the cervical esophagus. This portion of the esophagus contains skeletal muscle and the bolus moves quickly. In the thoracic segment, where it is under the influence of smooth muscle, it moves slowly.[16]

Motility studies in the normal esophagus show a primary wave of contraction that arises in the pharynx and continues along the entire length of the esophagus. Secondary waves begin in the body of the esophagus and continue to the stomach. The movement of the bolus is also controlled by the intrathoracic pressure changes associated with respiration. Inspiration enhances movement of the bolus, whereas the positive pressure of expiration slows it down. Coughing, from either primary respiratory problems or aspiration, may slow down or reverse the passage of the food bolus in the intrathoracic portion of the esophagus. This can aggravate existing problems with aspiration.

The final checkpoint for the bolus is at the gastroesophageal junction, where the esophageal and diaphragmatic musculatures are organized into the lower esophageal sphincter. Both the upper and the lower esophageal sphincters represent high intraluminal pressure zones, but the pressures decrease as the stripping wave passes through them. The lower esophageal sphincter is less competent in infants and young children than it is in adults, accounting for the frequent occurrence of gastroesophageal reflux in newborns and infants.

Central Nervous System Control

Stimulation studies have shown regions in the brain stem, specifically in the pons and the medulla, that evoke a swallowing reflex when stimulated. The motor nuclei for many of the muscles involved in swallowing also are located in the brain stem. However, direct stimulation of these motor nuclei produces a contraction of only a specific muscle group and does not generate a complete swallowing reflex. Therefore, the motor nuclei themselves are distal to the interneurons that are actually responsible for initiating the swallow reflex.

Within the pons, regions dorsal and ventral to the trigeminal nucleus evoke swallowing when stimulated. The dorsal region is a reticular formation that receives ascending sensory input from the pharynx and, in turn, transmits this information to the thalamus. The region ventral to the trigeminal nucleus is part of the descending cortical-subcortical pathway. Both of these regions are responsible for conveying information about swallowing, rather than its actual control.

Two areas lower in the brain stem are more closely associated with the control of swallowing. One of these, the nucleus tractus solitarius (NTS), lies in the dorsal medulla. Many of the peripheral nerves that initiate swallowing when stimulated, such as the superior laryngeal nerve, synapse in the NTS and in the adjacent reticular formation. The NTS also contains synapses from the cortical regions that evoke swallowing. Synapses to the interneurons here have very short latencies. When they fire, a burst of activity is sent to the motor nuclei with a specific timing sequence that evokes a coordinated swallow.[17]

Between the NTS and the dorsal motor nucleus of the vagus nerve is a separate region that receives input from pharyngeal receptors and is crucial for generating the esophageal phase of swallowing. Unilateral lesions here or in the NTS do not prevent a swallow if the contralateral superior laryngeal nerve is stimulated, implying that there is bilateral innervation of this control center (Fig. 51–2).

The second region in the medulla, lying more ventrally, that plays a role in swallowing is the nucleus ambiguus (NA). Stimulation of the NA produces the esophageal, but not the pharyngeal, phase of swallowing.

The NA receives sensory inputs from the superior laryngeal nerve, but the latencies of these signals are greater than for the NTS. Cortical input to this region is present and is more extensive than in the NTS. These cortical inputs are believed to be primarily involved in the modulation of activity during swallowing. The NA has multiple synaptic connections with ipsilateral and contralateral motor nuclei and brain stem regions that are involved in swallowing. The NA has been called the "switching" nuclei for swallowing, compared with the "master" neurons in the NTS.[15]

Role of the Cerebral Cortex

The cerebral cortex plays a major role in the initiation of the voluntary oral and pharyngeal phase of swallowing. Muscle contraction during the involuntary phase of swallowing has been considered to be primarily influenced by lower brain stem activity. Because these brain stem regions receive bilateral cortical input, bilateral injury was previously thought to be necessary to impair swallowing. Studies have shown, however, that the cortex may play a more significant role in facilitating swallowing and that unilateral lesions may be more damaging than were previously believed.[15]

Stimulation of a region immediately in front of the precentral cortex evokes swallowing that often is associated with mastication. Surface electrode stimulation of the lateral precentral and sylvian cortex during awake craniotomies for epilepsy surgery produces swallowing that is accompanied by orofacial movement, salivation, and vocalization. In experimental animals, the greatest disruption of swallowing was produced with lesions in the lowest part of the precentral gyrus and the posterior portion of the inferior frontal gyrus. These cortical regions are thought to modify the duration and intensity of swallowing and to coordinate the interaction of the facial, tongue, and masticatory muscles. The actions involved are related to tongue movement, elevation of the hyoid bone, adduction of the vocal folds, and contraction of the upper esophagus. Stimulation of these regions also produces swallowing that is associated with mastication. Reflex swallowing is facilitated by input from the hypothalamus and the midbrain ventral tegmental field; exposing these regions to dopamine increases this facilitation.[12, 15]

Development from Suckle Feeding to Mature Swallowing

The unique suckle reflex of the infant is regulated in the brain stem. It allows the infant a constant flow of milk from a natural or synthetic nipple while maintaining regular respirations.[8] The dynamics of the process involve alternating compression of the nipple with development of negative pressure in the oral cavity, which acts as a reservoir while normal respirations are occurring. The tongue empties the reservoir into the pharynx at regular intervals, and the pharyngeal phase of swallowing occurs with no interruption of the respiratory cycle.

From birth to 6 months, the predominant pattern of tongue movement is suckling, with primarily an anterior-posterior thrusting movement of the tongue. After 6 months, the pattern shifts to sucking predominantly characterized by a strong upward and downward movement of the tongue. During feeding, the sucking rate is approximately one suck per second, with a 1:1 relationship between sucking and swallowing.

Infants demonstrate a non-nutritive suckling reflex when a finger or plastic nipple is placed in the mouth. Non-nutritive sucking is important in the development of proper oral-motor coordination. Infants receiving nutrition through nasogastric or percutaneous feeding tubes need oral-motor stimulation to ensure that this development takes place.[1, 19]

In infants, the pharyngeal phase is of longer duration and the forward movement of the posterior pharyngeal wall is exaggerated compared with that of adults. Despite the prolonged transit time of the bolus through the pharynx, there is normally no aspiration seen in newborns and infants. This is probably a result of the soft cartilaginous laryngeal framework, which allows more efficient sphincter closure.[7]

The infantile swallow is characterized by protrusion of the tongue to the lower lip, slight parting of the jaws, and active contraction of the facial muscles. The first maturation, or transition, is when the tongue lies lower in the mouth and extends between the teeth laterally and the lips purse and pucker. At this stage, any solids introduced into the mouth cause the tongue to press against the hard palate.

The next transition is characterized by jaw closure and an approximation of the posterior alveolar ridges on swallowing. At 4 to 6 months of age, solid foods elicit a posterior stripping action of the tongue, followed by a swallow. Rhythmic biting occurs at 7 to 9 months of age, and facial muscle activity is less prominent. The masticatory effort increases after 12 months of age, coincident with the appearance of teeth. The tongue tip, which had been positioned between the incisors, moves posterior to them. At this age, the efficiency of mastication is low. By age 6 years, the efficiency of mastication increases to approximately 40% of the adult level, but it is not at the adult level until age 16 years. Children and teenagers tend to gulp their food and swallow large portions, but their digestive system is able to handle the larger pieces of food.[18]

Summary

The functions of the mouth, pharynx, and esophagus are related primarily to the digestive system. Their interface

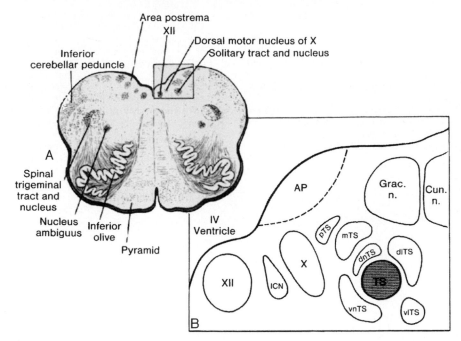

FIGURE 51–2. *A,* Major cell groups and tracts in the caudal medulla. The enclosed area in the dorsomedial portion of the diagram is shown in greater detail in part B. *B,* Subnuclei forming the nucleus of the solitary tract, which receives afferents from cranial nerves IX and X. AP, area postrema; Cun. n., cuneate nucleus; dlTS, dorsolateral nucleus of solitary tract; dnTS, dorsal nucleus of solitary tract; Grac. n., gracile nucleus; ICN, intercalated nucleus; mTS, medial nucleus of solitary tract; pTS, parvicellular nucleus of solitary tract; TS, solitary tract; vlTS, ventrolateral nucleus of solitary tract; vnTS, ventral nucleus of solitary tract; X, dorsal motor nucleus of vagus nerve; XII, hypoglossal nucleus. (From Parent A. Carpenter's Human Neuroanatomy, 9th ed. Philadelphia, Williams & Wilkins, 1996.)

with the respiratory system and the speech-producing mechanism further complicates the physiology of this region. This chapter outlines the relationships between these structures and the functional anatomic units that are derived from them. The physiologic changes that accompany maturation from the newborn period through infancy and childhood are presented.

Acknowledgments

The authors thank Gary L. Schechter, M.D., for his assistance in the preparation of this paper.

SELECTED REFERENCES

Conklin JL, Christensen J. Motor functions of the pharynx and esophagus. In Johnson L (ed). Physiology of the Gastrointestinal Tract. New York, Raven Press, 1994, pp 903–928.
   A thorough description of the upper aerodigestive tract, with an emphasis on the esophagus.
Perlman AL, Schulze-Delrieu K (eds). Deglutition and Its Disorders. San Diego, Singular, 1997.
   A comprehensive description of the anatomy, physiology, diagnosis, and treatment of a wide variety of swallowing disorders.

REFERENCES

1. Arvedson JC, Rogers BT. Swallowing and feeding in the pediatric patient. In Perlman AL, Schulze-Delrieu K (eds). Deglutition and Its Disorders. San Diego, Singular, 1997, pp 419–448.
2. Bass NH. The neurology of swallowing. In Groher M (ed). Dysphagia: Diagnosis and Treatment. Boston, Butterworth-Heinemann, 1997, pp 7–35.
3. Conklin JL, Christensen J. Motor functions of the pharynx and esophagus. In Johnson L (ed). Physiology of the Gastrointestinal Tract. New York, Raven Press, 1994, pp 903–928.
4. Cunning DM, Lipke N, Wax MK. Significance of unilateral submandibular gland excision on salivary flow in noncancer patients. Laryngoscope 108:812, 1998.
5. Goyal RK, Martin SB, Shapiro J, et al. The role of the cricopharyngeus muscle in pharyngoesophageal disorders. Dysphagia 8:252, 1993.
6. Hanson KM. Physiology of the oral cavity, oropharynx, and nasopharynx. In Cummings C, Fredrickson J, Harker L, et al (eds). Otolaryngology-Head and Neck Surgery, vol. 1. St Louis, CV Mosby, 1986, pp 1103–1116.
7. Harding R. Functions of the larynx in the fetus and newborn. Annu Rev Physiol 46:645, 1984.
8. Herbst JJ. Development of sucking and swallowing. In Lebenthal E (ed). Textbook of Gastroenterology and Nutrition in Infancy. New York, Raven Press, 1981, pp 97–107.
9. Kahrilas PJ. Functional anatomy and physiology of the esophagus.

In Castell D (ed). The Esophagus. Boston, Little, Brown, 1992, pp 1–29.

10. Kaplan MD, Baum BJ. The functions of saliva. Dysphagia 8:225, 1993.

11. Lawless H. Sensory development in children: research in taste and olfaction. J Am Diet Assoc 85:577, 1985.

12. Martin RE, Sessle MDS. The role of the cerebral cortex and swallowing. Dysphagia 8:195, 1993.

13. Miller A, Bieger D, Conklin JL. Functional controls of deglutition. In Perlman A, Schulze-Delrieu K (eds). Deglutition and Its Disorders. San Diego, Singular, 1997, pp 43–98.

14. Miller AJ. Neurophysiological basis of swallowing. Dysphagia 1:91, 1986.

15. Miller AJ. The search for the central swallowing pathway: the quest for clarity. Dysphagia 8:185, 1993.

16. Perlman AL, Christensen J. Topography and functional anatomy of the swallowing structures. In Perlman AL, Schulze-Delrieu K (eds). Deglutition and Its Disorders. San Diego, Singular, 1997, pp 15–42.

17. Perlman A, Schulze-Delrieu K (eds). Deglutition and Its Disorders. San Diego, Singular, 1997.

18. Schwartz JL, Niman CW, Gisel EG. Tongue movements in normal preschool children during eating. Am J Occup Ther 38:87, 1984.

19. Tuchman DN. Cough, choke, sputter: the evaluation of the child with dysfunctional swallowing. Dysphagia 3:111, 1989.

52

Methods of Examination

Lawrence W.C. Tom, M.D., William P. Potsic, M.D., and Steven D. Handler, M.D.

Examination of the oral cavity and pharynx in a child may be a traumatic experience for both patient and examiner if there has been inadequate preparation. Children are usually being examined in an unfamiliar environment by a stranger and frequently have unpleasant objects placed in their mouth and nose. To prevent a child from interpreting the examination as an attack, the practitioner first needs to establish rapport with the child. Children should be verbally and physically reassured. Allaying their fears often means the difference between a successful examination and a frustrating, unsuccessful one. Touching and playing with the child while talking is often relaxing and reassuring.

An explanation of the examination while it is being carried out may help to assure the patient that there will be no unexpected maneuvers or painful surprises. Use of familiar examining aids such as fingers, tongue blades, and flashlights first promotes continued cooperation as unfamiliar instruments are employed. Permitting children to touch and play with some instruments may be helpful. These should be introduced with a simple explanation of their use. Uncomfortable or potentially disquieting portions of the oropharyngeal examination (which may cause gagging) should be reserved until the end of the examination.

The oropharyngeal examination should be performed with the child in a secure, comfortable position that allows mobility for the patient, and the examiner should be comfortably seated and mobile. Children are frequently examined while they sit in their parent's lap. This gives them a feeling of security and allows the parent to assist in the examination (Fig. 52–1). For very young children, a pediatric examining table may be used. Visualization of the oral cavity requires good light, directed along the line of sight. This may be provided with a flashlight or otoscope, but we recommend a head light, which leaves the examiner's hands free to move the patient and handle instruments.

Oral Cavity and Oropharynx

Examination of the oral cavity begins with a general inspection of the face, which can reveal much about a child's emotional and physical state. The examiner may sense anxiety or note an expression of pain in the child's face. A careful and thorough examination permits detection of even the most subtle lesions (Fig. 52–2). Observation of lip color may indicate anemia (pallor) or cardiopulmonary disease (cyanosis). The parched, dry appearance of dehydration or the copious drooling of neuromuscular disorders, oropharyngeal infections or burns, or esophageal foreign bodies may be noted. A mouth that is open to breathe may indicate nasopharyngeal obstruction or generalized air hunger. Odor from the oral cavity should not be ignored because it can be an early sign of a metabolic disorder, tumor, or infection. Inability of the child to open the mouth may indicate lack of cooperation, dysfunction of the fifth cranial nerve, trismus secondary to a lesion (neoplastic or inflammatory) involving fascial spaces, or a subcondylar mandibular fracture. Asymmetrical pursing of the lips is seen with seventh cranial nerve paralysis.

The primary method of examination of the oral cavity and pharynx is inspection. The mouth is opened and exposure is obtained with the use of wooden tongue blades, instruments familiar to all children. A careful systematic inspection of the oral cavity is performed, including an assessment of the teeth, gingiva, buccal mucosa, undersurface of the tongue, floor of the mouth, palate, and orifices of the salivary glands. To expose the entire buccal mucosal surface, the lips and cheeks can be retracted using a tongue blade simultaneously in each hand; failure to do so may result in overlooking significant pathologic changes (Fig. 52–3).

Examination of the teeth and gingiva gives the observer an idea of the child's general hygiene as well as clues to assist in the detection of systemic disorders[4] (e.g., the notched teeth of congenital syphilis, gingival alterations with vitamin deficiencies or drug ingestion) (Fig. 52–4).

The child is then asked to extend the tongue, thus exposing both lateral borders and frequently bringing the posterior third of the tongue forward and into view. In some children, the epiglottis may also be visualized at this time. During tongue extension, the neuromuscular function of the tongue (cranial nerve XII) can be assessed. Fasciculation, atrophy, or deviation of the tongue may be noted. The full range of tongue mobility can be observed; limitation may occur with a short frenulum or neuromuscular disorders. Tongue strength can be assessed by ap-

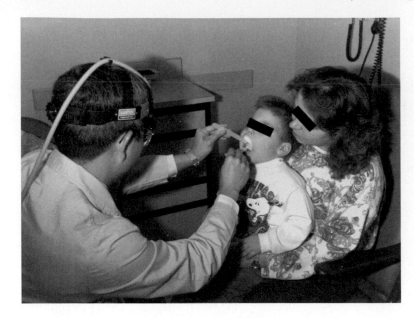

FIGURE 52–1. Young child being examined while on his mother's lap.

plying pressure with a finger against the patient's cheek when the tongue is pushed against the buccal surface.

Inspection of the palate is facilitated by extension of the head. The child is asked to say the familiar "ah," providing an opportunity to evaluate the neuromuscular function of the palate (cranial nerves IX and X). The examination may detect a bifid uvula, asymmetrical palatal retraction, or a palatomaxillary deformity such as a high-arched palate, torus palatinus, or cleft palate.

Inspection of the oropharynx is facilitated by depression of the tongue inferiorly and anteriorly. Care should be taken to place the tongue blade on the anterior two thirds of the tongue to avoid the gag reflex. With this maneuver, the posterior border of the palate, uvula, tonsils, and posterior pharyngeal wall can be seen. Tonsillar symmetry as well as surface appearance can be assessed. Care should be taken to place the child's head in the midline position, because head turning tenses the parapharyngeal muscles on the same side, displacing the tonsil medially. This displacement may give a false impression of asymmetry, thus mimicking unilateral tonsillar disease such as abscess or lymphoma (Fig. 52–5).

A complete examination of the oral cavity and pharynx includes palpation, which children usually accept without

difficulty because their own fingers are familiar objects to their mouths. Palpation of the tongue with a gloved finger offers valuable information about pathologic changes deep within its substance (lymphangioma) or surface anomalies (median rhomboid glossitis) (Fig. 52–6). Palpation of the palate is essential to detect submucous clefts, and anesthesia of the palate can be a sign of a destructive process involving the fifth cranial nerve at the foramen rotundum. Palpation of the posterior third of the tongue may reveal a lingual thyroid.

Bimanual palpation with a finger in the oral cavity and the opposite hand against the cheek permits evaluation of the quality and size of the parotid and submandibular salivary glands. Massage of the gland toward the duct orifice usually causes clear fluid to appear. Cloudy or sandy fluid is evidence of stasis and usually of inflammation. Salivary fluid can be collected, cultured, and examined microscopically. Immunoelectrophoresis may detect a rare immunoglobulin A deficiency.

Radiographic techniques are seldom used to evaluate

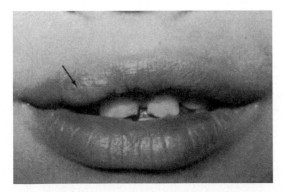

FIGURE 52–2. Hemangioma of the lip (*arrow*) that may be missed by a careless examiner.

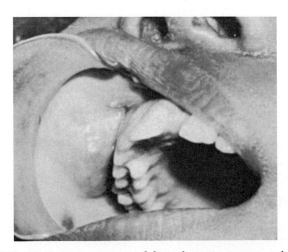

FIGURE 52–3. Hemangioma of buccal mucosa, seen only by retracting the lip.

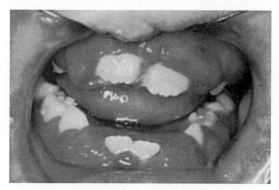

FIGURE 52–4. Gingival hypertrophy induced by phenytoin (Dilantin).

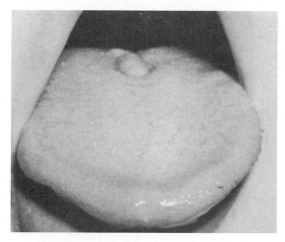

FIGURE 52–6. Median rhomboid glossitis.

the oral cavity and oropharynx because these areas are accessible to physical examination. A lateral neck radiograph permits evaluation of the base of the tongue and posterior pharynx. Ultrasonography, computed tomography (CT), and magnetic resonance imaging (MRI) can be used to evaluate suspected lesions. Radioisotopic scanning with iodine-123 or technetium Tc 99m is used to detect a lingual thyroid. Contrast videoradiography may outline masses or foreign bodies and can be used to assess the oropharyngeal phases of deglutition (modified barium swallow test). Videoradiography and nasopharyngoscopy provide the most useful information in the assessment of velopharyngeal competence. Videoradiography in the lateral and base projections during phonation provides a dynamic evaluation of the palate and the lateral pharyngeal walls and creates a permanent record of function to guide therapeutic intervention. This evaluation is best performed by a speech pathologist in cooperation with a radiologist. Nasopharyngoscopy with video recording provides similar information and avoids radiation exposure.

Nasopharynx

Examination of the nasopharynx is most frequently accomplished by visualization. The preferred method employs the flexible fiberoptic laryngoscope (Fig. 52–7),

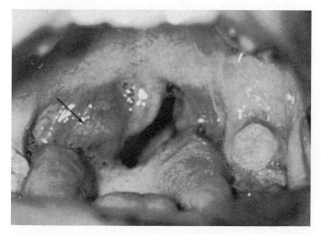

FIGURE 52–5. Lymphoma of the tonsil *(arrow)* manifesting as tonsillar asymmetry.

which has replaced both the nasopharyngeal mirror and the rigid telescope. Flexible telescopic examination provides a panoramic view of the nasopharynx and can be performed on many children in an office setting. Infants and small children have to be restrained by a parent or other adult. Older children and adolescents usually tolerate flexible nasopharyngoscopy. The examiner must explain the procedure and reassure the patient. If the examiner believes that the child is not a candidate for office nasopharyngoscopy or if attempts to perform the examination fail, general anesthesia may be required.

Before insertion of the telescope, a combination of a local anesthetic (lidocaine) and vasoconstrictive agent (oxymetazoline) is sprayed into the nose. After several minutes, the instrument is gently introduced into either nasal cavity and advanced under direct visualization (Fig. 52–8). The nasal cavity is inspected, and when the telescope enters the nasopharynx, the eustachian tube orifices, adenoids, and soft palate can be assessed. Palatal function can be evaluated, and lesions arising in or extending into the nasopharynx can be visualized. A video camera can be attached to the telescope, enabling several people to view the examination and providing an excellent teaching tool. Still photographs or the entire video can be obtained and included in the child's permanent record to document the presence of disease and, if serial examinations are performed, the progression or regression of disease.

Palpation of the nasopharynx is uncomfortable and difficult in the awake child but may be performed when the child is anesthetized. Assessment can be made of the adenoids, choanae, eustachian tube region, and any nasopharyngeal lesions.

Radiographic techniques provide extensive information about the nasopharynx and play an important role in the evaluation of this relatively inaccessible region. The lateral neck radiograph (Fig. 52–9) is an excellent screening study. It is easy to perform, involves little radiation, and provides valuable information regarding the adenoids, nasopharyngeal lesions, and the nasopharyngeal airway. Contrast radiography to outline the nasopharynx and evaluate the patency of the nasopharynx has rarely been used since the development of CT and MRI. Videofluoroscopy

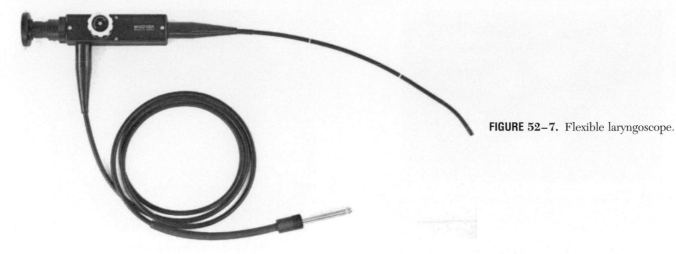

FIGURE 52-7. Flexible laryngoscope.

can be used to examine the palate and nasopharynx during the evaluation for velopharyngeal insufficiency.

CT and MRI provide the most complete evaluation of the nasopharynx.[6] CT is the study of choice to diagnose choanal atresia (Fig. 52–10) and may also detect intracranial communications such as nasopharyngeal encephaloceles. Both CT and MRI can identify masses in the nasopharynx and delineate their size and extent. MRI has several advantages and is preferred over CT for the evaluation of nasopharyngeal masses.[5] MRI (Fig. 52–11) is more sensitive to changes in contrast between the mass and normal tissue, providing superior resolution. It demonstrates better anatomic detail, has multiplanar capability, and involves no radiation exposure. The lack of bony artifact makes MRI especially useful in detecting lesions of the skull base and in revealing epidural and intradural spread, which CT may not demonstrate. CT, however, takes less time and is easier to perform, especially in young children. CT may complement MRI and, in some cases, be superior to MRI because CT will reveal bony involvement and intralesional calcifications (Fig. 52–12).

MRI can be combined with magnetic resonance angiography to delineate the vascularity of a mass and define the specific blood supply.[9] For some vascular lesions, arteriography may still be required to embolize individual vessels before instituting therapy.

Hypopharynx

As in the nasopharyngeal examination, the flexible fiberoptic laryngoscope is the instrument of choice for assessment of the hypopharynx. In addition to spraying the nose with a local anesthetic and vasoconstrictive agent, a local anesthetic is sprayed into the oral cavity and pharynx. The laryngoscope is introduced into the nose and advanced beyond the nasopharynx. This provides a panoramic and dynamic view of the hypopharynx, with visual-

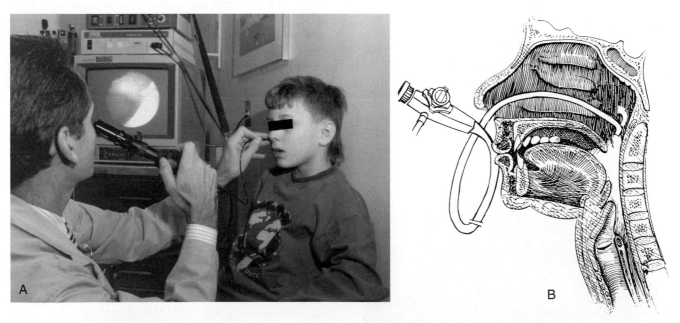

FIGURE 52-8. *A*, A flexible laryngoscope can be inserted into the nose (as pictured) or into the mouth. *B*, The distal tip can be deflected to view the nasopharynx or the larynx. The camera allows additional people to view the examination and permits it to be recorded.

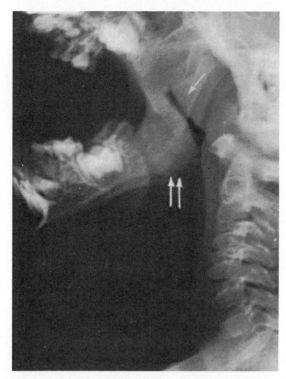

FIGURE 52–9. Lateral neck radiograph demonstrating enlarged adenoid pad *(single arrow)* and tonsils *(double arrows)*.

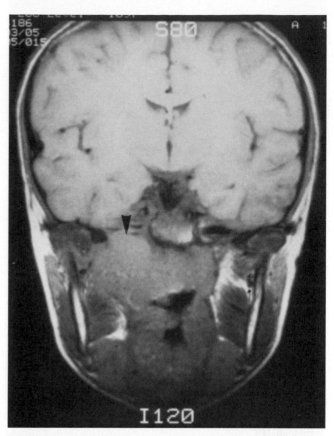

FIGURE 52–11. Magnetic resonance image demonstrating a carcinoma in the nasopharynx with intracranial extension *(arrow)*.

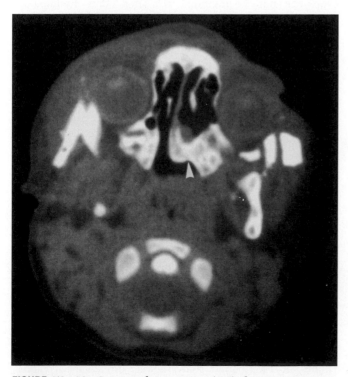

FIGURE 52–10. Computed tomogram (CT) demonstrating unilateral choanal atresia *(arrow)*.

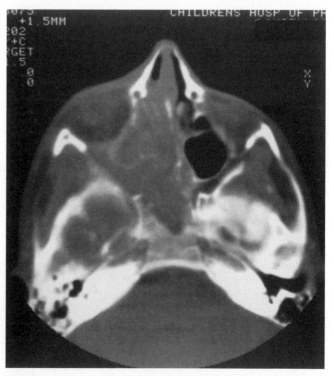

FIGURE 52–12. CT demonstrating a rhabdomyosarcoma involving the nasopharynx, nasal cavities, right maxillary sinus, and right pterygomaxillary fossa with destruction of the base of the skull.

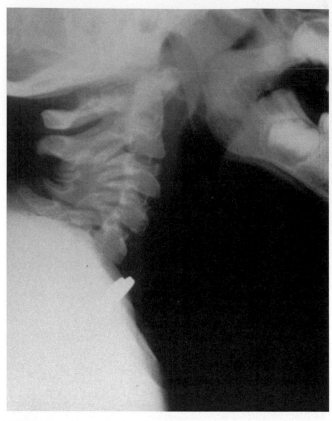

FIGURE 52–13. Lateral neck radiograph of a child demonstrating two coins in the esophagus. The second coin would not have been detected without the lateral view.

ization of the base of the tongue, the vallecula, the epiglottis, and the true and false vocal cords. A camera can be attached to the telescope for teaching, observation, and documentation. Video photographic recording can also be made but is of more value in the evaluation of the larynx than of the hypopharynx. A camera can also be attached to a rigid telescope. Although the optics may be superior to the flexible instrument, examination with the rigid telescope is more uncomfortable and, thus, more difficult to perform. These two methods have replaced the laryngeal mirror for assessment of the hypopharynx.

Direct visualization of the hypopharynx is usually done in conjunction with direct laryngoscopy. This examination may be performed in an office setting, but in most cases it is performed in the operating room under general anesthesia, allowing for a more thorough examination of the hypopharynx and adjacent structures and biopsy of any suspected lesions.

Palpation of the hypopharynx should not be performed in an awake child because it is uncomfortable, causes gagging, and may induce emesis. The laryngeal structures can also be injured. Foreign bodies may be forced into the mucosa, with subsequent perforation, or pushed into the larynx, resulting in airway obstruction.

Radiographic evaluation is useful. Lateral neck radiographs, CT, and MRI may yield valuable information regarding the anatomy of the hypopharynx. Contrast videoradiography may be especially helpful in demonstrating

neuromuscular dysfunction in deglutition, reflux into the nasopharynx, and laryngeal aspiration. The contrast may also outline masses.

Fiberoptic endoscopic evaluation of swallowing is another method for the evaluation and documentation of the pharyngeal stage of swallowing. It can be performed in children who tolerate flexible fiberoptic pharyngoscopy and compares favorably with videofluoroscopy. The endoscope is passed just beyond the palate, and structures and function of the pharynx and larynx are examined during speech and swallowing. Food coloring can be placed on the tongue, and its clearance is used to evaluate the child's ability to handle secretions. Pharyngeal clearance, coordination of swallowing, and aspiration can be assessed by the child's ability to swallow different amounts and textures of food.[8]

Esophagus

The definitive method of esophageal examination is esophagoscopy; however, radiography of the esophagus should precede endoscopy in nearly all cases. Radiographic studies help determine the nature and location of the pathologic changes to be evaluated. This is especially true in children with esophageal foreign bodies, strictures, congenital anomalies, or surgically produced anatomic variations (e.g., colon interposition). Careful radiographic evaluation before esophagoscopy can prevent serious complications such as esophageal perforation.

In children, anteroposterior and lateral views of the neck and chest are used to demonstrate the esophagus. These projections permit evaluation of the esophagus in the neck and mediastinum as well as its relationship to surrounding structures. In small children, the entire esophagus may be included in a single film. Radiopaque foreign bodies, subcutaneous emphysema from perforation, and displacement of structures may be seen on plain films. The anteroposterior and lateral projections are complementary, and, for the most thorough evaluation,

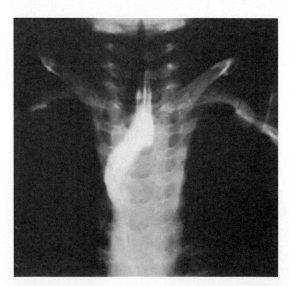

FIGURE 52–14. Contrast study showing extraluminal compression of the esophagus.

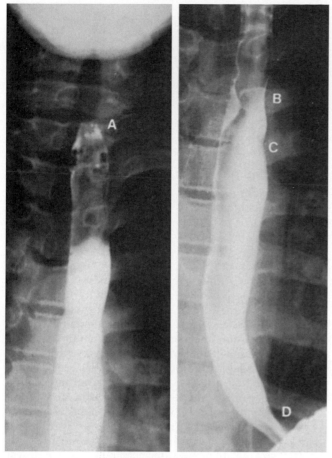

FIGURE 52–15. Normal esophagogram with narrowing at the thoracic inlet (A), aortic arch (B), take-off of the left mainstem bronchus (C), and gastroesophageal junction (D).

geal fistula[2] (Fig. 52–16). These patients are particularly susceptible to food impaction at the site of the stricture. The stricture may be improved by dilatation using an esophageal dilator.

Videofluoroscopy using barium provides a qualitative evaluation of the neuromuscular function of the esophagus and should be performed in all patients with suspected esophageal disease. The serial pictures also provide a permanent record to follow the progress of disease and response to therapy. When a clinical history of aspiration suggests a communication between the esophagus and the respiratory tract, as in a tracheoesophageal stricture, a water-miscible contrast material should be used. Oily contrast material causes severe pneumonitis if aspirated into the airway.

Esophageal manometry documents and quantitates the neuromuscular function of the esophagus and is used to demonstrate functional swallowing disorders.[7] The esophageal pH probe is used to diagnose gastroesophageal reflux, a condition that is being recognized with increasing frequency in children. Probes are placed at the gastroesophageal junction and at the level of the cricopharyngeal muscle to detect the presence of acid. Esophageal biopsy may also be used to diagnose this condition.

Esophagoscopy allows visualization of the entire esophagus and should be performed after a sufficient period of fasting (usually 8 hours) to ensure an empty stomach, thereby decreasing the risk of aspiration. Two types of esophagoscopes are currently available: rigid (Fig. 52–17) and flexible (Fig. 52–18). Both are available in sizes ap-

both should be obtained. Significant findings may be missed if both projections are not reviewed (Fig. 52–13).

Contrast videoradiography of the esophagus is particularly valuable because the esophagus can be outlined easily with varying thicknesses of barium. This allows evaluation of the mucosa, outlining of intrinsic masses and foreign bodies, and demonstration of compression by external masses (Fig. 52–14). Barium is well accepted by children, and young children often drink the contrast medium from a bottle quite readily.

Esophagography is performed with the child in the prone position and with a slight rotation of the body to the right. In this manner, the transit time of the contrast medium is slowed to allow a careful assessment of motility as the esophagus is projected away from the overlying vertebral column. The normal esophagus has five areas of constriction where foreign bodies can become lodged.[1] Most foreign bodies come to rest at the cricopharyngeal area (C6) or in the hiatal region (T10–T11). Other narrowed regions occur at the thoracic inlet (T1), the aortic arch (T4), and the tracheal bifurcation (T6), where the left mainstem bronchus crosses the esophagus (Fig. 52–15). Abnormal strictures may be seen in children with a history of caustic ingestion and after esophageal surgery, especially repair of esophageal atresia, and tracheoesopha-

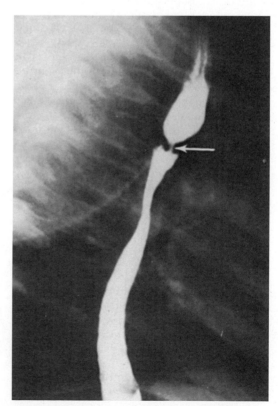

FIGURE 52–16. Esophageal stricture *(arrow)* after repair of esophageal atresia.

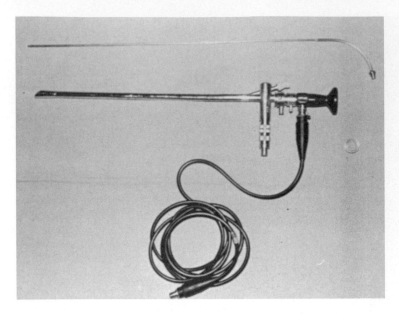

FIGURE 52–17. Rigid, open-ended esophagoscope (with Hopkins rod lens telescope).

propriate for pediatric patients, both use fiberoptic light sources, and both can be attached to cameras for teaching purposes.

Esophagoscopy in children is almost always carried out in the operating room with general anesthesia or in an endoscopy suite with the patient under sedation so that muscle relaxants may be used to decrease the risk of esophageal perforation. Lack of esophageal relaxation increases the risk of perforation.[3] Local anesthesia is not used for pediatric esophagoscopy. Children do not tolerate this uncomfortable procedure while awake, and their greater sensitivity to the toxicity of the local anesthetic agents makes this method potentially more dangerous.

If the flexible instrument is chosen, the patient is placed supine on the operating table, and a roll is placed under the shoulders to extend the neck. A lubricating agent such as water-soluble jelly is applied to the shaft of the endoscope. The instrument is inserted into the oral cavity and advanced while the examiner observes through the eyepiece (Fig. 52–19). The advancing end of the esophagoscope may be deflected in any direction to facilitate passage through the cricopharyngeal muscle and advancement through the esophageal lumen and into the stomach (Fig. 52–20). Air is insufflated through one of the channels to balloon out the esophagus in front of the advancing esophagoscope. The entire esophagus may be examined, as well as the stomach, if desired. Aspiration and biopsy can be performed through this instrument, but the size of the operating channel may limit the amount of tissue that can be obtained. Similarly, the retrieval of foreign bodies may be hampered by the size of the forceps. In addition, the foreign body cannot be drawn up into the lumen of the esophagoscope (as can be done in the rigid open esophagoscope) to protect the esophageal mucosa from injury as the instrument and foreign body are withdrawn.

When the rigid esophagoscope is used, the patient is again placed supine on the operating table, with a roll

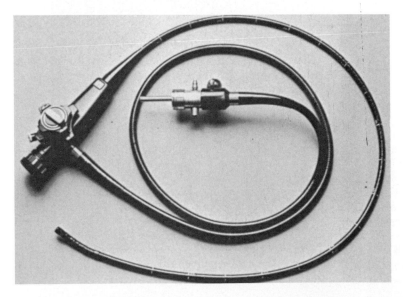

FIGURE 52–18. A 9-mm gastrointestinal fiberscope.

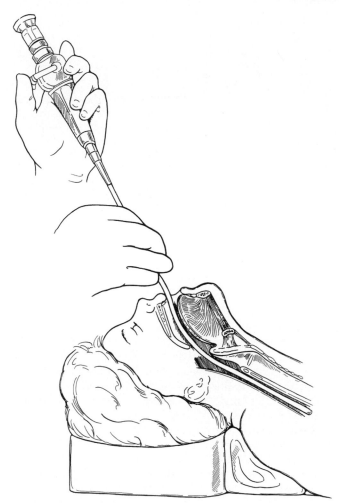

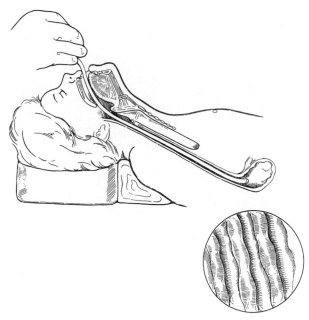

FIGURE 52–20. The distal tip of the esophagoscope can be deflected in any direction to facilitate the passage of the instrument through the esophagus and into the stomach. *Insert* depicts the rugae of the stomach.

FIGURE 52–19. The flexible esophagoscope is inserted into the mouth and advanced through the esophagus.

under the shoulders to extend the neck. The patient's mouth is opened with the endoscopist's left hand, and a moistened gauze sponge or rubber guard is placed over the upper lip and teeth to prevent injury by the instruments. A Jackson laryngoscope is used to facilitate identification of the esophageal inlet and to permit a complete examination of the oral cavity, the hypopharynx, and (if necessary) the larynx. The laryngoscope is held with the left hand and introduced into the oral cavity, which is examined in a systematic fashion. The instrument is advanced into the hypopharynx, which is thoroughly examined, and then into the postcricoid region to identify the esophageal inlet. To minimize the risk of perforation, the esophagoscope should not be introduced until the inlet is located. It is at this site that esophageal perforations most commonly occur.

When the inlet has been visualized, the proximal end of the rigid esophagoscope is grasped like a pencil with the right hand. The esophagoscope (with its distal shaft lubricated) is inserted into the oral cavity and, following the laryngoscope, introduced into the esophagus (Fig. 52–21). The laryngoscope is then removed, and the left

FIGURE 52–21. The rigid esophagoscope is inserted into the esophagus using a laryngoscope as a guide.

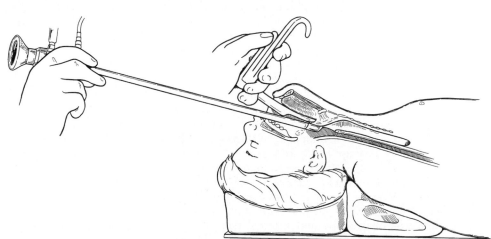

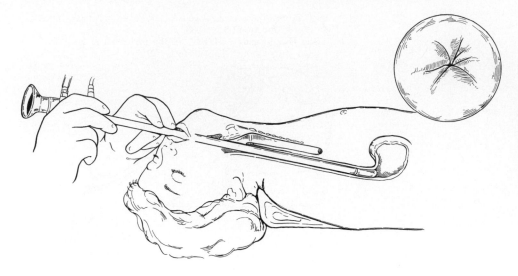

FIGURE 52–22. The patient's head is turned slightly to the right to facilitate passage of the esophagoscope into the stomach. *Insert* depicts the appearance of the esophageal lumen at the level of the gastroesophageal sphincter.

hand is held near the patient's mouth to steady and support the esophagoscope while keeping it away from the patient's lips and teeth. The esophagoscope is advanced slowly and carefully with the left hand as the right hand stabilizes the instrument.

If passage of the instrument is difficult, a soft filiform dilator or lumen finder may be inserted through the esophagoscope and into the esophagus. The esophagoscope is then advanced following the dilator under direct vision. If a cuffed endotracheal tube is used, it may be necessary to deflate the balloon to permit passage of the esophagoscope. Air may be insufflated to balloon the mucosa out in front of the esophagoscope and to aid in identifying the lumen. The esophagoscope is never advanced unless the lumen is in view. The instrument is gently advanced (never forced) through the thoracic esophagus and, in some patients, into the cardia of the stomach. Because the distal esophagus turns to the left and anteriorly before entering the stomach, the patient's head and shoulders must be lowered below the rest of the body, with the head turned slightly to the right to allow the esophagoscope to enter the stomach (Fig. 52–22). As the stomach is entered, gastric juice and rugal folds are visualized. The esophagus is examined again as the esophagoscope is removed. The esophagoscope is withdrawn using a circular motion to distend the mucosa, providing complete visualization of the esophagus. Aspiration, biopsy, and retrieval of foreign bodies can be performed through the open esophagoscope with a variety of special instruments.

Postoperative management is individualized. If the esophagoscopy was atraumatic, oral intake may be started when the child is awake. If a sharp foreign body was removed or the procedure was traumatic, difficult, or complicated, the patient is maintained on intravenous fluids and observed for symptoms and signs of esophageal perforation. Usually, no antibiotics and antipyretics are prescribed because they could mask signs and symptoms of perforation. When a cervical esophageal perforation occurs, signs and symptoms include sore throat immediately following esophagoscopy and cervical pain, tenderness, swelling, and crepitus. Perforation of the thoracic esophagus is more serious and is suggested by chest pain radiating to the back, high fever, hypotension, tachypnea, tachycardia, crepitus, and sternal tenderness.

If a perforation is suspected, the diagnosis may be confirmed by chest and neck radiographs that demonstrate cervical emphysema, pneumomediastinum, widening of the mediastinum, or pleural effusion. The site of the perforation may be localized by having the patient swallow a water-miscible, radiopaque dye.

Small cervical perforations without large tracts or pockets respond well to restricted oral intake and intravenous antibiotics. Larger tears and gross mediastinal involvement require surgical drainage. The catastrophe of esophageal perforation is best prevented by careful and cautious esophagoscopy. However, if perforation does occur, prompt recognition and treatment are key factors in preventing the significant morbidity and mortality that can accompany this complication.

Conclusion

Examination of the oral cavity, pharynx, and esophagus using basic physical diagnostic techniques, radiography, endoscopy, and a variety of other maneuvers can identify disease states. Proper evaluation of these areas requires the physician to be skilled both in the performance of these methods of examination and in the interpretation of their results.

SELECTED REFERENCES

Handler SD, Myer CM. Atlas of Ear, Nose, and Throat Disorders in Children. Ontario, Canada, BC Decker, 1998.
   An excellent atlas displaying disorders of the aerodigestive tract in children.
Schild JA, Snow JB. In Ballenger JJ, Snow JB (eds). Otorhinolaryngology Head and Neck Surgery, 15th ed. Philadelphia, Lea & Febiger, 1996.
   An excellent, concise treatise on all aspects of esophagology.
Valvassori GE, Mafee MF, Carter BL. Imaging of the Head and Neck. New York, Thieme, 1994.
   This text is a complete review of imaging of the head and neck.

REFERENCES

1. Atkins JP Jr, Keane WM. Esophagology. In English GM (ed). Otolaryngology, vol. 3. New York, Harper & Row, 1978, pp 1–28.
2. Benjamin B. Atlas of Paediatric Endoscopy: Upper Respiratory Tract and Oesophagus. New York, Oxford University Press, 1981.
3. Gans SL (ed). Pediatric Endoscopy. New York, Grune & Stratton, 1983.
4. Laskaris G. Color Atlas of Oral Disease. New York, Thieme, 1988.
5. Mafee MF, Campos M, Subba R, et al. Head and neck: high field magnetic resonance imaging versus computed tomography. Otolaryngol Clin North Am 21:513, 1988.
6. Reede DL. Imaging modalities for the evaluation of head and neck pathology. Otolaryngol Clin North Am 21:495, 1988.
7. Skinner DB, Belsey RH. Esophageal function tests. In Skinner DB, Belsey RH (eds). Management of Esophageal Disease. Philadelphia, WB Saunders, 1988, pp 81–96.
8. Willging JP. Endoscopic evaluation of swallowing in children. Int J Pediatr Otorhinolaryngol 32(Suppl):107, 1995.
9. Yuh WTC, Sato Y, Loes DJ, et al. Magnetic resonance imaging and computed tomography in pediatric head and neck masses. Ann Otol Rhinol Laryngol 100:54, 1991.

53

Sore Throat in Children: Diagnosis and Management

Margaret A. Kenna, M.D. and Sanjay R. Parikh, M.D.

Sore throat, or pharyngitis, is one of the most common presenting problems in the physician's office. Although most sore throats are infectious in nature, there are many other less common causes. The common anatomic structures involved in a sore throat include the lymphoid tissue of Waldeyer's ring, the tongue, and the hard and soft palates. Because the various types of sore throat differ significantly in etiology, management, and complications, a logical and straightforward approach to diagnosis and treatment is needed to minimize unnecessary therapy and maximize clinical outcome.

Etiology

The range of diagnoses associated with sore throat is broad (Table 53–1). Divided into infectious and noninfectious etiologies, the majority of sore throats are infectious in nature. One can further subdivide infectious sources into viral, bacterial, and fungal categories.

Respiratory viruses are the major cause of pharyngitis. Rhinovirus and coronavirus are the most common and generally cause fairly mild illness. Adenovirus and herpes simplex virus, while less common, often result in more clinically severe illness. Pharyngitis is a very common presentation in infectious mononucleosis, caused by the Epstein-Barr virus (EBV). Cytomegalovirus may resemble infectious mononucleosis and present with pharyngitis, although the clinical course is usually milder. Herpangina has been associated with many enteric viruses (including coxsackievirus group A types 1 to 10, 16, and 22 and group B types 1 to 5) and some enteric cytopathogenic human orphan (ECHO) viruses.[40] The hand, foot, and mouth syndrome is also associated with coxsackievirus group A type 16. The various influenza viruses frequently have moderate to severe pharyngitis as part of the symptom complex.[36, 54] Measles (caused by a paramyxovirus) and varicella may have pharyngitis as part of their symptom complex. Koplik spots, the pathognomonic enanthem of measles, emerge during the prodromal phase, first appearing as white spots on the buccal mucosa opposite the maxillary molars, but quickly spreading to involve most of the buccal and labial mucosa.

Bacteria account for 5% to 30% of all pharyngitis episodes, and there is marked overlap of signs and symptoms with viral pharyngitis. Group A beta-hemolytic streptococcus (GABHS) is the most commonly isolated bacterium by throat culture. The importance of GABHS infection is threefold: (1) marked short-term morbidity associated with the immediate illness, (2) rheumatic fever, found in the past to occur in 3% of untreated but documented GABHS pharyngitis cases,[24] and (3) acute poststreptococcal glomerulonephritis (AGN), found to occur after 10% to 15% of pharyngitis episodes caused by specific nephrogenic serotypes (type 12 being the most common). Other streptococci, notably groups C and G, but occasionally groups B and F, have also been shown to cause pharyngitis.[27, 31] However, non–group A beta-hemolytic streptococci do not cause rheumatic fever or AGN.[4, 40]

Many other bacteria have been implicated as causes of pharyngitis (see Chap. 60). *Staphylococcus aureus* is occasionally isolated on throat swabs; more recently, *Streptococcus pneumoniae, Haemophilus influenzae, Moraxella catarrhalis, Haemophilus parainfluenzae,* and *Arcanobacterium haemolyticum* have been isolated from surface or core tonsillar cultures.[17, 46, 74] Anaerobes may also be playing a larger role in both acute and chronic pharyngitis. Brook[13] and Tuner and Nord[72] have reported anaerobes present in both surface and core tonsillar cultures, with *Bacteroides* being the most common. Often, these bacteria elaborate beta-lactamase and are therefore penicillin resistant.[12] Other organisms from the tonsil that elaborate beta-lactamase include *H. influenzae* type B, *Fusobacterium,* and *S. aureus.* Organisms other than GABHS probably cause pharyngotonsillitis; multiple isolates are often found with careful culturing techniques. These anaerobes and other beta-lactamase–producing organisms may be at least partially responsible for the 10% to 30% failure rate of treatment for streptococcal tonsillitis. Finally, *Chlamydia* and *Mycoplasma pneumoniae* have been mentioned as possible pathogens leading to pharyngitis, although further confirmation is needed.[38, 54]

Less common bacterial causes of pharyngitis include *Corynebacterium diphtheriae,* more prevalent in nonvaccinated populations, and *Neisseria gonorrhoeae.* Fungus can cause pharyngitis, with *Candida albicans* being most commonly implicated. The microbiologic organisms associated with pharyngitis are listed in Table 53–1.

Other infectious causes of sore throat that do not have inflammation of the tonsils as a prominent feature are

TABLE 53–1. Microbiologic Causes of Acute Sore Throat

Viral
Rhinovirus
Adenovirus
Coronavirus
Herpes simplex virus
Parainfluenza virus
Influenza virus
Coxsackievirus
Epstein-Barr virus
Cytomegalovirus
Respiratory syncytial virus
Bacterial
Streptococcus pyogenes (group A beta-hemolytic streptococcus)
Groups C and G beta-hemolytic streptococcus
Haemophilus influenzae, all types
Moraxella catarrhalis
Arcanobacterium haemolyticum
Anaerobes
Corynebacterium diphtheriae
Corynebacterium haemolyticum
Corynebacterium ulcerans
Neisseria gonorrhoeae
Staphylococcus aureus
Bacterial (possible)
Chlamydia trachomatis
Mycoplasma pneumoniae
Fungal
Candida albicans

TABLE 53–2. Noninfectious Causes of Pharyngitis

Causes Associated with Other Medical Conditions
Foreign body
Allergy
Sinusitis
Gastroesophageal reflux
Malignancy
Leukemia
Lymphoma
Squamous cell carcinoma
Behçet syndrome
Reiter syndrome
Kawasaki disease
Other Causes
Trauma
Accidental
Child abuse
Burns
Chemical burns
Caustic ingestion
Medication-related (e.g., aspirin)
Thermal injury
Hot foods or liquids
Contact stomatitis
Toxins
Cigarette smoke
Marijuana smoke
Environmental pollutants (smog)

epiglottitis and uvulitis (which may have associated epiglottitis). *H. influenzae* type B is the major etiologic organism in both of these diseases. The sore throat in these cases is usually severe. In children, epiglottitis (and occasionally uvulitis) generally presents with airway obstruction as the prominent feature; in adults, however, sore throat is often the most common presenting symptom.

Finally, some noninfectious causes of pharyngitis must be considered. Allergy, exposure to irritating substances (e.g., cigarette smoke, marijuana smoke, smog), and sinusitis (either allergic or bacterial) with posterior nasal drainage may all produce the symptom of a "scratchy" throat. Severe pain and fever are usually not present, and there is a paucity of abnormal pharyngotonsillar findings on examination. This same scratchy throat may be associated with chronic nasal obstruction and mouth breathing as with adenoid hypertrophy. Malignancies, such as leukemia, may present with severe pharyngitis and oral cavity involvement. Lymphoma may manifest as a sore throat, often with asymmetrical tonsillar or parapharyngeal space enlargement. Squamous cell carcinoma and rhabdomyosarcoma, although rare, may involve the tonsils, adenoids, tongue, and surrounding structures. Persistent pain or localized areas of inflammation or ulceration that do not respond to local measures should raise the suspicion of malignancy (Table 53–2). Finally, a foreign body should always be suspected, especially if the usual findings of pharyngitis are not present but the child's symptoms do not resolve.

Kawasaki disease (KD), also known as mucocutaneous lymph node syndrome, a disease of unclear etiology, may have sore throat as a symptom, and acute rheumatic fever (ARF) and KD are the two leading causes of acquired heart disease in children. KD is a multisystem vasculitis that presents as an acute febrile illness that has, as two of its six diagnostic criteria, cervical lymphadenopathy and changes of the lips and oral cavity, including oropharyngeal erythema, strawberry tongue, and fissuring of the lips. There have been reports of simultaneous GABHS pharyngitis and KD, as well as retropharyngeal cellulitis as a complication of KD.[23, 41] Timely treatment of KD may prevent serious, long-term sequelae (e.g., coronary artery aneurysm); therefore, a high index of suspicion is necessary to include or exclude a diagnosis of KD, whether or not there is concurrent GABHS disease.

Of final note, the role of gastroesophageal reflux disease as a cause of sore throat is unclear. Certainly, gastroesophageal reflux disease is being more commonly diagnosed and treated in the pediatric population (see Chap. 69), and can cause caustic irritation of the pharynx.[19]

Epidemiology

Children begin to experience upper respiratory viral infections at about age 6 months, when maternal immunity wanes, although these infections can occur at any age. It has been estimated that children have between five and eight upper respiratory tract infections per year, and 30% to 70% of the time, pharyngitis accompanies an upper respiratory infection. The method of spread for most respiratory pathogens is by close contact, because the viruses are present in nasal secretions and sometimes in saliva. Use of objects on which the virus is present in heavy concentrations may also cause spread. Herpangina and infectious mononucleosis account for only about 1% of all cases of clinically apparent pharyngitis but can be associated with significant morbidity. Infection with EBV occurs mainly in older children and young adults. Infection with cytomegalovirus is often clinically mild in younger children but may mimic EBV infection in presentation in older children.

Most episodes of infectious pharyngitis occur during the colder months of the year. Some viruses have certain times of peak incidence, such as coronaviruses, which are most common in the winter, and rhinoviruses, which are more important in the spring and fall. Influenza often occurs in epidemics. Streptococcal pharyngitis appears most often in the late winter and early spring and is identified more commonly in children older than 3 years of age, although it is also recognized in younger children.[65] Streptococcal disease is also transmitted by close contact and is present in saliva and nasal secretions. Food and waterborne outbreaks of streptococcal disease have also been well documented.[4] The pharyngeal carriage rate of GABHS in schoolchildren is 15% to 20% and varies with the season and geographic location. The adult carriage rate is lower. However, it is generally accepted that carriers of streptococci in the oropharynx are not very contagious.

The incidence of diphtheria has decreased dramatically with the introduction of improved public health measures and vaccination, but diphtheria is still reported in the United States and many other countries. It should be especially strongly suspected in unvaccinated patients. Diphtheria can occur in all age groups but is most common in children younger than 10 years of age. Most reported deaths also occur in this age group.

Gonococcal pharyngitis should be suspected in children who have been abused and in sexually active adolescents. Infection may be asymptomatic or accompanied by only mild symptoms, so culture studies are needed for definitive diagnosis. The incidence of gonococcal disease is increasing, so this disease must be considered in prolonged or atypical cases, especially in the high-risk groups mentioned.

Fungal infections of the oral cavity, usually secondary to *Candida* infection, are much more common in neonates and in immunocompromised patients. This latter group includes children undergoing treatment for malignancies, children receiving immunosuppressive therapy (i.e., transplant patients), and children with acquired and congenital immunodeficiencies, especially the acquired immunodeficiency syndrome.

The incidence and prevalence of pharyngitis related to noninfectious causes vary according to the underlying etiology. Because the noninfectious causes may be underreported, it is possible that they are more common than is currently appreciated.

Complications

Suppurative Complications

The complications of infectious pharyngitis are related mainly to the rich lymphatic and blood supply of the para- and retropharyngeal spaces. Although the complication rate with viral infections is low, the recognized complications include cervical lymphadenopathy and bacterial superinfection. Bacterial infections include bacterial otitis media, sinusitis, and cervical adenitis. Mesenteric adenitis may accompany either viral or bacterial infections, causing abdominal pain and vomiting and, occasionally, mimicking appendicitis.[4, 40]

Streptococcal or other bacterial disease may lead to peritonsillar cellulitis or abscess, retropharyngeal abscess, cervical lymphadenitis, sinusitis, otitis media, or meningitis. Extension via the mastoid or the ethmoid sinus may produce meningitis, brain abscess, or thrombosis of the venous sinuses. Metastatic spread of streptococcal infection can also result in suppurative arthritis, endocarditis, meningitis, brain abscess, osteomyelitis, and abscesses in other organ systems (see Chaps. 27, 45, and 100).

In the 1990s, a toxic shock–like disease caused by toxins elaborated by GABHS was described. This syndrome in children has been associated with varicella, atopic dermatitis, and altered lymphatic drainage, as well as being secondary to apparent spontaneous bacteremia.[2, 6] Bradley and Chapnick and their associates have reported toxic streptococcal syndrome caused by exotoxins A and B in association with pharyngitis secondary to GABHS.[7, 20] This syndrome is similar to the toxic shock syndrome caused by staphylococcal organisms, and the management is also similar, using appropriate pressors, fluids, and antimicrobial agents.

Nonsuppurative Complications

Viral pharyngitis, especially when associated with herpangina; hand, foot, and mouth syndrome; or EBV infection, may be so severe as to cause markedly decreased oral intake and dehydration, occasionally requiring hospitalization of the patient. In patients with infectious mononucleosis, such marked tonsillar enlargement may develop that airway obstruction occurs, requiring the placement of a nasopharyngeal airway, or even intubation, for adequate ventilation.[67]

The two major nonsuppurative complications of streptococcal pharyngitis are rheumatic fever and acute glomerulonephritis.

Acute Rheumatic Fever and Acute Glomerulonephritis

ARF caused by GABHS was once a prevalent and devastating sequela of streptococcal pharyngitis. In 1950, Denny and colleagues[24] reported an incidence of 200,000 to 250,000 new cases of rheumatic fever per year in the United States. In the mid-1960s, the incidence rate in Nashville, Tennessee, was reported to be 25 cases per 100,000 population, and 55 cases per 100,000 in black children.[49] For the years 1977 to 1981 in Baltimore, Maryland, Gordis[35] reported a rate of 0.5 cases in 100,000 new cases in children. The reasons for the decline after World War II were thought to be improved living standards and the widespread use of antibiotics, especially penicillin.[51] Then, in 1987, several authors reported new outbreaks of ARF in Salt Lake City, Utah; Columbus and Akron, Ohio; Pittsburgh, Pennsylvania; San Diego, California; and Nashville, Tennessee.[22, 43, 75, 76] In the past, ARF was seen mainly in indigent patients from large urban areas living in crowded conditions with little access to medical care; in contrast, these new cases often occurred in rural or suburban middle-class populations with good access to medical care.[21] Additionally, many of the "new" patients reported no or very minor symptoms of pharyngitis before their diagnosis of ARF. Certain strains of GABHS appeared to be associated with these outbreaks, including M types 1, 3, and 18 and highly encapsulated mucoid colonies. These strains may be considered "rheumatogenic," just as there are certain "nephrogenic" strains that cause AGN. An article by Taubert and colleagues[70] evaluated these outbreaks and surveyed 505 U.S. hospitals, including all the children's hospitals. They found no overall increase in the numbers of patients discharged with the diagnosis from 1984 to 1987, when all hospital statistics were taken together. Rather, these appeared to be widely separated outbreaks that may have occurred in relation to the presence in the community of rheumatogenic strains of GABHS.

However, the rate of rheumatic fever in less developed countries can be high, with a reported incidence from Sri Lanka of 142 in 100,000 for 1972 to 1978.[3] More recently, reported rates include 5.7% among aboriginal northern Australians, 5 in 100,000 in Nazareth (Israel), and 0.73% among children in Ankara (Turkey).[18, 37, 57]

AGN occurs after pharyngitis or skin infection with certain serotypes of group A streptococcus. M type 12 is the most common serotype to cause AGN after pharyngitis, while type 49 is most frequently related to AGN after skin infection. In contrast to the situation with rheumatic fever, there is little evidence that the attack rate decreases significantly with penicillin treatment of the pharyngitis. Also, recurrences of ARF are common, up to 50%, while recurrences of AGN are rare.[4, 5]

The complications of epiglottitis, foreign bodies, and other unusual causes of sore throat are discussed in Chapters 63, 64, 66, 69, 71, and 85.

Diagnosis

One of the major goals in the diagnosis of pharyngitis is to distinguish cases of streptococcal pharyngitis from those caused by respiratory viruses or other etiologies. Unusual causes of pharyngitis should always be considered, especially if prompt resolution does not occur with routine medical management. The entire oral cavity and pharynx should always be examined. The nasopharynx and hypopharynx should also be evaluated, especially with prolonged or unusual symptoms.

The differentiation of viral pharyngitis from bacterial pharyngitis cannot be made with great accuracy on clinical grounds. However, the patient's history and physical examination and other epidemiologic factors may be helpful. Other family members may have colds or influenza. The time of year and the presence of a known epidemic may also be useful clues.

Certain viral illnesses have distinguishing features. In pharyngoconjunctival fever secondary to adenovirus infection, the patient may be more ill than would be expected with a common cold. One third to one half of the patients have conjunctivitis; this is follicular and bilateral

25% of the time. Herpetic pharyngitis may be mild but can be severe. Vesicles and shallow ulcers on the palate are characteristic and may also be present on the buccal and labial mucosa if there is associated gingivostomatitis. Herpangina is characterized by 1- to 2-mm vesicles on the soft palate, uvula, and anterior tonsillar pillars. The pain may be severe, causing dysphagia and resulting in dehydration. In the hand, foot, and mouth syndrome, vesicular lesions 3 to 7 mm in diameter appear on the hands and feet as well as on the oral mucosa.

The classic signs and symptoms of GABHS pharyngitis are pharyngeal pain, dysphagia, fever, exudate over the tonsils and posterior pharyngeal wall, and tender anterior cervical adenopathy. Headache may also be a prominent feature, and there may be an elevated white blood cell count. However, exudative pharyngotonsillitis with tender adenopathy and fever may also be a prominent finding in infectious mononucleosis or influenza. Knowledge of the patient's age and of the prevailing viral and streptococcal disease in the community can be helpful. However, in patients younger than 3 years of age, the symptoms of GABHS pharyngitis are often nonspecific, and a throat culture is definitely necessary for diagnosis.

Breese and Disney[11] and Breese[9] used a multifactorial rating system that took into account age, white blood cell count, and season, along with fever, sore throat, cough, headache, abnormal pharynx, and abnormal cervical lymph nodes. Using this system, they were able to predict 77.6% positive culture results (mean). Although other scoring systems have been suggested, none have been more accurate.[55, 62]

Although there is ongoing controversy over the best diagnostic test for GABHS, the mainstay is the throat culture. When it was established in 1950 that penicillin could prevent ARF if the preceding GABHS pharyngitis was adequately treated, throat culture was performed in nearly every person with a sore throat or upper respiratory infection.[24] Compared with anaerobic methods, the standard aerobic culture performed on sheep blood gives a sensitivity of 92% and specificity of 100%. Aerobic cultures are easier to perform in physicians' offices than are anaerobic cultures and have become the accepted standard method.[64] However, aerobic culture results are not available for 24 to 48 hours.

Faster methods of GABHS identification have been developed. These were initially based on fluorescent antibody staining of the throat swab. The tests currently in use are based on extracting the group A carbohydrate antigen from the throat swab and then assaying it with latex agglutination or enzyme-linked immunosorbent assay procedures.[26] If positive, these techniques provide faster diagnosis than either aerobic or anaerobic culture. Initial comparison of the antigen detection method with standard culture techniques indicated sensitivities of 72% to 95%, specificities of 88% to 100%, positive predictive values of 52% to 99%, and negative predictive values of 93% to 99%. However, Gerber and co-workers compared an enzyme fluorescent procedure with aerobic cultures for detection of GABHS.[33] They found it to be extremely inaccurate in identifying GABHS directly from throat swabs and did not recommend its use. Pichichero and colleagues[61] compared the reliability of clinical, culture, and antigen detection methods for GABHS and concluded that throat culture was still the gold standard. Wegner and colleagues[78] went even further and recommended that the two-plate method (both an aerobic and anaerobic culture plate) be used as the gold standard. The limitations of the "quick" tests include (1) inability to detect the presence of non-GABHS, or any other bacterial organism, (2) inability to detect smaller inoculum size, and (3) incorrect performance of the test by office personnel.[28, 39, 64] On the basis of the current information, the most cost-effective method for diagnosis, taking into consideration the "cost" of missed diagnosis, is to perform a quick test first; if it is negative, throat culture should be performed.[50] There is an increasing trend of using the quick test alone. Webb and associates,[77] in their review of 30,000 patients with pharyngitis over 4 years, demonstrated no increase in suppurative or nonsuppurative complications of GABHS despite switching from blood agar culture to antigen testing midway through their study.

Infectious mononucleosis can usually be identified by the presence of fever, sore throat, and cervical lymphadenopathy with associated fatigue, malaise, and headache. Mononuclear lymphocytosis is present in approximately 70% of cases and heterophil antibodies in 90%.

The patient with *C. diphtheriae* infection may exhibit no symptoms or may be very ill. This infection is most common in children between 5 and 14 years of age, especially those living in crowded conditions. The disease is characterized by a thin, tough membrane that becomes grayish green and may cover the tonsils, pharynx, uvula, and soft palate, extending to the tracheobronchial tree. Diagnosis is based on clinical signs and symptoms, because treatment should begin before culture results are available. Throat cultures of the tonsils, pharynx, and possibly the membrane should be obtained for confirmation.[53]

Infection with *N. gonorrhoeae* is usually asymptomatic and may be present in sexually abused children and sexually active adolescents. Culture and a high index of suspicion are needed for diagnosis.

Treatment

There is no specific treatment for most viral sore throats. Controversy exists in the literature regarding the use of antiviral agents and steroid therapy in the treatment of infectious mononucleosis. In a randomized, controlled trial of acyclovir-prednisone versus placebo, Tynell and coworkers[73] demonstrated that there was no difference in clinical outcome. In another meta-analysis of five randomized, controlled trials, Torre and colleagues[71] concluded that acyclovir should not be used for infectious mononucleosis despite good virologic activity of the drug. As for corticosteroid therapy alone, most researchers agree that there is a role in treatment for complications of infectious mononucleosis such as upper airway obstruction, but not for overall cure.[8, 44]

Most therapy is directed at the bacterial causes, the main one being GABHS. In 1950, when it was discovered that penicillin could prevent rheumatic fever, the main-

stay of treatment was intramuscular benzathine penicillin G.[24] Because of the rare but real possibility of anaphylaxis with intramuscular penicillin, oral penicillin V potassium (penicillin VK), given for 10 days, is now the more usual treatment. In the past, a positive throat culture for GABHS was required to start or to continue penicillin therapy. More recently, however, physicians either start antibiotic therapy empirically or may not discontinue treatment even if the cultures do not grow GABHS.[42] Continuing treatment despite a negative culture is thought to be justified by some because surface cultures do not always accurately reflect tonsillar core cultures and because of the physician's concern that appropriate treatment based on surface culture alone would be inadequate.

Bacteriologic failures after a 10-day course of oral penicillin approach 10% to 18%.[25] This raises several questions. Should all GABHS sore throats be treated? When should treatment begin? Should asymptomatic GABHS carriers be treated until eradication of the bacteria has been documented? What treatment regimen should be used? Should other bacteria be considered in treatment?

There continue to be two reasons why identified GABHS pharyngitis patients should receive treatment. First, medical therapy significantly shortens the period of subjective and objective morbidity, especially fever, cervical lymphadenitis, sore throat, and headache.[47, 63] This also enables the children to return to school earlier. Second, penicillin treatment definitely prevents rheumatic fever and may have a small effect on the development of AGN.[5]

Until recently, because of good documentation that treatment of GABHS pharyngitis could begin up to 9 days after the onset of illness without increasing the rate of ARF, physicians felt justified in waiting for culture results. If the culture results were negative, the patient would not be given antimicrobials, thus avoiding expense and possible drug allergy. With several studies now showing clinical improvement with earlier treatment, the 24- to 48-hour delay for culture results may no longer be reasonable. However, with the advent of faster diagnostic tools, it may be possible, especially in high-risk populations or when GABHS disease is strongly suspected, to start penicillin therapy sooner, thereby decreasing morbidity, suppurative complications, and possibly rheumatic fever and AGN.[36]

Since 1953, the standard length of penicillin treatment has been 10 days.[30] More recently, this duration has been challenged. Schwartz and co-workers[66] found that 10 days of oral penicillin V versus 7 days was significantly more effective in ridding the upper respiratory tract of GABHS. Meanwhile, Zwart[79] found that 7 days of penicillin V treatment was superior to 3 days or placebo in terms of resolving symptoms. Gerber and associates[30] compared 5 days of penicillin V therapy with 10 days and found that there were significantly more bacteriologic treatment failures in the 5-day group. Penicillin V given three times daily versus the same medicine given twice daily was found to have a similar failure rate.[28] However, penicillin V given twice daily was found to be superior to once-daily therapy.[48] There are numerous explanations for penicillin failure in the treatment of GABHS, including lack of compliance, the presence of beta-lactamase–producing copathogens, repeated exposure to infective agents, eradication of protective pharyngeal microflora, antibiotic suppression of immunity, penicillin tolerance, and streptococcal carriage. In many studies, recurrences and persistence of GABHS are not really known because repeated cultures are not serotyped.[59]

Many other antimicrobials have been evaluated for use instead of penicillin, most notably erythromycin, used in penicillin-allergic patients, and many cephalosporins. Bacteriologic failure rates were lower for cephalexin, clarithromycin, and cefadroxil than for penicillin V.[25, 29, 52] Failure rates were also lower with cefdinir; however, adverse reactions were found higher than for penicillin V.[56] Other cephalosporins that have proved safe and effective for GABHS pharyngitis include cefixime, loracarbef, cefpodoxime, cefuroxime axetil, and cefprozil.[1, 60] Amoxicillin-clavulanate has been shown in one study to be superior to penicillin in the eradication of streptococci from the pharynx.[15] The macrolides erythromycin, azithromycin, and clarithromycin have all proved effective and safe in the treatment of GABHS.[34] Most of these newer agents, however, are expensive, have potential side effects, and have a broader antimicrobial spectrum than may be needed. Also, only penicillin has been shown, in a controlled, prospective fashion, to reduce the incidence of rheumatic fever.

The question of what to do with GABHS carriers remains controversial. After documented penicillin treatment, the carriage rate (i.e., percentage of truly asymptomatic patients with throat cultures persistently positive for GABHS) may be as high as 20%. Initially, it was thought that these patients were at risk for development of rheumatic fever, but most of them appear to be at much less risk than those with true infection. Because of this, aggressive treatment to eradicate streptococcal carriage is not routinely advocated.[4, 25] Generally, in children with clinical resolution of GABHS pharyngitis, no further throat cultures are indicated unless they become symptomatic.[25] In certain high-risk groups, further attempts at eradication may be indicated. The high-risk factors include a history of rheumatic fever, a known rheumatic fever patient in the family, known rheumatic fever cases in the community, recurrent symptomatic GABHS disease in the immediate family or in a closed community, and known valvular heart disease or the presence of prosthetic heart valves in the patient.

Until recently, the streptococcal carrier state was defined as a positive throat culture with a negative serologic response to GABHS. Infection was defined as a positive throat culture and a positive serologic response. Nontreatment of the carrier state in most cases was based on this difference. An article by Gerber and colleagues[32] raises questions about the appropriateness of using antibody responses to define infection. They found a dramatic clinical response to penicillin V or cefadroxil in patients with positive throat cultures and signs and symptoms suggestive of GABHS infection but with negative serologic response. There is some evidence that treatment of presumed or proven GABHS infection early in its course blunts the antibody response. This makes use of the antibody response problematic in differentiating between true infection and the carrier state. Further work to define these states is clearly needed for optimal prevention of rheumatic fever.[32]

When a child has recurrent "strep" throats, does not respond to medical therapy, or does not seem to be "growing out" of the problem, tonsillectomy has been recommended, especially if the tonsils are very large and causing airway obstruction.[10] There is no evidence that tonsillectomy reduces the rate of rheumatic fever. In 1984, Paradise and colleagues[58] reported the results of a randomized trial of tonsillectomy versus no tonsillectomy for children meeting strict criteria for recurrent sore throat. The children who underwent surgery had less sore throat illness postoperatively than the control group. However, many of the children in the control group had a decrease in the number of sore throat illnesses over time. The conclusion was that carefully selected individuals may benefit from tonsillectomy for severe, recurrent sore throat. In children with less severe but recurrent GABHS sore throats, prophylaxis with penicillin has been advocated by several pediatricians.[10] In children with symptomatic recurrent GABHS, with the same serotype, evidence suggests that clindamycin or rifampin may be more effective for eradication than penicillin alone.[16, 68, 72]

For *C. diphtheriae*, diagnosis is made on clinical grounds, because effective treatment with toxoid needs to be started before culture results are known. Penicillin and erythromycin are effective both in treating the disease and in eradicating the carrier state.[53]

The usual treatment of oral candidiasis consists of nystatin. More recently, ketoconazole has been used when nystatin was ineffective. In children who are immunosuppressed or in whom the candidiasis is invasive, intravenous amphotericin may be necessary.

Finally, the role of anaerobes and of bacteria other than GABHS (copathogens) in the pathogenesis of pharyngotonsillitis needs further study. Evidence both for and against the role of beta-lactamase production by copathogens as a cause of penicillin failure has been published.[14, 45, 69] Currently, in clinical terms, if treatment with penicillin fails, coverage for other organisms with a broad-spectrum antimicrobial should be considered.

Probably one of the most important non-GABHS causes of pharyngitis to diagnose is KD. Prompt treatment with salicylates and gamma globulin helps prevent some of the serious sequelae and should be initiated as soon as the diagnosis is made (see Chapters 60, 61, 63, 64, and 69).

Summary

Many new findings have altered the diagnosis and management of pharyngitis in children. Cultures and serologic tests are better able to identify viruses and bacteria; diagnostic tests are becoming faster and more sophisticated. Bacteria other than GABHS are being given more credit for pharyngitis. Antimicrobials other than penicillin are being used with increasing frequency. The incidence of rheumatic fever has declined precipitously, although totally unexpected outbreaks continue to occur.[75] Because of these factors and many others, the approach to the pediatric patient with pharyngitis has changed and should continue to evolve.

SELECTED REFERENCES

Denny FW. Group A streptococcal infections. Curr Probl Pediatr 23: 179, 1993.

Denny FW, Wannamaker LW, Brink WR, et al. Prevention of rheumatic fever: treatment of preceding streptococcic infection. JAMA 143:151, 1950.

REFERENCES

1. Adam D, Scholz H, Helmerking M. Comparison of short-course (5 day) cefuroxime axetil with a standard 10 day oral penicillin V regimen in the treatment of tonsillopharyngitis. J Antimicrob Chemother 45:23, 2000.
2. Belani K, Schlievert PM, Kaplan E, Ferrieri P. Association of exotoxin producing group A streptococci and severe disease in children. Pediatr Infect Dis J 10:351, 1991.
3. Bisno AC. The rise and fall of rheumatic fever. JAMA 254:538, 1985.
4. Bisno AC. *Streptococcus pyogenes*. In Mandell GL, Douglas RG, Bennett JE (eds). Principles and Practice of Infectious Diseases. New York, John Wiley, 1985, pp 1124–1133.
5. Bisno AC. Nonsuppurative poststreptococcal sequelae: rheumatic fever and glomerulonephritis. In Mandell GL, Douglas RG, Bennett JE (eds). Principles and Practice of Infectious Diseases. New York, John Wiley, 1985, pp 1133–1141.
6. Bradley JS, Schlievert PM, Peterson BM. Toxic shock-like syndrome: a complication of sore throat. Pediatr Infect Dis J 10:790, 1991.
7. Bradley JS, Schlievert PM, Sample TG. Streptococcal toxic shock-like syndrome as a complication of varicella. Pediatr Infect Dis J 10: 77, 1991.
8. Brandfonbrener A, Epstein A, Wu S, Phair J. Corticosteroid therapy in Epstein-Barr virus infection. Effect on lymphocyte class, subset, and response to early antigen. Arch Intern Med 146:337, 1986.
9. Breese BB. A simple scorecard for the tentative diagnosis of streptococcal pharyngitis. Am J Dis Child 131:4514, 1977.
10. Breese BB, Denny FW, Dillon HC, et al. Consensus: difficult management problems in children with streptococcal pharyngitis. Pediatr Infect Dis J 4:10, 1985.
11. Breese BB, Disney GA. The accuracy of diagnosis of beta-hemolytic streptococcal infections on clinical grounds. J Pediatr 44:670, 1954.
12. Brook I. Role of beta-lactamase-producing bacteria in the failure of penicillin to eradicate group A streptococci. Pediatr Infect Dis J 4: 491, 1985.
13. Brook I. Pathogenicity and therapy of anaerobic bacteria in upper respiratory tract infections. Pediatr Infect Dis J 6:131, 1987.
14. Brook I. Emergence and persistence of beta-lactamase-producing bacteria in the oropharynx following penicillin treatment. Arch Otolaryngol Head Neck Surg 114:667, 1988.
15. Brook I. Treatment of patients with acute recurrent tonsillitis due to group A {beta}haemolytic streptococci: a prospective randomized study comparing penicillin and amoxicillin/clavulanate potassium. J Antimicrob Chemother 24:227, 1989.
16. Brook I, Hirokawa R. Treatment of patients with a history of recurrent tonsillitis due to group A beta-hemolytic streptococci. Clin Pediatr (Phila) 24:331, 1985.
17. Brook I, Yocum P, Friedman EM. Aerobic and anaerobic bacteria in tonsils of children with recurrent tonsillitis. Ann Otol Rhinol Laryngol 90:261, 1981.
18. Carapetis JR, Currie BJ, Mathews JD. Cumulative incidence of rheumatic fever in an endemic region: a guide to the susceptibility of the population? Epidemiol Infect 124:239, 2000.
19. Carr MM, Nguyen A, Nagy M, et al. Clinical presentation as a guide to the identification of GERD in children. Int J Pediatr Otorhinolaryngol 54:27, 2000.
20. Chapnick EK, Gradon JD, Lutwick LI, et al. Streptococcal toxic shock syndrome due to noninvasive pharyngitis. Clin Infect Dis 14: 1074, 1992.
21. Congeni BL. The resurgence of acute rheumatic fever in the United States. Pediatr Ann 21:816, 1992.
22. Congeni B, Rizzo C, Congeni J, Sreenivasan VV. Outbreak of acute rheumatic fever in Northeast Ohio. J Pediatr 111:176, 1987.
23. Cox F, Foshee W, Miller J, Moore S. Simultaneous Kawasaki disease and group A streptococcal pharyngitis. Clin Pediatr (Phila) 32: 48, 1993.
24. Denny FW, Wannamaker LW, Brink WR, et al. Prevention of rheumatic fever: treatment of preceding streptococcic infection. JAMA 143:151, 1950.
25. Dillon HC. Streptococcal pharyngitis in the 1980's. Pediatr Infect Dis J 6:123, 1987.
26. Drulak M, Bartholomew W, LaScolea L, et al. Evaluation of the modified Visuwell StrepA enzyme immunoassay for detection of group A streptococcus from throat swabs. Diagn Microbiol Infect Dis 14:281, 1991.
27. Dudley JP, Sercarz J. Pharyngeal and tonsil infections caused by non-group A streptococcus. Am J Otolaryngol 12:292, 1991.
28. Gerber MA, Markowitz M. Management of streptococcal pharyngitis reconsidered. Pediatr Infect Dis 4:518, 1985.
29. Gerber MA, Randolph MF, Chanatry J, et al. Once daily therapy for streptococcal pharyngitis with cefadroxil. J Pediatr 109:531, 1986.
30. Gerber MA, Randolph MF, Chanatry J, et al. Five vs ten days of penicillin V therapy for streptococcal pharyngitis. Am J Dis Child 141:224, 1987.
31. Gerber MA, Randolph MF, Martin NJ, et al. Community-wide outbreak of group G streptococcal pharyngitis. Pediatrics 87:598, 1991.
32. Gerber MA, Randolph MF, Mayo DR. The group A streptococcal carrier state. Am J Dis Child 142:562, 1988.
33. Gerber MA, Randolph MF, Tilton RC. Enzyme fluorescence procedure for rapid diagnosis of streptococcal pharyngitis. J Pediatr 108: 421, 1986.
34. Gooch WM. Alternatives to penicillin in the management of group A streptococcal pharyngitis. Pediatr Ann 21:810, 1992.
35. Gordis L. Changing risk of rheumatic fever. In Schulman ST (ed). Management of Pharyngitis in an Era of Declining Rheumatic Fever: Report of 86th Ross Conference on Pediatric Research. Columbus, Ohio, Ross Laboratories, 1984, pp 7–13.
36. Gwaltney JM. Pharyngitis. In Mandell GL, Douglas RG, Bennett JE (eds). Principles and Practice of Infectious Diseases. New York, John Wiley, 1985, pp 355–359.
37. Habib GS, Saliba WR, Mader R. Rheumatic fever in the Nazareth area during the last decade. Isr Med Assoc J 2:433, 2000.
38. Hammerschlag MR. The role of chlamydia in upper respiratory tract infections. Curr Infect Dis Rep 2:115, 2000.
39. Hayden GF, Turner JC, Kiselica D, et al. Latex agglutination testing directly from throat swabs for rapid detection of beta-hemolytic streptococci from Lancefield serogroup C. J Clin Microbiol 30:716, 1992.
40. Healy GB. Pharyngitis. In Cummings C, Frederickson J, Harker L, et al (eds). Otolaryngology-Head and Neck Surgery, vol. I. St Louis, CV Mosby, 1986, pp 1185–1188.
41. Hester TO, Harris JP, Kenny JF, Albernaz MS. Retropharyngeal cellulitis: a manifestation of Kawasaki disease in children. Otolaryngol Head Neck Surg 109:1030, 1993.
42. Holmberg SD, Faich GA. Streptococcal pharyngitis and acute rheumatic fever in Rhode Island. JAMA 250:2307, 1983.
43. Hosier DM, Craenen JM, Teske DW, Wheller JJ. Resurgence of acute rheumatic fever in Northeast Ohio. Am J Dis Child 141:730, 1987.
44. Jenson HB. Acute complications of Epstein-Barr virus infectious mononucleosis. Curr Opin Pediatr 12:263, 2000.
45. Kaplan EL, Johnson DR. Eradication of group A streptococci from the upper respiratory tract by amoxicillin with clavulanate after oral penicillin. J Pediatr 113:400, 1988.
46. Karpathios T, Drakoni S, Zervoudaki A, et al. *Arcanobacterium haemolyticum* in children with presumed streptococcal pharyngotonsillitis or scarlet fever. J Pediatr 121:735, 1992.
47. Krober MS, Bass JW, Michaels GN. Streptococcal pharyngitis: pla-

cebo-controlled double-blind evaluation of clinical response to penicillin therapy. JAMA 253:1271, 1985.

48. Lan AJ, Colford JM, Colford JM Jr. The impact of dosing frequency on the efficacy of 10-day penicillin or amoxicillin therapy for streptococcal tonsillopharyngitis: a meta-analysis. Pediatrics 105:E19, 2000.

49. Land MA, Bisno AC. Acute rheumatic fever: a vanishing disease in suburbia. JAMA 249:895, 1983.

50. Lieu TA, Fleisher GR, Schwartz JS. Cost-effectiveness of rapid latex agglutination testing and throat culture for streptococcal pharyngitis. Pediatrics 85:246, 1990.

51. Markowitz M. The decline of rheumatic fever: role of medical intervention. J Pediatr 106:545, 1985.

52. McCarty J, Hedrick JA, Gooch WM. Clarithromycin suspension vs penicillin V suspension in children with streptococcal pharyngitis. Adv Ther 17:14, 2000.

53. McCloskey RV. Corynebacterium (diphtheriae). In Mandell GL, Douglas RG, Bennett JE (eds). Principles and Practice of Infectious Diseases. New York, John Wiley, 1985, pp 1171–1177.

54. McMillan JA, Sandstrom C, Weiner LB, et al. Viral and bacterial organisms associated with acute pharyngitis in a school-aged population. J Pediatr 109:747, 1986.

55. Meland E, Digranes A, Skjaerven R. Assessment of clinical features predicting streptococcal pharyngitis. Scand J Infect Dis 25:177, 1993.

56. Nemeth MA, McCarty J, Gooch W III, et al. Comparison of cefdinir and penicillin for the treatment of streptococcal pharyngitis. Cefdinir Pharyngitis Study Group. Clin Ther 21:1873, 1999.

57. Olgunturk R, Aydin GB, Tunaoglu FS, Akalin N. Rheumatic heart disease prevalence among schoolchildren in Ankara, Turkey. Turk J Pediatr 41:201, 1999.

58. Paradise JL, Bluestone CD, Bachman RF, et al. Efficacy of tonsillectomy for recurrent sore throat infection in severely affected children. N Engl J Med 310:674, 1984.

59. Pichichero ME. Explanations and therapies for penicillin failure in streptococcal pharyngitis. Clin Pediatr (Phila) 31:642, 1992.

60. Pichichero ME. Cephalosporins are superior to penicillin for treatment of streptococcal tonsillopharyngitis: is the difference worth it? Pediatr Infect Dis J 12:268, 1993.

61. Pichichero ME, Disney FA, Green JL, et al. Comparative reliability of clinical, culture, and antigen detection methods for the diagnosis of group A beta-hemolytic streptococcal tonsillopharyngitis. Pediatr Ann 21:798, 1992.

62. Poses RM, Cebul RD, Collins M, et al. The accuracy of experienced physicians' probability estimates for patients with sore throats: implications for decision making. JAMA 254:925, 1985.

63. Randolph MF, Gerber MA, DeMeo KK, et al. Effect of antibiotic therapy on the clinical course of streptococcal pharyngitis. J Pediatr 106:870, 1985.

64. Roddey OF, Clegg HW, Clardy LT, et al. Comparison of a latex agglutination test and four culture methods for identification of group A streptococci in a pediatric office laboratory. J Pediatr 108:347, 1986.

65. Schwartz RH, Hayden GF, Wientzen RL. Children less than three years old with pharyngitis. Clin Pediatr (Phila) 25:185, 1986.

66. Schwartz RH, Wientzen RL, Pedreira F, et al. Penicillin V for group A streptococcal pharyngitis: a randomized trial of seven vs ten day therapy. JAMA 246:1790, 1981.

67. Snyderman N. Otolaryngologic presentation of infectious mononucleosis. Pediatr Clin North Am 28:1011, 1981.

68. Tanz RR, Shulman ST, Barthel MJ, et al. Penicillin plus rifampin eradicates pharyngeal carriage of group A streptococci. J Pediatr 106:876, 1985.

69. Tanz RR, Shulman ST, Stroka PA, et al. Lack of influence of beta-lactamase-producing flora on recovery of group A streptococci after treatment of acute pharyngitis. J Pediatr 117:859, 1990.

70. Taubert KA, Rowley AH, Shulman ST. Nationwide survey of Kawasaki disease and acute rheumatic fever. J Pediatr 119:279, 1991.

71. Torre D, Tambini R. Acyclovir for treatment of infectious mononucleosis: a meta-analysis. Scand J Infect Dis 31:543, 1999.

72. Tuner K, Nord CE. Impact of phenoxymethylpenicillin and clindamycin on microflora in recurrent tonsillitis. Ann Otol Rhinol Laryngol 94:278, 1985.

73. Tynell E, Aurelius E, Brandell A, et al. Acyclovir and prednisolone treatment of acute infectious mononucleosis: a multicenter, double-blind, placebo-controlled study. J Infect Dis 174:324, 1996.

74. Van Hare GF, Shurin PA. The increasing importance of Branhamella catarrhalis in respiratory infections. Pediatr Infect Dis J 6:92, 1987.

75. Veasy LG, Wiedmeier SE, Orsmond GS, et al. Resurgence of acute rheumatic fever in the intermountain area of the United States. N Engl J Med 316:421, 1987.

76. Wald ER, Dashefsky B, Feidt C, et al. Acute rheumatic fever in western Pennsylvania and the tristate area. Pediatrics 80:371, 1987.

77. Webb KH, Needham CA, Kurtz SR. Use of a high-sensitivity rapid strep test without culture confirmation of negative results: 2 years' experience. J Fam Pract 49:378, 2000.

78. Wegner DL, Witte DL, Schrantz RD. Insensitivity of rapid antigen detection methods and single blood agar plate culture for diagnosing streptococcal pharyngitis. JAMA 267:695, 1992.

79. Zwart S, Sachs AP, Ruijs GJ, et al. Penicillin for acute sore throat: randomized double blind trial of seven days versus three days treatment or placebo in adults. BMJ 320:150, 2000.

54

Dysphagia

Craig S. Derkay, M.D. and Randall L. Plant, M.D.

Dysphagia, or difficulty with swallowing, is defined as any defect in the intake or transport of endogenous secretions and nutriments necessary for the maintenance of life. The swallowing mechanism, by which food is transmitted to the stomach and digestive organs, is a complex action involving 26 muscles and five cranial nerves.

Understanding the swallowing mechanism in the neonate enhances the etiologic differentiation of dysphagia in older children; therefore, the basis for discussion of dysphagia is the swallowing mechanism as seen in the neonate and infant. Swallowing in the infant consists of three components: (1) the suck reflex is the delivery system and includes the orobuccal phase of deglutition, (2) the collecting system is the oropharynx, and (3) the transport system is the esophagus.[2] (See Chap. 51 for a detailed discussion of the physiology of swallowing.)

Swallowing may start in the fetus as early as the 12th week of pregnancy.[6] According to Brans, "Birth is only a stormy episode in what should otherwise be a smooth, continuous transition from aquatic to terrestrial life."[3] That swallowing and digestion may be important to fetal nutrition is suggested by the frequency of intrauterine growth retardation among fetuses who cannot swallow because of alimentary tract obstruction or neurologic damage.[3, 27] Approximately 5 mL/kg of body weight per hour, or up to a total of 850 mL, is swallowed daily by the fetus.[22]

Sucking and swallowing functions are vital to the newborn infant.[9] Both functions are established prenatally but are not fully developed until after birth. Sucking reflexively initiates swallowing in the infant by stimulation of the lips and deeper parts of the oral cavity. The mandible and maxilla (upper gums, lips, palate, and cheeks) are all necessary for compression of the nipple and expression of its contents. Infants born at term suckle in bursts of only three or four sucks for the first day or two before more effective sucking develops in bursts of 10 to 30 per day. In the newborn suckling infant, respirations and swallowing are intimately related to function and rhythm when the tongue, lips, and mandible move synergistically as a composite motor organ.[28] Swallowing inhibits respiration. Sucking, as a purely reflexive process, acquires complexity and conscious control as other functions emerge and mature.[2] Bosma[2] likens the tongue in infants to a piston within a cylinder, wherein the mouth is solely concerned with suckling, approximating, and orienting the nipple it encloses. For the first 3 months of life, infants fail to distinguish between liquids and solids and attempt to use the same sucking action for both. The mouth later acquires various new functions. The tongue, lips, and mandible achieve the independent functions of biting, chewing, moving food, and forming a bolus, functions that demand the learning of new motor patterns.

The normal infant has an arousal response when stimulated for feeding; when the lower lip is depressed, the tongue comes forward.[1] This response is an important characteristic of infants, unless they have been fed recently or are extremely fatigued.

Any defect of the lips, tongue, palate, mandible, maxilla, or cheeks creates problems for the first phase of deglutition, the delivery system of swallowing.[16] In older children, this may vary when they are fed manually. When reflex suckling initiates swallowing in the infant, the composite suckling and swallowing processes are subcortically controlled. As new oral skills, such as biting and chewing, enlist cortical levels for control, the initial phases of swallowing become voluntary. Successively acquired representations of the mouth are integrated with the maturing environmental orientation, intelligence, and motion of the growing child.[2]

Problem-Oriented Approach to Dysphagia

The differential diagnosis of dysphagia requires a detailed history and review of symptoms, a complete physical examination, a thorough evaluation of radiographic and special diagnostic studies, and, in most cases, endoscopy of the upper gastrointestinal and respiratory systems.

History

The history of a child with dysphagia should include details of the mother's pregnancy, a history of the child's birth, and a family history to uncover possible familial or genetic disorders. Details of the pregnancy that are important include maternal infections, bleeding, toxemia, intake of drugs, thyroid dysfunction, polyhydramnios, and fetal irradiation. Maternal ingestion of drugs during pregnancy, both licit and illicit, may obtund the infant's sensorium or cause nasal obstruction. Alcohol, cocaine, and antihypertensive drugs in particular may cause this problem. Polyhydramnios is frequently associated with esophageal anomalies and neurologic deficiencies[22, 27]; oligohydramnios is associated with intrauterine growth retardation and low birth weight. The birth history may direct attention to an anomaly or a causative factor for airway obstruction. It is important to document whether respirations and cry were spontaneous, resuscitation with or without intubation was required, a meningomyelocele was repaired, or a ventriculoperitoneal shunt was necessary. If such a repair or shunt was necessary, it may indicate possible vagal or other cranial nerve paralysis or both. If intubation was performed, airway obstruction from trauma to the larynx and trachea may have occurred, or the child may have suffered hypoxia or anoxia. Intubation trauma to the hypopharynx or upper esophagus may cause severe dysphagia by the production of a pseudodiverticulum.[17] Traumatic deliveries may be associated with airway obstruction from nasal septal trauma, central nervous system trauma, and vagal nerve paralysis. Familial neurologic problems should alert the examiner to the possibility of the infant's having a similar disease (e.g., myotonic dystrophy or myasthenia gravis).

In older infants and children, the history should include the age at onset of dysphagia; whether it is acute (sudden), progressive, or chronic; and whether the symptoms are periodic or constant. An important distinction should be made between dysphagia associated with eating and that which occurs between meals, or "nonfood" dysphagia. Equally important is whether the dysphagia differs for liquids and solids. A history of foreign body ingestion, corrosive substance ingestion, or medication-induced dysphagia should be suspected if the onset of the swallowing difficulty is sudden. If dysphagia is progressive, starting with solid foods and progressing to difficulty with liquids, a tumor or long-standing foreign body should be suspected. Reflux esophagitis, hiatal hernia, corrosive substance ingestion, or a collagen disease with prolonged vomiting and dysphagia suggests chronic esophagitis.

Dysphagia may be a manifestation of an underlying systemic disease. A careful review of systems is needed to look for evidence of autoimmune disease, endocrine disorders, multisystem infection, or impaired immunity. When all other anatomic and physiologic causes for dysphagia have been ruled out, the history should focus on psychological or behavioral abnormalities that may explain the symptoms.

Symptoms Accompanying Dysphagia

Dysphagia may be associated with a number of symptoms. Excessive salivation is rarely due to hypersecretion and should alert the physician to a swallowing problem. The normal infant can root, suck, breathe, swallow, gasp, and gag. The absence of any of these normal abilities indicates a potential problem with the swallowing mechanism. However, the absence of a gag reflex does not necessarily indicate a palatal or pharyngeal paralysis. Attempts to feed a child who has dysphagia from any cause may produce a choking spell, with coughing, gagging,

drooling, and flooding of the oral cavity, leading to cyanosis. Death may occur from drowning if persistent efforts are made to force the infant to feed as these symptoms progress. The only evidence of a swallowing problem may be the development of stridor during or after feeding. The stridor is usually expiratory but may be to-and-fro or wheezing in character. Aspiration ultimately causes recurrent or persistent bronchitis and pneumonia. The airway problem may be so dramatic that it may divert the physician's attention from the primary cause, which is the swallowing defect.

Odynophagia, or painful swallowing, is a serious complaint usually caused by an obstructive or neuromuscular disease. The association of weight loss with food-related dysphagia increases the likelihood that a significant organic process exists. The corollary to this is that nonfood dysphagia and the absence of weight loss usually indicate that there are no serious organic problems present.

Vomiting is an important symptom of dysphagia when it occurs soon after or during feeding. Nasopharyngeal regurgitation or contamination may be an early indicator of a neurologic deficiency, such as a cerebral palsy or an obstructive lesion in the upper alimentary tract.

The history may also help localize the site of the swallowing problems. Problems that occur in the initial 3 or 4 seconds after the initiation of swallowing are usually localized to the oral cavity, pharynx, or hypopharynx. Those occurring more than 4 seconds after initiation are most often due to a pathologic condition affecting the esophagus.

The history should also include information about the type, consistency, and temperature of food that cause the most difficulty. Liquids are the last to be affected by obstructing lesions, and the temperature of the food has little effect on the problem. Neuromuscular disorders, however, often manifest with aspiration of liquids first. Room temperature liquids, such as tap water, cause the most difficulty, whereas those of extreme temperatures cause the least.

Voice changes are an important historical factor relative to swallowing disorders. Children with reflux disorders with spillage of acid contents into the posterior laryngeal introitus often present with hoarseness that is worse in the morning and that improves as the day goes on.

An adolescent's psychosocial history is extremely important in the dysphagia work-up. However, it is best for the examining physician not to bring this up too early in the encounter because the patient and the family may have had negative experiences from being labeled anxious or hysterical by other physicians.

The premature infant whose dysphagia persists despite growth and development should undergo an intensive search for another cause of the swallowing problem. The airway is a frequent source of defects of swallowing. Stridor in an infant indicates airway obstruction. The site of any airway obstruction must be rapidly recognized, because correcting the obstruction may correct the swallowing problem. In an infant who has stridor after feedings, the airway obstruction is probably not the underlying problem. In these children, airway obstruction is usually a result of dysphagia.

Physical Examination

The otolaryngologist is usually consulted for endoscopic examination of the child's upper airway after a complete history and general physical examination have been performed. This is the appropriate time to fine tune the history and to perform a thorough head and neck examination, including a cranial nerve survey. The difficulties in determining the exact cause of dysphagia in infants make this problem a multidisciplinary project. A complete evaluation before endoscopic examination is essential to prepare the surgeon for management of any causes of the problem. This preliminary evaluation must include observing the infant feed.

The evaluation of the infant and child varies somewhat from that of the adult. Head size and shape, facial configuration, and pressure and size of the fontanelle may be important clues to the cause of an infant's swallowing problems. Laryngeal paralysis and other cranial nerve palsies are often associated with increased intracranial pressure after meningomyelocele repair. Low-set ears may indicate genetic defects or craniofacial and mandibulofacial disproportions. The otolaryngologist should be familiar with the craniofacial features of the more common genetic disorders, such as Down syndrome, Treacher Collins syndrome, Crouzon disease, Goldenhar and Apert syndromes, Pierre Robin sequence, Beckwith-Wiedemann syndrome, and the mucopolysaccharidoses. These disorders are associated with dysphagia because of defects of the facial skeletal structures that result in abnormalities of the oral cavity, palate, and pharynx.

A careful examination of the nasal airway to determine patency is essential (a 6-French catheter should easily pass through the nose into the nasopharynx in the normal, full-term infant). Examination of facial development and function, oral cavity anatomy, and neurologic function of the lips, tongue, palate, and pharynx is necessary.

The single most important issue relative to complaints of dysphagia is whether the difficulty in swallowing occurs during feeding, between meals, or both. A discussion with the nurse, parents, or guardians regarding observations they have made of the child during and after feedings is helpful. Before performing radiographic studies, the physician must observe the child feed.

Between-meal swallowing normally involves an effortless, nonconscious passage of saliva and nasal secretions through the pharynx into the esophagus. Obstructing disorders affect between-meal swallowing late in the course of the disease; neurologic disorders affect between-meal swallowing in the early stages.

Radiographic Examination

Radiologic examination should include fluoroscopy of the entire airway from the nasal cavity to the trachea. Radiographic films of the chest help diagnose tracheobronchial, pulmonary, cardiac, or mediastinal disorders that may contribute to the swallowing problem. Computed tomography scans or magnetic resonance imaging should be performed, when indicated, to assess masses affecting the head and neck.

A videofluoroscopic swallowing study is most commonly used and is considered to be the gold standard. This study is superior to the usual barium swallow study, which primarily focuses on the esophagus and stomach, because it evaluates all phases of swallowing and esophageal function. Having a speech/occupational therapist present to assist with the video swallow is ideal because he or she may help with proper positioning, feeding techniques, and suitable textures. This test should be performed with a nipple to determine the effectiveness of oropharyngeal function and laryngeal competence. The recording of an esophagogram with a feeding tube can obscure function of vital areas necessary to determine the site of the swallowing defect. When the child refuses to nipple feed, pharyngeal function can be studied by instillation of the radiopaque medium into the pharynx through a nasal catheter.

Esophageal anatomy and function can be studied after the competence of the oral, buccal, and pharyngeal components of the swallowing mechanism have been evaluated. In the older infant and child, test swallows generally include three consistencies of food substances: liquid, thickened paste, and a quarter cookie soaked in barium (the cookie is used to evaluate mastication). A cine-esophagogram is helpful when an unusual lesion or one that is difficult to demonstrate, such as an H-type fistula, is suspected. A normal esophagogram, however, does not necessarily rule out a small esophageal stricture or web, because overlapping contrast may obscure minimal disease.

Endoscopic Evaluation

In cases of progressive dysphagia, endoscopy is essential. Endoscopic procedures may include flexible or rigid laryngoscopy, bronchoscopy, or esophagoscopy, depending on the specific problem. The procedure may be diagnostic (to perform a biopsy or observe an abnormality) or therapeutic (to dilate a stricture, remove a foreign body, perform sclerotherapy, or remove a polyp). Flexible endoscopy of the airway allows a more dynamic assessment of function and requires less anesthesia (which could mask disease). Rigid aerodigestive tract endoscopy allows better airway control and better optics as well as superior ability to remove foreign bodies and control bleeding, but it requires general anesthesia. Flexible esophagogastroduodenoscopy, which in children is often performed with an endotracheal tube in place, is less likely to result in a perforation and allows biopsy and photography of the entire upper digestive tract.

Fiberoptic endoscopic evaluation of swallowing (FEES) in children may offer additional information with respect to the cause of dysphagia; however, its usefulness may be limited by the child's ability to cooperate. Advantages of the technique are that it avoids the risks of radiation, can be performed at the bedside, is good for evaluating "silent aspiration," uses regular foods, can be videotaped for review, and can be repeated serially. FEES is most useful for identifying "pharyngeal phase" dysphagia, aspiration, and aspiration risk. Clinically, FEES is used for making recommendations regarding when to resume oral feeding and what bolus consistencies to use for optimal swallowing success. So far, FEES has been more extensively used and studied in adults.

Differential Diagnosis of Dysphagia

A normal swallowing mechanism is essential if the respiratory tract is to be spared contamination, and a normal respiratory tract is necessary for normal deglutition. Protection of the lung, in addition to the cough reflex and laryngeal closure mechanism, is the normal, primary mechanism of the swallowing process. These facts are especially important to consider in dealing with the neonate and young infant.

Just as the respiratory and alimentary tracts arise from a common embryologic origin, they remain dependent on one another for normal function throughout life. Defects of development common to both systems create functional problems of swallowing and difficulty with maintenance of a normal airway.

A child with dysfunction of the swallowing mechanism presents a complex and often challenging problem. In some instances, the dysphagia is temporary and is due to either immaturity or a temporary central nervous system aberration that spontaneously subsides. A search for the cause is necessary in all cases, however, so that medical management or surgical intervention may be instituted early and serious complications prevented. During this search, alternative methods of feeding the child (i.e., nasogastric feeding tubes, percutaneous endoscopic gastrostomy, or hyperalimentation) are necessary.

Dysphagia in children is almost always due to one or a combination of factors (Table 54–1). Different causes of dysphagia lead to varying symptoms. The urgency to establish a cause for dysphagia is enhanced because delay can lead to severe pulmonary disease and failure to thrive. This is most likely to occur in the very young infant, in whom a poor cough mechanism leads to aspiration, bacterial contamination of the respiratory tract, airway obstruction, and possible irreversible lung disease. Malnutrition and death are the eventual outcomes of prolonged dysphagia and aspiration.

TABLE 54–1. Differential Diagnosis of Dysphagia in Children

Prematurity/Developmental Delays

Birth weight <1500 g or <32 weeks' gestation
Oral aversion/poor conditioning
Hypoxia and anoxia
Associated "intensive care unit factors"

Congenital Defects of Upper Airway

Nasal and Nasopharyngeal

Choanal atresia or stenosis (CHARGE association)
Septal deformity
NOWCA
Piriform aperture defect
Anotia
Anosmia

Oropharynx and Oral Cavity

Defects of lips and alveolar processes
Defects of palate (cleft and submucous cleft)
Craniofacial defects (e.g., Crouzon, Treacher Collins, Goldenhar)
Defects of tongue or floor of mouth (e.g., Beckwith-Wiedemann, Down syndrome, congenital ranula)

Hypophyarynx and Supraglottic Larynx

Craniofacial defects (Pierre Robin sequence)
Laryngomalacia
Congenital cysts

Congenital Defects of Larynx, Trachea, and Esophagus

Larynx

Vocal cord paralysis
Glottic and subglottic stenosis
Laryngeal cleft

Tracheoesophageal Fistula (H-Type) with Associated Atresia

Esophageal Anomalies, Atresia, and Strictures

Vascular Anomalies Causing Compression ("Vascular Ring")

Aberrant right subclavian artery
Double aortic arch
Right aortic arch with left ligamentum

Acquired Anatomic Defects

Trauma

External
Internal (intubation injury)
Iatrogenic (surgical injury to mucosa or nerves)

Foreign Body

Hypopharynx and oral cavity
Esophagus
Airway

Chemical Ingestion

Acids, alkalies, catalysts
Medication-induced

Postsurgical Effects

Tracheostomy
Laryngotracheal reconstruction
Stricture
Colonic or jejunal interposition

Inflammatory Conditions and Manifestations of Systemic Disease

Infection

Streptococcal and nonstreptococcal pharyngitis
Fungal (esophagitis)
Protozoan (Chagas disease)
Viral (acquired immunodeficiency syndrome)

Connective Tissue Disorders

Scleroderma
Lupus
Rheumatoid arthritis
Sjögren syndrome

Manifestations of Systemic Diseases

Diabetes
Thyroid disorders

Neoplastic Conditions

Benign (e.g., cystic hygroma, hemangioma, papilloma)
Malignant (e.g., adenocarcinoma, lymphoma)

Central Nervous System Conditions

Head trauma
Hypoxia and anoxia
Cortical atrophy, hypoplasia, agenesis
Arnold-Chiari malformation
Infection (meningitis, brain abscess)

Neuromuscular Diseases

Amyotonia (Duchenne muscular dystrophy)
Cerebral palsy
Guillain-Barré syndrome
Poliomyelitis (bulbar paralysis)
Botulinum toxin
Riley-Day syndrome (dysautonomia)

Behavioral/Psychological Factors

Globus
Food vs. nonfood dysphagia
Anorexia
Bulimia
Munchausen syndrome by proxy

Primary Gastrointestinal Disease

Upper Esophagus

Cricopharyngeal dysfunction
Nonsphincteric esophageal spasm
Achalasia
Zenker diverticulum

Lower Esophagus

Gastroesophageal reflux (chalasia)
Barrett esophagus
Esophageal varices

Stomach

Peptic ulcer
Gastritis

Small and Large Intestine

Crohn disease
Ulcerative colitis

NOWCA, nasal obstruction without choanal atresia.

Prematurity and Developmental Factors

Dysphagia due to prematurity is temporary and usually subsides with growth and development. Failure to acquire normal patterns of intake and swallowing may result from extreme prematurity, however, which leads to a long stay in an intensive care environment and the risk of repeated physical trauma to the mouth and esophagus. This situation may result in a conditioned avoidance of swallowing on repeated, less severe stimulations of the mouth or esophagus. Such a maladaptive pattern is referred to as *oral aversion* and requires intensive rehabilitative treatment.

The premature infant may be unable to take feedings normally and may require assistance with both respiration and feedings.[10] Gavage, gastrostomy, or hyperalimentation may be necessary. These infants have a weak suck reflex, fatigue easily, and tend to aspirate. They should not be fed by nipple. In infants with established feeding patterns, respirations are paced with sucking in a ratio of 1:1 or 1:2.[11] Irregularities in timing are useful clues to immaturity or an acquired impairment of central neurologic regulation of feeding and respirations.[20]

The premature neonate who has hypoxia or anoxia may suffer permanent neurologic damage, resulting in cerebral palsy. Cerebral palsy primarily affects the oral phase of swallowing. Inadequate function of the oral muscles interferes with the ability to maintain a lip seal and to transport ingested material to the pharyngeal area. Poor head control and impaired palatal function also affect the ability to swallow. Children with cerebral palsy commonly display tongue thrusting, prolonged and exaggerated bite reflex, hyperactive or hypoactive gag reflex, tactile hypersensitivity in the oral area, and drooling. The result is feeding problems from poor muscle coordination, lack of salivary control, gastroesophageal reflux, and upper extremity dysfunction. These problems require intensive rehabilitative services and frustrate parents and therapists alike.[19]

Congenital Defects of the Upper Airway

The neonate born with upper airway obstruction, whether nasal, oropharyngeal, or laryngeal, tends to have a poorly coordinated suck-breathe-swallow rhythm. This poor rhythm results in choking, aspiration, respiratory arrest, or, in a longer period, the development of lower airway disease (see Chap. 78).

The infant with airway obstruction usually has a normal arousal reflex, sucks eagerly, accepts feedings, and swallows well for a short time but soon fatigues. Whereas maintenance of a patent nasal and nasopharyngeal airway is of utmost importance in the neonate and young infant, it becomes less important for feeding in the older child.

A complete outline of the causes of nasal and nasopharyngeal obstruction is beyond the scope of this chapter, but a few causes may be mentioned. Nasal and nasopharyngeal obstruction can be caused by malformations of the nose ranging from absence to atresia or stenosis. Tumors rarely obstruct the nasal or nasopharyngeal areas sufficiently to produce dysphagia. Infection in the neonate or older child can produce serious airway obstruction, and

a specific bacteriologic cause should be determined by cultures of secretions so that appropriate therapy can be instituted. Bilateral choanal atresia produces serious airway obstruction, and normal feeding is virtually impossible without first establishing an appropriate airway. Unilateral atresia rarely produces airway or swallowing problems unless the normal side is obstructed by infection or other causes. Trauma to the nose with septal deflection rarely produces dysphagia unless it is severe, in which case correction is mandatory. Iatrogenic trauma from repeated attempts at establishing nasal patency with suction catheters can produce neonatal rhinitis (nasal obstruction without choanal atresia [NOWCA]) and is best treated with topical decongestants and steroids.[7] Gastroesophageal reflux into the nose may produce neonatal nasal obstruction with associated signs and symptoms of dysphagia in infants. Allergic rhinitis is rarely a cause of dysphagia in the neonatal period (see Chaps. 37, 42, 43, and 49).

Difficulty in swallowing is common among infants with craniofacial anomalies. Defects of the oropharyngeal area, such as deformities of the lips, alveolar processes, tongue, mandible, and hard and soft palate, produce problems for the normal piston-in-cylinder sucking reflex that initiates swallowing. Uncorrected cleft lip deformities affect the oral phase of swallowing with breast feeding and standard bottle feeding. This problem is overcome with specially designed nipples. The young child with an uncorrected cleft palate is susceptible to nasal cavity contamination by food products, with subsequent development of sinusitis and rhinitis. In other craniofacial and mandibulofacial disproportions (Treacher Collins syndrome, Crouzon disease, and Apert syndrome), airway obstruction and mandibular dysfunction produce dysphagia. As well, poor velopharyngeal closure impedes transfer of the food bolus from the oral cavity to the pharynx and results in nasal regurgitation. Clefts that occur as part of genetic disorders, such as Treacher Collins syndrome and Crouzon disease, further aggravate problems with swallowing because of the maxillary-mandibular disproportions and their deleterious effects on tongue function. Syndromes associated with macroglossia, such as Down and Beckwith-Wiedemann, can also produce dysphagia through interference with the tongue's function in sweeping the food bolus back into the pharynx. Poorly coordinated tongue function also hinders laryngeal protective measures, resulting in aspiration. Obstruction in the hypopharynx, seen with posterior displacement of the tongue in the Pierre Robin sequence, may also lead to aspiration by preventing posterior tilting of the epiglottis and anterosuperior laryngeal movement, which is necessary for the passage of the food bolus into the cervical esophagus. Severe laryngomalacia, in addition to producing airway distress in the neonate, may also impair closure of the laryngeal introitus and lead to aspiration.

Congenital Defects of the Larynx, Trachea, and Esophagus

The larynx is an important area to be considered in problems of dysphagia. The child with a congenital defect of the larynx, trachea, or esophagus usually has a normal arousal response, sucks eagerly and effectively, and has a normal suck-breathe-swallow rhythm. However, swallowing leads to aspiration, airway obstruction, and pneumonitis. The voice may be normal unless a laryngeal cleft, web, or cyst or adductor paralysis is present. In some children, the airway may be free of symptoms except for stridor that develops during and after feedings. If the airway and esophagus are both involved, as with the presence of vascular rings, bronchogenic cysts, or compression by a tumor, a to-and-fro stridor is aggravated by feedings. In some vascular abnormalities or compressive lesions, feeding in early infancy may be normal, but dysphagia develops when solid foods are added to the diet. In these cases, esophageal obstruction, or dysfunction, produces vomiting and aspiration during or soon after feedings (see Chaps. 67, 83, and 84).

Airway obstruction produced by webs, cysts, subglottic stenosis, midline paralysis, or tumors must be treated early. Defects of the larynx, such as clefts, with or without involvement of the tracheoesophageal septum, are causes of aspiration. Neurologic defects produce aspiration when they are associated with either abductor or bilateral adductor vocal cord paralysis or anesthesia of the larynx produced by superior laryngeal nerve involvement of peripheral or central origin.

Congenital defects of the trachea and esophagus produce swallowing problems because of obstruction of the airway; abnormal opening between the tracheobronchial tree and the esophagus; obstruction within the esophagus; compressive lesions involving the trachea, esophagus, or both; and neurologic disturbance of motility of the esophagus. The lesions to be considered are clefts of the larynx and tracheoesophageal septum, tracheoesophageal fistula, tracheal stenosis, vascular rings, bronchogenic cysts, duplications of the esophagus, atresia, and stricture of the esophagus. In many instances involving congenital defects, airway obstruction is aggravated by swallowing of endogenous secretions and by feedings. Congenital bronchobiliary fistula produces reflux into the lung from the biliary tract during feedings, particularly when fatty foods are given. Surgical correction of this condition is essential to preserve life.

Esophageal atresia is a surgical emergency. It occurs in 1 of 3000 to 4500 live births; three fourths of these cases are associated with a fistula between the trachea and the distal esophagus. Atresia should be suspected when there is history of maternal polyhydramnios; the infant has excessive oral and pharyngeal secretions; or choking, cyanosis, or coughing occurs with attempts at feeding. Additional congenital anomalies (cardiovascular anomalies being the most common) occur in at least 30% of infants with esophageal atresia. Early diagnosis and correction may be followed by airway obstruction, paralysis of the larynx, strictures of the esophagus, reflux esophagitis, hiatal hernia, and many other disorders.[5] The tracheal stenosis and abnormalities of the tracheobronchial tree are well documented. The neurogenic problem of the lower segment of the esophagus is well established and is a cause of foreign body obstruction and dysphagia. Children with this anomaly should be fed in an upright position. Endoscopic dilatations and removal of foreign bodies are frequently necessary in children who have had esophageal atresias with tracheoesophageal fistula repaired. Children who have undergone a successful tracheoesophageal fistula repair nearly always are left with some degree of dysphagia resulting from esophageal dysmotility and gastroesophageal reflux.

Other esophageal lesions that cause swallowing problems are cricopharyngeal lesions, stenosis or achalasia, congenital strictures of the esophagus, and reflux esophagitis. Reflux may be associated with a hiatal hernia and can lead to stricture formation. Congenital strictures produce swallowing problems and may be associated with recurrent bronchitis and pneumonia. Dysphagia in some children with congenital strictures may not occur until solid foods are given. A foreign body may be the first evidence of a congenitally strictured esophagus.

Acquired Anatomic Defects

The clinical picture in a child with an acquired anatomic defect varies with the site of the problem. If the lips, mouth, face, and oropharynx are involved, the suck reflex may be seriously impaired. If the lesion is in the larynx, trachea, or esophagus, dysphagia manifests as described in the discussion of congenital lesions. Trauma to the larynx and surrounding areas, when associated with dysphagia, can be indicative of potential serious airway problems. Foreign body obstruction is a common cause of dysphagia even in very young infants. When a foreign body causes obstruction, fluids may be tolerated without difficulty, yet solid foods may produce choking, vomiting, or both. In this category, the most important diagnostic factors are the history of exposure to chemicals, medications, foreign body ingestion, intubation, prior surgical procedures involving the aerodigestive tract, and possible iatrogenic surgical trauma. Ingestion of corrosive substances is self-evident when seen early; but when the physician is confronted with a child with progressive dysphagia, strictures due to this type of ingestion must be considered even in the absence of a report of such ingestion. Mediastinal disease, either infection or tumor, may extrinsically compress the esophagus and cause swallowing problems. Postsurgical effects from laryngotracheal reconstruction or esophageal replacement with colon or jejunum may lead to esophageal motility dysfunction and manifest with dysphagia (see Chaps. 70, 71, and 72).

Problems with dysphagia after tracheostomy are well described.[24] With improving salvage in neonates of young gestational age, an increasing number of survivors are requiring prolonged airway support and subsequent need for tracheostomy. These children may have dysphagia associated with laryngeal stents used for laryngeal reconstruction. They may have aspiration through the top of an Aboulker stent along with complaints of dysphagia.[25] Fortunately, these problems resolve with decannulation.

Inflammatory Conditions and Manifestations of Systemic Diseases

Inflammatory conditions, both infectious and noninfectious, affecting the gastrointestinal tract can produce dysphagia and odynophagia in the child. Adenoid and tonsillar hypertrophy are not infrequent causes for feeding problems because of associated airway obstruction. Acute streptococcal and nonstreptococcal pharyngitis, including Epstein-Barr viral mononucleosis, usually manifests with some degree of dysphagia or odynophagia. Deep neck infections are uncommon in infants, but just as in older children, they can cause severe dysphagia and need to be diagnosed and treated early. Infections in the larynx, especially supraglottic disease (epiglottitis), create a sudden onset of dysphagia and represent a serious problem in which early diagnosis and therapy are mandatory. Esophagitis in the immunocompromised host is increasingly being recognized as a cause of dysphagia. This may be due to tuberculous involvement of the esophagus, histoplasmosis, blastomycosis, actinomycosis, candidiasis, or bacterial esophagitis. The last two, in particular, should be considered in children with human immunodeficiency virus infection[8] or absolute neutropenia as a consequence of chemotherapeutic drug therapy. In immunocompromised hosts, opportunistic infections by viral agents must also be considered. Biopsies and brushings, looking for cytomegalovirus and herpesvirus, are indicated when an esophagogastroduodenoscopy is performed. Tuberculous involvement of the esophagus, either primarily or secondarily, is rare. Tertiary syphilitic lesions of the esophagus do not occur in children (see Chaps. 60 and 63).

Among the parasitic diseases producing dysphagia, Chagas disease is the most prominent. A major public health hazard in South and Central America, this disease is the result of infection by a protozoan, *Trypanosoma cruzi*, which targets the esophagus, heart, and colon. It produces a dilated, atonic esophagus and, with long-standing disease, megaesophagus.

Connective tissue disorders may be associated with dysphagia by altering esophageal motility. The site of the dysmotility varies with the connective tissue disorder. Progressive systemic sclerosis (scleroderma), mixed connective tissue disorder, systemic lupus erythematosus, and Raynaud disease primarily affect motility of the distal two thirds of the esophagus. Polymyositis and dermatomyositis affect the motility of the pharynx and proximal esophagus. Juvenile rheumatoid arthritis (Still disease) may affect the cricoarytenoid joints, producing dysphagia; Sjögren syndrome has its primary gastrointestinal manifestations in the salivary glands, producing xerostomia.

Endocrine disorders, such as diabetes and thyroid disease (hyperthyroidism and myxedema), have rarely been shown to produce esophageal abnormalities in children. Late manifestations of these disorders in adults produce dysphagia, reflux, esophagitis, autonomic neuropathy, and delayed esophageal and gastric emptying.

Neoplastic Conditions

Benign and malignant neoplasms of the aerodigestive tract can lead to dysphagia in children. With an obstructive lesion of the esophagus, liquids may be well tolerated while solid foods produce choking. Recurrent respiratory papillomas are the most common benign tumors affecting the larynx. These may cause aspiration in addition to stridor and airway distress. With aggressive disease, papillomatous growth in the esophagus may lead to total obstruction and a need for gastrostomy tube feeding. Congenital plunging ranulas can cause oropharyngeal and hypopharyngeal obstruction and require early surgical intervention if symptoms are severe. Hemangiomas and lymphangiomas (hygromas) may involve the oral cavity, floor of mouth, and neck and extend into the peritracheal and periesophageal area, causing severe feeding difficulties and airway obstruction.[23] Childhood esophageal adenocarcinoma is rare but has been reported to occur in the setting of Barrett esophagus.[12]

Central Nervous System Disease

It is not within the purview of this chapter to review in detail the neurologic problems causing dysphagia. Dysphagia may be one of the earliest signs of a neurologic deficiency. When an anatomic or acquired defect has been ruled out, a neurologic cause is all that remains to be considered, and one can be fairly certain that a central nervous system, peripheral nerve, neuromuscular, autonomic, or psychological defect is the cause of the swallowing problem. The physician, who is usually in search of an anatomic defect as the cause of swallowing problems, must include an evaluation of the child's neurologic status in the search for the cause of dysphagia. The child with a poor suck reflex and an absent arousal reflex who aspirates secretions and who cannot feed normally can be considered to have a central nervous system defect from trauma, hypoxia, dysgenesis of the brain, infection, or one of a number of neurologic deficiencies. Other evidence of neurologic disease may be present, such as poor muscle tone, poor head support, and poor gag reflex. Excessive saliva in the mouth or oropharynx and drooling are evidence of swallowing defects and are prominent symptoms in neurogenic dysphagia. Neurogenic dysphagia, especially when it results from a Chiari malformation, is uniformly progressive and precedes the onset of other severe brain stem signs.[21] With neurogenic dysphagia, widespread dysfunction of the swallowing mechanism is seen with a combination of pharyngoesophageal dysmotility, cricopharyngeal achalasia, nasal regurgitation, tracheal aspiration, and gastroesophageal reflux. Defects of swallowing may occur in association with amyotonia (Werdnig-Hoffmann syndrome), myotonic muscular dystrophy, myasthenia gravis, Guillain-Barré syndrome, and bulbar poliomyelitis. A neurologic consultation usually aids in arriving at the specific diagnosis. Therapy is directed toward the protection and support of the airway and the use of alternative methods of feeding. Early recognition of and intervention for treatable causes of neurogenic dysphagia correlate with a favorable neurologic outcome and avoid recurrent aspiration pneumonias and failure to thrive (see Chap. 73).

Neuromuscular Disease

Infants and children with neuromuscular disease may display protean manifestations of upper gastrointestinal dysfunction. This is particularly evident in children with

Duchenne muscular dystrophy. These children exhibit dysphagia, choking while eating, the need to clear the throat during or after eating, heartburn, and vomiting during or after meals out of proportion to age-matched healthy control subjects.[13] The Riley-Day syndrome (familial dysautonomia) manifests with disturbances in autonomic and peripheral sensory functions. In infants, Riley-Day syndrome is manifested by poorly coordinated swallowing movements, resulting in gagging, vomiting, and aspiration. In familial dysautonomia, dysphagia is associated with hypersecretion, recurrent bronchopneumonia from aspiration associated with disordered swallowing from delay in opening of the cricopharyngeal muscle, and marked changes in the motility of the esophagus with improper relaxation of the lower esophageal sphincter.[18] The prognosis is poor; most children succumb to pulmonary failure before adulthood.

Behavioral and Psychological Factors

Behavioral and psychological factors causing difficulty in swallowing can be manifested during infancy, although they are more commonly appreciated during the teenage and early adult years. There is a strong female predominance. As previously mentioned, newborns in an intensive care environment have been noted to exhibit oral aversion to feedings, resulting in hampered weight gain. Whether these are manifestations of behavioral conditioning or psychological disorders has not been determined.

The *globus sensation* refers to a situation in which the patient complains of a continuous sensation of a lump in the throat. This sensation is most prominent between swallows, or nonfood dysphagia. Gastroesophageal reflux is the most common underlying factor, but often an anatomic or physiologic abnormality may be found to account for globus sensation. After all anatomic and physiologic factors have been ruled out, psychological factors are considered.

Anorexia nervosa is an eating disorder in which the patient has a distorted body image and a fear of becoming obese. Typically a disorder of adolescent girls, anorexia nervosa is characterized by progressive weight loss to the point of emaciation. Dysphagia can be a consequence of the gastrointestinal manifestations affecting dentition, parotid gland enlargement, delayed gastric emptying, distorted esophageal motility, and colonic disease resulting from laxative abuse.

Bulimia nervosa is similar to anorexia nervosa in that an underlying distorted body image is present. Bulimia nervosa is typified by binge eating followed by self-induced vomiting. Bulimics generally maintain a normal body weight, although they, too, abuse cathartics and diuretics and enthusiastically fast and exercise. Dysphagia in bulimics may be a direct consequence of vomiting-induced esophagitis, but endoscopic findings tend to dispute this theory.[14]

When the history, physical examination, and radiologic findings in the pediatric patient do not correlate with the symptoms, Munchausen syndrome by proxy should be considered. This is a psychological disorder often resulting from some form of child abuse. This is often difficult to document, but the symptoms resolve whenever the child is removed from the presence of a suspected overly protective family member. Perseverance by the medical staff, possibly with the assistance of high-technology surveillance equipment within the hospital environment, may be necessary to establish this diagnosis and end the pattern of abuse.

Gastrointestinal Disease

Of great interest to the physician are the autonomic defects involving the esophagus. In many defects in this category, the oral and buccopharyngeal phases of the swallowing mechanism are normal. However, problems arise after secretions and feedings enter the esophagus, resulting in retention of secretions and food, esophagitis, megaesophagus, and vomiting. In cricopharyngeal dysfunction, food cannot enter the esophagus, and the child aspirates or regurgitates immediately after swallowing (i.e., at the end of the buccopharyngeal phase). The upper esophageal sphincter prevents swallowed material from reentering the pharynx and air from being drawn into the gastrointestinal tract with respiration. It normally remains contracted between swallows. Successful deglutition depends on coordination between pharyngeal contractions that propel the food bolus into the esophagus and relaxation of the upper esophageal sphincter. Patients with upper esophageal sphincter dysfunction (cricopharyngeal achalasia) demonstrate dysphagia in the form of choking, gagging, pharyngonasal regurgitation, or recurrent aspiration pneumonias. Hypopharyngeal diverticula (Zenker diverticula) are a common cause of dysphagia in older men as a result of cricopharyngeal dysfunction, but they are rarely seen in children or adolescents.

Diffuse esophageal spasm occurs when contractions in the smooth muscle portion of the distal two thirds of the esophagus are uncoordinated and nonperistaltic. This results radiographically in a spiral or corkscrew appearance with a dilated proximal esophagus. Dysphagia and chest pain are common presenting symptoms in adults, but this phenomenon is rarely seen in children and adolescents.

Megaesophagus or achalasia is primarily a condition of adults; children younger than 4 years of age constitute less than 5% of all patients. In achalasia, the swallowing mechanism is normal; however, with failure of the esophagus to empty, dilatation occurs and vomiting is common. Achalasia results from a lack of relaxation of the lower esophageal sphincter with swallowing, which causes a relative obstruction made worse by a lack of peristaltic waves in the esophagus. Symptoms include dysphagia, regurgitation of food, cough, and failure to thrive. When unrecognized, achalasia leads to esophagitis, and pulmonary infections develop owing to constant aspiration. Peptic acid disorders may be accompanied by dysphagia. In addition to the more traditional presentations, peptic ulcer disease in children and adolescents may present as dysphagia with hematemesis.

Although dysphagia, dyspepsia, and odynophagia are cardinal symptoms of gastroesophageal reflux in adults, they rarely occur in children in the absence of regurgitation or vomiting. The sensation of "food sticking," however, may be a presenting symptom of reflux esophagitis in children without a history suggestive of gastroesophageal reflux and without evidence of a peptic stricture.[26] In gastroesophageal reflux (chalasia), regurgitation is frequently seen after feeding, particularly when the child is recumbent, but is relieved by smaller feedings and an upright position. Gastroesophageal reflux disease in children may exacerbate many otolaryngologic conditions, and investigation is warranted when children with dysphagia, stridor, laryngomalacia, laryngitis, or sinusitis have failed to respond to usual treatments.

Esophageal varices may occur in children as a complication of portal hypertension. The principal signs are recurrent, profuse, bright red hematemesis and tarry stools, although dysphagia may be present in long-standing cases and as a consequence of sclerotherapy.

Crohn disease may involve the upper gastrointestinal tract in as many as 30% of affected children, with specific esophageal involvement documented by endoscopy in 6.5%.[15] Typical complaints of Crohn esophagitis are dyspepsia, dysphagia, chest pain, and weight loss. Pulmonary symptoms in the child with Crohn disease strongly suggest esophageal involvement. This is most commonly noted at or shortly after diagnosis of ileocolitis.

Neurotoxins may produce dysphagia. Botulinum toxin may seriously affect the motor function of the esophagus in infants.[4]

Management

Management decisions in infants and children with feeding and swallowing problems are best made through a team approach in which the caregivers participate with medical and educational professionals. The goal is to maximize the child's nutritional status in the context of safe and efficient feeding. Management decisions are best made after repeated observations and assessments of feedings in conjunction with a videofluoroscopic swallow study and a detailed medical history.

Principles of management for pediatric dysphagia include emphasizing a "whole child approach" (safety, comfort, enjoyment), through which adequate nutrition is achieved with a stable respiratory status. Gastroesophageal reflux, if present, must be well managed. Total oral feeding may not be a realistic goal for all children. After observing the feedings and making a video swallow assessment, recommendations may be offered in several areas. These may include changing the route of nutrition; changing posture or position during feeding; altering bolus size, consistency, shape, texture, or temperature; changing utensils; changing the feeding schedule and pacing during mealtimes; and instituting nutritional guidelines.

Caregivers of children beyond infancy who have behavioral components to their feeding problems are given "rules" regarding scheduling (mealtimes no longer than 30 minutes, nothing offered between meals except water), feeding environment (no game playing, food never given as reward, no forcing food), and feeding procedures (small portions, solids first, fluids last, food removed after 10 minutes if child plays without eating, meal terminated

if child throws food in anger). Advice is offered with regard to optimal positioning of the child (no single position is effective in all situations) and alterations in the various attributes of food and liquid (bolus volume, consistency, temperature, and taste). Adjustments are made in the feeding schedule and pacing during mealtimes to optimize intake and minimize aspiration risk. When appropriate, medical or surgical interventions may be offered to supplement the feeding therapy.

Summary

As the physician's exposure to swallowing problems in children increases, a tentative diagnosis is more likely to be made on the basis of clinical observation. With experience, the diagnosis is more accurately accomplished with a minimum of laboratory studies.

Unlike the adult patient with dysphagia who comes to the physician's office concerned about the possibility of cancer, the parents of the pediatric patient with dysphagia are mainly concerned with the child's failure to thrive. However, it is still important to address the issue of malignant neoplasia as a possibility and to assure the family that everything reasonable is being done to rule out a malignant process.

SELECTED REFERENCES

Arvedson JC. Management of pediatric dysphagia. Otolaryngol Clin North Am 31:453, 1998.
> *This article offers a contemporary approach to management from the perspective of the speech/occupational therapist.*

Bosma JF (ed). Third Symposium on Oral Sensation and Perception. Springfield, Ill, Charles C Thomas, 1972.
> *This symposium, edited by an experienced anatomist, physiologist, and researcher, is suggested reading for those interested in the development, physiology, and anatomy of the problems of deglutition.*

Darrow DH, Harley CM. Evaluation of swallowing disorders in children. Otolaryngol Clin North Am 31:405, 1998.
> *An excellent systematic review of swallowing disorders in children.*

Wagner ML, Rudolph AJ, Singleton EB. Neonatal defects associated with abnormalities of the amniotic fluid. Radiol Clin North Am 54:279, 1968.
> *This is an excellent review of prenatal physiology of fetal swallowing defects related to anomalies causing abnormal accumulation of amniotic fluid.*

REFERENCES

1. Ardran GM, Harker P, Kemp FH. Tongue size in Down's syndrome. Ment Defic Dis 16:160, 1972.
2. Bosma JF (ed). Third Symposium on Oral Sensation and Perception. Springfield, Ill, Charles C Thomas, 1972.
3. Brans Y. Neonatal nutrition, an overview. Postgrad Med 60:113, 1976.
4. Cannon RA. Differential effect of botulinal toxin on esophageal motor function in infants. J Pediatr Gastroenterol Nutr 4:563, 1985.
5. Choudhury SR, Ashcraft KW, Sharp RJ, et al. Survival of patients with esophageal atresia: influence of birth weight, cardiac anomaly and late respiratory complications. J Pediatr Surg 34:70, 1999.

6. Davis ME, Potter EL. Intrauterine respirations of the human fetus. JAMA 131:1194, 1946.

7. Derkay CS, Grundfast KM. Airway compromise from nasal obstruction in neonates and infants. Int J Pediatr Otorhinolaryngol 19:241, 1990.

8. Ezzell JH, Bremer J, Adamec TA. Bacterial esophagitis: an often forgotten cause of odynophagia. Am J Gastroenterol 95:296, 1990.

9. Gryboski JD. The swallowing mechanism of the neonate. Pediatrics 35:445, 1965.

10. Gryboski JD. Suck and swallow in the premature infant. Pediatrics 43:96, 1969.

11. Halverson HM. Mechanisms of early infant feeding. J Genet Psychol 64:185, 1944.

12. Hassall E, Dimmick JE, Magee JF. Adenocarcinoma in childhood Barrett's esophagus: case documentation and the need for surveillance in children. Am J Gastroenterol 88:282, 1993.

13. Jaffe KM, McDonald CM, Ingman E, Haas J. Symptoms of upper gastrointestinal dysfunction in Duchenne muscular dystrophy: case-control study. Arch Phys Med Rehabil 71:742, 1990.

14. Kiss A, Bergmann H, Stacher G, et al. Upper gastrointestinal endoscopy findings in patients with longstanding bulimia nervosa. Gastrointest Endosc 35:516, 1986.

15. Lenaerts C, Roy CC, Vaillancourt M, et al. Involvement in children with Crohn's disease. Pediatrics 83:7710, 1989.

16. Logan WJ, Bosma JF. Oral and pharyngeal dysphagia in infancy. Pediatr Clin North Am 14:47, 1967.

17. Lynch FP, Coran AG, Cohen SR, et al. Traumatic esophageal pseudodiverticula in the newborn. J Pediatr Surg 9:675, 1974.

18. Margulies SI, Brunt SW, Donner MW, et al. Familial dysautonomia. Radiology 90:107, 1968.

19. McPherson KA, Kenny DJ, Koheil R, et al. Ventilation and swallowing interactions of normal children and children with cerebral palsy. Dev Med Child Neurol 34:577, 1992.

20. Peiper A. Cerebral Function in Infancy and Childhood. New York, Consultants Bureau, 1963.

21. Pollack IF, Pang D, Kocoshis S, Putram P. Neurogenic dysphagia resulting from Chiari malformation. Neurosurgery 30:709, 1992.

22. Pritchard JA. Fetal swallowing and amniotic fluid volume. Obstet Gynecol 28:606, 1966.

23. Ricciordelli EJ, Richardson MA. Cervicofacial cystic hygroma. Arch Otolaryngol Head Neck Surg 117:546, 1991.

24. Sasaki CT, Suzuki M, Horiuchi M, Kirchner JA. The effect of tracheostomy on the laryngeal closure reflex. Laryngoscope 97:1428, 1987.

25. Smith ME, Mortelliti AJ, Cotton RT, Myer CM. Phonation and swallowing considerations in pediatric-laryngotracheal reconstruction. Ann Otol Rhinol Laryngol 101:731, 1992.

26. Tsou VM, Bishop PR. Gastroesophageal reflux in children. Otolaryngol Clin North Am 31:419, 1998.

27. Wagner ML, Rudolph AJ, Singleton EB. Neonatal defects associated with abnormalities of the amniotic fluid. Radiol Clin North Am 54:279, 1968.

28. Warner RA. Deglutition. Int J Orthod 13:19, 1975.

55

The Management of Drooling

William S. Crysdale, M.D.

Drooling, or sialorrhea, is the spillage of saliva out of the mouth. It is a common clinical problem among neurologically impaired children and adults. Drooling greatly increases the demands for patient care, in that frequent changes of wet clothing (four or five times a day) or bibs (15 to 20 per day) may be required. Furniture, rugs, and toys that have been soiled need to be repeatedly cleaned or replaced. Excoriated skin about the lips and chin requires management. Patient education and development are compromised because people are reluctant to interact with a child constantly wet with saliva. Toys, writing equipment, keyboards, and other communication devices become soaked in saliva, leading to further difficulties and restrictions in education and development. For children of normal intelligence, drooling is particularly distressing: it causes embarrassment, reduces self-esteem, and interferes with interpersonal relationships. As has been said to the author, "Nobody wants to hold and kiss a child covered in spit!"

The Production, Nature, and Role of Saliva

Approximately 1.5 L of saliva is secreted into the oral cavity each day, and all except a small amount produced by the minor salivary glands comes from the major salivary glands in the following ratios: parotid, 25%; submandibular, 70%; and sublingual, 5%. The rate of production varies significantly among the various major glands. The submandibular and sublingual glands secrete saliva at a steady rate throughout the waking hours, with a significant reduction in secretion during sleep, whereas parotid secretion is more episodic. Parotid gland secretion is increased six- or sevenfold with the presentation of a sialagogue (olfactory and gustatory); thus, during meals, parotid secretion increases significantly.

Saliva produced by the submandibular and sublingual glands and the parotid glands contains much the same constituents (Table 55–1), but the ratio of constituents is different between the two systems. Submandibular and sublingual secretions have a higher level of glycoproteins; thus, the saliva from these glands is more viscid. In contrast, the secretion from the parotid glands has more enzymes and fewer glycoproteins, so that the saliva tends to be more water-like. Clinically, it is the viscid saliva

("the stuff that hangs down") produced by the submandibular (and sublingual) glands that is the problematic saliva in the drooling child. The parotid glands are composed primarily of serous cells, whereas the submandibular and sublingual glands consist mostly of mucus-producing cells.

Saliva plays a vital role in the maintenance of oral health. This is most apparent when salivary flow is severely reduced after radiotherapy of the head and neck or during the long-term use of some tranquilizers. In such circumstances, the incidence of dental caries and gingival disease is greatly increased. Saliva maintains oral health by means of the following processes:

1. Mucous membrane lubrication and protection. Saliva lubricates the oral cavity, thus facilitating tongue mobility and chewing. The glycoprotein and mucoid constituents of saliva form a mechanical barrier that protects the oral mucosa from desiccation, irritants, and potential carcinogens.
2. Mechanical cleansing. Saliva enters the mouth from the salivary glands and leaves through the act of swallowing. This flow of saliva washes bacteria, cellular debris, and food particles from the oral cavity into the gastrointestinal tract.
3. Buffering. Saliva plays an important role in neutralizing acids produced by oral bacteria. This buffering action, due mainly to the bicarbonate found in saliva, maintains an oral pH of 6.0 to 7.4.
4. Tooth integrity. Saliva helps maintain healthy teeth. The minerals it contains aid tooth maturation and prevent tooth dissolution. The glycoprotein in saliva forms a film on teeth that helps to reduce wear.
5. Antibacterial activity. Lysozymes and immunoglobulin A give saliva a strong antibacterial function.

Neurologic control of the salivary glands is achieved via the autonomic nervous system through secretomotor (parasympathetic) fibers. Preganglionic fibers pass from the inferior salivary nucleus to the otic ganglion, with postganglionic fibers from this ganglion innervating the parotid gland. The submandibular and sublingual glands are innervated by fibers from the superior salivary nucleus, which synapse in the submandibular ganglion before feeding into the glands themselves.

TABLE 55–1. Constituents of Saliva Other than Water

Inorganic	Organic
Sodium	Lysozyme
Chloride	Amylase
Potassium phosphate	Carbonic anhydrase
Calcium	Mucoproteins
Bicarbonate	Glycoproteins
Copper	Lipids
Thiocyanate	Sugars
Magnesium	Amino acids
Iodide	Kallikrein
Bromide	Urea
Fluoride	Desquamated epithelial cells
Citrate	Microorganisms

TABLE 55–2. Quantitative Assessment of Drooling

Severity
1. Dry: never drools
2. Mild: only lips wet
3. Moderate: lips and chin wet
4. Severe: clothing soiled
5. Profuse: clothing, hands, and tray moist and wet

Frequency
1. Never drools
2. Occasional drooling (not every day)
3. Frequent drooling (every day)
4. Constant drooling

Physiology of Drooling

Drooling is a normal occurrence in young children, particularly during episodes of teething, but most children stop drooling by 2 years of age. Intermittent drooling up to 4 years of age is unusual but may occur in children who have no neurologic deficits.

Persistent drooling in children may be the result of either neuromuscular dysfunction or hypersecretion of saliva. In fact, most children with chronic drooling have at least some degree of neuromuscular pathology. Typically, in the drooling patient, the oral phase of swallowing is affected, resulting in pooling of saliva in the mouth and eventual spillover. While troublesome drooling may be seen in children with a variety of neurologic disorders, it is most commonly seen in those with cerebral palsy. The latter is defined as a nonprogressive disorder of neuromuscular function occurring in 1 of 300 newborns. Ten percent to 15% of children with cerebral palsy drool significantly.[2] The clinical manifestations of cerebral palsy are truly kaleidoscopic, reflecting very different degrees of clinical involvement in association with very significant differences of developmental delay (Figs. 55–1 and 55–2). Hypersecretion as a cause of drooling is less common. It may be seen in children with gingivitis, rabies, or mercury poisoning, or after anticholinesterase ingestion.[21]

Management: A Multidisciplinary Approach

Since 1976, the author has participated in a drooling management program at a pediatric rehabilitation center. From its inception until the end of 1999, a total of 1167 patients ranging from 2 to 68 years of age were assessed (Figs. 55–3 and 55–4). A multidisciplinary team approach[7, 8, 15] has been very effective in the evaluation and management of this patient population. Our team consists of an otolaryngologist (who acts as chairperson), a pediatric dentist, and speech pathologists. The speech pathologists document previous attempts at treatment, quantitate the present degree of drooling using the scales relating its severity and frequency (Table 55–2), and assess oromotor function. On the basis of experience, the speech pathologist can usually predict the effectiveness of remedial exercise programs for motor control. Through interviews with both parents and child, the otolaryngologist assesses the

quantity of saliva produced and the impact of the problem on the daily management and life of the child. With respect to the latter, we use indicators such as the frequency with which bibs have to be changed, the occurrence of skin problems that have arisen from excoriation by saliva, and difficulties with the use of keyboards and other communication devices because of contamination by saliva. Finally, we determine how all of these events impose restrictions on the child's life. Head and neck examination is completed and documented. Particular attention is paid to the position and control of head movements, the nature of the drooled saliva (viscid or waterlike), tongue size and mobility, and tonsil size. The dentist determines occlusion, the condition of the teeth and gums, and the configuration of the mandible and palate. All team members document their findings in a multipage form unique to this clinic.

After these individual evaluations, the team meets to reach a consensus on the management plan. Further evaluations are rarely required. Occasionally a neurologic consultation is sought if there is any doubt about the stability of the child's neurologic status. Radiographic swallow studies may be required if aspiration is a concern. As the treatment plan is applied, regular follow-up visits are arranged at 6- to 12-month intervals to assess the patient's progress. The follow-up differs from the initial assessments in that patients are evaluated simultaneously by team members. The outcome of treatment, as assessed both quantitatively (see Table 55–2) and qualitatively (Table 55–3), is documented. An up-to-date database file is maintained for all patients. Aside from demographic information, each patient's database file contains the initial date of assessment, initial management recommendation, dates and types of surgical procedures, complications of surgical procedures, and qualitative and quantitative outcome results at the time of the most recent assessment or survey.

Patients attending our drooling clinic are offered one

TABLE 55–3. Qualitative Assessment of Postoperative Outcome

Excellent: no saliva on chin
Good: saliva on chin, dribbling once a day
Fair: saliva on chin, dribbling at least once a day
Poor: no change

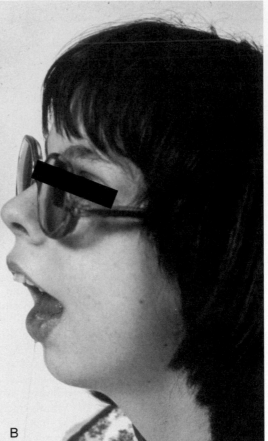

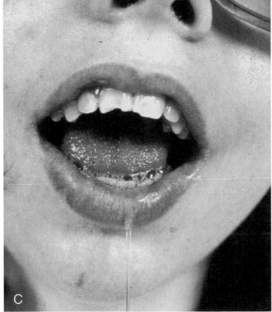

FIGURE 55–1. *A*, This 10-year-old girl with normal intelligence has focal cerebral palsy involving just the oral musculature; her otherwise neat appearance is marred by the fact that she wears a bib throughout the day because of profuse drooling. The side view (*B*) and close-up frontal view (*C*) not only document the drooling but demonstrate the anterior open bite and overjet secondary to the high anterior position and thrusting of the tongue commonly observed in many of these children.

of six management options (Table 55–4). Irradiation of salivary glands does reduce salivary flow and has proven helpful in the management of patients with sialectasis and salivary fistulas,[17] but we do not recommend it as a treatment option in this patient population because of the potential long-term risks of exposure to radiation.

No Treatment

No specific treatment is our recommendation for the following:

1. Children younger than 4 years of age who have only occasional drooling of a mild to moderate degree.

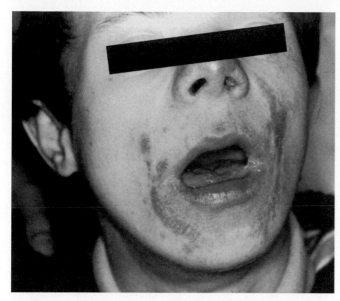

FIGURE 55–2. This 8-year-old boy with severe developmental delay in association with cerebral palsy and Down syndrome illustrates hypertrophic scarring of the facial skin secondary to chronic irritation as a result of profuse drooling associated with smearing of the saliva from mouthing of hands and other objects.

We know that normal children may occasionally drool until 4 years of age and have learned that children with neurologic deficits mature later. Drooling of a minor nature may disappear spontaneously in such a child by 6 to 8 years of age.

2. Children or adults with drooling resulting from an acquired lesion (e.g., a closed head injury) in whom the clinical status is improving. Intervention becomes an option when function has plateaued for at least 6 months.

3. Children or adults in whom drooling is but one problem of many that are of greater concern to parents or caregivers. For instance, a developmentally delayed child who is severely affected by cerebral palsy and has chronic aspiration with drooling as well is really not a candidate for intervention with respect to the drooling.

Oral Motor Training

Oral motor training intended to improve oral motor skills is the foundation for the nonsurgical management of drooling. That this was a primary recommendation in only 18% of our patients (see Table 55–4) reflects the fact that all our patients are referred and, in most instances, have already had considerable oral motor therapy.

In these programs, exercises are intended to improve lip closure, jaw elevation, and tongue mobility. These exercises are frequently initiated and monitored by speech and language pathologists or physiotherapists, but they most often need to be maintained on a daily basis by parents or caregivers. When intervention for drooling is recommended, almost all patients should have had the

benefit of at least 6 months of oral motor training before other forms of therapy are considered. The exception is in individuals (children or adults) who drool profusely and are severely developmentally delayed, because there is a lack of or inability for compliance with oral motor training in these patients.

Biofeedback

Biofeedback therapy involves using conditioning techniques to train the patient to swallow more frequently in response to an auditory stimulus. This therapeutic approach is time consuming for therapists, patients, and caregivers. Six to eight 2-hour sessions may be necessary to condition the child properly. When therapy is completed, it is anticipated that patients will function in their normal environment wearing a device that emits a sound every 30 seconds, stimulating a swallow (Fig. 55–5).

This treatment option is suitable only for a small number of patients evaluated: they must be older than 8 years of age with normal intelligence, they must have only mild to moderate drooling, and both patients and parents must be highly motivated to attend the conditioning sessions. Not only do few children meet these criteria, but also the improvement in drooling is often lost with the passage of time as the child either forgets to wear the device or becomes oblivious to the sound. This therapeutic option has been recommended less frequently during recent years.

Situational Factors

Correctable situational factors may contribute to the patient's drooling. Gingivitis and dental caries may require treatment by a dentist; both these conditions tend to increase salivary flow rates. Upper airway obstruction caused by adenotonsillar hypertrophy may require correction by the otolaryngologist, because this condition predisposes children to mouth breathing and increased drooling. To maximize swallowing, it is occasionally necessary to use a head-back wheelchair to reposition the patient's head. Even when all these factors have been corrected, however, only 10% of patients show significant improvement.[8]

Pharmacotherapy

We have infrequently recommended pharmacotherapy, but the use of drugs to control drooling has often been

TABLE 55–4. Patient Management Options*

No treatment: 195 (17%)
Oral motor training: 210 (18%)
Situational factors: 38 (3%)
Biofeedback: 52 (4%)
Pharmacotherapy: 11 (1%)
Surgery: 661 (57%)

* This table shows the distribution of primary management recommendations made to all 1167 patients at the author's clinic at the time of initial assessment to January 1, 2000.

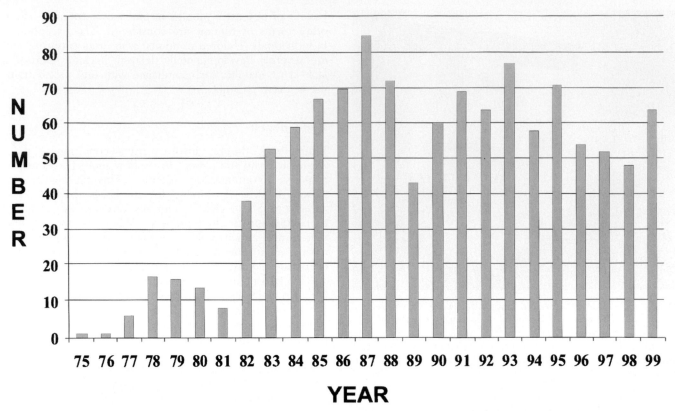

FIGURE 55–3. The number of new patients assessed each year in the Drooling Control Clinic at the Bloorview MacMillan Centre from 1976, a total of 1167 patients to January 1, 2000.

advocated by others. The efficacy of benzhexol hydrochloride,[16] transdermal scopolamine,[20, 22] and atropine sulfate[12] for short-term management of drooling has been demonstrated. The drawbacks of pharmacotherapy are that the patient needs to be on continuous medication for life, long-term therapy has potential side effects, and difficulties with compliance occur.

Surgery

Generally speaking, unless the patient has undergone intensive oral motor therapy since an early age, surgery is deferred until at least 6 years of age so that all the spontaneous maturation of function that may occur will have done so.

Surgery is recommended primarily for patients who have profuse constant drooling and who have significant cognitive impairment making nonsurgical therapy impractical from a compliance point of view. It is also recommended for those who have shown continued significant drooling despite appropriate nonsurgical therapy. As stated previously, each child should have a minimum of 6 months of oral training to improve oral motor skills. Such therapy should be continued and surgery deferred if there are any suggestions of significant improvement.

Surgery was the primary recommendation for 57% of the patients assessed in the author's clinic (see Table 55–4), reflecting both that many of the patients referred had undergone years of oral motor therapy and that a considerable number were profuse droolers with signifi-

cant developmental delays precluding the application of nonsurgical measures.

Surgery was a secondary recommendation in a significant proportion (up to one third) of patients in whom nonsurgical measures had initially been recommended.

Operative Procedures for Drooling

Operative procedures intended to eliminate drooling have evolved in two directions: those intended to reduce the amount of saliva produced and those intended to redirect the flow of saliva so that it may be swallowed more readily. Procedures recognized as reducing saliva production are tympanic neurectomy (division of the parasympathetic secretomotor nerve fibers to the major salivary glands), excision of the submandibular glands, and parotid duct ligation. Operations recognized as diverting saliva flow are submandibular duct relocation and parotid duct fistulization.

Tympanic neurectomy[5, 6] is accomplished through an endomeatal tympanotomy. Once the surgeon has entered the middle ear, the chorda tympani nerve conveying the secretomotor fibers to the submandibular and sublingual glands and the tympanic plexus that contains similar fibers destined for the parotid glands can be divided. This operation can be completed bilaterally in a relatively short time. Its advantages are that it is an easy procedure of short duration, associated with minimal patient morbidity and short hospitalization. Aside from the loss of taste, the principal disadvantage is that, within 6 months,

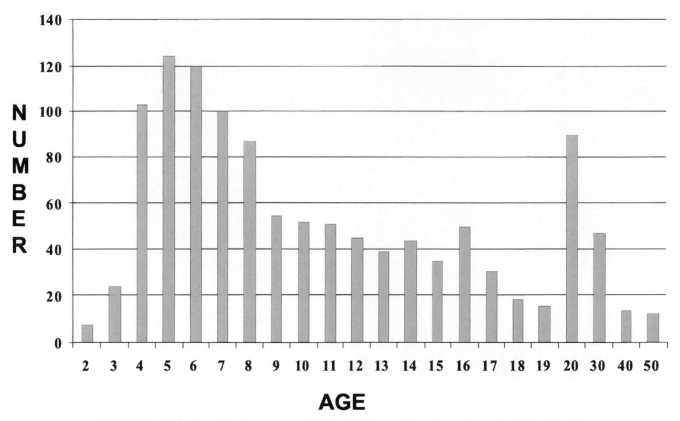

FIGURE 55–4. The age distribution of the 1167 patients in the Drooling Control Clinic at the time of initial assessment; 732 were male and 435 female; 85% were under 21 years of age. 20, patients 20 to 29 years of age inclusively; 30, patients 30 to 39 years of age inclusively; 40, patients 40 to 49 years of age inclusively; 50, all patients 50 years of age and older. The oldest patient assessed was actually 75 years of age.

drooling often returns to preoperative levels. Most clinicians dealing with this patient population have abandoned this procedure.

Excision of the submandibular glands with ligation of the parotid ducts is an approach advocated by some authors. Operative morbidity is greater and a longer hospital stay is necessary. A patient is also left with external neck scars.

Fistulization of the parotid ducts to the tonsillar fossae with excision of the submandibular glands was first described by Wilkie and Brody.[23, 24] This procedure helped control drooling but was associated with a wide array of complications, including septic parotitis, duct stenosis, and gingivitis. A refinement of the Wilkie procedure, combining parotid duct ligation with submandibular gland excision, reduces postoperative morbidity while maintaining a satisfactory outcome.[3] The disadvantages of these techniques include chronic sialadenitis, an external scar, and xerostomia. Because drooling involves saliva produced by the submandibular glands in most cases, we do not favor carrying out procedures on the parotid gland as part of the initial surgical intervention. Submandibular gland excision leaves the patient with two external scars.

Bilateral submandibular duct relocation, first described by Laage-Hellman in 1969,[14] has been our operation of first choice since 1978; as of January 1, 2000, this operation was undertaken in 516 patients. Tonsillectomy is also performed if the tonsils are large, filling the fossae to the

point where relocation of the submandibular ducts would be difficult, or if the tonsils contain a significant quantity of debris in their crypts. Since 1988, this procedure has been combined with bilateral sublingual gland excision in 291 patients. In 1999, surgical experience with submandibular duct ligation was reported[13] for the management of aspiration; certainly this procedure would be of interest for the management of drooling if it stands the test of time, in that it could be a simpler way of achieving significant clinical improvement with very low morbidity.

A summation of the surgical experience in our unit is presented graphically in Figure 55–6. From 1976 to 1979 we completed 36 primary tympanic neurectomies, but, as reported previously, we became disillusioned with that procedure because of poor long-term results. The nine neurectomies completed intermittently since that time were secondary procedures in patients who had significant persistent viscid sialorrhea despite submandibular gland excision (completed elsewhere) or submandibular duct relocation (completed by ourselves). In 1978, we began to perform submandibular duct relocation as our procedure of choice and have remained impressed with its effectiveness in most patients. In 1988, this procedure was combined with sublingual gland excision. Parotid duct fistulization was performed in three patients in 1984 for the management of persistent watery sialorrhea after submandibular duct relocation; morbidity was significant, and the ineffective operation was abandoned. Parotid duct li-

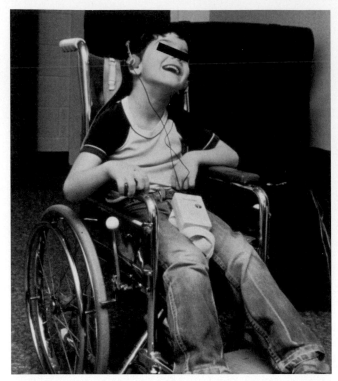

FIGURE 55–5. This 10-year-old boy has undergone biofeedback training to reduce drooling. The Walkman modified device in his lap emits through the earphones a low-pitched sound of 1 second's duration every 30 seconds. The volume can be adjusted.

gation, again for persistent watery sialorrhea after submandibular duct relocation, has been completed in 17 patients since 1987; this procedure is associated with much less morbidity and a much better outcome. In 1990, in one patient with persistent sialorrhea after submandibular duct relocation, parotid duct ligation was combined with sublingual gland excision; morbidity was significant and drooling only modestly reduced.

Surgical Technique of Submandibular Duct Relocation and Sublingual Gland Excision

This operation is carried out with the patient positioned as for a tonsillectomy, with general anesthesia maintained via a nasoendotracheal tube. Tonsillectomy, if indicated, is completed using the dissection technique complemented with electrocautery for hemostasis. The Boyle-Davis mouth gag is removed after tonsillectomy, and a self-retaining retractor is positioned on the incisors or molars to maintain a mouth-open position. The floor of the mouth anterior and posterior to the submandibular papillae is infiltrated with 1% lidocaine with 1:200,000 epinephrine. An elliptic incision is made surrounding the submandibular duct papillae, and this ellipse of mucosa is raised as an island containing the papillae (Fig. 55–7A). The submandibular ducts are identified (see Fig. 55–7B) and dissected posterior to the lingual nerve (see Fig. 55–7C). A chromic catgut suture is placed at the lateral edges of the mucosal island, and the island is sutured

temporarily to the undersurface of the tongue (see Fig. 55–7D). Attention is then given to removal of the sublingual glands. The mucosa of the floor of the mouth is divided posteriorly parallel to and 1 cm medial to the mandible almost to the tonsillar fossa. The anterior aspect of the sublingual gland is mobilized off the mandible, with blunt dissection posteriorly off the underlying mylohyoid and the medially positioned genioglossus muscles. Next, the mucosa between the tongue and sublingual gland is divided. The lingual nerve is identified and dissected free laterally. All gland tissue external to the lingual nerve is usually sublingual gland tissue. The soft tissue attachments remaining are carefully isolated, cauterized, and divided. The arterial supply to the sublingual gland is anterior to the lingual nerve emerging through the mylohyoid muscle near its posterior margin. After removal of the sublingual glands on both sides, the mucosal incisions are closed with interrupted No. 30 chromic catgut sutures.

Postoperative Care

After surgery, patients are nursed in a constant care environment (one nurse per four patients 24 hours a day). During the immediate postoperative period, particular attention is paid to the patient's airway, hydration, and pain control. While upper airway obstruction resulting from edema of the tongue and floor of the mouth is a potential problem, intervention has rarely been required. To minimize edema, intravenous steroids are given intraoperatively, followed by a single postoperative dose. Patients with marked retrognathic mandibles are at particular risk for development of respiratory distress from intraoral swelling. In reality, endotracheal intubation for management of immediate postoperative airway distress has been required in only two or three patients to date. One patient needed a tracheotomy 5 days postoperatively for a 10-day period to treat excessive airway secretion retention. Patients are maintained on intravenous fluids until they are drinking well, and prophylactic broad-spectrum antibiotic coverage is continued for 1 week. Because a high proportion of these patients are on anticonvulsant therapy, control of seizure activity during the postoperative period is very important, but this often proves difficult. The average length of hospital stay is 3.5 days.

Complications

Swelling of the submandibular glands is frequently observed in the immediate postoperative period. It is rarely symptomatic and usually subsides within the first week.

Since 1988, when we combined simultaneous sublingual excision with submandibular duct relocation, we have had a complication requiring additional surgery in only one patient—a teenager who required a tonsillectomy 6 months after submandibular duct relocation and sublingual gland excision for the removal of a cyst in the tonsil.

Before 1988, we dealt with two complications requiring additional surgery—lateral neck cysts and ranulas. Lateral cervical cyst formation (Fig. 55–8) occurred in six patients after submandibular duct relocation only.[10] Pa-

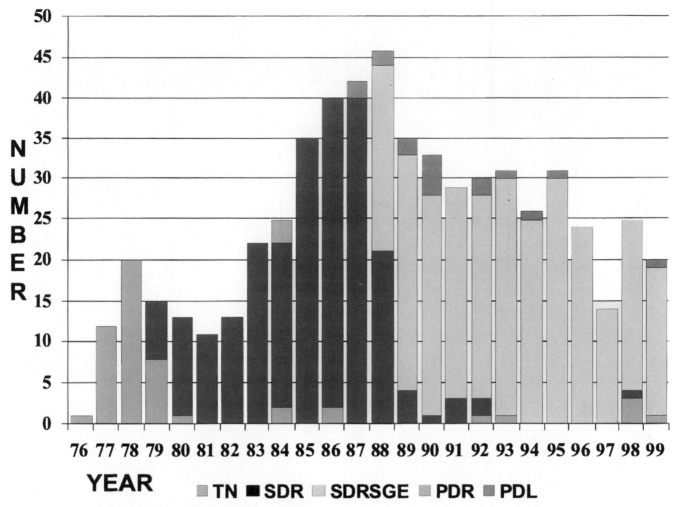

FIGURE 55–6. Distribution by year of the number of surgical procedures completed to control drooling to January 1, 2000. (Numbers following each group indicate total number of procedures completed.) SDR (submandibular duct relocation), 225; PDL (parotid duct ligation), 17; SDRSGE (submandibular duct relocation with simultaneous sublingual gland excision), 291.

tients characteristically presented with gradual swelling in the submandibular area within a few months of surgery. The cyst consists of a dilated submandibular duct and is believed to arise from obstruction of the relocated duct with continuing function of the gland. This problem was managed surgically with the removal of the cyst and the submandibular gland. Ranula formation (Fig. 55–9) occurred in 20 patients who underwent bilateral submandibular duct relocation only.[4, 9] Ranulas develop as extravasation pseudocysts arising from disrupted sublingual gland tissue. As a result, it has become standard practice in our unit to excise the sublingual glands simultaneously with relocation of the submandibular ducts; we have not witnessed a ranula since 1988.

Although an increase in the prevalence of caries after submandibular duct relocation has been reported,[1] with the mandibular incisor and canine teeth most at risk, our dental staff have not documented this as a problem.

Xerostomia has been reported after submandibular gland excision with parotid duct rerouting or ligation.[18, 19] Xerostomia has not been documented following our pri-

mary procedure of choice (submandibular duct relocation with simultaneous sublingual gland excision) but has occurred (as discussed later) after secondary parotid duct ligation for persistent sialorrhea.

The author's experience with complications following surgery is summarized in Table 55–5. From a statistical point of view, there is little doubt that submandibular duct relocation combined with simultaneous sublingual

TABLE 55–5. Complications Requiring Surgery*

Complication	SDR (226 Patients)	SDRSGE (249 Patients)
Ranula	20 patients	0
Lateral neck cyst	6 patients	0
Other	0	1 (tonsil cyst)

* This table illustrates that the complications requiring additional surgery have been significantly less frequent in those patients having simultaneous sublingual gland excision with submandibular duct relocation (SDRSGE) versus those patients just having submandibular duct relocation (SDR).

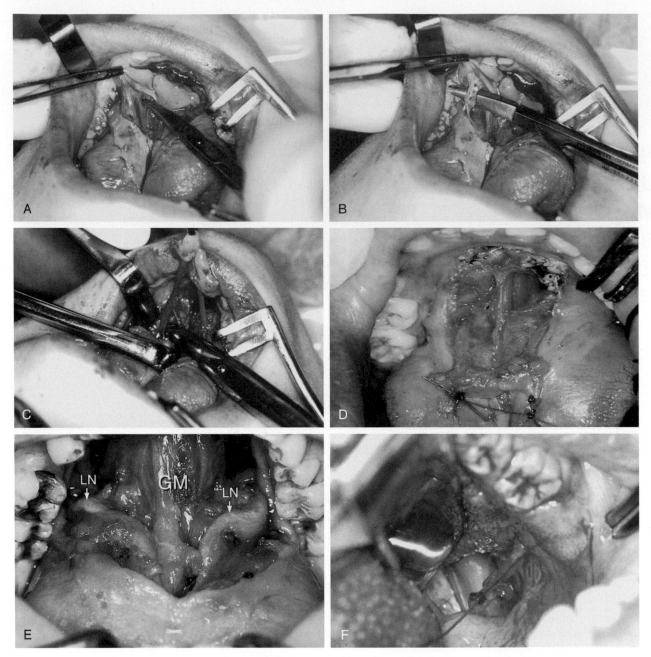

FIGURE 55–7. Stages of submandibular duct relocation with simultaneous sublingual gland excision. This is the surgeon's view from the head of the operating table. The self-retaining retractor has been inserted and the tip of the tongue is sutured back to the soft palate to facilitate exposure of the floor of the mouth. *A,* An island of mucosa encompassing the submandibular papillae; the submandibular duct is found with blunt scissor dissection. *B,* The left submandibular duct. *C,* Both submandibular ducts have been dissected back to their junction with the submandibular gland. *D,* The island of mucosa with both papillae is temporarily sutured to the undersurface of the tongue so that the ducts remain clearly in view while the sublingual glands are removed. *E,* The floor of the mouth after the sublingual glands have been removed. The island of mucosa has been released from the undersurface of the tongue, divided, and the submandibular ducts relocated to the ipsilateral tonsillar fossa. Note the lingual nerves (LN) and the genioglossus muscle (GM). *F,* The duct in the tonsillar fossae after repositioning before being sutured into place.

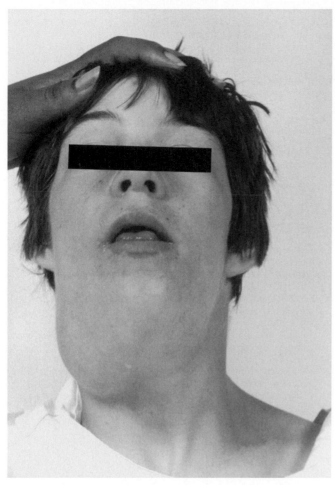

FIGURE 55–8. This 13-year-old girl slowly developed this large cystic swelling in the right side of the neck 3 months after submandibular duct relocation. Management consisted of excision of the cyst with the associated submandibular gland via an external excision.

gland excision has been associated with significantly fewer complications than submandibular duct relocation alone.

Results

Most patients who undergo submandibular duct relocation with or without sublingual gland excision show significant improvement, although drooling may still be present to some degree. A recently completed review,[13] which encompassed the author's patients who had sublingual

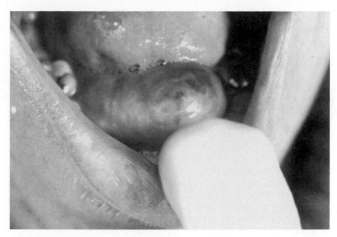

FIGURE 55–9. A large ranula in the floor of the mouth posterior to the lower dentition. Successful management required the removing of both sublingual glands via an intraoral approach.

glands removed simultaneously, has documented (Table 55–6) that there is no significant change in the outcome of the two groups of patients.

Those patients who continue to drool significantly 1 year after submandibular duct relocation are reviewed in our multidisciplinary clinic to determine what option (oromotor therapy, pharmacotherapy, surgery) might be appropriate. In the past, we offered one of two further surgical procedures, depending on the nature of the drooled saliva. For patients who had viscid saliva, we offered transtympanic neurectomy (a procedure which, in a secondary role, has proved modestly beneficial in approximately 50% of such cases). For patients who continued to drool but were losing water-like saliva as opposed to viscid saliva, we recommended parotid duct ligation. Since 1990, we have more often recommended parotid duct ligation regardless of the nature of the spilled saliva, because we have been impressed with the efficacy of this relatively simple procedure. However, it is in this latter group of patients (secondary parotid duct ligation after submandibular duct relocation with sublingual gland excision) that we have observed some cases of xerostomia. To date, caregivers have expressed a preference for xerostomia as opposed to residual drooling. My personal preference is to achieve optimal reduction of drooling but to maintain a moist, healthy oral cavity, which may mean the persistence of some drooling. As of January 1, 2000, a total of 14 of 225 patients who underwent submandibular duct relocation only (the earlier group of patients) and 8

TABLE 55–6. Quantitative Response to Surgery*

Patient Population Surveyed	Number of Responses	Time Postoperative (Years)	Preoperative Drooling Score	Postoperative Drooling Score	Change
SDR	107	1.6	8.2	4.8	3.4
SDRSGE	113	3.98	8.40	5.15	3.35

* This table illustrates that there is no significant difference in the quantitative response to surgery, either submandibular duct relocation only (SDR) or simultaneous sublingual gland excision with submandibular duct relocation (SDRSGE).

of 291 patients who had simultaneous sublingual gland excision with submandibular duct relocation (the latter group of patients) have had secondary surgery for persistent drooling.

REFERENCES

1. Arnrup K, Crossner CG. Caries prevalence after submandibular duct repositioning in drooling children with neurological disorders. Pediatr Dent 12:98, 1990.
2. Brown AS, Silverman J, Greenberg S, et al. A team approach to drool control in cerebral palsy. Ann Plast Surg 15:423, 1985.
3. Brundage SR, Moore WD. Submandibular gland resection and bilateral parotid duct ligation as a management for chronic drooling in cerebral palsy. Plast Reconstr Surg 83:443, 1989.
4. Burton MJ. The surgical management of drooling. Dev Med Child Neurol 33:1110, 1991.
5. Cotton RT, Richardson MA. The effect of submandibular duct rerouting in the treatment of sialorrhea in children. Otolaryngol Head Neck Surg 89:535, 1981.
6. Crysdale WS. The drooling patient: evaluation and current surgical options. Laryngoscope 90:775, 1980.
7. Crysdale WS. Drooling: experience with team assessment and management. Clin Pediatr 31:77, 1992.
8. Crysdale WS, Greenberg J, Koheil R, Moran R. The drooling patient: team evaluation and management. Int J Pediatr Otorhinolaryngol 9:241, 1985.
9. Crysdale WS, Mendelsohn JD, Conley S. Ranulas-mucoceles of the oral cavity: experience in 26 children. Laryngoscope 98:296, 1988.
10. Crysdale WS, White A. Submandibular duct relocation for drooling: a 10-year experience with 194 patients. Otolaryngol Head Neck Surg 101:87, 1989.
11. Crysdale WS, Raveh E, McCann C, et al. Management of drooling—surgical experience from 1103 patients assessed. Dev Med Child Neurol 43(6):379, 2001.
12. Dworkin JP, Nadal JC. Nonsurgical treatment of drooling in a patient with closed head injury and severe dysarthria. Dysphagia 6:40, 1991.
13. Klem C, Mair EA. Four duct ligation: a simple and effective treatment for chronic aspiration from sialorrhea. Arch Otol 125:796, 1999.
14. Laage-Hellman JE. Retroposition av glandula submandibularis utforsgang som behandling av dregling. Nord Med 27:1522, 1969.
15. Reddihough D, Johnson H, Ferguson E. The role of a saliva control clinic in the management of drooling. J Pediatr Child Health 28:395, 1992.
16. Reddihough D, Johnson H, Staples M, et al. Use of benzhexol hydrochloride to control drooling of children with cerebral palsy. Dev Med Child Neurol 32:985, 1990.
17. Robinson AC, Khoury GG, Robinson PM. Role of irradiation in the suppression of parotid secretions. J Laryngol Otol 103:594, 1989.
18. Rosen A, Komisar A, Ophir D, Marshak G. Experience with the Wilkie procedure for sialorrhea. Ann Otol Rhinol Laryngol 99:730, 1990.
19. Shott SR, Myer CM, Cotton RT. Surgical management of sialorrhea. Otolaryngol Head Neck Surg 101:47, 1989.
20. Siegel LK, Klingbeil MA. Control of drooling with transdermal scopolamine in a child with cerebral palsy. Dev Med Child Neurol 33:1013, 1991.
21. Stuchell RN, Mandel ID. Salivary gland dysfunction and swallowing disorders. Otolaryngol Clin North Am 21:649, 1988.
22. Talmi YP, Finkelstein Y, Zohar Y. Reduction of salivary flow with transdermal scopolamine: a four-year experience. Otolaryngol Head Neck Surg 103:615, 1990.
23. Wilkie TF. The problem of drooling in cerebral palsy. A surgical approach. Can J Surg 10:60, 1967.
24. Wilkie TF, Brody GS. The surgical treatment of drooling. Plast Reconstr Surg 59:791, 1977.

56

Congenital Malformations of the Mouth and Pharynx

Harlan R. Muntz, M.D., and Steven D. Gray, M.D.

It is imperative for the physician who evaluates congenital malformations of the mouth and pharynx to have an understanding of the normal embryology, anatomy, and physiology of this area. This information is important in the planning and timing of treatment for the individual patient and should not be considered to be just academic. The reader is referred to Chapters 1, 2, 50, and 51 for more complete discussions of embryology, anatomy, and physiology.

The major portion of embryonic development of the mouth and pharynx occurs in the fourth to eighth weeks of intrauterine life. The formation of the mouth begins in the early part of this period via the development of a depression on the ventral surface of the embryo cephalad to the first branchial arches. This depression is lined with ectoderm and is termed the *stomodeum*. The entoderm-lined primitive gut extends to the stomodeum, and these two structures are separated by the oropharyngeal communication. The tongue forms from the lateral tubercles and tuberculum impar, which are covered with ectoderm. The maxillary and mandibular processes extend above and below the stomodeum to form the supportive structures of the mouth and lower face.[38] The bony framework of the mouth is formed by the maxilla, mandible, and palatine bones. The soft tissues include the lips, tongue, soft palate, external facial muscles, mastication muscles, and lymphoid tissue of the Waldeyer ring. These important anatomic relationships are discussed in Chapter 50, and the reader is strongly encouraged to review this material.

The mouth and pharynx play important roles in life-sustaining functions of the individual, including respiration and intake of food and water. Obviously, severe disturbance of these functions is not compatible with life and must be treated promptly and appropriately. Additional functions of the oral cavity and pharynx are taste and speech.

Facial Clefts

The common cleft of the upper lip is thought to be due to a faulty union between the maxillary and globular processes during embryologic development. Other clefts that involve the mouth may develop owing to failure of the maxillary and mandibular processes to fuse. The etiologic and embryologic factors involved in many facial clefts are not completely understood, so classifications of such clefts have been difficult. The Tessier classification of facial clefts is provided (Fig. 56–1). The clefts are numbered 0 to 14. Many of these clefts involve the mouth, but it is the orbit that is generally regarded as the reference landmark. One of the more common clefts is a lateral facial cleft that results in macrostomia. It may be seen in isolation or in conjunction with mandibulofacial dysostosis and oculoauriculovertebral dysplasia.

Lips

Cleft lips may be paramedian, median, oblique, or transverse. Small mucosal sinus tracts or pits (as seen in Van der Woude syndrome) may also occur, usually symmetrically in the vermilion of the lower lip. They may be associated with cleft lip and palate. They communicate with or contain minor salivary glands, and simple excision is the treatment of choice.

There is a great deal of individual variability in the size of the oral opening; however, an abnormally large mouth (macrostomia) or an abnormally small mouth (microstomia) may be diagnosed.

The apparent double lip, which is seen when the lips are parted, particularly in smiling, is due to a redundancy of the mucosal lining. This deformity may occur in isolation or as a component of Ascher syndrome (double lip, blepharochalasis, and nontoxic thyroid enlargement).

Surgical management of the cleft lip deformity must ensure the appropriate reconstruction of the obicularis oris muscular ring. This allows normal animation and function. The lip reconstruction should attempt to restore the normal vermilion, white line, and Cupid's bow. Procedures include the rotation advancement flap as described by Millard and other straight line or triangular closures. A lip adhesion can be performed in infancy to convert the wide cleft to an incomplete cleft, with the hope that it will result in a nicer definitive lip repair and allow for deformational pressure on the alveolar segments. This procedure is used by many as the first stage in the lip reconstruction.

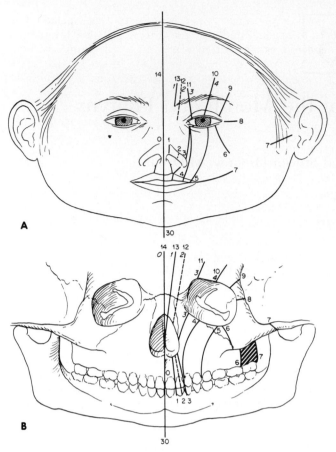

FIGURE 56–1. Diagram shows classification of facial clefts as described by Tessier. Note that the lateral facial cleft, or macrostomia, is type 7.

Palate

Cleft of the palate may occur in isolation or be associated with cleft of the alveolus and lip. Cleft palates may be divided into a cleft of the primary palate, a cleft of the secondary palate, or both. A cleft of both the primary and secondary palates associated with a cleft lip is the most common. Clefts of only the primary palate are rare and usually occur with a cleft of the alveolus and lip.

Anatomically, the palate is divided by the incisive foramen. The structures in front of the incisive foramen are referred to as the *primary palate,* and the structures posterior to the incisive foramen are often referred to as the *secondary palate.* These divisions are based on embryologic studies that show that the primary palate forms from mesoderm beneath the nasal pits and the secondary palate forms as a result of fusion of the palatal shelves.[41]

Abnormalities of the palate are frequently divided into syndromic and nonsyndromic categories. The determination of whether a cleft palate is syndromic is important, because it may lead not only to clues as to the etiology of the cleft and its inheritance pattern but also to the discovery or awareness of other associated problems. This may help in counseling of parents, treatment of the condition, and prognosis. All patients with cleft palate should be evaluated by a geneticist. Cleft palate is thought to occur from the interaction of both genetic and environ-

mental factors. Examples of cleft palates with a predominant genetic component are Treacher Collins syndrome (5q32-q33.1), Klippel-Feil syndrome (8q24.12), Van der Woude syndrome (1q32-q41), and chromosomal aberrations, including trisomies such as Down syndrome. Examples of environmental factors that increase the occurrence of cleft palate are maternal cigarette smoking,[24] inadequate prenatal folic acid consumption,[31] phenytoin,[17] and ethanol.[22]

Children afflicted with cleft palates should be followed by a craniofacial or cleft palate team from infancy. Conditions associated with cleft palate that require team care are the nearly universal incidence of middle-ear disease, including chronic otitis media with effusion and infection; velopharyngeal incompetence and disorders of articulation, phonology and language; orthodontic abnormalities; disturbed and retarded facial growth; and, occasionally, airway obstruction.

In the normal musculature of the soft palate, there is a transverse orientation to the levator veli palatini muscle. The main body of this levator muscle is in the posterior soft palate. The most anterior part of the soft palate contains an aponeurosis.[29] Other muscles of the soft palate that contribute to palatal movement are the palatopharyngeal muscle, tensor veli palatini muscle, palatoglossus muscle, and superior pharyngeal constrictor muscle. The musculus uvulae causes thickening of the central portion of the soft palate. Although the musculus uvulae was historically thought to be of little importance, patients can experience velopharyngeal incompetence based only on its absence.[7] The defect of the musculus uvulae can be seen well with nasopharyngoscopy and appears as a furrow or flattening of the soft palate. This is further covered in Chapter 106. The palatal muscles normally form a sling, which pulls the palate superiorly and posteriorly to abut the posterior pharyngeal wall. In some patients, the posterior pharyngeal musculature, the uppermost portion of the superior constrictor, can be contracted to move the posterior pharyngeal wall forward. When seen, this shelf-like projection is called the *Passavant ridge.*

In the cleft palate, the aponeurosis is nonexistent or almost nonexistent, and the muscles that form the muscular sling are oriented longitudinally and insert into the posterior edge of the hard palate (Fig. 56–2). This impairs any superior and posterior palatal motion. Surgical procedures to repair the palatal cleft have been designed not only to close the cleft palate but also to reorient the levator sling across the palate. The intravelar veloplasty and the Furlow double-reversing Z-plasty closure are used to accomplish this. The palate musculature seems to be more functional.

Surgery

Surgery on the cleft palate is performed when a child is healthy and, on the basis of the surgeon's experience, the palate can be closed safely. The usual time for palatal closure is 6 to 16 months. Wide palatal clefts may be closed later so the operation is easier to perform. Narrow clefts and soft palatal clefts are frequently closed at the

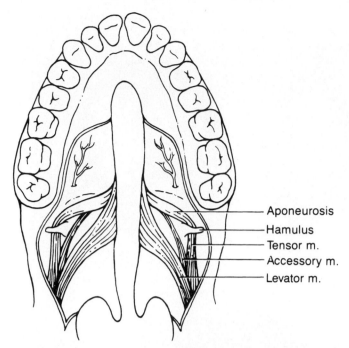

FIGURE 56-2. Sketch of cleft palate musculature. The muscles are attached to the posterior edge of the hard palate with a thin and narrow aponeurosis. The muscles are not located in the posterior portion of the soft palate, where a muscle sling would be most effective. The orientation of the muscle fibers is in an anterior-to-posterior direction instead of transverse.

Aponeurosis
Hamulus
Tensor m.
Accessory m.
Levator m.

earlier end of the time spectrum. Surgery may also be delayed in patients who are predisposed to airway difficulty, such as in Robin sequence, to allow further maturation of the upper airway. Closure of the cleft palate leads to postoperative airway edema, tongue swelling, and reduced upper airway, so these children are at risk for upper airway obstruction and must be monitored closely.

Various surgical techniques have been developed in an effort to obtain palatal closure and good palatal muscle function. This chapter deals with three of the more popular ways of closing cleft palates: (1) Furlow palatoplasty (also known as a double-reversing Z plasty), (2) Wardill-Kilner-Veau operation, and (3) two-flap palatoplasty.

The Wardill-Kilner-Veau operation is a V-Y lengthening operation (Fig. 56-3). Mucoperiosteal flaps are elevated off the hard palate. The muscular sling is detached from the posterior edge of the hard palate to provide increased length of the palate, and a V-Y closure is performed in which the two mucoperiosteal flaps are pushed posteriorly. For this to be adequate, the nasal mucosa must be cut so that the nasal surface can slide posteriorly. This can be done as described by Stark[40] and Cronin[8] or with island flaps[33] or flaps of buccal mucosa.[23] Despite these maneuvers, the palatal lengthening is frequently not successful; we therefore use this procedure for clefts of the secondary palate that have adequate soft palatal length.

The two-flap palatoplasty is useful for complete cleft palates and for wide clefts. In this approach, two palatal mucoperiosteal flaps are elevated back to the soft palate. The soft palatal musculature and aponeurosis are de-

tached from the posterior edge of the hard palate. The neurovascular bundle of the greater palatine foramen is dissected as needed to allow adequate closure without tension on the two flaps. The nasal mucosa is closed as the first layer. The soft palatal musculature is closed as a separate layer, and then the palatal mucosa is closed. The advantages of this procedure are the relatively simple design and its versatility. It can be used in many types and widths of palatal clefts and in bilateral or unilateral clefts (Fig. 56-4).

The double-reversing Z plasty has gained popularity because of two effects the surgery has on the soft palate. First, the soft palate gains considerable length as a result of the Z plasty. Second, the Z plasty tends to line up the soft palatal musculature so that the bulk of the musculature is in the posterior portion of the soft palate and the muscle bundles are lined up more transversely than in other types of palatal closure procedures. It appears that the speech results are as good as or better than those obtained with other surgical techniques of palatal closure. Many are using this as a standard for closure of the soft palate. The disadvantage to this technique is that it is difficult to perform on wide clefts, and the procedure is more time consuming than the previously described pro-

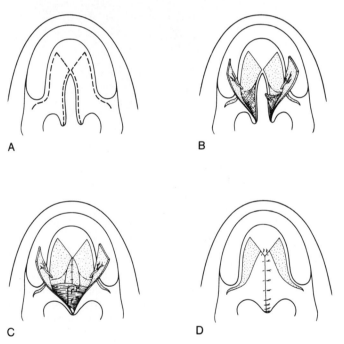

A   B

C   D

FIGURE 56-3. Wardill-Kilner-Veau palatal repair. *A,* Incisions are marked on a cleft of the secondary palate. At the apex of the cleft, the incision extends toward the area where the canine tooth will erupt. *B,* Mucoperiosteal flaps, which are based on the greater palatine artery, are elevated. The aponeurosis and muscle attachments of the soft palate are detached from the posterior edge of the hard palate. *C,* The nasal layer is closed, and then the soft palate musculature is sewn together. *D,* Mucoperiosteal flaps are sewn together and advanced posteriorly, thus providing the name *V-Y push-back.* This operation was designed to give more palatal length. However, without incision of the nasal layer, minimal push-back is actually achieved. (From Randall P, LaRossa D. Cleft palate. In McCarthy JG [ed]. Plastic Surgery, Vol 4. Philadelphia, WB Saunders, 1990, pp 2723–2752.)

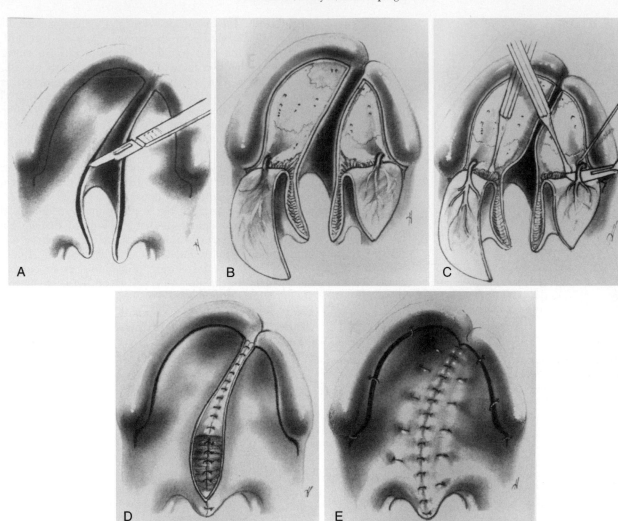

FIGURE 56–4. Two-flap palatoplasty. *A,* Incisions are outlined to proceed along the junction of the gingivopalatal mucosa. A 1- to 2-mm edge of nasal mucosa is left on the oral side to assist in nasal layer closure. *B,* The bilateral mucoperiosteal flaps based on the greater palatine artery are elevated. *C,* Three steps are shown: first, detaching the muscle from the posterior edge of the hard palate; second, elevating the nasal layer for closure; and third, dissecting the neurovascular bundle so that the mucoperiosteal flaps can be transposed more medially. If a knife is used as shown in this illustration, then an elevator needs to be placed between the bundle and the knife to protect the neurovascular supply. *D,* The nasal and muscle layer is closed. *E,* The oral layer is closed, occasionally with the use of vertical mattress sutures. Although the illustration shows the gingivopalatal incisions closed, this is not necessary and should be discouraged if it creates excess tension on the palatal closure. (From Bardach J, Salyer K. Cleft palate repair. In Surgical Techniques in Cleft Lip and Palate. Chicago, Year Book Medical Publishers, 1987. By permission of Mosby–Year Book, Inc.)

cedures. It does increase palatal length. It is exceptionally good for repairing submucous clefts (Fig. 56–5). Long-term outcome (5 years) has been good in the speech results for those nonsyndromic children with the Furlow as an initial repair.[25]

A bifid uvula is one of the major findings in submucous cleft palate. A bifid uvula, however, may occur in isolation with a normal palate. The frequency of bifid uvula is said to be about 1:80, and the frequency of submucous cleft palate is generally regarded as about 1:280.

If the bifid uvula is present, a more thorough examina-

tion of the palate is warranted. Other findings that may confirm the presence of a submucous cleft palate are a palpable notch in the midline of the hard palate, a bluish line in the midline of the soft palate (zona pellucida), and muscle bundles or ridges along the lateral sides of the submucous cleft. In the submucous cleft palate, a muscle ridge can be felt and seen on either side of the midline. The child with submucous cleft palate may be asymptomatic but may present with velopharyngeal insufficiency and middle-ear disease. The complication of velopharyngeal insufficiency after adenoidectomy is more often seen in patients with submucous cleft palate.

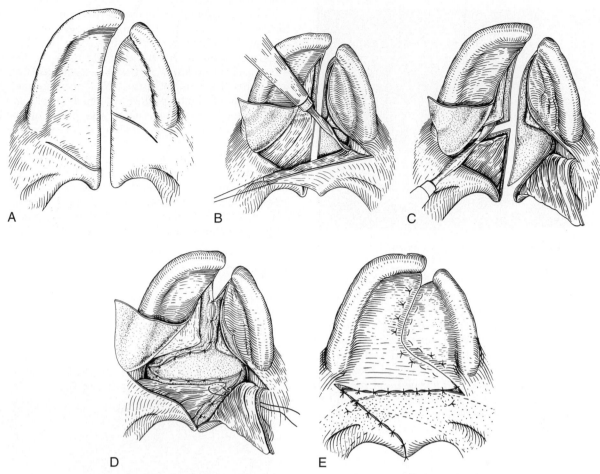

FIGURE 56–5. Furlow or double-reversing Z plasty repair. *A,* Oral Z plasty incisions are marked. *B,* On the right side, the incision is extended through the palatal aponeurosis, and a flap is elevated that includes the muscle and oral mucosa. The nasal mucosa is left as a separate layer. The right oral mucosa and muscle flap are posteriorly based. On the left side, only the oral mucosa is raised as a separate flap that is based anteriorly. *C,* Now the mirror Z plasty is performed on the nasal surface side. An incision is made through the nasal mucosa on the right side up to the hamulus. On the left side, the nasal mucosa and soft palate musculature are posteriorly based by dividing the aponeurosis from the hard palate to the hamulus. *D,* The left posteriorly based nasal mucosa and muscle flap are sutured across to the right side. The right anteriorly based nasal flap is sutured into the aponeurosis area. *E,* The right-sided oral mucosa and muscle flap are now laid over the previous muscle flap, and the remaining Z plasty is closed. Note that the two muscle areas are now overlapped, and they are pushed farther posteriorly. (From Furlow LT Jr. Cleft palate repair by double opposing Z-plasty. Plast Reconstr Surg 12:724, 1986.)

Pseudopalatal Clefts

Some patients have marked lateral hard palatal swellings. These are associated with a high-arched palate and a median furrow, which gives the appearance of a cleft palate. Careful examination reveals an intact palate. These are common in patients with Apert syndrome, as well as in patients with Crouzon disease. Usually, no treatment is needed.

Tongue

Variations in the size of the tongue are seen among individuals and ethnic groups. Congenital macroglossia is seen in association with other syndromes, such as Down syndrome and Beckwith-Wiedemann syndrome. It may also be isolated and idiopathic. Lymphangioma or hemangioma of the tongue may also result in macroglossia. The surgical reduction of an enlarged tongue should be planned in relation to the deformity. Resection of the dorsal midline, the anterior free tongue, or the lateral margins of the tongue can be performed.

Maldevelopment of the lingual frenulum results in mandibular ankyloglossia, or tongue-tie (Fig. 56–6). This is a relatively common condition and often a suspected cause of poor articulation in children. There also is debate as to its effect on feeding.[5]

The clinical evaluation of the child with tongue-tie should indicate the necessity for correction. Physical findings indicative of a need for surgical intervention include notching of the protruding tongue tip, inability of the

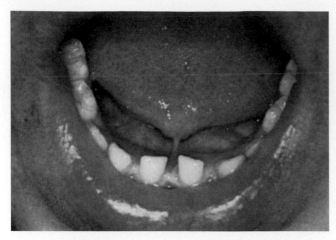

FIGURE 56–6. Ankyloglossia, or tongue-tie.

tongue tip to contact the maxillary alveolar ridge, restriction of lateral tongue motion, and restriction of tongue protrusion beyond the mandibular alveolus.[11]

Surgical correction depends on the extent of the malformation. Occasionally, the short lingual frenulum is a thin, filmy membrane that can be clipped with the patient under local anesthesia, with little risk of recurrence. In some cases, the membrane is thickened and requires a frenuloplasty to provide adequate lingual mobility and to prevent recurrent ankyloglossia. This may be achieved by a Z plasty, V-Y plasty, or horizontal-to-vertical plasty (Fig. 56–7).

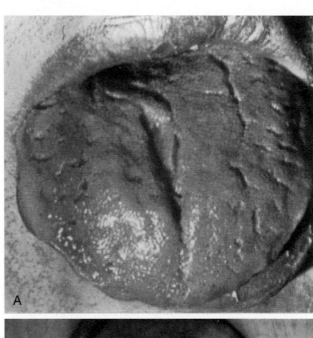

FIGURE 56–7. *A,* Horizontal-to-vertical repair of ankyloglossia. *B,* Z plasty repair of ankyloglossia.

Other congenital anomalies of the tongue include bifid tongue, fissured or scrotal tongue, geographic tongue, and median rhomboid glossitis (Fig. 56–8). The fissured tongue is seen in nearly all children with Down syndrome. This condition also occurs as an isolated finding with a positive familial history. Median rhomboid glossitis is a result of faulty posterior lingual development with papilla-free tissue appearing in the posterior medial aspect of the tongue in the region of the embryonic tuberculum impar.

Macroglossia may be symptomatic by causing airway obstruction, disturbing speech intelligibility, interfering with chewing and drinking, and causing drooling and cracking of the tongue and lips. When it is symptomatic, tongue reduction may be indicated. Various types of tongue resections have been proposed[30] (Fig. 56–9).

Lingual Thyroid

A mass lesion in the midline of the posterior tongue may represent a lingual or an undescended thyroid gland. Embryologically, the thyroid develops from the floor of the

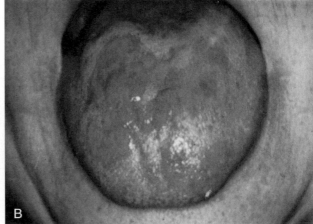

FIGURE 56–8. *A,* Fissured tongue. *B,* Geographic tongue.

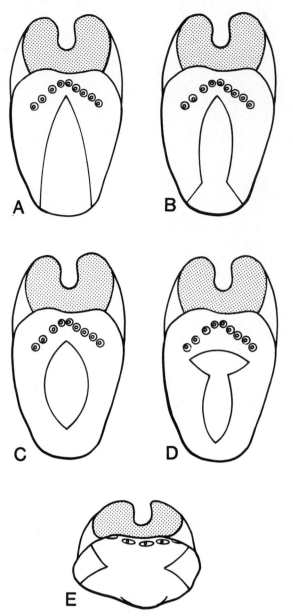

FIGURE 56–9. Various incisions that have been proposed for tongue reduction. *A* and *B* are both used to reduce length of the tongue. *C, D,* and *E* are more often used to reduce tongue width.

primitive pharynx and migrates anteriorly and inferiorly to reach its final adult location. Abnormality of this descent process can result in the development of a thyroglossal duct and cyst or, less commonly, in an undescended thyroid at the base of the tongue or superficial to the hyoid bone.

The lingual thyroid mass (Fig. 56–10) usually increases in size as the child becomes older because of the effect of thyroid-stimulating hormone on this marginally functioning thyroid tissue. The common symptoms are dysphagia, dysphonia, dyspnea, and, occasionally, pain.

The lingual thyroid may be the patient's only functioning thyroid tissue. Thyroid scanning with radioactive isotopes is necessary to make the diagnosis and to evaluate the amount of active thyroid tissue present so management can be planned. There also is an increased frequency of thyroid carcinoma in lingual thyroid tissue.

Management considerations include functional, metabolic, and cosmetic factors. If the patient is euthyroid and without functional or cosmetic problems, no therapy—with careful follow-up—is acceptable. If the patient is euthyroid or hyperthyroid with functional or cosmetic problems or both, suppressive thyroid hormone therapy should be initiated. If adequate regression of the mass occurs, this therapy can be continued; otherwise, surgical treatment is in order. Excision with subsequent thyroid hormone replacement or autotransplantation of the thyroid tissue to the neck or abdominal wall is the surgical technique that is used.[43]

Maxilla and Mandible

The development of the maxilla is in part related to airflow through the nose. Conditions that cause chronic nasal airway obstruction may result in a high-arched, narrow palate or occlusion problems, such as molar crossbite. High-arched palates are also seen in many of the previously discussed congenital syndromes. The palate may appear normal at birth and become high arched in the first 4 to 5 years of life.

Congenital asymmetries of the mandible and maxilla are uncommon as isolated findings. They may develop as a result of trauma or in relationship to other syndromes, such as facial hemihypertrophy or hemifacial atrophy.

Torus palatinus and torus mandibularis are rarely seen in the newborn but develop as the patient matures. There are bony exostoses on the center of the hard palate (palatinus) or on the lingual table of the mandible at the level of the canine and first premolar teeth (mandibularis). Their appearance is characteristic and their removal is not necessary, except possibly for the improvement of denture fitting.

Various cysts of the maxilla can be seen during the developmental years. These cysts are rarely congenital and usually occur in young adults. They occur mainly in the embryologic fusion lines of the premaxilla and maxilla. Examples include globulomaxillary, nasoalveolar, nasopalatine, and palatine cysts.

Congenital tumors may be present in the pharynx. Examples of these include Tornwaldt cyst, branchial cleft cyst, teratomas, chordomas, craniopharyngiomas, cystic hygromas, and hemangiomas.

During indirect laryngoscopy, small, yellowish, thin-walled cysts are frequently seen in the vallecula and hypopharynx. These usually require no therapy. A large vallecular cyst can occasionally result in dysphonia, dysphagia, and dyspnea, requiring surgical treatment. Recurrence after needle aspiration is common, and treatment by marsupialization or excision is preferred.

Obstructive sleep apnea can occur in children with congenital pharyngeal malformations; tonsil and adenoid hypertrophy in a congenitally small pharynx can also result in sleep apnea. Tonsil and adenoid removal is beneficial if obstructive hypertrophy exists.

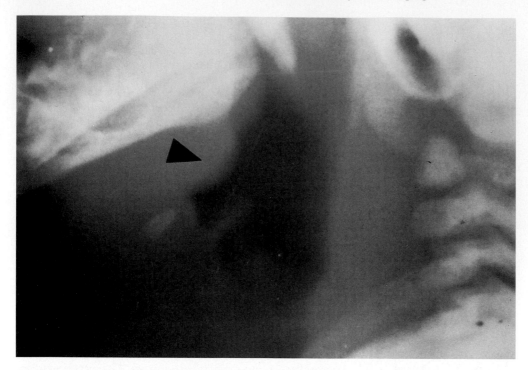

FIGURE 56–10. Note the mass effect above the vallecula (*arrow*) as the lingual thyroid is seen on a lateral soft tissue radiograph. (Courtesy of Dr. Gary Hedlund, Radiology, Primary Children's Medical Center, Salt Lake City, UT.)

Other Congenital Syndromes

There are many other congenital syndromes that involve the mouth and pharynx, including whistling face syndrome (Freeman-Sheldon syndrome), lingual malformations in Mohr syndrome, aglossia-adactylia syndrome, and others. The reader is referred to Gorlin and associates[15] for more extensive discussions of syndromes that involve the mouth and pharynx.

Management of Congenital Syndromes

The team approach to patients with multiple congenital abnormalities of the head and neck is most likely to result in an accurate assessment, a correct diagnosis, a rational plan of management, and an optimal prognosis. This team may include the pediatrician, otolaryngologist, neurologist, plastic surgeon, ophthalmologist, geneticist, speech pathologists, audiologists, social workers, and dental specialists. Other specialists may be required, depending on the individual patient's problems.

When a patient with a "head and neck syndrome" is first seen, it is important not to reach a premature diagnostic decision. Computed tomography (CT) scanning in multiple planes has replaced standard radiographic techniques in the assessment of patients with congenital head and neck syndromes.[10] Because the major malformations are bony, CT scanning provides better evaluation than magnetic resonance imaging. CT scanning in more than one plane or three-dimensional reconstructions of fine-cut axial CT can be helpful.

Special neurologic assessment of hearing, sight, facial motion, and deglutition may be necessary. It is frequently beneficial to obtain chromosome studies to aid in the diagnosis and to help provide a basis for genetic counseling. Each case needs to be compared with literature descriptions to correctly identify the syndrome. This can be accomplished only after a careful, accurate physical examination.

Once the diagnosis has been made, it is important to formulate and pursue an orderly, comprehensive plan of action. With the team approach, although many will have valuable input, it is necessary that one member of the team be responsible for the coordination of therapeutic events.

The "syndrome patient" needs to have his or her various malformations individually evaluated and corrected by the best-qualified member of the care team. The timing of correction is determined in a triage fashion, with the most serious and life-threatening problems being corrected first. Some malformation corrections may be delayed for several years but require special supportive care in the interim to enhance the ultimate prognosis. An example is the child with bilateral external auditory canal atresia. The planned reconstruction would occur at age 4 to 6 years; however, during infancy and before the time of correction, the child should be fitted with a hearing aid to facilitate speech and language development.

The ultimate prognosis is dependent on the sum of the expected results of treatment for the specific problems. The skills of the individual team members are important. The rehabilitative facilities and expertise available also contribute greatly to the ultimate prognosis. The concern and follow-through of the physician and team members are of crucial importance. In addition, the parents need to be a part of the team. Their attention to prescribed therapies and follow-up will ultimately affect the outcome of even the best care. Finally, the parents and physicians must face problems realistically. A patient with severe mental retardation will obviously have a social and vocational prognosis different from that of a patient with normal mental capabilities. It is important to be realistic in expectations but to always provide the parents with hope for the future.

The parents and other family members should not be forgotten in the care of the malformed child. Parents experience anxiety, apprehension, guilt, discouragement, and anger over the problems of their child. The parents need to be counseled, given support, and helped to understand their role in the care process. Social adjustments are often necessary to reduce the trauma the parents and siblings feel in coping with a malformed child. The psychiatrist, psychologist, and social worker can be beneficial in this regard. Family support groups provide supportive interactions that help families deal with their feelings and needs.

Congenital Syndromes Involving the Mouth and Pharynx

A large number of congenital and hereditary syndromes involve oropharyngeal structures. This section covers some of the more noteworthy syndromes the physician encounters. Many of the associated functional and cosmetic problems are best managed by the otolaryngologist on the craniofacial team (Chap. 4).

Cleft Palate, Micrognathia, and Glossoptosis (Pierre Robin Sequence)

This sequence may occur as an isolated problem or be associated with other congenital syndromes, such as Stickler syndrome (cleft palate, retinal detachment, and hereditary arthro-ophthalmopathy), cerebrocostomandibular syndrome (microcephaly, hypoplastic or absent ribs, and vertebral anomalies), camptomelic syndrome (ocular hypertelorism; flat face; and vertebral, scapular, and extremity anomalies), and persistent left superior vena cava syndrome. The Pierre Robin anomaly usually causes early respiratory embarrassment because the micrognathia and glossoptosis result in a narrowed pharyngeal airway. The anomaly was originally defined by the presence of three factors: palatal cleft, micrognathia (small jaw), and airway obstruction. Although this disorder is often called a syndrome, Gorlin and colleagues[13] use the term anomalad because the three factors do not represent a genetic syndrome but rather constitute a single malformation with its resulting effects. More accurately, this is termed a sequence. The retroposition or underdevelopment of the mandible leads to upward and posterior displacement of the tongue, causing arrest of the developing palatal shelves and eventually leading to cleft palate.[18] The retrognathia also results in tongue encroachment on the airway. Glossoptosis (tongue falling backward in the throat) may occur, although Sher and coworkers[39] have described other patterns of pharyngeal collapse in these patients that are not wholly the result of glossoptosis.

Frequently, the airway problems can be managed by placing the infant in a prone or side position. This throws the tongue forward to improve the airway. Gavage feedings may be required temporarily. Sher[38] suggests the use of a nasal trumpet for up to 6 weeks and reports that many infants may improve their airway sufficiently during this time so that surgical intervention is not needed.

In more severe cases, surgical correction may be required. Because feeding difficulties are most commonly due to the airway obstruction, improvement in the airway usually improves the feeding. Tracheotomy will effectively bypass the airway obstruction. Although many believe that this a drastic measure, it should be considered the most effective. Anterior glossopexy may be accomplished by a suture passed through the anterior arch of the mandible to the base of the tongue, across the base of the tongue, and back to the anterior mandible. The suture is passed through a rubber catheter or button across the base of the tongue and through a second rubber catheter placed anteriorly to prevent suture damage to the soft tissues. This anterior displacement of the tongue may be combined with a floor of mouth release.[1, 4] Other suggested techniques have included the formation of a lingual-labial flap.[19] Although the use of tongue displacement procedures is controversial, the controversy often seems to surround the selection of patients and the careful follow-up required. Sher and colleagues,[39] using nasopharyngoscopy, indicated that pharyngeal collapse patterns showing mainly glossoptosis probably respond to tongue displacement procedures, whereas pharyngeal collapse patterns showing circular airway collapse or velar collapse probably require tracheostomy. Freed and associates[12] presented the cases of four infants with documented apnea who improved after tongue-lip adhesion. Hyomandibulopexy has also been reported as a method of treatment for this apnea.[2, 16] It is not typically described in infants, and it pulls the mandible posteriorly and the larynx anteriorly, making intubation more difficult. Close follow-up is required postoperatively to ensure the apnea has resolved.

For patients with severe airway obstruction or associated neurologic or pulmonary disorders, or if intubation is difficult, we prefer tracheostomy.

The child represented in Figure 56–11, with Treacher Collins syndrome, had marked mandibular hypoplasia. Glossopexy was performed but did not provide an adequate pharyngeal airway, and a tracheostomy was necessary. The tracheostomy remained in place approximately 1 year.

As the child matures, the mandible usually increases its dimensions, unless the child has a syndrome that consists of long-term mandibular hypoplasia. The glossopexy procedure should be reversible so that normal anatomic relationships can be reestablished after growth and development of the mandible.[38] Surgical reversal of the glossopexy procedure or closure of the tracheostomy can usually be performed before the child's first birthday. Some children will require tracheostomy, especially or exclusively when sleeping, until the mandible grows sufficiently or surgical correction is performed to establish more normal mandibular positioning.

Distraction osteogenesis is being used for the care of the child with airway obstruction secondary to mandibular hypoplasia. In this technique, the child undergoes an osteotomy after the placement of distal and proximal pins or screws into the mandible. The mandibular segments are distracted, and the intervening gap is filled with new bone, allowing the elongation of the mandible. Rapid ex-

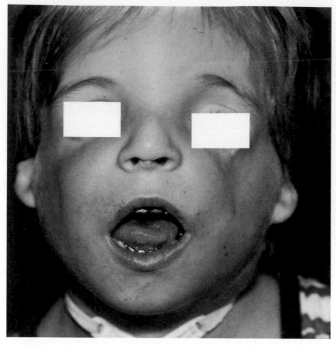

FIGURE 56–11. Child with Treacher Collins syndrome with airway obstruction due to retrognathia. (Courtesy of Dr. Louis Morales, Craniofacial and Plastic Surgery Associates, Primary Children's Medical Center, Salt Lake City, UT.)

pansion and the use of multidimensional devices have made this more effective in the early correction of the mandibular defect and thereby prevented the need for tracheotomy in many infants. Maxillary distraction can also be used in the older child when the bones are sufficient to retain the pins.

Close observation in the neonatal period allows the clinician to make a decision as to the need for surgical intervention for the airway. Social situations that make the care of a child with a tracheotomy more dangerous should be factored into that decision tree.

Craniofacial Dysostosis (Crouzon Disease [10q25.3-q26])

Dysostosis refers to a defect in the normal ossification process of the developing fetus. Craniofacial dysostosis has a pattern of autosomal dominant transmission. The syndrome involves premature craniosynostosis, most commonly involving the coronal, sagittal, and lambdoid sutures. The cranial shape depends on the extent and timing of suture involvement. The midface demonstrates the results of maxillary hypoplasia, with a short upper lip, parrot-beaked nose, relative mandibular prognathism, and hypertelorism (Fig. 56–12).

The maxillary hypoplasia results in obvious intraoral problems manifested mainly in the dental occlusion. Class III malocclusion is most commonly encountered, with crowding of the upper teeth, a high-arched palate, and crossbite.

Oral examination may reveal large lateral palatal swellings, which can give the appearance of a cleft palate. The lateral palatal swellings create a median furrow. Careful

examination reveals an intact palate. The midface hypoplasia may lead to sleep apnea, and tonsillectomy and uvulopalatopharyngoplasty or maxillary advancement may be needed to improve the airway. Patients with midface hypoplasia usually have a shallow anterior skull base. This is important in the treatment of sleep apnea because adenoidectomy or palatopharyngoplasty is less likely to result in velopharyngeal insufficiency. Of course, the presence of a cleft palate or submucous cleft palate affects palatal function. Fortunately, only about 3% of patients with craniofacial dysostosis have cleft palate.[28]

Mental deficiency may occur in some cases. This is possibly related to the increased intracranial pressure that frequently occurs in this syndrome. Conductive deafness has also been reported to occur as a result of associated atresia of the external auditory canal and anomalies of the middle-ear structures.

Mandibulofacial Dysostosis (Treacher Collins Syndrome [5q32-q33.1])

The inheritance pattern of this syndrome is autosomal dominant with variable expressivity. The gene for the syndrome has been located at 5q31-34.[9] Major involvement occurs in the structures that derive from the first and second branchial arches, groove, and pouch. Unlike Crou-

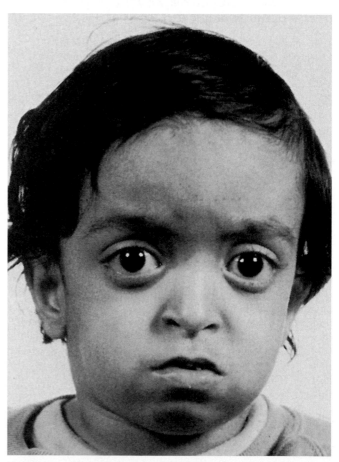

FIGURE 56–12. Child with Crouzon syndrome. (From Kaban LB. Pediatric Oral and Maxillofacial Surgery. Philadelphia, WB Saunders, 1990, p 450.)

zon disease, the cranial bones are essentially normal. The midface is involved with abnormal development of the malar bones, nonfusion of the zygomatic arches, defective orbital margins, and small or absent paranasal sinuses (see Fig. 56–11). The mandibular condyle is hypoplastic.[20] The ear canals and pinnae are usually malformed, with severe auricular deformities and, frequently, absence of the external auditory canals, with or without ossicular defects resulting in conductive deafness.[21]

The combination of these anomalies results in a characteristic facial appearance with depressed cheekbones, deformed pinnae, downward-sloping palpebral fissures, large fishlike mouth, and receding chin. Dental malocclusion is common, and there is a high frequency of associated high-arched palate or cleft palate. Mental retardation is reportedly present in less than 10% of patients.

Mandibular hypoplasia with relative glossoptosis can result in early pharyngeal respiratory embarrassment in these patients. Many have an associated Robin sequence. Oral examination reveals a cleft palate in about 35% of patients. Congenital palatal incompetence due to poorly mobile soft palate, submucous cleft palate, or short soft palate has been found in as many as 30% to 40% of additional patients.[37] Rarely, cleft lip is present. Macrostomia is present in about 15% of patients, and parotid glands have been reported to be absent or hypoplastic.[32]

Preaxial acrofacial dysostosis, more commonly referred to as *Nager syndrome,* has features similar to many of those found in mandibulofacial dysostosis. With both conditions, patients may be brought to the pediatric otolaryngologist for emergency airway control shortly after birth. Both may have a Robin sequence, and intubation may be extremely difficult. Patients with Nager syndrome have more marked micrognathia and may have complete mandibular ankylosis so that the mouth will not open. Laryngeal hypoplasia has been described.[27]

Acrocephalosyndactyly (Apert Syndrome [10q25.3-q26])

It has been suggested that this syndrome is caused by a defect in the tissues important in bone development before the fifth to sixth week of embryonic life.[35] Most cases have occurred sporadically and appear to be associated with increased parental age at the time of conception. Some hereditary patterns suggest autosomal dominant transmission.

Early fusion of the coronal area and a wide midline calvarial defect result in the characteristic brachycephalic or oxycephalic appearance. The maxilla is hypoplastic; hypertelorism and proptosis are usually present. The underdevelopment of the maxilla results in a relative prognathism of the mandible. The nose is small and underdeveloped. Frequently, there is a high-arched palate; this is constricted and may have a marked median furrow and lateral palatal swellings. A soft palate cleft is encountered in 25% to 30% of patients. Again, severe occlusion problems are encountered, with dental crowding and class III malocclusion. Retarded dental eruption is also a common finding.

Mental retardation may be encountered, although it usually is not as severe as that seen in Down syndrome. The associated deformities of the extremities include syndactyly of digits 2, 3, and 4. Digits 1 and 5 are occasionally involved. The upper extremities are short. Joint involvement may be seen at the elbow, shoulder, and hip.

Oculoauriculovertebral Dysplasia (Goldenhar Syndrome)

This syndrome involves the structures formed from the first and second branchial arches in conjunction with vertebral abnormalities. The majority of the cases occur sporadically; however, familial occurrence has been reported with different modes of inheritance. In addition to auricular deformity with agenesis of the external auditory canals, severe oral deformities are seen. The condition is often asymmetric, with one side of the face more severely involved than the other. The degree of the mandibular involvement is highly variable, ranging from minimal condylar abnormality to aplasia of the mandibular ramus. There may be associated macrostomia, agenesis of the ipsilateral parotid gland, salivary gland fistulas, lingual hypoplasia, and cleft lip or palate.

There usually are eye findings in these children; epibulbar dermoid is most often noted.

Beckwith-Wiedemann Syndrome (11p15.5)

Beckwith-Wiedemann syndrome is characterized by macroglossia, omphalocele, visceromegaly, and cytomegaly of the adrenal cortex (Fig. 56–13). Gorlin and colleagues[14] list it as an overgrowth syndrome with sporadic occurrence. The infant mortality rate is around 21% and is related to congestive heart failure or birth malformations. The associated growth rate is excessive, and most patients are above the 90% growth curve for age. These patients are of interest to the otolaryngologist because of the macroglossia. This may cause airway obstruction or chronic alveolar hypoventilation. Interestingly, in many patients, the macroglossia may regress. If airway management is needed, a tracheostomy is preferred over any tongue surgery during the early years of life.

Down Syndrome (Trisomy 21, Mongolism)

There are many different syndromes with basic chromosomal abnormalities and resultant orofacial manifestations. Down syndrome is the most common example of this group of abnormalities and reportedly accounts for approximately 15% of all patients institutionalized for mental deficiency. The frequency of Down syndrome is reportedly 1 : 600 to 700 births.

These children commonly have associated cardiorespiratory, gastrointestinal, musculoskeletal, and cutaneous abnormalities. A complete discussion of the associated anomalies is beyond the scope of this book; only the oral manifestations of this disease are emphasized.[6]

The lips are normal in size at birth; however, progressive enlargement of the lips is the usual clinical course. The tongue is enlarged; this enlargement may be a true macroglossia or a relative macroglossia due to a small oral

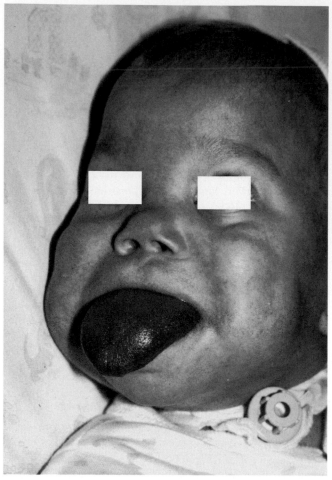

FIGURE 56-13. Macroglossia due to Beckwith-Wiedemann syndrome. (Courtesy of Dr. Louis Morales, Craniofacial and Plastic Surgery Associates, Primary Children's Medical Center, Salt Lake City, UT.)

cavity. Most patients with Down syndrome have fissuring of the tongue by the age of 5 years. The palate is high and tends to be narrow. Occasionally, bifid uvula and cleft lip and palate occur. The nasopharynx is narrow at least in part due to platybasia. Tongue resections may be successful in reducing tongue size and thereby improving oral hygiene, but convincing data that demonstrate improved speech after tongue reduction are lacking.[26, 36] Speech is affected by many factors in these patients and is not corrected by tongue reduction.

Chronic purulent rhinorrhea is often observed in the patient with Down syndrome. Chronic mouth breathing is also frequent. The adenoid tissue mass is often small to normal sized, and adenoidectomy in these children has been shown to have little effect on rhinorrhea and nasal breathing. Adenoidectomy has also had little effect on the course of ear pathologic changes in these children. Obstructive adenoid or tonsil hypertrophy or both can occur, and then excision is beneficial.[42]

Pharyngeal hypotonia as part of more generalized hypotonia is a feature of Down syndrome. The small oropharynx and hypotonia contribute to the risk and occur-

rence of sleep apnea in this syndrome. Congenital subglottic stenosis may also occur.[34]

There is lower-than-average frequency of dental caries in affected children; however, there is a high frequency of periodontal disease, a situation probably related to the poor oral hygiene frequently encountered in these patients. Retarded dental eruption is observed in both deciduous and permanent dentition, and missing teeth and small teeth are common in Down syndrome patients. In addition, their lingual papillae are often hypertrophied.

The middle third of the face is often hypoplastic, producing a relative mandibular prognathism and flattened facial appearance. The characteristic appearance includes brachycephaly, short neck, slanted and wide-set eyes, short nose, and abnormal earlobes. Mental retardation, which may be severe, is common.

Arachnodactyly (Marfan Syndrome [15q21.1])

Photographs and medical records of Abraham Lincoln suggest that he might have had Marfan syndrome. This major problem appears to be a defect in protein synthesis at the cellular level, especially involving collagen and elastin. The disorder is transmitted as an autosomal dominant trait with high penetrance and variable expressivity. The typical adult appearance is that of a tall, thin person with scoliosis, pectus excavatum, long fingers and toes, and subluxation of the ocular lenses. Sudden death may occur as a result of inherent dissecting aneurysm due to defects of the wall of the aorta.

Oral manifestations include a high palatal vault, occasionally a cleft palate or bifid uvula, dental malocclusion, and long, narrow teeth. Mandibular prognathism is also frequently associated with this syndrome.

Osteogenesis Imperfecta (Ekman Syndrome [7q22.1 and 17q21.31-q22.05])

This condition was described early as *brittle bone disease.* The most common form of the disorder is the "tarda" form, which is inherited as an autosomal dominant trait with a wide range of expressivity and incomplete penetrance. The basic defect appears to be a failure of collagen maturation.

The maxillofacial manifestations of this disease have been described[3] and include condylar deformity, prognathic mandible, frequent mandibular dislocation, hypoplastic hemimandible, depressed zygoma, and dentinogenesis imperfecta. Bergstrom[3] also pointed out that the facial bones are apparently more resistant to fractures than are the long bones, which can be attributed to the greater amount of elastic fiber content in facial bones. From 50% to 60% of patients with the tarda form of this syndrome have otosclerosis with stapedial fixation and resultant conductive hearing loss. Sensorineural hearing loss has also been reported in this disorder.

Hemifacial Atrophy (Romberg Syndrome)

This condition has also been known as *progressive facial hemiatrophy.* Involvement is usually restricted to the facial structures, although the entire half of the body may be involved in a small percentage of patients. Most cases occur sporadically; again, there are various theories regarding etiology, with trauma apparently playing a role in some patients. There may be some relationship between this disorder and scleroderma.

The condition is often not obvious at birth, but with the growth and development of the child, it becomes apparent during the first decade of life. The development of the hemiface is retarded, and the atrophy occurs in the cartilaginous and musculoskeletal structure of the face; facial distortion, unilateral enophthalmos, and maxillary and mandibular abnormalities with dental problems result. Hemiatrophy of the tongue also occurs.

Congenital Facial Diplegia (Möbius Syndrome [3q21-q22])

This condition consists of congenital bilateral cranial nerve palsies. The sixth and seventh cranial nerves are most commonly involved; however, nearly every cranial nerve can be affected. Facial nerve involvement may be asymmetric, and the lower divisions may be spared. The mouth is small. The tongue may demonstrate atrophy, fasciculation, or paralysis. Difficulty with feeding and speech are frequently important clinical aspects of this syndrome. Limb anomalies, chest wall defects, and mental retardation may be associated. Occurrence has been sporadic.

Mucopolysaccharidosis IH (Hurler Syndrome or Gargoylism [4p16.3])

Multiple inherited disorders of mucopolysaccharide metabolism have been reported. Hurler syndrome is a severe form of mucopolysaccharide abnormality and was one of the first to be described. The syndrome is inherited as an autosomal recessive trait.

The characteristic facial appearance begins to develop in the first 3 to 6 months of life and is usually apparent by the age of 3 years. The large head exhibits a flattened and small nose, prominent forehead, thick lips, and thick earlobes. The mouth is usually held open, with the tongue protruding. Lip and tongue enlargement is progressive. The mandible is short and broad. Motion at the temporomandibular joint may be limited because of condylar abnormality. Apnea may occur because of thickened pharyngeal tissues.

Cleidocranial Dysostosis (Cleidocranial Dysplasia [6p12])

This syndrome consists of clavicular aplasia or hypoplasia, delayed ossification of the fontanelles, and exaggerated development of the cranium. Autosomal dominance is the type of transmission. The palate is highly arched and may have a submucous cleft or even a complete cleft. Nonunion of the mandibular symphysis has been reported.

The apparent lack of teeth in patients with this syndrome has been shown to be due to delay in or failure of eruption of both the deciduous and permanent teeth, as shown on maxillary and mandibular radiographs. Premaxillary development has also been noted to be poor.

Cutaneous and Mucosal Pigmentation Associated With Gastrointestinal Polyposis (Peutz-Jeghers Syndrome)

This syndrome is representative of a group of syndromes with associated mucosal and cutaneous lesions. Its inheritance is autosomal dominant. The gastrointestinal polyposis component of the syndrome causes most clinical problems. Approximately 50% of these patients have brown to bluish black maculae present on the skin, particularly periorally, perinasally, or periorbitally. The oral mucosa may demonstrate similar maculae, which are usually 1 to 12 mm in size but may be confluent. Their pigmentation is similar to the pigmentation of the cutaneous lesions. The tongue and floor of the mouth are rarely involved. There is no correlation between the degree of mucocutaneous pigmentation and the severity of the gastrointestinal polyposis.

Van der Woude Syndrome (1q32-q41)

Van der Woude syndrome is an autosomal recessive condition and consists of combinations of cleft lip, cleft palate, and lip pits. Lip pits are caused by abnormal salivary glands. Although Van der Woude syndrome accounts for less than 1% of all cleft lips and palates, it is important because it represents a genetic condition in which cleft lips and palates are mixed with cleft palates. The lip pits occur on the lower lip and may be excised if they are symptomatic or present a cosmetic problem.

SELECTED REFERENCES

Bardach J, Salyer K. Surgical Techniques in Cleft Lip and Palate. Chicago, Year Book, 1987.
> A good description of cleft lip and palate surgery with the exception of the Furlow palatoplasty.

Cleft Palate Craniofac J 29, 1992.
> This volume is dedicated to Pierre Robin sequence. It provides a useful interdisciplinary approach to this condition.

Furlow LT Jr. Cleft palate repair by double opposing Z-plasty. Plastic Reconstr Surg 12:724, 1986.
> The original description of the double-opposing Z plasty.

Gorlin RJ, Cohen MM Jr, Levin LS. Syndromes of the Head and Neck, 3rd ed. New York, Oxford University Press, 1990.
> This comprehensive textbook describes syndromes of the head and neck.

Tewfik TL, Kaloustain VM. Congenital Anomalies of the Ear, Nose, and Throat. New York, Oxford University Press, 1997.
> Excellent comprehensive review of the congenital deformities of the head and neck, providing recent molecular and genetic information on different syndromes.

REFERENCES

1. Argamaso RV. Glossopexy for upper airway obstruction in Robin sequence. Cleft Palate J 29:232, 1992.

2. Bergoin M, Giraud JP, Chaix C. L'hyomandibulopexie dans le traitement des formes graves du syndrome de Pierre Robin. Ann Chir Infant (Paris) 12:85, 1971.
3. Bergstrom L. Osteogenesis imperfecta: otologic and maxillofacial aspects. Laryngoscope 87 (Suppl):6, 1977.
4. Caouette-Laberge L, Bayet B, Larocque Y. The Pierre Robin sequence: review of 125 cases and evolution of treatment modalities. Plast Reconstr Surg 93:934, 1994.
5. Catlin FI, DeHann V. Tongue-tie. Arch Otolaryngol 94:548, 1971.
6. Cohen MM Sr, Cohen MM Jr. The oral manifestations of trisomy G1 (Down syndrome). Birth Defects 7:241, 1971.
7. Croft CD, Shprintzen RJ, Daniller A, Lewin ML. The occult submucous cleft and the musculus uvulae. Cleft Palate J 15:150, 1978.
8. Cronin TD. Push back palatorrhaphy with nasal mucosal flaps. In Grabb WC, Rosenstein SW, Bzoch KR (eds). Cleft Lip and Palate: Surgical, Dental, and Speech Aspects. Boston, Little, Brown, 1971.
9. Dixon MJ, Read AP, Donnai P, Colley A. The gene for the Treacher Collins syndrome maps to the long arm of chromosome 5. Am J Hum Genet 49:17, 1991.
10. Fitz CR, Noyek AM. Contemporary radiology in congenital craniofacial disorders. Otolaryngol Clin North Am 14:65, 1981.
11. Fletcher SG, Daly DA. Sublingual dimensions in infants and young children. Arch Otolaryngol 99:292, 1974.
12. Freed G, Pearlman MA, Brown AS, Barot LR. Polysomnographic indications for surgical intervention in Pierre Robin sequence: acute airway management and follow-up studies after repair and takedown of tongue-lip adhesion. Cleft Palate J 25:151, 1988.
13. Gorlin RJ, Cohen MM Jr, Levin LS. Orofacial clefting syndromes: general aspects. In Syndromes of the Head and Neck, 3rd ed. New York, Oxford University Press, 1990, p. 714.
14. Gorlin RJ, Cohen MM Jr, Levin LS. Overgrowth syndromes and postnatal onset obesity syndromes. In Syndromes of the Head and Neck, 3rd ed. New York, Oxford University Press, 1990, pp 323–352.
15. Gorlin RJ, Cohen MM Jr, Levin LS (eds). Syndromes of the Head and Neck, 3rd ed. New York, Oxford University Press, 1990.
16. Guinard F, Morgon A, Deplagne H, et al. La necessité de la libération de la hyomandibulopexie dans le syndrome de Pierre Robin. Rev Laryngol Otol Rhinol (Bord) 106:385, 1985.
17. Hanson JW, Smith DW. The fetal hydantoin syndrome. J Pediatr 87:285, 1975.
18. Hanson J, Smith DW. U-shaped palatal defect in the Robin anomaly: development and clinical relevance. J Pediatr 87:30, 1975.
19. Hawkins DB, Simpson JV. Micrognathia and glossoptosis in the newborn. Clin Pediatr 13:1066, 1974.
20. Herring SW, Rowlatt UF, Pruzansky S. Anatomical abnormalities in mandibulofacial dysostosis. Am J Med Genet 3:225, 1979.
21. Hutchinson JC Jr, Caldarelli DD, Valvassori GE, et al. The otologic manifestations of mandibulofacial dysostosis. Trans Am Acad Ophthalmol 84:520, 1977.
22. Jones KL, Smith DW, Hall DB, et al. A pattern of craniofacial and limb defects secondary to aberrant tissue bands. J Pediatr 84:90, 1974.
23. Kaplan EN. Soft palate repair by levator muscle reconstruction and a buccal mucosal flap. Plast Reconstr Surg 56:129, 1975.
24. Khoury MJ, Gomez-Farias M, Mulinare J, Boring J. Does maternal cigarette smoking during pregnancy cause cleft lip palate in offspring? Presented at the Society of Epidemiology Research Annual Meeting, Vancouver, 1988 (abstract).
25. Kirschner RE, Wang P, Jawad AF, et al. Cleft palate repair by modified Furlow double-opposing Z-plasty: the Children's Hospital of Philadelphia experience. Plast Reconstr Surg 104:1998, 1999.
26. Klaiman P, Witzel MA, Margar-Bacal F, Munro I. Changes in aesthetic appearance and intelligibility of speech after partial glossectomy in patients with Down syndrome. Plast Reconstr Surg 82:403, 1988.
27. Krauss CM, Hassell LA, Gang DL, et al. Anomalies in an infant with Nager acrofacial dysostosis. Am J Med Genet 21:761, 1985.
28. Kreiborg S. Crouzon syndrome. Scand J Plast Reconstr Surg Suppl 18:1, 1981.
29. Latham RA, Long RE, Latham EA. Cleft palate velopharyngeal musculature in a five-month old infant: a three-dimensional histological reconstruction. Cleft Palate J 17:1, 1980.
30. Lemperle G. Down syndrome. In McCarthy JG (ed). Plastic Surgery. Philadelphia, WB Saunders, 1990, pp 3161–3174.
31. Loffredo LCM, Souza JMP, Freitas JAS, et al. Oral clefts and vitamin supplementation. Cleft Palate Craniofac J 38:76–83, 2001.
32. Markitziu A, Sela M, Seltzer R. Major salivary glands in branchial arch syndromes. Oral Surg Oral Med Oral Pathol 58:672, 1984.
33. Millard DR Jr. A new use of the island flap in wide palate clefts. Plast Reconstr Surg 56:129, 1986.
34. Miller R, Gray SD, Cotton RT, et al. Subglottic stenosis and Down syndrome. Am J Otolaryngol 11:274, 1990.
35. Park EA, Powers GF. Acrocephaly and scaphocephaly with symmetrically distributed malformations of the extremities. Am J Dis Child 20:235, 1920.
36. Parsons CL, Iacono TA, Rosner L. Effects of tongue reduction on articulation in children with Down syndrome. Am J Ment Defic 91:328, 1987.
37. Peterson-Falzone S, Pruzansky S. Cleft palate and congenital palatopharyngeal incompetency in mandibulofacial dysostosis: frequency and problems in treatment. Cleft Palate J 13:354, 1976.
38. Sher AE. Mechanisms of airway obstruction in Robin sequence: implications for treatment. Cleft Palate J 29:224, 1992.
39. Sher AE, Shprintzen RJ, Thorpy MJ. Endoscopic observations of obstructive sleep apnea in children with anomalous upper airways: predictive and therapeutic value. Int J Pediatr Otorhinolaryngol 11:135, 1986.
40. Stark DB. Nasal lining in partial cleft palate repair. Plast Reconstr Surg 32:75, 1963.
41. Stool S, Post JC. Craniofacial growth, development, and malformations. In Bluestone C, Stool S, Kenna M (eds). Pediatric Otolaryngology, 3rd ed. Philadelphia, WB Saunders, 1996.
42. Strome M. Down's syndrome: a modern otorhinolaryngology perspective. Laryngoscope 91:1581, 1981.
43. Wertz ML. Management of undescended lingual and subhyoid thyroid glands. Laryngoscope 84:507, 1974.

57

Primary Care of Infants and Children with Cleft Palate

Jack L. Paradise, M.D.

From birth onward, the child with a cleft palate faces a diversity of medical and medically related problems and presents substantial challenges to the physician and other health professionals involved in the child's care.[60] Initially, it is the child's parents who, on learning of the deformity, require understanding and support as they experience reactions that may range from dismay to grief, guilt, or resentment. Their questions about prognosis must be answered in detail, even though the prognosis may be in some respects uncertain.

Feeding difficulties of some degree are experienced by almost all infants with cleft palate. Those with associated mandibular hypoplasia and glossoptosis (Pierre Robin sequence) may have, in addition, episodic or chronic upper airway obstruction, which, in extreme instances, may be life-threatening or actually lethal. In virtually all patients with cleft palate, otitis media with effusion accompanied by some degree of hearing impairment persists, unless treated surgically, throughout infancy and often beyond, and there is risk that chronic middle-ear infection, permanent impairment of hearing, or both will develop. For all patients, periods of hospitalization associated with one or more reconstructive surgical procedures are inevitable. Various instructions received from professionals of various disciplines in the course of frequent visits to hospitals and clinics must be coordinated and incorporated into family scheduling. Finally, some patients experience continuing difficulties of differing degrees involving oral hygiene, dentition, and dental occlusion (see Chaps. 58 and 59); cosmesis; speech (see Chaps. 105 and 106); language; cognition; or social adjustment and emotional status. The assiduousness and skill with which all these medical, surgical, and rehabilitative problems are managed during infancy and childhood can be important determinants of adult attainment and adjustment; sophisticated management can usually be expected to result in gratifyingly good overall outcomes, whereas neglect or inept management may have the opposite effect.

This chapter focuses on three areas of particular importance to physicians responsible for the primary or general care—as distinct from reconstructive surgical care—of infants and young children with cleft palate: (1) feeding and nutrition, (2) glossoptotic airway obstruction in the Pierre Robin sequence, and (3) otologic and audiologic problems.

Feeding and Nutrition

Nature and Extent of the Problem

Feeding difficulty is encountered to some degree by most infants with cleft palate, especially during the first few weeks of life, and usually over the first few months. Sucking efficiency, which depends to a considerable extent on the generation of negative intraoral pressure, is impaired as a consequence of the relative inability of the deficient palate to seal off the nasal cavity and nasopharynx from the oral cavity and oropharynx. As a result, breast feeding is rendered particularly problematic, and usually impossible without resorting to the introduction of a prosthetic feeding appliance (see later discussion). Nasal regurgitation episodes, resulting from aspiration of milk into the respiratory tract, and choking further disrupt the feeding process. As a result of all these problems, individual feedings often are laborious and time consuming, and ingested volume often is inadequate. Both the parent and the infant are deprived of the usual physical and emotional gratification of the feeding process; the parent may be frustrated, disappointed, and anxious, and the infant may be hungry and inadequately nourished.[18, 91, 99] Most infants, unless specific intervention (described later) is undertaken, fail to gain weight adequately.[65] The elements of the feeding problem and their interrelationships in infants with cleft palate are shown schematically in Figure 57–1.

Management

Because an inability to generate effective oral suction is the major cause of the difficulty in feeding, compensation should be attempted through the use of one of various feeding devices that permit the direct expression of milk into the infant's mouth. Ideally, infants should receive breast milk for as much of the first year as possible, both on general principles and, as discussed later, in the hope specifically of minimizing the development of otitis me-

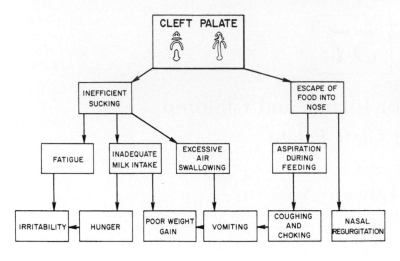

FIGURE 57–1. Elements of the feeding problem and their interrelationships in infants with cleft palate. (From Paradise JL, McWilliams BJ. Simplified feeder for infants with cleft palate. Pediatrics 53:566, 1974. Reproduced by permission of Pediatrics, copyright 1974.)

dia. Mothers willing to breast feed their infants but who—as is usually the case—are unable to do so satisfactorily, should be encouraged to pump their breasts, harvest their milk, and feed the milk to the baby using one of these feeding devices. Currently, the most satisfactory of these devices is the Mead Johnson Cleft Palate Nurser (Mead Johnson Nutritionals, Evansville, Ind), which consists of a soft, readily compressible plastic bottle and a soft rubber, cross-cut nipple (Fig. 57–2). (These nursers can be ordered by telephone by parents (1-800-BABY123) or by hospitals (1-800-457-3550). Also satisfactory, however, is a simple, compressible feeder consisting of a rigid plastic shell (several types are available commercially) into which is placed a disposable plastic bag (available commercially in convenient, rolls) to serve as a container for milk, and onto which a conventional nipple-carrying cap is screwed (Fig. 57–3). With a pocket knife or similar tool, slots wide enough to permit inserting a finger are cut into opposite sides of the shell. Through the slot, gentle pressure can then easily be applied to the bag of milk throughout the feeding process (Fig. 57–4).

With all feeders, soft rubber ("preemie") nipples with cross cuts are usually preferable to standard nipples with either standard or enlarged holes; however, cross-cut nipples generally require the limbs of the "X" to be lengthened slightly with a razor blade before the initial use to achieve effective flap valve function.

Using this type of compressible feeder, adequate amounts of milk can be fed to most infants with cleft palate in 15 to 20 minutes. In the author's experience, adoption of a compressible feeder for infants previously using standard bottles not only has greatly facilitated the feeding process but also has generally resulted in prompt upturns of weight toward normal. One clinical trial in which most infants also received palatal prostheses, as described later, showed no advantage in growth using a compressible feeder compared with a standard feeder,[10]

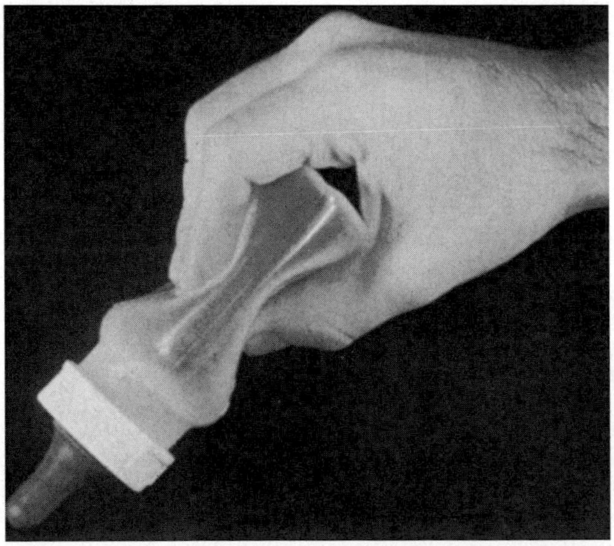

FIGURE 57–2. Mead Johnson cleft palate nurser, showing the compressible plastic bottle.

FIGURE 57–3. Plastic nursing shells that permit feeding from compressible, disposable bags. (From Paradise JL, McWilliams BJ. Simplified feeder for infants with cleft palate. Pediatrics 53: 566, 1974. Reproduced by permission of Pediatrics, copyright 1974.)

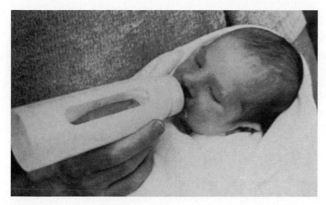

FIGURE 57–4. Mother feeding an infant with cleft palate, using a compressible feeder. (From Paradise JL, McWilliams BJ. Simplified feeder for infants with cleft palate. Pediatrics 53:566, 1974. Reproduced by permission of Pediatrics, copyright 1974.)

but in a more recent trial in which prostheses were not used, use of the compressible feeder resulted in superior weight gain.[78]

The compressible feeding device described here does nothing to prevent either aspiration or nasal regurgitation of milk. These problems usually can be avoided or minimized by keeping the infant in an upright position during feedings, avoiding excessive pressure on the compressible bag, and being alert to early signs of distress in the infant.

Some authors have advocated the use of prosthetic feeding appliances that obturate the palatal cleft.[11, 15, 38, 41, 91, 97, 99] Supporting data, however, have not been reported. Prosthodontic skill is required to fashion these appliances so that they fit and function properly. In this author's experience, when fitted early, prostheses have, in some instances, seemed effective but in other instances have been unacceptable to the infant and therefore not successful. The palatal prosthesis seems especially attractive as a potential facilitator of breast feeding, since, as noted previously, unaided breast feeding of infants with cleft palate generally proves unsuccessful.

"Ducky," lamb's, or other special nipples are also sometimes advised, but parents usually find them no more effective than standard nipples or actually disadvantageous.

Pierre Robin Sequence

The Pierre Robin sequence consists of (1) mandibular hypoplasia (commonly but less properly termed micrognathia), (2) glossoptosis and, virtually always, (3) a midline posterior cleft of the palate. Although the cause of the sequence is obscure, all of its elements probably result pathogenetically from a primary deficiency of mandibular development early in fetal life. The underdeveloped mandible holds the tongue posteriorly, such that it interferes with closure of the palatal shelves.[84] Usually, the Pierre Robin sequence occurs as an isolated triad of abnormalities, but occasionally it constitutes part of more complex clinical entities, such as the trisomy 18 and Stickler syndromes. Early recognition of the Stickler syn-

drome is important, so that the often associated high myopia can be managed with appropriate optical correction and so that retinal detachment, if it occurs, can be detected and treated promptly.[98] Because the diagnosis of the Stickler syndrome is not always evident, infants with the Pierre Robin sequence should routinely undergo early ophthalmologic evaluation. As with other craniofacial abnormalities, routine audiologic evaluation should also be carried out (see Chap. 16).

Airway Obstruction

Infants with mild forms of the Pierre Robin sequence present no airway-related problems. However, those with more severe forms encounter more difficulty and are at greater risk during the first few months of life than are infants with much more extensive palatal clefts but without the Pierre Robin sequence. Because of the small mandible in the Pierre Robin sequence, the tongue lies in an abnormally posterior position. It thereby becomes unusually susceptible to the negative-pressure forces of both deglutition and inspiration and tends to become easily aspirated and held in the hypopharynx in ball valve fashion, effectively obstructing the upper airway.[16, 23, 40] Evidence of airway obstruction usually becomes apparent immediately after birth but may first appear days or weeks later.[53] Infants so affected may die suddenly of asphyxia or, more commonly, have chronic partial obstruction with, in some cases, cor pulmonale,[14, 28, 36, 40] which may eventuate in congestive heart failure (see Chaps. 62 and 81).[40, 77]

Feeding and Nutritional Problems

In severely affected infants with the Pierre Robin sequence, the feeding and nutritional problems expected in any case as a consequence of the palatal cleft are compounded by the glossoptotic airway obstruction. Choking episodes during feeding, with aspiration of milk, may, in turn, further jeopardize respiration. Faced with increased energy needs imposed by the work of labored breathing, infants frequently fail to gain weight, or may lose weight and become progressively enfeebled.

Conservative Management

Because even severe airway obstruction in the Pierre Robin sequence almost always resolves spontaneously or at least improves markedly by 4 to 6 months of age, the cornerstone—indeed the sine qua non—of management for infants with obstruction of any appreciable degree is to assiduously maintain them in the prone position during the first few months in an effort to "buy time." The prone position exploits the influence of gravity on the tongue, so that it tends to fall forward out of the airway, thus becoming less susceptible to being aspirated. If the infant's condition permits, the supine position may be attempted for short periods to facilitate diapering, dressing, bathing, and the like, but in the most severe cases, all these functions are best carried out with the infant prone. Feeding can, in some cases, be satisfactorily accomplished using a compressible feeder as described earlier, but more often attempts at oral feeding are more or less unsuccessful and result in increased respiratory distress. Under such circumstances, gavage feeding via nasogastric or orogastric tube, with the infant kept prone, must be resorted to. Because most young infants are obligate nasal breathers, a nasogastric tube should be removed between feedings so as not to further compromise the already compromised airway. To institute and satisfactorily maintain this regimen, relatively long periods of hospitalization are sometimes necessary, but once the regimen has been successfully instituted, parents can usually be taught quickly to continue it at home.

Surgical Intervention

When, despite maintenance of the infant in the prone position, unacceptable respiratory distress persists, tracheostomy usually must be performed.[69, 70] Alternative measures, such as nasogastric, nasoesophageal, or nasopharyngeal intubation[20, 30, 86] or glossopexy (lip-tongue adhesion),[52] in the author's experience, have generally proved ineffective in severe cases, prompting speculation that the reported success of these measures had been achieved in infants who, in fact, had not been so severely affected and who might have fared equally well with a scrupulously executed conservative regimen. Greater success with the use of a nasopharyngeal tube may be possible in some cases when careful attention is accorded the length of the tube,[30] or when, in addition, the tube is modified so as to eliminate the connector and better anchor the tube in place.[12, 42] However, in the author's opinion, the risk of displacement or obstruction of a nasopharyngeal tube militates against its use in place of tracheostomy, except under intensive care conditions for short periods of time. The various complications of glossopexy[3] argue against its use as well. Beginning in the mid-1990s, mandibular distraction osteogenesis using either extraoral or intraoral devices has been used successfully to lengthen the mandible and thereby draw the tongue forward and relieve upper airway obstruction.[34, 51] However, because of potential complications (e.g., facial scarring, effects on dentition, and, in the case of the intraoral appliance, increased feeding difficulty),[34, 51] the role of mandibular distraction in the treatment armamentarium remains to be clarified.

Mechanism of Spontaneous Resolution of Airway Obstruction

Resolution of airway obstruction in infants with Pierre Robin sequence who survive the first few months of life has generally been attributed to gradual forward movement of the base of the tongue, assumedly due to progressive mandibular growth.[70] More likely, however, the underlying event responsible is the infant's acquisition, as a normal developmental phenomenon, of progressively increasing control of tongue musculature.[40]

Otologic and Audiologic Problems

More than a century ago (in 1893), Gutzmann[29] first reported that hearing impairment was a significant problem in about half the cleft palate population, and the proportion appears to have remained relatively constant since then.[6] If patients with relatively minor hearing losses were to be added to the count, the proportion would probably be considerably higher than 50%.[54, 93] Matching these observations regarding hearing, significant abnormalities of the tympanic membrane have been reported to occur in approximately three fourths of older children and adults with cleft palate.[2, 83] Those abnormalities have consisted mainly of scarring, distortion of normal architecture, adhesions, perforation, and cholesteatoma. Moreover, otologic difficulties in cleft palate patients appear not to be limited to the middle ear; sensorineural losses can also be found (see Chap. 26).[4]

Universality of Otitis Media in Affected Infants

In 1966, it was first observed that otitis media with middle-ear effusion is present in virtually all infants younger than 2 years of age with unrepaired clefts of the palate,[62, 88] an observation that has been repeatedly confirmed in studies in various parts of the world.* Presumably sterile, inflammatory effusions of varied viscosity are found in most infants,[39] but frank suppuration also occurs frequently. In some cases, granulation tissue fills the middle-ear cavity partially or completely,[18, 88] whereas in other cases, histologic evidence of inflammation of the middle-ear mucosa may be present before frank effusion develops.[49] Such circumstances may account for the occasional failure to find effusion at myringotomy in ears that otoscopically had been considered grossly abnormal. Following surgical repair of the palate, difficulties with otitis media often are reduced,[17, 61, 67, 75, 85, 92] but for most patients, middle-ear disease remains an important problem well into later life.

The occurrence of otitis media in association with submucous cleft palate appears not to have been studied systematically. In series of selected patients with submucous cleft palate, bifid uvula, or both, the proportions of patients with histories or findings of middle-ear disease have ranged from 34% to 80%.[76, 81, 87, 89, 90] Clearly, patients with submucous clefts deserve close, continuing observation for the development of persistent otitis media.

Pathogenesis of Otitis Media in Patients with Cleft Palate

Investigators interested in the pathogenesis of otitis media in patients with cleft palate have consistently focused on the eustachian tube. The hypothesis that middle-ear inflammation develops and persists because the tube, although patent anatomically, is unable to open properly

---

*See references 1, 5, 13, 17, 19, 25, 27, 37, 48, 57, 61, 67, 71, 85, 89, 92, 95, 96.

and ventilate the middle ear, has found support in investigations since the 1960s involving anatomic studies,[31–33, 43, 44, 46, 74, 79, 80, 82] histochemical studies,[45] impedance measurements,[68] roentgenographic[6, 8] and air pressure[7] studies, and endoscopic observations.[22] This presumed impairment of the opening mechanism of the eustachian tube may be a consequence of greater than normal compliance of the tubal wall. Another possible factor in the pathogenesis of otitis media in patients with cleft palate is defective velopharyngeal valving, which may result in disturbed aerodynamic and hydrodynamic relationships in the nasopharynx and proximal portions of the eustachian tubes. That actual middle-ear infection and related immunologic factors may also play a role in pathogenesis is suggested by the observation, in a prospective study of infants with cleft palate, that some who had received breast milk in differing quantities were free from middle-ear effusion from time to time, whereas freedom from effusion was only rarely found among exclusively formula-fed infants.[63]

Implications of Middle-Ear Disease

It seems reasonable to infer that some of the structural middle-ear damage—e.g., tympanic membrane retraction pockets and cholesteatoma—and associated conductive hearing losses noted in older cleft palate patients might be the end result of chronic middle-ear inflammation in earlier life. That the sensorineural losses also found in some cleft palate patients[4, 94] might similarly have originated from early-life, chronic otitis media is suggested by the observation that inflammation in the middle ear may lead to pathologic changes in the inner ear.[55]

Furthermore, in light of evidence that the persistent effusions of infants with cleft palate are usually accompanied by conductive hearing losses of variable degree,[21] it can be assumed that many infants with cleft palate experience persistent hearing impairment of some degree throughout infancy.

Finally, certain evidence suggests the possibility that mild, sustained hearing loss or fluctuating hearing loss during infancy and early childhood may adversely affect the development of speech, language, and cognitive function. Although this evidence is far from conclusive,[59, 66] it seems reasonable to speculate that the restrictions of language skill and the various psychological problems often found in older children with cleft palate[47] might be at least in part traceable to hearing loss accompanying longstanding otitis media during their infancy and early childhood. Other reports suggest that such hearing loss in children with cleft palate, when limited to the first few years of life, may not result in impaired language or psychological development but may contribute to impaired speech, especially the articulation of consonants.[35]

Management of Otitis Media in Infants with Cleft Palate

In infants with cleft palate, rational management of presumably nonsuppurative middle-ear effusion—as distinct from episodes of infection—is limited to one of two opposite approaches: (1) watchful waiting, having advised parents to take into account, in all aspects of child care, that the effusion may interfere with hearing, or (2) early myringotomy, aspiration of the effusion, and insertion of tympanostomy tubes, followed by repeat tube insertion as needed to maintain middle-ear ventilation. The latter approach has been advocated widely[24, 50, 56, 58, 61] because it offers maintenance, for the most part, of an effusion-free state[61] and normal hearing acuity,[21] with possibly favorable developmental implications, and because it has appeared to result in better long-term otologic, audiologic, and speech outcomes than had previously been achieved in children not receiving early tube insertion.[26, 31] Nonetheless, it remains uncertain whether these benefits sufficiently offset the difficulties and complications of the treatment regimen, namely, the necessity of frequent examination to determine whether tympanostomy tubes are in place and patent, the necessity to carry out repeat myringotomy on infants whose tubes have been extruded, the frequent occurrence of purulent otorrhea that is often fairly resistant to treatment,[9, 61] the frequent development of seemingly significant eardrum scarring, and the occasional development of eardrum perforations (see Chap. 26).[35, 48, 56, 61] In some cases, otorrhea that had persisted for long periods despite usual treatment methods has cleared only after closure of the soft palate.[9, 61] In view of the difficulties and complications of tube placement, Robinson et al[72] have recommended that children with cleft palate receive unilateral tube placement only, and Robson et al[73] and Rynnel-Dagöö et al[75] have recommended that tube placement in children with cleft palate be limited to those with more severe degrees of hearing loss, or with problematic speech or language development or behavior. The Robinson et al retrospective study,[72] in keeping with an earlier study in older children with repaired cleft palate,[48] found worse outcomes in ears treated with tubes than in those not so treated. However, various limitations of the two studies (e.g., possible selection bias, limited ascertainment, uncertain matching, use, in many of the children, of long-term tubes that may be particularly damaging, and lack of information about the adjunctive use of antimicrobials) detract from the conclusiveness of the studies.

Currently, it seems reasonable to recommend that infants with cleft palate and persistent middle-ear effusion receive myringotomy and tympanostomy tube insertion at a relatively early age—that is, within the first 12 months or so of life. In infants who also have cleft lip, 2 to 3 months may be a convenient age for the initial procedure because it is often at that age that lip repair is undertaken, and the two operations can then be accomplished with a single administration of anesthesia. In infants whose otitis remains relatively asymptomatic, the timing of initial tube insertion within the first year of life (i.e., whether at 3, 6, or 12 months of age) appears to have little effect on the occurrence of otitis media during the second, third, or fourth years of life.[64] Whether tube insertion can be advantageously delayed beyond 12 months of age, or indefinitely, in selected children who are being closely observed, whose hearing is little affected, and whose ears do not show progressive changes remains to be determined. On the other hand, if hearing acuity is markedly impaired or if discomfort or frequent bouts of infection are occurring, earlier rather than later tube placement seems advisable. After the tubes have been extruded, as is usually inevitable eventually, myringotomy and tube insertion may be repeated if middle-ear effusion recurs and remains persistent. The degree of aggressiveness of surgical management may be guided by the severity of the symptoms, particularly hearing impairment and recurrent infection. Further discussion of this problem may be found in Chapter 25.

SELECTED REFERENCES

McWilliams BJ, Morris HL, Shelton RL, et al. Speech, language, and psychological aspects of cleft lip and cleft palate: the state of the art. ASHA 9:1, 1973.
> *This is a comprehensive review of developmental issues in children with cleft palate.*

Paradise JL, Bluestone CD, Felder H. The universality of otitis media in 50 infants with cleft palate. Pediatrics 44:35, 1969.
> *This is one of the first references identifying the high prevalence of otitis media in infants with cleft palate.*

Paradise JL, Elster BA, Tan L. Evidence in infants with cleft palate that breast milk protects against otitis media. Pediatrics 94:853, 1994.
> *This report provides evidence that breast milk, even when fed artificially, provides infants with cleft palate a measure of protection against the development of otitis media.*

REFERENCES

1. Ahonan JE, McDermott JC. Extended high-frequency hearing loss in children with cleft palate. Audiology 23:467, 1984.
2. Aschan G. Hearing and nasal function correlated to postoperative speech in cleft palate patients with velopharyngoplasty. Acta Otolaryngol (Stockh) 61:371, 1966.
3. Augarten A, Sagy M, Yahav J, et al. Management of upper airway obstruction in the Pierre Robin syndrome. Br J Oral Maxillofac Surg 28:105, 1990.
4. Bennett M. The older cleft palate patient (a clinical otologic-audiologic study). Laryngoscope 82:1217, 1972.
5. Bess FH, Schwartz DM, Redfield NP. Audiometric, impedance, and otoscopic findings in children with cleft palates. Arch Otolaryngol 102:465, 1976.
6. Bluestone CD. Eustachian tube obstruction in the infant with cleft palate. Ann Otol Rhinol Laryngol 80(Suppl 2):1, 1971.
7. Bluestone CD, Paradise JL, Beery QC, et al. Certain effects of cleft palate repair on eustachian tube function. Cleft Palate J 9:183, 1972.
8. Bluestone CD, Wittel RA, Paradise JL. Roentgenographic evaluation of eustachian tube function in infants with cleft and normal palates. Cleft Palate J 9:93, 1972.
9. Braganza RA, Kearns DB, Burton DM, et al. Closure of the soft palate for persistent otorrhea after placement of pressure equalization tubes in cleft palate infants. Cleft Palate Craniofac J 28:305, 1991.
10. Brine EA, Rickard KA, Brady MS, et al. Effectiveness of two feeding methods in improving energy intake and growth of infants with cleft palate: a randomized study. J Am Diet Assoc 94:732, 1994.
11. Burston WR. The early orthodontic treatment of cleft palate conditions. Dent Pract 9:41, 1958.
12. Chang AB, Masters IB, Williams GR, et al. A modified nasopharyngeal tube to relieve high upper airway obstruction. Pediatr Pulmonol 29:299, 2000.
13. Chaudhuri PK, Bowen-Jones E. An otorhinological study of children with cleft palates. J Laryngol Otol 92:29, 1978.
14. Cogswell JJ, Easton DM. Cor pulmonale in the Pierre Robin syndrome. Arch Dis Child 49:905, 1974.
15. Drillien CM, Ingram TTS, Wilkinson EM. The Causes and Natural History of Cleft Lip and Palate. Baltimore, Williams & Wilkins, 1966, pp 102–140.
16. Fletcher MM, Blum SL, Blanchard CL. Pierre Robin syndrome: pathophysiology of obstructive episodes. Laryngoscope 79:547, 1969.
17. Frable MA, Brandon GT, Theogaraj SD. Velar closure and ear tubings as a primary procedure in the repair of cleft palates. Laryngoscope 95:1044, 1985.
18. Frans N, Scheuerle J, Bequer N, et al. Middle ear tissue mass and audiometric data from otologic care of infants with cleft palate. Cleft Palate J 25:70, 1988.
19. Freeland AP, Evans DM. Middle ear disease in the cleft palate infant: its effect on speech and language development. Br J Plast Surg 34:142, 1981.
20. Freeman MK, Manners JM. Cor pulmonale and the Pierre Robin anomaly: airway management with a nasopharyngeal tube. Anaesthesia 35:282, 1980.
21. Fria TJ, Paradise JL, Sabo DL, et al. Conductive hearing loss in infants and young children with cleft palate. J Pediatr 111:84, 1987.
22. Gereau SA, Stevens D, Bassila M, et al. Endoscopic observations of eustachian tube abnormalities in children with palatal clefts. In Lim DJ, Bluestone CD, Klein JO, et al (eds). Recent Advances in Otitis Media. Toronto, BC Decker, 1988, pp 60–63.
23. Goldberg MH, Eckblom RH. The treatment of the Pierre Robin syndrome. Pediatrics 30:450, 1962.
24. Goldman JL, Martinez SA, Ganzel TM. Eustachian tube dysfunction and its sequelae in patients with cleft palate. South Med J 86:1236, 1993.
25. Gopalakrishna A, Goleria KS, Raje A. Middle ear function in cleft palate. Br J Plast Surg 37:558, 1984.
26. Gould HJ. Hearing loss and cleft palate: the perspective of time. Cleft Palate J 27:36, 1990.
27. Grant HR, Quiney RE, Mercer DM, et al. Cleft palate and glue ear. Arch Dis Child 63:176, 1988.
28. Greenwood RD, Waldman JD, Rosenthal A, et al. Cardiovascular abnormalities associated with Pierre Robin anomaly. Pediatr Dig 19:31, 1977.
29. Gutzmann H. Zur Prognose und Behandlung der angeborenen Gaumendefekte. Mschr Sprachheilk, 1893.
30. Heaf DP, Helms PJ, Dinwiddie R, et al. Nasopharyngeal airways in Pierre Robin syndrome. J Pediatr 100:698, 1982.
31. Holborow CA. Deafness associated with cleft palate. J Laryngol Otol 76:762, 1962.
32. Holborow CA. The assessment of eustachian function. J Otolaryngol Soc Aust 2:18, 1969.
33. Honjo I, Okazakai N, Kumazawa T. Opening mechanism in the eustachian tube. Ann Otol Rhinol Laryngol 89(Suppl 68):25, 1980.
34. Howlett C, Stavropoulos MF, Steinberg B. Feeding complications in a six-week-old infant secondary to distraction osteogenesis for airway obstruction: a case report. J Oral Maxillofac Surg 57:1465, 1999.
35. Hubbard TW, Paradise JL, McWilliams BJ, et al. Consequences of unremitting middle-ear disease in early life: otologic, audiologic, and developmental findings in children with cleft palate. N Engl J Med 312:1529, 1985.
36. Jeresaty RM, Huszar RJ, Basu S. Pierre Robin syndrome. Am J Dis Child 117:710, 1969.
37. Koch HF, Neveling R, Hartung W. Studies concerning the problems of ear diseases in cleft palate children. Cleft Palate J 7:187, 1970.
38. Lifton JC. Methods of feeding infants with cleft palate. J Am Dent Assoc 53:22, 1956.
39. Lupovich P, Bluestone CD, Paradise JL, et al. Middle ear effusions: preliminary viscometric, histologic and biochemical studies. Ann Otol Rhinol Laryngol 80:342, 1971.
40. Mallory SB, Paradise JL. Glossoptosis revisited: on the development and resolution of airway obstruction in the Pierre Robin syndrome. New observations from a case with cor pulmonale. Pediatrics 64:946, 1979.
41. Malson TS. Prosthesis for the newborn. J Prosthet Dent 21:384, 1969.
42. Masters IB, Chang AB, Harris M, O'Neil MC. Modified nasopha-

ryngeal tube for upper airway obstruction. Arch Dis Child 80:186, 1999.

43. Matsune S, Sando I, Takahashi H. Insertion of the tensor veli palatini muscle into the eustachian tube cartilage in cleft palate cases. Ann Otol Rhinol Laryngol 100:439, 1991.

44. Matsune S, Sando I, Takahashi H. Abnormalities of lateral cartilaginous lamina and lumen of eustachian tube in cases of cleft palate. Ann Otol Rhinol Laryngol 100:909, 1991.

45. Matsune S, Sando I, Takahashi H. Elastin at the hinge portion of the eustachian tube cartilage in specimens from normal subjects and those with cleft palate. Ann Otol Rhinol Laryngol 101:163, 1992.

46. Maue-Dickson W, Dickson D, Rood S. Anatomy of the eustachian tube and related structures in age matched human fetuses with and without cleft palate. Trans Am Acad Ophthalmol Otolaryngol 82:159, 1976.

47. McWilliams BJ, Morris HL, Shelton RL, et al. Speech, language, and psychological aspects of cleft lip and cleft palate: the state of the art. ASHA 9:1, 1973.

48. Møller P. Hearing, middle ear pressure and otopathology in a cleft palate population. Acta Otolaryngol (Stockh) 92:521, 1981.

49. Møller P, Dalen H. Middle ear mucosa in cleft palate children: a scanning electron microscopic study. Acta Otolaryngol Suppl (Stockh) 360:198, 1979.

50. Moore IJ, Moore GF, Yonkers AJ. Otitis media in the cleft palate patient. Ear Nose Throat J 65:291, 1986.

51. Morovic CG, Monasterio L. Distraction osteogenesis for obstructive apneas in patients with congenital craniofacial malformations. Plast Reconstr Surg 105:2324, 2000.

52. Oeconomopoulos CT. The value of glossopexy in Pierre Robin syndrome. N Engl J Med 262:1267, 1960.

53. Ogborn MR, Pemberton PJ. Late development of airway obstruction in the Robin anomalad (Pierre Robin syndrome) in the newborn. Aust Paediatr J 21:199, 1985.

54. Pannbacker J. Hearing loss and cleft palate. Cleft Palate J 6:50, 1969.

55. Paparella MM, Oda M, Hiraide F, et al. Pathology of sensorineural hearing loss in otitis media. Ann Otol Rhinol Laryngol 81:632, 1972.

56. Paradise JL. Management of middle ear effusion in infants with cleft palate. Ann Otol Rhinol Laryngol 85(Suppl 25):285, 1976.

57. Paradise JL. Otitis media in infants with cleft palate. In Weit RJ, Coulthard SW (eds). Proceedings of the Second National Conference on Otitis Media. Columbus, Ohio, Ross Laboratories, 1979, pp 62–66.

58. Paradise JL. Otitis media in infants and children. Pediatrics 65:917, 1980.

59. Paradise JL. Otitis media during early life: how hazardous to development? A critical review of the evidence. Pediatrics 68:869, 1981.

60. Paradise JL, Alberti PWRM, Bluestone CD, et al. Pediatric and otologic aspects of clinical research in cleft palate. Clin Pediatr 13:587, 1974.

61. Paradise JL, Bluestone CD. Early treatment of the universal otitis media of infants with cleft palate. Pediatrics 53:48, 1974.

62. Paradise JL, Bluestone CD, Felder H. The universality of otitis media in 50 infants with cleft palate. Pediatrics 44:35, 1969.

63. Paradise JL, Elster BA, Tan L. Evidence in infants with cleft palate that breast milk protects against otitis media. Pediatrics 94:853, 1994.

64. Paradise JL, Elster BA. Timing of initial tympanostomy-tube placement in infants with cleft palate [abstract]. Pediatr Res 27:125A, 1990.

65. Paradise JL, McWilliams BJ. Simplified feeder for infants with cleft palate. Pediatrics 53:566, 1974.

66. Paradise JL, Rogers KD. On otitis media, child development, and tympanostomy tubes: new answers or old questions? Pediatrics 77:88, 1986.

67. Passy V. Middle-ear effusions in patients with velopalatal insufficiency. Ear Nose Throat J 57:490, 1978.

68. Paulsen JW. Studies on the hearing and the tubal function in a series of children with cleft palates. Acta Otolaryngol Suppl (Stockh) 188:36, 1964.

69. Pielou WD. Nonsurgical management of Pierre Robin syndrome. Arch Dis Child 42:20, 1967.

70. Pruzansky S, Richmond JB. Growth of mandible in infants with micrognathia. Am J Dis Child 88:29, 1954.

71. Riberti C, Baldo D, Tirone L, et al. Hearing changes in patients with cleft lip and palate: clinicostatistical contribution. Pediatr Med Chir 6:131, 1984.

72. Robinson PJ, Lodge S, Jones BM, et al. The effect of palate repair on otitis media with effusion. Plast Reconstr Surg 89:640, 1992.

73. Robson AK, Blanshard JD, Jones K, et al. A conservative approach to the management of otitis media with effusion in cleft palate children. J Laryngol Otol 106:788, 1992.

74. Rood S, Doyle W. Morphology of the tensor veli palatini, tensor tympani and dilator tubae muscles. Ann Otol Rhinol Laryngol 87:202, 1978.

75. Rynnel-Dagöö B, Lindberg K, Bagger-Sjoback D, Larson O. Middle ear disease in cleft palate children at three years of age. Int J Pediatr Otorhinolaryngol 23:201, 1992.

76. Saad EF. The bifid uvula in ear, nose and throat practice. Laryngoscope 85:734, 1975.

77. Shah CV, Pruzansky S, Harris WS. Cardiac malformations with facial clefts. Am J Dis Child 119:238, 1970.

78. Shaw WC, Bannister RP, Roberts CT. Assisted feeding is more reliable for infants with clefts—a randomized trial. Cleft Palate Craniofac J 36:262, 1999.

79. Shibahara Y, Sando I. Histopathologic study of eustachian tube in cleft palate patients. Ann Otol Rhinol Laryngol 97:403, 1988.

80. Shprintzen RJ, Croft CB. Abnormalities of the eustachian tube orifice in individuals with cleft palate. Int J Pediatr Otorhinolaryngol 3:15, 1981.

81. Shprintzen RJ, Schwartz RH, Daniller A, et al. Morphological significance of bifid uvula. Pediatrics 75:553, 1985.

82. Sief S, Dellon A. Anatomic relationships between the human levator and tensor palatini and the eustachian tube. Cleft Palate J 15:329, 1978.

83. Skolnik EM. Otologic evaluation in cleft palate patients. Laryngoscope 68:1908, 1958.

84. Smith DW. Recognizable Patterns of Human Malformation, 2nd ed. Philadelphia, WB Saunders, 1976, p 130.

85. Soudijn ER, Huffstadt AJC. Cleft palates and middle ear effusions in babies. Cleft Palate J 12:229, 1975.

86. Stern LM, Fonkalsrud EW, Hassakis P, et al. Management of Pierre Robin syndrome in infancy by prolonged nasoesophageal intubation. Am J Dis Child 124:78, 1972.

87. Stewart JM, Ott JE, Lagace R. Submucous cleft palate. Birth Defects 7:64, 1971.

88. Stool SE, Randall P. Unexpected ear disease in infants with cleft palate. Cleft Palate J 4:99, 1967.

89. Strupler W. Middle ear deafness in infants with cleft palate. Int J Pediatr Otorhinolaryngol 1:279, 1980.

90. Taylor GD. The bifid uvula. Laryngoscope 82:771, 1972.

91. Tisza VB, Gumpertz E. The parents' reaction to the birth and early care of children with cleft palate. Pediatrics 30:86, 1962.

92. Ushiro K, Honjo I, Haji T, et al. Middle ear diseases in cleft palate children. Nippon Jibiinkoka Gakkai Kaiho 85:805, 1982.

93. Walton WK. Audiometrically "normal" conductive hearing losses among the cleft palate. Cleft Palate J 10:99, 1973.

94. Watson DJ, Rohrich RJ, Poole MD, et al. The effect on the ear of late closure of the cleft hard palate. Br J Plast Surg 39:190, 1986.

95. Wayoff M, Chobaut JC, Simon C, et al. Oreille moyenne et division palatine (à propos de 230 observations). J Fr Otorhinolaryngol 29:665, 1980.

96. Webster JC, Eldis F. Ear disease in relation to age in the cleft palate child and adolescent. Clin Otolaryngol 3:455, 1978.

97. Williams AC, Rothman BN, Seidman IH. Management of a feeding problem in an infant with cleft palate. J Am Dent Assoc 77:81, 1968.

98. Wilson MC, McDonald-McGinn DM, Quinn GE, et al. Long-term follow-up of ocular findings in children with Stickler's syndrome. Am J Ophthalmol 122:727, 1996.

99. Zickefoose M. Feeding problems of children with cleft palate. Children 4:225, 1957.

58

Dental and Gingival Disorders

Brian S. Martin, D.M.D., Yasser Armanazi, D.M.D.,
Jerry Bouquot, D.D.S., M.S., and M. M. Nazif, D.D.S., M.D.S.

Interactions between the professions of dentistry and oto-laryngology are common in modern medical specialty practice. This chapter provides the reader with a clinically oriented review of dental development, oral pathology, and dental care for patients undergoing chemotherapy or other forms of cancer treatment.

Dental Development

The structures of the oral cavity are constantly evolving during infancy and childhood. From teething age through the transition between the primary and permanent dentition, the oral cavity provides easily visible signs of growth and development. Development of the dentition begins at approximately 6 weeks in utero.[52] As a result, the child's overall health profoundly affects the development of the orofacial complex.

Development of the Teeth

Tooth "buds" or *follicles* arise from three distinct entities. The dental organ, which produces tooth enamel, is derived from oral ectoderm. The dental papilla, which forms the tooth pulp, is derived from mesenchyme. Finally, the dental sac, which forms both cementum and the periodontal ligament, is also derived from oral mesenchyme.[37] Figure 58–1 presents a diagram of tooth development.

In general, development of any given subset of teeth (i.e., molars, premolars, canines, incisors) within the mandibular arch precedes the maxillary arch. Development proceeds from the incisal edge toward the root apex. Sex differences also exist, with the dentition of females developing faster than that of males.[52] Figure 58–2 illustrates normal position and nomenclature of the primary and permanent dentition.

Primary Dentition

The process of eruption begins after approximately half of a tooth's root is formed. As eruption proceeds, growth and development of the alveolar bone is directly related to the path of the erupting tooth. Dental development is normally symmetrical. At approximately age 6 months, the mandibular central incisors erupt. This event is often preceded by a period of increased salivation, local gingival irritation, and irritability. These symptoms may vary in intensity but respond well to analgesics and usually subside when the last primary tooth erupts into the oral cavity. Other symptoms, such as fever or diarrhea, have not been proven to be directly related to teething.[22] The timing and sequence of eruption show tremendous variability.[30] The lower incisors are soon followed by the maxillary central incisors and maxillary and mandibular lateral incisors. By the end of the first year, all eight anterior teeth are usually visible. By age 3 years, the primary dentition should be fully present and functional.

Any variation in the timing and sequence of eruption in an otherwise normal infant may call for an early dental referral. In general, children should undergo their first dental examination by age 1. Eruption of primary teeth is sometimes delayed for up to 8 months; this is considered a normal variation if the child is otherwise healthy. Retarded primary tooth eruption is associated with Down syndrome, hypothyroidism, hypopituitarism, achondroplastic dwarfism, osteopetrosis, rickets, or chondroectodermal dysplasia.[16] A significant variation affecting a single tooth or a few teeth should also be thoroughly investigated.

Permanent Dentition

Table 58–1 lists the development timing and sequence of the permanent dentition.

Eruption of the first permanent tooth marks the beginning of the "mixed" dentition. This developmental stage proceeds in three distinct stages. The early mixed dentition is characterized by the eruption of the permanent maxillary and mandibular incisors and first molar teeth, with concurrent exfoliation of their primary counterparts. Generally speaking, the early mixed dentition occurs from age 6 to 9. After these teeth have erupted, dental development becomes quiescent during what is known as the *intertransitional period,* from age 9 to 11. During this time, no further permanent teeth erupt. Finally, during

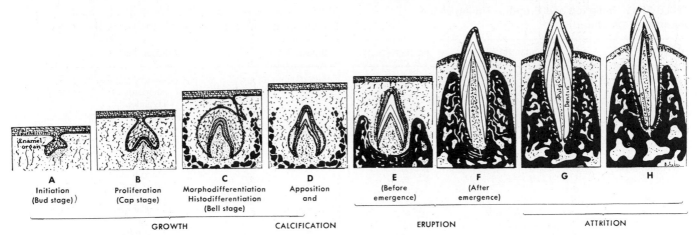

FIGURE 58–1. The life cycle of a tooth. (Modified from Schour I, Massler M. Studies in tooth development. J Am Dent Assoc 27:1785, 1940.)

the late mixed dentition, the permanent canines, premolars, and second molar teeth erupt, usually from age 11 to 13. Development of the third molars proceeds throughout the teenage years, with subsequent eruption in the late teens.

Developmental and Acquired Anomalies of the Teeth

It is important to note that disturbances within any of the developmental stages shown within Figure 58–1 can cause distinct pathologic clinical outcomes. Table 58–2 outlines the relationship between these growth stages and associated anomalies of the dentition.

Disturbances in Initiation and Proliferation: Hyperdontia, Hypodontia, and Anodontia

Disturbances in the initial stage of tooth development cause variations in the number of developing teeth. Clinically, this condition is classified into one of three categories: hyperdontia, hypodontia, or anodontia.

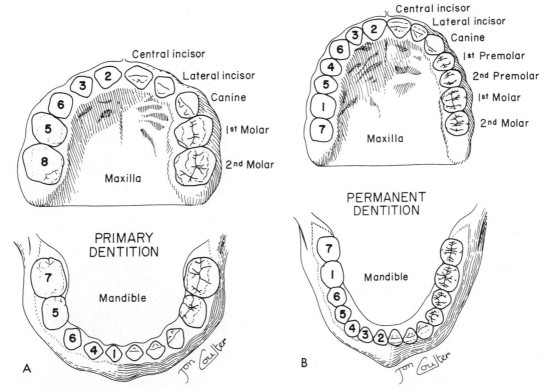

FIGURE 58–2. *A,* The eruption sequence and nomenclature of the primary dentition. *B,* The eruption sequence and nomenclature of the permanent dentition.

TABLE 58–1. Initiation and Eruption Timing of the Permanent Dentition

Tooth	Initiation (Month)	Eruption (Year)
Maxilla		
Central incisor	5–5.25 in utero	7–8
Lateral incisor	5–5.25 in utero	8–9
Canine	5.5–6 in utero	11–12
First premolar	Birth	10–11
Second premolar	7.5–8	10–12
First molar	3.5–4 in utero	10–12
Second molar	8.5–9	12–13
Third molar	3.5–4 (yr)	17–25
Mandible		
Central incisor	5–5.25 in utero	6–7
Lateral incisor	5.25 in utero	7–8
Canine	5.5–6 in utero	9–11
First premolar	Birth	10–12
Second premolar	7.5–8	11–12
First molar	3.5–4 in utero	6–7
Second molar	8.5–9	11–13
Third molar	3.5–4 (yr)	17–25

From Gorlin RJ, Cohen MM, Levine S. Syndromes of the Head and Neck, 4th ed. Oxford, Oxford University Press, 1994.

TABLE 58–2. Relationship Between Disturbance in Growth Stages and Resultant Anomalies of the Teeth

Growth Phase	Clinical Results

Initiation/proliferation	Abnormal number
	  Anodontia
	  Hypodontia
	  Hyperdontia

Histodifferentiation	Atypical structure
	  Amelogenesis imperfecta
	  Dentinogenesis imperfecta

Morphodifferentiation	Ayptical shape/size
	  Macrodontia
	  Microdontia
	  Gemination

Apposition	Abnormal quantity
	  Enamel hypoplasia
	  Dentin hypoplasia

Calcification	Abnormal hardness
	  Enamel hypocalcification
	  Intrinsic staining

Hyperdontia, or "supernumerary teeth," occurs in about 3% of the general population. The incidence is significantly higher among patients with cleft lip/palate or cleidocranial dysostosis.[7] There is a 2:1 male predominance. Ninety percent of cases occur in the anterior maxilla.[53] Supernumerary teeth may have the size and morphology of adjacent teeth or may be small and atypical in shape. They may erupt spontaneously or remain impacted. Early consideration of removal is justified because of complications such as impeded eruption, crowding, or resorption of permanent teeth; formation of cystic lesions; or ectopic eruption into the nasal cavity, the maxillary sinus, or other sites.[18] Figure 58–3 shows how a permanent central incisor is impacted because of a supernumerary tooth within its path of eruption.

Congenital absence of teeth (*anodontia* or *hypodontia*) is more common in the permanent dentition than in the primary. Most frequently missing are third molars, second premolars, and lateral incisors. Complete anodontia is rare.[31] Most cases are related to hereditary hypohydrotic ectodermal dysplasia. Hypodontia is also frequently associated with several ectodermal syndromes, such as anhidrotic ectodermal dysplasia and chondroectodermal dysplasia.[18]

Disturbances in Histodifferentiation: Atypical Structure

Amelogenesis Imperfecta

Amelogenesis imperfecta describes a group of genetically determined defects that involve the enamel of primary and permanent teeth without involving dentin, pulp, or cementum. The condition is caused by injury to the ameloblasts during enamel formation. The overall prevalence is 1:14000. Although the types of amelogenesis imperfecta

are numerous, major classifications describe hypocalcified, hypoplastic, or hypomaturation types.[51]

The hypocalcified type is the most common, with a prevalence of 1:20,000. The mode of transmission is autosomal dominant. The enamel of newly erupted teeth is chalky, poorly mineralized, and varied in color. The enamel quickly erodes with mastication, exposing underlying dentin.[45]

The hypoplastic type results in thin, pitted, or fissured enamel; however, the enamel present is appropriately mineralized and of good quality and consistency. The mode of transmission may be autosomal dominant or autosomal recessive.[45]

The hypomaturation type manifests as discolored enamel of normal thickness but decreased hardness that tends to chip away slowly, exposing underlying dentin.[13] Radiographic evaluation demonstrates decreased density of enamel. Treatment of this and the aforementioned

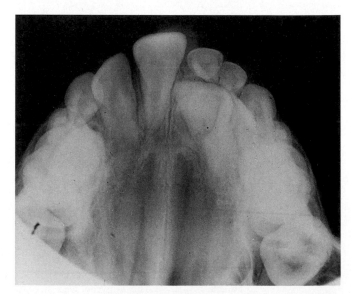

FIGURE 58–3. Impacted permanent central incisor secondary to the presence of a supernumerary tooth.

enamel conditions often requires full coverage restorations (crowns) of the affected teeth.[45]

Dentinogenesis Imperfecta

Dentinogenesis imperfecta results in dentin defects and is usually inherited as an autosomal dominant trait, with a prevalence of 1:8000. There are two basic subclassifications. *Type I dentinogenesis imperfecta* is associated with osteogenesis imperfecta. Autosomal dominant and recessive forms exhibit varied expressivity.[51] Teeth are blue to pinkish-brown and have an opalescent sheen. Despite normal enamel morphology, the crowns undergo rapid attrition or wearing (Fig. 58–4). The roots are shortened, and pulp cavities become calcified over time. Primary teeth are more severely affected than the permanent, although permanent teeth can be prone to fracture. *Type II dentinogenesis imperfecta,* or *hereditary opalescent dentin,* has no skeletal involvement. Clinical presentation is very similar to type I; both dentitions are equally affected.[18]

Treatment of both types of dentinogenesis imperfecta includes preservation of the integrity of the primary and permanent dentitions. Aesthetic restorative materials (crowns, tooth-colored filling materials) deserve special consideration whenever possible.

Disturbances in Morphodifferentiation: Alteration in Size and Shape

Teeth that are smaller or larger than normal are called *microdonts* and *macrodonts*, respectively. These teeth are genetic anomalies. They are clinically significant when a discrepancy between tooth and arch length results in severe crowding or spacing of the teeth. Size abnormalities are often localized to one tooth or a very small group of teeth.[3] Variations in shape also result from the joining of teeth or tooth buds. For example, the condition known as *gemination* occurs when the crowns of two teeth share a single root system.[26]

Disturbances in Apposition and Calcification: Hypoplasia and Hypocalcification

Numerous local and systemic insults can cause the enamel defects of hypoplasia and hypocalcification. The most common causes are local infections such as an abscessed primary tooth, which, when not properly treated, can damage the formation of the enamel of its permanent successor. Other causes include systemic infections associated with high fever, trauma, or chemical injury such as fluorosis. Other etiologic factors include nutritional deficiencies, allergies, rubella, cerebral palsy, embryopathy, prematurity, and radiation therapy. Hypoplasia results from an insult during active enamel matrix formation and clinically presents as pitting, furrowing, or thinning of enamel. Hypocalcification results from an insult during the mineralization of the tooth and appears as opaque, chalky, or white lesions.[18]

Discoloration of Teeth

Three major types of tooth discoloration are common: (1) discoloration from stains that adhere externally to the surfaces of the teeth (extrinsic), (2) discoloration from various pigments that are incorporated into the tooth structure during development (intrinsic), and (3) intrinsic discoloration secondary to hereditary defects, which were previously discussed.

Extrinsic discoloration is primarily limited to patients with poor oral hygiene, those receiving certain medications, those who heavily consume stain-containing foods or drinks, or those who smoke or chew tobacco or other

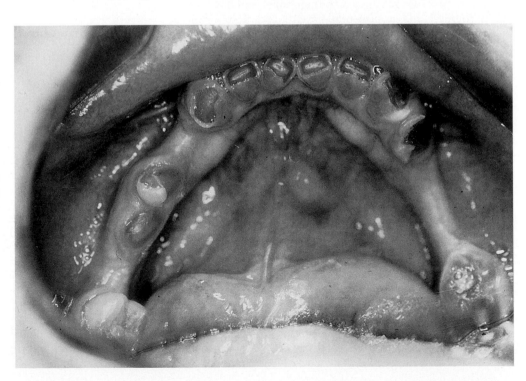

FIGURE 58–4. Dentinogenesis imperfecta. Severe attrition is visible on the crowns of affected teeth.

substances. Diagnosis requires appropriate medical, dental, and dietary histories that emphasize oral hygiene, food and drug intake, and tobacco habits. Treatment includes scaling, dental prophylaxis and polishing, and regular oral hygiene. Extrinsic stain colorations can range from brown/black to orange/green and can be caused by iron supplements, chromogenic bacteria and fungi, and other sources.

Intrinsic discoloration is usually induced during the calcification of dentin and enamel by excessive levels of the body's natural pigments, such as hemoglobin and bile, or by pigments introduced by the intake of chemicals, such as fluorides or tetracyclines. Occasionally, isolated intrinsic discoloration results from pulpal necrosis. Generalized intrinsic discoloration of primary teeth occurs in patients with advanced hepatic disease associated with persistent or recurrent jaundice and hyperbilirubinemia. The intensity of discoloration varies and may be related to the severity of the disease. Color ranges from brown to grayish brown and usually has no clinical significance unless it is associated with significant hypoplasia of the dentition. Teeth stained because of tetracycline therapy may vary in color from yellow to brown to dark gray. Staining occurs when the tetracycline is incorporated into calcifying teeth and bone. The enamel and, to a greater degree, the dentin that are calcifying at the time of intake incorporate tetracycline.[11] The severity of discoloration depends on the dose, duration, and type of tetracycline administered. As tetracyclines readily cross the placenta, they should not be prescribed to pregnant women or children under age 10.

Dental Caries

Dental caries is an infectious disease strongly influenced by diet. The causes involved in the caries process include cariogenic microorganisms, a fermentable carbohydrate "food source," and a susceptible tooth and host. Clinically, dental caries manifests itself through a progressive demineralization of tooth structure. Acidic byproducts of bacterial metabolism demineralize the enamel, causing microscopic cavitations. Saliva serves both as a pH buffer and source of dissolved mineral substrate for remineralization of the affected tooth structure. If the host's capacity for remineralization is overwhelmed, the carious lesion can progress through the enamel and into the dentin.[43] After infection, the dentinal tubules can serve as a microenvironment for the invading bacteria, transmitting metabolic byproducts and toxins toward the pulp. This can lead to pulpal necrosis, with subsequent acute infection such as dental abscess or, in the permanent dentition, formation of cystic lesions.

Role of Plaque in Dental Caries

Dental plaque is composed primarily of bacteria with lesser amounts of bacterial extracellular products, salivary glycoproteins, desquamated epithelial cells, and food debris. Studies have shown that *Streptococci mutans* is the bacteria responsible for dental decay. *S. mutans* orga-

nisms possess cariogenic traits that make them particularly pathogenic. For example, *S. mutans* creates an acidic environment during periods of low salivary secretion (such as sleep) by continuously synthesizing insoluble glucans and polysaccharides and releasing lactic acid, thereby contributing to the caries process.[43]

Diet and Early Childhood Caries

Any fermentable carbohydrate consumed by the child is a potential source of substrate for cariogenic bacteria. However, it is important to note that sucrose and fructose found in soda, fruit juice, and other prepackaged beverages are often the primary cause of early childhood dental caries, commonly known as *baby bottle syndrome.* Limited exposure to these fermentable carbohydrates is critical to preserve the health of the primary dentition.[43]

Soft Tissue Pathology

Gingival Disorders

The gingiva is the part of the oral mucous membrane attached to the teeth and alveolar processes of the jaws. Histologically, the gingiva is composed of keratinizing epithelium and connective tissue. Clinically and histologically, *gingivitis* refers to inflammation limited to the free gingiva. It specifically does not include any inflammatory process that may extend to the underlying bone or periodontal ligament. Marginal gingivitis often results from poor oral hygiene. Predominant organisms in the early stages of gingivitis include gram-positive rods such as *Actinomyces*. However, spirochetes (including *Treponema*) may also be involved.[46] Treatment simply involves improvement of oral hygiene, but systemic antibiotics may be required for treatment of acute episodes.[12]

Acute Necrotizing Ulcerative Gingivitis

Acute necrotizing ulcerative gingivitis (ANUG) is an acute gingivitis specifically linked to high bacterial populations of fusiform bacteria and spirochetes.[29] New research has also associated this condition with *Treponema pallidum.*[40] Factors contributing to ANUG include psychological stress, smoking, local trauma, poor oral hygiene, and deficient nutritional status. Specifically, stress is thought to alter the T4/T8 lymphocyte ratios while decreasing the response of neutrophil chemotaxis and phagocytic response. Patients who are immunocompromised are at increased risk for ANUG.

Clinically, ANUG is characterized by lymphadenopathy, fever, and malaise. Intraorally, the first areas affected are the interdental papillae. As the disease progresses, the papillae become necrotic, take on a blunt or "punched out" appearance, and are often covered with a gray pseudomembrane. A fetid odor, pain, spontaneous bleeding, and accumulations of necrotic debris complete the clinical picture.[19] Figure 58–5 shows a classic clinical example of ANUG. Treatment includes systemic antibiotics, debridement, and chlorhexidine rinses.[17]

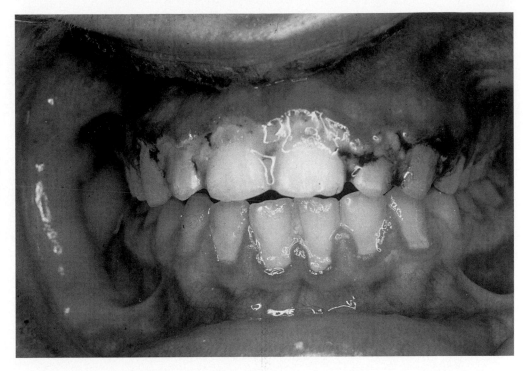

FIGURE 58–5. Acute necrotizing ulcerative gingivitis. White pseudomembrane is present, along with blunted gingival papillae.

Mouth Breathing Gingivitis

Gingivitis secondary to mouth breathing generally affects the maxillary anterior region. Xerostomia associated with anterior open-bite malocclusion can also cause this form of gingivitis. Definitive treatment must include correction of the malocclusion, often with a combination of orthodontic and orthognathic surgical therapy.

Gingival Hyperplasia

Hyperplasia, or overproliferation of keratinized gingival tissue, can result from drug reactions and hereditary factors.

Drug-Induced Gingival Hyperplasia

Examples of drug-induced gingival hyperplasia are phenytoin, calcium channel blockers (e.g., nifedipine), and immunosuppressant agents such as cyclosporine.[9] Severe phenytoin-induced gingival hyperplasia is shown in Figure 58–6. There is extreme gingival hypertrophy in the posterior segment. The degree of gingival enlargement correlates strongly with oral hygiene, patient susceptibility, and occlusion and more weakly with drug dosage.[4] Clinically, gingival hyperplasia usually appears 1 to 3 months after the initiation of drug therapy. The enlargements originate in the interdental papillae and subsequently spread laterally across the gingival margins. The affected gingiva is normal in color and appearance if oral hygiene is good; otherwise, secondary infection follows. Treatments include gingivectomy, chlorhexidine rinses, scrupulous oral hygiene, and discontinuation or substitution of the causative medication.[4]

Gingival Fibromatosis

Gingival fibromatosis is a rare progressive fibrous enlargement of the gingiva that is inherited as an autosomal dominant trait. The condition is characterized by a noninflammatory gingival enlargement and can affect both maxillary and mandibular gingiva. The distribution pattern can be localized or generalized. Treatment is surgical gingivectomy as spontaneous remission does not occur even with excellent oral hygiene.[41]

Periodontitis

Periodontitis, like gingivitis, is an inflammatory disease process that affects the supporting structures of the teeth, including the periodontal ligament, alveolar bone, and cementum. Chronic periodontitis can lead to progressive breakdown of these attachment structures, causing tooth mobility and possible loss.[38] The incidence of periodontitis in juvenile populations is quite low; the exception is *localized juvenile periodontitis,* which occurs in otherwise healthy adolescents and is not associated with any specific systemic disease process. It is characterized by pubertal onset, with a female predilection.[50] Clinically, this disorder involves localized alveolar bone destruction, specifically in the area of the first permanent molars and anterior teeth. Resorption is usually bilateral. Research has shown that 90% of adolescents who present with localized juvenile periodontitis have a chemotactic defect in neutrophils or monocytes, or both. The bacterium implicated is *Actinobacillus actinomycetemcomitans,* which has been isolated in 97% of reported cases. In addition, *Capnocytophaga* organisms have been isolated in 25% of patients.[50] Treatment includes surgical curettage, a systemic

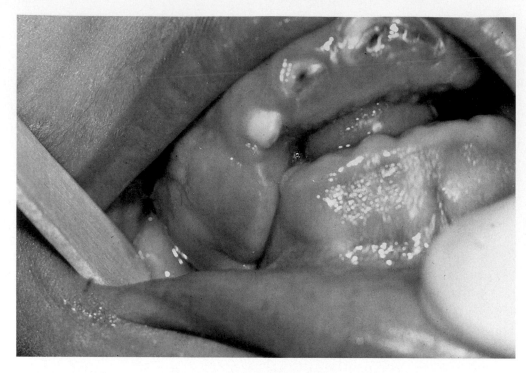

FIGURE 58–6. Phenytoin-induced gingival hyperplasia.

antibiotic such as tetracycline, and oral chlorhexidine rinses.[27]

Hard and Soft Tissue Cysts

Epithelium-lined hard and soft tissue cysts are common within the oral cavity and jawbones of children and adolescents. These growths may arise during the embryonic development of teeth (dentigerous cyst, odontogenic keratocyst), during eruption (eruption cyst), or from viable epithelial fragments embedded beneath the oral mucosa.

Dentigerous Cyst

The dentigerous cyst is associated with the crown of an unerupted or partially erupted tooth. The cyst usually surrounds the crown but may develop along only one surface of the tooth. It is the most common of the developmental odontogenic cysts of the jaws. The epithelial lining can arise from the epithelial cells associated with the embryonic development of the teeth. Dentigerous cysts may also be associated with the extraction of a nonvital or abscessed primary tooth.[2]

Malignant transformation can occur with dentigerous cysts but has been documented only in permanent teeth in the adult population.[20] The dentigerous cyst is rarely associated with a deciduous tooth. It is seen as an even, well-demarcated radiolucency around the crown of an impacted tooth. Figure 58–7 shows a dentigerous cyst, with a large radiolucency surrounding the lower-right first molar. Note the root destruction on the adjacent primary molar secondary to the cyst. The lesion is almost always asymptomatic unless secondarily infected, and smaller cysts can be found during routine radiographic examination. Large cysts may extend into the maxillary sinus or the ramus of the mandible before they are detected.

The *eruption cyst* appears clinically as a clear fluid-filled bulla on the crest of the alveolus and radiographically as a saucerized radiolucency, with the crown of the tooth extending centrally. Trauma of an eruption cyst often causes hemorrhage into the cyst lumen, resulting in a red or bluish clinical discoloration (*eruption hematoma*). This subtype of dentigerous cyst is superficial and often requires no treatment since spontaneous regression is common.

Dentigerous cysts are usually unilocular, but multilocular examples are not rare. Large lesions, or those which are multilocular or extend into the mandibular ramus, are more likely to represent the more aggressive odontogenic keratocyst (discussed elsewhere in this chapter) than dentigerous cysts.

Careful, conservative enucleation is the recommended treatment for the dentigerous cyst. The associated tooth is usually removed but may be salvaged by marsupialization. In this technique, the cyst is unroofed, part of the lining is removed, and the remaining lining is reattached to adjacent tissue. A patent opening is then maintained into the cystic lumen. This procedure typically results in slow shrinkage of the lesion.

Odontogenic Keratocyst

The odontogenic keratocyst is possibly the most aggressive of the jaw cysts. It is presumably a developmental phenomenon rather than a neoplasm, but its high recurrence rate and growth potential has made its status as a benign neoplasm controversial.[42] The lesion arises from epithelial rests persisting after embryogenesis and development of the teeth. It accounts for approximately 12% of all non-infectious odontogenic jaw cysts.[33] The mandible is much more often involved (80% of cases) than the maxilla, and there is a marked predilection for the molar

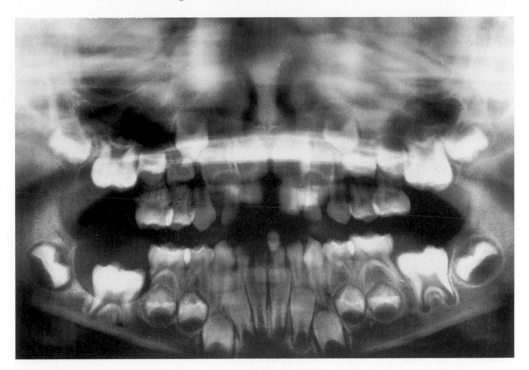

FIGURE 58–7. Dentigerous cyst surrounding mandibular right first molar.

and ramus area.[33] The cyst presents as a well-demarcated, usually multilocular radiolucency with a thin sclerotic rimming and anteroposterior growth pattern. Associated teeth are normal.

The microscopic appearance of the odontogenic keratocyst is unique and pathognomonic. The epithelium is usually thin, with a general loss of rete pegs, a thin corrugated surface of parakeratin or orthokeratin, polarization and hyperchromatism of the basal cells, and a pulling away from the basement membrane.

Odontogenic keratocysts are usually curetted as the initial treatment. This minor treatment is adequate for about 50% of the cases, but the keratocyst has a high recurrence rate.[33] More aggressive surgery, such as block resection, is performed for the persistent or recurrent lesion. Malignant transformation has been noted in adult populations. Long-term follow-up is necessary as cysts have occurred more than 10 years after surgery.

Soft Tissue Tumors of the Oral Cavity

Soft tissue tumors of the oral cavity are found in at least 1 of every 450 persons under age 20 (prevalence rate: 2.6 per 1000 persons).[24] These tumors may be associated with the gingiva, mucosal tissues, or other soft tissue structures, including the tongue.

Pyogenic Granuloma

Pyogenic granuloma of the oral cavity is essentially an inflamed mass of edematous granulation tissue.[5, 49] It is similar to its counterparts in other parts of the body. This pseudotumor is associated with local irritation and poor oral hygiene to produce a focal inflammatory enlargement of one or more gingival papillae. Pyogenic granuloma can occur at any mucosal location of trauma or infection. The gingiva is the most common location. Other sites of common involvement include the tongue, the lip mucosa and vermilion, and the buccal mucosa. Figure 58–8 is an example of pyogenic granuloma of the tongue. All ages and both genders are susceptible to the pyogenic granuloma. Among young persons, it is most commonly diagnosed in adolescents and teenagers.[5]

The pyogenic granuloma is usually a pedunculated, even, lobulated mass. It is bright or dark red, perhaps with white surface areas of ulceration, and tends to hemorrhage with palpation. It is composed of a rich profusion of anastomosing vascular channels, usually with plump endothelial cell nuclei (neovascularity). Older lesions are more fibrosed and less hemorrhagic and tend to be normal in color, with few surface ulcers.

Pyogenic granuloma is treated by conservative surgical excision with removal of potential traumatic or infective causes. The recurrence rate is approximately 15%, with gingival cases recurring much more frequently than lesions of other oral mucosal sites.[49]

Pericoronitis

Pericoronitis is an inflammatory mass of the soft tissues posterior to the last erupted tooth in the mandible.[6, 34] The mandibular retromolar pad or operculum often pushes against or overlaps the last molar in the arch. Food debris and bacteria may become entrapped between this pad and the tooth, resulting in acute infection and pain.

Pericoronitis typically occurs in teenagers and young adults, before or soon after the eruption of the second or third mandibular molars. It is characteristically an ery-

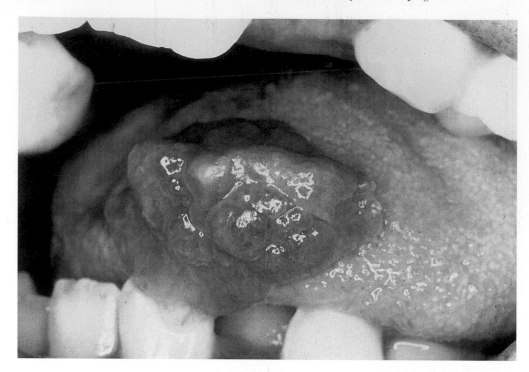

FIGURE 58–8. Pyogenic granuloma of the anterior tongue.

thematous, tender, sessile swelling of the retromolar pad, often with traumatic surface ulceration from the opposing maxillary molars. Pus may be expressed from the tissue/tooth interface, a foul taste may be present, and trismus may occur. Cervical lymphadenopathy, fever, leukocytosis, and malaise are common, as are ipsilateral tonsillitis and upper-respiratory infection.[32, 36]

Acute pericoronitis is treated by local antiseptic lavage and gentle curettage under the flap, with or without systemic antibiotics. Once the acute phase is controlled, the offending molar is extracted or a wedge of hyperplastic pad tissue is removed surgically. Recurrence is unlikely with either of these treatments.[6]

Peripheral Ossifying/Cementifying Fibroma

The peripheral ossifying fibroma is a unique inflammatory or reactive hyperplasia originating in the mesenchymal cells of the periodontal ligament. Bone, cementum, or both are produced above the cortex.[8]

The peripheral ossifying fibroma occurs at all ages but has a predilection for teenagers and young adults.[54] It occurs more frequently in persons with poor oral hygiene and, by definition, it can be found only at gingival sites. It is a painless, hemorrhagic, often lobulated mass of the gingiva, usually with large areas of surface ulceration. Early lesions are quite irregular and red, but older lesions may have a smooth salmon-pink surface and may be indistinguishable clinically from the more common *irritation fibroma*. Early growth is often rapid. Radiographs may show irregular scattered radiopacities in the body of the lesion.[8]

The peripheral ossifying fibroma is treated by conservative surgical excision followed by curettage of the wound bed and root planing of adjacent teeth.[21]

Congenital (Granular Cell) Epulis

The congenital epulis (mass on the gingiva) is a unique and rare congenital hyperplasia of the anterior jaws in infants (Fig. 58–9).[25, 35] The congenital epulis is almost exclusively found on the anterior alveolar ridges of newborns, although a few cases have reportedly developed shortly after birth. Approximately 90% of cases occur in girls and 10% are multiple, often involving both jaws. The epulis typically presents as a 0.5- to 2.0-cm, soft, pedunculated, and perhaps lobulated nodule of the alveolar mucosa, especially the mucosa of the maxilla. Prior to birth, the congenital epulis enlarges at a rate similar to that of the growing fetus, but after birth the mass tends to spontaneously regress and disappear over the first 8 months of life. There is no tenderness or surface change, and the lesion does not grow over time. In fact, many of the smaller masses spontaneously regress shortly after birth.[25, 35]

Residual remnants do not interfere with tooth eruption. Thus, treatment is unnecessary. The larger lesion may interfere with eating or drinking, requiring conservative excision as soon as the child is mature enough to safely undergo surgery. There is no tendency for recurrence, and malignant transformation has not been reported.

Oral Infections

Viral Infection of the Oral Cavity: Herpetic Gingivostomatitis

Primary herpetic gingivostomatitis, caused by herpes simplex type 1, is an extremely painful disease that affects children, especially between the ages of 6 months and 3 years.[23] The vesicular lesions of the lips, tongue, gingivae, and oral mucosa are preceded by fever, headache, regional lymphadenopathy, and gingival hyperemia and

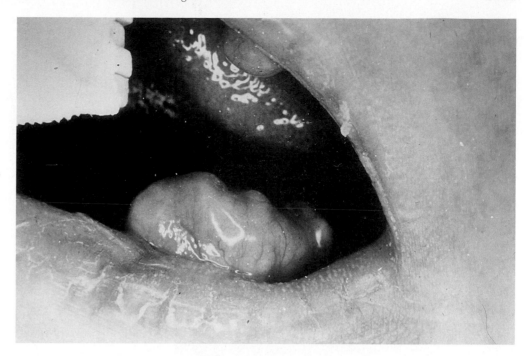

FIGURE 58–9. Congenital epulis of the newborn.

edema. These lesions tend to rupture quickly, leaving shallow ulcerations covered by a gray membrane and surrounded by an erythematous halo. The inflamed gingivae are friable and bleed easily. Lesions heal in 1 to 2 weeks without scarring.[23] Since inflammation makes brushing too painful, chlorhexidine or peroxide rinses can be used to maintain oral hygiene. A bland diet and rinsing with viscous lidocaine in equal parts diphenhydramine (Benadryl) and Maalox (in older children) in addition to oral analgesics can help to minimize discomfort. Systemic acyclovir may be indicated in moderate to severe cases.

Secondary, or recurrent, infections caused by reactivation of latent herpes simplex virus are fairly common. Lesions are few and more localized; systemic symptoms are absent unless the host is immunocompromised. Lesions are usually located on the lips, with prodromal symptoms of itching and burning preceding the development of thin-walled vesicles that rupture and become crusty.

When intraoral lesions occur, they manifest as small vesicles in a localized group on mucosa that is tightly bound to periosteum.[42]

Odontogenic Infections

Facial cellulitis secondary to bacterial infection in the pediatric population can be broadly classified as odontogenic or non-odontogenic. Unkle et al reported that odontogenic infections constitute a significant proportion (47%) of facial cellulitis in pediatric hospital patients (1997).[48] Because of the complex anatomical structures found within the region (sinuses, lymphatic tissue, and facial planes), management often involves the expertise of both pediatric dental and ENT personnel. Figure 58–10 shows buccal cellulitis secondary to dental infection.

Several diagnostic parameters can aid clinicians in the differential diagnosis of odontogenic versus non-odontogenic facial cellulitis:

- *Age.* Unkle et al reported that patients admitted for odontogenic infection had a mean age of 8.8 years, significantly older than the mean age for the non-odontogenic group (4.4 years).[48]
- *Temperature.* In the same study, body temperature was significantly higher in patients with maxillofacial infection of non-odontogenic origin (38.4°C) than in patients with odontogenic infection (37.5°C).[48]
- *Location.* Dodson et al reported that patients with upper-face infections were younger and more likely to have non-odontogenic disease than those with lower-face infections.[15] However, odontogenic origin predominated in lower-face infections. This finding is supported by Unkle et al.[48]
- *Complete blood count.* Travis and Steinle reported that CBC values are normal with dental infections until they reach the stage of acute facial cellulitis.[47] Once the patient presents with this condition, odontogenic infections exhibit generalized leukocytosis, specifically neutrophilia, monocytosis, eosinopenia, and basopenia. Unkle et al reported that in non-odontogenic cases, white blood cell counts are more likely to be greater than 15,000 /mm³.[48] Leukocytosis was more likely to be worse in cases of odontogenic origin.

The bacteriologic flora of odontogenic infection is polymicrobial, including both aerobes and anaerobes. It is well documented that anaerobic bacteria predominate in mixed cultures. Aderhold et al found anaerobic bacteria in 96% of cultured odontogenic infections.[1] Dominant organisms include *Bacteroides, Fusobacterium, Peptococcus,* and *Peptostreptococcus* species. With respect to aerobic species, α-hemolytic streptococci are most common. Unkle et al showed that in cases of odontogenic infection, α-hemolytic *Streptococcus* (47%), *Neisseria* (28%), and

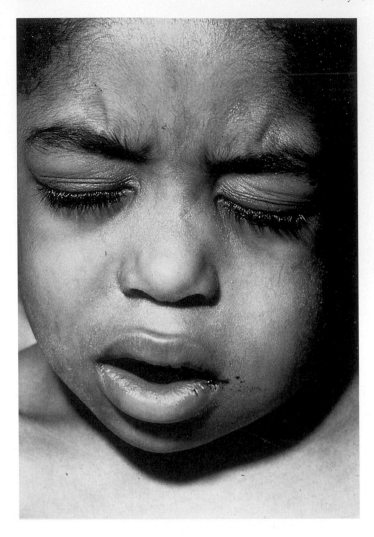

FIGURE 58–10. Facial cellulitis secondary to dental infection.

diphtheroids (25%) were the most commonly isolated microorganisms.[48]

A retrospective review of 113 children hospitalized with maxillofacial infection demonstrated bacteriologic differences between upper-face and lower-face infections.[15] Upper-face infections were found to grow *Haemophilus influenzae* and *Staphylococcus aureus,* the two most common penicillin-resistant organisms. Unkle et al also found *H. influenzae* organisms in upper-face infections, along with coagulase-negative *Staphylococcus.*[48] This phenomenon apparently is different in patients immunized against *H. influenzae,* in whom penicillin-susceptible bacteria are most common. Therefore, an immunization history for *H. influenzae* is helpful in the diagnosis and treatment of midface cellulitis. Although a non-odontogenic source of infection, the possibility of *H. influenzae* within patients presenting with facial cellulitis should alter treatment regimens as it is the organism most frequently associated with sepsis and meningitis.

Antibiotic Therapy

Initial antibiotic treatment of odontogenic infection is often empirical. According to Dodson et al, location of infection is a factor in selecting appropriate antibiotic therapy.[15] With an upper-face infection of unknown or uncertain cause, the child should be started on a second-generation cephalosporin. This regimen covers penicillin-resistant organisms, including *H. influenzae* and *S. aureus.* For patients who present with infection of a known odontogenic source, penicillin therapy is the antibiotic of choice, with clindamycin as the alternative for penicillin-sensitive patients. Lower-face infections are best treated with penicillins. Aderhold et al recommend clindamycin because of its effectiveness against anaerobes commonly found in odontogenic infection and its ability to penetrate alveolar bone.[1]

Surgical Treatment

Surgical management of odontogenic infection includes incision and drainage, endodontic (root canal) therapy, and possible tooth extraction. Removal of the odontogenic infectious cause is paramount. Treatment modalities are determined by the extent of the infection, medical status, presence of trismus, and anatomical factors. In addition to antibiotic therapy, effective pain control is an essential part of infection management.

Patients Undergoing Treatment for Cancer

The survival of patients with neoplasms during childhood has improved steadily in recent decades, largely because of advances in chemotherapy and radiation treatment. As a result, pediatric dentists and allied medical specialists are now presented with a group of patients with specific concerns and needs secondary to their medical condition and treatment modalities.

Dental Care for the Immunosuppressed Patient

Infection is a serious problem in immunosuppressed patients. The oral cavity is particularly vulnerable because of easy disruption of the integument of oral mucosa by mechanical and chemical means. Mucositis is a common complication when pathways are opened for invasion by bacteria, fungi, or viruses. Such invasion can be life-threatening because of inhibited immune mechanisms. Appropriate cultures and specimens should be obtained as early as possible, followed by aggressive antibiotic, antifungal, or antiviral treatment.

Dental treatment for this patient population is preventive. Careful and frequent monitoring of oral health status is recommended. Early dental evaluation, including radiographs, assessment of oral hygiene, and elimination of all foci of infection, is very important. Prophylactic antibiotic therapy may be indicated, depending on the patient's immune status, the procedure planned, and the risk of bacteremia. The prophylactic use of chlorhexidine mouth rinses during chemotherapy significantly reduces the incidence of mucositis, candidiasis, and herpes gingivostomatitis.[28]

Dental Care for Patients Receiving Radiation Therapy

Possible complications of dental care for patients receiving radiation therapy to the head and neck regions include:

Xerostomia. This condition is associated with reduced flow and increased viscosity of saliva. Xerostomia can be demonstrated in as little as 2 weeks after the initiation of radiation therapy. The buffering effects of saliva are reduced, while plaque adherence and activity is significantly increased, resulting in rapid caries destruction of the teeth.

Infection. A change in oral microflora occurs with potential increases in opportunistic microorganisms such as *Candida albicans* and the herpes viruses. Should an infection occur, appropriate culture and sensitivity tests should be obtained and appropriate treatment administered.

Osteoradionecrosis. This is the most serious potential side effect of radiation therapy, with morbidity increasing with both age and cumulative doses of radiation. Infected teeth should be extracted *prior* to irradiation.[14] If dental surgery is necessary after radiation therapy, aggressive intravenous antibiotic prophylaxis, followed by high doses of oral antibiotics after discharge, is indicated. The mandible is more prone to osteomyelitis than the maxilla.

Loss of Taste. This complication is usually transient, with taste sensation returning in most cases in less than 1 year.

All patients who are scheduled for radiation therapy of the head and neck should undergo a dental examination and have all necessary dental care completed; they should begin a strict oral hygiene regimen prior to the initiation of radiotherapy. Flouride mouth rinses are indicated for daily use to combat the effects of xerostomia.[39]

SELECTED READINGS

McDonald RE, Avery DR (eds). Dentistry for the Child and Adolescent, 7th ed. St Louis, Mosby-Year Book, 1999.

Pinkham JR, et al. (eds). Pediatric Dentistry: Infancy Through Adolescence, 3rd ed. Philadelphia, WB Saunders, 1999.

REFERENCES

1. Aderhold L, et al. The bacteriology of denogenous pyogenic infections. Oral Surg 52:583, 1981.
2. Aguilo L, Gandia JL. Dentigerous cyst of mandibular second premolar in a five-year-old girl, related to a non-vital primary molar removed one year earlier: a case report. J Clin Pediatr Dent 22:155, 1998.
3. Balit HL. Dental variation among populations. An anthropologic view. Dent Clin North Am 19:125, 1975.
4. Barclay S, Thomason JM, Seymour RA. The incidence and severity of nifedipine-induced gingival overgrowth. J Clin Periodontol 19:311, 1992.
5. Bhaskar SN, Jacoway JR. Pyogenic granuloma—clinical features, incidence, histology, and result of treatment: report of 242 cases. J Oral Surg 24:391, 1966.
6. Blakey GH, White RP, Offenbacher S, et al. Clinical/biological outcomes of treatment for pericoronitis. J Oral Maxillofac Surg 54:1150, 1996.
7. Bodin I, Julin P, Thomsson M. Hyperdontia. I. Frequency and distribution of supernumerary teeth among 21,609 patients. Dentomaxillofac Radiol 7:15, 1978.
8. Buchner A, Hansen LS. The histomorphologic spectrum of peripheral ossifying fibroma. Oral Surg Oral Med Oral Pathol 63:452, 1987.
9. Butler RT, Kalkwarf KL, Kaldahl WB. Drug induced gingival hyperplasia: phenytoin, cyclosporine, and nifedipine. J Am Dent Assoc 114:56, 1987
10. Brannon RB. The odontogenic keratocyst: a clinicopathologic study of 312 cases. Oral Surg Oral Med Oral Path 47:54, 1976.
11. Chiappinelli JA, Walton RE. Tooth discoloration resulting from long-term tetracycline therapy: a case report. Quintessence Int 23:539, 1992.
12. Ciancio SG. Agents for the management of plaque and gingivitis. J Dent Res 71:1450, 1992.
13. Collins MA, Mauriello SM, Tyndall DA, et al. Dental anomalies in amelogenesis imperfecta: a radiographic assessment. Oral Surg Oral Med Oral Pathol Oral Radiol Endod 88:358, 1999.
14. Dick V, et al. Osteomyelitis in infants and children. Am J Dis Child 129:1273, 1975.
15. Dodson TB, et al. Pediatric maxillofacial infections: a retrospective study of 113 patients. J Oral Maxillofac Surg 47:327, 1989.
16. Gorlin RJ, Cohen MM, Levine S. Syndromes of the Head and Neck, 4th ed. Oxford, Oxford University Press, 1994.
17. Hartnett AC, Shiloah J. The treatment of acute necrotizing ulcerative gingivitis. Quintessence Int 22:95, 1991.

18. Ingnelzi MA. Clinical Update: Developmental Anomalies and Pathology in Children. Ann Arbor, University of Michigan Press, 2000.

19. Johnson BD, Engel D. Acute necrotizing ulcerative gingivitis: a review of diagnosis, etiology, and treatment. J Periodontol 57:141, 1986.

20. Johnson L, Sapp JP, McIntyre DN. Squamous cell carcinoma arising in a dentigerous cyst. J Oral Maxillofac Surg 52:987, 1994.

21. Kenney JN, Kaugers GE, Abbey LM. Comparison between the peripheral ossifying fibroma and peripheral odontogenic fibroma. J Oral Maxillofac Surg 47:378, 1989.

22. King DL. Teething revisited. Pediatr Dent 16:179, 1994.

23. King DL, Steinhauer W, Garcia-Godoy F, Elkins CJ. Herpetic gingivostomatitis and teething difficulty in infants. Pediatr Dent 14:82, 1992.

24. Kleinman DV, Swango PA, Pindborg JJ. Epidemiology of oral mucosal lesions in United States schoolchildren 1986–87. Commun Dent Oral Epidemiol 22:243, 1994.

25. Lack EE, et al. Gingival granular cell tumors of the newborn (congenital "epulis"): a clinical and pathologic study of 21 patients. Am J Surg Pathol 5:37, 1981.

26. Levitas TC. Gemination, fusion, twinning, and concrescence. J Dent Child 32:93, 1965.

27. Lindhe J, Liljenberg B. Treatment of localized juvenile periodontitis: results after 5 years. J Clin Periodontol 11:399, 1984.

28. Lindquist SF. Dental management for the cancer chemotherapy patient. Cancer Bull 29:79, 1977.

29. Loesche WJ, et al. The bacteriology of acute necrotizing ulcerative gingivitis. J Periodontol 53:223, 1982.

30. Lunt RC, Law DB. A review of the chronology of calcification of deciduous teeth. J Am Dent Assoc 89:872, 1974.

31. Meon R. Hypodontia of the primary and permanent dentition. J Clin Pediatr Dent 16:121, 1992.

32. Meurman JH, Rajasuo A, Murtomaa H, Savolainen S. Respiratory tract infections and concomitant pericoronitis of the wisdom teeth. BMJ 310:834, 1995.

33. Myounr H, et al. Odontogenic keratocyst: review of 256 cases for recurrence and clinicopathologic parameters. Oral Surg Oral Med Oral Pathol Oral Radiol Endod 91:328, 2001.

34. Neissen LC. Pericoronitis as a cause of tonsillitis. Lancet 348:1602, 1996.

35. O'Brien FV, Pielou WD. Congenital epulis: its natural history. Arch Dis Child 46:559, 1971.

36. Olson JW, et al. Odontogenic carcinoma occurring in a dentigerous cyst: case report and clinical management. J Periodontol 71:1365, 2000.

37. Sider H (ed). Orban's Oral Histology and Embryology, 5th ed. St Louis, CV Mosby, 1966.

38. Rees JS, Midda M. Update on periodontology. I. Current concepts in the histopathology of periodontal disease. Dent Update 18:418, 1991.

39. Reynolds WR, et al. Dental management of the cancer patient receiving radiation therapy. Clin Prev Dent 2:5, 1980.

40. Riviere GR, et al. Identification of spirochetes related to *Treponema pallidum* in necrotizing ulcerative gingivitis and chronic periodontitis. N Engl J Med 325:539, 1991.

41. Rushton MA. Hereditary or idiopathic hyperplasia of the gums. Dent Pract Dent Rec 7:136, 1957.

42. Sapp JP, Eversole LR, Wysocki GP. Contemporary Oral and Maxillofacial Pathology, 1st ed. St Louis, CV Mosby, 1997.

43. Seow WK. Biological mechanisms of early childhood caries. Commun Dent Oral Epidemiol 26:8, 1998.

44. Seow WK. Clinical diagnosis and management strategies of amelogenesis imperfecta variants. Pediatr Dent 15:384, 1993.

45. Seow WK. Enamel hypoplasia in the primary dentition: a review. J Dent Child 58:441, 1991.

46. Stamm JW. Epidemiology of gingivitis. J Clin Periodontol 13:360, 1986.

47. Travis RT, Steinle CJ. The effects of odontogenic infection on the complete blood count in children and adolescents. Pediatr Dent 6:214, 1984.

48. Unkle JH, et al. Comparison of odontogenic and non-odontogenic facial cellulites in a pediatric hospital population. Pediatr Dent 19:476, 1997.

49. Vilmann A, Villmann P, Villmann H. Pyogenic granuloma: evaluation of oral conditions. Br J Oral Maxillofac Surg 24:376, 1986.

50. Watanabe K. Prepubertal periodontitis: a review of diagnostic criteria, pathogenesis, and differential diagnosis. J Periodont Res 25:31, 1990.

51. Witkop CJ. Amelogenesis imperfecta, dentinogenesis imperfecta, and dentin dysplasia revisited, problems in classification. J Oral Pathol 17:547, 1988.

52. Wright JT. Normal formation and developmental defects of human dentition. Pediatr Clin North Am 47:975, 2000.

53. Yusof WZ. Non-syndrome multiple supernumerary teeth. Literature review. J Can Dent Assoc 56:147, 1990.

54. Zain RB, Fei YJ. Fibrous lesions of the gingiva: a histopathologic analysis of 204 cases. Oral Surg Oral Med Oral Pathol 70:466, 1990.

59

Orthodontic Problems in Children

L'Tanya J. Bailey, D.D.S., M.S., Carroll-Ann Trotman, B.D.S., M.A., M.S., and
Donald W. Warren, D.D.S., M.S., Ph.D.

Growth of the Craniofacial Complex

The face of the infant is normally wide and short and, proportionally, the cranium is larger than the face. With continued growth, the middle portion of the face grows more rapidly, and the characteristics of the adult face become more apparent. According to Hellman,[15] the contrast between the infant face and the adult face is due to the growing of various parts at different rates at different times. Under the influence of genetic and environmental factors, growth is generally completed first in the depth of the face, then in the width of the face, and finally in the vertical length of the face (see Chaps. 1 and 2).

Contrasting Theories of Growth

Two basic types of bony movements appear to be involved in craniofacial growth. One is *deposition and resorption* on the surface of bones, which produces cortical drift and typically results in overall enlargement as well as remodeling.[12] The other involves *displacement*, or *translation*, of contiguous bones growing away from each other. As groups of bones enlarge, each becomes repositioned as a unit away from the others as all continue to grow and remodel by deposition and resorption.

Certain regions, such as the synchondroses of the cranial base and the nasal septal cartilage, are often considered to be sites of special importance in determining total skull growth. These regions are assumed to function as growth centers to regulate the rate and the amount of growth occurring at sites elsewhere.[35] The remodeling processes are considered to be secondary to growth at the centers. This view of skull growth emphasizes that intrinsic growth factors are present in the cartilage. Sutural growth is secondary and is influenced by synchondrosis proliferation. In contrast, the traditional theory of Sicher[40] suggests that intrinsic genetic factors are most important in skull growth, and modeling changes occur secondary to the influences of function and environmental factors.

A popular theory proposed by Moss[32] is that all growth of bone is secondary and that growth changes in bone reflect the growth and function of the tissue systems associated with the bones. These tissue systems are called *functional unit matrices*, and Moss distinguishes periosteal from capsular matrices: periosteal matrices include muscles and teeth, whereas capsular matrices include the volumes enclosed within the skull.

Enlow[12] has concluded that none of the previous theories of the control of bone growth were entirely satisfactory and that Limborgh's synthesis[24] of the major theories is presently the most accurate to explain growth of the craniofacial complex. His synthesis is as follows:

1. Chondrocranial growth is controlled mainly by intrinsic genetic factors.
2. Desmocranial (intramembranous) growth is controlled by only a few intrinsic genetic factors.
3. Growing skull cartilages are growth centers.
4. Sutural growth is controlled mainly by influences originating from the skull cartilages and from other adjacent head structures.
5. Periosteal growth is controlled mainly by influences originating from adjacent head structures.
6. Sutural and periosteal growth are additionally governed by local, nongenetic, and environmental influences and muscle forces inclusive.

Proffit and Ackerman[35] have stressed that, in deference to this synthesis, mandibular condylar cartilage growth is controlled largely by local, nongenetic environmental influences.

The Cranial Base

Growth of the cranial base occurs through sutural growth, elongation at the synchondroses, and direct cortical drift and remodeling. This combination of factors enables growth of the contours of the cranial base and maintains the housing for vessels and nerves. Growth occurs at the spheno-occipital, intersphenoid, and sphenoethmoidal synchondroses. Cartilage growth at these synchondroses primarily follows the neural growth curve (Fig. 59–1).

The spheno-occipital synchondrosis has traditionally been regarded as a region of major growth in the cranial base during the postnatal period. This synchondrosis ossifies at 13 to 16 years in boys and at 11 to 14 years in girls. Activity of the other synchondroses disappears either at birth or shortly thereafter.

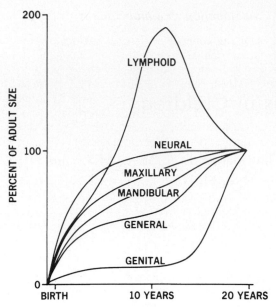

FIGURE 59–1. Differential growth rate for different body tissues. The mandible follows the general growth curve, and the neurocranium follows the neural growth curve. The maxilla falls between the general and neural curves. (Modified from Scammon RE. The Measurement of Man. Minneapolis, University of Minnesota Press.)

The Cranial Vault

The cranial vault grows primarily by proliferation and ossification at the sutural surfaces in conjunction with relatively small surface deposits on the ectocranial surfaces. More than 90% of calvaria development is achieved by the fifth year of life. Cranial vault growth is directly influenced by the developing brain.

The Maxilla

The developing facial skeleton is influenced by the growing cranial base and is translated downward and forward in relation to it. The maxilla actually grows in a variety of directions (Fig. 59–2). Addition of bone to the orbital surfaces and the supramaxillary sutures provides downward movement, and additions at the maxillary tuberosity provide forward displacement. Thus, the maxilla is *relocated,* or *translated,* as well as enlarged by the growth processes. Connective tissue proliferation with ossification at the sutural surfaces, apposition and resorption at other bony surfaces, and translation are the mechanisms for maxillary growth. The growth curve of the maxilla primarily follows the neural growth curve but is temporally behind (see Fig. 59–1). The nasomaxillary region expands in a forward and downward direction by interstitial growth of the cartilaginous nasal septum.

The Mandible

The mandible appears to grow in a similar forward and downward manner, but growth actually takes place in a number of directions. Although some growth occurs on the superior and inferior borders of the mandible, vertical

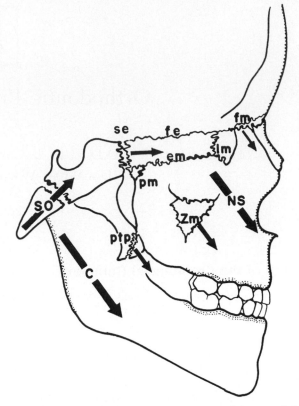

FIGURE 59–2. Growth directions of the cranial base and facial sutures during the first decade of life. Surface apposition and resorption are shown by the stippled area. SO, spheno-occipital synchondrosis growth; C, direction of translation of the mandible due to condylar growth; NS, nasal septum growth; se, sphenoethmoidal suture; fe, frontoethmoidal suture; fm, frontomaxillary suture; lm, lacrimofrontal suture; em, ethmoidomaxillary suture; pm, palatomaxillary suture; ptp, pterygopalatine suture; Zm, zygomaticomaxillary suture. (From Cohen SE. Growth and class II treatment. Am J Orthod 52:5–26, 1966.)

growth of the mandible is determined to a great extent by the growing mandibular condyle. Condylar growth is generally superior and posterior, which translates the mandible in an anteroinferior direction. The posterior vertical portion of the mandible is subjected to resorption on its anterior border and to deposition on its posterior border. This pattern of resorption and deposition lengthens the mandible. The changes in mandibular position ideally complement the changes occurring simultaneously in the maxilla. The growth curve of the mandible approximates both the general and neural growth curves (see Fig. 59–1).

Introduction to Orthodontic Concepts

Definition of Orthodontics

Orthodontics is a specialty of dentistry that is concerned with the supervision, guidance, and correction of the growing or mature dentofacial structures. Orthodontic treatment may be required for conditions that require the movement of teeth, the correction of malrelationships of teeth and their related structures, and the adjustment of

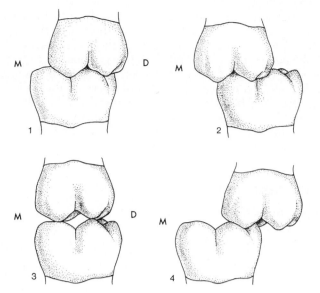

FIGURE 59–3. Angle's classifications of molar occlusion. M, mesial, the side of the tooth toward the midline following the curve of the dental arch; D, distal, away from the midline following the curve of the dental arch. 1, Class I; 2, Class II; 3, end to end; 4, Class III.

relationships among teeth and facial bones by the application of forces or the stimulation and redirection of functional forces within the craniofacial complex. Orthodontic therapy may involve orthopedic appliances, early guidance of tooth eruption, repositioning of teeth for function and aesthetics, and management of orthognathic surgical cases and temporomandibular joint problems.

The Goal of Orthodontic Treatment

The goal of orthodontic treatment is to position the teeth and jaws so as to obtain for each patient the optimal combination of masticatory function and dentofacial aesthetics. The concept of *optimal combination* is important, because it is not always possible to obtain both ideal function and ideal aesthetics for every patient. Thus, a relationship between the maxillary and mandibular teeth as they are brought into functional contact (the occlusion of the teeth) that is ideal is not always a treatment possibility and seldom occurs naturally.[21]

A second concept fundamental to an understanding of orthodontics is the differentiation between normal occlusion and abnormal occlusion, or malocclusion. Graber[13] states, "Normal in physiology is always a range, never a point." Normal occlusion and malocclusion should not be thought of as being opposite ends of a spectrum, but rather as overlapping frequency distributions. Malocclusion represents a range of normal human variation and should be used to describe only occlusal problems that could benefit from correction. Normal occlusion, while not necessarily ideal, requires no orthodontic treatment to improve function or aesthetics. Assessment of the variables that determine the need for orthodontic treatment is the essence of orthodontic diagnosis and is considered in subsequent sections.

The Classification of Malocclusion

Implicit in the concept of optimal masticatory function is the need to evaluate the teeth from a dynamic viewpoint, because the teeth function within the entire craniofacial system. Indeed, such an evaluation must be made in order to diagnose and properly treat any orthodontic problem. However, for simplicity in describing various types of malocclusions and for ease of communication among professionals, static descriptions are useful.

The most commonly used system of classification in orthodontics was devised by Edward Angle[4] at the beginning of the 20th century. Angle based his various classifications on the occlusal relationship between the maxillary and the mandibular first permanent molars. He defined three general classifications, class I, class II, and class III, which are shown in Figure 59–3.

Class I

Normal, or Angle class I, occlusion is defined as the relationship in which the mesial (side of the tooth toward the anterior dental midline following the curve of the dental arch) lateral (buccal, or toward the cheeks) projection (cusp) of the maxillary first permanent molar articulates in the mesial buccal groove of the mandibular first permanent molar (see Fig. 59–3, 1). If these teeth are in a class I relationship and all the other teeth are present, aligned with proper contacts, and of the proper size relationships, an ideal occlusion results.

Class II

Angle class II, or distocclusion, is defined as occurring when the mesial buccal groove of the mandibular first molar is posterior (distal, or away from the anterior dental midline) to the mesial buccal cusp of the maxillary first molar (see Fig. 59–3, 2). This posterior positioning of the mandibular first molar relative to the corresponding maxillary molar may be the result of any combination of maxillary skeletal or dental protrusion, or mandibular skeletal or dental retrusion.

Because there are several types of skeletal or dental displacement possibilities in a class II relationship, these cases are further subdivided into division 1 or 2. In a class II division 1 malocclusion, the molar teeth are in a class II relationship while the maxillary incisors are projected forward in a protrusive position (Fig. 59–4). This is the classic "bucktooth" appearance, which frequently demonstrates spacing between the maxillary incisors and an increased vertical overlap of the teeth (overbite) (Fig. 59–5).

In a class II division 2 malocclusion, the molar teeth are in a class II relationship, but the two maxillary middle (central) incisors are tipped posteriorly, usually contacting the mandibular incisors (Fig. 59–6). The adjacent maxillary lateral incisors often protrude and may appear to wrap around or "across" the maxillary central incisors. The mandibular incisors are usually very vertical, and the anterior overbite is usually excessive.

As seen in Figure 59–3, 3, the permanent first molars

may occlude in a position that is actually halfway between the class I and class II relationship; this is termed an *end-to-end relationship*. In children who have not yet lost (the mixed dentition stage of dental development) the primary ("baby") molar teeth, this relationship is normal. End-to-end molar occlusion is not normal in the permanent dentition and may be considered a less severe form of a class II malocclusion.

Class III

Angle class III, or mesiocclusion, occurs when the mesial buccal groove of the mandibular first molar is anterior to the mesial buccal cusp of the maxillary first molar (see Fig. 59–3, 4). In this situation, the mandibular incisors are usually forward of the maxillary incisors, and anterior crossbite or reverse overjet (see Fig. 59–5) results (Fig. 59–7). A class III malocclusion may be the result of any combination of maxillary skeletal or dental retrusion, or mandibular skeletal or dental protrusion.

The Classification of Skeletal Types and Patterns of Growth

When he devised his classification system, Angle assumed that the maxillary arch and the teeth within it were relatively stable in relation to the cranium. By relating the teeth to each other, he intended also to relate the maxilla to the mandible. Angle's assumptions are not always true, and variations in the positions of the jaws or positions of individual teeth within either jaw may occur. However, it is true that teeth generally reflect underlying skeletal relationships. For this reason, orthodontists have extended Angle classification beyond the dental arch to cover the skeletal relationship. Thus, two distinct classification schemes have resulted, Angle's dental classification (described earlier) and Angle's skeletal classification. In the skeletal classification, a patient with mandibular protrusion may be said to have a class III skeletal relationship. The Angle classification also may be extended to describe the pattern of growth by which any skeletal relationship develops, for example, a "class III growth pattern."

Orthodontic Diagnosis and Treatment Planning

Diagnosis and treatment planning depend on the accumulation of adequate diagnostic data from which to generate a problem list and treatment solutions. The Angle system is simple and well accepted but it is incomplete. It fails to consider dental and skeletal relationships in the transverse and vertical planes of space, considering only the anteroposterior (sagittal) plane. In addition, it does not consider how the relationship of the teeth to the face affects facial aesthetics.

Proffit and Ackerman[1, 35] have proposed a method of assessing and classifying malocclusions by which characteristics and their interrelationships are systematically evaluated. Using their method, the clinician can ascertain that all relevant factors are considered, with as little complication as possible.

In general, one should examine and describe the alignment and symmetry of the teeth in their respective jaws (the dental arches). Next, facial aesthetics, especially the influence of the teeth and the chin position on the profile, is assessed. Finally, the teeth are evaluated as they relate to each other and are described in the three planes of space (sagittal, transverse, and vertical), and a differentiation between skeletal and dental problems is made. In the following sections, analyses of these parameters will be discussed.

Alignment Analysis

First, the alignment and symmetry of the dental arches are evaluated by quantifying the presence of crowding or spacing of the teeth and by describing individually any severely malpositioned teeth. Usually, the question is whether there is enough space to accommodate all the teeth. The amount of crowding in the permanent dentition can be determined by measuring and comparing the size of the teeth with the space available. During the time the primary teeth are being lost and replaced by the permanent teeth (the mixed dentition stage of dental development), methods exist to estimate the size of the unerupted teeth.[17, 33, 34] In either case, a millimeter measurement of the amount of space deficiency or excess is determined.

Facial Form Analysis

Analysis in the Sagittal Plane

The second step in the systematic description is to assess the patient's facial aesthetics, giving attention to a description of both profile and full frontal view characteristics. The judgments desired in profile analysis are the same as those desired from an analysis of a lateral cephalometric radiograph. The relationships among the various parts of the face are determined.

The patient should be examined with his or her head held in the natural head position.[30] A patient naturally assumes this position when standing relaxed and looking off at the horizon or into his or her own eyes in a mirror. Ideal facial proportions are illustrated in Figure 59–8 and serve as a model with which to compare any particular patient.

In profile analysis, it is helpful for the clinician to form a mental image of the patient's face and imagine dividing the face into five separate anatomic units, as illustrated in the schematic face in Figure 59–9. In the ideal face, the cranium and the cranial base (see Fig. 59–9, 1), the skeletal maxilla (see Fig. 59–9, 2), the maxillary teeth (see Fig. 59–9, 3), the mandibular teeth (see Fig. 59–9, 4), and the skeletal mandible (see Fig. 59–9, 5) all line up in a relatively straight line. The analysis can then concentrate on the relationships of these five anatomic segments and can describe any deviation of any segment.

In particular, in profile analysis, three areas of special focus are important: (1) the anteroposterior position of the chin, (2) the degree of lip protrusion, and (3) the vertical height of the anterior face, especially the lower

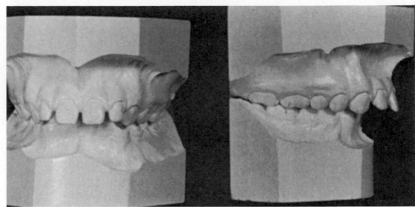

FIGURE 59–4. Study models of a patient with a Class II Division 1 malocclusion. The teeth are in a Class II relationship, and the maxillary incisors are flared forward and spaced. Overeruption of the mandibular incisors results in increased vertical overlap of the teeth.

OVERJET   OVERBITE   OPEN BITE

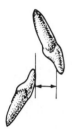

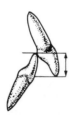

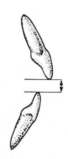

FIGURE 59–5. Schematic illustration of the terms overjet, overbite, and open bite. Overjet is the horizontal projection of the maxillary incisors in front of the mandibular incisors. Overbite is the extent to which the maxillary anterior teeth overlap the mandibular in a vertical direction. Open bite is the vertical distance between the maxillary and mandibular incisors when they do not overlap.

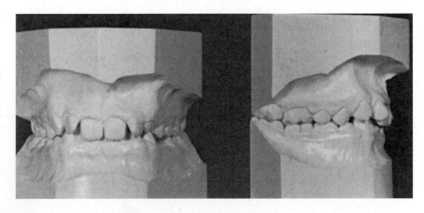

FIGURE 59–6. Study models of a patient with a Class II Division 2 malocclusion. The molars are in an end-to-end relationship, the maxillary central incisors are tipped palatally, and the maxillary lateral incisors protrude facially. Overeruption of the mandibular incisors results in a deep anterior overbite.

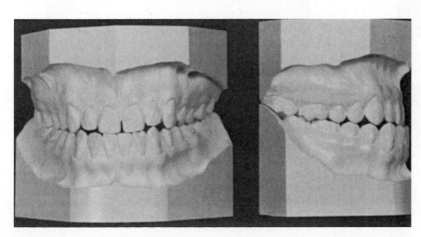

FIGURE 59–7. Study models of a patient with a Class III malocclusion. The teeth are in a Class III relationship, and an anterior crossbite exists.

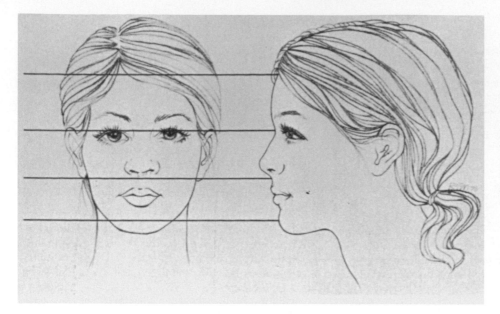

FIGURE 59–8. Full-face and profile views of ideal facial proportions. The face is divided into equal thirds vertically, and all facial features are in good proportion and balance.

third. The judgments required in determining the anteroposterior position of the chin are those involved in relating the chin to a vertical reference line, as illustrated in Figure 59–10. If one mentally projects such a reference line (a line perpendicular to the Frankfort horizontal from the soft tissue nasion) onto the patient's face, the relationships of the profile points become clear (see Fig. 59–10). Variations in the direction and degree of the maxilla, the mandible, and the teeth of either jaw are noted. Only by separating the face into its five basic units can these differential judgments be made.

Since the soft tissue thickness tends to be relatively constant over the face, lip contour (and especially the degree of lip protrusion) tends to reflect the support provided by the incisor teeth. Specifically, teeth that are positioned forward in the face cause increased lip protrusion, while those positioned more posteriorly offer less support and consequently a more retruded lip profile.

The amount of lip protrusion that is desirable is affected by definite racial and ethnic considerations: for instance, blacks and Asians normally show a greater degree of protrusion in comparison with whites.[2, 3] For pa-

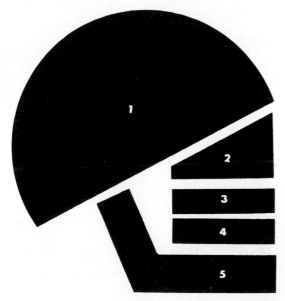

FIGURE 59–9. Schematic illustration of an ideal arrangement of the dentofacial and craniofacial structures. In the ideal face the cranium and cranial base (1), skeletal maxilla (2), maxillary teeth (3), mandibular teeth (4), and skeletal mandible (5) all align in a relatively straight line.

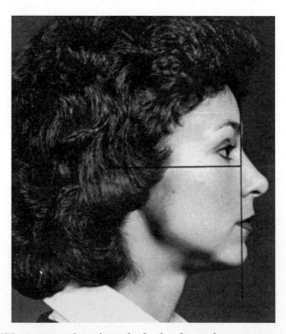

FIGURE 59–10. Clinical method of judging the anteroposterior position of the mandible. The chin should fall approximately on a vertical line drawn from the soft tissue nasion perpendicular to the Frankfort horizontal (ear-eye plane).

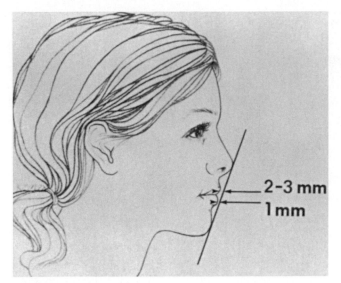

FIGURE 59–11. Ideal position of the lips relative to the chin and the nose.

tients of northern European ancestry, a good guide for judging lip position is the esthetic, or *e,* line illustrated in Figure 59–11.[37]

The e line, which extends from the tip of the nose to the most anterior point of the chin, describes the acceptable anterior limits of the lips in profile. By mentally projecting this line onto the patient's face, one can determine lip position. Ideally, the lower lip position should range from being on the line to being 1 mm behind it. The upper lip should be approximately 2 to 3 mm behind the line. Proffit and Ackerman[1, 35] suggest that lip posture and incisor prominence should be evaluated by viewing the patient's profile with the lips relaxed. They recommend the visual construction of a true vertical line passing through the concavity at the base of the upper lip and relating the upper lip to this line. A second true vertical line passes through the concavity between the base of the lower lip and chin to evaluate lower lip protrusion. If the lip is significantly forward of this line, it is judged to be prominent, and if it is behind this line, it is retrusive. Incompetent lips are separated by a distance of 3 to 4 mm at rest.

In an ideally proportioned face, the profile can be divided into approximately equal vertical thirds (see Fig. 59–8). The upper third, from the hairline to the bridge of the nose between the eyes (soft tissue nasion), is variable with the hairline and not subject to orthodontic modification. The middle third extends from the soft tissue nasion to directly under the nose (anterior nasal spine) and can be affected by orthodontic treatment, although it is not the area at which treatment is primarily directed. The lower third, from the anterior nasal spine to the chin, contains the alveolar-dental structures and is the area most affected by orthodontic treatment. Consequently, the vertical deviations most significant to orthodontics are seen in the lower third and should be noted

as an increase or a decrease in facial height. This is evaluated clinically by examining the angle formed by the lower border of the mandible (the mandibular plane) and the true horizontal. This angle is referred to as the *mandibular plane angle.* An increase in this angle correlates with a steep mandibular plane and long anterior facial height, which often accompanies an anterior open bite malocclusion (see Fig. 59–5). Conversely, a decrease in the mandibular plane angle is associated with a flat mandibular plane and deep bite malocclusion.[35] Such deviations influence anteroposterior relationships of the teeth and the jaws, as well as the amount of overbite or open bite. Cephalometric radiographic analysis may be used to quantitate any vertical discrepancy observed. Although orthodontists have typically placed more emphasis on profile analysis, analysis of facial proportions from a full frontal view is equally important. Without special effort, patients do not see themselves from a profile view; however, they are usually very aware of their appearance in a full-face view.

Analysis in the Frontal Plane

The analysis of full-face frontal aesthetics takes into account relationships and proportions in the vertical and transverse planes. In the frontal plane, the ideal face can again be divided into approximately equal thirds, just as was done in the profile analysis (see Fig. 59–8). Deviations in vertical balance should be noted and should agree with the assessment made in the profile analysis. A second important vertical determination to make is the relationship of the maxillary incisors to the upper lip. Normally, about 2 mm of the maxillary incisor teeth may be exposed with the lips slightly apart. In a full smile, all of the incisor's crown is exposed, along with perhaps a millimeter or two of gingiva. Variations in the amount of maxillary incisor displayed, whether excessive or deficient, are noted. Excessive vertical exposure of the maxillary incisors at rest, or of the teeth and gingival tissue during a smile, usually results in an unaesthetic appearance and smile line. This increased incisor display at rest or in function may result from an excessively large vertical dimension of the maxilla, a short upper lip, or a very mobile upper lip. The clinician must evaluate and determine the cause of the abnormal incisor display. Prominence of the maxillary incisors resulting from horizontal maxillary excess and its relative impact upon facial aesthetics also must be assessed.

Another important determination to be made from the frontal plane is transverse or left-right symmetry. The bridge of the nose, tip of the nose, philtrum of the upper lip, center of the lower lip, and center of the chin all should lie on the same vertical line. Assessment of transverse symmetry is concerned with describing any deviation of any of these facial features from this vertical reference line. If a mandibular asymmetry is noted, it must be determined whether a true skeletal asymmetry exists or whether the patient is merely shifting the mandible to one side while closing the teeth together. In the case of a shift, the face appears more symmetric when the mandible is slightly depressed and the teeth are apart.

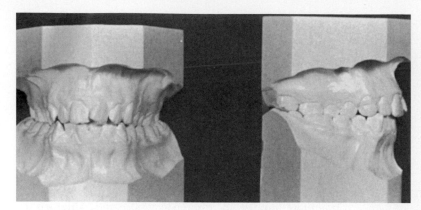

FIGURE 59–12. Study models of a patient illustrating a bilateral posterior crossbite. Note that the maxillary posterior teeth are positioned palatally and occlude inside the mandibular posterior teeth.

Occlusal Analysis

Analysis in the Sagittal Plane

The Angle classification of occlusion is used to describe the dental arches with regard to the sagittal plane of space. In addition, a determination of whether the problem is skeletal, dental, or a combination of skeletal and dental is made. Information gained from the profile analysis aids in this skeletal-dental differentiation.

Analysis in the Frontal Plane

Just as with the profile analysis, occlusal analysis must take into account relationships in both the vertical and the transverse planes. When the dental arches are viewed with regard to the vertical plane of space (see Fig. 59–5), the vertical overlapping of the teeth, especially the incisors, is referred to as *overbite*. The overbite is frequently quantitated as the percentage of the crown height of the lower incisor that is overlapped by the upper incisors. A normal degree of overbite may include an overlap that covers up to one third of the crown of the mandibular incisors. A complete lack of any vertical overlap of the incisors, termed an *open bite* (see Fig. 59–5), is not considered to be normal occlusion.

Abnormalities of the dental arches with respect to the transverse plane of space are referred to as posterior crossbites. Normally, the lateral (buccal) surfaces of the maxillary posterior teeth lie outside the corresponding surfaces of the mandibular posterior teeth. When the mandibular teeth are in the buccal, or outside, position, a posterior crossbite exists (Fig. 59–12). In addition, the situation in which the medial (palatal) surface of a maxillary tooth lies outside the buccal surface of a mandibular tooth is also termed a crossbite (or sometimes a "scissor bite").

Crossbites may be caused by any combination of maxillary or mandibular skeletal or dental deviations and may be either a unilateral or a bilateral problem. Crossbites may involve a single tooth, groups of teeth, or the entire dental arch. Frequently, crossbites can cause a lateral deviation of the mandible as the patient shifts to a more comfortable biting position, which is termed a *convenience bite*. A diagnosis pinpointing the cause of the crossbite and differentiating between the skeletal and dental causes is necessary for treatment.

Cephalometric Analysis

A cephalometric radiograph is actually a lateral skull radiograph obtained under highly standardized conditions. The distance from the radiographic source to the patient's midsagittal plane is 5 ft. The midsagittal plane is positioned parallel to and 11 cm from the film. Finally, the patient's head is positioned so that his or her Frankfort horizontal plane (ear-eye plane) is oriented parallel to the floor. Worldwide use of this standard technique permits comparison of cephalometric films with reasonable accuracy.

Cephalometric analyses are used to assess and compare the size and positional relationships of the various components of the craniofacial and dentofacial complexes. These comparisons may be used as an aid in treatment planning by describing a patient's skeletal and dental relationships at one point in time. In addition, by using serial cephalometric films, one can determine the magnitude and direction of any dentofacial changes resulting from growth over a period of time. Finally, serial cephalometric films can be used to evaluate changes in the positions of the jaws or teeth as a response to treatment.

Basically, cephalometric analyses are used to make either linear or angular measurements and comparisons between the following six relationships, in both the vertical and the sagittal planes of space: (1) maxilla to cranial base, (2) mandible to cranial base, (3) maxilla to mandible, (4) maxillary dentition to maxilla, (5) mandibular dentition to mandible, and (6) maxillary dentition to mandibular dentition.

Numerous cephalometric analyses have been devised to assess these relationships,[11, 31, 38, 42, 43] and compilations of mean cephalometric values have been published.[39]

When to Refer Children for Orthodontic Treatment

Health professionals working with children are frequently asked, "When is the best time to refer a child for orthodontic treatment?" The recommended age is 7 years. Because there is such variation among patients and problems, this age should not be viewed as a definite rule. Therefore, as soon as a problem is identified, no matter what age, the child should be referred for evaluation. It is generally agreed to be appropriate, in the absence of obvious problems, to see most patients for an initial examination after the eruption of the permanent incisor teeth—at approximately 7 to 8 years of age. No treatment may be indicated at this early age, but referral allows the orthodontist the opportunity to make the decision concerning proper treatment sequencing and timing.

Functional problems, such as a mandibular deviation caused by a posterior crossbite, generally are treated as soon as they are recognized. Similarly, problems involving skeletal growth discrepancies are frequently treated at earlier ages, because treatment may involve growth redirection and guidance with orthopedic forces. Most Angle class II or class III problems involve some element of skeletal discrepancy and should be referred early.

In children in the primary dentition stage of dental development, little orthodontic treatment is usually appropriate except for the maintenance of space for prematurely lost or missing primary teeth (space maintenance) and the elimination of functional problems. In the mixed-dentition stage, correction of functional problems and space maintenance are again indicated. In addition, treatment to correct skeletal discrepancies may begin in the late mixed-dentition stage: ages 8 to 11 years.

Most orthodontic treatment cannot be completed until all the permanent teeth erupt. Treatment should begin earlier only when such early treatment will eliminate a problem entirely or else significantly reduce its severity, allowing better and faster final correction later on.

Airway Obstruction and Malocclusion

Many attempts have been made to establish a causal relationship between dentofacial deformities and nasal airway inadequacy.[49, 57] The most prevalent view has been that mouth breathing resulting from an inadequate nasal airway is often associated with such deformities as retrognathic mandible, protruding maxillary anterior teeth, high palatal vault, constricted V-shaped maxillary arch, flaccid and short upper lip, flaccid perioral musculature, and a somewhat dull appearance due to a constant, open-mouthed posture.

Angle,[4] in a statement concerning class II division 1 malocclusion, noted that "this form of malocclusion is always accompanied and, at least in its early stages, aggravated, if indeed not caused, by mouth breathing due to some form of nasal obstructions." Allergists have expressed similar views in their concern for the allergic rhinitis patient and for the patients with enlarged adenoids.[28] Mouth breathing is a common finding in these patients, and there are reports of protruding maxillary anterior teeth or a constricted maxillary arch as well as other dental deformities. However, Hunter[18] did not find a relationship between allergic rhinitis and malocclusion. His data did demonstrate that the frequency of mouth breathing increases as nasal airway resistance increases. Eighty-three percent of his allergic subjects were classified as mouth breathers.

Several investigators[25, 26, 47] have described a special facial type as characteristic of persons with enlarged adenoids, mouth breathing, or both. Generally referred to as *adenoid facies,* this facial type reportedly is marked by a long, narrow face with pinched nostrils, a short upper lip, prominent maxillary incisors, and a lips-apart posture (see Chap. 61).

Joshi[20] suggested that dropping the mandible during mouth breathing may produce an exaggerated distal relationship between the mandible and maxilla by allowing overdevelopment of maxillary posterior alveolar processes. Moffatt[29] related protrusion of the maxillary incisors to mouth breathing. When the mouth is open, the lower lip tends to fall between the upper and the lower incisors, and in this retruded position, an anterior force is exerted on the upper incisors. However, Linder-Aronson and Backstrom[27] found no relationship between mouth breathing and either inclination of the upper incisors or overjet.

Similarly, Harvold and colleagues[14] have drawn attention to a possible association between palatal anatomy and impaired nasal breathing. These researchers simulated hypertrophied adenoids in primates with acrylic blocks and found that the palatal vault increased in vertical height, creating an anterior open bite in 9 to 15 months. Harvold believed that an open, clear nasal airway is a prerequisite to normal facial form and function.

On the other hand, Korkhaus[23] suggested that maxillary arch form is a primary factor in determining nasal cavity size and, hence, breathing mode. His studies indicated that alterations of the maxilla due to inhibition of growth or deformation are not a local symptom but rather characteristic of a complex anomaly that usually extends beyond the immediate region and that includes the nose and sinuses.

Further complicating our understanding are findings that demonstrate dentofacial deformities without airway inadequacy and airway inadequacy without dentofacial deformities. For example, Derichsweiler[10] argued against nasal obstruction as a primary etiologic factor in dentofacial deformity, based on three cases of choanal atresia with normally developed jaws and dentition. Similarly, Watson and associates[59] measured nasal airway resistance in orthodontic patients and noted that, when resistance was high, mouth breathing invariably resulted, but that skeletal deformity did not always occur. Interestingly, they noted that 23% of the mouth breathers did so out of habit rather than from physiologic need. A more recent study supports these findings.[52]

Apparently, individuals with a high, narrow palate and posterior dental crossbite often breathe through their mouths.[16] This type of malocclusion is often associated with high nasal airway resistance. Treatment of such cases with orthodontic appliances to expand the maxillary arch not only corrects the malocclusion but also, in many instances, significantly reduces the nasal stenosis as well.[16, 45] However, in many cases, the reduction is not enough to prevent continued obligatory mouth breathing.[53]

Advances in respirometric techniques have provided more objective information in this controversial area.[50, 54] Airway inadequacy can be defined in terms of nasal area, and mouth breathing can be measured in terms of percentage oral or nasal respiration. For example, in an 18-year-old patient, the minimal nasal airway size should be between 0.6 and 0.7 cm². If the area is less than 0.4 cm², there is a 97% chance of mouth breathing.[52] Since the size of the airway varies inversely with age, the dimensions would be smaller for younger persons.[51] The switching range from nasal to nasal-oral breathing seems to be an off-on phenomenon, that is, once the airway is impaired, some mouth breathing invariably occurs.[52]

The term *mouth breathing* should be used with caution, since even impaired nasal breathers demonstrate a wide range of nasal-oral volumes with each breath. While some may be oral breathers, many are predominantly oral, mixed, or even predominantly nasal breathers.[52] Perhaps the inability to link respiratory behaviors to dentofacial growth stems in part from this inconsistent and variable response. More important, recent findings indicate that exaggerated postural responses to impairment may be significant.[57, 58] When impaired nasal respiration results in postural changes of the head and neck[41] and changes in tongue and mandibular placement,[44] unfavorable dentofacial development may occur. The stimulus for exaggerated postural responses may relate to morphologic factors within the oropharynx. If a person has large tonsils, a long draping soft palate, a large tongue, or all three, an anterior displacement of the tongue and movement of the mandible forward and down may be necessary to open the oral airway adequately. If the oral airway were clear, only a slight parting of the lips would be necessary. Thus, the reason for possible morphologic changes may be multifactorial and may involve not only the nasal and nasopharyngeal airway but also, more important, the oropharyngeal airway.[56]

Speech and Malocclusion

The relationship between speech and malocclusion is complex and is complicated by the many factors that have to be considered in connection with speech disorders. In addition to malocclusion, such elusive considerations as intelligence, hearing acuity, motivation, and, in particular, an individual's ability to compensate may influence speech performance.[36] For example, even in severe malocclusion, speech may be perfectly normal as a result of compensatory adjustments of the articulatory structures. In another instance, even a slight malocclusion may be related to a speech problem because of an inability to compensate, as Benediktsson[5] pointed out.

Although there have been many attempts to explain the relationship between speech and dental disorders, the results are inconclusive. As Jensen[19] noted, there is general agreement that, except in the case of open bite malocclusion, there is probably no direct relationship between malocclusion and defective speech articulation. Studies supporting such a relationship generally reflect clinical impressions rather than objective data.

It is certainly possible that, while a particular malocclusion is not necessarily the cause of defective speech, it is a factor that can influence sound production. For example, Klechak and colleagues[22] saw evidence that the size of the opening in the anterior part of the mouth for sibilant production is modified in the presence of an open bite. Vallino and Tompson[48] noted that "regardless of the type of occlusal defect, errors occurred primarily on the

sibilants /s, z/ and 'sh, ch, j, dz,' which were characterized mostly by combined visual and auditory distortions." However, except for those with class III malocclusions, compensations usually occurred that provided acceptable sound production.

Speech performance may be affected by malocclusion in the presence of a cleft palate. Counihan[8] found that cleft palate patients with narrow maxillary arches did not perform as well as those with normal arches. Similarly, Claypoole and associates[7] reported that anterior malocclusion and spacing also appeared to affect speech performance in cleft palate patients. On the other hand, Bishara and co-workers[6] observed that individuals with cleft palate did not differ significantly in their facial and dental relations regardless of whether their articulation was good or poor. Dalston and Vig[9] investigated structural changes resulting from orthognathic surgery and found that such surgery did not result in perceptibly significant alterations of speech.

It is obvious that very few patients demonstrate a malocclusion severe enough to prevent them from acquiring adequate sound productions. The speech articulators have the potential to adapt to conditions in the oral cavity. Only severe open bite seems to affect articulation, and this is usually limited to sibilant sounds. Apparently, when articulation is distorted by a defect in the dentition, there is usually some other physical or psychologic factor involved.

Conference Issues to Consider with Parent/Patient

It is extremely important that the clinician not overlook the importance of including the patient and parents in the treatment planning process. Proffit and Ackerman[35] have suggested that the clinician is generally more influenced by the objective findings (i.e., the problem list), and the patients are more influenced by subjective findings (i.e., their perception of their needs and values). This dichotomy makes effective communication an essential tool when one is faced with the decision between orthodontic camouflage and surgical-orthodontic correction. The modern concept of patient autonomy vs. paternalism in orthodontic treatment planning shifts the role of the doctor from the sole decision maker in the treatment planning process toward inclusion of the patient as co−decision maker.

The patient/parent conference should have three components: (1) a description of the problem list by the orthodontist with input from the patient on the prioritization of the problem list, (2) a review of the risk-benefit considerations with the merits of treatment alternatives and the consideration of no treatment as an option (especially since most orthodontic treatment is elective), and (3) consideration of the patient's expectations and values. Informed consent requires not only gaining the patient's permission to treat after having explained the risks but also a dialogue between the clinician and patient in deciding on the final treatment plan. It is important that the patient and doctor openly communicate about the decision-making process because it has been documented that the patient's perception of the problem is not always the same as the doctor's understanding of the issue.

Proffit and Ackerman[35] have further recommended that the clinician not ignore the limitations of the soft tissues in guiding the treatment planning process. They have suggested that these soft tissue constraints are (1) the pressures exerted on the teeth by the lips, cheeks, and tongue that are a primary determinant of stability, (2) the periodontal attachment apparatus that is a primary consideration in oral health, (3) the temporomandibular muscular and connective tissue components that play a major role in function, and (4) the soft tissue integument of the entire face that determines aesthetics. Cephalometric values guiding the position of the incisors are restricted by racial, ethnic, and pretreatment positions, and thus orthodontic treatment should reflect the amount of incisor change that would occur relative to stability since the pretreatment position likely reflects the soft tissue influences. These authors have also suggested that expansion to the incisors anteroposteriorly more than 2 mm, or transverse expansion more than 4 or 5 mm, will likely be unstable. If macroglossia exists, there is the possibility that constriction of the lower arch to close spaces would not be maintained.

Previous guidelines have been published that outline the relationship between the periodontium and orthodontic treatment. Gingival recession and dehiscence of the alveolar bone may occur with orthodontic expansion when the attached gingiva is thin, especially when accompanied by plaque accumulation and inflammation. If there is inadequate attached gingiva, these authors recommend gingival grafting of the area to avoid recession.

Controversy continues to exist regarding the exact placement of the condyles within the fossae; however, it is relatively agreed upon that treatment which displaces the condyles more than a small distance from their most relaxed retruded position increases the potential for relapse toward a more comfortable location.

Ackerman and Proffit have clearly delineated the aesthetic guidelines that one should use when evaluating the dynamic soft tissue integument. These authors suggest that

1. Protraction of the incisors would be more preferable in a patient with a large nose or chin, as long as there would not be excessive deepening of the mentolabial fold.
2. Orthodontics alone can rarely correct severe midface deficiency or mandibular prognathism because these two conditions often are accompanied by unaesthetic lip position and neck form.
3. Moderate amounts of mandibular deficiency are often acceptable to patients, although the orthodontist might prefer more prominence of the lower face.
4. Maxillary incisors should never be retracted to the point that the inclination of the upper lip becomes negative to a true vertical line.
5. Short lower facial height or protrusion of the teeth may create an ill-defined labiomental sulcus as a result of the necessity to strain the lips in an effort to gain a lip seal.
6. Over-retraction of the maxillary incisors often tilts the occlusal plane down anteriorly, creating an excessive display of gingiva, which is considered unaesthetic. Patients do not mind if only moderate amounts of gingiva show on smiling.
7. When the lower lip is trapped under the maxillary incisors (such as in cases of excessive overjet), or when the mandibular incisors have been excessively proclined (such as in camouflage of skeletal class II malocclusions), then the resulting lip position is unacceptable.
8. Lack of a vermilion border (which often results from a concave profile with thinning of the upper lip) is not desirable. Tooth movement that proclines the incisor would create an aesthetically fuller lip.
9. Extreme bilabial protrusion is generally perceived as unacceptable, regardless of the racial or ethnic group.

The following case report illustrates the use of the diagnostic procedures presented in this chapter and demonstrates the type of treatment result that can be obtained for a patient with a severe dentofacial deformity.

1. Case Report

CASE STUDY: Patient L. P. was seen for evaluation at the age of 13 years and 8 months. Her chief complaints at that time were protruding maxillary teeth and an inability to incise and chew properly.

Facial Examination. Full-face examination indicated that facial features were symmetric except that her nasal tip deviated to the right. Lip closure was not possible (termed *lip incompetence*), and approximately 7 mm of maxillary central incisor crown was exposed when the lips were in the resting position; in a broad smile, she had a very high upper lip line, exposing 5 mm of gingival tissue. The lower third of her face was noted to be excessively long. Facial examination of the patient's profile indicated that she had a severely retru-

sive mandible, increased lower anterior facial height, and incompetent lip closure, with a deeply rolled lower lip (Fig. 59–13).

The intraoral examination revealed poor oral hygiene and generalized dental caries with severe involvement of the mandibular first molars. Her dentition was in a class II relationship, with a 12-mm overjet. She also had maxillary constriction and a 5-mm anterior open bite. Both the maxillary and the mandibular arches had 4 to 5 mm of crowding (Fig. 59–14).

Radiographic examination showed generalized shortening of root structures, especially in the maxillary incisors. Cephalometric analysis supported the clinical impression of a patient who had mandibular retrognathism, a severe skeletal open bite with excessive ver-

Continued on page 1195

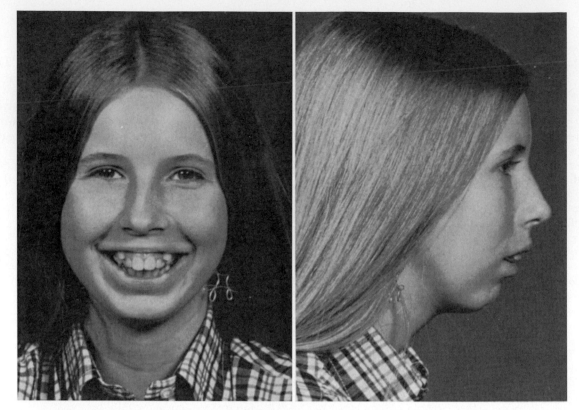

FIGURE 59–13. Pretreatment full-face and profile views that indicate a high lip line, increased lower facial height, retrognathia, and retrogenia.

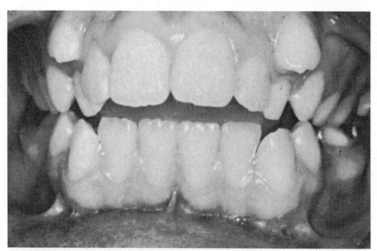

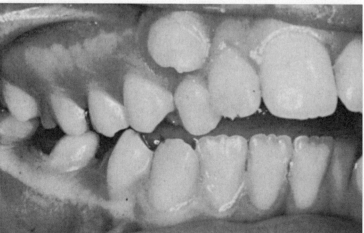

FIGURE 59–14. Pretreatment dental relationships demonstrating a Class II malocclusion with an anterior open bite, maxillary constriction, and arch length deficiency.

tical maxillary development, increased lower anterior facial height, and maxillary and mandibular dental protrusion.

Problem List. From the results of the clinical examination and analysis of the diagnostic records, the following problem list was generated:

1. Poor oral hygiene and dental caries with possible pulpal involvement of the mandibular first molars
2. Maxillary vertical excess causing a downward and backward rotation of the mandible, resulting in a subsequent anterior open bite, mandibular retrognathism, and a long lower facial height
3. Maxillary and mandibular dental protrusion
4. Bilateral maxillary constriction
5. Maxillary and mandibular crowding
6. Lack of chin projection (retrogenia)

Treatment Plan. This patient's facial aesthetic and malocclusion problems were judged to be too severe to be corrected with routine orthodontic treatment, and a combination orthodontic and surgical treatment plan was initiated.

The initial phase of orthodontic treatment involved the following:

1. Elimination of dental caries and extraction of both mandibular first permanent molars
2. Full banding of both arches with orthodontic appliances
3. Closure of the mandibular extraction sites and correction of crowding and rotations
4. Alignment of the maxillary dental arch
5. Vertical alignment of the maxillary teeth in three segments

The goal of the initial phase of orthodontic treatment was to position the teeth in the proper relationship to the basal bone of their respective jaws. It was realized that, following initial orthodontics, the patient's teeth would not occlude as well as they had previously and that facial aesthetics would be made worse. The patient was warned to expect these changes initially (Fig. 59–15).

The surgical treatment plan included the following:

1. Extraction of the maxillary first premolar teeth.
2. Total maxillary osteotomy and ostectomy, mobilizing the maxilla in two posterior segments and an anterior segment. The posterior segments were superiorly repositioned and expanded laterally while the anterior segment was superiorly repositioned and retracted into the premolar extraction sites.
3. Mandibular inferior border osteotomy to advance the chin.

Cephalometric prediction indicated that this treatment plan would result in closure of the open bite, correction of the maxillary protrusion, improvement of the tooth-to-lip relationship, and shortening of the anterior facial height (due to the upward rotation of the mandible allowed by the superior repositioning of the maxilla). The inferior border osteotomy was necessary to eliminate the deficiency in chin projection, further enhancing the aesthetic result.

Continued on page 1197

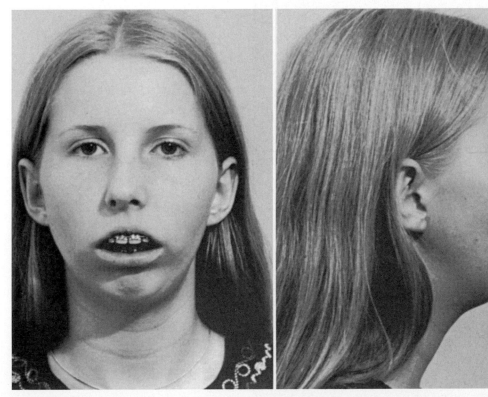

FIGURE 59–15. Presurgical full-face and profile views after initial orthodontic preparation.

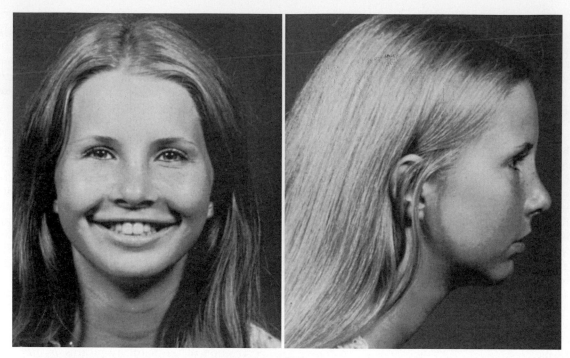

FIGURE 59–16. Post-treatment full-face and profile views.

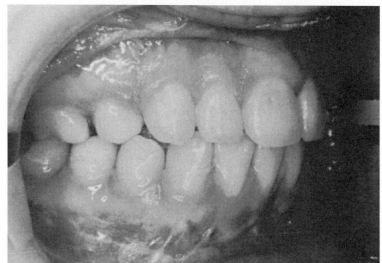

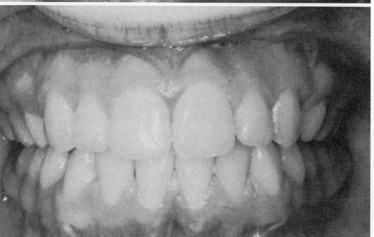

FIGURE 59–17. Post-treatment dental relationships.

With the patient under general anesthesia, the osteotomies were performed, and a portion of the nasal septum was resected to allow passive, superior repositioning of the maxillary segments. Surgical fixation was maintained by direct wiring of the segments and maxillomandibular fixation. Mandibular function was resumed after a 6-week period of immobilization. Rigid internal fixation, a recent advancement in the treatment of dentofacial deformities that uses small bone plates and screws for direct fixation of the bone segments,[46] was not used in this patient. This technique, when used, typically allows a reduction in the period of maxillomandibular fixation and jaw immobilization. Final orthodontic positioning of the teeth was accomplished in an additional 4 months.

Postsurgical facial and dental photographs (Figs. 59–16 and 59–17) show the improved aesthetic and functional relationships obtained from the combined orthodontic and surgical treatment of this patient. Comparison of preoperative and postoperative quantitative evaluations of nasal airway resistance revealed an increased capacity for nasal respiration as a result of surgical management of the nasal septal deviation and enlargement of the constricted nares.

SELECTED REFERENCES

Moore RN. Orthodontic management of the patient with cleft lip and palate. Ear Nose Throat J 65:46, 1986.

A good general review of orthodontic treatment in cleft patients written for physicians.

Posnick JC, Dagys AP. Bilateral cleft deformity: an integrated orthognathic and orthodontic approach. J Oral Maxillofac Surg 3:693, 1991.

A good chapter on orthodontic and integrated orthognathic surgery in patients with bilateral clefts in a text dedicated to treatment approaches for cleft patients.

Proffit WR, Turvey TA. Special problems in cleft-palate patients. In Proffit WR, White RP (eds). Surgical Orthodontic Treatment. St Louis, Mosby–Year Book, 1990, p 625.

This is an excellent chapter covering the orthodontic and surgical timing of treatment for cleft patients from one of the premier centers for cleft patients.

Warren DW, Spalding P. Dental morphology and breathing: a century of controversy. In Melsen B (ed). Controversies in Orthodontics. Berlin, Quintessenz, 1990, p 45.

A good review of past and present opinions concerning the upper airway and its effects on dentofacial growth and development.

REFERENCES

1. Ackerman JL, Proffit WR. Soft tissue limitations in orthodontics. Treatment planning guidelines. Angle Orthod 67:327, 1997.
2. Altemus LA. A comparison of cephalofacial relationships. Angle Orthod 30:223, 1960.
3. Altemus LA. Comparative integumental relationships. Angle Orthod 33:217, 1963.
4. Angle EH. Treatment of Malocclusion of the Teeth, 7th ed. Philadelphia, SS White, 1907.
5. Benediktsson E. Variations in tongue and jaw position in /s/ sound production in relation to the front teeth occlusion. Am J Orthod 40:149, 1954.
6. Bishara SE, Vandemark DR, Henderson WG. Relation between speech production and orofacial structures in individuals with isolated clefts of the palate. Cleft Palate J 12:452, 1975.
7. Claypoole WH, Warren DW, Bradley DP. The effects of cleft palate on oral port constriction during fricative productions. Cleft Palate J 11:95, 1974.
8. Counihan DT. A clinical study of the speech efficiency and structural adequacy of operated adolescent and adult cleft palate persons. PhD dissertation, Northwestern University, Chicago, 1956.
9. Dalston RD, Vig PS. Effects of orthognathic surgery on speech: a prospective study. Am J Orthod Dentofacial Orthop 86:291, 1984.
10. Derichsweiler H. Gaumennahrterweiterung. Munich, Karl Hanser, 1956.
11. Downs WB. The role of cephalometrics in orthodontic case analysis and diagnosis. Am J Orthod 38:162, 1952.
12. Enlow DH. Facial Growth, 3rd ed. Philadelphia, WB Saunders, 1990.
13. Graber TM. Orthodontics. Principles and Practice, 2nd ed. Philadelphia, WB Saunders, 1966.
14. Harvold EP, Vargervik K, Chierici G. Primate experiments on oral sensation and dental malocclusions. Am J Orthod 63:494, 1973.
15. Hellman M. The face in its developmental career. D Cosmos 77:685, 1935.
16. Hershey HG, Stewart BL, Warren DW. Changes in nasal airway resistance associated with rapid maxillary expansion. Am J Orthod 69:274, 1976.
17. Hixon EH, Oldfather RE. Estimation of the sizes of unerupted cuspid and bicuspid teeth. Angle Orthod 28:236, 1958.
18. Hunter BM. Nasal airway resistance, breathing patterns and dentofacial characteristics. MS thesis, University of North Carolina, Chapel Hill, 1971.
19. Jensen R. Anterior teeth relationship and speech. Acta Radiol 276:1(Suppl), 1968.
20. Joshi MR. A study of dental occlusion in nasal and oronasal breathers in Maharashtrian children. J All India Dent Assoc 36:219, 1964.
21. Kelly JE, Sanchez M, Van Kirk LE. An assessment of the occlusion of teeth of children. Data from the National Health Survey. National Center for Health Services, US Public Health Service. DHEW Publication No. (HRA) 74:1612, 1973.
22. Klechak TL, Bradley DP, Warren DW. Anterior open-bite and oral port constriction. Angle Orthod 46:232, 1976.
23. Korkhaus G. Present orthodontic thought in Germany: jaw widening with active appliances in cases of mouth breathing. Am J Orthod 46:187, 1960.
24. Limborgh JV. A new view on control of the morphogenesis of the skull. Acta Morphol Neerl Scand 8:143, 1970.
25. Linder-Aronson S. Adenoids: their effect on mode of breathing and nasal airflow and their relationship to characteristics of the facial skeleton and the dentition. Acta Otolaryngol Suppl (Stockh) 265:1, 1970.
26. Linder-Aronson S, Aschan G. Nasal resistance to breathing and palatal height before and after expansion of the median palatine suture. Orthod Rev 14:254, 1963.
27. Linder-Aronson S, Backstrom A. A comparison between mouth and nose breathers with respect to occlusion and facial dimensions. Orthod Rev 11:343, 1960.
28. Marks MB. Allergy in relation to orofacial dental deformities in children: a review. J Allergy 36:293, 1965.
29. Moffatt JB. Habits and their relation to malocclusion. Aust Dent J 8:142, 1963.
30. Moorrees CFA, Kean MR. Natural head position, a basic consideration in the interpretation of cephalometric radiographs. Am J Phys Anthropol 16:213, 1958.
31. Moorrees CFA, Lebret L. The mesh diagram in cephalometrics. Angle Orthod 32:214, 1962.
32. Moss ML. The primacy of functional matrices in orofacial growth. Dent Pract Dent Rec 19:65, 1968.
33. Moyers RE. Handbook of Orthodontics, 4th ed. Chicago, Mosby–Year Book, 1988, p 235.

1198   The Mouth, Pharynx, and Esophagus

34. Nance HN. The limitations of orthodontic treatment. Parts I and II. Am J Orthod 33:177, 253, 1947.
35. Proffit WR, Ackerman JL. Orthodontic diagnosis: the development of a problem list. In Proffit WR (ed). Contemporary Orthodontics, 2nd ed. St Louis, Mosby–Year Book, 1993, pp 139–185.
36. Rathbone JS. Appraisal of speech defects in dental anomalies. Angle Orthod 25:42, 1965.
37. Ricketts RM. Planning treatment on the basis of the facial pattern and an estimate of its growth. Angle Orthod 27:14, 1957.
38. Ricketts RM. Cephalometric analysis and synthesis. Angle Orthod 31:141, 1961.
39. Riolo ML, Moyers RE, McNamara JA, et al. An Atlas of Craniofacial Growth: Cephalometric Standards from the University of Michigan. Craniofacial Growth Series, No. 2. Ann Arbor, University of Michigan, 1974, pp 321–323.
40. Sicher H. Oral Anatomy. St Louis, CV Mosby, 1952.
41. Solow B, Krieborg S. Soft-tissue stretching: a possible control factor in craniofacial morphogenesis. Scand J Dent Res 85:505, 1977.
42. Steiner CC. Cephalometrics for you and me. Am J Orthod 39:729, 1953.
43. Steiner CC. Cephalometrics as a clinical tool. In Kraus BS, Riedel RA (eds). Vistas in Orthodontics. Philadelphia, Lea & Febiger, 1962, p 131.
44. Subtelny JD. Effect of diseases of tonsils and adenoids on dentofacial morphology. Ann Otol Rhinol Laryngol 84:50, 1975.
45. Timms DJ. The effect of rapid maxillary expansion on nasal airway resistance. Br J Orthod 13:221, 1986.
46. Tucker MR, White RP. Principles of surgical management for dentofacial deformity. In Proffit WR, White RP (eds). Surgical Orthodontic Treatment. St Louis, Mosby–Year Book, 1991, pp 226–247.
47. Tully WJ. Abnormal functions of the mouth in relation to the occlusion of the teeth. In Walther DP (ed). Current Orthodontics. Baltimore, Williams & Wilkins, 1966.
48. Vallino LD, Tompson B. Perceptual characteristics of consonant errors associated with malocclusion. J Oral Maxillofac Surg 51:850, 1993.
49. Warren DW. Aerodynamic studies of the upper airway: implications for growth, breathing and speech. In McNamara JA (ed). Naso-Respiratory Function and Craniofacial Growth. Ann Arbor, University of Michigan: Center for Human Growth and Development, 1980, pp 41–86.
50. Warren DW. A quantitative technique for assessing nasal airway impairment. Am J Orthod 86:306, 1984.
51. Warren DW, Duany LF, Fischer ND. Nasal airway resistance in normal and cleft palate subjects. Cleft Palate J 6:134, 1969.
52. Warren DW, Hairfield WM, Seaton D, et al. Relationship between nasal airway size and nasal-oral breathing. Am J Orthod Dentofacial Orthop 93:289, 1988.
53. Warren DW, Hershey GH, Turvey TA, et al. The nasal airway following maxillary expansion. Am J Orthod Dentofacial Orthop 91:111, 1987.
54. Warren DW, Hinton VA, Hairfield WM. Measurement of nasal and oral respiration using inductive plethysmography. Am J Orthod 89:480, 1986.
55. Warren DW, Hinton VA, Pillsbury HC, et al. Effects of size of the nasal airway on nasal airflow rate. Arch Otolaryngol Head Neck Surg 113:405, 1987.
56. Warren DW, Lehman MD, Hinton VA. Analysis of simulated upper airway breathing. Am J Orthod 86:197, 1984.
57. Warren DW, Spalding P. Dental morphology and breathing: a century of controversy. In Melsen B (ed). Controversies in Orthodontics. Berlin, Quintessenz, 1990, p 45.
58. Warren DW. Breathing behavior and posture. In McNamara JA Jr (ed). The Enigma of the Vertical Dimension. Craniofacial Growth series, vol. 36. Ann Arbor: Center for Human Growth and Development, University of Michigan, 2000.
59. Watson RM, Warren DW, Fischer ND. Nasal resistance, skeletal classification, and mouth-breathing in orthodontic patients. Am J Orthod 54:367, 1968.

60

Inflammatory Disease of the Mouth and Pharynx

Cuneyt M. Alper, M.D., and Jack L. Cluckman, M.D.

Various inflammatory conditions of the mouth and pharynx are commonly seen in children. Developing a differential diagnosis for an oral lesion requires a systematic approach including a thorough medical and dental history, clinical examination, and laboratory studies with appropriate cultures, biopsy, radiographs, blood tests, and other studies as indicated.

Most of the inflammatory conditions in children are infectious. The warm and moist environment of the mouth and pharynx is an ideal ground for a variety of microorganisms. Over 200 varieties of bacteria, yeast, viruses, and other microorganisms have been identified on the oral cavity. Most of them are opportunistic pathogens, but they may produce local or systemic infections under the right circumstances. Some of the common infections that cause sore throat are discussed in Chapter 53.

Many oral infections in pediatric patients are the result of neglected dental problems that are related to tooth decay, trauma, and periodontal disease (see Chap. 58). Many systemic infections or diseases may have oral manifestations (see Chap. 63). It should be remembered that, although they are rare in children, certain benign and malignant processes may have primary oral lesions that can resemble common oral infections (see Chap. 66).

This chapter includes an approach to the most common inflammatory conditions that affect the mucosa of the oral cavity and the pharynx (Table 60–1) that are likely to be found in the pediatric patient. Primary infections of the teeth and gingivae, infections of lymphoid tissue of the pharynx, and oral manifestations of systemic disease are addressed elsewhere (see Chaps. 53, 58, and 63).

Viral Infections

The most common viral agents of pharyngitis are rhinovirus, coronavirus, adenovirus, influenzaviruses A and B, and parainfluenza viruses. On the other hand, only a few produce specific syndromes—for example, acute lymphonodular pharyngitis due to coxsackievirus A (types 2, 4, 5, 6, 8, 10); pharyngoconjunctival fever due to an adenovirus; infectious mononucleosis; infection with cytomegalovirus that may mimic infectious mononucleosis; herpangina; and hand-foot-and-mouth disease. In the oral cavity,

herpetic infection (due to herpesvirus types 1 and 2) is the most common type of viral illness.

Pharyngitis occurs particularly in respiratory season or during colder months of the year. The peak prevalance of rhinoviruses is during spring and fall, coronaviruses and adenoviruses during the colder months, and other adenoviruses (pharyngoconjunctival fever) in the early summer.

Adenoviral pharyngitis is characterized by severe sore throat, malaise, headache, chills, myalgia, and fever. On examination, pharyngeal erythema and exudates are present. Conjunctivitis may also be present in 25% to 50% of patients with adenoviral pharyngitis.

With influenzal pharyngitis, severe sore throat is present with myalgia, headache, cough, coryza, and temperature elevation. Erythema of the pharynx is mild. Only mild pharyngeal irritation is found with rhinovirus infection.

Other viruses associated with pharyngitis include Epstein-Barr virus and human immunodeficiency virus (HIV). Pharyngitis with fever, myalgia, lethargy, and truncal maculopapular rash is characteristic of primary infection with HIV.

Herpes Simplex Virus

Infections due to herpes simplex virus (HSV) are of two varieties: (1) a primary infection that is usually subclinical but, when it does manifest, may be severe, and (2) a secondary or recurrent infection, which is the more common. HSV-1 primarily infects the nongenital sites, whereas HSV-2 primarily infects the genitalia. However, both may occur in both areas.

Primary Herpetic Gingivostomatitis

This infection most commonly manifests in children aged 2 to 5 years. Infants derive antibodies to HSV from the mother. Once circulating antibodies are no longer present, the child is susceptible to HSV infection. In most children, the initial HSV infection is subclinical. There is classically a prodromal period of several days with vague constitutional symptoms and signs. The stomatitis then develops and is characterized by an initial tingling in the mucosa followed by the development of erythema and edema. Primary infection with herpes simplex

TABLE 60–1. Classification of Stomatitis

Infection

Viral
   Herpes simplex infection
   Herpes zoster infection
   Herpangina
   Hand-foot-and-mouth disease
   Infectious mononucleosis
Bacterial
   Vincent stomatitis
   Streptococcal infection
   Diphtheria
   Gonococcal pharyngitis
   Syphilis
   Tuberculosis
Fungal
   Candidiasis
   Actinomycosis
   Histoplasmosis
   Mucormycosis

Other Inflammatory Conditions

Trauma-induced conditions
Contact stomatitis
Aphthous stomatitis
Behçet syndrome
Reiter syndrome
Periadenitis mucosa necrotica recurrens
Necrotizing sialometaplasia
Fixed drug reaction (stomatitis medicamentosa)

virus may present as acute painful pharyngitis with erythema and exudates; vesicles and shallow ulcers of both posterior (buccal) and anterior (labial) mucosa are helpful in the diagnosis if associated with gingival stomatitis. Fever, irritability, and regional lymphadenopathy may be present. Vesicles then form and rupture, resulting in superficial ulcers that spontaneously heal in 10 to 14 days. These ulcers may be discrete or may coalesce to cover a wide area. They are covered with a gray pseudomembrane. Although any area of the mucosa may be involved, the gingiva, lips, tongue, and palate are most commonly

infected. Uncommon sequelae include a skin eruption, meningoencephalitis, and disseminated herpes. Diagnosis is established by viral studies, and biopsy demonstrates intranuclear inclusion bodies. Chronic herpes simplex infection in immunocompromised hosts is characterized by progressive large, shallow, painful ulcers.

Treatment of primary herpetic stomatitis is symptomatic and supportive. Use of topical anesthetics is reserved for children who are having difficulty in maintaining adequate oral intake. Dyclonine hydrochloride 0.5% topical solution is used before meals when needed. Kaopectate or sucralfate may be used to coat the lesions.

Secondary or Recurrent Herpes

Once infection has occurred with HSV, the virus may lie dormant in the regional neuroganglia until reactivated by a number of factors to produce secondary lesions. The commonly described precipitating factors include sunlight, emotional stress, pyrexia of any origin, and immunodeficiency states.

After a prodromal period of burning and pruritus at the affected site, single or multiple vesicles develop and then rupture after a few hours, leaving a superficial ulceration that spontaneously heals in 10 to 14 days. While these lesions may occur on the vermilion border of the lips ("fever blisters" or "cold sores") (Fig. 60–1), they may occur intraorally on mucosa bound to bone (Fig. 60–2) or on the skin of the face. Secondary bacterial infection may develop, which complicates the clinical picture (Fig. 60–3).

Recurrent herpetic lesions are self-limiting, and treatment is symptomatic in healthy patients. Immunocompromised patients may need treatment with acyclovir.

Herpes Zoster

This infection is classically seen in patients who are immunocompromised. It is thought to be due to reactivation of the varicella virus lying dormant in the sensory ganglia.

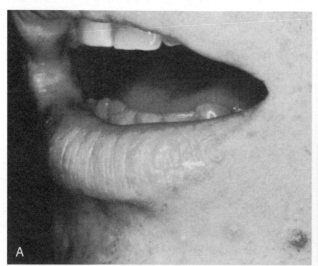 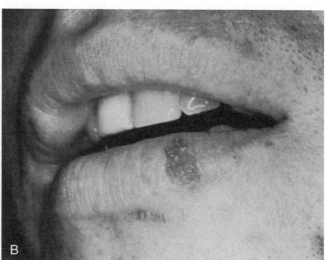

FIGURE 60–1. *A,* Herpetic vesicles on lips. *B,* Rupture of vesicles, with superficial ulceration.

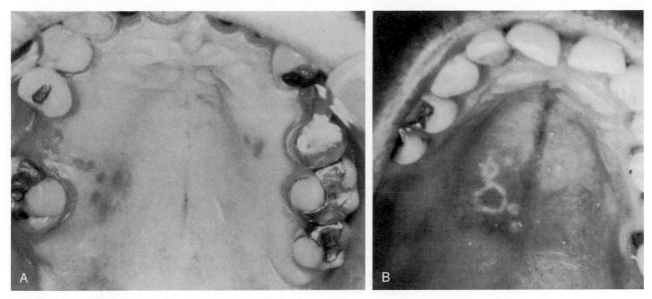

FIGURE 60–2. *A,* Discrete herpetic ulcers of the hard palate. *B,* Herpetic ulcers that have coalesced.

Oral lesions result when either the second or the third branch of the trigeminal nerve or both are involved. The presence of skin and mucosal lesions in the distribution of these nerves makes the diagnosis obvious (Fig. 60–4). Rarely, oral lesions alone may be the only manifestation of the disease. The classic clinical picture consists of the development of vesicles that rupture to form ulcers that coalesce.

Herpangina

This relatively common condition is frequently misdiagnosed as bacterial pharyngotonsillitis. It occurs in young children, with coxsackievirus A being the common etiologic organism, but has been associated with many enteric viruses, including coxsackievirus B and enteric cytopathogenic human orphan viruses (echoviruses).[2] It is characterized by the sudden onset of pyrexia, malaise, and other flulike symptoms with an intense sore throat.

Examination reveals congestion of the oropharynx and posterior oral cavity with erythema. Multiple small vesicles (1 to 2 mm) are typically seen only in the posterior pharynx (soft palate, uvula, and anterior tonsillar pillars) that rupture to form superficial ulcers. The gingiva and the rest of the oral cavity are usually not involved. The condition spontaneously resolves in approximately 1 week.

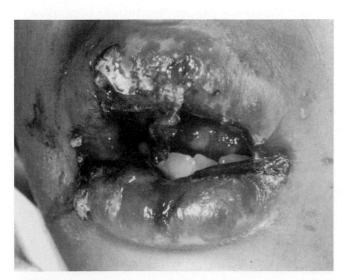

FIGURE 60–3. Secondary bacterial infection of a herpetic infection, which aggravates the clinical picture. (Courtesy of Dr. John McDonald.)

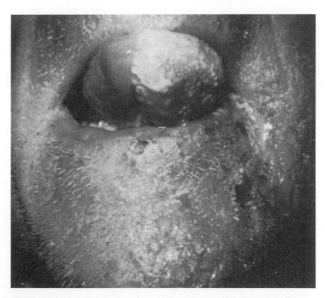

FIGURE 60–4. Intraoral lesions of herpes zoster in the distribution of the trigeminal nerve. Note the unilateral involvement of tongue and skin.

Hand-Foot-and-Mouth Disease

This viral illness, which is also due to a variety of coxsackieviruses A, mimics herpangina in every respect, with the addition of vesiculopapular lesions on the palms of the hands and the soles of the feet.[17] Children and young adults are usually affected. Spontaneous resolution occurs in 7 days.

Infectious Mononucleosis

This disease commonly occurs in adolescents and young adults. It is caused by the Epstein-Barr virus and is characterized by malaise, fatigue, generalized lymphadenopathy, and splenomegaly. Hepatitis with jaundice may occasionally complicate the clinical picture. The oral manifestations may include greatly enlarged tonsils, membranous pharyngotonsillitis, petechiae on the soft palate, and even severe ulceration of the oropharynx. The disease may be mild or severe, and although it classically lasts weeks, many patients complain of malaise for months. Diagnosis is made on the basis of the blood smear by the presence of atypical lymphocytes and by the heterophile antibody agglutination (monospot) test. However, some patients will have a negative monospot test response during the early phase of illness, and repeated testing or serologic study for Epstein-Barr virus is required to confirm the diagnosis. While supportive treatment is generally all that is required, secondary bacterial infection of the tonsils is relatively common and should be treated with antibiotics. Systemic steroids are indicated if the enlarged tonsils cause respiratory obstruction and in the presence of significant hepatitis.

Treatment of Viral Illness

At this time, there is no definitive antiviral therapy for viral stomatitis and pharyngitis. Therapy is symptomatic until the condition spontaneously resolves. Various cleansing mouthwashes can be used in an attempt to prevent secondary infection. Ceepryn 1:4000 or benzalkonium chloride (Zephiran) 1:1000 may be used for oral lavage. If such infection should occur, antibiotics may be of some value. In viral stomatitis, local anesthetic preparations applied to the affected areas may be helpful, particularly before eating. Great care should be paid to ensure adequate hydration, particularly in young children.

Great interest has been shown in the use of antiviral agents for HSV infections. Oral acyclovir (15 mg/kg five times a day with a maximum dose of 1 g/24 hours for 7 days) started within 72 hours of onset of lesions has significant benefits in children with primary herpetic gingivostomatitis by decreasing drooling, gum swelling, pain, eating and drinking difficulties, and duration of lesions.[1] Therapy of recurrent oral herpes with oral acyclovir has limited effects. Acyclovir is effective in herpes infections and is used topically for dendritic corneal ulcers.[7] In addition, oral acyclovir has been shown to prevent stomatitis from HSV reactivation during chemotherapy in bone marrow transplant patients.[23] Oral acyclovir has been used in genital herpes, but its value has not conclusively been confirmed in the pediatric group. Topical idoxuridine has

also been given, with some success when it is used during the prodromal phase. The key to management of recurrent herpetic infections appears to remain the avoidance of any precipitating event.

Bacterial Infections

Bacterial infection of the oral cavity is rare and is usually due to commensals of the oral cavity that become pathogenic when the host defense mechanisms are impaired. A child has a sterile mouth at birth, with the bacterial content increasing through childhood. Multiple types of spirochetes and bacteria are found, particularly in the crevices adjacent to teeth; the number and the type of bacteria are influenced by the amount of periodontal disease and the level of oral hygiene. Approximately 80% of the bacteria consists of facultative and anaerobic streptococci and diphtheroids. Among the organisms listed are *Streptococcus, Corynebacterium, Veillonella, Staphylococcus aureus* and other staphylococci, *Costobacillus, Leptothrix, Actinomyces, Bacteroides, Fusobacterium*, spirochetes, *Neisseria, Candida*, and protozoa.

Corynebacteria, including *Corynebacterium diphtheriae* and *C. ulcerans, Arcanobacterium haemolyticum* (formerly called *Corynebacterium haemolyticum*), *Yersinia enterocolitica, Neisseria gonorrhoeae*, mixed anaerobic infection (Vincent angina), and *Treponema pallidum* are less common causes of pharyngitis. Mycoplasma pneumonia rarely causes pharyngitis. An even less common potential cause is *Mycoplasma hominis*. The role of *Chlamydia trachomatis* is less established. In patients with recurrent pharyngotonsillitis, the possibility of beta-lactamase–producing bacteria (*Staphylococcus aureus, Haemophilus influenzae, Branhamella catarrhalis*, and *Bacteroides* species) should be considered.

Other bacteria may cause sore throats as part of a generalized illness, but these are not discussed in this chapter.

Vincent Stomatitis (Acute Necrotizing Ulcerative Gingivitis, Trench Mouth)

This acute infection is usually localized to the marginal gingiva but may also involve other areas of the oral cavity and oropharynx. The causative organisms are a complex of oral bacteria (fusospirochetal bacteria) consisting of an aerobic fusiform bacillus and a spirochete that are commensals in the oral cavity but become pathogenic during periods of decreased tissue resistance. While this condition is most commonly seen in young adults and rarely presents in childhood, it may well complicate systemic disease in childhood. Precipitating events include emotional stress, systemic disease, and immunosuppression.

The classic presentation is a sudden onset of acute inflammation of the gingiva leading to necrosis of the marginal gingiva and interdental papillae. This superficial ulceration is covered by a gray pseudomembrane surrounded by marked erythema. If the membrane is removed, a raw area is exposed that bleeds easily. In fact, gingival hemorrhage, either spontaneous or provoked by minimal trauma, is characteristic of this condition. There is marked halitosis and a foul taste in the mouth together with significant pain. There may be associated constitutional symptoms. If untreated, the disease may become chronic or relapsing. The disease may progress to involve the rest of the oral cavity, with increasing deterioration and gangrene, particularly in debilitated individuals (cancrum oris). While the process may spread to involve the oropharynx, occasionally it presents exclusively in the oropharynx (Vincent angina). Here it presents as a membranous pharyngotonsillitis and must be differentiated from other similarly presenting infections in this area.

The diagnosis is a clinical one. Culture results are not diagnostic, because the organisms isolated are normally found in periodontal pockets and other gingival infections. Likewise, biopsy results are not specific or diagnostic.

Treatment consists of ruling out any systemic underlying condition and alleviating any precipitating factor. Cleansing mouthwashes should be used regularly. A dentist should be consulted to perform dental prophylaxis and periodontal scaling. Penicillin is the antibiotic of choice.

Streptococcal Infection

Severe pharyngotonsillitis can result from infection by group A beta-hemolytic streptococci. It is unfortunate that the diagnosis of a "strep" throat is made all too frequently; probably only 10% to 15% of all presumptive streptococcal infections without culture are due to beta-hemolytic streptococci. Less often, groups B, C, and G beta-hemolytic streptococci are responsible for sore throat.

Streptococcal pharyngitis occurs during the colder months of the year, and infection rates are higher in late winter and early spring. From 15% to 20% of school children carry group A streptococci in their throat, but fewer than 10% have a sore throat.

The true streptococcal infection results in marked erythema of the pharynx and a yellow exudate. The oral cavity may be reddened but is usually uninvolved. Scarlet fever is likewise due to infection by group A beta-hemolytic streptococcus that, in addition, produces an erythrogenic toxin, resulting in a diffuse erythematous rash. There may be a circumoral pallor, which is believed to be diagnostic. The pharyngeal manifestations are similar to those of the routine streptococcal infection. However, there is also an associated glossitis (strawberry tongue), which is due to superficial desquamation of the papillae, with prominent fungiform papillae. This glossitis is, in fact, a nonspecific reaction to infection and pyrexia.

The treatment is supportive, and penicillin is the antibiotic of choice.

Diphtheria

Diphtheria is now well controlled in the United States by mass immunization; however, in many parts of the world, cases are still seen. The causative organism is *Corynebacterium diphtheriae*. Infection results in a necrotizing pharyngitis that is characterized locally by an intense erythema and thick pseudomembrane formation. Release of

a bacterial toxin often leads to severe systemic manifestations. While the oropharynx is the dominantly affected site, the process may involve the larynx and the trachea, with the membrane causing respiratory obstruction. The incubation period is 1 to 6 days, and thereafter the patient has a sore throat and disproportionate systemic symptoms. The exotoxin produced by the bacteria may result in a generalized toxemia or may have a direct effect on the heart and the nervous system. Diagnosis is made on the basis of the clinical picture and the identification of bacteria on staining of the membrane, but culture is also necessary because many strains of diphtheroids are commensals in the oral cavity. Treatment consists of early therapy with antitoxin and antibiotics (i.e., penicillin and erythromycin).

Gonococcal Pharyngitis

Obviously, in a discussion of causes of pharyngitis in the pediatric age group, gonococcal pharyngitis is not a dominant problem. However, gonococcal pharyngitis has been described in children[22] and therefore should always be borne in mind when a child with membranous pharyngitis is evaluated. Caused by *Neisseria gonorrhoeae*, this condition commonly affects the oropharynx, although any of the tissues of the oral cavity may be involved.

Infection in the newborn results from genital infection in the mother. Because other *Neisseria* organisms are found in the oral cavity, diagnosis by Gram stain is unsatisfactory, and the diagnosis is best made by culture on a Thayer-Martin culture plate. As antibiotic resistance continues to evolve, treatment will depend on the recommendations of the public health authorities.

Syphilis

After a dramatic decline in frequency, there has been an increase in the number of early cases of syphilis. Therefore, a high index of suspicion should exist.[11] In the pediatric group, both congenital and acquired forms of the disease may be seen.

Ten to 90 days after infection with *Treponema pallidum*, the primary lesion (chancre) presents as a painless, rapidly enlarging ulcer with marked surrounding induration, usually on the lips, tongue, and tonsils. This lesion heals spontaneously in a few weeks. Regional adenopathy is usually present.

If the primary lesion is not treated, the secondary form of the disease develops shortly thereafter as the mucous patch, which is characterized by superficial ulceration covered with a gray-white pseudomembrane (Fig. 60–5). Usually, there is associated diffuse infection of the oral cavity and oropharynx, and maculopapular lesions may be present at the commissure of the lips. The patient is contagious at this stage, which lasts 20 to 90 days. If untreated, the condition will spontaneously resolve; tertiary syphilis develops after a symptomless latent period in approximately one third of patients.

Tertiary syphilis of the oral cavity is characterized by the gumma, which is a granulomatous process that progresses to a punched-out ulcer of the hard palate and a

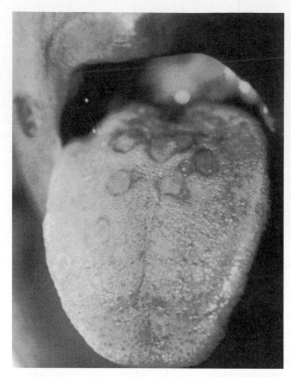

FIGURE 60–5. "Mucous patches" of secondary syphilis on the tongue. (Courtesy of Dr. John McDonald.)

diffuse syphilitic glossitis that leaves the tongue with an atrophic appearance. Leukoplakia may develop, with a predilection for malignant transformation.

The occurrence of congenital syphilis is unfortunately increasing in some large American cities, at least in part owing to inadequate prenatal screening.[16] The infection is acquired through an infected birth canal or by transplacental infection. The classic clinical features consist of notched central incisors, with generally hypoplastic teeth, interstitial keratitis, and eighth cranial nerve involvement (Hutchinson triad). Other described abnormalities include the saddle nose deformity, rhagades, atrophic glossitis, and a mucopurulent rhinitis (snuffles).

The diagnosis is made by dark-field microscopic examination of the primary and secondary lesions to demonstrate the presence of the spirochete. Serologic tests, including the screening nontreponemal and confirmatory treponemal tests, are needed for confirmation of the diagnosis; the results of these tests become positive shortly after the formation of the chancre.

Treatment consists of large doses of penicillin, which will result in resolution of all the oral lesions except the atrophic glossitis.

Tuberculosis

Tuberculosis of the oral cavity is rarely seen in the United States. It is rarely due to primary inoculation because the oral mucosa is resistant to invasion by *Mycobacterium tuberculosis,* and usually infection results from spread to the mucosa by the hematogenous route. When the oral mucosa, particularly the tongue, is the site of primary invasion, an ulcer with surrounding induration

may develop. If the patient has adequate resistance, the lesion will resolve. However, if the patient's resistance is low, disease spread will be to regional cervical nodes and may even be miliary.

A secondary lesion of the oral cavity manifests as a tuberculous ulcer or granuloma, which is usually seen on the tongue or the gingiva. Tuberculous osteomyelitis of the mandible may occasionally complicate miliary tuberculosis. A presumptive diagnosis is usually made on the basis of biopsy results and culture of the tissue. Treatment consists of a prolonged course of antituberculous chemotherapy. At least two drugs shown to be effective against the isolated strain are employed (e.g., isoniazid, rifampin, ethambutol). Results are excellent with completion of a full therapeutic course. Increasingly, resistant strains are being encountered, most associated with the HIV epidemic. Extended therapy using multiple drug regimens is often required for resistant organisms.

Fungal Infections

Candidiasis (Moniliasis, Thrush)

Candida albicans is a normal commensal of the oral cavity that causes overt infection only when there is a reduction in the competitive oral microflora (e.g., secondary to long-term, broad-spectrum antibiotic therapy) or a decrease in the host resistance (e.g., as a result of diabetes, debilitation from stress or malnutrition, prematurity, or conditions causing immunosuppression).

Candidiasis is essentially a disease of infants, but it can occur in any age group. The classic manifestation consists of white plaques covering the mucous membrane of the oral cavity, particularly the tongue, buccal mucosa, and hard palate, which easily rubs off to leave an underlying red, raw surface (Fig. 60–6). This membrane consists of an almost pure colony of the fungus. This lesion is confined to the surface mucosa and is not invasive. Only rarely, in the case of severe underlying debilitation, may a more aggressive generalized form develop with extensive oral mucosal lesions.

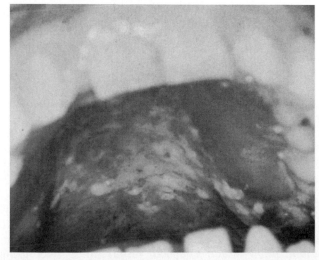

FIGURE 60–6. Candidiasis of the oral cavity. (Courtesy of Dr. John McDonald.)

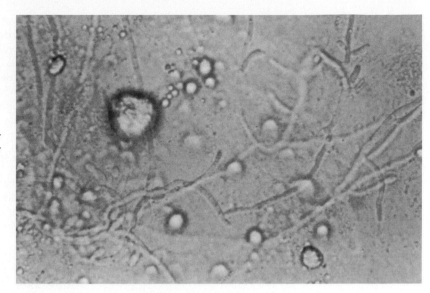

FIGURE 60-7. Hyphae of *Candida* seen after staining with 20% potassium hydroxide. (Courtesy of Dr. John McDonald.)

The diagnosis is usually made from the classic clinical features. However, if necessary, a smear of the plaque should be made, with a drop of 20% potassium hydroxide added, and the hyphae should be looked for to confirm the diagnosis (Fig. 60–7). Of course, the mere isolation of the organism in a diseased area of the oral cavity does not necessarily imply *Candida* infection because it is a commensal.

Before definitive therapy is discussed, it must be stressed that an underlying cause should always be sought and treated. For example, in one study, oral *Candida* lesions provided the earliest clinical evidence of HIV infection in children younger than 15 months.[13] The condition is most easily treated with 1 to 2 mL of topical nystatin oral suspension, 100,000 U/mL, applied to the mouth four times daily for 7 to 10 days). Nystatin should be retained in the mouth for several minutes. Nystatin is not absorbed systemically and must be in direct contact with the organism to be effective. The ointment form is useful for treatment of the commissures of the lips. Older children may use the tablet form in the mouth. Nystatin oral suspension may also be combined with Popsicle juice and frozen to make nystatin Popsicles. Nystatin vaginal suppositories used as a lozenge and allowed to dissolve in the mouth are also effective. Gentian violet 1% aqueous solution remains a popular therapy and is effective but is messy to use. Older children who are prone to repeated infections can be placed on chlorhexidine (Peridex) mouthwash twice daily to prevent infections. Alternative treatment may be done with clotrimazole 10-mg oral troches, which are allowed to dissolve in the mouth five times daily. In the rare instances when the disease process is resistant to these therapies, miconazole or keto-conazole may be needed. If a severe systemic infection exists, amphotericin can be used.

Actinomycosis

This infection is caused by the anaerobic organism *Actinomyces israelii,* a harmless commensal found in the tonsil crypts and periodontal pockets and activated only after necrosis of tissue (e.g., after trauma, particularly dental extraction). Most cases present as a granulomatous mass in the face or neck, with secondary sinus formation discharging the classic sulfur granules. Actinomycosis may occasionally present as a local ulcer in the oral cavity. Treatment consists of large doses of oral penicillin for up to 6 months.

Histoplasmosis

This condition is due to *Histoplasma capsulatum* and is endemic in the Mississippi and Ohio River valleys. Most infected individuals have relatively asymptomatic pulmonary infection; however, it rarely becomes disseminated and life threatening. In this progressive form of the disease, superficial, nonspecific ulcers may be seen in the oral cavity. Diagnosis is made by histologic examination and culture results. The treatment consists of systemic amphotericin for the progressive disseminated form of the disease.

Mucormycosis

Rarely, mucormycosis involves the oral cavity, with ulceration and granuloma formation, particularly on the palate. The condition is usually seen when an underlying debilitating condition or immunosuppression exists. The course of the disease is commonly fulminant. Thus, aggressive therapy with systemic amphotericin and wide surgical débridement is required.

Other Inflammatory Conditions

Trauma-Induced Conditions

Physical trauma is one of the most common causes of ulcers of the oral cavity in children. Typical examples include accidental cheek and tongue biting, irritation from a tooth, and laceration of the hard or soft palate mucosa secondary to direct injury from such objects as Popsicle sticks and toothbrushes. Occasionally, neurotic habits (e.g., habitual cheek and lip biting) may cause severe tissue damage. Bruxism may also result in chronic injury to the buccal mucosa. The lesion is, therefore, dependent on the severity and the chronicity of the injury. It commonly manifests as an ulcer that may be superficial or deep with marked surrounding induration, particularly if secondary infection complicates the picture. These ulcers are usually painful. The diagnosis is made on the basis of the history of the injury and by the site of the lesion—for example, an ulcer closely related to a carious tooth or area of induration or an ulcer on the buccal mucosa related to cheek biting. An unusual but potentially serious physical injury, particularly in children, is an electrical burn of the lips due to biting on an electric cord or placing the female end of an extension cord in the mouth, which causes arcing of the electric current.[14] This commonly results in injury to the commissure of the lips, with subsequent scarring. For prevention of stenosis, a long-term stent is needed and, ultimately, even a surgical procedure to release the fibrosis.[3]

Of the chemical burns, by far the most common is the "aspirin burn" due to the popular custom of placing an aspirin in contact with a painful area in the oral cavity (e.g., a sore tooth). This results in a superficial ulcer that may be painful. Of more serious consequence is the introduction into the mouth of noxious chemicals (e.g., alkali or acid), which produce intense reaction; if the reaction is severe enough, significant scarring can result, with limitation of movement of the tongue and trismus. Essentially, the treatment should consist of careful irrigation of the mouth, analgesics, and the use of topical or systemic steroids and antibiotics if the injury is severe enough. Careful emphasis on maintaining adequate hydration is mandatory. Because these children frequently swallow the corrosive substance, esophageal burns should be suspected and managed accordingly (see Chap. 70).

Thermal injury may result from hot food or liquids and may occur anywhere in the oral cavity. The best known of these is the "pizza burn" due to the melted cheese, which classically results in ulceration on the hard palate or the dorsum of the tongue. Similar injuries can occur from drinking hot chocolate or eating melted cheese sandwiches.

Treatment of traumatic ulcers consists of elimination of the precipitating event, supportive therapy, and use of a mild saline rinse or an oxidizing mouthwash (e.g., hydrogen peroxide 3%, diluted with two parts mouthwash or warm water) to aid healing and to prevent secondary infection. When this regimen is used, most traumatic ulcers heal in 7 to 10 days.

Contact Stomatitis (Stomatitis Venenata)

This uncommon condition is due to sensitization of the oral mucosa by previous contact with the causative agent. This sensitization may occur after a single previous exposure or even after multiple previous exposures, which makes identification of the causative agent difficult. The local reaction may vary from mild erythema to superficial ulceration or even a vesiculobullous reaction. There is no associated systemic reaction. Many substances have been implicated, including chewing gum, candy, cough drops, antiseptic lozenges, mouthwashes (particularly if used undiluted), toothpaste,[12] and topical or injected local anesthetic agents.

Treatment consists of identifying the causative substance and discontinuing its use. In addition to supportive therapy, antihistamines may occasionally be of value during the acute episode.

Aphthous Stomatitis

This condition may develop at any age and exhibits a slight female preponderance. While commonly seen in teenagers and young adults, it is not uncommon in children younger than 10 years. The etiology is unknown, but the disease is thought to be immunologically mediated. In one study, patients with recurrent aphthous ulcers demonstrated decreased cellular immune function, which persisted after resolution of the oral lesions.[21] Also, increased activity in the antibody-dependent cellular cytotoxicity mechanism has been implicated as the cause of local tissue damage, but the triggering event for this reaction is unclear.[15]

This disease is characterized by the development of ulcers of the oral mucosa and varies in severity from mild symptoms, with lesions developing once or twice a year, to situations in which the patient is almost never free of ulcers, with new ulcers forming as the old ones heal. Local trauma, vitamin B deficiency, emotional stress, and debilitating disease have all been noted as precipitating factors.

Usually, there is a prodromal period of tingling in the area, followed by the development of single or multiple ulcers. Note that there is no stage of vesicle formation. These are painful superficial ulcers with slightly raised borders and erythematous halos. The ulcers occasionally coalesce. Healing occurs in 10 to 14 days, without scarring. Classically, these lesions develop on the mucous membrane of the oral cavity not bound to bone (Fig. 60–8), compared with herpetic stomatitis, which occurs on mucosa bound to bone.

There is no known definitive therapy for this condition. The best that can be recommended is to keep the area clean and to prevent secondary infection by using cleansing mouthwashes—for example, chlorhexidine mouth rinse, which has been shown to reduce mucositis in chemotherapy patients by decreasing oral microbial flora.[5] The application of topical local anesthetic before meals may be helpful. Cauterization with silver nitrate or cryosurgery has been used in an effort to diminish the pain. While this does seem to be effective to some degree, the healing time appears to be prolonged by this therapy. Topical steroids have been advocated, but there is no real evidence that this alters the course of the disease in any way. The case is similar with the intralesional injection of steroids. Systemic steroids may be helpful in severe stomatitis.

Behçet Syndrome

This rare syndrome consists of recurrent aphthous ulceration of the oral cavity together with painful ulcers of the

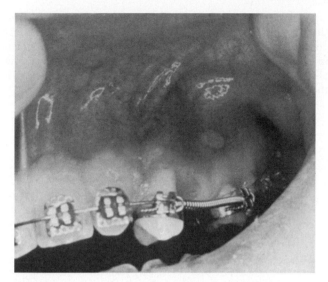

FIGURE 60–8. Aphthous ulcers developing on mucosa *not* bound to bone. (Courtesy of Dr. John McDonald.)

eyes (uveitis and iridocyclitis) and genitalia.[8] Although the etiology is unknown, association between Behçet syndrome and several HLA antigens suggests a genetic basis for this disease.[20] It is seen rarely in Western countries but is relatively more common in the Middle East, Korea, China, and Japan. The diagnosis may be difficult to make at the initial examination because multifocal involvement may not be present. Therapy is the same as that for aphthous stomatitis.

Reiter Syndrome

This syndrome is similar to Behçet syndrome and is rarely reported in children. The classic triad of Reiter syndrome consists of urethritis, conjunctivitis, and arthritis. Oral lesions, when present, are small and whitish and do not resemble aphthous ulcers.[18] Reiter syndrome in adults usually follows an infection with *Chlamydia*, whereas in children, gram-negative enteric infections are most commonly responsible. The pathophysiologic mechanism of this disease involves an autoimmune process triggered by cross-reactivity between host and bacterial antigens in a genetically susceptible individual.[4] Most children recover in a few months without sequelae, although some have a chronic relapsing condition. Permanent disability is unusual. Treatment consists of anti-inflammatory medications.

Periadenitis Mucosa Necrotica Recurrens (Sutton Disease)

This syndrome is the most severe type of aphthous stomatitis and is characterized by large (frequently greater than 1 cm) painful ulcers on the oral mucosa. Like aphthous ulcers, they may be single or multiple, and the clinical course may vary from sporadic occurrence to persistent ulceration lasting months. Because the ulcer is deep and has surrounding induration with raised broad borders (Fig. 60–9), it must be differentiated from malig-

nant neoplasm. The ulcers usually heal with scarring, which may even result in trismus. Sutton disease is difficult to treat. Stanley recommended cleaning the lesions with warm saline solution and then coating the lesions with a thick layer of potent steroid in emollient dental paste.[19] He also recommended systemic steroid therapy for patients whose lesions are too large, too numerous, or too difficult to reach for topical treatment. In 40 patients with oral and genital aphthae and Sutton disease, thalidomide (100 to 300 mg/day for 1 to 3 months) yielded remission in 15 patients and marked improvement in 15 other patients.[6]

Necrotizing Sialometaplasia

This benign condition of unknown etiology is characterized by the development of a large ulcer on the hard palate. The ulcers are usually 1 to 2 cm in size, unilateral, and painless. Ulcerations occur less frequently in other oral cavity sites but are also seen in the nasal cavity and larynx.

On microscopic examination, the lesion is characterized by pseudoepitheliomatous hyperplasia of the epithelium, necrosis of salivary gland tissue, and squamous metaplasia of involved salivary ducts and acini. In adults, these histologic findings may resemble squamous cell carcinoma.

This condition requires only supportive therapy and resolves spontaneously. Biopsy establishes the diagnosis.[7]

Fixed Drug Reaction (Stomatitis Medicamentosa)

This condition is characterized by reaction of the oral mucosa to a systemically administered drug. In general, any drug may produce any type of reaction, from the most mild to the most severe (Stevens-Johnson syndrome). The various types of reactions can be categorized as follows[10]:

1. Pharmacologic: This reaction is due to the deposition of heavy metals in the gingiva (e.g., bismuth,

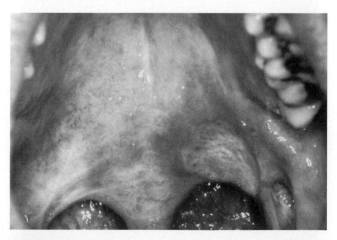

FIGURE 60–9. Periadenitis mucosa necrotica recurrens (PMNR). Note the large ulcer with surrounding induration. (Courtesy of Dr. John McDonald.)

lead). A line on the gingiva due to the precipitation of the metal salt is characteristic.

2. Toxic: A toxic reaction is classically seen in patients receiving chemotherapy (e.g., methotrexate). A combination of direct toxic effect on the oral mucosa and local factors promoting mucosal breakdown results in stomatitis. Reactions can vary from mild to severe superficial ulceration. If there is an associated agranulocytosis, the stomatitis may be even more severe.

3. Intolerance-based and idiosyncratic: Examples of these reactions include gingival hyperplasia due to phenytoin (Dilantin). This represents an idiosyncratic reaction to the drug. A granulomatous reaction has been described in some patients receiving iodides and bromides.

4. Allergic: In the classic allergic reaction, urticaria may occur in response to the drug. In the fixed drug eruption, diffuse stomatitis may result, or the reaction may be confined to one area of the mucosa because of the presence of fixed antibodies. It may manifest as erythema, superficial ulcers, or even vesiculobullous eruptions (Fig. 60–10). The classic "target" lesion is characterized by a central bulla surrounded by urticarial reaction and may be found on the mucosa and the skin. Drugs that are classically associated with allergic reaction in the pediatric group are antibiotics, barbiturates, tranquilizers, and salicylates.

5. Ecologic: This reaction is seen secondary to broad-spectrum antibiotic use and is characterized by *Candida* overgrowth. Denuded papillae of the tongue and a painful beefy tongue result.

6. Indirect: If bone marrow suppression occurs secondary to drug administration, a severe stomatitis usually characterized by marked ulceration may result.

In general, treatment should consist of identification of the drug and cessation of its use. Supportive therapy consisting of mouth rinses and topical local anesthesia is usually all that is necessary. Antihistamines are occasionally of some value, and systemic steroids can be used if the reaction is severe.

SELECTED REFERENCES

Carter AB. Infections of the Oral Cavity. In Kaplan SL (ed). Current Therapy in Pediatric Infectious Disease, 3rd ed. St Louis, BC Decker, 1993, pp 21–26.

A useful review of the odontogenic and nonodontogenic infections of the oral cavity.

Cherry JD. Pharyngitis (pharyngitis, tonsillitis, tonsillopharyngitis, and nasopharyngitis). In Feigin RD, Cherry JD (eds). Textbook of Pediatric Infectious Diseases, 4th ed. Philadelphia, WB Saunders, 1998, pp 148–156.

A detailed review of common infectious diseases of the mouth, and pharynx.

Fenton SJ, Unkel JH. Viral infections of the oral mucosa in children: a clinical review. Pract Periodont Aesthetic Dent 9(6):683-90, quiz 692, 1997.

A review of the common viral infections in the pediatric age group.

Levin LS, Johns M. Lesions of the oral mucous membranes. Otol Clin North Am 19:87, 1986.

A good overview of common oral lesions and disease seen by otolaryngologists, including lesions due to viral infection, drug reactions, exposure to environmental agents, and idiopathic causes.

McNulty JS, Fassett RL. Syphilis. An otolaryngologic perspective. Laryngoscope 91:889, 1981.

A useful review of the head and neck manifestations of both acquired and congenital syphilis. This article has particular relevance in view of the AIDS epidemic and the increasing frequency of congenital syphilis in some large American cities.

Moniaci D, Cavallari M, Greco D, et al. Oral lesions in children born to HIV-1 positive women. J Oral Pathol Med 22:8, 1993.

This cohort study of 69 children born to HIV-positive mothers found that oral candidiasis may be the earliest clinical sign of HIV infection in children younger than 15 months.

REFERENCES

1. Amir J, Harel L, Smetana Z, Varsano, I. Treatment of herpes simplex gingivostomatitis with acyclovir in children: a randomized double blind placebo controlled study. BMJ 314:1800, 1997.
2. Cherry JD, John CL. Herpangina: the etiologic spectrum. Pediatrics 36:632, 1965.
3. Colcleugh RG, Ryan JE. Splinting electrical burns of the mouth in children. Plast Reconstr Surg 58:239, 1976.
4. Cuttica RJ, Scheines EJ, Garay SM, et al. Juvenile onset Reiter's syndrome. A retrospective study of 26 patients. Clin Exp Rheumatol 10:285, 1992.
5. Ferretti G, Ash R, Brown A, et al. Chlorhexidine for prophylaxis against oral infections and associated complications in patients receiving bone marrow transplants. J Am Dent Assoc 114:461, 1987.
6. Grinspan D. Significant response of oral aphthosis to thalidomide treatment. J Am Acad Dermatol 12:85, 1985.
7. Hirsch MS, Swartz MN. Antiviral agents. N Engl J Med 302:903, 1980.
8. Lehner T. Pathology of recurrent oral ulceration and oral ulceration

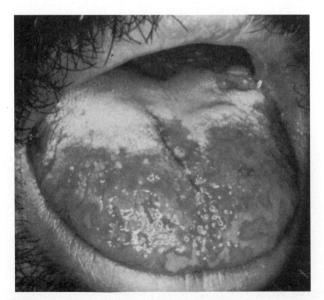

FIGURE 60–10. Stomatitis medicamentosa due to erythromycin. (Courtesy of Dr. John McDonald.)

in Behçet's syndrome: light, electron and fluorescence microscopy. J Pathol 97:481, 1969.

9. Levin LS, Johns M. Lesions of the oral mucous membranes. Otol Clin North Am 19:87, 1986.

10. McCarthy PL, Shklar G. Oral manifestations of systemic drug reactions. In McCarthy PL, Shklar G (eds). Diseases of the Oral Mucosa. Philadelphia, Lea & Febiger, 1980, pp 241–255.

11. McNulty JS, Fassett RL. Syphilis. An otolaryngologic perspective. Laryngoscope 91:889, 1981.

12. Millard LG. Contact sensitivity to toothpaste. Br Med J 1:676, 1973.

13. Moniaci D, Cavallari M, Greco D, et al. Oral lesions in children born to HIV-1 positive women. J Oral Pathol Med 22:8, 1993.

14. Palin WE Jr, Sadove AM, Jones JE, et al. Oral electrical burns in a pediatric population. J Oral Med 42:17, 1981.

15. Porter SR, Scully C. Aphthous stomatitis—an overview of aetiopathogenesis and management. Clin Exp Dermatol 16:235, 1991.

16. Rawstron SA, Jenkins S, Blanchard S, et al. Maternal and congenital syphilis in Brooklyn, N.Y. Epidemiology, transmission, and diagnosis. Am J Dis Child 147:727, 1993.

17. Richardson HB, Leibovitz A. Hand, foot, and mouth disease in children. J Pediatr 67:6, 1965.

18. Sharp JT. Reiter's syndrome. Curr Probl Dermatol 5:157, 1973.

19. Stanley HR. Management of patients with persistent recurrent aphthous stomatitis and Sutton's disease. Oral Surg Oral Med Pathol 35: 174–179, 1973.

20. Sun A, Lin SE, Chu CT, et al. HLA-DR and DQ antigens in Chinese patients with Behçet's disease. J Oral Pathol Med 22:60, 1993.

21. Ueta E, Umazume M, Yamamoto T, et al. Leukocyte dysfunction in oral mucus membrane diseases. J Oral Pathol Med 22:120, 1993.

22. Wiesner PJ, Tronca E, Bonin P. Clinical spectrum of pharyngeal gonococcal infections. N Engl J Med 288:181, 1973.

23. Woo S, Sonis S, Sonis A. The role of herpes simplex virus in the development of oral mucositis in bone marrow transplant recipients. Cancer 66:2375, 1990.

Tonsillectomy and Adenoidectomy

Jack L. Paradise, M.D.

No practice involving health care for children in the 20th century has excited more heated controversy among health professionals than has surgical removal of the tonsils and adenoids. Long the most common major operation carried out on children, tonsillectomy and adenoidectomy (T&A) continues to constitute a treatment whose benefits in relation to costs and risks have yet to be thoroughly assessed and whose indications have begun to be clarified only in the past two decades. Nonetheless, the persistently high rate of performance of T&A, despite substantial declines over the past three decades, attests to its hold on the minds of many physicians and parents as a treatment of importance and value. In 1996, an estimated 248,000 children younger than 15 years of age underwent T&A, an estimated 39,000 children underwent tonsillectomy alone, and an estimated 129,000 children underwent adenoidectomy alone.[89] Annual expenditures for tonsil and adenoid surgery in the United States probably exceed one and one half billion dollars.

While T&A is often thought of as, and most often carried out as, a single, combined operation, it is obvious that in considering indications for operating, each of the two components—tonsillectomy and adenoidectomy—requires attention individually.

History

Tonsillectomy has been known as a surgical procedure for at least two millennia, a technique for the operation having been described by Celsus as early as 50 AD.[60] Adenoidectomy, by contrast, was probably not undertaken until the latter half of the 19th century, when Wilhelm Meyer of Copenhagen suggested that adenoid vegetations were responsible not only for nasal symptoms but also for impaired hearing.[82] The two operations began increasingly to be carried out together early in the 20th century, as the then-popular "focus of infection" theory attributed various systemic disorders, most notably "rheumatism," to diseased tonsils and adenoids, and as enthusiasts proceeded even further to recommend T&A as a treatment for such diverse conditions as anorexia, mental retardation, and enuresis, or simply as a general measure to promote good health.[53, 60] Perhaps the ultimate in enthusiasm for T&A was manifested, in certain communities, in

wholesale surgery on entire populations of school children in public school buildings.[8]

Skepticism regarding the propriety of subjecting such large numbers of children to T&A began to be voiced increasingly in the 1930s[3, 60] and 1940s.[9] This skepticism received powerful reinforcement as (1) epidemiologic studies pointed to a natural decline in the incidence of upper respiratory infections in children after the first few years in school[7, 75, 122, 123, 126]; (2) recognition spread, in the period preceding the development of an effective vaccine, that individuals who had recently undergone tonsillectomy were at increased risk of developing poliomyelitis, particularly of the bulbar type[5, 40, 43, 44, 68]; (3) a succession of effective antimicrobial agents became available for treating bacterial respiratory infections; and (4) a number of studies were published that purported to show that tonsil and adenoid surgery was, after all, ineffective.[25, 76, 104]

Antipathy toward T&A, particularly in pediatric circles, mounted, exacerbated by frequent instances in which surgery had been undertaken for obviously insubstantial indications. Occasional newspaper accounts of family-wide tonsillectomy (Fig. 61–1) added to collective righteous indignation about unnecessary surgery on children. During the 1950s, a major health care program, the United Mine Workers Welfare and Retirement Fund, hoping to both improve quality of care and reduce costs, instituted as a requirement for paying for a tonsil or adenoid operation prior endorsement of the procedure by one of a select panel of pediatricians or internists. In the late 1960s, an account in a standard pediatric textbook questioned the very existence of indications for tonsillectomy,[39] while a critical review in a prestigious journal termed tonsillectomy "ritualistic surgery."[14] As recently as 1976, the suggestion was made that tonsil and adenoid surgery be suspended entirely until such time as its efficacy could be established in properly conducted trials.[112]

Notwithstanding this climate ranging from skepticism to outright condemnation, support for T&A continued throughout many segments of the medical community. This support derived variously from (1) attitudes acquired during training; (2) judgments drawn from personal clinical experience; (3) later studies, embodying for the first time randomized, clinical trials, which despite their limitations suggested that the operations *are* in some degree efficacious[74, 77, 78, 111]; (4) contentions by orthodontists that

FIGURE 61-1. Newspaper photograph of five children in one family who underwent tonsillectomy and adenoidectomy on the same day. (Courtesy of the Pittsburgh Post-Gazette.)

sustained mouth breathing due to large adenoids may cause abnormalities in the growth and development of the facial skeleton and dentition[65, 66, 118]; and (5) accumulating reports of instances of life-threatening airway obstruction attributable to enlarged tonsils and adenoids that was relieved by their removal.[63, 69, 70, 81, 86]

Over the years, striking variability in tonsil and adenoid surgery rates has been noted between nations,[105] between regions within nations,[19, 27, 64, 80, 84] and even between adjoining communities of similar population make-up.[10, 48, 50, 72, 129] Underlying these differences in surgical rates have been wide differences of opinion concerning how extensive, severe, and long-standing various tonsil- or adenoid-related conditions should be to justify surgery. Opinions have also differed as to whether, under various clinical circumstances, surgery should consist of tonsillectomy only, or adenoidectomy only, or the combined procedure. Tonsillectomy has generally been considered the component of tonsil and adenoid surgery that is efficacious with regard to recurrent throat infection,[59, 77] and adenoidectomy the component efficacious with regard to disease of the middle ear.[32, 34, 54, 59, 78, 82] Nonetheless, when either operation alone has appeared indicated for a specific category of illness, the other operation often has been added to the procedure to "take advantage" of the hospitalization and anesthesia, and in the belief that more was to be gained than lost by performing maximal removal of pharyngeal lymphoid tissue. A survey of Blue Cross/Blue Shield programs and practicing otolaryngologists in 1991 indicated that not only adenoidectomy but also T&A continued to be commonly performed because of recurrent or persistent otitis media.[94] Similarly, more recent reports indicate that tonsillectomy in young children is usually accompanied by adenoidectomy.[89, 124]

That the presence or absence of financial incentives may have been an additional factor that has influenced physicians' decisions to perform tonsil and adenoid surgery is suggested by the comparatively low frequency with which such surgery was performed in certain group practice, prepayment insurance programs, in which the

surgeon's income was not geared to the volume of surgery performed.[61, 106]

The substantial variations in attitude and practice that have existed in the medical community concerning tonsil and adenoid surgery are not surprising in light of the striking disparities that have existed in the recommendations of authorities. Contrast, for example, the mid-1970s American Academy of Pediatrics[2] and AMA-PSRO[4] criterion for tonsillectomy of "four or more episodes of tonsillitis with cervical adenitis within the preceding year," with this statement in a then relatively contemporaneous standard pediatric textbook: "Since the frequency with which episodes of acute pharyngitis or tonsillitis occur is not decreased by tonsillectomy, 'frequent sore throat' is not a valid indication."[13]

One need not search far for an explanation of the long-standing controversies concerning tonsil and adenoid surgery. It lies simply in the lack, until relatively recently, of convincing evidence that T&A in the conditions for which it has most commonly been undertaken, is more efficacious than conservative management. Such evidence can come only from properly designed and carefully conducted clinical trials. The first clinical trials of T&A were reported in 1963 by McKee.[77, 78] Trials reported in the succeeding two decades were not only relatively few but, for the most part, inadequate and inconclusive. Many of their methodologic limitations and flaws in experimental design have previously received extensive discussion[42, 56, 90, 92, 95] and will not be reviewed here in detail. One of the major shortcomings was the exclusion from most of the studies, on ethical grounds, of severely affected children, and the inclusion of children who were only mildly affected and in whom, therefore, the benefits of surgery could at best be slight.

The more recent Children's Hospital of Pittsburgh study, to be discussed later, was designed to avoid the various limitations of earlier studies. In particular, by employing stringent surgical criteria, it focused on children who were severely affected and who therefore should have been optimally positioned to show meaningful improvement if tonsil and/or adenoid surgery were indeed efficacious.

Patterns of Performance

Current Trends

Table 61–1 shows representative data concerning the numbers of tonsil and adenoid operations carried out on persons of all ages in the United States during the 25-year period from 1971 to 1996. Striking declines have occurred in the frequency of both tonsillectomy and T&A, whereas the frequency of adenoidectomy-only procedures has increased almost threefold. Throughout that period, most of the tonsillectomy-only procedures were performed on people older than 15 years of age (in 1996, 72.9%[89]), whereas most of the T&As and adenoidectomy-only procedures were performed on children younger than 15 years of age (in 1996, 90.5% and 94.9%, respectively[89]). (Because, until recently, available national statistics on surgical operations in the United States were limited to those performed on hospital inpatients, and because, increasingly since the early 1980s, tonsil and/or adenoid surgery has been performed on an outpatient basis, reliable estimates of the *total* number of tonsil and adenoid operations performed were not possible for the period extending from about 1983 to 1995.)

Age

As noted, age is an important factor in tonsil and adenoid surgical statistics. In 1996, 75.1% of all the operations were performed on children younger than 15 years of age.[89] Tonsillectomy alone is infrequently performed in children younger than 3 years of age, and adenoidectomy alone is infrequently performed in individuals older than 14 years of age.

Sex

Sex also influences surgical rates. In 1996, the rate of adenoidectomy-only was 1.7 times as high in males as in females, whereas the rate of tonsillectomy-only was 1.7 times as high in females as in males. The rate of T&A—the procedure most commonly performed in both sexes—was slightly higher in females.[89]

Why Tonsil and Adenoid Surgery Is Performed

Most indications used by those practitioners recommending or performing tonsil and adenoid surgery are encompassed by two categories of problems affecting the upper respiratory tract: infection that is recurrent or chronic, and obstruction. The infections involve variously the middle ears, mastoid air cells, nose, nasopharynx, adenoids, paranasal sinuses, oropharynx, tonsils, peritonsillar tissues, and cervical lymph nodes. The obstructions involve the nasopharyngeal and oropharyngeal airways and the oropharyngeal deglutitory pathway.

Certain variations on the themes of infection and obstruction are often cited in the case of the middle ear: adenoidectomy or T&A may be performed because of concern about persistent otitis media with effusion (OME; nonsuppurative, secretory, or serous otitis media), a condition in which infection is generally thought to play an initiating but not necessarily continuing role. Here the surgery is intended not only to eliminate presumed sources of infection in the adenoids or tonsils, or both, but also, in the case of adenoidectomy, to relieve presumed eustachian tube obstruction.[12]

Other, more general complaints, such as poor appetite or slow weight gain, that used to be widely accepted as indications for tonsil and adenoid surgery, may still occasionally be invoked as justifying surgery, but whether and how often this occurs is impossible to determine.

Costs Versus Benefits of Tonsil and Adenoid Surgery

The efficacy of an operation is a familiar concept for physicians, but the cost/benefit ratio of an operation or of withholding an operation may not be, and this subject deserves brief attention. The costs and potential benefits of tonsil and adenoid surgery are summarized in Table 61–2.

If surgery is resorted to, involved are not only financial costs but also, and more importantly, risks of potentially lethal or damaging anesthetic or surgical mishaps such as malignant hyperthermia, cardiac arrhythmia, hemorrhage, airway obstruction, bronchopulmonary infection, and transient or lasting velopharyngeal insufficiency.[108, 113, 115, 116] There may also be other risks, such as immunologic ones,[88] that have yet to be elucidated fully.

Offsetting costs and risks, however, are potential benefits that could be substantial. Reductions in the frequency of episodes of ear, nose, and throat illness would involve corresponding reductions for children in discomfort, in-

TABLE 61–1. Frequency, in Thousands, of Tonsillectomy, Adenoidectomy, and Adenotonsillectomy (T&A) for Persons of All Ages in the United States

Year	Tonsillectomy, n	Adenoidectomy, n	T&A, n	Total, n
1971	227	52	740	1019
1979	198	83	303	584
1996	144	136	274	554

Data from National Center for Health Statistics: National Hospital Discharge Survey, 1998.

TABLE 61–2. Costs and Potential Benefits of Tonsillectomy or Adenoidectomy or Both

Costs	Potential Benefits
$4265 (total cost [hospital plus professional fees] at Children's Hospital of Pittsburgh for adenotonsillectomy in 2001)°	Reduction in frequency of ear, nose, or throat illness and thus in
Risk of anesthetic accidents	Discomfort
Malignant hyperthermia	Inconvenience
Cardiac arrhythmia	School absence
Vocal cord trauma	Parental anxiety
Aspiration with resulting bronchopulmonary obstruction or infection	Work missed by parents
Risk of miscellaneous surgical or postoperative complications	Costs of physician visits and drugs
Hemorrhage	Reduction in nasal obstruction with improved
Airway obstruction due to edema of tongue, palate, or nasopharynx, or to retropharyngeal hematoma	Respiratory function
Central apnea	Comfort
Prolonged muscular paralysis	Sleep
Dehydration	Craniofacial growth and development
Palatopharyngeal insufficiency	Appearance
Otitis media	Reduction in hearing impairment
Nasopharyngeal stenosis	Improved growth and overall well-being
Refractory torticollis	Reduction in long-term parental anxiety
Facial edema	
Emotional upset	
Unknown risks	

° Costs for tonsillectomy alone and adenoidectomy alone are somewhat lower.

convenience, and school absence and for parents in anxiety, time missed from work, the costs and inconveniences of physician office visits, and the costs of medications. A reduction in nasal obstruction, if it were to occur, might result in improved respiratory function, lower incidence or lesser severity of upper respiratory infections, improved comfort, more restful sleep, more normal craniofacial growth and development, and more generally acceptable facial appearance. The remaining potential benefits shown in Table 61–2—for children, reduction in hearing impairment and improvement in growth and overall well-being, and for parents, reduction in overall anxiety—would, if they in fact resulted, obviously be important.

Most of the benefits listed in Table 61–2 might reasonably be termed *improved quality of life.* Applying actual monetary values to such benefits constitutes an exercise termed by economists *shadow pricing*, and it is used by them in attempting to translate into economic terms value judgments that are biosocial in nature.[1, 41] This is an approach that merits the attention of clinicians but is beyond the scope of the present discussion. Attempts at economic quantification aside, it is certain that physicians would be better able to judge whether the overall biosocial benefits of a tonsil or adenoid operation appear likely to outweigh its risks and costs if data were available regarding the degree of improvement the operation could be expected to bring about—that is, its efficacy.

To summarize, to arrive at rational indications for tonsil and adenoid surgery, groups of children had first to be defined who had particular symptom complexes severe enough to justify particular operations; in those groups, the efficacy of the operations then had to be tested by means of an integrated group of randomized, controlled trials; finally, if the operations proved efficacious, their overall impact had to be assessed as critically as possible

in relation to their risks and costs. It was with this frame of reference that the Children's Hospital of Pittsburgh Tonsil and Adenoid Study was designed and undertaken.

Recent Clinical Studies

The Children's Hospital of Pittsburgh Tonsil and Adenoid Study

Goals, Design, and Methods

The Children's Hospital of Pittsburgh Tonsil and Adenoid Study was conducted from 1971 to 1994, supported mainly by the National Institutes of Health. The study addressed a number of questions involving both the natural history of presumably tonsil- and adenoid-related problems and the results of tonsil and adenoid surgery.[91–93, 95] In particular, the study focused on three main problems: (1) the efficacy of tonsillectomy in reducing the frequency and severity of episodes of pharyngitis; (2) the efficacy of adenoidectomy in reducing the frequency and severity of episodes of otitis media; and (3) the effect of adenoidectomy on the course of nasal obstruction due to large adenoids.

Salient characteristics of the study included a dedicated study team; stringent entry criteria for separate clinical trials of tonsillectomy and of adenoidectomy; routine screening allergy skin tests and determination of serum immunoglobulin levels; standardized systems for quantifying or rating relevant clinical findings and diagnoses; ongoing testing of interobserver reliability; assessment of middle-ear status based on combined otoscopic, tympanometric, and audiometric examinations; standardized cephalometric radiographs to assess adenoid size; and standardized monitoring of subjects at frequent intervals.

Findings to Date

Limitations of Undocumented Histories of Recurrent Throat Infection. Many of the children initially referred to the study as potential candidates for the tonsillectomy trial had histories of recurrent throat infection episodes that appeared to meet all the criteria for entry as listed in Table 61–3 except for full documentation. Those children were enrolled in the study and followed prospectively, and if at least two observed episodes of throat infection then developed with patterns of frequency and clinical features that matched or exceeded those described in their presenting histories, the children became eligible for the tonsillectomy trial. However, a large majority of the children who lacked full documentation failed to develop frequent or severe episodes of throat infection.[97] From this experience, one may reasonably conclude that histories of recurrent throat infection that are undocumented do not validly forecast subsequent experience and hence do not constitute an adequate basis for subjecting children to tonsillectomy.

Efficacy of Tonsillectomy for Recurrent Throat Infection: The Initial and Subsequent Clinical Trials. Over a period of 11 years, the researchers studied the efficacy of tonsillectomy in 187 children with recurrent throat infection who met the stringent entry criteria described in Table 61–3. Of these children, 91 were assigned randomly to either surgical or nonsurgical treatment groups and 96 were assigned according to parental preference. In both the randomized and the nonrandomized trials, the incidence of throat infection during the first 2 years of follow-up was significantly lower ($p < .05$) in the surgical groups than in the corresponding nonsurgical groups. For example, in the randomized trial, during the first and second years, respectively, 92% and 84% of surgical subjects developed no episodes of throat infection rated clinically as moderate or severe, compared with 34% and 41% of control subjects. Third-year differences, although in most cases not statistically significant, also consistently favored the surgical groups. On the other hand, in each follow-up year, many subjects in the nonsurgical groups had fewer than three episodes of infection, and most

TABLE 61–3. Children's Hospital of Pittsburgh Adenotonsillectomy Study: Criteria for Entering First Controlled Trial of Tonsillectomy on the Basis of Recurrent Throat Infection

1. At least three episodes in each of 3 years, or five episodes in each of 2 years, or seven episodes in 1 year.
2. Each episode must have been characterized by one or more of the following:
   a. Oral temperature of 101°F (38.3°C) or higher
   b. Enlarged (>2 cm) or tender anterior cervical lymph nodes
   c. Tonsillar exudate
   d. Positive culture for group A beta-hemolytic streptococcus
3. Apparently adequate antibiotic therapy must have been administered for proven or suspected streptococcal episodes.
4. Each episode must have been confirmed by examination and its qualifying features described in a clinical record at the time of occurrence.

episodes among subjects in the nonsurgical groups were mild. Of the 95 subjects treated with surgery, 13 (14%) had surgery-related complications, all of which were readily managed or self-limited.[98]

The authors concluded that these results warrant the election of tonsillectomy for children meeting the trials' stringent eligibility criteria, but also provide support for nonsurgical management. It appeared to the researchers that treatment for such children should be individualized, with decisions for or against tonsillectomy taking into account the potential adverse consequences of surgery previously described, as well as various other factors, including the parents' and the child's respective preferences, anxieties, and tolerance of illness; the child's tolerance of antimicrobial drugs; the child's school performance in relation to illness-related absence; the accessibility of health care services; out-of-pocket costs; and the nature of available anesthetic and surgical services and facilities.

Because the findings in these trials cannot properly be extrapolated to children with throat infection experiences that are less extreme or less well documented, the researchers conducted a subsequent trial in which somewhat less severely affected children were enrolled and randomly assigned to one of three treatment groups: tonsillectomy, T&A, or control. Results of this latter trial indicate substantially less efficacy for surgery than was found in the original trials.[101] The researchers interpreted these results as indicating that the surgical criteria used in this latter trial were insufficiently stringent for general clinical use, and that the more stringent criteria of the original trials should ordinarily be adhered to in practice.

Efficacy of Adenoidectomy for Otitis Media: The Initial and Subsequent Clinical Trials. The researchers initially studied the efficacy of adenoidectomy in 213 children defined as being at high risk for otitis media in that each had received myringotomy with tympanostomy-tube placement and, subsequent to tube extrusion, had developed a recurrence of either OME or (less often) acute otitis media (AOM), or both.[102] Of these children, 99 were assigned randomly to either adenoidectomy or nonadenoidectomy treatment groups and 114 were assigned according to parental preference. In both trials, over a period of at least 2 years, the results favored subjects who underwent adenoidectomy. In the randomized trial, during the first and second years, respectively, adenoidectomy subjects had 47% and 37% less time with otitis media than control subjects and 28% and 35% fewer AOM episodes than control subjects. Nonetheless, many of the adenoidectomy subjects continued having episodes of otitis media. The researchers concluded from these results that adenoidectomy is justified on an individualized basis for children who develop recurrent otitis media after extrusion of tympanostomy tubes, with individual decisions for or against surgery taking into account the same factors as those noted previously regarding tonsillectomy for recurrent throat infection.

These original adenoidectomy trials did not address three important, related questions: the efficacy of tonsiladenoid surgery in children who had not previously undergone tube placement, the efficacy of such surgery in children who had had troublesome histories of recurrent AOM (as distinct from persistent OME), and the extent to which adding tonsillectomy to adenoidectomy affects the outcome. To address these questions, the researchers undertook a subsequent study consisting of two parallel randomized clinical trials.[103] Children were eligible for this study if they had *not* undergone tube placement and if they had experienced at least three episodes of AOM during the preceding 6 months or four episodes during the preceding 12 months, or at least 180 days of middle-ear effusion during the preceding 12 months.

In one of the two trials, 304 children without appreciable tonsil-related illness were assigned to one of three treatment groups: adenoidectomy, T&A, or control. In the other trial, 157 children who had, in addition to appropriate middle-ear disease histories, either tonsillar hypertrophy or recurrent throat infection that met specified criteria, were assigned to one of only two treatment groups—T&A or control.[100] Virtually all of the children enrolled in each of the two trials were enrolled on the basis of recurrent AOM rather than on the basis of persistent middle-ear effusion (although many of those enrolled on the basis of recurrent AOM had also had middle-ear effusion for considerable periods, but less than 180 days cumulatively during the preceding 12 months). In both trials, the efficacy of surgery—whether adenoidectomy or T&A—proved to be modest and limited mainly to the first follow-up year. The largest differences in that year were found in the three-way trial between the T&A group and the control group: mean annual rate of episodes of AOM, 1.4 vs. 2.1 ($p < .001$); and mean estimated percentage of time with otitis media, 18.6% vs. 29.9% ($p = .002$). Perioperative and postoperative complications occurred not infrequently, but more often in children who underwent T&A than in children who underwent adenoidectomy. Given the limited benefit both of adenoidectomy and of T&A in these trials, and the risks, morbidity, and costs of the operations, the researchers concluded that neither operation should be undertaken in children who had not previously undergone tube placement and whose only indication for surgery is recurrent AOM. On the other hand, because of the lim-

ited number of enrolled children who met the trials' entry criteria regarding persistent middle-ear effusion, no conclusions were possible regarding such children concerning the efficacy of either adenoidectomy or T&A.

The Clinical Trial of Adenoidectomy for Nasal Obstruction. Children were admitted to the researchers' clinical trials of adenoidectomy for nasal obstruction only if the obstruction was appreciable and could be shown with reasonable certainty to be due wholly or mainly to large adenoids (Fig. 61-2). Full results of these trials have not yet been reported. However, the children who underwent adenoidectomy appear to have experienced good results persisting for at least 2 years. In the control group, spontaneous improvement of some degree developed within the first year or two in some of the subjects, but complete resolution of nasal obstruction developed in relatively few.[99] The children providing these observations were mainly 5- and 6-year-olds.

It is important to consider whether the significantly greater relief of nasal obstruction achieved in the children who underwent adenoidectomy resulted in benefits that offset the costs and risks of the operation (see Table 61-2). In an effort to test the development of one such benefit—improved nasal function—the researchers assessed olfaction in a group of study children using various concentrations of phenylethyl alcohol, a roselike odorant. The researchers found that children rated as having no nasal obstruction showed almost uniformly good olfactory function, whereas most of those with severe obstruction showed poor function.[47]

Other Recent Trials of Adenoidectomy for Otitis Media

During the last two decades, a number of clinical trials of the efficacy of adenoidectomy for otitis media have been reported from other centers. Of these, two are most noteworthy. Maw[73] randomly assigned 103 children with bilateral middle-ear effusion to undergo adenoidectomy, T&A, or neither operation. In addition, each subject received unilateral myringotomy with tube placement. Results of the trial were based on findings in the unoper-

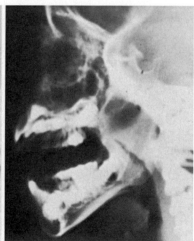

FIGURE 61-2. Lateral radiographs of children showing normal adenoids and adequate airway *(left)* and adenoids encroaching on the nasopharyngeal airway *(right)*.

ated ears only. Rates of clearance of effusion from those ears during the first year of follow-up were higher in subjects who underwent adenoidectomy or T&A than in subjects who underwent neither operation (at 1 year, 72% and 62%, respectively, versus 26%). However, data were not provided on the possible adjunctive use of antimicrobial treatment by the subjects' primary care physicians or on findings in the ears that had received tympanostomy tubes. Accordingly, the validity of the results seems questionable. Even if valid, the results bear on the *treatment* of middle-ear effusion, rather than its *prevention,* which is the issue of greater practical interest. Finally, the applicability of the results seems questionable because most surgeons probably would not leave long-standing middle-ear effusion unevacuated in an anesthetized child undergoing adenoidectomy.

Gates et al[46] reported results from a carefully executed trial involving 578 children with chronic middle-ear effusion. Adenoidectomy combined with myringotomy or with tympanostomy-tube placement proved to be more efficacious than myringotomy or tube placement alone in preventing recurrences of otitis media over a 2-year period. The authors recommended adenoidectomy combined with myringotomy as "the initial surgical treatment" in children with persistent effusions like the children they studied. However, the differences favoring adenoidectomy with myringotomy over tube placement were relatively small (e.g., mean cumulative times with effusion in the two treatment groups over the 2-year follow-up period were 31 and 36 weeks, respectively) and, in many instances, not statistically significant. Accordingly, one might conclude that tympanostomy-tube placement would be the more appropriate first surgical recourse for such children, with adenoidectomy reserved for those in whom otitis media continues to be a problem after tubes have been extruded.[96]

Adenoidectomy and Facial Growth

Other hoped-for outcomes of adenoidectomy remain to be evaluated. For example, certain orthodontists have attributed presumably abnormal growth patterns—long and narrow faces, low tongue placement, narrow upper jaws, steep mandibles, and open anterior bites—to large adenoids and have advocated surgery to prevent or ameliorate the so-called adenoid facies.[65, 66, 118] In keeping with earlier reports reviewed by Solow,[117] researchers in the Children's Hospital of Pittsburgh study found larger measures of anterior facial height and other open bite indicators in children with marked adenoidal obstruction of the nasopharyngeal airway than in carefully matched control subjects.[79] Some studies have described improvement in dentofacial measurements, dental arch morphology, and dental position following adenoidectomy[66, 67] or tonsillectomy,[55] but the studies failed to include unoperated control subjects. Solow[117] has reported normalization following adenoidectomy of the increased craniocervical angle found in children with adenoidal obstruction. Certain other hoped-for outcomes of adenoidectomy, such as an increased sense of comfort in breathing and improved facial appearance, are essentially subjective and not easily quantifiable, but nonetheless important and deserving of investigation.

Currently Acceptable Surgical Indications and Surgical Decision-Making

Removal of the tonsils or adenoids, or both, is clearly indicated in a small number of severely affected children and is clearly not indicated in the great majority of children in whom the degree of tonsil- or adenoid-related illness or disability is insubstantial. Between these extremes lies an intermediate group who meet minimum criteria for tonsil or adenoid surgery but who are not so severely affected that surgery is mandatory. These children have what might be termed *reasonable* surgical indications. As a group, these children would receive near-term benefit from surgery, but most would also sooner or later improve spontaneously, "outgrowing" their problems. Currently there would appear to be no satisfactory way to predict whether an individual child within this intermediate group would, without surgery, have a satisfactory near-term outcome, or instead continue for some period to experience the difficulty that the surgery is likely to ameliorate.

Definite Surgical Indications

Operation is clearly indicated in those relatively unusual circumstances in which massive hypertrophy of tonsils or adenoids or both results in unquestioned dysphagia, extreme discomfort in breathing, clinically significant obstructive sleep apnea (see Chapter 62) or, even more extremely, alveolar hypoventilation or cor pulmonale.[62, 63, 69, 70, 81, 86]

Alveolar hypoventilation is a diagnosis that may be difficult to establish, short of documenting the presence of hypoxia or hypercarbia during sleep, as in polysomnography,[16] or finding clinical, radiographic, or electrocardiographic evidence of cor pulmonale.[71] Extremely stertorous breathing when a child is awake and frequently occurring episodes of obstructive apnea during sleep are signs that should lead to a high index of suspicion for the presence of alveolar hypoventilation. The persistent presence of these signs alone—even without further evidence of alveolar hypoventilation—should occasion removal of the adenoids or tonsils, or both, depending on their respective size. Diagnostic polysomnography may be particularly useful in the occasional child with a history suggestive of obstructive sleep apnea but with only mild or moderate adenotonsillar hypertrophy.[85, 109] Although the reports must be interpreted with caution because the studies were not controlled, surgical relief of pronounced obstruction has been followed in some children by rapid improvement in weight,[131] and in others by improvement in nocturnal enuresis[128] or in overall behavior.[51]

Even in children with symptoms or signs of appreciable obstruction, however, surgery should not be resorted to immediately and automatically. Seemingly dramatic obstructive manifestations, even when long-standing, may sometimes be due to edema accompanying relatively inapparent infection, rather than to fixed structural changes.

Such obstructive symptoms may sometimes lessen considerably when vigorous antimicrobial treatment is applied. Accordingly, a trial of an appropriate antimicrobial agent is often advisable before deciding finally whether surgery is mandatory or even reasonably indicated. Finally, Demain and Goetz[35] recently reported reductions in adenoidal hypertrophy and associated obstructive symptoms after 24 weeks of treatment with aqueous nasal beclomethasone spray, and Brouillette et al[17] reported improvement in children with obstructive sleep apnea after 6 weeks of treatment with nasal fluticasone spray. As these authors indicated, further study is required to determine both the optimal duration of treatment and the likelihood of lasting improvement. Nonetheless, in children with obstructive sleep apnea that seems not so severe as to require urgent surgery, a trial of topical steroid treatment would certainly appear to be worthwhile.

Two other rare conditions constitute definite indications for tonsillectomy: malignant tumors of the tonsil and uncontrollable hemorrhage from tonsillar blood vessels.

Reasonable Indications for Surgery

Tonsillectomy

At present, recurrent throat infection may be considered a reasonable indication for tonsillectomy, provided that the conditions specified in Table 61–3 are met. Certain other nonurgent conditions may also be reasonable indications for tonsillectomy, even though their response to surgery has not been tested in controlled trials. These conditions include chronic (as distinct from recurrent acute) tonsillitis unresponsive to antimicrobial treatment (a condition that is rare if not nonexistent in young children); obstructive symptoms such as "hot potato" voice; halitosis due to debris in tonsillar crypts when conservative measures, such as gargling or pharyngeal douche, have proved ineffective; and peritonsillar abscess when the condition has developed more than once or has developed in a child with a substantial history of recurrent throat infection.

Adenoidectomy

Nonurgent conditions justifying adenoidectomy include obstructive adenoidal hypertrophy, persistent or recurrent otitis media, and chronic sinusitis. In the two former instances, the conditions of children considered for surgery should meet stringent standards of severity or duration, or both, comparable to those previously described for the Children's Hospital of Pittsburgh clinical trials.

In children with well-established adenoidal obstruction, adenoidectomy is certainly appropriate, although a short trial of antimicrobial treatment followed by a more protracted trial of topical nasal steroid treatment, as noted earlier, may be worthwhile before surgery is considered. If adenoidectomy is being considered as a component of orthodontic management, there should be objective evidence of adenoidal obstruction of the nasopharyngeal airway.

In children who have previously received tympanostomy-tube placement because of recurrent or persistent otitis media (see Chapter 25) and who, after tubal extrusion, continue to be troubled with recurrent AOM or OME, adenoidectomy is appropriate because, as noted previously, it reduces the risk of subsequent recurrences. Accordingly, in children scheduled to receive a second tube-placement procedure, the addition of adenoidectomy seems particularly advisable. On the other hand, for children in whom recurrent AOM has not been associated with persistent OME, and who have not previously received tube placement, the benefit of adenoidectomy, also as noted previously, is considerably more limited. For that reason, in such children in whom recurrences of AOM have become intolerable, tube placement alone seems a more reasonable first surgical recourse.

For children whose middle-ear problems consist mainly of persistent OME, who have not previously received tube placement, and in whom surgical intervention is deemed desirable, the advisability of adenoidectomy remains debatable. As noted previously, Gates et al[46] found that adenoidectomy combined with myringotomy or with tube placement was more efficacious than myringotomy or tube placement alone, but the reported differences were small. More recently, in an analysis of hospital discharge records in Ontario, Canada, Coyte et al[31] found that in 37,316 children who received tympanostomy tubes, adjuvant adenoidectomy and, especially, adjuvant T&A were associated with substantially reduced risks of the reinsertion of tympanostomy tubes and of rehospitalization for conditions related to otitis media. However, because the children who received adjuvant surgery were older than children who did not (median ages, 4 years and 2 years, respectively), and because the two groups may have differed in other important ways, the findings cannot be considered conclusive. In this author's view, if surgical intervention of any kind is to be undertaken for persistent OME in a child who has not previously received tube placement, the intervention should be limited to tube placement alone.

Finally, in the occasional child with chronic sinusitis whose symptoms have failed to respond satisfactorily to appropriate antimicrobial therapy, adenoidectomy may prove beneficial as an adjunctive procedure and may obviate the need for consideration of endoscopic sinus surgery.[18, 120, 125] However, before undertaking surgery of any kind, a search should be made for the presence of underlying conditions such as ciliary dysmotility syndromes[30] and immunodeficiencies.[107]

General Considerations

Given the current limitations of knowledge, modifications of the standards described in the foregoing paragraphs may be appropriate provided that they preserve intact the standards' general principles. For example, in a child about to undergo adenoidectomy for unequivocal indications, it would seem reasonable to add tonsillectomy if the tonsils have also been to some degree problematic, even if not to the degree that the criteria for tonsillectomy discussed previously would have required.

On the other hand, the fact that a child indeed meets the outlined criteria should not necessarily lead to a deci-

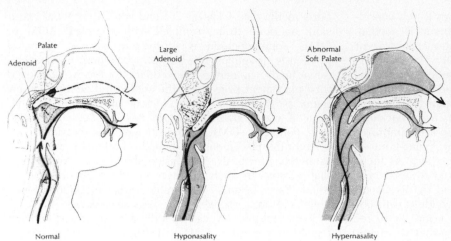

FIGURE 61-3. Functional and anatomic relationships in nasality. Normally, the soft palate reaches the posterior pharyngeal wall during production of sibilant and plosive sounds (*solid arrow, left*). With other sounds, the passage is open enough for normal nasal resonance (*dashed arrow, left*). Large adenoids (*center*) interfere with airflow and produce hyponasality. Velopharyngeal insufficiency (as in the submucous cleft) lets sound escape through the nose and produces hypernasality (*right*). (Figure by Donner C. In Paradise JL, Bluestone CD. Toward rational indications for tonsil and adenoid surgery. Hosp Pract 11(2):79–87, 1976.)

sion in favor of surgery. As noted previously, each decision should be individualized. Exemplifying the need for individualized decision making, one report argued in favor of tonsillectomy for the patient with rheumatic heart disease who has large tonsils and in whom antistreptococcal prophylaxis cannot be maintained with confidence.[42]

Contraindications to Tonsil and Adenoid Surgery

Contraindications to surgery are in four general categories: velopharyngeal, hematologic, immunologic, and infectious.

A number of abnormal conditions that result in velopharyngeal insufficiency constitute contraindications to adenoidectomy. These include overt cleft of the palate; submucous (covert) cleft of the palate; neurologic or neuromuscular abnormalities leading to impaired palatal function; and the unusually capacious pharynx. In each of these conditions, the presenting complaint is likely to be hypernasality, a symptom that the unwary observer may fail to distinguish from hyponasality. If adenoidectomy is undertaken to improve the nasal speech of such children, the symptom may worsen markedly, since the adenoids had been helping to fill the relative velopharyngeal void and thus facilitate normal speech production (Fig. 61–3). Suspicion should be aroused that a submucous cleft of the palate is present when a bifid uvula is observed or when widening and attenuation of the median raphe of the soft palate are present. The question can be clarified by the examiner's palpating along the junction of the hard and soft palates, where a V-shaped midline notch, rather than the normal rounded curve, strongly suggests the presence of a submucous cleft (Fig. 61–4). This examination should be performed on all children, with or without hypernasality, for whom adenoidectomy is being considered. Irrespective of the findings, if hypernasality due to velopharyngeal insufficiency is suspected, it is advisable to refer the patient to an individual or a team skilled in cleft palate evaluation and management.

Hematologic contraindications to tonsil or adenoid surgery consist of (1) anemia and (2) disorders of hemosta-

sis. Surgery should not be undertaken electively if the hemoglobin concentration is less than 10 g/dL or if the hematocrit is less than 30%. When surgery is being considered, careful inquiry should always be made about a family or past history of unusual bleeding or bruising, because certain rare hemostatic disorders may not be detectable with readily available tests. Routine preoperative studies may include measurements of the hemoglobin level or hematocrit, prothrombin time, and partial thromboplastin time and an estimate of the platelet level, usually from a stained blood smear, although the predictive value of these tests is limited.

In the view of some clinicians, the existence of frank respiratory allergy that has not been treated for at least 6 months constitutes a contraindication to tonsil or adenoid

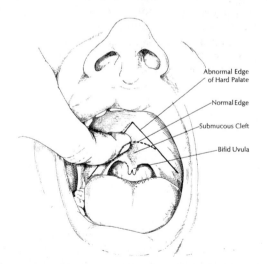

FIGURE 61-4. In patients with cleft palate, either overt or submucous, adenoidectomy is usually contraindicated, since it would tend to worsen hypernasality. Palpation for diagnosis of submucous cleft palate, which may be easily overlooked, is diagrammed. Bifid uvula, widening and attenuation of the median raphe of the soft palate, and a V-shaped midline notch, rather than a smooth curve, are diagnostic and should be sought. (Figure by Donner C. In Paradise JL, Bluestone CD. Toward rational indications for tonsil and adenoid surgery. Hosp Pract 11(2):79–87, 1976.)

surgery unless urgent, obstructive symptoms are present.[6] The opinion that tonsil or adenoid surgery in allergic children may precipitate the development of asthma[26] has not been tested in clinical studies. Certainly in children with nonurgent obstructive symptoms who have both upper respiratory allergy and large tonsils or adenoids, a reasonable trial of antiallergic management seems prudent as a precursor to considering surgery.

Tonsillectomy or adenoidectomy should not be undertaken in the face of local infection unless urgent obstructive symptoms are present or unless appropriate, prolonged antimicrobial treatment has been maintained unsuccessfully, or, in the view of some practitioners,[15] unless a peritonsillar abscess is present. Ordinarily, an interval of at least 3 weeks after an episode of acute infection both allows general recuperation and reduces the risk of operative hemorrhage.

Adverse Effects of Tonsil and Adenoid Surgery: Real and Potential

Any physician who recommends tonsil or adenoid surgery must weigh the possibility that harm will result. The possible adverse consequences range from death to nonfatal direct and indirect anesthetic and surgical complications to hypothetical interference with immunologic defense mechanisms. It is unfortunate that accurate statistics regarding mortality and morbidity in large patient populations are not available.

The death of a child as a consequence of tonsil or adenoid surgery is tragic in any circumstance but particularly so if, as is usually the case, the operation was elective in nature. Case fatality rates have been variously reported during the past quarter century as ranging from 1 in 1000 to 1 in 27,000,[6, 11, 87] but the validity of some of these reports is open to question. No deaths occurred among 35,710 children who underwent tonsillectomy, adenoidectomy, or T&A at the Pittsburgh Eye and Ear Hospital between 1954 and 1974,[114] whereas one death, from hemorrhage, occurred among 7743 children undergoing these operations in a hospital in Austria between 1979 and 1992.[83] Except for a probably irreducible minimum of anesthesia-related deaths (the anesthesia-related mortality rate unadjusted for age has been reported at 1 in 14,000[6]), death as a result of tonsil or adenoid surgery should be almost entirely preventable under present-day circumstances of care.

The possible nonfatal complications of tonsil or adenoid surgery are summarized in Table 61–2. Unfortunately, velopharyngeal insufficiency can sometimes develop after adenoidectomy even in children who preoperatively showed no evidence of palatal insufficiency.[132]

The risk of hemorrhage can be minimized by avoiding surgery during or immediately after episodes of infection, by careful attention to surgical technique,[37] and by avoiding the use of aspirin for the relief of postoperative pain. Preoperative screening for bleeding disorders by means of both history and laboratory tests can occasionally identify patients at heightened risk of hemorrhage, and in many centers these screening procedures are carried out routinely. Unfortunately, however, the procedures have both low positive predictive value (few of the abnormal histories or abnormal test results portend eventual hemorrhage) and low sensitivity (few of the children who develop hemorrhage will have had abnormal preoperative histories or laboratory values).[20] Hemorrhage, either primary (within 24 hours of surgery) or secondary (more than 24 hours after surgery), is thus bound to occur in some cases, and transfusion is occasionally required. In recent reports, the rate of primary hemorrhage has ranged from 0.2% to 2.2% and the rate of secondary hemorrhage from 0.1% to 3%.[21, 23, 24, 28, 33, 113]

Airway complications include both obstructive and central apnea, the latter particularly likely to occur in children younger than 3 years of age who had had obstructive symptoms preoperatively.[121, 130] Children who receive succinylcholine before intubation, and who happen to have cholinesterase deficiency, may develop prolonged muscular paralysis and require assisted ventilation.[98] Dehydration may result from reduced oral intake both pre- and postoperatively. Otitis media has been reported as a not infrequent postoperative complication,[77, 78] but it is not clear that the risk is higher than in comparable patients not operated upon. Rare complications of tonsil or adenoid surgery include nasopharyngeal stenosis,[29] refractory torticollis,[36] transient facial edema,[110] and bacterial tracheitis.[38]

Whether tonsil or adenoid surgery imposes immunologic risks of any practical consequence remains uncertain. The heightened risk of poliomyelitis that was an important deterrent to surgery before the advent of an effective vaccine, and for which an immunologic basis was later elucidated,[88, 119] is no longer of practical concern in this era of virtually universal immunization. In the Children's Hospital of Pittsburgh study, in subjects meeting specified surgical criteria, serum levels of immunoglobulins G, A, and M were measured at baseline and at intervals after the receipt or nonreceipt of tonsil and/or adenoid surgery. Decreases in levels of immunoglobulin G, but not in levels of immunoglobulin A or M, tended to occur more commonly and to be of greater magnitude in children who underwent tonsillectomy or T&A than in corresponding control subjects. However, in both surgical and control subjects, the subsequent incidence of throat infection showed no relationship to either contemporaneous immunoglobulin levels or changes from baseline levels. No significant changes in immunoglobulin levels developed in subjects who underwent adenoidectomy only.[45] The authors concluded that a decline in serum immunoglobulin levels following tonsillectomy did not constitute—as had been suggested by others[22]—a risk factor for developing respiratory infection but instead reflected a reduction in antigenic stimulation. Finally, the concern that tonsillectomy might predispose to the development of Hodgkin disease[127] appears to have been dispelled by later epidemiologic investigations.[49, 52, 58] Although it remains possible that the removal of the immunologically active tonsils and adenoids will someday prove to undermine resistance to disease of some sort, the likelihood at present seems small.

Preparation for Hospitalization and Surgery and Care in the Hospital

Children who are to undergo surgery should be prepared specifically for the experience well in advance. Parents should describe the expected course of events in as much detail and as frankly as possible, commensurate with the child's ability to comprehend. Children should be told that a certain amount of discomfort will occur but that every effort will be made by hospital personnel to minimize it. Many hospitals permit advance visits so that children can see first-hand the facilities and equipment that will be used and become acquainted with some of the personnel. Coloring or story books can also be helpful in the familiarization process. Once admitted to the hospital, children should have free and unlimited access to parents or parental surrogates. In any event, one or both parents or other caregivers should remain with the child during the period immediately preceding the trip to the operating room and should be at the bedside when the child returns. Careful preparation and kind, thoughtful management of the entire process of hospitalization and surgery should virtually eliminate the risk of untoward psychological consequences in previously well-adjusted children. For the child who is emotionally disturbed, the same general principles apply, but in addition, specialized professional advice may be appropriate to help minimize the risk of the child's neurotically misinterpreting the operative event.[57]

REFERENCES

1. Abt CC. The issue of social costs in costbenefit analysis of surgery. In Bunker JP, Barnes BA, Mosteller F (eds). Costs, Risks, and Benefits of Surgery. New York, Oxford University Press, 1977, pp 40–55.
2. American Academy of Pediatrics, Committee on Hospital Care. Pediatric Model Criteria Sets. Evanston, IL, American Academy of Pediatrics, 1975–1976, p 32.
3. American Child Health Association. Physical Defects: The Pathway to Correction. New York, American Child Health Association, 1934, pp 80–96.
4. American Medical Association. Sample Criteria for Short-Stay Hospital Review: Screening Criteria to Assist PSROs in Quality Assurance. Chicago, American Medical Association, 1976, pp 457–458.
5. Anderson GW, Rondeau JL. Absence of tonsils as a factor in the development of bulbar poliomyelitis. JAMA 155:1123, 1954.
6. Avery AD, Harris LJ. Tonsillectomy, adenoidectomy, and tonsillectomy with adenoidectomy: assessing the quality of care using short-term outcome measures. In Quality of Medical Care Assessment Using Outcome Measures: Eight Disease-Specific Applications. Santa Monica, CA, Rand, 1976, pp 651–727.
7. Badger GF, Dingle JH, Feller AE, et al. A study of illness in a group of Cleveland families. II. Incidence of the common respiratory diseases. Am J Hyg 58:31, 1953.
8. Baker SJ. Fighting for Life. New York, Macmillan, 1939, pp 140–141.
9. Bakwin H. Pseudodoxia pediatrica. N Engl J Med 232:691, 1945.
10. Bloor MJ, Venters GA, Samphier ML. Geographical variation in the incidence of operations on the tonsils and adenoids: an epidemiological and sociological investigation. Part I. J Laryngol Otol 92:791, 1978.
11. Bluestone CD, Paradise JL, Kass EH, et al. The workshop on tonsillectomy and adenoidectomy. Ann Otol Rhinol Laryngol 84:1, 1975.
12. Bluestone CD, Wittel RA, Paradise JL, et al. Eustachian tube function as related to adenoidectomy for otitis media. Trans Am Acad Ophthalmol Otolaryngol 76:1325, 1972.
13. Boat TF, Doershuk CF, Stern RC, et al. Tonsils and adenoids. In Behrman RE, Vaughn VC III (eds). Nelson Textbook of Pediatrics, 12th ed. Philadelphia, WB Saunders, 1983, pp 1019–1022.
14. Bolande RP. Ritualistic surgery—circumcision and tonsillectomy. N Engl J Med 280:591, 1969.
15. Brandow EC Jr. Immediate tonsillectomy for peritonsillar abscess. Trans Am Acad Ophthalmol Otolaryngol 77:1412, 1973.
16. Brouilette R, Hanson D, David R, et al. A diagnostic approach to suspected obstructive sleep apnea in children. J Pediatr 105:10, 1984.
17. Brouillette RT, Manoukian JJ, Ducharme FM, et al. Efficacy of fluticasone nasal spray for pediatric obstructive sleep apnea. J Pediatr 138:838, 2001.
18. Buchman CA, Yellon RF, Bluestone CD. Alternative to endoscopic sinus surgery in the management of pediatric chronic rhinosinusitis refractory to oral antimicrobial therapy. Otolaryngol Head Neck Surg 120:219, 1999.
19. Bunker JP. Surgical manpower: a comparison of operations and surgeons in the United States and in England and Wales. N Engl J Med 282:135, 1970.
20. Burk CD, Miller L, Handler SD, et al. Preoperative history and coagulation screening in children undergoing tonsillectomy. Pediatrics 89:691, 1992.
21. Canter RJ, Rogers J. Tonsillectomy: home after 24 hours? J Laryngol Otol 99:177, 1985.
22. Cantini A, Bellioni P, Salvinelli F, et al. Serum immunoglobulins and secretory IgA deficiency in tonsillectomized children. Ann Allergy 57:413, 1986.
23. Capper JWR, Randall C. Postoperative haemorrhage in tonsillectomy and adenoidectomy in children. J Laryngol Otol 98:363, 1984.
24. Carmody D, Vamadevan T, Cooper SM. Posttonsillectomy hemorrhage. J Laryngol Otol 96:635, 1982.
25. Chamovitz R, Rammelkamp CH, Wannamaker LW, et al. The effect of tonsillectomy on the incidence of streptococcal respiratory disease and its complications. Pediatrics 26:355, 1960.
26. Clein NW. Influence of tonsillectomy and adenoidectomy on children with special reference to the allergic implications of respiratory symptoms. Ann Allergy 10:568, 1952.
27. Close GR, Rushworth RL, Rob MI, et al. Variation in selected childhood surgical procedures: the case of tonsillectomy and management of middle ear disease. J Paediatr Child Health 29:429, 1993.
28. Colclasure JB, Graham SS. Complications of outpatient tonsillectomy and adenoidectomy: a review of 3,340 cases. Ear Nose Throat J 69:155, 1990.
29. Cotton RT. Nasopharyngeal stenosis. Arch Otolaryngol 111:146, 1985.
30. Cowan MJ, Gladwin MT, Shelhamer JH. Disorders of ciliary motility. Am J Med Sci 321:3, 2001.
31. Coyte PC, Croxford R, McIsaac W, et al. The role of adjuvant adenoidectomy and tonsillectomy in the outcome of the insertion of tympanostomy tubes. N Engl J Med 344:1188, 2001.
32. Crowe SJ, Watkins SS, Rothholz AS. Relation of tonsillar and nasopharyngeal infections to general systemic disorders. Bull Johns Hopkins Hosp 28:2, 1917.
33. Crysdale WS, Russel D. Complications of tonsillectomy and adenoidectomy in 9409 children observed overnight. Can Med Assoc J 135:1139, 1986.
34. Dealing with fluid in the middle ear [editorial]. Lancet 1:1297, 1978.
35. Demain JG, Goetz DW. Pediatric adenoidal hypertrophy and nasal airway obstruction: reduction with aqueous nasal beclomethasone. Pediatrics 95:355, 1995.
36. Derkay CS, Kenna MA, Pang D. Refractory torticollis: an uncommon complication of adenotonsillectomy. Int J Pediatr Otorhinolaryngol 14:87, 1987.
37. DeWeese DD, Saunders WH. Textbook of Otolaryngology, 3rd ed. St Louis, CV Mosby, 1968, pp 72–78.
38. Eid NS, Jones VF. Bacterial tracheitis as a complication of tonsillectomy and adenoidectomy. J Pediatr 125:401, 1994.
39. Einhorn AH. The nose, paranasal sinuses and pharynx. In Barnett

HL (ed). Pediatrics, 14th ed. New York, Appleton-Century-Crofts, 1968, pp 1675–1677.

40. Eley RC, Flake CG. Acute anterior poliomyelitis following tonsillectomy and adenoidectomy with special reference to the bulbar form. J Pediatr 13:63, 1938.

41. Enthoven AC. Shattuck lecture. Cutting cost without cutting the quality of care. N Engl J Med 298:1229, 1978.

42. Feinstein AR, Levitt M. The role of tonsils in predisposing to streptococcal infections and recurrences of rheumatic fever. N Engl J Med 282:285, 1970.

43. Fisher AE, Lucchesi PF, Marks HH, et al. Poliomyelitic paralysis and tonsillectomy. JAMA 186:873, 1963.

44. Francis T Jr, Krill CE, Toomey JA, et al. Poliomyelitis following tonsillectomy in five members of a family. JAMA 119:1392, 1942.

45. Friday GA Jr, Paradise JL, Rabin BS, et al. Serum immunoglobulin changes in relation to tonsil and adenoid surgery. Ann Allergy 69:225, 1992.

46. Gates GA, Avery CA, Prihoda TJ, et al. Effectiveness of adenoidectomy and tympanostomy tubes in the treatment of chronic otitis media with effusion. N Engl J Med 317:1444, 1987.

47. Ghorbanian SN, Paradise JL, Doty RL. Odor perception in children in relation to nasal obstruction. Pediatrics 72:510, 1983.

48. Gittelsohn AM, Wennberg JE. On the incidence of tonsillectomy and other common surgical procedures. In Bunker JP, Barnes BA, Mosteller F (eds). Costs, Risks, Benefits of Surgery. New York, Oxford University Press, 1977, pp 91–106.

49. Gledovic Z, Radovanovic Z. History of tonsillectomy and appendectomy in Hodgkin's disease. Eur J Epidemiol 7:612, 1991.

50. Glover JA. The incidence of tonsillectomy in school children. Proc R Soc Med 31:1219, 1938.

51. Goldstein NA, Post C, Rosenfeld RM, Campbell TF. Impact of tonsillectomy and adenoidectomy on child behavior. Arch Otolaryngol Head Neck Surg 126:494, 2000.

52. Gutensohn N, Li FP, Johnson RE, et al. Hodgkin's disease, tonsillectomy and family size. N Engl J Med 292:22, 1975.

53. Hays HM. Diseases of pharynx, nasopharynx and hypopharynx. In Abt IA (ed). Pediatrics, 3rd ed. Philadelphia, WB Saunders, 1924, pp 217–218.

54. Howard WA. The tonsil and adenoid problem. In Ferguson CF, Kendig EL Jr (eds). Pediatric Otolaryngology, 2nd ed. Philadelphia, WB Saunders, 1972, p 1093.

55. Hultcrantz E, Larson M, Hellquist R, et al. The influence of tonsillar obstruction and tonsillectomy on facial growth and dental arch morphology. Int J Pediatr Otorhinolaryngol 22:125, 1991.

56. Illingworth RS. Discussion on the tonsil and adenoid problem. Proc R Soc Med 43:317, 1950.

57. Jessner L, Blom GE, Waldfogel S. Emotional implications of tonsillectomy and adenoidectomy in children. Psychoanal Stud Child 7:126, 1952.

58. Johnson SK, Johnson RE. Tonsillectomy history in Hodgkin's disease. N Engl J Med 287:1122, 1972.

59. Kaiser AD. Results of tonsillectomy: a comparative study of 2200 tonsillectomized children with an equal number of controls three and ten years after operation. JAMA 95:837, 1930.

60. Kaiser AD. Children's Tonsils In or Out? Philadelphia, JB Lippincott, 1932, pp vii, 2, 3, 8–10.

61. Klevit HD, Oleinick A. The decline of tonsillectomy in a prepayment practice. Proceedings of the 13th International Congress of Pediatrics, Vienna, 1971, pp 135–140.

62. Kravath RE, Pollak CP, Borowiecki B. Hypoventilation during sleep in children who have lymphoid airway obstruction treated by nasopharyngeal tube and T and A. Pediatrics 59:865, 1977.

63. Levy AM, Tabakin BS, Hanson JS, et al. Hypertrophied adenoids causing pulmonary hypertension and severe congestive heart failure. N Engl J Med 277:506, 1967.

64. Lewis CE. Variations in the incidence of surgery. N Engl J Med 281:880, 1969.

65. Linder-Aronson S. Adenoids: their effect on mode of breathing and nasal airflow and their relationship to characteristics of the facial skeleton and the dentition. Acta Otolaryngol (Stockh) 265:1, 1970.

66. Linder-Aronson S. Effects of adenoidectomy on dentition and nasopharynx. Am J Orthod 65:1, 1974.

67. Linder-Aronson S, Woodside DG, Hellsing E, et al. Normalization of incisor position after adenoidectomy. Am J Orthod Dentofac Orthop 103:412, 1993.

68. Lucchesi PF, LaBoccetta AC. Relationship of tonsils and adenoids to the type of poliomyelitis: an analysis of four hundred and thirty-two cases. Am J Dis Child 68:1, 1944.

69. Luke MJ, Mehrizi A, Folger GM Jr, et al. Chronic nasopharyngeal obstruction as a cause of cardiomegaly, cor pulmonale, and pulmonary edema. Pediatrics 37:762, 1966.

70. Macartney FJ, Panday J, Scott O. Cor pulmonale as a result of chronic nasopharyngeal obstruction due to hypertrophied tonsils and adenoids. Arch Dis Child 44:585, 1969.

71. Mandel EM, Paradise JL, Bluestone CD, et al. Large tonsils without large adenoids as a cause of upper airway obstruction, alveolar hypoventilation, and cor pulmonale [abstract]. Pediatr Res 14:647, 1980.

72. Massachusetts Department of Public Health. Tonsillectomy and adenoidectomy in Massachusetts. N Engl J Med 285:1537, 1971.

73. Maw AR. Chronic otitis media with effusion (glue ear) and adenotonsillectomy: prospective randomized controlled study. Br Med J 287:1586, 1983.

74. Mawson SR, Adlington P, Evans M. A controlled study evaluation of adenotonsillectomy in children. J Laryngol Otol 81:777, 1967.

75. McCammon RW. Natural history of respiratory tract infection patterns in basically healthy individuals. Am J Dis Child 122:232, 1971.

76. McCorkle LP, Hodges G, Badger GF, et al. A study of illness in a group of Cleveland families. VIII. Relation of tonsillectomy to incidence of common respiratory disease in children. N Engl J Med 252:1066, 1955.

77. McKee WJE. A controlled study of the effects of tonsillectomy and adenoidectomy in children. Br J Prev Soc Med 17:49, 1963.

78. McKee WJE. The part played by adenoidectomy in the combined operation of tonsillectomy with adenoidectomy: second part of a controlled study in children. Br J Prev Soc Med 17:133, 1963.

79. McKibben DH, Marasovich WA, Paradise JL, et al. Facial skeletal morphology in children with and without nasal obstruction. Abstracts, Sixth Annual Meeting, American Society of Pediatric Otolaryngology, Waikoloa, Hawaii, May 9–11, 1991, p 56.

80. McPherson K, Wennberg JE, Hovind OB, et al. Small-area variations in the use of common surgical procedures: an international comparison of New England, England, and Norway. N Engl J Med 307:1310, 1982.

81. Menashe VD, Ferrehi C, Miller M. Hypoventilation and cor pulmonale due to chronic upper airway obstruction. J Pediatr 67:198, 1965.

82. Meyer W. On adenoid vegetations in the nasopharyngeal cavity: their pathology, diagnosis, and treatment. Medicochirurg Trans (London) 53:191, 1870.

83. Mutz I, Simon H. Blutungs-Komplikationen nach Tonsillektomie und Adenotomie: Erfahrungen über 7743 Operationen in 14 Jahren. Wien Klin Wochenschr 105:520, 1993.

84. Nickerson RJ, Colton T. Area studies: surgery in the United States. In Zuidema GD (ed). A Summary Report of the Study on Surgical Services for the United States. Baltimore, RR Donnelley, 1975, pp 36–55.

85. Nieminen P, Tolonen U, Löppönen H. Snoring and obstructive sleep apnea in children: a 6-month follow-up study. Arch Otolaryngol Head Neck Surg 126:481, 2000.

86. Noonan JA. Reversible cor pulmonale due to hypertrophied tonsils and adenoids: studies in two cases. Circulation 32:164, 1965.

87. Office of Population Censuses and Surveys. London, 1980.

88. Ogra PL. Effect of tonsillectomy and adenoidectomy on nasopharyngeal antibody response to poliovirus. N Engl J Med 284:59, 1971.

89. Owings MF, Kozak LJ. Ambulatory and inpatient procedures in the United States, 1996. Vital Health Stat 13 (139). Hyattsville, MD, National Center for Health Statistics. 1998, p. 49.

90. Paradise JL. Why T&A remains moot. Pediatrics 49:648, 1972.

91. Paradise JL. Pittsburgh tonsillectomy and adenoidectomy study: differences from earlier studies and problems of execution. Ann Otol Rhinol Laryngol 84:15, 1975.

92. Paradise JL. Clinical trials of tonsillectomy and adenoidectomy: limitations of existing studies and a current effort to evaluate efficacy. South Med J 69:1049, 1976.

93. Paradise JL. T and A: nature of the controversy and steps toward its resolution. Int J Pediatr Otorhinolaryngol 1:201, 1979.

94. Paradise JL. Adenoidectomy and adenotonsillectomy for recurrent

or persistent otitis media: still commonly performed and still controversial [abstract]. Pediatr Res 31:99A, 1992.

95. Paradise JL, Bluestone CD. Toward rational indications for tonsil and adenoid surgery. Hosp Pract 11:79, 1976.

96. Paradise JL, Bluestone CD. Adenoidectomy and chronic otitis media [letter]. N Engl J Med 318:1470, 1988.

97. Paradise JL, Bluestone CD, Bachman Z, et al. History of recurrent sore throat as an indication for tonsillectomy: predictive limitations of histories that are undocumented. N Engl J Med 298:409, 1978.

98. Paradise JL, Bluestone CD, Bachman RZ, et al. Efficacy of tonsillectomy for recurrent throat infection in severely affected children: results of parallel randomized and nonrandomized clinical trials. N Engl J Med 310:674, 1984.

99. Paradise JL, Bluestone CD, Carrasco MM. Nasal obstruction due to adenoid hypertrophy: two-year course with and without adenoidectomy. Abstracts, 18th Annual Meeting of the Ambulatory Pediatric Association, New York City, April 25, 1978, p 43.

100. Paradise JL, Bluestone CD, Colborn DK, et al. Adenoidectomy and adenotonsillectomy for recurrent otitis media: parallel randomized clinical trials in children not previously treated with tympanostomy tubes. JAMA 282:945, 1999.

101. Paradise JL, Bluestone CD, Colborn DK, et al. Tonsillectomy and adenotonsillectomy for recurrent throat infection in moderately affected children. Pediatrics 110:7, 2002.

102. Paradise JL, Bluestone CD, Rogers KD, et al. Efficacy of adenoidectomy for recurrent otitis media in children previously treated with tympanostomy-tube placement: results of parallel randomized and nonrandomized trials. JAMA 263:2066, 1990.

103. Paradise JL, Bluestone CD, Taylor FH, et al. Adenoidectomy with or without tonsillectomy for otitis media (T&A II study). Ann Otol Rhinol Laryngol 92:36, 1983.

104. Paton JHP. Tonsil-adenoid operation in relation to health of group of school girls. Q J Med 2:119, 1943.

105. Pearson RJ, Smedley B, Berfenstam R, et al. Hospital caseloads in Liverpool, New England, and Uppsala: an international comparison. Lancet 2:559, 1968.

106. Perrott GS. The Federal Employees Health Benefits Program: Seventh Term (1967) Coverage and Utilization. Selected data prepared for Group Health Association annual meeting, Washington DC, March 21, 1970.

107. Polmar SH. The role of the immunologist in sinus disease. J Allergy Clin Immunol 90:511, 1992.

108. Rasmussen N. Complications of tonsillectomy and adenoidectomy. Otolaryngol Clin North Am 20:383, 1987.

109. Rosenfeld RM, Green RP. Tonsillectomy and adenoidectomy: changing trends. Ann Otol Rhinol Laryngol 99:187, 1990.

110. Rowlands JK. Head and neck swelling after tonsillectomy. Anaesth Intensive Care 13:336, 1985.

111. Roydhouse N. A controlled study of adenotonsillectomy. Arch Otolaryngol 92:611, 1970.

112. Shaikh W, Vayda E, Feldman W. A systematic review of the literature on evaluative studies of tonsillectomy and adenoidectomy. Pediatrics 57:401, 1976.

113. Siodlak MZ, Gleeson MJ, Wengraf CL. Posttonsillectomy secondary hemorrhage. Ann R Coll Surg Engl 67:167, 1985.

114. Smith RB, Petruscak J. Tonsillectomy mortality. JAMA 227:557, 1974.

115. Smith RM. Anesthesia for Infants and Children, 4th ed. St Louis, CV Mosby, 1980, pp 587–615.

116. Snow JC, Healy GB, Vaughan CW, et al. Malignant hyperthermia during anesthesia for adenoidectomy. Arch Otolaryngol 95:442, 1972.

117. Solow B. Upper airway obstruction and facial development. In Davidovitch Z (ed). The Biological Mechanisms of Tooth Movement and Craniofacial Adaptation. Columbus, Ohio, The Ohio State University College of Dentistry, 1992, pp 571–579.

118. Subtelny JD. The significance of adenoid tissue in orthodontia. Angle Orthod 24:59, 1954.

119. Surjan L, Surjan L Jr, Surjan M. Further investigation into the immunological role of the tonsils. Acta Otolaryngol (Stockh) 73:222, 1972.

120. Takahashi H, Honjo I, Fujita A, Kurata K. Effects of adenoidectomy on sinusitis. Acta Otorhinolaryngol Belg 51:85, 1997.

121. Tom LWC, DeDio RM, Cohen DE, et al. Is outpatient tonsillectomy appropriate for young children? Laryngoscope 102:277, 1992.

122. Townsend JG, Sydenstricker E. Epidemiological study of minor respiratory disease. Public Health Rep 42:99, 1927.

123. Tucker D, Coulter JE, Downes J. Incidence of acute respiratory illness among males and females at specific ages. Milbank Mem Fund Q 30:42, 1952.

124. Valtonen HJ, Blomgren KEV, Qvarnberg YH. Consequences of adenoidectomy in conjunction with tonsillectomy in children. Int J Pediatr Otorhinolaryngol 53:105, 2000.

125. Vandenberg SJ, Heatley DG. Efficacy of adenoidectomy in relieving symptoms of chronic sinusitis in children. Arch Otolaryngol Head Neck Surg 123:675, 1997.

126. Van Volkenburgh VA, Frost WH. Acute minor respiratory diseases prevailing in a group of families residing in Baltimore, Maryland, 1928–1930: prevalence, distribution, and clinical description of observed cases. Am J Hyg 17:122, 1933.

127. Vianna NJ, Greenwald P, Davies JNP. Tonsillectomy and Hodgkin's disease: the lymphoid tissue barrier. Lancet 1:431, 1971.

128. Weider DJ, Sateia MJ, West RP. Nocturnal enuresis in children with upper airway obstruction. Otolaryngol Head Neck Surg 105:427, 1991.

129. Wennberg JE, McPherson K, Caper P. Will payment based on diagnosis-related groups control hospital costs? N Engl J Med 311:295, 1984.

130. Wiatrak BJ, Myer CM III, Andrews TM. Complications of adenotonsillectomy in children under 3 years of age. Am J Otolaryngol 12:170, 1991.

131. Williams EF III, Woo P, Miller R, et al. The effects of adenotonsillectomy on growth in young children. Otolaryngol Head Neck Surg 104:509, 1991.

132. Witzel MA, Rich RH, Marger-Bacal F, et al. Velopharyngeal insufficiency after adenoidectomy: an 8-year review. Int J Pediatr Otorhinolaryngol 11:15, 1986.

62

Obstructive Sleep Disorders

Bruce R. Maddern, M.D., and Cheryl S. Cotter, M.D.

Obstructive sleep disorders and sleep-associated airway obstruction are becoming more frequently recognized by physicians as a significant health problem in children. Perhaps 40% of snoring children referred to specialists may have obstructive sleep disorders and some estimate a 3% overall prevalence.[18]

Obstructive sleep apnea or obstructive sleep apnea syndrome (OSAS) is part of a clinical spectrum of obstructive sleep disorders. The clinical significance of sleep-related respiratory obstruction is not completely understood. Many questions remain unanswered. One of the areas of vigorous research and controversy is the clinical significance of snoring and OSAS in altering a child's potential for growth and development. Furthermore, there are dilemmas in diagnostic testing and therapeutic choices. There are key differences between adults and children with OSAS in pathophysiology, diagnosis, and management. These differences are summarized in Table 62–1 and are highlighted throughout this chapter.

As the indications for adenotonsillectomy have evolved over the past 20 to 30 years, airway obstruction has become a more frequent indication for surgery.[25, 32] It has been argued that the incidence of upper airway obstruction caused by adenotonsillar hypertrophy has increased.[19] To appropriately treat upper airway obstruction in this increasing population of affected patients, it is first necessary to understand the processes involved.

Historical Perspective

A review of the literature surrounding sleep-related upper airway obstruction illustrates the long process of unraveling the pathophysiology and etiology involved. In 1837, Dickens described an obese hypersomnolent boy named Joe in *The Posthumous Papers of the Pickwick Club*. Dickens carefully described the clinical features and behavior of his corpulent character, which was the model for many subsequent descriptions of these patients.[11] In 1889, Hill wrote "the stupid looking lazy child who frequently suffers from headache at school, breathes through his mouth instead of his nose, snores and is restless at night . . . is well worthy of the solicitory attention of the school medical officer."[22]

In 1918, Osler[40] coined the term "pickwickian" to describe hypersomnolent and morbidly obese patients. Kerr and Lagen[24] associated these pickwickian patients with significant cardiovascular changes such as cor pulmonale and right-sided heart failure. Gastaut and colleagues[17] described the occurrence of repeating episodes of sleep apnea in these patients. It was not until 1965, when Menashe and associates[36] reported two nonobese children with adenotonsillar hypertrophy and cardiovascular changes who underwent successful treatment with adenotonsillectomy, that treatment was described for obstructive sleep disorders. Since these original discussions, a large body of literature has developed to describe obstructive sleep apnea and its causes, pathophysiology, and therapies.

Pathogenesis

Obstructive sleep apnea is manifested by repeated episodes of decreased breathing (airflow) of upper airway origin occurring during sleep. In obstructive sleep apnea, there is a decreased airway caliber resulting from anatomic, neuromuscular, or other factors. To maintain adequate airflow through a diminished lumen, the patient must increase respiratory effort. This attempt to increase airflow requires increasing intraluminal airway pressure. Because of the Bernoulli effect, increased intraluminal negative pressure, and a compliant airway structure, collapse of the airway and cessation of airflow result. Increasing negative airway pressure paradoxically causes further airway collapse and increased resistance to airflow.

Three physical parameters relate directly to the ease of airway collapse. First, compliance or elasticity of the soft tissues allows distensibility. Second, spatial relationships and anatomic narrowing of the available lumen contribute because of flow volume dynamics. Third, there are sleep-associated neurophysiologic changes that lead to a decrease in muscle tone and support of the airway.

Peripheral and central neuromuscular regulation of respiratory function also contributes to the development of obstructive sleep disorders. There is a normal sleep regulatory cycle–related decrease in the activity of respiratory muscles such as the genioglossus and diaphragm. Obstructive apneas occur more frequently during these periods of decreased electromotor activity.[39]

During sleep, a repeating sequence of events occurs in which negative inspiratory pressure overcomes the ability

TABLE 62–1. Comparison of Childhood and Adult Obstructive Sleep Apnea Syndrome

Parameter	Adult	Children
Feature		
Obesity	Frequent	Rare
Underweight/failure to thrive	Rare	Frequent
Excessive daytime sleepiness	Frequent	Rare
Mouth breathing	Rare	Frequent
Gender	Male	Female, male
Adenotonsillar hypertrophy	Rare	Frequent
Sleep Pattern		
Obstruction	Apnea	Apnea and hypopnea
Arousal	Common	Rare

Modified from Carroll JL, Loughlin GM. Diagnostic criteria for obstructive sleep apnea syndrome in children. Pediatr Pulmonol 14:71, 1992.

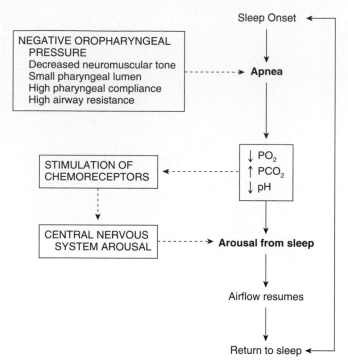

FIGURE 62–1. Primary sequence of events in obstructive sleep apnea and mechanisms that contribute. (Modified from Bradley TD, Phillipson EA. Pathogenesis of sleep apnea. Med Clin North Am 69:1169, 1985.)

of the airway to maintain patency, resulting in cessation of airflow. The cessation of airflow causes obvious physiologic changes, including acidosis, hypercapnia, and hypoxemia. Once sufficient changes in the partial pressure of oxygen (PCO_2), the partial pressure of carbon dioxide (PCO_2), and the pH occur, central and peripheral chemoreceptors and baroreceptors are stimulated to cause arousal and awakening from sleep (Fig. 62–1). This repeating cycle of sleep, sleep awakenings, and restless sleep may occur many times in a night.

The duration and frequency of apnea vary according to each patient's ability to tolerate and compensate for these physiologic changes. This repeating cycle of disordered sleep, along with chronic hypoxemia, acidosis, and hypercapnia, induces secondary physiologic changes. Certain clinical features and symptoms are directly related to these chronic pathophysiologic changes (Fig. 62–2).

Sleep disturbances cause decreased amounts of rapid eye movement and non–rapid eye movement sleep. The quality of sleep, both physiologic and psychologic restful sleep, is markedly disturbed. This may lead to behavioral disturbances such as hyperactivity, aggression, and depression and to hypersomnolence and learning difficulties.[2]

Secondary cardiovascular changes may occur, including arrhythmias, ectopy, right-sided heart failure, and cor pulmonale. Many of these conditions can be reversed with appropriate therapy.[36]

Long-standing obstructive sleep apnea may impair growth and development. Some children with sleep apnea have decreased growth hormone secretion.[34] Children with obstructive sleep apnea may also have failure to thrive, which can be a result of both increased caloric expenditure during sleep and decreased growth hormone secretion.[49] These are probably responsible for the observation that most young children with OSAS are underweight, whereas adults with OSAS are obese.

Several studies have reported that poor performance in school and poor weight and height gains can be dramatically altered by therapy.[5, 28, 31] It is believed that, after treatment, there is decreased caloric expenditure for sleep-associated work of breathing. A significantly in-

creased nocturnal growth hormone secretion allows children to resume more normal growth and development.

Etiology

Adenotonsillar hypertrophy is the most common cause of respiratory obstruction of upper airway origin during sleep in children. However, numerous other anatomic, congenital, neuromuscular, and miscellaneous causes are well documented (Table 62–2). Any anatomic obstruction of the upper airway may potentially contribute to the development of obstructive sleep apnea. The site of obstruction and airway collapse is different for each patient. Other causes of airway obstruction, such as laryngotracheal abnormalities, may produce stridor and apnea, but they are not considered in this discussion.

Richardson and associates,[46] using videofluoroscopy, demonstrated four mechanisms in the upper airway that contribute to obstruction during sleep: (1) collapse of the hypopharynx, (2) descent of the tonsil, (3) posterior tongue placement, and (4) occlusion of the velopharyngeal sphincter. These probably do not occur in isolation but may all contribute, depending on each patient's anatomic and neuromuscular characteristics.

Patients with craniofacial syndromes such as Crouzon, Apert, Treacher Collins, Pierre Robin, and Cornelia de Lange syndromes often have abnormalities of the upper airway. These patients frequently have a history of snoring and disordered breathing during sleep. Although a broad range of phenotype expression of the classic features for each syndrome is common, when evaluating

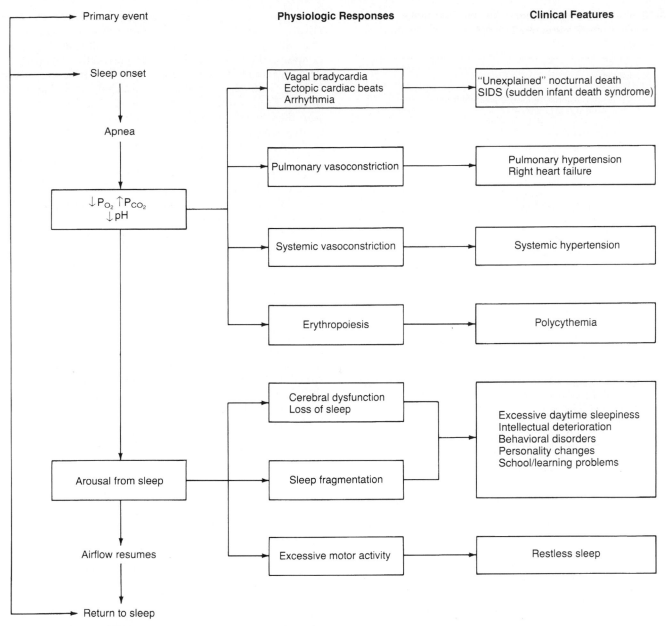

FIGURE 62–2. Clinical features and physiologic changes seen in obstructive sleep apnea. (Modified from Bradley TD, Phillipson EA. Pathogenesis of sleep apnea. Med Clin North Am 69:1169, 1985.)

these patients, the otolaryngologist should be suspicious of OSAS.

The site of airway obstruction in dysmorphic patients is usually multifactorial. Bony restrictions of the skull base and velopharyngeal musculature and neuromusculature control may contribute. Common findings vary with different syndromes and may include maxillary hypoplasia, nasal septal deflection, micrognathia, retrognathia, choanal atresia, choanal stenosis, platybasia, and macroglossia.[53]

Down syndrome patients are prone to obstructive sleep disorders. This is due to characteristic anatomic craniofacial features and, importantly, to neuromuscular control problems. These children have a small oropharynx and nasopharynx along with a relative macroglossia. Poor gross motor and fine motor control of the velopharyngeal mechanism and tongue are common in these patients.[13]

Children with mucopolysaccharide storage diseases frequently have nasal and pharyngeal airway obstruction resulting from deposition of storage material in soft tissues. This alters lumen size, as well as control of the airway.[52]

Neuromuscular difficulties that contribute to airway obstruction are less common. Decreased muscle tone, regardless of etiology, may potentially cause narrowing of the upper airway. Iatrogenic causes of obstructive sleep disturbance are well documented. Repair of cleft palate and velopharyngeal flap surgery can obstruct an already compromised airway. Snoring and nasal obstruction are

TABLE 62–2. Etiology of Upper Airway Obstruction Associated with Obstructive Sleep Apnea and Related Disorders

I. Anatomic
  A. Nasal
    1. Anterior nares (fetal warfarin syndrome)
    2. Nasal septal hematoma
    3. Trauma—septal deviation
  B. Nasopharyngeal
    1. Choanal atresia, stenosis
    2. Choanal polyp
    3. Nasopharyngeal cyst
    4. Adenoid hypertrophy
    5. Cleft palate repair
    6. Velopharyngeal repair
  C. Oropharyngeal
    1. Tonsillar hypertrophy
    2. Macroglossia (Down syndrome)
    3. Retrognathia, micrognathia
      a. Pierre Robin, Cornelia de Lange syndromes
      b. Achondroplasia
  D. Supraglottic
    1. Laryngotracheomalacia
    2. Vallecular cyst
  E. Craniofacial syndromes
    1. Crouzon
    2. Apert
    3. Treacher Collins
    4. Down
II. Neuromuscular
  A. Cerebral palsy
  B. Down syndrome
  C. Myotrophic dystrophy
  D. Arnold-Chiari malformation
    1. Type I with Klippel-Feil syndrome
    2. Type II with spina bifida
  E. Syringomyelobulbia
III. Miscellaneous
  A. Congenital myxedema
  B. Prader-Willi syndrome (mental retardation, short stature, obesity, hypogonadic hypogonadism)
  C. Obesity
    1. Endogenous
    2. Exogenous
  D. Sickle-cell disease

common postsurgical findings in these patients and warrant evaluation.

Obstructive Sleep Disorders in Neonates and Young Infants

Neonates and young infants represent a special and increasing group of patients with obstructive sleep disorders, due, in part, to differences in respiratory physiologic responses exhibited by neonates.

Roloff and Aldrich[48] described several mechanisms in premature infants that are responsible. Central neuropathways that control ventilation are not completely developed, leading to hypoventilation, central apnea, and periodic breathing. Physiologic responses to hypoxemia and hypercapnia are not fully developed due to chemoreceptor immaturity. Other neuromuscular control mechanisms, such as laryngeal abduction and diaphragmatic coordination, are incompletely developed.

Assessment techniques and treatment options in this group are different than those used in older children. History in neonates is largely observational, which makes reliability and interpretation of events difficult. Signs and symptoms in young infants with obstructive sleep disorders may include respiratory distress, stridor, cyanosis, feeding difficulties, pectus excavatum, and failure to thrive. These events are different and perhaps more severe than those seen in older children.

In young infants, an association between gastroesophageal reflux (GER) and apnea has been described. GER can cause airway occlusion by reflux of acid material directly into the glottis or secondary to central apnea by vagally mediated reflexes that inhibit respiration.[50] Considerable debate wages about causal relationships of GER and apnea. GER is common in all infants. Central nervous system disorders may also lead to GER and obstructive sleep apnea by separate mechanisms. An association has been suggested between GER, an apparently life-threatening event, and obstructive apnea. Obstructive sleep apnea has been implicated in sudden infant death syndrome. Autopsy studies have shown signs of upper airway obstruction in some patients.[1] Guilleminault and co-workers[20] have documented five "near miss" sudden infant death syndrome cases, in which OSAS was subsequently identified. There was no suspicion of airway obstruction before evaluation of sudden infant death syndrome. Even though central apnea is certainly the leading cause of sudden infant death syndrome, it may be that some infants cannot tolerate the acute physiologic changes in oxygen saturation and acid-base balance that occur with obstructive sleep apnea.

Diagnosis

The diagnosis of OSAS is based on a thorough history and physical examination along with appropriate ancillary studies. The evaluation of the patient with potential obstructive sleep apnea is frequently complex. It is often difficult to correlate the severity of symptoms with the history and physical findings. Signs and symptoms that occur at night, when the patient and parents are asleep, are not well recorded. Parental concerns and descriptions of breathing activities may not be clinically accurate. Likewise, sometimes only subtle findings may be overlooked or only evident during the day.

Because obstructive sleep disorders are frequently chronic, the patient may become accustomed to certain signs and symptoms and parents may fail to recognize these changes. Growth and development may be altered as a means of compensation.

Snoring is a universal feature of OSAS. Approximately 10% of children snore during an average night's sleep. Most of these children have primary snoring characterized by snoring during sleep without associated apnea, hypoventilation, or sleep disturbance.

Children with suggested upper airway resistance syndrome snore and have partial sleep-associated upper airway obstruction. Daytime symptoms and sleep disruption may occur, but apnea, hypopnea, or gas exchange abnormalities as seen in OSAS do not occur. These patients do

TABLE 62–3. Classification of Obstructive Sleep Disorders and Related Disorders Based on Clinical Features and Symptoms

I. Primary snoring (alone)
   Excessive oropharyngeal noise associated with sleep. More prominent with inspiration
   Respirations orderly and regular
II. Snoring with
   Respiratory pattern changes
   Irregular breathing cycle
   Irregular breathing with short pauses (up to 5 seconds)
III. Snoring with
   Breathing pauses up to 6 seconds
   Periodic breathing (three or more pauses of 3 seconds in a 20-second period)
   Hypopnea (limitation of airflow)
IV. Obstructive sleep apnea syndrome
   A. Obstructive apnea (cessation of airflow for >6 seconds)
      Airway obstruction
      Apnea, 20–30 episodes of obstructive type per evening (obstructive sleep apnea syndrome)
   B. Snoring with behavioral changes
      Hyperactivity, excessive daytime somnolence, aggression, depression
      Deteriorating school performance due to poor attentiveness, behavior changes, or hypersomnolence
   C. Obstructive apnea with major clinical features
      Poor growth and development
      Heart failure
      Cor pulmonale
      Hypertension (other primary causes of hypertension ruled out)
      Hypoxemia with sleep

not meet the diagnostic criteria for OSAS by polysomnography (PSG).[22] They have a wide variety of clinical presentations and therapeutic options remain controversial.

Patients with snoring and obstructive sleep apnea may be classified according to the severity of symptoms and associated clinical features (Table 62–3). This suggested scheme takes into account signs, symptoms, and clinical features to help aid the clinician in determining the severity of obstructive sleep disorders. Treatment options can then be outlined.

In the evaluation of obstructive sleep disorders, the assistance of pediatric subspecialists from pulmonary medicine, neonatology, radiology, and neurology is often valuable. A multidisciplinary team approach in management, especially in complex cases, is recommended and should include anesthesia as well as critical care medicine.

History

Several symptoms and complaints, which can occur either in the daytime or nocturnally, occur with regularity in OSAS (Table 62–4). Snoring, mostly inspiratory in character, is a cardinal finding. The history often reveals a chronic and gradually worsening condition, which suggests upper airway obstruction during sleep. Parents describe frank apnea with gasping for air following an episode of obstruction in their child.

Severity of snoring does not imply severity of the disorder. Loud snorers may have little or no apnea, whereas quiet snorers may have extended periods of apnea. This

may be especially true in infants. Pauses in breathing of greater than 6 seconds are considered apnea in children.

Nocturnal enuresis, or bed-wetting, is a common complaint in children. OSAS is one of many causes. The mechanism involved is probably similar to that for upper airway muscular control, in which marked decreases in neuromuscular tone occur during sleep and may be worsened with OSAS. Enuresis in patients with documented OSAS is often corrected with therapy for obstructive sleep apnea.[56]

Other nocturnal complaints include frequent awakenings, restless sleep, diaphoresis, and night terrors. Diaphoresis is a result of the hypercapnia and secondary vasodilatation that occurs with obstructive sleep apnea.

In obtaining a nighttime history from parents about their child, it is important to determine frequency and chronicity, association with upper respiratory infections, character of the respiratory noise, and any other associations elicited from a complete history. Because of sleep dynamics, sleep behavior should be observed at intervals throughout the sleep cycle, not merely from the first 5 minutes of active sleep, which is what parents frequently report. A video or audio tape can accurately record sleep behaviors and overcome the inadequacy of parental observations.

Daytime complaints frequently include mouth breathing and behavior problems. Excessive daytime sleepiness or hypersomnolence may be interpreted in a young child as the normal need for a nap and makes this difficult to assess. In an older child, this may indicate a poor nocturnal sleep pattern. Daytime hypersomnolence is a rare finding in children with OSAS. Behavioral problems associated with OSAS include aggression, poor attention span, and worsening school performance.

Mouth breathing is a frequent finding and often associated with a hyponasal speech quality. Both of these are due to the nasopharyngeal obstruction seen with adenoid hypertrophy. Articulation errors are common with phonemes such as /m/, /n/, and /ng/. These require nasal escape of air for proper formation, can easily be assessed in a clinical setting, and give an indication of nasal ob-

TABLE 62–4. Symptoms and Features Often Found in Obstructive Sleep Apnea Syndrome

Nocturnal	Daytime
Snoring	Mouth breathing
Pauses with breathing at night	Hypersomnolence (excessive daytime sleepiness)
Frequent awakenings from sleep, restless sleep	Poor school performance
Nightmares	Abnormal daytime behavior
Nocturnal enuresis	Aggression
Nocturnal diaphoresis	Hyperactivity
	Discipline problems
	Morning headache
	Weight problem (failure to thrive or obesity)
	Frequent upper respiratory tract infections
	Chronic rhinorrhea
	Difficulty swallowing

struction. The validity of clinical history in determining the diagnosis of OSAS has received extensive discussion. Brouillette and colleagues[6] have suggested that thorough history and physical examination are adequate for the diagnosis to be made. Other authors[7, 27, 30] have fostered the idea that history alone is not sufficient because of the confusing nature of this disorder. They conclude that parents, as well as physicians, overestimate the severity of the disease and, therefore, other ancillary testing is necessary to confirm the diagnosis.

Physical Examination

Physical examination should include a complete otolaryngologic and head and neck evaluation, with particular attention to potential sites of airway obstruction. Although pickwickian complex is one of the most well-known presentations of obstructive sleep apnea, it is not the most common clinical picture seen in children. Children with obstructive sleep apnea are more often slender and frequently lag in growth and development.[20] Observation should be made of any anatomic or functional limitations, as well as any anomalies suggestive of orofacial or craniofacial syndromes.

Examination should include observation of the patient's breathing pattern and quality of speech. Obvious mouth breathing, a dry lower lip, and a hyponasal speech pattern are commonly found in patients with adenotonsillar hypertrophy.

Oropharyngeal examination should assess pharyngeal dimensions, anatomy, and function. Neuromuscular assessment of velopharyngeal functions should be carefully assessed. Sphincter closure, appearance of the Passavant ridge, lateral and anteroposterior velar mobility, and gross and fine motor control of the tongue are all important determinations. Assessment should be made of pharyngeal dimensions, noting tonsil size and lingual anatomy.

Brodsky and colleagues[3] demonstrated that patients with airway obstruction caused by adenotonsillar hypertrophy had several significant changes in anatomic relationships. The distance between the medial surfaces of the tonsils, the distance between the lateral pharyngeal walls, and the distance between the soft palate and posterior pharyngeal wall were significantly decreased in obstructed patients when compared with individuals without obstruction. The weight of the tonsils removed from these patients at surgery was increased in those patients with obstruction as well. This supports the opinion that large tonsils in a smaller or narrow airway may cause obstruction.

Intranasal examination should include assessment of the nasal airway with particular attention to the nasal septum, nasal mucosa, and adenoids. A cervical and thoracic examination is necessary to rule out any processes that may contribute to or aggravate potential upper airway obstruction. A neuromuscular examination, including cranial nerves V, IX, X, XI, and XII, is warranted to assess motor control and coordination of swallowing, phonation, and respiration.

When evaluating craniofacial dysmorphic patients, the otolaryngologist should be suspicious of airway problems and obstructive sleep disturbance. Specific abnormalities that should be considered in craniofacial syndromes are micrognathia, maxillary hypoplasia, choanal atresia, choanal stenosis, cranial base anomalies, macroglossia, and pharyngeal hypotonia.

Ancillary Studies

Radiography. Soft tissue, lateral, or sinus series x-ray films are frequently ordered when one suspects adenoid hypertrophy. However, these are two-dimensional and their usefulness has not been determined. Lateral and anteroposterior views of the head are included with a routine sinus radiography series. This may be a more cost-effective choice in many of these patients and provides more information. Assessment of overall craniofacial anatomy, airway dimensions, and adenotonsillar hypertrophy can easily be made. Sinus series radiography may be an important adjunct in evaluations, along with a complete history and examination.

Cephalometric Study. Cephalometric studies are an accurate recording of bony landmarks; they provide precise dimensions but do not record soft tissue abnormalities, which are frequently the cause of airway difficulty. These studies are not part of the usual work-up for OSAS but may be indicated in patients with craniofacial syndromes or suspected facial dysmorphia. This study is expensive and not all centers have the necessary equipment readily available.

Computed Tomography. Computed tomographic scanning is an accurate and expensive method of recording bony and soft tissue landmarks but provides little information about functional problems. These studies may be indicated in complex cases.

Sleep Audio/Video Recording. A frequently used, inexpensive study is the nighttime recording of the child sleeping using an audio or video tape recorder. This provides information regarding sleep behavior: snoring, pauses, apnea, and restlessness. Its disadvantages are background noise, necessity for parental compliance, and difficulty in distinguishing true apnea from depressed respiration or hypopnea. Lamm and associates[26] published their results with home audio tapes in children referred for possible OSAS. They concluded that the home audio tape was helpful, especially if a "struggle sound" was heard. With new developments in video technology, many families have VHS or 8-mm recording capability for home use. A nighttime recording may be helpful in accurately visualizing sleep behavior and correlating sleep sounds.

Polysomnography. PSG, or sleep study, is the gold standard for the diagnosis of sleep apnea and associated sleep disorders. It consists of multiple physiologic and neurophysiologic simultaneous recordings of different variables, which include at least (1) electroencephalogram with minimum two or three electrode placements, (2) electrocardiogram, (3) assessment of nasal and oral airflow by thermistors, (4) oxygen saturation monitoring, and (5) chest strain gauges or esophageal manometry to assess thoracic respiratory movements. Technical considerations for performing PSG in children must take into account the child's age and size.

In addition, often the sleep study includes an electro-oculogram to assess rapid eye movement or non–rapid eye movement sleep stages, an electromyogram of the chin to assess muscle tone and activity, a recording of end-tidal P_{CO_2} by nasal sampling, and a videotape recording of sleep. The sleep study can determine frequency, duration, type, and severity of apneic episodes. By monitoring oxygen saturation and P_{CO_2}, an assessment of physiologic changes associated with apnea can be made and the type of apnea, either central or obstructive (peripheral), can be determined.[7] Apnea is defined as cessation of airflow for at least 10 seconds in adults. The definition of apnea in children remains controversial. Authors have suggested a 6-second limit standard in children

because of higher oxygen consumption needs, which may lead to more rapidly developing hypoxemia, even with brief apneic periods and higher respiratory rates. Others have suggested cessation of airflow for two breaths or with a change of 4% oxygen saturation.[9, 33] Apnea has been observed in some patients with OSAS to last 70 seconds or more.[13]

Central apnea implies central nervous system dysfunction. The sleep study demonstrates lack of respiratory movements, along with apneic episodes. This is an important distinction from obstructive apnea, in which respiratory movements continue despite the cessation of airflow, implying upper airway obstruction. The mixed pattern, which begins as central and then progresses to obstructive apnea, is frequently seen in OSAS and young children. Figure 62–3 illustrates the different types of apnea

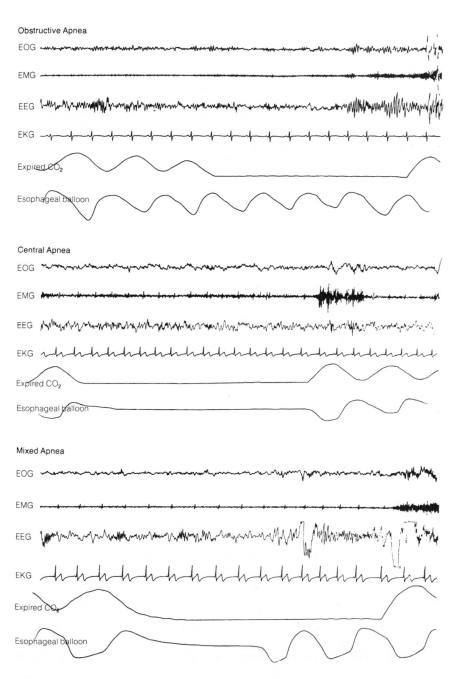

FIGURE 62–3. Types of apnea and their typical polysomnographic recordings. EOG, electro-oculogram; EMG, electromyogram; EEG, electroencephalogram; EKG, electrocardiogram. (From Hauri PJ. Current Concepts: The Sleep Disorders. Kalamazoo, Mich, Upjohn, 1982.)

and their typical polysomnographic recordings. Interpretation of PSG is difficult in children and normative PSG data remains controversial. Variations due to age, neurologic, or cardiac status make interpretation difficult. Some centers lack pediatric standards or adapt adult protocols for pediatric use. Data that may be statistically significant may not have clinical correlation. There are no standard guidelines for classifying the severity of childhood OSAS.

The disadvantages of PSG are that it is expensive, cumbersome to perform, and not universally available. It usually requires a one-night hospitalization and is better tolerated by adults than by children. The sleep study is not practical in the routine evaluation of the snoring child. Some authors have studied the utility of portable PSG, which may be combined with video monitoring in the home. Most authors found in-home sleep testing to be accurate and of practical use in evaluating sleep apnea.[8, 10, 14, 23] Currently, in-home PSG is geographically limited and not universally available, especially for pediatric patients.

Indication for PSG is another area of controversy or specialty preferences; referral patterns and payer reimbursement issues contribute to this problem. Some groups have argued that all children who snore should have a PSG before definitive (surgical) therapy. Others believe PSG should be confined to use in confusing patient scenarios or high-risk patients.[37]

The sleep study may be indicated when apnea is strongly suspected but history and physical examination findings are confusing. Often, the neurologically impaired child is being assessed and there is a need to distinguish between central and obstructive apnea, as well as to determine the severity of OSAS before recommending appropriate therapy. PSG is also indicated if one is considering tracheostomy in complex cases. Sleep study has many other uses in the evaluation of behavioral, psychiatric, and neurologic disorders.

Modified in-hospital studies have been used where there is a lack of available formal PSG with newer and universally available monitoring. These studies are performed in a monitored hospital bed, such as intensive care or respiratory care unit, and use available monitoring such as oxygen and carbon dioxide saturation, apnea bradycardia, and a respiratory diary. The parent or nursing staff log nighttime events in correlation with recorded physiologic changes.

Sleep Sonography. This technique may provide a practical, noninvasive measure to assist with managing snoring patients. The equipment consists of an anesthesia-type precordial stethoscope with a 100-Hz frequency filter linked to an audiocassette recorder. The stethoscope is placed on the suprasternal notch, and, after the child is asleep, a 2-hour recording of respiratory sounds is made. The recording is examined by computer analysis to determine depth of respiration and duration and frequency of apnea.[43] This instrument is as yet investigational, but, compared with PSG, it has a high degree of accuracy in predicting apnea and severity of disease.[42] This may be more acceptable to families because of decreased expense, convenience of at-home use, and noninvasive qualities. Availability of this testing remains a problem.

Videofluoroscopy. Videofluoroscopy involves cineradiographic recording of a patient's sleep while sedated. This can be coupled with several polysomnographic measurements and can give a valuable assessment of functional airway problems, especially in younger children and infants. Often, the location of obstruction can be accurately determined and a direct recording of apneic episodes with airway obstruction can be obtained. Videofluoroscopy requires the skills of an experienced radiologist and does expose the patient to radiation. Because the child is sedated, this is not normal physiologic sleep and recordings may not correlate with nighttime findings.

Endoscopy. Flexible fiberoptic nasopharyngoscopy may provide useful anatomic and functional information. It can be performed in a clinical setting with minor coaxing and topical anesthesia. Newer, thinner fiberscopes make this especially useful in young children and neonates. Excellent visualization of static and dynamic components of the upper airway are possible and can greatly aid in the evaluation of all age patients for OSAS.

Rigid endoscopy is indicated in the patient with craniofacial abnormalities to determine nasopharyngeal, oropharyngeal, or supraglottic abnormalities and to rule out laryngotracheal problems. It may also be helpful in removing or correcting certain lesions that impinge on the upper airway.

Miscellaneous. Assessment with chest radiography, echocardiography, and electrocardiography may be helpful in the evaluation of complex cases and their use should be determined on an individual basis.

Therapy

Many different therapeutic options are available for the treatment of obstructive sleep disorders in children (Table 62–5). A thorough understanding of each option and of the risks versus benefits for each is necessary when treating these complicated cases.

Management decisions in obstructive sleep disorders can be surgical, medical, or airway position therapies. To make an appropriate therapeutic choice, the clinician needs to take into account the exact etiology and severity of the problem. Anatomic, craniofacial dysmorphism, neurologic status, and patient compliance issues are important considerations.

Therapeutic choices vary according to the age of the patient. Young infants and neonates with obstructive sleep disorders may only be amenable to certain treatment options because of size and growth considerations. Conversely, teenagers may receive effective treatment using the same algorithm as adults.

Surgery remains the mainstay of treatment in children. Newer, nonsurgical choices have become more available but remain more useful in adults.

Medical (Nonsurgical) Therapies

Nonsurgical options have included (1) medications such as medroxyprogesterone, steroids, protriptyline, theophylline, and acetazolamide, (2) dietary measures or weight

TABLE 62–5. Therapeutic Options for Upper Airway Obstruction in Obstructive Sleep Apnea Syndrome and Related Disorders in Children

Removal of Obstruction
Adenoidectomy
Tonsillectomy
Adenotonsillectomy
Uvulopalatopharyngoplasty
Hyoidplasty
Aryepiglottiplasty
Septorhinoplasty
Choanal atresia repair
Tongue reduction

Bypass of Obstruction
Oral airway (for neonates)
Nasopharyngeal airway
Tracheostomy

Positional Manipulation of Airway
Orthognathic surgery (e.g., maxillary or mandibular osteotomies)
Oral prosthesis (e.g., SNOAR)
Tongue suspension (e.g., Repose)

Medical (Nonsurgical)
Medications—medroxyprogesterone, steroids, protriptyline, acetazolamide
Diet or weight reduction
Nasal continuous positive airway pressure
Nasal bilevel positive airway pressure
Thyroid replacement (for congenital hypothyroidism)
Chemotherapy (Hodgkin disease)

reduction, (3) nasal continuous positive airway pressure or nasal bilevel positive airway pressure measures, and (4) oral prosthetics (e.g., SNOAR). These measures are useful in a specific few patients, but are largely not effective in the majority of children with sleep-related airway obstruction.[20, 44]

Nasal positive airway pressure, either continuous or biphasic, is being used in children with increasing frequency. Advances in equipment and mask design have allowed young children and previously noncompliant patients greater ease in usage. Like in adults, morbidly obese children, those undergoing weight reduction, and those in whom surgery has failed are the most successful users.[4, 21] Long-term use and patient compliance remain problems, but this nonsurgical technology is gaining wider acceptance for use in children.

Weight loss in morbidly obese patients may have some usefulness.[29] Although used primarily in adults, its importance in young children is unknown. In patients with endogenous obesity, such as Prader-Willi syndrome, the obesity may not be the underlying difficulty and weight reduction may be of limited benefit.

Surgical Therapy

Preoperative, operative, and postoperative management of patients with obstructive sleep apnea requires careful evaluation, an interdisciplinary team approach, and postoperative monitoring. These cases are frequently complex and need to be treated as such. Preoperative discussion ensures as safe a procedure as possible and encourages a team approach in management.

Perioperative management should be individualized. The surgeon may consider chest radiography, electrocardiography, and anesthesia consultation in patients with confirmed OSAS. If cardiomegaly, right ventricular hypertrophy, or electrocardiographic abnormality is noted, cor pulmonale should be suspected and cardiology evaluation is warranted. An echocardiogram is useful in diagnosing cardiac status. Patients with cerebral palsy, spastic diplegia, and static encephalopathy may need preoperative assessment by a neurologist, because these patients have poor neuromuscular control and are therefore more susceptible to complications.

Surgery in patients with complex craniofacial dysmorphism and severe OSAS should be discussed well in advance with anesthesia colleagues. Decisions about airway management, anesthetic techniques, and postanesthesia care need to be agreed to collaboratively before the procedure.[55] Children with OSAS have diminished ventilatory response to CO_2 stimulation, which may contribute to respiratory complications postoperatively.[38, 54] Judicious use of narcotics is recommended.

Parental discussions about informed consent should include topics of reasonable risks, benefits, success, and failure of the recommended procedure. Discussion with parents should include the required preoperative evaluation and postoperative care, including added testing, monitoring, and the risk of airway obstruction in the child with obstructive sleep apnea.

Surgical interventions are directed toward relieving the site of obstruction or bypassing the obstruction. Because adenotonsillar hypertrophy is by far the most common cause of obstructive sleep apnea, adenotonsillectomy is the most frequently performed procedure. This procedure is very successful in relieving symptoms and correcting pathophysiologic changes due to OSAS.

Children with a compromised airway from anatomic or neuromuscular causes, such as Down syndrome, may be more susceptible to airway obstruction from even moderately enlarged adenoids or tonsils. Adenotonsillectomy may be definitive therapy in these borderline cases.[12] In addition, adenotonsillectomy may be appropriate initial management for complex or borderline cases before committing the patient and family to more long-term and invasive options such as tracheostomy.

The surgical procedure for obstructive sleep disease is identical to adenotonsillectomy performed for other reasons. Care should be taken to remove all adenoid tissue, especially superiorly against the posterior nasal choanae. Palatoglossus and palatopharyngeus musculature needs to be preserved as well as possible to minimize the risk of postoperative velopharyngeal incompetence.

Tracheotomy is an alternative to definitive correction of the obstructive lesion of the airway. This procedure bypasses the obstruction and can be a temporary solution used in combination with other future surgical reconstructive procedures. In complex craniofacial patients, this option may be especially helpful. Tracheotomy as a temporary solution is also used in conjunction with weight reduction therapy in morbidly obese patients.

In some patients, tracheotomy is a permanent treatment modality. This is appropriate treatment in patients in whom other procedures have failed, in patients with multiple, medically complex situations who are not candidates for other procedures, and in patients who refuse other treatment options.[20]

Uvulopalatopharyngoplasty (UPPP) has been popularized, especially for adults with OSAS.[15] This technique, or a modification of it, may be indicated in the child with redundant or poorly functioning pharyngeal soft tissues. Uvulopalatopharyngoplasty has been used increasingly in children with severe handicaps, such as static encephalopathy and neuromuscular oromotor dysfunction. These patients have poor palatal control and redundant nonfunctional soft tissues. Simple removal of adenoids and tonsils in these patients may fail to relieve the obstruction and uvulopalatopharyngoplasty should be considered.[51] Conservative removal of soft tissue is warranted because postoperative velopharyngeal insufficiency may be especially detrimental in these patients.

Midline laser glossectomy has been used in adults with some success.[15, 16] This technique has been helpful in a specific subset of patients in whom surgery (e.g., uvulopalatopharyngoplasty) has failed and in patients with tongue base disproportions.[16] Experience in children is limited. Midline laser glossectomy may be a helpful alternative or addition in the child with macroglossia, such as Beckwith-Wiedemann and Down syndromes.

A wide variety of procedures have demonstrated some success in the management of OSAS in children with complex craniofacial disorders. Orthognathic surgery, including maxillary or mandibular advancement, tongue-hyoid suspension, and mandibular distraction, have been outlined.[47] Tracheotomy may be avoided in some of these difficult to manage cases. These techniques may not be practical in small children and may interfere with active bone growth centers and tooth buds.

Postoperative care of the patient with documented obstructive sleep apnea requires monitoring.[35] These children are at risk for postoperative edema, bleeding, and airway obstruction. Acute pulmonary edema is an uncommon complication that may occur after relief of longstanding upper airway obstruction.[38] The onset is variable, ranging from within minutes of intubation to hours after surgery. The key to management is early recognition, adequate oxygenation, and careful monitoring of the airway. Continuous positive airway pressure or mechanical ventilation is sometimes necessary, as is careful fluid management. The process is usually self-limiting, resolving within 12 to 24 hours.

Surgeons should consider performing adenotonsillectomy for OSAS as an inpatient or overnight monitored hospital stay.[45] The risk of respiratory compromise is increased in children younger than 3 years and in those with neuromuscular disorders, chromosomal abnormalities, and severe OSAS. Pulse oximetry, cardiorespiratory monitoring, or both aid in the immediate identification of respiratory compromise. Nursing and support staff need to be aware that OSAS patients are not routine postoperative adenotonsillectomy patients. Postoperative care protocols and training of hospital staff are key to effective management and improved patient safety. Humidification, oxygen support, and judicious use of narcotics are advocated. A single dose of intravenous dexamethasone can decrease postoperative edema, nausea, and vomiting.[41]

SELECTED REFERENCES

Brouillette R, Hanson D, David R, et al. A diagnostic approach to suspected obstructive sleep apnea in children. J Pediatr 105:10, 1984.
The authors describe a clinically useful approach to the evaluation of snoring patients. A useful table of the signs and symptoms in OSAS is based on an exhaustive statistical analysis.
Guilleminault C, Korobkin R, Winkle R. A review of 50 children with obstructive sleep apnea syndrome. Lung 159:275, 1981.
Koopman C, Moran W. Sleep apnea. Otolaryngol Clin North Am 23(4): 571, 1990.
A complete reference on sleep disorders with well-written chapters on pathophysiology, polysomnography, and medical and surgical therapy. The chapter on sleep apnea in children is an excellent review and is highly recommended.

REFERENCES

1. Ariagno RL, Guilleminault C. Apnea during sleep in the pediatric patient. Clin Chest Med 6:679, 1985.
2. Bradley TD, Phillipson EA. Pathogenesis and pathophysiology of obstructive sleep apnea syndrome. Med Clin North Am 69:1169, 1985.
3. Brodsky L, Moore L, Stanievich J. A comparison of tonsillar size and oropharyngeal dimensions in children with obstructive adenotonsillar hypertrophy. Int J Pediatr Otorhinolaryngol 13:149, 1987.
4. Brooks LJ, Crooks RL, Sleeper GP. Compliance with nasal CPAP by children with obstructive sleep apnea [abstract]. Am Rev Respir Dis 145:A556, 1992.
5. Brouillette, RT, Fernbach SK, Hunt CE. Obstructive sleep apnea in infants and children. J Pediatr 100:31, 1982.
6. Brouillette RT, Hanson D, David R, et al. A diagnostic approach to suspected obstructive apnea in children. J Pediatr 105:10, 1984.
7. Brouillette RT, Morielli A, Leimanis A, et al. Nocturnal pulse oximetry as an abbreviated testing modality for pediatric obstructive sleep apnea. Pediatrics 105:405, 2000.
8. Brouillette RT, Jacob SV, Waters KA, et al. Cardiorespiratory sleep studies for children can often be performed in the home. Sleep 19(10 Suppl):S278, 1996.
9. Carroll JL, Loughlin GM. Diagnostic criteria for obstructive sleep apnea syndrome in children. Pediatr Pulmonol 14:71, 1992.
10. Davidson TM, Do KL, Justus S. The use of ENT-prescribed home sleep studies for patients with suspected obstructive sleep apnea. Ear Nose Throat J 78:754, 1999.
11. Dickens C. The Posthumous Papers of the Pickwick Club. London, Chapman and Hall, 1837.
12. Donalson JD, Redmond WM. Surgical management of obstructive sleep apnea in children with down syndrome. J Otolaryngol 17:398, 1988.
13. Frank Y, Dravath RE, Pollack CP, et al. Obstructive sleep apnea and its therapy: clinical and polysomnographic manifestations. Pediatrics 71:737, 1983.
14. Fry JM, DiPhillipo MA, Curran K, et al. Full polysomnography in the home. Sleep 21:635, 1998.
15. Fujita S, Conway W, Zorick F, et al. Surgical correction of anatomic abnormalities in OSAS: uvulopalatopharyngoplasty. Otolaryngol Head Neck Surg 89:923, 1981.
16. Fujita, S, Woodson BT, Clark JL, et al. Laser midline glossectomy as a treatment for obstructive sleep apnea. Laryngoscope 101:805, 1991.
17. Gastaut H, Tassinari CA, Duron B. Etude polygraphique des manifestations episodiques (hypnigues et respiratoires) diurnes et nocturnes, du syndrome de Pickwick. Rev Neurol 112:568, 1964.

18. Gislason T, Benediktsdottir B. Snoring, apneic episodes, and nocturnal hypoxemia among children 6 months to six years old: an epidemiologic study of lower limit of prevalence. Chest 107:963, 1995.
19. Grundfast, KM, Wittich DJ. Adenotonsillar hypertrophy and upper airway obstruction in evolutionary perspective. Laryngoscope 92:650, 1982.
20. Guilleminault C, Korobkin R, Winkle R. A review of 50 children with obstructive sleep apnea syndrome. Lung 159:275, 1981.
21. Guilleminault C, Nino-Murcia G, Heldt G, et al. Alternative treatment to tracheostomy in obstructive sleep apnea syndrome: nasal continuous positive airway pressure in young children. Pediatrics 78:797, 1986.
22. Hill W. On some causes of backwardness and stupidity in children and the relief of these symptoms in some instances by NP scarification. BMJ 2:711, 1889.
23. Jacob SV, Morielli A, Mogress MA, et al. Home testing for pediatric obstructive sleep apnea syndrome secondary to adenotonsillar hypertrophy. Pediatr Pulmonol 20:241, 1995.
24. Kerr WJ, Lagen JB. The postural syndrome of obesity leading to postural emphysema and cardiorespiratory failure. Ann Intern Med 10:569, 1936.
25. Kravath RE, Pollack CP, Borowiecki B. Hypoventilation during sleep in children who have lymphoid airway obstruction treated by nasopharyngeal tube and T and A. Pediatrics 59:865, 1977.
26. Lamm C, Mandeli J, Kattan M. Evaluation of home audiotapes as an abbreviated test for obstructive sleep apnea syndrome (OSAS) in children. Pediatr Pulmonol 27(4):267, 1999.
27. Leach J, Olson J, Hermann J, et al. Polysomnographic and clinical findings in children with obstructive sleep apnea. Arch Otolaryngol 118:741, 1992.
28. Lind MG, Lundell BPW. Tonsillar hyperplasia in children. Arch Otolaryngol 108:650, 1982.
29. Lombard RM, Zwillich CW. Medical therapy of obstructive sleep apnea. Med Clin North Am 69:1317, 1985.
30. Loughlin GM, Brouillette RT, Rosen C. Standards and indications for sleep studies in children. Am J Respir Crit Care Med 153:866, 1996.
31. Maddern BR, Reed HT, Ohene-Frempong K, Beckerman RC. Obstructive sleep apnea syndrome in sickle cell disease. Ann Otol Rhinol Laryngol 98:174, 1989.
32. Mangat D, Orr WC, Smith RO. Sleep apnea, hypersomnolence and upper airway obstruction secondary to adenotonsillar enlargement. Arch Otolaryngol 103:383, 1977.
33. Marcus CL, Brouillette RT, Gozal D, et al. Cardiorespiratory sleep studies in children. Workshop summary of American Thoracic Society. Am J Respir Crit Care Med 160:1381, 1999.
34. Marcus CL, Carroll JL, Koerner CB, et al. Determinants of growth in children with the obstructive sleep syndrome. J Pediatr 125:556, 1994.
35. McColley SA, April MD, Carroll JL, et al. Respiratory compromise after adenotonsillectomy in children with obstructive sleep apnea. Arch Otolaryngol 118:940, 1992.
36. Menashe V, Farrehi C, Miller M. Hyperventilation and cor pulmonale due to chronic upper airway obstruction. J Pediatr 67:198, 1965.
37. Messner AH. Evaluation of obstructive sleep apnea by polysomnography prior to pediatric adenotonsillectomy. Arch Otolaryngol Head Neck Surg 125:353, 1999.
38. Motamed M, Djazaeri B, Marks R. Acute pulmonary oedema complicating adenotonsillectomy for obstructive sleep apnea. Int J Clin Pract 53:230, 1999.
39. Onal E, Lopata M, O'Connor T. Pathogenesis of apneas in hypersomnia-sleep apnea syndrome. Am Rev Respir Dis 125:167, 1982.
40. Osler W. The Principles of Practice and Medicine. New York, Appleton, 1918.
41. Pappas AS, Sukhani R, Hotaling A, et al. The effect of preoperative dexamethasone on the immediate and delayed postoperative morbidity in children undergoing adenotonsillectomy. Anesth Analg 87:57, 1998.
42. Potsic WP. Comparison of polysomnography and somnography for assessing regularity of respiration during sleep in adenotonsillar hypertrophy. Laryngoscope 97:1430, 1987.
43. Potsic WP, Marsh RR, Pasquariello PS. Recorder for assessment of upper airway disorder. Otolaryngol Head Neck Surg 91:584, 1983.
44. Potsic WP, Pasquariello PS, Baranak CC, et al. Relief of upper airway obstruction by adenotonsillectomy. Otolaryngol Head Neck Surg 94:476, 1987.
45. Price SD, Hawkins DB, Kahlstrom EJ. Tonsil and adenoid surgery for airway obstruction: perioperative respiratory morbidity. Ear Nose Throat J 72:526, 1993.
46. Richardson MA, Seid AB, Cotton RT, et al. Evaluation of tonsils and adenoids in sleep apnea syndrome. Laryngoscope 90:1106, 1980.
47. Riley RW, Guilleminault C, Powell NB. Maxillofacial surgery and obstructive sleep apnea: a review of 80 patients. Otolaryngol Head Neck Surg 101:353, 1989.
48. Roloff DW, Aldrich MS. Sleep disorders and airway obstruction in newborns and infants. Otolaryngol Clin North Am 23:639, 1990.
49. Saini J, Krieger J, Brandenbrger G, et al. Continuous positive airway pressure treatment. Effects on growth hormone, insulin and glucose profiles in obstructive apnea patients. Horm Metab Res 25:375, 1993.
50. See CS, Newman LJ, Berezin S, et al. Gastroesophageal reflux-induced hypoxemia in infants with apparent life-threatening event(s). Am J Dis Child 143:951, 1989.
51. Seid AB, Martin PJ, Pransky SM, Kearns DB. Surgical therapy of obstructive sleep apnea in children with severe mental insufficiency. Laryngoscope 100:507, 1990.
52. Shapiro J, Strome M, Crocker AC. Airway obstruction and sleep apnea in Hurler and Hunter syndromes. Ann Otol Rhinol Laryngol 94:458, 1985.
53. Shprintzen RJ. Palatal and pharyngeal anomalies in craniofacial syndromes. Birth Defects Original Article Series 18:53, 1982.
54. Strauss SG, Lynn AM, Bratton SL, Nespeca MK. Ventilatory response to CO_2 in children with obstructive sleep apnea from adenotonsillar hypertrophy. Anesth Analg 89:328, 1999.
55. Warwick JP, Mason DG. Obstructive sleep apnoea syndrome in children. Anaesthesia 53:571, 1998.
56. Weider DJ, Hauri PJ. Nocturnal enuresis in children with upper airway obstruction. Int J Pediatr Otorhinolaryngol 9:173, 1985.

63

Oropharyngeal Manifestations of Systemic Disease

Laura N. Sinai, M.D.

Pathologic findings affecting the oropharynx often herald systemic disease in both the pediatric and adult populations. This chapter lists many pediatric systemic illnesses that have significant oropharyngeal findings (Tables 63–1 and 63–2). In order to avoid delays in the diagnosis of many serious diseases, awareness of these signs and symptoms is important for the otolaryngologist. Some of the specific disorders are described elsewhere in this text (see Chaps. 53, 54, 60, 64, 66, and 73).

Infections

Candida albicans

Oral infection with *Candida albicans* may be a localized problem (thrush) or may be associated with many diseases such as hypoparathyroidism, diabetes mellitus, adrenal insufficiency, leukemia, or immunodeficiency such as acquired immunodeficiency syndrome (AIDS) or DiGeorge syndrome. Thrush is a normal pediatric finding until the age of 6 to 12 months, or at any age following antibiotic treatment. In most other settings, the diagnosis of an oral candidal infection warrants a more in-depth evaluation. Treatment regardless of the associated illness is with oral nystatin.

Mucocutaneous Candidiasis

Mucocutaneous candidiasis disease is characterized by persistent monilial infections of the mucous membranes, nails, and skin, without systemic symptoms. About one half of patients also have an endocrinopathy. In contrast to patients with DiGeorge syndrome, these patients have normal reactions to viral infections and vaccines. These patients also mount normal responses to infections by bacteria and other fungi. However, over time, these patients' general immunity may wane, making them more widely susceptible to disease. The onset of illness is variable. Treatment is with oral nystatin or intravenous amphotericin and newer antifungal agents. Unfortunately, symptoms usually recur after treatment is terminated. There are reports of the successful use of transfer factor.

Human Immunodeficiency Virus

At least 40 oral manifestations of human immunodeficiency virus (HIV) infection have been recorded so far.[19] They can best be classified as fungal, viral, bacterial, neoplastic, and idiopathic lesions. Some lesions have been noted only in adults; others are more common in children.

Fungal Infections

Oral candidiasis is the most common infection of the HIV-infected patient. In children, the prevalence ranges from 20% to 75%, depending on the source cited. This infection can present in one of four forms: the atrophic form, which is most common; the chronic hypertrophic form; the pseudomembranous (thrush) form; or the angular cheilitis form. Candidiasis can also progress to hairy tongue, which is an elongation of filiform papillae of the dorsum of the tongue. Esophageal candidiasis is one of the diagnostic features of AIDS. Oral nystatin is the usual treatment.[2, 6]

Viral Infections

Herpes simplex virus (HSV) infection, the most common viral infection seen in children with HIV infection, causes intraoral and perioral lesions as well as systemic symptoms of fever, malaise, and cervical lymphadenopathy. Recurrent herpetic lesions on the vermilion border are common in the normal host, whereas recurrent herpetic lesions inside the mouth suggest immunocompromise. Diagnosis is based on cytologic findings and immunostaining. HSV infection can be a devastating disease in the neonatal period with the possibility of significant CNS destruction regardless of HIV status. Affected newborns are most often symptomatic between 7 and 21 days of life. Oral acyclovir is the usual treatment for localized disease, whereas intravenous acyclovir is used in sicker children or disseminated disease.

Hairy leukoplakia, which is not to be confused with hairy tongue, is almost always indicative of HIV infection. Twenty-two percent of patients present with this finding. Hairy leukoplakia is a white corrugated lesion found on the lateral borders of the tongue bilaterally. Electron mi-

TABLE 63–1. Common Oropharyngeal Findings That Are Part of Systemic Disease

Dryness
 Dehydration
 Bulimia
 Atropine poisoning
 Tricyclic antidepressant use
 Inflammatory disease
Large tongue
 Hemangioma
 Hypothyroidism
 Down syndrome
 Neurofibromatosis
Salivary gland swelling
 Mumps
 HIV infection
 Cystic fibrosis
 Eating disorder
 Sialectasia
Enlarged tonsils
 Infectious mononucleosis
 Gonorrhea
 Leukemia
Bleeding
 Idiopathic thrombocytopenic purpura
 Leukemia
 Hemophilia
 Von Willebrand disease
 Sepsis
Paleness
 Anemia
 Leukemia

croscopy of the lesion reveals the presence of the Epstein-Barr virus (EBV). Treatment is with acyclovir.[19]

Bacterial Infections

Bacterial infections of the upper respiratory tract such as draining otitis media and sepsis are quite common in patients with HIV infection. These infections are distinguished from those occurring in the general pediatric population by their persistence and severity. Acute necrotizing ulcerative gingivitis (ANUG) is rare under the age of 10 years in the United States; however, it is seen in children in India and Africa. Treatment includes antibiotics aimed at the offending microorganism, and improving oral hygiene.[6]

Neoplastic Involvement

Oral Kaposi sarcoma usually presents on the palate but may involve any area of the mouth. Non-Hodgkin lymphoma is also associated with HIV infection and may present as a firm painless swelling anywhere in the oral cavity. These neoplasms are very rare in children and have been noted to date only in adults with HIV.

Idiopathic Involvement

Persistent diffuse parotitis is frequently seen in children with HIV infection. From 14% to 30% of children are affected, whereas only 5% of adults have this finding. The enlargement may be recurrent or persistent. The salivary

gland involvement is almost always associated with xerostomia in adults, but children usually escape this complication. The cause is unclear, but there are reports of resolution of parotitis with steroid therapy.[6]

Unusual Oral Manifestations Seen Only in Adults to Date

Papillomavirus warts, condyloma acuminatum, histoplasmosis, and *Toxoplasma gondii, Cryptococcus neoformans,* cytomegalovirus, and *Mycobacterium avium-intracellulare* infections have been seen in the oropharynx of adults with HIV infection.[17]

Tuberculous oral ulcers with tuberculous cervical adenitis, oral lesions of cat-scratch disease, persistent aphthous-like ulcers of the pharynx and esophagus, and gangrenous stomatitis are occasionally seen in association with HIV. A facial palsy resembling Bell palsy has also been reported in several patients with HIV infection. Other cranial nerve neuropathies, especially involving cranial nerves V and VIII, have also been reported. Oral hyperpigmentation consisting of brown or brown-black macules has been documented as well.[17]

Common Childhood Infections

The widespread use of immunizations and the improvement of living conditions have contributed to a decrease in the incidence of some of the common infectious diseases in children. Still present, these infections have sys-

TABLE 63–2. Classifications of Oropharyngeal Manifestations of Systemic Disease

Infections
 Candida albicans
 Mucocutaneous candidiasis
 Human immunodeficiency virus (HIV); fungal, viral, bacterial, neoplasm, idiopathic, rare findings
 Common childhood infections
  Varicella (chickenpox)
  Rubeola (measles)
  Infectious mononucleosis
Tumors
 Leukemia
 Histiocytosis
 Neurofibromatosis
 Tumor therapy
Bleeding disorders
 Idiopathic thrombocytopenic purpura
 Hemophilia
 Von Willebrand disease
Inflammatory diseases
 Kawasaki disease
 Systemic lupus erythematosus
 Sjögren syndrome
 Crohn disease
 Ulcerative colitis
 Pemphigus vulgaris
Congenital anomalies
 DiGeorge syndrome
 Fetal alcohol syndrome
 Genetic disease
Endocrine
Nutritional deficiencies
Eating disorders

temic manifestations as well as significant oral findings. Some infections, such as certain specific group A beta-hemolytic streptococcal infections of the pharynx, lead to an immune complex disease that affects the collagen vascular system, with emphasis on the heart in rheumatic fever, or on the kidney in acute poststreptococcal glomerulonephritis. Both of these illnesses present several weeks after the primary pharyngeal infection has abated. Several of the more common childhood infections such as varicella (chickenpox), rubeola (measles), and infectious mononucleosis are discussed in this section, emphasizing the systemic aspects of these infections.

Varicella Zoster

Varicella (chickenpox) is transmitted by aerosolized droplets and has an incubation period of 11 to 21 days. The contagious period begins 24 hours before the rash appears and ends 6 to 7 days later, after the vesicular lesions are all crusted. The lesions usually start on the trunk and spread to the head and extremities. Vesicles can be found on any mucous membrane. The vesicles in the mouth rapidly become macerated and may form shallow ulcers. When the larynx is involved, respiratory distress may develop. The most common complication of chickenpox is secondary bacterial infection, usually staphylococcal or streptococcal. Both impetigo and cellulitis are frequently seen. Varicella pneumonia, rare in children, is a serious and, at times, fatal complication. Other complications include myocarditis, pericarditis, endocarditis, hepatitis, and glomerulonephritis. Ten percent of Reye syndrome (encephalopathy with fatty degeneration of the liver) cases occur after chickenpox. Other central nervous system involvement of varicella includes encephalitis, cerebellar ataxia, transverse myelitis, and ascending paralysis (Guillain-Barré syndrome).

Herpes zoster is a localized re-emergence of the varicella-zoster virus. Disease occurs most often in a single dermatome. Zoster produces oral ulcerations when the virus involves the third division of the trigeminal nerve.

To prevent the development of varicella in individuals at risk, such as newborns, those with malignancies, and those on immunosuppressive drugs, varicella-zoster immune globulin (VZIG) may be given within 72 hours of exposure. Acyclovir is modestly effective if given within 24 hours of initial symptoms; however, it is reserved for individuals at risk and adults who usually have a more severe course than children. Otherwise, treatment is symptomatic for the relief of pruritus. The varicella vaccine was licensed for use in early 1995. The current recommendations are for universal immunization of children, which has resulted in marked decline in the incidence of chickenpox in the United States.

Measles (Rubeola)

Measles, characterized by a cough, coryza, conjunctivitis, a generalized maculopapular rash, and Koplik spots in the mouth, usually has an incubation period of 10 to 12 days. Infected individuals are contagious from the fifth day of incubation to several days after the rash appears. Immunization is highly effective at preventing disease.

Typically, the patient has a cough and fever and malaise similar to those of a common upper respiratory infection. From 24 to 48 hours before the rash, the typical Koplik spots (red lesions with a bluish-white speck in the center) appear on the buccal mucosa (Fig. 63–1). The most common location for Koplik spots is opposite the lower molars. Over time, the cough becomes more brassy or harsh and persists when the rash and conjunctivitis recede.

The major systemic reactions are in the respiratory tract and the central nervous system. Otitis media, cervical lymphadenitis, laryngotracheobronchitis, and pneumonia may develop. The viral pneumonia, characterized by giant cell infiltration, may take several weeks to resolve and is often fatal in the immunocompromised host. Bacterial superinfection is a serious complication.

Encephalitis develops in 0.1% of measles patients. Up to 50% of the cases of encephalitis result in permanent damage such as mental retardation, epilepsy, neuromuscular dysfunction, and deafness.

Infectious Mononucleosis

Infectious mononucleosis is characterized by fever, pharyngitis, cervical adenopathy, and splenomegaly. Caused by the Epstein-Barr virus, infectious mononucleosis has a variable incubation period (average of 50 days). The symptoms include a sore throat accompanied by a gray exudate and an edematous soft palate with petechiae. In one third of affected patients, group A beta-hemolytic streptococcus can be cultured from the throat

Lymphadenopathy, a central feature of the disease, involves the tonsils, cervical nodes, spleen, and other lymph nodes in the body. The nodes in the cervical area may become so prominent that a "bull neck" appearance results. Splenomegaly occurs in about 50% and hepatitis in about 10% of patients. Other systemic involvement includes pneumonia, aseptic meningitis, en-

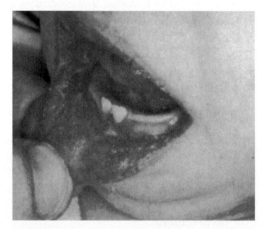

FIGURE 63–1. Koplik spots in an uncommon location with involvement of the buccal and lower labial mucosa. (From Cherry JD. Cutaneous manifestations of systemic infections. In Feigin RD, Cherry JD. Textbook of Pediatric Infectious Diseases, 2nd ed. Philadelphia, WB Saunders, 1987.)

cephalitis, coma, and transverse myelitis. Many EBV infections occur in children without the complete clinical picture of infectious mononucleosis.

Evidence supporting the diagnosis includes 10% to 20% atypical lymphocytes on a complete blood cell count and a positive Monospot test. Since the Monospot test is not specific in young children, EBV titers confirm the diagnosis. Nearly diagnostic is the erythematous rash that erupts when a patient with infectious mononucleosis takes amoxicillin for presumed "strep" throat.

The treatment is usually supportive, but in cases of massive adenitis and pharyngeal edema that compromise the airway and cause respiratory distress, corticosteroids are very helpful.

Tumors

Tumors limited to the oropharynx are rare; these tumors are discussed in other chapters. Three generalized tumor conditions that deserve mention include leukemia, histiocytosis, and neurofibromatosis.

Leukemia

Oral lesions often represent the first manifestations of many acute hematologic disorders in previously healthy individuals. Findings often include pale mucosa, mucosal hemorrhages, ulcerative gingivitis, and dentalgia. Leukemia in particular causes a significant number of oropharyngeal changes in addition to those listed here. An infiltration of leukemic cells into the gums causes them to become edematous, erythematous, and soft. Infiltration can also occur in the palate and other tissues. These infiltrations can result in the deceptive appearance of simple hypertrophy. Gingivitis is common in the patient with leukemia, usually secondary to an infection with oral flora. This can lead to widespread necrosis and ulcer formation. Ischemic necrosis of the gums usually results from local thrombosis of vessels by leukemic cell proliferation.[21]

Langerhans Cell Histiocytosis (Histiocytosis X)

Reticuloendothelial cells, found in all tissues of the body, have phagocytic functions, form antibodies, and play an important role in local and systemic reactions to infection. Formerly, three separate syndromes involving this cell line were recognized: Hand-Schuller-Christian, Letterer-Siwe, and eosinophilic granuloma. Today, these syndromes are considered a spectrum of the basic disease process of the reticuloendothelial cells and are labeled Langerhans cell histiocytosis. The clinical symptoms depend on the involved organ system and range from an isolated lesion of bone or soft tissue to a widespread systemic malignant process. It is unclear whether this disease is an abnormality in immune function or a true malignancy.

In the acute disseminated form, many organs are involved, especially gingival mucosa, skin (eczematoid rash), spleen, liver, lungs, lymph nodes, and bone marrow. In the mouth, there is gingival swelling, ulceration, bleeding, and infection. The teeth may be loose, and frequently,

unexplained loss of teeth is an early complaint. This generalized involvement is usually found in young children and is associated with an early death.

A more chronic and milder form of this disease is seen in older children (over 5 years). The major organs involved are skin, bones, middle ear, spleen, liver, and lymph nodes. Lytic lesions may be seen in all bones and lead to symptoms such as loose teeth, exophthalmos, pituitary dysfunction, labyrinthine dysfunction, and pseudotumor cerebri. The variable course ranges from solitary lesions that resolve spontaneously to disseminated disease that may or may not respond to chemotherapy or radiation.

Tissue biopsy is diagnostic. Treatment by chemotherapy is most promising. Radiotherapy or surgical excision is effective in isolated lesions.

Neurofibromatosis (von Recklinghausen Disease)

Neurofibromatosis, an autosomal dominant disorder, consists of characteristic pigmentation of the skin plus neurofibromas of the cranial, spinal, and peripheral nerves. Neurofibromas can cause macroglossia or can present as postpharyngeal masses that press down on the soft palate and cause speech with a nasal escape sound. They can also appear as solitary or multiple nodules elsewhere in the oropharynx. Other central nervous system tumors found in neurofibromatosis include meningiomas, astrocytomas, gliomas, and spinal cord ependymomas. For the uncomplicated neurofibroma, there is no special treatment. The tumor should be removed if it causes pressure symptoms.

Effect of Tumor Treatment

Chemotherapy and radiation therapy take their toll on many organ systems of the oncology patient. The otolaryngologist needs to be aware of the specific problems faced by oncology patients regardless of their type of cancer or its location.

Cancer treatment itself causes several oral changes to occur. Mucositis is a red swelling of the oral mucosa due to thinning of the epithelium. This may or may not be painful. It can progress to cell desquamation, resulting in painful ulcerations. Cancer treatment often leads to thrombocytopenia and intraoral petechiae and hematomas. When platelet counts are extremely low, tooth brushing is ill advised and oral hygiene should be limited to saline rinses. Lips often become dry and chapped and then easily infected with oral flora in the defenseless host. Radiation and certain forms of chemotherapy also result in a reduced salivary flow rate. This can cause dysphagia and a change in oral flora.[4]

Radiotherapy and chemotherapy can also result in abnormally formed or absent teeth. The teeth may be dwarfed, tapered, prematurely calcified, or even noted to erupt prematurely as a result of their insult. The particular sequela is dependent on both the dose of the agent and the stage of tooth development at the time of injury. Facial anomalies include abnormal mandibular and maxillary development.[11]

Bleeding Disorders

The mouth is frequently subject to minor and major trauma. The mouth therefore can provide early evidence of a bleeding disorder. Apparent coagulation problems in the mouth may reflect decreased platelet counts (generalized sepsis, systemic lupus erythematosus, leukemia, chemotherapy, idiopathic thrombocytopenic purpura [ITP]) or coagulation defects (hemophilia, von Willebrand disease, and vitamin K deficiency). ITP and coagulation defects will be discussed here.

Idiopathic Thrombocytopenia

Idiopathic thrombocytopenic purpura (ITP) is an immunologic disorder in which platelets are first sensitized and then destroyed by the reticuloendothelial system, usually in the spleen. Clinical symptoms include epistaxis, diffuse petechiae or ecchymoses in the skin, bleeding gums, sublingual hematoma, or postpharyngeal bleeding. The peripheral blood smear shows decreased or absent platelets. The prothrombin time (PT) and partial thromboplastin time (PTT) are normal, and bone marrow examination shows an increased number of megakaryocytes. Most cases remit spontaneously. Current therapy includes intravenous gamma globulin, which usually results in a rapid rise of the platelet count, thereby avoiding any complications associated with hemorrhage. Corticosteroids also raise the platelet count and are used in chronic disease. From 2% to 10% of cases progress to chronic thrombocytopenia, requiring corticosteroid therapy and at times splenectomy.

Hemophilia

The hemophilias are genetic disorders of the clotting cascade that may be sex-linked, autosomal dominant, or autosomal recessive. Factor VIII deficiency is the most common form of hemophilia. Less frequently, factor V, VII, IX, X, XI, XII, or XIII may be deficient.

Bleeding may be spontaneous, cyclic, or the result of minor trauma, most often to the joints or soft tissue. Oropharyngeal bleeding usually occurs after trauma or with dental disease. The PTT, PT, bleeding time (BT), or thrombin time (TT) may be abnormal depending on the missing factor. The diagnosis is confirmed with a specific factor assay. Hemophilia is treated with replacement of the missing factor (if available), with cryoprecipitate, or with fresh-frozen plasma. For bleeding of oral mucosa, seen often with classic hemophilia, epsilon-aminocaproic acid, an inhibitor of the fibrinolytic system, is used with factor VIII concentrates.

von Willebrand Disease

Von Willebrand disease (pseudohemophilia) is an autosomal dominant disease that involves dysfunction of the platelets and decreased levels of factor VIII complex. The clinical symptoms are epistaxis and mucous membrane and skin bleeding. Bleeding may also occur after dental procedures and oral trauma. Unlike the bleeds in classic hemophilia, joint and large soft tissue involvement is rare. Laboratory findings reveal a prolonged BT and PTT. Platelet aggregation is abnormal. The mildest form of von Willebrand disease is type I, constituting 65% to 80% of cases. The treatment of choice for type I is desmopressin, or 1-deamino-8-D-arginine vasopressin (DDAVP), which results in increased levels of von Willebrand factor for a duration of 12 hours. Some of the other types of von Willebrand disease are responsive as well, but DDAVP can actually worsen disease in certain instances. When DDAVP is ineffective, treatment is with cryoprecipitate. Commercial factor VIII preparations do not correct the bleeding.[10]

Cyclic Neutropenia

Cyclic neutropenia is a potentially life-threatening disease characterized by periodic episodes of fever, oral ulcers, and profound neutropenia. The disease usually has its onset in the first decade of life. The cycles can be quite frequent, from 2 to 4 weeks apart. Most children have a benign course although they are at risk for catastrophic complications during the neutropenic periods.

Inflammatory Diseases

The oropharynx is frequently involved in systemic inflammatory or collagen vascular diseases. Symptoms include ulcerations secondary to vasculitis, dryness if the salivary glands are involved, and bleeding if the bone marrow is affected or platelet antibodies depress the platelet count (see Chap. 60).

Kawasaki Disease

Kawasaki disease (mucocutaneous lymph node syndrome), a disease of unclear etiology, has many different modes of presentation. The classic appearance includes five of the following six categories: fever for 5 days, lymphadenopathy (usually of the anterior cervical chain), rash, peripheral edema, bilateral conjunctival injection (without discharge), and oral mucous membrane involvement. The common oropharyngeal manifestations are an injected pharynx, dry fissured lips, and a strawberry tongue.

Kawasaki disease often presents in an atypical form. Some unusual initial manifestations include clinical mimicry of a suppurative infection of the parapharyngeal space, infectious mononucleosis, or an infected branchial cyst. Kawasaki disease has also been reported to cause necrotic pharyngitis and deep neck space cellulitis. Two reported unusual presenting symptoms of Kawasaki disease are severe uvulitis and supraglottitis.[3]

In these noted cases, the correct diagnosis was delayed because of the incorrect but convincing initial diagnosis. Early treatment can prevent coronary artery aneurysm, the most debilitating sequela. Treatment consists of high-dose intravenous gamma globulin and oral aspirin. Management also includes echocardiography and close cardiac follow-up.

Systemic Lupus Erythematosus

Systemic lupus erythematosus (SLE) most frequently affects adolescent and adult women. Oral lesions occur in about 25% of patients affected with lupus. The initial symptoms are fatigue, weakness, fever, and weight loss. Systemic involvement includes photosensitivity, arthritis, vasculitis of many organs, changes of the skin, and the classic butterfly rash over the malar area (although any area of the skin can be involved). Alopecia is common. Vasculitic changes in the brain may produce seizures or personality changes. Cardiac involvement can result in cardiomyopathy, tachycardia, pericardial effusion, and endocarditic vegetations. In children, the type and the severity of the associated renal involvement determine the prognosis.

The oropharyngeal lesions are found on the tongue, hard palate, and mucosa of the lips and cheeks. The typical lesions are white plaques with dark reddish-purple margins. There is also a tendency for oral bleeding, petechiae, and superficial ulcerations. Xerostomia is brought on by chronic inflammation of the salivary glands that results in occlusion and atrophy of the ducts. Patients experience difficulties in chewing, eating, swallowing, and taste. There is often significant lymphadenopathy. Temporomandibular joint involvement with arthritis is common. Patients with lupus often demonstrate the same oropharyngeal features as do those with Sjögren syndrome.[14, 16]

The diagnosis of lupus is made by clinical findings and a panel of tests that include a positive antinuclear antibody (ANA) screen, positive systemic lupus erythematosus preparations, and antibodies to double-stranded DNA. The patients may have anemia and a decreased platelet count, complement disorders, a positive Coombs test, and a false-positive serologic test result for syphilis (RPR).

The treatment depends on the severity of the problem. Rarely do salicylates control the symptoms in children, as they do in adults. More frequently, corticosteroids are required for children. If renal involvement is extensive, cyclophosphamide (Cytoxan) is added. The prognosis is variable and is dependent largely on renal involvement and the susceptibility to infection.

Sjögren Syndrome

Sjögren syndrome involving the salivary and lacrimal glands presents with keratoconjunctivitis and xerostomia. The salivary and lacrimal glands are progressively destroyed by infiltrating lymphocytes. In 50% of the cases in children, rheumatoid arthritis or another connective tissue disorder is also present. In addition, there is an associated decrease in secretions in the tracheobronchial tree, upper gastrointestinal tract, and pancreas.

The major symptoms include dry mouth and difficulty in chewing, swallowing, and speaking. Dental caries are common, and ulcers of the tongue, lips, and mucous membranes are present. There is also photosensitivity, dryness of the eyes, and keratoconjunctivitis.

The laboratory tests show nonspecific evidence of an inflammatory process. There is anemia; an elevated sedimentation rate; positive tests for ANA and rheumatoid factor; and a positive Coombs test. Specific anti-salivary duct antibody can be demonstrated by immunofluorescent techniques.

Treatment is symptomatic. The eyes must be lubricated. Corticosteroids may be used to control the associated systemic involvement. The prognosis is related to the associated diseases that occur with Sjögren syndrome, such as lupus, rheumatoid arthritis, and malignancy (see Chap. 65).

Crohn Disease

Crohn disease is an inflammatory disease characterized by granulomatous inflammation of the gastrointestinal tract. Involvement can be found from mouth to anus. Only 9% of patients with Crohn disease will reveal oral findings. However, in this subgroup oral signs and symptoms are the initial manifestation of the disease in up to 60% of patients.[13] Oral symptoms include edema, ulcers, pustules, and papules of the mucosa. Cheek swelling, angular stomatitis, gingivitis, pain, fever, and facial distortion may also be found. Multiple exacerbations of oral Crohn disease afflict over half of the affected patients. Findings of lesions suspicious of Crohn disease should lead to a thorough bowel investigation. Treatment is with topical or systemic steroids and/or azathioprine.[12]

Ulcerative Colitis

Ulcerative colitis is an inflammatory bowel disease usually limited to the large intestine. Symptoms include bloody diarrhea, weight loss, iron deficiency anemia, and abdominal pain. However, like Crohn disease, certain oral pathologies are associated with this disease, specifically chronic oral ulcers and the less common mucosal pustules called pyostomatitis vegetans.

Pemphigus Vulgaris

Pemphigus vulgaris is a serious vesiculobullous disease of autoimmune origin. It is most common in middle age but does occur in children. In a study by Laskaris and Stoufi,[5] the oral mucosa was the site of onset in almost all reported pediatric cases. The lesions usually take the form of oral mucosal erosions. Histologic and immunofluorescence examinations are necessary to establish the proper diagnosis.[5]

Multiple Congenital Anomaly Syndromes
DiGeorge Syndrome

DiGeorge syndrome, or the third and fourth pharyngeal pouch syndrome, is an absence or hypoplasia of the thymus and parathyroid.[7] This syndrome is characterized clinically by neonatal tetany, relapsing hypocalcemia, oral and cutaneous moniliasis, increased susceptibility to infection, failure to thrive, malformation of the ear, micrognathia, blunted nose, neck anomalies, great vessel lesions such as a double aortic arch, and cardiac lesions such as endocardial cushion defects.

The cause is unclear, but it is related to a defect in the third and fourth pharyngeal pouches from which the parathyroid and thymus normally evolve. The range of symptoms and laboratory findings is related to the amount of thymus and parathyroid tissue that is present. Diagnosis can be delayed in cases in which there is subclinical hypocalcemia and noncritical cardiac involvement. In those cases, immune dysfunction, resulting in candidiasis and other persistent infections, may be the first sign of illness.

The laboratory findings in this disease are related to the amount of thymus and parathyroid tissue that is present. Usually, the levels of immunoglobulins are normal, but the thymus-dependent functions are affected, leading to delayed skin reaction to antigens (*Candida*) and inability to reject a skin graft, depressed proliferative responsiveness of peripheral blood lymphocytes to phytohemagglutination, and depressed antibody response to specific immunization.

Children with this syndrome have difficulty with fungal and viral diseases and may succumb to live virus immunization. Fetal thymus transplantation has been helpful.

Fetal Alcohol Syndrome

Alcohol intake by pregnant women causes harmful effects to the fetus, including prenatal onset and persistent growth deficiency, as well as alterations in morphogenesis. Findings include short palpebral fissures, epicanthal folds, maxillary hypoplasia, micrognathia, a flattened philtrum, and a thin upper lip. A cleft lip and palate, a high arched palate, and small teeth have been reported in the fetal alcohol syndrome by some authors. Minor joint and limb abnormalities, cardiac septal defects, and mental deficiency are the other systemic findings. The ill effects are thought to be due to acetaldehyde, a by-product of ethanol metabolism, rather than to the ethanol itself. No specific therapy exists, and the prognosis is poor. Prevention is of paramount importance.[1]

Genetic Disorders

Darier disease is a rare inherited disorder of keratinization that produces a typical skin eruption of scattered brownish keratotic papules. Mucosal lesions affecting the mouth, pharynx, eyes, and vagina have been reported with this disease. Salivary gland swelling has also been noted, but usually without xerostomia. In its mild form, palatal Darier disease resembles nicotinic stomatitis. In the more severe form, it may resemble papillary hyperplasia of the palate. Oral warty dyskeratoma, found without skin lesions, resembles Darier disease and most likely represents a localized form. Oral Darier disease does not warrant specific treatment.[9]

Endocrinopathies

Endocrine imbalance states have potential for multisystem involvement, with many findings in the head and neck. In particular, hypercortisolism is associated with pathologic fractures of the mandible or maxilla secondary to osteoporosis. Similarly, fracture healing is delayed. Moon facies is seen secondary to fatty tissue deposition. In Addison disease (hypoadrenocorticism), "bronzing" hyperpigmentation of the skin is seen, especially in sun-exposed areas, e.g., the face. In addition, oral mucosal melanosis is found, particularly on the buccal mucosa. Diabetes mellitus can result in xerostomia, sialadenosis, altered taste, and burning mouth syndrome.

Nutritional Deficiencies

Nutritional deficiencies arise from one of three causes: inadequate intake, increased losses, or impaired absorption. Findings associated with specific deficiencies include cheilosis and angular fissures associated with niacin and vitamin B_6; spongy, bleeding red gums associated with vitamin C; red raw fissured tongue associated with folate, niacin, iron, and vitamins B_6 and B_{12}; and pale, atrophic tongue associated with iron and folate.[20] Identifying a nutritional deficiency in the United States should always initiate an in-depth evaluation for an underlying disease state, including social deprivation and poverty.

Other Disorders

Eating disorders are an unfortunately widespread problem in females between the ages of puberty and approximately 30. Cases of eating disorders in males do occur, but with a markedly smaller incidence. The prevalence of these disorders ranges from 1% to 20% in high-risk groups. A number of medical complications result from disorders of eating. They include dehydration from fluid losses, electrolyte abnormalities including hypochloremia and alkalosis, gastric dilatation, abdominal pain, neuromuscular symptoms, and amenorrhea. Specific to anorexia nervosa are problems with hypotension, hypothermia, cardiac arrhythmia, hypothalamic pituitary disturbances, growth of lanugo hair, and leukopenia. All eating disorders have enormous psychosocial consequences.

The ritual vomiting noted in patients with bulimia or combined anorexia and bulimia results in many oropharyngeal problems. Tooth destruction is the most obvious manifestation and proceeds in the following manner. First, there is loss of enamel, and then dentin, on the lingual surfaces of the teeth. As the severity increases, loss at the occlusal surfaces takes place. This results in severe hypersensitivity of the teeth, which leads to poor oral hygiene and ultimately to caries.[18]

Women with bulimia are also at great risk for xerostomia and parotid gland hypertrophy. The submandibular gland may be involved as well. While the xerostomia is thought to be due at least in part to the decreased total fluid volume, the cause of the salivary gland hypertrophy is unclear.[18]

Treatment is unfortunately difficult and prolonged. Patients with the above-listed oropharyngeal findings should be questioned about their eating habits. On average, patients have had an eating disorder for 5 years before coming to medical attention.

SELECTED REFERENCES

Behrman RE, Kliegman RM, Nelson WE, Vaughan VC III. Nelson Textbook of Pediatrics, 14th ed. Philadelphia, WB Saunders, 1992.

> *This complete pediatric textbook, written by more than 100 contributors, is an excellent general reference, with a listing of additional references.*

Feigin RD, Cherry JD. Textbook of Pediatric Infectious Diseases, 3rd ed. Philadelphia, WB Saunders, 1992.

> *This text outlines in detail the important infectious diseases that affect the head and neck as well as other organ systems. It has good illustrations, diagrams, and references.*

Nathan DG, Oski FA. Hematology of Infancy and Childhood, 4th ed. Philadelphia, WB Saunders, 1992.

> *This text, well-written and comprehensive, describes the pathophysiology and clinical aspects of children's blood problems.*

REFERENCES

1. Jackson IT, Hussain K. Craniofacial and oral manifestations of fetal alcohol syndrome. Plast Reconstr Surg 85:505, 1990.
2. Katz MH, Mastrucci MT, Leggott PJ, et al. Prognostic significance of oral lesions in children with perinatally acquired human immunodeficiency virus infection. Am J Dis Child 147:45, 1993.
3. Kazi A, Gauthier M, Lebel MH, et al. Uvulitis and supraglottitis: early manifestation of Kawasaki disease. J Pediatr 120:564, 1992.
4. Krywulak ML. Dental considerations for the pediatric oncology patient. J Can Dent Assoc 58:125, 1992.
5. Laskaris G, Stoufi E. Oral pemphigus vulgaris in a 6-year old girl. Oral Surg Oral Med Oral Pathol 69:609, 1990.
6. Leggott PJ. Oral manifestation of HIV infection in children. Oral Surg Oral Med Oral Pathol 73:187, 1992.
7. Lischner H. DiGeorge syndrome. J Pediatr 81:1042, 1972.
8. Long RG, Hlousek L, Doyle JL. Oral manifestations of systemic diseases. Mt Sinai J Med 65:309, 1998.
9. MacLeod RI, Munro CS. The incidence and distribution of oral lesions in patients with Darier's disease. Br Dent J 171:133, 1991.
10. Nathan DG, Oski FA. Hematology of Infancy and Childhood, 4th ed. Philadelphia, WB Saunders, 1992, pp 1613, 1623–1631.
11. Okano T, Tanaka T, Sun H, et al. Oral manifestations of radiation therapy in infancy. Oral Surg Oral Med Oral Pathol 71:517, 1991.
12. Plauth M, Jenss H, Meylee J. Oral manifestations of Crohn's disease. An analysis of 79 cases. J Clin Gastroenterol 13:29, 1991.
13. Rehberger A, Puspok A, Stallmeister T, et al. Crohn's disease masquerading as aphthous ulcers. Eur J Dermatol 8:274, 1998.
14. Rhodus NL, Johnson DK. The prevalence of oral manifestations of systemic lupus erythematosus. Quintessence Int 21:461, 1990.
15. Scully C, Porter S. Orofacial disease: Update for the dental clinical team. 2. Ulcers, erosions and other causes of sore mouth. Dent Update 26:31, 1999.
16. Scully C. Orofacial manifestations in the rheumatic diseases. Dent Update 16:240, 1989.
17. Scully C, Laskaris G, Porter SR. Oral manifestations of HIV infection and their management. II. Less common lesions. Oral Surg Oral Med Oral Pathol 71:167, 1991.
18. Spigset O. Oral symptoms in bulimia nervosa. A survey of 34 cases. Acta Odontol Scand 49:335, 1991.
19. Terezhalmy GT. A checklist of common oral manifestations of HIV infection. Cleve Clin J Med 59:56, 1992.
20. Touger-Decker, R. Oral manifestations of nutrient deficiencies. Mt Sinai J Med 65:355, 1998.
21. Weckx LLM, Hidal LBT, Marcucci G. Oral manifestations of leukemia. Ear Nose Throat J 69:341, 1990.

64

Idiopathic Conditions of the Mouth and Pharynx

George H. Conner, M.D., and Kay Chang, M.D.

Idiopathic conditions of the mouth and pharynx include disorders that vary from those that are frequently seen to those that are very rare. A classification of idiopathic oral and pharyngeal disease based on clinical presentation is summarized in Table 64–1.

Ulcerative Diseases

Ulcerative diseases of the mouth are common; in frequency they are second only to gingivitis.[45] The patients characteristically describe an abrupt onset of painful ulcerations that last from 1 to 3 weeks. Most oral ulcers may be diagnosed by their clinical appearance; however, in some instances, a biopsy may be necessary.

Systemic diseases with oral manifestations, especially blood dyscrasias or nutritional deficiency states, should always be considered.[34]

Acute Necrotizing Ulcerative Gingivitis (Vincent Infection, Vincent Stomatitis, Trench Mouth)

Natural History. Most cases of acute necrotizing ulcerative gingivitis occur in teenagers or young adults; the condition is less common in older persons. When it is found in younger children, a thorough investigation for debilitating systemic disease, particularly for blood dyscrasias, should be carried out. Systemic signs and symptoms such as fever, pallor, and fatigue may be prominent.[45]

Etiology. The exact cause of this type of gingivitis is unknown, although poor oral hygiene, food impactions, malocclusion, and local dental diseases may contribute. Since many patients with acute necrotizing ulcerative gingivitis are high school or college students, unusual physical or emotional stress may play a role (see Chap. 58).[45] Similarly, dietary imbalances and fatigue may also be of significance. Underlying systemic disease, such as nutritional deficiency states and blood dyscrasias seen with this condition, may represent only lowered local tissue resistance to bacterial invasion.

There are no specific confirmatory laboratory tests for this condition. The presence of Vincent microorganisms is not definite proof of the existence of acute recurrent ulcerative stomatitis, since 80% of healthy individuals

have these organisms within their mouths. It is probably not possible to transmit this disease to a healthy mouth.[45]

Clinical Picture. Most patients present with a complaint of painful, bleeding gums, a bad taste in the mouth, or a foul mouth odor. Examination reveals the presence of gingivitis of variable severity. Ulcerations at the base of the teeth are covered by dirty, gray, necrotic membranes that adhere loosely. Removal of this necrotic slough reveals a painful ulceration at the base of the tooth. Occasionally, the buccal mucosa or other tissues of the mouth become involved (Fig. 64–1).

Management. The treatment of acute necrotizing ulcerative gingivitis consists of (1) searching for and eliminating any local or systemic contributing disorder and (2) gentle mechanical cleansing of involved areas, improvement of oral hygiene, and antibiotics. Water irrigating devices and oxidizing oral rinses are helpful.

Prognosis. Provided that there is no underlying systemic condition, local measures should result in gradual improvement. In rare instances, infection of a severe degree has been known to invade the underlying bone, leading to marked tissue destruction and necrosis that is sometimes severe enough to expose bone.[45] In the majority of cases, however, the prognosis is good.

Recurrent Aphthous Stomatitis

Natural History. Recurrent aphthous stomatitis (RAS) may appear on the oral mucosa as minor aphthous ulcerations, major aphthae, or herpetiform ulcers. RAS is most prevalent in childhood and lasts from 1 to 4 weeks. The ulcers are painful and are often recurrent.

Etiology. The cause of RAS is not clear. A family history positive for this condition may be present. There may be predisposing factors, such as vitamin deficiencies, nutritional deficiencies, or altered immunity. In women, aphthae may appear before menses. Stress and trauma can also be associated with aphthae.

Clinical Picture. RAS is a common problem affecting at least 20% of the population at one time or another. There are three types of RAS: RAS with minor aphthae

TABLE 64–1. Idiopathic Conditions of the Mouth and Pharynx

I. Ulcerative diseases
   A. Acute necrotizing ulcerative gingivitis
   B. Recurrent aphthous stomatitis (RAS)
      1. Minor aphthous stomatitis (MiRAS)
      2. Major aphthous stomatitis (MaRAS)
      3. Herpetiform ulceration (HU)
   C. Sweet syndrome
   D. Behçet disease
   E. Angular stomatitis
   F. Noma
   G. Geographic tongue
   H. Cheilitis granulomatosa
   I. Eosinophilic ulcer
II. Vesiculobullous diseases
   A. Erythema multiforme
   B. Epidermolysis bullosa
      1. Simplex
      2. Dystrophica
      3. Acquisita
   C. Pemphigus vulgaris
   D. Mucous membrane pemphigoid
   E. Bullous pemphigoid
   F. Linear IgA disease
III. Keratotic diseases
   A. Lichen planus
   B. Hereditary keratosis
      1. Familial white folded dysplasia
      2. Keratosis follicularis
   C. Chronic discoid lupus erythematosus

(MiRAS), RAS with major aphthae (MaRAS), and herpetiform ulceration (HU).

The minor aphthae in MiRAS are the most common and are usually 2 to 4 mm in diameter, with an erythematous halo and a dirty necrotic base. The aphthae are usually located on the mucosal surfaces of the lips, cheeks, floor of the mouth, and lateral aspects of the tongue. Less common sites include the gingivae, palate, and dorsum of the tongue. The aphthae usually occur a few at a time, healing in 7 to 10 days and recurring at variable intervals. Small aphthae heal without scar. Most aphthae occur in those aged 10 years or older.

The major aphthous ulcers in MaRAS, sometimes referred to as Sutton ulcers, are larger, are more painful, last longer, and are more prone to recur than the ulcers of MiRAS. These large aphthae may occur anywhere on the oral mucosa, including the palate and dorsum of the tongue. Healing occurs slowly and may result in considerable scar formation.[40]

Herpetiform ulcers in HU usually begin as a crop of small vesicles that progress into multiple discrete ulcers at any oral site. As the ulcers increase in size, they may coalesce into large, ragged ulcers that heal slowly. Their resemblance to herpetic stomatitis gives rise to their name, but there is no evidence of a herpetic viral origin. HU has a slight female predominance and occurs in a slightly older age group than RAS.[32]

Management. There is no specific management for RAS. Underlying disorders, deficiencies, or altered immune status should be ruled out. Biopsies may be necessary to rule out malignancy. Topical steroids,[19] topical tetracycline, and analgesics are of some benefit.

Prognosis. The overall prognosis is good; however, the recurrent painful nature of the aphthae, especially the larger ones, may be debilitating. Occasionally, scarring may be severe enough to distort oral tissues and interfere with oral functions.[45]

Sweet Syndrome (Acute Febrile Neutrophilic Dermatosis)

Natural History. Sweet syndrome (SS) manifests as a febrile illness with leukocytosis, oral aphthous ulcerations, and raised painful plaques on the skin of the neck, face, and limbs.[37] There are also associated genital and conjunctival lesions and arthralgias. Underlying conditions, such as rheumatoid arthritis, colitis,[37] Sjögren syndrome, and leukemias, may be present.

Etiology. The cause of SS is unknown. Its association with other autoimmune disorders suggests a causal relationship. SS resembles Behçet disease in many ways and could represent an acute phase of that disorder.[25]

Clinical Picture. SS manifests as a febrile illness. Aphthous oral ulcerations, as well as genital mucosal ulcers and uveitis, may be present. Joint pains, erythema nodosum–like skin plaques, and folliculitis may also occur.[2] There may be frequent recurrences.[25]

Management. Underlying conditions, especially malignancies, should be ruled out. Treatment with systemic steroids and colchicine has been reported to be effective in causing remissions.[25] Dapsone has also been reported to be successful.[2]

Prognosis. The overall prognosis for SS should be good, provided that there is no life-threatening underlying illness. Recurrences over many years remain a problem.

Behçet Disease

Natural History. Behçet disease is a rare condition characterized by a triad of symptoms involving ocular inflam-

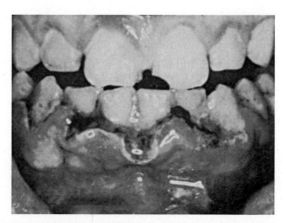

FIGURE 64–1. Acute necrotizing ulcerative gingivitis. Ulcerations at the base of the teeth are covered with a dirty, gray, necrotic membrane. There is associated local pain and bleeding, with a foul mouth odor. (Courtesy of Bailliere's Medical Transparencies, London.)

mation with aphthous ulceration of the oral mucosa and external genitalia.[10] It is seen in young adults of either sex. Ulcerations involving the oral and genital areas are discrete and resemble the lesions of aphthous stomatitis.[40] Such lesions may be recurrent for many years. Neurologic involvement may occur in as many as 25% of patients.[43] Eye manifestations, such as uveitis, iridocyclitis, and hypopyon, which eventually lead to blindness, may also occur.[26] Other systems with involvement include esophageal ulceration with chest pain,[12, 17] recurrent pneumonia with hemoptysis, arthralgia, erythema nodosum, colitis, vasculitis, thrombophlebitis, large artery aneurysms, and encephalitis.[26]

Etiology. The cause of Behçet disease is unknown, although the possibility of a specific virus or an immune response[10, 41] to an unknown substance has been debated.[26] The occurrence of arthralgias and erythema nodosum suggests an autoimmune defect.[32]

Clinical Picture. The usual presenting complaint is a painful ulcer in the mouth. Such ulcers may resemble aphthous ulcerations or the lesions of recurrent ulcerative stomatitis. The ulcers may be multiple, small, and shallow and covered with a yellow serofibrous exudate. Larger ulcers may be somewhat depressed in the center, with elevated rims. The mouth lesions per se are not specific and are not diagnostic.[45] In most cases, mouth lesions are accompanied by genital or eye lesions, and the diagnosis is made on the basis of these multiple-site lesions. The genital lesions are similar in appearance to those of the mouth and affect the vulvar folds or vaginal canal in females and the scrotal sac or penis in males. The eye lesions may consist of purulent conjunctivitis and uveitis, iridocyclitis, or hypopyon. When the eye is involved, progression to blindness is almost the rule.[20]

Occasionally, the skin is involved with a cutaneous vasculitis. The joints may exhibit synovitis, and the central nervous system involvement may be manifested by paresis, cerebellar ataxia, pseudobulbar palsy, or ocular palsies.[26]

Management. Remissions may occur with vigorous therapy, including systemic corticosteroids, azathioprine, chlorambucil,[20] and transfer factor.[42] Levamisole, dapsone, acyclovir, and cyclosporine have all been tried with some degree of success.[32] Exacerbations may occur when steroid dosages are reduced.[26] Chlorambucil should be given for at least 6 months after complete remission has occurred.[20]

Prognosis. Behçet disease is usually a recurrent disease that lasts for years. The more benign forms may respond to early systemic steroids. Long-term combination therapy may be curative. Deaths have been reported when neurologic involvement has occurred. The most significant complication is that of extensive scarring about the eye, with resultant diminished vision or blindness. This complication occurs an average of 3.36 years after the onset of eye symptoms.[20]

Angular Stomatitis

Natural History. Angular stomatitis is the occurrence of an inflammatory lesion at the corner of the mouth. The usual lesion begins at the mucocutaneous junction and extends onto the skin (Fig. 64–2).

Etiology. Angular stomatitis is an easily recognized condition and in most cases has an underlying cause, such as a riboflavin deficiency. It is referred to as cheilosis in such instances.[24] However, occasionally, no apparent cause can be found.

Pseudocheilosis is a term used to describe a situation in which a decrease in the intermaxillary distance results in an accentuation of the transverse folds of the skin at the angle of the mouth with pooling of the saliva in the corners, leading to drying and crusting that cause local inflammation. This condition is usually a result of loss of dentition and is more common in the elderly.[45]

The lesions at the angle of the mouth may be complicated by secondary invasion by microorganisms of the oral flora, particularly streptococci, staphylococci, and *Monilia*. When *Candida albicans* is predominant, the condition is referred to as perlèche.[24]

Angular stomatitis may also be due to an allergic or toxic reaction to such substances as lipsticks, other cosmetics, or ointments.

Management. Every attempt should be made to determine the underlying cause of the inflammation. Nutritional deficiency states, mechanical problems, and allergic disorders should all be investigated. In cases in which there is a secondary invasion by local microorganisms, the topical application of antibiotic or antifungal ointments is often successful. In the occasional case in which there is no clear-cut cause of the angular stomatitis, symptomatic improvement may be observed with topical corticosteroid medications.[45]

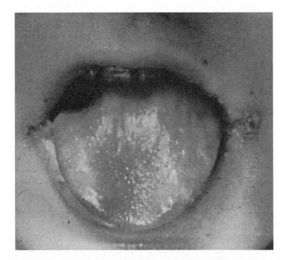

FIGURE 64–2. Angular stomatitis in a child with nutritional deficiency. Such areas can become secondarily invaded by normal oral flora or *Candida albicans*. (From Dreizen S. The Mouth in Medicine. Multi-Media Postgraduate Medicine, 1971.)

Prognosis. The prognosis is good, provided that there is no serious underlying disorder.

Noma (Gangrenous Stomatitis, Cancrum Oris)

Natural History. Noma is a gangrenous disease that involves the lips, cheek, face, maxilla, or mandible and occurs most commonly in children. Although rare in the Western world,[16] it is still a major health problem in many developing countries.[38]

Noma may be initiated by necrotic foci developing in areas of preexisting inflammation, such as partially erupted teeth. The acute lesion develops into an indolent ulcer that rapidly increases in depth and size. Acute inflammation occurs in the overlying skin, followed by necrosis and sloughing. The gangrenous area may rapidly expand, with indistinct margins between the necrotic tissue and the surrounding inflammation. Perforation of the lips or cheeks occurs early and is often accompanied by a foul odor. There is a significant mortality rate if treatment is delayed or unsuccessful. In fatal cases, there is a downhill course with the development of aspiration pneumonia, septicemia, and death.[45]

Etiology. The specific cause of noma is unknown, although it is seen in debilitative states, with malnutrition,[16] or following an acute infectious process or exanthem. Most cases are reported in areas of the world where malnutrition and avitaminosis are prevalent. Often, measles precedes the onset of the disease. No specific organisms are ordinarily found in the necrotic material.

Clinical Picture. The picture is usually that of a toxic child with an acute inflammation that often involves the buccal mucosa adjacent to a sharp, carious, or partially impacted tooth. An ulceration appears with pain, edema, and acute inflammation involving the overlying skin. This is followed by rapid necrosis with the formation of a grayish or black purulent slough that expands rapidly. Perforation of the lips or cheeks is the forerunner of a steadily worsening course of pneumonia and septicemia, leading to death.

Management. Vigorous treatment with antibiotics[16] and supportive measures, with extensive local debridement, may be successful. Severe disfigurement with ankylosis of the jaw requiring surgical correction at a later date is often typical in survivors.[27]

Geographic Tongue

Natural History. Geographic tongue is a common condition that is seen in all age groups. It may occur suddenly and last for many weeks or even years. Often, there is an associated fissuring of the tongue.

Etiology. There is no known cause of this condition.

Clinical Picture. The involved areas of the tongue are smooth and red, and the fungiform papillae are easily observable. This is due to a loss of filiform papillae in well-defined areas, which are surrounded by an elevated zone of white exudate. The symptoms are usually mild and are accompanied by differing degrees of discomfort (Fig. 64–3).

Management. Therapy for geographic tongue is directed toward providing local comfort. Topical anesthetic agents and the avoidance of hot or spicy foods may be helpful. The prognosis is good.[45]

Cheilitis Granulomatosa

Natural History. Cheilitis granulomatosa begins as a diffuse swelling of the lips, more commonly involving the lower lip. It is a rare condition that results in chronic and persistent enlargement of the lips.

Clinical Picture. The lower lip is usually involved. The swelling is firm and elastic to touch. Scaling and fissuring may be present. Microscopically, there is chronic, nonspecific inflammation with local granuloma formation. When the condition is associated with facial paralysis and a congenitally fissured tongue, it is known as Melkersson-Rosenthal syndrome.[24]

Management. Since there is no known cause, there is no reliable or specific therapy. However, the prognosis for resolution of the problem is good.

Eosinophilic Ulcer

Natural History. Eosinophilic ulcer occurs most commonly on the tongue, although it can occur anywhere on

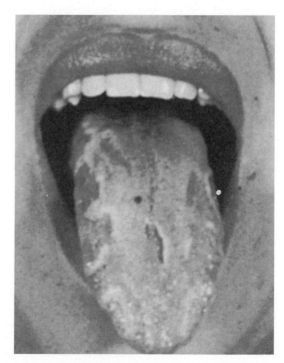

FIGURE 64–3. Geographic tongue. Patchy areas of loss of filiform papillae result in the appearance of smooth, red areas surrounded by zones of elevated, white exudate. Often, there is an associated fissuring.

the oral mucosa.[35] It is a self-limited benign lesion. Diagnosis is made by biopsy. The lesion may heal spontaneously or, if excised, it tends not to recur.

Etiology. Although trauma has been suggested as causal, the cause remains obscure.

Clinical Picture. Eosinophilic ulcer manifests as a rather large ulceration, usually on the dorsum of the tongue, that has raised indurated margins and a pseudomembranous cover. Other ulcers may appear on the lips or palate, or elsewhere on the oral mucosa. The ulcer may persist for weeks or months. Because of the clinical resemblance to other lesions, biopsy is necessary for a definitive diagnosis.

Management. No specific therapy is required; however, because of the resemblance to carcinomas, chancres, tuberculous ulcers, necrotizing sialometaplasia, lethal midline granulomas, and Wegener granulomatosis, biopsy is of critical importance. The lesion may heal spontaneously after biopsy. If healing seems delayed, the lesion may be excised.

Prognosis. The prognosis for this benign lesion is good.

Vesiculobullous Disorders

Erythema Multiforme

Natural History. Erythema multiforme is an acute inflammatory disease that may be accompanied by a variety of skin lesions that are often self-limiting. Oral lesions are often present, involving the lips with bullae, which then form ulcers and are covered by hemorrhagic exudate.[11] The skin lesions begin as macules and papules that eventually become vesicles and bullae and break down to become erosions and ulcerations. An iris-like target lesion on the skin is diagnostic.[1] The condition comes on acutely and may recur frequently. In the mild form, it may heal spontaneously in about 2 weeks. There may be seasonal variations, with the disorder occurring more often in the winter and the early spring.

Etiology. The cause of erythema multiforme is not known, although it frequently occurs following inflammatory disorders, especially herpes simplex, and after vaccinations. It may also be precipitated by a variety of agents, such as penicillin, barbiturates, sulfonamides, and others.[3, 31] *Mycoplasma pneumoniae* has been cultured from the throat and bullae of some patients, but it is not known what role, if any, it may play in the disease. *Candida* has been cultured from many patients, and they have responded to antifungal therapy, suggesting a possible fungal cause.

Clinical Picture. Erythema multiforme usually has an abrupt onset, accompanied by fatigue, malaise, and fever. The latter, however, may be absent when the eruptions are restricted to the mouth (Fig. 64–4).

The oral mucosal lesions of erythema multiforme may be large and irregular with a raw base. Necrotic sloughs that are firmly adherent may occur. The lips are covered by a hemorrhagic exudate.[11] Iris-like target lesions may

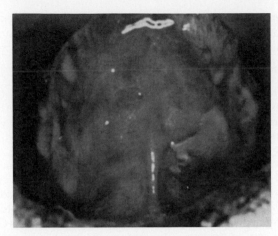

FIGURE 64–4. Erythema multiforme involving the tongue. Superficial necrotic sloughs may be multiple within the mouth. The lesions may be large and irregular with a raw base. (Courtesy of Bailliere's Medical Transparencies, London.)

occur on the skin, especially on the palms of the hands, and are diagnostic. In severe cases, when associated with purulent conjunctivitis, fever, leukopenia, macular erythematous necrotic skin lesions, and bullous stomatitis, the name Stevens-Johnson syndrome is given to this disorder.

Management. Treatment of erythema multiforme is palliative in mild cases, with antihistamines,[5] and local moist compresses for erosive lesions. Hydrogen peroxide (3%) mouthwash and topical anesthetic agents are helpful for the oral lesions. Tetracycline or erythromycin may be used for suspected *M. pneumoniae* infections.[11] Treatment for possible *Candida* infection may be beneficial. Systemic corticosteroids are indicated when involvement is more severe.

In cases of Stevens-Johnson syndrome, treatment should include immediate hospitalization, intravenous fluids, and systemic corticosteroids in high doses given initially and tapered off over a 2- to 3-week period. Levamisole and azathioprine may also be helpful at this time. Additionally, local care as outlined above for skin lesions should be instituted. This form of the disorder runs a 1- to 4-week course, usually ending with the recovery of the individual. Fatalities may occur, particularly with severe pulmonary involvement.[45]

Complications. Severe purulent conjunctivitis, sometimes resulting in blindness, has been reported.

Epidermolysis Bullosa

Natural History. Epidermolysis bullosa is a rare connective tissue disorder in which there is a lack of adherence of the epidermis to the dermis, which results in a separation, leading to bullous formations.

Oral lesions occur as a result of minor trauma or even normal oral activity, such as sucking. Any trauma to the skin causes vesicles and bullae to develop.

Etiology. In most cases, there is a family history of the disorder.

Clinical Picture. Epidermolysis bullosa is divided into three types: epidermolysis bullosa simplex, epidermolysis bullosa dystrophica, and childhood epidermolysis bullosa acquisita.

Epidermolysis bullosa simplex is the milder form of the disorder, appearing at birth or shortly thereafter. Small bullae containing serous fluid appear on areas of trauma, especially over joints and on the hands and feet. These areas heal without scarring unless secondary infection becomes a problem. Oral lesions frequently occur. The first evidence may be on the lips of an infant as a result of forceful or prolonged sucking. Later, any traumatic experience results in lifting of the epidermis and subsequent erosion.

Epidermolysis bullosa dystrophica is the serious form of the disease; it appears in infancy and rapidly leads to death. Bullae appear following minor trauma. The area may then become hemorrhagic. Large sheets of epidermis may come loose, denuding much of the surface of the body and allowing rapid fluid and protein loss and secondary infection. In such cases, the oral lesions may be so severe as to prevent feeding, thus contributing to the rapid demise of the infant.

Childhood epidermolysis bullosa acquisita is the third form, occurring during childhood, and is characterized by blistering of the skin, oral mucosa, and anogenital mucosa. The initial clinical and histologic findings resemble those of mucous membrane pemphigoid, from which it can be differentiated by immunofluorescent techniques.[30]

Management. Treatment is directed at protecting the individual from any form of traumatic experience. This is likely to be successful only in the milder or epidermolysis bullosa simplex cases.

Systemic therapy with steroids, dapsone, azathioprine, and cyclophosphamide, singly or in combination,[30] may be helpful in simplex or acquisita forms of the disease.

Prognosis. In the dystrophic form of the disease, the prognosis is poor.

Pemphigus Vulgaris

Natural History. Pemphigus vulgaris is uncommon in childhood[14] and may be clinically indistinguishable from erythema multiforme, mucous membrane pemphigoid,[4] bullous pemphigoid, or epidermolysis bullosa acquisita. All are part of a spectrum of subepithelial autoimmune bullous diseases that present with oral blisters or erosions with immune deposits in the epithelial basement membrane zone.[32] All have been reported in children.

In pemphigus vulgaris, oral lesions are present about 60% of the time. Blisters rapidly break down, leaving painful erosions that may be recalcitrant to therapy.

Etiology. Pemphigus vulgaris is believed to be most likely an autoimmune disorder.

Management. Systemic steroids and immunosuppressants,[4] such as azathioprine, are indicated.

Prognosis. The prognosis for pemphigus vulgaris, when actively treated, is good.

Mucous Membrane Pemphigoid

Natural History. Mucous membrane pemphigoid (MMP) is a chronic disease primarily involving the oral mucosa. While this disease most commonly affects middle-aged and older women, it has been seen rarely in teenagers.

Etiology. MMP is most likely an autoimmune disorder.[39] Causative factors remain unknown. There is no apparent family history or relationship to food products, drugs, or microbial agents.

Clinical Picture. The gingival mucosa is the most common site of involvement and is characterized by erythema and pseudomembrane-covered painful ulcerations. The eye may become involved, with a symblepharon that may be progressive. Remission is rare. Biopsy reveals a separation of the epithelial layer from the underlying connective tissue; however, diagnosis may be elusive.[21]

Management. Systemic or topical steroids help produce remission. When the minimal effective dose of prednisone cannot be tolerated, a lower effective dose can be attained by combining prednisone with azathioprine. Prognosis is good concerning survival; however, the disease may last for years.

Linear IgA Disease

Natural History. Linear IgA disease (LAD) is a rare blistering dermatosis characterized by a cutaneous eruption consisting of bullae that are often arranged in an annular configuration.[13] The oral mucosa and conjunctiva may be involved.

Etiology. The cause of LAD is unknown, but it is thought to be autoimmune.[15]

Clinical Picture. Patients with LAD present with cutaneous blisters and bullae that may be in an annular configuration. Ulceration and erosion of the oral mucosa may be present, as well as widespread erosive gingivitis and erosive cheilitis. Conjunctival adhesions between the lid and the globe may occur, as well as corneal opacification. Diagnosis is confirmed by immunofluorescent techniques.

Management. Dapsone and prednisone have been found to be effective for this disorder.

Prognosis. The prognosis for LAD is good, although remissions and exacerbations may persist for years.

Keratotic Diseases

Lichen Planus

Natural History. Lichen planus is a fairly common dermatologic disorder involving the mucous membranes and the skin.[33] It occurs in older children and young adults, as well as in older populations. It is seen with equal frequency in males and females. The lesions are usually discovered accidentally when the patient sees or feels them, or when they are noted by a dentist or physician.

Etiology. The cause of lichen planus is unknown, although trauma, emotional disturbances, toxic reactions, and infections have been implicated. A relationship to systemic lupus erythematosus has been suggested.[8, 29]

Clinical Picture. The mouth is the most frequently affected site, with the buccal mucosa and tongue most commonly involved. The lesions may vary in size from a papule a few millimeters in diameter to involvement of the entire buccal mucosa. Often, the lesions appear in a reticular pattern, although papules, plaques, and ulcerative forms may occur.[33] The reticular pattern is the most easily recognized and occurs most often on the buccal mucosa (Fig. 64–5). This pattern is composed of narrow, slightly elevated gray-white lines that join each other at angles to form a network-like pattern. The papular pattern consists of pinhead-sized, slightly raised, glistening white spots that occur in groups or diffusely over the oral mucosa. Frequently, the lesion takes the form of a solid, raised, white plaque. Magnified examination of such plaques reveals them to be composed of large numbers of tiny papules.

The symptoms of lichen planus are variable. The patient may be symptom-free; however, if ulcerations are present, local discomfort and burning sensations occur. The history is usually one of remission and exacerbation for years.[49]

The diagnosis is confirmed by a biopsy specimen that shows keratosis and parakeratosis with a moth-eaten pattern of destruction of the basal cells. A broad band of inflammatory cells, usually lymphocytes, is located directly beneath the basal epithelium.

Management. There is no known effective treatment. Reassurance that the condition is benign and not precancerous is important. When the condition is ulcerative, systemic corticosteroids are occasionally effective. Intralesional injection of steroids may also promote healing.[9]

Prognosis. The prognosis is good, although symptoms may persist indefinitely.

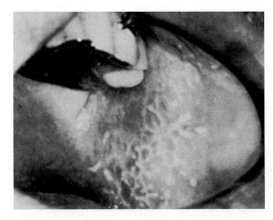

FIGURE 64–5. Lichen planus involving the buccal mucosa with a reticular pattern. Other lesions may consist of glistening white papules or plaques. (Courtesy of Bailliere's Medical Transparencies, London.)

Hereditary Keratoses

By definition, hereditary disorders cannot be considered idiopathic and are technically out of place in this chapter. However, for the purpose of differential diagnosis, two keratotic disorders of the mouth are covered briefly: (1) familial, white folded dysplasia (white sponge nevus) and (2) keratosis follicularis (Darier disease).

White Folded Dysplasia

Natural History. White folded dysplasia is probably a hereditary condition that can be noted at birth. Lesions of gray-white spongy areas with fissures and folds may be noted on the tongue or buccal mucosa. Progressive involvement continues until adolescence, when the extent of the disorder tends to stabilize. Lesions of a similar nature may also be found on the vaginal, rectal, or nasal mucosa.

Clinical Picture. The lesions are white, soft, and spongy and resemble diffuse leukoplakia. The entire oral mucosa tends to be involved, with the most obvious lesions in the buccal mucosa, the floor of the mouth, and the ventral surface of the tongue. The lesions are entirely asymptomatic.

Diagnosis is dependent on the clinical appearance and the presence of a similar condition in a sibling, parent, or grandparent. The histologic findings are those of thickening of the epithelium with acanthosis with an intact basal cell layer. Intracellular edema and vacuolization of the prickle cell layer is present. There is little or no cornification.

Management. There is no specific therapy, and since these patients are virtually symptom-free, generally no therapy is needed. Reassurance that this is not a malignant condition and that it will usually arrest itself during adolescence is given. There usually are no complications or sequelae.[24]

Keratosis Follicularis (Darier Disease)

Natural History. This rare hereditary condition involves the epidermis of the skin and mucous membranes. The disease is generally slowly progressive, with periods of remission and exacerbation. The mucous membranes tend to be less frequently involved than the skin.

Clinical Picture. The skin lesions may appear as small, firm, red papules that may ulcerate, coalesce, and form crusts. The skin lesions are most commonly found on the face, neck, shoulders, and axillae. Secondary infections are common, especially during warm, humid weather. Remissions may occur, usually during the winter months. The oral lesions are firm nodules or papules, usually on the palate, although the tongue and buccal mucosa may be involved. The mouth lesions are usually asymptomatic.

Etiology. Nothing is known about the cause of Darier keratosis follicularis except for its familial tendency.

Management. There is no known effective treatment;

however, some improvement with vitamin A therapy has been reported.[24]

Chronic Discoid Lupus Erythematosus

Natural History. This collagen disorder involves the skin and the mucous membranes. It is rare in childhood. It is included in this section because the oral manifestations demonstrate areas of patchy hyperkeratosis.

The natural course of the disease is one of pronounced chronicity with periods of remission and exacerbation. There is a tendency for gradual remission, and eventually many cases seem to burn out over a period of years.

With chronic discoid lupus erythematosus, there are very few associated signs or symptoms, and generally this does not progress to the acute or disseminated forms of the disease. Occasionally, it is seen with lichen planus.[8]

Etiology. The cause of chronic discoid lupus erythematosus is unknown, although it is believed that it is in some way related to the autoimmune disorders.

Clinical Picture. Chronic discoid lupus erythematosus is a mucocutaneous disorder that affects either sex, with a slight predilection for females. It is rare in childhood, being seen usually between the ages of 20 and 40 years. About 25% of the patients show lesions on the oral mucosa, with the buccal mucosa the most common site. Photosensitivity may exist.[28]

The characteristic oral lesion is usually a well-defined area of irregular configuration with loss of epithelium mixed with patches of hyperkeratosis and exudates. A unique radial arrangement of capillaries at the periphery of the lesion extending into the surrounding tissues is present. Scarring occurs with older lesions along with irregular white patches.

Patients with oral lesions almost invariably have skin manifestations. Usually, these take the form of the characteristic butterfly configuration over the nose and cheeks.

Histologically, the oral lesions demonstrate hyperkeratosis, parakeratosis, and degeneration of the stratum germinativum with hyaline-like degeneration of the connective tissue collagens and lymphocytic infiltration in clumps, usually in a perivascular pattern. The periodic acid–Schiff staining procedure for mucopolysaccharides reveals an intense reaction in the areas of collagen degeneration.[24] Immunofluorescence techniques may be helpful in establishing a diagnosis.[8]

Management. The treatment of chronic discoid lupus erythematosus consists of the use of antimalarial drugs, such as chloroquine, antipyrine, and primaquine, as well as topical and systemic steroids. The overall prognosis for this ailment is good.

SELECTED REFERENCES

Lund WS. Treatment of superficial lesions of the mouth and pharynx. J Laryngol Otol 90:101, 1976.

This brief, concise article clearly describes virtually all the lesions that commonly occur in the mouth. Up-to-date treatment is also discussed.

O'Duffy JD, Goldstein NP. Neurologic involvement in seven patients with Behçet's disease. Am J Med 61:170, 1976.

An extremely readable article on this subject, this is probably the most complete article on neurologic disorders of Behçet disease, and it has excellent coverage of all manifestations and current treatments.

Tempest MN. Cancrum oris. Br J Surg 53:949, 1966.

An excellent and very complete article about all the ravages of this severe disorder, it contains numerous illustrations and recommendations for immediate and rehabilitative therapy.

Three books are worthy of mention and deserve to be in the library of any physician interested in diseases of the mouth:

McCarthy PL, Gerald S. Diseases of the Oral Mucosa. New York, McGraw-Hill, 1964.

Pindborg JJ. Atlas of Diseases of the Oral Mucosa, 5th ed. Philadelphia, WB Saunders, 1992.

Zagarelli EV, Kutscher AH, Hyman GA. Diseases of the Mouth and Jaws. Philadelphia, Lea & Febiger, 1969.

Together, these texts provide a complete reference source for virtually all diseases of the mouth.

REFERENCES

1. Ackerman AB, Penneys NS, Clark WH. Erythema multiforme exudativum: distinctive pathological process. Br J Dermatol 84:554, 1971.
2. Aram H. Acute febrile neutrophilic dermatosis (Sweet's syndrome). Arch Dermatol 120:245, 1984.
3. Baer RL. Perspective: erythema multiforme—1976. Am J Med Sci 271:119, 1976.
4. Bean SF, Jordan RE. Chronic non-hereditary blistering disease in children. Arch Dermatol 110:941, 1974.
5. Bhargava RK, Singh V, Soni V. Erythema multiforme resulting from insecticide spray. Arch Dermatol 113:686, 1977.
6. Bjornberg A, Hellgren L. Treatment of chronic discoid lupus erythematosus with betamethasone 17,21-dipropionate. Curr Ther Res 19:442, 1976.
7. Colvard DM, Robertson DM, O'Duffy JD. The ocular manifestations of Behçet's disease. Arch Ophthalmol 95:1813, 1977.
8. Davies MG, Gorkiewicz A, Knight A, et al. Is there a relationship between lupus erythematosus and lichen planus? Br J Dermatol 96:145, 1977.
9. Ferguson MM. Treatment of erosive lichen planus of the oral mucosa with depot steroids. Lancet 2:771, 1977.
10. Haim S. Behçet's disease: etiology and treatment. Dermatologica 150:163, 1975.
11. Haskell R. Oral vesiculo-bullous lesions. J Laryngol Otol 90:101, 1976.
12. Kaplinsky N, Neumann G, Harzahav Y, et al. Esophageal ulceration in Behçet's syndrome. Gastointest Endosc 23:160, 1977.
13. Kelly SE, Frith PA, Millard PR, et al. A clinicopathological study of mucosal involvement in linear IgA disease. Br J Dermatol 119:161, 1988.
14. Laskaris G, Sklavounou A, Stratigos J. Bullous pemphigoid, cicatricial pemphigoid, and pemphigus vulgaris. Oral Surg 54:656, 1982.
15. Leonard JN, Haffenden GP, Ring NP, et al. Linear IgA disease in adults. Br J Dermatol 107:301, 1982.
16. Limongelli WA, Clark MS, Williams AC. Noma-like lesion in a patient with chronic lymphocytic leukemia. Oral Surg 41:40, 1976.
17. Lockhart JM, McIntyre W, Caperton EM Jr. Esophageal ulceration in Behçet's syndrome. Ann Intern Med 84:572, 1976.
18. Lozada-Nur F, Gorsky M, Silverman S Jr. Oral erythema multiforme: clinical observations and treatment of 95 patients. Oral Surg 67:36, 1989.
19. Lund WS. Treatment of superficial lesions of the mouth and pharynx. J Laryngol Otol 90:105, 1976.
20. Mamo JG. Treatment of Behçet's disease with chlorambucil. Arch Ophthalmol 94:580, 1976.

21. Manton SL, Scully C. Mucous membrane pemphigoid: an elusive diagnosis? Oral Surg 66:37, 1988.
22. Marra LM, Wunderlee RC. Oral presentation of toxic epidermal necrolysis. J Oral Maxillofac Surg 40:59, 1982.
23. Martin S. Clarification of lichen planus actinicus. Arch Dermatol 113:1615, 1977.
24. McCarthy PL, Gerald S. Diseases of the Oral Mucosa. New York, McGraw-Hill, 1974.
25. Mizoguchi M, Chikakane K, Goh K, et al. Acute febrile neutrophilic dermatosis (Sweet's syndrome) in Behçet's disease. Br J Dermatol 116:727, 1987.
26. O'Duffy JD, Goldstein NP. Neurologic involvement in seven patients with Behçet's disease. Am J Med 61:170, 1976.
27. Oluwasanmi JO, Lagundoye SB, Akinyemi O. Ankylosis of the mandible from cancrum oris. Plast Reconstr Surg 57:342, 1976.
28. Prystowsky SD, Gilliam JN. Antinuclear antibody studies in chronic cutaneous discoid lupus erythematosus. Arch Dermatol 113:183, 1977.
29. Romero RW, Nesbitt LT Jr, Reed RJ. Unusual variant of lupus erythematosus or lichen planus. Arch Dermatol 113:741, 1977.
30. Rubenstein RE, Esterley NB, Fine JD. Childhood epidermolysis bullosa acquisita. Arch Dermatol 123:772, 1987.
31. Safai B, Good RA, Day NK. Erythema multiforme: report of two cases and speculation on immune mechanisms involved in the pathogenesis. Clin Immunol Immunopathol 7:379, 1977.
32. Scully C. Inflammatory disorders of the oral cavity. In English GM (ed). Otolaryngology, vol III. Philadelphia, JB Lippincott, 1993.
33. Scully C, El-Kom M. Lichen planus: review and update of pathogenesis. J Oral Pathol 14:431, 1985.
34. Scully C, Grattan CEH. Oral ulceration: a diagnostic problem. Br Med J 292:1093, 1986.
35. Sklavounou A, Laskaris G. Eosinophilic ulcer of the oral mucosa. Oral Surg 58:431, 1984.
36. Silverman S Jr, Gorsky M, Lozada-Nur F, et al. Oral mucous membrane pemphigoid. Oral Surg 61:233, 1986.
37. Sweet RD. An acute febrile neutrophilic dermatosis. Br J Dermatol 76:349, 1964.
38. Tempest MN. Cancrum oris. Br J Surg 53:949, 1966.
39. Venning VA, Frith PA, Bron AJ, et al. Mucosal involvement in bullous and cicatricial pemphigoid. A clinical and immunopathological study. Br J Dermatol 118:7, 1988.
40. Walker DM, Dolby AE. Recurrent aphthous ulceration. Int J Dermatol 15:589, 1976.
41. Williams BD, Lehner T. Immune complexes in Behçet's syndrome and recurrent oral ulceration. Br Med J 1:1387, 1977.
42. Wolf RE, Fudenberg HH, Welch TM, et al. Treatment of Behçet's syndrome with transfer factor. JAMA 238:869, 1977.
43. Wolf SM, Schotland DL, Phillips LL. Involvement of nervous system in Behçet's syndrome. Arch Neurol 12:315, 1965.
44. Wray D, Ferguson MM, Mason DK, et al. Recurrent aphthae: treatment with vitamin B_{12}, folic acid, and iron. Br Med J 1:490, 1975.
45. Zagarelli EV, Kutscher AH, Hyman GA. Diseases of the Mouth and Jaws. Philadelphia, Lea & Febiger, 1969.

65

Diseases of the Salivary Glands

Charles M. Bower, M.D., and Robin A. Dyleski, M.D.

Disorders originating in or involving the salivary glands are uncommon in children. However, these disorders include a number of interesting and diverse pathologic states, the diagnosis of which is made difficult by the similarities of their clinical manifestations, and their management is hampered by the complex regional anatomy and the indolent but tenacious nature of many of these problems. With the exception of viral parotitis (mumps), all salivary gland disorders are more common in adults than in children: effective immunization against the mumps virus will probably remove this exception as well. Inflammatory diseases are more common than neoplasms in childhood salivary gland lesions. Even though benign tumors are more common than malignant tumors, the probability of a solid mass being malignant is higher in children than in adults.

Most pediatric salivary gland problems are characterized by a painful swelling of the gland or, less commonly, a painless mass within the gland. Infectious, inflammatory, systemic, autoimmune, congenital, neoplastic, and traumatic disorders may be diagnosed in the salivary glands. The general nature of the problem is usually apparent after history and physical examination, although precise diagnosis may require the use of invasive techniques.

This chapter describes the relevant clinical features and treatment of salivary gland problems likely to be seen by the pediatrician and pediatric otolaryngologist. Basic information about the anatomy and physiology of the glands is included. Evaluation and diagnostic testing is covered, followed by disease-specific diagnosis and treatment. Diseases of the minor salivary glands are also discussed in Chapter 66.

Salivary Gland Anatomy and Physiology

The parotid gland fills the irregular space between the ear canal and the mandible. The gland extends across the lateral mandibular surface where its duct crosses the masseter muscle and then opens in the mouth opposite the second maxillary molar. The deep lobe extends medial to the mandible. The external parotid fascia is tightly bound to the adjacent structures, preventing the borders of the normal gland from being seen or felt. When swollen by a diffuse pathologic condition, the external contour of the gland can be seen anterior and inferior to the external ear, often pushing the lobule superiorly. Rarely, parotid masses may enlarge medially, displacing the tonsil and soft palate toward the midline as the mass encroaches upon the parapharyngeal space. Gland enlargements do not, as a rule, cause swelling of the cheek except in the immediate preauricular area. The gland parenchyma is divided into noncommunicating compartments by fascial septa.

The submandibular gland may be seen and felt as a smooth bulge in the submandibular triangle, in both the normal and pathologic states. It is possible to palpate the gland bimanually, intraorally and externally. Enlargements or masses of the gland are confined below the lower border of the mandible because of its mandibular fascial attachments. Intraorally, the duct is seen under the mucosa in the floor of the mouth, where it opens into a papilla just lateral to the midline frenulum of the tongue. The duct exits the gland at a right angle and then travels superiorly to the floor of the mouth.

The neural relationships of the glands aid in diagnosis and therapy. Paralysis or even weakness of associated nerves is prima facie evidence of malignancy. This situation is more common in the parotid; the facial nerve is vulnerable as it passes through the gland parenchyma. By contrast, the lingual and hypoglossal nerves lie outside the capsule of the submandibular gland and are infrequently affected. The secretomotor fibers to both glands traverse the tympanic cavity: the chorda tympani nerve innervates the submandibular gland; the tympanic plexus innervates the parotid gland.

Physiology

General

The function of the salivary glands is to produce saliva, a complex fluid of variable composition that has the following functions: (1) to moisten the mouth for hygiene, protection, speech, and chewing; (2) to lubricate the food for mastication, taste sensation, and deglutition; and (3) to initiate the preliminary phase of starch digestion by alpha-amylase. The salivary glands indirectly participate in water regulation because dehydration leads to diminished salivary flow and the subsequent oral dryness stimulates the sensation of thirst.

Production

Saliva formation is the result of the separate activities of the acini and ducts. The acini are the source of the water and various protein components of saliva; the ducts are concerned largely with ion transport (Fig. 65–1). The primary fluid has the composition of an isotonic ultrafiltrate of serum. It enters the acinar lumen by the intracellular transport mechanisms of pinocytosis and active ion pumping. The proteins in the acinar secretions consist primarily of the salivary amylases, glycoproteins, and mucopolysaccharides. Submandibular gland saliva also contains the blood group antigens. Proteins enter the acinar lumen by disruption of the secretory (zymogen) granules at the apical ends of the acinar cells. The acinar fluid is carried distally by a pressure gradient and contraction of the myoepithelial cells surrounding the acinus.

In the striated duct, hyperosmolar reabsorption of electrolytes leaves a fluid that is hypotonic; low in sodium, chloride, calcium, and bicarbonates; and high in potassium. Electrolyte composition, except for potassium, is dependent on the flow rate: low flow rates allow greater reabsorption of electrolytes, whereas high flow rates prevent ductal ion reabsorption. The basal saliva flow rate approximates 0.05 mL/minute and reaches rates of 0.5 mL/minute under conditions of physiologic stimulation. The parotid and submandibular glands provide almost 90% of the total saliva.[46] Continuous lubrication of the oral cavity results from the constant secretion of the minor salivary glands of the palate, cheeks, tongue, and lips. The major glands secrete only in response to reflex stimuli, primarily tactile and gustatory, but also olfactory.[21]

Regulation of Salivary Secretion

Gland secretion and salivary flow are under autonomic control. Parasympathetic saliva flow is watery, copious, and persists indefinitely, whereas sympathetic saliva flow is thick, viscid, and low volume, even gradually ceasing despite prolonged stimulation. It is generally thought that, in humans, reflex salivation occurs largely as the result of parasympathetic discharge and that sympathetic stimulation results in expulsion of preformed saliva.[4]

Pathophysiology

Disturbances in gland function are uncommon but are generally severe. Hyposalivation leading to xerostomia is more common than hypersalivation. Functional disturbances may result in alterations in both the composition of saliva and total saliva volume.

Hyposalivation

Causes of decreased salivation are protean but may be divided into four main categories: dehydration, gland disease, radiation effects, and side effects of drugs. Cessation or decrease in salivation is one of the first sequelae of dehydration and hypovolemia. This leads to dryness of the oral mucous membranes and the sensation of thirst, which, in the normal individual, results in increased water intake. Dehydration, in the debilitated or unconscious patient, is an important predisposing cause for acute suppurative parotitis.

Congenital agenesis of the major salivary glands, caus-

SALIVARY GLAND UNIT

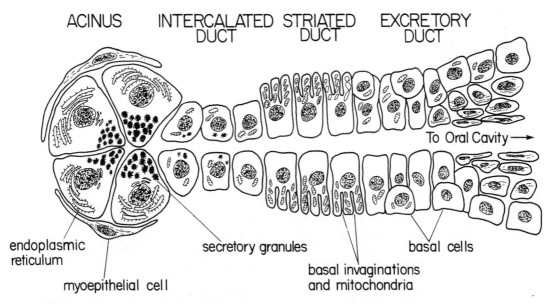

FIGURE 65–1. The secretory unit: Several acinar cells are depicted around a central lumen, which empties into the intercalated duct, thence into the striated duct, and finally into the excretory duct.

ing severe xerostomia, has been reported.[62] The lacrimal glands may also be absent. This rare condition can be confirmed by radionuclide imaging or magnetic resonance imaging (MRI). Xerostomia of this degree inevitably leads to severe caries and dental problems.

Most inflammatory conditions, both acute and chronic, of the salivary glands can result in at least temporary hyposalivation. Resumption of salivary flow occurs as the condition subsides. Alterations in ion composition of the saliva may occur in conjunction with saliva volume and flow rate. For example, the salivary volume in chronic parotitis is diminished and noted to be more viscid and opalescent, while in Sjögren syndrome there is a moderate to severe hyposalivation with increased sodium and chloride ion concentration. Many systemic disorders are associated with dry mouth due to hyposalivation, including poorly controlled diabetes,[38] hypertension, and some hypogeusic conditions.[30] In individuals with well-controlled diabetes mellitus, salivary gland function is not significantly impaired.[13] Anxiety and fear produce a severe dry mouth, presumably as the result of increased circulating catecholamines.[32] Some genetic disorders, such as Prader-Willi syndrome, are associated with diminished salivary secretion.[29]

Severe xerostomia (dry mouth) is a common side effect of ionizing radiation to the salivary glands and oral cavity (e.g., that used in the treatment of head and neck cancer) as well as in patients receiving total body irradiation before bone marrow transplantation for treatment of leukemia.[33] This severe xerostomia has a devastating effect on the teeth, often resulting in rampant dental caries.

Many drugs inhibit saliva production as an unwanted side effect. Drugs possessing anticholinergic activity, such as atropine, are most notable, but postganglionic sympathetic blocking agents have a similar effect. Antidepressants, such as the dibenzepin derivatives imipramine and amitriptyline, exert an atropine-like effect on the salivary glands. In some cases, the xerostomia may be severe enough to cause ulcerative stomatitis and require drug discontinuation. Sympathomimetic agents used for nasal decongestion, antihistamines for allergic rhinitis, and ganglionic blocking agents used for hypertension also produce variable degrees of oral dryness.

Hypersalivation

True hypersalivation is rare and usually occurs as the result of painful or noxious stimuli from oral disease or from heavy metal poisoning in which oral irritation is a prominent factor. Hypersalivation and drooling (sialorrhea) are common in children during teething and in children with cerebral palsy. In cerebral palsy, there is a decreased ability to sense, to swallow, and to clear the oral secretions. Salivary suppressant medication may be inappropriate for long-term use because of the additional side effects of tracheobronchial mucosal dryness, urinary retention, constipation, and blurred vision. Children with cerebral palsy and severe sialorrhea that is unable to be controlled with medical or behavioral therapy may benefit from surgical treatment. Additional information on the management of drooling may be found in Chapter 55.

Altered Composition

Changes in the chemical or physical nature of saliva occur but are seldom noticed or a problem to patients. Saliva is normally tasteless because of the low concentration of sodium and glucose. Active secretion of drugs or other compounds (e.g., certain iodine-containing materials) into saliva may produce peculiar taste sensations. Certain systemic illnesses can affect the saliva composition. Cystic fibrosis is associated with excessive amounts of salivary calcium and phosphorus, which predisposes to dental calculi but not to salivary calculi.[72] Salivary uric acid levels increase in gout and may be associated with uric acid salivary calculi.[10]

Diagnosis

History

As in most areas of medicine, the time-related events surrounding a particular illness involving the salivary glands are generally easy to establish by direct inquiry and provide important diagnostic perspective. For example, was the particular episode of enlargement the first or merely one of a series of problems? As an example, viral parotitis (mumps) occurs only once in each person. The time of onset, duration, and severity of symptoms should be documented. Enlargement related to eating indicates a lesion obstructing salivary outflow; this is confirmed by subsidence of pain and swelling in the first two postprandial hours. Inflammatory lesions do not subside so promptly. Progressive or recurring swelling may be present. Progressively enlarging masses usually are neoplastic in nature, although some granulomas can behave this way. An aggressive malignant lesion can grow so fast that one suspects inflammation as the cause.

Salivary gland infections are usually diagnosed by history and physical examination. Fever and chills may suggest an inflammatory process. A history of recent surgery, especially abdominal surgery and repair of hip fractures, significantly increases the risk of suppurative sialadenitis. Dehydration and malnutrition also increase the risk of sialadenitis. The etiology of salivary gland infections is often suggested by looking for evidence of associated respiratory tract infections, ocular inflammation, or face or scalp lesions. A history of animal bites or scratches may suggest cat-scratch disease. A history of external or oral trauma, or prior surgical management in the region, is important.

Systemic diseases can affect the salivary glands, and review of systems should include a search for immune system dysfunction, autoimmune disease (e.g., Sjögren syndrome), systemic infection (e.g., infection with human immunodeficiency virus [HIV]), diabetes, allergy, and pulmonary or gastrointestinal dysfunction (e.g., cystic fibrosis). Medications taken should be reviewed because many can affect salivary gland function.

Physical Examination

Examination of the salivary glands includes visual inspection as well as careful bimanual palpation (Fig. 65–2). It

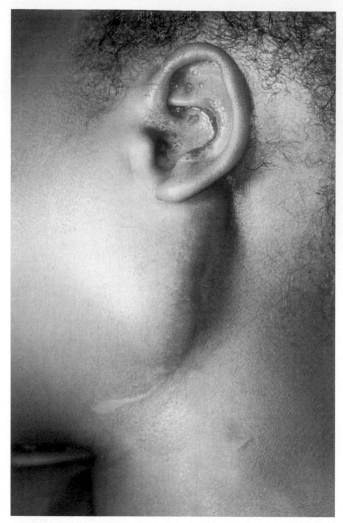

FIGURE 65–2. A large mass in the parotid region is noted to displace the ear lobule superiorly. Note the prior parotidectomy incision. This lobular hard mass is a recurrent neurofibroma.

is important to determine whether one or more glands are involved; whether the entire gland or just a part of it is enlarged; whether the mass is in or around the glands; and whether the mass is solid, cystic, or inflammatory. Local tenderness, erythema, and edema, as well as the texture of the mass, should be noted, such as whether it is soft, spongy, hard and wooden-like, smooth, or irregular. The mass may be mobile or fixed. Bilaterally symmetrical enlargement of the entire gland that is soft and non-nodular suggests a search for an underlying metabolic problem, particularly diabetes. Diffuse enlargement of a single parotid gland is generally of greater concern; one should search for an underlying granuloma, such as tuberculosis or sarcoid, by appropriate skin tests, laboratory examination, and biopsy. A discrete mass within the parotid suggests an inflamed lymph node, congenital lesion, or neoplasm. Progressive diffuse enlargement of the submandibular glands is seen in cystic fibrosis and as a side effect of drug therapy with adrenergic blocking agents. Less commonly, this gland may be involved along with the parotids in Sjögren syndrome. Enlargement of a single submandibular gland is of concern, and neoplasm

should be suspected. Unlike the parotid, in which a discrete mass is easily discerned because the gland is attached to surrounding structures, the more mobile submandibular gland conforms to the pressure of the enlarging mass within it.

The ductal orifice should be inspected, and the nature of the saliva should be noted. Saliva can be expressed with manual massage of the gland. Normal saliva is crystal clear. Redness of the punctum and clear saliva suggest viral infection. Purulent secretions are seen in cases of bacterial infection. Opalescent saliva is common in many types of chronic glandular dysfunction. Palpation of the duct may reveal a stone, but dilatation of the punctum and insertion of a probe into the lumen is often more helpful; the probe encounters the stone and imparts a feeling of resistance or gritty sensation to the examiner. A stricture of the duct or punctum is readily evident on attempting to dilate before probing.

Cranial nerve function should be assessed in evaluating salivary gland problems. Facial movement and symmetry (cranial nerve VII), and tongue movement and sensation (cranial nerves V and XII) are most important. Facial paralysis associated with a parotid mass indicates a neoplasm until proven otherwise; benign lesions do not, as a rule, disrupt neural function. A similar rule can be made for the submandibular gland because the adjacent nerves (marginal mandibular branch of the seventh cranial nerve, lingual nerve, and hypoglossal nerve) are some distance away from the gland; neural findings may indicate a nonresectable tumor.

Laboratory Examination

A variety of diagnostic tests can be performed in patients with salivary gland disease. Acute inflammatory disease can be followed up with a complete blood count. HIV testing is occasionally indicated for bilateral cystic swelling of the parotids. The suspicion of tuberculosis (Tb) or atypical Tb suggests the need for a chest radiography study and purified protein derivative (PPD) skin test. Specific testing for diabetes, cystic fibrosis, and autoimmune disease is necessary when clinically indicated.

Three examinations can be done on saliva: culture, cytologic study, and sialochemical analysis. The validity of culture data is greatest when the specimen is carefully obtained. Ideally, needle aspiration (after careful skin preparation) or intraductal aspiration by a catheter should be attempted. Cultures made from specimens obtained by simple swabbing of the duct opening may grow oral flora, which may be misleading.

Cytologic and chemical examinations of saliva are best done on fluid obtained from an intraductal catheter or a vacuum-held collection cup placed over the orifice. In this way, fluid from abnormal glands is obtained undiluted by saliva from the other glands. Fluid flow should be stimulated by applying 6% citric acid or whole lemon juice to the tongue.

In cases of neoplasm, cytologic examination reveals tumor cells in more than two thirds of cases; if interpreted by an experienced cytopathologist, the results may provide a histologic diagnosis before biopsy. Chemical examination of the saliva is not useful for the diagnosis of salivary gland disorders, but it is used as a research tool in pharmacology and toxicology.

Salivary Gland Imaging

Current techniques of salivary gland imaging include the older modalities of radiographic plain films and contrast sialography and the newer modalities of high-resolution ultrasonography, including Doppler scanning, computed tomography (CT), and MRI. A discussion of the advantages and limitations of each technique follows. There is little, if any, role for radionuclide scans in pediatric salivary gland disease problems, with the possible exception of the rare congenital agenesis of major salivary glands.

Plain films are readily available and are useful in detecting radiopaque duct stones (80% of submandibular, 20% of parotid). Intraoral dental films and multiple views may be helpful. Dystrophic calcification and adjacent bony structures are visualized. Disadvantages of plain films include the difficulty in evaluation of the soft tissues, the use of ionizing radiation, and the need for a motionless patient.

With the development of high-resolution ultrasonography, sialography is rarely indicated. Sialography is still the definitive diagnostic tool for salivary duct abnormalities, such as stricture, stones, and sialectasis (Figs. 65–3 and 65–4). Salivary secretory status may be studied by using a sialogogue (e.g., lemon juice) after filling the ducts with contrast material; clearance of the contrast material is monitored. A major disadvantage of sialography is the requirement for a general anesthetic or deep sedation in a young uncooperative child for cannulation of the duct. Discomfort or mild pain is often experienced when the intraglandular ducts are filled with contrast material.

High-resolution ultrasonography has revolutionized imaging of the parotid gland. Morphologic details of the parotid gland can be exquisitely visualized. Anatomic

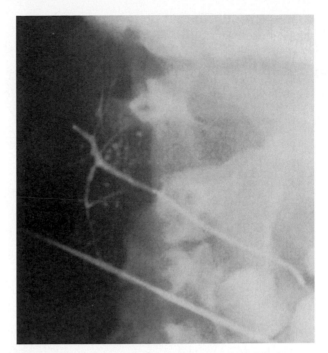

FIGURE 65–4. Sialogram demonstrating punctate sialectasis.

landmarks, including the mastoid tip, sternocleidomastoid muscle, styloid process, posterior facial vein, internal jugular vein, and external carotid artery, can be easily identified in the parotid gland.[57] Ultrasonography can be extremely helpful in diagnosing sialectasis, which has a characteristic pattern of small punctate echogenic densities throughout the gland.[19, 48] Salivary gland stones greater than 2 mm in size can be detected as an echo-dense spot in greater than 90% of cases. Salivary stone detection is as successful with ultrasonography as by sialography.[67] Ultrasonography can also determine whether apparent parotid swelling is due to intraparotid or extrinsic causes. Ultrasound examination is useful to follow a nodal abnormality within the parotid or in adjacent enlarged nodes to determine abscess formation in adenitis.[47] Nodes not responding to medical management and developing abscesses have a characteristic ultrasound appearance, the walls becoming echogenic and the center hypoechoic, with loss of central hilar vessels on color flow Doppler imaging. Ultrasonography is useful in demonstrating whether masses, adjacent to or within the parotid, are vascular by use of Doppler duplex scanning.

Ultrasonography is the diagnostic test choice for vascular malformations because of the ease of use, safety, and accuracy of diagnosis. Ultrasonography of deep hemangiomas reveals a well-defined hypoechoic mass lesion with heterogeneous echotexture and the presence of cystic and sinusoidal spaces within, as well as the occasional presence of phleboliths.[73] Color flow Doppler imaging is very important in diagnosis of vascular lesions on ultrasound. Hemangiomas demonstrate high flow and a mixed arterial and venous flow pattern without shunting. Venous malformations demonstrate more heterogeneous echogenicity with a hypoechoic lacunar pattern, with either no flow or low flow on Doppler imaging. Ultrasonography uses no ionizing radiation, requires no sedation or intravenous

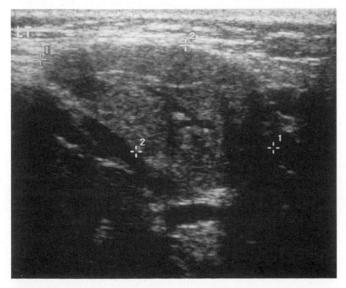

FIGURE 65–3. An ultrasound of the submaxillary gland reveals an echogenic stone in the hilum of the gland, with dilatation of the surrounding ducts.

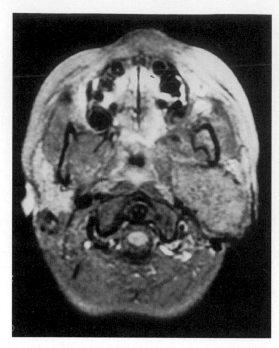

FIGURE 65–5. An MRI in the axial plane of the patient shown in Figure 65–2 demonstrates a large mass replacing the left parotid gland. Excisional biopsy revealed a large neurofibroma.

contrast agent, and is inexpensive to perform in comparison with CT or MRI.

CT may also be used to image the parotid gland in children.[12, 51] CT scanning, like MRI, not only assesses the pathology of the gland but also provides accurate anatomic detail, which can assist with surgical planning. CT can easily demonstrate whether a mass is intrinsic or extrinsic and can detect early abscess formation with ring enhancement about an area of inflammation. Intravenous contrast material is required to evaluate tumor vascularity and abscess formation. The disadvantages of CT are the use of ionizing radiation and the need for sedation.

MRI supplies the best soft tissue detail of the salivary glands. MRI is the only imaging technique capable of direct imaging of the facial nerve within the parotid gland.[64] Its enhanced soft tissue contrast resolution and the ability to manipulate multiplanar images aid in precise localization of lesions and their relationship to surrounding structures. For example, prestyloid space tumors, almost always pleomorphic adenomas, can be identified readily. Variations in signal intensity (T_1- and T_2-weighted images) provide additional information about tumor type, although detection of calcification is poor (Fig. 65–5).[63] Hemangiomas, the most common masses in the parotid gland, are high-flow, parenchymatous lesions of intermediate intensity on T_1-weighted images and of high intensity on T_2-weighted images. Flow voids are usually seen on both T_1- and T_2-weighted images. MRI is the diagnostic procedure of choice to confirm hemangioma if ultrasonography and physical examination are inconclusive.[31] MRI of the parotid gland often requires sedation in children because the patient must be motionless during the examination. Intravenous contrast material is not neces-

sary, however, and the patient receives no ionizing radiation. Ultimately, the value of all three imaging modalities (ultrasonography, MRI, and CT) is dependent on the expertise of the technicians performing them.

Biopsy

Open biopsy is necessary in some parotid masses to make an accurate diagnosis. Incisional biopsy of salivary glands is rarely indicated. If a histologic diagnosis is required when, for example, neoplasm is suspected, excisional biopsy is preferred for several reasons: (1) the pathologist usually needs to study the entire tumor to make an accurate diagnosis; (2) complete excision avoids cutting and spillage of the tumor; (3) for most cases, complete excision is indicated for treatment; and (4) formal excisional biopsy avoids the hazards of accidental nerve injury from limited exposure approaches. Incisional biopsy may be helpful in the presence of an obvious, advanced malignant neoplasm to determine the cell type before radiation therapy or chemotherapy. To confirm a diagnosis of Sjögren syndrome, an incisional biopsy of the minor salivary glands of the labial or buccal mucosa is usually sufficient because these glands often show the same histologic abnormality as in the major glands.

Fine-needle aspiration biopsy of salivary gland masses is another useful outpatient procedure in cooperative older children. Sensitivity and specificity are on the order of 50% to 85% and 85% to 92%, respectively, with an overall diagnostic accuracy of 84%.[2, 41] While advocated as a diagnostically efficient and cost-effective procedure,[22, 39] its overall clinical utility has been challenged by other investigators.[5, 9] Ultrasonography may be useful to guide needle biopsies in deep masses.

Clinical Pathology

The salivary glands may be involved in many pathologic processes, ranging from inflammation to systemic autoimmune processes, generalized endocrine and metabolic dysfunction, generalized exocrine gland dysfunction (cystic fibrosis), congenital abnormalities, trauma, and benign and malignant neoplastic diseases (Table 65–1). This section describes the various clinical conditions, diagnostic tests, and therapeutic management options for salivary gland disorders seen mainly in children.

Inflammatory Disorders

Bacterial Sialadenitis

An acute suppurative bacterial sialadenitis may develop in any of the major salivary glands. The parotid gland is the most commonly affected major salivary gland, with the submandibular and lingual glands less often involved. The composition of the saliva affects the infection rate, with the saliva of the submandibular gland (higher in mucin) being more protective than the serous saliva of the parotid.[60] Parotitis or acute suppurative sialadenitis occurs in infants, children, and adolescents, but less frequently in

TABLE 65–1. Salivary Gland Diseases

Inflammatory
　Acute
　　Bacterial
　　　Suppurative sialadenitis
　　　Lymphadenitis/abscess
　　Viral
　　　Mumps
　　　Human immunodeficiency virus
　　　Other
　Chronic
　　Obstructive
　　　Sialectasis
　　　Sialolithiasis
　　　Mucocele or cyst
　　Granulomatous
　　　Mycobacterial
　　　Actinomycosis
　　　Cat-scratch disease
　　　Sarcoid
　　　Toxoplasmosis
　　Necrotizing sialometaplasia
Neoplastic
　Benign
　　Hemangioma
　　Lymphangioma
　　Vascular malformation
　　Pleomorphic adenoma
　　Other
　Malignant
　　Mucoepidermoid carcinoma
　　Acinic cell carcinoma
　　Other
Congenital
　Dermoid cyst
　Branchial cleft cyst
　Branchial pouch cyst
　Congenital ductal cyst
　Agenesis of the salivary gland
Traumatic
　Penetrating cheek trauma
　Blunt trauma
　Radiation injury
Autoimmune
　Benign lymphoepithelial disease
　Sjögren syndrome
Other
　Allergy
　Chronic sialorrhea
　Cystic fibrosis
　Drug induced
　Pneumoparotitis
　Systemic conditions

adults. It may be seen as a single episode or as a series of recurrent infections.

Acute parotitis manifests with a diffusely swollen and painful parotid gland with rapid onset. It is often associated with fever, poor oral intake, and difficulty chewing because of pain during mastication. Often, parotitis occurs in debilitated, dehydrated individuals because the decrease in salivary flow and dry oral mucosa predisposes to bacterial infection. The purulent secretions expressed from the Stensen duct are often diagnostic. It is unusual to require additional diagnostic testing, other than culture of the purulent saliva, once the clinical diagnosis is made.

Acute suppurative parotitis is most commonly due to a bacterial infection. *Staphylococcus aureus* and *Streptococ-cus viridans* account for most cases of parotitis. Infrequently, other organisms, such as *Streptococcus pneumoniae*, *Haemophilus influenzae*, and *Bacteroides* sp., may cause parotitis.[44]

Most cases of parotitis resolve with appropriate antibiotics, usually an antistaphylococcal antibiotic, based on culture of the purulent salivary secretions. Conservative medical management of parotitis consists of hydration, warm compresses, gland massage (to increase salivary flow and diminish stasis of saliva), and sialogogues (such as lemon drops and wedges) to promote and increase salivary flow. Debilitated and severely dehydrated persons may benefit from intravenous antibiotics and fluid replacement.

When acute suppurative parotitis does not improve with antibiotics, coalescence of the infected gland parenchyma may occur and progress to parotid abscess. In this condition, the gland remains diffusely, often tensely, swollen and painful with overlying erythematous skin. Although submandibular sialadenitis may progress to abscess, it is seen rarely. Improvement rarely occurs with intravenous antibiotics alone, and surgical drainage is usually necessary.[54] Parotid abscess is best diagnosed with CT or high-resolution ultrasound. The advantage of CT is in localizing the multiple abscess sites commonly found within the parotid, resulting from the fascial septa dividing the parenchyma, including the deep lobe (which is more difficult to visualize with ultrasound).

Surgical drainage is performed via a standard parotidectomy incision with flap elevation. Abscesses are drained via multiple fascial incisions made parallel to the course of the branches of the facial nerve; drains may be needed. If there is preoperative facial nerve paresis, it usually completely resolves after complete treatment of the infection.

Recurrent Parotitis

Some children have recurrent episodes of acute suppurative parotitis, with intervening normal intervals. Factors that may increase the likelihood of recurrent infection include a congenital anomaly of the duct system, dental trauma to the papilla of the Stensen duct, sialoliths, and dehydration. Young children (ages 3 to 6 years) are most commonly affected; boys are affected more often than girls. The organisms isolated in recurrent parotitis in children are commonly *S. pneumoniae* and *H. influenzae*, with *S. viridans* occurring less often.[27]

As is recommended for isolated suppurative parotitis, acute treatment for recurrent parotitis is conservative and consists of antibiotics and supportive care as previously described. In most cases of recurrent parotitis, there is marked decrease in the frequency of infection by adolescence.[14] Ultrasonography is usually diagnostic in demonstrating punctate sialectasis seen in recurrent parotitis. Ultrasonography has been recommended as the diagnostic modality of choice over sialography, because serial sonography is capable of detecting changes in duct architecture more sensitively than sialography.[59] If ductal stricture, calculi, or both are identified as the predisposing etiology, then dilatation is recommended for primary management because many parotid stones are small and can pass through the newly dilated duct. In the rare refractory case, total parotidectomy may be required; removal of the deep lobe of the parotid is required to prevent recurrence in that region.[1]

Viral Infections

Mumps

Before the development of the mumps vaccine, mumps virus was the most common cause for acute swelling and tenderness of the parotid, and, less commonly, the submandibular glands in children. As a result of the nearly universal immunization (seroconversion rate is greater than 95%) with mumps vaccine in the United States, there has been a significant reduction in the number of viral mumps cases, down to about 1500 cases annually.[42, 52]

Mumps is an acute contagious viral illness that usually is associated with fever and (usually) painful parotid enlargement. It is transmitted by droplet and direct contact with an infected person's saliva. Organ system involvement may occur with meningoencephalitis, orchitis (15% to 25%) or oophoritis (5%), pancreatitis, or deafness (usually unilateral). There is an 18- to 21-day incubation period and a 1- to 3-day prodromal period of malaise before the parotitis develops. The saliva contains shed virus up to 6 days before and up to 9 days after parotid swelling.[16] In some cases, parotitis may be absent; in others, all four glands may become affected. Rarely, only one gland is affected.

Involvement of the central nervous system can be variable, ranging from the commonly seen mild headache and lassitude to aseptic meningoencephalitis and seizures. Meningoencephalitis can be seen in up to 2.5% of patients.[42] Pancreatitis is probably more common than suspected. The sensation of vertigo and nausea may be due to central nervous system involvement, pancreatitis, or labyrinthitis, which commonly results in unilateral deafness with or without detectable loss of vestibular function. Death from mumps is extremely rare.

Treatment of mumps is generally supportive (liquid or soft diet, antipyretics, and analgesics), with expected resolution of symptoms. Respiratory isolation and disposal of items contaminated with saliva are recommended to decrease risk of transference of the illness for 9 days after onset of symptoms. Viral parotitis may predispose the gland to secondary bacterial infection, usually with *S. aureus*, which should be treated with an antistaphylococcal antibiotic.[50] Immunity, either from immunization or from contracting the disease, is considered lifelong.

Human Immunodeficiency Virus

Involvement of the parotid gland in HIV infection is common. Up to 30% of HIV-infected children may have parotid gland enlargement because of lymphocytic infiltration (Fig. 65–6).[40, 70] Intraglandular lymph node disease includes HIV lymphadenopathy, various infectious processes, and HIV-related malignant neoplasms, especially B-cell, non-Hodgkin lymphoma as well as the usual parotid malignant tumors.[36] Parotid enlargement resulting from multiple lymphoepithelial cysts, as diagnosed by CT or MRI, appears to be unique to HIV infection. On histologic examination, they consist of squamous or cuboid epithelial lining cells surrounded by lymphoid cells with germinal centers. These cysts contain serous fluid with some lymphocytes and macrophages. There is no evidence that the cysts become malignant or affect the overall prognosis of the disease. Open biopsy or parotidectomy should be reserved for atypical cases and aspiration considered for uncomfortable lesions.

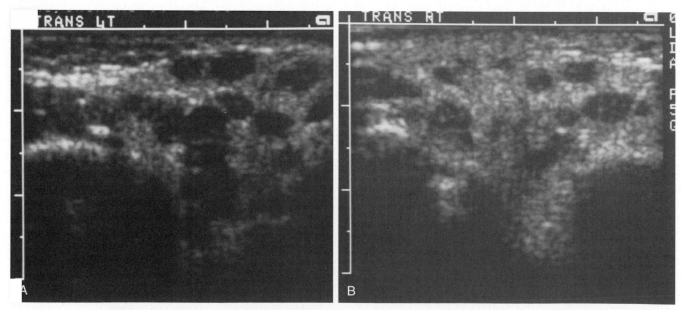

FIGURE 65–6. *A* and *B*, Ultrasound from a 4-year-old child with bilateral parotid swelling. Note the hypoechoic (dark) areas consistent with intraparotid adenopathy and cysts.

Other Viral Diseases

Other viruses are infrequent causes of salivary gland infection. Although the Epstein-Barr virus, the cause of infectious mononucleosis, is known to be present in high concentration in the saliva, it is not known to directly cause enlargement of the salivary gland. Because Epstein-Barr virus is a known cause of lymph gland enlargement, apparent parotid enlargement may actually be due to periparotid lymph gland enlargement.

Cytomegalovirus (CMV) has been reported to cause parotitis in infants and young children. The presence of parotitis is a sign of disseminated CMV disease and the complications seen with CMV infection. Brain stem involvement and lymphocytic infiltration of the liver and kidney are also commonly present when parotitis is present, especially in infants.[66]

Chronic Inflammatory Diseases

Sialectasis

Saccular dilatation of the small, intercalated ducts that connect the acini with the striated ducts is a commonly seen congenital anomaly of the salivary glands. Because there is no obstruction to flow, the term non-obstructive sialectasis has been used to differentiate this condition from dilatation of the larger ducts that occurs with distal ductal obstruction (obstructive sialodochiectasis). Although both parotids usually display the typical radiographic findings on sialography and ultrasound (see Fig. 65–4), the symptoms are most often confined to one gland and are due to recurrent secondary bacterial infection rather than the sialectasis. Submandibular gland involvement is rare.

The clinical presentation is one of painful gland enlargement associated with systemic signs of fever and leukocytosis. With repeated infection, the gland becomes permanently enlarged, and the ductal ectasia may worsen. Control of infection with appropriate antibiotics, manual expression of saliva by massage, maintenance of good hydration, and administration of sialogogues can help treat episodes and prevent progression. When conservative measures are ineffective, total parotidectomy may become necessary.[44]

Stricture

Narrowing of a major salivary duct may result in chronic sialadenitis and enlargement of the salivary gland. The stricture may result from faulty chewing habits (which traumatize the punctum) or from external trauma to the duct. Rarely, infection involving the duct may occur causing one or multiple stricture sites. The presence of a foreign body, such as a calculus, within the duct can induce a stricture to develop or may predispose to calculus formation (secondary to salivary stasis). Dilatation of the duct proximal to the stricture can be seen in long-standing cases (obstructive sialodochiectasis) as a result of weakening of the duct wall from persistent salivary pressure and intermittent inflammation.

Swelling of the parotid or submandibular gland is noted during or soon after a meal as the reflex secretory pressure and salivary flow maximize. This acute swelling may be painful enough to cause the person to stop eating. The reflex salivary secretion eventually ceases, and the gland and ductal system slowly empty through the stricture, usually with resolution of symptoms in about 2 hours.

Strictures can be readily diagnosed by sialography. In many cases, the stricture responds to simple dilatation of the duct. Reconstruction of the salivary duct is an option if the stricture fails to respond to dilatation; stenting of the duct is usually required. Gland excision with nerve preservation may become necessary if symptoms progress or cannot be controlled conservatively.

Sialolithiasis

Salivary gland duct stones (sialoliths) develop in response to local salivary gland causes rather than conditions that cause stones in other body areas, such as renal stones in hyperparathyroidism. Sialoliths are found in children less commonly than in teenagers and adults.

The submandibular gland is more susceptible to stones (80%) than the parotid (20%) because of specific anatomic and chemical differences. The distinct right-angle turn at the submandibular gland hilum and the relatively long upward course of the duct affect the salivary flow rate and the ability of sialoliths to develop. The submandibular saliva, as compared with parotid saliva, is more alkaline and more viscous, and has a higher concentration of calcium and phosphorus compounds. Precipitation of these salts occurs upon a nidus as a result of stasis or increased concentration of salts. Most salivary stones contain calcium and are thus radiopaque.[54] Interestingly, children with cystic fibrosis do not have increased salivary stones, despite the abnormally high calcium concentration in their salivary secretions.[72]

The main symptom of a sialolith is painful enlargement of the affected gland after reflex salivary secretion, which then slowly subsides over 2 to 3 hours, similar to the symptoms of salivary duct stricture. The intraductal calculi are usually smooth, elongated, and elliptic and can move within the duct by means of the increased salivary flow of mealtime salivation to impinge upon the punctum. The symptoms gradually worsen as the stone enlarges but may only become noticeable when the stone becomes large enough to obstruct the hilum or orifice of the duct. Symptoms may worsen if infection develops in the obstructed duct or if strictures are generated from the stone within the duct.

Diagnosis of a submandibular sialolith is often made with oral visual and bimanual examination (Fig. 65–7). The stone may be seen or palpated within the duct in the floor of the mouth. These stones may extrude through the punctum or fistulize through the duct wall spontaneously, with immediate resolution of symptoms. If this does not occur spontaneously, then the stone is surgically removed via duct incision or marsupialization.

Sialoliths within the gland or near the hilum may not be readily seen or palpated, even bimanually. These stones tend to be large, irregular, and fixed. They are less likely to cause intermittent painful swelling, rather caus-

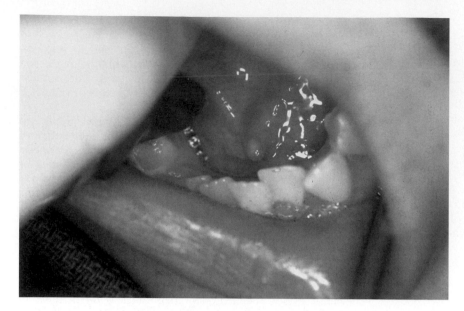

FIGURE 65–7. A small white stone is noted in the papilla of the submandibular gland duct.

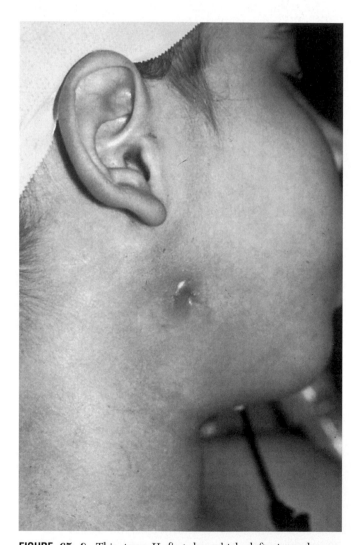

FIGURE 65–8. This type II first branchial cleft sinus demonstrates skin erythema, edema, and a draining sinus anterior and inferior to the ear.

ing chronic tender enlargement of the gland. Dental occlusive x-ray films or ultrasonography are useful in diagnosing these stones. Submandibular gland excision is the preferred treatment for symptomatic intraparenchymal and hilar sialoliths.

Parotid stones are far less common than submandibular stones. This is a reflection of the differences in anatomy and salivary composition of the two glands. Parotid stones are usually radiolucent as a result of their tendency to be composed of noncalcium compounds. If the stone is within the duct, it can often be palpated or seen on oral visual examination. Stones near the duct orifice may be removed via duct incision with enlargement and stenting of the duct. Parenchymal stones may rarely require parotidectomy with facial nerve preservation for complete resolution of symptoms.[54]

Cysts

Most cystic lesions occur in the parotid gland. Approximately 2% of all parotid masses are cystic lesions. Cysts may be congenital, trauma-related, or inflammatory (as seen in HIV infection), or they may be caused by degeneration of neoplasms.

Branchial cleft remnants include cysts, sinuses, and fistulas. The most common congenital cyst affecting the parotid is the first branchial arch cyst, containing epithelium only (type I) or epithelium and adnexal structures (type II).[71] First branchial cleft remnants, both Work type I and II, may manifest as parotid masses. Type I first branchial cleft anomalies are duplication anomalies of the ear canal. They often occur in the postauricular sulcus or concha bowl, but sometimes they occur as a mass or sinus in the preauricular region. Surgical excision may be difficult because the tract may course along the ear canal and insinuate between the cartilage folds of the auricle.

Type II anomalies are more complex and less common. They typically course anteriorly and inferiorly from the ear and extend into the upper neck just behind the angle of the mandible (Fig. 65–8). The tract always

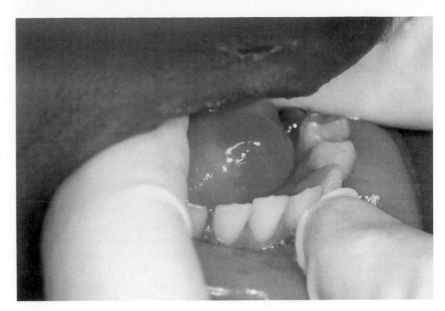

FIGURE 65–9. Ranulas present as a cystic mass in the floor of mouth.

passes in close approximation to the facial nerve; in one case reported by Work,[71] the tract passed through a split in the facial nerve main trunk. Abscess formation or a chronically draining sinus is a common manifestation, but asymptomatic cysts can occur.[6]

In most cases, CT or MRI distinguishes and delineates the type of cyst. Surgical excision requires superficial parotidectomy with facial nerve dissection to safely remove the anomaly, because the fistula tract may course deep to, around, or superficial to the facial nerve.

Ranula

Mucous retention cysts are common in the minor salivary glands and occur as small fluctuant masses on the lips, buccal mucosa, and tongue. Surgical excision of the cyst and underlying salivary gland is curative.

Ranulas are mucous retention cysts of the sublingual gland. These often manifest as a soft, bluish swelling in the anterior floor of mouth (Fig. 65–9). Larger ranulas may extend posterior and deep to the mylohyoid muscle and manifest as a soft mass in the submandibular triangle (plunging ranula). Surgical excision or marsupialization of these thin-walled cysts with excision of the sublingual gland is usually necessary.

Lymphatic Involvement

The parotid gland has many lymph nodes within its parenchyma and closely associated with its fascial borders. These lymph nodes may become involved by lymphoma, or bacterial or granulomatous infections (e.g., cat-scratch disease, atypical mycobacteria, and actinomycosis), leading to the appearance of an enlarged, tender parotid gland. Although the tissues over the submandibular gland contain fewer nodes than the parotid, these lymph glands are more commonly affected by atypical mycobacterial infection. The clinical distinction between a lymph node disorder and a salivary gland disorder may be difficult. Imaging studies, including ultrasonography, CT, or MRI, are

helpful in this differentiation (Fig. 65–10). Biopsy of the lesion may be required for definitive diagnosis, with care taken to protect associated neurovascular structures.

Endocrine and Systemic Disorders

Salivary gland enlargement occurs by fatty infiltration in some diabetics and grossly obese persons, by a functional hypertrophy in persons who consume an exclusively carbohydrate diet, and by autoimmune processes in Sjögren syndrome. Transient benign symmetrical parotid hypertrophy is commonly seen in up to 30% of individuals suffering from the eating disorder bulimia.[17]

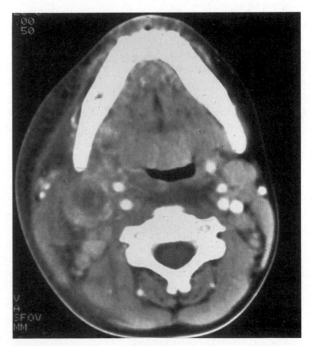

FIGURE 65–10. A CT scan in the axial plane reveals a ring-shaped enhancing mass deep to the right parotid consistent with a deep abscess.

Sjögren syndrome is an uncommon autoimmune disorder that is typified by progressive enlargement of the salivary glands, lacrimal glands, or both, resulting in dryness of the oral and conjunctival membranes. Parotitis is a common symptom when this disorder manifests in childhood.[3] One must be suspicious for this condition because the classic clinical manifestations may be absent, especially in children. Sialograms or ultrasound reveals the sialectasis that is frequently present. Test results for antinuclear antibody and SS-A and SS-B autoantibodies may be positive. Histologic examination reveals acinar atrophy and marked mixed lymphocyte infiltration, often with germinal centers. The disorder is progressive; steroid therapy is of little help in the amelioration of symptoms. Patients require close follow-up because the incidence of benign and malignant lymphoproliferative disorders (especially non-Hodgkin B-cell lymphoma) is increased.[23]

In cystic fibrosis, the salivary composition is altered with elevated calcium and phosphorus content.[72] Although sodium and chloride levels in other body fluids are elevated, this is inconsistently manifested in the saliva, and altered levels are more related to flow rate.[34] Persons with cystic fibrosis are not seen to have elevated incidence of salivary stones. More than 90% of persons with cystic fibrosis demonstrate asymptomatic idiopathic submandibular gland enlargement.[8]

Primary Neoplasms

The most common tumors of the salivary glands in children are of vascular origin: hemangioma and lymphangioma. If vascular lesions are excluded and only the solid or firm masses are considered, only 3.2% of all salivary gland neoplasms occur in persons younger than 15 years of age. Of these, up to 57% have been reported as malignant.[46, 58] This high incidence of malignant disease has been challenged by Camocho and colleagues,[11] who found an inflammatory process in greater than 50% of their series of 22 patients. Only one child had a malignant tumor. The authors emphasize that although the true incidence of parotid gland malignant disease is unknown, the safest course in a solid parotid mass is to obtain the diagnosis by biopsy. Submandibular and minor salivary gland tumors are more likely to be malignant than are parotid neoplasms.[46]

Clinically, salivary gland tumors fall into three groups: benign, low-grade malignant, and high-grade malignant. In adults, the ratios of these three types are 70:20:10; in children, they are 43:35:22. In children, there is essentially only one benign salivary gland epithelial tumor: the mixed tumor. All other benign lesions are rare and are usually of supporting tissue origin. The low-grade malignant neoplasms are the mucoepidermoid carcinoma and acinar cell carcinoma. The high-grade malignant group consists of mucoepidermoid carcinoma and of a variety of adenocarcinomas and sarcomas (see Chap. 66).

Primary Epithelial Neoplasms

An enlarging mass in or about the parotid gland most frequently is a neoplasm. Congenital cysts, benign lym-phadenopathy, and granulomas are occasionally found. The safest rule to follow is to consider that all parotid masses are neoplastic until proven otherwise. After appropriate studies have been done, such as skin tests, imaging, and routine hematologic tests, one must decide whether the clinical picture is probably that of a benign or a malignant neoplasm. If the usual criteria are met (i.e., slow, painless growth; no nerve involvement; no fixation to surrounding structures), an excisional biopsy should be performed. This is, in fact, the definitive treatment for the majority of cases because the specimen containing the tumor consists of the bulk of the gland; no further surgery is necessary for the benign tumor or for the small, low-grade malignant neoplasm.

This approach, wherein definitive treatment is carried out before a tissue diagnosis, has become standard practice for salivary gland neoplasms because incisional biopsy leads to tumor recurrence by tumor cell spillage and "seeding of the wound." A pathologic frozen section is obtained to confirm the diagnosis.

On occasion, the pathology report on the permanent section differs from that on the frozen section. If the diagnosis is revised to that of a high-grade malignant neoplasm where a benign or low-grade lesion was clinically suspected, further surgery, postoperative radiotherapy, or both can be carried out as indicated. If the initial frozen section indicates malignant change in the absence of clinical verification, the operation is terminated after the excisional parotid biopsy and further treatment is delayed until the permanent sections have been thoroughly studied. In general, radical surgery, including nerve sacrifice, is not performed on the basis of frozen section interpretation because a report of suspicious findings may be contradicted by later findings.

Solid Tumors

Benign Tumors

Several neoplasms of epithelial origin arise in salivary glands: the mixed tumor (pleomorphic adenoma), the Warthin tumor, an oncocytoma, a variety of adenomas, and the lymphoepithelial lesion. Of these, only the mixed tumor occurs with any regularity in children; it accounts for 4.5% of all mixed tumors,[56] and it is the single most common solid salivary gland tumor seen in pediatric patients.

The mixed tumor is composed of two cellular elements that are derived from the intercalated duct reserve cell: the epithelial cell and the myoepithelial cell.[53] There is usually a distinct stromal component. The capsule is thin, and the surface is often irregular and lobulated.

This type of tumor usually arises in the lateral portion of the gland, grows slowly, is painless, and, on average, has been present for 15 months before removal in most children. The average age of children undergoing an operation for this problem is 9.5 years. The mass averages 2.7 cm in diameter, it is firm and freely mobile, and there is no evidence of facial nerve weakness associated with the tumor.

Large, deep, or ill-defined masses should be assessed by ultrasonography, CT, or MRI to aid in surgical plan-

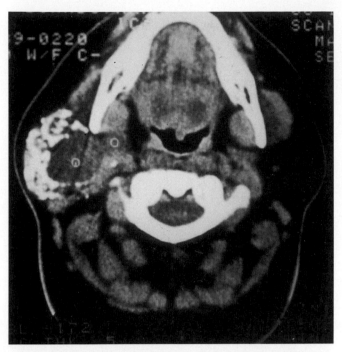

FIGURE 65–11. This homogeneous mass noted in the body of the right parotid on CT scan was proved to be a benign mixed tumor (pleomorphic adenoma) on excisional biopsy.

ning (Fig. 65–11). Fine-needle aspiration biopsy can help direct therapy in some patients. Obtaining an incisional biopsy specimen is contraindicated because of facial nerve risk and tumor seeding. The treatment of mixed tumors is surgical excision, typically, a superficial parotidectomy with facial nerve preservation. The risk of recurrence of benign mixed tumors can approach 20%.[58]

Other solid, benign tumors, such as Warthin tumor, basal cell adenoma, neurofibroma, xanthoma, neurilemoma, and lipoma occur rarely in the salivary glands.

Low-Grade Malignant Neoplasms

Two low-grade malignant neoplasms appear occasionally in children: mucoepidermoid carcinoma and acinar cell carcinoma (acinic cell carcinoma). Both lesions have a generally benign course in most cases, but, because some occasionally exhibit malignant behavior, it is inappropriate to classify either one as completely benign or malignant.

The biologic and clinical behavior of acinar cell carcinoma cannot be predicted from histologic features.[7] For mucoepidermoid carcinoma, however, local invasiveness, regional metastasis, and overall prognosis correlate with the degree of differentiation of the tumor.[15]

The mucoepidermoid carcinoma is composed of epithelial cells derived from the excretory duct. These may be differentiated into predominantly squamous cells in the high-grade tumor and mucous cells in the low-grade tumor. The presence of intracellular mucin as detected by Alcian blue or other stains is necessary to establish the diagnosis and to distinguish the high-grade tumor from a squamous cell carcinoma.

The acinar cell carcinoma may be recognized histologically by its uniform, large, round clear cells, which have abundant basophilic or clear cytoplasm. These cells are thought to arise from precursors of the acinar cell. The 5-year control rate of this tumor is excellent, but control decreases to 50% after 25 years.[20]

Both lesions tend to be clinically similar to the mixed tumor: a solitary, firm, mobile, slow-growing, painless mass in the parotid (most commonly) or submandibular gland. Clinical evidence of malignant transformation, such as rapid growth, pain, fixation, or facial paralysis, is uncommon and should alert the clinician to the probability that the lesion is not a mixed tumor.

Diagnostic testing is the same as described for benign tumors. For low-grade neoplasms, surgical excision by superficial parotidectomy with facial nerve preservation is usually curative. Facial nerve sacrifice with nerve grafting is necessary only for complete nerve entrapment. Postoperative radiation or chemotherapy is usually not indicated.

High-Grade Malignant Neoplasms

High-grade malignant neoplasms tend to occur at a younger age (average 5.3 years) than do the low-grade and benign tumors (9.7 and 9.5 years average, respectively).[49, 56] The most common high-grade malignant neoplasm is mucoepidermoid carcinoma (55%), followed by adenocarcinoma (27%), adenoid cystic carcinoma (9%), and malignant mixed tumor (9%). The rate of growth and the severity of local symptoms are generally more pronounced than in the benign and low-grade tumors. Facial paralysis and fixation are the classic physical findings of malignant parotid tumors; in the submandibular gland, fixation and involvement of the lingual, hypoglossal, or marginal mandibular branch of the facial nerve similarly indicate advanced disease. Metastases to the regional lymph nodes are common, and hematogenous spread to the lungs, liver, and bone may occur. Excisional biopsy, when technically feasible, or incisional biopsy when not, is essential for proper diagnosis. Treatment of high-grade mucoepidermoid carcinoma is wide surgical excision with facial nerve preservation unless the nerve is not dissectible from the tumor.[37] Simple enucleation for malignant parotid tumors is inadequate treatment. Neck dissection is indicated for lymph nodes that are positive for metastasis. Postoperative radiation therapy is generally recommended.[24] Five-year survival rate approaches 80%, but is considerably less for stage II and III tumors.[61]

Rhabdomyosarcomas can occur in the region of the parotid gland and rarely manifest as a parotid mass (Fig. 65–12).[55] Diagnosis is suggested by fine-needle aspiration, and usually requires incisional or excisional biopsy for confirmation. Surgical excision with radiation and chemotherapy planned before therapy, in some cases, and for salvage after treatment for large tumors, is usually recommended. Survival is strongly dependent on tumor stage.

Primary lymphoma of the salivary glands is rare; Regezi and Batsakis[53] reviewed six reported series composed of 2924 parotid neoplasms, of which 7 were lymphomas. Many of these were associated with Sjögren syndrome, and the prognosis was poor. The non-Sjögren patients had favorable outcomes. The reported cases have all occurred in the parotid gland.

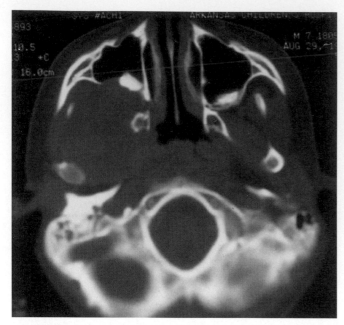

FIGURE 65–12. This large mass with compression of the posterior wall of the maxillary sinus noted on a CT scan presented as a parotid mass. Biopsy revealed a rhabdomyosarcoma.

The parotid gland is a common site for metastases of primary neoplasms of the scalp, face, cheek, orbit, and external nose. One should search for a primary lesion outside of the gland in all cases of suspected malignant disease. The clinical behavior of metastatic tumors reflects the biologic features of the primary neoplasm.

Submandibular Gland

The principles of management outlined for neoplasms of the parotid gland are equally applicable to those arising in the submandibular gland. Because tumors of the submandibular gland are so uncommon in children, they are generally misdiagnosed, and adequate treatment is not planned for.

Hemangioma and Lymphangioma

Approximately 60% of all pediatric salivary gland masses are hemangiomas or, less frequently, lymphangiomas. These masses usually appear in the first few months or weeks after birth and many enlarge rapidly. Most are solitary lesions, but multiple lesions occur in 20% of patients. Of the salivary gland hemangiomas, 80% occur in the parotid gland, 18% in the submandibular gland, and 2% in the minor salivary glands. Many hemangiomas regress spontaneously but are unpredictable. Early involution tends to be more complete.

The hemangioma is composed of solid masses of cells and of capillary-like vascular spaces that have replaced the secretory tissue of the gland, leaving only widely spaced ducts. The tumor usually infiltrates the entire gland, limited only by the fascial envelope of the gland, which results in a characteristic appearance (Fig. 65–13). The mass is warm, soft, and compressible; does not trans-

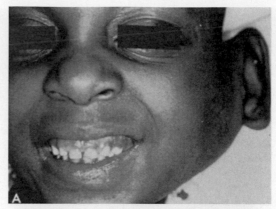

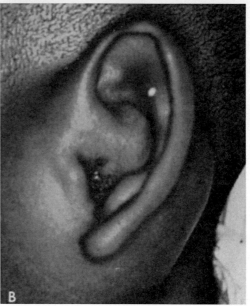

FIGURE 65–13. *A,* Anterior view of a left parotid hemangioma. Note the normal facial motion. *B,* Lateral view of a left parotid hemangioma.

illuminate; and grows more tense with crying or straining. If large, it extends into the upper neck. There is no facial weakness. The skin overlying the gland may be normal; subtly involved, with hemangioma with an erythematous or telangiectatic macule; or grossly involved, with typical raised bright-red hemangioma. The saliva is usually normal.

Diagnosis of these masses is usually evident from physical examination. Ultrasonography of hemangiomas demonstrates a well-defined hypoechoic mass lesion with heterogeneous echotexture and the presence of cystic and sinusoidal spaces within, as well as the occasional presence of phleboliths (Fig. 65–14). If the diagnosis remains in question, an MRI scan of the parotid should be obtained.[31] Rarely is a biopsy indicated to make an accurate diagnosis.

Treatment is not necessary for small, uncomplicated hemangiomas. For rapidly progressing hemangiomas or for complications (ulceration, infection, bleeding), a trial of steroids (prednisone, 3 to 5 mg/kg per day) for several weeks should be tried as initial therapy. Resection by an experienced parotid surgeon is indicated when there are

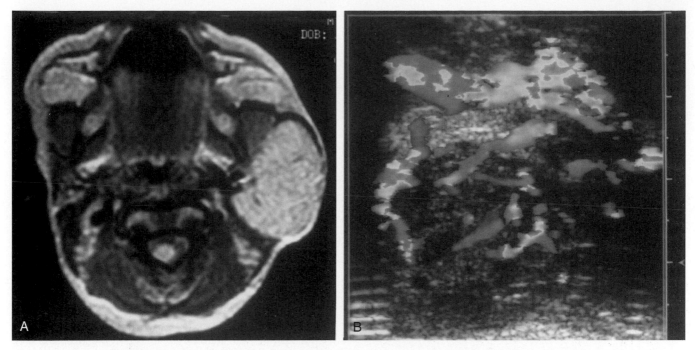

FIGURE 65–14. *A,* MRI of a left parotid hemangioma reveals a large homogeneous mass replacing the parotid with large vessel flow voids. *B,* Ultrasonography of a parotid hemangioma reveals a highly vascular, well-defined hypoechoic mass.

complications of extremely rapid growth, such as infection or hemorrhage, despite medical management. Resection can often be delayed to allow spontaneous regression of the hemangioma to occur and to let the child grow. The complications of parotidectomy for hemangioma that have been reported,[69] such as facial paralysis, residual tumor, and postoperative deaths, are persuasive of the adoption of a "wait and see" approach.

Lymphangioma (cystic hygroma) occurs less commonly, is softer and more diffuse, and transilluminates more readily than a hemangioma. Approximately 50% of lymphangiomas are present at birth, and 90% become apparent by 1 year of age. In gross appearance, the mass extends beyond the anatomic borders of the gland and invades rather than replaces the gland. On microscopic examination, lymphangiomas may be composed of small, capillary-sized spaces, cavernous dilated spaces, or both. When the lesion is large and composed more of loculated lymph cysts than of channels, the term *cystic hygroma* has been used. While there may be some fluctuation in size, especially associated with upper respiratory infections, complete spontaneous regression is rare, if it occurs at all. Ultrasonography, CT, and MRI all demonstrate cystic areas with septa. Biopsy is rarely indicated. Excision of the lymphangioma is often incomplete because of its diffuse and invasive growth pattern, but subtotal removal is usually sufficient to relieve the patient of the symptoms of the mass.

Dermoids are small congenital squamous-epithelial–lined cysts with associated skin appendages. Dermoids are discrete, slowly enlarging masses within or in the soft tissue overlying the gland. Complete excision is curative.

Agenesis of the major salivary glands has been reported and is associated with xerostomia and rampant dental carries.[25, 28, 62] Proper oral hygiene is the only treatment.

Trauma

Blunt and penetrating trauma to the face can cause injury to the major salivary glands. Injury of the gland parenchyma usually does not require specific management beyond wound closure and possibly drainage. Facial nerve injury and salivary duct injury should be recognized and repaired. Wounds deep to the parotid fascia with facial nerve injury should be repaired within 72 hours. Only facial nerve injury occurring within 2 cm of the end muscle has a high probability of reinnervation. Injuries anterior to a vertical line extending from the lateral canthus to the mental foramen should be in this "safe" region. For injuries posterior to this line, the wound should be explored and the proximal and distal stumps identified. The proximal portion may require identification of the main trunk and dissection of the nerve branches. Identification of the distal stump is facilitated by electrical stimulation. The nerve is usually reanastomosed without difficulty, although nerve grafting is occasionally needed.

The parotid duct can be injured with lacerations posterior to the anterior border of the masseter. Duct injury may be obvious by wound exploration. If the degree of injury is uncertain, a probe can be placed through the Stensen duct for identification of the duct. Primary reanastomosis is possible in most cases. Many authors recommend repairing the duct over a small indwelling Silastic or polyethylene tubing stent. If reanastomosis is not possible, the duct may be rerouted intraorally or the proximal end ligated, which usually leads to gland atrophy.

Blunt trauma to the gland may result in hematoma or salivary pseudocyst. A history of trauma and subsequent development of a mass acutely (hematoma) or delayed (cyst) is usually diagnostic. Ultrasonography can be helpful. Aspiration or incision and drainage with pressure dressing is sometimes necessary. Pneumoparotiditis is an uncommon finding in children, but may occur in musicians, glass blowers, or other patients in whom increased intrabuccal pressure is noted. Treatment is usually not necessary.

Xerostomia is a known complication of radiation therapy in the region of the salivary glands. Artificial saliva is helpful for severe symptoms, and pilocarpine has been shown to decrease the sensation of oral dryness. Artificial saliva preparation frequently instilled into the mouth facilitates deglutition and helps with oral hygiene. One such formula is methylcellulose 4%, 20 mL; glycerine, 10 mL; and lemon oil, 1 drop. Sialogogues, such as sour lemon drops, are also helpful. The incidence of secondary malignancies of the salivary glands is increased after even low-dose radiation.[35, 45]

Drooling (Sialorrhea)

Drooling occurs most commonly in neurologically impaired children, usually with cerebral palsy (see Chap. 55). In addition to cosmetic and emotional problems for the child, there are increased risks for perioral infection, dehydration, and inability to eat a regular diet.[43] Significant time and effort may be required of the caregiver to keep these children dry.

A multidisciplinary assessment of these patients is advocated by Crysdale and Richardson.[18] Evaluation should include determination of nasal airway patency, dental examination, and assessment of swallowing by esophagogram. Treatment modalities are both surgical and nonsurgical. Nonsurgical methods include physical therapy, usually employed in an adjunctive role, and anticholinergic drugs. Drug therapy is poorly tolerated on a long-term basis because of troublesome side effects, such as constipation, urinary retention, blurred vision, and restlessness.

Surgical procedures consist of gland denervation, gland excision, duct ligation, and duct repositioning, usually performed in various combinations. Radiation to produce gland atrophy is no longer recommended because of the risk of inducing neoplasia. Tympanic neurectomy requires bilateral procedures and produces a thick, mucoid saliva. If the chorda tympani nerve is sacrificed also, there is loss of taste from the anterior two thirds of the tongue. In addition, an especially bothersome type of xerostomia has been reported after tympanic neurectomy.[18] Late failures are due to regrowth of preganglionic fibers. Duct rerouting consists of transposing either Stensen duct (Wilkie procedure) or the submandibular duct into the tonsillar fauces. Wilkie and Brody[68] reported 10-year follow-up of 123 patients who underwent parotid duct rerouting and submandibular gland excision. Initial results were good in 86% of patients. Twenty patients required reoperation because of stenosis. Other late complications included

parotid cysts with intermittent swelling and infection. Reoperation for cyst excision or marsupialization may be required.[65] Submandibular duct repositioning is associated with ranula formation. Crysdale advocates concomitant excision of sublingual glands to eliminate this problem.

The preferred surgical treatment at present appears to be bilateral submaxillary gland excision and parotid duct ligation.[44] Although this produces external scars, it is well tolerated with minimal morbidity. In the authors' experience, parotid swelling and discomfort have been transient and mild. Recent data suggest not only the benefit of decreased drooling but also improved pulmonary status with fewer infections, presumably from decreased aspiration of saliva.[26]

REFERENCES

1. Afzelius LE, Walter CG: The surgical treatment of chronic parotitis. J Laryngol Otol 96:1131, 1982.
2. Al-Khafaji BM, Nestok BR, Katz RL. Fine needle aspiration of 154 parotid masses with histologic correlation; ten-year experience at the University of Texas MD Anderson Cancer Center. Cancer 84:153, 1998.
3. Anaya JM, Ogawa N, Talal N. Sjögren's syndrome in childhood. J Rheumatol 22:1152, 1995.
4. Arglebe C, Eysholdt U, Chilla R. Pharmacological inhibition of salivary glands: a possible therapy for sialosis and sialoadenitis. Effect of experimentally induced beta-receptor block on the rat parotid gland. ORL J Otorhinolaryngol Relat Spec 38:218, 1976.
5. Atula T, Greenman R, Laippala P, Klemi PJ. Fine-needle aspiration biopsy in the diagnosis of parotid gland lesions: evaluation of 438 biopsies. Diagn Cytopathol 15:185, 1996.
6. Baader WM, Lewis JM. First branchial cleft cysts presenting as parotid tumors. Ann Plast Surg 33:72, 1994.
7. Baker S, Malone B. Salivary gland malignancies in children. Cancer 55:1730, 1985.
8. Barbero G, Sibinga M. Enlargement of the submaxillary salivary glands in cystic fibrosis. Pediatrics 29:788, 1962.
9. Batsakis JG, Sneige N, El-Naggar AK. Fine-needle aspiration of salivary glands: its utility and tissue effects. Ann Otol Rhinol Laryngol 101:185, 1992.
10. Blatt IM, Denning RM, Zumberge JH, et al. Studies in sialolithiasis. The structure and mineralogical composition of salivary gland calculi. Ann Otol Rhinol Laryngol 67:595, 1958.
11. Camocho AE, Goodman ML, Eavey RD. Pathologic correlation of the unknown solid parotid mass in children. Otolaryngol Head Neck Surg 101:566, 1989.
12. Casselman JW, Mancuso AA. Major salivary gland masses: comparison of MR imaging and CT. Radiology 165:183, 1987.
13. Cherry-Peppers G, Sorkin J, Anders R, et al. Salivary gland function and glucose metabolic status. J Gerontol 47:130, 1992.
14. Chitre VV, Premchandra DJ. Recurrent parotitis. Arch Dis Child 77: 359, 1997.
15. Conley J, Tinsley P. Treatment and prognosis of mucoepidermoid carcinoma in the pediatric age group. Arch Otolaryngol 111:322, 1985.
16. Control of Communicable diseases in man. In Benenson AS (ed). Washington, DC, American Public Health Association, 1985.
17. Coulthard SW. Nonneoplastic salivary gland diseases. In Meyerhoff WL, Rice DTT (eds). Otolaryngology—Head and Neck Surgery. Philadelphia, WB Saunders, 1992.
18. Crysdale WS, Richardson MA. The effect of submandibular duct rerouting in the treatment of sialorrhea in children. Laryngoscope 90:775, 1980.
19. Cvetinovic M, Jovic N, Mijatovic D. Evaluation of ultrasound in the diagnosis of pathologic processes in the parotid gland. J Oral Maxillofac Surg 49:147, 1991.

20. Eneroth CM, Hamberger CA. Principles of treatment of different types of parotid tumors. Laryngoscope 84(Suppl):1732, 1974.

21. Enfors BO. The parotid and submandibular secretion in man. Quantitative recordings on the normal and pathological activity. Acta Otolaryngol Suppl (Stockh) 172:1, 1962.

22. Frable MA, Frable WJ. Fine-needle aspiration biopsy of salivary glands. Laryngoscope 101:245, 1991.

23. Freimarle B, Fantozzi R. Detection of clonally expanded salivary gland lymphocytes in Sjögren's syndrome. Arthritis Rheum 32:859, 1989.

24. Garden AS, el-Naggar AK, Morrison WH, et al. Postoperative radiotherapy for malignant tumors of the parotid gland. Int J Radiat Oncol Biol Phys 37:79, 1997.

25. Gelbier MJ, Winter GB. Absence of salivary glands in children with rampant dental caries: report of seven cases. Int J Paediatr Dent 5:253, 1995.

26. Gerber ME, Gaugler MD, Myer CM 3rd, Cotton RT. Chronic aspiration in children. When are bilateral submandibular gland excision and parotid duct ligation indicated? Arch Otol Head Neck Surg 122:1368, 1996.

27. Giglio MS, Landaeta M, Pinto ME. Microbiology or recurrent parotitis. Pediatr Infect Dis J 16:386, 1997.

28. Gomez RS, Aguiar MJ, Ferreira AP, Castro WH. Congenital absence of parotid glands and lacrimal puncta. J Clin Pediatr Dent 22:247, 1998.

29. Hart PS. Salivary abnormalities in Prader-Willi syndrome. Ann N Y Acad Sci 15;842:125, 1998.

30. Henkin RI, Schechter RJ, Hoye R, et al. Idiopathic hypogeusia with dysgeusia, hyposmia, and dysosmia. A new syndrome. JAMA 217:434, 1971.

31. Huchzermeyer P, Birchall MA, Kendall B, Bailey CM. Parotid haemangiomas in childhood: a case for MRI. J Laryngol Otol 108:892, 1994.

32. Jenkins GN, Dawes C. The psychic flow of saliva in man. Arch Oral Biol 11:1203, 1966.

33. Jones LR, Toth BB, Keene HJ. Effects of total body irradiation on salivary gland function and caries—associated oral microflora in bone marrow transplant patients. Oral Surg Oral Med Oral Pathol 73:670, 1992.

34. Kaiser D, Schoni M, Drack E. Anionen- and Lationenausscheidung per Parotis in Abhangigkeit von der Fliessrate bei Mukoviszidosepartienten and Gesunden. Helv Pediatr Acta 29:145, 1974.

35. Kaste SC, Hedlund G, Pratt CB. Malignant parotid tumors in patients previously treated for childhood cancer: clinical and imaging findings in eight cases. AJR Am J Roentgenol 162:655, 1994.

36. Lee KC, Chung SW. Evaluation of the neck mass in human immunodeficiency virus infected patients. Otolaryngol Clin North Am 25:1287, 1992.

37. Leverstein H, van der Wal JE, Tiwari RM, et al. Malignant epithelial parotid gland tumors: analysis and results in 65 previously untreated patients. Br J Surg 85:1267, 1998.

38. Liu FT, Lin HS. Role of insulin in body growth and in the growth of salivary and endocrine glands in rats. J Dent Res 48:559, 1969.

39. Mathew S, Ali SZ. Parotid fine-needle aspiration: a cytologic study of pediatric lesions. Diagn Cytopathol 17:8, 1997.

40. Medelena L, Dragan I, Mihordea M. Clinical and immunological features of the HIV infection associated with chronic hypertrophic parotitis in children. Rom J Virol 46:135, 1995.

41. Megerian CA, Maniglia AJ. Parotidectomy: a ten year experience with fine needle aspiration and frozen section biopsy correlation. Ear Nose Throat J 73:377, 1994.

42. Modlin JF. Current status of mumps in the United States. Infection 132:106, 1975.

43. Myer C. Sialorrhea. Recent advances in pediatric otolaryngology. Pediatr Clin North Am 36:1495, 1989.

44. Myer CM III. Salivary gland disease in children. In Gates GA (ed). Current Therapy in Otolaryngology—Head and Neck Surgery, vol. 4. Philadelphia, BC Decker, 1990.

45. Myer CM III. Second primary malignancies of the head and neck in children. Am J Otolaryngol 16:415, 1995.

46. Myer C, Cotton RT. Salivary gland disease in children: a review. Part 1. Acquired non-neoplastic disease. Clin Pediatr 25:314, 1985.

47. Na DG, Lim HK, Byun HS, et al. Differential diagnosis of cervical lymphadenopathy: usefulness of color Doppler sonography. AJR Am J Roentgenol 168:1311, 1997.

48. Nozaki H, Harasawa A, Hara H, et al. Ultrasonographic features of recurrent parotitis in childhood (see comments). Pediatr Radiol 24:98, 1994, 25:402, 1995.

49. Ogata H, Ebihara S, Mukai K. Salivary gland neoplasms in children. Jpn J Clin Oncol 24:88, 1994.

50. Pershall K, Koopmann CF Jr, Coulthard SW. Sialadenitis in children. Int J Pediatr Otorhinolaryngol 11:199, 1986.

51. Rabinov K, Kell T Jr, Gordon PH. CT of the salivary glands. Radiol Clin North Am 22:145, 1984.

52. Red Book 1997. American Academy of Pediatrics. Mumps. In Peter G (ed). 1997 Red Book: Report of the Committee on Infectious Diseases, 24th ed. Elk Grove Village, Ill, American Academy of Pediatrics, 1997, pp 366–369.

53. Regezi JA, Batsakis JG. Histogenesis of salivary gland neoplasms. Otolaryngol Clin North Am 10:297, 1977.

54. Rice DH. Non-neoplastic diseases of the salivary glands. In Paparella MM, et al (eds). Otolaryngology. Philadelphia, WB Saunders, 1991.

55. Salomao DR, Sigman JD, Greenebaum E, Cohen MB. Rhabdomyosarcoma presenting as a parotid gland mass in pediatric patients: fine-needle aspiration biopsy findings. Cancer 84:245, 1998.

56. Schuller DE, McCabe BF. Salivary gland neoplasms in children. Otolaryngol Clin North Am 10:399, 1977.

57. Seibert RW, Seibert JJ. High resolution ultrasonography of the parotid gland in children. Pediatr Radiol 16:374, 1986.

58. Shikhani AH, Johns ME. Tumors of the major salivary glands in children. Head Neck Surg 10:257, 1998.

59. Shimizu M, Ussmuller J, Donath K, et al. Sonographic analysis of recurrent parotitis in children: a comparative study with sialographic findings. Oral Surg Oral Med Oral Pathol Oral Radiol Endo 86:606, 1998.

60. Spatt J. Etiology and therapy of acute pyogenic parotitis. Surg Gynecol Obstet 112:391, 1961.

61. Sprio RH, Huvos AF, Strong EW. Cancer of the parotid gland. A clinicopathologic study of 288 primary cases. Am J Surg 130:452; 1975.

62. Sucupira MS, Weinreb JW, Camargo EE, Wagner HN Jr. Salivary gland imaging and radionuclide dacrocytography in agenesis of salivary glands. Arch Otolaryngol Head Neck Surg 109:197, 1983.

63. Tabor EK, Curtin HD. MR of the salivary glands. Radiol Clin North Am 379:27, 1989.

64. Teresi LM, Kolin E, Lufkin RB, Hanafee WN. MR imaging of the intraparotid facial nerve: normal anatomy and pathology. AJR Am J Roentgenol 148:995, 1987.

65. Tunkel DE, Furin MJ. Salivary cysts following parotid duct translocation for sialorrhea. Otolaryngol Head Neck Surg 105:127, 1991.

66. Variend S, O'Neill D, Arnold P. The possible significance of cytomegaloviral parotitis in infant and early childhood deaths. Arch Pathol Lab Med 121:1272, 1997.

67. van der Akker HP. Diagnosis imaging in salivary gland disease. Oral Surg Oral Med Oral Pathol 66:625, 1988.

68. Wilkie TF, Brody GS. The surgical treatment of drooling. A ten year review. Plast Reconstr Surg 59:791, 1977.

69. Williams HB. Hemangiomas of the parotid gland in children. Plast Reconstr Surg 56:29, 1975.

70. Williams MA. Head and neck findings in pediatric acquired immune deficiency syndrome. Laryngoscope 97:713, 1987.

71. Work WP. Newer concepts of first branchial cleft defects. Laryngoscope 82:1581, 1972.

72. Wotman S, Mercadente J, Mandel ID, et al. The occurrence of calculus in normal children, children with cystic fibrosis, and children with asthma. J Periodontol 44:278, 1973.

73. Yang WT, Ahuja A, Metreweli C. Sonographic features of head and neck hemangiomas and vascular malformations: review of 23 patients. J Ultrasound Med 16:39, 1997.

66

Tumors of the Mouth and Pharynx

Carlos Gonzalez, M.D.

Oral tumors in children constitute approximately 3% of all tumor-like growths in the oral cavity, jaws, and salivary glands in all age groups. The overwhelming majority of those tumors are benign (Table 66–1). However, the wide variety of congenital and acquired oral and pharyngeal neoplasms encountered in the pediatric age group underscores the need for the otolaryngologist to have a systematized diagnostic approach to these lesions (Table 66–2).

The head and neck area, excluding the central nervous system, is the site of 5% to 10% of all childhood malignant neoplasms.[50] Malignant tumors arising in the oral cavity, oropharynx, or hypopharynx are more often of mesodermal than of ectodermal or endodermal origin. This tendency, however, is less marked than the 9:1 ratio of sarcomas to carcinomas described for all tumors in all sites in children.[27] The occurrence of 40 of 48 reported cases of epidermoid carcinoma in children in the mouth and pharynx emphasizes the relative frequency of this tumor type in the mouth and pharynx.[42]

The diagnostic identification of an oral or pharyngeal mass in a youthful patient can often be made with considerable accuracy by combining historical information with careful inspection and palpation of the lesion.

Important historical data should include information regarding age of the patient at onset of the mass; rapidity of growth and extension; subsequent size increase, decrease, or stability; relationship of tumor growth rate to growth rate of the child; random fluctuations in size; presence or absence of inflammation, ulcerations, bleeding, or drainage; alterations in color, texture, or consistency; presence of pain; local or regional paresthesia or anesthesia; presence of similar contiguous or distant lesions; and family history of similar lesions.

Physical examination should take note of the precise site, size, color, and texture of the tumor; whether it is sessile or pedunculated, fixed or mobile, tender or painless, mucosal or submucosal, and ulcerated or infected; and whether it blanches on pressure, transilluminates, is fluctuant, has a bruit, extends to or from neighboring structures, or tends to interfere with deglutition, speech, or respiration.

In consequence, history and physical examination alone can identify a number of pediatric oral or pharyngeal tumors with considerable certainty (e.g., cavernous he-mangiomas and torus palatinus) and others with a high probability (e.g., sublingual dermoid and lingual thyroid). Those lesions that continue to enlarge, interfere with function, cause persistent symptoms, or remain diagnostically obscure should be excised if they are accessible, or a biopsy specimen should be obtained to determine the need for additional therapy.

It is difficult in dealing with certain individual lesions of the oral and pharyngeal tissues in children to determine whether the mass is a true tumor and, if so, what its subsequent biologic behavior will be. An attempt is made to identify these problem areas and to indicate if clarifying evidence is available.

Oral Cavity

In a study of 293 oral tumors in children, Bhaskar[6] found that 91% were benign and 9% were malignant. Thirty-nine percent of the tumors were found in the first 4 years of life, whereas the remaining 61% appeared between ages 5 and 14 years. Boys and girls were about equally affected (47.5% and 52.5%, respectively). More than two thirds of the lesions arose from the oral soft tissues, with 27% being derived from the jaws and 5% from the salivary glands. The four most common benign oral tumors were vascular and lymphatic (27%), fibrous (15%), odontogenic (15%), and nonodontogenic (12%). Further, in order of decreasing frequency, epithelial lesions, hamartomas or choristomas, salivary gland hemangiomas, miscellaneous soft tissue tumors, and a variety of other salivary gland masses were reported. The relatively large proportion of jaw lesions in this particular series may well reflect the dental origin of much of the patient material.

Benign Tumors of the Oral Soft Tissues

Hemangiomas

Hemangioma is the single most common head and neck tumor of childhood. Together, lymphangioma and hemangioma compose approximately 30% of oral tumors in children. In a survey of 293 cases, the lip was the most common site, with involvement of the cheek and the tongue following in frequency.[6] In unusual instances,

TABLE 66-1. Estimated Relative Frequency of Tumors of the Mouth and Pharynx in Children

Tumor Type	Frequency°	Tumor Subtypes	Frequency°	Comment
Benign	92%	Mesenchymal	78%	
		Hemangioma	30%	Most common tumor
		Epulis	27%	
		Hamartoma	7%	
		Epithelial	14%	
		Papilloma	8%	Most common epithelial tumor
Malignant	8%	Sarcoma	Sarcoma predominates; number of reported cases too small to produce meaningful figures	Most common primary malignant neoplasm
		Rhabdomyosarcoma		
		Other sarcomas		
		Lymphoma/leukemia		Least common single type
		Carcinoma		

° Percentage of all tumors.

other oral or pharyngeal structures may harbor a hemangioma.

Hemangiomas are usually classified histologically as cellular (juvenile), capillary, cavernous, or mixed. There is, however, considerable overlap in the features of these hemangiomas, and this classification may indeed be somewhat artificial. It has been proposed on the basis of transition areas in some lesions that there may be a "maturation" of cellular type to the capillary and thence to the cavernous variety.[4] Clinical behavior can rarely be predicted on the basis of microscopic appearance alone.

Most oral hemangiomas are diagnosed in early infancy and should be differentiated from other inflammatory lesions with a dominant vascular component, which usually become evident in later childhood. Pyogenic granuloma is an exaggerated vascular response to relatively minor trauma. Found in a universal distribution in the body, it is common in the oral cavity (Fig. 66-1).

The oral lesions may be small and superficial, in which case they occur as blue or purplish, sessile, compressible masses. More deeply seated hemangiomas are generally more extensive and are often recognized by age 5 years. They are firm, are less well defined, and may exhibit only irregular bluish discoloration through the overlying mucosa. Extensive replacement of the lip (macrocheilia) or tongue (macroglossia) has been described. Diffuse lingual hemangioma as a cause of macroglossia can almost always be distinguished from other forms of symmetric enlargement of the tongue on the basis of its obvious vascular nature. Macroglossia may also represent an isolated congenital anomaly; may be due to lymphangiomatosis, plexiform neurofibromatosis, or mucopolysaccharidosis; or may be part of Beckwith-Wiedemann syndrome (visceromegaly, omphalocele, and hypoglycemia).[5]

A number of syndromes may be recognized by associated vascular lesions. The angiomatous lesions of heredi-

TABLE 66-2. Classification of Benign and Malignant Tumors of the Mouth and Pharynx in Children

Oral Cavity

Oral Soft Tissues	Gingiva and Jaws	Pharynx
Benign tumors	Benign tumors	Benign tumors
Hemangioma	Gingiva	Primary tumors
Lymphangioma	Congenital epulis	External compression tumors
Fibrous tumors	Melanotic neuroectodermal tumor	Malignant tumors
Epithelial tumors	Giant cell reparative granuloma	Lymphoma
Papilloma	Pyogenic granuloma	Rhabdomyosarcoma
Dermoid	Gingival hypertrophies	
White sponge nevus	Odontogenic tumors	
Cystic tumors	Cysts	
Ranula	Cementomas	
Thyroglossal duct cyst	Ameloblastoma	
Branchial cysts	Central fibromas	
Hamartomas and choristomas	Nonodontogenic tumors	
Miscellaneous tumors	Hemorrhagic cyst	
Malignant tumors	Aneurysmal bone cyst	
Rhabdomyosarcoma	Fibrous dysplasia	
Other sarcomas	Cherubism	
Epidermoid carcinoma	Malignant tumors	
Miscellaneous malignant neoplasms	Gingiva and jaw	
	Burkitt lymphoma	
	Fibrosarcoma	
	Osteogenic sarcoma	
	Ewing sarcoma	
	Chondrosarcoma	

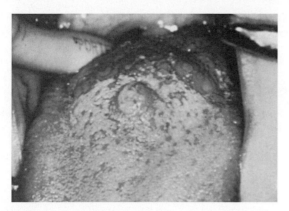

FIGURE 66–1. Pyogenic granuloma of the tongue. The sessile, fleshy, vascular appearance of the lesion is typical.

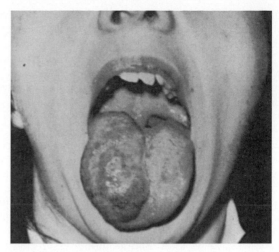

FIGURE 66–2. Extensive cavernous hemangioma of the tongue. The entire right half of the tongue is replaced by an irregularly nodular, purplish, compressible vascular mass.

tary hemorrhagic telangiectasia appear frequently at the labial mucocutaneous junction or on the anterior tongue as friable, small, abnormal collections of vessels that may be spider-like, punctiform, or nodular in type. Batsakis[4] also mentions that the Sturge-Weber, Maffucci, and von Hippel–Lindau syndromes can include oral vascular lesions. Juvenile nasopharyngeal angiofibroma has been described as having the palate eroded. There is no convincing evidence that benign lesions give rise to malignant vascular tumors.

Typically, hemangiomas are noted at birth or in the first few weeks of life. They usually enlarge during the first year, then undergo some degree of spontaneous regression in the next several years. Many will have virtually disappeared by age 5 years. For this reason, conservative management is usually advocated. Active therapy is indicated when hemangiomas cause uncontrolled hemorrhage, pain, infection, ulceration, airway obstruction, thrombocytopenia, or cardiovascular decompensation.

Treatment of oral hemangiomas has included surgical excision, irradiation, sclerosing agents, cryosurgery, corticosteroid therapy, and carbon dioxide laser excision. Corticosteroid therapy has been demonstrated to decrease the size of hemangiomas and appears to hasten spontaneous resolution in some.[24] However, the need for prolonged therapy and the risk of complications still limit its usefulness. The use of carbon dioxide laser excision has been advocated owing to decreased intraoperative bleeding and good local control. Blood vessel diameter limits its usefulness to well-defined lesions of the tongue and oral mucosa and would contraindicate its use in large deforming lesions of the cavernous type.[2, 14] Extensive lesions have also been successfully treated with one or several applications of cryosurgery (Figs. 66–2 and 66–3). Promising results have recently been reported with endovascular embolization of large hemangiomas that would be considered unresectable.[32, 54]

Lymphangiomas

Lymphangiomas involve the oral cavity more often than any other area of the body. Within the oral cavity, the tongue is more frequently involved.[6] Between 50% and 60% are recognized at birth, and 80% to 90% are evident

by the end of the second year of life, corresponding to the period of greatest lymphatic growth.[4]

Lymphangiomas have been classified into three groups: simplex or capillary, composed of thin-walled lymphatic channels; cavernous, composed of dilated lymphatic spaces; and cystic hygroma, composed of cysts varying in size from a few millimeters to several centimeters in diameter. It is likely that all represent different stages of the same disease. The morphologic variations may be due to differences in anatomic location. This unified concept has been proposed by Bill and Sumner.[8] In addition, combinations of patterns are frequently seen in neighboring parts of the same tumor. In this respect, lymphangiomatous malformations of the tongue are often seen with cystic hygromas of the neck.

Oral lymphangiomas generally appear as whitish or pink, fluctuant, superficial lesions that transilluminate. Larger and deeper tumors are usually ill-defined and woody with little mucosal color change.

The tongue is a fairly frequent site of lymphangiomatous involvement. The cavernous type is by far the most common, and more than two thirds of the lymphangiomas of the tongue are of this type. By contrast, most lymph-

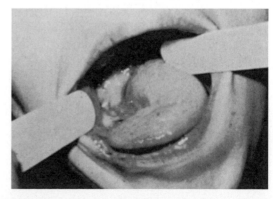

FIGURE 66–3. Cavernous hemangioma of the tongue. Same lesion as in Figure 66–2, 18 days after cryosurgery. The tumor has sloughed, and healing is satisfactory.

angiomas of the floor of the mouth contain a mixture of lymphangioma and cystic hygroma.[8] An isolated lymphangioma of the tongue or floor of the mouth often causes both some asymmetry and restriction of tongue movement. The lesion is somewhat rubbery on palpation. The surface mucosa may be pale and may contain small translucent cysts.

Diffuse involvement of the tongue may result in macroglossia. If the lingual involvement has been of long duration, a true open-bite malocclusion may occur; cephalometric analysis may show anterior incisal displacement. Cystic hygroma of the neck is an associated finding in 7% of tongue lymphangiomas.

Surgical excision is the mainstay of treatment. All other modalities, such as needle aspiration, incision and drainage, electrocautery, application of sclerosing agents, and irradiation, have yielded disappointing results. A high mortality rate is associated with extensive lesions, especially when emergency treatment is necessary during the early days or weeks of life. The optimal age for surgery appears to be between 18 months and 2 years.

The purpose of surgery is to remove the tumor entirely if possible, preserving normal function of the involved surrounding structures. Because of a poorly defined interphase with surrounding tissue, excessive or radical surgery will not necessarily guarantee complete elimination of disease and may be harmful. At times, planned staged excision may be beneficial. In smaller lesions, carbon dioxide laser excision has also demonstrated satisfactory results.[14] Some of the smaller lesions may undergo spontaneous fibrous obliteration.

Cystic Lesions

A ranula is a large, lateralized retention cyst of the floor of the mouth usually caused by obstruction of the sublingual or another major salivary gland duct. A few may represent cervical sinus remnants.[4] The lesion is mucosa covered and typically has a translucent, bluish white, frog belly appearance (Fig. 66–4). Secondary salivary gland inflammation is rare. Treatment of the enlarging mass commonly takes the form of marsupialization, thus avoiding widespread dissection in the floor of the mouth.

Thyroglossal duct cysts may rarely occur in the substance of the midline base of tongue. It is important to

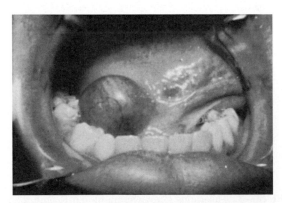

FIGURE 66–4. Ranula. The pale, cystic, translucent nature of this lesion of the floor of the mouth is evident.

distinguish this lesion from the more common lingual thyroid. Sublingual branchial cleft cysts have also been reported.[48]

Fibrous Tumors

The histologic complexity of fibrous tumors has made a unified concept of classification hard to achieve. This situation produces difficulty in predicting prognosis as well as in treatment for the great diversity of fibrous tumors. Treatment is therefore often determined by the lesion's location, size, and biologic behavior.

Dehner and Askin[18] described 66 children with tumors of fibrous tissue origin, of which 33% arose in the head and neck region. Five of the 22 head and neck lesions occurred in the oral cavity, three on the tongue, and one each on maxillary gingiva and retromolar trigone. The average age of the 22 patients was 5.7 years. Thirty-two percent of the treated lesions recurred, and 4% of the patients died of their disease. It was stated that adequate local surgery was generally successful.

Lesions arising from the musculoaponeuroses form a group of fibrous tumors known as desmoids. Because this term does not convey the diversity of cellularity encountered in different desmoid tumors, Batsakis prefers the term fibromatosis. Masson and Soule[37] noted that 12% of 284 desmoid tumors were encountered in the head and neck region. As a group, these lesions are noted for their local aggressiveness and high recurrence rate. Erosion of bone or actual invasion of bone may occur. Aggressive surgical treatment is usually required.

True oral fibromas are probably unusual. It is at least difficult to distinguish histologically between true benign fibrous neoplasms and induced hyperplasia.

Epithelial Tumors

Oral squamous papillomas are a familiar mucosal lesion. Whereas the viral etiology of oral papillomatous lesions in animals has been demonstrated, this hypothesis has not been proved with respect to human oral papilloma. In a study of 464 oral papillomas, 8.3% were in patients younger than 10 years.[1] The palatal complex was involved in 34.3% of cases, followed by the tongue in 23.5% and the lips in 13.8%. Although the potential for premalignant transformation has been reported in other parts of the body, this has not been demonstrated in oral lesions.[6] These lesions are frequently accompanied by chronic inflammatory changes. They respond well to local excision, and recurrences are rare.

Multiple papillomas of the lips, oral cavity, and oropharynx are also seen in association with multiple hamartomas of the skin, other mucosas, breast, gastrointestinal tract, and thyroid in Cowden disease. Finally, Darier disease is an inherited abnormality in which crusted hyperkeratotic oral papular lesions exist in the absence of systemic findings.[23]

White sponge nevus is a rare familial form of epithelial hyperplasia of the oral mucosa. The abnormality has been reported only in whites, and boys and girls are equally affected. Fewer than 50 cases have been recorded.[28] The lesion appears at birth or in later childhood as a diffuse, whitish, thickened, folded-appearing, asymptomatic lesion, particularly involving the buccal mucosa, lips, floor of the mouth, and ventral surface of the tongue. Epithelial thickening and parakeratosis are seen microscopically. The lesion tends to progress but is thought to be entirely benign and to require no treatment.

Focal epithelial hyperplasia (Heck disease) is a familial form of epithelial hyperplasia found in children of American Indian parentage.[55] Single cases have been reported in children of other races. Multiple soft, pale papules and confluent patches are evident on the oral mucosa, particularly the lower lip. Acanthosis and parakeratosis are prominent histologically. No serious late sequelae have been identified.

Approximately 1.6% of all dermoids and 20% of head and neck dermoids occur in the oral cavity, and most of these lesions are in the anterior part of the floor of the mouth. The tumor may be evident at birth or may not become manifest until the second or third decade of life.[47] The sexes are equally affected. Dermoids in the floor of the mouth may be located above the mylohyoid diaphragm and may displace the tongue upward, or they may appear below the mylohyoid where they produce a double-chin effect. The lesions are found in or close to the midline. Seemingly aberrant dermoids are believed to be choristomas in most if not all cases. Complete excision is the preferred treatment.

A small number of dermoid cysts of the lip and palate have been presented in the literature. They usually occur at or near the midline as globular submucosal masses of moderate size with a doughy feeling on palpation. Intraoral excision is usually indicated.

Hamartomas and Choristomas

The tongue is the most common oral site for hamartomas. Tissue indigenous to the area composes these tumor-like masses. Some authors consider granular cell myoblastoma to be a hamartoma. Choristomas of the region contain unexpected tissue, such as glandular acini, glial tissue, cartilage, or bone.[34] Oral cysts containing gastric mucosa occur in the tongue or floor of the mouth of infants or young children and are believed to be choristomas.[21] Choristomas, particularly if highly cellular, may be diagnostically confusing initially. Hamartomas and choristomas can generally be excised without difficulty.

Lingual thyroid represents a rest of thyroid tissue that is found in the midline of the dorsum of the base of tongue between the foramen cecum and the vallecula. The mass is globular, reddish, highly vascular, smooth or lobulated, and firm or soft; it may have intact or superficially ulcerated mucosa covering it. The tumor may become clinically apparent at any time from birth through adulthood. Females are predominantly affected. Dysphagia is the most common presenting symptom, although a muffled voice, dyspnea, orthopnea, and hemorrhage are also seen. Normally functioning thyroid tissue is usually present in the mass. About 3% of all lesions have malignant changes. Uptake and scan studies are requisite to demonstrate the functional status of the mass and the presence or absence of functioning thyroid tissue elsewhere in the neck. Taking a biopsy specimen may induce necrosis and is not advised. Symptomatic masses may be handled by ablation and replacement therapy or by removal and autotransplantation of the tissue into a suitable skeletal muscle bed.

Miscellaneous Tumors

Mucoceles are commonly occurring lesions of the oral cavity. The lesions are usually painless, freely mobile, smooth, soft, fluctuant masses varying in size from a few millimeters to several centimeters. Larger lesions are usually located in the floor of the mouth or in the substance of the tongue. Mucoceles involving the base of tongue region can enlarge enough to cause airway compromise. In a series of 594 cases, Cataldo and Mosadomi[10] noted that almost half the lesions were in patients younger than 20 years. On histologic examination, the walls of most of the specimens are composed of granulation tissue, and rarely is an epithelial lining identified. Computed tomography may be beneficial to assess the true extent of a mass appearing in the oral cavity (Fig. 66–5). Treatment consists of surgical excision and marsupialization of larger ones.

Multiple neuromas of the lip (bumpy lip syndrome), tongue, and larynx have been observed in association with pheochromocytomas, medullary carcinoma of the thyroid gland, and hyperparathyroidism (Sipple syndrome).[3] Neurofibromas, either solitary or representing the oral manifestations of von Recklinghausen syndrome, are seen occasionally in pediatric patients. The plexiform type may be particularly difficult to control locally.[51] Oral mucosal neurofibromas are also found in the neuropolyendocrine

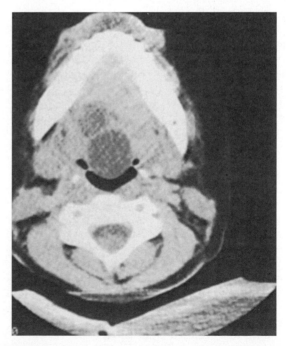

FIGURE 66–5. Computed tomography scan demonstrating vallecular mucocele with involvement of the deep musculature of the tongue. Differential diagnosis would include lymphangioma.

syndrome along with multiple endocrine adenomas and medullary carcinoma of the thyroid gland. Neurilemoma occurs rarely.

Leiomyomas occur in the tongue as well as elsewhere in the oral cavity.[12] Origin from undifferentiated mesenchyme, from smooth muscle of local blood vessels, or from both sources has been postulated.

Fordyce disease (Fordyce granules) is a relatively common developmental abnormality in which ectopic sebaceous glands occur submucosally in the oral cavity, typically beneath the posterior buccal mucosa near the line of occlusion. The glands appear as 1- to 2-mm yellowish masses. They have no clinical significance.

Malignant Tumors of the Oral Soft Tissues

Malignant tumors of the oral cavity are notably unusual in the pediatric age group. Approximately 5% to 10% of all tumors in childhood fall into this category. The accumulated experience with many tumor types is so small that no meaningful generalizations can be made regarding relative incidence, biologic behavior, therapy, or prognosis. Three groups of lesions are sufficiently common to permit the formulation of some useful conclusions. In descending order of frequency, these are rhabdomyosarcoma, other sarcomas, and epidermoid carcinoma.

Rhabdomyosarcoma

Rhabdomyosarcoma is an embryonic malignant neoplasm of skeletal muscle. The most common primary site for rhabdomyosarcoma, the head and neck region, accounts for approximately 38% of these tumors.[41] Of those occurring in the head and neck, 30% are found in the oral, pharyngeal, and nasopharyngeal cavities.[19]

Epidemiologically, rhabdomyosarcoma has two age peaks, the first in children 2 to 6 years of age and a second during adolescence. Tumors in the head and neck region occur primarily during the first peak. Li and colleagues[36] found five families among 698 patients in which a second child had a soft tissue sarcoma and in which other close relatives had a high frequency of early-onset breast and other cancers, suggesting a familial syndrome of multiple primary neoplasms. They also noted that the tumor was not associated with congenital defects, as are many other neoplasms of early inception, and that there are no variations of occurrence with time or place that might suggest environmental influences.

Within the oral cavity, the tongue, palate, and cheek are relatively common sites of origin (Fig. 66–6). Among other structures reportedly involved have been gingiva, retromolar trigone, floor of the mouth, and lip. Jones and Campbell[27] state that rhabdomyosarcoma is the most common primary malignant neoplasm of the tongue in children. In most instances, the tumor appears during the first decade of life; about 40% are seen before age 6 years. A small number of cases are congenital (less than 5%), and a few occur in older age groups. Racial distribution is predominantly white.

Rhabdomyosarcoma nearly always occurs as a mass that may have an innocent polypoid appearance, but sub-

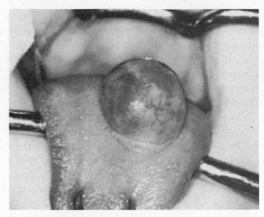

FIGURE 66–6. Rhabdomyosarcoma of the tongue in a 10-month-old infant. The tumor appears innocent but had appeared recently and grown rapidly.

sequently, rapid growth, ulceration, and bleeding suggest the diagnosis. The bulk of the tongue tends to mask the tumor so that any asymmetric expanding mass of that organ in a young child must be considered possible rhabdomyosarcoma. On the order of half the cases have until recently shown local recurrence, distant metastases, or both; nodal metastases are not necessarily regional, and lung and bone spread is also common.

A microscopically embryonal tumor and a more differentiated pleomorphic subtype of tumor are recognized. Alveolar and botryoid varieties have also been described, but these may represent variants of the embryonal tumor. The embryonal subtype is the most frequently observed histologic subtype in children, accounting for approximately 60% to 70% of rhabdomyosarcomas in childhood.[44] However, most tongue lesions tend to have pleomorphic characteristics.

Before the use of adjuvant chemotherapy and radiation therapy, survival rates were discouragingly low.[38, 39] Of the 170 cases studied by Dito and Batsakis,[19] there was a 15.8% 3-year survival rate and an 8.2% 5-year survival rate. In 1973, Donaldson and colleagues[20] reported that 74% of 19 patients were alive 2 years after therapy consisting of local excision if possible, 6000 rad of radiotherapy, and chemotherapy.

Currently, the therapeutic plan for patients with rhabdomyosarcoma is determined by the primary site of involvement; the pathologic changes; and the clinical findings, including location as well as residual disease after attempted surgical excision and the presence of metastatic disease. All children with rhabdomyosarcoma require multimodality therapy. Before administration of adequate radiation therapy and chemotherapy, surgical excision was the mainstay of therapy. However, more recently, local therapy with use of surgical excision, chemotherapy, and radiation therapy has yielded promising results, with remission rates as high as 87%. Within the oral cavity and pharynx, aggressive surgical resection is seldom used because clear surgical margins without unacceptable functional consequences are difficult to achieve. Radiation therapy is an effective method of achieving local control of tumor for patients with microscopic or gross residual disease following initial surgical resection. The timing of radiation therapy generally allows for chemotherapy to be given for 2 to 3 months prior to the initiation of radiation therapy, with the exception of patients with parameningeal disease and evidence of meningeal extension in whom radiation therapy usually begins at the time of diagnosis.[40] Multimodality therapy has yielded excellent results. Data suggest that most patients who are disease-free at 2 years will remain in remission; however, if relapse occurs, the chance of long-term disease-free survival is poor.[46]

Other Oral Sarcomas

The epidemiologic study of 696 childhood sarcomas by Chabalko and associates[11] pointed out that the tumors were found primarily in the head and neck in younger children and in the lower extremities in adolescents. This might be related to differences in the timing of rapid growth phases. Fifty-seven of 297 sarcomas studied in hospitalized patients were in the head and neck. Among the specific sarcomas reported in pediatric patients have been fibrosarcoma (tongue and gingiva), leiomyosarcoma (palate, floor of the mouth, tongue, and gingiva), angiosarcoma (lip and tongue), Kaposi sarcoma (unspecified secondary involvement), reticulum cell sarcoma (sites unspecified), and undifferentiated sarcoma (lip, cheek, palate, and tongue). In general, therefore, almost any type of sarcoma can appear in the oral cavity of a child. The patient is usually in the earlier years and is found to have a bulky, infiltrating, often submucosal mass. Kaposi sarcoma of the oral cavity is extremely rare; however, its presence should alert the clinician to the possibility of acquired immunodeficiency syndrome (AIDS).[49] The long-term results of combined surgery, radiotherapy, and chemotherapy are usually fair to poor. Exceptions, as with well-differentiated fibrosarcoma, exist.

Epidermoid Carcinoma

The relative rarity of epidermoid carcinoma in this region is reflected in Conley's series of head and neck malignant tumors in children, in which only four of 88 tumors were of this type.[13] In a study of 14,253 cases of oral squamous cell carcinoma, Krolls and Hoffman[33] found that 0.05% of the total occurred in patients up to 14 years of age and another 0.15% in patients between 15 and 19 years of age. Further, in 1958, Moore[42] found a total of 40 cases of squamous cancer of the mouth and pharynx in children in the literature, of which eight were in the oral cavity (tongue, four; lip, two; gingiva, one; and unspecified site, one). Fourteen years later, Pichler and co-workers[45] identified a total of 11 reported cases of tongue carcinoma.

Despite the restricted number of cases, Jones[26] believed that certain generalizations could be made: tumor growth rate is rapid in the growing host, symptom duration is usually measured in weeks, regional metastases occur early, and no exogenous etiologic factors are obvious. Preexisting ectodermal defects may predispose a child to tumor formation.[35]

The tongue is the site of predilection, particularly at the junction of the anterior two thirds and the base.

Involvement of lip, palate, and gingiva has also been reported.

Treatment is comparable to that in the adult, but salvage rates are certainly not as good.

Miscellaneous Oral Malignant Neoplasms

Other malignant neoplasms rarely found in the oral cavity of the child include malignant mesenchymoma, neuroblastoma, neuroepithelioma, malignant paraganglioma, hemangiopericytoma, Hand-Schüller-Christian disease, lymphoma, mucoepidermoid carcinoma, adenoid cystic carcinoma, and melanoma. Li and associates[36] found 19 second primary tumors in 414 long-term survivors of other childhood malignant tumors. Seventeen of the 19 patients had received radiotherapy.

Benign Tumors of the Gingiva and Jaws

A wide variety of mass lesions may arise from the gingival soft tissues or from the mandible or maxilla. Those arising within the mandible or maxilla are divided into odontogenic and nonodontogenic. The precise incidence of these major types of lesions is difficult to ascertain largely because the smaller and more common lesions either are not treated or do not come to the attention of the pathologist. In general, however, it appears that gingival lesions are most common, odontogenic neoplasms occur next most frequently, and nonodontogenic tumors of the jaws are least common.

Further confusion arises both from inaccurate classification of some of these lesions and from the continued use of ill-defined clinical terms, such as *epulis* and *epignathus*. Epulis literally means "in the gum" and has been applied to congenital epulis (granular cell tumor), vascular epulis (hemangioma), fibrous epulis (pyogenic granuloma), epulis of pregnancy (granuloma gravidarum), and giant cell epulis (giant cell reparative granuloma). Thus, it is obvious that the term *epulis* is used to refer to any localized, fleshy, small to moderately sized gingival mass regardless of its cause or histologic characteristics. *Epignathus* can indicate any mass present at birth and attached to the jaw or jaws, the hard palate, or both. This term has been variously used to describe hamartomas, choristomas, or teratomas of the region present at birth and believed to be monozygotic in origin or thought to be examples of incomplete dizygotic twinning, whether these abnormalities arose in the jaws, palate, or nasopharynx.

Gingival Tumors

Localized benign tumors include giant cell reparative granuloma, pyogenic granuloma, congenital epulis, and melanotic neuroectodermal tumor of infancy.

Peripheral giant cell reparative granuloma is a sessile, reddish mass of young vascular connective tissue containing multinucleated giant cells. It usually bleeds easily and may occur on the gingiva of either jaw. Frequency of occurrence in boys and girls is equal.[17] The gingiva anterior to the premolars is most often involved. Duration of the lesion is usually a few weeks to a few months. Often there is a history of recent trauma. Excision or curettage is usually curative, but the question of possible recurrence has not been settled.

Pyogenic granuloma is thought to represent an overzealous response to relatively minor local trauma. The lesion usually occurs as an elevated, soft, pedunculated growth with a smooth red surface that bleeds easily. Gingival lesions involve the maxilla more often than the mandible and the buccal aspect more frequently than the lingual aspect of the jaws. On histologic examination, they are composed of numerous small capillaries and are often confused with hemangioma. Treatment consists of local excision; the recurrence rate is 16%.

Congenital epulis is a rare, benign gingival tumor of the newborn that affects girls 80% of the time and occurs on the anterior maxillary gingiva in about 70% of cases. Multiple lesions are seen occasionally. The mass is generally pink, spherical, lobulated, pedunculated, and mucosa covered. It may range from 5 mm to 9 cm in greatest diameter.[15] On microscopic examination, the component cells resemble those of granular cell myoblastoma, although ultrastructural studies have suggested that the lesion may represent an abortive ameloblastoma.[29] Local resection is indicated. Recurrences are unknown.

Melanotic neuroectodermal tumor of infancy has in the past been referred to by such terms as melanotic progonoma, retinal anlage tumor, and pigmented ameloblastoma. Approximately 158 cases have been reported. In most instances, the lesion becomes evident during the first 6 months of life as a 1- to 3-cm mass of the anterior maxilla near the junction of the globular and maxillary processes. The circumscribed mass is covered with mucosa through which gray, tan, brown, or black pigment is visible in some cases.[30] The mandible and remote sites are involved occasionally. Girls are more commonly affected than boys. On histologic examination, a moderately vascular fibrous stroma divides the tumor cells into islands, which contain irregular, slitlike alveoli. The alveoli are lined with large cells, the abundant cytoplasm of which contains melanin. Smaller cells with dark nuclei and little cytoplasm fill the alveoli. Neuroectodermal derivation appears to be the favored histogenic theory. Complete local excision is required. Recurrence rates have been reported to be between 10% and 15%. Cutler and associates[16] report five cases of malignant melanotic neuroectodermal tumor, although it is classically described as a benign tumor.

Epstein pearls are small keratin cysts seen on the alveoli or palate of newborn infants. The lesions exfoliate within a few weeks.

In Caffey disease, bilateral, firm soft tissue swellings occur over the mandible, along with local new bone formation, hyperirritability, and fever.[22]

Diffuse enlargement of the gingiva may be either generalized or localized. Hereditary gingival fibromatosis is transmitted as an autosomal dominant trait and leads to generalized gingival hypertrophy, usually at the time of permanent tooth eruption, owing to collagenous fibrous connective tissue accumulation. Hypertrichosis or cherubism is associated at times. Sporadic cases are termed idiopathic.

Acquired generalized gingival hypertrophy may be due to poor oral hygiene, phenytoin (Dilantin) ingestion, leukemia, the Sturge-Weber syndrome, cyclic neutropenia, or scurvy. Massive hyperplasia may be seen several months after phenytoin therapy is begun and regresses if the drug is discontinued. At least one third of children with leukemia exhibit gingival enlargement that is spongy and friable and may be associated with other oral ulcerations or infiltrations. The Sturge-Weber syndrome can also lead to highly vascular gingival hypertrophy.[43]

Localized gingival enlargement takes the form of bilateral involvement in the region of maxillary or mandibular tuberosities as a hereditary or an idiopathic abnormality.[56] It may be found as a randomly located, sporadic lesion in response to local irritation.

Persistent forms of gingival enlargement that do not respond to therapy in patients with good prognosis may require periodontal treatment and surgery.

Odontogenic Tumors

In a small percentage of cases, any of a multitude of lesions of certain or probable odontogenic origin may expand intraorally to manifest as oral tumors. Among the lesions to be considered are odontogenic cysts, cementoma, dentinoma, odontoma, ameloblastoma, odontogenic myxoma, and odontogenic fibroma.

Odontogenic cysts may be periodontal, dentigerous, or primordial.[31] Primordial cysts arise in the enamel organ before the formation of calcified structures, and they are more common in the mandible than in the maxilla. The third molar region is a site of predilection. The tooth of origin is missing. The cyst may attain considerable size and extend through the cortex of the jaw. Dentigerous cysts arise in the enamel organ after amelogenesis is complete, and the posterior mandible is again a frequent site. The formed associated teeth are unerupted, or their eruption is delayed. These cystic lesions may enlarge beyond the confines of the jaw of origin.

Periodontal cysts that result from root canal infection are relatively rare in children, and only a small percentage of that number enlarge to the point of producing external deformity of the bone.

In the basal cell nevus syndrome, both jaws, particularly the mandible, often contain many keratocysts, which may reach several centimeters in size.

Unusual lesions in childhood are cementomas, consisting of a mass of cementum around a tooth root apex; dentinoma, made up of a small paradental collection of dentin; and odontoma, a probably hamartomatous mixture of ameloblastic epithelium, dentin, cementum, and connective tissue. Rarely, if ever, do these lesions become large enough to impinge on the oral cavity.

Ameloblastoma is a benign odontogenic neoplasm that is seen at times in children, particularly in tropical countries. Blacks are somewhat more commonly affected. The mandible is the area of involvement in approximately 80% of cases. The tumor is multicystic, osteolytic, and expansile, and the diagnosis may be made by the onset of a soft swelling in the mouth. Complete surgical excision is recommended. Recurrence rates as high as 60% are reported when only "conservative" excision is performed.

Most myxomas of the jaws are believed to be odontogenic in origin. Two thirds of myxomas of the jaws become apparent between 10 and 29 years of age, and the two jaws are equally affected, usually posteriorly. Not infrequently, myxoma leads to loosening of the teeth locally and bulging of the contiguous bone. The tumor is locally aggressive and must be treated by wide excision if the reported 25% recurrence rate is to be avoided.

Central fibroma of the jaws (usually the maxilla) has been reported in a small number of cases. Although most investigators agree that it is a rare lesion, Bhaskar[6] reports fibroma to constitute 23% of odontogenic tumors. Treatment is by enucleation.

Nonodontogenic Tumors of the Jaws

Tumors and cysts that do not arise from the dental lamina or its derivatives are classified as nonodontogenic. A considerable number of nonodontogenic cystic and solid tumors may occur in the mandible and maxilla of the young patient and can enlarge sufficiently to produce an intraoral mass.

Nonodontogenic cysts include fissural, hemorrhagic, and aneurysmal types. Fissural cysts are presumed to arise from epithelial inclusions in embryonic lines of closure or from epithelial rests. These cysts are subclassified as globulomaxillary, nasoalveolar, median alveolar, median palatine, or nasopalatine, according to their anatomic locations.[7] Enucleation of the offending cysts is predictably curative.

Hemorrhagic cyst (solitary or traumatic bone cyst) is an idiopathic cavity most commonly found in the posterior portion of the mandible or the incisor region in males 10 to 20 years of age. In excess of 150 cases have been recorded.[25] The cyst appears radiographically as a large area of radiolucency with a scalloped outline that may expand the cortex of the jaw. The cause may be local trauma, and painless enlargement is the usual mode of presentation. Surgical obliteration may be required.

Aneurysmal bone cyst is rare and occurs most often as a honeycombed, enlarging mass in the body of the mandible in females. The cyst may result from vascular changes initiated by a preexisting primary lesion of bone.[9] On radiographic examination, a radiolucency is noted, which is usually multilocular, giving it a soap bubble appearance. The jaw is usually expanded, but the cortex is not destroyed. The lesion is highly vascular and responds in most cases to curettage.

Solid, nonodontogenic jaw tumors, which have been reported to manifest or conceivably can manifest as intraoral swellings, include isolated osteoma, the multiple osteomas of Gardner syndrome, exostosis (torus mandibularis), hemangioma, lipoma, neurogenous tumors, the nonodontogenic varieties of fibroma and myxoma, fibrous histiocytoma, the fibrous gingival tumors associated with tuberous sclerosis, central giant cell reparative granuloma, bony involvement by histiocytosis X (particularly eosinophilic granuloma), the bone lesions of hyperparathyroidism, fibrous dysplasia, and cherubism. Space does not permit a detailed description of the clinical, radiologic, and pathologic features that help differentiate these tumors. However, if one encounters a youthful patient with an expansile lesion of the mandible or maxilla in whom there is no convincing clinical evidence of an odontogenic lesion, this nonodontogenic group of neoplasms should be considered.

Fibrous dysplasia of the jaw is usually monostotic and is not associated with the other stigmas of Albright syndrome. The process appears to be a hamartomatous replacement of bone with collagen, fibroblasts, and osteoid and exhibits its phase of rapid growth in the period from early childhood to adolescence. The lesion is generally unilateral and involves the maxilla more frequently than the mandible. Maxillary lesions tend to expand into the canine fossa and zygomatic areas and, in addition, may lead to proptosis. The mandibular angle is the common site of involvement of that bone, and painless swelling is the typical mode of clinical presentation. The dentition is usually not affected, and the lesion tends to stabilize with maturity. Deformity, pain, and interference with function are reasons for conservative subtotal resection. Complete resection of the involved area often results in considerable functional and cosmetic defects and is not recommended. Malignant change in fibrous dysplasia is unusual, but the true frequency has been difficult to determine. A late growth spurt may herald sarcomatous change. Most reported cases of sarcomatous change have followed radiation therapy for the fibrous dysplasia.

Cherubism is a developmental process of familial occurrence in which bone is replaced by fibrous tissue with giant cells. It is thought to be an autosomal dominant disorder with a 100% penetrance in males, a 50% to 70% penetrance in females, and a variable expressivity. The lesion is somewhat clinically similar to but histologically different from fibrous dysplasia and reparative granuloma. The process classically begins as a symmetric fullness of both mandibular angle regions in the second or third year of life. Enlargement of the involved portions of the bones is greatest during the following 1 to 2 years and ceases at about 10 years of age, with considerable regression of the lesion after puberty. Maxillary involvement is seen in approximately two thirds of cases. The deciduous teeth are shed prematurely, and the permanent teeth often fail to erupt into the mouth. The cherub-like appearance results from a combination of the rounded face and retraction of the lower eyelids, producing an effect of the eyes "raised to heaven."[4] Pain or functional disability seldom occurs, although reactive cervical lymph node hyperplasia is common. Surgical recontouring of the cosmetically disturbed areas is the only therapy required in most patients. Occasional cases may be unilateral or otherwise atypical.

Central giant cell reparative granuloma is seen predominantly in patients between 10 and 20 years of age. This lesion is endosteal and involves the mandible more often than the maxilla. Clinically, the lesion may be asymptomatic or may occur as a localized jaw deformity. Radiographic evaluation reveals radiolucent areas, and a multicystic, soap bubble appearance may be noted at times. Simple surgical excision or curettage is the treatment of choice. Irradiation is contraindicated.

A torus is an exophytic, benign, bony overgrowth that most often arises in the oral cavity (in about 20% of the general population), often at puberty, in the midline of

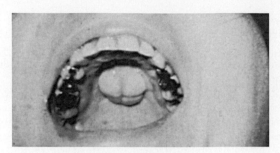

FIGURE 66–7. Torus palatinus. This bony, hard, midline palatal mass is lobulated and mucosa covered.

the hard palate.[4] There is, in addition, an 8% incidence of tori on the lingual aspect of the mandible in the premolar region. The mass may be lobulated (Fig. 66–7). Although these are clearly not mucosal lesions, the overlying mucosa is ulcerated occasionally.

Malignant Tumors of the Jaws

Malignant jaw tumors tend to become clinically evident by causing some combination of expansion of the gingiva, loosening and displacement of teeth, soft tissue ulceration, toothache and local pain, paresthesia or anesthesia in the area, or trismus.

These tumors are uncommon. For example, only four of the 189 head and neck childhood malignant neoplasms studied by Sutow and Montague[53] involved the jaws. It is, therefore, not possible to characterize the behavior of most specific tumor types. As a rule, these lesions resemble their counterparts in other parts of the body. The lesions involved are essentially all mesodermal, and the ultimate prognosis is believed to be poor.

Sporadic reports have indicated that osteogenic sarcoma, fibrosarcoma, osteochondrosarcoma, chondrosarcoma, myxofibrosarcoma, Burkitt sarcoma, Ewing sarcoma, malignant fibrous histiocytoma, or carcinoma occurs in the jaws of children. Wilms tumor metastatic to the mandible has also been documented.

Burkitt lymphoma was originally described as a process in children of Central Africa that often began as a jaw tumor and later became generalized. It is now recognized that both the age and geographic distribution are much broader. Jaw involvement is not universal and attains its highest frequency at age 3 years. Boys are more often affected, and the maxilla is involved twice as often as the mandible. A single posterior maxillary lesion is most often seen first, although multiple lesions of the maxilla or of both jaws may be present, especially if searched for roentgenographically. The tumor is osteolytic and is seen clinically as a whitish mass that expands the paresthesia. Untreated patients die in 4 to 6 months. High-dose alkylating agent chemotherapy has induced remission in more than 90% of cases. However, relapse occurs in approximately two thirds of these patients. Judicious surgical debulking in addition to chemotherapy may improve chances of successful remission. A 20% to 25% long-term remission rate is induced, which may relate as much to the patient's immunologic response as to the therapy.

Most oral fibrosarcomas are periosteal in origin. More

rarely, a medullary-endosteal type occurs. The tumor is osteolytic and is associated with a high local recurrence and metastatic rate.

Osteogenic sarcoma appears to affect boys predominantly. Often affecting the mandible, it is usually a painful, osteolytic, multicystic malignant tumor with a poor prognosis.

Ewing sarcoma is also more often found in the mandible. It probably originates in marrow and has a 5-year survival rate of about 15%.

Chondrosarcoma tends to involve either the anterior maxilla or the posterior (angle) mandible. High recurrence rate, aggressive local extension, and fatal metastases are indicative of its poor prognosis.

Pharynx

Neither the oropharynx nor the hypopharynx is a common site for tumor formation. As a result, most of the available information consists of isolated case reports and anecdotal statements. Only a few lesions, most notably malignant lymphoma of the oropharynx, have been reported often enough to justify any meaningful statements regarding their specific behavior. Benign lesions are more frequently encountered than malignant lesions.

Benign Tumors

An impressive variety of benign lesions may exist in the pharynx of the child. These lesions may represent developmental errors, acquired neoplasia, reaction to local irritation or inflammation, or impingement on the pharyngeal cavity by masses in contiguous areas.

Tumors that have been reported include hamartoma, choristoma, hemangioma, melanotic neuroectodermal tumor, granular choristoma, granular cell myoblastoma, leiomyoma, lipoma, myxoma, fibrous histiocytoma, papilloma, teratoma, pleomorphic adenoma, neurofibroma, localized fibrous lesions, fibromatous polyp, and pyogenic granuloma. Fibromatous polyp is generally seen as a sessile mass of variable size projecting from the posterior hypopharyngeal wall. It probably represents herniation of adipose or fibrous tissue through a portion of the pharyngeal wall weakened by injury or inflammation. Pyogenic granuloma may appear anywhere in the pharynx as a reaction to minor trauma, but such lesions in the tonsillar region can specifically be caused by endotracheal intubation.

The wall of the pharynx can be impinged on by branchial cleft cysts, neurofibromas, or other cervical or parapharyngeal space masses. In addition, any number of nasopharyngeal tumors may occur in the oropharynx; this group includes dermoids (hairy polyp), other teratomas, gliomas, and, on rare occasions, angiofibroma, antralchoanal polyp, or chordoma.

If any of the benign tumors primary in the oropharynx or hypopharynx are enlarging, are symptomatic, or otherwise cause concern, an excisional biopsy should be obtained.

Malignant Tumors

Malignant lymphoma and rhabdomyosarcoma are the two most frequently encountered oropharyngeal or hypopharyngeal cancers. Sporadic reports have been made of other lesions, such as fibrosarcoma of the oropharynx or epidermoid carcinoma of the hypopharynx or tonsil in childhood. Epidermoid carcinoma appears to exhibit a more rampant and rapidly fatal outcome in children than in older patients. Aggressive surgical and radiotherapeutic measures with possible adjuvant immunotherapy are, therefore, often recommended.[52]

Malignant lymphoma is most frequently diagnosed as a tumor of the oropharynx in children 5 to 10 years of age. The tumor may be found in the structures of the Waldeyer ring (tonsil or base of the tongue) or the pharyngeal wall proper. If the Waldeyer ring is involved, cervical nodes usually also exhibit abnormal findings. In either case, no conclusion can be reached about possible infradiaphragmatic disease without a specific search for disseminated tumor. The diagnosis is suggested by a bulky, enlarging oropharyngeal mass, particularly if one tonsil is involved. There may be difficulty swallowing, snoring, a muffled voice, or stridor. If a tonsil is the site of the tumor, its normal cryptic appearance is often replaced by a cauliflower-like neoplasm, the surface of which may be ulcerated or hemorrhagic. Cervical nodes, especially the jugulodigastric, may well be palpable. An excisional biopsy of the affected tonsil is indicated. If the process is limited to the pharynx, radiotherapy is effective. Chemotherapy is reserved for systemic disease.

Rhabdomyosarcoma of the pharynx is of the embryonal type in most cases. The region is one of the least often affected in the head and neck. In the oropharynx, the tumor may arise beneath the tonsil and pharyngeal wall and thus initially mimic peritonsillar, retropharyngeal, or lateral pharyngeal abscess. Treatment is the same as for the tumor in other sites.

SELECTED REFERENCES

Batsakis JG. Tumors of the Head and Neck, 2nd ed. Baltimore, Williams & Wilkins, 1979.

> Most of the head and neck tumors commonly encountered in infants and children are described in a concise and accurate way. A number of controversial groups of lesions are covered effectively.

Jones PG, Campbell PE. Tumors of the head and neck. In Jones PG, Campbell PE (eds). Tumors of Infancy and Childhood. London, Blackwell, 1976, pp 295–396.

> This chapter provides a well-organized, complete, and clear overview of the spectrum of pediatric head and neck tumors, including an extensive list of references.

REFERENCES

1. Abbey LM, Page DG, Sawyer DR. The clinical and histopathologic features of a series of 464 oral squamous cell papillomas. Oral Surg 49:419, 1980.
2. Apfelberg DB, Morton MR, Lash H, et al. Benefits of the CO_2 laser in oral hemangioma excision. Plast Reconstr Surg 75:46, 1985.
3. Bartley PC, Lloyd HM, Aitken RE. Medullary carcinoma of the thyroid, multiple pheochromocytoma, mucosal neuromas, Marfanoid habitus and other abnormalities (Sipple's syndrome). Med J Aust 2: 1973, 1976.
4. Batsakis JG. Tumors of the Head and Neck, 2nd ed. Baltimore, Williams & Wilkins, 1979.
5. Beckwith JB. Macroglossia, omphalocele, adrenal cytomegaly, gigantism and hyperplastic visceromegaly. Birth Defects 5:188, 1969.
6. Bhaskar SN. Oral tumors of infancy and childhood. J Pediatr 63: 195, 1963.
7. Bhaskar SN. Oral lesions in infants and newborn. Dent Clin North Am July:421, 1966.
8. Bill AH Jr, Sumner DS. A unified concept of lymphangioma and cystic hygroma. Surg Gynecol Obstet 120:79, 1965.
9. Buraczewski J, Dabska M. Pathogenesis of aneurysmal bone cyst: relationship between the aneurysmal bone cyst and fibrous dysplasia of bone. Cancer 28:597, 1971.
10. Cataldo E, Mosadomi A. Mucoceles of the oral mucous membrane. Arch Otolaryngol 91:360, 1970.
11. Chabalko JJ, Creagan ET, Fraumeni JF Jr. Epidemiology of selected sarcomas in children. J Natl Cancer Inst 53:675, 1974.
12. Cherrick HM, Dunlap CE, King OH Jr. Leiomyomas of the oral cavity. Oral Surg 35:54, 1973.
13. Conley J. Concepts in Head and Neck Surgery. New York, Grune & Stratton, 1970, p 187.
14. Crockett DM, Healy GB, McGill TJI, et al. Benign lesions of the nose, oral cavity, and oropharynx in children: excision by carbon dioxide laser. Ann Otol Rhinol Laryngol 94:489, 1985.
15. Custer RP, Fust JA. Congenital epulis. Am J Clin Pathol 22:1044, 1952.
16. Cutler LS, Chaudhry AP, Topazian R. Melanotic neuroectodermal tumor of infancy. Cancer 48:257, 1981.
17. Dehner LP. Tumors of the mandible and maxilla in children. I. Clinicopathological study of 46 histologically benign lesions. Cancer 31:364, 1973.
18. Dehner LP, Askin FB. Tumors of fibrous tissue origin in childhood. Cancer 38:888, 1976.
19. Dito WR, Batsakis JG. Intra-oral, pharyngeal and nasopharyngeal rhabdomyosarcomas. Arch Otolaryngol 77:123, 1963.
20. Donaldson SS, Castro JR, Wilbur JR, et al. Rhabdomyosarcoma of head and neck in children. Cancer 31:26, 1973.
21. Gorlin RJ, Jirasek JE. Oral cysts containing gastric or intestinal mucosa. Arch Otolaryngol 91:594, 1970.
22. Gorlin RJ, Pindborg JJ. Syndromes of the Head and Neck. New York, McGraw-Hill, 1964, pp 325–330.
23. Greer RO Jr, Pooper HA, DeMento FJ. Cowden's disease (multiple hamartoma syndrome). Report of a limited mucocutaneous form. J Periodontol 47:531, 1976.
24. Hawkins DB, Crockett DM, Kahlstrom EJ, et al. Corticosteroid management of airway hemangiomas: long term follow-up. Laryngoscope 94:633, 1984.
25. Huebner GR, Turlington EG. So-called traumatic (hemorrhagic) bone cysts of the jaws. Oral Surg 31:354, 1971.
26. Jones JH. Oral carcinoma in the young patient with a report of two cases. Br J Oral Surg 8:159, 1970.
27. Jones PG, Campbell PE. Tumors of the head and neck. In Jones PG, Campbell PE (eds). Tumors of Infancy and Childhood. London, Blackwell Scientific Publications, 1976, pp 295–396.
28. Kamalamma MK, Prabhu SR, Shetty JN, et al. The white sponge nevus. Oral Surg 30:51, 1970.
29. Kay S, Elzay R, Willson M. Ultrastructural observations on a gingival cell tumor (congenital epulis). Cancer 27:674, 1971.
30. Kaye BL, Robinson DW, Masters FW, et al. Tumors of the premaxilla in children: report of two unusual cases and a review. Plast Reconstr Surg 37:131, 1966.
31. Killey HC, Kay LW. Benign Cystic Lesions of the Jaws. Edinburgh, E & S Livingstone, 1966.
32. Komiyama M, Nakajima H, Kitano S, et al. Endovascular treatment of huge cervicofacial hemangioma, complicated by Kasabach-Merrit syndrome. Pediatr Neurosurg 33(1):26, 2000.
33. Krolls SO, Hoffman S. Squamous cell carcinoma of the oral soft tissues: a statistical analysis of 14,253 cases by age, sex and race of patients. J Am Dent Assoc 92:571, 1976.

34. Krolls SO, Jacoway JR, Alexander WN. Osseous choristomas (osteomas) of intraoral soft tissues. Oral Surg 32:588, 1971.
35. Lancaster L, Fournet LF. Carcinoma of the tongue in a child. J Oral Surg 27:269, 1969.
36. Li FP, Cassady JR, Jaffe N. Risk of second tumors in survivors of childhood cancer. Cancer 35:1230, 1975.
37. Masson JK, Soule EH. Desmoid tumors of the head and neck. Am J Surg 112:615, 1981.
38. Maurer HM, Foulkes M, Gehan EA, et al. Intergroup Rhabdomyosarcoma Study. (IRSII preliminary report.) Proc Am Soc Clin Oncol 2:70, 1983.
39. Maurer HM, Moon TE, Donaldson M, et al. The Intergroup Rhabdomyosarcoma Study. Cancer 40:2015, 1977.
40. Maurer HM, Gehan EA, Beltangady M, et al. The Intergroup Rhabdomyosarcoma Study—II. Cancer 71(5):1904, 1993.
41. Miser JS, Pizzo PA. Soft tissue sarcomas in childhood. Pediatr Clin North Am 32:779, 1985.
42. Moore C. Visceral squamous cancer in childhood. Pediatrics 21:573, 1958.
43. Mostehy MR, Stallard RE. The Sturge-Weber syndrome: its periodontal significance. J Periodontol 40:243, 1969.
44. Newton WA, Soule EH, Hamoudi AB, et al. Histopathology of childhood sarcomas. J Clin Oncol 6(1):67, 1988.
45. Pichler AG, Williams JR, Moore JA. Carcinomas of the tongue in childhood and adolescence: report of a case and review of the literature. Arch Otolaryngol 95:178, 1972.
46. Raney RB, Crist WM, Maurer HM, et al. Prognosis of children with soft tissue sarcoma who relapse after achieving a complete response: a report from the Intergroup Rhabdomyosarcoma Study. Cancer 52:44, 1983.
47. Resouly A. Sublingual dermoids. J Laryngol Otol 90:487, 1976.
48. Robins RB. Sublingual branchial cleft cyst: a case report. Laryngoscope 79:288, 1969.
49. Rubinstein A. Pediatric AIDS. Curr Probl Pediatr 16:363, 1986.
50. Rush BF Jr, Chambers RG, Ravitch MM. Cancer of the head and neck in children. Surgery 53:210, 1963.
51. Smith RF, Toomey JM, Snyder GG III. Facial plexiform neurofibroma. Laryngoscope 87:2101, 1977.
52. Son YH, Kapp DS. Oral cavity and oropharyngeal cancer in a younger population. Cancer 55:441, 1985.
53. Sutow WW, Montague ED. Pediatric tumors. In MacComb WS, Fletcher GH (eds). Cancer of the Head and Neck. Baltimore, Williams & Wilkins, 1967, pp 428–446.
54. Webb CJ, Porter G, Spencer MG, Sissons GR. Cavernous haemangioma of the nasal bones: an alternative management option. J Laryngol Otol 114:287, 2000.
55. Witkop CJ, Niswander JD. Focal epithelial hyperplasia in Central and South American Indians and Latinos. Oral Surg 20:213, 1965.
56. Zagarelli EV, Kutscher AH, Lichtenthal R. Idiopathic gingival fibromatosis: report of 20 cases. Am J Dig Dis 8:782, 1963.

67

Congenital Malformations of the Esophagus

Stephen E. Morrow, M.D., and Don K. Nakayama, M.D.

Congenital malformations of the esophagus are usually first recognized in infancy or childhood because of respiratory or feeding difficulties. However, they may remain asymptomatic until later in life and may be difficult to detect without appropriate diagnostic tests. Physicians need to be familiar with the diagnosis of these entities so that corrective surgery can take place before complications ensue. This chapter highlights the essential features of two common congenital abnormalities of the esophagus: esophageal atresia (EA), with or without tracheoesophageal fistula (TEF), and duplications of the esophagus.

Esophageal Atresia and Tracheoesophageal Fistula

The first description of EA was published by Durston in 1670,[12] while Gibson was the first to record a case of EA with TEF.[15] These anomalies received little attention until 1929, when Vogt published his classification system, which was modified soon afterward by Gross for clinical use.[17, 48] Sadly, these defects were invariably fatal until 1939, when Ladd and Leven independently reported the first survivors. These innovative pioneers used a staged approach with initial gastrostomy followed by fistula ligation. Later, they restored enteric continuity with antethoracic skin tubes.[28, 29] Haight was the first to successfully perform direct repair of EA using a transthoracic approach.[18] The basic operative techniques used by these brilliant surgeons have withstood the test of time. Advancements in the last 60 years have chiefly been those of improved perioperative management, anesthesia, and nutritional support.

Embryology

According to Smith,[43] TEF and EA develop as a result of incomplete separation of the respiratory and digestive divisions of the primitive foregut. According to this traditional explanation, at the 22nd day of gestation (in a 3-mm embryo) a ventral diverticulum develops from the primitive foregut distal to the pharyngeal pouches. This diverticulum, the future larynx and trachea, separates from the underlying esophagus by midline migration of the lateral foregut grooves. Aberrant growth of these grooves causes EA, while failure of the two grooves to fuse in the midline leads to TEF.[9] However, Kluth,[26] using electron microscopy to study chick embryos, failed to find any sign of lateral foregut grooves. From these more recent observations, he concluded that the esophagus and trachea develop by simple reduction of the size of the foregut, and that the pathogenesis of isolated atresias and fistulas is not caused by faulty foregut development. Rather, these lesions are the result of defective development occurring *after* complete tracheal and esophageal differentiation. By this theory, EA might arise from insufficient circulation and subsequent hypoxia (known to be a factor in the pathogenesis of intestinal atresias), while TEF would result from an abnormally ventral location of the differentiated esophagus, causing it to fuse with the trachea (see Chap. 50).

Classification and Incidence

TEF/EA in various forms is found in approximately 1 in 3000 live births, with a slight male predominance.[9] Although a comprehensive atlas of some 96 variants of this anomaly has been published by Kluth,[25] five types predominate: atresia with fistula involving the distal esophageal pouch (~85%), atresia without fistula (~7%), fistula without atresia (~4% to 5%), atresia with fistula to the proximal pouch only (~1% to 2%), and atresia with fistula to both pouches (~1% to 4%) (Fig. 67–1). As one might expect for a defect occurring at such a critical stage of embryologic development, other anomalies accompany TEF/EA in slightly more than 50% of cases. The VACTERL (vertebral/vascular, anorectal, cardiac, tracheoesophageal, radial/renal, limb deformities) syndrome describes a constellation of associated anomalies that can occur in various combinations in these children.[23] Other abnormalities, such as Down syndrome and low birth weight, also occur with increased frequency (Table 67–1). TEF/EA occasionally occurs in a familial setting.[20]

Presentation and Diagnosis

TEF/EA is sometimes encountered prenatally on obstetric ultrasonography. Accurate diagnosis is difficult, however, even among experienced examiners. Polyhydramnios, a nonspecific finding, suggests possible upper

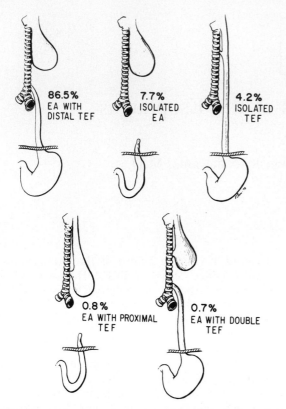

FIGURE 67–1. Esophageal atresia and tracheoesophageal fistula: schematic of the most common variants of these anomalies with the approximate incidence of each. EA, esophageal atresia; TEF, tracheoesophageal fistula.

gastrointestinal obstruction. More than 90% of fetuses with EA will have polyhydramnios due to diminished ability of swallowed fluid to reach the stomach. The esophageal pouch may be prominent, suggesting EA, and the absence of liquid-filled loops of bowel further supports this diagnosis (Fig. 67–2).

Newborn infants with TEF/EA usually have early feeding and respiratory difficulties. Babies with EA cannot swallow saliva or feedings and therefore drool excessively. They may aspirate the contents of the upper esophageal pouch, causing choking, apnea, or pneumonia. Similarly, the abnormal communication with the airway in isolated TEF may cause aspiration as swallowed material enters the trachea, or stomach contents may reflux into the lungs through a distal TEF. With positive-pressure ventilation, delivered breaths from a mask or endotracheal tube may force air into the esophagus and distal gastrointestinal tract, causing abdominal distention.

Associated anomalies (VACTERL) may be obvious at birth and may prompt investigation for tracheoesophageal deformity. Conversely, if tracheoesophageal deformity is discovered, a careful search for other anomalies is mandatory. Ultrasonography is useful to examine the heart and kidneys for associated pathology.

The first diagnostic step is to demonstrate the presence of EA by attempting to pass a tube from the mouth into the stomach. If passage is impossible or if gastric juice is not obtained, anteroposterior and lateral chest films should be obtained to visualize the position of the

catheter, which is typically coiled in the proximal esophageal pouch (Fig. 67–3). The administration of contrast material is neither necessary nor recommended.

In the presence of EA, air in the bowel implies a distal fistula (Fig. 67–4). If the abdomen is gasless (i.e., no air-filled stomach or bowel loops are seen), the baby is presumed to have an isolated EA. However, mucous plugs can sometimes occlude a distal fistula, leading to an erroneous conclusion about a gasless abdomen seen on plain films.[16] Bronchoscopy may help locate fistulas and guide operative strategy. Kosloske and associates[27] recommend routine preoperative bronchoscopy because it changed patient management in 31% of cases. Among such changes cited were an unsuspected cervical fistula repaired by a cervical approach, unusual variants of TEF (trifurcation, quadrifurcation) requiring specific dissection, congenital stenosis of the right mainstem bronchus needing postoperative dilatation, and severe tracheobronchitis contraindicating thoracotomy.

The so-called H-type fistula, or isolated TEF, may elude diagnosis without a high index of suspicion. Its presence should be considered in babies with recurrent pneumonias or a history of choking with feeding. It is noteworthy that the opening in the trachea is typically more cephalad than the opening in the esophagus. This arrangement consequently gives an "N" rather than a horizontal "H" configuration that is directly visible from the trachea during bronchoscopy. Contrast esophagograms are frequently employed to demonstrate TEFs, but the slanted orientation of the N configuration may prevent reflux into the fistula and produce a false-negative result (Fig. 67–5). TEFs may vary in size, from the width of a mainstem bronchus to a small punctum in the posterior tracheal wall. A ureteral stent or Fogarty catheter may be helpful in probing small fistulas (see Chap. 76).

TABLE 67–1. Associated Anomalies in 1058 Patients with Esophageal Atresia and/or Tracheoesophageal Fistula

Anomalies	No.	%	
None	553	52	
Associated anomalies	505	48	
(849 anomalies)			
Congenital heart disease	201	19	
Gastrointestinal	134	13	
Intestinal atresia		38	3.6
Malrotation		21	2.0
Genitourinary	109	10	
Imperforate anus	99	9.4	
Musculoskeletal	91	8.6	
Arm and hand		45	4.3
Hemivertebrae		19	1.8
Face	53	5.0	
Cleft lip and/or palate		28	2.6
Central nervous system	35	3.3	
Down syndrome	28	2.6	
Larynx, trachea, and lung	19	1.8	
Diaphragm	17	1.6	
Vascular	11	1.0	
Liver and spleen	8	0.8	
Miscellaneous	43	4.1	

Data from Holder TM, Cloud DT, Lewis JE Jr, et al. Esophageal atresia and tracheoesophageal fistula. A survey of its members by the Surgical Section of the American Academy of Pediatrics. Pediatrics 34:542, 1964.

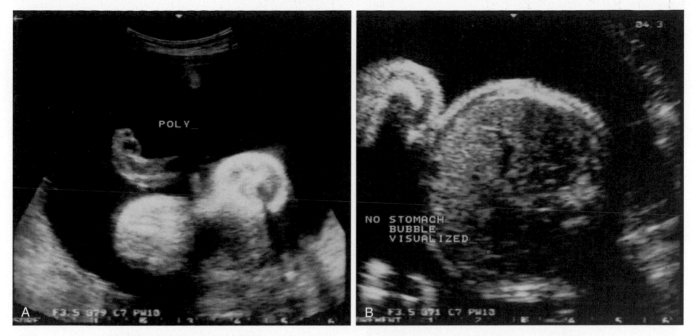

FIGURE 67–2. Prenatal diagnosis of EA by ultrasonography. *A* shows polyhydramnios, indicating possible enteric obstruction. *B* shows the absence of a fluid-filled stomach or intestines, a finding highly suspicious for EA. (Courtesy of Dr. Nancy Chescheir, Department of Obstetrics and Gynecology, University of North Carolina, Chapel Hill, NC.)

Treatment

Specific interventions should be initiated immediately after diagnosis to prevent aspiration and gastric reflux. A sump catheter should be placed into the upper esophageal pouch and connected to constant suction. The baby should be placed in a prone, head-up position on a flat platform to minimize gastroesophageal reflux. Traditionally, a gastrostomy was used routinely to decompress the stomach and allow access for feedings before definitive repair. In 1989, however, the routine use of this procedure was challenged,[47] and most surgeons currently reserve gastrostomy for severely ill or low–birth-weight babies who cannot undergo urgent primary repair. In this setting, gastric decompression is usually beneficial. However, in babies with noncompliant lungs on positive-pressure ventilation, a gastrostomy may actually compromise ventilation by offering a path of least resistance through the fistula. Emergency division of the TEF then becomes necessary.[47]

The timing of operative intervention has traditionally been based on the Waterston risk criteria, which place babies with TEF/EA into one of three categories based on body weight (weight greater than 2.5 kg, between 2.0 and 2.5 kg, and less than 2.0 kg) and the presence or absence of pneumonia or associated anomalies. Those infants with lowest risk (Waterston class A, weight over 2.5 kg, no complicating conditions) underwent immediate repair, while those in the intermediate-risk category (Waterston class B, weight between 2.0 and 2.5 kg, no associated problems) were treated with "delayed primary repair," consisting of gastrostomy followed by thoracotomy, after pneumonia or other, more urgent anomalies had been controlled. Infants in the high-risk category (Water-

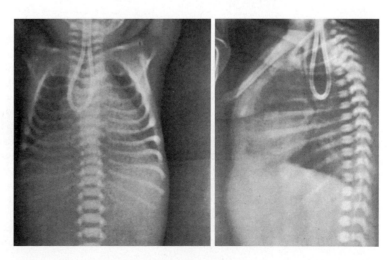

FIGURE 67–3. EA demonstrated by the curled catheter in the upper esophageal pouch. This simple technique is the initial diagnostic maneuver of choice. Note the gasless abdomen, which strongly suggests the absence of a fistula.

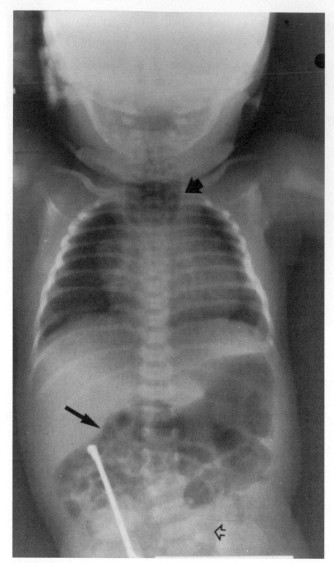

FIGURE 67–4. Plain film showing air in the upper esophageal pouch *(thick arrow)* as well as in the intestinal tract *(thin arrow)*. This classic pattern is typical of EA with a distal TEF, which is by far the most common variant of this disorder. Note also the vertebral abnormality *(open arrow)*, a common accompaniment of EA/TEF. (Courtesy of Dr. David Merten, Department of Radiology, University of North Carolina, Chapel Hill, NC.)

ston class C, weight under 2.0 kg, or presence of pneumonia or cardiac anomalies) were treated in a staged fashion with sequential gastrostomy, fistula ligation, and reconstruction. However, advances in neonatal intensive care have prompted a revision of the traditional approach to TEF/EA in recent years. Today, even ill, low–birth-weight babies undergo primary repair successfully. Accordingly, a new risk classification has been proposed recognizing that prognosis in cases of TEF/EA is influenced primarily by ventilator dependence and severe associated anomalies.[36] The presence of either, or low birth weight, places the baby into a high-risk category. While most infants undergo early primary repair, reasons for delay include severe associated anomalies (such as cardiac defects that may have a priority in management), severe

pneumonia or respiratory distress, and a long gap between esophageal pouches.

Although the technical details of the repair are beyond the scope of this chapter, several points warrant consideration. An extrapleural approach through a right thoracotomy usually affords the best exposure of the middle and upper esophagus. However, if a right-sided aortic arch is present, the left chest is chosen for the incision. Most surgeons prefer to preserve the integrity of the pleural space by carefully peeling the parietal pleura off the chest wall. Should a postoperative anastomotic leak occur, the pleural space is protected from soilage, and pleural empyema and scarring are thus avoided. The fistula is identified and divided, leaving a cuff of esophagus on the trachea to be oversewn with interrupted sutures. This maneuver reduces the risk of tracheal stenosis. The proximal pouch is mobilized with the help of the anesthesiologist, who pushes gently on the upper pouch with a Hurst bougie. During this maneuver the surgeon should carefully examine the proximal pouch for a fistula. Whereas branches of the inferior thyroid artery supply the proximal pouch in an axial fashion and allow extensive mobilization, the distal pouch has a segmental blood supply from intercostal vessels and therefore must be mobilized cautiously. Most surgeons prefer a single-layer anastomosis, accepting a higher leak rate (17% versus 6% for double-layer repairs) in return for a lower stricture rate (4% versus 23%).[32] As in all anastomoses, a tension-free approximation with adequate blood supply is critical for a successful outcome.

"Long-Gap" Atresia and Esophageal Replacement

If the space between pouches cannot be closed without undue tension, extramucosal circular myotomies can lengthen the upper pouch. Up to three myotomies, each creating about 1 cm of extra length, may allow a primary anastomosis.[30] The best approach to the "long-gap" problem may be to recognize its presence preoperatively and to delay repair. The gap spontaneously narrows to about 1.5 to 2 cm in the first 2 to 3 weeks of life.[10] Puri and colleagues[37] state that maximal growth and hypertrophy of the segments will have occurred by approximately 8 weeks and recommend operation after that age. Others recommend stretching the pouches with bougies from above and below to encourage growth. Once the gap narrows to about 2 cm or less, anastomosis is possible.

If the gap persists, or if significant esophageal complications ensue (usually aspiration, apnea, or bradycardia), replacement of the esophagus is necessary. The upper pouch is exteriorized to the left lateral neck as a cervical esophagostomy, commonly referred to as a "spit fistula." The baby's skin at the site of the esophagostomy must be protected from excoriation and breakdown until the time of esophageal reconstruction. Most surgeons prefer to delay esophageal replacement until the child reaches 1 year of age. Viable options in babies include colon interposition, construction of a gastric tube, and gastric interposition. Jejunal interposition is infrequently attempted in children owing to the small size of the mesenteric vessels, which are too short to extend into the thorax and are

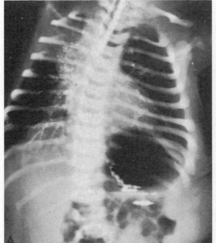
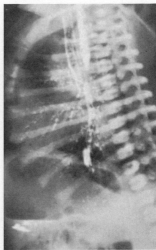
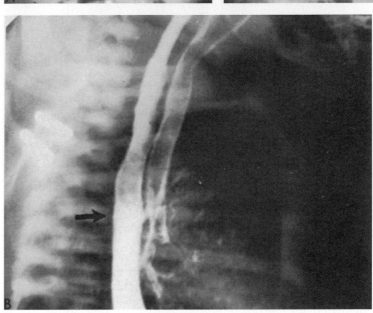

FIGURE 67–5. The father of this 6-week-old girl had been operated on 21 years previously for EA with TEF. Since birth the baby had had several episodes of apparent aspiration when feeding, as well as multiple bouts of abdominal distention with crying. A barium swallow did not demonstrate any fistula. Suddenly, on this examination, the fistula opened, generously outlining the trachea and causing some aspiration. Only a mild pneumonia occurred. *A,* Anteroposterior and lateral films do not definitely demonstrate the fistula. *B,* Cineradiographic study nicely demonstrates the fistula, which is considerably lower than usual *(arrow).*

prone to spasm. Colon interposition has been the traditional procedure of choice. Construction of a gastric tube using the greater curvature has also proved successful over the long term.[13] Anderson and colleagues[1] compared these two procedures and found no difference in patient acceptance, nutrition, growth, or complications. The gastric transposition, frequently used in adults, has been largely avoided in children because of problems with respiratory embarrassment caused by a disproportionately large stomach lodged within a restricted mediastinum. However, Spitz and colleagues[45, 46] reported that gastric pull-up in the posterior mediastinal position is successful in infants. Their results compare favorably with those from colon interposition. During esophageal replacement, it is important to excise or ablate the native esophagus to prevent mucocele and subsequent respiratory compromise.[21]

Complications

Although complications occur relatively frequently, patients without severe associated anomalies have an excel-

lent chance of leading normal lives. Chetcuti and Phelan,[6] in a series of 334 repaired TEF/EA patients, found that two thirds required hospitalization postoperatively, and one half needed one or more additional operations. The operations most frequently performed were esophageal dilatation (47%), foreign body removal (29%), fundoplication (13%), and resection of esophageal stricture (11%).

Anastomotic leaks usually resolve with parenteral nutrition and posterior drainage, although repeat thoracotomy is required if healing does not occur. Unfortunately, strictures and recurrent fistulas often (in 25% of cases) follow anastomotic leaks.

Strictures are the most common complication and have been associated with tension on the anastomosis, two-layer closure, use of silk sutures, end-to-side anastomoses, and gastroesophageal reflux.[7] They are sufficiently common to warrant a barium contrast study or esophagoscopy before hospital discharge in all patients.[40] Although strictures may respond to bougienage, concomitant reflux usually mandates an antireflux procedure (Fig. 67–6). Children with a history of long-gap atresia are more prone to reflux than those without such a history (32% versus 3%).[33]

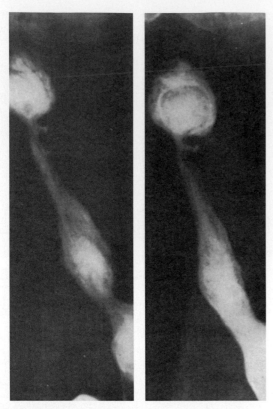

FIGURE 67–6. Esophageal anastomotic stricture and ulcer caused by reflux. This child underwent repair of EA and TEF. A persistent anastomotic narrowing was noted to recur repeatedly, and an ulcer developed at the anastomosis. Gastrointestinal series demonstrated reflux on several occasions. Gastric fundoplication resulted in prompt resolution of the stricture.

Antireflux procedures are frequently needed in TEF/EA patients.[5, 31] Wheatley and associates[50] found a 33% incidence of recurrent reflux in TEF/EA children who had undergone Nissen fundoplication, compared with 10% in children without TEF/EA undergoing the same procedure. Prolonged dysmotility and dysphagia, seen in two thirds of children after repair of TEF/EA, usually resolves by 5 years of age (see Chaps. 52 and 69).[6]

Respiratory problems arise in 46% of TEF/EA patients.[8] While gastroesophageal reflux is the most common cause, 10% to 20% develop tracheomalacia,[14, 32] which requires bronchoscopy to distinguish it from reflux.[8] Aortopexy affords excellent long-term relief of symptoms for severe tracheomalacia.[22] If aortopexy fails, the patient may require an airway splint or tracheostomy.

These frequent delayed complications involving both the esophagus and the trachea mandate regular surveillance for all TEF/EA patients through adulthood.

Duplications of the Esophagus

This interesting anomaly was first described nearly 300 years ago.[3, 49] Although rare (with an estimated incidence of 1 in 8200 births), esophageal duplications are the most common esophageal tumor in infancy and are second in incidence only to leiomyomas among benign esophageal tumors in all age groups.[2] Embryologists believe that these lesions result when vacuolated cells in the solid primitive esophagus fail to coalesce properly while forming the lumen. Duplications are cystic or tubular in shape and consist of two layers of smooth muscle enveloping a mucosa-lined cavity.[11] Kirwan and associates[24] state that true duplications are characterized by a double layer of smooth muscle, lack of cartilaginous elements, and absence of vertebral anomalies. These features distinguish them from bronchogenic cysts and enteric cysts. Bronchogenic cysts are caused by defective lung budding and contain cartilage, whereas enteric cysts are thought to arise from an anomalous split notochord and therefore connect to the vertebral column. Esophageal duplications occur multiply in 15% of cases[4, 41] and usually do not communicate with the true esophageal lumen, although they often share a common wall. In their review of the literature, Arbona and colleagues[2] found that 60% of these lesions occur in the lower third of the esophagus.

Clinical Manifestation and Diagnosis

Lesions in the lower esophagus are usually asymptomatic in childhood, but upper esophageal lesions may cause respiratory symptoms in infants.[19] Other associated anomalies are common, such as vertebral defects, TEF/EA, and duplications elsewhere in the digestive tract.

The mucosal lining of these duplications is varied, and complications frequently arise in untreated lesions according to their mucosal type. For example, respiratory mucosa often creates a mucocele that may slowly enlarge and cause respiratory embarrassment from extrinsic airway compression. Infection represents the most common sequela of untreated cases.[24] Gastric mucosa may cause peptic ulceration, bleeding, and perforation.[34] Both exocrine and endocrine pancreatic tissues have been found in these cysts.[38] Malignant transformation has also been described, although cases have been restricted to older age groups.[35]

The evaluation of these lesions is usually prompted either by respiratory symptoms or by the incidental finding of a posterior mediastinal mass on chest film.[44] A contrast esophagogram typically shows extrinsic compression or displacement of the esophagus. Although esophagoscopy can confirm extrinsic compression and rule out mucosal ulceration, this examination is rarely diagnostic.[39] Computed tomographic (CT) scans with contrast show enhancement of the wall of the lesion, thereby distinguishing esophageal duplications from neurogenic tumors. Magnetic resonance imaging, superior to CT for soft tissue imaging, can accurately delineate the margins of the lesion and eliminate spinal communication from consideration.[39] If doubt persists, myelography should be used to resolve this important issue. Holcomb and colleagues[22] recommend an abdominal sonogram to search for synchronous enteric duplications.

Treatment

The preferred management for this disorder is surgical excision,[22] which definitively treats the symptoms, prevents complications, and excludes malignancy. It is preferable to completely excise the lesion without entering the true esophageal lumen. If communication with the true esophageal lumen exists, this must be closed. The surgeon must be prepared for communication with the dura and attachment to the vertebral column. This feature is specifically sought on preoperative scans. It is important to dissect with care to avoid injury to important adjacent structures, such as the recurrent nerve, trachea, and great vessels, which at times are adherent as a result of inflammation. The safest course is often to open the cyst, remove the mucosa, and leave the remainder of the lesion in situ.

SELECTED REFERENCES

Boix-Ochoa J, Marhuenda C. Gastroesophageal reflux. In Ashcraft KW, Holder TM (eds). Pediatric Surgery, 3rd ed. Philadelphia, WB Saunders, 2000, pp 370–390.

> *The author covers the subject of reflux disease in detail and also describes the relative merits and limitations of both the Nissen and Thal fundoplications.*

Jolley SG. Current surgical considerations in gastroesophageal reflux disease in infancy and childhood. Surg Clin North Am 72:1365, 1992.

> *This excellent review of the diagnosis and management of gastroesophageal reflux is written by a pediatric surgeon who is considered a leading authority on the subject.*

Harmon CM, Coran AG. Congenital anomalies of the esophagus. In O'Neill JA, Rowe MI, Grosjild JL, et al (eds). Pediatric Surgery, 5th ed. St. Louis, Mosby, 1998, pp 941–967.

> *This work, directed primarily toward the pediatric surgeon, is widely regarded as the most comprehensive textbook on pediatric surgery currently available.*

REFERENCES

1. Anderson KD, Noblett H, Belsey R, et al. Long-term follow-up of children with colon and gastric tube interposition for esophageal atresia. Surgery 111:131, 1992.
2. Arbona JL, Figueroa F, Mayoral J. Congenital esophageal cysts: case report and review of the literature. Am J Gastroenterol 79:177, 1984.
3. Blasius G. Observationes medicae anatomae rariores. Amestelodami Langerach, 1711.
4. Bower RJ, Sieber WK, Kiesewetter WB. Alimentary tract duplications in children. Ann Surg 188:66, 1977.
5. Boyle JT. Gastroesophageal reflux in the pediatric patient. Gastroenterol Clin North Am 18:317, 1989.
6. Chetcuti P, Phelan PD. Gastrointestinal morbidity and growth after repair of oesophageal atresia and tracheo-oesophageal fistula. Arch Dis Child 68:163, 1993.
7. Chittmittrapap S, Spitz L, Kiely EM, et al. Anastomotic stricture following repair of esophageal atresia. J Pediatr Surg 25:508, 1990.
8. Delius RE, Wheatley MJ, Coran AG. Etiology and management of respiratory complications after repair of esophageal atresia with tracheoesophageal fistula. Surgery 112:527, 1992.
9. de Lorimier AA, Harrison MR. Esophageal atresia: embryogenesis and management. World J Surg 9:250, 1985.
10. de Lorimier AA, Harrison MR. Long gap esophageal atresia. Primary anastomosis after esophageal elongation by bougienage and esophagomyotomy. J Thorac Cardiovasc Surg 79:138, 1980.
11. Dresler CM, Patterson GA, Taylor BR, et al. Complete foregut duplication. Ann Thorac Surg 50:306, 1990.
12. Durston WA. A narrative of monstrous birth in Plymouth October 22, 1670; together with the anatomical observations taken thereupon by William Durston, Doctor in Physick, and communication to Dr. Tim Clerk. Philos Trans R Soc V:2096, 1670.
13. Ein SH, Shandling B, Stephens CA. Twenty-one year experience with the pediatric gastric tube. J Pediatr Surg 22:77, 1987.
14. Filler RM, Messineo A, Vinograd I. Severe tracheomalacia associated with esophageal atresia: results of surgical treatment. J Pediatr Surg 27:1136, 1992.
15. Gibson T. The Anatomy of Humane Bodies Epitomized, 6th ed. London, Awnsham & Churchill, 1703.
16. Goh DW, Brereton RJ, Spitz L. Esophageal atresia with obstructed tracheoesophageal fistula and gasless abdomen. J Pediatr Surg 26:160, 1991.
17. Gross RE. Surgery of Infancy and Childhood. Philadelphia, WB Saunders, 1953.
18. Haight C, Towsley HA. Congenital atresia of the esophagus with tracheoesophageal fistula: extrapleural ligation of fistula and end-to-end anastomosis of esophageal segments. Surg Gynecol Obstet 76:672, 1943.
19. Haller JA, Shermeta DW, Donahoo JS, et al. Life-threatening respiratory distress from mediastinal masses in infants. Ann Thorac Surg 19:364, 1975.
20. Hausmann PF, Close AS, Williams LP. Occurrence of tracheoesophageal fistula in three consecutive siblings. Surgery 41:542, 1957.
21. Heiss K, Wesson D, Bohn D, et al. Respiratory failure due to retained esophagus: a complication of esophageal replacement. J Pediatr Surg 26:1359, 1991.
22. Holcomb GW, Gheissari A, O'Neill JA, et al. Surgical management of alimentary tract duplications. Ann Surg 209:167, 1989.
23. Holder TM, Cloud DT, Lewis JE Jr, et al. Esophageal atresia and tracheoesophageal fistula. A survey of its members by the Surgical Section of the American Academy of Pediatrics. Pediatrics 34:54, 1964.
24. Kirwan WO, Walbaum PR, McCormack RJM. Cystic intrathoracic derivatives of the foregut and their complications. Thorax 28:424, 1973.
25. Kluth D. Atlas of esophageal atresia. J Pediatr Surg 11:901, 1976.
26. Kluth D, Steding G, Seidl W. The embryology of foregut malformations. J Pediatr Surg 22:389, 1987.
27. Kosloske AM, Jewell PF, Cartwright KC. Crucial bronchoscopic findings in esophageal atresia and tracheoesophageal fistula. J Pediatr Surg 23:466, 1988.
28. Ladd WE. The surgical treatment of esophageal atresia and tracheoesophageal fistulas. N Engl J Med 230:625, 1944.
29. Leven NL. Congenital atresia of the esophagus with tracheoesophageal fistula. Report of successful extrapleural ligation of fistulous communication and cervical esophagostomy. J Thorac Surg 10:648, 1941.
30. Livaditis A, Radberg L, Odensjo G. Esophageal end-to-end anastomosis. Reduction of anastomotic tension by circular myotomy. Scand J Thorac Cardiovasc Surg 6:206, 1972.
31. Malthaner RA, Newman KD, Parry R, et al. Alkaline gastroesophageal reflux in infants and children. J Pediatr Surg 26:986, 1991.
32. Manning PB, Morgan RA, Coran AG, et al. Fifty years' experience with esophageal atresia and tracheoesophageal fistula. Ann Surg 204:446, 1986.
33. McKinnon LJ, Kosloske AM. Prediction and prevention of anastomotic complications of esophageal atresia and tracheoesophageal fistula. J Pediatr Surg 25:778, 1990.
34. Nakahara K, Fujii Y, Miyoshi S, et al. Acute symptoms due to a huge duplication cyst ruptured into the esophagus. Ann Thorac Surg 50:30, 1990.
35. Olsen JB, Clemmensen O, Andersen K. Adenocarcinoma arising in a foregut cyst of the mediastinum. Ann Thorac Surg 51:497, 1991.
36. Poenaru D, Laberge J-M, Neilson IR, et al. A new prognostic classification for esophageal atresia. Surgery 113:426, 1993.
37. Puri P, Ninan GK, Blake NS, et al. Delayed primary anastomosis for esophageal atresia: 18 months' to 11 years' follow-up. J Pediatr Surg 27:1127, 1992.
38. Qazi FM, Geisinger KR, Nelson JB, et al. Symptomatic congenital gastroenteric duplication cyst of the esophagus containing exocrine and endocrine pancreatic tissues. Am J Gastroenterol 85:65, 1990.
39. Rafal RB, Markisz JA. Magnetic resonance imaging of an esophageal duplication cyst. Am J Gastroenterol 86:1809, 1991.

40. Harmon CM, Coran AG. Congenital anomalies of the esophagus. In O'Neill JA, Rowe MI, Grosjild JL, et al (eds). Pediatric Surgery, 5th ed. St. Louis, Mosby, 1998, pp 941–967.

41. Robison RJ, Pavlina PM, Scherer LR, et al. Multiple esophageal duplication cysts. J Thorac Cardiovasc Surg 94:144, 1987.

42. Shaul DB, Schwartz MZ, Marr CC, et al. Primary repair without routine gastrostomy is the treatment of choice for neonates with esophageal atresia and tracheoesophageal fistula. Arch Surg 124:1188, 1989.

43. Smith EI. The early development of the trachea and esophagus in relation to atresia of the esophagus and tracheoesophageal fistula. Contrib Embryol Carnegie Inst Wash 24:36, 1957.

44. Snyder ME, Luck SR, Hernandez R, et al. Diagnostic dilemmas of mediastinal cysts. J Pediatr Surg 20:810, 1985.

45. Spitz L. Gastric transposition via the mediastinal route for infants with long-gap esophageal atresia. J Pediatr Surg 19:149, 1984.

46. Spitz L, Kiely E, Sparnon T. Gastric transposition for esophageal replacement in children. Ann Surg 206:69, 1987.

47. Templeton JM, Templeton JJ, Schnaufer L, et al. Management of esophageal atresia and tracheoesophageal fistula in the neonate with severe respiratory distress syndrome. J Pediatr Surg 20:39, 1985.

48. Vogt EC. Congenital esophageal atresia. Am J Roentgenol 22:463, 1929.

49. O'Neill JA, Rowe MI, Grosjild JL, et al (eds). Pediatric Surgery, 5th ed. St. Louis, Mosby, 1998, pp 941–967.

50. Wheatley MJ, Coran AG, Wesley JR. Efficacy of the Nissen fundoplication in the management of gastroesophageal reflux following esophageal atresia repair. J Pediatr Surg 28:53, 1993.

68

Functional Abnormalities of the Esophagus

Andrew J. Hotaling, M.D., and Atul M. Vaidya, M.D.

In recent years, functional disorders of the esophagus have gained recognition in the diagnosis and management of children with feeding abnormalities. The wide range of clinical presentations from simple food refusal to life-threatening apneic events and aspiration pneumonia reflect the diversity of these pathologic entities.

This chapter reviews the anatomy and physiology of swallowing, then describes the signs and symptoms of pediatric dysphagia. The diagnostic work-up is then summarized, and the manometric and radiographic findings that characterize many of the functional disorders of the esophagus are emphasized. Finally, the most common disease entities and their management are reviewed, with focus on the primary esophageal motility disorders and complications of gastroesophageal reflux disease (GERD). Mechanical abnormalities, including mass lesions, congenital anomalies, caustic strictures, and foreign bodies, are reviewed elsewhere in this text.

Anatomy

The esophagus is a muscular tube connecting the pharynx and stomach. It is lined by stratified, nonkeratinizing epithelium and is composed of a two-layer muscle wall. The inner layer consists of circular fibers; the outer fibers are longitudinally orientated. There is no serosal layer. The proximal esophagus is composed of striated muscle, while more than half of the distal esophagus is smooth muscle. A cadaveric study demonstrated the following muscle compositions of the esophagus: the first 4.1% to 5.6% of the proximal esophagus is striated muscle; the next 32.4% to 41.9% of the esophagus is a mixture of striated and smooth muscle; the distal 54% to 62% is smooth muscle[1] (Fig. 68–1).

The primary functions of the esophagus are to serve as a conduit for food transfer from the pharynx to the stomach and to protect the pharynx and larynx from refluxed gastric contents. Both physiologic and anatomic barriers carry out the protective function of the esophagus. The physiologic barriers are specialized muscular structures known as the upper esophageal sphincter (UES) and lower esophageal sphincter (LES). Four discrete anatomic structures prevent gastroesophageal reflux (GER) from entering the distal esophagus: diaphragmatic crura, phrenoesophageal ligament, gastroesophageal angle with its mu-

cosal flap valve, and intra-abdominal segment of the esophagus. From an animal model, the diaphragm is believed to contribute 25% of LES competence.[2] The phrenoesophageal ligament is a fibroelastic membrane fixing the esophagus in the diaphragmatic hiatus. It may be involved in holding or pulling the esophagus inferiorly, thus helping to establish an intra-abdominal esophageal segment.[3] The gastroesophageal angle is formed when the esophagus enters the cardia; it creates a 180-degree mucosal fold preventing reflux in the presence of a low LES pressure in adults.[4] The length of the intra-abdominal esophagus is paramount in preventing GER. From the physical laws governing the behavior of soft tubes, the longer the length of the tube, the lower the pressure required to collapse the tube and thus prevent reflux[5] (see Chap. 50).

Physiology

Upper Esophageal Sphincter

The esophagus is collapsed at rest. The UES is composed of striated muscle, primarily from the cricopharyngeal muscle (CPM) and, to a lesser extent, the inferior constrictor muscle (ICM).[6] The CPM is tonically contracted to protect the larynx and pharynx from refluxed esophageal contents. It also blocks respired air from distending the esophagus and allows controlled venting of air by belching. The nucleus ambiguus supplies basal neural input via the vagus nerve and the neurotransmitter acetylcholine. When released at the neuromuscular junction, acetylcholine activates a nicotinic-cholinergic receptor on a single striated muscle cell.[7] Similar to striated muscle, the UES contracts much faster than the distal smooth muscle. When viewed from above, the UES appears as a slitlike structure lying in the axial plane. It is narrowest in the midline but widens laterally in the parasagittal planes. This radial asymmetry can be demonstrated manometrically, where the highest pressures result from the midline anterior attachment of the CPM to the cricoid cartilage. UES sphincter pressure is labile; augmentation is demonstrated electromyographically during phonation, respiration, changes in head posture, intraluminal distention, and psychological stress.[8]

Bolus transfer through the UES requires its transient

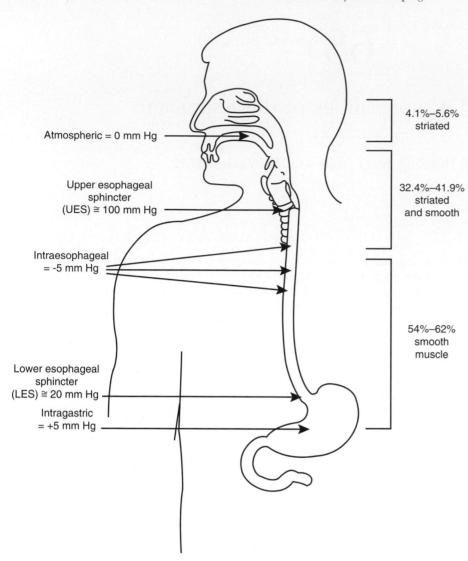

Atmospheric = 0 mm Hg

Upper esophageal
sphincter
(UES) ≅ 100 mm Hg

Intraesophageal
= -5 mm Hg

Lower esophageal
sphincter
(LES) ≅ 20 mm Hg

Intragastric
= +5 mm Hg

4.1%–5.6%
striated

32.4%–41.9%
striated
and smooth

54%–62%
smooth
muscle

FIGURE 68–1. Esophageal segmental manometric pressures and muscle composition. (Adapted from Castell DO. Anatomy and physiology of the esophagus and its sphincters. In Castell DO, Castell JA (eds). Esophageal Motility Testing, 2nd ed. Norwalk, CT, Appleton & Lange, 1994; and Meyer GW, Austin RM, Castell DO. Muscle anatomy of the human esophagus. J Clin Gastroenterol 8:131, 1986.)

relaxation in coordination with the pharyngeal phase of swallowing. These events are controlled by the medullary swallowing center, first conceptualized in 1968 by Robert Doty, who theorized that sensory input from the periphery triggers a "central pattern generator" in the central nervous system, which sequentially activates all of the motor neurons needed to effect a swallow.[9] The central pattern generator consists of three parts. The first is the afferent limb of the pattern generator, localized to the solitary tract and receiving input from cranial nerves V, VII, IX, and X and from sympathetics C1 to L3.[10] The second component is the "intermediate coordinating region," with two anatomically discrete parts. The dorsal region near the solitary tract is involved in the initiation and organization of the pharyngeal swallow. The ventral region near the nucleus ambiguus includes "switching neurons" that temporally sequence proximally to distally the output of the motor neurons involved in the pharyngeal and esophageal phases of swallowing.[9] The third part, which is the efferent limb, encompasses the trigeminal, facial, and hypoglossal nuclei as well as the nucleus ambiguus of the vagus for esophageal striated muscle and

the dorsal motor nucleus of the vagus for esophageal smooth muscle[10] (see Chap. 51).

Tubular Esophagus

Although the medullary swallowing center initiates volitional swallowing and directly controls the striated muscle, progression of peristalsis through the smooth muscle is programmed by the enteric nervous system, that is, the myenteric plexus of Auerbach. The enteric nervous system is independent of the central nervous system. The cranial-to-caudal control by the enteric nervous system of esophageal peristalsis can be initiated by commands from the medullary swallowing center or from stretch receptors within the smooth muscle segment.[7, 11] *Primary peristalsis* occurs after central stimulation of the enteric nervous system by the medullary swallowing center and requires approximately 8 to 10 seconds to reach the distal esophagus. *Secondary peristalsis* originates in the enteric nervous system after mechanical distention of the smooth muscle and can be demonstrated experimentally in vitro after disruption of all connections to the central nervous system. *Tertiary contractions* represent pathologic non-peristaltic contractions of unknown etiology.[6, 7]

Lower Esophageal Sphincter

The LES fulfills two physiologic roles: to prevent GER by tonic contraction and to relax appropriately with swallowing to allow bolus passage into the stomach. Resting LES sphincter tone is believed to be an intrinsic property of the muscle because complete chemical denervation with the neurotoxin tetrodotoxin does not extinguish LES tone.[6] Increased calcium ion leakage has been implicated in electrophysiologic studies showing that the resting membrane potential of the LES is less negative compared with the membrane potential in other esophageal segments. In addition, calcium antagonists have been shown to diminish resting tone. However, the exact cellular mechanism is not known.[7]

LES relaxation during swallowing, in contrast, is a neural event because it occurs via vagal stimulation. There are both excitatory and inhibitory vagal neurons, and stimulation of the vagal inhibitory neurons results in release of nitric oxide. Nitric oxide is well accepted as an inhibitory neurotransmitter in the gastrointestinal tract. Specifically, it has been shown to be one of the neurotransmitters that mediate relaxation of the LES. By administering NG-monomethyl-L-arginine (L-NMMA), a specific nitric oxide synthase inhibitor, the production of nitric oxide is blocked. This decrease in nitric oxide production results in a diminished transient relaxation in LES tone normally induced by gastric distention. Other neurotransmitters are also involved in LES tone, including vasoactive intestinal polypeptide–mediated relaxation of LES tone and muscarinic receptor–mediated contraction of the LES. Thus, maintenance of LES tone is controlled by a combination of base line neural resting tone and the influence of multiple neurotransmitters.[12–14]

Phases of Swallowing

The swallow is divided into four phases: oral preparatory, oral, pharyngeal, and esophageal. The oral preparatory stage does not occur in unweaned infants, who make the transition naturally to this stage in the first year of life. At birth, deglutition occurs as a reflexive suck and swallow mechanism.

The Suck and Swallow

Suck and swallowing begins in utero as early as the 12th gestation week and matures by 34 to 35 weeks of gestation. After birth, the suck and swallow mechanism centers around the infant's ability to lip-seal around a nipple and appose the posterior tongue musculature to the soft palate to seal the oral cavity. The nipple is positioned between the tongue and hard palate. As the mandible depresses and elevates, the nipple is compressed, creating suction to strip milk from the nipple. The oral cavity fills with short bursts of sucking until this milk reservoir is full. When the bolus spills onto the base of tongue, the swallow reflex is triggered.

The Mature Swallow

During the first year of life, the liquid diet changes to a soft and then solid consistency. The infant must learn how to prepare a solid food bolus. In the oral preparatory stage, the lips close after the bolus is accepted. The labial and buccal muscles contract to close the anterior and lateral sulci. The bolus is held between the alveolar ridges by the lateral rolling action of the tongue to facilitate mastication. Respiration continues nasally during mastication by anterior soft palate movement, which seals the oral cavity and opens the nasopharyngeal airway.[15]

During the oral stage, the bolus is propelled posteriorly to the palatoglossal arch by the pumping action of the tongue. The pharyngeal stage is controlled by the medullary swallowing center and is triggered reflexively by the mechanical stimulation of the sensory receptors of cranial nerves V, VII, IX, and X. The medullary swallowing center initiates involuntary responses including closures of the velopharyngeal port and of the laryngeal aditus, orad (toward the mouth) movement of the larynx to distend the UES, active relaxation of the UES, and pharyngeal peristalsis.[16]

The esophageal phase usually lasts 8 to 10 seconds and consists of primary and secondary peristalsis, as described previously.[6]

History

The otolaryngologist is often consulted for abnormalities in pediatric alimentation. The clinical manifestations are myriad and may include food refusal or selectivity, choking, gagging, regurgitation, rumination, failure to thrive, and weight loss. Respiratory complications of dysphagia also occur and may necessitate emergent otolaryngologic intervention. These include coughing or choking, desaturation, bradyarrhythmia, apnea, recurrent bronchospasm, and pneumonia. These symptoms must be viewed in the context of the maturation of the child's swallowing behavior. Therefore, an accurate developmental history is essential to the evaluation of pediatric dysphagia.[17]

The developmental history begins with a prenatal survey. Polyhydramnios is noteworthy because it may represent the earliest sign of esophageal disease.[18] The maternal history includes reviews for maternal infection, thyroid disease, and toxemia. Peripartum events such as traumatic delivery, prolonged hypoxemia with low Apgar scores, and intubation may also be relevant.[19] Successful adaptation to the bottle and to the spoon and cup in oral feeding as well as mastery of progressive textures (purees, junior foods, table foods) should be recorded.[17] A complete family history must also be obtained with particular emphasis on familial neurologic disorders and congenital anomalies.[20]

With older children, the patient's complaint may implicate a specific stage of swallowing. Oral dysphagia indicates a problem in the initiation of swallowing. Its differential diagnosis includes neurogenic disorders, decreased salivary flow, and painful oropharyngeal lesions. Children with pharyngeal dysphagia complain of sticking of the food bolus at or above the suprasternal notch. Additional complaints include nasal regurgitation, inability to clear the throat, and symptoms of aspiration. Most pharyngeal dysphagia is due to neuromuscular disorders; however, structural narrowing due to a mucosal web or Zenker diverticulum should be ruled out. Finally, patients with esophageal dysphagia localize the problem from the suprasternal notch to the epigastrium. While the patient's perception of location can help to differentiate the affected stage of swallowing, one can be misled because epigastric or retrosternal disease can be referred to the neck region.[21] Two general pathologic processes present as esophageal dysphagia: structural narrowing of the lumen (e.g., Schatzki ring, peptic stricture) and motility disorders (e.g., achalasia, diffuse esophageal spasm)[22] (see Chap. 54).

Physical Examination

A complete head and neck examination is performed, with emphasis on neurologic and craniofacial abnormalities. A detailed neurologic evaluation includes a general assessment of the child's level of consciousness and a thorough cranial nerve examination. Dysmorphic features and structural lesions of the nose, oral cavity, and pharynx are sought. Palatal integrity and function, tongue size and function, and adequacy of lip closure are assessed. In the cooperative child, rigid or flexible pharyngeal endoscopy can evaluate vocal fold and pharyngeal mobility, pooling of secretions, and aspiration.[17, 19, 20] In the young child, observing the parent or primary caregiver in the act of feeding the infant can be informative (see Chap. 52).

Diagnostic Work-up

Plain Chest Radiograph

In evaluation of for esophageal disorders, chest x-ray is important to search for concomitant aspiration pneumonia. In addition, an esophageal air-fluid level without gastric air bubble may indicate a motility disorder. On a lateral film, a dilated esophagus may obscure the posterior cardiac silhouette.[23]

Contrast Studies

The barium esophagogram has been used since the 1930s to image the esophagus. When coupled with videofluoroscopy, contrast studies can evaluate the morphologic features and function of the oral, pharyngeal, and esophageal phases of swallowing as well as gastric emptying.[24]

To examine the esophagus, four radiographic techniques are used: (1) full-column technique, (2) mucosal relief technique, (3) double-contrast technique, and (4) motion recording methods.[25]

Full-Column Technique

In this classic examination of the esophagus, the patient is in the prone oblique position and takes barium through a straw or is given barium by nasogastric tube to demonstrate primary peristalsis. Esophageal narrowing from a mucosal ring or peptic stricture may be visualized and is best seen by using a solid bolus (e.g., barium tablets/marshmallow) or by halting primary peristalsis with chilled barium or rapid sequential swallowing.[25, 26]

Mucosal Relief Technique

This examination follows the full-column technique when the esophagus is collapsed and coated with barium. Subtle mucosal abnormalities such as esophagitis and varices can be visualized.[27]

Double-Contrast Technique

This examination can be performed in older children. In the upright position, the patient rapidly gulps dense barium along with effervescent pills or powder, followed by 10 to 15 mL of water to provide gaseous distention of the esophagus, which allows simultaneous evaluation of the distended esophagus and its mucosal surface. Local esophageal narrowing, esophagitis, and subtle mucosal lesions again may be visualized.[25]

Videofluoroscopic Swallowing Study

The videofluoroscopic swallowing study (VFSS) allows dynamic evaluation of the oral, pharyngeal, and esophageal phases of swallowing. Oral dysfunction involves either delayed oral transit with retained oral residual or premature spilling into the pharynx, both of which disrupt pharyngeal peristalsis and may cause aspiration. The usual cause is neurogenic and is due to impaired lingual or facial movement; however, decreased salivation, mucosal lesions, and mass lesions should be ruled out.[28]

Pharyngeal dysfunction has several manifestations, including nasal regurgitation, hypopharyngeal pooling, and aspiration. Nasal regurgitation occurs when apposition of the soft palate and superior constrictor fails because of incomplete elevation of the soft palate or incomplete formation of Passavant ridge. Hypopharyngeal pooling has several causes, including abnormal pharyngeal peristalsis, diminished superoanterior excursion of the hyoid and larynx, and impaired relaxation of the CPM. Finally, aspiration may be seen before, during, or after the pharyngeal swallow. Early aspiration results from premature spillage of the bolus during the oral stage. Aspiration during a swallow is usually neurogenic in origin because of a deficiency of intrinsic laryngeal musculature. Late aspiration results from residual material collecting in the hypopharynx secondary to impaired peristalsis, abnormal CPM relaxation, or esophagopharyngeal regurgitation.[24, 28]

Esophageal dysfunction occurs when the normal aboral (away from the mouth) contraction, which strips the food bolus inferiorly, is disrupted. Primary motility disorders include achalasia, diffuse esophageal spasm, nutcracker esophagus, hypertensive LES, and nonspecific esophageal motility disorder. Each of these disorders results in distinct videofluoroscopic findings, which are discussed later.[25]

Videoendoscopic Swallowing Study

An important adjunct to the videofluoroscopic examination is the videoendoscopic swallowing study. This evaluation surveys the structure and function of the palate, pharynx, and larynx, directly visualizing the patient's swallowing ability with various food consistencies by use of a fiberoptic nasolaryngoscope. In a cooperative older child, the technique allows assessment of a bedridden child unable to travel to a radiology suite and can be used for frequent reassessment when the swallowing function is rapidly changing. Repeated VFSS examinations would be impractical and would expose a patient to excessive radiation.[29, 30]

Invasive Techniques

Esophageal Manometry

The first manometric studies were reported in 1883 by Kronecker and Meltzer; the modern era began with Fyke et al in 1956, when the LES was identified manometrically.[31] Many technologic refinements followed and currently allow reliable quantification of esophageal peristalsis and sphincter pressures.

Primary equipment consists of an esophageal manometry tube, either a water-infusion type with external transducers or a solid-state type with internal microtransducers. The water-infusion system consists of small capillary tubes receiving distilled water at a constant rate (0.5 mL/min). The capillary tubes connect to external transducers linked to a strip recorder. The capillary tubes are placed into side holes in the manometry tube. These side holes are occluded by a peristaltic wave or by the sphincter action, which results in an increase in pressure in the water-filled capillary tubes. The pressure change is detected by the external transducer and noted by the strip recorder.[32] In the solid-state manometer, the microtransducers abut mucosa directly, allowing direct pressure measurements.[32] Indications for manometric studies are summarized in Table 68–1. Young children and infants may require sedation and restraint.

Measurement of Pressures

Measurements of LES pressure are made in reference to base line gastric pressure, arbitrarily assigned a value of 0 mmHg. The catheter is withdrawn from the stomach to the high-pressure zone created by the LES. In practice, two techniques are used. In the "station pull-through," the catheter is withdrawn in 0.5- to 1.0-cm increments with momentary pauses to record pressures. In the "rapid pull-through," the catheter is rapidly withdrawn through the LES while the patient suspends respiration. Greater reliability is achieved with multiple trials to generate an

TABLE 68–1. Clinical Applications of Esophageal Manometry

Investigation of Dysphagia
Primary esophageal motility disorder
   Achalasia
   Diffuse esophageal spasm
   Hypertensive LES
   Nutcracker esophagus
   Nonspecific esophageal motility disorders
   UES/pharyngeal manometry for pharyngeal dysphagia
Secondary esophageal motility disorders
   Collagen-vascular diseases (e.g., scleroderma)
Evaluation of Possible Gastroesophageal Reflux Disease
Measure LESP to identify high-risk patients (LESP < 6 mm Hg)
Support diagnosis in difficult case
   Atypical symptoms
   Failure of medical therapy
Rule out defective peristalsis
Rule out connective tissue disease (scleroderma)
Assist with placement of pH probe
Evaluation of Patients with Noncardiac Chest Pain
Rule out Esophageal Cause for Possible Eating Disorder

LES, lower esophageal sphincter; LESP, lower esophageal sphincter pressure; UES, upper esophageal sphincter.
Adapted from Castell DO. Historical perspectives and current use of esophageal manometry. In Castell DO, Castell JA. Esophageal Motility Testing, 2nd ed. Norwalk, Conn, Appleton & Lange, 1994.

average LES pressure because this system is sensitive to mild perturbations, such as a Valsalva maneuver.[31, 33]

Normal basal LES pressure ranges from 10 to 45 mmHg. Relaxation is recorded by a trough-shaped depression from the resting tone, followed by a contraction that often exceeds the normal basal resting tone of the LES (i.e., postrelaxation overshoot). Classic diseases of the LES include achalasia and GERD. Given the wide range of normal values, only measurements at the extremes are diagnostically significant. For example, an LES pressure of less than 6 mmHg may predict GER.[6, 31, 34]

Technical improvements have increased the accuracy of measurements in the tubular esophagus. Formerly, 40 mmHg was thought to be an abnormally high pressure; however, it has come to be known that normal contractions vary from 40 to 100 mmHg.[31]

The pharyngoesophageal segment posed several problems to the traditional, water-infusion manometers. Until recently, these obstacles have precluded meaningful studies and include fast response rate, UES radial asymmetry, and UES movement with deglutition. The solid-state, computerized manometer was developed to meet these challenges. The first challenge is the rapid contraction rate of the striated muscle in the UES and pharynx compared with the slower rates of the smooth muscle in the distal esophagus. Computerized recordings and microtransducers directly contacting muscle fibers allow measurement of rapid sphincter pressure changes. However, satisfactory characterization of sphincter and pharyngeal coordination remains elusive.[35] Second, the UES is radially asymmetric because of CPM attachments to the cricoid cartilage, as stated earlier. The highest pressures are recorded in the midline, while lower pressures are found laterally. Solid-state manometry measurements are independent of catheter position because internal transducers contact the esophageal wall and measure circumferential pressures directly.[35] Third, manometric measurements of the UES pressure recordings must adapt to its anterosuperior movement (1 to 2 cm with the hyoid bone and larynx in adults) during swallowing. The catheter is positioned superior to the UES at rest. During the swallow, the UES moves anterosuperiorly onto the transducer. An initial pressure elevation is seen, followed by a decrease as the bolus passes. A second pressure increase occurs as the UES regains basal tone, followed by a second decrease as the UES goes below the transducer with return of the larynx to its resting position. A characteristic "M" pattern is generated. The M configuration is used to corroborate correct placement of the catheter for UES measurement. This sequence of events has been confirmed by videofluoroscopic studies.[36, 37] Despite these advances, a wide range of UES pressures are found in normal patients. Normative UES pressure values have not yet been determined.[37]

Ambulatory 24-Hour Motility Monitoring

With the advent of solid-state catheters and computerized recordings, ambulatory studies of esophageal motility are possible. Extended studies are more physiologic and less likely to miss intermittent motor abnormalities. Adult studies, particularly with simultaneous pH monitoring, have reported promising results. Stein et al[38] demonstrated either functional or secretory abnormalities in 84% of the adult patients; GERD, esophageal motility disorders, and prolonged postprandial alkalinization of the gastric pH were among the abnormalities found[38, 39] (see Chap. 69).

pH Studies

Tuttle and Gross first reported the measurement of esophageal pH in conjunction with manometry in 1958, allowing direct diagnosis of GER.[40] GER is defined as the retrograde passage of gastric contents into the esophagus. This refluxate can be acidic, basic, or neutral. GER is either physiologic (normal) or pathologic (disease). Physiologic GER, henceforth known as GER, is usually asymptomatic, rarely occurs during sleep, and is frequent during the postprandial state. Pathologic reflux is symptomatic, can be identified and measured diagnostically, can cause pathologic changes in the upper aerodigestive tract, and is defined as GERD.

Twenty-four–hour pH probe studies are considered the gold standard for the diagnosis of GER.[40] Varty et al[41] demonstrated the prognostic value of the pH probe in a study of 57 children with GERD. Using more than 18% of study time at a pH less than 4, they identified patients requiring surgery with a specificity and sensitivity of 92% and 70%, respectively, for patients with GERD alone and 80% and 86%, respectively, for children with GERD resulting from esophageal atresia, tracheoesophageal fistula, or neurologic disease.

A normal pH study, however, does not rule out GER. In 1958, Tuttle and Gross found that their patients reported symptoms of heartburn when the intraesophageal pH went below 4.0. These authors selected a pH less than 4 as the diagnostic threshold for GERD, and it is the definition currently used by most laboratories.[40] Therefore, by definition, a pH study ignores neutral or basic reflux. False-negative results can occur in the following situations: neutral reflux, basic reflux, refluxed gastric contents buffered by an infant's milk, and increased salivary flow rates stimulated by the nasogastric probes.[42]

Finally, a double-electrode system is available. Here, probes are placed both in the lower esophageal body and in the hypopharynx. The proximal probe detects pharyngoesophageal reflux, identifying infants at risk for respiratory complications.[43]

Gastroesophageal Radionuclide Scintiscan (Milk Scan)

The esophageal scintiscan is used to diagnose GER of any pH. The patient swallows a liquid (milk) bolus tagged with a gamma-emitting radionuclide. The passage of the bolus is monitored in the postprandial period with a gamma camera and computer quantified. The rate of gastric emptying is calculated, and late imaging of the lung fields can detect aspiration. The gastroesophageal scintiscan, with a sensitivity of 90%, has been shown to be an accurate, noninvasive method of diagnosing and measuring GER in a more physiologic manner than with the pH probe.[44] In more recent studies, investigators have used the scintiscan to quantify esophageal transport in patients with motility disorders, measure pharyngeal transit times, and assess the efficacy of treatment.[45, 46]

Electromyography

Simultaneous recordings of electromyographic (EMG) activity and intraluminal pressures were performed experimentally to better select adult patients with oropharyngeal dysphagia for cricopharyngeal myotomy. EMG needle electrodes were placed in the cricopharyngeal and inferior constrictor muscles; pressure recordings were made by a water-infusion catheter with external transducers. Two patterns of EMG abnormalities were identified. In patients with motor neuron disease, the burst of EMG activity in the ICM was not seen with swallowing, demonstrating pharyngeal muscle weakness. In patients with idiopathic dysphagia, the resting EMG activity of the CPM was higher than that of control subjects and may indicate an abnormally high level of tonic CPM contraction. Although not yet performed in children, EMG studies will certainly add to the diagnosis and management of functional disorders of the esophagus.[47, 48]

Esophagoscopy and Esophageal Biopsy

Esophageal endoscopy is primarily used to rule out esophagitis in the context of GERD; however, a mass lesion (e.g., leiomyoma) can also be ruled out. The mucosal pathologic change of GERD, including edema, erythema, erosions, stricture, and Barrett esophagus, is directly visualized. Given the 40% frequency of microscopic esophagitis with normal-appearing mucosa on endoscopy, biopsy is routinely performed.[44, 49]

Direct Laryngoscopy and Bronchoscopy

At endoscopy, direct laryngoscopy and bronchoscopy may also be performed. Laryngeal sequelae of GERD are sought, including interarytenoid edema, arytenoid fixation, vocal cord changes, and subglottic stenosis. Finally, aspirates of the tracheobronchial tree may contain lipid-laden macrophages. While lipid-laden macrophages are seen with a variety of irritative phenomena, their sensitivity for GER is 85%.[50] However, their absence does not rule out GER.

Disease Entities

Functional disorders of the esophagus may be organized by pathologic categories, which are summarized in Table 68–2. Emphasis is placed on the primary motility disorders and GERD.

TABLE 68–2. Differential Diagnosis of Dysphagia

Esophageal Disease
*Primary Motility Disorders—
Proximal Esophagus*
Cricopharyngeal achalasia
Upper esophageal sphincter hypotension
Pharyngeal incoordination of the newborn
*Primary Motility Disorders—
Distal Esophagus*
Achalasia
Diffuse esophageal spasm
Nutcracker esophagus
Hypertensive lower esophageal sphincter
Nonspecific esophageal motility disorders
Gastroesophageal Reflux Disease Secondary Motility Disorders
Structural problems
  Stenosis, strictures, esophageal atresia, tracheoesophageal fistula
  Diverticulum
  Extrinsic compression (e.g., vascular anomalies)
  Hiatal hernia
  Perforations
  Varices
  Lacerations (e.g., Mallory-Weiss syndrome)
Esophagitis
  Acute chemical
  Drug-induced (e.g., FeSO$_4$, antibiotic)
  Pemphigus
  Lichen planus
  Stevens-Johnson syndrome
  Uremia
  Behçet syndrome
	Collagen-vascular diseases
	  Dermatomyositis
	  Mixed connective tissue disease
	  Polymyositis
	  Rheumatoid arthritis
	  Scleroderma
	  Systemic lupus erythematosus
	Infections
	  Bacterial
	  Fungal
	  Viral
	  Tuberculosis
	  Actinomycosis
	  Syphilis
	Mass lesions
	  Leiomyoma
	  Cancer
	Neurologic Disease
	Central Nervous System
	Cerebral palsy
	Arnold-Chiari malformation
	Head injury
	Amyotrophic lateral sclerosis
	Other motor neuron diseases
	Myasthenia gravis
	Multiple sclerosis
	Huntington chorea
	Progressive cerebellar degeneration
	Cranial Nerve Deficits
	Diabetes mellitus
	Diphtheria
	Rabies
	Lead poisoning
	Tetanus
	Other neurotoxins

Primary Motility Disorders of the Proximal Esophagus

Cricopharyngeal Achalasia

Pharyngeal dysphagia is attributed to an abnormality in the initiation of the swallowing reflex. In infants and children, pharyngeal dysphagia can present with coughing, coughing and choking with eating, regurgitation, nasal reflux, and poor eating. A common cause of pharyngeal dysphagia is cricopharyngeal achalasia, which is thought to involve spasm or incomplete relaxation of the CPM. On radiographic examination, a prominent bar is commonly seen on VFSS in patients with cricopharyngeal achalasia. Reichert et al[51] argue that it reflects a spastic CPM. The clinical significance of this bar is debated, however, because the extent of the contribution of the CPM to the UES is uncertain. For example, simultaneous radiographic and manometric studies have shown that the CPM composes only the distal third of the UES pressure zone and that peak UES pressures are recorded proximal to the CPM.[52] In contrast, EMG studies by Elidan et al[47, 48] emphasize the sphincteric functions of the CPM and ICM; minimal activity of the ICM was demonstrated at rest, while the CPM exhibited marked activity at rest. On deglutition, these roles reversed with a burst of ICM activity and a marked reduction of CPM activity.

As well, the mere presence of the cricopharyngeal bar does not predict manometric abnormalities of the UES, and it has been seen in normal children.[52] The cricopharyngeal bar may represent muscular hypertrophy or fibrosis.[24] Regardless of etiology, the cricopharyngeal bar does decrease the lumen of the CPM. Both elevated intraluminal pressures, consistent with proximal obstruction, and delayed pharyngeal transit times are associated with the presence of the bar. CPM myotomy has been proposed as reasonable treatment of pharyngeal dysphagia.[52] Dilation therapy is also reported to be effective for cricopharyngeal dysfunction secondary to a bar in childhood.[53]

Upper Esophageal Sphincter Hypotension with Gastroesophageal Reflux Disease

Technologic advancements in microtransducer manometry have improved the ability to evaluate the UES, particularly with respect to esophagopharyngeal reflux in pediatric GERD. Low basal UES tone was believed to cause esophagopharyngeal reflux in GERD and its complications of nasal regurgitation, vomiting, failure to thrive, and aspiration pneumonia. Using prolonged measurement periods in unsedated children 2 to 81 months old, Willing et al[54] found that esophageal distention caused by GERD triggered transient UES relaxations. UES pressure varied with the child's level of arousal but not with esophageal acidification. Further miniaturization of the manometric catheter is needed for the study of infants younger than 2 months[54] (see Chap. 69).

Pharyngeal Incoordination of the Newborn

Transient pharyngeal dysphagia occurs but is rarely considered in the differential diagnosis of respiratory distress in the first days of life. Usually, premature infants are affected. Treatment is conservative, consisting of nasogastric tube feedings and reflux precautions. Symptoms usually resolve within 2 weeks. If the dysphagia persists, other neurologic and anatomic defects should be considered.[55]

Primary Motor Disorders of the Distal Esophagus

Achalasia

Achalasia is the best known primary motility disorder of the esophagus. It is rare in childhood; patients younger than 15 years account for only 4% to 5% of all the cases. Achalasia is usually sporadic, but several familial cases have been reported.[56, 57] In contrast to the slowly progressive dysphagia for both liquids and solids in adults, children often have dramatic presentations, with marked retardation of growth and development and a history of chronic pulmonary disease and typically repeated aspiration pneumonias.[58] Delay in diagnosis of 2 to 3 years is common and may result in severe sequelae.[59] The etiology is unknown; absent or reduced number of ganglion cells in the enteric nervous system has been implicated in the pathogenesis. However, this pathologic defect is inconsistently seen. The absence of ganglion cells may simply reflect the duration of the disease, resulting from wallerian degeneration.[59]

Achalasia is a neuromuscular disease. Whether the defect is primarily intra- or extraesophageal is not known; there is evidence for both theories. Varicella-zoster virus may play an intraesophageal role; a serologic study demonstrated that its DNA titers were significantly higher in the myenteric plexus of patients with achalasia than in control subjects.[60] In contrast, achalasia in the context of familial neurogenic diseases, including familial dysautonomia, familial glucocorticoid deficiency, and Rozycki syndrome, is secondary to extrinsic neural abnormalities.[59]

The diagnosis of achalasia is made radiographically and manometrically. A plain chest film may reveal a widened mediastinum; the barium swallow demonstrates the characteristic "bird-beak" deformity with a dilated proximal esophagus followed by the smooth distal tapering of the distal esophagus. A midesophageal air-fluid level without a gastric air-fluid level is often seen. Endoscopy is required to rule out a mass lesion and peptic stricture. The diagnosis is confirmed with manometry. Three characteristic findings are observed: (1) abnormally high tonic LES pressure, (2) failure of the LES to relax on swallowing, and (3) absence of primary peristalsis in the tubular esophagus.[61]

Treatment of achalasia is aimed at relieving the functional obstruction of the LES. Behavioral, pharmacologic, and invasive interventions are described. The recommended behavioral changes are straightforward: soft diet and gravity-enhancing positioning (i.e., eating and sleeping with the head elevated) to encourage esophageal emptying.[62]

Pharmacologic treatment of esophageal motility disorders uses agents that either reduce sphincter hypertonicity or enhance (i.e., prokinetic) weak, peristaltic contrac-

tions. Medical treatment of achalasia includes isosorbide dinitrate, which has been shown to significantly lower LES pressure in adults; however, severe side effects (e.g., headaches) prevent its long-term use. Calcium antagonists such as nifedipine and verapamil have also been shown to significantly decrease LES pressure; however, concomitant clinical improvement has not been demonstrated. Therefore, medical therapy in achalasia plays, at most, a temporizing role until dilation or surgery can be performed.[63]

In adults, a trial of one to two dilations is routinely performed before esophageal myotomy. The role of dilation in children is controversial. On the basis of a series of 20 children, Azizkhan et al[58] recommend a pneumatic dilation as first-line therapy in older children. In patients younger than 9 years, this technique was uniformly ineffective. In contrast, Nakayama et al[64] argue that pneumatic dilation is a logical first step in all patients, given their experience with 19 children. Finally, Nihoul-Fekete et al[59] reported 35 cases of achalasia in which no children were "subjected to forceful or pneumonic dilation" because of the poor evidence for effectiveness in the literature, only 45% for pneumatic dilation versus 84% for esophageal myotomy.

In children, pneumatic dilation may be performed under local sedation or general anesthesia. After dilator placement under fluoroscopy, 300 mmHg of pressure is typically maintained. Reported complications include aspiration pneumonia, persistent chest pain, and reflux esophagitis resulting from LES incompetence.[62] No case reports of esophageal perforation in children were identified; however, a 4% leak rate was seen in the extensive review of 899 adult patients by Okike et al.[65]

Heller reported the first operation for achalasia in 1913. His double (anterior and posterior walls) esophagomyotomy was limited to the anterior wall of the esophagus in 1918 by Groeneveld. This modified Heller procedure has become the operation of choice for achalasia in childhood.[59] The procedure can be transthoracic or transabdominal and includes a longitudinal myotomy of the distal 2 cm of esophagus and 1 to 2 cm of the anterior gastric wall to the submucosal layer. The modified Heller procedure is effective in alleviating clinical symptoms in 90% of patients.[58, 59, 65]

The most prominent complication of esophageal myotomy is postoperative GER. Sufficient preservation of the LES to prevent GER is difficult if an adequate myotomy is performed. As a result, postoperative GER rates of 10% to 60% have been reported.[62] Subsequent esophagitis may be seen in about 20% of GER-complicated esophageal myotomies in children. Therefore, several authors advocate combining an antireflux procedure (usually a Nissen fundoplication) with the esophageal myotomy. Using this protocol, Nihoul-Fekete et al[59] performed 31 consecutive procedures without evidence of postoperative GER.

Other Primary Esophageal Motility Disorders

The remaining primary esophageal motility disorders include diffuse esophageal spasm, nutcracker esophagus, hypertensive LES, and the nonspecific esophageal motility disorders.

Patients with diffuse esophageal spasm have dysphagia and noncardiac substernal chest pain. Symptoms are often triggered by hot or cold foods and exacerbated by emotional stress. Although rare in children, the bronchopulmonary complications of diffuse esophageal spasm—aspiration pneumonia, apnea, bradycardia—have appeared in several case reports in the pediatric literature in the past 10 years.[66] Simultaneous esophageal contractions accounting for more than 10% of wet swallows (i.e., liquid or solid food bolus), intermixed with normal peristalsis, is the pathognomonic manometric pattern of diffuse esophageal spasm. Several associated manometric findings of diffuse esophageal spasm, including repetitive contractions (more than three peaks), prolonged duration of contractions, high-amplitude contractions, frequent spontaneous contractions, and LES abnormalities of incomplete relaxation or high resting pressures, may also been seen in diffuse esophageal spasm. However, these findings are not diagnostic of diffuse esophageal spasm.[67] Radiographic confirmation with a barium swallow or VFSS demonstrates delayed bolus transit resulting from the nonpropulsive, simultaneous contractions.[62]

The fundamental defect in diffuse esophageal spasm is unknown. In contrast to achalasia, the ganglion cells of the enteric nervous system are preserved, but gross thickening of the distal esophageal muscle has been a consistent pathologic finding.[67]

Treatment of diffuse esophageal spasm is conservative. Behavioral changes include avoiding hot or cold foods and eating in the upright position. Pharmacologic intervention with anticholinergics, nitrates, and calcium antagonists has not shown sustained benefit.[63] Surgery, usually esophageal myotomy, is reserved for severe refractory cases. Most surgical series report a 75% success rate in mitigating symptoms.[68]

The remaining primary motility disorders—nutcracker esophagus, hypertensive LES, and nonspecific esophageal motility disorders—are relatively new clinical entities. Identification of these disorders resulted from the evaluation of an increasing number of patients with noncardiac chest pain. Nutcracker esophagus and hypertensive LES are manometrically defined; the nutcracker esophagus has a mean peristaltic pressure greater than 180 mmHg and hypertensive LES has a mean peristaltic pressure greater than 45 mmHg. Both values are more than 2 standard deviations above normal. Nonspecific esophageal motility disorders describe a diverse set of manometric abnormalities that differ from the other primary motility diseases.[69]

Although less commonly evaluated than adults, children with chest pain have demonstrated significant manometric esophageal disease. For example, Glassman et al[70] performed manometry and esophagogastroscopy on 83 children (1 to 20 years of age) with chest pain and found that 44% of the patients' symptoms were esophageal in origin. The most common motility disorder was diffuse esophageal spasm (33%) followed by nutcracker esophagus (10%). In a study of 27 children with chest pain, Berezin et al[71] found that 78% had an esophageal cause.

Gastroesophageal Reflux Disease

GERD is a common pediatric disorder and the most frequent esophageal disorder in young children. Symptoms range from a benign postprandial vomiting to complications including failure to thrive, esophagitis, and airway obstruction. While GERD can cause disease in normal children, certain populations have greater morbidity and mortality risks. High-risk factors include tracheoesophageal fistula, esophageal atresia, colonic interposition, chronic pulmonary disease, subglottic stenosis, and neurologic impairment.

The pathogenesis of GERD is multifactorial and includes hiatal hernia, Zenker diverticulum, decreased LES pressure, transient LES relaxations, impaired mucosal barrier, delayed esophageal acid clearance, delayed gastric emptying, UES dysfunction, and neuromuscular immaturity. The complications resulting from these GERD impairments are reviewed here. For a complete discussion of the natural history and pathophysiology of GERD, refer to Chapter 69.

Complications of Gastroesophageal Reflux Disease

Both extraesophageal and esophageal complications of GERD have been reported. With respect to extraesophageal entities, GERD has been implicated in the pathogenesis of asthma, stridor, apnea, chronic pulmonary diseases, reflux laryngitis, apparent life-threatening events, and sudden infant death syndrome.[72–79]

The pathophysiologic process of GERD-related airway disease has been postulated to include three mechanisms: (1) macroaspiration with chemical pneumonitis, (2) microaspiration with chemical pneumonitis or stimulation of laryngeal protective reflexes, possibly involved in the pathogenesis of apnea or apparent life-threatening events, and (3) stimulation of esophageal receptors causing bronchial hyperactivity.[80]

Esophageal Complications

Esophagitis. Esophagitis is a common sequela of GERD. Its pathogenesis is multifactorial and includes an increased number of transient LES relaxations, reduced esophageal peristaltic amplitudes, and decreased clearing efficacy of both primary and secondary peristalsis.[81] These factors predispose children to longer periods of esophageal acid exposure, resulting in higher rates of esophagitis. O'Neill et al[82] noted a stricture rate of 15% to 30% in children for both peptic esophagitis and GERD in their literature review.

Esophageal Strictures. Benign fibrous esophageal strictures can result from continued esophageal acid exposure, with histologic findings of chronic superficial esophagitis, fibrous infiltration of the submucosa, and obliteration of the normal esophageal architecture. The signs and symptoms of esophagitis or esophageal stricture formation usually present late in the course of the disease, after the infant's diet has progressed to solids. Dysphagia may be the only presenting symptom in GERD children who otherwise display no symptoms of reflux or esophageal stricture.[83] Catto-Smith et al[83] investigated 16 children with dysphagia and found that 12 had histologic evidence of esophagitis as a cause for dysphagia.

Rode et al[84] reported that 12% of 130 children undergoing an antireflux operation had a stricture in the middle to lower esophageal region. These children had a mean delay in diagnosis of 22.4 months after the onset of symptoms. The authors concluded that the preferred preoperative management was aggressive nutritional support on an inpatient basis.

Once the child's nutritional deficiencies have been corrected, a surgical antireflux procedure should be performed. Preoperative or intraoperative esophageal dilation, combined with an antireflux procedure and postoperative dilations, has resulted in a 76% to 88% stricture resolution in 48 children with a median age of 2.5 to 6.3 years.[82, 84, 85] Complications included two esophageal perforations, two disrupted fundoplications, and a 50% postoperative redilation rate.

Barrett Esophagus. Barrett esophagus is a glandular metaplastic change in the distal esophagus, clinically recognized as a cephalad migration of the squamocolumnar junction, present in 2.5% to 13% of children with GERD.[86] Adenocarcinoma may develop within these metaplastic areas and occurs in 5% to 10% of adults.[87] Cheu et al[88] reviewed 180 cases of pediatric Barrett esophagus. Of the 180, two children younger than 14 years had adenocarcinoma, and ten patients younger than 25 years had adenocarcinoma. There is a single case report of partial Barrett esophagus regression after an antireflux operation in a child.[89]

Children with Barrett esophagus need to be observed yearly with esophageal biopsies to rule out dysplasia or early malignant change, regardless of symptoms.[88] Adenocarcinoma has been reported to occur in Barrett esophagus after successful antireflux surgery in adults, indicating that once the metaplastic changes occur, they may never regress, leaving the patient at lifelong risk for development of adenocarcinoma.[88]

Esophageal Bleeding. Hematemesis may be one of the first manifestations of GERD in the infant. It is well known that GERD can cause esophagitis with mucosal erosions.[74] Bleeding follows diffuse mucosal thinning and exposure of the blood vessels at the level of the rete pegs. Slow bleeding can cause iron deficiency anemia; profuse bleeding can present as massive gastrointestinal hemorrhage.

While pharmacologic treatment is indicated for nonemergent hemorrhage, life-threatening hemorrhage requires urgent evaluation and hemodynamic support. Flexible or rigid endoscopy allows control of bleeding with cautery, neodymium:yttrium-aluminum-garnet laser, or injection therapy of various agents. Endoscopic treatment has been shown to be effective in reducing active bleeding, transfusion requirement, rebleeding rates, and length of hospitalization.

Secondary Disorders of the Esophagus

Multiple systemic diseases affect the pharyngeal and esophageal stages of swallowing. Examples from each diagnostic category are found in Table 68–2 (see Chaps. 54 and 73).

Proximal Esophagus—Cerebral Palsy

VFSS has allowed a more complete assessment of the oropharyngeal swallowing defects in children with cerebral palsy. Early VFSS observations in small series of children with cerebral palsy identified slow oropharyngeal transit time with poor bolus formation as prominent abnormalities.[90] A larger study of 90 children with cerebral palsy revealed swallowing defects in more than 90% of patients, including poor tongue control and delayed oral phase (90%), inefficient swallows (83%), pharyngeal residue (58%), and aspiration (38%). More important, 97% of the aspiration events were clinically silent. Incoordination of respiration and deglutition is also implicated in the pathophysiology of aspiration in cerebral palsy. The therapeutic benefit of VFSS in tailoring the speech pathologist's interventions is also demonstrated.[91]

Distal Esophagus—Scleroderma

Scleroderma is a connective tissue disorder characterized by periarteriolar inflammation and the formation of hyalinized and thickened collagenous tissue. Esophageal abnormalities, demonstrated either radiographically or manometrically, are seen in 75% to 85% of patients with scleroderma. Classic esophageal symptoms include heartburn and regurgitation secondary to the characteristic manometric findings of weak to absent distal peristalsis with decreased LES pressure. The resultant GERD can lead to ulcerative esophagitis, stricture, aspiration pneumonia, malnutrition, and growth failure. Therapy is directed at pharmacologic or surgical prevention of GERD.[92, 93]

SELECTED REFERENCES

Allescher HD, Ravich WJ. Medical treatment of esophageal motility disorders. Dysphagia 8:125, 1993.

Baron TH, Richter JE. The use of esophageal function tests. Adv Intern Med 38:361, 1993.

A description of various testing methods and indications for their use.

Dodds WJ, Stewart ET, Logemann JA. Physiology and radiology of the normal oral and pharyngeal phases of swallowing. AJR Am J Roentgenol 154:953, 1990.

Feussner H, Kauer W, Siewert JR. The surgical management of motility disorders. Dysphagia 8:135, 1993.

Goyal RK, Martin SB, Shapiro J, et al. The role of cricopharyngeus muscle in pharyngoesophageal disorders. Dysphagia 8:252, 1993.

Kramer SS, Eicher PM. The evaluation of pediatric feeding abnormalities. Dysphagia 8:215, 1993.

A clinical approach to feeding difficulties in children.

REFERENCES

1. Meyer GW, Austin RM, Brady CE, Castell DO. Muscle anatomy of the human esophagus. J Clin Gastroenterol 8:131, 1986.
2. Rodmark T, Petterson GB. The contribution of the diaphragm and an intrinsic sphincter to the gastroesophageal anti-reflux barrier. An experimental study in the dog. Scand J Gastroenterol 24:85, 1989.
3. Watanabe Y, Lister J. Development of the human fetal-esophageal membrane and its role in the anti-reflux mechanism. Surgery Today Jpn J Surg 23:722, 1993.
4. Hill LD, Kraemer SJ. Does modern technology belong in GI surgery: a step from subjective perception to objective information. World J Surg 16:341, 1992.
5. Bonavina L, Evander A, DeMeester TR, et al. Length of a distal esophageal sphincter and competency of the cardia. Am J Surg 151:25, 1986.
6. Castell DO. Anatomy and physiology of the esophagus and its sphincters. In Castell DO, Castell JA (eds). Esophageal Motility Testing, 2nd ed. Norwalk, Conn, Appleton & Lange, 1994.
7. Conklin JL. Control of esophageal motor function. Dysphagia 8:311, 1993.
8. Cook IJ. Cricopharyngeal function and dysfunction. Dysphagia 8:244, 1993.
9. Miller AJ. The search for the central swallowing pathway: the quest for clarity. Dysphagia 8:185, 1993.
10. Diamant NE. Physiology of the esophagus. In Sleisenger M, Fordtran J (eds). Gastrointestinal Disease: Pathophysiology, Diagnosis, Management, 5th ed. Philadelphia, WB Saunders, 1993.
11. Hendrix TR. Coordination of peristalsis in pharynx and esophagus. Dysphagia 8:74, 1993.
12. Hornby PJ, Abrahams TP. Central control of lower esophageal sphincter relaxation. Am J Med 108(Suppl 4a):90s, 2000.
13. Hirsch DP, Holloway RH, Tytgat GN, Boechxstaens GE. Involvement of nitric oxide in human transient lower esophageal sphincter relaxations and esophageal primary peristalsis. Gastroenterology 115:1374, 1998.
14. Kim CD, Goyal RK, Mashimo H. Neuronal nitric oxide synthase provides nitrergic inhibitory neurotransmitter in mouse lower esophageal sphincter. Am J Physiol 277(2 Pt 1):G280, 1999.
15. Dodds WJ, Stewart ET, Logemann JA. Physiology and radiology of the normal oral and pharyngeal phases of swallowing. AJR Am J Roentgenol 154:953, 1990.
16. Castell JA, Castell DO. The upper esophageal sphincter. In Castell DO, Castell JA (eds). Esophageal Motility Testing, 2nd ed. Norwalk, Conn, Appleton & Lange, 1994.
17. Kramer SS, Eicher PM. The evaluation of pediatric feeding abnormalities. Dysphagia 8:215, 1993.
18. Scott JS, Wilson JK. Hydramnios as an early sign of oesophageal atresia. Lancet 21:569, 1957.
19. Weiss MH. Dysphagia in infants and children. Otolaryngol Clin North Am 21:727, 1988.
20. Shapiro J, Healy GB. Dysphagia in infants. Otolaryngol Clin North Am 21:737, 1988.
21. Jones B, Ravich WJ, Donner MW, et al. Pharyngoesophageal interrelationships: observation and working concepts. Gastrointest Radiol 10:225, 1985.
22. Hendrix TR. Art and science of history taking in the patient with difficulty swallowing. Dysphagia 8:69, 1993.
23. Stark P, Thordarson S, McKinney M. Manifestations of esophageal disease on plain chest radiographs. AJR Am J Roentgenol 155:729, 1990.
24. Jones B, Donner MW. How I do it: examination of the patient with dysphagia. Dysphagia 4:162, 1989.
25. Ott DJ. Radiographic techniques and efficacy in evaluating esophageal dysphagia. Dysphagia 5:192, 1990.
26. Ott DJ, Gelfand DW, Wu WC, et al. Esophagogastric region and its rings. AJR Am J Roentgenol 142:281, 1984.
27. Baron TH, Richter JE. The use of esophageal function tests. Adv Intern Med 38:361, 1993.
28. Dodds WJ, Logemann JA, Stewart ET. Radiologic assessment of abnormal oral and pharyngeal phases of swallowing. AJR Am J Roentgenol 154:965, 1990.
29. Bastian RW. Videoendoscopic evaluation of patients with dysphagia: an adjunct to the modified barium swallow. Otolaryngol Head Neck Surg 104:339, 1991.
30. Bastian RW. The videoendoscopic swallowing study: an alternative and partner to the videofluoroscopic swallowing study. Dysphagia 8:359, 1993.
31. Castell DO. Historical perspectives and current use of esophageal manometry. In Castell DO, Castell JA (eds). Esophageal Motility Testing, 2nd ed. Norwalk, Conn, Appleton & Lange, 1994.
32. Castell JA, Dalton CB. The esophageal motility laboratory: materials and equipment. In Castell DO, Castell JA (eds). Esophageal Motility Testing, 2nd ed. Norwalk, Conn, Appleton & Lange, 1994.
33. Dalton CB, Castell JA. The manometric study. In Castell DO, Castell JA (eds). Esophageal Motility Testing, 2nd ed. Norwalk, Conn, Appleton & Lange, 1994.
34. Feussner H, Kauer W, Siewert JR. The place of esophageal manometry in the diagnosis of dysphagia. Dysphagia 8:98, 1993.
35. Castell JA, Castell DO. Modern solid state computerized manometry of the pharyngoesophageal segment. Dysphagia 8:270, 1993.
36. Kahrilas PJ, Dodds WJ, Dent J, et al. Upper esophageal sphincter function during deglutition. Gastroenterology 95:52, 1988.
37. Castell JA, Castell DO. The upper esophageal sphincter. In Castell DO, Castell JA (eds). Esophageal Motility Testing, 2nd ed. Norwalk, Conn, Appleton & Lange, 1994.
38. Stein HJ, Eypasch EP, DeMeester TR, et al. Circadian esophageal motor function in patients with gastroesophageal reflux disease. Surgery 108:769, 1990.
39. Stein HJ. Clinical use of ambulatory 24-hour esophageal motility monitoring in patients with primary esophageal motor disorders. Dysphagia 8:105, 1993.
40. Jamieson GG, Duranceau A. Diagnostic assessment of gastroesophageal reflux. In Jamieson GG, Duranceau A (eds). Gastroesophageal Reflux. Philadelphia, WB Saunders, 1988.
41. Varty K, Evans D, Kapila L. Paediatric gastro-esophageal reflux: prognostic indicators from pH monitoring. Gut 34:1478, 1993.
42. Cucchiara S, Stiano A, Casali LG, et al. Value of 24-hour intraoesophageal pH monitoring in children. Gut 31:129, 1990.
43. Contencin P, Narcy P. Gastropharyngeal reflux in infants and children—a pharyngeal pH monitoring study. Arch Otolaryngol Head Neck Surg 118:1028, 1992.
44. Fisher RS, Mamud LS, Roberts GS, et al. Gastroesophageal (GE) scintiscanning to detect and quantitate GE reflux. Gastroenterology 70:301, 1976.
45. Hamlet SL, Muz J, Patterson R, et al. Pharyngeal transit time: assessment with videofluoroscopic and scintigraphic techniques. Dysphagia 4:4, 1989.
46. Stacher G, Bergmann H. Scintigraphic quantitation of gastrointestinal motor activity and transport: oesophagus and stomach. Eur J Nucl Med 19:815, 1992.
47. Elidan J, Shochina M, Gonen B, et al. Manometry and electromyography of the pharyngeal muscles in patients with dysphagia. Arch Otolaryngol Head Neck Surg 116:910, 1990.
48. Elidan J, Shochina M, Gonen B, et al. Electromyography of the inferior constrictor and cricopharyngeal muscles during swallowing. Ann Otol Rhinol Laryngol 99:466, 1990.
49. Ismail-Beigi F, Horton PF, Pope CF. Histological consequences of gastroesophageal reflux in man. Gastroenterology 58:163, 1970.
50. Nussbaum E, Maggi JC, Mathis R, et al. Association of lipid-laden macrophages and lactose assay as markers of aspiration in neonates with lung disease. J Pediatr 110:190, 1987.
51. Reichert TJ, Bluestone CD, Stool SE, et al. Congenital cricopharyngeal achalasia. Ann Otol 86:603, 1977.
52. Goyal RK, Martin SB, Shapiro J, et al. The role of cricopharyngeus muscle in pharyngoesophageal disorders. Dysphagia 8:252, 1993.
53. Dinari G, Danziger Y, Mimouni M, et al. Cricopharyngeal dysfunction in childhood: treatment by dilatations. J Pediatr Gastroenterol Nutr 6:212, 1987.
54. Willing J, Davidson GP, Dent J, et al. Effect of gastro-oesophageal reflux on upper oesophageal sphincter motility in children. Gut 34:904, 1993.
55. Frank MM, Baghdassarian Gatewood OM. Transient pharyngeal incoordination in the newborn. Am J Dis Child 111:178, 1966.
56. Kaar TK, Waldron R, Ashraf MS, et al. Familial infantile oesophageal achalasia. Arch Dis Child 66:1353, 1991.
57. O'Brien CJ, Smart HL. Familial coexistence of achalasia and non-

achalasic oesophageal dysmotility: evidence for a common pathogenesis. Gut 33:1421, 1992.

58. Azizkhan RG, Tapper D, Eraklis A. Achalasia in childhood: a 20-year experience. J Pediatr Surg 15:452, 1980.

59. Nihoul-Fekete C, Bawab F, Lortat-Jacob S, et al. Achalasia of the esophagus in childhood: surgical treatment in 35 cases with special reference to familial cases and glucocorticoid deficiency association. J Pediatr Surg 24:1060, 1989.

60. Robertson CS, Martin BAB, Atkinson M. Varicella-zoster virus DNA in the oesophageal myenteric plexus in achalasia. Gut 34:299, 1993.

61. Troshinsky MB, Castell DO. Achalasia. In Castell DO, Castell JA (eds). Esophageal Motility Testing, 2nd ed. Norwalk, Conn, Appleton & Lange, 1994.

62. Herbst JJ. Achalasia and other motor disorders. In Wyllie R, Hyams JS (eds). Pediatric Gastrointestinal Disease: Pathophysiology, Diagnosis, Management. Philadelphia, WB Saunders, 1993.

63. Allescher HD, Ravich WJ. Medical treatment of esophageal motility disorders. Dysphagia 8:125, 1993.

64. Nakayama DK, Shorter NA, Boyle JT, et al. Pneumatic dilatation and operative treatment of achalasia in children. J Pediatr Surg 22:619, 1987.

65. Okike N, Payne WS, Neufeld DM, et al. Esophagomyotomy versus forceful dilation for achalasia of the esophagus: results in 899 patients. Ann Thorac Surg 28:119, 1979.

66. Perisic VN, Tomomasa T, Kuroume T, et al. Recurrent pneumonia caused by diffuse oesophageal spasm. Eur J Pediatr 150:139, 1990.

67. Richter JE. Diffuse esophageal spasm. In Castell DO, Castell JO (eds). Esophageal Motility Testing, 2nd ed. Norwalk, Conn, Appleton & Lange, 1994.

68. Feussner H, Kauer W, Siewert JR. The surgical management of motility disorders. Dysphagia 8:135, 1993.

69. Castell DO. The nutcracker esophagus, the hypertensive lower esophageal sphincter and nonspecific esophageal motility disorders. In Castell DO, Castell JA (eds). Esophageal Motility Testing, 2nd ed. Norwalk, Appleton & Lange, 1994.

70. Glassman MS, Medow MS, Berezin S, et al. Spectrum of esophageal disorders in children with chest pain. Dig Dis Sci 37:663, 1992.

71. Berezin S, Medow MS, Glassman MS, et al. Chest pain of gastrointestinal origin. Arch Dis Child 63:1457, 1988.

72. Berquist W, Rachelefsky GS, Kadden M, et al. Gastro-esophageal reflux–associated recurrent pneumonia and chronic asthma in children. Pediatrics 68:29, 1981.

73. Mansfield LE. Gastroesophageal reflux and asthma. Postgrad Med 86:265, 1989.

74. Contencin P, Narcy P. Gastropharyngeal reflux in infants and children—a pharyngeal pH monitoring study. Arch Otolaryngol Head Neck Surg 118:1028, 1992.

75. Nielson DW, Heldt GP, Tooley WH. Stridor and gastro-esophageal reflux in infants. Pediatrics 85:1034, 1990.

76. Ramet J, Egreteau L, Cruzi-Dascalova L, et al. Cardiac, respiratory, and arousal responses to an esophageal acid infusion test in near-term infants during active sleep. J Pediatr Gastroenterol Nutr 15:135, 1992.

77. Putnam PE, Orenstein SR. Hoarseness in a child with gastroesophageal reflux. Acta Paediatr 81:635, 1992.

78. Bethmann O, Couchard M, Ajuriaguerra M, et al. Role of gastroesophageal reflux and vagal overactivity in apparent life-threatening events: 160 cases. Acta Paediatr 389(Suppl 82):102, 1993.

79. Jolley SG, Halpern LM, Tunell WP. The risk of sudden infant death from gastroesophageal reflux. J Pediatr Surg 26:691, 1991.

80. Burton DM. Pediatric airway manifestations of gastro-esophageal reflux. Ann Otol Rhinol Laryngol 101:742, 1992.

81. Orenstein SR. Gastroesophageal reflux. In Wyllie R, Hyams JS (eds). Pediatric Gastrointestinal Disease: Pathophysiology, Diagnosis, Management. Philadelphia, WB Saunders, 1993.

82. O'Neill JA, Betts J, Ziegler MM, et al. Surgical management of reflux strictures of the esophagus in childhood. Ann Surg 196:453, 1982.

83. Catto-Smith AG, Machida H, Butzner JD, et al. The role of gastroesophageal reflux in pediatric dysphagia. J Pediatr Gastroenterol Nutr 12:159, 1991.

84. Rode H, Miller AW, Brown RA, et al. Reflux strictures of the esophagus in children. J Pediatr Surg 27:462, 1992.

85. Hicks LM, Christie DL, Hall DG, et al. Surgical treatment of esophageal strictures secondary to gastroesophageal reflux. J Pediatr Surg 15:863, 1980.

86. Snyder JD, Goldman H. Barrett's esophagus in children: a consequence of chronic gastroesophageal reflux. Gastroenterology 80:318, 1984.

87. Yakshe PN, Fleischer DE. Neoplasms of the esophagus. In Castell DO (ed). The Esophagus. Boston, Little, Brown, 1992.

88. Cheu HW, Grosfeld JL, Heifetz SA, et al. Persistence of Barrett's esophagus in children after anti-reflux surgery: influence on follow-up care. J Pediatr Surg 27:260, 1992.

89. Hassall E, Weinstein WM. Partial regression of childhood Barrett's esophagus after fundoplication. Am J Gastroenterol 87:1506, 1992.

90. Jones PM. Feeding disorders in children with multiple handicaps. Dev Med Child Neurol 31:404, 1989.

91. Rogers B, Arvedson J, Buck G, et al. Characteristics of dysphagia in children with cerebral palsy. Dysphagia 9:69, 1994.

92. Hill JL. Neuromotor esophageal disorders. In Welch KJ, Randolph JG, Ravitch MM, et al (eds). Pediatric Surgery, vol. I, 5th ed. Chicago, Year Book, 1986.

93. Scobey MW, Castell DO. Secondary esophageal motility disorders. In Castell DO, Castell JA (eds). Esophageal Motility Testing, 2nd ed. Norwalk, Conn, Appleton & Lange, 1994.

69

Gastroesophageal Reflux Disease

Robert F. Yellon, M.D., and Robin T. Cotton, M.D.

Recently, evidence has been accumulating to suggest that gastroesophageal reflux disease (GERD) contributes to many types of otolaryngic manifestations and pathologic conditions in infants and children. The symptoms may be intermittent and vary in time course and severity. A high index of suspicion for GERD, and for the concept of "silent" GERD (GERD without overt symptoms such as regurgitation or heartburn) is necessary for accurate diagnosis and treatment of otolaryngic manifestations of GERD in these patients. In this chapter, the conclusions of the Gastroesophageal Reflux Guidelines Committee of the North American Society for Pediatric Gastroenterology and Nutrition are presented.[121] The document produced by this committee is an excellent evidence-based review and clinical guideline, and its conclusions and recommendations are cited extensively in this chapter. The literature regarding the effects of gastroesophageal reflux disease on otolaryngic disorders in infants and children is also reviewed.

Pathophysiology

Gastroesophageal reflux is a normal process in infants and children. It occurs when stomach contents pass into the esophagus. Regurgitation occurs when the refluxate passes into the mouth. Gastroesophageal reflux occurs in 67% of 4-month-olds but only in 5% of 10- to 12-month-olds.[102]

The primary mechanism of gastroesophageal reflux is believed to be transient relaxation of the lower esophageal sphincter. GERD occurs when the refluxate produces symptoms. Many factors contribute to the pathogenesis of GERD, including frequency and duration of reflux events, the acidity and content of the refluxate, esophageal clearance mechanisms, gastric emptying, integrity of mucosal barriers, and responsiveness of the target organs such as the esophagus, the larynx, the large airways, and the lungs. The acid and pepsin in gastric juice have been demonstrated to be injurious to mucosa. Esophageal clearance mechanisms include both esophageal peristalsis and the swallowing of saliva, which is alkaline and helps to neutralize the acid in gastric juice.

Diagnosis

Although children may present with chief symptoms or complaints of rhinosinusitis, cough, laryngitis, globus pharyngeus, dysphagia, airway obstruction, apnea, asthma, recurrent croup, laryngomalacia, stridor, or subglottic stenosis, a possible concomitant underlying factor and possible etiologic factor is GERD. The diagnosis of GERD is straightforward in a child with otolaryngic symptomatology that clearly coincides with episodes of spitting up and irritability, or in an older child with heartburn. In many cases, however, the diagnosis is less clear, and additional diagnostic studies are required.

The diagnosis may be made by the primary care physician, the otolaryngologist, or the gastroenterologist. When the clinical scenario suggests GERD and if airway symptoms are not significant, a trial of empiric therapy may be useful in selected cases for both diagnosis and treatment. The treatments discussed subsequently, such as dietary changes, positioning, or administration of H_2-receptor blockers, are easy and relatively benign. If there is a good response to empiric therapy, and if the symptoms return upon withdrawal of therapy, then a presumptive diagnosis has been established, and expensive and time-consuming tests have been avoided.

A number of diagnostic studies are available for cases in which the diagnosis is less clear, and the following discussion may help to guide selection of the most appropriate test. Each test for GERD addresses a specific question and each has advantages and limitations.

The 24-hour pH probe is considered to be the gold standard for the diagnosis of GERD.[121] The double electrode pH probe with distal esophageal plus pharyngeal or proximal esophageal electrodes is considered the best examination tool for diagnosis of otolaryngic manifestations of gastropharyngoesophageal reflux.[35] The exact placement of the second electrode in the pharynx or upper esophagus is variable, and techniques are not standardized. This lack of standardization may limit valid comparisons between studies. It is also important to define whether a pH probe study will be performed with the child on or off antisecretory or prokinetic agents. The pH probe is unable to detect nonacidic reflux.

A reflux event is defined as a drop in esophageal pH to less than 4 for a specified period of time, such as 15 to 30 seconds.[52, 121] The pH probe study can measure acid reflux over a prolonged period of time, which increases the sensitivity of the test. The total percentage of time that the esophageal pH is less than 4 is called the reflux index. The Gastroesophageal Reflux Guidelines Commit-

TABLE 69–1. Results of the Children's Hospital of Pittsburgh Esophageal Biopsy Study

Problem	Positive Biopsy, n (%)	Negative Biopsy, n (%)	Total, n (%)
Asthma	21 (75)	7 (25)	28
Recurrent croup	12 (75)	4 (25)	16
Cough	30 (81)	7 (19)	37
Apnea	33 (75)	11 (25)	44
Sinusitis	10 (100)	0 (0)	10
Stridor	42 (63)	25 (27)	67
Laryngomalacia	21 (75)	7 (25)	28
Subglottic stenosis	23 (68)	11 (32)	34
Posterior glottic erythema	20 (83)	4 (17)	24
Posterior glottic edema	17 (81)	4 (19)	21

From Yellon R, Cotticchia J, Dixit S, Lee D. Esophageal biopsy for the diagnosis of gastroesophageal reflux-associated otolaryngologic problems in children. Am J Med 108 (suppl 4a):131S, 2000.

tee of the North American Society for Pediatric Gastroenterology and Nutrition has defined the upper limit of normal as 12% for the first year of life and 6% for older children.[121] With esophageal pH monitoring, it can be determined whether the patient's symptoms, such as stridor, cough, or apnea, are correlated temporally with reflux events. In a particular child, the reflux index may be normal but GERD may still cause problems that occur infrequently, such as apnea or aspiration pneumonia. The pH probe study has the disadvantage of not being able to detect nonacidic reflux, and placement of the electrodes and wires may not be well tolerated by children.

Esophageal biopsy is another very useful diagnostic test for GERD. Esophageal biopsy can be performed during rigid or flexible esophagoscopy or by suction biopsy without esophagoscopy.[159] A positive esophageal biopsy showing histologic esophagitis may preclude the need for more costly and time-consuming pH probes or gastric scintiscans. The finding of endoscopic or histopathologic esophagitis is strongly correlated with pH study results. If ulcerations or erosions of the esophageal mucosa are found, there is a 95% chance that the reflux index determined by pH probe will be abnormal.[19, 39, 146] Esophagoscopy and biopsy are a rapid way to make a diagnosis, especially if they are performed at the time of direct laryngoscopy, rigid bronchoscopy, or other procedures, such as adenotonsillectomy or tympanostomy tube placement.

Under normal conditions, esophageal mucosa does not contain neutrophils or eosinophils, and their presence is indicative of GERD-induced esophagitis.[19, 132] Epithelial basal zone hyperplasia and increased papillary height correlate with increased acid exposure.[19, 154] The presence of more than seven eosinophils per high-powered field suggests the presence of eosinophilic esophagitis, which may be a primary disease or secondary to food allergy and not related to GERD.[92, 123]

The procedure of esophagoscopy and biopsy requires a general anesthetic and carries a small risk of esophageal perforation. If the esophageal biopsy examination has negative results and clinical suspicion of GERD is high, then pH probe or scintiscan may be required.

The safe and successful application of esophageal biopsy as a technique used by the otolaryngologist for the diagnosis of GERD has recently been reported.[159] Rigid esophagoscopy with biopsies or suction biopsy[118] may be

performed at the time of other concomitant otolaryngic procedures.

Esophageal biopsy specimens can be taken from the distal one third of the esophagus, with the use of up-biting cup forceps during rigid esophagoscopy. Suction biopsies[118] may be performed by the Pediatric Gastroenterology service when it is judged that the airway is too tenuous for a rigid esophagoscopy, which might cause airway edema and further airway compromise. The suction esophageal biopsy catheter is small and causes less potential airway edema than the larger rigid esophagoscope. Biopsy specimens are evaluated for histologic esophagitis based on well-accepted published criteria.[42]

Table 69–1 shows the results of the Children's Hospital of Pittsburgh esophageal biopsy study.[159] The esophageal biopsy data suggest that children who present to the otolaryngologist with the selected diagnoses and endoscopic findings listed in the table have a high incidence of GERD. A positive biopsy finding may preclude the need for more costly and time-consuming pH probes and scintiscans.

At the Children's Hospital Medical Center in Cincinnati, McMurray and colleagues[98] compared the results of dual pH probe studies (upper and lower esophagus) with results of biopsies of the laryngeal interarytenoid area, postcricoid area, and upper and lower esophagus in patients being evaluated for laryngotracheal reconstruction. They observed that biopsies of the larynx were statistically correlated with biopsies of the esophagus in terms of the presence or absence of mucosal changes. This was in contrast to lack of correlation between biopsies of the larynx and dual pH probe testing. The authors concluded that laryngeal mucosal biopsies may be the most sensitive test for mucosal injury from GERD.

Bronchoscopy and bronchoalveolar lavage with measurement of lipid-laden macrophages can be performed at the time of esophagoscopy to document aspiration, which may be related to GERD[104] or may be an independent event. The finding of many lipid-laden macrophages on a bronchoalveolar lavage specimen is sensitive for aspiration, but other types of pathologic lesions can also increase the percentage of lipid-laden macrophages.

Nuclear medicine gastric scintiscans (milk scans) have the advantage of detecting aspiration, delayed gastric emptying, and acidic and nonacidic reflux.[124] Radiolabeled contrast material is administered to the patient by mouth, and scintiscans are performed periodically to detect the location of the ingested material. Radiolabled material found in the respiratory system indicates primary aspiration or aspiration secondary to reflux. Infrequently occurring events such as occasional aspiration may not be detected on a limited scintiscan.[53] The Gastroesophageal Reflux Guidelines Committee of the North American Society for Pediatric Gastroenterology and Nutrition reported that the sensitivity and specificity of gastric scintiscan for the diagnosis of GERD when compared with pH monitoring are 15% to 59% and 83% to 100%, respectively.[121] The techniques of gastric scintscan are often not standardized, and comparisons between studies are therefore limited.

Barium contrast radiography, including barium swallow and upper gastrointestinal series, may show GERD, but negative results on a barium contrast study do not preclude GERD, since the swallow only detects the occurrence of GERD during a small window of time. The modified barium swallow does provide information about the functional aspects of swallowing, such as aspiration, and will provide information related to the presence of strictures, webs, achalasia, and other structural problems. When compared with pH monitoring, the Gastroesophageal Reflux Guidelines Committee of the North American Society for Pediatric Gastroenterology and Nutrition found that the sensitivity, specificity, and positive predictive value of upper gastrointestinal series to detect GERD range from 31% to 86%, 21% to 83%, and 80% to 82%, respectively.[31, 64, 100, 121, 131, 138, 142]

A new method of evaluation of swallowing function and aspiration that is useful in children with GERD and possible aspiration has been developed at the Children's Hospital Medical Center, Cincinnati. This new method is fiberoptic endoscopic evaluation of swallowing and neurosensory testing.[11, 93] With this technique, the airway can be evaluated for laryngomalacia, vocal cord mobility, or other lesions as well as for swallowing function and aspiration. Additionally, the threshold for the laryngeal closure reflex is determined by delivery of a controlled stimulus (puff of air) to the supraglottis as part of the neurosensory testing.

Manometric studies may be required to characterize motility disorders or chronic low tone of the lower esophageal sphincter.

Ear, Nose, and Throat Disorders and Other Presentations Associated with Gastroesophageal Reflux Disease

The following discussion reviews the literature concerning selected GERD-associated problems in the pediatric population.

Sandifer Syndrome

Sandifer syndrome occurs in children with GERD. Although it is not a true otolaryngic problem, it is included in this review because awareness of this entity may aid in the diagnosis of GERD in patients who do have associated otolaryngic problems. Children with Sandifer syndrome are irritable, have frequent regurgitation following feeds, and often have episodes of arching, crying, and torticollis. Arching and torticollis are believed to be related to esophageal discomfort induced by GERD, and the posturing may help to clear esophageal acid.[117]

Reflux Rhinitis and Chronic Sinusitis

Contencin and Narcy[35] performed nasopharyngeal pH monitoring on 14 children with chronic rhinopharyngitis and GERD and on 18 control subjects without rhinopharyngitis. There was a significantly higher incidence of nasopharyngeal pH below 6 in the rhinopharyngitis group. It is provocative that all 10 patients with sinusitis in the Children's Hospital of Pittsburgh esophageal biopsy series[159] had positive esophageal biopsies. In adults, DiBaise et al[48] performed esophagoscopy with biopsy, esophageal manometry, and pH probes on 18 patients with chronic sinusitis that was refractory to medical and surgical treatment. Eleven of 16 patients (69%) tested with manometry were found to have a hypotensive lower esophageal sphincter, and 14 of 18 patients (78%) tested with pH probes had abnormal results. Patients were treated with a proton pump inhibitor ($n = 12$), or proton pump inhibitor plus prokinetic agent ($n = 4$), and 2 underwent laparoscopic fundoplication. Twelve of the 18 patients (67%) reported improvement in their sinus symptoms following GERD treatment. Bothwell et al[23] reported that treatment of GERD in a series of 28 children with sinusitis that met criteria for endoscopic sinus surgery resulted in improvement and avoidance of surgery in 25 patients (89%).

Reflux of gastric contents into the nasal cavity is believed to cause chronic inflammation. Other possible mechanisms to explain an association between GERD and sinusitis include GERD-induced alterations in mucosal bacterial adherence or lymphatic drainage. Children with chronic sinusitis have multiple causes for their disease, and GERD may be a component; however, viral upper respiratory infections, adenoid hypertrophy, allergic rhinitis, anatomic factors, and immunodeficiency also contribute to this complex problem, and these other factors must also be investigated.

Chronic Cough

Holinger and Sanders[71] studied 72 infants and children with cough of at least 1 month's duration and normal chest radiographic findings. Diagnostic testing included complete blood count with differential, cytology of nasal and bronchial washings, upper gastrointestinal studies (barium esophagram, reflux scan, pH probe, or esophagoscopy), sinus and soft tissue upper airway radiography, pulmonary function testing, direct laryngoscopy, and bronchoscopy. For the overall group, cough variant asthma (32%) was the most common cause of chronic cough, followed by sinusitis (23%), GERD (15%), aberrant innominate artery with tracheal compression (12%), and psychogenic cough (10%). In children younger than 18 months of age, aberrant innominate artery was the most common cause. In the Children's Hospital of Pittsburgh esophageal biopsy series,[159] the incidence of positive esophageal biopsy was 81% in 37 children with chronic cough.

Asthma

Although asthma is not a true otolaryngic problem, it is not uncommon in an otolaryngology practice to see patients with asthma that is possibly related to GERD. For example, it is not uncommon to see a child with airway obstruction secondary to adenotonsillar hypertrophy who also has asthma and GERD. These children often improve following surgery with relief of airway obstruction and treatment of GERD diagnosed by esophagoscopy and esophageal biopsy showing histologic esophagitis. Several studies have documented an association between asthma and GERD. Esophageal instillation of acid was shown to induce bronchospasm and significantly decrease peak expiratory flow rates in adults with and without both asthma and GERD.[129] Twenty-four-hour pH probes were used to document GERD in 12 infants with persistent wheezing that improved significantly following medical or surgical treatment of GERD.[50] GERD was found using pH probes in 27 of 36 (75%) asthmatic children who had no overt GERD symptomatology.[144] These results are in excellent agreement with the Children's Hospital of Pittsburgh esophageal biopsy study[159] in that 21 of 26 (75%) of the children with a history of asthma had positive esophageal biopsy results. In a study of 186 adult asthmatic patients, endoscopy and esophageal biopsy were used to document GERD-induced esophagitis in 39% of these patients, and 58% were found to have hiatal hernia.[134]

Globus Pharyngeus

Globus pharyngeus, or the sensation of having a lump in the throat, may be caused by reflux pharyngitis in some patients. Curran et al[41] used 24-hour pH monitoring to document GERD in 8 of 21 adult patients with globus pharyngeus. The differential diagnosis includes osteophytes of the spine, foreign body, cricopharyngeal hyperactivity, large tonsils, goiter, postcricoid web, cervical lymph nodes, or mass in the pharynx or esophagus. Physical examination, anteroposterior and lateral neck radiographs, barium swallow, and endoscopy should help to make the diagnosis. No published data exist showing an association between globus pharyngeus and GERD in the pediatric population.

Dysphagia

Oropharyngeal dysphagia is difficulty of passage of solids or liquids from the mouth to the upper esophagus. The causes include central neurologic problems, peripheral neurologic problems, primary muscular problems, cricopharyngeal dysfunction, and local factors. Local factors include those listed for globus pharyngeus. Donner et al[49] found that certain adults have an acid-sensitive esophagus in which acidic barium promotes motility disturbance with spastic contractions or an abnormally propagated peristaltic wave. Antacid was found to relax the esophagus. No published data exist showing an association between oropharyngeal dysphagia and GERD in the pediatric population.

Chronic Pharyngitis

Reflux of gastric contents into the pharynx with mucosal inflammation may be a cause of chronic sore throat in children. It usually is worse in the morning, since the reflux has been greater in the supine position while sleeping. Erythema of the pharynx, tonsils, uvula, and larynx may be observed. The sore throat is unresponsive to antimicrobial therapy and throat cultures are negative. Flexible laryngoscopy may reveal erythema and edema of the posterior glottis and pharynx, or of the tongue base or lingual tonsils. No published studies exist showing an association between chronic pharyngitis and GERD in the pediatric population.

Otalgia and Otitis

Referred otalgia may also occur secondary to pharyngitis from GERD.[96] The differential diagnosis of chronic otalgia also includes otitis media and temporomandibular joint problems. Although there are anecdotal reports of otitis secondary to gastropharyngeal reflux with eustachian tube inflammation as the cause, there is no conclusive evidence that GERD causes otitis.

Airway Obstruction and GERD

There appears to be an association between airway obstruction and GERD. A study in rats showed that partial upper airway obstruction resulted in a powerful thoracoabdominal end-expiratory pressure gradient, which may contribute to GERD by overcoming the antireflux barrier mechanism.[151] Thus, children with partial airway obstruction may progress to more severe airway obstruction when exposure of airway mucosa to gastric contents contributes to mucosal thickening.[161] Additionally, coughing associated with aspiration that frequently occurs during airway obstruction increases intra-abdominal pressure, which further promotes GERD.

Laryngomalacia

Laryngomalacia, which is caused by prolapse of floppy supraglottic tissues into the glottic airway during inspiration, has been considered the most common cause of stridor in infants. The usual presentation includes inspiratory stridor that is worsened with crying and placement in the supine position. It is classically improved by placing the child in the prone position.

Belmont and Grundfast[14] reported that 16 of 20 children (80%) with laryngomalacia had GERD documented by barium esophagram. Polonovski et al[116] documented, with barium swallow studies and esophagoscopy, a 50% incidence of GERD in 39 children with severe laryngomalacia requiring surgical intervention. Bouchard et al[24] reported that 61% of 18 children with laryngomalacia had

GERD documented with pH probes. Eighty percent of these children improved with medical treatment (H₂ blocker and prokinetic agent). We observed in the Children's Hospital of Pittsburgh esophageal biopsy study[159] that 21 of 28 children (75%) with endoscopically proven laryngomalacia had positive esophageal biopsy results.

If the duration and severity of the stridor have been impressive enough to warrant endoscopy, a complete airway evaluation in the operating room is indicated. Flexible nasopharyngolaryngoscopy with topical intranasal anesthesia is performed with the child awake or minimally sedated to evaluate for laryngomalacia and vocal cord mobility. Many of these children have erythematous and edematous supraglottic structures. Rigid bronchoscopy is also performed to assess the subglottis and tracheobronchial tree. The incidence of finding a second airway lesion that is synchronous with laryngomalacia is 17%,[60] and thus we prefer to perform rigid bronchoscopy for these patients to avoid missing a possible second, potentially life-threatening airway lesion. During bronchoscopy, bronchoalveolar lavage is also performed to look for increased amounts of lipid-laden macrophages, which may indicate aspiration related to GERD or primary aspiration.[104]

At the time of endoscopy, if the airway is robust, then rigid esophagoscopy and esophageal biopsy are performed to determine whether there is gross or histologic esophagitis. If the airway is tenuous, then rigid esophagoscopy is deferred and the gastroenterology service is consulted for esophageal suction biopsy; or a pH probe study or scintiscan is obtained to decrease the chances of airway edema. Arytenoid edema may result from rigid esophagoscopy, which should be avoided with a tenuous airway. Many of these children improve significantly as airway mucosal thickening resolves with lifestyle changes or pharmacotherapy for GERD. If the children have continued life-threatening airway obstruction or cannot gain weight, then supraglottoplasty or tracheotomy is performed.

Reflux-Induced Stridor and "Pseudolaryngomalacia"

Several reports have documented that GERD can induce stridor. With laryngomalacia, the stridor tends to be consistent when the child is crying or lying supine and improved with prone positioning and cessation of crying, as discussed earlier. In contrast, with reflux-induced stridor or "pseudolaryngomalacia," the stridor may be intermittent, has a variable temporal pattern, and is not significantly affected by changes in position. This clinical picture, plus a history of frequent spitting-up and possibly irritability, is consistent with reflux-induced stridor. Orenstein et al[112] and Nielson et al[103] have reported cases of infants who had intermittent stridor only during episodes of GERD that were documented by esophageal pH probe and resolved with pharmacotherapy. Henry and Mellis[68] reported on two children whose stridor resolved completely following Nissen fundoplication. Orenstein et al[109] also documented with the modified Bernstein test that esophageal instillation of acid could cause stridor in some children. Direct exposure of the glottis to gastric contents may result in laryngospasm; however, esophageal

instillation of acid has also been reported to result in laryngospasm via reflex pathways.[69, 111] Another mechanism of stridor may be related to agitation and more rapid or forceful breathing associated with esophageal pain during GERD leading to a "relative airway narrowing."[111]

Bouchard et al[24] reported that 58% of 31 children with stridor had GERD documented with pH probes. Eighty-three percent of these children improved with medical treatment (H₂ blocker and prokinetic agent). In the Children's Hospital of Pittsburgh esophageal biopsy series,[159] when children with a complaint of stridor resulting from all causes were combined, we observed that 42 of 67 of these children (63%) had positive esophageal biopsy results.

If the history and physical findings are clear-cut and mild, then empiric lifestyle changes or GERD pharmacotherapy, or both, can be tried. For more severe airway obstruction, the work-up would proceed as described under the section for laryngomalacia, including airway endoscopy. The typical laryngoscopic findings with pseudolaryngomalacia are edematous and erythematous arytenoids and posterior commissure. Many of these children respond to lifestyle changes or pharmacotherapy, but fundoplication may be required for severe refractory cases.

Apnea

Apneic episodes induced by GERD can be life-threatening. Herbst et al[69] and Gorrotxategi et al[61] documented apnea associated with GERD using pH probes in infants. There are two possible mechanisms of GERD-induced apnea. The first mechanism is related to GERD followed by aspiration of stomach contents into the glottis, subglottis, or tracheobronchial tree. This event will usually be followed by an episode of laryngospasm of varying duration. The second mechanism is reflex related. Herbst et al[69] have described the use of esophageal pH monitoring to document reflex apnea induced by acid reflux in the distal esophagus.

Ing et al[74] reported a significant association between GERD and obstructive sleep apnea in adults. When the GERD was treated with medication, there was a significant decrease in the apnea index. Additionally, when patients were treated with continuous positive airway pressure, there was a significant decrease in both GERD and the apnea index. In the Children's Hospital of Pittsburgh esophageal biopsy study,[159] 33 of 44 children with apnea (75%) had positive esophageal biopsy results, suggesting an association between apnea and GERD. Apneic episodes may respond to medical therapy, but severe, refractory, life-threatening episodes require fundoplication.

Recurrent Croup and Spasmodic Croup

Spasmodic croup has been purported to be caused by viral infection, allergy, and psychological factors, but the cause is often not clear in these difficult cases. It is likely that at least some cases of spasmodic croup are associated with recurrent bouts of reflux-induced stridor.

Waki et al[150] used scintiscan, pH probe, esophagoscopy, and barium swallow studies to document GERD in 15 of 32 (47%) children with recurrent croup. Contencin and Narcy[34] found pharyngeal and esophageal reflux with a double pH probe in eight of eight children with recurrent croup. In another series of 15 children with recurrent croup,[7] GERD was documented by pH probe in 7 (47%). In the Children's Hospital of Pittsburgh esophageal biopsy series,[159] 12 of 16 children (75%) with a history of recurrent croup had positive esophageal biopsy results. The explanation for these observations may be that children with GERD and baseline airway edema and inflammation, when challenged with a viral upper respiratory infection, have additional edema that causes significant airway obstruction.

Endoscopy to rule out additional anatomic airway anomalies is important in selected cases of recurrent croup. Waki et al[150] found that 8 of 32 (25%) of their patients had anatomic airway anomalies, including laryngomalacia and subglottic stenosis.

Subglottic Stenosis

The causes of subglottic stenosis in animal models have included trauma, infection,[22, 128, 139] and GERD.[59, 87, 96, 160] In canine studies, trauma to the subglottic perichondrium resulted in subglottic stenosis[22] that was more severe when gastric juice was applied.[94] Wynne et al[157] developed a murine model in which animals who aspirated gastric juice had desquamation of the superficial tracheal cell layer and delayed regeneration as compared with saline and acid (pH of 1.5) without gastric juice controls. Gaynor[59] irrigated rabbit tracheas with synthetic gastric juice (pH of 4 or 1.4) for periods of 1 to 4 hours and observed ulceration and necrosis. Koufman[85] reported, in a canine model, that healing of subglottic mucosal injuries was delayed by repeated painting of the injury with an acid plus pepsin solution as compared with saline and acid solution without pepsin controls.

At the Children's Hospital of Pittsburgh, a porcine model was developed to study the effects of brief gastric juice exposure on intact subglottic mucosa.[161] In the gastric juice group, basal cell hyperplasia, squamous metaplasia, moderate submucosal edema, and mucosal ulceration were seen. The saline control group did show squamous metaplasia and mild edema, but no basilar hyperplasia or ulceration was found. Messenger RNA measurement (reverse transcriptase-polymerase chain reaction) showed that application of gastric juice to the intact subglottis resulted in significantly lower expression of message for epidermal growth factor receptor compared with controls.

Koufman[85] also demonstrated, with 24-hour esophageal pH monitoring, a 78% incidence of GERD in 32 adult patients with laryngeal and tracheal stenosis. Jindal et al[76] reported that seven of seven adult female patients with idiopathic subglottic stenosis required GERD treatment for resolution. In a series of 36 children with subglottic stenosis who underwent laryngotracheal reconstruction at the Children's Hospital of Pittsburgh, 21 of 26 patients tested (80%) had at least one positive test for GERD.[160] A diagnosis of GERD was made following a positive finding on at least one of the following: barium swallow

study, 24-hour pH probe, esophageal biopsy, or radionuclide gastric emptying scan. At the Children's Hospital Medical Center, Cincinnati, Walner et al[149] used pH probes to evaluate for GERD in 74 children with subglottic stenosis. They found distal esophageal pH of less than 4.0 for at least 5% of the study period in 50% of these children. Fifty-five of these children underwent dual pH probe study (upper and lower esophagus). Proximal esophageal pH of less than 4.0 for at least 1% of the study period was detected in 49% of these children. As discussed in the section on the diagnosis of GERD, this same group[93] compared the results of dual pH probe studies (upper and lower esophagus) with results of biopsies of the interarytenoid area, postcricoid area, and upper and lower esophagus in patients being evaluated for laryngotracheal reconstruction. They observed that results of biopsies of the larynx were statistically correlated with biopsies of the esophagus. This was in contrast to lack of correlation between biopsies of the larynx and dual pH probe testing. The authors concluded that laryngeal mucosal biopsies may be the most sensitive test for mucosal injury from GERD. In the Children's Hospital of Pittsburgh series[159] of children who underwent esophageal biopsies, we found that 23 of 34 (68%) of children with subglottic stenosis had positive esophageal biopsy results. The estimated incidence of pathologic GERD is only 20% in infants[10] and only 8% after 12 months of age.[146] The increased incidence of GERD in patients with subglottic stenosis suggests that GERD may play a role in the etiology of subglottic stenosis, although cause and effect have not been conclusively demonstrated.

In a report concerning laryngotracheal reconstruction for subglottic stenosis by Zalzal et al,[162] it was concluded that there was no benefit from GERD testing or treatment. There were only seven patients in the group with documented GERD who were not treated with anti-GERD medication. Thus, the absence of statistical significance may simply be a result of inadequate sample size.

Other Laryngeal Manifestations of Gastroesophageal Reflux Disease (Reflux Laryngitis, Hoarseness, Vocal Cord Nodules, Throat Clearing, Vocal Cord Granulomas, and Ulcers)

Reflux of gastric contents up to the glottis can lead to inflammation that may result in hoarseness or throat clearing. Putnam and Orenstein[119] reported a case of a child with hoarseness and GERD documented by esophagoscopy, esophageal biopsy, and pH probe, whose hoarseness resolved with GERD pharmacotherapy. Hanson et al[66] reported on a series of 182 adults with endoscopically documented chronic laryngitis. Ninety-six percent responded to antireflux precautions, famotidine, or omeprazole. Endoscopically, a red or edematous posterior glottis is noted. There may be vocal cord edema.

In children with chronic throat clearing and vocal abuse, vocal cord nodules may develop. Kuhn et al[86] reported an association between vocal cord nodules and GERD documented by pH probe, with a higher incidence of GERD in the vocal cord nodules group compared with a control group. Bouchard et al[24] documented an incidence of GERD of 56% in 16 children with laryngitis. Eighty-six percent improved with medical (H_2 blocker and prokinetic agent) treatment for GERD. In the Children's Hospital of Pittsburgh esophageal biopsy series,[159] if an erythematous or edematous posterior glottis was noted, the esophageal biopsy finding was positive 83% and 81% of the time, respectively. Allergic rhinitis or sinusitis with postnasal drip may also contribute to these laryngeal problems and must be considered in the differential diagnosis.

Cherry and Margulies[32] reported three cases of refractory contact ulcer of the larynx in adults that resolved only after treatment of GERD. In 1968, Delahunty and Cherry[44] reported a canine model in which they repeatedly painted the posterior glottis with gastric juice, resulting in posterior glottic ulcers and granulation tissue. Airway mucosal trauma, vocal abuse, and infection are also possible causes of vocal cord granulomas and ulcers. Surgical removal of vocal cord granulomas may be followed by recurrence if the associated GERD is not treated.

Treatment

Treatments for GERD include lifestyle changes, pharmacotherapy, and surgery. Lifestyle changes for GERD in infants includes changes in the formula or sleep position. Lifestyle changes for older children include specific food avoidance (chocolate, caffeine, spicy foods),[4, 104, 148, 159] avoidance of overeating, weight loss for obese children, and avoidance of alcohol and smoking for adolescents.[36, 58, 78, 106, 153]

Changes in the formula composition are not usually successful as a treatment for GERD, except in infants who have true cow's milk protein allergy.[29, 30, 57, 69, 72] A trial of hypoallergenic formula may be useful in some infants.

Thickening of formula with rice cereal does not decrease the reflux index but does decrease vomiting.[12, 110, 147] Use of thickened formula may increase cough.[113] The increased caloric intake associated with the use of thickened feeds may be beneficial to infants with malnutrition secondary to GERD. The opening in the nipple used for thickened feeds must be enlarged (cross-cut) to allow the material to pass easily.

Although supine positioning is recommended to decrease the chances of sudden infant death syndrome,[1, 75, 115, 133] prone positioning is recommended when the risk of death from severe complications of GERD such as massive aspiration is greater. It is important to have tight bed sheets and no pillows to decrease the chances of sudden infant death syndrome in the prone position. The reflux index is decreased in the prone position as compared with the supine position.[99] Placement in an infant seat increases GERD.[114] For older children, left-sided positioning and elevation of the head of the bed may decrease GERD, as it does in adults,[65, 77, 137] but this has not been formally studied in children.

Pharmacotherapy includes acid neutralizers such as antacids, blockers of acid secretion such as H_2-receptor antagonists or gastric proton pump inhibitors, and proki-

netic agents. H_2-receptor blockers include ranitidine[38] and cimetidine.[37, 87] The H_2-receptor antagonists have been shown to be effective for relief of symptoms and healing of esophagitis.[33, 38, 97, 125, 136]

Proton pump inhibitors are the most effective acid suppressants and include omeprazole.[108] These drugs inactivate the gastric parietal cell H^+,K^+-ATPase pump.[155] Since these drugs require acid in the stomach to work best, they are most effective when given one half hour prior to a meal.[155] The indication for proton pump inhibitor therapy in children is failure of GERD to improve in response to H_2-receptor antagonists. Omeprazole has been demonstrated to normalize esophageal pH monitoring[63] and effectively treat esophagitis in infants and children.[5, 43, 80, 141] One randomized controlled study found that omeprazole was equally effective as very high dose ranitidine in improving symptoms, histologic esophagitis, and pH study results.[38] Many case series have suggested that in children with GERD that persisted despite the administration of H_2-receptor antagonists, omeprazole treatment improved both symptoms and endoscopic findings.[5, 43, 63, 82, 144]

There is some concern regarding the safety of prolonged omeprazole use and resultant hypergastrinemia. The concerns are related to reports of development of gastric polyps, expansion of the parietal cell zone, dilatation of gland lumina, and lingular pseudohypertrophy of individual parietal cells in adults and children.[15, 47, 62, 67, 126, 140] No cases of malignancy have been reported. Studies in adults with follow-up averaging 6.5 years demonstrated that omeprazole was both effective and safe, although Barrett's metaplasia of the esophagus (a premalignant condition) may still develop despite omeprazole treatment.[84]

Antacids neutralize gastric acid. High doses of the combination of magnesium hydroxide and aluminum hydroxide were shown to be as effective as cimetidine for peptic esophagitis in children.[40, 73] However, aluminum-containing antacids have been shown to increase plasma aluminum concentrations to toxic levels,[143] which may be associated with osteopenia, anemia, and neurotoxicity.[6, 83, 129] Since safe and effective alternatives are available, the Gastroesophageal Reflux Guidelines Committee of the North American Society for Pediatric Gastroenterology and Nutrition has not recommended their use for pediatric patients.[121] The exception to the recommendations is the use of antacids for children who have only occasional heartburn.

Prokinetic agents are designed to increase the resting tone of the lower esophageal sphincter, decrease transient lower esophageal sphincter relaxations, increase esophageal peristalsis, and accelerate gastric emptying. Prokinetic agents include cisapride,[79, 105, 144] metoclopramide, and bethanechol.[51, 121] Cisapride is considered the best prokinetic agent; it is less likely to worsen bronchospasm than bethanechol and less likely to cause extrapyramidal side effects than metoclopramide.[108] Cases of prolonged Q-T interval and fatal arrhythmias have been associated with cisapride used concomitantly with certain other drugs. Concomitant administration of cisapride with macrolide antimicrobials or imidazole antifungal agents must be avoided to prevent these arrhythmias.[2, 25, 82, 91, 107, 158]

Because of reports of fatalities related to cisapride, its use has been discontinued except for rare patients with severe GERD who must use the special protocol, as follows.

The Gastroesophageal Reflux Guidelines Committee of the North American Society for Pediatric Gastroenterology and Nutrition has recommended that cisapride be used only for selected infants and children who have failed lifestyle and antisecretory therapy. The recommendations include a special protocol including repeated venipuncture and electrocardiograms, which decrease the practicality of this approach. The Guidelines Committee concluded that there is insufficient evidence that prokinetic agents other than cisapride are effective in the treatment of GERD in infants and children.[121]

Metaclopramide is a dopamine antagonist but is also an acetylcholine and serotonin agonist. Two studies suggested that metaclopramide decreased vomiting in children,[46, 89] whereas two other studies showed no effect.[13, 95] A major disadvantage of metaclopramide is the potential for serious neurologic complications, including parkinsonian reactions, acute dystonic reactions, and tardive dyskinesia.[120]

Bethanechol, an acetylcholine agonist, was found in one study to decrease vomiting,[26] but a second study found no effect.[90] For domperidone, one study found improvement in symptoms and pH scores[46] and two other studies showed no effect.[18, 27]

The surface agent sucralfate adheres to gastric ulcers and protects the esophageal mucosa against the effects of gastric juice. A randomized study in children showed that it was as effective as cimetidine for esophagitis.[9] However, it contains aluminum and thus its safety in children has not been determined in view of the potential for aluminum toxicity in children.[6, 83, 130]

Pediatric cases of GERD that are still refractory to maximal medical therapy or will not tolerate discontinuation of medical therapy may require surgical fundoplication.[54, 55, 56, 88] There are numerous case series reporting favorable results for fundoplication in infants and children. In these surgeries, a portion of the gastric fundus is wrapped totally or partially around the distal esophagus to increase the tone of the lower esophageal sphincter. Studies were not well controlled and varied in technique and may or may not have included pyloroplasty. Medical therapy and diagnostic testing prior to fundoplication were variable.[3, 16, 17, 20, 21, 27, 45, 54, 55, 122, 135, 148, 152]

Success rates varied from 57% to 92%. Mortality as a complication of surgery ranged from 0% to 4.7%, while the complication rate varied from 2.2% to 45%. Complications include breakdown of the wrap, small bowel obstruction, gas bloat syndrome, infection, atelectasis, pneumonia, perforated viscus, esophageal stricture, esophageal obstruction, dumping syndrome, incisional hernia, and gastroparesis.[3, 16, 17, 20, 21, 27, 45, 54, 55, 81, 122, 127, 135, 148, 152]

With regard to fundoplication in the pediatric population, the recommendations of the Gastroesophageal Reflux Guidelines Committee of the North American Society for Pediatric Gastroenterology and Nutrition are as follows. For chronic esophagitis, both upper endoscopy and biopsy and prolonged pH monitoring are recommended to confirm the diagnosis of GERD and to rule out other pathologic conditions, such as eosinophilic esophagitis. For respiratory complications of GERD, the recommended diagnostic studies include radiographic studies, bronchoalveolar lavage, esophageal pH monitoring, and swallowing studies.[121] The authors of this chapter recommend the addition of flexible and direct laryngoscopy and bronchoscopy to rule out significant concomitant airway pathologic lesions such as laryngeal cleft, laryngomalacia, vocal cord paralysis, subglottic stenosis, or vascular compression of the trachea.

Conclusion

Associations between GERD and several other important pediatric problems are suggested by review of clinical studies and animal model results. Although GERD has not definitively been shown to cause all of these problems, the associations that have been documented suggest that testing for GERD should be considered in selected children who carry diagnoses and endoscopic findings that include asthma, recurrent croup, chronic cough, apnea, sinusitis, stridor, laryngomalacia, subglottic stenosis, laryngitis, and posterior glottic edema or erythema. Although substantial evidence is accumulating, further prospective clinical and basic studies are needed to conclusively demonstrate cause and effect between GERD and these problems and to determine whether treatment improves the outcomes for these patients.

SELECTED READINGS

Rudolph CD, Mazur LJ, Liptak GS, et al: Guidelines for evaluation and treatment of gastroesophageal reflux in infants and children: Recommendations of North American Society for Pediatric Gastroenterology and Nutrition. J Pediatr Gastroenterol Nutr 32:1, 2001.
   An excellent evidence-based review of the spectrum of GERD-associated conditions, as well as diagnostic and treatment modalities.

REFERENCES

1. Adams EJ, Chavez GF, Steen D, et al. Changes in the epidemiologic profile of sudden infant death syndrome as rates decline among California infants: 1990–1995. Pediatrics 102:1445, 1998.
2. Ahmad SR, Wolfe SM. Cisapride and torsades de pointes. Lancet 345:508, 1995.
3. Ahrens P, Heller K, Beyer P, et al. Antireflux surgery in children suffering from reflux-associated respiratory diseases. Pediatr Pulmonol 28:89, 1999.
4. Allen ML, Mellow MH, Robinson MG, et al. The effect of raw onions on acid reflux and reflux symptoms. Am J Gastroenterol 85:377, 1990.
5. Alliet P, Raes M, Bruneel E, et al. Omeprazole in infants with cimetidine-resistant peptic esophagitis. J Pediatr 132:352, 1998.
6. American Academy of Pediatrics, Committee on Nutrition. Aluminum toxicity in infants and children. Pediatrics 97:413, 1996.
7. Andrieu-Guitrancourt J, Dehesdin D, Luyer BL, et al. Role du reflux gastro-esophagien au cours des dyspnées laryngées aigues recidivantes de l'enfant. Ann Otolaryngol 101:141, 1984.
8. Andze GO, Brandt ML, St. Vil D, et al. Diagnosis and treatment of gastroesophageal reflux in 500 children with respiratory symptoms: the value of pH monitoring. J Pediatr Surg 26:295, 1991.

9. Arguelles-Martin F, Gonzalez-Fernandez F, Gentles MG. Sucralfate versus cimetidine in the treatment of reflux esophagitis in children. Am J Med 86:73, 1989.
10. Aronow E, Silverberg M. Normal and abnormal GI motility. In Silverberg M (ed). Pediatric Gastroenterology. New York, Medical Examination Publishing, 1983, p 214.
11. Aviv JE, Kim T, Saco RL, et al. FEESST: a new bedside endoscopic test of the motor and sensory components of swallowing. Ann Otol Rhinol Laryngol 107:378, 1998.
12. Bailey DJ, Andres JM, Danek GD, et al. Lack of efficacy of thickened feeding as treatment for gastroesophageal reflux. J Pediatr 110:187, 1987.
13. Bellissant E, Duhamel JF, Guillot M, et al. The triangular test to assess the efficacy of metoclopramide in gastroesophageal reflux. Clin Parmacol Ther 61:377, 1997.
14. Belmont JR, Grundfast K: Congenital laryngeal stridor (laryngomalacia): etiologic factors and associated disorders. Ann Otol Rhinol Laryngol 93:430, 1984.
15. Berlin RG. Omeprazole: gastrin and gastric endocrine cell data from clinical studies. Dig Dis Sci 36:129, 1991.
16. Bensoussan AL, Yazbeck S, Carceller-Blanchard A. Results and complications of Toupet partial posterior wrap: 10 years' experience. J Pediatr Surg 29:1215, 1994.
17. Bergmeijer JH, Harbers JS, Molenaar JC. Function of pediatric Nisses-Rossetti fundoplication followed up into adolescence and adulthood. J Am Coll Surg 184:259, 1997.
18. Bines JE, Quinlan JE, Treves S, et al. Efficacy of domperidone in infants and children with gastroesophageal reflux. J Peditr Gastroenterol Nutr 14:400, 1992.
19. Black DD, Haggitt RC, Orenstein SR, et al. Esophagitis in infants: morphometric histological diagnosis and correlation with measures of gastroesophageal reflux. Gastroenterology 98:1408, 1990.
20. Blane CE, Turnage RH, Oldham KT, et al. Long-term radiographic follow-up of the Nissen fundoplication in children. Pediatr Radiol 19:523, 1989.
21. Bliss D, Hirschl R, Oldham K, et al. Efficacy of anterior gastric fundoplication in the treatment of gastroesophageal reflux in infants and children. J Pediatr Surg 29:1071, 1994.
22. Borowiecki B, Croft BC. Experimental model of subglottic stenosis. Ann Otol 86:835, 1977.
23. Bothwell MR, Parsons DS, Talbot A, et al. Outcome of reflux therapy on pediatric chronic sinusitis. Otolaryngol Head Neck Surg 121:255, 1999.
24. Bouchard S, Lallier M, Yazbeck S, Bensoussan A. The otolaryngologic manifestations of gastroesophageal reflux: when is a pH study indicated? J Pediatr Surg 34:1053, 1999.
25. Bran S, Murray WA, Hirsch IB, Palmer JP. Long QT syndrome during high-dose cisapride. Arch Intern Med 155:765, 1995.
26. Buler AR. Use of bethanechol for the treatment of gastroesophageal reflux. J Pediatr 96:321, 1980.
27. Caniano DA, Ginn-Pease ME, King DR. The failed antireflux procedure: analysis of risk factors and morbidity. J Pediatr Surg 25:1022, 1990.
28. Carroccio A, Iacono G, Montalto G, et al. Domperidone plus magnesium hydroxide and aluminum hydroxide: a valid therapy in children with gastroesophageal reflux. A double-blind randomized study versus placebo. Scan J Gastroenterol 29:300, 1994.
29. Cavataio F, Iacono G, Montalto G, et al. Gastroesophageal reflux associated with cow's milk allergy in infants: which diagnostic examinations are useful? Am J Gastroenterol 91:1215, 1996.
30. Cavataio F, Iacono G, Monalto G, et al. Clinical and pH-metric characteristics of gastro-esophageal reflux secondary to cows: milk protein allergy. Arch Dis Child 75:51, 1996.
31. Chen M, Ott D, Sinclair J, et al. Gastroesophageal reflux disease: correlation of esophageal pH testing and radiographic findings. Radiology 185:483, 1992.
32. Cherry J, Margulies SI: Contact ulcer of the larynx. Laryngoscope 78:1937, 1968.
33. Chiba N, De Gara CJ, Wilkinson JM, Hunt RH. Speed of healing and symptom relief in grade II to IV gastroesophageal reflux disease: a meta-analysis. Gastroenterology 112:1798, 1997.
34. Contencin P, Narcy P: Gastropharyngeal reflux in infants and children. Arch Otolaryngol Head Neck Surg 118:1028, 1992.
35. Contencin P, Narcy P: Nasopharyngeal pH monitoring in infants

and children with chronic rhinopharyngitis. Int J Pediatr Otorhinolaryngol 22:249, 1991.
36. Cook DG, Strachan DP. Health effects of passive smoking—10: Summary of effects of parental smoking on the respiratory health of children an implications for research. Thorax 54:357, 1999.
37. Cucchiara S, Gobio-Casali L, Balli F, et al. Cimetidine treatment of reflux esophagitis in children: an Italian multicentric study. J Pediatr Gastroenterol Nutr 8:150, 1989.
38. Cucchiara S, Minella R, Iervolino MR, et al. Omeprazole and high dose ranitidine in the treatment of refractory reflux oesophagitis. Arch Dis Child 69:655, 1993.
39. Cucchiara S, Staiano A, Gobio Casali L, et al. Value of the 24-hour intraesophageal pH monitoring in children. Gut 311:29, 1990.
40. Cucchiara S, Staiano A, Romaniello G, et al: Antacids and cimetidine treatment for gastro-oesophageal reflux and peptic oesophagitis. Arch Dis Child 1984, 59:842.
41. Curran AJ, Barry MK, Callanan V, Gormley PK: A prospective study of acid reflux and globus pharyngeus using a modified symptom index. Clin Otolaryngol 20:552, 1995.
42. Dahms BB. Reflux esophagitis and sequelae in infants and children. In Dahms BB, Qualman SJ (eds). Gastrointestinal Diseases: Perspectives in Pediatric Pathology, Vol. 20. Basel, Karger, 1997, pp 14–34.
43. De Giacomo C, Bawa P, Franceschi M, et al. Omeprazole for severe reflux esophagitis in children. J Pediatr Gastroenterol Nutr 24:528, 1997.
44. Delahunty JE, Cherry J. Experimentally produced vocal cord granulomas. Laryngoscope 78:1941, 1968.
45. Dalla Vecchia LK, Grosfeld JL, West KW, et al. Reoperation after Nissen fundoplication in children with gastroesophageal reflux: experience with 130 patients. Ann Surg 226:315, 1997.
46. De Loore I, Van Ravensteyn H, Ameryckx L. Domperidone drops in the symptomatic treatment of chronic paediatric vomiting and regurgitation: a comparison with metoclopramide. Postgrad Med J 55:40, 1979.
47. Dent J, Yeomans ND, Mackinnon M, et al. Omeprazole v. ranitidine for prevention of relapse in reflux oesophagitis: a controlled double blind trial of their efficacy and safety. Gut 35:590, 1994.
48. DiBaise J, Huerter J, Quigley E. Sinusitis and gastroesophageal reflux disease. Ann Intern Med 129:1078, 1998.
49. Donner MW, Silbiger ML, Hookman P, et al. Acid barium swallows in the radiographic evaluation of clinical esophagitis. J Laryngol Otol 87:220, 1966.
50. Eid NS, Shepherd RW, Thomson MA: Persistent wheezing and gastroesophageal reflux in infants. Pediatr Pulmomol 18:39, 1994.
51. Euler AR. Use of bethanechol for the treatment of gastroesophageal reflux. J Pediatr 96:321, 1980.
52. Euler AR, Byrne WJ. Twenty-four hour esophageal intraluminal pH probe testing: a comparative analysis. Gastroenterology 80:957, 1981.
53. Fawcett HD, Hayden CK, Adams JC, et al. How useful is gastroesophageal reflux scintigraphy in suspected childhood aspiration? Pediatr Radiol 18:311, 1988.
54. Fonkalsrud EW, Ashcraft KW, Coran AG, et al. Surgical treatment of gastroesophageal reflux in children: a combined hospital study of 7467 patients. Pediatrics 101:419, 1998.
55. Fonkalsrud EW, Burstorff-Silva J, Perez CA, et al. Antireflux surgery in children under 3 months of age. J Pediatr Surg 34:527, 1999.
56. Fonkalsrud EW, Ellis DG, Shaw A, et al: A combined hospital experience with fundoplication and gastric emptying procedure for gastroesophageal reflux in children. J Am Coll Surg 180:449, 1995.
57. Forget P, Arends JW. Cow's milk protein allergy and gastro-esophageal reflux. Eur J Pediatr 144:298, 1985.
58. Fraser-Moodie CA, Norton B, Gornall C, et al. Weight loss has an independent beneficial effect on symptoms of gastro-oesophageal reflux in patients who are overweight. Scan J Gastroenterol 34:337, 1999.
59. Gaynor EB: Gastroesophageal reflux as an etiologic factor in laryngeal complications of intubation. Laryngoscope 98:972, 1988.
60. Gonzales C, Reilly JS, Bluestone CD: Synchronous airway lesions in infancy. Ann Otol Rhinol Laryngol 96:77, 1987.
61. Gorrotxategi P, Eizaguirre I, Saenz de Ugarte A, et al. Characteristics of continuous esophageal pH metering in infants with gastro-

esophageal reflux and apparent life-threatening events. Eur J Pediatr Surg 5:136, 1995.

62. Graham JR. Gastric polyposis: onset during long-term therapy with omeprazole. Med J Aust 157:287, 1992.

63. Gunasekaran TS, Hassail EG. Efficacy and safety of omeprazole for severe gastroesophageal reflux in children. J Pediatr 123:148, 1993.

64. Gupta JP, Kumar A, Jain AK, et al. Gastro-eophageal reflux disease (GERD): an appraisal of different tests for diagnosis. J Assoc Physicians India 38:699, 1990.

65. Hamilton JW, Boisen RJ, Yamamoto DT, et al. Sleeping on a wedge diminishes exposure of the esophagus to refluxed acid. Dig Dis Sci 33:518, 1988.

66. Hanson DG, Kamel PL, Kahrilas PJ: Outcomes of antireflux therapy for the treatment of chronic laryngitis. Ann Otol Rhinol Laryngol 104:550, 1995.

67. Hassall E. Wrap session: is the Nissen slipping? Can medical treatment replace surgery for severe gastroesophageal reflux disease in children? Am J Gastroenterol 90:1212, 1995.

68. Henry RL, Mellis CM: Resolution of inspiratory stridor after fundoplication: case report. Aust Paediatr J 18:126, 1982.

69. Herbst JJ, Minton SD, Book LS: Gastroesophageal reflux causing respiratory distress and apnea in newborn infants. J Pediatr 95:763, 1979.

70. Hill DJ, Cameron DJ, Francis DE, et al. Challenge confirmation of late-onset reactions to extensively hydrolyzed formulas in infants with multiple food protein intolerance. J Allergy Clin Immunol 96:386, 1995.

71. Holinger LD, Sanders AD: Chronic cough in infants and children: an update. Laryngoscope 101:596, 1991.

72. Iacono G, Carroccio A, Cavataio F, et al. Gastroesophageal reflux and cow's milk allergy in infants: a prospective study. J Allergy Clin Immunol 97:822, 1996.

73. Iacono G, Carroccio A, Montalto G, et al. [Magnesium hydroxide and aluminum hydroxide in the treatment of gastroesophageal reflux.] Minerva Pediatr 43:797, 1991.

74. Ing A. Obstructive sleep apnea and gastroesophageal reflux. Am J Med 108(suppl 4a):120S, 2000.

75. Jeffery HE, Megevand A, Page M. Why the prone position is a risk factor for sudden infant death syndrome. Pediatrics 104:263, 1999.

76. Jindal JR, Milbrath MM, Hogan WJ, et al. Gastroesophageal reflux disease as a likely cause of "idiopathic" subglottic stenosis. Ann Otol Rhinol Laryngol 1994, 103:186.

77. Johnson LF, DeMeester TR. Evaluation of elevation of the head of the bed, bethanechol, and antacid from tables on gastroesophageal reflux. Dig Dis Sci 26:673, 1981.

78. Kadakia SC, Kikendall JW, Maydonovitch C, et al. Effect of cigarette smoking on gastroesophageal reflux measured by 24-h ambulatory esophageal pH monitoring. Am J Gastroenterol 90:1785, 1995.

79. Kamel PL, Hanson D, Kahrilas PJ: Omeprazole for the treatment of posterior laryngitis. Am J Med 96:321, 1994.

80. Kato S, Ebina K, Fujii K, et al. Effect of omeprazole in the treatment of refractory acid-related diseases in childhood: endoscopic healing and twenty-four-hour intragastric acidity. J Pediatr 128:415, 1996.

81. Khoshoo V, Roberst PL, Loe WA, et al. Nutritional management of dumping syndrome associated with antireflux surgery. J Pediatr Surg 29:1452, 1994.

82. Klausner MA. Dear Doctor letters. Pharmaceutria Research Foundation. Feb. 3, 1995; Oct. 14, 1995.

83. Klein GL. Metabolic bone disease of total parenteral nutrition. Nutrition 14:149, 1998.

84. Klinkenberg-Knol EC, Nelis F, Dent J, et al. Long-term omprezole treatment in resistant gastroesophageal reflux disease: efficacy, safety and influence on gastic mucosa. Gastroenterology 118:661, 2000.

85. Koufman JA: The otolaryngologic manifestations of gastroesophageal reflux disease (GERD): a clinical investigation of 225 patients using ambulatory 24 hour pH monitoring and an experimental investigation of the role of acid and pepsin in the development of laryngeal injury. Laryngoscope 101:1, 1991.

86. Kuhn J, Toohill R, Ulualp S, et al. Pharyngel acid reflux evnts in patients with vocal cord nodules. Laryngoscope 108:1146, 1998.

87. Lambert J, Mobassaleh M, Grand RJ. Efficacy of cimetidine for gastric acid suppression in pediatric patients. J Pediatr 120:474, 1992.

88. Leape LL, Ramenofsky ML: Surgical treatment of gastroesophageal reflux in children. Am J Dis Child 134:935, 1980.

89. Leung C, Lai W. Use of metoclopramide for the treatment of gastroesophageal reflux in infants and children. Curr Ther Res 36:911, 1984.

90. Levi P, Marmo P, Saluzzo C, et al. Bethanechol versus antacids in the treatment of gastroesophageal reflux. Helv Paediatr Acta 40:349, 1985.

91. Lewin MB, Bryant RM, Fenrich AL, Grifka RG. Cisapride-induced long QT interval. J Pediatr 128:279, 1996.

92. Liacouras CA, Wenner WJ, Brown K, et al. Primary eosinophilic esophagitis in children: successful treatment with oral corticosteroids. J Pediatr Gastroenterol Nutr 26:380, 1998.

93. Link DT, Willging JP, Miller CK, et al. Pediatric laryngopharyngeal sensory testing during FEES: feasible and correlative. Ann Otol Rhinol Laryngol 109:899, 2000.

94. Little FB, Koufman JA, Kohut RI, Marshall RB. Effect of gastric acid on the pathogenesis of subglottic stenosis. Ann Otol Rhinol Laryngol 94:516, 1985.

95. Machida HM, Forbes DA, Gall DG, et al. Metoclopramide in gastroesophageal reflux of infancy. J Pediatr 112:483, 1988.

96. Malherbe WD. Otalgia with esphageal hiatus hernia. Lancet 1:1368, 1958.

97. McCarty-Dawson D, Sue SO, Morrill B, et al. Ranitidine versus cimetidine in the healing of erosive esophagitis. Clin Ther 18:1150, 1996.

98. McMurray JS, Gerber M, Stern Y, et al. Role of laryngoscopy, dual pH probe monitoring, and laryngeal mucosal biopsy in the diagnosis of pharyngoesophageal reflux. Ann Otol Rhinol Laryngol 110:299, 2001.

99. Meyers WF, Herbst JJ. Effectiveness of positioning therapy for gastroesophageal reflux. Pediatrics 69:768, 1982.

100. Meyers WF, Roberts CC, Johnson DG, et al. Value of tests for evaluation of gastroesophageal reflux in children. J Pediatr Surg 20:515, 1985.

101. Murphy DW, Castell DO. Chocolate and heartburn: evidence of increased esophageal acid exposure after chocolate ingestion. Am J Gastroenterol 83:633, 1988.

102. Nelson SP, Chen EH, Syniar GM, et al. Prevalence of symptoms of gastroesophageal reflux during infancy: a pediatric practice-based survey. Pediatric Practice Research Group. Arch Pediatr Adolesc Med 151:569, 1997.

103. Nielson DW, Heldt GP, Tooley WH: Stridor and gastroesophageal reflux in infants. Pediatrics 85:1034, 1990.

104. Nussbaum E, Maggi JC, Mathis R, Galant SP: Association of lipid-laden alveolar macrophages and gastroesophageal reflux in children. J Pediatr 110:190, 1987.

105. Olafsdottir E: Gastro-oesophageal reflux and chronic respiratory disease in infants and children: treatment with cisapride. Scand J Gastroenterol 30(Suppl 211):32, 1995.

106. Oliveria SA, Christos PJ, Talley NJ, et al. Heartburn risk factors, knowledge, and prevention strategies: a population-based survey of individuals with heartburn. Arch Intern Med 159:1592, 1999.

107. Olsson S, Edwards IR. Tachycardia during cisapride treatment. BMJ 305:748, 1992.

108. Orenstein SO. Management of GER in childhood asthma. Pediatr Pulmonol Suppl 11:57, 1995.

109. Orenstein SR, Kocoshis SA, Orenstein DM, Proujansky R: Stridor and gastroesophageal reflux: diagnostic use of intraluminal esophageal acid perfusion (Bernstein Test). Pediatr Pulmonol 3:420, 1987.

110. Orenstein SR, Magill HL, Brooks P. Thickening of infant feedings for therapy of gastroesophageal reflux. J Pediatr 110:181, 1987.

111. Orenstein SR, Orenstein DM: Gastroesophageal reflux and respiratory disease in children. J Pediatr 112:847, 1988.

112. Orenstein SR, Orenstein DM, Whitington P: Gastroesophageal reflux causing stridor. Chest 84:301, 1983.

113. Orenstein SR, Shalaby TM, Putnam PE. Thickened feedings as a cause of increased coughing when used as therapy for gastroesophageal reflux in infants. J Pediatr 121:913, 1992.

114. Orenstein SR, Whitington PF, Orenstein DM. The infant seat as treatment for gastroesophageal reflux. N Engl J Med 309:70, 1983.

115. Oyen N, Markestad T, Skaerven R, et al. Combined effects of

sleeping position and prenatal risk factors in sudden infant death syndrome: the Nordic Epidemiological SIDS Study. Pediatrics 100: 613, 1997.

116. Polonovski JM, Contencin P, Viala P, et al. Aryepiglottic fold excision for the treatment of severe laryngomalacia. Ann Otol Rhinol Laryngol 99:625, 1990.

117. Puntis JW, Smith HL, Buick RG, Booth IW. Effect of dystonic movements on oesophageal peristalsis in Sandifer's syndrome. Arch Dis Child 64:1311, 1989.

118. Putnam P, Orenstein S: Blind esophageal suction biopsy in children less than 2 years of age. Gastroenterol 102:A149, 1992.

119. Putnam PE, Orenstein SR: Hoarseness in a child with gastroesophageal reflux. Acta Paediatr 81:635, 1992.

120. Putnam PE, Orenstein SR, Wessel HB, et al. Tardive dyskinesia associated with use of metoclopramide in a child. J Pediatr 121: 983, 1992.

121. Rudolph C, Mazur LJ, Liptak GS, et al. Gastroesophageal Reflux Guidelines Committee of the North American Society for Pediatric Gastroenterology and Nutrition. Pediatrics 2001 (in press).

122. Randolph J. Experience with the Nissen fundoplication for correction of gastroesophageal reflux in infants. Ann Surg 198:579, 1983.

123. Ruchelli E, Wenner W, Boytek T, et al. Severity of esophageal eosinophilia predicts response to conventional gastroesophageal reflux therapy. Pediatr Dev Pathol 2:15, 1999.

124. Ruth M, Carlsson S, Mansson I, et al. Scintigraphic detection of gastro-pulmonary aspiration in patients with respiratory disorders. Clin Physiol 13:19, 1993.

125. Sabesin SM, Berlin RG, Humphries TJ, et al. Famotidine relieves symptoms of gastroesophageal reflux disease and heals erosions and ulcerations: results of a multicenter, placebo-controlled, dose ranging study. USA Merck Gastroesophageal Reflux Disease Study Group. Arch Intern Med 151:2394, 1991.

126. Sachs G. The safety of omeprazole: true or false? Gastroenterology 106:1400, 1994.

127. Samuk I, Afrait R, Horne T, et al. Dumping syndrome following Nissen fundoplication, diagnosis, and treatment. J Pediatr Gastroenterol Nutr 23:235, 1996.

128. Sasaki CT, Horiuchi M, Koss N. Tracheostomy-related subglottic stenosis: bacteriologic pathogenesis. Laryngoscope 89:857, 1979.

129. Schan CA, Harding SM, Haile JM, et al. Gastroesophageal reflux induced bronchoconstriction. Chest 106:731, 1994.

130. Sedman A. Aluminum toxicity in childhood. Pediatr Nephrol 6:383, 1998.

131. Seibert JJ, Byrne WJ, Euler AR, et al. Gastroesophageal reflux— the acid test: scintigraphy or the pH probe? AJR Am J Roentgenol 140:1087, 1983.

132. Shub MD, Ulshen MH, Hargrove CB, et al. Esophagitis: a frequent consequence of gastroesophageal reflux in infancy. J Pediatr 107:881, 1985.

133. Skadberg BT, Morild I, Markestad T. Abandoning prone sleeping: effect on the risk of sudden infant death syndrome. J Pediatr 132: 340, 1998.

134. Sontag SJ, Schnell TG, Miller TQ, et al. Prevalence of oesophagitis in asthmatics. Gut 33:872, 1992.

135. Spillane AJ, Currie B, Shi E. Fundoplication in children: experience with 106 cases. Aust N Z J Surg 66:753, 1996.

136. Stacey JH, Miocevich ML, Sacks GE. The effect of ranitidine (as effervescent tablets) on the quality of life of GERD patients. Br J Clin Pract 50:190, 1996.

137. Stanciu C, Bennett JR. Effects of posture on gastro-oesophageal reflux. Digestion 15:104, 1977.

138. Stephen TC, Younoszai MK, Massey MP, et al. Diagnosis of gastropharyngeal reflux in pediatrics. J Ky Med Assoc 92:188, 1994.

139. Squire R, Brodsky L, Rossman J. The role of infection in the pathogenesis of acquired tracheal stenosis. Laryngoscope 100:765, 1979.

140. Stolte M, Bethke B, Ruhl G, et al. Omeprazole-induced pseudohypertrophy of gastric parietal cells. Z Gastroenterol 30:134, 1992.

141. Strauss RS, Calenda KA, Dayal Y, et al. Histological esophagitis: clinical and histological response to omeprazole in children. Dig Dis Sci 44:134, 1999.

142. Thompson JK, Koehler RE, Richter JE. Detection of gastroesophageal reflux: value of barium studies compared with 24-hr pH monitoring. AJR Am J Roentgenol 162:621, 1994.

143. Tsou VM, Young RM, Hart MH, et al. Elevated plasma aluminum levels in normal infants receiving antacids containing aluminum. Pediatrics 87:148, 1991.

144. Tucci F, Resti M, Fontana R, et al. Gastroesophageal reflux and bronchial asthma: prevalence and effect of cisapride therapy. J Pediatr Gastroenterol Nutr 17:265, 1993.

145. Vandenplas Y, De Wolf D, Sacre L. Influence of xanthines on gastroesophageal reflux in infants at risk for sudden infant death syndrome. Pediatrics 77:807, 1986.

146. Vandenplas Y, Franckx-Goossens A, Pipeleers-Marichal M, et al. Area under pH 4: advantages of a new parameter in the interpretation of esophageal pH monitoring data in infants. J Pediatr Gastroenterol Nutr 9:34, 1989.

147. Vandenplas Y, Sacre L. Milk-thickening agents as a treatment for gastroesophageal reflux (published erratum appears in Clin Pediatr [Phila] 26:148, 1987). Clin Pediatr (Phila) 26:66, 1987.

148. Veit F, Schwagten K, Auldist AW, et al. Trends in the use of fundoplication in children with gastro-oesophageal reflux. J Paediatr Child Health 31:121, 1995.

149. Walner DL, Stern Y, Gerber ME, et al. Gastroesophageal reflux in patients with subglottic stenosis. Arch Otolaryngol Head Neck Surg 124:551, 1998.

150. Waki EY, Madgy DN, Belenky WM, Gower VC: The incidence of gastroesophageal reflux in recurrent croup. Int J Pediatr Otorhinolaryngol 32:223, 1995.

151. Wang W, Tovar J, Eizaguirre I, et al. Airway obstruction and gastroesophageal reflux: an experimental study on the pathogenesis of this association. J Ped Surg 28:995, 1993.

152. Weber TR. Toupet fundoplication for gastroesophageal reflux in childhood. Arch Surg 134:717, 1999.

153. Wilson LJ, Ma W, Hirschowitz BI. Association of obesity with hiatal hernia and esophagitis. Am J Gastroenterol 94:2840, 1999.

154. Winter HS, Madara JL, Stafford RJ, et al. Intraepithelial eosinophils: a new diagnostic criterion for reflux esophagitis. Gastroenterology 83:818, 1982.

155. Wolfe MM, Sachs G. Acid suppression: optimizing therapy for gastroduodenal ulcer healing, gastroesophageal reflux disease, and stress-related erosive syndrome. Gastroenterology 118:S9, 2000.

156. Wright LE, Castell DO. The adverse effect of chocolate on lower esophageal sphincter pressure. Am J Dig Dis 20:703, 1975.

157. Wynne JW, Ramphal R, Hood CI: Tracheal mucosal damage after aspiration. Am Rev Respir Dis 124:728, 1981.

158. Wysowskl DK, Bacsanyi J. Cisapride and fatal arrhythmia [letter]. N Engl J Med 335:290, 1996.

159. Yellon R, Cotticchia J, Dixit S, Lee D. Esophageal biopsy for the diagnosis of gastroesophageal reflux-associated otolaryngologic problems in children. Am J Med 108(suppl 4a):131S, 2000.

160. Yellon R, Parameswaran M, Brandom B. Decreasing morbidity following laryngotracheal reconstruction in children. Int J Ped Otol 41:145, 1997.

161. Yellon R, Szeremeta W, Grandis J, et al. Subglottic injury, gastric juice, corticosteroids, and peptide growth factors in a porcine model. Laryngoscope 108:854, 1998.

162. Zalzal GH, Choi SS, Patel KM. The effect of gastroesophageal reflux on laryngotracheal reconstruction. Arch Otolaryngol Head Neck Surg 122:297, 1996.

70

Burns and Acquired Strictures of the Esophagus

Keith H. Riding, M.D., and Cuneyt M. Alper, M.D.

Esophageal injuries may result in strictures that limit or prevent passage of food or liquids. The most common cause of an acquired stricture of the esophagus is a burn from a caustic ingestion. Every effort should be made to prevent accidental ingestion of caustic substances. When ingestion has occurred, accurate assessment of the injury and prompt treatment may help reduce some of the severe sequelae that lead to significant morbidity or mortality.

It has been estimated that there are 26,000 caustic ingestions per year in the United States.[43] Children in the first decade of life constitute the largest group affected, with an especially high incidence in the first 3 years; most of these cases are accidental. As many as 5000 accidental lye ingestions by children younger than 5 years of age are reported per year in the United States.[40, 50, 59] Adults attempting suicide form another group, with females outnumbering males. Laboratory accidents may account for a few cases each year.

Oral, pharyngeal, laryngeal, or esophageal injuries may occur from various substances including alkalis, acids, or bleaches. In all reported series, the substances causing burns most frequently were the alkalis (60% to 80%). The remainder was caused by such substances as Lysol (phenol), Clorox, and acids.[2, 6, 16, 32, 52, 66]

History. Toward the end of the 19th century and the beginning of the 20th century, lye products became commercially available for domestic use, primarily as drain cleaners.[28] Coincident with the increasing availability of these products in the home was the increasing number of children with esophageal burns caused by accidental ingestion. Chevalier Jackson saw the need for publicity campaigns warning mothers of the dangers of lye products and for labeling such products as poisonous.[36] After several years of effort and against a certain amount of opposition, he was able to initiate a law that required lye products to be labeled as poisonous and to have antidote advice on the label. This law was the Federal Caustic Act of 1927, enacted by President Coolidge on March 2 of that year.

Laws. Since 1927, further regulations have come into being: the Poison Prevention Packaging Act (1970) and the Federal Hazardous Substances Act (1972). Both are administered by the U.S. Consumer Product Safety Commission. These laws require child-resistant packaging for sodium hydroxide (NaOH) or potassium hydroxide (KOH) in the dry form or in solutions greater than 2%. As well as containing the manufacturer's name, the chemical name, and the words "Keep out of the reach of children," labels for solutions of NaOH or KOH of between 2% and 5% concentration should contain the word "Danger" and possibly also the words "Fatal if swallowed." For solutions of more than 10%, the label should have the word "Poison" instead of "Danger." On every label, suitable handling and antidote procedures must be listed. Acids and other caustic substances are to be treated similarly.

Under the Federal Food, Drug, and Cosmetic Act, the Food and Drug Administration has authority over lye products that are not commercially available. These include such products as Clinitest tablets, which contain NaOH.

Action on Drains. In 1970 a consumer organization investigated drain cleaners.[13] The action of NaOH or KOH on a blocked U-shaped trap under a sink is first to generate intense heat when it comes into contact with water, and then to attack fat and other substances by reacting with them. The intense reaction causes spattering of the chemical into the air around the sink, and it was recommended that most lye products were acceptable only if the user wore rubber or plastic gloves, rubber or plastic aprons, and goggles or face masks. Most products were inefficient at removing the obstruction. Complete banning of most household drain cleaners was recommended.

Types of Corrosives

Alkalis

Alkalis are bases that dissolve in water. They contain a positive radical and a hydroxyl group. The common alkalis are NaOH, KOH, and ammonium hydroxide (NH_4OH).

Common alkali-containing substances are lyes, ammonia, hair-relaxing agents, nonphosphate detergents, dishwasher soaps, and disk batteries.

Lyes are alkaline agents that contain NaOH, KOH, or $Ca(OH)_2$. Lyes are used as farm cleaning products, in soap making, and as drain pipe cleaners. Lyes can be in liquid, solid, or granular form.

Ammonia (NH_4OH) does not usually cause esophageal

injury unless it is more concentrated than usual house-hold solutions (<4%). However, there is a potential for pharyngeal or laryngeal edema leading to upper airway obstruction.

Hair stiffeners or *relaxing agents* usually contain calcium or lithium hydroxide and the activator guanidine carbonate, which, when mixed, turn into the product guanidine hydroxide with a pH of up to 13. Although the ingestion of these products, which are usually in non-childproof containers, is becoming more prevalent, serious injuries or sequelae are rare, making the need for hospitalization and esophagoscopy of these cases controversial.[1, 14]

Non-phosphate– or *low phosphate–containing detergents* may cause mucosal injury but rarely result in esophageal stricture.

Disk batteries have been featured in several reports of esophageal burns.[41] Of 125 batteries ingested during 114 episodes between August 1982 and June 1983, 33.9% were ingested by hearing-impaired children from their own hearing aids. Most batteries pass through the gastro-intestinal tract without causing any harm, but if they become lodged in the esophagus, they can cause severe burns. Apparently, an electrochemical current develops across the battery's seal when the battery becomes lodged in the esophagus, and leakage of the contents occurs. Usually the battery contains a 45% solution of KOH or NaOH. Immediate endoscopic removal is indicated. Attempts at retrieval from the stomach are not recommended.

Acids

Acids are compounds that contain hydrogen and one or more nonmetals. Most are soluble in water. Common acids are hydrochloric, sulfuric, and nitric (HCl, H_2SO_4, and HNO_3). Commonly ingested acidic substances are toilet bowl cleaners, swimming pool cleaners, and rust removers.

Other corrosives commonly encountered include:

Phenol or hydroxybenzene (C_6H_5OH), a crystalline, acidic compound that is very caustic. When a little water or alcohol is added to it, it is sold as carbolic acid or Lysol in drugstores.

Bleach, in which the active ingredient is hypochlorous acid ($HClO$), is usually sold as a salt (e.g., Clorox) that is 5.25% sodium hypochlorite. When it gives up its oxygen, hydrochloric acid is formed. Bleach is usually available in low concentration and almost neutral pH. Ingestion of household bleach therefore does not usually result in esophageal burn.[27] More concentrated preparations, however, may cause esophageal injury.

Other substances, such as kerosene, creosote, potassium permanganate, and sodium dichromate.

Pathology

Effects of Corrosives on the Esophagus. Krey[39] reviewed the literature and experimented on rabbits with lye. From this excellent article, the natural history of the burned esophagus can be followed. The extent of corrosive ulcers and the degree of penetration into the esophageal wall depend on the type, concentration, amount, and time of contact of the corrosive agent.

Types of Corrosive. Acids cause a coagulation necrosis from which an eschar forms. This tends to keep the corrosive from penetrating to deeper layers of tissues. Alkalis, on the other hand, produce liquefaction necrosis with an edematous loosening of the tissue and with diffusion of the corrosive into the deeper layers. Lesions caused by acids are thus more superficial and have a more favorable prognosis than the deeper alkali lesions.

Concentrations of Corrosive. The concentration of NaOH required to produce a lesion is between 0.5% and 1%. If a solution is stronger than this, it is likely to cause a lesion. For example, 3.8% NaOH (1N) causes necrosis of the mucosa and submucosa, with some involvement of the inner longitudinal fibers; 10.7% NaOH (3N) causes necrosis extending into the circular muscle layer; 16.9% (5N) causes necrosis extending into the outer longitudinal muscle; and solutions greater than 22.5% cause necrosis through the whole esophageal wall and also affect the periesophageal connective tissue.

Weeks and Ravitch[62] reported an experiment in which cats were exposed to liquid chlorine bleach (sodium hypochlorite 0.05%, NaOH 5.25%). This solution resulted in burns of the stomach and esophagus, with late stricture formation in some animals. It was suggested that the damage was done by oxidation rather than by chlorination. Ashcraft and Padula[5] used sulfuric acid, in a concentration of less than 10%, in cats and produced severe esophageal damage after a 30-second exposure.

Amount. Leape and associates[40] reported that 1 mL of highly concentrated liquid lye solution produced esophageal lesions in cats. Ashcraft and Padula[5] reported that even small amounts of concentrated NaOH caused lesions in children; in one case, a patient placed a discarded cap from a bottle of drain cleaner in her mouth and suffered esophageal burns.

Time of Contact. Krey[39] showed that areas of physiologic narrowing of the esophagus—the cricopharyngeal opening, the crossing of the aorta and left mainstem bronchus, and also the fundus where the esophagus passes through the diaphragm—were often more severely affected because of the longer amount of time spent by the corrosive at these sites. Leape and associates[40] showed that highly concentrated liquid lye caused ulceration and eventual stricture of the esophagus in cats after even 1 second of exposure.

Pathologic Stages of Burn

Krey[39] was able to observe by the naked eye and by microscopic examination the progress of discrete burns in the esophagus caused by varying concentrations of NaOH. On the first day, the edge of the lesion is poorly defined, but after a few days, a distinct ulcer is seen that is covered by a crust and has discrete edges. After 15 to 20 days, the necrotic area is shed, leaving granulation tissue in the ulcer with patches of irregular epithelialization. Thirty to 40 days later, the ulcer is still not covered by epithelium, but the wall around the ulcer is thickened. Microscopically, no epithelial remnants can be found after 24 hours, and the connective tissue of the submucosa remains as a few degenerated connective tissue fibrils. The muscle fibers are slightly swollen and held apart by a leukocyte-rich inflammatory exudate. The inflammatory process is not limited to the immediate vicinity of the necrotic area but extends for some distance into the surrounding esophageal wall and into the periesophageal connective tissue. After 2 to 4 days, granulation tissue consisting of newly formed blood vessels and young connective tissue develops between the necrotic area and the intact tissue. By 5 to 8 days, a well-marked necrotic area can be seen as a result of the increase in granulation tissue. By 10 days, the greater part of the ulcer is filled with granulation tissue, which forces the necrotic area into the esophageal lumen. By 15 days, the whole ulcer is filled with granulation tissue, and the necrotic tissue can remain adherent to the surface of the ulcer for up to 30 to 40 days. The esophageal wall at the site of the lesion is greatly thickened into the rich development of granulation tissue, which is transformed into connective tissue in the deeper layers. After 20 to 25 days, the surface of the ulcer is covered with a purulent, fibrinous exudate in which necrotic particles can be seen. The fibrous conversion of the granulation tissue in the deeper layers of the wound begins to predominate over the cellular components. After 30 to 40 days, complete epithelialization of the ulcer has still not taken place. The underlying connective tissue becomes richer in collagen, and this eventually forms the scar, which contracts and leads to constriction of the lumen.

From the pathology, three stages are seen: acute, intermediate, and late. These stages correspond clinically to the following: (1) immediate pain and discomfort on swallowing and difficulty swallowing, gradually easing over the first 2 weeks, (2) a relatively asymptomatic period lasting for 1 week or more, and (3) a period of increasing difficulty in swallowing, leading in some cases to a complete inability to swallow as strictures develop.

Cardona and Daly[9] classified patients into five categories, depending on the severity of their burns, for the purpose of comparing results and evaluating the effect of treatment. Their classification was based on both clinical observation and esophagoscopy.

Mild Nonulcerative Esophagitis. These patients have very little discomfort on swallowing. Esophagoscopy shows hyperemia of the esophageal mucosa without ulceration.

Mild Ulcerative Esophagitis. These patients usually have discomfort on swallowing and difficulty swallowing. They have shallow ulcers in the esophagus that seem to involve the mucosa only. These may form strictures, and the patient goes through the three clinical stages of esophageal burns.

Moderate to Severe Ulcerative Esophagitis. These patients have lesions that produce deep craters. The muscle layers of the esophagus and sometimes even the entire wall are involved. There may be a single ulceration, or there may be multiple ulcers with viable mucosa in between. If these cases go untreated, strictures inevitably develop.

Severe Ulcerative, Uncomplicated Esophagitis. Most of the esophageal mucosa is involved, with very few areas of intact mucosa remaining. Sloughing and necrosis are deep, involving most of the layers.

Severe Ulcerative Esophagitis with Complications. In these cases, perforation occurs, resulting in mediastinitis or localized mediastinal abscesses. Perforation of the stomach or duodenum may also occur, leading to peritonitis. In addition, the larynx may be burned, leading to upper airway obstruction, and there may be acid-base metabolic disturbances.

Management

Management of the patient with caustic ingestion is based on the timing of presentation, the degree of the burn, and the pathologic stage of the esophageal burn.

Emergency Management

Most patients present during the acute stage. The severity of signs and symptoms at this stage may vary from completely normal to severe with complications. The initial tasks are to accurately assess the vital signs, to obtain the history of the ingestion, to assess the severity of symptoms and signs, to manage emergency complications, and to decide and prepare for endoscopic assessment of the degree of the esophageal burn.

Pediatric caustic ingestion is usually accidental, involving small children. Caustic ingestion in teenagers may be due to a suicide attempt and may involve a large amount of substance with a potential risk of severe burn and complication. Initial steps of management immediately after the ingestion may have an impact on the outcome. It is important to reduce the time of contact of the concentrated substance. Irrigating the contact sites as well as having the child drink either milk or water serves this purpose. Vomiting can increase the degree of esophageal injury and should be avoided. The amount of liquid given should not be so much that it results in vomiting.

In the emergency department, it is important to find out the type of substance that was ingested or suspected to have been ingested. Most often, the parents or the people accompanying the patient can provide only the name of the substance. In this case, information as to the constitution and concentration of the substance can be obtained from the nearest poison center. An attempt should be made to estimate how much of the substance was ingested. In children, this is usually difficult. It should be emphasized that even small amounts of caustic products can cause severe damage to the esophagus and that once a substance has touched a child's tongue, the natural reflex leads to swallowing. Thus, parents should not be reassured that no damage has been done until the child has been fully examined. It is important to know whether the patient vomited or was made to vomit after the ingestion, because vomiting increases the length of time the esophagus is exposed to the agent.

Examination of the patient, especially a child, may reveal burns on the lips, chin, hands, or chest as a result of manipulation of the substance and possible regurgitation. Patients may be in severe pain and unable to swallow even their own saliva. There may be burns in the mouth, which do not necessarily correlate with burns in the esophagus; thus, it should not be assumed that, if there are no burns in the mouth, then esophageal burns are improbable, and vice versa. The complications of acute laryngitis that lead to airway obstruction, such as stridor, hoarseness, and cough, should be sought. Mediastinitis from rupture of the esophagus may cause severe chest pains, especially on respiration. The abdomen should also be examined for signs of peritonitis from stomach perforation. Abdominal pain and rigidity may suggest a perforation.

A chest x-ray study in posteroanterior and lateral views should be obtained in all cases as a base line and to detect evidence of mediastinitis or aspiration pneumonia. At the same time that the intravenous line is being established, blood should be drawn for electrolyte estimation.

Complications

The mortality rate of patients in the severe, complicated esophageal burn group is high. Christesen[11] suggested that lye ingestion, intentional ingestion, and multiple positive signs or symptoms of substance ingestion, as well as esophageal findings of deep or circumferential burns were the predictors of a complication after a caustic ingestion.

Shock and metabolic acid-base disturbance is treated along basic surgical principles, with intravenous replacement therapy and correction of acid-base balance. The larynx may have been burned to a varying degree. Edema and inflammation may cause an upper airway obstruction, which is relieved by tracheostomy. The larynx may be affected in the same way as the esophagus, with substantial tissue destruction leading to subsequent stricture formation. This may require laryngeal surgery at a later date.

Mediastinitis is due to perforation of the esophagus and may lead to the development of small, localized abscesses around the esophagus or to full-blown mediastinitis. In the case of small, localized abscesses, the help of a thoracic surgeon may be necessary to place a drain in the chest. Severe mediastinitis may require immediate esophagectomy. Ritter and co-workers[55] recommended radical treatment for these patients, since the mortality rate is so high. *An immediate esophagectomy is sometimes recommended, leaving the patient with a cervical esophagostomy and gastrostomy.* This means that a colon interposition would be required at a later date. However, radical surgery is reserved for the most severely perforated esophagus.

A burn of severity sufficient to cause mediastinitis may also cause perforation of the stomach, duodenum, or both, leading to peritonitis. In these cases, again, immediate esophagogastrectomy is recommended to remove dead and necrotic tissue and reduce the morbidity and mortality rates.

Medical Management

Once it is established that there is no airway obstruction, mediastinitis, or peritonitis, certain measures are taken. The aim of management is to prevent strictures forming in the esophagus. Any form of management that reduces the amount of granulation tissue, the number and activity of fibroblasts, or both contributes to this end. A dilemma is in knowing whether to treat all cases of children with a history of caustic ingestion (Fig. 70–1) or just those with symptoms. It is difficult to predict which children have suffered burns, so all symptomatic patients are treated until esophagoscopy confirms the diagnosis. Most children who are asymptomatic may have either no burn or a first-degree burn, and, in most (or all) of these cases, strictures do not develop. Some physicians would opt for no treatment in these children.

Analgesics. Intramuscular or intravenous narcotics appropriate to age and weight may be administered.

Antibiotics. Krey[39] showed that epithelialization occurred more quickly when animals were given antibiotics. By reducing the number of bacteria present in the burn tissue, granulation tissue can be reduced. It is usual to

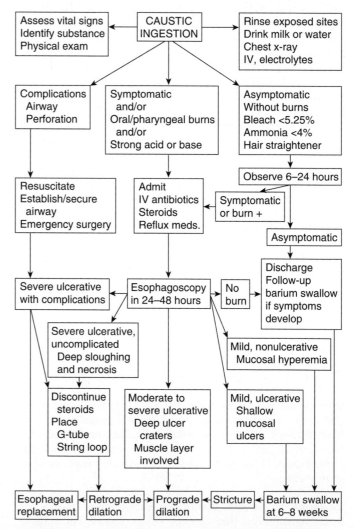

FIGURE 70–1. Algorithm for management of a caustic burn.

use ampicillin, 50 to 100 mg/kg per day intravenously, or, if the patient can swallow, amoxicillin orally, where it has both a local and a systemic effect.

Alimentation. The patient, if able to swallow, should be allowed only clear liquids. Krey[39] showed that particles of food become caught up in necrotic tissue and produce more granulation tissue. If the patient is unable to swallow or when the patient is given nothing by mouth before the esophagoscopy, fluids are given intravenously.

Steroids. There is no general agreement over the use, dosage, or length of steroid treatment.

Spain and associates[60] showed that, when cortisone was given to a group of mice with wounds on their backs, compared with control mice, they exhibited an almost complete lack of exudate and fibrin in the wounds, together with marked diminution of cellular elements. However, if the steroids were given more than 48 hours after the wound occurred, there was no significant difference between the group receiving the drug and the control group. Johnson[37] experimented on dogs and showed that steroid therapy, if started early, definitely inhibited the inflammatory response and granulation tissue formation, with a subsequent decrease in stricture formation. Anderson and associates,[3] in a controlled study, concluded that although steroids appear to decrease the stricture formation in moderate to severe burns with caustic substances and reduced the need for esophageal replacement, the differences did not reach a statistical significance because of the small number of patients. Howell and co-workers,[35] in a statistical analysis of past studies, concluded that steroids were not indicated for children with first-degree burns and that further trials were needed to evaluate their efficacy in children with second- or third-degree burns. In a review of 214 cases, Hawkins and colleagues[29] concluded that steroids were effective in preventing strictures in moderately severe burns. Many patients with caustic burns of the esophagus have been given steroids combined with antibiotics. Various authors[26, 49, 54, 56–58, 63, 66, 67] have applied treatment of a combination of antibiotics and steroids and found the incidence of stricture formation to be much lower than previously.

Prednisone, 2 mg/kg per day to a maximum of 60 mg/day, is recommended to be given intravenously initially, then orally after a few days as the ability to swallow returns. This dosage is continued for 21 days and then tapered over the next 21 days, so that the total time on steroids is 6 weeks. To be effective, steroids must be given within the first 8 hours of the injury. The extent of the injury cannot be judged until an esophagoscopy is performed, usually 24 to 48 hours later. Some physicians may therefore opt to treat all cases with steroids initially, stopping them if no burn is found during esophagoscopy.

Antacids. Intermittent acid and pepsin exposure on burned esophageal mucosa is shown to delay healing in an animal model.[48] Aggressive antireflux treatment with H_2-receptor blockers or proton pump inhibitors should be started as soon as possible and continued all through the observation or treatment period with or without esopha-

geal dilatations. There may be increased gastroesophageal reflux during or after the dilatations.

Use of lathyrogens in the management of esophageal burns is controversial. Lathyrogens are chemicals that inhibit the covalent cross-links between collagen. These cross-links are thought to be important in the physical characteristics of newly formed collagen. It might be possible either to prevent dense scarring or to soften well-established scarring by use of these chemicals. Butler[7] and Madden[44] and their associates used beta-aminopropionitrile in dogs and showed greater benefit from its use than from steroids in reducing scarring. This drug is not approved for human clinical trials. Penicillamine was shown by Gehanno and Guedon[23] to have good results in rats. Liu and Richardson[42] pointed out that N-acetyl-L-cysteine, another lathyrogen, is commercially available and is approved for clinical use in various bronchopulmonary disorders for its mucolytic properties, and in acetaminophen and arsenic overdosage. They described a study of the use of N-acetyl-L-cysteine in caustic burns of the esophagus in a few rats.

Assessment of Social and Mental Status

Assessment of social and mental status of a child and establishment of support may be critical in continued care and prevention. Sobel[59] studied 367 families whose children had been involved in accidental poisonings and found that the frequency of poisoning was unrelated to the accessibility of toxic substances, which, he pointed out, was contrary to common sense. There was also found to be no relation among the level of motor development, the intelligence of the child, birth complications, and parental accident-proneness. There was, however, significant association between accidental poisoning and measures of maternal psychopathology, such as the mother's marital dissatisfaction, mental illness, poor ego strength, and sexual dissatisfaction. His data suggested that a negative role performance on the mother's part generates a power struggle with the child, which may eventually result in the ingestion of forbidden substances by the child as an act of defiance and rebellion. Accidental poisoning, therefore, should always be treated as a symptom of family disturbance. It is considered that psychiatric consultation is essential for giving emotional support to mothers who are unable to cope with the stress placed on them by their maternal and marital roles.

The mental trauma, both for child and family, in a severe case of poisoning also warrants psychiatric support, as does the prolonged treatment necessary if a stricture develops, with frequent and, to a young child, often unpleasant visits to the hospital. In cases in which suicide has been attempted by an older child, psychiatric consultation is mandatory (see Chapter 109).

Esophagoscopy

Direct visualization is the only accurate way to diagnose esophageal burns. Cardona and Daly[9] emphasized the poor correlation between oral or pharyngeal ulcerations and esophageal ulcerations. Gaudreault and co-workers[22] state that the signs or symptoms do not adequately predict the presence or severity of an esophageal lesion following a caustic ingestion. Crain and co-workers[15] subsequently confirmed this and suggested that patients with two or more serious signs, such as drooling, vomiting, and stridor, may be more reliably predicted to have esophageal burns. Gorman and co-workers[24] suggested that esophagoscopy was not required in asymptomatic patients and agreed that patients with two or more signs of oral burns, such as dysphagia, pain, and vomiting, were more likely to have esophageal burns.

Suggestions concerning the appropriate timing of the initial esophagoscopy vary from within 24 hours to 36 to 72 hours later. If esophagoscopy is performed within the first 24 hours, a lesion may be overlooked, since, in nearly all animal experiments, it took at least 24 hours for lesions to become visible to the naked eye. However, Wijburg and colleagues[64] advocate flexible fiberoptic esophagoscopy within the first 24 hours. Esophagoscopy performed later than 72 hours after the event may result in unnecessary medical treatment and hospitalization if no burns of the esophagus are found.

Controversy also exists over the instrument to use for esophagoscopy. Some physicians prefer rigid esophagoscopes while others prefer flexible esophagoscopes. Each group claims that the other instrument is more likely to perforate the esophagus. Most physicians advocate performing a rigid esophagoscopy of symptomatic patients 24 to 72 hours after ingestion.

The esophagoscope should not be advanced beyond the first area of a severe burn, since the danger of perforation becomes greater. However, advancement of an esophagoscope with a telescope or of a fiberoptic flexible esophagoscope may be performed when a mild burn is visualized in the proximal esophagus, since a severe burn may be present in the distal esophagus.

Management after Esophagoscopy

Many aspects of management of esophageal burns are controversial, particularly regarding whether to place a nasogastric tube, stent, or string; whether to continue use of steroids; whether to perform gastrostomy; whether to plan for prograde or retrograde dilatation; and whether to resect the esophagus with a pull-up, a colon, or a jejunal graft. If no burn is seen on esophagoscopy, medication is discontinued and an esophagogram is obtained before the patient is discharged from the hospital, both as a base line and as a precaution in case a lesion is overlooked. The patient is discharged from the hospital but should be seen again in 6 to 8 weeks for a second esophagogram. If the results are normal and the patient is still asymptomatic, no follow-up is necessary.

If, on the basis of the esophagoscopic results, the patient is considered to have either mild or moderate ulcerative esophagitis, the combination of antibiotic and steroid therapy should be continued for 3 to 6 weeks (see earlier discussion). The child should be maintained on clear liquids or intravenous fluids for the first few days, but then may begin a soft diet. At this stage, the child may be nursed at home. After about 3 weeks, the steroids can be tapered. An esophagogram should be obtained in 6 to 8 weeks, and the patient should be seen every 3 months for 1 year. If the child has difficulty in swallowing or the esophagogram shows evidence of early stricture formation, dilatation may be necessary.

Patients with severe burn are initially treated the same as less severely burned patients, but as soon as the extent of the burn is realized by esophagoscopy, the steroids are discontinued. To continue steroid treatment would increase the danger of perforation in cases in which the whole wall of the esophagus is necrotic.

There is a significant risk of stricture formation in patients with severe burn. The goal is either to keep a tube or stent in place to prevent the stricture, or to perform repeated dilatations until scar formation is mature. In case of a severe esophageal burn, the esophagus must be rested with a gastrostomy or jejunostomy. If a safer retrograde dilatation is preferred, a string loop is inserted that utilizes the gastrostomy. Contrary to all the aforementioned methods, nasogastric intubation is advocated by some groups as the sole method of treatment of caustic burns.

"Special" Nasogastric Tube. Wijburg and co-workers[64] inserted nasogastric tubes under endoscopic control and decided when to remove them by endoscopy. They intubated when deep, circular esophageal burns were encountered and stated that, of 32 patients undergoing this treatment, strictures developed in only two. Subsequently, Wijburg and co-workers[65] advocated the passage of a "special" nasogastric tube after esophagoscopy, within 24 hours of the ingestion.

Coln and Chang[12] and Estrera and co-workers[21] advocate passing an esophageal "stent," creating a gastrostomy, and passing a transgastric jejunal tube at the time of assessment by esophagoscopy. They emphasize leaving the stent in place until healing is complete. Weekly assessment by esophagoscopy may be needed. De Peppo and co-workers[18] suggested that, with stent placement, esophageal replacement should rarely be necessary.

Krey[39] found that the best results in reducing stricture formation were obtained by resting the esophagus, which may be accomplished by performing a gastrostomy and using antibiotics. He advocated passing a string through the esophagus and bringing it out through the gastrostomy. The upper end of the string is brought out through the nose and tied to the lower end so that there is a continuous loop of string through the esophagus. If possible, the patient should facilitate placement of the string by swallowing it. If not, it can be done during esophagoscopy. Retrograde bougienage may be started after 3 weeks, when the gastrostomy stoma is mature enough and when there is less risk of perforation.

Management of Acquired Strictures

An example of an esophageal stricture is shown in Figure 70–2. Such strictures may develop from other causes apart from caustic burn damage. Attempts at surgical repair of the strictured esophagus by direct end-to-end anastomosis (after excising the stenotic segment), gastric pull-up, or esophagogastric or esophagocolic anastomosis

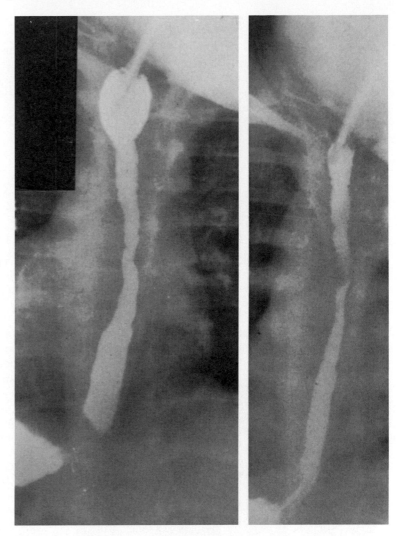

FIGURE 70-2. Example of esophageal stricture due to a caustic burn.

(from colon interposition) may also lead to stricturing at the repair site. Holinger and Johnston[31, 33] mentioned that one of the major problems after repair of congenital esophageal atresia is stenosis at the site of anastomosis.

Esophageal strictures may be managed in several ways. One of the more popular and successful ways is the use of the Grüntzig balloon under radiographic control. Mc-Lean and LeVeen[46] pointed out that dilatation in a radial direction should be less likely to tear the esophagus than prograde or retrograde dilatation, which generates longitudinal forces.

Dilatation by Balloon

A significant change in the ability of physicians to treat esophageal strictures occurred in 1974, when a balloon dilatation catheter was described by Grüntzig and Hopff[25] (Fig. 70-3), originally to dilate atheromatous narrowing of arteries. The dilatation is performed under radiographic control, with the child under general anesthesia or local anesthesia and heavy sedation. The technique is well described by Dawson and associates.[17] Myer and coworkers[51] suggested balloon dilatation as the procedure of choice for the management of most esophageal strictures in children. Balloon dilatation catheters are available in a range of sizes: from 10 to 20 mm in diameter and from 4 to 8 cm in length. The advantage of using this form of dilatation is that the catheter can be passed through a narrow stricture, and the balloon, when inflated, dilates in a radial direction (Fig. 70-4). Several dilatations may be necessary, depending on the return of symptoms of obstruction, which, in turn, depend on the length and density of the stricture.

Prograde Dilatation

Several types of dilators are used for prograde dilatation. The Jackson silk-woven bougies are passed through a rigid esophagoscope under direct vision with the patient under general anesthesia. Emerson[20] described Teflon dilators that are used in the same way. Other methods require the use of a string with a gastrostomy under general anesthesia. For example, the Plummer method uses metal olives passed over a string. Hine and coworkers[30] compared the Eder-Puestow method with that used for the Celestin Neoplex dilator. Both methods require passage of a guidewire first, either under fluoroscopic control or through the biopsy channel of a flexible esophagoscope. Fogarty vascular balloon catheters have

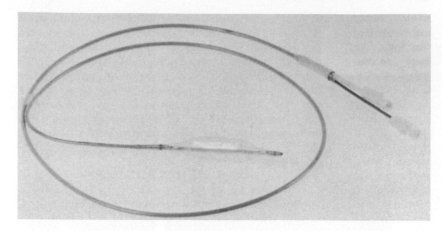

FIGURE 70–3. Example of a Grüñtzig catheter balloon partially inflated.

also been used, and the Grüntzig balloon dilatation method is described earlier. Hurst or Maloney dilators can be used without a general anesthetic.

Dilatation may be carried out using Hurst mercury bougies without the need for general anesthesia in very young children, who must, however, usually be wrapped in a blanket and held upright on the lap of an assistant

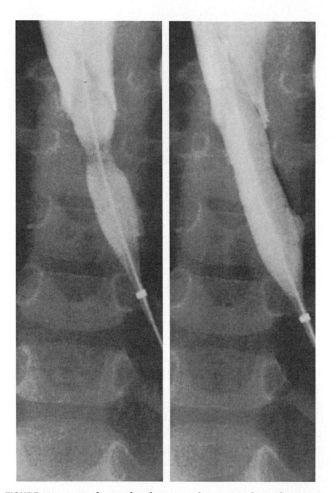

FIGURE 70–4. Radiographs showing a lower esophageal stricture with a Grüñtzig balloon in position, partially inflated on the left and fully inflated on the right. The indentation of the balloon on the left is the stricture. Dilatation of this stricture by the balloon is in a radial direction.

(Fig. 70–5). A bougie of suitable size may be selected at the time of esophagoscopy. The tip of the dilator should be inserted into the patient's mouth and held high above his or her head so that the weight of the mercury encourages the passage of the tube down the esophagus. It is unfortunate that, in some of the smaller-sized bougies, the weight of the mercury is not great enough to carry the bougie down the esophagus, so that gentle insertion of the bougie by the operator may be necessary. The size of the dilator is then increased until one size is found that will not pass down the esophagus. The intervals between dilatations are governed by how well the patient can swallow food. These patients will probably need dilatation for the rest of their lives, but the length of time between dilatations should increase as they grow. Periodically throughout this time, esophagography and esophagoscopy should be performed to follow the extent of the disease.

Esophageal perforations resulting from esophageal dilatations are not uncommon. Karnak and co-workers[38] re-

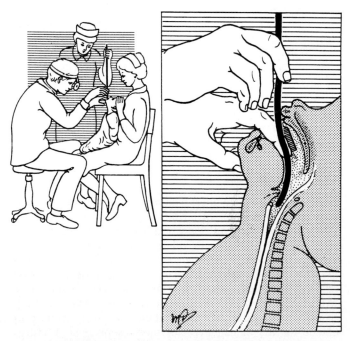

FIGURE 70–5. Prograde esophageal dilatation.

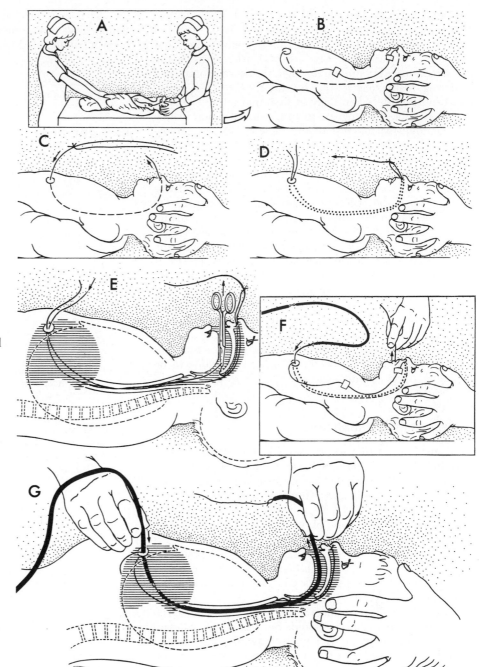

FIGURE 70–6. Retrograde esophageal dilatation.

ported a 17.4% esophageal perforation rate during dilatation of caustic esophageal strictures in children with a spectrum from a minimal periesophageal leakage to massive rupture with pneumothorax and sudden death.

Retrograde Dilatation

Hawkins[28] compared antegrade with retrograde dilatation of strictures and emphasized the greater degree of safety with Tucker dilators used in a retrograde fashion. Retrograde bougienage may be performed while the patient is awake, even in a very young child, although the procedure is generally distressing for both child and operator

(Fig. 70–6A). The technique, described by Tucker,[61] should be such that the string is always present in the esophagus (see Fig. 70–6B). The loop is first cut, and two pieces of string are tied to the lower end (see Fig. 70–6C). By pulling on the upper end, two new pieces are pulled out through the nose (see Fig. 70–6D). The upper end of one of these pieces of string is tied to the lower end of the same string; this is the loop that remains in the esophagus after dilatation. The second loop is brought out through the mouth with forceps (see Fig. 70–6E). A Tucker dilator is tied to the lower end of the string, and by a combination of pulling on the upper string and pushing the dilator, it can be passed up the esophagus and into the mouth (see Fig. 70–6F). Dilators of increasing size can be tied end to end like a string of sausages, and the whole string can be pulled right out through the mouth (see Fig. 70–6G). Alternatively, the first dilator can be pulled through the gastrostomy, and the string reattached to the second dilator. This procedure can be undertaken daily at first, and after a while it may be possible to progress to prograde dilatation, which may continue for the rest of the patient's life, at varying intervals. Periodic esophagoscopy and esophagography are necessary to follow the course of the disease.

Mendelsohn and Maloney[47] suggested injection of steroids into the stricture at esophagoscopy. They found this to be useful if the stricture was resistant and if progress toward increasing the lumen was slow by prograde dilatation. They used 1.5 to 2 mL hydrocortisone acetate or triamcinolone acetonide (40 mg/mL) injected through the esophagoscope with a long needle; 1 mL hyaluronidase is mixed with this steroid to act as a spreading agent. This is followed by immediate dilatation, using dilators 2 or 4 French sizes greater than those used in previous dilatations. Bleeding is a warning sign to stop the dilatation. The researchers had no problems with infection, abscess, or perimediastinitis. They believed that the stricture was softened and that this procedure enabled dilatation to be carried out more rapidly.

Replacement of Esophagus

Esophagectomy with various choices of reconstruction is advocated by some authors because of the high risk for esophageal carcinoma after severe esophageal burns. Appelqvist and Salmo[4] and Hopkins and Postlethwait[34] pointed out that up to 7% of patients with esophageal carcinoma have a history of caustic ingestion in childhood. It is estimated that, after caustic ingestion, there is a 1000-fold increase in the likelihood of development of esophageal carcinoma. The interval between injury and development of the squamous cell carcinoma varies between 13 and 71 years.

If dilatation fails, esophageal replacement may be the alternative. Every effort should be made to maintain esophageal function for as long as possible. Panieri and co-workers[53] reported only 41% success with dilatation therapy. They reported the early factors predictive of failure of conservative treatment as (1) delay in presentation of more than 1 month, (2) severe pharyngoesophageal burns requiring a tracheotomy, (3) esophageal perforation, (4) stricture longer than 5 cm, and (5) inability to pass appropriate size dilators in early bougienage. Choi and co-workers[10] suggested that children who have hypopharyngeal scarring and obliterated esophageal inlet could undergo colonic esophageal replacement with high pharyngocolic anastomosis.

Campbell and co-workers[8] reported cases of colon interposition. They stressed that achievement of good functional results with low complication rates depends on experience and the technique employed rather than on whether stomach or colon is used. They favored intrathoracic colon interposition. McCaffrey and Fisher[45] described three cases of repair of cervical esophageal stenosis by means of microvascular free jejunum transfer. Esophageal replacement with gastric tube conduit has been recommended with good results.[19]

SELECTED REFERENCES

Hawkins DB. Dilation of esophageal strictures: comparative morbidity of antegrade and retrograde methods. Ann Otol Rhinol Laryngol 97: 460, 1988.

This article summarizes the different techniques of esophageal dilation and lists a number of references on the topic.

Jackson C. The Life of Chevalier Jackson (An Autobiography). New York, Macmillan, 1931.

An interesting perspective on the historical background of caustic burns.

Johnson EE. A study of corrosive esophagitis. Laryngoscope 73:1651, 1963.

An excellent article describing experimental studies on dogs using controlled, immediate antibiotic therapy, immediate steroid therapy, immediate steroid-antibiotic therapy, delayed antibiotic-steroid therapy, and other treatment. It provides the basis of current clinical management.

Krey H. On the treatment of corrosive lesions in the esophagus: an experimental study. Acta Otolaryngol (Stockh) Suppl 102, 1952.

Another recommended article that reviews the literature up to 1952. It describes a series of experiments on rabbits by which the natural history of esophageal burns can be followed, together with various treatment modalities in a controlled series. From this stems the procedure of antibiotic therapy and resting the esophagus.

Spain DM, Molomut N, Haber A. The effect of cortisone on the formation of granulation tissue in mice. Am J Pathol 268:710, 1950.

On the basis of the findings reported in this very short article, steroids were used to treat caustic burns of the esophagus.

REFERENCES

1. Ahsan S, Haupert M. Absence of esophageal injury in pediatric patients after hair relaxer ingestion. Arch Otolaryngol Head Neck Surg 125:953, 1999.
2. Alford BR, Harris HH. Chemical burns of the mouth, pharynx, and esophagus. Ann Otol Rhinol Laryngol 68:122, 1959.
3. Anderson KD, Rouse TM, Randolph JG. A controlled trial of corticosteroids in children with corrosive injury of the esophagus. N Engl J Med 233:637, 1990.
4. Appelqvist P, Salmo M. Lye corrosion carcinoma of the esophagus—a review of 63 cases. Cancer 45:2655, 1980.
5. Ashcraft KW, Padula RT. The effect of dilute corrosives on the esophagus. Pediatrics 53:226, 1974.
6. Bikhazi HB, Thompson ER, Shumrick DA. Caustic ingestion: current status, a report of 105 cases. Arch Otolaryngol 89:112, 1969.
7. Butler C, Madden JW, Davis WM, et al. Morphologic aspects of experimental esophageal lye strictures. II. Effect of steroid hormones, bougienage and induced lathyrism on acute lye burns. Surgery 81:431, 1977.
8. Campbell JR, Webber BR, Harrison MW, et al. Esophageal replacement in infants and children by colon interposition. Am J Surg 144: 29, 1982.
9. Cardona JC, Daly JF. Current management of corrosive esophagitis. Ann Otol Rhinol Laryngol 80:521, 1971.
10. Choi RS, Lillehei CW, Lund DP, et al. Esophageal replacement in children who have caustic pharyngoesophageal strictures. J Pediatr Surg 32:1083, 1997.
11. Christesen HBT. Prediction of complications following caustic ingestion in adults. Clin Otolaryngol 20:272, 1995.
12. Coln D, Chang JHT. Experience with esophageal stenting for caustic burns in children. J Pediatr Surg 21:588, 1986.

13. Consumer Reports. Drain cleaners. Consumer Reports 35:481, 1970.
14. Cox AJ, Eisenbeis JF. Ingestion of caustic hair relaxer: is endoscopy necessary? Laryngoscope 107:897, 1997.
15. Crain EF, Gershel JC, Mezey AP. Caustic ingestions. Symptoms as predictors of esophageal injury. Am J Dis Child 138:863, 1984.
16. Daly JF, Cardona JC. Acute corrosive esophagitis. Arch Otolaryngol 74:41, 1968.
17. Dawson SL, Mueller PR, Ferrucci JT, et al. Severe esophageal strictures: indications for balloon catheter dilatation. Radiology 153:631, 1984.
18. De Peppo F, Zaccara A, Dall'Oglio L, et al. Stenting for caustic strictures: esophageal replacement replaced. J Pediatr Surg 33:54, 1998.
19. Ein SH. Gastric tubes in children with caustic esophageal injury: a 32-year review. J Pediatr Surg 33:1363, 1998.
20. Emerson EB. Teflon esophageal dilators. Arch Otolaryngol 81:213, 1965.
21. Estrera A, Taylor W, Mills LJ, Platt MR. Corrosive burns of the esophagus and stomach: a recommendation for an aggressive surgical approach. Ann Thorac Surg 41:276, 1986.
22. Gaudreault P, Parent M, McGuigan MA, et al. Predictability of esophageal injury from signs and symptoms: a study of caustic ingestion in 378 children. Pediatrics 71:767, 1983.
23. Gehanno P, Guedon C. Inhibition of experimental esophageal lye strictures by penicillamine. Arch Otolaryngol 107:145, 1981.
24. Gorman RL, Khim-Maung-Gyi MT, Klein-Schwartz W, et al. Initial symptoms as predictors of esophageal injury in alkaline corrosive ingestions. Am J Emerg Med 10:189, 1992.
25. Grüntzig A, Hopff H. Perkutane Rekanalisation chronischer arterieller Verschlüsse mit einen neuen Dilatationskatheter. Modifikation der Dotter-Technik. Dtsch Med Wochenschr 99:2502, 1974.
26. Haller JA, Bachman K. The comparative effect of current therapy on experimental caustic burns of the esophagus. Pediatrics 34:236, 1964.
27. Harley EH, Collins DM. Liquid household bleach ingestion in children: a retrospective review. Laryngoscope 107:122, 1997.
28. Hawkins DB. Dilation of esophageal strictures: comparative morbidity of antegrade and retrograde methods. Ann Otol Rhinol Laryngol 97:460, 1988.
29. Hawkins DB, Demeter MJ, Barnett TE. Caustic ingestion: controversies in management. A review of 214 cases. Laryngoscope 90:98, 1980.
30. Hine KR, Hawkey CJ, Atkinson M, Holmes GKT. Comparison of the Eder-Puestow and Celestin techniques for dilating benign esophageal strictures. Gut 25:1100, 1984.
31. Holinger PH. Endoscopic aspects of esophagitis and esophageal hiatal hernia. JAMA 172:313, 1960.
32. Holinger PH, Johnston KC. Caustic strictures of the esophagus. Illinois Med J 98:246, 1950.
33. Holinger PH, Johnston KC. Postsurgical endoscopic problems of congenital esophageal atresia. Ann Otol Rhinol Laryngol 72:1035, 1963.
34. Hopkins RA, Postlethwait RW. Caustic burns and carcinoma of the esophagus. Ann Surg 194:146, 1981.
35. Howell JM, Dalsey WC, Hartsell FW, Butzin CA. Steroids for the treatment of corrosive esophageal injury: a statistical analysis of past studies. Am J Emerg Med 10:421, 1992.
36. Jackson C. The Life of Chevalier Jackson (An Autobiography). New York, Macmillan, 1931, pp 208–211.
37. Johnson EE. A study of corrosive esophagitis. Laryngoscope 73:1651, 1963.
38. Karnak I, Tanyel FC, Buyukpamukcu N, Hicsonmez A. Esophageal perforations encountered during the dilation of caustic esophageal strictures. J Cardiovasc Surg 39:373, 1998.
39. Krey H. On the treatment of corrosive lesions in the esophagus: an experimental study. Acta Otolaryngol (Stockh) Suppl 102, 1952.
40. Leape LL, Ashcraft KW, Scarpelli DG, et al. Hazard to health; liquid lye. N Engl J Med 284:578, 1971.
41. Litovitz TL. Battery ingestions: product accessibility and clinical course. Pediatrics 75:469, 1985.
42. Liu AJ, Richardson MA. Effects of N-acetylcysteine on experimentally induced esophageal lye injury. Ann Otol Rhinol Laryngol 94:477, 1985.
43. Lovejoy FH Jr. Corrosive injury of the esophagus in children. N Engl J Med 323:668, 1990.
44. Madden JW, Davis WM, Butler C, et al. Experimental esophageal lye burns. II. Correcting established strictures with beta-aminopropionitrile and bougienage. Ann Surg 178:277, 1973.
45. McCaffrey TV, Fisher J. Repair of traumatic cervical esophageal stenosis using microvascular free jejunum transfer. Ann Otol Rhinol Laryngol 93:512, 1984.
46. McLean GK, LeVeen RF. Shear stress in the performance of esophageal dilation: comparison of balloon dilation and bougienage. Radiology 172:983, 1989.
47. Mendelsohn HJ, Maloney WH. The treatment of benign strictures of the esophagus with cortisone injection. Ann Otol Rhinol Laryngol 79:900, 1970.
48. Messner AH, Browne JD, Geisinger KR. Effect of intermittent acid and pepsin exposure on burned esophageal mucosa. Am J Otolaryngol 17:45, 1996.
49. Middelkamp JN, Ferguson TB, Roper CL, et al. The management of problems of caustic burns in children. J Thorac Cardiovasc Surg 57:341, 1969.
50. Moore WR. Caustic ingestions. Pathophysiology, diagnosis and treatment. Clin Pediatr (Phila) 25:192, 1986.
51. Myer CM III, Ball WS Jr, Bisset GS III. Balloon dilatation of esophageal strictures in children. Arch Otolaryngol Head Neck Surg 117:529, 1991.
52. Owens H. Chemical burns of the esophagus; the importance of various chemicals as etiologic agents in stricture formation. Arch Otolaryngol 60:482, 1954.
53. Panieri E, Rode H, Millar AJW, Cywes S. Oesophageal replacement in the management of corrosive strictures: when is surgery indicated? Pediatr Surg Int 13:336, 1998.
54. Ray ES, Morgan DL. Cortisone therapy of lye burns of the esophagus. J Pediatr 49:394, 1956.
55. Ritter FN, Gago O, Kirsh M, et al. The rationale of emergency esophagogastrectomy in the treatment of liquid caustic burns of the esophagus and stomach. Arch Otolaryngol 80:513, 1971.
56. Ritter FN, Newman MH, Newman DE. A clinical and experimental study of corrosive burns of the stomach. Ann Otol Rhinol Laryngol 67:830, 1968.
57. Rosenberg N, Kunderman PJ, Vroman L, et al. Prevention of experimental lye strictures of the esophagus by cortisone. Arch Surg 63:147, 1951.
58. Rosenberg N, Kunderman PJ, Vroman L, et al. Prevention of experimental esophageal stricture by cortisone. Arch Surg 66:593, 1953.
59. Sobel R. The psychiatric implications of accidental poisoning in childhood. Pediatr Clin North Am 17:653, 1970.
60. Spain DM, Molomut N, Haber A. The effect of cortisone on the formation of granulation tissue in mice. Am J Pathol 268:710, 1950.
61. Tucker G. Cicatricial stenosis of the esophagus with particular reference to treatment by continuous string, retrograde bougienage with the author's bougie. Ann Otol Rhinol Laryngol 69:118, 1924.
62. Weeks R, Ravitch MM. Esophageal injury by liquid chlorine bleach: experimental study. J Pediatr 73:911, 1969.
63. Weisskopf A. Effects of cortisone on experimental lye burn of the esophagus. Ann Otol Rhinol Laryngol 68:681, 1952.
64. Wijburg FA, Beukers MM, Bartelsman JF, et al. Nasogastric intubation as sole treatment of caustic esophageal lesions. Ann Otol Rhinol Laryngol 94:337, 1985.
65. Wijburg FA, Heymans HSA, Urbanus NAM. Caustic esophageal lesions in childhood: prevention of stricture formation. J Pediatr Surg 24:171, 1989.
66. Yarington CT Jr, Bales GA, Frazer JP. A study of the management of caustic esophageal trauma. Ann Otol Rhinol Laryngol 73:1130, 1964.
67. Yarington CT Jr, Heatley CA. Steroids, antibiotics, and early esophagoscopy in caustic esophageal trauma. N Y State J Med 63:2960, 1963.

71

Foreign Bodies of the Pharynx and Esophagus

Scott C. Manning, M.D., and Sylvan E. Stool, M.D.

The Problem

Toddlers and young children are naturally inclined toward oral exploration of their environment, and foreign body aspiration or ingestion is a particular problem in this age group. Humans are unique among mammals in their anatomic separation of nose and larynx, allowing a space for resonating vocal sounds for evolution of language. This shared space, however, creates a potential for choking. The separation of nose and larynx is complete by age 1 year, about the same time the child becomes more mobile.

Contributing factors in ingestions and aspirations include male sex, lack of molars before age 4 years for fine chewing, and immature coordination of swallowing and laryngeal sphincter control.[39] Other risk factors include neurologic disorders such as mental retardation and seizure disorder and a history of anatomic or functional motility disorder of the esophagus (patients with a history of tracheoesophageal fistula repair share both the later risk factors).[26] Inadequate parental care or an abusive environment has also been found to increase risk for aerodigestive foreign bodies, and unusual presentations such as young age, multiple foreign bodies, or repeated episodes should raise suspicion for child abuse.[7, 28] Simply stated, risk = hazard × exposure (personal communication, Gene Rider, Inchcape Testing Services Risk Analysis and Management, Moonachie, NJ, 1994).

According to the National Safety Council, suffocation from foreign body ingestion and aspiration is the third leading cause of accidental death in children younger than 1 year and the fourth leading cause in children between 1 and 6 years old. Ingestions are often asymptomatic, unrecognized, and self-resolving. But, because retained esophageal foreign bodies are so much more common than aspirations, procedures for removal outnumber those for aspirated foreign bodies.

Presentation and Natural History

Probably a majority of pediatric foreign body ingestions are not witnessed by parents. Studies of poison centers reveal that a large percentage of parents of witnessed ingestions do not seek medical advice beyond calling the poison center, and, in fact, the most common advice currently given after ingestion of coins in asymptomatic children is to observe the child and check the stools. If the coin fails to appear within 14 days or if the child becomes symptomatic, then parents are advised to seek medical attention for imaging.

Caravati et al[11] reported on a series of 162 cases of pediatric coin ingestion where the family was advised by a Poison Control Center in 1989 to seek medical attention. In fact, 60% of families elected not to seek medical attention; these children remained asymptomatic as determined by follow-up telephone call after 24 hours (no mention was made of long-term follow-up). Of the patients following the advice for evaluation, 20% were found on imaging to have swallowed coins (and 2 of these 13 patients were asymptomatic). Ten years later, Conners et al[15] reported on 67 asymptomatic pediatric coin ingestion patients whose families were given a scripted Poison Control Center message not to seek medical attention unless the child became symptomatic. Two thirds of parents sought medical attention despite this advice. One child in the group (who subsequently became symptomatic) underwent endoscopy for an image-proven retained esophageal coin.

In studies of proven esophageal foreign bodies, generally 75% to 80% of patients are children, most commonly ages 18 to 48 months.[37] In about 75% of pediatric cases, the ingested foreign bodies are coins, and in 15% of cases, the foreign bodies are food or bones. The remaining percentage is made up of buttons, other plastic items, marbles, crayons, batteries, screws, and pins. Adult risk factors for esophageal foreign body retention include psychiatric illness and prisoner or edentulous status. Food bolus and bones are the most common adult problems. Only 14% of pediatric cases of esophageal foreign body retention are seen in children older than age 5 years, and food bolus and school supplies are more common in older children.[24]

Series of pediatric patients seen in the health care system (beyond the Poison Control Center telephone call) with esophageal foreign bodies show that approximately 65% of patients are younger than age 3 years, 75% of events are witnessed, and up to 40% of patients are asymptomatic.[16, 20] Sixty percent to 70% of patients are seen in less than 24 hours, and 5% are seen more than 1 week past ingestion. The predominantly liquid and soft diet of young children can sometimes allow them to retain an esophageal foreign body for months before obstruction becomes manifest. Symptoms and signs in children are often vague but may include vomiting, dysphagia, ptyalism, gagging, poor feeding, and irritability. Large foreign bodies or long-standing foreign bodies with periesophageal inflammation may cause airway symptoms such as wheezing, stridor, cough, and recurrent aspiration via anterior displacement of the common posterior tracheal wall and inability to effectively swallow secretions. As Chevalier Jackson pointed out, in the most severely complicated cases of esophageal foreign bodies, the diagnosis is often never considered until late in the course of management of the patient.[22]

In pediatric series, 63% to 84% of foreign bodies are retained at the level of the cricopharyngeus muscle (upper esophageal sphincter), 10% to 17% at the level of the aortic crossover at the midesophagus, and 5% to 20% at the lower esophageal sphincter.[37] Quarters (24 mm) are inevitably located at the cricopharyngeus, while dimes (17 mm) and pennies (18 mm) may appear more distally. Three percent to 5% of patients have an initially unsuspected second (or multiple) foreign body, sometimes an adherent coin.[34]

Complications of Esophageal Foreign Bodies

Foreign body ingestion is an extremely common occurrence in pediatric patients, and prolonged retention of unsuspected objects is rare. However, unrecognized esophageal foreign bodies inevitably lead to devastating complications, and this fact underscores the dilemmas faced in all management paradigms.

Reilly et al[29] described a 1.7% overall rate of secondary complications in a national survey of 702 esophageal foreign bodies. Esophageal foreign bodies retained for more than 1 week can result in severe complications, including death.[17] Gilchrist et al[19] described five cases of delayed diagnosis of esophageal foreign body (2 months to 2 years) out of a cohort of 100 consecutive children undergoing esophagoscopy for removal of foreign body. The retained objects included coins, a heart pendent, and a toy soldier. All five patients suffered significant complications including esophageal diverticulum, lobar atelectasis, mediastinitis, and bronchoesophageal fistula. One patient died after esophagoscopy as a result of massive hemorrhage from an aortoesophageal fistula. In retrospect, diagnostic clues to the diagnosis of retained esophageal foreign body included new onset asthma, recurrent "upper respiratory tract infections," and excessive salivation. Useful adjuncts in making the diagnosis of retained foreign body included chest radiographs (posteroanterior and lateral) and barium swallow.

Imaging

Most authors recommend that all patients suspected of harboring an esophageal or pharyngeal foreign body undergo anteroposterior and lateral neck and chest radiography. Hodge et al,[21] in a retrospective review of 80 children with a history of coin ingestion, found that 31% had an esophageal coin demonstrated by radiographs, including 44% of patients who were asymptomatic at the time. All symptomatic children were found to have coins in the esophagus.

Faintly radiopaque objects, such as eggshells and bones, are often seen best on lateral views because they tend to orient in the coronal plane in the esophagus. The presence of radiolucent objects, such as plastics and aluminum, may be inferred by signs of periesophageal inflammation or by hyperinflation of the hypopharynx and proximal esophagus. Chest films may also demonstrate complications such as mediastinitis, pneumothorax, or aspiration pneumonia.

Hand-held metal detectors are 95% to 100% sensitive and specific compared with radiographs in documenting the presence of esophageal coins.[2, 6] These devices are especially useful in monitoring passage of a metallic foreign body into the stomach, eliminating the time, expense, and radiation exposure of further radiographs. The child must be examined in a metal-free environment because the devices are sensitive enough to pick up even metal in undergarments of parents holding the patient.

When plain films are normal or equivocal in a symptomatic patient, additional diagnostic procedures may be considered. Esophagograms may demonstrate radiolucent foreign bodies as persistent filling defects, but such studies pose the risk of aspiration of contrast material, and residual contrast material may obscure the foreign body at later endoscopy. Barium esophagograms may be helpful in revealing vascular compression or intrinsic stricture as the predisposing factor for foreign body entrapment. Computed tomography is excellent at showing periesophageal soft tissue inflammation and abscess formation. In one recent study of symptomatic adults with a history of fish or chicken bone ingestion, computed tomography was 100% sensitive and specific in diagnosing esophageal foreign body by demonstrating either the bone itself or surrounding esophageal wall inflammation.[18] Magnetic resonance imaging is excellent for soft tissue abnormalities but may require general anesthesia for young children. Negative results of imaging do not definitely rule out the presence of a foreign body, and endoscopy may be indicated for persistent symptoms.

Management Issues

Coins

Coins have remained at the top of the list of foreign bodies most frequently ingested by children. Most ingested coins pass spontaneously through the body and never come to the attention of the physician. Patients seen for medical evaluation can be divided into a simple or favorable group versus a complex group. Persons in the *simple* group are first seen within 24 hours of ingestion and have no history of esophageal anatomic or motility disorder and no respiratory symptoms. Several authors recommend observing patients with documented esophageal coins in the simple or favorable category for 24 hours with subsequent radiographs or metal detector imaging because there is an approximate 30% rate of spontaneous passage into the stomach.[35] Coins in the distal esophagus have the greatest likelihood of spontaneous passage.[14]

For retained coins in patients in the *complex* category, removal of the foreign body should be accomplished in a timely fashion. Traditionally, otolaryngologists have advocated rigid endoscopy with its advantages of better visualization and control of foreign body manipulation. However, rigid endoscopy carries with it the risk of general anesthesia and an overall 2% risk of other complications ranging from minor lip abrasion to esophageal perforation. With increasing pressure for better time efficiency and for lower costs in medicine, authors are reporting increasing numbers of ingested coins managed with other techniques.

Flexible endoscopy has been used frequently for removal of coins and other blunt or smooth esophageal foreign bodies. Even though most advocates use general anesthesia in children, they claim a lower overall complication rate than for rigid endoscopy.[4] Bendig[3] reported on a series of 23 cases in children managed with flexible esophagoscopy with intravenous sedation only. The coin was removed successfully in 18 patients and pushed distally into the stomach in five.

Balloon extraction of esophageal coins was first reported in the 1960s, and several pediatric tertiary care centers report this method as their first choice of extraction for smooth foreign bodies. At the conservative end of the balloon extraction spectrum, the technique is limited to restrainable patients in the simple or favorable category with proximal esophageal coins. A Foley catheter (number 8, 10, 12, or 14, depending on the size of the patient) is placed transnasally and then advanced distal to the coin under fluoroscopic guidance with the child in a supine position. The child is then rotated to a lateral decubitus or prone position and the balloon is inflated with 3 to 5 cc of air or contrast and then removed if no resistance is encountered. No sedation or local anesthesia is used, and surgeons or experienced anesthesiologists are in attendance with McGill grasping forceps available to assist in removing the coin from the hypopharynx if the child is unable to spit it out unaided.[12] Morrow et al[27] described a series of 173 children with smooth esophageal foreign bodies at varying esophageal levels and with no respiratory symptoms. A total of 146 patients had successful extraction with the balloon technique under fluoroscopic guidance, 12 patients experienced spontaneous passage into the stomach, and 15 patients required subsequent removal with rigid endoscopy after failure of the balloon technique. The only complication in the series was one episode of epistaxis.

Kelly et al[23] described a series of patients managed with balloon extraction in the emergency department without fluoroscopic guidance. The approach was limited to patients with proximal coins, and a small percentage required rigid endoscopy after initial failure of the Foley technique. Likewise, Agarwala et al[1] have reported a series of 302 children with esophageal coins managed by the blind Foley technique in the emergency department. The technique was successful in 94%.

Schunk et al[32] described their philosophy of balloon extraction even in children with esophageal abnormalities

or more prolonged foreign body retention. In a retrospective review of 415 cases, they found an overall high success rate for Foley extraction but more failures in patients with esophageal disease or with a history of retention greater than 4 days. They found an overall 1% rate of significant complications, including an esophageal laceration requiring open repair and an episode of postoperative temporary airway edema.

Because complications are rare once coins have passed to the stomach, one interesting management option receiving more attention is esophageal bougienage. Blunt-tipped weighted esophageal bougies are passed to advance the coin into the stomach, and the patient is then reexamined by radiograph or metal detector. Calkins et al[10] described a consecutive series of 27 patients with retained esophageal foreign bodies evaluated for bougie technique. Twelve patients met the authors' criteria of a single coin, symptoms less than 24 hours, no esophageal abnormalities, and no respiratory distress. The coin was successfully advanced to the stomach in 10 of the 12 patients with no complications in the series.

Management of esophageal coins in uncomplicated cases represents an interesting situation in which expense and risk are directly proportional among varying techniques. Bougienage has close to a 0% complication rate and relatively low cost compared to rigid endoscopy with general anesthesia. Balloon extraction falls somewhere in the middle, with expense dependent upon use of fluoroscopy, among other things.[13, 36] Many management paradigms have been proposed recommending bougienage for uncomplicated patients with more distal coins, balloon extraction for more proximal coins, and rigid endoscopy for patients with airway symptoms, prolonged retention, or esophageal abnormalities, or when other techniques fail.[23, 33] These recommendations apply only to the ideal situation in which the interest, availability, equipment, and experience for every technique exists. Proponents of bougienage and balloon techniques emphasize lower cost and complication rates. Proponents of rigid endoscopy (including most otolaryngologists) emphasize the discomfort of esophageal procedures in unsedated patients with the risk of airway obstruction in the unintubated patient. In the real world, decisions must be guided by the experience and culture of the institution (Fig. 71–1).

Batteries

As disk and button batteries have become ubiquitous, the number of pediatric ingestions has grown dramatically. Disk batteries are of four types: mercury, manganese, silver, and lithium manganese. Problems related to ingestions can include direct caustic injury, absorption of toxins, pressure necrosis, and tissue necrosis from electrical discharge.[31] Vottler et al,[38] in a dog model study, demonstrated esophageal mucosal ulceration within 4 hours and penetration within 6 hours of alkaline battery ingestion. Injury results from leakage of caustic chemical or from low-voltage direct current, which releases intracellular potassium, resulting in cell death.

Recent studies have found that large 3-volt lithium

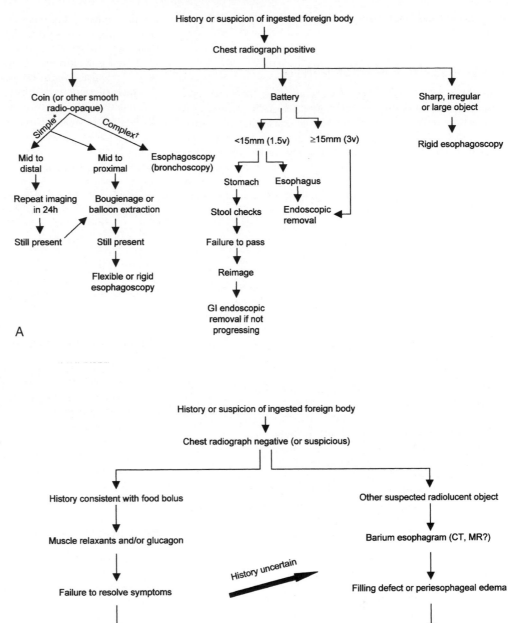

FIGURE 71–1. *A* and *B*, Example of a management paradigm for esophageal foreign bodies assuming available expertise and experience for all techniques. °Simple refers to healthy patient with no respiratory symptoms. †Complex refers to prolonged retention of foreign body, history of previous foreign body retention, or history of anatomic or neuromuscular esophageal abnormality.

batteries account for a disproportionate percentage of bad outcomes in battery ingestion series, even though they constitute a minority of batteries produced. The current generated by the 3-volt batteries is enough to cause tissue necrosis via cellular electrolyte flux. The generally safer 1.5-volt button batteries are usually 7.9 to 11.6 mm in diameter, whereas the 3-volt lithium batteries (which may be found in the soles of children's athletic shoes) are usually 20 to 23 mm.[25] All batteries lodged in the esophagus should be regarded as emergencies and treated accordingly, and most authors recommend the use of careful rigid endoscopy for extraction. Smaller disk batteries, which have passed beyond the gastroesophageal sphincter, are generally followed up with stool checks or radiographs, with flexible endoscopic removal reserved for bat-

teries that fail to pass rapidly. Because of the increased risk for tissue necrosis and gut perforation with 3-volt lithium batteries, some authors recommend removal of all batteries greater than 15 mm in diameter, no matter where they appear in the gastrointestinal tract.

Food

Standard practice in many emergency departments includes the use of muscle relaxants or intravenous glucagon as initial medical therapy for patients with impacted esophageal food boluses. However, medical therapy is often ineffective in patients with underlying stricture or motility disorder.[26] In various series of patients with esophageal food bolus, up to 70% have esophageal abnormalities.[24]

Sharp, Irregular, and Large Objects

Sharp, irregular, and large objects are less likely to pass spontaneously and are more likely to lead to esophageal perforation with the potential for mediastinitis or aorto-esophageal fistula.[9] Esophageal foreign bodies of this type call for emergency rigid esophagoscopy under general anesthesia. Anesthesia allows for deep muscle relaxation and rigid scopes afford the opportunity to "capture" points or sharp edges within the scope, allowing for safe advancement back up the proximal esophagus.

Choking

Choking with asphyxiation is the fourth most common cause of pediatric injury death, after homicide, suffocation, and motor vehicle accident. The incidence of choking deaths has decreased during the past decade by 4.6% per year, perhaps, in part, because of changes in consumer product law. Risk factors for accidental death in general include low birth weight, young parents, and low level of parental education.[8]

Rimell et al[30] examined Consumer Product Safety Commission data regarding characteristics of objects causing death or injury. They found that conforming or spherical objects presented the greatest danger. Balloons accounted for approximately one third of all deaths (including two cases of balloons made from examination gloves in doctors' offices). Other objects resulting in fatal asphyxiation included marbles, balls, bottle caps, buttons, coins, and pen caps. Several objects were large enough to have passed the Federal Hazardous Substances Act Small Parts Fixture test with diameters greater than 3.17 cm.

Endoscopy

Endoscopy remains the preferred technique for esophageal foreign body removal for most otolaryngologists, especially when control of the airway, manipulation of the object, and excellent visualization are necessary. Few esophageal foreign bodies are such emergencies that preoperative preparations cannot be completed before their removal. In addition to discussing the situation with the child's parents and performing a thorough medical evaluation of the child, the surgeon should practice techniques for removal of a duplicate foreign body and plan the procedure carefully with the endoscopic team before the actual operation.

Discussion with Parents

The family of a child who will undergo endoscopy for removal of a foreign body must be made aware of the limitations and possible complications of the procedure. Most children who have swallowed or could have swallowed a foreign body have been seen first by another physician before being referred to the otolaryngologist, but unless the child has swallowed a sharp object, many families have not been told of the complications that can arise during attempted removal. The parents should be told that endoscopy is not always successful, especially for long-standing foreign bodies with surrounding granulation. A decision may be made to abort the procedure in the face of poor visualization resulting from inflammation or because of stricture and to obtain further imaging studies while treating the patient with antibiotics.

Medical Evaluation

Although the focus of the family and the endoscopist is on the foreign body problem, a careful general history must be taken and a physical examination performed on each child who presents with possible foreign body in the esophagus. Special attention should be given to airway disease, seizure disorder, muscle disease, medications, hydration, and nutritional status. Consultation with a pediatrician is routine in many institutions.

Practice on a Duplicate

Unless the foreign body has been identified as a common item such as a coin, it is highly desirable for the endoscopist to practice removing a duplicate foreign body from a dummy (or at least from a cup). Many unexpected problems of forceps purchase, rotation, and changes in presentation or position of the foreign body, and insecure fit of the endoscopic equipment can become obvious. Solutions to these problems can be developed in a practice session.

Anesthesia

The anesthesiologist is a vital part of the management team and should be included in planning from the earliest stages. Aspiration presents a significant risk in patients with esophageal foreign bodies when the obstructing lesion does not allow for passage of secretions and swallowed liquids. For this reason, some anesthesiologists prefer to use rapid sequence technique with cricoid pressure until the airway is secured through intubation, at least for cases of high aspiration risk such as a food impaction caused by esophageal stricture. Cricoid pressure should not be used with large or sharp foreign bodies in the proximal esophagus behind the cricoid. Succinylcholine chloride is used by many as a means of short-acting muscle relaxation for rapid sequence, but it carries the risk of prolonged muscular weakness in a patient with undiagnosed muscular dystrophy (infant male). Rocuronium bromide is another choice for muscular relaxation, but its duration is much longer.

Otherwise healthy children with recent coin ingestion present little aspiration risk, and most anesthesiologists manage these patients with standard halothane induction for intubation. Another choice for induction for patients in the favorable category is intravenous propofol with a short-acting narcotic such as alfentanil hydrochloride or remifentanil hydrochloride.

Esophagoscopes

In general, esophagoscopes differ from bronchoscopes in having a smooth, flared leading edge designed for gently spreading apart esophageal mucosa instead of a sharper shovel tip designed for spreading apart the vocal cords. Esophagoscopes are engineered for the job of esophagoscopy, and bronchoscopes should not be used in their stead.

Short esophagoscopes, such as the Forbes esophageal speculum, can be ideal for the common problem of foreign body lodged in the proximal esophagus at the level of the cricopharyngeus muscle. Longer esophagoscopes are necessary for removal of more distal foreign bodies. The largest instrument that will pass easily should be used to allow for maximum visualization and ease of instrumentation. The patient should be positioned in a neutral sniffing position with the cervical spine straight to allow for easy passage over the cervical kyphosis.

Classic rigid esophagoscope designed with distal light carriers include the Hollinger and Jesberg models. The Jesberg esophagoscopes allow for a larger working area but lack suction channels. The Storz system affords greatly enhanced visualization by means of the Hopkins rod-lens telescope and is preferred by many endoscopists. The Storz endoscopes lack a separate suction channel, but a flexible, small suction catheter can be introduced via a side port. The system includes separate optical telescope grasping forceps with alligator and peanut designs.

Flexible endoscopic systems are more expensive and may require a separate technician for help with suction, video monitoring, and forceps operation. They provide the potential advantages of excellent visualization combined with the ability to go past the gastroesophageal sphincter into the stomach. Early flexible esophagoscopes could not be used to remove sharp objects because they had no mechanism to sheath a point, but newer instruments are equipped with hoods that permit safe removal of most foreign bodies.[5] Nevertheless, for removal of most foreign bodies above the gastroesophageal junction, and especially for removal of foreign bodies with complicated shapes and sharp points, rigid endoscopy is still probably the safest technique in the context of the expertise available at most institutions.

Illustrative Cases

The following case histories illustrate typical foreign bodies causing aerodigestive injury and their management.

1. Esophageal Coin—Two Cents' Worth of Trouble

A 9-month-old boy has a 1-week history of new onset reactive airways disease and a 2-day history of inspiratory stridor and croupy cough. A chest radiograph obtained in the pediatrician's office reveals a proximal esophageal circular foreign body with an apparent notched circumference (Fig. 71–2). Because there is a history of airway symptoms, the patient is taken as an emergency to the operating room where two adjacent pennies are easily removed with rigid esophagoscopy (Fig. 71–3). Bronchoscopy shows anterior displacement of the posterior tracheal wall as a result of periesophageal edema. The penny itself is extremely corroded (Fig. 71–4), characteristic of newer U.S. pennies with high zinc content, which possibly present a greater risk of mucosal inflammation than other coins. Airway symptoms resolve rapidly, and the patient is discharged home the next day.

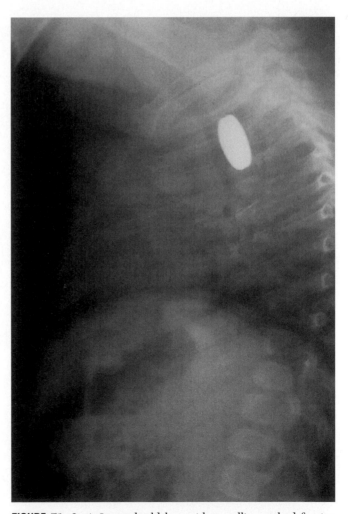

FIGURE 71–2. A 9-month-old boy with metallic notched foreign body in the esophagus.

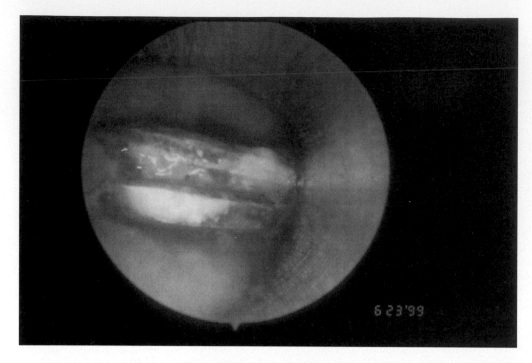

FIGURE 71–3. Endoscopic view of two pennies in the proximal esophagus.

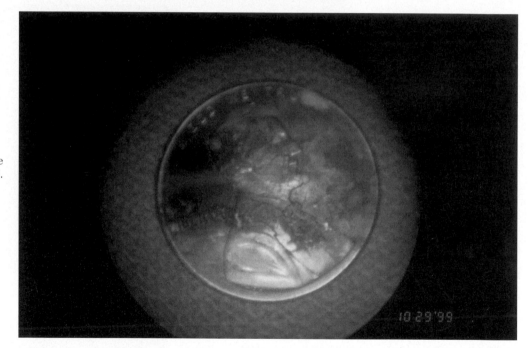

FIGURE 71–4. Corrosion of the newer high zinc content U.S. pennies.

2. Disk Battery

A 10-month-old boy has a history of new onset croup (no history of ingestion), and anteroposterior chest radiograph demonstrates an apparent quarter in the proximal esophagus (Fig. 71–5). Lateral radiograph shows periesophageal edema with anterior displacement of the trachea (Fig. 71–6). Rigid endoscopy is used to successfully remove the object, which proves to be a 23-mm 3-volt lithium disk battery closely matching the dimensions of a quarter (24 mm). The patient has extensive esophageal mucosal inflammation and is maintained for 24 hours with nasogastric tube feedings. Airway symptoms resolve rapidly.

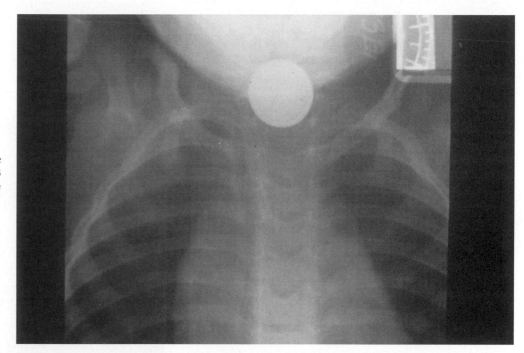

FIGURE 71–5. Large metallic disk-shaped foreign body (3 volt lithium battery) in the proximal esophagus.

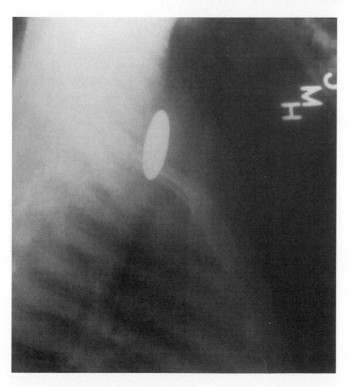

FIGURE 71–6. Lateral view showing periesophageal edema and anterior displacement of the trachea.

3. Plastic

A 1½-year-old boy undergoes a barium swallow as part of an evaluation for progressive stridor. The anteroposterior view shows the barium outline of a disk-shaped object in the midesophagus (Fig. 71–7). The lateral view shows a filling defect at the same level, above a posterior esophageal indentation (from a vascular anomaly that proves to be a double aortic arch) (Fig. 71–8). The patient is then taken to the operating room, where bronchoscopy shows pronounced anterior displacement of the posterior tracheal wall (Fig. 71–9), and rigid esophagoscopy is successful in removing a plastic eye from the midesophagus (Fig. 71–10).

When shown the plastic foreign body, the parents recalled that a teddy bear had been missing an eye for about 1 year. This case illustrates the facts that vascular anomalies compressing the esophagus may predispose to impaction of ingested material, and that young children can remain well nourished despite the presence of a long-standing foreign body, due primarily to their liquid and soft diet. The case also shows that very inert materials such as plastic can potentially remain impacted for long periods before manifesting symptoms resulting from esophageal inflammation.

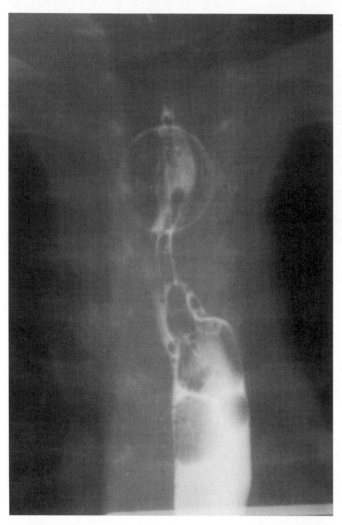

FIGURE 71–7. An 18-month-old boy with progressive stridor. Anterior view barium swallow shows a circular filling defect in the mid-esophagus.

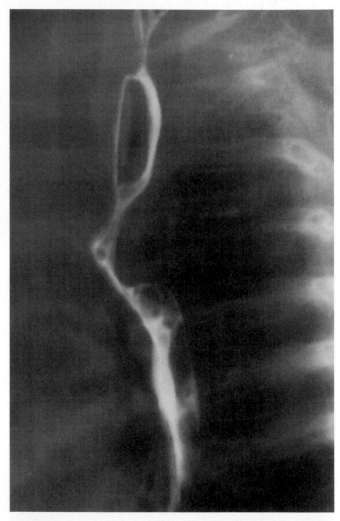

FIGURE 71–8. Lateral view barium swallow demonstrates a disk-shaped esophageal foreign body above a vascular compression (double aortic arch).

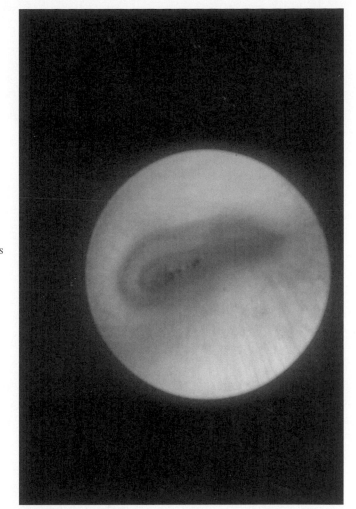

FIGURE 71–9. Same patient as Figure 71–8. Bronchoscopy shows anterior displacement of the posterior tracheal wall.

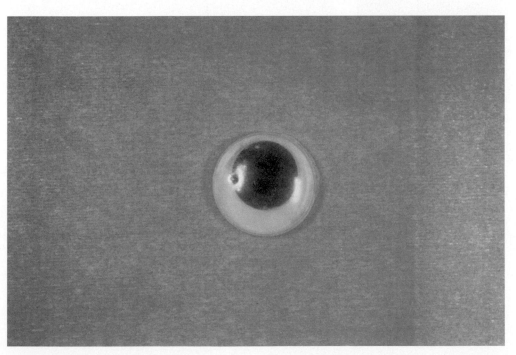

FIGURE 71–10. The esophageal foreign body proved to be a teddy bear eye, missing for approximately one year.

4. Meat Bolus

A 7-year-old girl with Down syndrome undergoes her ninth procedure for removal of impacted meat bolus at the level of the midesophagus. The patient has a known mild midesophageal narrowing and mild dysmotility, but her parents have had increasing difficulty in preventing her from eating large pieces of meat. A number 5 bronchoscope is used as the rigid endoscope, and no abnormalities are noted other than her known mild midesophageal narrowing. The patient is discharged home immediately after the procedure but returns the following day with chest pain and fever.

Chest radiographs are interpreted as mild right perihilar infiltrate only and the patient is admitted and given intravenous antibiotics. The patient's symptoms intensify, and further radiographs the next day show a right pneumohydrothorax (Fig. 71–11). A barium esophagram demonstrates a leak of contrast into the right chest (Fig. 71–12), and the patient is taken to surgery for a right thoracotomy. A small midesophageal fistula is closed primarily in two layers and a chest tube is placed. Recovery with further intravenous antibiotics is uneventful, and subsequent barium swallow shows no further leak (Fig. 71–13).

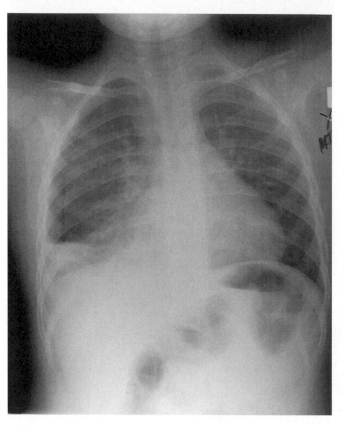

FIGURE 71–11. Right hydropneumothorax following rigid endoscopic removal of a meat impaction in a child with Down syndrome with known mild mid-esophageal stricture.

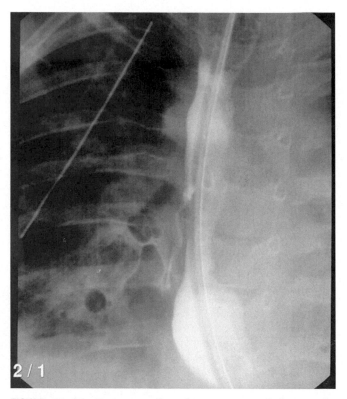

FIGURE 71–12. Barium swallow demonstrates a leak into the right chest from the esophageal perforation.

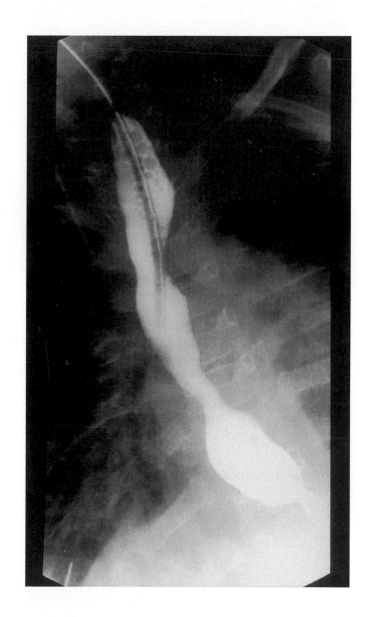

FIGURE 71–13. Imaging after repair shows no leak.

5. Open Safety Pin

Figure 71–14 shows chest radiographs of a 16-month-old boy who swallowed an open safety pin. The presenting complaint is that the child "won't eat and is irritable." At surgery, a number 4 Hollinger esophagoscope is used to pass ring rotation forceps, which are used to grasp the spring of the safety pin. Because the pin's presenting part is the keeper, the object is advanced into the stomach and then extracted by version.

All methods of removing a safety pin from the esophagus (straightening, endogastric version, point sheathing, and closing) are based on the dictum "advancing points perforate: trailing points do not." Various techniques should be practiced before one or more is attempted in vivo, and fluoroscopic guidance can be helpful.

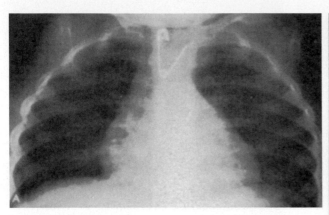
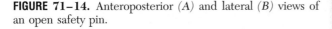
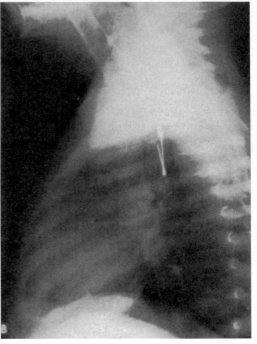

FIGURE 71–14. Anteroposterior (A) and lateral (B) views of an open safety pin.

Acknowledgments

The authors thank Gene Rider, Inchcape Testing Services Risk Analysis & Management, Moonachie, NJ.

SELECTED REFERENCES

Calkins CM, Christians KK, Sell LL. Cost analysis in the management of esophageal coins: endoscopy versus bougienage. J Pediatr Surg 34: 412, 1999.

A good overview of management paradigms.

Litovitz TL, Schmitz BF. Ingestion of cylindrical and button batteries: an analysis of 2382 cases. Pediatrics 89:747, 1992.

This article is of great value in giving details of this potentially fatal foreign body.

Schunk JE, Harrison AM, Corneli HM. Fluoroscopic Foley catheter removal of esophageal foreign bodies in children: experience with 415 episodes. Pediatrics 94:709, 1994.

A large series of balloon extraction technique.

REFERENCES

1. Agarwala S, Bhatnagar U, Mitra DK. Coins can be safely removed from the esophagus by Foley's catheter without fluoroscopic control. Indian Pediatr 33:109, 1996.
2. Bassett KE, Schunk JE, Logan L. Localizing ingested coins with a metal detector. Am J Emerg Med 17:338, 1999.
3. Bendig DW. Removal of blunt esophageal foreign bodies by flexible endoscopy without general anesthesia. Am J Dis Child 140:789, 1986.
4. Berggreen PJ, Harrison E, Sanowski RA, et al. Techniques and complications of esophageal foreign body extraction in children and adults. Gastrointest Endosc 39:626, 1993.
5. Bertoni G, Pacchione D, Sassatelli R, et al. A new protector device for safe endoscopic removal for sharp gastroesophageal foreign bodies in infants. J Pediatr Gastroenterol Nutr 16:393, 1993.
6. Biehler JL, Tuggle D, Stacy T. Use of the trasmitter-receiver metal detector in the evaluation of pediatric coin ingestions. Pediatric Emerg Care 9:208, 1993.
7. Binder L, Anderson WA. Pediatric gastrointestinal foreign body ingestions. Ann Emerg Med 13:61, 1984.
8. Brenner RA, Overpeck MD, Trumble AC, et al. Deaths attributed to injuries in infants, United States 1983–1991. Pediatrics 103:968, 1999.

9. Bullaboy CA, Derkal WM, Johnson DH, et al. False aneurysm of the aorta secondary to an esophageal foreign body. Ann Thorac Surg 39:275, 1985.
10. Calkins CM, Christians KK, Sell LL. Cost analysis in the management of esophageal coins: endoscopy versus bougienage. J Pediatr Surg 34:412, 1999.
11. Caravati EM, Bennett DL, McElwee NE. Pediatric coin ingestion. A prospective study on the utility of routine roentgenograms. Am J Dis Child 143:549, 1989.
12. Carlson DH. Removal of coins in the esophagus using a Foley catheter. Pediatrics 50:475, 1977.
13. Connors GP. A literature-based comparison of three methods of pediatric esophageal coin removal. Pediatr Emerg Care 13:154, 1997.
14. Conners GP, Chamserlain JM, Ochsenschlager DW. Symptoms and spontaneous passage of esophageal coins. Arch Pediatr Adolesc Med 149:36, 1995.
15. Conners GP, Cobaugh DJ, Feinberg R, et al. Home observation for asymptomatic coin ingestion: acceptance and outcomes. The New York State Poison Control Center Coin Ingestion Study Group. Acad Emerg Med 3:213, 1999.
16. Crysdale WS, Sendi KS, Yoo J. Esophageal foreign bodies in children, 15-year review of 484 cases. Ann Otol Rhinol Laryngol 100:320, 1991.
17. Dahiya M, Denton JS. Esophagoaortic perforation by foreign body (coin) causing sudden death in a 3 year-old child. Am J Forensic Med Pathol 20:184, 1999.
18. Eliashar R, Dano I, Dangoor E, et al. Computed tomography diagnosis of esophageal bone impaction: a prospective study. Ann Otol Rhinol Laryngol 108:708, 1999.
19. Gilchrist BF, Valerie EP, Nguyen M, et al. Pearls and perils in the management of prolonged, peculiar, penetrating esophageal foreign bodies in children. J Pediatr Surg 32:1429, 1997.
20. Hawkins DB. Removal of blunt foreign bodies from the esophagus. Ann Otol Rhinol Laryngol 99:935, 1990.
21. Hodge D, Tecklenburg F, Fleisher G. Coin ingestion: does every child need a radiograph? Ann Emerg Med 14:443, 1985.
22. Jackson C, Jackson CL. Diseases of the Air and Food Passages of Foreign Body Origin. Philadelphia, WB Saunders, 1936.
23. Kelly JE, Leech MH, Carr MG. A safe and cost effective protocol for the management of esophageal coins in children. J Pediatr Surg 28:898, 1993.
24. Lemberg PS, Darrow DH, Holinger LD. Aerodigestive tract foreign bodies in the older child and adolescent. Ann Otol Rhinol Laryngol 105:267, 1996.
25. Litovitz TL, Schmitz BF. Ingestion of cylindrical and button batteries: an analysis of 2382 cases. Pediatrics 89:747, 1992.
26. Mazzadi S, Salis GB, Garcia A, et al. Foreign body impaction in the esophagus: are there underlying motor disorders? Dis Esophagus 11:51, 1998.
27. Morrow SE, Bickler SW, Kennedy AP, et al. Balloon extraction of esophageal foreign bodies in children. J Pediatr Surg 33:266, 1998.
28. Nolte KB. Esophageal foreign bodies as child abuse. Potential fatal mechanisms. Am J Forensic Med Pathol 14:323, 1993.
29. Reilly J, Thompson S, MacArthur C, et al. Pediatric aerodigestive foreign body injuries are complications related to timeliness of diagnosis. Laryngoscope 107:17, 1997.
30. Rimell FL, Thome A Jr, Stool S, et al. Characteristics of objects that cause choking in children. JAMA 274:1763, 1995.
31. Samad L, Ali M, Ramzi H. Button battery ingestion: hazards of esophageal impaction. J Pediatr Surg 34:1527, 1999.
32. Schunk JE, Harrison AM, Corneli HM. Fluoroscopic Foley catheter removal of esophageal foreign bodies in children: experience with 415 episodes. Pediatrics 94:709, 1994.
33. Schweich PJ. Management of coin ingestion: any change? Pediatr Emerg Care 11:37, 1995.
34. Smith SA, Conners GP. Unexpected second foreign bodies in pediatric esophageal coin ingestions. Pediatr Emerg Care 14:261, 1998.
35. Soprano JV, Fleisher GR, Mandl ZD. The spontaneous passing of esophageal coins in children. Arch Pediatr Adolesc Med 153:1073, 1999.
36. Soprano JV, Mandl KD. Four strategies for the management of esophageal coins in children. Pediatrics 105:e5, 2000.
37. Stack LB, Munter DW. Foreign bodies in the gastrointestinal tract. Emerg Med Clin North Am 14:493, 1996.
38. Vottler TP, Nash JC, Rutledge JC. The hazard of ingested alkaline disc batteries in children. JAMA 249:2504, 1983.
39. Wiseman N. The diagnosis of foreign body aspiration in childhood. J Pediatr Surg 19:531, 1984.

72

Injuries of the Mouth, Pharynx, and Esophagus

Roberto L. Barretto, M.D., Mark Marunick, D.D.S, M.S., Terry L. Donat, M.D.,
Robert H. Maisel, M.D., and Robert H. Mathog, M.D.

Injuries to the mouth, pharynx, and esophagus require careful and complete evaluation for appropriate treatment of the injury and associated early complications as well as prevention of later problems in speech and eating. Early and precise diagnosis of the location and extent of tissue damage is essential and often requires imaging studies and general anesthesia with peroral endoscopy. Intubation or tracheostomy may be necessary to assist in the evaluation and to prevent airway obstruction.

The early wound care, debridement, and repair of soft tissue depend on the location and cause of the injury. Ingested foreign bodies must be accurately localized and extracted to prevent airway obstruction, infection, and visceral penetration. Burns require observation for a time to determine the extent of tissue destruction. Generalized debilitation from malnutrition requires correction before definitive reconstruction. The goals in all treatment are a rapid rehabilitation, a short period of hospitalization, the preservation of normal psychosocial development, and the prevention of environmental circumstances resulting in these injuries.

Injuries from Accidents

Accidents are the major cause of death and injury in children and include intraoral penetration by foreign bodies and compressed gases; automobile accidents; animal or human bites; and injuries from knives, guns, and endoscopic instruments. These injuries may involve the upper digestive and respiratory tracts, but the lip and cheek are frequently involved. Curiosity, belligerence, and carelessness commonly lead to accidents resulting in intraoral penetration. In many cases, parental neglect and abuse have also been factors and necessitate a careful survey of associated injuries with detailed medical documentation and social service evaluation.

Oral and Pharyngeal Injuries Caused by Foreign Bodies

Probably the most common injuries to the upper aerodigestive tract are those that occur from foreign objects placed in the mouth, from a fall in which the gaped mouth makes contact with an object, or from a bite into soft tissue. Toys, sticks, pencils, eating utensils, and similar objects cause contusions, lacerations, and puncture wounds of the oral and pharyngeal mucosa. Teeth and tooth fragments must never be overlooked as endogenous sources of foreign bodies that may be swallowed, aspirated, or embedded in oral wounds after full-thickness bite penetration.[18] It is important to determine the mechanism and magnitude of force involved when the severity of the injury is evaluated on physical examination, because even innocuous injuries have been associated with severe respiratory and neurologic complications.

The injuries are most often minor, requiring only careful inspection, removal of any retained fragments, hemostasis, approximation of large lacerations involving nondevitalized tissue, and oral administration of antibiotics (along with tetanus toxoid, if indicated) to prevent infection.

A higher suspicion for severe injury should be maintained for penetrating or blunt injuries near vital structures, such as to the lateral soft palate and peritonsillar areas, overlying the carotid artery, and the posterior pharynx, overlying the cervical spine and retropharyngeal space. Contusion of the carotid artery between the penetrating object and the cervical vertebral transverse processes with intimal disruption and thrombosis is a rare complication, usually developing within 48 hours, that may be suspected if neurologic sequelae without other cause develop.[28] In the presence of a lateral palatal or peritonsillar wound highly suggestive of carotid trauma or with the development of neurologic signs, initial noninvasive assessment with Doppler ultrasonography and ocular pneumoplethysmography is advised to document vascular flow and the presence and extent of injury. Magnetic resonance angiography has demonstrated equal or greater sensitivity for carotid injuries and may obviate the need for invasive testing.[38] Carotid arteriography should be used when there are equivocal Doppler ultrasonography or magnetic resonance angiography findings and progressive neurologic signs. Although it is an invasive procedure with inherent risks, arteriography is advantageous in that it can definitively delineate a vascular injury and determine the treatment approach if vascular flow is diminished or if intraluminal thrombosis or occlusion is present.[14] Treatment, whether medical with thrombolytics or surgical, is controversial.[33, 38]

In apparent minor injuries without neurovascular sequelae, admission for observation should be based on the proximity of the patient's home to the hospital and the reliability of adult caretakers. However, neurovascular involvement may not become clinically apparent for days, and signs such as fever, poor oral intake, lethargy, or vision changes warrant immediate reevaluation.[33]

Other early major complications may include soft tissue edema, deep cervical emphysema, or hematoma development in the tongue or pharynx that may lead to respiratory embarrassment and obstruction. Later, retained foreign material (visible on plain radiographs if it is radiopaque) may incite a foreign body tissue reaction or lead to abscess, both of which require removal of the foreign material; in addition, abscess requires external neck drainage with healing by secondary intention. Inpatient observation is warranted if signs of the early, rare complications exist, if there is inability to maintain adequate oral intake, or if the parents are unreliable caretakers.

Oropharyngoesophageal Barotrauma

Blast trauma to the upper aerodigestive tract is a relatively rare event that may arise from expulsion of the lid and contents of overpressurized carbonated beverage containers or from the accidental expulsion of contents from pressurized tanks, hoses, and tires in proximity to the oral cavity.[8] Most carbonated beverages are packaged at 2 atmospheres of pressure, which may increase to nearly 6 atmospheres of pressure in the presence of high temperature, agitation,[21] or the introduction of dry ice for rapid cooling.[6] The injudicious use of teeth by children in removing the container cap leads to the blast of the cap and liquid contents into the oral cavity. Superficial mucosal injuries may be simply observed. Deeper injuries involving the parapharyngeal soft tissues and development of cervical surgical emphysema, pneumomediastinum, or pneumothoraces on plain radiography require high-risk airway observation and intubation for respiratory compromise; intravenous administration of broad-spectrum antibiotics; endoscopy and a diatrizoate meglumine (Gastrografin) pharyngoesophagogram to determine the sites of injury; and primary repair with mediastinal drainage at the site of cervical, tracheal, pharyngeal, or esophageal perforation. Tracheotomy is recommended in the event of tracheal injury. Pneumothoraces are managed by thoracostomy tube placement, and nutrition is supplied by parenteral or nasogastric enteral routes. Thoracic esophageal perforation requires thoracotomy repair and drainage.

Vehicle Accidents

Automobile and bicycle accidents often result in injuries of the head and neck, causing facial fractures as well as soft tissue damage. Many states have legislated the proper use of three-point seat belt restraints and mandatory infant child seats, which has reduced the frequency of outright deaths and the seriousness of adult, infant, and young child trauma. In the older child and early adolescent, the effects of these preventive measures are less certain, owing to restraints that are often too loose, and the shoulder strap poses a strangulation hazard to a child. Likewise, a relative increase in facial soft tissue trauma is seen among the increased number of survivors. Infant seats are currently either built in or recommended for use in conjunction with existing restraining systems, but they may not always be adequate to prevent the release and propulsion of the child.

In vehicle-caused accidents involving injury to the head and neck, the location and extent of damage to the child must be evaluated. The primary concern must be maintenance of an adequate airway and observation for possible edema of the oropharyngeal airway and subsequent respiratory distress. In the presence of a mandibular fracture, support of the tongue is reduced, and retrodisplacement of the tongue may result in obstruction. Swelling caused by tissue edema or hematoma at the base of the tongue or in the pharyngeal walls may present similar difficulties. In cases in which the larynx is injured by a direct blunt or penetrating mechanism, the airway may rapidly become compromised. Secretions and blood in the pharynx of the awake or obtunded individual compound any respiratory difficulties and must be cleared by suction.

The airway, if compromised, is the initial priority and is preferably secured by suctioning of secretions and endotracheal tube placement. Transnasal intubation for nasopharyngeal and nasotracheal ventilation or nasogastric suction catheter placement should be avoided in cases of suspected midfacial fractures to prevent the possibility of intracranial positioning. Cricothyrotomy and tracheostomy should be reserved for instances of cervical spine injury, anticipated long-term intubation, and severe laryngotracheal injury in which intubation may cause more trauma or in which oral intubation is otherwise unsuccessful or impossible. Cricothyrotomy should be converted to tracheostomy as soon as possible, preferably within 24 hours, because it may result in long-term complications related to damage of the subglottic airway. Subsequent general trauma survey must include chest evaluation for possible pneumothorax and hemothorax; cervical spine films delineate subluxation or fracture.

The evaluation and repair of facial fractures are discussed in Chapter 47. In cases of laceration or avulsion soft tissue injury, the site should be irrigated with copious amounts of normal saline and inspected for extent of the injury and presence of foreign bodies. Dead tissue should be conservatively debrided, whereas viable tissue should be retained. All landmarks should be marked with Bonney's Blue or similar marking solution before infiltration with local anesthetics and primary wound repair.

Lip Injury

Lip lacerations and small avulsions up to one third of the lip length, whether full or partial thickness, should be repaired by direct primary approximation or wedge-type excision (Fig. 72–1, top). Partial-thickness wounds are advantageous because of their lack of loss of lip length and potential ability for closure without wedge resection

AVULSION OF LIP

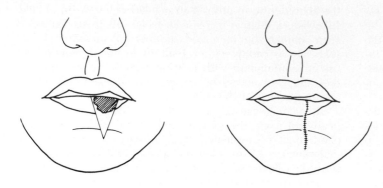

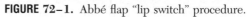

FIGURE 72–1. Abbé flap "lip switch" procedure.

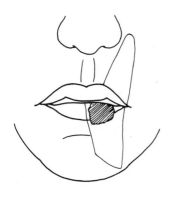

Wedge Excision

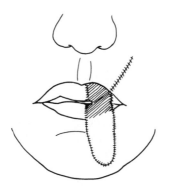

loss of lip length. In cases involving loss of the vermilion and mucocutaneous junction, reconstruction can be effected by use of a labially based V-Y subcutaneous advancement flap in conjunction with a twin submucosal advancement flap, without loss of lip length.[36] A V-shield–like extension of the wound or a W-incision made inferiorly to the defect is frequently useful to close the wound when wedge resection closure methods are employed. Of functional importance is the required repair of the lacerated orbicularis oris muscle with absorbable suture to maintain muscle continuity and avoid retraction deformity. Only after this layer is satisfactorily approximated may further closure be completed. Exact alignment of the vermilion border is the first priority with use of nonabsorbable sutures, which are then used to conclude the cutaneous closure. The mucocutaneous approximation is similarly performed with absorbable suture.

When avulsions extend from one third to two thirds of the lip, full-thickness local flaps must be used for repair. The preferred flaps are the Gillies fan flap and Karapandzic flap for repair of midline upper or lower lip injury, the Abbé flap for medial or lateral lip injury without commissural involvement (see Fig. 72–1, *bottom*), and the Estlander flap for lateral injury with commissural involvement. The single-stage Gillies fan flap uses bilateral, horizontal, and medially directed lateral lip advancement flaps, facilitated with crescentic excision of perialar or cheek skin, for the midline defect repair. The single-stage Karapandzic flap similarly uses direct horizontal advance-

ment but with facilitation by circumoral skin and subcutaneous incisions, with orbicularis oris muscle mobilization allowing rotation of opposing lip portions to effect the closure. The Abbé flap is constructed akin to the Estlander flap; the height of the flap equals the defect's height, and the width of the flap equals half the defect's width to ensure symmetric lip length reduction. Abbé flap vermilion border approximation must be exact with conclusion of the second-stage pedicle release. The single-stage Estlander flap may be based inferiorly or superiorly; the superiorly based flap incorporates the nasolabial fold for improved cosmesis. A secondary commissuroplasty to correct microstomia may be necessary later. Both cross-lip flaps provide superior cosmesis to the Gillies flap, which may result in a "fishmouth" deformity requiring further correction.[31] Single-stage procedure healing should be allowed to proceed for 3 to 6 months before any corrective procedures are planned because this allows the evaluation of the final appearance of the commissures after wound contracture.

In upper and lower lip injuries involving greater than two thirds or total lip destruction, local and regional flaps are useful in successful reconstruction. If there is adequate, viable adjacent cheek tissue, closure of midline defects may be effected by any of several large-volume advancement flaps as described independently by Burow, Bernard, Dieffenbach, and Webster.[31] Karapandzic flaps can also be constructed in conjunction with Abbé or Estlander flaps. Large lateral defects may be closed by full-thickness nasolabial transpositional flaps. Additional flaps derived from the temporal forehead, medial forehead, or neck areas may be needed for reconstruction up to and including replacement of the entire upper and lower lips when adjacent cheek tissue is unsuitable for use. These flaps are less cosmetic with respect to texture and color match, compared with adjacent cheek tissue, and secondary donor site deficiencies are more pronounced.

Tongue Injury

Reconstruction of laceration or avulsion tongue injuries is not usually required; primary wound healing often occurs rapidly because of the rich vascular supply to the tongue. Only with lacerations larger than 2 cm or with difficulties in obtaining hemostasis is it necessary to effect closure. In the child, this must usually be performed with use of heavy parenteral sedation or under general anesthesia, because it is difficult to immobilize the tongue for local anesthetic infiltration and subsequent suturing, using absorbable suture. Loss of the lateral tongue or tongue tip from extensive injury usually produces no permanent deficit, since the tongue hypertrophies to rebulk itself in a period of 6 months. Injuries involving the tongue base are more likely to affect function in the event of hypoglossal nerve injury or late fibrosis from large, transecting lacerations. Many times, a laceration in which a flap of muscle is elevated may be ignored; this results in some distortion of the tongue, which is of concern to the parent and, later, to the child. Good oral hygiene and antibiotics directed against oral flora are advisable.

A special group of injuries to the tongue are those that occur in children with coagulopathies. These tend to heal slowly, and, although they may heal primarily, the process may take weeks in a child who has hemophilia. Suture repair of relatively small injuries in these cases may expedite healing and is advisable, since it is necessary to maintain these children with replacement coagulation factors. Dental fabrication of a smooth splint for the prevention of wound irritation by the maxillary teeth is additionally warranted.

For effective function after the proper repair of the lip and tongue, early motion is advisable. Within several days after removal of the sutures, the patient should be executing stretching exercises. Contracture of the lips, commissure, and buccal areas can be prevented by passive opening of the mouth with tongue blades or a commercial device (e.g., Therabite). These exercises should be continued until the tissues soften and the period of wound contracture has passed.

Palate Injuries

The hard palate, because of its firm, bony support, is rarely penetrated by sharp objects, but it may be sagittally fractured in the median or paramedian position with a severe injury that involves a maxillary fracture, often resulting in malocclusion. Intermaxillary fixation and bone plating or palatal splinting, with coordinated reduction of associated maxillary fractures, are required.[41]

The soft palate, composed of muscle and mucosa, is occasionally penetrated or partially avulsed by intraoral foreign bodies as previously discussed. The injury may produce acute oral bleeding, but an examination usually shows only a mucosal tear and, occasionally, complete penetration to the nasopharynx or lateral pharyngeal wall. These injuries are usually not sutured if near approximation is present and the bleeding stops expeditiously. Lacerations of the mucous membrane heal spontaneously when kept clean, and the only repair should be secondary in cases of persistent fistula. Rare but severe complications of this type of injury are associated with contusion or penetration through the lateral soft palate and superior peritonsillar region with injury of the venous plexus surrounding the carotid artery, which requires tamponade, or direct carotid injury with the development of hemorrhage or neurologic signs, as previously discussed.

Pharyngeal Injury

Lacerations, avulsions, and fractures involving the pharynx, whether caused by blunt or penetrating, transoral or external trauma, require careful evaluation of the extent and location of the primary injury and any concurrent esophageal or laryngotracheal injuries via laryngoscopy, bronchoscopy, esophagoscopy, and imaging studies (e.g., esophagogram, computed tomographic scan), with intubation or tracheostomy as indicated in the presence of impending airway obstruction. Injuries of this type may be recognized by symptoms of dysphagia, odynophagia, dysphonia, progressive respiratory distress with stridor and hemoptysis, and physical signs of cervical tenderness and edema, with or without a visible external neck wound, crepitance, or displacement or palpable fractures of the hyoid bone and thyroid or cricoid cartilages. Plain radiographic evidence of cervical or mediastinal emphysema has been noted in as many as 95% of cases. In cooperative children, fiberoptic nasopharyngolaryngoscopy is useful as part of the initial examination. Computed tomographic scan with contrast enhancement is the standard imaging modality used for laryngeal trauma to delineate injury and plan treatment approach but should not preclude airway stabilization. Initially, if injury is present and the airway compromised, oral intubation may be attempted. If the airway is distorted, rigid endoscopic airway control is recommended, with subsequent tracheostomy.

Management of pharyngeal injury, including involvement of the piriform sinuses, is identical to that discussed for barotraumatic injuries. The child's larynx lies higher in the neck, is smaller absolutely, and is less prominent than the adult's, affording it relatively greater protection by the mandible. Unfavorably, though, blunt trauma is less sustainable by the pediatric larynx because of the relative pliability of its cartilage, the laxity of the suspensory soft tissues, and the narrow endolaryngeal lumen, all of which enhance the potential for soft tissue destruction and edema to yield early airway compromise in these injuries. A further discussion of laryngotracheal injuries is made in Chapter 88.

Penetrating Injury

Damage from guns and knives used irresponsibly or with provocation, and available to children through carelessness, is commonly observed. Most civilian gunshot wounds are caused by low-velocity projectiles, which cause moderate soft tissue destruction and bone injury in their path. Often these projectiles are deflected by arteries, nerves, and fascial planes, without their injury, to yield an erratic path with little relation to implied wound trajectories. These projectiles can subsequently penetrate fixed structures, such as the pharynx and esophagus. Although compressed air- and carbon dioxide-propelled target handguns and rifles are considered short range and often "toylike," their potential to produce penetrating low-velocity, small-projectile, fatal injuries remains present.

In contrast, high-velocity rifle and shotgun wounds cause extensive destruction of all soft tissue along a sustained initial entry trajectory, frequently involving arterial and neural structures or shattering the mandible and maxilla with significant loss of bone. Knife wounds are extremely dangerous, and although the entry wound may not be large, these sharp instruments may easily lacerate nerves and other vital structures along their direct trajectory to depths greater than anticipated for the length of the knife because of external soft tissue compression at maximal penetration.

In cases of neck wounds penetrating beyond the platysma, the patient should be admitted to the hospital and should be evaluated systematically, especially for signs of neurovascular compromise or aerodigestive injury. Further discussion regarding management of penetrating neck injuries is found in Chapter 103.

An esophageal injury must be suspected in any midline injury or injury crossing midline and evaluated immediately. The extent and location of esophageal lacerations and avulsions can be evaluated only by endoscopy with a rigid endoscope and radiologic fluoroscopic studies. If a torn viscus is suspected, use of the locally toxic Hypaque contrast material should be avoided. If the physician suspects a tracheoesophageal fistula or aspiration, iso-osmolar, nonionic contrast material, such as Omnipaque, is the indicated agent. Barium and water-soluble hyperosmolar ionic agents should be avoided when there is a risk of chemical pneumonitis or the potential pleural space delivery of barium.

With all tears and lacerations of the digestive system, broad-spectrum antibiotic treatment is necessary. Exploration through the neck or through a combined neck-chest incision is desirable to drain any abscesses. If there is mediastinitis, chest tubes may be placed and irrigated with antibiotics. Small, uncomplicated pharyngeal tears are ordinarily allowed to heal by secondary intention, whereas early cervical and thoracic esophageal injuries should be explored surgically.[20]

Instrument Injuries

Instruments are a common cause of injury to the esophagus. These injuries can occur during the removal of foreign bodies, biopsies, dilatations, or diagnostic evaluations. Injury may also occur with the aggressive use of suction catheters or during placement of nasogastric tubes in the pediatric population. Although the flexible endoscope may reduce the likelihood of such complications, the rigid endoscope is often required to carry out many of these procedures.

The most common site of injury to the esophagus during endoscopy is at the cricopharyngeus. The hypopharynx and piriform sinuses just proximal to the cricopharyngeus may also be injured during endoscopy or attempted intubation. Poor visualization and the use of excessive force greatly contribute to this type of injury. It is not clear whether the use of local or general anesthesia affects the frequency of such a complication. Occasionally, the injury goes unnoticed until the patient complains of chest pain. Widening of the mediastinum, development of a left pleural effusion or infiltrate on radiographs, fever, tachycardia, subcutaneous emphysema, and elevation of the white blood cell count are symptoms of the injury and indicate the possibility of mediastinitis.

Hypopharyngeal injury has already been discussed in this chapter. The treatment of esophageal tears consists of immediate administration of antibiotics and evaluation of the extent of the tear. Gastrografin esophagography and endoscopy are complementary studies that in combination yield a sensitivity of greater than 90%. If the injury appears to be significant by the presence of extravasation, early drainage of the mediastinum may be indicated. In cases in which the infection progresses to an abscess, drainage is essential to treat this life-threatening complication.[26]

Animal and Human Bites

Animal bites may also be a cause of injuries to the upper digestive and respiratory tracts. Approximately 8% of animal bites occur in the head and neck and primarily affect the middle and lower face. Most of the bites are ascribed to family dogs or at least a dog known in the neighborhood that is provoked by removal of food or a litter. In some cases, kissing and playing with the animal have accounted for the injuries. Most human bites result from either altercations or amorous encounters. In contrast to automobile accidents, animal and human bites frequently involve soft tissues and spare bony structures.

The types of injuries observed with human and animal bites are usually puncture wounds, lacerations, and avulsions. All areas of injury should be cleansed and copiously irrigated with benzalkonium chloride[17] or normal saline, preferably by gentle pressure irrigation. The mild, acute swelling that may occur with these mucosal injuries may be treated with cold compresses and steroids to reduce the inflammation. Wound repair management remains controversial, but, in general, puncture wounds require no closure. Clean, nonhuman lacerations may be closed primarily if they are seen within 5 hours. Severe human bite lacerations and bite avulsion injuries of any source should be managed by topical dressing changes with delayed primary closure when the wound appears clinically clean, usually in 2 to 5 days. Antibiotics are administered for 10 days in all cases. The primary choices are amoxicillin-clavulanic acid orally for outpatient management in primarily repaired wounds, and ampicillin-sulbactam or ticarcillin-clavulanic acid combinations intravenously for delayed wound management, plus completion of the oral antibiotic course after repair.[37]

Tetanus prophylaxis is prescribed when there are entry wounds on the face, lips, or neck. Recommendation by the U.S. Public Health Service is also made for postexposure rabies prophylaxis for bites involving dogs, cats, and most wild mammals and carnivores, other than livestock and rodents, aside from woodchucks. It is accomplished by thorough wound cleansing with soap and water and the administration of human rabies immune globulin (HRIG) and active vaccination with human diploid cell vaccine (HDCV) or rabies vaccine adsorbed (RVA). If the animal is available for 10-day observation or pathologic examination, prophylaxis should be withheld until the animal's development of symptoms or laboratory confirmation. If the animal is known to be or highly suspected of being rabid, or is unavailable for examination, prophylaxis should be given immediately. HRIG, 20 IU/kg, is administered with half infiltrated around the wounds and the remainder intramuscularly injected in the gluteal region. HDCV or RVA, 1.0 mL intramuscularly, is administered into the deltoid area (only acceptable site in adults or older children; lateral thigh acceptable in young children and infants).

Injury from Heat

Electrical Burns

In the United States, injuries from electricity account for 2400 emergency department admissions annually, 3% to 5% of burn patient admissions, and 1500 deaths per year.[42] About one third of major electrical accidents occur in electrical workers, one third in construction workers, and the remaining third in the home, especially among children.[42] Electrical burns of the head and neck, and especially those of the mouth, account for a significant number of childhood injuries,[7] but low-voltage injuries (<1000 volts) are declining[29] as a result of improved safety of electrical systems in the home.

Electrical burns usually occur in children between 2 and 5 years of age. More than 50% of the injuries are due to sucking on the female end of a live extension cord[40]; the remainder of the injuries occur when the child places the junction between two cords into the mouth or sucks on an open structural socket (Fig. 72–2). Rarely does the child ever bite through the cover of a live wire, although injury from sucking on an exposed wire has been reported.[15]

The location of tissue injury is determined by the current (amperage) of the line. The current (I) is calculated from the voltage (V) and resistance (R) according to Ohm's law (I = V/R). Since most household voltage is 110 or 220 volts, current flow and current intensity vary according to the local and distant resistances. Electric current (especially alternating current such as that used in U.S. households) can be fatal if it flows throughout the body, and in the case of the less likely contact burn found with dry contact and improved grounding, cardiac rhythm is disrupted. Local damage occurs primarily if the

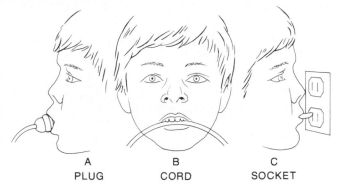

FIGURE 72–2. Thirst and dryness may be factors that cause children to chew or suck on electric cords. (From Small A. Early surgery for electrical mouth burns. AORN J 23:128, 1976. Reproduced with permission from the Association of Operating Room Nurses and Allen Small, M.D.)

current flows only through one area of reduced resistance.[40]

The degree of injury from electricity is related to the thermal energy expended, which varies with resistance and the square of the current ($H = I^2R$). Current, which is the most important factor, depends on the local tissue's electrical resistance. Dry skin has a high resistance of 40,000 to 100,000 ohm/cm^2 and allows minimal current flow; but mucous membrane resistance may be as low as 100 ohm/cm^2, allowing high current flow. Thus, the low resistance of mucosa may lead to intense oral burns (Fig. 72–3). The high resistance distally accounts for the low 2% incidence of death and 5% incidence of cardiac arrhythmia and respiratory failure in these children.

The oral burn results from the arc conduction of current from the electrical source to the low-resistance saliva-coated mucosa with the production of heat up to 3000°C. This subsequently causes tissue destruction with eventual necrosis. The lower lip is usually more severely burned than the upper lip, and most damage of the lip occurs at the vermilion border. Approximately 25% of all electrical lip burn injuries occur to the middle of the lip; the remainder involves the commissure, with involvement of either or both the upper and lower lip. Extensive burns may involve the labial and lingual mucosa and extend into the alveolar process. In such cases, the burn can devitalize deciduous teeth and cause mucous membrane and periosteal necrosis. Alveolar bone exposure and sequestration can occur, often with significant pain. Curiously, the unerupted permanent dentition is never destroyed in these children. The tongue is involved between 30% and 40% of the time by the burn, and its destruction may later cause loss of mobility, with poor speech and difficulty in deglutition. Deeper structures in the oral cavity usually show minimal damage except when they are the sites of exit of the electric current.

The early appearance of an oral burn wound is similar to that of any third-degree burn; a gray central depression or ulcer is surrounded by a pale elevation of the skin. Hyperemia haloes the immediately adjacent skin. The lesions are usually avascular, cold, and relatively painless, owing to cauterization of the sensory nerves. On histologic examination, coagulation necrosis extends be-

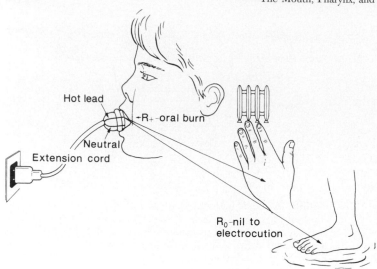

FIGURE 72–3. Mechanism of an oral burn. When regional resistance is low and peripheral resistance is high (R_+), oral burn results. When regional resistance is low and peripheral resistance is low (R_0), tingling or electrocution results. (From Thomson HG. Electric burns to the mouth in children. Plast Reconstr Surg 35:466, 1965.)

yond the gross margins of the wound. The media of blood vessel walls is often destroyed and may cause late, brisk bleeding, with a frequency of 20%. An exposed, eroded labial artery can bleed extensively, either within 10 days after the injury or later, with the sloughing of the eschar over the burn site. In either event, it may initially be managed by direct compression.

In the acute care phase, to encourage development of a "clean" eschar, the burn injury is treated with antibiotic ointment and frequent hydrogen peroxide swabbings. Tetanus prophylaxis is administered, and fluids are permitted if swallowing is satisfactory. Supplemental intravenous infusions are used if needed. Systemic antibiotics in the form of penicillin are recommended until the slough of the necrotic tissue occurs. Inpatient management should be considered in those cases of injury with inability to tolerate oral intake, where home care delivery may prove inadequate, or when the initial management of a labial artery bleed would be overwhelming to the particular parents.

The timing of surgical repair and debridement of these wounds is a topic of debate. Classicists advocate local conservative care so that the burn will demarcate before excision. Approximately 1 to 2 weeks are needed for the coagulation necrosis to become obvious. Advocates of the conservative school note that early surgery may cause removal of the otherwise viable and vital tissues, which are needed for the repair. The proponents of acute surgical debridement and excision claim that the occurrence of labial artery bleeding can be prevented by early surgery. Moreover, these surgeons believe that when the wound is excised and approximated, healing from secondary intention is avoided, contracture is minimized, and ultimately less scarring will occur.

The method of repair depends on the degree of destruction and availability of local tissues. Minimal burns of the lip heal satisfactorily by first intention. More extensive injuries may require reconstructive surgery (see Chap. 41 for more details).

In 1976, Colcleugh and Ryan described splinting of oral commissure burns. In the ensuing years, predominantly two types of splinting appliances have been used.

The first is a nondynamic or fixed splint that is anchored to the maxillary teeth and either the maxillary arch or, if necessary, the facial bones (Fig. 72–4). The acrylic post-extensions are positioned using measurements from the unaffected commissure to the midline (Fig. 72–5).[9, 34] The measurements are made with the patient at rest and with the patient smiling. The distal of the maxillary canines is used to determine the mesiodistal width and the incisal edges of the maxillary canines for locating the vertical position of the acrylic posts. These dental landmarks are extremely important to determine the configuration of the acrylic posts, especially when both commissures are involved.[12, 16, 32]

The splint is worn 24 hours a day and is removed for eating and cleaning the teeth. The splint is worn until the burn scar is soft and pliable. An additional 4 to 6 months of nighttime wear is advisable. Modifications in contour and tension can be developed until optimal tissue contours are achieved. Favorable results have been reported; only two patients of the 59 cases reported required subsequent reconstructive surgery.

Removable dynamic splints provide adjustable traction between oral commissures.[13, 19] These types of splints present problems for eating and speaking because they traverse the oral opening. Extraoral dynamic splints using oral commissure retractors with circumcranial and orthodontic headgear traction can avoid these problems.[11, 30]

Both kinds of appliances exert continuous pressure on the oral commissures to prevent microstomia formation during healing. These types of appliances have reduced the duration of hospitalization, and many patients no longer require multiple-stage reconstruction.[1, 27]

Splinting to prevent microstomia is now considered first-line therapy in mild to moderate burns of the oral commissure.[39] Splinting has been sufficient to allow healing, with restoration of a functioning oral commissure and decrease of the need for late operative scar revision[9, 10] (Fig. 72–6). The duration of time required for the appliance to be in place is 2 to 12 months, and patients have been treated up to age 13 years.

The prevention of lip burns is extremely important. Easy access to sources of electricity is probably the most

FIGURE 72–4. Removable acrylic post commissure burn splint on table top. Dental portion has been relined with a temporary soft material to enhance the retention of the splint.

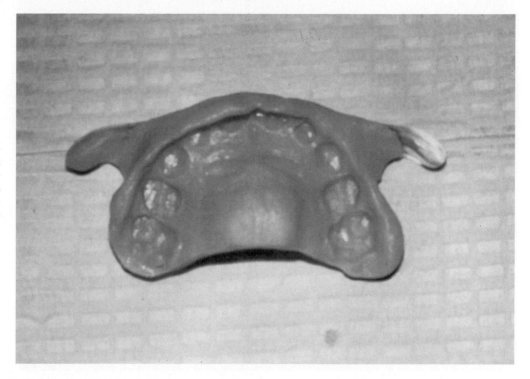

significant problem with children. New electrical safety devices in common use in newer homes, such as ground fault circuit interrupters (GFCIs) and better insulated extension cords,[29] have made it less dangerous for children to put plugs into their mouths. Parental education is still important in keeping the young child away from live extension cords, maintaining socket caps, and keeping the child from tampering with electric-powered equipment.

Inhalation and Scald Burns

Injuries from fire burns are usually limited to the lips, tongue, pharynx, and supraglottic airway. Below the level of the glottis and hypopharynx, burn damage to the airway and digestive tract is unusual. Hot air and other gases carry relatively little thermal energy, unless the ignition of a flammable gas has occurred; thus, with increasing distance from the source, damage is minimal to the cool, moist, surface epithelium. Hot liquids and steam can transfer large quantities of heat and can cause respiratory tract and esophageal burns, but fortunately these burns are rare. The increased use of household microwave ovens poses a significant threat for this type of injury in children; liquids can be rapidly heated to a superheated state (greater than 100°C without vapor bubble production), which can be deceptively consumed, or suddenly "bump" to a violent boil. Development of airway edema is a significant risk in these patients, and it must be identified and treated early if it occurs.[4] In the majority of these cases, the exposure of the glottic aperture to heat causes reflex vocal cord closure and protection of the trachea; similar spasm prevents thermal damage to the esophagus.

The burn injury can become complicated beyond just surface damage. In a confined area, the patient exposed to thermal sources may be forced to inhale smoke and toxic gases. These substances irritate and inflame the bronchial mucosa and cause protein to be exuded from lung epithelium, which obstructs alveoli and bronchioles. Casts of the bronchi or trachea may be formed, and respiratory death can occur owing to pulmonary edema, lower airway obstruction, or both. Extensive surface burns of the face and neck can also cause thermal injury and swelling of the deep tissues of the pharynx and oral cavity. The inflamed area usually responds quickly to treatment, but airway control is needed during the early phases.

The mechanism of injury from burns has been studied

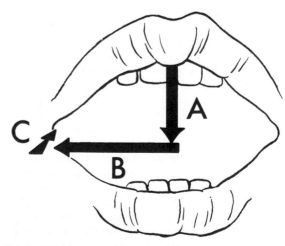

FIGURE 72–5. Measurements necessary to locate the commissure of the unaffected side. These are used to position the posts of the splint appliances. (From Czerepak CS. Oral splint therapy to manage electrical burns of the mouth in children. Clin Plast Surg 11:687, 1984.)

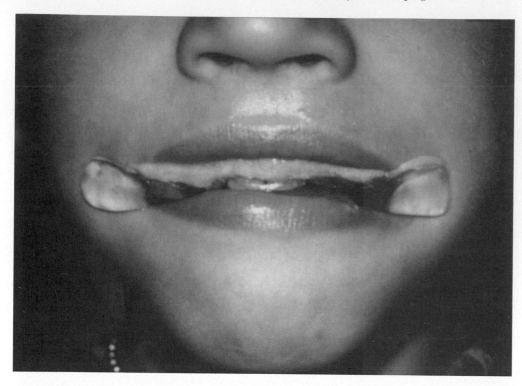

FIGURE 72–6. Six-year-old boy status post–8-weeks electrical burn to the left commissure with removable acrylic post burn splint in place.

extensively. After the initial injury, cell membranes become abnormally permeable, and molecules of molecular weight to 125,000 escape to the extravascular space. Plasma, protein, and fibrinogen enter the extravascular and extracellular spaces. Fluids shift into these spaces with the protein; these shifts are significant for burns over more than 10% of the body surface area and require aggressive intravenous replacement of 2 to 4 mL/kg per percentage of body surface area within the first 24 hours.[24] Burns confined to the head and neck body surface area in infants and children to age 15 years are maximally 21% and 11%, respectively, as determined by the Lund-Browder chart,[2] although comprising only 9% in adults. Plasma and extracellular fluid losses occur mostly during the first 12 hours after injury and continue for only 5 to 12 hours beyond that time. The shifts in fluid may cause soft tissue edema, obstruction of the airway, and difficulty in swallowing.[3]

During the acute phase after smoke inhalation, the main problems are bronchospasm and airway edema. Intubation or tracheostomy must be performed in the burn patient who has a compromised upper airway. Some studies have shown that pulmonary sepsis in burn patients is six times more common in patients with tracheostomy than in those who did not require such a procedure. Bacteria identical to those in the burn wound can be cultured from the endotracheal aspirate. To avoid infection, nasal or oral intubation is usually preferred, and tracheostomy is even more carefully considered than in the usual airway obstruction before the operation is undertaken.

Some of the indications for early intubation in the burn patient include charring, edema of the posterior

pharynx with the threat of upper airway obstruction, full-thickness burns of the entire face, severe hoarseness or stridor, and obvious smoke inhalation with pathognomonic signs of pulmonary contamination by the production of carbonaceous sputum, along with pulmonary wheezing, rales, and rhonchi.[23] Severe orofacial burns and coma at the time of admission similarly suggest the need for airway control. In patients with smoke inhalation without a severe burn, the main indication for intubation is evidence of central nervous system depression, symptomatic of hypoxia. Clark et al[5] have produced a reliable mortality probability assessment for burns, which includes inhalational injuries and may be used in triage for early intensive treatment. Airway observation of thermal injury patients must account for conditions of hypovolemia, with little or no evidence of mucosal edema, progressing to airway obstruction on adequate rehydration.[22] Delay in intubation makes the procedure difficult because of upper airway edema, and tracheostomy may then be necessary. Patients can be intubated for several days, although the possibility of eventual scarring of the larynx and subglottis must be considered in the presence of an upper airway burn. Laryngoscopy, bronchoscopy, and, if indicated, esophagoscopy should be performed as soon as cardiovascular stabilization is attained. Xenon-133 lung scans and pulmonary function tests may also be useful to assess injury.[22]

The effectiveness of steroids in the treatment of smoke inhalation is still a matter of debate. It appears that early in the course of the disease, steroids with high glucocorticoid activity, such as methylprednisolone and dexamethasone, are helpful. Mineralocorticoid drugs, such as cortisone or hydrocortisone, have been found to be ineffective in animal studies and may cause sodium retention and possible fluid overload.

Significant burns of the lip with tissue destruction are reconstructed by the techniques described for repair after electric injury. Pharyngeal contractures usually need no late treatment, but when they are significant in extent, they are treated best by split-thickness skin graft repair and rotation mucosal flaps. Esophageal injuries resulting from thermal energy and smoke inhalation are rare, and these stenoses are best managed by dilatation.

Chemical Injuries

Although the evaluation and treatment of caustic burns are discussed in Chapter 70, it should be noted that acid and alkali are common causes of injury to the lips, oral cavity, hypopharynx, and larynx, with the larynx being involved in nearly 50% to 75% of cases.[25] The frequency of oropharyngeal burns bears no relationship to the presence of esophageal burns, nor does the absence of oropharyngeal burns preclude esophageal burns. Signs and symptoms are identical to those seen with esophageal burns; additionally, there may be hoarseness, stridor, and the potential for rapidly progressive airway obstruction resulting from supraglottic edema. In this instance, obstruction is effectively alleviated by intubation.

Injury from chemicals is initially evaluated by direct laryngoscopy and esophagoscopy within 24 hours for extent and depth; after 24 to 48 hours, necrosis may become more apparent. As with more distal esophageal injuries, the patient with a pharyngeal burn is immediately started on a broad-spectrum intravenous antibiotic, and steroids may be administered to patients with more significant injury to limit airway edema and prevent excessive stenoses. Steroids are rarely used in patients with oral burns. Steroids are frequently used in pharyngeal burns and are the usual treatment in esophageal burns that show erosion deeper than the mucosa, although steroid use remains controversial for deeply penetrating burns into the esophageal musculature because of the potential for impaired wound healing and resultant perforation. A nasogastric tube is inserted carefully to maintain a feeding schedule. Treatment for pharyngeal stenoses after the healing phases would require skin grafts, flaps, Z plasty, or a combination of these procedures.

SELECTED REFERENCES

Colcleugh RC, Ryan JR. Splinting electrical burns of the mouth in children. Plast Reconstr Surg 58:239, 1976.

> *This important article led the specialty into a new and better therapy for oral burns.*

Moncrief JA. Burns. N Engl J Med 288:444, 1973.

> *Military and university centers headed by this author are unparalleled in treatment of burns, and his recommendations are logical and universally respected.*

Thomson H, Juckes AW, Farmer AW. Electric burns to the mouth in children. Plast Reconstr Surg 35:466, 1965.

> *This article summarizes the authors' extensive experiences with this problem and describes the etiology of this type of injury.*

REFERENCES

1. Al-Qattan MM, Gillet D, Thomson HG. Electrical burns to the oral commissure: does splinting obviate the need for commissuroplasty? Burns 22:555, 1996.
2. Artz CP, Moncrief JA. The Treatment of Burns, 2nd ed. Philadelphia, WB Saunders, 1969.
3. Beal DD. Respiratory tract injury: a guide to management following smoke and thermal injury. Laryngoscope 80:25, 1970.
4. Bjork L, Svensson H. Upper airway obstruction—an unusual complication following minor scalding injury. Burns 19:85, 1993.
5. Clark CJ, Reid HR, Gilmour WH, et al. Mortality probability in victims of fire trauma: revised equation to include inhalation injury. BMJ 292:1303, 1986.
6. Conlan AA, Wessels A, Hammond CA, et al. Pharyngoesophageal barotrauma in children: a report of six cases. J Thorac Cardiovasc Surg 88:452, 1984.
7. Crikelair GF, Dhaliwal AS. The cause and prevention of electrical burns of the mouth in children. Plast Reconstr Surg 58:206, 1976.
8. Curci MR, Dibbins AW, Grimes CK. Compressed air injury to the esophagus: a case study. J Trauma 29:1713, 1989.
9. Czerepak CS. Oral splint therapy to manage electrical burns of the mouth in children. Clin Plast Surg 11:685, 1984.
10. Dado DV, Polley W, Kernahan DA. Splinting of oral commissure electrical burns in children. J Pediatr 107:92, 1985.
11. Denton B, Shaw S. Mouth conformer for the prevention and correction of burn scar contracture. Phys Ther 56:683, 1975.
12. Grissius R, Moore D. Miscellaneous prostheses. In Beumer J, Curtis T, Maunnick M (eds). Maxillofacial Rehabilitation Prosthodontic and Surgical Considerations, 2nd ed. St Louis, Ishiyaku Euro America, Inc., 1996.
13. Hartford C, Kealey O, Lavelle W, Buckner H. An appliance to prevent and treat microstomia burns. J Trauma 15:356, 1975.
14. Hengerer AS, DeGroot TR, Rivers RJ, et al. Internal carotid artery thrombosis following soft palate injuries: a case report and review of 16 cases. Laryngoscope 94:1571, 1984.
15. Leake JE, Curtin JW. Electrical burns of the mouth in children. Clin Plast Surg 11:669, 1984.
16. Marunick M. Prosthetic management for electrical burns to the oral commissures. J Michigan Dent Assoc 6:529, 1986.
17. Mathog RH, Wurman I, Pollak D. Animal bites to the head and neck. In Sisson GA, Tardy ME (eds). Plastic and Reconstructive Surgery of the Face and Neck, vol. 2. Rehabilitative Surgery. Proceedings of the Second International Symposium. New York, Grune & Stratton, 1977.
18. McDonnell DG, McKiernan EX. Broken tooth fragments embedded in the tongue: a case report. Br J Oral Maxillofac Surg 24:464, 1986.
19. McGowan RH. Prevention of microstomia following facial burns. Br Dent J 149:83, 1980.
20. McInnis WB, Cruz AB, Aust JB. Penetrating injuries to the neck: pitfalls in management. Am J Surg 130:416, 1975.
21. Meycrovitch J, Ami TB, Rozenman J, et al. Pneumatic rupture of the esophagus caused by carbonated drinks. Pediatr Radiol 18:468, 1988.
22. Miller EP, Gray SD, Cotton ET, et al. Airway reconstruction following laryngotracheal thermal trauma. Laryngoscope 98:826, 1988.
23. Moncrief JA. Tracheotomy in burns. Arch Surg 79:45, 1959.
24. Moncrief JA. Burns. N Engl J Med 288:444, 1973.
25. Moulin D, Bertrand J, Buts J, et al. Upper airway lesions in children after ingestion of caustic substances. J Pediatr 106:408, 1985.
26. Paparella MM, Shumrick DA. Otolaryngology, 3rd ed. Philadelphia, WB Saunders, 1991.
27. Port RM, Cooley RO. Treatment of electrical burns of the oral and perioral tissues in children. J Am Dent Assoc 112:352, 1986.
28. Radkowski D, McGill TJ, Healy GB, et al. Penetrating trauma of the oropharynx in children. Laryngoscope 103:991, 1993.
29. Rai J, Jeschke MG, Barrow RE, et al. Electrical injuries: a 30-year review. J Trauma 46:933, 1999.
30. Reisberg D, Fine L, Fattore L, Edmonds D. Electrical burns of the oral commissure. J Prosthet Dent 49:71, 1983.
31. Renner GJ, Zitsch RP. Reconstruction of the lip. Otolaryngol Clin North Am 23:975, 1990.
32. Ryan JE. Prosthetic treatment for electrical burn of the oral cavity. J Prosthet Dent 42:434, 1979.

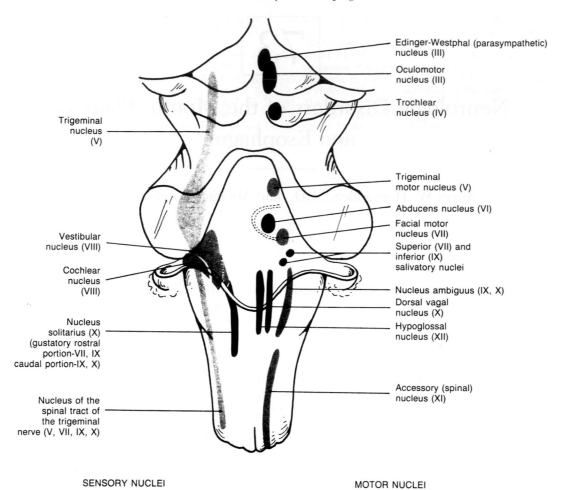

FIGURE 73–1. Brain stem with the nuclei of the cranial nerves (dorsal view).

The gag reflex may be lost in lesions of the glossopharyngeal or vagus nerves. Loss of the gag reflex has considerable localizing value if there is unilateral loss. Because there is great variability in the gag reflex, however, a bilaterally diminished response may be a variation of normal. Despite bilateral lesions of the vagus or glossopharyngeal nerves, the gag response may be partially intact as a result of function of the tensor veli palatini muscle innervated by the trigeminal nerve.[21] Although the tensor veli palatini functions primarily as the dilator of the eustachian tube,[13] it does play a role in the gag reflex. Although the gag and swallowing reflexes involve the same sensory and motor pathways, presence or absence of a gag reflex may not reflect swallowing integrity.[40]

Swallowing can be divided into three phases. In the initial oral phase, food is propelled toward the pharynx with the tongue and buccal musculature. In the second or pharyngeal phase, the nasopharynx closes with elevation of the soft palate, and the larynx closes with elevation of the hyoid bone and adduction of the vocal cords. Food is propelled toward the upper esophageal sphincter (cricopharyngeal muscle) by pharyngeal constrictors. The cricopharyngeal muscle relaxes reflexively, and the third phase of swallowing is characterized by esophageal peristalsis followed by opening of the lower esophageal sphincter.

Cricopharyngeal malfunction is seen in a variety of neurologic disorders.[20] Typically, central nervous system problems impair cricopharyngeal relaxation; peripheral neuromuscular abnormalities reduce sphincter pressure. In peripheral neuromuscular disorders, relaxation may nevertheless be incomplete because of impaired elevation of the hyoid bone as peripheral neuromuscular disease involves all pharyngeal muscles nonselectively. The traction force delivered by the elevation of the hyoid is required for complete opening of the sphincter.[7] Symptoms of neurogenic dysphagia include prolonged feeding, drooling, nasal regurgitation, cough, and choking during feeding, which eventually result in failure to thrive. Dysphagia for liquids precedes dysphagia for solids and is characteristic of neurologic impairment of swallowing. The investigation of the dysphagia should include cinefluorography and manometry to differentiate the structural abnormalities from neurogenic causes.[11]

Hiccups (singultus) are a common phenomenon; but rarely, intractable hiccups can herald a serious underlying neurologic disorder. The inspiration starting with the involuntary and spasmodic contractions of the diaphragm ends abruptly with the closure of the glottis. The afferent arm of this reflex includes the vagus and the phrenic nerves. Peripheral irritation of various branches of these two nerves, or a central nervous system disease affecting the area near the respiratory center in the medulla, may cause hiccups.[39]

Swallowing (deglutition) syncope is an uncommon condition that may be seen in children and adults. It is characterized by a decrease in cardiac output in response to swallowing. This phenomenon is thought to be a vaso-vagal reflex causing bradycardia and heart block resulting in cerebral hypoperfusion and loss of consciousness. It may be precipitated by cold drinks and large bolus of food, among other factors.[29, 65]

Disorders of taste, phonation/articulation, and dysphagia due to anatomic abnormalities are not addressed in this chapter. Neurologic disorders affecting the mouth, pharynx, and esophagus are discussed in two groups. Primary neurologic illnesses leading to functional impairment because of direct effects on innervation are presented first, followed by disorders in which structural abnormalities in the mouth, pharynx, and esophagus coexist with neurologic abnormalities.

Primary Neurologic Illnesses Leading to Functional Disorders

In light of the complex neuroanatomic connections, it is evident that neurologic disorders at different anatomic levels can be responsible for a variety of functional problems. These abnormalities are reviewed according to their functional disorder.[41]

Dysphagia

Table 73–1 summarizes the main causes of dysphagia by neuroanatomic localization. Impairment of cortical control on brain stem nuclei due to bilateral corticobulbar lesions is the most common upper motor neuron problem affecting the mouth, pharynx, and esophagus. Unilateral lesions uncommonly impair bulbar function because bulbar centers receive bilateral input.

Among several diffuse conditions affecting the brain, perinatal hypoxic injury, and prematurity-related cerebral injuries (periventricular leukomalacia and subependymal hemorrhage) are frequent causes of poor oropharyngeal coordination (sucking and swallowing). Aspiration pneumonias are a common occurrence in patients with these lesions. Congenital malformations of the brain, such as Chiari type II, microcephaly, holoprosencephaly, schizencephaly, and hydrocephalus, also lead to nutritional problems through the same mechanism.

Postinfectious leukoencephalopathies, acute demyelinating encephalomyelitis, and leukodystrophies are the principal demyelinating conditions affecting swallowing in the young. Multiple sclerosis frequently affects bulbar musculature, but this entity is rare in childhood.

Children with epilepsy may manifest oral and pharyngeal symptoms caused by distinctly different mechanisms. Frequent seizures may be responsible for a progressive encephalopathy and poor suck-swallow function. Certain seizures may present with isolated mouth-related symptoms, such as prolonged intermittent drooling and oral

TABLE 73–1. Causes of Dysphagia

Secondary to Cerebral Cortex Disorders

Perinatal hypoxic-ischemic injury
Prematurity-related cerebral injuries
Periventricular leukomalacia
Subependymal hemorrhages
Congenital malformation of the brain
  Microcephaly
  Holoprosencephaly
  Schizencephaly
  Hydrocephalus
Postinfectious leukoencephalopathy
Acute disseminated encephalomyelitis
Leukodystrophies
Epilepsy
Benzodiazepines
Metabolic disorders
Wilson disease
Infantile Gaucher disease
Alexander disease
Hexosaminidase A deficiency (Tay-Sachs disease)

Secondary to Brain Stem Disorders

Posterior fossa tumors
Brain stem gliomas
Ischemic lesions
Vertebral dissections
Vascular malformations
Poliomyelitis
Bulbospinal muscular atrophy (Brown-Vialetto-VanLaere syndrome)
Progressive bulbar palsy (Fazio-Londe disease)
Möbius syndrome
Chiari malformation
  Type I
  Type II
Basilar impression
Platybasia
Syringobulbia
Klippel-Feil syndrome

Secondary to Neuropathic Disorders

Miller-Fisher syndrome
Malignancies
Leukemia
Lymphoma
Rhabdomyosarcoma
Jugular fossa syndrome (Vernet syndrome)
Paragangliomas/schwannomas
Diphtheria
Vitamin E deficiency
Craniofacial syndrome (trigeminal and glossopharyngeal neuralgias)
Isolated hypoglossal nerve palsy

Secondary to Neuromuscular Junction Disorders

Myasthenia gravis
Transient neonatal myasthenia
Botulism
Infantile botulism
Lambert-Eaton myasthenic syndrome
Tetanus

Secondary to Muscle Disorders

Dermatomyositis
Fascioscapulohumeral dystrophy
Myotonic dystrophy
Oculopharyngeal dystrophy
Congenital muscular dystrophy

motor dyspraxia.[55] Chewing and lip smacking movements are typical automatisms in complex partial seizures associated with impairment in consciousness during the seizure.

Anticonvulsant treatment with the benzodiazepines is known to cause excessive drooling secondary to impaired swallowing. Nitrazepam has been associated with cricopharyngeal achalasia, abnormal esophageal peristalsis, and bronchospasm. This mechanism may be related to the propensity of nitrazepam to promote parasympathetic overactivity.[36]

Bruxism commonly occurs in mentally retarded children. Although it is not common, destruction of the teeth or supportive structures can occur. Treatment with interdental splints may be effective in some cases.[52]

Metabolic illnesses affecting the central nervous system predominantly cause supranuclear bulbar symptoms usually late in the course of the disease process, but symptoms may occasionally manifest early in the course of these diseases. Several metabolic disorders are prominent in causing supranuclear oropharyngeal symptoms.

Wilson disease is an autosomal recessive disorder of copper transport metabolism causing hepatolenticular degeneration. Neurologic manifestations usually occur after the second decade but may be seen earlier and include abnormal speech, dystonic smile, and impaired swallowing. Tongue dyskinesia may be among the early manifestations of this disorder.[35]

Infantile Gaucher disease usually manifests before 6 months of age with hypotonia, difficulties in sucking and swallowing, and oculomotor palsies. Head retraction is an early and typical sign. Splenomegaly and early demise are the rule.[6]

Alexander disease is a leukoencephalopathy characterized by megalencephaly, seizures, developmental delay, and spasticity. This disorder is an abnormality of astrocyte metabolism resulting in a characteristic pathologic finding of Rosenthal fibers diffusely distributed throughout the brain. A rare subtype of Alexander disease presents with predominantly brain stem involvement resulting in swallowing difficulties and nasal speech.[56]

Infants with hexosaminidase A deficiency (Tay-Sachs disease) typically present with developmental regression and a characteristic retinal abnormality referred to as the cherry red spot. There is, however, a spectrum of different patterns, one of which mimics bulbar palsy and lower motor neuron disease.[27]

Posterior fossa tumors constitute approximately half of the brain tumors encountered in the pediatric age group, and brain tumors are the second most common tumor type in children. Brain stem gliomas manifest with early bulbar involvement in association with corticospinal and cerebellar abnormalities. Progressive multiple bulbar neuropathies may be present as the only manifestation of brain stem gliomas before cerebellar and corticospinal tract signs develop. Cerebellar astrocytomas, medulloblastomas, and ependymomas of the fourth ventricle manifest with increased intracranial pressure and cerebellar abnormalities rather than lower cranial neuropathies.

Brain stem ischemic lesions in children are rare, but vertebral dissection or vascular malformations are occasionally responsible for bulbar nuclear impairment. Ischemic lesions in the medulla usually cause long tract signs as well as sensory changes except in Avellis syndrome (palatopharyngeal hemiplegia), which may occur after ischemic or traumatic injury.[32]

Poliomyelitis causes bulbar paralysis but is now relatively rare because of worldwide immunization efforts.

Spinobulbar muscular atrophies are progressive illnesses of the anterior horn cells and involve bulbar motor neurons, particularly the hypoglossal nucleus.

Fazio-Londe disease is a rare hereditary disorder with progressive bulbar paralysis secondary to degeneration of the brain stem motor neurons in association with pyramidal system involvement. Manifestation is usually between 1 and 5 years of age with stridor, dysphagia, facial palsy, tongue wasting, and fasciculations.[44]

Brown-Vialettovan-Laere syndrome manifests with progressive sensorineural deafness in the first decade of life but is followed after a latent period by cranial nerve palsies, particularly of the fifth, seventh, and twelfth cranial nerves.[18]

Congenital agenesis of the brain stem nuclei is known as Möbius syndrome. Typical Möbius syndrome is characterized by bilateral facial and abducens palsies, but variants with involvement of other cranial nerve nuclei are known.

Chiari malformation, specifically type II but also type I, may manifest with lower cranial neuropathies. Neurogenic dysphagia may be the initial manifestation causing failure to thrive, nasal regurgitation, and tracheal aspiration before further symptoms of bulbar dysfunction develop. Chiari type II malformation includes cerebellar herniation, medullary prolongation with kink, and abnormalities of the midbrain tectum. Chiari I malformation is isolated herniation of the cerebellar tonsils. With brain stem compression, symptoms such as facial palsy, central apnea, and bilateral vocal cord paralysis may occur. Early cranial cervical decompression should be performed to prevent irreversible injury.[53]

Basilar impression or invagination is characterized by upward dislocation of the margins of the foramen magnum and the odontoid process with varying degrees of compression of the medulla. Acquired forms of basilar impression are due to softening of bone and are seen in illnesses such as Paget's disease, hyperparathyroidism, rickets, achondroplasia, rheumatoid arthritis, and Hurler syndrome. Congenital basilar impression is a developmental defect of the chondrocranium and is often associated with occipitalization of the atlas, Klippel-Feil anomaly, Chiari malformation, and syringobulbia. The term *platybasia* refers to an abnormally obtuse angle of the clivus with the anterior cranial fossa. Isolated platybasia is neurologically insignificant, but if it is associated with invagination,[47] nuchal pain, vertigo, gait abnormalities, and lower cranial nerve palsies[1] may be seen. Symptoms are usually delayed to the second to fourth decade of life, but this disorder has been reported in infancy.[61] Syringobulbia is the term clinically applied to brain stem symptoms caused by central cavities in the medulla. Common symptoms include occipital headaches, vertigo, dysarthria, and dysphagia as well as palatal and glossal impairment.[48]

The Klippel-Feil syndrome is characterized by an abnormally short neck associated with limited neck movement due to abnormal fusion and a reduced number of

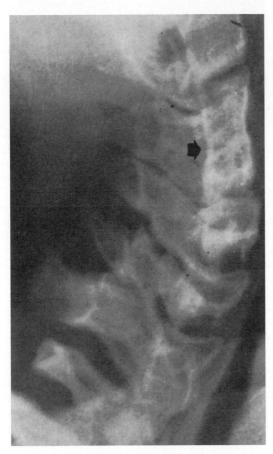

FIGURE 73–2. Cervical spine radiograph of a patient with Klippel-Feil syndrome. Note bony fusion (*arrow*).

cervical vertebrae (Fig. 73–2). Klippel-Feil syndrome may be associated with Chiari malformation, basilar impression, hydrocephalus, and syringomyelia.[50] Not infrequently, cleft palate and bifid tongue are seen with the Klippel-Feil syndrome.[64]

The Miller-Fisher variant of Guillain-Barré syndrome typically involves cranial nerves, causing ophthalmoplegia and bulbar palsies. The pathophysiologic mechanism is thought to be autoimmune after viral infection. Progression is gradual and may require prolonged support until spontaneous recovery begins. No therapy of benefit has been documented, but recommendations include the administration of intravenous immunoglobulins or plasmapheresis.

Nerve invasion by malignant neoplasms may also result in bulbar palsy. Meningeal infiltration of leukemias or direct invasion of bulbar cranial nerves by lymphoma or rhabdomyosarcoma may lead to various symptoms. The treatment of malignant neoplasms, in particular by vincristine, is known to cause peripheral neuropathy, but cranial neuropathy[15] and orofacial pain[43] have been noted rarely. Irradiation of head and neck tumors may induce mucositis, hyposalivation, trismus, caries, and osteonecrosis.[25] Wegener midline granulomatosis is an inflammatory condition but acts much like a malignant neoplasm, invading the skull base and encasing lower cranial nerves. Pneumonitis invariably accompanies Wegener disease.

Jugular fossa syndrome (Vernet syndrome) is characterized by gradual or rapid loss of ninth, tenth, and eleventh cranial nerve function caused by a tumor in the jugular foramen. Paragangliomas and Schwannomas are more common than the invasive nasopharyngeal carcinoma or meningioma of the elderly.[54]

Diphtheria has become a rare entity, but outbreaks still occur in developing countries. A small portion of infected children will have progressive systemic polyneuropathy that may be associated with cranial neuropathies.

Vitamin E deficiency, particularly in abetalipoproteinemia, biliary atresia, or cystic fibrosis, typically manifests with ataxia, visual loss, and ophthalmoplegia. Bulbar involvement, however, may be seen along with the other manifestations of these disorders.[34, 36]

Craniofacial pain syndrome (trigeminal and glossopharyngeal neuralgia) is rarely reported in children. The pain is sharp and lancinating, triggered by certain contacts, and lasts seconds. Involvement of the tongue is rare despite the fact that the anterior two thirds of tongue sensation is supplied by the trigeminal nerve. Mucolipidosis type IV may be an underlying cause of craniofacial pain in childhood.

Isolated hypoglossal nerve palsy (Fig. 73–3) is rarely encountered but may manifest as a transient mononeuropathy similar to Bell palsy.[60] Internal jugular vein puncture, radiation, internal carotid artery dissection, infectious mononucleosis, birth trauma, tonsillectomy, and third molar extractions have also been associated with isolated or bilateral hypoglossal palsies.[59] Similarly, isolated unilateral paralysis of the soft palate may manifest with abrupt onset of hypernasal speech and nasal regurgitation.[8]

Myasthenic syndromes and botulism are the two illnesses commonly affecting the neuromuscular junction. Tetanus is less common. Eaton-Lambert syndrome (a paraneoplastic condition) is not observed in children.

Several types of myasthenic illnesses are observed during childhood. The typical form of myasthenia gravis is an autoimmune disease affecting the acetylcholine receptors. Ocular, bulbar, or generalized involvement can be seen in

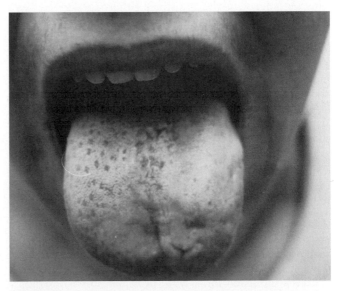

FIGURE 73–3. Unilateral hypoglossal involvement with atrophy.

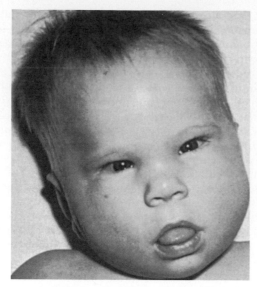

FIGURE 73–4. Myotonic dystrophy in a neonate. Note tented upper lip.

any combination. Fatigability increases dramatically with exercise. Symptomatic treatment with pyridostigmine (Mestinon) and treatment with steroids and thymectomy, both directed against the autoimmune process, can improve the patient's function.

Transient neonatal myasthenia is observed in newborns of myasthenic mothers, and symptoms such as poor sucking and swallowing in association with diffuse weakness can last up to several weeks.

Botulism is acquired through improperly processed food products or from contamination of open wounds with *Clostridium botulinum.* Onset of symptoms is within 36 hours, producing ophthalmoplegia, bulbar paralysis, and generalized weakness. Early administration of antitoxin in association with supportive treatment is the cornerstone of management.

Infantile botulism differs from botulism seen in older individuals because the toxins are acquired through germinating spores in the intestine. Honey intake has been associated with this entity. Onset may be insidious, with weakness and poor feeding. Constipation and ptosis are frequently encountered. Treatment is supportive. Dysphagia is due to the involvement of the striated pharyngeal and upper esophageal muscles, rather than the smooth muscles of the esophagus.[5]

Trismus and dysphagia in association with a general irritability and spasms are characteristic of tetanus; dysphagia may be a presenting manifestation. The diagnosis of tetanus is purely clinical and dependent on the observation of its varying manifestations.[63]

A variety of congenital and acquired myopathies involve bulbar musculature.

Dermatomyositis typically presents with a heliotrope rash on the face and knuckles. Painful proximal muscle weakness and, in advanced cases, dysphagia due to pharyngoesophageal involvement characterize this disorder.

Facioscapulohumeral dystrophy characterized by facial weakness in association with proximal upper extremity

weakness is usually associated with sensory motor deafness.

Myotonic dystrophy may involve the face, but this is rarely evident in childhood; impaired pharyngeal and esophageal motility are commonly encountered in childhood. Newborns of mothers with undiagnosed myotonic dystrophy sometimes present with profound generalized and facial weakness at birth (Fig. 73–4). Prolonged nasogastric feeding with gastric tube placement may be necessary in infants who manifest severe pharyngoesophageal dysmotility. Temporomandibular joint dysfunction, occlusal alterations, and swallowing and mastication difficulties are also reported with older patients.[51]

Oculopharyngeal dystrophy is typically described in adults of French Canadian origin but appears infrequently in teenage years. Initial symptoms are usually bilateral ptosis followed by oropharyngeal dysphagia, which may respond to cricopharyngeal myotomy. Esophageal motility is normal in this disorder.[10]

Cricopharyngeal achalasia is another cause of dysphagia, and it is usually a manifestation of diffuse central nervous system or neuromuscular disease (Table 73–2), but isolated primary neonatal cricopharyngeal achalasia has been reported.[58] Cricopharyngeal myotomy can be helpful in a select group of patients who have satisfactory pharyngeal motion and no evidence of cricopharyngeal muscle relaxation.[2] A work-up with cinefluoroscopy and manometry is crucial to determine these two factors. New data have shown that botulinum toxin may be helpful in the diagnosis and management of cricopharyngeal achalasia.[3, 9]

Dysarthria

Articulation consists of contractions of the pharynx (cranial nerves, or CN, IX and X), palate (CN V to X), tongue (CN XII), and lips (CN VII), which interrupt or alter the vocal sounds. Vowels are laryngeal in origin, and consonants are formed for the most part during articulation. The consonants *m, b,* and *p* are labial, *l* and *t* are

TABLE 73–2. Causes of Cricopharyngeal Achalasia

Secondary to Cerebral Cortex Disorders
Hypoxic-ischemic injury
Chiari type II malformation
Congenital malformations
Microcephaly
Holoprosencephaly
Hydrocephalus
Secondary to Brain Stem Disorders
Syringobulbia
Cervical syrinx
Progressive bulbar palsy (Fazio-Londe syndrome)
Secondary to Muscle Disorders
Myotonic dystrophy
Oculopharyngeal dystrophy
Congenital muscular dystrophies

lingual, and *ne* and *ng* are pharyngeal (throat and soft palate).

Defective articulation is easily recognized by listening to the patient speak during an ordinary conversation. A quick bedside test to bring out a particular abnormality is to ask the patient to repeat sounds, e.g., *la-la-la-la* (lingual), *k-k-k-k* (pharyngeal), *me-me-me-me* (labial).

Causes of dysarthria are summarized in Table 73–3. In neuropathic dysarthria there is special difficulty in articulation of lingual and labial consonants due to flaccidity of the musculature. When the larynx is involved, the voice is breathy, inspiration is quite audible, and phrases are short. Dysphonia (alteration of the voice to a rasping monotone due to vocal cord paralysis) may be seen as well (Table 73–4).

The spastic (cortical or bulbar) dysarthric speech is characterized as slow, low in pitch, thick, and incomprehensible due to clustering of consonant sounds.

The speech with acute or chronic cerebellar lesions (ataxic dysarthria) is marked by two major defects: articulatory and prosodic. It is characterized by slow rate, slurring, monotony, and scanning (unnatural intervals between syllables or words) of phrases.

Palatal myoclonus is discussed here because it may interfere with articulation of words. It occurs after lesions of the central tegmental pathway lead to transsynaptic degeneration and hypertrophy of the inferior olivary nucleus. The lesion usually involves the ipsilateral central tegmental tract or the contralateral dentate nucleus. The cause of these lesions is usually vascular but may be neoplastic.[33] Palatal myoclonus is characterized by bilateral or unilateral oscillations of the soft palate, often in association with other muscles in the pharynx, mouth, lower face, and eyes. This disease is uncommonly seen in

TABLE 73–3. Causes of Dysarthria

Secondary to Neuropathic or Neuromuscular Junction Disorder (Flaccid)
Miller-Fisher/Guillain-Barré syndrome Myasthenia gravis Poliomyelitis Diphtheria
Secondary to Cortical or Bulbar Disorders (Spastic)
Hypoxic-ischemic insult Progressive bulbar palsy Demyelinating diseases Leukodystrophies Multiple sclerosis Acute disseminated encephalomyelitis Vascular (ischemic or hemorrhagic) lesions Hallervorden-Spatz disease
Secondary to Acute or Chronic Cerebellar Disorders (Ataxic)
Acute or chronic cerebellar lesions Multiple sclerosis Anoxic encephalopathy Ataxia-telangiectasia Episodic ataxia (Hereditary paroxysmal cerebellar ataxia) Spinocerebellar ataxias Friedreich's ataxia

TABLE 73–4. Causes of Dysphonia

Secondary to Upper Motor Neuron Disorder
Juvenile Parkinson disease Posterior fossa tumors Spasmodic dysphonia (adults)
Secondary to Lower Motor Neuron Disorder
Myasthenia gravis Miller-Fisher/Guillain-Barré syndrome

childhood.[17] Presentation may be a complaint of tinnitus due to rapid clicking (10 to 200 per minute) secondary to rapid opening and closing of the eustachian tube.[37] Spontaneous resolution usually occurs, but treatment options include the use of antiepileptic medications.[16] Isolated lingual myoclonus has been reported with good response to sodium valproate.[19]

Structural Changes Associated with Neurologic Illness

Ulcerative Lesions

The appearance of ulcerative lesions in the mouth, in most instances, is a secondary occurrence resulting from nonspecific viral or traumatic causes, but several specific illnesses manifest with oral ulcerations in association with neurologic disease (see Chaps. 60 and 64).

Ataxia telangiectasia is an autosomal recessive disorder manifesting with oculocutaneous telangiectasias (Fig. 73–5), progressive ataxia, choreoathetosis, and recurrent sinopulmonary infections. Ataxia is usually noted at the time children begin to walk. Recurrent respiratory infections develop between 3 and 8 years of age, and oral inflammatory lesions are observed at this time. Mental retardation is present in 30% to 50% of children with ataxia telangiectasia.

Chédiak-Higashi disease is characterized by dramatic depigmented areas of the skin, hair, and irises; pancytopenia; and atopy. These children also demonstrate nystagmus, weakness, and peripheral neuropathy. Decreased resistance to infection due to impaired granulocyte function results in recurrent oral inflammatory lesions. Disease be-

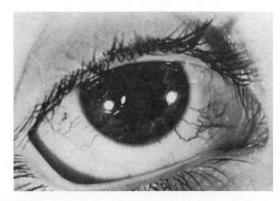

FIGURE 73–5. Ocular telangiectasia in ataxia telangiectasia.

comes evident in the first 2 years of life, and symptoms resemble those seen in familial spinocerebellar degeneration.

Behçet disease is characterized by the triad of uveitis with oral and genital ulcers. Oral ulcerations may be painful, while those ulcers in the genital region are typically painless. Central nervous system involvement is characterized by combinations of increased intracranial pressure, stroke, and vasculitic lesions. Oral ulcerations are usually the first manifestations of this disorder, and esophageal ulcerations are occasionally seen.[38]

Oral ulcerations are frequently seen in central nervous system infections related to herpes simplex virus, coxsackievirus, and echovirus. Herpes encephalitis is usually a fulminant illness. Characteristic hemorrhagic lesions have a predilection for the temporal and orbital frontal regions of the brain. Multiple oral vesicular lesions frequently accompany the encephalitis. The oral lesions progress through ulcerative, hemorrhagic, crusted, and confluent stages.[49] Among the enteroviruses causing meningoencephalitis in late summer and fall, coxsackieviruses and echoviruses are known to produce oral lesions. The typical lesions of coxsackievirus are on the anterior tonsillar pillar and soft palate; those of echovirus infection are less predictable in their location. Epstein-Barr virus (EBV) is frequently associated with a gamut of central nervous system abnormalities including meningoencephalitis, myelitis, and multiple cranial neuropathies.[42] EBV typically produces exudative tonsillitis associated with high fever and lymphadenopathy.

Histoplasmosis, actinomycosis, and blastomycosis are significant infections in immunocompromised patients. Typical mucosal lesions appear nodular and later ulcerate. In disseminated disease, central nervous system involvement is characterized by meningoencephalitis, and multiple small abscesses develop.

Vitamin deficiencies, especially of thiamine (B_1), riboflavin (B_2), pyridoxine (B_6), and niacin (B_3), are responsible for oral ulcerative lesions. The tongue and buccal mucosa are red, swollen, and fissured. Central nervous system abnormalities are protean, consisting of encephalopathy, ophthalmoparesis, and peripheral neuropathies. These deficiencies are seen in circumstances of malnutrition, which may be encountered in malignant neoplasms, malabsorptive syndromes, pernicious vomiting, and, of course, starvation.

A number of heavy metal intoxications are known to cause oral mucosal lesions in association with neurologic signs and symptoms.[14] Mercury, bismuth, lead, thallium, and arsenic poisoning produce inflammation and discoloration of the oral mucosa. Arsenic is found in some insecticides (especially ant pastes) and may contaminate unwashed fruits and vegetables. This metal results in intense abdominal pain, bloody diarrhea, a garlic odor to the breath, and acute hemorrhagic encephalopathy that may be associated with polyneuropathy. Lead encephalopathy manifests with lethargy, vomiting, colicky abdominal pain, seizures, and coma. In a minority of children, the gingivae are stained blue-black in a linear fashion. Thallium is present in a variety of depilatory agents and certain pesticides. Ingestion produces green-black discoloration of the tongue; central nervous system manifestations include ir-

ritability, convulsions, and choreoathetosis. Alopecia is often a clue to the presence of thallium. In chronic mercury poisoning, mucosal ulceration, salivation, gingivitis, and stomatitis are frequently present in association with tremor and erethism (insomnia, shyness, emotional lability, and memory loss). Encephalopathy or a neuropathy mimicking Guillain-Barré syndrome may be present. Bismuth intoxication caused by ingestion of therapeutic preparations, such as Pepto-Bismol, in large quantities is associated with a reversible encephalopathy, stomatitis, and black punctate lesions of the oral mucosa.[22]

Pigmentary and Vascular Lesions

Pigmentary and vascular lesions are not infrequently early manifestations of specific neurologic illnesses. Adrenoleukodystrophy is a peroxisomal disorder characterized by progressive neurologic deterioration of motor and cognitive function associated with adrenal atrophy. Increased pigmentation of nonexposed body surfaces, including buccal, gingival, and lingual mucosa, is an early feature of this illness.[57]

The vascular nevus of Sturge-Weber disease often extends to involve the mouth. The port wine nevus, capillary in nature, is seen in the distribution of the ophthalmic division of the fifth nerve with variable combinations of involvement of the second and third divisions. The slow flow capillary angioma present in the meninges causes ischemia of the overlying cerebral cortex, resulting in cortical gliosis and calcification. Involvement of the gyri with sparing of the sulci results in the characteristic "railroad track" or "tram track" calcification pattern seen on skull films. The central nervous system calcifications, however, are most readily detected by computed tomographic scan.

Rendu-Osler-Weber disease characteristically produces small angiomas over the buccal and lingual mucosae. This autosomal dominant illness presents with recurrent epistaxis and gastrointestinal bleeding. Subarachnoid hemorrhage and hydrocephalus are seen, as well as unruptured intracranial angiomas. Brain abscess secondary to pulmonary arteriovenous fistulas may be encountered.[4]

Fabry disease is a sex-linked recessive storage disease caused by absence of alpha-galactosidase A. Red-purple angiokeratomas are characteristically present over the scrotum and umbilical region and may be seen in the oral mucosa. The accumulation of alpha-galactosidase A in the corneas, peripheral nerves, kidneys, brain, and spinal cord leads to a painful peripheral neuropathy, encephalopathy, seizures, myelopathy, and renal failure.

Hypoalphalipoproteinemia (Tangier disease) is characterized by a pathognomonic yellow-orange enlargement of the tonsils. Asymmetric polyneuropathy characterized by relapsing weakness and sensory loss is seen in childhood.

Abnormalities of the Teeth and Gingivae

Embryologically, teeth develop from neural crest cells, and hormones play a major role in dental development. These two factors explain the association of certain cen-

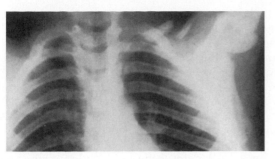

FIGURE 73-6. Cleidocranial dysostosis: partial clavicular agenesis.

tral nervous system abnormalities with disturbed dentition.

Delayed dentition is seen with tumors involving the hypothalamus as well as developmental disorders such as cleidocranial dysostosis. Not infrequently, delayed eruption of deciduous teeth is followed by failure to shed, resulting in crowding of primary and secondary teeth. These abnormalities may precede the more common manifestations of these disorders and present the opportunity for early recognition (see Chap. 58).

Craniopharyngioma is characterized by impaired growth, visual field defects, and eventual increased intracranial pressure. Cleidocranial dysostosis is characterized by a partial or complete absence of the clavicles, presence of the wormian bones of the skull, and relative macrocephaly (Figs. 73-6 and 73-7). Basilar impression frequently present in cleidocranial dysostosis results in lower cranial neuropathies, syringomyelia, and hydrocephalus. Impaired palatal and tongue function as well as hydrocephalus and spastic paraparesis result. Supernumerary teeth are a related dental anomaly.[26]

Conic defects of teeth are also seen in incontinentia

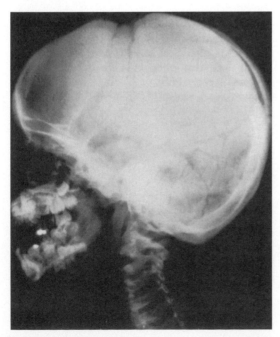

FIGURE 73-7. Cleidocranial dysostosis: wormian bones of the skull.

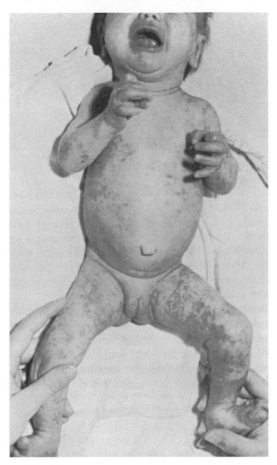

FIGURE 73-8. Bullous eruption on the neonate with incontinentia pigmenti.

pigmenti, Rieger syndrome, and Williams syndrome. Incontinentia pigmenti manifests with a papular or vesicular eruption following a dermatomal linear pattern in the newborn period (Fig. 73-8). These lesions evolve into a pigmented, whorled spidery pattern later in childhood. Dystrophic nails are frequently noted, and patients may demonstrate mental retardation and seizures. A third of these patients have hypodontia, delayed eruption, or malformation of the teeth (Fig. 73-9). Rieger syndrome consists of dysplasia of the iris, hypodontia, and partial adontia. A variable number of patients with this syndrome have associated myotonic dystrophy. Williams syndrome is

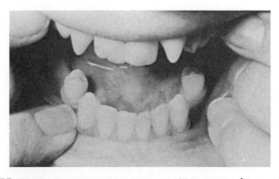

FIGURE 73-9. Incontinentia pigmenti. Note conic bicuspid defects and partial adontia.

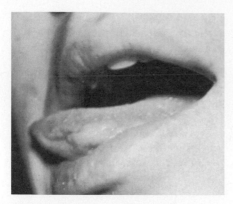

FIGURE 73–10. Neurofibroma of the tongue.

characterized by neonatal hypercalcemia, elfin facies with a fishshaped mouth, supravalvular aortic stenosis, and mental retardation. Partial adontia and malformed teeth are frequently seen in these patients.[30, 32]

Tuberous sclerosis typically consists of hypopigmented skin lesions, seizures, adenoma sebaceum, and mental retardation. Neurologic manifestations of tuberous sclerosis may be subtle, and recognizing oral manifestations such as hypoplasia and hypocalcification of the teeth, angiomas in the mouth, and pits in the enamel becomes important.[23, 62]

Neurofibromatosis type 1 is also associated with hypodontia and occasional oral neurofibromas with cutaneous neurofibromas and café au lait spots.[24] Macroglossia is a common manifestation (Fig. 73–10).

Lesch-Nyhan syndrome is characterized by choreoathetosis, mental retardation, seizures, and self-mutilation. The self-mutilation characteristically involves chewing of the lip and buccal mucosa. Dental dysplasia has been reported with this syndrome.

Both pseudohypoparathyroidism and hypoparathyroidism are characterized by seizures, tetany, and muscle cramps. These disorders may be mistaken for epilepsy, but dental abnormalities are often a clue to the correct underlying diagnosis. In pseudohypothyroidism, patients are short and stout with round facies. Characteristically, the fourth metacarpal bones are unusually short. Central nervous system calcifications are frequently seen. Teeth are frequently hypoplastic but erupt in the normal sequence of tooth development.

Mucopolysaccharidoses and mucolipidoses are genetically distinct metabolic abnormalities but phenotypically share the characteristics of coarse features, variable mental retardation, and ocular and bony abnormalities. Dental abnormalities are also frequently observed in these disorders.

Structural Changes of the Tongue

Melkersson-Rosenthal syndrome is characterized by recurrent facial palsy and edema of the lips and face. Facial palsy may be unilateral or bilateral. Prominent furrowing of the tongue (lingua plicata) is frequently associated with this syndrome but is not pathognomonic. Swelling, erythema, and painful erosions affecting the gingiva, buccal mucosa, and palate are seen.[66]

Familial dysautonomia (Riley-Day syndrome) is a neurologic disorder manifesting with hypotonia in infancy, dysregulation of the body temperature, and blotchy discoloration of the skin. This familial form of autonomic neuropathy is seen in Ashkenazi Jews; further disturbances include alacrimation, areflexia, sensory deficits, and mental retardation. Mental retardation becomes prominent with age. The tongue shows a striking absence of fungiform papillae, which are the clearly visible red projections among the more numerous gray filiform papillae. The red coloration is due to high vascularity. Patients with Riley-Day syndrome typically cannot distinguish between acidic and sweet solutions. Neuropathy and autonomic dysfunction result in dysphagia due to pharyngeal dyscoordination and delay in cricopharyngeal opening.[31]

Structural Changes in the Palate

Cleft palate and lip are frequent developmental abnormalities seen in the mouth and face. The location of the cleft relative to the incisive foramen separates anterior clefts involving the lip and primary palate (including the alveolar ridge) from posterior clefts of the secondary palate (posterior portion of the hard palate and soft palate). Anterior and posterior clefts are embryologically distinct, but the combination of these two abnormalities is not rare. Inheritance is multifactorial.[45]

A number of chromosomal abnormalities are reported with cleft. Trisomy 13 and trisomy 18 are the most common ones and most frequently are associated with profound mental retardation. Two percent of cleft palate patients also have Klippel-Feil anomaly. Occipital or frontal encephaloceles may be associated with cleft palate (Fig. 73–11). The cyst may extend to the oral cavity and should not be mistaken for a nasal polyp or adenoidal mass.

Median clefts rather than bilateral clefts are more

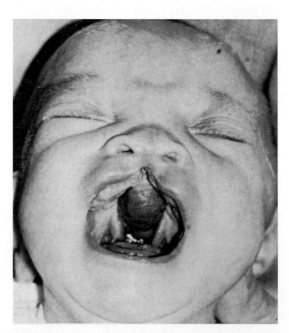

FIGURE 73–11. Child with cleft palate and a nasofrontal encephalocele.

commonly associated with midline central nervous system anomalies. A midline cleft of the upper lip and tongue is characteristic of Mohr syndrome (oral-facial-digital syndrome, type II) associated with conductive hearing loss and normal intelligence. Type II is in contrast to oral-facial-digital syndrome type I, which includes irregular clefts, hypoplastic nasal cartilages, asymmetrically short digits, and mental retardation.[28]

Duane syndrome, characterized by fibrosis of the lateral rectus muscle of the eye causing impaired ocular abduction, may occasionally be seen in association with cleft palate.

Awareness of the variety of neurologic illnesses associated with oral, pharyngeal, and esophageal lesions will, it is hoped, alert specialists to specific diagnoses and allow them to undertake appropriate investigations, genetic counseling, and treatment.

SELECTED REFERENCES

Cook IJ. Cricopharyngeal function and dysfunction. Dysphagia 8:244, 1993.

This article provides an up-to-date review of oropharyngeal and specifically cricopharyngeal physiology.

Kilman WJ, Goyal RK. Disorders of pharyngeal and upper esophageal sphincter motor function. Arch Intern Med 136:592, 1976.

This article presents a clear review of oropharyngeal physiology and several associated neurologic illnesses.

Lapresle J. Palatal myoclonus. Adv Neurol 43:265, 1986.

Palatal myoclonus is a complex pathologic process with a unique clinical presentation. The anatomic basis of this complexity is well outlined in this paper.

Mackey RW. Clinical neurologic disorders in children with special otolaryngologic relationships. Otolaryngol Clin North Am 20:13, 1987.

This article reviews neurologic illnesses with otolaryngologic manifestations.

Pollack IF, Pang D, Kochosis S, Putnam P. Neurogenic dysphagia resulting from Chiari malformations. Neurosurgery 30:709, 1992.

This common posterior fossa anomaly and its relation to swallowing is discussed in a series of 15 patients.

Remley KB, Latchaw RE. Imaging of cranial nerves 9, 10 and 11. Neuroimaging Clin North Am 3:171, 1993.

In this paper, radiology of the posterior fossa, nerve pathways, anatomic correlations, and clinical examples are presented in detail.

REFERENCES

1. Bassi P, Corona C, Contri P, et al. Congenital basilar impression: correlated neurological syndromes. Eur Neurol 32:238, 1992.
2. Berg HM, Persky MS, Jacobs JB, Cohen NL. Cricopharyngeal myotomy: a review in patients with cricopharyngeal achalasia of neurogenic origin. Laryngoscope 95:1337, 1985.
3. Blitzer A, Brin MF. Use of botulinum toxin for diagnosis and management of cricopharyngeal achalasia. Otoryngol Head Neck Surg 116:328, 1997.
4. Boynton RC, Morgan BC. Cerebral arteriovenous fistula with possible hereditary telangiectasia. Am J Dis Child 125:99, 1973.
5. Cannon RA. Differential effect of botulinum toxin on esophageal motor function in infants. J Pediatr Gastroenterol Nutr 4:563, 1985.
6. Conradi N, Kyllerman M, Mansson JE, et al. Late infantile Gaucher disease in a child with myoclonus and bulbar signs: neuropathological and neurochemical findings. Acta Neuropathol 82:152, 1991.
7. Cook IJ. Cricopharyngeal function and dysfunction. Dysphagia 8:244, 1993.
8. Crovetto MA, Aguirre JM, Perez-Rojo A, Saint-Gerons S. Idiopathic paralysis of the palate in childhood. Br J Oral Maxillofac Surg 26:241, 1988.
9. Del Rosario JF, Orenstein SR. Common pediatric esophageal disorders. Gastroenterologist 6:104, 1998.
10. Dobrowski JM, Zajtchuk JT, Lapiana FG, Hensley SD. Oculopharyngeal muscular dystrophy: clinical and histopathologic correlations. Otolaryngol Head Neck Surg 95:131, 1986.
11. Donner MW, Siegel CI. The evaluation of pharyngeal neuromuscular disorders by cinefluorography. AJR 94:299, 1965.
12. Doty RW, Richmond WH, Storey AT. Effect of medullary lesions on coordination of deglutition. Exp Neurol 17:91, 1967.
13. Doyle WJ, Casselbrant ML, Swarts JD, Bluestone CD. Observations on a role for the tensor veli palatini muscle in intrinsic palatal function. Cleft Palate J 27:317, 1990.
14. Ellenhorn MJ, Barceloux DG. Metals and related compounds. In Ellenhorn MJ, Barceloux DG (eds). Medical Toxicology. New York, Elsevier, 1988.
15. Erdmann H. Unilateral paralysis of the recurrent nerve caused by vincristine. Med Klin 85(Suppl 1):154, 1990.
16. Fitzgerald DC. Palatal myoclonus-case report. Laryngoscope 94:217, 1984.
17. Fox GN. Palatal myoclonus in children. Neurology 39:877, 1989.
18. Francis DA, Ponsford JR, Wiles CM, et al. Brown Vialetto-Van Laere syndrome. Neuropathol Appl Neurobiol 19:91, 1993.
19. Gobernado JM, Galaretta M, DeBlas G, et al. Isolated continuous rhythmic lingual myoclonus. Mov Disord 7:367, 1992.
20. Goyal RK. Disorders of the cricopharyngeus muscle. Otolaryngol Clin North Am 17:115, 1984.
21. Hanson MR, Sweeney PJ. Lower cranial neuropathies. In Bradley WG, Becker DP (eds). Neurology in Clinical Practice. London, Butterworth-Heinemann, 1989, pp 217–229.
22. Hasking G, Duggan J. Encephalopathy from bismuth subsalicylate. Med J Aust 2:167, 1982.
23. Hoff M. Enamel defects associated with tuberous sclerosis. Oral Surg 40:261, 1975.
24. Holt GR. Von Recklinghausen's neurofibromatosis. Otolaryngol Clin North Am 20:179, 1987.
25. Jansma J, Vissink A, Bouma J, et al. A survey of prevention and treatment regimens for oral sequelae resulting from head and neck radiotherapy used in Dutch radiotherapy institutes. Int J Radiat Oncol Biol Phys 24:359, 1992.
26. Jensen BL, Kreiborg S. Development of the dentition in cleidocranial dysplasia. J Oral Pathol Med 19:89, 1990.
27. Johnson WG. The clinical spectrum of hexosaminidase deficiency diseases. Neurology 31:1453, 1981.
28. Jones KL. Smith's Recognizable Patterns of Human Malformations. Philadelphia, WB Saunders, 1988, pp 220–223.
29. Kadish AH, Wechsler L, Marchlinski FE. Swallowing syncope: observations in the absence of conduction system or esophageal disease. Am J Med 81:1098, 1986.
30. Kelly JR, Barr EJ. The elfin facies syndrome. Oral Surg 40:205, 1975.
31. Kilman WJ, Goyal RK. Disorders of pharyngeal and upper esophageal sphincter motor function. Arch Intern Med 136:592, 1976.
32. Kitanaka C, Sugaya M, Yamada H. Avellis syndrome after minor head trauma: report of two cases. Surg Neurol 37:236, 1992.
33. Lapresle J. Palatal myoclonus. Adv Neurol 43:265, 1986.
34. Larsen PD, Mock DM, O'Conner PS. Vitamin E deficiency associated with vision loss and bulbar weakness. Ann Neurol 18:725, 1985.
35. Liao KK, Wang SJ, Kwan SY, et al. Tongue dyskinesia as an early manifestation of Wilson disease. Brain Dev 13:451, 1991.
36. Lim HC, Nigro MA, Beierwaltes P, et al. Nitrazepam induced cricopharyngeal dysphagia, abnormal esophageal peristalsis and associated bronchospasm: probable cause of nitrazepam related sudden death. Brain Dev 14:309, 1992.
37. Litman RS, Hausman SA. Bilateral palatal myoclonus. Laryngoscope 92:1187, 1982.
38. Lockhart JM, McIntyre W, Caperton EM. Esophageal ulceration in Behçet's syndrome. Ann Intern Med 84:572, 1976.
39. Loft LM, Ward RF. Hiccups. A case presentation and etiologic review. Arch Otolaryngol Head Neck Surg 118:1115, 1992.

40. Logeman J. Evaluation and Treatment of Swallowing Disorders. San Diego, College Hill Press, 1983, pp 11–36.
41. Mackey RW. Clinical neurologic disorders in children with special otolaryngologic relationships. Otolaryngol Clin North Am 20:13, 1987.
42. Maddern BR, Werkhaven J, Wessel HB, Yunis E. Infectious mononucleosis with airway obstruction and multiple cranial nerve paresis. Otolaryngol Head Neck Surg 104:529, 1991.
43. McCarthy GM, Skilling JR. Jaw and other orofacial pain in patients receiving vincristine for the treatment of cancer. Oral Surg Oral Med Oral Pathol 74:299, 1992.
44. McShane MA, Boyd S, Harding B, et al. Progressive bulbar paralysis of childhood. Brain 115:1189, 1992.
45. Menezes AH, Van Gilder JC. Anomalies of the craniovertebral junction. In Youmans JR (ed). Neurological Surgery. Philadelphia, WB Saunders, 1990, pp 1359–1420.
46. Monrad-Krohn GH. The Clinical Examination of the Nervous System, 12th ed. New York, Harper & Row, 1964, pp 62–80.
47. Moore K. The branchial apparatus and the head and neck. In Moore K (ed). Developing Human: Clinical Human Embryology. Philadelphia, WB Saunders, 1988, pp 195–203.
48. Morgan D, Williams B. Syringobulbia: a surgical approach. J Neurol Neurosurg Psychiatry 55:1132, 1992.
49. Muller J. Viral infections of the skin and mouth. Oral Surg 32:752, 1971.
50. Nagib MG, Maxwell RE, Chou SN. Klippel-Feil syndrome in children: clinical features and management. Child Nerv Syst 1:255, 1985.
51. Pennarocha M, Bagan JV, Vilchez J, et al. Oral alterations in Steinert's myotonic dystrophy: a presentation of two cases. Oral Surg Oral Med Oral Pathol 69:698, 1990.
52. Peterson JE, Schneider PE. Oral habits. A behavioral approach. Pediatr Clin North Am 38:1289, 1991.
53. Pollack IF, Pang D, Kochosis S, Putnam P. Neurogenic dysphagia resulting from Chiari malformations. Neurosurgery 30:709, 1992.
54. Remly KB, Latchaw RE. Imaging of cranial nerves 9, 10, and 11. Neuroimaging Clin North Am 3:171, 1993.
55. Roulet E, Deonna T, Despland PA. Prolonged intermittent drooling and oromotor dyspraxia in benign childhood epilepsy with centrotemporal spikes. Epilepsia 30:564, 1989.
56. Russo LS, Aron A, Anderson PJ. Alexander's disease: a report and reappraisal. Neurology 26:607, 1976.
57. Schaumburg HH, Powers JM, Raine CS, et al. Adrenoleukodystrophy: a clinical and pathologic study of 17 cases. Arch Neurol 32:577, 1975.
58. Skinner MA, Shorter NA. Primary neonatal cricopharyngeal achalasia: a case report and review of the literature. J Pediatr Surg 27:1509, 1992.
59. Smoker WRK. Hypoglossal nerve. Neuroimaging Clin North Am 3:193, 1993.
60. Sugama S, Matsunaga T, Ito F, et al. Transient, unilateral, isolated hypoglossal nerve palsy. Brain Dev 14:122, 1992.
61. Teodori JB, Painter MJ. Basilar impression in children. Pediatrics 74:603, 1982.
62. Tillman JJ, DeCaro F. Tuberous sclerosis. Oral Surg Oral Med Oral Pathol 71:301, 1991.
63. Wang L, Karmody CS. Dysphagia as the presenting symptom of tetanus. Arch Otolaryngol Head Neck Surg 111:342, 1985.
64. Widgerow AD. Klippel-Feil anomaly, cleft palate and bifid tongue. Ann Plast Surg 25:219, 1990.
65. Woody RC, Kiel EA. Swallowing syncope in a child. Pediatrics 78:507, 1986.
66. Zimmer WM, Rogers RS, Reeve CM, Sheridan PJ. Orofacial manifestations of Melkersson Rosenthal syndrome. A study of 42 patients and review of 220 cases from literature. Oral Surg Oral Med Oral Pathol 74:610, 1992.

The Larynx, Trachea, Bronchi, Lungs, and Esophagus

74

Developmental Anatomy and Physiology of the Larynx, Trachea, and Esophagus

Glenn Isaacson, M.D.

The complex structure and physiology of the upper aerodigestive tract mirror the considerable demands placed on it by the developing human. In utero, the immature larynx has a single but important chore—to modulate fetal breathing in an aqueous medium, a function essential to orderly lung development. Suddenly, at birth, the larynx must assume three difficult and contradictory tasks. It must control respiration, protect the lower airway from contamination, and produce the first cry. All this can be accomplished despite an immature central nervous system because of several remarkable structural adaptations. The larynx of a growing child permits eating, breathing, and speaking to proceed with ever greater efficiency and overlap as neural control and anatomy are refined with time.

The esophagus is called on to perform contradictory tasks as well. It must relax, then rhythmically contract to propel a food bolus toward the stomach during swallowing yet maintain sufficient tone to prevent reflux between swallows.

The trachea's structural modifications allow it sufficient rigidity to resist collapse during inspiratory airflow while remaining flexible enough to stretch with negative intrathoracic pressure, to absorb the pounding of the brachiocephalic artery anteriorly, and to permit the passage of food boluses at its party wall with the esophagus.

This chapter highlights the events in human upper aerodigestive development from these structures' appearance to their maturation in the second decade of life. At each point, the interaction of structure and function helps explain how they succeed in a healthy body and how they fail in disease states.

The Embryo

The embryology of the larynx, trachea, and esophagus was well studied during the first half of this century and is described in detail by Soulie and Bardier,[30] Lisser,[20] Hast,[10] O'Rahilly and Tucker,[24] and Tucker and Tucker.[33]

In the 2-mm embryo, a median pharyngeal groove presages the first appearance of the respiratory tract (Fig. 74–1). The anlagen of the larynx, trachea, bronchi, and lungs arise from a ventromedial diverticulum of the foregut called the tracheobronchial groove at about 25 days of intrauterine life. The lining of the larynx and trachea is thus derived from the same endoderm as that of the gut. The cartilage of the trachea and the connective tissue and muscle of both the trachea and esophagus come from splanchnic mesenchyme. Lateral furrows develop on each side of the ventromedial diverticulum, deepen, and join to form the tracheoesophageal septum that will become the layers of tissue between the trachea and esophagus (Figs. 74–2 and 74–3). At 33 days of life, the distal esophagus can be distinguished from the stomach, and the laryngeal primordia appear (Fig. 74–4). The laryngeal aditus or slit is altered by the growth of three tissue

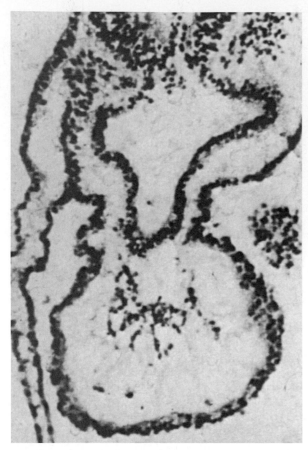

FIGURE 74–1. Section through the pharynx and the heart of a human embryo at 3 weeks' gestational age, 1.38 mm in length. The median pharyngeal groove can be seen immediately dorsal to the heart. In the heart, the so-called epimyocardial mantle, the cardiac mesenchyme ("jelly"), and the endocardium can be identified. (From Tucker JA, O'Rahilly R. Observations on the embryology of the human larynx. Ann Otol Rhinol Laryngol 81: 520, 1972. Carnegie Collection, 5074.)

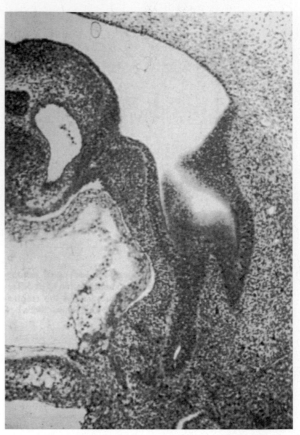

FIGURE 74–2. Median section through the pharyngeal region at 5 weeks' gestational age (4.5 mm). The respiratory diverticulum can be seen descending from its origin in the foregut. Its close relationship to the heart is evident. The site of the tracheoesophageal septum is clearly visible. (From Tucker JA, O'Rahilly R. Observations on the embryology of the human larynx. Ann Otol Rhinol Laryngol 81:520, 1972. Carnegie Collection, 9297.)

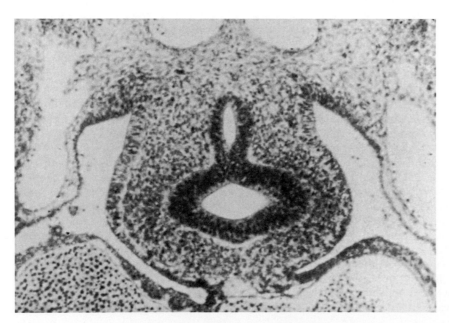

FIGURE 74–3. Five weeks' gestational age. Horizontal section through the hypopharynx at the junction of the respiratory canal and digestive canals. (Carnegie Collection, 836.)

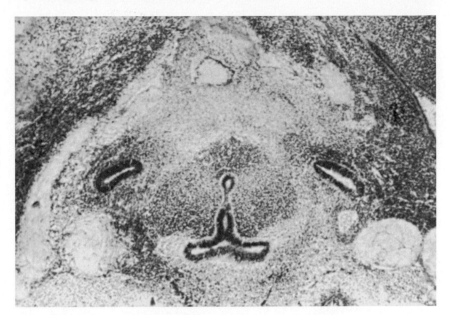

FIGURE 74-4. Five and one-half weeks' gestational age. Laryngeal primordium. Triangular condensation of undifferentiated mesenchyme around the respiratory canal. (Carnegie Collection, 8929.)

masses: anteriorly, the primordium of the epiglottis (from the hypobranchial eminence, arches III and IV) and laterally from the precursors of the arytenoid cartilages (ventral ends of arch VI). The aditus is now T shaped. In the fifth and sixth weeks, the tracheoesophageal septum extends to the first tracheal ring. In the 13- to 17-mm embryo, laryngeal cartilage and muscle development is clearly identifiable, and lateral cricoid condensation is under way. By the seventh week of development, the cricoid ring is complete, and the cartilaginous hyoid is visible below the epiglottis (Fig. 74-5). Definitive tracheal cartilages appear at this stage, and the esophagus has four discrete layers. By the end of the embryonic period (27 to 31 mm crown-rump length), the larynx, trachea, and esophagus are well-formed organs (Fig. 74-6).

The complex structure of the larynx and its numerous folds and outpouchings predispose this region to congenital malformations. Congenital laryngoceles and saccular cysts arise in the region of the laryngeal ventricle. Laryngoceles are outpouching of saccular mucosa. They may remain within the confines of the cartilaginous larynx (internal laryngoceles) or extend through the thyrohyoid membrane to present as neck masses (combined laryngoceles). Saccular cysts occur in the laryngeal ventricle as well but are isolated from the interior of the larynx and do not contain air. They are submucosal and covered by normal mucous membrane.[4]

It has been theorized that failure of epithelial growth in the vestibule and subglottic regions results in laryngeal atresia. These atresias can be divided into three types. Type 1 consists of a supraglottic obstruction, absent vestibule, and stenotic subglottis. Type 2 is a supraglottic obstruction that separates the primitive vestibule from the normal subglottis. In type 3, a perforated membrane

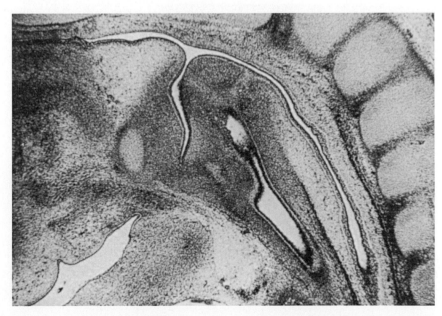

FIGURE 74-5. Sagittal section near the median plane at 7 weeks' gestational age (18 mm). The base of the skull and the vertebral center are evident. The forming epiglottis is evident. The cartilaginous hyoid is seen below the epiglottis. (From Tucker JA, O'Rahilly R. Observations on the embryology of the human larynx. Ann Otol Rhinol Laryngol 81:520, 1972. Carnegie Collection, 8226.)

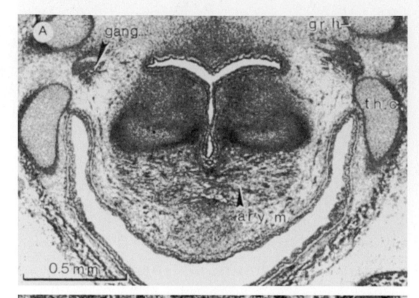

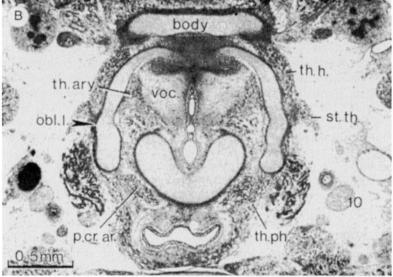

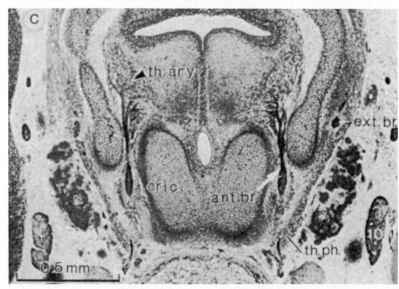

FIGURE 74–6. *A,* The greater horn of the hyoid and the thyroid lamina can be seen on each side. The laryngeal cavity is T shaped; that of the pharynx is U shaped. Behind the arytenoid cartilages, the transverse arytenoid muscle is evident. In the region between the hyoid and the thyroid, the ganglion is identifiable bilaterally (×76). *B,* The body of the hyoid, thyroid laminae, and cricoid cartilages are clearly visible, as are the laryngeal cavity and that of the laryngopharynx. The submandibular and thyroid glands can be seen bilaterally. The thyrohyoid and sternothyroid muscles and the oblique line of the thyroid cartilage are indicated, as is the posterior cricoarytenoid muscle. The blastema of the vocal ligament is marked. The internal jugular vein, vagus nerve, common carotid artery, and sympathetic trunk are identifiable on each side, and a parathyroid gland shows well on the left-hand side of the photomicrograph (×49). *C,* Portions of the thyroid and cricoid cartilages, as well as the thyroid gland, are evident. On each side, the anterior branch of the inferior laryngeal nerve can be seen passing forward in the vicinity of the cricothyroid joint and ending in the thyroarytenoid muscle (silver preparation, ×76). (From Müller F, O'Rahilly R, Tucker J. The human larynx at the end of the embryonic period proper. 2. The laryngeal cavity and the innervation of its lining. Ann Otol Rhinol Laryngol 94:607, 1985.)

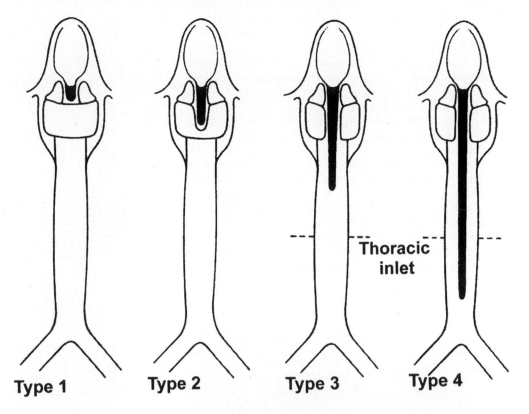

FIGURE 74–7. Benjamin-Inglis classification of laryngotracheoesophageal clefts. (Modified after Benjamin B, Inglis A. Minor congenital laryngeal clefts: diagnosis and classification. Ann Otol Rhinol Laryngol 98:417, 1989, by permission.)

Type 1   **Type 2**   **Type 3**   **Type 4**

Thoracic inlet

partly obstructs the glottis.[35, 37] Laryngeal atresia presents with asphyxia and death at the time of birth in most cases. Because the imperforate larynx cannot be intubated, emergent tracheotomy in the first minutes of life has accounted for the few reported survivors of this malformation.

Failed fusion of the two lateral growth centers of the posterior cricoid cartilage at 6 to 7 weeks of fetal life could result in a posterior laryngeal cleft. Further aborted development of the tracheoesophageal septum might result in a laryngotracheoesophageal cleft that could extend to the carina.[19, 21] Several staging systems have been proposed for laryngotracheoesophageal clefts. Occult clefts can be appreciated only by palpation and measurement of the interarytenoid height. Type 1 clefts are limited to the supraglottic, interarytenoid area. Type 2 clefts show partial clefting of the posterior cricoid cartilage, sometimes with a mucosal bridge across the cartilaginous gap. Type 3 clefts involve the entire cricoid and the cervical portion of the tracheoesophageal membrane, stopping above the thoracic inlet. Type 4 clefts involve a major portion of the intrathoracic tracheoesophageal wall[3] (Fig. 74–7).

Three mechanisms have been proposed for the origin of tracheoesophageal fistulas: epithelial occlusion, in which occlusion of the esophageal lumen might occur; intraembryonic pressure, in which pressure from the heart, great vessels, or developing lung causes a disruption of esophageal growth; or differential growth, in which abnormalities of cellular proliferation cause the trachea to outgrow the esophagus in length. In each of these theoretic situations, the earlier the disruption, the more severe is the extent of the malformation.[12, 29]

The Fetus

The upper aerodigestive tract forms in the embryonic period. In the fetal period, it grows, refines its structure, and develops the basic neurologic reflexes necessary for postnatal life.

In the third month, the thyroid laminae fuse, the cartilaginous vocal processes of the arytenoids are seen, and the ventricle and saccule are identifiable. Fetal breathing movements have been visualized in utero by ultrasonography toward the end of the third month.

Myenteric plexuses and ganglion cells are differentiated by 13 weeks of gestation, and the esophageal muscularis is well formed, suggesting the potential for peristalsis. Primitive swallowing movements have been observed in aborted fetuses of 75-mm length.[13] Studies of radioactive colloidal gold or red blood cells injected into the amniotic fluid have shown that a 16-week fetus swallows 2 to 7 mL of fluid each day and that this amount increases with gestational age. The role of fetal swallowing in the regulation of amniotic fluid volume is controversial, but polyhydramnios can complicate pregnancies in which fetal swallowing is impaired by neurologic disorders, mass lesions, or esophageal atresia.[9]

In the fourth month, goblet cells appear in the laryngeal submucosa and the trachea is fully ciliated. The esophageal lining cells are also ciliated at this point. Conversion to mature squamous esophageal epithelium begins in the fifth month. Fibroelastic cartilage appears in the epiglottis in the fifth and sixth months, and the cuneiform and corniculate cartilages develop.

During the second trimester, fetal breathing becomes

a more mature activity, and laryngeal coordination and regulation are apparent. By use of antenatal ultrasonography with simultaneous color flow Doppler imaging, this activity can be seen and measured. Fetal diaphragmatic movements result in tracheal and laryngeal exchange of amniotic fluid with inspiratory and expiratory velocities on the order of 0.1 to 0.2 m/sec.[15] The pharynx shows rhythmic expansion 200 msec before the onset of inspiration, stenting the tongue and pharynx open to allow the passage of fluid. Similarly, the larynx is seen to open 100 msec before the onset of inspiratory flow and to relax on expiration, narrowing the glottic chink and modulating expiratory flow and duration. The timing and duration of these activities are similar to those observed during air exchange after birth.

A third-trimester fetus is prepared for extrauterine life. Although the larynx is small, it is ready to perform its protective, respiratory, and phonatory functions (Figs. 74–8 and 74–9).

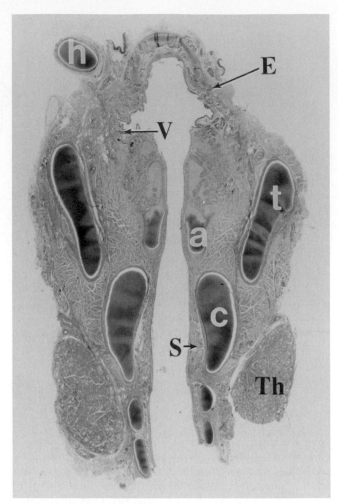

FIGURE 74–9. Coronal histologic section through the anterior hyolaryngeal complex. Note the glandular elements in the submucosa of the aryepiglottic folds (E), laryngeal ventricles (V), and subglottis (S). These may give rise to congenital cysts in these locations. h, hyoid; t, thyroid cartilage; a, arytenoid; c, cricoid; Th, thyroid gland.

The Infant

A neonate's larynx is different in form and position from that of an adult (Figs. 74–10 to 74–12). The pharynx is vertically short, and the structures associated with it are high within the cervical area (Fig. 74–13). The inferior margin of the cricoid cartilage is at the level of the fourth cervical vertebra (C4), and the tip of the epiglottis is at C1. The close apposition of the epiglottis and soft palate is thought to permit suckling and simultaneous respiration in the newborn and contributes to a baby's obligate nasal breathing.[6] The hyolaryngeal skeleton is vertically compact, compared with that of an adult. The thyroid cartilage is within the arch of the hyoid and slightly inferior to it. The vocal cords are oriented transversely in a newborn, the epiglottis is short, and the aryepiglottic folds are thick and bulky. The arytenoids are comparatively large and expanded by a thick areolar submucosa. All these features give a neonate's larynx a different endoscopic appearance from that of an older child or adult.[32] On introduction of a laryngoscope, the larynx appears anteri-

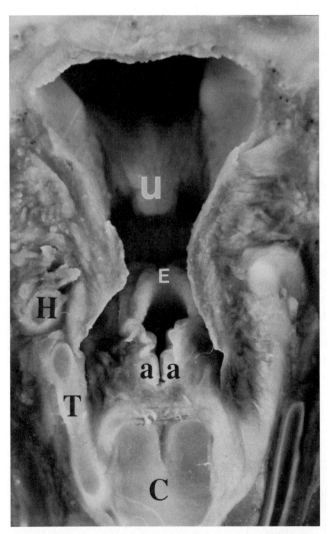

FIGURE 74–8. Coronal section through the posterior pharynx of a second-trimester fetus. Note close approximation of the uvula (u) and epiglottis (E), the prominent arytenoids (a), and the short epiglottic height. H, hyoid; T, thyroid cartilage; C, posterior cricoid lamina.

Mature   Infant

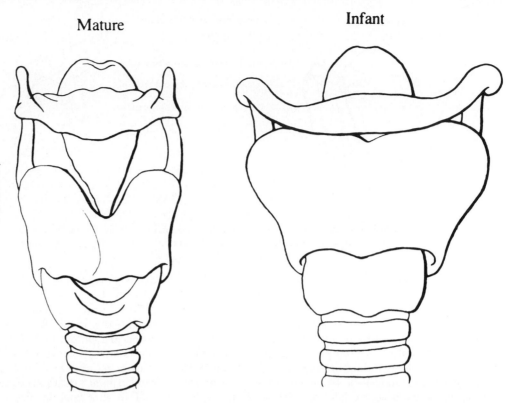

FIGURE 74–10. Anterior view of the hyolaryngeal complex. (From Bosma JF. Anatomy of the Infant Head. Baltimore, Johns Hopkins University Press, 1986, pp 366–367.)

orly displaced, the arytenoids are prominent, and the membranous portion of the vocal folds is short.

A newborn's glottis is 7 mm in anteroposterior and 4 mm in lateral dimension. The subglottis is the narrowest portion of a newborn's airway, with a diameter of 4 to 5 mm. It has a thick submucosa and is rich in mucus-producing glands. The relative resistance of a newborn's subglottis to injury from prolonged intubation has been attributed to this high proportion of cross-sectional soft tissue. These mucus-producing glands can be injured during such a period of intubation and are thought to be the source of acquired subglottic cysts (see Fig. 74–9).

Mature   Infant

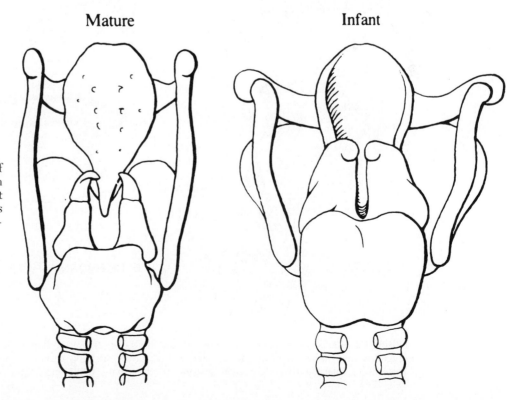

FIGURE 74–11. Posterior view of the hyolaryngeal complex. (From Bosma JF. Anatomy of the Infant Head. Baltimore, Johns Hopkins University Press, 1986, pp 366–367.)

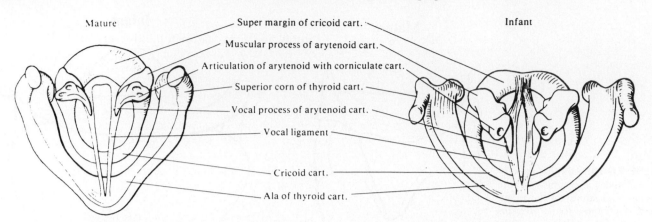

FIGURE 74–12. Superior view of the hyolaryngeal complex. (From Bosma JF. Anatomy of the Infant Head. Baltimore, Johns Hopkins University Press, 1986, pp 366–367.)

Although the larynx of a healthy newborn can perform the basic protective, respiratory, and phonatory functions, these actions are inefficient. Immediately after birth, the closure reflex, which protects the lungs from contamination during eating, works poorly, leaving a neonate susceptible to aspiration. As time passes, the airway becomes more capable of excluding foreign matter. An infant's glottis closes in response to tactile, thermal, or chemical stimulation of the laryngeal inlet or trachea. Further, glottic closure can be triggered by irritation of distal esophageal afferents (as in reflux) or by stimulation of any of the major cranial nerves. The larynx should open again as soon as the stimulus disappears. In the immature larynx, glottic closure may continue long after the stimulus disappears—this is the phenomenon of laryngospasm.[31] Laryngospasm that routinely terminates in adults as blood oxygen decreases and carbon dioxide increases may persist in a neonate and has been implicated in the etiology of sudden infant death syndrome.[2, 26]

Two abnormal developmental conditions of the larynx, laryngomalacia and vocal cord paralysis, are worthy of mention here. Among the many causes of stridor in a

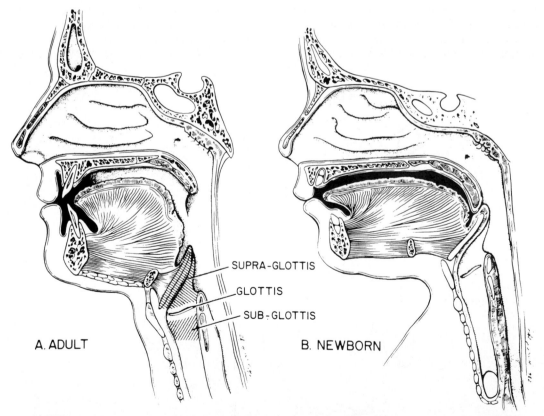

SUPRA-GLOTTIS
GLOTTIS
SUB-GLOTTIS

A. ADULT   B. NEWBORN

FIGURE 74–13. Sagittal section of adult (A) and newborn (B) heads. Note apposition of the epiglottis and the soft palate, an adaptation that favors suckling without aspiration. (From Sasaki CT, Isaacson GC. Functional anatomy of the larynx. Otolaryngol Clin North Am 21: 595, 1988.)

newborn, these two abnormalities make up the bulk of diagnoses. Increasing evidence shows that laryngomalacia and vocal cord paralysis, when presenting in otherwise healthy children (i.e., those free of central nervous system diseases), represent maturational abnormalities in central nervous system control of laryngeal musculature. Laryngomalacia shows no histologic abnormalities in cartilage development, is frequently associated with swallowing difficulties, and routinely resolves with time, thus suggesting a neurologic cause. Further, laryngomalacia can develop in previously normal patients after central nervous system lesions.[1, 36] Likewise, many "idiopathic" vocal cord paralyses resolve spontaneously by the first year of life.[16] Such paralyses may be intermittent, showing normal function on one inspiration and incoordinate or absent movement on other breaths. Electromyography may demonstrate abnormal rather than absent innervation.[8] Thus, some vocal cord paralyses seem to represent incoordination of the opposing adductor and abductor function rather than an absence of innervation as is seen in acquired palsies.

The trachea of a newborn tends to collapse easily. Its compliance is three times that of a 1-year-old's trachea and six times that of an adult's. The mechanical resistance of the trachea is partly due to the strength of its cartilages and partially attributable to the tone of the smooth muscle in its posterior wall.[34] Resistance to airflow in animal preparations with compressed tracheas and in children with tracheomalacia decreases when smooth muscle tone is increased with methacholine.[25]

The common occurrence of postprandial regurgitation has focused much attention on the esophageal function in a newborn. About one third of infants demonstrate significant reflux on barium swallow, and this proportion may be higher with use of more sensitive techniques such as 24-hour pH probes and radionuclide milk scans. Esophageal motility in premature infants shows poor coordination with deglutition. Contractions are rapid and often not peristaltic, with simultaneous contractions along the entire esophagus. Lower esophageal sphincter pressure is low in newborns but increases with age, as does the coordination of peristalsis.[9]

The Child

The position, structure, and function of the larynx continue to change throughout childhood.[28] By the age of 2 years, the lower border of the larynx has descended in the neck to the level of the fifth cervical vertebra (C5). It has reached C6 by age 5 years, and its definitive position (C6–7) is achieved at around 15 years.[23] The thyroid cartilage and hyoid bone, which overlap in a newborn, separate during laryngeal descent.

Growth of the larynx is rapid from birth to 3 years of age, then slows until puberty.[18] Growth in the various laryngeal dimensions from birth to puberty is linear and proportional; thus, the general configuration of the larynx changes little during this time. Exceptions are the epiglottis and vocal folds. The epiglottis increases in curvature until age 3 years, then gradually flattens toward its adult configuration. Sixty to 75% of the vocal fold length is attributable to the vocal process of the arytenoid at

birth. This configuration favors respiration over phonation and is similar to that seen in other mammals. By a child's third birthday, the membranous portion of the vocal fold is dominant in size.[7] The internal and external landmarks of the larynx maintain their relationships during this period of growth as well. Specifically, throughout childhood, the level of the true vocal folds is halfway between the thyroid notch and the lower border of the thyroid cartilage, the upper border of the cricoid maintains a 30-degree angle with the true cords, and the arytenoids are one third the anterior height of the thyroid cartilage.[14]

The growth of the larynx is accompanied by a gradual lowering of the vocal pitch. The fundamental frequency of a newborn's cry is 500 Hz and descends to 286 Hz by 7 years of age. Until puberty, the vocal characteristics of males and females are similar.

The trachea measures 4 cm in length in a newborn and increases to 12 cm by adulthood. Growth in childhood is divided proportionally between the tracheal cartilages and the annular ligaments that divide them. After puberty, growth is restricted to the annular ligaments, so the cartilages of a child are more closely approximated than are those of an adult. The upper edge of the trachea remains at the level of the sixth cervical vertebra throughout life.[5]

The Teenager

The larynx undergoes remarkable changes in configuration in the second decade of life. The thyroid cartilage grows in size and changes its shape, producing the prominence of the Adam's apple. The arytenoids grow slowly compared with the rest of the larynx, assuming adult proportions. The vocal folds elongate with only minor growth in the vocal processes of the arytenoids. In this way, the voice-producing membranous portion of the vocal fold comes to occupy six tenths of the total length of the cord. This represents a compromise of respiratory function in favor of voice, as the 3:10 ratio of membranous/cartilaginous lengths has been shown to be optimal for respiration and is more closely approximated in a neonate.[22]

Ossification of the thyroid cartilage does not begin until the end of the second decade and is seen first near the inferior horn.[11] The distribution of hyaline and elastic cartilage remains fairly constant through life.[27]

The most dramatic changes in the second decade are those associated with male voice mutation. Between the ages of 11 and 16 years, a clear sexual dimorphism is seen. Similar in appearance to the female larynx in prepuberty, the male larynx exceeds its counterpart in all dimensions by puberty. The angle of the thyroid laminae decreases from 120 to 90 degrees in both sexes as the anteroposterior length of the glottis increases, but the male thyroid eminence becomes much more prominent. Boys' vocal folds grow twice as fast as girls' in length during this period.[17] This increase in length and mass of the vocal fold is thought to account for the drop in fundamental frequency from 286 Hz in the child to 207 Hz in the average woman and 120 to 130 Hz in the average man.

Darwin's evolutionary theories were questioned. How could a structure as complex as the eye, for instance, evolve and at each point in phylogeny represent a reproductive advantage for the creature that possessed it? If ontogeny recapitulates phylogeny, then the upper aerodigestive tract is a magnificent example of how evolving structures can successfully serve their host at all points of growth and development.

This chapter is dedicated the memory of James F. Bosma, M.D. (1916–2001), whose exceptional contributions to the study of infant development enlightened us all.

SELECTED READINGS

Bosma JF. Anatomy of the Infant Head. Baltimore, MD, The Johns Hopkins University Press, 1986.

Crelin ES. Development of the upper respiratory system. Clin Symp 28: 3, 1976.

Kirchner JA. The vertebrate larynx: adaptations and aberrations. Laryngoscope 103:1197, 1993.

Sasaki CT, Isaacson G. Functional anatomy of the larynx. Otolaryngol Clin North Am 21:595, 1988.

REFERENCES

1. Archer SM. Acquired flaccid larynx: a case report supporting the neurologic theory of laryngomalacia. Arch Otolaryngol Head Neck Surg 118:654, 1992.

2. Bauman NM, Sandler AD, Schmidt C, et al. Reflex laryngospasm induced by stimulation of distal esophageal afferents. Laryngoscope 104:209, 1994.

3. Benjamin B, Inglis A. Minor congenital laryngeal clefts: diagnosis and classification. Ann Otol Rhinol Laryngol 98:417, 1989.

4. Civantos FJ, Holinger LD. Laryngoceles and saccular cysts in infants and children. Arch Otolaryngol Head Neck Surg 118:296, 1992.

5. Crelin ES. Functional Anatomy of the Newborn. New Haven, CT, Yale University Press, 1973, pp 37–38.

6. Crelin ES. Development of the upper respiratory system. Clin Symp 28:3, 1976.

7. Eckel HE, Keobke J, Sittel C, et al. Morthology of the human larynx during the first five years of life studied on whole organ serial sections. Ann Otol Rhinol Laryngol 108:232, 1999.

8. Gartlan MG, Peterson KL, Hoffman HT, et al. Bipolar hooked-wire electromyographic technique in the evaluation of pediatric vocal cord paralysis. Ann Otol Rhinol Laryngol 102:695, 1993.

9. Grand RJ, Watkins JB, Torti FM. Development of the human gastrointestinal tract, a review. Gastroenterology 70:790, 1976.

10. Hast MH. The developmental anatomy of the larynx. Otolaryngol Clin North Am 3:413, 1970.

11. Hately W, Evison G, Samuel E. The pattern of ossification in the laryngeal cartilages: a radiological study. Br J Radiol 38:585, 1965.

12. Holinger PH, Zimmermann AA, Parchet VN, Johnston KC. A correlation of the embryonic development of the trachea and lungs with congenital malformations. Adv Otorhinolaryngol 3:1, 1955.

13. Humphrey T. The development of mouth opening and related reflexes involving the oral area of human fetuses. Ala J Med Sci 5:126, 1968.

14. Isaacson G. Extraliminal arytenoid reconstruction: laryngeal framework surgery applied to a pediatric problem. Ann Otol Rhinol Laryngol 99:616, 1990.

15. Isaacson G, Birnholz JC. Human fetal upper respiratory tract function as revealed by ultrasonography. Ann Otol Rhinol Laryngol 100: 743, 1991.

16. Isaacson G, Moya F. Hereditary congenital laryngeal abductor paralysis. Ann Otol Rhinol Laryngol 96:701, 1987.

17. Kahane JC. A morphological study of the human prepubertal and pubertal larynx. Am J Anat 151:11, 1978.

18. Klock LE, Beckwith JB. Appendix: Dimensions of the human larynx during infancy and childhood. In Bosma JF (ed). Anatomy of the Infant Head. Baltimore, MD, Johns Hopkins University Press, 1986, pp 368–371.

19. Lim TA, Spanier SS, Kohut RI. Laryngeal clefts. A histopathologic study and review. Ann Otol 88:837, 1979.

20. Lisser H. Studies on the development of the human larynx. Am J Anat 12:27, 1911.

21. Moungthong G, Holinger LD. Laryngotracheoesophageal clefts. Ann Otol Rhinol Laryngol 106:1002, 1997.

22. Negus VE. The Comparative Anatomy and Physiology of the Larynx. London, Heinemann, 1949.

23. Noback GJ. The developmental topography of the larynx, trachea and lungs in the fetus, newborn, infant and child. Am J Dis Child 26:515, 1923.

24. O'Rahilly R, Tucker JA. Early development of the larynx in staged human embryos. Ann Otol Rhinol Laryngol 82:3, 1973.

25. Panitch HB, Keklikian EN, Motley RA, et al. Effect of altering smooth muscle tone on maximal expiratory flows in patients with tracheomalacia. Pediatr Pulmonol 9:170, 1990.

26. Sasaki CT. Development of laryngeal function: etiologic significance in sudden infant death syndrome. Laryngoscope 3:420, 1979.

27. Sato K, Kurita S, Hirano M, Kiyokawa K. Distribution of elastic cartilage in the arytenoids and its physiologic significance. Ann Otol Rhinol Laryngol 99:363, 1990.

28. Schwartz DS, Keller MS. Maturational descent of the epiglottis. Arch Otolaryngol Head Neck Surg 123:627, 1997.

29. Smith EI. The early development of the trachea and esophagus in relation to atresia of the esophagus and tracheoesophageal fistula. Contrib Embryol Carnegie Inst Wash 31:43, 1957.

30. Soulie A, Bardier E. Recherches sur le developpment du larynx chez l'homme. J Anat Physiol 43:137, 1907.

31. Suzuki M, Sasaki CT. Laryngeal spasm: a neurophysiologic redefinition. Ann Otol Rhinol Laryngol 86:1, 1977.

32. Tucker G. The infant larynx: direct laryngoscopic observations. JAMA 99:1899, 1932.

33. Tucker JA, Tucker GF. Some aspects of fetal laryngeal development. Ann Otol Rhinol Laryngol 84:1, 1975.

34. Wailoo M, Emery JL. Structure of the membranous trachea in children. Acta Anat 106:254, 1980.

35. Walander A. The mechanisms of origin of congenital malformations of the larynx. Acta Otolaryngol (Stockh) 45:426, 1955.

36. Woo P. Acquired laryngomalacia: epiglottis prolapse as a cause of airway obstruction. Ann Otol Rhinol Laryngol 101:314, 1992.

37. Zaw-Tun HIA. Development of congenital laryngeal atresias and cleft. Ann Otol Rhinol Laryngol 97:353, 1988.

75

Physiology of the Larynx, Airways, and Lungs

Robert E. Wood, Ph.D., M.D.

The Larynx

Structure

The larynx is composed of the cricoid, thyroid, and arytenoid cartilages; the epiglottis; the vocal cords; and associated muscles and ligaments. The details of laryngeal structure can be found in any standard anatomy text and in Chapter 74.

Intrinsic Laryngeal Musculature

There are four important functions of the intrinsic laryngeal muscles.[1] The glottis is opened by rotation of the arytenoid cartilages, which are moved by the posterior cricoarytenoid muscles.[2] The glottis is closed by the action of the lateral cricoarytenoid muscles, which rotate the arytenoids in a direction opposite to that which opens the glottis. This action is supplemented by that of the arytenoid muscle, which approximates the arytenoids and shortens the posterior commissure. In addition, the cricothyroid muscle tenses the vocal cords and thus may also participate in glottic closure.[3] Vocal cord tension is regulated by two sets of muscles. The cricothyroid muscle tilts the cricoid cartilage backward, tensing and lengthening the vocal cords. This is important in phonation as well as in glottic closure. The thyroarytenoid muscle relaxes the cords and shortens them. The vocal muscle, a part of the thyroarytenoid, "fine tunes" vocal cord tension and is thus important in phonation.[4] The fourth muscle function of the larynx is that of lowering and raising the epiglottis. The aryepiglottic muscle lowers the epiglottis to cover the glottic orifice; the thyroepiglottic muscle, extending from the anterior portion of the epiglottis to the thyroid cartilage, raises the epiglottis, thus exposing the glottis.

Innervation

Innervation of the larynx, both motor and sensory, is from the tenth cranial nerve via the superior and inferior (recurrent) laryngeal nerves. Since there is bilateral cortical representation to each side, motor paralysis of the larynx is almost always due to a peripheral lesion. Innervation to all the intrinsic muscles of the larynx is by the recurrent laryngeal nerves, except for the cricothyroid muscle, which is innervated by the external branch of the superior laryngeal nerve. The sensory supply of the epiglottis, the aryepiglottic folds, and the laryngeal mucosa (including the subglottic space) comes from the internal branch of the superior laryngeal nerve.

There are many laryngeal reflexes, some of which are poorly defined and understood. Reflexes arising in the larynx may affect the cardiovascular system, the lower airways, or the respiratory center in the brain, producing bradycardia, apnea, laryngospasm, and bronchoconstriction. In addition, systemic alterations, such as hypoxemia and hypercapnia, may reflexively alter laryngeal muscle tone. Many of the laryngeal reflexes may be abolished or modified by topical anesthetics or vagolytic drugs.

Function

The larynx serves three important functions: it acts as an airway, it serves as an instrument of phonation, and it protects the lower airways. The larynx is the narrowest portion of the entire airway system and therefore is particularly vulnerable to obstruction. The subglottic space is entirely surrounded by the cricoid cartilage, which serves a protective function but may also contribute to airway obstruction should mucosal edema occur, since the only direction in which the mucosa may swell is into the airway lumen. Complete or partial closure of the glottis during expiration results in increased intrathoracic pressure. This is essential for coughing or for forceful expulsion of abdominal contents (Valsalva maneuver) and may improve airway dynamics or gas exchange in pathologic conditions, as discussed later.

The vocal function of the larynx is a complex subject that is not addressed here.

The larynx protects the airway in several ways. Most important, it effects complete and automatic closure of the glottis during swallowing. The epiglottis, contrary to popular belief, is not essential for glottic closure or for prevention of aspiration. During swallowing, the vocal cords close completely, and the epiglottis is brought down over the glottis, deflecting the bolus of swallowed material to either side and posteriorly into the esophageal orifice. The other major protective function of the larynx is its role in the cough reflex, which is triggered by sensitive receptors in the larynx and the subglottic space. Stimulation of these receptors results in immediate closure of the glottis, which is followed by an explosive cough. This reflex mechanism is essential to life.

Important Physiologic Derangements in Laryngeal Function

Vocal Cord Paralysis

Paralysis of the vocal cords usually results from injury to the recurrent laryngeal nerves. Because of the longer course of the left recurrent laryngeal nerve (which passes around the aortic arch), it is more susceptible to injury than the right recurrent nerve, and it may also be involved by mediastinal lesions. Birth trauma is a relatively common cause of transient cord paralysis. Abductor paralysis (paralysis of the posterior cricoarytenoid muscles) leaves the cords in a paramedian position, with resulting airway obstruction. Phonation and cry are often fairly normal, although the patient usually has stridor, and older patients may complain of dyspnea. Adductor paralysis (paralysis of the lateral cricoarytenoid and arytenoid muscles) results in the inability to close the glottis, thus leading to aspiration, aphonia, and an ineffective cough. Unilateral adductor paralysis may lead to aspiration, whereas unilateral abductor paralysis is often relatively asymptomatic.

Obstruction

Laryngeal obstruction may result from abductor paralysis, as noted previously, or, more commonly, from infection or trauma leading to edema. Laryngeal edema may be generalized, as with thermal burns, or it may be localized to either the subglottic or the supraglottic region. Supraglottic edema is most often associated with acute infectious epiglottitis and is discussed elsewhere in this text. Subglottic edema may result from viral infections (croup) or mechanical trauma (such as intubation or bronchoscopy). Other causes of laryngeal obstruction include foreign bodies, congenital or acquired lesions (such as laryngeal webs, cysts, or other masses), and subglottic stenosis, which are discussed in other chapters of this text (see Chaps. 83, 89, and 90).

Laryngomalacia is an important laryngeal obstructive lesion in infancy, the physiology of which is instructive. This condition is usually benign and self-limited but may be severe enough to require surgical intervention to achieve an adequate airway. The most common findings associated with laryngomalacia are a floppy epiglottis, large redundant aryepiglottic folds, and large or redundant arytenoid processes. Any of these supraglottic structures may fall into the glottis during inspiration, thus causing obstruction; stridor associated with laryngomalacia is thus predominantly inspiratory. There is usually little obstruction during expiration, as the supraglottic structures are pushed out of the way during expiration. During crying, the stridor may decrease, because increased laryngeal muscle tone may stiffen the supraglottic structures. However, stridor due to subglottic obstruction (such as croup) is usually more severe when the rate and depth of respiration are increased, as in crying or with exercise. Two factors contribute to this phenomenon: (1) because

of the Bernoulli effect (lateral pressure in a flowing stream decreases as the velocity of flow increases), the laryngeal structures tend to collapse inward, producing more obstruction as the airflow velocity increases; (2) higher flow velocity increases the turbulence of the flow and therefore the noise of respiration. During quiet breathing (as in sleep), flow velocities may be so low that no stridor may be apparent.

Severe laryngeal obstruction leads to alveolar hypoxia. This, in turn, leads to pulmonary arteriolar constriction and elevation of pulmonary arterial pressure. Eventually, permanent changes may occur in the pulmonary arterial tree that lead to irreversible pulmonary hypertension, cor pulmonale, and death.

The Airways

Structure

One of the most important features of the structure of the airways is their ability to remain patent despite relatively large shifts in intrathoracic pressure during respiration. This characteristic is due to the fact that central airways have enough cartilage to maintain their shape. In the trachea and major bronchi, the cartilage is in the form of roughly C-shaped rings; but in more peripheral airways, the cartilage becomes more irregular and less prominent. Only in the subglottic space does the cartilage (cricoid) completely encircle the airway. Smaller airways are supported entirely by the elastic properties of the pulmonary parenchyma, and surfactant may play an important role in maintaining patency of airways smaller than about 2 mm. Larger airways are surrounded by strands of smooth muscle, particularly between the ends of the cartilaginous rings, contraction of which decreases the diameter of the airways and increases resistance to airflow.

The epithelium of the respiratory mucosa from the posterior laryngeal commissure to the smaller airways is pseudostratified and ciliated. At the bronchiolar level, the epithelium becomes more cuboid in nature, and the number of cilia is decreased. No cilia are found in the respiratory bronchioles or smaller airways. Mixed seromucous glands are numerous in the larger airways (approximately one gland per square millimeter) but become sparse after the first several generations of airways. Goblet cells are numerous in the upper airway and extend further into the respiratory tree than do the glands; under normal circumstances, however, they are not present in the smaller airways.

The airways are lined with a thin (perhaps discontinuous) layer of mucus that overlies the tips of the cilia on the epithelial cells. Secretion of mucus and fluid by the mucosal glands is under parasympathetic nervous control; goblet cells discharge their contents (mucus) primarily in response to irritative phenomena. Surrounding the cilia is a fluid the precise composition of which is unknown, but which, for hydrodynamic reasons, must have a low viscosity. The volume and the composition of the periciliary fluid are regulated by active ion transport at the apical surface of the airway epithelial cells.

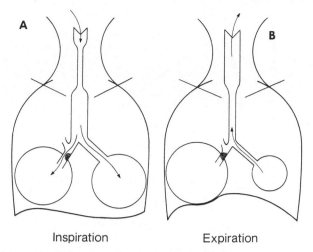

Inspiration   Expiration

FIGURE 75–1. *A,* During inspiration, intrathoracic pressure is lower than atmospheric pressure, thus leading to distention of the intrathoracic airways. The extrathoracic portion of the trachea is surrounded by atmospheric pressure and may become narrower. *B,* During expiration, intrathoracic pressure is higher than atmospheric pressure, and intrathoracic airways narrow, while the extrathoracic trachea may distend or remain at normal caliber. The dimensional changes on this diagram are exaggerated. The lower airways are not as well supported as the trachea, and their change in size with respiration may be more pronounced. This diagram illustrates that in the presence of partial bronchial obstruction (as by a foreign body), air may be able to enter the lung distal to the obstruction during inspiration but may not exit during exhalation, thus leading to air trapping and overinflation of that part of the lung (obstructive emphysema).

Innervation

Sensory innervation of the trachea and the airways is entirely via the vagus nerve. The receptors are primarily irritant receptors, stimulation of which results in effects similar to those seen with stimulation of the larynx. Motor innervation is both vagal and sympathetic, as is the nerve supply of the mucosal glands.

Function

The major function of the airways is air conduction. The velocity of airflow at any point depends on respiratory frequency, tidal volume, airway diameter, and difference in pressure between the atmosphere and the pleural space. In normal adults, tracheal airflow velocity is approximately 1.5 m/sec during quiet breathing. With an effective cough, the peak tracheal airflow velocity may approach two thirds the speed of sound (more than 200 m/sec). The total cross-sectional area of the airways increases dramatically with distal branching, and thus the linear airflow velocity decreases in peripheral airways. In the central airways (except perhaps the trachea), airflow patterns are turbulent or nearly so, and it is this turbulent flow that produces normal breath sounds. In smaller airways, airflow becomes laminar, and at the level of the alveolar ducts and alveoli, linear airflow velocity is so low that molecular diffusion may account for a significant proportion of gas movement.

Inspiration occurs when intrathoracic pressure is lower than atmospheric pressure, and expiration occurs when intrathoracic pressure becomes greater than atmospheric pressure. The airways have some degree of compliance, increasing in diameter during inspiration and decreasing in diameter during expiration (Fig. 75–1). Because of this, the shear force exerted by the air on the secretions on the airway walls is greater during expiration than during inspiration, a fact that may play some role in keeping the airways clear of secretions. This phenomenon is exaggerated during hyperventilation, which helps explain the effectiveness of exercise in stimulating a productive cough. Narrowing of the lumen of the larger airways during coughing (by active muscle contraction as well as by increased intrathoracic pressure) increases the linear airflow velocity and thus leads to a more effective cough.

The ventilatory function of the lung can be described in terms of volumes, flow rates, and airway resistance (the most common parameters of pulmonary function measured in the laboratory). Total lung capacity is divided into several components (Fig. 75–2). The reference point for all volume measurements is functional residual capacity: the volume of gas contained in the lung when all forces acting on the lung are in equilibrium. In practice, this occurs at the end of a quiet, relaxed, normal exhalation. Residual volume is the volume of gas remaining in the lung at the end of a maximal exhalation. Vital capacity (total lung capacity minus residual volume) and its subdivisions (inspiratory capacity and expiratory reserve volume) are usually measured with a simple spirometer. Measurements of absolute lung volumes (functional residual capacity, residual volume, and total lung capacity) require more sophisticated methods. The simplest technique for measurement of functional residual capacity is to have the patient rebreathe from a closed container of helium. After rebreathing and equilibration (usually for 7

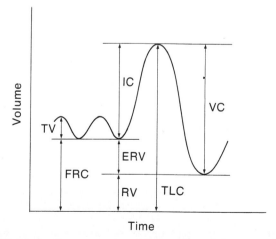

FIGURE 75–2. This spirogram indicates the subdivisions of lung volume. Tidal volume (TV), vital capacity (VC), expiratory reserve volume (ERV), and inspiratory capacity (IC) are relative volumes and can be measured with a simple spirometer. The absolute lung volumes, total lung capacity (TLC), functional residual capacity (FRC), and residual volume (RV), cannot be determined by use of a simple spirometer but must be measured by gas dilution or plethysmographic techniques.

minutes), the volume of gas contained in the lungs can be calculated from the ratio of the initial and final helium concentrations and the initial volume of the container. Measurement of functional residual capacity with a body plethysmograph, although requiring more complex and expensive equipment, has the advantage of rapid measurement and is more accurate in patients with poor gas mixing in the lung (as with significant airway obstruction). Helium dilution will underestimate functional residual capacity in the presence of airway obstruction; the difference between lung volumes measured by helium dilution and those measured by body plethysmography is the volume of "trapped" gas that does not participate in gas exchange.

Flow rates are affected by the neuromuscular and mechanical components of ventilation. The most common measurement of flow is the forced expiratory volume in the first second (FEV_1), which is measured with a spirometer (Fig. 75–3). Normally, the FEV_1 is at least 80% of the vital capacity. Decreased FEV_1 may be due to poor effort or muscle weakness but is usually a manifestation of airway obstruction. The FEV_1 may not reflect significant increases in airflow resistance in airways less than about 2 mm in diameter.

A spirometric tracing shows expired volume versus time. Plotting the first derivative of the spirometric tracing (i.e., volume per unit time) against expired volume yields the so-called flow/volume curve (Fig. 75–4). From this graphic presentation of the expiratory flow maneuver, inferences may be made about the state of the small and large airways. The slope of the flow/volume curve below approximately 50% of vital capacity is relatively independent of effort. In contrast, the FEV_1 is highly effort dependent. Small airway obstruction is manifested primarily by lower flow rates at low lung volumes, thus giving a concave flow/volume curve. Obstruction at the larynx or in the trachea yields a curve with a truncated peak (see Fig. 75–4). Flow/volume curves are ordinarily generated

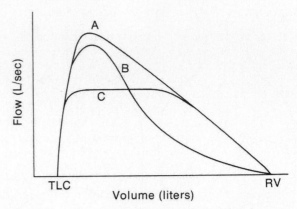

FIGURE 75–4. The expiratory flow/volume curve presents the same data as are shown in a conventional spirogram but in a more easily interpreted form. Curve A is a normal tracing in which the peak flow is achieved after 10% to 15% of the vital capacity has been exhaled; the remainder of the curve has a nearly constant slope. The tail of the curve is relatively effort-independent. Curve B is a tracing obtained from a patient with lower airway obstruction. Flow rates at low lung volumes are markedly decreased, while the peak flow is maintained at a near normal level. Curve C is a tracing obtained in a patient with high airway obstruction (tracheal or laryngeal) in which the expiratory flow is limited at high lung volumes but not at lower lung volumes. RV, residual volume; TLC, total lung capacity.

with an electronic pneumotachometer in which flow rate is measured directly and is integrated against time to yield volume.

Airway resistance is defined by the pressure required to produce a given flow rate and is expressed in units of centimeters of water pressure per liter per second of airflow. Airway resistance is measured in a body plethysmograph. Airway resistance at low lung volumes is higher than that measured at high lung volumes owing to the increase in the diameter of the airways during inspiration. This can be taken into account by multiplying the airway resistance by the lung volume at which the measurements were taken; the resulting measurement is called the *specific airway resistance*. Measurements of airway resistance primarily reflect changes in the larger, central airways; the peripheral airways, although small, have a relatively large total cross-sectional area and contribute approximately one fourth or less of the total pulmonary resistance.

Another important function of the airways is humidification of inspired air. At 37°C, air saturated with water vapor contains 43 mg of water per liter; at room temperature, air contains only 10 to 15 mg of water per liter, depending on the relative humidity. Thus, a large amount of water must be added to the inspired air. During normal nasal breathing, a major portion of the humidification occurs in the upper airway (above the glottis), but further warming and humidification take place in the trachea and mainstem bronchi. When the nose is bypassed, by mouth breathing or an artificial airway, the lower airways must assume a much greater role in humidification and warming. Failure to achieve adequate humidification may result in airway obstruction by inspissated secretions.

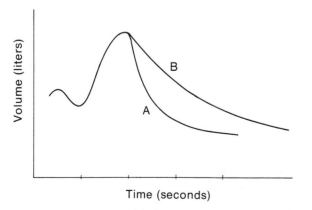

FIGURE 75–3. This spirogram shows forced expiratory maneuvers. Curve A represents a normal tracing, in which approximately 86% of the vital capacity (VC) is expelled in the first second (FEV_1 [expiratory flow rate]/VC = 0.86). Curve B is an abnormal tracing recorded from a patient with airway obstruction (FEV_1/VC = 0.49). The administration of a bronchodilator will usually result in an increase in FEV_1 in a patient with physiologic airway obstruction.

Important Derangements in Airway Function

Mechanical obstruction of the airways may be the result of extrinsic compression (as by mass lesions or enlarged great vessels) but more commonly is due to an intrinsic airway lesion. There are many causes of intrinsic airway obstruction, including endobronchial masses, airway stenosis (congenital or acquired), aspirated foreign body, mucosal edema, and increased tracheobronchial secretions. The single most common cause of chronic obstruction is increased secretions associated with decreased airway clearance (as in chronic bronchitis or cystic fibrosis).

Physiologic obstruction is most often the result of increased bronchomotor tone (bronchospasm). This is usually transient and reversible but may be intractable and life-threatening (status asthmaticus). In an asthma attack, several mechanisms operate to produce obstruction, including increased bronchomotor tone, increased secretions, increased viscosity of secretions, mucosal edema, and impaired mucociliary transport. Bronchomotor tone is increased by parasympathetic effectors and may be decreased by beta-adrenergic–stimulating agents or by parasympatholytic agents such as atropine. Physiologic airway obstruction may also be the result of decreased bronchomotor tone, which may produce increased compliance of the airway walls. If the airways are too compliant, as in bronchiectasis or bronchomalacia, collapse may occur during exhalation, and air is trapped in the lung. Diffuse distal airway obstruction, as occurs with asthma or bronchiolitis, may lead to airway collapse with air trapping because of the increased intrathoracic pressure generated in the effort to overcome the expiratory resistance. This may to some extent be overcome by partial glottic closure during exhalation ("grunting") or pursed-lip breathing so that the major pressure drop occurs at the glottis or lips. In much the same way and for the same reasons, an infant with surfactant deficiency grunts to maintain a higher intrathoracic pressure during exhalation. During mechanical ventilation of patients with distal airway obstruction or surfactant deficiency, elevation of the end-expiratory pressure may help maintain airway patency and improve gas exchange.

The dynamics of the trachea are different from those of other airways, since part of the trachea lies outside the thorax. The extrathoracic trachea is, in effect, surrounded by atmospheric pressure, which remains constant, in contrast to the intrathoracic trachea, which is surrounded by the varying pressures of the intrathoracic space. The extrathoracic trachea tends to collapse during inspiration, whereas the intrathoracic trachea tends to collapse during expiration (see Fig. 75–1). Thus, a patient with tracheomalacia may have both inspiratory stridor and expiratory wheeze. Relaxation of the smooth muscle of the tracheal wall may increase the compliance of the membranous portion of the wall, which normally tends to invaginate when intrathoracic pressure is increased. Because of this, patients with tracheomalacia may have increased expiratory obstruction after administration of a bronchodilator, owing to loss of tracheal (and large airway) muscle tone.

The Pulmonary Parenchyma

The pulmonary parenchyma can be considered to consist of the terminal airways, alveoli, pulmonary capillary bed, and their supporting tissues. The functional unit of the lung is the alveolar/capillary interface, across which gas exchange takes place.

Structure

Alveoli first appear as outpouchings in the walls of respiratory bronchioles; they are more numerous in the alveolar ducts, which terminate in a cluster of alveolar sacs. Each alveolus is a rough hexagon, with one side open to the alveolar duct. The number of alveoli increases about tenfold from birth to adulthood, when it averages 300 to 400 million, with a total surface area of 40 to 100 m². The alveolar walls, or septa, are composed of two types of epithelial cells, reticular and elastic fibers, a thin basement membrane, and the capillary endothelium. Capillaries make up the majority of the septa. Small holes in the septa between adjacent alveoli (alveolar pores) provide an alternative route for movement of gases. Type I alveolar epithelial cells have a thin cytoplasm through which gases diffuse readily. Type II alveolar epithelial cells are rich in mitochondria and endoplasmic reticulum and actively synthesize and secrete surfactant.

The patency of the smallest airways is dependent on the elastic properties of the lung parenchyma, since these airways have no cartilaginous support. When lung elasticity is reduced, as in old age or with emphysema, collapse of the smaller airways during exhalation may result in air trapping and impaired ventilation.

Function and Major Derangements of Pulmonary Parenchyma

The major function of the lungs and respiratory system is gas exchange, for which there are three major requirements: pulmonary capillary blood flow, alveolar ventilation, and diffusion of gases across the alveolar capillary membrane.

Perfusion

Under normal circumstances, the entire right ventricular output passes through the pulmonary arteries before returning to the left atrium. The regional distribution of pulmonary blood flow is regulated by the pulmonary arterioles, which in turn respond to the partial pressure of oxygen in the adjacent alveoli. Alveolar hypoxia results in pulmonary arteriolar constriction, which helps maintain a uniform ratio of perfusion to ventilation. Gravitational effects may also be important, as blood flow to dependent portions of the lung is increased.

Ventilation

The diaphragm and the accessory muscles of respiration interact with the rigid chest wall to produce the negative intrathoracic pressure that is necessary for flow of air into the lungs. Relaxation of the muscles combined with elastic recoil of the lung parenchyma increases intrathoracic pressure and results in exhalation. Forced exhalation is accomplished by contraction of the abdominal muscles and the internal intercostal muscles.

The regional distribution of ventilation depends on several factors: distribution of pressures, distribution of resistance and compliance, and rate and depth of respiration. In unilateral diaphragmatic paralysis, intrathoracic pressure on the paralyzed side is less negative, and therefore ventilation is impaired on that side. Areas of the lung with high airway resistance or low compliance are relatively poorly ventilated. At low respiratory frequencies, the distribution of ventilation is relatively even regardless of the distribution of airway resistance; however, as respiratory frequency increases, ventilation is shunted preferentially to the areas of the lung having the lowest airway resistance. Deeper inspirations not only result in a larger tidal volume but also tend to open relatively less compliant areas of lung, thus increasing their ventilation.

Compliance is defined as the change in lung volume per unit change in transpulmonary pressure. In practice, compliance is more useful as a concept than as data, since its accurate measurement is relatively complex. Compliance is decreased by the normal elastic forces in the lung and by surface tension in the alveoli as well as by pathologic processes such as pneumonia, pulmonary edema, and interstitial fibrosis. Surfactant reduces surface tension, thus increasing pulmonary compliance.

Because the alveoli are so small (the average diameter is approximately 0.25 mm), they have a significant amount of surface tension, which tends to make them collapse. This is countered by the presence of surfactant, which markedly reduces surface tension, especially during deflation of the lung. Surfactant is composed mostly of dipalmitoyl lecithin and a protein component and is synthesized in type II alveolar cells. The metabolic pathway matures at approximately 32 to 33 weeks in the human fetus, and infants born before that time usually have surfactant deficiency with the clinical syndrome of hyaline membrane disease (respiratory distress syndrome). The stress of birth or prolonged labor results in the induction of the enzymes of this pathway in the immature newborn, as does exogenous administration of corticosteroids. Approximately 24 to 48 hours are required for full induction of the pathway and synthesis of sufficient surfactant to prevent hyaline membrane disease. Hypoxia and metabolic acidosis interfere with both enzyme induction and surfactant production and may contribute to the development of surfactant deficiency in a mature infant.

Surfactant deficiency increases alveolar surface tension and reduces pulmonary compliance, so more inspiratory effort is required to achieve adequate tidal volume. The functional residual capacity is decreased, and many alveoli may become completely atelectatic during expiration. Atelectasis and low functional residual capacity result in intrapulmonary shunting of blood and reduced arterial oxygen tension despite increased inspired oxygen concentrations. Alveolar collapse may be reduced or prevented by application of a constant positive distending pressure to the alveoli (continuous positive airway pressure or continuous negative pressure applied to the thorax). This increases pulmonary compliance and reduces the work of breathing. In patients whose ventilation is being assisted mechanically, positive end-expiratory pressure accomplishes the same goal. The maintenance of a constant distending pressure, regardless of the mechanism by which it is produced, has greatly reduced mortality due to neonatal respiratory distress. Constant distending pressure is also used effectively in patients beyond the neonatal period who for some reason have lost surfactant (e.g., as a result of shock lung) or who have poor compliance.

Matching of perfusion and ventilation is a factor of major importance in gas exchange. "Wasted" ventilation occurs when areas of lung are ventilated but not perfused, but this does not contribute to arterial desaturation. Wasted perfusion (areas of the lung are perfused but not ventilated) results in arterial hypoxemia by mixing of the unoxygenated pulmonary arterial blood with the pulmonary venous return. Pulmonary arteriolar constriction in response to low alveolar oxygen tension is the most important mechanism for maintaining even distribution of perfusion and ventilation. Ventilation/perfusion mismatching due to uneven distribution of ventilation is the most common cause of hypoxemia.

Another major factor in gas exchange is the ratio of anatomic or physiologic dead space to tidal volume. Physiologic dead space is the volume of air contained in the conducting airways that does not reach the alveoli and in the areas of the lung that are ventilated but not perfused. Normally, the dead space is approximately 30% of tidal volume. With disease that decreases the tidal volume or results in wasted ventilation, this ratio increases, and the per minute volume must be increased to maintain the same effective alveolar ventilation. Examples of conditions that may produce an increased ratio of dead space to tidal volume include restrictive lung disease, severe obstructive lung disease, chest trauma, pneumothorax, and hypoventilation due to depressant drugs.

The regulation of respiration rate as well as tidal volume can be considered to have three major components: sensors (chemoreceptors and mechanical receptors), effectors (lungs and respiratory muscles), and the controller (the central nervous system).

Arterial chemoreceptors in the carotid and aortic bodies respond to changes in the arterial oxygen tension by increasing their output when the arterial oxygen tension decreases. Likewise, acidosis or an increase in arterial carbon dioxide tension results in increased chemoreceptor activity. Central chemoreceptors in the medulla respond to changes in cerebrospinal fluid pH. Since the cerebrospinal fluid bicarbonate concentration equilibrates slowly with that in the blood, the medullary chemoreceptor is essentially a carbon dioxide sensor. With long-standing hypercapnia and metabolic compensation (increased bicarbonate), the response of this chemoreceptor may be blunted, leaving the oxygen receptors as the primary functioning sensor. Since the activity of the peripheral arterial oxygen sensor begins to fall off rapidly as the arterial oxygen tension rises above 100 Torr, it is evident that administering oxygen to chronically hypercapnic patients may deprive them of much of their respiratory drive.

Pulmonary stretch receptors within the airway smooth

muscle are activated by inflation of the lungs and reflexively inhibit inspiration (the Hering-Breuer reflex). Central control of respiration may be a voluntary, cortical function, but automatic respiration is a brain stem function. A number of different nuclei and tracts are involved in the generation of respiratory rhythm, the integration of efferent and afferent signals, and the responses to various respiratory stimuli.

Under normal circumstances, arterial carbon dioxide tension is the most important factor controlling overall ventilatory function; as it rises, so does minute ventilation. In most healthy subjects, minute ventilation increases by at least 1 L/minute per Torr of carbon dioxide; the sensitivity to carbon dioxide is greater in younger subjects. The hypoxic respiratory drive is a nearly linear function of the desaturation of arterial hemoglobin, even though the chemoreceptors respond directly to changes in arterial oxygen tension. The individual response to hypoxia is variable and may be diminished in patients with chronic hypoxia.

Diffusion

The final essential component to effective gas exchange is diffusion. Both oxygen and carbon dioxide must diffuse across the alveolar capillary membrane. The rate of diffusion of carbon dioxide is much greater than that of oxygen (by approximately 20-fold) and is usually not limited by diffusion. On the other hand, diffusion of oxygen may be impaired when the alveolar capillary membrane is thickened by disease (e.g., interstitial pneumonitis or fibrosis, or pulmonary edema), and arterial hypoxemia may result. The diffusing capacity of the lung for oxygen (DLO_2) is estimated by measuring the diffusing capacity for carbon monoxide ($DLCO$).

Pulmonary Defense Mechanisms

Pulmonary defense mechanisms can be divided into four different categories: mechanical, neurologic, humoral, and cellular.

Mechanical Defense Mechanisms

Mechanical defense mechanisms begin at the nares, where the nasal hairs provide an important filtration function for large particulates. Turbulent airflow over the turbinates results in the deposition of many particles on the nasal mucosa. The particles that survive in the airstream beyond the nose (usually smaller than about 10 μm) are then trapped in the mucus layer lining the airways, either by impaction or (in peripheral airways) by sedimentation. The depth to which particles penetrate the lung is a function of the size and density of the particles. Particles trapped in the mucus layer are removed from the lung by mucociliary transport, coughing, or both. Particles that reach the alveolar spaces are removed by phagocytic cells. Another vitally important mechanical defense is cough, which may remove aspirated fluid as well as particles and secretions.

Mucociliary transport serves to remove not only inhaled particulate matter but also secretions and cellular debris from the airways. The importance of mucociliary transport in maintaining pulmonary homeostasis is emphasized by patients with immotile cilia, who have chronic bronchitis, sinusitis, and bronchiectasis at an early age. These patients also have chronic otitis because of failure of ciliary transport in the eustachian tube.

Effective mucociliary transport requires the concurrent function of a number of elements, including the number and distribution of cilia (or ciliated cells). Areas of squamous metaplasia may occur after various forms of insult and result in diminished mucus transport. Ciliary beat frequency (normally 15 to 20 beats per second) and the direction of coordinated ciliary beat are important aspects of effective mucociliary function. The mucus layer (sometimes referred to as the "gel" layer) floats on the periciliary fluid and is propelled along by the tips of the cilia. High viscosity and effective intermolecular cross-bridging between the adjacent mucous glycoprotein molecules are necessary for effective mucociliary transport. This has clinical relevance, since the administration of mucolytic agents such as N-acetylcysteine may liquefy mucus and result in pooling of secretions rather than normal clearance. The periciliary fluid must have appropriate viscoelastic properties and must be of the correct depth. If this layer is relatively dehydrated, the tips of the cilia may be crushed by the overlying mucus. If this layer is too deep, the mucus may float above the tips of the cilia. In either case, mucociliary transport is impaired.

Many extrinsic factors may affect mucociliary transport. Trauma to the mucosa, as may occur with intubation or bronchoscopy, may impair transport until the mucosal damage has been repaired. Some viral infections, particularly influenza, produce a marked sloughing of ciliated cells, and many weeks may be required to achieve normal function again (which may explain the high incidence of bacterial superinfections associated with influenzal pneumonia). Bacterial infection or nonspecific inflammation may also interfere with mucus transport.

Dehydration of the tracheobronchial secretions reduces mucociliary transport. Thus, it is important to provide additional humidification of inspired air when normal humidification is impaired (as during intubation). Cigarette smoking and many disease states also interfere with effective mucociliary function. These include chronic bronchitis, cystic fibrosis, asthma, vitamin A deficiency, and immotile cilia syndrome.

Mucociliary function may be improved by the administration of beta-adrenergic–stimulating agents, by restoring normal humidification, by correcting nutritional or metabolic abnormalities, and by eliminating extrinsic factors such as cigarette smoking.

Neurologic Defense Mechanisms

Neurologic pulmonary defense mechanisms primarily involve avoidance reflexes. A noxious odor stimulates bronchospasm or even apnea to reduce the penetration of the offending material into the lung. On a more integrated basis, an organism will attempt to remove itself from a noxious environment.

Cough is also a neurologic defense mechanism in that it is a reflex involving the participation of the larynx, airways, and respiratory musculature and may be impaired by blocking of the sensory pathways.

Humoral Defense Mechanisms

Humoral defense mechanisms in the lung involve both local and systemic immune responses. Secretory immunoglobulin, produced locally in the upper airways, does not fix complement, nor does it have much opsonizing activity, but it is important in neutralization of viruses and toxins. In addition, it may agglutinate bacteria and reduce bacterial attachment to tissue.

Large amounts of lysozyme are secreted in the epithelium of the upper airways and may be important in antibacterial defenses.

In the lower airways, IgG is the predominant immunoglobulin. There is both local production (mediated by the bronchial-associated lymphoid tissue) and transudation from the vascular bed. Other proteins, such as IgM and complement, are found in small quantities in the pulmonary secretions, but all proteins enter the secretions more readily in the presence of inflammation.

Cellular Defense Mechanisms

The cellular defense mechanisms of the lung include alveolar macrophages, lymphocytes, and polymorphonuclear leukocytes. The alveolar macrophage is derived from blood monocytes, which are in turn derived from the bone marrow. The alveolar macrophage is a highly specialized cell and, in contrast to macrophages elsewhere in the body, is critically dependent on oxidative metabolism, becoming essentially nonfunctional at oxygen concentrations less than about 25 mm Hg. Alveolar macrophages are primarily responsible for removal of particulate debris, including dead or damaged cells, from the alveoli and terminal airways.

Alveolar macrophages depend to a great extent on chemotactic factors produced by lymphocytes, which invite macrophages (and neutrophils) into the lung and then make them feel at home. Mechanical factors may also result in mobilization of macrophage-particulate loads (such as are produced with cigarette smoking), which leads to a great increase in the number of macrophages recoverable from the lung by saline lavage. Activation of macrophages by lymphocyte factors results in increased production of lysosomal enzymes, enhanced phagocytosis, and other phenomena. Alveolar macrophages may in turn stimulate lymphocytes by initial processing of antigens to which the lymphocytes then respond specifically. Macrophages are very important in killing intracellular organisms (such as *Mycobacterium* and *Toxoplasma* organisms) as well as fungi, bacteria, and viruses. Activated macrophages are capable of recognizing and killing tumor cells.

Infections or other inflammatory reactions in the lung attract large numbers of polymorphonuclear leukocytes. These cells may be more important in dealing with established infection than are alveolar macrophages, since they are less dependent on oxygen and thus can operate within masses of secretions or hypoxic tissue.

REFERENCES

1. Afzelius BA. The immotilecilia syndrome: a microtubule associated defect. Crit Rev Biochem 19:63, 1985.
2. Berger AJ, Mitchell RA, Severinghaus JW. Regulation of respiration (three parts). N Engl J Med 29:194, 1977.
3. Derene JPH, Macklem PT, Roussos CH. The respiratory muscles: mechanics, control, and pathophysiology (two parts). Am Rev Respir Dis 118:119, 1978.
4. Ellis H, Feldman S. Anatomy for Anaesthetists, 3rd ed. Oxford, Blackwell Scientific Publications, 1977.
5. Green GM, Jakab GJ, Low RB, et al. Defense mechanisms of the respiratory membrane. Am Rev Respir Dis 115:479, 1977.
6. Proctor DF. The upper airways. I. Nasal physiology and defense of the lungs. Am Rev Respir Dis 115:97, 1977.
7. Proctor DF. The upper airways. II. The larynx and trachea. Am Rev Respir Dis 115:315, 1977.
8. Thurlbeck WM. Postnatal growth and development of the lung. Am Rev Respir Dis 111:803, 1975.
9. Wanner A. Clinical aspects of mucociliary transport. Am Rev Respir Dis 116:73, 1977.
10. West JB. Ventilation-perfusion relationships. Am Rev Respir Dis 116:919, 1977.
11. Wilmott RW, Khurana-Hershey G, Stark JM. Current concepts on pulmonary host defense mechanisms in children. Curr Opin Pediatr 12:187, 2000.

76

Methods of Examination

Margaretha L. Casselbrant, M.D., Ph.D. and Cuneyt M. Alper, M.D.

In the evaluation of the pediatric airway, the history and physical examination and radiographic and laboratory evaluations differ greatly from those of the adult patient. It is the purpose of this chapter to bring together information from different sources and to organize it in a framework that the otolaryngologist can use to facilitate evaluation of the pediatric patient's airway.

Any examination of the airway should answer three questions: Is the airway normal? If the airway is abnormal, is the pathologic condition in the upper or lower airway? If the airway is abnormal, what is the nature of the pathologic condition?

To answer the first question, the physician must evaluate the airway in terms of air movement (respiratory effort), ventilation (the intake of oxygen and the exhalation of carbon dioxide), the quality of the vocal output (including cry and cough), and the ease of swallowing (freedom from drooling or evidence of aspiration) (see Chapter 78).

If the airway is abnormal, it is extremely important for the physician to determine whether the abnormality is in the upper or the lower airway and then to establish a differential diagnosis. This chapter seeks to help the physician acquire an airway examination technique that will provide the answers to the three key questions so that a diagnosis and a treatment plan can be made.

History

The general difficulty in obtaining a careful and precise history from the pediatric patient is widely appreciated. The necessary historical information must be obtained from the child's parents, from other physicians who have seen the child, and from all other appropriate sources.

The physician should immediately start gathering information on the potential urgency of the airway compromise. This should precede starting a detailed history and complete physical examination. In the presence of clues for potential urgency, a focused history should target and rule out some of the relatively common emergencies of the pediatric age group.

A quick way to rule out most of the emergency conditions is to ask these questions: (1) Is the condition of recent onset? (2) Is it progressive? (3) Is the patient newborn? A negative answer to all three questions would most likely allow enough time to obtain a detailed history and perform a complete physical examination. A positive answer to any of these questions, on the other hand, should alert the physician to a potential airway emergency, and targeted history taking should accompany rapid assessment of vital functions with focused examination of the airway. Along with obtaining more information from the parents or caregivers, rapid assessment of certain signs and symptoms should include the patient's skin color; chest movements; retractions; presence, severity, and phase of the stridor; adequacy of air exchange; level of consciousness; heart rate; intraoral signs of infection, swelling, or poor handling of secretions; use of accessory muscles of respiration; and nasal flaring. The history and physical examination should aim to rule out pediatric airway emergencies such as foreign body, acute epiglottitis, croup, laryngeal papillomatosis, congenital abnormalities, and respiratory distress due to nonobstructive causes. If any of these diagnoses are suspected, steps for further management should be started according to the diagnosis and severity of the condition. Decisions for urgent airway management should cover immediate supportive treatment (oxygen, heliox, racemic epinephrine, steroid), imaging, admission, intubation, transport, or taking the patient to the operating room for endoscopy or tracheotomy. Once the focused history and examination have ruled out a potential emergency, the complete history and physical examination should be obtained.

Age of the patient at presentation, or age of onset of symptoms, provides critical information on differential diagnosis. The pediatric patient's history begins with the nature of the mother's pregnancy and the delivery of the patient. In dealing with a newborn infant, it is important to recognize the significance of medications the mother may have taken or infections she may have had during pregnancy. Prematurity is an important factor in establishing a diagnosis of respiratory distress syndrome in the neonate. A traumatic delivery is known to be a factor in some cases of vocal cord paralysis or nasal trauma, either of which may result in airway obstruction in the neonate.

Respiratory distress that presents at birth suggests bilateral choanal atresia, laryngeal web, or laryngeal atresia, which are rare. Distress presenting 1 to 3 weeks after delivery suggests subglottic stenosis, or cysts of the subglottis, vallecula, or saccule (see Chapter 84). When respiratory distress presents 1 to 3 months after delivery, a subglottic hemangioma should be suspected and careful examination made for cutaneous manifestations of this disorder, which is found in approximately half of these neonates (see Chapter 91). Laryngomalacia often progresses and becomes severe at 2 to 3 months of age. Laryngeal papillomas can be found in infants but are usually diagnosed in older children.

A history of respiratory distress with feeding during the neonatal period suggests the possibility of a congenital anomaly resulting in nasal obstruction, difficulty in swallowing or aspiration, such as choanal atresia, a tracheoesophageal fistula, vocal cord paralysis, congenital posterior cleft of the larynx, cricopharyngeal achalasia, or gastroesophageal reflux disease (see Chapters 69 and 83).

If the onset of respiratory distress has occurred immediately after a surgical procedure with intubation, one may suspect that inspissated subglottic mucus or possibly subglottic edema is the cause of the problem. However, if several hours pass after intubation before distress develops, the obstruction is more likely to be related to traumatic edema of the glottic and subglottic region. Development of distress within 2 to 3 weeks after intubation may indicate an early subglottic stenosis. Respiratory distress or hoarseness 2 to 3 months after intubation raises the possibility of vocal cord granuloma formation.

Stridor that occurs after an apparently simple upper respiratory tract infection with cough lasting for a few days is indicative of laryngotracheobronchitis. The onset of supraglottitis (epiglottitis) is usually rapid and can occur within a few hours. Immunization of children with *Haemophilus influenzae* type b (Hib) vaccine has reduced the incidence of epiglottitis dramatically. There are children, particularly immigrants, however, who have not received the Hib vaccine. Also, although extremely rare, the same clinical presentation caused by other bacteria can be seen in immunocompromised children. A child with epiglottitis is usually in an older age group (3 to 6 years) than a child with laryngotracheobronchitis (6 months to 3 years). Episodic coughing associated with wheezing and dyspnea should lead the physician to evaluate the patient for asthma (see Chapter 86), aspiration, or gastroesophageal reflux disease.

Physical Examination

General Pediatric Examination

In some instances, a child is observed to have respiratory distress not associated with laryngotracheal abnormality. For example, several supralaryngeal conditions can produce respiratory distress. Bilateral complete choanal atresia usually produces severe respiratory distress immediately at birth, because the newborn infant is an obligatory nose breather. The micrognathia and macroglossia of the Robin sequence also produce respiratory distress secondary to upper airway obstruction. Hypertrophy of the tonsils and adenoids has been shown to obstruct the airway and in more severe cases can result in cor pulmonale. Retropharyngeal and parapharyngeal abscesses, as well as abscess formation in the floor of the mouth, may compro-

mise the oropharyngeal airway and result in respiratory distress (see Chapters 62 and 100).

Neck masses, such as a large lymphangioma or hemangioma, may compress the laryngeal and cervical tracheal airway. A large thyroglossal duct cyst, lingual thyroid gland, or branchial cleft cyst may also produce compression of the airway. Pressure from a foreign body in the cervical segment of the esophagus can result in respiratory distress from airway compression (see Chapters 71 and 97).

Extrinsic compression of the trachea by vascular anomalies such as a complete vascular ring, innominate artery, or left aberrant pulmonary artery can cause respiratory distress (see Chapter 84). Congenital anomalies involving the central nervous system, such as the Arnold-Chiari malformation, as well as inflammatory and neoplastic diseases involving the central nervous system, can cause respiratory distress (see Chapter 87). In particular, Arnold-Chiari malformation is associated with bilateral vocal cord paralysis. Certain systemic disorders, including high fever and anemia, severe biochemical alterations such as the metabolic acidosis occurring with diarrhea or diabetes, and respiratory alkalosis (e.g., salicylate toxicity), produce tachypnea. Metabolic alkalosis, resulting from pyloric stenosis and other causes of intractable vomiting, and respiratory acidosis, resulting from the ingestion of opiates or tranquilizers, can produce a marked slowing of the respiratory rate (bradypnea).

Airway and Respiration in General

Inspection

The shape of the thorax varies with age. In the newborn and infant, the thorax is round when viewed from above, but with increasing age it becomes more oval and appears flatter anteriorly and posteriorly. Asymmetry of thoracic expansion may be observed with unilateral obstruction of one mainstem bronchus. The side with diminished motion may appear to be underinflated in the presence of a complete obstruction or overinflated in the presence of a ball valve obstruction. Paradoxical movement of half of the thorax occurs when one side of the thorax moves out of phase with the other. This may result from obstruction of a mainstem bronchus or may be seen in association with pneumothorax. It arises when there is a negative intrathoracic pressure on inspiration without subsequent inflation of the lung. Congenital malformation of the thorax, such as Jeune syndrome or fused ribs, can occur but is rare.

This element of the examination begins with observation of the respiratory rate, which is most accurately measured when the child is asleep or completely relaxed. The normal respiratory rate varies with the age of the child, being rapid in the neonate and much slower in the adolescent. Tachypnea is an increased rate of respiration. This is seen normally after exertion or when the child is anxious but is also seen with a high fever, severe anemia, metabolic acidosis, or respiratory alkalosis. Tachypnea also occurs with bronchiolitis, or in lung parenchymal diseases such as pneumonia, pleural effusion, asthma, and pulmonary edema. Bradypnea is an abnormally slow respiratory rate and is seen in children with metabolic alkalosis, respiratory acidosis, and certain disorders of the central nervous system.

After measuring the rate, the examiner should observe and document the respiratory rhythm. Abnormalities of respiratory rhythm include periodic breathing, in which the patient breathes normally for about 15 seconds and then stops breathing for a period of 5 to 10 seconds, and apneic spells, in which the nonbreathing interval is greater than 10 seconds. Apnea occurring during sleep is called *sleep apnea*, and the presence or absence of respiratory efforts during the apnea episodes suggests an obstructive versus a central cause, respectively (see Chapter 62). Cheyne-Stokes breathing is a waxing and waning of the depth of respiration followed by periods of apnea. This is observed in children with congestive heart failure, cerebral injury, and increased intracranial pressure. Biot breathing is a condition in which the child takes one or two breaths followed by long periods of apnea; it is associated with severe brain damage from trauma or encephalitis.

Next, the examiner should note the depth of respiration. Variations from normal include hyperpnea (generally seen with tachypnea) and hypopnea (generally seen with bradypnea). Trepopnea is the condition in which the affected person finds it much easier to breathe when lying on one side. The child lies with the better side upward.

Finally, the examiner should note the ease of respiration. The normal child has relatively effortless respiration, known as *eupnea*. With some respiratory disorders, the child finds it much easier to breathe while sitting in the upright position (orthopnea), whereas in other disorders, breathing is difficult in all positions (dyspnea).

Observation of these features of the general respiratory pattern is followed by careful inspection of the child for other signs of respiratory distress. Specific features that may be seen in respiratory distress are head movement with respiration (head bobbing), flaring of the nasal alae with inspiration, circumoral pallor, and suprasternal and intercostal retractions. Intercostal retraction is a primary sign of respiratory obstruction and results from the unusually high negative pressure associated with labored inspiration.

Palpation

The infant larynx and trachea are soft and compressible. The larynx and hyoid are quite high in the neck and are thus protected by the mandible from injury. The most prominent landmark in an infant or a young child is the anterior cricoid arch rather than the thyroid lamina. With increasing age, the cartilaginous framework of these structures becomes firmer, and they gradually descend to their adult location. Landmarks such as the superior notch of the thyroid cartilage then become easier to identify. The hyoid bone also becomes a prominent landmark structure.

The trachea may normally be located very slightly to the right of the midline at the root of the neck. Deviation of the trachea from the midline can occur as a result of pathologic processes in the neck or inside the thorax. The first step is to determine whether the deviation is dynamic or fixed. In the case of a dynamic deviation, there is a perceptible movement in the trachea with respiration (like a pendulum) as the mediastinum shifts owing to overinflation or underinflation of one lung. The trachea may be deviated from the midline in a fixed or static manner by pathologic processes that push or pull it to one side. Examples of the latter condition include tracheal displacement secondary to a large branchial cyst, cervical or mediastinal lymphadenopathy, or neoplasms of the thyroid or thymus.

Fracture of the larynx is unusual in the pediatric age group because of the high location and protection behind the mandible as well as the elasticity of the airway cartilages and the great mobility of these structures in the child. Laryngeal fracture or laryngotracheal separation may result from a very forceful impact, such as striking the dashboard of an automobile during an accident, particularly with the head extended (padded dashboard syndrome). There are also numerous accounts of laryngotracheal separation associated with motorbike and snowmobile accidents. Palpation of the larynx reveals areas of localized tenderness and may disclose palpable abnormalities of the laryngeal cartilage together with crepitus. It should be remembered that such severe trauma might also cause esophageal and cervical spine injuries.

Neck masses involving the larynx and cervical trachea are uncommon, but when they occur, they may be of any consistency to the touch, from totally compressible to hard. A compressible mass adjacent to the larynx suggests the possibility of a laryngocele (rare in children), while a soft mass adjacent to the larynx may represent a congenital cyst or a laryngomucopyocele. A firm mass adjacent to the larynx or cervical trachea might be a chondroma or chondrosarcoma (see Chapter 97).

Subcutaneous emphysema is characterized by a distinctive crepitant sensation on palpation of the neck in a child with apparent neck swelling. It indicates a break in the integrity of the airway at some point between the pharynx and the terminal bronchioles, which may have resulted from trauma, instrumentation, or spontaneous rupture of the pulmonary alveoli (as may occur in emphysema). Radiographic and endoscopic evaluation are necessary in most instances to localize the area of airway injury. Clostridial infection may result in gas accumulation in the neck, but this is extremely rare. Tracheal foreign bodies may cause a "palpatory thud," owing to a freely moving foreign body, which is best felt with a finger on the trachea.

Auscultation

Voice, Cry, and Cough

Important diagnostic information can sometimes be obtained by listening carefully to the child's voice, cry, and cough. Variations from the normal voice should be characterized precisely as muffled, coarse (gruff), breathy (aspirate), or high-pitched.

Supraglottic. A muffled quality to the voice ("hot potato voice") suggests the presence of a supraglottic obstructive process that is altering the normal modulation of the sound produced at the glottic level. A muffled voice may be noted in patients with acute epiglottitis, a large supraglottic laryngeal cyst, a retropharyngeal abscess, large tonsils, or a peritonsillar abscess.

Glottic. A coarse or "gruff" voice suggests excessive vocal cord bulk either from swelling of the cords, or a tumor or papilloma that is interfering with the normal vibratory pattern of the true cord. Examples of this type of problem are acute and chronic laryngitis, hemangioma, and certain endocrine disorders, such as myxedema.

A breathy vocal quality is produced by the presence of a lesion that interferes with normal vocal cord approximation. This can be caused by recurrent respiratory papillomatosis, postintubation granuloma, vocal nodules, or a foreign body. A breathy (aspirate) vocal quality is also produced by vocal cord paralysis (especially unilateral).

A high-pitched voice suggests excessive vocal cord tension or anatomically shortened vocal folds. A high-pitched voice is heard in children with a congenital web at the anterior commissure or with underdevelopment of the larynx.

Aphonia (inability to vocalize) is extremely rare. It may result from the presence of a foreign body lodged between the vocal cords, may be due to cricoarytenoid joint fixation, or may be a manifestation of a psychogenic disorder.

The cri du chat syndrome is a chromosomal disorder in which the newborn infant cry is quite similar to the mewing sound of a cat.

Subglottic. Subglottic lesions usually do not cause any changes in the voice. A dry, barking, or brassy cough in infants and young children is usually associated with obstruction of the larger airways, as with subglottic stenosis, aberrant innominate artery, tracheomalacia, or croup. In older children, such a cough is most commonly psychogenic. A loose productive cough is most probably associated with an infectious process of the lower tracheobronchial tree, as in pneumonia or chronic bronchitis. Cough associated with throat clearing may be related to asthma, gastroesophageal reflux disease, or postnasal drainage.

Upper Airway

The respiratory sounds heard when the stethoscope is placed over the larynx and cervical trachea are described as *tubular.* These are high pitched and harsh.

Stridor is a harsh, high-pitched, loud sound produced by high-velocity airflow through a small passage. It may occur predominantly during the inspiratory phase of respiration or during exhalation. Since the upper airway effectively decreases in size during inspiration, most obstructive lesions of the larynx and cervical trachea are associated with inspiratory stridor. Expiratory stridor is usually associated with intrathoracic lesions or tracheobronchomalacia but may occur associated with inspiratory stridor with subglottic stenosis or glottic stenosis. Although stridor is audible without the aid of a stethoscope, this instrument may be used to localize the area of maximum obstruction.

Laryngomalacia (congenital laryngeal stridor) is the most commonly seen obstructive disorder in the newborn but is rarely severe enough to require surgical intervention. Most of these children are better by 12 to 18 months of age.

Croup (infectious laryngotracheobronchitis) and acute epiglottitis are characterized by the relatively sudden onset of inspiratory stridor and respiratory distress (see Chapter 85). Subglottic hemangioma is characterized by the slow onset of inspiratory stridor (most commonly between the ages of 1 and 3 months). Juvenile papillomatosis of the larynx presents the same slow onset of inspiratory stridor plus hoarseness, usually between the ages of 1 and 3 years. A congenital web or cyst of the larynx may be suspected when there is noisy inspiration or abnormal cry at birth (see Chapter 83).

Lungs

Auscultation of a child's lungs is best accomplished with an adult stethoscope. This is not only more convenient but also provides more auditory information than is usually obtained with a pediatric stethoscope.

Foreign bodies can be localized in some patients by careful auscultation. There may be a wheezing sound that is maximal over the foreign body, as a reflection of diminished airway diameter and associated airflow turbulence. This asthmatoid wheeze is best heard when the patient is breathing with the mouth open. There may also be diminished breath sounds peripheral to the foreign body, and, on occasion, there may be an audible slap caused by the foreign body's moving with respiration, which is also best heard when the patient's mouth is open.

Breath sounds are noted to change as one moves from the tracheal airway to the periphery of the lungs. Tracheal sounds are high pitched, harsh, and tubular, whereas bronchial, bronchovesicular, and vesicular breath sounds are lower pitched, soft on inspiration, and usually absent on expiration. The latter are actually vibrations produced by the movement of air through the tubular tracheobronchial tree; they vary with the size of the tubular passage and the intensity or velocity of the airflow.

Suppressed breath sounds (softer than normal) indicate underventilation, a condition that occurs in atelectasis of the newborn with respiratory insufficiency; it may or may not be associated with dullness to percussion.

Rales, or crackles, are produced by small amounts of air bubbling through liquid. They are classified as fine (usually in the larger bronchioles) or coarse and are audible as a discontinuous crackling sound. It should be remembered that rales are not significant if they clear with coughing.

Rhonchi, or wheezes, are produced by air flowing past an obstruction at a high velocity, usually in association with some air turbulence. Rhonchi are classified as sibilant (high pitched) or sonorous (low pitched). They are persistent and musical and are usually heard during the expiratory phase in the lower airway, as opposed to the stridor heard in the upper airway. This is because lower-airway structures are larger during the inspiratory phase than during the expiratory phase.

A friction rub is a high-pitched squeaking sound that is

produced by movement of the inflamed pulmonary and thoracic pleural layers against each other. This condition is occasionally heard in children with pneumonia.

Percussion is useful in the detection of areas of decreased aeration. Dullness to percussion in a localized area suggests the presence of atelectasis, and hyper-resonance indicates overinflation of the underlying tissue and may be found in children with a foreign body that is functioning as a ball valve or in children with pneumothorax. It is also useful in the detection of a mediastinal shift.

Office Examination

Direct Examination

The examiner can see the epiglottis in most children by having the child open the mouth, protrude the tongue, and say "aah." Further depression of the tongue with a wooden blade may improve the view. A swollen, red epiglottis seen in this manner is occasionally all that is needed to make the diagnosis of acute epiglottitis. However, this procedure can provoke acute, total respiratory obstruction, which is to be avoided; in the presence of drooling and increased quantities of saliva in the pharynx and significant stridor, the examiner should avoid this procedure and proceed to the operating room to secure the airway.

Indirect Examination

Indirect examination of the larynx can be accomplished in most children older than 4 years of age if the child's confidence is obtained by careful explanation and reassurance. If the child has been properly prepared, it is usually unnecessary to spray the pharynx with a topical anesthetic. The patient should sit upright, in a chair with a light source behind it, while the examiner is in a position so that the light reflected from the head-mirror (head light) can be focused on the patient's mouth. The laryngeal mirror should be warmed and the temperature of the instrument tested on the skin of the physician. The child protrudes the tongue, which is then held in a piece of gauze between the examiner's thumb and index finger. The patient is asked to breathe in as relaxed a fashion as possible while the mirror is inserted into the patient's mouth to rest on the soft palate. The back of the tongue should not be touched by the mirror. The examiner, by focusing the light onto the mirror, is able to see the tongue base, hypopharynx and larynx, which should be examined systematically. The movement of the larynx and vocal cords can be seen when the patient vocalizes the sounds "aah" and "eee."

Endoscopy

Endoscopic examination in the office or in the hospital ward can be accomplished with some of the newer instruments. These include fiberoptic laryngoscopes and optical lens-mirror systems, which provide an excellent view of the larynx in a cooperative child.

The decision of whether to perform an office flexible

nasolaryngoscopic examination depends on the age and cooperation of the child as well as on the possible or likely sites of concern in the child's airway. If there is a suspicion that the airway obstruction is below the vocal cords, or if the severity of the signs or symptoms are such that it would not be safe to perform a flexible examination, a complete airway evaluation including flexible nasopharyngolaryngoscopy plus direct laryngoscopy and bronchoscopy and possible esophagoscopy in the operating room is warranted. Although a flexible nasolaryngeal examination could diagnose a supraglottic or glottic abnormality, a second airway abnormality below the vocal cords would be missed. Even if the likely site of the airway lesion is supraglottic or glottic, and symptoms and signs are not severe, it may not be possible to perform flexible nasolaryngoscopy with an uncooperative child. The child's response to the nasal examination or application of topical anesthesia via a spray or cotton may be good predictors of compliance with the flexible examination.

The fiberoptic laryngopharyngoscope using the Hopkins rod lens system with a 90-degree telescope can be used in the older child.[10] This method, like the mirror examination, demands cooperation from the patient. It has the advantage of uniform bright illumination and a wide-angle field. The patient is positioned as for mirror examination, sitting upright in a chair with the tongue held forward, and the instrument is passed through the mouth to rest on the palate. This provides an excellent view of the larynx and hypopharynx. However, to a large extent it has been replaced by the flexible fiberoptic nasopharyngolaryngoscope.

The flexible fiberoptic nasopharyngolaryngoscope is available in a number of sizes and is valuable in examination of the larynx and supralaryngeal area.[3, 9] The flexible nasopharyngolaryngoscope gives a good view of the nose, nasopharynx, and larynx and also allows a dynamic assessment of the palate and laryngeal function. A flexible nasopharyngolaryngoscope (Machida) with an outer diameter of 1.9 mm can easily be used to examine infants and young children. However, these very thin scopes have no side channel for suction or instrumentation and are easily damaged. General anesthesia is not required, although some children may require sedation. Figure 50–8 illustrates the flexible nasopharyngolaryngoscope.

Before endoscopy, one of the nasal passages is anesthetized with 2% lidocaine or tetracaine and decongested with phenylephrine or oxymetazoline. The instrument is then passed along the floor of the nasal passage into the nasopharynx. It is helpful at this stage if the patient can breathe through the nose to allow the palate to drop down, thereby exposing the epiglottis. The instrument is further advanced to reveal the larynx, which can now be examined with particular reference to appearance and mobility. Swallowing by the patient usually eliminates any saliva, which may impair the view. The examiner must be sure that a significant pathologic state is not missed by an incomplete examination due to an uncooperative child. The airway below the vocal cords may not be examined. Gonzalez et al[4] showed that in 18% of 103 children who underwent diagnostic laryngoscopy and bronchoscopy for airway obstruction, stridor, or both, two or more synchronous airway lesions were detected. Prinja and Manoukian[8] reported that 59 neonates in an intensive care unit who required rigid bronchoscopy were found to have an airway lesion and 75% of these lesions were found below the vocal cords. Synchronous airway lesions were found in 27 neonates and 41% of these lesions were also below the vocal cords. Thus these lesions would probably not have been identified with flexible nasopharyngolaryngoscope as the only procedure. Bluestone et al[1, 2] have strongly recommended against using awake flexible nasolaryngoscopy as the only procedure to assess the airway in neonates, infants, and children because of concerns for safety and missing airway lesions below the vocal cords.

Documentation

Both the flexible fiberoptic and the Hopkins rod lens systems permit documentation by still photography and video recording. Continuous video monitoring during a procedure improves the communication between the anesthesiologist and the surgeons. In addition, it is an excellent tool for teaching residents and other students in the operating room, and video recordings can also be used in more didactic sessions. If repeat evaluations of the airway are performed, previous documentation obtained by video recordings or prints can be used to determine improvement or deterioration of an airway condition. Also, parents and referring physicians can get a better understanding of the child's problem by having access to the photographic documentation.

Radiographic Evaluation

Radiographic studies of the larynx and tracheobronchial tree can be extremely valuable in supplementing the information obtained from the history and physical examination.

Plain radiographs of the upper and lower airway can provide information about the contour of the airway passages. A lateral, soft tissue radiograph of the neck is useful in the diagnosis of retropharyngeal abscess or acute epiglottitis (see Chapter 81). These views are taken with the patient's neck in the extended position and during inspiration, as flexion produces a marked widening of the normal retropharyngeal soft tissue shadow, simulating retropharyngeal infection and expiration.

The posteroanterior retropharyngeal view of the larynx and trachea can provide useful information. The normal, slight deviation of the trachea to the right may be exaggerated during expiration. When films are obtained during phonation and deep respiration, they may be useful in documenting a vocal cord paralysis. Asymmetry of the subglottic region is noted with a unilateral subglottic hemangioma (more common on the left side). Other irregularities in the contour of the airway can indicate external compression by vascular abnormalities or tumors, inflammatory narrowing of the subglottis (steeple sign) such as croup, tracheal stenosis, or a foreign body (see Chapter 81). Aluminum objects do not show up well on a radiograph, even though they are metallic. This is important in regard to the flip tops from aluminum cans, as they may

not be seen easily on radiographs unless they are viewed end-on.

Plain radiographs of the lower airway are useful in the detection of three types of atelectasis: that of the newborn (see Chapter 82); that due to a foreign body; and that which occurs postoperatively. Interstitial disease, such as pneumonia or an abscess, can also be seen on plain radiographs of the chest (see Chapter 85). Other diseases are characterized by the presence of hyperaeration, visible on the chest radiograph. This usually results from partial obstruction of the airway, which may be produced by asthma, cystic fibrosis, bronchiolitis, or the presence of a foreign body, with trapping of air.

Ball valving by a bronchial foreign body produces obstructive emphysema of the involved lung on the expiratory chest radiograph, and inspiration and expiration radiographs may help diagnose a nonradiopaque foreign body (see Chapter 90). Cinefluoroscopy is helpful in evaluating the dynamics of respiration and may be particularly helpful in the evaluation and localization of a foreign body. However, a normal study would not exclude a foreign body. Rigid bronchoscopy still has to be performed when a foreign body is suspected (see Chapter 90).

Xeroradiography provides a very crisp image of the airway wall by virtue of its ability to enhance the contrast between air and soft tissue. One disadvantage of this technique is that it exposes the child to more radiation than plain radiography.

Ultrasonography of the larynx provides a good analysis of cartilage and endolaryngeal structures and can also show the dynamic aspects of the larynx. It has been used for assessing vocal cord paralysis. Also it is useful in differentiating between a solid mass, a fluid-filled space such as a cyst, and an abscess and in evaluation of vascular anomalies in the chest (see Chapter 84).

Computed tomography (CT) has essentially replaced polytomography, as CT far surpasses polytomography in the ability to differentiate one tissue from another and also involves less radiation exposure (see Chapter 81). The air-bone and air–soft tissue interfaces are much clearer. The bone algorithm allows an excellent depiction of bone and soft tissue margins. CT also allows better definition of the cross-sectional area of the airway and has been used in the evaluation of laryngotracheal stenosis, laryngeal hemangioma, or laryngocele in the neonate. Intravenous contrast enhancement frequently provides a better depiction of inflammatory masses to differentiate between cellulitis and abscess. Markedly enhancing masses on CT may suggest a vascular lesion such as hemangioma, juvenile angiofibroma, arteriovenous malformation, or aneurysm.

Magnetic resonance imaging (MRI) is an excellent noninvasive method for evaluation of airway obstruction in children (see Chapter 81). MRI is far better than CT in soft tissue imaging and depiction of detailed anatomic structures in several planes without ionizing radiation or intravenous contrast media. However, the imaging time is much longer than for CT. MRI demonstrates well the trachea and its relation to surrounding mediastinal vascular structures. The cause of the tracheal compression and the degree and location of the collapse can be identified. Close correlation with the endoscopic findings and MRI is very useful in evaluating vascular compressions of the trachea and differentiating between vascular rings and slings, innominate artery compression, aortic arch anomalies, and pulmonary artery sling (see Chapter 84).

The use of CT and MRI may require sedation or sometimes general anesthesia in young children. The airway should always be secured before imaging studies are performed in a child with airway distress.

Contrast studies of the trachea and bronchus (tracheogram and bronchogram) are sometimes necessary to evaluate the nature and extent of certain pulmonary diseases (see Chapter 84). These studies are rarely indicated and should be done only when the results are important for decisions in major aspects of therapy. CT, MRI, and bronchoscopy have to a large extent replaced these studies.

Contrast studies of the esophagus (esophagograms) are often indicated in children with respiratory problems. These studies are useful in the detection of a vascular ring or sling, a tracheoesophageal fistula, which is best shown in the left oblique position, and in some cases of primary aspiration or persistent aspiration secondary to gastroesophageal reflux disease.

Angiography is the gold standard for assessing airway compression from a vascular anomaly, such as a right aortic arch, vascular duplication, or an anomalous vascular ring. However, owing to the risk of complications, it should be reserved for evaluation prior to cardiothoracic surgery if indicated. Instead, excellent noninvasive studies, such as magnetic resonance angiography and echocardiography, are preferred as first-line imaging methods.

Endoscopic Examination

The indications for endoscopy are both diagnostic and therapeutic. The diagnostic uses are to inspect structural or functional abnormalities and to obtain cultures and biopsy specimens. The therapeutic uses include removal of foreign bodies, removal of thickened secretions and bronchial lavage, removal of tumors (e.g., papillomas), dilatation of strictures, and provision of an airway in the obstructed child.

Direct Laryngoscopy

Direct laryngoscopy in the operating room is the primary technique for the definitive diagnosis and management of laryngeal disease. There is still some discussion of whether general anesthesia is required for direct laryngoscopy in infants. In the neonate and infant, the endoscopist may obtain an adequate assessment of the structures and mobility of the larynx without the use of anesthesia. However, flexible nasolaryngoscopy is a better method for assessing supraglottic and glottic structures and function than direct laryngoscopy, avoiding the distortion of the position and function of the structures. For example, assessment of the site and degree of supraglottic collapse in laryngomalacia may be inaccurate when the blade of the laryngoscope placed in the vallecula lifts the epiglottis up. It has been alleged that there is an increased likelihood of apnea in the obstructed child when general anesthesia

is used, but with modern anesthetic techniques this problem can be managed successfully.

With flexible nasolaryngoscopy, children, including neonates and infants, can easily and atraumatically be examined without general anesthesia. Local anesthesia of the nose can be obtained using 2% lidocaine or tetracaine and decongestion can be obtained with phenylephrine or oxymetazoline. With the child awake and firmly held, vocal cord mobility and dynamic function of the supraglottic and glottic areas can be assessed. In some children, the evaluation may be difficult because of increased secretion, a floppy epiglottis, or a very anteriorly placed larynx.

Direct laryngoscopy and bronchoscopy should be performed in the operating room or in a well-equipped endoscopy room. When general anesthesia is used, it is important that both the endoscopist and the anesthesiologist are cognizant of the aims and the technical details of the procedure. The individual role of each physician must be discussed in advance and be understood by the other. This facilitates the team approach that is necessary to achieve a controlled, safe airway. The patient under general anesthesia does not move, so the endoscopist should be able to perform a careful assessment of the airway, and biopsy or surgery can be carried out more precisely. The cardiovascular and respiratory functions of the child are monitored, as for any other operative procedure. Halothane is the most commonly used anesthetic, but it is useful to augment it with topical anesthetic, such as 2% lidocaine spray applied to the larynx. Mask ventilation alone can be used if the procedure is short. The vocal cord mobility can be assessed in spontaneously breathing children under general anesthesia. If the vocal cords are immobile, a passive vocal cord mobility test is performed by palpating the arytenoids with a laryngeal spatula or suction to rule out posterior glottic stenosis and cricoarytenoid joint fixation. In addition, the posterior larynx should be evaluated for a laryngeal cleft. Laryngoscopy can be performed with an endotracheal tube in place; this provides a secure airway, but vocal cord mobility cannot be assessed and a laryngeal abnormality may be missed.

In some conditions, the Venturi jet ventilation apparatus can be used. This includes situations in which the endotracheal tube obstructs the surgeon's view of the larynx and would interfere with any surgery being performed, including laser surgery. It is important to obtain paralysis of the vocal cords when using the Venturi jet ventilation, so that a glottic opening is always available for the passage of air (both inhalation and exhalation). Sudden trapping of air can cause bilateral pneumothorax.

There are three main types of laryngoscopes, each of which has a fiberoptic light carrier attached to a xenon light source (Fig. 76–1). The standard laryngoscope permits a good assessment of the glottic area and anterior commissure. An even better view of the subglottic region can be obtained with the subglottic scope. The anterior commissure laryngoscope with the widened lumen allows binocular vision to be utilized with the microscope, and so microsurgical procedures can be performed with greater ease.

Before the procedure is begun, the instruments to be used should be assembled and tested. It is important to remember that the entire procedure should be carried

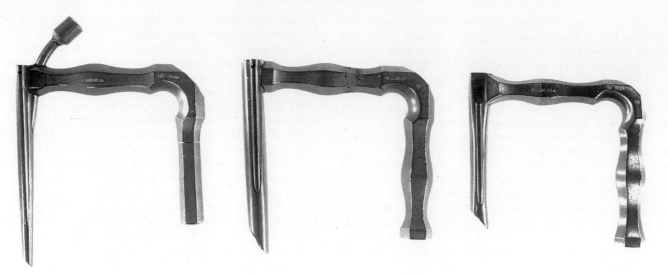

FIGURE 76–1. Three different laryngoscopes *(left to right)*: anterior commissure laryngoscope, standard laryngoscope, and subglottic laryngoscope.

out with extreme gentleness to avoid edema. The patient is positioned with the head extended on the flexed neck. The upper teeth or gingivae are protected by a guard or gauze and should not be used as a fulcrum; the doctor's forefinger and thumb are used to support the endoscope. The laryngoscope is held in the left hand, and the distal end of the laryngoscope is lubricated and introduced on the right side of the tongue with the blade rotated about 90 degrees counterclockwise. The tongue is swept to the left. The tip is inserted into the vallecula, the blade is rotated back to normal position, and the epiglottis is examined. One exposes larynx by pulling the tongue and epiglottis forward and not prying on the teeth (Fig. 76–2). It is important to use this approach when assessing the mobility of the vocal cords in an awake or lightly anesthetized child, as there is, at this stage, no restraining pressure from the laryngoscope. The glottis is also seen when the laryngoscope is advanced below (posterior to) the epiglottis. A rod lens telescope can be used for an enhanced view of the larynx, and a camera can be attached for documentation.

Each area of the hypopharynx and larynx should be

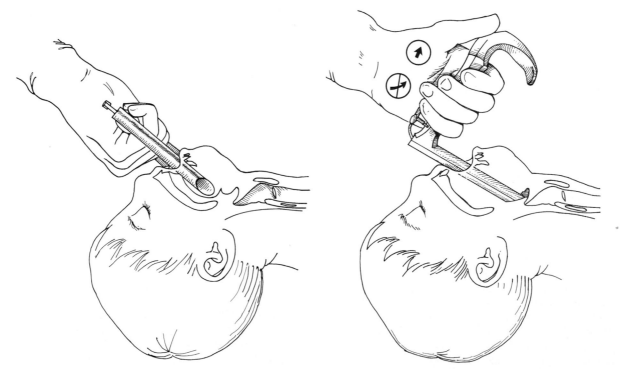

FIGURE 76–2. Introduction of the laryngoscope. (From Chan KH, Riding KH, McGowan FX, Stool SE. Endoscopic surgery of the upper aerodigestive tract. In Bluestone CD, Stool SE (eds). Atlas of Pediatric Otolaryngology. Philadelphia, WB Saunders, 1994, pp 427–428.)

methodically and carefully examined. One should note the appearance of the supraglottic structures, keeping in mind the possibility that an omega-shaped epiglottis (as in laryngomalacia), a cyst, or a web might be present. Subglottic stenosis can be viewed through the cords as an annular constriction. Hemangiomas usually occur in the left subglottic region and appear as bluish swellings protruding from the laryngeal wall. As they partially empty under general anesthesia, their size shrinks and the mucosa acquires a more normal color. This makes the smaller hemangiomas more difficult to diagnose.

The operating microscope enables any surgical procedure, including laser surgery, to be performed more precisely. When surgical procedures are performed, the laryngoscope is held in place with the suspension apparatus, and the larynx is viewed through the microscope using a 400 mm objective lens (see Chapter 92).

Electromyography

Electromyography is used for assessment of immobile vocal cords to differentiate between true paralysis or paresis and vocal cord immobility due to posterior glottic stenosis or cricoarytenoid joint ankylosis as well as for monitoring immobile vocal cords over time. Because awake laryngeal electromyographic examination requires full cooperation from the patient, intraoperative electromyography under general anesthesia can be performed and is more suitable for children. Bipolar hook wire electrodes are inserted into the midportion of the vocal cords, while the larynx is suspended with a laryngoscope suspension unit. Although voluntary activity cannot be recorded, appropriate laryngeal function can be assessed by recording of muscle activity from the thyroarytenoid muscle during reflexive coughing or swallowing and withdrawal of muscle relaxation as activity returns. Typical intraoperative electromyographic patterns with progressive recruitment of larger motor units during emergence from anesthesia are seen in a normal and an ankylotic vocal fold but not in paralyzed vocal folds.[12]

Bronchoscopy

Rigid Bronchoscopy

The question of whether bronchoscopy should be performed with the patient under general or local anesthesia can be answered with the arguments used in the section on direct laryngoscopy. The authors perform most of their bronchoscopies with the patient under general anesthesia, using the bronchoscope to ventilate the patient; they feel that because modern anesthetic techniques are so safe, there is very little place for bronchoscopy using local anesthesia in the child. However, if local anesthesia is used, it is imperative that the child be wrapped firmly and the head held to prevent any movements. Spontaneous breathing during the rigid bronchoscopy allows an accurate assessment of the presence and degree of compression and collapse of the intrathoracic tracheobronchial tree.

In children, the rigid bronchoscopes with the rod-lens optical telescopes are most commonly used and provide

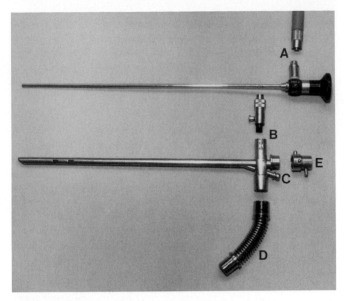

FIGURE 76–3. Bronchoscope with Hopkins optical system. *A*, Light source and attachment to telescope; *B*, prismatic light deflector and attachment to light source; *C*, aspiration and instrumentation channel; *D*, connector to anesthesia; *E*, telescope bridge.

excellent views of the trachea and bronchi while maintaining a secure airway and allowing the passage of instruments for the aspiration of secretions, tissue biopsy sampling, and the removal of foreign bodies. In addition, the rigid endoscopes have a ventilating connector that can be attached to the anesthetic equipment so that ventilation can safely be performed during the procedures.

The Storz endoscope (Fig. 76–3) with the Hopkins rod-lens optical system was introduced in 1966 and has replaced the Jackson and Holinger endoscopes to a large extent. The rod-lens telescopes have the advantages of good illumination, magnification, and angled views. The pediatric Storz rigid bronchoscopes are available in three lengths and different sizes: 20 cm (2.5 to 3.5) for premature and neonatal infants, 26 cm (3.0 to 4.0) for neonates and young infants, and 30 cm (3.5 to 6.0) for older children (Fig. 76–4, Table 76–1). A variety of forceps, in-

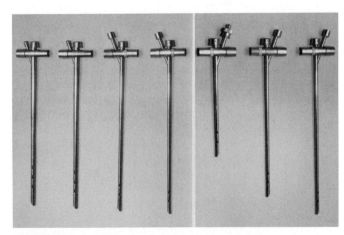

FIGURE 76–4. Different bronchoscope sizes (3.5 to 6.0) *(left)* and different lengths (20, 26, and 30 cm) *(right)*.

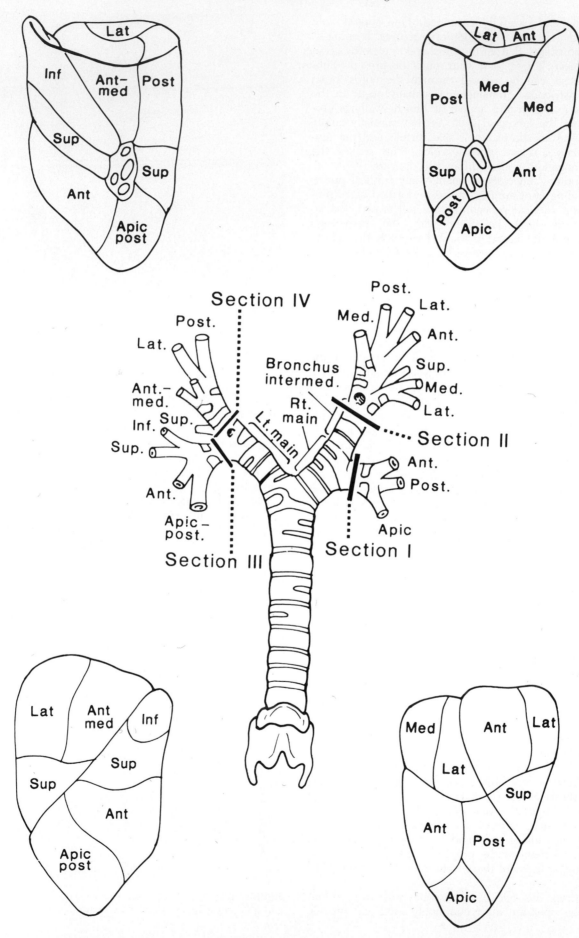

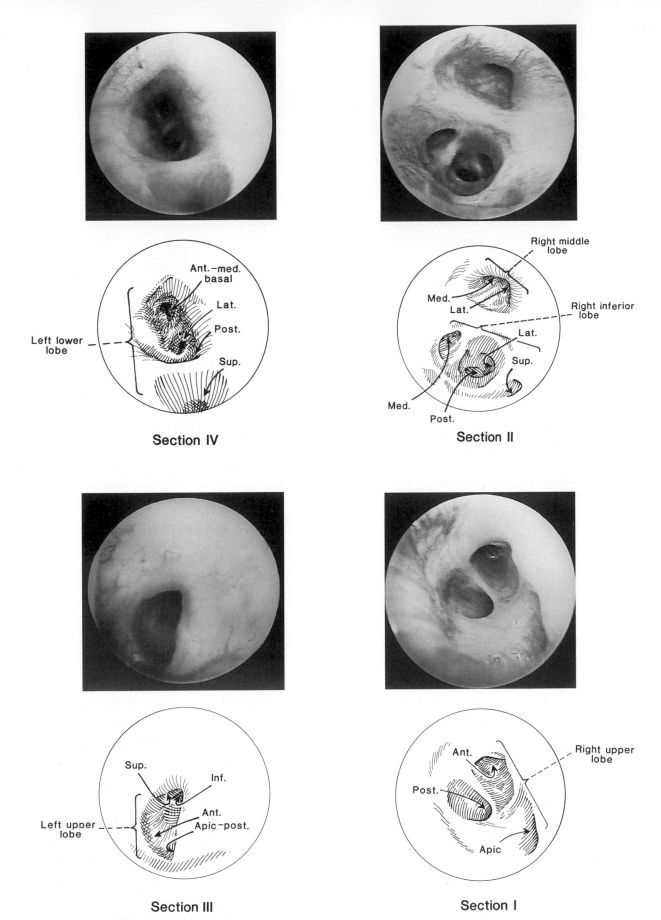

FIGURE 76-5. Schematic drawing of subdivision of lobes into bronchopulmonary segments and four cross-sectional bronchoscopic views. Section I: right upper lobe; section II: right middle and lower lobes; section III: left upper lobe; and section IV: left middle and lower lobes. For details, see text.

TABLE 76–1. Different Storz Bronchoscope Sizes (Diameter and Length) and Suggested Use According to Age of the Patient

Size	Length	ID, mm	OD, mm	Age
2.5	20	3.5	4.2	Premature
3.0	20, 26	4.3	5.0	Premature, newborn
3.5	20, 26, 30	5.0	5.7	Newborn–6 mo
3.7	26, 30	5.7	6.4	6 mo–1 yr
4.0	26, 30	6.0	6.7	1–2 yr
5.0	30	7.1	7.8	3–4 yr
6.0	30, 40	7.5	8.2	5–7 yr
6.5	43	8.5	9.2	Adult

ID, inner diameter; OD, outer diameter.

cluding optical forceps (cup, alligator, peanut) that enhance the view, are available for biopsy and removal of foreign bodies (see Chapter 90). The straightforward (0-degree), oblique (30-degree), and lateral (70-degree) telescopes enable closer inspection of areas that cannot be seen with the bronchoscope tube alone. Specifically, they are useful to view the right and left upper bronchial orifices, the right middle bronchial orifices, and the basal bronchi.

As with direct laryngoscopy, successful and safe bronchoscopy can be attributed to good preparation and gentleness during the procedure. The time taken to carry out the bronchoscopy should be as short as possible, especially in the infant, because the subglottic area may be traumatized during prolonged examinations, resulting in obstructive edema. The bronchoscope should be the size that affords the physician the best possible view while causing the least trauma at the glottic and subglottic regions (see Table 76–1). When glottic or subglottic edema is anticipated or experienced because of the instrumentation, intravenous administration of steroid (0.6–1 mg/kg dexamethasone) should be considered. One can inspect the subglottic area and trachea by using the telescope alone to avoid any trauma to the airway. However, the airway is then not secured.

Before the procedure, the surgeon should check the instruments to be used to ensure proper function. The appropriate size of bronchoscope (length and diameter) and the telescope that gives the best optical resolution but the most favorable airway resistance should be selected.[6] In addition, one or two sizes of smaller bronchoscopes should be available for use if needed. The appropriate size (width and length) of suctions, forceps, and other instruments should have been selected and prepared for use prior to initiation of the procedure. Radiographic evidence of a lesion should be translated into the anatomy of the tracheobronchial tree as viewed through the bronchoscope (Fig. 76–5).

The child should be positioned with the head extended on the flexed neck. In the older child, a shoulder roll can be helpful. It is usually not necessary to have a person to hold the head of the young child, but a headrest should be used. The same care of the teeth and gingivae should be taken as in direct laryngoscopy. The forefinger and the thumb of the physician's left hand are used to support the instrument. Figure 76–6 illustrates the technique used to introduce the bronchoscope. It is considerably

easier to use the Jackson laryngoscope with its slide or a regular anesthesia laryngoscope to introduce the bronchoscope in the child. The laryngoscope is introduced, as previously described, until the glottis is in sight. The selected bronchoscope is then passed through, or next to, the lumen of the laryngoscope to the level of the true vocal cords. Next, the bronchoscope is turned 90 degrees to align the leading edge of the bronchoscope with the axis of the vocal cords. This positions the tip of the bronchoscope in the glottis. A gentle twisting motion while advancing the bronchoscope allows entry into the subglottic area (Fig. 76–7).

If the laryngoscope is not used, it is possible for the physician to lose his or her way. However, in the older child or adolescent, the bronchoscope can be introduced on its own. The instrument is passed to the back of the mouth, where the vallecula and epiglottis are seen. The epiglottis is lifted forward on the beak of the bronchoscope, and with the examiner taking care to keep the bronchoscope in the midline, the glottis is approached and entered as described previously.

The subglottic area and the trachea are inspected. Attention should be paid to the lumen, mucosa, and secretions. Features such as narrowing, tumors, differences in mucosal coloration, pulsation, and collapsibility of the trachea should be noted and investigated appropriately. Abnormal secretions are collected for culture using a Luki (Davis and Geck) trap. The suction apparatus should be washed through with nonbacteriocidal saline so that all the secretions are collected in the Luki trap. The secretions are sent for cytologic inspection and culture for bacteria, including acid-fast organisms, and fungi.

The bronchoscope is further advanced to the carina. This movement should be easy, but if there is any resistance, the physician should check that the head and neck are correctly positioned, that the lips are not caught on the bronchoscope, and that the jaw is freely open. The physician should also ensure that the correct size of bronchoscope is being used. The carina should appear as a sharp, vertical spur dividing the entry into the two mainstem bronchi. Its appearance changes with respiration, becoming more blunt on expiration. Widening or decreased movement may be caused by pathologically enlarged hilar nodes.

The right mainstem bronchus is the easier to enter because it meets the trachea at an angle of about 25 degrees, whereas the left mainstem bronchus is at a 75-

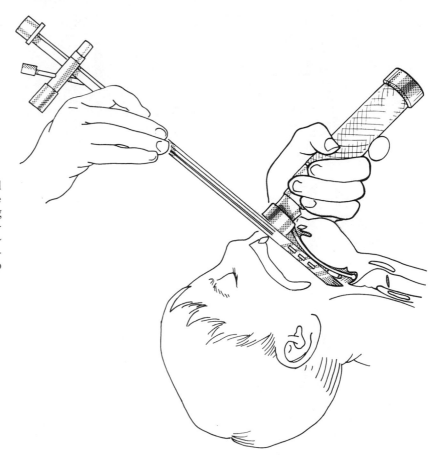

FIGURE 76–6. Insertion of bronchoscope and telescope, which is usually performed with the laryngoscope in place. (From Chan KH, Riding KH, McGowan FX, Stool SE. Endoscopic surgery of the upper aerodigestive tract. In Bluestone CD, Stool SE (eds). Atlas of Pediatric Otolaryngology. Philadelphia, WB Saunders, 1994, p 436.)

degree angle to the trachea. Both sides of the lower respiratory tree should be inspected. The examiner should look for abnormalities and variations in the bronchial structure such as a tracheal bronchus on the right side. Any abnormality in secretions or mucosal color and any tumors or pulsatile masses causing narrowing of the lumen should be noted. It is advisable to complete the total bronchoscopic evaluation of both lung fields before performing any biopsy, as any resultant bleeding will make the subsequent examination more difficult. Secretions are aspirated from both mainstem bronchi, and, occasionally, bronchoalveolar washings are obtained by instilling nonbacteriocidal saline into the endoscope and bronchi and suctioning it back into the sterile Luki trap. Bronchoalveolar lavage sample may be sent for culture and sensitivity testing and testing for the presence and proportion of lipid-laden macrophages, which may be associated with aspiration and gastroesophageal reflux disease (see Chapter 69).

One enters the right mainstem bronchus by turning the lip of the bronchoscope in the direction of the bronchus and turning the head of the patient slightly to the left. A better view is always obtained if the axis of the bronchus to be viewed and the bronchoscope are coincident. The right upper lobe bronchus exits from the lateral wall of the mainstem bronchus (see Fig. 76–5). As in other parts of the bronchial tree, it is not uncommon to see variations in its anatomy, such as a right tracheal bronchus. The normal tripartite division of the upper lobe into anterior, apical, and posterosuperior lobe bronchi can

be seen with a lateral telescope. The right mainstem bronchus (bronchus intermedius) divides into the middle and lower lobe bronchi. Just below the upper lobe bronchus, the superior bronchus of the lower lobe can be seen in the posterior wall. The bronchial divisions to the four basal segments of the lower lobe then can be identified and can be more carefully inspected using the straightforward telescope.

The left bronchial tree should then be examined. Because of the angle that the left mainstem bronchus makes with the trachea, the head of the patient has to be turned toward the right shoulder to give easy access to this area. The obliquely lying division between the left upper lobe bronchus and the lower lobe bronchus is seen running from a position of 12 o'clock to 8 o'clock on an imaginary clock face. It is sometimes possible to enter the left upper bronchus with the bronchoscope, but on other occasions the lateral viewing telescope must be used. The upper lobe bronchus quickly divides into its upper and lingular divisions. The bronchus leading to the lingular lobe then divides into its superior and inferior segments.

The left lower bronchus is longer than the right, with a relatively higher origin for the posteriorly placed left superior lower bronchus. The basal branches are a mirror image of the right except that the medial basal branch arises from the anterior basal branch.

At the completion of the examination, the bronchoscope should be removed with as much care as was used in its insertion, under direct vision to avoid any unnecessary trauma.

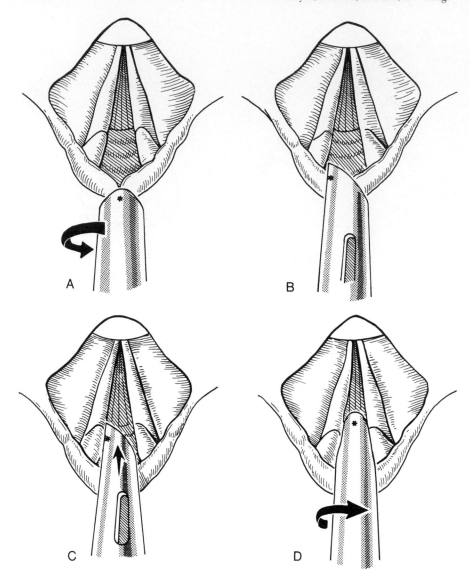

FIGURE 76–7. Sequence of passing the bronchoscope through the larynx. The *asterisks* indicate the orientation of the bronchoscope, and the *arrows* indicate the rotation and the direction of the bronchoscope. (From Chan KH, Riding KH, McGowan FX, Stool SE. Endoscopic surgery of the upper aerodigestive tract. In Bluestone CD, Stool SE (eds). Atlas of Pediatric Otolaryngology. Philadelphia, WB Saunders, 1994, p 437.)

Flexible Bronchoscopy

Flexible bronchoscopy allows evaluation of peripheral parts of the tracheobronchial tree and dynamic assessment during spontaneous respiration. It is particularly useful for evaluation of tracheomalacia and bronchomalacia. The use of flexible bronchoscopy in children has been limited to the older child because the instrument obstructs a considerable part of the airway and thus interferes with ventilation. With improved technology, however, smaller instruments have been designed, and neonates and infants can also be evaluated safely using flexible bronchoscopy.[7]

Flexible bronchoscopy should be performed in the operating room or in an endoscopy room with the aid of an anesthesiologist who is in charge of the monitoring and sedation. The physician, standing at the head of the table, usually introduces the flexible bronchoscope through the nose, which should be anesthetized and decongested with 2% lidocaine or tetracaine and phenylephrine or oxymetazoline. When the instrument reaches the nasopharynx, the tip is angulated downward and the instrument is slowly passed toward the larynx and through the glottis into the trachea. Additional lidocaine can be instilled through the side channel for topical anesthesia of the larynx and tracheobronchial tree. The instrument can also be passed orally through a special mouthpiece, which prevents trauma to the instrument from the child's biting.

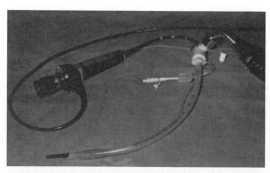

FIGURE 76–8. Flexible fiberoptic bronchoscope passing through an endotracheal tube.

The flexible bronchoscope can also be introduced through an endotracheal tube in a child under general anesthesia or through a tracheostomy tube (Fig. 76–8). A special adaptor (Bodai Bronch-Safe Double Swivel, Sontele Medical) can be connected to the endotracheal or tracheotomy tube, so ventilation can be continued during the procedure (Fig. 76–9). The approach through the endotracheal tube or tracheostomy tube permits easy access directly into the trachea but does not give a view of the larynx.

Most flexible bronchoscopes have an optical channel and a channel for aspiration, biopsy, and brushings for cytologic examination. The slimmest flexible bronchoscope with a side channel (Olympus) has an external diameter of 2.8 mm and a side channel of 1.2 mm. This instrument can be passed through a 4.5 endotracheal tube or a 4.5 Shiley pediatric tracheotomy tube. The slimmest flexible nasopharyngoscope with an external diameter of 1.9 mm (Machida) does not have a suction channel but can pass through a 3.0 endotracheal tube and a 3.0 Shiley neonate pediatric tracheotomy tube. This instrument is excellent for neonates and infants, but it has some limitation in its usefulness because of the absence of a side channel. It can also be used for evaluation of the endotracheal or tracheotomy tube position and may decrease the need for repeated chest radiography.

The flexible bronchoscope is directed by adjusting the tip by remote control and rotating the whole instrument. It should be remembered that these are delicate instruments, the fibers of which can easily be broken by excessive bending or torque during rotation of the bronchoscope. The bronchoscope is passed systematically through the lower respiratory tract, and attention is paid to the same details of anatomy as when the rigid bronchoscope is used. Specimens for cytologic examination can be obtained by aspirating secretions and collecting the results of brushings from the bronchial wall. Biopsy specimens can also be taken. The flexible bronchoscope should not be used if foreign bodies are suspected.

The otolaryngologist should attempt to acquire familiarity with the use of both rigid and flexible bronchoscopes, as each has a part to play in the examination and treatment of the lower respiratory tract.

FIGURE 76–9. Adapter that connects the endotracheal tube or tracheotomy tube to the anesthesia equipment so that the patient can be ventilated during the examination.

Complications

The complication rate for rigid endoscopy has been reported as 2% to 3%.[5, 11] The complications of endoscopic examination are trauma to the teeth and gums, arytenoid dislocation, laryngospasm, trauma to the glottic or subglottic area resulting in edema and obstruction, bronchospasm, bleeding, or perforation. The surgeon can avoid these complications by as gentle and methodical an examination as possible and by working in close collaboration with the anesthesiologist. Early recognition of problems is essential to avoid possible loss of airway control, which can lead to hypoxia, causing brain damage or death.

Conclusions

In children, direct laryngoscopy and rigid bronchoscopy are used for both diagnostic and therapeutic reasons. However, improvements in technology have made it possible to perform flexible endoscopy in infants and neonates. Flexible endoscopy can be performed under local anesthesia and permits examination of the tracheobronchial tree during spontaneous respiration. Rigid endoscopy has the advantage of controlling the airway and providing secure ventilation and is the only safe technique for the removal of foreign bodies.

SELECTED REFERENCES

Chan KH, Riding KH, McGowan FX, Stool SE. Endoscopic surgery of the upper aerodigestive tract. In Bluestone CD, Stool SE (eds). Atlas of Pediatric Otolaryngology. Philadelphia, WB Saunders, 1995, pp 419–446.

Hulka GF, Wilmott RW, Cotton RT. Evaluation of the airway. In Myers CM III, Cotton ET, Shove SR (eds). Pediatric Airway: An Interdisciplinary Approach. Philadelphia, JB Lippincott, 1995, pp 25–44.

Potsic WP, Cotton RT, Handler SD. Surgical pediatric otolaryngology: head and neck surgery. In Endoscopy, Part VII. New York, Thieme Medical Publishers, 1997, pp 506–551.

REFERENCES

1. Bluestone CD, Healy GB, Cotton RT. Diagnosis of laryngomalacia is not enough! Arch Otolaryngol Head Neck Surg 122:1417, 1996.
2. Bluestone CD, Healy GB, Cotton, RT. Neonatal upper airway assessment by awake flexible laryngoscopy. Ann Otol Rhinol Laryngol 8:733, 1998.
3. Fan LL, Flynn JW. Laryngoscopy in neonates and infants: experience with the flexible fiberoptic bronchoscope. Laryngoscope 91: 451, 1991.
4. Gonzalez C, Reilly JS, Bluestone CD. Synchronous airway lesions in infancy. Ann Otol Rhinol Laryngol 96:77, 1987.
5. Hoeve LJ, Rombout J, Meursing AE. Complications of rigid laryngo-bronchoscopy in children. J Ped Otorhinolaryngol 26:47, 1993.
6. Marzo SJ, Hotaling AJ. Trade-off between airway resistance and optical resolution in pediatric rigid bronchoscopy. Ann Otol Rhinol Laryngol 104:282, 1995.
7. Perez CR, Wood RE. Update on pediatric flexible bronchoscopy. Pediatr Clin North Am 41:385, 1994.
8. Prinja N, Manoukian JJ. Neonatal/infant rigid bronchoscopy. J Otolaryngol 27:31, 1998.

9. Silberman HD. The use of the flexible fiberoptic nasopharyngolaryn-goscope in the pediatric upper airway. Otolaryngol Clin North Am 11:365, 1978.

10. Ward PH, Berci G, Calcaterra TC. Advances in endoscopic examination of the respiratory system. Ann Otol Rhinol Laryngol 83:754, 1974.

11. Wiseman NE, Sanchez I, Powell RE. Rigid bronchoscopy in the pediatric age group: diagnostic effectiveness. J Ped Surg 27:1294, 1992.

12. Woo P, Arandia H. Intraoperative laryngeal electromyographic assessment of patients with immobile vocal folds. Ann Otol Rhinol Laryngol 101:799, 1992.

77

Cough

Andrew J. Hotaling, M.D. and George T. Moynihan, M.D.

The cough is the watchdog of the lungs.
— *Chevalier Jackson, 1920*[24]

Cough is a common, but frequently misunderstood, sign of illness. It is the most common symptom of respiratory tract disease, but it is not a diagnosis. Cough is the principal reason for more than 16 million physician office visits per year in the United States.[19] The majority of diseases that occur in the first decade of life are respiratory in origin. It is estimated that respiratory illness causes one half of all illnesses and is responsible for two thirds of all infections in the first 5 years of life.[11] The rational treatment of cough requires that a diagnosis be made. The more accurate and the more precise the ·diagnosis, the greater the opportunity for accurate and precise therapy.

The goals of this chapter are first to discuss the mechanism and pathophysiology of cough; then to review pertinent elements in the history and evaluation of cough in children; and finally to discuss the differential diagnosis of cough with attention to specific causes in childhood.

Mechanics and Pathophysiology of Cough

Coughing is one of the four protective mechanisms for the respiratory system. The second is the gag reflex.[19] The third is the mucociliary escalator, which is able to clear all parts of the lungs down to the alveolar ducts. The fourth is the phagocytic and lymphatic systems, which are the only effective clearance mechanisms beyond the terminal bronchiole level (see Chapter 75).

Coughing has two functions: to expel foreign material from the airway and to remove excessive secretions from the airway. In the healthy person, the primary system for the performance of these functions is the mucociliary escalator. Coughing becomes a factor only when there is an abnormal type or quantity of material to be removed or when the mucociliary system has become ineffective. The stimuli for cough can be classified into four groups: chemical, mechanical, thermal, and inflammatory. Examples of these stimuli are cigarette smoke; vascular ring; cold, dry air; and increased mucus, respectively.

The afferent pathway begins with receptors located in the upper levels of the respiratory tract and extending to the level of the terminal nonrespiratory bronchioles. It is believed that there are four types of receptors: slowly adapting receptors, rapidly adapting receptors, C-fiber re-

ceptors, and pulmonary stretch receptors. The slow and rapidly adapting receptors are located at the level of the carina and larger bronchi; these respond to mucosal tactile stimulation. The C-fiber receptors extend from the larynx to the alveoli and respond to chemical and mechanical stimulation. Pulmonary stretch receptors are located in the smooth muscle of the respiratory tree and are stimulated by mechanical forces in the airway.[33] The highest concentration of receptors is found in the larynx, the lower half of the trachea, the carina, and the midsized bronchi. Of these, the carina is the most sensitive.[14] The afferent stimuli from these receptors travel via cranial nerves IX and X. Tactile stimulation of the Arnold nerve, a branch of cranial nerve X innervating the external auditory canal and tympanic membrane, can result in cough. These afferent signals are carried to the upper brain stem and pons level. However, no discrete cough center has been identified.

The efferent pathway for cough is transmitted via cranial nerve X and spinal motor nerves C2 to S2, including the phrenic nerve. The efferent signals can result in stimulation of the diaphragmatic, pharyngeal, laryngeal, intercostal, abdominal wall, and pelvic muscle groups. Regardless of the mode of afferent stimulation, all coughs are generated by this efferent pathway. These afferent and efferent pathways are illustrated in Figure 77–1.[19] There is also cortical input, and cough can be initiated or suppressed by an awake patient. Voluntary suppression is common in adolescent patients with lung disease.[10]

Thus, multiple elements are required for the generation of a cough, including an intact sensory apparatus, neural processing, timing and distribution of neuromuscular activity, and an adequate musculoskeletal system.[28] Cough is noted to be less vigorous in newborns than in older children. When stimulated by direct laryngoscopy, only 25% of premature infants cough, versus 50% of full-term infants.[28]

The mechanism of cough production can be divided into four phases: inspiratory, contractive, compressive, and expulsive.[10] The inspiratory phase usually begins with a gasping inspiration, terminated by glottic closure. Coughing at higher lung volumes is more effective than at low volumes because of earlier airway closure at low volumes. The contractive phase involves the various muscles of expiration receiving appropriate neural stimuli and

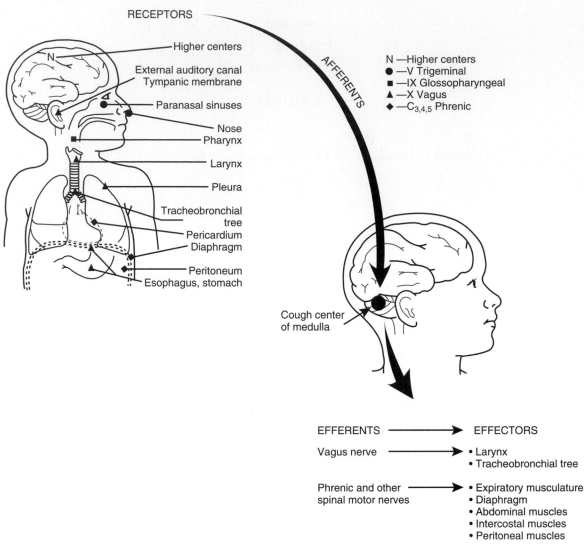

FIGURE 77-1. Afferent and efferent pathways of cough stimulation. (From Holinger LD, Sanders AD. Chronic cough in infants and children: an update. Laryngoscope 101:597, 1991.)

subsequently contracting against closed glottic or supraglottic sphincters, or both.[1] These muscular contractions lead to the compressive phase, in which there is a marked elevation of alveolar, pleural, and subglottic airway pressures. The final phase is expiratory, in which the glottis opens quickly, resulting in a release of trapped air at high flow rates, causing movement of secretions and foreign material from the larger airways into the pharynx or beyond. This sudden movement has been described as the *bechic blast* by Jackson.[33] The peak flow approaches 25,000 cm/sec, approximately Mach 0.75 (Mach 1 is the speed of sound).[25] The peak flow continues after glottic opening, owing to dynamic collapse of the larger airways and continued intrathoracic compression of gas.[10] With prolonged expiration, the subsequent compression of pulmonary parenchyma into airways squeezes more distal secretive material into larger airways, termed the *tussive squeeze* by Jackson.[33]

It appears that increased secretions are necessary for effective cough. In a study by Camner et al,[3] small tagged particles were instilled in the airways of healthy patients.

Coughing by healthy patients did not eliminate particles from the airway; however, patients with lung disease were able to eliminate the particles by coughing. It was concluded that increased tracheobronchial secretions are a necessary component for effective coughing. Glottic closure is not essential for coughing.[15] Coughing can occur in intubated patients. However, the peak flow rate occurs earlier and is submaximal in comparison with the cough in patients with a competent glottis. The endotracheal tube prevents tracheal compression, permitting high flow rates only after full inspiration and only in the initial phases of coughing.

History, Physical Examination, and Laboratory Studies

History

An accurate history may give the diagnosis. If it does not lead to the specific diagnosis, the history will certainly narrow the differential diagnosis (Table 77-1).

TABLE 77-1. Key Historical Findings of Cough

Aspiration
Choking episode (foreign body)
Coughing with feeding
Immunization status
Malabsorption
Pollution
Seasonal variation
Wheezing

The age of the patient may suggest a diagnosis. Coughing in the neonatal group is unusual and suggests significant abnormality such as a congenital anomaly, gastroesophageal reflux, cystic fibrosis, or chlamydial pneumonia. Attendance at a day care center increases exposure to respiratory pathogens. Seasonal variation of cough in an older child may suggest an allergic cause. Malabsorption, poor growth despite a large appetite, rectal prolapse, and nasal polyps raise the possibility of cystic fibrosis. Bordetella pertussis and pertussis-like viral infections can result in cough that has been described as the "100-day cough."[33] Infants with pertussis may not have the classic inspiratory whoop. Coughing associated with feeding suggests gastroesophageal reflux, aortic arch anomaly, or an abnormal connection between the respiratory tract and the digestive tract. In any age group, particularly the toddler, the possibility of a foreign body must be investigated. Cough is the single most common symptom of a bronchial foreign body, present in up to 94% of cases.[33] Recurrent viral upper respiratory infection is probably the most common cause of acute and chronic recurrent cough in children, with an average of eight or more episodes per year in preschool children.[1, 33]

The possible effects of environmental pollution as well as indirect smoking must be considered. In a prevalence study of respiratory symptoms in secondary school children, the incidence of cough without cold was 14.8% in a high-pollution region versus 8.2% in a low-pollution region.[17] In an Italian study, with the use of cooking fuels other than natural gas and with heating appliances other than central heating, there appeared to be a mild adverse health effect in a general population sample.[37] In another study, materially deprived children suffered worse respiratory illness in childhood, with evidence presented that the sequelae persisted into adulthood.[39] There is additional evidence that the experience of respiratory illness early in life is associated with increased respiratory morbidity later in childhood and in adulthood. Additionally, even mild illnesses such as coughs and colds can have a detrimental effect on cognitive performance.[39]

In a large study of more than 2000 infants followed for the first 5 years of life, the lowest incidence of pneumonia and bronchitis in the first year of life was recorded in the situation in which both parents were nonsmokers.[7] In the first 12 months of life, exposure to cigarette smoke in the home doubled the risk of pneumonia and bronchitis for the infant. In an adolescent with coughing, the possibility that the child has been smoking must be considered. Another study demonstrated reduction of pulmonary function and increased frequency of cough in teenage athletes subjected to passive smoking. There was a fourfold increase in lower forced expiratory flow (FEF), 25% to 75%, or cough in teenage athletes exposed to passive smoking. Boys were more often affected than girls, but girls were affected to a greater extent.[36] A survey of respiratory symptoms in childhood was repeated 24 years after an initial survey.[38] The prevalence of persistent wheezes, daytime and nighttime cough, and phlegm increased despite a substantial reduction in outdoor air pollution levels.

Specific features of the cough should be determined: quality, timing, duration, and productivity. A chronic cough is usually defined as persisting for at least 2 to 3 weeks. A "seal-like bark" is typical of croup (laryngotracheobronchitis), whereas a loud Canada goose-like honk suggests a psychogenic cause. A paroxysmal cough with repeated coughs in quick succession, followed by a rapid inspiration ("whoop"), suggests pertussis. However, an infant with pertussis may present with no cough or a cough that leads to facial plethora or cyanosis. The paroxysm may terminate with vomiting or apnea. A whoop is uncommon in this age group. A staccato cough is heard in patients with chlamydial pneumonia.

The timing of the cough is important. Gastroesophageal reflux is considered when the cough occurs postprandially or during sleep. Coughing with feeding suggests an abnormal tracheoesophageal connection (i.e., laryngotracheoesophageal cleft, tracheoesophageal fistula) or an aortic arch anomaly. Cough variant asthma is suggested by a cough occurring with exercise, cold exposure, or laughing, and during sleep. The duration of the cough can be helpful. Often, it is difficult to distinguish between recurrent episodic coughing and persistent coughing. The most common causes of persistent coughing are reactive airway disease (asthma) and bronchitis, whereas recurrent episodic coughing is usually associated with recurrent upper respiratory infections. A productive cough usually occurs with a suppurative process, such as bacterial pneumonia. However, it is unusual for a young child to expectorate sputum, since the sputum is usually swallowed. If significant amounts of sputum are swallowed, vomiting may occur. A nonproductive or dry, hacking cough may be associated with a focal lesion in the airway. The association of coughing with hemoptysis is unusual in children. In such patients, one should consider bronchiectasis, cystic fibrosis, foreign bodies, pulmonary hemosiderosis, and tuberculosis. Sonorous breathing or snoring and rhinorrhea in the absence of upper respiratory infection suggest nasal obstruction.

Physical Examination

The physical examination begins with the vital signs, height, and weight. The presence of a fever usually indicates an infectious or inflammatory process. A growth delay or weight not meeting the expected level for a given height may suggest a chronic respiratory problem such as cystic fibrosis or uncontrolled asthma. The presence of a rash suggests an allergic or infectious cause. The presence of allergic shiners can indicate the venous congestion seen with a variety of upper respiratory tract disorders. Adenoidal facies can be seen with chronic upper airway obstruction. Asymmetry of the chest is found in congenital and destructive processes. Digital clubbing is seen in chronic suppurative lung diseases such as cystic fibrosis, hypersensitivity pneumonia, and bronchiectasis but is rarely, if ever, seen with reactive airway disease (asthma).

Examination of the chest includes inspection, palpation, percussion, and auscultation. The rate, depth, and symmetry of breathing should be noted. Young children with pulmonary disease increase tidal volume by increasing the respiratory rate; thus, an increased respiratory rate is a sensitive indicator of pulmonary disease in the young population.[25] The use of accessory muscles and nasal flaring are also noted. Percussion may indicate areas of dullness due to consolidation or due to pleural effusions. The normal inspiratory/expiratory ratio is 1:2.5 to 1:3. Most children 4 to 5 years of age or older, and some younger children, are able to cough on demand. The presence of wheezes, rales, and rhonchi is noted. A forced expiration may bring on wheezing, suggesting asthma. The presence of coughing with stridor suggests a partial upper airway obstruction. Auscultation of the neck is useful to locate more precisely the level of obstruction.

The ear, nose, and throat examination can be very helpful. The presence of a foreign body in the external auditory canal, excessive cerumen, or hair touching the tympanic membrane can stimulate the Arnold nerve, producing a cough. The nasal examination may suggest rhinitis of various forms, sinusitis, or polyps. The presence of nasal polyps in the pediatric patient mandates that a sweat test be performed to rule out cystic fibrosis. Sniffing, throat clearing, and hyponasal speech indicate chronic nasal, sinus, or adenoidal disease. A positive "99" test indicates significant nasal obstruction. The word *nine* is one of the few words in the English language that has an obligate nasal sound. The child is instructed to say "ninety-nine." The nose of the child is then occluded, and the child repeats the word. If there is no change in the nasality of the sound, there is a significant nasal obstruction. The allergic, or nasal, salute, usually made by passing the back of the hand across the tip of the nose, can result in a transverse nasal crease in the supratip region. The salute is found in patients with various chronic nasal disorders, including allergy. The oropharynx may demonstrate postnasal drip or signs of chronic irritation, including the presence of prominent lymphoid follicles on the posterior pharyngeal wall (known as cobblestoning). Acute pharyngitis can be associated with cough. Examination of the larynx indirectly with a mirror or a flexible nasopharyngoscope may show irritation consistent with aspiration or gastroesophageal reflux, a laryngeal cyst, or vocal cord paralysis. Sinusitis should be considered when palpation and percussion of the paranasal sinuses produce point tenderness. Transillumination is not useful in most children (see Chapter 35).

Laboratory Studies

Ancillary studies may be helpful. Radiographic studies include posteroanterior and lateral chest radiographs, screening sinus computed tomography, lateral soft tissue neck radiographs, barium swallow studies, a milk scan or nuclear scintiscan reflux study, and inspiratory/expiratory or lateral decubitus chest radiographs. If the child can produce a sputum sample, gross and microscopic examination can be beneficial. For example, clear mucoid sputum is consistent with an allergic or asthmatic cause, in contrast to cloudy sputum, which suggests a respiratory tract infection. The sputum in cystic fibrosis is frequently purulent but rarely foul smelling. The nasal smear is a simple, fast, reliable test to differentiate allergic rhinitis from vasomotor or infectious rhinitis. A Hansel stained slide showing greater than 5% eosinophils suggests allergic disease. Additional laboratory tests may include a sweat test, complete blood count with differential, eosinophil count, pulse oximetry or arterial blood gas test, erythrocyte sedimentation rate, tuberculin skin test, sputum culture and sensitivity test, pulmonary function test including methacholine challenge, and flow volume loop examinations. These tests are selected on the basis of history and physical examination findings.

Differential Diagnosis

The differential diagnoses of cough are presented in three different arrangements. Table 77–2 gives the differential diagnosis by cause in five categories: congenital, inflammatory, infectious, neoplastic, and miscellaneous. Table 77–3 gives the differential diagnosis by anatomic location. Table 77–4 lists the differential diagnosis by age.

A brief discussion of some causes follows.

Foreign Body

Chest radiographs are often normal in the first 24 hours in patients with tracheobronchial foreign bodies. The decision to perform an endoscopy is frequently based on the history, as there may not be physical or radiologic findings in the early postaspiration period. A child of any age can be suspected of having a foreign body; however, most frequently, the child is a toddler. Foreign bodies in the esophagus can present with airway symptoms, including cough, due to tracheal compression (see Chapter 90).

Aspiration

Aspiration may be a cause of cough. However, aspiration is not a specific diagnosis but rather a sign of another problem. The differential diagnosis includes neuromuscular weakness, tracheolaryngoesophageal cleft, type H tracheoesophageal fistula, gross gastroesophageal reflux, uncoordinated swallow, and disorders of the laryngeal innervation, including the internal and external branches of the superior laryngeal nerve and the recurrent laryngeal nerve (see Chapter 78).

TABLE 77–2. Differential Diagnosis of Cough by Cause

Congenital Cause	**Infectious Cause**
Aberrant innominate artery	Adenoiditis
Achalasia	Adenovirus
Aspiration	Bronchiectasis
Bronchogenic cyst	Bronchitis, chronic
Bronchomalacia	*Chlamydia trachomatis* infection
Bronchopulmonary dysplasia (child also with wheeze)	Congenital rubella
Ciliary dyskinesia	*Cryptococcus neoformans* infection (immunocompromised host)
Congenital heart disease	Cytomegalovirus
Congenital subglottic stenosis	Human immunodeficiency virus
Cystic fibrosis	Measles (classic triad: cough, coryza, conjunctivitis)
Elongated uvula	*Mycoplasma pneumoniae* infection
Esophageal duplication	Parasites[35]
Esophageal incoordination	Pertussis, parapertussis
Gastroesophageal reflux disease	Pharyngitis (chronic Waldeyer ring infection)
Immunodeficiency	Pneumonia
Kartagener syndrome (situs inversus, bronchiectasis, sinusitis)	Sinusitis
Laryngotracheomalacia	Tuberculosis
Lung cyst	**Neoplastic Cause**
Tracheal and bronchial stenosis	*Primary benign*
Tracheoesophageal fistula	Bronchial adenoma
Tracheolaryngoesophageal cleft	Cystic hygroma
Tracheomalacia	Mediastinal mass
Vascular ring	Recurrent respiratory papillomatosis
Vocal cord paralysis	Subglottic hemangioma
Inflammatory Cause	Teratoma
Allergy	*Primary malignant*
Asthma	Lymphoma
Bronchopulmonary fistula[32]	T cell leukemia
Cigarette smoking	Thymic neoplasm
Environmental (indirect cigarette smoke, industrial pollutants)	*Metastatic malignant*
External auditory canal cerumen	Hepatoblastoma
External auditory canal foreign body	Osteogenic sarcoma
External auditory canal hair on tympanic membrane	Wilms tumor
Foreign body	**Miscellaneous Cause**
Gastroesophageal reflux disease	Congestive heart failure
Laryngeal cyst	Drug (beta-adrenergic receptor antagonist, angiotensin-converting enzyme inhibitors)
Subacute thyroiditis[22]	Habit cough (psychogenic cough, cough tic)
Vallecular cyst	Mitral stenosis
	Ortner syndrome (cardiomegaly and recurrent laryngeal nerve paralysis)
	Rheumatic fever
	Vocal cord paralysis

Gastroesophageal Reflux Disease

Gastroesophageal reflux disease (GERD) frequently presents with a cough in the neonate or infant. One pediatric study estimates the incidence of GERD causing cough in the presence of a normal chest radiograph as 10%.[2] In an adult study by Irwin et al,[21] 49 patients with chronic cough were examined. After work-up, 10% of these patients had cough attributable to GERD. A suspected diagnosis of GERD in a child must be systematically evaluated. Studies can include a barium esophagogram, an upper gastrointestinal tract scintigraphy study, a pH probe, direct laryngoscopy, bronchoscopy, esophagoscopy, esophageal biopsy, and staining of tracheal aspirate for lipid-laden macrophages. Treatments include positioning maneuvers to maintain the stomach in a dependent position with respect to the mouth; lower esophageal sphincter tone-enhancing and prokinetic drugs such as metoclopramide; H_2 blockers such as ranitidine; proton pump inhibitors such as lansoprazole; and fundoplication (see Chapter 69).

Laryngomalacia

Laryngomalacia or, more appropriately, supraglottic laryngomalacia, is the most common congenital diagnosis of the larynx. Ten percent of patients with laryngomalacia present with cough, although stridor is a more frequent sign. Usually, a positional history can be obtained in which the noise is exacerbated or is present only when the patient is in the supine position with increased activity. If there are no other airway anomalies, the patients usually do not require any treatment, and the parents can be reassured that the child will outgrow the process (see Chapters 81 and 83).[8] However, 5% of children with laryngomalacia may have an associated subglottic stenosis.[16] These disorders can sometimes be diagnosed with

TABLE 77–3. Differential Diagnosis of Cough by Anatomic Location

Ear Acute otitis media Foreign body, cerumen, hair (Arnold reflex) Neoplasm **Nose and Nasopharynx** Adenoiditis Allergy (atopic upper airway disease) Environmental pollutants (active and passive cigarette smoke, industrial pollutants) Foreign body **Paranasal Sinus** Allergy Environmental pollutants (cigarette smoke, industrial pollutants) Kartagener syndrome (complete situs inversus, chronic sinusitis, bronchiectasis) Sinusitis **Oropharynx** Elongated uvula Pharyngitis Vallecular cyst **Hypopharynx, Larynx** Aspiration Croup (laryngotracheal bronchitis) Foreign body Laryngeal cyst Laryngomalacia Tracheolaryngoesophageal cleft Vocal cord paresis or paralysis **Large Airway** Bronchiectasis Bronchitis *Chlamydia trachomatis* infection Cigarette smoking Croup Foreign body Kartagener syndrome (complete situs inversus, chronic sinusitis, bronchiectasis) Pertussis Tracheobronchomalacia Tracheoesophageal fistula	**Small Airway** Asthma Bronchiolitis Congenital rubella Cystic fibrosis Cytomegalovirus infection Lung cyst **Parenchyma** Alveolar disease (e.g., pulmonary hemosiderosis) Pneumonia **Gastrointestinal Tract** Esophageal foreign body Gastroesophageal reflux disease Tracheoesophageal fistula (H-type) **Central Nervous System** Arnold-Chiari malformation Gilles de la Tourette syndrome (20% with cough) Habit cough (psychogenic cough, cough tic) **Mediastinum** Cardiomegaly Cystic hygroma Hepatoblastoma Lymphoma Ortner syndrome (cardiomegaly and recurrent laryngeal nerve paralysis) Osteogenic sarcoma Sarcoidosis T cell leukemia Teratoma Thymic neoplasm Wilms tumor **Miscellaneous** Aortic arch anomaly Habit cough (psychogenic cough, cough tic) Innominate arterial compression Trauma Vocal cord paralysis **Environmental** Low humidity Overheating Passive smoking, pollution

fluoroscopy but may require flexible fiberoptic nasopharyngoscopy or direct laryngoscopy and bronchoscopy.

Cough with Feeding

In the neonate or young infant, cough with feeding suggests aortic arch anomalies and tracheoesophageal connections such as cleft larynx and tracheoesophageal fistula. Some of these disorders can be diagnosed with a barium esophagogram, but others require direct laryngoscopy (see Chapters 67 and 83).

Postnasal Drip

Postnasal drip is a disputed cause of cough. Studies performed in the 1930s showed that dye placed in the nasopharynx does not enter the larynx but enters the esophagus instead.[27] However, many clinicians believe that postnasal drip can precipitate cough. Irwin and Pratter[20] evaluated adult patients and found that 29% had postnasal drip as the sole cause of chronic persistent cough, and an additional 18% had postnasal drip combined with asthma as the cause of chronic persistent cough. In another study, 52% of 202 children with chronic cough had postnasal drip.[40] Sources for the postnasal drip include the nose, paranasal sinuses, and adenoids. In a separate study, Irwin et al[23] examined nine patients with chronic cough secondary to postnasal drip. Flow volume loop studies demonstrated extrathoracic upper airway obstruction. The coughs resolved following specific therapy. Two theories are available to explain why postnasal drip causes cough. The first is that the postnasal drip into the hypopharynx irritates the larynx, leading to cough. The second theory is that an irritated upper airway, the result of postnasal drip, causes cough and may irritate the larynx to the extent that edema occurs in the true vocal cords, leading to a partial obstruction (see Chapter 37).

TABLE 77–4. Differential Diagnosis of Cough by Age

Newborn	School-Age Child
Adenoiditis	Adenoiditis
Aortic arch anomaly (vascular ring)	Allergy
Arnold-Chiari malformation	Asthma
Aspiration	Bronchiectasis
Bronchiectasis	Cigarette smoking
Bronchopulmonary dysplasia	Cystic fibrosis
Chlamydia trachomatis infection[8]	Environmental (passive cigarette smoke, industrial pollutants)
Congenital rubella	Foreign body
Croup	Habit cough (psychogenic cough, cough tic)
Cystic fibrosis	Kartagener syndrome (complete situs inversus, chronic sinusitis, bronchiectasis)
Cytomegalovirus infection	*Mycoplasma pneumoniae* infection (most common age group)
Environmental (passive cigarette smoke, industrial pollutants)	Pharyngitis
Gastroesophageal reflux disease	Pneumonia
Kartagener syndrome (complete situs inversus, chronic sinusitis, bronchiectasis)	Rhinitis
Laryngotracheobronchomalacia	Sinusitis
Laryngotracheoesophageal cleft	Tuberculosis
Pertussis	Viral bronchitis
Pharyngitis	**Uncommon Causes**
Pneumonia	Alveolitis
Tracheoesophageal fistula (H-type)	Pulmonary fungal infections (*Aspergillus*)
Tuberculosis	Emphysema
Viral bronchiolitis	Alpha$_1$ antitrypsin deficiency
Vocal cord paralysis	Ciliary dyskinesia
Preschooler	Pleural effusion
Adenoiditis	Pulmonary edema
Allergy (atopic upper airway disease)	Tuberculosis
Asthma	
Bronchiectasis	
Bronchitis (viral)	
Croup	
Cystic fibrosis	
Environmental (passive cigarette smoke, industrial pollutants)	
Foreign body	
Gastroesophageal reflux disease	
Pertussis	
Pharyngitis	
Pneumonia	
Rhinitis	
Sinusitis	
Tuberculosis	

Cough Variant Asthma

Reactive airway disease (asthma) is one of the most frequent causes of cough in the pediatric population. Most asthmatic children develop asthma within the first 5 years of life.[30] Classically, the presentation of asthma is wheezing. Cough variant asthma was first noted in an adult study and later in a pediatric study.[4, 31] Chronic cough was the only presenting manifestation of bronchial asthma in a second adult study.[9] An epidemiologic study of wheeze, doctor-diagnosed asthma, and cough showed that 11% of children had been formally diagnosed as having asthma, with a somewhat higher prevalence of 12.7% in boys versus 9.2% in girls. The cumulative prevalence of asthma increased significantly with age. However, some children present with cough as the first sign. This cough typically is present with exertion and during sleeping. Frequently, such children do not have wheezing. In a detailed study by Hannaway and Hopper,[18] 32 pediatric patients with chronic cough were examined. These children had had cough for more than 2 months. The majority were younger than 10 years of age. In 23 of 32

patients, the cough was nocturnal. In 25, there was cough with exercise. Fourteen of 32 subjects had cough with exposure to cold air. All histories suggested that the cough was triggered by an upper respiratory infection. Forty percent of the children had a positive family history of asthma. Fifty-five percent of the children had positive skin test reactions to two or more inhalants. On physical examination, approximately one third had subtle expiratory wheezes with prolonged expirations. Twenty of these patients underwent pulmonary function tests, the results of all of which were normal. All the patients had a positive response to bronchodilator therapy, with resolution of cough. Of the 24 children followed long-term, 18 went on to develop classic asthma.

Some authors advocate a methacholine challenge to identify patients likely to benefit from bronchodilator therapy for cough variant asthma.[12, 13] Other disease processes can also give a positive methacholine challenge: a viral upper respiratory infection, allergic rhinitis, sarcoidosis, and congestive heart failure. A total eosinophil count has been advocated as an excellent screening device to predict patients who will benefit from bronchodilator therapy for cough variant asthma.[6] If all tests are negative or inconclusive, some practitioners advocate a diagnostic/therapeutic trial of systemic corticosteroids.[13]

The mechanism of cough variant asthma is unknown.[18] A theory is that cough receptors become more reactive after changes in the tight junctions between epithelial surface cells due to conditions such as allergic exposure and infection.[18] Because the cough receptors are primarily located in the large airways, the response to stimulation is cough, in contrast to the wheezing that occurs in small airway disease. The diagnosis of asthma is usually made by exercise testing, histamine challenge, or methacholine challenge. The diagnosis of asthma, both classic and cough variant, cannot be excluded unless the proper dose of medication was prescribed and taken (see Chapter 86). The treatment of reactive airway diseases is begun with a beta$_2$-adrenergic agonist given orally or by inhalation.

Cystic Fibrosis

Cough is the most constant symptom of pulmonary involvement in cystic fibrosis.[8] Cystic fibrosis should be considered in any child with chronic cough. Additionally, there may be a history of malabsorption. A negative sweat test performed by the pilocarpine iontophoresis method of Gibson and Cooke in a hospital cystic fibrosis center is required to exclude this disease as a cause of cough. Genetic testing is also available.

Bronchitis

Bronchitis usually exists in association with other respiratory diseases. Frequently, the trachea is involved concurrently. Acute tracheobronchitis is usually of viral origin. It can also occur with influenza, measles, typhoid, pertussis, diphtheria, and scarlet fever. Bacterial infections usually occur secondarily and may include infection with *Streptococcus pneumoniae* and *Haemophilus influenzae*. Chronic bronchitis is unusual in the absence of underlying pulmonary or systemic disease, such as cystic fibrosis or immotile cilia.

Bronchitis presents with a chronic nonproductive or slightly productive cough following a respiratory infection (croup, pneumonia, mild upper respiratory infection). The cough may last for weeks and is exacerbated in a dry environment. Infectious bronchitis is very common and typically of viral origin. Seasonally, fall and winter are the times of highest incidence, with the infection occurring in children aged 5 to 7 years and usually resolving in fewer than 10 days. If the bronchitis persists more than 14 days, consideration should be given to bacterial cause, atelectasis, asthma, cystic fibrosis, immunodeficiency, and the presence of a foreign body (see Chapter 90).

Bronchiolitis

Bronchiolitis is common in the lower respiratory tracts of children through the first 2 years of life. The cause is viral, with respiratory syncytial virus being the most com-

mon causative agent. The cough is described as paroxysmal and wheezy. Frequently, there is associated tachypnea of 80 to 90 respirations per minute, which may interfere with adequate feeding.

Bronchiectasis

The term *bronchiectasis* describes dilatation of bronchi due to inflammatory changes of the bronchial wall, with accumulation of secretions. Rarely, the process is congenital. More commonly, the process is acquired, usually secondary to chronic pulmonary infections. Most commonly, the cause is cystic fibrosis. GERD can also produce bronchiectasis. A chronic productive cough is described, often with a history of repeated episodes of pneumonia involving the same lung segment, commonly the left lower lobe. Initially, the process may be insidious, with a normal initial physical examination. Hemoptysis may occur in approximately 50% of patients with bronchiectasis, and digital clubbing may be found.[9] Bronchiectasis can be the sequela to pertussis, measles, cystic fibrosis, asthma, tuberculosis, pneumonia, foreign body, hypergammaglobulinemia, and congenital tracheobronchial malformations. It is one of the components of Kartagener syndrome, which also includes the situs inversus, otitis, and chronic sinusitis (see Chapter 86).

Allergy

Allergy may be a predisposing factor for upper airway disease manifesting with cough. A response to antihistamine therapy indicates causative atopic upper airway disease. Cough or sneezing may be the presenting sign of a latex allergy in the spina bifida population, via an immunoglobulin E–mediated immediate hypersensitivity reaction that may progress to generalized anaphylaxis or cardiovascular collapse (see Chapter 47).[34]

Pertussis

Because of poor compliance with recommended immunization schedules, pertussis outbreaks have occurred in many areas. The cough may begin without anticipation in an afebrile patient. There is a distinctive paroxysmal cough followed by a whoop. However, in an infant or in a patient older than 5 years, the typical whoop may not be present. Apnea may be a prominent feature in the infant.[8] Typically, the child is red-faced and occasionally cyanotic at the end of the paroxysm. The paroxysmal stage lasts 2 to 4 weeks or longer. Clinically, there is a repetitive series of 5 to 20 forceful coughs in the course of a single expiration. Frequently, vomiting occurs with the cough paroxysm. If a child presents with this history, pertussis must be considered. Infection occurs in epidemic cycles, at a frequency of 2 to 4 years. Paroxysmal coughing without whooping can be found in patients with pneumonia secondary to infection with adenovirus or *Chlamydia* (see Chapter 85).

Habit Cough

Synonyms of habit cough include *psychogenic cough* and *psychosomatic cough*. The typical presentation is a bright-eyed child, worried parents, and a harassed physician.[8] This cough may occur without the signs and symptoms of respiratory tract disease or with a disease that should be benign. Classically, the cough is described as sounding like the honk of a Canada goose. The key feature of the cough is that it is not present while the patient is asleep. The most common cause is thought to be a conversion or hysterical reaction to a school phobia. The posture is classically described as the chin placed on the chest with the hand held against the throat as if supporting the larynx. Successful treatment has been reported with a variety of therapies. The cough can resolve immediately and for a long term with a single session of appropriate suggestion therapy using the distractor of diluted nebulized topical anesthesia.[29] Other authors report successful treatment with 24 to 48 hours of bedsheet wrapping of the chest to support "weak chest muscles" as a face-saving but deceptive mechanism.[5] Benign neglect with no parental reinforcement may also be beneficial. Frequently, one or both parents may resist the diagnosis.

Chlamydia trachomatis *Infection*

Chlamydial infection frequently presents as a pneumonia occurring in the first 6 months of life, usually associated with a prolonged afebrile illness featuring congestion, cough, tachypnea, rales, hyperinflated lungs with diffuse interstitial alveolar infiltrates, peripheral eosinophilia, and elevated levels of serum immunoglobulins.[8] The cough is described as staccato and can cause cyanosis and emesis. There is a brief inspiration followed by a cycle of staccato cough and then a brief inspiration with the cycle repeating itself. There may be a preceding conjunctivitis.

Congenital Rubella or Cytomegalovirus Infection

Congenital rubella and cytomegalovirus infections can cause cough for weeks to months after birth.

Mycoplasma pneumoniae *Infection*

The initial presentation of *Mycoplasma pneumoniae* infection is a dry cough, but this cough rapidly progresses to become a mucoid or mucopurulent cough. Commonly, there are paroxysms of coughing while the patient is sleeping. School-age children are at highest risk.

Immunocompromised Host

If the host is known to be immunocompromised, unusual causes should be sought, including infection with *Pneumocystis carinii, Cryptococcus neoformans,* and cytomegalovirus. With the last organism, the cough is often nonproductive or scantily productive. In cases in which no other cause of cough can be found, the possibility of an immunocompromised host should be considered. The differential diagnosis of immunocompromise includes immunoglobulin deficiency and human immunodeficiency virus infection.

Cough Syncope

Coughing can lead to syncopal episodes,[26] typically in children with asthma. The usual sequence is paroxysmal coughing, with facial congestion, turgidity, and cyanosis. Loss of consciousness occurs within seconds, with recovery in seconds to minutes. Pulmonary function tests demonstrate reversible bronchospasm.

Vocal Cord Paralysis

The differential diagnosis of vocal cord paralysis includes Arnold-Chiari syndrome, Ortner syndrome, and idiopathic causes (see Chapter 87). Penetration or aspiration associated with vocal cord paralysis may result in chronic cough.

SELECTED REFERENCES

Beardsmore CS, Simpson H. Cough in children. J Asthma 28:309, 1991.
> *A comprehensive review of cough in children.*

Chang AB. Cough, cough receptors, and asthma in children. Pediatr Pulmonol 28:59, 1999.

Chang AB, Powell CV. Non-specific cough in children: diagnosis and treatment. Hosp Med 59:9, 1998.

Corrao WM. Chronic persistent cough: diagnosis and treatment update. Pediatr Ann 25:3, 1996.

Holinger LD. Chronic cough in infants and children. Laryngoscope 96:316, 1986.
> *Emphasis on the prevalence of cough variant asthma as a cause of chronic cough and support for the usefulness of endoscopy in the diagnosis of chronic cough.*

Holinger LD, Sanders AD. Chronic cough in infants and children: an update. Laryngoscope 101:596, 1991.
> *An update of the 1986 article, again emphasizing the frequency of cough variant asthma as the most common cause of cough.*

Irwin RS, Curley FJ, French CL. Chronic cough: the spectrum and frequency of causes, key components of diagnostic evaluation, and outcome of specific therapy. Am Rev Respir Dis 141:640, 1990.
> *Although written for the adult literature, this article gives an excellent overview of cough.*

Kamei RK. Chronic cough in children. Pediatr Clin North Am 38:593, 1991.
> *An excellent discussion of chronic cough in children.*

REFERENCES

1. Beardsmore CS, Simpson H. Cough in children. J Asthma 28:309, 1991.
2. Brashear RE. Cough: diagnostic considerations with normal chest roentgenograms. J Fam Pract 15:979, 1982.
3. Camner P, Mossberg B, Philipson K, et al. Elimination of test particles from the human tracheobronchial tract by voluntary coughing. Scand J Respir Dis 60:56, 1979.
4. Cloutier MM, Loughlin GM. Chronic cough in children, a manifestation of airway hyperreactivity. Pediatrics 67:6, 1981.
5. Cochlan SW, Stone SM. The cough and the bedsheet. Pediatrics 74:11, 1984.
6. Cohen RM, Grant W, Lieberman P, et al. The use of methacholine skin testing, distilled water inhalation challenge and eosinophil counts in the evaluation of patients presenting with cough and/or nonwheezy dyspnea. Ann Allergy 56:308, 1986.
7. Colley JRT, Holland WW, Corkhill RT. Influence of passive smoking and parental phlegm on pneumonia and bronchitis in early childhood. Lancet 2:1031, 1974.
8. Cooper DM. Chronic cough. In Kelly VC (ed). Practice of Pediatrics, Vol 2. New York, Harper & Row, 1987, pp 1–10.

9. Corrao WM, Braman FF, Irwin RS. Chronic cough as the sole presenting manifestation of bronchial asthma. N Engl J Med 300: 633, 1979.
10. Davis HL. Chronic cough. In Conn RB (ed). Current Diagnosis, Vol 7. Philadelphia, WB Saunders, 1985, pp 12–17.
11. Dawson KP. The child with a chronic or recurrent cough. N Engl J Med 96:1013, 1983.
12. de Benedictis FM, Canny GJ, Levison H. Methacholine inhalation challenge in the evaluation of chronic cough in children. Asthma 23: 303, 1986.
13. Doan T, Patterson R, Greenberger PA. Coughvariant asthma: usefulness of diagnostic therapeutic trial with prednisone. Ann Allergy 69:505, 1992.
14. Evans JN, Jaeger MJ. Mechanism aspects of coughing. Pneumonologie 152:253, 1975.
15. Gal TJ. Effects of endotracheal intubation on normal cough performance. Anesthesiology 52:324, 1980.
16. Gonzales C, Reilly JS, Bluestone CD. Synchronous airway lesions in infancy. Ann Otol Rhinol Laryngol 96:77, 1987.
17. Goren AJ, Hellman SC. Prevalence of respiratory symptoms and disease in school children living in a polluted and a low polluted area in Israel. Environ Res 45:28, 1988.
18. Hannaway PJ, Hopper GDK. Cough variant asthma in children. JAMA 247:206, 1982.
19. Holinger LD, Sanders AD. Chronic cough in infants and children: an update. Laryngoscope 101:596, 1991.
20. Irwin RS, Pratter MR. Postnasal drip and cough. Clin Notes Respir Dis 18:11, 1980.
21. Irwin RS, Corrao WM, Pratter MR. Chronic persistent cough in the adult: the spectrum and frequency of causes and successful outcome of specific therapy. Am Rev Respir Dis 123:413, 1981.
22. Irwin RS, Pratter MR, Halmolsky MW. Chronic persistent cough: an uncommon presenting complaint of thyroiditis. Chest 81:386, 1982.
23. Irwin RS, Pratter MR, Holland PS, et al. Postnasal drip causes cough and is associated with reversible upper airway obstruction. Chest 85:346, 1984.
24. Jackson C. Postulates on cough reflux in some of its medical and surgical phases. P Ther Gaz 44:609, 1920.
25. Kamai RK. Chronic cough in children. Pediatr Clin North Am 38: 593, 1991.
26. Katz RM. Cough syncope in children with asthma. J Pediatr 77:48, 1970.
27. Landau LI. Letter to editor. Does postnasal drip cause cough? Clin Notes Respir Dis 18:7, 1979.
28. Leith DE. Development of cough. Am Rev Respir Dis 111:S39, 1985.
29. Lokshin B, Lindgren S, Weinberger M, et al. Outcome of habit cough in children treated with a brief session of suggestion therapy. Ann Allergy 67:579, 1991.
30. Luyt DK, Burton PR, Simpson H. Epidemiologic study of wheeze, doctor diagnosed asthma, and cough in preschool children in Leicestershire. Br Med J 306:1386, 1993.
31. McFadden ER. Exertional dyspnea and cough as preludes to attacks of asthma. N Engl J Med 292:555, 1975.
32. Pappas FC, Sasaki A, Minuk GY. Bronchobiliary fistula presenting as cough with yellow sputum [letter]. N Engl J Med 307:1027, 1982.
33. Reisman JJ, Canny GJ, Levison H. The approach to chronic cough in childhood. Ann Allergy 61:163, 1988.
34. Schneck FX, Bellinger MF. The "innocent" cough or sneeze: a harbinger of serious latex allergy in children during bladder stimulation and urodynamic testing. J Urol 150:687, 1993.
35. Shookhoff HB. Cough [letter]. Arch Intern Med 138:1305, 1978.
36. Tsimoyianis GV, Jacobson MS, Feldman JG, et al. Reduction in pulmonary function and increased frequency of cough associated with passive smoking in teenage athletes. Pediatrics 80:32, 1987.
37. Viegi G, Paoletti P, Carrozzi L, et al. Effects of home environment on respiratory symptoms and lung function in a general population sample in North Italy. Eur Respir J 4:580, 1991.
38. Whincup PH, Cook DG, Strachan DP, et al. Time trends and respiratory symptoms in childhood over a 24-year period. Arch Dis Child 68:729, 1993.
39. Wyke S, Hewison J, Hey EN, et al. Respiratory illness in children: do deprived children have worse coughs? Acta Paediatr Scand 80: 704, 1991.
40. Yun DJ, Hong CH, Oh KK. Chronic cough in sinusitis in children. Yonsei Med J 24:67, 1983.

78

Aspiration

R. Casey Strahan, M.D. and Arlen D. Meyers, M.D., M.B.A.

Human survival depends on eating, and the ability of humans to swallow food without aspirating it represents an advanced evolutionary event. The fact that the respiratory and digestive systems share a common conduit demands the use of unique physiologic adaptations. All normal people experience some clinically insignificant aspiration.[48] Aspiration becomes a problem when the aspirated material cannot be cleared or when it is significantly toxic or voluminous. This chapter focuses on the pathogenesis, diagnosis, and management of recurrent aspiration that causes pulmonary compromise.

In children, any important dysfunction of the swallowing mechanism impairs the function of the respiratory tract.[20] To understand the causes and treatment of chronic aspiration, therefore, the physician must be acquainted with the anatomy and physiology of the swallowing mechanism and with those morbid and pathophysiologic events that alter it.

A thorough history and physical examination often reveal the underlying cause of the aspiration. In more complex cases, additional studies, including imaging studies and endoscopy, are needed to further elucidate the disease process. The treatment of aspiration must account for the severity of the problem and should be directed at both preventing permanent lung damage and resolving the underlying disease.

Anatomy and Physiology

The anatomy and physiology of the mouth, pharynx, and esophagus are discussed in detail in Chapters 50 and 51. However, certain points should be stressed with regard to disorders of swallowing and aspiration in children.

The swallowing mechanism can be divided into four phases: the preparatory phase, the oral phase, the pharyngeal phase, and the esophageal phase.[32, 65] The first two phases are under voluntary control, and the second two are reflexes. In the preparatory phase, food is taken into the oral cavity and prepared into a bolus held between the hard palate and central anterior two thirds of the tongue. While food is being chewed, it is prevented from passing into the pharynx by apposition of the base of the tongue with the soft palate. During the oral phase, the anterior tongue elevates and contacts the hard palate, the soft palate closes off the nasopharynx, and the food bolus is pushed into the pharynx. Several investigators have discussed the physiologic aspects of sucking and swallowing in normal and abnormal infants.[1, 6, 8, 10, 27, 37, 41, 68, 73, 77, 93] Squeezing the liquid from the nipple seems to be part of the infant's oral phase. Indeed, it appears that sucking is only half as effective as squeezing liquid from a nipple.[1]

The pharyngeal phase begins reflexively when the bolus passes the tonsillar pillars. A conduit, the *palatopharyngeal partition*,[30] is formed by the apposing pharyngeal constrictors, palate, and palatopharyngeus. This conduit directs the food into the hypopharynx. At this point, the tongue base elevates against the posterior pharyngeal wall, the pharynx and larynx elevate, and the prepared food is engulfed.

Opening of the cricopharyngeus muscle initiates the fourth phase of swallowing, the esophageal phase.[1, 43] As this phase begins, several events occur. The cricopharyngeus relaxes, respiration stops, the glottis closes, the nasopharynx is occluded by the velum, and peristalsis begins.[89]

The last two phases of swallowing are reflex actions. The afferent limb consists of sensory and proprioceptive fibers in the glossopharyngeal, trigeminal, and superior laryngeal nerves. Impulses are transmitted to the *swallowing center* in the floor of the fourth ventricle. The efferent limb begins in the nucleus ambiguus of the medulla and descends in the vagus.

There are three limbs to the mechanism of airway protection in the normal person. First, the larynx acts as a sphincter that guards the respiratory tract from particulate invasion. There are three tiers to this sphincter, and these are, from superior to inferior, the epiglottis and aryepiglottic folds, the false vocal folds, and the true vocal folds. The second limb of airway protection is cough, initiated by sensory receptors in the epithelium of the large and small airways. During a cough, air leaves the trachea at high speeds, assisting in the mucociliary clearance of debris deposited in the tracheobronchial tree. The last limb of protection is swallowing, which clears material from the larynx and oropharynx.

The swallowing mechanism of children varies in several ways from that of adults.[1, 30] Because the hard palate is relatively closer to the base of the skull in children, angulation of the soft palate during nasopharyngeal closure is not a prominent feature. The adenoid pad also contributes to closure in children. In addition, the tonsils

TABLE 78-1. Disease Processes Associated with Aspiration

I. Anatomic or Mechanical Anomalies

Congenital Abnormalities

Partial or complete mandibular agenesis
First and second branchial arch syndromes
Cleft palate
Short palate
Macroglossia[23]
Microglossia
Ankyloglossia superior[97]
Choanal atresia
Laryngeal cleft[7, 29, 30]
Laryngeal ptosis
Esophageal absence
Esophageal stenosis, webs, atresia
Esophageal duplication
Tracheoesophageal fistula
Cardiovascular anomalies (e.g., vascular rings)
Pharyngeal diverticulum or pouch[12, 18]

Traumatic

Pseudodiverticulum of the pharynx[71]
Foreign body (including endotracheal or tracheostomy tube)
Laryngeal endotracheal tube damage or other trauma during intubation[39, 55]

Neoplasm

Infection or Edema of Laryngeal Structures

II. Neuromuscular or Functional Disorders

Central

Tumor or degenerative disorders of CNS[20, 41]
Immaturity of newborn[6, 37]
Cerebral palsy[35]
Agenesis of nucleus ambiguus
Bulbar paralysis[20]
Dysautonomia
Hydrocephalus
Seizures

Neuromuscular

Cricopharyngeal achalasia[85]
Muscular dystrophy
Tetanus[3]
Myasthenia gravis
Superior or recurrent laryngeal nerve paralysis

Functional

Gastroesophageal reflux
Collagen vascular diseases (scleroderma, dermatomyositis)

---

act as directors of small quantities of food into the oropharynx and help to keep the airway open until the child is ready to swallow. Because the larynx is relatively higher in the neck in children, there is less upper and posterior movement of the hyoid and larynx. Finally, the swallowing frequency during sleep in the adult is one sixtieth that of the sleeping preterm infant (six swallows per minute).

Common Causes

Pulmonary aspiration is not a primary pathologic process but rather the sequela of an abnormality in the swallowing or airway protective mechanism, or both. Thus, aspiration requires treatment of the pulmonary sequelae as well as a work-up to uncover its underlying cause.

Pulmonary aspiration can be classified first by the site of origin of the aspirate. There are three main categories of aspirated material: orally ingested material, oral and upper-airway secretions, and regurgitated gastric contents. Aspiration can be further classified into mechanical versus functional causes (Table 78-1). Mechanical causes include those anatomic, traumatic, neoplastic, and infectious abnormalities that result in an alteration in the structure of the upper aerodigestive tract such that the normal swallowing and airway protective mechanisms are compromised. Foremost in this category for children are congenital abnormalities of the upper aerodigestive tract. Functional causes of aspiration include neuromuscular disorders that interfere with normal swallowing and laryngeal function.

Abnormalities associated with chronic pulmonary aspiration are summarized in Table 78-1. The most common abnormality associated with chronic pulmonary aspiration is gastroesophageal reflux (GER).[4] The complex relationship between GER and aspiration has been the subject of a considerable amount of literature in the last 10 years.[81] Thus, GER as a cause of aspiration deserves special mention. Signs of aspiration due to GER may be as obvious as postprandial cough, regurgitation, or emesis, or they may be as seemingly unrelated as bronchospasm, laryngospasm, central apnea, or bradycardia.[81] However, one cannot assume that the coexistence of both diseases implies a causal relationship. Indeed, it is often necessary to treat the reflux and then wait and see if the pulmonary condition improves.[81]

An association of GER with sudden infant death syndrome (SIDS) and apparent life-threatening events (ALTEs) has been postulated. Although the role of GER in these diseases has not been fully defined and much controversy exists in this area, considerable evidence links these syndromes. The pathophysiology of SIDS and ALTEs appears to be multifactorial, and several studies implicate GER as one of these factors, especially in the case of ALTEs.[28, 66] The incidence of significant GER in patients with ALTEs (20% to 70%, depending on the study) is much higher than in normal infants, and GER has been temporally linked to apneic events.[51, 66, 67] Reflux is postulated to cause bradycardia, central apnea, and laryngospasm via reflexes involving the stimulation of distal esophageal receptors as well as laryngeal receptors.[5, 53]

GER is covered in detail in Chapter 69.

Diagnosis

As mentioned earlier, aspiration of small amounts of oropharyngeal secretions is normal, especially during sleep.[48] Aspiration that results in pulmonary sequelae represents disease. The work-up of this disease must therefore establish (1) that aspiration is significant and (2) that pulmonary function is compromised or threatened. As there is no single test or combination of tests that can establish this with 100% sensitivity and specificity, a great deal of clinical judgment is often necessary. Often, the clinician can only prove that aspiration is occurring and must then infer that this aspiration is causing the child's problems, often by the exclusion of other possibilities.

History

The approach to a patient with recurrent aspiration begins with a thorough history designed to uncover those symptoms suggestive of anatomic or physiologic abnormalities of the mouth, laryngopharynx, esophagus, or respiratory tract.[35] The presence of certain risk factors can predispose an infant to aspiration. These include a depressed level of consciousness (as in coma or sleep), deficient swallowing mechanisms, sickness or debilitation, and preterm birth.[92]

The feeding history is often key in the evaluation of aspiration. Poor sucking habits or nasopharyngeal reflux during feedings suggests at least oropharyngeal discoordination and may indicate poor swallowing coordination. Poor sucking habits may manifest as the need for an enlarged nipple hole, the inability to breathe and suck at the same time, and frequent choking and gagging. The association of respiratory symptoms during or shortly after feeding is highly suggestive of aspiration and warrants thorough investigation. Failure to thrive can be due to chronic feeding problems associated with aspiration. It is important to note methods of improving a feeding problem. If an infant aspirates only liquids, attention should be directed to the extent of glottic competence as the basic problem.

The child's prenatal and birth history are also important. Hydramnios can be associated with defects of the esophagus such as esophageal atresia, tracheoesophageal fistula, and ectatic esophagus.[44, 95] A traumatic delivery, including forceps delivery, predisposes the infant to unilateral or bilateral recurrent laryngeal nerve injury. Upper-airway instrumentation, although usually benign, can lead to significant injury, including pseudodiverticulum formation and pneumothorax.[33, 71] Near-miss SIDS may be a manifestation of GER with aspiration during sleep.[44, 67]

The patient's family history should also be investigated, with special attention to a history of neurologic disease.

Physical Examination

Methods of examining the mouth, pharynx, and esophagus are discussed in Chapter 52. Inspection and palpation of all mucous membranes of the nose, oral cavity, and oropharynx are essential in dealing with children who aspirate chronically. The examiner should observe the child during feeding. Insertion of the examiner's finger into the child's mouth can reveal information about the strength and coordination of sucking, as well as the resistance to deep finger insertion. A hyperactive or hypoactive gag reflex may be elicited. Specific information about feeding and feeding reflexes can be gained if the physician bottle feeds the patient.[35] Signs such as unusual feeding movements, difficulty in breathing, and drooling should be noted. Some authors think that auscultation of the pharynx yields valuable information.[35] Several anatomic abnormalities can result in aspiration and should be noted (see Table 78–1).

Auscultation of the lungs may reveal findings nonspecific for aspiration. Aspiration pneumonia typically occurs in the dependent lobes. Examination before and after feeding may reveal differences suggesting aspiration.

In addition, a general physical examination with attention to the neurologic system is basic to the evaluation of children with feeding problems, as several syndromes of neurologic dysfunction are commonly associated with dysphagia and subsequent aspiration. Drooling and excess accumulation of secretions in the mouth may be manifestations of swallowing disorders or tracheoesophageal fistula. Gaseous abdominal distention also occurs with tracheoesophageal fistula.

Ancillary Tests and Examinations

If the history and physical examination leave the physician in doubt as to the cause of the aspiration, ancillary studies are indicated (Table 78–2). A lateral neck film and plain chest films are usually the initial studies of choice. The lateral neck film may reveal structural abnormalities of the upper aerodigestive tract. In patients with chronic aspiration, the chest film appearance may vary from normal to one of diffuse, severe involvement. In a group of 22 patients with recurrent aspiration, Colombo reported localized infiltrates in 41%, diffuse infiltrates in 27%, bronchial wall thickening in 18%, and a normal appearance in 14%.[21]

The modified barium swallow is usually the next examination of choice (Fig. 78–1). Several techniques for performing cineradiography in children have been described.[1, 80, 87, 95] Characteristic abnormalities of pharyngeal motion are readily visualized.[31, 35, 77, 83] Generally, aspiration occurs in one of two ways[35]: (1) directly, at the time of swallowing, or (2) later, with barium running into the trachea after the preceding swallow during inspiration or expiration. Besides aspiration, a barium swallow may reveal functional abnormalities of swallowing such as nasopharyngeal reflux or cricopharyngeal achalasia[54] or structural abnormalities such as a laryngotracheoesophageal cleft or tracheoesophageal fistula. Finally, GER or a hiatal hernia may be revealed. However, the barium esophagogram has been shown to be only 50% to 85% sensitive in detecting GER, with a false-positive rate of 25% to 30%.[2, 69, 72]

Methods of detecting GER are discussed in detail in Chapter 69. Briefly, these include prolonged monitoring of esophageal pH, gastric scintiscan, barium swallow, and esophagoscopy with esophageal biopsy. It must be kept in mind, however, that the demonstration of reflux alone does not prove aspiration or a causal link to known aspiration or pulmonary disease.

A newer method for detecting GER and aspiration is radionuclide scintigraphy. Several variations of this method

TABLE 78–2. Studies Useful in the Evaluation of Aspiration

Lateral soft tissue radiograph of neck
Chest radiograph
Modified barium swallow
Esophageal pH probe
Gastroesophageal scintigraphy
Lipid-laden macrophage index
Endoscopy with or without biopsies

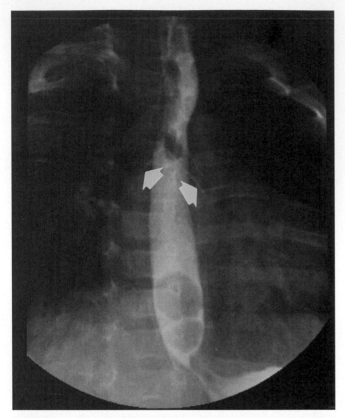

FIGURE 78–1. Thin liquid barium swallow demonstrating aspiration of barium into the trachea. The arrows indicate barium in the right and left mainstem bronchi.

have been described.[9, 45, 46, 70, 94] In general, a radioisotope is mixed with oral or gastric feedings, and the esophagus or tracheobronchial tree, or both, are examined for radioactivity some time later. The advantage of this method is that radioactivity in the lungs or tracheal washings must have originated wherever the radioisotope was instilled, giving a clue as to where the aspiration is originating (e.g., oral versus gastric contents). The sensitivity of this test is highly dependent on several technical aspects of its performance, including the timing of the scanning.[46, 70] However, this test can be very useful in linking GER to aspiration and has been used in the study of near-miss SIDS.[9]

The examination of respiratory secretions can also give clues linking GER to aspiration. Several studies have linked the finding of lipid-laden macrophages in pulmonary secretions to aspiration due to GER.[22, 24, 79] However, this finding is not specific to aspiration and can be found in cases of bronchial obstruction and intravenous lipid infusion.[19, 84] Bronchoalveolar lavage fluid can also be examined microscopically for meat and vegetable fibers, indicating aspiration of gastric contents.[25, 86] Lastly, for patients with artificial airways in place, oral or gastric feedings can be labeled with colored dyes, and tracheal secretions can be examined for the presence of staining.[13, 17, 39] However, positive findings correlate directly with the volume of dye used; thus, this test should be interpreted carefully.

Finally, high levels of antibodies against bovine milk may suggest recurrent aspiration in infants and children fed cow's milk.[78]

In the case of known or suspected neurologic disorders, computed tomography or magnetic resonance imaging of the brain is usually indicated.

Endoscopy

Endoscopy in children is discussed in Chapter 76. If the history, physical examination, and ancillary test results fail to reveal the cause of chronic aspiration, direct laryngoscopy, esophagoscopy, and bronchoscopy are indicated. Endoscopy often complements many of these tests. For example, laryngotracheoesophageal cleft may be differentiated from a tracheoesophageal fistula only after both a barium swallow and rigid endoscopy. Similarly, GER may be suggested on barium swallow but only confirmed by esophageal biopsy. A vascular ring is a rare cause of dysphagia that may predispose to aspiration and that may be suspected only after endoscopy.

The choice of flexible versus rigid endoscopy depends on the individual patient and the information desired. Flexible laryngoscopy and bronchoscopy can be performed in the awake child and are valuable in assessing the function of various structures. Rigid endoscopy requires a general anesthetic and is excellent for assessing structural abnormalities and obtaining biopsies.

Treatment

Treatment of chronic aspiration should follow a stepwise approach, with the severity of the aspiration dictating the degree of intervention necessary.

Underlying abnormalities predisposing to aspiration should be corrected first whenever possible. In the case of anatomic anomalies, correction may require surgical intervention, such as closure of a tracheoesophageal fistula or laryngotracheoesophageal cleft. Airway foreign bodies such as endotracheal tubes or tracheotomy tubes should be removed as soon as it is safe to do so. The treatment of GER is covered in detail in Chapter 69 and is summarized in Table 78–3. Initial treatment involves positioning, thickening of feedings, use of small and frequent feedings in infants, and fasting before bedtime in older children. In infants, the optimal position is upright or prone, and sitting may actually exacerbate the reflux.[82] When these measures fail, pharmacologic therapy is indicated. This typically involves the use of metoclopramide (Reglan) to increase lower esophageal sphincter tone and increase gastric emptying and H_2 blockers to increase the pH of the reflux material. Bethanechol can also be used to increase lower esophageal sphincter tone and gastric emptying, but it must be used cautiously as it can precipitate bronchospasm in patients with reactive airways. Sucralfate may be used in a case of GER related to delayed gastric emptying due to ulcers in or near the pylorus. According to most authors, failure of 6 weeks of medical therapy is an indication for antireflux surgery.[4, 11, 52]

When the treatment of underlying diseases is inadequate or impossible (e.g., as most neurologic disorders), steps can be taken to minimize the aspiration or at least

TABLE 78–3. Treatment of Symptomatic GER

Medical
   Thickened feedings
   Positioning (prone or upright)
   Metoclopramide
   Bethanechol
   H$_2$ blockers
   Sucralfate
Surgical
   Fundoplication
      Partial—Thal procedure
      Complete—Nissen procedure
   Pyloroplasty
   Gastric tube

TABLE 78–4. Surgical Treatment Options for Chronic Aspiration in Infants and Children

Alimentary procedures
   Feeding gastrostomy or jejunostomy
   Fundoplication
   Cricopharyngeal myotomy
Laryngeal incompetence procedures
   Tracheostomy
   Vocal fold medialization
   Glottic closure or epiglottoplasty
   Laryngeal diversion or separation

the damage done by the aspiration. In the setting of aspiration pneumonia, antibiotic coverage and pulmonary toilet measures are necessary. The choice of antibiotics depends on the suspected pathogens, with particular attention paid to whether the infection was acquired in the hospital or not. Broad anaerobic coverage is recommended. In a child with teeth, maintenance of good oral hygiene may help reduce the damage done by aspirated saliva. Dietary and swallowing therapy may be of benefit in a child with chronic swallowing dysfunction. Speech and swallowing therapists performing the modified barium swallow may be able to recommend changes in food consistency and patient positioning to minimize aspiration. If the aspiration appears to be self-limited or temporary,[71] measures such as nasogastric tubes, gastrostomy, esophagotomy, parenteral feeding, or tracheotomy may be of benefit until the abnormality is corrected. Patients with neurologic or neuromuscular abnormalities frequently benefit from a program of physical therapy directed toward retraining damaged pharyngeal or oral muscles. Several techniques for feeding and teaching patients with swallowing disabilities have been described and should be used before surgery is considered.[14, 15, 38, 42, 47, 59]

The otolaryngologist is often consulted when these measures fail or when aspiration is life-threatening—i.e., when surgical intervention is contemplated. The choice of surgical procedure depends on many factors, including the severity of the aspiration, underlying disorders, the potential for rehabilitation, the presence of neurologic dysfunction, and the degree of malnutrition. These procedures can be alimentary procedures that reduce GER or bypass the upper aerodigestive tract during feedings, or laryngeal incompetence procedures that protect the airway directly (Table 78–4).

Alimentary procedures include feeding gastrostomy or jejunostomy, fundoplication, and cricopharyngeal myotomy. Feeding gastrostomy or jejunostomy tubes are the most common procedures for severe or irreversible swallowing dysfunction. They are especially indicated when chronic aspiration becomes associated with malnutrition. However, these tubes do not in themselves prevent GER or aspiration of oral secretions. Gastric fundoplication is indicated for severe GER that has not responded to conservative therapy. This procedure lengthens the intra-abdominal portion of the esophagus and attempts to create a one-way valve at the lower esophageal sphincter by wrapping the upper portion of the stomach around the lower portion of the esophagus. This procedure is highly effective in controlling GER, but it does not prevent aspiration of oral secretions. Cricopharyngeal achalasia may be treated with esophageal dilations in mild cases or with cricopharyngeal myotomy in severe cases.[85, 90] This condition is usually diagnosed by means of a modified barium swallow or esophageal manometry. The myotomy procedure uses a lateral cervical approach to divide the cricopharyngeus over an esophageal bougie, taking care to preserve the esophageal mucosa.

Laryngeal incompetence procedures include tracheotomy, laryngectomy, vocal-fold medialization, laryngeal closure, and laryngeal diversion or separation. Tracheotomy provides a temporary means of increasing pulmonary toilet and may be helpful as a temporary measure for severe aspiration with pulmonary complications. Tracheotomy, however, does not prevent aspiration, and in the setting of chronic aspiration a more definitive procedure is required.[17] Laryngectomy does permanently separate the air and food passages but is usually reserved for adults with oropharyngeal cancer.

Simpler and less deforming procedures have been devised for diverting the air and food passages in the absence of cancer. Vocal-fold medialization procedures are indicated for incomplete glottic closure, usually due to vocal-fold paralysis. This can be accomplished either endoscopically or via an external approach.[26] Endoscopically, various materials, including polytetrafluoroethylene (Teflon) and Gelfoam, are injected into the vocal fold to medialize the fold.[61, 62, 88] In the setting of bilateral vocal-fold paralysis, however, bilateral vocal-fold injection has been shown to be ineffectual.[60] Externally, a type I thyroplasty is performed via a window in the thyroid cartilage. The vocal fold is medialized by augmentation with either cartilage or a silicone-based (Silastic) implant.[49, 50, 76] In the setting of congenital recurrent laryngeal nerve paralysis, including bilateral paralysis, it is recommended that surgical procedures on the larynx be delayed several years, as the nerve often recovers.[36]

Many techniques have been described for laryngeal closure or to increase laryngeal competence. However, most of these come from studies on adults who have undergone surgical procedures for ablative cancer. These include suspension of the larynx, posterior cricoid resection, epiglottoplasty, glottic closure, and laryngeal stents.[16, 40, 56, 57, 75, 96] Few, if any, of these procedures appear applicable to children.

Laryngeal diversion and separation are the most definitive procedures for chronic aspiration. These procedures

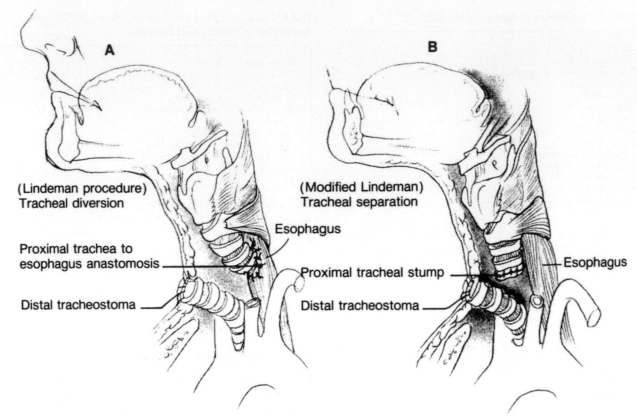

FIGURE 78–2. Diagram of the Lindeman procedure (laryngeal diversion) and its modification (laryngeal separation). (From Dunham ME, Holinger LD. Stridor, aspiration, and cough. In Bailey BJ, Johnson JT, Kohut RI, et al [eds]. Head and Neck Surgery–Otolaryngology. Philadelphia, JB Lippincott, 1993, p 686.)

are indicated for severe aspiration due to laryngeal incompetence that is not expected to recover.[34] They are thus especially useful in cases of central neurologic defects. Lindeman first described the procedure in which the trachea is divided just below the larynx, the proximal stump is anastomosed to the esophagus, and the distal stump is brought out to the skin as a permanent tracheostoma.[63] This technique was later modified by creating a blind pouch with the proximal stump (Fig. 78–2).[58, 74] Neither procedure is technically difficult, and both are highly effective in preventing aspiration. Successful reversal of these procedures has been reported in cases in which the patient regained laryngeal function.[64, 91]

Conclusions

Children with chronic aspiration most commonly have associated anatomic or neurologic abnormalities that interfere with normal swallowing or airway protection, or both. Defining the cause frequently requires a thorough history and physical examination as well as complete radiographic and endoscopic evaluation. Although some patients have transient dysfunction, most have permanent abnormalities that require treatment. GER is commonly associated with aspiration in children. Nutritional support and pulmonary toilet are of paramount importance. Although physical therapy and medical therapy can be ben-

eficial, many patients continue to aspirate and may require appropriate surgical intervention.

SELECTED REFERENCES

Bauer ML, Figueroa-Colon R, Georgeson K, Young DW. Chronic pulmonary aspiration in children. South Med J 86:789, 1993.

This article summarizes the authors' approach to the pediatric patient with suspected aspiration and reviews the pathophysiology, work-up, and treatment of chronic aspiration in children.

Bosma JF. Deglutition, pharyngeal stage. Physiol Rev 37:275, 1957.

Although somewhat dated, this article presents a comprehensive review of the physiology of the oral and pharyngeal stages of swallowing. It presents a nice framework of the neurologic pathways of deglutition, abnormalities of which are frequently found in newborns with aspiration.

Lewis WS, Wikholm RP, Passy V. Bilateral vocal cord Teflon injection: an ineffective treatment for recurrent aspiration pneumonia. Arch Otolaryngol Head Neck Surg 117:427, 1991.

Although the proposed procedure proved to be ineffectual, the authors present an excellent review of the various surgical options for the treatment of chronic aspiration. Most of the literature reviewed pertains to adults.

Reichert TJ, Bluestone CD, Stool SE, et al. Congenital cricopharyngeal achalasia. Ann Otol Rhinol Laryngol 76:603, 1977.

The authors present in this article 13 cases of cricopharyngeal achalasia in children with comments on their management. The physiology and anatomy of the cricopharyngeal muscle are reviewed.

Thack BT, Menon A. Pulmonary protective mechanisms in human infants. Am Rev Respir Dis 131:555, 1985.

A good review of infantile swallowing physiology, particularly during sleep, during prolonged apnea, and during and following postfeeding regurgitation.

REFERENCES

1. Andross GM, Kemp FH, Lind J. A cineradiographic study of bottle feeding. Br J Radiol 31:11, 1958.
2. Arasu TS, Wyllie R, Fitzgerald JF, et al. Gastroesophageal reflux in infants and children-comparative accuracy of diagnostic methods. J Pediatr 96:798, 1980.
3. Atharale VB, Pai PN. Tetanus-clinical manifestations in children. J Pediatr 65:590, 1964.
4. Bauer ML, Figueroa-Colon R, Georgeson K, et al. Chronic pulmonary aspiration in children. South Med J 86:789, 1993.
5. Bauman NM, Sandler AD, Schmidt C, et al. Reflex laryngospasm induced by stimulation of distal esophageal afferents. Laryngoscope 104:209, 1994.
6. Benson PF. Transient dysphagia due to muscular incoordination. Proc R Soc Med 55:237, 1962.
7. Berkoritz RNP, Bos CE, Struben WH. Congenital laryngotracheoesophageal cleft. Arch Otolaryngol 100:442, 1974.
8. Bishop HC. Cricopharyngeal achalasia and childhood. J Pediatr Surg 9:775, 1974.
9. Boonyaprapa S, Alderson P, Garfinkel D, et al. Detection of pulmonary aspiration in infants and children with respiratory disease: concise communication. J Nucl Med 21:314, 1980.
10. Bosma JF. Deglutition, pharyngeal stage. Physiol Rev 37:275, 1957.
11. Boyle JT. Gastroesophageal reflux in the pediatric patient. Gastroenterol Clin North Am 18:315, 1989.
12. Britnall ES, Kridelbaugh WW. Congenital diverticulum of the posterior hypopharynx simulating atresia of the esophagus. Am J Surg 131:564, 1950.
13. Browning D, Graves S. Incidence of aspiration with endotracheal tubes in children. J Pediatr 102:582, 1983.
14. Buckley JE, Addicka CL, Maniglia J. Feeding patients with dysphagia. Nurs Forum 15:69, 1976.
15. Bullock J. Dysphagia. Nurs Time 71:1928, 1975.
16. Calcaterra TC. Laryngeal suspension after supraglottic laryngectomy. Arch Otolaryngol 94:306, 1971.
17. Cameron J, Reynolds J, Zuidema G. Aspiration in patients with tracheostomies. Surg Gynecol Obstet 136:68, 1973.
18. Clay B. Congenital lateral pharyngeal diverticulum. Br J Radiol 45:863, 1972.
19. Cohen A, Cline M. In vitro studies of the foamy macrophage of postobstructive endogenous lipoid pneumonia in man. Am Rev Respir Dis 106:69, 1972.
20. Cohen SR. Congenital dysphagia: neurogenic considerations. Laryngoscope 65:515, 1955.
21. Colombo JI. Pulmonary aspiration. In Hilman BC (ed). Pediatric Respiratory Disease: Diagnosis and Treatment. Philadelphia, WB Saunders, 1993, pp 429–436.
22. Colombo JL, Hallberg TK. Recurrent aspiration in children: lipid-laden alveolar macrophage quantitation. Pediatr Pulmonol 3:86, 1987.
23. Combs JT, Grunt JA, Brandt IK. A new syndrome of neonatal hypoglycemia: association with visceromegaly, macroglossia, microcephaly, and abnormal umbilicus. N Engl J Med 275:236, 1965.
24. Corwin R, Irwin R. The lipid-laden alveolar macrophage as a marker of aspiration in parenchymal lung disease. Am Rev Respir Dis 132:576, 1985.
25. Crausaz F, Favez G. Aspiration of solid food particles into lungs of patients with gastroesophageal reflux and chronic bronchial disease. Chest 93:376, 1988.
26. Crumley RL. Teflon versus thyroplasty versus nerve transfer: a comparison. Ann Otol Rhinol Laryngol 99:759, 1990.
27. Culley JRT, Creamer B. Sucking and swallowing in infants. Br Med J 2:422, 1958.
28. De Bethmann O, Couchard M, de Ajuriaguerra M, et al. Role of gastro-esophageal reflux and vagal overactivity in apparent life-threatening events: 160 cases. Acta Paediatr Suppl 82:102, 1993.
29. Delahunty JE, Cherry L. Congenital laryngeal cleft. Ann Otol Rhinol Laryngol 78:96, 1969.
30. Del Monico ML, Hoar JG. Bifid epiglottis. Arch Otolaryngol 96:178, 1972.
31. Donner MW. Swallowing mechanism and neuromuscular disorders. Semin Roentgenol 9:273, 1974.
32. Dunham ME, Holinger LD. Stridor, aspiration, and cough. In Bailey BJ, Johnson JT, Kohut RI, et al (eds). Head and Neck Surgery–Otolaryngology. Philadelphia, JB Lippincott, 1993.
33. Edison B, Holinger PH. Traumatic pharyngeal pseudodiverticulum in the newborn infant. J Pediatr 82:483, 1973.
34. Eisele DW, Yarington CT, Lindeman RC. Indications for the tracheal esophageal diversion procedure and the laryngotracheal separation procedure. Ann Otol Rhinol Laryngol 97:471, 1988.
35. Ekdahl C, Mansson I, Sandberg N. Swallowing dysfunction in the brain-damaged with drooling. Acta Otolaryngol (Stockh) 78:141, 1974.
36. Emery PJ, Fearon B. Vocal cord palsy in pediatric practice: a review of 71 cases. Int J Pediatr Otorhinolaryngol 8:147, 1984.
37. Frank MM, Baghdassrian-Gatewood OM. Transient pharyngeal incoordination in the newborn. Am J Dis Child 111:178, 1966.
38. Gaffney TW, Campbell RP. Feeding techniques for dysphagic patients. Am J Nurs 74:2194, 1974.
39. Goitein K, Rein A, Gornstein A. Incidence of aspiration in endotracheally intubated infants and children. Crit Care Med 12:19, 1984.
40. Goode RL. Laryngeal suspension in head and neck surgery. Laryngoscope 86:349, 1976.
41. Graham PJ. Congenital flaccid bulbar palsy. Br Med J 2:26, 1964.
42. Griffin KM. Swallowing training for dysphagic patients. Arch Phys Med Rehab 55:467, 1974.
43. Hendrix TR. The motility of the alimentary canal. In Mountcastle UB (ed). Medical Physiology. St Louis, CV Mosby, 1974.
44. Herbst JJ, Book LS, Bray PF. Gastroesophageal reflux in the "near miss" sudden infant death syndrome. Pediatrics 92:73, 1978.
45. Heyman S, Respondek M. Detection of pulmonary aspiration in children by radionuclide "salivagram." J Nucl Med 30:697, 1989.
46. Heyman S, Kirkpatrick J, Winter H, Treves S. An improved radionuclide method for the diagnosis of gastroesophageal reflux and aspiration in children (milk scan). Radiology 131:479, 1979.
47. Holser-Beuhler P. The Blanchard method of feeding the cerebral palsied. Am J Occup Ther 20:31, 1966.
48. Huxley E, Viroslav J, Gray W, et al. Pharyngeal aspiration in normal adults and patients with depressed consciousness. Am J Med 64:564, 1978.
49. Isshiki N, Okamura H, Ishikawa T. Thyroplasty type I (lateral compression) for dysphonia due to vocal cord paralysis or atrophy. Acta Otolaryngol (Stockh) 80:465, 1975.
50. Isshiki N, Taira T, Kojima H, et al. Recent modifications in thyroplasty type I. Ann Otol Rhinol Laryngol 98:777, 1989.
51. Jeffery HG, Rahilly P, Read DJ. Multiple causes of asphyxia in infants at high risk for sudden infant death. Arch Dis Child 58:92, 1983.
52. Jolley SG, Johnson DG, Herbst JN, et al. The significance of gastroesophageal reflux patterns in children. J Pediatr Surg 16:859, 1981.
53. Kernigsberg K, Griswold PG, Buckley BJ, et al. Cardiac effects of oesophageal stimulation: possible relationship between gastroesophageal reflux and sudden infant death syndrome (SIDS). J Pediatr Surg 18:542, 1983.
54. Kilman WJ, Rajk G. Disorders of the pharyngeal and upper-esophageal sphincter motor function. Arch Intern Med 136:592, 1976.
55. Krajina Z, Vecerina S. Act of swallowing in the fixed larynx. Acta Otolaryngol (Stockh) 81:323, 1976.
56. Krespi YP, Sisson GA. Reconstruction after total or subtotal glossectomy. Am J Surg 146:488, 1983.
57. Krespi YP, Pelzer HJ, Sisson GA. Management of chronic aspiration by subtotal and submucosal cricoid resection. Ann Otol Rhinol Laryngol 94:580, 1985.
58. Krespi YP, Quataz VC, Sisson GA, et al. Modified tracheoesophageal diversion for chronic aspiration. Laryngoscope 94:1298, 1984.
59. Larsen GL. Rehabilitation for dysphagia paralytica. J Speech Hear Disord 37:187, 1972.
60. Lewis WS, Wikholm RP, Passy V. Bilateral vocal cord Teflon injec-

tion: an ineffective treatment for recurrent aspiration pneumonia. Arch Otolaryngol Head Neck Surg 117:427, 1991.

61. Lewy RB. Teflon injection of the vocal cord: Complications, errors, and precautions. Ann Otol Rhinol Laryngol 92:473, 1983.

62. Lewy RB. Glottic rehabilitation with Teflon injection: the return of voice, cough, and laughter. Acta Otolaryngol (Stockh) 58:215, 1964.

63. Lindeman RC. Diverting the paralyzed larynx: a reversible procedure for intractable aspiration. Laryngoscope 85:157, 1975.

64. Lindeman RC, Yarington CT, Sutton D. Clinical experience with the tracheoesophageal anastomosis for intractable aspiration. Ann Otol Rhinol Laryngol 85:609, 1976.

65. Logemann JA. Manual for the videofluorographic study of swallowing. San Diego, College Hill Press, 1986.

66. MacFadyen UM. Regurgitation and sudden infant death syndrome. Acta Paediatr Suppl 82 389:98, 1993.

67. MacFadyen UM, Hendry GMA, Simpson H. Gastroesophageal reflux in near-miss sudden infant death syndrome or suspected aspiration. Arch Dis Child 58:87, 1983.

68. Margulies SE, Brunt PW, Donner MW, et al. Familial dysautonomia. Radiology 90:107, 1968.

69. McCauley RG, Darling DB, Leonidas JC, et al. Gastroesophageal reflux in infants and children: a useful classification and reliable physiologic technique for its demonstration. AJR 130:47, 1978.

70. McVeagh P, Howman-Giles R, Demp A. Pulmonary aspiration studied by radionuclide milk scanning and barium swallow roentgenography. Am J Dis Child 141:917, 1987.

71. Meyers A, Lillydahl P, Brown G. Hypopharyngeal perforations in neonates. Arch Otolaryngol 104:51, 1978.

72. Meyers WF, Roberts CC, Johnson DG, et al. Value of tests for evaluation of gastroesophageal reflux in children. J Pediatr Surg 20:515, 1985.

73. Mistretta CM, Bradley RM. Taste and swallowing in utero. Br Med Bull 31:80, 1975.

74. Montgomery WW. Surgery to prevent aspiration. Arch Otolaryngol 101:679, 1975.

75. Montgomery WW. Surgical laryngeal closure to eliminate chronic aspiration. N Engl J Med 292:1390, 1975.

76. Montgomery WW, Blaugrund SM, Varvares MA. Thyroplasty: a new approach. Ann Otol Rhinol Laryngol 102:571, 1993.

77. Moosa A. The feeding difficulty in infantile myotonic dystrophy. Dev Med Child Neurol 16:824, 1974.

78. Muller W, Rieger C, von der Hardt H. Increased concentrations of milk antibodies in recurrent pulmonary aspiration in infants and young children. Acta Paediatr Scand 74:660, 1985.

79. Nussbaum E, Maggi J, Mathis R, Galant S. Association of lipid-laden alveolar macrophages and gastroesophageal reflux in children. J Pediatr 110:190, 1987.

80. O'Connor AF, Ardran GM. Cineradiography in the diagnosis of pharyngeal palsies. J Laryngol Otol 90:1015, 1976.

81. Orenstein SR, Orenstein DM. Gastroesophageal reflux and respiratory disease in children. J Pediatr 112:847, 1988.

82. Orenstein SR, Whitington PF. Positioning for prevention of infant gastroesophageal reflux. J Pediatr 103:534, 1983.

83. Penchaszadeh V. Oculopharyngeal muscular dystrophy. Birth Defects 7:118, 1971.

84. Recalde A, Nickerson B, Vegal M, et al. Lipid-laden macrophages in tracheal aspirates of newborn infants receiving intravenous lipid infusions: a cytologic study. Pediatr Pathol 2:25, 1984.

85. Reichert TJ, Bluestone CD, Stool SE, et al. Congenital cricopharyngeal achalasia. Ann Otol Rhinol Laryngol 76:603, 1977.

86. Ristagno R, Kornstein M, Hansen-Flaschen J. Diagnosis of occult meat aspiration by fiberoptic bronchoscopy. Am J Med 80:154, 1986.

87. Rossato RG. Dionosil swallow: a test of laryngeal protection. Surg Neurol 7:24, 1977.

88. Schramm VL, May M, Lavorato AS. Gelfoam paste injection for vocal cord paralysis: temporary rehabilitation of glottic incompetence. Laryngoscope 88:1268, 1978.

89. Sessle BJ, Hannam AG (eds). Mastication and Swallowing. Toronto, University of Toronto Press, 1976.

90. Skinner MA, Shorter NA. Primary neonatal cricopharyngeal achalasia: a case report and review of the literature. J Pediatr Surg 27:1509, 1992.

91. Snyderman CH, Johnson JT. Laryngotracheal separation for intractable aspiration. Ann Otol Rhinol Laryngol 97:466, 1988.

92. Thach BT, Menon A. Pulmonary protective mechanisms in human infants. Am Rev Respir Dis 131:855, 1985.

93. Utiam HL, Thomas RG. Cricopharyngeal incoordination in infancy. Pediatrics 43:402, 1969.

94. Valat C, Demont F, Pegat MA, et al. Radionuclide study of bronchial aspiration in intensive care newborn children. Nucl Med Comm 7:593, 1986.

95. Weathers RM, Becker MH, Genieser NB. Improved technique for study of swallowing function in infants. Radiol Technol 46:98, 1974.

96. Weisberger EC, Huebsch SA. Endoscopic treatment of aspiration using a laryngeal stent. Otolaryngol Head Neck Surg 90:215, 1982.

97. Wilson RA, Klimen MR, Hardyment AF. Ankyloglossia superior (palatoglossal adhesion in the newborn infant). Pediatrics 31:1051, 1963.

79

Hoarseness

Jacob Friedberg, M.D., F.R.C.S.(C.) and Hamdy El-Hakim, F.R.C.S.Ed., O.R.L.

Hoarseness is a common clinical complaint. The abnormal qualities of the hoarse voice may be described as breathy or harsh, husky or rough, or strident or coarse. The term *hoarse* may also describe the quality of a conversational voice, the simple cry of a newborn infant, or any vocalization. By definition it does not indicate resonance, pitch, or loudness problems.[10]

The incidence of voice disorders in children as estimated by most surveys is in the approximate range of 6% to 9%.[41] Although speech and language pathologists and phoniatricians will care for a major share of patients with these conditions, the otolaryngologist will be responsible for the management of some of the most challenging of them.

Hoarseness always indicates some abnormality of structure or function. Because of the precision of laryngeal mechanisms, hoarseness may result from a remarkably small lesion and thus represent an early sign in the course of a disease process. Conversely, if the lesion's origin is remote from the vocal cords, hoarseness may be a late sign. In contrast to adult hoarseness, the pediatric patient's symptom seems to be met with less enthusiasm, probably because of the rarity of malignant diagnosis and the relative difficulty of examination of larynges in patients of that age group.[6]

This chapter approaches hoarseness, when it presents as a primary symptom to the otolaryngologist, in terms of its character, its associated symptoms and signs, the age of the patient at onset, and the mode of its onset. Indications for extended investigation are discussed, as well as those aspects of diagnosis pertinent to the evaluation of these lesions.

Pathogenesis

Although many lesions produce hoarseness, they can do so in a limited number of ways.

In most general terms, the intensity of the voice varies with the subglottic air pressure maintained against glottic resistance. Vocal pitch and timbre are affected by the length and tension of the vibrating segment of the vocal cords and by their mass and posture and strength of movement. The shape of the free vocal cord margins also plays a role in determining voice quality.

Apart from alteration in the structure of these vocal components or the control of their functions, hoarseness may be the result of a mutational voice disorder or a psychosomatic problem (Table 79–1).

Clinical Evaluation

Establishing a differential diagnosis[6, 21, 25, 28, 29, 36] of the causes of hoarseness is a lengthy process, and statistically most of these lesions are innocuous and self-limiting. Thus, because of the potential hazards of some of the diagnostic techniques, before proceeding beyond the clinical examination, one must first decide how important it really is to establish a firm diagnosis of the cause of hoarseness.

The quality of the hoarseness[23] will give limited but valuable clues to its cause, whereas other characteristics, such as age of the patient at onset, rate of progression, associated infection, history of trauma or surgery, and the presence of respiratory or cardiac distress, may be of much greater significance.

A low-pitched, coarse, fluttering voice suggests a supraglottic or even hypopharyngeal lesion; a more high pitched, cracking voice, or an aphonic or breathy voice suggests a cordal problem. An associated high-pitched stridor also suggests a glottic or subglottic lesion. Hoarseness that is altered by a position change suggests a mobile lesion, such as a vallecular or aryepiglottic cyst or pedunculated polyp (see Chapter 74).

General examination is often helpful. A head and neck lymphangioma or hemangioma strongly suggests the possibility of a similar laryngeal lesion as the source of hoarseness, although these lesions rarely present primarily with hoarseness.

Central nervous system depression as with birth trauma or other head injury, diminished level of consciousness, abnormal muscle tone or coordination, increased intracranial pressure, or a meningocele should alert the clinician to the possibility of laryngeal nerve palsy.

Associated dysphagia, regurgitation, aspiration, and pooling of laryngeal secretions in the absence of esophageal obstruction or fistula should also suggest a neurologic lesion, usually bulbar, as a cause of hoarseness. Neck masses, tracheal shift, and abnormal heart sounds and murmurs should direct the examiner to look for recurrent

TABLE 79–1. Differential Diagnosis of Hoarseness in Children

Congenital

Laryngeal anomalies
  Laryngomalacia
  Glottic webs
  Subglottic stenosis
  Vocal cord sulcus
  Laryngotracheoesophageal cleft
Cystic lesions
  Laryngocele
  Mucous retention cyst
  Thyroglossal duct cyst
Aspirational disorders
  Tracheoesophageal fistula
  Pharyngoesophageal dyskinesia
Angiomas
  Lymphangioma (cystic hygroma)
  Hemangioma
  Arteriovenous malformation
Cri du chat syndrome

Neurogenic (Congenital and Acquired)

Supranuclear, e.g., hydrocephalus, subdural hematoma, pseudobulbar palsy, meningocele
Nuclear, e.g., brain stem compression (due to Arnold-Chiari malformation, Dandy-Walker cyst, meningocele), bulbar poliomyelitis, Guillain-Barré syndrome
Peripheral, e.g., cardiovascular anomalies, mediastinal cysts and tumors, neuropathies (lead, arsenic, diphtheria, postinfectious), myasthenia gravis, recurrent laryngeal nerve trauma, invasion by tumor
Psychogenic hoarseness

Vocal Abuse

Vocal cord polyps, nodules

Neoplasia

Papilloma
Squamous cell carcinoma
Others

Physical Voice Change of Puberty

Inflammatory

Infectious
  Simple laryngitis
  Diphtheria
  Laryngotracheitis
  Supraglottitis (epiglottitis)
Noninfectious
  Chronic laryngitis
  Allergic laryngitis
  Angioneurotic edema
  Rheumatoid arthritis
  Relapsing polychondritis
  Smoking: active and passive

Traumatic

Hematoma
Laryngeal cartilage fracture
Arytenoid dislocation
Impacted foreign body
Postintubation
  Cord avulsion
  Granuloma
  Glottic web: anterior or interarytenoid
  Cricoarytenoid joint fixation
Recurrent laryngeal nerve injury
  Thyroidectomy
  Tracheoesophageal fistula repair
  Cardiac surgery
  Segmental tracheal resection
  Penetrating neck wound
  Neoplastic infiltration
Tracheotomy

or superior laryngeal nerve involvement. Palpation of the neck and larynx may define some of the above problems. Examination of the oropharynx and hypopharynx may reveal a vallecular cyst or parapharyngeal mass. Particular care should be taken in the presence of potential airway obstruction unless one is fully prepared to establish an airway (see Chapter 81).

The Neonate

A number of congenital anomalies may affect voice, airway, or both,[12, 13] each in varying degrees, depending on the precise location and extent of the lesion. If the airway is significantly occluded, the resultant stridor, both inspiratory and expiratory, may be sufficiently noisy to obscure any vocal sounds. This stridor may disappear at rest, but so will any active sounds in the small infant. The distinction is less than academic, and the primary problem in such cases is airway management, if indicated (see Chapter 81).

Congenital laryngeal stridor or laryngomalacia is characterized by a coarse inspiratory stridor, but usually with a normal voice. With redundancy of the arytenoid and aryepiglottic mucosa, the infant's cry may have a rough component to it, which is relieved in the prone position. Similarly, the infant with subglottic stenosis usually has a good voice that may be obscured by the stridor. With

sufficient stenosis, the air exchange is so poor that the cry is weak, if not truly hoarse. A posterior laryngeal stenosis may be rigid enough to fix the cords partially, giving the cry a breathy as well as a stridorous quality.

A variety of cysts occur in or about the larynx.[11, 22] All are capable of affecting the voice or airway. Most of these are simple retention cysts of seromucinous glands, commonly occurring in the valleculae or aryepiglottic folds where they would not affect the voice or cause a mottled quality if the cysts are large. Occasionally, these may be subglottic, and clinically indistinguishable from a fibrous subglottic stenosis. Still less common is the laryngocele[22] that results from a functional occlusion of the neck of the saccule and subsequent dilatation with air. If fluid filled, the cyst is called a saccular cyst. Hoarseness is an early sign of a laryngocele, but with enlargement, and particularly with infection of the sac, an acute airway problem may be precipitated. When recognized, simple aspiration and marsupialization of the cyst can manage most of these cases, with dramatic relief of the symptoms. Recurrences should be resected via a laryngofissure approach.

Laryngeal webs,[22] commonly glottic, vary in extent from a simple mucosal fold at the anterior commissure to a complete fibrous obliteration of the glottis (atresia). The latter is obviously incompatible with life unless tracheotomy is performed immediately after birth. The remainder may cause varying degrees of impairment, from mild hoarseness to aphonia, and various respiratory signs, from minimal stridor and croupy cough to gross obstruction and severe distress. Diagnosis is by endoscopic examination. The smaller, thinner webs often respond well to lysis or dilatation. The more extensive lesions require a tracheotomy for airway control and more definitive surgery, including incision and repeated dilatation, resection via laryngofissure and keel insertion, or carbon dioxide laser excision.

Gastroesophageal reflux disease (GERD) is the symptomatic retrograde movement of gastric contents into the esophagus. It is common in children and infants. Classic symptoms include emesis, dysphagia, sleep disturbance, and failure to thrive, among others, but GERD is often silent. Despite being a common denominator to many respiratory and laryngeal manifestations, the relation between airway disease and GERD is complex and controversial. Not only are various mechanisms implicated (e.g., direct contact of respiratory mucosa with acid, vagal reflex with bronchospasm) but also, in some cases, respiratory disorders and therapies can cause GERD (e.g., induction of positive abdominal pressure, lower esophageal relaxation by methyl-xanthines, beta-adrenergic agonists, or nasogastric tube feeds).[40] To date, pH monitoring fails to give a significant statistical relationship between pH levels and laryngeal manifestations.[8]

There is no single investigative method that can, in addition to demonstrating the reflux and its severity, identify it as the cause of the child's symptoms (pH monitoring, upper gastrointestinal tract series, nuclear medicine scintiscan, esophagoscopy with or without biopsy, bronchoscopy with lipid-laden macrophages, and modified Bernstein test). Currently, the most accepted method for diagnosing GERD is ambulatory pH monitoring in conjunction with suggestive history, especially as the sensitivity of barium swallows is low for reflux, and the absence of mucosal changes on endoscopy is not exclusive.[4] Common laryngeal abnormalities found in association with GERD include posterior laryngitis, hypertrophic interarytenoid tissue, edematous vocal folds, diffuse supraglottic edema, vocal cord granulomas, and subglottic inflammation. Only one study has demonstrated by pH monitoring an incidence of gastroesophageal reflux disease of 62% in a cohort of children with chronic hoarseness, suggesting an association between the two entities.[18]

Tracheoesophageal fistula, with or without atresia, must be considered and is readily diagnosed clinically, radiologically, and endoscopically. The much less common posterior laryngotracheal cleft is less easy to recognize. The patient's cry is weak, and aspiration is a constant problem. On direct examination, the endoscopist may miss the cleft unless the larynx is observed during vocal cord abduction, or unless the endoscopist gently but deliberately applies pressure to the posterior commissure, thus opening the cleft. To avoid the problems of chronic aspiration, these lesions should be repaired at the earliest possible date after diagnosis, either endoscopically or via a lateral pharyngotomy or laryngofissure.

Cri du chat syndrome[26] is a rare chromosomal syndrome notorious for being a cause of an abnormal cry. The cry is weak and high pitched, characteristically like the mewing of a cat. The larynx is seen to be narrow, with a diamond-shaped glottis during inspiration and a persistent posterior glottic chink on expiration, resulting in constant air leakage. Many abnormalities, including gross retardation, microcephaly, and hypotonia, are also present. The literature points out that many other syndromes are associated with abnormal phonation. Other genetic syndromes such as achondroplasia (high pitched), Apert (hoarse, breathy), the CHARGE association (hoarseness), mechanically inducing syndromes as Hurler and Hunter, and trisomy 21[39] are associated with abnormal phonation.

Dysphonia in a neonate may be a clue to far-reaching damage to the vagus nerve system[33] from supranuclear to peripheral lesions, plus associated difficulty with deglutition and aspiration of secretions. Vocal cord movement is the simplest of the vagus nerve functions to recognize clinically and as such is a useful guide to the diagnosis of more extensive neurologic lesions. Diagnosis is best made endoscopically, with care taken not to restrict cord movement with the laryngoscope. Flexible fiberoptic laryngoscopy is best for assessing vocal cord motion. Unilateral cord palsy usually results in hoarse cry only. This may improve in time, if not by recovery of function then by compensatory movement of the opposite cord. Airway obstruction is seldom a problem unless precipitated by minor swelling from an otherwise uneventful endotracheal intubation or respiratory tract infection. The patient with a bilateral palsy, on the other hand, will have a clear but weak cry; however, dyspnea and stridor may be marked, and extensive central neuropathy, such as the Arnold-Chiari malformation, is usually apparent. Again, airway management takes priority and is usually in the form of a tracheotomy; if recovery is not forthcoming, some form of cord lateralization is indicated.

Neonatal myasthenia gravis may be seen in the newborn infant of a mother with myasthenia. The larynx is commonly affected, resulting in a weak cry, which may, however, be overshadowed by widespread signs of neuromuscular weakness. Fortunately, this tends to regress in a few weeks (see Chapters 80, 81, 82, and 87).

The Older Child

Many congenital lesions can manifest themselves at any age. Trauma and infection resulting in hoarseness can also affect children of any age. The older child is subject to essentially the same causes of hoarseness as is the adult[34] (see Chapters 80, 81, and 87).

The Progressive Lesion

Hoarseness in children tends to be overlooked or at least accepted until it reaches a certain level of severity. An accurate history of progression is often lacking but should be sought. The most common lesions[1, 43] in this group are the simple laryngeal nodule, polyp, or keratosis of the vocal cord caused by voice abuse. In addition to the progression of hoarseness, there is a fluctuation in the severity of the symptoms, which are aggravated by vocal abuse and respiratory tract infections and relieved by periods of rest. Thus, hoarseness may be worse at the end of the day, but the voice will be near normal at the beginning of the day. Dramatic deterioration may occur because of sudden swelling of a polyp with infection or hemorrhage. This is seen in the vocally aggressive child, who may share the disease with other members of the immediate family. For this self-limiting and self-correcting lesion, treatment should be conservative unless the voice is socially or educationally unacceptable. Speech therapy may be both correcting and reassuring,[42] but it is often more time consuming than the symptom merits. Surgery is seldom necessary. In any event, unless underlying speech habits are corrected, the nodules are likely to recur. If there is any possibility that the lesion is anything other than a nodule, biopsy is mandatory.

Relentlessly progressive hoarseness should suggest neoplasia, of which recurrent respiratory papillomatosis is by far the most common lesion. The treatments are legion and are not dealt with here, except to recommend that representative biopsy specimens always be taken. Although the clinical appearance is usually typical, it may be indistinguishable from that of rare but much more ominous laryngeal squamous cell carcinoma of childhood. Conversely, the rare but benign granular cell myoblastoma may present in the larynx. Inadequate biopsy specimens may be interpreted as malignant because of pseudoepitheliomatous hyperplasia overlying these lesions.

Progressive hoarseness due to recurrent nerve invasion by malignancy is occasionally seen in children, particularly from thyroid carcinoma.

Physiologic voice change at puberty should not be forgotten. The rapidly developing adolescent may require many months to gain control of his new larynx; however, such individuals are not immune to neoplasia and palsies, and a thorough clinical examination is still warranted.

Recurrent laryngeal nerve involvement, and thus hoarseness and breathiness, may be seen as part of a host of peripheral neuropathies (see Chapter 87), including heavy metal poisoning, deficiency states, diabetes, postinfectious polyneuropathy, collagen vascular diseases, and infections such as diphtheria, leprosy, and infectious mononucleosis. Hoarseness is often the least dramatic sign in such conditions but should alert the clinician to possible airway or aspiration problems.

Idiopathic unilateral and bilateral vocal cord palsies are seen in childhood and are often diagnosed as tracheitis, simple laryngitis, or even functional. When these conditions fail to resolve as expected, cord palsy must be ruled out.

Inflammatory Lesions

Hoarseness due to various laryngeal inflammations, including simple infective laryngitis, laryngotracheitis, supraglottitis, and associated exanthemas, is seldom a diagnostic or therapeutic problem. The concern is with the airway, and the voice change is viewed as incidental. Occasionally, the systemic manifestations of the disease are mild, with the voice change an early sign and airway obstruction comparatively late, catching the clinician unawares. Even epiglottitis may run a course of 2 or 3 days, with mild

dysphagia and a "hot potato" voice being the only initial symptoms (see Chapter 85).

Diphtheria, although now admittedly rare as a cause of acute laryngitis, is nevertheless still with us and, with the growing degree of laxity by the population regarding primary immunization, may once again become a serious consideration.

Fungal laryngitis is occasionally seen in children taking inhaled steroids[37] or in immunocompromised children.[19] In the former group, the condition should be self-limiting once the medication is discontinued. In the immunocompromised patient, hoarseness may indicate a life-threatening invasive candidiasis or aspergillosis.

The noninfectious cricoarytenoid joint inflammation of rheumatoid arthritis or relapsing polychondritis is seldom recognized in children. It is potentially reversible before permanent fixation with voice and airway changes occurs. Hoarseness, vocal discomfort, and dysphagia should suggest the diagnosis in the young arthritic patient; inflammatory changes in the arytenoid mucosa may also be apparent on laryngoscopy.

The presence of rhinosinusitis or chest infection from any cause is commonly reflected in the laryngeal mucosa and associated voice changes. In the presence of chronic laryngeal irritation, a history of smoking or passive tobacco smoke exposure should always be sought, regardless of the child's age.

Idiopathic atrophic changes of the respiratory tree may occur in the pediatric age group and may affect not only the nose in classic atrophic rhinitis but also the larynx and trachea. Loss of normal cilia, squamous cell metaplasia, secondary chronic infection, and retained secretions result in persistent hoarseness and may be readily assessed by indirect laryngoscopy (see Chapter 85).

Post-traumatic Hoarseness

In the newborn, laryngeal trauma may begin in the nursery. Common causes of laryngeal problems include frequent overaggressive pharyngeal aspiration in the newborn and repeated passage of a feeding tube. A weak cry should be a warning for the nursing personnel to be more gentle in their management (see Chapter 88).

Blunt laryngeal trauma[14] is not common in children but is sometimes the result of play injury in preadolescents. A backhand from a bat or a racket, a fall on bicycle handlebars, and a blow from a swing set are typical mischances that may result in laryngeal trauma. In recent years, use of snowmobiles and all-terrain vehicles has resulted in accidents that are a significant cause of laryngeal trauma, even in the pediatric age group. Gross signs of injury may be obvious, but even a minor change in voice quality should lead the physician to suspect a possible thyroid or cricoid fracture or arytenoid dislocation with its associated odynophagia. Fortunately, children of this age group are usually readily examined, and when there is a good airway, normal laryngeal mobility, and apparent laryngeal asymmetry, they can often be treated conservatively. Hoarseness associated with surgical emphysema, however, should warn the examiner of a more serious situation: the mucosa has obviously been breached, and the progression of emphysema may result in local airway obstruction, pneumomediastinum, and pneumothorax. Careful observation is therefore mandatory in these cases.

Postoperative Hoarseness

Considering the frequency with which direct laryngoscopy and intubation are performed, often without the advantage of anesthesia, it is gratifying that injury occurs so rarely. Nevertheless, it does occur, even when the procedures are performed with utmost care (see Chapter 88).

The newborn who becomes dysphonic or totally aphonic after intubation for assisted ventilation may have suffered an arytenoid dislocation. If recognized, this can be reduced by manipulation with an anterior commissure laryngoscope. Such a sign during a transfer from the obstetric to the neonatology department may go unrecognized. In these cases, direct laryngoscopy would be both diagnostic and therapeutic.

Prolonged orotracheal intubation or the use of too large a tube may lead to varying degrees of ulceration of the larynx, damage to soft tissue and cartilage, granuloma formation and subsequent stenosis, webbing or airway obstruction, and even vocal cord palsy. Immediate postextubation vocal huskiness and croupy cough are common in these cases and indicate an impending complication. If all is proceeding well, this hoarseness should resolve in a few days; if not, direct visualization of the larynx should be considered.

With the increasing sophistication of ventilatory and resuscitative techniques, the performance of tracheotomies has become uncommon; consequently, the expertise gained in this technique over the last few decades will likely be lost. Injury to the recurrent laryngeal nerves or the cricoid and subglottic areas, although rare, may not be recognized until extubation is attempted, by which time irreversible damage may have been sustained. Coincidental with this trend is the increasing use of percutaneous needles or trochars into the larynx for topical anesthesia or for the establishment of an emergency airway. Here, too, the injury may go unrecognized until long after the acute episode is over, but damage to the voice should be minimal. Although the risk of local damage from these techniques may be small, adjacent structures are vulnerable; indeed, even the cervical spinal cord has been injured.

Thyroid surgery is today primarily reserved for malignancy or suspected malignancy. When it is performed, postoperative hoarseness may be the result of recurrent laryngeal nerve injury, making routine pre- and postoperative visualization of the larynx critical. Late onset of the hoarseness (months or even a year after thyroid surgery) should suggest the development of a delayed palsy, presumably from fibrosis or ischemia or, in the case of malignancy, from recurrent disease. A remarkably good voice may be preserved even in the presence of a bilateral recurrent nerve injury. If not truly hoarse, the voice is at least weak and slightly breathy, depending on the precise vocal cord position.

The vulnerability of the recurrent laryngeal nerves in the surgical repair of tracheoesophageal fistula,[2, 32] with or without atresia, by direct anastomosis or by segmental replacement by a gastric tube or colon, is obvious. The apparently low incidence of such injury may simply reflect lack of follow-up investigations. Many infants who undergo repair of a tracheoesophageal fistula have an endotracheal or nasogastric tube in place for a prolonged time, so any transient voice problems may go unnoticed. Compensation with a unilateral palsy is usually excellent, and no treatment is indicated. Persistent hoarseness or breathiness, however, requires a direct examination. Bilateral palsy usually demands that a tracheotomy be performed.

Vocal changes after cardiac surgery, particularly for the repair of a patent ductus, a double aortic arch, or pulmonary artery anomalies, should not automatically be attributed to intubation. The left recurrent laryngeal nerve is at risk, as it passes around the arch of the aorta, and should be assessed in these cases.

Indications for Investigation

Certainly not every child with a hoarse voice or cry merits investigation beyond an assessment of symptoms. In the presence of hoarseness with respiratory distress, tachypnea, decreased air entry, tachycardia or cyanosis, however, the larynx *must* be visualized and a firm diagnosis of the cause of the hoarseness made. A laryngeal examination should be carried out when hoarseness is associated with recognized cardiac,[7] esophageal, or nervous system disease. Such an examination may well precipitate an acute airway obstruction, necessitating intubation. Facilities for rigid bronchoscopy or tracheotomy should be available. As much as one may wish to avoid such instrumentation, it should at least occur at the time and place chosen by the examiner under a controlled situation with minimal risk to life, rather than on an emergency basis.

Progressive hoarseness also merits investigation, and one need not wait until total aphonia or airway problems occur. Progression usually indicates an acquired lesion such as a laryngeal or hypopharyngeal cyst, a neoplasm such as a papilloma, a proliferative lesion such as a hemangioma, or indeed, the occasional malignancy. Hoarseness in the presence of lesions such as cutaneous hemangiomas or head and neck lymphangioma should lead the examiner to exclude the presence of a similar lesion in or about the larynx.

Social embarrassment or poor intelligibility of speech, particularly in the school-age child, does merit thorough assessment and, whenever possible, correction.[31] Hoarseness after external trauma or an otherwise uneventful intubation should also not go unchecked. Many granulomas resolve in time if untreated, but a dislocated arytenoid, once fixed out of position, will never again be made normally functional.

Hoarseness that has been, according to the history, "present since birth" is difficult to evaluate in regard to infant and childhood vocal quality. So often, one discovers the offending lesion to be simple vocal cord nodules, probably due to vocal abuse and hardly congenital. A true history of congenital presentation should prompt an investigation to rule out laryngeal web, cyst, palsy, or hemangioma, all of which may be treated readily but which have the potential to obstruct the airway. In these cases, a diagnosis should be made.

Diagnostic Imaging

Imaging, rather than endoscopy, will play a principal role in the differential diagnosis of hoarseness in this age group in a few situations. Namely, where a central nervous system cause is high on the list, where there is a history of trauma, or where there is an extensive lesion with a suspected extralaryngeal extension.

Xeroradiography,[24, 30] because of its properties of edge enhancement, is particularly helpful in visualizing lesions encroaching on the airway. Unfortunately, the radiation dose in this technique is about four times that of conventional radiographs, and the technique is currently seldom used for airway evaluation.

Ultrasonographic examination has been proposed recently as an attractive tool in the assessment of the pediatric larynx. Because the cartilages are not ossified in the pediatric patient, the use of a small probe permits internal laryngeal structures to be observed through axial slices at different levels during quiet breathing and phonation. The results of using computerized equipment suggest it as a sensitive modality for diagnosing vocal fold paralysis.[15] It also can demonstrate laryngeal edema and space-occupying lesions and analyze the arytenoid movement.[16] Despite noninvasiveness, safety, and good patient tolerance, it is rarely used, as its sensitivity is highly dependent on the expertise of the examiner.

A plain chest radiograph may demonstrate any one of a number of mediastinal lesions, including inflammatory or neoplastic lymph nodes, neurogenic tumors, and bronchial or esophageal cysts or duplications, as well as a number of cardiac and vascular anomalies that may affect the recurrent laryngeal nerves.

Computed tomography (CT) accurately defines the caliber of the airway and documents the site and extent of caliber changes as well as giving detailed information about the tissues adjacent to the airway.[27] Modern imaging techniques, which include spiral CT, permit rapid acquisition of data, greatly reducing the need for sedation in young children.[9] The likely indications for a CT scan of the larynx are congenital cysts, solid tumors, and external laryngeal trauma. Also, ultrafast CT is sometimes used for assessing laryngeal paralysis and vestibular or subglottic hemangioma.[27]

Magnetic resonance imaging can reveal mass lesions as intra- or extralaryngeal hemangiomas, cystic hygromas, cysts, and other benign and malignant lesions, as well as abnormal aortic arches and other mediastinal lesions. Sagittal sections reveal particularly well any deviation or narrowing of the airway lumen at all levels.[9] However, this method is limited by motion artifact in pediatric patients unless they are sedated or intubated, either of which may be unacceptable.

Flexible Fiberoptic Nasopharyngolaryngoscope

In the past, flexible fiberoptic and endoscopic equipment was too large for widespread use in children.[35, 40] Instruments ranging from 2.7 to 3.6 mm in diameter have since become available that, even in the newborn,[3] can usually be passed nasally for visualization of the hypopharynx and larynx. Instruments 2.2 mm in diameter and even smaller are available but are expensive, inordinately fragile, and of limited life expectancy in most clinical settings. Topical anesthesia and decongestants can be applied by spray (nonaerosolized), dropper, or pledget, bearing in mind that dosages may be critical in the small infant (e.g., a maximum of 3 to 4 mg/kg lidocaine). This permits observation of the larynx without the shortcomings of general anesthesia or the fixation artifacts of the rigid endoscopes. Visualization is far superior to that obtained with conventional mirror examination, but the subglottic airway is difficult to thoroughly examine, especially in patients with severe glossoptosis, severe laryngomalacia, or vocal cord paresis or paralysis, and in infants, especially those with pooling of secretions. Patient cooperation is required even with good topical anesthesia. In infants this is not an issue, and children older than 6 or 7 years of age can usually be coopted into the examination. The intermediate age group may be less amenable and may tax the skill of the most experienced clinician. All are worth a try (see Chapter 76). The success rate of this examination reaches well over 90% with gentle technique and nonthreatening manner[5, 20] and could be supplemented with video-recording for documentation and demonstration of the pathologic lesion to parents and children. This may allow a stroboscopic examination if the child can tolerate it.[17] Flexible endoscopy is not advisable in the presence of a tenuous airway, arrhythmias, or bleeding disorders.

Indirect Laryngoscopy

Indirect laryngoscopy can provide all necessary information required but may be rapidly becoming a lost art. With patience and gentleness, children from 4 years of age, and occasionally those younger, can be examined. The alcohol flame for mirror warming is frightening and should be avoided. As defogging solutions are often foul tasting, warm water can be used for demisting mirrors, although most modern examination consoles incorporate a source of warm air that renders the process fairly inconspicuous. Also, aerosolized topical anesthetic spray may be startling; these too should be avoided, and the anesthetic can generally be applied with cotton-tipped applicators. Because of the relatively high position of the child's larynx and narrow epiglottis, a small web or papilloma at the anterior commissure may be missed, but an adequate view of the remaining structures can readily be obtained (see Chapter 76).

Direct Laryngoscopy

The diagnostic information provided by a properly conducted direct laryngoscopic examination supported by operating microscope and/or Hopkins rod telescope visualization is still without an equal. More important is the control the examiner has over the possibly compromised airway and the ability to immediately relieve or correct a significant number of the lesions that may be encountered. Direct laryngoscopy is generally a safe procedure, but it is not without some risk to maxillofacial and pharyngeal structures, as well as the cervical spine, larynx, and airway. It should therefore not be undertaken merely out of curiosity. With few exceptions, if there is significant airway obstruction, a general anesthetic should not be used.

Even with a compromised airway, the maintenance of normal oropharyngeal muscle tone and spontaneous respiration provides a great safety factor in the awake patient. In the neonate or small infant, anesthesia is not necessary. Structural lesions such as webs, cysts, and polyps are readily appreciated; however, functional disorders, such as cordal spasm or paresis, may be difficult to appreciate, particularly if obscured by struggling swallowing movements, coughing, irregular respiration, and secretions. After physical obstruction has been ruled out, and the examiner is confident of his or her ability to establish and

maintain an airway, anesthesia can be induced with the patient breathing spontaneously. Topical anesthesia will eliminate any tendency to laryngospasm. Quiet respiration facilitates the use of the operating microscope, which may reveal lesions not apparent to the naked eye, such as small capillary malformations of the cord, perhaps indicative of a more extensive underlying hemangioma. Similarly, a pinpoint nodule on the free margin of the cord, which may result in an extraordinary degree of hoarseness for its size, can be seen readily. Palpation of the cords for passive mobility may be carried out at this time to rule out cricoarytenoid fixation and posterior glottic stenosis.

As the patient is awakened, the cords may be examined at leisure for mobility, with care taken not to inadvertently fix one or both cords with an improperly placed laryngoscope. Passive movement with increasing depth of respiration may be mistaken for active cord movement by the inexperienced examiner, who should learn to coordinate visualization of cord movement with chest movement. Passive abduction is in the expiratory phase, whereas active abduction is inspiratory. Similarly, the marked abduction with coughing should not be mistaken

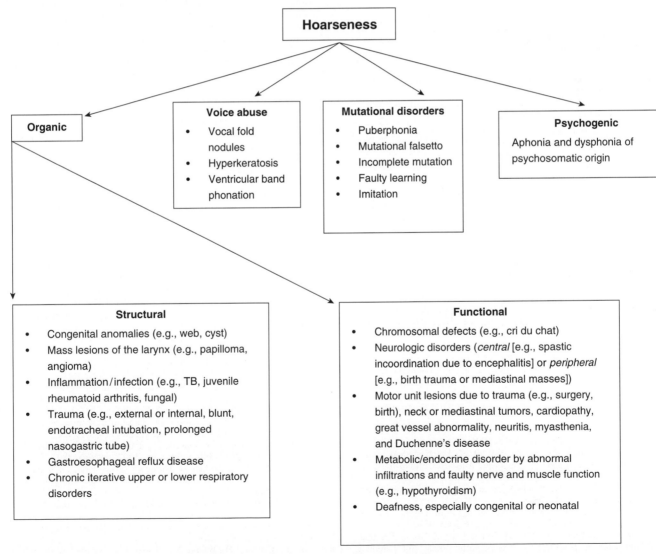

FIGURE 79–1. Differential diagnosis of hoarseness in children.

for active movement on awakening. It bears repeating that, at all times during the course of this examination, one should be prepared to establish an airway by orotracheal intubation or bronchoscopy and to institute appropriate resuscitative measures.

Conclusions

The list of lesions capable of causing hoarseness in childhood has not been exhausted here. More often, the problem is innocuous, self-limiting, and reversible. Some causes of hoarseness are progressive, potentially life threatening, or symptomatic of extensive disease, which is why a precise diagnosis of the cause is required (Fig. 79–1).

Acknowledgment

We would like to thank Dr. Susan Blaser, Staff Radiologist at the Hospital for Sick Children of Toronto, for her help and advice in the preparation of this manuscript, especially the section pertaining to imaging of the airway.

SELECTED REFERENCES

Ferguson CF. Congenital abnormalities of the infant larynx. Otolaryngol Clin North Am 3:185, 1970.

Holinger PH. Clinical aspects of congenital anomalies of the larynx, trachea, bronchi and esophagus. J Laryngol 75:1, 1961.

> These two articles, based on the authors' best clinical experiences, provide a most comprehensive view of many of the lesions responsible for hoarseness in the infant.

Rontal M, Rontal E. Lesions of the vagus nerve: diagnosis, treatment and rehabilitation. Laryngoscope 87:72, 1977.

> The multiplicity of vocal cord problems has been dealt with in a convenient and useful fashion, providing the clinician with an orderly approach to this sometimes confusing subject.

REFERENCES

1. Arnold GE. Vocal nodules and polyps: laryngeal tissue reaction to habitual hyperkinetic dysphonia. J Speech Hear Disord 27:205, 1962.
2. Bedard T, Girvan DP, Shandling B. Congenital H-type tracheoesophageal fistula. J Pediatr Surg 9:63, 1974.
3. Berkowitz RG. Neonatal upper airway assessment by awake flexible laryngoscopy. Ann Otol Rhinol Laryngol 107:75, 1998.
4. Burton DM, Pransky SM, Katz RM, et al. Pediatric airway manifestations of gastroesophageal reflux disease. Ann Otol Rhinol Laryngol 101:742, 1992.
5. Chait DH, Lotz WK. Successful pediatric examinations using nasoendoscopy. Laryngoscope 101:1016, 1991.
6. Cohen SR, Thomson JW, Geller KA, et al. Voice change in the pediatric patient: a differential diagnosis. Ann Otol Rhinol Laryngol 92:437, 1983.
7. Condon LM, Katkov H, Singh A, et al. Cardiovocal syndrome in infancy. Pediatrics 76:22, 1985.
8. Contencin P, Narcy P. Gastroesophageal reflux in infants and children. Arch Otolaryngol Head Neck Surg 118:1028, 1992.
9. Contencin P, Gumpert LC, De Gaudemar I, et al. Non-endoscopic techniques for the evaluation of the pediatric airway. Int J Pediatr Otolaryngol 41:347, 1997.
10. Dejonckere PH. Voice problems in children: pathogenesis and diagnosis. Int J Pediatr Otolaryngol 49(Suppl 1):311, 1999.
11. Desanto LW, Devine KD, Weilhand LH. Cysts of the larynx: classification. Laryngoscope 80:145, 1970.
12. Fearon B. Respiratory distress in the newborn. Otolaryngol Clin North Am 1:147, 1968.
13. Ferguson CF. Congenital abnormalities of the infant larynx. Otolaryngol Clin North Am 3:185, 1970.
14. Fitz-Hugh GS, Powell JB. Acute traumatic injuries of the oropharynx and the laryngopharynx and cervical trachea in children. Otolaryngol Clin North Am 3:375, 1970.
15. Friedman EM. Role of ultrasound in the assessment of vocal cord function in infants and children. Ann Otol Rhinol Laryngol 106:199, 1997.
16. Garel C, Hassan M, Elmaleh M, et al. Laryngeal ultrasonography in infants and children: pathological findings. Pediatr Radiol 21:164, 1991.
17. Gray SD, Smith ME, Schneider H, et al. Voice disorders in children. Pediatr Clin North Am 43:1357, 1996.
18. Gumpert L, Kalach N, Dupont C, Contencin P. Hoarseness and gastroesophageal reflux in children. J Laryngol Otol 112:49, 1998.
19. Hass A, Hyatt AC, Kattan M, et al. Hoarseness in immunocompromised children: association with invasive fungal infection. J Pediatr 111:731, 1987.
20. Hawkins DB, Clarke RW. Flexible laryngoscopy in neonates, infants and young children. Ann Otol Rhinol Laryngol 96:81, 1987.
21. Holinger PH. Clinical aspects of congenital anomalies of the larynx, trachea, bronchi and esophagus. J Laryngol 75:1, 1961.
22. Holinger PH, Brown WT. Congenital webs, cysts, laryngocele and other anomalies of the larynx. Ann Otol Rhinol Laryngol 76:744, 1967.
23. Holinger PH, Johnson KC, MacMahon RJ. Hoarseness in infants and children. Eye Ear Nose Throat Monthly 31:247, 1952.
24. Holinger PH, Lotterbeck EF, Bulger R. Xeroradiography of the larynx. Ann Otol Rhinol Laryngol 81:806, 1972.
25. Holinger PH, Schild JA, Weprin L. Pediatric laryngology. Otolaryngol Clin North Am 3:625, 1970.
26. LeJeune J. Cri du chat syndrome, chromosomal deletion causes severe retardation. JAMA 197:40, 1966.
27. Liu P, Danman A. Computed tomography of intrinsic laryngeal and tracheal abnormalities in children. J Comput Assisted Tomogr 8:662, 1984.
28. Lore JM Jr. Hoarseness in children. Arch Otolaryngol Head Neck Surg 51:814, 1950.
29. Murphy RS. Hoarseness. Nova Scotia Med Bull 46:177, 1967.
30. Noyek AM, Friedberg J, Steinhardt MI, et al. Xeroradiography in the assessment of the pediatric larynx and trachea. J Otolaryngol 5:468, 1976.
31. Putney FJ. Hoarseness: management of common causes. Med Clin North Am 49:1295, 1965.
32. Robertson JR, Birck HG. Laryngeal problems following infant esophageal surgery. Laryngoscope 86:72, 1977.
33. Rontal M, Rontal E. Lesions of the vagus nerve: diagnosis, treatment and rehabilitation. Laryngoscope 87:72, 1977.
34. Schwatz L, Noyek AM, Naiberg D. Persistent hoarseness. N Y State J Med 66:2658, 1966.
35. Selkin SG. Clinical use of pediatric flexible fiberscope. Int J Pediatr Otorhinolaryngol 10:75, 1985.
36. Senturia BH, Wislon FE. Otolaryngologic findings in children with voice deviation. Ann Otol Rhinol Laryngol 77:1027, 1968.
37. Settipane BH, Kalliel JN, Klein DE. Re-challenge of patients who developed oral candidiasis or hoarseness with beclomethazone dipropionate. N Engl Reg Allergy Proc 8:95, 1987.
38. Silberman HD, Wolf H, Tucker JA. Flexible fiberoptic nasopharyngolaryngoscope. Ann Otol Rhinol Laryngol 85:640, 1976.
39. Shprintzen RJ. Genetics, syndromes, and communication disorders. San Diego, Singular Publishing Group, 1997, pp 205–280.
40. Van Den Abeele T, Bruhier N, Narcy P. Severe laryngeal manifestations of gastroesophageal reflux in children. Pediatr Pulmonol Suppl 16:237, 1997.
41. Wilson DK. Voice Problems in Children, 3rd ed. London, Williams & Wilkins, 1987, pp 99–101.
42. Wilson DK. Voice therapy for children with laryngeal dysfunction. South Med J 611:956, 1968.
43. Yairi E, Currin LH, Bulian N. Incidence of hoarseness in school children over a one year period. J Commun Disord 7:321, 1974.

80

Voice

Marshall E. Smith, M.D. and Steven D. Gray, M.D.

This work was supported by grant K08 000132 and DC 04336 from the National Institute on Deafness and Communicative Disorders (NIDCD).

Introduction

The voice is one of the first signs of life. Then, throughout life, the voice is a primary means of expression and communication. It is an indicator of health, sickness, emotion, and age. The voice may provide the means to earn a living. It may convey great artistic expression through skillful use. The voice has lifelong importance to normal oral communication and social well-being. *Voice* may be defined in a broad (synonymous with speech) or narrow sense.[128] This chapter focuses on voice in a narrow way, particularly voice production. Other terms used in this context include *vocalization*, the sound produced by vocal-fold vibration, and *phonation*, the physical and physiologic processes of vocal-fold vibration. Phonation is a key component of speech production in conjunction with the functions of respiration, articulation, and resonance.

This chapter covers developmental anatomy and physiology of the larynx as they pertain to phonation before proceeding to a clinical review of the topic of voice. Disorders of phonation (or *dysphonias*) that occur in the pediatric age group and their evaluation are presented. Treatment of pediatric voice disorders, particularly medical and surgical approaches, is discussed. These topics necessarily overlap with other chapters on laryngeal diseases throughout this book, for which any voice problem may be a symptom. The reader is referred to this material when appropriate.

Developmental Laryngeal/Phonatory Anatomy

Endolaryngeal/Histologic Studies

The elegant studies of Hirano et al[65] provide much insight into the development of the phonatory larynx. They studied 88 normal larynges in patients whose ages ranged from a few hours after birth to 69 years. Several gross anatomic and histologic variables were studied. The length of the entire vocal fold and the length of the membranous portion (anterior fold) and the cartilaginous portion (posterior fold, including vocal process and arytenoid) were measured. It was found that up to the age of 10 years, the length of the vocal fold did not vary much between boys and girls (6 to 8 mm) (Fig. 80–1A). From age 10 years to age 20 years, the length of the membranous portion of the vocal fold gradually increased in males. In girls, the vocal fold increases in length to 8.5 to 12 mm by age 20 years. In boys, the length more than doubles to 14.5 to 18 mm by age 20 years. The length increase occurs gradually during adolescence (Fig. 80–1B). The study by Kahane[71] on morphologic features of the prepubertal and pubertal larynx also documented the changes in vocal-fold length with puberty. On measurement of the entire vocal-fold length (membranous and cartilaginous portions) before and after puberty, the average increase in female vocal folds was 4.2 mm; in males it was 10.9 mm, more than twice as much.

The cartilaginous portion of the vocal fold also grows with age (Fig. 80–1C).[65] It increases from about 1.25 mm in newborns to 3 mm in males and 2.5 mm in females. The ratio of the length of the membranous portion to that of the cartilaginous portion of the vocal fold is about 1.5 in newborns (Fig. 80–2). It increases to about 4.0 in adult women and 5.5 in adult men. This ratio has value in understanding the functions of the larynx in children. In children, a larger portion of the glottis composes the posterior glottis. Hirano et al[64] call this portion the *respiratory glottis*. Indeed, respiratory and protective functions of the larynx play a larger role than phonation in infants and children. The membranous portion of the vocal folds is more susceptible to edema in children than in adults, yet because the membranous fold (the *anterior* or *phonatory glottis*) composes a smaller percentage of the entire glottal area, these obstructive effects are minimized, serving as a relative protection.

Hirano and Kakita studied the histologic appearance of the vocal folds in the developing larynx. They reported extensively on the layered structure of the vocal fold.[63] It is described as having five distinct layers. The first two layers, the vocal fold epithelium and superficial layer of the lamina propria (also known as Reinke space), compose the *cover*. Underneath this are the intermediate and deep layers of the lamina propria (or vocal ligament) and the thyroarytenoid (or vocal) muscle. The deeper layers are called the *body*. The complex interaction between the

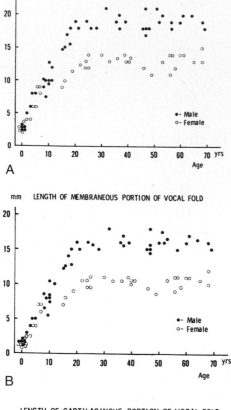

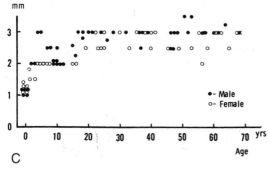

FIGURE 80–1. Various measures of the vocal fold taken from 48 males and 40 females ranging in age from a few hours to 69 years. *A,* Length of the entire vocal fold measured in millimeters. *B,* Length of the membranous portion of the vocal fold measured in millimeters. *C,* Length of the cartilaginous portion of the vocal fold measured in millimeters. (From Hirano M, Kurita S, Nakashima T. In Bless DM, Abbs JH [eds]. Vocal Fold Physiology: Contemporary Research and Clinical Issues. San Diego, College-Hill Press, 1983, pp 22–43.)

cover and body facilitates phonation through its range of pitches, loudness, and registers. This layered structure goes through extensive maturational changes.[65] Up to age 4 years, the intermediate and deep layers of the lamina propria are not well differentiated. After 4 years, the vocal ligament is immature. Fibroblasts throughout the lamina propria are much more dense in children than in adults.

This change in density is gradual, with some children developing more differentiated lamina propria at different ages. Figure 80–3 shows an infant vocal fold compared

with an adult one. In this case, even the 6-month-old infant shows some developing vocal ligament (elastin fibers). Note how the vast portion of the infant fold is not very fibrous but rather a loose lamina propria, reminiscent of the superficial layer of the lamina propria in adults, but this similarity has not been histologically investigated.

Figure 80–4 shows the results of cross-sectional studies of lamina propria components.[47, 51, 52] Note that elastin concentration goes up with age, while collagen amount depends more on gender than on age. Furthermore, although pediatric patients were not involved in the study, evidence in the adult population supports the idea that the surgical plane of dissection between the superficial layer and middle layer of the lamina propria gets more superficial with age. In other words, the surgical layer, or superficial layer, is relatively thicker in younger subjects.

The cellular biology of the vocal fold in the pediatric patient has not been well described. Developmental biology and genomic research suggests that influences on cellular differentiation and gene expression are divided into three basic categories: genetics, cellular microenvironment (i.e., sun exposure, trauma, organ system architecture, humidity), soluble factors (i.e., hormones, pharmaceutical agents), and mechanical forces (i.e., vibration, vocal-fold stretch, exercise). All of these factors probably help to determine maturation of the vocal folds, scar potential of the folds, voice quality, and healing capability. Studies of cellular biology in the vocal folds of mice across age groups have found that pediatric folds show a high degree of protein turnover and remodeling.[33, 34] In mice, both protein production and enzymatic destruction are increased in pediatric folds (Fig. 80–5). Pediatric folds are metabolically much more active than adult folds. Although some have inferred from this datum that pediatric folds have a higher propensity for scar, clinical studies and observations do not support this. Indeed, the proportionally large amount of superficial layer-like lamina propria may help or perhaps protect the pediatric patient from surgical, traumatic, and infectious injuries.

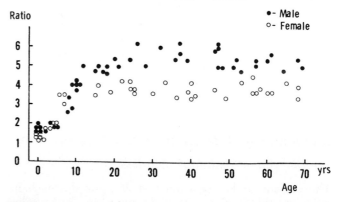

FIGURE 80–2. Ratio of length of membranous portion to the cartilaginous portion of vocal fold for 48 males and 40 females ranging in age from a few hours to 69 years. (From Hirano M, Kurita S, Nakashima T. In Bless DM, Abbs JH [eds]. Vocal Fold Physiology: Contemporary Research and Clinical Issues. San Diego, College-Hill Press, 1983, pp 22–43.)

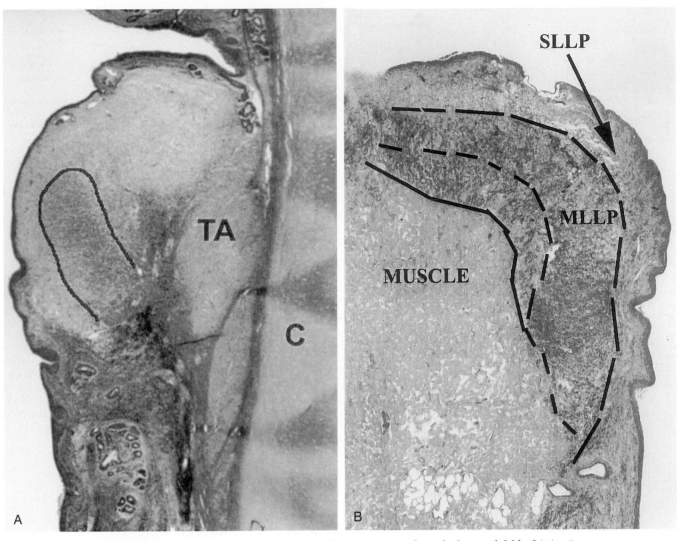

FIGURE 80–3. This figure shows a mid-membranous section through the vocal fold of (A) a 6-month-old male and (B) a 46-year-old male. Vocal folds have been stained for elastin fibers (*small black dots* in the lamina propria). Note the very rudimentary collection of elastin fibers in the 6-month-old child, whereas the older man has a more organized and complete structure. TA, thyroarytenoid muscle; C, cartilage; SLLP, superficial layer of the lamina propria; MLLP, middle layer of the lamina propria.

By age 16 years, the layered structure of the adult is in place. With growth and continual exposure to the mechanical forces of phonation, elastic fibers of the intermediate layer develop and fibroblasts decrease while collagen fibers of the vocal ligament form.

The structure of the larynx itself changes markedly with age. In two reports, Klock[77, 78] published extensive measurements on the anatomic dimensions of the larynx in infancy and childhood. In general, the growth of the overall dimensions of the larynx is linearly related (directly proportional) to crown–heel length (somatic height). Laryngeal growth thus relates to age only as overall body growth relates—that is, a sigmoid curve with acceleration between birth and 3 years, then deceleration, then rapid growth phase at puberty, especially in boys. The thyroid alae in infancy are positioned in a curving semicircle of about 130 degrees. This narrows to 120 degrees in prepubertal girls and 110 degrees in boys.[71, 72]

Kahane also documented the changes in external laryngeal anatomy resulting from puberty.[72] Significant regional growth localized to the anterior aspect of the thyroid cartilage was measured in laryngeal specimens of pubertal boys, i.e., formation of the "Adam's apple." This results in both an increase in length of the anterior vocal folds and a change in the angle of the thyroid alae to 90 degrees. Other external laryngeal measurements showed less dramatic differences between pubertal boys and girls.

Additional Considerations

Voice production occurs because the tissue in the vocal folds oscillates. The ease with which this tissue oscillates depends on many variables that are beyond the scope of this chapter.[128] One important factor is the mucociliary blanket that covers the larynx. This moving layer of water,

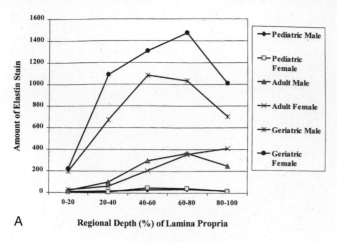

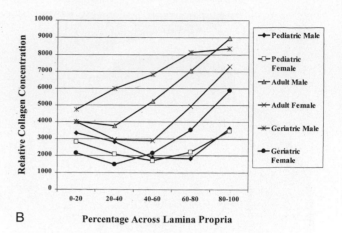

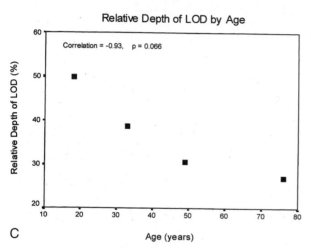

FIGURE 80–4. A, The relative concentration of elastin fibers at various depths into the lamina propria. This assessment was performed using a histologic stain for elastin fibers. B, The same information for collagen fibers. Note that in the middle layer of the lamina propria, the elastin fiber concentration increases but for collagen it stays the same or decreases. C, The relative depth of a blunt surgical plane of dissection in the lamina propria becomes thinner with age. In essence, this study suggested that the "cover" (epithelium and superficial layer of the lamina propria) is thicker in the pediatric population and becomes thinner with age.

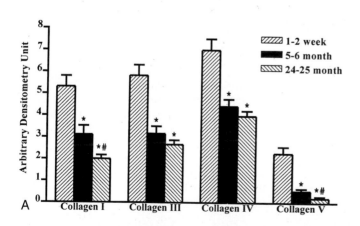

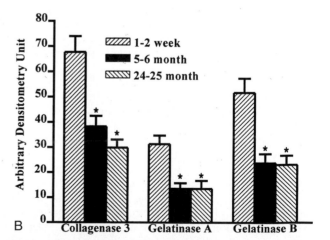

FIGURE 80–5. These two graphs display the expression (mRNA) for genes that regulate collagen production and breakdown in the vocal folds of infant, young adult, and geriatric mice. A, The expression for collagen genes is increased in the infant mice, with significant differences in the decreased gene expression for collagen in older mice. B, Addition of the dimension of genes that enzymatically destroy the various types of collagen. Note that these genes also are increased in the infant mice. Taken together, these graphs show that collagen turnover is much higher in the vocal folds of infant mice compared with adults.

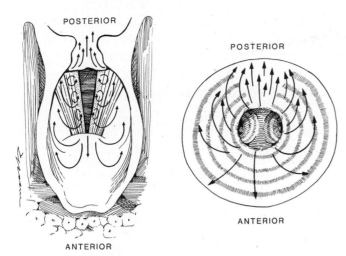

FIGURE 80–6. The flow and direction of the mucous blanket across the larynx and trachea. The majority of mucus flow occurs posteriorly because of the ciliary motion of the trachea. See text.

proteins, electrolytes, and other molecules keeps the tissue moist and healthy and adds protection against infectious, traumatic, or environmental injury. Keeping this mucociliary system healthy is important. Understanding how it works helps clinicians to better anticipate disease location and diagnosis. The mucociliary blanket of the trachea moves superiorly and posteriorly. Although the entire trachea is lined with cilia, the majority of mucus travels up the posterior portion. Figure 80–6 is a diagram of this motion. By the time the blanket reaches the larynx, most of the pulmonary secretions are tracking along the posterior wall and consequently through the posterior glottis. The posterior glottis is the only portion that is consistently and widely ciliated. The anterior glottis also has a small narrow strip of epithelium that is ciliated, but because the trachea cilia move all the mucus posteriorly, little mucus from the lungs tracks through the anterior glottis.[39, 45]

The result of mucus from the lung traveling predominantly through the posterior glottis is that agents of pulmonary infectious diseases are concentrated in the posterior glottis. Tuberculosis and fungal disease often have a posterior glottic manifestation while the vocal folds are relatively uninvolved. When extraesophageal signs of reflux focus attention on posterior glottic disease, remember that the posterior glottis does have important functions and is attacked by various diseases.

Developmental Physiology of the Voice

Phonation Mechanisms

The acoustic output of the phonatory larynx is produced by vibration of the anterior membranous edges of the vocal folds, which periodically interrupts the airstream from the lungs. This fundamental aspect of phonation is creation and maintenance of mucosal traveling waves and their entrainment with the airflow.[7] Vibration, or oscillation, is self-sustained by (1) the elastic recoil of vocal fold

mucosa and (2) alternating pressures within the glottis that separate and bring together the folds.[24, 127, 128] This traveling mucosal wave, observed with high-speed cinematography or stroboscopy, is created by the interaction of the airflow with the vocal-fold mucosal cover. The inferior-to-superior movement of the traveling wave is influenced by the pressure of the airstream (lung pressure), the thickness of the vocal folds, the approximation of the vocal folds, and the elasticity of vocal-fold tissue.

While vocal-fold oscillation is described as periodic — that is, repeating itself at regular intervals — it is increasingly recognized that this does not precisely occur in the voices of children and adults. Cycle-to-cycle variations in frequency and amplitude periodicity (termed *jitter* and *shimmer*, respectively) have been measured in normal children's voices[42, 43] as well as in adults.[3] Other types of sudden qualitative changes in vibration, known as *bifurcations*, create unusual repeating patterns or aperiodicity.[128] Studies have observed these patterns in voices of normal adults,[76] infants,[95] and disordered voice populations.[60] These features describe a system that is "chaotic" (both deterministic and unpredictable), and vocal-fold vibration is now being investigated in these terms.[70, 102, 129]

Pitch (Frequency)

The most notable feature of the pediatric voice is pitch change. The pitch drops throughout infancy, childhood, and adolescence in both males and females. The frequency of the infant's cry is about 500 Hz, and this drops by about half by age 8 to 10 years. Several investigators have measured differences in the frequency of voices in prepubescent boys and girls[42, 58] beginning at 5 to 8 years. Wilson's composite data suggest that the frequency of the male voice is 5 to 10 Hz lower than the female voice beginning at about age 8 years.[135] Given the observation of Hirano et al[65] that membranous fold length is similar at these ages, the explanation for these findings is unclear but may be related to height/weight differences, vocal tract changes, or cultural factors.[42] Since adrenal androgens begin secretion in boys between 6 and 10 years of age,[126] subtle hormonal influences may also be present. The decrease in pitch continues through adolescence for males and females, with the male voice change at puberty most noticeable. Titze[128] has shown how the changes in pitch are due mostly to changes in membranous length of the vocal folds (Fig. 80–7). There are interesting irregularities in the curve at the ages of 3 and 10 years that may be related to changes in tissue stiffness as the vocal ligament develops.

The male adolescent voice goes through a transition, usually between ages 13 and 14 years, when the pitch drops. This is due to the anterior growth of the thyroid cartilage in response to testosterone, which causes an increase in vocal-fold length.[55] An additional change in laryngeal structure is an increase in bulk of the thyroarytenoid muscle. This increases the vertical thickness of the vocal fold and causes bulging of its medial contour.[128] With this change, glottal closure occurs over a larger portion of the glottal cycle, and amplitude of vocal-fold vibration increases, resulting in a richer voice.

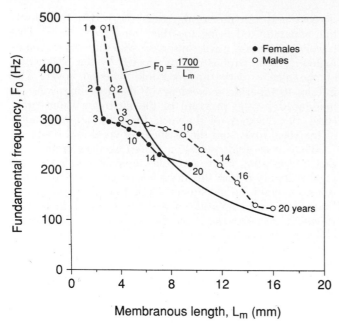

FIGURE 80–7. Fundamental frequency as a function of the membranous length of the vocal fold, with age as a parameter. (From Titze IR. Principles of Voice Production. Englewood Cliffs, NJ, Prentice-Hall, 1994, p 180. ©1994 by Ingo Titze. Reproduced by permission of the author.)

Loudness (Intensity), Aerodynamics, and Breathing

The cry of an infant or scream of a distressed child attests to the fact that children can create loud voices. Further consideration reveals that levels of acoustic power (averaging 70 dB for conversational speech) comparable to that of adults are generated with a much smaller phonatory and respiratory mechanism. Several physiologic principles underlie this, including the dependence of vocal intensity on frequency and lung pressure and the differences in the pediatric respiratory system. Titze[128] explained that vocal intensity increases about 8 to 9 dB per octave increase in fundamental frequency. A 3-year-old child speaking at 300 Hz is doubling the 150-Hz frequency of the adult. However, other issues play into the ability to drive shorter vocal folds at a faster rate, namely, lung pressure.

Stathopoulos and Sapienza studied variations in vocal intensity during phonation in 4-year-old and 8-year-old children and adults.[124] They found that for comparable soft, comfortable, and loud phonation tasks, the children generated lung pressures 50% to 100% greater than those of the adults. In association with this, rib-cage excursion for 4-year-olds was equal to that of adults; for 8-year-olds, it was nearly twice that of adults. Because lung volume excursion in children is about half that in adults, the authors explained that children are required to move their rib cages more to achieve the same lung volume displacement and have greater lung volume excursion relative to vital capacity during phonation. Similar findings, also reported in speech breathing research by Hoit et al,[67] led to the conclusion that children work harder to use their voice. They have a shorter maximal phonation time than adults do[54, 135] and take more frequent breaths during speech.[67] This increased respiratory effort expended decreases to adult-like patterns by age 10 years.[67]

Causes of Voice Problems

When is the voice a problem? This question is not always straightforward, since the child often does not perceive dysphonia. Although acute voice changes prompt concern, parents and family members may not regard a child's voice as dysphonic when it has not changed suddenly. Voice problems become noticeable to others when the child enters a larger social circle, such as starting school.

Voice problems are usually categorized as abnormalities in vocal quality, pitch, or loudness.[135] By far, the most common are abnormalities in quality—that is, a voice that is hoarse, rough, harsh, or breathy. Pitch abnormalities relate to voice that is thought to be too high or low, not corresponding to the child's age or gender. Loudness abnormalities relate to a voice that is too soft or too loud. Frequently, a perceived voice problem is actually a problem with speech resonance (i.e., hypernasality or hyponasality). In the series reported by Campbell and Stool,[12] of 203 children who were referred to a specialty clinic for a voice problem, 38 (19%) were found to have velopharyngeal insufficiency.

Incidence

Nearly all studies on the incidence of voice disorders in children have involved school-age children.[135] Such studies state that voice disorders are fairly common, occurring in 6% to 23% of children,[4, 116, 118] with an average rate of 6% to 9%.[135] These data were corroborated by McAlister et al,[91] who twice recorded the voices of 58 10-year-old children at 2-month intervals. Perceptual ratings identified eight with hoarseness (14%). All were boys. Other researchers have confirmed this preponderance of male over female schoolchildren with voice problems, usually in ratios of 2 or 3 to 1.[4, 84, 116] Voice disorders are severe enough to warrant clinical treatment in 2% to 3% of cases.[135] This rate corresponds to the average percentage of voice patients in the caseload seen by school-based speech pathologists.[135]

As in other areas of pediatric otolaryngology, the causes of pediatric voice disorders include a few common entities (e.g., vocal nodules) and a large list of uncommon diagnoses. These have been separated by Cohen et al[21] into neurologic, congenital, and genetic anomalies; tumors; infection and granulomatous diseases; trauma; endocrine and metabolic disorders; and physiologic, psychogenic, and iatrogenic categories. It is similarly helpful to separate causes of voice disorders into those likely to be encountered in various age groups, including newborn to 6 months, 6 months to 5 years, 5 to 13 years, and 13 to 18 years (Table 80–1). Although not comprehensive, this classification gives the clinician direction in sorting through a large differential diagnosis.

In the newborn with an abnormal cry, with or without stridor, dysphonia may have a variety of causes. Congenital laryngeal abnormalities include anterior glottic web,[18]

TABLE 80-1. Differential Diagnosis of Common Pediatric Voice Problems Categorized by Age

0 to 6 Months	6 Months to 5 Years	5 Years to 13 Years	13 Years to 18 Years
Traumatic: intubation Iatrogenic: surgical Neurogenic: central or peripheral neuropathy Neoplastic: hemangioma, cysts Congenital: web, cleft Infectious: herpes	Traumatic: foreign bodies, intubation Infectious: respiratory Neoplastic: papillomas Behavioral: nodules Inflammatory: extraesophageal reflux	Behavioral: nodules Infectious: respiratory Inflammatory: allergy, extraesophageal reflux	Behavioral *Male:* mutational/transitional voice *Female:* nodules Functional: muscle tension dysphonia, aphonia Infectious: respiratory Inflammatory: allergy, extraesophageal reflux

laryngeal clefts (posterior[17] or anterior[20]), laryngeal anomalies associated with genetic defects such as cri du chat syndrome,[133] and lipoid proteinosis.[114] The neurogenic causes of vocal-fold paralysis are various. Generally, bilateral vocal-fold paralysis has a central neurologic origin, such as Chiari malformation, meningomyelocele, or hydrocephalus. Airway concerns predominate in these cases. Unilateral vocal-fold paralysis (UVFP) causing dysphonia is often of peripheral origin. It may be related to cardiac disease,[23, 117] birth trauma (e.g., neck traction during forceps delivery),[19] or iatrogenic trauma. Any surgical procedure in the chest or neck that encounters the course of the vagus or laryngeal nerves, such as tracheoesophageal fistula repair, esophageal atresia repair, or surgery of the great vessels, may cause vocal-fold paralysis. Ductus arteriosus ligation has been reported to cause left vocal-fold paralysis in 4% to 7.4% of cases.[31, 37, 142] Low–birth-weight infants are at much higher risk for this complication.[142] Right vocal-fold paralysis has occurred after the Blalock-Taussig shunt procedure (M. Smith, personal observation, 1994). Traumatic causes of dysphonia in infants usually relate to the sequelae of intubation injuries with granuloma, laryngeal stenosis, or arytenoid dislocation. Neoplastic causes include hemangioma, papilloma, cystic hygroma, and saccular or other laryngeal cysts. Neonatal infectious laryngitis related to herpesvirus infection has been reported.[104]

In the infant and young child (6 months to 5 years), other causes of dysphonia may become manifest. A variety of viral and bacterial infectious illnesses often result in temporary hoarseness. Any other *acute* voice change in these patients, especially if it is associated with persistent cough or stridor, requires consideration of foreign-body aspiration.[53, 106] Laryngeal papillomas may manifest as hoarseness in this age group. Behavioral causes of dysphonia can begin at early ages with vocal nodule formation (Fig. 80–8).

In children 5 to 13 years old, vocal nodules predominate as the major cause of dysphonia.[35] Other patients with a high frequency of vocal nodules are those with velopharyngeal inadequacy.[94] They may develop laryngeal hyperfunction as part of compensatory efforts to close the velopharyngeal sphincter. Infectious and inflammatory causes of dysphonia are common. Chronic hoarseness from extraesophageal reflux–induced laryngitis is now increasingly recognized as a cause of voice problems in adults[103, 132] and children.[108]

In the adolescent years, behavioral and psychogenic causes of chronic dysphonia predominate. The frequency of vocal nodules in boys drops abruptly; however, both boys and girls are still at fairly equal risk.[35] In boys, problems with voice transition at puberty may yield hoarseness and persistent high pitch, called *puberphonia* or *mutational (adolescent male transitional) voice disorder.* Psychogenic and functional voice disorders may also occur.[38, 57, 119]

Several special categories of children with voice problems should be recognized. In immunosuppressed children being treated for leukemia, voice problems may be related to fungal infection[59] or chemotherapy-induced la-

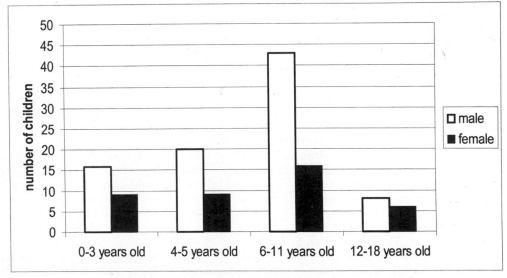

FIGURE 80–8. Vocal nodules in children grouped by age and sex. (Data from Dobres R, Lee L, Stemple JC, et al: Description of laryngeal pathologies in children evaluated by otolaryngologists. J Speech Hear Disord 55:526, 1990.)

ryngeal neuropathy.[2] Traumatic brain injury may cause voice problems in connection with speech deficits, often characterized by decreased loudness.[92, 93] Likewise, children with cerebral palsy may have a variety of voice problems related to voicing interruptions, abnormal speech breathing, impaired pitch control, breathiness, or hyperfunction.[135] Children with mental retardation also have voice problems. The most examined group in this regard is children with Down syndrome. Their voices may be rough or harsh or have excessive pitch variability.[135] Children with hearing loss are well known to demonstrate abnormalities in voice, which are greatly dependent on the severity and age at onset of the hearing loss and the associated language and articulation difficulties.[135] Their voices are described as high-pitched, monotone, harsh, breathy, and tense.[136] Hearing-impaired persons who receive a cochlear implant show a reduction in vocal pitch, lowered intensity, and reduced nasality.[98]

Evaluation of Voice Problems

The approach to evaluation of a child with a voice problem differs from that of the adult in several respects.[76, 109] Voice disorders in children often coexist with speech, language, and developmental delays. Children have a limited ability to cooperate, so any procedures or assessment techniques must be performed in the least invasive and nonthreatening manner. Parents, family members, and other caregivers are included in the acquisition of historical information and are involved with therapy.

The assessment of voice problems requires a comprehensive medical and behavioral evaluation. This requires specialists from a variety of disciplines: otolaryngology–head and neck surgery, speech/language pathology, pediatrics, psychology, and social work. Other medical specialties that may be involved include neurology, gastroenterology, genetics, and endocrinology.

The history of a voice problem often involves persons other than the child, such as parents and school teachers. In detailing the history of a voice problem, the questionnaire described by Maddern et al is useful.[90] The otolaryngologist performs a complete examination. A hearing test is obtained. In cases of adolescent male dysphonias, physical maturity is assessed.[56]

Laryngeal examination is crucial to voice evaluation. The flexible fiberoptic laryngoscope has become the tool of choice for evaluating voice problems in adults and children.[80] Even young children can tolerate this examination well with proper preparation of the child and parent, use of topical nasal anesthesia, and an engaging and nonthreatening atmosphere. These methods have been well described.[14, 30, 87] The use of video equipment has advantages of engaging the child's attention, providing visual feedback for the parent, and facilitating communication between the physician and speech pathologist and others.

Several points may be emphasized in the course of this examination. After the fiberscope is passed beyond the turbinates, the velopharynx is examined for velopharyngeal insufficiency. The adenoid pad and tonsils are visualized as the fiberscope passes beyond the nose into the pharynx. In the hypopharynx, the laryngeal and pharyngeal mucosa are inspected for erythema and mucosal thickening, especially the arytenoid mucosa, posterior glottis, and true vocal-fold mucosa. Edema of the vocal folds or subglottic mucosa, called *pseudosulcus*, may be present.[61] These are signs of extraesophageal reflux. Diffuse edema of the laryngeal mucosa, "cobblestoning" of the posterior pharynx, and edematous nasal mucosa may be a sign of allergy. Vocal-fold mobility is inspected, including observation during coughing and sniffing maneuvers. The larynx is observed during connected speech, such as counting to 10 or repeated phrases. These tasks are helpful for observing supraglottal hyperfunction in both functional dysphonias and as compensatory behavior in organic lesions.[80] The vocal folds themselves are examined for irregularities, swelling, or lesions. Such abnormalities of the vocal fold, when unilateral, should be inspected for congenital cysts.[10, 97] During sustained phonation of the vowel /i/, the glottal closure is visualized. Incomplete posterior glottal closure (posterior "chink") is common in children, as it is in many adult women.[43, 62]

During endoscopic visualization, one can decide whether stroboscopic lighting would help elucidate the problem (e.g., suspicion of abnormal mucosal-wave vibration due to scar or sulcus in the absence of nodules; unilateral cord lesion). Laryngostroboscopy has limitations in young children, who may not be able to phonate long enough for stroboscopic pictures to be obtained (the child's maximal phonation time should be at least 5 seconds). Older children can sometimes tolerate well a rigid oral telescopic examination of the larynx. A 70-degree rod lens telescope is usually used. This yields a more detailed view of the vocal fold and laryngeal mucosa, which is helpful for examining vocal-fold mass lesions, inflammation, and stroboscopy. Only sustained vowel phonation can be seen, usually while having the patient say the vowel /i/ with the mouth open and tongue extended. The disadvantage of this method is that it does not permit a view during connected speech and sometimes yields a less adequate view of vocal-fold movement. Sensitive gag reflex precludes transoral laryngeal examination of some patients.

The voice assessment by the speech/language pathologist is ideally conducted during the same visit to the otolaryngologist. The child's voice is rated perceptually during a variety of speech tasks and sustained vowels. The voice is recorded for acoustic measures. Aerodynamic and glottographic measurements may also help elucidate the problem and are easily obtained with current instrumentation. These measurements have certain advantages: documentation of the problem, corroboration of findings with the laryngeal imaging examination, documentation of treatment efficacy, and use as biofeedback during therapy.

Direct visualization of the larynx under anesthesia is sometimes required for diagnosis of pediatric dysphonia. Indications include (1) an inability to examine the larynx with fiberoptic endoscope, (2) when detailed visualization is required to determine the presence of glottic web, laryngeal cleft, arytenoid fixation, or vocal-fold lesion (such as papilloma, sulcus vocalis, cyst), and (3) laryngeal electromyography for paralysis assessment.[8, 41, 79, 137, 138] Laryngeal electromyography does not appear to have much utility in the prognostic assessment of congenital vocal-fold paralysis,[8, 137] but it has been helpful in selected cases of pediatric new-onset paralysis, tumors affecting laryngeal nerves, or decannulation decisions.[137]

Management of Voice Problems

The management of voice problems requires an understanding of the pathophysiology and mechanism of dysphonia as well as the natural history of the problem. The severity of the voice problem is also taken into account— whether the voice calls attention to itself, interferes with communication, or causes the speaker to be unhappy. The multifactorial nature of causes of dysphonia, in a biopsychosocial perspective, may require consideration.[109] This information guides answers to the questions of if, when, and how to intervene. Management options include behavioral, medical, and surgical therapies. Treatment of the common causes of pediatric dysphonia (vocal nodules, reflux laryngitis, laryngeal paralysis, congenital glottic webs, laryngeal papillomas, and laryngeal stenosis) is considered in this context.

Vocal Nodules and Functional Voice Disorders

Given that vocal nodules are an organic manifestation of laryngeal hyperfunction,[82] the mainstay of treatment of vocal nodules is behavioral voice therapy. A study by Murry and Woodson[101] confirmed this. They studied 59 adult patients treated with (1) combined voice therapy (speech pathologist and otolaryngologist), (2) voice therapy (speech pathologist only), or (3) vocal nodule surgery followed by voice therapy. By post-treatment perceptual analysis of voice recordings, overall improvement was highest in the first group, followed by the second group. No patients in the first two groups underwent surgery. The surgical group had the poorest outcome. Behavioral voice therapy is clearly indicated in adolescents and adults, but the decision to treat is less clear in children, in whom vocal nodules can occur at quite young ages (see Fig. 80–8).

Clinical experience of the natural history of vocal nodules in children suggests spontaneous remission by puberty.[130] However, Mori reported that 12% of children with vocal nodules did not experience voice improvement according to a parental survey performed after the child had reached puberty.[100] There are fewer data to document the efficacy of behavioral treatment of vocal nodules in children. Because of these factors, "therapeutic nihilists" advocate no intervention.[74, 90, 130] Some behavioral treatment programs have reported success by various means of assessment. In a retrospective survey review of 120 children with vocal nodules treated by several methods, Mori found that those treated with vocal hygiene advice only did not improve.[100] Voice therapy did show improvement in many patients, and the degree of improvement was related to the number of therapy sessions attended: 69% of patients that attended more than seven sessions reported an improvement in voice. So, patient and parent motivation appear to be a factor in voice therapy outcome. Voice therapy is more likely to have a

successful outcome with improved compliance in a 9- or 10-year-old child than a 5- or 6-year-old. The topic is one of active debate.[73, 113] Common behavioral therapy strategies for vocal nodules are outlined in approaches by Maddern et al,[90] Wilson,[135] and Andrews.[1]

Surgery is rarely recommended owing to risks of vocal-fold scarring, but some authors advocate surgical treatment of vocal nodules by use of microdissection techniques when nodules are identified, after a trial of voice therapy.[5, 10] The optimal age for voice surgery in these children is considered to be 9 to 11 years,[10] at which age compliance with therapy to limit voice abuse is considered improved. Bouchayer and Cornut[10] also reported a high frequency of congenital cysts, polyps, and sulci seen only on microlaryngoscopy in children previously thought to have vocal nodules. Mori's survey results imply that other factors are responsible for the dysphonia and presumed "vocal nodules" after puberty in some children.[100] It seems reasonable to recommend that other factors be considered when fiberoptic laryngoscopy reveals a unilateral lesion since typical vocal nodules come in pairs. In contrast with the European approach to voice therapy followed by surgery (if warranted), the United States is home to a variety of conflicting philosophies. A survey of 535 otolaryngologists on management of pediatric vocal nodules found that surgery followed by voice therapy was recommended by 9.4% and that surgery alone was recommended by 0.8% of respondents; 59% recommended voice therapy alone, and 31% recommended no intervention or other treatment.[99] At this time, we recommend voice therapy for children who are old enough to comply with behavioral management, and we view surgical treatment as an uncommon exception.

While vocal nodules may be considered a functional voice disorder with organic manifestations, functional voice disorders without lesions may also occur in children, presenting as dysphonia or aphonia.[11, 38, 57, 119] Another functional voice disorder in this age group is the transitional male adolescent dysphonia (puberphonia). Voice therapy is indicated but may require a prolonged course in aphonic children, especially adolescents.[57, 119] Psychosocial considerations should be addressed in the treatment of these patients.[110]

Reflux Laryngitis

Problems with voice related to extraesophageal reflux of stomach contents into the laryngopharynx are being recognized with increasing frequency. This problem can cause a multitude of throat-related complaints, including throat pain, hoarseness, cough, and dysphagia. Typically, the patient has no gastrointestinal complaints that are usually associated with gastroesophageal reflux. Hoarseness in adults is thought to result from glottic inflammation secondary to exposure of laryngopharyngeal structures to the gastric contents.[81]

There is little reference to this phenomenon in the pediatric and adolescent population. Putnam and Orenstein reported an 8-year-old girl with a 4-year history of hoarseness and nocturnal cough attributed to gastroesophageal reflux that resolved with metoclopramide and cimetidine therapy.[108] Gumpert et al studied 21 children, aged 2 to 14 years (mean age, 8 years) with chronic hoarseness.[50] Fiberoptic laryngoscopy revealed inflammation with at least one of the following features: interarytenoid erythema, edema, granuloma or vocal-fold nodules. None had typical signs or symptoms of gastroesophageal reflux. Dual-channel 24-hour pH probe monitoring revealed gastroesophageal reflux in 13 patients (62%) based on established adult parameters. We have seen this problem as well. We studied nine children at our institution who presented with chronic hoarseness. Results of esophageal pH probe testing were positive in five of six patients. Five of nine who underwent upper gastrointestinal endoscopy had signs of esophagitis. Seven of nine had a positive response to antireflux medication. Five of these patients had vocal nodules. A high association of reflux in adults with vocal nodules has been reported.[83] This problem requires further study to determine optimal methods to diagnose the condition and its effective treatment.

Laryngeal Paralysis

UVFP and associated glottal insufficiency may be a cause of dysphonia in children. Associated airway and feeding concerns are managed initially. Several large reviews have reported that the natural history of laryngeal paralysis is toward spontaneous "recovery." Cohen et al described 38 children with UVFP; although 14 were lost to follow-up, 13 recovered completely.[19] Emery and Fearon reported 30 cases of UVFP in children.[36] Peripheral nerve injuries usually recovered (60% of cases). In laryngeal paralysis, it is important to distinguish between neurogenic (return of vocal-fold movement) and phonatory (improvement in voice) recovery, since they do not always equate.[66] This is demonstrated in the series of Emery and Fearon[36]: in eight patients observed for an average of 6 years, vocal-fold mobility did not return, yet the voice recovered in six of the eight patients. Only one patient underwent surgery (Teflon injection). The infrequent reports of surgical management of dysphonia in children from laryngeal paralysis attest to the trend toward natural improvement in voice through compensatory means, with or without recovery of vocal-fold movement (see Chapter 85).

Surgical management of glottal insufficiency and laryngeal paralysis has received much attention. Although Teflon injection of the vocal fold is commonly performed in adults, it has several disadvantages in children, including irreversibility and unknown long-term effects.[131] A variety of phonosurgical techniques have been popularized as alternatives to Teflon injection of the vocal cords.[68] These laryngeal framework procedures have had some limited application in children.[40, 86, 120] Link et al reported on eight patients with UVFP treated with type I medialization thyroplasty for dysphonia or aspiration symptoms.[86] The arytenoid adduction procedure,[69] while appropriate in theory for closure of posterior glottic defects, has technical problems that preclude its use in young children.[120] This procedure is recommended in adolescents with UVFP and large glottal gap if concomitant aspiration symptoms are present. These procedures are usually performed under local anesthesia in adults. This is not possi-

ble in most children. The use of laryngeal mask airway and intraoperative fiberoptic laryngoscopy to adjust implant location has been reported in two children.[40]

Reinnervation of the paralyzed larynx is another surgical option for dysphonia from UVFP. Two variations of this approach have been investigated: ansa hypoglossi to recurrent laryngeal nerve anastomosis,[29] and ansa-strap nerve–muscle pedicle implantation into laryngeal muscle (lateral cricoarytenoid or thyroarytenoid).[44] Both of these techniques aim to reinnervate laryngeal muscle to prevent atrophy, increase tone, and improve glottal adduction and voice. In the series reported by Tucker of eight children with UVFP, three underwent the nerve–muscle pedicle procedure, in addition to voice therapy, with "good" voice results.[131] In older preteens and adolescents with UVFP, we have used the technique of combining arytenoid adduction with reinnervation of the ansa hypoglossi.[15] This approach combines the benefits of framework surgery to close the posterior glottis and reinnervation to increase adductor muscle tone.

Laryngeal Papillomas

Recurrent respiratory papillomatosis is the most common benign laryngeal neoplasm in children. These papillomas can cause hoarseness, stridor, and respiratory distress, which may necessitate surgical intervention to maintain an adequate airway.[49] The voice may improve because of recurrent respiratory papillomatosis or the treatment. While the disease is present, the voice may be affected because of interference of the papilloma with vocal-fold closure. However, after the disease is in remission, the voice may be affected as a complication of the surgical treatment previously used. Crockett et al described glottic complications as a result of surgical intervention for recurrent respiratory papillomatosis.[28] Glottic scarring (anterior and posterior glottic webbing) occurred in patients who had frequent and multiple procedures.

One of the difficulties in treating recurrent respiratory papillomatosis is that aggressive removal of the papillomas to provide the best airway may result in eventual injury to the vocal folds. Since severe papilloma disease obscures normal anatomic laryngeal landmarks and structures, it can be difficult to limit the surgical excision to the epithelial layers. This can be particularly true in the anterior glottis, the posterior glottis, and the membranous vocal folds. Wetmore and colleagues reported that the frequency of soft tissue complications increased in patients who required six or more laser operations.[134] The authors concluded that deep vaporization of papilloma resulted in a higher frequency of glottic complications. Papilloma removal in the 1980s focused on the concept of total or near-total eradication with each surgery.[28, 134] In the late 1980s, we conducted a study of voice characteristics in eight patients who had experienced extensive, repeated surgery for removal of papilloma and were then in remission for at least 2 years.[46] Results demonstrated reduced frequency and intensity range and laryngeal stroboscopic findings consistent with stiff vocal folds due to scar. Subjectively, patients did not feel that their voice was normal. Such findings raised concerns about whether the voice difficulty experienced by these patients arose from the disease or from the treatment.

An awareness of these voice disorders has led some surgeons to a more conservative approach for papilloma removal.[6] This approach is directed at two points of surgical technique. The first is use of more precise instrumentation for papilloma to minimize damage to the underlying subepithelial tissues, e.g., lamina propria. Advances have been made in reducing the laser spot size, using a micromanipulator, and adjusting laser parameters to minimize tissue destruction.[105] The second consideration involves sparing a small area of papilloma unilaterally at the anterior and posterior glottis if that area is involved. Small cup forceps may be used to debulk papilloma from these areas, avoiding laser injury.[6]

Using this approach, Ossoff et al reported on 22 patients (14 children and 8 adults) in whom the delayed soft tissue complications were significantly reduced.[105] Only three children had problems related to posterior glottic web or vocal-fold scar. From this study, the authors concluded that these problems in patients undergoing papilloma surgery are related to the surgical technique used and not to the number of procedures performed. This report underscores the need to consider the effect of these endoscopic laryngeal procedures on the voice, although the focus of the treatment involves airway and papilloma management (see Chapter 90). Adjuvant therapies to reduce papilloma regrowth received continued attention. These include vocal-fold injection of papilloma with the antiviral cidofovir[107] and oral ingestion of indole-3-carbinol, a modifier of estrogen metabolism.[22] The tissue effects of cidofovir on vocal-fold tissue are unknown. Vocal quality outcomes in these patients might improve to the extent that the number of laryngeal procedures is reduced.

Congenital Glottic Web

Congenital glottic webs are rare in children and are nearly always located in the anterior glottis. In the largest series reported by Cohen, 51 patients with congenital anterior glottic webs were seen over 32 years.[18] A voice problem at birth was the most commonly reported symptom. Cohen categorized glottic webs on the basis of observation and estimation of web extent in the glottic lumen. Those involving less than 35% often required no treatment. Airway symptoms increased with increasing web size. Only 4 of 32 patients with 50% or less of the glottis involved underwent tracheotomy, but all 16 patients with greater than 50% involvement did so. Treatment of the web involved a combination of endoscopic treatment with dilation, division, or laser. Twelve patients underwent laryngofissure and placement of McNaught or Silastic keel.

Dedo reported success in treating a newborn with anterior glottic web using an endoscopically placed Teflon keel.[32] In this patient, however, problems with development of posterior glottic stenosis were encountered from keel irritation in the posterior commissure and arytenoids. Cohen recommended waiting until age 3 years, when the larynx is large enough to avoid this complication of keel

placement.[18] He also emphasized that normal voice quality was rarely attained in his series. Most patients had a hoarse or husky voice, a weak voice, or "double voice." Laryngeal webs often accompany congenital subglottic stenosis.[96] The current treatment of both the airway and the voice problem caused by congenital laryngeal web often involves laryngotracheal reconstruction with cartilage grafting.[9] The comments of Zalzal et al on voice problems after pediatric laryngotracheal reconstruction also apply to these patients.[140] The voice problems from the underlying abnormality may be compounded by surgery to correct the disease.

Laryngotracheal Reconstruction

Surgical techniques for repair of glottic and subglottic stenosis have advanced in many ways.[26] These procedures, generally known as laryngotracheal reconstruction (LTR), are particularly applicable to the pediatric population, in which laryngotracheal stenosis has been a prevalent clinical problem. The goal of these procedures is to restore the airway. However, it can readily be appreciated that laryngeal surgery designed to address one aspect of laryngeal function may necessarily affect other functions of the larynx, such as phonation.[123]

Voice problems have been associated with cartilage graft LTR procedures in some children.[16, 88, 115, 122, 140, 141] For example, Smith et al described eight patients with voice problems after LTR.[122] The voices were frequently rough, low-pitched, or breathy. Two patients exhibited reverse or inhalatory phonation. Fiberoptic laryngoscopy and laryngostroboscopy demonstrated supraglottal phonation in three, glottal incompetence in two, arytenoid fixation in two, anterior commissure blunting or widening in three, vertical asymmetry of the vocal folds in two, and vocal fold scarring (i.e., absent mucosal wave) in three. Most patients exhibit more than one abnormal finding. Although the study was not controlled and was probably representative of LTR patients with more severe voice problems, it is comparable to other reports.[16, 75, 140, 141]

LTR may adversely affect phonation in various ways. Stenosis at the level of the free margin of the vocal folds and scarring of the superficial lamina propria inhibit vocal-fold vibration and are difficult to reconstruct. It is also apparent that surgery designed to enlarge the laryngeal airway may adversely affect phonation, which requires glottal closure. Trends from studies indicate some additional factors that appear to increase risk for a poor postoperative voice result in children who undergo LTR. These include the use of posterior cricoid cartilage grafts, combined use of anterior and posterior grafts, long-term placement of endolaryngeal stents, and multiple LTR procedures.[16, 27, 123, 140, 141]

Posterior glottic and subglottic stenosis can be successfully treated with posterior cricoid cartilage grafts.[27, 139] This technique can also be used for treatment of impaired vocal-fold mobility, such as bilateral vocal-fold paralysis.[48] In the series reported by Zalzal, 12 patients were treated for posterior laryngeal stenosis with posterior cricoid cartilage grafts.[139] The patient's voice quality was assessed by a household member who spent the most

TABLE 80–2. Factors in Laryngotracheal Reconstruction that Affect Voice

Laryngotracheal Reconstruction Procedures	Potential Adverse Effects on Phonation	Techniques
Anterior laryngotracheal split or graft	Anterior commissure disruption Vocal fold vertical asymmetry Cricothyroid muscle dysfunction Supraglottic collapse	Avoid complete laryngofissure, if possible Avoid graft placement in anterior commissure Perform exact alignment of anterior commissure
Posterior laryngotracheal split or graft	Increased glottic gap Impaired arytenoid adduction Arytenoid subluxation	Avoid excessive graft width Gentle retraction of hemi-cricoid
Stents	Scarring of vocal fold mucosa Impaired arytenoid mobility Rounded scarring of vocal fold edge	Minimize stenting time Use single-stage laryngotracheal reconstruction, if possible Stent below vocal folds, if possible
Cricotracheal resection	Vocal fold paralysis from recurrent laryngeal nerve injury Cricothyroid muscle dysfunction Arytenoid prolapse	Dissect closely to cricoid and trachea anterior to cricothyroid joint, and inside the outer cricoid perichondrium

time with the patient before and after surgery (subjective perceptual assessment). Of the eight patients with preoperative normal voice quality, postoperative voice quality was normal in only two; six patients were described as having a hoarse or husky voice. In another series reported by Zalzal et al, 16 patients underwent formal assessment of voice quality.[140] Only four of the nine patients who received posterior grafts had breathiness, yet these four were the only patients with a breathy postoperative voice. Smith et al described 15 patients who underwent "single-stage" LTR (no tracheotomy tube employed or removal of the tracheotomy tube at initial surgery).[123] In the 12 patients who were successfully extubated, informal voice quality assessment performed 3 to 6 months postoperatively showed that seven had a normal voice, four had moderate dysphonia, and one had severe dysphonia. All five of these patients underwent placement of both anterior and posterior cricoid cartilage grafts. For three of these five, the surgery was a revision procedure.

The use of endolaryngeal stents to secure cartilage grafts in place has been well described. However, these stents appear to injure the voice, especially when used in the long term. In Cotton's large series of 61 patients who underwent posterior cricoid graft LTR, the duration of stenting was found to be correlated with postoperative voice assessment in that better voice results occurred when the duration of stenting was 12 weeks or less.[27] In a series of 20 children who underwent LTR, Maddalozzo and Holinger[89] reported that hoarseness was not an infrequent problem in those who required stenting. In the report of Zalzal et al, all 16 patients underwent stent placement and 15 had aberrant voice quality.[140] However, the authors failed to find a correlation between stenting duration and postoperative voice quality.

Several animal studies have examined the effects of stent/intubation on the larynx, with implications for voice problems.[85, 121] In a goat animal study of the effect of long-term endolaryngeal stents on the larynx, disruption of laryngeal mucosa and underlying tunica elastica, particularly in the posterior glottis, was observed in preparations that underwent endolaryngeal stent placement for 3 months.[121] Squamous metaplasia of the posterior glottic mucosa occurred, as did erosion of the vocal process of

the arytenoid. Epithelial hyperplasia and fibrous proliferation in the submucosa anterior to the vocal process were observed. This has potential implications for injury to the membranous folds. Because of the abundant and diffuse distribution of fibroblasts throughout the superficial and deep lamina propria, the membranous folds (phonatory glottis) of the pediatric larynx may be more susceptible to voice injury from surgical trauma, stents, or intubation.

Techniques of LTR may alter the position and anatomy of the vocal folds and endolaryngeal structures through external surgical manipulation of their support, the thyroid cartilage and arytenoids. In this way, these procedures may also be viewed as laryngeal framework surgery, examples of which are seen in the commonly employed techniques of LTR. Cartilage grafts, usually from autogenous rib, are popularly used in LTR.[25, 27] These grafts may be placed in the anterior or posterior cricoid region. Anterior cartilage grafts alter the laryngeal framework by immobilizing the action of the cricothyroid muscles, which lengthen and tense the vocal folds. Highly placed anterior cartilage grafts may disrupt the anterior commissure and splay the vocal folds. Posterior cricoid cartilage grafts widen the posterior commissure. This separates the arytenoids and affects the ability of the vocal folds to approximate at the vocal processes. Posterior cricoid grafts may also impair action of the interarytenoid muscle. These effects on glottal closure could be more pronounced in the pediatric larynx since it has a relatively larger posterior glottis. Cricotracheal resection places the recurrent laryngeal nerves at risk, transects the cricothyroid muscle, and can cause arytenoid prolapse.[111, 112, 125] All these factors can affect the voice outcome.

A summary of suggestions for minimizing or preventing phonation problems in laryngeal framework cartilage graft surgery for pediatric laryngotracheal stenosis is given in Table 80–2.

Conclusions

The pediatric otolaryngologist is called on to manage the voice in a variety of settings: from the newborn period to adolescence, from the common to the obscure, and from the severely developmentally impaired child to the aspiring vocal professional. This chapter emphasizes several points. The diagnosis and treatment of voice problems are approached from (1) a firm understanding of the anatomy and physiology of phonation, (2) a knowledge of the myriad disease processes that affect phonation, and (3) a realization of the complex behavioral and neuromotor development of the laryngeal valve as a sound source for purposes of communication. The biopsychosocial model of disease is pertinent in the approach to many voice problems.[109] In treatment, the pediatric otolaryngologist realizes that (1) most voice problems are not managed surgically but behaviorally and medically, and (2) any surgical procedure on the larynx may affect the voice, sometimes adversely. In the context of communication, the voice has a pivotal role. The goal of maximizing and preserving lifelong healthy vocal use is important. According to Casper, the voice's function, as part of our means of oral communication, "is basic to social/emotional development, to learning, to career choice, to interpersonal relationships, in sum, to all the things we are and do as human beings."[13]

REFERENCES

1. Andrews ML. Voice Therapy for Children. San Diego, Singular Publishing Group, 1991.
2. Annino DJ, MacArthur CJ, Friedman EM. Vincristine-induced recurrent laryngeal nerve paralysis. Laryngoscope 102:1260, 1992.
3. Baken RJ, Orlikoff RF. Clinical Measurement of Speech and Voice, 2nd ed. San Diego, Singular Publishing Group, 1999.
4. Bayes RA. An incidence study of chronic hoarseness among children. J Speech Hear Disord 31:171, 1966.
5. Benjamin B, Croxson G. Vocal nodules in children. Ann Otol Rhinol Laryngol 96:530, 1987.
6. Benjamin B, Parsons DS. Recurrent respiratory papillomatosis: a ten-year study. J Laryngol Otol 102:1022, 1988.
7. Berke GS, Gerratt BR. Laryngeal biomechanics: an overview of mucosal wave mechanics. J Voice 7:123, 1993.
8. Berkowitz RG. Laryngeal electromyography findings in idiopathic congenital bilateral vocal cord paralysis. Ann Otol Rhinol Laryngol 105:207, 1996.
9. Biavati MJ, Wood WE, Kearns DB, Smith RJ. One-stage repair of congenital laryngeal webs. Otolaryngol Head Neck Surg 112:447, 1995.
10. Bouchayer M, Cornut G. Microsurgical treatment of benign vocal fold lesions: indications, technique, results. Folia Phoniatr (Basel) 44:155, 1992.
11. Bridger MWM, Epstein R. Functional voice disorders: A review of 109 patients. J Laryngol Otol 97:1145, 1983.
12. Campbell TF, Stool S. Principles of assessment of the child with a voice disorder. Thesis. University of Pittsburgh School of Medicine, Pittsburgh, 1993.
13. Casper J. Disorders of speech and voice. Pediatr Ann 14:220, 1985.
14. Chait DH, Lotz WK. Successful pediatric examinations using nasoendoscopy. Laryngoscope 101:1016, 1991.
15. Chhetri DK, Gerratt BR, Kreiman J, Berke GS. Combined arytenoid adduction and laryngeal reinnervation in the treatment of vocal fold paralysis. Laryngoscope 109:1928, 1999.
16. Clary RA, Pengilly A, Bailey M, et al. Analysis of voice outcomes in pediatric patients following surgical procedures for laryngotracheal stenosis. Arch Otolaryngol Head Neck Surg 122:1189, 1996.
17. Cohen SR. Cleft larynx: a report of seven cases. Ann Otol Rhinol Laryngol 84:747, 1975.
18. Cohen SR. Congenital glottic webs in children: a retrospective review of 51 patients. Ann Otol Rhinol Laryngol 94:1, 1985.
19. Cohen SR, Geller KA, Birns JW, et al. Laryngeal paralysis in children: a long-term retrospective study. Ann Otol Rhinol Laryngol 91:417, 1982.
20. Cohen SR, Thompson JW. Ventral cleft of the larynx: a rare congenital laryngeal defect. Ann Otol Rhinol Laryngol 99:281, 1990.
21. Cohen SR, Thompson JW, Geller KA, Birns JW. Voice change in the pediatric patient: a differential diagnosis. Ann Otol Rhinol Laryngol 92:437, 1983.
22. Coll DA, Rosen CA, Auborn K, et al. Treatment of recurrent respiratory papillomatosis with indole-3-carbinol. Am J Otolaryngol 18:283, 1997.
23. Condon LM, Katkov H, Singh A, Helseth HK. Cardiovocal syndrome in infancy. Pediatrics 76:22, 1985.
24. Cooper DS. The laryngeal mucosa in voice production. Ear Nose Throat 67:332, 1988.
25. Cotton RT. In Myers EN, et al (eds). Advances in Otolaryngology–Head and Neck Surgery. St Louis, CV Mosby, 1987, pp 241–260.
26. Cotton RT. In Myers EN, et al (eds). Advances in Otolaryngology—Head and Neck Surgery. St Louis, CV Mosby, 1987, pp 241–260.
27. Cotton RT. The problem of pediatric laryngotracheal stenosis: a clinical and experimental study on the efficacy of autogenous cartilaginous grafts placed between the vertically divided halves of the posterior lamina of the cricoid cartilage. Laryngoscope 101(Suppl 56):1, 1991.
28. Crockett DM, McCabe BF, Shive CJ. Complications of laser surgery for recurrent respiratory papillomatosis. Ann Otol Rhinol Laryngol 96:639, 1987.
29. Crumley RL. In Cummings CW, et al (ed). Otolaryngology–Head and Neck Surgery, Update II. St Louis, CV Mosby, 1991, pp 100–106.
30. D'Antonio LL, Chait DH, Lotz WK, et al. Pediatric videonasoendoscopy for speech and voice disorders. Otolaryngol Head Neck Surg 94:578, 1986.
31. Davis JT, Baciewicz FA, Suriyapa S, et al. Vocal cord paralysis in premature infants undergoing ductal closure. Ann Thorac Surg 46:214, 1988.
32. Dedo HH. Endoscopic Teflon keel for anterior glottic web. Ann Otol Rhinol Laryngol 88:467, 1979.
33. Ding H, Gray SD. Senescent expression of genes coding collagens, collagen-degrading metalloproteinases, and tissue inhibitors of metalloproteinases in rat vocal folds: comparison with skin and lungs. J Gerontol A Biol Sci Med Sci 56:B145, 2001.
34. Ding H, Gray SD. Senescent expression of genes coding tropoelastin, elastase, lysyl oxidase, and tissue inhibitors of metalloproteinases in rat vocal folds: comparison with skin and lungs. J Speech Lang Hear Res 44:317, 2001.
35. Dobres R, Lee L, Stemple JC, et al. Description of laryngeal pathologies in children evaluated by otolaryngologists. J Speech Hear Disord 55:526, 1990.
36. Emery PJ, Fearon B. Vocal cord palsy in pediatric practice: a review of 71 cases. Int J Pediatr Otorhinolaryngol 8:147, 1984.
37. Fan LL, Campbell DN, Clarke DR, et al. Paralyzed left vocal cord associated with ligation of patent ductus arteriosus. Int J Pediatr Otorhinolaryngol 8:147, 1989.
38. Froese AP, Sims P. Functional dysphonia in adolescence: two case reports. Can J Psychiatry 32:389, 1987.
39. Fukuda H, Kawaida M, Tatchara T, et al. In Fujimura O (ed). Vocal Physiology: Voice Production, Mechanisms and Functions. New York, Raven Press, 1988, pp 83–92.
40. Gardner GM, Altman JS, Balakrishnan G. Pediatric vocal fold medialization with silastic implant: intraoperative airway management. Int J Pediatr Otorhinolaryngol 52:37, 2000.
41. Gartlan MG, Peterson KL, Luschei ES, et al. Bipolar hooked-wire electromyographic technique in the evaluation of pediatric vocal cord paralysis. Ann Otol Rhinol Laryngol 102:695, 1993.
42. Glaze LE, Bless DM, Milenkovic P. Acoustic characteristics of children's voice. J Voice 2:312, 1988.
43. Glaze LE, Bless DM, Susser RD. Acoustic analysis of vowel and loudness differences in children's voice. J Voice 4:37, 1990.
44. Goding GS. Nerve-muscle pedicle reinnervation of the paralyzed vocal cord. Otolaryngol Clin North Am 24:1239, 1991.
45. Gray SD. Cellular physiology of the vocal folds. Otolaryngol Clin North Am 33:679, 2000.

46. Gray SD, Barkmeier J, Shive C, et al. Vocal Function in Papilloma Patients. Waikoloa, HI, 1991.
47. Gray SD, Chan KJ, Turner B. Dissection plane of the human vocal fold lamina propria and elastin fibre concentration. Acta Oto-Laryngol 120:87, 2000.
48. Gray SD, Kelly SM, Dove H. Arytenoid separation for impaired pediatric vocal fold mobility. Ann Otol Rhinol Laryngol 103:510, 1994.
49. Green GE, Bauman NM, Smith RJ. Pathogenesis and treatment of juvenile onset recurrent respiratory papillomatosis. Otolaryngol Clin North Am 33:187, 2000.
50. Gumpert L, Kalach N, Dupont C, Contencin P. Hoarseness and gastroesophageal reflux in children. J Laryngol Otol 112:49, 1998.
51. Hammond TH, Gray SD, Butler J, et al. Age and gender-related elastin distribution changes in human vocal folds. Otolaryngol Head Neck Surg 119:314, 1998.
52. Hammond TH, Gray SD, Butler JE. Age- and gender-related collagen distribution in human vocal folds. Ann Otol Rhinol Laryngol 109:913, 2000.
53. Hanukoglu A, Fried D, Segal S. Loss of voice as sole symptom of subglottic foreign-body aspiration. Am J Dis Child 140:973, 1986.
54. Harden JR, Looney NA. Duration of sustained phonation in kindergarten children. Int J Pediatr Otorhinolaryngol 7:11, 1984.
55. Harries M, Hawkins S, Hacking J, Hughes I. Changes in the male voice at puberty: vocal fold length and its relationship to the fundamental frequency of the voice. J Laryngol Otol 112:451, 1998.
56. Harries ML, Walker JM, Williams DM, et al. Changes in the male voice at puberty. Arch Dis Child 77:445, 1997.
57. Harris C, Richards C. Functional aphonia in young people. J Laryngol Otol 106:610, 1992.
58. Hasek C, Singh S, Murray T. Acoustic attributes of children's voices. J Acoust Soc Am 68:1262, 1980.
59. Hass A, Hyatt AC, Kattan M, et al. Hoarseness in immunocompromised children: association with invasive fungal infection. J Pediatr 111:731, 1987.
60. Herzel H, Berry D, Titze IR, Saleh M. Analysis of vocal disorders with methods from nonlinear dynamics. J Speech Hear Res 37:1008, 1994.
61. Hickson C, Simpson CB, Falcon R. Laryngeal pseudosulcus as a predictor of laryngopharyngeal reflux. Laryngoscope 111:1742, 2001.
62. Hirano M, Bless DM. Videostroboscopic Examination of the Larynx. San Diego, Singular Publishing Group, 1993.
63. Hirano M, Kakita Y. In Daniloff RG (ed). Speech Science. San Diego, College-Hill Press, 1985, pp 1–46.
64. Hirano M, Kurita S, Kiyokawa K, et al. Posterior glottis: morphological study in excised human larynges. Ann Otol Rhinol Laryngol 95:576, 1986.
65. Hirano M, Kurita S, Nakashima T. In Bless DM, Abbs JH (eds). Vocal Fold Physiology: Contemporary Research and Clinical Issues. San Diego, College-Hill Press, 1983, pp 22–43.
66. Hirano M, Nozoe I, Shin T, Maeyama T. In Hirano M, Kirchner JA, Bless DM (eds). Neurolaryngology: Recent Advances. Boston, College-Hill Press, 1987, pp 232–248.
67. Hoit JD, Hixon TJ, Watson PJ, et al. Speech breathing in children and adolescents. J Speech Hear Res 33:51, 1990.
68. Isshiki N. In Myers EN, et al (eds). Advances in Otolaryngology–Head and Neck Surgery, vol 5. St Louis, CV Mosby, 1991, pp 37–56.
69. Isshiki N, Tanabe M, Sawada M. Arytenoid adduction for unilateral vocal cord paralysis. Arch Otolaryngol 104:555, 1978.
70. Jiang JJ, Zhang Y, Stern J. Modeling of chaotic vibrations in symmetric vocal folds. J Acoust Soc Am 110:2120, 2001.
71. Kahane JC. A morphological study of the human prepubertal and pubertal larynx. Am J Anat 151:11, 1978.
72. Kahane JC. Growth of the human prepubertal and pubertal larynx. J Speech Hear Res 25:446, 1982.
73. Kahane JC, Mayo R. The need for aggressive pursuit of healthy childhood voices. Lang Speech Hear Serv Schools 20:102, 1989.
74. Kay NJ. Vocal nodules in children—aetiology and management. J Laryngol Otol 96:731, 1982.
75. Kearns DB, Grace AR, Parsons DS, et al. Laryngeal characteristics after reconstruction for subglottic stenosis: a clinical correlation. J Laryngol Otol Suppl 17:39, 1988.
76. Klatt DH, Klatt LC. Analysis, synthesis, and perception of voice quality vibrations among female and male talkers. J Acoust Soc Am 87:820, 1990.
77. Klock LE. 1968, University of Washington, Seattle.
78. Klock LE, Beckwith JB. In Bosma JF (ed). Anatomy of the Infant Head. Baltimore, Johns Hopkins University Press, 1987.
79. Koch BM, Milmoe G, Grundfast KM. Vocal cord paralysis in children studied by monopolar electromyography. Pediatr Neurol 3:288, 1987.
80. Koufman JA. Approach to the patient with a voice disorder. Otolaryngol Clin North Am 24:989, 1991.
81. Koufman JA. The otolaryngologic manifestations of gastroesophageal reflux disease (GERD): a clinical investigation of 225 patients using ambulatory 24-hour pH monitoring and an experimental investigation of the role of acid and pepsin in the development of laryngeal injury. Laryngoscope 101(4 part 2, suppl 53):1, 1991.
82. Koufman JA, Blalock PD. Functional voice disorders. Otolaryngol Clin North Am 24:1059, 1991.
83. Kuhn J, Toohill RJ, Ulualp SO, et al. Pharyngeal acid reflux events in patients with vocal cord nodules. Laryngoscope 108(8 part 1):1146, 1998.
84. Leeper HA, Leonard JE, Iverson RL. Otorhinolaryngologic screening of children with vocal quality disturbances. Int J Pediatr Otorhinolaryngol 2:123, 1980.
85. Leonard R, Senders C, Charpied G. Effects of long-term intubation on vocal fold mucosa in dogs. J Voice 6:86, 1992.
86. Link DT, Rutter MJ, Liu JH, et al. Pediatric type I thyroplasty: an evolving procedure. Ann Otol Rhinol Laryngol 108:1105, 1999.
87. Lotz WK, D'Antonio LL, Chait DH, Netsell RW. Successful nasoendoscopic and aerodynamic examinations of children with speech/voice disorders. Int J Pediatr Otorhinolaryngol 26:165, 1993.
88. MacArthur CJ, Kearns GH, Healy GB. Voice quality after laryngotracheal reconstruction. Arch Otolaryngol Head Neck Surg 120:641, 1994.
89. Maddalozzo J, Holinger LD. Laryngotracheal reconstruction for subglottic stenosis in children. Ann Otol Rhinol Laryngol 96:665, 1987.
90. Maddern BR, Campbell TF. Pediatric voice disorders. Otolaryngol Clin North Am 24:1125, 1991.
91. McAlister A, Sederholm E, Sundbert J, Gramming P. Relations between voice range profiles and physiological and perceptual voice characteristics in ten-year-old children. J Voice 8:230, 1994.
92. McHenry M. Acoustic characteristics of voice after severe traumatic brain injury. Laryngoscope 110:1157, 2000.
93. McHenry MA, Wilson RL, Minton JT. Management of multiple physiologic system deficits following traumatic brain injury. J Med Speech Lang Pathol 2:59, 1994.
94. McWilliams BJ, Lavorato AS, Bluestone CD. Vocal cord abnormalities in children with velopharyngeal valving problems. Laryngoscope 83:1745, 1973.
95. Mende W, Herzel H, Wermke K. Bifurcations and chaos in newborn infant cries. Phys Lett [A] 145:418, 1990.
96. Milczuk HA, Smith JD, Everts EC. Congenital laryngeal webs: surgical management and clinical embryology. Int J Pediatr Otorhinolaryngol 52:1, 2000.
97. Monday LA, Cornut G, Bouchayer M, et al. Epidermoid cysts of the vocal cords. Ann Otol Rhinol Laryngol 92:124, 1983.
98. Monini S, Banci G, Barbara M, et al. Clarion cochlear implant: short-term effects on voice parameters. Am J Otol 18:719, 1997.
99. Moran MJ, Pentz AL. Otolaryngologists' opinions of voice therapy for vocal nodules in children. Lang Speech Hear Serv Schools 18:172, 1987.
100. Mori K. Vocal fold nodules in children: preferable therapy. Int J Pediatr Otorhinolaryngol 49(Suppl 1):S303, 1999.
101. Murry T, Woodson GE. A comparison of three methods for the management of vocal fold nodules. J Voice 6:271, 1992.
102. Neubauer J, Mergell P, Eysholdt U, Herzel H. Spatio-temporal analysis of irregular vocal fold oscillations: biphonation due to desynchronization of spatial modes. J Acoust Soc Am 110:3179, 2001.
103. Olson NR. Laryngopharyngeal manifestations of gastroesophageal reflux disease. Otolaryngol Clin North Am 24:1201, 1991.
104. Opitz JC, Kettrick MA, Sullivan BJ. Recurrent neonatal herpes presenting initially with hoarseness. Am J Perinatol 6:307, 1989.
105. Ossoff RH, Werkhaven JA, Dere H. Soft-tissue complications of

laser surgery for recurrent respiratory papillomatosis. Laryngoscope 101:1162, 1991.

106. Phillips DE, Childs D, Walsh S. Hoarse cry with fatal outcome. Br Med J 299:847, 1989.

107. Pransky SM, Brewster DF, Magit AE, Kearns DB. Clinical update on 10 children treated with intralesional cidofovir injections for severe recurrent respiratory papillomatosis. Arch Otolaryngol Head Neck Surg 126:1239, 2000.

108. Putnam PE, Orenstein SR. Hoarseness in a child with gastroesophageal reflux. Acta Paediatr 81:635, 1992.

109. Rammage L, Morrison J, Nichol H. In Management of the Voice and Its Disorders, 2nd ed. San Diego, Singular Publishing Group, 1991.

110. Roy N, Bless DM, Heisey D. Personality and voice disorders: a multitrait-multidisorder analysis. J Voice 14:521, 2000.

111. Rutter MJ, Hartley BE, Cotton RT. Cricotracheal resection in children. Arch Otolaryngol Head Neck Surg 127:289, 2001.

112. Rutter MJ, Link DT, Hartley BE, Cotton RT. Arytenoid prolapse as a consequence of cricotracheal resection in children. Ann Otol Rhinol Laryngol 110:210, 2001.

113. Sander EK. Arguments against the agressive pursuit of voice therapy for children. Lang Speech Hear Serv Schools 20:94, 1989.

114. Savage MM, Crockett DM, McCabe BF. Lipoid proteinosis of the larynx: a cause of voice change in the infant and young child. Int J Pediatr Otorhinolaryngol 15:33, 1988.

115. Sell D, MacCurtain F. Speech and language development in children with acquired subglottic stenosis. J Laryngol Otol Suppl 17:35, 1988.

116. Senturia BH, Wilson FB. Otorhinolaryngic findings in children with voice deviations. Preliminary report. Ann Otol Rhinol Laryngol 77:1027, 1968.

117. Shankargouda S, Krishnan U, Murali R, Shah MJ. Dysphonia: a frequently encountered symptom in the evaluation of infants with unobstructed supracardiac total anomalous pulmonary venous connection. Pediatr Cardiol 21:458, 2000.

118. Silverman EM, Zimmer CH. Incidence of chronic hoarseness among school-age children. J Speech Hear Disord 40:211, 1975.

119. Smith ME, Darby KP, Kirchner K, Blager FB. Simultaneous functional laryngeal stridor and functional aphonia in an adolescent. Am J Otolaryngol 5:366, 1993.

120. Smith ME, Gray SD. In Myers EN, et al (eds). Advances in Otolaryngology–Head and Neck Surgery, vol 8. St Louis, CV Mosby, 1994.

121. Smith ME, Gray SD, O'Connor DM, et al. Endolaryngeal trauma associated with long-term endolaryngeal stents. Otolaryngol Head Neck Surg 105:206, 1991.

122. Smith ME, Marsh JH, Cotton RT, Myer CM. Voice problems after pediatric laryngotracheal reconstruction: videolaryngostroboscopic, acoustic and perceptual assessment. Int J Pediatr Otorhinolaryngol 25:173, 1993.

123. Smith ME, Mortelliti AJ, Cotton RT, Myer CM. Phonation and swallowing considerations in pediatric laryngotracheal reconstruction. Ann Otol Rhinol Laryngol 101:731, 1992.

124. Stathopoulos ET, Sapienza C. Respiratory and laryngeal measures of children during vocal intensity variation. J Acoust Soc Am 94:2531, 1993.

125. Stern Y, Gerber ME, Walner DL, Cotton RT. Partial cricotracheal resection with primary anastomosis in the pediatric age group. Ann Otol Rhinol Laryngol 106:891, 1997.

126. Tanner JM. Sequence, tempo, and individual variation in the growth and development of boys and girls aged twelve to sixteen. Daedalus 100:907, 1971.

127. Titze IR. Comments on the myoelastic-aerodynamic theory of phonation. J Speech Hear Res 23:495, 1980.

128. Titze IR. Principles of Voice Production. Englewood Cliffs, NJ, Prentice-Hall, 1994.

129. Titze IR, Baken RJ, Herzel H. In Titze IR (ed). Vocal Fold Physiology: New Frontiers in Basic Science. San Diego, Singular Publishing Group, 1993, pp 143–188.

130. Toohill RJ. The psychosomatic aspects of children with vocal nodules. Arch Otolaryngol 101:591, 1975.

131. Tucker HM. Vocal cord paralysis in small children: principles of management. Ann Otol Rhinol Laryngol 95:618, 1986.

132. Ward PH, Berci G. Observation on the pathogenesis of chronic nonspecific pharyngitis and laryngitis. Laryngoscope 92:1377, 1982.

133. Ward PH, Engel E, Nancy WE, et al. The larynx in the cri du chat (cat cry) syndrome. Trans Am Acad Ophthalmol Otolaryngol 72:90, 1968.

134. Wetmore SJ, Key JM, Suen JY. Complications of laser surgery for laryngeal papillomatosis. Laryngoscope 95:798, 1985.

135. Wilson DK. Voice Problems in Children, 3rd ed. Baltimore, Williams & Wilkins, 1987.

136. Wirz S. In Fawcus M (ed). Voice Disorders and Their Management, 2nd ed. San Diego, Singular Publishing Group, 1992.

137. Wohl DL, Kilpatrick JK, Leshner RT, Shaia WT. Intraoperative pediatric laryngeal electromyography: experience and caveats with monopolar electrodes. Ann Otol Rhinol Laryngol 110:524, 2001.

138. Woo P, Arandia H. Intraoperative laryngeal electromyographic assessment of patients with immobile vocal fold. Ann Otol Rhinol Laryngol 101:799, 1992.

139. Zalzal GH. Rib cartilage grafts for the treatment of posterior glottic and subglottic stenosis in children. Ann Otol Rhinol Laryngol 97:506, 1998.

140. Zalzal GH, Loomis SR, Derkay CS, et al. Vocal quality of decannulated children following laryngeal reconstruction. Laryngoscope 101:425, 1991.

141. Zalzal GH, Loomis SR, Fischer M. Laryngeal reconstruction in children: assessment of voice quality. Arch Otolaryngol Head Neck Surg 119:504, 1993.

142. Zbar RI, Chen AH, Behrendt DM, et al. Incidence of vocal fold paralysis in infants undergoing ligation of patent ductus arteriosus. Ann Thorac Surg 61:814, 1996.

81

Stridor and Airway Obstruction

Christopher J. Hartnick, M.D., and Robin T. Cotton, M.D.

Stridor is a physical sign characterized by a harsh, high-pitched musical sound produced by turbulent airflow through the upper airways. Evaluation must be tailored to the clinical situation; stridor can range from mild to severe and life-threatening. In the latter scenario, urgent decision making and treatment are required. This chapter reviews the pertinent physiology related to stridor and then discusses the evaluation process and differential diagnosis.

Physiology

The larynx is a complex evolutionary structure that permits the trachea and the bronchi to be joined to the pharynx as a common aerodigestive pathway. The larynx serves the essential functions of (1) ventilation of the lungs, (2) protection of the lungs during deglutition by its sphincteric mechanisms, (3) clearance of secretions by a vigorous cough, and (4) vocalization. An infant's survival is predicated on the structural and neurologic integrity of the larynx, and prompt diagnostic and surgical intervention for airway management are mandatory.

Pathophysiology

To understand the sign of stridor, a brief review of certain pertinent physical principles as well as some understanding of the anatomy of the pediatric airway is helpful. As relates to any system of tubular fluid dynamics, flow within the system is related to the radius of the tube to the fourth power according to the Poiseuille law ($Q = [\Pi \, d^4 \, (P1-P2)]/128v$; Q = flow, d = diameter, P = pressure).[10] It follows then that resistance is related to the inverse of the radius to the fourth power. This law explains why even a minor obstruction in the airway is potentially more significant for a child than for an adult. A neonate's glottis measures approximately 7 mm in the sagittal plane and 4 mm in the coronal plane. The vocal cords are 6 to 8 mm long, and the posterior aspect is composed of the cartilaginous process of the arytenoid. The subglottic diameter measures approximately 4.5 by 7 mm. Narrowing the subglottic diameter by 1 mm increases airway resistance by 16-fold and decreases the cross-sectional area by 75%. A similar 1-mm narrowing in an adult would increase airway resistance by twofold

while decreasing the cross-sectional area by only 30% (Fig. 81–1).

The other physical law that is crucial to a proper understanding of pediatric stridor is the Bernouilli law, which states that as velocity increases through a constant area, the pressure on the wall of the lumen decreases ($W = PAv$; W = work, P = pressure, A = area, v = velocity). In other words, airflow dynamics dispose a region where there is an anatomic narrowing to collapse further dynamically with increased turbulent airflow through that region. The resulting stridor can be localized to discrete areas of the airway according to the nature of the sound in relationship to the phase of breathing. These discrete regions can be divided into three zones: (1) a supraglottic and supralaryngeal zone (including the pharynx), (2) an extrathoracic tracheal zone (including both glottis and subglottis), and (3) an intrathoracic tracheal zone (including primary and secondary bronchi).[7, 9, 10] Supraglottic lesions often cause stridor during inspiration, whereas lesions of the intrathoracic trachea or bronchi are aggravated during expiration (Table 81–1).

The first zone, which is composed of the supraglottis, tongue, and pharynx, is relatively loosely supported and often falls into the airway or is drawn into it during inspiration. Inspiration is initiated by the expansion of the thorax, lung tissue, and intrathoracic bronchi. Vigorous inspiratory efforts, particularly when associated with air hunger requiring accessory muscle use, create a relative decrease in pharyngeal pressure. As air passes through the narrowed, diseased supraglottis, the Bernouilli forces and pharyngeal pressures have a combined effect that constricts the airway. Stridor for this zone is generally inspiratory and high pitched. Expiration has the opposite effect on the supraglottic regions, forcing the airway open.

The second, or extrathoracic, trachea is a neutral zone, affected equally by both inspiration and expiration. The vocal ligament tightly supports the vocal cords between the thyroid and arytenoid cartilages and, in the absence of neural stimulation, is rigid. Similarly, the subglottic region is unyielding because of the cricoid ring. The airflow in both the vocal ligament and the subglottis is less dependent on fluid dynamics. Airflow is regulated by absolute lumen size, because the airway cannot contract or expand dynamically. When stridor develops in this zone, the glottic and subglottic lumen has reached a critically

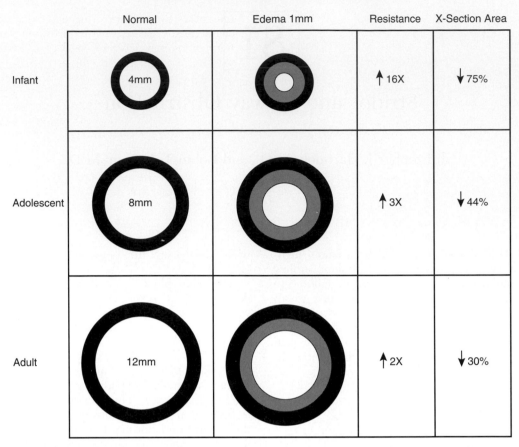

FIGURE 81-1. The effects of airway edema on cross-sectional area and diameter according to the age of the individual.

small diameter. Stridor produced in this region is often biphasic, being heard during both inspiration and expiration, and is of intermediate pitch. Breathing requires tremendous effort to move air through a pinpoint opening, and biphasic stridor often heralds respiratory collapse.

In the third, or intrathoracic, bronchial zone, exhalation commences by the contraction of the thorax. The relative positive pressures of expiratory forces within the chest wall narrow the bronchial lumen in normal children. As air moves during expiration, the Bernouilli principle again adds a constricting force. The intrathoracic forces and the Bernouilli forces act jointly to close the lumen against a foreign body or other lesion. The resultant sound is expiratory in phase and less harsh than stridor but retains a musical quality and is often called a wheeze. The term wheeze is derived from an Old Norse word meaning to hiss and by common usage has come to

be associated with, but is not restricted to, the hard breathing of asthma.

As a consequence of chronically increased negative pleural pressures during inspiration, retraction of the costal cartilages, sternum, and suprasternal tissues occurs. The degree of retraction is determined by the relative amount of negative pleural pressure and the compliance of the rib cage. Young children have a highly compliant rib cage, and sternal retraction thus is particularly marked.

Aside from the association of the sound of stridor with breathing, the characteristics of the sound itself can also help to localize an airway lesion.[9, 23] The well-trained ear can differentiate classic stridor from the wheeze described earlier as well as from stertor, which represents a low-pitched inspiratory sound produced by nasal or nasopharyngeal obstruction.

TABLE 81-1. Obstructive Symptoms and Their Relationship to Site of Obstruction

Location	Voice	Stridor	Retraction	Feeding	Cough
Laryngeal: supraglottic	Muffled "Hot potato"	Snoring Inspiratory fluttering	None until late	Difficult to impossible	Not noted
Laryngeal: subglottic	Normal Occasionally hoarse	Inspiratory-expiratory snoring	Intercostal early, then xyphoid	Normal	Barking (no other place in the airway)
Tracheal	Normal	Expiratory and wheezing	None, except in severe obstruction	Normal	Brassy

Initial History and Evaluation

Evaluation of a child with stridor requires a carefully taken history and thorough physical examination, as discussed previously, as well as knowledge of the functional anatomy of the upper airway. Stridor may result from obstruction at one of several sites in the upper airway, as discussed earlier.

History and Physical Examination

Common causes of noisy breathing in infants are outlined in Table 81–2.

Clinical assessment is of the utmost importance. An immediate assessment of the urgency of the situation should be made. Acute stridor in an older child may be due to foreign body or acute infection. Laryngomalacia is

TABLE 81–2. Causes of Stridor in Children According to Site of Obstruction

Pharynx
Congenital anomalies
  Lingual thyroid
  Choanal atresia
  Craniofacial anomalies (Apert syndrome, Down syndrome, Robin syndrome)
  Cysts (dermoid, thyroglossal)
Inflammatory
  Abscess (parapharyngeal, retropharyngeal, peritonsillar)
  Allergic polyps
Neoplasm (benign and malignant)
Adenotonsillar hyperplasia
Foreign body

Larynx
Congenital anomalies
  Laryngomalacia
  Webs, cysts, laryngocele
  Cartilage dystrophy
  Subglottic stenosis
  Cleft larynx
Inflammatory
  Croup
  Epiglottis
  Miscellaneous; tuberculosis, diphtheria
Vocal cord paralysis (many causes)
Trauma
  Intubation (laryngeal or subglottic edema, subglottic stenosis)
  Neck trauma
  Foreign body
Neoplasm
  Subglottic hemangioma
  Laryngeal papilloma
  Cystic hygroma (neck)
  Malignant (rhabdomyosarcoma, chondrosarcoma)
Laryngospasm (hypocalcemic tetany)

Trachea and Bronchi
Congenital
  Vascular anomalies
  Webs, cysts
  Tracheal stenosis
Foreign body (tracheal or esophageal)
Neoplasm (benign and malignant)
  Tracheal
  Compression by neoplasm of adjacent structure (thyroid, thymus, esophagus)
Trauma
  Tracheal stenosis secondary to intubation or tracheotomy

the most common cause of congenital stridor and has a characteristic history.[16–18, 24] Birth injury or neurologic abnormalities may indicate vocal cord paralysis. Age of onset and duration of stridor are important indicators of which of the congenital causes of stridor is most likely. A history of intubation may indicate subglottic stenosis.[4]

Careful inspection of the patient is the first priority. The child should remain in the parent's arms, and the physician can judge the respiratory rate and degree of distress. The physician should look for tachypnea or the onset of fatigue that may portend respiratory collapse. Flaring of the nasal alae and the use of accessory neck or chest muscles demonstrate the degree of respiratory effort needed to maintain an oxygenated state. Increasing cyanosis and air hunger, particularly from supraglottic infection or a foreign body, cause a patient to sit with the neck hyperextended in an attempt to improve airflow. The patient should be permitted to maintain such posture.

In a gravely ill child, additional examination should not be undertaken lest it precipitate respiratory arrest. The child requires prompt transport to an appropriate hospital.

In a well-oxygenated, stable child, additional examination can then proceed. An important part of the examination is auscultation, which is performed both with the ear and with the aid of a stethoscope. Sequential listening over the nose, open mouth, neck, and chest should be performed to localize its probable site of production by its heightened intensity. Attention is next directed to the respiratory cycle, which normally is composed of a shorter inspiratory phase and a longer expiratory phase. Which phase is prolonged or shortened by an obstruction? Are stridulous sounds present during that phase? Supraglottic obstruction is usually associated with inspiratory noises, whereas bronchial obstruction has characteristic expiratory noises or wheezes. Similarly, in laryngeal and supraglottic obstruction, the time of inspiration is greatly lengthened, whereas in bronchial obstruction, expiration tends to be prolonged. Tracheal and glottic obstruction is often marked by both inspiratory and expiratory stridor.[13]

An infant should also be placed in various positions to determine their effect on the stridor. The stridors of laryngomalacia, micrognathia, macroglossia, and vascular compression diminish when the baby lies prone with the neck extended.

The presence and quality of the voice or cry can help

TABLE 81–3. Items Included in History and Physical Examination for Stridor

History	Physical Examination
Time of onset—gradual, progressive, or sudden	Stridor, pitch, duration, and timing of the stridulous sound
Characteristics of cry	
Relationship of cry	Careful inspection of the patient in the parent's arms
Relationship of stridor to feeding	Respiratory rate and degree of distress
Aspiration or reflux	
Cyanosis	Tachypnea and onset of fatigue
Previous intubation	Flaring of nasal alae and other signs of respiratory effort
Careful repeated questioning for aspirated foreign body	Auscultation of stridor

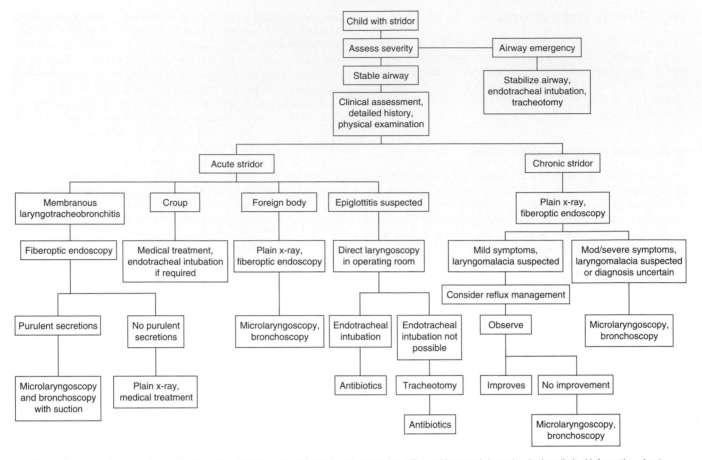

Fiberoptic examination is performed in the awake child and gives information about cord mobility and laryngeal dynamics. It gives limited information about structural defects below the level of the vocal cords.

Rigid endoscopy using Hopkins rod lens telescopes allows detailed examination of the subglottis, trachea, and bronchi while maintaining a stable airway. The combination of fiberoptic and rigid endoscopy will accurately diagnose most congenital and acquired abnormalities of the pediatric airway.

FIGURE 81–2. Clinical algorithm for evaluating a child with stridor.

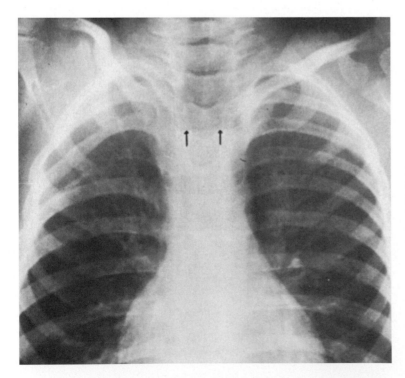

FIGURE 81–3. Anteroposterior radiograph demonstrating an air-fluid level in the esophagus secondary to food impaction in the thoracic esophagus at the site of a tracheoesophageal repair.

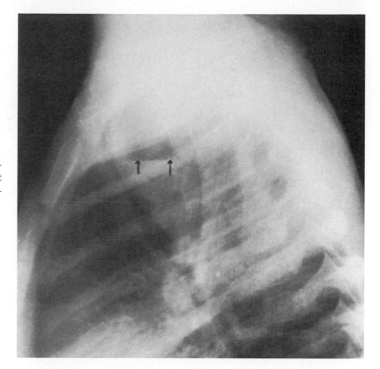

FIGURE 81–4. Lateral radiograph of the patient shown in Figure 81–3. The tracheal lumen is considerably narrowed just below the air-fluid level owing to the pressure of the esophageal contents.

to identify laryngeal causes of stridor. A weak cry may be related to vocal cord disorders or to conditions with poor pulmonary function, such as neuromuscular disorders. Although laryngeal lesions are most often accompanied by voice changes, a normal voice does not rule out a laryngeal cause of stridor. For example, bilateral vocal cord paralysis is most often associated with a normal voice in addition to the marked airway obstruction.[3, 5] In this situation, the vocal cords may be able to adduct but not abduct.

Certain maneuvers can be performed to determine the nature of the obstruction; these actions may be both diagnostic and therapeutic. If stridor is present at birth, the first maneuver should be to open the neonate's mouth and pull the mandible and tongue forward. If the stridor lessens, the obstruction is at the level of the larynx or higher. Nasal catheters should be passed to determine the patency of the nasopharyngeal airway. In patients with choanal atresia, the placement of an oral airway helps to diagnose the disorder and to bypass the obstruction.[11] Introduction of a laryngoscope supports the laryngeal structures and decreases the stridor of laryngomala-

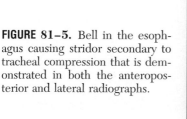

FIGURE 81–5. Bell in the esophagus causing stridor secondary to tracheal compression that is demonstrated in both the anteroposterior and lateral radiographs.

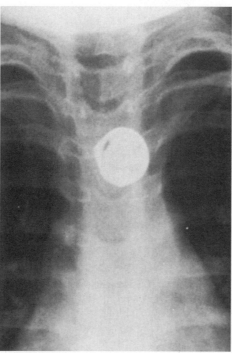

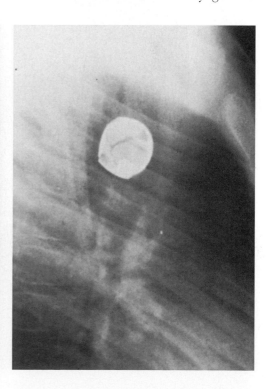

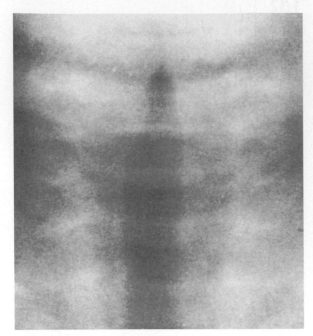

FIGURE 81–6. Anteroposterior radiograph of the neck demonstrating an asymmetric appearance of the subglottic walls, a finding of subglottic hemangioma or subglottic cysts in an infant.

cia but does not relieve the obstruction of vocal cord paralysis or subglottic stenosis. Pulling the mandible and tongue forward often relieves the obstruction seen in the Robin syndrome, and emergency placement of a nasopharyngeal airway maintains the patient until a long-term care decision can be made. Choices include keeping the nasopharyngeal airway in place or performing a tracheot-

omy to secure the airway for the first 6 to 8 months of life.[2] Placement of an orogastric tube may also be a useful temporizing measure. Important points in the history and physical examination are summarized in Table 81–3. An algorithm for stridor is presented in Figure 81–2.

It must be emphasized that no history for stridor would be complete without a high suspicion of an aspirated foreign body, as well as careful repeated questioning about such a possibility.[6] The time of onset of the stridor may indicate the underlying pathologic condition. Immediate onset of stridor, often accompanied by a choking spell, is strongly suggestive of a foreign body. It is important to realize that severe apnea and aphonia in an infant or child not only are signs of a laryngeal foreign body but also can herald an upper esophageal foreign body. The laryngeal cartilages and trachea are so compressible that airway problems develop rapidly after esophageal obstruction. Figure 81–3 is an anteroposterior radiograph of a 3-year-old child in whom food has lodged at the site of a previous esophageal repair for tracheoesophageal fistula. On the lateral view (Fig. 81–4), compression of the tracheal air column is clearly evident. Compression of the trachea in both the anteroposterior and lateral views is noticeable in the radiograph of a 2-year-old child with a bell in the esophagus (Fig. 81–5). Neonates can swallow bells or coins inadvertently fed to them by an innocent older sibling, and such objects can be undetected for months or years (Chapters 71 to 90).

Endoscopy—Flexible

Indirect examination of the larynx with a laryngeal mirror is no longer necessary. Instead, the advent of smaller

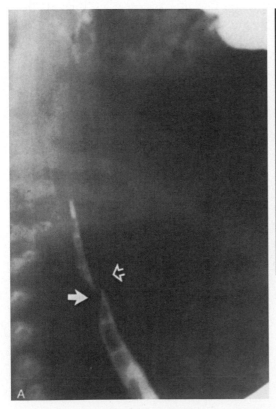
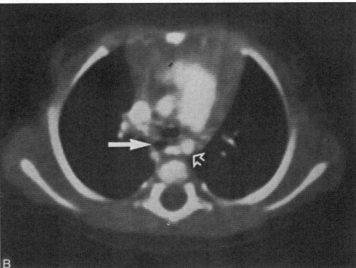

FIGURE 81–7. *A,* Barium esophagogram (lateral) in a 3-month-old infant demonstrating posterior esophageal compression *(solid arrow)* and anterior tracheal compression *(open arrow)* from the vascular ring. *B,* Axial computed tomographic scan of the chest with vascular enhancement, confirming a left aortic arch with right retroesophageal subclavian artery *(open arrow)* in a 3-month-old child with stridor (esophagus, *solid arrow*). (Courtesy of Department of Radiology, Children's Hospital of Alabama.)

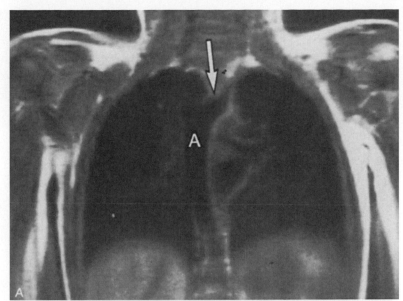
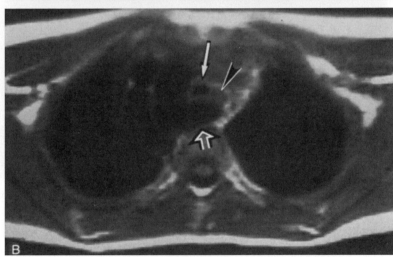

FIGURE 81–8. *A,* Magnetic resonance image (MRI) showing the right aortic arch (A) and descending aorta. The *arrow* points to an aberrant left subclavian artery in a 5-month-old child with stridor. *B,* MRI (transverse, T-weighted) confirming the narrowed trachea *(solid arrow)* as well as the esophagus *(arrowhead).* The aberrant left subclavian artery *(open arrow)* appears to be passing behind the esophagus. (Courtesy of Department of Radiology, Children's Hospital of Alabama.)

flexible endoscopy instruments makes direct examination of the larynx possible even in the smallest children. Vocal cord mobility, laryngeal masses, laryngomalacia, and other laryngeal problems are easily assessed with transnasal flexible endoscopy, which is usually performed in an office or clinic setting using appropriate (for age) topical anesthesia for the nose. A variation of this technique can be used to observe the process of swallowing. With the tip of the flexible endoscope just at the posterior margin of the soft palate, colored food or liquid can be observed passing through the oropharynx and into the esophagus. The information obtained from this evaluation of swallowing is comparable to that obtained from a modified barium swallow without requiring exposure to radiation.[8, 22]

All patients with suspected airway pathology should undergo a flexible fiberoptic nasopharyngoscopy while awake. The examination begins in the anterior nasal cavity to rule out a pyriform aperture stenosis[1] and moves posteriorly in the nose to rule out a choanal stenosis or atresia. The nasopharynx can be examined for adenoid hypertrophy or other mass lesions. Hypopharyngeal visu-

alization illustrates the hypopharyngeal tone. The epiglottis and arytenoid cartilages can be assessed for edema or erythema consistent with gastroesophageal reflux disease or infection.[12] In addition, any evidence of laryngomalacia can be noted. Determining the mobility of the true vocal cords is an essential part of this evaluation. A subglottic view is occasionally possible with a flexible scope, but in general, only the anatomy from the true vocal cords and superior can be visualized using this method.

Radiographic Evaluation

Radiographic evaluation gives excellent information about the subglottis, trachea, and larger bronchi and therefore complements the flexible endoscopic examination. Lateral and anteroposterior plain films of the neck provide significant information about the patency of the airway lumen and the presence of mass lesions.[20] The anteroposterior high-kilovoltage technique is particularly useful for depicting the upper airway, because it enhances the tracheal air column and de-emphasizes the bony cervical spine (Fig.

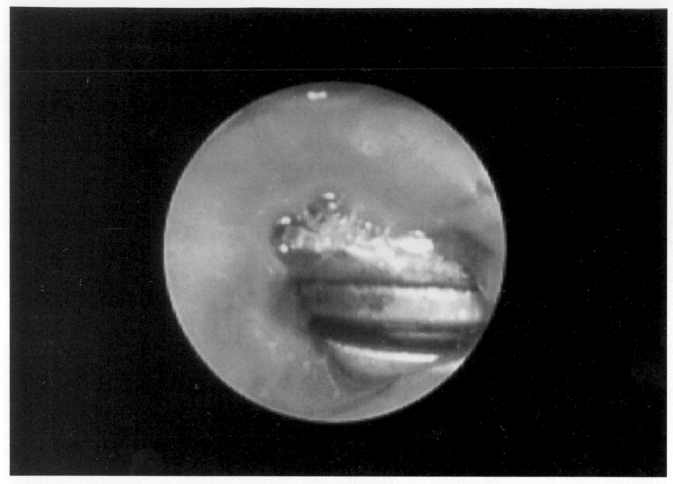

FIGURE 81-9. Endoscopic view of coins impacted in the esophagus.

81-6). Videofluoroscopy is helpful for evaluating dynamic airway problems such as hypopharyngeal collapse and tracheomalacia. As an adjunct to the flexible endoscopic evaluation of swallowing described earlier, the barium swallow is useful to detect both aspiration related to vocal cord paralysis, posterior laryngeal cleft, or H fistula and external compression from vascular lesions. Computed tomography and magnetic resonance imaging are useful for obtaining specific information in selected cases, e.g., vascular compression of tracheobronchial tree, but are no substitute for endoscopic evaluation[15, 21] (Figs. 81-7 and 81-8).

TABLE 81-4. Indications for Flexible or Rigid Bronchoscopy

Indications for Fiberoptic Laryngoscopy Evaluation of stridor Hoarseness or weak cry Difficult pre-extubation of epiglottitis	**Indications for Fiberoptic Bronchoscopy** ***Diagnostic*** Stridor Tracheotomy surveillance
Indications for Rigid Microlaryngoscopy and Bronchoscopy Stridor Tracheotomy surveillance Foreign body evaluation/management Interval evaluation following laryngotracheal reconstruction Chronic cough Severe hemoptysis Management of severe laryngotracheal infections Airway trauma Assessment of toxic inhalation/aspiration Evaluation of laryngeal pathology Management of mass lesions of the airway, including recurrent respiratory papillomatosis	Persistent wheezing Persistent atelectasis Persistent pneumonia/diffuse infiltrates Chronic cough Infiltrates in the immunocompromised host bronchoalveolar lavage Mild hemoptysis Lung lesion of unknown cause Selective bronchography Assessment of toxic inhalation/aspiration Monitor after lung transplantation ***Therapeutic*** Confirmation of endotracheal tube position Acute lobar atelectasis Cystic fibrosis management Removal of mucous plugs

TABLE 81–5. Expected Subglottic Size

Age	Minimum Internal Diameter (mm)
0–3 mo	3.5
3–9 mo	4.0
9–24 mo	4.5
2–4 yr	5.0
4–6 yr	5.5
6–8 yr	6.0
8–9 yr	6.5
10–12 yr	7.0
12–13 yr	7.5

Adapted from Mustafa SM. Variations in subglottic size in children. Proc R Soc Med 69:793, 1976.

Endoscopy—Rigid

By the time a patient has had a history and physical examination followed by flexible endoscopic examination of the airway above the vocal cords and study of appropriate anteroposterior and lateral radiographs of the trachea, the diagnosis most likely is established. In some cases, diagnostic rigid endoscopy is still needed if (1) the diagnosis remains in question, (2) the previous evaluation suggests a subglottic lesion, and (3) a second significant distal lesion in the airway is suspected in addition to the diagnosis of a more obvious proximal lesion in the upper airway. Rigid airway endoscopy may also be necessary for therapy such as for removal of foreign bodies (Fig. 81–9).

Flexible and rigid endoscopy are to some extent complementary, and both should often be performed at the same examination. Fiberoptic examination of an infant's larynx is possible when the child is awake and gives useful information about cord mobility and laryngeal dynamics. Only by rigid endoscopy under controlled conditions of general anesthesia can a magnified, leisurely view of the larynx and lower airways be made. The cords can be viewed with a binocular microscope, affording a stereoscopic view. Only the use of a rigid endoscope allows the lower airway to be inspected safely and in minute detail while maintaining complete and secure control over ventilation. Flexible bronchoscopes do not allow such control and in a small infant will cause significant if not total airway obstruction. The image quality obtained by rigid telescopes is superior to that obtained by flexible fiberoptic bundles, especially in the smaller sizes, and therefore documentation is clearer. Flexible instruments are most useful in the examination of the dynamics of the tracheobronchial tree. A listing of the indications for flexible and rigid bronchoscopy is presented in Table 81–4.

The operating room is the safest place to perform rigid upper-airway endoscopy. Atropine (0.02 mg/kg with minimum 0.1 mg; maximum dose for child, 0.5 mg/kg) is given before the induction of anesthesia. This drug sup-

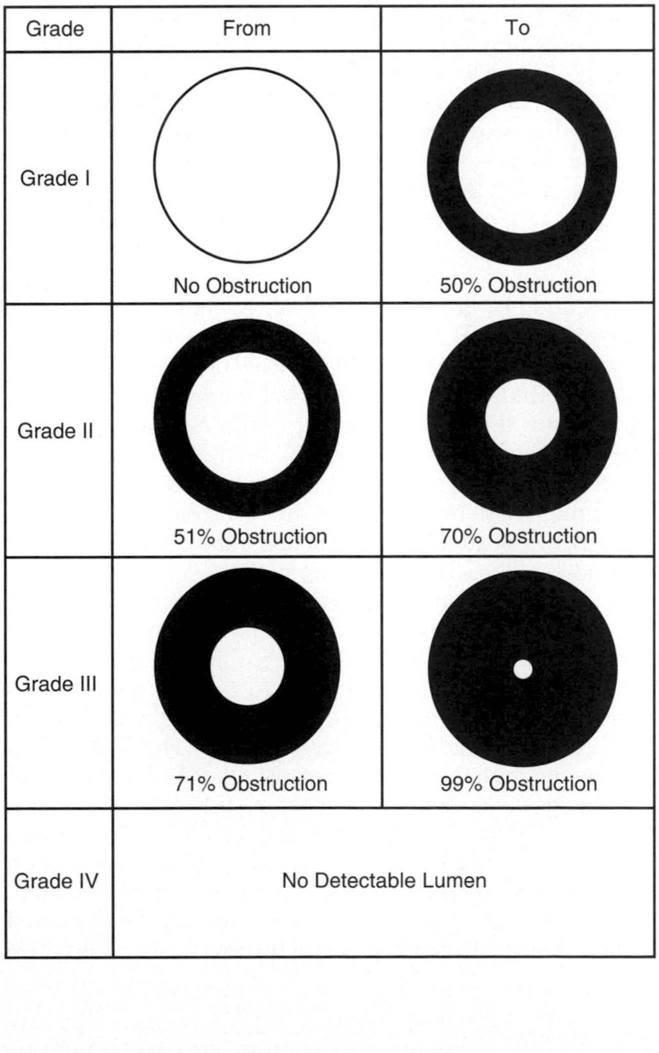

FIGURE 81–10. Myer-Cotton grading system for subglottic stenosis.

presses the salivary secretions and the vagal reflexes, minimizing the risk of bradycardia. Slow masked inhalation induction is useful to preoxygenate the infant and is often necessary to saturate the tissues with oxygen, so the endoscopist surgeon must be patient and vigilant. Lidocaine may be applied topically to the larynx to prevent laryngospasm. Rigid endoscopy can be accomplished using the spontaneous ventilation anesthesia technique[19]; other techniques include Venturi jet ventilation and apneic techniques.

Before the induction of anesthesia, the surgeon and operating room team must select the proper size bronchoscope and ascertain that all ancillary equipment, including lenses, side arm ventilation, suction tips, and forceps, is functioning properly. Subglottic size must be estimated either from knowledge of tables (Table 81–5) or from calculating the age-appropriate endotracheal tube size ([16 + age]/4) and then choosing the proper endoscope with this knowledge.

Laryngoscopy is performed using a straight blade (Miller blade or Parsons laryngoscope) and an open-lumen bronchoscope. This examination should proceed carefully but promptly. The ventilating bronchoscope is then passed through the glottis under direct vision. The essential procedures can then be carried out. These are (1) measurement of the size of the air passage, especially the subglottis, (2) inspection of anatomic and mucosal contour, and (3) maintenance of a channel to the lungs both to ventilate and to enable instrumentation to obtain a biopsy specimen, aspirate, or remove an obstruction. With reference to the size of the airway, the Myer-Cotton grading system is used to establish a common lexicon.[14] Endotracheal tubes are used to grade the severity of the stenosis because they are universally available. The endotracheal tube is advanced so that the second graduated mark is at the level of the vocal cords. The endotracheal tube is then connected to the anesthesia machine, and the pressure valve is closed. The glottis is visualized, and the appearance of bubbles around the endotracheal tube or the audible presence of a leak is noted. The individual's endotracheal tube size is defined as the largest endotracheal tube that permits a leak of less than 30 cm H_2O. The individual's endotracheal tube size is then compared with the age-appropriate endotracheal tube size. The Myer-Cotton grading system divides subglottic stenosis into four groups: grade I stenosis, 0 to 50% obstruction; grade II stenosis, 51% to 70% obstruction; grade III stenosis, 71% to 99% obstruction; and grade IV, total obstruction (Fig. 81–10).

If the child can be examined bronchoscopically (the critical outer diameter size is 3.5 mm), intubation is then possible. After intubation, a safe esophagoscopy or nasopharyngoscopy can be performed to rule out masses, foreign bodies, or fistulas. Biopsies to diagnose reflux esophagitis may be performed during esophagoscopy. After endoscopic examination is completed, administration of anesthetics is discontinued, and as the anesthesia level becomes lighter, the laryngoscope can be reintroduced into the vallecula before extubation to permit inspection of vocal cord mobility during emergence from sedation. This is the last step and may be essential. As discussed earlier, however, flexible laryngoscopy is an alternative

approach and is often performed before and/or after the patient has emerged from general anesthesia to avoid laryngospasm. Active, bilateral movement must be observed. Passive movement and fluttering do not give information on the status of the laryngeal nerves.

With efficient teamwork between surgeon and anesthesiologist and with gentle instrumentation, edema of the larynx should rarely occur during endoscopy. If this is observed, postendoscopy treatment should include the use of a cool mist tent and vaporized administration of racemic epinephrine for immediate relief. Dexamethasone can be administered to prevent delayed swelling, and the child should be closely observed for possible reintubation or tracheotomy. The child should remain hospitalized until the airway is stable.

Conclusion

The diagnosis, care, and protection of a child's airway should always be the cardinal concern of a responsible physician. A thorough understanding of respiratory dynamics, airflow, and the presence of abnormal lung sounds such as stridor remains as critical today as in the day of Laënnec.

SELECTED READINGS

Cotton RT. The management and prevention of subglottic stenosis in infants and children. Adv Otolaryngol Head Neck Surg 1:241, 1987.
The author presents a thorough overview of both the causes and the surgical treatment of subglottic injury.
Murray JF. The Normal Lung. Philadelphia, WB Saunders, 1986.
An excellent review of prenatal and postnatal development of the lung, as well as modern concepts of pulmonary physiology.

REFERENCES

1. Brown OE, Myer CMD, Manning SC. Congenital nasal pyriform aperture stenosis. Laryngoscope 99(1):86, 1989.
2. Caouette-Laberge L, Bayet B, Larocque Y. The Pierre Robin sequence: review of 125 cases and evolution of treatment modalities. Plast Reconstr Surg 93:934, 1994.
3. Cohen SR, Geller KA, Birns JW, et al. Laryngeal paralysis in children: a long-term retrospective study. Ann Otol Rhinol Laryngol 91:417, 1982.
4. Cotton RT. Pediatric laryngotracheal stenosis. J Pediatr Surg 19:699, 1984.
5. de Jong AL, Kuppersmith RB, Sulek M, et al. Vocal cord paralysis in infants and children. Otolaryngol Clin North Am 33:131, 2000.
6. Friedman EM. Tracheobronchial foreign bodies. Otolaryngol Clin North Am 33:179, 2000.
7. Friedman EM, Vastola AP, McGill TJ, et al. Chronic pediatric stridor: etiology and outcome. Laryngoscope 100:277, 1990.
8. Hartnick CJ, Hartley BEJ, Miller C, et al. Pediatric fiberoptic endoscopic evaluation of swallowing. Ann Otol Rhinol Laryngol 109:996, 2000.
9. Hirschberg J. Acoustic analysis of pathological cries, stridors and coughing sounds in infancy. Int J Pediatr Otorhinolaryngol 2:287, 1980.
10. Holinger LD, Lusk RP, Green CG. Pediatric Laryngology and Bronchoesophagology. Philadelphia, Lippincott-Raven, 1997, p 402.
11. Maniglia AJ, Goodwin WJ Jr. Congenital choanal atresia. Otolaryngol Clin North Am 14:167, 1981.

12. Matthews BL, Little JP, McGuirt WF, et al. Reflux in infants with laryngomalacia: results of 24-hour double-probe pH monitoring. Otolaryngol Head Neck Surg 120:860, 1999.

13. Mussell MJ. The need for standards in recording and analysing respiratory sounds. Med Biol Eng Comput 30:129, 1992.

14. Myer CM 3d, O'Connor DM, Cotton RT. Proposed grading system for subglottic stenosis based on endotracheal tube sizes. Ann Otol Rhinol Laryngol 103:319, 1994.

15. Myer CM 3d, Auringer ST, Watrak BJ, et al. Magnetic resonance imaging in the diagnosis of innominate artery compression of the trachea. Arch Otolaryngol Head Neck Surg 116:314, 1990.

16. Olney DR, Grenwald JH, Smith RJ, et al. Laryngomalacia and its treatment. Laryngoscope 109:1770, 1999.

17. Rowe LD. Airway obstruction in the pediatric patient. Prim Care 9:317, 1982.

18. Shah UK, Wetmore RF. Laryngomalacia: a proposed classification form. Int J Pediatr Otorhinolaryngol 46:21, 1998.

19. Stern Y, et al. Spontaneous respiration anesthesia for respiratory papillomatosis. Ann Otol Rhinol Laryngol 109:72, 2000.

20. Walner DL, Ouanounous S, Donnelly LF, et al. Utility of radiographs in the evaluation of pediatric upper airway obstruction. Ann Otol Rhinol Laryngol 108:378, 1999.

21. Wiatrak BJ, Myer CMD, Cotton RT. Atypical tracheobronchial vascular compression. Am J Otolaryngol 12:347, 1991.

22. Willging JP. Endoscopic evaluation of swallowing in children. Int J Pediatr Otorhinolaryngol 32(suppl):S107, 1995.

23. Zalzal GH. Pediatric stridor and airway compromise. J Med Liban 42:221, 1994.

24. Zalzal GH. Stridor and airway compromise. Pediatr Clin North Am 36:1389, 1989.

82

Respiratory Disorders of the Newborn

Saroj K. Parida, M.D., M.R.C.P.

Respiratory disorders of the newborn present with multiple symptoms, which range from mild respiratory distress that does not require any treatment to acute respiratory failure requiring critical management in a neonatal intensive care unit. Not only can respiratory distress be a manifestation of an underlying respiratory illness, but it can also result from a wide variety of nonrespiratory causes involving other systems (e.g., cardiac, neurologic). Pediatric otolaryngologists have a significant role in the acute management of such cases when procedures such as tracheostomy or endoscopy are required. Pediatric otolaryngologists also play a significant role in the management of chronic respiratory problems, such as laryngeal or tracheal granulation or stenosis due to prolonged endotracheal intubation. A number of infants with severe and recurrent otitis media have underlying chronic pulmonary disease that may have originated in the newborn period. Thus, a concise review of respiratory disorders in newborns should help the otolaryngologist to recognize the impact of specific management techniques.

Ontogeny of the Lung

The primordial lung bud appears on day 26 of gestation as a ventral epithelial outgrowth from the foregut. Subsequently, continuous dichotomous branching leads to progressive caudal penetration of the lung mesenchyme. The pulmonary artery appears by about 37 days, but venous structures appear somewhat later. There are five phases of lung development:

1. *Embryonic period* (4 to 6 weeks): This is the stage in which proximal airways form. The right and left main bronchi appear at 4 weeks, the five lobar bronchi at 5 weeks, and 10 segmental bronchi at 6 weeks.
2. *Glandular period* (7 to 16 weeks): Conducting airways are formed during this stage. Cartilage appears at 7 weeks in the trachea and develops peripherally. The pleural membranes and pulmonary lymphatics develop between 8 and 10 weeks. By the end of this phase, a total of 20 generations of conducting airways have developed, the last 8 of which are called bronchioles.
3. *Canalicular period* (17 to 24 weeks): The first intra-

acinar respiratory bronchioles develop by dichotomous branching, marking the birth of the gas-exchange part of the lung. Granular pneumocytes, the site of production of surfactant, are distinguished at 20 weeks by the appearance of lamellar inclusions. The lamellar bodies appear later. Apposition of capillary endothelial cells and alveolar lining cells occurs with sporadic points of fusion at 19 to 20 weeks.
4. *Saccular period* (27 to 35 weeks): At about 27 to 28 weeks, secondary crests appear, which herald the division of primary saccules into subsaccules or primitive alveoli. This is the stage of expansion of gas-exchange sites.
5. *Alveolar period* (36 weeks to 3 years post term): This is the phase of expansion of the surface area of the lung. At term, about 50 million alveoli are present, accounting for the majority of terminal air spaces. A rapid increase in the number of alveoli ensues, and the adult number of about 300 million alveoli is reached by age 3 years.

Physiology

In fetal life, the airways and terminal air spaces of the lung are filled with liquid, produced by the lungs, that contains surface-active lipoproteins. The secretion of lung liquid is important for fetal lung growth. The uptake of oxygen and the elimination of carbon dioxide are carried out via the placenta. At birth, pressures as high as 40 cm H_2O may be necessary to initiate the introduction of air into the airless lung. After the first few breaths, inflation pressures lessen considerably. The fluid in the lung is rapidly cleared during delivery and by the pulmonary circulation and lymphatics. When alveoli are filled with air, alveolar stability is maintained, especially at the low transpulmonary pressures of end expiration, through the presence of a surface-active phospholipid known as *surfactant*. The lungs are perfused by only 7% of the cardiac output. The rest of the combined ventricular output bypasses the lungs via the foramen ovale and ductus arteriosus. At birth, pulmonary vascular resistance decreases, the foramen ovale and ductus arteriosus close, and the total cardiac output perfuses the lungs.

Surfactant

Synthesized in the smooth endoplasmic reticulum of the granular pneumocytes, the insoluble surfactant phospholipids are composed of 90% lipids, 8% proteins, and 2% carbohydrates. The lipids are composed of 45% saturated phosphatidylcholine, 25% unsaturated phosphatidylcholine, 5% phosphatidylglycerol, 10% neutral lipids, and 5% other phospholipids. The functions of these insoluble phospholipids are (1) to stabilize the lung during deflation, (2) to prevent high-surface-tension pulmonary edema, (3) to protect the lung against epithelial damage, and (4) to defend against infection.

Acute Disorders

Respiratory Distress Syndrome

Respiratory distress syndrome (RDS) is the most common form of respiratory distress in the newborn. The condition is an acute illness that usually affects preterm infants of less than 32 weeks' gestation. Males are more commonly affected, and the condition is a significant cause of morbidity.

Pathophysiology

RDS is also called *hyaline membrane disease* or *surfactant deficiency disorder*. Hyaline membranes develop in the alveolar ducts, caused by the leakage of plasma proteins. During recovery, these membranes are removed by macrophages and by the process of fibrinolysis. Underlying the pathophysiology of this disease is the immaturity of the lungs, especially the surfactant synthesis system. Surfactant prevents the collapse of alveoli at end expiration. When surfactant is absent, alveolar collapse occurs. This leads to reduced compliance of the lungs.[10] The work of breathing is increased, and an expiratory grunt is evident reflecting the infant's attempt to maintain adequate lung volumes for optimal gas exchange by maintaining positive end expiratory pressure.[32] After 36 to 48 hours, surfactant appears and compliance of the lung improves and is normal in 6 to 7 days if no complications develop. The infant is hypoxemic, a hallmark of RDS, because of ventilation-perfusion mismatch in the lungs, i.e., an intrapulmonary right-to-left shunt occurs. In addition, some degree of pulmonary hypertension persists because of acidosis, hypoxemia, and hypercarbia, and this promotes right-to-left shunting through the ductus arteriosus and foramen ovale. Carbon dioxide retention occurs because of hypoventilation due to the atelectatic lungs and an increase in dead-space ventilation.

Clinical Presentation

The infant with RDS is usually premature. Symptoms begin within 4 hours of delivery. The infant presents with rapid respirations, chest-wall retractions, nasal flaring, and a characteristic grunt. Nasal flaring decreases the work of breathing. Grunting results from forced expiration through a partially closed glottis to compensate for the increased work of breathing. The infant is cyanotic in room air. Over the next 24 to 36 hours, the infant tires and the distress worsens. Slowing of the infant's breathing with apnea is a sign of respiratory failure. The infant may be hypotensive because of myocardial depression and a relatively low blood volume. The very-low-birth-weight infant is prone to hypoglycemia. Metabolic and respiratory acidosis may be present. The differential diagnosis includes pneumonia and heart failure.

Radiographic Findings

The chest films show a characteristic diffuse opacity known as *white out* of the lung fields, with fine reticular granular pattern and air bronchograms in the involved lung fields (Fig. 82–1).

Treatment

The primary goal of therapy is to relieve the hypoxemia. Oxygen is administered to maintain an arterial partial pressure of oxygen (PaO_2) of 55 to 75 mm Hg or an oxygen saturation of approximately 94% or greater. With adequate perfusion, this level of oxygenation should ensure adequate oxygen delivery to the brain and other vital

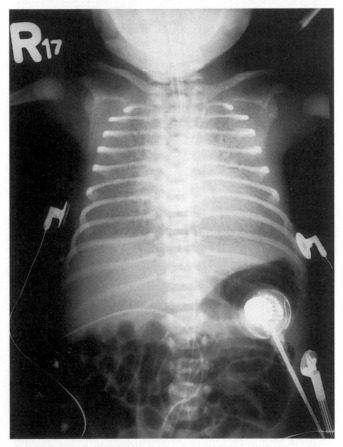

FIGURE 82–1. Chest radiograph of a premature infant with hyaline membrane disease showing diffuse granular opacification ("white out") in both the lung fields. Note the air bronchograms visualized bilaterally.

organs while avoiding excessive blood oxygen levels and the possible retinopathy of prematurity. Oxygen is usually provided initially with an *oxygen hood.* In the spontaneously breathing infant, respiratory distress may be aggravated by a nasogastric tube obstructing half of the upper airway.[18] With worsening of the disease, i.e., increasing hypoxemia and work of breathing, adequate levels of oxygen in the blood may be achieved with continuous positive airway pressure (CPAP) applied via nasal prongs. Should the infant not respond adequately to this maneuver, tracheal intubation and mechanical ventilation are required to prevent hypoxemia as well as an increase in CO_2 levels and respiratory acidosis. Metabolic acidosis may also develop. The pH is kept above 7.25 to avoid the deleterious effects of acidosis on myocardial contractility and diaphragmatic activity. The initial phase of the disease may be difficult to distinguish from sepsis, and RDS and sepsis can coexist. Thus, antibiotics are administered initially, and pending positive identification of sepsis in cultures, antibiotics are maintained.

Instillation of artificial surfactant into the lungs in very-low-birth-weight infants has been shown to reduce the mortality of RDS.[23] The marked improvement in oxygenation allows one to titrate the inspired oxygen concentrations to safe lower levels and decrease ventilation pressures and thus lessen the potential for bronchopulmonary dysplasia. Stabilizing the infant hemodynamically includes the administration of fluids, as the infants may be hypovolemic, and in the very sick patient, inotropic support, e.g., dopamine, may be necessary to maintain an adequate blood pressure. Other supportive measures are carried out, e.g., maintaining a normal body temperature, electrolyte balance, and a normal blood glucose level and optimizing nutritional support.

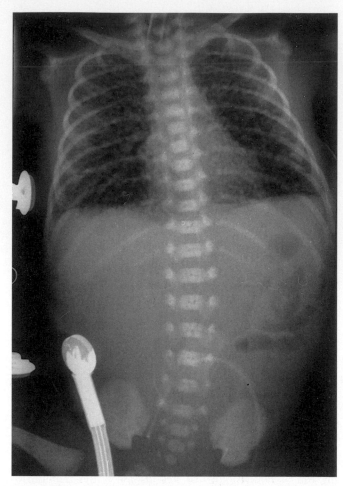

FIGURE 82–2. Chest radiograph of an infant with hyaline membrane disease showing air leak into the pulmonary interstitium, resulting in multiple radiolucent areas bilaterally. These changes are designated pulmonary interstitial emphysema (PIE).

Complications

The complications resulting from RDS and its treatment can be primarily categorized into acute and chronic types.

Acute

Air Leaks, Pneumothorax, Pulmonary Interstitial Emphysema. Air leaks occur predominantly in infants on mechanical ventilation.[30] Any sudden worsening in the infant's condition suggests the possibility of an air leak (Fig. 82–2). Pulmonary interstitial emphysema and pneumomediastinum are often precursors of a life-threatening tension pneumothorax. Air dissection occasionally leads to a pneumopericardium or pneumoperitoneum. Pneumothorax is related to increasing peak inspiratory pressure and increasing mean airway pressure. It is also related to the infant's breathing against the ventilator during a prolonged inspiratory phase. If the pneumothorax is severe, the infant's respiratory status and cardiovascular status are compromised. Oxygen levels fall, and heart rate and blood pressure decrease. The $PaCO_2$ may be abnormal. A tension pneumothorax (Fig. 82–3) or pericardial tamponade may develop, requiring urgent treatment.

Once pneumomediastinum and pulmonary interstitial emphysema develop, the ventilator settings are adjusted

to reduce the mean airway pressures. A high-frequency ventilator, particularly the oscillator, has been employed in this situation to limit pulmonary interstitial emphysema and allow resolution of the air leak. This modality of ventilation has an active expiratory phase, which is beneficial in air leaks.

Patent Ductus Arteriosus. A patent ductus arteriosus is a frequent finding in low–birth-weight infants with RDS. A large left-to-right shunt across the ductus may lead to congestive heart failure and delay the infant's weaning from the ventilator. In some infants, the ductus closes with simple measures such as restricting fluid intake and giving diuretics. Indomethacin, a prostaglandin inhibitor, is successful in causing closure of the ductus in the majority of cases.[22] In the relatively few cases in which the drug therapy fails or is contraindicated, surgical ligation becomes necessary.

Intraventricular and Periventricular Hemorrhage. Intraventricular hemorrhage is initiated in the germinal matrix layer of the lateral ventricle. The hemorrhage usually manifests on the third or fourth day of life with apnea, bradycardia, cardiovascular collapse, seizures, or

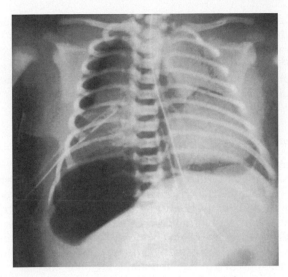

FIGURE 82–3. Chest radiograph of a newborn showing a massive right-sided tension pneumothorax with shift of the mediastinum, including the heart, to the right. Note the depression of the left hemidiaphragm and herniation of the left lung into the right hemithorax. These changes occurred in an infant with severe respiratory distress syndrome.

sudden onset of anemia. There are four grades of intraventricular hemorrhage based on the ultrasonographic findings. Small hemorrhages may be asymptomatic, but larger hemorrhages are responsible for serious morbidity in the form of significant neurologic sequelae. Post-hemorrhagic hydrocephalus may follow intraventricular hemorrhage.[17]

Chronic

Chronic Lung Disease. Most infants recover fully from RDS. However, some very-low-birth-weight infants experience the changes of chronic lung disease previously designated bronchopulmonary dysplasia (BPD)—usually after a prolonged period of ventilator support with high concentrations of inspired oxygen (>50%). Pneumothorax has been associated with an increased incidence of BPD. BPD may progress with the development of right-ventricular heart failure. Infants with BPD have more respiratory infections. Approximately 50% of infants weighing less than 1.5 kg at birth require hospital readmission in the first year after discharge from the neonatal intensive care unit.[36] The major problems are respiratory and neurologic. Long-term neurologic sequelae are more common in ventilated infants with RDS than in control infants.

Endotracheal-Tube Complications. Endotracheal intubation in some infants produces significant trauma to the glottis and subglottic areas. When trauma is prolonged, granulomas may occur on the vocal cords. In the subglottic area, ischemic necrosis from compression may result in scarring, with resultant subglottic stenosis. This complication may be limited by choosing an endotracheal tube that has a fit with a slight leak. In addition, the use of tubes especially tested to minimize irritation to the mucosa is recommended. Nasotracheal intubation may be associated with ischemia and necrosis of the nares and, in some cases, the nasal septum with subsequent loss of the septal cartilage (see Chapter 87).

Prevention

The most important factor in reducing the incidence of RDS is the prevention of prematurity. Since prematurity cannot be fully prevented, the next best modality would be induction of lung maturation. Based on sheep studies that showed evidence of lung maturation after fetal as well as maternal corticosteroid treatment, human trials using prenatal maternal corticosteroids have conclusively shown beneficial effects on fetal lung maturation. The incidence of RDS has decreased by about 50%, and RDS tends to be less severe. This preventive modality of administering glucocorticoids to the mother for 24 hours before delivery has been the most effective factor in reducing neonatal morbidity and mortality in recent years.[8, 12]

Pneumonia

Pneumonia in infants in the perinatal period is a significant cause of mortality. The lungs are the most common site for the establishment of sepsis in the neonate. Such infection, whether bacterial or viral, may be acquired before or at the time of birth or in the early postnatal period. Since bacterial pneumonia carries a substantial mortality in the neonate, an extremely high index of suspicion must be maintained for all infants, preterm and term alike, in whom signs of respiratory distress are observed.

Transplacental viral pneumonias are caused by cytomegalovirus, herpes simplex virus, varicella-zoster virus, and human immunodeficiency virus (HIV). Pneumonia acquired during labor and delivery is most commonly due to group B *Streptococcus* (GBS). The organism is present in the female genitourinary tract, and while many infants are colonized, infection and disease occur in relatively few. Gram-negative enteric bacilli may also cause pneumonia.

Pneumonia may also complicate preexisting lung disease such as that occurring with RDS, BPD, meconium aspiration syndrome, and aspiration pneumonitis. Pneumonia may result from the newborn's exposure to humidified incubators and respiratory equipment. Organisms responsible include *Pseudomonas, Klebsiella,* and *Serratia marcescens. Staphylococcus aureus* outbreaks have resulted from lapses in hand washing by the caretaking staff, cytomegalovirus and herpes simplex virus infections, and outbreaks of echovirus and coxsackievirus B. Recurrent pneumonia may suggest gastroesophageal reflux disease or tracheoesophageal fistula (see Chapters 65 and 67).

Clinical Course

Pneumonia may be part of a systemic disease. The nonspecific nature of the clinical signs that are characteristic of neonatal sepsis make a high index of suspicion the key to early diagnosis. In some cases of severe pneumonia, infants may be totally lacking in pulmonary symptoms and present only mild or severe neurologic depression. Other alerting features include thermal instability, apneic spells, abdominal distention, poor feeding, or irritability. The presence of tachypnea, cyanosis, or other signs of respiratory distress may focus attention on the lungs in these infants. Chest radiograph findings range from unilateral or bilateral streaky densities, which may progress to confluent mottled opacified areas, to a diffusely granular appearance with air bronchograms. Thus, it may be impossible to radiographically differentiate bacterial pneumonia from RDS.

Problems also may be experienced in differentiating severe neonatal pneumonia on radiographs from widespread meconium aspiration or primary cardiac conditions that cause profound pulmonary venous congestion, such as those associated with total anomalous pulmonary venous return. The difficulty in making a definitive diagnosis of neonatal pneumonia by radiograph has led to the widely accepted practice of administering antibiotics to infants with respiratory distress after appropriate cultures have been obtained. White blood cell count with differential, platelet count, or a Gram stain of tracheal aspirate may be useful in the diagnosis of neonatal sepsis. However, the Gram stain of tracheal aspirates may not differentiate overt pulmonary infection from early colonization although the presence of many neutrophils suggests active infection.

GBS pneumonia is a significant cause of morbidity and mortality. GBS is common in the genital tract of pregnant women. Infants are often colonized; however, only approximately 1% experience invasive disease. *Early-onset GBS* presents as septicemia, meningitis, and pneumonia with the infant in respiratory distress. Chest radiograph signs may be indistinguishable from those of RDS. Pulmonary vascular hypertension and severe hypoxemia are often present. If the disease process is not controlled early and adequately, it may result in more fulminant systemic disease with septic shock that may be associated with disseminated intravascular coagulation. *Late-onset GBS* infection presents between the ages of 1 and 6 weeks. The disease is often associated with meningitis. Diagnosis is confirmed by identification of the organism in blood cultures and cerebrospinal fluid. While blood culture results are awaited, a latex particle agglutination test may provide a preliminary diagnosis. Antibiotic therapy is carried out for 10 to 14 days. A definitive diagnosis of GBS sepsis still must be established through direct culture of the organism.

If congenital intrauterine infection is suspected, appropriate serologic tests should be performed and cord blood immunoglobulins should be measured, although not all infants with intrauterine pneumonia have elevated IgM levels. *Chlamydia trachomatis* causes pneumonia that manifests between the ages of 2 and 12 weeks. The infant's illness commences with nasopharyngitis or otitis media followed by a cough and respiratory distress. Some infants have conjunctivitis. Chest films show hyperinflated lungs with interstitial infiltrates. Chlamydial pneumonitis may be diagnosed by culturing nasopharyngeal or tracheobronchial secretions under appropriate laboratory conditions. *Ureaplasma* and *Mycoplasma* infections can also occur later in an infant's life, just as with chlamydial infections, and reveal similar findings on chest radiographs. *Staphylococcus epidermidis* is most prevalent in small premature infants weighing less than 1500 g.

Treatment

Treatment almost invariably is instituted before the pathogenic organism is identified and its antibiotic sensitivities determined. Broad-spectrum coverage, including a penicillin and an aminoglycoside, is the initial line of treatment. For pneumonia of later onset, agents specific for staphylococcal infection should be added. In small premature infants with *S. epidermidis* pneumonia, the addition of vancomycin to the antibiotic regimen may be warranted. Once the responsible bacterium has been isolated and antibiotic sensitivities identified, the most effective drug or combination of antibiotics should be continued for 10 days or longer, depending on the infant's clinical course.[40] The duration of chlamydial pneumonia in the neonate appears to be shortened by a 14-day course of oral erythromycin. Although antibiotics form the mainstay of treatment, good supportive care is essential. This must include careful fluid management, blood gas monitoring, and ventilatory assistance, as indicated.

Congenital Diaphragmatic Hernia

Congenital diaphragmatic hernia has an incidence of 1 per 2500 live births. The condition results from the premature return of the midgut to the abdominal cavity during its embryonic development before the diaphragm has completely formed. As a result, the abdominal viscera appear in the chest. This usually includes the stomach, the small or large intestine, and occasionally the liver and spleen. There may be associated malrotation of the gut. The herniation occurs most often through the pleuroperitoneal sinus (foramen of Bochdalek) on the left; much less commonly, the herniation occurs through the substernal sinus (foramen of Morgagni). Pulmonary hypoplasia occurs on the affected side and in some cases in the opposite lung as well. Severe pulmonary hypoplasia is usually the cause of death in these infants. However, if the herniation occurs later in the development of the lungs, there is more functional lung tissue and the outcome is more favorable.

The hypoplastic lungs have a diminished surface area for gas exchange because of significant reduction in alveoli and capillaries. The pulmonary arteries are fewer and have an abnormally thick muscular coat that is extremely sensitive to mediators of vasoconstriction. Pulmonary hypertension and right-ventricular failure occur. Blood is shunted through the ductus arteriosus and foramen ovale, aggravating the hypoxemia and acidosis. Approximately one in four newborns with congenital diaphragmatic hernia has associated congenital anomalies. Premature infants with severe anomalies have a high mortality rate.

Clinical Presentation

The diagnosis may be made prenatally by ultrasonography. Immediately after birth, the infant is noted to be in respiratory distress with tachypnea, chest-wall retractions, and cyanosis. There is decreased chest movement on the affected side, with a shift of the cardiac impulse to the opposite side. The abdomen is scaphoid because of displacement of the bowels into the chest. On occasion, respiratory distress may not appear until some hours or even days after birth. The infant is severely hypoxemic, as reflected by the poor blood gas concentrations. Hypercapnia and acidemia may also be prominent. Further respiratory compromise may be the result of a pneumothorax from the contralateral lung, which may occur before, during, or after surgery and is frequently unsuspected. A decreasing incidence of pneumothorax has been correlated with improving survival with congenital diaphragmatic hernia. Radiographic studies are diagnostic, showing gas-filled loops of bowel in the chest with a marked shift of the mediastinum to the opposite side and compression of the contralateral lung (Fig. 82–4). This appearance may be confused with congenital cystic lung disease.

Treatment

The infant is stabilized by endotracheal intubation. Muscle relaxants are administered to prevent agitation of the infant that may displace the bowel loops into the chest. Gentle ventilation is performed to avoid injury to the hypoplastic lungs. Right-to-left shunting via the ductus arteriosus and foramen ovale occurs with low postductal

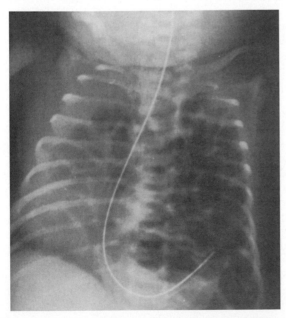

FIGURE 82–4. Chest radiograph showing the variety of diaphragmatic hernia that commonly occurs on the left side. The multiple circular radiolucent areas visible on the entire left hemithorax and partially on the right hemithorax are due to the herniated bowel loops. Note the mediastinal shift to the right side. A nasogastric tube has been placed to decompress the bowel loops in the chest.

PaO_2. If the hypoxemic state persists, there is potential for irreversible damage to the liver, gut, and kidneys. Every effort is made to ensure adequate perfusion through intravascular volume expansion and inotropic drugs so that relatively low PaO_2 levels are tolerated without serious sequelae. Factors that produce pulmonary artery vasoconstriction, e.g., hypoxemia, acidosis, hypercarbia, and hypothermia, are avoided. Noxious stimuli, such as pain and endotracheal suctioning, may increase pulmonary vascular tone.

A number of maneuvers may aid maximal pulmonary vasodilation. Maximizing oxygenation, inducing hyperventilation to achieve a pH greater than 7.5, and administering sodium bicarbonate to achieve a metabolic alkalosis promote pulmonary vasodilation. The infant's response to therapy as monitored by PaO_2, $PaCO_2$ and pH predicts survival.[4, 28]

Until recently, emergency surgery, i.e., reduction of the hernia, was routine. However, it was found that all too often initial stabilization was rapidly followed by marked deterioration due to intense and unremitting pulmonary vasoconstriction. Emergency surgery has now been replaced by a more conservative approach that aims at stabilizing the infant physiologically for 24 hours, when pulmonary vasculature may be more stable.[28]

Pharmacologic vasodilator therapy of the pulmonary vasculature was until recently a trial of various vasodilators, e.g., tolazoline, isoproterenol, and prostaglandins, all of which were anecdotally reported to be successful. However, their use was often associated with serious systemic vasodilation and cardiovascular collapse. The recent use of nitric oxide—a selective pulmonary vasodilator administered by inhalation through the ventilator circuit—has shown promising effects in reversing pulmonary vasoconstriction in selected patients.[38, 39] When progressive hypoxemia is unresponsive to all the above measures, extracorporeal membrane oxygenation (ECMO) has been successfully employed.[7, 25] The outcome after surgical repair largely depends on the degree of the underlying pulmonary hypoplasia. Those with severe hypoplasia may have impaired ventilation and are liable to experience severe complications with any respiratory infection. Continuation of the developmental process of the lung growth for approximately the first 8 years of life compensates somewhat for the underdevelopment of the lungs.

Persistent Pulmonary Hypertension of the Newborn

In 1969 Gersony et al described three term newborn infants with severe central cyanosis caused by right-to-left shunting of blood through fetal channels in the absence of underlying congenital heart disease.[13–15] These were the first reported cases of persistent pulmonary hypertension of the newborn (PPHN), which at that time was designated *persistent fetal circulation*. Two years later, Siassi et al provided a more extensive description of this syndrome, labeling it *persistent pulmonary vascular obstruction of the newborn*.[40] These initial reports stimulated many other investigators to document their experience with such infants, producing a consistent picture of severe central cyanosis, with varying degrees of respiratory distress, in the absence of major pulmonary disease.

In 1976 Riemenschneider et al emphasized the frequency with which varying degrees of myocardial dysfunction were associated with pulmonary hypertension in these infants. Both global myocardial dysfunction and transient tricuspid insufficiency have been demonstrated in infants with PPHN.[2] One often forgets that PPHN presents as a spectrum that varies from mild transient neonatal cyanosis with little or no myocardial dysfunction to severe persistent cyanosis, hypoxemia, and significant myocardial dysfunction.[3] The clinical picture depends on the response of the individual infant's pulmonary vascular bed and the myocardium to stress. The exact incidence of PPHN is uncertain since statistics vary markedly with the criteria that have been previously used in the diagnosis at various centers. However, most recent statistics indicate that PPHN accounts for approximately 2% to 9% of admissions to neonatal intensive care units and occurs in 1 in 522 to 1 in 1454 live births.[20-22, 43]

The failure of transition from a high pulmonary vascular resistance to a normal low pulmonary vascular resistance may be a primary problem or be associated with a number of conditions, i.e., meconium aspiration syndrome, severe intrapartum asphyxia, infection (especially GBS), or pulmonary hypoplasia (congenital diaphragmatic hernia), or it may be secondary to congenital heart disease. A number of factors may contribute to pulmonary vasoconstriction, including hypoxia, acidosis, and alterations in nitric oxide and arachidonic acid metabolism. Muscularization of the pulmonary arterial system occurs; the musculature is abnormally thickened and reactive. These changes are completely reversible if the disease process is captured in a timely fashion.

Clinical Presentation

The infant is usually near term or postmature and presents with severe hypoxemia—often labile—that is disproportionate to any existing lung disease. A history of meconium aspiration, pneumonia/infection, or severe birth asphyxia is common. The infant's distress progresses, and the infant shows extreme sensitivity to minimal stimulation, i.e., marked decreases in arterial oxygen saturation levels. Echocardiography is diagnostic and is also helpful in ruling out structural heart disease. Positive findings include right-ventricular pressure at or above the systemic pressure, and right-to-left shunting across the patent ductus and foramen ovale.[41]

Treatment

The goal of therapy is to augment pulmonary blood flow by lowering pulmonary vascular resistance and thus decreasing the right-to-left shunt. Inducing respiratory or metabolic alkalosis has a significant effect on lowering pulmonary vascular resistance and improving oxygenation. The critical pH may need to be as high as 7.55. However, hyperventilation may provoke barotrauma, and metabolic alkalosis may be induced if sodium bicarbonate

is used to achieve the required pH level.[47] The potential benefits of these maneuvers are balanced against possible adverse effects, namely, hyperventilation and an associated decrease in cerebral blood flow, and the effects of alkalosis, which shifts the hemoglobin-oxygen dissociation curve in a direction that would decrease the release of oxygen at the cellular level. Increasing the systemic vascular resistance by volume expansion or using vasopressors such as dopamine helps reverse the right-to-left shunt, which improves tissue oxygenation.

Pharmacologic agents such as tolazoline and nitroprusside have been used to reduce pulmonary vascular resistance.[16] However, these agents have vasodilating effects on the systemic circulation as well, often with resulting complications (severe hypotension) that may outweigh the benefits. If tolazoline is used via the endotracheal route, the systemic side effects are minimized.[16, 37] Recently, nitric oxide by inhalation has been effective in producing pulmonary vascular dilation without any effect on the systemic circulation.[26] ECMO has been effective in treating infants with life-threatening PPHN when the infant has not responded to conventional mechanical ventilation and a trial of nitric oxide inhalation.

Meconium Aspiration Syndrome

Meconium aspiration syndrome (MAS) is primarily a disease of term and post-term infants; the incidence increases significantly with postmaturity. Although knowledge of the pathophysiologic stimuli in the fetus that govern the passage of meconium in response to stress is still incomplete, this phenomenon is seldom observed before a gestational age of 34 weeks. The passage of meconium in utero accompanies 8% to 20% (average, 12%) of all deliveries and predominantly occurs in small-for-gestational-age and postmature infants, as well as those with cord complications or other factors compromising the in utero placental circulation. MAS is thought to occur in about 4% of deliveries complicated by meconium-stained fluid. Many infants with meconium-stained amniotic fluid exhibit no signs of depression, although some brief period of asphyxia could have induced the passage of meconium before delivery.

Meconium is a green viscid material consisting of inspissated fetal intestinal secretions. Meconium may be aspirated before, during, or immediately after delivery. Infants who are asphyxiated and pass meconium during delivery have been found to have higher levels of motilin, a substance that is produced mainly in the jejunum and that stimulates peristalsis. Fetal hypoxia stimulates fetal gasping movements, which promote amniotic fluid aspiration. Postnatally, the infant is liable to aspirate meconium from the mouth and pharynx. Passage of meconium may occur normally, particularly in breech presentation; however, its significance is that it may be associated with fetal asphyxia.

The effects of meconium aspiration, especially when the aspirated amniotic fluid has a large amount of thick meconium, are on the lungs and pulmonary vasculature. The associated effects of severe birth asphyxia also contribute to morbidity. The effects on the lung consist of a marked rise in airway resistance. The thick meconium plugs the airways so that air is unable to be exhaled, leading to gas trapping and possible pneumothorax. The meconium is irritating to the lungs, causing pneumonitis and lung damage. Secondary bacterial infection may follow. Meconium also switches off surfactant production, thus promoting alveolar collapse.

The effect on the pulmonary vasculature results in increased pulmonary artery pressure, which can be markedly resistant to therapy. The infant presents the classic features of PPHN. The often-associated severe asphyxia contributes to significant sequelae, i.e., renal failure, cardiac failure, and hypoxemic-ischemic encephalopathy.

Clinical Presentation

The clinical effects range from mild respiratory distress to serious life-threatening hypoxemia and pulmonary hypertension. The infant in distress is markedly tachypneic, with chest-wall retractions. Breathing is labored because of the increase in airway resistance and the reduced lung compliance. The infant may be severely hypoxemic. The hypoxemia results from a combination of ventilation-perfusion mismatch in the lungs and right-to-left shunt through the foramen ovale and ductus arteriosus due to persistent pulmonary hypertension.

The chest radiograph shows coarse irregular pulmonary densities with areas of diminished aeration or consolidation. If such infiltrates are a manifestation of retained lung fluid, they would be expected to clear within 24 to 48 hours. Pneumothorax and pneumomediastinum are common in infants with severe MAS. Hyperinflation of the chest may be noted radiographically with flattening of the diaphragm. Cardiomegaly also may be detected, possibly as a manifestation of the underlying perinatal hypoxia.

Treatment

The presence of meconium in the amniotic fluid necessitates careful supervision of labor and close monitoring of fetal well-being. The delivery team must be alerted to the possibility of a depressed fetus, and personnel skilled in newborn resuscitation must be present in the delivery room. With appropriate management of the airway, MAS and its complications can be substantially reduced.

Immediately after birth, the mouth and pharynx are aspirated. Intubation and suctioning of the trachea in infants born with thick meconium may be helpful in reducing the morbidity and mortality associated with MAS. Depending on the severity of the condition, the treatment is primarily supportive to ensure adequate oxygenation for the infant while the lung macrophages clear the aspirated meconium and allow lung function to normalize.

In severe cases, tracheal intubation and ventilation support are required. The use of positive end-expiratory pressure (PEEP) is carefully evaluated, as increases in PEEP may aggravate the underlying hyperinflation. Careful monitoring for possible pneumomediastinum and pneumothorax is carried out. If PPHN occurs, it should be managed appropriately as mentioned earlier. High-

frequency ventilation has been employed in selective cases.[6] In life-threatening MAS that are refractory to conventional therapy, i.e., mechanical ventilation, ECMO has been a life-saving maneuver.

Deaths from MAS are rare. However, serious morbidity may follow. Of particular concern are the effects of severe hypoxemic-ischemic encephalopathy. Long-term effects on the lungs have also been reported, with late-childhood morbidity from abnormal lung function caused by asthma.

Apnea

Apnea is common in the premature infant, particularly before 30 weeks of gestation.[35] Apnea is defined as cessation of breathing for more than 20 seconds. After 20 seconds, bradycardia (heart rate < 100 beats per minute) and cyanosis develop; after 30 to 45 seconds, the infant experiences pallor, hypotonia, and unresponsiveness to tactile stimulation. Apneic spells persist for variable periods postnatally but generally cease by 37 weeks' postconceptional age.

Periodic breathing consists of regular clusters of 4 to 10 breaths followed by an apneic interval of up to 12 seconds not associated with cyanosis or bradycardia. Apneic spells leading to hypoxemia and ischemia of the central nervous system may result in brain injury.

Apnea is primarily divided into the following: *central, obstructive,* and *mixed* (a combination of central and obstructive apnea). In central apnea, the neural drive to the inspiratory muscles is interrupted. In obstructive apnea, upper-airway closure is defective during breathing, resulting in ineffective movement of air following respiratory muscle and diaphragmatic contractions. Mixed apnea involves both central and peripheral (obstructive) causes.[31] It appears that the apneic episode may start from a central cause, but with collapse of the soft tissues of the upper airway, the obstructive component becomes progressively more significant. During apneic spells, laryngeal closure has also been detected by endoscopy in apneic infants. It has been noted that infants have significantly more central and mixed apnea in the supine than in the prone position.[27]

Etiology

The causes of apnea are multiple. Apnea of prematurity usually occurs after the first 1 to 3 days of life. If apnea occurs within the first 24 hours of life, it usually has a pathologic basis such as sepsis, birth asphyxia, intracranial hemorrhage, seizures, hypothermia and hyperthermia, hypoglycemia, and depression from medications. It may also result from other conditions, such as anemia and gastroesophageal reflux disease.[42]

Treatment

It is essential to rule out secondary disorders that may present with apnea. Most apneic spells requiring stimulation are associated with a decrease in oxygen saturation, and therefore infants with recurrent attacks should be monitored with a pulse oximeter and oxygen should be administered should desaturation occur. At times, bag-and-mask resuscitation is required. In some cases, especially in the very immature infant, CPAP or mechanical ventilation may be required. CPAP stabilizes the airway by mechanically splinting it and ensuring air movement.

Theophylline and caffeine are most commonly used to treat apnea of prematurity. Theophylline is methylated in the body to caffeine. The intravenous route is used if the infant cannot tolerate oral feeds. Theophylline has a higher incidence of side effects in the form of tachycardia and tremors. Caffeine has a longer half-life, and therefore the compliance rate is better. Theophylline and caffeine are equally efficacious.

After a history of recurrent apnea, some infants have experienced poor neurologic development. Possible causes include underlying periventricular hemorrhage or other adverse factors related to prematurity that are associated with a poor prognosis. Of concern in the treatment of these infants is that life-threatening postoperative apnea may occur in an otherwise healthy infant.[29] For this reason, minor surgical procedures should not be carried out on an ambulatory basis. These infants should be monitored postoperatively for 12 to 24 hours.

Congenital Lobar Emphysema

Congenital lobar emphysema is characterized by overinflation and air trapping in the affected lobe with compression atelectasis of the adjacent lung parenchyma and displacement of the mediastinum (Fig. 82–5).[46] The upper and middle lobes are more commonly involved, especially the left upper lobe.

The cause is not apparent in about half of cases. Bronchial obstruction may be from intrinsic congenital defi-

ciency of bronchial cartilage, leading to bronchial-wall collapse. Intrinsic bronchial stenosis or extrinsic vascular compression from a pulmonary artery sling may also result in bronchial obstruction. Associated congenital anomalies may also be found, especially congenital heart disease. The hyperinflated lobe does not deflate. In some cases, it appears that increased rigidity of the alveolar walls (due to abnormal collagen deposits) prevents normal deflation.

Clinical Presentation

Acute presentation takes the form of progressive respiratory distress in the newborn period or during early infancy. Tachypnea, retractions, wheezing, and cyanosis are noted. Rapid deterioration may occur, requiring urgent surgery. The emphysematous lobe displaces the mediastinum to the opposite side and causes compression atelectasis of the contralateral lung. The shift of the mediastinum and increased intrathoracic pressure also impede venous return and lead to decreased cardiac output. The emphysematous lobe does not participate in gas exchange, and, with atelectasis of the opposite lung, gas exchange is severely compromised.

Chronic presentation is in the form of recurrent chest infections and failure to thrive in an infant or older child. Congenital lobar emphysema should be differentiated from postpneumonic pneumatocele, pulmonary cystic disease, and tension pneumothorax. Additional studies may be helpful in clarifying the diagnosis. Computed tomography may define a bronchial obstruction that is either intrinsic or extrinsic. A ventilation-perfusion scan demonstrates markedly reduced ventilation of the affected lobe and decreased perfusion as a result of vascular compression by the expanding lobe.

Treatment

In the neonate, surgical excision of the lobe is urgent if it is expanding rapidly. In the older infant with few symptoms, nonsurgical treatment may be considered, although this is controversial. Conservative therapy, including bronchoscopy, may relieve obstruction due to a mucus plug.

Congenital Pulmonary Cysts

Congenital pulmonary cysts maybe classified as (1) *bronchogenic*, (2) *alveolar*, or (3) a *combination of bronchogenic and alveolar*. Acquired cystic disease, however, is much more common. Embryologically, congenital cystic disease is thought to arise as an anomalous development of the bronchopulmonary system. The cyst arises from expiratory obstruction through bronchiolar narrowing. The more common form is a single, peripheral, air-filled cyst with tracheobronchial communication. Cysts may be multiple. The cyst is air-filled, either directly through the tracheobronchial communication or through the pores of Kohn, and the air becomes trapped. At times, the cyst may be fluid-filled. An increase in the size of the cyst leads to compression of normal lung with a shift of the mediastinum and a decrease in functioning lung tissue.

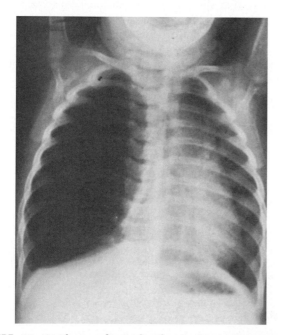

FIGURE 82–5. Chest radiograph of an infant with congenital lobar emphysema revealing massive hyperinflation of the right upper lobe with compression of the right middle and lower lobes. The mediastinum is shifted to the left.

Contralateral atelectasis occurs. The cyst readily becomes infected because of inadequate drainage, and re-infection of the cyst is common.

Clinical Presentation

The clinical findings depend on the degree of distention of the cyst with air. Tension pneumothorax may develop. There is severe cardiopulmonary distress, and emergency treatment is critical. In late infancy and childhood, infection of the cyst occurs with symptoms of fever, cough, sputum production, and possibly hemoptysis, with the cyst developing into a lung abscess.

A chest radiograph shows a large distended cyst with mediastinal shift. There is compression atelectasis of upper and lower lobes, and the radiographic picture may resemble that of lobar emphysema. A CT scan of the chest helps differentiate the two conditions. Diaphragmatic hernia may occasionally resemble multiple lung cysts. A staphylococcal pneumatocele may also resemble a congenital lung cyst. However, pneumatoceles resolve with treatment.

Treatment

Thoracotomy and surgical resection of the cyst are indicated because of the potential for serious complications, such as tension pneumothorax, bronchopleural fistula, and abscess formation. If the patient is in severe respiratory distress, needle aspiration of the chest may be required.

Chronic Lung Disease, or Bronchopulmonary Dysplasia

Chronic lung disease, or BPD, represents a state of pulmonary insufficiency in an infant who remains oxygen-dependent after 28 postnatal days and whose chest x-ray appears abnormal. It is most commonly associated with prematurity and may develop in 50% of very-low-birth-weight infants. BPD is usually associated with barotrauma from mechanical ventilation when peak inflating pressures are high, i.e., greater than 35 cm H_2O, and from oxygen toxicity. Other factors that are associated with BPD include patent ductus arteriosus and fluid overload, infection, air leaks, and conditions associated with abnormal surfactant synthesis.

Hyper-reactivity of the airways is increased in BPD. This may in part be genetic and in part due to mediator release from neutrophils, which are more commonly found in the airways of infants with RDS and BPD than in controls. The mediators include leukotrienes, which are potent bronchoconstrictors. Infants at risk for BPD show an enhanced inflammatory reaction in the lungs and an increase in pulmonary microvascular permeability.[19]

Clinical Presentation

The infant typically exhibits a delay in recovery from RDS and remains oxygen-dependent and, in some cases,

ventilator-dependent after 28 postnatal days. The infant has frequent episodes of increased respiratory distress associated with wheezing and profuse secretions. Chronic CO_2 retention occurs, and pulmonary hypertension, followed by right-ventricular failure (cor pulmonale), may occur. Marked hypoxemia may also occur.

The radiograph shows hyperinflation, with streaky densities and small cystic changes (Fig. 82–6). The degree of abnormality found on x-ray films is an indicator of the degree of functional abnormality in the infant.

Pathology

The lungs are emphysematous, with cystic areas interspersed with atelectatic areas. There is bronchiolar metaplasia and hyperplasia, which are partly responsible for the increased airway resistance. Over months, fibrous tissue in the lungs increases and pulmonary vascular disease becomes evident.

Treatment

Oxygen is administered to maintain a saturation of greater than 90% while excessive oxygen therapy and the risks of retinopathy of prematurity are avoided. Mechanical ventilation is carried out, with emphasis on providing adequate time for expiration and low end-expiratory pressures to minimize air trapping. Elevated levels of CO_2 are well tolerated, provided the pH is maintained above 7.25. Weaning from the respirator can be a prolonged and difficult effort. Trials of extubation may be followed by deterioration due to atelectasis from the profuse secretions that often accompany this disease. Prolonged intubation may lead to tracheal or subglottic stenosis, usually at the cricoid level. The infant presents with stridor and

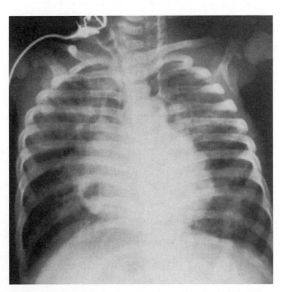

FIGURE 82–6. Chest radiograph of an infant with chronic lung disease showing multiple cystic changes called bronchopulmonary dysplasia. Alternating areas of atelectasis and hyperaeration result in an overall volume expansion of the lungs.

marked respiratory distress. Infants with BPD require increased caloric intake to cope with their respiratory distress. Feeding may be compounded by aspiration and gastroesophageal reflux disease. Infants with BPD frequently experience pulmonary hypertension, and some go on to experience cor pulmonale.[1]

Diuretics are commonly employed. Acute management consists of administration of furosemide (Lasix), which has been associated with an increase in lung compliance and a decrease in airway resistance with an improvement in blood gas concentrations.[7] Furosemide has some potential adverse side effects, i.e., increased urinary excretion of sodium, chloride, potassium, and calcium. This agent may also produce ototoxicity, especially when administered with aminoglycosides. Its long-term use may result in nephrocalcinosis. Chronic diuretic therapy using hydrochlorothiazide and spironolactone, either alone or in combination, is a standard treatment to control excessive fluid accumulation in the lungs.

Theophylline may be beneficial in BPD because of its bronchodilator effect and also because it improves diaphragmatic contractility. Infants with BPD have peribronchiolar smooth muscle hypertrophy, and bronchodilator therapy in the form of inhaled aerosols, e.g., albuterol, may be beneficial in some infants.

Steroid therapy has been found to improve the course of BPD. In the studies of steroid therapy in which steroids were given for over 1 month, infants were weaned from mechanical ventilation and oxygen earlier.[9] The steroids have been well tolerated, with no apparent increase in infection.

Some infants recovering from BPD require continuous oxygen therapy at home for a number of months. Oxygen saturation levels maintained at 95% have been associated with better weight gains and decreased rates of readmission to hospitals.[11] The morbidity and mortality associated with BPD are significant. Infant growth may be severely retarded, and neurodevelopmental and learning abnormalities are more frequent than in controls. Increased airway resistance persists in some of these infants: the children exhibit wheezing, and pulmonary function test results are abnormal. Respiratory infection is more common. Less severe cases improve such that by age 1 year, lung function may be normal.

SELECTED READINGS

Corbet A, Hansen T, Ballard RA. The respiratory system. In Textbook of Diseases of the Newborn, 6th ed. Philadelphia, WB Saunders, 1991, pp 461–563.
Greenough A, Morley CJ, Roberton NRC. Acute respiratory disease in the newborn. In Roberton NRC (ed). Textbook of Neonatology, 2nd ed. New York, Churchill Livingstone, 1992, pp 385–504.
Taeusch HW, Ballard RA, Avery ME, et al. Chronic lung disease. In Avery GB, Fletcher MA, MacDonald MG (eds). Neonatology-Pathophysiology and Management of the Newborn, 4th ed. Philadelphia, JB Lippincott, 1994, pp 453–477.
Whittsett JA, Pryhuber GS, Rice WR, et al. Acute respiratory disorders. In Avery GB, Fletcher MA, MacDonald MG (eds). Neonatology-Pathophysiology and Management of the Newborn, 4th ed. Philadelphia, JB Lippincott, 1994, pp 429–452.

REFERENCES

1. Abman SH, Wolfe RE, Accurso FJ, et al. Pulmonary vascular response to oxygen in infants with severe bronchopulmonary dysplasia. Pediatrics 75:80, 1985.
2. Abman SH. Pathogenesis of neonatal and post neonatal pulmonary hypertension. Curr Opin Pediatr 6:239.
3. Adams R, Gardner TH. Persistent pulmonary hypertension of the newborn. Am J Dis Child 138:592, 1984.
4. Bohn DJ. Ventilation and blood gas parameters in pediatric survival in congenital diaphragmatic hernia. Pediatr Surg Int 2:336, 1987.
5. Cassin S, Tod M, Philips J, et al. Effects of prostaglandin D2 on the perinatal circulation. Am J Physiol 240:H755, 1981.
6. Clark RH. High-frequency ventilation. J Pediatr 124:661, 1994.
7. Connors RH, Tracy T, Bailey PV, et al. Congenital diaphragmatic hernia repair on ECMO. J Pediatr Surg 25:1043, 1990.
8. Crowley P, Chalmers I, Keirse M. The effect of corticosteroid administration before preterm delivery: an overview of the evidence from controlled trials. Br J Obstet Gynaecol 97:11, 1990.
9. Cummings JJ, D'Eugenio DB, Gross SJ. A controlled trial of dexamethasone in preterm infants at high risk for bronchopulmonary dysplasia. N Engl J Med 320:1505, 1989.
10. Dreizzen E, Migdal M, Praud JP, et al. Passive compliance of total respiratory system in preterm infants with respiratory distress syndrome. J Pediatr 112:778, 1988.
11. Garg M, Kurxner SI, Bautista DB, et al. Clinically unsuspected hypoxia during sleep and feeding in infants with bronchopulmonary dysplasia. Pediatrics 81:635, 1988.
12. Garrite JJ, Rumney PJ, Btiggs GG, et al. A randomized placebo-controlled trial of betamethasone for the prevention of respiratory distress syndrome at 24–28 weeks gestation. Am J Obstet Gynecol 166:646, 1992.
13. Gersony WM, Duc GV, Adams A, Gardner TH. Persistence pulmonary hypertension of the newborn. Am J Dis Child 138:592, 1984.
14. Gersony WM, Duc GV, Sinclair JC. "PFC" syndrome (persistence of the fetal circulation). Circulation 40(Suppl III):87, 1969.
15. Gersony WM, Duc GV, Sinclair JC. "PFC" syndrome [abstract]. Circulation 40(Suppl III):87, 1969.
16. Goetzman BW, Riemenschneider TA. Persistence of the fetal circulation. Pediatr Rev 2:37, 1980.
17. Graham M, Levene M, Trounce JQ, Rutter N. Prediction of cerebral palsy in very low birthweight infants: prospective ultrasound study. Lancet 1:593, 1987.
18. Greenspan IS, Wolfson ME, Holt WJ, Shaffer TH. Neonatal gastric intubation: differential respiratory effects between nasogastric and orogastric tubes. Pediatr Pulmonol 8:254, 1990.
19. Groneck P, Gdtze-Speer B, Opperman M, et al. Association of pulmonary inflammation and increased microvascular permeability during the development of bronchopulmonary dysplasia. Pediatrics 93:712, 1994.
20. Gryglewski RJ, Korbut R, Ocetkiewicz A. Generation of prostacyclin by lungs in vitro and its release into the arterial circulation. Nature 273:765, 1978.
21. Hammerman C, Lass N, Strales E, et al. Prostanoids in neonates with persistent pulmonary hypertension. J Pediatr 110:470, 1987.
22. Heyman MA. Prostaglandins and leukotrienes in the perinatal period. Clin Perinatol 14:857, 1987.
23. Jobe AH. Pulmonary surfactant therapy. N Engl J Med 328:861, 1993.
24. Kao CC, Durand DJ, Phillips BP, et al. Oral theophylline and diuretics improve pulmonary mechanics in infants with bronchopulmonary dysplasia. J Pediatr 111:439, 1987.
25. Kanto WP. A decade of experience with neonatal extracorporeal membrane oxygenation. J Pediatr 124:335, 1994.
26. Kinsella JP, Abman SH. Inhalational nitrous oxide therapy for persistent pulmonary hypertension of the newborn. Pediatrics 91:997, 1993.
27. Kurlak LO, Ruggins NR, Stephenson TJ. Effect of nursing position on the incidence, type and duration of clinically significant apnea of preterm infants. Arch Dis Child 71:F16, 1994.
28. Langer JC, Filler RM, Bohn DJ, et al. Timing of surgery for congenital diaphragmatic hernia: is emergency operation necessary? J Pediatr Surg 23:731, 1988.

29. Liu LMP, Cote CJ, Goudsouzian NG, et al. Life threatening apnea in infants recovering from anesthesia. Anesthesiology 59:506, 1983.
30. Madansky DL, Lawson EE, Chernick V, et al. Pneumothorax and other forms of pulmonary air leak in the newborn. Am Rev Respir Dis 120:729, 1979.
31. Martin RJ, Miller MJ, Carlo WA. Pathogenesis of apnea in preterm infants. J Pediatr 109:733, 1986.
32. McCann EM, Goldman, SL, Brady JP. Pulmonary function in the sick newborn infant. Pediatr Res 21:313, 1987.
33. Meadows W, Meus P. An animal model of neonatal sepsis: early and late hemodynamic and metabolic sequelae of Group B beta strep (GBS) sepsis in piglet. Pediatr Res 15:1973, 1981.
34. Meyrick B, Reid L. Pulmonary hypertension: anatomic and physiologic correlates. Clin Chest Med 4:1997, 1983.
35. Miller MJ, Faranoff AA, Martin RJ. In Faranoff AA, Martin RJ (eds). Neonatal-Perinatal Medicine, 5th ed. St Louis, Mosby–Year Book, pp 848–853, 1992.
36. Mutch L, Newdick M, Lodwick A, et al. Secular changes in rehospitalization of very low birthweight infants. Pediatrics 78:164, 1986.
37. Parida SK, Baker S, Desai N, et al. Endotracheal tolazoline in persistent pulmonary hypertension of the newborn (PPHN). J Perinatol 17:461, 1997.
38. Roberts JD, Polaner DM, Lang P, et al. Inhaled nitric oxide in persistent pulmonary hypertension in the newborn. Lancet 340:818, 1992.
39. Roberts JD, Shaul PW. Advances in the treatment of persistent pulmonary hypertension of the newborn. Pediatr Clin North Am 40:983, 1993.
40. Siassi B, Goldberg SJ, Emmanouilides GC, et al. Persistent pulmonary vascular obstruction in newborn infants. J Pediatr 78:610, 1971.
41. Spitzer AR, Davis J, Clarke WT, et al. Pulmonary hypertension and fetal circulation in the newborn. Clin Perinatol 15:389, 1988.
42. Spitzer AR, Fox WW. Infant apnea. Pediatr Clin North Am 33:561, 1986.
43. Stenmark K, Janes S, Voekel N. Leukotriene C4 and D4 in neonates with hypoxemia and pulmonary hypertension. N Engl J Med 309:77, 1983.
44. Walsh Sukys MC. Persistent pulmonary hypertension of the newborn. The black box revisited. Clin Perinatol 20:127, 1993.
45. Wegeman ME. Annual summary of vital statistics—1990. Pediatrics 88:1081, 1991.
46. Wesley JR, Heidelberger KP, DiPietro MA, et al. Diagnosis and management of congenital cystic disease of the lungs in children. J Pediatr Surg 21:202, 1986.
47. Zayek M, Cleveland D, Morin FC. Treatment of persistent pulmonary hypertension in the newborn lamb by inhalational nitrous oxide. J Pediatr 122:743, 1993.

83

Congenital Laryngeal Anomalies

Mark E. Gerber, M.D., and Lauren D. Holinger, M.D.

The larynx functions as a breathing passage, provides airway protection during swallowing, aids in the clearance of secretions (through cough), and allows for vocalization. It follows that symptoms of laryngeal anomalies are those of airway obstruction, difficulty in feeding, and abnormalities of phonation. These symptoms vary and are characteristic of individual anomalies.

The signs and symptoms of a child with airway obstruction are usually different, depending on the location and severity of obstruction. Being able to assess and localize the potential site and cause of the obstruction is essential. Airway obstruction at the level of the nasopharynx or oropharynx produces the inspiratory low-pitched sound called *stertor*, or snoring. Dynamic supraglottic and glottic obstructions tend to produce inspiratory stridor due to collapse of these structures with negative inspiratory pressure. Intrathoracic airway lesions cause expiratory obstruction. Stridor caused by fixed subglottic laryngeal and cervical tracheal lesions is most often biphasic. Obstructive symptoms can vary from mild stridor to severe obstruction with increased work of breathing (retractions), tachypnea, episodes of apnea, and cyanosis.

The larynx provides a three-tiered system of "sphincters" that contribute to airway protection during swallowing: the epiglottis, aryepiglottic folds, and arytenoids (first level), the false vocal folds (second level), and the true vocal folds (third level). Anomalies that affect any of these protective barriers can result in aspiration. Symptoms of swallowing dysfunction and aspiration include coughing, choking, and gagging episodes during and after feedings, stasis of secretions, and recurrent pneumonias.

Phonatory abnormalities differ depending on the level of laryngeal anomaly present. A muffled cry is suggestive of supraglottic obstruction. A high-pitched or absent cry is associated with glottic abnormalities such as webs or atresia.

Laryngomalacia

Laryngomalacia is the most common congenital laryngeal anomaly and the most frequent cause of stridor in children. Sixty percent of congenital laryngeal anomalies in children with stridor result from laryngomalacia.[28] Large

series of congenital laryngeal anomalies cite a 50% to 75% incidence for laryngomalacia.[20, 35, 52]

Terminology

Laryngomalacia is a specific disease state with an ill-defined pathogenesis manifested by derangements of supraglottic anatomy, histology, or neurologic function. The term *laryngomalacia* was first used by Jackson and Jackson[38] in 1942 to describe the inward collapse of supraglottic structures during inspiration. Prior to that, the general term *congenital laryngeal stridor* had been used.[73] *Laryngomalacia* is a term that reflects the flaccidity of supraglottic laryngeal tissues without implying a specific pathophysiologic mechanism. A few authors still prefer not to use the term *laryngomalacia*, suggesting that it implies a chronic degenerative process or an inherent abnormality of laryngeal cartilage.[21] Stridor is a symptom and not a specific disease state, however, and there are many congenital laryngeal disorders that can cause stridor.

Symptoms

Intermittent, low-pitched inspiratory stridor is the hallmark of laryngomalacia. Symptoms usually appear within the first 2 weeks of life, although, rarely, onset occurs months after birth.[70] This delay is interesting because laryngomalacia is presumed to be congenital. An increase in the severity of stridor over the initial few months usually is followed by a gradual improvement. Symptoms usually are at their worst by 6 months of age, when they plateau and begin to resolve gradually. Although most patients are symptom-free by 18 to 24 months of age,[34] stridor can persist for years.[70]

Typically, stridor is exacerbated by an exertion, such as crying, agitation, feeding, or supine positioning. Substernal retractions indicate severe obstruction, and pectus excavatum is a complication of extreme chronic obstruction.[42] Moderate to severe cases may be complicated by feeding difficulties, gastroesophageal reflux, failure to thrive, cyanosis, intermittent complete obstruction, or cardiac failure (as seen in obstructive sleep apnea).[37, 64, 76] If untreated, the infant with severe laryngomalacia may asphyxiate and die. Reardon reported seven deaths resulting from laryngomalacia.[58]

Pathophysiology

Anatomic, neurologic, and inflammatory factors all may contribute to the development of laryngomalacia. Anatomic or mechanical abnormalities are variable, with one or more often occurring simultaneously and with one aspect dominating (Fig. 83–1). Some investigators consider the omega shape of the epiglottis to be a factor that contributes to stridor. However, the omega shape often is present in the absence of obstructive symptoms and is normal in infancy.[46] The omega shape itself probably is not responsible for stridor[1] but may become a contributing factor when pathologically exaggerated. Regularly identified anatomic abnormalities include the following:

1. Inward collapse of the aryepiglottic folds, primarily the cuneiform cartilages, which often are enlarged.
2. A long tubular epiglottis (a pathologic exaggeration of the normal omega shape).
3. Anterior, medial collapse of the arytenoid cartilages.
4. Posterior inspiratory displacement of the epiglottis against the posterior pharyngeal wall or inferior collapse to the vocal folds.
5. Short aryepiglottic folds.[64]

Laryngeal cartilage immaturity, with resultant weakness and a tendency to collapse on inspiration, has been suggested as a contributing factor.[42] However, this theory is weakened by the fact that the incidence of laryngomalacia is not increased in premature infants as compared with full-term infants.[40] Conclusive evidence of histologic abnormalities has not been found.[42] Keleman[40] discerned no uniform differences between specimens from stridulous infants and from normal infants. Histopathologic examination of specimens from patients with severe laryngomalacia requiring surgical intervention revealed predominantly normal microanatomy in one study of 10 patients[76] or

pervasive subepithelial edema in a more recent study of nine patients.[8] Because only a few reports document altered histologic structure,[7, 42, 67] the evidence currently does not support microscopic structural pathology as the sole cause of laryngomalacia.

Immature or defective neuromuscular control is another pathophysiologic mechanism thought to play a role in laryngomalacia. McSwiney et al[47] noticed delayed speech in 4 of 21 children with laryngomalacia. Associations among laryngomalacia, central apnea, hypotonia, mental retardation, and early speech problems have been reported, adding further support to the theory of a delayed development in neuromuscular control. Belmont and Grundfast[1] proposed that an active neuromuscular support system, made up of the stylopharyngeus, palatopharyngeus, hyoglossus, and digastric muscles, is necessary to exert a dilatory effect on the supraglottic structures. They believe that hypotonia of these muscles, secondary to neuromuscular dysfunction, is manifested by stridor and varying degrees of airway obstruction and dysphagia.

Gastroesophageal reflux is frequently associated with laryngomalacia. The increased negative intrathoracic pressure generated on inspiration with a partially collapsed supraglottic larynx can increase the retrograde flow of gastric contents into the esophagus. The reverse may also occur with pharyngoesophageal reflux inducing posterior supraglottic edema. The edematous supraglottic mucosa collapses into the laryngeal introitus during inspiration.

Diagnosis

The diagnosis of laryngomalacia is made with awake fiberoptic laryngoscopy identifying the pathologic features. When dysphagia is present, a fiberoptic endoscopic evaluation of swallowing or a videofluoroscopic swallow study can be obtained. Plain chest radiographs (posteroanterior and lateral) and soft tissue neck radiographs (high KV

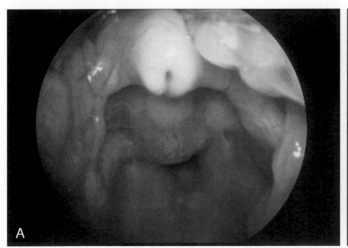
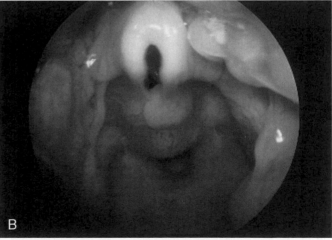

FIGURE 83–1. Direct laryngoscopy of a child with laryngomalacia under a general anesthetic with spontaneous ventilation. *A,* During inspiration with collapse of the supraglottic larynx. *B,* During expiration with passive opening of the supraglottic larynx.

anteroposterior and lateral) are used to assist in evaluating the subglottic and tracheal airway. When symptoms and findings are severe enough to warrant surgical intervention, a thorough endoscopic evaluation of the entire respiratory tract should be made at the time of surgery to evaluate for the possibility of synchronous lesions (which exist in up to 27% of patients with laryngomalacia).[23]

Treatment

Expectant observation is suitable for most cases of laryngomalacia. Most patients' symptoms resolve spontaneously without intervention. A few patients have such severe symptoms, however, that intervention becomes necessary. Severe symptoms necessitating intervention include apparent life-threatening events,[37] cor pulmonale,[76] failure to thrive, and feeding difficulties. Medical management includes treatment of any primary or secondary gastroesophageal reflux. Historically, tracheostomy was the standard therapy for the patient with severe laryngomalacia.

This allowed for the pathologic lesion to be bypassed until the child outgrew it. The morbidity and mortality of tracheostomy are not inconsequential, however. Before the 1980s, there were only scattered case reports of alternative surgical approaches. Early efforts focused on modification of the obstruction of the epiglottis. In 1922, Iglauer[37] performed the first successful surgical alteration of the supraglottic larynx for laryngomalacia by amputating the redundant epiglottis with a wire snare, which resulted in resolution of the child's severe cyanotic and apneic episodes. In 1944, Schwartz[63] removed a V-shaped wedge of tissue from the epiglottis, which resulted in an immediate improvement in a patient. Fearon and Ellis[19] successfully decannulated a patient with severe laryngomalacia shortly after suturing the epiglottis to the base of the tongue. Also in 1971, hyomandibulopexy (suspension of the hyoid bone to the symphysis of the mandible) was used successfully to create anterosuperior displacement of the obstructing epiglottis.[6]

The current management of severe laryngomalacia involves conservative excision of the obstructing supraglottic

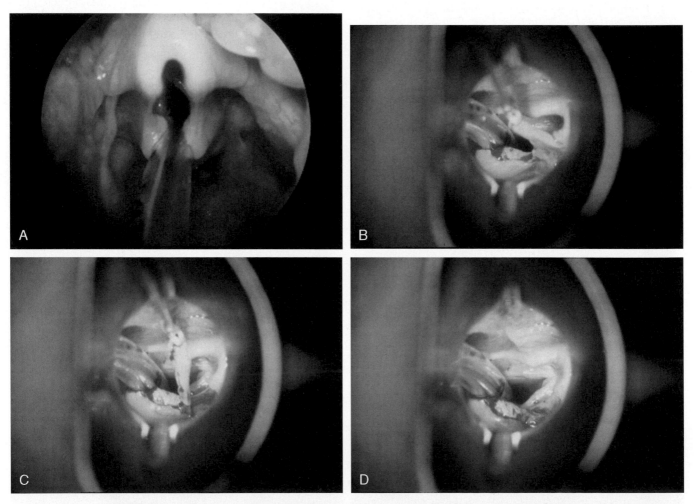

FIGURE 83–2. The same patient as in Figure 83–1, now intubated for supraglottoplasty. *A*, Contributing features include the shortened aryepiglottic folds and prominent cuneiform cartilages. *B*, Grasping of the right aryepiglottic fold with trimming of the cuneiform cartilage and aryepiglottic fold mucosa. *C*, Completing the wedge excision of the aryepiglottic fold with the anterior incision along the free edge of the epiglottis. *D*, The improved view of the glottis after completion of the right side of the procedure.

tissues. In 1984, Lane et al[42] first described the use of microcupped forceps and Bellucci scissors to remove obstructing structures of the posterior supraglottic region. In 1985, Seid et al[64] successfully treated three patients by dividing shortened aryepiglottic folds with the CO_2 laser. Zalzal et al[76] subsequently described "epiglottoplasty," the trimming of mucosa from the lateral edges of the epiglottis, the aryepiglottic folds, and the arytenoids and corniculate cartilages with microlaryngeal scissors. The term *supraglottoplasty* may be more appropriate, as it can be used to describe any of these surgical procedures that modify the flaccid obstructing supraglottic tissues. The location and extent of resection are adapted to fit individual mechanical problems (Fig. 83–2). Both the CO_2 laser and microlaryngeal scissors can be successfully used.

Complications

Although complications of supraglottoplasty are unusual, an overly aggressive approach may lead to supraglottic stenosis or an exacerbation of dysphagia with aspiration. Conservative excision minimizes the probability of postoperative complications. If the excision proves inadequate, the child can always be returned to the operating room for additional removal of tissue. In rare cases, massive collapse of the entire supraglottic framework may require tracheotomy placement.

Laryngoceles and Saccular Cysts

The laryngeal ventricle is a fusiform fossa bounded by the vocal folds and false vocal cords. The anterior part of the roof of the ventricle leads up into a cecal pouch of mucous membrane called the *saccule*. The laryngeal saccule rises vertically between the false vocal cord, the base of the epiglottis, and the inner surface of the thyroid cartilage. Below the surface of its mucous membrane are delicate muscles that compress it to express its secretions on the vocal folds. A variety of abnormalities of the laryngeal saccule can occur (Fig. 83–3).[30] A laryngocele is an abnormal dilatation or herniation of the saccule. It communicates with the lumen of the larynx and is filled with air but on occasion may be temporarily distended and filled with mucus. An internal laryngocele is confined to the interior of the larynx and extends posterosuperiorly into the area of the false vocal cord and aryepiglottic fold. An external laryngocele extends cephalad to protrude laterally into the neck through the thyrohyoid membrane. When an external laryngocele is combined with a symptomatic dilatation of the internal portion, it is termed a *combined laryngocele*. The diagnosis of a laryngocele can be made when an ectatic, dilated saccule is symptomatic, palpable, or observed to extend above the superior margin of the thyroid cartilage by indirect or direct laryngoscopy, radiography, or dissection (at surgery or autopsy).[14, 30]

Laryngoceles become clinically perceptible only when distended by air or temporarily filled with a collection of fluid. In the latter situation, it is apparent that laryngoceles and saccular cysts are often indistinguishable from each other. Therefore, a fluid-filled, smooth mass distending the aryepiglottic fold may be a saccular cyst or a laryngocele.

The pathogenesis of laryngoceles is variable. The extent to which congenital or acquired factors may be implicated must be assessed in each individual case. Laryngoceles observed in newborns are certainly congenital. The apparently increased incidence of laryngoceles observed in individuals whose occupations or hobbies involve prolonged periods of increased pressure within the laryngeal lumen (e.g., players of wind instruments) suggests that acquired factors contribute to laryngocele formation in some cases.[36, 43, 45, 57] In infants and children, a congenital defect or anatomic variation of the saccule must be implicated to a greater degree. A spectrum exists: a laryngocele may be purely congenital (as in the newborn); may represent a congenital defect made apparent or exacerbated by habitual, increased intralaryngeal pressure; or may be acquired solely on the basis of prolonged increased intralaryngeal pressure.

The saccular cyst (congenital cyst of the larynx, laryngeal mucocele) is distinguished from the laryngocele in that its lumen is isolated from the interior of the larynx and it does not contain air. Saccular cysts are distinctly submucosal and are covered with normal mucous membrane.[14] There are two types of saccular cysts. The lateral saccular cyst extends posterosuperiorly into the false vocal cord and aryepiglottic fold from the nonpatent orifice of the saccule. The anterior saccular cyst extends medially and posteriorly from its origin at the nonpatent orifice of the saccule to protrude into the laryngeal lumen between the true and false vocal cords.

Several mechanisms have been proposed to explain the formation of saccular cysts, but given their constant anatomic location, these cysts almost certainly result from a developmental failure to maintain patency of the saccular orifice.[53] Saccular cysts can be congenital or acquired, as inflammation, trauma, or tumors may occlude the saccular orifice with the same result.

The laryngopyocele is an infected laryngocele, saccular cyst, or large saccule in which the orifice may have become occluded as a result of the infectious process.[14] The term first was coined and applied to an infected laryngocele, but it can describe any of the pus-containing saccular dilatations, most of which are clinically similar in appearance.

Symptoms

Symptoms of laryngoceles include intermittent hoarseness and dyspnea that may increase with crying. A weak cry or aphonia also may occur. Saccular cysts usually cause respiratory distress, typically with inspiratory stridor. An inaudible or muffled cry may also be present. Dysphagia is occasionally encountered.

Diagnosis

The diagnosis of a laryngocele or saccular cyst is suggested by flexible laryngoscopy. Laryngoceles can be identified with high KV soft tissue radiographs of the neck. Both with laryngoscopy and with radiography, however, if

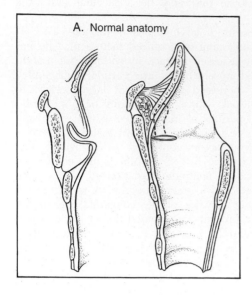

A. Normal anatomy

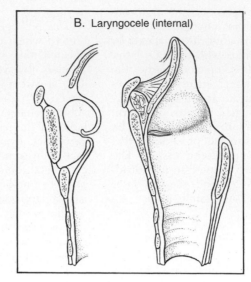

B. Laryngocele (internal)

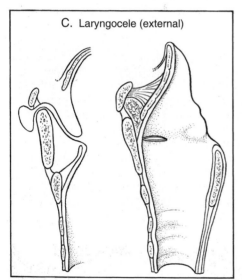

C. Laryngocele (external)

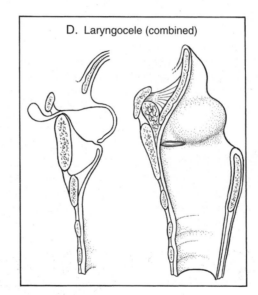

D. Laryngocele (combined)

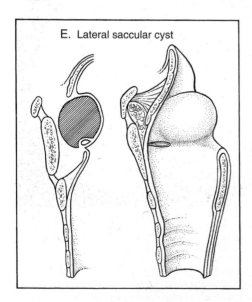

E. Lateral saccular cyst

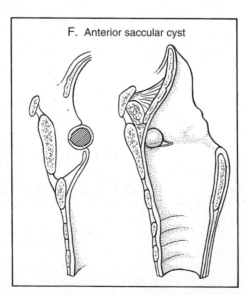

F. Anterior saccular cyst

FIGURE 83–3. Coronal and sagittal views illustrate the anatomy and pathology of the laryngeal saccule and ventricle. Schematic coronal sections are taken through the anterior larynx at the level of the saccular orifice. (From Holinger L. Congenital laryngeal anomalies. In Holinger L, Lusk R, Green C (eds). Pediatric Laryngology and Bronchoesophagology. Philadelphia, Lippincott-Raven, 1997, pp 137–164.)

the laryngocele is not distended with air at the time of the evaluation, no significant abnormalities will be visualized. In the older child or adolescent, the diagnosis of a combined laryngocele is suspected by a mass in the neck produced with a modified Valsalva maneuver.

Treatment

Needle aspiration of lateral saccular cysts confirms the diagnosis but rarely obviates the need for more definitive therapy. Recurrence can be managed by aspiration or unroofing with a cup forceps or CO_2 laser. However, repeated endoscopic procedures may be required.[8] Therefore, if a cyst recurs after diagnostic aspiration, endoscopic excision is undertaken dissecting the cyst to its base at the orifice of the saccule, removing any remnants with the CO_2 laser. Thereafter, if there is a recurrence, excision through a lateral cervical approach should be considered. Incising the thyrohyoid membrane along the superior margin of the thyroid cartilage while protecting the superior laryngeal nerve exposes the cyst, allowing for its excision after dissection, after the base is ligated. It is rarely necessary to remove a portion of the thyroid cartilage. Tracheostomy can usually be avoided, but occasionally intubation will be needed for a few days until the perioperative edema subsides.

Neurologic Lesions

Neurologic lesions (vocal cord paralysis) are the third most common congenital laryngeal anomaly producing stridor in infants and children.[31] Only laryngomalacia and congenital subglottic stenosis are more common. Unilateral and bilateral vocal cord paralysis occur with equal frequency. Vocal cord paralysis in infants is largely congenital in origin, or is the result of congenital anomalies of the central nervous system. Of those cases of congenital vocal cord paralysis, approximately 50% are associated with other anomalies. Of cases of acquired vocal cord paralysis, nearly 70% are secondary to congenital neurologic abnormalities (such as meningomyelocele, Arnold-Chiari malformation, and hydrocephalus) or the neurosurgical efforts to treat them.[31] The origin of unilateral vocal cord paralysis may be associated with cardiovascular anomalies, and the left side is more commonly affected.

Symptoms

Bilateral paralysis of the vocal folds typically produces high-pitched, inspiratory stridor: a phonatory sound or inspiratory cry. The vocal folds can appear to function as a one-way valve, being drawn during inspiration but opening passively during expiration (paradoxical motion).

Unilateral vocal fold paralysis produces much less prominent symptoms in the neonate. Stridor is uncommon. Usually, the cry is weak and occasionally breathy. Children with unilateral paralysis may have problems with feeding secondary to laryngeal penetration and aspiration.

Diagnosis

The diagnosis of vocal fold paralysis is made by awake flexible laryngoscopy. Because of the rapid respiratory rate of infants, recording the endoscopy is helpful for slow-motion replay to confirm the diagnosis.

Once the diagnosis of paralysis of one or both vocal folds has been made, a thorough investigation for the underlying cause is carried out. Imaging of the head and chest is recommended to evaluate for possible associated cardiovascular or neurologic abnormalities. When an associated laryngeal lesion is suspected, it is important to completely evaluate the larynx and trachea with the patient under general anesthesia to assess passive arytenoid mobility and to visualize any possible webbing or scarring.

Treatment

If treated early, paralysis caused by increased intracranial pressure often responds to cerebrospinal shunting or posterior fossa decompression. Vocal fold paralysis in infants usually resolves within 6 to 18 months. However, function is unlikely to return if there is no sign of improvement within 2 to 3 years. Because of this fact, a watchful waiting approach is appropriate management for the initial 2 or more years. Unilateral vocal cord paralysis rarely requires surgical intervention. The occasional child with feeding difficulties can usually be managed with thickening of liquids. Rarely is airway support needed.

With bilateral vocal cord paralysis, a temporary tracheotomy is usually, but not always, necessary. When managing an infant without a tracheostomy, frequent reassessment to prevent failure to thrive is needed, as airway requirements will increase with growth of the child.

The wide variety of possible surgical approaches to improve the airway in patients with bilateral vocal fold paralysis suggests that no one procedure is ideal. The goal is to restore the glottic airway by lateralizing one or both of the paralyzed vocal cords. Reinnervation techniques are of unclear utility and are currently rarely employed.

Surgical lateralization procedures for bilateral vocal fold paralysis are to some degree injurious to the developing larynx. Excisional procedures, in which tissue is removed from the posterior glottis, can be performed in an open fashion or endoscopically with the surgical laser. Experience with laser arytenoidectomy or posterior cordotomy has been good,[15, 39, 56, 59] with most patients being decannulated after a single treatment. Since the tissue excision is primarily within the posterior larynx, long-term voice results are typically acceptable. Also, if care is taken to avoid overly aggressive resection, aspiration is rarely a problem. The most common late complication is failure to achieve an adequate airway. More consistent results can be obtained using external approaches in children.[5] Possible options include arytenoidectomy,[5] arytenoidopexy,[69] or laryngeal expansion with costal cartilage augmentation to the posterior cricoid plate.[24]

Congenital Laryngeal Webs and Atresia

Congenital laryngeal webs are uncommon. Most are glottic and occur with extension into the subglottic larynx.

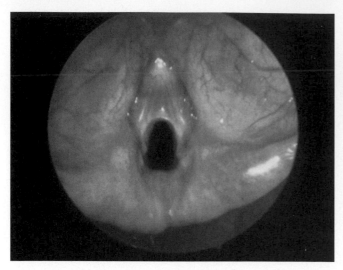

FIGURE 83–4. Anterior thick glottic web.

The symptom complex and severity depend on where the webs are located and the degree of involvement. Virtually all infants and children with laryngeal webs have some degree of vocal dysfunction. When there is a thin anterior glottic web, the vocal folds are usually visible through these thin webs and there is little obstruction of the airway associated with mild hoarseness. As the webs become thicker and begin to extend into the subglottic larynx, there is increasing airway obstruction and the voice becomes weaker (Fig. 83–4). When more than 75% of the glottis is involved by a thick web, or with significant subglottic extension, the infant may be aphonic and airway obstruction severe, requiring tracheostomy soon after birth (Fig. 83–5).[10]

Isolated subglottic webs are less common than glottic webs. Supraglottic webs are also rare. Most supraglottic webs probably represent fusion of the ventricular bands anteriorly and typically cause mild symptoms of airway obstruction. When the larynx is difficult to visualize and vocal cord mobility is limited, the larynx needs to be assessed for the possibility of a posterior supraglottic or interarytenoid web.[2, 3]

Complete congenital laryngeal atresia is incompatible with life unless an emergency tracheotomy is carried out in the delivery room. Associated tracheal and esophageal anomalies are present in affected patients.[33]

Treatment

Management of laryngeal webs is based on the extent of the lesion and the severity of symptoms. A thin anterior glottic web may require only incision or dilatation to realize a significant improvement in the voice. More significant webs that are still isolated to the glottis may respond adequately to dilatation after incision along the margin of one vocal fold. In this case, however, revisions may be needed to obtain an optimal result. When there is involvement of the subglottic larynx, the anterior cricoid plate is usually abnormal and needs to be addressed for adequate results to be achieved. This requires an external approach with division of the web and the cricoid plate. Along with reorienting the rotated anterior cricoid plate, one can use a cartilage graft if expansion is needed or place a laryngeal keel for 7 to 14 days. Occasionally, the anterior cricoid plate is not amenable to repositioning and can be resected submucosally, followed by anterior costal

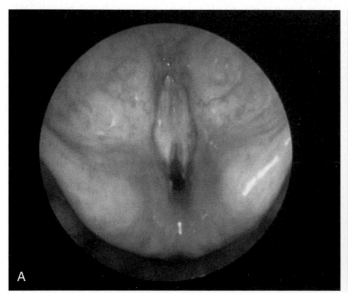

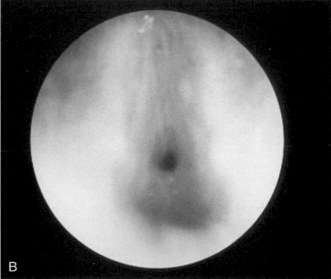

FIGURE 83–5. Partial laryngeal atresia in a 5-year-old child who underwent tracheostomy placement immediately after birth. *A*, View of supraglottis and glottis. *B*, View of subglottis through an anterior commissure laryngoscope, which was used to separate the posterior aspect of the vocal cords, allowing visualization of the small pinhole posterior subglottic opening.

cartilage augmentation[4] or completion of a partial crico-tracheal resection in severe cases.

Congenital Subglottic Stenosis

Congenital subglottic stenosis is the second most common cause of stridor in neonates, infants, and children.[28] Congenital subglottic stenosis involves narrowing of the sub-glottic lumen in the absence of trauma (intubation). The normal full-term newborn larynx has a diameter of at least 5 mm. A subglottic lumen of less than 4 mm in a full-term newborn (3 mm in a premature infant) represents subglottic stenosis. The origin of congenital sub-glottic stenosis is believed to be incomplete recanalization of the laryngeal lumen during embryogenesis.

Congenital subglottic stenosis can be divided by histo-pathologic criteria into cartilaginous and membranous types. By endoscopic examination, the membranous type is usually circumferential and generally soft and dilatable. The mucosal lining is markedly thickened, either secondary to an increase in the fibrous connective tissue layer in the submucosa or as a result of hyperplasia and dilatation of the mucous glands in the subglottis.[18, 74]

In contrast to the membranous type of stenosis, the cartilaginous variety is more variable in appearance. Mild stenoses usually have a normal shape but a smaller than normal size. More commonly, the cricoid cartilage has an abnormal shape, with prominent lateral shelves giving an elliptical appearance to the subglottic lumen (Fig. 83–6).[18]

Symptoms

Symptoms of upper airway obstruction predominate. Stridor is primarily inspiratory, progressing to biphasic with increasing severity of obstruction. With severe obstruction

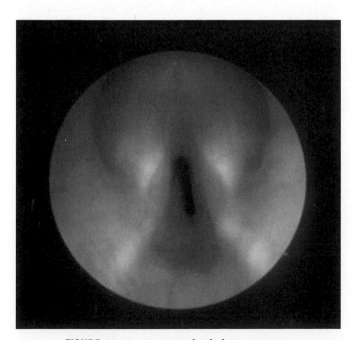

FIGURE 83–6. Congenital subglottic stenosis.

during the neonatal period, intubation is often necessary, which necessitates the change in classification from congenital to acquired. More mild to moderate stenosis may be asymptomatic until an upper respiratory tract infection results in additional subglottic edema, which narrows the airway and leads to symptoms of croup. Patients with this condition often have a history of recurrent and prolonged croup episodes.

Diagnosis

The diagnosis of subglottic stenosis is made by rigid endoscopy with the patient under general anesthesia. The entire larynx is examined to determine the areas involved (supraglottis, glottis, subglottis) and the nature of the stenosis (soft is membranous, and firm is cartilaginous). The remainder of the tracheobronchial tree is then examined to assess for possible synchronous lesions. Thereafter, an objective measure of the stenosis severity is obtained. An endotracheal tube is passed (starting small so as to not unintentionally dilate the stenosis) through the stenosis and attached to the anesthetic circuit. The circuit is closed and pressure is permitted to rise gradually in the airway while the endoscopist is visualizing the subglottis with the endoscope. The pressure that causes a visible or audible leak is recorded. If there is a leak at less than 10 cm H_2O pressure, then the next larger size of endotracheal tube is passed and the procedure repeated. The endotracheal tube size that permits a leak between 10 and 25 cm H_2O pressure is considered to be an accurate measure of the airway size. Comparison can then be made to the expected normal size for age to identify the percentage of the airway that is obstructed. The grading system most commonly used today is based on this endotracheal tube sizing: grade I, less than 50% obstruction; grade II, 51% to 70% obstruction; grade III, 71% to 99% obstruction; grade IV, no detectable lumen (Table 83–1).[51]

Treatment

The treatment of subglottic stenosis must be individualized, as each patient presents with multiple variables that require consideration in addition to the degree of stenosis, including the amount of extension out of the subglottis and the patient's general medical condition, swallowing ability, age, and weight. Congenital subglottic stenoses are often less severe than acquired stenoses. In patients with grade I stenosis (<50% obstruction), supportive care is usually adequate until sufficient laryngeal growth is spontaneously achieved. Most patients with greater than 50% obstruction require at least some level of intervention, however. Options for surgical management include endoscopic techniques, expansion procedures (including splits and cartilage grafting), and partial cricotracheal resection.

Many endoscopic techniques have been advocated in the past, including microcauterization,[41] cryosurgery,[61] and serial electrosurgical resection. These modalities have largely been replaced by carbon dioxide and the KTP lasers because of their precise tissue characteristics. The

TABLE 83-1. Classification of Laryngotracheal Stenosis by Endotracheal Tube Sizing*

Patient Age		ID 2.0	ID 2.5	ID 3.0	ID 3.5	ID 4.0	ID 4.5	ID 5.0	ID 5.5
Premature		40							
		58	30						
0-3 mo		68	48	26		No Obstruction			
3-9 mo		75	59	41	22				
9 mo-2 yr		80	67	53	38	20			
2 yr	No	84	74	62	50	35	19		
4 yr	Detectable	86	78	68	57	45	32	17	
6 yr	Lumen	89	81	73	64	54	43	30	16
	Grade IV	Grade III			Grade II		Grade I		

* Used for characterizing firm, mature subglottic stenosis. The size is determined by placement of an endotracheal tube that leaks between 10 and 25 cm H_2O.
ID, interior diameter
Adapted from Meyer CI, O'Connor D, Cotton R. Proposed grading system for subglottic stenosis based on endotracheal tube sizes. Ann Otol Rhinol Laryngol 108:319, 1994.

laser is useful for treating early intubation injury with granulation tissue accumulation, subglottic cysts, thin circumferential webs, and crescent-shaped bands. Factors that predispose to failure in treating subglottic stenosis with laser include previous failed endoscopic procedures, significant loss of the cartilaginous framework, thick, circumferential cicatricial scarring greater than 1 cm in vertical dimension, and posterior commissure involvement. In addition, exposure of perichondrium or cartilage during laser excision predisposes to perichondritis and chondritis that may induce extensive scar formation. Given that the majority of congenital stenoses are cartilaginous in nature, management with the laser is not usually advocated.

Open surgical reconstruction is recommended when endoscopic methods to establish an airway are inappropriate or have failed. In general, grade I stenosis is best corrected by endoscopic methods. Grade II stenosis can be approached with either endoscopic or open methods. Grade III and IV lesions almost always require open surgical reconstruction.

Anterior laryngotracheal decompression (cricoid split) is utilized predominantly in the neonate or young child with anterior subglottic or glottic narrowing who has failed multiple attempts at extubation in spite of an adequate pulmonary reserve. In this situation, successful extubation has been obtained in 66% to 78% of cases.[11] The procedure has also been used in similar children with progressive airway obstruction and in those who already had a tracheotomy, with an overall decannulation or extubation rate of 75% to 78%.[32]

Many open procedures are used to expand the stenotic pediatric laryngeal framework. Many methods have comparable success when used in the appropriate situation. When there is anterior fibrous subglottic stenosis without loss of cartilaginous support (grade II and some grade III cases), the authors prefer to consider options that include anterior laryngotracheal split with above-stoma stenting or a single-stage technique, or reconstruction using anterior autogenous costal or auricular cartilage grafting (with or without stenting). When there is posterior glottic or subglottic involvement, or in cases of more severe grade III

and grade IV stenosis, the authors prefer to consider the following: anterior, posterior, and possibly lateral laryngotracheal decompression (split) with long-term (8-12 weeks) above-stoma stenting, reconstruction with autologous costal cartilage graft to the posterior cricoid and possibly anterior cricoid regions with 2- to 4-week stent placement, or partial cricotracheal resection. Single-stage reconstruction is considered when the reconstructed airway will have adequate cartilaginous support, eliminating the need for long-term stenting.

The ultimate goal of laryngotracheal reconstruction is tracheotomy decannulation or prevention. The rate of decannulation varies with the severity of stenosis and the method of reconstruction. Patients with grade II stenosis can be decannulated, or tracheotomy can be avoided in 81% to 88% with a single reconstructive procedure and in up to 97% after two procedures.[44] The single-procedure success rate in patients with grade III stenosis is 78% to 81% and increases up to 91% after revision surgery.[54] The results for surgical repair of 100% stenotic lesions (grade IV) have improved significantly with the more recent use of partial cricotracheal resection, with decannulation obtained in more than 90% of patients with a single procedure.[72] Earlier reports for 100% lesions using cartilage expansion were uniformly worse, with decannulation rates of 37% to 50% after a single attempt, and up to 72% after multiple procedures.[12]

Laryngeal and Laryngotracheoesophageal Clefts

Congenital laryngeal and laryngotracheoesophageal clefts are rare conditions that can be characterized by a posterior midline deficiency in the separation of the larynx and trachea from the hypopharynx and esophagus. The incidence is less than 0.1% and the majority of cases are sporadic. There is a strong association with other anomalies (56%), most commonly tracheoesophageal fistula in 20% to 27% of cases.[17] Of special interest is that more than 6% of children with tracheoesophageal fistula have a coexisting laryngeal cleft. Of the children who present with tracheoesophageal fistula, the laryngeal cleft goes undetected in three of four cases until persistent aspiration in spite of successful tracheoesophageal fistula repair prompts further investigation.[17] Laryngeal or laryngotracheoesophageal cleft is also part of the Pallister-Hall syndrome (autosomal dominant, hypothalamic hamartoblastoma, laryngeal cleft, hypopituitarism, imperforate anus, and polydactyly), as well as G syndrome/Opitz-Friaz syndrome (dysphagia, hypospadias, hypertelorism, cleft lip and palate).[16]

The degree of clefting may be relatively minor, involving only a failure of interarytenoid muscle development, or can extend to the carina and even into the mainstem bronchi. Several classification systems have been used to describe laryngeal clefts. Independent from the numbering system used, it is useful to differentiate the length of the cleft as laryngeal (interarytenoid only, partial cricoid, or complete cricoid), and laryngotracheoesophageal clefts that extend into the cervical trachea, or the intrathoracic trachea.

Symptoms and Diagnosis

Patients with laryngeal or laryngotracheoesophageal clefts may present with inspiratory stridor, cyanotic attacks associated with feeding, aspiration, and recurrent pulmonary infections. As the length of the cleft increases, so does the severity of presenting symptoms, with aspiration present in 100% of laryngotracheoesophageal clefts. Although radiographic contrast studies may suggest aspiration, the best single study for identifying a laryngeal cleft is careful endoscopic examination. The arytenoids need to be parted to obtain adequate visualization, as the larynx may be obscured by redundant esophageal mucosa prolapsing into the glottic and subglottic lumen (Fig. 83-7). Smith et al[71] introduced a new instrument for measuring interarytenoid notch height relative to the vocal folds when a minor laryngeal cleft is suspected.

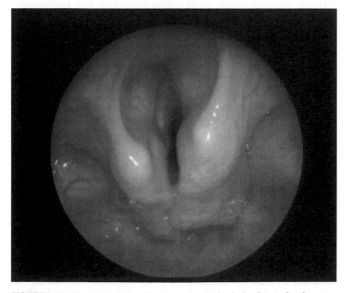

FIGURE 83-7. Laryngotracheoesophageal cleft through the cricoid and into the first two tracheal rings.

Treatment

Most clefts that are limited to the supraglottic larynx do not require surgical intervention. Treatment methods include evaluation and treatment of gastroesophageal reflux and swallowing therapy.[17] When surgical intervention is required, endoscopic repair is successful in more than 80% of cases, with open repair reserved for endoscopic failures.[3, 17]

In contrast to the interarytenoid clefts, surgical repair is required for nearly all laryngeal clefts that extend below the vocal cords. A complete discussion of the surgical options is beyond the scope of this chapter. However, an anterior approach through a laryngeal fissure is most commonly used (Fig. 83-8). The advantage of this approach is excellent exposure of the entire defect without risk to laryngeal innervation. Complete laryngotracheoesophageal clefts that extend to the carina may require a posterolateral approach to allow for a two-layer closure, usually without requiring intraoperative extracorporeal circulation. In most circumstances, a tracheotomy is present prior to, or placed at the time of, reconstructive surgery. However, single-stage repair with endotracheal intubation as a short-term stent is increasingly being used.

The mortality associated with laryngeal clefts is usually from accompanying congenital anomalies or an excessive delay in making the diagnosis, and the reported rate has been between 11%[17] and 46%.[62] The reported mortality rate associated with intrathoracic laryngotracheoesophageal clefts has been as high as 93%.[62] The incidence of required revision surgery also increases with the severity of the cleft,[17] with an overall incidence of 11%.[60] In addition to length of the cleft, insufficiently treated gastroesophageal reflux may also be associated with a decreased success rate.[27]

Congenital Neoplasms

Vascular Anomalies

In 1982, Muliken and Glowacki presented a systematic biologic classification of vascular anomalies of infancy and childhood based on physical findings, clinical behavior, and cellular kinetics.[50] The classification correctly describes two major types of pediatric vascular lesions: hemangiomas and vascular malformations. The suffix -oma once referred to any swelling or tumor but today denotes a tumor characterized by cellular hyperplasia. A subglottic hemangioma, therefore, is a tumor characterized by increased cell turnover of endothelium, mast cells, fibroblasts, and macrophages. In contrast, vascular malformations are not neoplastic lesions. They have a normal rate of endothelial turnover and are errors of vascular morphogenesis manifesting as various channel abnormalities.[22] Vascular malformations are categorized by their predominant channel type (capillary, venous, arterial, lymphatic, or a combination thereof). Lesions such as arteriovenous malformations that have arterial components are termed *fast-flow malformations*. *Slow-flow malformations* are anomalies with capillary, lymphatic, or venous components. These formerly and incorrectly were called capil-

23. Gonzalez C, Reilly J, Bluestone C. Synchronous airway lesions in infancy. Ann Otol Rhinol Laryngol 96:77, 1987.
24. Gray S, Kelly S, Dove H. Arytenoid separation for impaired pediatric vocal fold mobility. Ann Otol Rhinol Laryngol 103:510, 1994.
25. Hawkins D, et al. Corticosteroid management of airway hemangiomas: long-term follow-up. Laryngoscope 94:633, 1984.
26. Healy G, et al. Treatment of subglottic hemangioma with the carbon dioxide laser. Laryngoscope 90:809, 1980.
27. Hof E, et al. Deleterious consequences of gastroesophageal reflux in cleft larynx surgery. J Pediatr Surg 22:197, 1987.
28. Holinger L. Etiology of stridor in the neonate, infant, and child. Ann Otol Rhinol Laryngol 89:397, 1980.
29. Holinger L. Congenital laryngeal anomalies. In Holinger L, Lusk R, Green C (eds). Pediatric Laryngology and Bronchoesophagology. Philadelphia, Lippincott-Raven, 1997, pp 137–164.
30. Holinger L, Barnes D, Smid L. Laryngocele and saccular cysts. Ann Otol Rhinol Laryngol 87:675, 1978.
31. Holinger L, Holinger P, Holinger P. Etiology of bilateral abductor vocal cord paralysis: a review of 389 cases. Ann Otol Rhinol Laryngol 85:428, 1976.
32. Holinger L, Stankiewicz J, Livingston G. Anterior cricoid split: the Chicago experience with an alternative to tracheotomy. Laryngoscope 97:19, 1987.
33. Holinger L, Tansek K, Tucker GJ. Congenital laryngeal anomalies associated with tracheal agenesis. Ann Otol Rhinol Laryngol 96:505, 1987.
34. Holinger P, Brown W. Congenital webs, cysts, laryngoceles, and other anomalies of the larynx. Ann Otol Rhinol Laryngol 76:744, 1967.
35. Holinger P, Johnson K, Schiller F. Congenital anomalies of the larynx. Ann Otol Rhinol Laryngol 63:581, 1954.
36. Holinger P, Steinem E. Congenital cysts of the larynx. Pract Otorhinolaryngol 9:129, 1947.
37. Iglauer S. Epiglottidectomy for the relief of congenital laryngeal stridor. Laryngoscope 32:56, 1922.
38. Jackson C, Jackson C. Diseases and Injuries of the Larynx., New York, MacMillan, 1942, p 63.
39. Kashima H. Bilateral vocal fold motion impairment: pathophysiology and management by transverse cordotomy. Ann Otol Rhinol Laryngol 100:717, 1991.
40. Keleman G. Congenital laryngeal stridor. Arch Otolaryngol 58:245, 1954.
41. Kirchner F, Toledo P. Microcauterization in otolaryngology. Arch Otolaryngol 99:198, 1974.
42. Lane R, et al. Laryngomalacia: a review and case report of surgical treatment with resolution of pectus excavatum. Arch Otolaryngol 110:546, 1984.
43. Larrey D. Exercee particulirement dans les camps et les hopitaux militares depuis 1792 jusqu'en 1829. In Clinique Chirugicale. Paris, Chef Gabon, 1829, p 81.
44. Lusk R, Kang D, Muntz H. Auricular cartilage grafts in laryngotracheal reconstruction. Ann Otol Rhinol Laryngol. 102:247, 1993.
45. MacFie W. Asymptomatic laryngoceles in wind-instrument bandsmen. Arch Otolaryngol 83:270, 1866.
46. McGill T. Congenital diseases of the larynx. Otolaryngol Clin North Am 17:57, 1984.
47. McSwiney P, Cavanagh M, Languth P. Outcome in congenital stridor (laryngomalacia). Arch Dis Child 52:215, 1977.
48. Meeuwis J, et al. Subglottic hemangiomas in infants: treatment with intralesional corticosteroid injection and intubation. Int J Pediatr Otorhinolaryngol 19:145, 1990.
49. Mulder J, van den Broek P. Surgical treatment of infantile subglottic hemangioma. Int J Pediatr Otorhinolaryngol 17:57, 1989.
50. Mulliken J, Glowacki J. Hemangioma and vascular malformation of infants and children. A classification based on endothelial characteristics. Plast Reconstr Surg 69:412, 1982.
51. Myer CI, O'Connor D, Cotton R. Proposed grading system for subglottic stenosis based on endotracheal tube sizes. Ann Otol Rhinol Laryngol 108:319, 1994.
52. Narcy P, et al. Anomalies laryngies du nouveau: ne apropos de 687 observations. Ann Otolaryngol Chirur Cervicofac 101:363, 1984.
53. Niparko J, Moran M, Baker S. Laryngeal saccular cyst: an unusual clinical presentation. Otolaryngol Head Neck Surg 97:576, 1987.
54. Ochi J, Evans J, Bailey C. Pediatric airway reconstruction at Great Ormond Street: a ten-year review. I. Laryngotracheoplasty and laryngotracheal reconstruction. Ann Otol Rhinol Laryngol 101:465, 1992.
55. Ohlms L, et al. Interferon alfa-2a therapy for airway hemangiomas. Ann Otol Rhinol Laryngol 103:1, 1994.
56. Ossof R, et al. Endoscopic laser arytenoidectomy revisited. Ann Otol Rhinol Laryngol 99:764, 1994.
57. Pietrantoni L, Felisanti D, Finzi A. A laryngocele and laryngeal cancer. Ann Otol Rhinol Laryngol 68:100, 1959.
58. Reardon T. Congenital laryngeal stridor. Am J Med Sci 134:242, 1907.
59. Remsen K, et al. Laser lateralization for bilateral vocal cord abductor paralysis. Otolaryngol Head Neck Surg 93:645, 1985.
60. Robie D, et al. Operative strategy for recurrent laryngeal cleft: a case report and review of the literature. J Pediatr Surg 26:971, 1991.
61. Rodgers B, Talbert J. Clinical application of endotracheal cryotherapy. J Pediatr Surg 13:662, 1978.
62. Roth B. Laryngotracheoesophageal cleft, clinical features, diagnosis, and therapy. Eur J Pediatr 140:41, 1983.
63. Schwartz L. Congenital laryngeal stridor (inspiratory laryngeal collapse): a new theory as to its underlying cause and the desirability of a change in terminology. Arch Otolaryngol 39:403, 1944.
64. Seid A, et al. Laser division of the aryepiglottic folds for severe laryngomalacia. Int J Pediatr Otorhinolaryngol 10:153, 1985.
65. Seid A, Pransky S, Kearns D. The open surgical approach to subglottic hemangioma. Int J Pediatr Otorhinolaryngol 22:85, 1991.
66. Sharp H. Hemangioma of the trachea in an infant, successful removal. J Laryngol Otol 63:413, 1949.
67. Shulman J, et al. Familial laryngomalacia: a case report. Laryngoscope 86:84, 1976.
68. Sie K, McGill T, Healy G. Subglottic hemangioma: ten years' experience with the carbon dioxide laser. Ann Otol Rhinol Laryngol 103:167, 1994.
69. Singer M, Haymaker R, Miller S. Restoration of the airway following bilateral recurrent laryngeal nerve paralysis. Laryngoscope 95:1204, 1985.
70. Smith G, Cooper D. Laryngomalacia and inspiratory obstruction in later childhood. Arch Dis Child 56:345, 1981.
71. Smith R, Neville M, Bauman N. Interarytenoid notch height relative to the vocal folds. Ann Otol Rhinol Laryngol 103:753, 1994.
72. Stern Y, et al. Partial cricotracheal resection with primary anastomosis in the pediatric age group. Ann Otol Rhinol Laryngol 106:891, 1997.
73. Sutherland G, Lack H. Congenital laryngeal obstruction. Lancet 2:653, 1897.
74. Tucker G, et al. Histopathology of the congenital subglottic stenosis. Laryngoscope 89:866, 1979.
75. Wiatrak B, et al. Open surgical excision of subglottic hemangioma in children. Int J Pediatr Otorhinolaryngol 34:191, 1996.
76. Zalzal G, Anon J, Cotton R. Epiglottoplasty for the treatment of laryngomalacia. Ann Otol Rhinol Laryngol 96:72, 1987.

84

Congenital Malformations of the Trachea and Bronchi

Erica C. Bennett, M.D., and Lauren D. Holinger, M.D.

Congenital anomalies of the trachea and bronchi may be due to a primary embryologic disturbance in the formation of these structures or may be associated with an abnormality in the surrounding cardiovasculature or digestive tracts. Symptoms usually begin within the first few days or weeks of life, but some children may live a full life without symptoms. The severity varies from mild, vague symptoms to severe respiratory obstruction and death. Some of the more subtle presentations require a high index of suspicion and an organized method of diagnosis and treatment. A classification of congenital tracheobronchial anomalies is outlined in Box 84–1.

Tracheal Anomalies

Tracheomalacia

A classification system for tracheomalacia was proposed by Benjamin (Box 84–2).[4] Tracheomalacia accounts for almost half of all cases of patients with congenital tracheal anomalies who present with stridor.[15] The severity, duration, and location of tracheomalacia determine the presenting symptoms. Intrathoracic tracheomalacia usually produces expiratory wheezing or stridor, a harsh barking cough, neck hyperextension, and recurrent respiratory infections. In severe cases, patients may have cyanosis, respiratory distress, and attacks of reflex apnea that are associated with tracheal compression due to cardiovascular anomalies.[4] Premature infants usually present with extubation failure. Those who are otherwise normal may present in the first few weeks of life.

Expiratory lateral chest radiograph may show tracheal narrowing, but the diagnosis is confirmed during bronchoscopy (Fig. 84–1). During spontaneous respiration, the widened posterior membranous trachea collapses anteriorly during expiration, possibly completely obliterating the lumen. Contrast computed tomography (CT) is used to diagnose the cause in cases of discrete collapse.

The normal trachea has a cartilaginous to membranous ratio of about 4.5 to 1 (Fig. 84–2A). In primary tracheomalacia, the ratio may be 3 to 1 or 2 to 1 and is not due to extrinsic compression (Fig. 84–2B). Primary tracheomalacia usually resolves by 18 to 24 months of age, but

severe cases may require tracheotomy with continuous positive pressure ventilation.

Secondary tracheomalacia may be due to compression by cardiac or vascular structures (Fig. 84–2C) and congenital cysts, or it may be associated with tracheoesophageal fistulae (Fig. 84–2D).

Congenital Vascular and Cardiac Anomalies (Box 84–3)

Vascular malformations of the fourth and sixth branchial arch vessels rarely cause aerodigestive symptoms. An estimated 3% of the population at autopsy have an abnormality of the aortic arch system, but few have aerodigestive compromise.[20, 23] Fourth arch anomalies form either complete or incomplete vascular rings encircling the trachea or esophagus. Sixth arch defects result in anomalous left pulmonary artery development. Symptoms usually develop in the neonatal period and may include stridor, chronic cough, recurrent pneumonia, and dysphagia. Severe cyanotic episodes with apnea, or "dying spells," may necessitate cardiopulmonary resuscitation. Plain airway or chest radiographs may suggest compression of the airway by a vascular ring with a widened superior mediastinum, consolidation, hyperaeration, or narrowing of the tracheal air column. Barium esophagram is often diagnostic. CT scan with contrast provides the cardiovascular surgeon with the precise anatomy for preoperative planning.[20] Bronchoscopy is essential to document the precise area and degree of compression and to rule out any concomitant airway abnormalities.

Aberrant Innominate Artery

Innominate artery compression of the trachea may cause expiratory or biphasic wheezing or stridor, barking cough, recurrent "croup," and pneumonia, in addition to reflex apnea or apparently life-threatening events. Other causes of these events include central apnea and gastroesophageal reflux with apnea.

Bronchoscopy reveals the characteristic triangular shape of the compressed trachea in the upper portion

Box 84–1. Classification of Congenital Anomalies of the Trachea and Bronchi

I. Tracheal anomalies
  A. Tracheomalacia
    1. Primary
      a. In otherwise normal infants
      b. In premature infants
    2. Secondary
      a. Tracheoesophageal fistula and esophageal atresia
      b. External compression
        i. Vascular:
          Innominate artery compression
          Double aortic arch and right aortic arch
          Pulmonary artery sling
          Aberrant right subclavian artery
        ii. Cardiac: enlargement of the left atrium, pulmonary veins, and arteries
        iii. Congenital cysts
      c. Dyschondroplasia
  B. Agenesis and atresia
  C. Stenoses and webs
    1. Congenital stenosis with complete tracheal rings
    2. Tracheal cartilaginous sleeve
    3. Congenital stenoses and webs
II. Foregut cysts
  A. Bronchogenic cysts
  B. Intramural esophageal cysts (duplication)
  C. Enteric cysts
III. Bronchial anomalies
  A. Bronchomalacia
  B. Atresia and stenosis
  C. Abnormal bifurcation
  D. Bronchomegaly
IV. Pulmonary anomalies
  A. Pulmonary sequestration
  B. Pulmonary vascular anomalies
  C. Congenital lobar emphysema
  D. Congenital cystic adenomatoid malformation

Box 84–2. Classification of Tracheomalacia[4]

I. Primary tracheomalacia
  A. In otherwise normal infants
  B. In premature infants
II. Secondary tracheomalacia
  A. Tracheoesophageal fistula and esophageal atresia
  B. External compression: vascular, cardiac, congenital cyst, neoplasm
  C. Bony thorax abnormality: pectus excavatum, kyphoscoliosis
  D. Dyschondroplasias

(Fig. 84–3 and see Figs. 84–1*B* and 84–2*C*). The right brachial or carotid pulse will diminish when pressure is placed on the anterior tracheal wall with the tip of the bronchoscope. There is usually a widened membranous trachea with a normal diameter and accumulation of secretions distal to the obstruction.

Most symptoms are self-limited and resolve with growth. When symptoms are severe, suspension of the innominate artery and aorta to the posterior aspect of the sternum, or innominate arteriopexy, is the treatment of choice. Symptoms usually improve, but the associated tracheomalacia is still present and will become less symptomatic with time.

Double Aortic Arch

A vascular ring results from the abnormal development of the aortic arch complex. Complete vascular rings encircle the trachea and esophagus, with compression of both structures. Vascular rings include double aortic arch and right aortic arch with left ligamentum arteriosum. The most common complete vascular ring is a double arch, in

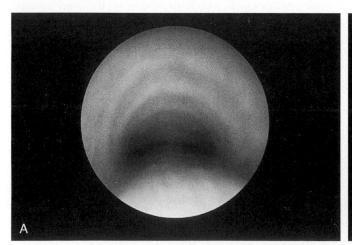

FIGURE 84–1. Tracheomalacia. *A,* Endoscopic view of a 14-month-old boy demonstrating the wide posterior membranous trachea, which collapses anteriorly during expiration. *B,* Right anterolateral compression of the mid-trachea due to an aberrant innominate artery. (From Holinger LD, Lusk RP, Green CG [eds]: *Pediatric Laryngology and Bronchoesophagology.* Philadelphia, Lippincott-Raven, 1997.)

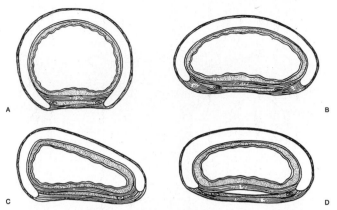

FIGURE 84–2. Axial sections of the trachea. *A,* Normal trachea. The ratio of the cartilaginous trachea to the posterior membranous trachea is 4 or 5 to 1. *B,* Primary tracheomalacia. Ratio of 2 or 3 to 1. *C,* Secondary tracheomalacia with a triangular shape due to right anterolateral compression of the trachea from an innominate artery. *D,* Tracheomalacia associated with tracheoesophageal fistula. (From Holinger LD, Lusk RP, Green CG [eds]: *Pediatric Laryngology and Bronchoesophagology.* Philadelphia, Lippincott-Raven, 1997.)

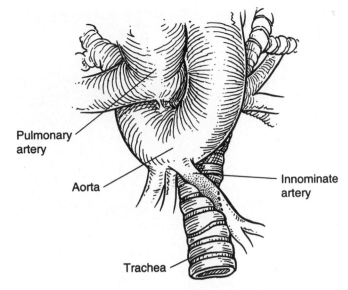

FIGURE 84–3. Endoscopist's perspective of an aberrant innominate artery compressing the right anterolateral aspect of the trachea. (From Holinger LD, Lusk RP, Green CG [eds]: *Pediatric Laryngology and Bronchoesophagology.* Philadelphia, Lippincott-Raven, 1997.)

which the ascending aorta bifurcates to surround both the trachea and the esophagus, then rejoins to form the descending aorta (Fig. 84–4). The double arch results from a failure of resorption of the right ventral fourth branchial arch.

Symptoms may begin at birth and are usually present by 3 months of age. Biphasic stridor that is exacerbated by feeding, as well as dysphagia, cyanotic spells, and recurrent respiratory infections are present. Significant dysphagia is seen only with solid food intake.

Barium esophagography demonstrates the posterior indentation of the esophagus (Fig. 84–5). With bronchoscopic examination, the tracheal lumen has a teardrop appearance with compression of the lower trachea. Chest CT with contrast is performed prior to surgical division. Usually one arch is dominant. The smaller arch is divided and most of the symptoms improve, but symptoms secondary to the resultant tracheomalacia may persist for some time.

Pulmonary Artery Sling

In a pulmonary artery sling, an aberrant left pulmonary artery arises from the right pulmonary artery, encircles the lower trachea and right main bronchus, and passes between the trachea and the esophagus, producing a right-sided compression of the lower trachea and right main bronchus (Fig. 84–6). Failure of normal development of the left pulmonary artery from the left sixth branchial arch results in this anomaly.

Most infants develop respiratory distress in the first year of life. Barium esophagography may demonstrate some compression. Bronchoscopy reveals narrowing of the lower trachea from the right and compression of the right main bronchus. The most common associated anomaly is complete tracheal rings.[6] Surgical division and reimplantation of the anomalous left pulmonary artery improves symptoms. When complete tracheal rings cause

---

Box 84–3. Congenital Vascular and Cardiac Anomalies

I. Aberrant innominate artery
II. Vascular rings
   A. Double aortic arch
      1. Right arch dominant
      2. Left arch dominant
      3. Balanced arches
   B. Right aortic arch with left ligamentum arteriosum
      1. Retroesophageal left subclavian artery
      2. Mirror-image branching
III. Pulmonary artery sling
IV. Aberrant right subclavian artery
V. Congenital cardiac defects

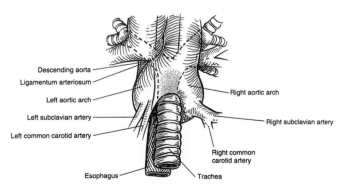

FIGURE 84–4. Double aortic arch encircling both the trachea and the esophagus (endoscopist's perspective). (From Holinger LD, Lusk RP, Green CG [eds]: *Pediatric Laryngology and Bronchoesophagology.* Philadelphia, Lippincott-Raven, 1997.)

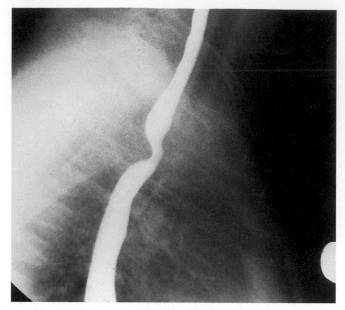

FIGURE 84–5. Barium esophagram showing the posterior indentation of the esophagus due to a double aortic arch that encircles the trachea and the esophagus. (From Holinger LD, Lusk RP, Green CG [eds]: *Pediatric Laryngology and Bronchoesophagology*. Philadelphia, Lippincott-Raven, 1997.)

severe airway compromise, tracheoplasty is performed at the same time.

Other Vascular Anomalies

Another common vascular anomaly is the aberrant right subclavian artery (Fig. 84–7). It is due to persistence of the right dorsal aorta and compresses only the esophagus. Patients are usually asymptomatic but may have dysphagia and recurrent aspiration.[23]

A right aortic arch develops with resorption of the left ventral fourth arch. When it is associated with a left descending aorta and a left ductus or ligamentum arteriosum, the left subclavian and carotid arteries cause anterior tracheal compression (Fig. 84–8). With a right descending aorta and a right ductus or ligamentum arteriosum, an aberrant left subclavian artery is usually found arising from the descending aorta and passing posterior to the esophagus. Ligation and division of the ligamentum arteriosum are usually sufficient to decompress both of these rings.

Other congenital defects of the cardiac, genitourinary, gastrointestinal, and endocrine systems may be present in patients with vascular anomalies and must be investigated.[23]

Congenital Cardiac Anomalies

Cardiac disease may cause left main bronchus compression. The left main bronchus lies in contact with the left atrium and left pulmonary veins. It is encircled by these structures and the left pulmonary artery (Fig. 84–9A). In

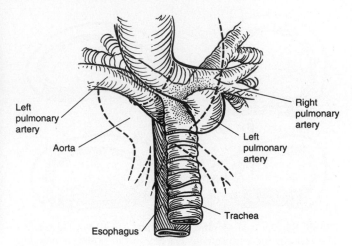

FIGURE 84–6. Pulmonary artery sling. The left pulmonary artery arises from the right, encircles the trachea, and passes between the trachea and the esophagus, causing right-sided compression of the lower trachea and right main bronchus. (From Holinger LD, Lusk RP, Green CG [eds]: *Pediatric Laryngology and Bronchoesophagology*. Philadelphia, Lippincott-Raven, 1997.)

infants and children with ventricular septal defects or a patent ductus arteriosus, right-to-left shunts are present, causing pulmonary hypertension and left atrial enlargement. This hypertension leads to increased size of the pulmonary arteries that, along with the enlarged atrium, may compress the left main or right middle lobe bronchi (Fig. 84–9B).

Symptoms vary in severity and may include wheezing, recurrent pneumonia, atelectasis, or lobar emphysema. Left main bronchial compression is seen by endoscopy

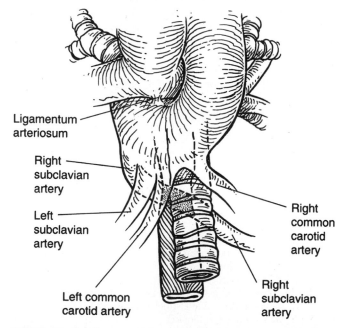

FIGURE 84–7. Aberrant right subclavian artery originating from the aortic arch on the left traversing the mediastinum posterior to the esophagus. (From Holinger LD, Lusk RP, Green CG [eds]: *Pediatric Laryngology and Bronchoesophagology*. Philadelphia, Lippincott-Raven, 1997.)

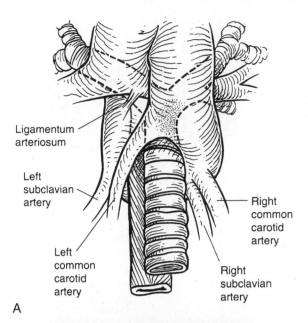

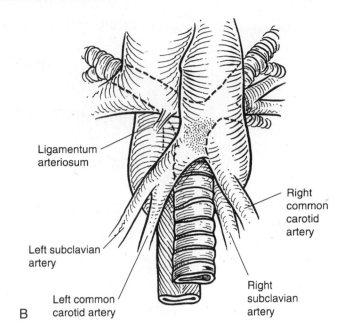

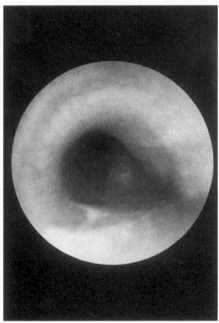

FIGURE 84–8. Right aortic arch with left ligamentum arteriosum. *A*, With retroesophageal left subclavian artery. *B*, With mirror-image branching. *C*, Endoscopic view in a 10-month-old boy with characteristic right anterolateral tracheal compression. (From Holinger LD, Lusk RP, Green CG [eds]: *Pediatric Laryngology and Bronchoesophagology.* Philadelphia, Lippincott-Raven, 1997.)

(Fig. 84–10). Post-contrast chest CT scans, magnetic resonance imaging (MRI), or cardiac catheterization is used to diagnose the underlying condition. Treatment is surgical correction of the underlying pathologic lesion combined with pulmonary artery plication or arteriopexy, if indicated.

Tracheoesophageal Fistula and Esophageal Atresia

Tracheoesophageal fistula (TEF) and esophageal atresia (EA) occur in approximately 1 in 3000 to 5000 live-born infants. Neonates present with excessive mucus and saliva in the oral or nasal cavities, respiratory difficulty, and feeding difficulty with persistent aspiration. There may be a history of maternal polyhydramnios, and about one

third of these neonates weigh less than 2250 g. About half have additional congenital anomalies of the cardiovascular, intestinal, skeletal, and genitourinary systems.[3] There are five types of EA and TEF (Fig. 84–11).

The diagnosis of EA is suggested when a catheter cannot be passed to the stomach. An EA will allow passage of a catheter only to about 9 cm from the lips. With distal TEF, gas can be seen in the stomach on the radiograph. Contrast studies carry a risk of aspiration of the contrast media. Endoscopy prior to repair delineates the pathologic anatomy while revealing associated airway anomalies such as cleft larynx, subglottic or tracheal stenosis, tracheomalacia, and second or upper pouch fistula. Vocal fold mobility is assessed in the awake infant followed by laryngoscopy and bronchoscopy. Usually, a large opening is seen in the posterior tracheal wall in the midline or just to the left of midline. A small catheter placed

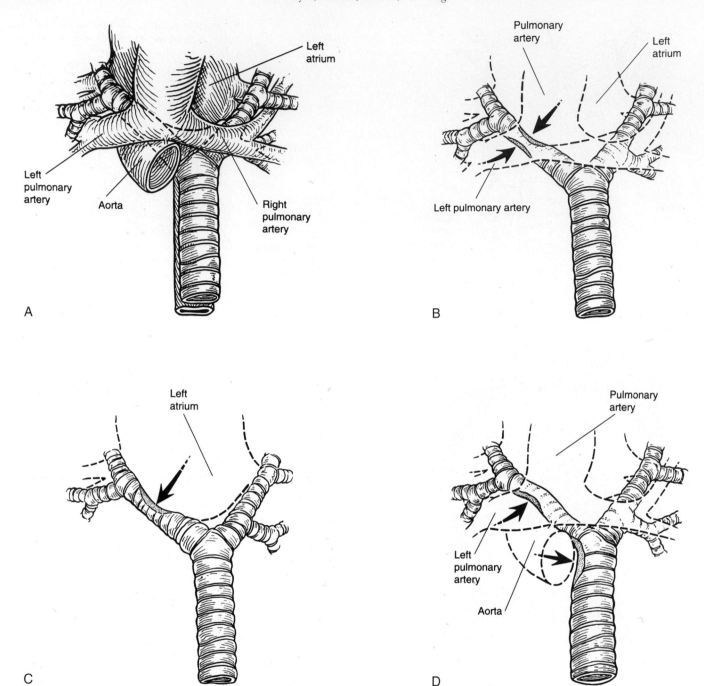

FIGURE 84–9. Congenital cardiac anomalies. *A*, Normal anatomy. *B*, The left main bronchus is narrowed by enlargement of the left atrium and pulmonary artery. *C*, Compression of the left main bronchus due to isolated enlargement of the left atrium. *D*, Compression of the left main bronchus due to isolated enlargement of the pulmonary artery, also displacing the aorta superomedially causing a narrowing of the lower trachea from the left. (From Holinger LD, Lusk RP, Green CG [eds]: *Pediatric Laryngology and Bronchoesophagology.* Philadelphia, Lippincott-Raven, 1997.)

through the fistula assists in identification during thoracotomy and repair. Esophagoscopy is used to determine the length of the upper esophageal pouch and to rule out an upper pouch fistula. Prerepair endoscopy gives important information about the pathologic anatomy, may modify the approach, and provides information that assists in the postoperative care.

The tracheomalacia associated with TEF is a congenital anomaly that is part of the whole malformation and often involves one or both main bronchi.[3] Symptoms are retention of infected secretions, barking cough, aspiration, atelectasis, and cyanotic and apneic spells. Endoscopic examination shows the typical triad of widened tracheal cartilages, ballooning of the posterior membranous wall,

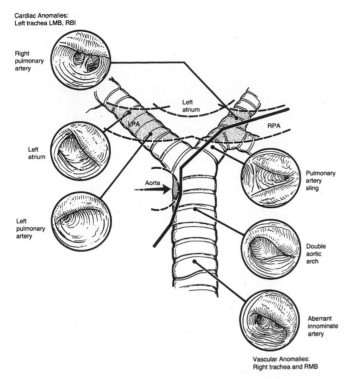

FIGURE 84–10. Endoscopic perspective of the trachea and main bronchi showing areas of compression caused by congenital vascular anomalies and cardiovascular disease. The heavy solid line separates the mainly right-sided compression due to vascular anomalies from the mainly left-sided compression due to cardiac anomalies. Cardiac anomalies may also compress the right bronchus intermedius and middle lobe bronchus. (From Holinger LD, Lusk RP, Green CG [eds]: *Pediatric Laryngology and Bronchoesophagology*. Philadelphia, Lippincott-Raven, 1997.)

and collapse with partial loss of the lower tracheal lumen. Tracheotomy may be indicated in severe cases or in those associated with additional laryngeal or upper airway anomalies.

Squamous epithelium has been demonstrated in the tracheas of children with TEF who clinically have sputum retention. Other factors that contribute to the respiratory obstruction and secretion retention include tracheal compression by the innominate artery, foreign body or food obstructing the esophageal lumen, collapse of the trachea during coughing, and aspiration due to disordered esophageal peristalsis or gastroesophageal reflux.[3]

Thoracotomy with division and oversewing of the fistula tract and repair of the atresia is the usual treatment. The survival rate in patients without additional anomalies is greater than 90%. Postoperative problems include tracheomalacia, gastroesophageal reflux, recurrent fistula, and esophageal stricture. Fistulae recur or persist in approximately 5% of cases.[3] Endoscopic closure of these fistulae has been accomplished.[14] The tract is roughened with a bronchial brush, then plugged with fibrin tissue adhesive.

H-Type Fistula

The H-type fistula is rare but is suspected in infants who have symptoms of coughing, choking, or cyanosis during feeding soon after birth. Copious tracheal secretions, recurrent respiratory tract infections, gurgling respirations, and abdominal distension may be present. Nasogastric tube feeding improves the symptoms.

The best method of diagnosis is to combine endoscopic and radiographic assessment. Contrast esophagography with water-soluble material may show extravasation into the trachea. Bronchoscopy combined with esophagoscopy with a telescope usually will localize the esophageal fistula opening. It may appear as a small slit in an inverted V shape in the anterior upper esophagus more distal to the tracheal opening. The tracheal opening will have a round shape surrounded by prominent blood vessels in the midline of the cervical portion of the posterior membranous wall.

Tracheal Agenesis and Atresia

Tracheal agenesis is a rare developmental anomaly, is untreatable, and is incompatible with life. It is most likely a defect in differentiation in the third or fourth week of embryogenesis. Floyd et al[11] described three types with varying degrees of agenesis and communication with the esophagus.

The neonate has severe respiratory distress at birth and attempts ventilation through the esophageal commu-

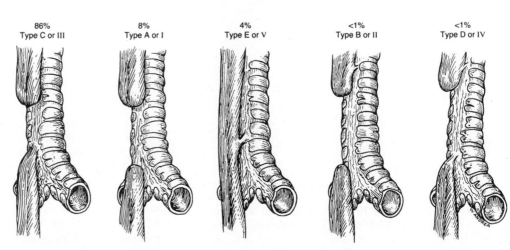

FIGURE 84–11. Tracheoesophageal fistula and esophageal atresia. Type III is the most common, accounting for approximately 86%. (From Holinger LD, Lusk RP, Green CG [eds]: *Pediatric Laryngology and Bronchoesophagology*. Philadelphia, Lippincott-Raven, 1997.)

nication. Attempts to intubate are unsuccessful, and laryngoscopy may reveal coincidental laryngeal anomalies, including laryngeal cleft or elliptical cricoid cartilage.[17] Temporary ventilation may be possible with intubation of the esophagus. Tracheotomy is not successful. Delineation of the tracheoesophageal communication and bronchial tree is possible with endoscopy or contrast infusion through the esophagus, but there have been no survivors.[18]

Tracheal Stenosis

Webs

Discrete congenital stenoses of the soft tissue of the tracheal lumen are rare. Symptoms include biphasic stridor or expiratory wheezing of severity dependent on the degree of narrowing. Simple dilatation is often the only required treatment.

Cartilaginous Stenosis

Complete Tracheal Rings

Congenital tracheal stenosis with complete tracheal rings usually presents in the first year of life, often during an acute respiratory illness. Symptoms may be present at birth and include stridor, retractions, cyanosis, wheezing, and recurrent pneumonia or "croup."

Tracheal narrowing can often be seen on plain radiographs (Fig. 84–12). CT and MRI studies may diagnose the specific length and degree of narrowing and will also detect commonly associated cardiovascular anomalies.[9] In-

volvement ranges from a single ring to the entire length of the trachea.

Treatment is determined by the severity of symptoms. Proximal stenoses are more amenable to surgical repair. Short stenoses may be treated with resection and end-to-end anastomosis. For more lengthy stenoses, pericardial patch repair, slide tracheoplasty, and, more recently, tracheal autograft repair are used. There are larger series of data on pericardial patch repair, but recent data on the autograft technique are promising.[1] Bronchoscopy is used to delineate the stenotic segment and to assess the post-repair site and endotracheal tube placement. Some patients have a difficult prolonged postoperative course requiring multiple bronchoscopic procedures for dilatation and removal of granulation tissue. The overall survival rate is approximately 80%.[1, 9] Between 1996 and 2000, 13 infants at Children's Memorial Hospital in Chicago underwent free tracheal autograft for congenital tracheal stenosis with complete tracheal rings. Twelve of the children were alive and well 2 to 57 months postoperatively. There was one early death due to severe cardiac anomalies and sepsis. Two children have tracheotomies.

Tracheal Cartilaginous Sleeve

Congenital tracheal cartilaginous sleeve is a rare malformation in which the individual tracheal arches are not formed. The trachea appears as a cylinder of vertically fused cartilage with or without a membranous portion (Fig. 84–13). Tracheal cartilaginous sleeve is often associated with craniosynostosis syndromes such as Apert, Pfeiffer, Crouzon, and Goldenhar.[19]

Symptoms may present soon after birth or with acute respiratory illness and consist of biphasic stridor with respiratory distress, cough, and recurrent croup or respiratory infections. Because of the tracheal rigidity, the infants may have difficulty clearing secretions.

Bronchoscopy reveals a smooth anterior tracheal wall without the normal appearance of tracheal arches. The membranous posterior tracheal wall may be normal, reduced, or absent. CT and MRI delineate the lesion. Treatment may include a tracheotomy for pulmonary toilet or removal of obstruction but often is not necessary with early diagnosis and aggressive management of concomitant anomalies and respiratory infections.

Foregut Cysts

Bronchogenic Cysts

Bronchogenic cysts result from abnormal budding of the bronchial tree in which a portion of the lung bud develops independently. The cysts often have cartilage within the cyst wall and are lined with ciliated columnar epithelium. Infants most often present with respiratory distress and may have cough, chest pain, or wheezing. A plain chest radiograph may suggest the diagnosis, but a CT scan and barium esophagram are helpful. The lesions tend to enlarge to cause airway obstruction. The treatment is surgical excision.

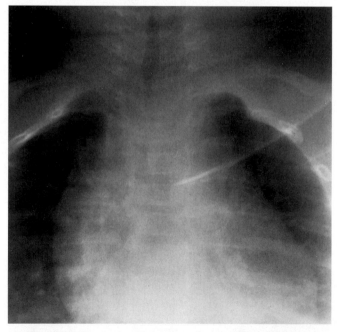

FIGURE 84–12. Chest radiograph of a 7-month-old girl with congenital tracheal stenosis with complete tracheal rings. The air column is narrowed in the middle one third of the trachea. (From Holinger LD, Lusk RP, Green CG [eds]: *Pediatric Laryngology and Bronchoesophagology.* Philadelphia, Lippincott-Raven, 1997.)

lar wall similar to intestine. Symptoms are similar to those of other foregut cysts. Chest radiographs may show the vertebral anomaly with a caudally located cyst.[7]

Bronchial Anomalies

Bronchomalacia

Bronchomalacia is abnormal collapsibility of a main bronchus. The affected bronchus lacks rigidity because of insufficient cartilage or extrinsic compression, and severity depends on the stability and strength of the bronchial wall and the transmural airway pressure. It may be unilateral, bilateral, or associated with tracheomalacia.

Patients usually present in the first 6 months of life after the first upper respiratory infection. In mild cases, there may be no symptoms with quiet respiration. Symptoms may include expiratory wheezing, chronic "congestion" with retained bronchial secretions, and recurrent pneumonia due to poor clearance of secretions. On auscultation, a low-pitched wheeze is audible. Symptoms persist between illnesses, and severity may increase with concomitant small airway disease or cardiac disease. Symptoms typically decrease as the child ages and the diameter of the bronchi increases. Asthma is a common misdiagnosis. Bronchoscopy is often necessary to distinguish bronchomalacia from reactive airway disease refractory to medical therapy.

Plain radiographs usually have normal findings. Barium esophagram is helpful to rule out a vascular ring. Pulmonary function tests show flattening of the flow-volume loop at high lung volumes and have normal results at low lung volumes. Bronchoscopy during spontaneous breathing is diagnostic and may reveal flaccid bronchial walls or a widened membranous portion.

Severe bronchomalacia has been treated with tracheotomy and positive end-expiratory pressure ventilation, endobronchial stenting in life-threatening situations, chest physiotherapy, and prophylactic antibiotics for recurrent pneumonia.[10, 12]

Abnormal Bifurcation

Tracheal Bronchus

The right upper lobe bronchus joins the lower trachea rather than the right main bronchus in approximately 2% of humans. It is the normal anatomy in the pig, cattle, sheep, and other ruminants. The location is above the level of the carina on the right lateral wall and may be segmental, lobar, or supernumerary.[6] It is usually an incidental finding on bronchoscopy performed for other indications and is asymptomatic. Suspicion of this anomaly may arise when decreased right upper lobe breath sounds persist despite the apparently correct location of the endotracheal tube.

High Bifurcation

A short trachea with a high bifurcation has fewer tracheal rings than normal. It has been identified in patients with DiGeorge syndrome, skeletal dysplasias, congenital heart

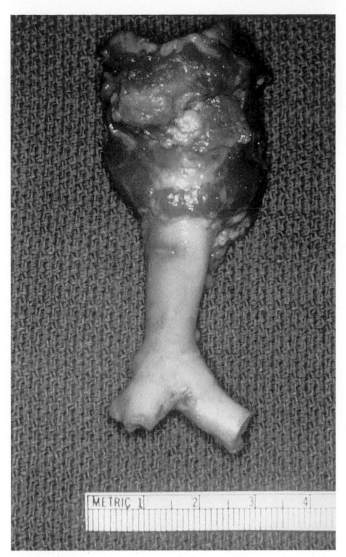

FIGURE 84–13. Congenital tracheal cartilaginous sleeve. An autopsy specimen shows a solid sleeve of cartilage extending from the larynx to involve the main bronchi. (From Holinger LD, Lusk RP, Green CG [eds]: *Pediatric Laryngology and Bronchoesophagology.* Philadelphia, Lippincott-Raven, 1997.)

Intramural Esophageal Cysts (Esophageal Duplication)

Intramural esophageal cysts are true duplications of the esophagus and result from defects in the vacuolation process. They are less common than bronchogenic cysts, lie in close proximity to the esophageal wall, and are lined with ciliated columnar epithelium. Symptoms include airway obstruction, epigastric pain, and vomiting. Diagnosis and treatment are the same as for bronchogenic cysts.

Enteric Cysts

Enteric cysts are usually found in the posterior mediastinum and are commonly associated with vertebral abnormalities. They are usually attached to the vertebral body by fibrous tissue as part of the split notochord syndrome. They have variable types of epithelial lining and a muscu-

disease, and myelomeningocele. The abnormally high carina (T3 or above) can be seen on a posteroanterior chest radiograph. Accidental bronchial intubation is common in a patient with such an anomaly.[6]

Bridging Bronchus

The bridging bronchus was first described in 1976 by Gonzalez-Crussi et al.[13] It is an abnormal branching in which the bronchial drainage of the right middle and lower lobes is provided by a large bronchial branch originating from the left main bronchus and bridging the mediastinum to the left lung. A number of reports of this condition have since been published, but most have been postmortem diagnoses. Wells et al[24] identified four patterns of tracheobronchial branching in patients with pulmonary artery sling. They described bronchial abnormalities in which the middle and lower lobes of the right lung, or entire right lung, are supplied by a bronchus arising more distally in the airway than normal. Often the bridging bronchus and trachea are narrowed by long-segment tracheal stenosis with complete tracheal rings. Patients with bridging bronchi usually have other congenital anomalies such as vascular and cardiac anomalies and imperforate anus. CT, bronchography, bronchoscopy, and echocardiography have all been used to diagnose this lesion. Treatment is surgical, if clinically indicated, during repair of the cardiovascular anomalies.

Bronchial Stenosis

The causes of bronchial stenoses are similar to those of tracheal stenosis. Compressive vascular, cardiac, and congenital cystic lesions and soft tissue or cartilaginous stenoses are causes. Symptoms and treatment depend on the location and severity of the lesion.

Bronchial Agenesis and Atresia

Congenital absence of a bronchus is more common than tracheal agenesis and is compatible with life. There may be complete agenesis of the lung, bronchus, and their vascular supply; aplasia, in which there is a rudimentary bronchus and absent lung; or hypoplasia, in which there is a hypoplastic lung and rudimentary bronchus. Bronchoscopy, CT, and bronchography are used for diagnosis. Other congenital anomalies of the skeletal, cardiovascular, gastrointestinal, and genitourinary systems may also be present. Therapy and prognosis depend on the symptomatology, precise anatomy, and associated anomalies.[2]

Williams-Campbell Syndrome

Williams-Campbell syndrome is a rare congenital absence of cartilage in subsegmental bronchi leading to distal airway collapse and bronchiectasis. Patients usually present in early childhood with cough, wheezing, and recurrent pulmonary infections. Physical findings are typical of chronic lung disease. Chest radiography and bronchography demonstrate thin-walled cystic bronchiectasis with

enlargement of smaller bronchi on inspiration and collapse with expiration. Inspiratory and expiratory CT images can demonstrate the syndrome. Prognosis is variable, and there is no known treatment. Lung transplantation has been attempted.[21]

Bronchomegaly

Mounier-Kuhn syndrome is a syndrome in which the trachea and bronchi are enlarged. It may be associated with Ehlers-Danlos syndrome. Symptoms are recurrent pneumonia, bronchitis, and chronic cough with poor clearance of secretions.

Pulmonary Anomalies

Pulmonary Sequestration

Pulmonary sequestration is a mass of abnormal pulmonary tissue lacking a normal connection to the tracheobronchial tree and can be classified as intralobar or extralobar. An abnormal arterial supply arises from the systemic circulation below the diaphragm. The extralobar type is contained in its own pleural envelope and usually has systemic venous drainage. The intralobar sequestration is within the pulmonary parenchyma and drains into the pulmonary venous system. Patients present with recurrent infection, mass effect, or hemoptysis. Plain radiography may reveal a posteromedial lower lobe mass, typically on the right. Ultrasonography, CT, or MRI may show variable cystic and solid components. Angiography confirms the aberrant blood supply. Treatment is surgical excision.

Congenital Cystic Adenomatoid Malformation

Congenital cystic adenomatoid malformation is a rare lesion characterized by cystic spaces of varying sizes. The most accepted classification system divides the lesions into three types based on histologic findings and the gross size of the cysts. Large lesions that cause mediastinal shift resulting in cardiovascular compromise, contralateral lung hypoplasia, maternal polyhydramnios, and fetal hydrops have a poor prognosis and often result in intrauterine death. Early diagnosis with ultrasonography makes possible in utero treatment with thoracocentesis, thoracoamniotic shunt, or surgical excision.[5]

REFERENCES

1. Backer CL, Mavroudis C, Dunham ME, et al. Intermediate-term results of the free tracheal autograft for long segment congenital tracheal stenosis. J Pediatr Surg 35:813, 2000.
2. Baktai G, Szekely E, Kadar L. Bronchial agenesia, aplasia and hypoplasia: analysis of 32 cases. Chest 112:134S, 1997.
3. Benjamin B. Endoscopy in esophageal atresia and tracheoesophageal fistula. Ann Otol Rhinol Laryngol 90:376, 1981.
4. Benjamin B. Tracheomalacia in infants and children. Ann Otol Rhinol Laryngol 93:438, 1984.
5. Cha I, Adzick NS, Harrison MR, et al. Fetal congenital cystic

adenomatoid malformations of the lung: a clinicopathologic study of eleven cases. Am J Surg Pathol 21:537, 1997.

6. Chen JC, Holinger LD. Congenital tracheal anomalies: pathology study using serial macrosections and review of the literature. Pediatr Pathol 14:513, 1994.

7. Cohen SR, Geller KA, Birns JW, et al. Foregut cysts in infants and children: diagnosis and management. Ann Otol Rhinol Laryngol 91:622, 1982.

8. Dayan SH, Dunham ME, Backer CL, et al. Slide tracheoplasty in the management of congenial tracheal stenosis. Ann Otol Rhinol Laryngol 106:914, 1997.

9. Dunham ME, Holinger LD, Backer CL, et al. Management of severe congenital tracheal stenosis. Ann Otol Rhinol Laryngol 103:351, 1994.

10. Finder JD. Primary bronchomalacia in infants and children. J Pediatr 130:59, 1997.

11. Floyd J, Campbell DC, Dominy DE. Agenesis of the trachea. Am Rev Respir Dis 86:557, 1962.

12. Furman RH, Backer CL, Dunham ME, et al. The use of balloon-expandable metallic stents in the treatment of pediatric tracheomalacia and bronchomalacia. Arch Otolaryngol Head Neck Surg 125:203, 1999.

13. Gonzalez-Crussi F, Padilla LM, Miller JK, et al. Bridging bronchus. Am J Dis Child 130:1015, 1976.

14. Hoelzer DJ, Luft JD. Successful long-term endoscopic closure of a recurrent tracheoesophageal fistula with fibrin glue in a child. Int J Pediatr Otorhinolaryngol 48:259, 1999.

15. Holinger LD. Etiology of stridor in the neonate, infant, and child. Ann Otol 89:397, 1980.

16. Holinger LD, Green CG, Benjamin B, et al. Tracheobronchial tree. In Pediatric Laryngology and Bronchoesophagology. Philadelphia, Lippincott-Raven, 1997, pp 187–213.

17. Holinger LD, Volk MS, Tucker GFJ. Congenital laryngeal anomalies associated with tracheal agenesis. Ann Otol Rhinol Laryngol 96:505, 1987.

18. Koltai PJ, Quiney R. Tracheal agenesis. Ann Otol Rhinol Laryngol 101:560, 1992.

19. Lin SY, Chen JC, Hotaling AJ, et al. Congenital tracheal cartilagionous sleeve. Laryngoscope 105:1213, 1995.

20. McLaughlin RB, Wetmore RF, Tavill MA, et al. Vascular anomalies causing symptomatic tracheobronchial compression. Laryngoscope 109:312, 1999.

21. Palmer SM, Layish DT, Kussin PS, et al. Lung transplantation for Williams-Campbell syndrome. Chest 113:534, 1998.

22. Pu WT, Chung T, Hoffer FA, et al. Diagnosis and management of agenesis of the right lung and left pulmonary artery sling. Am J Cardiol 78:723, 1996.

23. Smith RJH, Smith MCF, Glossop LP, et al. Congenital vascular anomalies causing tracheoesophageal compression. Arch Otolaryngol 110:82, 1984.

24. Wells TR, Gwinn JL, Landing BH, et al. Reconsideration of the anatomy of sling left pulmonary artery: the association of one form with bridging bronchus and imperforate anus: anatomic and diagnostic aspects. J Pediatr Surg 23:892, 1988.

85

Infections of the Lower Respiratory Tract

Patricia A. Hughes, D.O., Paul G. Comber, M.D., Ph.D., and Martha L. Lepow, M.D.

Infections of the respiratory tract constitute the most common cause of morbidity and mortality in infants and young children. This chapter includes infections of the retropharyngeal space, epiglottis, larynx, trachea, bronchi, bronchioles, and lungs.

The etiologic agents of disease and anatomic predisposition to infection are age related. Since the lower airway in a young child is small, obstruction may be a significant problem. Children in the 1- to 3-year-old age group have the greatest frequency of illness attributable to respiratory viruses[13] and bacteria such as *Streptococcus pneumoniae* (pneumococcus), *Haemophilus* species, and *Moraxella catarrhalis*. The first infection with these organisms frequently leads to more severe disease in which both the upper and the lower portions of the respiratory tract are affected. Reexposure later in childhood usually leads to milder disease because of preexisting immunity. Table 85–1 lists the more common infectious agents and the anatomic sites of predilection. It is apparent that the same pathogen may infect more than one site. The anatomic location of the infectious process is the most important factor in management as well as in predicting the outcome of the illness. There is also convincing evidence that passive smoke inhalation either in the home or in day care settings markedly increases a child's risk of respiratory illness.[35]

Acute Epiglottitis

Incidence and Etiology

Epiglottitis is almost always bacterial in origin, and *Haemophilus influenzae b* (HIB) previously accounted for more than 90% of cases. With licensure of conjugate HIB vaccines in 1991 and close to universal infant immunization, the incidence of systemic HIB disease and carrier state has declined precipitously.[2] The incidence of epiglottitis due to HIB has decreased 80% to 90% since the introduction of this vaccine. Infection by group A beta-hemolytic streptococcus now accounts for the majority of the rare cases of epiglottitis that are seen.[29]

Clinical Features

Acute epiglottitis usually has a sudden onset and a rapidly progressive course. Typically, the child develops a high fever with respiratory distress, drooling, and painful swallowing. The patient classically sits hunched forward with neck extended and mouth open (sniffing position). The illness may quickly progress to respiratory obstruction. Manipulation of the pharynx (with tongue depressor or swab) or airway may result in complete obstruction of the larynx and therefore should be avoided. A lateral radiograph of the neck to assess the retropharyngeal space and remainder of the upper airway should be done only if the diagnosis is uncertain. An individual capable of emergency intubation or tracheostomy should always accompany the patient going for radiographs.

The classic radiographic features include edema of the epiglottis and a ballooning of the hypopharynx (Fig. 85–1). Epiglottitis is a medical emergency and requires the establishment of an airway by intubation or tracheotomy. A protocol for the management of epiglottitis should be in place in all hospitals caring for children. The method of airway intervention that is selected depends on the expertise of the staff caring for the patient. Intubation requires sedation and the constant availability of personnel capable of reintubating the patient should extubation occur. On the other hand, a tracheotomy requires continuous attention to be sure the secretions are cleared. This is especially important in the very small child, in whom the tube may easily become occluded, resulting in asphyxia. Complications of properly performed intubation or tracheotomy are infrequent (see Chap. 81). A single dose of steroid can be used prior to extubation.

Laboratory Features

Blood cultures should always be obtained, although bacteremia is uncommon with either group A streptococcus or pneumococcus. At the time of intubation, culture samples should be taken from the epiglottis. The white blood cell count is usually elevated, and the differential count shows a predominance of polymorphonuclear leukocytes. Meningitis or infection at other sites is uncommon.

Management

After an artificial airway has been placed, it should remain until spasm and edema have subsided and the infection is under control. This usually requires 2 to 3 days.

TABLE 85–1. Association of Etiologic Agent with Anatomic Site in Childhood Respiratory Tract Infection

Anatomic Site	Bacteria	Viruses
Nose (sinuses)	*Branhamella catarrhalis*	Rhinoviruses
	Beta-hemolytic streptococci	
	Streptococcus pneumoniae	Influenza viruses A and B
	Haemophilus influenzae	
	Staphylococcus aureus	
	Corynebacterium diphtheriae	
Pharynx and tonsils	Beta-hemolytic streptococci	Adenoviruses
	C. diphtheriae	Epstein-Barr virus
		Parainfluenza viruses 1 and 2
		Coxsackievirus and echovirus
Epiglottis	*S. pneumoniae*	
	Beta-hemolytic streptococci	
Larynx	*C. diphtheriae*	Parainfluenza viruses 1 and 2
		Influenza viruses A and B
		Rubella
		Varicella-zoster
Trachea	*S. aureus*	Parainfluenza viruses 1 and 2
	H. influenzae type B	Influenza viruses A and B
Bronchi and bronchioles	*S. pneumoniae*	Respiratory syncytial virus
	Bordetella pertussis	Adenoviruses
	Chlamydia pneumoniae	Parainfluenza viruses 1, 2, and 3
		Rhinoviruses
		Measles virus

The clinical state of the patient and appearance with direct visualization should determine when extubation or decannulation should occur. Antibiotics should always be used. Initial treatment with cefuroxime, cefotaxime, or ceftriaxone is recommended. These antibiotics are effective against pneumococcus and group A streptococcus (Table 85–2). Vancomycin is an alternative if the patient cannot tolerate cephalosporins or if resistant pneumococcus is suspected. Therapy can be modified after the susceptibility of the offending organism is known. Pneumococci resistant to penicillin and trimethoprim-sulfamethoxazole have been increasing.[11, 44] Sensitivity studies should be carried out on all pneumococci associated with invasive disease. Group A streptococci are sensitive to penicillin; azithromycin is an alternative.

Acute Croup

Acute croup, or laryngotracheobronchitis, is another obstructive disease of the subglottic airway that may be spasmodic or follow an upper respiratory tract infection.

Etiology and Epidemiology

Infectious croup almost always has a viral cause (see Table 85–1). Parainfluenza and influenza viruses are frequently implicated pathogens, although measles, varicella, and other viruses can cause similar symptoms. Diagnosis is based on the clinical features.

Parainfluenza virus, especially type 1, frequently induces croup in clusters of cases in the spring and fall. It is generally benign and occurs primarily in children 1 to 3 years of age. Infection may extend from the larynx to the trachea, bronchi, and bronchioles (Figs. 85–2 and 85–3).

Clinical Features

The patient usually has a low-grade or moderate fever, and there may be antecedent upper respiratory tract symptoms. Respiratory distress occurs with an increased respiratory rate, inspiratory stridor, hoarseness, a barking cough, and expiratory rhonchi. The larynx alone may be affected or the lower airway may also be involved. Although many children can be managed as outpatients, children with stridor at rest will probably benefit from observation and treatment in a hospital setting. If there are retractions and restlessness or significant tachypnea,

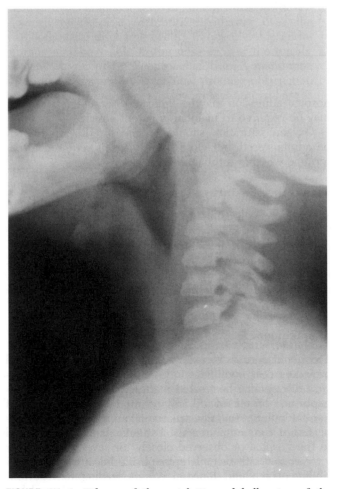

FIGURE 85–1. Edema of the epiglottis and ballooning of the hypopharynx in a case of epiglottitis (the "thumb" sign).

tive immunity, and recipients had more severe disease (including two deaths) when subsequently infected with RSV.[39] Recently, vaccines using purified RSV viral proteins have been in clinical trials.[37]

Passive immunity with high-titer human pooled anti-RSV intravenous immunoglobulin has been successfully used to prevent severe RSV infection in high-risk infants but is contraindicated in children with congenital heart disease.[50] Further work with passive RSV immunity has led to the licensure of the first humanized monoclonal antibody for clinical use, palivizumab. When given to premature infants (born at less than 32 weeks' gestation) and infants with chronic lung disease, it significantly reduces RSV hospitalization.[60] The dose is 15 mg/kg given as a monthly intramuscular injection during the RSV season. All high-risk infants younger than 6 months of age at the start of the RSV season should receive passive immunization throughout the entire RSV season.

Pneumonia

Definition

Pneumonia is a lower respiratory tract illness that involves the lung parenchyma, including the alveoli, the interstitial spaces, and the distal bronchioles. Clinically, it is characterized by fever, cough, and tachypnea. Causative agents are listed in Table 85–3.

Nonbacterial Pneumonia

Unlike infections in adults, the majority of episodes of acute pneumonia in infants and children younger than 4 years old are caused by viruses, specifically RSV, parainfluenza viruses, and influenza A[45] (see Table 85–3). Peak attack rates occur between 2 and 4 years of age, and there is a slight male predominance. Seasonal epidemics occur corresponding to the times when these viruses are circulating. Crowding and group settings, such as day care centers, enhance transmission. Previously, varicella pneumonia would be included in the differential diagnosis, but with widespread immunization, the disease will likely be rare.

Pathogenesis

The pathogenesis of viral pneumonia primarily involves a descending infection from an initial upper respiratory infection. Loss of ciliated epithelium and damage to surfactant-producing cells in the alveoli characterize this distal spread. As infection progresses, mononuclear cells begin to invade the area, and the infected epithelium sloughs into the lumen of the bronchioles, causing obstruction. With adenovirus infections, submucosal tissue can be injured and a necrotizing pneumonitis can occur. More commonly, the primary tissues involved are peribronchial, causing a diffuse interstitial inflammation.

Clinical Features

Clinically, viral pneumonia has a gradual onset preceded by several days of upper respiratory symptoms and low-grade fever. In infants, apnea may be the only presenting sign. Nonspecific rashes, loss of appetite, and vomiting can occur. Fever rarely exceeds 39°C. Auscultatory findings are extremely variable and may even be normal. An interstitial process with hyperinflation and areas of atelectasis are the most common radiographic findings; however, a recent report indicated that as many as one third of culture-proven viral pneumonia cases had an alveolar pattern on chest radiographic examination.[1] The white blood cell count is extremely variable and can even be normal, although lymphocytosis may indicate viral pneumonia.

The differential diagnosis of acute viral pneumonia includes recurrent aspiration, especially with gastroesophageal reflux, asthma, foreign body aspiration, and congenital abnormalities (such as lung sequestration and lobar emphysema).

Supportive care is the mainstay of therapy for viral pneumonia. Oxygen, humidified air, and therapy to aid in mobilizing secretions are all extremely important. Influenza vaccination is recommended for children younger than 6 months of age with immunodeficiencies (including those with symptomatic HIV infection), chronic lung diseases, hemodynamically significant cardiac defects, and hemoglobinopathies who may be at risk for more severe pneumonia. There are insufficient data to recommend amantadine or ranitidine for prophylaxis in children with influenza A. Zanamivir and oseltamivir, new antivirals, are approved for use only in persons older than 12 years and older than 18 years, respectively. When given for acute infections, these agents must be used within 24 to 48 hours of symptoms onset to achieve efficacy. They may also help prevent secondary spread among family members.[33]

TABLE 85–3. Most Common Causes of Pneumonias by Patient Age

Age	Viruses	Bacteria
Newborn	Herpes simplex virus	Group B streptococcus
	Cytomegalovirus	*Escherichia coli*
	Adenovirus	*Chlamydia trachomatis*
		Listeria monocytogenes
Infant–5 years	Respiratory syncytial virus	*Mycoplasma pneumoniae*
	Parainfluenza viruses 1 and 3	*Streptococcus pneumoniae*
	Influenza virus A	*Haemophilus influenzae*
	Adenoviruses	
Greater than 5 years	Influenza viruses A and B	*M. pneumoniae*
		S. pneumoniae
		Beta-hemolytic streptococcus
		Staphylococcus aureus
		Chlamydia pneumoniae

Bacterial Pneumonia

Pathogenesis

Bacterial pneumonia remains a significant cause of respiratory disease, particularly in young infants and older children. In the newborn, the primary bacterial pathogens responsible for pneumonia are group B streptococci, gram-negative *Enterobacteriaceae*, and chlamydial pneumonia, reflecting those organisms encountered in the maternal genital tract that can be aspirated at birth (see Table 85-3). Beyond the newborn period until age 5, *S. pneumoniae* is the most common bacterial isolate in children. In school-age children, *Mycoplasma pneumoniae* is the most frequent cause of pneumonia. *Chlamydia pneumoniae* TWAR strain is an important pathogen, especially in adolescents. The symptoms are similar to those of mycoplasma infection.[41]

Group A streptococci and, rarely, *Staphylococcus aureus* can cause pneumonia. *Legionella pneumophila* is an infrequent bacterial pathogen with an incidence of infection in children of 1 case per 1 million inhabitants per year.[43] *Legionella* infection historically has most often occurred in epidemics because of contamination of potable water sources, but sporadic cases, especially in immunosuppressed patients, are increasingly being reported.[48] The symptoms of *Legionella* infection are similar to those of pneumococcal pneumonia and tend to be more acute in onset than infection with *Mycoplasma* or *Chlamydia*.

The bacterial pathogens that cause pneumonia in older infants and children are the normal inhabitants of the upper respiratory tract, and spread is usually from droplets. It is rare to find epidemics of bacterial pneumonia, although the incidence of pneumococcal pneumonia is reported to increase after periods of epidemic viral pneumonia, especially influenza. *Mycoplasma pneumoniae* infection is generally endemic within a given community, but localized outbreaks can occur.

Because of ciliated respiratory epithelium, the cough reflex, alveolar macrophages, and lymphatic drainage, the lung is usually well protected from invading bacteria. It is speculated that a preceding viral illness may predispose the host to bacterial pneumonia, perhaps by affecting ciliary motility, especially in the case of influenza.[24]

Clinical Features

In contrast to viral pneumonias, bacterial pneumonias are more sudden in onset, rapidly progressive, and accompanied by high fevers, often associated with rigors or sweats. Tachypnea and a productive cough are usually present in the older child. In younger children, however, the signs of pneumonia may be nonspecific, and extrapulmonary signs such as abdominal pain may be the only presenting complaint. Lower lobe pneumonia can cause emesis and abdominal pain without significant pulmonary symptoms in patients of any age. Blood culture samples should be obtained in cases of pneumonia; however, the likelihood of obtaining an etiologic organism in the blood in children is less than in adults.[15] Usually the total white blood cell count is elevated, with a predominance of polymorphonuclear leukocytes.

The chest radiographic examination in acute bacterial pneumonia most commonly reveals a lobar consolidation, particularly when *Pneumococcus* is the cause, although a bronchiolar and even an interstitial pattern can occur. Pneumatoceles on chest radiographic films are characteristic of infection with *S. aureus*. *M. pneumoniae* infection usually produces acute bilateral interstitial pneumonia but can also appear as lobar pneumonia.[16]

It is difficult to make a definitive bacteriologic diagnosis in infants and young children. Older cooperative children can produce sputum that aids in defining the etiologic agent. Younger children, however, usually swallow their secretions. Characteristic findings on chest radiographs along with systemic manifestations and an elevated white blood cell count may support a presumptive diagnosis of bacterial pneumonia. The nonspecific cold agglutination test and specific immunoglobulin M serologic tests for *M. pneumoniae* may aid in making this diagnosis. Polymerase chain reaction testing of throat or tracheal secretions can be useful in the diagnosis of *M. pneumoniae* infection. More invasive techniques such as bronchoscopy or biopsy are generally reserved for children who are critically ill and are failing to respond to conventional therapy. If pleural fluid is present, a sample should be obtained by thoracentesis and sent for culture.

Treatment

The proper choice of antibiotics requires knowledge of expected pathogens according to age. In newborns, ampicillin and gentamicin or cefotaxime are appropriate initial agents for the treatment of the most likely pathogens (see Table 85-2). In children from 1 month to 5 years old, it is important first to assess the need for hospitalization. For outpatient management, amoxicillin at doses to produce efficacy against the resistant pneumococcus (80 mg/kg per day) is an appropriate initial antibiotic choice. Also, second-generation cephalosporins such as cefuroxime axetil, amoxicillin/clavulanate, or a macrolide may also be appropriate.[34] If hospitalization is necessary because of the severity of illness in the child, parenteral antibiotics such as cefuroxime or ceftriaxone with efficacy against pneumococcus should be given. If there is failure of response, vancomycin should be added in the event of cephalosporin resistance. If clinical signs or radiographic findings suggest *S. aureus* pneumonia, a penicillinase-resistant penicillin (such as oxacillin) should be used. If *M. pneumoniae* or *C. pneumoniae* is the suspected etiologic agent, erythromycin is indicated. New macrolides (e.g., clarithromycin, azithromycin) may also be useful but have yet to be proven equally efficacious. If a specific pathogen is recovered, therapy should be appropriately narrowed. The recently licensed conjugate pneumococcal vaccine will undoubtedly decrease the incidence of pneumococcal pneumonia in children, as has been demonstrated in preliminary studies.[6]

Parapneumonic effusions are frequently associated with bacterial pneumonias caused by pneumococcus, HIB, *S. aureus*, *M. pneumoniae*, and group A beta-hemolytic streptococcus.[25] Thoracentesis should be performed on all nonloculated effusions of 10 mm or greater in a lateral decubitus chest radiograph. The pH, glucose level, lactate dehydrogenase activity, protein level, cell count, and Gram stain with culture provide useful information for therapy. Open chest tube drainage is indicated for loculated effusions or empyema defined as pus in the pleural space or positive culture in the pleural fluid. The most frequent bacterial isolates in pleural effusions (in decreasing order of prevalence) are *Streptococcus pneumoniae* (including penicillin-resistant pneumococcus), *Staphylococcus aureus*, and anaerobic organisms.[7, 10, 32] A large series of fungal empyemas was recently reported from Taiwan[40]; however, a fungal cause is uncommon in the United States. The need for surgical management of empyema in childhood remains controversial. Chest tube drainage and antibiotics alone produced favorable outcomes in some series.[46] However, complicated effusions (low pH or glucose level, high protein or lactate dehydrogenase level) usually require the instillation of streptokinase through the chest tube or surgical decortication, or both.[17]

Aspiration Pneumonia

Aspiration of gastric contents, hydrocarbons, oropharyngeal secretions, foreign bodies, or water, as in cases of near drowning, can result in pneumonia. It may be chronic, as in cases of neurologic or muscular impairment of swallowing. In cases of large-volume aspiration or foreign body aspirations, bronchoscopy is indicated. In the acute case of aspiration, therapy with penicillin or clindamycin may be useful, since oral bacteria will predominate. Gentamicin, cefotaxime, or ceftriaxone may also be useful for gram-negative flora.

Uncommon Infections in Normal Hosts

Rarely, exposure to *Histoplasma capsulatum* or *Coccidioides immitis* may result in pneumonia that mimics viral infections or malignancies. Serologic examination, analysis of urine for antigen, sputum for smear and culture, and occasionally lung biopsy may be necessary to make a diagnosis. When there has been exposure to a wild small mammal, *Francisella tularensis* should be considered, and psittacosis may occur when there is avian exposure.

Tuberculosis

Both the advent of the HIV epidemic and the emergence of multidrug-resistant strains have caused a resurgence of interest in *Mycobacterium* tuberculosis.

From 1985 through 1992, the number of reported cases of tuberculosis in the United States steadily increased. The children who are most susceptible to infection with tuberculosis are those who live with adults who are at high risk for acquiring the disease. Children younger than 14 years of age do not produce enough sputum to transmit tuberculosis, unless a cavity can be seen on a chest radiograph. Mantoux tuberculin skin testing with 5 μ PPD is still the best screening test for mycobacterial tuberculosis. In children who have contact

with an adult with known tuberculosis or who are infected with HIV, an induration of 5 mm should be considered positive. Ten millimeters of induration is considered positive in children younger than 4 years of age with underlying chronic diseases or who come from a foreign country where tuberculosis is endemic. An induration of greater than 15 mm is positive for children older than 4 years who have no other risk factors. However, 10% to 20% of children with tuberculosis may fail to respond to skin testing because of anergy.

Microbiologic documentation of tuberculosis is difficult to obtain in children but should always be attempted. Gastric lavage obtained in the morning is more sensitive than bronchial lavage, but the combined lavage findings are positive in only about 40% of children with pulmonary tuberculosis. It is therefore important to identify the adult contact case to obtain bacteriologic diagnosis and drug susceptibility. A high index of suspicion for pulmonary tuberculosis should be maintained in any child with hilar adenopathy or an indolent segmental pneumonia with or without effusion. The recommended treatment is shown in Table 85-2. Isoniazid daily for 9 months is recommended for children with latent infection, defined as a positive skin test but no evidence of disease.

The Immunocompromised Child

Pneumonia in the immunocompromised child presents a diagnostic dilemma for the clinician.[51] All classes of microbes as well as malignancy, radiation, or chemotherapeutic toxicities or cardiac failure can produce infiltrates in the lung.

Susceptibility to particular pathogens depends on which part or parts of the immune system are deficient, the cause of the immunodeficient state, the length of time the patient has been in such a state, and the source of transplanted organs (Table 85-4). Also, common respiratory viruses such as RSV, parainfluenza, or influenza can cause serious disease in the immunocompromised host. Children with deficiencies in humoral immunity or complement or with asplenia are susceptible to infection with encapsulated bacteria, such as *Pneumococcus*. These children are candidates for the pneumococcal vaccine, and this should decrease the incidence of this disease.

The child with an underlying hematologic malignancy has multiple risk factors for pneumonia. Neutropenia caused by the underlying disease or chemotherapy predisposes the child to common bacterial pneumonias, alpha-hemolytic streptococci, and gram-negative pathogens. On chest radiographs, these pneumonias generally have a lobar distribution. Prolonged neutropenia increases the susceptibility to fungi, including *Candida*, *Aspergillus*, and *Mucor*, which appear as a diffuse interstitial process or as a fluffy round infiltrate "fungal ball." Included in the differential diagnosis of interstitial pneumonias in these children is infection with *Pneumocystis carinii*. Since prophylactic trimethoprim-sulfamethoxazole has become standard with children with hematologic malignancy, the incidence of disease due to *P. carinii* has fallen dramatically. However, if compliance is questionable or the child has a

TABLE 85-4. Pulmonary Pathogens Associated with Immunodeficient States

Disorder	Bacteria	Viruses	Fungi	Protozoa	Noninfectious Agents
Neutrophil disorders	*Staphylococcus aureus* *Haemophilus influenzae* type B *Pneumococcus*		*Candida*		
Oncologic treatment or chemotherapy	Alpha-hemolytic streptococci *Pneumococcus* Gram-negative organisms	Cytomegalovirus Herpes simplex Varicella Epstein-Barr	*Candida* *Mucor*	*Pneumocystis carinii*	Graft-vs-host-disease Chemical or radiation exposure Malignancy
B-cell disorders	*H. influenzae* type B *Pneumococcus*		*Aspergillus*		
T-cell disorders (especially HIV)	*Pneumococcus* *Mycobacteria* species	Cytomegalovirus Herpes simplex	*Candida* *Cryptococcus*	*Pneumocystis carinii* *Toxoplasma gondii*	Lymphocytic interstitial pneumonitis
Solid organ transplant	*S. aureus* Gram-negative organisms	Cytomegalovirus Herpes simplex	*Candida* *Aspergillus* *Mucor*	*Pneumocystis carinii*	

dry cough, hypoxia, or an increase in serum lactate dehydrogenase levels, the diagnosis of *Pneumocystis* infection should be entertained.

The recipient of a bone marrow transplant has similar susceptibilities to infection as the child with hematologic malignancies but also has additional risks associated with the graft. The immunosuppressive agents used to decrease the graft rejection puts this child at increased risk for certain viral pathogens, particularly cytomegalovirus, herpes simplex virus, Epstein-Barr virus, adenoviruses, and *P. carinii*. These generally produce a diffuse interstitial pattern on chest radiographs. Graft-versus-host disease is another major contributor to pneumonia in bone marrow transplant patients and may present with infiltrates at any time following transplant. In children with solid organ transplants, cytomegalovirus is the most significant pathogen, causing interstitial disease.

Children infected with HIV represent an increasing population of immunocompromised hosts. The most common initial acquired immunodeficiency syndrome–defining illness in children is *P. carinii* pneumonia[64]; however, with early identification of infected infants, prophylaxis, and institution of antiretroviral therapy, the incidence of *P. carinii* pneumonia has been markedly decreased. Another respiratory illness that seems to be uniquely associated with HIV in children is lymphocytic interstitial pneumonitis. This disease is characterized by a diffuse alveolar process on chest radiographs and pathologically by migration of lymphocytes into the interstitial spaces. Often, extrapulmonary lymph node enlargement is present. Steroid therapy is indicated for exacerbations of this disease. Mycobacteria, cytomegalovirus, and *Toxoplasma gondii* can also cause disease in these children, although less commonly than occurs in HIV-infected adults.

Pneumonitis from varicella-zoster virus can be seen in any immunosuppressed patient exposed to children with varicella. It has even been reported in otherwise immunocompetent asthmatic patients being treated with a short course of oral steroids.[22] It is characterized by fever, cough, dyspnea, tachypnea, and an interstitial pattern on the chest radiograph. Patients with varicella pneumonitis are usually extremely ill, and the mortality rate is 10% to 20%.[23]

Flexible bronchoscopy with lavage is the primary method of diagnosis of pneumonia in the immunocompromised patient. Bronchoalveolar lavage specimens can be examined by many methods, including bacterial and viral culture, Gomori methenamine silver stain (for fungus and *Pneumocystis*), polymerase chain reaction, immunofluorescence, and in situ hybridization (for cytomegalovirus and other viruses).[19] Open lung biopsy is usually reserved for critically ill patients without a diagnosis. Transbronchial biopsy is technically limited in pediatric patients and is possible only in adolescents. Inducing sputum with aerosolized hypertonic saline may be helpful in the older cooperative child but is ineffective in younger children. Analysis of sputum samples by polymerase chain reaction for *Pneumocystis* is currently being explored to aid in the diagnosis of *P. carinii* pneumonia.[57]

Therapy is usually begun empirically and is directed at the suspected pathogens. For the neutropenic patient, broad-spectrum antibiotics effective against gram-positive and gram-negative organisms are given. Erythromycin and amphotericin may need to be added. More invasive diagnostic procedures are reserved for the child who fails to respond to therapy. Ganciclovir (5 mg/kg IV q 12 h) is used to treat suspected cytomegaloviral pneumonia, while acyclovir (1500 mg/m² per day, divided, q 8 h) is used for varicella pneumonia.

For the HIV-infected child with diffuse bilateral interstitial disease, therapy with high-dose trimethoprim-sulfamethoxazole (20 mg/kg) should be started. If there is failure to respond, more invasive techniques may be necessary to establish a diagnosis. If sulfonamides are not tolerated, intravenous pentamidine at 4 mg/kg per day may be used.

Lung Abscess

Lung abscess is extremely uncommon in children. Necrosis of lung tissue may occur because of aspiration, obstruction by a foreign body, or infection of congenital cystic lesions. If the sputum smells foul, anaerobes are probably the cause. Otherwise, aerobic pyogenic organisms are the most likely cause.

Bronchoscopy may be necessary, regardless of cause, for diagnosis and treatment and possible drainage. Clindamycin is the drug of choice. Percutaneous drainage is not usually recommended because of the risk of fistula formation.

Bronchiectasis

Definition

Bronchiectasis, or dilatation of bronchi, may be congenital, from postnatal arrest in development, or acquired. Acquired bronchiectasis results most frequently from antecedent infection, such as pertussis, rubeola, recurrent pneumonia, or presence of a foreign body. A triad described by Kartagener consists of sinusitis, bronchiectasis, and situs inversus. This syndrome is autosomal recessive and results from structurally abnormal respiratory cilia. Abnormal or absent cilia can be found without the full triad and frequently results in bronchiectasis. Ciliary biopsy confirms the diagnosis.

Bronchiectasis is also a common finding in cystic fibrosis patients with moderate to severe disease. Patients with asthma, hypogammaglobulinemia, sinusitis, tuberculosis, and repeated pulmonary infections may rarely develop bronchiectasis.

Pathogenesis and Pathology

Inflammation secondary to obstruction of bronchi is most important. In areas that are atelectatic as a result of obstruction, bronchial secretions favor both aerobic and anaerobic growths. The greatest damage is to the cartilage of the bronchi. Columnar cells are replaced by cuboid ones, and cilia are scanty. The left lower lobe is most frequently involved, followed by the right middle lobe.

Clinical Features

The onset may be acute or insidious. The most frequent symptom is productive cough. Hemoptysis may occur from erosion of the bronchial wall. The height of a fever is variable, and dyspnea is a late feature.

Radiographic Findings

Persistence of atelectasis and failure of the chest radiographic appearance to return to normal after appropriate therapy is suspicious for underlying bronchiectasis. The radiographic finding of a bronchus that is larger than the adjacent bronchial artery ("tram tracking") is pathognomonic for bronchiectasis. A high-resolution computed tomography scan is the most sensitive diagnostic test.

Treatment

Medical management includes postural drainage and other mechanisms for decreasing obstruction and atelectasis. Prompt treatment of exacerbations with antibiotics is recommended, but controversy exists about the use of continuous prophylactic antibiotics in these children because of concerns about antibiotic resistance and side effects. Segmental disease that is not controlled after an appropriate period of chemotherapy may require bronchoscopy or surgical resection. Bronchoscopy may also be indicated to clear obstruction for patients with localized atelectasis.

SELECTED REFERENCES

Klassen TP. Recent advances in the treatment of bronchiolitis and laryngitis. Pediatr Clin North Am 44:249, 1997.
> This is an excellent review of the treatment options for bronchiolitis and croup.

McCracken GH. Diagnosis and management of pneumonia in children. Pediatr Infect Dis J 19:924, 2000.
> This is a recent review of pathogens, epidemiology, clinical features, and treatment of pneumonia in children.

REFERENCES

1. Abzug MJ, Beam AC, Gyorkos EA, et al. Viral pneumonia in the first month of life. Pediatr Infect Dis J 9:881, 1990.
2. Adams WG, Deaver KA, Cochi SL, et al. Decline of childhood Haemophilus influenzae type b (Hib) disease in the Hib vaccine era. JAMA 269:221, 1993.
3. American Academy of Pediatrics. Respiratory syncytial virus. In Pickering LK (ed). 2000 Red Book: Report of the Committee on Infectious Diseases, 25th ed. Elk Grove Village, IL, American Academy of Pediatrics, 2000, pp 483–487.
4. Ausejo M, Saenz A, Pham B, et al. The effectiveness of glucocorticoids in treating croup: meta-analysis. BMJ 319:595, 1999.
5. Berger I, Argaman Z, Schwartz SB, et al. Efficacy of corticosteroids in acute bronchiolitis: short-term and long-term follow-up. Pediatr Pulmonol 26:162, 1998.
6. Black S, Shinefield H, Fireman B, et al. Efficacy, safety and immunogenicity of heptavalent pneumococcal conjugate vaccine in children. Northern California Kaiser Permanente Vaccine Study Center Group. Pediatr Infect Dis J 19:187, 2000.
7. Brook I. Microbiology of empyema in children and adolescents. Pediatrics 85:722, 1990.
8. Bulow SM, Nir M, Levin E, et al. Prednisolone treatment of respiratory syncytial virus infection: a randomized controlled trial of 147 infants. Pediatrics 104:e77, 1999.
9. Cade A, Brownlee KG, Conway SP, et al. Randomised placebo controlled trial of nebulised corticosteroids in acute respiratory syncytial viral bronchiolitis. Arch Dis Child 82:126, 2000.
10. Campbell JD, Nataro JP. Pleural empyema. Pediatr Infect Dis J 18:725, 1999.
11. Castillo EM, Rickman LS, Brodine SK, et al. Streptococcus pneumoniae: bacteremia in an era of penicillin resistance. Am J Infect Control 28:239, 2000.
12. Chapman RS, Henderson FW, Clyde WA Jr, et al. The epidemiology of tracheobronchitis in pediatric practice. Am J Epidemiol 114:786, 1981.
13. Cherry JD. Newer respiratory viruses: their role in respiratory illness of children. Adv Pediatr 20:225, 1973.
14. Chomel JJ, Remilleux MF, Marchand P, et al. Rapid diagnosis of

influenza A. Comparison with ELISA immunocapture and culture. J Virol Methods 37:337, 1992.

15. Chumpa A, Bachur RG, Harper MB. Bacteremia-associated pneumococcal pneumonia and the benefit of initial parenteral antimicrobial therapy. Pediatr Infect Dis J 18:1081, 1999.

16. Cockcroft DW, Stilwell GA. Lobar pneumonia caused by Mycoplasma pneumoniae. Can Med Assoc J 124:1463, 1981.

17. Davies RJ, Traill ZC, Gleeson FV. Randomised controlled trial of intrapleural streptokinase in community acquired pleural infection. Thorax 52:416, 1997.

18. De Lorenzo RA, Singer JI, Matre WM. Retropharyngeal abscess in an afebrile child. Am J Emerg Med 11:151, 1993.

19. Delvenne P, Arrese JE, Thiry A, et al. Detection of cytomegalovirus, Pneumocystis carinii, and aspergillus species in bronchoalveolar lavage fluid. A comparison of techniques. Am J Clin Pathol 100:414, 1993.

20. Dobson JV, Stephens-Groff SM, McMahon SR, et al. The use of albuterol in hospitalized infants with bronchiolitis. Pediatrics 101:361, 1998.

21. Donnelly BW, McMillan JA, Weiner LB. Bacterial tracheitis: report of eight new cases and review. Rev Infect Dis 12:729, 1990.

22. Dowell SF, Bresee JS. Severe varicella associated with steroid use. Pediatrics 92:223, 1993.

23. Feldman S. Varicella-zoster virus pneumonitis. Chest 106:22S, 1994.

24. Finland M, Barnes MW, Sampler BA. Influenza virus isolations and serologic studies made in Boston during the winter of 1943–44. J Clin Invest 24:192, 1945.

25. Freij BJ, Kusmiesz H, Nelson JD, et al. Parapneumonic effusions and empyema in hospitalized children: a retrospective review of 227 cases. Pediatr Infect Dis 3:578, 1984.

26. Galazka A. Implications of the diphtheria epidemic in the Former Soviet Union for immunization programs. J Infect Dis 181:S244, 2000.

27. Gay BB Jr, Atkinson GO, Vanderzalm T, et al. Subglottic foreign bodies in pediatric patients. Am J Dis Child 140:165, 1986.

28. Geelhoed GC, Macdonald WB. Oral and inhaled steroids in croup: a randomized, placebo-controlled trial. Pediatr Pulmonol 20:355, 1995.

29. Gorelick MH, Baker MD. Epiglottitis in children, 1979 through 1992. Effects of Haemophilus influenzae type b immunization. Arch Pediatr Adolesc Med 148:47, 1994.

30. Hahn DL, Dodge RW, Golubjatnikov R. Association of Chlamydia pneumoniae (strain TWAR) infection with wheezing, asthmatic bronchitis, and adult-onset asthma. JAMA 266:225, 1991.

31. Hall CB. Respiratory syncytial virus: a continuing culprit and conundrum. J Pediatr 135:2, 1999.

32. Hardie W, Bokulic R, Garcia VF, et al. Pneumococcal pleural empyemas in children. Clin Infect Dis 22:1057, 1996.

33. Hayden FG, Gubareva LV, Monto AS, et al. Inhaled zanamivir for the prevention of influenza in families. N Engl J Med 343:1282, 2000.

34. Heffelfinger JD, Dowell SF, Jorgensen JH, et al. Management of community-acquired pneumonia in the era of pneumococcal resistance: a report from the Drug-Resistant Streptococcus Pneumoniae Therapeutic Working Group. Arch Intern Med 160:1399, 2000.

35. Holberg CJ, Wright AL, Martinez FD, et al. Child day care, smoking by caregivers, and lower respiratory tract illness in the first 3 years of life. Group Health Medical Associates. Pediatrics 91:885, 1993.

36. Johnson DW, Jacobson S, Edney PC, et al. A comparison of nebulized budesonide, intramuscular dexamethasone, and placebo for moderately severe croup. N Engl J Med 339:498, 1998.

37. Kahn JS. Respiratory syncytial virus vaccine development. Curr Opin Pediatr 12:257, 2000.

38. Kellner JD, Ohlsson A, Gadomski AM, et al. Efficacy of bronchodilator therapy in bronchiolitis: a meta-analysis. Arch Pediatr Adolesc Med 150:1166, 1996.

39. Kim HW, Canchola JG, Brandt CD, et al. Respiratory syncytial virus disease in infants despite prior administration of antigenic inactivated vaccine. Am J Epidemiol 89:422, 1969.

40. Ko SC, Chen KY, Hsueh PR, et al. Fungal empyema thoracis: an emerging clinical entity. Chest 117:1672, 2000.

41. Kuo CC, Jackson LA, Campbell LA, et al. Chlamydia pneumoniae (TWAR). Clin Microbiol Rev 8:451, 1995.

42. Landry ML, Ferguson D. SimulFluor respiratory screen for rapid detection of multiple respiratory viruses in clinical specimens by immunofluorescence staining. J Clin Microbiol 38:708, 2000.

43. Marston BJ, Lipman HB, Breiman RF. Surveillance for Legionnaires' disease: risk factors for morbidity and mortality. Arch Intern Med 154:2417, 1994.

44. Mason EO Jr, Lamberth LB, Kershaw NL, et al. Streptococcus pneumoniae in the USA: in vitro susceptibility and pharmacodynamic analysis. J Antimicrob Chemother 45:623, 2000.

45. McCracken GH Jr. Diagnosis and management of pneumonia in children. Pediatr Infect Dis J 19:924, 2000.

46. McLaughlin FJ, Goldmann DA, Rosenbaum DM, et al. Empyema in children: clinical course and long-term follow-up. Pediatrics 73:587, 1984.

47. Menon K, Sutcliffe T, Klassen TP. A randomized trial comparing the efficacy of epinephrine with salbutamol in the treatment of acute bronchiolitis. J Pediatr 126:1004, 1995.

48. Plouffe JF. Importance of atypical pathogens of community-acquired pneumonia. Clin Infect Dis 31:S35, 2000.

49. Postma DS, Jones RO, Pillsbury HCD. Severe hospitalized croup: treatment trends and prognosis. Laryngoscope 94:1170, 1984.

50. PREVENT Study Group. Reduction of respiratory syncytial virus hospitalization among premature infants and infants with bronchopulmonary dysplasia using respiratory syncytial virus immune globulin prophylaxis. Pediatrics 99:93, 1997.

51. Rivkin MJ, Aronoff SC. Pulmonary infections in the immunocompromised child. Adv Pediatr Infect Dis 2:161, 1987.

52. Rodriguez WJ. Management strategies for respiratory syncytial virus infections in infants. J Pediatr 135:45, 1999.

53. Schuh S, Johnson D, Canny G, et al. Efficacy of adding nebulized ipratropium bromide to nebulized albuterol therapy in acute bronchiolitis. Pediatrics 90:920, 1992.

54. Sethi S. Infectious etiology of acute exacerbations of chronic bronchitis. Chest 117:380S, 2000.

55. Shay DK, Holman RC, Newman RD, et al. Bronchiolitis-associated hospitalizations among US children, 1980–1996. JAMA 282:1440, 1999.

56. Sigurs N, Bjarnason R, Sigurbergsson F, et al. Respiratory syncytial virus bronchiolitis in infancy is an important risk factor for asthma and allergy at age 7. Am J Respir Crit Care Med 161:1501, 2000.

57. Sing A, Trebesius K, Roggenkamp A, et al. Evaluation of diagnostic value and epidemiological implications of PCR for Pneumocystis carinii in different immunosuppressed and immunocompetent patient groups. J Clin Microbiol 38:1461, 2000.

58. Tibballs J, Shann FA, Landau LI. Placebo-controlled trial of prednisolone in children intubated for croup. Lancet 340:745, 1992.

59. Tilley PA, Kanchana MV, Knight I, et al. Detection of Bordetella pertussis in a clinical laboratory by culture, polymerase chain reaction, and direct fluorescent antibody staining; accuracy; and cost. Diagn Microbiol Infect Dis 37:17, 2000.

60. Top FH Jr, Connor EM, Carlin DA. Prophylaxis against respiratory syncytial virus in premature infants. IMpact-RSV Study Group. Lancet 355:1014, 2000.

61. Van Bever HP, Wieringa MH, Weyler JJ, et al. Croup and recurrent croup: their association with asthma and allergy. An epidemiological study on 5–8-year-old children. Eur J Pediatr 158:253, 1999.

62. Visentin DE, Yang WH, Karsh J. C1-esterase inhibitor transfusions in patients with hereditary angioedema. Ann Allergy Asthma Immunol 80:457, 1998.

63. Waecker NJ Jr, Shope TR, Weber PA, et al. The Rhino-Probe nasal curette for detecting respiratory syncytial virus in children. Pediatr Infect Dis J 12:326, 1993.

64. Working Group on Antiretroviral Therapy: National Pediatric HIV Resource Center. Antiretroviral therapy and medical management of the human immunodeficiency virus-infected child. Pediatr Infect Dis J 12:513, 1993.

86

Noninfectious Disorders of the Lower Respiratory Tract

Jonathan D. Finder, M.D.

Virtually every disorder of the respiratory tract is influenced by infection, so it is somewhat arbitrary to divide noninfectious from infectious respiratory tract disorders. In infectious disorders a normal host is attacked by an infectious organism, as occurs in tuberculosis. Noninfectious disorders involve in some manner an abnormal host. Such abnormalities range from gross structural disorders (e.g., bronchomalacia) to disorders of cell biology (the epithelial cell with immotile cilia in Kartagener syndrome) to molecular defects (the electrophysiologically abnormal epithelial cell of the cystic fibrosis patient).

This chapter focuses on the structural disorders of the lower respiratory tract. All parenchymal lung disease is divided into disorders of (1) airway, (2) alveolar space, (3) interstitium, and (4) vascular space. Of these four anatomic spaces in the lung parenchyma, the majority of pediatric lung diseases fall in the first category, airway diseases. Indeed, this category is the predominant focus of the pediatric otolaryngologist. Airway diseases can be further divided into diseases of the small (peripheral) airway and those of the large (central) airway. Diseases of the alveolar space tend to be infectious (e.g., pneumonia) and are discussed in Chapter 85, although a few noninfectious diseases of the alveolar space are included here. Interstitial diseases are quite rare and are often related to autoimmune processes and are discussed here. Vascular diseases, although also unusual in the pediatric population, are discussed as well. The other anatomic spaces not included in the list of parenchymal lung disease locations include pleural space and chest wall/diaphragm. The involvement of the pleural space in pediatric respiratory disease is largely infectious (i.e., parapneumonic effusion and empyema) and thus is discussed in Chapter 85. The chest wall and diaphragm are briefly discussed here.

Airway Diseases

Airway diseases are by far the most prevalent respiratory diseases seen by pediatric specialists and nonspecialists alike. In the infant and child under the age of 5 years, there is a significant proportion of patients with large airway diseases masquerading as asthma in whom one must have a heightened suspicion for congenital lesions of the large airway. Still, the large majority of airway diseases in all age groups affect the smaller, peripheral airways. The history and physical examination can be quite different for patients with large compared to small airway diseases and can help the clinician differentiate these diseases.

History

In general, large airway disorders are congenital in nature, and become symptomatic within the first 6 months of life. Small airway diseases, on the other hand, tend to be acquired and generally require some trigger to produce symptoms. Patients with lesions of the central airway tend to have chronically noisy, congested-sounding breathing. Parents of such patients will often report that their child was "born with a cold." Laryngeal disorders tend to give the patient a noisy, stridorous inspiratory phase, whereas disorders of the trachea and bronchi have predominantly expiratory noise. An astute observer may be able to report this difference. The noisy breathing is often inapparent when the child is brought in for a scheduled consultation. Thus, the parents' history becomes as important as your physical examination, if not more so. I always inquire whether the parents can feel a vibration in the back of the infant or child when holding him or her. Palpable fremitus suggests central airway disease. Is the problem present all the time or only intermittently? Most of the airway diseases that are constantly symptomatic are large airway lesions; small airway diseases generally are symptomatic with colds.

What has been the response to therapy? By the time a patient with airway disease has been referred to a specialist, he or she has usually been given a number of therapies, such as antibiotics, bronchodilators, and corticosteroids. A good response to antibiotics suggests the possibility of humoral immunodeficiency (IgA and IgG subclasses, typically), cystic fibrosis, ciliary dyskinesia—all diseases that lead to increased bacterial infection in the lower airways. No response to antibiotics is the norm, since most airway diseases do not involve bacterial infection in children. While a good response to a bronchodilator suggests asthma, no response or a worsening to bronchodilator leads one to consider diagnoses involving the larger airways.

Ask about the nature of the cough. The typical cough of the pediatric asthma patient is dry and hacking. A wet-sounding cough suggests excessive secretions in the lower airways, or a pooling of such secretions due to impaired clearance. Diseases that predispose to bacterial infections of the respiratory tract (cystic fibrosis, immotile cilia, and humoral immunodeficiency) typically are associated with wet or productive cough.

One must always inquire about the environment in children with chronic respiratory complaints. Second-hand tobacco smoke exposure is very common and can cause a chronic bronchitis in affected children, as well as lead to increased frequency of asthma, pneumonia, and otitis media. It appears to paralyze the cilia, leading to poor mucociliary clearance, bacterial stasis, overgrowth, and, subsequently, infection. Other environmental pathogens (particularly for the atopic patient) include animal danders, molds, house dust mites, and cockroaches. A dusty environment may be responsible for ongoing symptoms in the allergic child.

Finally, inquire about symptoms of gastroesophageal reflux disease (GERD). These symptoms depend on age of the child. Frequent effortless vomiting, especially at night, pain behaviors (crying and arching, generally at night), and recurrent croup are all symptoms of GERD. Laryngomalacia and inspiratory stridor may be associated with GERD. GERD is often accompanied by bronchospasm. These children have an incomplete response to an antiasthma regimen at best.

Physical Examination

A careful physical examination can help sort out large from small airway diseases. Since the examination is often normal between illness in most airway diseases, parents should be encouraged to bring their children to the clinic when they are sick so that the worst symptoms can be evaluated. The chest physical examination can be broken down into inspection, palpation, percussion, and auscultation.

Inspection. Because of the compliance of the chest wall of infants, the air trapping that accompanies small airway diseases usually results in an indrawing of the lower end of the rib cage during periods of lower airway obstruction. This occurs because the diaphragm, whose fibers normally are apposed to (up against) the inner surface of the chest wall, has been pushed away from the chest wall, so that they pull inward on their insertion at the lower end of the rib cage. This indrawing results in a subcostal retraction. Chronic lower airway obstruction can lead to an increased anteroposterior diameter of the chest.

Palpation. The hyperinflation that results in a subcostal retraction can also be perceived by palpation: one can feel the rib cage pulling inward during inspiration. A palpable vibration (fremitus) with tidal breathing suggests

a central airway obstruction, such as tracheo- or bronchomalacia, foreign body, or even a mucus plug. Unilateral fremitus is suggestive of bronchial rather than tracheal obstruction.

Percussion. One reliable sign in children younger than age 5 is that the level of the domes of the diaphragms upon percussion is at the scapular tip in normal lungs. This finding requires the child to be upright and with the arms down. Obstructive diseases of the peripheral airways frequently result in air trapping, which depresses the position of the diaphragm. Large airway diseases seldom result in air trapping and, thus, depressed position of the diaphragm, unless the obstruction is high grade. The finding of a depressed position of the diaphragm is a reliable indicator of small airways obstruction in infants and children younger than age 5 but less so after that age. An elevated hemidiaphragm suggests unilateral diaphragmatic paresis, paralysis, or eventration.

Auscultation. Auscultatory findings depend on where and when one listens. Breath sounds emanate from branch points in the airways, where there is turbulence of flow. Thus, more sounds come from the central airways, where there is more turbulence. Breath sounds over the trachea are tubular and equally loud during the expiratory and inspiratory phases. As one listens more peripherally, the inspiratory sounds become louder than the expiratory sounds. Tubular sounds over the central airways become more bronchial and finally vesicular over the distal lung segments. Over the peripheral portions of lung, the breath sounds are much louder during inspiration and nearly silent during expiration.

Contrary to a commonly held belief, all breath sounds emanate from the airway and none from the airspace. The most common abnormal breath sounds are crackles and wheezes. The way to differentiate these sounds is to determine whether the sound is continuous or discontinuous. A wheeze is a continuous sound made by the walls of a narrowed airway vibrating against one another. Wheezes can be either inspiratory or expiratory, but more often are expiratory. Wheezes of multiple pitches are called polyphonic and those of a single pitch are called monophonic. Polyphonic wheezes are typical of asthma and bronchiolitis; monophonic wheezes are heard in central airway obstructive diseases such as tracheomalacia or when a foreign body is present in the airway. Crackles are discontinuous sounds made as a pressure wave moves down an airway and pops through a fluid meniscus. Crackles are generally inspiratory but can be expiratory as well. Airway diseases associated with expiratory crackles include bronchiectasis.

Large Airway Disorders

Extrinsic Lesions

Please see Chapter 84, Congenital Malformations of the Trachea and Bronchi.

Intrinsic Lesions

Primary Tracheomalacia and Bronchomalacia

Insufficient airway rigidity is among the more common problems causing referral of a patient to a subspecialist. Most commonly found are primary tracheomalacia and bronchomalacia (TBM). These disorders are the result of insufficient cartilage within the airway wall, usually as a developmental anomaly. The bronchus can be involved (bronchomalacia), or the trachea (tracheomalacia), or a combination of the two (tracheobronchomalacia). Not infrequently there is concomitant laryngomalacia. Although the exact incidence of these disorders is unknown, TBM comprises a substantial proportion of patients referred for bronchoscopy and is generally viewed as common. The typical patient with primary TBM presents within the first 6 months of life. Although the sound is best described as a low-pitched, monophonic wheeze generally audible without a stethoscope, parents tend to use the term "congestion" in describing affected children. The wheeze frequently is present at base line and exacerbated by viral respiratory infections. Parents may also describe feeling a vibration in the child's back. With bronchomalacia, the vibration is often felt predominantly in one hemithorax. The fremitus to palpation is particularly apparent when there are increased lower airway secretions. Collapse of the central airway with coughing impedes mucociliary clearance and predisposes these patients to pneumonia. Unless there is concomitant asthma, the lung volumes are normal to percussion and on chest radiograph. Unless there are life-threatening complications of TBM, no intervention is necessary, and with supportive care most patients will resolve this disease between ages 2 and 5.[12] Surgical intervention has included aortopexy,[4, 21] bronchopexy,[1, 26, 34] sleeve resection,[46] tracheotomy and constant positive airways pressure,[33, 36] and internal mesh stent placement.[10–13] These interventions are very much the exception rather than the rule in TBM, and have been used in cases of persistent lobar or pulmonary atelectasis, severe pneumonia, and recurrent intubation for respiratory distress. Stent placement, which has been recently described in the pediatric population, requires experience and careful patient selection. The most common complication of the internal mesh stent (most commonly, the Palmaz stent) is development of granulation tissue obstructing the lumen of the airway. Laser coagulation of this tissue is relatively contraindicated since heating the metal stent can cause a thermal burn and make the stent impossible to remove subsequently. Death from erosion into adjacent aorta has also been described.[3]

Secondary Tracheomalacia and Bronchomalacia

Even after correction of a primary problem, such as a vascular ring, bronchogenic cyst, or tracheoesophageal fistula, the airway remains abnormal for a time. The length of this period depends on the severity of the lesion and the delay in intervention. The site of a correction of a tracheoesophageal fistula frequently remains persistently abnormal and deficient in cartilage. Bronchomalacia is frequently found in patients with congenital cardiac disease even after surgical correction. This finding is more than merely a bronchoscopic oddity, since this finding will markedly change management. Excessive use of beta agonists can worsen the airway compromise in such patients because relaxation of smooth muscle in areas deficient in cartilage will worsen airway floppiness.[42]

Small Airway Diseases

The term *small airways* is used here to refer to the peripheral airways, as opposed to the central airways. *Lower airways* in this chapter refers to all airways below the glottis. Diseases characterized by small airways obstruction (Table 86–1) manifest in a manner distinct from those of the large airways. Significant small airways disease frequently results in enough ventilation-perfusion mismatch to cause hypoxemia, as opposed to uncomplicated large airways obstruction, in which normoxemia is the rule. In most cases, small airways diseases have periods in which the patient is asymptomatic. Commonly there is overlap of small and large airway diseases, making both diagnosis and management challenging.

Asthma

As many as 20% of children have a wheezing illness at least once during childhood. Asthma is the most common reason for lost school days and hospital admission, and occurs in as much as 10% of children. In differentiating the child with a single wheezing illness from the child with asthma, "the three Rs" can be useful: reactivity, recurrence, and responsiveness.

The first R, reactivity, reminds one that asthma is a response of the host lung to an external stress. The most common trigger of asthma in younger children and infants is respiratory viral infections. After age 4 or so there is an increase in allergic disease, but even in the allergic child, viral respiratory infections remain important triggers of asthma. In an environment such as a day care center in which a dozen infants are exposed to the same virus, it is interesting to see how different children react differently. Two may require hospitalization for bronchiolitis, most develop rhinitis and cough, and a few may have minor wheezing. What distinguishes those who develop severe bronchiolitis from those who merely develop rhinorrhea is not clear. Evidence suggests that those infants at risk for developing bronchiolitis with a viral lower respiratory infection have an asymptomatic decrease in pulmonary function.[30] These children subsequently develop normal pulmonary function by age 6.[31] There appear to be two subgroups of early childhood asthmatics: those who develop an atopic phenotype and those who do

TABLE 86–1. Small Airways Diseases

Asthma
Gastroesophageal reflux
Bronchiolitis
Cystic fibrosis
Obliterative bronchiolitis
Chronic aspiration

not.[15] The so-called "allergic asthmatics" tend to develop their symptoms later in childhood than those without allergy.

The second R, recurrence, reminds one that a single wheezing illness does not make a diagnosis of asthma. Three episodes of wheezing are generally required before one can define a patient as having asthma. Unfortunately, wheezing is not always evident, and so the asthmatic is often diagnosed as having recurrent pneumonia—especially if there is atelectasis on a chest radiograph—or recurrent bronchitis. One may need to inquire about illnesses with prolonged coughing or periods of retractions. Bronchiolitis, which is discussed elsewhere, may lead to subsequent episodes of wheezing, and should raise one's index of suspicion for asthma.

The last R, reversibility, is critical for a diagnosis of asthma. Frequently, children with other airway diseases like bronchomalacia or vascular ring are diagnosed with asthma prior to the establishment of a correct diagnosis. A clue that the initial diagnosis is incorrect is a failure of response to therapy. Most patients with a fixed or dynamic upper airway obstruction show no improvement when treated with beta-adrenergic agonists and may in fact worsen. Since asthma has both early and late mediators of inflammation, it is important to remember that only the early stage of asthma achieves near full restoration of pulmonary function with a beta agonist. Later, one may need to administer a course of systemic steroids to reverse the airways obstruction. The gold standard for determining reversibility of airways obstruction is the pulmonary function test. Children under age 5 (too young to perform pulmonary function testing) require assessment of clinical response such as decreased cough, retractions, and wheeze. Improvement in oxygenation is also a clue to reversibility.

Asthma therapy for pediatric patients has improved recently, especially with the improvement in anti-inflammatory topical therapies available to infants and toddlers. Therapies include intermittent administration of beta-adrenergic agonists via metered-dose inhaler or nebulizer. Patients with frequent symptoms require assessment of "triggers" (allergies, gastroesophageal reflux, and viral infections) and usually daily anti-inflammatory therapy. Such base line therapies include (1) nebulized cromolyn sodium or budesonide and (2) metered-dose inhaler corticosteroids (fluticasone, budesonide, beclomethasone, and flunisolide, to name a few), nedocromil, and cromolyn sodium. Leukotriene modifiers have recently become standard therapy, especially oral leukotriene D4 receptor antagonists (LTRA). Montelukast and zafirlukast have been used as either monotherapy or as an addition to a topical anti-inflammatory therapy. There exists some controversy as to whether the LTRAs are truly anti-inflammatory agents and whether they should be used as first-line agents in asthma.[6, 51] LTRAs have grown in acceptance and are increasingly used in the pediatric age group.

Gastroesophageal Reflux–Induced Bronchospasm

In the child with difficult to control asthma, the diagnosis of gastroesophageal reflux disease (GERD) should be entertained. In a questionnaire, Orenstein found that 40% of infants had daily regurgitation, despite only a minority of them having true gastroesophageal reflux disease.[41] How one differentiates pathologic reflux from normal GER depends on clinical and laboratory findings. Symptoms of GERD include pain behaviors (excessive crying, particularly at night), arching, hoarseness, cough, wheeze, and recurrent croup. Recurrent wheeze and subcostal retractions are signs of GER-induced bronchospasm. Laryngomalacia is frequently associated with GERD.

The cause of respiratory disease in GERD is not entirely clear. Most patients cannot be demonstrated to have frank aspiration of gastric contents. In adults, acidification of the lower esophagus can induce bronchospasm in a laboratory setting (the Bernstein test) in the absence of aspiration. Aspiration of a tiny amount of gastric contents, however, can induce intense bronchospasm. Microaspiration, or the aspiration of essentially undetectable amounts of gastric acidity, is thus probably the cause of much of the GERD-induced bronchospasm. Patients with GERD-induced bronchospasm generally are unresponsive to traditional anti-asthma therapies such as inhaled corticosteroids or cromolyn. Blockers of acid production (H_2 blockers or proton pump inhibitors) are critical to their management.

Work-up of the patient with potential GERD includes a careful history and physical examination. Subtle signs of airway obstruction include hyperinflation to percussion, subcostal retractions, tachypnea, and use of abdominal muscles on expiration. Barium swallow studies are not useful in diagnosis of GERD and should not be ordered unless there is concern for malrotation, feeding problems, or anterograde aspiration. A pH probe study is useful in patients whose diagnosis is in question. Direct laryngoscopy and bronchoscopy are valuable in assessing the upper airway. Typical findings include (1) erythema and edema of the laryngeal structures, (2) laryngomalacia, (3) erythema and edema of the trachea and bronchi with blunting of the normal landmarks, and (4) occasionally, numerous lipid-laden macrophages on bronchoalveolar lavage. Biopsy of the lower esophagus can be performed at the same time to demonstrate changes consistent with GERD-induced esophagitis. Gastric emptying or radionuclide milk scan is also useful for diagnosis of GERD. Delayed gastric emptying is a frequently associated finding, and one that can act as a multiplier of disease in GERD. Identification of delay in gastric emptying and treating this aspect of the reflux can be extremely important in the success of a therapeutic regimen.

Obliterative Bronchiolitis

Obliterative bronchiolitis (OB) is a rare cause of peripheral airways obstruction. In the 21st century, this diagnosis is most commonly made in association with transplantation of either bone marrow or lung.[19, 27] In OB, a progressive, irreversible obliteration of the bronchioles is associated with an immune response that is centered on the airway epithelium. In bone marrow transplantation patients, OB is a form of graft-versus-host disease. Lung transplantation patients manifest OB as a form of chronic rejection.[23] Prior to the age of transplantation, OB was associated with a number of common infections, including influenza, mycoplasma, and adenovirus. Swyer-James-MacLeod syndrome is characterized by a unilateral hyperlucent lung due to unilateral OB following a respiratory infection (most often, mycoplasma).

OB is suspected when there is irreversible airflow obstruction on a pulmonary function test. There is little or no response to bronchodilator or systemic corticosteroids. Diagnosis generally relies upon histologic evaluation of the lung parenchyma, obtained at open lung biopsy or thoracoscopically. Clinical course varies with cause. In patients with OB following adenovirus, there can be varying degrees of symptoms for months before the disease "burns out." Persistent airflow obstruction is the rule, and symptoms depend on the degree of airway obstruction. Bronchiectasis is a frequent accompanying factor. Patients with OB following transplantation may develop worsening airflow obstruction to the point of respiratory failure.

Bronchiectasis

Bronchiectasis is most commonly associated with cystic fibrosis, which is discussed elsewhere. Bronchiectasis is defined as chronic infection of airways, leading to destruction of airway walls, with abnormally widened, floppy, and thickened peripheral airways.[16] Ciliary clearance is often abnormal before the development of bronchiectasis but is uniformly abnormal in bronchiectatic lung parenchyma. Poor airway clearance is the rule in bronchiectasis, which leads to stasis of bacteria and chronic infection. A purulent bronchiolitis/bronchitis results, leading to a chronic cough productive of purulent sputum. Prior to the antibiotic era, bronchiectasis was far more commonly encountered. Aside from the population of patients with cystic fibrosis, other patients with bronchiectasis include those with primary ciliary dyskinesia (PCD). PCD is a heterogeneous group of disorders in which the ciliary function is impaired. In the prototypic type of PCD, called Kartagener syndrome, the outer dynein arm of the cilia is absent, and the cilia are immotile. These patients also have chronic otitis media and sinusitis. Male infertility in these patients is due to immotile spermatozoa. Dextrocardia occurs in half of patients with PCD (and is one of the cardinal features of Kartagener syndrome). Other causes of bronchiectasis include prolonged retention of foreign body (in which the bronchiectasis is limited to the affected lobe), and severe previous infection with destruction of ciliated epithelium. Bronchiectasis is also seen in association with OB, as the scarring process destroys normal airway epithelium.

Diagnosis of bronchiectasis is best made with high-resolution computed tomography of the chest. Bronchoscopy for culture of lower airway secretions is a useful adjunct in patients too young to produce sputum and allows the clinician to tailor antibiotic therapy.

Bronchopulmonary Dysplasia

The term *bronchopulmonary dysplasia* (BPD) was introduced in 1967 by Northway et al[39] to describe a new chronic pulmonary syndrome associated with the use of positive-pressure ventilation and high oxygen concentrations for longer than 6 days. BPD has become the most common form of chronic lung disease in infancy in the United States. It is a chronic disease occurring in prematurely born infants treated with positive-pressure ventilation and oxygen supplementation for respiratory insufficiency. The principal factors in the pathogenesis of BPD are premature birth, respiratory failure, toxic effects of oxygen, and barotrauma.[8] Prematurity is associated with immature lung structure, lack of surfactant, inadequate respiratory drive, and insufficient antioxidant activity to protect against increased oxygen radicals. Respiratory failure is critical in pathogenesis in that it requires treatment with mechanical ventilation and oxygen. Positive-pressure mechanical ventilation is important in pathogenesis because of its stretching effects on the premature airway and its delivery of oxygen. BPD was originally thought to occur only with hyaline membrane disease, but it may actually occur in any condition in premature infants causing respiratory failure.

Our understanding of the structural changes in the lungs of BPD patients is largely the result of autopsy studies, which thus have a selection bias for the most severely affected patients. In an often-quoted paper, Margraf et al[29] reported that both the large and small airways are affected. They reported that central airways were scarred and narrowed, and had increased amounts of smooth muscle in their walls. Smooth muscle hypertrophy and peribronchiolar fibrosis narrowed the lumen of the bronchioles, although the small airways were better preserved than the large airways. There was squamous metaplasia of the bronchial mucosa. Total alveolar number was decreased, and the acinar structure was greatly simplified, resulting in a fall in the total surface area of the lung and a decrease in the cross-sectional area of the vascular bed. The vascular space was further limited by arteriolar smooth muscle hypertrophy.

Patients with BPD have increased airway resistance and reactivity. Decreased surface area for gas exchange leads to poor pulmonary reserve, and poor tolerance of any lower respiratory tract infection. Bronchospasm is common, especially in the setting of viral respiratory tract infections. GERD (including chronic aspiration[43]) is uniformly present in patients with BPD; recognition and treatment are critical to successful management. Tracheomalacia and bronchomalacia are also common.[7] Treatment of BPD includes use of oxygen to keep hemoglobin saturation above 92%, inhaled beta-agonists and often inhaled ipratropium bromide, inhaled anti-inflammatory agents (nebulized cromolyn sodium or budesonide), oral diuretics in severely affected patients with sensitivity to fluid overload (a minority of patients), and careful attention to nutrition. Patients with BPD have increased caloric requirements[28] and may require gastrostomy feedings for nutrition adequate for growth. Patients with BPD are at high risk of severe complications of respiratory syncytial virus infection. Monthly injections of an anti-RSV monoclonal antibody is efficacious in the prevention of RSV infections in patients at risk[48] but is not effective in treatment of documented RSV infection.

Improvements in the treatment of respiratory distress

syndrome and BPD, such as limitation of peak inspiratory pressures and oxygen concentrations, as well as surfactant replacement and dexamethasone therapy have resulted in a decrease in the number of patients with severe BPD. There has been a decrease in the incidence of BPD in neonates with birth weights above 1000 g and especially in those above 1500 g. However, because of increased occurrence of BPD in neonates of birth weights below 1000 g, the overall incidence of BPD has not changed owing to increased survival of this last group of low–birth-weight neonates in recent years. Many infants with BPD require supplemental oxygen for months to years. Adolescents and young adults with prior BPD, when tested, often show measurable pulmonary dysfunction even though they are asymptomatic.[37, 38]

Vascular Diseases

Vascular diseases of the chest are rare in the pediatric age group. Primary diseases of the pulmonary vasculature include primary pulmonary hypertension (which can include arterial occlusive disease and pulmonary veno-occlusive disease), pulmonary embolic disease, and malformations of the pulmonary vasculature. Other vascular diseases seen include those complicating congenital cardiac disease. Primary diseases of the pulmonary vasculature often are diagnosed relatively late since their presentation can be subtle and challenging. Persistent pulmonary hypertension of the neonate is discussed elsewhere.

Treatment for primary pulmonary hypertension (PPH) has improved significantly since the early 1990s but remains a devastating and often fatal illness.[44] Before effective therapies became available, median survival was less than 3 years from diagnosis. Even in the face of improved therapy, PPH is quite often fatal. PPH most commonly manifests with syncope with exertion. Dyspnea out of proportion to the level of exertion may be apparent before the first syncopal episode. Seizure, which is another manifesting sign, can actually delay diagnosis since the concern becomes the central nervous system rather than the pulmonary vasculature. Incidence is quite low, approximately 1 to 2 per million. Pathologic study of biopsy and post-mortem tissue demonstrates plexiform lesions, neointimal proliferation, and medial hypertrophy. Treatments include continuous intravenous prostacyclin, inhaled nitric oxide, inhaled iloprost (a prostacyclin analog)[18], anticoagulation, calcium channel blockers, and oxygen. The most promising therapy at present is prostacyclin and its analogs, which is most effective in younger children. Lung transplantation is another treatment for PPH.

A poorly understood disease worth mentioning in the context of vascular disease is fibrosing mediastinitis, more often associated with pulmonary vascular obstruction. Fibrosing mediastinitis has been associated with pulmonary tuberculosis and histoplasmosis.[20] In this disease, there is a progressive proliferation of fibrous tissue in the mediastinum, leading to obstruction of vascular structures, most commonly the pulmonary veins.

Pulmonary embolism[14] (PE) can occasionally be seen in the pediatric population but is seldom suspected. Risk factors for PE in adolescents include obesity, oral contraceptive usage, and cigarette smoking. Early presentation of PE is worrisome for a hypercoagulable state, such as protein S or C deficiency, or the factor V Leiden mutation. Patients with PE often present with sudden onset of chest pain and dyspnea. Syncope is occasionally seen. Hemoptysis is rare in pediatric patients. The chest radiograph is usually normal, and diagnosis requires either ventilation-perfusion scan or pulmonary angiogram. Treatment is usually a prolonged course of anticoagulation. In cases of massive PE, surgical removal of the embolism has been successfully performed.

Airspace Diseases

Atelectasis

The most common pediatric disease of the alveolar space, pneumonia, is discussed elsewhere in this text. After pneumonia, the most common disorder of the alveolar space is a loss of alveolar volume. This process is referred to as atelectasis. The most common cause of atelectasis is mucus plugging, often in association with asthma. Patients with weakened muscles of respiration, such as those with muscular dystrophy, are at especially high risk for development of atelectasis. Atelectasis can also be seen after pneumonia with resorption of the inflammatory fluid. Persistent collapse of a lung segment can be seen radiographically for months. We generally do not routinely perform bronchoscopy on patients with atelectasis unless a foreign body or mucus plug is suspected. Most cases of atelectasis have no bronchoscopic findings and no identifiable cause. Obstructive atelectasis may result from extrinsic compression or intrinsic occlusion of a bronchial lumen.

Atelectasis may result from a long-present foreign body, especially those, such as nuts, which produce a mucosal reaction. Mucus plugs associated with asthma can produce a picture identical to that of aspirated foreign bodies: partial obstruction creating emphysema, leading to total obstruction and atelectasis. Postoperative atelectasis is usually due to mucus plug obstruction in combination with nonobstructive factors discussed in the following text.

Nonobstructive atelectasis results from insufficient pulmonary surfactant or inadequate expansion of the thorax. Surfactant is the surface tension-lowering substance present in the alveolar lining layer. It is a complex mixture of proteins and phospholipids. The predominant phospholipid is lecithin, the molecules of which are arranged so that they form a highly compressible, tension-lowering film. Without surfactant, alveolar inflation would be determined according to the Laplace relationship for a sphere:

$$\text{Pressure} = \frac{(2)\,(\text{surface tension})}{\text{radius}}$$

On expiration, when both alveolar radius and pressure are low, surface tension would promote collapse of alveoli. The presence of a substance that lowers alveolar surface tension prevents this occurrence. Surfactant deficiency is the cause of diffuse atelectasis associated with hyaline membrane disease of neonates. Surfactant deficiency also plays a role in adult respiratory distress syndrome (ARDS), in which the alveolar lining film and cells are damaged.[2] Limited expansion of the chest may result from discomfort, as after injuries or after surgery; it may also result from either congenital or acquired neuromuscular dysfunction, or from chest wall deformities. Except in cases of massive atelectasis that causes severe dyspnea, the symptoms of atelectasis are the same, with perhaps slight accentuation, as those of the underlying condition. The diagnosis is usually made by chest radiograph, the collapsed portion having increased density and sometimes a contracted appearance with concave borders.

Treatment of atelectasis is directed toward the underlying disease. Atelectasis associated with pulmonary infections in childhood usually clears with resolution of the infection. Chest physiotherapy and postural drainage aid in clearing mucus from the obstructed bronchus. Bronchoscopy and removal of mucus plugs are indicated if atelectasis is impeding the child's recovery or if it persists after clearing of the infection. If a foreign body is the suspected cause, early bronchoscopy is indicated. Longstanding atelectasis of months or years duration that is unresponsive to medical treatment and bronchoscopy may require surgical resection if it is a site of repeated infections.

Pulmonary Alveolar Proteinosis

Pulmonary alveolar proteinosis can be congenital or acquired. The congenital form, most commonly caused by deficiency of surfactant protein B, is seen as a form of hyaline membrane disease developing in children not at risk for this disease.[52] This disease is generally fatal unless lung transplantation is performed. Acquired pulmonary alveolar proteinosis has an entirely different course from the congenital form. The diagnosis is suspected based on classic computed tomographic findings of interlobular septal thickening and patchy involvement of the alveolar space with a ground-glass appearance. The characteristic finding with bronchoalveolar lavage is milky fluid with sediment. The sediment contains granules that on electron microscopy prove to be compacted surfactant. The cause of alveolar proteinosis is unknown. Recent data suggest a role for granulocyte-macrophage colony-stimulating factor (GM-CSF).[22, 25, 47, 49] The mainstay of treatment is repeated pulmonary lavage to clear out the alveoli. Duration of survival has increased greatly with the introduction of modern flexible bronchoscopy techniques. An occasionally noted familial occurrence suggests that a genetic etiology exists.

Pulmonary Alveolar Microlithiasis

This disease is characterized by the formation of tiny calcium carbonate stones within pulmonary alveoli. The mechanism by which the stones are formed is not known; the patients appear to have no identifiable metabolic abnormalities. Radiographic examination shows fine granular densities scattered throughout the lungs. Lung biopsy is required for definitive diagnosis. The disease begins in childhood and progresses slowly, and the patients usually die of cardiopulmonary failure in mid-adult life. There is a familial occurrence that suggests a genetic etiologic basis.

Air Leak Syndromes: Pneumothorax, Pneumomediastinum, and Subcutaneous Emphysema

Pneumomediastinum and pneumothorax may develop from any condition causing a break in the wall of the air or food passages within the neck or thorax. Subcutaneous emphysema is often associated with pneumomediastinum and pneumothorax. Spontaneous pneumothorax is rare in children; it occurs occasionally with acute asthma. The most common causes of pneumomediastinum and pneumothorax in children are mechanical ventilation, surgical procedures in the neck, injuries occurring during endoscopy or endotracheal intubation, foreign bodies, and injuries to the neck or chest. Although pneumomediastinum and pneumothorax may be found in the neonate after a difficult delivery or with pulmonary diseases such as hyaline membrane disease or meconium aspiration, most cases result from mechanical ventilation. For example, the incidence of pneumothorax in hyaline membrane disease without ventilator management is less than 5%, whereas it is 20% with mechanical ventilation.[8] The initial break in the airway with artificial ventilation is rupture of an alveolus, producing pulmonary interstitial emphysema. Air dissects along the perivascular and peribronchial spaces to the mediastinum. If enough air leaks from the alveolus, it can dissect through the superior mediastinum into the subcutaneous tissues of the neck.[32] It can also break through into the pleural space and produce pneumothorax. Tracheotomy is the most common surgical procedure causing pneumomediastinum and pneumothorax.

Pneumomediastinum alone seldom causes significant symptoms, even though a large amount of mediastinal air can be seen on radiographs of the chest. Symptoms of pneumothorax depend on its extent; a small pneumothorax will be asymptomatic, whereas a progressively enlarging tension pneumothorax (i.e., an enlarging mass of air within the pleural cavity compressing the adjacent lung) can produce severe respiratory distress. Limited respiratory excursions may be noted on the side of the chest in which the pneumothorax has developed. Breath sounds are diminished over an area of pneumothorax. A peculiar sound, referred to as the mediastinal crunch, may be heard by auscultation over the mediastinum in patients with pneumomediastinum.

If the pneumothorax is large, or if it is a tension pneumothorax, it must be decompressed. In some cases, one needle aspiration is sufficient; in other cases, a chest tube must be inserted for continuous closed drainage until the air leak into the pleural cavity seals. In patients with rapidly developing tension pneumothorax and increasing respiratory distress, prompt needle aspiration of pleural air may be lifesaving. A chest tube should be inserted in these patients at the time of initial needle aspiration.

Pneumomediastinum without pneumothorax usually requires no specific treatment. Its presence, however, may indicate that there is an underlying condition that needs treatment.

Interstitial Lung Diseases

The pulmonary interstitium is a potential space between the vascular endothelium and the alveolar epithelium. As much of the endothelium shares a common basement membrane with the alveolar epithelium (and is thereby fused), the normal lung contains very little interstitium. The interstitium is predominantly noncellular (collagen, fibronectin, elastin). The few cellular elements are fibroblasts and occasional tissue macrophages. In disease, this space can widen and fill with inflammatory cells and connective tissue. This leads to two important physiologic sequelae: diffusion block and decreased pulmonary compliance. Early in the course of disease these changes can be inapparent and asymptomatic. Hypoxemia may only be present with vigorous exercise. As the diffusion block worsens, exercise tolerance progressively worsens. The increasingly stiff lungs lose vital capacity, and the patient must breath more rapidly to achieve the same ventilation. Retention of carbon dioxide occurs only late in course, while hypoxemia occurs much earlier. This difference is due to the increased solubility of carbon dioxide in tissues.

The prototypic interstitial lung disease, idiopathic pulmonary fibrosis, is quite rare in pediatric patients but has been reported.[35, 45] More commonly, interstitial processes are seen in the setting of viral pneumonitis (discussed elsewhere). The radiographic findings range from a subtle reticular pattern on chest radiograph to peripheral cystic changes, best seen on computed tomography of the chest, late in the course. Pneumothorax and pneumomediastinum are frequent complications.

Interstitial lung disease is seen as a complication of treatment for childhood cancers, generally secondary to chemotherapy. The agents involved in this complication include bleomycin-anthracyclines and carmustine.[9, 40] Radiation therapy involving the chest can be an important multiplier in this process.

Other interstitial diseases seen rarely in pediatric patients include sarcoidosis, desquamative interstitial pneumonitis, and lymphocytic interstitial pneumonitis (LIP). LIP is most commonly associated with AIDS and is a feature that helps to define pediatric AIDS.

The pulmonary hemorrhage syndromes are an important and diverse group of interstitial diseases.[5] This group of diseases includes idiopathic pulmonary hemosiderosis (IPH), Goodpasture syndrome, and Wegener granulomatosis. In IPH there is intermittent cough, hemoptysis, pulmonary infiltrates, and anemia. Bronchoscopy with bronchoalveolar lavage demonstrates hemosiderin-laden macrophages. Lung biopsy is generally recommended in such cases to differentiate different causes of the pulmo-

nary hemorrhage. An association of IPH and cow's milk sensitivity (Heiner syndrome) has been described. IPH is a diagnosis of exclusion, and careful serologic evaluation for Wegener granulomatosis and Goodpasture syndrome is required.

Goodpasture syndrome is "pulmonary-renal" syndrome[50] caused by an autoantibody to basement membrane collagen (antibodies are directed against the noncollagenous domain of the alpha 3 chain of type IV collagen).[24] Isolated pulmonary disease has been described.[17] The typical patient with Goodpasture syndrome has pulmonary hemorrhage and hematuria. The renal disease can be progressive and lead to death.

Wegener granulomatosis (WG) is a disease well known to otolaryngologists. WG is a vasculitis with multisystem involvement, including sinus, pulmonary, and renal disease. It is associated with antineutrophil cytoplasmic antibodies (ANCA). Pulmonary hemorrhage occurs, as does hematuria. Otitis media and subglottic stenosis have been reported in association with WG. Renal failure in WG can be the cause of death. Cytotoxic therapy with cyclophosphamide and glucocorticoids has improved prognosis in this disease.

REFERENCES

1. Ahel V, Severinski S, Vukas D, Rozmanic V. Primary bronchomalacia and patent ductus arteriosus: simultaneous surgical correction in an infant. Tex Heart Inst J 26:215, 1999.
2. Beaufils F, Mercier J, Farnoux C, et al. Acute respiratory distress syndrome in children. Curr Opin Pediatr 9:207, 1997.
3. Cook CH, Bhattacharyya N, King DR. Aortobronchial fistula after expandable metal stent insertion for pediatric bronchomalacia. J Pediatr Surg 33:1306, 1998.
4. Corbally MT, Spitz L, Kiely E, et al. Aortopexy for tracheomalacia in oesophageal anomalies. Eur J Pediatr Surg 3:264, 1993.
5. Dearborn D. Pulmonary hemorrhage in infants and children. Curr Opin Pediatr 9:219, 1997.
6. Drazen JM, Israel E. Should antileukotriene therapies be used instead of inhaled corticosteroids in asthma? Yes. Am J Respir Crit Care Med 158:1697, 1998.
7. Duncan S, Eid N. Tracheomalacia and bronchopulmonary dysplasia. Ann Otol Rhinol Laryngol 100:856, 1991.
8. Farrell P, Fiascone J. Bronchopulmonary dysplasia in the 1990's: a review for the pediatrician. Curr Probl Pediatr 27:133, 1997.
9. Fauroux B, Meyer-Milsztain A, Boccon-Gibod L, et al. Cytotoxic drug-induced pulmonary disease in infants and children. Pediatr Pulmonol 18:347, 1994.
10. Filler RM, Forte V, Chait P. Tracheobronchial stenting for the treatment of airway obstruction. J Pediatr Surg 33:304, 1998.
11. Filler RM, Forte V, Fraga JC, Matute J. The use of expandable metallic airway stents for tracheobronchial obstruction in children. J Pediatr Surg 30:1050, 1995.
12. Finder JD. Primary bronchomalacia in infants and children. J Pediatr 130:59, 1997.
13. Furman RH, Backer CL, Dunham ME, et al. The use of balloon-expandable metallic stents in the treatment of pediatric tracheomalacia and bronchomalacia. Arch Otolaryngol Head Neck Surg 125:203, 1999.
14. Goldhaber SZ. Pulmonary embolism. N Engl J Med 339:93, 1998.
15. Halonen M, Stern DA, Lohman C, et al. Two subphenotypes of childhood asthma that differ in maternal and paternal influences on asthma risk. Am J Respir Crit Care Med 160:564, 1999.
16. Hansell D. Bronchiectasis. Radiol Clin North Am 36:107, 1998.
17. Harrity P, Gilbert-Barness E, Cabalka A, et al. Isolated pulmonary Goodpasture syndrome. Pediatr Pathol 11:635, 1991.

18. Hoeper MM, Schwarze M, Ehlerding S, et al. Long-term treatment of primary pulmonary hypertension with aerosolized iloprost, a prostacyclin analogue. N Engl J Med 342:1866, 2000.

19. Kaditis A, Gondor M, Nixon P, et al. Airway complications following pediatric lung and heart-lung transplantation. Am J Respir Crit Care Med 162:301, 2000.

20. Kalweit G, Huwer H, Straub U, Gams E. Mediastinal compression syndromes due to idiopathic fibrosing mediastinitis–report of three cases and review of the literature. Thorac Cardiovasc Surg 44:105, 1996.

21. Kamata S, Usui N, Sawai T, et al. Pexis of the great vessels for patients with tracheobronchomalacia in infancy. J Pediatr Surg 35:454, 2000.

22. Kavuru MS, Sullivan EJ, Piccin R, et al. Exogenous granulocyte-macrophage colony-stimulating factor administration for pulmonary alveolar proteinosis. Am J Respir Crit Care Med 161:1143, 2000.

23. Kelly K, Hertz M. Obliterative bronchiolitis. Clin Chest Med 18:319, 1997.

24. Kelly P, Haponik E. Goodpasture syndrome: molecular and clinical advances. Medicine (Baltimore) 73:171, 1994.

25. Kitamura T, Tanaka N, Watanabe J, et al. Idiopathic pulmonary alveolar proteinosis as an autoimmune disease with neutralizing antibody against granulocyte/macrophage colony-stimulating factor. J Exp Med 190:875, 1999.

26. Kosloske AM. Left mainstem bronchopexy for severe bronchomalacia. J Pediatr Surg 26:260, 1991.

27. Kurland G, Orenstein DM. Complications of pediatric lung and heart-lung transplantation. Curr Opin Pediatr 6:262, 1994.

28. Kurzner S, Garg M, Bautista D, et al. Growth failure in bronchopulmonary dysplasia: elevated metabolic rates and pulmonary mechanics. J Pediatr 112:73, 1988.

29. Margraf LR, Tomashefski JF Jr, Bruce MC, Dahms BB. Morphometric analysis of the lung in bronchopulmonary dysplasia. Am Rev Respir Dis 143:391, 1991.

30. Martinez FD, Morgan WJ, Wright AL, et al. Diminished lung function as a predisposing factor for wheezing respiratory illness in infants. N Engl J Med 319:1112, 1988.

31. Martinez FD, Wright AL, Taussig LM, et al. Asthma and wheezing in the first six years of life. The Group Health Medical Associates. N Engl J Med 332:133, 1995.

32. Maunder RJ, Pierson DJ, Hudson LD. Subcutaneous and mediastinal emphysema. Pathophysiology, diagnosis, and management. Arch Intern Med 144:1447, 1984.

33. Miller RW, Pollack MM, Murphy TM, Fink RJ. Effectiveness of continuous positive airway pressure in the treatment of bronchomalacia in infants: a bronchoscopic documentation. Crit Care Med 14:125, 1986.

34. Mutabagani KH, Menke JA, McCoy KS, Besner GE. Bronchopexy for congenital bronchomalacia in the newborn. J Pediatr Surg 34:1300, 1999.

35. Nagai S, Kitaichi M, Izumi T. Classification and recent advances in idiopathic interstitial pneumonia. Curr Opin Pulm Med 4:256, 1998.

36. Neijens HJ, Kerrebijn KF, Smalhout B. Successful treatment with CPAP of two infants with bronchomalacia. Acta Paediatr Scand 67:293, 1978.

37. Northway W. Bronchopulmonary dysplasia: twenty-five years later. Pediatrics 89:969, 1992.

38. Northway W, Moss R, Carlisle K, et al. Late pulmonary sequelae of bronchopulmonary dysplasia. N Engl J Med 323:1793, 1990.

39. Northway W, Rosan R, Porter D. Pulmonary disease following respirator therapy of hyaline-membrane disease. Bronchopulmonary dysplasia. N Engl J Med 276:357, 1967.

40. O'Driscoll B, Hasleton P, Taylor P, et al. Active lung fibrosis up to 17 years after chemotherapy with carmustine (BCNU) in childhood. N Engl J Med 323:378, 1990.

41. Orenstein SR, Shalaby TM, Cohn JF. Reflux symptoms in 100 normal infants: diagnostic validity of the infant gastroesophageal reflux questionnaire. Clin Pediatr (Phila) 35:607, 1996.

42. Panitch HB, Keklikian EN, Motley RA, et al. Effect of altering smooth muscle tone on maximal expiratory flows in patients with tracheomalacia. Pediatr Pulmonol 9:170, 1990.

43. Radford PJ, Stillwell PC, Blue B, Hertel G. Aspiration complicating bronchopulmonary dysplasia. Chest 107:185, 1995.

44. Rubin LJ. Primary pulmonary hypertension. N Engl J Med 336:111, 1997.

45. Ryu JH, Colby T, Hartman T. Idiopathic pulmonary fibrosis: current concepts. Mayo Clin Proc 73:1085, 1998.

46. Smith KP, Cavett CM. Segmental bronchomalacia: successful surgical correction in an infant. J Pediatr Surg 20:240, 1985.

47. Tanaka N, Watanabe J, Kitamura T, et al. Lungs of patients with idiopathic pulmonary alveolar proteinosis express a factor which neutralizes granulocyte-macrophage colony stimulating factor. FEBS Lett 442:246, 1999.

48. The IMpact-RSV Study Group. Palivizumab, a humanized respiratory syncytial virus monoclonal antibody, reduces hospitalization from respiratory syncytial virus infection in high-risk infants. Pediatrics 102:531, 1998.

49. Thomassen MJ, Yi T, Raychaudhuri B, et al. Pulmonary alveolar proteinosis is a disease of decreased availability of GM-CSF rather than an intrinsic cellular defect. Clin Immunol 95:85, 2000.

50. von Vigier R, Trummler S, Laux-End R, et al. Pulmonary renal syndrome in childhood: a report of twenty-one cases and a review of the literature. Pediatr Pulmonol 29:382, 2000.

51. Wenzel SE. Should antileukotriene therapies be used instead of inhaled corticosteroids in asthma? No. Am J Respir Crit Care Med 158:1699, 1998.

52. Whitsett JA, Nogee LM, Weaver TE, Horowitz AD. Human surfactant protein B: structure, function, regulation, and genetic disease. Physiol Rev 75:749, 1995.

87

Neurogenic Diseases of the Larynx

Douglas D. Dedo, M.D., and Herbert H. Dedo, M.D.

Isolated neurologic disorders of the upper respiratory and gastrointestinal tracts are unusual in the pediatric population. However, unilateral and occasionally bilateral recurrent nerve paralysis is seen in the newborn or infant. It may be a manifestation of a multisystem anomaly, or, if there is no apparent cause, it is presumably due to stretching of the recurrent laryngeal nerves at delivery. Early detection of these neurogenic disorders is based on a high index of suspicion and is important for prevention of catastrophes during periods of acute respiratory embarrassment.

Clinical Symptoms

Acquired or congenital neurogenic laryngeal disorders affect one or all of the normal functions of the larynx. An abnormal cry or voice, respiratory obstruction, and difficulty swallowing are the symptoms of altered laryngeal function. A neonate with a weak or absent cry may have a laryngeal anomaly whether or not respiration is impaired. Unilateral vocal cord paralysis tends to produce a breathy and weak cry. In bilateral vocal cord paralysis, the cry is normal, but significant airway obstruction is ordinarily present; expiratory air passing through the glottis with the cords in a median or paramedian position produces a normal cry and voice, even though both cords are paralyzed. A muffled cry usually signifies a problem of pharyngeal origin, such as a vallecular cyst, lingual thyroid, or pharyngeal abscess.

Stridor, the harsh respiratory sound produced when air passes a partially vibrating obstruction (the vocal cords), is the most frequent symptom of children with cord paralysis for which parents seek advice.[2] When the stridor is associated with a normal cry, the most common cause (confirmed by direct laryngoscopy) is congenital laryngomalacia (soft cartilage or floppy epiglottis). Unilateral or bilateral vocal cord paralysis, laryngotracheobronchitis, web, foreign body, cricoarytenoid joint fixation, and tumor must be ruled out in these stridulous patients.

Abnormal deglutition is frequently associated with disorders of the larynx. Drooling, recurrent choking, and aspiration of pharyngeal secretions suggest either a developmental anomaly of the laryngopharynx, such as a posterior cleft larynx or a tracheoesophageal fistula, or a peripheral or central lesion of the ninth or tenth cranial nerves. Pharyngeal and vocal cord paralysis have been reported to occur together.[10]

Etiology of Laryngeal Paralysis

Laryngeal paralysis may be congenital or acquired in the neonate or infant, but in older children, as in adults, trauma is the usual cause. The following outline lists the myriad sources of laryngeal paralysis in neonates and infants.

I. Congenital
  A. *Central nervous system*
    1. Cerebral agenesis
    2. Hydrocephalus
    3. Encephalocele
    4. Meningomyelocele
    5. Meningocele
    6. Arnold-Chiari malformation
    7. Nucleus ambiguus dysgenesis
    8. Associated multiple congenital anomalies
      a. Mental retardation
      b. Down syndrome
      c. Other cranial nerve palsies
  B. *Peripheral nervous system*
    1. Congenital defect in peripheral nerve fiber at neuromuscular junction, as in myasthenia gravis
    2. Platybasia
  C. *Cardiovascular anomalies*
    1. Cardiomegaly
      a. Interventricular septal defect
      b. Tetralogy of Fallot
    2. Abnormal great vessels
      a. Vascular ring
      b. Dilated aorta
      c. Double aortic arch
      d. Patent ductus arteriosus
      e. Transposition of the great vessels
  D. *Associated with other congenital anomalies*
    1. Tumors or cysts of mediastinum (bronchogenic cyst)
    2. Malformation of the tracheobronchial tree
    3. Esophageal malformation
      a. Cyst
      b. Duplication
      c. Atresia

       d. Tracheoesophageal fistula
    4. Diaphragmatic hernia
    5. Erb palsy
    6. Cleft palate
    7. Laryngeal anomalies
       a. Laryngeal cleft
       b. Subglottic stenosis
       c. Laryngomalacia
II. Acquired
   A. *Trauma*
    1. Birth injury
    2. Postsurgical correction of cardiovascular or esophageal anomalies
   B. *Infections*
    1. Whooping cough encephalitis
    2. Polyneuritis
    3. Polioencephalitis
    4. Diphtheria
    5. Rabies
    6. Syphilis
    7. Tetanus
    8. Botulism
    9. Tuberculosis
   10. Guillain-Barré syndrome
   C. *Supranuclear and nuclear lesions*
    1. Kernicterus
    2. Multiple sclerosis

In older children and adolescents, the etiology is similar to that in most adult series. The cause is usually traumatic: (1) thoracic or head and neck surgery; (2) external neck trauma; (3) intubation for general anesthesia.

Congenital

Vocal cord paralysis is the second most common laryngeal anomaly of the neonate. (The most common is laryngomalacia.) Unilateral or bilateral paralysis together account for approximately 10% of all congenital laryngeal lesions.[9] The majority of these infants have multiple congenital defects. The overall incidence for each of the congenital causes of vocal cord paralysis is rare and mirrors the respective incidence of the associated congenital anomalies. Because the larynx is not routinely examined in these patients, the vocal cord paralysis may remain undiagnosed for a long time.

The Arnold-Chiari malformation is frequently seen with hydrocephalus, meningocele, and myelomeningocele (cervical, lumbar, or sacral).[7] The anatomy of the malformation is illustrated in Figure 87–1. The medulla and cerebellum protrude through the foramen magnum into the spinal canal so that the tenth cranial nerves exit the brain stem in the spinal canal. The abnormal course of the vagal nerves—traveling superiorly through the fora-

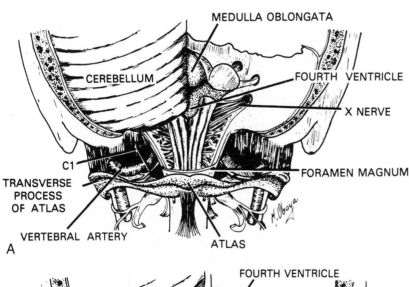

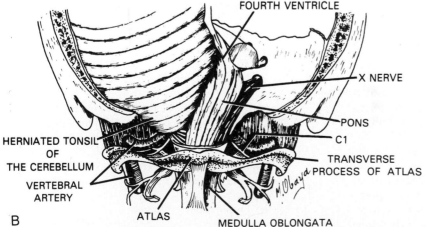

FIGURE 87–1. *A,* Normal dorsal view of the posterior fossa; left cerebellar hemisphere is in place, and right cerebellar hemisphere is removed. *B,* Arnold-Chiari malformation showing herniation and inferior displacement of brain stem, with subsequent abnormal course of vagus nerves, superiorly through foramen magnum to exit the jugular foramen.

men magnum to exit the jugular foramen—leaves them vulnerable to injury. The subsequent caudal displacement of the brain stem by increasing intracranial pressure stretches the vagi and causes tenth cranial nerve, and therefore recurrent nerve and vocal cord, paralysis.

Hemorrhages and infarcts have been found at autopsy in the medulla of children clinically diagnosed with the Arnold-Chiari malformation.[17] The altered vascular supply to the malformed medulla may contribute to or even be a more important source of vocal cord paralysis than stretching of the tenth cranial nerve.

Other developmental anomalies of the central nervous system, such as encephalocele, cerebral agenesis, mental retardation, and nucleus ambiguus dysgenesis, have been reported with vocal cord paralysis.

Vocal cord paralysis with or without other bulbar palsies has been described with other progressive congenital and acquired neuromuscular disorders.[8,10,18] Benign congenital hypotonia, Werdnig-Hoffman disease, leukodystrophy, and Charcot-Marie-Tooth disease have all been complicated by laryngeal paralysis. The causal relationship between the disease and the paralysis has not been defined.

Myasthenia gravis is a disease affecting all age groups. It is characterized by weakness and abnormal fatigability of skeletal muscles. The return of normal muscle strength after fatigue is prolonged. Neonatal myasthenia gravis may manifest with bulbar symptoms. These children, whose mothers have myasthenia gravis, are noted to have marked inability to suck or swallow.[21] An absent or weak cry and facial weakness are also common symptoms. Tracheotomy is performed on those infants unable to swallow or to cough effectively.

Congenital or juvenile myasthenia gravis affects those children with normal mothers. Although the presenting symptom is usually ptosis of the eyelids, dysphagia or dysphonia may also be exhibited. These symptoms occur because of weak pharyngeal and tongue muscles.[14] The diagnosis is established by the use of anticholinesterase drugs.

Skeletal malformations may damage the peripheral cranial nerves. Platybasia is a flattening of the base of the skull on the cervical spine. Subsequent stretching of the cranial nerves may produce vocal cord paralysis. The diagnosis is readily made with skull radiographs.[15]

A wide variety of congenital cardiovascular anomalies have been associated with vocal cord paralysis. Although the left recurrent nerve is more vulnerable to injury than the right because of its longer course, right vocal cord paralysis has been seen with cardiovascular defects. Cardiomegaly due to an interventricular septal defect or tetralogy of Fallot may stretch the left recurrent nerve. Abnormalities of the great vessels, such as a vascular ring, dilated aorta, double aortic arch, transposition, and patent ductus arteriosus, have all been associated with vocal cord paralysis.[10]

The intimate embryologic development of the laryngopharynx, esophagus, and tracheobronchial tree from the third, fourth, fifth, and sixth visceral arches accounts for the associated congenital anomalies in these structures. Esophageal cysts, duplication or atresia of the esophagus, diaphragmatic hernia, and tracheoesophageal fistula have been reported with laryngeal paralysis. Bronchogenic cysts of the mediastinum and tracheobronchial malformations have also been complicated by vocal cord paralysis. Similarly, congenital defects of the larynx, including subglottic stenosis, laryngomalacia, and laryngeal clefts, may have associated unilateral or bilateral vocal cord paralysis. Several other congenital disorders and syndromes, such as Down syndrome, arthrogryposis multiplex congenita,[4] and cleft palate, have been reported with laryngeal paralysis as one facet of the anomaly (see Chap. 83).

Acquired

The acquired neurogenic lesions of the larynx in the pediatric patient may be divided into three broad categories: traumatic, infectious, and miscellaneous. Injury to the recurrent laryngeal nerves at birth has been implicated. For a significant number of pediatric patients with vocal cord paralysis, as in any adult series, no apparent cause of the problem can be found. It has been suggested that, in these cases, the recurrent nerves have been unavoidably stretched during delivery, as with a breech presentation with twisting and stretching of the neck to deliver the head. Hyperextension of the neck to the right or left in the vertex position to rotate and deliver the shoulders may also produce recurrent laryngeal nerve injury. The anatomy of the recurrent laryngeal nerves makes them vulnerable to injury as they course around the subclavian artery on the right and the aorta on the left. During delivery, the vessels provide countertraction against the nerves, thus stretching them, with subsequent paralysis that may be temporary or permanent. Tracheotomy is usually necessary for bilateral but not for unilateral paralysis (see Chap. 93).

Surgical correction of many of the thoracic and cardiovascular anomalies may be complicated by injury to the recurrent laryngeal nerves. Because vocal cord paralysis has been reported after repair of patent ductus arteriosus, tracheoesophageal fistula, and other similar anomalies, preoperative visualization of the larynx to determine vocal cord mobility is useful.

Antibiotics and immunizations (vaccinations) have greatly reduced the infectious types of vocal cord paralysis. Whooping cough encephalitis, poliomyelitis, diphtheria, rabies, tetanus, syphilis, and botulism have been sources of laryngeal paralysis that are rarely seen in present-day pediatric practice.[2] Any bacterial or viral encephalitis may be complicated by bulbar paresis. Similarly, an ascending paralysis, as in the Guillain-Barré syndrome, occasionally involves the bulbar nuclei with subsequent laryngeal or chest paralysis, or both, requiring cuffed tracheotomy and assisted ventilation for several days or weeks. Infectious mononucleosis has a neurologic complication rate of 1% to 2%. Meningoencephalitis and peripheral neuritis with pharyngeal and laryngeal paralysis have been reported with mononucleosis.[16]

Idiopathic vocal cord paralysis occasionally follows a viral infection[7] and is usually in the form of a peripheral neuritis similar to Bell palsy. Return of vocal cord mobility in 2 to 6 months can occur. In unusual cases, tracheotomy is necessary to relieve the airway obstruction.

Tumors of the central nervous system may occur with bulbar paralysis. Ross and Chambers[20] reported a case of an infant with a chondroma at or near the nucleus ambiguus that caused laryngeal nerve paralysis. Similar paresis from a spongioblastoma multiforme of the right cerebellar hemisphere confluent with the pons and medulla has also been reported.[11]

A broad category of miscellaneous causes for acquired neurogenic disorders includes those diseases in which the laryngeal nerve may be involved along its anatomic course.[19] The supranuclear areas and nuclei may be involved in kernicterus and multiple sclerosis. Holinger[10] reported a case of mediastinitis resulting from an esophageal foreign body that caused bilateral recurrent nerve paralysis.

In adolescence, the incidence of vocal cord paralysis decreases, and the causes reflect those of most adult series. In this age group, the most frequent cause of vocal cord paralysis is trauma to the recurrent laryngeal nerves. In addition, head and neck or thoracic surgery may be complicated by a postoperative vocal cord paralysis. Blunt neck trauma from motor vehicle accidents may generate forces sufficient to stretch or even to avulse the recurrent laryngeal nerves, with subsequent vocal cord paralysis. Postintubation vocal cord paralysis has been reported in adults but never in children, infants, or neonates. The mechanism of injury is thought to be the result of the endotracheal tube cuff compressing the recurrent laryngeal nerve against the thyroid cartilage.[3] The use of non-cuffed tubes in pediatric surgery or the extreme elasticity of the thyroid cartilage may account for its not being reported in the pediatric population.

Diagnosis and Management

In the neonate, the diagnosis of a vocal cord paralysis is frequently overlooked because of a more severe associated central nervous system or cardiovascular anomaly. A newborn or infant with an airway problem, feeding difficulties, weak or absent cry, deglutition abnormalities, or known anomaly of the esophagus, heart, or central nervous system should have a laryngeal examination.

Preliminary examination of the larynx in the neonate or newborn is best scheduled in the neonatal intensive care unit. After a history is obtained from the neonatologist or pediatrician, the newborn receives nothing by mouth for 6 hours. The pediatric endoscopy equipment is brought from the operating room to the neonatal intensive care unit. In general, the pediatric specialists are much more comfortable starting intravenous lines, sedating, and managing these patients than are the anesthesiologists in the operating rooms, unless well-trained pediatric anesthesiologists are available. If a tracheotomy becomes necessary, it can be done over an endotracheal tube or bronchoscope.

Flexible fiberoptic laryngoscopy with nasal decongestion and topical anesthesia is the method of choice to evaluate vocal cord mobility in the neonate and newborn. Direct laryngoscopy without anesthesia is an alternative method to evaluate vocal cord mobility in the neonate and newborn. Oxygen, pediatric (2.5:3.0) endotracheal tubes, Ambu bag, and suction are laid out on a clean surgical field for immediate accessibility if needed. The Hopkins laryngoscope blade is placed in the vallecula and tilted forward. Laryngeal movement must be evaluated during inspiration and phonation or crying. Passage of the pediatric rigid telescope alongside the laryngoscope, to lie just above the arytenoids, greatly enhances the examination. After assessment of laryngeal movement, the configuration of the vocal cords, anterior commissure, and subglottic surface is observed. Cyanosis, apnea, and the cardiac status of the infant may require administration of oxygen throughout the examination, with interruption for oral ventilation if required.

If there is no apparent pathologic condition to explain the stridor or partial upper airway obstruction, microlaryngoscopy under general anesthesia should be done. Subglottic lesions not visible with direct laryngoscopy when the infant is awake are sometimes visible under magnification by focusing the microscope through the cords when they are fully relaxed. In fact, confirmation of any laryngeal disease initially diagnosed in the neonatal unit is done under general anesthesia in the operating room. This allows the passive movement of the arytenoid with a small probe or suction to confirm a vocal cord paralysis as opposed to cricoarytenoid joint fixation.

Once the infant is discharged from the hospital, flexible laryngoscopy with the smaller pediatric scope may be done in the office. However, a child with severe stridor, cardiac anomalies, or compromise is best examined in the hospital with controlled conditions for rapid intubation or tracheotomy if acute obstruction occurs. In an infant with hoarseness for which papilloma is even faintly suggested, flexible nasal endoscopy is contraindicated because of the possibility of seeding the mucosa with the papillomavirus.

When the recurrent laryngeal nerve and superior laryngeal nerve are paralyzed on the same side, the vocal cord lies in the intermediate position, and the arytenoids do not come together. The posterior larynx is rotated to the side of paralysis. During inspiration, when the moving vocal cords open, the edge of the paralyzed vocal cord is not a straight line. The tip of the vocal process sticks out because the membranous cord is more atrophic. When both recurrent laryngeal nerves are paralyzed, on inspiration the maximal glottic chink will be less than the width of either membranous cord (i.e., less than a 3-mm glottic chink). To estimate the width of the chink, compare the chink to the width of the membranous cord. One third, two thirds, or three thirds of the width of the membranous cord translates into a 1-, 2-, or 3-mm glottic chink, respectively.

Spastic dysphonia may be considered a neurogenic disease of the larynx. The two youngest patients given such a diagnosis were 9 and 17 years. After the diagnosis was confirmed with local infiltration and paralysis of the recurrent laryngeal nerve, the two patients subsequently underwent recurrent laryngeal nerve section.[6] Botulinum toxin injections are now used for spastic dysphonia.

When other congenital anomalies of the respiratory or digestive systems are suspected, bronchoscopy (complemented with the Hopkins telescope) and esophagoscopy should be part of the management protocol.

Which radiologic studies are appropriate is largely determined by the presence of other congenital anomalies. Posterior, anterior, and lateral radiographs of the chest and neck can be helpful. Skull films and dye studies of the larynx, trachea, esophagus, and cardiovascular system may be required to document and evaluate associated defects.[12] A specific radiographic study of the larynx to evaluate mobility is the positive contrast laryngogram with videography in the posteroanterior view. Magnetic resonance imaging and computed tomography of the larynx are of limited value.

Treatment

The initial treatment of a child with a neurogenic disorder of the larynx is primarily symptomatic. Maintenance of the airway and adequate nutrition are of prime importance. Cavanaugh[2] and Holinger[10] reported a 50% incidence of tracheotomy in children with bilateral vocal cord paralysis; the incidence of tracheotomy for unilateral vocal cord paralysis was 20%. After the condition of the patient is stabilized, the search for the cause of the paralysis may proceed. A diagnosis is usually obvious in 90% of the cases,[5] whereas the remaining 10% are classified as idiopathic.

When the diagnosis of a laryngeal paralysis has been made and the etiology investigated, the patient must be carefully observed for the next several weeks to months. Cavanaugh[2] and Holinger[10] both reported spontaneous resolution of the paresis in a few cases. Bluestone and colleagues[1] emphasized the importance of close cooperation between the neurosurgeon and the otolaryngologist in treating children with the Arnold-Chiari malformation due to myelomeningocele. In these children, when the increased intracranial pressure was corrected by a shunt within 24 hours of onset of the vocal cord paralysis, reversal to normal vocal cord mobility was seen to occur up to 2 weeks later. A delay in diagnosing the increased intracranial pressure and subsequent laryngeal paralysis could result in irreversible vocal cord paralysis. Because of the possibility of spontaneous recovery with any vocal cord paralysis, 6 months to a year should elapse before any definitive therapy is planned.

Correction of an incompetent glottis in unilateral recurrent laryngeal paralysis and tracheal decannulation after relieving the airway obstruction in bilateral vocal cord paralysis are the two major treatment problems in these children. The optimal age of the child for either procedure is unknown. Priest and colleagues[18] have successfully performed the classic Woodman and Pennington[22] procedure in children 5, 6, and 14 years of age with bilateral vocal cord paralysis. Laser arytenoidectomy may allow decannulation in small children. Similarly, polytetrafluoroethylene (Teflon) injection has been used by one of the authors (H. Dedo) in a 9-year-old girl for correction of an incompetent glottis due to laryngeal nerve paralysis after open heart surgery.

Laryngoplastic phonosurgery to correct incompetent airways and paralyzed vocal cords in the pediatric population is still experimental. The long-term effects of these procedures in the pediatric population on the growing larynx are unknown.[13]

Unfortunately, the management of these children is complex and not limited to the realm of the otolaryngologist. For instance, parental instruction in maintaining a tracheotomy in an infant cannot be taken for granted. Because of the associated pharyngeal paralyses, a gastrostomy is often necessary.

The associated central nervous system or cardiovascular anomalies make many of these patients long-term nursing problems, never able to be discharged from the hospital.

Prognosis

The acquired forms of vocal cord paralysis have a more favorable outcome than those of congenital origin. The latter are dependent on the course of the underlying central nervous system or cardiovascular anomaly. Unilateral vocal cord paralysis involves the left more commonly than the right because of its longer course and associated cardiac anomalies; the prognosis is also poorer for left-sided than for right-sided paralysis. In general, the right-sided paresis is an isolated finding, with laryngeal function being found ultimately to be good.

Bilateral vocal cord paralyses have a worse prognosis than unilateral paralyses. The children who require a tracheotomy for obstruction and who do not die of their other anomalies may sometimes not be decannulated. The exception is the child with a traumatic delivery in whom the paralysis resolves spontaneously 4 to 6 months after birth.

SELECTED REFERENCES

Cavanaugh F. Vocal palsies in children. J Laryngol Otol 69:399, 1955.
> *This important work was one of the first to draw attention to vocal cord paralysis in children. The author reviews the case reports in the literature through 1955 and then adds several cases of her own. It is an article referenced by all authors writing on pediatric vocal cord paralysis.*

Holinger PH. Clinical aspects of congenital anomalies of the larynx, trachea, bronchi, and esophagus. J Laryngol Otol 75:1, 1961.
> *A perspective of the relative incidences of the different anomalies of the upper airway is gained from this excellent paper. A large series of vocal cord paralyses with management and long-term follow-up is presented.*

REFERENCES

1. Bluestone CD, Delerme AN, Samuelson GH. Airway obstruction due to vocal cord paralysis in infants with hydrocephalus and meningomyelocele. Ann Otol 81:778, 1972.
2. Cavanaugh F. Vocal palsies in children. J Laryngol Otol 69:399, 1955.
3. Cavo JW. True vocal cord paralysis following intubation. Laryngoscope 95:1352, 1985.
4. Cohen SR, Isaacs H Jr. Otolaryngological manifestations of arthrogryposis multiplex congenita. Ann Otol Rhinol Laryngol 85:484, 1976.
5. Dedo HH. Paralyzed larynx: electromyographic study in dogs and humans. Laryngoscope 80:1455, 1970.

6. Dedo HH. Surgery of the Larynx and Trachea. Philadelphia, BC Decker, 1990.

7. Graham MD. Bilateral recurrent laryngeal nerve paralysis associated with upper respiratory infection. J Laryngol Otol 76:535, 1962.

8. Hart CW. Functional and neurological problems of the larynx. Otolaryngol Clin North Am 3:609, 1970.

9. Holinger LD, Holinger PC, Holinger PH. Etiology of bilateral abductor vocal cord paralysis—a review of 389 cases. Ann Otol Rhinol Laryngol 85:428, 1976.

10. Holinger PH. Clinical aspects of congenital anomalies of the larynx, trachea, bronchi, and esophagus. J Laryngol Otol 75:1, 1961.

11. Jackson C, Jackson CL. Larynx and Its Diseases. Philadelphia, WB Saunders, 1937, p 289.

12. Kahn A, Baran D, Sephl N, et al. Congenital stridor in infancy. Clin Pediatr 16:19, 1977.

13. Koufman JA, Isaacson G. Laryngoplastic phonosurgery. Otolaryngol Clin North Am 24:1151, 1991.

14. Maxwell S, Locke JL. Voice and myasthenia gravis. Laryngoscope 78:1902, 1968.

15. Merritt HH. A Textbook of Neurology. Philadelphia, Lea & Febiger, 1963, p 424.

16. Montandon L, Rauch S, Reytan T. Mononucleosis, Guillain-Barré syndrome and paralysis of the posterior cricoarytenoid muscle. Acta Otolaryngol (Stockh) 46:35, 1956.

17. Papasozomenos S, Roessmann U. Respiratory distress and Arnold-Chiari malformation. Neurology 31:97, 1981.

18. Priest RE, Ulvestad HS, Van de Water F, et al. Arytenoidectomy in children. Ann Otol Rhinol Laryngol 69:869, 1966.

19. Rontal M, Rontal E. Lesions of the vagus nerve: diagnosis, treatment and rehabilitation. Laryngoscope 87:72, 1977.

20. Ross DE, Chambers DC. Recurrent laryngeal nerve paralysis occurring in the infant. Am J Surg 94:513, 1957.

21. Stuart WD. Otolaryngological aspects of myasthenia gravis. Laryngoscope 75:112, 1963.

22. Woodman D, Pennington CL. Bilateral abductor paralysis. Ann Otol Rhinol Laryngol 85:437, 1976.

88

Injuries to the Lower Respiratory Tract

Susan E. Pearson, M.D., Franklin Rimell, M.D., and James Sidman, M.D.

Blunt and penetrating laryngotracheal trauma is rare in adults and even more unusual in children. The reported incidence is between 0.00003% and 0.0001% of all pediatric emergency room trauma patients and 0.5% of admitted pediatric trauma patients.[12, 49] Although it is rare, when it does occur, it frequently results in significant morbidity or in mortality. This is due to the fact that minor direct trauma to the larynx or trachea, in the pediatric population, usually results in serious injury.[24]

Pediatric laryngotracheal injuries are different from the commonly observed adult injuries. This is because of the unique anatomic features of the pediatric larynx. Some protective features of the pediatric larynx include relatively soft, pliable cartilages and a high position of the larynx in the neck, shielded by the mandible (Fig. 88-1).[43, 22] These differences result in fewer laryngeal injuries, especially fractures. The unfavorable characteristics of the pediatric larynx include its size and shape and the immaturity of the membranes. The pediatric larynx is much smaller than the adult larynx.[24] It is funnel-shaped and is narrowest at the subglottic region. The epiglottis is narrower and has an omega-like shape, and there is a posterior tilt to the cricoid. These differences bring the aryepiglottic folds closer to the midline and result in a narrowed laryngeal inlet. The intercartilaginous fibers and membranes are weaker and thus more susceptible to rupture in the pediatric population.[2] Because of these differences, similar injuries have more severe consequences in children.[41]

Types of Injuries

Trauma may be blunt or penetrating. Blunt injuries are more common than penetrating injuries. Bicycle accidents account for the majority of the blunt injuries in children, whereas penetrating injuries are caused by gunshot wounds, knife or scissor stab wounds, or falls onto sharp objects. Although the use of seat belts and airbags has resulted in lower fatality rates associated with motor vehicle accidents, there is a growing amount of literature on injuries caused by seat belt restraint or airbag deployment. Most automobile passengers sustain minor injuries, but there are reported adult and child fatalities.[16]

Blunt Injuries

Blunt laryngotracheal trauma in a child is typically sustained while the child is riding a bicycle or motorbike. Falling onto the handlebars with the neck extended causes compression of the larynx and trachea against the cervical vertebral column.[12] Injuries resulting from riding a motorbike or all-terrain vehicle into a clothesline have also occurred. The force of such a blow is imparted on the laryngotracheal complex. An extensive variety of injuries can result, including hyoid fractures (Fig. 88–2), vocal cord avulsion or paralysis, laryngeal fractures, arytenoid cartilage dislocation, thyroepiglottic ligament disruption, posterior tracheal lacerations, mucosal edema, submucosal hematoma, tracheobronchial ruptures, and laryngotracheal separation.[12] Other mechanisms of injury include child abuse, suicide attempts (hangings) (Fig. 88–3), and athletic injuries. Children of all ages are involved in blunt laryngotracheal injuries, with a mean age of approximately 10 years, and boys are affected more frequently than girls are.[12]

Presenting complaints may be quite minimal with blunt airway injuries. Frequent symptoms include neck pain and some degree of respiratory distress. Children may also present with odynophagia, dysphagia, voice change, hemoptysis, cervical or mediastinal subcutaneous emphysema, and ecchymosis.[22]

Laryngotracheal separations and tracheobronchial ruptures are uncommon, but are more common in children than in adults. Mortality rates of up to 30% have been reported. Half of the children who die do so within 1 hour of the trauma event.[13] The elasticity of the chest wall in children allows massive external forces directly onto the mediastinum without disruption of the integrity of the chest wall. Rib fractures, present in approximately 90% of adults with tracheobronchial injury, are present in only approximately 24% of children with similar injuries.[13] Thus, absence of rib fractures does not rule out major intrathoracic injuries in children. The pathogenesis of tracheobronchial rupture is a rapidly increased intrabronchial pressure caused by compression of the chest against a closed glottis.[10] Air dissects through the rupture and into the retropharynx and mediastinum.[50] Other explanations include shear forces, traction, and crush of the airways between the chest and the vertebrae.[10] Successful

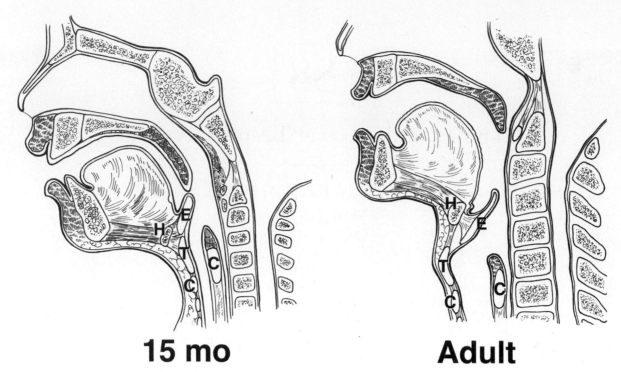

15 mo   Adult

FIGURE 88-1. Differences between the adult's and the child's upper airway anatomy. E, epiglottis; H, hyoid; T, thyroid cartilage; C, cricoid cartilage.

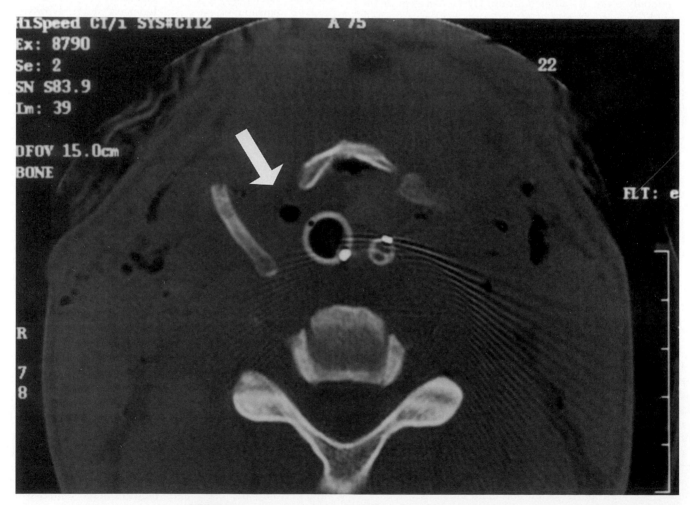

FIGURE 88-2. Computed tomographic scan of a hyoid fracture.

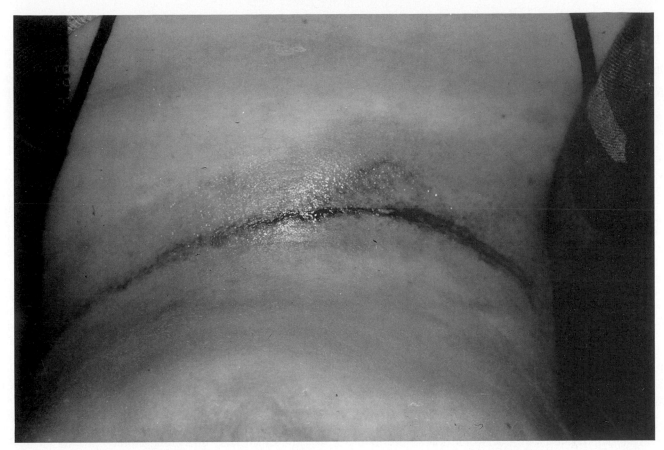

FIGURE 88–3. Neck injury and resulting hematoma secondary to hanging.

management of airway disruptions is based on prompt recognition of airway compromise along with rapid treatment to maintain effective ventilation. Traumatic pneumothorax or pneumomediastinum is usually present. Continued air leak despite decompression of the pneumothorax with a chest tube is the key to suspecting possible tracheobronchial disruption.[13]

The location of tracheobronchial injuries has been found to be relatively consistent: 80% involve the mainstem bronchi, 15% involve the trachea, and 5% involve the distal bronchi.[20, 39]

Blunt trauma to the laryngotracheal complex may also result in tears of the esophagus. Hypopharyngeal and esophageal tears can occur without disruption of the laryngeal skeleton. The greater cornu of the thyroid cartilage can lacerate the pharyngeal mucosa.[30]

The morbidity and mortality associated with blunt neck injuries are most often related to a delay in diagnosis. A possible reason for the delay in diagnosis of laryngotracheal injury is the fact that the relatively stiff cervical fascia and tracheal cartilage may initially preserve the airway continuity until soft-tissue swelling or hematoma formation leads to signs and symptoms of airway compromise.[9]

Penetrating Injuries

Penetrating laryngotracheal injuries in children are even less common than blunt injuries; however, these injuries are associated with significant morbidity and mortality rates.[40] Boys are injured more frequently than girls are, and the children tend to be older than those affected by blunt trauma injury, with a mean age of 12 years.[18] The mechanisms of injury include gunshot wounds, knife or scissors stab wounds, and glass injuries.[7, 18]

Predominant clinical findings on presentation include air bubbling through the wound, subcutaneous crepitus, respiratory distress or stridor, shock or hemorrhage, neurologic signs, hemoptysis, hematemesis, dysphonia or hoarseness, and expanding hematoma. Unlike blunt laryngotracheal trauma, associated chest, digestive tract, and vascular injuries are common.[8, 14] Approximately 10% of these patients must have emergency surgery secondary to instability.[35] Typical indications for emergency surgery include bleeding, open airway, and expanding hematoma.

Airway compromise and exsanguination from major vascular injury are the major factors contributing to early mortality in patients with penetrating neck injuries. Late mortality is generally secondary to undiagnosed esophageal injuries.[8] Esophageal injuries are rare but are the most commonly missed associated injury.[51] There is an associated digestive tract injury in 15% to 50% of these patients. Esophageal injuries have significant associated morbidity and a mortality rate reaching 19.5%.[40] Associated esophageal injuries are difficult to diagnose because they may be 3 to 4 cm away from the tracheal injury. This is because of the extensive esophageal mobility.[38] Odynophagia, hematemesis, and subcutaneous emphysema are the most common findings of esophageal injury.[8]

Diagnostic Techniques

History and Physical Examination

Any child sustaining anterior cervical injury should be examined for the presence of laryngotracheal injury. Symptoms of injury include increasing airway obstruction with stridor or dyspnea, cough, dysphonia or aphonia, dysphagia or odynophagia, hemoptysis or hematemesis, and neck pain.[31]

A thorough and careful history should be obtained and an accurate physical examination performed, including determining the mechanism of injury. The patient should be quickly but meticulously examined for respiratory difficulty, stridor, loss or change in voice, and swallowing abnormalities. The child's voice may initially be muffled, hoarse, or aphonic or may be normal and deteriorate gradually. Neurologic deficits, especially cervical spine injuries, should be ruled out. The neck should be inspected for palpable laryngeal cartilage fractures, obliteration of external laryngeal anatomic landmarks, tenderness, crepitus, hematoma formation, and swelling.

Diagnostic Tests

Several diagnostic tests contribute to the diagnosis of these injuries. It must be underscored that if respiratory distress symptoms are progressive, endotracheal intubation or tracheostomy followed by an orderly evaluation may be necessary.

The definitive diagnostic step for discerning the extent of the injury and determining the necessity for open exploration and repair is endoscopy.[11] In experienced hands, flexible laryngoscopy is a very valuable tool for evaluating laryngeal anatomy and function. A 2 to 3 mm pediatric flexible scope can easily identify vocal cord mobility, mucosal tears, hematoma, or arytenoid dislocations without endangering the cervical spine. One must remember, however, that in an already traumatized larynx, irreversible laryngospasms may occur if the scope is advanced too close to the larynx. Direct laryngoscopy may be needed to further evaluate the larynx but requires a general anesthetic and may exacerbate mucosal tears or miss a dislocated epiglottis.[33, 45]

The patient with dyspnea, hemoptysis, subcutaneous emphysema, or a pneumothorax refractory to the insertion of chest tubes needs an immediate bronchoscopy, with possible control of the distal airway if a tracheobronchial separation is found.[5] In children, who have smaller airways, fiberoptic bronchoscopy has been invaluable in the diagnosis of tracheal and bronchial injuries. A fiberoptic bronchoscope may be inserted through the endotracheal tube and is helpful in aspirating material, mucous plugs, and thick secretions.[3] Fiberoptic bronchoscopy also allows the selective stenting of the transected or lacerated trachea or selective intubation of the right or left mainstem bronchus, allowing controlled ventilation prior to an immediate thoracotomy by a thoracic surgeon.[5] Minor air-

way lesions may be overlooked unless the endoscopy is completed by an examination with increased intratracheal pressure, thus stenting open the airway. This additional maneuver is recommended whenever a tracheal wall lesion is suspected but is not seen by endoscopy.[19] Bronchoscopy is the most reliable means of establishing the diagnosis and determining the site, nature, and extent of tracheobronchial injury.[20]

Esophagoscopy is the procedure of choice in the evaluation of a possible concomitant esophageal injury. The presence of a hematoma or blood usually suggests an underlying injury, and visualization of the perforation confirms the diagnosis. When the procedure is performed under general anesthesia with positive-pressure breathing, bubbles often form in the field, making it easier to detect small perforations. Although a negative esophagoscopic finding does not definitively rule out a perforation, the addition of an esophagram improves the yield.[14]

The initial radiologic examination may include the lateral soft tissue radiograph of the neck, cervical spine series, and a chest radiograph. It is best to obtain portable films in the emergency department. These are low cost, straightforward, rapidly obtainable, and highly useful diagnostic procedures that have long been regarded as standard of airway examination.[21] They may provide valuable information about fractured or displaced laryngeal cartilages, soft tissue swelling or emphysema, pneumothorax or pneumomediastinum, and cervical spine injuries. Unfortunately, the cartilage of the airway in children is not ossified, and thus these studies provide an inadequate evaluation of cartilaginous damage.

Computed tomography (CT) adds a three-dimensional component to the understanding of the laryngeal and tracheal anatomy. Only hemodynamically stable patients without airway compromise should undergo CT evaluation. In the acute setting, at most institutions, CT of the neck is used to evaluate for possible bony and cartilaginous fractures and soft tissue injuries (Fig. 88–4). This is especially needed when laryngoscopic examination is difficult. Indications for CT usually include neck trauma with signs and symptoms of cervical and laryngeal injury or a mechanism of trauma known to cause such injuries.[32]

Helical CT represents a recent major improvement in the evaluation of trauma patients. It differs from conventional single-section CT in that the x-ray source continuously circles the patient as he or she is moved through the tube for a predetermined distance at a predetermined speed. Scanning time through the neck is substantially reduced, because data are continuously collected. Short scan times, in turn, reduce the likelihood of motion artifacts and result in the higher quality of reformatted and three-dimensional reconstructed images.[1]

In children, the airway is a complex, three-dimensional, variably ossified structure. Frequently, three-dimensional CT provides significant additional information for patients with suspected laryngotracheal injury. It can confirm subtle injuries suggested on two-dimensional CT and may reveal additional unsuspected pathologic lesions. No additional scanning time is needed, and it takes only minutes for most current CT software to reconstruct the images. Thus, it tends to increase diagnostic accuracy and

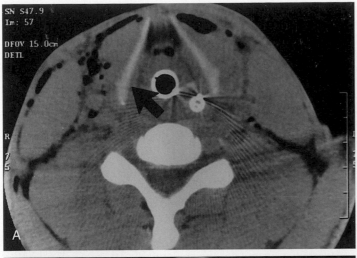

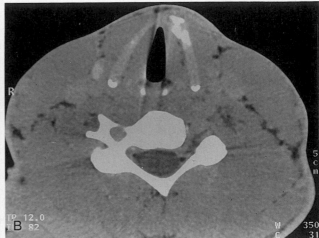

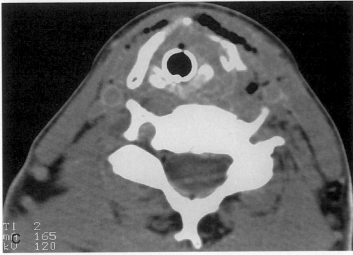

FIGURE 88–4. Computed tomographic scan of varying degrees of laryngeal fractures, from nondisplaced to severely comminuted (**A–C**). Note the subcutaneous air in each of the fractures, regardless of the severity.

may be helpful in preoperative planning.[36] The results obtained by spiral CT with color-coded three-dimensional reconstruction have recently been compared to those obtained with magnetic resonance angiography and are as informative yet less costly, with a shorter examination period.[25]

Magnetic resonance imaging (MRI) studies of children with laryngotracheal trauma are generally not performed in the acute setting, because of the sensitivity of MRI to motion and the longer examination time. The availability of the MRI scanner and its costs are also limiting factors. Yet, in the evaluation of subacute or chronic laryngotracheal injuries, MRI is capable of better soft tissue contrast than CT and can offer coronal and sagittal views.[6] This offers excellent visualization of the airway with the additional advantage of no exposure to radiation. It has obviated the need for angiography in many patients. Because of the extended examination time, a disadvantage of MRI is that most children need sedation or general anesthesia.

A gastrografin swallow study may need to be performed to rule out an esophageal tear. The sensitivity of a swallow study alone is reportedly between 50% and 90%.[23, 52] Water-soluble contrast agents should be used to help prevent barium sulfate–induced mediastinitis. The use of fluoroscopy with multiple views in addition to the standard anteroposterior and lateral projections increase the yield of esophagography.[14]

Treatment

The literature is limited in reports of the management of pediatric laryngotracheal trauma, although it generally parallels adult management. Immediate airway management followed by timely diagnosis of associated injuries is essential for effective treatment and the avoidance of complications. The goal of treatment should be the restoration of a normal airway and voice.[24]

Securing the airway is the most important first step in the management of victims of penetrating or blunt laryngotracheal trauma, yet there is controversy regarding the best method. Some authors avoid intubation because of concern about further iatrogenic injury by converting a small tear or partial transection into a complete transection. They cite possible neck manipulation during intubation with exacerbation of a cervical spine injury, and the danger of persistent airway edema, and suggest a tracheotomy.[37, 48] Also, the failure to establish an airway would mean that an emergency tracheotomy would have to be performed under less than ideal conditions. If possible, children should have their airways secured in an operating room after induction with inhalation general anesthesia.[41, 28]

In contrast, other authors recommend endotracheal intubation by a skilled physician, preferably over a flexible bronchoscope, especially in infants and small children.[9, 17, 50] In this patient population, whose airways are smaller and less defined, there is an increased rate of tracheotomy complications. Other disadvantages of tracheotomy include possible further damage to the posterior tracheal wall by the rigid nature of most tracheotomy tubes.[50] If endotracheal intubation is attempted, one should always be prepared to perform an emergency tracheotomy if the airway becomes compromised.

Endoscopic examination of the larynx should be performed to look for exposed or fractured cartilage, injury to vocal cords, or other signs of damage to the larynx. Children with isolated laryngeal injury with no exposed cartilage can be managed conservatively, provided they are closely monitored. Medical management, including humidification of the inspired air, elevation of the head of the bed, broad-spectrum antibiotics, H2 blockers, and intravenous steroids, is most effective during the acute phase.[4] A patient with laryngeal trauma that is managed

conservatively should be reevaluated in 7 to 14 days when the swelling subsides. Subtle cricoarytenoid joint dysfunction may then become more evident. Vocal cord hematomas (Fig. 88–5) and edema are slower to resolve and may cause persistent dysphonia.[5]

Laryngeal problems must be corrected prior to any attempted tracheal repair.[34] Exposed laryngeal cartilage should be covered with mucosa to decrease the likelihood of chondritis.[34] The avulsed mucosa can usually be sutured back to its normal anatomic position. Otherwise, local mucosal flaps should be rotated. Closure should be performed with absorbable sutures, with the knots buried to prevent granulation formation and possible obstruction.[4] Fractures need to be reduced and plated, usually with absorbable plates and screws, as soon as possible.[53]

A crushed larynx, although rare, requires meticulous reduction and airway maintenance. A stent may be inserted to maintain the reduction and is usually kept in place for 2 to 6 weeks.[42, 48] The stent provides internal stenting, maintains the lumen of the larynx, helps prevent adhesions, and helps maintain the scaphoid shape of the anterior commissure, all of which are essential for normal vocalization.[48] Laryngeal repair within 24 to 48 hours of injury has been shown to improve outcome.[4, 29] Dislocated, subluxed, or avulsed arytenoids should be positioned back onto the cricoarytenoid facet. Early endoscopic reduction is preferred, although delayed reduction

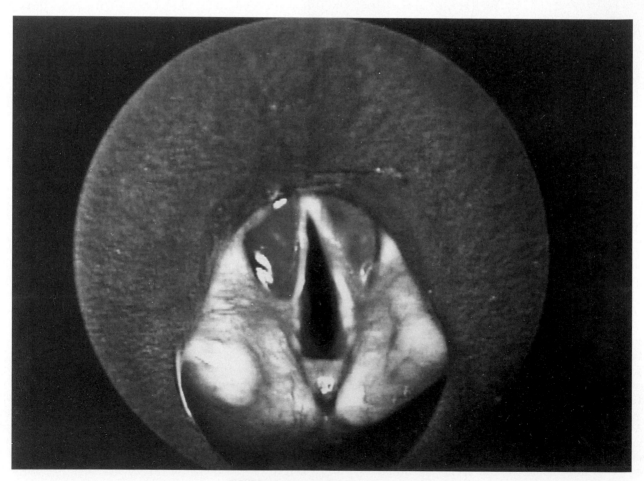

FIGURE 88–5. Vocal fold hematoma.

should still be attempted, despite the possibility of suboptimal return of function.[47] The completely avulsed arytenoid should be preserved and repositioned to provide bulk in the posterior glottis and help prevent aspiration.[5]

The treatment of tracheal injuries is primarily surgical. Lesions less than one third the circumference of the trachea may be associated with the full expansion of the lung and early cessation of the air leak after chest tube placement, and nonoperative medical management may be sufficient. This is especially true if the laceration is of the posterior wall and has well-opposed edges with no soft tissue loss (Fig. 88–6).[20, 26, 44] Endoscopically, the wound edges can be sealed with fibrin glue, provided the wound edges can be reapproximated without tension.[19] Alternatively, an endotracheal tube placed distal to a tracheal lesion for 48 hours may help seal the wound, although this is not standard practice.[8] These nonsurgical treatment options are important because lower tracheal injuries require a thoracotomy or an inferior cervical incision, which have higher rates of complications.[19]

Larger lacerations of the trachea should be repaired with absorbable 4-0 suture material using the interrupted technique. Local muscle flaps can be used to reinforce these suture lines.[34] Placement of a tracheotomy tube through a simple anterior laceration should be avoided, unless long-term intubation is expected.[34]

In managing extensive tracheal wounds, it is imperative to acquire a tension-free, well-vascularized anastomosis. The blood supply to the trachea enters primarily from the lateral aspects; thus, mobilization should be performed by anterior and sometimes posterior dissection with preservation of the adjacent lateral tissues.[8, 15] Extensive tracheal injuries require débridement of devitalized tissue. Conservation of viable tracheal tissue is essential. Careful end-to-end anastomosis is done using interrupted 4-0 absorbable suture.[34] Interrupted absorbable sutures are used exclusively to allow growth and to avoid the granuloma problems associated with nonabsorbable sutures.[13] Sutures are placed around the cartilage at a submucosal level, with the knots tied outside the lumen.[13] Complete tracheal separations are often closed by passing of an endotracheal tube across the lacerated trachea. The repair is then completed over the endotracheal tube.[5] Lung or laryngeal mobilization to reduce anastomotic tension is rarely needed in children, although the anastomosis must be tension-free.[13] Laryngeal mobilization can result in an increase in the length of the trachea of up to 5 cm.[2] The results of end-to-end anastomoses are satisfactory in more than 90% of the cases.[27]

Traumatic esophageal perforation carries high rates of morbidity and mortality, although there is a better prognosis for children than adults. Children also tolerate delayed repair better than adults do. Esophageal injuries should be closed in two layers with a vascularized flap of tissue interposed between the trachea and the esophagus. This will help prevent tracheoesophageal fistulas. Sternocleidomastoid muscle, omohyoid muscle, other strap muscles, pleura, pericardium, and intercostal muscle flaps have all been used.[35]

Complications

Severe injuries, injuries that go undiagnosed, and injuries that are poorly managed may lead to significant complications. These include glottic or subglottic stenosis, glottic webs or scarring, vocal cord paralysis, esophageal stricture or stenosis, or tracheoesophageal fistulas. Stridor or dyspnea on exertion may indicate stenosis. Dysphonia or aphonia may result from glottic webs or scarring, vocal cord paralysis, or arytenoid damage. Dysphagia and weight loss may signal an esophageal stricture or stenosis. Tracheoesophageal fistula, vocal cord paralysis, or arytenoid damage may be diagnosed after a child has repeated bouts of aspiration pneumonia.

The surgical treatment of vocal cord paralysis is usually delayed for a year. This allows adequate time for the return of vocal cord function. During this period of time, electromyography can be used to follow any nerve progress. The paralyzed vocal cord can be temporarily injected with Gelfoam or fat to help reduce the chance of aspiration. If the paralysis continues after 1 year, thyroplasty or laryngeal reinnervation can be performed.

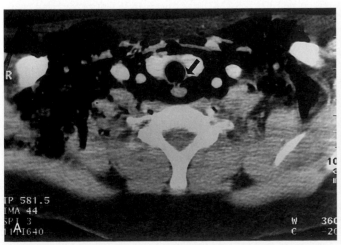
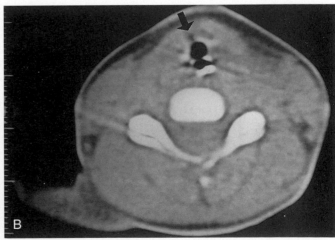

FIGURE 88–6. Tracheal tears. Note the presence of subcutaneous air.

Conclusion

Laryngotracheal trauma is rare in the pediatric population but extremely challenging because of the size of the airway and the potential threat to life. Early diagnosis and careful, aggressive, individualized treatment are the key elements of a successful outcome.

REFERENCES

1. Alexander AE Jr, Lyons GD, Fazekas-May MA, et al. Utility of helical computed tomography in the study of arytenoid dislocation and arytenoid subluxation. Ann Otol Rhinol Laryngol 106:1020, 1997.
2. Alonso WA, Pratt LL, Zollinger WL, et al. Complications of laryngotracheal disruption. Laryngoscope 84:1276, 1974.
3. Becmeur F, Donato L, Horta-Geraud P, et al. Rupture of the airways after blunt chest trauma in two children. Eur J Pediatr Surg 10:133, 2000.
4. Bent JP, Porubsky ES. The management of blunt fractures of the thyroid cartilage. Otolaryngol Head Neck Surg 110:195, 1994.
5. Chagnon FP, Mulder DS. Laryngotracheal trauma. Chest Surg Clin North Am 6:733, 1996.
6. Chui L, Lufkin R, Hanafee W. The use of MRI in the identification of post-traumatic laryngeal deformities. Clin Imaging 14:127, 1990.
7. Cooper A, Barlow B, Niemirska M, et al. Fifteen years' experience with penetrating trauma to the head and neck in children. J Pediatr Surg 22:24, 1987.
8. Demetriades D, Asensio JA, Velmahos G, et al. Complex problems in penetrating neck trauma. Surg Clin North Am 76:661, 1996.
9. Ford HR, Gardner ML, Lynch JM. Laryngotracheal disruption from blunt pediatric neck injuries: impact of early recognition and intervention on outcome. J Pediatr Surg 30:1–5, 1995.
10. Gaebler C, Mueller M, Schramm W, et al. Tracheobronchial ruptures in children. Am J Emerg Med 14:279, 1996.
11. Ganzel TM, Mumford LA. Diagnosis and management of acute laryngeal trauma. Am Surgeon 55:303, 1989.
12. Gold SM, Gerber ME, Shott SR, et al. Blunt laryngotracheal trauma in children. Arch Otolaryngol Head Neck Surg 123:83, 1997.
13. Grant WJ, Meyers RL, Jaffe RL, et al. Tracheobronchial injuries after blunt chest trauma in children-hidden pathology. J Pediatr Surg 33:1707, 1998.
14. Grewal H, Rao PM, Mukerji S, et al. Management of penetrating laryngotracheal injuries. Head Neck 17:494, 1995.
15. Grillo HC. Surgery of the trachea. Current Prob Surg 3:59, 1970.
16. Grisoni ER, Pillai SB, Volsko TA, et al. Pediatric airbag injuries: the Ohio experience. J Pediatr Surg 35:160, 2000.
17. Gussack GS, Jurkovich GJ, Luterman A. Laryngotracheal trauma: a protocol approach to a rare injury. Laryngoscope 96:660, 1986.
18. Hall JR, Reyes HM, Meller JL. Penetrating zone-Il neck injuries in children. J Trauma 3:1614, 1991.
19. Hager J, Gunkel AR, Riccabona U. Isolated longitudinal rupture of the posterior tracheal wall following blunt neck trauma. Eur J Pediatr Surg 9:104, 1999.
20. Hancock BI, Wiseman NE. Tracheobronchial injuries in children. J Pediatr Surg 26:16, 1991.
21. Herdman RC, Saeed SR, Hinton EA. The lateral soft tissue neck X-ray in accident and emergency medicine. Arch Emerg Med 9:149, 1992.
22. Humar A, Pitters C. Emergency department management of blunt cervical tracheal trauma in children. Pediatr Emerg Care 7:291, 1991.
23. Jurkovich GJ, Zingarelli W, Wallace J, et al. Penetrating neck trauma: diagnostic studies in the asymptomatic patient. J Trauma Injury Infect Crit Care 25:819, 1985.
24. Kadish H, Schuck J, Woodward GA. Blunt pediatric laryngotracheal trauma: case reports and review of the literature. Am J Emerg Med 12:207, 1994.
25. Katz M, Konen E, Rozenman J, et al. Spiral CT and 3D image reconstruction of vascular rings and associated tracheobronchial anomalies. J Comp Assist Tomogr 19:564, 1995.
26. Kielmovitch IH, Friedman WH. Lacerations of the cervical trachea in children. Int J Pediatr Otorhinolaryngol 15:73, 1988.
27. Kirsh MM, Orringer MB, Behrendt DM, et al. Management of tracheobronchial disruption secondary to nonpenetrating trauma. Ann Thorac Surg 22:93, 1976.
28. Kurien M, Zachariah N. External laryngotracheal trauma in children. Int J Pediatr Otorhinolaryngol 49:115, 1999.
29. Leopold DA. Laryngeal trauma: a historical comparison of treatment methods. Arch Otolaryngol 109:106, 1983.
30. Lusk RP. The evaluation of minor cervical blunt trauma in the pediatric patient. Clin Pediatr 25:445, 1986.
31. Mace SE. The unstable occult cervical spine fracture: a review. Am J Emerg Med 10:611, 1992.
32. Maceri DR, Mancuso AA, Canalis RF. Value of computed axial tomography in severe laryngeal injury. Arch Otolaryngol 108:449, 1982.
33. Maran AG, Stell PM. Acute laryngeal trauma. Lancet 2:1107, 1970.
34. Mathisen DJ, Grillo HC. Laryngotracheal trauma. Ann Thorac Surg 43:254, 1987.
35. McConnell DB, Trunkey DD. Management of penetrating trauma to the neck. Adv Surg 27:97, 1994.
36. Meglin AJ, Biedlingmaier JF, Mirvis SE. Three-dimensional computerized tomography in the evaluation of laryngeal injury. Laryngoscope 101:202, 1991.
37. Merritt RM, Bent JP, Porubsky ES. Acute laryngeal trauma in the pediatric patient. Ann Otol Rhinol Laryngol 107:104, 1998.
38. Minard G, Kudak KA, Croce MA, et al. Laryngotracheal trauma. Am Surg 58:181, 1992.
39. Mordehai J, Kurzbart E, Kapuller V, et al. Tracheal rupture after blunt trauma in a child. J Pediatr Surg 32:104, 1997.
40. Mulder DS, Barkun JS. Injury to the trachea, bronchus and esophagus. Trauma 343, 1991.
41. Myer CM, Orobello P, Cotton RT, et al. Blunt laryngeal trauma in children. Laryngoscope 97:1043, 1987.
42. Myers EM, Iko BO. The management of acute laryngeal trauma. J Trauma Injury Infect Crit Care 27:448, 1987.
43. Nahum AM, Seigel AW. Biodynamics of injury to the larynx in automobile collisions. Ann Otol Rhinol Laryngol 76:781, 1967.
44. Ngakane H, Muckart DJ, Luvuno FM. Penetrating visceral injuries of the neck: results of a conservative management policy. Br J Surg 77:908, 1990.
45. O'Keeffe LI, Maw AR. The dangers of minor blunt laryngeal trauma. J Laryngol Otol 106:372, 1992.
46. Roberts D, Pexa C, Clarkowski B, et al. Fatal laryngeal injury in an achondroplastic dwarf secondary to airbag deployment. Pediatr Emerg Care 15:260, 1999.
47. Sataloff RT, Rao VM, Hawkshaw M, et al. Cricothyroid joint injury. J Voice 12:112, 1998.
48. Schaeffer SD. The acute management of external laryngeal trauma: a 27-year experience. Arch Otolaryngol Head Neck Surg 118:598, 1992.
49. Schaeffer SD. The treatment of acute external laryngeal injuries. Arch Otolaryngol Head Neck Surg 117:35, 1991.
50. Schoem SR, Choi SS, Zalzal GH. Pneumomediastinum and pneumothorax from blunt cervical trauma in children. Laryngoscope 107:351, 1997.
51. Shama DM, Odell J. Penetrating neck trauma with tracheal and esophageal injuries. Br J Surg 71:534, 1984.
52. Weigelt JA, Thal ER, Snyder WH, et al. Diagnosis of penetrating cervical esophageal injuries. Am J Surg 154:619, 1987.
53. Woo P. Laryngeal framework reconstruction with miniplates. Ann Otol Rhinol Laryngol 99:772, 1990.

89

Management and Prevention of Subglottic Stenosis in Infants and Children

Michael J. Rutter, F.R.A.C.S, Robert F. Yellon, M.D., and Robin T. Cotton, M.D.

Congenital subglottic stenosis and laryngeal webs are well recognized as causes of stridor in the newborn.[45] However, since the mid-1960s, acquired subglottic stenosis secondary to prolonged intubation has become more prevalent. This is a direct consequence of the introduction by McDonald and Stocks[56] in 1965 of prolonged intubation for management of the premature respiratory system. Although this revolutionized the care of the premature infant, there was a marked corresponding increase in the incidence of acquired subglottic stenosis, which in turn established the field of pediatric airway reconstruction.

Acquired subglottic stenosis differs from congenital subglottic stenosis in three ways: first, it is a complication of medical treatment; second, the child is much less likely to outgrow the lesion; and third, it is generally more severe, leading to greater problems in management. Treatment of established subglottic stenosis is often difficult and challenging, and the most effective intervention is prevention, with the pathogenesis of subglottic injury discussed in the following section.

Etiology and Pathophysiology

The cause of severe congenital subglottic stenosis is inadequate recanalization of the laryngeal lumen after completion of normal epithelial fusion at the end of the third month of gestation. The final pathologic condition depends on the degree of recanalization and varies from complete laryngeal atresia; through varying degrees of incomplete atresia, stenosis, and laryngeal webs; to the mildest form of congenital stenosis, in which the cricoid ring is merely somewhat smaller in diameter or altered in shape compared with a normal one.

The cause of acquired laryngeal stenosis secondary to intubation is not well understood, however, and many questions concerning the pathogenesis of neonatal acquired subglottic stenosis remain unanswered. If the pressure from an endotracheal tube exceeds the capillary perfusion pressure, mucosal ischemia, edema, erosion, and ulceration rapidly occur. Autopsy data show that there is a period of progressive ulceration and necrosis of cricoid mucosa in the first hours and days after intubation,[31, 39, 48] which may lead to full-thickness destruction of the cricoid cartilage. This is usually associated with granulation tissue formation around the endotracheal tube at both the glottic and the subglottic levels. After this, there is a 3-week period of healing and re-epithelialization, even though the endotracheal tube remains in place.[32, 74] This observation explains why most neonates do not develop subglottic stenosis after prolonged intubation, but it does not explain what happens to the 1% to 8% of those neonates who do develop stenosis.[35, 67, 70, 76]

There is no clear evidence of a single principal cause of the stenosis in these neonates.[2] There are several probable factors, and their effects are probably synergistic. The primary site of the damage is at the cricoid, the smallest part of the upper airway in the neonate (Fig. 89–1) and the only point at which the airway is surrounded completely by cartilage. The posterior cricoid is especially vulnerable. The endotracheal tube causes ischemic necrosis from pressure, and this process is presumed to be worse the tighter the fit. The two variables are the size of the tube and the size of the cricoid. Recommendations for the use of appropriately small tubes are well heeded, but if the cricoid is already congenitally small, even the smallest tube becomes a tight fit. It is probable, though conjectural, that a proportion of the 1% to 8% of neonates who do develop acquired stenosis have a congenitally small cricoid.[63]

Movement of the endotracheal tube, sometimes associated with poor fixation, can cause traumatic ulceration after re-epithelialization has occurred. The duration of intubation has been blamed, because it is thought that pressure and movement continue to be of influence as long as the tube remains in place. Although this may be true of the larynx of the older child and the adult, histologic data of the neonatal larynx suggest that after the first week, the degree of injury is not proportional to the length of intubation.[74] It is evident that infants who develop stenosis are intubated for longer than those who do not, but early development of subglottic injury leads to failed extubation and, therefore, inevitably to longer periods of intubation.

Initial failures of extubation may be caused by other problems in the infant (e.g., pulmonary disease, severe

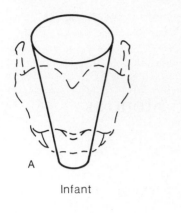
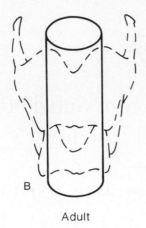

Infant   Adult

FIGURE 89–1. The narrowest portion of the infant's airway is the subglottic space.

laryngomalacia) and not by stenosis; a formal diagnosis of stenosis is not made until direct laryngoscopy. This usually occurs some weeks after the true onset of laryngeal damage, and accurate retrospective dating of the onset of the stenosis is difficult. In many cases, prolonged intubation may be the result, not the cause, of subglottic stenosis. Reintubation should be minimized, because each passage of the endotracheal tube increases the risk of mucosal injury.[39]

The route of intubation does not appear to be a factor, and there are no data to show that either nasotracheal or orotracheal intubation has a significant effect on the incidence of subglottic stenosis. Tube design and materials are important; only disposable, sterile endotracheal tubes made of implant-tested polyvinyl chloride or Silastic should be used for intubation.[64]

Although prematurity, cardiac disease, and other congenital anomalies are responsible for most prolonged intubations in the neonatal population, in the pediatric population, sepsis, other serious illness, and trauma are most common. Trauma may be direct laryngeal, inhalational (including caustic lye ingestion), or nonlaryngeal, requiring prolonged intubation (e.g., closed head injury). The pediatric larynx is not as tolerant of prolonged intubation as the neonatal larynx, and if intubation for over a week is anticipated, consideration of tracheotomy is appropriate.

Superimposed bacterial infection compounds mechanical mucosal trauma by increasing the inflammatory response and scar tissue formation.[82] Although the clinical relationship between subglottic stenosis and gastroesophageal reflux (GER) has not been established clearly, numerous reports have implicated GER as a potentially complicating factor,[34, 50, 104–106] especially in combination with prolonged intubation and the resultant laryngotracheal injury.

Other causes of subglottic stenosis in children include inflammatory and autoimmune conditions, including Wegener granulomatosis. Although iatrogenic causes may include external beam radiotherapy, most are surgically induced. Endoscopic laryngeal surgery, especially prolonged or extensive use of cautery or laser, risks formation of or worsening of subglottic stenosis. High tracheotomy

(through the thyroid, cricoid, or first tracheal ring), especially for a prolonged period, is a potent risk factor for subglottic stenosis,[46] though short-term cannulation carries a lesser risk.[4, 57] Past reconstruction of the subglottis also carries a risk of exacerbating subglottic stenosis. This may result from inappropriate operative selection, uncontrolled GER, bacterial infection, exuberant granulation tissue, or stenting problems. Often, acquired subglottic stenosis is the result of the synergist effects of more than one factor, with the effects of an endotracheal tube being compounded by the presence of GER, an injured larynx, a sick patient, a congenitally small cricoid, and so on.

In animals, subglottic stenosis has been reproduced by one of two methods: either the subglottic mucosa is removed by a single act of abrasion,[3] or it is injured by prolonged intubation for days or weeks.[55, 96] The purpose of these studies has been to examine the pathologic process of stenosis rather than to study the pathogenic factors. A satisfactory animal model for the study of subglottic stenosis still has not been developed.

Management of established subglottic stenosis is potentially complex, and not without risk to the patient. Prevention of subglottic stenosis is infinitely preferable, if not always achievable. In a child requiring long-term intubation, the size and composition of the endotracheal tube are the most critical factors, but stability of the tube, length of intubation, and control of reflux and infection are also important considerations. The ideal endotracheal tube size is not the largest that fits, but rather the smallest that permits adequate ventilation. If a leak exists around an endotracheal tube at less than 25 cm H_2O pressure, the risk of subglottic stenosis falls dramatically.

Diagnosis

The evaluation of a child with suspected subglottic stenosis depends on whether the child is intubated or unintubated or already has a tracheotomy. Assessment includes a combination of history and physical examination, radiologic evaluation, and endoscopic examination.

Clinical Picture

Although the diagnosis of subglottic stenosis is suggested by the inability to extubate the patient, in an intubated neonate or child, initial airway assessment may have to wait until the child is sufficiently medically stable. In some cases, this may not occur until a tracheotomy has already been placed.

In the intubated child, relevant information includes the reasons for intubation, the length of intubation, the size of the endotracheal tube, and whether any difficulties were encountered on intubation. Evaluation should include an assessment of the child's ongoing need for airway support, and whether this primarily relates to the airway or to the underlying medical condition that required intubation (e.g., pulmonary disease). The leak pressure around the endotracheal tube is important and ideally should be less than 25 cm H_2O. A trial of extubation is usually appropriate, and if the child is still struggling to maintain the airway, flexible nasopharyngoscopy may give valuable information on glottic abduction, vocal cord function, and glottic granulation. However, the definitive assessment is with rigid endoscopy, though in an intubated child, final judgment may require reassessment after several days of extubation or tracheotomy to allow the larynx to recover. A marginal airway usually temporarily deteriorates after extubation owing to reactive edema and granulation tissue, and racemic epinephrine and steroid administration (dexamethasone repeated up to 6 times hourly in a child with a tenuous airway) may be beneficial.

In the unintubated child, mild to moderate subglottic stenosis, whether congenital or acquired, is usually asymptomatic until an upper respiratory infection causes additional narrowing of the airway, resulting in respiratory distress. These children may have recurrent or atypical croup with upper respiratory infections. Severe congenital subglottic stenosis usually presents at birth, although even grade III (see Table 89–3) congenital subglottic stenosis may not present for weeks or months. In acquired stenosis, there is a history of laryngeal injury (intubation). The symptoms and signs usually occur 1 to 4 weeks after the original injury, although the latent period occasionally is longer.

The main symptoms and signs of laryngeal stenosis relate to airway, voice, and feeding. Progressive respiratory difficulty is the prime symptom of subglottic airway obstruction, with biphasic stridor, exertional dyspnea, air hunger, and vigorous efforts at breathing with suprasternal, intercostal, and diaphragmatic retractions. Disturbed sleep and nocturnal apnea may occur. Abnormal cry, aphonia, or hoarseness occurs when the vocal folds are affected, although this is unusual in isolated subglottic stenosis. Dysphagia and feeding abnormality with recurrent aspiration and pneumonia can occur. Cyanosis is a late and deeply concerning sign. Cyanosis owing to subglottic stenosis in a child with a normal heart and lungs may herald acute decompensation and should be considered an emergency. Chronic airway obstruction may present with failure to thrive.

In a child already tracheotomy-dependent, evaluation of the airway is required to differentiate children with an adequate airway who can proceed directly to decannulation from children who require a period of observation or airway reconstruction. The general health status of the child, including pulmonary reserve and aspiration history, is important. The size of the tracheotomy tube and the child's ability to use a speaking valve or to produce any voice at all are relevant, as is whether the child can tolerate plugging of the tracheotomy tube and, if so, for how long.

A complete physical examination of the upper aerodigestive tract should be performed to rule out associated congenital anomalies or acquired injuries.

Radiologic Evaluation

Radiologic evaluation is helpful in the nonintubated child. It contributes to the assessment of the exact site and length of the stenotic segment, especially in obliterated airways. Several studies may be helpful.

Soft Tissue X-Ray Examination of the Neck, Including Lateral and High-Kilovoltage Anteroposterior Projections. The pre-endoscopic lateral soft tissue x-ray film is the single most important view in children. The anteroposterior high-kilovoltage technique adds to the visibility of the upper airway by enhancing the tracheal air column while de-emphasizing the bony cervical spine.[25] It may show subglottic steepling or may provide a valuable warning of an unsuspected tracheal stenosis warranting especially gentle endoscopic assessment.

Inspiratory and Expiratory Lateral Soft Tissue X-Ray Examination of the Neck, Together with Fluoroscopy. If the airway is sufficiently patent, fluoroscopy is very helpful for studying airway dynamics, including hypopharyngeal, laryngeal, and tracheal collapse.

Chest X-Ray Examination. Chest x-ray examination is essential because it rules out other concomitant respiratory problems and secondary effects of upper respiratory tract obstruction on the lower airway.

Barium Swallow. A barium swallow should be used to identify associated esophageal abnormality, including vascular compression or GER. A modified barium swallow may provide valuable information on a child's ability to swallow and risk for aspiration. Occasionally, it may alert the clinician to be vigilant for a posterior laryngeal cleft or "H" type tracheoesophageal fistula.

Magnetic Resonance Imaging. Magnetic resonance imaging (MRI) is particularly useful for the confirmation of a suspected vascular compression component contributing to the obstruction; it should be done with contrast enhancement or with magnetic resonance arteriography or magnetic resonance venography. Cine MRI may replace fluoroscopy in dynamic assessment of the upper airway in selected children.

Computed Tomography. Standard computed tomography (CT) has limited application for the study of subglottic stenosis in children, as does linear tomography. Spiral CT scanning is superior, but both CT and MRI evaluation of the subglottis have the potential to be misleading.

Other Radiologic Modalities. Despite the high quality of the images produced, neither positive-contrast laryngography nor xeroradiography is currently used. Xeroradiography, in particular, requires longer exposure to radiation than any of the other techniques.[22, 55, 68] PET scanning has no current airway application. Radionuclide studies have a place in children with associated thyroid disease and when assessing silent salivary aspiration (radionuclide spit study).

Radiologic airway evaluation is a valuable complement to airway endoscopy but does not replace it.

Endoscopic Evaluation

Indirect laryngoscopy alone is inadequate to fully evaluate the airway, and direct visualization of the larynx is essential for accurate diagnosis. The thickness and length of the stenosis should be assessed, as well as the mobility of the vocal folds (ruling out fixation or paralysis). Diagnostic biopsies can be obtained to exclude lesions other than fibrosis, and coexisting airway abnormalities should be identified. Ideally, both flexible and rigid endoscopy should be performed. In a child with a potentially unstable airway, this should not be considered a minor surgical procedure, and surgeon, anesthesiologist, and nurse need to work as a team and have complete familiarity with the instruments and techniques to best optimize a child's care.

Awake flexible fiberoptic endoscopy assesses the dynamics of vocal cord function, and an impression may be gained of subglottic narrowing. However, for a detailed assessment of the subglottic stenosis, the child must be anesthetized and the larynx carefully examined using the operating microscope or Hopkins rod telescope. Ideally, the anesthetic should be with spontaneous ventilation, with at least part of the assessment being with the patient lightly anesthetized, to allow an adequate appreciation of dynamic lesions such as laryngomalacia and tracheomalacia. A rigid Storz-Hopkins optical telescope is used to examine the stenosis and, if possible, is passed through the stenosis into the trachea and bronchi to exclude a second airway lesion. Using the telescope alone is usually adequate, but a ventilating bronchoscope may be required, particularly in a tortuous airway or in a child with glossoptosis. It is important that the size of the airway be carefully measured by passing an endotracheal tube of known outer dimensions, then measuring the leak pressure according to a standard protocol. With a conservatively chosen endotracheal tube in place, the audible leak pressure is determined in cooperation with the anesthesiologist. If a tracheotomy tube is present, it should be removed and the tracheostoma occluded during the airway sizing. If the audible leak pressure is less than approximately 10 cm H_2O, the tube is removed and replaced with the next larger size. If the resultant leak pressure is between 10 and 25 cm H_2O, this tube is compared with the expected size for the patient's age to obtain the percentage obstruction. If the leak pressure for the larger tube exceeds 25 cm H_2O, the smaller tube is used for comparison and grading.[65] The original Cotton subglottic grading system was revised into the Myer-Cotton grading system in 1994 (see Table 89–3). This grading scale relates only to subglottic stenosis. The normal diameter of the subglottic lumen in the full-term neonate is 4.5 to 5.5 mm; in premature babies, it is about 3.5 mm. Subglottic stenosis in a term neonate is defined as an airway diameter of less than 4 mm—a useful reference is the outer diameter of a standard Mallinckrodt 3.0 endotracheal tube (4.2 mm). The 3 mm measures the inner diameter of endotracheal tubes, while stents and T-tubes are sized according to their outer diameter. The appropriate endotracheal tube size for a child between the ages of 2 and 12 years with a normal airway is given by the formula

$$(Age\ in\ Years) + 16 \div 4$$

In a child with subglottic stenosis and without a tracheotomy, it is critical that endoscopy and airway sizing be performed gently. Rough instrumentation risks sub-

glottic edema, and because flow is inversely proportional to the fourth power of the radius, even 1 mm of edema in a nonstenotic infant larynx may compromise flow by more than 60%. In a child with subglottic stenosis and no tracheotomy, preoperative dexamethasone should be administered.

Differential Diagnosis

The differential diagnosis of subglottic stenosis is important because treatment may be contingent on identification of the precise anatomic abnormality.

Subglottic stenosis is considered to be congenital in the absence of a history of endotracheal intubation or other apparent causes of acquired stenosis. The diagnosis may be difficult to substantiate, and it is not known how many intubated premature infants who fail extubation have an underlying congenital stenosis. By best approximation, then, congenital subglottic stenosis is the third most common congenital disorder of the larynx after laryngomalacia and recurrent laryngeal nerve paralysis. Acquired subglottic stenosis is now more common than congenital stenosis as a result of the increased use of prolonged endotracheal intubation.

Congenital subglottic stenosis is divided into membranous and cartilaginous types.[27, 98] The membranous type is a fibrous soft tissue thickening of the subglottic area, owing to either increased fibrous connective tissue or hyperplastic dilated mucous glands with no inflammatory reaction. It is usually circumferential, with the narrowest area 2 to 3 mm below the true vocal folds, sometimes extending upward to include the true vocal fold.

The cartilaginous types are more variable, but a common type is a thickening or deformity of the cricoid cartilage that causes a shelflike plate of cartilage, partially filling the concave inner surface of the cricoid ring and extending posteriorly as a solid rigid sheet, leaving only a small posterior opening.[27, 58] Other variations include the elliptical cricoid cartilage and the trapped first tracheal ring.[42, 83]

Congenital subglottic stenosis is a clinical endoscopic diagnosis that describes a variety of histopathologic conditions that produce narrowing of the subglottic airway[62, 98] (Table 89–1). Some forms of subglottic stenosis are recognizable endoscopically: the firm cicatricial scar is easily

TABLE 89–1. Histopathologic Classification of Subglottic Stenosis

Soft Tissue Stenosis	Cartilaginous Stenosis
Granulation tissue	Cricoid cartilage deformity
Submucosal hyperplasia	Normal shape
	Small for infant's size
Submucosal fibrosis	Abnormal shape
	1. Large anterior lamina
	2. Large posterior lamina
	3. Generalized thickening
	4. Elliptical shape
	5. Submucous cleft
	6. Other congenital cricoid stenosis
	Trapped first tracheal ring
	Combined stenosis

recognized, as is stenosis owing to a reparative process; the congenital stenosis owing to submucosal fibrosis with a normal cricoid is distinguishable from that owing to an abnormally shaped cartilage. However, the endoscopic diagnosis of cricoid stenosis owing to normal shape but small size is difficult unless tubes of precise diameter are used to measure the endolarynx.

Many stenoses are not purely one type or another; in particular, a larynx with an underlying congenital subglottic stenosis is more likely than a normally sized larynx to be complicated by submucosal fibrosis or granulation tissue acquired from endotracheal intubation. The clinical importance of diagnosing cartilaginous stenosis is that such a stenosis is not responsive to dilation or laser therapy but is treatable by the anterior cricoid split or external laryngotracheoplasty.

Although endoscopic evaluation often gives clues to the type of subglottic stenosis, the clinicopathologic determination is made either at the time of laryngotomy for reconstructive surgery or at postmortem examination by whole-section organ mounts of the larynx. A case in point is the trapped first tracheal ring, where the first tracheal ring has failed to descend and is trapped inside the lower cricoid cartilage. This condition may be difficult to distinguish endoscopically from a congenitally small cricoid (see Chap. 74).

Posterior glottic stenosis also results from prolonged endotracheal intubation and may occur in isolation or in association with subglottic stenosis. It may closely mimic bilateral vocal cord paralysis, and careful evaluation with rigid endoscopy is required to confirm the diagnosis. Palpation of the arytenoids to assess for mobility and fixation of the posterior glottis is the key to making the diagnosis of posterior glottic stenosis. If associated with subglottic stenosis, both lesions require intervention to achieve decannulation.

Treatment of Acquired Subglottic Stenosis

Neonatal Management

In the neonate in whom extubation has failed and other causes of airway obstruction have been eliminated (e.g., choanal atresia, hypoplasia of the mandible, laryngomalacia, tracheomalacia), there are three possible courses of action, depending on the degree of subglottic injury. Findings in mild injury include edema only, less than 30% of the subglottic lumen showing de-epithelialization, a few individual polyps or granulomas, or subglottic cysts.[19, 44, 97] In such patients, reintubation for several days may allow subglottic edema to subside, especially if a treatable infection is apparent in the subglottis and chest. Systemic steroids have been used, but their value has not been formally assessed. Dilation is of little use in edema enclosed by the complete cricoid ring,[71] but individual polyps or granulomas can be removed with forceps, the carbon dioxide laser,[41] or the KTP (potassium titanyl phosphate) laser.

Alternatively, in cases of severe subglottic injury with extensive de-epithelialization and granulation tissue, an anterior cricoid split[13] may be performed in an attempt to increase the circumference of the subglottis and to allow

TABLE 89-2. Criteria for Performing an Anterior Cricoid Split Procedure

1. Extubation failure on at least two occasions secondary to laryngeal pathologic conditions
2. Weight greater than 1500 g
3. No assisted ventilation for 10 days before evaluation
4. Supplemental O_2 requirement less then 35%
5. No congestive heart failure for 1 month before evaluation
6. No acute upper or lower respiratory tract infection at the time of evaluation
7. No antihypertensive medication for 10 days before evaluation

healing without the need for a tracheotomy. Criteria for performing the anterior cricoid split procedure in the intubated neonate are listed in Table 89-2. This procedure should be attempted only when excellent neonatal intensive care unit support facilities and personnel are available.

Tracheotomy may be performed either at once or after failure of any or all of the maneuvers previously described. If in addition to severe subglottic injury, there is substantial glottic and/or tracheal abnormality, a tracheotomy is indicated. After tracheotomy and without the endotracheal tube to act as a stent, the stenosis becomes more severe with contraction of the scar tissue. During the next year or two, the airway may widen sufficiently to permit decannulation. However, more commonly, the stenosis is so severe that the child is dependent on the tracheotomy for respiration and requires surgical reconstruction of the subglottis to achieve decannulation.

The anterior cricoidectomy as conceived by the original authors[17] and supported by others[8, 14, 24, 29, 36, 43, 72, 87] is an effective treatment for acquired subglottic stenosis in the neonate in the absence of substantial glottic and tracheal pathologic conditions and in the presence of adequate pulmonary reserve.

Anterior Laryngotracheal Decompression Procedure (Anterior Cricoid Split)

Vocal fold paralysis and causes of airway obstruction other than subglottic stenosis must be excluded before any surgical procedure. For rigid endoscopy, atropine is the only preoperative medication given. General inhalation anesthesia with spontaneous respiration is required. The larynx is sprayed with lidocaine (Xylocaine), the endotracheal tube withdrawn into the hypopharynx, and anesthesia maintained using the insufflation technique.[41] This allows an unobstructed view of the larynx using the zero-degree Hopkins rod telescope. The supraglottic structures, glottis, trachea, and bronchi are examined, ruling out any other obstructing lesions of the airway. If information from flexible endoscopy is unavailable, vocal fold paralysis can be ruled out during rigid endoscopy under light general anesthesia. Any discrete lesions such as granulomas, cysts,[19, 97] and asymmetric subglottic swellings[44] may be removed. Unless there is more generalized subglottic damage, the patient is then carefully reintubated and an anterior cricoid split is performed.

The patient is positioned as for a tracheotomy, and a

horizontal skin incision is made over the cricoid to expose the cricoid and the upper two tracheal rings. A single vertical incision is made through the anterior cartilaginous ring of the cricoid and through the mucosa to expose the endotracheal tube. The incision is extended inferiorly to divide the upper two rings in the midline (Fig. 89–2). When the incision is made through the cricoid, the cricoid springs open and the endotracheal tube is readily visible in the lumen. The incision in the larynx is extended superiorly in the midline to include the lower two thirds of the thyroid cartilage. The insertion of the anterior commissure lies at the junction of the upper two thirds and lower third of the internotch distance of the anterior thyroid cartilage; therefore, the upper part of the thyroid cartilage incision should be through cartilage but not the underlying soft tissue to prevent disruption of the anterior commissure. Stay sutures of 4-0 Prolene are placed in each side of the incised cricoid. If the endotracheal tube becomes dislodged in the early postoperative period, these sutures can be used as retractors to allow reinsertion of the endotracheal tube through the incision until orotracheal intubation is re-established. The skin is loosely approximated around an elastic band drain. In acquired subglottic stenosis, the endotracheal tube is left in place for 7 to 10 days, acting as a stent while the mucosal swelling subsides and the split cricoid and tracheal rings heal. Very careful measures are taken to avoid inadvertent extubation during the first 5 postoperative days. Sedation is routinely used, and, occasionally, paralysis with assisted ventilation may be necessary. Thus, the support of an outstanding neonatal intensive care unit staff of nurses, physicians, and respiratory therapists is essential. The main hazard of inadvertent extubation is that during reintubation the tube may be passed between the vocal folds and anteriorly through the laryngotracheal incision. If such misplacement is not recognized, subcutaneous emphysema, pneumomediastinum, and pneumothorax result. Should accidental extubation occur, reintubation may be performed via the neck. The infant is then reintubated via the nasotracheal route, with anterior pressure over the cricoid to prevent tube penetration into the soft tissues of the neck.

Endoscopy is not performed at extubation. Dexamethasone is administered 12 hours before extubation and is continued for 5 days. Humidification and chest physical therapy are used after extubation. If respiratory distress develops acutely, racemic epinephrine is given by nebulizer. If airway obstruction progresses, the child is returned to the operating room for endoscopic evaluation under general anesthesia. Aspiration of secretions, laryngeal dilation, and excision of granulation tissue by forceps or laser may obviate the need for reintubation. If this fails, repeated anterior cricoid split or tracheotomy is the only alternative.

A modification of the anterior cricoid split is to place a cap graft over the split in an effort to allow the airway to seal more rapidly and allow earlier extubation. Thyroid alar cartilage and auricular cartilage are both excellent, though auricular cartilage may cause donor site deformity in this young age group.

Pediatric Management

There are many approaches to pediatric laryngotracheal reconstruction (LTR), and surgeons need to be familiar with a variety of procedures to ensure the best care for their patients.[9, 11, 12, 66, 69] Each case is different and must be individualized according to the pathologic condition, age, and general condition of the patient and the degree of stenosis. No single procedure can adequately address all manifestations of laryngeal stenosis. Important questions in planning treatment include type of stenosis (firm fibrous tissue or loss of cartilaginous framework), length of stenosis, glottic involvement, location of stenosis (anterior, posterior, circumferential), and whether more than one level of airway compromise exists (e.g., coexistent cord paralysis). It is most important to assess the lower trachea and to recognize coexisting tracheal problems such as complete rings of the trachea or vascular compression of the trachea.

There are three basic approaches in the management of pediatric subglottic stenosis, namely, a wait-and-see approach, a medical approach, and a surgical approach planned to enlarge the subglottis sufficiently to permit decannulation. Depending on the severity of the subglottic stenosis, this may be either endoscopic or open reconstruction.

Wait-and-See Approach

The wait-and-see approach advocates nonintervention in the hope that normal growth will be sufficient to allow decannulation. This approach was advocated for cases of congenital subglottic stenosis (severe enough to require a tracheotomy). However, acquired subglottic stenosis is generally associated with more airway compromise than congenital stenosis, and a more aggressive approach is required.

There are three main reasons for this:

1. To reduce the risk of mortality associated with tracheotomy in children in whom the airway is severely obstructed above the tracheotomy.
2. To permit phonation and the development of spoken language. Many children, even those with a severe stenosis, are able to force air through their larynx, either by "chin dipping" or with the aid of a speaking valve. However, some children, and in particular those with a complete stenosis, are unable to phonate. In these patients, surgery is necessary to create an airway. Until the airway is open enough for phonation, language development should be supported by a formal signing program.[88]
3. To permit decannulation. Children with tracheotomies are a constant worry to parents and others who look after them, and supervision at school may create problems.

A waiting period is also appropriate in children in whom airway reconstruction is premature and in whom time may permit a better prognosis for reconstruction. Examples include children with significant oxygen needs, usually related to bronchopulmonary dysplasia (and that

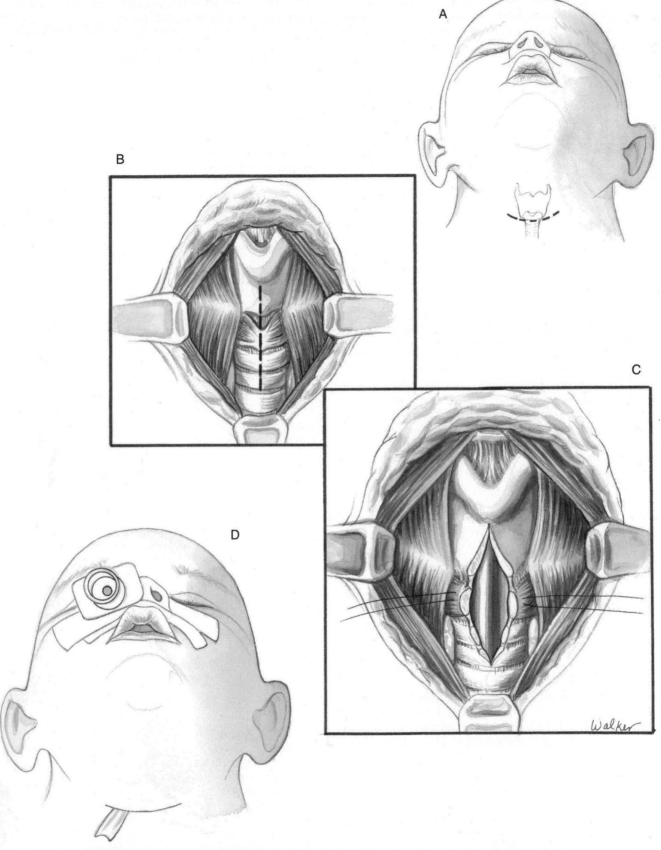

FIGURE 89–2. *A,* Skin incision over the cricoid cartilage. *B,* Incision through the cricoid, upper two tracheal rings, and thyroid cartilage (excluding the notch). *C,* Stay sutures through the cut edges of the cricoid cartilage. *D,* Wound loosely approximated, with drain and nasotracheal intubation.

should significantly improve with time) and children with an "active" larynx, particularly when not related to reflux disease. Although weight under 10 pounds is undesirable, this is a relative contraindication.

Medical

Soft tissue subglottic stenosis may be improved by medical therapy in some children. This is especially true in the small proportion of children with severe gastrolaryngeal reflux disease, and histamine H_2 blockers, proton pump inhibitors, or fundoplication may permit spontaneous improvement of subglottic stenosis. This may allow decannulation without laryngeal reconstruction, may permit a less extensive procedure to be performed, or may improve the prognosis after reconstruction.

An increasingly recognized cause of subglottic stenosis exacerbation is non–reflux-related allergic eosinophilic esophagitis. In these children, an active larynx is seen, despite a normal dual-probe pH study. Esophageal or laryngeal biopsies show sheets of eosinophils. The underlying cause is often found to be a food allergy, frequently to milk products. Therapy is directed at allergy testing, an elimination diet, and topical steroid therapy in some cases (fluticasone sprayed in the mouth and swallowed, rather than inhaled).

In children with inflammatory subglottic disease such as Wegener granulomatosis or similar conditions, medical therapy to stabilize the active subglottic disease before reconstructive surgery is prudent. In some cases, medical therapy alone may permit decannulation. Steroids, cyclophosphamide, and trimethoprim/sulfamethoxazole may all be beneficial.

Although medical therapy may improve an inflammatory soft tissue subglottic stenosis, it will not improve cicatricial scarring or cartilage deformity. However, it may improve the prognosis after reconstruction.

Surgery

Acquired subglottic stenosis after prolonged intubation often requires tracheotomy to permit extubation. After extubation, the stenosis usually worsens, with healing and scarring in the extubated subglottis. In these children, spontaneous improvement is not to be expected, and laryngeal reconstructive surgery is usually required to permit decannulation.

The degree of stenosis provides a valuable guide to intervention (Table 89–3). Most grade I and many grade II airways do not require any intervention or may be amenable to endoscopic management. Many grade II and

TABLE 89–3. Grading Scale of Laryngotracheal Stenosis

Grade	Laryngeal Lumen Obstruction (%)
Grade I	≤50
Grade II	51–70
Grade III	71–99
Grade IV	No detectable lumen

TABLE 89–4. Factors Predisposing to Failure in Treating Subglottic Stenosis Using CO_2 Laser

1. Failure of previous endoscopic procedures
2. Significant loss of cartilaginous framework
3. Combined laryngotracheal stenosis
4. Circumferential cicatricial scarring
5. Fibrotic scar tissue in the interarytenoid area of the posterior commissure
6. Abundant scar tissue greater than 1 cm in vertical dimension
7. Severe bacterial infection of trachea following tracheotomy
8. Exposure of perichondrium or cartilage during CO_2 laser excision predisposing to perichondritis and chondritis

all grade III and IV airways require open reconstruction to permit decannulation. If two children have identical grade II subglottic stenosis, but one child has a tracheotomy while the other does not, the child with the tracheotomy will probably require airway reconstruction, whereas the child without a tracheotomy may require no intervention.

Endoscopic Methods

A variety of methods of endoscopic excision have been proposed, including microcauterization,[49] cryosurgery,[78] and serial electrosurgical resection.[23, 47] These modalities have been supplanted by the carbon dioxide laser, which is the recommended endoscopic tool. Lasers allow the surgeon to vaporize scar tissue with precision, producing minimal damage to healthy areas.[41, 89]

The value of laser excision surgery is precision, and tissue destruction is directly related to the amount of energy delivered by the laser and the duration of the exposure. If minimal energy is delivered over a short time to destroy existing scar tissue, damage to the underlying and normal surrounding structure is minimized. However, if the laser is employed at high energy levels over for a long time, it acts much like any other uncontrolled method of tissue destruction, such as diathermy and cryosurgery, and stenosis may be created or worsened.[18]

The laser is useful for treating early intubation injury with granulation tissue and may improve the airway without causing significant bleeding or edema, thus avoiding the need for a tracheotomy. Several authors have reported adequate results in treating early or mild subglottic stenosis using the carbon dioxide laser,[30, 40, 51, 53, 90, 95] generally with multiple procedures.

Factors associated with a poor result or failure with this technique have been identified (Table 89–4). In general, these represent more advanced cases of subglottic stenosis. When these factors are present, the surgeon should proceed directly to an open reconstructive procedure. Some endoscopic failures present a major surgical challenge because of either loss of cartilaginous support or ossification of scar and surrounding cartilage. Under these circumstances, it is difficult to evaluate whether the case was unsuitable for endoscopic surgery in the first place or whether the endoscopic attempts worsened the initial pathologic condition.

Prophylactic systemic antibiotic therapy is recommended in endoscopic management of subglottic stenosis.

Systemic steroids and mitomycin C may retard the reformation of scar tissue after a laser procedure.[85, 100]

Airway dilatation rarely has a role in the management of established subglottic stenosis but may be useful in combination with subglottic laser surgery or after open reconstruction if the airway is in danger of restenosing.

External Surgical Methods

Surgical reconstruction is recommended in mature cases of subglottic stenosis when conservative efforts to establish a satisfactory airway are inappropriate or have failed. Open surgery may be required in patients who are not tracheotomy dependent, usually in the presence of increasing exercise intolerance and no apparent growth of the airway framework.

Before surgical correction of acquired subglottic stenosis, careful evaluation of the patient will permit optimal management decisions to be made. The goal of open reconstructive surgery is to achieve early decannulation with minimal detrimental effect on the voice.[27, 54, 91, 110]

Contraindications to open reconstructive surgery are

1. General anesthesia (absolute contraindication).
2. Conditions in which, even if the laryngeal stenosis were relieved, tracheotomy would still be necessary. There are some exceptions to this (e.g., patients with grade IV stenosis on a ventilator in whom reconstruction may be performed for phonation and communication reasons).
3. Severe incompetence of the esophagogastric junction, with esophageal reflux. This condition must be controlled either medically or surgically before corrective laryngeal surgery is undertaken.

Preoperative Evaluation

Once subglottic stenosis is confirmed, and a decision is made that open reconstruction is required, a more thorough evaluation designed to optimize the operative outcome is needed. The most important aspects of this are an evaluation of GER and intervention if required. No single investigation has the desired level of sensitivity and specificity, and therefore a combination of dual-probe pH probe placement, esophagogastroduodenoscopy, and esophageal biopsy[104] is ideally required to evaluate the risk and severity of reflux. Ideally, the patient should be evaluated off acid suppression medicine. Gastric scintiscan may also be useful to demonstrate GER (including nonacid GER), aspiration, and delayed gastric emptying. Even a small number of episodes of acid reflux to the upper esophagus or pharynx may be significant, but normative data for reflux in relation to the pediatric airway do not exist. If there is evidence of reflux, initial management with H_2 blockers or proton pump inhibitors is appropriate, with re-evaluation a few weeks later. If reflux is still evident, fundoplication may be required. Medication can control acid secretion, but in some children with gross reflux, nonacid reflux may still be highly irritating to the larynx.

Successful LTR requires more than merely re-establishing an adequate subglottic airway. Aspiration must be avoided, as in the long term this will have potentially far greater consequences than tracheotomy dependency. Most children at risk of postoperative aspiration have preoperative risk factors. If a child already aspirates, airway reconstruction is more likely to exacerbate the problem than resolve it. Aspiration may be assessed by flexible bronchoscopy with bronchoalveolar lavage, looking for lipid-laden macrophages. This is not reliable in a child who is purely G-tube fed. A chest CT scan may show chronic changes associated with aspiration. Modified barium swallow (videofluoroscopy) and functional endoscopic evaluation of swallowing (FEES) are complementary modalities for assessing aspiration risk, laryngeal sensation, and laryngeal protective mechanisms. Functional endoscopic evaluation of swallowing may be combined with sensory testing (FEESST) and also allows an excellent appreciation of dynamic vocal cord function. A child who shows no preoperative evidence of aspiration or risk for aspiration may still aspirate after reconstruction, but this is usually temporary and self-limiting. Particular care should be taken with children with grade IV subglottic stenosis because they are incapable of aspirating until reconstructed. A risk of aspiration does not preclude airway reconstruction. A period of feeding therapy and time may allow enough improvement to warrant reconstruction. In some children, a choice of ostomies may be required, and in an effort to achieve decannulation a child may require a gastrostomy and a drool procedure before airway reconstruction. After decannulation, to minimize the risk of aspiration, the child may be totally reliant on nutrition via the gastrostomy.

Syndromic Considerations

Children born with congenital anomalies are at higher risk of prolonged intubation and therefore subglottic stenosis. Some syndromes are associated with airway anomalies, whereas others need special consideration before airway reconstruction. Congenital high airway obstructive syndrome (CHAOS) has an occluded upper airway, usually at the glottic or subglottic level, that in turn gives rise to the other anomalies associated with the syndrome—namely, pulmonary hypoplasia and diaphragmatic and abdominal wall abnormalities. Other syndromes associated with airway anomalies include Down, cri du chat, Pfeiffer, VATER/VACTERYL, velocardiofacial, Hurler, Pierre Robin sequence, and CHARGE association.

Down syndrome is associated with congenital subglottic stenosis, and prolonged intubation is a risk factor for superimposed acquired stenosis. The age-appropriate tube for a child with Down syndrome is one full size less than that for a normal child of the same age (e.g., a 4-year-old Down syndrome child requires a 4.0 endotracheal tube, whereas a normal 4-year-old requires a 5.0 endotracheal tube).[86] Cardiac anomalies are present in 50%.

Most children with cri du chat syndrome are too impaired for airway reconstruction to be a consideration. If the child merits reconstruction, the laryngeal abnormalities that produce the characteristic cry do not preclude reconstruction, but there may be a risk of aspiration.

Pfeiffer syndrome appears to carry a higher risk of

airway stenosis than other midfacial deformities (e.g., Crouzon, Apert, Treacher Collins, Goldenhar). As with all midfacial hypoplasia children, the supraglottic airway must be adequate before airway reconstruction and may require midfacial advancement or mandibular advancement if glossoptosis is severe. Pfeiffer syndrome is usually associated with tracheal anomalies, though the typical tortuous trachea rarely requires intervention.

VATER and VACTERYL association may present with severe embryologic airway defects including laryngeal atresia, tracheal agenesis, posterior laryngeal cleft, congenital subglottic stenosis, and tracheoesophageal fistula. These children may have multifaceted problems requiring extensive interdisciplinary care. Airway evaluation and reconstruction should be performed with care to prevent injury to the cervical spine.

Velocardiofacial syndrome is common and may be subtle. Although few children with velocardiofacial syndrome have a laryngeal anomaly, the majority of children with partial laryngeal atresia (anterior glottic web) have velocardiofacial syndrome, and therefore all children with a laryngeal web should be tested for velocardiofacial syndrome. A laryngeal web may be the only obvious manifestation of the syndrome. Partial laryngeal atresia implies not only a glottic web, but also a cartilaginous subglottic stenosis.

Pierre Robin sequence may require placement of a tracheotomy tube for retrognathia and glossoptosis. However, decannulation may require airway reconstruction because there is a predilection for suprastomal collapse, which may be further complicated by segmental tracheomalacia, and an increased risk for the development of subglottic stenosis.

Children with CHARGE association frequently require tracheotomy, even after choanal atresia repair, and have a higher incidence of subsequent subglottic stenosis than would otherwise be expected. Airway reconstruction should be approached with caution because there is a high incidence of aspiration postoperatively.

Other syndromes may not be directly associated with airway anomalies but put the patient at risk of developing subglottic stenosis and require consideration if airway reconstruction is contemplated. For example, in Noonan syndrome, abnormal lymphatic vasculature may compromise reconstruction and result in persistent postoperative subglottic edema.[103] Several syndromes are associated with a potentially unstable cervical spine, including acromegaly and Down, Hunter, Hurler, and Larsen syndromes.

Graft Materials

Expansion LTR requires prolonged stenting, grafting, or both. The four-quadrant split with prolonged stenting has been replaced by the cricotracheal resection, while expansion cartilage grafting remains the workhorse for subglottic reconstruction. Graft materials include costal cartilage, thyroid alar, and auricular cartilage.

Costal cartilage is an excellent, abundant, and robust material to work with, and several decades of experience have confirmed its efficacy.[109] The usual donor site is the right fifth or sixth rib, with the scar placed in the anticipated breast crease in girls to prevent breast deformity and to hide the scar. Contiguous ribs may be harvested through the same incision if needed. Care is required to preserve the inner perichondrium at the donor site to allow the potential for some cartilage regeneration. Although this also reduces the risk of pneumothorax, a Valsalva maneuver before closure of the chest wound and a postoperative chest x-ray are mandatory. The outer perichondrium is preserved on the graft to line the luminal aspect of the airway. The graft may be carved with flanges to prevent prolapse into the airway, and grafts more than 3 cm long may be placed if required. Costal cartilage may be used for any grafting application.

Thyroid alar cartilage is available within the surgical field and is useful if only a small amount of graft material is required. However, it is usually not possible to flange the graft. The graft should be harvested from the superior thyroid alar on one side, preserving 1 mm of cartilage above the level of the vocal fold on that side. It is ideal as a posterior cartilage graft or as an anterior cricoid graft to prevent the need for costal cartilage (for example, if the cricoid is found to be small during removal of a subglottic hemangioma or repair of a laryngeal cleft).

Auricular cartilage is the weakest grafting material. It is not suitable as an insertion graft between cut edges of the cricoid but is ideal as a capping graft. In older children, there is no donor site deformity, but in the neonatal age group, asymmetric ears may result. Suprastomal collapse is well managed by an overlay auricular cartilage graft, with the incised suprastomal region pexed up to the graft.

Other grafting options include nasal septal cartilage, pedicled hyoid bone interposition, and clavicular periosteum pedicled on sternocleidomastoid. The last option has application in the older child with gross cartilage damage and loss of structural support of the airway. The clavicular periosteum may be used to reconstruct the airway over a T-tube stent, and after 6 to 12 months it will have partially ossified, permitting decannulation.

Stents

The airway usually requires postoperative stenting after reconstruction to facilitate healing, prevent graft prolapse, and maintain a lumen. The different stenting options and the appropriate time to stent are important preoperative considerations. If only short-term (less than 2 weeks) stenting is required, a single-stage procedure using an endotracheal tube as the stent may be desirable (discussed later). Otherwise, a two-stage procedure (retaining a tracheotomy) is required. With a flanged anterior costal cartilage graft, no stent at all may be needed. However, posterior and anteroposterior cartilage grafts require stenting. A suprastomal Teflon stent (Aboulker) stabilized with a transfixion suture is reliable.[1] The lower end of the stent must not overlap the tracheotomy, or the new tracheotomy tube may be impossible to reinsert during a tracheotomy tube change. Very little air can flow through a suprastomal stent. Granulation at the cut lower end of a suprastomal stent is common, but if the stent remains in place for less than 6 weeks, it will spontaneously involute once the stent is removed.

The more scarred or unstable the airway, the longer the period of stenting required. This is particularly true for salvage airway surgery where previous airway reconstruction has not achieved an adequate airway. Although a suprastomal stent remains an option, there is a risk of developing tracheal stenosis between the lower end of the stent and the tracheotomy. Longer-term stenting options include a full-length Teflon stent with a metal tracheotomy tube wired into it. This was the mainstay of reconstruction for many years and is reliable. However, the potential for stent fracture or inappropriate management by other health care professionals unfamiliar with the technique has led to the wired-in stent being less frequently used. A T-tube is the other long-term stenting option and may be maintained for months or years if necessary. After subglottic reconstruction, the upper limb of the T-tube must lie above the level of the vocal cords (ideally, at the level of the arytenoids). The result is a tendency to aspirate, but this resolves rapidly in most children once they are taught a supraglottic swallowing technique. T-tubes require a meticulous cleaning regimen to prevent airway obstruction from crusting of secretions because they cannot be easily removed. Although T-tubes are available in sizes as small as 5 mm (outer diameter), we do not use T-tubes smaller than 8 mm. An 8-mm T-tube can be used in a child as young as 4 years.

Single-Stage Reconstruction

Single-stage reconstruction using an endotracheal tube as a short-term stent is an important technique for reconstruction of grade I and II stenoses and selected grade III stenoses and is especially useful in cases with associated suprastomal collapse.[102] It is also useful in children without preoperative tracheotomy dependency. Single-stage reconstruction has both advantages and disadvantages. Advantages include avoidance of a tracheotomy and removal of the tracheotomy during reconstruction. Disadvantages include the need for sedation in young children, the risk of accidental extubation, and the potential for replacement of the tracheotomy if the airway is still compromised on extubation. Absolute requirements for single-stage reconstruction are complete confidence in the nursing, anesthetic, and intensive care resources available at your institution and the expectation that the child will do well without a tracheotomy.[15, 37, 52, 73, 84, 93]

Although the optimal duration of intubation is not definitively established, general recommendations are that anterior cartilage grafts and cricotracheal resections be intubated for 2 to 7 days, whereas posterior and anteroposterior grafts are intubated for 10 to 14 days. The older the child, the larger the airway and the briefer the period of intubation required. The more complex the surgery, or the more unstable the cricoid, the longer the period of intubation required.

Airway maintenance in the intensive care unit is critical. Accidental extubation and self-extubation should be avoided by securely taping the nasotracheal tube and by using arm restraints and sedation in young children. Most children younger than 3 years require sedation, whereas most children older than 3 years do not. This is further influenced by the cognitive abilities of the child and the willingness of the parents to maintain a constant bedside vigil. Paralysis is an option, but in the event of accidental extubation, immediate reintubation is required because the child can no longer support his or her own airway. A fully awake child is preferable because there is less need for supported ventilation and less potential for the iatrogenic complications associated with prolonged sedation, including lung atelectasis, pneumonia, and withdrawal.

Single-stage reconstruction is relatively contraindicated in children requiring complex airway reconstruction, especially those with multiple levels of airway pathology, those with grade IV stenosis, and those requiring salvage airway reconstruction. Adequate pulmonary reserve is also advisable. Children in whom reintubation is difficult should also be approached with caution, including children with craniofacial anomalies (especially Pierre Robin sequence) and children with vertebral anomalies.

Twenty-four hours before planned extubation, microlaryngoscopy and bronchoscopy are performed to assess the condition of the airway, the position of the graft, the progress of epithelialization, and the suitability of the airway for extubation. Occasionally, the removal of granulation tissue may be required, using optical cup forceps or carbon dioxide laser. If the airway is in satisfactory condition, extubation is planned for the next day. A dose of systemic steroids is administered, and the endotracheal tube is replaced with one of the next smaller size. Extubation is performed in the intensive care unit, where the patient remains for at least 24 hours. Prolonged simultaneous administration (more than 48 hours) of neuromuscular blockers and corticosteroids must be avoided to prevent postextubation weakness and myopathy.[105] Close supervision of the patient is maintained, and endoscopic evaluation is repeated approximately 10 days after extubation.

On extubation, there may still be airway compromise. This may result from inadequate surgical repair but more commonly relates to glottic edema and granulation or oversedation. Racemic epinephrine, dexamethasone, and helium/oxygen may be beneficial, as may surgical removal of granulation tissue, but the best solution for a larynx irritated by an endotracheal tube is trying to avoid reinserting the tube. If this cannot be achieved, the child is reintubated with a smaller endotracheal tube, and extubation is attempted again a few days later with the child fully awake and premedicated with dexamethasone. If there is still airway compromise, formal re-evaluation of the airway under anesthesia is recommended, and a decision should be made as to whether to attempt a further trial of extubation or to place a tracheotomy. If no obvious obstruction is seen at endoscopy, the anesthesia is lightened and the airway inspected during spontaneous respiration to see if any dynamic collapse is contributing to the obstruction.[80] A trial of continuous positive airway pressure (CPAP) for a few days may be helpful in this situation. If tracheotomy is required, the tracheotomy should be placed to avoid violating the reconstructed subglottis, if possible. If glottic granulation and edema were responsible for the need for tracheotomy, decannulation may be attempted a few weeks later, after broncho-scopic re-evaluation. Cultures should be taken to direct antimicrobial coverage because bacterial infection may contribute to granulation tissue formation.

Operation Selection

The most appropriate reconstructive technique is para-mount. Although an excellent assessment of the airway may be obtained endoscopically, the final decision on which reconstructive technique is best suited to the indi-vidual child may not be made until the airway is fully exposed during open surgery. Therefore, allowing leeway for a modification of the preoperative plan is prudent; for example, if a thyroid alar graft is planned, the right chest should still be prepared and draped to allow costal carti-lage to be easily harvested if required. Similarly, it is in the patient's best interest that the surgeon be familiar with differing reconstructive techniques and be able to apply this knowledge on an individualized basis, even with intraoperative modifications as necessary.

The options available for open subglottic reconstruc-tion include anterior cricoid cartilage grafting, posterior cricoid cartilage grafting, anterior and posterior cricoid cartilage grafting, and cricotracheal resection. Anterior cricoid grafting is the simplest of these procedures, whereas cricotracheal resection is the most technically challenging. All yield comparable success when used for the correct indications. Not infrequently, subglottic steno-sis is not an isolated entity but may coexist with a second-ary airway lesion such as posterior glottic stenosis or su-prastomal collapse, and the choice of procedure must account for this.

Anterior Cricoid Cartilage Grafting

This procedure is recommended for isolated anterior sub-glottic stenosis without glottic extension and is well suited to most grade I and II and some grade III stenoses.[11, 26] An intact posterior cricoid skeleton is a prerequisite for the success of this operation. Single-stage reconstruction or two-stage reconstruction without a stent is appropriate in most cases.

Autogenous costal cartilage is the graft material of choice, especially when there is little identifiable cricoid cartilage remaining anteriorly.[6] Because of the abundance of costal cartilage available, any length of cartilage re-quired can be obtained to graft the subglottis and the trachea. If coexistent suprastomal collapse exists, a long anterior graft overlapping a second distal transverse graft placed at the tracheotomy site (the so-called T graft; see Fig. 89–3E) will repair both problems. This is ideally done as a single-stage reconstruction.

General anesthesia is achieved through the existing tra-cheotomy. A shortened oral RAE endotracheal tube sewn to the skin of the anterior chest is more convenient than a tracheotomy tube to deliver anesthetic gases. The pa-tient is placed supine, with the neck hyperextended using a shoulder bolster. Usually, the fifth or sixth right costal cartilage is selected for the graft, and a 4-cm length of cartilage is removed, leaving the lining perichondrium on

one side of the graft. The larynx is exposed via a horizon-tal skin incision centered over the cricoid cartilage and incorporating the superior aspect of the previous tracheo-otomy (Fig. 89–3A). The cricoid cartilage is split verti-cally in the midline, and the incision is deepened through the intraluminal scar and lining mucosa to enter the sub-glottic lumen. The vertical incision is extended superiorly in the midline of the thyroid cartilage to a point immedi-ately below the anterior commissure, which is left undis-turbed. The vertical incision is extended inferiorly in the midline through the upper tracheal rings. In most cases, the incision incorporates the tracheotomy site (Fig. 89–3B and C). The intraluminal scar and lining mucosa are incised along the length of the stenotic segment, strictly in the midline. No attempt is made to remove the scar. The lateral edges of the costal cartilage graft are beveled and mortised to prevent the graft from settling into the lumen (Fig. 89–4). Without thinning, the largest cartilage graft that can be placed easily between the cut edges of the thyroid, cricoid, and tracheal cartilages is used, with its perichondrial surface facing toward the lu-men. The bare surface of the graft, without perichon-drium, is exposed to the strap muscles from which nutri-ents are supplied to the graft. The graft is sewn into position using 4–0 Prolene suture in an extramucosal mattress fashion (Fig. 89–3D and E), and Vicryl sutures are used to approximate the cut edge of the scar tissue to the perichondrium of the graft. The wound is closed in layers, over a small Penrose drain.

Careful tracheal suction is done, and immediate endos-copy is performed to assess the increase in the subglottic and upper tracheal diameters. If this is not satisfactorily increased, the graft must be repositioned at this stage. Six to eight weeks postoperatively, endoscopy is performed to assess the size of the subglottis. If it is adequate, a short trial period of plugging the tracheotomy tube day and night is undertaken, and decannulation is achieved.[7] Post-operatively, the child's voice is expected to be normal because the incision does not involve the anterior com-missure.

Posterior Cricoid Cartilage Grafting

Although subglottic stenosis principally affecting the pos-terior cricoid may necessitate a posterior cricoid cartilage graft, more frequently, the indication is posterior glottic stenosis or posterior glottic stenosis coexistent with sub-glottic stenosis. An anterior cricoid cartilage graft is not required if the subglottic lumen is adequate after the placement of the posterior graft. This is determined by placing a 4-cm segment of age-appropriate endotracheal tube in the subglottis and then assessing whether the anterior airway will easily close over it. If it will not, an anterior graft is also required (discussed later).

Anteroposterior Cricoid Cartilage Grafting

Anteroposterior grafting of the cricoid cartilage is re-quired for most grade III and IV stenoses and for grade II stenoses with associated posterior glottic stenosis.[7, 9, 13, 21, 77, 107] It is particularly effective in children with sub-

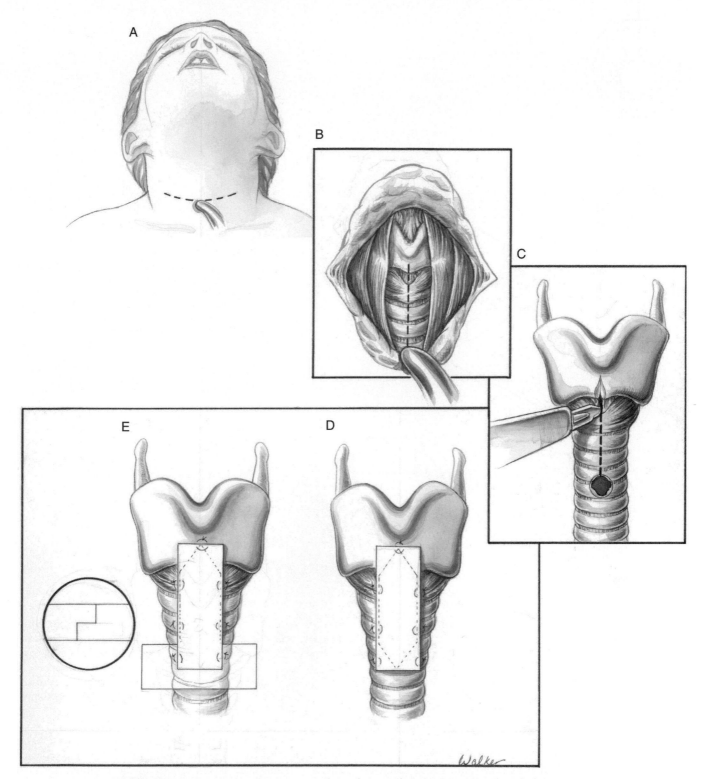

FIGURE 89–3. Anterior autogenous costal cartilage graft (CCG). *A*, Horizontal skin incision incorporating the superior aspect of the tracheotomy. *B* and *C*, Midline incision through the lower thyroid cartilage (inferior to the true vocal cords), cricoid, and upper tracheal rings, extending through scar tissue to the lumen. *D*, CCG to augment the anterior wall of the cricoid and upper trachea with lining perichondrium facing internally. *E*, Catgut sutures are used to approximate the cut edge of the scar to the perichondrium; 4–0 Prolene or PDS sutures are used to suture the graft to the cut edges of the trachea and cricoid. (*E*, From Cotton RT. Pediatric laryngotracheal reconstruction. Op Tech Otolaryngol Head Neck Surg 3: 169, 1992.)

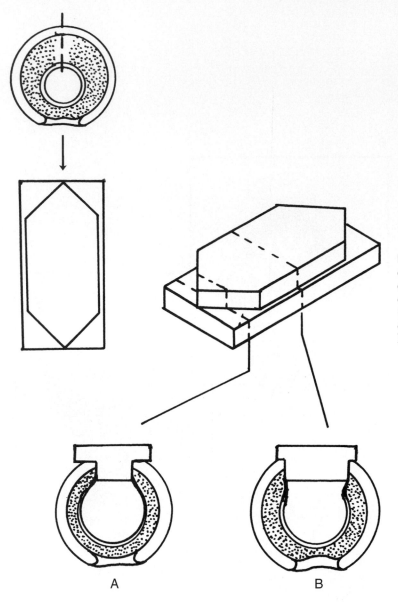

FIGURE 89–4. Schematic drawing of an anterior costal cartilage graft. The technique allows flanges at each end of the graft to lie over the cut margin of the thyroid cartilage superiorly and the tracheal wall inferiorly (*cross-section A*). Smaller mortises along the middle edges of the graft remain outside the border of the laryngotracheal fissure (*cross-section B*).

glottic stenosis owing to lateral cricoid shelves. A variation is an anterior graft with a posterior split (similar to the original Réthi procedure).[7, 16, 20, 28, 33, 61, 77] A prolonged period of stenting is required, except in the very young child. The great advantage of a posterior graft over a posterior split is that it allows a much shorter period of stenting, with even single-stage procedures permissible.[9, 108] As with the anterior cricoid graft, it is important to emphasize that scar removal is generally unnecessary or limited with anteroposterior cricoid cartilage grafting.

The operation is effective in both adults and children of all ages. With the patient under general anesthesia administered via the tracheotomy, a horizontal skin incision is made, incorporating the upper portion of the stoma (Fig. 89–5A and B). Subplatysmal flaps are elevated superiorly and inferiorly, and the strap muscles are retracted laterally, exposing the thyroid, cricoid, and upper tracheal rings. A midline anterior incision is made in the larynx and the upper trachea, extending from the superior thyroid notch to the tracheotomy site (Fig.

89–5C and D). Particular care is taken to split the anterior commissure exactly in the midline, and an assistant providing endoscopic guidance with a 30-degree rod telescope and video monitor is recommended. In a child older than 8 years, it may be possible to graft the posterior cricoid without performing a complete laryngofissure, leaving the anterior commissure intact.

After injection of 1% lidocaine with epinephrine 1:100,000 into the posterior larynx, the posterior scar and full length of the posterior lamina of the cricoid are divided, taking care to cut strictly in the midline, down to the level of the hypopharyngeal mucosa. The laryngeal scar should not be excised. The incision is carried superiorly into the interarytenoid area as far as the inferior border of the interarytenoid muscle and inferiorly into the membranous tracheoesophageal septum just below the border of the cricoid (Fig. 89–5E). If the interarytenoid muscle is found to be fibrosed, this is divided; otherwise, the muscle is left intact. The divided halves of the posterior cricoid lamina are distracted laterally. Although

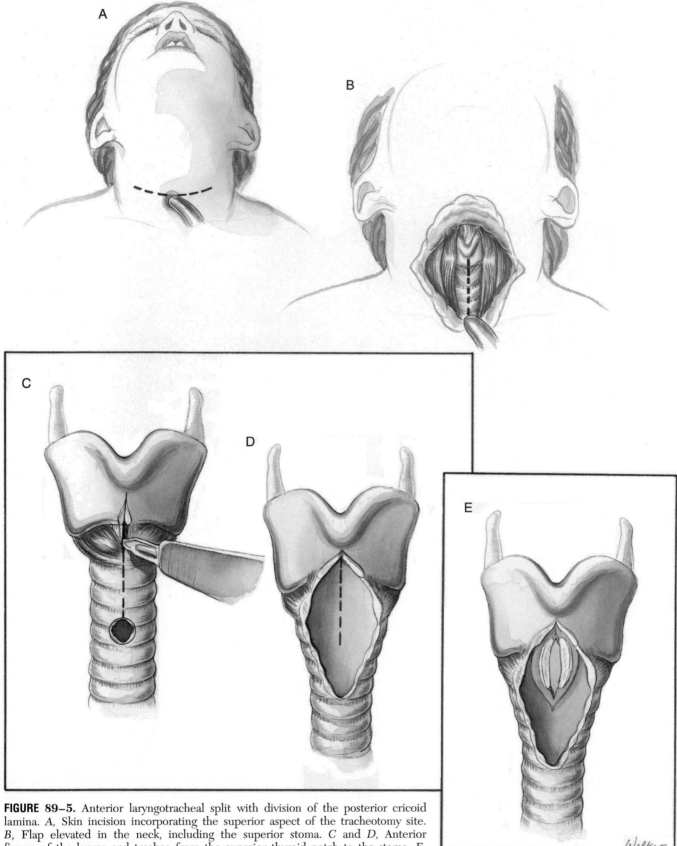

FIGURE 89–5. Anterior laryngotracheal split with division of the posterior cricoid lamina. *A*, Skin incision incorporating the superior aspect of the tracheotomy site. *B*, Flap elevated in the neck, including the superior stoma. *C* and *D*, Anterior fissure of the larynx and trachea from the superior thyroid notch to the stoma. *E*, Division of the posterior lamina of the cricoid. (Modified from Cotton RT. Pediatric laryngotracheal reconstruction. Op Tech Otolaryngol Head Neck Surg 3:166, 1992.)

approximately 1 mm of distraction per year of age up to 10 years may be obtained between the cut edges of the divided cricoid lamina, rarely is a graft wider than 5 to 6 mm required.

An autogenous costal cartilage graft is sewn posteriorly between the cut ends of the cricoid lamina using 4-0 or 5-0 Prolene or Monocryl suture (Fig. 89–6A and B, Fig. 89–7, and Fig. 89–8). A beveled posterior cartilage graft may be used and may be sufficiently stable to preclude the need for posterior sutures in some cases. If it is not possible to close the anterior laryngotracheal fissure incision satisfactorily (over an age-appropriate endotracheal tube; see Posterior Cricoid Cartilage Grafting), anterior cartilage grafting in addition to the posterior graft is advised (Fig. 89–6C). Stenting may be long-term above the tracheotomy (Fig. 89–6D) or by short-term nasotracheal intubation (see Fig. 89–6C and the section on single-stage LTR).

If long-term stenting is required, the Teflon Aboulker stent is the stent of choice and is inserted to maintain the diastasis of the divided cricoid lamina and the position of the graft. If a softer stent is required, the upper limb of a Montgomery T-tube is a good alternative to a Teflon stent but should be sewn shut at the proximal end to prevent aspiration. The size of the stent selected is the one that fits comfortably into the lower tracheal segment. The upper placement of the stent is crucial; the stent is correctly positioned when its bevel lies just above the vocal folds and the tip of the stent is immediately above the arytenoid cartilage. The stent is cut to allow placement of an appropriately sized tracheotomy tube below the inferior aspect of the stent. The stent's position must be checked endoscopically before closure of the airway, and the stent should be repositioned if necessary. It is most important that the stent be sufficiently high. It is fixed in position by a 2-0 Prolene suture placed through the lateral tracheal wall, through the stent, out the opposite side, and tied over the strap muscles through a short length of Angiocath tubing. The stent is removed endoscopically, usually by 6 weeks depending on the severity of the stenosis. A full-length wired-in stent may be left for several months if required.

Cricotracheal Resection

Although used in the management of adult subglottic stenosis for many years, cricotracheal resection has only comparatively recently been accepted as a viable method of managing pediatric subglottic stenosis. Initial reservations included the risk of dehiscence of the anastomosis; the risk of damage to the recurrent laryngeal nerves; the possible interference with laryngeal and tracheal growth, limiting the options for future reconstructive surgery; and the technical difficulty of the operation. It is now apparent that cricotracheal resection does not inhibit normal laryngotracheal growth and that it need not be considered an end-stage procedure because future laryngeal reconstruction may still be performed if necessary after cricotracheal resection. Although cricotracheal resection remains technically challenging, and the risk of anastomotic dehiscence and recurrent laryngeal nerve damage is real,

the potential advantages of cricotracheal resection often outweigh the potential risks.[5, 13, 59, 60, 75, 79, 94, 99, 101]

At the commencement of the procedure, the airway is re-evaluated endoscopically and an esophageal bougie placed. Using the same initial approach as for a laryngotracheoplasty, the airway is exposed anteriorly and the provisional margins of resection planned (Fig. 89–9A). The anterior cricoid is entered with a vertical incision (Fig. 89–9B), with care taken to incise only a minimal portion of the thyroid cartilage. Similarly, only the upper one or two tracheal rings are incised to preserve as many normal tracheal rings as possible. If the decision is made to sacrifice the old stoma site, further tracheal resection may be performed later in the operation. Up to this point, it is still possible to convert to a standard laryngotracheoplasty (if, for example, the scar is found to approximate the vocal cords). The lateral cricoid is then sacrificed (Fig. 89–9C), which greatly enhances exposure of the stenotic lesion. After infiltration of the posterior mucosa with 1% lidocaine with epinephrine 1:100,000, the posterior mucosa and scar are incised transversely with a beaver blade through the perichondrium, and subperichondrial dissection is commenced, both superiorly (to a level above the scar but below the cricoarytenoid joints) and inferiorly. Inferiorly, the flap is dissected to the distal aspect of the cricoid cartilage, and then the septum between the trachea and esophagus is entered. The scarred portions of each mucosal flap are then sacrificed, and the posterior cricoid cartilage is thinned with a diamond drill or a scalpel, taking care not to disrupt the cricoarytenoid joints (Fig. 89–9D). Retraction sutures are then placed in the distal tracheal segment and the distal trachea is mobilized (Fig. 89–9E). The perichondrium is hugged laterally to protect the recurrent laryngeal nerves, and the trachea is elevated off the esophagus. Although extensive dissection may be accomplished laterally and anteriorly, more limited dissection should be performed in the tracheoesophageal septum so as not to devitalize the trachea. At this point, a decision is made on whether to sacrifice the old stoma site (Fig. 89–9F); if normal tracheal rings are present above the stoma, then the stoma need not be sacrificed. The upper tracheal segment, including the stoma, should not be sacrificed unless the surgeon is confident that a tension-free anastomosis can be achieved. A suprahyoid release may be performed to lower the larynx at this time. Whether sacrificing only the stenotic segment of upper trachea or also sacrificing the old stoma, a generous amount of the trachealis should be preserved at this time. This allows retraction of the tip of the flap in tissue that will ultimately be sacrificed when the flap is trimmed before to the posterior mucosal anastomosis. A segment of normal tracheal ring may be preserved anteriorly to insert into the lower aspect of the thyroid cartilage (Fig. 89–9G). Although this assists in expanding the lower aspect of the thyroid cartilage and therefore helps the larynx match the size of the tracheal, it is not mandatory. Detensioning 2-0 Prolene sutures are then placed laterally between the trachea and thyroid cartilage and loosely tied so that the posterior mucosal anastomosis may be performed without tension (Fig. 89–9H). At this time, the stent of choice may be placed (endotracheal tube, T-tube, suprastomal stent, or no stent

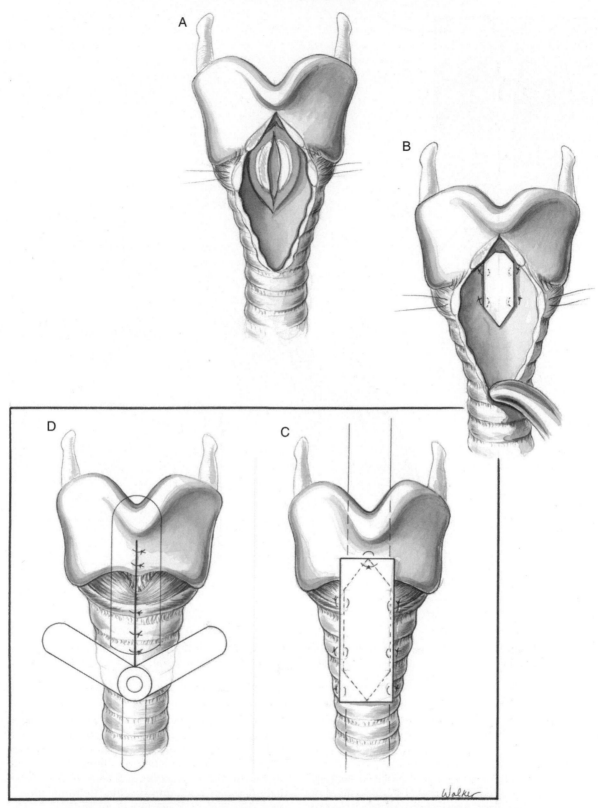

FIGURE 89–6. Laryngotracheal reconstruction with division of the posterior cricoid lamina and posterior autogenous CCG. *A,* Anterior and posterior divisions complete with distraction of the divided posterior cricoid lamina. *B,* Posterior graft of autogenous costal cartilage in place between the divided lamina of the posterior cricoid cartilage. *C,* Anterior CCG in addition to a posterior graft with nasotracheal intubation for short-term stenting. *D,* Modified Aboulker stent and tracheotomy tube in position for longer-term stenting, with closure of the anterior laryngofissure. (*B* and *D,* Modified from Cotton RT. Pediatric laryngotracheal reconstruction. Op Tech Otolaryngol Head Neck Surg 3:168, 1992.)

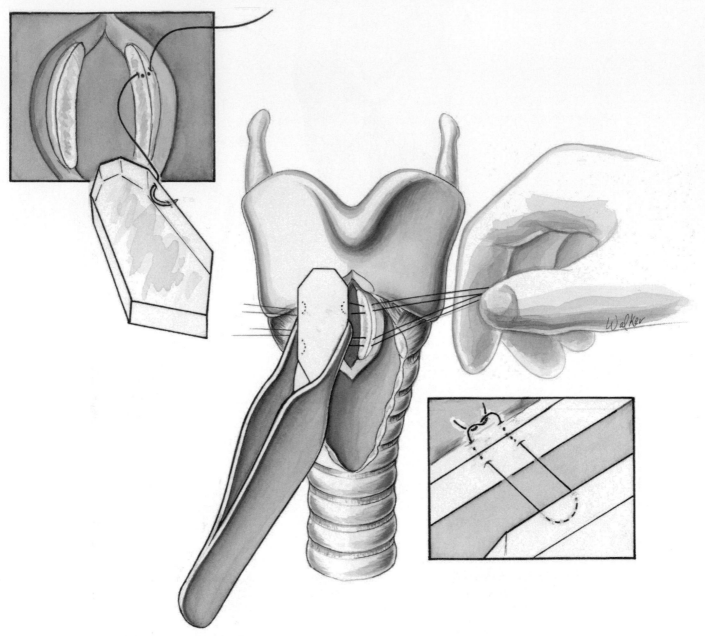

FIGURE 89–7. Placement of a graft of costal cartilage in the divided posterior lamina of the cricoid cartilage. (From Cotton RT. Pediatric laryngotracheal reconstruction. Op Tech Otolaryngol Head Neck Surg 3:168, 1992.)

at all). The other anastomotic sutures may then be placed and tied (Fig. 89–9*I*). Ideally, the remaining cricoid should be nearly flat, with most of the lateral cricoid sacrificed, so that the trachea sits *on* (rather than *in*) the posterior cricoid. Quilting sutures may be placed laterally between the posterior cricoid and the posterior aspect of the tracheal rings, but great care should be taken not to damage the recurrent laryngeal nerves as they travel medially near the cricothyroid joints. The wound is then closed in layers over a Penrose drain, and the chin is sutured to the chest to keep the head flexed.

For comparable severe subglottic lesions, cricotracheal resection results are superior to those seen with standard expansion laryngotracheal reconstructive techniques. This is most notably true for those children with the most difficult airways. Standard expansion techniques usually do not allow decannulation of a grade IV subglottic stenosis with a single procedure, whereas cricotracheal resection permits operation-specific decannulation in most cases. Similarly, salvage airway surgery after failed expansion LTR is also well suited to cricotracheal resection.

Therefore, the indications for cricotracheal resection include severe subglottic stenosis (grade III and IV lesions) and revision laryngotracheoplasty. With grade III lesions, concentric subglottic stenosis is best suited to cricotracheal resection, whereas subglottic lateral shelves

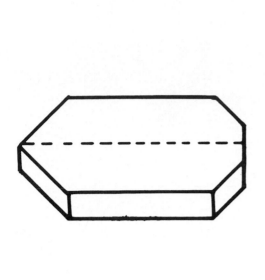
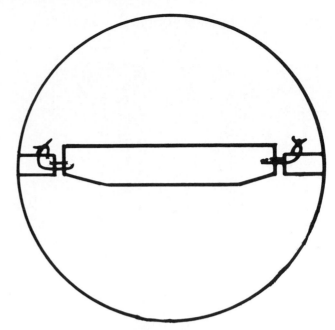

FIGURE 89–8. Longitudinal cross-section of a graft of costal cartilage in the divided posterior lamina of the cricoid cartilage.

are still best managed with anterior and posterior cricoid cartilage grafting. Other indications include severely damaged or deficient cartilage of the anterior cricoid and inflammatory lesions of the subglottis (particularly Wegener granulomatosis). The attraction of cricotracheal resection is that damaged or diseased subglottic cartilage and mucosa are removed and discarded, rather than augmented.

The contraindications to cricotracheal resection are all relative. Generally, the operation is not justified in grade I and II subglottic stenosis because standard LTR is simpler and offers a high success rate for these lesions. Ideally, 4 mm of normal airway below the vocal cords is desirable, as is a normal glottis. However, glottic and high subglottic involvement do not preclude cricotracheal resection; rather, they increase the technical difficulty of the procedure and the risk of complications and have a correspondingly poorer success rate.

Revision Laryngotracheal Reconstruction

Reconstruction of the pediatric airway is not always successful. Factors associated with a higher risk of failure include severe stenosis (grades 3 and 4), more than one level of airway pathology (for example, subglottic stenosis and tracheal stenosis), and an active larynx. Causes of an active larynx include reflux esophagitis, eosinophilic esophagitis, and idiopathic inflammation of the larynx. Coexistent tracheomalacia may also compromise decannulation.[80] Laryngeal inflammation from an endotracheal tube may compromise single-stage reconstruction, requiring replacement of a tracheotomy tube. The other very significant risk factor for failure of LTR to achieve decannulation is previous failure of LTR to achieve decannulation.

Previous failure of LTR is not a contraindication to further LTR. In most circumstances, revision LTR is the most appropriate intervention after failed LTR. However, it is prudent to allow the larynx to lie quiescent for a few months before undertaking further reconstruction.

Revision surgery has a higher risk of failure, and therefore optimization of the patient before surgery is desirable. If the reason for previous failure is apparent, then the cause should be addressed. If the cause of failure is not apparent, reassessment to exclude esophagitis is warranted. Assessment should also be made of cord function and supraglottic compromise. Repeated surgery to the larynx risks dynamic collapse of the supraglottis with epiglottic petiole prolapse or arytenoid prolapse.[81]

In revision surgery using expansion cartilage grafts, it is not necessary to excise previously placed graft material unless it is infected or unhealthy, which is unusual. The airway should be incised in the midline with the incision passing straight through the old cartilage grafts if required. Further cartilage grafts can be introduced between the cut edges of the old cartilage grafts without detriment. In an airway that has failed reconstruction on two or more previous occasions, consideration should be given to cricotracheal resection unless it is otherwise contraindicated.

In cricotracheal resection, the recurrent laryngeal nerves are not routinely identified. This is especially relevant in cricotracheal resection after failed LTR because the recurrent nerves may be embedded in scar tissue and therefore especially vulnerable. The tracheal cartilages should be the guide for dissection, although the classically described subperiosteal dissection is often not possible owing to scarring. Particular care should be taken to avoid the area of the cricothyroid joint, with both dissection and suture placement.

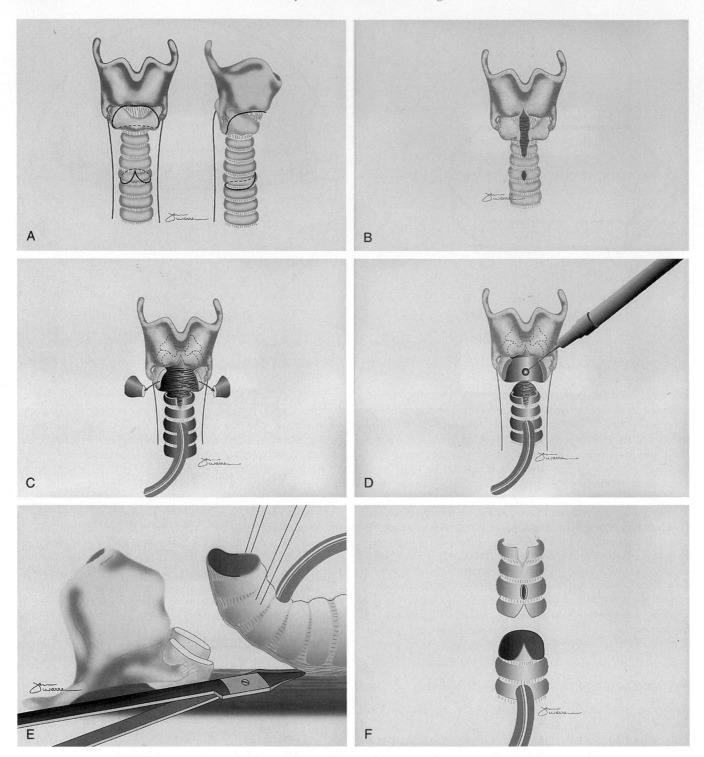

FIGURE 89–9. Cricotracheal resection. *A*, Proposed margins of resection. *B*, Anterior vertical incision through cricoid and subglottic stenosis. *C*, Sacrifice of lateral cricoid. *D*, Removal of scar tissue and thinning cartilage, posterior cricoid. *E*, Elevation of trachea off esophagus. *F*, Sacrifice of upper trachea.

Figure continues on opposite page.

Adjunctive Procedures

Subglottic stenosis may coexist with a variety of other airway pathologies, and these may need to be surgically addressed at the same time as the subglottic reconstruction. Suprastomal collapse may require cartilage grafting, with lowering of the tracheotomy site for a two-stage procedure or with obliteration of the stoma for a single-stage procedure. Vocal cord paralysis or cricoarytenoid joint fixation may require lateralization of the vocal process and/or arytenoidectomy. Posterior glottic stenosis

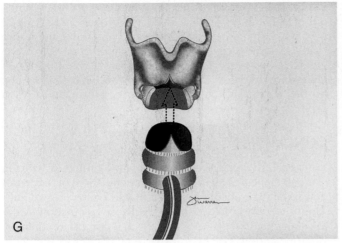

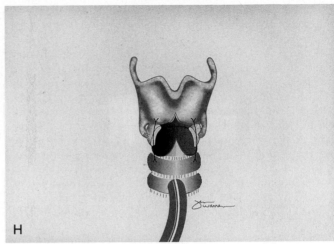

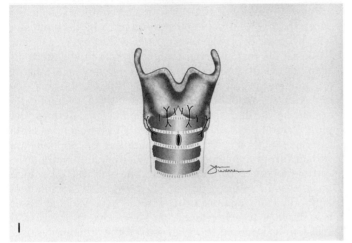

FIGURE 89-9 *Continued. G,* Proposed anastomosis. *H,* Posterior mucosal anastomosis. *I,* Anterior and lateral cartilage anastomosis.

may require a posterior cartilage graft. Arytenoid prolapse may require partial arytenoidectomy with the laser.

In some circumstances, the subglottic stenosis may be a secondary problem that requires management at the same time as the primary problem is corrected. This may be seen with anterior glottic webs, laryngotracheal esophageal clefts, and subglottic hemangiomas.[38] The more extensive the adjunctive operations required, the less advisable a single-stage reconstruction becomes.

Complications

Children requiring airway reconstruction compose a high proportion of children with additional significant medical problems. Most have acquired subglottic stenosis after prolonged intubation, usually for extreme prematurity. These children are at high risk for bronchopulmonary dysplasia, GER, and feeding problems and have a predisposition to aspiration. Children of this complexity are more prone to complications after any surgery, but especially after LTR.

Complications may be considered intraoperative, early postoperative, intermediate postoperative, late postoperative, or associated with single-stage reconstruction.[10] Intraoperative complications include hypoxia, usually owing to air leaking around an endotracheal tube, displacement of an endotracheal tube, or blood compromising the distal airway. Pneumothorax may occur, particularly during harvest of costal cartilage, but it is usually due to a breach in the parietal pleura rather than lung damage. Recognition is key because the patient may be easily managed by placing a pursestring suture around the breach in the pleura and closing the suture during a Valsalva maneuver. A chest drain is rarely required. Tracheal resection and cricotracheal resection also carry a small risk of pneumothorax from breach of the pleura in the mediastinum during distal tracheal mobilization. Cricotracheal resection also carries a risk of damage to the recurrent laryngeal nerve.

In the early postoperative phase, if air leaks from the repaired airway, there is a risk of subcutaneous emphysema, pneumothorax, pneumomediastinum, and aerocele formation. This is more likely to occur if high ventilatory pressures are required postoperatively or if a tracheotomy tube is inadvertently displaced into the soft tissues anterior to the trachea. Penrose drains allow the air to escape safely.

Perioperative bacterial wound infections and pneumonia may be prevented by use of prophylactic broad-spectrum antimicrobial agents.[105]

The intermediate postoperative phase may be complicated by displacement or resorption of the graft or dislodgment of a stent in the airway. Graft resorption may be seen with injudicious use of postoperative steroids.

However, steroids may be required to manage glottic or subglottic granulation tissue, especially after single-stage reconstruction.

Late complications include a poor voice, which may occur if the anterior commissure has not been divided precisely in the midline and then reconstructed precisely in the midline. Supraglottic compromise may be seen with arytenoid prolapse or prolapse of the epiglottic petiole in children who have had repeated airway reconstruction. A persistent tracheocutaneous fistula may be at the old tracheotomy site, and though it is usually the result of a long-standing, mature tracheotomy, it may also be a warning sign of a persistent mild airway obstruction. Therefore, it is best to be patient and to avoid surgical closure of a persistent tracheocutaneous fistula for 6 to 12 months.

Single-stage reconstruction carries its own particular risks; these include obstruction of an endotracheal tube, unplanned extubation, difficulty with sedation, and narcotic withdrawal. In some children, the larynx is very sensitive to intubation, particularly if the child is restless, and glottic edema and granulation tissue may preclude extubation and require replacement of the tracheotomy tube, at least temporarily. Narcotics should be weaned as early as possible.

Many complications can be anticipated and therefore avoided. When complications do occur, early recognition is desirable. The most common serious complication is early restenosis of the airway, requiring revision of LTR.

Follow-Up

After single-stage reconstruction of the airway and before extubation, it is desirable to formally reassess the airway in the operating room and downsize the endotracheal tube so that any possible problems with extubation can be anticipated. After extubation, the airway should be reinspected on at least one further occasion before the patient's discharge. A tenuous airway may require several re-evaluations before the patient's airway has stabilized and the patient is able to return home.

In two-stage reconstructions, if a suprastomal stent has been used, it should ideally be removed within 6 weeks to prevent scarring distal to the stent. Once the stent has been removed, the highest risk of restenosis occurs during the next week, and formal reassessment of the airway is recommended within a week of stent removal. Although the management of any particular child must be individualized appropriately, our guideline is that the child return in 4 to 6 weeks for further re-evaluation of the airway. If the reconstruction appears to have been successful at that time, the tracheotomy tube is downsized and capped, and the patient is observed in the hospital for 48 hours. If this proceeds well, the patient is allowed to return home, plugging the tracheotomy tube during the day but not at night (unless continuous pulse oximetry and responsible caregivers are available). After an additional 6 weeks, the patient is reassessed, and if clinical progress has been good, the patient is decannulated and observed for a further 48 hours. Another bronchoscopy is performed 6 weeks after decannulation to ensure that granuloma formation has not occurred at the old tracheotomy site. The child is normally reassessed at ever-increasing intervals (every 1 or 2 years) to ensure that the airway continues to grow appropriately for the child. In our experience, approximately 5% to 10% of children grow faster than their airway after reconstruction of the subglottis, and some may require late revision LTR.

CONCLUSION

Laryngeal stenosis is a relatively rare problem, with an estimated incidence in the adult population of 1.5 cases per 1 million patients per year in the United Kingdom.[92] There are no estimates in the pediatric population. Mild-to-moderate cases respond well to appropriate therapy, whether endoscopic or external reconstructive, but more advanced problems remain a major surgical challenge. More than 90% of patients can expect to be decannulated within 1 year of airway reconstructive surgery.[7]

Based on anatomic and pathologic principles, the traditional tenets of the treatment of chronic laryngeal stenosis are minimal excision of scar tissue, thus minimizing new raw surfaces; adoption of the principle of widening the cricoid by dividing the posterior lamina (the Réthi principle); restoration of skeletal support with autogenous costal cartilage; and allowing epithelialization of raw mucosal surfaces from adjoining respiratory epithelium without resorting to other mucosal grafts. The survival of autogenous costal cartilage grafts has been well documented both clinically and experimentally.[109] In selected cases, cricotracheal resection offers an alternative approach with excision (as opposed to expansion) of the stenotic lesion.

The management of patients with chronic laryngeal stenosis is a continual learning process, and, with a thoughtful approach, surgeons will continue to improve their techniques and results.

REFERENCES

1. Aboulker P, Sterkers JM, Demaldent JE, et al. Modifications apportées à l'intervention de Réthi. Intérêt dans les stenoses laryngotrachéales et trachéales. Ann Otolaryngol Chir Cervicofac (Paris) 83:98, 1966.
2. Albert DM, Mills RP, Fysh J, et al. Endoscopic examination of the neonatal larynx at extubation: a prospective study of variables associated with laryngeal damage. Int J Pediatr Otorhinolaryngol 20: 203, 1990.
3. Borowiecki B, Croft CB. Experimental animal model of subglottic stenosis. Ann Otol Rhinol Laryngol 86:835, 1977.
4. Brantigan CO, Grow JB Sr. Cricothyroidotomy: elective use in respiratory problems requiring tracheotomy. J Thorac Cardiovasc Surg 1976;71:72.
5. Conley JJ. Reconstruction of subglottic air passage. Ann Otol Rhinol Laryngol 62:477, 1953.
6. Cotton RT. Management of subglottic stenosis in infancy and childhood. Review of a consecutive series of cases managed by surgical reconstruction. Ann Otol Rhinol Laryngol 87:649, 1978.
7. Cotton RT. Pediatric laryngotracheal stenosis. J Pediatr Surg 19: 699, 1984.
8. Cotton RT. Prevention and management of laryngeal stenosis in infants and children. J Pediatr Surg 20:845, 1985.
9. Cotton RT. The problem of pediatric laryngotracheal stenosis: a clinical and experimental study on the efficacy of autogenous carti-

laginous grafts placed between the vertically divided lamina of the cricoid cartilage. Laryngoscope 101(suppl 56):1, 1991.

10. Cotton RT. Management of subglottic stenosis. Otol Clin North Am 33:111, 2000.

11. Cotton RT, Evans JNG. Laryngotracheal reconstruction in children. Five year followup. Ann Otol Rhinol Laryngol 90:516, 1981.

12. Cotton RT, Gray SD, Miller RP. Update of the Cincinnati experience in pediatric laryngotracheal reconstruction. Laryngoscope 99: 1111, 1989.

13. Cotton RT, Manoukian JJ. Glottic and subglottic stenosis. In Cummings CW, Fredrickson JM, Harker LA, et al (eds). Otolaryngology—Head and Neck Surgery. St Louis, CV Mosby, 1986, p 2159.

14. Cotton RT, Myer CM 3rd, Bratcher GO, et al. Anterior cricoid split. Arch Otolaryngol 114:1300, 1992.

15. Cotton RT, Myer CM 3rd, O'Connor DM. Innovations in pediatric laryngotracheal reconstruction. J Pediatr Surg 27:196, 1992.

16. Cotton RT, Richardson MA, Seid AB. Panel discussion: the management of advanced laryngotracheal stenosis. Management of combined advanced glottic and subglottic stenosis in infancy and childhood. Laryngoscope 91:221, 1981.

17. Cotton RT, Seid AB. Management of the extubation problem in the premature child: anterior cricoid split as an alternative to tracheotomy. Ann Otol Rhinol Laryngol 89:508, 1980.

18. Cotton RT, Tewfik TL. Laryngeal stenosis following carbon dioxide laser in subglottic hemangioma. Ann Otol Rhinol Laryngol 94:494, 1985.

19. Couriel JM, Phelan PD. Subglottic cysts: a complication of neonatal endotracheal intubation? Pediatrics 68:103, 1981.

20. Crysdale WS. Laryngeal and tracheal stenosis in children. Otolaryngol Clin North Am 12:817, 1979.

21. Crysdale WS. Subglottic stenosis in children. A management protocol plus surgical experience in 13 cases. Int J Pediatr Otorhinolaryngol 6:23, 1983.

22. Crysdale WS, Crepeau J. Surgical correction of subglottic stenosis in children. J Otolaryngol 11:209, 1982.

23. Downing TP, Johnson DG. Excision of subglottic stenosis with the urethral resectoscope. J Pediatr Surg 14:252, 1979.

24. Drake AF, Babyak JW, Niparko JK, et al. The anterior cricoid split. Arch Otolaryngol Head Neck Surg 114:1404, 1988.

25. Dunbar JS. Upper respiratory tract obstruction in infants and children. AJR Am J Roentgenol 109:227, 1970.

26. Evans JN, Todd GB. Laryngotracheoplasty. J Laryngol Otol 88:589, 1974.

27. Fearon B, Cotton RT. Subglottic stenosis in infants and children: the clinical problem and experimental surgical correction. Can J Otolaryngol 1:281, 1972.

28. Fearon B, Crysdale WS, Bird R. Subglottic stenosis of the larynx in the infant and child. Methods and management. Ann Otol Rhinol Laryngol 87:645, 1978.

29. Frankel LR, Anas NG, Perkin RM, et al. Use of the anterior cricoid split operation in infants with acquired subglottic stenosis. Crit Care Med 12:395, 1984.

30. Friedman EM, Healy GB, McGill TJ. Carbon dioxide laser management of subglottic and tracheal stenosis. Otolaryngol Clin North Am 16:871, 1983.

31. Gould SJ, Howard S. The histopathology of the larynx in the neonate following endotracheal intubation. J Pathol 146:301, 1985.

32. Gould SJ, Young M. Subglottic ulceration and healing following endotracheal intubation in the neonate: a morphometric study. Ann Otol Rhinol Laryngol 101:815, 1992.

33. Grahne B. Operative treatment of severe chronic traumatic laryngeal stenosis in infants up to three years old. Acta Otolaryngol (Stockh) 72:134, 1971.

34. Gray S, Miller R, Myer CM 3rd, et al. Adjunctive measures for successful laryngotracheal reconstruction. Ann Otol Rhinol Laryngol 96:509, 1987.

35. Grundfast KM, Camilon FS Jr, Pransky S, et al. Prospective study of subglottic stenosis in intubated neonates. Ann Otol Rhinol Laryngol 99:390, 1990.

36. Grundfast KM, Coffman AC, Milmoe G. Anterior cricoid split: a simple surgical procedure and a potentially complicated care problem. Ann Otol Rhinol Laryngol 94:445, 1985.

37. Gustafson LM, Hartley BE, Liu, JH, et al. Single-stage laryngotracheal reconstruction in children: a review of 200 cases. Otolaryngol Head Neck Surg 123:430, 2000.

38. Hartley JH Jr, Schatten WE: Cavernous hemangioma of the mandible. Plast Reconstr Surg 50:287, 1972.

39. Hawkins DB. Hyaline membrane disease of the neonate, prolonged intubation in management: effects on the larynx. Laryngoscope 88: 201, 1978.

40. Healy GB, McGill T, Simpson GT, et al. The use of the carbon dioxide laser in the pediatric airway. J Pediatr Surg 14:735, 1979.

41. Holinger LD. Treatment of severe subglottic stenosis without tracheotomy. Ann Otol Rhinol Laryngol 91:407, 1982.

42. Holinger LD, Oppenheimer RW. Congenital subglottic stenosis: the elliptical cricoid cartilage. Ann Otol Rhinol Laryngol 98:702, 1989.

43. Holinger LD, Stankiewicz JA, Livingston GL. Anterior cricoid split: the Chicago experience with an alternative to tracheotomy. Laryngoscope 97:19, 1987.

44. Holinger LD, Toriumi DM, Anandappa EC. Subglottic cysts and asymmetrical subglottic narrowing on neck radiograph. Pediatr Radiol 18:306, 1988.

45. Holinger PH, Kutnik SL, Schild JA, et al. Subglottic stenosis in infants and children. Ann Otol Rhinol Laryngol 85:591, 1976.

46. Jackson C. High tracheotomy and other errors as the chief causes of chronic laryngeal stenosis. Surg Gynecol Obstet 1921;32:392.

47. Johnson DG, Stewart DR. Management of acquired tracheal obstructions in infancy. J Pediatr Surg 10:709, 1975.

48. Joshi VV, Mandavia SG, Stern L, et al. Acute lesions induced by endotracheal intubation. Occurrence in the upper respiratory tract of newborn infants with respiratory distress syndrome. Am J Dis Child 124:646, 1972.

49. Kirchner FR, Toledo PS. Microcauterization in otolaryngology. Arch Otolaryngol 99:198, 1974.

50. Koufman JA. The otolaryngologic manifestations of gastroesophageal reflux disease (GERD): a clinical investigation of 225 patients using ambulatory 24 hour pH monitoring and an experimental investigation of the role of acid and pepsin in the development of laryngeal injury. Laryngoscope 101(suppl 53):1, 1991.

51. Koufman JA, Thompson JN, Kohut RI. Endoscopic management of subglottic stenosis with the CO_2 surgical laser. Otolaryngol Head Neck Surg 89:215, 1981.

52. Lusk RP, Gray S, Muntz HR. Single stage laryngotracheal reconstruction. Arch Otolaryngol Head Neck Surg 117:171, 1991.

53. Lyons GD, Owens R, Lousteau RJ, et al. Carbon dioxide laser treatment of laryngeal stenosis. Arch Otolaryngol 106:255, 1980.

54. MacArthur CJ, Kearns GH, Healy GB. Voice quality after laryngotracheal reconstruction. Arch Otolaryngol Head Neck Surg 120: 641, 1994.

55. Marshak G, Doyle WJ, Bluestone CD. Canine model of subglottic stenosis secondary to prolonged endotracheal intubation. Laryngoscope 92:805, 1982.

56. McDonald IH, Stocks JG. Prolonged nasotracheal intubation. Br J Anaesth 1965;37:161.

57. McGill J, Clinton JE, Ruiz E. Cricothyroidotomy in the emergency department. Ann Emerg Med 1982;11:361.

58. McMillan WG, Duvall AJ. Congenital subglottic stenosis. Arch Otolaryngol 87:272, 1968.

59. Monnier P, Savary M, Chapuis G. Partial cricoid resection with primary tracheal anastomosis for subglottic stenosis in infants and children. Laryngoscope 103:1273, 1993.

60. Monnier P, Lang F, Savary M. Partial cricotracheal resection for severe pediatric subglottic stenosis: update of the Lausanne experience. Annals Otol Rhinol Laryngol 107:961–968, 1998.

61. Montgomery WW. Chronic subglottic stenosis. Otolaryngol Clin North Am 17:107, 1984.

62. Morimitsu T, Matsumoto I, Okada S, et al. Congenital cricoid stenosis. Laryngoscope 91:1356, 1981.

63. Mostafa SM. Variation in subglottic size in children. Proc Rev Soc Med 69:793, 1976.

64. Motoyama EK. Endotracheal intubation. In Motoyama EK, Davis PJ (eds). Smith's Anesthesia for Infants and Children. St. Louis, CV Mosby, 1990, p 269.

65. Myer CM 3rd, O'Connor DM, Cotton RT. Proposed grading system for subglottic stenosis based on endotracheal tube sizes. Ann Otol Rhinol Laryngol 103:319, 1994.

66. Narcy P, Contencin P, Fligny I, et al. Surgical treatment for laryngotracheal stenosis in the pediatric patient. Arch Otolaryngol Head Neck Surg 116:1047, 1990.

67. Nicklaus PJ, Crysdale WS, Conley S, et al. Evaluation of neonatal

subglottic stenosis: a 3 year prospective study. Laryngoscope 100: 1185, 1990.

68. Noyek AM, Friedberg J, Steinhardt MI, et al. Xeroradiography in the assessment of the pediatric larynx and trachea. J Otolaryngol 5: 468, 1976.

69. Ochi JW, Evans JN, Bailey CM. Pediatric airway reconstruction at Great Ormond Street: a ten-year review. I. Laryngotracheoplasty and laryngotracheal reconstruction. Ann Otol Rhinol Otolaryngol 101:465, 1992.

70. Papsidero MJ, Pashley NR. Acquired stenosis of the upper airway in neonates. Ann Otol Rhinol Laryngol 89:512, 1980.

71. Pashley NR. Serial dilation compared to elective laryngotracheoplasty in the treatment of acquired subglottic stenosis in children. Int J Pediatr Otorhinolaryngol 5:59, 1983.

72. Pashley NR. Anterior cricoidotomy for congenital and acquired subglottic stenosis in infants and children. J Otolaryngol 13:187, 1984.

73. Prescott CAJ. Protocol for management of the interposition cartilage graft laryngotracheoplasty. Ann Otol Rhinol Laryngol 97:239, 1988.

74. Quiney RE, Gould SJ. Subglottic stenosis: a clinicopathological study. Clin Otolaryngol 10:315, 1985.

75. Ranne RD, Lindley S, Holder TM, et al. Relief of subglottic stenosis by anterior cricoid resection: an operation for the difficult case. J Pediatr Surg 26:255, 1991.

76. Ratner I, Whitfield J. Acquired subglottic stenosis in the very low birthweight infant. Am J Dis Child 137:40, 1983.

77. Réthi A. An operation for cicatricial stenosis of the larynx. J Laryngol Otol 70:283, 1956.

78. Rodgers BM, Talbert JL. Clinical application of endotracheal cryotherapy. J Pediatr Surg 13:662, 1978.

79. Rutter MJ, Hartley BE, Cotton RT. Cricotracheal resection in children. Arch Otolaryngol Head Neck Surg 127:289, 2001.

80. Rutter MJ, Link DT, Liu JH, et al. Laryngotracheal reconstruction and the hidden airway lesion. Laryngoscope 110:1871, 2000.

81. Rutter MJ, Link DT, Hartley BE, et al. Arytenoid prolapse as a consequence of cricotracheal resection in children. Ann Otol Rhinol Laryngol 110:210, 2001.

82. Sasaki CT, Horiuchi M, Koss N. Tracheostomyrelated subglottic stenosis: bacteriologic pathogenesis. Laryngoscope 89:857, 1979.

83. Schlesinger AE, Tucker GF Jr. Elliptical cricoid cartilage: a unique type of congenital subglottic stenosis. AJR Am J Roentgenol 146: 1133, 1986.

84. Seid AB, Pransky SM, Kearns DB. One stage laryngotracheoplasty. Arch Otolaryngol Head Neck Surg 117:408, 1991.

85. Shapsay SM, Rahbar R. Mitomycin: effects on laryngeal and tracheal stenosis, benefits, and complications. Ann Otol Rhinol Laryngol 110:1, 2001.

86. Shott SR. Down syndrome: analysis of airway size and a guide for appropriate intubation. Laryngoscope 110:585, 2000.

87. Silver FM, Myer CM 3rd, Cotton RT. Anterior cricoid split update 1991. Am J Otolaryngol 12:343, 1991.

88. Simon BM, Fowler SM, Handler SD. Communication development in young children with long term tracheostomies: preliminary report. Int J Pediatr Otorhinolaryngol 6:37, 1983.

89. Simpson GT, Healy GB, McGill T, et al. Benign tumors and lesions of the larynx in children. Surgical excision by CO_2 laser. Ann Otol Rhinol Laryngol 88:479, 1979.

90. Simpson GT, Strong MS, Healy GB, et al. Predictive factors of success or failure in the endoscopic management of laryngeal and tracheal stenosis. Ann Otol Rhinol Laryngol 91:384, 1982.

91. Smith ME, Mortelliti AJ, Cotton RT, et al. Phonation and swallowing considerations in pediatric laryngotracheal reconstruction. Ann Otol Rhinol Laryngol 101:731, 1992.

92. Stell PM, Maran AG, Stanley RE, et al. Chronic laryngeal stenosis. Ann Otol Rhinol Laryngol 94:108, 1985.

93. Stenson K, Berkowitz R, McDonald T, et al. Experience with one stage laryngotracheal reconstruction. Int J Pediatr Otorhinolaryngol 27:55, 1993.

94. Stern Y, Walner DL, Gerber ME, Cotton RT. Partial cricotracheal resection with primary anastomosis in the pediatric age group. Annals Otol Rhinol Laryngol 106:891–896, 1997.

95. Strong MS, Healy GB, Vaughan CW, et al. Endoscopic management of laryngeal stenosis. Otolaryngol Clin North Am 12:797, 1979.

96. Supance JS, Reilly JS, Doyle WJ, et al. Acquired subglottic stenosis following prolonged endotracheal intubation. Arch Otolaryngol 108: 727, 1982.

97. Toriumi DM, Miller DR, Holinger LD. Acquired subglottic cysts in premature infants. Int J Pediatr Otorhinolaryngol 14:151, 1987.

98. Tucker GF, Ossoff RH, Newman AN, et al. Histopathology of congenital subglottic stenosis. Laryngoscope 89:866, 1979.

99. Vollrath M, Freihorst J. [Surgery of acquired laryngotracheal stenoses in childhood. Experiences and results from 1988–1998. II: The cricotracheal resection]. Hno 1999; 47(7):611–622.

100. Ward RF, April MM. Mitomycin-C in the treatment of tracheal cicatrix after tracheal reconstruction. Int J Pediatr Otorhinolaryngol 44:221, 1998.

101. Wiatrak BJ, Cotton RT. Anastomosis of the cervical trachea in children. Arch Otolaryngol Head Neck Surg 118:58, 1992.

102. Willis R, Myer CM 3rd, Miller R, et al. Tracheostomy decannulation in the pediatric patient. Laryngoscope 97:764, 1987.

103. Yellon RF. Complications following airway surgery in Noonan syndrome. Arch Otolaryngol Head Neck Surg 123:1341, 1997.

104. Yellon R, Cotticchia J, Dixit S, Lee D. Esophageal biopsy for the diagnosis of gastroesophageal reflux–associated otolaryngologic problems in children. Am J Med 108:131S–138S, 2000.

105. Yellon R, Parameswaran M, Brandom B. Decreasing morbidity following laryngotracheal reconstruction in children. Int J Pediatr Otolaryngol 141:145–154, 1997.

106. Yellon R, Szeremeta W, Grandis J, et al. Subglottic injury, gastric juice, corticosteroids, and peptide growth factors in a porcine model. Laryngoscope 108:854–862, 1998.

107. Zalzal GH. Rib cartilage grafts for the treatment of posterior glottic and subglottic stenosis in children. Ann Otol Rhinol Laryngol 97:506, 1988.

108. Zalzal GH. Use of stents in laryngotracheal reconstruction in children: indications, technical considerations, and complications. Laryngoscope 98:849, 1988.

109. Zalzal GH, Cotton RT, McAdams AJ. The survival of costal cartilage grafts in laryngotracheal reconstruction. Otolaryngol Head Neck Surg 94:204, 1986.

110. Zalzal GH, Loomis SR, Derkay CS, et al. Vocal quality of decannulated children following laryngeal reconstruction. Laryngoscope 101:425, 1991.

┌─────┐
│ 90 │
└─────┘

Foreign Bodies of the Larynx, Trachea, and Bronchi

David H. Darrow, M.D., D.D.S., and Lauren D. Holinger, M.D.

On March 27, 1897, whilst eating some soup, [J.W.] aspirated a bone. This accident was followed by attacks of violent cough and dyspnoea, which, however, became gradually less. . . . On direct laryngeal examination by means of Kirstein's spatula, the patient being seated with his head strongly deflected to the left, I saw in the right principal bronchus a white mass. On the following day I introduced, under cocaine anaesthesia, a straight tube of 9 millimetres diameter and of 25 centimetres length through the larynx and the trachea until I came near the foreign body. The curvature of the trachea was thus removed, and the foreign body could be seen distinctly. I had had great difficulty in catching hold of the foreign body, using a pair of slender forceps which had specially and quickly been made. The difficulties were great, as at that time . . . I was still without the necessary practice which enables one to look easily, and even more to operate, through long tubes. Eventually I succeeded in catching the bone and in extracting it. The patient was able to return home on the following day.

Gustav Killian, 1902[24]

Despite significant advances in prevention, first aid, and endoscopic technology, foreign bodies of the pediatric airway remain a diagnostic and therapeutic challenge. In the United States, over the last 35 years, there has been a dramatic downturn in the number of childhood deaths from asphyxiation by ingested objects.[40, 41] Nevertheless, the incidence of foreign body aspiration has not changed significantly and is unlikely to do so as long as children continue to use their mouths to explore their surroundings. Long-standing airway foreign bodies are still associated with considerable morbidity, and early diagnosis therefore remains the key to successful and uncomplicated management of these accidents.

History

Prior to the 20th century, a foreign body in the lung led to a long and torturous illness, frequently ending in death. In his 1854 paper, "A Practical Treatise on Foreign Bodies in the Air Passages," Dr. Samuel D. Gross of the University of Louisville compiled more than 200 cases of foreign body aspiration and demonstrated a significant rate of morbidity and mortality in victims of such accidents.[10] He described the early management of airway

foreign bodies, including the use of emetics, sternutatories, expectorants, purgatives, and blood-letting. Gross, however, favored surgical treatment of foreign bodies, emphasizing the "important practical precept to resort to bronchotomy in all cases, the minute it is known that there is a foreign substance in the windpipe."[10] An alternative open approach was proposed by Jameson, who in 1823 reported that occlusion of the trachea by a sponge placed through a tracheotomy produced an expiratory effort sufficiently violent to expel the offending foreign body.[10] However, in a series of 937 foreign body cases reported by Weist in 1882, bronchotomy was associated with a mortality rate of 27%, while observation without intervention resulted in death in 23% of cases.[59] As a result, the popularity of surgical intervention diminished.

Although intubation of the trachea was practiced as early as the era of Hippocrates, endoscopic visualization of the airway was not accomplished until the 1800s. During an early rigid esophagoscopy using indirect lighting, Rosenheim accidentally passed the esophagoscope through the larynx and stumbled upon the carina.[10] In 1895, Gustav Killian successfully examined the bronchus of an adult male using a 9 mm rigid tube, and subsequently used his tube to perform the first endoscopic removal of a foreign body from the airway in 1897.[24] Distal illumination for esophagoscopy was introduced by Einhorn in 1902, and then modified for bronchoscopic use by Dr. Chevalier Jackson.

Jackson is credited with the development of the armamentarium and techniques that made endoscopic removal of foreign bodies from the airway a safe and successful procedure.[22] Collaborating with such manufacturers as the Pilling Company of Fort Washington, Pennsylvania, he designed a wide variety of extraction forceps. Jackson also described appropriate preparation of patients and optimal supine positioning for foreign body extraction. By 1936, he reported that the mortality rate associated with foreign bodies had been reduced from 24% to 2%, and that bronchoscopic removal was successful in 98% of cases.[23] Jackson further influenced foreign body management throughout the world by disseminating his knowledge and experience through assistants and students, such as Gabriel Tucker, Louis Clerf, C.L. Jackson, Paul H. Holinger, Lyman Richards, Edwin Broyles, and Charles Norris.

The next 50 years saw small modifications in the tech-

1543

nique of bronchoscopic removal of foreign bodies. Negus added a glass shield at the proximal end of the bronchoscope to protect the operator's eye.[33] In the early 1940s, Broyles improved magnification and lighting, using a set of bronchoscopic telescopes and proximal magnifiers, and later introduced the use of fiberoptic illumination in bronchoscopy.[33] Holinger developed the standard bronchoscopic anaesthesia adapter.[33] However, the addition of the Hopkins rod lens telescope to bronchoscopy in 1968 again revolutionized the procedure, bringing vastly improved illumination and visualization.[19, 33] Using glass rods instead of small lenses and glass fibers to carry the light, this instrumentation produced increased depth of field, a wider angle of vision, and a brighter image using less space. With the design of special extraction forceps capable of carrying the telescope into the bronchi, visualization during foreign body removal was also improved, and the rate of associated complications was diminished.[21]

While the instruments and techniques of bronchoscopy have improved much since Chevalier Jackson's time, improved results of treatment for these patients are also due to better diagnosis of the problem. As Ryland wrote in 1838,[9] "The diagnosis of the [foreign body] accident claims the most minute attention and we must avail ourselves of every circumstance at all calculated to throw light upon the subject."

Acute Airway Obstruction and Foreign Bodies

The most serious sequela of foreign body aspiration is complete obstruction of the airway. In such cases, the foreign body becomes lodged in the larynx or trachea, leaving little room peripherally for air exchange. Globular food objects such as hot dogs, candies, nuts, and grapes are the most frequent offenders, while rubber balloons, balls, marbles, and other toys (Fig. 90–1) are most common among nonfood objects.[27, 51, 53]

In the United States, the death toll from foreign body aspiration among all age groups has remained at about 3000 per year for the last 20 years. In contrast, the incidence of asphyxiation in the pediatric population has demonstrated a progressive decline. Among children between birth and 4 years of age, 650 died from foreign body ingestion in 1968; however, by 1997, this number had decreased to 140.[40, 41] This trend has most likely resulted from improved public awareness and prevention, from the development of rapid response paramedic teams, and from the introduction of the Heimlich maneuver.[16] Indeed, in a study of 103 paramedic runs for acute obstruction in choking children, the airway was cleared prior to the arrival of Emergency Medical Services personnel in 85%.[1]

Recognition of the child with complete airway obstruction is critical to the success of first aid efforts. Coughing, gagging, and throat clearing are reflexes that protect the airway and indicate that obstruction is not yet complete. First aid delivered to such a child is unnecessary and potentially dangerous. Probing the hypopharynx with a finger may impact a loose foreign body tightly into the larynx, thus transforming partial obstruction into complete obstruction. The foreign body may also be forced into the esophagus, where compression of the trachea against the upper sternum causes an obstruction that cannot be relieved even by tracheotomy. Similarly, back blows with the victim inverted are also ill-advised in the incompletely obstructed child. Such treatment may cause a bronchial or lower tracheal foreign body to impact in the glottis from below, precipitating complete obstruction. Alterna-

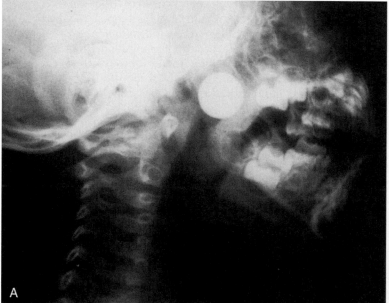
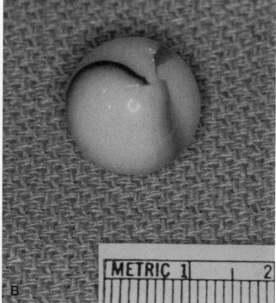

FIGURE 90–1. Lateral radiograph (A) demonstrating a foreign body in the nasopharynx of a 2-year-old boy. After radiographs were obtained, the object fell into the hypopharynx, causing complete occlusion of the laryngeal inlet. Direct laryngoscopy was performed in the operating room without anesthesia, and the object, identified as a marble (B), was removed with McGill forceps.

Box 90–1. First Aid for the Choking Child: Recommendations of the American Heart Association and the International Liaison Committee on Resuscitation[12]

Relief of foreign body airway obstruction in the *responsive infant*:

1. Infant is held prone with the head slightly lower than the chest, resting on the forearm of the rescuer. The rescuer's forearm is rested on the thigh with the hand supporting the jaw.
2. Five back blows are administered forcefully with the heel of the hand between the infant's shoulder blades.
3. If obstruction is not relieved, the infant is turned supine as a unit onto the free forearm with the hand supporting the occiput of the head. The forearm is again rested on the thigh with the head lower than the trunk.
4. Five rapid chest thrusts are administered over the lower third of the sternum, one finger's breadth below the inter-mammary line. Chest thrusts are delivered at a rate of 1 per second.
5. If the airway remains obstructed, the sequence is repeated until the object is removed or the victim becomes unresponsive.

Relief of foreign body airway obstruction in the *responsive child*:

1. Rescuer stands or kneels behind victim, arms under the victim's axillae, encircling the torso.
2. Rescuer places flat, thumb side of one fist against victim's abdomen in the midline slightly above the navel and well below the tip of the xiphoid process.
3. Rescuer grabs fist with other hand and exerts a series of five quick inward and upward thrusts. The xiphoid process and lower portions of the rib cage are avoided, since force applied to these structures may damage internal organs. Each thrust should be a separate, distinct movement, delivered with the intent to relieve the obstruction.

4. If the airway remains obstructed, the series may be repeated, or back blows and chest thrusts may be substituted as described for the unresponsive infant. The rescue attempt continues until the foreign body is expelled or the victim becomes unresponsive.

Relief of foreign body airway obstruction in the *unresponsive infant or child*:

1. Rescuer opens victim's airway with tongue-jaw lift and looks for an object in the pharynx. If the object is visible, it is removed with a finger sweep. *Blind finger sweep should not be performed.*
2. Rescuer opens the airway with a head tilt–chin lift and attempts to provide rescue breaths. If the breaths are not effective, the head is repositioned and ventilation reattempted.
3. If breaths are still not effective:
   - *For infant:*
     a. Rescuer performs sequence of five back blows and five chest thrusts.
     b. Steps 1 through 3a are repeated until the object is dislodged and the airway is patent, or for approximately 1 minute. If the infant remains unresponsive after approximately 1 minute, rescuer activates EMS system.
   - *For child:*
     a. Rescuer performs sequence of five abdominal thrusts.
     b. Steps 1 through 3a are repeated until the object is retrieved or rescuer breaths are effective.
4. Once effective breaths are delivered, rescuer assesses for signs of circulation and provides additional cardiopulmonary resuscitation as needed or places the infant or child in a recover position if he or she demonstrates adequate breathing and signs of circulation.

---

tively, a foreign body from a lower lobe bronchus may be shifted to an upper lobe bronchus, where anatomic factors complicate its removal.

Complete airway obstruction can be recognized in the conscious child as sudden respiratory distress, followed by an inability to speak or cough. Older children may use the distress signal of choking, which is the gesture of clutching the neck between the thumb and index finger. When complete obstruction is identified, prompt delivery of first aid is indicated.

Appropriate management of the child with airway obstruction due to foreign body aspiration is controversial and evolving. In 2000, the American Heart Association, in collaboration with the International Liaison Committee on Resuscitation revised its policy statement on first aid for the child with foreign body obstruction of the airway.[12] Although inspection of the oral cavity for foreign body is still recommended, blind finger sweeps and manipulations to visualize foreign bodies are no longer advocated. Rescuers are advised to perform cardiopulmonary resuscitation for 1 minute prior to activating the Emergency Medical Services system, since such maneuvers often generate sufficient pressure to expel a foreign body. Back blows and chest thrusts remain the primary therapy for children younger than 1 year of age, due to the potential for intra-abdominal injury in these children by

the abdominal thrust (Heimlich) maneuver. In older children, abdominal thrusts are the mainstay of treatment. Current recommendations for management of foreign body airway obstruction in infants and children by lay personnel are given in Box 90–1.

In the presence of skilled rescuers and appropriate equipment, laryngoscopy may reveal a foreign body that can be removed to reestablish the airway. If the obstruction is below the level of the vocal folds, ventilation can be temporarily established using an 18-gauge needle or intravenous catheter introduced through the cricothyroid membrane. Urgent tracheotomy can also be performed if surgically trained personnel are present.

Epidemiology

In the pediatric age group, most victims of foreign body aspiration are older infants and toddlers. According to case series from the last decade, children younger than 5 years of age account for approximately 84% of cases (range, 74–96%), and children younger than 3 years account for 74% of cases (range, 52–90%).* Boys are affected more frequently than girls, by a ratio of about 2:1.

---

*5, 6, 20, 26, 28, 31, 36, 39, 42, 43, 45, 46, 55, 57, 60

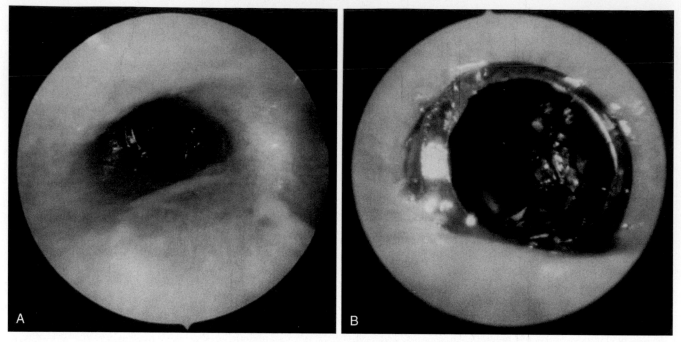

FIGURE 90–2. Endoscopic views of a plastic Lego block in the right main bronchus of a 5-year-old boy. The hollow, conical toy was removed with the hollow-object forceps.

The reason for the male predominance remains unclear, but the high incidence in this age group reflects the tendency of these children to explore their world using their mouths. Furthermore, these children have not yet developed a full posterior dentition, and neuromuscular mechanisms for swallowing and airway protection may not be fully mature. As a result, chunks of food are often too large and may cause gagging. If they cannot be moved into the hypopharynx, they may obscure the laryngeal inlet when the child inspires.

Types of Airway Foreign Bodies

The spectrum of airway foreign bodies varies somewhat from country to country, depending on the diet and customs of the population in question. Nevertheless, vegetable matter is uniformly the most common foreign body found in the pediatric airway. Such material is found in 55% to 95% of cases, with peanuts and other nuts alone accounting for an average of 39% (range, 7–58%).* Carrot pieces, beans, sunflower seeds, and watermelon seeds are also found frequently. Nuts with oils on the surface tend to stimulate a robust inflammatory mucosal response. Dried beans may also be associated with greater morbidity because of their tendency to swell when exposed to secretions in the airway.

Metal foreign bodies, once quite common because of the use of safety pins with diapers, have fallen to an incidence of 5% to 15% in the era of disposable diapers. In contrast, plastic foreign bodies have risen in frequency to 5% to 15% because of the widespread use of this material in the toy industry. These objects are inert, and some of the plastics, such as the polyethylenes, have no

incorporated radiopaque substances.[47] Because of their nonirritating and radiolucent qualities, plastics may remain as foreign bodies in the tracheobronchial tree for prolonged periods of time (Fig. 90–2). Other common foreign bodies include stones, bones, and glass.

School supplies have been implicated in foreign body aspiration in older children. Lemberg et al[26] reported that half of the aspiration events in children older than 5 years of age involved school supplies, and the importance of aspirated ballpoint pen parts in this age group has been observed by Garcia-Iriarte et al.[14]

Location of Airway Foreign Bodies

Most foreign bodies pass through the larynx and trachea to become lodged more peripherally in the airway. However, large foreign bodies or those with sharp, irregular edges may become lodged in the laryngeal inlet. This occurrence is particularly common in infants younger than 1 year of age. Such objects account for 1% to 7% of airway foreign bodies.[3, 5, 15, 20, 32, 36, 43, 46, 58]

Once a foreign object traverses the larynx and enters the trachea, its final resting place is determined by several factors. Tracheal foreign bodies, found in 3% to 12% of cases,* are more likely if the tracheal lumen is narrowed by tracheomalacia or previous surgery, or if the patient's respiratory effort is weak. Occasionally, a long-standing esophageal foreign body may erode through the party wall and present in the trachea. In most cases, however, the foreign body finds its way into one of the main bronchi, the right being more frequently involved than the left in most series. Explanations for the predominance of the right main bronchus include its greater

---

*2, 3, 5, 6, 20, 26, 28, 29, 31, 36, 39, 42, 43, 45, 46, 55, 57

*3, 5, 20, 28, 29, 32, 36, 43, 45, 46, 57, 58, 60

diameter, its smaller angle of divergence from the tracheal axis, greater airflow through the right lung, and the position of the carina to the left of the midline. In a study of adult cadavers in which peanuts were passed into the trachea and the final site of lodgment noted, only the position of the carina was felt to correlate with foreign body location.[30]

Presentation

Aspiration of foreign bodies usually causes significant coughing, choking, gagging, and wheezing in a short time, thus calling attention to the problem. However, in many cases the diagnosis is delayed, usually because the ingestion was not witnessed, because there were no symptoms or signs, or because the presence of a foreign body was not suspected when symptoms and signs did appear. Foreign bodies may be the cause of a variety of acute and chronic diseases of the lung and should be considered in differential diagnoses. Also, when no signs or symptoms are present, the physician may be misled into assuming that an object has been swallowed and will safely pass through the digestive tract. The mucosa of the larynx, trachea, and bronchi rapidly adapts to the presence of foreign objects, and the physician must be aware that symptoms and signs may not appear immediately.

The practice of treating asthmatic or "croupy" children with antibiotics or steroids may well obscure signs and symptoms that would normally be expected with a retained foreign object. Clearing of symptoms with these agents cannot always be assumed to be diagnostic of a specific disease process. The fact that a wheeze disappears or that a pneumonic process clears may merely mean that a patient's reaction to the presence of the foreign object has been temporarily controlled. The recurrence of "asthma" after the withdrawal of therapy should heighten the physician's suspicion of a foreign object as the possible underlying cause of distress.

Clinical Stages of Foreign Body Aspiration

Signs and symptoms associated with foreign body aspiration are observed in three stages. In the initial stage, there is a history of a choking episode, followed by violent paroxysms of coughing, gagging, and, occasionally, complete airway obstruction. Such a history may be elicited in about 80% of cases (range, 48–100%).* In a series of 100 cases of foreign body aspiration, a choking crisis was the most sensitive clinical parameter (97%) and had reasonable specificity as well (63%), in contrast to other symptoms and radiography, which were sensitive (88% and 85%, respectively), but not specific (9%).[4] Unfortunately, many parents tend to downplay the significance of such an episode or do not recount the history until after the foreign body has been removed.

An asymptomatic interval generally follows the aspiration, during which time the foreign body becomes lodged, the reflexes become fatigued, and the immediate irritating symptoms subside. This stage is most treacher-

ous and accounts for a large percentage of delayed diagnoses or overlooked foreign bodies. Twenty to 50% of foreign bodies are not detected for more than a week,[2, 31, 39, 42, 43, 46, 57, 60] generally because the parent or the referring physician has, in the absence of symptoms and signs, minimized the possibility of a foreign body accident. Longer delays in diagnosis appear to correlate with increasing age.[2]

The third stage is characterized by symptoms of complications. It is the stage in which obstruction, erosion, or infection develops to again direct attention to the presence of the foreign body. Cough, hemoptysis, pneumonia, lung abscess, fever, and malaise may develop with foreign bodies of the airway.

Laryngeal Foreign Body

As mentioned previously, foreign bodies lodging in the larynx that are completely obstructive usually cause sudden death. Objects that are only partially obstructive and thus compatible with life are usually flat and thin and lodge between the vocal folds in the sagittal plane (Fig. 90–3). Such objects will commonly cause hoarseness, croupy cough, stridor, and varying degrees of dyspnea, all of which increase as edema and infection develop. Odynophagia may be present if the foreign body has sharp edges. These symptoms and signs may also be present due to laryngeal inflammation following migration of a foreign body from the larynx to the trachea, or from digital or instrumental attempts at removal. If the foreign body is in fact lodged in the esophagus, there may still be sufficient periesophageal reaction and obstruction to cause secretions to overflow through the larynx and cause the outlined symptoms and signs as secondary manifestations of the presence of a foreign body.

Tracheal Foreign Body

Foreign bodies of the trachea present in a manner similar to those of the larynx, with the exception that hoarseness is a less common finding. Three additional features originally described by Jackson and recounted by McCrae[35] are pathognomonic for tracheal foreign body. The *audible slap* results from the impact of a mobile foreign body against the wall of the trachea on deep inspiration or coughing and is best heard at the open mouth. The same movement also creates a simultaneous *palpatory thud*, which can be felt with one finger on the trachea. *The asthmatoid wheeze* is in fact higher in pitch and more intense than that of bronchial asthma. It is best heard at the open mouth or with a stethoscope over the trachea and is poorly heard over the chest.

Bronchial Foreign Body

The initial symptoms of bronchial foreign body are those mentioned previously, including choking, coughing, and wheezing. However, in one large series,[28] 33% of patients with bronchial foreign bodies presented with none of these symptoms. Choking and coughing were found to be highly suggestive of foreign body aspiration (specificity of

---

*2, 3, 28, 29, 32, 36, 37, 39, 42, 45, 46, 55, 58, 60

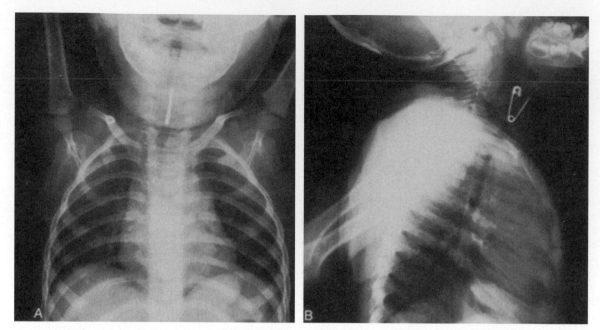

FIGURE 90–3. Posteroanterior (*A*) and lateral (*B*) radiographs of an open safety pin in the larynx of an infant. She had typical symptoms and signs of a hoarse cry, odynophagia, and airway obstruction.

91% and 80%, respectively), but the diagnostic sensitivity of both was considerably lower (less than 40%). Such data lend credence to the aphorism, "A positive history must never be ignored, while a negative history may be misleading."

Common physical signs of bronchial foreign body include expiratory wheezing and decreased air entry on the affected side. Use of a two-headed stethoscope can enhance subtle differences in the intensity, phase, and quality of respiratory sounds heard on the two sides of the chest.[44] However, although such differences often suggest the presence of a foreign body, they are an unreliable means of localizing the object, as conditions in the airway may vary over time. Secretions, whether normal or pathologic, may shift from one location to another. The foreign body itself may shift in position, and thus there may be variation in the aeration distal to the foreign object. Foreign bodies in the lower trachea may give rise to a variety of signs and symptoms as the foreign body shifts its position in the region of the carina.

Respiratory distress is a relatively uncommon finding in children with bronchial foreign bodies, but such patients require immediate attention and intervention. Dry vegetables and beans that swell as they become moist from bronchial secretions are often responsible in these cases. Hemoptysis, also a rare finding, suggests the presence of granulation tissue.

Late manifestations may be obscured by the prior treatment of the patient with steroids or antibiotics. Obstructive bronchial foreign bodies classically cause emphysema, atelectasis, pneumonia, and, eventually, pulmonary abscess. Organic materials are apt to cause a relatively violent reaction, with symptoms of laryngotracheobronchitis, toxemia, cough, and irregular fever.

Imaging

Radiographic examination for airway foreign bodies consists of anteroposterior and lateral views of the extended neck for soft tissue visualization and posteroanterior and lateral radiographs of the chest. Smaller children may undergo lateral chest radiography with the arms behind the back, the neck flexed, and the head extended to allow for visualization of the entire airway from the mouth to the carina. Radiographs of the chest in inspiration and expiration are the most useful radiographs for demonstrating unilateral air trapping. Because these views are difficult to obtain in children, lateral decubitus radiographs are often performed in order to use the patient's body weight to promote expiratory excursion. Dynamic imaging by fluoroscopy is useful for studying partial obstruction of the lung in real time; complete ventilation of the lung may be demonstrated if given enough time. Videofluoroscopy offers the additional advantage of multiple reviews without prolonged radiographic exposure.

When a foreign body is present at the orifice of a main bronchus, obstruction may be partial or complete. In partial *bypass valve* obstruction, air is exchanged in both inspiration and expiration, resulting in a normal radiographic study. *Check valve* obstruction is commonly associated with acute bronchial foreign bodies. In such cases, air can move past the foreign body on inhalation but not on expiration due to the normal physiologic decrease in bronchial diameter. The result is hyperinflation of the obstructed lung and mediastinal shift to the opposite side (Fig. 90–4). Foreign bodies of long standing cause edema and granulation tissue, resulting in complete, or *stop valve*, obstruction and a chest radiograph that demonstrates collapse of the affected segment. *Ball valve* ob-

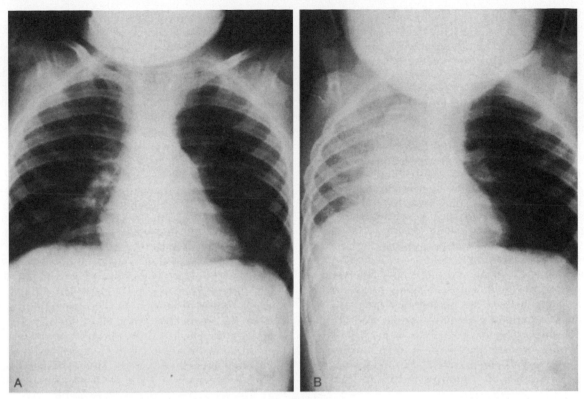

FIGURE 90–4. Inspiratory (*A*) and expiratory (*B*) chest radiographs of a 2½-year-old child who aspirated a peanut fragment. The foreign body lodged in the left main bronchus, where it obstructed egress of air from the left lung and produced obstructive emphysema, apparent only on the expiratory film (*B*).

struction, rarely seen in cases of bronchial foreign body, allows egress of air from the lung but prevents entrance of air on inhalation. Such obstruction leads to atelectasis and mediastinal shift toward the obstructed side.

Bronchograms are occasionally helpful in outlining a radiolucent foreign body that is too peripheral for endoscopic visualization. Frequently, only obstruction of a segment of lung is demonstrated because the foreign body has created enough reaction to occlude an orifice. Bronchograms may also be necessary to evaluate and follow bronchiectasis caused by a long-standing foreign body. Computed tomography may also be useful for cases in which standard radiographic studies fail to demonstrate a foreign body.

Diagnostic Accuracy

Complete radiographic assessment is often diagnostic in cases of laryngeal foreign body. In series reported by Silva et al[54] and Halvorson et al,[15] cervical radiographs were considered diagnostic in 7 of 10 patients with laryngeal foreign bodies. Of 19 patients with laryngotracheal foreign bodies reported by Esclamado and Richardson,[13] 13 patients underwent radiography of the neck and 12 of these radiographs (92%) demonstrated a subglottic density or swelling. In contrast, chest radiographs were normal in 11 of 19 patients (58%). Mu et al[38] reported abnormal radiographic findings in only 8 of 40 children with laryngotracheal foreign bodies; however, the foreign

body was tracheal in more than 90% of these children. Zerella et al[61] reported only 19% sensitivity for foreign bodies of the trachea. Thus, posteroanterior and lateral neck radiographs are considered an essential part of the evaluation for stridor and airway obstruction and are obtained when foreign body aspiration is suspected but not confirmed by radiographs of the chest. They are frequently diagnostic in cases of laryngeal foreign body, but normal films cannot be used to discount an object in the trachea.

In cases of suspected bronchial foreign body, chest radiography is less often diagnostic but is vital to the assessment of the patient's pulmonary status and the potential for complications. Air trapping (obstructive emphysema) is the most common radiographic finding, noted in 32% to 66% of cases.° Atelectasis and pneumonia are somewhat less common. A radiopaque foreign body is identified in fewer than one fourth of patients.† Normal chest radiographs can be seen in up to 40% of cases.[39, 57]

The accuracy of chest radiography in the diagnosis of tracheobronchial foreign bodies was studied by Svedstrom et al[56] in 83 consecutive cases of suspected foreign body aspiration. Among the 34 patients (41%) in whom a foreign body was removed, preoperative radiographs demonstrated air trapping in 50%, signs of infection in 18%, and signs of atelectasis in 12%. In 21%, a radiopaque foreign

---

°2, 3, 6, 28, 32, 39, 42, 43, 45, 55, 61

†2, 3, 5, 6, 28, 29, 32, 36, 39, 42, 43, 45, 46, 55, 57, 61

body could be identified. No radiographic abnormality was found in 24% of cases. The authors computed a diagnostic accuracy of 67%, a sensitivity of 68%, and a specificity of 67% and concluded that plain radiography is neither sufficiently sensitive nor sufficiently specific for the diagnosis of foreign body aspiration. Studying foreign bodies throughout the airway, Silva et al[54] found a sensitivity and specificity of 73% and 45%, respectively, and arrived at the same conclusion.

It should be concluded that, in cases of tracheobronchial foreign body, history and physical examination, and not radiographs, determine the indication for bronchoscopy.[54] At many institutions, time and resources are wasted on fluoroscopy or inspiratory/expiratory films, when a history of witnessed choking or an examination revealing decreased breath sounds on one side clearly suggests the need for endoscopic assessment. Bronchoscopy should be considered the definitive diagnostic intervention as well as the preferred therapeutic intervention; radiographs provide additional information in cases associated with pneumonia or other suspected causes of airway obstruction and should be limited to posteroanterior and lateral films of the chest.

Management

The treatment of choice for foreign bodies in the upper respiratory tract is prompt endoscopic removal under conditions of maximum safety and minimum trauma. Too often, foreign bodies are considered dire emergencies, leading to hasty, inadequate study and poorly prepared, improper attempts at removal. However, unless actual or potential airway obstruction is present, a foreign body is not an acute emergency. The majority of patients with foreign bodies who come to the otolaryngologist have already passed the acute phase. When there is no imminent danger to the patient's life, the problem is approached with complete and thoughtful consideration of the physiologic and mechanical factors involved. The endoscopic removal can be scheduled when trained personnel are available, when instruments have been checked, and when techniques have been tested.

Often, the primary physician may delay referral for endoscopy unless there is strong evidence of a foreign body. Endoscopy, however, is a form of physical examination (inspection) and is, therefore, both a diagnostic and a therapeutic technique. If the history or physical findings are suspicious, endoscopic examination may be indicated to establish the diagnosis and to provide relief of symptoms.

Postural drainage (chest physical therapy) and bronchodilator therapy were proposed by Burrington and Cotton[7] as an alternative to bronchoscopic removal of foreign bodies. This technique purports to dislodge the foreign body to facilitate its expulsion by the patient's own cough reflex. However, control of the object is lost, and complete obstruction of the airway may result.[52] Of the first 52 patients treated using this technique, 4 suffered sudden respiratory arrest, 1 of whom also experienced transient cortical blindness.[7, 11] As a result of these complica-

tions, the authors discontinued the use of postural drainage in the treatment of foreign bodies of the main bronchi, and limited its use to peripherally located foreign bodies. In a subsequent series of 28 such cases, only 18 were successfully treated with this therapy; bronchoscopic removal salvaged 8 of the 10 failures.[8] Postural drainage is therefore a procedure to be avoided, and bronchoscopic extraction remains the first-line therapy for all cases of tracheobronchial foreign bodies.

Planning for Endoscopy

Parental Consultation

Consultation with the child's parents is an essential part of the preparation for endoscopy. Risks of the procedure, including complete airway obstruction, injury to the tracheobronchial tree, and failed extraction, are discussed but in such a way that the parents do not delay the procedure unnecessarily. The consultation also provides an opportunity to learn from the parents the topographic details of the foreign body or to obtain from them a duplicate on which to practice. Postoperatively, if extraction is successful, the parents are instructed to abstain from feeding nuts and seeds to young children and to keep small, potentially ingestible objects out of their reach.

Medical Evaluation

A thorough medical history and physical examination is necessary prior to endoscopy. Patients with a history of asthma prior to the aspiration are carefully evaluated by specialists in pulmonary medicine or allergy and by the anesthesiologist. A history of poor oral intake or vomiting may suggest a concomitant esophageal foreign body, while symptoms of aspiration may herald an associated tracheoesophageal fistula. Further attention is given to other preexisting illnesses and medications the child is taking.

Analysis of the Problem

Extraction of a foreign body from the tracheobronchial tree is a mechanical problem that requires study and advance planning. The shape, texture, location, and possible orientation of the object are all considered in the selection and use of instruments. A duplicate foreign body obtained from the parents is extremely useful for this purpose, and practice on a mannequin board results in a smoother procedure. As stated by Holinger[18] in 1961, "If two hours are spent in such preparation, the safe endoscopic removal may only take two minutes. But if only two minutes are taken for preparation, the endoscopist may find himself attempting makeshift ineffective procedures for the next two hours."

Selection of Instruments

A complete instrumentarium is essential in foreign body extraction. Many of the complications and failures of attempted foreign body removal arise because the endoscopist lacks the instrument specifically designed for the problem. This is not a valid excuse but rather a regrettable explanation for the failure. If a full range of laryngoscopes, open-tube bronchoscopes, and foreign body forceps is not available, the procedure should not be attempted. Equipment must be in perfect repair and working order.

Visualization of the larynx prior to bronchoscopy simplifies passage of the bronchoscope and allows the endoscopist to assess the laryngeal inlet for the presence of a foreign body and for postaspiration trauma. This is best accomplished with a laryngoscope of appropriate size designed for use in the vallecula (Table 90–1). Laryngoscopes in common use for this purpose include the Parsons laryngoscope (Karl Storz) and the Tucker side-slide laryngoscope (Pilling). An anesthesia laryngoscope fitted with a MacIntosh blade may also be used.

The rigid bronchoscope is unquestionably the instrument of choice for working in the tracheobronchial tree. The major drawbacks to the use of flexible instruments are lack of control of the foreign body and inadequate control of the airway. The rigid instruments afford a much greater range of size and variety of forceps, better exposure of the foreign body, and the ability to shield pointed and sharp foreign body parts within the tube during extraction. The flexible bronchoscope may be of some help in the occasional older child or adult with a foreign body lodged far into the periphery of the lung, or in a patient who is unable to extend the head and neck for any reason.

The Holinger ventilating fiber-illuminated bronchoscopes (Pilling) or Doesel-Huzly bronchoscopes with Hopkins rod-lens telescopes (Karl Storz) are the instruments most commonly employed for foreign body extraction. A 3.5 mm by 25 cm or 4 mm by 30 cm bronchoscope (Pilling) or a 3.7 mm by 30 cm (Karl Storz) is most often used, but, like the laryngoscope, the bronchoscope is selected on the basis of patient age and size (see Table 90–1). As a general rule, it is wise to use the largest bronchoscope that can be passed without resistance; this permits use of a larger telescope for better visualization and increase the likelihood that the object can be withdrawn through the bronchoscope. Two laryngoscopes and two bronchoscopes are lighted and ready; should a light fail or a forceps become jammed in a scope, a back-up will be available immediately. An additional bronchoscope

is also useful in cases of fragmented foreign bodies, so that the airway can be rapidly reestablished and the procedure continued after the equipment from the initial pass is handed off to the scrub technician.

Positive-action (center-action) forceps are most commonly used in extraction of airway foreign bodies, owing to the popularity of the optical forceps system fitted with the Hopkins rod-lens telescope (Karl Storz) (Fig. 90–5C). The optical forceps are manufactured in appropriate lengths for the bronchoscopes with which they are used and are available in the peanut-grasping, forward-grasping ("alligator"), and cup forceps varieties. Other nonoptical types are also available (Fig. 90–5B) and are used with distal illumination through light carriers (Pilling) or proximal illumination using a glass prism (Storz). Positive-action forceps may be particularly helpful in dilating the bronchial wall to create forceps spaces when a foreign body is wedged in a distal bronchus. Passive-action forceps offer a greater range of blades for the various types of mechanical problems. A specific forceps of one of the four major types (forward-grasping, rotation, ball bearing, or hollow object forceps) can be selected in most cases (Fig. 90–5A). No fewer than 60 variations of these four types have been designed.

For a particular foreign body, the forceps are selected and tried with a duplicate object on a mannequin board or lung model. The forceps should be smooth in operation, and the blades should be adjusted so that they close completely when the handles are closed. The shaft of the forceps must be straight to provide proper visualization and to prevent friction between the forceps and the lumen of the tube. Two varieties of forceps are made available for removal of any foreign body. Although a forceps may be chosen that is apparently best suited for the job, unexpected circumstances may arise after the procedure is under way and may require the use of a second variety of forceps.

The Fogarty embolectomy catheter is another instrument that has found its way into the foreign body armamentarium at some institutions.[25] This small catheter fitted with a balloon can be passed through a bronchoscope, positioned distal to the foreign body, inflated with saline, and withdrawn to trap the presenting part of the object within the lumen of the bronchoscope. The bronchoscope, catheter, and foreign body are then removed from the patient as a single unit. This technique, however, compromises control of the object.

TABLE 90–1. Suggested Endoscope Sizes for Infants and Children

Patient Age	Parsons Laryngoscope*	Tucker Laryngoscope*	Storz Bronchoscope Size	Outside Diameter (mm)
Premature infant	8	8	2.5	4.2
Newborn–3 mo	8	8	3.0	5.0
3–18 mo	9	9 or 10.5	3.5	5.7
1–3 yr	9 or 11	10.5	3.7	6.4
3–5 yr	11 or 13.5 (Benjamin)	10.5 or 12	4.0	6.7
5–10 yr	13.5 (Benjamin)	12	5.0	7.8
>10 yr	13.5 (Benjamin)	16	6.0	8.2

* Sizes indicate length of blade in centimeters.

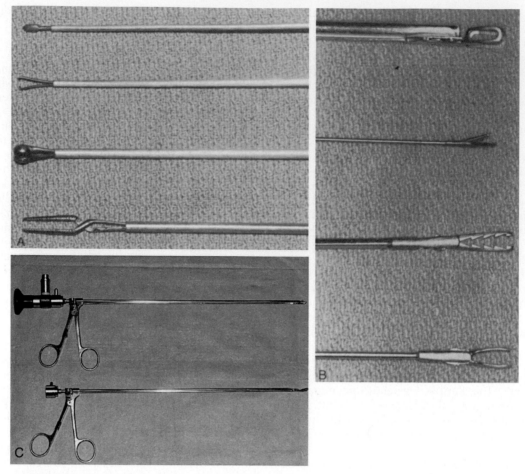

FIGURE 90–5. *A,* Passive-action forceps. *From top to bottom:* forward-grasping forceps, rotation forceps, globular-object forceps, and hollow-object forceps. *B,* Positive (center-action) forceps. *From top to bottom:* optical peanut forceps and three varieties of forward-grasping forceps. *C,* Optical forceps. *Top:* peanut forceps with telescope mounted. *Bottom:* alligator forceps with telescope mounted.

The Surgical Team

A team approach to foreign body removal cannot be overemphasized. The anesthesiologist, the scrub technician, the circulating nurse, and the endoscopist must all have experience with extraction of foreign bodies. If this is not the case, consideration is given to delaying the procedure until experienced personnel are available. A plan for orderly removal of the object is discussed with each member of the team and his or her role in that plan clearly delineated. The procedure is not begun until all members of the team are prepared and positioned appropriately.

Anesthesia

In cases of severe airway obstruction, foreign bodies are usually located in the larynx or upper trachea. In such cases, the child may be mummified, and the object removed through a laryngoscope placed without anesthesia. Oxygenation may be supported intraoperatively by insufflation through a nasal catheter.

For most foreign body extractions, however, general anesthesia provides a more controlled setting. Spontaneous ventilation is preferable to apneic technique, since the patient has already demonstrated that he can ventilate himself by generating negative intrathoracic pressure. Changing the system to positive-pressure ventilation under apneic conditions may render the patient unable to ventilate owing to obstruction by the foreign body. While spontaneous ventilation technique precludes the use of the rapid sequence induction, no cases of aspiration on induction have been reported.

Preoperative sedation, which can potentially depress the patient's respiratory drive, is avoided. During induction in the operating suite, standard monitoring is initiated, including an electrocardiogram, a precordial stethoscope, a blood pressure cuff, a pulse oximeter, an end-tidal carbon dioxide monitor, and a thermometer. An anticholinergic agent (usually glycopyrrolate) is administered intravenously prior to the procedure to reduce secretions and the risk of bradycardia. Induction of anesthesia is by mask using halothane or sevoflurane and oxygen. Nitrous oxide may be used to facilitate a smooth induction but should be discontinued prior to the procedure so that the patient remains adequately saturated with oxygen during the foreign body extraction. Following induction, the laryngoscope is passed by the endoscopist to ensure that no foreign body is present in the larynx. If the laryngeal inlet is clear, the larynx is sprayed with a solution of 2% lidocaine to desensitize the larynx and reduce the risk of laryngospasm.

The bronchoscope is then inserted, and the tracheobronchial tree is inspected while the patient is ventilated and anesthetized through the bronchoscope side arm. Spontaneous ventilation is maintained through a closed system created using an eyeglass or telescope to occlude the proximal end of the bronchoscope. The inhaled agent may be changed to isoflurane, supplemented by propofol as needed. Positive-pressure ventilation is avoided, because this tends to drive the foreign body further peripherally. Use of the rod-lens system within the bronchoscope reduces the lumen through which the patient is ventilated and may result in transient desaturation. When this occurs, temporary replacement of the telescope with an eyeglass allows the child to be adequately saturated with oxygen before proceeding. As the anesthesia lightens, an occasional cough may actually help move the foreign body toward the bronchoscope.

Endoscopic Technique

Endoscopic extraction of foreign bodies in children is a gentle, delicate procedure. Adequate protection is applied to the eyes and superior alveolar ridge. The laryngoscope is placed atraumatically into the right side of the mouth, with the tongue gently pushed to the left. The tip of the scope is positioned in the vallecula. The bronchoscope is inserted with care taken not to injure the laryngeal structures. One must never force a scope, forceps, or foreign body.

Once the bronchoscope has been advanced into the upper trachea, ventilation through the side arm is established and confirmed by the endoscopist. The tracheobronchial tree is completely inspected, as multiple foreign bodies may be present. Inspection begins with the normal bronchus, and all secretions are removed to ensure optimal respiratory function when the involved side is inspected. When a foreign body is seen, its shape, position, and forceps spaces are assessed. The suction is used to remove secretions from around the foreign body but is inadequate to hold foreign bodies and is not used for attempted removal. The presentation of the foreign body is studied, with special attention to the location of unseen parts, such as sharp points, which may be buried deep within the mucosa.

Prior to extraction, the orientation of the object may be modified with the tip of the scope, a technique especially helpful when establishing forceps spaces between the object and lumen walls. When possible, the foreign body is rotated into the sagittal plane, since this is the largest diameter of the laryngeal lumen. One must be cautious not to drive the foreign body further down.

Forceps spaces, the spaces where the blades of the forceps can safely be placed, may be obliterated if granulations are present or if the surrounding mucosa is swollen. If granulations are present proximal to the foreign body, the bronchoscope can be pushed past the granulations, or the granulations can be removed. If bleeding makes manipulation unsafe, topical epinephrine diluted 1:30,000 or topical oxymetazoline can be applied with a sponge-carrier.

When the foreign body is grasped, an effort is made to place the tips strategically. In grasping globular foreign bodies, the blades must pass beyond the equator of the object to avoid stripping off. Vegetable foreign bodies such as peanuts are grasped lightly to avoid fragmentation. Use of a peanut forceps with light, delicate blades facilitates such gentle handling. Once firmly within the forceps, the object is dislodged and gently withdrawn. The scope is then advanced to the foreign body, and the object anchored against the tube mouth to protect the grasp. The foreign body, scope, and forceps are then removed as a unit.

Immediately following removal of the foreign body, the laryngoscope is reinserted and a second pass made with the bronchoscope. This procedure ensures that there is no retained foreign body in the airway and allows for reassessment of airway patency in the region previously occupied by the object. Bleeding can be controlled with topical vasoactive agents, granulation tissue can be resected as necessary, and purulent secretions can be more effectively cleared.

Postoperative use of antibiotics is indicated in patients with fever, and when evidence of pneumonia is present. Steroids are not usually necessary unless there has been significant trauma to the airway. In one study, the routine use of steroids was associated with a higher incidence of persistent pneumonia and atelectasis.[36] In cases in which granulation tissue causes significant narrowing of the airway, steroids may reduce the risk of permanent bronchial stenosis.

Special Situations

"Stripping off"

Several factors may cause the foreign body to be stripped from the forceps' grasp. Three of these are related to the forceps: faulty application of forceps, improper forceps for the problem, and mechanically imperfect forceps (poorly adjusted or poorly constructed). Three additional factors are related to the foreign body: improper orientation of the object, failure to anchor the foreign body against the tube mouth, and a foreign body that is too large for the lumen. In the last situation, it may be necessary to fragment the foreign body or to remove it through a tracheotomy.

If a foreign body is stripped off in the larynx, the airway is reestablished immediately, either by removal of the object or by pushing it down into one bronchus (preferably the one in which it had been lodged). The faulty technique is corrected, and the object is relocated. A foreign body lost in the trachea will most probably enter the opposite bronchus. This occurs because a previously obstructed lung or lobe moves little air and the foreign body will be carried into the normal bronchus. If the foreign body cannot be located readily, it may be found next to the scope below the vocal folds or in the mouth, hypopharynx, or nasopharynx.

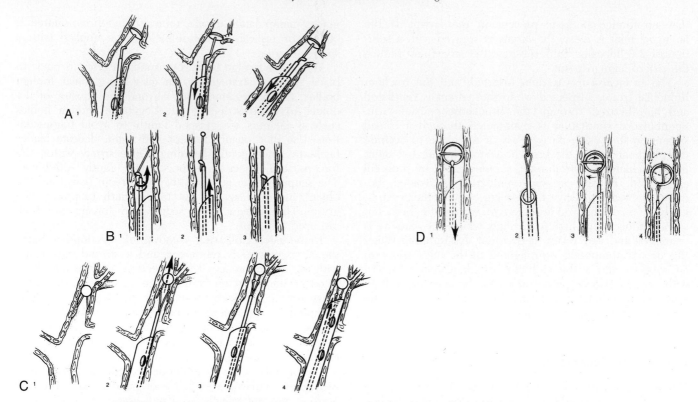

FIGURE 90–6. Techniques for endoscopic removal of sharp and penetrating foreign bodies. *A,* Long-axis traction is particularly important for pointed objects with large heads. The point may be easily located (1), but the greater hazard lies in the risk of tearing the bronchial wall with the head of the tack (2). Positioning the patient's head toward the opposite side straightens the axis of the airway, permitting relatively safe, slow, steady withdrawal of the object (3). *B,* An inward rotation method is used for pins or needles with an embedded point. Side-grasping forceps capture the pin near its point. A corkscrew motion is used to push the pin distally while rotating it clockwise, freeing the point and aligning it with the long axis of the forceps (1). The scope is advanced over the point to sheathe it (2) for extraction (3). *C,* Double-pointed objects can be converted to a single point, then sheathed for extraction. *D,* Rotation forceps: Forward-grasping forceps fix a foreign body (1), increasing the likelihood of laceration. However, the two pointed, opposing blades of rotation forceps (2) allow foreign bodies with sharp points or jagged edges to rotate (3), so hazardous parts trail harmlessly during extraction (4). (From Holinger LD. Foreign Bodies of the Airway Bronchoesophagology. Philadelphia, Lippincott Williams & Wilkins, 1997, p 248.)

Pointed Objects

The first priority in removing pointed objects from the airway is to locate the point and then to release and sheath it within the scope (Fig. 90–6A *and* B). One accomplishes this by advancing the scope over the foreign body, rather than by pulling the foreign body into the tube. Double-pointed objects can be bent and converted to a single point for extraction; alternatively, a wide (staple) forceps, scope, or both can be used to protect both points simultaneously during the extraction maneuver (Fig. 90–6C). The operator releases the point, then sheathes it by advancing the scope over it. The forceps, foreign body, and scope are removed as a unit. If the point cannot be sheathed, the foreign body can be withdrawn with the point trailing. Rotation forceps can be used to allow points to rotate and trail, thus avoiding perforation (Fig. 90–6D).

Peripheral and Upper Lobe Foreign Bodies

Peripheral and upper lobe foreign bodies are occasionally difficult to visualize and access by standard bronchoscopic technique. As previously mentioned, flexible fiberoptic bronchoscopy may be used for this purpose, preferably via an indwelling open-tube bronchoscope or endotracheal tube. Fluoroscopic guidance is also useful in these cases. In particular, the use of simultaneous biplane fluoroscopy in the angiography suite results in rapid and precise localization of the object. One must proceed cautiously, however, because the fluoroscope does not visualize the tissues that lie between the forceps blades and the foreign body. Bronchography, topical vasoconstrictors (oxymetazoline), and Fogarty catheter extraction have also been used successfully in managing inaccessible foreign bodies.[17] A wire with a magnetic tip may be useful in extracting distal ferromagnetic foreign bodies.[34]

Unsuccessful Endoscopic Removal

Employing the techniques just described, the endoscopist can successfully extract foreign bodies on the first attempt in the vast majority of cases. In cases involving significant granulation tissue and bleeding or multiple small fragments that migrate distally, a second procedure may be required to complete the extraction. Similarly, complicated foreign bodies such as burs and crab claws may not be expeditiously removed. If the foreign body cannot be removed within about 60 minutes, the procedure should be temporarily aborted.

Inflammation of the airway is proportional to the time the bronchoscope is in the larynx, the trauma of the procedure, and the size of the bronchoscope in relation to the size of the child's larynx. When stridor and dyspnea result from the endoscopy, treatment with humidity, high-dose intravenous steroids (dexamethasone, 1–1.5 mg/kg, up to a 30 mg bolus), racemic epinephrine, and elevation of the head is usually effective within 24 hours. Repeat bronchoscopy can be attempted once residual laryngeal symptoms have resolved. Should a second attempt at extraction fail, thoracotomy with bronchotomy or segmental lobectomy may be necessary.

Complications

Complications associated with airway foreign bodies have been defined by Inglis and Wagner[21] as conditions or actions before or during bronchoscopy leading to ongoing postoperative morbidity. Of 119 patients treated by these authors between 1984 and 1989, minor complications, such as postoperative atelectasis, wheezing, and stridor from subglottic trauma, were present in 12%. Major complications, defined as those requiring more than 1 week of hospitalization postoperatively or those requiring open surgery, were present in 3%. This overall complication rate of 15% represented a significant improvement over that of 44% identified in a similar group of patients 20 years earlier. The authors attributed this change to the development of the rod-lens optical system, which led to a reduction in missed or incompletely removed foreign bodies. In addition, the authors identified an increased risk of complications with increasing duration of the foreign body in situ. Complication rates in other recent reports range from 0% to 25%.[2, 37, 42]

Laryngeal edema and traumatic laryngitis are common sequelae of airway foreign bodies and their removal. Stridor resulting from foreign body extraction can be treated with steroids and racemic epinephrine, as previously described. Persistent pneumonia and atelectasis are most common following removal of long-standing foreign bodies. Intravenous antibiotics, bronchodilators, and chest physical therapy may be useful for several days postoperatively in such cases. Bronchospasm and postobstructive pulmonary edema, which occur less frequently, may also require aggressive medical management. Further surgical intervention may be required in cases of persistent granulation tissue, laryngotracheal or bronchial stenosis, bronchial hemorrhage, pneumothorax, pneumomediastinum, bronchial fistula, and lung abscess. Fatal complications of airway foreign bodies include complete obstruction of the airway and cardiac arrest induced by prolonged hypoxia. Fortunately, these are exceedingly rare.

Prevention

Avoidance of objects that are easily aspirated or readily lodge in the pediatric airway is the ultimate prevention against all foreign body accidents. However, it is impractical to assume that even the most vigilant parents and caretakers can make all such objects inaccessible to children. Continuing education through child advocates such as the American Academy of Pediatrics, the American Society of Pediatric Otolaryngology, and individual providers of pediatric medical services is essential if such accidents are to be reduced in frequency. Well-child visits are an ideal opportunity to advise parents and caretakers to avoid feeding nuts, popcorn, seeds, and spherical candies to children younger than 4 or 5 years of age. Hot dogs and grapes should be cut into tiny pieces before being fed to young children. Children should also be supervised during playtime, since they may obtain dangerous objects from a sibling or from a location in the home that has not been childproofed. Balloons are a significant airway risk in children of all ages.

Federal regulations enacted over the last 25 years have been directed at controlling the size and shape of objects intended for use by children. In 1979, the Consumer Product Safety Commission established the minimum size criteria for manufacture of new toys used by children younger than 3 years of age [16 CFR Section 1500 18(a)(9)]. Based on modeling of the pediatric airway and historical data, these dimensions were established at 31.7 mm in diameter and 25.4 to 57.1 mm in length.[48] These measurements were used to create the Small Parts Test Fixture, a truncated plastic cylinder into which the product or any of its detachable parts must *not* fit (Fig. 90–7).[48] In a series of 534 aerodigestive tract foreign body events accumulated by Reilly et al[50] over the 2-year period of 1988 to 1989, 99% of the involved objects failed the small parts test and just 6% were toys or toy parts, supporting the continued use of the test device. However, 37% of the events in this study, and 31% in another recent series by Rimell et al,[51] occurred in children older than 3 years, suggesting that the age group considered to be at risk should be expanded. That study also included computer analysis of 101 objects causing asphyxiation, of which 5 had diameters larger than the Small Parts Test Fixture and 9 had dimensions longer than the Small Parts Test Fixture. All five with passing diameters and one with a passing length were toys with at least one spherical part. In addition, a Consumer Product Safety Commission review of choking events occurring between 1973 and 1983 identified 195 choking events in children aged 3 months to 4 years caused by items that would have passed the small parts test.[48] Of these, 37 children (19%) died as a result of the event. Spherical objects were recovered in 66%. Based on these data and the sizes of the offending objects, it has been recommended that the passing criteria for diameter of spherical

PATIENT INITIAL: ____ DATE OF SURGERY: _____ SURGEON: _____
PATIENT ID # _____ INSTITUTION _____

1. How long since the last papilloma surgery? ___ days, ___ weeks, ___ months, ___ years,
                              ___ don't know, ___ this is the child's first surgery
2. Counting today's surgery, how many papilloma surgeries in the past 12 months? _____
3. Describe the patient's voice today:
       normal___(0), abnormal___(1), aphonic___(2)
4. Describe the patient's stridor today:
       absent___(0), present with activity___(1), present at rest___(2)
5. Describe the urgency of today's intervention:
       scheduled___(0), elective___(1), urgent___(2), emergent___(3)
6. Describe today's level of respiratory distress:
       none___(0), mild___(1), Mod___(2), severe___(3), extreme___(4)

Total score for questions 3–6 =

FOR EACH SITE, SCORE AS: 0 = NONE, 1 = SURFACE LESION, 2 = RAISED LESION,
3 = BULKY LESION

LARYNX:
       Epiglottis
              Lingual surface _____ Laryngeal surface _____
       Aryepiglottic folds: Right ___ Left ___
       False vocal cords: Right ___ Left ___
       True vocal cords: Right ___ Left ___
       Arytenoids: Right ___ Left ___
       Anterior commissure _____
       Posterior commissure _____
       Subglottis _____

FIGURE 91–2. Coltera/Derkay staging and severity scheme. (From Derkay CS. Recurrent respiratory papillomatosis. Laryngoscope 111:57, 2001.)

TRACHEA:
       Upper one-third _____
       Middle one-third _____
       Lower one-third _____
       Bronchi: Right ___ Left ___
       Tracheotomy stoma _____

OTHER:
       Nose   _____
       Palate   _____
       Pharynx   _____
       Esophagus   _____
       Lungs   _____
       Other   _____

TOTAL SCORE ALL SITES: _____

TOTAL CLINICAL SCORE: _____

view, firstborn children of teenage mothers with visible condylomata acuminata have a higher risk of RRP.[56] It is in this group of women that a cesarean delivery should be seriously considered.

The immunologic status of a small number of patients with RRP has been investigated, but the results have been inconclusive. Perrick and colleagues[86] found that two of four patients had subnormal functional natural killer activity. One of the two received interferon for 4 months, and although natural killer function normalized, no effect on the papillomatosis was seen. Bent and Probusky[12] prospectively evaluated the immune status of four patients and reported that the two patients who had subnormal natural killer function had a more prolonged disease course than did the other two with normal natural killer function.

It has been presumed that hormones have some influence on the disease process of RRP. This notion is based on the observation that the growth rate of genital condylomas is increased during pregnancy[11] and that some cases of spontaneous regression have been observed during puberty. However, others do not believe that the onset of puberty has any effect on remission.[10]

HPV has been identified in clinically nondiseased epithelium in both active RRP patients and those in clinical remission.[2, 113, 115] One study detected HPV DNA in nondiseased sites almost as frequently as in gross papillomas—40% versus 50%.[87] Studies of sites of predilection for RRP have revealed that they occur at squamociliary junctions: the nasal vestibule, nasopharynx, palate, epiglottis, larynx, trachea, bronchi, and lung. HPV has not been demonstrated in ciliated epithelium.[56] Traumatized ciliated epithelium usually heals as nonciliated epithelium and results in an iatrogenic squamociliary junction. Thus, injury to the tracheal mucosa by surgical instrumentation (suction tip, forceps, or laser) or by an endotracheal tube can create mucosal changes and a squamociliary junction, thereby increasing the chance of infection developing at these sites. This finding explains the recognized propensity of papillomas to recur in sites of previous excision or epithelial injury. Similarly, tracheostomy leads to epithelial injury and to squamous metaplasia, which in turn leads to the formation of a squamociliary junction and the commonly observed development of tracheal papillomas after tracheotomy.

Current therapeutic regimens for RRP stress maintenance of a patent airway and acceptable voice while preventing complications. Surgical therapy should be based on the principle of preservation of nondiseased tissue to prevent the complication of laryngeal scarring or stenosis while attempting total removal of the papilloma. Since no therapeutic regimen is presently available that can reliably and permanently eradicate HPV, in an area where removal of the lesion would cause long-term iatrogenic damage (such as the anterior commissure web), incomplete excision of papillomas is preferred.

Surgical treatment in the past has included the use of thermal cautery, cryosurgery, US, and removal of papillomas with cup forceps.[93] Presently, the most widely used procedure is microsuspension laryngoscopy with the CO_2 laser or microforceps (or both) to remove papillomas. The advantage of the laser is its superior precision and inherent hemostatic properties. Microforceps are used for biopsy, as well as for removing the bulk of the disease. Thorough knowledge of laser application has resulted in fewer operative complications such as airway fires, pneumothorax, and anesthetic complications. However, reports of delayed local tissue damage have ranged from a low of 13% to as high as 35%.[23, 85, 125] The majority of problems involve the delayed formation of laryngeal webs, most commonly at the anterior commissure, followed by the posterior commissure and then the interarytenoid bands. Data suggest that the number of laser procedures and the severity of disease have a linear relationship to the frequency and severity of complications. Using a microspot CO_2 laser at lower settings and shorter bursts, as well as accepting residual disease at anatomically vulnerable locations, can reduce the frequency of complications. The aim of therapy in extensive disease should be to reduce the tumor burden, decrease the spread of disease, create a safe and patent airway, improve voice quality, and increase the time interval between surgical procedures. Overaggressive use of the laser may result in injury to nonaffected tissue and create an environment suitable for the implantation of viral particles. These concerns, as well as an animal study demonstrating that CO_2 laser ablation causes a greater delay in healing and denser fibrosis than is the case with microforceps,[28] have recently led to the pursuit of nonlaser surgical therapy. The recent introduction of the laryngeal microdebrider may enable the surgeon to better achieve these surgical goals. The laryngeal microdebrider is an adaptation of endoscopic sinus instruments. Once the surgeon adjusts to manipulation of the telescope and the debrider in a suspended larynx, con-

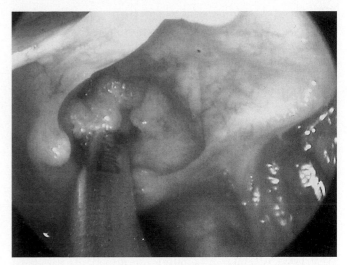

FIGURE 91–3. Removal of a papilloma with a microlaryngeal debrider.

trolled removal of gross papillomas is possible with minimal risk to normal tissue (Fig. 91–3). We have routinely used this technique recently and prefer it to laser ablation in most cases of papilloma surgery.

The variety of attempts at medical control of this disease reflects the difficulty in finding a definitive curative therapy for this disease process. Previous unsuccessful therapeutic trials to control the underlying viral infection have included antibiotics, hormones, steroids, the topical antiviral agent podophyllin, antimetabolites (5-fluorouracil and methotrexate), and transfer factors. Radiation therapy has the potential for malignant transformation and is contraindicated.[93] Ongoing adjunct therapeutic trials include interferon alfa, indole-3-carbinol (I3C)/diindolylmethane (DIM), photodynamic therapy (PDT), cidofovir, acyclovir, ribavirin, cis-retinoic acid, and mumps vaccine.

Interferons are a class of proteins manufactured by cells in response to a variety of stimuli, including viral infection. Interferon binds to specific membrane receptors and then alters cell metabolism. It has antiviral, antiproliferative, antitumor, and immunomodulatory effects. The exact mechanism of interferon's action on laryngeal papillomatosis is not known, but it is thought that it affects the production of enzymes such as protein kinase and endonuclease, thereby leading to the inhibition of viral protein synthesis and to breakdown of viral DNA.[7] Preliminary reports in the early 1980s were quite encouraging.[38, 42, 70] Several prospective studies using interferon in association with the CO_2 laser found a mixed response. Patients who did benefit experienced either complete eradication of the disease or a decrease in tumor growth and a resultant reduction in the number of surgical procedures necessary to control the disease.[67, 68] Healy[47] reported results from a multi-institutional study that showed that human leukocyte interferon helps control disease in the first 3 to 6 months of treatment but that its effectiveness is questionable after 6 months of therapy. A different study group using lymphoblastoid interferon at a much higher dose found that the response lasted beyond 6 months and could be reinduced after a period of no interferon treatment.[63, 64] Mullooly and associates[81] observed a dose-related response of RRP to interferons as well. Toxicity associated with interferon includes the acute reactions of fever and generalized influenza-like symptoms (chills, headache, myalgias, and nausea), which diminish over time, and the chronic effects of a decrease in the growth rate of children (although an increase in the growth rate is noted when therapy is ceased). Transient increases in transaminase levels, leukopenia, and thrombocytopenia have been reported, as have rashes, dry skin, alopecia, generalized pruritus, and systemic lupus erythematosus.[22, 118] Fatigue, which appears to be dose related, is the most noteworthy of the adverse reactions. Spastic diplegia has been reported in those who received interferon before gross motor development, so precautions should be taken when using this agent in infants. Neurologic and developmental assessment, especially in infants, should be performed before beginning therapy. HPV DNA is inhibited by interferon in patients who have recurrence during therapy,[114] possibly because of the formation of blocking antibodies. Recombinant interferon is thought to be more prone to this effect as a result of its monoclonal purity. In addition, latent infection is not eliminated by interferon. The response to interferon does vary, but in the treatment of recalcitrant RRP, it is presently the most widely used adjuvant to surgical therapy. We recommend the higher doses of 5 million U/m² per day for 1 month, followed by the same dose three times weekly for 5 months. Monitoring by complete blood count, platelets, urinalysis, and liver function studies should be performed before beginning therapy and every 1 to 2 months while receiving therapy. If a response is followed by latent recurrence, another therapeutic trial could be instituted.

I3C is derived from cruciferous vegetables (cabbage, broccoli, Brussels sprouts, cauliflower) and appears to be effective in controlling the growth of new laryngeal papillomas.[94] I3C seems to affect papilloma growth through its effect on estrogen metabolism. Rosen and colleagues[94] found that a third of RRP patients who received oral I3C had complete arrest of new papilloma growth, another third had a reduced papilloma growth rate, and the rest did not have any benefit. A high correlation was noted between the urinary estrogen metabolite ratio (2-hydroxylestrone to 16-alpha-hydroxylestrone) and response. Interestingly, most (five of six) of the complete response group were adults whereas most (five of six) of the nonresponders were children. DIM is a natural product of I3C acid digestion in the stomach and is thought to be the active metabolite of I3C. Animal studies have demonstrated that I3C, when injected intravenously to bypass stomach acid digestion, does not produce an estrogen metabolite effect whereas DIM is equally effective when administered by direct injection or ingestion. I3C seems to be relatively safe, with very few reports of significant adverse effects from long-term use. Rare reports have described low bone density in children who have been maintained on a high dose of I3C. However, studies in mice did not show any change in bone density with the use of I3C. The only side effect appears to be disequilibrium associated with higher doses. Larger studies of I3C/DIM with prolonged follow-up are needed. Presently, it appears to be a viable option as an adjunct to surgery.

PDT with dihematoporphyrin ether (DHE) uses the propensity of this substance to concentrate in papillomas versus surrounding normal tissue. When activated by light with the appropriate wavelength (630 nm), DHE produces cytotoxic agents that selectively destroy cells containing the DHE. The proposed mechanism of cell destruction is via production of toxic oxygen radicals that cause disruption of the cell membrane by lipid or protein sulfhydryl oxidation. Vascular damage in the form of microcirculatory disruption of rapidly dividing tissue also occurs.[108] In a randomized prospective study, Abramson and colleagues[1] found that PDT produced a notable improvement in respiratory papillomatosis, the effect was dependent on the DHE dose, and the benefit was maintained at a 3-year follow-up. Mullooly and associates[80] found that the only side effect of PDT in 26 patients was photosensitivity, which usually occurred within 2 weeks of therapy. None of the patients were reported to have any difficulty with airway obstruction or required tracheotomy. Abramson and Mullooly reported the use of a new agent at the Long Island Jewish Medical Center, m-tetrahydroxyphenylchlorinn (mTHPC), which has a much shorter period of photosensitivity. It has shown good responses in the majority of patients who have been monitored for 12 to 18 months. Unfortunately, the PDT response is not as apparent in tracheal lesions, and it has no effect on parenchymal lesions[8] or on the persistence of HPV DNA. PDT has a beneficial effect in modifying the RRP disease process and should be especially considered in more aggressive cases that do not respond to other techniques.

Cidofovir is an antiviral agent with a broad spectrum of activity against a wide variety of DNA viruses, including HPV. It has a propensity to be selectively absorbed by cells with HPV. The cell converts it into active agents that cause early death of the cell. It has been used in human immunodeficiency virus–induced cytomegalovirus retinitis in an intravenous form. Snoeck and associates in 1998 described its use for severe laryngeal papillomatosis in adults.[111] They initially reported complete disappearance of papillomas in 14 of 17 patients. Reports of malignancy in 2 of 36 adult patients, however, raised concern about the safety of this agent, but subsequent review at the Armed Forces Institute revealed evidence of carcinoma before initiation of treatment with cidofovir. Pransky and co-workers[89] reported good results with cidofovir in five children with severe disease requiring very frequent surgical procedures. Four of the five patients were significantly improved or disease free. A follow-up report continued to reveal good response at 18 to 22 months.[88] An additional five patients also had a good response. No toxicity has occurred, and biopsy specimens have not revealed any malignant transformation. The use of a more concentrated solution of 5 mg/mL was recommended (versus the 2.5 mg/mL in the original series). Patients should be well hydrated, and they should be monitored by a complete blood count, urinalysis, blood urea nitrogen, creatinine, and liver function tests. Other reports have stated that cidofovir injection results in regression of papillomas without surgical removal—the only agent that is reported to cause regression of papillomas as opposed to cessation of their growth. A prospective multi-institutional trial using cidofovir in papillomatosis is presently being organized.

Results of a trial of retinoic acid have been inconclusive, with some significant toxicity.[12] After a report of apparent success with acyclovir in three RRP patients,[4] Morrison and colleagues[76] administered acyclovir to four patients and concluded that acyclovir does not influence the RRP disease process. They stated that papilloma viruses lack the key enzyme, thymidine kinase, that is necessary for acyclovir activity and do not recommend the use of acyclovir in RRP. Another antiviral agent, ribavirin in an aerosol form, was used to treat a child with RRP involving the tracheobronchial tree; ribavirin resulted in a significant reduction in the frequency of therapeutic endoscopy.[76] Long-term studies are needed to evaluate this agent. Mumps vaccine has been reported to show some effectiveness in decreasing the rate of recurrence after direct injection into papillomas, but the data are from a small series of uncontrolled patients, and a prospective clinical trial with a larger number of patients is needed. Lastly, a new therapeutic approach is undergoing evaluation using immune modulation with heat shock protein for RRP. No data are available.

Factors associated with spontaneous remission of RRP are not well understood. It is likely that HPV becomes dormant rather than being eradicated inasmuch as RRP has recurred after many years of quiescence. RRP may also behave in an extremely aggressive fashion, a form labeled "invasive papillomatosis" by Fechner and co-workers.[31] In these cases, spread of papilloma into the pulmonary parenchyma, soft tissue of the neck, and even the regional lymph nodes has been described.[96] These cases of invasive papillomatosis represent benign disease that has become locally aggressive. A variety of reports of squamous cell carcinoma arising within RRP have also appeared. Initially, the malignant degeneration was documented in association with radiation therapy. Later reports demonstrated squamous cell carcinoma in RRP patients who had not received radiation therapy (and who did not smoke).[13, 25, 96, 97, 112] Furthermore, these reports have demonstrated the potential for distant metastases. Irradiated patients have a 16-fold increase in the risk of a carcinoma developing in the respiratory tract.[66] Carcinoma developing from preexisting papilloma arises much earlier if irradiated (average duration of disease of 10 years) than if not irradiated (average of 30 years). Irradiated patients have a much worse prognosis, with the carcinoma being fatal in most cases, whereas most non-irradiated patients survive.[57] Cocarcinogens, host immunocompetence, the type of HPV infection (types 16 and 18), and the duration of infection all play a role, but exact understanding of the interaction of these factors is limited.

Subglottic Hemangioma

Subglottic hemangioma occurs in infants and is a relatively rare, benign, congenital vascular malformation that stems from mesodermal rests. Like any obstructive tumor in the airway, it can be life threatening. Classically, symptoms of airway obstruction with inspiratory or biphasic

stridor are present and can progress to acute respiratory distress. Symptoms do not normally begin at birth but occur within the first few weeks to months of life. Eighty-five percent of cases occur before 6 months of age.[15] The stridor is frequently exacerbated by excitement or crying, which causes vascular engorgement, and is reduced with rest. Upper respiratory tract infections worsen the symptoms, and episodic exacerbations may result in an erroneous diagnosis of recurrent croup. Other symptoms include feeding problems, cough, cyanosis, and rarely, hoarseness. Slow and progressive growth of the lesion can lead to almost complete obstruction of the subglottic airway. Fifty percent of children with subglottic hemangiomas are found to have cutaneous hemangiomas, especially in the face. As a corollary, a high association is noted between facial hemangiomas with a "beard" distribution and symptomatic hemangiomas of the upper airway. One series found that 63% of children with multiple facial hemangiomas had symptomatic airway hemangiomas.[84] Most series report a female-male ratio in subglottic hemangioma as high as 2:1.

In an infant with obstructive airway symptoms such as stridor, dyspnea, cyanotic episodes, or feeding problems, endoscopy is performed to establish the diagnosis. Adjunctive radiographic measures that are helpful preoperatively include high-kilovoltage anteroposterior neck films, which may demonstrate asymmetric subglottic narrowing (50% according to Cooper and colleagues[19]), and an esophagogram, which helps rule out other congenital vascular anomalies. After bronchoscopy has determined that the only airway lesion present is in the subglottis, microsuspension laryngoscopy will confirm the diagnosis. The classic appearance is one of an asymmetric, smooth, submucosal, pink or blue compressible subglottic mass (Fig. 91–4). Most authorities report a left-sided predominance, although the lesion may occur on the right or be bilateral. Hemangiomas have also been reported to extend into the

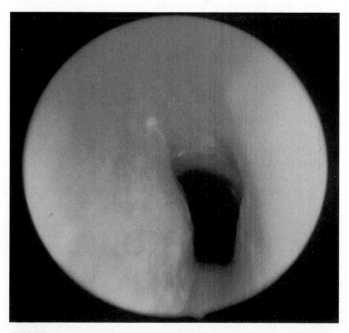

FIGURE 91–4. Subglottic hemangioma.

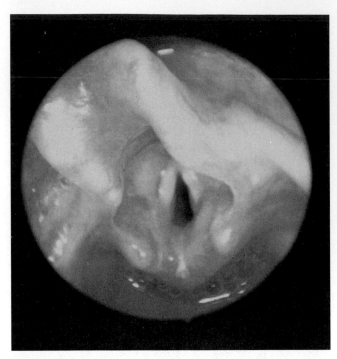

FIGURE 91–5. Subglottic hemangioma with a glottic and supraglottic blush.

posterior commissure and to the upper part of the trachea. Hemangiomas that exhibit a "blush" or staining of the supraglottic, glottic, or tracheal mucosa suggest a significant extent of disease (Fig. 91–5). Goldsmith and co-workers[39] reported a postcricoid hemangioma that caused failure to thrive and recurrent pneumonia. Biopsy is controversial: it is the only way of proving the diagnosis histologically, but it is theoretically dangerous because of the possibility of uncontrollable hemorrhage. Shikhani and associates[106] reported few problems, and most experts believe that the risk of bleeding is minimal. However, the diagnosis is frequently based on the history and endoscopic findings alone. To provide maximal evidence for the diagnosis, photographic documentation of the lesion at each endoscopic procedure should be obtained. CT or MRI of the neck and mediastinum can be considered for larger subglottic hemangiomas, especially those associated with cutaneous hemangiomas in the head and neck area.

Because of the rarity of this lesion and the reluctance to perform a biopsy on these lesions, most of the pathologic description comes from cutaneous hemangiomas. It would appear that subglottic hemangiomas behave similarly to cutaneous hemangiomas. Histologically, the tumor shows tubules of plump, proliferating endothelial cells surrounding narrow vessels and an abundance of mast cells.[98] The natural history of these lesions is variable, but many lesions appear to spontaneously involute after 12 to 18 months. Cutaneous hemangiomas are said to have two involutional rates—early and late. Early involuters go through the proliferation phase during the first 6 to 12 months and then start to involute, with involution completed by 3 to 5 years of age. Late involuters do not complete their involution until 12 years of age, and most of the lesions do not involute completely.

Many different therapies have been advocated as treatment of subglottic hemangioma. Mild cases that cause few symptoms can be closely observed. The question then remains how to best deal with potential life-threatening airway compromise until involution occurs.

The first decision that needs to be made in symptomatic cases is the necessity of tracheotomy. If the lesion is recognized early, a tracheotomy can be avoided and the hemangioma can be treated by other means, thus obviating the known morbidity associated with infantile tracheotomy. In severe, life-threatening cases, tracheotomy can be performed to establish an airway. In these cases, the hemangioma should still be treated aggressively to shorten the time before decannulation.

Independent of the tracheotomy, treatment options include systemic and intralesional corticosteroids, laser surgery, open surgical excision, and interferon alfa. Former treatments include radiation therapy, radioactive gold implantation, injection of sclerosing agents, and cryotherapy. Systemic steroid therapy has frequently been used during the proliferative stage, with a good initial response. The mechanism of the effect of steroids on hemangiomas is not clear, however. One theory suggests that steroids occupy estradiol receptor sites, thus inhibiting some supportive function of estradiol on the hemangioma.[46] On the basis of the experimental observation that cortisone and hydrocortisone inhibit angiogenesis in the presence of a fragment of heparin, prednisone is thought to have an effect on the hemangioma during the proliferative stage.[121] Some suggest that corticosteroids may increase the sensitivity of vessels to other natural vasoconstrictors.[95] Therefore, steroid use may result in shrinkage of the vascular mass. Cohen and Wang[17] and Kveton and Pillsbury[60] have had good success with this form of therapy, but other reports have not been as encouraging.[9] Hawkins and co-workers[46] reported that steroid therapy successfully improved the airway in eight patients and tracheotomy was necessary in only one. However, they encountered some of the known complications of prolonged steroid use, such as some degree of growth suppression and the development of cushingoid features. Prednisone can be given at 4 mg/kg per day or 8 mg/kg every other day for 6 to 12 weeks and then tapered slowly. A second course can be used after a few weeks in those with resumption of hemangioma growth. If long-term steroid use is contemplated, treatment should be administered every other day, at a lower dose of 1 mg/kg per day, to decrease the possibility of untoward effects of the steroid. Steroids can play an additional beneficial role of reducing inflammation in acute respiratory infections or in milder cases with only intermittent respiratory distress. Caution should be exercised because the hemangioma may recur after withdrawal of the steroids. Meeuwis and associates[73] administered intralesional steroids to six infants with subglottic hemangiomas and found all infants to be symptom free after 3 months. Three patients needed only one injection, two needed three injections, and one needed five injections. Postoperative intubation was necessary, usually for 1 week. No patients required tracheotomy. Steroids may also be helpful when used in concert with other forms of therapy. Narcy and colleagues[82] advocated a trial of steroids in association with endotracheal intubation. Hawkins and co-workers[46] suggested using steroids either alone or in conjunction with CO_2 laser therapy.

CO_2 laser treatment has been used for the treatment of subglottic hemangioma. It was initially described as a modality that resulted in little morbidity and effectively removed the obstructing lesion.[48] This therapy can be used for unilateral lesions or staged for smaller bilateral lesions and has been shown to be able to prevent the need for tracheotomy. A follow-up report on 31 patients showed good success rates with the CO_2 laser.[49] Eighteen of 31 patients had complete remission with one laser treatment, whereas 9 patients required two procedures and 3 patients required three applications of the laser. Of 19 patients without tracheotomies at the time of laser surgery, only 1 required a tracheotomy for airway maintenance. Cotton and Tewfik[20] reported three cases in which postoperative subglottic stenosis occurred after laser therapy and advocated careful selection of patients. They noted that as the lesion involutes with time, any treatment to decrease tumor size must be performed in a manner that leaves the larynx functionally normal. Guidelines to be kept in mind with laser therapy include the use of intense postoperative humidification to avoid crust formation, use only on capillary-type lesions (because cavernous lesions have vascular spaces too large for the hemostatic properties of the laser), use in patients with subglottic lesions only and not in those with diffuse hemangioma extending to the trachea, and staged resection of large subglottic lesions to prevent the apposition of raw mucosal surfaces. When these precautions are observed, CO_2 laser therapy is thought to be a safe, effective treatment of isolated subglottic hemangiomas.[75] Both the neodymium:yttrium-aluminum-garnet (Nd-YAG) and argon lasers have been used to treat subglottic hemangiomas, but with limited success and a high rate of complications.[71] The potassium titanyl phosphate (KTP) laser has a practical advantage over the CO_2 laser in that it can be delivered through a fiberoptic cable. It also has the advantage of an absorption spectrum corresponding to blood. These advantages allow more direct delivery of laser energy, especially to distal subglottic hemangiomas and distal tracheobronchial tumors. It has the potential advantage that more focused delivery of lower laser energy could lead to less damage to adjacent mucosa and thus possibly less chance than the CO_2 laser of the development of subglottic stenosis after laser therapy.[29, 69] The authors recommend and prefer the use of KTP at low settings (less than 2 W) rather than CO_2 when a laser is used for subglottic hemangioma.

Open surgical excision, which is generally thought to be associated with greater morbidity and postoperative scarring, has been gaining support.[79] Seid and associates[102] were able to successfully decannulate two infants and recommended that open surgical excision be considered when other therapeutic attempts have failed. Others have since reported success with the open surgical approach to subglottic hemangiomas.[50, 126]

The incidental finding of recombinant interferon alfa being effective in Kaposi sarcoma and pulmonary hemangiomatosis, as well as the in vitro observation of inhibition of capillary endothelium locomotion, has led to a trial of this drug for hemangiomas. Ezekowitz and associates[30] treated corticosteroid-resistant life- or vision-threatening hemangiomas in 20 neonates and infants with interferon alfa-2a and had 90% of the hemangiomas regress at least 50% after an average of about 8 months of treatment. Four of these patients had a laryngeal lesion. Side effects of interferon, which included fever, neutropenia, and skin necrosis, were transient and minimal. Ohlms and colleagues[83] reported their experience with the use of interferon alfa-2a in 15 patients with airway-obstructing hemangiomas unresponsive to laser or corticosteroid therapy. Interferon at three million U/m^2 body surface was given subcutaneously daily until 50% or greater regression in tumor size occurred and the airway was stable. All of the patients previously treated without tracheotomy (8 of 15) responded and did not require tracheotomy after starting interferon therapy. Six of the seven patients who had tracheotomy before interferon therapy were decannulated after the completion of therapy. They did not report any long-term morbidity associated with interferon therapy and recommend prolonged therapy for 9 to 14 months. The reports of spastic diplegia in young infants after the use of interferon as presented in the previous papillomatosis section is especially relevant in the treatment of subglottic hemangioma since most of these patients are infants. Interferon should be considered when traditional therapeutic modalities such as steroids and the CO_2 laser fail and especially when subglottic hemangioma is part of a massive life-threatening cervicofacial hemangioma. Further investigation is needed to determine whether interferon would be useful alone or in conjunction with traditional therapy in less severe and limited cases.

Radiation therapy has been used in the past but is no longer thought to be appropriate because of concern for inducing malignant changes in adjacent neck structures. Benjamin and Carter,[9] in a report of 23 patients, treated 11 with radioactive gold grain implants. The radioactive grain is inserted via microsurgical technique and produces local radiation with minimal effect on surrounding tissue. Endoscopic reassessment of the airway is performed 8 to 10 weeks after insertion of the implant and permits removal of shrunken residual tissue. Of note is that all these patients had tracheotomies and were able to be successfully decannulated 2 to 5 months after therapy. Other therapies that have been used include injection of sclerosing agents, which is unsuccessful in bringing about tumor regression and associated with a risk of hemorrhage and tracheobronchitis, and cryotherapy. The latter technique has been reported to be successful[3, 54] but requires a tracheotomy because of postoperative swelling. Concern regarding cryotherapy involves potential damage to normal tissue and perichondrial injury that may result in tracheomalacia or luminal narrowing.

In summary, multiple modalities are available for the treatment of subglottic hemangiomas, and frequently, a combination of therapies is used. When an infant has obstructive symptoms from hemangioma, a careful systematic approach to ablation of the hemangioma should be undertaken to obviate the need for tracheotomy or to allow for early decannulation in those who require tracheotomy because of severe airway compromise. Corticosteroids and laser treatment, CO_2 or KTP, are the main modalities of therapy. For more extensive and resistant lesions, open excision or interferon alfa-2a should be considered.

Neurogenic Tumors of the Larynx

Neurogenic tumors of the larynx are rare, with only approximately 120 cases reported in both children and adults. They occur in all age groups and are slightly more common in female patients. They tend to occur in the supraglottic region or the posterior of the larynx, and most of the benign neoplasms can be removed by transoral excision. Some of more common neurogenic tumors that have been reported to occur in the larynx include neurofibroma, neurilemoma, granular cell tumor, and carcinoid tumor.[113]

Neurofibroma and neurilemoma are neoplasms of Schwann cell origin. Although they are similar in their clinical features, some characteristics may be used to distinguish between neurofibroma and neurilemoma.[104] Neurilemomas are typically solitary and encapsulated, whereas neurofibromas are nonencapsulated and are more frequently multiple, especially in association with neurofibromatosis (von Recklinghausen disease). Histologically, neurilemoma, also known as benign schwannoma or neurinoma, has two characteristic cellular patterns: Antoni A and B. The Antoni A pattern designates cellular areas composed of a compact arrangement of bipolar cells whose nuclei occasionally line up in vertical palisades (Verocay body), whereas the Antoni B pattern consists of loosely organized nonaligned cells in a myxoid matrix.[55]

Endolaryngeal neurofibromas may be solitary endolaryngeal lesions or may occur in association with systemic neurofibromatosis. The systemic association seems to be more common in children.[113] The youngest patient reported had the diagnosis made at 3 months of age.[120] Crowe and colleagues[24] estimated the incidence of multiple neurofibromatosis to be 1 in 3000 births. The diagnosis of von Recklinghausen disease is made with the presence of six or more café au lait spots greater than 1.5 cm in diameter. Symptoms of laryngeal neurofibroma are dyspnea, voice change or hoarseness, cough, noisy sleeping or stridor, and less commonly, dysphagia. Nearly all the tumors described involve the arytenoids or the aryepiglottic folds. Although they often appear to be well encapsulated, microscopic extension along nerve roots is the rule. If a submucosal mass is discovered in the larynx, especially in a patient with other manifestations of neurofibromatosis, a biopsy specimen should be obtained for diagnosis. Complete surgical excision of the lesion is recommended[117] but, in reality, may be difficult to achieve. For complete excision, a radical open surgical procedure is often required, and recurrence is frequent. Thus, multiple procedures may be necessary to completely excise the tumor. This problem is especially apparent in plexiform neurofibromas, which differ from nonplexiform lesions in that the former are highly infiltrating, more diffuse, and poorly localized and involve multiple nerves. Total removal may not be possible, even with total laryn-gectomy. Sidman and associates[109] reported no successful cases of complete excision of plexiform neurofibromas of the larynx. Thus, repeated local excision may be necessary as the lesion encroaches on the airway. It is important to remember that this lesion is benign (albeit with malignant potential) and that judicious subtotal removal is indicated when vital structures are involved.

Granular cell tumor in the pediatric larynx is very rare, and only 20 cases have been reported in the literature.[18, 52, 62] Granular cell tumor occurs more commonly in the 4th to 6th decade of life and can develop in any part of the body. The most common site of involvement is the tongue. The larynx is reported to be involved in about 7% to 10%.[62] It was originally thought to be a neoplasm of muscular origin, but most experts presently believe the origin of the tumor to be neurogenic, either Schwann cell or primitive neuroectodermal cell. Histologically distinctive, the cells are polymorphic with abundant acidophilic and granular cytoplasm. Nuclei are small, vesicular, and centrally located. Mitosis is rare. The common unique phenomenon of pseudoepitheliomatous hyperplasia in adult laryngeal granular cell tumor (50% to 60%) has not been found in pediatric cases. In adults, superficial biopsy of tumors with this phenomenon can lead to the misdiagnosis of squamous cell carcinoma. In pediatric patients, the initial symptoms are usually hoarseness, stridor, and respiratory difficulty. The sites of origin in children are principally confined to the glottis and subglottis, in contrast to adults, in whom subglottic involvement is rare. Clinically, the lesions appear as a polypoid or sessile mass that may be solitary or multiple. A 10% to 15% rate of multicentricity is reported. This tumor generally takes a benign course, and most pediatric patients have responded well to the treatment of choice, local endoscopic excision. The recurrence rate is low, 2% to 8%, even in those with incomplete excision. However, 2 of the 18 reported patients had extensive enough tumor to require laryngectomy. Although malignant granular cell tumors have a reported incidence of 2% to 3%, only one tumor has been reported in the larynx, and none of the pediatric cases have been malignant.

Miscellaneous Benign Laryngeal Tumors

Fibrous histiocytoma is a mesenchymal neoplasm that is extremely rare in the larynx. Just 18 cases have been reported, only 2 of which have involved children. Controversy exists regarding the cell of origin in this tumor, as reflected by the confusing and variable nomenclature used. Most authorities believe that the histiocyte is the cell of origin, whereas some think that the cell of origin is a primitive, undifferentiated mesenchymal stem cell.[32] The confusion is underscored by Blitzer and colleagues,[14] who list 21 different synonyms for fibrous histiocytoma. The differential diagnosis includes other benign and malignant mesenchymal neoplasms such as fibromatosis, fibrosarcoma, myoblastoma, and pleomorphic rhabdomyosarcoma. Differentiating these various diseases can be quite difficult, and electron microscopy is usually necessary to confirm the diagnosis. Wetmore[124] described a 6-year-old child with fibrous histiocytoma. At the time of initial diagnosis a biopsy was performed, followed by laser resection of the subglottic mass. Repeat endoscopy with biopsy indicated no recurrence of the tumor, and the patient was then lost to follow-up. Cohen and colleagues[16] treated a 2-year-old child by endoscopic removal of a tracheal fibrous histiocytoma. Based on the results in these cases and the difficulty in differentiating between benign and malignant disease, close, long-term follow-up is recommended with routine repeat endoscopy and biopsy. Recurrence of the lesion would then demand more aggressive surgical extirpation.

Keen and associates[58] reported an inflammatory pseudotumor of the subglottis that caused obstructive upper airway symptoms. Histologically, this lesion is composed of mesenchymal and inflammatory infiltrates. Involvement of the airway with this lesion is usually in the pulmonary parenchyma. When the upper airway is involved, endoscopic removal or open surgical excision of the lesion should be performed.

Malignant Laryngeal Tumors

Malignant tumors of the larynx are uncommon in children. Ferlito and co-workers[33] reviewed the last 20 years and found 47 laryngeal malignancies in children and adolescents. Their survey revealed that the type of laryngeal malignancies in children has evolved from epithelial origin to mostly mesenchymal origin. Most of them (20/47 cases) were rhabdomyosarcomas, predominantly the embryonal type. Squamous cell carcinomas were the next most common at 13 of 47 cases. The rest of the cases were synovial sarcoma, malignant fibrous histiocytoma, non-Hodgkin lymphoma, chondrosarcoma, Ewing sarcoma, fibrosarcoma, malignant schwannoma, mixed sarcoma, mucoepidermoid carcinoma, and primitive neuroectodermal tumor. Mesenchyme-derived cancers accounted for 33 of the 47 malignancies, so over two thirds were of nonepithelial origin. This result is in contrast to a 1980 report in which it was revealed that the majority of laryngeal malignancies were of epithelial origin, such as squamous cell carcinoma.[36] In that review of 54 cases of carcinoma of the larynx in children, only 1 was an adenocarcinoma from a minor salivary gland, with all other cases being squamous cell carcinoma. Ferlito and colleagues[33] did not find that children with laryngeal cancer had the usual risk factors such as exposure to radiation therapy, chemicals, or active/passive smoking. This finding is in contrast to the series of Gindhart and associates, where radiation therapy for benign tumors such as RRP, active and passive smoking, cancer malformation syndrome, intrauterine exposure to ionizing radiation, and chemical carcinogens were common risk factors among children in their series. This difference in risk factors probably reflects the recent realization of the high risk of cancer associated with these agents and the subsequent avoidance of these agents. The male-female ratio was about 3:1, as compared with 3:2 in the previous series. The average age for the development of rhabdomyosarcoma was younger than that for squamous cell carcinoma, 9 versus 12 years. The most frequent site was supraglottic at 37%, followed by glottic at 22%. The most common symptoms were dyspnea, hoarseness, and dysphagia. Direct laryngoscopy and bronchoscopy with biopsy are essential in establishing the type of malignancy, as well as defining its extension. A metastatic work-up, including a skeletal survey, bone scan, and bone marrow biopsy, as well as chest CT, is important, particularly for rhabdomyosarcomas. The choice of treatment depends on the histologic type, clinical stage, and available treatment regimen. For rhabdomyosarcoma, a combination of radiation and multiagent chemotherapy is usually recommended, surgery generally being reserved for biopsy and debulking only. For squamous cell carcinoma, treatment with radiation or surgery, or both, is indicated. When radiation therapy is used in children, the possibility of growth arrest and radiation-induced malignancy must be factored into selection of the method of treatment. Unlike younger adults, pediatric laryngeal squamous carcinomas are well-differentiated keratinizing carcinomas, and survival is relatively good.[99] Using both CT and MRI preoperatively enhances one's ability to more accurately determine the extent of extirpation necessary. Prompt recognition plus treatment of any abnormal laryngeal mass in a young child with hoarseness is critical. The overall survival of children seems to be at least as good as that of adults.

In all these pediatric laryngeal malignancies, the principle of early identification of unusual laryngeal findings in children with hoarseness or voice change is stressed.

Tumors of the Trachea

Primary tumors of the trachea are rare. Desai and co-authors[27] reviewed the literature for the period from 1965 to 1995 and found that 36 primary neoplasms of the trachea were reported in children and adolescents (Table 91–2). Some differences were noted in the occurrence of the various types of tracheal neoplasms in children in comparison to the previous review by Gilbert and associates,[34, 35] who found 42 tracheal tumors in children reported between 1908 and 1952. Desai and co-workers

TABLE 91–2. Primary Tracheal Tumors in Children

Benign	
Hemangioma	5
Granular cell tumor	4
Benign fibrous histiocytoma	4
Papilloma	3
Neurofibroma	3
Pleomorphic adenoma	2
Hemangioendothelioma	1
Neurilemoma	1
Total benign	23 (64%)
Malignant	
Malignant fibrous histiocytoma	4
Mucoepidermoid carcinoma	3
Adenoid cystic carcinoma	2
Rhabdomyosarcoma	2
Squamous cell carcinoma	1
Carcinoid	1
Total malignant	13 (36%)
Total	36 (100%)

From Desai DP, Holinger LD, Gonzalez-Crussi F. Tracheal neoplasms in children. Ann Otol Rhinol Laryngol 107:790, 1998.

found that only 64% of the tracheal tumors were benign, whereas Gilbert and colleagues found that over 90% were benign. The predominant benign tracheal tumors were hemangiomas, granular cell tumors, and benign fibrous tumors (benign fibrous histiocytoma and mesenchymoma), while Gilbert and associates reported papilloma, followed by fibroma and angioma. Tracheal papillomas accounted for almost 60% (23/39) of the benign tracheal tumors in Gilbert and colleagues' review and only 13% (3/23) in Desai and co-workers' report. This significant change may be more a reflection of a change in reporting bias and not a true change in histopathology. Malignant tracheal tumors in children include malignant fibrous histiocytoma, mucoepidermoid carcinoma, adenoid cystic carcinoma, rhabdomyosarcoma, squamous cell carcinoma, and carcinoid. Gilbert and coauthors reported only three tracheal malignancies, all sarcomas. The wider histopathology found in the more recent literature probably represents evolution of the pathologic classification. Grillo and Mathisen[41] reviewed their experience of 198 primary tracheal tumors over a 26-year period and found just 12 patients younger than 19 years (6%), only 4 of whom were younger than 10 years. Whereas 80% of the primary tracheal tumors in adults were either squamous cell carcinoma or adenoid cystic carcinoma, none of the pediatric cases had these diagnoses.

Desai and colleagues found that tracheal tumors occur most frequently in the cervical trachea and that malignant tumors occur distally, in the intrathoracic trachea. The available data showed that the tracheal tumors most commonly originated from the posterior wall of the trachea. Malignant tumors tended to develop later, with 11 of the 13 malignancies occurring during adolescence. The initial symptoms were most commonly wheezing (56%), stridor (36%), cough (33%), and dyspnea (9%). Other symptoms include hemoptysis, especially in malignant lesions, hoarseness, and dysphagia. Symptoms from tracheal obstruction are not generally manifested until significant obstruction is present, at least 50%, so a delay in the diagnosis of tracheal neoplasms is expected. Desai and associates found that lesions obstructed 50% to 95% of the lumen by the time that they were diagnosed.

The diagnostic work-up should begin with radiographs of the airway, neck, and chest, possibly followed by CT or MRI (or both) of the neck and chest to evaluate intraluminal and extraluminal spread of the disease. Other tests of assistance include barium swallow, especially for those with dysphagia, angiography, and pulmonary function tests (flow-volume curve). A definitive diagnosis requires direct laryngoscopy, bronchoscopy, and possibly esophagoscopy to determine the extent of disease, obtain a biopsy specimen for tissue diagnosis, and ensure an adequate airway.

The rarity and the variety of the tumors limit the experience in treating pediatric tracheal tumors. In general, surgical excision appears to be the mainstay of therapy and may be performed either endoscopically through a tracheal fissure or by tracheal resection. As dictated by histopathology, radiotherapy and chemotherapy may be added. Close follow-up with CT/MRI, as well as serial bronchoscopy, is necessary.

Other Rare Tumors of the Trachea

Fibrous histiocytoma of the trachea is very rare, with only 10 patients being reported, 7 of whom were younger than 18 years.[100] Just as for fibrous histiocytoma of the larynx, histologic identification can be difficult. The histologic criteria differentiating malignant from benign lesion are not well demarcated. Localization of the tumor in the lower part of the trachea is more commonly reported, with symptoms being related to this region (i.e., noisy breathing, progressive dyspnea, and hemoptysis). This location causes difficulty in airway management inasmuch as tracheotomy may not bypass the obstruction. Laser bronchoscopy offers the most efficacious means of debulking. Local resection, frequently under bronchoscopic control, is the mode of treatment; recurrence is common, however. In malignant cases, tracheal resection will be needed.

Bronchial Tumors

Although primary bronchial tumors in children are rare, they are more common than primary tracheal neoplasms. Unlike tracheal tumors, the majority of bronchial neoplasms are malignant. A large variety of benign lesions have been identified.

Benign Tumors

Inflammatory Pseudotumor

Hartman and Shochat[44] reported that inflammatory pseudotumor is the most common benign bronchial tumor in children. It consists of a proliferation of reticuloendothelial cells that arise from an inflammatory response to a previous insult, such as infection or trauma. Approximately 50 cases have been reported in children younger than 16 years. The youngest child was 1 year of age at diagnosis, although most lesions are identified in children older than 5 years. Symptoms are usually rare and nonspecific, such as fever or cough. Occasionally, pain, hemoptysis, or pneumonitis is encountered. The natural history is slow growth with a tendency to local invasiveness. Treatment generally requires excisional surgery with bronchoplasty.[74]

Hamartomas

These lung lesions consist of an abnormality in the proportion or arrangement of normal pulmonary elements. Approximately 15 cases have been reported in children. The lesion is mostly parenchymal in nature, is often quite large, and causes significant symptoms or severe respiratory distress. A triad of tumors consisting of pulmonary hamartoma, extra-adrenal paraganglioma, and gastric smooth muscle tumors have been identified in young women. Thus, if any young female is identified as having any one of these three lesions, one must search for the other two.[44]

Malignant Tumors

Bronchial Adenomas

Unfortunately, the term "bronchial adenoma" is a misnomer that allows clinicians to believe that they are dealing with a benign disease. This term refers to a heterogeneous group of lesions with significant malignant potential. Included in this category are bronchial carcinoids, mucoepidermoid carcinoma, and adenoid cystic carcinoma. They are generally slow growing, and symptoms include recurrent pneumonia, hemoptysis, wheezing, chest pain, pleural effusion, persistent cough, and dyspnea. The differential diagnosis includes asthma, foreign bodies, tuberculosis, aspergillosis, hamartoma, bronchiectasis, and cystic fibrosis.

Bronchial carcinoids are the most commonly reported bronchial tumors in children. Hause and Harvey[45] found 86 cases in their literature review and added 3 more. Of these, approximately 10% to 15% have metastatic disease. Carcinoid syndrome was noted to develop in one patient with metastatic disease.[61] Typical bronchial carcinoids have low malignant potential, whereas atypical carcinoids are much more aggressive lesions that are capable of lymphatic invasion and distant metastases. They are in the amine uptake and decarboxylase (APUD) group of tumors and are derived from multipotential neural crest cells known as Kulchitsky cells.

Signs and symptoms in children are wheezing and atelectasis, in addition to the classic triad of cough, pneumonitis, and hemoptysis described in adults. The diagnosis is made by endoscopy, and the tumor appears as a polypoid mass that is either partially or totally obstructing the bronchus.[72] Biopsy is necessary but may cause significant bleeding. Because of concern for recurrence (60% to 75% recurrence rate with endobronchial excision), as well as metastatic spread, endoscopic resection is not recommended. Conservative surgical resection with removal of any involved lymphatics is the treatment of choice.[6] Follow-up is performed with repeat bronchoscopy and CT/MRI examination. The prognosis after complete excision is good, with a reported survival rate of 90%.[45]

Mucoepidermoid carcinoma occurs less frequently than bronchial carcinoids, with approximately 24 cases reported in children.[119] These lesions are histologically identical to the more common mucoepidermoid carcinomas of the salivary glands and can be classified into low-, intermediate-, and high-grade tumors. Recurrent pneumonia is the most common initial symptom. These tumors tend to be of low malignancy in children, and only one case of metastatic spread to the regional lymph nodes has been reported.[103] The tumor is noted to arise from the mainstem bronchus or the proximal portion of the lobar bronchus. The lesions are usually covered with normal mucosa, so bronchial washings are not useful in diagnosis. Conservative surgical resection is the treatment of choice, and no recurrence has been reported after complete resection. Adjuvant chemotherapy or radiation therapy is not necessary if the resection is complete.[45, 122]

Only four cases of adenoid cystic carcinoma have been noted in children. These tumors are locally aggressive lesions, and they disseminate through lymphatic channels. En bloc resection with hilar lymphadenectomy appears to be the best approach to these tumors.

Bronchogenic Carcinoma

Bronchogenic carcinoma has been identified in children, with approximately 50 cases noted in the literature. Undifferentiated carcinoma and adenocarcinoma account for 80% of the lesions. Unfortunately, the disease is frequently disseminated at the time of diagnosis, and such dissemination is the reason for its poor prognosis. If the lesion is identified early, surgical and adjunctive therapies can be curative. Two cases of bronchogenic carcinoma have been noted in congenital cystic malformations. This finding is somewhat disturbing, so it is recommended that patients with asymptomatic congenital cystic malformations who do not undergo surgical resection be closely monitored.[44]

Miscellaneous Tumors

A variety of other malignant lesions have been identified in the tracheal bronchial tree of children, including pulmonary blastoma, leiomyosarcoma, rhabdomyosarcoma, hemangiopericytoma, malignant teratoma, plasmacytoma, and myxosarcoma. Symptomatic children are more likely to have a malignant lesion than those who have their tumor identified by routine screening. If it is at all suspected that a lesion is present, bronchoscopy can reveal most tumors and thus allow for earlier diagnosis and treatment. An improved prognosis depends on early identification and prompt surgical intervention.

SELECTED REFERENCES

Cripe TP. Human papillomaviruses: pediatric perspectives on a family of multifaceted tumorigenic pathogens. Pediatr Infect Dis J 9:836, 1990.

This article is an excellent broad review of HPV infection in disease and is especially informative in the role of maternal fetal transmission in recurrent respiratory papillomatosis.

Derkay CS. Recurrent respiratory papillomatosis. Laryngoscope 111:57, 2001.

A thorough review of the current state-of-the-art knowledge in recurrent respiratory papillomatosis.

Greene GE, Bauman NM, Smith RJ. Pathogenesis and treatment of juvenile onset recurrent respiratory papillomatosis. Otolaryngol Clin North Am 33:187, 2000.

This article is a comprehensive review article of recurrent respiratory papillomatosis. It has very informative sections on the etiologic agent HPV and the latest information on ongoing therapeutic trials, including contact information.

Kashima H, Mounts P, Leventhal B, Hruban RH. Sites of predilection in recurrent respiratory papillomatosis. Ann Otol Rhinol Laryngol 102:580, 1993.

This article describes how the recurrent respiratory papillomas have a definite pattern of anatomic predilection for the squamociliary epithelial junction, natural or iatrogenically created. This observation explains the phenomenon of RRP occurring along the tracheotomy tract and emphasizes the importance of avoiding injury to nondiseased ciliated epithelia.

Ohlms LA, Jones DT, McGill TJI, Healy GB. Interferon alfa-2a therapy for airway hemangiomas. Ann Otol Rhinol Laryngol 103:1, 1994.

This article describes the usefulness of interferon alfa-2a in the management of life-threatening airway lesions.

Shikhani AH, Jones MM, Marsh BR, Holliday MJ. Infantile subglottic hemangiomas: an update. Ann Otol Rhinol Laryngol 95:336, 1986.

This review article discusses 323 reported cases of subglottic hemangiomas between 1913 and 1985. It covers the various treatment modalities available and the authors' recommendation for management.

WWW.RRPF.ORG and WWW.RRPWEBSITE.ORG

In these are two websites, patients and some professionals discuss treatment and results. The latest information is likely to show up here first, although the information may be anecdotal.

REFERENCES

1. Abramson AL, Shikowitz MJ, Mullooly VM, et al. Clinical effects of photodynamic therapy on recurrent laryngeal papillomas. Arch Otolaryngol Head Neck Surg 118:25, 1992.
2. Abramson AL, Steinberg BM, Winkler B. Laryngeal papillomatosis: Clinical, histopathologic and molecular studies. Laryngoscope 97:678, 1987.
3. Adzick NS, Strome M, Gang D, Donahoe PK. Cryotherapy of subglottic hemangioma. J Pediatr Surg 19:353, 1984.
4. Aguado DL, Perez PB, Betancor L, et al. Acyclovir in the treatment of laryngeal papillomatosis. Int J Pediatr Otorhinolaryngol 21:269, 1991.
5. Armstrong LR, Derkay CS, Reeves WC. Initial results from the national registry for juvenile-onset recurrent respiratory papillomatosis. RRP Task Force. Arch Otolaryngol Head Neck Surg 125:743, 1999.
6. Attar S, Miller JE, Hankins J, et al. Bronchial adenoma: a review of 51 patients. Ann Thorac Surg 30:126, 1985.
7. Avidano MA, Singleton GT. Adjuvant drug strategies in the treatment of recurrent respiratory papillomatosis. Otolaryngol Head Neck Surg 112:197, 1995.
8. Basheda SG, Mehta AC, De Boer G, Orlowski JP. Endobronchial and parenchymal juvenile laryngotracheobronchial papillomatosis. Effect of photodynamic therapy. Chest 100:1458, 1991.
9. Benjamin B, Carter P. Congenital laryngeal hemangioma. Ann Otol Rhinol Laryngol 92:448, 1983.
10. Benjamin B, Parsons DP. Recurrent respiratory papillomatosis: a 10 year study. J Laryngol Otol 102:1022, 1988.
11. Bennett RS, Powell KR. Human papillomaviruses: associations between laryngeal papillomas and genital warts. Pediatr Infect Dis J 6:229, 1987.
12. Bent JP, Porubsky ES. Recurrent respiratory papillomatosis. Insights Otolaryngol 8:1, 1993.
13. Bewtra C, Krishnan R, Lee SS. Malignant changes in non-irradiated juvenile laryngotracheal papillomatosis. Arch Otolaryngol 108:114, 1982.
14. Blitzer A, Lawson W, Biller HF. Malignant fibrous histiocytoma of the head and neck. Laryngoscope 87:1479, 1977.
15. Choa DI, Smith MCF, Evans JNG, Bailey CM. Subglottic hemangioma in children. J Laryngol Otol 100:447, 1986.
16. Cohen SR. Fibrous histiocytoma of the trachea. Ann Otol Rhinol Laryngol (Suppl) 87:2, 1978.
17. Cohen SR, Wang C. Steroid treatment of hemangiomas of the head and neck in children. Ann Otol Rhinol Laryngol 81:584, 1972.
18. Conley SF, Milbrath MM, Beste DJ. Pediatric laryngeal granular cell tumor. J Otolaryngol 21:6, 1992.
19. Cooper M, Slovis TL, Madgy DN, Levitsky D. Congenital subglottic hemangioma: frequency of symmetric subglottic narrowing on frontal radiographs of the neck. AJR Am J Roentgenol 159:1269, 1992.
20. Cotton RT, Tewfik TL. Laryngeal stenosis following carbon dioxide laser in subglottic hemangioma: Report of three cases. Ann Otol Rhinol Laryngol 94:494, 1985.
21. Cripe TP. Human papillomaviruses: pediatric perspectives on a family of multifaceted tumorigenic pathogens. Pediatr Infect Dis J 9:836, 1990.
22. Crockett DM, Lusk RP, McCabe BF, Mixon JH. Side effects and toxicity of interferon in the treatment of recurrent respiratory papillomatosis. Ann Otol Rhinol Laryngol 96:601, 1987a.
23. Crockett DM, McCabe BF, Shive CJ. Complications of laser surgery for recurrent respiratory papillomatosis. Ann Otol Rhinol Laryngol 96:639, 1987.
24. Crowe F, Schull W, Neel J. Multiple Neurofibromatosis. Springfield, IL, Charles C Thomas, 1956.
25. Dallimore NS. Squamous bronchial carcinoma arising in a case of multiple juvenile papillomatosis. Thorax 40:797, 1985.
26. Derkay CS. Recurrent respiratory papillomatosis. Laryngoscope 111:57, 2001.
27. Desai DP, Holinger LD, Gonzalez-Crussi F. Tracheal neoplasms in children. Ann Otol Rhinol Laryngol 107:790, 1998.
28. Durkin GE, Duncavage JA, Toolhill RJ, et al. Wound healing of true vocal cord squamous epithelium after CO_2 laser ablation and cup forceps stripping. Otolaryngol Head Neck Surg 95:273, 1986.
29. Edmonds J, Pransky S, Carvalho D, Homicz M. KTP laser treatment of subglottic hemangioma. Poster presented at the annual meeting of the American Broncho-Esophagological Association at Orlando, FL, 2001.
30. Ezekowitz RA, Mulliken JB, Folkman J. Interferon alfa-2a therapy for life-threatening hemangiomas of infancy. N Engl J Med 326:1456, 1992.
31. Fechner RE, Goepfert H, Alford BR. Invasive laryngeal papillomatosis. Arch Otolaryngol 99:147, 1974.
32. Ferlito A, Nicolai P, Recher G, Narne S. Primary laryngeal malignant fibrous histiocytoma: Review of the literature and report of seven cases. Laryngoscope 93:1351, 1983.
33. Ferlito A, Renaldo A, Marioni G. Laryngeal malignant neoplasms in children and adolescents. Int J Pediatr Otorhinolaryngol 49:1, 1999.
34. Gilbert JG, Kaufman B, Mazzarella LA. Tracheal tumors in the infant and children. J Pediatr 35:63, 1949.
35. Gilbert JG, Mazzarella LA, Feit LJ. Primary tracheal tumors in the infant and adult. Arch Otolaryngol 58:1, 1953.
36. Gindhart TD, Johnston WH, Chism SE, Dedo HH. Carcinoma of the larynx in childhood. Cancer 46:1683, 1980.
37. Gissman L, Wolnik L, Ikenberg H, et al. Human papillomavirus types 6 and 11 DNA sequences in genital and laryngeal papillomas and in some cervical cancer. Proc Natl Acad Sci U S A 80:560, 1983.
38. Goepfert H, Sessions RB, Gutterman JU, et al. Leukocyte interferon in patients with juvenile laryngeal papillomatosis. Ann Otol Rhinol Laryngol 91:431, 1982.
39. Goldsmith MM, Strope GL, Postma DS. Presentation and management of postcricoid hemangiomata in infancy. Laryngoscope 97:851, 1987.
40. Greene GE, Bauman NM, Smith RJ. Pathogenesis and treatment of juvenile onset recurrent respiratory papillomatosis. Otolaryngol Clin North Am 33:187, 2000.
41. Grillo HC, Mathisen DJ. Primary tracheal tumors: Treatment and results. Ann Thorac Surg 49:69, 1990.
42. Haglund S, Lundquist P, Cantrell K, Strander H. Interferon therapy in juvenile laryngeal papillomatosis. Arch Otolaryngol 107:327, 1981.
43. Hallden C, Majmudar B. The relationship between juvenile laryngeal papillomatosis and maternal condyloma acuminata. J Reprod Med 31:804, 1986.
44. Hartman GE, Shochat SJ. Primary pulmonary neoplasms of childhood: a review. Ann Thorac Surg 36:108, 1983.
45. Hause DW, Harvey JC. Endobronchial carcinoid and mucoepidermoid carcinoma in children. J Surg Oncol 46:270, 1991.
46. Hawkins DB, Crockett DM, Kahlstrom EJ, MacLaughlin EF. Corticosteroid management of airway hemangiomas: long-term follow-up. Laryngoscope 94:633, 1984.
47. Healy GB. Personal communication, 1988.
48. Healy GB, Fearon G, French R, McGill T. Treatment of subglottic hemangioma with the carbon dioxide laser. Laryngoscope 90:809, 1980.
49. Healy GB, McGill T, Friedman EM. Carbon dioxide laser in subglottic hemangioma: an update. Ann Otol Rhinol Laryngol 93:370, 1984.

50. Hoeve LJ, Kuppers GL, Verwoerd CD. Management of infantile subglottic hemangioma: laser vaporization, submucous resection, intubation, or intralesional steroids? Int J Pediatr Otorhinolaryngol 42:179, 1997.
51. Holinger PH. Benign tumors of the trachea and bronchi. Otolaryngol Clin North Am 3:219, 1968.
52. Holland RS. Granular cell tumor of the larynx in a six-year-old child: case report and review of the literature. Ear Nose Throat J 77:652, 1998.
53. Irwin BC, Hendrickse WA, Pincott JR, et al. Juvenile laryngeal papillomatosis. J Laryngol Otol 100:435, 1986.
54. Jokinen K, Palva A, Karja J. Cryocauterization in the treatment of subglottic hemangioma in infants. Laryngoscope 91:79, 1981.
55. Jones SR, Myers EM, Barnes L. Benign neoplasms of the larynx. Otolaryngol Clin North Am 17:151, 1984.
56. Kashima H, Mounts P, Leventhal B, Hruban RH. Sites of predilection in recurrent respiratory papillomatosis. Ann Otol Rhinol Laryngol 102:580, 1993.
57. Kashima H, Wu TC, Mounts P, et al. Carcinoma ex-papilloma: histologic and virologic studies in whole-organ section of the larynx. Laryngoscope 98:619, 1988.
58. Keen M, Cho HT, Savetisky L. Pseudotumor of the larynx: An unusual cause of airway obstruction. Otolaryngol Head Neck Surg 94:243, 1986.
59. Kramer S, Wehunt WD, Stocker JT, Kashima H. Pulmonary manifestations of juvenile laryngotracheal papillomatosis. Am J Radiol 144:687, 1985.
60. Kveton JF, Pillsbury HD. Conservative treatment of infantile subglottic hemangioma with corticosteroids. Arch Otolaryngol 108:117, 1982.
61. Lack EE, Harris GBC, Eraklis AJ, Vawter GF. Primary bronchial tumors in childhood: a clinicopathologic study of six cases. Cancer 51:492, 1983.
62. Lazar RH, Younis RT, Kluka EA, et al. Granular cell tumor of the larynx: Report of two pediatric cases. Ear Nose Throat J 71:440, 1992.
63. Leventhal BG, Kashima HK, Mounts P, et al. Long-term response of recurrent respiratory papillomatosis to treatment with lymphoblastoid interferon alfa-n1. N Engl J Med 325:613, 1991.
64. Leventhal BG, Kashima HK, Weck PW, et al. Randomized Surgical Adjuvant Trial of Interferon Alfa-n1 in Recurrent Papillomatosis. Arch Otolaryngol Head Neck Surg 114:1163, 1988.
65. Lindeberg H, Elbrond O. Laryngeal papillomas: the epidemiology in a Danish subpopulation 1965–1984. Clin Otolaryngol 15:125, 1990.
66. Lindeberg H, Elbrond O. Malignant tumours in patients with a history of multiple laryngeal papillomas: The significance of irradiation. Clin Otolaryngol 16:149, 1991.
67. Lundquist PG, Haglund S, Carlsoo B, et al. Interferon therapy in juvenile laryngeal papillomatosis. Otolaryngol Head Neck Surg 92:386, 1984.
68. Lusk RP, McCabe BF, Mixon JH. Three-year-experience of treating recurrent respiratory papilloma with interferon. Ann Otol Rhinol Laryngol 96:158, 1987.
69. Madgy D, Ahsan SF, Kest D, Stein I. The application of the potassium-titanyl-phosphate (KTP) laser in the management of subglottic hemangioma. Arch Otolaryngol 127:47, 2001.
70. McCabe BF, Clark KF. Interferon and laryngeal papillomatosis: the Iowa experience. Ann Otol Rhinol Laryngol 92:2, 1983.
71. McCaffrey TV, Cortese DA. Neodymium:YAG laser treatment of subglottic hemangioma. Otolaryngol Head Neck Surg 94:382, 1986.
72. McDougall JC, Gorenstein A, Unni K, O'Connell EJ. Carcinoid and mucoepidermoid carcinoma of bronchus in children. Ann Otol Rhinol Laryngol 89:425, 1980.
73. Meeuwis J, Bos CE, Hoeve LJ, van der Voort E. Subglottic hemangiomas in infants: treatment with intralesional corticosteroid injection and intubation. Int J Pediatr Otorhinolaryngol 19:145, 1990.
74. Messineo A, Mognato G, D'Amore ES, et al. Inflammatory pseudotumors of the lung in children: conservative or aggressive approach? Med Pediatr Oncol 31:100, 1998.
75. Mizono G, Dedo HH. Subglottic hemangiomas in infants: treatment with CO$_2$ laser. Laryngoscope 94:638, 1984.
76. Morrison GAJ, Kotecha B, Evans JNG. Ribavirin treatment for juvenile respiratory papillomatosis. J. Laryngol Otol 107:423, 1993.
77. Mounts P, Kashima H. Association of human papillomavirus subtype and clinical course in respiratory papillomatosis. Laryngoscope 94:28, 1984.
78. Mounts P, Shah KV, Kashima H. Viral etiology of juvenile and adult-onset squamous papillomas of the larynx. Proc Natl Acad Sci U S A 79:5425, 1982.
79. Mulder JJS, van den Broek P. Surgical treatment of infantile subglottic hemangioma. Int J Pediatr Otorhinolaryngol 17:57, 1989.
80. Mullooly VM, Abramson AL, Shikowitz MJ. Dihematoporphyrin ether–induced photosensitivity in laryngeal papilloma patients. Laser Surg Med 10:349, 1990.
81. Mullooly VM, Abramson AL, Steinberg BM, Horowitz MS. Clinical effects of alpha-interferon dose variation on laryngeal papillomas. Laryngoscope 98:1324, 1988.
82. Narcy P, Contencin P, Bobin S, Manac'h Y. Treatment of infantile subglottic hemangioma: a report of 49 cases. Int J Pediatr Otolaryngol 9:157, 1985.
83. Ohlms LA, Jones DT, McGill TJI, Healy GB. Interferon alfa-2a therapy for airway hemangiomas. Ann Otol Rhinol Laryngol 103:1, 1994.
84. Orlow SJ, Isakoff MS, Blei F. Increased risk of symptomatic hemangiomas of the airway in association with cutaneous hemangiomas in a "beard" distribution. J Pediatr 131:643, 1997.
85. Ossoff RH, Werkhaven JA, Dere H. Soft-tissue complications of laser surgery for recurrent respiratory papillomatosis. Laryngoscope 101:1162, 1991.
86. Perrick D, Wray BB, Leffell MS, et al. Evaluation of immunocompetency in juvenile laryngeal papillomatosis. Ann Allergy 65:69, 1990.
87. Pignatari S, Smith EM, Gray SD, et al. Detection of human papillomavirus infection in diseased and nondiseased sites of the respiratory tract in recurrent respiratory papillomatosis patients by DNA hybridization. Ann Otol Rhinol Laryngol 101:408, 1992.
88. Pransky SM, Brewster DF, Magit AE, et al. Clinical update on 10 children treated with intralesional cidofovir injections for severe recurrent respiratory papillomatosis. Arch Otolaryngol Head Neck Surg 126:1239, 2000.
89. Pransky SM, Magit AE, Kearns DB, et al. Intralesional cidofovir for recurrent respiratory papillomatosis in children. Arch Otolaryngol Head Neck Surg 125:1143, 1999.
90. Quick CA, Kryzek R, Watts S, et al. Relationship between condylomata and laryngeal papillomata: clinical and molecular virological evidence. Ann Otolaryngol 89:467, 1980.
91. Quiney RE, Hall D, Croft CB. Laryngeal papillomatosis: analysis of 113 patients. Clin Otolaryngol 14:217, 1989.
92. Reid R, Laverty CR, Copplesen M, et al. Noncondylomatous cervical wart virus infection. Obstet Gynecol 55:476, 1982.
93. Robbins KT, Woodson GE. Current concepts in the management of laryngeal papillomatosis. Head Neck Surg 6:861, 1984.
94. Rosen CA, Woodson GE, Thompson JW, et al. Preliminary results of the use of indole-3-carbinol for recurrent respiratory papillomatosis. Otolaryngol Head Neck Surg 118:810, 1998.
95. Sadan N, Wolach B. Treatment of hemangiomas of infants with high doses of prednisone. J Pediatr 128:141, 1996.
96. Schnadig VJ, Clark WD, Clegg TJ, Yao CS. Invasive papillomatosis and squamous carcinoma complicating juvenile laryngeal papillomatosis. Arch Otolaryngol Head Neck Surg 112:966, 1986.
97. Schouten DJ, Broeck PVD, Cremers WRJ, et al. Interferons and bronchogenic carcinoma in juvenile laryngeal papillomatosis. Arch Otolaryngol 109:289, 1983.
98. Schwager K, Waner M, Hohmann D. Hemangioma: differential diagnosis and necessary early laser treatment. Adv Otorhinolaryngol 49:70, 1995.
99. Schwartz DA, Katin L, Lesser RD, et al. Juvenile laryngeal carcinoma: correlation of computed tomography and magnetic resonance imaging with pathology. Ann Clin Lab Sci 20:225, 1990.
100. Sculerati N, Mittal KR, Greco MA, Ambrosino MM. Fibrous histiocytoma of the trachea: management of a rare cause of upper airway obstruction. Int J Pediatr Otorhinolaryngol 19:295, 1990.
101. Sedlack TV, Lindheim S, Eder C, et al. Mechanism for human papillomavirus transmission at birth. Am J Obstet Gynecol 161:55, 1989.
102. Seid AB, Pransky SM, Kearns DB. The open surgical approach to subglottic hemangioma. Int J Pediatr Otorhinolaryngol 22:85, 1991.
103. Seo S, Warren J, Mirkin LD, et al. Mucoepidermoid carcinoma of

When a population of atoms are in their lowest energy transition state, it is called the *ground state*. An atom in the ground state can interact with a photon, absorb energy, and be promoted to a higher energy state, or an excited state. Once this atom is in the higher energy state, it can undergo transition back to the ground state with the spontaneous release of electromagnetic radiation (or photon), a process called *spontaneous emission*. Stimulated emission occurs in a system where this photon then interacts with another atom that already exists in a higher energy state. This photon can cause the transition from a higher energy level to a lower energy level with the emission of a second photon from the second atom. For this process to occur, the potential transition state of the second atom must exactly match the energy state of the incident photon. Thus, two photons are released from the system, the original photon and the second, emitted photon. These two photons are of equivalent wavelength and are coherent (coordinated in space and time). Coordination in space and time means that both the incident and the emitted photons are traveling in the same direction with their wavelengths in phase.[24]

Within a laser, an external energy source must be applied to the lasing medium to raise the atoms within the medium to the excited energy state. For the process of developing a laser beam to proceed, more than half the population of atoms within the lasing medium must be in the excited state, a phenomenon called *population inversion*. The energy can be input into the lasing medium in several ways. Typically, an electric current, radiofrequency energy source, or flashlamp is used to deliver energy into the lasing medium. With many of the atoms in the lasing medium in a higher energy state, spontaneous emission occurs frequently and in a random spacial orientation. The last requirement for a surgical laser, therefore, is an optical cavity to redirect, focus, and amplify the spontaneous emission of photons into a concentrated, usable output. To accomplish this, the lasing medium is placed inside an optical cavity. Typically, the optical cavity is a space between two special mirrors. One mirror is completely reflecting, and the other mirror is only partially reflecting, therefore allowing a portion of the generated laser beam to pass through the mirror and thus be available for use. The cascade effect begins when a photon is spontaneously emitted along the axis of the optical cavity. Photons are reflected between the two mirrors, and, as the photons interact with other excited atoms, another photon is generated that is coherent with the incident photon. Thus, one photon generates two, two generate four, and so on. This cascade effect would rapidly deplete the atoms existing in a stimulated state were it not for the constant input of energy from the electric current, radiofrequency excitation, or flashlamp. For the laser to function in a continuous mode, energy must be continuously applied to the lasing medium to keep the medium in a state of population inversion.[6]

Another important characteristic of the optical cavity is that its length must be an integer or multiple of the wavelength that is desired. This is necessary to create a standing wave within the cavity, allowing the photons to propagate. A nonintegral wavelength of the optical cavity would allow cancellation of energy by destructive interference of the wavelengths. The energy that is released through the partially reflective mirror is termed the *laser beam*. This energy is coherent (i.e., the photons are all in phase with one another and parallel in direction). This results in the unique characteristics of the laser beam, which are monochromaticity, intensity, collimation, and coherence. Once the beam exits the optical cavity, it may then be redirected into delivery devices that are specific for each surgical application. The mid-infrared wavelength of the CO_2 laser is not transmitted through an optical fiber but is redirected by a series of mirrors down a hollow articulated arm system. This maintains the beam's coherence, collimation, and intensity. At the end of the articulated arm assembly, the beam may then be passed through a lens, which serves to focus the beam to an extremely small spot size. Other laser-visible and near-infrared wavelengths are capable of being transmitted through flexible optical fibers. The bending and flexing of the fiber result in the internal reflection of the beam within the fiber and the loss of the collimation of the beam. This loss of collimation is seen as beam divergence as it exits the fiber tip; the quality of the fiber determines the degree of divergence, typically between 8 and 30 degrees.

Surgical lasers allow the operator to select power (watts) and exposure time (seconds). In addition, through manipulation of the fiber or the end-stage delivery device of an articulated arm (microspot micromanipulator or bronchoscopic coupler), the surgeon may also control the spot size. The surgical tissue effects of the laser are dependent on the amount of energy delivered to the tissue and the absorption of that particular wavelength within the tissue.

Power density is a measure of the concentration of laser energy and is represented as power (watts) per square centimeter. Radiant exposure is expressed as power density × time and is represented as joules per centimeter squared (joules = power [watts] × time).

Power density can vary linearly, as the power output of the laser is changed, or logarithmically, as the size of the laser spot is changed. Laser spot size may be changed by defocusing the fiber or pulling it away from the surgical field or by changing the site of focus of a micromanipulator or bronchoscopic coupler. Radiant exposure is a measure of the total energy delivered to the tissue and allows comparison of tissue effects for individual wavelengths at different energy exposures. As a general rule, the concept of power density (watts/cm²) is a more useful measurement for the surgeon. Generally, the higher the power density, the faster the vaporization of tissue occurs; conversely, the lower the power density, the slower vaporization or coagulation occurs.[7]

Tissue Effects

The photons of light or laser energy can interact with tissue in one of several possible reactions. First, the photons may be reflected from the surface of the tissue and have no further interaction. Second, another reaction may be transmission through tissue. This can be compared with the phenomenon seen when a flashlight is used to shine through a patient's fingers or hands to localize superficial veins. A potential application of this concept of transmission is diaphanography, in which a bright pulse of light is directed through breast tissue to localize breast masses that are more dense than surrounding fibrofatty tissue. Third, photons of light may be scattered within tissue, either by individual atoms or by variations in tissue structure such as sheets of collagen or muscle fibers. This scattering can redirect the photons of light back out of the tissue (indirect reflectance) or may allow further transmission through the tissue (indirect transmission).

Finally, the photon of light may be absorbed by various chromophores within the tissue. Chromophores may be specific atoms, molecules, or macromolecular structures. Once a photon of light energy is absorbed, it elevates the chromophore to a higher energy level. Either a thermal effect is caused by the higher kinetic energy of the chromophore or the re-emission of energy of a lower wavelength results in a phenomenon named *fluorescence*. It is the absorption of energy by chromophores within the tissue, with the resultant increase in kinetic energy that is the basis for application of most surgical lasers. The absorption of kinetic energy results in coagulation or vaporization of tissue.

The absorption of energy by a chromophore is wavelength dependent. This concept results in the various specific tissue thermal effects from lasers of different wavelengths. The CO_2 laser operating at 10,600 nm is absorbed well by one of the bending modes of the water molecule. Therefore, its tissue effects are best in tissues with high water content and are correspondingly less in tissues with low water content, such as bone. The neodymium:yttrium-aluminum-garnet (Nd:YAG) laser is poorly absorbed by most tissues in the body and, therefore, has one of the deepest optical penetration depths. The 1064-nm wavelength is not absorbed well by any specific chromophore but is absorbed in a nonspecific fashion by multiple compounds within tissue, and this results in a deep thermal coagulative effect. The argon laser with its main output wavelengths at 488 nm and 514 nm is absorbed by tissue proteins, melanin, and hemoglobin. The strong absorption by melanin and hemoglobin results in an intermediate optical penetration depth and good coagulation. The KTP/532 laser operating at 532 nm is absorbed less specifically by proteins, melanin, and hemoglobin but has an optical penetration depth and a thermocoagulation similar to those of the argon laser. The flashlamp-excited dye laser at 585 nm and the argon yellow dye laser of the same wavelength represent the first lasers designed to be absorbed by a specific chromophore. The wavelength was selected to be high enough to minimize protein and melanin absorption while still allowing adequate absorption by the chromophore hemoglobin. This results in specific absorption in vascular tissue.[30]

In summary, the surgical effect of a laser is due to the absorption of specific wavelengths of light, and the rate of surgical effect is determined by the power density or the rate at which energy is directed into the tissue.

Lasers in Common Surgical Application

The common surgical lasers, in order of increasing wavelength, are the argon laser, KTP/532 laser, flashlamp-excited dye laser, argon pump dye laser, Nd:YAG laser, and CO_2 laser. Each of these lasers has been around for many years and has demonstrated its usefulness for specific clinical applications. New applications and new lasers are constantly being developed and evaluated, and this list is subject to change. The next sections discuss some lasers with potential clinical applications.

Argon Laser

The argon laser uses a direct-current energy source to excite argon ions. The energy requirement to create argon ions from atoms and then stimulate them to a high energy state is relatively inefficient. These lasers generally need a flowing water cooling system because of the high heat generated. The argon ion laser is a multiple wavelength output laser with its two main output wavelengths at 488 nm and 514 nm in the blue and blue-green region of the visible spectrum. This laser can operate in a continuous mode with a fiberoptic delivery system. Early argon ion lasers had a power output limitation of less than 5 watts and initially found application only in dermatology. Newer argon ion lasers now have power output capabilities up to 20 watts for tissue vaporization and cutting.

KTP/532 Laser

The KTP/532 laser uses a crystal matrix of Nd:YAG, whose laser output is directed through a potassium-titanium-phosphate (KTP) frequency-doubling crystal to decrease the wavelength from 1064 to 532 nm. This laser was initially developed in response to the low power output available with older-generation argon ion lasers. The 532-nm wavelength was shown to be well absorbed by hemoglobin and nonspecifically absorbed by melanin to a lesser extent than the argon laser. The output is through a fiberoptic delivery system. The high peak powers, up to 20 watts, allow coagulation and vaporization of tissue, which initially were not possible with the argon laser. Since the development of the KTP/532 laser, specific improvements to the device have expanded its potential applications. Modifications to the device itself allow the surgeon to operate not only with the 532-nm wavelength but also with the 1064-nm wavelength of the central Nd:YAG crystal. Beam delivery devices have been optimized for use with this laser for dermatologic applications, and a dye module, which may be added to the laser, allows production of other wavelengths dependent on the dye selected.

Flashlamp-Excited Dye Laser

The flashlamp-excited dye laser represents the first laser designed for a specific application. Dermatologic applications of the argon laser especially demonstrated some long-term complications of pigmentation changes owing to melanin absorption and textural changes owing to non-specific thermal coagulation effects within the dermis. The flashlamp-excited dye laser was specifically designed for absorption by the chromophore hemoglobin. The wavelength was determined to be 585 nm for maximal absorption, and the optimal duration of the beam was experimentally determined to be 400 μsec.[33] The tissue effect resulting from the use of this laser is coagulation of small vascular structures. This laser has found widespread application and acceptance in the treatment of cutaneous vascular lesions, such as port-wine stains and hemangioma. Delivery output is through a fiberoptic cable directed into a handpiece with a fixed 3- or 5-mm spot size.

Argon Pump Dye Laser

The argon pump dye laser was first used as a research tool. An argon laser is directed into a dye module, and the dye is excited to emit a laser output. Because of the macromolecular design of the dye, the output is tunable over a limited range, which is specific for each type of dye. Although this laser began as a research tool to allow investigation of tissue effects of various wavelengths, it found clinical applications in photodynamic therapy. An exogenous chromophore, such as hematoporphyrin derivative, is given to a patient and allowed to localize within target tissues. The absorption of ultraviolet wavelengths of light by this dye results in the fluorescence of the dye, allowing localization of the dye within the target tissue. Stimulation of a hematoporphyrin derivative at 633 nm in the red visible wavelengths results in absorption by the dye and production of singlet oxygen. The singlet oxygen results in a chemical cascade reaction, causing cell death of the target tissue.[35] The laser itself, because of its use of an argon exciting source, has high power and cooling requirements and can be delivered through a fiberoptic cable.

Nd:YAG Laser

The Nd:YAG laser is a flashlamp-excited crystalline matrix laser. The Nd atom is embedded in a YAG crystal and emits a wavelength at 1064 nm. The earliest Nd:glass laser emitted a wavelength at 1060 nm, and this variation in laser output illustrates the effect that surrounding environment may have on constraining the quantum states available to an atom and crystal lattice. As noted earlier, the absorption of the 1064-nm wavelength is nonspecific in tissue, resulting in a deep thermocoagulation. The delivery output from this laser is through a fiberoptic cable.

Carbon Dioxide Laser

The CO_2 laser has become the general-purpose laser within the field of otolaryngology–head and neck surgery. Since its initial endoscopic laryngeal applications by Jako[12] in 1972, this laser has found widespread applications, both endoscopically and macroscopically. The output wavelength of 10,600 nm is produced by direct current or radiofrequency excitation of a gas mixture of CO_2, nitrogen, and helium. The output of the laser is coupled to an articulated arm system, which, in turn, may be attached to a microspot micromanipulator for the microscope, a bronchoscopic coupler for the bronchoscope, or a handpiece. Output devices of a wave-guide nature with outside diameters as small as 1 mm have been developed, but these have limited bend radius and length. Because of the mid-infrared nature of the output wavelength, an FDA-acceptable fiberoptic cable does not yet exist. This wavelength may be transmitted through silver halide fibers, but these fibers are extremely brittle and crack easily, with resultant decrease in fiber transmission. Endoscopic applications with the microspot micromanipulator have been facilitated with the development of smaller spot sizes. The newer units available have spot sizes as small as 250 μm at 400-mm focal length and afford greater precision in the larynx than do older units.[28] Macroscopic applications using the laser handpiece have found acceptance in oral cavity, head, and neck surgery. At the author's institution, the CO_2 laser is employed for almost 90% of all cases in which a laser is used.

Laser Safety and Anesthetic Considerations

Each type of laser has a unique wavelength and tissue effect. Therefore, it is the responsibility of the surgeon to obtain training in the safe use of the equipment as well as in the potential clinical applications. Although many clinical applications are being developed and no specific training courses exist for them, courses exist to train the surgeon in the safe use of the laser and to give hands-on experience in the tissue effects. The courses that are offered cover various types of lasers and, as a mandate, include instruction in basic laser physics and in tissue interaction and safety.

Safety considerations include those for the patient, the surgeon, and all operating room personnel. Safety issues encompass the hazards of stray laser exposure to all personnel within the operating room; the hazards of exposure to laser by-products, such as the laser smoke plume; and the hazards of laser exposure to anesthetic instruments, such as the endotracheal tube.

The highest principle of medicine holds that no untoward harm befall the patient. To this end, the patient should be protected against any stray laser exposure. Eye protection varies by laser and, at a minimum, includes lubricating the eyes with a water-soluble lubricant (oil-based lubricants may have the potential for ignition), taping the eyes closed, and then protecting the eyes with saline-soaked gauze pads. This ocular exposure protection is adequate for the CO_2 laser, but for visible-wavelength lasers and the Nd:YAG laser, which may penetrate easily through water, the added protection of aluminum foil over the eye pads is required. The operative field should be draped as well as possible and surrounded with moist towels; in appropriate circumstances, aluminum foil protection from stray laser exposure may also be required.

All personnel within the operating room should wear protective eye shields that are specific for the laser wavelength being used. All laser-safe eye shields are imprinted with the optical density at the appropriate wavelength; if the glasses or goggles are not specifically marked as such, they are generally not acceptable. Ocular protection should include side shields to protect from stray laser exposure laterally. The windows in the operating room should be covered with an opaque material whenever visible-wavelength lasers are used, but the glass in a window will stop transmission of a CO_2 mid-infrared laser. A sign should be posted outside the operating room warning that laser operations may occur within the confines of the operating room. In addition, a spare set of safety glasses is usually left outside the door for operating personnel who wish to come inside the room while the laser is in operation.

Although the fiberoptic transmission of certain laser beams has been said to be generally safe when within a body cavity, it is still prudent to be cautious. Although remote, the possibility does exist for accidental breakage of the optical fiber between the coupler and the operating field, with subsequent unplanned exposure to operating personnel.

The hazards of exposure to the laser smoke plume have been recognized as a concern. When surgical lasers are used in the vaporization mode, the initial velocity of material ejected from the wound may be as high as several meters per second.[18] The smoke plume can be seen to rise high above the operative field to the level of the surgeon's and assistant's heads, and, therefore, they may be exposed directly to laser plume products. Special laser masks with extremely small pores should be worn to minimize exposure to this laser plume. Studies have examined the contents of the laser plume, and although the studies were unable to demonstrate viable cells, intact fragments of DNA were demonstrated.[1, 8] The remote theoretical possibility exists for these fragments to be inhaled by operating room personnel. A survey of more than 2000 laser users was unable to conclusively demonstrate transmission of papillomavirus to operating otolaryngologists, gynecologists, or podiatrists, but the prudent approach dictates caution. A high-volume smoke evacuator should be used in the operating field to collect the laser plume. Other studies have looked at the effects of the plume itself in causing pulmonary inflammation and have demonstrated that the plume from use of the electrosurgical unit is at least as inflammatory as that from use of the surgical lasers.[36] In light of all these facts, it appears that the most judicious course would also be to use smoke evacuation whenever an electrosurgical unit is in use.

Anesthesia for Laser Procedures

The otolaryngologist, by virtue of the site of the specialty, must share access to the patient with the anesthesiologist. Use of lasers in the head and neck region is accompanied by the risk of accidental laser exposure to anesthetic equipment and endotracheal tubes. The early use of the CO_2 laser resulted in some unfortunate cases in which the endotracheal tube was ignited, with a resultant fire and blowtorch effect within the patient's airway. Some of these cases had disastrous outcomes. Whenever the laser is to be used within the region of the anesthetic equipment, laser-safe endotracheal tubes should be used, and the anesthetic equipment as best as possible should be shielded with aluminum foil to prevent stray laser exposure. In the oral cavity, oropharynx, and glottis, a laser-resistant endotracheal tube must be used that is specific for the wavelength of laser that is being applied. Situations do occur, however, in which the endotracheal tube is too large or obstructs exposure to the operative field, and alternatives must be considered. Appropriate alternatives include the use of jet ventilation in the glottis, as well as the apneic technique, whereby the endotracheal tube is removed intermittently and work is performed while the patient's oxygen saturation is monitored.[20] It is an interesting counterpoint, and one of concern, that hospitals that require surgeons to have demonstrated instruction in safety and use of lasers do not require anesthesiologists to be likewise informed. With the proliferation of multiple-wavelength lasers and newer applications, this is an oversight that many within the field of otolaryngology would like to see rectified.

Clinical Applications of Lasers in Pediatric Otolaryngology

It is a true axiom that children are not just "small adults." Many laser applications initially developed for use on adult patients require reduction in size and modification of certain delivery instruments to make them available for use in pediatric patients. This is not the only difference. Because of reduced size, vital structures may be closer or more adjacent to each other and thus be at greater risk from scattered laser illumination. Healing and potential scarring are also often different compared with those of the adult patient. Examples of all these differences are illustrated in the following paragraphs; these differences serve to emphasize the justifiably conservative application of lasers within the pediatric population until all the data and effects are well known.

Otologic Applications

The argon, KTP, and CO_2 lasers are used for otologic applications in the general adult population. The most common application of lasers is for stapedotomies and revision stapedotomy procedures. Several papers have analyzed the thermal effects of the various lasers, and some controversy still exists over which is the ideal unit to use for this procedure.[14, 15] In theory, the visible wavelengths of the argon and the KTP lasers may be transmitted through a stapedotomy hole and damage structures within the vestibule.[34] In practice, this has not been noted, which may in part be due to the divergence of the laser beam once it leaves the end of the fiber. From an engineering standpoint, it is somewhat more convenient for the surgeon to use the fiberoptic handpieces of the argon and the KTP lasers versus the microspot micromanipulator of the CO_2 laser, but all three units have their advocates. For the occasional stapedotomy surgeon, it appears that the learning curve for a laser-assisted stapedotomy is easier than that for classic techniques, and, therefore, this procedure allows the occasional surgeon more consistent results.[23] No independent studies dedicated to the use of these lasers for stapedotomy in the pediatric population have been published, but many otologists have anecdotal reports of performing this procedure in older children and teenagers with good results. These lasers have also been used in middle-ear exploration work to remove granulation tissue. They have proved a valuable adjunct to chronic ear surgery by the atraumatic and hemostatic removal of granulation tissue to allow better visualization. Again, the experience in children is limited, and concerns about laser exposure to the facial nerve and to the promontory must be considered.

Various lasers have been used to perform a myringotomy. In theory, the vaporization of the tympanic membrane with cauterization of the edges should allow a myringotomy hole to be performed hemostatically and quickly. It was originally thought that laser-performed myringotomy incisions would stay open an intermediate length of time between a cold steel myringotomy and a pressure equalization tube insertion (i.e., 30 to 60 days). Results have not shown that laser-performed myringotomy incisions stay open any appreciable length of time, which has significantly limited the usefulness of this procedure.[9] Reports in the literature on the use of the laser for tympanoplasty welding have not documented its use in children. In this technique, a low-power argon, KTP, or CO_2 laser is used to thermally fuse the graft to the edges of the perforation. The reports have indicated that although this technique is successful, the overall graft success rate is not significantly different from that for conventional techniques. Therefore, it appears that there is minimal benefit to be obtained from the use of lasers for tympanomeatal flap or tympanic membrane welding.[10]

Rhinologic Applications

The rhinologic applications of lasers in the pediatric population have closely paralleled those in adults. In addition, the use of lasers for repair of choanal atresia has been investigated for many years. The limited exposure available in the pediatric nose encourages the development of less invasive techniques, for which the laser is of great potential benefit. However, especially in children, there may be significant disadvantages related to the proximity of vital structures to each other as well as to the thinness of tissue, which allows deeper optical scattering with potential harm to the orbit.

Choanal stenosis has traditionally been repaired with a transpalatal or transnasal approach. The use of small sinus endoscopy telescopes has significantly reduced the number of patients who undergo transpalatal repair. Soft tissue stenosis may be repaired straightforwardly either by elevation of mucosal flaps and removal of soft tissue or by serial dilation and placement of indwelling stents. Lasers have been used to vaporize soft tissue choanal stenosis, with significant reduction in blood loss and with no difference in success or in morbidity. The argon, KTP, and CO_2 lasers have all been used to perform vaporization of the soft tissue component of choanal stenosis. The advantage of the argon and KTP units is the fiberoptic delivery, which allows simultaneous endoscopic visualization of the operative site. The CO_2 laser, because of its need for an articulated arm delivery system on a microspot micromanipulator, requires visualization through the microscope. The advantages of high magnification are somewhat offset by the inconvenience of delivery of the CO_2 beam to the posterior aspect of the nose.[11] The success rates for repair of soft tissue stenosis by the three types of lasers are roughly equivalent. Potential difficulties arise when the choanal stenosis is of a bony nature. In these cases, none of the three lasers has been demonstrated to be beneficial in the removal of the bone. In particular, use of the CO_2 laser results in a significant amount of char and thermal spread laterally to the point of laser impact. It would appear, therefore, that the use of argon, KTP, or CO_2 laser for repair of bony stenosis has no advantages. The holmium:YAG laser at 2.1 μm, however, has shown initial benefit in these cases. The holmium:YAG laser can ablate both soft tissue and bone with a minimum of thermal char to the bone. Anecdotal reports suggest that this laser may be effective for this application, but larger prospective trials are necessary.

The argon, KTP, Nd:YAG, and CO_2 lasers have all been used for inferior turbinate reduction. The lasers are used in their coagulation or minimal vaporization mode to reduce the soft tissue hypertrophy over the inferior turbinate.[17] Care must be taken in the use of these lasers to leave islands of normal mucosa to allow remucosalization, or the development of exposed bone and bony sequestrations may result. In addition, technical care must be exercised to avoid reflectance from the tissue surface with potential coagulation of septal mucosa.

The KTP/532 laser has been extensively promoted for use in endoscopic sinus surgery. The potential advantages of hemostasis with improved visualization and decreased tissue trauma have been promoted on the basis of procedures performed in adults. There are no reported ocular injuries in adults owing to transmission of the beam through the lamina papyracea. However, in children, there are anecdotal reports of diplopia resulting from medial rectus edema, presumably owing to the optical penetration of the beam through normal lamina papyracea. Because of the relative thinness of tissue in children and the proximity of vital structures to each other, it appears that the prudent and conservative approach would be to withhold application of the laser for endoscopic sinus surgery. The holmium:YAG laser, with its relatively shallow optical penetration depth, may have some potential applications, but studies have not yet been performed in children.[27]

Oral/Oropharyngeal Applications

Within the oral cavity and oropharynx, the surgical lasers have found application for removal of tongue lesions and floor of mouth lesions, glossal reductions, and lingual tonsil and thyroid resections. The operative exposure in this region is such that any of the lasers can be used with their handpieces, including the CO_2 laser. The Nd:YAG laser in contact mode has been found to be especially useful, but all surgical lasers are beneficial because of their hemostasis and lack of muscular artifact compared with resection with an electrosurgical unit.

Tongue lesions, such as granulomas and small hemangiomas, can be removed completely. In operations on the tongue, the laser avoids the distortion the electrosurgical unit causes by contraction of the muscle. If the resection area is small, the area may be left to heal secondarily, whereas large resections may require primary closure. Vascular malformations and lymphangiomas may be photocoagulated with superficial illumination from the Nd:YAG laser because of its deep coagulative effect. Multiple treatments may be required, but hemiglossectomy or tongue resection may not be an option. The contact Nd:YAG laser has been especially useful in resection of ranulas of the floor of the mouth. Marsupialization results in an unacceptably high recurrence rate. The contact Nd:YAG laser allows resection of the cyst by allowing the surgeon to stay close to the cyst with good hemostasis and less than 1 mm of thermal coagulation lateral to the vaporization. Noncontact argon and KTP/532 laser use may result in 2 to 3 mm of thermal coagulation and, if the cyst extends deep, has the potential for lingual nerve injury. Although the CO_2 laser has been used for resections of ranulas, the tactile control of the contact Nd:YAG laser makes this procedure slightly easier technically.

All the surgical lasers can be used efficaciously for glossal reduction in Beckwith-Wiedemann or Down syndrome. Either a stellate or a keyhole pattern resection is done in the midline of the tongue. In this resection, the lasers are especially useful because they do not cause muscular artifact that would be seen with electrosurgical units and therefore allow a more precise resection pattern. Hemostasis is generally good, and the wound is closed primarily.

Incidence of chronic lingual tonsillitis is uncommon in younger children but presents with increasing frequency throughout the teens. Occasional lingual tonsil hypertrophy may result in airway obstruction and sleep apnea. Endoscopic removal of lingual tonsils may be performed with the CO_2 laser and microspot micromanipulator. With the patient on suspension, the beam is defocused, and the lingual tonsils are ablated rather than resected. This results in much better hemostasis than would incision and resection.[39] Another acceptable technique for resection of lingual tonsils is transoral resection using of the argon, KTP, or contact Nd:YAG laser with the tongue retracted far inferiorly. Exposure is usually adequate. Lingual thy-

roid has been removed when it has caused obstruction and dysphagia and is unresponsive to thyroid suppression.[16] Hemostasis is generally good with all the surgical laser systems.

Tonsillectomy

No other procedure within the field of otolaryngology has generated as much controversy as the performance of tonsillectomy using laser. All commonly used surgical lasers have been promoted at one time or another for this procedure. The argon, CO_2, KTP, and Nd:YAG lasers in both contact and noncontact modes have been used to perform tonsillectomy. Proponents have claimed decreased blood loss with better hemostasis, faster operating times, and decreased pain as beneficial effects of using laser. Each of the lasers being used is employed for its thermocoagulation properties and its simultaneous vaporization of tissue. The technique is to place the tonsil under tension and, staying carefully on the tonsil capsule, to vaporize the areolar tissue holding the tonsil to the underlying constrictor muscle. Depending on the laser used, as the perforating vessels are encountered, the laser may need to be defocused to cauterize these vessels, or, when the CO_2 laser is used, electrocautery must be employed for the larger vessels. Unfortunately, lasers have been marketed as "painless" surgery, and some patients request the use of the laser for tonsillectomy in the misguided belief that their procedure will be completely without pain.

The depth of thermocoagulation for the CO_2 laser is on the order of 200 μm. The thermocoagulation depth of the *contact* KTP and Nd:YAG lasers is slightly deeper. Only when the argon or KTP/532 laser is used in a *noncontact* mode are thermocoagulation depths on the order of 1 to 2 mm approached with consistent sealing of blood vessels and minimal bleeding. Clinical situations exist, such as von Willebrand disease and hemophilia, in which this is desirable. This deeper thermocoagulation is associated with a delayed healing time, however, because the tissue takes 7 to 10 days longer to slough than in a standard cold steel or electrosurgical tonsillectomy. The delayed eschar slough occasionally results in postoperative bleeding as late as 14 to 20 days, but the incidence of postoperative bleeding is less.

Proponents of decreased pain with laser tonsillectomy cite the sealing of nerves with resultant lack of axoplasmic leakage as the reason for reduced postoperative pain. Patients' subjective reports of pain comparing a standard tonsillectomy on one side with laser tonsillectomy on the other side have yielded inconsistent trends. Objective measurements of oral intake of patients having laser tonsillectomy compared with patients having standard treatment have not shown statistically significant differences. Many of the studies comparing the laser techniques with traditional techniques of tonsillectomy are flawed by the numbers of patients who are too small to generate statistically significant data.

The cost of the use of the laser is often passed on to the patient as an amortization cost. In addition, the use of an optical fiber is often charged to the patient as a direct cost. This results in an increase in the overall cost of the procedure to the patient, which, in the current era of negotiated global prices for procedures, must be absorbed by the hospital and cannot be passed on to the patient.

Current recommendations take into consideration the small potential benefit for increased hemostasis and decreased blood loss with the concomitant increased cost to the patient. The use of the KTP/532 or argon laser appears justified in those patients with a documented bleeding disorder, such as hemophilia or von Willebrand disease. In addition, the laser may be used for those patients in whom the surgeon wishes to avoid the potential electromagnetic interference with cardiac pacing units associated with use of electrosurgical units.[19]

Glottic and Tracheal Applications

The CO_2 laser was the first surgical laser to be used for endoscopic applications, beginning with Jako's report[12] of laryngeal surgery in 1972. Since that time, the CO_2 laser has become the most commonly used surgical laser in otolaryngology–head and neck surgery, and most CO_2 laser procedures are performed endoscopically within the larynx or trachea. The laser is uniquely beneficial in endoscopic applications because of its hemostasis, precision, and hands-off approach. Other surgical lasers have specific, although limited, applications, but newer applications are being investigated. Despite all the potential advantages of the laser for endoscopic applications, most procedures can still be performed with cold steel techniques.

The CO_2 laser has been demonstrated to be the treatment of choice for palliation for recurrent laryngeal papillomatosis.[29] The advantages of the CO_2 laser of precision, hemostasis, and minimal thermal effect have resulted in a decrease in surgical complications, such as anterior glottic webs and scarring.[22] There have been reports of the use of the KTP/532 laser for palliation of papilloma, but the depth of thermocoagulation lateral to the impact is a theoretical concern. A clinical trial is under way for photodynamic therapy for cure, and early results are encouraging, but final results are not yet available.

Excision of glottic lesions can easily be performed with the CO_2 laser. Epiglottic, glottic, and subglottic cysts may be either excised or marsupialized if they are exceedingly large. Hemorrhagic polyps may be removed avascularly.[13] Vocal nodules are rarely removed in children; when strong indications exist for their removal, they may be shave-excised with the CO_2 laser, but conventional cold steel techniques are probably more appropriate and result in less scarring.

The microtrapdoor flap to preserve overlying mucosa is useful in the treatment of anterior and posterior glottic webs as well as of subglottic stenosis. With this technique, the laser is used to make an incision in the scar, and dissection raises a mucosal flap. The laser is then used to vaporize the substance of the scar tissue, and the flap is replaced to give immediate coverage and prevent reformation of scar. This has been successfully used in treatment of anterior and posterior glottic webs as a one-stage procedure and in a serial fashion for sequential repair of subglottic stenosis of Cotton grades I and II.[2, 38]

Subglottic hemangiomas present a difficult challenge. Many of these hemangiomas are capillary hemangiomas; therefore, the thermal coagulation afforded by the CO_2 laser is adequate. The depth of the hemangioma is sometimes difficult to determine, and it may extend through the cricothyroid membrane or may have destroyed some of the cartilaginous support of the cricoid. Sequential excision with the CO_2 laser is the conservative approach to spare lateral tissue, but vessels with significant vascular engorgement may be beneficially treated with the KTP/532 or argon laser. The 3- to 4-mm thermocoagulation depth from the Nd:YAG laser may cause unwanted damage to the underlying cricoid cartilage.

Excision of suprastomal granulation tissue after tracheotomy can be performed with the CO_2 laser under direct vision and relatively avascularly. Excision of granuloma is usually not performed until the patient is ready to be decannulated because the routine excision of granulomas does not prevent their recurrence owing to the indwelling tracheotomy tube's causing reformation. Excision of granuloma can be performed with the subglottoscope or the ventilating CO_2 laser bronchoscope.[37]

Tracheal applications of surgical lasers are infrequently done but can be performed safely with the CO_2, argon, and KTP/532 lasers. Obstructing endotracheal or endobronchial tumors may be ablated with surgical laser. When lesions are especially vascular, the KTP laser with a small fiber may be useful for vaporization with coagulation lateral to the impact point. For greatest thermal precision, the CO_2 laser is the laser of choice. Excision of scar tissue and granulation tissue is best performed with the CO_2 laser ventilating bronchoscope.[21] One difficulty with the use of this instrument is that the smallest size requires the trachea to be large enough to admit a 7-mm diameter bronchoscope. Infants in whom this size of bronchoscope cannot be inserted must be treated with a surgical laser using fiberoptic delivery, such as the KTP/532 or argon laser. In these cases, fiberoptic delivery can be achieved through the side channel on the ventilating bronchoscope.

Cutaneous Applications

Hemangiomas and vascular malformations are common in children. The clinical distinction between these two entities is related to the rate of growth. Vascular malformations grow proportionately with the child. Many common hemangiomas demonstrate spontaneous involution in early childhood.

Early results with ruby and argon lasers in children (especially those younger than 12 years) were disappointing. Textural irregularities, scarring, and hyper- and hypopigmentation were potential complications. In theory, they were due to nonspecific absorption by melanin and proteins in the dermis.[3] To overcome these problems, the flashlamp-excited dye laser was developed with a peak operating wavelength of 585 nm and a 400-μsec pulse duration to allow a compromise between coagulation and thermal diffusion.

Bandage Scissors

Bandage scissors, preferably with a blunt end, are needed to cut the tracheostomy tape.

Humidifier

A mist humidifier should be kept in the child's room, and adequate humidity should be maintained. The humidifier should be cleaned periodically. Humidification for the entire house should be provided if feasible. Proper humidification can decrease the tendency for other members of the family to have upper respiratory tract infections and provides a more healthful atmosphere for the child.

Devices to improve humidification to the tracheostomy tube, such as an artificial nose, are also available. These adapters attach to the standard 15 mm tracheostomy connector and provide excellent humidification, especially when the child is mobile.

Syringes

Syringes or droppers are used to drop saline into the tracheostomy tube to liquefy secretions. The size of syringe depends on the age of the child.

Normal Salt Solution

A normal saline solution can be purchased or made by mixing 2 teaspoons of noniodized salt in 1 quart of boiled water.

Intercom

A portable intercom system can be purchased from an electronics store. This item permits the attendant to detect from a remote location if the child is in distress. Because the child is unable to cry with a tracheotomy, small bells may be attached to the bed or to the infant's shoes to make noise when the infant becomes distressed.

Monitors

Apnea monitors are of limited use in detecting obstruction. An obstructed child will likely demonstrate increased chest movement and tachycardia, and the monitor is likely to detect poor chest movement only when the child nearly reaches asphyxiation. Cardiac monitoring is helpful in detecting a child in distress; however, the child may be severely hypoxic by the time the alarm sounds. Pulse oximetry is the best airway monitor, although it is twice as costly to rent as an apnea monitor. While there are a frequent number of false-positive alarms, pulse oximetry gives the quickest indication of hypoxia due to an airway accident.

Nursing Technique

Irrigation

The intervals for irrigation depend on the child's needs. These are often related to the age of the child and the length of time the tracheotomy is in place. The intervals usually lengthen as the child grows older and a more efficient cough reflex develops. Usually, when the child first goes home, the hospital routine of irrigation every 3 or 4 hours is followed, but the child may rapidly adapt to the family routine and sleep through the night.

Suction Technique

Whenever possible, the child should be encouraged to cough and clear accumulated mucus. However, when suctioning is necessary, the catheter should be inserted just past the end of the tracheostomy tube. The catheter is usually occluded so that suction is not applied as it is inserted; it is then withdrawn slowly with a rotating motion, using suction to clear the airway. The catheter should be rinsed in saline solution after each aspiration. The duration of suctioning should not be more than 30 seconds; the child may become hypoxic if suctioning is prolonged.

Percussion

When the child first goes home, chest physiotherapy is usually continued on the same routine as in the hospital. After a child develops a strong cough reflex, however, percussion is usually necessary less frequently or not at all.

Changing the Tube

Because the tracheostomy tube is a foreign body, it can be a source of chronic infection and plugging. For this reason, the tube should be replaced or cleaned regularly. This is probably the most traumatic problem of the home program. At least two adults must be present when the tube is changed, especially when the child first goes home and when the child becomes stronger and resists the tube change. Parents can expect the child to become tense and cough or cry as a normal protest. The occasional child, however, is cooperative and may assist in the tracheostomy tube change. The frequency of changing the tube depends on the child's age, the amount of secretions, and the type of tube used. With most of the newer silicone rubber tubes, weekly changes are sufficient. The parents should not be led to understand that a weekly change is a universally adopted time schedule, however. The parent should discover the best time to change the tube. Generally, it is advisable to avoid changing the tube at meal time. Occasionally, the child can be awakened from a deep sleep and the tube can be changed before the child fully awakens.

To change the tube, one parent should position the child so that the neck can be seen clearly. Good lighting is essential. The child can be wrapped in a towel or sheet to restrain the arms and legs, and the shoulders should be elevated to hyperextend the neck. All the equipment necessary for the tube change as well as emergency equipment should be available. The attendant removes the tube by cutting the tape holding the tube and allowing the child to cough it out, or it may be removed by the attendant. The new tube is quickly inserted. A smaller tube should be readily available in case the tube of the same size as that which was removed cannot be reinserted. An emergency small and longer tube, such as an endotracheal tube, should be available to establish an airway if the tracheostomy tube cannot be inserted. In children who resist the tube change by tightening their neck muscles, it may be necessary to use a length of catheter as a guide for insertion of the tube; a 12 to 15 cm length of catheter is inserted into the stoma, which usually causes the child to cough, thus relaxing the neck muscles. The tracheostomy tube can then be threaded over this catheter, and the catheter guide can be removed.

Skin Care

The area where a tracheotomy has been established usually forms an epithelial-lined tract, and minimal skin care is necessary. However, areas of irritation may develop beneath the tube. These can usually be cleaned with cotton balls and hydrogen peroxide. Occasionally, antibiotic ointment is desirable, and, if granulation tissue develops around the tube, antibiotic ointment with steroids is useful. Granulation tissue can also be removed with chemical cautery, such as silver nitrate. The care of the tube depends on the material from which it is constructed; however, as soon as the tube is removed, it is usually wise to clean it with pipe cleaners and to soak it in germicide solution, or, if the tube is metal, to boil it for 5 minutes.

Adjustment to Tracheotomy

The physicians must help the parents accept the tracheotomy and responsibilities for its care. The initial appearance of a child who has just undergone a tracheotomy may be a shock to the parents. Their fear is eased through adequate explanations, which many times must be repeated and reinforced. The child's loss of voice strength can cause extreme emotional distress, and the parents must be reassured that it is not permanent. When the child goes home, it is important to emphasize that care of the child should be shared by all members of the family and that a certain amount of emotional stress is inevitable for a task that requires constant attention.

It is important to emphasize to the family that relatives and friends may not understand the operation and that they may ask questions that seem indiscreet. Usually, the adjustment occurs rapidly and satisfactorily. It is important that the child should attempt to live as normal a life as possible. There should be little restriction on active play, although the child should be watched around sandboxes and swimming pools.

Helpful Hints

The child should not be permitted to submerge in the bathtub, and, during hair washing, water must be kept from the tracheotomy. Spray attachments for the faucet are valuable for rinsing the hair.

Clothing

Turtleneck sweaters and blouses may not be advisable, but thin scarves or loosely knit bibs may be of value, especially on windy days, to prevent particles from entering the trachea.

Feeding

Feeding by breast, bottle, or spoon in usually perceived as a problem. However, even with mild aspiration, most children aliment themselves quite well. However, when children begin to feed themselves, a small bib over the neck may keep food from falling into the tracheostomy tube.

Sleeping

If possible, the parents should maintain their normal sleeping arrangements and should install a portable intercom between the child's room and their own. Bells attached to the child's bed or to the child's limbs usually alert the parents to the child's distress, because a child in respiratory distress thrashes around. The monitor alarms should also be audible in the parents' room.

Traveling

It is possible to carry an aspirator or a hand suction unit when traveling. Usually, the aspirator can be connected to an electrical outlet in service stations, toll booths on expressways, or other business establishments. Battery units are also available. For traveling on airplanes, permission forms from physicians may be required, and permission from the airline may be necessary.

Schooling

Children with tracheotomies may attend public schools, but each situation should be considered individually. Parents may need a letter from the physician stating that the child may attend school. Someone should be in attendance in the school who is trained to care for a tracheostomy tube if it becomes plugged or displaced.

Entertainment

A third person should be trained to care for the child so the parents can leave home for recreational purposes. The physician should encourage the family to entertain and seek entertainment as they normally would. As the child adapts to the tracheotomy, the care of the tracheotomy becomes more routine, and it is usually possible for parents to assume a more normal lifestyle.

Detection of Complications

Complications of tracheotomy can be seen by changes in the color and consistency of the mucus. Unusual sounds may herald airway obstruction, with coughing or wheezing if there is a foreign body in the tracheobronchial tree. Unusual odors may arise from the wound site if the tube needs to be changed, and irritation around the skin, with development of granuloma or bleeding, may be due to irritation from the tracheostomy tube or superficial skin infections.

Emergency Procedures

Preparation for emergencies should be made before the child is discharged from the hospital. The community police department, fire department, or ambulance or rescue squad should be contacted to ascertain the best source of equipment and personnel in case there is a respiratory emergency. Telephone numbers for the best sources of this equipment should be posted in plain view near the home telephone. The names of physicians who are familiar with the child should be available to the parents; these telephone numbers should be posted in several places throughout the house. If the child lives a distance from the hospital, several local physicians should know about the child so that they can respond in an emergency. Spare keys to the family's car should be located near the door. The parents should be taught mouth-to-mouth resuscitation as well as be provided with a large catheter or endotracheal tube that can be inserted into the stoma for resuscitation.

Emergency suction equipment should be available for electrical failures. It is also advisable to notify the local electric company that the residents should be on a priority panel in case of power failure. Parents should know where emergency power is available; in many communities, the fire department has a mobile generator that is adaptable to house current.

Checklist for Home Care

The steps for arranging for home care are to (1) instruct parents in tracheostomy techniques; (2) notify referring physicians and other agencies that the patient is to be discharged; (3) arrange home care service contacts, such as a visiting nurse, and have agencies evaluate the home for its suitability as an aftercare setting for the child; (4) assemble appropriate equipment; (5) have parents provide tracheostomy care within the hospital setting; (6) evaluate and arrange for emergency care; and (7) arrange for appropriate follow-up care after discharge.

SELECTED REFERENCES

Yellen R. Technique and complications of tracheotomy in the pediatric age group. In Myers EN, Johnson JT, Murray T (eds). Tracheotomy: Airway Management, Communication, and Swallowing. San Diego, Singular, 1998.
This is a comprehensive text of all aspects of tracheotomy.
Bleile KM (ed). The care of children with longterm tracheostomies. San Diego, Singular, 1993.
This excellent text encompasses all aspects of care for the child with a long-term tracheotomy.

Wetmore RF, Marsh RR, Thompson ME, Tom LWC. Pediatric tracheostomy: a changing procedure? Ann Otol Rhinol Laryngol 108: 695, 1999.
This is a significant series of more than two decades' experience from a large children's hospital.

REFERENCES

1. Altman KW, Wetmore RF, Marsh RR. Congenital airway abnormalities requiring tracheotomy: a profile of 56 patients and their diagnoses over a 9 year period. Int J Pediatr Otorhinolaryngol 41:199, 1997.
2. Arcand P, Granger J. Pediatric tracheostomies: changing trends. J Otolaryngol 17:2, 1988.
3. Attia RR, Battit GE, Murphy JD. Transtracheal ventilation. JAMA 234:1152, 1975.
4. Benjamin B, Curley JWA. Infant tracheotomy—endoscopy and decannulation. Int J Pediatr Otorhinolaryngol 20:113, 1990.
5. Bonanno PC. Swallowing dysfunction after tracheostomy. Ann Surg 174:29, 1971.
6. Cameron JL, Reynolds J, Zuidema GD. Aspiration in patients with tracheostomies. Surg Gynecol Obstet 136:68, 1973.
7. Carron JD, Derkay CS, Strope GL, et al. Pediatric tracheotomies: changing indications and outcomes. Laryngoscope 110:1099, 2000.
8. Cohen SR, Eavey RD, Desomond MS, et al. Endoscopy and tracheotomy in the neonatal period. Ann Otol Rhinol Laryngol 86:577, 1977.
9. Cote C, Eavey R, Jones RD, Todres ID. Cricothyroid membrane puncture: oxygenation and ventilation in a dog model using an intravenous catheter. Crit Care Med 16:615, 1988.
10. Cote CJ, Ryan JF, Todres ID, Goudsouzian NG. A Practice of Anesthesia for Infants and Children, 2nd ed. Philadelphia, WB Saunders, 1992.
11. Crysdale WS, Feldman RI, Naito K. Tracheotomies: a 10-year experience in 319 children. Ann Otol Rhinol Laryngol 97:439, 1988.
12. Crysdale WS, Forte V. Posterior tracheal wall disruption: a rare complication of pediatric tracheotomy and bronchoscopy. Laryngoscope 96:1279, 1986.
13. Davies IJ, Belam OH. Minitracheostomy. Practitioner 199:76, 1967.
14. Deutsch ES. Early tracheostomy tube change in children. Arch Otolaryngol Head Neck Surg 124:1237, 1998.
15. DeVito MA, Wetmore RF, Pransky SM. Laryngeal diversion in the treatment of chronic aspiration in children. Int J Pediatr Otorhinolaryngol 18:139, 1989.
16. Diamant H, Kinnman J, Okiman L. Decannulation in children. Laryngoscope 71:404, 1961.
17. Dorland's Illustrated Medical Dictionary, 27th ed. Philadelphia, WB Saunders, 1988.
18. Downes JJ, Schreiner MS. Tracheostomy tubes and attachments in infants and children. Int Anesthesiol Clin 23:4, 1985.
19. Eckhauser FE, Billtoe J, Burke JF, et al. Tracheostomy complicating massive burn injury: a plea for conservatism. Am J Surg 127: 418, 1974.
20. Forbes GB, Salmon G, Herweg JC. Further observations on posttracheotomy, mediastinal emphysema and pneumothorax. Pediatrics 31:172, 1947.
21. Friedberg J. Tracheotomy revision in infants: to facilitate extubation and restore phonation. Int J Pediatr Otorhinolaryngol 13:61, 1987.
22. Galloway TC. Tracheotomy in bulbar poliomyelitis. JAMA 123:1096, 1943.
23. Gluth MB, Maska S, Nelson J, Otto RA. Postoperative management of pediatric tracheostomy: results of a nationwide survey. Otolaryngol Head Neck Surg 122:701–705, 2000
24. Goldberg JD, Mitchell N, Angrist A. Mediastinal emphysema and pneumothorax following tracheotomy for croup. Am J Surg 56:448, 1942.
25. Goodall EW. The story of tracheotomy. Br J Child Dis 31:167, 1934.
26. Gray RF, Todd NW, Jacobs IN. Tracheostomy decannulation in children: approaches and techniques. Laryngoscope 108:8–12, 1998.
27. Greene NM. Fatal cardiovascular and respiratory failure associated with tracheotomy. N Engl J Med 261:846, 1959.

28. Greenway RE. Tracheostomy: surgical problems and complications. Int Anesthesiol Clin 10:151, 1972.
29. Griggs WM, Worthley LIG, Gilligan JE, et al. A simple percutaneous tracheostomy technique. Surg Gynecol Obstet 170:543, 1990.
30. Handler SD. The difficult decannulation. In Gates G (ed). Current Therapy in Otolaryngology—Head and Neck Surgery. Philadelphia, BC Decker, 1986.
31. Hawkins DB, Williams EH. Tracheostomy in infants and young children. Laryngoscope 86:331, 1976.
32. Holinger PH, Brown WT, Maurizi DG. Tracheostomy in the newborn. Am J Surg 109:771, 1965.
33. Hughes RK, Davenport C, Williamson H. Needle tracheostomy: further evaluation. Arch Surg 95:295, 1967.
34. Jackson C. High tracheotomy and other errors: the chief causes of chronic laryngeal stenosis. Surg Gynecol Obstet 32:392, 1921.
35. Jacobs HB. Emergency percutaneous transtracheal catheter and ventilator. J Trauma 12:50, 1972.
36. Jacoby JJ, Hamelberg W, Ziegler CH, et al. Transtracheal resuscitation. JAMA 162:625, 1956.
37. Johnson JT. Antibiotics in tracheostomy. In Myers EN, Stool SE, Johnson JT (eds). Tracheotomy. New York, Churchill Livingstone, 1985.
38. Kaler J, Kaler H. Michael had a tracheostomy. Am J Nurs 74:852, 1974.
39. Kanter RK, Watchko JF. Pulmonary edema associated with upper airway obstruction. Am J Dis Child 138:356, 1984.
40. Kessler A, Wetmore RF, Marsh RR. Childhood epiglottitis in recent years. Int J Pediatr Otorhinolaryngol 25:155, 1993.
41. Line WS, Hawkins DB, Kohlstrom EJ, et al. Tracheotomy in infants and young children: the changing perspective 1970–1985. Laryngoscope 96:510, 1986.
42. Lusk RP, Gray S, Muntz HR. Singlestage laryngotracheal reconstruction. Arch Otolaryngol Head Neck Surg 117:171, 1991.
43. MacLachlan RF. Decannulation in infancy. J Laryngol Otol 83:991, 1969.
44. Mallory GB, Reilly JS, Motoyama EK, et al. Tidal flow measurement in the decision to decannulate the pediatric patient. Ann Otol Rhinol Laryngol 94:454, 1985.
45. Mathog RH, Kenan PD, Hudson WR. Delayed massive hemorrhage following tracheostomy. Laryngoscope 81:107, 1971.
46. McGill J, Clinton JE, Ruiz E. Cricothyrotomy in the emergency department. Ann Emerg Med 11:361, 1982.
47. Merritt RM, Bent JP, Smith RJH. Suprastomal granulation tissue and pediatric tracheotomy decannulation. Laryngoscope 107:868–871, 1997.
48. Myers EN, Stool SE, Johnson JT. Technique of tracheotomy. In Myers EN, Stool SE, Johnson JT (eds). Tracheotomy. New York, Churchill Livingstone, 1985.
49. Oppenheimer P. Needle tracheotomy. Otorhinolaryngol Digest 39:9, 1977.
50. Park JY, Suskind DL, Prater D, et al. Maturation of the pediatric tracheostomy stoma: effect on complications. Ann Otol Rhinol Laryngol 108:1115, 1999.
51. Potondi A. Pathomechanism of hemorrhages following tracheotomy. J Laryngol Otol 83:475, 1969.
52. Rabuzzi D, Reed GF. Intrathoracic complications following tracheotomy in children. Laryngoscope 81:939, 1971.
53. Reilly JS, Myer CM. "How I do it": excision of suprastomal granulation tissue. Laryngoscope 95:1545, 1985.
54. Rogers LA, Osterhout S. Pneumonia following tracheostomy. Am Surg 36:39, 1970.
55. Rosnagle RS, Yanagisawa E. Aerophagia: an unrecognized complication of tracheotomy. Arch Otolaryngol 89:537, 1969.
56. Ruben RJ, Newton L, Chambers H, et al. Home care of the pediatric patient with a tracheotomy. Ann Otol Rhinol Laryngol 91:633, 1982.
57. Sasaki CT, Gaudet PT, Peerless A. Tracheostomy decannulation. Am J Dis Child 132:266, 1978.
58. Sasaki CT, Suzuki M, Horiuchi M, et al. The effect of tracheostomy on the laryngeal closure reflex. Laryngoscope 87:1428, 1977.
59. Schachner A, Ovil Y, Sidi J, et al. Percutaneous tracheotomy: a new method. Crit Care Med 17:1052, 1989.
60. Schild JA. Tracheostomy care. Int Anesthesiol Clin 8:649, 1970.
61. Schreiner MS, Downes JJ, Kettrick RG. Chronic respiratory failure in infants with prolonged ventilatory dependency. JAMA 258:3398, 1987.
62. Simon BM, Fowler SM, Handler SD. Communication development in young children with long term tracheostomies: preliminary report. Int J Pediatr Otorhinolaryngol 6:37, 1983.
63. Stool SE, Beebe JK. Tracheotomy in infants and children. Curr Probl Pediatr 3:3, 1973.
64. Stool SE, Tucker J. Larynx, trachea and endoscopy. In Brenneman's Practice of Pediatrics. Hagerstown, MD, Harper & Row, 1972.
65. Sullivan MJ, Horn DB, Passamani PP, et al. An unusual complication of tracheostomy. Arch Otolaryngol Head Neck Surg 113:198, 1987.
66. Tom LWC, Miller L, Wetmore RF, et al. Endoscopic assessment in children with tracheotomies. Arch Otolaryngol Head Neck Surg 119:321, 1993.
67. Tunkel DE, McColley SA, Baroody FM, et al. Polysomnography in the evaluation of readiness for decannulation in children. Arch Otolaryngol Head Neck Surg 122:721–724, 1996.
68. Wetmore RF, Handler SD. Epiglottitis: evolution in management during the last decade. Ann Otol Rhinol Laryngol 88:822, 1979.
69. Wetmore RF, Handler SD, Potsic WP. Pediatric tracheostomy: experience during the past decade. Ann Otol Rhinol Laryngol 91:628, 1982.
70. Wetmore RF, Marsh RR, Thompson ME, Tom LWC. Pediatric tracheostomy: a changing procedure. Ann Otol Rhinol Laryngol 108:695, 1999.
71. Willis R, Myer C, Miller R, Cotton RT. Tracheotomy decannulation in the pediatric patient. Laryngoscope 97:764, 1987.
72. Wind J. Reflections on difficult decannulation. Arch Otolaryngol 94:426, 1971.

94

Intensive Care Management of Infection-Related Acute Upper Airway Obstruction in Children

Joseph Carcillo, M.D.

Acute airway obstruction secondary to infection remains a life-threatening but reversible event in children. The otolaryngologist/anesthesiologist/intensivist team is needed for these children to survive their otherwise lethal condition. The epidemiology of this condition is ever-changing. Although the development of more effective bacterial immunization technology has reduced the incidence of epiglottitis, the concomitant development of immunosuppressant therapies and strategies in diseases of childhood has increased the incidence of opportunistic infection–related acute upper airway obstruction.

Anatomy is the reason why airway obstruction is a relatively common, though reversible, cause of death in children as compared with adults. The smallest diameter of the airway is the size of one's little finger. Babies have little fingers and airways of very small diameter. Poiseuille's law dictates that the surface area of a circle is related to the cube of the radius. No matter how small the reduction in radius from edema, it results in the cube of that reduction in airway size. The narrowest part of the airway in children is in the subglottic region; hence, this is the most common site of acute airway obstruction in children with laryngotracheitis. Children have other important anatomic considerations: The adenoids, tonsils, and epiglottis are all relatively large compared with the nasopharyngeal and supraglottic airways in children. Although it is very rare for adenotonsillar hypertrophy or supraglottitis to result in life-threatening airway obstruction in adults, it is a relatively common occurrence in children.

Remember! In children with acute, life-threatening disease, it is usually the airway and breathing, not the circulation, that is the primary problem. Kids are different from adults!

The Immunocompetent Child

Nasopharyngeal Obstruction from Adenotonsillitis

The most common cause of acute nasopharyngeal obstruction in children is infection-related adenotonsillar hypertrophy. The most common cause is Epstein-Barr virus. Children usually have a history of a viral prodrome. They present with Epstein-Barr virus and, frequently, secondary infection with group A streptococci. They have difficulty breathing, particularly when supine, but have improved air movement when sitting forward.

Positioning in the sitting or prone position is often helpful. In some cases, mild jaw thrust or chin lift may be necessary as well. Helium-oxygen mixtures can be delivered by face mask to decrease air flow turbulence and obstruction. The maximum effect on reducing gas viscosity occurs with more than 70% helium mixture; there is little effect with less than 60% helium mixture. Advanced airway management can usually be secured with a nasopharyngeal airway. The airway length should be chosen to bypass adenotonsillar obstruction while minimizing the gag reflex. The airway should be suctioned as needed. Patency can be assessed by holding a mirror or metal surface at the external opening of the airway. Condensation with exhalation implies air movement. On occasion, the nasopharyngeal airway is not adequate, and endotracheal or nasotracheal intubation is required.

Medical management is not well studied, but case series suggest that intravenous steroids and penicillin are the treatments of choice. The disease process usually improves in 24 to 48 hours, likely because the disease is usually caused by a viral infection and a secondary bacterial superinfection.

Airway Obstruction from Supraglottitis

Acute epiglottitis was once a scourge of childhood. Bacterial infection, usually caused by *Haemophilus influenzae*, resulted in progressive inflammation of the supraglottis and glottis, which caused acute airway obstruction and death. One of the great achievements of 20th century medicine was the determination that tracheostomy could cure this dread disease. It is not surprising that many were reluctant to forgo tracheotomy for nasotracheal intubation. Thus, controversy existed throughout the 1970s and into the 1980s on whether one should perform a tracheostomy or a nasotracheal intubation in the child with life-threatening epiglottitis. In the 1980s, the conjugated *H. influenzae* vaccine was developed. Before the use of this vaccine, *H. influenzae* was the leading cause of bacterial sepsis, meningitis, and epiglottitis. *H. influenzae* epiglottitis was more common than meningitis during this time! Since use of the vaccine began, the incidence of *H. influenzae* in immunized children has all but disappeared.

Children with epiglottitis may have fever, drooling, dysphagia, and dyspnea with chest wall retractions. The lateral neck film shows a classic "thumb" sign owing to loss of the aryepiglottic folds from soft tissue swelling. Suspicion of epiglottitis should be handled with a team-oriented approach that includes anesthesiologist and otolaryngologist. The child should be taken to the operating room, and induction should be maintained with mask inhalational anesthetic so that nasotracheal intubation can be performed during spontaneous ventilation. The native airway is often completely obscured, and only air bubbles emitted during exhalation direct proper placement of the endotracheal tube. Nasotracheal tube size should be chosen on the basis of nares size and age considerations. On rare but frightening occasions, the airway cannot be visualized, and emergency tracheotomy is required. Although controversy once existed, it is generally agreed that nasotracheal intubation is the treatment of choice, with tracheotomy reserved only for intubation failures.

Once intubated, the child can be returned to the pediatric intensive care unit (PICU) with spontaneous respiration and minimal sedation if the airway is tolerated, or with mechanical ventilation, maximal sedation, and perhaps even neuromuscular blockade if the airway is not tolerated. The majority of these children have *H. influenzae* infection, with lesser numbers having *Streptococcus pneumoniae* or *Staphylococcus aureus*. From the 1970s to the 1980s, ampicillin was the antibiotic of choice, but emerging *H. influenzae* ampicillin resistance has led to the use of cephalosporins (e.g., cefuroxime). Cultures can be obtained at the time of tube placement from the airway and blood.

The length of intubation for epiglottitis is relatively short, with most children able to be safely extubated within 12 to 48 hours of intubation. There is no documented need for steroids for successful extubation in this population. Several techniques have been used to ensure success; some use a leak test (20 cm H_2O airway pressure), others use laryngoscopy to ensure resolution of swelling, and still others recommend use of x-ray findings to guide extubation. There have been no head-to-head studies of these techniques. There does not appear to be any need for follow-up examination of the airway after successful extubation and patient discharge from the hospital (Table 94–1).

Airway Obstruction from Laryngotracheobronchitis

Acute airway obstruction from viral laryngotracheobronchitis, or croup, is the most common form of acute air-

TABLE 94–1. Review of Acute Epiglottitis Literature

Study	Airway	Airway Type (Mean Duration of Intubation)	Mortality/Other Outcomes
Alho et al, 1999	40/46		0/46
Damm et al, 1996	24		3/24 (prehospital arrests)
Berg et al, 1996	72% of 306 0–19 y: 3.2/100,000; 0–4 y: 14.7/100,000		5/306
Henry et al, 1994	40/44	40 nasotracheal (22 h)	0/44
Andreassen et al, 1992	111 3.2/100,000		2/111
Emmerson et al, 1991	174/234		2.1% pulmonary edema, 2/234 died
Arndal et al, 1988	74% of 92	92% intubated, 8% tracheotomy	
Crockett et al, 1988	80	100% nasotracheal	
Butt et al, 1988	87% of 349	83% spontaneous, 1% mechanical ventilation	
Sendi et al, 1987	242	Tracheotomy common before 1976; after 1976, 85% nasotracheal	5/242 deaths and 4/242 neurologic sequelae, all before airway
Gonzalez et al, 1986	100	100% nasotracheal (48 h)	
Gerber et al, 1986	137	100% nasotracheal (28 h)	1.9% mortality (preairway arrest); 1 polyp, 1 chronic hoarseness
Vernon et al, 1986	78	100% nasotracheal	0% in ED, but 20% (preairway) mortality in transferred patients
DiTirro et al, 1994	148	Before 1975 tracheotomy, after 1975 nasotracheal	
Rundcrantz, 1983	86	3 tracheotomy, 83 nasotracheal	0%
Kinnefors, 1983	102	79 tracheotomy, 23 nasotracheal (2.3 vs. 2.9 d)	
Andreasson et al, 1981	70/141	100% nasotracheal (41 h)	
Diaz et al, 1981	104	100% nasotracheal	
Schulz et al, 1982	16/26	100% nasotracheal (15/16 extubated at 48 h)	0%
Bottenfeld et al, 1980	90	100% nasotracheal	
Schloss et al, 1980	204	Promotes nasotracheal vs. tracheotomy	9%
Faden et al, 1979	47/48	100% nasotracheal (3.3 d)	
Greenberg et al, 1979	21	100% nasotracheal	
Hans et al, 1978	33	100% tracheotomy	

ED, emergency department.

way obstruction in childhood. It is a beguiling condition because it is common and is usually remedied by conservative management, but on occasion it is deadly. Most children present with a viral prodrome and a low-grade temperature. The notable exception is spasmodic croup, which is a condition that occurs in an otherwise healthy child. Pediatricians usually advise parents to hold the child next to a running shower to provide mist. Although there are no available studies showing that this treatment is effective (not even studies proposing why it might work), it remains the most common form of treatment. In children who fail mist therapy, other approaches are implemented. Some, but not all, clinicians use a Croup Score to direct therapy and proper patient placement for care. The general approach is to treat the patient who has retractions and or cyanosis and to observe the patient who does not.

Racemic epinephrine remains a mainstay of therapy. Inhaled epinephrine is thought to stimulate the alpha$_1$-receptor and cause vasoconstriction of tissue beds, leading to decreased swelling. There is an evident "rebound" phenomenon associated with the elimination phase of epinephrine from the tissue. Apparently, reperfusion occurs into a relatively dilated vascular bed when the high-dose alpha$_1$-agonist effect resolves. The use of racemic epinephrine should be treated with respect, not only because of its rebound effect, but also because it can mislead the practitioner. Even a child with life-threatening airway edema may respond well enough to racemic epinephrine that he or she appears well to the inexperienced practitioner. When the drug effect diminishes, however, the life-threatening edema recurs, leaving the child in dire condition. Practitioners who use racemic epinephrine should not allow the child to be outside close medical observation until several hours have passed.

For many years, controversy surrounded the use of inhaled, enteral, or systemic steroids in children with croup. The "pro" argument suggested that virus-mediated edema was inflammation induced and would therefore respond to an anti-inflammatory steroid. The "con" argument stated that steroid use would prolong infection and swelling by preventing the immune system from killing the virus. The con argument also suggested that steroids could cause gastrointestinal bleeding and hypertension. The use of steroids is the best-studied issue in management of children with infection-related acute upper airway obstruction. The consensus of the literature is that inhaled budesonide, or systemic dexamethasone or prednisolone, reduces the need for racemic epinephrine and the need for intubation in children with croup. Most practitioners now treat children with croup with inhaled or systemic steroids; however, their use can be associated with gastric bleeding and hypertension.

Helium-oxygen mixtures also have a role in children with croup. They can reduce work of breathing by reducing gas viscosity and improving air flow. Younger children, however, may not tolerate face mask administration.

When children have retractions, cyanosis, or ongoing increased work of breathing, the decision to rescue the airway is necessary. It is again ideal to intubate with inhaled anesthetic induction so that spontaneous respirations are maintained, but it is also acceptable to intubate

in a controlled setting after using sedation and rapid sequence technique with neuromuscular blockade if the airway is thought to be easily visualized. Unlike the supraglottitis airway, which is obscured, the croup airway is usually easily visualized because edema and obstruction occur below the vocal cords. It is paramount that the otolaryngologist be present, capable, and ready to perform an emergency tracheotomy if intubation is not successful. Choosing an endotracheal tube size is difficult because the narrow airway will likely not allow intubation with an age-appropriate size. I suggest having several endotracheal tubes available below the age-appropriate size. It is likely prudent to use uncuffed tubes.

Once intubated, the child should be brought to the PICU with spontaneous respirations and minimal sedation if she or he is tolerating the tube, or ventilated with increased sedation and perhaps even neuromuscular blockade if she or he is not tolerating the tube. The length of intubation required with intubated croup is longer than that with epiglottitis. The literature suggests that the use of steroids reduces both the length of intubation and the need for reintubation in children with viral laryngotracheobronchitis.

Several studies suggest a higher incidence of airway abnormalities, particularly subglottic stenosis, in children with viral croup who require intubation. Therefore, it is recommended by more than one author that laryngoscopy and bronchoscopy be considered on extubation of these children (Table 94–2).

Airway Obstruction from Bacterial Tracheitis: A Deadly Disease

Studies suggest that the majority of patients with laryngotracheitis who require intubation and do not have an underlying airway abnormality (subglottic stenosis) are suffering from bacterial tracheitis. The most common bacteria are *S. aureus* and *S. pneumoniae*. Many of these patients also have positive airway virus cultures. This has led to the suggestion that the children have viral laryngotracheobronchitis that is secondarily superinfected with bacteria. Children with bacterial tracheitis uniformly require intubation.

The insidious character of this disease is disturbing. My most recent encounter with this disease was unfortunate. Two parents observed their child at home with croup and misinterpreted slowing of what had been rapid breathing as a sign of improvement. The child soon died of airway obstruction. Examination of his airway revealed purulent secretions and *S. aureus*. This too-common experience has fueled the controversy about use of antibiotics in children with fever and croup. Although the conjugate vaccine for *H. influenzae* and the new vaccine for *S. pneumoniae* have reduced and will continue to reduce the incidence of acute bacterial epiglottitis, the incidence of *S. aureus*-induced bacterial tracheitis will remain unchanged.

Children with bacterial tracheitis almost always require intubation, particularly when they are not treated with antibiotics. This disease should be considered in any child with fever and croup that have required the use of race-

TABLE 94–2. Review of Viral Laryngotracheobronchitis (Croup) Literature

Study	Therapy	Airway Type (Mean Duration of Intubation)	Outcome
Durward et al, 1998	Budesonide inhaled	34 croup (5 d) 10 subglottic stenosis (7 d)	Budesonide reduced need for intubation
Sumboonnanonda et al, 1997	RCT: 14 dexamethasone 0.5 mg/kg/d × 3 d, 18 placebo		Lower incidence of intubation with dexamethasone
Anene et al, 1996	RCT: 66 dexamethasone 0.5 mg/kg q 6 h IV vs. saline 6–12 h before extubation	Endotracheal intubation	Fewer required racemic epinephrine (4/31 vs. 22/32) or reintubation (0/31) vs. 7/32) 1 GI bleed, 1 hypertension
Fitzgerald et al, 1996	RCT: 35 budesonide, 31 racemic epinephrine	Endotracheal intubation	Improvement in both groups in need for reintubation
Tibbals et al, 1993	RCT: prednisolone (38) 1 mg/kg q 12 h or placebo (32) png	Endotracheal intubation Prednisolone (98 h) Placebo (138 h) ($p < .05$)	34% placebo vs. 5% prednisolone required Reintubation ($p < .05$)
Sendi et al, 1992	377/1727 (22%) admitted from ED 120/1727 (22%) received racemic epinephrine 17/1727 received steroids	12/1727 (0.7%) endotracheal intubation	0% mortality
Dawson et al, 1991	44/894 (4.9%) admitted to ICU	12/894 (1.3%) intubated (170 h)	0% mortality, 1 gastric ulceration, questions need for steroids on ward
McEniery et al, 1991	208	181/208 (87%) nasotracheal, 27/208 (13%) tracheotomy (10 for subglottic narrowing, 17 for trauma)	Suggest selective endoscopy and tracheostomy
Freezer et al, 1990	416/2623 (16%) to PICU	176/2623 (6%) intubated	59/117 needed reintubation, steroids associated with successful 2nd extubation
Prescott et al, 1990		4.6% of 3500 croup patients received tracheotomy	
Kairys et al, 1989	Metanalysis of 9 RCT evaluating effects of steroids on croup score and need for intubation		Steroids improved croup score OR 2.25 at 12 h, 3.19 at 24 h Reduced need for intubation OR 0.21, >25 mg cortisone or 100 mg hydrocortisone more improvement
Mitchell et al, 1980	2567	65/2567 airway, 45/2567 intubated (6 d), 30/2.567 tracheotomy (11 d)	1/2567 from ETT obstruction
Duncan et al, 1979	7 patients with decreased work of breathing after use of helium		
Wesley et al, 1975		58 intubated children	Recommend intubation for 2 or more of following; HR > 170, RR > 55, Paco$_2$ > 37, Pao$_2$ < 50, cardiac failure or severe lower respiratory infection
Schuller et al, 1975	815 croup, 55 acute epiglotittis	6.5% croup patients intubated (88 h), 60% epiglottitis patients (55 h) intubated	0% mortality from intubation, 1.6% complication rate (postextubation symptoms)

mic epinephrine. Sustained or recurrent lack of response to racemic epinephrine should heighten one's suspicion. Progression to complete obstruction can occur if these children are sent home from the emergency department or the office. Unfortunately, there are no good discriminating tests for diagnosing bacterial tracheitis versus febrile viral laryngotracheobronchitis.

Intubation in these patients is complicated by purulent secretions that require frequent suctioning to maintain patency of the endotracheal tube. Antibiotic therapy should be directed to cover *S. aureus*. The length of intubation is longest in this disease. There are no studies documenting benefit of steroids for extubation success.

Most clinicians use the leak test (positive air leak at 20 cm H$_2$O) to direct extubation. There are no strong recommendations either way on the need for laryngoscopy and bronchoscopy after extubation (Table 94–3).

Airway Obstruction from Pseudomembranous Tracheitis

This disease has been reported, for the most part, in children who have been intubated and ventilated with higher airway pressures. The x-ray shows a shaggy radiopaque lining of the trachea. Bronchoscopy reveals a mu-

TABLE 94–3. Review of Bacterial Tracheitis Literature

Study	Incidence/Cause	Airway Type (Mean Duration of Intubation)	Outcome
Damm et al, 1996	12 bacterial tracheitis, 21 acute epiglottitis	76% nasotracheal intubation, 5% tracheostomy	Recommend fiberoptic endoscopy
Tan et al, 1992	500 children with croup symptoms, 2% bacterial tracheitis, 98% croup	All bacterial croup required intubation and endoscopy, 6% of croup required intubation.	Suggest laryngoscopy and bronchoscopy for high incidence of bacterial tracheitis or subglottic stenosis in intubated croup patients
Sofer et al, 1991	743 children with croup symptoms, 1.9% bacterial tracheitis	16/74 PICU patients NT intubation, 10/16 bacterial tracheitis	9/10 survived, PICU stay 3–14 days
Kasian et al, 1989	14 patients: *S. aureus, Branhamella catarrhalis, S. pneumococcus, Haemophilus influenzae,* 2 with concomitant virus	13 nasotracheal intubation (7.6 d)	1 PICU death
Labay et al, 1984	4 membranous LTB, measles (2), *S. aureus* (1)	NT intubation, bronchoscopic clearing	
Liston et al, 1983	17 children with unresponsive croup, 6 *S. aureus,* 7 alpha-hemolytic streptococci	4 observation, 13 tracheostomy	4/4 cardiac arrest, 2/4 died with observation, 1/13 died with tracheostomy
Henry et al, 1983	7 with pseudomembranous croup, *S. aureus* most common	All intubated	Recommend antibiotics, bronchosopic clearing

copurulent pseudomembrane, and investigators have recorded positive airway cultures for both measles virus and *S. aureus*. The children frequently experience life-threatening occlusion of the endotracheal tube. Many authors recommend bronchoscopic removal of the membranous secretions.

Hypoxia after Relief of Airway Obstruction: Pulmonary Edema? Pneumothorax? Or Pneumonia?

The only experience more frightening than being unable to secure an airway in a child with end-stage airway obstruction is observing worsening hypoxia after resolution of airway obstruction. The differential diagnosis includes an ineffective airway (nasogastric intubation, main stem intubation, or intubation of a tissue plane), pulmonary edema, pneumothorax, and pneumonia.

Pulmonary edema is a well-recognized and reported complication of acute airway obstruction and can become most prominent after resolution of obstruction with an endotracheal tube or tracheostomy. The pathophysiology is not well understood, but some theories exist. Pulmonary edema before relief of the obstruction may be a result of left heart failure owing to severe hypoxia and stress. Pulmonary edema after relief of the obstruction has been attributed to sudden change in intrapleural and intrathoracic pressures. During obstruction, extreme negative pressures occur in the intrapleural and thoracic compartments. Intubation results in sudden equalization of pressures. It is hypothesized that this results in transudation of fluid and pulmonary edema. This condition usually resolves in 24 to 48 hours. Pulmonary edema can be reversed with positive end-expiratory pressure and diuretics. *Pneumothorax* has been less frequently reported and can be exacerbated to the degree of tension with positive pressure breathing. This life-threatening complication can be managed with chest tube placement. Pneumonia can also cause hypoxia, but it is unlikely to cause worsening hypoxia after intubation (Table 94–4).

The Immunocompromised Child

Continuing technology breakthroughs in immunizations and immunosuppressive therapies, the "yin and yang" of infection-related disease, dictate a decreasing incidence of immunocompetent children with airway obstruction and

TABLE 94–4. Review of Airway Obstruction-Associated Pulmonary Edema Literature

Study	Therapy	Airway Type	Outcome
Emmerson et al, 1991	174 intubated epiglottitis patients	Nasotracheal intubation	2.1% incidence of pulmonary edema
Schere et al, 1988	PEEP	Intubation	
Galvis et al, 1987	20 patients treated with PEEP	Intubation	
Kanter et al, 1984	153 patients with croup or epiglottitis, 34 required intubation	Pulmonary edema in 4/34 after intubation	PaO$_2$ <50 in 38%, pneumothorax in 24%. Can require oxygen, mechanical ventilation, PEEP, and chest tube.

an increasing incidence of immunocompromised children with acute airway obstruction.

Airway Obstruction Associated with Nasopharyngeal Obstruction

Malignant adenotonsillar hypertrophy associated with Epstein-Barr virus has been observed and reported in children with transplantation-associated lymphoproliferative disease. These children are frequently unable to have obstruction relieved by a nasopharyngeal airway because they often have concomitant supraglottic (but not epiglottic) involvement. They have very significant lymphadenopathy associated with uncontrolled lymphoproliferation. It is remarkable that a disease once referred to as lymphoma is now euphemistically called lymphoproliferation.

The treatment for this life-threatening disease is an emergency airway. The visualization of the airway is often obscured, and it can be prudent to intubate these children with inhaled anesthetic induction that allows spontaneous respiration. It is also prudent to have fiberoptic laryngoscopy and tracheotomy as available therapies if intubation fails. The ultimate treatment is patient specific. If immunosuppression can be rapidly tapered, or if agents can be used to treat lymphoma (e.g., trials with a monoclonal antibody to the B-lymphocyte have been encourag-

ing), then the adenopathy may decrease with prolonged intubation. When these options are not available, adenotonsillectomy and/or tracheotomy may be needed.

Airway Obstruction Associated with Epiglottitis or Tracheitis

Immunocompromised patients, particularly those with neutropenia, have been reported to have epiglottitis or tracheitis from penicillin-resistant *S. pneumoniae*, *S. aureus*, *Candida*, or cytomegalovirus. These conditions present more insidiously than in immunocompetent hosts but do progress to complete airway obstruction if not recognized. Infection in these children can spread to the paraglottic planes as well as to the submandibular and submental regions. Lack of response to antibiotics and immune-stimulating therapies (e.g., granulocyte colony–stimulating factor, intravenous immunoglobulin G, white blood cell transfusion) may signify the need for surgical drainage or débridement of these tissue planes. A more prolonged course of airway edema and obstruction can be expected because these children cannot kill their infection effectively. Esophagitis can also accompany this process. Therefore, inability to culture organisms from the epiglottis or trachea may be overcome using esophageal culture or biopsy.

The Neck

95

The Neck: Embryology and Anatomy

Mark A. Richardson, M.D., and Kathleen C. Y. Sie, M.D.

The neck is a complex region that is the passageway for communication between the head and the trunk. The tremendous variety of pathologic conditions that may occur in this region makes an understanding of the embryology and anatomy of the neck a vital part of the otolaryngologist's knowledge. This chapter emphasizes the embryology of the major vessels, nerves, muscles, and thyroid and parathyroid glands as they relate to clinical problems. The surface anatomy of the neck with reference to the triangles of the neck and lymphatic drainage are discussed, as are the fascial planes and related spaces.

Embryologic Development of Arteries of the Neck

Symmetry is a fundamental principle in embryologic development. In accordance with this principle, the arteries start as a paired symmetric system that is altered during development by the fusion or atrophy of their various parts.

As the heart is displaced caudally and the pharyngeal arches are formed, six pairs of pharyngeal arteries develop in succession. Not all six pairs of pharyngeal vessels are present at the same time. The mandibular and hyoid arch vessels disappear before the fifth and sixth pharyngeal arch vessels have differentiated.

Figure 95–1 shows the pharyngeal arch arteries arising ventrally from the aortic sac and terminating laterally in the dorsal aorta of the corresponding side. At a more caudal level, the two dorsal aortas fuse to form a single midline dorsal aorta. The initial arrangement of the arch vessels is subsequently transformed during development.

The first and second pharyngeal arch vessels disappear at about the time the third and fourth arch vessels mature and increase in size. The remnant of the first arch artery is the maxillary artery, and the stapedial artery (when present) represents a remnant of the second arch. The ventral portions of the first and second arch vessels may also contribute to the development of the external carotid artery (see Fig. 95–1).[2, 4]

The third pharyngeal arch vessels differentiate into the internal carotid arteries. The fourth arch vessels form the arch of the aorta on the left side and contribute to the proximal aspect of the subclavian artery on the right. The left subclavian artery arises by hypertrophy of a branch of the left dorsal aorta (see Fig. 95–1).[12]

Abnormalities of the great vessels are among the most common developmental anomalies. With the growth of the body and changes in the vascular patterns, certain channels may persist that normally undergo regression, or vessels that normally persist may disappear. In most cases, these variations have little effect on function, and circulation is not impaired. In some cases, however, variations in the aortic arch development may be of greater clinical significance. For instance, persistence of the right and left fourth arches and dorsal aortic root results in an "aortic ring," which may compress the trachea and esophagus. The resulting interference with swallowing may require ligation of one of the two arches.

Another arch abnormality that produces clinical symptoms and signs is the aberrant right subclavian artery. In this case, the vessel passes from the dorsal aortic root across the midline behind the esophagus. It may then exert enough pressure to interfere with swallowing, although usually not as great a pressure as occurs with

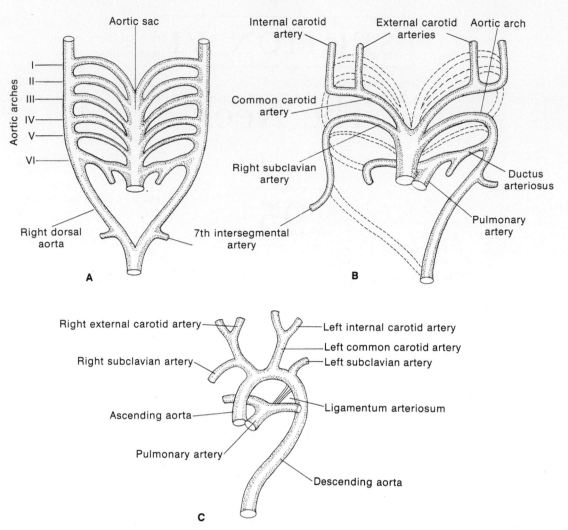

FIGURE 95-1. *A,* Aortic arches before transformation into a definitive vascular pattern. *B,* Aortic arches after transformation. *C,* The great arteries in the adult. (After Langman J. Medical Embryology: Human Development—Normal and Abnormal. Baltimore, Williams & Wilkins, 1969.)

aortic ring malformation. Other abnormalities in the development of the branchial arch vessels are discussed in major embryologic texts.[10, 15]

Hematoma formation within the stapedial artery stem in mouse embryos results in varying degrees of ear (outer and middle), mandibular, parotid, and facial nerve anomalies. This vascular phenomenon results in craniofacial microsomia in animal models and is the presumed cause in nongenetic human craniofacial microsomia.[17]

Veins of the Neck

The superficial veins, subcutaneous veins, and external and anterior jugulars are especially variable in size and course, and their connections between the deep veins also vary.

External Jugular

The external jugular vein begins in the substance of the parotid gland where it is most often formed by the union of the posterior facial and posterior auricular veins. In this region of the parotid gland, it may receive a communication from the internal jugular vein. The external jugular vein runs vertically downward across the superficial surface of the sternomastoid muscle and courses inferiorly to pierce the fascia of the posterior triangle of the neck, just above the clavicle. It also receives the transverse cervical, the suprascapular, and, frequently, the anterior jugular veins. The external jugular vein usually terminates in the subclavian vein but, in one third of instances, may terminate in the internal jugular vein.

Anterior Jugular

The anterior jugular vein usually begins in the suprahyoid region, through the confluence of variable superficial veins, or it may arise more laterally. It has variable communications with the internal jugular or the facial vein and descends on the infrahyoid musculature. In the lower portion of the neck above the sternum, the two veins are commonly united by a transversely disposed jugular venous arch, which is one of the vessels that may be encountered in a tracheostomy incision. Below this jugular venous arch, each anterior jugular vein courses laterally to empty into the terminal portion of the external jugular vein or into the subclavian vein between the external and internal jugulars.

Internal Jugular

The right internal jugular vein is usually the larger of the jugular veins, and it begins at the jugular foramen as the continuation of the sigmoid and inferior petrosal sinuses. This confluence forms the jugular bulb in the floor of the tympanic cavity. The jugular bulb is usually covered by bone and generally lies inferior to the level of the annulus. A high jugular bulb extends into the mesotympanum and can be dehiscent or covered with bone. It is usually seen as a bluish mass in the posterior tympanum on otoscopic examination. These lesions can cause tinnitus and hearing loss or can be asymptomatic. Inadvertent puncture of a high jugular bulb during middle-ear surgery or myringotomy can cause significant hemorrhage.[18] A minute bit of apparent chemoreceptor tissue from which tumors may arise is located against the jugular bulb.

The jugular vein lies posterior to the internal carotid artery, from which it is separated by the 9th, 10th, and 11th cranial nerves as they emerge from the anterior portion of the jugular foramen. At its superior end, the internal jugular vein receives the inferior petrosal sinus, which passes through the anterior aspect of the jugular foramen. The middle meningeal veins and the vein of the cochlear aqueduct also enter it here. As the jugular vein courses into the neck, it lies lateral to the internal and common carotid arteries. As the vein assumes the position lateral to the artery, the vagus nerve lies posterior and somewhat between the two vessels. The internal jugular vein is intimately related to the deep cervical lymph nodes that are embedded in that portion of the carotid sheath surrounding the vein. At about the level of the hyoid bone, the internal jugular vein receives the facial vein and a part of the posterior facial vein. As it courses inferiorly, the internal jugular vein typically receives the superior thyroid vein and, often, the pharyngeal and lingual veins (Fig. 95–2). Its termination joins the subclavian vein to form the brachiocephalic, or innominate, vein on each side. The thoracic duct on the left and the right lymphatic duct or its constituent vessel on the right open between the internal jugular and subclavian vessels. The subclavian vein lies anterior to the corresponding artery and at a slightly lower level. Anteriorly, the vein passes deep to the clavicle and superficial to the anterior scalene

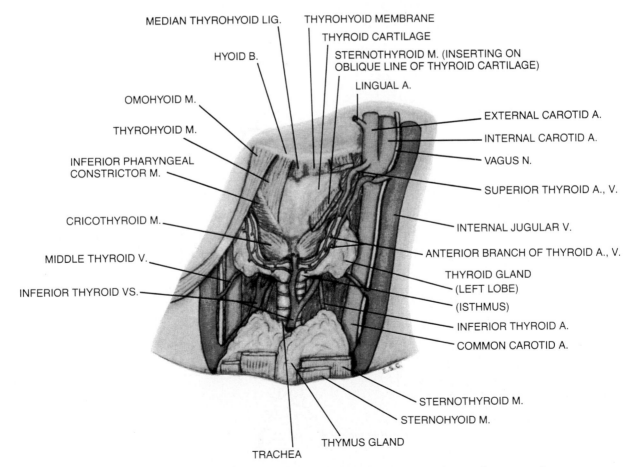

FIGURE 95–2. Deep veins and thymus. (From Crelin ES. Anatomy of the Newborn: An Atlas. Philadelphia, Lea & Febiger, 1969.)

muscle. The subclavian artery passes deep to the scalene muscle. (Normally, the phrenic nerve passes deep to it but sometimes the accessory phrenic nerve courses anterior to the vein.)

Thoracic and Right Lymphatic Ducts

Thoracic Duct

As the thoracic duct enters the inferiormost portion of the neck, it lies somewhat to the right of the subclavian artery and behind the left common carotid artery (Fig. 95–3). From this position between the esophagus and the left pleura and deep to the left common carotid artery and left vagus nerve, it arches anterosuperiorly and laterally. In so doing, the thoracic duct emerges between the left common carotid and the left subclavian artery. As the thoracic duct arches above the level of the subclavian artery, it passes between the internal jugular vein and the anterior scalene musculature, generally to terminate near the junction of the internal jugular vein on the left and the subclavian vein. Typically, the thoracic duct drains both lower limbs, most of the abdomen and its contents, and the left side of the head and neck. The actual termination of the thoracic duct varies, and it may terminate in the subclavian vein, the internal jugular vein, or the innominate vein.

It appears that there is at least a potential anastomosis between the thoracic duct and the right lymphatic duct. If the thoracic duct becomes obstructed in the neck, the anastomosis may have a functional significance. Injuries to the thoracic duct occurring during surgery can frequently be treated by temporary pressure. Ligation may be necessary if the leak does not stop with pressure.

Right Lymphatic Duct

The right lymphatic duct receives lymph from the right side of the head and neck, from the right upper extremity, and from the right side of the thorax. This duct usually terminates into the angle of union between the subclavian and the internal jugular veins or directly into one of these veins. Like the thoracic duct, the right lymphatic duct has two valves at its opening into the venous system to prevent retrograde mixing of venous blood.

Lymphatic channels are thought to originate by endothelial buds derived from the lining of jugular sacs. Disorders of the formation of the lymphatic system can lead to lymphatic malformations. Although the term "-oma" suggests a tumor, these malformations are not tumors and include a spectrum of lesions ranging from cystic hygromas to lymphangiomas. The cystic hygroma is a purely lymphatic channel entity in which there is anomalous lymphatic drainage. The sequestered lymphatic tissue gives rise to cysts lined with endothelium that enlarge greatly when infected. The close relationship of the developing lymphatic and venous systems sometimes leads to lymphaticovenous malformations. Grossly, lymphatic malformations consist of multiloculated cysts containing serous fluid. They are commonly located in the neck but may appear in the axilla, thorax, groin, or abdomen. Large posterior cervical cystic hygromas have been associated with Turner syndrome.[5, 19] Treatment requires operative excision.

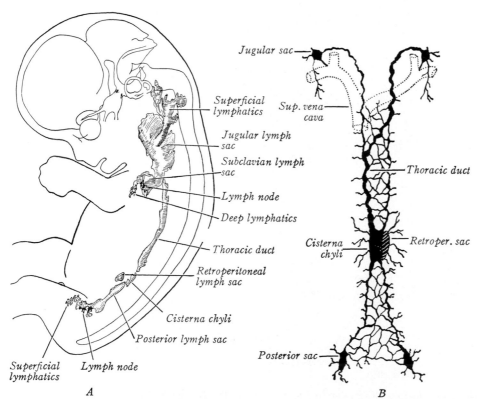

FIGURE 95–3. Development of the lymphatic vessels. *A*, Human embryo at 9 weeks, showing the primitive lymph sacs and the developing vessels (after Sabin). *B*, Ventral view of formation of the single thoracic duct from the primitive paired lymphatic plexus. (*B*, From Arey LB. Developmental Anatomy, 7th ed. Philadelphia, WB Saunders, 1974.)

Embryologic Development of Neck Muscles

The muscles of the body develop from mesoderm. Segmentation of the para-axial mesoderm into somites is followed by subsequent differentiation into the myotome (which gives rise to muscle mass), dermatome (which gives rise to integumentary tissues), and sclerotome (which gives rise to the axial skeleton). Unlike the voluntary musculature of other parts of the body, most of the segmental musculature of the neck is formed by the differentiation of branchial arch mesenchyme, with some contributions from the cervical somites. The extensor musculature of other parts of the body and most of the segmental musculature of the neck is formed from the epaxial divisions of the cervical myotomes. The hypaxial portions of these myotomes form the scalene, prevertebral, geniohyoid, and infrahyoid muscles.[15]

In general, the muscles of branchiomeric origin retain the innervation characteristic of the arch. Therefore, the muscles that are derived from the mesenchyme of the mandibular, or first, arch are supplied by fibers of the trigeminal nerve. This group includes the muscles of mastication, the mylohyoid muscle, and the anterior belly of the digastric muscle as well as the tensor veli palatini and tensor tympani muscles. The second arch is associated with the hyoid and the ossicular chain lateral to the stapes footplate. The muscles of the second arch include the muscles of facial expression, the platysma, and the anterior portion of the base of tongue. The artery and nerve of this arch are the stapedial artery and facial nerve, respectively. The third arch gives rise to the stylopharyngeus and part of the pharyngeal constrictor muscles. They are innervated by the glossopharyngeal nerve. The primordial muscle masses of the fourth and fifth arches give rise to the muscles of the larynx and part of the pharyngeal constrictors. These muscles are innervated largely by the vagus nerve.

Anomalies of the branchial apparatus can result from incomplete closure of the branchial clefts, failure of obliteration of the cervical sinus of His, or entrapment of epithelial rests within lymph nodes. These developmental anomalies can result in formation of a sinus, a fistula, or a cyst. These are discussed in Chapter 98. Third branchial cleft anomalies may rarely manifest as recurrent thyroiditis resulting from an intrathyroid cyst that communicates with the piriform sinus.[14]

The precise development of the sternocleidomastoid and trapezius muscles is difficult to establish. Most researchers think that this muscle group is formed primarily from branchiomeric tissue but that the migration of muscle cells from the occipital somites contributes to part of this development. The innervation of these muscles is from the spinal accessory nerve. The infrahyoid muscles of the anterior aspect of the neck are of somitic origin. These muscles are innervated by a branch of the hypoglossal nerve with fibers from the first and second cervical nerves, the ansa cervicalis. Early in embryonic development, the infrahyoid muscle mass was closely associated with the mass that gives rise to the diaphragmatic musculature. This helps explain the origin of the innervations of the infrahyoid muscles from the cervical nerves.[12]

Embryology of Thyroid and Parathyroid Glands and Thymus

Thyroid Gland

The thyroid gland originates early in embryonic development as a thickening of the endoderm of the floor of the pharynx in the midline between the first and second pouches, near the portion that becomes the tuberculum impar. This tissue mass forms a diverticulum with a bilobed, flasklike appearance. This thyroid primordium (Fig. 95–4) soon begins to descend, but a thin connection, the stalklike thyroglossal duct, remains attached to the oropharynx. This point of attachment marks the origin of the thyroid gland and may be seen in the adult as the foramen caecum. When the thyroid primordium descends, it consists of two lobes extending to either side of the midline, with a narrow isthmus of tissue joining them medially. This tissue mass reaches the level of the laryngeal primordium at about the seventh week of gestation. The thyroglossal tract is normally obliterated but, when it persists, may increase the likelihood of the formation of thyroglossal duct cysts (Fig. 95–5). A persistent thyroglossal duct may track medial to the central portion of the hyoid cartilage as it descends toward the thyroid gland.[9] Furthermore, the superior portion of the persistent duct may have several finger-like projections to the tongue base, predisposing to recurrent lesions.[11] Accessory thyroid tissue may be found along the path of migration of the thyroid gland. When the primordial thyroid fails to descend, it may persist in the tongue musculature as a lingual thyroid (Fig. 95–6).[12, 15]

Parathyroid Glands

Two pairs of parathyroid glands develop from separate pouches. The inferior pair is derived from the third and the superior from the fourth pharyngeal pouch. They are frequently designated as parathyroids 3 and parathyroids 4. At the seventh week of development, the parathyroid primordia free themselves from the pouches and move caudally. Although they initially move in close association with each other, parathyroids 3 remain attached to the thymus and migrate farther caudally than do parathyroids 4. Occasionally during their migration, fragmentation of the parathyroid tissue takes place, resulting in the formation of accessory parathyroid glands. Parathyroids 4 usually adhere to the thyroid capsule and may become embedded in the substance of the thyroid gland (see Fig. 95–6). Further details of the embryology and developmental abnormalities of the thyroid and parathyroid are discussed in Chapter 98.

Thymus

The thymus also is derived from the third pharyngeal pouch and moves caudally with parathyroids 3 to a level lower than the thyroid tissue, eventually migrating to the superior mediastinum. Remnants of thymus tissue can remain in the neck to form thymic cysts or accessory

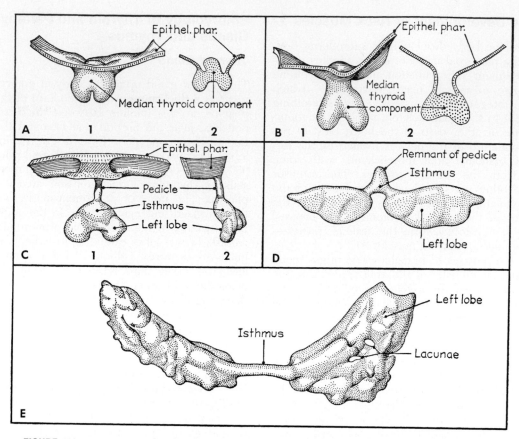

FIGURE 95–4. Stages in the development of the thyroid gland. *A, 1,* the thyroid primordium and pharyngeal epithelium of a 4.5-mm human embryo; *2,* section through the same structure, showing raised central portion. *B, 1,* thyroid primordium of a 6.5-mm embryo; *2,* section through the same structure. *C, 1,* thyroid primordium of an 8.2-mm embryo, beginning to descend; *2,* lateral view of the same structure. *D,* Thyroid primordium of an 11-mm embryo. The connection with the pharynx is broken, and the lobes are beginning to grow laterad. *E,* Thyroid gland of a 13.5-mm embryo. The lobes are thin sheets curving around the carotid arteries. Several lacunae are present in the sheets, which are not to be confused with follicles. (From Weller GL. Development of the thyroid, parathyroid, and thymus glands in man. Contrib Embryol Carnegie Inst Wash 24:93, 1933.)

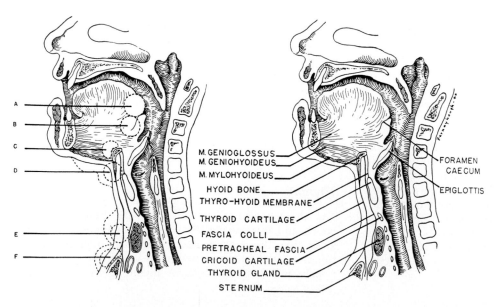

FIGURE 95–5. Various locations of thyroglossal duct cysts. *A,* In front of the foramen caecum; *B,* at the foramen caecum; *C,* above the hyoid bone; *D,* below the hyoid bone; *E,* in the region of the thyroid gland; *F,* at the suprasternal notch. About 50% of the cysts are at *D,* below the hyoid bone. (From Ward GE. Thyroglossal tract abnormalities. Cysts and fistulas. Surg Gynecol Obstet 89:727, 1949. By permission of Surgery, Gynecology, and Obstetrics.)

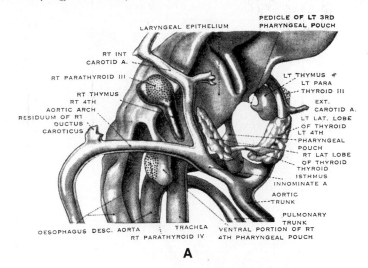

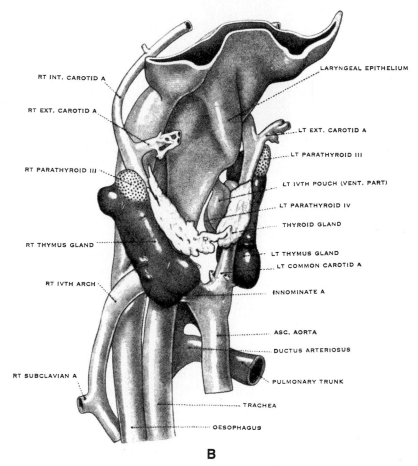

FIGURE 95–6. Reconstruction of the pharyngeal pouches, their derivatives, and related aortic arches. *A*, At 13.5 mm (beginning of seventh week); *B*, at 16.8 mm (beginning of eighth week).

Illustration continued on following page

lobes of thymus; these usually lie below the thyroid cartilage.

Surface Anatomy of the Neck

The neck may be divided into an anterior region, or the cervix, and a posterior region, or the nucha. The nuchal division is more properly related to the back and is represented by the vertebral column with its paravertebral musculature. The cervical division is of greater interest to the otolaryngologist. When viewed from the lateral aspect, it has a quadrilateral outline. It is bounded superiorly by the mandible and mastoid process, inferiorly by the clavicle, anteriorly by the midline of the neck, and posteriorly by the anterior border of the trapezius muscle.

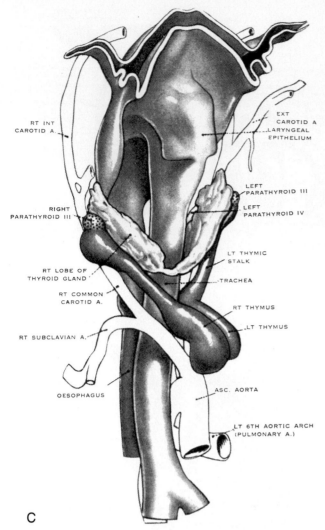

RT INT
CAROTID A.

EXT
CAROTID A
LARYNGEAL
EPITHELIUM

RIGHT
PARATHYROID III

LEFT
PARATHYROID III

LEFT
PARATHYROID IV

RT LOBE OF
THYROID GLAND

LT THYMIC
STALK

TRACHEA

RT COMMON
CAROTID A.

RT THYMUS

LT THYMUS

RT SUBCLAVIAN A.

OESOPHAGUS

ASC. AORTA

C

LT 6TH AORTIC ARCH
(PULMONARY A.)

FIGURE 95–6 *Continued. C,* At 23 mm (end of eighth week). (From Hamilton WJ, Mossman HW. Human Embryology, 4th ed. Baltimore, Williams & Wilkins, 1972. After Weller, 1933.)

Triangles of the Neck

The sternocleidomastoid muscle is a prominent landmark in the neck and divides it into anterior and posterior parts, or triangles, as it courses from the mastoid tip to the medial aspect of the clavicle (Fig. 95–7).

The Posterior Triangle

The posterior triangle is bounded posteriorly by the trapezius muscle, anteriorly by the sternocleidomastoid muscle, and inferiorly by the middle third of the clavicle. Its floor is formed by the deep layer of the deep cervical fascia, which covers the scalene muscle, the levator muscle of the scapula, and the splenius capitis muscle. The roof of the triangle is the superficial layer of the deep cervical fascia (see Fig. 95–7).

The most important contents of the posterior triangle are the subclavian artery, brachial plexus, spinal accessory

nerve, and posterior cervical lymph nodes. The omohyoid muscle crosses the posterior triangle and divides it into a superior occipital triangle and an inferior subclavian triangle.[7, 16]

The Anterior Triangle

The anterior triangle is bounded posteriorly by the sternocleidomastoid muscle, anteriorly by the midline of the neck, and superiorly by the lower border of the mandible. Its floor (deep border) is formed by the mylohyoid and hyoglossus muscles and by parts of the thyrohyoid and pharyngeal constrictor muscles. Its roof (superficial border) is formed by the superficial layer of the deep cervical fascia and the platysma muscle. The anterior triangle is crossed by the digastric, stylohyoid, and omohyoid muscles, which subdivide this area into smaller triangles: the submandibular, carotid, submental, and inferior carotid triangles. The chief contents of the anterior triangle are the common, external, and internal carotid arteries; the internal jugular vein; the laryngeal, pharyngeal, vagal, and recurrent laryngeal nerves; the submandibular gland; and lymphatic tissue (see Fig. 95–7).

Lymph Nodes of the Neck

The lymph nodes of the neck include five main groups: submandibular, submental, superficial cervical, anterior cervical, and deep cervical nodes (Fig. 95–8).[7, 8]

The submandibular nodes, which are inferior to the body of the mandible in the submandibular triangle, are chiefly superficial to the submandibular gland. Small lymph nodes are sometimes found on the undersurface of the submandibular gland. These nodes drain the cheek, the medial canthal region, the lateral aspect of the nose, the upper lip, the gingiva, and the anterolateral aspect of the tongue. The submandibular nodes drain subsequently into the superior deep cervical nodes.

The submental nodes are between the anterior bellies of the digastric muscles. These nodes drain the central aspect of the lower lip and floor of the mouth and the mobile tongue. The submental nodes drain subsequently into the submandibular nodes and into the deep cervical node group at the level of the hyoid cartilage.

The superficial cervical nodes lie adjacent to the external jugular vein and superficial to the sternocleidomastoid muscle. These nodes drain the inferior aspects of the auricular and parotid regions and drain subsequently into the superior deep cervical nodes (Figs. 95–8 and 95–9).

The anterior cervical nodes lie ventral to the larynx and trachea and drain the lower part of the larynx, the thyroid gland, and the cervical aspect of the trachea. Efferents from this node group pass deeper into the deep cervical nodes, which are larger, more numerous, and lie along the carotid sheath. The deep cervical nodes are frequently divided into two groups: the superior deep cervical nodes and the inferior deep cervical nodes.

The superior deep cervical nodes lie deep to the sternocleidomastoid muscle and in close association with the

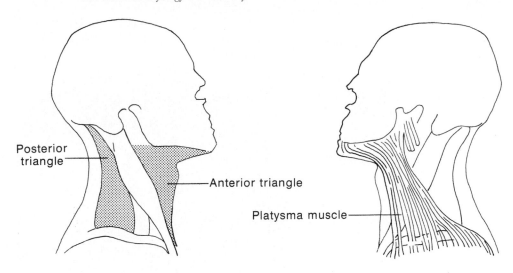

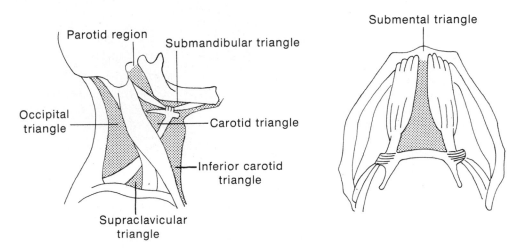

FIGURE 95–7. Triangles of the neck.

internal jugular vein and spinal accessory nerve. These nodes drain the occipital region, the back of the neck, the auricle, most of the tongue, the larynx, thyroid gland, trachea, nasopharynx, nasal cavities, palate, and esophagus. They also receive efferent vessels from a major portion of the other nodes of the head and neck.

The inferior deep cervical nodes lie deep to the sternocleidomastoid muscle in the supraclavicular area and are in close proximity to the brachial plexus and subclavian vein. This inferior node group drains the back of the scalp and neck as well as part of the pectoral region. The inferior deep cervical nodes receive lymphatic drainage from the superior deep cervical nodes. The deep cervical node groups on the right side form a large lymphatic vessel, the jugular trunk, which joins the venous system at the junction of the internal jugular and subclavian veins. On the left side, the jugular trunk joins the thoracic duct.

The retropharyngeal nodes are an important nodal chain in the pediatric patient. Infection and subsequent suppuration in these nodes cause retropharyngeal abscess formation. These nodes lie in the buccopharyngeal fascia, between the posterior pharynx and the cervical vertebrae. They drain the nasal cavities, the nasopharynx, and Waldeyer's ring. Efferents from this group pass to the superior deep cervical nodes (Fig. 95–10) (see Chap. 99).

Fascial Layers of the Neck

It is important to understand the position of the lymph nodes relative to the fascial layers and compartments of the head and neck. The lymphatic system drains three areas of infection in the head and neck. Subsequent suppuration and necrosis in the involved node may lead to the accumulation of purulent material, which may spread through one or more continuous fascial compartments. Thus, infections that originate from one site in the skin or in the pharynx may subsequently spread to involve specific lymphatics of the neck with subsequent deep neck infection.[6]

A knowledge of the anatomy of the cervical fascia is essential to the understanding of the pathophysiology and treatment of infectious and noninfectious diseases of the head and neck.

Cervical Fascia

The neck is enveloped by two basic fascial layers, the superficial and deep cervical fascias. These fascial layers both unite and separate various important structures. In so doing, certain fascial planes and compartments are formed.

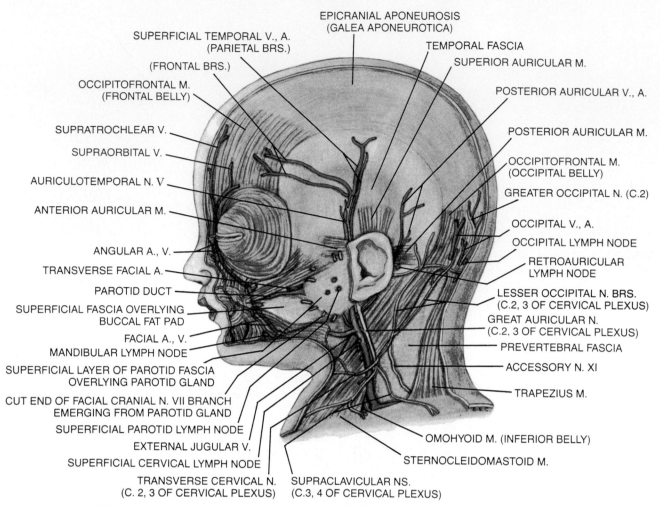

EPICRANIAL APONEUROSIS
(GALEA APONEUROTICA)

SUPERFICIAL TEMPORAL V., A.
(PARIETAL BRS.)

TEMPORAL FASCIA

(FRONTAL BRS.)

SUPERIOR AURICULAR M.

OCCIPITOFRONTAL M.
(FRONTAL BELLY)

POSTERIOR AURICULAR V., A.

SUPRATROCHLEAR V.

POSTERIOR AURICULAR M.

SUPRAORBITAL V.

OCCIPITOFRONTAL M.
(OCCIPITAL BELLY)

AURICULOTEMPORAL N. V

GREATER OCCIPITAL N. (C.2)

ANTERIOR AURICULAR M.

OCCIPITAL V., A.

ANGULAR A., V.

OCCIPITAL LYMPH NODE

TRANSVERSE FACIAL A.

RETROAURICULAR
LYMPH NODE

PAROTID DUCT

LESSER OCCIPITAL N. BRS.
(C.2, 3 OF CERVICAL PLEXUS)

SUPERFICIAL FASCIA OVERLYING
BUCCAL FAT PAD

GREAT AURICULAR N.
(C.2, 3 OF CERVICAL PLEXUS)

FACIAL A., V.

PREVERTEBRAL FASCIA

MANDIBULAR LYMPH NODE

ACCESSORY N. XI

SUPERFICIAL LAYER OF PAROTID FASCIA
OVERLYING PAROTID GLAND

TRAPEZIUS M.

CUT END OF FACIAL CRANIAL N. VII BRANCH
EMERGING FROM PAROTID GLAND

SUPERFICIAL PAROTID LYMPH NODE

EXTERNAL JUGULAR V.

OMOHYOID M. (INFERIOR BELLY)

SUPERFICIAL CERVICAL LYMPH NODE

STERNOCLEIDOMASTOID M.

TRANSVERSE CERVICAL N.
(C. 2, 3 OF CERVICAL PLEXUS)

SUPRACLAVICULAR NS.
(C.3, 4 OF CERVICAL PLEXUS)

FIGURE 95–8. Superficial veins and muscles of the neck. (From Crelin ES. Anatomy of the Newborn: An Atlas. Philadelphia, Lea & Febiger, 1969.)

By understanding the contents of these spaces together with their position in the neck and their relationships to other structures, the differential diagnosis of a neck mass may be made more easily, and potential complications from deep neck infections may be anticipated. The surgeon must be fully familiar with these structures and their relationships if the surgical approach to and drainage of deep neck infections is to be effective.[8]

The superficial cervical fascia surrounds the neck and is continuous with the superficial fascia of the pectoral, deltoid, and back regions inferiorly and the fascia of the muscles of facial expression superiorly. Within this layer are the thin sheets of platysma muscle as well as the external jugular vein and superficial lymph nodes. The more important deep cervical fascia is in three layers: a superficial investing layer, a middle layer, and a prevertebral layer (Fig. 95–11).

The superficial layer of the deep cervical fascia completely surrounds the neck like a stocking. Posteriorly, it is attached to the spinal processes of the cervical vertebra and to the ligamentum nuchae. It passes forward and divides to ensheathe the trapezius muscle and then forms a single layer as it passes over the posterior triangle of the neck. After dividing again to ensheathe the sternocleidomastoid muscle, the fascia continues across the neck as

a single layer to join the corresponding layer of the opposite side in the anterior midline. The superficial layer is attached to the hyoid bone in the anterior triangle and is divided into suprahyoid and infrahyoid portions. The suprahyoid portion splits to envelop the submandibular and parotid glands. Between these two glands, the fascia unites to form the stylomandibular ligament, which attaches to the lingual surface of the angle of the mandible and to the styloid process. Thus, the superficial layer of the deep cervical fascia separates the submandibular and parotid glands from each other and from the rest of the neck. The superficial layer continues superiorly to ensheathe the posterior body of the mandible. Its medial extension ensheathes the internal and external pterygoid muscles.

The infrahyoid portion of the superficial layer of the deep cervical fascia splits inferiorly to attach to the anterior and posterior aspects of the manubrium, where it forms the suprasternal space of Burns. This space contains the anterior jugular veins with their communicating veins and a few lymph nodes (see Fig. 95–11).

The middle, or pretracheal, layer of the deep cervical fascia is composed of two layers: a superficial muscular layer and a deep visceral layer. The more superficial muscular layer ensheathes the strap muscles—the sternohy-

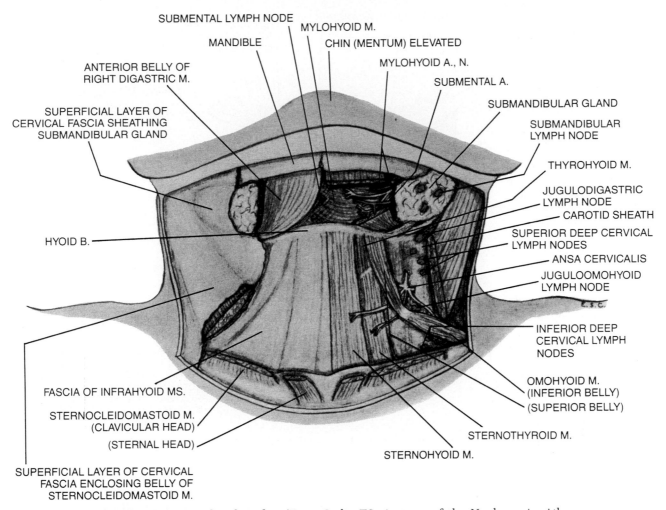

SUBMENTAL LYMPH NODE

MYLOHYOID M.

MANDIBLE

CHIN (MENTUM) ELEVATED

ANTERIOR BELLY OF
RIGHT DIGASTRIC M.

MYLOHYOID A., N.

SUBMENTAL A.

SUPERFICIAL LAYER OF
CERVICAL FASCIA SHEATHING
SUBMANDIBULAR GLAND

SUBMANDIBULAR GLAND

SUBMANDIBULAR
LYMPH NODE

THYROHYOID M.

JUGULODIGASTRIC
LYMPH NODE

CAROTID SHEATH

HYOID B.

SUPERIOR DEEP CERVICAL
LYMPH NODES

ANSA CERVICALIS

JUGULOOMOHYOID
LYMPH NODE

INFERIOR DEEP
CERVICAL LYMPH
NODES

FASCIA OF INFRAHYOID MS.

OMOHYOID M.
(INFERIOR BELLY)
(SUPERIOR BELLY)

STERNOCLEIDOMASTOID M.
(CLAVICULAR HEAD)

(STERNAL HEAD)

STERNOTHYROID M.

STERNOHYOID M.

SUPERFICIAL LAYER OF CERVICAL
FASCIA ENCLOSING BELLY OF
STERNOCLEIDOMASTOID M.

FIGURE 95–9. Deep lymph nodes. (From Crelin ES. Anatomy of the Newborn: An Atlas. Philadelphia, Lea & Febiger, 1969.)

oid, sternothyroid, thyrohyoid, and omohyoid muscles. The deeper visceral layer surrounds the trachea, thyroid gland, and esophagus. Both layers are attached to the thyroid cartilage superiorly and extend downward to the posterior aspect of the sternum, where they blend with the tissue between the pericardial sac and great vessels and with that of the sternum. The lateral aspect of this layer contributes to the formation of the carotid sheath before fusing with the outer superficial fascial layer. The posterosuperior portion of this visceral fascial layer envelops the constrictor muscles and attaches to the base of the skull, forming the anterior aspect of the retropharyngeal space. This portion of the visceral layer is also referred to as the buccopharyngeal fascia (see Fig. 95–11).[1]

The deep, or prevertebral, layer of the deep cervical fascia, like the superficial layer, begins in the posterior midline and completely surrounds the neck. As the fascial layer proceeds forward from the ligamentum nuchae and the cervical spine, it covers the prevertebral musculature, forming the floor of the posterior cervical triangle, and covers the brachial plexus and subclavian artery. After attaching to the transverse process of the cervical vertebrae, this fascial layer splits into two layers in front of the vertebral column, forming the "danger space." Both layers of this prevertebral fascia originate at the base of the

skull, but the anterior layer fuses with the fascia of the esophagus in the superior mediastinum, forming the posterior wall of the retropharyngeal space. The posterior lamina continues further down through the mediastinum and retroperitoneum to the coccyx. An anterior extension of this layer to the carotid sheath, called the alar fascia, separates the retropharyngeal space from the pharyngomaxillary space (see Fig. 95–11).

The Carotid Sheath

The carotid sheath is the condensation of fascia that invests the carotid artery, internal jugular vein, and vagus nerve. It has contributions from all three layers of the deep cervical fascia. The cervical sympathetic trunk lies behind the sheath superficial to the prevertebral fascia. The carotid sheath extends from the base of the skull through the pharyngomaxillary space, superficial to the deep layer of the deep cervical fascia, into the superior mediastinum (see Fig. 95–11).

Potential Neck Spaces

Although the interfascial spaces of the neck are shown as anatomically absolute and distinct, almost all these spaces

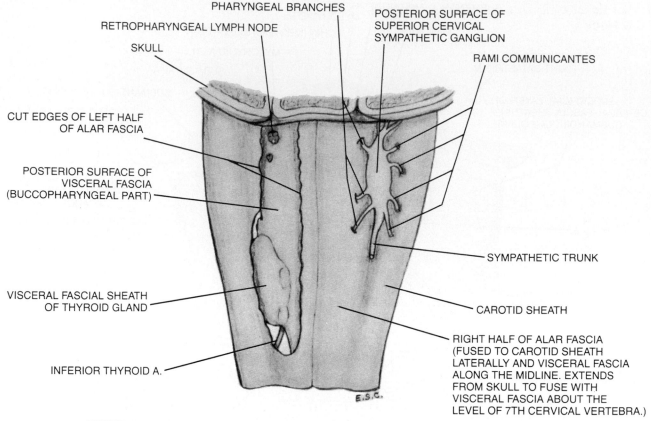

PHARYNGEAL BRANCHES

RETROPHARYNGEAL LYMPH NODE

SKULL

POSTERIOR SURFACE OF
SUPERIOR CERVICAL
SYMPATHETIC GANGLION

RAMI COMMUNICANTES

CUT EDGES OF LEFT HALF
OF ALAR FASCIA

POSTERIOR SURFACE OF
VISCERAL FASCIA
(BUCCOPHARYNGEAL PART)

VISCERAL FASCIAL SHEATH
OF THYROID GLAND

INFERIOR THYROID A.

SYMPATHETIC TRUNK

CAROTID SHEATH

RIGHT HALF OF ALAR FASCIA
(FUSED TO CAROTID SHEATH
LATERALLY AND VISCERAL FASCIA
ALONG THE MIDLINE. EXTENDS
FROM SKULL TO FUSE WITH
VISCERAL FASCIA ABOUT THE
LEVEL OF 7TH CERVICAL VERTEBRA.)

FIGURE 95-10. Retropharyngeal nodes. (From Crelin ES. Anatomy of the Newborn: An Atlas. Philadelphia, Lea & Febiger, 1969.)

may communicate with each other by way of defects in fascial integrity produced by perforating vessels and nerves, developmental aberrations, or destruction secondary to a disease process. For this reason, variations in the clinical behavior of certain diseases of the head and neck may take place.[8, 13]

The hyoid bone serves as a point of attachment for the fascial layers and, as such, divides the fascial spaces into a suprahyoid and infrahyoid group. Those spaces whose ensheathing fascia are not bound to the hyoid run through the entire length of the neck. Insofar as these fascial layers limit the spread of infection, the hyoid bone represents an important structure in the control of certain diseases (see Chap. 100).

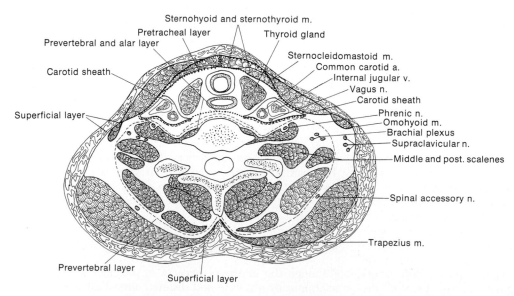

FIGURE 95-11. Transverse section of the neck at the level of the larynx, showing fascial layers. (After Hollinshead WH. Textbook of Anatomy, 3rd ed. Hagerstown, Md, Harper & Row, 1974.)

Spaces Extending through the Entire Length of the Neck

Retropharyngeal Spaces

The retropharyngeal space may be divided anatomically into three separate spaces: the retroesophageal, prevertebral, and danger spaces (Figs. 95–11 and 95–12).

The retroesophageal space lies between the middle layer of the deep cervical fascia anteriorly and the prevertebral layer of the deep cervical fascia posteriorly. It extends from the base of the skull superiorly into the superior mediastinum to the level of T1 where the middle and deep layers fuse. This space contains the retropharyngeal lymph nodes, which are typically present in children younger than 4 years of age. Infection in the adenoids, nasal cavities, nasopharynx, and posterior ethmoid sinuses may spread via lymphatics to involve these nodes. Nodal necrosis may result in abscess formation within this retroesophageal space.

The prevertebral space is located between the prevertebral layer of the deep cervical fascia and the bodies of the cervical vertebrae. Extending from the base of the skull along the spinal column to the coccyx, this potential space allows for the spread of infection from the neck to the psoas muscle. Tuberculosis involving the cervical vertebrae with extension into this space was seen before the development of effective tuberculosis therapy (see Figs. 95–11 and 95–12).

The danger space lies within the two layers of the prevertebral fascia and extends from the base of the skull downward through the mediastinum. Infection within this space may spread as far inferiorly as the diaphragm. The close relationship of this potential space to the prevertebral, retroesophageal, and lateral pharyngeal spaces may allow for infection in the pharynx to spread into the mediastinum or beyond. The potential danger of infection in this area is great (see Chap. 100).

The Vascular Space

The visceral vascular space is the potential space within the carotid sheath and extends from the base of the skull into the superior mediastinum. Because all three layers of the deep cervical fascia contribute to the formation of this space, infection in any other fascial space may ultimately involve this space. Thrombosis of the internal jugular vein and erosion of the carotid artery represent serious complications of infection within the carotid sheath; it is thus most important that the clinician recognize and treat carotid space infections (see Figs. 95–11 and 95–12).

Suprahyoid Spaces

Submandibular Space

The submandibular space is divided by the mylohyoid muscle into the sublingual space superiorly and the submaxillary space inferiorly. The submandibular gland extends into and communicates with both of these spaces. The central compartment of the submaxillary space, which is medial to the anterior belly of the digastric muscle, is termed the submental space (Fig. 95–13).

The entire submandibular space is bounded superiorly by the mucosa of the floor of the mouth, laterally and anteriorly by the mandible, posteriorly and inferiorly by the intrinsic muscles of the base of the tongue and hyoid bone, and inferiorly by the superficial layer of the deep cervical fascia.

The submandibular gland protrudes around the posterior border of the mylohyoid muscle to enter and become a passageway between the superior sublingual compartment and the submaxillary space. Infection in the submental space may spread freely beneath the anterior belly of the digastric muscle and into the submaxillary space and then via the submandibular gland into the sublingual space. Because of this free intercommunication, these spaces should be considered as a single unit. This concept was discussed by Ludwig, and multispace infection is the hallmark of Ludwig angina (see Fig. 95–13) (see Chaps. 65 and 100).

Pharyngomaxillary Space

The pharyngomaxillary space is also called the parapharyngeal or lateral pharyngeal space. This lateral, cone-

FIGURE 95–12. Longitudinal section through the neck showing spaces and fascial layers. (After Hollinshead WH. Textbook of Anatomy, 3rd ed. Hagerstown, Md, Harper & Row, 1974.)

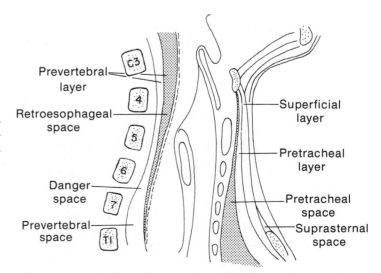

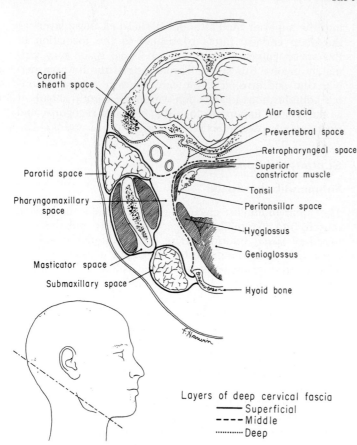

Layers of deep cervical fascia
——— Superficial
- - - - Middle
·········· Deep

FIGURE 95–13. Oblique section through the neck. (From Everts EC, Echevarria J. The pharynx and deep neck infections. In Paparella MM, Shumrick DA [eds]. Otolaryngology, Vol 3. Philadelphia, WB Saunders, 1973.)

shaped potential space has its base along the sphenoid bone at the base of the skull and its apex at the hyoid bone. It is bounded medially by the buccopharyngeal fascia, which covers the superior constrictor muscle. Its lateral limit is formed by the superficial layer of the deep cervical fascia covering the mandible, by the internal pterygoid muscle, and by the deep lobe of the parotid. The pterygomandibular raphe limits it anteriorly, and the prevertebral fascia limits it posteriorly. The styloid process and its attachments divide this space into two compartments: an anterior muscular compartment and a posterior neurovascular compartment. The posterior compartment contains the carotid sheath and cranial nerves IX through XII. The anterior compartment contains no vital structures and extends upward between the lateral wall of the pharynx and the medial surface of the internal pterygoid muscle (Fig. 95–14). Penetrating trauma of the oropharynx, lateral to the tonsil, may violate the carotid sheath.

The pharyngomaxillary space communicates with several other spaces in the neck. The inferomedial submandibular space, the posteromedial retropharyngeal space, the lateral parotid and masticator spaces, and the posterior carotid sheath all communicate with the parapharyngeal space and, in so doing, may influence the spread of infection in the head and neck. The adenoids, tonsils, nasal cavities, and paranasal sinuses represent sources of infection in this space. Mastoid infection may progress to a coalescent mastoiditis and erode through the mastoid

tip at the digastric ridge, producing a Bezold abscess (see Fig. 95–14) (see Chaps. 26, 99, and 100).

Masticator Space

The masticator space is anterior and lateral to the pharyngomaxillary space. It contains the masseter muscle, the internal and external pterygoid muscles, the ramus of the mandible, the tendon of the temporalis muscle, and the inferior alveolar neurovascular bundle. The masticator space is bounded by the superficial layer of the deep fascia, which divides around the mandible. The outer layer surrounds the masseter muscle and attaches to the zygoma. The inner layer ensheathes the internal and external pterygoid muscles. These two layers then reunite around the posterior and anterior bodies of the mandibular ramus. Infections in this space most commonly arise from molar teeth, but infection in the region of the zygoma, temporal bone, or mandible may also spread to this space (see Fig. 95–13) (see Chap. 100).

Parotid Space

The parotid space is formed by the superficial layer of the deep cervical fascia as it splits to enclose the parotid gland. The space is separated from the submandibular space inferiorly by the stylomandibular ligament. Connective tissue septa radiate from the surface of the capsular

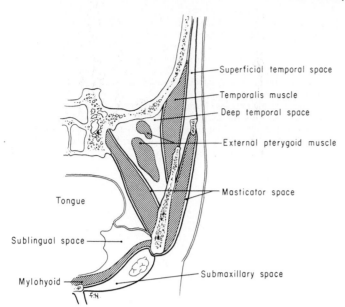

FIGURE 95–14. Coronal section through the head. (From Everts EC, Echevarria J. The pharynx and deep neck infections. In Paparella MM, Shumrick DA [eds]. Otolaryngology, Vol 3. Philadelphia, WB Saunders, 1973.)

sheath into the surrounding connective tissue. Similar septa perforate the gland itself and internally bind the gland to its capsule. The medial aspect of this parotid capsule is incomplete and allows direct communication of the parotid space with the pharyngomaxillary space. Therefore, infections in the parotid space pose a significant threat because they may spread readily into the pharyngomaxillary space and then to the prevertebral space (see Fig. 95–14) (see Chaps. 65 and 100).[3, 12]

Peritonsillar Space

The peritonsillar space lies between the capsule of the faucial tonsil medially, the superior constrictor muscle laterally, and the tonsillar pillars anteriorly and posteriorly. Infection in this space may spread into the pharyngomaxillary space, and involvement of the carotid sheath with subsequent thrombosis of the internal jugular vein may occur (see Fig. 95–14) (see Chaps. 61 and 100).

Anterior Visceral Space

The anterior visceral space is the pretracheal portion of the visceral compartment and is bounded by the visceral fascia, which surrounds the trachea from the thyroid gland superiorly to the anterior portion of the mediastinum at the level of the arch of the aorta inferiorly. This space communicates freely with the posterior visceral space. Penetration of the cervical esophagus by instruments or a foreign body may cause infection in this space, with subsequent extension into the mediastinum (see Figs. 95–11 and 95–12).

The fascial layers and compartments in the infant do not differ significantly in anatomy from those of the adult. The fascia of the infant may be somewhat thinner and less well developed than that of the adult, but the fascial layers and compartments contain the same structures and have the same anatomic relationships as do those of the adult. The less well developed neck musculature of the infant and child may not supply the same degree of support as is found in the adult and so may be more prone to displacement and distortion from disease processes. Therefore, infection in the deep neck spaces may interfere with breathing and swallowing to a greater degree in the child than in the adult.

Fascial layers may become quite thickened and well defined in response to chronic infection, so what may represent a flimsy layer of fascia in the uninfected neck may become a thickened fascial layer that serves as an effective barrier to the spread of infection in response to chronic infection in this area.

SELECTED REFERENCES

Anson BJ, McVay CB. Surgical Anatomy, 5th ed. Philadelphia, WB Saunders, 1971.

> *A surgical anatomy text with fine illustrations and a discussion of the anatomy of the neck that relates well to the surgical approach to pathologic processes in this region.*

Crelin ES. Development of the upper respiratory system. Clin Symp 28: 4, 1976.

> *Clear and concise review that covers comparative anatomy as well as embryology of the head and neck. Also instructive drawings by Dr. Frank Netter.*

Levitt GW. Cervical fascia and deep neck infections. Laryngoscope 80: 409, 1970.

Patten BM. Human Embryology, 3rd ed. New York, McGraw-Hill, 1968.

> *A clear presentation of human embryology with fine illustrations.*

REFERENCES

1. Anson BJ, McVay CB. Surgical Anatomy, 5th ed. Philadelphia, WB Saunders, 1971.
2. Arey LB. Developmental Anatomy: A Textbook and Laboratory Manual of Embryology, 7th ed. Philadelphia, WB Saunders, 1974.
3. Beck AL. Surgical approaches to deep neck infection. Ann Otol Rhinol Laryngol 64:91, 1955.
4. Crelin ES. Development of the upper respiratory system. Clin Symp 28:4, 1976.
5. Edwards MJ, Graham JM Jr. Posterior nuchal cystic hygroma. Clin Perinatalol 17:611, 1990.
6. Everts EC, Echevarria J. The pharynx and deep neck infections. In Paparella MM, Shumrick DA (eds). Otolaryngology, vol 3. Philadelphia, WB Saunders, 1973.
7. Gray H. Anatomy of the Human Body, 27th ed. Philadelphia, Lea & Febiger, 1959.
8. Hollinshead WH. Textbook of Anatomy, 3rd ed. Hagerstown, Md, Harper & Row, 1974.
9. Horisawa M, Niinomi N, Ito T. Anatomical reconstruction of the thyroglossal duct. J Pediatric Surg 26:776, 1991.
10. Jaffe BF. The branchial arches—normal development and abnormalities. In Ferguson CF, Kendig EL (eds). Pediatric Otolaryngology, vol 2. Philadelphia, WB Saunders, 1972.

11. Kim MK, Pawel BR, Isaacson G. Central neck dissection for the treatment of recurrent thyroglossal duct cysts in childhood. Otolaryngol Head Neck Surg 121:543, 1999.
12. Langman J. Medical Embryology: Human Development—Normal and Abnormal, 2nd ed. Baltimore, Williams & Wilkins, 1969.
13. Levitt GW. Cervical fascia and deep neck infections. Laryngoscope 80:409, 1970.
14. Miller D, Hill JL, Sun CC, et al. The diagnosis and management of pyriform sinus fistulae in infants and young children. J Pediatr Surg 18:377, 1983.
15. Patten BM. Human Embryology, 3rd ed. New York, McGraw-Hill, 1968.
16. Pernkopf E. Atlas of Topographical and Applied Human Anatomy, vol 1. Philadelphia, WB Saunders, 1963.
17. Poswillo DE. Etiology and pathogenesis of first and second branchial arch defects: the contribution of animal studies. In Converse JM, McCarthy JG, WoodSmith D (eds). Symposium on Diagnosis and Treatment of Craniofacial Anomalies, vol 20. New York, New York University, 1976, pp 86–99.
18. Suarez PA, JG Batsakis. Nonneoplastic vascular lesions of the middle ear. Ann Otol Rhinol Laryngol 102:738, 1993.
19. van der Putte SC. Lymphatic malformation in human fetuses. A study of fetuses with Turner's syndrome or status Bonnevie Ullrich. Virchows Arch [Pathol Anat] 376:233, 1977.

96

Methods of Examination

Joseph Haddad Jr., M.D.

The neck of a child changes during the first decade of life. Fat accumulations in the superficial fascial compartments are initially prominent but begin to resorb at 9 months of age. The cartilaginous framework of the infantile larynx is not prominent and is located higher in the neck. As the child grows and the neck elongates, anatomic structures such as the sternocleidomastoid muscle become more reliable landmarks (Fig. 96–1). A careful history and physical examination should guide the physician in choosing among a wide array of diagnostic procedures.

History

A careful history combines information taken from the patient, family, and referring physician and includes the onset of the problem and its duration, location, severity, and progression. The information should lead to a differential diagnosis chosen from the basic types of pathologic conditions found in the neck. Congenital lesions may be symptomatic at birth or, like branchial cleft cysts, may become obvious with infection or slow filling with mucus. Acute inflammatory processes may occur with fever, pain, and swelling; chronic inflammatory processes, such as with granulomatous disease, have varying symptoms and signs. Neoplastic neck masses may slowly enlarge without causing significant symptoms. Interference with air or food passage or neural involvement may be late symptoms.

Temporal associations should be considered. Neck pain or swelling during meals suggests salivary duct obstruction by stricture or stones. Neck mass enlargement with exercise, straining, or crying may indicate a vascular or lymphatic abnormality or a laryngocele.

Environmental exposures should be determined. In a child with a neck mass, previous contact with a cat suggests cat-scratch disease. Medications such as diphenylhydantoin (Dilantin) may promote cervical lymphadenopathy. Radiation therapy to the head and neck is associated with an increased risk of thyroid carcinoma in later years. Children on cyclosporine or FK506 therapy after organ transplantation are at risk for lymphoproliferative disorders, with diffuse cervical lymphadenopathy.

Physical Examination

Examination is begun when the child is comfortable with the physician. The young patient may sit in the parent's lap to be examined.

Most examiners divide the neck into anatomic areas for better definition of a differential diagnosis and to facilitate description of the problem among physicians. For example, midline neck lesions may represent a congenital problem (Fig. 96–2). Landmarks are outlined in Chapter 97, Figure 97–3.

Inspection

In good light, the following normal landmarks should be identified: the jaw, the sternocleidomastoid muscles, the clavicles, and the cartilaginous larynx and trachea. Asymmetry, vascular marks, skin discolorations, scars, fistulas, and abnormal pulsations should be recorded. If a neck mass is present, its location and size should be noted, as should changes with swallowing, tongue protrusion, and head lowering. Thyroglossal duct cysts are attached to the hyoid muscle, usually in the midline, and may move with tongue protrusion. Head lowering causes venous congestion, which may cause cavernous hemangiomas to increase in size. Transillumination of a neck mass is sometimes helpful in superficial, cystic, or fluid-filled masses. Many neck masses change in size and appearance over time, and serial examinations may be necessary for adequate evaluation. Photographs may be useful.

Palpation

Using both hands, the examiner gently palpates the areas of the neck. Notable features include mobility, consistency, tenderness, pulsation, and crepitus. Sebaceous cysts are attached to the epidermis; benign lymph nodes are rubbery, well defined, and mobile; hemangiomas and lymphangiomas have a "bag of worms" consistency due to the presence of loculated fluid chambers (Fig. 96–3).

Palpation should include careful evaluation of the following structures in the neck: salivary glands, lymph nodes, sternocleidomastoid muscle, thyroid gland, and

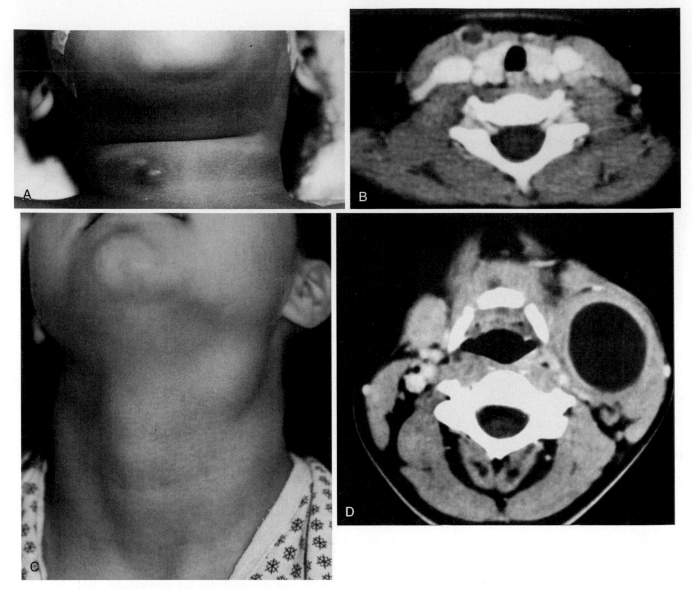

FIGURE 96–1. Maturational differences in neck examination and imaging. *A* shows an infected branchial cleft cyst in a 2-year-old child; *B* shows a computed tomographic (CT) scan in the same child. It is difficult to diagnose the neck mass in this child on the basis of neck landmarks. In the teenager shown in *C* the landmarks are prominent, and a large branchial cleft cyst is seen anterior to the sternocleidomastoid muscle; CT demonstrates the large cystic lesion in *D*.

larynx. The laryngeal examination is discussed in Chapter 76.

Salivary Glands

The parotid glands are usually not palpable in normal children. The Stensen duct should be examined since pus may be expressed in acute parotitis. Bilateral parotid enlargement is common in mumps; when recurrent, it may represent benign parotitis of childhood. Most parotid masses in children are benign lymphangiomas and hemangiomas; they are usually soft and diffuse. Cystic masses have been reported in children and adolescents infected with human immunodeficiency virus. Solid masses in children carry a higher risk for neoplasm. Cat-scratch disease may manifest with intraparotid lymphadenopathy.

The submandibular and sublingual glands are best examined with bimanual palpation (Fig. 96–4). Palpation of the submandibular gland may reveal the presence of stones.

Oral cavity examination is discussed in Chapter 52.

Lymph Nodes

Lymphadenopathy is common in children and usually represents inflammation after an upper respiratory tract

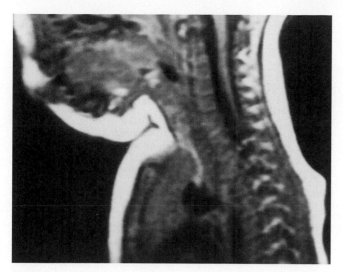

FIGURE 96-9. Sagittal view on magnetic resonance imaging (MRI) demonstrating a large thymus in an infant with a suprasternal mass.

of moving sources (protons in flowing blood) without the injection of a contrast agent. The images may be stacked and rotated in a computer display to obtain a three-dimensional representation of the larger, faster flowing vessels. The lesion, however, may not be visualized unless it is coarsely vascular and has a high flow. Since the vessels, along with the lesion, can usually be discerned on conventional MRI slices, MRA is not often necessary. MRA is sensitive to motion artifacts, especially swallowing, and is likely to require sedation in children (Fig. 96-10).

Gadolinium (Gd) injection usually enhances (brightens) the signal of a neck mass on MRI. Because adjacent fat planes are already bright, especially on the most frequently obtained (T_1-weighted) pulse sequences, enhancement may actually decrease the conspicuousness of a lesion. Conspicuousness increases when gadolinium is used in conjunction with a "fat suppression" pulse sequence that darkens fat planes adjacent to the lesion. These sequences are exquisitely sensitive to motion artifact, however, and for most neck masses in children, conventional T_1-weighted images in multiple planes, supplemented by a T_2-weighted sequence for further characterization of the lesion, may be sufficient. Some sedation may be necessary even in these cases.

Nuclear Scintigraphy

The thyroid gland is easily evaluated by nuclear medicine procedures using isotopes. Even though thyroid masses are rare in children, when they do occur, they are more likely to be malignant than they are in adults, and nuclear imaging plays an important role in their detection. In the past decade, technetium-99m (^{99m}Tc) has replaced radioactive iodine for scanning the thyroid gland. Sodium pertechnetate ^{99m}Tc is concentrated within the thyroid gland by the same trapping mechanism that stores iodine, but this isotope is not incorporated into the precursors of thyroxine. Nonfunctioning (cold) nodules are demonstrated as filling defects within the image of the gland; functioning (hot) nodules are demonstrated as areas of increased activity. If only the nodules concentrate the radioactive isotope, then the thyroid gland must be stimulated by thyroid-stimulating hormone (TSH) and the pa-

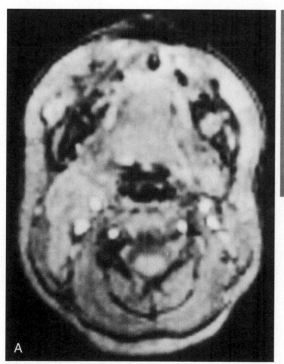

FIGURE 96-10. MRI of a 4-month-old infant with a right neck mass. *A,* Mass adjacent to the carotid on an axial view. *B,* Magnetic resonance angiographic reconstruction of the neck vessels, with deviation of the carotid. Excisional biopsy revealed ectopic thymus of the right neck.

tient is scanned again. After TSH stimulation, a normal thyroid gland is seen, with the autonomous thyroid nodule evident in the normal tissue.

The same techniques can be used to evaluate the salivary glands, but the results are nonspecific. Degenerative diseases such as Sjögren disease show decreased uptake of radioisotope. Neoplastic or inflammatory masses that destroy or replace the gland display focally decreased uptake. Warthin tumor and oncocytoma, rare in children, may concentrate the isotope.

^{99m}Tc diphosphonate is a bone-imaging agent that is normally taken up in the cervical spine. This agent may also be absorbed in areas of necrosis or calcification within the soft tissues of the neck. Neuroblastomas take up bone-scanning agents, even when calcification of this tumor cannot be demonstrated radiographically.

The use of gallium for evaluation of neck masses requires a relatively high radiation dose and is discouraged in children.

Arteriography

The use of angiography has diminished dramatically with the widespread use of CT. Its main uses are limited to the diagnosis of vascular neck masses and cervical trauma with vascular injury. The vascular neck masses include chemodectomas and nasopharyngeal angiofibromas, which show numerous enlarged arteries and staining in the capillary phase of the study. Arteriovenous malformations are characterized by large feeding vessels and show prompt filling of large draining veins during the arterial phase. Cavernous hemangiomas have a slow flow and are rarely demonstrated. Digital subtraction angiography is widely used and employs a digital format for computer image enhancement. With this modality, exposure to contrast and radiation is usually reduced.

Arteriography has taken on an important role in preoperative evaluation and embolization of vascular malformations in the neck. A variety of embolic materials has been employed, including plastic, Gelfoam, metal, coils, absolute alcohol, blood clots, and muscle. Vascular thrombosis distal to the embolic material reduces vascularity and flow of the malformation and operative blood loss.

Other Imaging Techniques

With the advent of CT scanning, sialography is rarely used in children. Xeroradiography exposes the child to approximately four times the radiation of conventional neck radiography and is not routinely used in children.[4]

SELECTED REFERENCES

The following articles provide background information to the topic discussed in this chapter.

Carter BL, Karmody CS, Blickman JR, Panders AK. Computed tomography and sialography: I. Normal anatomy. J Comput Assist Tomogr 5:42, 1981.

Cole DR, Bankoff M, Carter BL. Percutaneous catheter drainage of deep neck infections guided by CT. Radiology 152:224, 1984.

Dietrich MB, Lufkin R, Kangarloo H, et al. Head and MR imaging in the pediatric patient. Radiology 159:769, 1986.

Faerber EN, Swartz JD. Imaging of neck masses in infants and children. Crit Rev Diagn Imaging 31:283, 1991.

Fiori-Ratti L, DeCampora E, Senin U. Sequence scintigraphy: a morphological and functional study of the salivary glands. Laryngoscope 87:1086, 1977.

Frable WJ. Thin needle aspiration biopsy. Am J Clin Pathol 65:168, 1976.

Friedman AP, Haller JO, Goodman JD, Nager H. Sonographic evaluation of noninflammatory neck masses in children. Radiology 147:693, 1983.

Gatenby RA, Mulhern CB Jr, Strawitz J. CT-guided percutaneous biopsies of head and neck masses. Radiology 146:717, 1983.

Gay SB, Pevarski DR, Phillips CD, Levine PA. Dynamic CT of the neck. Radiology 180:284, 1991.

Harnsberger HR, Mancuso AA, Muraki AS, et al. Branchial cleft anomalies and their mimics: computed tomographic evaluation. Radiology 152:739, 1984.

Leboeuf G, Ducharme JR. Thyroiditis in children. Diagnosis and management. Pediatr Clin North Am 13:19, 1966.

Ravindranath T, Janakiraman N, Harris V. Computed tomography in diagnosing retropharyngeal abscess in children. Clin Pediatr 32:242, 1993.

Solbiati L, Cioffi V, Ballarati E. Ultrasonography of the neck. Radiol Clin North Am 30:941, 1992.

Swartz JD, Yussen PS, Popky GL. Imaging the soft tissues of the neck: nonnodal acquired disease. Crit Rev Diagn Imaging 31:471, 1991.

Weber AL, Baker AS, Montgomery WM. Inflammatory lesions of the neck, including fascial spaces-evaluation by computed tomography and magnetic resonance imaging. Isr J Med Sci 28:241, 1992.

Yousem DM. Dashed hopes for MR imaging of the head and neck: the power of the needle. Radiology 184:25, 1992.

REFERENCES

1. Brodeur AE, Silberstein MD, Graviss ER. Direct microfocus magnification: its many advantages in pediatrics. Am J Dis Child 134:245, 1980.

2. Gould LV, Summings CW, Rabuzzi DD, et al. Use of computerized axial tomography of the head and neck region. Laryngoscope 87:1270, 1977.

3. Kraus R, Han B, Babcock D, Oestreich A. Sonography of neck masses in children. AJR Am J Roentgenol 146:609, 1986.

4. Smith C, Ramsey RG. Xeroradiography of the lateral neck. Radiographics 2:306, 1982.

5. Stark D, Moss A, Gamsu G, et al. Magnetic resonance imaging of the neck. Radiology 150:447, 1984.

97

Neck Masses

Paul W. Bauer, M.D., and Rodney P. Lusk, M.D., F.A.C.S.

Neck masses in children are common. The etiology is often assigned to one of three categories: inflammatory, congenital, or neoplastic. In adults, most neck masses are categorized as neoplastic. By comparison, the frequency of benign inflammatory adenopathy in children is high.[106] Most of these children are never seen by an otolaryngologist, and the incidence of significant lymphadenopathy requiring biopsy is low. The evaluation of neck masses warrants special concern in children because there is an 11% potential for malignancy; 29% of biopsied benign-appearing masses are malignant.[99] Therefore, vigilance is warranted in the evaluation of neck masses in children.

The approach to each case should be organized and systematic. The history and physical examination direct diagnostic studies or intervention to confirm the diagnosis. This chapter provides an overview of the initial evaluation and differentiation of neck masses in children.

History

A thorough history often indicates a likely diagnosis before the physical examination. The history should establish the age of onset, the duration of signs and symptoms, and the involvement of other organ systems.

A neck mass present at birth is congenital. Although the lesions are present at birth, not all congenital lesions are recognized in the neonatal period. Some are not seen until adulthood after an infection has caused inflammation and rapid enlargement. Congenital lesions are rarely malignant.

The natural history of cervical adenitis is gradual regression after treatment and resolution of the primary infection.[27] Cervical adenopathy that persists raises concern of a possible malignancy. In the evaluation of inflammatory neck masses, environmental information regarding exposure to cats, nondomestic animals, insects, unusual travel, and humans with tuberculosis should be obtained to exclude uncommon granulomatous etiologies.

Slowly growing masses are probably benign or congenital lesions manifesting after birth. Masses that fluctuate in size are compatible with an inflammatory process or late-appearing congenital lesion. A rapidly growing mass that develops over days suggests an inflammatory process. A mass that grows rapidly over a period of 4 to 8 weeks should raise suspicion of a malignancy.[48]

Constitutional symptoms such as fatigue, weight loss, fever, and night sweats raise concern of possible malignancy. In addition, a history of unilateral otitis media, otorrhea, rhinorrhea, and nasal obstruction may accompany a malignancy that may manifest primarily or metastasize to the neck. These early signs and symptoms can also be seen in immune-mediated inflammatory processes or granulomatous infections, such as tuberculosis or nontuberculous mycobacterium (NTM). Most malignant neck masses in children manifest as an asymptomatic mass.[29] A painful mass is most often inflammatory; however, hemorrhage into a necrotic tumor or cystic mass may also lead to complaints of pain. The ability to distinguish malignant from benign adenopathy based on the clinical history is limited.[27]

It is import to solicit any history of ionizing radiation exposure, for example, in patients from areas of the world where known nuclear accidents have occurred. A causative association for neoplastic transformation in thyroid and salivary glands exposed to ionizing radiation has been described.[88, 100]

Some populations have a higher risk of malignancy. Neoplasms such as neuroblastoma and medullary thyroid carcinoma are associated with known genetic origins.[17, 59] Nasopharyngeal carcinoma is more common in patients from Southeast Asia and may occur as a metastatic neck mass. DNA from the Epstein-Barr virus (EBV) has been isolated from both nasopharyngeal carcinoma and Burkitt lymphoma.[67]

A thorough family history aids in the diagnosis of lesions with a genetic origin. Congenital cysts can be associated with syndromes, such as branchio-otorenal syndrome.[66]

Physical Examination

Techniques of physical examination are described in Chapter 96. In evaluating a child with a neck mass, it is important to perform a systematic, thorough examination of the head and neck, quality of the mass, and the entire body.

A thorough head and neck examination initially directed away from the mass is important to avoid overlooking a potential primary lesion. One sixth of malignant neck lesions in children manifest with a primary or asso-

TABLE 97-1. Diagnosis of Neck Masses by Location

Parotid (Preauricular) Region

Inflammatory

Lymphadenitis from upper face and anterior scalp
Parotitis
    Viral—puncta red, secretions clear
    Bacterial—puncta normal, secretions purulent
    Granuloma
    Tuberculosis and nontuberculous mycobacterium
    Sarcoidosis

Congenital

Lymphatic malformation, hemangioma

Traumatic

Sialocele

Neoplastic

Benign—pleomorphic adenoma
Malignant—mucoepidermoid carcinoma
Lymphoma

Idiopathic

Sjögren syndrome—sialogram shows "bunch of grapes" pattern
Sarcoidosis (uveo-parotid fever)

Postauricular Region

Congenital

First branchial cleft anomalies (type I)

Inflammatory

Lymphadenitis from posterior scalp

Submental Region

Congenital

Thyroglossal duct cyst or ectopic thyroid
Lymphatic malformation
Dermoid cyst
Vascular malformation

Inflammatory

Lymphadenitis from oral or nasal cavity

Neoplastic

Thyroglossal duct papillary carcinoma

Submandibular Region

Congenital

Lymphatic or vascular malformation

Inflammatory

Lymphadenitis from cheek or midoral cavity
Sialadenitis
Cystic fibrosis—submandibular gland enlarged

Neoplastic

Salivary gland neoplasms

Other

Plunging ranula

Jugulodigastric Region

Normal

Transverse process of C_2 or styloid process

Congenital

First or second branchial cleft cyst
Vascular or lymphatic malformation

Inflammatory

Lymphadenitis from oropharyngeal

Neoplastic

Parotid neoplasms
Lymphoma

Midline Neck Region

Congenital

Thyroglossal duct cyst or ectopic thyroid, dermoid cyst

Inflammatory

Lymphadenitis

Neoplastic

Thyroid malignancy

Anterior Border Sternocleidomastoid Muscle

Congenital

Branchial cleft anomalies, laryngocele, lymphatic or vascular malformation, sternocleidomastoid tumor of infancy, thymic cyst or ectopic thymus

Neoplastic

Carotid body tumor
Lymphoma
Sarcoma

Spinal Accessory Region

Congenital

Lymphatic or vascular malformation

Neoplastic

Lymphoma
Metastatic (from nasopharynx)

Inflammatory

Lymphadenitis (from nasopharynx)

Paratracheal Region

Inflammatory

Lymphadenitis
Thyroiditis

Congenital

Thyroglossal duct cyst
Branchial cleft anomalies

Neoplastic

Thyroid or parathyroid neoplasms

Supraclavicular Region

Congenital

Lymphatic or vascular malformation

Neoplastic

Lipoma
Lymphoma
Metastatic lesion (lung, esophagus, renal, testicular)

Suprasternal Region

Congenital

Dermoid cyst
Thymic cyst or ectopic thymus

Neoplastic

Lipoma
Metastatic lesion

From May M. Neck masses in children: diagnosis and treatment. Pediatr Ann 5:8, 1976.

ciated lesion in the oropharynx, hypopharynx, or nasopharynx.[53] Inspection of these areas can be accomplished with a mirror or flexible scope in a cooperative child. Some children may require an examination under general anesthesia with rigid endoscopy to exclude nasopharyngeal or pharyngeal pathology. All other noninvasive means of evaluating the child should be completed before proceeding with an examination and biopsy under general anesthesia. This allows coordinated planning among the other medical and surgical services that may also need to perform invasive procedures such as bone marrow aspiration, central venous catheter insertion, or lumbar puncture.

In directing the examination toward the mass, bimanual palpation, when possible, should be performed to assess the consistency and character of the mass and to determine its relationship to surrounding structures. Noting the anatomic location of the mass helps to further differentiate the lesion. May[71] described the diagnosis of neck masses by 11 anatomic locations and generated a differential diagnosis based on the location (Table 97–1). The sternocleidomastoid muscle divides the neck into anterior and posterior triangles. Most cervical masses are found in the anterior triangle. Masses in the anterior triangle have a lower incidence of malignancy compared with masses in the posterior triangle. Careful attention should be given to persistent palpable supraclavicular masses. In one study of children who had undergone surgical biopsy, 35% of patients with a supraclavicular mass had lymphoma.[99] Masses other than lymphangiomas and hemangiomas that occupy both triangles have the highest incidence of malignancy. The regions of the neck described by May also encompass the lymphatic drainage pattern of the head and neck. An example of the lymphatic drainage pattern is Parinaud oculoglandular syndrome, which is the combination of unilateral conjunctivitis and preauricular adenopathy that can be seen in cat-scratch disease.[21, 46]

A thorough examination of the entire body should be performed to identify systemic disease. The skin should be carefully inspected for suspicious cutaneous lesions. In cervical adenitis, the scalp should be thoroughly examined for a possible primary site of infection. Cutaneous hemangiomas can be associated with synchronous masses in the head and neck. Café au lait spots may be seen in cases of neurofibromatosis. In cat-scratch disease, an inoculation papule at the site of the scratch is seen in approximately half of patients (see Fig. 97–5A). Close attention should also be directed to the abdomen, axillary, and inguinal areas since head and neck malignancy may be a part of a systemic process involving these regions. Specifically, palpation should include axillary and inguinal nodes and assessment of liver and spleen enlargement.

Diagnostic Studies

After completing a thorough history and physical examination, the differential diagnosis should be significantly narrowed to allow selection of appropriate diagnostic studies. The diagnostic approach is based on the clinical assumption of the mass being inflammatory, congenital, or neoplastic. Torsiglieri et al[99] found that children with nonspecific lymph node hyperplasia underwent the largest number of laboratory and radiologic studies, the majority of which were normal. They believed that this demonstrated a lack of diagnostic direction in evaluating children with cervical adenopathy. Because of increasing health care costs, this emphasizes the need for a meticulous history and physical examination that will appropriately direct the diagnostic studies.

Laboratory Evaluation

A complete blood count with differential analysis is appropriate in most patients who present with a neck mass. The cellular response that is demonstrated by this test might provide clues to the nature of an offending organism or possibly to the presence of neoplastic cells. In masses confined to the midline of the neck or related to the thyroid gland, thyroid function testing may be appropriate. In lesions with a systemic effect, renal and liver function testing should be considered. Isolated cervical adenopathy is a common manifestation of tuberculosis, with or without chest radiographic findings. Therefore, in a patient with multiple firm nodes, an exposure history, or a suppressed immune status, or in a patient from an endemic area, purified protein derivative (PPD) testing with controls is warranted. The importance of a thorough history regarding travel and animal exposure is demonstrated in the selection of serologic testing. In the setting of an appropriate history, serologic testing for *Bartonella* (cat-scratch disease), tularemia, EBV, *Borrelia* (Lyme disease), toxoplasmosis, mumps, cytomegalovirus, brucellosis, histoplasmosis, or coccidioidomycosis should be considered.

Radiologic Evaluation

The use of diagnostic radiology in the head and neck has grown. In addition to assisting in narrowing the differential diagnosis of a neck mass, imaging techniques can define the extent of the lesion to assist in preoperative planning, localize recurrent disease, and serve as an adjunct to interventional techniques.

Plain Radiographs

More advanced imaging techniques have supplanted the use of plain radiographs, except when soft tissue–air interfaces provide sufficient information to determine the site and degree of airway narrowing. Neck films that can quickly substantiate the clinical diagnosis of crepitus in the setting of anaerobic necrotizing cellulitis may be lifesaving and support the need for emergency surgical intervention.

Traditionally, soft tissue lateral neck radiographs have been used to quickly evaluate neck swelling associated with airway distress as the site of a parapharyngeal or retropharyngeal inflammatory process can be defined with plain radiographs. Standards have been defined for what constitutes prevertebral soft tissue thickening. The thickness of the prevertebral soft tissue measured at the C2-C3 sagittal level is compared with the sagittal diameter of C2 at its lower border. The maximum normal ratio is 1.0 at birth to age 1 year and decreases to 0.4 at ages 6 to 10 years.[63] Another method has defined the normal sagittal soft tissue limits of the prevertebral soft tissue in a child as between 4 and 7 mm at the C2 level and less than 14 mm at the anteroinferior aspect of C6 (Fig. 97–1A).[76] In addition to showing prevertebral soft tissue thickening, lateral neck radiographs can show straightening of the normal cervical lordotic curve resulting from muscle

spasm. The degree of muscle spasm from acute inflammation may be so great as to suggest subluxation.[63]

These films are not always easy to interpret. The superimposed normal shadow of the earlobe and the normal tonsil can both appear to be an abnormal pharyngeal mass. In addition, these films are technique dependent. Prevertebral thickening may be falsely interpreted as the result of the phase of respiration, positioning, crying, or swallowing.

Plain radiographs may also include the chest in selected patients. Children with granulomatous neck disease

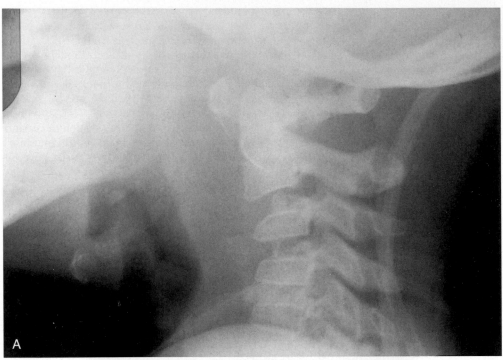

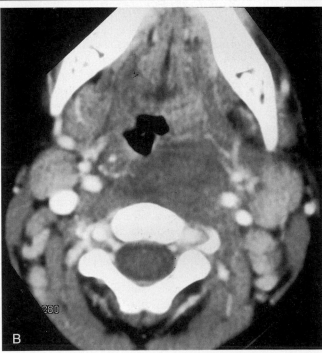

FIGURE 97–1. Five-year-old boy presenting with a deep neck abscess. *A,* Plain airway film reveals thickening of the prevertebral soft tissue and straightening of the normal cervical lordotic curve. *B,* Contrast enhanced CT confirms a left deep neck abscess with rim enhancement.

may have cavitary or calcified pulmonary lesions or may have evidence of mediastinal widening as a result of lymphadenopathy. Suspected malignant neoplasms may have a primary pulmonary etiology and generalized systemic disease such as lymphoma may have a widened mediastinum.

Ultrasonography

Ultrasonography (US) is an attractive option in children because of its simplicity, decreased cost, immediate results, and absence of radiation, often alleviating the need for sedation. US can determine the size, define the borders, and show the relationship of a neck mass to adjacent structures such as the great vessels or trachea. US characterizes the echogenic patterns of a mass, classifying them as cystic, solid, or complex in nature, thus narrowing the differential diagnosis of the neck mass. The sonographic findings must be correlated with the clinical presentation to arrive at the correct diagnosis. For example, in a branchial cleft cyst, acute inflammation can alter the characteristic sonographic echogenic pattern.[90]

In evaluating thyroid gland lesions, US is an accurate presurgical tool that can differentiate between thyroiditis, multinodular goiter, and follicular adenomas.[43] In the case of a presumed thyroglossal duct cyst, US can confirm the presence of thyroid tissue in the normal location; a radioisotope scan is needed to assess the function of the thyroid tissue.

The sonographic characteristic patterns of some lesions have been well defined. A lymphangioma appears as a multilocular, predominantly cystic mass with linear septa of various thicknesses, depending on the amount of connective tissue, muscle, and fat between the cysts (see Fig. 97–3A).[91] A sternocleidomastoid tumor of infancy appears as an ovoid or fusiform homogeneous mass within the sternocleidomastoid muscle, which moves with the muscle and has no significant internal vascular flow.[104]

All large inflammatory lesions must be evaluated for sequestration of abscess fluid. Abscesses are seen as distinct cystic masses using US (see Fig. 97–5B). Color flow Doppler US demonstrates enhanced peripheral and central vascular flow in inflammatory adenopathy; in suppurated nodes the central vascularity is lost. Using color flow Doppler imaging, US can define the great vessels or the presence of a thrombophlebitis.[73] In select pediatric patients, US can be used to guide aspiration of a potential abscess, and complete drainage of a deep neck abscess has been described.[80, 90]

US is limited by an air–soft tissue interface and bone. Probing inflamed areas may lead to significant patient discomfort and necessitate sedation. Glasier et al[44] showed that US was more predictive than computed tomography (CT) for finding an abscess at the time of drainage. However, surgeons are often not able to easily interpret sonographic images and the lack of a surgical "roadmap" often leads to the acquisition of CT confirmation before surgical intervention, despite clear sonographic evidence of a deep neck abscess.

Computed Tomography

Contrast enhanced CT is the standard means of imaging for rapid, accurate diagnosis of the acute deep neck abscess.[51, 65, 76, 77, 101] On CT scan, cellulitis is defined as soft tissue swelling with the obliteration of regional fat planes. An abscess is defined with a contrast CT with an area of low attenuation and a rim of contrast enhancement surrounded by cellulitis (see Figs. 97–1B and 97–5C).[65] This same pattern can be seen in neoplasms with a necrotic center, but the clinical and laboratory findings usually lead to the correct diagnosis. Nagy and Backstrom[76] compared the sensitivity of lateral neck radiographs and CT scanning in evaluating patients with clinically suspected deep neck infections. They found that lateral neck radiographs offered no benefit in the work-up of children who clinically were strongly suspected to have a deep neck infection. They found that CT scans with contrast were 100% sensitive in determining the presence and location of an infectious process in the lateral or retropharyngeal space.[76]

CT allows assessment of abscess size, location, and position in relation to the great vessels. In cases of internal jugular vein thrombophlebitis, diffuse inflammatory changes are seen in the surrounding tissues, the lumen of the vein does not enhance with contrast (the wall of the vein may enhance), and the vein itself may be distended (Fig. 97–2).[51] The location of the abscess in relation to the great vessels may help direct surgical management. When the abscess is located medial to the great vessels, a transoral approach to incision and drainage may be ap-

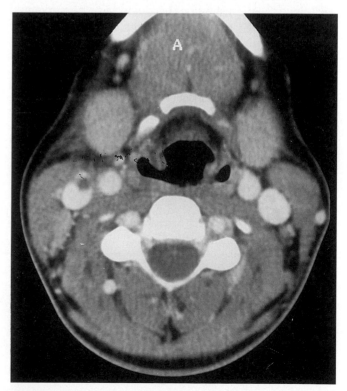

FIGURE 97–2. Contrast enhanced CT demonstrating thrombus formation in the right internal jugular vein.

propriate.[77] A CT with contrast is the only way a surgeon can effectively determine the best approach for intervention. In the assessment of deep neck infections, CT has been shown to be 100% sensitive in determining the presence of an infectious process (phlegmon or suppuration); however, the sensitivity of CT for demonstrating suppuration when suppuration is surgically present is only between 88% and 92%.[65, 76, 101] Therefore, the sensitivity for detecting an abscess is good but not perfect. This emphasizes the importance of correlating radiologic findings with clinical findings before proceeding with surgical intervention. The CT scan can say nothing about the duration of the mass.

In evaluating a noninflammatory neck mass, contrast enhanced CT can be used to differentiate solid from cystic masses. CT can also provide sufficient detail to strongly suggest the type of bone reaction (e.g., erosion, lysis, or passive bowing), invasion of contiguous structures, or intracranial extension of the lesion. As is often the case in congenital lesions, CT is used to preoperatively define the extent of the lesion and its relationship to vital structures of the neck rather than diagnostically differentiate the lesion.

Magnetic Resonance Imaging

Either CT or magnetic resonance imaging (MRI) can be used in the assessment of most neck masses in children (Fig. 97–3B and C). The decision as to which technique to use is often based on availability, need for sedation, compatibility of life support devices with the technique, and familiarity of the surgeon and radiologist with the technique.[56] An institution may not have the required nursing support and dedicated equipment necessary to sedate and monitor children with marginal airways for lengthy MRI examinations. CT scans frequently require no sedation or a shorter period of sedation.

MRI provides exquisitely sensitive soft tissue imaging with excellent anatomic detail in any anatomic plane (see Fig. 97–3C, D, and E). It is the procedure of choice for evaluating and differentiating vascular and lymphatic neoplasms in the pediatric neck (Table 97–2).[3, 56, 105] It is useful for assessing extension into the mediastinum in the coronal plane and the degree of airway impingement in

the axial plane and vascular compromise can be seen (on axial images) with magnetic resonance angiography (MRA) or venography.[56]

MRI has not been shown to be more successful than CT in distinguishing cellulitis or phlegmon from a true abscess collection.[51, 56] Contrast enhanced CT remains the standard imaging technique for the evaluation of the acute neck abscess.[51, 56, 65, 76, 77, 101] The MRI scan can, however, elegantly show vascular complications, such as venous thrombophlebitis or carotid artery narrowing.

MRI cannot show bone but can be used to assess the periosteum and the extent of involvement of marrow-containing spaces; it is the preferred technique for evaluating intracranial extension of tumor. In addition, special fat saturation techniques and intravenous contrast MRI allow earlier detection of perineural spread of disease, before any bulky tumor or bone destruction is seen on CT.[56] On occasion, the seriousness of the lesion dictates that both MRI and CT be performed.

Positron-Emission Tomography

Positron-emission tomography (PET) scanning has been used extensively to study the metabolic activity of the brain. The radionuclide tracers used in PET scanning rely on glycolytic metabolism in tumor cells. Tumor cells prefer glycolysis to oxidative metabolism. PET scanning can be used to determine whether a mass is neoplastic, the extent of disease, and the response of the tumor to therapy, and, following therapy, it can be used to determine whether residual mass is tumor or scar. Neuroblastoma, rhabdosarcoma, and lymphoma are all pediatric neck masses that may be imaged using PET scans. The radiation burden is comparable to conventional nuclear medicine and, because the procedure is long, sedation is needed for most infants and children.[92]

Radionuclide Scans

In evaluating patients with a midline neck mass, US can confirm the location of the normal thyroid gland; however, in select patients, a technetium-99m (^{99m}Tc) or iodine-123 (^{123}I) scan to confirm the location of functioning

TABLE 97–2. MRI Features of Lymphatic and Vascular Malformations and Hemangiomas

Lesion	Soft-Tissue Component	Flow Voids	Contrast Enhancement
Lymphatic malformations (macrocystic)	Minimal	None	None
Lymphatic malformations (microcystic)	+	None	Septal enhancement
Vascular malformations (venous)	+ (Phleboliths)	None	Diffuse (variable)
Vascular malformations (arteriovenous)	None	+++	Intense (++)
Hemangioma	+++	++	Intense (+++)

Adapted from Jones BV, Koch BL. Magnetic resonance imaging of the pediatric head and neck. Top Magn Reson Imaging 10:348–361, 1999.

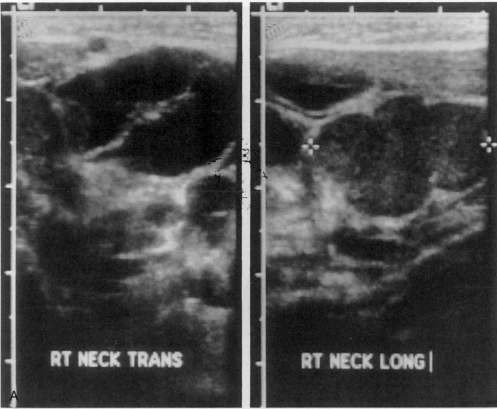

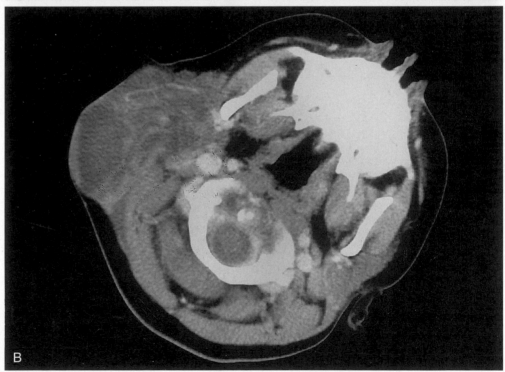

FIGURE 97–3. Three-year-old boy with a lymphatic malformation involving the right neck. *A,* Ultrasound reveals the characteristic multilocular, predominantly cystic nature of the mass. The varied echogenic pattern of the fluid within the cyst correlates with the complex nature of these lesions. *B,* Contrast enhanced CT reveals the adjacent bony architecture and complex nature of the lesion.

Illustration continued on following page

thyroid tissue may be indicated.[87] These techniques are also often used in the evaluation of thyroid nodules.[4] ^{99m}Tc scanning tests only the transport of iodine, but it can be performed in a day, is simple, and involves a relatively low dose of radiation. In comparison, ^{123}I tests both the transport and organification of iodine; however, it is more expensive, involves a higher dose of radiation, and requires 2 days to complete. Thyroid scanning does not allow differentiation between benign and malignant thyroid nodules.[72]

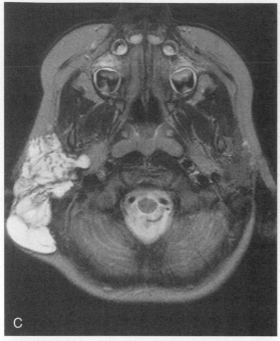

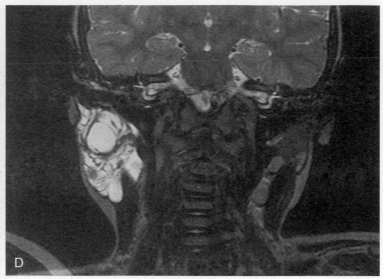

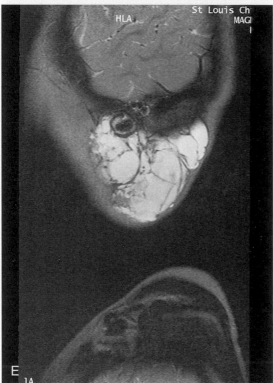

FIGURE 97–3 *Continued. C,* T$_2$-weighted axial MRI highlights the fluid-filled nature of the cyst and provides exquisite anatomic detail of the surrounding soft tissue structures. *D,* T$_2$-weighted coronal MRI of the same lesion. *E,* T$_2$-weighted sagittal MRI of the same lesion. The coronal and sagittal views demonstrate the ability of MRI to examine masses in multiple anatomic planes.

Angiography/Interventional Radiology

Angiography is rarely indicated in the evaluation or treatment of neck masses in children. The advancement of magnetic resonance technology with multiplanar capability, MRA, and magnetic resonance venography has allowed the diagnosis of vascular lesions to be confidently established. Interventional radiography may be required for children with arteriovenous malformations or angiofibromas. The need for treatment of neck hemangiomas and vascular malformations is based on interference with function, growth, and development; potential for hemorrhage; and cosmetic stigma.[3] Arteriovenous malformations are preferably embolized before surgery, but, because of functional and cosmetic concerns in the head and neck, surgery is not always practical and embolization may be the only intervention available.[3]

Head and neck hemangiomas are typically managed conservatively. Intervention may be indicated when the location leads to airway compromise or functional impairment, or threatens life.[36] Interventional treatment of hemangiomas involves embolization of vessels feeding the vascular bed.[3] Because tissue is expected to swell from tissue ischemia after embolization, care should be taken to appropriately secure the airway.

Arterial complications from deep neck infections are rare; however, carotid artery rupture or pseudoaneurysm formation may occur. Preoperative angiography is dictated if CT or MRI indicates expansion of the carotid lumen, a lack of enhancement in the lumen is seen, or the patient has unexplained neurologic deficits.[51]

Prenatal Imaging

The widespread use of prenatal US has led to the detection of intrauterine congenital head and neck abnormalities. The mortality rate associated with massive congenital neck masses (such as cervical teratomas and lymphatic malformations) in the neonatal period can be high. An association has been observed between sonographic evidence of polyhydramnios and acute airway obstruction at birth.[98] Fetal MRI can provide a more accurate diagnosis, greater anatomic detail, and a larger field of view, and it can better define the anatomic relationship to surrounding normal structures than US.[50, 68] Reports differ as to whether sonographic-guided needle drainage may offer a more favorable outcome in select cases of fetal lymphatic malformations.[25, 26] Prenatal detection of life-threatening fetal neck masses allows formulation of a controlled delivery plan. The EXIT (ex utero intrapartum treatment) procedure is an example of a technique designed to secure the infant airway while uteroplacental gas exchange is preserved.[68] The mother undergoes general anesthesia to achieve maximum uterine relaxation to preserve uteroplacental circulation and fetal gas exchange. The fetus is delivered through cesarean section with the head and

shoulders delivered through the hysterotomy while the umbilical cord and lower torso remain in the uterus. The fetal airway is then secured either through endotracheal intubation or tracheostomy (Fig. 97–4).[68, 98]

Fine-Needle Aspiration

Fine-needle aspiration (FNA) is reported to be an easily performed, low morbidity, accurate, and safe technique that is commonly practiced in adults and is probably underused in children.[74] The availability of an experienced and competent cytopathologist with expertise in evaluating the morphologic characteristics of specimens obtained from pediatric neck masses may limit the use of this technique. A negative result of a needle aspirate should never be conveyed as indicating the absence of malignancy.[74]

FNA is not limited to differentiating benign from malignant disease. The use of ancillary studies such as electron microscopy, lymphocyte marker analysis, immunoperoxidase stains, DNA flow cytometry, and molecular hybridization often allows an accurate diagnosis regarding specific tumor subtype to be established.[74] Where these studies are available, the diagnosis of lymphoma, rhabdomyosarcoma, and thyroid malignancy can be established without open incisional or excisional biopsy.[34, 62, 74] The role of FNA in evaluating pediatric thyroid nodules is still under investigation. The higher incidence of malignancy seen in pediatric thyroid nodules has resulted in recommendations for aggressive surgical excision for all pediatric solitary thyroid nodules.[42, 52] Recent studies have demonstrated the high diagnostic accuracy of thyroid FNA and the role FNA can play in improving pediatric patient selection for surgery.[62, 86]

FNA can assist in the assessment and treatment of inflammatory neck masses. In children with cervical

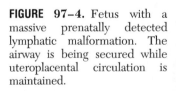

FIGURE 97–4. Fetus with a massive prenatally detected lymphatic malformation. The airway is being secured while uteroplacental circulation is maintained.

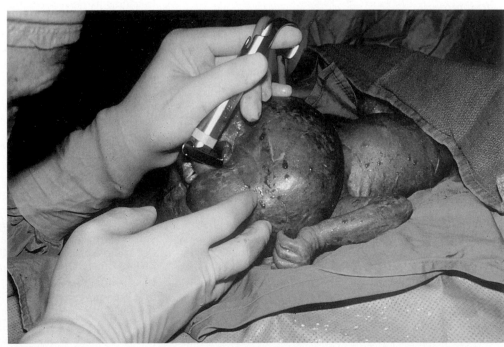

lymphadenitis, a lymph node aspirate can be cultured to direct antibiotic therapy.[10] In cases of abscess formation, FNA with or without US guidance may serve either a diagnostic or therapeutic role. In the diagnosis of granulomatous neck masses, *Mycobacterium tuberculosis* polymerase chain reaction for mycobacterial DNA sequences has been performed on material from FNA and has successfully diagnosed cervical tuberculous lymphadenitis.[6]

Biopsy

The appropriateness of performing an open incisional or excisional biopsy frequently arises during the evaluation of a neck mass. Failure to diagnose a malignancy is often a concern when evaluating neck masses in children. If the diagnosis is unclear from laboratory data, radiologic studies, or FNA, or if there has been no significant resolution with a short course of conservative therapy, then a biopsy should be performed. When the lesion is clinically thought to be malignant, a multidisciplinary team should plan the approach and staging procedures before the biopsy. Depending on the location and size of the mass, the biopsy is incisional or excisional. An excisional biopsy may be both diagnostic and therapeutic.

Diagnosis

A more thorough discussion of the differential diagnosis and management of specific neck masses follows in Chapters 98 to 103. The location of the mass provides valuable information about the most likely diagnosis. After the history, physical examination, and diagnostic studies are completed, most lesions can be classified as inflammatory, congenital, or neoplastic, thus directing further management.

Inflammatory

The most common neck mass in children is inflammatory cervical lymphadenopathy. Clinically palpable cervical lymph nodes are a normal finding in at least 40% of infants younger than 1 year of age.[8] By far, the most common etiology of palpable cervical nodes in children is a viral or bacterial upper respiratory tract infection.[15, 27, 99, 106] These nodes are characteristically tender. Bacteria-infected nodes may suppurate and, in children, are common causes of deep neck infections. *Staphylococcus aureus* followed by group A beta-hemolytic streptococcus is the organism most frequently cultured from the involved nodes.[10, 19, 77] Cervical adenopathy present for a short duration of time and associated with a recent upper respiratory infection warrants a trial of conservative therapy (observation or oral antibiotic therapy) unless there is evidence of abscess formation. In cases of massive adenopathy, an empirical trial of intravenous antibiotic may be appropriate. If no clinical improvement is seen over 48 hours or if obvious signs of suppuration develop, a drainage procedure is warranted.[77] Needle aspiration, transoral incision and drainage, or external incision and drainage, each combined with intravenous antibiotics,

have all demonstrated effectiveness.[18, 77] The most appropriate approach to drainage should be determined by what is best for the individual patient. Deep neck infections rarely recur after surgical incision and drainage. Even though most deep neck infections are the result of suppurative adenitis, the recurrence of a deep neck infection should prompt investigation of a possible underlying congenital cystic mass.[79]

Mycobacterium cervical adenitis is a relatively common cause of inflammatory lymphadenopathy in children. Suspicion is often prompted when patients fail standard antibiotic management. Infection is more often from NTM, with *Mycobacterium avium-intracellulare* being the most commonly cultured organism.[40, 64, 83] The typical clinical presentation is in a preschool-aged girl who presents with an upper cervical or submandibular mass with overlying violaceous skin.[40, 103] The natural history of untreated NTM is unknown. Infected nodes may suppurate, develop fibrocalcific scarring, or remain subclinical. However, when the nodes become prominent enough to prompt the parent to seek medical attention, progression of the disease to suppuration and spontaneous sinus formation is the usual course if not treated.[103] PPD testing can help to differentiate between tuberculous and nontuberculous etiologies, but positive cultures are needed to confirm the diagnosis. Treatment has included complete excision, incision and drainage with or without curettage, needle aspiration, and medical management.[1, 14, 40, 61] The treatment of choice for NTM is complete surgical excision.[14, 40] This can be limited by the proximity of disease to branches of the facial nerve (a common finding in NTM), and, in difficult operative conditions, it is preferable to leave disease than to inflict irreversible neural injury.[85] The postoperative management of remaining disease with clarithromycin plus rifabutin may be of benefit in preventing or treating sinus formation.[14]

Infectious mononucleosis is due to EBV and classically includes cervical lymphadenopathy, fever, malaise, and tonsillitis as part of the manifestation. Positive heterophile reaction or EBV antibody titers can confirm the diagnosis. Other etiologies of inflammatory adenopathy that may mimic EBV-related infectious mononucleosis are cytomegalovirus, human immunodeficiency virus, toxoplasmosis, brucellosis, or tularemia.[71, 106]

Bartonella henselae is the most common causative organism of cat-scratch disease; *Bartonella quintana* is seen less often. Lymphadenopathy is a prerequisite for the diagnosis, the location of which is dependent on the site of inoculation (Fig. 97–5A). In most patients, an inoculation papule can be found. It is typically round, red to brown, and nontender, manifesting in the line of a cat scratch 3 to 10 days after inoculation and persisting for as long as 2 to 3 weeks.[12, 21] In the immunocompetent patient, cat-scratch disease is a self-limited granulomatous and suppurative response lasting for 2 to 3 months. The head and neck is the location of the adenopathy in 26% of cases.[21] There is seasonal variation in the presentation of cat-scratch disease, with most cases manifesting in the last 6 months of the year.[21] The standard for establishing the diagnosis of cat-scratch disease is serologic testing for the presence of antibodies to *Bartonella*; the most appropriate management is medical. Promising results have

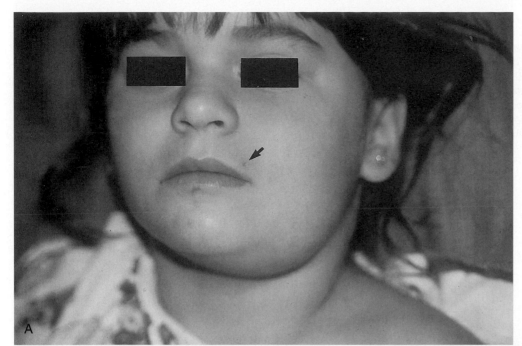

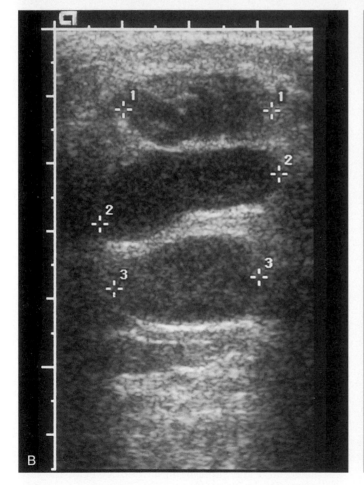

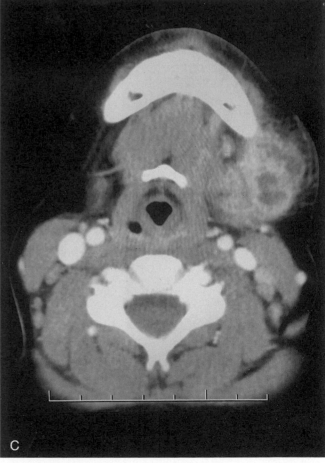

FIGURE 97–5. Five-year-old girl with cat scratch disease. *A,* The *arrow* points to the healing inoculation papule. The skin overlying the left submandibular mass is brightly erythematous and the mass is fluctuant. *B,* Color flow Doppler ultrasound demonstrated a loss of central vascularity in the two most superficial nodes consistent with suppuration of the contents. The deepest node demonstrated central vascular flow consistent with inflammatory adenopathy. *C,* Contrast enhanced CT reveals a multilocular left submandibular abscess with rim enhancement. Owing to the cutaneous changes, the abscess was incised and drained.

been seen with a 5-day course of azithromycin, which has been demonstrated to provide clinical benefit as measured by a total decrease in the lymph node volume on US.[11] The role of surgery is less clear. Bass et al[11] concluded that suppuration with resorption of the liquefied nodal contents was the natural course of cat-scratch disease based on their serial ultrasonographic observations. They found that surgical intervention for even large suppurative nodal masses was not needed, and they reserved intervention for suppurative nodes when spontaneous rupture was imminent. Approximately 10% of cases progress, with the development of overlying erythema, fluctuation, and eventual spontaneous rupture of the suppurated node (see Fig. 97–5B and C).[12]

Uncommon systemic etiologies of inflammatory cervical lymphadenopathy include diphtheria, sarcoidosis, Kawasaki disease (mucocutaneous lymph node syndrome), Kikuchi-Fujimoto disease, and Castleman disease (giant lymph node hyperplasia).[41, 55, 89, 106]

Congenital

In a large series of excised cervical masses, congenital lesions were diagnosed in more than half the patients.[99] Of the 445 children who underwent excision of a cervical

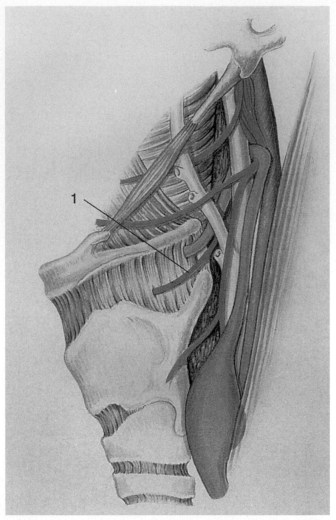

FIGURE 97–7. Anatomic course of third branchial cleft anomalies. 1) Superior laryngeal nerve. (From Petcu LT, Sasaki CT. Surgery for benign lesions of the neck. In Panje WR, Herberhold C [eds]. Head and Neck Surgery: Vol 3: Neck, 2nd ed. New York, Thieme, 1998 pp 5–26.)

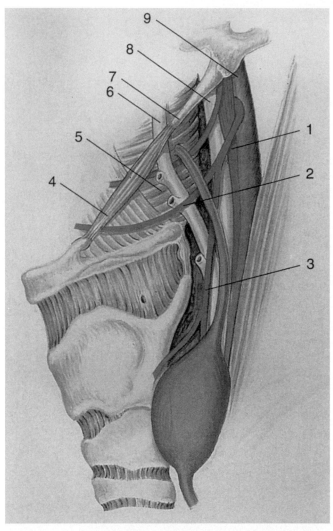

FIGURE 97–6. Anatomic course of second branchial cleft anomalies. 1) Vagus nerve. 2) Hypoglossal nerve. 3) Descending branch of hypoglossal nerve. 4) Stylohyoid muscle. 5) Middle pharyngeal constrictor muscle. 6) External carotid artery. 7) Stylohyoid process. 8) Internal carotid artery. 9) Internal jugular vein. (From Petcu LT, Sasaki CT. Surgery for benign lesions of the neck. In Panje WR, Herberhold C [eds]. Head and Neck Surgery: Vol. 3: Neck, 2nd ed. New York, Thieme, 1998 pp 5–26.)

mass, 17% had a branchial cleft cyst excised, and 16% had a thyroglossal duct cyst excised.[99]

Branchial anomalies can occur in conjunction with the first, second, third, or forth branchial cleft or pouch and can manifest as a fistula, sinus, or cyst. A fistula is an epidermal lined tract that communicates the pharynx to the skin, whereas a sinus is an epidermal based duct that can communicate either externally or internally. A cyst is a retained epidermal lined space of ectodermal origin without communication to the skin or mucosa. The course of branchial anomalies can be predicted based on embryologic development. In general, a branchial cleft anomaly lies inferior to all embryologic derivatives of its associated arch and superior to all derivatives of the next arch. Second, third, and fourth branchial anomalies all lie deep to the platysma and, if they communicate with the skin, open anterior to the sternocleidomastoid muscle, and all pass superior to the hypoglossal nerve. Second branchial anomalies track superior and lateral to the common carotid artery, ascend with the carotid sheath to pass medially between the external and internal carotid arteries, pass lateral and superior to the glossopharyngeal and hypoglossal nerves, and penetrate the middle pharyngeal constrictor muscle to open into the tonsillar fossa (Fig. 97–6). Third branchial anomalies track along the carotid sheath, pass posteriorly behind the internal carotid artery, pass superior to the hypoglossal nerve, and then pass anteriorly, inferiorly, and medially to penetrate the thyrohyoid membrane superior to the superior laryngeal nerve, opening within the lateral wall of the piriform sinus (Fig. 97–7). Fourth branchial anomalies would have to track in a course that would pass inferior to the recurrent laryngeal nerve.

Anomalies of the second branchial cleft are by far the most common (Fig. 97–8A).[22] Cysts typically manifest differently than a sinus or fistula. Cysts typically manifest along the upper third of the anteromedial border of the sternocleidomastoid muscle in the second through fourth decades of life. A sinus or fistula typically occurs along the lower third of the neck, is almost always seen in infants, and can occur bilaterally in one third of cases.[22] If the cysts become large, they may cause a sensation of pressure or fullness, dysphagia, stridor, and dyspnea. The treatment is surgical excision because there is a high incidence of secondary infections (see Fig. 97–8B and C). Carcinoma occurring in a branchial cleft cyst has been reported but is rare. The diagnosis is controversial because of the difficulty in histologically distinguishing a branchial cleft cyst from the cystic degeneration of a metastatic cervical node.[94] Demonstration of an epithelial lined cyst with gradual transition to invasive squamous cell carcinoma and 5-year disease-free survival is needed to establish the diagnosis.[94] The number of malignant cases reported is probably not as high as the literature indicates, because many cases do not fit absolute criteria for branchial cleft cysts.[94] Although pediatric case reports exist, malignant degeneration usually does not occur until adulthood.

First branchial cleft anomalies (FBCAs) can be divided into types I and II, but this is not a particularly clinically useful classification. Type I FBCAs are considered to be a duplication of the membranous external auditory canal and are of only ectodermal origin. Type I FBCAs do not manifest as a neck mass. Type II FBCAs consist of both ectoderm and mesoderm and can be a fistulous tract extending from the floor of the external auditory canal to the submandibular area. A sinus or fistulous tract opening into the submandibular area or external auditory canal is highly suggestive of a type II FBCA.[93] A myringeal web is a fibrous band that extends from the fistula orifice in the floor of the external auditory canal to the umbo and is present only in type II FBCA (Fig. 97–9).[93]

Both third and fourth branchial cleft anomalies are rare, and their existence and clinical distinction from one another are controversial.[33, 45, 79, 97] The fistula orifice in both third and fourth branchial cleft anomalies has been reported to open into the piriform sinus. There does seem to be an association between the thyroid gland and

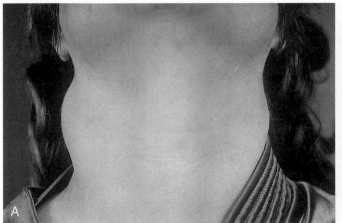

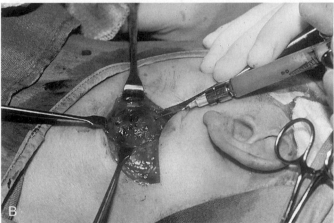

FIGURE 97–8. *A,* Fourteen-year-old girl with a right second branchial cleft cyst. *B,* Surgical excision of a left second branchial cleft cyst. Decompression of the cyst facilitated complete excision without violating the cyst wall. *C,* The specimen was opened after excision, revealing the squamous lining of the cyst.

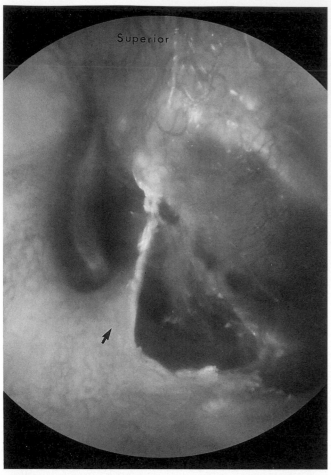

FIGURE 97–9. Left tympanic membrane with a band (*black arrow*) of tissue extending from the anterior/inferior aspect of the external auditory canal to the manubrium—a "myringeal web." This clinical finding is pathognomonic of a type II FBCA.

the diagnosis of a third or fourth cleft anomaly, with the majority of the lesions being reported on the left side.[33, 45, 79, 97] In a child with a solitary thyroid nodule, branchial cleft cyst should be included in the differential diagnosis.[97]

A firm, mobile midline neck mass is usually a thyroglossal duct cyst; however, the differential diagnosis includes dermoid cyst, lipoma, an enlarged thyroid isthmus or pyramidal lobe of the thyroid, and lymph nodes (Fig. 97–10). A dermoid cyst is the second most common midline neck mass.[5] By holding the mass as the patient swallows, congenital thyroid anomalies, which are fixed to the hyoid or visceral fascia, can be felt to move in the vertical axis on swallowing or tongue extrusion. Lymph nodes and dermoid cysts do not move because they are not attached to the underlying structures. Dermoid cysts usually are attached to and move with the skin. Location alone cannot be used to differentiate a thyroglossal duct cyst, which may manifest as a lateral neck mass.[97] In addition, a midline neck mass may represent ectopic thyroid tissue, which may be the only functioning thyroid tissue. Ectopic thyroid tissue is uncommon; it is most commonly located in the base of the tongue, is usually the only functioning thyroid tissue, and is far more common in female patients.[24] Concern that a midline neck mass may represent the only functioning thyroid has led to debate over appropriate preoperative evaluation. Some clinicians advocate preoperative US to document the presence of thyroid tissue in the normal location (assuming that if thyroid tissue is present in the normal location that the midline mass is not the only functioning thyroid), limiting radionuclide scans to patients with clinical or laboratory evidence of hypothyroidism.[87] However, not all patients with an ectopic thyroid are hypothyroid; ectopic thyroid tissue can produce sufficient thyroid hormone to sustain the patient.[47, 84] Therefore, some authors recom-

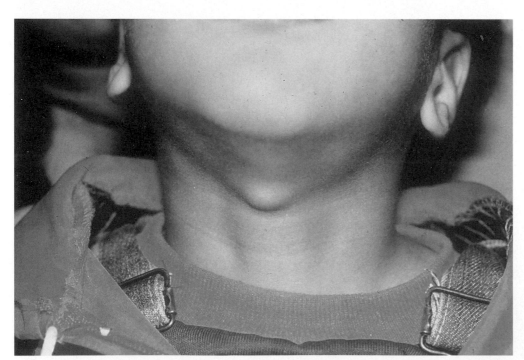

FIGURE 97–10. Four-year-old boy presenting with a midline neck mass.

mend that a thyroid scan be performed before surgery to ensure that the thyroglossal duct cyst does not contain the only functional thyroid tissue.[30, 84]

The treatment of a thyroglossal duct cyst is surgical removal of the cyst in conjunction with the central portion of the hyoid bone with a cuff of the base of the tongue musculature—the Sistrunk procedure.[95] Resection of only the cyst results in an unacceptably high recurrence rate. In one series, only 1 of 64 patients who underwent the Sistrunk procedure required a second excision, whereas five of five patients who underwent simple cystectomy required a second excision.[57]

We recommend a preoperative ultrasound to confirm the presence of thyroid tissue in the normal location and complete surgical excision using the Sistrunk technique.

Thyroid carcinoma can occur in a thyroglossal duct cyst. The most common pathologic finding is papillary carcinoma.[49]

Lymph nodes, dermoid cysts, and lipomas require only local excision and do not recur. They are usually easy to identify at the time of the excision, and the central portion of the hyoid does not require excision.

Thymic anomalies are a rare etiology of neck masses in children and are seldom included in the differential diagnosis. They can occur as a cystic lesion or ectopic rest and are found predominantly on the left.[58, 60, 78] They probably develop from the third pharyngeal pouch and can occur anywhere along the line of descent of the thymus. Thymic cysts are rarely diagnosed preoperatively and can be confused with branchial cleft anomalies or lymphangiomas.[78] The differentiation of a possible thymic cyst is important for surgical planning in that approximately 50% extend into the mediastinum either by direct extension or by fibrous cord.[58, 78] The diagnosis depends on the presence of thymic tissue remnants in the cyst wall with pathognomonic Hassall corpuscles.

Lymphangiomas most often involve the head and neck region, where they can cause significant functional deficits, airway compromise, and cosmetic deformity. One third of lesions are diagnosed at birth and the majority by 2 years of age.[16, 81] They manifest as soft tissue masses that are slow growing, fluctuant, and painless, and can be transilluminated on physical examination. Upper respiratory infections may cause rapid enlargement that diminishes with resolution of the infection. Reports of spontaneous regression may be related to the regression in size seen after infections. However, most investigators agree that lymphangiomas do not spontaneously involute and, left untreated, all eventually recur and enlarge.[16, 81, 96] The options for treatment include surgical excision or sclerotherapy. The treatment and decision to operate must be individualized because of risk to surrounding neural and vascular structures. Aspiration may reduce the size and serve as a temporizing measure while definitive therapy is planned. Recently, favorable results have been obtained in macrocystic lesions using OK432 as a sclerosing agent.[96] OK432 is produced by the lyophilization of group A *Streptococcus pyogenes* and induces sclerosis by damaging the endothelial lining cells of individual cysts. Direct inoculation into the cyst is needed for sclerosis to occur.[96] Currently, complete surgical excision, although rarely accomplished with large lesions, remains the treatment of choice for lymphangiomas.[16, 81] The elective sacrifice of normal structures, such as neural and vascular structures, is not warranted. Multiple-staged procedures may be considered in infants with very large infiltrating lesions that surround vital structures.[99] If gross cystic disease is left in an area because of potential functional deficit, consideration should be given to unroofing the remaining cyst to promote local scarring that may help to limit recurrences.[16]

Hemangioma has been used as a generic term that encompasses an array of vascular lesions. A clinically useful classification system based on histopathologic features differentiates between only two major types of vascular lesions: hemangiomas and vascular malformations.[75] Hemangiomas manifest during the late fetal or early neonatal period, with rapid growth during the proliferative phase (histologically characterized by hypercellularity), and usually undergo a slow involution phase (histologically characterized by fibrosis and diminished cellularity). Vascular malformations are present at birth, grow commensurably, fail to regress, and are histologically characterized by normal endothelial mitotic activity. Vascular malformations may have capillary, venous, arterial, or lymphatic components or any combination of these. Clinically, vascular malformation may enlarge as a result of changes in pressure and flow, ectasia, collateral formation, shunting, or hormonal modulation.[75] A vascular malformation should increase in size and firmness when the child strains or cries.

Hemangiomas are the most common occurring congenital vascular abnormalities in the head and neck (Fig. 97–11).[48, 99] Treatment must be individualized, because the natural history of hemangiomas is complete resolution in more than 50% of children by the age of 5 years, 70% by the age of 7 years, and continued improvement can be expected in the remaining children until 10 to 12 years of age.[37] A conservative approach is appropriate unless function is significantly impaired, vital structures are compromised, uncontrollable bleeding occurs, a consumptive coagulopathy develops, or the child's life is threatened as a result of complications.[36, 48] The use of steroids remains limited because of the high rate of spontaneous regression, the known side effects, and the lack of sustained improvement. Sclerosing agents and cryotherapy have been used on extensive lesions, resulting in considerable scarring and unpredictable success. Favorable results have been reported using either alpha$_{2a}$- or alpha$_{2b}$-interferon in children with life-threatening hemangiomas.[23, 37] Follow-up data have led to confusion regarding the utility of interferon and have shed light on the potential neurologic, hepatic, and systemic toxicity associated with this therapy.[9, 23, 38] Interventional radiology may play a role in the management of select lesions with endovascular obliteration of the vascular bed.[3] Postembolization swelling resulting from tissue ischemia is a significant concern; care should be taken to appropriately secure the airway. Preoperative embolization may also assist in decreasing intraoperative blood loss.[3] Surgical intervention is warranted in children with significant functional impairment, airway compromise, uncontrollable bleeding, consumptive coagulopathy, and life-threatening lesions. After involution, residual hemangioma may cause disfigurement and warrant surgical excision or laser therapy.

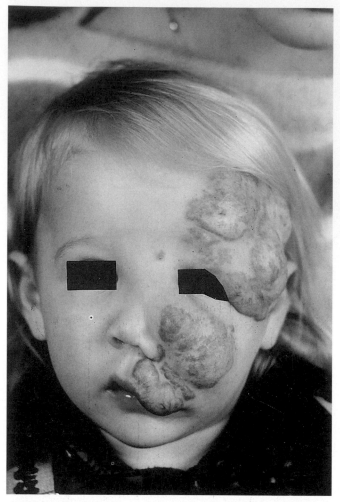

FIGURE 97–11. Two-year-old boy with a hemangioma involving the left side of the face, parotid area, and left submandibular area. The lesion was managed conservatively with observation. He required cosmetic refinement after regression of the lesion.

Neoplastic

The failure to diagnose a potential malignancy remains a concern that often guides the evaluation of a child with a neck mass. This concern is potentiated by the paucity of history and examination findings in cases of malignancy. An asymptomatic neck mass is the most typical presentation of malignancy of the head and neck in children.

Lymphomas are the most common malignancy of the head and neck in children, accounting for as many as 55% to 59% of cases.[29, 53] In general, non-Hodgkin lymphoma is far more common than Hodgkin disease in children. However, Hodgkin disease is more commonly seen in the head and neck. In one series, of the 85 patients presenting with Hodgkin disease, all presented with a neck mass.[29] In both types of lymphoma, asymptomatic, unilateral lymphadenopathy is the most common manifestation. Extranodal disease involving the lymphoid tissue in the area of the Waldeyer ring and systemic disseminated disease is more commonly seen at presentation in children with non-Hodgkin lymphoma.[29, 53, 99] Systemic symptoms such as fever, weight loss, night sweats, weakness, and pruritus are typically not seen until late in the course of disease and are generally not seen in children with disease localized to the neck.[29]

Soft tissue sarcomas, of which rhabdomyosarcoma is most frequently seen, are the second most common malignancy in the head and neck of children (Fig. 97–12).[29, 53] In the head and neck, rhabdomyosarcoma is seen in the orbit, nasopharynx, temporal bone, parotid, and neck.[29] As with other malignancies, rhabdomyosarcoma usually mani-

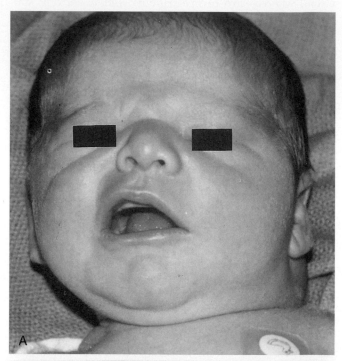

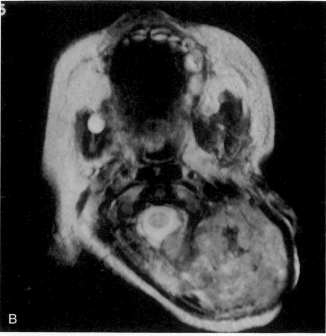

FIGURE 97–12. Newborn child with disseminated rhabdomyosarcoma. *A,* Asymmetry of facial motion on physical examination indicates involvement of the left facial nerve. *B,* MRI reveals the soft tissue extent of the mass.

fests as an asymptomatic mass or with symptoms and signs related to the primary location of the mass (see Fig. 97–11A). The use of combined chemotherapy, radiation therapy, and surgery has significantly improved overall survival rates.[28, 70] Surgery for rhabdomyosarcoma is often limited to incisional biopsies or debulking because of the location and extent of the tumor. Complete surgical resection of localized disease in the head and neck accomplished without long-term surgical morbidity may allow children to avoid radiation therapy with its associated long-term complications, with no compromise in survival.[31]

Thyroid carcinoma is the third most common neck malignancy in children and accounts for a significant proportion of all neck masses seen in adolescent girls. Thyroid carcinoma has been estimated to be two to three times more common in girls than in boys.[42] Between 25% and 55% of palpable thyroid nodules in children contain a malignancy, most commonly papillary carcinoma.[42, 52] Children tend to present with advanced disease. In children, cervical lymph node metastases, larger primary tumors, and pulmonary metastases are all more commonly seen than in adults. Even so, in appropriately managed children, the prognosis is excellent.

An association has long been established between radiation exposure and thyroid carcinoma. Important points of the clinical history include not only a history of prior radiation therapy but also possible environmental exposure, as is seen in citizens from the Ukraine who may have been exposed to the Chernobyl nuclear accident. The younger the patient at the time of radiation exposure, the more likely is the development of thyroid carcinoma.[39] Thyroid carcinoma after radiation exposure is usually papillary carcinoma and tends to be more aggressive, with a high frequency of lymph node metastases, venous invasion, and extrathyroidal extension.[100] With the current trend toward less surgically invasive procedures and because of the increased use of radiation therapy to the head and neck for the treatment of cancer, careful attention should be given to the thyroid gland because of the risk for late development of radiation-induced thyroid carcinoma.[32]

A much less common but more often studied lesion is medullary thyroid carcinoma. The interest has been generated by the discovery of genetic and biochemical markers of the disease. There are four distinct groups of patients in whom medullary thyroid carcinoma develops: type IIa multiple endocrine neoplasia (MEN), type IIb MEN, familial non-MEN, and sporadic cases. Approximately 75% of cases are sporadic. Hereditary forms are inherited in an autosomal dominant pattern with near complete penetrance. Genetic screening for the RET germline mutation has allowed early detection and treatment of these patients.[59] Immunoradiometric assays for the monomeric form of serum calcitonin serve as a precise tumor marker, allowing early preoperative diagnosis and the detection of postoperative recurrent disease.[35] Early or prophylactic surgery for medullary thyroid carcinoma includes total thyroidectomy and central neck dissection.

Salivary gland neoplasms are uncommon in children. Most cases occur in the parotid gland. If vascular and lymphatic neoplasms are excluded, approximately 50% are malignant and approximately 50% of malignant pediatric salivary gland neoplasms are mucoepidermoid carcinoma.[7, 20, 72] As in adults, poor outcomes are associated with high tumor grades, perineural invasion, local extraglandular extension, perivascular and perilymphatic extension, and lymph node metastases.[7, 20] Treatment must be tailored to the individual patient and may require a combination of surgery, radiotherapy, and chemotherapy. In cases of malignant neoplasms, a total parotidectomy may be required.

The true incidence of benign salivary gland malignancies is difficult to ascertain. Variations in reporting of pediatric age groups and referral patterns make interpretation of the data difficult. In analyzing the distribution of salivary gland tumors by age, hemangiomas and lymphatic malformations are most common in neonates and infants.[69] Epithelial tumors (both benign and malignant) occur later in childhood.[69] The most common benign epithelial tumor in older children is a pleomorphic adenoma, accounting for greater than 90% of these lesions.[20, 54, 69, 82] Other benign epithelial tumors commonly seen in adults, such as a Warthin tumor, are uncommon in the pediatric population. One epithelial salivary gland neoplasm that is unique to children is the embryoma.[13] Recognized only in newborns or during the first year of life, embryomas are thought to be an embryonic anlage tumor of the major salivary glands. Special consideration should also be given to the potential that an asymptomatic firm salivary gland mass might represent an inflammatory process. Children with viral sialadenitis, chronic recurrent sialadenitis, and granulomatous sialadenitis may all present in this manner.[82, 102]

Other less common malignant tumors of the head and neck in children include neurogenic sarcoma, nasopharyngeal carcinoma, and neuroblastoma. All of these lesions require biopsy to make the diagnosis.

One other group of diseases, Langerhans cell histiocytosis, is not a malignancy, but has a propensity for benign proliferation that mimics malignancy. Patients can be grouped at presentation as having localized disease, multifocal disease, or disease involving vital organs.[2] The skull and mandible are typical sites of manifestation in the head and neck. Patients with multifocal disease may present with cervical lymphadenopathy.[2] Treatment of children with multifocal and systemic disease is focused toward decreasing morbidity because eradication of disease is uncommon.

All tumors of the head and neck must be treated and followed up by a multidisciplinary team to ensure the best possible outcome. See Chapter 101 for a discussion of tumors of the neck in children.

SELECTED REFERENCES

Cunningham MJ, Myers EN, Bluestone CD. Malignant tumors of the head and neck in children: a twenty-year review. Int J Pediatr Otorhinolaryngol 13:279, 1987.

Jaffe BF, Jaffe N. Head and neck tumors in children. Pediatrics 51:731, 1973.

Jones BV, Koch BL. Magnetic resonance imaging of the pediatric head and neck. Topics Magn Reson Imaging 10:348, 1999.

Mulliken JB, Glowacki J. Hemangiomas and vascular malformations in infants and children: a classification based on endothelial characteristics. Plast Reconstr Surg 69:412, 1982.

Torsiglieri AJ, Tom LWC, Ross AJ III, et al. Pediatric neck masses: guidelines for evaluation. Int J Pediatr Otorhinolaryngol 16:199, 1988.

REFERENCES

1. Alessi DP, Dudley JP. Atypical mycobacteria-induced cervical adenitis. Treatment by needle aspiration. Arch Otolaryngol Head Neck Surg 114:664, 1988.
2. Angeli SI, Alcalde J, Hoffman HT, et al. Langerhans' cell histiocytosis of the head and neck in children. Ann Otol Rhinol Laryngol 104:173, 1995.
3. Armstrong DC, ter Brugge K. Selected interventional procedures for pediatric head and neck vascular lesions. Neuroimaging Clin North Am 10:271, 2000.
4. Ashcraft MW, van Herle AJ. Management of thyroid nodules. II: scanning techniques, thyroid suppressive therapy, and fine needle aspiration. Head Neck Surg 3:297, 1981.
5. Athow AC, Fagg NLK, Drake DP. Management of thyroglossal cysts in children. Br J Surg 76:811, 1989.
6. Baek CH, Kim SI, Ko YH, et al. Polymerase chain reaction detection of Mycobacterium tuberculosis from fine-needle aspirate for the diagnosis of cervical tuberculous lymphadenitis. Laryngoscope 110:30, 2000.
7. Baker SR, Malone B. Salivary gland malignancies in children. Cancer 55:1730, 1985.
8. Bamji M, Stone RK, Kaul A, et al. Palpable lymph nodes in healthy newborns and infants. Pediatrics 78:573, 1986.
9. Barlow CF, Priebe CJ, Mulliken JB. Spastic diplegia as a complication of interferon alfa-2a treatment of hemangiomas of infancy. J Pediatr 132:527, 1998.
10. Barton LL, Feigin RD. Childhood cervical lymphadenitis: a reappraisal. J Pediatr 84:846, 1974.
11. Bass JW, Freitas BC, Freitas AD, et al. Prospective randomized double blind placebo-controlled evaluation of azithromycin for treatment of cat-scratch disease. Pediatr Infect Dis J 17:447, 1998.
12. Bass JW, Vincent JM, Person DA. The expanding spectrum of Bartonella infections: II. Cat-scratch disease. Pediatr Infect Dis J 16:163, 1997.
13. Batsakis JG, Mackay B, Ryka AF, et al. Perinatal salivary gland tumours (embryomas). J Laryngol Otol 102:1007, 1988.
14. Berger C, Pfyffer GE, Nadal D. Treatment of nontuberculous mycobacterial lymphadenitis with clarithromycin plus rifabutin. J Pediatr 128:383, 1996.
15. Bergman KS, Harris BH. Scalp and neck masses. Pediatr Surg 40:1151, 1993.
16. Brock ME, Smith RJH, Parey SE, et al. Lymphangioma. An otolaryngologic perspective. Int J Pediatr Otorhinolaryngol 14:133, 1987.
17. Brodeur GM, Seeger RC. Gene amplification in human neuroblastomas: basic mechanisms and clinical implications. Cancer Genet Cytogenet 19:101, 1986.
18. Brodsky L, Belles W, Brody A, et al. Needle aspiration of neck abscesses in children. Clin Pediatr 31:71, 1992.
19. Brook I. Microbiology of abscesses of the head and neck in children. Ann Otol Rhinol Laryngol 96:429, 1987.
20. Callender DL, Frankenthaler RA, Luna MA, et al. Salivary gland neoplasms in children. Arch Otolaryngol Head Neck Surg 118:472, 1992.
21. Carithers HA. Cat-scratch disease: an overview based on a study of 1,200 patients. Am J Dis Child 139:1125, 1985.
22. Chandler JR, Mitchell B. Branchial cleft cysts, sinuses, and fistulas. Otolaryngol Clin North Am 14:175, 1981.
23. Chang E, Boyd A, Nelson CC. Successful treatment of infantile hemangiomas with interferon-α-2b. J Pediatr Hematol Oncol 19:237, 1997.
24. Chanin LR, Greenberg LM. Pediatric upper airway obstruction due to ectopic thyroid: classification and case reports. Laryngoscope 98:422, 1988.
25. Chen CP, Jan SW, Liu FF, et al. Echo-guided lymphatic drainage by fine-needle aspiration in persistent isolated septated fetal nuchal cystic hygroma. Fetal Diagn Ther 11:150, 1996.
26. Chen CP, Wang W, Lin SP, et al. Favorable outcome in a fetus with an early-onset extensive cystic hygroma colli and intralesional hemorrhage. Am J Perinatol 15:601, 1998.
27. Connolly AAP, MacKenzie K. Paediatric neck masses—a diagnostic dilemma. J Laryngol Otol 111:541, 1997.
28. Crist W, Gehan EA, Ragab AH, et al. The third intergroup rhabdomyosarcoma study. J Clin Oncol 13:610, 1995.
29. Cunningham MJ, Myers EN, Bluestone CD. Malignant tumors of the head and neck in children: a twenty-year review. Int J Pediatr Otorhinolaryngol 13:279, 1987.
30. Damiano A, Glickman AB, Rubin JS, et al. Ectopic thyroid tissue presenting as a midline neck mass. Int J Pediatr Otorhinolaryngol 34:141, 1996.
31. Daya H, Chan HSL, Sirkin W, et al. Pediatric rhabdomyosarcoma of the head and neck. Is there a place for surgical management? Arch Otolaryngol Head Neck Surg 126:468, 2000.
32. de Vathaire F, Hardiman C, Shamsaldin A, et al. Thyroid carcinomas after irradiation for a first cancer during childhood. Arch Intern Med 159:2713, 1999.
33. Edmonds JL, Girod DA, Woodroof JM, et al. Third branchial anomalies. Avoiding recurrences. Arch Otolaryngol Head Neck Surg 123:438, 1997.
34. Eisenhut CC, King DE, Nelson WA, et al. Fine-needle biopsy of pediatric lesions: a three-year study in an outpatient biopsy clinic. Diagn Cytopathol 14:43, 1996.
35. Engelbach M, Görges R, Forst T, et al. Improved diagnostic methods in the follow-up of medullary thyroid carcinoma by highly specific calcitonin measurements. J Clin Endocrinol Metab 85:1890, 2000.
36. Enjolras O, Riche MC, Murland JJ, et al. Management of alarming hemangiomas in infancy: a review of 25 cases. Pediatrics 85:491, 1990.
37. Ezekowitz RAB, Mulliken JB, Folkman J. Interferon alfa-2a therapy for life-threatening hemangiomas of infancy. N Engl J Med 326:1456, 1992.
38. Ezekowitz RAB, Mulliken JB, Folkman J. Additional corrections: interferon for hemangiomas of infancy. N Engl J Med 333:595, 1995.
39. Farahati J, Demidchik EP, Biko J, et al. Inverse association between age at the time of radiation exposure and extent of disease in cases of radiation-induced childhood thyroid carcinoma in Belarus. Cancer 88:1470, 2000.
40. Flint D, Mahadevan M, Barber C, et al. Cervical lymphadenitis due to non–tuberculous mycobacteria: surgical treatment and review. Int J Pediatr Otorhinolaryngol 53:187, 2000.
41. Garcia CE, Girdhar-Gopal HV, Dorfman DM. Kikuchi-Fujimoto disease of the neck update. Ann Otol Rhinol Laryngol 102:11, 1993.
42. Geiger JD, Thompson NW. Thyroid tumors in children. Otolaryngol Clin North Am 29:711, 1996.
43. Gianfelice D, Jequier S, Patriquin H, et al. Sonography of neck masses in children: is it useful? Int J Pediatr Otorhinolaryngol 11:247, 1986.
44. Glasier CM, Stark JE, Jacobs RF, et al. CT and ultrasound imaging of retropharyngeal abscesses in children. AJNR Am J Neuroradiol 13:1191, 1992.
45. Godin MS, Kearns DB, Pransky SM, et al. Fourth branchial pouch sinus: principles of diagnosis and management. Laryngoscope 100:174, 1990.
46. Grando D, Sullivan LJ, Flexman JP, et al. Bartonella henselae associated with Parinaud's oculoglandular syndrome. Clin Infect Dis 28:1156, 1999.
47. Grant DB, Hulse JA, Jackson DB, et al. Ectopic thyroid: residual function after withdrawal of treatment in infancy and later childhood. Acta Paediatr Scand 78:889, 1989.
48. Handler SD, Raney RB Jr. Management of neoplasms of the head and neck in children. I. Benign tumors. Head Neck Surg 3:395, 1981.
49. Heshmati HM, Fatourechi V, van Heerden JA, et al. Thyroglossal duct carcinoma: report of 12 cases 72:315, 1997.

50. Hubbard AM, Crombleholme TM, Adzick NS. Prenatal MRI evaluation of giant neck masses in preparation for the fetal exit procedure. Am J Perinatol 15:253, 1998.

51. Hudgins PA. Nodal and nonnodal inflammatory processes of the pediatric neck. Neuroimaging Clin North Am 10:181, 2000.

52. Hung W, August GP, Randolph JG, et al. Solitary thyroid nodules in children and adolescents. J Pediatr Surg 17:225, 1982.

53. Jaffe BF, Jaffe N. Head and neck tumors in children. Pediatrics 51:731, 1973.

54. Jaques DA, Krolls SO, Chambers RG. Parotid tumors in children. Am J Surg 132:469, 1976.

55. Johnson JT, Oral A, Nalesnik M. Giant lymph node hyperplasia: clinical and immunohistologic correlation of an intermediate variant. Ear Nose Throat J 64:249, 1985.

56. Jones BV, Koch BL. Magnetic resonance imaging of the pediatric head and neck. Topics Magn Reson Imaging 10:348, 1999.

57. Josephson GD, Spencer WR, Josephson JS. Thyroglossal duct cyst: the New York Eye and Ear Infirmary experience and a literature review. Ear Nose Throat J 77:642, 1998.

58. Kacker A, April M, Markentel CB, et al. Ectopic thymus presenting as a solid submandibular neck mass in an infant: case report and review of literature. Int J Pediatr Otorhinolaryngol 49:241, 1999.

59. Kebebew E, Ituarte PHG, Siperstein AE, et al. Medullary thyroid carcinoma. Clinical characteristics, treatment, prognostic factors, and a comparison of staging systems. Cancer 88:1139, 2000.

60. Kelley DJ, Gerber ME, Willging JP. Cervicomediastinal thymic cysts. Int J Pediatr Otorhinolaryngol 39:139, 1997.

61. Kennedy TL. Curettage of nontuberculous mycobacterial cervical lymphadenitis. Arch Otolaryngol Head Neck Surg 118:759, 1992.

62. Khurana KK, Labrador E, Izquierdo R, et al. The role of fine-needle aspiration biopsy in the management of thyroid nodules in children, adolescents, and young adults: a multi-institutional study. Thyroid 9:383, 1999.

63. Kuhn JP, Slovis TL, Silverman FN, Kuhns, LR. The neck and respiratory system: neck and upper airway In Silverman FN, Kuhn JP (eds). Caffey's Pediatric X-ray Diagnosis: An Intergrated Imaging Approach, 9th ed. St Louis, Mosby, 1993, pp 355–377.

64. Lai KK, Stottmeier KD, Sherman IH, et al. Mycobacterial cervical lymphadenopathy. Relation of etiologic agents to age. JAMA 251: 1286, 1984.

65. Lazor J, Cunningham M, Eavey R, et al. Comparison of computed tomography and surgical findings in deep neck infections. Otolaryngol Head Neck Surg 111:746, 1994.

66. Legius E, Fryns JP, Van Den Berghe H. Dominant branchial cleft syndrome with characteristics of both branchio-oto-renal and branchio-oculo-facial syndrome. Clin Genet 37:347, 1990.

67. Levine PH. Immunologic markers for Epstein-Barr virus in the control of nasopharyngeal carcinoma and Burkitt lymphoma. Cancer Detect Prevent Suppl 1:217, 1987.

68. Liechty KW, Crombleholme TM, Flake AW, et al. Intrapartum airway management for giant fetal neck masses: the EXIT (ex utero intrapartum treatment) procedure. Am J Obstet Gynecol 177: 870, 1997.

69. Luna MA, Batsakis JG, El-Naggar AK. Salivary gland tumors in children. Ann Otol Rhinol Laryngol 100:869, 1991.

70. Maurer HM, Gehan EA, Beltangady M, et al. The intergroup rhabdomyosarcoma study-II. Cancer 71:1904, 1993.

71. May M. Neck masses in children: diagnosis and treatment. Pediatr Ann 5:517, 1976.

72. Mazzaferri EL. Thyroid cancer in thyroid nodules: finding a needle in a haystack. Am J Med 93:359, 1992.

73. Miskin M, Noyek AM, Kazdan MS. Diagnostic ultrasound in otolaryngology. Otolaryngol Clin North Am 11:513, 1978.

74. Mobley DL, Wakely PE, Frable MAS. Fine-needle aspiration biopsy: application to pediatric head and neck masses. Laryngoscope 101:469, 1991.

75. Mulliken JB, Glowacki J. Hemangiomas and vascular malformations in infants and children: a classification based on endothelial characteristics. Plast Reconstr Surg 69:412, 1982.

76. Nagy M, Backstrom J. Comparison of the sensitivity of lateral neck radiographs and computed tomography scanning in pediatric deep-neck infections. Laryngoscope 109:775, 1999.

77. Nagy M, Pizzuto M, Backstrom J, et al. Deep neck infections in children: a new approach to diagnosis and treatment. Laryngoscope 107:1627, 1997.

78. Nguyen Q, deTar M, Wells W, et al. Cervical thymic cyst: case reports and review of the literature. Laryngoscope 106:247, 1996.

79. Nusbaum AO, Som PM, Rothschild MA, et al. Recurrence of a deep neck infection. A clinical indication of an underlying congenital lesion. Arch Otolaryngol Head Neck Surg 125:1379, 1999.

80. Ochi K, Ogino S, Fukamizu K, et al. US-guided drainage of deep neck space abscess. Acta Otolaryngol (Stockh) Suppl 522:120, 1996.

81. Orvidas LJ, Kasperbauer JL. Pediatric lymphangiomas of the head and neck. Ann Otol Rhinol Laryngol 109:411, 2000.

82. Orvidas LJ, Kasperbauer JL, Lewis JE, et al. Pediatric parotid masses. Arch Otolaryngol Head Neck Surg 126:177, 2000.

83. Pang SC. Mycobacterial lymphadenitis in Western Australia. Tubercle Lung Dis 73:362, 1992.

84. Pinczower E, Crockett DM, Atkinson JB, et al. Preoperative thyroid scanning in presumed thyroglossal duct cysts. Arch Otolaryngol Head Neck Surg 118:985, 1992.

85. Pransky SM, Reisman BK, Kearns DB, et al. Cervicofacial mycobacterial adenitis in children: endemic to San Diego? Laryngoscope 100:920, 1990.

86. Raab SS, Silverman JF, Elsheikh TM, et al. Pediatric thyroid nodules: disease demographics and clinical management as determined by fine needle aspiration biopsy. Pediatrics 95:46, 1995.

87. Radkowski D, Arnold J, Healy GB, et al. Thyroglossal duct remnant. Preoperative evaluation and management. Arch Otolaryngol Head Neck Surg 117:1378, 1991.

88. Schneider AB, Favus MJ, Stachura ME, et al. Salivary gland neoplasms as a late consequence of head and neck irradiation. Ann Intern Med 87:160, 1977.

89. Seicshnaydre MA, Frable MA. Kawasaki disease: early presentation to the otolaryngologist. Otolaryngol Head Neck Surg 108:344, 1993.

90. Sherman NH, Rosenberg HK, Heyman S, et al. Ultrasound evaluation of neck masses in children. J Ultrasound Med 4:127, 1985.

91. Sheth S, Nussbaum AR, Hutchins GM, et al. Cystic hygromas in children: sonographic-pathologic correlation. Radiology 162:821, 1987.

92. Shulkin BL. PET applications in pediatrics. Q J Nucl Med 41:281, 1997.

93. Sichel JY, Halperin D, Dano I, et al. Clinical update on type II first branchial cleft cysts. Laryngoscope 108:1524, 1998.

94. Singh B, Balwally AN, Sundaram K, et al. Branchial cleft cyst carcinoma: myth or reality? Ann Otol Rhinol Laryngol 107:519, 1998.

95. Sistrunk WE. Technique of removal of cysts and sinuses of the thyroglossal duct. Surg Gynecol Obstet 46:109, 1928.

96. Smith RJH, Burke DK, Sato Y, et al. OK-432 therapy for lymphangiomas. Arch Otolaryngol Head Neck Surg 122:1195, 1996.

97. Sonnino RE, Spigland N, Laberge JM, et al. Unusual patterns of congenital neck masses in children. J Pediatr Surg 24:966, 1989.

98. Stocks RMS, Egerman RS, Woodson GE, et al. Airway management of neonates with antenatally detected head and neck anomalies. Arch Otolaryngol Head Neck Surg 123:641, 1997.

99. Torsiglieri AJ, Tom LWC, Ross AJ III, et al. Pediatric neck masses: guidelines for evaluation. Int J Pediatr Otorhinolaryngol 16:199, 1988.

100. Tronko MD, Bogdanova TI, Komissarenko IV, et al. Thyroid carcinoma in children and adolescents in Ukraine after the Chernobyl nuclear accident. Statistical data and clinicomorphologic characteristics. Cancer 86:149, 1999.

101. Wetmore RF, Mahboubi S, Soyupak SK. Computed tomography in the evaluation of pediatric neck infections. Otolaryngol Head Neck Surg 119:624, 1998.

102. White AK. Salivary gland disease in infancy and childhood: non-malignant lesions. J Otolaryngol 21:422, 1992.

103. Wolinsky E. Mycobacterial lymphadenitis in children: a prospective study of 105 nontuberculous cases with long-term follow-up. Clin Infect Dis 20:954, 1995.

104. Youkilis RA, Koch B, Myer CM III. Ultrasonographic imaging of sternocleidomastoid tumor of infancy. Ann Otol Rhinol Laryngol 104:323, 1995.

105. Yuh WTC, Sato Y, Loes DJ, et al. Magnetic resonance imaging and computed tomography in pediatric head and neck masses. Ann Otol Rhinol Laryngol 100:54, 1991.

106. Zuelzer WW, Kaplan J. The child with lymphadenopathy. Semin Hematol 12:323, 1975.

98

Developmental Anomalies of the Neck

Collin S. Karmody, M.D.

The complex embryology of the neck almost guarantees a plethora of congenital anomalies. Developmental aberrations might be obvious at birth or might manifest later, even in the fourth or fifth decade of life. Anomalies of the neck are sometimes difficult to diagnose and, at times, even more problematic or dangerous to treat. Because anomalies might primarily affect any embryonic tissue layer of the neck, they are described according to tissue systems as follows: anomalies of the skeletal system, muscles, skin, blood vessels, lymphatics, and branchial apparatus.

Skeletal Anomalies

Skeletal anomalies are caused by any one or a combination of the following mechanisms: (1) failure of differentiation, (2) defective segmentation, (3) failure of fusion of ossification centers, (4) failure of migration, (5) supernumerary parts, and (6) structural defects or deformities. A few of the possible anomalies of the skeleton are discussed here.

Congenital Synostosis of the Cervicothoracic Vertebrae (Klippel-Feil Syndrome)

Klippel-Feil syndrome is a rare malformation caused by dysmorphism of the spine in which there is a variety of maldevelopments of the vertebrae, particularly the cervical spine, with fusion of vertebral bodies, hemivertebrae, and, in some cases, the atlanto-occcipital joint (Fig. 98–1).[36] In their original paper, Klippel and Feil described a case in which the thoracic cage was immediately under the cranial base, which is a most apt description of the clinical picture of these patients.[56] Feil classified this syndrome into four types, of which type II is the most frequent. Although the Klippel-Feil syndrome is genetically heterogeneous, there is some evidence of a familial predisposition in type II.[20]

The disorder, which occurs more frequently in girls, is caused by failure of segmentation of the mesodermal somites during early fetal life, resulting in widened, flattened, fused vertebral bodies. Cervical spina bifida is common.

Clinical manifestations vary according to the severity of the deformity, and milder deformities might be diagnosed incidentally. Severe deformities, however, give the impression of an extremely short neck with the head sitting directly on the thorax and a very low-set occipital hairline.[36] There is usually marked limitation of motion of the cervical spine, but flexion and extension of the head, which take place at the atlanto-occipital joints, might be unrestricted. Webbing of the lateral soft tissues of the neck and a torticollis are not uncommon. Other congenital anomalies of the skeleton might be associated, such as cervical ribs, scoliosis, and kyphosis.[91] Anomalies of soft tissues in other parts of the body have been reported, including cleft palates and intraventricular septal defects. Approximately 24% to 70% of patients with Klippel-Feil syndrome have sensorineural, conductive, or mixed hearing losses.[43]

Treatment of Klipppel-Feil syndrome varies with the extent of the anomalies. In the early stages, passive stretching exercises are recommended to maintain maximum mobility. Surgery, however, is sometimes necessary for stabilizing the spine and for preventing or treating neurologic problems.[7, 51]

Anomalies of the Clavicle

Mutational Dysostosis (Cleidocranial Dysostosis) (MIM 119600)

Cleidocranial dysplasia (CCD), or Scheuthauer-Marie-Sainton syndrome (dysostosis cleidocranialis), is an autosomal dominant skeletal dysplasia particularly of membranous bone. It is characterized by abnormal clavicles, patent sutures and fontanelles, supernumerary teeth, short stature, and a variety of other skeletal changes. The disease gene has been mapped to chromosome 6p21 within a region containing the osteoblast-specific transcription factor CBFA1.[72, 100]

The right clavicle is almost always affected, but bilateral agenesis has been reported. The absent clavicular strut allows for a characteristic abnormal adduction of the shoulders to almost meet in the midline (Figs. 98–2 and 98–3). Mental retardation is commonly associated. Humans with CCD have severely retarded ossification of the cranial base, strongly suggesting that both intramembranous ossification and endochondral ossification are affected. In addition to the multiple supernumerary teeth

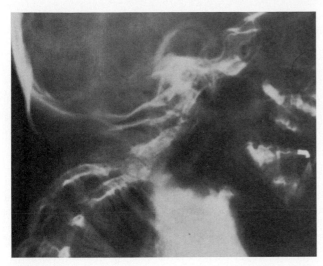

FIGURE 98–1. Radiograph of a 3-year-old child with Klippel-Feil syndrome. The bodies of the cervical vertebrae are fused and the neck is shortened. There was gross limitation of lateral motion of the neck.

and delayed tooth eruption, there are deformities of the facial skeleton.[58, 79] The clavicular defects can be diagnosed prenatally by ultrasonography.[88]

Approximately one third of patients with CCD have sensorineural hearing loss.[42, 50] In addition to the anomalies associated with CCD, the clavicles might have pseudarthroses. The absent segments of the clavicle rarely cause problems with function.

Congenital Pseudarthrosis of the Clavicle

Congenital pseudarthrosis of the clavicle is a rare, nonfamilial anomaly that results from failure of fusion of the primary centers of ossification of the clavicle. The condition usually manifests as a mass just lateral to the middle of the right clavicle, which is frequently obvious soon after birth. The right subclavian artery rides high and is at risk during any surgical maneuvers.[62] The deformity increases with growth and might become unsightly, in which case a bone grafting procedure can be performed. The clinical significance of this problem is primarily cosmetic at first, and a thoracic outlet syndrome may de-

velop in patients with both pseudarthrosis and CCD as they age.

Anomalies of the Scapula

Scapula Elevata (Sprengel Deformity)

The scapula begins as a cervical appendage, then descends to the upper posterior thorax toward the end of the third fetal month. If it fails to descend, the result is an abnormally high scapula known as the Sprengel deformity.

In the Sprengel deformity, which is usually unilateral and diagnosed at birth, the scapula is high, small, distorted, rotated forward, and might be attached to the cervical vertebrae by fibrous tissue, cartilage, or even bone (omovertebral bone). The musculature of the shoulder girdle is usually defective, and the trapezius muscle is sometimes weak or absent. There might be other associated anomalies, for instance, absence or fusion of ribs, cervical ribs, spina bifida, or a hypoplastic clavicle.

Early passive and active stretching of the musculature is useful in increasing function and mobility of the abnormal scapula. Various surgical maneuvers have been described for repositioning the scapula inferiorly.[11, 40]

Anomalies of the Cervical Muscles

Congenital Muscular Torticollis

Congenital muscular torticollis is caused by unilateral contracture of the sternocleidomastoid muscle, which tilts the head to the ipsilateral side and rotates the chin to the opposite side. The immediate cause is fibrosis within the sternocleidomastoid muscle, with subsequent contracture and shortening of the muscle. Experimental evidence suggests venous occlusion as the cause of the fibrosis.

The deformity may be noted at birth or may become evident soon thereafter. Within the first 2 weeks of life, a nontender, "fibrous tumor" becomes palpable in the substance of the muscle (Fig. 98–4). The tumor consists of fibrous tissue and grossly looks white. This mass progresses to maximum size in about 1 month, then regresses, leaving a contracted muscle. This is the typical description, but histologic studies in large cohorts indicate diffuse involvement of the whole muscle in 75% of

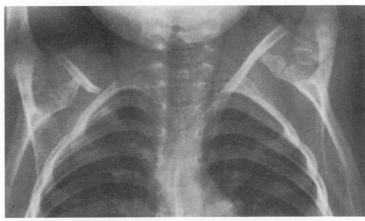

FIGURE 98–2. Radiograph of a patient with cleidocranial dysostosis. The medial half of the right clavicle has failed to develop.

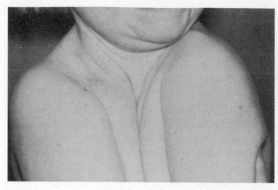

FIGURE 98–3. The patient with cleidocranial dysostosis shown in Figure 98–2. There is excessive adduction of the shoulders.

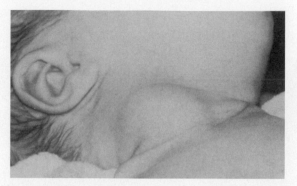

FIGURE 98–4. This 2-week-old child developed a mass in the right sternocleidomastoid muscle 5 days after birth. The mass was very firm and nontender, was not enlarging, and represented a "fibrous tumor," which is the first stage in the development of congenital muscular torticollis.

cases.[18] The mass can be easily evaluated by ultrasonography,[48] computed tomography(CT), or magnetic resonance imaging (MRI). Diagnosis can be confirmed by fine-needle aspiration biopsy.[6, 35] Sixty percent to 70% of children with persistent congenital torticollis have cranial or facial asymmetry and ocular imbalance.[92] There is evidence, however, that the mild ipsilateral hemifacial microsomia might be part of the developmental syndrome rather than secondary to the torticollis.[46] Soon after diagnosis is confirmed, passive stretching exercises must be performed four to six times daily. If conservative treatment is begun before age 3 months and is carried out assiduously, then there is a 90% chance of success.[22] If conservative management fails, the sternal and clavicular heads of the sternocleidomastoid muscle are divided surgically.[19] Postoperatively, the neck is splinted, and stretching exercises are continued until the situation stabilizes.

Anomalies of the Skin

Developmental abnormalities of the skin of the neck might be localized or might be part of a generalized ectodermal defect. Two anomalies are discussed here: pterygium colli and midline cervical cleft.

Pterygium Colli (Wing Neck)

A pterygium is a flat fold of skin and connective tissue that extends from the region of the mastoid process to the point of the shoulder. Pterygia are found in the following conditions: Turner syndrome (45,X), leopard syndrome, Noonan syndrome, and multiple pterygium syndrome. Turner syndrome and the other syndromes are the result of chromosomal abnormalities and are associated with a high intrauterine mortality rate. These syndromes are characterized in utero by nuchal hydrops (lymphedema), which is easily seen on ultrasonography.

45,X Syndrome (Turner Syndrome)

Turner syndrome is caused by monosomy of the sex chromosomes. The classic features of Turner syndrome are short stature, pterygium colli, absence of sexual maturation, and a broad, shield-like chest with widely spaced nipples (Fig. 98–5). Aortic stenosis is a frequently associated anomaly.[95]

Multiple Lentigines (Leopard) Syndrome

Leopard syndrome is an autosomal dominant trait characterized by numerous lentigines on the neck and trunk, electrocardiographic defects, hypertelorism, pulmonary stenosis, genital abnormalities, retardation of growth, sensorineural deafness, and, frequently, pterygia colli.

Turner Phenotype with Normal Karyotype (Noonan Syndrome)

The Noonan and leopard syndromes have many features in common, such as hypertelorism, small stature, pulmonary stenosis, abnormal electrocardiograms, and pterygium colli.[74]

Multiple Pterygium Syndrome

In multiple pterygium syndrome, folds of skin cross the angles of most of the joints, such as the knee joints, elbows, and metacarpophalangeal joints, and prominent pterygium colli are present.[1] Cosmetically unacceptable pterygia can be surgically improved by Z plasty.

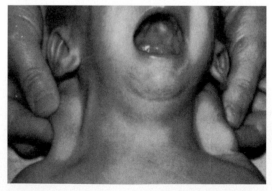

FIGURE 98–5. A 10-month-old child with Turner syndrome. The pterygium colli are being stretched by the examiner's fingers.

Midline Cervical Clefts

Midline cervical clefts are rare anomalies caused by abnormal fusion of the branchial arches in the ventral midline of the neck, which is, instead, represented by a band of fibrous tissue that extends from the mandibular symphysis to the sternal manubrium. In the neonate, cervical clefts appear as a linear vertical area of thin, erythematous, raised skin about 10 mm wide, characteristically with a cephalad skin tag, a mucosal surface, and a caudal sinus.[9] The fibrous band extends from the surface to the pretracheal fascia and is frequently attached to a spur on the mandible. Gargan et al[33] found that, of 12 patients, 11 were girls. Untreated, the fibrous band, which does not have the capacity to grow, anchors the symphysis to the sternum, fixing the neck in flexion. Midline clefts should be excised earlier rather than later, preferably through single or double horizontal incisions.

Anomalies of the Blood Vessels

Arterial Anomalies

The development of the cervical arterial system is described in Chapter 95. All vascular lesions must be studied as thoroughly as possible by contrast imaging before making any attempt at treatment, particularly surgical maneuvers. Because these patients frequently have associated cardiac anomalies, thorough investigation of the heart is also mandatory. CT, MRI, angiography, Doppler ultrasonography, echocardiography, and barium studies may all be used individually or collectively to define the extent of the problem.[67, 68] A multidisciplinary team is highly recommended.

Most of the aberrations of the major vessels can be demonstrated by magnetic resonance angiography. Direct invasive contrast angiography, although still a useful tool, is necessary in a smaller percentage of cases. When there is respiratory difficulty, the vascular anomaly can frequently be identified on bronchoscopy.[37]

Major vessel anomalies are discussed in Chapter 82.

Anomalies of the Major Arteries

Most of the anomalies of the major vessels in the neck manifest with respiratory symptoms such as acute or chronic stridor, wheezing, and recurrent infections. Some have isolated or concurrent dysphagia.

The major vessel anomalies mainly involve the carotid and subclavian systems, rarely the vertebral system. In the neck, only three anomalies are clinically important: high bifurcation of the common carotid artery, left-sided origin of the right subclavian artery, and left-sided origin of the innominate artery.

High bifurcation of the common carotid artery is not rare and is usually not significant except when a chemodectoma develops or when there are penetrating wounds of the neck.

When the right subclavian artery (brachiocephalic trunk) arises from the left side of the aortic arch or when a left subclavian vessel arises from a right-sided aortic arch, the vessel usually runs posterior to the esophagus or

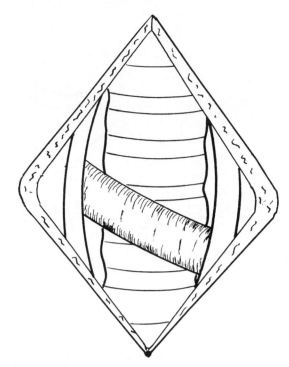

FIGURE 98–6. Diagram of findings at tracheostomy in a 3-year-old girl with multiple congenital anomalies. The innominate artery is at the level of the third and fourth tracheal rings.

between the esophagus and trachea, in which position it compresses the trachea or esophagus, resulting in difficulty with breathing or swallowing.[65] Symptomatic large vessel anomalies can be managed by suspension away from the airway or by reimplantation of the vessel to a different site. Ligation and division of the vessel carries a significant risk of morbidity or even mortality.

When the innominate artery (brachiocephalic trunk) arises from the left side of the aortic arch, it courses upward and to the right into the neck before bifurcating. In this position, the vessel is unusually high; it might compress the trachea or be directly in the path of a tracheostomy (Fig. 98–6), or it might be susceptible to erosion after placement of a tracheostomy tube. If this situation is encountered during tracheostomy, the vessel can be ligated and sectioned, a maneuver that might cause hemiplegia. Alternatively, the sternohyoid muscle can be detached from the hyoid bone and the free end passed between the vessel and the trachea. The free end is then sutured to the lowest point of the sternal head of the sternocleidomastoid muscle to form a tissue barrier and downward sling for the innominate artery (Fig. 98–7). I have used this technique successfully in a 3-year-old child with multiple congenital anomalies.

Anomalies of Minor Vessels

Abnormalities of the vascular system have long presented problems with terminology, as witnessed by the myriad of names applied to these lesions. Mulliken and Glowacki[71] have classified minor vessel lesions into two broad categories based on the activity of the endothelial cells: heman-

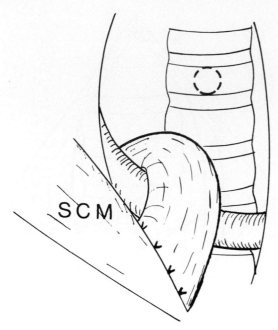

FIGURE 98–7. Explanatory diagram of the surgical maneuver performed on the patient described in Figure 98–6. The sterno-hyoid muscle was detached from the hyoid. The muscle was then looped around the innominate artery, and its free end was firmly sutured to the lower sternocleidomastoid muscle (SCM). A tracheostomy was placed at the second tracheal ring.

giomas and vascular malformations. This classification is accepted internationally as the standard.

Hemangiomas are tumors with increased activity of endothelial and mast cells during the growth phase. Characteristically, hemangiomas are usually not obvious at birth but appear within a few weeks. They tend to expand rapidly for 6 to 12 months, and then slowly involute. With involution, the numbers of both cell types return to normal. During the growth phase, hemangiomas are somewhat invasive.

Hemangiomas tend to be multicentric. The larger lesions might involve the full thickness of the neck, extending from skin to mucosa. In the head and neck, the parotid area is a frequent site. Because of the tendency for multicentricity, all patients with vascular lesions should be thoroughly evaluated, paying particular attention to the airway because subglottic lesions can be problematic.

In vascular malformations, the complement of endothelial and mast cells is normal, and their rate of division is also normal. Vascular malformations are usually present but are not always obvious at birth. They grow slowly with the child's growth pattern and do not involute. They are always larger than suggested by clinical examination and should be thoroughly assessed by Doppler ultrasonography and contrast radiography.[31] Therapeutically it is important to distinguish between hemangiomas and vascular malformations. Recently, North et al[75] found increased immunoreactivity of GLUT1 in juvenile hemangiomas but not in vascular malformations. This test, therefore, has the potential for distinguishing between the two entities, which is pertinent to their future management.

Initially, vascular lesions are treated only if they are life threatening. If vascular lesions do not regress spontaneously after a prolonged period, they should be treated. Hemangiomas are treated, for the most part, by judicious observation. Systemic corticosteroids or alpha-interferon frequently causes significant reduction in size, but too early withdrawal of treatment might result in regrowth. Subglottic lesions are ablated with lasers.

Surgery is usually the treatment of choice for most vascular lesions, but the approach to excision must be practical, realistic, and undertaken only after careful study. Sclerosing therapy by intralesional injection of various agents is the choice in a number of centers and, presently, the most popular agent is polidocanol.[98]

Venous Malformations

Venous malformations are the most frequent of the vascular malformations and have a predilection for the head and neck, mainly affecting the face and head. About 20% of patients with extensive superficial venous malformations have cerebral venous malformations, and 50% have anomalies of the deep veins, particularly phlebectasia.[25] Therefore, it is important to search for cerebral lesions when confronted with a cervicofacial venous malformation.

Venous malformations manifest as blue-colored, soft, compressible swellings with indistinct margins. Prominent veins might or might not be visible in the surrounding skin. Most venous malformations are low-flow lesions and expand slowly. A few might involute by spontaneous thrombosis.

Venous anomalies can be assessed by CT, MRI, or ultrasonography. After initial investigation, the lesions can be followed up with periodic ultrasound studies.[94] The preferred treatment of venous malformations varies in different centers.

Surgical extirpation carefully performed is the standard method for the treatment of vascular malformations in most institutions, but these procedures might be technically difficult because of bleeding, or they may lead to significant functional morbidity from nerve damage. Alternatively, sclerotherapy has proven to be a successful modality for these lesions, as demonstrated by Pappas et al[77] in a study of 57 patients using ethanol, and by Berenguer et al[8] using alcohol and sodium tetradecyl sulfate. Others prefer to use polidocanol.

Treatment of venous malformations with lasers, particularly the Nd:YAG (neodymium:yttrium-aluminium-garnet), has also been successful for superficial lesions.[16] Recently, Jacob et al[49] reported good results in treating larger lesions with intralesional, Doppler-guided laser therapy.

In the management of all vascular malformations, staged treatment is frequently necessary, and long-term follow-up is mandatory because of the propensity for recurrence.

Arteriovenous Malformations

Arteriovenous malformations are the most severe forms of the spectrum of vascular malformations and are most

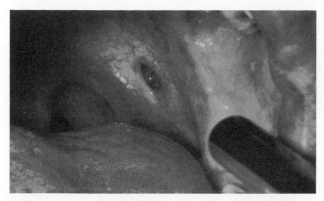

FIGURE 98–19. This 28-year-old man complained of recurrent sore throat. On examination, there was a clean opening in the left anterior tonsillar pillar that communicated with a blind tract that coursed through the tonsil and ended at the level of the base of the tongue.

artery on the right, and returning to the neck to a more superficial position lateral to the hypoglossal nerve. Such an entity has not yet been reported.

Rarely, the fourth pouch persists as a cul-de-sac from the piriform sinus (Fig. 98–19). More than 90% of these sinuses are on the left side.[34] If the sac becomes infected, it first manifests as an inflammatory mass in the anterior lower neck, which is usually diagnosed as suppurative thyroiditis. If this abscess is incised or drains spontaneously, a tract is formed that runs directly from the skin to the piriform sinus (Fig. 98–20). Usually, the external exit is in the lower neck near the thyroid gland. Therefore, a persistent fourth branchial pouch must be considered in the differential diagnosis of recurrent abscesses of the anterior neck.

The internal opening in the piriform sinus can usually be identified by a barium swallow or on direct endoscopy.[60, 73, 80]

Fourth pouch sinuses that are recurrently infected require excision. If there is an external opening, the tract is first delineated by injecting a coloring agent such as methylene blue (Fig. 98–21). An elliptical incision is made around the external opening, and the tract is carefully followed superiorly and medially to the piriform sinus where it is divided and ligated. In the course of dissection, great care must be taken to first identify and protect the recurrent laryngeal nerve. It might be necessary to resect a segment of the lamina of the thyroid cartilage.

Cervical Thymic Rests

Thymic rests in the neck are rare but are being reported with increasing frequency. They occur as either solid or, more frequently, cystic masses in the neck, sometimes extending to the thorax and might be otherwise asymptomatic or cause respiratory distress. A few thymic rests manifest acutely as cystic inflammatory swellings.[14, 44, 66, 70, 81] Graeber et al,[38] in their series of 46 patients with thymic cysts, found seven in the neck and 39 in the mediastinum. Two of the masses were malignant.

The consensus of these reports is that no characteristic

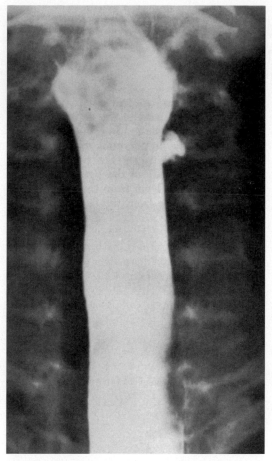

FIGURE 98–20. A 7-year-old girl presented with a recurrent abscess in the anterior neck for which numerous surgical procedures had been performed. A barium swallow demonstrated a fistulous tract from the left piriform sinus. This obviously was a persistent fourth pouch sinus.

feature defines these masses preoperatively. They have occurred in the midline anterior neck and in the paramedian or lateral planes. Most of these are de novo cystic or begin as solid masses that are prone to cystic degeneration. They are frequently associated with hypertrophy of the adjacent parathyroid gland.[10] Diagnosis is made by histologic examination with identification of Hassall corpuscles. These masses can be studied by ultrasonography, CT, or MRI. A few of these cysts have been associated with disordered calcium metabolism. In the neonate, small child, or even the older patient, the superior mediastinum should be examined.

Thymic rests should be treated with surgical excision, which may be urgent in the neonate.

Anomalies of the Branchial Arches

There are many developmental variations of the mesodermal derivatives of the branchial arches. Some of these anomalies, such as hemifacial microsomia, are sporadic, whereas others are genetically determined and inherited, such as in the Treacher Collins syndrome, first and second arch syndrome, and the branchio-otorenal (BOR) syndrome.[54, 69]

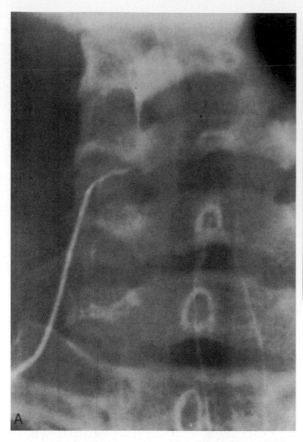

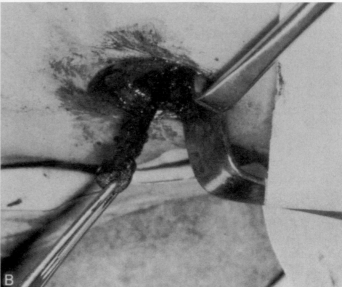

FIGURE 98–21. This 11-year-old girl presented at age 2 years with a mass in the right lower neck. After three surgical procedures, she was left with a draining opening on the incision. A fistulogram demonstrated a tract leading to the ipsilateral piriform sinus (*A*). At surgery, the tract was first injected with methylene blue and then cleanly excised (*B*).

Thyroglossal Duct Cysts

The thyroid gland begins from a median thickening in the floor of the embryonic pharynx just caudal to the tuberculum impar. The thickening forms the thyroid diverticulum, which descends anterior to the developing respiratory tract. The superior segment of the tract remains connected to the foramen caecum of the tongue as the thyroglossal duct. By the eighth week of embryonic life, the bilobed thyroid gland has attained its final position in front of the trachea. The upper end of the thyroglossal duct usually disappears, but the tissue around the lower end sometimes persists as the pyramidal lobe of the thyroid gland. During the descent of the thyroid gland and the thyroglossal duct, the second branchial arch grows forward, and the Reichert cartilage, which eventually becomes the hyoid bone, comes into close relationship with the thyroglossal duct. The hyoid bone might completely surround the duct or might displace the duct forward so that the duct lies anterior to the hyoid bone, or the duct might end at the hyoid bone.

If the duct persists, local expansions form thyroglossal duct cysts anywhere from the foramen caecum to the thyroid gland. If a cyst becomes infected and ruptures on the skin, a thyroglossal duct sinus results.

Thyroglossal duct cysts are more common in children but can occur in adults. The cysts usually manifest as asymptomatic swelling in the midline of the neck at the level of or just inferior to the hyoid bone. Frequently, however, they are lateral and superior or much inferior to the hyoid bone. The possible locations of thyroglossal duct cysts are shown in Figure 98–22, and their actual

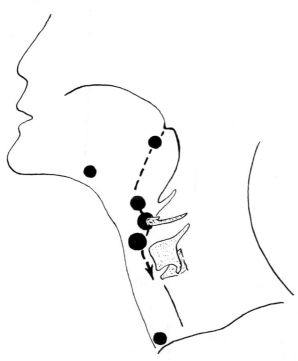

FIGURE 98–22. Possible sites of thyroglossal duct cysts (see Table 98–1). The arrow represents the embryologic path of the thyroglossal duct.

TABLE 98–1. Location of Thyroglossal Duct Cysts in 72 Patients

Location	Number
Lingular	0
Submental	2
Suprahyoid	18
Transhyoid	2
Infrahyoid	45
Suprasternal	5

From Ward PH, Strahan RW, Acquarilli M, et al. The many faces of cysts of the thyroglossal duct. Trans Am Acad Ophthalmol Otolaryngol 74:310, 1970.

locations in 72 patients are listed in Table 98–1. Several cases of papillary adenocarcinoma of the thyroglossal duct cyst have been reported.

Thyroglossal duct cysts are easily diagnosed clinically. It is, however, always wise to confirm the diagnosis by CT scan or ultrasonography to rule out the possibility of an ectopic thyroid gland, which can occur in the same position.[13]

The treatment of thyroglossal duct cysts is excision. The standard technique is the Sistrunk procedure.[76, 86] Because of the intimate embryologic relationship with the hyoid bone and the tongue, to ensure complete removal, the tract must be dissected free of the hyoid bone, or a block of the central bone must be excised in continuity, and the potential tract in the tongue must also be excised.

A horizontal incision is made at the level of the hyoid bone. The soft tissues of the neck are divided, and the cystic mass is identified and carefully dissected from the surrounding tissue, taking great care to prevent its rupture. There is usually a tract that runs to the central body of the hyoid bone. This is dissected free but left attached to the hyoid bone. The upper ends of the sternohyoid and the thyrohyoid muscles are released from the central 2 cm of the body of the hyoid bone, and the hyoid bone is divided 1 cm from the midline on both sides. A block of tissue from the central hyoid to the foramen caecum of the tongue is then cored from the substance of the tongue. An assistant's finger pressing on the dorsum of the tongue helps during this part of the dissection. The upper end of this core is clamped and ligated superiorly at the level of the foramen caecum, thus ensuring complete removal of the thyroglossal duct.

Incomplete excision of a thyroglossal duct almost guarantees recurrence.

Anomalies of the Branchial Arch Cartilages

Most of the branchial arch cartilages disappear except for the parts that contribute to bony structures or ligaments. Occasionally, however, remnants of arch cartilages persist as small, triangular masses deep to the skin along the anterior border of the sternocleidomastoid muscle (Fig. 98–23). These manifest only cosmetic problems and are easily removed.

Heterotopic Cervical Salivary Gland Tissue

Heterotopic salivary gland tissue in the neck is comparatively rare but might manifest as a cervical mass or in association with a draining sinus.

Heterotopic salivary glands have been described by a number of authors.[59] They usually occur as draining sinuses along the anterior border of the sternocleidomastoid muscle. Joseph et al[52] and Shvero et al[85] found heterotopic salivary gland tissue associated with draining cervical sinuses in patients with branchial cleft syndromes. The sinuses also exited at along the anterior border of the sternocleidomastoid muscle. Gudbrandsson et al[41] described two adults with solid middle neck masses along the anterior border of the sternocleidomastoid muscle. In one patient, the mass was salivary glands; in the other, the mass was a pleomorphic adenoma presumably arising from heterotopic glandular tissue. Ferlito et al[29] and others also reported neoplasms arising from heterotopic salivary glands in the neck.

The diagnosis of heterotopic salivary gland tissue is made by histologic examination of excised tissue; there are no specific clinical features for preoperative identification. The origin of heterotopic salivary glands is still not known but does seem to be related to the development of the branchial arches.

Primary Branchiogenic Carcinoma

Carcinoma arising in a branchial anomaly continues to be a controversial concept. A number of authors have described convincing cases, while others believe that these cases are cystic metastases. Park and Karmody[78] described a case of squamous cell carcinoma arising in a first branchial cleft duplication anomaly in a young woman. Other cases have been documented.[55, 57, 82] I am convinced that branchial arch anomalies can become malignant, although they rarely do so.

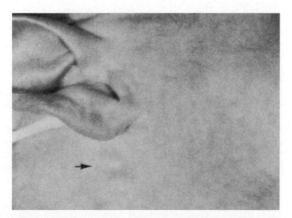

FIGURE 98–23. This small mass *(arrow)* inferior to the lobule of the ear was firm and contained a triangular mass of cartilage, the remnant of a branchial arch cartilage.

SELECTED REFERENCES

Albers GD. Branchial anomalies. JAMA 183:399, 1963.
A classic paper on the branchial arch apparatus.

Cheng JC, Tang SP, Chen TM. Sternocleidomastoid pseudotumor and congenital muscular torticollis in infants: a prospective study of 510 cases. J Pediatr Surg 34:549,1999.

A detailed study of a vast experience of muscular torticollis.

Ford GR, Balakrishnan A, Evans JNG, Bailey CM. Branchial cleft and pouch anomalies. J Laryngol Otol 106:137, 1992.

An excellent review of branchial anomalies.

Karmody CS. Anomalies of the first and second branchial arches. In English GM (ed). Otolaryngology. Philadelphia, Harper & Row, 1983, pp 1–18.

A review of anomalies of the arch apparatus with a new classification of first groove anomalies.

Mulliken JB, Glowacki J. Hemangiomas and vascular malformations in infants and children: a classification based on endothelial characteristics. Plast Reconstr Surg 62:412,1982.

The classic paper on the classification of vascular anomalies.

Tom LWC, Rossiter JL, Sutton LM, et al. Torticollis in children. Otolaryngol Head Neck Surg 105:1, 1991.

A good review of torticollis and its differential diagnosis.

Ward PH, Strahan RW, Acquarelli M, et al. The many faces of cysts of the thyroglossal duct. Trans Am Acad Ophthalmol Otolaryngol 74: 310, 1970.

This article is a concise and orderly presentation of the embryology, clinical manifestations, and anatomic distributions of thyroglossal duct cysts.

Work WD. Newer concepts of first branchial cleft defects. Laryngoscope 82:1581, 1972.

A classic article on duplication anomalies of the first branchial cleft. Excellent anatomic descriptions are included.

REFERENCES

1. Aarskog D. Pterygium syndrome. Birth Defects 7:232, 1971.
2. Agaton-Bonilla FC, Gay-Escoda C. Diagnosis and treatment of branchial cleft cysts and fistulae. A retrospective study of 183 patients. Int J Oral Maxillofac Surg 25:449, 1996.
3. Androulakis M, Johnson JT, Wagner RL. Thyroglossal duct and second branchial cleft anomalies in adults. Ear Nose Throat J 69: 318, 1990.
4. Albers GD. Branchial anomalies. JAMA 183:399, 1963.
5. Aldred AJ. Congenital pseudarthrosis of the clavicle. J Bone Joint Surg 45:312, 1963.
6. Apple SK, Nieberg RK, Hirschowitz SL. Fine needle aspiration diagnosis of fibromatosis colli. A report of three cases. Acta Cytol 41(4 Suppl):1373, 1997.
7. Baba H, Maezawa Y, Furusawa N, et al. The cervical spine in the Klippel-Feil syndrome. A report of 57 cases. Int Orthop 19:204, 1995.
8. Berenguer B, Burrows PE, Zurakowski D, Mulliken JB. Sclerotherapy of craniofacial venous malformations: complications and results. Plast Reconstr Surg 104:1, 1999.
9. Bill AH, Summer DS. A unified concept of lymphangioma and cystic hygroma. Surg Gynecol Obstet 120:79, 1965.
10. Bergevin MA, Shefis S, Myer C, McAdam AJ. Congenital midline cervical cleft. Pediatr Pathol 9:731, 1989.
11. Borges JL, Shah A, Torres BC, Bowen JR. Modified Woodward procedure for Sprengel deformity of the shoulder: long-term results. J Pediatr Orthop 16:508, 1996.
12. Brewis C, Pracy JP, Albert DM. Treatment of lymphangiomas of the head and neck in children by intralesional injection of OK-432 (Picibanil). Clin Otolaryngol 25:130, 2000.
13. Brewis C, Mahadevan M, Bailey CM, Drake DP. Investigation and treatment of thyroglossal cysts in children. J R Soc Med 93:18, 2000.
14. Buchanan G, Gregory MM. Giant functioning cervical mediastinal parathyroid cyst. Ann Otol Rhinol Laryngol 88:545, 1979.
15. Carroll WR, Zappia JJ, McClatchey KD. Branchiogenic carcinoma. J Otolaryngol 22:26, 1993.
16. Chang CJ, Fisher DM, Chen YR. Intralesional photocoagulation of vascular anomalies of the tongue. Br J Plast Surg 52:178, 1999.
17. Charabi B, Bretlau P, Bille M, Holmelund M. Cystic hygroma of the head and neck–a long-term follow-up of 44 cases. Acta Otolaryngol Suppl 543:248, 2000.
18. Cheng JC, Tang SP, Chen TM. Sternocleidomastoid pseudotumor and congenital muscular torticollis in infants: a prospective study of 510 cases. J Pediatr Surg 34:549, 1999.
19. Cheng JC, Tang SP. Outcome of surgical treatment of congenital muscular torticollis. Clin Orthop 362:190, 1999.
20. Clarke RA, Catalan G, Diwan AD, Kearsley JH. Heterogeneity in Klippel-Feil syndrome: a new classification. Pediatr Radiol 28:967, 1998.
21. Contencin P, Augui O, de Gaudemar I, Helardot P. Recurrent thyroid abscess in children and malformations of the pyriform sinus. Ann Chir 51:76, 1997.
22. Demirbilek S, Atayurt HF. Congenital muscular torticollis and sternomastoid tumor: nonoperative treatment. Arch Phys Med Rehabil 80:637, 1999.
23. DiGeorge AM. Congenital absence of the thymus and its immunologic consequences: concurrence with congenital hypoparathyroidism. In Bergsma D, Good RA (eds). Birth Defects: Original Article Series. Immunologic Deficiency Diseases in man. New York, The National Foundation—March of Dimes 4:116, 1968.
24. Eastlack JP, Howard RM, Frieden IJ. Congenital midline cervical cleft: case report and review of the English language literature. Pediatr Dermatol 17:118, 2000.
25. Eifert S, Villavicencio JL, Kao TC, et al. Prevalence of deep venous anomalies in congenital vascular malformations of venous predominance. J Vasc Surg 31:462, 2000.
26. Enbom H, Widstrom A, Magnusson P. Lateral fistulae and cysts of the neck. Heredity and diagnosis. Acta Otolaryngol Suppl 360:64, 1979.
27. Engel D. The etiology of the undescended scapula and related syndromes. J Bone Joint Surg 45:613, 1943.
28. Enjolras O, Riche MC, Merland JJ. Superficial vascular (arterial and venous) malformations: clinical aspects and complementary tests. Ann Chir Plast Esthet 36:271, 1991.
29. Ferlito A, Bertino G, Rinaldo A, et al. A review of heterotopia and associated salivary gland neoplasms of the head and neck. J Laryngol Otol 113:299, 1999.
30. Ford GR, Balakrishnan A, Evans JNG, Bailey CM. Branchial cleft and pouch anomalies. J Laryngol Otol 106:137, 1992.
31. Fordham LA, Chung CJ, Donnelly LF. Imaging of congenital vascular and lymphatic anomalies of the head and neck. Neuroimaging Clin N Am 10:117, 2000.
32. Frazer JE. Nomenclature of disease states caused by certain vestigial structures of the neck. Br J Surg 11:131, 1923.
33. Gargan TJ, McKinnon M, Mulliken JB. Midline cervical cleft. Plast Reconstr Surg 76:225, 1985.
34. Godin MS, Kearns DB, Pransky SM, et al. Fourth branchial pouch sinus: principles of diagnosis and management. Laryngoscope 100: 174, 1990.
35. Gonzales J, Ljung BM, Guerry T, Schoenrock LD. Congenital torticollis evaluation by fine-needle aspiration biopsy. Laryngoscope 99:651,1989.
36. Gorlin RJ, Cohen MM, Levin LS (eds). Syndromes of the Head and Neck, 3rd ed. New York, Oxford University Press, 1990, pp 886–890.
37. Gormley PK, Colreavy MP, Patil N, Woods AE. Congenital vascular anomalies and persistent respiratory symptoms in children. Int J Pediatr Otorhinolaryngol 51:23, 1999.
38. Graeber GM, Thompson LD, Cohen DJ, et al. Cystic lesions of the thymus. An occasionally malignant cervical and/or anterior mediastinal mass. J Thorac Cardiovasc Surg 87:295, 1984.
39. Greinwald JH Jr, Burke DK, Sato Y, et al. Treatment of lymphangiomas in children: an update of Picibanil (OK-432) sclerotherapy. Otolaryngol Head Neck Surg 121:38, 1999.
40. Greitemann B, Rondhuis JJ, Karbowski A. Treatment of congenital elevation of the scapula. 10 (2–18) year follow-up of 37 cases of Sprengel's deformity. Acta Orthop Scand 64:365, 1993.
41. Gudbrandsson FK, Liston SL, Maisel RA. Heterotopic salivary tissue in the neck. Otolaryngol Head Neck Surg 90:279, 1982.
42. Hawkins HB, Shapiro R, Petrillo CJ. The association of cleidocranial dysostosis with hearing loss. Am J Roentgenol Radium Ther Nucl Med 125:944, 1975.

43. Helmi C, Pruzansky S. Craniofacial and extracranial malformations in the Klippel-Feil syndrome. Cleft Palate J 17:65, 1980.
44. Hendrickson M, Azarow K, Ein S, et al. Congenital thymic cysts in children—mostly misdiagnosed. J Pediatr Surg 33:821, 1998.
45. Hoffmann MH, Vadstrup S. DiGeorge syndrome. Velocardiofacial syndrome/chromosome 22q11 deletion syndrome. Ugeskr Laeger 162:2736, 2000.
46. Hollier L, Kim J, Grayson BH, McCarthy JG. Congenital muscular torticollis and the associated craniofacial changes. Plast Reconstr Surg 105:827, 2000.
47. Hong R. The DiGeorge anomaly. Immunodefic Rev 3:1, 1991.
48. Hsu TC, Wang CL, Wong MK, et al. Correlation of clinical and ultrasonographic features in congenital muscular torticollis. J Pediatr 134:712, 1999.
49. Jacob R, Frommeld T, Maurer J, Mann W. Duplex ultrasonography-controlled Nd:Yag laser therapy of vascular malformations. Ultraschall Med 20:191, 1999.
50. Jaffee IS. Congenital shoulder-neck-auditory anomalies. Laryngoscope 78:2119, 1968.
51. Johnson MC. Klippel-Feil syndrome revisited: diagnostic pitfalls impacting neurosurgical management. Childs Nerv Syst 8:322, 1992.
52. Joseph MP, Goodman ML, Pilch BZ, et al. Heterotopic cervical salivary gland tissue in a family with probable branchiootorenal syndrome. Head Neck Surg 8:456, 1986.
53. Karmody CS. Anomalies of the first and second branchial arches. In English GM (ed). Otolaryngology. Philadelphia, Harper & Row, 1983, pp 1–18.
54. Karmody CS, Feingold M. Autosomal dominant first and second branchial arch syndrome. A new inherited syndrome. In Birth Defects: Original Article Series. Malformation Syndromes. New York, The National Foundation—March of Dimes 10:31–40, 1974.
55. Khafif RA, Prichep R, Minkowitz S. Primary branchiogenic carcinoma. Head Neck 11:153, 1989.
56. Klippel M, Feil A. Anomalie de la colonne vertebrale par absence des vertebres cervicales: cage thoracique remontant jusqu'a la base du crane. Bull Soc Anat Paris 87:185, 1912.
57. Knobber D, Lobeck H, Steinkamp HJ. Does malignant lateral cervical cyst still exist? HNO 43:104, 1995.
58. Kreiborg S, Jensen BL, Larsen P, et al. Anomalies of craniofacial skeleton and teeth in cleidocranial dysplasia. J Craniofac Genet Dev Biol 19:75, 1999.
59. Lassaletta-Atienza L, Lopez-Rios F, Martin G, et al. Salivary gland heterotopia in the lower neck: a report of five cases. Int J Pediatr Otorhinolaryngol 43:153, 1998.
60. Lee FP. Occult congenital pyriform sinus fistula causing recurrent left lower neck abcess. Head Neck 21:671, 1999.
61. Liston SL. Fourth branchial fistula. Otolaryngol Head Neck Surg 89:520, 1981.
62. Lloyd-Roberts GC, Apley AG, Owen R. Reflections upon the aetiology of congenital pseudarthrosis of the clavicle. With a note on cranio-cleido dysostosis. J Bone Joint Surg Br 57:24, 1975.
63. McCrae RG, Lee KJ, Goertzen E. First branchial cleft anomalies and the facial nerve. Otolaryngol Head Neck Surg 91:197, 1983.
64. McGaughran JM, Kuna P, Das V. Audiological abnormalities in the Klippel-Feil syndrome. Arch Dis Child 79:352, 1998.
65. McLaughlin RB Jr, Wetmore RF, Tavill MA, et al. Vascular anomalies causing symptomatic tracheobronchial compression. Laryngoscope 109:312, 1999.
66. McLeod DM, Karandy EJ. Aberrant cervical thymus. Arch Otolaryngol 107:180, 1981.
67. Mahboubi S, Harty MP, Hubbard AM, Meyer JS. Innominate artery compression of the trachea in infants. Int J Pediatr Otorhinolaryngol 35:197, 1996.
68. Mahboubi S, Meyer JS, Hubbard AM, et al. Magnetic resonance imaging of airway obstruction resulting from vascular anomalies. Int J Pediatr Otorhinolaryngol 28:111, 1994.
69. Melnick M, Bixler D, Nance WE, et al. Familial branchio-oto-renal dysplasia: a new addition to the branchial arch syndromes. Clin Genet 9:25, 1976.
70. Millman B, Pransky S, Castillo J 3rd, et al. Cervical thymic anomalies. Int J Pediatr Otorhinolaryngol 47:29, 1999.
71. Mulliken JB, Glowacki J. Hemangiomas and vascular malformations in infants and children: a classification based on endothelial characteristics. Plast Reconstr Surg 62:412, 1982.
72. Mundlos S. Cleidocranial dysplasia: clinical and molecular genetics. J Med Genet 36:177, 1999.
73. Nicollas R, Ducroz V, Garabedian EN, Triglia JM. Fourth branchial pouch anomalies: a study of six cases and review of the literature. Int J Pediatr Otorhinolaryngol 44:5, 1999.
74. Noonan JA. Hypertelorism with Turner phenotype: a new syndrome with associated congenital heart disease. Am J Dis Child 116:373, 1968.
75. North PE, Waner M, Mizeracki A, Mihm MC Jr. GLUT1: a newly discovered immunohistochemical marker for juvenile hemangiomas. Hum Pathol 31:11, 2000.
76. Organ GM, Organ CH Jr. Thyroid gland and surgery of the thyroglossal duct: exercise in applied embryology. World J Surg 24:886, 2000.
77. Pappas DC Jr, Persky MS, Berenstein A. Evaluation and treatment of head and neck venous vascular malformations. Ear Nose Throat J 77:914, 918, 1998.
78. Park SS, Karmody CS. The first branchial cleft carcinoma. Arch Otolaryngol Head Neck Surg 118:969, 1992.
79. Richardson A, Deussen FF. Facial and dental anomalies in cleidocranial dysplasia: a study of cases. Int J Paediatr Dent 4:225, 1994.
80. Rosenfeld RM, Biller HF. Fourth branchial pouch sinus: diagnosis and treatment. Otolaryngol Head Neck Surg 105:44, 1991.
81. Rosevear WH, Singer MI. Syptomatic cervical thymic cyst in a neonate. Otolaryngol Head Neck Surg 89:73, 1981.
82. Sandiford JA, Chun BK, Potter JF. Branchiogenic carcinoma. J R Coll Surg Edinb 32:148, 1987.
83. Sergi C, Serpi M, Muller-Navia J, et al. CATCH 22 syndrome: report of 7 infants with follow-up data and review of the recent advancements in the genetic knowledge of the locus 22q11. Pathologica 91:166, 1999.
84. Shenoy PK, David VC. Cervical thymic cyst—a case record. J Laryngol Otolaryngol 107:950, 1993.
85. Shvero J, Mardar T, Abraham A, et al. Heterotopic salivary tissue and branchial sinuses. J Laryngol Otolaryngol 100:243, 1986.
86. Sistrunk WE. Technique of removal of cysts and sinuses of the thyroglossal duct. Surg Gynecol Obstet 46:109, 1928.
87. Smith CS, Clark SK. Cervical congenital arteriovenous malformation. Laryngoscope 88:1522, 1978.
88. Stewart PA, Wallerstein R, Moran E, Lee MJ. Early prenatal ultrasound diagnosis of cleidocranial dysplasia. Ultrasound Obstet Gynecol 15:154, 2000.
89. Taylor PH, Bicknell PG. Stripping of branchial fistulae, a new technique. J Laryngol Otolaryngol 91:141, 1977.
90. Thomas RA, Landing BH, Wells TR. Embryologic and other developmental considerations of thirty-eight possible variants of the DiGeorge anomaly. Am J Med Genet Suppl 3:43, 1987.
91. Thomsen MN, Schneider U, Weber M, et al. Scoliosis and congenital anomalies associated with Klippel-Feil syndrome types I–III. Spine 22:396, 1997.
92. Tom LWC, Rossiter JL, Sutton LM, et al. Torticollis in children. Otolaryngol Head Neck Surg 105:1, 1991.
93. Triglia JM, Nicollas R, Ducroz V, et al. First branchial cleft anomalies: a study of 39 cases and a review of the literature. Arch Otolaryngol Head Neck Surg 124:291, 1998.
94. Trop I, Dubois J, Guibaud L, et al. Soft-tissue venous malformations in pediatric and young adult patients: diagnosis with Doppler-US. Radiology 212:841, 1999.
95. Turner HH. A syndrome of infantilism, congenital webbed neck, and cubitus valgus. Endocrinology 23:566, 1938.
96. Ward PH, Strahan RW, Acquarelli M, et al. The many faces of cysts of the thyroglossal duct. Trans Am Acad Ophthalmol Otolaryngol 74:310, 1970.
97. Wild G, Mischke D, Lobeck H, Kasatenbauer E. The lateral cyst of the neck: congenital or acquired. Acta Otolaryngol (Stockh) 103:546, 1987.
98. Winter H, Drager E, Sterry W. Sclerotherapy for treatment of hemangiomas. Dermatol Surg 26:105, 2000.
99. Work WD. Newer concepts of first branchial cleft defects. Laryngoscope 82:1581, 1972.
100. Zhou G, Chen Y, Zhou L, et al. CBFA1 mutation analysis and functional correlation with phenotypic variability in cleidocranial dysplasia. Hum Mol Genet 8:2311, 1999.

99

Cervical Adenopathy

Richard M. Rosenfeld, M.D., M.P.H

Almost every person has had cervical adenopathy to a greater or lesser degree at some time during childhood. About one third of asymptomatic neonates have palpable lymph nodes, rising to nearly two thirds by infancy.[12] Although cervical adenopathy in children is rarely malignant, neck masses still merit precise diagnosis because therapy may be required for conditions of lesser risk. Neck masses can result from nodal and non-nodal processes, but only the former are discussed in this chapter. Non-nodal neck masses are thoroughly discussed elsewhere in this text (see Chap. 97).

Cervical adenopathy can be defined as "swelling and morbid change in the lymph nodes of the neck."[121] This is a broad definition, including many important pathologic entities. One way to systematically approach this problem is to review briefly the embryology, anatomy, and physiology of the lymph nodes and then to discuss the congenital, inflammatory, neoplastic, and iatrogenic causes of cervical adenopathy. Inflammatory adenopathy is by far the most common, and can be subdivided into viral, bacterial, fungal, parasitic, and noninfectious categories. This chapter will conclude with a recommended clinical approach to the child with undiagnosed cervical adenopathy.

Embryology

Lymph node development begins after the formation of the primary lymphatic vascular system by dilatation of areas of lymph channels into lymphatic sacs. Mesenchyme then invaginates into these spaces to eventually form the primordial lymph node, which is later populated by B- and T-lymphocytes. This process occurs late in fetal development and continues for some time after birth.

Anatomy

The lymphoid system is composed of lymphocytes and supporting cellular structures, which include epithelial and stromal cells.[27] These lymphoid structures may be fully encapsulated, as in the case of lymph nodes, or diffuse, as in Peyer patches (which are found in the wall of the intestine).

Lymphoid Tissue

Lymphocytes differentiate from stem cells in the primary lymphoid tissue. In humans, T-lymphocytes are produced in the thymus, and B-lymphocytes are produced in the fetal liver and bone marrow. After the stem cells proliferate and mature, they migrate into the secondary lymphoid organs. The secondary, or peripheral, lymphoid organs include the lymph nodes, Waldeyer ring (adenoids, palatine tonsils, lingual tonsils, and lateral pharyngeal bands), thoracic duct, spleen, and regional lymphoid systems (gut-, skin-, and bronchus-associated). Filtration of antigenic materials from tissue fluid or the environment takes place at these sites.

Lymph Nodes of the Head and Neck

The intricate lymphatic system of the head and neck contains nearly 300 of the body's total of 800 lymph nodes, varying in size from 1 to 25 mm in diameter. The afferent lymphatic channel drains into the subcapsular or marginal sinus. This tissue fluid, containing lymphocytes and antigenic material, percolates through the cortex (B-cells) and paracortex (T-cells). Peripheral lymph nodes are 60% T-lymphocytes and 40% B-lymphocytes. As lymph passes through the node, the majority of the antigenic material is phagocytized and destroyed by the macrophages. However, small amounts of this antigen are trapped on the surface of the specialized follicular dendritic cells. The antigen may then interact with B- or T-lymphocytes to form immunologically activated lymphocytes and antibodies. These activated cells leave the lymph nodes via the efferent lymphatic vessel found in the hilum of the node. The lymphatics and lymph nodes of the head and neck form various networks, which eventually rejoin the blood circulation by draining into the thoracic duct.

Patterns of Lymphatic Drainage

Networks of lymphatic channels and nodes are fairly discrete and may be of diagnostic value in pinpointing the various sites of head and neck infections (Fig. 99–1). The major groups of lymph nodes in the head and neck are pre- and postauricular; occipital; pre- and intraparotid;

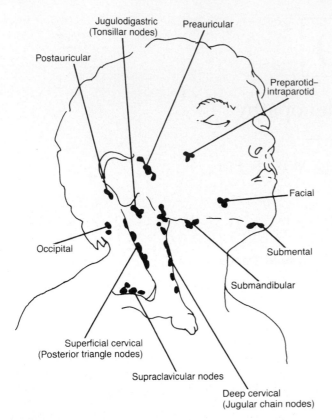

FIGURE 99–1. Surface anatomy of the lymph nodes of the head and neck.

TABLE 99–1. Lymph Nodes of Head and Neck

Lymph Node Groups	Areas Drained
Occipital	Posterior scalp
Postauricular	Temporal and parietal scalp
Preauricular	Skin anterior to ear, entire pinna
Preparotid-intraparotid	Forehead and temporal scalp, midface, external auditory canal, buccal mucosa, gums, parotid gland
Retropharyngeal (Rouvier)	Nasopharynx, oropharynx, palate, nasal fossa, paranasal sinuses, middle ear
Facial	Eyelids, conjunctiva, skin of nose, nasal mucosa, cheek
Submandibular	Cheek, nose, lips, anterior tongue, submandibular gland
Submental	Central lower lip, floor of mouth
Superficial cervical	Ear and parotid gland
Superior deep cervical	Posterior scalp, posterior neck, tonsil, tongue, larynx, thyroid, palate, nose, esophagus, paranasal sinuses
Inferior deep cervical	Dorsal scalp and neck, superficial pectoral region of arm, superior deep cervical nodes

facial; submandibular; submental; superficial cervical; superior deep cervical; inferior deep cervical; and retropharyngeal (Table 99–1). More than 80% of children with cervical adenitis have submandibular or deep cervical involvement because most of the head and neck lymphatic drainage goes to these areas.

Pathophysiology

Lymph nodes serve as filter, removing infectious agents from lymphatics draining bacterial or antigenic material from areas of acute inflammation. Local inflammatory and immune tissue responses partially inactivate and degrade this material via polymorphonuclear and macrophage phagocytosis. After transport to local nodes via afferent vessels, the material interacts with the B- and T-lymphocytes in the node, producing multiple germinal centers and active cell proliferation. In resting nodes, plasma cells (activated B-cells) compose 1% to 3% of the cell population. However, in the activated nodes, their numbers are greatly increased and account in part for the increased size of the reactive lymph node in the face of infection or antigenic stimulus (e.g., lymphadenopathy). Acute lymphadenitis produces swelling and hyperplasia of sinusoidal lining cells and the infiltration of leukocytes. Chronic lymphadenitis causes a proliferative response with hyperplasia of reticuloendothelial cells, prominent germinal centers, and dilated lymph sinuses filled with mononuclear cells.

Congenital Disorders

A few rare, congenital disorders display both cervical and generalized adenopathy. Congenital agammaglobulinemia and dysgammaglobulinemia are rare X-linked recessive hereditary disorders caused by the absence or deficiency of gamma globulin. They are seen only in males, who usually have severe recurrent bacterial infections during infancy. The clinical response to viral infections is usually normal, but immunologic response to blood typing or immunization fails to occur. Treatment consists of close surveillance and early treatment of infectious disease and periodic gamma globulin injections.

Primary immunodeficiencies include disorders of complement, T-lymphocytes, B-lymphocytes, and the phagocytic system. Of these disorders, only phagocytic deficiencies are commonly associated with lymphadenopathy and lymphadenitis. Chédiak-Higashi syndrome is an autosomal recessive disorder in which phagocytes have an abnormal membrane fluidity. Diagnosis is based on identification of characteristic giant cytoplasmic granules in the patient's leukocytes. In contrast, phagocytes from patients with chronic granulomatous disease fail to generate superoxide anion and other oxygen radicals in response to phagocytosis. The nitroblue tetrazolium dye-reduction test is diagnostic. Children with phagocytic disorders also have recurrent otitis, rhinitis, sinusitis, and infections of the skin and soft tissues.[2, 109]

Familial storage disorders may also be associated with generalized and cervical adenopathy. In Gaucher disease, an enzymatic defect causes excess storage of glucocerebroside in reticuloendothelial cells. Hepatosplenomegaly, skeletal lesions, anemia, jaundice, thrombocytopenia, and neurologic lesions may be present. Niemann-Pick disease (sphingomyelin lipidosis) is another storage disease of infancy; its features include generalized adenopathy, hepatosplenomegaly, neurologic involvement, foam cells in bone marrow, and early childhood death.

TABLE 99-4. Distinguishing Features of Childhood Mycobacterial Infections

Feature	Nontuberculous (Atypical) Mycobacteria	Mycobacterium Tuberculosis
Prevalence in children	90–95% of scrofula	5–10% of scrofula
Age group	Preschoolers and young children	Older children
Typical host	Whites in rural communities	African-Americans and Asians in urban settings
Transmission	Aspiration or inoculation of contaminated soil, food, or water	Person-to-person
Tuberculosis contact history	Negative	Positive
Cervical lymphadenitis	Unilateral; submandibular or mandibular	Bilateral; superior cervical or preauricular
Local complications	More common	Less common
PPD skin test (5 TU)	0–15 mm	Greater than 15 mm
Abnormal chest roentgenogram	Rare (less than 5%)	Common (25–70%)
Treatment	Excision, aspiration, or curettage	Chemotherapy

tection of MTB target sequences by a molecular probe.[118] Sensitivity and specificity are 95% to 98% for sputum samples that are positive on acid-fast staining, but the positive predictive value is no better than skin testing for acid-fast negative sputum. Accuracy declines further with gastric aspirates, including false-positive reactions with *M. avium-intracellulare* disease. Consequently, NAA tests have a limited role in evaluating nonimmunocomprised children with MTB. Histologic examination of biopsied lymph nodes reveals granulomas with caseating necrosis for both MTB and NTM. Despite suggestive pathologic appearances,[92] culture results remain the definitive method for distinguishing between NTM and MTB when serologic and clinical findings are nondiagnostic.

Nontuberculous Mycobacterial Adenitis

Nontuberculous scrofula usually affects children aged 1 to 5 years, most often in the submandibular and jugulodigastric nodes. Lymph nodes generally remain less than 3 cm in diameter, with a pink hue and a fragile appearance of the overlying skin. About 50% of nodes are firm, and about 25% are adhesive or tender.[69] Less common manifestations of NTM infection include otitis media, cutaneous lesions, osteomyelitis, and pulmonary disease. The clinical course is generally indolent and self-limited unless there is an underlying immunodeficiency syndrome. Therefore, any child with severe or disseminated NTM infection should undergo HIV testing following informed consent.

Surgical excision is the treatment of choice because of excellent healing, cosmesis, and cure rates.[37, 55, 128] Moreover, prompt excision yields better cosmesis than does delayed excision.[69] Incision and drainage are avoided because of chronic drainage and persistent sinus tracts.[119] In contrast, a draining fistula (Fig. 99-5) requiring secondary excision occurs in less than 10% to 20% of cases treated with primary excision.[88, 110] When complete excision is prevented by extensive skin involvement or by proximity to the facial nerve (typically the marginal mandibular branch), treatment by curettage[59, 128] or by repeated needle aspirations[3] are safe alternatives. Curettage employs a small incision over the fluctuant area of the lesion, with thorough removal of necrotic tissue using orthopedic curettes. Skin is not excised, but the underlying surface is curetted to remove adherent debris.

Wounds are packed overnight and allowed to heal secondarily. Parents are counseled that initial treatment with curettage may require a second surgical procedure for cure or cosmesis.[128]

Multidrug therapy for NTM is reserved for children with AIDS, other immunodeficiencies, or with infections caused by *M. kansasii* or *M. fortuitum*. In contrast, chemotherapy does not usually benefit otherwise healthy children with infection caused by *M. scrofulaceum* or *M. avium* complex. Exceptions include cases in which the family refuses surgery, a recurrence after surgery occurs, or extensive disease precludes safe excision.[117] Clarithromycin and azithromycin have activity against *M. avium* complex organisms in vitro,[45] but should not be used as monotherapy because of rapid resistance in vivo; rifampin or rifabutin is commonly used as a second drug. The recommended duration of therapy ranges from 1 to 6 months. Delayed cosmetic surgery may be necessary for children with masses, skin discoloration, or nonhealing wounds that persist without improvement several months after medical or surgical therapy.

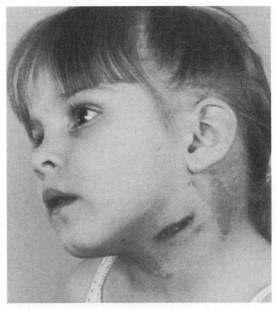

FIGURE 99-5. A draining postsurgical fistula in a child with *Mycobacterium intracellulare* infection.

Tuberculous Mycobacterial Adenitis

Tuberculous scrofula usually affects older children with AIDS or contact with a tuberculosis-infected individual. Cervical adenopathy occurs up to 6 months after initial infection with MTB in 4% to 12% of children, most often in children aged 5 years or older.[66, 123] Massive bilateral adenopathy may require a temporary tracheotomy for extrinsic airway compression. Additional manifestations of MTB include atelectasis, pleural effusion, hilar or mediastinal adenopathy, and segmental or lobar pulmonary involvement. Extrapulmonary disease (bone, renal, joint, miliary, or meningeal) occurs in about 20% of pediatric patients. For suspected MTB adenitis, INH and rifampin are given until culture results and antibiotic susceptibilities are known or until healing is complete; pyrazinamide is administered concurrently for the first 2 months. If the diagnosis is confirmed by a positive culture, a 6-month regimen of therapy is completed.[116] Residual adenopathy (exceeding 10 mm diameter) is present in 30% of children after therapy, and should be biopsied if persistent. Therapy beyond 6 months is required for HIV-positive individuals. HIV testing (with informed consent) is recommended for all children with MTB disease.

Cat-Scratch Disease

Cat-scratch disease (CSD) accounts for approximately 3% of lymph node procedures performed on patients younger than 15 years. The estimated annual incidence of disease in ambulatory patients is 9.3 per 100,000, with most cases reported in September through January.[52] About 90% of patients with CSD report contact with cats, and most have been scratched. After 3 to 10 days a round, redbrown, nontender papule develops in the scratch line and may persist up to 2 to 3 weeks.[17] Adenopathy can develop several weeks after inoculation and may be accompanied by fever or mild systemic symptoms. The area around the nodes may be noninflamed but is often warm, tender, erythematous, and indurated; up to 30% of affected nodes will suppurate spontaneously.[104] More serious systemic involvement occurs in 10% of cases, including encephalitis, pneumonia, hepatitis, osteomyelitis, and Parinaud oculoglandular complex (unilateral conjunctivitis and preauricular adenitis secondary to indirect eye inoculation; 6% incidence). Imaging studies reveal asymmetric adenopathy with a dominant node.

CSD is caused by infection with *Bartonella henselae*.[104] Risk factors for CSD include owning a pet kitten aged 12 months or younger, having been scratched or bitten by a kitten, and having at least one kitten with fleas. Fleas are the major vector by which the cat becomes infected, and are more prevalent in warm and humid climates. Serologic testing for antibodies to *B. henselae* is the most widely used diagnostic test, and has superseded skin testing. Polymerase chain reaction assays are available on a limited basis in some commercial laboratories. If lymph node, skin, or conjunctival tissue is available, the catscratch bacillus may be identified by the Warthin-Starry silver impregnation stain. The histopathologic picture is nondiagnostic. Culture is rarely useful because of a 6-week incubation period.

Management of CSD is usually symptomatic, although aspiration of a suppurative node is occasionally required. Complete resolution may require several months. Excision of necrotizing lymph nodes is not recommended because suppuration may persist for weeks through the operative incision. Anecdotal reports suggest that antibiotics (aminoglycosides, oral ciprofloxacin, rifampin, and trimethoprim-sulfamethoxazole) shorten the duration of illness, but convincing evidence of antimicrobial efficacy is lacking.[52] In one trial[18] patients randomly assigned to 5 days of oral azithromycin showed greater decrease in lymph node size during the first 30 days of illness than did placebo control subjects.

Less Common Bacterial Diseases

Tularemia is caused by the bacillus *Francisella tularensis*, which is transmitted to humans through rabbits, ticks, or contaminated drinking water.[83] Infection in children is incidental and usually results from interaction with biting or blood-sucking insects, wild animals, or their environment. Children present with lymphadenopathy (96%), fever (87%), and less often (39%) with myalgias or arthralgias.[53] Tularemia should be considered in the differential diagnosis of cervical adenopathy in the southeastern to midwestern United States, with highly endemic areas including Oklahoma, Missouri, and Arkansas. Inflamed lymph nodes are painful, may drain spontaneously, and may be associated (45%) with a painful ulcer or papule at the port of entry. Conjunctival innoculation (2% of cases) results in ocular infection with preauricular lymphadenopathy (Parinaud complex). Diagnosis is usually confirmed by serology; culture and isolation of *F. tularensis* are difficult. Virtually all strains are susceptible to streptomycin and gentamicin.[53]

Bubonic plague is a rare cause of fever and painful lymphadenitis; about 12 cases occur annually in the United States. Fleas and rodents are the reservoir for *Yersinia pestis*; cats, dogs, and squirrels transmit the infection to humans. Outbreaks on Indian reservations in the western United States have been attributable to flea bites from infected carrier rodents (prairie dogs and rats). Approximately 25% of cases occur in children 6 years or younger.[24] The diagnosis is usually made by Gram stain and culture of material from the suppurating nodes (buboes), although serologic testing is also used. Treatment involves strict isolation and tetracycline, chloramphenicol, or streptomycin.

Brucellosis is caused by several species of the genus *Brucella*, which are small, aerobic, gram-negative bacilli. Although primarily a disease of animal handlers and farmers, pediatric cases have been caused by the ingestion of unpasteurized cow's or goat's milk. Fatigue, malaise, fever, and mild cervical or generalized adenopathy are the usual signs and symptoms; most pediatric cases are mild and self-limited. Blood culture is diagnostic during the acute phase, and enzyme immunoassay is widely used for serologic diagnosis. Rifampicin is the treatment of choice for uncomplicated pediatric disease, with co-trimoxazole as an alternative.[28]

Other Infectious Diseases

Occasionally reported infective agents causing cervical adenopathy include *Mycoplasma pneumoniae* and *Actinomyces israelii*. Lymphadenopathy caused by *M. pneumoniae* is almost always associated with cough secondary to a subacute tracheobronchitis. Erythromycin is the preferred treatment for children younger than 9 years of age; tetracycline is preferred for older children. Cervicofacial actinomycosis is a rare cause of chronic, indurated, neck masses in infants and children[38]; a draining sinus tract may be present. Direct tissue invasion by *A. israelii*, a component of the endogenous oral flora, is the usual cause. FNA reveals the typical beaded colonies[47]; prolonged high-dose penicillin is curative.[111] Cervical adenopathy may also accompany infection with *Chlamydia pneumoniae* or *Treponema pallidum*.

Fungal Infections

Mycotic cervical lymphadenitis is clinically indistinguishable from adenitis of viral or bacterial origin, but primarily affects immunocompromised patients. Although cervical lymphadenitis may be the presenting symptom of deep fungal infection, most children have multisystem fungal abscesses demonstrable by computed tomography.[106] Congenital disorders of the immune system (agammaglobulinemia, dysgammaglobulinemia, and congenital granulocyte dysfunction) and acquired defects of the immune system caused by chemotherapy, immunosuppression to prevent transplant rejection, and AIDS all place the patient at risk for a variety of infections not seen in individuals with an intact immune system. The most common opportunistic fungal infections include candidiasis, histoplasmosis, aspergillosis, and cryptosporidiosis; aspergillus adenopathy can rarely affect otherwise healthy children.[71] Therapy with systemic antifungal agents is used in conjunction with interventions to correct the underlying immune defect.

Parasitic Infections

Cervical adenopathy caused by parasitic infections other than *Toxoplasma gondii* is rare and includes visceral larva migrans, African trypanosomiasis, and filariasis. These diseases have usually been seen in adopted children arriving in the United States from tropical countries.

Toxoplasmosis

Acquired *T. gondii* infection causes 3% to 7% of clinically significant lymphadenopathy. About 80% of patients have cervical lymph node involvement of the posterior and/or anterior triangles.[72] Nodes are usually solitary, discrete, rarely suppurate, vary in firmness, and do not ulcerate; tenderness may or may not be present. Humans become infected by consumption of poorly cooked meat or by ingestion of oocytes excreted in cat feces. Infection in an immunocompetent host is usually asymptomatic and self-limited, but may include malaise, fever (uncommon), sore throat, and myalgia; myocarditis and pneumonitis are possible complications. Serologic tests are diagnostic up to 6 months after clinical onset,[76] but a microscopy of fine-needle aspirate smears can be highly suggestive.[54] Mild cases are self-limited; pyrimethamine and sulfonamides are used for more severe illness.

Noninfectious Inflammatory Disorders

Kawasaki Disease

Kawasaki disease (mucocutaneous lymph node syndrome) is an acute, multisystem vasculitis of unknown etiology usually seen in children under 5 years of age.[133] Most children are aged 1 to 2 years, with peak incidence in the late winter and spring seasons. Diagnosis is strictly clinical, requiring fever (up to 40°C) for at least 5 days and four or more of the following signs: (1) nonexudative conjunctivitis; (2) oral cavity changes including erythema, strawberry tongue, and fissuring of the lips; (3) rash, primarily on the trunk; (4) changes in the extremities including erythema of the palms and soles, edema of the hands and feet, and periungual desquamation of the fingers and toes (after 10 days); and (5) acute cervical adenopathy greater than 1.5 cm (seen in 50% to 75% of patients; the presenting symptom in 12% of patients).

Cervical adenopathy may precede changes in the skin and mucous membranes by up to 5 days, resulting in over 40% of children initially misdiagnosed as having bacterial adenitis.[6] Prompt diagnosis of Kawasaki disease is essential, however, since 20% of untreated children develop coronary artery abnormalities (aneurysm or diffuse dilatation), and up to 0.5% have a myocardial infarction. Diagnostic clues include thrombocytosis, nonsuppurative adenitis, persistent high fever despite antibiotics, and pericardial effusion or coronary artery dilatation on echocardiogram.[93] Peritonsillar abscess has been reported.[99] Morbidity is significantly reduced by intravenous gamma globulin during the acute phase (7 to 14 days) and low-dose aspirin in the subacute phase[103, 133]; corticosteroids given in the acute phase may further decrease fever and coronary sequelae.[108] A base line echocardiogram is obtained, followed by routine annual echocardiograms over the next 5 years.

Kikuchi-Fujimoto Disease

Kikuchi-Fujimoto disease (histiocytic necrotizing lymphadenitis) is a rare cause of persistent cervical adenopathy unresponsive to antibiotic therapy. The typical patient is a young Asian woman with localized unilateral or bilateral cervical adenopathy, occasionally tender to palpation.[126] Most patients are aged 20 to 40 years, with only sporadic reports of patients younger than 10 years of age.[65] Lymph node biopsy is diagnostic, and is often necessary to exclude malignant disease. The characteristic histology shows necrotizing lymphadenitis with karyorrhexis and an absence, or paucity, of granulocytes; misdiagnosis as non-Hodgkin lymphoma is common and can result in unnecessary chemotherapy.[13, 65] Although the cause is unknown, practically all reported cases have resolved spontaneously within 6 months.[39, 48]

Kimura Disease

Kimura disease is an allergic inflammatory disorder of unknown cause, seen primarily in Asian males during the second and third decades of life[75]; children under 10 years of age are rarely affected.[26] Lymphadenopathy is accompanied by nontender subcutaneous swellings in the head and neck region, predominantly in the preauricular and submandibular areas. Diagnosis is suggested by elevated serum IgE and peripheral eosinophilia (usually >10%), but lymph node biopsy or excision is needed for confirmation. The histologic picture reveals normal tissue architecture with a dense eosinophilic infiltrate and prominent germinal centers. Treatment involves complete excision, when possible, but regrowth is common. Local irradiation is effective in older patients.

Sarcoidosis

Sarcoidosis is a multisystemic granulomatous disease of unknown etiology. Children are rarely affected, but when involvement occurs most cases manifest between 13 and 15 years of age.[107] Sarcoidosis should be strongly suspected in any child with roentgenographic evidence of bilateral hilar lymphadenopathy.[58] The "typical" child is a black adolescent or preadolescent, and may have peripheral lymphadenopathy (70%) or parotid gland enlargement (12%). Supraclavicular lymphadenopathy is almost always present. There is no laboratory test for sarcoidosis, but the diagnosis is confirmed by demonstrating a typical noncaseating granuloma on a biopsy specimen. Childhood sarcoidosis with multisystem involvement is treated with corticosteroids; low-dose methotrexate has also been recommended.[107]

Sinus Histiocytosis with Massive Lymphadenopathy (Rosai-Dorfman Disease)

Sinus histiocytosis with massive lymphadenopathy (SHML) is an uncommon idiopathic disorder characterized by massive, nontender, bilateral cervical adenopathy.[23] Most cases occur in children 10 years of age or younger, and 43% have at least one site of extranodal localization (often the nasal cavity or paranasal sinuses). Most SHML is pathologically diagnosed and rarely suspected by clinical evaluation. Lymph node architecture is preserved early in the disease course, but later changes include dilated sinuses, large numbers of plasma cells, and marked proliferation of sinusoidal histiocytes. Treatment is generally unnecessary, but some patients may require surgery, radiation therapy, or chemotherapy because of disseminated disease.[23, 120] Endoscopic surgery is the optimal treatment for extranodal nasal involvement.

PFAPA Syndrome

PFAPA (periodic fevers with aphthous stomatitis, pharyngitis, and cervical adenitis) syndrome is an increasingly common cause of cervical adenopathy in young children. Diagnosis is based on the following clinical criteria: (1) regularly recurring fevers with an early age of onset (<5 years of age); (2) constitutional symptoms in the absence of upper respiratory infection with at least one of the following clinical signs: aphthous stomatitis, cervical lymphadenitis, or pharyngitis; (3) exclusion of cyclic neutropenia; (4) completely asymptomatic between episodes; and (5) normal growth and development.[124] Fever is usually of abrupt onset, ranges from 38.9 to 41.1°C, and lasts a mean of 3.8 days. The mean symptom-free interval is 28 days, with recurrences for several years.

Laboratory tests for PFAPA syndrome are normal, except for leukocytosis and a mildly elevated erythrocyte sedimentation rate during the episodes. Antibiotics are ineffective, but oral or topical steroids may shorten episodes; cimetidine prevents attacks for some children.[35, 124] A dramatic symptomatic response to a single oral dose of prednisone (2 mg/kg) has been proposed as a diagnostic criterion.[87] Tonsillectomy (with or without adenoidectomy) has led to remission in a limited number of patients.[1, 124]

Giant Lymph Node Hyperplasia (Castleman Disease)

Giant lymph node hyperplasia (GLH) is a rare, benign lymphoproliferative disorder with no predilection for sex or age.[132] The usual manifestation is a chronic, asymptomatic, solitary enlarging neck mass which may be fixed to the overlying skin. Excisional biopsy is diagnostic and therapeutic. Histologic examination reveals proliferation of small blood vessels within the interfollicular areas, with a characteristic concentric "onion skinning" of mantle zone lymphocytes around the germinal centers. Nearly all head and neck cases (98%) are the hyaline vascular type, for which excision is curative with no reported recurrence.

Miscellaneous Inflammatory Diseases

Acute rheumatoid arthritis and systemic lupus erythematosus have been associated with generalized adenopathy and cervical masses. There have also been reports of posterior cervical adenopathy caused by chronic dermatitis from a nickel allergy to earring posts. The dermatitis and adenopathy resolved with removal of the earring posts.[9] Amyloidosis has been reported to cause extensive cervical lymphadenopathy with respiratory compromise.[63]

Neoplastic Disorders

Most malignant tumors of the head and neck region in children occur in the lymph nodes, except for sarcoma and neuroblastoma. Malignant nodes are firm, enlarge rapidly, and are typically posterior or supraclavicular. Cervical adenopathy accounts for about two thirds of pediatric lymph node biopsies,[112] with 10% to 15% reported as malignant.[60, 79] Cunningham and co-workers[29] noted the following distribution of tumor types: Hodgkin disease and non-Hodgkin lymphoma (60%), rhabdomyosarcoma (15%), thyroid tumors (10%), neuroblastoma (5%), and nasopharyngeal carcinoma (5%). Soldes and colleagues[112] found a similar predominance of Hodgkin disease and non-Hodgkin lymphoma; other metastatic tumors were uncommon.

Painless, persistent cervical lymphadenopathy (>2 cm) can be the manifesting sign of leukemia, lymphoma, or metastatic disease.[134] Hodgkin disease manifests commonly with asymptomatic cervical or supraclavicular lymphadenopathy, which may fluctuate over time.[50] Two thirds of patients also have mediastinal node involvement, but constitutional symptoms (fever, night sweats, weight loss) occur in only 25% to 30%. Non-Hodgkin lymphoma manifests less often with cervical adenopathy,[105] but when adenopathy does occur (50% to 80% of patients), it is often exclusively supradiaphragmatic (i.e., involving the neck, supraclavicular regions, and axillae). Conversely, a neck mass is often the only manifesting sign of pediatric thyroid carcinoma, with palpable lymph nodes in 60% to 80% of patients.[36] Neuroblastoma of the head and neck almost always (>96%) represents metastatic disease.[40]

In young children, Langerhans cell histiocytosis, formerly called histiocytosis X, is more common than the lymphomas.[101] Langerhans cell histiocytosis typically manifests with unifocal or multifocal bony lesions; only about 10% of patients initially have isolated cervical nodes. It is not a true malignancy, but a reactive process characterized by proliferation of the monocyte/macrophage line. Biopsy of affected lymph nodes or skin is diagnostic. Treatment consists primarily of surgical excision for localized lesions, and of drug therapy, with or without irradiation and surgery, for multifocal disease.[31, 74, 98]

Iatrogenic Disorders

Serum sickness is usually caused by an allergic reaction to an ingested or injected drug. Systemic antigen-antibody complexes provoke cervical and generalized lymphadenitis. Other symptoms include malaise, fever, urticaria, swollen joints, arthralgias, and hepatosplenomegaly. The symptoms usually subside 1 to 2 weeks after cessation of the offending agent.

Bacille Calmette-Guérin (BCG) vaccination against tuberculosis produces lymphadenopathy in 1% of children.[77] Diagnosis is suggested by axillary (97%), cervical (2%), or clavicular (1%) adenitis ipsilateral to the vaccine site with no other detectable cause; a cutaneous sinus drainage tract may be present at the site of injection. Mean age at presentation is 7 months, with onset of adenitis weeks to months following inoculation. Treatment is supportive, with excisional biopsy reserved for large nodes (3 cm or greater) or those that show rapid enlargement and induration during follow-up.[85] Suppurative nodes are managed with needle aspiration, which is done subcutaneously 2 to 3 cm from the periphery of the node to avoid iatrogenic sinus formation.[14]

Diptheria, tetanus, and pertussis (DTP)–induced cervical lymphadenitis is a rare complication of DTP inoculation. The etiology is obscure. Spontaneous resolution generally occurs within several weeks.[86]

Drug-induced cervical adenopathy has been reported with phenytoin,[127] isoniazid, pyrimethamine, allopurinol, and phenylbutazone. In addition, immunosuppressive agents such as cyclosporine and FK 506 may produce cervical adenopathy as part of post-transplant lymphoproliferative disease.[7, 81] Once biopsy has established the diagnosis, discontinuation of immunosuppressive therapy will generally reverse the disease progression.

Clinical Approach

Initial Evaluation

History and Physical Examination

The duration and laterality of the adenopathy provide important diagnostic clues. Acute unilateral adenitis is generally caused by streptococcal, staphylococcal, or, less often, viral infection; the pharynx and tonsils are the most common sources of primary involvement. Conversely, acute bilateral adenitis is most often a response to systemic infection or a localized reaction to nonspecific viral pharyngitis. When a bacterial etiology is suspected for acute adenitis, 7 to 10 days of an oral cephalosporin or semisynthetic penicillin should be prescribed as a diagnostic trial.[61] Persistent acute adenitis despite oral antibiotics in an older child may indicate infectious mononucleosis; in very young children, the possibility of Kawasaki disease must be considered. The most common causes of subacute or chronic adenitis are mycobacterial infections, cat-scratch disease, and toxoplasmosis. AIDS must also be considered in an at-risk child. Nontender adenopathy of any duration is suspicious for malignancy.

A targeted history and physical examination are essential for accurate diagnosis. The history should probe for fever, recent travel, regional infections, fluctuations in size, dental problems (actinomycosis), exposure to cats (CSD, toxoplasmosis), contact with rabbits (tularemia), daily use of medications (e.g., Dilantin), antecedent vaccination (BCG, DTP), family history of infections (tuberculosis), and use of unpasteurized dairy products (brucellosis). Physical examination should begin with accurate notes regarding the size, location, mobility, consistency, and tenderness of any masses present as well as any changes in the overlying skin. A search should be made for lesions of the scalp, skin, pharynx, or conjunctiva. Flexible fiberoptic endoscopy is used, as needed, to detect mucosal lesions of the nasopharynx, hypopharyx, and larynx. The presence or absence of otitis media, dental caries, pneumonia, noncervical lymphadenopathy, and hepatosplenomegaly should be noted. Last, bacterial cultures are performed of the throat and any impetiginous lesions of the scalp or face.

Differential Diagnosis

The differential diagnosis of cervical adenopathy includes congenital anomalies, sialadenitis, and benign and malignant tumors of the head and neck. Certain congenital masses of the head and neck may go unnoticed until secondary infection occurs, making distinction from bacterial adenitis or deep neck infection difficult.[80] A history of a previous noninflamed mass or external fistula at the same site may indicate a cystic hygroma, a branchial cleft anomaly, or an infected thyroglossal duct cyst. Recurrent deep neck infection or suppurative thyroiditis suggests a persistent internal sinus of the third or fourth branchial pouch.[102] Relapsing acute or subacute pre- or infra-auricular swelling is characteristic of recurrent parotitis of childhhood, an idiopathic but self-limited disorder.[34] Episodes of parotitis are most often unilateral, and accompanied by fever, pain, and malaise. Last, submandibular sialadenitis must be distinguished from adenitis in the submandibular region.

The relative probability of different diagnoses varies by child age and mass location. Occipital and postauricular adenopathy is a common nonspecific finding in infancy, but is rare beyond 2 years of age.[46] Cervical and submandibular node involvement is rare in infants under 12 months, but is common in older children. Supraclavicular node enlargement is probably pathologic at any age. Preauricular lymphadenopathy (oculoglandular syndrome) can occur secondary to granulomatous nodular conjunctival infection caused by tularemia, CSD, listeriosis, sporotrichosis, and lymphogranuloma venereum. Midline or paramedian neck masses are most often a thyroglossal duct cyst (52%), epidermoid cyst (26%), or cervical adenopathy (16%). Preoperative diagnosis, however, is correct in less than two thirds of the cases,[60] and biopsy is often indicated. Masses completely anterior to the sternocleidomastoid muscle are generally benign, with the exception of metastatic thyroid carcinoma. In contrast, supraclavicular or posterior cervical masses have a higher risk of malignancy.[59, 79]

Additional Diagnostic Tests

A complete blood count with differential blood cell count, reticulocyte count, and lactate dehydrogenase level is warranted for any suspicous neck mass.[134] Leukemia is suggested by blast cells on the peripheral smear and by unexplained anemia, especially if accompanied by reticulocytopenia or abnormalities of platelets or leukocytes. Lymphoma can produce high serum lactate dehydrogenase levels. Intradermal skin tests for tuberculosis are recommended early in the diagnostic evaluation, including NTM antigens when available. A chest x-ray is helpful in diagnosing MTB, sarcoidosis (hilar adenopathy), M. pneumoniae, and AIDS (30% to 50% of AIDS patients have lymphoid interstitial pneumonitis). An abnormal chest x-ray is also suspicious for malignancy, particularly if supraclavicular adenopathy is also present.[112]

When adenopathy persists despite a trial of antibiotics, and the diagnosis is not apparent from FNA, recommended tests include a heterophile count, antistreptolysin O (ASO) titers, and serologic evaluation. Serologic tests are available for EBV (monospot or viral antibody titers), CSD, herpes simplex virus, cytomegalovirus, HHV-6, HIV, toxoplasmosis, tularemia, Brucella, histoplasmosis, and coccidioidomycosis.

Imaging Studies

Imaging studies help define the size, number, location, and composition of enlarged cervical nodes.[49, 56] CT and magnetic resonance imaging (MRI) offer similar information, but MRI is slightly more sensitive for soft tissue abnormalities.[100] Compared with MRI and CT, ultrasound offers the advantages of lower cost and portability, but provides inferior soft tissue details. Nonetheless, ultrasound can determine if a lesion is cystic or solid, help monitor disease progression, and serve as a guide for FNA.[32] Large or invasive masses are least suitable for sonography.

To standardize the description of cervical adenopathy, a simplified, regional classification scheme has been adopted by the radiologic community (Table 99–5). The scheme divides the anatomic spaces of the neck into seven nodal levels to facilitate communication between clinicians and radiologists.[56] The first, and most commonly used, criterion for distinguishing benign and malignant nodes is size. Normal nodes are up to 10 mm with a longitudinal to transverse diameter ratio of 2:1 or higher. Larger nodes are abnormal, particularly if the ovoid shape is not preserved. Central nodal necrosis with a rim of irregular enhancement strongly suggests tumor infiltration, and is abnormal regardless of lymph node size. Necrosis, however, is uncommon in lymphomatous nodes.

Lymph node enhancement on CT or MRI can be caused by acute infection, lymphoma, or tuberculosis; other less common causes include vascular metastases, Kikuchi-Fujimoto disease, Kimura disease, and giant lymph node hyperplasia. Tuberculous adenitis most often produces multiple, low-density nodes with thick rims of peripheral rim enhancement; calcification may be present. Calcifications in lymph nodes can also occur with other forms of granulomatous adenopathy, lymphoma (primarily after irradiation or chemotherapy), in metastatic disease (thyroid and mucin-producing carcinomas), and following healed viral or bacterial infection. Diffuse cervical lymphadenopathy with multiple parotid cysts suggests HIV infection and may be seen before the patient tests posi-

TABLE 99–5. Radiologic Classification Scheme for Cervical Lymph Nodes

Classification	Description
Level I	Submental and submandibular nodes
Level II	Superior internal jugular chain (posterior belly of digastric to level of hyoid bone)
Level III	Middle internal jugular chain (hyoid bone to inferior aspect of cricoid cartilage)
Level IV	Inferior internal jugular chain (inferior aspect of cricoid cartilage to clavicle)
Level V	Posterior triangle (spinal accessory chain)
Level VI	Juxtavisceral (pretracheal, paratracheal)
Level VII	Tracheoesophageal groove

tive for HIV.[100] Imaging may also detect an occult naso-pharyngeal primary tumor and aid in directed biopsies.[84]

Fine-Needle Aspiration

FNA is indicated for acute adenitis that persists or progresses despite antimicrobial therapy, and for subacute or chronic adenopathy of unknown cause. FNA for acute cervical lymphadenitis will culture an etiologic agent in 60% to 88% of cases.[15, 21, 131] The largest and/or most fluctuant node is selected for aspiration. After cleansing with betadine and alcohol, the overlying skin is anesthetized with 2% lidocaine or procaine. Aspiration is performed with an 18- or 20-gauge needle attached to a 20-mL syringe. If no aspirate is obtained, 1 to 2 mL of sterile nonbacteriostatic saline are injected into the node and then reaspirated.[15] The aspirate is inoculated directly onto appropriate media for aerobes, anaerobes, fungi, and mycobacteria; Gram and acid-fast stains are also performed.

Early use of FNA to evaluate noninflammatory adenopathy can help guide additional diagnostic tests, including imaging studies and excisional biopsy.[97] FNA is rapid, well-tolerated, and extremely safe provided that the infant or child is adequately restrained. Aspiration is performed with a 22-gauge needle attached to a 10-mL syringe. The plunger is withdrawn to 1 mL prior to insertion and moved using a rapid in-and-out motion within the lesion. Suction applied during motion increases the likelihood of adequate sampling.[4] The aspirate is spread on two prelabeled slides placed directly in ethanol or sprayed with fixative. When properly performed, FNA has an extremely low false-positive rate and can achieve a diagnostic sensitivity of 92% and specificity over 99%.[33] A recently described alternative to FNA is ultrasound-guided cutting-needle biopsy.[10] Although a core of tissue is obtained with this technique, the potential risks are greater than with FNA and appropriate indications have yet to be delineated.

Excisional Biopsy

Early biopsy of cervical adenopathy should be considered when the risk of serious disease is high. Indications for early biopsy[61, 112] include (1) supraclavicular or low neck adenopathy; (2) prolonged systemic symptoms, such as fever, weight loss, night sweats; (3) hard or fixed mass; (4) abnormal chest x-ray; and (5) rapid or progressive growth in the absence of inflammation. Biopsy is also indicated for a persistent mass of unknown cause following the additional studies described here. If the adenopathy is confined to a single anatomic group of nodes, then the largest intact node is removed. When multiple sites are involved, specimens from the lower neck and supraclavicular areas provide the highest diagnostic yield.[61]

Excised nodes are submitted fresh in saline, *not* formalin, for bacteriologic studies, routine histologic examination, and for Giemsa, acid-fast, Warthin-Starry, periodic acid–Schiff (PAS), and methenamine silver stains. Frozen section may be performed but is not helpful for the

diagnosis of lymphoma. A biopsy result of non-Hodgkin lymphoma should prompt a complete otolaryngologic examination because one third of children who present with cervical node adenopathy may have unsuspected extranodal disease in the Waldeyer ring.[78]

Several situations warrant additional precautions prior to performing excisional biopsy. A suspicious, firm, solitary node caused by toxoplasmosis can mimic a neoplasm; preoperative serologic testing may prevent unnecessary biopsy.[72, 76] In neonates, sternomastoid tumor of infancy[125] is a benign, self-limited mass that can be mistaken for a malignancy. Absent at birth, but usually detected by 3 to 6 weeks of age, it manifests as a firm, nontender, spindle-shaped nodule in the lower one third of the sternomastoid muscle. In AIDS patients, biopsy may be necessary for HIV-related neoplasm or for opportunistic infection. Proposed indications for cervical lymph node biopsy in adults with AIDS include marked constitutional symptoms, progressive localized or unilateral lymphadenopathy, and the presence of a single disproportionately large node larger than 3 cm.[64] In pediatric AIDS, however, the relative incidence of secondary neoplasms and opportunistic infections is lower than in adults, and open biopsy is less often indicated.

Midline and periauricular lesions require special considerations. Because up to 2% of midline neck masses are ectopic thyroid,[96] a preoperative thyroid scan is recommended to confirm the presence of a functioning gland in the lower neck.[96] Midline lesions should be aspirated intraoperatively prior to complete removal; mucoid or serous contents indicate a thyroglossal duct cyst, and a Sistrunk procedure is recommended even if a connection to the hyoid bone is inapparent.[60] In contrast to the midline mass, lesions in the pre- or infra-auricular region may represent anomalies of the first branchial cleft, with the potential for facial nerve injury during biopsy.[73] Last, excisional biopsy of preauricular lesions is most easily accomplished through a supra-auricular approach to the temporalis fascia when a pit or sinus is encountered.[95]

REFERENCES

1. Abramson JS, Givner LB, Thompson JN. Possible role of tonsillectomy and adenoidectomy in children with recurrent fever and tonsillopharyngitis. Pediatr Infect Dis J 8:119, 1989.
2. Adamkiewicz T, Quie PG. When to evaluate a child with recurrent infections for immunodeficiency. Rep Pediatr Infect Dis 2:26, 1992.
3. Alessi DP, Dudley JP. Atypical mycobacteria-induced cervical adenitis: treatment by needle aspiration. Arch Otolaryngol Head Neck Surg 114:664, 1988.
4. Allen SM, Boon AP, Brownridge DM, et al. Fine needle cytology of palpable head and neck lesions: a comparison of sampling methods with and without suction. Cytopathology 10:97, 1999.
5. American Academy of Pediatrics. Data from Report of the Committee on Infectious Diseases, 25th ed. Elk Grove Village, Ill, American Academy of Pediatrics, 2000.
6. April MM, Burns JC, Newburger JW, Healy GB. Kawasaki disease and cervical adenopathy. Arch Otolaryngol Head Neck Surg 115: 512, 1989.
7. Armitage JM, Fricker FJ, Kurland G, et al. Pediatric lung trans-

plantation: the years 1985 to 1992 and the clinical trial of FK 506. J Thor Cardiovasc Surg 105:337, 1993.

8. Armstrong KL, James RW, Dawson DJ, et al. *Mycobacterium haemophilum* causing perihilar or cervical lymphadenitis in healthy children. J Pediatr 121:202, 1992.

9. Ashkenazi S, Mimouni M. Superficial cervical lymphadenopathy after insertion of earrings. Am J Dis Child 138:1147, 1984.

10. Bain G, Bearcroft PW, Berman LH, Grant JW. The use of ultrasound-guided cutting-needle biopsy in paediatric neck masses. Eur Radiol 10:512, 2000.

11. Baker CJ. Group B streptococcal cellulitis-adenitis in infants. Am J Dis Child 136:631, 1982.

12. Bamji M, Stone RK, Kaul A, et al. Palpable lymph nodes in healthy newborns and infants. Pediatrics 78:573, 1986.

13. Banani SA, Alborzi A. Needle aspiration for suppurative post-BCG adenitis. Arch Dis Child 71:446, 1994.

14. Banerjee MLP, Edmondson D, Harris M. Histiocytic necrotizing lymphadenitis (Kikuchi-Fulimoto disease): continuing diagnostic difficulties. Histopathology 33:248, 1998.

15. Barton LL, Feigin RD. Childhood cervical lymphadenitis: a reappraisal. J Pediatr 84:846, 1974.

16. Barton LL, Ramsey RA, Raval DS. Neonatal group B Streptococcal cellulitis-adenitis. Pediatr Dermatol 10:58, 1993.

17. Bass JW, Vincent JM, Person DA. The expanding spectrum of *Bartonella* infections: II. Cat-scratch disease. Pediatr Infect Dis J 16:163, 1997.

18. Bass JW, Freitas BC, Freitas AD, et al. Prospective randomized double blind placebo-controlled evaluation of azithromycin for treatment of cat-scratch disease. Pediatr Infect Dis J 17:447, 1998.

19. Black BG, Chapman JS. Cervical adenitis in children due to human and unclassified mycobacteria. Pediatrics 33:887, 1964.

20. Brodsky L, Belles W, Brody A, et al. Needle aspiration of neck abscesses in children. Clin Pediatr 31:71, 1992.

21. Brook I. Aerobic and anaerobic bacteriology of cervical adenitis in children. Clin Pediatr 19:693, 1980.

22. Campadelli-Fiume G, Mirandola P, Menotti L. Human herpesvirus 6: an emerging pathogen. Emerging Infect Dis 5:353, 1999.

23. Carbone A, Passannante A, Gloghini A, et al. Review of sinus histiocytosis with massive lymphadenopathy (Rosai-Dorfman disease) of the head and neck. Ann Otol Rhinol Laryngol 108:1095, 1999.

24. Centers for Disease Control. Plague—United States, 1992. JAMA 268:3055, 1992.

25. Chen AY, Ohlms LA, Stewart MG, Kline MW. Otolaryngologic disease progression in children with human immunodeficiency virus infection. Arch Otolaryngol Head Neck Surg 122:1360, 1996.

26. Chusid MJ, Rock AL, Sty JR, et al. Kimura's disease: an unusual cause of cervical tumour. Arch Dis Child 77:153, 1997.

27. Claman HN. The biology of the immune response. JAMA 268:2790, 1992.

28. Corbel MJ. Brucellosis: an overview. Emerg Infect Dis 3:213, 1997.

29. Cunningham MJ, Myers EN, Bluestone CD. Malignant tumors of the head and neck in children: a twenty-year review. Int J Pediatr Otorhinolaryngol 13:279, 1987.

30. Dajani AS, Garcia RE, Wolinsky E. Etiology of cervical lymphadenitis in children. N Engl J Med 268:1329, 1963.

31. DiNardo LJ, Wetmore RF. Head and neck manifestations of histiocytosis-X in children. Laryngoscope 99:721, 1989.

32. Dubois J, Patriquin H. Doppler sonography of head and neck masses in children. Neuroimaging Clin NA 10:215, 2000.

33. Eisenhut CC, King DE, Nelson WA, et al. Fine-needle biopsy of pediatric lesions: a three-year study in an outpatient biopsy clinic. Diagnostic Cytopathol 14:43, 1996.

34. Ericson S, Zetterlund B, Ohman J. Recurrent parotitis and sialectasis in childhood: clinical, radiologic, immunologic, bacteriologic, and histologic study. Ann Otol Rhinol Laryngol 100:527, 1991.

35. Feder HM. Cimetidine treatment for periodic fever associated with aphthous stomatitis, pharyngitis and cervical adenitis. Pediatr Infect Dis J 11:318, 1992.

36. Feinmesser R, Lubin E, Segal K, Noyek A. Carcinoma of the thyroid in children—a review. J Pediatr Endocrinol Metabol 10:561, 1997.

37. Flint D, Mahadevan M, Barber C, et al. Cervical lymphadenitis

38. Friduss ME, Maceri DR. Cervicofacial actinomycosis in children. Henry Ford Hosp Med J 38:28, 1990.

39. Garcia CE, Girdhar-Gopal HV, Dorfman DM. Kikuchi-Fujimoto disease of the neck: update. Ann Otol Rhinol Laryngol 102:11, 1993.

40. Haase GM. Head and neck neuroblastoma. Sem Pediatr Surg 3:194, 1994.

41. Hadfield PJ, Birchall MA, Novelli V, et al. The ENT manifestations of HIV infection in children. Clin Otolaryngol 21:30, 1996.

42. Har-El G, Josephson JS. Infectious mononucleosis complicated by lingual tonsillitis. J Laryngol Otol 104:651, 1990.

43. Haverkos HW, Amsel Z, Drotman DP. Adverse virus-drug interactions. Rev Infect Dis 13:697, 1991.

44. Hawkins DB, Austin JR. Abscesses of the neck in infants and young children: a review of 112 cases. Ann Otol Rhinol Laryngol 100:361, 1991.

45. Hazra R, Robson CD, Perez-Atayde RA, Husson RN. Lymphadenitis due to nontuberculous mycobacteria in children: presentation and response to therapy. Clin Infect Dis 28:123, 1999.

46. Herzog LW. Prevalence of lymphadenopathy of the head and neck in infants and children. Clin Pediatr 22:485, 1983.

47. Hong IS, Mezghebe HM, Gaiter TE, Lofton J. Actinomycosis of the neck: diagnosis by fine-needle aspiration biopsy. J Natl Med Assoc 85:145, 1993.

48. Hoyt DJ, Fishher SR. Kikuchi's disease causing cervical lymphadenopathy. Otolaryngol Head Neck Surg 102:755, 1990.

49. Hudgins PA. Nodal and nonnodal inflammatory processes of the pediatric neck. Neuroimaging Clin NA 10:181, 2000.

50. Hudson MM, Donaldson SS. Hodgkin's disease. Pediatr Clin North Am 44:891, 1997.

51. Huebner RE, Schein MR, Cauthen GM, et al. Usefulness of skin testing with mycobacterial antigens in children with cervical lymphadenitis. Pediatr Infect Dis J. 11:450, 1992.

52. Jackson LA, Perkins BA, Wenger JD. Cat scratch disease in the United States: an analysis of three national databases. Am J Pub Health 83:1707, 1993.

53. Jacobs RF. Tularemia. Adv Pediatr Infect Dis 12:55, 1996.

54. Jayaram N, Ramaprasad AV, Chethan M, Sujay AR. Toxoplasma lymphadenitis: analysis of cytologic and histopathologic criteria and correlation with serologic tests. Acta Cytol 41:653, 1997.

55. Joshi W, Davidson PM, Jones PG, et al. Non-tuberculous mycobacterial lymphadenitis in children. Eur J Pediatr 148:751, 1989.

56. Kaji AV, Mohuchy T, Swartz JD. Imaging of cervical lymphadenopathy. Semin Ultrasound CT MRI 18:220, 1997.

57. Kelly CS, Kelly RE Jr. Lymphadenopathy in children. Pediatr Clin North Am 45:875, 1998.

58. Kendig EL. The clinical picture of sarcoidosis in children. Pediatrics 54:289, 1974.

59. Kennedy TL. Curettage of nontuberculous mycobacterial cervical lymphadenitis. Arch Otolaryngol Head Neck Surg 118:759, 1992.

60. Knight PJ, Hamoudi AB, Vassy LE. The diagnosis and treatment of midline neck masses in children. Surgery 93:603, 1983.

61. Knight PJ, Mulne AF, Vassy LE. When is lymph node biopsy indicated in children with enlarged peripheral nodes? Pediatrics 69:391, 1982.

62. Lai KK, Stottmeier KD, Sherman IH, McCabe WR. Mycobacterial cervical lymphadenopathy: relation of etiologic agents to age. JAMA 251:1286, 1984.

63. Leach DB, Hester TO, Farrell HA, Chowdhury K. Primary amyloidosis presenting as massive cervical lymphadenopathy with severe dyspnea: a case report and review of the literature. Otolaryngol Head Neck Surg 120:560, 1999.

64. Lee KC, Cheung SW. Evaluation of the neck mass in human immunodeficiency virus-infected patients. Otolaryngol Clin North Am 25:1287, 1982.

65. Lerosey Y, Lecler-Sarcella V, Francois A, Guitrancourt JA. A pseudo-tumoral form of Kikuchi's disease in children: a case report and review of the literature. Int J Pediatr Otorhinolaryngol 45:1, 1998.

66. Lobato MN, Cummings K, Royce S. Tuberculosis in children and adolescents: California, 1985 to 1995. Pediatr Infect Dis J 17:407, 1998.

67. Lucente FE. Impact of the acquired immunodeficiency syndrome

epidemic on the practice of laryngology. Ann Otol Rhinol Laryngol 102(suppl 161):1, 1993.

68. Maddern BR, Werkhaven J, Wessel HB, Yunis E. Infectious mononucleosis with airway obstruction and multiple cranial nerve paresis. Otolaryngol Head Neck Surg 104:529, 1991.

69. Maltezou HC, Spyridis P, Kafetzis DA. Nontuberculous mycobacterial lymphadenitis in children. Pediatr Infect Dis J 18:968, 1999.

70. Margileth AM. Cat scratch disease and nontuberculous mycobacterial disease: diagnostic usefulness of PPD-Battey, PPD-T and cat scratch skin antigens. Ann Allergy 68:149, 1992.

71. Mazzoni A, Ferrarese M, Manfredi R, et al. Primary lymph node invasive aspergillosis. Infection 39:24, 1996.

72. McCabe RE, Brooks RG, Dorfman RF, Remington JS. Clinical spectrum in 107 cases of toxoplasmic lymphadenopathy. Rev Infect Dis 9:754, 1987.

73. McLelland J, Broadbent V, Yeomans E, et al. Langerhans cell histiocytosis: the case for conservative treatment. Arch Dis Child 65:301, 1990.

74. McRae RG, Lee KJ, Goentzer E. First branchial cleft anomalies and the facial nerve. Otolaryngol Head Neck Surg 91:197, 1983.

75. Messina-Doucet MT, Armstrong WB, Pena F, et al. Kimura's disease: two case reports and a literature review. Ann Otol Rhinol Laryngol 107:1066, 1998.

76. Montoya JG, Remington JS. Studies on the serodiagnosis of toxoplasmic lymphadenitis. Clin Infect Dis 20:781, 1995.

77. Mori T, Yamauchi Y, Shiozawa K. Lymph node swelling due to bacille Calmette-Guerin vaccination with multipuncture method. Tubercle Lung Dis 77:269, 1996.

78. Morton RP, Sillars HA, Benjamin CS. Incidence of "unsuspected" extranodal head and neck lymphoma. Clin Otolaryngol 17:373, 1992.

79. Moussatos GH, Baffes TG. Cervical masses in infants and children. Pediatrics 32:251, 1963.

80. Myers EN, Cunningham MJ. Inflammatory presentations of congenital head and neck masses. Pediatr Infect Dis J 7:S162, 1988.

81. Nazer H, al-Sabban E, Harfi H, et al. FK 506 associated disorders in liver transplantation. J Gastroenterol Hepatol 7:257, 1992.

82. Niederman JC, Liu CR, Kaplan MH, Brown NA. Clinical and serological features of human herpesvirus-6 infection in three adults. Lancet 2:817, 1988.

83. Nordahl SHG, Hoel T, Scheel O, Olofsson J. Tularemia: a differential diagnosis in oto-rhino-laryngology. J Laryngol Otol 107:127, 1993.

84. Norton KI, Som PM, Shugar JM. Persistent cervical adenitis and nasopharyngeal carcinoma in children. J Computed Tomogr 11:275, 1987.

85. Oguz F, Mujgan S, Alper G, et al. Treatment of bacillus Calmette-Guerin associated lymphadenitis. Pediatr Infect Dis J 11:887, 1992.

86. Omokoku B, Castells S. Post-DPT inoculation cervical lymphadenitis in children. N Y State J Med 81:1667, 1981.

87. Padeh S, Brezniak N, Zemer D, et al. Periodic fever, aphthous stomatitis, pharyngitis, and adenopathy syndrome: clinical characteristics and outcome. J Pediatr 135:98, 1999.

88. Pang SC. Mycobacterial lymphadenitis in Western Australia. Tubercle Lung Dis 73:362, 1992.

89. Patamasucon P, Siegel JD, McCracken GH. Streptococcal submandibular cellulitis in young infants. Pediatrics 67:378, 1981.

90. Patterson SB, Larson EB, Corey L. Atypical generalized zoster with lymphadenitis mimicking lymphoma. N Engl J Med 302:848, 1980.

91. Peter J, Ray G. Infectious mononucleosis. Pediatr Rev 19:276, 1998.

92. Pinder SE, Colville A. Mycobacterial cervical lymphadenitis in children: can histological assessment help differentiate infections caused by non-tuberculous mycobacteria from Mycobacterium tuberculosis? Histopathology 22:59, 1993.

93. Pontell J, Rosenfeld RM, Kohn B. Kawasaki disease mimicking retropharyngeal abscess. Otolaryngol Head Neck Surg 110:428, 1994.

94. Powers GF, Boisvert PL. Age as a factor in streptococcosis. J Pediatr 25:481, 1944.

95. Prasad S, Grundfast K, Milmoe G. Management of congenital preauricular pit and sinus tract in children. Laryngoscope 100:320, 1990.

96. Radkowski D, Arnold J, Healy GB, et al. Thyroglossal duct rem-

nants: preoperative evaluation and management. Arch Otolaryngol Head Neck Surg 117:1378, 1991.

97. Ramadan HH, Wax MK, Boyd CB. Fine-needle aspiration of head and neck masses in children. Am J Otolaryngol 18:400, 1997.

98. Ranney RB, D'Angio GJ. Langerhans' cell histiocytosis (histiocytosis X): experience at the Children's Hospital of Philadelphia, 1970–1984. Med Pediatr Oncol 17:20, 1989.

99. Ravi KV, Brooks JR. Peritonsilar abscess—an unusual presentation of Kawasaki disease. J Laryngol Otol 111:73, 1997.

100. Reede DL, Som PM. Lymph nodes. In Som PM, Bergeron RT (eds). Head and Neck Imaging, 2nd ed. St. Louis, Mosby-Year Book, 1991, pp 565–577.

101. Robinson LD, Smith RJH, Rightmire J, et al. Head and neck malignancies in children: an age-incidence study. Laryngoscope 98:11, 1988.

102. Rosenfeld RM, Biller HF. Fourth branchial pouch sinus: diagnosis and treatment. Otolaryngol Head Neck Surg 105:44, 1991.

103. Rowley AH, Shulman ST. Kawasaki syndrome. Clin Microbiol Rev 11:405, 1998.

104. Schutze GE. Diagnosis and treatment of Bartonella henselae infections. Pediatr Infect Dis J 19:1185, 2000.

105. Shad A, Magrath I. Non-Hodgkin's lymphoma. Pediatr Clin North Am 44:863, 1997.

106. Shenep JL, Kalwinsky DK, Feldman S, Pearson TA. Mycotic cervical adenitis following oral mucositis in children with leukemia. J Pediatr 106:243, 1985.

107. Shetty AK, Gedalia A. Sarcoidosis: a pediatric perspective. Clin Pediatr 37:707, 1998.

108. Shinohara M, Sone K, Tomomasa T, Morkiawa A. Corticosteroids in the treatment of the acute phase of Kawasaki disease. J Pediatr 135:465, 1999.

109. Shyur SD, Hill HR. Immunodeficiency in the 1990s. Pediatr Infect Dis J 10:595, 1991.

110. Sigalet D, Lees G, Fanning A. Atypical tuberculosis in the pediatric patient: implications for the pediatric surgeon. J Pediatr Surg 27:1381, 1992.

111. Smego RA, Foglia G. Actinomycosis. Clin Infect Dis 26:1255, 1998.

112. Soldes OS, Younger JG, Hirschl RB. Predictors of malignancy in childhood peripheral lymphadenopathy. J Pediatr Surg 34:1447, 1999.

113. Spark RP, Fried ML, Bean CK, et al. Nontuberculous mycobacterial adenitis of childhood: the ten-year experience at a community hospital. Am J Dis Child 142:106, 1988.

114. Stettner-Gloning R, Jager G, Gloning H, et al. Lymphadenopathy in connection with human herpes virus type 6 (HHV-6) infection. Clin Invest 70:59, 1992.

115. Stevenson DS, Webster G, Stewart IA. Acute tonsillectomy in the management of infectious mononucleosis. J Laryngol Otol 106:989, 1992.

116. Starke JR, Correa AG. Management of mycobacterial infection and disease in children. Pediatr Infect Dis J 14:455, 1995.

117. Starke JR. Management of nontuberculous mycobacterial cervical adenitis. Pediatr Infect Dis J 19:674, 2000.

118. Starke JR. Diagnosis of tuberculosis in children. Pediatr Infect Dis J 19:1095, 2000.

119. Stewart MG, Starke JR, Coker NJ. Nontuberculous mycobacterial infections of the head and neck. Arch Otolaryngol Head Neck Surg 120:873, 1994.

120. Stones DK, Havenga C. Sinus histiocytosis with massive lymphadenopathy. Arch Dis Child 67:521, 1992.

121. Taber's Cyclopedic Medical Dictionary, 15th ed. Philadelphia, FA Davis Co, 1985.

122. Tacy JB, Tilawi I, Goldman M. Herpes simplex adenitis. An unusual presentation with necrosis and viral particles. Arch Pathol Lab Med 109:1043, 1985.

123. Talmi YP, Cohen AH, Finkelstein Y, et al. Mycobacterium tuberculosis cervical adenitis: diagnosis and management. Clin Pediatr 28:408, 1989.

124. Thomas KT, Feder HM, Lawton AR, Edwards KM. Periodic fever syndrome in children. J Pediatr 135:15, 1999.

125. Thomsen JR, Koltai PJ. Sternomastoid tumor of infancy. Ann Otol Rhinol Laryngol 98:955, 1989.

126. Thongsuksai P, Kayasut K. Histiocytic necrotizing lymphadenitis

(Kikuchi's disease): clinicopathologic characteristics of 23 cases and literature review. J Med Assoc Thai 82:812, 1999.

127. Treyve EL, Duckert LG. Phenytoin-induced lymphadenopathy appearing as a nasopharyngeal malignant neoplasm. Arch Otolaryngol 107:392, 1981.

128. Tunkel DE. Surgery for cervicofacial nontuberculous mycobacterial adenitis in children: an update. Arch Otolaryngol Head Neck Surg 125:1109, 1999.

129. Woods WA, Carter CT, Schlager TA. Detection of group A streptococci in children under 3 years of age with pharyngitis. Pediatr Emerg Care 15:338, 1999.

130. Wright JE, Reid IS. Acute cervical lymphadenitis in children. Austral Pediatr J 23:193, 1987.

131. Yamauchi T, Ferrieri P, Anthony BF. The aetiology of acute cervical adenitis in children: serological and bacteriological studies. J Med Microbiol 13:37, 1980.

132. Yi AY, deTar M, Becker TS, Rice DH. Giant lymph node hyperplasia of the head and neck (Castleman's disease): a report of five cases. Otolaryngol Head Neck Surg 113:462, 1995.

133. Yoskovitch A, Tewfik TL, Durry CM, Moroz B. Head and neck manifestations of Kawasaki disease. Int J Pediatr Otorhinolaryngol 52:123,2000.

134. Young G, Toretsky JA, Campbell AB, Eskenazi AE. Recognition of common childhood malignancies. Am Fam Physician 61:2144, 2000.

100

Head and Neck Space Infections

Robert F. Yellon, M.D.

Infections of the deep spaces of the head and neck have been reported since the time of Hippocrates, Galen, and other authors under the names "morbus strangulatorius," "cynanche" (Greek for suffocation), and "angina maligna."[34, 53] It is reported that George Washington died after suffering a type of deep neck infection called "cynanche trachealis."[39] Substantial progress has been made since Wilhelm Fredrick von Ludwig recommended the application of leeches and a piece of silver nitrate to the middle of the area of swelling during a case of the deep neck infection that bears his name (Ludwig angina).[13] However, even in this era of antibiotic therapy, thorough knowledge of the important anatomic, etiologic, bacteriologic, and clinical factors, as well as the diagnostic and therapeutic modalities required for the proper care of deep head and neck space infections in children, is essential to ensure rapid resolution and avoid complications.

The following discussions of the anatomy of the fascial planes and deep head and neck spaces are adapted from the classic textbook by Hollinshead,[25] with more recent critical review by Som and Curtin[51] and Myers and Johnson (personal communication, Eugene Myers and Jonas Johnson, 2000). This chapter describes the typical clinical features of deep head and neck space infections, medical versus surgical management, and important complications of these infections. Previous treatment of deep head and neck space infections with antimicrobial agents and the increasing prevalence of immunocompromised patients may lead to atypical manifestations and pathogens; thus, the clinician must be vigilant in making the correct diagnosis and prescribing the correct treatment.

Etiology of Head and Neck Space Infections

Knowledge of the most common sources of head and neck space infections is important so that infection in the fascial space, as well as at the original site, can be eradicated. Retropharyngeal space infection frequently originates from an infection in the nose, paranasal sinuses, or nasopharynx that drains to the retropharyngeal lymph nodes. These nodes may undergo suppurative adenitis with the subsequent formation of a retropharyngeal abscess. Trauma to the pharynx can also provide a portal of entry for infection of the retropharyngeal and lateral pharyngeal spaces. Tuberculous infection of the vertebral bodies (Pott abscess), as well as nontuberculous infection, can lead to prevertebral (retropharyngeal) space infections.

The tonsils and adenoids are a source of infection of the lateral pharyngeal space. Infection of the temporal bone with extension of infection from the inferior aspect of the petrous apex into the lateral pharyngeal space may occur. A Bezold abscess (Fig. 100–1) develops when infection in the mastoid tip erodes through the mastoid cortex, usually on its medial side, and occupies the space between the mastoid tip and the mandible. This infection may also extend medially into the lateral pharyngeal space (Fig. 100–2) or anteriorly into the submandibular space (see Chap. 26). Tonsillar infection can lead to peritonsillar space infection. Peritonsillar infection, in turn, can extend through the pharyngeal constrictor muscle into the lateral pharyngeal space. Iatrogenic causes of lateral pharyngeal space infections include local anesthesia given for tonsillectomy and superior alveolar nerve block (see Chap. 58).

Dental and gingival infection can lead to deep head and neck infections spontaneously or iatrogenically. Infection of the mandibular teeth usually leads to infection of the mandibular, submandibular, masseteric, parotid, and lateral pharyngeal spaces.[60] Infection of the maxillary teeth generally spreads to the masticator space. Buccal space infection may occur secondary to infection of the maxillary or mandibular teeth, the parotid gland, or the skin overlying the buccal space or from adenitis of the nodes overlying the adjacent masseter muscle. In children younger than 3 years, buccal space infection may arise secondary to bacteremia from *Haemophilus influenzae* type B in the absence of another locus of infection. These children often have a high fever present for 24 hours before clinical signs of buccal space infection become apparent. Canine space infection results from maxillary canine tooth infection as its root abscess erodes through the anterior cortex of the maxilla into the canine space.

Infection of the parotid space and space of the submandibular gland can result from infection of the glands themselves or be secondary to suppurative adenitis of the lymph nodes within these spaces. Parotid space infection may also be a complication of the acute parotitis that can occur postoperatively after major surgery, or it may result from calculi or tumors encroaching on the lumina of the

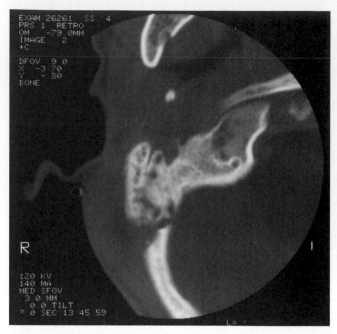

FIGURE 100–1. Computed tomographic scan of the right temporal bone showing erosion of the mastoid cortex in a child with a Bezold abscess.

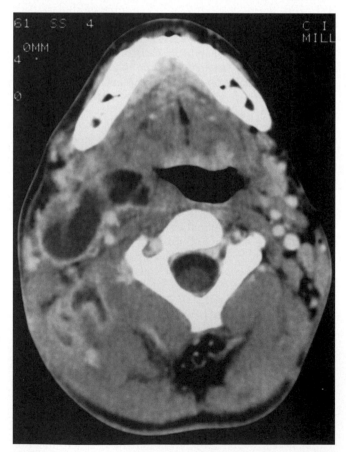

FIGURE 100–2. Computed tomographic scan of the neck showing an abscess in the right lateral pharyngeal space associated with the Bezold abscess seen in Figure 100–1.

ductal system. Trauma or infection of the tonsils, laryngotracheal complex, hypopharynx, and esophagus can provide a source of infection for the visceral and pretracheal spaces.

Infection of cystic hygromas and branchial cleft remnants can extend into the adjacent deep neck spaces. The structures of the carotid sheath may become infected by extension from adjacent deep neck spaces and suppurative adenitis. Intravenous drug abuse and iatrogenic causes, such as central venous catheter placement, may lead to infection within the carotid sheath or other spaces. Deep neck space infections may also arise secondary to anatomic connections with abscesses in the mediastinum (see Chap. 95).

Bacteriology of Head and Neck Space Infections

Both aerobic and anaerobic pathogenic bacteria have been isolated from head and neck space infections. Of the gram-positive aerobic pathogens in our series of 117 children ($N = 78$ cultures obtained) treated for head and neck space infections at the Children's Hospital of Pittsburgh from 1986 to 1992 (Table 100–1), beta hemolytic streptococci (18%) and *Staphylococcus aureus* (18%) were most prevalent. Of the anaerobic pathogens, *Bacteroides melaninogenicus* (16.7%) and *Veillonella* species (14%) predominated.[57] The gram-negative pathogen *Haemophilus parainfluenzae* was found in 14% of cultures. If all gram-negative pathogens are included, these organisms were present in 17.9% of cultures. Many of these abscesses are polymicrobial, and many of these organisms

TABLE 100–1. Bacteriology of Head and Neck Space Infections in 78 Infants and Children at Children's Hospital of Pittsburgh: January 1986 through June 1992

	Number of Cases (%)
Beta hemolytic *Streptococcus*	14 (18)
Staphylococcus aureus	14 (18)
Bacteroides melaninogenicus	13 (16.7)
Veillonella species	11 (14)
Haemophilus parainfluenzae	11 (14)
Bacteroides intermedius	6 (7.7)
Micrococcus species	6 (7.7)
Peptostreptococcus species	4 (5)
Fusobacterium species	4 (5)
Candida albicans	4 (5)
Staphylococcus, coagulase negative	2 (2.6)
Beta *Streptococcus* group C	2 (2.6)
Haemophilus haemolyticus	2 (2.6)
Haemophilus influenzae (nontypable)	2 (2.6)
Bacteroides bivius	2 (2.6)
Eikenella corrodens	2 (2.6)
Escherichia coli	1 (1.3)
Alpha hemolytic *Streptococcus*	34 (44)
Neisseria species*	17 (22)
Diphtheroid species*	9 (11.5)
Other†	16 (20.5)
No growth	7 (9)

* Normal oropharyngeal flora.

† Other organisms consisted of 16 species considered to be normal oropharyngeal flora (one isolate of each species).

produce beta-lactamase.[2, 11] Gas-forming bacteria may cause emphysema and crepitus. Buccal space infections with or without preseptal cellulitis of the orbit secondary to *H. influenzae type B* may occasionally occur in children younger than 3 years in the absence of a previous locus of infection.

Mycobacterium tuberculosis, atypical mycobacteria, and cat-scratch disease can cause infection of cervical nodes with adenopathy and occasional abscess and fistula formation.[1, 14, 28] Infections caused by atypical mycobacteria and the cat-scratch disease bacillus *Rochalimaea henselae* tend to differ from infections caused by the other typical pathogens already listed in that fever and pain are usually absent.[61, 62] The fever and massive adenopathy that can be associated with Kawasaki disease (mucocutaneous lymph node syndrome) may simulate bacterial deep neck space infection. Kawasaki disease may be differentiated from bacterial deep neck space infection by the associated findings of conjunctivitis, strawberry tongue, rash, desquamation of the skin of the hands and feet, and coronary artery vasculitis. Other causes of adenopathy in children include infection with viruses (Epstein-Barr virus, human immunodeficiency virus), fungi, brucellosis, plague, tularemia, and lymphogranuloma venereum. Noninfectious causes of adenopathy in children include sarcoidosis, drug reaction (phenytoin), and malignancy[6] (see Chap. 99).

Antimicrobial Therapy for Head and Neck Space Infections

After appropriate cultures are obtained, intravenous antimicrobials are indicated for infection of the head and neck spaces. Oral antibiotics may be adequate in selected patients, such as adolescents with adequately drained peritonsillar abscesses, minimal trismus, and good oral intake. Penicillin was used most frequently to treat these infections, but because beta-lactamase–producing bacteria are common, agents that are beta-lactamase stable or those that inhibit beta-lactamase are more desirable. We have had considerable success with the use of clindamycin plus cefuroxime for initial empirical therapy in such patients. Clindamycin is an appropriate choice for gram-positive organisms and anaerobes. However, clindamycin is not recommended as monotherapy if gram-negative organisms are suspected, in which case the combination of clindamycin and cefuroxime is preferred. In our series (see Table 100–1), gram-negative aerobic pathogens were found in 17.9% of cultures from children with head and neck space infections.[57] *H. parainfluenzae* was found in 14% and *H. influenzae* (nontypable) was found in 2.6% of 78 cultures from 117 children. More recently, the combination ampicillin-sulbactam has been recommended for its excellent in vitro activity against the usual pathogens.[44, 46, 50] Our experience with ampicillin-sulbactam has been excellent. The optimal duration of antimicrobial therapy has not been formally studied, but a minimum of 10 to 14 days is recommended. When the patient has improved sufficiently to change from intravenous to oral therapy, amoxicillin-clavulanate is an appropriate agent. Cefuroxime axetil, cefprozil, and clindamycin are other good

choices. For children with allergy to penicillin or cephalosporin, clindamycin or the combination of erythromycin and sulfisoxazole is an alternative.

Diagnostic Studies

Studies appropriate for most patients with head and neck space infections include a complete blood count with differential, prothrombin time, partial thromboplastin time, electrolytes, and possibly, urine specific gravity. Throat, blood, and sputum cultures may be needed. Fungal and acid-fast cultures may be indicated for immunocompromised patients. Cultures should be obtained before antibiotic therapy is begun.

Anteroposterior and lateral soft tissue radiographs of the neck and pharynx may be indicated. The lateral soft tissue neck and pharyngeal film should be taken with the child's neck in extension and during inspiration. If this film is taken with the child's neck in flexion or during expiration, spurious thickening of the retropharyngeal and retrotracheal spaces may be seen, especially in young children. If the retropharyngeal space measures more than 7 mm and the retrotracheal space more than 13 mm, an infection in this space is probable.[21] The presence of a retropharyngeal abscess usually causes loss of the normal cervical spine curvature with resultant straightening. A gas-fluid level confirms the presence of an abscess. A lateral neck radiographic film may also demonstrate a radiopaque foreign body. Gas-forming bacteria (Fig. 100–3) and penetrating lesions of the upper aerodigestive tract may produce emphysema in the soft tissue. Sialoliths that cause obstruction may be identified in the salivary glands. Lesions that erode bone, such as a Bezold abscess eroding the mastoid tip, may be observed (see Fig. 100–1). Panorex films may identify areas of osteomyelitis of the mandible with bone erosion, as well as dental infection, abscesses, or granulomas. A chest radiograph may identify concomitant pneumonia or mediastinal involvement.

If the aforementioned studies are not diagnostic and it is possible that an abscess is present rather than cellulitis or adenopathy, further imaging techniques may be indicated. In some cases, needle aspiration of inflammatory head or neck masses may be diagnostic of an abscess if frank pus is aspirated. Needle aspiration is particularly useful for differentiating between peritonsillar abscess and cellulitis in selected, cooperative patients.

In recent years, computed tomography (CT) has been the most widely used imaging procedure. Axial CT should be performed with 4- to 5-mm sections from the base of the cranium to the upper portion of the mediastinum. The lateral pharyngeal space, oral cavity, and submandibular and submental spaces may also require examination with 4-mm coronal sections.[59] Advantages of CT include delineation of both osseous and soft tissue structures. Intravenous contrast may help identify an abscess as a "rim-enhancing lesion" with a low-density center. A gas-fluid level or gas bubbles are also diagnostic of an abscess. Multilocular abscesses may be present. Intravenous contrast also helps delineate vascular structures, thrombosis of the jugular vein, and lymph node anatomy. The use

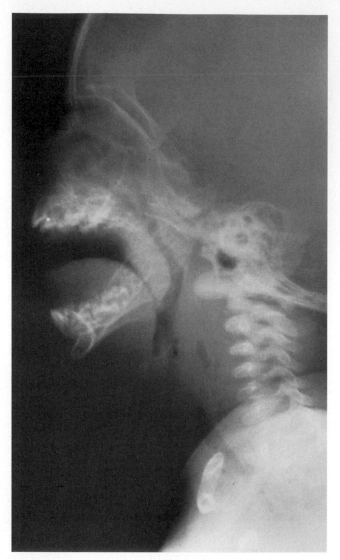

FIGURE 100–3. A lateral neck film of a child with an abscess in the retropharyngeal space shows significant thickening of the prevertebral soft tissues and gas in the retropharyngeal space.

of contrast, however, carries the risk of occasional allergic reaction and renal insult.

In one study involving 22 children and adults with both benign and malignant neck masses, CT was used to correctly identify surgically proven abscesses in 6 patients.[26] Six additional patients with CT findings of adenopathy or cellulitis were surgically explored and found to have only inflammatory tissue without abscesses. Thus, no false-positive or false-negative results for abscess occurred in that series. Another study assessed the value of CT in the differentiation of abscess from adenopathy or cellulitis in 31 children and adults with deep head and neck space infections.[42] The CT findings agreed with the intraoperative findings in 23 of the 25 patients who underwent surgical exploration. In our study of 117 deep head and neck space infections treated at the Children's Hospital of Pittsburgh, a series of 16 CT scans were available from children who had also undergone either open surgical exploration or needle aspiration.[57] The sensitivity of CT in our study for the detection of head and neck space ab-

scesses when reviewed by a neuroradiologist in a blinded fashion was 91% with a specificity of 60%. The positive predictive value of CT for identifying abscesses was 91% (Table 100–2). The two patients with false-negative results underwent needle aspiration only; thus, with needle aspiration, some abscesses may not have been detected. Choi et al[16] found abscesses at surgical exploration in 76% of 45 children in whom retropharyngeal or parapharyngeal space abscesses (or both) were diagnosed by CT. In a similar study,[32] 38 adults and children underwent surgical exploration of the retropharyngeal or lateral pharyngeal space within 48 hours after CT scanning. Twenty-nine patients (76%) had surgical confirmation of CT-identified abscesses. In five patients (13%), the CT scan suggested abscesses, but no abscesses were found at surgery. Four patients (11%) had CT scans negative for abscess, but when they failed to improve with intravenous antimicrobial therapy, surgical exploration documented abscesses. The sensitivity of CT for identification of abscesses was 88%, the false-positive rate was 13%, and the false-negative rate was 11%. In a small series of eight children with CT findings consistent with lateral pharyngeal abscesses,[49] the authors found that three patients had frank pus at surgical exploration, two had negative findings at surgical exploration, and in three the abscesses resolved with intravenous antimicrobial therapy alone. The authors concluded that children who are severely ill or have complications should be surgically drained. However, in the absence of severe illness, complications, or CT evidence of abcess, intravenous antimicrobial agents should be used as initial treatment, with surgical drainage reserved for those who do not improve after 48 hours.

Some authors have recommended the use of magnetic resonance imaging (MRI) to help differentiate head and neck abscesses from cellulitis. The use of MRI has the advantage of examination in multiple planes, including the axial, coronal, and sagittal planes. Five-millimeter sections using T_1-weighted sequences help delineate the major anatomic structures, while the inflammatory tissue has low to intermediate signal intensity. T_2-weighted images can characterize inflammatory tissue and abscess cavities because these tissues have high-intensity signals. The use of gadolinium contrast may help identify abscess cavities by demonstrating "rim enhancement." Sagittal MRI sec-

TABLE 100–2. Sensitivity and Specificity of Computed Tomography Scans in Distinguishing Cellulitis Versus Abscesses in Head and Neck Space Infections in 16 Infants and Children at Children's Hospital of Pittsburgh: January 1986 through June 1992

		Abscess Found at Surgery	
		Yes	*No*
CT scan	*Positive*	10	2
	Negative	1	3

Sensitivity = 10/11 = 91%
Specificity = 3/5 = 60%
Positive predictive value = 10/11 = 91%
Negative predictive value = 3/4 = 75%

tions may be particularly valuable for evaluation of retropharyngeal and lateral pharyngeal space infections.[59]

Ultrasonography (US) has also been recommended as a method to differentiate between cellulitis or adenopathy and abscesses in head and neck space infections (Fig. 100–4). One study in children compared the efficacy of US and CT in the diagnosis of retropharyngeal adenopathy or cellulitis versus abscess.[17] All 10 patients in this study had CT scans that were interpreted as showing abscesses. Real-time US identified only 3 of 10 of these patients as having abscesses. In patients who had US evidence of abscess, intraoperative US guidance allowed surgical drainage of the three abscess cavities. Two additional children who had CT evidence of abscess but only adenopathy on US examination underwent US-guided needle aspiration of the center of the mass, and no pus could be aspirated. A study in adults compared physical examination and US for differentiation between deep neck adenopathy and abscess.[30] Of 40 patients in this study, 34 underwent surgical exploration and 24 were found to have abscesses. Physical examination had a sensitivity of 33% and a specificity of 81% in detecting the presence of an abscess; US had a sensitivity of 95% and a specificity of 75%. The authors point out that false-positive results may occur with US because inflammatory or lymphomatous adenopathy can occasionally appear to be cystic on US. False-negative US examinations for abscesses can occur because a truly cystic lesion may appear solid with US if the fluid within the cyst is atypical and contains crystals or proteinaceous debris. One study reported correct identification of retropharyngeal adenitis or cellulitis by US in seven children whose infections all resolved with antibiotic therapy alone.[7] In a series of 12 children, US correctly differentiated between abscess and adenopathy/cellulitis.[29] Intraoral US was recently used to identify peritonsillar abscesses in 12 patients.[20]

Thus, the role of US in the evaluation of head and neck space infections in children has not been fully determined. If CT or MRI is not available, US is indicated to aid in the diagnosis. US may also be valuable when CT, MRI, or the clinical picture is not clear regarding the presence of an abscess versus cellulitis or adenopathy. We speculate that the combination of US with CT or MRI may provide the best information in equivocal cases. Finally, US appears to be useful for intraoperative localization of abscesses.[17, 33] In some patients, such as older cooperative children with head and neck space infections (e.g., peritonsillar space infection), needle aspiration is faster and more cost effective than imaging studies in determining the presence of an abscess.

Clinical Features of Head and Neck Space Infections

Certain signs and symptoms are common in children with head and neck space infections. In the series of 117 children with head and neck space infections evaluated at our institution, the most common symptom was fever (73%), followed by sore throat (47%), dysphagia (37.6%), trismus (36%), decreased appetite (22.2%), and voice change (18%).[57] Because many of these patients may have previously been treated with antimicrobials, the clinical manifestations may be atypical.

Airway Management for Head and Neck Space Infections

In children with any type of head and neck space infection, a stable airway must be maintained. Airway stability may be accomplished when necessary by endotracheal intubation or tracheostomy. If trismus or massive soft tissue edema precludes endotracheal intubation, tracheotomy is necessary. Establishment of an artificial airway in a child with a tenuous airway should be strongly considered before the child depletes all respiratory reserve or progresses to complete obstruction or respiratory failure, which necessitates a more risky emergency tracheotomy. In extreme circumstances, cricothyroidotomy may be required. Securing the airway by initial endotracheal intubation or with a rigid bronchoscope followed by conversion to a tracheotomy is important in patients at risk for postoperative extubation and difficult reintubation. Unsuccessful attempts at intubation may also precipitate acute airway obstruction, and thus tracheotomy under local anesthesia has occasionally been performed. A nasopharyngeal or oral airway may be useful to avoid intubation

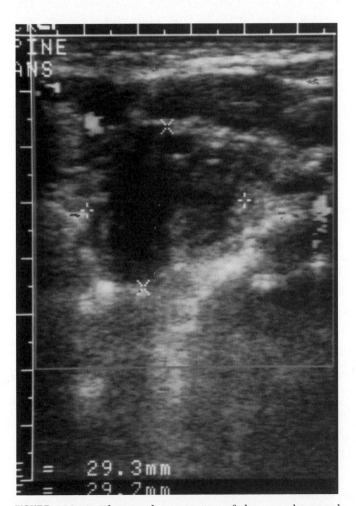

FIGURE 100–4. Ultrasound examination of the retropharyngeal space in a child with a retropharyngeal abscess.

1686   The Neck

or tracheotomy and may be a helpful temporizing measure in selected cases (see Chap. 93).

Superficial Fascia of the Neck

The superficial fascia of the neck is composed of subcutaneous tissue. This fascial layer contains fat, and in its deep portion, it covers voluntary muscles such as the platysma and the muscles of the head and face.

Deep Fascia of the Neck

Superficial Layer

The superficial or anterior layer of the deep cervical fascia is distinct from the superficial fascia of the neck because it is a deeper structure. The superficial layer of the deep cervical fascia arises from the vertebral spinous processes and ligamentum nuchae on both sides of the neck (Fig. 100–5). It then travels between and encircles the trapezius, sternocleidomastoid, and omohyoid muscles and subsequently travels anterior to and between the strap muscles. It is attached to the hyoid bone superiorly. This fascial layer splits inferiorly to attach to both the anterior and posterior surfaces of the sternum, thereby creating the suprasternal space (of Burns) between the inferior portions of the sternocleidomastoid muscles.

Middle Layer

Anterolaterally, the middle, pretracheal, or visceral layer of the deep cervical fascia is continuous with the superficial layer of the deep cervical fascia at the lateral borders of the strap muscles. The middle layer then passes posterior to the strap muscles and anterior to the trachea and thyroid gland, hence the name pretracheal fascia (see Fig. 100–5). This fascial layer travels posteriorly to envelop the pharynx and esophagus, hence the name visceral fascia. The middle layer of the deep cervical fascia is continuous with the buccopharyngeal fascia. Superiorly, the middle cervical fascia fuses with the hyoid bone and thyroid cartilage. Inferiorly, this layer travels deep to the sternum and extends over the fibrous pericardium and great vessels in the superior mediastinum.

Posterior Layer

Similar to the superficial and middle layers, the posterior or prevertebral layer of the deep cervical fascia arises on the vertebral spinous processes and ligamentum nuchae. It then passes deep to the trapezius muscles and covers the scalene muscles, levator scapulae, longus coli, brachial plexus, and phrenic nerve. This layer also covers the vertebral column and attaches to the clavicles inferiorly. The portion of this fascia that covers the vertebral bodies and longus coli muscles is described as being composed of two distinct layers[19, 25] (Figs. 100–6 and 100–7). The

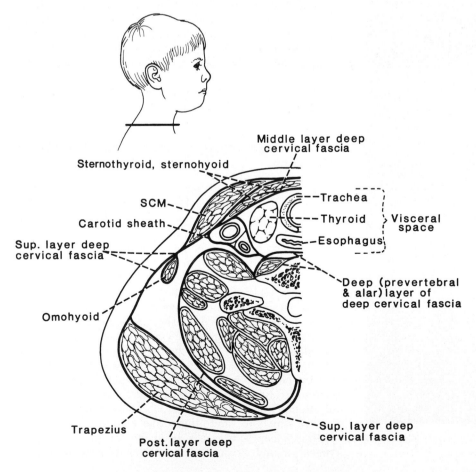

FIGURE 100–5. Major fascial layers and anatomic structures seen in an axial section of the lower part of the neck. Note the carotid sheath and visceral space. SCM, sternocleidomastoid muscle.

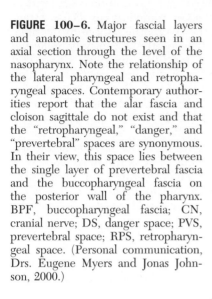

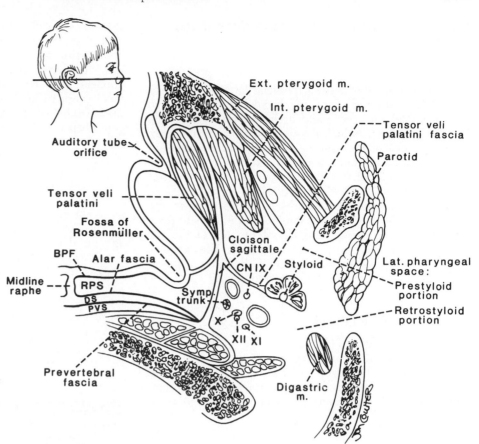

FIGURE 100–6. Major fascial layers and anatomic structures seen in an axial section through the level of the nasopharynx. Note the relationship of the lateral pharyngeal and retropharyngeal spaces. Contemporary authorities report that the alar fascia and cloison sagittale do not exist and that the "retropharyngeal," "danger," and "prevertebral" spaces are synonymous. In their view, this space lies between the single layer of prevertebral fascia and the buccopharyngeal fascia on the posterior wall of the pharynx. BPF, buccopharyngeal fascia; CN, cranial nerve; DS, danger space; PVS, prevertebral space; RPS, retropharyngeal space. (Personal communication, Drs. Eugene Myers and Jonas Johnson, 2000.)

more posterior prevertebral portion is directly applied to the vertebral bodies and muscles, while the more anterior portion is called the alar fascia. Other researchers question the existence of the alar layer and instead describe a fascial structure called the cloison sagittale (see Fig. 100–6), which is discussed further in the section on the danger space and the cloison sagittale.[15, 51] In contrast, more contemporary head and neck anatomists state that the fascia in this region is composed of only a single layer of prevertebral fascia with no alar fascia or cloison sagittale (personal communication, Eugene Myers and Jonas Johnson, 2000).

FIGURE 100–7. Fascial layers and deep neck spaces seen in a midline sagittal section.[16, 22] (Personal communication, Drs. Eugene Myers and Jonas Johnson, 2000.)

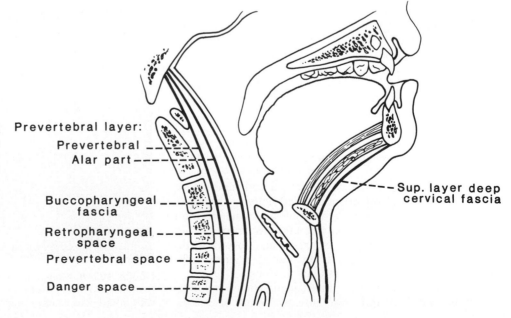

Fascia of the Upper Part of the Neck, Face, and Head

Superficial Layer

Above the hyoid bone, the superficial layer of the deep cervical fascia extends from the hyoid bone inferiorly to the mandible and zygomatic arch superiorly (see Fig. 100–7). This fascia, which lies deep to the platysma muscle, splits to cover both the medial and lateral surfaces of the mandible. Anteriorly, it covers the mylohyoid muscle and anterior belly of the digastric muscle. At the level of the submandibular gland, it divides to form a capsule around this structure. Posteriorly, it divides to cover the lateral aspect of the masseter muscle, and it splits to form a capsule on the medial and lateral surfaces of the parotid gland on its way to the zygoma. It also sends a lamina to cover the medial aspect of the internal pterygoid muscle on its way to the pterygoid plate.

Buccopharyngeal Fascia

The buccopharyngeal fascia covers the pharynx and is continuous with the tunica adventitia or visceral fascia (middle layer of the deep cervical fascia) covering the esophagus. It also covers the lateral surface of the buccinator muscle and attaches to the mandible at the pterygomandibular raphe.

Anatomy, Clinical Manifestations of Infections, and Open Surgical Procedures

Peritonsillar Space

Lying between the capsule of the palatine tonsil and the pharyngeal muscles, the peritonsillar (or paratonsillar) space is the most common site of head and neck space infections. This space is filled with loose connective tissue. It extends anterior and posterior to the tonsillar pillars. Superiorly, it may extend to the level of the hard palate or torus tubarius. Inferiorly, it may extend as low as the piriform fossa. Although the anatomic boundaries of the peritonsillar space do not include the lateral pharyngeal space, peritonsillar infection often extends into the lateral pharyngeal space with involvement of the internal pterygoid muscle, a combination that results in trismus. In the Children's Hospital of Pittsburgh series, 63% of 61 children with peritonsillar space infection were reported to have had trismus.[57]

Clinical findings in children with peritonsillar space infections include pain, fever, dysphagia, and cervical adenopathy. An oropharyngeal examination is important to make the diagnosis. The hallmark of peritonsillar space infection is swelling of the tissues lateral and superior to the tonsil, with consequent medial and anterior displacement of the tonsil. Displacement of the uvula to the contralateral side of the pharynx may also occur. The tonsils may be erythematous, enlarged, and covered with exudate. The breath is fetid. If an abscess is present, it usually forms at the superior pole of the tonsil.

In the management of peritonsillar infections, cellulitis should be differentiated from abscess. Some abscesses may be clinically obvious; others are less obvious, and clinical distinction is more difficult. An initial 12- to 24-hour trial of appropriate intravenous antibiotics is reasonable in selected patients with peritonsillar infection and no clear evidence of abscess, airway compromise, septicemia, severe trismus, or other complications. When extension of infection from the peritonsillar space to the adjacent deep neck spaces is suspected, CT may be indicated (Fig. 100–8). If improvement does not occur after a trial of intravenous antimicrobial therapy, needle aspiration may be attempted to identify an abscess. Intraoral US evaluation correctly identified 12 of 12 cases of peritonsillar abscess in 10 adults and 2 children and was a useful guide for needle aspiration.[20]

The use of needle aspiration versus incision and drainage for definitive treatment of a peritonsillar abscess is controversial. The traditional treatment of peritonsillar abscess has been incision and drainage via a curvilinear incision through the anterior tonsillar pillar, followed by blunt dissection into the abscess cavity with a hemostat or tonsil clamp. If indicated, interval tonsillectomy is then performed 4 to 12 weeks later.[43] Some surgeons advocate immediate tonsillectomy ("quinsy tonsillectomy," "tonsillectomy a chaud") as definitive treatment to ensure com-

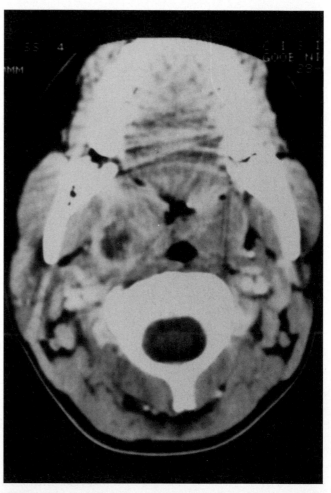

FIGURE 100–8. Computed tomographic scan showing a right peritonsillar abscess. Note the "rim enhancement" of the abscess with intravenous contrast material.

plete drainage of the abscess and to obviate the need for a second hospitalization to perform an interval tonsillectomy.[5, 18, 35, 47, 52] The incidence of bleeding after quinsy tonsillectomy in adults and children ranged from 0% to 7% with an overall incidence of 1% in 1027 patients from five series[5, 18, 35, 47, 52] (Table 100–3). In a study involving 55 children who underwent quinsy tonsillectomy, no patient had postoperative or delayed bleeding.[47] In a military population, essentially no difference was noted in the amount of intraoperative or postoperative bleeding in patients treated with quinsy tonsillectomy and those treated with interval tonsillectomy.[35]

Needle aspiration has been used successfully as definitive treatment of peritonsillar abscesses. In one study, 90% of 41 patients (age not specified) were successfully managed with needle aspiration of peritonsillar abscesses at the point of maximum bulging or, if the first aspiration was unsuccessful, 1 cm lower.[24] In a second series of 74 patients (adults and children) with peritonsillar infections who underwent needle aspiration of the superior, middle, and inferior peritonsillar areas, pus was aspirated in 70% of cases. A second series of aspirations was required for seven patients (10%) on the following day.[48]

In a series of 29 children, the incidence of recurrent peritonsillar abscess and recurrent tonsillitis after peritonsillar abscess was 7% each.[27] Recurrence rates for peritonsillar abscess in series including adults and children ranged from 6% to 36%, with an overall incidence of 17% in 526 patients from six studies[5, 22, 27, 35, 41, 52] (Table 100–4). Rates of recurrent tonsillitis occurring before or after peritonsillar abscess ranged from 7% to 50%, with an overall incidence of 28% in 345 patients from four studies[5, 22, 27, 41] (see Table 100–4). In one study, the incidence of recurrent peritonsillar abscess or recurrent tonsillitis after incision and drainage of the initial peritonsillar abscess was 63% in 27 patients younger than 30 years.[41]

In the treatment of peritonsillar abscess, quinsy tonsillectomy, incision and drainage with or without interval tonsillectomy, and needle aspiration are all safe and effective. Each therapeutic modality has advantages in certain situations. In patients with peritonsillar abscess and significant airway obstruction and in those who have associated complications such as lateral pharyngeal space abscess, quinsy tonsillectomy is appropriate. If incision and drainage or needle aspiration fail to adequately drain an abscess, quinsy tonsillectomy is also indicated. Additionally, for patients with a previous history of recurrent periton-

TABLE 100–3. Incidence of Perioperative or Delayed Hemorrhage Associated with Quinsy Tonsillectomy

Reference	Number of Patients	Number with Hemorrhage (%)
Grahne (1958)	725	0 (0)
Beeden and Evans (1970)	100	5 (5)
McCurdy (1977)	28	2 (7)
Templer et al (1977)	119	2 (2)
Richardson and Birck (1981)	55	0 (0)
TOTAL	1027	9 (1)

TABLE 100–4. Incidence of Prior or Subsequent Recurrent Tonsillitis or Recurrent Peritonsillar Abscess Associated with Peritonsillar Abscess

Reference	Number PTA	Number Recurrent PTA (%)	Number Recurrent Tonsillitis (%)
Beeden and Evans (1970)	111	18 (16)	56 (50)
McCurdy (1977)	62	4 (6)	
Templer et al (1977)	119	11 (9)	
Herbild and Bonding (1981)	161	36 (22)	32 (20)
Holt and Tinsley (1981)	29	2 (7)	6 (21)
Nielsen and Greisen (1981)	44	16 (36)	3 (7)
TOTAL	526	87/526 (17)	97/345 (28)

PTA, peritonsillar abscess.

sillar abscess or recurrent tonsillitis severe enough to warrant tonsillectomy, quinsy tonsillectomy should be considered. In this last scenario, incision plus drainage followed by interval tonsillectomy (4 to 6 weeks later) is also a reasonable choice. For a child in whom tonsillectomy is indicated on the basis of recurrent peritonsillar abscess, recurrent tonsillitis, or chronic airway obstruction secondary to tonsillar hypertrophy, quinsy tonsillectomy may be the most cost-effective treatment because it obviates a second period of hospitalization, anesthesia, and morbidity.

Needle aspiration of peritonsillar abscesses, when successful, is the least invasive and least painful of the various treatment modalities. In older and cooperative children without associated complications, needle aspiration of peritonsillar abscesses is safe and effective. For children with a bleeding diathesis who are not allowed blood transfusion for religious reasons or whose general condition is too poor to tolerate a general anesthetic, needle aspiration is the treatment of choice.

Retropharyngeal Space

The retropharyngeal space is the superior continuation of the retrovisceral space. According to Grodinsky and Holyoke[19] and Hollinshead,[25] it lies posterior to the buccopharyngeal fascia (middle layer of the deep cervical fascia) covering the pharynx and anterior to the prevertebral fascia (alar layer) (see Figs. 100–6 and 100–7). Many contemporary head and neck anatomists consider the retropharyngeal space to be synonymous with the prevertebral and danger spaces; they report that these latter two spaces do not exist as separate entities and that the alar layer of the prevertebral fascia does not exist (personal communication, Eugene Myers and Jonas Johnson, 2000).

The superior limit of the retropharyngeal space is the cranial base. Inferiorly, the retrovisceral space extends into the mediastinum to approximately the level of the tracheal bifurcation. The buccopharyngeal fascia is adherent to the prevertebral fascia in the midline, so infections

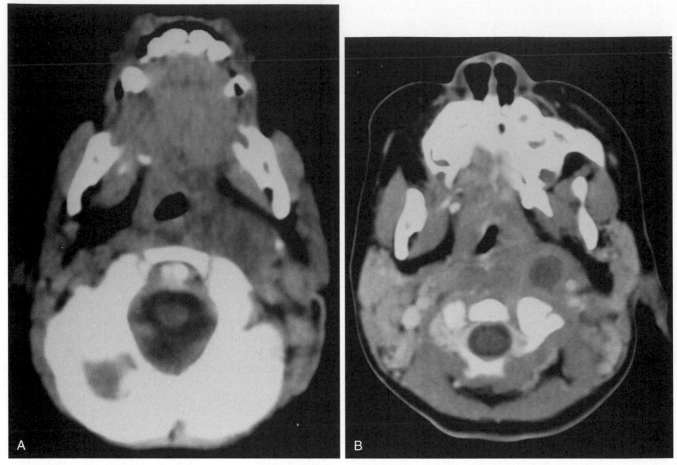

FIGURE 100–9. Computed tomographic scans showing left retropharyngeal cellulitis without an abscess *(A)* and a left retropharyngeal abscess *(B)*.

in the retropharyngeal space are unilateral. Lateral neck films (see Fig. 100–3), CT (Fig. 100–9), MRI, or US (see Fig. 100–4) may help ascertain whether cellulitis or a true abscess is present. Two chains of lymph nodes are present on either side of the midline in the retropharyngeal space. They receive drainage from the nose, paranasal sinuses, pharynx, and eustachian tube. These lymph nodes may be prominent in children, and some may persist into adulthood. In the interpretation of Grodinsky and Holyoke[19] and Hollinshead,[25] infections in the prevertebral space (between the vertebral bodies and the prevertebral layer of fascia) bulge in the midline and are bilateral.

Children with an infection in the retropharyngeal space are usually irritable and have fever, dysphagia, muffled speech or cry, noisy breathing, a stiff neck, and cervical lymphadenopathy. As the infection progresses, stridor and drooling develop. In our series of 27 children with retropharyngeal infections, 9 (33%) had torticollis.[57] The most important diagnostic sign is the presence of unilateral posterior pharyngeal swelling when the child's pharynx is inspected. Although retropharyngeal space infections clinically appear to be unilateral, imaging studies show some edema of the contents of the contralateral retropharyngeal space in its medial aspect. A child who is uncooperative or unable to cooperate should be re-

strained. If the patient is in acute respiratory distress, this part of the examination should be performed in the operating room because the child will probably require an artificial airway (endotracheal intubation or tracheotomy). In addition, the child might have supraglottitis (epiglottitis) if fever, stridor, drooling, and dysphagia are of sudden onset. This part of the examination is important in the differential diagnosis because a prevertebral infection is manifested as a midline mass and peritonsillar cellulitis or abscess does not involve the posterior pharyngeal wall, except in rare instances when both the peritonsillar and retropharyngeal spaces are involved. Swelling of the lateral pharyngeal wall more likely represents infection in the lateral pharyngeal space than in the retropharyngeal space. The child may have lymphadenitis in the posterior pharynx, which can usually be distinguished from retropharyngeal cellulitis or abscess. A localized unilateral swelling is most frequently indicative of involvement of one of the retropharyngeal lymph nodes, whereas generalized unilateral posterior pharyngeal swelling that extends from high in the nasopharynx to the upper esophageal area is usually either cellulitis or an abscess.

A transoral approach is recommended for incision and drainage of abscesses in the retropharyngeal space. The patient must be intubated orally, which can be performed safely by introducing the tube on the side opposite the abscess. To avoid aspiration of purulent material if the abscess ruptures during intubation, the patient should be in the head-down Trendelenburg position. The position and mouth gag used to perform tonsillectomy are preferred for adequate exposure and to secure the endotracheal tube. Before the incision and drainage, needle aspiration of the abscess should be performed to prevent tracheal aspiration of pus during the incision and to obtain material for Gram stain, culture, and antimicrobial sensitivity studies. After the aspiration procedure, a small vertical incision is made in the lateral aspect of the posterior pharyngeal wall at a point between the junction of the lateral third and medial two thirds of the distance between the midline of the pharynx and the medial aspect of the retromolar trigone. The space is then opened gently with a hemostat to drain the abscess and avoid possible vascular injury. No drain is placed because it could potentially be aspirated or swallowed postoperatively. If the infection also involves the lateral pharyngeal space, the procedure should be performed through an external neck incision as described in the section Open Surgical Approach to Deep Neck Space Infections. On rare occasion, both transoral and external neck approaches are needed to provide adequate drainage. If the child has early recurrence of the abscess or if the abscess does not resolve rapidly after a transoral drainage procedure, an external cervical approach should be carried out.

Danger Space and Cloison Sagittale

As described by Grodinsky and Holyoke[19] and cited by Hollinshead,[25] the portion of the deep layer of the cervical fascia that covers the vertebral bodies and longus coli muscles is composed of two distinct layers. The anterior portion is called the alar fascia, and the more posterior portion that is in direct contact with the vertebral bodies is called the prevertebral fascia. The space between the two layers is called the danger space[19] (see Figs. 100–6 and 100–7). This space extends from the cranial base to the diaphragm.

The existence of the danger space and the alar layer of the prevertebral fascia is debated. Some authorities argue that the danger space and the alar layer do not exist and that a structure called the cloison sagittale is the important fascial structure in this region.[15, 51] The cloison sagittale is described as a thin layer of fascia that runs in an anterior-to-posterior plane from the pterygoid plate to the prevertebral fascia and separates the lateral aspects of the retropharyngeal space from the lateral pharyngeal space on either side of the neck (see Fig. 100–6). Thus, the cloison sagittale prevents the spread of infection from the retropharyngeal space to the lateral pharyngeal space.

Contemporary authorities report that based on dissections in pharyngeal cancer patients, the alar fascia and cloison sagittale do not exist and the retropharyngeal, danger, and prevertebral spaces are synonymous. In their view, this space lies between the single layer of prevertebral fascia and the buccopharyngeal fascia on the posterior wall of the pharynx (personal communication, Eugene Myers and Jonas Johnson, 2000).

Prevertebral Space

In the opinion of Grodinsky and Holyoke[19] and Hollinshead,[25] the prevertebral space lies posterior to the prevertebral fascia and anterior to the vertebral bodies and is the most posterior of the spaces (see Figs. 100–6 and 100–7). Infection in this space is seen as a bulging mass in the midline of the pharynx, with extension to both sides of the pharynx because of the absence of a midline raphe. The prevertebral space extends from the base of the cranium to the diaphragm. Infection in this space is best approached surgically as described in the section Open Surgical Approach to Deep Neck Infections rather than by the transoral approach because the external approach avoids the possibility of a persistent draining fistula in the pharynx with the potential for aspiration. Needle aspiration via the transoral route may be useful for localization of an abscess. These infections may require prolonged antimicrobial therapy for associated osteomyelitis or tuberculous infection of the vertebral bodies.[4]

Currently, many head and neck surgeons consider the retropharyngeal, danger, and prevertebral spaces to be synonymous and that this space lies anterior to the single layer of prevertebral fascia and posterior to the buccopharyngeal fascia on the posterior pharyngeal wall (personal communication, Eugene Myers and Jonas Johnson, 2000). In their opinion, the alar fascia and cloison sagittale do not exist.

Mandibular Space

Filled with loose connective tissue, the space of the body of the mandible is an actual space rather than a potential one. This space is formed by splitting of the two leaflets of the superficial layer of the deep cervical fascia. These two leaflets attach to the inferior border of the mandible on its lateral surface and the medial surface of the mandible at the level of the mylohyoid muscle. This space is limited anteriorly by the attachment of the anterior belly of the digastric muscle and posteriorly by the attachment of the medial pterygoid muscle to the mandible.

Mandibular space infections usually follow dental infection, trauma, or surgery. The suppurative dental process erodes through the lingual cortex of the mandible to create an abscess between the mandible and the inner leaflet of the superficial layer of the deep cervical fascia. This intraoral swelling lies more anterior than swelling that occurs during infection of the medial portion of the masticator space. Pain and intraoral swelling are present, but not external facial swelling unless the process extends to involve the dependent lymphatics in the submandibular space. Mandibular space abscesses may be drained via an intraoral incision along the medial surface of the body of the mandible.

Masticator Space

The masticator space is created by splitting of the superficial layer of the deep cervical fascia around the masseter and internal pterygoid muscles (Fig. 100–10). Also contained in this space are the ramus of the mandible, the temporalis muscle, fat, and loose connective tissue. This

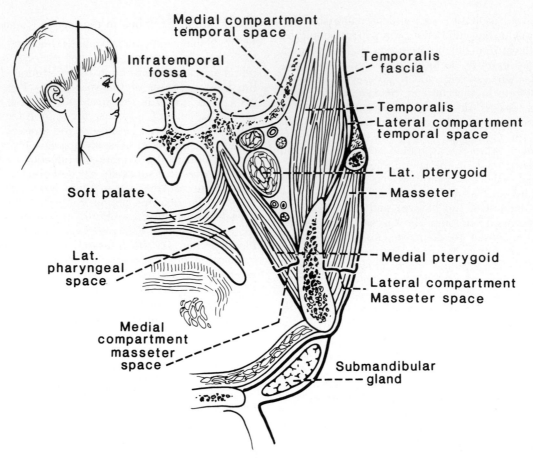

FIGURE 100–10. Major structures seen in a coronal section of the head at the level of the soft palate, along with the anatomic relationships of the masticator space.

space extends anteriorly as the fascia covers the buccal fat pad and then ends as the fascia attaches to the maxilla and buccinator muscle fascia. The space ends posteriorly as the two laminae of the fascia fuse along the posterior border of the mandible. Superiorly, the medial aspect of the masticator space is limited by the origin of the temporalis muscle from the skull; laterally, it is limited by the temporalis fascia. It extends medially to include the pterygopalatine fossa. The mandibular nerve and the internal maxillary artery are also found in this space. Infection in the masticator space most commonly arises from the mandibular teeth but may also extend from infection in the temporal or zygomatic bones. Infection in this space may be limited to the medial portion of the space that lies medial to the mandible or in the portion that lies lateral to the mandible, or both. The superior portion of the masticator space is sometimes referred to as the temporal space, with compartments both medial and lateral to the temporalis muscle.

Infections of the masticator space are usually related to dental infection, trauma, or surgery. Localized osteomyelitis or subperiosteal abscess of the mandible may be present, as may cellulitis of the gingiva. The major symptom of masticator space infection is deep pain along the ascending ramus of the mandible. Trismus is an early and prominent finding. Sore throat, dysphagia, and pain on moving the tongue are often present. Signs depend on whether the medial, lateral, or both compartments of the

masticator space are involved. Swelling is present in the area of the retromolar trigone if the medial compartment is involved. This swelling may be mistaken for a peritonsillar abscess. If the lateral compartment is involved, swelling will be present externally, overlying the masseter muscle and mandible. Infection may also extend superiorly and lie medial or lateral to the temporalis muscle.

When masticator space infections require incision and drainage, the approach depends on whether the medial or lateral portion is involved. If the lateral portion is involved, an incision may be made below and parallel to the body of the mandible, with incision of the platysma and fascial capsule of the submandibular gland. The facial vein and possibly the facial artery are then identified and ligated, and the vessels along with the fascial capsule of the gland, platysma, and marginal mandibular nerve are carefully elevated to the level of the inferior border of the mandible. The tendon of the masseter muscle is then detached from the mandible, and the lateral portion of the masticator space is entered and drained. Iodophor-impregnated packing is placed.

The medial portion of the masticator space is approached via an intraoral incision medial to the ascending ramus of the mandible in the area of the retromolar trigone. In some instances, both intraoral and external drainage may be required.

Superior extension of masticator space infections into the temporal portion of the masticator space that require drainage may be approached in the following manner: incisions are made along the hairline through the temporalis fascia to reach abscesses lateral to the temporalis muscle. To reach medially located abscesses, incisions are made through the temporalis fascia and muscle. Packing is placed.

Buccal Space

Lateral to the buccinator muscle lies the buccopharyngeal fascia, which forms the medial wall of the buccal space. The skin of the cheek is the lateral boundary. Limiting the buccal space inferiorly is the lower border of the mandible; the posterior limit is the pterygomandibular raphe. The buccal space contains the buccal fat pad, the Stensen duct, and the facial artery.[55]

Infections in the buccal space are characterized by marked swelling of the cheek, which is warm, tender, and red. Trismus from inflammation of the adjacent masseter muscle is often observed. Subcutaneous fluctuation may be found with an abscess. Usually, little intraoral swelling is evident. Buccal space infections may occasionally extend to involve the maxillary sinus, the orbit, the preseptal orbital tissues, or the cavernous sinus.

Buccal space abscesses usually occur subcutaneously in the cheek. These abscesses may be drained by a skin incision, followed by blunt dissection in a direction parallel to the branches of the facial nerve. Packing may be placed.

Canine Space

The canine space is a potential space anterior to the maxillary canine fossa, superior to the origin of the levator anguli oris muscle, and inferior to the origin of the levator labii superioris muscle on the face of the maxilla.

A toothache usually precedes canine space infection. Swelling is present lateral to the nares; thus, canine space infection may be mistaken for dacryocystitis. The infection may occasionally drain just inferior to the medial canthus of the eye. If the infection extends inferior to the origin of the levator anguli oris muscle, swelling is also present in the labial sulcus.

Abscesses in the canine space may be approached by an incision in the maxillary labial sulcus down through the periosteum. Blunt dissection superiorly is then performed to enter and drain the abscess. Treatment of the associated dental infection may include apicoectomy and curettage of purulent granulation tissue from the bony defect over the canine root, pulp extirpation, or extraction, for which dental consultation is recommended.[55]

Other Dental Infections

An apical abscess of the roots of any tooth can erode through the inner or outer bony cortices of the mandible or maxillary alveolus and cause a subperiosteal abscess. The location depends on the involved tooth. Toothache, local swelling, and possibly fever and fluctuation may be present. Surgical treatment of an abscess in these areas requires incision and drainage, followed by appropriate

dental care as described in the section Canine Space (see Chap. 58).

Parotid Space

Similar to the space of the submandibular gland, the parotid space is formed by splitting of the superficial layer of the deep cervical fascia to cover the medial and lateral surfaces of the parotid gland. The parotid space also contains the periparotid lymph nodes and the facial nerve and may contain the auriculotemporal nerve, the external carotid and superficial temporal arteries, and the retromandibular vein. In contrast to the thick fascia covering the lateral surface of the parotid gland, the fascia covering the medial surface of the gland is thin, thus allowing parotid space infection to extend into the adjacent lateral pharyngeal space.

Pain, redness, and edema over the parotid area are typical of parotid space infection. Even when an abscess is present, the tough, tense fascia covering the lateral aspect of the gland prevents the palpation of fluctuation in the parotid space. It is nearly always unilateral.

Parotid space abscesses may be approached through a standard parotidectomy-type incision, including an incision around the base of the lobule, or via a "hockey stick" incision in a preauricular crease, with extension of the incision below the angle of the mandible toward the tip of the hyoid bone. Anterior and posterior flaps are elevated for a short distance in the plane of the parotid capsule superiorly and in the subplatysmal plane inferiorly. The parotid fascia is then detached from the anterior surface of the tragal cartilage and sternocleidomastoid muscle and is superficially incised to drain the parotid space. If necessary, the dissection anterior to the tragus and bony external auditory canal is carefully continued in a medial direction until the main trunk of the facial nerve is identified. Blunt dissection can then be used to drain an abscess that lies in the posterosuperomedial aspect of the parotid space above the main trunk of the nerve. The parotid gland may then be detached from the posterior belly of the digastric muscle. Blunt medial dissection superior to the posterior belly of the digastric muscle and posterior to the mandible allows drainage of the lateral pharyngeal space, which may be secondarily involved because of the propensity for parotid space infection to traverse the thin layer of fascia on the medial surface of the gland. When necessary, the lateral pharyngeal space may also be approached via blunt dissection inferior to the posterior belly of the digastric muscle and anterior to the sternocleidomastoid muscle. Abscesses within the parenchyma of the gland may be drained by gentle blunt dissection in a direction parallel to the branches of the facial nerve (see Chap. 19).

Open Surgical Approach to Deep Neck Space Infections

Achieving and maintaining adequate drainage of loculated collections of pus are the goals of open surgical procedures for the treatment of deep head and neck space infections. Associated foci of infection such as abscesses of tooth roots or infections of the temporal bone must also be identified and treated by the surgeon. The classic description of the open surgical approach to deep pus in the neck written by Mosher[38] in 1929 is useful today with minor modifications. This approach is useful for drainage of visceral, submandibular, lateral pharyngeal, and prevertebral space infections, infections of the carotid sheath, and selected infections of the retropharyngeal space. Most uncomplicated retropharyngeal abscesses may be drained transorally as previously described. Choi et al[16] recommended that abscesses in the retropharyngeal or lateral pharyngeal spaces that lie medial to the great vessels be drained via a transoral approach and that abscesses lying lateral to the great vessels and those involving multiple spaces be approached via an external cervical approach.

Mosher's first recommendation was to make a large T-shaped incision, which has been modified by most contemporary surgeons so that the horizontal limb is slightly lower in relation to the body of the mandible and the vertical limb is omitted entirely (Fig. 100–11). The remainder of Mosher's technique is unchanged. After making a horizontal neck incision through the skin and platysma, dissection is carried out between the anterior border of the sternocleidomastoid muscle and the posterior and inferior aspects of the submandibular gland. The fascial layers may be extremely thickened. The facial artery should be avoided or ligated during elevation of the submandibular gland. If the abscess is limited to the space of the submandibular gland, the fascial capsule of the gland can simply be incised along its lower border for

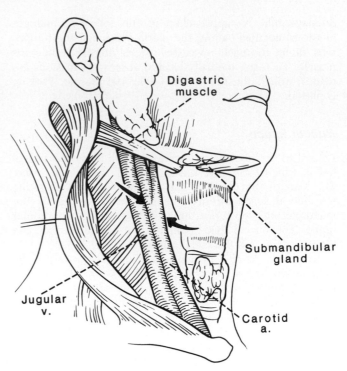

FIGURE 100–12. Lateral neck anatomy seen with posterolateral retraction of the sternocleidomastoid muscle. *Arrows* show how the carotid sheath and retropharyngeal, lateral pharyngeal, and visceral spaces can be approached.

drainage, or the entire gland may be excised. The carotid sheath structures are identified opposite the tip of the greater horn of the hyoid bone, and the sheath may require incision and drainage if an abscess is present. Finger dissection superiorly along the carotid sheath allows drainage of the lateral pharyngeal space up to the cranial base. Blunt dissection medial to the carotid sheath in an inferior direction allows drainage of both the pretracheal and retrovisceral portions of the visceral space (Fig. 100–12). Iodophor-impregnated packing is placed for several days, and the wounds are closed loosely. The packing is slowly removed over a period of several days.

Head and neck space abscesses that are obviously pointing may be surgically managed by simple skin and subcutaneous tissue incision, evacuation of purulent material, and blunt or digital exploration of the abscess cavity to open and drain any areas of loculated pus. Packing is then placed.

Lateral Pharyngeal Space

According to the descriptions of Hollinshead,[25] the lateral pharyngeal space is continuous with the retropharyngeal space in its lateral aspect. In contrast, reports of Som and Curtin[51] and Charpy[15] describe the existence of a fascial band called the cloison sagittale that separates the retropharyngeal space from the lateral pharyngeal space (see Fig. 100–6). The lateral pharyngeal space has also been called the parapharyngeal, peripharyngeal, pharyngomaxillary, pterygopharyngeal, pterygomandibular, and pharyngomasticatory space. This space is shaped like an inverted pyramid. Superiorly, the lateral pharyngeal space extends

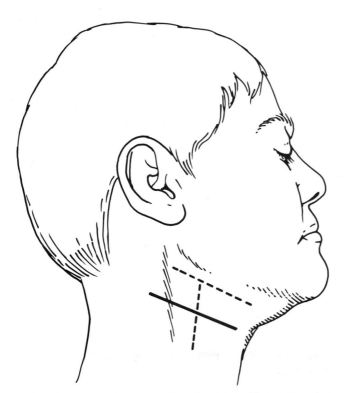

FIGURE 100–11. The incision for open surgical procedures to drain deep neck space infections is shown by the *solid line.* The outdated T incision of Mosher with an unnecessary vertical limb is shown by the *dotted line.*

to the cranial base. The inferior limit of this space is the place where the hyoid bone joins the fascia of the submandibular gland and the sheaths of the stylohyoid muscle and the posterior belly of the digastric muscle. It lies lateral to the buccopharyngeal fascia on the pharynx and medial to the pterygoid muscles and fascia on the medial surface of the parotid gland. The lateral pharyngeal space extends anterosuperiorly to the pterygomandibular raphe and posteriorly to the posterior surface of the carotid sheath. Infection may spread to the lateral pharyngeal space from the tongue, retropharyngeal space, teeth, submandibular gland, parotid gland, masticator space, tonsils, and peritonsillar areas. The styloglossus and stylopharyngeus muscles cross the lateral pharyngeal space.

The styloid process and attached fascia of the tensor veli palatini muscle divide the lateral pharyngeal space into a prestyloid compartment that contains the internal maxillary artery, the maxillary nerve, and the tail of the parotid gland and a post-styloid compartment that contains the carotid artery, internal jugular vein, cervical sympathetic chain, and cranial nerves IX, X, XI, and XII (see Fig. 100-6). Pain, fever, and a stiff neck are the usual initial complaints of a child with a lateral pharyngeal space infection. Trismus is present when the anterior (prestyloid) compartment is involved because of inflammation of the internal pterygoid muscle, but trismus may be absent when only the posterior (post-styloid) compartment is involved. Perimandibular edema occurs frequently and can involve the parotid and submandibular areas. As described, oropharyngeal examination can be helpful in making the diagnosis in those with lateral pharyngeal wall swelling, which is frequently posterior to the tonsil. The tonsil is usually medially and anteriorly displaced. CT, MRI, or US may help differentiate an abscess from cellulitis in the lateral pharyngeal space (Figs. 100-2 and 100-13). When infection is severe and extensive, airway obstruction may be present. One or more of the cranial nerves or the cervical sympathetic chain (Horner syndrome) in the posterior compartment may be involved. Because other potential spaces of the head and neck may be primarily or secondarily involved, the examination must include these areas. Infections in the lateral pharyngeal space requiring surgical intervention are best drained by the open surgical approach already described.

Carotid Sheath

Within the carotid sheath are the carotid artery, internal jugular vein, and the vagus nerve. The anterolateral wall of the carotid sheath is derived from the anterior layer of the deep cervical fascia. A contribution from the middle layer of the deep cervical fascia is present anteriorly. The medial and posterior walls are derived from the anterior layer of the deep cervical fascia as it sends a lamina medial to the great vessels, and then posterior to them, to overlie the posterior layer of the deep cervical fascia. Posteromedially, a portion of the carotid sheath is attached to a lamina from the posterior layer (see Fig. 100-5).

Infections in adjacent deep neck spaces, suppurative adenitis, tumor masses, hypercoagulable states, intrave-

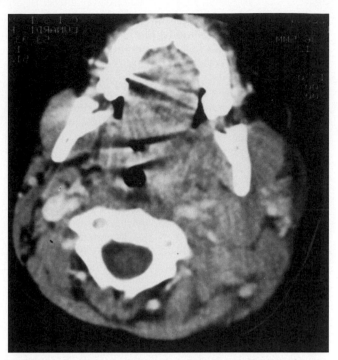

FIGURE 100-13. Computed tomographic scan of the neck of a child with left lateral pharyngeal space cellulitis and no abscess.

nous drug abuse, and iatrogenic causes such as placement of a central venous catheter may lead to infection of the structures within the carotid sheath. Stiffness and swelling of the anterolateral aspect of the neck and torticollis are present. With thrombosis of the internal jugular vein, spiking ("picket fence" pattern) fevers may occur as septic emboli seed the pulmonary circulation. The open surgical approach to this deep neck space was described earlier.

Visceral Space

Contents of the visceral space include the thyroid gland, trachea, and esophagus (see Fig. 100-5). It is divided into pretracheal and retrovisceral spaces, which are in continuity superiorly. Above the level where the inferior thyroid artery enters the thyroid gland there is only one visceral compartment, and it is surrounded by the middle layer of the deep cervical fascia anteriorly, the fascia of the carotid sheath laterally, and the posterior layer of the deep cervical fascia posteriorly. Below the level where the inferior thyroid artery enters the thyroid gland, dense connective tissue attaches the lateral aspect of the esophagus to the prevertebral layer, thus creating the anterior portion of the visceral space or the pretracheal space anterior to the esophagus and the retrovisceral space posteriorly. The pretracheal portion extends superiorly to the attachments of the strap muscles to the thyroid cartilage and hyoid bone. Inferiorly, the pretracheal portion of the visceral space extends to the anterior mediastinum at the level of the arch of the aorta and fibrous pericardium. The retrovisceral portion extends superiorly to become the retropharyngeal space, which continues to the cranial base. Inferiorly, the retrovisceral space extends into the mediastinum to approximately the level of the tracheal bifurcation, a common pathway for neck infection to spread into the mediastinum. The esophagus is enclosed in a tunica adventitia that is continuous with the middle layer of the deep cervical fascia (buccopharyngeal fascia) covering the pharynx.

Infections in the visceral space are serious. Early symptoms include sore throat, dysphagia, and a hoarse or muffled quality of the voice. The sore throat is a manifestation of edema and inflammation of the pharyngeal structures. Changes in vocal quality are due to laryngeal or supraglottic edema. This edema may progress to aphonia and airway obstruction. Perforation of viscera can lead to emphysema and crepitus in the neck, as well as mediastinal emphysema and pneumothorax. Dyspnea, possibly related to bronchopneumonia, may be prominent. Tenderness may be present over the lateral aspects of the hyoid bone and larynx. Neck swelling, with or without fluctuation, may occur. Open surgical therapy is required.

Submandibular Space Infections and Ludwig Angina

In continuity with the lateral pharyngeal space at its most anterior extent is the submandibular space. The limits of the submandibular space are the mucosa of the floor of the mouth and the tongue superiorly and the superficial layer of the deep cervical fascia as it runs from the hyoid bone inferiorly to the mandible superiorly (Figs. 100–14 and 100–15). According to Hollinshead,[25] the portion of the submandibular space that lies below the level of the mylohyoid muscle is referred to as the submaxillary space. This space is further divided into the submental space, which lies medial to the anterior bellies of the digastric muscles, and the subsidiary submaxillary space, which lies

lateral and posterior to these muscles. The sublingual space is superior to the mylohyoid muscle in the submandibular space and contains the sublingual glands, the lingual and hypoglossal nerves, and a portion of the submandibular gland and duct.

Contemporary head and neck anatomists consider some of these terms to be outdated. Instead, they divide the submandibular space into a supramylohyoid portion (equivalent to the sublingual space) and an inframylohyoid portion, which contains the structures in the submandibular triangle lateral to the digastric muscle and medial to the mandible and also contains the submental space medial to the anterior bellies of the digastric muscles (personal communication, Eugene Myers and Jonas Johnson, 2000). The supramylohyoid and inframylohyoid portions are in continuity posterior to the mylohyoid muscle (see Fig. 100–14). The space of the submandibular gland lies within the submandibular triangle.

Infections in this area often arise from mandibular dental disease, but they may also result from sialoadenitis, suppurative adenitis, or tonsillar disease. Early in the course, the infection is localized to the gingiva, floor of the mouth, and tongue. Later, infection may extend to involve all portions of the submandibular space on one side. Induration and edema of the floor of the mouth are noted with infection of the supramylohyoid portion of the submandibular space. If the inframylohyoid portion of the submandibular space is involved, induration and edema are palpable inferior and medial to the mandible. Infections in these spaces may progress to abscess formation (Fig. 100–16), with or without fluctuation, or persist as cellulitis. Trismus may be present as the infection extends to involve the suprahyoid musculature and internal pterygoid muscle.

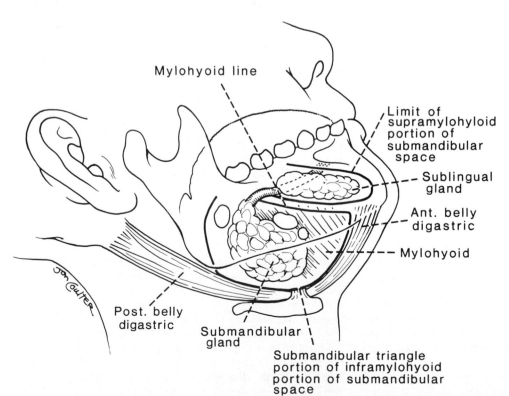

FIGURE 100–14. Selected structures seen in an anteroinferior oblique view of the submandibular space. Note how the supramylohyoid portion of the submandibular space is in continuity with the inframylohyoid portion and how the submandibular duct passes posterior to the mylohyoid muscle.

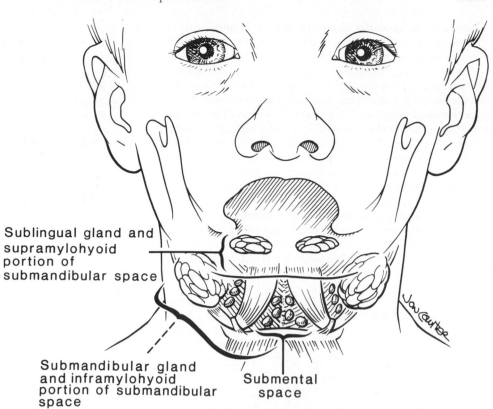

FIGURE 100–15. Anterior view of the submandibular space showing the relationship of the supramylohyoid, inframylohyoid, and submental portions of the submandibular space.

Sublingual gland and supramylohyoid portion of submandibular space

Submandibular gland and inframylohyoid portion of submandibular space

Submental space

Bilateral involvement of the submandibular spaces can lead to massive edema of the tongue and floor of the mouth, with posterior displacement of the tongue. Trismus from involvement of the internal pterygoid muscles combines with edema of the floor of the mouth and tongue to cause respiratory compromise. The patient has halitosis and difficulty handling secretions. The tissues of the supramylohyoid and inframylohyoid portions of the submandibular spaces are extremely indurated. This constellation of signs and symptoms is called Ludwig angina.

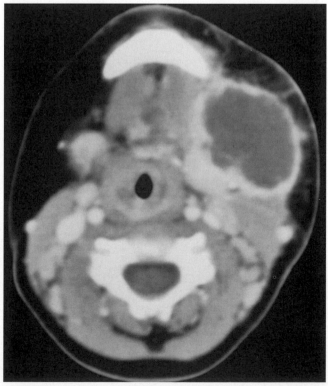

FIGURE 100–16. Computed tomographic scan of the neck in a child with a large abscess involving the left submandibular triangle area of the inframylohyoid portion of the submandibular space.

Bilateral involvement is always present in Ludwig angina. Laryngeal or supraglottic edema may occur and lead to vocal changes or airway obstruction.

In a true case of Ludwig angina, cellulitis with tension on soft tissues may be noted; an abscess may or may not be present. In Ludwig angina, release of tension is the basic surgical principle.[56] However, it is important to perform adequate exploration for abscesses and drain them. Even if imaging studies do not show an abscess, open surgical intervention is recommended in all but an exceptionally mild, early case. Again, early control of the airway should be strongly considered in all but exceptional mild, early cases. Tracheotomy is preferred. The surgical approach to Ludwig angina includes a generous horizontal incision approximately 1 cm above the hyoid bone (Fig. 100–17). This incision may be extended laterally to explore the space of the submandibular gland, with incision of the capsule if an abscess is suspected. The platysma is divided horizontally, while the superficial layer of the deep cervical fascia is incised vertically in the midline from the mandibular symphysis to the hyoid bone (Fig. 100–18). The digastric, mylohyoid, and a variable portion of the tongue muscles are divided in the midline sagittal plane to decompress the floor of the mouth. Blunt or finger dissection between the layers of muscles in a lateral direction is useful to identify and drain any abscesses. Iodoform-impregnated packing is placed for several days, and the wounds are left open.

Space of the Submandibular Gland

As the superficial layer of the deep cervical fascia splits to form a capsule around the submandibular gland, the space of the submandibular gland is formed. This space contains the submandibular gland as well as lymph nodes. On its medial surface, the fascia is perforated by the

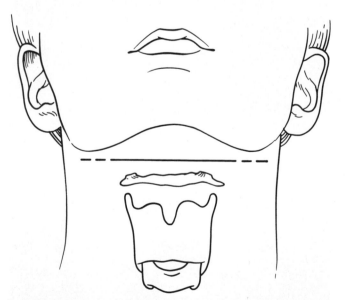

FIGURE 100–17. Incision for the surgical approach to Ludwig angina. Note that the central incision (*solid line*) can be extended laterally (*dotted lines*) to allow exploration and drainage of the space of the submandibular gland if an abscess in this space is suspected.

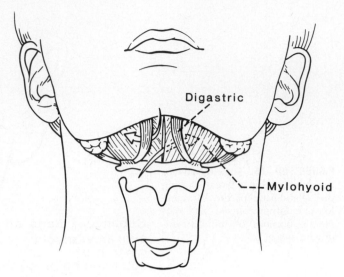

FIGURE 100–18. Surgical approach to Ludwig angina. After horizontal division of the platysma, the superficial layer of the deep cervical fascia, the mylohyoid, and a portion of the tongue muscles are divided in the midline. Blunt dissection is performed between the muscle layers in a lateral direction to drain any abscesses that may be present.

submandibular duct, which allows easy spread of infection to the supramylohyoid portion of the submandibular space (see Fig. 100–14). The space of the submandibular gland is part of the larger inframylohyoid portion of the submandibular space and is contained within the submandibular triangle, medial to the mandible and lateral to the digastric muscle. It may be drained by the open surgical approach described earlier.

Surgical versus Nonsurgical Therapy

Debate continues regarding the need for and timing of surgical intervention in head and neck space infections. With the availability of newer antimicrobial agents, some clinicians advocate withholding surgical intervention in patients with an abscess and providing treatment with a prolonged course of antimicrobial therapy. In our opinion, antimicrobial therapy is effective in treating most patients who have uncomplicated cellulitis or adenopathy in the head and neck spaces and who lack the signs and symptoms of airway obstruction. When patients have a compromised airway or fail to rapidly improve after antimicrobial therapy, incision and drainage are indicated, despite the lack of evidence from imaging that an abscess is present. If no improvement is seen over a reasonable period, such as 24 to 72 hours, and antimicrobial therapy is continued without surgical intervention, catastrophic events can occur (see Complications later). For patients with obvious abscesses, as determined by clinical examination and imaging studies, incision and drainage should be performed in the operating room. When imaging studies are negative or equivocal for the diagnosis of an abscess, an initial trial of medical management is appropriate. Repeated imaging studies during the course of medical treatment can be helpful, especially in a child who is not rapidly improving. The initial imaging studies may have been negative or equivocal, but the follow-up study may be positive. The most effective method to determine the causative organisms and select the most appropriate antimicrobial agents is to obtain material for culture during fine-needle aspiration of the inflammatory mass or during incision and drainage in the operating room. Incision and drainage are indicated when the child fails to rapidly improve after empirical treatment, when complications such as airway compromise occur, or when an unusual organism is suspected, such as in a patient who is immunocompromised. Needle aspiration in an awake infant or young child is not feasible and can be dangerous. However, needle aspiration for diagnosis and for evacuating purulent material can be performed in selected older children and adolescents. In one study, the combination of one or two needle aspirations plus intravenous antimicrobial therapy for neck abscesses in children was successful in 56% of 18 abscesses in 17 children.[10] Children with unilocular and small abscesses had a higher response rate to needle aspiration than did those with multilocular and large abscess cavities, which more often required incision and drainage. Needle aspiration has also been reported to be successful in the treatment of nonperitonsillar head and neck abscesses in adults.[23]

One author reported resolution of seven small, early, CT-documented retropharyngeal and lateral pharyngeal abscesses in children who were administered intravenous antibiotics as the sole treatment.[12] Successful treatment of a child with Ludwig angina and airway compromise by endotracheal intubation and intravenous antibiotics has been reported.[40] In a series involving 65 children with retropharyngeal abscesses, 73% were treated with incision and drainage and 27% were treated medically.[54] In another series of 17 children with retropharyngeal abscesses, 81% were treated with incision and drainage and 19% with antibiotics alone.[37]

For abscesses associated with airway obstruction, septicemia, or complications and for those that fail to respond to needle aspiration, incision and drainage are indicated. For noncomplicated head and neck space abscesses, the choice of using intravenous antibiotics alone versus needle aspiration or incision and drainage plus intravenous antibiotics is up to the clinician, although we strongly recommend incision and drainage.

Complications

Complications of head and neck space infections include airway obstruction, septicemia, carotid artery rupture, thrombosis of the internal jugular vein, mediastinitis with subsequent rupture of one of the great vessels into the chest, and rupture of an abscess into the pharynx, all of which can be fatal. Sentinel bleeding from the pharynx or ear may be a harbinger of arterial erosion and massive hemorrhage. Arteriography may be indicated to identify the bleeding vessel if the clinical course allows time for such an examination. Obtaining access to the great vessels for ligation to control hemorrhage is critical in this situation. Reisner et al[45] reported that internal carotid pseudoaneurysm complicated a staphylococcal lateral pharyngeal space abscess. Symptoms included a pulsatile neck mass,

Horner syndrome, hemoptysis, and hemorrhagic shock. The pseudoaneurysm was managed by angiography and endovascular occlusion.

Britt et al[9] reviewed the literature from the last 30 years and found that 29 cases of Ludwig angina in children were reported. Five of the 29 (17%) children died of causes that included airway obstruction, mediastinitis, empyema, pneumonia, and sepsis.

Complications that occur during the course of a head and neck space infection require an open surgical approach for drainage of the space. An intrathoracic complication during the course of a head and neck space infection requires consultation with a chest surgeon.

Thrombosis of the internal jugular vein is characterized by spiking fevers, chills, and facial and orbital swelling, with evidence of septic emboli in the pulmonary and, occasionally, the systemic circulation. The diagnosis of internal jugular vein thrombosis may be made on the basis of the typical clinical picture plus evidence of thrombosis as detected by CT with contrast, US, or MRI with flow-sensitive pulse sequences.[3, 36] Arteriography and venography appear to be unnecessarily invasive for the diagnosis of most cases of internal jugular vein thrombosis because the previously listed methods are reliable and safer (personal communication, Charles Fitz, 2001). Internal jugular vein thrombosis in the course of head and neck space infection may require systemic anticoagulation or even ligation with possible excision of the vein.[3]

An abscess may rupture into the pharynx or trachea and cause asphyxiation, pneumonia, lung abscess, or empyema. Inflammatory torticollis with cervical vertebral subluxation requiring cervical traction and fusion to prevent spinal cord injury has been reported to occur during head and neck space infections.[8] Neuropathies involving cranial nerves IX, X, XI, and XII may complicate lateral pharyngeal space infections.[31] Horner syndrome may occur during lateral pharyngeal space infections.[58] Because life-threatening complications can develop, the clinician must make the diagnosis as rapidly as possible and institute the most effective methods of management.

SELECTED REFERENCES

Hollinshead W (ed). Anatomy for Surgeons, vol 1, 3rd ed. Philadelphia, Harper & Row, 1982, pp 269–289.
> *An excellent description of the fascia and fascial spaces of the head and neck. This chapter should be studied by all physicians involved in the care of patients with head and neck space infections.*

Holt GR, Tinsley PP. Peritonsillar abscesses in children. Laryngoscope 91:1226, 1981.
> *This retrospective study of 41 children with peritonsillar abscesses discusses the incidence of recurrent tonsillitis and recurrent peritonsillar abscess. It clearly describes the indications for tonsillectomy associated with peritonsillar abscess but does not address the timing of tonsillectomy.*

Mosher H. The submaxillary fossa approach to deep pus in the neck. Trans Am Acad Ophthalmol Otolaryngol 34:19, 1929.
> *Although Mosher's T-shaped neck incision has been abandoned for the more cosmetic horizontal neck incision, his classic description is an excellent guide to the open surgical approach to drainage of infection in the fascial spaces of the neck.*

Richardson KA, Birck H. Peritonsillar abscess in the pediatric population. Otolaryngol Head Neck Surg 89:907, 1981.

In this retrospective study, 55 children underwent immediate tonsillectomy for peritonsillar abscess and had lower morbidity and a shorter hospital stay than did 60 children treated by incision and drainage. The safety and the advantages of immediate versus interval tonsillectomy are described. Selection criteria for immediate tonsillectomy in the treatment of peritonsillar abscess are not addressed by these authors.

Weber AL, Baker AS, Montgomery WW. Inflammatory lesions of the neck, including fascial spaces—evaluation by computed tomography and magnetic resonance imaging. Isr J Med Sci 28:241, 1992.

A concise description of the anatomy of the fascial spaces of the head and neck is provided along with pertinent CT and MRI criteria that help identify cellulitis, abscesses, and internal jugular vein thrombosis.

REFERENCES

1. Alvi A. *Mycobacterium chelonei* causing recurrent neck abscess. Pediatr Infect Dis J 12:617, 1993.
2. Asmar BI. Bacteriology of retropharyngeal abscess in children. Pediatr Infect Dis J 9:595, 1990.
3. Bach MC, Roediger JH, Rinder HM. Septic anaerobic jugular phlebitis with pulmonary embolism: problems in management. Rev Infect Dis 10:424, 1988.
4. Battista RA, Baredes S, Krieger A, Fieldman R. Prevertebral space infections associated with cervical osteomyelitis. Otolaryngol Head Neck Surg 108:160, 1993.
5. Beeden AG, Evans JNG. Quinsy tonsillectomy—a further report. J Laryngol Otol 84:443, 1970.
6. Behrman R, Vaughan V, Nelson W (eds). Nelson Textbook of Pediatrics, 13th ed. Philadelphia, WB Saunders, 1987, pp 529, 632, 638–639, 710–711.
7. BenAmi T, Yousefzadeh DK, Aramburo MJ. Presuppurative phase of retropharyngeal infection: contribution of ultrasonography in the diagnosis and treatment. Pediatr Radiol 21:23, 1990.
8. Bredenkamp JK, Maceri DR. Inflammatory torticollis in children. Arch Otolaryngol Head Neck Surg 116:310, 1990.
9. Britt J, Josephson G, Gross C. Ludwig's angina in the pediatric population: report of a case and review of the literature. Int J Pediatr Otorhinolaryngol 52:79, 2000.
10. Brodsky L, Belles W, Brody A, et al. Needle aspiration of neck abscesses in children. Clin Pediatr (Phila) 31:71, 1992.
11. Brook I. Microbiology of abscesses of the head and neck in children. Ann Otol Rhinol Laryngol 96:429, 1987.
12. Broughton RA. Nonsurgical management of deep neck infections in children. Pediatr Infect Dis J 11:14, 1992.
13. Burke J. Angina ludovici: a translation, together with a biography of Wilhelm Fredrick von Ludwig. Bull Hist Med 7:115, 1939.
14. Carithers HA. Cat-scratch disease: an overview based on a study of 1200 patients. Am J Dis Child 139:1124, 1985.
15. Charpy A. Aponeuroses de cou. In Poirier P, Charpy A (eds). Traite de Anatomic Humaine, vol 2, f. 1. Paris, Masson, 1912, pp 258–280.
16. Choi S, Vezina L, Grundfast K. Relative incidence and alternative approaches for surgical drainage of different types of deep neck abscesses in children. Arch Otolaryngol Head Neck Surg 123:1271, 1997.
17. Glasier CM, Stark JE, Jacobs RF, et al. CT and ultrasound imaging of retropharyngeal abscesses in children. AJNR Am J Neuroradiology 13:1191, 1992.
18. Grahne B. Abscess tonsillectomy. Arch Otolaryngol 68:332, 1958.
19. Grodinsky M, Holyoke E. The fasciae and fascial spaces of the head, neck and adjacent region. Am J Anat 63:367, 1938.
20. Haeggstrom A, Gustafsson O, Engquist S, Engstrom CF. Intraoral ultrasonography in the diagnosis of peritonsillar abscess. Otolaryngol Head Neck Surg 108:243, 1993.
21. Haug RH, Wible RT, Lieberman J. Measurement standards for the prevertebral region in the lateral soft-tissue radiograph of the neck. J Oral Maxillofac Surg 49:1149, 1991.
22. Herbild O, Bonding P. Peritonsillar abscess: recurrence rate and treatment. Arch Otolaryngol 107:540, 1981.
23. Herzon FS. Management of nonperitonsillar abscesses of the head and neck with needle aspiration. Laryngoscope 95:780, 1985.
24. Herzon FS. Permucosal needle drainage of peritonsillar abscesses. Arch Otolaryngol 110:104, 1984.
25. Hollinshead W (ed). Anatomy for Surgeons, vol 1, 3rd ed. Philadelphia, Harper & Row, 1982, pp 269–289.
26. Holt GR, McManus K, Newman RK, et al. Computed tomography in the diagnosis of deep-neck infections. Arch Otolaryngol 108:693, 1982.
27. Holt GR, Tinsley PP. Peritonsillar abscesses in children. Laryngoscope 91:1226, 1981.
28. Kennedy TL. Curettage of nontuberculous mycobacterial cervical lymphadenitis. Arch Otolaryngol Head Neck Surg 118:759, 1992.
29. Kraus R, Han BK, Babcock DS, Oestreich AE. Sonography of neck masses in children. Am J Radiol 146:609, 1986.
30. Kreutzer EW, Jafek BW, Johnson ML, Zunkel DE. Ultrasonography in the preoperative evaluation of neck abscesses. Head Neck Surg 4:290, 1982.
31. Langenbrunner DJ, Dajani S. Pharyngomaxillary space abscess with carotid artery erosion. Arch Otolaryngol 94:447, 1971.
32. Lazor JB, Cunningham MJ, Eavey RD, Weber AL. Comparison of computed tomography and surgical findings in deep neck infections. Otolaryngol Head Neck Surg 111:746, 1994.
33. Lewis GJS, Leithiser RE, Glasier CM, et al. Ultrasonography of pediatric neck masses. Ultrasound Q 7:315, 1989.
34. McCaskey CH. Ludwig's angina. Arch Otolaryngol 36:467, 1942.
35. McCurdy JA. Peritonsillar abscess: a comparison of treatment by immediate tonsillectomy and interval tonsillectomy. Arch Otolaryngol 103:414, 1977.
36. Merhar GL, Colley DP, Clark RA, Herwig SR. Computed tomographic demonstration of cervical abscess and jugular vein thrombosis. Arch Otolaryngol 107:313, 1981.
37. Morrison JE, Pashley NRT. Retropharyngeal abscesses in children: a 10-year review. Pediatr Emerg Care 4:9, 1988.
38. Mosher H. The submaxillary fossa approach to deep pus in the neck. Trans Am Acad Ophthalmol Otolaryngol 34:19, 1929.
39. Muckleston HS. Angina ludovici and kindred affections: an historical and clinical study. Ann Otol Rhinol Laryngol 37:711, 1928.
40. Nguyen VD, Potter JL, Hersch-Schick MR. Ludwig angina: an uncommon and potentially lethal neck infection. AJNR Am J Neuroradiol 13:215, 1992.
41. Nielsen VM, Greisen O. Peritonsillar abscess. I. Cases treated by incision and drainage: a follow-up investigation. J Laryngol Otol 95:801, 1981.
42. Nyberg DA, Jeffrey RB, Brant-Zawadzki M, et al. Computed tomography of cervical infections. J Comput Assist Tomogr 9:288, 1985.
43. Paparella MM, Shumrick DA, Meyerhoff WL, Seid AB (eds). Otolaryngology, vol 3, 2nd ed. Philadelphia, WB Saunders, 1980, pp 2272–2273.
44. Reinhardt JF, Johnston L, Ruane P, et al. A randomized, double-blind comparison of sulbactam/ampicillin and clindamycin for the treatment of aerobic and aerobic-anaerobic infections. Rev Infect Dis 8(Suppl 5):569, 1986.
45. Reisner A, Marshall G, Bryant K, et al. Endovascular occlusion of a carotid pseudoaneurysm complicating deep neck-space infection in a child. Case report. J Neurosurg 91:510, 1999.
46. Retsema JA, English AR, Girard A, et al. Sulbactam/ampicillin in vitro spectrum, potency, and activity in models of acute infection. Rev Infect Dis 8(Suppl 5):528, 1986.
47. Richardson KA, Birck H. Peritonsillar abscess in the pediatric population. Otolaryngol Head Neck Surg 89:907, 1981.
48. Robson CD, Hazra R, Barnes PD, et al: Nontuberculous mycobacterial infection of the head and neck in immunocompetent children. AJNR Am J Neuroradiol 20:1829, 1999.
49. Schechter GL, Sly DE, Roper AL, Jackson RT. Changing face of treatment of peritonsillar abscess. Laryngoscope 92:757, 1982.
50. Sichel J, Gomori JM, Saah D, Elidan J. Parapharyngeal-space abscess in children: the role of CT for diagnosis and treatment. Int J Pediatr Otorhinolaryngol 35:213, 1996.
51. Som P, Curtin H. The fasciae and spaces of the head and neck: an analysis of the confusion in the literature with new anatomic correlation. Unpublished manuscript, 1993.

52. Syriopoulou V, Bitsi M, Theodoridis C, et al. Clinical efficacy of sulbactam/ampicillin in pediatric infections caused by ampicillin-resistant or penicillin-resistant organisms. Rev Infect Dis 8(Suppl 5): 630, 1986.
53. Templer JW, Holinger LD, Wood RP, et al. Immediate tonsillectomy for the treatment of peritonsillar abscess. Am J Surg 134:596, 1977.
54. Thomas TT. Ludwig's angina: an anatomical, clinical and statistical study. Univ Pennsylvania Med Bull 21:2, 1908.
55. Thompson JW, Cohen SR, Reddix P. Retropharyngeal abscess in children: a retrospective and historical analysis. Laryngoscope 98: 589, 1988.
56. Topazian R, Goldberg M (eds). Management of Infections of the Oral and Maxillofacial Regions. Philadelphia, WB Saunders, 1981, pp 196–199.
57. Tschiassny K. Ludwig's angina—a surgical approach based on anatomical and pathological criteria. Ann Otol Rhinol Laryngol 56:937, 1947.
58. Ungkanont K, Yellon R, Weissman J, et al. Head and neck space infections in infants and children. Otolaryngol Head Neck Surg 112: 375, 1995.
59. Varghese S, Hengerer AS, Putnam T, Colgan MT. Neck abscess causing Horner's syndrome. N Y State J Med 82:1855, 1982.
60. Weber AL, Baker AS, Montgomery WW. Inflammatory lesions of the neck, including fascial spaces—evaluation by computed tomography and magnetic resonance imaging. Isr J Med Sci 28:241, 1992.
61. Yonetsu K, Izumi M, Nakamura T. Deep facial infections of odontogenic origin: CT assessment of pathways of space involvement. AJNR Am J Neuroradiol 19:123, 1998.
62. Zangwill KM, Jamilton DH, Perkins BA, et al. Cat scratch disease in Connecticut: epidemiology, risk factors, and evaluation of a new diagnostic test. N Engl J Med 329:8, 1993.

101

Malignant Tumors of the Head and Neck

Kenneth R. Whittemore, Jr., M.D., and Michael J. Cunningham, M.D.

Physicians who treat children must have a working knowledge of the neoplasms that may occur in the head and neck region in the pediatric population. Cancer ranks second only to trauma as a cause of mortality in children 1 to 14 years of age, accounting for approximately 1500 childhood deaths annually.[203] An estimated 5% of primary malignant tumors in children originate in the head and neck, with this figure approximating 50% in infants.[399] One of every four malignancies in the pediatric age group eventually involves the head and neck region.[362]

Five extensive reviews of head and neck malignancies in the pediatric population have been published.[77, 82, 172, 182, 360] A 28-year review at the University of Pittsburgh identified 411 children with malignancies arising or initially manifesting within the head and neck region (Table 101–1). The most striking observation made by all series is the rarity of epidermoid carcinoma in children in comparison with adults. Lymphomas, especially Hodgkin disease, are the predominant neoplasms in this region. Soft tissue sarcomas, specifically rhabdomyosarcomas, are the next most common. Bone sarcomas are comparatively rare.[182] Thyroid carcinomas and salivary gland malignancies are the most common neoplasms of glandular origin, with papillary carcinoma and mucoepidermoid carcinoma being the most prevalent in each gland, respectively.[182] Nasopharyngeal carcinoma (NPC) is the principal epithelial malignancy; melanoma and other skin cancers are rare. Neuroblastoma and germ cell neoplasms may occur as either primary or metastatic lesions in the head and neck.

The distribution of the histologic types of malignancy in the head and neck varies with patient age and sex. Age-specific presentation patterns are listed in Table 101–2. Malignant teratomas are primarily congenital lesions. Neuroblastomas tend to occur in infants.[399] Sarcomatous neoplasms span the entire pediatric age range, with the majority of rhabdomyosarcomas occurring in the preschool years. The non-Hodgkin lymphomas (NHLs) likewise demonstrate a broad age range, predominantly clustered slightly later in childhood, that is, during the school-age years.[159, 182] Hodgkin lymphoma (HL) usually occurs in early adolescence[182]; it rarely occurs in children younger than 5 years of age. Thyroid carcinoma, NPC, and salivary gland neoplasms also occur predominantly in adolescents. Thyroid carcinoma is more common in girls, whereas HL and NHL are more common in boys.[145, 182]

The survival rate of children with head and neck cancer, particularly those with lymphoma and sarcoma, has improved significantly over the last 30 years (Table 101–3).[41, 345] This improvement can be attributed to a combination of earlier disease recognition, the evolution of coherent and aggressive clinicopathologic staging systems, the establishment of multimodality treatment protocols, and the improvement in craniofacial resection techniques for previously unresectable neoplasms.

Early recognition requires a knowledge of those historical factors known or strongly suspected to increase the risk of malignancy in a child. Examples include a family history of childhood cancer, a previous primary neoplasm, a known systemic cancer predisposition, and exposure to radiation therapy or to carcinogenic or immunosuppressive drugs.[240, 256]

The most common manifestation of a malignancy of the head and neck in the pediatric age group is an asymptomatic mass. The neck is the most common anatomic site of manifestation (Table 101–4). The oropharynx, nasopharynx, orbit, salivary glands, face and scalp, and auricular region follow in descending order of frequency. Early signs and symptoms such as lymphadenopathy, otalgia, otorrhea, rhinorrhea, nasal obstruction, and headache are also common to the benign illnesses affecting this age group. More recognizable symptoms heralding upper aerodigestive tract compromise include voice change, hoarseness, stridor, dysphagia, and hemoptysis. These typically occur late in the course of malignant disease. Clinical factors that increase the risk that a mass may be malignant include onset in the neonatal period, history of rapid or progressive growth, skin ulceration, fixation to underlying structures, or a firm mass greater than 3 cm in diameter.[238] Despite the comparatively high frequency of reactive cervical lymphadenopathy, congenital lesions, and benign neoplasms in the pediatric age group, a firm neck mass in a child without the usual signs of inflammation should be considered possibly malignant until proven otherwise.

A child suspected of having a malignancy in the head and neck region requires a complete otolaryngologic and systemic evaluation. Particular attention during the physical examination should be directed at the abdominal, axillary, and inguinal areas owing to the frequency with which head and neck malignancy is part of a generalized

TABLE 101–1. Histopathologic Features of 411 Pediatric Head and Neck Malignancies

Pathologic Diagnosis and Histopathologic Subtype	Subtotal	No. of Children	Percentage of Total
Hodgkin lymphoma (HL)		131	32.0
Nodular sclerosis (NS)	63		
Mixed cellularity (MC)	28		
Lymphocyte predominance	15		
Both NS and MC	12		
Paragranuloma°	6		
Granuloma°	3		
Unclassified	3		
Lymphocyte depletion	2		
Non-Hodgkin lymphoma (NHL)		117	28.5
Lymphoblastic	59		
Lymphocytic, poorly differentiated	20		
Undifferentiated, Burkitt	14		
Histiocytic	12		
Undifferentiated, non-Burkitt	8		
Mixed lymphocytic-histiocytic	2		
Unclassified	2		
Rhabdomyosarcoma (RMS)		53	13.0
Embryonal	46		
Alveolar	4		
Unclassified	3		
Other sarcomas		19	4.5
Mesenchymal chondrosarcoma	3		
Ewing sarcoma	4		
Fibrosarcoma	2		
Malignant fibrohistiocytoma	2		
Synovial sarcoma	2		
Neurogenous sarcoma	1		
Chondromyxoid sarcoma	2		
Osteogenic sarcoma	2		
Unclassified	1		
Thyroid carcinoma (TC)		38	9.0
Papillary adenocarcinoma	21		
Mixed papillary–follicular	11		
Follicular adenocarcinoma	4		
Medullary carcinoma	1		
Mixed medullary and papillary	1		
Nasopharyngeal carcinoma (NPC)		18	4.5
Squamous cell carcinoma	6		
Undifferentiated carcinoma	8		
Nonkeratinizing carcinoma	4		
Neuroblastoma		20	5.0
Salivary gland malignancies (SGM)		10	2.0
Mucoepidermoid carcinoma	7		
Adenocarcinoma	3		
Malignant teratoma		3	1.0
Other uncommon tumors		2	.05
Squamous cell carcinoma of the skin	1		
Parathyroid adenoma	1		
TOTALS		411	100

Histopathologic subtype classifications used are as follows: HL, Rye classification[222] and Jackson and Parker classification[171]; NHL, modified Rappaport classification[126]; RMS, Intergroup Rhabdomyosarcoma Study classification; NPC, World Health Organization classification[340]; TC and SGM, standard tumor nomenclature.

process involving these regions. The importance of a thorough otolaryngologic examination is underscored by the observation that one of every six children with a malignant neck mass has a primary oronasopharyngeal lesion.[174] Otologic, nasal, oral, and neck examinations are easily performed in most children. Visualization of the nasopharynx, hypopharynx, and larynx may be accomplished by flexible fiberoptic nasopharyngoscopy in children of all ages. Laryngoscopy and pharyngoscopy under general anesthesia are required for those children who cannot be examined satisfactorily in the outpatient setting.

Axial and coronal computed tomography (CT) and magnetic resonance imaging (MRI) are the radiologic studies of choice in evaluating suspected neoplasms of the head and neck.[291] CT can help differentiate between solid and cystic masses; it also allows documentation of bone erosion, invasion of contiguous structures, and intracranial extension. Advantages of MRI include better contrast of tissues of similar densities, better delineation of neoplasms from surrounding soft tissue structures, the ability to obtain multiplanar images, and the avoidance of ionizing radiation or intravenous iodinated contrast material. Disadvantages of MRI include prolonged imaging times with the need to keep children restrained and sometimes sedated, high sensitivity to motion, poor distinction of bone, and imaging prohibition resulting from the pres-

TABLE 101–2. Age Distribution of 411 Children with Head and Neck Malignancies

	Average Age (Yr)	Age Range (Yr)
Malignant teratoma	—	NB
Neuroblastoma	1.9	NB–5
Rhabdomyosarcoma	6.4	NB–17
Non-Hodgkin lymphoma	8.0	2–18
Other sarcomas	8.1	NB–18
Hodgkin lymphoma	11.8	4–18
Thyroid carcinoma	12.4	6–18
Nasopharyngeal carcinoma	14.4	9–18
Salivary gland malignancies	15.2	7–8

NB, newborn.
From University of Pittsburgh, Children's and Eye and Ear Hospitals, 1965 to 1993.

ence of metallic foreign bodies or implants.[83] Radionuclide scan and uptake studies may be warranted in the evaluation of suspected thyroid neoplasms.[91] Systemic neoplastic evaluation may require skeletal survey, bone scan, liver spleen scan, or intravenous pyelogram. Positron emission tomography (PET) has also recently been used to evaluate primary tumors, tumor response to treatment, and evidence of local disease recurrence.[143] The primary goals of the radiologic assessment are (1) to more precisely define the primary lesion and (2) to detect metastatic disease for accurate clinical staging.

Examination under general anesthesia complements radiographic studies in defining the extent of the primary tumor and allowing for adequate tissue sampling for histopathologic diagnosis. Biopsy of pharyngeal and laryngeal lesions is performed under direct visualization at the time of operative examination. Biopsy of external head and neck lesions is done in either an excisional or incisional fashion, depending on the size and location of the mass. An excisional biopsy may be therapeutic as well as diagnostic. Fine-needle aspiration (FNA) for cytologic study is useful in the assessment of suspected thyroid gland lesions, salivary gland lesions, and additional selected neck masses (e.g., metastatic nodes).[91, 92, 238, 250] The reliability of FNA is highly dependent on the expertise of the cytopathologist. The use of monoclonal antibody techniques and DNA amplification with polymerase chain reaction has improved the reliability, sensitivity, and specificity of making an accurate cytopathologic diagnosis.[110, 250] A negative needle biopsy still requires open biopsy for confir-

mation if the clinician has a high index of suspicion. Other histopathologic studies of potential benefit include bone marrow and cerebral spinal fluid evaluations, blood assays for tumor-produced substances such as alpha-fetoprotein and beta-human chorionic gonadotropin (hCG) in suspected germ cell tumors, and genetic testing for markers such as n-*myc* in suspected neuroblastomas.[159] Communication between the surgeon and the pathologist regarding the clinical presentation is essential for establishing the correct diagnosis.[113]

The treatment of malignant neoplasms of the head and neck in the pediatric age group is dictated by the histopathologic diagnosis and the extent or stage of the disease. Coordination of treatment often requires the interaction of many pediatric specialties and support services because most solid malignancies require multimodality therapy.[159, 299] Radiation therapy and multidrug chemotherapy are the two primary treatment modalities for the lymphoid and sarcomatous pediatric malignancies. Surgical resection is the primary treatment of glandular neoplasms and has a primary therapeutic role for mesenchymal tumors that are accessible to complete excision. Surgical biopsy is required for initial diagnostic purposes and sometimes for staging. Surgery may additionally be required for debulking and salvage procedures, for airway maintenance, for follow-up endoscopic or operative examination purposes, and for routine and specialized otolaryngologic care.

Hodgkin Lymphoma

HL is a malignant neoplasm of the lymphoreticular system with a bimodal distribution; one peak occurs in adolescence and young adulthood and another peak at age older than 50 years. In contrast to NHL, HL is uncommon in preadolescent children and rarely occurs in children younger than 5 years of age.[211, 253] There is an approximate 2:1 male predominance. Although no definitive causal factors are known, there is an association of HL with prior Epstein-Barr virus (EBV) infection such as infectious mononucleosis.[4] An increased incidence of positive EBV titers is documented in patients with HL.[166]

HL is distinguished morphologically from the NHLs by the diagnostic presence of Reed-Sternberg (RS) cells.[184] RS cells have multinucleated nuclei, large nucleoli, and a "halo" clear zone around the nucleolus.[166] Al-

TABLE 101–3. Survival Trends of Children Younger than Age 15 for Five Most Common Malignancies in Head and Neck Region

	Relative 5-Year Survival Rate (%)					
	1960–1963	1970–1973	1974–1976	1977–1979	1983–1988	1989–1994
Hodgkin disease	52	90	79	83	88	92
Non-Hodgkin lymphoma	18	26	44	56	69	78
	—	44	57	67	—	—
Soft tissue sarcomas	—	34	53	64	—	—
Rhabdomyosarcoma	25	40	49	52	55	69
Neuroblastoma						

Adapted from Silverberg E, Lubera J. Cancer statistics, 1988; and CA Cancer J Clin 38:21, 1988; Boring CC, Squires TS, Tong T. Cancer statistics, 1993. CA Cancer J Clin 43:7, 1993; Landis SH, Murray T, Bolden S. CA Cancer J Clin 49:8, 1999.

TABLE 101–4. Anatomic Locations of 411 Pediatric Head and Neck Malignancies

Site	Pathologic Diagnosis	Subtotal	No. of Children	Percentage of Total
Neck			286	70.0
	Hodgkin lymphoma	131		
	Non-Hodgkin lymphoma	78		
	Thyroid carcinoma	38		
	Neuroblastoma	20°		
	Rhabdomyosarcoma	5		
	Other sarcomas	10		
	Teratoma	3		
	Parathyroid adenoma	1		
Oronasopharynx			71	17.0
	Non-Hodgkin lymphoma	33		
	Nasopharyngeal carcinoma	18		
	Rhabdomyosarcoma	18		
	Fibrohistiocytoma	2		
Orbit/paranasal sinuses			21	5.0
	Rhabdomyosarcoma	19		
	Chondrosarcoma	2		
Parotid			14	3.0
	Mucoepidermoid carcinoma	5		
	Non-Hodgkin lymphoma	5		
	Adenocarcinoma	2		
	Rhabdomyosarcoma	2		
Facial region			10	2.5
	Rhabdomyosarcoma	3		
	Synovial sarcoma	2		
	Osteogenic sarcoma	2		
	Chondrosarcoma	2		
	Non-Hodgkin lymphoma	1		
Ear/temporal bone			6	1.5
	Rhabdomyosarcoma	5		
	Squamous cell carcinoma	1		
Tongue			3	1.0
	Mucoepidermoid carcinoma	2		
	Adenocarcinoma	1		
TOTALS			411	100

° Fifteen neuroblastomas were likely cervical metastases from the abdomen.
From University of Pittsburgh, Children's and Eye and Ear Hospitals, 1965 to 1993.

though these cells represent the common malignant component of the diverse histologic subtypes of HL, the histogenesis of the RS cell remains an enigma. The Rye classification system recognizes four HL subtypes: lymphocyte predominance, lymphocyte depletion, nodular sclerosis, and mixed cellularity (Table 101–5).[222] The lymphocyte predominance category is characterized by an abundance of mature lymphocytes with only occasional RS cells and most closely resembles reactive hyperplasia.[166] The lymphocyte depletion group demonstrates few lymphocytes in association with an abundance of pleomorphic RS cells, disorderly fibrosis, or both. In the nodular sclerosis variant, broad bands of collagen divide the

involved lymph node into cellular nodules. The cellular proliferation within these nodules is characterized by the presence of "lacunar cells," variant RS cells with well-defined cellular borders surrounded by a clear space. In the mixed cellularity subtype, the lymph node is obliterated by a heterogeneous population of cells, including lymphocytes, plasma cells, eosinophils, neutrophils, and frequent RS cells. Mixed cellularity HL is the subtype most commonly associated with human immunodeficiency virus (HIV) infection.[166] About two thirds of pediatric patients have nodular sclerosis disease at the time of presentation; lymphocyte predominance and mixed cellularity disease are relatively more common in children age

TABLE 101–5. Histopathologic Classifications of Hodgkin Disease

Jackson and Parker (1944)	Lukes and Butler (1966)	Rye (1966)
Paragranuloma	Lymphocytic and/or histiocytic (a) Nodular (b) Diffuse	Lymphocytic predominance
	Nodular sclerosis	Nodular sclerosis
Granuloma	Mixed diffuse fibrosis	Mixed cellularity
Sarcoma	Reticular	Lymphocytic depletion

From Kapadia S. Hematologic diseases: malignant lymphomas, leukemias, plasma cell dyscrasias, histiocytosis X, and reactive lymph node lesions. In: Barnes L, ed. Surgical Pathology of the Head and Neck. New York, Marcel Dekker, 1985, p 1075.

TABLE 101–6. Real Classification

"Classic" Hodgkin lymphoma	Lymphocyte rich Nodular sclerosis Mixed cellularity Lymphocyte depletion

Nodular lymphocyte predominant Hodgkin lymphoma (NLPHL)
Adapted from Harris NL. Hodgkin's lymphoma: classification, diagnosis, and grading. Semin Hematol 36:220, 1999; Harris NL, Jaffe ES, Stein H, et al. A revised European-American classification of lymphoid neoplasms: a proposal from the International Lymphoma Study Group. Blood 84:1361, 1994, 1999; ref. Harris, et al., 1994.

10 years or younger; the lymphocyte depletion subtype is rarely encountered in children.[75, 211] A pathologic classification, called the REAL classification system (Revised European-American Lymphoma), divides HL into two broad categories, "classical" HL and nodular lymphocyte predominant HL (NLPHL) (Table 101–6).[150, 151] The rationale for this classification system is the recognition that NLPHL is clinically less aggressive than classic HL, with a decreased incidence of systemic symptoms and mediastinal involvement as well as typical manifestation at an earlier stage.[150]

Hodgkin disease arises within lymph nodes in more than 90% of childhood and adult cases.[95] The typical patient with HL has asymmetric lymphadenopathy that is firm, rubbery, and nontender. The cervical and supraclavicular lymph nodes are the most frequent sites of manifestation (Fig. 101–1).[166] Axillary, inguinal, and generalized lymphadenopathy are uncommon. Extranodal primary sites are rare. Extranodal involvement does occur with progression of the disease. The spleen, liver, lung, bone, and bone marrow are the common organ systems affected.

Unlike NHL, HL of Waldeyer ring is rare. Mediastinal node involvement, however, is common, particularly in association with right supraclavicular nodal disease.[211, 253] Obstruction of the superior vena cava or tracheobronchial tree may occur as a complication of such mediastinal lymphadenopathy. Laparotomy reveals retroperitoneal and abdominal lymph node involvement in approximately 40% of HL patients.[131] The spleen is the most frequent extranodal site of HL. There is a strong association between splenic and abdominal lymph node involvement.[130] Similarly, hepatic involvement occurs almost exclusively in the presence of splenic disease. Pulmonary involvement is often due to extranodal spread from contiguous mediastinal and hilar lymph node disease.[123] Bone and bone marrow involvement, in contrast, represent hematogenous metastases.[275] Neutropenia, thrombocytopenia, and anemia may occur with advanced bone marrow infiltration. At presentation, children with HL have nonspecific systemic symptoms, termed B-symptoms, in 25% to 30% of cases; these may include unexplained fever, night sweats, weight loss, weakness, anorexia, and pruritus.[166, 211]

The diagnosis of HL is made by lymph node biopsy. Once the diagnosis is established, it is essential to define the full extent of disease in each patient before instituting specific treatment. The Ann Arbor staging system (Table 101–7) is based on the premise that HL arises in a unifocal lymph node site, spreads via lymphatics to contiguous lymph node groups, and involves extralymphatic

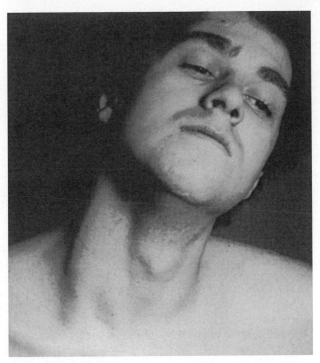

FIGURE 101–1. Hodgkin disease occurring in typical fashion as a mass in the right neck of a 17-year-old male.

sites, including the spleen, principally by hematogenous dissemination.[56, 204] The system recognizes that localized extralymphatic spread may occur and that such patients do as well as comparable patients of the same stage without local extralymphoid disease. Such involvement is denoted by the letter E after the stage designation. Constitutional symptoms of unexplained fever, night sweats, and weight loss are also considered significant in the staging of the disease and are designated A when absent and B when present.

Clinical staging (CS) includes history, physical examination, radiologic procedures, and laboratory tests other

TABLE 101–7. Ann Arbor Staging Classification of Hodgkin Disease*

Stage	Definition
I	Involvement of a single lymph node region or a single extralymphatic organ or site (IE)
II	Involvement of two or more lymph node regions or localized involvement of an extralymphatic site and one or more lymph node regions on same side of the diaphragm (IIE)
III	Involvement of lymph node regions on both sides of the diaphragm, which may also be accompanied by involvement of the spleen (IIIS) or an extralymphatic organ or site (IIIE)
IV	Diffuse or disseminated involvement of one or more extralymphatic organs or tissues, with or without associated lymph node involvement

* Each stage is subdivided into A and B categories indicating the absence or presence, respectively, of documented unexplained fever, night sweats, or weight loss (>10% of body weight in the prior 6 months).
From Carbone P, Kaplan H, Musshoff K, et al. Report of the Committee on Hodgkin's Disease Staging Classification. Cancer Res 31:1860, 1971.

than biopsies. Evaluation of the lungs and mediastinum by CT for extranodal disease is important because 50% of previously untreated patients have disease discovered on CT that had been undetected on plain films.[320] If a mediastinal mass is present, the ratio of the maximum diameter of the mass to the maximum intrathoracic diameter should be calculated because masses more than one third of the thoracic diameter carry a poor prognosis.[312, 319] If high cervical nodes are involved, CT scan of the neck to include Waldeyer ring may be indicated because Waldeyer ring may be difficult to evaluate on physical examination.[211] CT is also used to assess abdominal and pelvic disease but is inaccurate because of a lack of contrasting retroperitoneal fat in children; in one pediatric series, CT had a sensitivity of only 40% in detecting abdominal adenopathy.[22] PET has been found to be more accurate than CT for staging and can also be useful for evaluating bone marrow and extranodal involvement.[28, 385] PET has also been used to follow disease response to therapy and was predictive of disease relapse.[385, 405] MRI can also be used to assess for soft tissue extranodal disease extension and bone marrow involvement.[28]

Laparotomy remains the gold standard for pathologic staging.[293] The use of systemic therapy for early stage disease and newer imaging techniques have made pathologic staging less necessary. Bone marrow biopsy is reserved for patients with CS III or IV disease, patients of any stage with B-symptoms, and those with recurrence.[166] The yield of an abnormal bone marrow finding in a patient with newly diagnosed CS I-IIA disease is so low as to negate its use.[211] Bone marrow aspirate and biopsy are important because histologic documentation of bone marrow involvement in and of itself denotes stage IV disease.[275] Thoracotomy for pulmonary parenchymal biopsy is also occasionally necessary.[123] When surgical staging is performed, the pathologic staging differs from the clinical stage in 40% to 50% of patients; in 20% to 30% the clinical stage is advanced and in 10% to 20% it is lessened.[180] In a study of 133 children staged clinically, a change in stage of 28% after laparotomy was noted; 10 children were downstaged and 27 upstaged.[324] PET scanning has been compared with routine staging using combined CT, bone scanning, bone marrow biopsy, and laparotomy; PET scanning has been found to alter the stage, with most patients being upstaged based on the PET scan result.[29]

The treatment of HL varies according to stage. In children, the trend is to treat in multimodality fashion so as to reduce the morbidity and mortality associated with the higher doses of chemotherapy or radiation therapy needed for single modality treatment. CS IA and IIA disease may be treated with a combination of low-dose multiagent chemotherapy and radiation therapy to the involved field.[166, 293] The event-free survival rate in these patients is generally greater than 90%. Given this excellent response, current efforts are directed at tailoring treatments to minimize morbidity while maintaining an excellent prognosis.[293] A potential area to reduce treatment morbidity in low-risk stage IA and IIA disease is to hold adjuvant radiation therapy in patients who are complete responders after chemotherapy. Intermediate risk patients include those with stage IIIA disease or stages I

or II disease with B-symptoms, bulky disease, or spleen involvement. These patients require an increased number of cycles of chemotherapy and either increased dose or volume of radiation therapy.[293] Total nodal irradiation is a therapeutic choice for patients with stages IB and IIB disease[164]; localized radiotherapy supplemented with chemotherapy, however, appears to offer the same therapeutic advantages of total nodal irradiation without the deleterious side effects.[98] Stage IIIA patients are treated with a combination regimen of extended field radiation therapy and chemotherapy. For patients with high-risk advanced stages IIIB and IV HL, multiagent chemotherapy alone or in combination with radiation therapy is used.[293] The addition of either involved or extended field radiation therapy in the setting of advanced disease is desirable if it allows a decrease in the total dose of chemotherapy required.[166] The recent management of HL distinguishes between children who have obtained full growth and those who are still growing in an attempt to limit the high doses and extended fields of radiation therapy that cause considerable long-term morbidity for children and young adolescents. Similarly, chemotherapeutic regimens have been changed to reduce the risks of sterility, pulmonary toxicity, and secondary malignancies. HL patients who relapse may be retreated with chemotherapy, combination therapy, or autologous stem cell transplantation.[166, 167, 380]

With current treatments, greater than 90% of all HL patients, regardless of stage, initially achieve a complete remission. Prolonged remission and cure is achieved in approximately 90% of patients with early stage I and II disease and in 35% to 60% of patients with advanced stage III and IV disease.[75, 211] Histopathologic findings also have prognostic implications; patients with lymphocyte predominance lesions have the most favorable survival statistics, followed in prognostic order by the nodular sclerosis, mixed cellularity, and unfavorable lymphocyte depletion subtypes.[95]

As mentioned previously, the long-term survival of successfully treated HL patients has resulted in additional problems. Older children and adolescents subjected to radiation therapy and chemotherapy have experienced growth arrest, hypothyroidism, sterility, and pulmonary fibrosis.[140, 240] Sepsis is a risk in patients after undergoing splenectomy or bone marrow transplantation. All HL survivors, particularly those treated in multimodality fashion, are at risk for the development of second malignancies involving the lung, gastrointestinal tract, breast, and thyroid as well as acute nonlymphoblastic leukemia and NHL.[94, 183, 363, 377]

Non-Hodgkin Lymphoma

NHL designates a heterogeneous group of solid primary neoplasms of the lymphoreticular system. In children, NHL most commonly occurs between the ages of 2 and 12 years and, as in HL, demonstrates a male predilection.[12, 396] The incidence of NHL increases steadily with age and the subtypes vary; high-grade NHL predominates in children.[326] Both congenital and acquired immunodeficiency disorders predispose to the development of

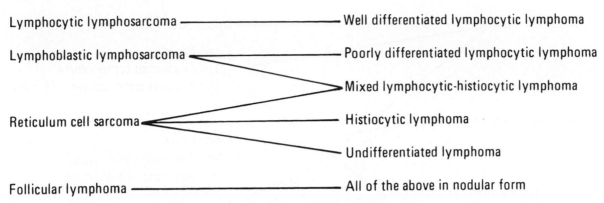

FIGURE 101-2. Histopathologic classifications of non-Hodgkin lymphoma. (From Howard D, Batsakis J. Non-Hodgkin's lymphomas: contemporary classification and correlates. Ann Otol Rhinol Laryngol 94:326, 1985.)

NHL,[127, 224] with a clear documented increased incidence in children with acquired immunodeficiency syndrome (AIDS).[185] Other immunodeficiencies that predispose to NHL include common variable immunodeficiency, combined variable immunodeficiency, ataxia-telangiectasia, Wiskott-Aldrich syndrome, X-linked lymphoproliferative disorder, and immunosuppression for transplantation.[102, 224, 364]

The classification of NHL is confusing and controversial (Fig. 101–2). Older classification systems used the categories of lymphoblastic lymphosarcoma, lymphocytic lymphosarcoma, and reticulum cell sarcoma. These terms were used to differentiate the lymphomas on a morphologic basis, with lymphosarcoma being small cell differentiated lymphomas and reticulum cell sarcoma being large cell undifferentiated lesions. A separate classification recognizing the favorable prognostic significance of a nodular histologic pattern was termed *follicular lymphoma*.[165] Rappaport and associates[307] modified the older classification systems by recognizing the resemblance of malignant lymphoma cells to their benign lymphocytic or histiocytic counterparts. Within the lymphocytic category, the importance of cellular differentiation was retained, as was the distinction between nodular and diffuse histologic patterns. Categories were created to encompass lesions with more than one cell type and lesions whose cells appeared undifferentiated. Clinicopathologic studies demonstrated the Rappaport classification to be a useful guide in management and prognosis of NHL.[181]

Subsequent advances in the development of immunologic markers for lymphocytic subtypes have led to further changes in NHL classification.[221] Immunologic typing allows separation of NHL into categories of B-cell, T-cell, and true histiocytic origins. The B- and T-cell lymphomas are further subdivided based on their morphologic appearance and degree of lymphocytic transformation (Fig. 101–3).[165] In an attempt to allow correlation between the several histologic classification systems, a working formulation was developed.[271] This classification scheme groups the lymphomas according to their natural histories and responsiveness to therapy (Table 101–8). However, these groups represent a spectrum of disease, and already new

subgroups have been identified that do not fit well into this classification scheme.[12]

Ninety percent of children with NHL have high-grade disease consisting of three types: small noncleaved cell lymphoma, large cell lymphoma, and lymphoblastic lymphoma.[326] The small noncleaved cell lymphoma is of B-cell origin. Lymphoblastic lymphoma is generally of T-cell origin. Large cell lymphoma may express B- or T-cell markers or both.

The clinical features of NHL reflect the site of origin of the primary tumor and the extent of local and systemic disease. Asymptomatic lymphadenopathy is the most common initial presentation and 45% of patients are found to have neck involvement at diagnosis.[179, 206] Inguinal, axillary, and generalized nodal presentations are less frequent. Nodal growth may be rapid, but insidious presentations more often occur. Frequently, the presenting signs and symptoms are dependent on the location of the tumor and the rapidity of its enlargement. Signs and symptoms that have been described include swelling, pain from nerve compression, loose teeth, epistaxis, nasal blockage, rhinorrhea, dysphagia, and other neurologic findings, including cranial nerve deficits or central nervous system (CNS) symptoms.[206, 338] There may be associated anterior mediastinal adenopathy, which may cause superior vena cava syndrome, dyspnea caused by airway compression, or pleural effusion. Extranodal sites of origin include the oronasopharynx (Fig. 101–4), orbit (Fig. 101–5), ileocecal region, skin, bone, breast, parotid, and ovary.[119] Such extranodal NHL sites, especially Waldeyer ring, are particularly common in children.[82] The early detection of NHL involving Waldeyer ring may be difficult because it may mimic benign adenotonsillar hypertrophy. A biopsy via adenoidectomy or tonsillectomy may be warranted if there is asymmetry, discoloration, or evidence of systemic symptoms.

Childhood NHL additionally differs from that in adults in that it has a diffuse rather than a nodular histologic presentation, a greater likelihood of being composed of prognostically unfavorable (Rappaport classification) cell types, and a tendency toward leukemic transformation,

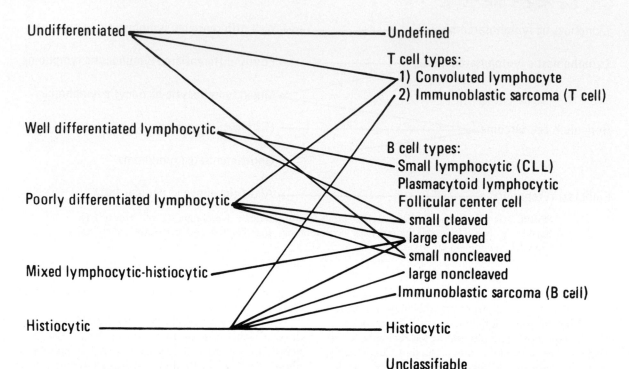

FIGURE 101–3. Immunohistopathologic classifications of non-Hodgkin lymphoma. (From Howard D, Batsakis J. Non-Hodgkin's lymphomas: contemporary classification and correlates. Ann Otol Rhinol Laryngol 94:327, 1985.)

hematogenous dissemination, and CNS involvement.[397] In children, almost all NHLs are small noncleaved cell, lymphoblastic, or diffuse large cell tumors.[326, 338] Constitutional signs and symptoms correlate with advanced disease and include fever, weight loss, malaise, pancytopenia resulting from bone marrow infiltration, and neurologic manifestations.

The Ann Arbor staging classification for HL (see Table 101–6) may be applied to patients with NHL. Alternative systems accounting for the characteristic extranodal pre-

sentations and tendency toward hematogenous dissemination in childhood NHL have also been proposed.[216, 257, 344] One proposal takes into account the dissemination of disease and possible involvement of the bone marrow and the CNS (Table 101–9).[258] The clinical staging of NHL requires a chest radiograph, skeletal survey, bone scan or bone marrow biopsy, and cerebrospinal fluid analysis in addition to a comprehensive history, physical examination, HIV testing, lactate dehydrogenase levels, and complete blood count. Abdominal CT with contrast or ultrasound

TABLE 101–8. Characteristics of the Subtypes of Non-Hodgkin Lymphoma According to the Working Formulation

Subtype	Frequency (%)	Growth Pattern	Cell Type	Immunophenotype	
				B-Cell	T-Cell
Low grade					
Small lymphocytic	4	Diffuse	Small round cells	99	1
Follicular small cleaved cell	23	Follicular	Small cleaved cells	100	0
Follicular mixed cell	8	Follicular	Small cleaved cells; intermediate number of large cells	100	0
Intermediate grade					
Follicular large cell	4	Follicular	Many large cleaved and noncleaved cells	100	0
Diffuse small cleaved cell	7	Diffuse	Small cleaved or small irregular cells	90	10
Diffuse mixed cell	7	Diffuse	Mixed small and large cells	60	40
Diffuse large cell	20	Diffuse	Predominantly large cleaved or noncleaved cells	90	10
High grade					
Immunoblastic (large cell)	8	Diffuse	Predominantly immunoblasts	80	20
Lymphoblastic	4	Diffuse	Round or convoluted lymphoblasts	5	95
Small noncleaved cell	5	Diffuse	Uniform, intermediate size, round cells	100	0

From the non-Hodgkin lymphoma classification project sponsored by the National Cancer Institute, 1982.

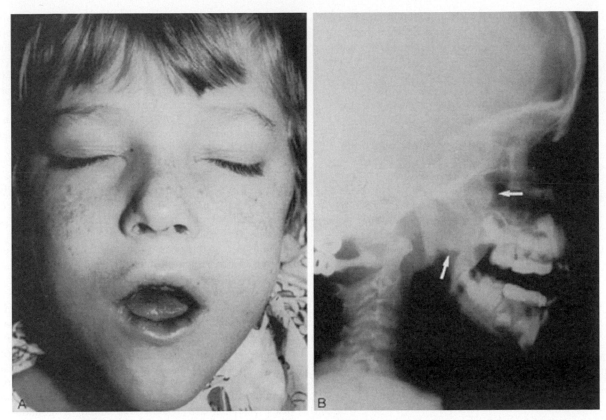

FIGURE 101-4. *A,* This 7-year-old child with non-Hodgkin lymphoma of the nasopharynx had serous otitis media in addition to nasal obstruction. *B,* Lateral radiograph reveals complete soft tissue obstruction of the nasopharynx *(arrows).* Nasopharyngeal rhabdomyosarcoma and carcinoma may present in similar fashion. (Courtesy of Sylvan Stool, M.D., Children's Hospital of Denver.)

may be used to assess for mesenteric lymph node involvement. More recently, gallium-67 scanning and PET with 18-F-fluoro-2-deoxy-D-glucose have been used for disease staging and for following disease progression during treatment.[28] Laparotomy is not a routine procedure in the staging of patients with NHL.[64]

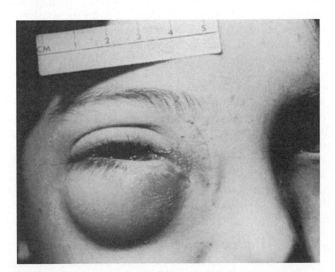

FIGURE 101-5. The orbit is another common extranodal site of origin of non-Hodgkin lymphoma. Orbital rhabdomyosarcoma presents in similar fashion.

The purpose of a staging system for a disease for which moderately effective treatments are available is to identify patients who are more or less likely to respond to treatment. Recently, factors other than the Ann Arbor staging classification have been shown to have prognostic importance. These include the maximum diameter of the largest tumor, immunologic characteristics of the lymphoma, specific extranodal sites of involvement, tumor proliferation rate, the patient's performance status, and serum lactate dehydrogenase concentrations.[12, 224, 344] Children more often present with widespread disease secondary to hematogenous spread; hence, stage I disease is rare in the pediatric age group. Approximately 80% of children with NHL are found to have advanced stage II, III, or IV disease.[82, 257]

Diagnosis requires biopsy, often by excision of a suspicious cervical node. Surgery plays little additional role in NHL treatment. Surgical debulking may be indicated in selected cases of aerodigestive tract compression; reduction of tumor load by surgical debulking may lower the risk of development of tumor lysis syndrome.[175, 390] Approximately 80% of children with NHL have disseminated disease at the time of diagnosis and therefore the treatment is generally chemotherapy for all stages; the rapid doubling time of high-grade NHL makes it very chemoresponsive.[206] Radiation therapy has a limited role in the treatment of NHL and is generally reserved for selected anatomic sites such as the CNS.[338] CNS prophy-

TABLE 101–9. Staging of Non-Hodgkin Lymphoma

Stage I	Single tumor (extranodal) or involvement of a single anatomic area with exclusion of the mediastinum and abdomen
Stage II	Single tumor (extranodal) with regional node involvement
	Two or more nodal areas on the same side of the diaphragm
	Two single extranodal tumors with or without regional node involvement on the same side of the diaphragm
	A primary gastrointestinal tract tumor with or without involvement of mesenteric nodes that is completely resectable
Stage III	Two single tumors (extranodal) on opposite sides of the diaphragm
	Two or more nodal areas above and below the diaphragm
	Any primary intrathoracic tumor (mediastinal, pleural, thymic)
	Extensive primary intra-abdominal disease
	Any paraspinal or epidural tumor independent of other sites of involvement
Stage IV	Any of the above findings with the initial involvement of the central nervous system, bone marrow, or both

° Adapted from Sandlund JT, Downing JR, Crist WM. Non-Hodgkin's lymphoma in childhood. N Engl J Med 334:1238, 1996; Murphy SB. Classification, staging, and end results of childhood non-Hodgkin's lymphomas: dissimilarities from lymphoma in adults. Semin Oncol 7:332, 1980.

laxis in children with high-grade NHL can be achieved with intrathecally administered chemotherapy alone. Treatment for relapse consists of high-dose chemotherapy; bone marrow transplantation may be considered.[326, 338]

Both early and late complications can occur in the setting of chemotherapy. Early complications generally are a result of rapid lysis of tumor cells, resulting in electrolyte abnormalities. Long-term complications are generally the development of secondary malignancies. Current efforts in treatment of NHL are directed at limiting chemotherapeutic exposure to that necessary to obtain excellent cure rates while attempting to reduce the chance of development of secondary malignancies.[215]

The overall 5-year survival rate for NHL is 70%.[206] The event-free survival rate for stage I and II disease is 85% to 95% and for stage III and IV disease is 50% to 85%, depending on the histologic type.[326] Prognosis is associated with disease stage, and children with CNS disease at the time of presentation do particularly poorly.[115, 396] The potential role of immunotherapy, given the observation that most childhood NHL is characterized by T- or B-cell differentiation, is speculative.[12, 378]

Burkitt Lymphoma

Burkitt lymphoma (BL) is an NHL that has distinct epidemiologic and clinical features.

Epidemiologic differences separate BL into an endemic African and a nonendemic American type. BL is a disease almost exclusively involving children; the peak age range of presentation is between 5 and 10 years of age.[225] There is a male predominance reported as 2 or 3 to 1.[225, 247] The limited geographic distribution of African BL suggests an infectious etiology, with evidence supporting a role for EBV. Almost all African BL patients demonstrate high antibody titers to EBV determinant antigens, and 80% to 90% of their tumor cells contain copies of the EBV DNA genome. In contrast, only 15% to 20% of patients with the American form of BL demonstrate this serologic and histopathologic EBV association.[187, 403] BL is of B-cell origin.[338] The B cells express EBV-latent proteins and thus EBV may be involved in the pathogenesis of BL.[135] There is an increased incidence of BL in patients with HIV infection.[404]

The diagnostic histopathologic pattern of BL is a diffuse proliferation of uniform, undifferentiated cells containing small, noncleaved nuclei and a discrete rim of amphophilic cytoplasm.[184] The so-called starry sky pattern produced by the presence of large macrophages interspersed among these neoplastic cells is highly characteristic but not pathognomonic. Genetic translocations have been found in BL, which affect the regulation of the proto-oncogene c-*myc*.[225]

The clinical presentation characteristic of African BL is different from that of the histologically similar lesion affecting children in North America.[49, 187] African BL characteristically occurs as a facial mass originating from the jaw.[225] The maxilla is more frequently involved than the mandible. Loose dentition, facial distortion, trismus, and proptosis are common manifestations. Abdominal masses, when present, are typically of renal or gonadal origin. Splenic and lymph node involvement is rare.

Most American BL patients, in contrast, have an abdominal mass or symptoms of abdominal obstruction, with presentation in the jaw being rare.[225] The abdominal lymphoma is usually of mesenteric lymph node or ileocecal origin. Asymptomatic cervical lymph node enlargement is most common; nasopharyngeal and tonsillar involvement is also reported.[212] Bone marrow involvement is more common in American BL, with approximately 20% at initial presentation as compared with 8% in African BL.[225]

BL has rapid proliferative potential and tumors may reach a large size quickly. Rapid diagnosis, staging, and treatment are advocated. Staging work-up is similar to that used in other NHLs. A greater emphasis is placed on CT scanning to localize abdomen and head and neck masses, and surgical staging is reserved for cases in which a tissue sample must be obtained for diagnosis.[355] Gallium scans and lactate dehydrogenase levels are useful to quantitate tumor burden and to follow up patients serially.[225, 403] Two clinical staging systems are used for BL (Table 101–10). Both are based on the premise that the anatomic sites of predilection of BL do not conform readily to the conventional Ann Arbor NHL staging classification.[212, 403]

Chemotherapy is the treatment of choice for both American and African BL.[403] Surgery has a limited role in the treatment of BL. The diagnosis can often be made by FNA.[189, 247] Surgery may be required when presenting symptoms are secondary to increased tumor bulk.[247] Radiation therapy is less useful as a treatment modality as a result of poor tumor response in comparison with the responsiveness of BL to chemotherapy.[225] Multiagent chemotherapeutic regimens using combinations of cyclophosphamide, vincristine, prednisone, and cytosine arabi-

TABLE 101–10. Staging Classifications of Burkitt Lymphoma

Stage	Extent of Tumor
A	Single extra-abdominal site
B	Multiple extra-abdominal sites
C	Intra-abdominal tumor
D	Intra-abdominal tumor with involvement of multiple extra-abdominal sites
AR	Stage C but with >90% of tumor surgically resected
Stage	**Extent of Tumor**
I	Single tumor mass: extra-abdominal (IA) or abdominal (IB)
II	Two separate tumor masses either above or below the diaphragm
III	More than two separate tumor masses above and below the diaphragm
IV	Pleural effusion, ascites, or involvement of central nervous system or bone marrow

Top: From Ziegler JL. Burkitt's lymphoma. N Engl J Med 305:735, 1981. Bottom: From Kapadia S. Hematologic diseases: malignant lymphomas, leukemias, plasma cell dyscrasias, histiocytosis X, and reactive lymph node lesions. In Barnes L (ed). Surgical Pathology of the Head and Neck. New York, Marcel Dekker, 1985, p 1065.

noside are used for BL.[326] Prophylactic intrathecal methotrexate is added to decrease CNS relapse rates.[403]

Three- and 5-year event-free survival rates are 85% to 95% for limited disease and 75% to 85% for advanced disease.[326] Relapse rates are lower and survival rates significantly higher in patients with a smaller tumor burden at presentation.[226] The majority of recurrences occur in the first year; this is a poor prognostic factor.[225] Children younger than 12 years of age do significantly better than older patients, and high anti-EBV antigen titers in American BL patients appear to be associated with a more favorable prognosis.[212]

Rhabdomyosarcoma

Rhabdomyosarcoma is the most common soft tissue malignancy in the pediatric age group, accounting for 50% to 70% of all childhood sarcomas.[96, 223, 248] According to the first and second Intergroup Rhabdomyosarcoma Studies (IRS I and IRS II), 35% of pediatric rhabdomyosarcomas occur in the head and neck. Approximately 70% of these children have disease before 12 years of age, and 43% are younger than 5 years of age. There is no apparent sex predilection; however, rhabdomyosarcoma is four times more common in white children than in any other racial group.[237]

Rhabdomyosarcoma has a wide spectrum of histopathologic subtypes; the recent IRS histopathologic classification lists embryonal, alveolar, botryoid, spindle cell, and undifferentiated.[16, 284] In IRS III, the frequency of occurrence of the histopathologic subtypes is as follows: embryonal, 54%, alveolar, 18.5%, undifferentiated, 6.5%, and botryoid, 4.5%. Spindle cell was not included.[81] Botryoid rhabdomyosarcoma is a variant of embryonal rhabdomyosarcoma that occurs when the growth of embryonal rhabdomyosarcoma is unrestricted in a body cavity such as the nasopharynx; it tends to become polypoid, resembling a bunch of grapes, so-called sarcoma botryoids. Histopa-

thology has been found to have prognostic significance; subtypes can be categorized as favorable prognosis (botryoid, spindle cell), intermediate prognosis (embryonal), and unfavorable prognosis (alveolar and undifferentiated).[16, 284] The characteristic microscopic appearance of embryonal rhabdomyosarcoma is that of small, dark, spindle-shaped cells in a loose myxoid background. Round cells resembling lymphocytes are also occasionally seen. Cytologic structures indicative of rhabdomyoblasts may be identified but are not considered necessary for histopathologic confirmation.

Rhabdomyosarcomas of the head and neck region are categorized as orbital, parameningeal, and nonparameningeal.[81, 88] Parameningeal sites include the nasopharynx, paranasal sinuses, middle ear, and the infratemporal fossa. Nonparameningeal sites include all other "superficial" areas of the head and neck.[392] This categorization has prognostic significance (see later discussion). Within the head and neck region, the most common sites of origin, in descending order of frequency, are the orbit, nasopharynx, middle ear–mastoid region, and sinonasal cavities.[30] Orbital rhabdomyosarcoma is the most frequent neoplasm of the orbit in children.[196, 354] Localized orbital disease is common. Rapidly progressive, unilateral proptosis in a child younger than 10 years of age is the typical presentation. CNS extension with associated pain, headache, and irreversible visual loss is infrequent. Rhabdomyosarcoma occurs in the nasopharynx in preschool children in less obvious fashion, with symptoms of unilateral otitis media, rhinorrhea, and nasal obstruction. In one series, only 4 of 20 primary rhabdomyosarcomas of the nasopharynx remained confined to the nasopharynx. A delay in diagnosis of several months after onset of symptoms is common.[55] Rhabdomyosarcoma of the paranasal sinuses may have manifestations analogous to either nasopharyngeal or orbital rhabdomyosarcoma. Headache and pain are the more common symptoms and are often mistaken for those of sinusitis. Other signs and symptoms include nasal obstruction, facial edema, and epistaxis.[53] Patients with rhabdomyosarcoma of the ear typically have unilateral otorrhea and a hemorrhagic, soft tissue mass in the external auditory meatus, middle ear, or both. An initial diagnosis of otitis media or otitis externa is often mistakenly made.[331] Approximately 50% of patients with aural rhabdomyosarcoma have neurologic findings by the time the proper diagnosis is determined, with the facial nerve being most commonly involved.[89] Multiple cranial nerve palsies suggest extension of disease to the base of the skull or CNS.[214] This is also true of nasopharyngeal and sinonasal sites of origin.[117] All head and neck rhabdomyosarcomas arising in parameningeal sites require CT or MRI radiologic evaluation, or both, as well as lumbar puncture with cerebrospinal fluid cytologic study to assess for skull base erosion or CNS involvement.[87, 116, 304]

Metastatic spread occurs by both lymphatic and hematogenous routes.[116, 125, 248] The incidence of cervical lymph node metastases varies with the primary site, being notably rare with orbital rhabdomyosarcoma. In IRS I and IRS II, no patients with orbital primary lesions presented with clinically positive neck nodes, whereas 7% of patients with other head and neck primary tumors had positive nodes.[208] The most common sites of hematogenous

TABLE 101-11. Staging of Rhabdomyosarcoma According to the Intergroup Rhabdomyosarcoma Study

Group I	Localized disease with tumor completely resected and regional nodes not affected
	Confined to muscle or organ of origin
	Contiguous involvement-infiltration outside the muscle or organ of origin
Group II	Localized disease with microscopic residual disease or regional disease with no residual or with microscopic residual disease
	Grossly resected tumor with microscopic residual disease (nodes negative)
	Regional tumor completely resected (nodes positive or negative)
	Regional disease with involved nodes grossly resected but with evidence of microscopic residual disease
Group III	Incomplete resection or biopsy with gross residual disease
Group IV	Metastatic disease present at onset

From Barnes L. Tumors and tumorlike lesions of the soft tissues. In Barnes L (ed). Surgical Pathology of the Head and Neck. New York, Marcel Dekker, 1985, p 796.

metastatic disease are the lung, bone, and bone marrow. About 13% of patients with rhabdomyosarcomas of the head and neck present with distant metastases, except for orbital primary lesions, which have a comparatively low 4% incidence.[361] Lesions arising in parameningeal sites have an additional increased incidence of meningeal extension.[214, 303] Skeletal survey, bone scan, and bone marrow aspirate or biopsy are necessary for complete systemic evaluation.

The treatment of patients with rhabdomyosarcoma is determined by the primary site of involvement and the clinicopathologic stage of disease as established by the IRS (Table 101-11). This clinical staging system is based on extent of disease (localized, regional, or systemic) at presentation and whether excision of local-regional disease is accomplished.[235] A recurring problem with this essentially postoperative staging system is that surgical definitions of disease resectability vary between institutions; hence, the IRS grouping of any particular lesion may also vary. An alternative preoperative TNM (tumor, node, metastasis) staging has been proposed (Table 101-12).[97, 287] This system places emphasis on local invasiveness as opposed to size criteria in determining the tumor stage. The TMN staging system is being evaluated prospectively in the IRS IV. Preliminary results examining

the TNM system in extremity RMS reveals it to have prognostic significance.[223, 265, 301] A similar study of head and neck RMS shows that parameters such as primary lesion size, local invasiveness, nodal metastasis, and distant metastasis do have prognostic significance.[199]

Treatment guidelines have come from the IRS. The IRS established the superiority of multimodality therapy—surgery, radiotherapy, and chemotherapy—over single modality therapy in treating this disease. Before the IRS, the 5-year survival rate for rhabdomyosarcoma of the head and neck, all sites considered, ranged from 8% to 20%. The average survival rate was 15 months for orbital rhabdomyosarcoma, 7 to 12 months for middle ear-mastoid rhabdomyosarcoma, and 17 months for rhabdomyosarcoma arising in the soft tissues of the face and the neck.[30] In IRS I using multimodality treatment principles, the 3-year relapse-free survival rates increased to 91% for orbital primary disease, 46% for parameningeal (middle ear-mastoid, sinonasal, nasopharyngeal, and infratemporal fossa) primary disease, and 75% for other head and neck sites.[361]

Surgical extirpation of the primary tumor is indicated when such removal imposes no major functional disability and when excision of the primary tumor permits either the elimination of postoperative radiation therapy or a reduction in radiation dose. This is true of many of the nonorbital and nonparameningeal head and neck sites.[391] Biopsy alone is advocated for orbital rhabdomyosarcoma because combined radiotherapy and chemotherapy have resulted in excellent long-term survival with limited morbidity.[361] When only partial tumor resection is possible, as is often true of parameningeal sites, initial surgery is limited to biopsy. Some institutions advocate complete resection of some parameningeal tumors if surgically feasible in order to obviate the need for radiotherapy. In one study, the successful resection of parameningeal tumors in selected sites including the occiput and infratemporal fossa was possible.[88] Possible complications of such surgical management include cranial nerve injury, cosmetic deformity, and trismus.[88] Surgery may also play a role in categorizing patients as partial or complete responders for possible additional therapy.[81] For example, in IRS III, patients in group III confirmed to be partial responders at the time of a "second look" surgical procedure received additional chemotherapy with prophylactic benefit.[80, 81, 284]

Because many rhabdomyosarcomas of the head and neck are not amenable to complete resection because of

TABLE 101-12. TNM Classification of Rhabdomyosarcoma Modified by the Intergroup Rhabdomyosarcoma Study Group

Stage	Site	T	Size	N	M
I	Orbit, head, and neck, excluding parameningeal sites, genitourinary but not bladder or prostate	T1 or T2	A or B	Any N	M0
II	Bladder, prostate, T1 or T2 extremity, cranial parameningeal sites, other	T1 or T2	A	N0 or Nx	M0
III	Bladder, prostate, T1 or T2 extremity, cranial parameningeal sites, other	T1 or T2	A	N1	M0
			B	Any N	M0
IV	All	T1 or T2	A or B	N0 or N1	M1

Where TNM and the size of the tumor are defined as: T1 is confined to the site of origin; T2 has extension or fixation to surrounding structures; A is a tumor ≤5 cm; B is a tumor >5 cm; N0 is no clinically involved lymph nodes; N1 is regionally involved lymph nodes; Nx is clinical status of lymph nodes unknown; M0 is no distant metastasis; M1 is metastasis present; TNM, tumor, nodes, metastasis.

Adapted from Pappó AS, Shapiro DN, Crist WM. Biology and therapy of pediatric rhabdomyosarcoma. J Clin Oncol 13:2123, 1995.

anatomic location, radiation therapy is commonly required, and almost all patients with head and neck rhabdomyosarcoma receive systemic chemotherapy. Chemotherapy is typically administered postoperatively to patients with small resectable lesions. Preoperative chemotherapy is given initially to patients with larger lesions to decrease tumor volume before local treatment. Such local treatment may require a combination of surgical resection and radiation. Radiation therapy is also indicated for group II, III, and IV tumors. Radiotherapy is directed at the primary site. Wide portals are determined by the extent of tumor on pretreatment clinical and roentgenographic examination.[365] The clinically negative neck requires no treatment beyond chemotherapy and observation. Children with a clinically positive neck benefit from neck dissection with additional radiation therapy.[235] Chemotherapy protocols vary principally with the stage of disease.[233, 234] The IRS III found that patients in groups I, II, and III (specifically those with orbit or nonparameningeal tumors with favorable histology) did well with the omission of cyclophosphamide from the chemotherapy protocol and thus recommended omission of cyclophosphamide.[81]

Complications of radiotherapy in the treatment of head and neck RMS include osteoradionecrosis, xerostomia, maxillofacial hypoplasia, malocclusion, dental disease, and the development of secondary malignancies, particularly additional sarcomas.[53, 199] Chemotherapy has both short- and long-term complications, including anemia, neutropenia, thrombocytopenia, neural and cardiac toxicity, and the potential development of acute myeloid leukemia.[285] One of the main goals of further investigation of RMS therapy is to modify treatment so as to minimize deleterious side effects, especially the development of secondary malignancies, without compromising survival.

The primary site is a very important prognostic indicator for several reasons. First, the location of the primary tumor determines the signs and symptoms that lead to diagnosis or delay in diagnosis. Second, the likelihood of lymphatic spread and hematogenous dissemination varies with primary site.[208] Third, the location has implications concerning resectability. The histopathologic subtype is also an important variable. Children with alveolar rhabdomyosarcoma and undifferentiated sarcoma have a poor survival rate compared with those with embryonal rhabdomyosarcoma.[156] A number of chromosomal abnormalities in RMS have been identified and are being investigated to determine their significance as prognostic indicators.[284] The most meaningful prognostic variable is the response to treatment because those children who do not achieve complete response will not survive.[375]

In IRS I, patients with distant metastases (group IV) or evidence of base of skull and CNS extension as with parameningeal sites with gross residual disease (group III) did particularly poorly. Survival in these groups was typically less than 12 months.[234] The meninges also proved to be the most common site of tumor recurrence (relapse), whether or not there was initial evidence of CNS disease.[361] These observations led to protocol changes in the second IRS (IRS II) in which an attempt was made to protect the CNS in high-risk patients with parameningeal disease by the addition of prophylactic cranial irradiation

and intrathecal triple-drug chemotherapy. This approach proved to be efficacious.[300] In IRS III, patients with parameningeal tumors without obvious intracranial extension were found to have a similar survival outlook whether they received solely radiotherapy to the tumor with a 2-cm margin or prophylactic CNS treatment. Therefore, the use of intrathecal chemotherapy and whole brain radiation therapy has been limited to those children with parameningeal RMS who also have intracranial extension, evidence of cerebrospinal fluid involvement, bony erosion, or cranial nerve deficits.[81] Control of disease in patients with distant metastases remains difficult. The IRS IV protocol addresses this distant metastases problem with trials of pairs of chemotherapeutic agents before the introduction of standard chemotherapy and radiation therapy.[302] Early results from IRS IV show an increased survival rate compared with IRS III with the use of increased doses of alkylating agents in patients with stage I embryonal tumors of the head and neck.[21] The failure-free survival was 90% in IRS IV compared with 53% in IRS III.

Children with orbital rhabdomyosarcoma and those with localized disease have the best outcome. The overall 5-year survival rate in IRS III was 71%, which has improved from IRS II by a statistically significant 8%.[81] This overall improvement was attributed principally to the benefit of intensification of chemotherapy in patients in group III, not including special pelvic, orbit, and nonparameningeal sites. The 5-year survival rate in IRS-III for select groups is as follows: group I favorable histology, 93%; group I unfavorable histology and group II, 54% to 81%; group III, 74%; group IV, 27% to 31%.[81, 282] Individuals who are free of recurrence 2 years after treatment are probably cured.[298]

Soft Tissue Sarcomas Other Than Rhabdomyosarcoma

Soft tissue sarcomas other than rhabdomyosarcoma account for approximately 3% of all malignant neoplasms in children younger than 15 years of age.[248] A bimodal age distribution curve with one incidence peak in children younger than 4 to 5 years of age and another peak in adolescence is characteristic of almost all these lesions.[63] The soft tissue sarcomas of infants and young children primarily occur in the head and neck region, whereas lesions in adolescents predominantly arise in the trunk and extremities. Because of their relative rarity, the study of the natural history of these neoplasms and the development of effective treatment regimens require multi-institution collaboration. In general, with the exception of fibrosarcoma, soft tissue sarcomas demonstrate a tendency toward both local recurrence and metastatic hematogenous spread. This behavior dictates a multimodality therapeutic approach similar to that used in rhabdomyosarcoma patients.[100, 176, 328, 381] In general, complete surgical excision is the treatment of choice with radiation and chemotherapy reserved for cases of incomplete resection.[263] In a study of 33 cases of nonrhabdomyosarcoma sarcomas of the head and neck, prognostic factors included extent of resection, grade of the tumor, disease bulk, and location, with tumors of the oral cavity and pharynx having the most favorable prognosis.[263] In another study of 88 pediatric patients with nonrhabdomyosarcomas not limited to the head and neck, a margin of greater than 1 cm was found to correlate with decreased risk of local recurrence; this was noted to be independent of tumor grade.[39] Postoperative radiation therapy was efficacious in those nonrhabdomyosarcoma cases in which surgical margins were less than 1 cm and the tumor was high grade. This observation is of particular importance in the head and neck region where it may be difficult to obtain a 1-cm margin without extensive morbidity.

Fibrosarcoma

Fibrosarcoma is the most common sarcomatous neoplasm after rhabdomyosarcoma, accounting for 11% of all soft tissue sarcomas of childhood.[248, 249] Although fibrosarcoma is primarily a malignancy of the extremities in adolescents, approximately 15% to 20% of fibrosarcomas occur in the head and neck region, predominantly in infants and young children.[63] The most common time of presentation in childhood is within the first 6 months of life.[282] Fibrosarcoma may also arise in older children as a secondary neoplasm following radiation therapy.[388]

Histopathologically, fibrosarcomas consist of malignant fibroblasts associated with variable collagen or reticulin production. Demonstrative evidence of local infiltration distinguishes well-differentiated fibrosarcoma from nonmalignant juvenile fibromatosis. This distinction can be difficult.[30, 34] Fibrosarcoma of infancy histologically appears the same as in older patients but is less aggressive.[282] The etiology of fibrosarcoma in children is speculative.[352]

The more common sites of occurrence of fibrosarcoma in the head and neck include the neck, oral cavity, scalp, auriculoparotid region, nose and paranasal sinuses, larynx, face, cheek, and hypopharynx.[30] A slowly enlarging, painless, firm mass is the typical presentation. Symptoms result from local extension and pressure on surrounding structures. Plain radiographs reveal a soft tissue density, frequently with associated bone destruction. Tracheobronchial airway lesions may manifest with various pulmonary signs and symptoms including stridor, recurrent pneumonia, cough, and hemoptysis.[289, 292] CT evaluation of fibrosarcomas in parameningeal locations is important to assess for base of skull erosion and intracranial extension.[218]

Fibrosarcoma is unique among the soft tissue sarcomas in that metastatic disease in infants and young children is infrequent. The incidence of local recurrence varies greatly between 17% and 43%.[282] Lymph node metastases occur in less than 10% of patients. The incidence of hematogenous metastasis to lung and bone is reported to be less than 10% for children younger than 10 years of age, whereas rates approach 50% in patients older than 15 years.[66, 358] Therapy is primarily directed at local disease control. Complete surgical excision, when possible, is advocated. Maintenance of function at the expense of inadequate margins or incompletely resected disease is often necessary in childhood head and neck cases. In such situations, gross tumor resection is followed by local radiation therapy. Adjuvant chemotherapy is of uncertain

value and is not used routinely because of the low incidence of distant metastases. Preoperative chemotherapy may be used to decrease the size of the tumor in an attempt to make it completely resectable.[282] The 5-year survival rate of infants and young children with fibrosarcoma is between 80% and 90%.

Synovial Sarcoma

Synovial sarcomas account for approximately 5% of all pediatric soft tissue sarcomas. Synovial sarcoma is primarily a malignancy of the extremities; the occurrence of this tumor in the head and neck is rare, with fewer than 50 cases reported.[30, 201, 252] There is a slight female predominance.[201] Synovial sarcoma is thought to arise from synovioblastic differentiation of mesenchymal stem cells; this derivation accounts for the presence of synovial sarcomas in head and neck sites, which have no normal synovial structures.[218]

Anatomically, these lesions have been reported in the larynx, pharynx, tongue, tonsil, and orofacial soft tissues. The most common location is the neck, where they occur as firm, gradually enlarging parapharyngeal or retropharyngeal masses, which become symptomatic by compromising contiguous structures. There is often a delay in diagnosis of up to 1 year.[201] Radiographically, synovial sarcomas appear as soft tissue masses, usually without adjacent bone erosion. The presence of multiple foci of calcification can be a helpful diagnostic feature.

Treatment of local disease consists of the widest possible surgical excision followed by radiation therapy.[58] Five-year survival rates following combined surgical and radiation treatment regimens approximate 50%; children with small localized lesions have the best outcome.[248, 321] Local recurrence and metastases to lymph nodes, bone marrow, and lung occur in approximately 50% of patients.[32] Because of the documented tumor regression following chemotherapy and because of the poor prognosis associated with systemic, particularly lung, metastases, multimodality treatment regimens similar to those used for childhood rhabdomyosarcoma are advocated to treat this disease.[297] In a study of 31 patients with synovial sarcoma treated by surgical resection followed by both chemotherapy and radiation therapy, the 5-year survival rate was an improved 74%[201]; the anatomic location of these lesions was not limited to the head and neck.

Neurofibrosarcoma (Malignant Schwannoma)

Neurofibrosarcoma, a malignant tumor of neural sheath origin, accounts for approximately 3% of all soft tissue sarcomas of childhood.[249] This malignant counterpart of a neurofibroma is the most common malignancy arising within peripheral nerves.[136] Children with von Recklinghausen neurofibromatosis (NF1) are at increased risk for the development of this lesion; neurofibrosarcoma develops in approximately 3% to 16% of these children.[114, 132]

Although similar in appearance to fibrosarcoma, neurofibrosarcoma is a vastly more aggressive lesion that must be histopathologically distinguished from the less malignant fibrosarcoma. Approximately 10% of all neurofibrosarcomas occur in the head and neck region.[33] The most common site is the neck, where neurofibrosarcoma may arise from the cranial nerves, cervical plexus, or sympathetic chain. An enlarging cervical mass is the common presentation; associated symptoms may include pain, paresthesias, or muscle weakness. Other symptoms may be associated with nerve involvement or mass effect and include dysphonia, dysphagia, facial nerve paresis, or muscle fasiculations.[90] Work-up should include CT or MRI and histopathologic examination with special stains to determine whether the tumor is of neurogenic origin.[90]

Wide surgical excision is advocated. Cranial nerve deficits after resection of cervical neurogenic tumors is common.[90] Local recurrence and hematogenous pulmonary metastases are common. Adjuvant radiotherapy and multidrug chemotherapy are potentially beneficial.[304] Patients with extensive local disease or distant metastases do poorly despite aggressive multimodality therapy; cure rates are highest in patients with completely resectable local disease.[249, 303, 374] Malignant schwannomas occurring in patients with von Recklinghausen disease tend to be particularly aggressive. The 5-year survival rate for this group of patients is 15% to 30% compared with 27% to 75% for patients whose neurofibrosarcomas are not associated with this syndrome.[33]

Hemangiopericytoma

Hemangiopericytomas account for 3% of the total number of childhood soft tissue sarcomas.[249] Approximately 5% to 15% of hemangiopericytomas are seen in the pediatric age group.[17, 104, 186] Two types of childhood hemangiopericytomas are recognized. Congenital or infantile hemangiopericytomas occur within the first year of life and invariably follow a benign course despite malignant histopathologic characteristics.[72, 104, 314] Hemangiopericytomas in children older than 1 year behave in a clinical fashion similar to that observed in adults; approximately 20% to 35% prove to be malignant.[186] Most lesions are solitary, but multiple congenital hemangiopericytomas have been reported in the head and neck. Hemangiopericytoma has been diagnosed in utero on ultrasonography, which allows for interdisciplinary planning regarding potential airway compromise at birth.[138]

Hemangiopericytomas arise from the pericytes of Zimmermann, cells that lie external to the reticulin sheath of capillaries. Microscopically, they consist of uniform round or spindle-shaped cells intimately associated with a vascular background. Special stains reveal a characteristic histopathologic reticulin pattern, which distinguishes hemangiopericytomas from hemangiosarcomas and other richly vascular soft tissue tumors.[30] Infantile hemangiopericytomas may differentiate and mature into a benign tumor.[314] Findings suggestive of malignancy include increased mitotic index, hemorrhage, calcification and necrosis.[104]

The nasal cavity and paranasal sinuses are the most common head and neck location of hemangiopericytomas; less frequent sites include the orbital region, parotid gland, and neck.[32] Sinonasal hemangiopericytomas frequently occur as a polypoid mass causing nasal obstruction and epistaxis. Congenital hemangiopericytoma has

been reported as midline nasal mass.[325] The characteristic presentation in other locations is that of a slowly enlarging, painless mass of firm, fibrous consistency. When hemangiopericytomas occur in the oral cavity, the most common location is the tongue.[153]

Hemangiopericytomas are generally not well encapsulated. Surgical excision with wide margins is the principal accepted therapeutic approach.[104, 325] Surgery alone is recommended for infantile hemangiopericytoma because of the low local recurrence rates and the low likelihood that metastatic disease will develop. In older children, adjuvant chemotherapy should be considered if there is gross residual tumor or metastatic disease. Chemotherapeutic responses have been documented in children with the use of vincristine, cyclophosphamide, doxorubicin, Adriamycin, and methotrexate. Radiation therapy, in combination with chemotherapy, is used in cases of unresectable or incompletely resectable local disease.

A high incidence of both local recurrence and lung metastases characterizes hemangiopericytoma of all sites, including the head and neck.[17, 20] The small number of cases reported in children does not allow for age-specific survival figures, although infantile hemangiopericytoma has a better prognosis. The overall survival rate at 5 years in adult series varies between 50% and 70%.[20, 105] Patients with unresectable local disease or metastatic disease at the time of presentation do poorly.

Kaposi Sarcoma

Kaposi sarcoma is a rare neoplasm that histologically demonstrates a variable mixture of vascular and sarcomatous components.[31, 255] This disease is rare in children. Classic Kaposi sarcoma is distinguishable from Kaposi sarcoma associated with AIDS. Most children with classic Kaposi sarcoma have been of African descent.[276] Classic Kaposi sarcoma is characterized by generalized lymphadenopathy with a predilection for head and neck glandular sites. The lacrimal, parotid, and submandibular glands are commonly involved and skin lesions are sparse. The distinguishing laboratory features of classic Kaposi sarcoma are that such children have a normal T4/T8 lymphocyte ratio and lack antibody to the human T-cell lymphotropic virus.[154]

Most cases of Kaposi sarcoma in the pediatric age group in the United States occur in infants with AIDS born to mothers with established or suspected HIV infection.[47, 178, 323] Such HIV-infected children with Kaposi sarcoma are rare.[147, 255, 296] These infants clinically demonstrate a disseminated lymphadenopathic form of Kaposi sarcoma. They differ from their African counterparts in several respects. They typically have demonstrable failure to thrive and developmental delay. They are also highly susceptible to opportunistic infections such as *Pneumocystis carinii* pneumonia, mucocutaneous candidiasis, and disseminated herpesvirus infection. They have profound lymphocyte depletion and a reversed T4/T8 lymphocyte ratio.[323, 393]

The manifestation of Kaposi sarcoma in the setting of HIV infection depends on whether it was acquired congenitally or later in childhood.[255] Children who became infected by vertical transmission usually present with the lymphadenopathic form, and children who acquired it later present with the cutaneous form. Adolescents with Kaposi sarcoma associated with AIDS present in a fashion similar to that of adults.[286] Skin and mucosal lesions are prominent, most frequently on the arms, face, and neck as well as on the oropharyngeal mucous membranes. The lesions appear purple, red, or brown with an oval appearance and a distinct border.[255] Multiple lesions are the rule, and generalized lymphadenopathy and visceral involvement are common.

Surgical excision and radiation therapy have been the traditional treatments of choice of localized Kaposi sarcoma. Immunotherapy and systemic chemotherapy have been used to treat disseminated disease.[286] Both classic Kaposi sarcoma and that associated with AIDS in childhood are aggressive, invariably fatal diseases.[47, 368] Experience with the treatment of Kaposi sarcoma in childhood is limited because of its rarity. The data from adults suggest that vincristine, etoposide, doxorubicin, and alpha-interferon may be effective antineoplastic agents.[217, 384]

Extraskeletal Ewing Sarcoma

Extraskeletal Ewing sarcoma (EES), also called *primitive neuroectodermal tumor*, is a malignant soft tissue tumor identical in histologic appearance to Ewing sarcoma of bone. The specific cell of origin of EES is suspected to be a primitive mesenchymal stem cell.[378] Histologic differentiation of EES from undifferentiated embryonal rhabdomyosarcoma is sometimes difficult because both are small, round, blue cell malignancies. Most individuals with EES are younger than 30 years of age at the time of diagnosis, with an average age at presentation of 15 years.[1]

In the head and neck region, EES typically arises within soft tissues adjacent to the cervical spine.[146] Cases of EES of the scalp, neck and paraspinal muscles in the pediatric population have been reported.[1, 65] Symptoms may include pain, tenderness, and neurologic disturbances related to spinal cord compression. Of 42 patients with EES reported by the Mayo clinic, 75% presented with a palpable mass and 66% with pain. On radiographic evaluation, the vertebrae adjacent to the soft tissue mass may show periosteal thickening and new bone formation.

Treatment of EES generally consists of surgical excision alone or in combination with radiotherapy or chemotherapy. Mortality is high, due in part to both local recurrence as well as pulmonary and osseous metastases. The multimodality IRS protocols used in the treatment of rhabdomyosarcoma have been applied to both adults and children with EES.[1, 318, 351] In a study of 24 patients treated in multimodality fashion with variable combinations of surgical resection, chemotherapy, and radiation therapy, the 5-year survival rate was 61%[1]; predictors of improved survival included age greater than 16 years and attempted surgical resection, whether complete or partial. The most important prognostic factor for children with EES appears to be the absence of clinically detectable metastatic disease at diagnosis.[1]

Additional Soft Tissue Sarcomas

Additional soft tissue sarcomatous neoplasms of the head and neck region in children include malignant hemangioendothelioma, leiomyosarcoma, liposarcoma, alveolar soft sarcoma, and malignant fibrous histiocytoma.[30, 248, 249, 310] The use of surgery and radiation therapy to control local disease, with the adjuvant administration of systemic chemotherapy to prevent metastases, appears applicable to these rare lesions as well.

Thyroid Carcinoma

Carcinoma of the thyroid gland is uncommon in the pediatric population. Data from the National Cancer Institute reveal an annual incidence of five cases per million per year for children age 19 years or younger in the United States.[401] Thyroid carcinoma represents approximately 1.5% of all tumors before the age of 15 years and 7% of the tumors of the head and neck in childhood.[9] The reported incidence of thyroid nodules in the pediatric population is 0.2% to 2.0%,[169, 295] with malignancy documented in 14% to 40% of solitary nodules.[170, 194] Although demonstrating an increased incidence at puberty, thyroid cancer can occur at any childhood age, including the neonatal period.[394] The female preponderance of adult thyroid carcinoma persists but is less marked in children, with an average male-to-female ratio for thyroid carcinoma in the pediatric population of 1:1.32.[111]

This discrepancy may be due in part to the historical common exposure of many pediatric thyroid carcinoma patients to ionizing radiation to the head and neck.[157, 270] In one study of 30 children with solitary thyroid nodules, 20 were girls and 10 were boys, with an incidence of malignancy of 45% in the girls and 30% in the boys.[194]

Previous exposure to radiation has historically been the single most important factor responsible for the occurrence of thyroid cancer in childhood.[108] The subsequent abandonment of radiotherapy for benign diseases has drastically reduced its etiologic importance. Children are still occasionally exposed to radiation as a result of external disasters such as the Chernobyl incident. The incidence of well-differentiated thyroid carcinoma in the pediatric population increased 62 times in the area surrounding Chernobyl.[270] The radiotherapy treatment of HL and other head and neck malignancies also increases the risk of development of thyroid carcinoma.[273, 327, 376] Concern also exists regarding the subsequent development of thyroid cancer after repeated radiodiagnostic studies[290] or following the radioiodine treatment of childhood Graves disease.[120]

Histopathologically, the majority of pediatric thyroid malignancies are well-differentiated papillary or mixed papillary-follicular adenocarcinomas.[394] Pure follicular, medullary, anaplastic, and undifferentiated carcinomas are rare. Although the incidence of multicentricity of thyroid cancer is higher after previous radiation therapy,[120] there is no evidence that the natural history of radiation-induced thyroid cancer differs from that of papillary or follicular carcinoma occurring spontaneously. The mortality rate and the recurrence rate in patients exposed to

mal in children with thyroid carcinoma.[14, 220, 245] Antithyroid and antimicrosomal antibody titers, if elevated, may suggest an inflammatory component but do not rule out malignancy. Thyroglobulin levels have little initial diagnostic value, although they may be useful in following up patients after treatment. In patients with medullary thyroid carcinoma, base line calcitonin levels are often elevated, and such levels increase further after stimulation by pentagastrin or calcium. These provocative tests historically had been used to screen family members for occult medullary carcinoma, but genetic screening for the MEN syndrome is now alternatively available.

Plain film radiography is of limited value in the workup of local thyroid disease but is important in the detection of asymptomatic pulmonary and bone metastases. CT, MRI, or ultrasonography of the neck allows evaluation of the size, position, and multiplicity of thyroid lesions and aids in determining their cystic or solid character. CT and MRI provide additional information regarding the absence or presence of cervical metastases and may be useful for evaluating tracheal displacement or compression from a large thyroid mass. The ultrasonographic characteristics of thyroid carcinoma can vary.[124] In general, a cystic lesion suggests benign disease, but thyroid carcinoma can have a cystic component. The combined use of ultrasonography, FNA, and cytopathologic evaluation has permitted greater operative selectivity of adult patients with thyroid masses.[15] Recently, FNA of thyroid nodules has been investigated in the pediatric population with a reported accuracy rate of diagnosing thyroid carcinoma and follicular adenoma of 87.5%.[192] The false-negative rate approximates 2% to 3%.[192, 294] Some clinicians advocate definite histopathologic diagnosis by thyroid lobectomy, even in the setting of a benign FNA, because of the high rate of malignancy in pediatric thyroid nodules. Serial examinations have alternatively been recommended in the setting of a benign FNA result.[192] Thyroid scanning, using technetium or iodine-123, is an additional diagnostic technique that can be used to evaluate children with solid thyroid nodules. The majority of thyroid cancers are nonfunctioning.[281] The management of nodules with varying degrees of isotope uptake is more controversial. Some investigators advocate open surgical biopsy of all solid nodules in children.[91] Others vary their approach to warm and hot nodules, depending on the presence or absence of antithyroid antibodies, response to thyroxine suppression therapy, or needle aspiration cytologic findings (Fig. 101–7).[308] This use of thyroid hormone suppression to help determine whether a nodule is benign or malignant is controversial[128] in that thyroid carcinoma can respond to suppression therapy with a reduction in tumor volume; hence, suppression does not rule out malignancy.

Thyroid lobectomy with intraoperative frozen section tissue diagnosis is the most accurate means to determine whether the child's thyroid mass is benign or malignant. Although definitive surgery may be dictated by frozen section results, certain thyroid lesions are difficult to diagnose accurately on frozen section. The distinction between follicular adenoma and well-differentiated follicular carcinoma is particularly troublesome[243] because it is diffi-

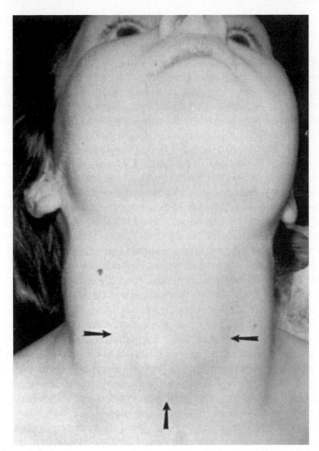

FIGURE 101–6. A firm, mobile mass in the anterior neck (arrows) is the common presentation of thyroid carcinoma as illustrated in this 10-year-old girl.

radiation are the same as in those not exposed.[270] Those cases of medullary carcinoma that do occur tend to be of the familial type associated with multiple endocrine neoplasia (MEN) syndrome types 2a and 2b.[316]

Most children with thyroid carcinoma present with a firm, otherwise asymptomatic neck mass (Fig. 101–6). The mass may be central or just lateral to the midline in location if arising from the thyroid gland, further lateral if representing a cervical lymph node metastasis, or present in both regions.[245] The suspicion of malignancy is increased when there is a history of rapid growth, hoarseness, dysphagia, or fixation of the mass to surrounding tissues.[91] Benign cystic nodules are usually mobile, soft, nontender, and solitary.[220] Palpable cervical lymph node metastases are present in 45% to 75% of patients at the time of initial evaluation.[245, 268] This incidence is higher in patients previously exposed to radiation.[270] Systemic metastases, typically to lung and bone, are also initially present in 15% and 5% of children, respectively.[107] In cases of familial medullary carcinoma associated with MEN syndrome, symptoms due to pheochromocytoma, hyperparathyroidism, or both may additionally be manifest.[188]

From a laboratory standpoint, thyroid hormone levels, including thyroxine (T4), triiodothyronine (T3), and thyroid-stimulating hormone (TSH), are nearly always nor-

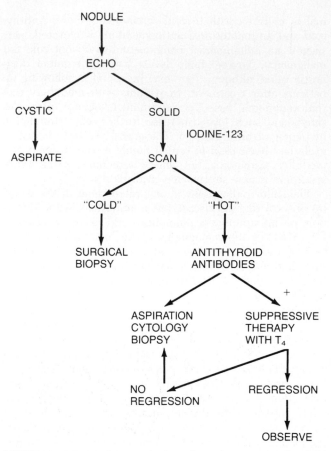

FIGURE 101–7. An alternative plan of management for the child with a thyroid nodule. (From Reiter E, Root A, Retting K, Vargus A. Childhood thyromegaly: recent developments. J Pediatr 99:515, 1981.)

cult to determine capsular and vascular invasion. When the pathologist is uncertain of the diagnosis, initial surgery should be limited to thyroid lobectomy pending review of permanent sections.

Most thyroid malignancies in children are well-differentiated adenocarcinomas of the papillary or mixed papillary-follicular types. Controversy regarding the surgical treatment of these children concerns the extent of surgery necessary to be assured of complete ablation of the carcinoma. In well-differentiated thyroid carcinoma without metastases, the decision is whether to perform a partial, total, or near-total thyroidectomy.[91, 389] The sequelae of total thyroidectomy include the need for lifelong thyroid hormone replacement as well as the potential risk of recurrent laryngeal nerve injury or permanent hypoparathyroidism. Ablation of metastatic or residual disease by radioactive iodine-131 (^{131}I) therapy is much more successful following near-total or total thyroidectomy. In particular, the use of near-total thyroidectomy plus ablation of remaining thyroid tissue with radioactive iodine has achieved excellent results while minimizing hypoparathyroidism.[134] Total thyroidectomy is always indicated when there is documented bilobed disease, regional or distant metastases, or gross carcinomatous infiltration into local tissues. Laryngectomy and tracheoesophageal resection

are contraindicated even in the presence of tumor infiltration.

Elective lymph node dissection in the absence of regional nodal metastases is not warranted.[134, 334] Modified neck dissection is advocated when cervical metastases are suspected based on physical examination or radiologic evaluation. Classic radical neck dissection should be used only in those children with gross extranodal extension of disease.

Current indications for the use of radioactive iodine therapy include ablation of residual normal thyroid tissue and ablation of functioning metastasis.[400] The effective use of postoperative ^{131}I therapy to eradicate residual disease requires prior near-total thyroidectomy.[347] The dose of ^{131}I needed to ablate any residual thyroid tissue in the neck depends largely on the size of the remaining thyroid remnant; dosimetry measurements are recommended.[400] After ablation of local thyroid tissue has been completed, the child can later be evaluated for recurrence or metastases by periodic ^{131}I total body scanning.[15] If recurrence or metastases occur, therapeutic options include salvage surgery if the disease is accessible or ablation with higher doses of ^{131}I. Documented side effects of high-dose ^{131}I therapy include lung fibrosis when extensive pulmonary metastases are present, temporary bone marrow suppression, reversible spermatogenic damage, nausea, emesis, sialadenitis, and a questionable increased incidence of leukemia.[91, 240, 400]

Postoperatively, all patients should receive thyroxine to maintain a euthyroid state and thereby achieve maximal suppression of thyroid-stimulating hormone. Thyroid-stimulating hormone is believed to have a growth promoting effect on well-differentiated thyroid cancers.[69] Thyroxine is usually used for suppression therapy rather than triiodothyronine because of its longer half-life. Until ^{131}I therapy is completed, the shorter half-life of triiodothyronine may be desirable.[68]

Suggested follow-up of thyroid carcinoma patients includes annual physical examination, thyroglobulin level checks, and periodic scanning with technetium or ^{123}I seeking local/regional recurrence or systemic metastases.[128] The prognosis for children with well-differentiated thyroid carcinoma is excellent, with one review finding a mortality rate of 2.4% over a follow-up period of 12 to 33 years, despite a recurrence rate of 10% to 35%.[111] It has been reported that the prognosis in children is better than that of the adult population, but this appears to be true only when the adult population is greater than 40 years old; the survival curve of adults younger than 40 years of age and children are similar.[251]

Medullary Thyroid Carcinoma

Medullary thyroid carcinoma (MTC) accounts for approximately 10% of thyroid malignancies in children.[202] MTC may be sporadic or familial. The familial form occurs in the setting of MEN syndrome types 2a and 2b, and it has been associated with Hirschsprung disease.[202] In children, the manifestation of MTC is far more common in the familial forms; the sporadic form does not typically manifest until 30 years of age or older.[128] The detection of

MTC in younger patients has historically been the result of screening. Elevated base line levels and pentagastrin-stimulated levels of thyrocalcitonin have been sought in patients "at risk" because of a family history of MEN 2 syndrome. An even earlier diagnosis of MEN 2 syndrome is possible by screening for the RET proto-oncogene on chromosome 10.[343] Such early detection has implications regarding the role of prophylactic thyroidectomy in this at-risk pediatric population.

Current treatment of MTC depends on the stage of the disease at the time of diagnosis. In the setting of a normal examination and positive genetic screening, some centers advocate a prophylactic total thyroidectomy with or without a central neck dissection because the penetrance of MTC in MEN 2 syndrome is nearly 100%.[202, 277] The treatment of a child with histopathologically confirmed MTC consists of a total thyroidectomy, with the addition of a modified radical neck dissection if there are clinically evident cervical metastases or intraoperative frozen section evidence of micrometastases on regional node sampling. Mediastinal lymphadenopathy, in the absence of other metastatic disease, requires mediastinal lymphadenectomy with sternotomy.[366]

MTC associated with MEN 2b is generally a more aggressive disease with a poorer prognosis than that associated with MEN 2a. MTC associated with MEN 2b may manifest before 1 year of age and is usually advanced at the time of diagnosis with a higher incidence of nodal metastases. The cause-specific mortality rate in familial associated MTC has been reported as 7% at 18 years in comparison to 23% for sporadic MTC over the same time course.[277]

Thyroglossal Duct Cyst with Carcinoma

The incidence of carcinoma arising in thyroglossal duct cysts is estimated at approximately 1%, with the majority of such lesions being papillary carcinoma.[207, 370] Follicular, mixed papillary-follicular, and squamous cell carcinomas are less commonly seen.[10, 93, 149, 372] The median age for manifestation of thyroglossal duct carcinoma (TGDC) is 40 years old, but pediatric cases have been reported.[191] Malignancy is typically identified incidentally at the time of the removal of a thyroglossal duct cyst and usually is not suspected preoperatively. Thyroglossal duct cysts are usually unilocular or multilocular, and the presence of a predominant solid component should raise suspicion of malignancy. Documentation of TGDC within a thyroglossal duct cyst dictates careful examination of the thyroid gland for any intrathyroidal abnormalities that may suggest metastatic disease.

The treatment for thyroid carcinoma arising in thyroglossal duct remnants is an en bloc resection via the so-called Sistrunk procedure. The need to perform a thyroidectomy is debated.[10, 372] If the TGDC focus is microscopic without invasion of the cyst wall and if there are no palpable masses in the thyroid or neck, then an en bloc resection without thyroidectomy should suffice.[191] Advocates of total thyroidectomy point to an associated 25% incidence of papillary carcinoma in thyroid glands removed in the setting of TGDC. In the setting of carcinoma in the thyroid gland or cervical lymph nodes, a total thyroidectomy seems warranted. Modified neck dissection should be considered in the setting of palpable cervical lymphadenopathy. The reported cure rate is 95% for TGDC.[207]

Parathyroid Carcinoma

Primary hyperparathyroidism due to adenoma, hyperplasia, or carcinoma of the parathyroid gland is uncommon in the pediatric population. Parathyroid carcinoma (PTC) is rare in all age groups and represents 0.005% of all cancer.[168] The few reported cases of PTC in the pediatric population have principally occurred in adolescents.[242] The epidemiology, presentation, treatment, and prognosis of PTC is based on experience in adults because of the paucity of pediatric cases. There is no apparent predilection for PTC based on race, ethnicity, or geographic location.[168] Some reports suggest an increased incidence in women.[74, 79] PTC is associated with familial isolated hyperparathyroidism, a condition unrelated to the MEN syndromes.[228, 382]

Histologic findings of PTC include fibrous trabeculae, capsular and vascular invasion, a high number of mitoses, and uniform-appearing cells.[74] Frozen section diagnosis is difficult. The initial suspicion of PTC may be based solely on intraoperative findings, as discussed later.

Patients with PTC present with a variety of signs and symptoms related to either the presence of a neck mass or to hypercalcemia secondary to hyperparathyroidism. The neck mass may be the primary tumor or a cervical lymph node metastasis. Adherence of the mass to surrounding cervical structures is indicative of malignancy. Supportive intraoperative findings of a parathyroid mass that may suggest malignancy include invasion of surrounding structures, fibrosis, and a gray appearance of the lesion as opposed to the normal tan color.[74]

Hypercalcemia may cause systemic problems including but not limited to the kidneys, digestive tract, and nervous system. Malaise, irritability, weakness, and fatigue may develop, appearing to be related to suppression of neuromuscular excitability.[5] Gastrointestinal atony results in constipation, emesis, and nausea. Renal calculi, chronic renal failure, osteoporosis, and depression may result from hypercalcemia.[74, 79] Manifestations of hypercalcemia in the musculoskeletal system of children include bone demineralization, primarily in the actively growing long bones, with resultant stunted growth, bowed legs, abnormal gait, and bone and joint pain.[306] Markedly elevated calcium levels may cause CNS encephalopathic changes, including behavior disturbances, altered state of consciousness, and seizure activity.[402] In general, the presence of a firm, adherent neck mass, elevated parathyroid hormone levels, and hypercalcemia suggests the possible diagnosis of PTC,[232] especially in the setting of additional palpable cervical adenopathy. The incidence of cervical lymph node metastases is 15% to 32%.[339] Bone and lung metastasis occur in approximately 33% and 11% of patients, respectively.[79]

From a laboratory standpoint, children with primary hyperparathyroidism are usually hypophosphatemic, show mildly elevated alkaline phosphatase levels, and are characteristically but not invariably hypercalcemic.[8] The serum calcium concentration of patients with adenomas generally averages 12 mg/100 mL. Patients with PTC have an average serum calcium level of 14.3 mg/100 mL and a parathyroid hormone level of 7.2 times normal.[79] Hypercalcuria can usually be demonstrated.

Ultrasonography, angiography, and technetium-thallium scanning have been used in adult patients for preoperative localization of parathyroid adenomas and carcinomas.[37, 163] Ultrasonography appears to have merit in the work-up of primary hyperparathyroidism in children because of its noninvasiveness and its efficacy in detecting large adenomas.[313] Additional imaging studies, specifically in the setting of suspected PTC, may include CT, thallium-technetium pertechnetate subtraction scanning, or a technetium-99 methoxy-isobutyl isonitrile scan. The use of these studies is generally not helpful in distinguishing between an adenoma and carcinoma and may be more useful in identifying lesions in reoperative cases.[79] Also, selective catheterization of neck veins for immunoreactive parathyroid hormone determinations has been used to localize hypersecreting lesions. This technique, along with digital subtraction angiography, is typically reserved for the detection of ectopic or residual tissue in children who have persistent or recurrent disease following surgical treatment.[5]

Treatment of PTC includes surgical excision of the lesion[232] with surrounding structures that are adherent, including an ipsilateral thyroid lobectomy. The lymph nodes of the central compartment, particularly of the tracheoesophageal groove, should be sampled.[74] Modified neck dissection is reserved for cases in which there is palpable lymphadenopathy suggestive of metastases. There is no defined role for radiotherapy. Patients may suffer systemic manifestations secondary to hypercalcemia in the setting of disease refractory to treatment and these patients may be treated with pamidronate. Distant metastases may be resected with some benefits.[274]

The most common complication of parathyroid surgery is temporary hypocalcemia of several days' to months' duration. Severe sequelae may include permanent hypoparathyroidism or vocal fold paralysis. The more extensive the dissection, the greater is the likelihood of recurrent laryngeal nerve injury.[288] Permanent hypoparathyroidism, even despite treatment, leads to diminished linear growth in children.[240]

In a study of 286 principally adult patients with PTC, the 5-and 10-year survival rates were 85.5% and 49.1%, respectively.[168] From this study, there was no apparent prognostic relationship to tumor size or lymph node status. For this reason, the TNM staging system is typically not applied.

Cancer of the Salivary Glands

Malignant neoplasms of the salivary glands in children are uncommon. An Armed Forces Institute of Pathology review of 10,000 salivary gland lesions revealed only 54 malignancies in the pediatric age group.[200] Other major oncologic institutions have likewise compiled individual totals of only 10 to 25 malignant salivary gland cases in young patients.[22, 50, 85, 330] The majority of malignant salivary gland neoplasms occur in older children and adolescents; cases involving infants and young children are rare.[158, 379] An estimated 2% of salivary gland malignancies occur in children younger than 10 years old, with approximately 16% occurring in patients younger than 30 years of age.[311] When vascular neoplasms are excluded, approximately 50% of reported salivary gland neoplasms in children are malignant[330]; this percentage decreases to 30% when vascular lesions are included[67] and further decreases to 4% to 16% when infectious and inflammatory lesions are considered.[54, 279] As in adults, pleomorphic adenoma is the most common benign nonvascular neoplasm.[229] Individuals exposed to radiation are at increased risk for the development of salivary gland malignancies; for example, the treatment of childhood cancer with radiotherapy to the head and neck region increases the risk for development of mucoepidermoid carcinoma of the major salivary glands.[315]

The World Health Organization has categorized 12 benign and 22 malignant neoplasms of primary salivary gland origin.[335] The histopathologic findings in malignant salivary gland neoplasms in children are similar to those in the adult population.[330] The relative frequency of occurrence of the various histologic types, however, does vary. Mucoepidermoid carcinoma, followed by acinic cell carcinoma, are the most common salivary gland malignancies in children.[67] The incidence of undifferentiated carcinoma is higher in children. Adenocarcinoma, adenoid cystic carcinoma, malignant mixed tumors, and salivary duct carcinoma are comparatively less common. Salivary gland manifestations of sarcomas and lymphoid malignancies can occur but are infrequent; rhabdomyosarcoma is most likely with seventh cranial nerve involvement in 50% of cases.[315] Mucoepidermoid, acinic cell, and adenocarcinoma may vary from low to high grade depending on patient-specific histopathology.[311] Salivary duct and undifferentiated carcinoma are considered high-grade tumors.

More than 90% of pediatric malignant tumors of salivary gland origin arise in the parotid gland.[395] Malignant tumors originating in the submandibular gland in children are extremely rare.[23, 62] The most common presentation is an asymptomatic, firm mass in the preauricular facial region (Fig. 101–8).[315] Rapid growth raises concern of malignancy as do facial weakness, pain, and ipsilateral cervicofacial lymphadenopathy.

The initial evaluation of a salivary gland neoplasm may include CT scan or MRI. If the tumor is large and there is a concern of bone involvement or entry into neural foramina, then a CT scan is most useful. MRI is useful for determining the soft tissue boundaries of the tumor and its probable site of origin.

The relatively high risk of malignancy, as outlined previously, dictates a histopathologic examination of all firm salivary gland masses. FNA with cytologic diagnosis is used in adults for this purpose[346]; in one study of 341 FNAs of salivary gland neoplasms in adults, the sensitivity for diagnosing a benign lesion was 97% and for a malignant lesion was 87%.[357] FNA of salivary gland lesions has been performed less frequently in the pediatric population[101, 383]; in one study of 15 patients, there was one

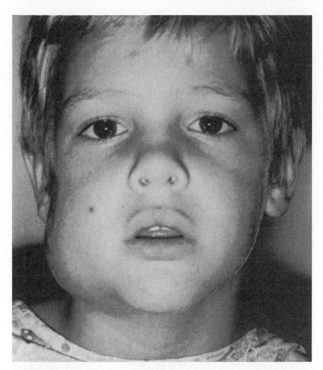

FIGURE 101–8. An asymptomatic mass in the lateral facial region is the most common presentation of a salivary gland neoplasm in children.

malignancy falsely diagnosed as benign. Although FNA has potential benefits, its role in children as the basis for determining management decisions is controversial.[92, 250, 259] Limitations to cytologic diagnosis include the wide variety of salivary gland malignancies as well as the fact that some malignancies are further differentiated on the basis of tissue invasion, which cannot be determined by FNA.[387]

Incisional biopsy is generally condemned because of the potential risk of injury to the facial nerve.[103] The exception to this rule is a clinically unresectable lesion for which diagnostic biopsy alone is needed. Under most circumstances, excisional biopsy is advocated. Superficial parotidectomy with preservation of the facial nerve, or total excision of the submandibular gland, are the preferred initial procedures.[330]

The mainstay of treatment of salivary gland neoplasms in children, as in adults, is surgery. Superficial or subtotal parotidectomy, or submandibular gland excision represents adequate therapeutic resection when the lesion in question is localized to the superficial parotid lobe or submandibular gland and subsequent histopathologic examination reveals a benign or low-grade malignancy. Deep-lobe parotid lesions and suspected or confirmed high-grade malignancies require total parotidectomy. Resection of the facial nerve or its branches is recommended only when there is gross anatomic or histopathologic evidence of nerve involvement (invasion) at the time of surgery; resection is not performed simply based on tumor type or grade.[50, 315] When resection of the nerve is necessary, immediate facial reanimation by means of primary anastomosis or free nerve graft is advocated.[78]

The role of neck dissection in salivary gland cancer in the pediatric age group is debatable. This is less so when there is documented cervical lymph node metastases. The presence of nodal metastases increases the mortality rate; therefore, a modified radical neck dissection, often followed by postoperative radiation therapy depending on histopathology, is recommended.[241] The diagnostic problem is that the presence of lymph node hyperplasia is so common in children that confusion may arise in some cases.[78] In the absence of confirmed cervical lymph node metastases, most centers limit neck dissection to patients with a high-grade malignancy[23] or advocate periglandular node dissection at the time of initial superficial parotidectomy or submandibular gland excision, proceeding with neck dissection if there are confirmed periglandular metastases.[50, 52] Factors that increase the risk of lymph node metastases include facial nerve involvement, high-grade histopathology, perilymphatic invasion, and extraparotid spread.[118] Because patients with these findings are typically treated with radiation therapy to the primary site, some centers advocate treating even the neck regardless of lymph node metastasis status simultaneously with radiotherapy or a prophylactic neck dissection under such circumstances.[241]

Radiation therapy is additionally used in the management of salivary gland malignancies in certain clinical situations. Positive margins following primary surgical excision increase the incidence of local recurrence and require either additional resection if anatomically feasible or postoperative radiation therapy.[373] Facial nerve invasion, extraglandular extension of tumor, or cervical metastases are histopathologic indications for postoperative radiotherapy at some centers,[50, 52] as are high-grade tumors such as high-grade mucoepidermoid carcinoma, adenoid cystic carcinoma, malignant mixed tumor, adenocarcinoma, and undifferentiated carcinoma.[311] Palliative radiation therapy may be the sole treatment of undifferentiated salivary gland malignancies that are beyond the control of surgical excision at the time of presentation.

Chemotherapy is being explored for use in palliation and as adjuvant therapy in the treatment of high-grade salivary gland cancer.[359] Because most studies have small numbers of patients with a large variety of salivary gland malignancies, there are no conclusions regarding the role of chemotherapy. The combination of cyclophosphamide, doxorubicin, and cisplatin is the most extensively studied chemotherapy regimen.[177] Cisplatin has shown particular promise in the treatment of adenoid cystic carcinoma.[337] Chemotherapy is usually reserved for patients with metastatic or local/regional disease refractory to resection and radiation. Multiagent chemotherapy is better than monotherapy in improving pain and local disease control but does not appear to offer any survival benefit.[2] Those rare cases of salivary gland involvement by rhabdomyosarcoma are treated with a combination of surgery, radiotherapy, and chemotherapy as dictated by the IRS protocols.[86]

The survival of children with salivary gland malignancies is chiefly determined by histopathology.[50] Children with low-grade malignancies such as grade I and grade II mucoepidermoid carcinoma, well-differentiated adenocarcinoma, and acinic cell carcinoma tend to do well. Those with high-grade malignancies such as grade III mucoepidermoid carcinoma, poorly differentiated adenocarcinoma, and undifferentiated tumors do poorly. The long-term follow-up of adenoid cystic lesions makes survival assessment of this group of patients difficult. The prognosis for children with mucoepidermoid and acinic cell carcinomas is particularly good, with 5-year survival rates of greater than 90%.[62, 78, 213] In cases of recurrent disease, the rate of distant metastasis is 60%, and the salvage rate in this population is 22%.[373] Submandibular gland malignancies with fixation have a particularly poor prognosis in a predominately adult population.[121]

Neuroblastoma

Neuroblastoma is a common malignancy of infancy and early childhood and is the most common malignancy in infants younger than 1 year of age.[260, 345] Neuroblastoma accounts for 8% to 10% of all pediatric cancers and is responsible for 15% of childhood cancer deaths.[61, 231] Ninety percent of these tumors occur in patients younger than 10 years of age, with birth to 5 years representing the usual age range.[105] There is a slight male predominance.[61] Neuroblastoma is categorized as one of the small round blue cell tumors with a histopathologic appearance similar to Ewing sarcoma, NHL, primitive neuroectodermal tumors, and rhabdomyosarcoma.

Neuroblastomas arise from undifferentiated sympathetic nervous system precursor cells of neural crest origin. The adrenal gland is the most common site of origin; additional sites include the sympathetic chain in the retroperitoneum, posterior mediastinum, and cervical regions. Only 2% to 4% of all neuroblastomas are primary cervical neck lesions. Metastatic disease to the head and neck from sites of origin below the diaphragm is much more common and must be excluded. At the time of diagnosis, 60% to 70% of neuroblastoma patients have systemic metastases to lungs, lymph nodes, liver, or bone.[70] Metastases to cervical lymph nodes, skull, orbit, and jaw are particularly common (Fig. 101–9).[46]

Patients with primary cervical neuroblastoma typically present during the first years of life with a firm mass in the lateral neck. Occasionally, ipsilateral Horner syndrome or heterochromia may be a manifesting sign.[173] The Horner syndrome is secondary to cervical sympathetic chain involvement, whereas the heterochromia reflects anomalous neural crest cell derivation. Respiratory distress and feeding difficulties may occur due to direct tracheal or esophageal compression or may reflect involvement of cranial nerve IX, X, XI, or XII. Cervical neuroblastoma spreads locally by invading surrounding tissues; neural foramina extension into the spinal canal is possible with neurologic sequelae. Neuroblastoma also has a high propensity for lymphatic spread; when including all primary sites, the rate of regional lymph node metastatic disease approximates 35%.[61] Systemic physical examination is necessary to rule out an abdominal mass. Hematogenous dissemination to the skin, bone marrow, and liver is present at the time of diagnosis in 68% of patients older than 1 year and in 25% of patients younger than 1 year of age.[45, 61]

Radiographic work-up, including intravenous pyelogram, abdominal ultrasound, abdominal CT, or a combination thereof, is directed toward ruling out an abdominal

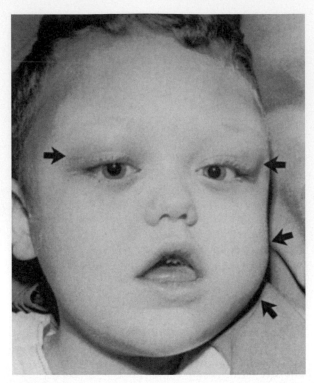

FIGURE 101–9. Neuroblastoma typically originates in sites below the diaphragm and commonly metastasizes to the skull and facial bones *(arrows)*, as demonstrated in this child. (Courtesy of Sylvan Stool, M.D., Children's Hospital of Denver.)

primary tumor. Tumors in the thoracic region are detected in the posterior mediastinum on plain chest radiographs or CT. Head and neck CT scanning allows evaluation for retropharyngeal or skull base extension or both. Metastatic evaluation includes skeletal survey, bone scan, or both, liver-spleen scan, and bone marrow biopsy.[254] A special diagnostic feature of neuroblastoma is the finding of elevated catecholamine levels in the urine. The substance usually measured is vanillylmandelic acid; the most accurate determination requires a 24-hour urine collection with elevated urine catecholamines documented in 90% to 95% of patients.[61] The examination of biopsy specimens by molecular genetic techniques (including proto-oncogene n-*myc* amplification, DNA ploidy, deletion of chromosome 1p, and expression of the TRK gene) appears to have prognostic significance, allowing stratification of patients into low-, intermediate-, or high-risk groups.[6, 7, 43, 60, 61, 122, 231, 262, 333] Some patients have an inherited predisposition to the development of neuroblastoma; current investigations are aimed at determining the genetic basis.[231]

The choice of single modality or multimodality therapy depends on the risk stratification of the patient. Surgery is used to obtain tissue to establish a diagnosis and to stage the disease; it may also be curative in localized cervical neuroblastoma.[84] There is evidence to suggest that, in low-risk patients, surgery alone may be adequate, even in the setting of residual disease.[57, 61] Chemotherapy is generally indicated in patients after incomplete resection of a primary neck neuroblastoma as well as in patients with metastases to the head and neck from other primary sites. Multiagent chemotherapy using cyclophosphamide, ifosfamide, doxorubicin, etoposide, cisplatin, and carboplatin is usually used.[61] The role of radiation therapy is not well defined and carries the risk of secondary thyroid carcinoma. Radiation therapy is reserved for unresectable primary lesions, or to treat these lesions or to treat intraspinal tumors. Immunotherapy, via a viral vector, is currently being investigated for the treatment of patients with refractory disease.[44]

The prognosis of neuroblastoma is influenced by age, stage, histology, primary tumor site, and DNA ploidy.[7, 43, 60, 61, 105, 262, 333, 356] Patients are categorized as low, intermediate, or high risk based on these parameters. Infants fare better than older children; this may simply be due to a greater proportion of favorably staged cases in the younger age group or to a higher incidence of unfavorable molecular characteristics in older children.[57, 60, 105] For young patients with resectable disease, complete excision offers the best chance for cure with at least a 90% survival rate in patients younger than 1 year of age. Primary neuroblastoma of the head and neck has a better prognosis than that of other sites, most likely attributable to an earlier stage presentation.[57] The current staging of neuroblastomas proposed by the International Neuroblastoma Staging System Committee (INSS) takes into account the status of the lymph nodes and the resectability of the tumor (Table 101–13).[61, 106] Neuroblastomas have also been classified according to histopathologic findings, which have been found to have prognostic significance.[342] Three-year event-free survival rates for INSS stage I, II, and IV-S disease range from 75% to 90%.[61] In infants, rates for stages III and IV disease are 80% to 90% and 60% to 75%, respectively.[61] For children older than 1 year, the rates are 50% and 15% for stage III and IV disease, respectively.[61] There is a tendency for widespread metastatic stage IV-S disease to undergo spontaneous resolution in children younger than 1 year of age.[378]

Paraganglioma

Paragangliomas are neoplasms arising from cells of neural crest origin. Paragangliomas of the head and neck arise specifically from collections of these cells associated with cranial or sympathetic nerves. The most common are the carotid body, intravagal, or aorticosympathetic paraganglioma. Such lesions are rare in children. Such familial paragangliomas have an increased incidence of multicentricity (78%) compared with nonfamilial paragangliomas (23%).[266] The inheritance pattern appears to be autosomal dominant with genomic imprinting.[236] Paragangliomas in the familial setting occur most commonly in the late adolescent years; biannual screening is recommended beginning at age 16 years with MRI and urine metabolite testing.[236] Malignant paragangliomas are noted in 4% to 19% of cases in adult series[104]; only case reports exist in the pediatric population.[269]

The majority of paragangliomas in the pediatric age group have been familial, occurring in association with an adrenal pheochromocytoma.[76, 129, 309] Children typically present with a neck mass and systemic evidence of catecholamine hypersecretion; elevated epinephrine, metanephrine, and vanillylmandelic acid levels can be confirmed using 24-hour urine collection. CT and MRI are useful in determining tumor extension, including soft tissue and bony involvement with particular attention to the skull base. Carotid angiography is both diagnostic and potentially therapeutic from a preoperative standpoint. Systemic evaluation is directed toward identifying a likely accompanying adrenal pheochromocytoma.

The treatment of choice of cervical paraganglioma in both children and adults is surgical excision.[129] The surgical approach is variable and dictated by the anatomic bounds of the tumor. Embolization may be performed preoperatively to reduce intraoperative bleeding. Transabdominal resection of an adrenal pheochromocytoma may be required first. Preoperative preparation with alpha (phenoxybenzamine) and beta (propranolol) adrenergic blocking agents is often necessary to prevent perioperative cardiovascular complications. The principal surgical risk is cranial nerve injury. In one study, the resection of carotid body tumors less than 5 cm had a 14% risk of cranial nerve injury, whereas in tumors larger than 5 cm, the risk increases to 67%.[236] The rate of cranial nerve injury after resection of glomus jugulare tumors was 100%. The sequelae of vagus nerve injury can be particularly severe with dysphagia and aspiration. Treatment options may include observation, swallow therapy, medialization laryngoplasty, or gastrostomy tube placement.[266] Treatment of paraganglioma with radiation therapy may control tumor growth and give a degree of palliation in unresectable or incompletely resectable cases.[139]

Nasopharyngeal Carcinoma

One percent of malignancies in children occur in the nasopharynx.[109] The principal neoplasms are rhabdomyo-

TABLE 101–13. International Neuroblastoma Staging System

Stage 1	Local tumor confined to the area of origin
	Complete resection with or without microscopic residual disease
	Ipsilateral and contralateral lymph nodes without tumor
Stage 2a	Unilateral with incomplete gross resection
	Ipsilateral and contralateral lymph nodes without tumor
Stage 2b	Unilateral with complete or incomplete gross resection
	Ipsilateral node with tumor and contralateral node without tumor
Stage 3	Tumor extending across the midline with or without regional lymph node involvement or unilateral tumor with contralateral lymph node involvement or midline tumor with bilateral lymph node involvement
Stage 4	Dissemination of tumor to distant lymph nodes, bone marrow, or other organs except as defined in Stage 4s
Stage 4s	Localized primary tumor as defined in stage 1 or 2 with disseminated disease to the liver, skin, or bone marrow

Adapted from Castleberry, R. P. 1997. Biology and treatment of neuroblastoma. Pediatr Clin North Am 44:919.

sarcoma and NPC, with NPC accounting for approximately one third.[109, 369] Major institutional reviews reveal an incidence of less than one case per year, principally in the adolescent age group.[82, 112, 174] There is no apparent sex predilection in children; however, there does appear to be an ethnicity factor, with an increased incidence of NPC among black teenagers.[99, 140]

NPC originates from epithelial cells within the nasopharynx. The World Health Organization classifies NPC into three groups: type 1 is keratinizing squamous cell carcinoma, type 2 is nonkeratinizing carcinoma, and type 3 is undifferentiated carcinoma.[386] An older term, lymphoepithelioma, describes the random histopathologic interrelationship between malignant undifferentiated carcinoma cells and normal lymphoid cells in the nasopharynx. The large majority of NPCs in young patients are type 3 undifferentiated carcinomas.[13] Histopathologic distinction of these lesions from rhabdomyosarcoma and NHL can be difficult.

A strong serologic relationship exists between both undifferentiated (type 3) and nonkeratinizing (type 2) NPC and EBV antibody titers, suggesting an infectious etiology; this is not true of Type 1 NPC.[264] The EBV genome and EBV proteins can be detected in approximately 100% of poorly differentiated NPC.[73] EBV titers usually correlate with tumor burden and decrease with successful therapy. Titers also tend to increase before the appearance of recurrent disease, making them useful indicators of disease activity. Rising titers after treatment for NPC is associated with a poor prognosis.[148]

Children present with a variety of signs and symptoms secondary to nasopharyngeal obstruction, including nasal congestion, snoring, epistaxis, otitis media, tinnitus, otalgia, and cranial nerve palsies; children may also present with a neck mass secondary to cervical metastases.[13, 109] Cranial nerve involvement and head pain are particularly suggestive of skull base involvement. Most children with NPC have metastatic disease in the neck[112, 350] (as high as 67% of patients in one pediatric study[369]); the superior deep cervical lymph nodes are most commonly involved. Delay in NPC diagnosis occurs frequently because many of its signs and symptoms mimic upper respiratory tract infection. An average of 18 weeks may elapse from the time of initial onset of symptoms to the actual diagnosis.[24]

Nasopharyngeal examination and biopsy is required for tissue diagnosis before the initiation of therapy. NPC has been found to mimic angiofibromas grossly and radiographically.[48] CT or MRI examination allows for precise evaluation of primary tumor extension, particularly with respect to the skull base and CNS. Systemic evaluation is directed toward ruling out hematogenous metastases, particularly to bone and liver.[350] Radionuclide bone scanning and CT of the chest and abdomen should be done to search for metastatic disease. If there is invasion of the tumor through the base of the skull, an examination of the cerebrospinal fluid should be performed.

Current staging of NPC as suggested by the American Joint Committee on Cancer is listed in Table 101–14. This staging system has been shown to correlate well with survival statistics.[280] NPC has traditionally been considered nonresectable because of its anatomic location. With

TABLE 101–14. American Joint Committee on Cancer 1997, Staging and Classification of Nasopharyngeal Carcinoma

AJCC 1997	T1	T2	T3	T4
N0	I	II	III	IV
N1	II	II	III	IV
N2	III	III	III	IV
N3	IV	IV	IV	IV

Where I, II, III, and IV are the stages of disease.

current craniofacial surgical techniques, this is no longer categorically true. In children, various approaches have been used, including transzygomatic, orbital, transoral, transmandibular, transpetrous, transbasal, and translabyrinthine.[205] Undifferentiated NPC is a radiosensitive tumor and demonstrates an excellent response to radiation therapy. Such therapy is limited to the primary tumor and its regional metastatic spread. Adjuvant chemotherapy is required in patients with disseminated systemic disease.[350] Although some series of NPC in childhood have reported increased survival rates with chemotherapy compared with historical control subjects, there has been no adequate demonstration of increased survival rates in randomized trials.[193, 219, 283, 317] Potential complications of radiotherapy include mucositis, xerostomia, weight loss, neck fibrosis, and panhypopituitarism.[13, 109] The overall 5-year survival rate of children with NPC approaches 40%.

Skin Malignancies

The incidence of malignant skin lesions in the pediatric population has been reported as 0.15 per 1000 patients seen in a general pediatric hospital.[278] In children, primary skin malignancies are more common than skin metastases. Basal cell carcinoma is most common, followed by melanoma and squamous cell carcinoma. Delay in diagnosis is typical. A heightened clinical suspicion is necessary in children at increased risk for skin cancer. Risk factors include radiation exposure and genetic or familial predisposition.

Basal Cell Carcinoma

Cutaneous de novo basal cell carcinoma is rare in the head and neck region in children.[36, 210] Most cases have occurred in pediatric patients with predisposing genetic defects or exposure to ultraviolet light or radiation. Genetic defects include basal cell nevus syndrome, xeroderma pigmentosum, and nevus sebaceus.[210] Multiple basal cell carcinomas occur in association with odontogenic cysts and other skeletal, dermatologic, and soft tissue anomalies in the inherited nevoid basal cell carcinoma syndrome.[137, 353] The nevi in this syndrome usually do not become malignant until after the first decade of life. Radiation therapy–associated basal cell carcinomas generally have occurred in children and adolescents treated for acute lymphoblastic leukemia or for HL. Surgical excision with possible Mohs technique is the treatment of choice for basal cell carcinoma.[332]

Melanoma

Melanoma is an uncommon malignancy in children with the majority of cases occurring in adolescents.[40, 305] Melanoma accounts for less than 1% of all childhood malignancies including rare presentations such as neurocutaneous melanosis and primary leptomeningeal melanoma.[227] A congenital form of generalized metastatic melanoma has also been described.[348] Giant congenital nevi can also locally transform into melanoma[349]; generally, this occurrence is in the first decade of life, leading to the recommendation to excise giant congenital nevi at a young age.[329] The familial occurrence of melanoma in patients with dysplastic nevus syndrome has also been recognized.[141, 142, 198] A positive familial history for melanoma and the generalized skin disorder xeroderma pigmentosum are additional predisposing factors.[362] Patients at increased risk should be followed up closely and a low threshold for biopsying abnormal lesions should be maintained.

Certain benign nevi termed *Spitz nevi*, *spindle* and *epithelioid cell nevi*, or *atypical juvenile nevi* may simulate melanoma in histologic appearance. Strict histopathologic criteria allow differentiation of these benign lesions from melanoma in most cases, making clinical evidence of malignancy in the form of regional or distant metastases unnecessary.[40] Two systems that are commonly used to classify primary melanoma lesions are the Clark and the Breslow classifications. The Clark system depends upon the histopathologic depth of penetration, whereas the Breslow classification measures the thickness of the lesion from its superficial surface.

Nevi that should raise suspicion of melanoma are characterized by an increase in size, bleeding, color change, or itching. Asymptomatic lesions may be detected on routine physical examination. Most melanomas are found on the trunk and extremities with the next most common site being the head and neck.[305, 367] Melanoma in the head and neck region in children and adolescents most commonly involves the face, particularly the cheek[341]; the forehead, ear, nose, scalp, and neck are less frequent sites of origin. Regional lymph node metastases are frequently palpable at presentation. The incidence of nodal metastases increases as the tumor thickness increases as measured by Clark level.[305] Disseminated metastatic melanoma is unusual outside of infancy.

Once the diagnosis of melanoma is established, further evaluation is necessary to rule out regional cervical and systemic pulmonary, bone, or visceral metastases. Liver function tests might suggest hepatic metastatic disease. Imaging studies should particularly focus on the hepatic, pulmonary, and central nervous systems. Biopsy of the sentinel lymph node by gamma probe localization has been used in adults for staging disease to determine the need for a regional lymph node dissection.[3] Such sentinel node mapping has only recently been performed in pediatric melanoma patients.[267]

Treatment of the primary lesion is complete removal of all microscopic disease. The exact type of surgery depends on the site, size, level of invasion, and extent of tumor (stage). The surgical approach is individualized for each child in accordance with the general principle that the treatment of children should be the same as in adults because the biologic behavior of melanoma appears to be identical in all age groups.[341] The margin of resection is dictated by the anatomic location. Melanomas that are less than 2 mm thick, and especially those that are 1 mm thick, can be excised with a margin of 1 cm without increasing the risk of local recurrence or affecting patient survival. Melanomas that are 1 to 4 mm thick may be excised with a 2-cm margin.[26] Superficial parotidectomy, modified radical neck dissection, or both are indicated when regional periauricular, parotid, or cervical metastases are present.[51] The role of these procedures on an elective basis in the absence of palpable lymphadenopathy is controversial.[25, 261] Elective neck dissection in the setting of a tumor 1 to 2 mm thick and with no lymph node metastases in the neck demonstrated improved 5-year survival rates in those adult patients who had an elective regional lymph node dissection compared with observation.[26] The role of chemotherapy and immunotherapy in melanoma patients is undetermined.[59, 152, 160] The adjuvant use of interferon alpha-2b appears to improve disease-free and overall survival rates in patients with high-risk disease.[195]

Survival rates of children with melanoma, all sites considered, is approximately 40% to 50%.[40] Survival rate varies depending on the presence of regional metastases and correlates with the depth of invasion of the primary lesions as graded by the Clark or Breslow levels.[71, 197, 305, 367] The survival rate of children and adolescents with melanoma was initially thought to be better than that of adults, but this may have been a result of the inclusion of Spitz nevi in original studies.[329] When cases of Spitz nevi are excluded, the aggressiveness of melanoma in the pediatric population is equal to that of adults.

Squamous Cell Carcinoma

Outside of the nasopharynx, the diagnosis of squamous cell carcinoma in children is extremely rare. Previously published reviews of head and neck malignancies in the pediatric age group reveal only sporadic cases.[77, 172, 360] Potential anatomic sites of involvement include the larynx, oral cavity, paranasal sinuses, facial skin (particularly the periauricular region and the upper lip), and skin of the neck.[36] Although de novo laryngeal squamous cell carcinoma has been documented in children without apparent risk factors, the majority of cases occur in pediatric patients irradiated for recurrent respiratory papillomatosis.[239] An association between squamous cell carcinoma and previous exposure to immunosuppressive drug therapy has also been noted.[70, 209] Squamous cell carcinoma is one of the malignancies that may appear in burn scars.[190, 272] Use of smokeless tobacco products by adolescents is increasing, and the use of smokeless tobacco has been associated with squamous cell carcinoma in adults.[161, 398]

Probably the greatest risk for development of cutaneous squamous cell carcinoma in children is preexisting xeroderma pigmentosum.[362] Xeroderma pigmentosum is an autosomal recessive condition in which a defective DNA repair mechanism makes the patient extremely susceptible to the carcinogenic effects of ultraviolet radiation; multiple skin cancers occur in sun-exposed areas. The principles of management of squamous cell carcinoma in the head and neck region in children are the same as in the adult population.

Malignant Teratoma

Teratomas are neoplasms that contain three germ cell layers. Teratomas occur with an incidence of 1 in 4000 births and are thought to be derived from pluripotential cells.[162] Approximately 7% to 9% of childhood teratomas are localized to the head and neck region.[18, 35] The ovaries, testes, anterior mediastinum, retroperitoneum, and especially the sacrococcygeal region are more common sites of origin. Extragonadal tumors are more common in young children. The incidence of malignancy arising in teratomas is estimated at 20%, with considerable variation among primary sites.[144] Malignant teratomas of the cervical region in neonates are rare.[19]

Teratomas have been found in numerous locations within the head and neck region and can be solid, cystic, or both. The neck, pharynx, nasopharynx, orbit, and paranasal sinuses are relatively frequent sites of origin.[133, 246] Oropharyngeal and nasopharyngeal teratomas occur almost exclusively in neonates and young infants. Most cervical teratomas are present at birth, appearing as large neck masses causing respiratory distress and dysphagia (Fig. 101–10).[155] Affected infants have an increased incidence of polyhydramnios, stillbirth, and prematurity. Large cervical teratomas may be detected in utero on ultrasonography and may result in neonatal airway compromise; a medical-surgical team should be organized to be present at birth to secure an airway and maintain adequate oxygenation as needed.[18, 322] Teratomas produce alpha-fetoprotein and beta hCG, which can act as tumor markers and decrease to normal levels after complete surgical resection.[11] Even though most pediatric cervical teratomas are histologically benign, morbidity and mortality are significant. Cervical and pharyngeal teratomas can cause aerodigestive tract compromise.[133] Orbital and paranasal sinus teratomas tend to manifest as massive unilateral proptosis. Teratomas can be classified as mature or immature depending on the degree of differentiation. The immature type may have elements of malignancy and generally have a poorer prognosis than the mature type.[230]

The treatment of mature and immature teratomas is surgical resection. Surgical resection of immature teratomas results in a 3-year tumor-free survival rate of 93%.[230] The use of salvage chemotherapy for recurrent disease results in a tumor-free 3-year survival rate of 98.6%.[230] Because malignant degeneration in head and neck teratomas in children is so rare, much of the experience in managing pediatric germ cell malignancies has been achieved in treating these lesions in gonadal and other

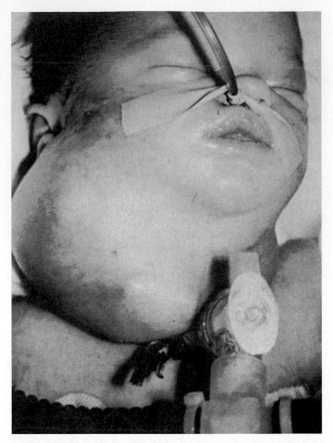

FIGURE 101–10. Respiratory distress requiring airway management results from tracheal compression by large cervical teratomas. The teratoma in this newborn demonstrated actual tracheal invasion and histopathologic evidence of malignancy. (Courtesy of Sylvan Stool, M.D., Children's Hospital of Denver.)

extragonadal locations. Metastasis from childhood teratomas is rare.[371] In this setting, therapy may consist of surgical resection, if possible, followed by a prolonged course of multidrug chemotherapy. Patients with unresectable or residual disease also receive irradiation to the primary site. Almost all patients demonstrate an initial response to therapy. Two-year disease-free survival rate approximates 50%.[144] Prolonged, careful follow-up of all children who have undergone resection of a teratoma, regardless of primary site and histopathologic state, is necessary. Follow-up should include physical examination and, when clinically warranted, alpha-fetoprotein and beta-hCG levels, CT and MR imaging, and nasopharyngoscopy.[11]

SELECTED REFERENCES

Cunningham MJ, Myers EN, Bluestone CD. Malignant tumors of the head and neck in children: a twenty year review. Int J Pediatr Otorhinolaryngol 13:279, 1987.

This review of pediatric head and neck malignancies at a single institution over a 20-year period complements the previous publications of Sutow (1964), Conley (1970), and Jaffe (1973) in terms of outlining the histopathology and mode of presentation of the various lesions in this region.

DeKeyser L, Van Herle A. Differentiated thyroid cancer in children. Head Neck Surg 8:100, 1985.

A well-written, excellent update, which focuses on the management of children with thyroid nodules as well as the treatment of those with established thyroid cancer.

Meadows A, Silher J. Delayed consequences of therapy for childhood cancer. CA Cancer J Clin 35:271, 1985.

Required reading for any physician who cares for pediatric cancer patients.

Miser J, Pizzo P. Soft tissue sarcomas in childhood. Pediatr Clin North Am 32:779, 1985.

A succinct, informative overview of the sarcomatous malignancies of childhood, including rhabdomyosarcoma. It is systemic in scope; however, the head and neck region is frequently a focus of discussion.

Winship T, Bosvoll R. Childhood thyroid carcinoma. Cancer 14:734, 1961.

The classic article on this subject.

REFERENCES

1. Ahmad R, Mayol BR, Davis M, et al. Extraskeletal Ewing's sarcoma. Cancer 85:725, 1999.
2. Airoldi M, Brando V, Giordano C, et al. Chemotherapy for recurrent salivary gland malignancies: experience of the ENT department of Turin University. ORL J Otorhinolaryngol Relat Spec 56:105, 1994.
3. Alex JC, Krag DN, Harlow SP, et al. Localization of regional lymph nodes in melanomas of the head and neck. Arch Otolaryngol Head and Neck 124:135, 1998.
4. Alexander FE, Jarrett RF, Lawrence D, et al. Risk factor for Hodgkin's disease by Epstein-Barr virus (EBV) status: prior infection by EBV and other agents. Br J Cancer 82:1117, 2000.
5. Allo M, Thompson N, Harness J, Nishiyama R. Primary hyperthyroidism in children, adolescents, and young adults. World J Surg 6:771, 1982.
6. Alvardo CS, London WB, Look AT, et al. Natural history and biology of stage A neuroblastoma: a pediatric oncology group study. J Pediatr Hematol Oncol 22:197, 2000.
7. Ambros IM, Zellner A, Roald B, et al. Role of ploidy, chromosome 1p, and Schwann cells in the maturation of neuroblastoma. N Engl J Med 334:1505, 1996.
8. Anast C. Parathyroid disorders in children. Pediatr Ann 9:28, 1980.
9. Anderson A, Bergdhal L, Boquist L. Thyroid carcinoma in children. Am J Surg 43:159, 1977.
10. Androulakis M, Johnson JT, Wagner BL. Thyroglossal duct and second branchial cleft anomalies in adults. Ear Nose Throat J 69:318, 1990.
11. April MM, Ward RF. Garelick JM. Diagnosis, management, and follow-up congenital head and neck teratomas. Laryngoscope 108:1398, 1998.
12. Armitage JO. Treatment of non-Hodgkin's lymphoma. N Engl J Med 328:1023, 1993.
13. Arush MW, Stein ME, Rosenblatt E, et al. Advanced nasopharyngeal carcinoma in the young: The Northern Israel Oncology Center experience, 1973–1991. Pediatr Hematol Oncol 12:271, 1995.
14. Ashcraft M, Van Herle A. Management of thyroid nodules. 1: History and physical examination, blood tests, x-ray tests, and ultrasonography. Head Neck Surg 3:216, 1981.
15. Ashcraft M, Van Herle A. Management of thyroid nodules. II: Scanning techniques, thyroid suppressive therapy, and fine needle aspiration. Head Neck Surg 3:297, 1981.
16. Asmar, Gehan E, Newton WA, et al. Agreement among and within groups of pathologists in the classification of rhabdomyosarcoma and related childhood sarcomas. Cancer 74:2579, 1994.
17. Atkinson J, Mahour G, Isaacs H Jr, Ortega J. Hemangiopericytoma in infants and children: a report of six patients. Am J Surg 148:372, 1984.
18. Azizhan RG, Caty,MG. Teratomas in childhood. Curr Opin Pediatr 8:287, 1996.
19. Azizkhan RG, Haase GM, Applebaum H, et al. Diagnosis, management, and outcome of cervicofacial teratomas in neonates: a children's cancer group study. J Pediatr Surg 30:312, 1995.
20. Backwinkel K, Diddams J. Hemangiopericytoma: report of a case and comprehensive review of the literature. Cancer 25:896, 1970.
21. Baker KS, Anderson JR, Link MP, et al. Benefit of intensified therapy for patients with local or recurrent embryonal rhabdomyosarcoma: results from the Intergroup Rhabdomyosarcoma Study IV. J Clin Oncol 18:2427, 2000.
22. Baker LL, Parker BB, Donaldson SS, et al. Staging of Hodgkin's disease in children: comparison of CT and lymphography with laparotomy. AJB 154:1251, 1990.
23. Baker S, Malone B. Salivary gland malignancies in children. Cancer 55:1730, 1985.
24. Baker S, McClatchey K. Carcinoma of the nasopharynx in childhood. Otolaryngol Head Neck Surg 89:555, 1981.
25. Balch CM, Milton GW, eds. Cutaneous Melanoma: Clinical Management and Clinical Results Worldwide. Philadelphia, JB Lippincott, 1985, p 31.
26. Balch CC, Soong SJ, Bartolucci AA, et al. Efficacy of an elective regional lymph node dissection of 1 to 4 mm thick melanomas for patients 60 years of age or younger. Ann Surg 224:255, 1996.
27. Balch CM, Urist MM, Karakousis CP. et al. Efficacy of 2-cm surgical margins for intermediate-thickness melanomas (1 to 4 mm) Ann Surg 218:262, 1993.
28. Bangerter M, Griesshammer M, Bergmann L. Progress in medical imaging of lymphoma and Hodgkin's disease. Curr Opin Oncol 11:339, 1999.
29. Bangerter M, Moog F, Buchmann I, et al. Whole-body 2-[^{18}F]-fluoro-2-deoxy-D-glucose positron emission tomography (FDG-PET) for accurate staging of Hodgkin's disease. Ann Oncol 9:1117, 1998.
30. Barnes L. Tumors and tumorlike lesions of the soft tissues. In Barnes L (ed). Surgical Pathology of the Head and Neck. New York, Marcel Dekker, 1985, pp 725–880.
31. Barnes L, Gnepp D. Miscellaneous disorders of the head and neck. In Barnes L (ed). Surgical Pathology of the Head and Neck. New York, Marcel Dekker, 1985, pp 1834–1836.
32. Barnes L, Peel B. Soft tissue tumors with special emphasis on the head and neck. American Society of Clinical Pathologists Workshop No. 1074, Orlando, Fla, October 1986.
33. Barnes L, Peel B, Verbin B. Tumors of the nervous system. In Barnes L (ed). Surgical Pathology of the Head and Neck. New York, Marcel Dekker, 1985, pp 659–724.
34. Beck JC, Devaney KO, Weatherly RA, et al. Pediatric myofibromatosis of the head and neck. Arch Otolaryngol Head Neck 125:39, 1999.
35. Berry C, Keeling J, Hilton C. Teratomata in infancy and childhood: a review of 91 cases. J Pathol 98:41, 1969.
36. Bhatia P, Gupta O, Samant II, Mehrotra M. Juvenile epithelial malignancy of head and neck. J Otolaryngol 6:208, 1977.
37. Biller H, Strashun A, Goldsmith S, Bergman D. Preoperative parathyroid adenoma localization by the technetium-thallium subtraction scan. Laryngoscope 96:1363, 1986.
38. Black P, Straaten A, Gutjahr P. Secondary thyroid carcinoma after treatment for childhood cancer. Med Pediatr Oncol 31:91, 1998.
39. Blakely ML, Spurbeck WW, Pappo AS, et al. The impact of margin resection on the outcome in pediatric nonrhabdomyosarcoma soft tissue sarcomas. J Pediatr Surg 34:672, 1999.
40. Boddie A Jr, Smith J Jr, McBride C. Malignant melanoma in children and young adults: effect of diagnostic criteria on staging and end results. South Med J 71:1074, 1978.
41. Boring CC, Squires TS, Tong T. Cancer statistics, 1993. CA Cancer J Clin 43:7, 1993.
42. Boswell WC, Zoller M, Williams JS, et al. Thyroglossal duct carcinoma. Am Surg 9:650, 1994.
43. Bown N, Cotterill S, Lastowska M, et al. Gain of chromosome arm 17q and adverse outcome in patients with neuroblastoma. N Engl J Med 340:1954, 1999.
44. Brenner MK, Heslop H, Krance R, et al. Phase I study of chemokine and cytokine gene-modified autologous neuroblastoma cells for treatment of relapsed/refractory neuroblastoma using an adenoviral vector. Hum Gene Ther 11:1477, 2000.
45. Brodeur GM, Castleberry RP, Pizzo PA, et al. Principles and Practice of Pediatric Oncology: Neuroblastoma. Philadelphia, JB Lippincott, 1997, p 771.

46. Brown B, Syzmula N, Lore J. Neuroblastoma of the head and neck. Arch Otolaryngol 104:395, 1978.

47. Buck B, Scott G, Valdes-Dapena M, Parks W. Kaposi sarcoma in two infants with acquired immune deficiency syndrome. J Pediatr 103:911, 1983.

48. Burkey B, Koopmann CF, Brunberg J. The use of biopsy in the evaluation of pediatric nasopharyngeal masses. Int J Pediatr Otolaryngol 20:169, 1990.

49. Burkitt D, O'Conner G. Malignant lymphoma in African children. I. A clinical syndrome. Cancer 14:258, 1961.

50. Byers B, Piorkowski R, Luna M. Malignant parotid tumors in patients under 20 years of age. Arch Otolaryngol 110:232, 1984.

51. Byers R, Smith J Jr, Russell N, Rosenberg V. Malignant melanoma of the external ear. Am J Surg 140:518, 1980.

52. Callender DL, Frankenthaler BA, Luna MA, et al. Salivary gland neoplasms in children. Arch Otolaryngol 118:472, 1992.

53. Callender TA, Weber RS, Janjan N, et al. Rhabdomyosarcoma of the nose and paranasal sinuses in adults and children. Otolaryngol Head Neck Surg 112:252, 1995.

54. Canacho AE, Goodman ML, Eavey RD. Pathologic correlation of the unknown solid parotid mass in children. Otolaryngol Head Neck Surg 101:566, 1989.

55. Canalis H, Jenkins H, Hemenway W, Lincoln C. Nasopharyngeal rhabdomyosarcoma: a clinical perspective. Arch Otolaryngol 104: 122, 1978.

56. Carbone P, Kaplan H, Musshoff K, et al. Report of the Committee on Hodgkin's Disease Staging Classification. Cancer Res 31:1860, 1971.

57. Carlsen N, Schroeder H, Bro P, et al. Neuroblastoma treated at the four major oncologic clinics in Denmark 1943–1980: an evaluation of 180 cases. Med Pediatr Oncol 13:180, 1985.

58. Carson J, Harwood A, Cummings B. The place of radiotherapy in the treatment of synovial sarcoma. Int J Radiat Oncol Biol Phys 7: 49, 1981.

59. Cassel W, Murray D, Phillips II. A phase II study on the postsurgical management of stage II malignant melanomas with a Newcastle disease virus oncolysate. Cancer 52:856, 1983.

60. Castleberry RP. Predicting outcome in neuroblastoma. N Engl J Med 340:1992, 1999.

61. Castleberry RP. Biology and treatment of neuroblastoma. Pediatr Clin North Am 44:919, 1997.

62. Castro E, Huvos A, Strong E, Foote F. Tumors of the major salivary glands in children. Cancer 29:312, 1972.

63. Chabalko J, Creagan E, Fraumeni J Jr. Epidemiology of selected sarcomas in children. J Natl Cancer Inst 53:675, 1974.

64. Chabner B, Fisher R, Young B, DeVita V. Staging of non-Hodgkin's lymphoma. Semin Oncol 7:285, 1980.

65. Chao TK, Chang YL, Sheen TS. Extraskeletal Ewing's sarcoma of the scalp. J Larnygol Otol 114:73, 2000.

66. Cheung E, Enzinger F. Infantile fibrosarcoma. Cancer 38:729, 1976.

67. Chong GC, Beahrs OH, Chen MLC, et al. Management of parotid gland tumors in infants and children. Mayo Clinic Proc 50:279, 1975.

68. Clark OH. TSH suppression in the management of thyroid nodules and thyroid cancer. World J Surg 85:39, 1981.

69. Clark O, Castner B. Thyrotropin receptors in normal and neoplastic human thyroid tissue. Surgery 85:624, 1979.

70. Clark B, Rosen I, Laperriere N. Malignant tumors of the head and neck in a young population. Am J Surg 144:459, 1982.

71. Clark WII Jr, Ainsworth AM, Bernandino EA, et al. The developmental biology of primary human malignant melanomas. Semin Oncol 2:83, 1975.

72. Cohen J, Landon C, Byers B. Pathologic quiz case 1. Arch Otolaryngol 113:562, 1987.

73. Cohen J I. Epstein-Barr virus infection. N Engl J Med 343:481, 2000.

74. Cohn K, Silverman M, Corrado J. et al. Parathyroid carcinoma: the Lahey Clinic experience. Surgery 98:1095, 1985.

75. Colby T, Hoppe B, Warnke B. Hodgkin's disease: a clinicopathologic study of 659 cases. Cancer 49:1848, 1981.

76. Cone T Jr. Recurrent pheochromocytoma: report of a case in a previously treated child. Pediatrics 21:994, 1958.

77. Conley J. Tumors of the head and neck in children. In Conley J (ed). Concepts in Head and Neck Surgery. New York, Grune & Stratton, 1970, pp 181–187.

78. Conley J, Tinsley P Jr. Treatment and prognosis of mucoepidermoid carcinoma in the pediatric age group. Arch Otolaryngol 111: 322, 1985.

79. Cordeiro AC, Montenegro FL, Kulcsar MAV, et al. Parathyroid carcinoma. Am J Surg 175:52, 1998.

80. Corpon CA, Andrassy RJ. Surgical management of rhabdomyosarcoma in children. Curr Opin Pediatr 8:283, 1996.

81. Crist W, Gehan EA, Ragab AH, et al. The third intergroup rhabdomyosarcoma study. J Clin Oncol 13:610, 1995.

82. Cunningham MJ, Myers EN, Bluestone CD. Malignant tumors of head and neck in children: a twenty year review. Int J Pediatr Otorhinolaryngol 13:279, 1987.

83. Curtin HD, Tabor EK. Radiologic evaluation. In Myers EN, Suen JY (eds). Cancer of the Head and Neck. New York, Churchill Livingstone, 1989, pp 39–74.

84. Cushing B, Slovis T, Philippart A, et al. A rational approach to cervical neuroblastoma. Cancer 50:785, 1982.

85. Dahlqvist A, Ostberg Y. Malignant salivary gland tumors in children. Acta Otolaryngol 94:175, 1982.

86. Daou B, Schloss M. Childhood rhabdomyosarcoma of the head and neck: 2 case reports on salivary glandular and paraglandular involvement. J Otolaryngol 11:52, 1982.

87. Das Narla L, Walsh JW. Diagnostic imaging in rhabdomyosarcoma. In Maurer HM, Ruymann FB, Pochedly C (eds). Rhabdomyosarcoma and Related Tumors in Children and Adolescents. Boca Raton, Fla, CRC Press, 1991, pp 125–137.

88. Daya H, Chan HSL, Sirkin W, et al. Pediatric rhabdomyosarcoma of the head and neck: is there a place for surgical management? Arch Otolaryngol Head Neck Surg 126:468, 2000.

89. Debner L, Chen K. Primary tumors of the external and middle ear. A clinicopathologic study of embryonal rhabdomyosarcoma. Arch Otolaryngol 104:399, 1978.

90. deCampora E, Radici M, deCampora L. Neurogenic tumors of the head and neck in children. Int J Pediatr Otolaryngol 49:S231, 1999.

91. DeKeyser L, Van Herle A. Differentiated thyroid cancer in children. Head Neck Surg 8:100, 1985.

92. Derias NW, Chong WH, O'Connor AFF. Fine needle aspiration cytology of a head and neck swelling in a child: a non-invasive approach to a diagnosis. J Laryngol Otol 106:755, 1992.

93. Deshpande A, Bobhate SK. Squamous cell carcinoma in thyroglossal duct cyst. J Laryngol Otol 109:1001, 1995.

94. DeVita V Jr. The consequences of the chemotherapy of Hodgkin's disease: the Tenth David A. Karnofsky Memorial Lecture. Cancer 47:1, 1981.

95. DeVita V Jr, Hellman S. Hodgkin's disease and non-Hodgkin's lymphomas. In DeVita V Jr, Hellman S, Rosenberg S (eds). Cancer: Principles and Practice of Oncology. Philadelphia, JB Lippincott, 1982, pp 1331–1401.

96. Donaldson SS. Rhabdomyosarcoma: contemporary status and future directions. Arch Surg 124:1015, 1989.

97. Donaldson S, Belli J. A rational clinical staging system for childhood rhabdomyosarcoma, J Clin Oncol 2:135, 1984.

98. Donaldson SS, Link MP. Combined modality treatment with low-dose radiation and MOPP chemotherapy for children with Hodgkin's disease. J Clin Oncol 5:742, 1987.

99. Easton JM, Levine PH, Hyams VJ. Nasopharyngeal carcinoma in the United States: a pathologic study of 177 US and 30 foreign cases. Arch Otolaryngol 106:88, 1980.

100. Eavey RD, Janfaza P, Chapman PH, et al. Skull base dumbbell tumor: surgical experience with two adolescents. Ann Otol Rhinol Laryngol 101:939, 1992.

101. Eisenhut CC, King DE, Nelson WA, et al. Fine-needle biopsy of pediatric lesions: a three year study in an outpatient biopsy clinic. Diagn Cytopathol 14:43, 1996.

102. Ellaurie M, Wiznia A, Berstein L, et al. Lymphoma in pediatric HIV infection. Pediatr Res 25:150, 1989.

103. Eneroth C, Hamberger C. Principles of treatment of different types of parotid tumors. Laryngoscope 84:1732, 1974.

104. Enzinger F, Smith B. Hemangiopericytoma: an analysis of 106 cases. Hum Patrol 7:61, 1976.

105. Evans A, D'Angio G, Koop C. Diagnosis and treatment of neuroblastoma. Pediatr Clin North Am 23:161, 1976.

106. Evans A, D'Angio G, Randolph J. A proposed staging for children with neuroblastoma. Cancer 27:374, 1971.

107. Exelby P, Frazell E. Carcinoma of the thyroid in children. Surg Clin North Am 49:249, 1969.

108. Favus M, Schneider A, Stachura M, et al. Thyroid cancer occurring as a later consequence of head and neck irradiation: evaluation of 1056 patients. N Engl J Med 294:1019, 1976.

109. Fearon B, Forte V, Brama I. Malignant nasopharyngeal tumors in children. Laryngoscope 100:470, 1990.

110. Feimesser R, Miyazaki I, Cheung R, et al. Diagnosis of nasopharyngeal carcinoma by DNA amplification of tissue obtained by fine-needle aspiration. N Engl J Med 326:17, 1992.

111. Feinmesser R, Lubin E, Segal K, et al. Carcinoma of the thyroid in children—a review. J Pediatr Endocrinol Metab 10:561, 1997.

112. Fernandez C, Cangir A, Samaan N, Rivera R. Nasopharyngeal carcinoma in children. Cancer 37:2787, 1976.

113. Ferreiro JA, Weiland LH. Pediatric surgical pathology of the head and neck. Semin Pediatr Surg 3:169, 1994.

114. Fienman N, Yakovac W. Neurofibromatosis in childhood. J Pediatr 76:339, 1970.

115. Finlay JL, Bunin NJ, Sinniah D. Non-Hodgkin's lymphoma. In D'Angio GJ, Sinniah D, Meadows AT, et al (eds). Practical Pediatric Ontology. New York, John Wiley, 1992, pp 269–277.

116. Flamant F, Luboinski B, Couanet D, McDowell H. Rhabdomyosarcoma in children: clinical symptoms, diagnosis, and staging. In Maurer HM, Ruymann FB, Pochedly C (eds). Rhabdomyosarcoma and Related Tumors in Children and Adolescents. Boca Raton, Fla, CRC Press, 1991, pp 91–124.

117. Fleischer A, Koslow M, Rovit R. Neurological manifestations of primary rhabdomyosarcoma of the head and neck in children, J Neurosurg 43:207, 1975.

118. Frankenthaler RA, Luna MA, Lee SS, et al. Prognostic variables in parotid gland cancer. Arch Otolaryngol Head Neck Surg 117:1251, 1991.

119. Freeman C, Berg J, Cutler S. Occurrence and prognosis of extranodal lymphomas. Cancer 29:252, 1972.

120. Freitas J, Swanson D, Gross M, Sisson J. Iodine [131]I: optimal therapy for hyperthyroidism in children and adolescents? J Nucl Med 20:847, 1979.

121. Friedman M, Levin B, Grybauskas V, et al. Malignant tumors of the major salivary glands. Otolaryngol Clin North Am 19:625, 1986.

122. Frostad B, Martinsson T, Tani E, et al. The use of fine-needle aspiration cytology in the molecular characterization of neuroblastoma in children. Cancer 87:60, 1999.

123. Fuller LM, Madoc-Jones H, Gamble J, et al. New assessment of the prognostic significance of histopathology in Hodgkin's disease for laparotomy-negative stage I and stage II patients. Cancer 39:2174, 1977.

124. Garcia CJ, Daneman A, Thorner P, et al. Sonography of multinodular thyroid gland in children and adolescents. Am J Dis Child 146:811, 1992.

125. Garnsey LA, Gehan EA. Prognostic factors in rhabdomyosarcoma. In Maurer HM, Ruymann FB, Pochedly C (eds). Rhabdomyosarcoma and Related Tumors in Children and Adolescents. Boca Baton, Fla, CRC Press, 1991, pp 139–154.

126. Garvin A, Simon B, Young RC, et al. The Rappaport classification and non-Hodgkin's lymphomas: a closer look using other proposed classifications. Semin Oncol 7:234, 1980.

127. Gatti R, Good R. Occurrence of malignancy in immunodeficiency diseases. Cancer 28:89, 1971.

128. Geiger JD, Thompson NW. Thyroid tumors in children. Otolaryngol Clin North Am 29:711, 1996.

129. Gibbs M, Carney J, Hayles A, Telander R. Simultaneous adrenal and cervical pheochromocytomas in childhood. Ann Surg 185:273, 1977.

130. Gladstein E, Guersney J, Rosenberg S, Kaplan H. The value of laparotomy and splenectomy in the staging of Hodgkin's disease. Cancer 24:709, 1969.

131. Gladstein E, Trueblood H, Enright L, et al. Surgical staging of abdominal involvement in unselected patients with Hodgkin's disease. Radiology 97:425, 1970.

132. Glover TW, Stein CK, Legius E, et al. Molecular and cytogenic analysis of minors in von Recklinghausen neurofibromatosis. Genes Chromosome Cancer 3:62, 1991.

133. Gnepp D. Teratoid neoplasms of the head and neck. In Barnes L (ed). Surgical Pathology of the Head and Neck. New York, Marcel Dekker, 1985, pp 1411–1433.

134. Goepfort It, Dichtel W, Samaan N. Thyroid cancer in children and teenagers. Arch Otolaryngol 110:72, 1984.

135. Goldsby RE, Carroll WL. The molecular biology of pediatric lymphomas. J Pediatr Hematol Oncol 20:282, 1998.

136. Gooder P, Farrington T. Extracranial neurilemomata of the head and neck. J Laryngol Otol 94:243, 1980.

137. Gorlin R, Goltz B. Multiple nevoid basal cell epithelium, jaw cysts and bifid rib: a syndrome. N Engl J Med 292:908, 1960.

138. Gotte K, Hormann K, Schmoll J, et al. Congenital nasal hemangiopericytoma: Intrauterine, intraoperative and histologic findings. Laryngoscope 108:589, 1999.

139. Grabb W Jr, Lampe I. The role of radiation therapy in the treatment of chemodectomas of the glomus jugulare. Laryngoscope 75:1861, 1965.

140. Greene MH, Franmeni JF, Hoover R. Nasopharyngeal cancer among young people in the United States: racial variations by cell type. J Natl Cancer Inst 58:1267, 1977.

141. Greene MH, Clark WH Jr, Tucker MA, et al. Acquired precursors of cutaneous malignant melanoma: the familial dysplastic nevus syndrome. N Engl J Med 10:91, 1985.

142. Greene MH, Clark WH Jr, Tucker MA, et al. High risk of malignant melanoma in melanoma-prone families with dysplastic nevi. Ann Intern Med 102:458, 1985.

143. Greven KM, Keyes JW Jr, Williams DW, et al. Occult primary tumors of the head and neck: lack of benefit from positron emission tomography imaging with 2-[F-18]fluoro-2-deoxy-D-glucose. Cancer 86:114, 1999.

144. Grosfeld J, Billmire D. Teratomas in infancy and childhood. Curr Probl Cancer 9:1, 1985.

145. Grovas A, Fremgen A, Rauck A, et al. The National Cancer Data Base Report of childhood cancers in the United States. Cancer 80:2321, 1997.

146. Gustafson R, Maragos N, Reiman H. Extraskeletal Ewing's sarcoma occurring as a mass in the neck. Otolaryngol Head Neck Surg 90:491, 1982.

147. Gutierrez-Ortega P, Hierro-Orozco S, Sanchez-Cisneros R, Montana LF. Kaposi's sarcoma in a 6-day-old infant with human immunodeficiency virus. Arch Dermatol 125:432, 1989.

148. Halprin J, Scott AL, Jacobson LJ, et al. Enzyme-linked immunosorbent assay of antibodies to Epstein-Barr virus nuclear and early antigens in patients with infectious mononucleosis and nasopharyngeal carcinoma. Ann Intern Med 104:331, 1986.

149. Hanna E. Squamous cell carcinoma in a thyroglossal duct cyst (TGDC): clinical presentation, diagnosis, and management. Am J Otolaryngol 17:353, 1996.

150. Harris NL. Hodgkin's lymphomas: classification, diagnosis, and grading. Semin Hematol 36:220, 1999.

151. Harris NL, Jaffe ES, Stein H, et al. A revised European-American classification of lymphoid neoplasms: a proposal from the International Lymphoma Study Group. Blood 84:1361, 1994.

152. Harwood AR. Role of radiation therapy in the treatment of melanoma. In Larson DL, Ballantyne J, Guillamondegui OM, (eds). Cancer in the Neck: Evaluation and Treatment. New York, Macmillan, 1986, pp 243.

153. Hasson O, Kirsch G, Lustmann J. Hemangiopericytoma of the tongue in an 11-year-old girl: case report and literature review. Pediatr Dent 16:49, 1994.

154. Haverkos H, Drotman D. Prevalence of Kaposi's sarcoma among patients with AIDS. N Engl J Med 312:1518, 1985.

155. Hawkins D, Park R. Teratoma of the pharynx and neck. Ann Otol Rhinol Laryngol 81:848, 1972.

156. Hays DM, Newton W Jr, Soule EH, et al. Mortality among children with rhabdomyosarcomas of the alveolar histologic subtype. J Pediatr Surg 18:412, 1983.

157. Hempelman L, Hall W, Phillips M, et al. Neoplasms in persons treated with x-rays in infancy: fourth survey in 20 years. J Natl Cancer Inst 55:519, 1975.

158. Hendrick J. Mucoepidermoid carcinoma of the parotid gland in a one-year-old child. Am J Surg 108:907, 1964.

159. Herrera JM, Krebs A, Harris P, et al. Childhood tumors. Surg Clin North Am 80:747, 2000.

160. Hill G, Moss GE, Golomb FM, et al. DTIC and combination

therapy for melanoma: DTIC (NSC 453881). Surgical Adjuvant Study—COG Protocol 7040. Cancer 47:2556, 1981.

161. Hoffmann D, Harley NH, Fisenne I, et al. Carcinogenic agents in snuff. J Natl Cancer Inst 76:435, 1986.

162. Holt G, Holt J, Weaver R. Dermoids and teratomas of the head and neck. Ear Nose Throat J 58:520, 1979.

163. Hoover L, Blacker J, Zuckerbraun L, Lee R. Surgical strategy in hyperparathyroidism. Otolaryngol Head Neck Surg 96:542, 1987.

164. Hoppe R. Radiation therapy in the treatment of Hodgkin's disease. Semin Oncol 7:144, 1980.

165. Howard D, Batsakis J. Non-Hodgkin's lymphomas: contemporary classification and correlates. Ann Otol Rhinol Laryngol 94:326, 1985.

166. Hudson MM, Donaldson SS. Hodgkin's disease. Pediatr Clin North Am 44:891, 1997.

167. Hudson MM, Donaldson SS. Treatment of pediatric Hodgkin's lymphoma. Semin Hematol 36:313, 1999.

168. Hundahl SA, Fleming ID, Fremgen AM, et al. Two hundred eighty six cases of parathyroid carcinoma treated in the U.S. between 1985–1995. Cancer 86:538, 1999.

169. Hung BW. Nodular thyroid disease and thyroid cancer. Pediatr Ann 21:50, 1992.

170. Hung BW, August GP, Randolph JG, et al. Solitary thyroid nodules in children and adolescents. J Pediatr Surg 17:225, 1982.

171. Jackson H Jr, Parker F Jr. Hodgkin's disease. 2. Pathology. N Engl J Med 231:34, 1944.

172. Jaffe B. Pediatric head and neck tumors: a study of 178 cases. Laryngoscope 83:1644, 1973.

173. Jaffe N, Cassady R, Filler R, et al. Heterochromia and Homer's syndrome associated with cervical and mediastinal neuroblastoma. J Pediatr 87:75, 1975.

174. Jaffe B, Jaffe N. Head and neck tumors in children. Pediatrics 51:731, 1973.

175. Janus C, Edwards BK, Sariban E, et al. Surgical resection and limited chemotherapy for abdominal undifferentiated lymphomas. Cancer Treat Rep 68:599, 1984.

176. Jenkin D, Sonley M. Soft tissue sarcomas in the young: medical treatment advances in perspective. Cancer 46:621, 1980.

177. Johns ME, Goldsmith MM. incidence, diagnosis and classification of salivary gland tumors. Oncology 3:47, 1989.

178. Joncas J, Delage C, Chad Z, LaPointe N. Acquired (or congenital) immunodeficiency syndrome in infants born to Haitian mothers. N Engl J Med 308:842, 1983.

179. Jones S. Clinical features and course of non Hodgkin's lymphoma. Clin Haematol 3:131, 1974.

180. Jones S. Importance of staging in Hodgkin's disease. Semin Oncol 7:126, 1980.

181. Jones S, Fuks Z, Bull M, et al. Non Hodgkin's lymphomas: IV. Clinicopathologic correlation in 405 cases. Cancer 31:806, 1973.

182. Josephson GD, Wohl D. Malignant tumors of the head and neck in children. Curr Opin Otolaryngol Head Neck. 7:61, 1999.

183. Kaldor JM, Day NE, Clarke A, et al. Leukemia following Hodgkin's disease. N Engl J Med 322:7, 1990.

184. Kapadia S. Hematologic diseases: malignant lymphomas, leukemias, plasma cell dyscrasias, histiocytosis X, and reactive lymph node lesions. In Barnes L (ed). Surgical Pathology of the Head and Neck. New York, Marcel Dekker, 1985, pp 1045–1209.

185. Kaplan LD, Abrams DI, Feigal E, et al. AIDS-associated non-Hodgkin's lymphoma in San Francisco. JAMA 261:719, 1989.

186. Kauffman S, Stout A. Hemangiopericytoma in children. Cancer 13:695, 1960.

187. Kearns D, Smith R, Pitcock J. Burkitt's lymphoma. Int J Pediatr Otorhinolaryngol 12:73, 1986.

188. Keiser H, Beaven M, Doppman J. Sipple's syndrome: medullary thyroid carcinoma, pheochromocytoma and parathyroid disease. Ann Intern Med 78:561, 1973.

189. Kemeny M, Magrath I, Brennan M. The role of surgery in the management of American Burkitt's lymphoma. Ann Surg 196:82, 1982.

190. Kennedy AW, Hart WR. Multiple squamous-cell carcinoma in Fanconi's anemia. Cancer 50:811, 1982.

191. Kennedy TL, Whitaker M, Wadih G. Thyroglossal duct carcinoma: a rational approach to management. Laryngoscope 108:1154, 1998.

192. Khurana KK, Labrador E, Izquierdo R, et al. The role of fine-needle aspiration biopsy in the management of thyroid nodules in children, adolescents and young adults: a multi-institutional study. Thyroid 9:383, 1999.

193. Kim TH, McLaren N, Alvarado CS, et al. Adjuvant chemotherapy for advanced nasopharyngeal carcinoma in childhood. Cancer 63:1922, 1989.

194. Kirkland RT, Kirkland JL, Rosenberg HS, et al. Solitary thyroid nodules in 30 children and report of a child with a thyroid abscess. Pediatrics 51:85, 1973.

195. Kirkwood JM, Strawderman MH, Ernstoff MS, et al. Interferon alfa-2b adjuvant therapy of high-risk resected cutaneous melanoma: the Eastern Cooperative Oncology Group Trial EST 1684. J Clin Oncol 14:7, 1996.

196. Knowles D, Jacobiec F, Jones I. Rhabdomyosarcoma. In Jones I, Jacobiec F (eds). Diseases of the Orbit. Hagerstown, Md, Harper & Row, 1979, pp 435–459.

197. Koh HK. Cutaneous melanoma. N Engl J Med 325:171, 1991.

198. Kopf AW, Hellman LJ, Rogers GS, et al. Familial malignant melanoma. JAMA 256:1915, 1986.

199. Kraus DH, Saenz C, Gollamudi S, et al. Pediatric rhabdomyosarcoma of the head and neck. Am J Surg 174:556, 1997.

200. Krolls S, Trodahl J, Boyers R. Salivary gland lesions in children: a survey of 430 cases. Cancer 30:459, 1972.

201. Ladenstein R, Treuner J, Koscielniak E, et al. Synovial sarcoma of childhood and adolescence: Report of the German CWS-81 study. 71:3647, 1993.

202. Lallier M, St-Vil D, Giroux M, et al. Prophylactic thyroidectomy for medullary thyroid carcinoma in gene carrieres of MEN 2 syndrome. J Pediatr Surg 33:846, 1998.

203. Landis SH, Murray T, Bolden S, et al. Cancer statistics, 1999. Ca Cancer J Clin 49:8, 1999.

204. Lange BJ. Hodgkin's disease. In D'Angio GJ, Sinniah D, Meadows AT, et al (eds). Practical Pediatric Oncology. New York, John Wiley, 1992, pp 261–267.

205. Lang DA, Neil-Dwyer G, Evans BT, et al. Craniofacial access in children. Acta Neurochir (Wein) 140:33, 1998.

206. LaQuaglia MP. Non-Hodgkin's lymphoma of the head and neck in childhood. Semin Pediatr Surg 3:207, 1994.

207. LaRouere MJ, Drake AF, Baker SR, et al. Evaluation and management of a carcinoma arising in a thyroglossal duct cyst. Am J Otolaryngol 8:351, 1987.

208. Lawrence W Jr, Hays HM, Heyn R, et al. Lymphatic metastases with childhood rhabdomyosarcoma: a report from the Intergroup Rhabdomyosarcoma Study. Cancer 60:910, 1987.

209. Lee YW, Gisser SD. Squamous cell carcinoma of the tongue in a nine year renal transplant survivor: a case report with a discussion of the risk of development of epithelial carcinoma in renal transplant survivors. Cancer 41:1, 1978.

210. Lesueur BW, Silvis NG, Hansen RC. Basal cell carcinoma in children. Arch Dermatol 136:370, 2000.

211. Leventhal BG, Donaldson SS. Hodgkin's disease. In Pizzo PA, Poplaek DG (eds). Principles and Practice of Pediatric Oncology, 2nd ed. Philadelphia, JB Lippincott, 1993, pp 577–594.

212. Levine P, Komarciu L, Connely R, et al. The American Burkitt's Lymphoma Registry: eight years' experience. Cancer 49:1016, 1982.

213. Levine S, Pestle W. Acinic cell carcinoma of the parotid gland in children. Int J Pediatr Otorhinolaryngol 11:281, 1986.

214. Leviton A, Davidson R, Gilles E. Neurologic manifestations of embryonal rhabdomyosarcoma of the middle ear cleft. J Pediatr 80:596, 1972.

215. Link ME, Donaldson SS, Berard CW, et al. Results of treatment of childhood localized non-Hodgkin's lymphoma with combination chemotherapy with or without radiotherapy. N Engl J Med 322:1169, 1990.

216. Link ME, Shuster JJ, Donadlson SS, et al. Treatment of children and young adults with early stage non-Hodgkin's lymphoma. N Engl J Med 337:1259, 1997.

217. Litenbaum RC, Ratner L. Systemic treatment of Kaposi's sarcoma: current status and future directions. AIDS 8:141, 1994.

218. Littman P, Raney B, Zimmerman R, et al. Soft-tissue sarcomas of the head and neck in children. Int J Radiat Oncol Biol Phys 9:1367, 1983.

219. Lobo-Sanahuja F, Garcia I, Carranza A, Camacho A. Treatment and outcome of undifferentiated carcinoma of the nasopharynx in childhood: a 13-year experience. Med Pediatr Oncol 14:6, 1986.

220. Lugo-Vicente H, Ortiz VN, Irizarry H, et al. Pediatric thyroid nodules: management in the era of fine needle aspiration. J Pediatr Surg 33:1302, 1998.
221. Lukes B, Collins B. Immunologic characterization of human malignant lymphomas. Cancer 34:1488, 1974.
222. Lukes B, Craver L, Hall T, et al. Report of the Nomenclature Committee. Cancer Res 26:1311, 1966.
223. MacArthur CJ, McGill TJI, Healy GB. Pediatric head and neck rhabdomyosarcoma. Clin Pediatr 31:66, 1992.
224. Magrath I. Malignant non-Hodgkin's lymphomas in children. In Pizzo PA, Poplack DC (eds). Principles and Practice of Pediatric Oncology. Philadelphia, JB Lippincott, 1993, pp 537–575.
225. Magrath IT. African Burkitt's lymphoma: history, biology, clinical features and treatment. Am J Pediatr Hematol Oncol 13:222, 1991.
226. Magrath I, Lee Y, Anderson T, et al. Prognostic factors in Burkitt's lymphoma: importance of total tumor burden. Cancer 45:1507, 1980.
227. Makin GWJ, Eden OB, Lashford LS, et al. Leptomeningeal melanoma in childhood. Cancer 86:878, 1999.
228. Mallette LE, Bilezikian JP, Ketcham AS, et al. Parathyroid carcinoma in familial hyperparathyroidism. Am J Med 57:642, 1974.
229. Malone B, Baker S. Benign pleomorphic adenomas in children. Ann Otol Rhinol Laryngol 93:210, 1984.
230. Marina N, Cushing B, Giller R, et al. Complete surgical excision is effective treatment for children with immature teratomas with or without malignant elements: a pediatric oncology group/children's cancer group intergroup study. J Clin Oncol 17:2137, 1999.
231. Maris JM, Matthay KK. Molecular biology of neuroblastoma. J Clin Oncol 17:2264, 1999.
232. Mashburn M, Chonkich G, Chase D, Petti G Jr. Parathyroid carcinoma: two new cases—diagnosis, therapy, and treatment. Laryngoscope 97:215, 1987.
233. Maurer H. The Intergroup Rhabdomyosarcoma Study II: objectives and study design. J Pediatr Surg 15:371, 1980.
234. Maurer H, Donaldson M, Gehan E. The Intergroup Rhabdomyosarcoma Study: update, November 1978. Natl Cancer Inst Monogr 56:61, 1981.
235. Maurer H, Moon T, Donaldson M, et al. The Intergroup Rhabdomyosarcoma Study: a preliminary report. Cancer 40:2015, 1977.
236. McCaffery TV, Meyer FB, Michels VV, et al. Familial paragangliomas of the head and neck. Arch Otolaryngol Head Neck 120:1211, 1994.
237. McGill T. Rhabdomyosarcoma of the head and neck: an update. Otolaryngol Clin North Am 22:631, 1989.
238. McGuirt WF. The neck mass: a diagnostic and therapeutic approach. In Johnson JT, Blitzer A, Ossoff RH, Thomas JR (eds). Instructional Courses. St Louis, Mosby–Year Book, 1990, pp 107–117.
239. McQuirt WF, Little JP. Laryngeal cancer in children and adolescents. Otolaryngol Clin North Am 30:207, 1997.
240. Meadows A, Silber J. Delayed consequences of therapy for childhood cancer. CA Cancer J Clin 35:271, 1985.
241. Medina JE. Neck dissection in the treatment of major salivary glands. Otolaryngol Clin North Am 31:815, 1998.
242. Meier DE, Snyder III WH, Dickson BA, et al. Parathyroid carcinoma in a child. J Pediatr Surg 34:606, 1999.
243. Meissner W. Frozen section: follicular carcinoma of the thyroid. Am J Surg Pathol 1:171, 1977.
244. Michaluart P Jr, Ferra AR. Parathyroid carcinoma. Am J Surg 175:52, 1998.
245. Millman B, Pellitteri PK. Thyroid carcinoma in children and adolescents. Arch Otolaryngol Head Neck 121:1261, 1995.
246. Mills R, Hussain S. Teratomas of the head and neck in infancy and childhood. Int J Pediatr Otorhinolaryngol 8:177, 1984.
247. Miron I, Frappaz D, Brunat-Mentigny M, et al. Initial management of advanced Burkitt lymphoma in children: is there still a place for surgery? Pediatr Hematol Oncol 14:555, 1997.
248. Miser J, Pizzo P. Soft tissue sarcomas in childhood. Pediatr Clin North Am 32:779, 1985.
249. Miser JS, Triche TJ, Pritchard DJ, Kinsella TJ. The other soft tissue sarcomas of childhood. In Pizzo PA, Poplack DG (eds). Principles and Practice of Pediatric Oncology, 2nd ed. Philadelphia, JB Lippincott, 1993, pp 823–840.
250. Mobley DL, Wakely PE Jr, Frable AS. Fine-needle aspiration biopsy: application to pediatric head and neck masses. Laryngoscope 101:469, 1991.
251. Moir CR, Telander RL. Papillary carcinoma of the thyroid in children. Semin Pediatr Surg 3:182, 1994.
252. Moore D, Berke G. Synovial sarcoma of the head and neck. Arch Otolaryngol 113:311, 1987.
253. Moran E, Ultmann JE. Clinical features and course of Hodgkin's disease. Clin Haematol 3:91, 1974.
254. Moss TJ, Reynolds CP, Sather TIN, et al. Prognostic value of immunocytologic detection of bone marrow metastases in neuroblastoma. N Engl J Med 324:219, 1991.
255. Mueller BU, Oizzo PA. Malignancies in pediatric AIDS. Curr Opin Pediatr 8:45, 1996.
256. Mulvihill JJ. Childhood cancer, the environment, and heredity. In Pizzo PA, Poplack DG (eds). Principles and Practice of Pediatric Oncology. Philadelphia, JB Lippincott, 1993, pp 11–27.
257. Murphy S. Childhood non-Hodgkin's lymphoma. N Engl J Med 299:1446, 1978.
258. Murphy SB. Classification, staging, and end results of childhood non-Hodgkin's lymphomas: dissimilarities from lymphoma in adults. Semin Oncol 7:332, 1980.
259. Myer CM III. Salivary gland disease in children. In Gates GA (ed). Current Therapy in Otolaryngology Head and Neck Surgery. Toronto, BC Decker, 1990, pp 174–176.
260. Myer CM III, Mortelliti AJ, Yank GA, et al. Malignant and benign tumors of the head and neck in children. In Smith JD, Bumstead RM (eds). Pediatric Facial Plastic and Reconstructive Surgery. New York, Raven Press, 1993, pp 235–262.
261. Myers JN. Value of neck dissection in the treatment of patients with intermediate thickness cutaneous malignant melanoma of the head and neck. Arch Otolaryngol Head Neck 125:110, 1999.
262. Nakagawara A, Arima-Nakagawara M, Scavarda NJ, et al. Association between high levels of expression of the TRK gene and favorable outcomes in human neuroblastoma. N Engl J Med 328:847, 1993.
263. Nasri S, Mark RJ, Sercarz JA, et al. Pediatric sarcomas of the head and neck other than rhabdomyosarcoma. Am J Otolaryngol 16:165, 1995.
264. Neel HB, Pearson GR, Taylor WF. Antibodies to Epstein-Barr virus in patients with nasopharyngeal carcinoma and in comparison groups. Ann Otol Rhinol Laryngol 93:477, 1984.
265. Nelville HL, Andrassy RJ, Lobe TE, et al. Preoperative staging: factors, and outcome for extremity rhabdomyosarcoma: a preliminary report from the intergroup rhabdomyosarcoma study IV (1991–1997). J Pediatric Surg 35:317, 2000.
266. Netterville JL, Jackson CG., Miller FR, et al. Vagal paraganglioma: a review of 46 patients treated during a 20-year period. Arch Otolaryngol Head Neck 124:1133, 1998.
267. Neville HL, Andrassy RJ, Lally KP, et al. Lymphatic mapping with sentinel node biopsy in pediatric patients. J Pediatr Surg 35:961, 2000.
268. Newman KD, Black T, Heller G, et al. Differentiated thyroid cancer: determinants of disease progression of patients <21 years of age at diagnosis. Ann Surg 227:533, 1998.
269. Nguyen QA, Gibbs PM, Rice DH. Malignant nasal paraganglioma: a case report and review of the literature. Otolaryngol Head Neck Surg 113:157, 1995.
270. Nikkiforo Y, Gnepp DR. Pediatric thyroid cancer after the Chernobyl disaster: Pathomorphologic study of 84 cases (1991–1992) from the Republic of Belarus. Cancer 74:748, 1994.
271. The Non-Hodgkin's Lymphoma Pathologic Classification Project. National Cancer Institute sponsored study of classifications of non-Hodgkin's lymphomas: summary and description of a working formulation for clinical usage. Cancer 49:2112, 1982.
272. Novick M, Gard DA, Hardy SB, Spira M. Burn scar carcinoma: a report and analysis of 46 cases. J Trauma 17:809, 1977.
273. Nygaard R, Garwicz S, Haldorsen T, et al. Second malignant neoplasms in patients treated for childhood leukemia. Acta Paediatr Scand 80:1220, 1991.
274. Obara T, Okamoto T, Ito Y, et al. Surgical and medical management of patients with pulmonary metastasis from parathyroid carcinoma. Surgery 114:1040, 1993.
275. O'Carroll D, McKenna B, Brunning B. Bone marrow manifestations of Hodgkin's disease. Cancer 33:1717, 1976.

276. Okweny C, Kaddumukasa A, Atine I, et al. Childhood Kaposi's sarcoma: clinical features and therapy. Br J Cancer 33:555, 1976.

277. O'Rordain DS, O'Brien T, Weaver AL, et al. Medullary thyroid carcinoma in multiple endocrine neoplasia types 2A and 2B. Surgery 116:1017, 1994.

278. Orozco-Covarrubias ML, Tamayo-Sanchez L, Duran-McKinster C, et al. Malignant cutaneous tumors in children. J Am Acad Dermatol 30:243, 1994.

279. Orvidas LJ, Kasperbauer JL, Lewis JE, et al. Pediatric parotid masses. Arch Otolaryngol Head Neck 126:177, 2000.

280. Ozyar E, Yildiz F, Akyol FH, et al. Comparison of AJCC 1988 and 1997 classifications for nasopharyngeal carcinoma. American Joint Committee on Cancer. Int J Radiat Oncol Biol Phys 44:1079, 1999.

281. Paltiel HJ, Summerville DA, Treves ST. Iodine-123 scintigraphy in the evaluation of pediatric thyroid disorders: a ten year experience. Pediatr Radiol 22:251, 1992.

282. Palumbo J S, Zwerdling T. Soft tissue sarcomas of infancy. Semin Perinatol 23:299, 1999.

283. Pao WJ, Hustu HO, Douglass EC, et al. Pediatric nasopharyngeal carcinoma in long-term follow-up of 29 patients. Int J Radiat Oncol Biol Phys 17:299, 1989.

284. Pappo AS, Shapiro DN, Crist WM, et al. Biology and therapy of pediatric rhabdomyosarcoma. J Clin Oncol 13:2123, 1995.

285. Pappo AS, Shapiro DN, Crist WM. Rhabdomyosarcoma biology and treatment. Pediatr Clin North Am 44:953, 1997.

286. Patow C, Steis R, Longo D, et al. Kaposi's sarcoma of the head and neck in the acquired immunodeficiency syndrome. Otolaryngol Head Neck Surg 92:255, 1984.

287. Pedrick T, Donaldson S, Cox R. Rhabdomyosarcoma: the Stanford experience using a TMN staging system. J Clin Oncol 4:370, 1986.

288. Petti G. Hyperparathyroidism: a study of 100 cases. Otolaryngol Head Neck Surg 90:413, 1982.

289. Picard E, Udassin R, Ramu N, et al. Pulmonary fibrosarcoma in childhood: a fiberoptic bronchoscopic diagnosis and review of the literature. Pediatr Pulmonol 27:347, 1999.

290. Pillay R, Garham-Pole J, Miraldi K, et al. Diagnostic x-irradiation as a possible etiologic agent in thyroid neoplasms in children. J Pediatr 101:566, 1982.

291. Postic W, Tom L, Zimmerman R. Computed tomography in pediatric otolaryngology. Trans Pa Acad Ophthalmol Otolaryngol 32:32, 1979.

292. Postovsky S, Peleg H, Ben-Itzhak O, et al. Fibrosarcoma of the trachea in a child: case report and review of the literature. Am J Otolaryngol 20:332, 1999.

293. Potter R. Peadiatric Hodgkin's Disease. Eur J Cancer 35:1466, 1999.

294. Raab SS, Silverman JF, Elsheikh TM, et al. Pediatric thyroid nodules: disease demographics and clinical management by fine-needle aspiration biopsy. Pediatrics 95:46, 1995.

295. Rallison ML, Dobyns BM, Heating FR, et al. Thyroid nodularity in children. JAMA 233:1069, 1975.

296. Ramos-Gomez FJ, Flaitz C, Catapano P, et al. Classification, diagnostic criteria, and treatment recommendations for orofacial manifestations in HIV-infected pediatric patients. J Clin Pediatr Dent 23:85, 1999.

297. Raney R Jr. Synovial sarcoma. Med Pediatr Oncol 6:41, 1981.

298. Raney R Jr, Crist W, Maurer H, Foulkes M. Prognosis of children with soft tissue sarcoma who relapse after achieving a complete response: a report from the Intergroup Rhabdomyosarcoma Study I. Cancer 52:44, 1983.

299. Raney RB Jr, Handler SD. Management of neoplasms of the head and neck in children. II. Malignant tumors. Head Neck Surg 3:500, 1981.

300. Raney RB Jr, Schnaufer L, Zeigler M, et al. Treatment of children with neurogenic sarcoma. Cancer 59:1, 1987.

301. Raney RB Jr, Tefft M, Hays DM, Triche TJ. Rhabdomyosarcoma and the undifferentiated sarcomas. In Pizzo PA, Poplaek DG (eds). Principles and Practice of Pediatric Oncology, 2nd ed. Philadelphia, JB Lippincott, 1993, pp 769–794.

302. Raney RB Jr, Tefft M, Maurer HM, et al. Disease patterns and survival rate in children with metastatic soft tissue sarcoma: a report from the Intergroup Rhabdomyosarcoma Study (IRS)-I. Cancer 62:1257, 1988.

303. Raney R Jr, Tefft M, Newton W, et al. Improved prognosis with intensive treatment of children with cranial soft tissue sarcomas arising in nonorbital parameningeal sites: a report from the Intergroup Rhabdomyosarcoma Study II. Cancer 59:147, 1987.

304. Raney R Jr, Zimmerman R, Bilaniuk L, et al. Management of craniofacial sarcoma in childhood assisted by computed tomography. Int J Radiat Oncol Biol Phys 5:529, 1979.

305. Rao BN, Hayes FA, Pratt CB, et al. Malignant melanoma in children: its management and prognosis. J Pediatr Surg 25:198, 1990.

306. Rapaport D, Ziv Y, Rubin M, et al. Primary hyperparathyroidism in children. J Pediatr Surg 21:395, 1986.

307. Rappaport H, Winter W, Hicks E. Follicular lymphoma: a reevaluation of its position in the scheme of malignant lymphomas, based on a survey of 253 cases. Cancer 9:792, 1956.

308. Reiter E, Root A, Retting K, Vargus A. Childhood thyromegaly: recent developments. J Pediatr 99:507, 1981.

309. Resler D, Snow J Jr, Williams G. Multiplicity and familial incidence of carotid body and glomus jugulare tumors. Ann Otol Rhinol Laryngol 75:114, 1966.

310. Restrepo J, Handler S, Saull S, Raney R Jr. Malignant fibrous histiocytoma. Otolaryngol Head Neck Surg 96:362, 1987.

311. Rice DH. Malignant salivary gland neoplasm. Otolaryngol Clin North Am 32:875, 1999.

312. Robinson B, Kingston J, Nogueira-Costa R, et al. Chemotherapy and irradiation in childhood Hodgkin's disease. Arch Dis Child 59:1162, 1984.

313. Rodriguez-Cueto G, Manzano-Sierra C, Villalpando-Hernandez S. Preoperative ultrasonographic diagnosis of a parathyroid adenoma in a child. Pediatr Radiol 14:47, 1984.

314. Rodriquez-Galindo C, Ramsey K, Jenkins JJ, et al. Hemangiopericytoma in children and infants. Cancer 88:198, 2000.

315. Rogers DA, Rao BN, Bowman L, et al. Primary malignancy of the salivary gland in children. J Pediatr Surg 29:44, 1994.

316. Root AW, Diamond FB, Duncan JA, et al. Ectopic and Entopic Peptide Hormone Secreting Neoplasms of Childhood. Chicago, Year Book, 1985, pp 369–415.

317. Roper HP, Essex-Cater A, Marsden HB, et al. Nasopharyngeal carcinoma in children. Pediatr Hematol Oncol 3:143, 1986.

318. Rosen G, Caparros B, Mosende C, et al. Curability of Ewing's sarcoma and considerations for future therapeutic trials. Cancer 41:888, 1978.

319. Roskos RB, Evans RC, Gilchrist GS, et al. Prognostic significance of mediastinal mass in childhood Hodgkin's disease. Cancer Treat Res 66:961, 1982.

320. Rostock RA, Siegelman SS, Lenhard RE, et al. Thoracic CT scanning for mediastinal Hodgkin's disease: results and therapeutic implications. Int J Radiat Oncol Biol Phys 9:1451, 1983.

321. Roth SA, Enzinger FM, Tannenbaum M. Synovial sarcoma of the neck: a follow-up study of 24 cases. Cancer 35:1243, 1975.

322. Rothschild MA, Catalano P, Urken M, et al. Evaluation and management of congenital cervical teratoma. Arch Otolaryngol Head Neck 120:444, 1994.

323. Rubinstein A, Sicklick M, Gupta A, et al. Acquired immunodeficiency with reversed T4/T8 ratios in infants born to promiscuous and drug-addicted mothers. JAMA 249:2350, 1983.

324. Russell KJ, Donaldson SS, Cox RS, Kaplan LIS. Childhood Hodgkin's disease: patterns of relapse. J Clin Oncol 2:80, 1984.

325. Sabini P, Josephson GD, Yung RT, et al. Hemangiopericytoma presenting as a congenital midline nasal mass. Arch Otolaryngol Head Neck 124:202, 1998.

326. Sandlund JT, Downing JR, Crist WM. Non-Hodgkin's lymphoma in childhood. N Engl J Med 334:1238, 1996.

327. Sankila R, Garwicz S, Dollner H, et al. Risk of subsequent malignant neoplasm among 1,641 Hodgkin's Disease patients diagnosed in childhood and adolescence: a population based cohort study in the five Nordic countries. J Clin Oncol 14:1442, 1996.

328. Sanroman JF, De Hoyo A Jr, Diaz FJ, et al. Sarcomas of the head and neck. Br J Oral Maxillofac Surg 30:115, 1992.

329. Sasson M, Mallory SB. Malignant primary skin tumors in children. Curr Opin Pediatr 8:372, 1996.

330. Schuller D, McCabe B. Salivary gland neoplasms in children. Otolaryngol Clin North Am 10:399, 1977.

331. Schwartz R, Movassaghi N, Marion E. Rhabdomyosarcoma of the middle ear: a wolf in sheep's clothing. Pediatrics 65:1131, 1980.

332. Schwartz SI, Shires GT, Spencer FC. Principles of Surgery. New York, McGraw-Hill, 1994, p 553.

333. Seeger C, Brodeur GM, Sather H, et al. Association of multiple copies of the n-*myc* oncogene with rapid progression of neuroblastoma. N Engl J Med 313:1111, 1985.

334. Segal K, Sidi J, Levy R, Abraham A. Thyroid carcinoma in children and adolescents. Ann Otol Rhinol Laryngol 94:346, 1985.

335. Seifert G, Sobin LH. The World Health Organization's histologic classification of salivary gland tumors. Cancer 70:379, 1992.

336. Sercarz JA, Mark RJ, Nasri S, et al. Pediatric rhabdomyosarcoma of the head and neck. Int J Pediatr Otolaryngol 31:15, 1995.

337. Sessions RB, Lehane DE, Smith RJ, et al. Intra-arterial cisplatin treatment of adenoid cystic carcinoma. Arch Otolaryngol 108:221, 1982.

338. Shad A, Magrath I. Non-Hodgkin's lymphoma. Pediatr Clin North Am 44:863, 1997.

339. Shaha AR, Shah JP. Parathyroid carcinoma: a diagnostic and therapeutic challenge. Cancer 86:378, 1999.

340. Shanmugaratnam K, Sobin L. Histologic typing of upper respiratory tract tumors. International Histologic Typing of Tumors. No. 19. Geneva, World Health Organization, 1978.

341. Shannon E, Samuel Y, Adler A, et al. Malignant melanoma of the head and neck in children: review of the literature and report of a case. Arch Otolaryngol 192:244, 1976.

342. Shimada H, Ambros IM, Dehner LP, et al. The international neuroblastoma pathology classification (the Shimada system). Cancer 86:364, 1999.

343. Shimotake T, Iwai N, Inoue K, et al. Germline mutations of the RET proto-oncogene in pedigree with MEN type 2A: DNA analysis and its implications for pediatric surgery. J Pediatr Surg 31:779, 1996.

344. Shipp MA, Harrington DP, Anderson JR, et al. A predictive model for aggressive non Hodgkin's lymphoma. N Engl J Med 329:987, 1993.

345. Silverberg E, Lubera J. Cancer statistics, 1987. CA Cancer J Clin 37:2, 1987.

346. Sismanis A, Strong M, Merriam J. Fine needle aspiration biopsy diagnosis of neck masses. Otolaryngol Clin North Am 13:421, 1980.

347. Sisson G. Applying the radioactive eraser: I-131 to ablate normal thyroid tissue in patients from whom thyroid cancer has been resected. J Nucl Med 24:743, 1983.

348. Skov-Jensen T, Hastrup J, Lambrethsen S. Malignant melanoma in children. Cancer 19:620, 1966.

349. Smith J Jr. Problems related to pigmented nevi and melanoma in children. Cancer Bull 24:22, 1972.

350. Snow J. Carcinoma of the nasopharynx in children. Ann Otol 84:817, 1975.

351. Soule E, Newton W Jr, Moon T. Extraskeletal Ewing's sarcoma: a preliminary review of 26 cases encountered in the Intergroup Rhabdomyosarcoma Study. Cancer 42:259, 1978.

352. Soule E, Pritchard D. Fibrosarcoma in infants and children: a review of 110 cases. Cancer 40:1711, 1977.

353. Southwick GJ, Schwartz RA. The basal cell nevus syndrome: disasters occurring among a series of 36 patients. Cancer 44:2294, 1979.

354. Stefanyszyn MA, Handler SD, Wright JE. Pediatric orbital tumors. Otolaryngol Clin North Am 21:103, 1988.

355. Stein JE, Schwenn MR, Jacir NN, et al. Surgical restraint in Burkitt's lymphoma in children. J Pediatr Surg 26:1273, 1991.

356. Stephenson SR, Cook BA, Mease AD, Ruymann FB. The prognostic significance of age and pattern of metastases in stage IV-S neuroblastoma. Cancer 58:372, 1986.

357. Stewart CJ, MacKenzie K, McGarry GW, et al. Fine-needle aspiration cytology of salivary gland: a review of 341 cases. Diagn Cytopathol 22:139, 2000.

358. Stout AP. Fibrosarcoma in infants and children. Cancer 15:1028, 1962.

359. Suen J, Johns M. Chemotherapy for salivary gland cancer. Laryngoscope 92:235, 1982.

360. Sutow W. Cancer of the head and neck in children. JAMA 199:414, 1964.

361. Sutow W, Lindberg R, Gehan E, et al. Three-year relapse-free survival rates in childhood rhabdomyosarcoma of the head and neck. Cancer 49:2217, 1982.

362. Sutow W, Montague E. Pediatric tumors. In MacComb W,

Fletcher G (eds). Cancer of the Head and Neck. Baltimore, Williams & Wilkins, 1967, pp 428–446.

363. Swerdlow AJ, Barber JA, Vaughan-Hudson G, et al. Risk of second malignancy after Hodgkin's disease in a collaborative British cohort: the relation to age at treatment. J Clin Oncol 18:498, 2000.

364. Taylor AMR, Metcalfe JA, Thick J, et al. Leukemia and lymphoma in ataxia-telangectasia. Blood 87:423, 1996.

365. Tefft M, Lindberg R, Gehan E. Radiation therapy combined with systemic chemotherapy of rhabdomyosarcoma in children: local control in patients enrolled in the Intergroup Rhabdomyosarcoma Study. Natl Cancer Inst Monogr 56:75, 1981.

366. Telander R, Moir CR. Medullary thyroid carcinoma in children. Semin Pediatr Surg 3:188, 1994.

367. Temple WJ, Mulloy RH, Alexander F, et al. Childhood melanoma. J Pediatr Surg 26:135, 1991.

368. Templeton A, Bhana D. Prognosis in Kaposi's sarcoma. J Natl Cancer Inst 55:1301, 1975.

369. Tom LWC, Anderson GJ, Womer RB, et al. Nasopharyngeal malignancies in children. Laryngoscope 102:509, 1992.

370. Topf P, Fried MP, Strome M. Vagaries of thyroglossal duct cysts. Laryngoscope 98:740, 1988.

371. Touran T, Applehaum H, Frost DB, et al. Congenital metastatic cervical teratoma: diagnostic and management considerations. J Pediatr Surg 24:21, 1989.

372. Trail ML, Zeringue GP, Chicola JP. Carcinoma in thyroglossal duct remnants. Laryngoscope 87:1685, 1977.

373. Tran L, Sadeghi A, Hanson D, et al. Major salivary gland tumors: treatment results and prognostic factors. Laryngoscope 96:1139, 1986.

374. Treuner J, Gross U, Maas E, et al. Results of the treatment of malignant schwannoma: a report from the German soft tissue sarcoma group (CWS). Med Pediatr Oncol 19:399, 1991.

375. Treuner J, Suder J, Keim M, et al. The predictive value of initial cytostatic response in primary unresectable rhabdomyosarcoma in children. Acta Oncologica 28:67, 1989.

376. Vane D, King D, Boles T Jr. Secondary thyroid neoplasms in pediatric cancer patients: increased risk with improved survival. J Pediatr Surg 19:855, 1984.

377. vanLeeuwen FE, Klokman WJ, Veer MB, et al. Long-term risk of second malignancy in survivors of Hodgkin's disease treated during adolescence or young adulthood. J Clin Oncol 18:487, 2000.

378. Variend S. Small cell tumors in childhood: a review. J Pathol 145:1, 1984.

379. Vawter G, Tefft M. Congenital tumors of the parotid gland. Arch Pathol 82:242, 1966.

380. Verdeguer A, Pardo N, Madero L, et al. Autologous stem cell transplantation for advanced Hodgkin's disease in children. Bone Marrow Transplant 25:31, 2000.

381. Wanebo HJ, Koness RJ, MacFarlane JK, et al. Head and neck sarcoma: report of the Head and Neck Sarcoma Registry. Head Neck Surg 14:1, 1991.

382. Wassif WS, Moniz CF, Freidman E, et al. Familial isolated hyperparathyroidism: a distinct genetic entity with an increased risk of parathyroid cancer. J Clin Endocrinol Metab 77:1485, 1993.

383. Webb AJ. Cytologic diagnosis of salivary gland lesions in adult and pediatric surgical patients. Acta Cytol 17:51, 1973.

384. Webster GF. Local therapy for mucocutaneous Kaposi's sarcoma in patients with acquired immunodeficiency syndrome. Dermatol Surg 21:205, 1995.

385. Weidmann E, Baican B, Hertel A, et al. Positron emission tomography (PET) for staging and evaluation of response to treatment in patients with Hodgkin's disease. Leuk Lymphoma 34:545, 1999.

386. Weiland L. Nasopharyngeal carcinoma. In Barnes L (ed). Surgical Pathology of the Head and Neck. New York, Marcel Dekker, 1985, pp 453–466.

387. Westra WH. The surgical pathology of salivary gland neoplasms. Otolaryngol Clin North Am 32:919, 1999.

388. Wexler H, Helman LJ. Pediatric soft tissue sarcomas. CA Cancer J Clin 44:211, 1994.

389. Weyl M, Arush B, Stein ME, et al. Pediatric thyroid carcinoma: 22 years of experience at the Northern Israel Oncology Center (1973–1995). Pediatr Hematol Oncol 17:85, 2000.

390. Whalen TV, LaQuaglia MP. The lymphomas: an update for surgeons. Semin Pediatr Surg 6:50, 1997.

391. Wharam M, Foulkes M, Lawrence W Jr, et al. Soft tissue sarcoma

of the head and neck in childhood: nonorbital and nonparameningeal sites. Cancer 53:1016, 1984.

392. Wiener ES. Head and neck rhabdomyosarcoma. Semin Pediatr Surg 3:203, 1994.

393. Williams M. Head and neck findings in pediatric acquired immune deficiency syndrome. Laryngoscope 97:713, 1987.

394. Winship T, Rosvoll R. Childhood thyroid carcinoma. Cancer 14:734, 1961.

395. Winslow C, Batuello S, Chan KC. Pediatric mucoepidermoid carcinoma of the minor salivary gland. Ear Nose Throat J 77:390, 1998.

396. Wollner N. Non-Hodgkin's lymphoma in children. Pediatr Clin 23:371, 1976.

397. Wollner N, Burchenal J, Lieberman P, et al. Non-Hodgkin's lymphoma in children: a comparative study of two modalities of therapy. Cancer 37:123, 1976.

398. Wray A, McGuirt WE. Smokeless tobacco usage associated with oral carcinoma: incidence, treatment, outcome. Arch Otolaryngol Head Neck Surg 119:929, 1993.

399. Xue H, Horwitz JR, Smith MB, et al. Malignant solid tumors in neonates: a 40-year review. J Pediatr Surg 30:543, 1995.

400. Yeh SDJ, LaQuaglia M. ^{131}I Therapy for pediatric thyroid cancer. Semin Pediatr Surg 6:128, 1997.

401. Young J, Percy C, Asire A, eds. Surveillance, epidemiology, and end results: incidence and mortality data, 1973–77. Natl Cancer Inst Monogr 57:15, 1981.

402. Young T, Saltzstein E, Boman D. Parathyroid carcinoma in a child: unusual presentation with seizures. J Pediatr Surg 19:194, 1984.

403. Ziegler JL. Burkitt's lymphoma. N Engl J Med 305:735, 1981.

404. Ziegler JL, Beckstead JA, Volderding PA, et al. Non-Hodgkin's lymphoma in 90 homosexual men. N Engl J Med 311:565, 1984.

405. Zinzani PL, Magagnoli M, Chierichetti F, et al. The role of positron emission tomography (PET) in the management of lymphoma patients. Ann Oncol 10:1181, 1999.

102

Thyroid

John Maddalozzo, M.D., F.A.C.S., and Erica C. Bennett, M.D.

Thyroid disease is uncommon in the pediatric population. Not only is it less frequent than in adults, but the distribution of disease processes, causes, and treatment strategies are quite different. In infants, thyroid disease is more likely to result from a congenital anomaly, inborn error of metabolism, or exposure to toxins or antibodies in utero. Nodular thyroid disease is also less common in children, but the percentage of malignant nodules is higher than in adults, requiring a more aggressive surgical approach to diagnosis and management.

Embryology/Anatomy

The thyroid primordium develops from an outpouching in the base of the tongue, located in the area of the foramen caecum. This anlage, known as the thyroglossal duct, descends into the neck during the sixth to eighth weeks of gestation. During its descent, it assumes an intimate association with the hyoid bone, which is concomitantly undergoing anterior fusion. After formation of the thyroid gland, the duct should involute. Persistent remnants of this thyroglossal duct may result in a thyroglossal duct cyst. Thyroglossal duct cysts and ectopic thyroid can occur anywhere along the path of the normal thyroid's descent.

The thyroid is a bilobed gland, with each lobe located lateral to the upper trachea and inferior larynx. The lobes are joined by the isthmus, which overlies the second to fourth tracheal rings. Some patients have superior extension of the isthmus. This structure is named the pyramidal lobe (Fig. 102–1).

The superior laryngeal nerve divides into internal and external branches near the hyoid cornu and is in close proximity to the superior thyroid artery. The recurrent laryngeal nerve is nonrecurrent approximately 1% of the time and will be near the superior thyroid vessels as well. Usually, the recurrent nerve is located 1 to 2 cm lateral to the trachea inferiorly and may pass anterior or posterior to the inferior thyroid artery as it ascends to enter the larynx between the inferior cornu of the thyroid cartilage and the arch of the cricoid, the cricothyroid notch. Many slight variations in branching patterns between patients and between right and left sides of the same patient can occur, requiring a systematic approach to identification and preservation.[29]

The vascular supply of the thyroid gland consists of two arteries and three veins associated with each lobe. The superior thyroid artery, a branch of the external carotid artery, enters the superior pole of the thyroid gland. It is located just lateral and inferior to the external branch of the superior laryngeal nerve. The inferior thyroid artery is a branch of the thyrocervical trunk and may branch and interdigitate with the recurrent laryngeal nerve prior to entering the thyroid gland.

Superior and middle thyroid veins drain into the internal jugular vein, and the inferior thyroid vein drains into the innominate vein.

The lymphatic drainage of the upper portion of the thyroid is into the superior pretracheal and cervical lymph nodes. The paratracheal and lower deep cervical nodes drain the lower portion of the gland.

The superior parathyroid glands, derivatives of the fourth branchial pouch, are most often located on the posterior aspect of the thyroid gland near the cricothyroid joint. The inferior parathyroid glands, third branchial pouch derivatives, have a longer course of migration and, therefore, a more variable location. They are usually found near the inferior pole of the thyroid and are supplied by the inferior thyroid vessels, but they may also be found near the carotid bifurcation or in the superior mediastinum.

Congenital Diseases of the Thyroid Gland

Thyroglossal Duct Cyst

Thyroglossal duct cysts are the most common cysts in the neck and second only to lymphadenopathy as a cause of pediatric neck masses. Approximately 7% of the population are thought to have remnants of the thyroglossal duct.[45] For details of thyroglossal duct cyst, see Chapter 98.

Carcinoma arising in a duct cyst is thought to occur in less than 1% of thyroglossal duct remnants.[45] The mean age at diagnosis is 40 years, with few pediatric reports. The etiology of the disease process is controversial. Theories include metastasis, direct extension through the thyroglossal duct, or primary development of carcinoma in the cyst wall or ectopic thyroid tissue. Sixty-two percent of surgical thyroglossal duct cyst specimens are found to

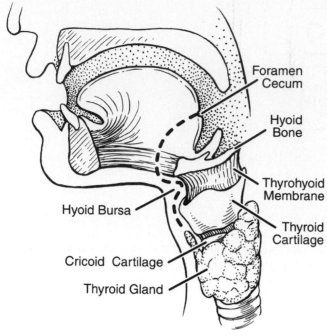

FIGURE 102–1. A figure demonstrating a normal thyroid and surrounding anatomic structures. The path of the thyroglossal duct is also demonstrated (*dotted line*).

have nests of thyroid cells, lending evidence to the primary development or de novo theory. The majority of lesions are papillary carcinoma, but follicular, squamous cell, and Hürthle cell carcinomas have been reported. The only lesion that has not been found to arise in a thyroglossal duct remnant is medullary carcinoma, which also adds support to the de novo theory, since there are no parafollicular cells in ectopic thyroid. Up to 30% of patients have synchronous carcinoma in the normally located thyroid gland, probably representing the multifocal nature of the disease and not necessarily metastasis. Most authors advocate total thyroidectomy with selective neck dissection, if clinically indicated, followed by postoperative radioiodine therapy. Others believe excision via Sistrunk procedure is adequate, as long as there is only a small focus of tumor without invasion of the cyst wall or metastasis and a clinically normal thyroid gland. All patients require close postoperative follow-up.[17]

Ectopic Thyroid

Ectopic thyroid is any functioning thyroid tissue found outside the normal gland location. It is usually located along the normal path of descent, but has been found in the mediastinum, heart, esophagus, and diaphragm. The incidence of primary congenital hypothyroidism is 1 in 4200 live births. Of these, about 23% of patients have an ectopic thyroid; most are located at the base of the tongue, a lingual thyroid. The true incidence of ectopic thyroid is unknown owing to the lack of symptoms in some people. The ectopic thyroid is the only functioning tissue in 70% of patients with a lingual thyroid. Some ectopic glands may function normally, but approximately 33% of patients with ectopic thyroid have hypothyroidism.

Hyperthyroidism is rare. Ectopic tissue is often discovered in the evaluation for congenital hypothyroidism diagnosed by neonatal screening. In cases of a large ectopic gland at the base of the tongue, airway obstruction may occur. Other symptoms include foreign body sensation, dysphagia, and dysphonia. Enlargement due to goiter may develop when the circulating thyroid hormone levels are insufficient. Manifestation may not occur until times of increased metabolic activity, such as puberty, pregnancy, menopause, infection, trauma, or surgery when the gland attempts to keep up with metabolic needs. Treatment with thyroid hormone replacement and/or suppression is usually sufficient, but rarely, surgical excision is necessary. Ultrasound and/or thyroid scan should be done prior to surgical intervention to locate additional functioning tissue.[7, 49]

Functional Diseases of the Thyroid Gland

Hypothyroidism

The incidence of congenital hypothyroidism is 1 in every 3000 to 5000 live births. It is characterized by low thyroid hormone and elevated thyrotropin levels at birth.[12, 16] Agenesis and dysgenesis of the thyroid gland are the most frequent causes. About 20% of patients have a normally developed and positioned gland. Hypothyroidism in these patients is due to chronic lymphocytic thyroiditis (diagnosed by elevated thyroid antibodies) or dyshormonogenesis, including thyroglobulin synthesis defects. Thyroglobulin is the matrix protein in which thyroid hormone is synthesized and stored.[40] Abnormality in the migration of the thyroid may lead to ectopy. The blood supply to the ectopic gland usually is not adequate to support normal thyroid function. This may lead to an enlargement of the gland in compensation and may result in normal enzymes or clinical hypothyroidism.

Congenital hypothyroidism is one of the most common causes of preventable mental retardation and requires prompt diagnosis and treatment with thyroid hormone replacement. The most common cause is sporadic thyroid dysgenesis, which occurs in 1 in 4000 live births. Congenital hypothyroidism is due to thyroid agenesis in 30%, ectopic tissue in 60%, and a defect in thyroid hormone synthesis in 10% of patients. Other causes are less frequent, with incidence approximately 1 in 30,000 live births. Infants may not present clinically until complications ensue. Clinical signs include a large posterior fontanel, jaundice, macroglossia, hoarseness, umbilical hernia, edematous facies, cold extremities, constipation, and hypotonia. Growth and neurodevelopmental retardation occurs without adequate treatment.

Preterm infants may have a transient hypothyroidism. Acquired hypothyroidism in the pediatric patient is rare (<1%) and usually has an autoimmune etiology.

Hyperthyroidism

The incidence of Graves disease in childhood is unknown, but it is usually reported as less than 5% of cases of hyperthyroidism. Neonatal Graves disease is extremely rare, occurring in less than 1% of cases of hyperthyroidism, and is usually associated with maternal disease. The incidence is higher in girls and increases with age. Most pediatric cases occur between the ages of 10 and 15 years.[42]

Placental transfer of thyroid-stimulating immunoglobulin may cause fetal and neonatal Graves disease, usually from active maternal Graves disease. The maternal immunoglobulins may still be produced after therapeutic surgery, radioiodine, or in Hashimoto thyroiditis. Fetal hyperthyroidism may be associated with fetal hydrops, intrauterine growth retardation, craniosynostosis, and intrauterine death. Neonatal Graves disease may manifest between birth and 4 to 6 weeks of age. This type usually regresses spontaneously between 20 and 48 weeks without treatment.[47] A second type of neonatal Graves disease manifests later in infancy, is associated with a strong family history, and usually requires medical management. Children tend to present with similar findings as adults with Graves disease. Goiter is the most common finding, along with tachycardia, nervousness, and increased pulse pressure, which are present in more than 80% of patients. Eye findings are present in more than 50% of cases and include stare, periorbital edema, lid retraction, and proptosis. Additional findings are low birth weight, diarrhea, poor weight gain, restlessness, irritability, warm skin, cardiomegaly, and heart failure. Thyromegaly, which is usually present, may cause tracheal compression.

Three main forms of therapy are used for hyperthyroidism: antithyroid medications, radioiodine, and surgical excision.

Propylthiouracil (PTU) and methimazole block the incorporation of oxidized iodide into tyrosine or thyroglobulin. PTU also inhibits the peripheral conversion of T4 to T3, so is often used when treating patients with severe hyperthyroidism. There is a delay in effect until thyroid hormone stores are depleted over 6 to 12 weeks. This medical therapy is effective in more than 95% of patients, but duration of therapy is difficult to determine because of high recurrence rates after termination of treatment. Toxicity due to medication occurs in 5% to 45% of patients and includes rash, agranulocytosis, and arthralgias. Noncompliance is common. Treatment for fetal hyperthyroidism is antithyroid medications given to the mother. Neonates are treated with antithyroid medications, beta-blockers, iodine, and occasionally, glucocorticoids and digoxin.[48]

Radioactive iodine (^{131}I) is rarely used in children because of fears of increased risk of mutagenesis, although a number of studies have proven otherwise. There is, however, a very high risk of permanent hypothyroidism.[43]

Surgery is indicated in hyperthyroidism after failure of medical therapy, for patients who are noncompliant with antithyroid medications, and to avoid the complications of medications. These complications may include arthralgia, dermatitis, urticaria, leukopenia, and agranulocytosis.[13]

Neonatal Graves disease is usually amenable to PTU treatment and does not require surgical intervention.[27]

Total thyroidectomy is recommended for Graves disease in older patients for rapid and predictable control.[6] The persistence of hyperthyroidism can be as high as 25% to 50% after subtotal resection,[13] and recurrence rates have been reported to be as high as 10% to 15%, but hyperthyroidism may not recur until 10 to 25 years after resection.[6] Secondary operations in patients with recurrence are technically more difficult and increase the complication rate. Total thyroidectomy also prevents progression of ophthalmopathy and excludes the possibility of carcinoma development.[13]

Multinodular Goiter

Multinodular thyroid disease defined as more than one thyroid nodule is uncommon in the pediatric population. In isolation, it is characterized by the formation of new follicles of unknown etiology. It is more common in girls and near puberty. A multinodular goiter may also be associated with McCune-Albright syndrome, Hashimoto thyroiditis, and rarely, carcinoma.

The incidence of malignancy in multinodular glands is reported to be 1% to 7%, compared with 10% to 25% in solitary nodules.[10]

Hashimoto Thyroiditis

Hashimoto thyroiditis is the most common cause of thyroid disease in children. It is an inflammatory autoimmune disorder with the development of thyroid autoantibodies and has an unknown etiology.[10] Patients with Hashimoto thyroiditis usually present with diffuse thyroid enlargement, but they may have a nodular gland.

Neoplasms of the Thyroid

Multiple reports on the subject of pediatric thyroid carcinoma appear in the literature, but since the disease is rare in children, randomized prospective data regarding incidence and therapy are limited; therefore, it is difficult to draw absolute conclusions.

Thyroid neoplasms represent 1% to 1.5% of all pediatric malignancies and 5% to 5.7% of malignancies in the head and neck. The lesions most commonly are papillary and follicular carcinomas. Thyroid nodules occur in 4% to 7% of adults but only in 1% 2% of children. However, only 5% of nodules in adults and 33% of nodules in children are malignant. Follicular adenoma is the most common cause of pediatric solitary nodules of the thyroid. An aggressive surgical approach is recommended for pediatric patients.[9, 10, 18, 23]

Pediatric thyroid malignancies are usually well differentiated papillary or papillary-follicular subtype, but all histologic types have been seen. Children usually present clinically with advanced disease and extensive regional nodal involvement (70% of cases) and distant metastasis (10% to 20% of cases), usually to the lungs. Pediatric patients have higher local and distant recurrence rates but tend to respond rapidly to therapy. The prognosis for children is excellent, with mortality rates between 0 and 10%. Since pediatric thyroid carcinoma is rare, data regarding appropriate therapy are limited.[44]

Exposure to radiation in childhood is a risk factor in the development of thyroid disease. These diseases include hypothyroidism (most commonly), hyperthyroidism, and neoplasia.[2, 33] Thyroid carcinoma is a known sequela of radiation exposure. From the 1920s to the 1960s, prior to recognition of its carcinogenic effects, external beam radiation was used for treatment of benign lesions such as tinea capitis, tonsillar hypertrophy, acne, and thymic enlargement.[5, 14, 24, 25, 39, 41] The Chernobyl disaster, in 1986, sparked an increased incidence of pediatric thyroid carcinoma up to 100-fold in the population exposed. Cases are almost exclusively papillary carcinoma.[25, 39]

Carcinoma of the thyroid gland in pediatric patients usually manifests as an asymptomatic mass. The mass is incidentally noted by parents, the patient, or by a physician during routine physical examination. The subsequent diagnostic work-up is aimed at assessing whether the lesion represents a malignancy. Data collected can be useful in preoperative planning if surgery is indicated.

Imaging studies can be particularly useful in the evaluation of a thyroid mass. Traditionally, ultrasound has been used in order to distinguish the lesion as being solid or cystic. Cystic lesions are considered by many investigators to represent benign lesions and are thought to represent hemorrhage into or degeneration of an adenomatous nodular goiter. However, approximately 8% of cystic lesions represent malignancies.[46]

Thyroid lobectomy is the initial procedure of choice for most solitary, benign thyroid lesions to adequately remove the pathology and spare enough thyroid tissue to maintain a euthyroid state.[6]

A near-total thyroidectomy with radical lobectomy on the side of the primary lesion and subtotal removal of the contralateral lobe is indicated if the lesion is proven or suspicious for well-differentiated carcinoma.[15] Near-total or subtotal thyroidectomy decreases the incidence of complications, such as recurrent nerve injury and parathyroid devascularization, although these structures still need to be identified and preserved.[13]

Although total thyroidectomy has not been proven to decrease recurrence, remaining thyroid tissue may interfere with the use of radioactive iodine both in the postoperative diagnostic scanning and in the treatment of microscopic regional and distant disease. Residual thyroid tissue also provides a source of thyroglobulin that diminishes the specificity of the test as a tumor marker postoperatively.[1]

Radioactive iodine therapy (^{131}I) is indicated postoperatively to ablate residual normal thyroid and treat functioning metastases in differentiated thyroid tumors. There have been very few reports of solid tumors or leukemia associated with ^{131}I treatment. Since cases are few and the general prognosis is excellent, ^{131}I is recommended only for pediatric patients with extensive, unresectable cervical nodal involvement, invasion of vital structures, or distant metastases.[44]

Medullary thyroid carcinoma (MTC) is usually associated with multiple endocrine neoplasia (MEN) type II in the pediatric population, but it may occur sporadically or as familial MTC without other associated endocrine abnormalities. MEN type II consists of MTC and pheochromocytoma and either hyperparathyroidism (IIa) or mucosal neuromas (IIb). MTC associated with MEN IIb is more virulent and may occur and metastasize early in infancy.

MTC arises from the thyroid parafollicular or C cells which secrete calcitonin and are derived from the neural crest and ultimobranchial body. Hyperplasia of the C-cells is thought to represent a precancerous state. Traditional screening for both MTC and C-cell hyperplasia is performed by measuring calcitonin levels before and after pentagastrin stimulation. Screening for MEN type II is now possible with DNA analysis for specific mutations in the *ret* proto-oncogene. Genetic testing should be performed at birth in children at risk for MEN IIb and no later than 1 year of age for MEN IIa.[32, 34]

Total thyroidectomy is the only effective treatment for MTC and, when performed early in childhood, prior to local or distant metastasis, provides the best chance for cure.[32] Owing to the increased virulence of MTC in those with MEN IIb, prophylactic total thyroidectomy should be performed as early as possible and before 5 years of age in those with MEN IIa.[19, 21]

Evaluation of the Thyroid Gland

Laboratory Studies

Serum T3, T4, and TSH are routine in the work-up of thyroid disease and are usually normal in malignancy. Antithyroid antibodies are helpful in diagnosing chronic lymphocytic thyroiditis. Thyroglobulin may be elevated in differentiated thyroid carcinoma and may be helpful in postoperative monitoring.

Traditional screening for both MTC and thyroid C-cell hyperplasia is performed by measuring calcitonin levels before and after pentagastrin stimulation. Screening for MEN II is now possible with DNA analysis for specific mutations in the *ret* proto-oncogene. Genetic testing should be performed at birth in children at risk for MEN IIb and no later than 1 year of age for those at risk for IIa.[32, 34]

Ultrasound/CT

Ultrasound is useful in differentiating solid from cystic lesions and detecting nonpalpable lesions. It provides information about the size, shape, location, and internal consistency of the mass. Cystic lesions are considered benign by many investigators and are thought to represent hemorrhage into or degeneration of an adenomatous nodular goiter. A solid nodule has a higher chance of being malignant. However, up to 50% of malignant lesions may have a cystic component, and approximately 8% of cystic lesions represent malignancies.[3, 46] The incidence of malignancy in multinodular goiter is 1% to 7% and 10% to 73% in solitary nodules in children.[10, 30, 31]

Ultrasound can be used to confirm the cystic nature of a thyroglossal duct cyst and the presence of a normal-appearing thyroid gland overlying the trachea. It can also be used to guide percutaneous needle biopsy.[30, 31]

CT scans can add useful information in cases of substernal extension, local invasion, or lymph node metastasis.

Radionucleotide Scan

Thyroid scintiscans are most useful in evaluating tissue function in thyroglossal duct cysts and in thyroid in a normal location, and in diagnosing ectopic thyroid, but have not proven very useful in distinguishing malignant from benign disease. "Cold" nodules or radiotracer deficient areas are most often benign adenomas in adults, but a larger number of them are carcinomas in children.[11]

Fine Needle Aspiration

Fine needle aspiration biopsy is the gold standard tool in the diagnostic work-up of adult thyroid nodules. Several studies report its efficacy in the pediatric population. High diagnostic accuracy with experienced pathologists improves selection of pediatric patients for surgery and is an adjunct guide to further management.[8, 18, 22, 28]

Surgical Approach to the Thyroid Gland

The Viscerovertebral Angle and the Operation

The viscerovertebral angle (VVA) is an anatomical abstraction modeled into a surgical reality and defined by the intersection of two planes, the first of which is determined by the prevertebral soft tissues and the second by the tangent to the lateral salient of the cervical viscera. The VVA thus established segregates the cervical viscera which comprise an aerodigestive/endocrine complex (larynx-trachea; pharynx-esophagus; thyroid-parathyroids-thymus) from the neurovascular conduits (vagus, descendens hypoglossi, sympathetic chain; common, internal, and external carotid arteries; internal jugular vein; lymphatic ducts) which flank on either side (Fig. 102–2).

Included amongst the structures which traverse the VVA from the base of skull to the diaphragm which are of particular interest to the thyroid surgeon are the superior laryngeal vessels, the superior and inferior thyroid vessels, the middle thyroid vein, the internal and external branches of the superior laryngeal nerve, and the recurrent laryngeal nerve with its inferior laryngeal termination.[35–38]

Although the thyroid and parathyroid glands are in the anterior aspect of the neck, their anatomic disposition is not so much in the midline as anterolateral. Consequently, the direct approach to them comes from an anterolateral aspect.

The thrust of the operative effort is the surgical realization of the anatomic abstraction the VVA, and its appli-

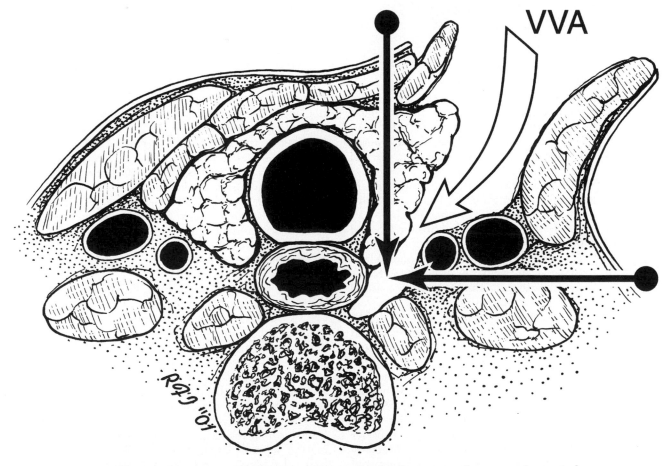

FIGURE 102–2. Cross-sectional diagram showing that the direct surgical access to the cervical viscera (the aerodigestive-endocrine complex composed of the larynx, trachea, pharynx, esophagus, thyroid, parathyroid glands, and thymus) and the great neurovascular bundle (composed of the internal jugular vein, lymphatic duct, carotid arteries, and descendens hypoglossi and vagus nerves and the cervical sympathetic chain) is an anterolateral approach. The sides of the viscerovertebral angle (VVA) are formed by the areolar tissue overlying the prevertebral musculature and the tangent to the lateral salient of the cervical viscera.

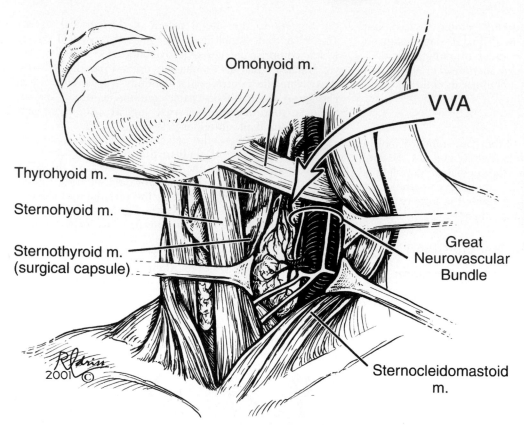

Thyrohyoid m.

Sternohyoid m.

Sternothyroid m.
(surgical capsule)

Omohyoid m.

VVA

Great
Neurovascular
Bundle

Sternocleidomastoid
m.

FIGURE 102-3. Separation of the medial margin of the sternocleidomastoid muscle from the tendinous sternal origin to the hyoid initiates the approach to the viscerovertebral angle (VVA). M, muscle.

cation as an operative system. In the process, the cervical viscera (larynx, pharynx, trachea, esophagus, thyroid, parathyroids, and thymus) are segregated from the great neurovascular bundle (descendens hypoglossi, vagus, sympathetic chain, jugular vein, lymphatic duct, and carotid arteries).

The topographic boundaries of the surgical field are the hyoid bone above, the neurovascular bundles laterally, and the sternoclavicular junction and sternal notch below.

The surgical incision is oriented horizontally and placed in a supramanubrial location. Its lateral extent is determined by the extremes of the hyoid bone, which also coincide topographically with the external tendinous origin of the manubrial head of the sternocleidomastoid muscle.

The depth of the incision is subplatysmal yet superficial to the anterior jugular and communicating veins. The superior limit of the surgical flap is the hyoid bone and the inferior boundary is the sternoclavicular junction and the angle of Louis. The lateral margin of the hyoid and the tendinous manubrial origin of sternocleidomastoid muscle limit the lateral extent. The medial margin of the sternocleidomastoid muscle is mobilized from its tendinous origin to the hyoid bone and reflected. The superior belly of the omohyoid muscle is then exposed and is skeletonized from its tendon to the hyoid and retracted superolaterally.

Immediately beneath are the descendens hypoglossi nerve and the internal jugular vein. Decollement of the sternohyoid muscle from its retromanubrial origin to its hyoid insertion follows, while observing the integrity of its neurovascular bundle, the descendens hypoglossi nerve.

Rarely, the sternohyoid and sternothyroid muscles may not be well segmented developmentally and may exist as an amorphous muscle plate (Fig. 102-3).

Whereas the sternohyoid muscle is linear and slender and meets its mate in the midline, the sternothyroid muscle is broad and just fails to contact its counterpart. It surgically encapsulates the thyroid lobes, and therefore must extend laterally to the internal jugular vein and its neurovascular companions. It, too, undergoes decollement from its retromanubrial origin to its insertion in the oblique line of the thyroid cartilage. Thus, the three infrahyoid muscles are liberated, each from tendon to tendon.

The anterior trachea surface, thyroid isthmus, and inferior thyroid veins are sought and demonstrated.

Development of the VVA proceeds with surgical transection of the middle thyroid vein. The dissection continues to the depth of the area of tissue that overlies the prevertebral musculature. The lobe of the thyroid is retracted medially, exposing the inferior pharyngeal constrictor muscle and esophagus while identifying and sparing the recurrent laryngeal nerve and the inferior and superior thyroid vessels. The thyroid lobe is separated from the pharyngeal constrictor, identifying and preserving the superior laryngeal nerve. The great cervical neurovascular bundle is consequently laterally disposed. The cervical viscera are mobilized and the prevertebral musculature is visualized.

The usual disposition of the parathyroid glands is in the following general pattern. The superior gland lies in the sulcus between the posteromedial aspect of the thyroid gland and the inferior constrictor muscle at the level

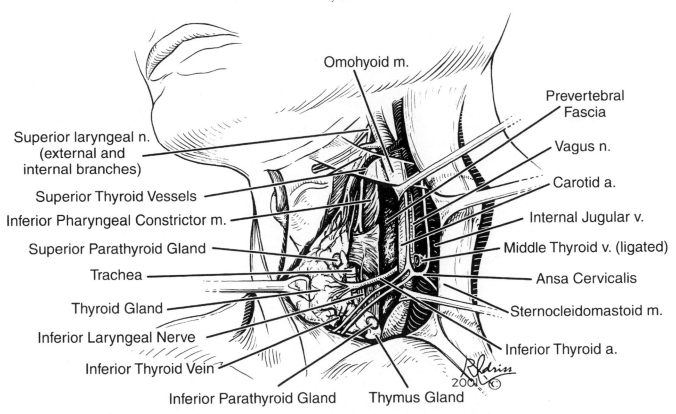

FIGURE 102–4. The superior belly of the omohyoid muscle is mobilized from its tendon to its hyoid insertion, exposing the great neurovascular complex. Separation of the sternohyoid and sternothyroid muscles from their manubrial origins to their respective insertions into the hyoid bone and thyroid cartilage, while preserving their innervation from the descendens hypoglossi nerve, provides access to the cervical viscera. Medial rotation of the cervical viscera from the great neurovascular bundle, and dissolution of the intervening gossamer areolar tissue, opens an avenue to the fascia overlying the prevertebral musculature. The viscerovertebral angle (VVA) is thereby constructed, providing exposure of the entire anterior cervical contents from the hyoid bone above and continuing into the superior mediastinum. Crossing the angle are the superior laryngeal nerves, the superior, middle, and inferior thyroid vessels, and the inferior laryngeal nerve. a, artery; m, muscle; n, nerve; v, vein.

of the inferior thyroid cartilage cornu and the superior rim of the cricoid cartilage. The inferior gland is often found in proximity to the intersection of the inferior thyroid vessels and the recurrent laryngeal nerve. Not infrequently, both superior and inferior glands are nearly juxtaposed at this neurovascular crossing. The parathyroid glands are identified and preserved.

The surgical field, in its depth, is now bounded laterally by the common carotid vessels converging through the thoracic inlet and inferiorly by the innominate vessels. Crossing the angle are the superior and inferior thyroid vessels, which now require transection and hemostatic control. The thyroid lobe can be mobilized off the central viscera and transected with or without the isthmus. If total thyroidectomy is required, the procedure can be repeated on the opposite side (Fig. 102–4).

The approach is astonishingly bloodless. It provides for exposure and exploration of the entire anterior neck contents as well as access to the superior mediastinum. It also provides for identification and visualization of the recurrent laryngeal nerve in the tracheoesophageal groove, well inferior to the thyroid gland. This provides for an easier dissection and preservation of this structure.

If a full nodal neck dissection is required, extension of the surgical incision is all that is needed.

Neck Dissection

Neck dissection in pediatric thyroid surgery is indicated for regional lymph node metastasis. A unilateral selective neck dissection should be performed, during which lymph nodes should be inspected in the paratracheal region, tracheoesophageal groove, and laterally, and excised if suspicious for pathology.[15]

Formal neck dissection has not been shown to improve outcome and has increased risk of minor surgical complications.[20]

Complications

Surgical complications include recurrent laryngeal nerve injury, hypoparathyroidism, hypothyroidism, and wound infection. The most common complication of a total thyroidectomy in children is parathyroid gland injury in 6% to 15% of cases, resulting in permanent hypoparathyroidism.[19, 20, 32, 34] A euthyroid state in all patients after total thyroidectomy is maintained with thyroid hormone replacement. After a subtotal thyroidectomy, hypothyroidism occurs in 6.5% to 49% of patients. Secondary operations are more hazardous.[6]

Postoperative Therapy

Pediatric patients have higher local and distant recurrence rates than adults, but tend to respond rapidly to therapy. The prognosis for children is excellent, with mortality rates between 0 and 10%. In patients younger than 10 years of age, the recurrence-free 20-year survival rate is 10.1%, and the rate is 48.3% in those older than 10 years. The overall 20-year survival rate is 92% to 100%. Some studies report young age as the major determinant of recurrence in pediatric differentiated thyroid carcinoma, which suggests a difference in tumor biology. Rearrangements in *ret* and *ntrk1* proto-oncogenes have been seen, which suggests the possibility of future gene therapy.[1]

Postoperative suppression of TSH with thyroid hormone may decrease recurrence of carcinoma and is more effective in papillary and papillary-follicular types. TSH-suppressive doses (150–200 μg) of thyroxine are begun postoperatively.[15]

A control thyroid scan 2 to 3 weeks postoperatively is usually performed. [131]I is given only with extensive neck disease or distant metastases.

Thyroid carcinoma has been found to recur up to 33 years after treatment. Patients should receive close follow-up with pulmonary function tests, chest x-rays, and CT scans as well as thyroid function tests.[4] Thyroglobulin levels should be followed for medullary carcinoma.

Local postoperative radiation is not recommended due to a possible carcinogenic effect in children.

REFERENCES

1. Alessandri AJ, Goddard KJ, Blair GK, et al. Age is the major determinant of recurrence in pediatric differentiated thyroid carcinoma. Med Pediatr Oncol 35:41, 2000.
2. Atahan IL, Yildiz F, Ozyar E, et al. Thyroid dysfunction in children receiving neck irradiation for Hodgkin's disease. Radiat Med 16:359, 1998.
3. Bajpai M, Ramaswamy S, Gupta DK, et al. Solitary thyroid nodule. Indian Pediatr 29:116, 1992.
4. Ben Arush MW, Stein ME, Perez Nahum M, et al. Pediatric thyroid carcinoma: 22 years of experience at the Northern Israel Oncology Center (1973–1995). Pediatr Hematol Oncol 17:85, 2000.
5. Bhatia S, Ramsay NK, Bantle JP, et al. Thyroid abnormalities after therapy for Hodgkin's disease in childhood. Oncologist 1:62, 1996.
6. Bryarly RC, Shockley WW, Stucker FJ. The method and management of thyroid surgery in the pediatric patient. Laryngoscope 95:1025, 1985.
7. Di Benedetto V. Ectopic thyroid gland in the submandibular region simulating a thyroglossal duct cyst: a case report. J Pediatr Surg 32:1745, 1997.
8. Eisenhut CC, King DE, Nelson WA, et al. Fine-needle biopsy of pediatric lesions: a three-year study in an outpatient biopsy clinic. Diagn Cytopathol 14:43, 1996.
9. Festen C, Otten BJ, van de Kaa CA. Follicular adenoma of the thyroid gland in children. Eur J Pediatr Surg 5:262, 1995.
10. Garcia CJ, Daneman A, Thorner P, et al. Sonography of multinodular thyroid gland in children and adolescents. Am J Dis Child 146:811, 1992.
11. Geiger JD, Thompson NW. Thyroid tumors in children. Otolaryngol Clin North Am 29:711, 1996.
12. Gordon B, Yaakob W, Willi S, et al. Congenital thyroid disease revisited: migrational anomalies and dyshormonogenesis. J Nucl Med Technol 27:282, 1999.
13. Herzog B. Thyroid gland diseases and tumours. Surgical aspects. Prog Pediatr Surg 16:15, 1983.
14. Jensen MO, Antonenko D. Thyroid and thymic malignancy following childhood irradiation. J Surg Oncol 50:206, 1992.
15. Joppich I, Roher HD, Hecker WC, et al. Thyroid carcinoma in childhood. Prog Pediatr Surg 16:23, 1983.
16. Kaiserman I, Siebner R, Sack J. Regional and temporal fluctuations in the incidence of congenital hypothyroidism in Israel. J Endocrinol Invest 18:595, 1995.
17. Kennedy TL, Whitaker M, Wadih G. Thyroglossal duct carcinoma: a rational approach to management. Laryngoscope 108:1154, 1998.
18. Khurana KK, Labrador E, Izquierdo R, et al. The role of fine-needle aspiration biopsy in the management of thyroid nodules in children, adolescents, and young adults: a multi-institutional study. Thyroid 9:383, 1999.
19. Lallier M, St-Vil D, Giroux M, et al. Prophylactic thyroidectomy for medullary thyroid carcinoma in gene carriers of MEN2 syndrome. J Pediatr Surg 33:846, 1998.
20. La Quaglia MP, Corbally MT, Heller G, et al. Recurrence and morbidity in differentiated thyroid carcinoma in children. Surgery 104:1149, 1988.
21. La Quaglia MP, Telander RL. Differentiated and medullary thyroid cancer in childhood and adolescence. Semin Pediatr Surg 6:42, 1997.
22. Lugo-Vicente H, Ortiz VN. Pediatric thyroid nodules: insights in management. Bol Asoc Med P R 90:74, 1998.
23. Lugo-Vicente H, Ortiz VN, Irizarry H, et al. Pediatric thyroid nodules: management in the era of fine needle aspiration. J Pediatr Surg 33:1302, 1998.
24. Metayer C, Lynch CF, Clarke EA, et al. Second cancers among long-term survivors of Hodgkin's disease diagnosed in childhood and adolescence. J Clin Oncol 18:2435, 2000.
25. Nikiforov Y, Gnepp DR. Pediatric thyroid cancer after the Chernobyl disaster. Pathomorphologic study of 84 cases (1991–1992) from the Republic of Belarus. Cancer 74:748, 1994.
26. Pinczower E, Crockett DM, Atkinson JB, et al. Preoperative thyroid scanning in presumed thyroglossal duct cysts. Arch Otolaryngol Head Neck Surg 118:985, 1992.
27. Postellon DC, Hale PM. Diagnosis and treatment of thyroid disease in infants. Compr Ther 17:57, 1991.
28. Raab SS, Silverman JF, Elsheikh TM, et al. Pediatric thyroid nodules: disease demographics and clinical management as determined by fine needle aspiration biopsy. Pediatrics 95:46, 1995.
29. Reed AF. Relations of inferior laryngeal nerve to inferior thyroid artery. Anat Rec 85:17, 1943.
30. Schneider K. Sonographic imaging of the thyroid in children. Prog Pediat Surg 26:1, 1991.
31. Sherman NH, Rosenberg HK, Heyman S, et al. Ultrasound evaluation of neck masses in children. J Ultrasound Med 4:127, 1985.
32. Skinner MA, Wells SA. Medullary carcinoma of the thyroid gland and the MEN 2 syndromes. Sem Pediatr Surg 6:134, 1997.
33. Solt I, Gaitini D, Pery M, et al. Comparing thyroid ultrasonography to thyroid function in long-term survivors of childhood lymphoma. Med Pediatr Oncol 35:35, 2000.
34. Telander RL, Moir CR. Medullary thyroid carcinoma in children. Semin Pediatr Surg 3:188, 1994.
35. Tenta LT, ed. Surgery of the Thyroid and Parathyroid Glands. Otolaryngol Clin North Am (Feb) 1980.
36. Tenta LT, Maddalozzo J. Parathyroid conservation and the viscerovertebral angle: a downsized view. Operative Tech Otolaryngol Head Neck Surg 5:137, 1994.
37. Tenta LT, Keyes GR. The viscerovertebral angle the surgical avenue of the neck. Clin Plast Surg 12:313, 1985.
38. Tenta, LT, Keyes GR. Transcervical parathyroidectomy with microsurgical autotransplantation and the viscerovertebral angle. Otolaryngol Clin North Am 13:169, 1980.

39. Thomas GA, Bunnell H, Cook HA, et al. High prevalence of *RET/PTC* rearrangements in Ukrainian and Belarussian post-Chernobyl thyroid papillary carcinomas: a strong correlation between *RET/PTC3* and the solid-follicular variant. J Clin Endo Metab 84:4232, 1999.

40. van de Graaf SA, Cammenga M, Ponne NJ, et al. The screening for mutations in the thyroglobulin cDNA from six patients with congenital hypothyroidism. Biochimie 81:425, 1999.

41. Vane D, King DR, Boles ET, Jr. Secondary thyroid neoplasms in pediatric cancer patients: increased risk with improved survival. J Pediatr Surg 19:855, 1984.

42. Waldhausen JHT. Controversies related to the medical and surgical management of hyperthyroidism in children. Semin Pediatr Surg 6:121, 1997.

43. Ward L, Huot C, Lambert R, et al. Outcome of pediatric Graves' disease after treatment with antithyroid medication and radioiodine. Clin Invest Med 22:132, 1999.

44. Yeh SD, La Quaglia MP. I131 therapy for pediatric thyroid cancer. Semin Pediatr Surg 6:128, 1997.

45. Yoo KS, Chengazi VU, O'Mara RE. Thyroglossal duct cyst with papillary carcinoma in an 11-year-old girl. J Pediatr Surg 33:745, 1998.

46. Yoskovitch A, Laberge JM, Rodd C, et al. Cystic thyroid lesions in children. J Pediatr Surg 33:866, 1998.

47. Zimmerman D. Fetal and neonatal hyperthyroidism. Thyroid 9:727, 1999.

48. Zimmerman D, Lteif AN. Thyrotoxicosis in children. Endocrinol Metab Clin North Am 27:109, 1998.

49. Zoller DC, Silverman BL, Daaboul JJ. Lingual thyroid. Arch Pediatr Adolesc Med 154:843, 2000.

103

Injuries of the Neck

Peggy E. Kelley, M.D., and Bruce W. Jafek, M.D.

Injury is the most common cause of childhood death and is responsible for more childhood deaths than all other causes combined. It has been estimated that approximately 25,000 deaths and 600,000 hospital admissions are due to pediatric injury each year in the United States.[4] Passengers, pedestrians, and cyclists in motor vehicle accidents account for the largest group of pediatric fatalities, followed by drowning, house fires, and firearm injuries. Falls and vehicular crashes account for almost 80% of all pediatric injuries, although the number of penetrating injuries is increasing in certain large cities. Multisystem injury is the rule rather than the exception, and all organ systems must be evaluated and treated.[1] Most injuries occur in children between the ages of 2 and 7 years, which represents the time of transition between total parental protection and adequate education for self-preservation. Approximately 10% to 15% of serious injuries in children are neck injuries.[11, 17]

General Principles

Pediatric injuries differ from those in the adult, not only in the nature of the injuries sustained but also in the emotional reaction of the patient to trauma and often in the management and response to therapy. Children have smaller body mass than adults and closer proximity of vital structures. Linear forces incurred from motor vehicle accidents or falls are therefore applied with greater energy per unit of body area. The pediatric skeleton is incompletely calcified and is more pliable than the adult skeleton. Internal injuries may occur without associated fracture of bone. A child's body surface area–to–volume ratio is highest at birth and decreases with age. These factors are important when considering blood loss, fluid resuscitation, or hypothermia during treatment of the pediatric trauma patient.[4]

Injuries of the neck may be categorized clinically into four types according to the immediacy of the treatment requirements[27]:

1. Injuries that interfere with vital physiologic function (e.g., hemorrhage, shock)
2. Injuries that are severe but not immediately life threatening
3. Injuries whose severity is occult, requiring additional evaluation or observation to determine the correct therapy
4. Injuries that are minor and superficial in character

The severity of neck injuries in traumatized children is related to the kinetic energy ($\frac{1}{2}$ mass $\times$ velocity^2) involved. Typically, motor vehicle accidents and falls are of relatively large mass and slow velocity. As the velocity of the applied force increases, the severity of resultant injury increases as a function of its square. Secondary missile injuries may be produced by disrupted bone, thereby increasing the resultant "cone of injury." Gunshot wounds at close range may produce their effects by blast injury as well as by missile injury.

Major neck injuries in the pediatric age range are most common in the aerodigestive system (pharynx, esophagus, larynx, and trachea) and are discussed elsewhere (Chaps. 68 to 70 and 86). Other serious injuries are less common and include those of the major blood vessels, spine, spinal cord, and peripheral nerves that pass through the neck. Significant injuries of the endocrine glands of the neck or thoracic duct are rare.

Early diagnostic and treatment efforts must avoid converting a lesser injury to one of greater severity. The child's parents or other next of kin should be notified of the injury and a progress report should be given as soon as possible after the injury and at appropriate intervals during acute management.

Anatomic Differences Between Children and Adults

Several anatomic differences between pediatric and adult head and neck structures contribute to a different spectrum of injuries in children.

1. The child's larynx is located much higher in the neck, largely beneath the protection of the mandible, and is less frequently injured. Descent of this structure occurs gradually and is complete by early adulthood.
2. The child's head is proportionally larger, relative to the rest of the body, than the adult's. The supporting neck structures are therefore more susceptible to sudden acceleration or deceleration injuries owing to "whipping" of the unrestrained head. These

structures, however, have more elasticity, allowing greater compensation without serious injury.[10]

3. The child's total weight is less; therefore, a lesser force is applied to the neck or body in deceleration or acceleration injuries (as in automobile accidents), with more rapid dissipation of the force.
4. The younger child's bones contain a greater percentage of cartilage, allowing proportionately more flexibility and resulting in less breaking of the bones. Fractures are therefore less frequent than in the adult.
5. Children are exposed to different types of traumatic risk than adults. Blunt trauma is responsible for 80% to 90% of serious external cervical injuries in children, whereas penetrating injuries are more common in the adult.[1]

Multisystem Involvement

Figures 103–1 and 103–2 illustrate the multiplicity of systems that may be involved in severe neck trauma and show that there is a need to be aware of other possible injuries.

Initial Diagnostic Approach

The general approach to a child with major trauma and neck injury includes rapidly obtaining a sufficient history to determine (as certainly as possible) the degree and type of injury and any serious coexistent medical problems. Sequential emergency management begins with a primary survey in which life-threatening conditions are identified and management is instituted simultaneously. The ABCDEs taught in Advanced Trauma Life Support (ATLS) should be followed. Some differences exist in the pediatric patient and are outlined briefly.

A. *Airway and cervical spine protection.* If the airway

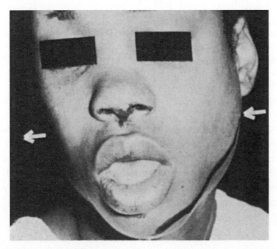

FIGURE 103–1. This 16-year-old was shot with a .22-caliber bullet. *Arrows* show entrance (left neck) and exit (right neck) wounds. Complications, including hematomas of the neck and oropharynx, odontoid fracture, left internal carotid artery occlusion with cerebral infarct, and epistaxis, demonstrate multisystem involvement of serious neck injuries.

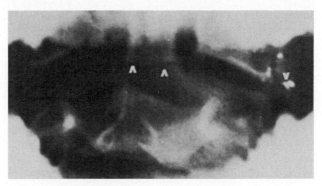

FIGURE 103–2. "Open mouth" radiograph shows nondisplaced odontoid fracture (*double arrows*) and retained bullet fragment (*single arrow*).

cannot be maintained by oxygenation or jaw thrust maneuvers, orotracheal intubation with adequate immobilization and protection of the cervical spine is preferred. Chin tilt is contraindicated in the trauma patient. Cricothyroidotomy is indicated only in children older than 11 years. A tracheostomy may be needed, but in the unintubated child, performing a tracheostomy is particularly difficult secondary to the softness of the cartilage, which prevents easy palpation of landmarks.

B. *Breathing and ventilation.* Note that the infant requires 40 to 60 breaths per minute, whereas the older child breathes 20 times per minute. Hypoventilation is the most common cause of cardiac arrest in the child, so management of ventilation as well as perfusion is critical to maintain a normal pH and prevent secondary sequelae of the injury.

C. *Circulation with hemorrhage control.* Significant blood loss is common in children because of their smaller blood volume. The seriousness of the situation may initially be underestimated because of the child's increased physiologic reserve compared with the adult. Early signs of impending circulatory collapse include tachycardia, increased capillary refill time, and decreased peripheral pulses. Late signs are bradycardia, mental status changes, and decreased blood pressure. In children, blood pressure will remain normal until 25% to 30% of blood volume is lost. Vascular access using two large-bore intravenous lines is needed for effective replacement. Interosseous access is also used when intravenous access is limited.

D. *Disability: neurologic status.* The result of the neurologic examination can be recorded by the modified Glasgow Coma Scale for Infants and Children or, more simply, by AVPU, in which A is alert, V is voice response only, P is pain response only, and U is unresponsive.

E. *Exposure/environmental control.* The child is especially sensitive to hypothermia. All resuscitative fluids should be warmed. Complete examination is needed so that less obvious injury is not missed.

Following the initial assessment and resuscitation, continued monitoring of vital signs and fluid dynamics is maintained until diagnosis and treatment of injuries found on secondary survey are completed. Children with multi-system injuries can deteriorate rapidly and develop serious complications. Therefore, such patients should be reassessed often and transferred early to a facility capable of managing the child with multisystem injuries.

Soft Tissue Injuries

The nature of the injury (e.g., laceration of skin, depth of penetration, velocity of injuring force, contamination, subcutaneous emphysema, hematoma formation or swelling, devitalized or missing tissue) should be documented. High-velocity–missile injuries are often accompanied by a surrounding cone of tissue injury that may not be immediately apparent. The differences in the diagnosis and management of penetrating versus blunt injury will be discussed.

Upper Aerodigestive Injuries

Cervical subcutaneous emphysema, dysphagia, odyno-phagia, hematemesis, hemoptysis, respiratory distress, stridor, hoarseness, cyanosis, tracheal deviation, or sucking wound may accompany upper aerodigestive tract injuries but may remain undiagnosed in the presence of other serious injuries. A complete secondary survey minimizes the chance of overlooking injuries to the esophagus, larynx, or upper trachea. For a more detailed discussion of the diagnosis and treatment of these injuries, see Chapters 68, 70, and 86.

Neurologic Injuries

The relatively large head size of children and the lack of strong neck muscles to control the head position in space place children at higher risk than adults for traumatic brain injury (TBI) and cervical spinal cord injury.

Patients with loss of consciousness or concussion and those noted to be "dazed" at the scene of the accident must be presumed to have some degree of TBI. Children with TBI may be combative and confused, requiring sedation for their own safety. Sedation, however, clouds any further neurologic evaluation and should be delayed for as long as possible. It should be remembered that confusion and combativeness may be signs of oxygen hunger, rather than neurologic injury, and sedation may compromise an airway already at risk. It can be particularly difficult to differentiate airway hunger from neurologic injury until a pulse oximeter is available and the patient can be controlled enough to get a reliable reading. Computed tomography (CT) is used to evaluate intracranial injury, and hyperventilation and mannitol are often recommended in the early treatment of TBI to prevent secondary injury from brain edema.

Spinal cord injury after neck trauma may be complete or incomplete. A complete neurologic examination, including motor, sensory, and autonomic function, is needed to diagnose a child with a spinal cord injury. It is important to note that any sedation used before complete neurologic examination or the presence of associated TBI can obscure the physical findings. It is also important to

know that children can have mild or moderately severe spinal cord injury without fracture of the bony cervical spine. Spinal cord injury in the child occurs secondary to hyperflexion or lateral flexion injury because of the increased flexibility of the child's neck and the decreased muscle strength compared with the adult. Therefore, a normal CT scan of the bony spine does not rule out significant spinal cord injury. A complete neurologic examination is more indicative of the presence or absence of injury than the radiologic examination.

Peripheral neurologic injury may also occur. Injury patterns may be specific to nerve roots or plexuses that run through the neck such as the recurrent laryngeal nerve, stellate ganglion, brachial plexus, or phrenic nerve. Injury of the peripheral nerves of the neck may be secondary to either blunt or penetrating trauma in the situation of multisystem injury. Diagnosis and treatment recommendations follow in the sections specific for blunt or penetrating trauma.

Vascular Injuries

Vascular injuries in the multiply injured child may result in local or distal sequelae. Hematoma may be palpated locally from either blunt or penetrating injury. Internal propagation of the clot may result in distal ischemic injury to the arm or brain. Ischemia also occurs as a consequence of blood flow interruption secondary to vessel laceration or intimal tears.

In addition to inspection and palpation of the major vessels of the neck (arterial as well as venous), pulsation in the peripheral branches (superficial temporal, facial, and ophthalmic, by ophthalmoscopy) should be checked. If neck exploration is not performed immediately, peripheral pulses should be followed closely when occult injury to the major arteries is suspected. Doppler monitoring may be helpful in these cases.[6] The "gold standard" for the diagnosis of vascular injury is arteriography. In children, ultrasound is not typically performed because normal vessel flow rates and diameters of vessels are not known for each age group.

Osseous Injuries

The initial examination should be kept to a minimum, attempting only to elicit point tenderness with the child's neck stabilized, until a complete neurologic examination and radiologic evaluation of the cervical vertebrae can be performed. To avoid iatrogenic injury to the spinal cord, the child's neck should not be manipulated unless absolutely necessary until the evaluation is complete. These precautions are especially important (and occasionally overlooked) when the neck injury is complicated by an acute airway problem.

Glandular Injuries

Endocrine abnormalities as the result of tissue loss or shock may become apparent as a late manifestation of acute cervical injury but are uncommon and seldom need emergency treatment.

Specific Cervical Injuries

Injuries of the upper aerodigestive tract (larynx, trachea, pharynx, and esophagus) are discussed in Chapters 68 to 70 and 86.

Penetrating Wounds of the Neck

Penetrating wounds of the neck may be caused by bites, gunshots, knives, or impalement with a variety of objects during play or vehicular trauma. Penetrating wounds frequently cause injuries to the soft tissues and the vascular, nervous, visceral, and bony structures of the neck.

Low-velocity missiles (such as pistol bullets and flying glass) may be deflected by deep neck structures and may end up in the head or chest. Injury to these adjacent areas must be considered in all penetrating wounds of the neck.

Clinical presentations and management of penetrating wounds of the neck differ according to the anatomic level of injury.[22] Zone I extends from the sternum and clavicles to the cricoid cartilage and contains the subclavian vessels, domes of the pleura, esophagus, great vessels of the neck, recurrent nerves, thoracic duct, and trachea. Zone II extends from the cricoid cartilage to the angle of the mandible and contains the larynx, pharynx, base of tongue, carotid artery, jugular vein, and cranial nerves X through XII. Surgical access in zone II is less difficult than in zone I or III. Zone III extends from the angle of the mandible to the base of skull and contains the internal and external carotid arteries, vertebral arteries, and cranial nerves IX through XII. Zone III is the most difficult to expose surgically.[29] Table 103–1 lists the zones of the neck with their anatomic ranges and important structures.

Clinical assessment of zone I and III penetrating neck injuries is more difficult, and arteriography is recommended preoperatively to pinpoint the site of the injury.

Although all penetrating neck wounds extending deep to the platysma were traditionally explored surgically, experience has shown that selective surgical exploration is equally effective in dealing with major complications as long as serial examinations and immediate surgical treatment are available.[28] Indications for immediate exploration include evidence of active bleeding (epistaxis, hemoptysis, expanding hematoma), vascular occlusion (loss

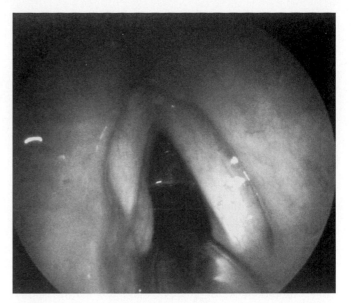

FIGURE 103–3. Direct laryngoscopic view of a fractured larynx revealing asymmetry of the true vocal folds.

of pulse, progressive central nervous system deficit), dysphagia, and respiratory distress.[29] Injury to the root of the neck or to the neck above the angle of the mandible quite often presents asymptotically with rapid decompensation at a future time.

Children with penetrating injuries may require further diagnostic evaluation to determine the need for exploration when stable. Injury of certain neurologic structures is often associated with occult but significant injury of juxtaposed vascular structures: the hypoglossal nerve affects the facial artery and vein; the Horner syndrome affects the carotid artery; and the glossopharyngeal, vagus, and accessory nerves affect the jugular vein and the internal carotid artery. Arteriography is indicated with such neurologic deficits. Arteriography is also undertaken if vascular injury is strongly suspected but not apparent on examination (as happens with bruit and aneurysm and when the wound is near a major vessel). Although not yet proved in pediatric patients, duplex sonography may be used in some centers for mid-neck vascular injury questions.[21]

Rigid endoscopy is performed if aerodigestive tract involvement is suspected (crepitus, dyspnea, stridor, dysphagia, or odynophagia). Figure 103–3 shows a direct laryngoscopic view of a child struck by a softball. True vocal fold asymmetry secondary to a laryngeal fracture is apparent. Flexible endoscopy is also quite effective in identifying mucosal disruption or extent of injury. Dye contrast pharyngoesophagogram may be beneficial but can potentiate mediastinitis or parapharyngitis. The decision to explore the neck is based on diagnostic studies and condition of the patient.

Soft Tissue Injuries

A *laceration* is a tissue disruption. Consideration should be given to penetration of underlying structures of a laceration, regardless of how small the laceration appears. A *puncture wound* may extend to some depth with minimal

TABLE 103–1. Zones of the Neck

Zone	Anatomic Range	Important Structures
I	Sternum and clavicles to cricoid cartilage	Subclavian vessels, domes of pleura, esophagus, carotid artery, jugular vein, recurrent nerves, thoracic duct, and trachea
II	Cricoid cartilage to angle of mandible	Larynx, pharynx, base of tongue, carotid artery, jugular vein, cranial nerves X through XII.
III	Angle of mandible to base of skull	Internal and external carotid arteries, vertebral arteries, cranial nerves IX through XII

surrounding tissue damage; *gunshot wounds* with a similar entrance wound as a laceration may produce their effects at some distance because of the surrounding cone of injury, production of secondary missiles of bone or missile fragments, or ricochet.

In the management of lacerations of the neck, the child's current tetanus immunization status should be determined. Depending on previous immunization status, age, and type and extent of injury, tetanus prophylaxis may be required.[5]

Simple lacerations above the level of the platysma should be cleaned to remove clots and foreign materials, scrubbed with aqueous iodine solution, and irrigated carefully. Local anesthesia (1% lidocaine with 1:200,000 epinephrine) is recommended, but general anesthesia may be required for more extensive lacerations.

Once the laceration has been cleansed, devitalized tissue should be conservatively débrided with scissors or a sharp scalpel back to clean, bleeding tissue. The wound edges should be at right angles, and the closure should be planned to lie in natural skin lines if possible.

After appropriate evaluation of lacerations extending deep to the platysma, the deeper tissues should be approximated with absorbable sutures in layers. The skin is closed with evenly placed, nonabsorbable, monofilament sutures. Smaller lacerations can often be closed with a running subcuticular suture, which can be removed more easily in small children. In either case, the skin edges should be reapproximated accurately with slight eversion. Interrupted sutures can be removed from the neck after 4 to 5 days, with tape reinforcement used for another 3 to 4 days.

Primary closure of cervical lacerations can be accomplished as long as 12 to 18 hours after injury because of the excellent blood supply of the neck. Beyond that time, or in grossly contaminated wounds, closure should be delayed for 72 hours. The laceration can then be sutured loosely or closed with adhesive strips if clean. Subsequent scar revision will likely be required. Gunshot wounds, because of their zone of injury, may need to be loosely closed initially and may require multiple débridement as the wound declares itself.

Neck scars, in general, may widen slightly in children because their tissue elasticity is increased; parents should be so forewarned.

Management of animal and human bites to the neck is varied and controversial. Stucker and colleagues[30] recommended the following standardized approach for bites to the head and neck:

1. Immediate cleaning, scrubbing, and high-pressure lavage are required to decrease the inoculum.
2. Medical therapy consisting of appropriate tetanus vaccine, rabies prophylaxis, and antibiotics is given. Antibiotics of choice are ticarcillin and clavulanic acid for intravenous use and amoxicillin with clavulanic acid for oral use. A full 10-day course is recommended.
3. Clean, nonhuman laceration bites can be safely closed if seen within 5 hours of injury.
4. Severe human bites are best treated in a delayed manner. Wound care consists of soaks with povidone-iodine solution.

Kountakis et al[18] found that all animal bites healed without wound infection when closed primarily, even in those who did not receive antibiotic prophylaxis. Human bites should always receive antibiotic prophylaxis, commonly intravenously.

Vascular Injuries

Vascular injuries are the most common cause of death following penetrating wounds of the neck. Acute management of injuries to cervical vessels includes direct pressure to control bleeding, establishment of two large-bore intravenous lines, and replacement of lost blood. Vital signs should be monitored closely, and blood must be drawn for type and crossmatch, initial hematocrit, and appropriate chemistry tests. The wound should not be probed in the emergency department.

Once the child is stabilized and evaluated, open exploration with control of bleeding is indicated. The tract of injury is followed to its depth with a systematic examination of each structure in or adjacent to the tract. The bleeding site is identified, and vascular control is secured proximally and distally by passing umbilical tape around the vessel. Clots are evacuated, and the wound is thoroughly cleansed and evaluated. The cut vessel edges are freshened, and vascular repair or ligation is accomplished.

Injuries to the internal and common carotid, subclavian, and innominate arteries should be repaired if possible. Although it has been stated that mortality and morbidity rates owing to carotid (common or internal) ligation are low in younger patients, the opposite has also been said to be true. Furthermore, statistics cannot be applied to individual cases.

Arteriorrhaphy of the common or internal carotid artery may be accomplished relatively easily using interrupted 4–0 Tevdek sutures in the cleanly penetrating, sharp missile wound of the neck (i.e., by razor or knife), but it gets progressively more difficult with more contamination or tissue loss.

When compromise of the vessel lumen is a potential problem with simple closure, a patch graft of autogenous vessel or synthetic material may be required. More extensive injuries may also require such a graft. Autograft vein interposition (using the internal jugular vein, for instance) is superior to synthetic grafting in contaminated wounds.[26]

Specific problems include the following:

1. An internal or external shunt (Javid) may be required during carotid arteriorrhaphy, although partial occlusion with a curved vascular clamp (Satinsky) may be possible.
2. Operative manipulation in the region of the bifurcation should be preceded by infiltration of the bulb with 1% lidocaine to avoid reflex hypotension owing to stimulation of the carotid pressor receptors. If this occurs inadvertently, atropine can reverse the effects of such stimuli.
3. Injury to the vertebral artery can be controlled only with great difficulty. Arteriorrhaphy is usually impossible (and unnecessary secondary to extensive

collateral flow), and control can be established only by pressure, bone wax, and suture ligation.

4. Control of subclavian or innominate hemorrhage may be established with difficulty and may require resection of the medial third of the clavicle, the entire clavicle, or the head of the sternocleidomastoid muscle, or it may require splitting the superior sternum (manubrium). The sternal incision may be carried laterally into the third intercostal space to avoid opening the full mediastinum unnecessarily and may be closed with stainless steel wire.

5. Lacerated major veins of the neck, aside from the effects of hemorrhage, introduce the risk of air embolism. Prompt pressure (either in the emergency department or subsequently in the operating room) and putting the patient in a slight Trendelenburg position should prevent the occurrence of air embolism.

6. The internal jugular vein may be repaired if it has been ligated unilaterally without sequelae. Other venous bleeders are ligated with silk.

Neurologic Injuries

Pediatric cervical neurologic injuries can be divided into those of the peripheral nerves and those of the central nervous system (cervical spinal cord).

Peripheral nerve injuries are usually caused by penetrating or lacerating trauma. Injuries to the cervical vertebrae or the skull may result in paresis or paralysis, which may be permanent (e.g., in injuries owing to crushing or laceration) or temporary (e.g., in concussive injuries).

Types of peripheral nerve injuries were described by Seddon as follows: *neurapraxia*, an intact nerve with physiologic block (complete recovery expected); *axonotmesis*, division of an axon only, with intact supporting structures (partial spontaneous recovery); and *neurotmesis*, division of the entire nerve.[21]

Peripheral nerve function, including the brachial and cervical plexuses, the phrenic nerve (proximal branch of the cervical plexus), and the regional cranial nerves (IX, X, XI, and XII), is first checked systematically.

Cranial nerve injuries are often overlooked and may offer important information as to the nature and location of deeper injuries. They may be checked quickly as follows: glossopharyngeal (IX), the soft palate rising in the midline with an intact gag reflex; vagus (X), intact vocal cord function without hoarseness; spinal accessory (XI), intact trapezius and sternocleidomastoid muscle function; and hypoglossal (XII), intact tongue motion without fasciculation.

Injuries to the cervical plexus, which is formed by the ventral primary divisions of the upper four cervical nerves, may produce sensory or motor deficits. The sensory deficits may occur over the posterior scalp (lesser occipital branch), auricle (greater auricular branch), or anterior neck and chest (cervical cutaneous and supraclavicular branches). Deep muscular branch deficits may be more obvious (phrenic branches) or less obvious, depending on the extent of total involvement.

In clean, open injuries, severed or lacerated nerves should be débrided and repaired primarily (neurorrhaphy) using interrupted, fine, nonreactive sutures to meticulously reapproximate the perineurium. Microsurgical techniques provide a useful adjunct to this type of repair.

Secondary repair may be necessary when the injury is extensively contaminated or seen after a delay. Each case should be treated individually.

Sutureless techniques using Micropore adhesive or glues have been popularized in Europe; however, these are not commonly used in the United States.

When there is an extensive area of missing or deficient nerve, especially in a motor nerve, an expendable regional sensory nerve, such as the greater auricular nerve, may be interposed as an autograft to facilitate the anastomosis without tension.

The treatment of brachial plexus injuries is also expectant, except when there is progression of the injury or when the insulting injury is to the middle third of the clavicle where direct bony impingement on the nerve may be expected and should be relieved. Otherwise, little benefit can be expected from neurolysis or exploration.

Partial division of a nerve should be repaired without interrupting the intact segment by freshening the divided bundle ends, ensuring a clean bed for the injured nerve. The incidence of neuroma and causalgia is increased relative to repair of a completely divided nerve, but the functional result is improved by not interrupting intact nerve fibers.[15]

Cervical spinal cord injuries in children are uncommon and rarely occur as a result of direct penetration.

Injury to the spinal cord is caused (1) directly, by bullets or other high-velocity missiles that strike it, resulting in concussion or laceration of the cord; (2) secondarily, by producing missiles composed of splintered fragments of vertebra or other bone, or (3) indirectly, through the concussive effects of the cylinder of transmitted energy.

Stab wounds, being of lower velocity, tend to injure only the directly penetrated spinal cord substance, although there may be adjacent areas of contusion, edema, or hematoma formation with resultant deficits. The most common injury is a hemisection of the cord with resultant Brown-Séquard syndrome (distal ipsilateral hemiplegia and hyperesthesia with contralateral hemianesthesia), but complete transection of the spinal cord may occur. Secondary injury to the spinal cord owing to compression by fragments of dislodged lamina or vertebral body is less common.[10]

Glandular Injuries

The thyroid gland is a richly vascular structure, and compromise of its endocrine status owing to trauma is uncommon. When there has been major tissue loss in this region, however, subsequent signs of hypothyroidism should be sought by history (symptoms such as tiredness, constipation, or dull hair), as well as by appropriate blood studies.

When injury to the gland is seen at the time of neck exploration, devitalized tissue should be débrided and hemostasis secured. The recurrent nerves should be evaluated carefully, as should the parathyroid glands. Traumatic loss of the entire thyroid would result in major vascular (carotid) and airway (trachea) injury, and survival in the acute stage is improbable.

Simultaneous injury to all parathyroid glands is uncommon because of their separate distribution in the neck. A substernal position of these glands is most uncommon, and total loss would lead to major vascular and airway injury with probable immediate death of the child. If a parathyroid gland is identified in a devitalized area of the neck, it should be reimplanted in an adjacent muscle.

Salivary gland injuries should be handled by débridement, control of bleeding, and drainage of the wound. The submandibular gland can be removed, but vital nerves should be spared if they are intact. Treatment of parotid gland injuries is not a consideration of cervical injuries except when the tail of the parotid extends into the neck. In this case, the preceding principles of débridement of devitalized tissue, hemostasis, nerve repair, and drainage should be followed.

Thoracic Duct

Wounds in the left lower neck near the junction of the internal jugular and subclavian veins may cause injury to the thoracic duct as well. Injury to this structure is identified by pooling of lymph (chyle) in the wound. Simple ligation of the duct is sufficient may be difficult because the identification of the duct may be a problem. Additionally, the thoracic duct may enter the vein as several tributaries, each of which must be identified, if injured, and ligated.

Injury on the right side of the neck may also injure a thoracic duct that uncommonly occurs on that side. Again, the treatments of choice are identification and ligation of the duct.

Complications

Late complications include infection, fistula (salivary or digestive), vascular occlusion, and bleeding, as well as other specific problems related to the structure indicated. These are uncommon if emergency treatment and diagnostic evaluation have been meticulous and if care has been given according to the principles already stated.

Specific injuries to the larynx and trachea are discussed in Chapter 86.

Blunt Trauma

Blunt trauma often occurs in children who are in motor or recreational vehicle accidents, diving accidents, or other sports-related accidents. Blunt trauma also occurs in the setting of strangulation, either accidental (when the child becomes entangled in bed sheets or clothing)[25] or purposeful (in a case of child abuse).[20]

Although penetrating injuries are responsible for most cervical vascular injuries, 3% to 10% of cervical vascular injuries occur secondary to blunt trauma and have a high morbidity and mortality rate.[9]

Soft Tissue Injuries

An *abrasion* is a superficial wound produced by friction (large-mass, low-velocity injury that dissipates energy tangentially). A *contusion* is a deeper injury with tissue damage (primarily vascular) without surface disruption. Deeper abrasions should be scrubbed under local or general anesthesia to remove all foreign material. Foreign bodies such as wood should be meticulously sought and removed. Greases can be removed more easily if a mild detergent is used. Organic iodine solutions such as povidone-iodine do not cause additional tissue injury and are excellent cleaning solutions. Aqueous solutions of 0.5% to 1.0% are suitable and less irritating than the tincture.[13] Hydrogen peroxide is irritating and is not recommended.

Cervical sprain is usually accompanied by a dull, aching pain in the back of the neck that may be diffuse or discrete. Radiographic findings are negative, and treatment is limited to cervical collar immobilization and heat and analgesic therapy.

In children who survive an accidental hanging or throttling, there may be hemorrhagic ecchymoses and abrasions about the neck. There are also signs of vascular congestion such as subconjunctival, gingival, and oral mucosal petechial hemorrhages. These cases require no special treatment except referral to an appropriate agency to evaluate abuse potential.[20]

Vascular Injuries

In strangulation, the arteries and veins of the neck are compressed. Strangulation cases should be treated the same as cases of penetrating trauma to vascular structures (i.e., signs of bleeding and obstruction should be sought).

Vascular injury can also occur without evidence of contusion or acute bleeding by intimal tearing. The decision to use anticoagulation, antiplatelet therapy, or observation is controversial with no outcome data available to guide therapeutic decisions.[19]

Neurologic Injuries

Blunt cervical spinal cord injuries in children are often caused by indirect, violent displacement. Displacement injuries may cause injury through dislocation, transient spinal cord compression, or avulsion. Closed injuries to the spinal cord are of two types: those accompanied by bony injury or dislocation and those resulting from violent vertebral column displacement without obvious fracture or displacement.

Injuries accompanied by bony fractures are the most common.[10] Injury may occur to the vertebral body, lamina, or pedicle, resulting in bony fragments being driven into or across the spinal cord. Soft tissue injuries to the intervertebral disk or connecting ligaments, sometimes accompanied by avulsion injuries of the vertebrae, are less common.

In either case, plain and CT radiologic studies may be unrevealing because fracture fragments may be too small to be seen, or compression of the spinal cord may be by the nonradiopaque parts of the vertebral column.[14, 32] Magnetic resonance imaging (MRI) has been found to be effective in finding many injuries previously missed, even in the comatose or obtunded patient.[16]

Vertebral fractures occur in predictable and reproducible patterns. In the cervical region, there are three basic mechanisms of injury: flexion, extension, and rotational.

Definitive operative treatment of spinal cord injuries is not ordinarily delegated to the otolaryngologist or pediatrician. Neurosurgery consult is needed because reduction of cervical dislocation, laminectomy, spinal cord decompression, or extensive rehabilitative measures may be required. Decompression is warranted when there is (1) progression of the neurologic deficit, (2) manometric (Queckenstedt) or myelographic block, or (3) radiographic evidence of bone fragments (or disk, with contrast studies) projecting into the spinal canal.[24]

Osseous (Cervical Vertebral) Injuries

Fractures or dislocations of the cervical spine are rare in children except in cases of extreme violence.[24] Compared with similar injuries in adults, cervical spine injuries in children are less likely to cause spinal cord transection and are less likely to result from whiplash injury. They occur more frequently as the result of diving accidents or football injuries. Radiographic evaluation is somewhat more difficult because of the presence of apophyses, growth centers, points of fusion, and congenital anomalies. Comparison of the radiographs with age-related standards is recommended.[24] The treatment is generally the same as for the adult, except there is somewhat accelerated healing.

If other signs of external trauma are absent, neurologic evaluation (see the section on neurologic injuries) and examination for point tenderness often provide an indication of the site of injury.

Prevention of extension of neurologic (spinal cord or peripheral nerve) injury and repair of the existing injury, if possible, are the goals of management of the vertebral injury. Spinal cord injury must be assumed until there is proof that none has occurred. Concomitant injury to the spinal cord may be expected in 25% of cases of severe injury to the cervical spine. Irrevocable cord damage and death may occur by careless handling of the child with cervical vertebral injury and resultant instability. The greatest permanent disability caused by trauma to the cervical spine is due to the associated injury to the spinal cord.

The main objectives of physical examination of the cervical vertebrae are observation for evidence of external trauma (e.g., points of missile penetration), neurologic evaluation (see section on neurologic injuries) and careful palpation of the spine for areas of point tenderness.

Cervical sprains, dislocations, or fracture-dislocation combinations may be identified and require early orthopedic or neurosurgical consultation (Figs. 103–4, 103–5 and 103–6). Temporary in-line stabilization is indicated until proper positioning can be secured with skeletal traction, bracing, or both. Open reduction and arthrodesis may be required if closed reduction and stabilization are unsuccessful.

Peripheral nerve root injuries may be expected in 25%

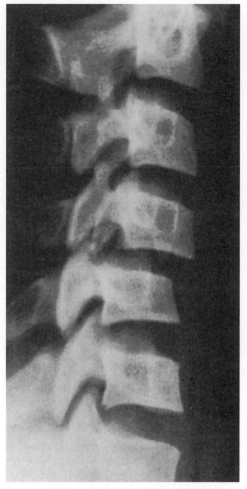

FIGURE 103–4. Lateral radiograph of the cervical spine of a 14-year-old injured in a trampoline accident, showing unilateral fracture and dislocation of the cervical fourth and fifth vertebrae. Quadriplegia developed, with greater involvement of lower extremities (acute central cervical cord injury).

of severe injuries to the cervical spine and are usually due to fracture or dislocation of the vertebral body or posterior displacement of the intervertebral disk. Initially, stabilization is indicated with possible subsequent exploration.

BURNS

Burns are the leading cause of non–motor vehicle deaths in children age 1 to 4 years and the second most common cause in children age 5 to 14 years. Approximately 80% of fire- and burn-related deaths result from house fires, usually in private residences without working smoke detectors.[4] Scalding occurs more frequently in the infant and toddler, whereas contact burns occur more frequently in older children.[7] Child abuse should be considered in burn injuries.

The severity of the burn depends on the duration of exposure, the intensity of the burning agent, and the body's response. Noncombustible liquids usually create second-degree burns because of their short exposure time. Combustible liquids and flames usually create third-

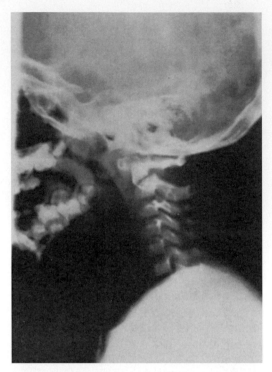

FIGURE 103–5. Lateral cervical spine radiograph of a 5-year-old injured in a diving accident shows a fracture of the odontoid process with slight displacement. There were no neurologic findings.[8]

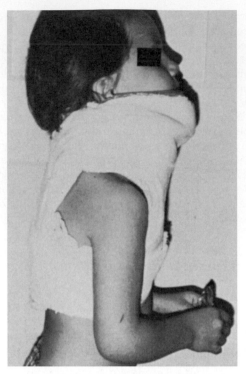

FIGURE 103–6. Minerva cast applied to a patient provides excellent cervical stabilization.

degree burns as a result of prolonged exposure and intensity of heat. Inhalation injury must also be evaluated in injuries associated with an open flame or smoky environment. With burns from high-voltage current, the underlying tissues suffer more destruction than the skin.[8]

Early treatment and evaluation of burn victims are discussed in Chapter 70. Children with burns on 10% or more of total body surface area require significant resuscitation. A consideration in evaluating burns in children is that the head and the neck compose about 20% of body surface area (BSA) in infants, more than double the BSA percentage of the adult head and neck. The percentage gradually decreases until the child is 10 years old, when it approximates that of the adult (10%). The American Burn Association recommends that any child younger than 10 years with partial and full-thickness burns greater than 10% of the BSA or full-thickness burns greater than 5% of the BSA be referred to a burn center.[4]

In a child with burns involving the neck, inspiration of flame or products of combustion must be suspected. Resultant damage to tracheal or laryngeal mucosa can lead to edema severe enough to cause airway obstruction or death. The onset of the clinical evidence of airway injury may be subtle and may take more than 24 hours to develop. Early intubation is critical to prevent the need for an emergent tracheostomy to bypass the upper airway obstruction. In the acute phase of injury to the neck, eschar forms over the areas of third-degree burn, and constriction of the neck skin can cause secondary respiratory distress. Escharotomy from chin to sternal notch is indicated.

The use of tracheostomy versus long-term intubation

has been debated.[23] Barret et al[2] found that tracheostomy did not increase the infection rate in 290 ventilated pediatric burn patients. One recommendation is to consider tracheostomy in patients with severe upper airway injury and in inhalation/burn patients who have been intubated more than 10 days.

Longer-term management of contractures of neck burns includes full-thickness skin grafting, compression, local and regional skin flaps, and free flaps.[31] Good function and good cosmesis should be the goals of the technique chosen.

Finally, patterns of contracture follow positions of comfort. Therefore, children with neck burns should not be allowed pillows, and their necks should be in hyperextension to prevent contracture.[12]

SELECTED REFERENCES

Advanced Trauma Life Support. Chicago, American College of Surgeons, 1997.
> *This well-known text has a succinct review of initial management of pediatric trauma.*

Eichelberger MR. Pediatric trauma :prevention, acute care, rehabilitation. St. Louis, Mosby–Year Book, 1993.
> *This covers all aspects of trauma in the pediatric patient.*

Miller RH, Duplechain JK. Penetrating wounds of the neck. Otolaryngol Clin North Am 24:15–29, 1991.
> *This article reviews penetrating wounds of the neck, including discussion of selective neck exploration. It is a good general reference.*

Pediatric Advanced Life Support. American Heart Association, 1997.
> *Pediatric resuscitation differs from resuscitation of the adult. Certifi-*

cation and course completion by anyone treating children is recommended.

Tornetta P, Cramer K (guest eds). Children's Fractures. Philadelphia, Lippincott, Williams & Wilkins, 2000.

An excellent review of pediatric fractures with a listing of pertinent references.

REFERENCES

1. Advanced Trauma Life Support. Chicago, American College of Surgeons, 1997.
2. Barret JP, Desai MH, Herndon DN. Effects of tracheostomies on infection and airway complications in pediatric burn patients. Burns 26(2):190–3, 2000.
3. Berkheiser EJ, Seidler F. Nontraumatic dislocations of the atlantoaxial joint. JAMA 96:517, 1931.
4. Chameides L, Hazinski MF. Pediatric Advanced Life Support. American Heart Association, 1997.
5. De Biasi RL, Simocs EA. Immunizations. In Hay WW, Hayward AR, Levin MJ, et al (eds). Current Pediatric Diagnosis and Treatment, 15th ed. New York, McGraw-Hill, 2001.
6. Demetriades D, Theodorou D, Cornell E 3rd, et al. Penetrating injuries of the neck in patients in stable condition. Physical examination, angiography, or color flow Doppler imaging. Arch Surg 13:971–975, 1995.
7. Durtschi MB, Kohler RE, Finleay A, et al. Burn injury in infants and young children. Surg Gynecol Obstet 150:651, 1980.
8. Edlich RF, Nichter LS, Morgan RF, et al. Burns of the head and neck. Otolaryngol Clin North Am 17:361, 1984.
9. Fakhry SM, Jaques PF, Proctor HJ. Cervical vessel injury after blunt trauma. J Vasc Surg 8:501–508, 1988.
10. Hall DE, Boydston W. Pediatric neck injuries. Pediatr Rev 20:13–20, 1999.
11. Haller JA, Talbert JL. Trauma and the child. In Ballinger WF, Rutherford RB, Zuidema GD (eds). The Management of Trauma, 2nd ed. Philadelphia, WB Saunders, 1973, p 719.
12. Hammond JS, Ward CG. Burns of the head and neck. Otolaryngol Clin North Am 16:679, 1983.
13. Harvey SC. Antiseptics and disinfectants. In Goodman LS, Gillman A (eds). The Pharmacological Basis of Therapeutics, 9th ed. New York, McGraw-Hill, 1996.
14. Herr CH, Ball PA, Sargent SK, et al. Sensitivity of prevertebral soft tissue measurement of C3 for detection of cervical spine fractures and dislocations. Am J Emerg Med 16:346–349, 1998.
15. Hoopes JE. Soft tissue injuries of the extremities. In Zuidema GD, Rutherford BB, Ballinger WF (eds). The Management of Trauma, 4th ed. Philadelphia, WB Saunders, 1985, p 543.
16. Keiper MD, Zimmerman RA, Bilaniuk LT. MRI in the assessment of the supportive soft tissues of the cervical spine in acute trauma in children. Neuroradiology 40:359–363, 1998.
17. Kelly M. Trauma to the neck and larynx. CRNA 8:22–30, 1997.
18. Kountakis SE, Chamblee SA, Maillard AA, et al. Animal bites to the head and neck. Ear Nose Throat J 77:216–220, 1998.
19. Kuzniec S, Kauffman P, Molnar LJ, et al. Blunt vascular injuries of the head and neck: is heparinization necessary? J Trauma Inj Inf Crit Care 45:997–1004, 1998.
20. Line WS Jr, Stanley LIB Jr, Choi JH. Strangulation: a full spectrum of blunt neck trauma. Ann Otol Rhinol Laryngol 94:542, 1985.
21. Montalvo BM, LeBlang SD, Nunex DB, et al. Color Doppler sonography in penetrating injuries of the neck. Am J Neuroradiol 17:943–951, 1996.
22. Mutabagani KH, Veaver BL, Cooney DR, et al. Penetrating neck trauma in children: a reappraisal. J Pediatr Surg 30:341–344, 1995.
23. Prater ME, Deskin RW. Bronchoscopy and laryngoscopy findings as indications for tracheotomy in the burned child. Arch Otolaryngol 124:1115–1117, 1998.
24. Rachesky I, Boyce WT, Duncan B, et al. Clinical prediction of cervical spine injuries in children. Am J Dis Child 141:199–201, 1987.
25. Rauchschwalbe R, Mann NC. Pediatric window-cord strangulations in the United States. JAMA 277(21):1696–1698, 1997.
26. Rutherford RB, Van Way CW 3rd. Peripheral vascular injuries. In Zuidema GD, Rutherford RB, Ballinger WF (eds). The Management of Trauma. Philadelphia, WB Saunders, 1985, p 631.
27. Shires GT. Initial care of the trauma patient. In Shires GT (ed). Principles of Trauma Care, 3rd ed. New York, McGraw-Hill, 1985.
28. Sofianos C, Degiannis E, Van den Aardweg MS, et al. Selective surgical management of zone II gunshot injuries of the neck: a prospective study. Surgery 120:758, 1996.
29. Stiernberg CM, Jahrsdoerfer RA, Gillenwater A, et al. Gunshot wounds to the head and neck. Arch Otolaryngol Head Neck Surg 118:592–597, 1992.
30. Stucker FJ, Shaw GY, Boyd S, et al. Management of animal and human bites in the head and neck. Arch Otolaryngol Head Neck Surg 116:789–793, 1990.
31. Waymack JP. Release of burn scar contractures of the neck in paediatric patients. Burns 12:422–426, 1986.
32. Woodring JH, Lee C. The role and limitations of computed tomographic scanning in the evaluation of cervical trauma, J Trauma 33:698–708, 1992.

104

Pediatric Skull Base Surgery

Ivo P. Janecka, M.D., Silloo B. Kapadia, M.D., and Charles Margozian, M.D.

Skull base surgery is a new field of medicine focusing its treatment efforts on the anatomic junction of the neurocranium and the facial viscerocranium. Pediatric skull base surgery has developed as a logical outgrowth of technical advances in adult cranial base surgery. Breakthroughs in radiologic imaging, advances in neuroanesthesia, and conceptual progress in surgical techniques are easily applicable to the pediatric patient. There are, however, also significant differences that must be considered in the surgical management of skull base lesions in the pediatric patient. Neoplastic lesions as well as surgically manipulated tissue dynamically interact with the growth potential of the regional anatomy before and after treatment. This impact on growth is an important distinction between pediatric and adult skull base surgery that has to be considered during oncologic surgery as well as in reconstruction. This chapter focuses on selected neoplastic and congenital lesions encountered at the skull base and their management.

Tumors and tumor-like lesions at the pediatric skull base can be broadly categorized into *congenital lesions* (nasal glioma, encephalocele, and dermoid cyst, as well as teratoma, hamartoma, and choristoma) and *true neoplasms* (olfactory neuroblastoma, angiofibroma, nasopharyngeal carcinoma, and rhabdomyosarcoma). Clinical evaluation often gives significant clues as to the nature of skull base disease. The time of onset (at birth or postnatally), the location (near the lines of fusion or not), and the tumor progression (static or enlarging) all contribute to the accuracy of diagnosis. Computed tomography (CT), magnetic resonance imaging (MRI), and angiography are often used in combination as the mainstay of the diagnostic evaluation of skull base lesions.

Congenital Lesions

Nasal glioma represents heterotopic mature glial tissue found in or around the nose. The term is a misnomer because it implies a neoplasm; however, it is not a neoplasm but a congenital abnormality in which there is anterior displacement of glial tissue. In spite of its origin from glial tissue, it is isolated from the cranial cavity and does not contain cerebrospinal fluid. It is usually present at birth, and male patients predominate by a factor of 3:1. About 30% of nasal gliomas are found intranasally,

60% extranasally, and only 10% in both locations. The nasal glioma is usually firm, noncompressible, and nonpulsatile. The main differential diagnosis is from a nasal encephalocele, but a nasal dermoid cyst or an inflammatory nasal polyp or several possible malignant tumors may also be clinically considered in the differential diagnosis. Histologic examination reveals neuroglial tissue (astrocytes and connective tissue) without a true capsule. Neurons are usually absent.

Nasal encephalocele represents a localized herniation of intracranial content through a defect in the skull. It is thought to represent an outgrowth of a neural tube that prevented closure of the cranium. Only about 15% to 20% of encephaloceles involve the skull base. Most of these are found at the frontoethmoidal or sphenoethmoidal junctions. Associated facial anomalies or deformities may also be present. As in nasal glioma, histologic examination reveals neuroglial tissue (astrocytes and connective tissue) without a true capsule. Neurons are usually present, but differentiation from a nasal glioma may be difficult on histologic examination alone because encephaloceles of long standing may develop fibrosis with a paucity of neurons. Therefore, the distinction between these two congenital lesions is best made on radiographic imaging (CT and MRI). Demonstration of a skull defect and intracranial connection is diagnostic of an encephalocele, whereas absence of a skull defect or any intracranial connection favors a nasal glioma. It must be emphasized that radiographic imaging should be performed in any congenital nasofrontal mass before biopsy, because biopsy of an encephalocele may lead to cerebrospinal fluid leak and fatal meningitis.

Dermoid cyst at the skull base is found in the midline and has potential intracranial connection through an open folliculus nasofrontalis or a foramen caecum. It may be located at any point from the glabella to the base of the columella. Histologic examination shows that tissues of ectodermal origin predominate (the cyst is lined by squamous epithelia replete with dermal appendages). Unlike dermoids at other sites, such as the ovary, nasal dermoids are congenital anomalies and do not represent a benign cystic teratoma. Nasal dermoid does not have malignant potential.

Teratoma, hamartoma, choristoma, and dermoid are distinguished by representation of germ layer origin. According to Batsakis,[4] *teratoma* is composed of tissue foreign to the site of origin and has histologic representation of all three germ layers. *Hamartoma*, on the other hand, contains tissue that is indigenous to its site of growth. *Choristoma* is similar to hamartoma in terms of normal tissue outgrowth, but it is at a foreign location. Teratoma has unlimited growth potential and is mostly found in the head and neck region—in the nasopharynx, face, and orbit. It is often diagnosed at birth. With involvement of the nasopharynx and oropharynx, severe respiratory distress may be encountered. In gross appearance, it may be solid or cystic. On histologic examination, it is composed of tissues formed from all three germ layers and is classified as either mature or immature. Immature tissues of neuroectodermal origin may resemble neuroblastoma or retinoblastoma. About 70% of head and neck teratomas have a neural component, and less than 5% have malignant areas.

Benign Tumors

Angiofibroma is a benign, vascular, and locally invasive tumor. It is found almost exclusively in males, primarily in adolescent boys between the ages of 10 and 17 years. They often present with symptoms of nasal obstruction and epistaxis in localized tumors, but extensive tumors often extend to the cheek. The site of origin of angiofibroma is thought to be the posterolateral aspect of the nasal cavity. This tumor is firm and nodular on gross examination and has no true capsule. Histologic examination reveals a fibrous stroma containing irregular (staghorn-shaped) vascular channels lined with endothelial cells without elastic membrane, and smooth muscle is often absent, irregular, or incomplete. This finding probably contributes to the profuse bleeding some patients experience with this tumor, and it is thought to be caused by the lack of contractility of injured tumor vessels. In the differential diagnosis, a vascular fibrosed inflammatory nasal polyp, lobular capillary hemangioma (so-called pyogenic granuloma), or hemangiopericytoma should be considered. Immunohistologic studies suggest that angiofibroma is composed primarily of myofibroblastic and vascular elements. The presence of androgen-receptor protein has been identified in this tumor, but it has no estrogen or progesterone receptors. Histologic evaluation gives no indication of either benign or aggressive clinical behavior. Flow cytometric evaluation by Barnes et al[3] showed all studied tumors to be diploid whatever their clinical behavior. Sarcomatous transformation is rare and has been reported mainly after radiation therapy in the treatment of angiofibroma.

The presence of a basic fibroblast growth factor (bFGF) in angiofibromas has been previously demonstrated. We studied the urinary excretion of bFGF in patients with angiofibromas. Our hypothesis involved three questions: (1) How frequently is there a measurable urinary bFGF excretion in patients with angiofibroma? (2) Is there change in the level of urinary bFGF after embolization and after surgery? and (3) Is there a correlation with tumor recurrence? We studied the urinary excretion of bFGF in 14 patients (13 had angiofibroma, and 1 had hemangiopericytoma). Urine was collected before and after embolization as well as before and after surgery and during follow-up (3 years). We found that the majority of patients who underwent preoperative tumor embolization (80%) had significantly increased urinary secretion of bFGF (average, 420%). Subsequent surgery, when total tumor resection was accomplished, reduced the bFGF levels to normal within several days postoperatively. Our tumor recurrence rate has been quite low (under 5%). We postulate that wide surgical access allowed by the facial translocation system of approaches we use significantly increases the chances for total tumor removal. Authors who use more limited surgical approaches report higher recurrence rates. We conclude that most angiofibromas become highly angiogenic when embolized. This is reflected in high levels of urinary bFGF observed in these patients after embolization. Rapid tumor regrowth can be anticipated if an incomplete resection is performed. Maximal surgical visualization is thus highly desirable.

Malignant Tumors

Olfactory neuroblastoma is a rare malignant tumor of the olfactory epithelium that originates from neuroectodermal stem cells. The olfactory epithelium is normally found in the superior third of the nasal septum, the cribriform plate, and the superior turbinate. It is composed of three types of cells: bipolar sensory neurons, supporting cells, and basal cells. The tumor is thought to originate from the basal cells. Approximately 250 cases of olfactory neuroblastoma have been reported in the literature; patients range in age from 3 to 88 years (mean age, 45 years; 20% occur in the 11- to 20-year-old age group). Patients with olfactory neuroblastoma usually present with unilateral nasal obstruction and epistaxis owing to a red-gray polypoid mass found high in the nasal cavity. Radiologic imaging reveals a soft tissue mass, possibly with some areas of bone destruction. Histologic examination reveals the tumor to be composed of round cells that grow in nests or lobules. Their nuclei are hyperchromatic, but mitotic activity is rare. Homer-Wright pseudorosettes (tumor cells surrounding a central space with pink fibrillar material) are typically seen in focal areas. About 60% to 70% of tumors have a variable amount of fibrillary stroma. Also, necrosis, dystrophic calcification, and vascular or lymphatic invasion may be found. A histologic grading system has been proposed by Hyams and colleagues (Table 104–1), and a clinical one has been proposed by Kadish et al.[17] In the differential diagnosis, the pathologist and the clinician must consider other round cell malignant neoplasms (sinonasal undifferentiated carcinoma, lymphoma, melanoma, plasmacytoma, embryonal rhabdomyosarcoma, Ewing sarcoma, and metastatic neuroblastoma). About 40% of patients develop local recurrence, and about 50% develop nodal and distant metastases.

Whether olfactory neuroblastoma is a member of the Ewing sarcoma/peripheral primitive neuroectodermal tumors (ES/PNET) has been debated. However, olfactory neuroblastomas are immunonegative for the P30/32

TABLE 104-1. Hyams' Grading System for Olfactory Neuroblastoma

Feature	Grade I	Grade II	Grade III	Grade IV
Architecture	Lobular	Lobular	± Lobular	± Lobular
Mitotic activity	Absent	Present	Prominent	Marked
Nuclear pleomorphism	Absent	Moderate	Prominent	Marked
Fibrillary matrix	Prominent	Present	Minimal	Absent
Rosettes	± HW	± HW	Flexner	Absent
Necrosis	Absent	Absent	± Present	Common

HW, Homer Wright.
Modified from Hyams VJ. Olfactory neuroblastoma (case 6). In Batsakis JG, Hyams VJ, Morales AR (eds). Special Tumors of the Head and Neck. Chicago, ASCP Press, 1982, pp 24–29.

MIC2 (12E7) antibody, a specific marker for ES/PNET. In addition, rarely, if ever, is olfactory neuroblastoma associated with the chromosomal translocation t(11;22)(q24;q12), which is characteristic of ES/PNET. Furthermore, molecular techniques for the presence of the EWS/FLI1 fusion transcript, such as reverse transcriptase–polymerase chain reaction, have shown that olfactory neuroblastomas are negative. These findings show that olfactory neuroblastoma is not a member of the ES/PNET family.

Nasopharyngeal carcinoma, a malignant tumor derived from surface epithelium of the nasopharyngeal mucosa, has a wide age range and is mainly a tumor of adults. However, 20% of all cases of nasopharyngeal carcinoma occur in children. Race, genetic susceptibility, and environmental factors, including the ubiquitous Epstein-Barr virus (EBV), play a role in its etiology. The World Health Organization's revised classification (Table 104–2) considers only two categories of nasopharyngeal carcinoma: squamous cell carcinoma (keratinizing) and nonkeratinizing carcinoma (differentiated and undifferentiated). The undifferentiated type of nasopharyngeal carcinoma is the most predominant type found in children. It has a bimodal age distribution in the second and sixth decades. All types of nasopharyngeal cancer have male predominance. They often present clinically with cervical adenopathy in the posterior cervical triangle and ear symptoms (otitis media, hearing loss) that are the result of eustachian tube obstruction. Cranial nerve neuropathy may be found as well. The keratinizing squamous cell carcinoma represents only about 25% of all nasopharyngeal malignant neoplasms in this country and, contrary to the nonkeratinizing variety, has a weak or absent relationship to EBV. The therapeutic response to conventional radiotherapy is poor, with only a 20% 5-year survival rate. The differentiated nonkeratinizing tumors have a slightly better 5-year survival of 35%. The best therapeutic response to radiotherapy is seen in the undifferentiated type, with 60% 5-year survival. In the differential diagnosis, lymphoma, Hodgkin disease, or eosinophilic granuloma should be considered. EBV infection has been strongly associated with the development of nonkeratinizing nasopharyngeal carcinomas.

Because of advances in skull base surgery, our treatment protocol now also includes surgery as a primary or salvage oncologic therapeutic modality. Primary surgery is offered to patients with a localized keratinizing carcinoma. Both the lateral and the posterior wall of the nasopharynx can now be resected en bloc. This is possible by use of a facial translocation approach to the skull base. Reconstruction of the surgical defect in the nasopharynx is done with the transfer of the temporalis muscle. Nonkeratinizing nasopharyngeal cancer is still being treated with primary radiotherapy because of a good response rate. For recurrent localized tumors, however, surgery is again considered. The patient's follow-up after radiotherapy consists of a baseline MRI at 6 weeks after completion of radiation. If any persistent tissue irregularity is found in the nasopharynx, an endoscopy-directed biopsy is carried out. Subsequent imaging and endoscopic evaluation of the nasopharynx are carried out in 3- to 6-month intervals. One study suggested that a high cure rate may be attained for locally advanced, undifferentiated nasopharyngeal carcinoma in children after a combined modality of treatment, using both local radiation therapy and systemic chemotherapy. Chemotherapy may be useful in the prevention of systemic metastases.

Rhabdomyosarcoma is a malignant neoplasm of striated muscle origin. It is the most common soft tissue sarcoma in children younger than 15 years. Approximately 75% of all head and neck soft tissue sarcomas in children are rhabdomyosarcomas.[21, 25, 26, 31] The orbit, nasopharynx, nasal cavity, paranasal sinuses, and middle ear are the most common sites involved by this aggressive tumor that rapidly invades adjacent tissues, including bone and meninges. The orbital rhabdomyosarcoma, the most frequent tumor in the head and neck (20% to 40%), presents as a rapidly enlarging mass in the inner and upper orbital quadrant. This causes proptosis. The temporal bone rhabdomyosarcomas, on the other hand, present with obstructive ear symptoms (hearing loss, otalgia, discharge). Cranial neuropathy (e.g., facial paralysis) often signifies extensive disease. Histologically recognizable types of rhabdomyosarcoma by the pattern of growth and cytologic features can be assigned to one of three prognostic

TABLE 104-2. Classification of Nasopharyngeal Carcinoma: World Health Organization (1991)

Squamous cell carcinoma
Nonkeratinizing carcinoma
   Differentiated nonkeratinizing carcinoma
   Undifferentiated carcinoma

groups: botryoid and spindle cell subtypes of embryonal rhabdomyosarcoma (superior prognosis, 95% at 5 years); embryonal rhabdomyosarcoma (intermediate prognosis, 64% at 5 years), and alveolar rhabdomyosarcoma and undifferentiated sarcoma (poor prognosis, 53% and 47% at 5 years, respectively). The pleomorphic subtype has been deleted from the new International Classification of Rhabdomyosarcoma (ICR) because it does not occur with any regularity in children. According to the new ICR by the Intergroup Rhabdomyosarcoma Study group, 49% of patients were diagnosed as embryonal, 6% as its botryoid subtype, and 3% as its spindle cell subtype. The ICR identified 32% as the alveolar type. The remaining 10% were undifferentiated sarcomas or rhabdomyosarcomas with rhabdoid features.

Embryonal rhabdomyosarcoma may occur in children from birth to the age of 15 years. The alveolar type is found in an older age group (10 to 25 years) and is often accompanied by the presence of a distant metastatic disease. Embryonal rhabdomyosarcoma exhibits a considerable variation in cytology from primitive fusiform or stellate mesenchymal cells with scant cytoplasm to highly differentiated muscle cells having fusiform cell bodies and moderate amounts of eosinophilic cytoplasm with cross striations. This is a moderately cellular neoplasm with loose myxoid stroma. The nuclei are smaller than those of alveolar rhabdomyosarcoma, with a lighter chromatin pattern, and nucleoli are not prominent. The botryoid subtype is characterized by a grapelike gross configuration in most cases with characteristic microscopic features, including a subepithelial condensation of tumor cells or cambium layer with a varying degree of rhabdomyoblastic maturation and a loosely cellular myxoid stroma.

Alveolar rhabdomyosarcoma is characterized histologically by fibrovascular connective tissue septa forming an alveolar pattern lined by tumor cells. The alveolar spaces may be densely packed with tumor cells. In 10% the alveolar pattern may be focal with the remaining tumor showing an embryonal pattern. The tumor cells and nuclei are generally round with coarse nuclear chromatin pattern, one to several nucleoli and scant eosinophilic cytoplasm.

In the differential diagnosis, the following tumors are considered: round and spindle cell sarcomas, Ewing's sarcoma/PNET, neuroblastoma, and lymphoma, especially when cross-striations of rhabdomyoblasts are difficult to find. Rhabdomyosarcomas show muscle markers by immunohistochemistry. Diagnostic chromosomal translocation t(2;13)(q35;q14) has been found in about 90% of alveolar rhabdomyosarcomas. In contrast, embryonal rhabdomyosarcomas do not contain this translocation but demonstrate loss of genetic material on the short arm of chromosome 11. The treatment is multidisciplinary. After a biopsy, a decision is made regarding surgery or primary chemotherapy and radiation treatment. In general, resection of the lesion with clear surgical margins followed by adjuvant chemotherapy gives the patient the best chance for a cure. Other treatment combinations—for example, incomplete tumor resection followed by chemotherapy and radiotherapy, or chemotherapy and radiotherapy only—have lesser expected cure rates. Additional potential improvement in the group of patients treated initially with chemotherapy and radiotherapy may be gained from the use of surgery for resection of residual disease. The pathologic subtype is strongly predictive of survival, in addition to the known prognostic factors of the primary site (orbit, nonparameningeal, and nonbladder/nonprostate genitourinary sites are favorable compared with extremity, bladder/prostate and cranial parameningeal sites), clinical group, and tumor size (<5 cm is better than >5 cm).

Chordoma is a rare, slow-growing, locally aggressive neoplasm of bone that arises from embryonic remnants of the notochord. This tumor typically occurs in the axial skeleton and has a predilection for the spheno-occipital region of the skull base and sacral regions. Craniocervical chordomas most often involve the dorsum sellae, clivus, and nasopharynx. The clinical presentation depends on the site of origin and direction of growth. Chordomas can occur at any age, but less than 5% occur in children.[7, 8, 18, 32] The mean age of chordomas at all sites is between 40 and 50 years. Most patients have headache and intermittent diplopia. Invasion of the cavernous sinus produces diplopia and facial numbness. Lower clivus tumors initially compress the lower cranial nerves; brain stem compression may follow. The diagnosis of a clival chordoma is often delayed because the symptoms are vague. MRI is the best technique for assessing the extent of tumor, but CT is important for demonstrating local bone destruction.[10] Imaging studies usually result in a working diagnosis, but biopsy is necessary for a specific diagnosis.

Chordomas are divided into conventional, chondroid, and dedifferentiated types. Conventional chordomas are the most common and are characterized by the absence of cartilaginous or additional mesenchymal components. Chondroid chordomas account for 5% to 15% of all chordomas and up to 33% of cranial chordomas. They contain both chordomatous and chondromatous features and have a predilection for the sphenooccipital region of the skull base. Chondroid tumors occur in a slightly younger age group, but the two lesions have similar survival rates. Dedifferentiation occurs in 2% to 8% of conventional chordoma, either at the onset of disease or later. On gross examination, chordomas are gelatinous, pink or gray masses with solid and cystic areas. Chondroid chordomas show both chordomatous components and variable degrees of benign or malignant cartilaginous components. Histologically, chordomas are composed of lobules containing epithelioid tumor cells arranged in cords or clusters and separated by fibrous strands in a mucinous matrix. Tumor cells have vesicular nuclei and abundant vacuolated, soap bubble–like cytoplasm (physaliphorous cells) that contains glycogen or mucin. Nuclear pleomorphism and mitoses are uncommon. Ultrastructurally, chordomas exhibit epithelial features with prominent desmosomes. Chordomas are typically positive for vimentin, cytokeratin, epithelial membrane antigen (EMA), and S-100 protein.[7, 8, 23]

The differential diagnosis includes chondrosarcoma, myxopapillary ependymoma, and mucinous adenocarcinoma.[7, 8, 23] Chondrosarcoma occurs in an older age group. S-100 protein expression is present in both chordoma and chondrosarcoma. However, unlike chordomas, tumor cells in chondrosarcoma and myxopapillary ependymoma are negative for cytokeratin and EMA. Only myxopapillary ependymoma is positive for glial fibrillary acidic protein (GFAP) in addition to S-100 protein; the other two histologies are negative. The differentiation of adenocarcinoma from chordoma may be difficult because both neoplasms are cytokeratin and EMA positive. Although vimentin and S-100 protein positivity supports the diagnosis of chordoma, this finding should be interpreted with caution because rare adenocarcinomas may be S-100 positive.

Surgery is performed to obtain diagnostic tissue and to reduce the tumor burden, which increases the effectiveness of radiotherapy. Complete resection, although desirable, is not achieved in most cases because of anatomic constraints to surgical access and the proximity of adjacent critical normal tissue. For this reason, postoperative radiation therapy is frequently used.[5, 12]

Conventional photon irradiation appears to result in poor local control in those with macroscopic residual disease after surgery. The local control rate with conventional megavoltage radiation is only 25%, but 85% of patients achieve useful and prolonged palliation of pain; median survival is 62 months. Local tumor control is essential for long-term survival, because salvage treatment after local recurrence is rarely successful. Charged particle beams, such as protons, permit delivery of higher radiation doses to intracranial tumor while limiting the dose to the surrounding structures and have led to improvements in local control (76%), with 5-year survival of 79%, depending on the volume of residual disease after surgery.[5] Patients who relapse locally have a poor prognosis, but both radiation and surgery can be used as salvage therapy. Subtotal resection can result in stable or improved status in as many as 50% of patients who relapse after primary therapy.

Surgical Considerations

Preoperative anesthesia evaluation consists of a complete history and physical examination. The history not only informs the anesthesiologist as to what has happened in the past but also may indicate how things should be done in the future. Management of a difficult airway may be delineated in previous anesthetic records, indicating a way to handle the airway in later procedures. Sometimes, understanding past operative procedures may alter the way one handles the anesthetic. A previous normal airway may now be difficult because the past surgical approach included traversing the temporomandibular joint, causing decreased opening later.

Although these examples pertain to airway management, there are some specific treatment modalities that may affect future anesthetics.

In particular, a history of chemotherapy can have future anesthetic implications depending on the agents used.[6] Use of doxorubicin and other toxic cardiac agents whose effects are dose dependent may require cardiac evaluation including an echocardiogram. Decreased cardiac function alters the types of anesthetic agents used and may require the use of a pulmonary catheter for monitoring. Neurotoxic agents may lessen the dose of

muscle relaxants or cause their duration of action to be prolonged. Bleomycin has been associated with pulmonary fibrosis at higher oxygen concentrations. These are just a few of the potential problems that demonstrate that the anesthesiologist must be aware of potential interactions with all chemotherapeutic agents.

Another factor that can have several implications is prior radiation therapy. Systemic problems secondary to radiation are rare unless pituitary function has been affected by radiation to the base of the skull. Should the pituitary gland be damaged, it can give rise to the problems of panhypopituitarism, including hypothyroidism, hypoadrenocorticism, and diabetes insipidus. Previous radiation to the operative site may also increase blood loss. There may be secondary radiation fibrosis, which makes surgical dissection more difficult and time consuming. It can also necessitate the use of microvascular flaps to close the surgical site. The location of the donor site and the potential anastomotic sites must be considered when positioning the patient.

Evaluation of the head and neck is the part of the physical examination that gets the most attention. A very high percentage of patients with craniofacial abnormalities have structural problems, making intubation of the trachea difficult, or require a tracheostomy tube for airway control.[28] Fortunately, this is not usually the case with patients with skull base lesions. Although intubation may not be as problematic, the route and fixation of the endotracheal tube (ETT) must be given consideration. For lesions where there is a midline surgical approach, oral intubation is the obvious route. If the lesion does not cross the midline, an oral or nasal approach may be used. Nasal endotracheal tubes may be secured by use of a heavy suture through the nasal septum and around the ETT. Oral endotracheal tubes may be secured by wiring the tube to the teeth, by suturing it to the gingival periosteum, or by using a circummandibular wire.

Standard anesthesia practice includes using the blood pressure cuff, appropriate electrocardiogram (ECG) monitoring, oxygen saturation probe, and temperature probe. Additional monitoring includes a Foley catheter to measure urine output, an intra-arterial line for direct blood pressure measurement and blood gas sampling, and a precordial Doppler to detect air embolism. Rarely, electroencephalogram (EEG) or evoked potential monitoring may be used. Venous access is secured by at least two intravenous (IV) catheters, a large-bore IV line for fluid volume administration and another IV line for medication or infusions. If a central line catheter is placed for air embolism, it should be a multi-orifice type and be placed at the superior vena cava–right atrial junction if the thought is to use it to treat an air embolism.[1] A chest x-ray should always be taken to verify central line placement.

The actual choice of anesthetic agents remains with the anesthesiologist, but it is usually some combination of inhalational agents and intravenous narcotics. Some anesthetists prefer to use an inhalational gas as the main component with additional narcotics for pain control and to smooth out hemodynamic responses. Others may prefer a technique of narcotic infusion with a background of under 0.5% volatile agent, which provides for good cardiovascular control and pain relief. The volatile agent at this concentration helps ensure amnesia. In an emergency, the narcotic may also be reversed, allowing the patient to breath spontaneously if muscle relaxants have not been given. The use of muscle relaxants deserves a mention at this point.

There are some procedures in which the surgeon needs to identify the facial nerve, either during the initial approach or during the dissection later in the case. It is during these procedures that the use of muscle relaxants is avoided. There are two main methods of inducing anesthesia and intubating the trachea in this scenario. One can induce anesthesia and continue with inhalational agent until the patient is adequately anesthetized, after which tracheal intubation can proceed. An alternative

technique is to induce anesthesia with IV propofol, to intubate immediately thereafter, and to continue with volatile agent and any fixed drugs. Muscle relaxants may be given later if nerve stimulation is not needed.

As with other craniofacial procedures, blood loss may become an issue. All patients should have a sample in the blood bank for type and cross-match as well as blood products set up in advance. Often family members donate blood (directed donor) in advance. This directed donor blood is identified and used first if blood is needed. Some institutions have programs for autologous blood donation. This blood is stored in advance as frozen red cells. Other methods of minimizing use of allogeneic blood have also been carried out. In larger patients with normal hematocrit, one technique is the use of modest hemodilution. At

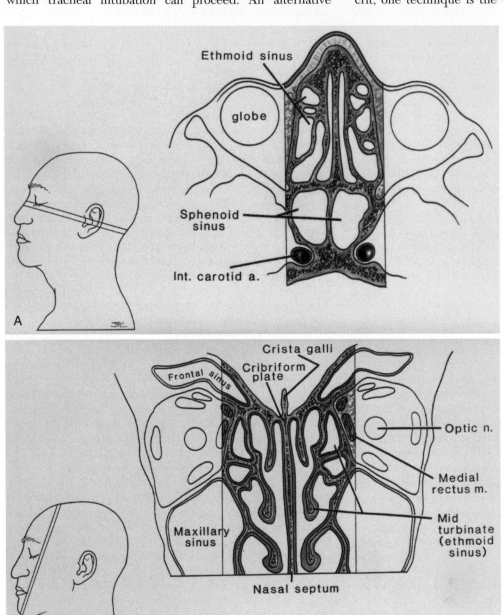

FIGURE 104–1. *A*, Schema of axial anatomy of the anterior cranial fossa; central skull base is highlighted. *B*, Schema of coronal anatomy of the same region. (From Sekhar L, Janecka IP [eds]. Surgery of Cranial Base Tumors. New York, Raven Press, 1993.)

the start of the surgery, a unit of blood is collected from the patient in a standard blood donation bag. After the bag is filled, it should be labeled and placed in the refrigerator for later use. Crystalloid or colloid can be used to replace the volume of blood removed. Serial blood gases are drawn every hour to follow the hematocrit. Allogeneic packed red blood cells are given if the hematocrit falls below 25% during the procedure with the possibility of ongoing loss. If no further blood loss is expected, the autologous unit can be returned to the patient or one can wait until the surgeon is closing the wound. This blood is rich in clotting factors and platelets and should help in hemostasis. In some cases, deliberate hypotension can help reduce the potential for massive blood loss or be indicated for surgical reasons such as clipping of an aneurysm. In this situation, hemodilution is avoided so as not to compromise oxygen delivery with potential adverse

consequences. Blood salvage techniques, such as Cell Saver, are usually not appropriate, given that most surgical sites are not approached through sterile approaches and that oxidized cellulose is used for hemostasis.

Most pediatric skull base surgery involves either the midline region of the anterior cranial fossa (Fig. 104–1) or the anterolateral skull base (Fig. 104–2). A useful technique to reach this area surgically is the facial translocation approach.[17] The principal "facial unit" is depicted in Figure 104–3. It is a versatile procedure that can be expanded either posteriorly to include the posterior fossa or anteriorly to include the central or even the entire contralateral facial region. The modular concept of the approach is reflected in the ability of the surgeon to use only a fraction of the total approach for limited tumors (Fig. 104–4). The reconstruction is accomplished with the return of the displaced facial tissues to their normal

FIGURE 104–2. *A,* Schema of axial anatomy of the anterolateral skull base. *B,* Schema of coronal anatomy of the same region. (From Sekhar L, Janecka IP [eds]. Surgery of Cranial Base Tumors. New York, Raven Press, 1993.)

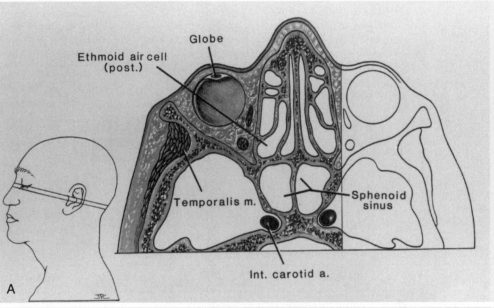

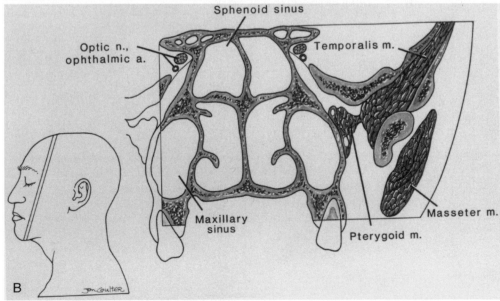

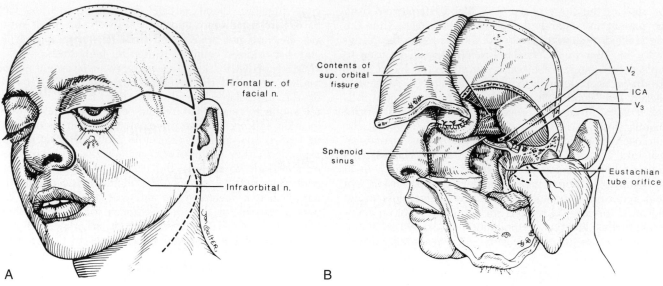

FIGURE 104–3. *A,* Outline of basic incisions of the facial translocation approach. *B,* Exposure achieved at the skull base; lip split is optional. Facial skeleton, including the palate, may also be included with the facial skin as a single composite unit that is then translocated. ICA, internal carotid artery; V₂, trigeminal nerve, 2nd division; V₃, trigeminal nerve, 3rd division. (From Sekhar L, Janecka P [eds]. Surgery of Cranial Base Tumors. New York, Raven Press, 1993.)

anatomic position. The stability of the craniofacial skeleton is ensured with micro/miniplating systems. Frequently, a temporalis muscle is used for defect reconstruction (Fig. 104–5). The potential for complications in skull base surgery (Table 104–3) can be lessened by using intraoperative neurophysiologic monitoring (Table 104–4).

Case Examples

A 7-year-old child had a right cheek mass. CT evaluation revealed a cystic mass with widening of the orbital fissures and foramen rotundum. A suspected meningocele was operated on with the use of the facial translocation approach. The mass was identified in the infratemporal

TABLE 104–3. Potential Complications in Skull Base Surgery

Category	Complication	Treatment Options
Mass lesions	Brain edema	Mannitol, diuretics, barbiturate coma, occasionally lobectomy
	Hematomas	Evacuation
Vascular	Carotid or vertebral artery rupture	Re-exploration and repair or occlusion
	Arterial thrombosis	Microvascular bypass
		Anticoagulation
	Arterial dissection	Anticoagulation
	Cerebral infarction	Induced hypertension
	Venous thrombosis	Volume hypertension
		Volume expansion
		Diuretics, heparinization
	Air embolism	Left lateral decubitus position, occlusion of venous defect
Other cerebral	Seizures	Anticonvulsants
Cerebrospinal fluid	Cerebrospinal fluid leakage—wound, ear, nose, nasopharynx	Re-exploration and repair; spinal fluid drainage; vascularized flap
Infections	Meningitis	Antibiotics
	Wound abscess	Drainage
	Epidural, subdural, or brain abscess	Antibiotics
Wound	Flap necrosis	Local or distant flap repair
Cranial nerve palsies	Cranial nerves I to XII	Nerve reconstruction
		Compensatory procedures (e.g., vocal cord injection)
		Rehabilitation
Metabolic	Diabetes insipidus	Fluid replacement, vasopressin
	Syndrome of inappropriate antidiuretic hormone secretion	Fluid restriction, hypertonic saline

From Janecka IP, Sekhar LN. Cranial base tumors. In Myers EN, Suen J (eds). Cancer of the Head and Neck. New York, Churchill Livingstone, 1989.

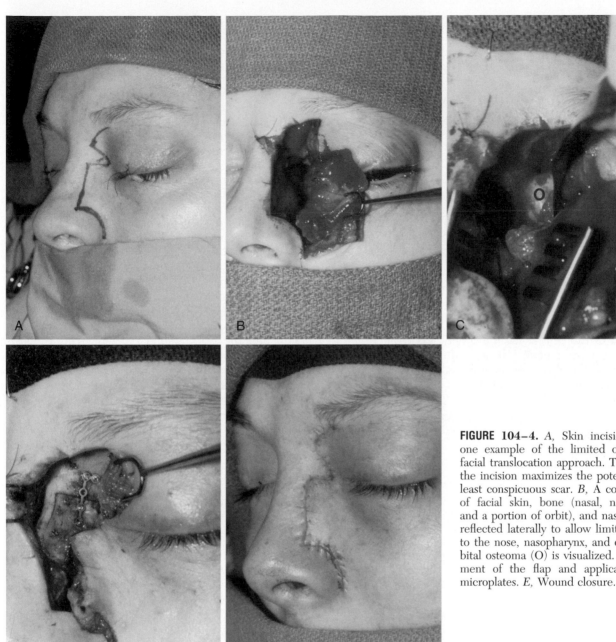

FIGURE 104–4. *A,* Skin incisions used in one example of the limited or segmental facial translocation approach. The design of the incision maximizes the potential for the least conspicuous scar. *B,* A composite flap of facial skin, bone (nasal, naxomaxillary, and a portion of orbit), and nasal mucosa is reflected laterally to allow limited exposure to the nose, nasopharynx, and orbit. *C,* Orbital osteoma (O) is visualized. *D,* Replacement of the flap and application of the microplates. *E,* Wound closure.

fossa and traced to the skull base bony defect. The lesion was resected, and the dural defect was repaired. The gross examination of the mass revealed a smooth lining of the cavity. Histologic evaluation with special stains revealed this mass to be a meningoencephalocele. The lining of the mass was positive for glial tissue (Fig. 104–6).

A 5-year-old child also presented with a painless cheek swelling causing significant proptosis and loss of vision. CT evaluation suggested another meningocele. A surgical resection included orbital exenteration and reconstruction with titanium plates. Postoperatively, an orbital prosthesis was fashioned. Histologic evaluation of the specimen confirmed the presence of a meningocele with an addition, however, of neurofibroma in its wall (Fig. 104–7).

A 12-year-old boy had symptoms of nasal airway ob-

struction, cheek swelling, and slight proptosis. MRI evaluation revealed an extensive tumor of the anterolateral skull base, including the sphenoid sinus, the orbit, the middle fossa, and the infratemporal fossa. Because of the patient's age, sex, and MRI appearance (multiple signal voids), angiography and tumor embolization were done of this suspected angiofibroma. Through a facial translocation approach, the tumor was removed, including the portion from the cavernous sinus region (Fig. 104–8).

An 8-year-old patient also had symptoms of nasal airway obstruction, primarily on his left side. MRI evaluation revealed a soft tissue mass filling the entire left nasal cavity and involving the cribriform plate. After a biopsy, a craniofacial resection was performed by use of a limited transfacial approach beside a frontal craniotomy. The re-

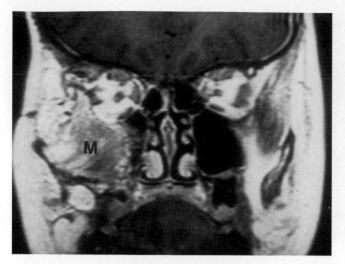

FIGURE 104–5. Temporalis muscle (M) transferred into the infratemporal fossa and orbital region to fill surgical defect after resection of rhabdomyosarcoma.

construction of the central facial anatomy was done with microplates and split cranial bone graft. The histologic examination of the final specimen revealed it to be an olfactory neuroblastoma (Fig. 104–9).

New Horizons

Surgical Navigation

Complex skull base anatomy demands the utmost precision. The traditional intraoperative orientation with visible or palpable landmarks cannot always be used owing to tumor extent or approach limitation. In such cases, an electronic navigation system based on the patient's own CT scan can be very useful. The principle is simple: a preoperative CT scan is obtained with defined special markers. This scan is downloaded to a workstation, which is available in the operating room (OR). At the time of surgery, re-registration of the patient's head takes place. During surgery, when verification of some critical landmark is necessary, a wireless pointer placed on the landmark in question identifies this point directly on the CT.

We have used an optical system with encouraging results (Figs. 104–10, 104–11, and 104–12). The main computational error (the difference between the patient's head position in the CT scanner and on the OR table) is generated with the registration sequence. We favor a tight-fitting headset with metallic markers to skin-pasted fiducials for use during the CT scan. In the OR, with the patient under general anesthesia, the identical headset is placed back on the patient's head in the same position as in the CT scanner. When its accuracy is verified, four additional bony affixed fiducials are inserted and registered as secondary fiducials. Now the head frame can be removed, and surgery can proceed without head fixation. For subsequent guidance system orientation, the pointer touches the four bony fiducials, thus re-registering the head. After that, any point touched with the pointer is immediately seen on the CT, thus immensely increasing the accuracy of surgery.

The optical system has a disadvantage in that the line of sight needs to be open between the pointer, the signal generator, and the work station receptor. This is, however, not a major hindrance, because the guidance system needs to be used only a few times during surgery for key orientation, and thus the optical communication of all the component parts can be maintained. Any re-registration during surgery takes only several minutes, and the estimated overall registration error ranges within 1 to 2 mm.

Tumor Assay

In vitro drug testing on tumor cells is in its infancy and is not a perfect predictor of clinical response. However, treatment with assay "positive" drugs seems to be more strongly associated with clinical response than treatment with assay "negative" drugs. We have obtained assays on several tumors and want to share the laboratory findings here. Clinical conclusions cannot be drawn at this early stage and such findings may be used only as guidance when chemotherapy options must be considered.

TABLE 104–4. Intraoperative Neurophysiologic Monitoring Techniques

Structure Monitored	Monitoring Modality	Usefulness
Cranial nerve II	Visual evoked response	Investigational
	Direct optic nerve potential	Investigational
Cranial nerves III, IV, VI	Ocular muscle EMG nerve stimulation	Useful
Cranial nerve VII	Facial muscle EMG with direct nerve stimulation	Very useful
Cranial nerve VIII	Cochlear action potential	Investigational
	BSER	Useful
	Direct nerve action potential	Very useful
Cranial nerve X	Sound-activated monitoring of vocal cord	Investigational
Cranial nerve XI	Trapezius muscle EMG	Useful
Cranial nerve XII	Tongue EMG	Useful
Temporal lobe (during retraction)	BSER from opposite side	Very useful
Brain stem	BSER from contralateral side	Very useful
Cervicomedullary junction	SSEP	Useful

EMG, electromyography; BSER, brain stem evoked response; SSEP, somatosensory evoked potential.
From Janecka IP, Sekhar LN. Cranial base tumors. In Myers EN, Suen J (eds). Cancer of the Head and Neck. New York, Churchill Livingstone, 1989.

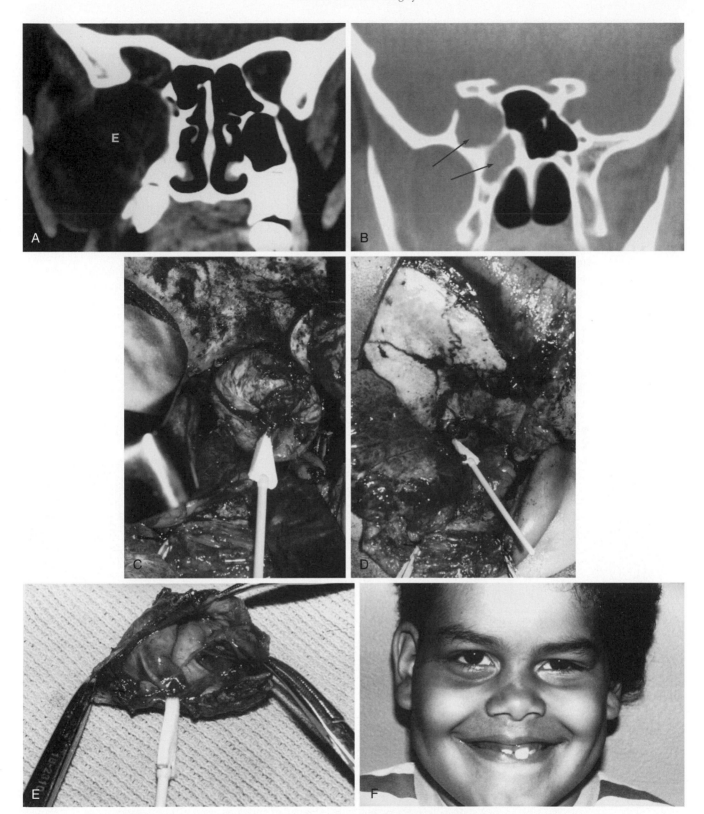

FIGURE 104–6. *A,* Coronal computed tomogram (CT) demonstrating a cystic mass (E) extending from widened inferior orbital fissure to the infratemporal fossa and cheek. *B,* Coronal CT (bone algorithm) more posterior to *A* showing widened superior orbital fissure and the foramen rotundum *(arrows). C,* Cystic mass (meningoencephalocele) identified in the right infratemporal fossa, lateral orbit, and skull base *(arrow). D,* Site of dural repair *(arrow)* after resection. *E,* Lumen of the mass (surgical specimen). *F,* Patient's postoperative result several months after right facial translocation for a spheno-orbital meningoencephalocele. (From Janecka J. Surgical approaches to skull base. Neuroimaging Clin North Am 4:639, 1994.)

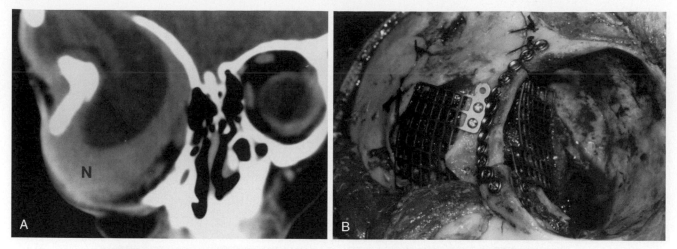

FIGURE 104–7. *A,* Coronal CT with contrast enhancement demonstrating an extensive meningocele accompanied by neurofibroma (N). *B,* Multiple titanium miniplates used in reconstructing right temporal fossa and orbit.

Case 1: Chordoma of clivus. The tumor assay showed sensitivity to cisplatin and ifosfamide.

Case 2: Myxoid fibrosarcoma. The tumor assay showed sensitivity to gemcitabine + cisplatin, gemcitabine + melphalan, and gemcitabine + melphalan + high-dose tamoxifen.

Case 3: Meningioma, middle and infratemporal fossa. The tumor assay showed sensitivity to paclitaxel.

Case 4: Chordoma of clivus. The tumor assay showed sensitivity to docetaxel, gemcitabine + cisplatin, gemcitabine + cisplatin + high-dose tamoxifen, gemcitabine + melphalan + high-dose tamoxifen, and vinorelbine + high-dose tamoxifen.

Case 5: Synovial cell sarcoma of upper neck. The tumor assay showed sensitivity to doxorubicin, gemcitabine + melphalan + high-dose tamoxifen, and ifosfamide.

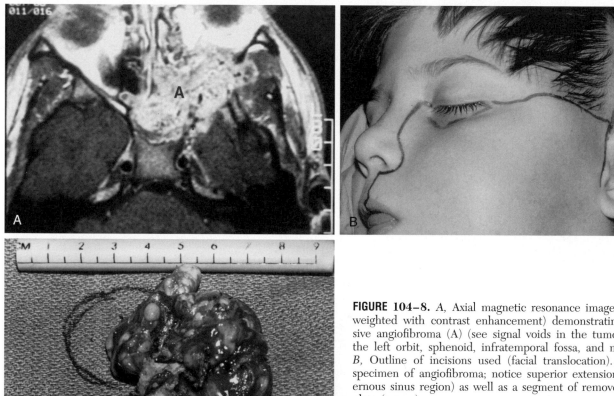

FIGURE 104–8. *A,* Axial magnetic resonance image (MRI) (T_1-weighted with contrast enhancement) demonstrating an extensive angiofibroma (A) (see signal voids in the tumor) involving the left orbit, sphenoid, infratemporal fossa, and middle fossa. *B,* Outline of incisions used (facial translocation). *C,* Surgical specimen of angiofibroma; notice superior extension (from cavernous sinus region) as well as a segment of removed pterygoid plate *(arrow).*

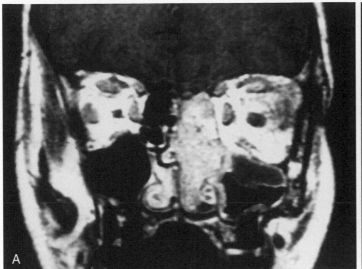

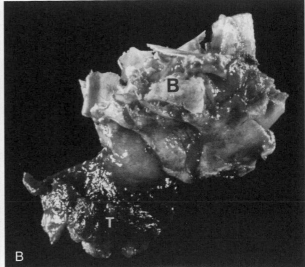

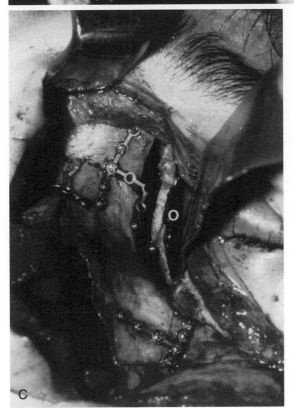

FIGURE 104–9. *A*, Coronal magnetic resonance image (T$_1$-weighted with contrast enhancement) showing an enhancing mass in the left nasal cavity with involvement of the cribriform plate. *B*, Left lateral view of the surgical specimen incorporating the intranasal portion of the tumor (T) as well as the anterior cranial base (B). *C*, A close-up view of left naso-orbital region being reconstructed with split cranial graft for medial orbital wall (O) and fixation of the nasofrontal complex with microplates. (From Janecka I. Surgical approaches to skull base. Neuroimaging Clin North Am 4:639, 1994.)

Case 6: Squamous cell carcinoma, maxilla. The tumor assay showed sensitivity to bleomycin, cisplatin, gemcitabine, gemcitabine + cisplatin, docetaxel, irinotecan + cisplatin, irinotecan + cisplatin + high-dose tamoxifen, and topotecan + cisplatin.

Case 7: Neuroendocrine carcinoma, ethmoid sinuses. The tumor assay showed sensitivity to trimetrexate.

Case 8: Meningioma, orbit, middle, and infratemporal fossae. The tumor assay showed sensitivity to extramusine, dacarbazine, and taxanes.

Case 9: Myxoid fibrosarcoma, orbit, infratemporal fossa, skull base. Tumor assay showed sensitivity to doxorubicin, epirubicin, gemcitabine, gemcitabine + cisplatin, gemcitabine + doxorubicin + high-dose tamoxifen,

gemcitabine + ifosfamide, and gemcitabine + melphalan.

Conclusion

Pediatric skull base surgery has evolved from the foundation of pediatric craniofacial and adult skull base surgery. It focuses primarily on the treatment of neoplastic and congenital lesions. The knowledge of not only regional anatomy but also embryology is essential in the diagnostic and therapeutic process concerning these lesions. The frequent use of multimodality therapy in pediatric patients puts additional emphasis on anticipation and pre-

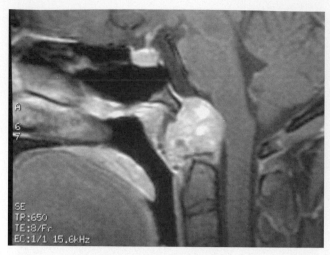

FIGURE 104–10. Sagittal magnetic resonance image (T1 with contrast) demonstrating enhancing chordoma of clivus with effacement of the brain stem.

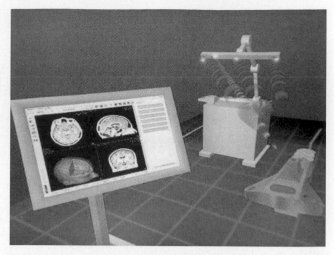

FIGURE 104–12. Schema of optical navigational system with the three basic components: the probe (the pointer), the optical signal and receptor generator, and the workstation panel.

vention of growth-related problems. In addition, the longer potential life span of younger patients highlights the need for the most tumor-specific treatment without systemic consequences. Many potential side effects can appear as the treated child becomes an adult. This is where surgery has a significant advantage over chemotherapy and radiotherapy because it does not contribute to the creation of the biologic environment conducive to possible second neoplasia. The disadvantages of surgery can be lessened by advanced reconstructive techniques emphasizing function and aesthetics. Microsurgery and microplating are examples of surgical refinements directly applicable to the pediatric patient that are intended for

the most advantageous long-term results. A close interdisciplinary collaboration with all clinical disciplines treating children and with basic scientists is essential. It provides the foundation for continuing advances in understanding of skull base disease and application of the best treatment to a specific disease. For most congenital lesions of the skull base, surgery is the primary treatment modality. The oncologic results with skull base surgical techniques can also offer significant benefits.[17, 22]

SELECTED REFERENCES

Guyuron B, Dagys P, Munro IR, Ross RB. Effect of irradiation on facial growth: a 7–25 year follow-up. Ann Plast Surg 11:423, 1988.

> *This article clearly demonstrates the relationship between the dose of radiation and the effect on facial growth. It highlights the broad spectrum of the effect of ionizing radiation not only on bony growth but also on growth of soft tissue with much lower dosages than previously suspected.*

Kawamoto HK Jr. Elective osteotomies and bone grafting of irradiated midfacial bones. J Craniomaxillofac Surg 15:199, 1987.

> *This article sets the principles for performing elective osteotomies in the craniofacial region after previous external beam radiotherapy.*

Moss ML. The functional matrix concept and its relationship to temporomandibular joint dysfunction and treatment. Dent Clin North Am 27:445, 1983.

> *Mel Moss is the originator of the concept of the "functional matrix" of facial growth. The hypothesis postulates that growth of the craniofacial skeleton is based on the function of its surrounding soft tissue (e.g., brain, muscles). This is in contradistinction to another concept of craniofacial growth, presumably only from "growth centers" (e.g., suture lines). It is possible that both hypotheses will be combined to explain craniofacial growth.*

Tessier P. The definitive plastic surgical treatment of the several facial deformities of craniofacial dysostosis: Crouzon's and Apert's disease. Plast Reconstr Surg 48:419, 1971.

> *This 1971 article by Paul Tessier updates his experience with craniofacial surgery for congenital deformities with applicability to congenital defects of the skull.*

Tessier P, Guiot G, Rougerie J, et al. Osteotomies cranio-naso-orbitofaciales hypertelorisme. Ann Chir Plast 12:103, 1967.

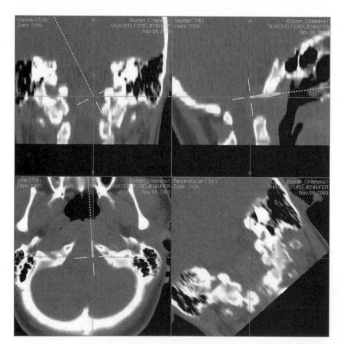

FIGURE 104–11. Surgical reach demonstrated with the navigational probe (cross-hair on multiplanar computed tomography) after chordoma resection.

Paul Tessier, the founder of modern craniofacial surgery, demonstrated the feasibility of mobilizing, transferring, and fixing large segments of craniofacial skeletons with subsequent expected healing and growth. A number of osteotomies that he designed for correction of congenital deformities are still being used in skull base surgery.

REFERENCES

1. Albin M: Venous air embolism. In Atlee J (ed). Complications in Anesthesia. Philadelphia, WB Saunders, 1999, pp 726–729.
2. Barnes L (ed). Surgical Pathology of the Head and Neck. New York, Marcel Dekker, 2000.
3. Barnes L, Weber PC, Krause JR, et al. Angiofibroma: a flow cytometric evaluation of 31 cases. Skull Base Surg 2:195, 1992.
4. Batsakis JB. Pathology consultation: nomenclature of developmental tumors. Ann Otol Rhinol Laryngol 93:95, 1984.
5. Catton C, O'Sullivan B, Bell R, et al. Chordoma: long-term follow-up after radical photon irradiation. Radiother Oncol 41:67, 1996.
6. Chung F. Cancer, chemotherapy, and anaesthesia. Can Anaesth Soc J 29:364, 1982.
7. Coffin CM, Swanson PE, Wick MR, et al. Chordoma in childhood and adolescence. A clinicopathologic analysis of 12 cases. Arch Pathol Lab Med 117:927, 1993.
8. Coffin CM, Swanson PE, Wick MR, Dehner LP. An immunohistochemical comparison of chordoma with renal cell carcinoma, colorectal adenocarcinoma, and myxopapillary ependymoma: a potential diagnostic dilemma in the diminutive biopsy. Mod Pathol 6:531, 1993.
9. Devaney K, Wenig BM, Abbondanzo SL. Olfactory neuroblastoma and other small round cell lesions of the sinonasal region. Mod Pathol 9:658, 1996.
10. Doucet V, Peretti-Viton P, Figarella-Branger D, et al. MRI of intracranial chordomas. Extent of tumour and contrast enhancement: criteria for differential diagnosis. Neuroradiology 39:571, 1997.
11. Douglass EC, Shapiro DN, Valentine M, et al. Alveolar rhabdomyosarcoma with the t(2;13): cytogenetic findings and clinicopathologics. Med Pediatr Oncol 21:83, 1993.
12. Fagundes MA, Hug EB, Liebsch NJ, et al. Radiation therapy for chordomas of the base of skull and cervical spine: patterns of failure and outcome after relapse. Int J Radiat Oncol Biol Phys 33:579, 1995.
13. Hirose T, Scheithauer BW, Lopes MBS, et al. Olfactory neuroblastoma: an immunohistochemical, ultrastructural and flow cytometric study. Cancer 76:4, 1995.
14. Hwang HC, Mills SE, Patterson K, Gowan AM. Expression of androgen receptors in nasopharyngeal angiofibroma: an immunohistochemical study of 24 cases. Mod Pathol 11:1122, 1998.
15. Janecka IP, Sen C, Sekhar LN, et al. Cranial base surgery: results in 183 patients. Otolaryngol Head Neck Surg 110:539, 1994.
16. Janecka IP, Sen C, Sekhar LN, Nuss DW. Facial translocation approach to the nasopharynx, clivus and infratemporal fossa. In Sekhar LN, Janecka IP (eds). Surgery of Cranial Base Tumors. New York, Raven Press, 1993, pp 245–261.
17. Kadish S, Goodman M, Wang CC. Olfactory neuroblastoma: a clinical analysis of 17 cases. Cancer 37:1571, 1976.
18. Kaneko Y, Sato Y, Iwaki T, et al. Chordoma in early childhood: a clinicopathologic study. Neurosurgery 29:442, 1991.
19. Kapadia SB, Janecka IP. Nasopharyngeal carcinoma. In Advances in Otolaryngol Head and Neck Surgery, vol. 9. St. Louis, Mosby, 1995, pp 247–261.
20. Kapadia SB, Popek EJ, Barnes L. Pediatric otorhinolaryngologic pathology: diagnosis of selected lesions. In Rosen PP, Fechner RE (eds). Pathology Annual. Norwalk, Connecticut, Appleton & Lange, 1994, pp 159–210.
21. Mezzelani A, Tornielli S, Minoletti F, et al. Esthesioneuroblastoma is not a member of the primitive peripheral neuroectodermal tumour-Ewing's group. Br J Cancer 81:586, 1999.
22. Mills SE, Gaffey MJ, Frierson JR. Tumors of the upper respiratory tract and ear. In Atlas of Tumor Pathology, Third Series, vol. 26. Washington, DC, Armed Forces Institute of Pathology, 2000, pp 153–163.
23. Mitchell A, Scheithauer BW, Unni KK, et al. Chordoma and chondroid neoplasms of the spheno-occiput. An immunohistochemical study of 41 cases with prognostic and nosologic implications. Cancer 72:2943, 1993.
24. Nelson RS, Perlman EJ, Askin FB. Is esthesioneuroblastoma a peripheral neuroectodermal tumor? Hum Pathol 26:639, 1995.
25. Newton WA, Gehan EA, Webber BL, et al. Classification of rhabdomyosarcomas and related sarcomas. Pathologic aspects and proposal for a new classification—an Intergroup Rhabdomyosarcoma Study. Cancer 76:1073, 1995.
26. Qualman SJ, Coffin CM, Newton WA, et al. Intergroup Rhabdomyosarcoma Study: Update for pathologists. Pediatr Dev Pathol 1: 550, 1998.
27. Ringborg U, Henle W, Henle G, et al. Epstein-Barr virus–specific serodiagnostic tests in carcinomas of the head and neck. Cancer 52: 1237, 1983.
28. Sculerati N, Gottlieb MD, Zimbler MS, et al. Airway management in children with major craniofacial anomalies. Laryngoscope 108: 1806, 1998.
29. Shanmugaratnam K, Sobin LH, Barnes L, et al. World Health Organization International Histologic Classification of Tumours: Histologic Typing of Tumors of the Upper Respiratory Tract and Ear, 2nd ed. Berlin, Springer-Verlag, 1991.
30. Shanmugaratnam K, Sobin LH, Bauer WC, at al. World Health Organization International Histological Classification of Tumours, No. 19: Histological Typing of Upper Respiratory Tract Tumours. Geneva, World Health Organization, 1978.
31. Whang-Peng J, Knutsen T, Theil K, et al. Cytogenetic studies in subgroups of rhabdomyosarcoma. Genes Chromosom Cancer 5:299, 1992.
32. Wold LE, Laws ER Jr. Cranial chordomas in children and young adults. J Neurosurgery 59;1043, 1983.
33. Zubizarreta PA, D'Antonio G, Raslawski E, et al. Nasopharyngeal carcinoma in childhood and adolescence. A single-institution experience with combined therapy. Cancer 89:690, 2000.

Communication Disorders

105

Disorders of Language, Phonology, Fluency, and Voice in Children: Indicators for Referral

Thomas F. Campbell, Ph.D., Christine A. Dollaghan, Ph.D., and J. Scott Yaruss, Ph.D.

Diagnosing speech, language, fluency, and voice disorders in children is a complex but crucial task. It is complex because communication development requires the interaction of multiple systems (e.g., sensory, motor, cognitive, and socioemotional) and comprises a variety of skills and functions. It is crucial because communication skills serve as the cornerstone for a host of intellectual, academic, and interpersonal achievements.

Comprehensive assessment of pediatric speech and language disorders is a time-intensive process involving numerous special procedures and analyses. The observations of parents and physicians are often instrumental in ensuring that children with communication deficits gain access to such services, particularly during the preschool years. The primary goal of this chapter is to provide physicians and other health care providers with a set of "referral indicators" that can be used to identify children for whom detailed speech and language evaluation is warranted. Because the physician's role in identifying children with communication disorders is likely to be greatest in the years before the child enters school, we have emphasized referral indicators for children ranging from 12 months to 5 years of age. All of the referral indicators can be observed readily in a reasonably brief encounter with a child or described by the parents. We have taken care to include only referral indicators that unequivocally mark the child as functioning outside the wide range of normal variation that characterizes this age group (i.e., at or below the 10th percentile).

In addition to providing a set of referral indicators, the secondary goal of this chapter is to offer an overview of four major classes of pediatric communication disorders,

including information about their symptoms, causes, and prevalence. Briefly described are some of the major diagnostic procedures that are likely to be used by certified speech-language pathologists to conduct an exhaustive assessment of children who have been referred by physicians, other health care providers, or parents. Finally, the major approaches to providing treatment to children with these disorders are summarized, as is available information on prognoses.

At the outset, we want to emphasize the importance of hearing assessment in efforts to diagnose and treat pediatric communication disorders. The hearing status of all children referred for suspected communication disorders should be verified, regardless of anecdotal reports or observations that suggest that hearing is normal. In addition, the frequency of temporary conductive hearing loss in children makes it important to verify adequate hearing sensitivity on the day of any speech and language testing.

The four communication disorders to be addressed are disorders of *language*, of *phonology*, of *fluency*, and of *voice*. The section on each disorder is organized as follows: (1) definition, description, and prevalence; (2) causal factors; (3) referral indicators; (4) information expected from a full evaluation; (5) major treatment approaches; (6) prognosis.

Language Disorders

Definition, Description, and Prevalence

A developmental language disorder can be defined as a significant limitation in a child's ability to acquire his or her first (or native) language. "Language impairment," "language disorder," "language delay," and "childhood aphasia/dysphasia" are among the terms that have been applied to such deficits. "Specific language impairment" is a term used for language disorders that are not accompanied by deficits in such associated areas as neurologic, cognitive, emotional, perceptual, or motor development.[65, 111] Acquired language disorders are those in which the previously normal course of language development is disrupted by some form of neurologic damage (e.g., cerebrovascular accident, traumatic brain injury).

Language disorders can impede children's ability to comprehend language and to produce language. Children with language comprehension (or receptive language) disorders have difficulty understanding the words, phrases, or sentences that they hear. If the language comprehension deficit is not severe, such children may give the impression that they understand much more than they do, because they rely on various nonlinguistic cues that often accompany linguistic input. For example, nonlinguistic cues such as gestures, facial expressions, and simple knowledge of predictable events may enable children to construct a likely interpretation and to respond appropriately even when they do not understand the specific words and sentences they hear. The use of such nonlinguistic cues by children as young as 8 months of age is one reason why parents (and others) typically overestimate the amount of language that children understand.[24] For this reason, diagnosing a language comprehension disorder requires thorough testing under controlled conditions, rather than an impression based on the child's behavior in a "cue-filled" conversation.

Language production disorders, also known as expressive language disorders, result in significant deficits in speaking or producing language. Children with language production disorders may be delayed in beginning to use words and may deploy an extremely limited set of speech sounds in their early words.[50, 90, 109] They are likely to add new words to their vocabularies more slowly than their peers and to begin combining words later than their peers.[40, 91] During the preschool years, children with expressive deficits are likely to speak less often and to convey less information than their peers.[81, 83] They are likely to have restricted vocabularies, and their sentences are likely to be short and simple, with a marked tendency toward mistakes or omissions involving acoustically weak but grammatically important words and forms (e.g., "is" and "the").[9, 66] A growing body of evidence suggests that, on reaching school age, such children are likely to encounter difficulties in learning to read.[23, 60]

The prevalence of language impairment depends on what criteria are used to identify affected individuals. Converging evidence from several recent epidemiologic studies suggests that 12% to 15% of English-speaking children have some type of language disorder.[11, 115] The prevalence rate decreases to approximately 7% for specific language impairments, in which the language disorder is not accompanied by neurologic, cognitive, perceptual, motoric, or socioemotional deficits.[114] Although a male-to-female ratio of 2:1 has been reported in studies of general language disorders, a ratio of 1.33:1 was found in one recent epidemiologic study of specific language impairment.[114]

Causal Factors

Efforts to pinpoint a single cause for developmental language disorders have not been successful. It appears that a number of variables, singly or in combination, may operate to precipitate or maintain pediatric language disorders.[80] Among the obvious risk factors for developmental language disorders are neurologic dysfunction, hearing impairment, cognitive impairment, emotional dysfunction, and oral mechanism deficit. There is substantial evidence that a family history of speech, language, or reading difficulties is also a risk factor for the disorder.[107, 113] Efforts to determine the contribution of genetic variables are in progress.[112] Children with language disorders appear to have weaknesses in the areas of information processing, conceptual development, and auditory perception, but the underlying mechanisms for such difficulties remain to be identified.[14, 49] It has also been suggested that children with language disorders are at increased risk for a variety of emotional disorders,[10, 22] but the importance of language to socioemotional development makes it difficult to determine the direction of any causal relationship between the two types of impairment.[87]

Referral Indicators

The behaviors that indicate that a child is in need of referral for a suspected language disorder change during the preschool years. Parental observations and concerns are particularly important sources of information for young children[63] who might not provide evidence of their capabilities with unfamiliar adults in unfamiliar situations. Parents' perceptions are particularly important when the child in question is bilingual or when the family's sociodemographic profile differs from that of the clinician. Because general communicative interaction styles as well as specific language forms vary across language communities and other sociodemographic groups, identification of a language disorder requires the use of measures that allow the child's performance to be compared with sociodemographically similar peers or use of assessment tools that are free of bias.[20, 37, 38]

A full evaluation is indicated if, at 12 months of age, a child does not respond to at least one familiar word or phrase in a familiar situation.[41] Similarly, a full evaluation is warranted if a 12-month-old shows little interest in communicating with a familiar caregiver (i.e., if the child does not look at, gesture to, or vocalize to a familiar person in order to obtain a desirable object). For 2-year-olds we recommend use of the Language Development Survey,[88, 89] a screening measure based on a parental checklist that requires minutes to complete and score. The Language Development Survey has excellent psychometric properties, and, by contrast with other such instruments, its validity has been established with parents from a broad range of socioeconomic, educational, and ethnic backgrounds. Based on the Language Development Survey, a referral is indicated for children 24 to 36 months of age who use fewer than 50 different words or do not combine words into phrases, particularly if the parent reports being worried about the child's language development.[63] Data suggest that approximately 50% to 60% of children who meet this criterion at age 2 years will have expressive language skills at or below the 10th percentile at age 3, age 4, and age 5 years.[82, 83, 91]

By 36 months of age, children's expressive language typically consists of combinations of three or more words.[72] A child of this age is expected to produce many multiword sentences in talking with a familiar person for at least 10 minutes.[38] A 3-year-old child whose utterances are primarily limited to single words in such a situation is functioning well below the level expected for his or her age. Similarly, a 4-year-old who is unable to carry on a simple conversation about "here and now" topics using utterances that contain an average of three words needs a full evaluation.

Information Expected from a Full Evaluation

In addition to obtaining an adequate case history, information on any other affected family members, an audiologic evaluation, and an evaluation of the structure and function of the oral mechanism, the physician who refers a child for a language evaluation should expect information in at least the following areas: general developmental or cognitive status, language comprehension status, and language production status.

General Developmental or Cognitive Status. General developmental or cognitive status is measured by instruments that do not require that the child understand or produce language. A child with a developmental delay is likely to be delayed in producing language as well.[68] The child's nonverbal developmental status provides a yardstick against which to measure the significance of the language impairment. Measures of general and cognitive development should be free of language demands to ensure that the child's performance is not adversely affected by language deficits. A truly "language-free" measure of cognition requires neither language comprehension nor language production from the child during the test; such measures typically depend on the child's ability to see relationships (e.g., "odd one out") among visual patterns and to respond by pointing. Such measures cannot be taken as comprehensive indices of cognitive status, but they at least enable the child's abilities in another sphere to be judged independently of any language difficulties.[64]

Language Comprehension Status. For children 24 months of age and younger, a full language evaluation should provide information on the ability to understand single, familiar words without nonlinguistic cues (a skill expected of 10- to 12-month-olds). For children 24 months and older who understand individual words, a full evaluation would also be expected to provide evidence on the child's comprehension of simple two- and three-word combinations (e.g., "Mommy's nose," "Tickle Ernie"), again in the absence of nonlinguistic cues.[73, 74] Between 30 and 36 months of age, the child's single word comprehension may be compared with that of his or her peers via a norm-referenced test. In addition, by 36 months of age, information on multiword comprehension can be obtained from several norm-referenced tests.

Language Production Status. A full evaluation of language production status should reveal information on the quantity and quality of the language produced spontaneously by the child, in play or conversation with a familiar adult (for young children). Typically, a 10- to 30-minute sample of the child's language is audiotaped during interaction with an adult; the vocabulary, speech sound, grammatical, and communicative features of the child's language are then analyzed and compared with developmental expectations. Of interest are the child's *semantic* or *lexical skills*, as reflected in the number and diversity of words used,[38, 118] the child's *morphosyntactic skills,* as seen in the grammatical complexity and correctness of utterances,[71] and the child's *pragmatic skills* (i.e., the extent to which the child engages appropriately in conversational interaction, as by asking and answering questions, making comments, and introducing new topics smoothly).[25]

Major Approaches to Treatment

Direct treatment for a child with a language disorder may take a number of forms, depending on several factors. Chief among these is the extent to which the child's disorder appears to be limited to language (i.e., a specific language impairment). During the preschool years, treatment for specific language impairment has the following primary objectives: (1) increasing the clarity, salience, and frequency of targeted language forms presented to the child, in an effort to facilitate the child's awareness of and familiarity with them, and (2) providing the child with more frequent opportunities to employ the targeted forms and skills, initially with adult assistance in the form of demonstrations or cues. Treatment activities and settings for preschoolers are likely to be as natural (i.e., "everyday") as possible, often being grounded in play or daily routines to facilitate the child's transfer of new language skills to situations outside the treatment context.[43, 80] Considerable evidence shows the efficacy of such programs in improving specific aspects of language comprehension and production in preschool children with language disorders.[17, 26, 44, 45, 78]

Prognosis

The prognosis for measurable improvement in targeted language skills following a treatment program is excellent, but the prognosis for complete mastery of age-appropriate language for children with language disorders is much more guarded. There is considerable evidence that children who have language impairments during the preschool years are at increased risk for reading disabilities when they reach school age.[23, 60, 110] One follow-up study of 20 adolescents who as preschoolers had been treated for language disorders revealed that the majority required some form of special academic assistance through high school.[6] A recent prospective longitudinal study of 103 children with language disorders at age 5 years showed that more than 70% continued to exhibit significant language, cognitive, and academic deficits both in early (age 12 to 13 years) and late (18 to 20 years) adolescence.[60] Similar results were reported for 71 children who had specific language disorders at 5½ years of age[110]; at age 15 years, 70% continued to have language disorders, and more than 90% showed literacy deficits. Several studies have suggested more positive outcomes for children with higher nonverbal intelligence scores.[6, 110] However, generalizations about long-term prognosis are unwarranted because of the heterogeneity of the population of children with language disorders.

Phonologic Disorders

Definition, Description, and Prevalence

Children with phonologic disorders are significantly less skilled than other children of the same age at producing the consonant or vowel sounds of their language. Historically, such disorders have been described by a number of definitions and terms that reflect varying theoretical perspectives on the underlying causes of the speech deficit. The two most frequently used terms are "functional articulation disorders" and "developmental phonologic disorders." Before 1980, "articulation disorder" was the term most frequently used to describe the phenomenon of speech-sound production errors. This term emphasized the physical and motor abilities required to produce speech sounds correctly. Over the past 2 decades, clinicians and researchers have adopted the expression "phonologic disorders," which implies a broader perspective on speech-sound production deficits. Phonologic disorders currently consist of problems in the physical articulation of sounds, in applying the linguistic rules for organizing and classifying speech sounds, and in the higher-level cognitive processes that support perception and production of speech.

The speech characteristics of children with phonologic deficits vary considerably. For example, their consonants or vowels may be deleted altogether (e.g., "bo" for "boat," "moke" for "smoke"), replaced by incorrect sounds (e.g., "tee" for "key"), or produced imprecisely, resulting in speech-sound distortions (e.g., the sound s produced with tongue against the upper teeth, resulting in a frontal lisp). The listener's ability to understand the child's speech, referred to as "speech intelligibility," depends on a number of factors in addition to the type and frequency of speech-sound errors. These include the child's language abilities, intonation and prosodic characteristics, voice and resonance quality, and the complexity of the speaking task (e.g., single words, short phrases, or longer stretches of speech). In general, children who produce sound distortions are judged to be more intelligible than children who produce a comparable number of substitution and omission errors.[98]

In children, the prevalence of phonologic disorders of no identifiable cause varies from 2% to 13%, depending on chronologic age and the criteria used to define the speech disorder.[11, 59, 84, 103, 104, 123] For example, if one includes only children who display multiple articulation errors that result in significant speech intelligibility deficits, the incidence rate is close to 2% to 3%, whereas, if school-aged children who incorrectly produce later developing sounds such as r and s are included, the percentage is closer to 9%. Incidence estimates are higher for boys than for girls, the male-to-female ratio being 2 to 3:1. In a recent study of speech-sound production disorders in 6-year-old children, Shriberg et al[103] reported that the prevalence of speech delay was 3.8%, with the disorder being 1.5 times more prevalent in boys. However, as expected, prevalence rates are higher in younger children; the prevalence of speech delay in a sample of 241 3-year-old children was 14.4%.[21]

Finally, the prevalence of phonologic and related speech deficits increases for children with known cognitive, neurologic, or structural disabilities. For example, children with known neurologic lesions may exhibit motor-based speech disorders such as apraxia of speech (i.e., difficulty with the motor planning aspects of speech production) or dysarthria (i.e., difficulty with the motor execution aspects of speech production). Children are sometimes given the diagnosis of apraxia of speech even in the absence of confirmed neurologic damage. The speech of such children typically is characterized by multiple inconsistent errors and abnormal prosody; they also have difficulty performing volitional nonspeech oral movements (e.g., smiling and puckering) in isolation or in sequence. It should be noted, however, that the use of this label for children with no known neurologic damage is controversial.[32]

Causal Factors

There is no single cause of phonologic disorders in children; however, a number of related factors are known to have important effects on phonologic development. Shriberg et al[99–101] proposed a diagnostic classification system that is based on a number of potential causal correlates of phonologic disorders. These include "mechanism" variables (e.g., hearing deficits, craniofacial abnormalities, velopharyngeal inadequacy, motor speech deficits), cognitive-linguistic variables (e.g., intellectual impairment, attention or memory deficits, language disorder, academic or learning deficits), and psychosocial variables (e.g., behavior management, maturity and affect of the child, family stability). Although these and other factors clearly influence phonologic development, it is rarely possible to identify a single cause for a child's phonologic deficit. However, new data suggest that in addition to gender and variety of neurologic and structural abnormalities, factors such as a positive family history of speech and language deficits and maternal education less than high school increase the risk of phonologic deficit.[21] In evaluating and treating phonologic disorders of children, it is important to consider the potential impact of all of these associated factors on speech-sound production.

Referral Indicators

Children's phonologic skills increase dramatically over the preschool years. Even as infants, most children experiment with producing a variety of speech sounds, but there is a great deal of individual variability in the earliest stages of speech-sound production. Such variability decreases between 2 and 3 years of age.[109] By 24 months of age, a normally developing child is able to use 10 different consonant sounds appropriately, although these sounds are used more frequently in word-initial position (i.e., as the first sound in the word) than in word-final position.[109] For example, a 24-month-old is likely to say "bo" rather than "boat." By 36 months, the typical child is using many sounds in word-final position; he or she is also likely to produce nearly all vowel sounds correctly. By 48 months of age, the child's speech-sound inventory has expanded to include the majority of consonant sounds, although errors may continue on certain "late-acquired" sounds, such as r, l, s, sh, and th.[97]

It is not feasible for physicians to make specific judgments about the type and frequency of sound errors in children's speech, and parents are not likely to make accurate judgments about specific sound errors. Such judgments require audiotaping and detailed transcription and analysis. To identify preschoolers in need of referral for a full speech evaluation, we suggest that physicians make use of a simple procedure described by Coplan and Gleason[30] in which parents are asked to respond to the following question: How much of your child's speech can a stranger understand? Answers include (1) less than half, (2) about half, (3) three quarters, and (4) all or almost all. Based on the results of their standardization and validation studies, Coplan and Gleason recommend a full speech evaluation if a parent estimates that a stranger can understand less than 50% of a child's speech at 22 months of age, less than 75% at 37 months of age, and less than 100% at 47 months of age.

Information Expected from a Full Evaluation

After referring for evaluation, the physician should expect the following information about the child's phonologic capabilities: oral speech motor function, description and analysis of speech-sound errors, description and analysis of speech prosody, and rating of speech intelligibility.

Oral Speech Motor Function. Because a sizable subgroup of children with phonologic disorders have associated speech motor deficits, an evaluation of the entire motor speech system, including respiratory, laryngeal, velopharyngeal, and articulatory function, is crucial. Deficits in one or more of these areas can have important implications for intervention. For children between 24 and 60 months of age, The Oral Speech Motor Control Protocol for Children provides quantitative and qualitative information about the structure and function of all the subsystems that support speech production.[94]

Description and Analysis of Speech-Sound Errors. The cornerstone of every phonologic evaluation is a comprehensive description of the child's speech-sound system. A single word articulation test and a spontaneous connected speech sample provide the data for the speech analyses. First, it is important to provide a description of the

child's *phonemic inventory*. This is accomplished by determining which of the 24 consonant and 12 vowel sounds of the English language the child is able to produce, regardless of whether it is produced in the appropriate position of the word. Second, it is important to have information about the range of *syllable shapes* the child is able to produce. The treatment plan and objectives for a phonologically disordered child who has a restricted number of syllable shapes (e.g., the child who produces words that consist of only a consonant and a vowel) is different from the one for a child who is able to produce more complex syllable shapes (e.g., words that consist of a consonant-consonant-vowel-consonant sequence). Third, the frequency and type of speech-sound *deletions, substitutions,* and *distortions* in specific positions of words should be calculated. Information on consistent patterns of phonologic errors (sometimes referred to as "phonologic processes") should also be specified. Finally, any fluctuation in the child's speech-sound production abilities during different speaking conditions should be noted. For school-aged children, comparison of samples from less and more demanding speaking contexts often reveals difficulties in speech-sound production when processing demands are high. This information often aids in interpreting the variability observed by parents and teachers in the speech production abilities of some children.

Description and Analysis of Speech Prosody. The ability to produce speech sounds correctly is only one variable that affects speech intelligibility. Some children are able to produce the majority of consonant and vowel sounds correctly, but still display inadequate speech intelligibility owing to a very slow or fast speaking rate, inappropriate phrasing of sentences, or incorrect placement of word and sentence stress. Therefore, a full phonologic evaluation should also include analysis of speech prosody. We often use the Prosody-Voice Screening Profile to identify potential deficits in prosody.[97, 102] This procedure is constructed so that it can be administered quickly and repeatedly, and it provides information about the child's speaking rate, phrasing of sentences, application of word and sentence stress, and voice and resonance characteristics. Depending on the results of this measure, specific aspects of prosody and voice may be targeted for more detailed analysis (e.g., speaking rate measured in syllables per second).

Rating of Speech Intelligibility. A full phonologic evaluation is not complete without an estimate of the listener's ability to understand the child in a spontaneous speaking situation. To accomplish this, the speech-language pathologist typically rates the child's speech intelligibility on a continuum using degrees such as mildly, moderately, and severely unintelligible; this judgment may be corroborated by calculating the percentage of consonants produced correctly in a sample of spontaneous connected speech.[98, 101] In addition to an intelligibility rating, the speech-language pathologist should specify which aspects of speech production are contributing to the child's unintelligible speech (e.g., incorrect production of specific sounds, slow or fast speaking rate, inappropriate voice or resonance).

Major Approaches to Treatment

The objective of any phonologic treatment program is to help the child learn to produce the speech sounds of a language correctly. To achieve this goal, an intervention plan must be developed based on the factors that are associated with the phonologic deficit. For example, a treatment plan for a child who lacks the motor abilities required to plan and execute speech-sound production is different from that for a child who lacks the phonologic knowledge and rules necessary to organize and produce the phonemes of the language.

Phonologic approaches to intervention emphasize the fact that the production of speech sounds for linguistic purposes involves more than an isolated motor event. The child must know the rules for organizing and combining speech sounds to form various word structures and must learn that speech sounds are used to contrast meanings of words. Phonologic intervention procedures focus primarily on expanding the child's inventory of phonemes and syllable shapes and on establishing various phonologic contrasts.[39, 58] Emphasis is also placed on improving intelligibility of speech.

Motor or articulatory approaches to treatment attempt to develop the speech motor skills necessary for correct speech-sound production. Intervention procedures often focus on facilitating the appropriate placement of the articulators during the production of specific sounds produced in isolation, words, phrases, and spontaneous speech. Emphasis is placed on improving the precision of articulatory movement rather than on expanding the child's phonologic knowledge of the sound system.[96, 122]

However, clinical experience and research have shown that many phonologically disordered children have deficits at several levels of the speech production system. Therefore, more eclectic and broader-based approaches to treatment have been developed since the mid-1980s. These broad-based intervention approaches include procedures that develop both the motor articulatory and phonologic skills required for normal speech-sound production.[57, 58]

Prognosis

For most children, the prognosis for measurable improvement in speech-sound production after treatment is excellent. The prognosis for attainment of normal speech intelligibility depends on a number of factors, including the type and severity of the speech deficit, the age of the child, and the frequency of intervention. For example, Campbell[18] has shown that children with apraxia of speech require significantly more individual treatment sessions than children with severe phonologic deficits to achieve a similar speech intelligibility outcome.

Evidence also exists that children with both articulation and language disorders have a less favorable prognosis for developing normal speech intelligibility than children with only articulation deficits.[54]

Fluency Disorders

Definition, Description, and Prevalence

Stuttering refers to a communication disorder typically characterized by disruptions in the forward flow of speech, as well as associated affective and cognitive reactions to the difficulties in communicating. The term *stuttering* is also commonly used to refer to specific types of disruptions in speech that are judged to be atypical for children's normal speech and language development. The use of the same term to refer to both the disorder and the primary symptom of the disorder has led to confusion regarding appropriate diagnostic labels and referral indicators. In this chapter, a distinction is made between the broad communication disorder known as stuttering and the speech disruptions, or "speech disfluencies," that most often characterize it.

Speech disfluencies can take several forms. In children who stutter, disfluencies most often consist of "part-word" repetitions (i.e., repetitions of sounds or syllables, "li- li-li- like this"), prolongations of sounds ("lllllike this"), or complete stoppages of speech production or "blocks" ("l—ike this").[28, 62, 127, 138] In addition to these so-called "core" disfluency types, accessory behaviors may also develop as children attempt to control their speech. Examples of these secondary behaviors, which rapidly become incorporated into the stuttering pattern, include physical tension and struggle in the speech musculature, changes in the rhythm or pitch of repetitions, eye blinking or breaking eye contact, and even movements of the head or limbs (e.g., tapping the mouth or throat where the child feels the blockage, stomping feet, or snapping fingers).

All children produce speech disfluencies when they are learning to speak, though not all disfluencies indicate a risk for development of a stuttering disorder.[3, 62, 125] For example, interjections (e.g., "um," "er") and revisions ("I want- I need that") are disfluencies that typically represent normal speech and language processes, unless they are specifically used by the speaker to avoid less typical types of speech disfluencies or are accompanied by physical tension or struggle.

Many children also develop significant emotional reactions to their speech disfluencies, such as feelings of embarrassment, frustration, anxiety, and shame, as well as low self-esteem.[2, 35, 52, 70, 77] In addition to the personal consequences of these negative reactions, anxiety or fear about a given speaking situation can increase the likelihood that a child will be disfluent, thereby creating the impression that children stutter when (or because) they are nervous. In actuality, however, the relationship between anxiety and stuttering is complex and interactive.[31] Negative affective and cognitive reactions may also cause children to try to hide their disfluencies or to avoid speaking in certain situations (e.g., talking on the telephone, talking to adults, or answering questions in school), and result in significant limitations in the child's ability to participate and succeed in interpersonal and academic activities.[137] For these reasons, the observable characteristics of the stuttering disorder (i.e., the speech disfluencies themselves) do not provide a complete indication of the severity or extent of the child's speaking difficulties.

Stuttering typically begins between the ages of 2½ and 5 years, although later onset in the school-age or teen years is sometimes reported.[4, 62, 126] The onset of stuttering often occurs during a period of otherwise normal or even advanced speech and language development,[13] although many stuttering children exhibit concomitant deficits in other aspects of speech and language development.[16] Most notably, children who stutter are significantly more likely to exhibit difficulties with speech-sound (phonologic) development than children who do not stutter; estimates of comorbidity of stuttering and speech-sound disorders average approximately 30%.[124, 138]

The onset of stuttering is typically assumed to follow a gradual pattern, with children initially producing repetitions with minimal physical tension, then gradually moving into prolongations and, ultimately, blocks, as children's reactions to their stuttering and the associated physical tension increase over time.[28, 116, 128] Some children, however, may exhibit a more sudden onset of severe stuttering behaviors.[116, 128, 129, 132] The onset of stuttering is almost never associated with a specific traumatic event, even in cases where onset appears to be sudden.

The prevalence of stuttering in the general population is generally estimated to be 1%, with a lifetime incidence of approximately 5%.[4, 16] Accurate determination of incidence and prevalence is complicated by the fact that many children exhibit speech disfluencies when learning to talk, combined with disagreements regarding the definition of stuttering and criteria for judging the presence of the disorder. Still, the difference between incidence and prevalence indicates that many children recover from stuttering, either naturally or following intervention.[34, 130] This recovery frequently occurs within 6 months of the initial onset of stuttering, but may occur up to 18 months or more after onset.[130] There is some evidence that children are less likely to experience a complete recovery the longer they continue to stutter, or if they are still stuttering after approximately age 7 years.[4] Beyond age 7 years, it is still possible for children to exhibit complete recovery; however, it is increasingly likely that they will continue to deal with stuttering in some fashion throughout their lives.

The ratio of men to women who stutter is typically cited as 3:1 for adults.[16] In young children close to the onset of stuttering, however, the ratio may be closer to 1:1, suggesting that more girls than boys recover from early stuttering.[128] There is also evidence that the onset of stuttering tends to occur somewhat earlier for girls.[47, 128, 138]

Causal Factors

There is no single cause of stuttering. For decades, researchers in the field attempted to identify a single factor (e.g., motor development, environmental factors) that could explain the onset and development of stuttering (see review in Ref. 15). The most influential theories of the 1950s and 1960s held that stuttering was almost exclusively the result of learning factors or environmental mislabeling of otherwise normal disfluencies.[61] These unidimensional explanations, now known to be largely inadequate, contributed to widespread public and professional misperception that stuttering is primarily an emotional disorder, and are the source of the common but inappropriate suggestion that parents and others should ignore or not "draw attention" to a child's stuttering.

Current theories about the onset and development of stuttering focus on multiple factors, emphasizing interactions between linguistic and motoric development, as well as between environmental and genetic factors.[106, 108] Current theories do not necessarily assume a specific deficit in language or motor development. Rather, they focus on the *interaction* between domains. For example, one of the most widely cited models suggests that there is a mismatch between a child's abilities in a variety of communication-related domains (motoric, linguistic, cognitive, and socioemotional development) and the demands placed on them in those domains, both by their environments and by themselves.[108]

Although such current multifactorial theories represent an advance in understanding of the etiology of stuttering, the causes of stuttering are still not well understood. Considerable debate continues throughout the field about appropriate models and theoretical explanations of stuttering, and research is ongoing in a number of relevant domains. For example, results of several recent studies indicate that there is a clear genetic component to stuttering, although it is not clear exactly what is inherited.[42, 131] Most theorists suggest that there is a specific predisposition to early stuttering, associated with the child's linguistic and motoric abilities, and, perhaps, with the child's temperament. These predispositions interact with factors in the child's environment, such as communication time pressures or the language model provided by the child's caregivers.

Another area of active research involves brain imaging studies with adults who stutter. Preliminary findings indicate that language functions may be distributed more bilaterally in adults who stutter, rather than unilaterally in the left hemisphere as is seen in normally fluent speakers.[36, 48] Because stuttering typically begins in childhood, and because of well-known changes in brain functioning associated with experience and maturation, it is impossible to determine whether these differences may be causal or are simply the result of a lifetime of stuttering. Still, these studies, combined with ongoing efforts to evaluate specific motoric, linguistic, and temperamental aspects of children's development, have contributed significantly to understanding of the etiology of the disorder.

Referral Indicators

One of the most important hallmarks of stuttering is variability. Fluctuations in the occurrence of speech disfluencies, as well as the resulting affective and cognitive reactions, can cause the observable characteristics of stuttering to change significantly from day to day and from situation to situation.[53, 56, 136] Indeed, many children and adults who stutter experience extended periods of near-normal fluency. This apparent fluency does not necessarily indicate recovery from stuttering; it is simply an expression of the normal variability that is characteristic of this communication disorder.

Numerous factors affect children's production of speech disfluencies in a given situation, such as excitement, fatigue, anxiety, the speech characteristics of their conversational partner, and the linguistic characteristics of their own utterances. For this reason, it is difficult, if not impossible, to make an accurate determination of the risk for stuttering through casual observation. Thus, even if the physician does not hear any disfluencies during a routine office visit, this does not necessarily mean that the child's speech fluency is developing normally.

Clinical experience indicates that caregivers are rarely inaccurate in their reporting of their children's disfluencies.[33] Accordingly, the presence of relevant risk factors indicating a need for a full evaluation of a child's speech fluency can typically be confirmed through caregiver report. Referral is warranted if the caregivers report observing any of the following: (1) frequent "part-word" disfluencies (repetitions of sounds or syllables, sound prolongations, or blocks), (2) noticeable physical tension or struggle during fluent or disfluent speech, or (3) any sign that the child is frustrated, concerned, or afraid about his or her speaking difficulties (e.g., avoidance of speaking situations, or questions such as "Why can't I talk right?"). In addition, referral is indicated if the child appears to exhibit any concomitant disorders of speech or language development.

Because of the significant variability in disfluency behaviors, there is no set "percentage" of disfluency or degree of physical tension that is clearly indicative of the need for referral, although several proposals of such guidelines have been made.[1, 138] For the purposes of routine clinical practice, if the disfluencies or indicators of frustration occur frequently enough for caregivers to become concerned, there is probably sufficient reason to conduct a more detailed evaluation to assess the broad range of risk factors associated with the development of childhood stuttering.

Information Expected from a Full Evaluation

Because multiple risk factors play a role in the development of stuttering, a full evaluation of a child's risk for continuing to stutter should provide information in several areas.[27] Perhaps the most basic information is a description of the observable characteristics of the child's speech disfluencies. Common measures include the frequency of disfluencies (i.e., the average number of disfluencies produced by the child per 100 words or syllables of speech), the average duration of disfluencies, and the distribution of disfluency types produced by the child (e.g., the percent of total disfluencies that are repetitions, prolongations, and blocks). As noted earlier, the occurrence of disfluencies is highly variable, so these measures

should be collected in more than one speaking situation. In many cases, multiple observations over an extended period of time may also be required to determine whether a child is at risk for continuing to stutter.

These measures of the observable characteristics of stuttering are typically combined to provide an overall estimation of stuttering severity.[92] Importantly, however, initial severity does not accurately predict the likelihood that a child will continue to stutter—some children may exhibit severe initial stuttering and still exhibit a complete recovery, whereas others may exhibit mild stuttering at onset but experience a gradual increase in severity over time, ultimately leading to chronic stuttering.[128] A better estimation of the child's overall risk for continuing to stutter can only be obtained through a more comprehensive evaluation of the child's overall linguistic and motoric development, as well as specific aspects of the child's communication environment, temperament, and family history of speech and language concerns.[28, 47, 138]

Some of the most pertinent information is obtained from a detailed diagnostic interview with the child's caregivers. Examples of topics typically discussed include approximate time since the onset of disfluencies, changes in the nature or frequency of disfluencies since onset, whether there is a family history of stuttering or other speech or language concerns, *any* indications that the child is concerned or frustrated about the disfluencies, signs of avoidance of sounds or speaking situations, and the nature of the caregivers' attempts to modify the child's fluency as well as the child's reactions to these attempts. Intervention is generally recommended if there is a positive family history of stuttering, if the child has been stuttering for 3 to 6 months or more, if the frequency of stuttering seems to be increasing over time, if the child has begun to produce more prolongations than repetitions, or if the child is reacting negatively to the disfluencies.

Information from the caregiver interview is typically supplemented with diagnostic testing of the child's development in the areas of receptive and expressive language and vocabulary, speech-sound production, and the ability to rapidly and precisely move the oral articulators. A deficit in any of these domains—or a mismatch among domains—generally indicates a greater risk for continuing to stutter and a clear need for treatment.

Major Treatment Approaches

The primary goal of treatment for early childhood stuttering (e.g., ages 3 to 6 years) is the elimination of atypical speech disfluencies and a return to normal speech fluency. Based on early theories suggesting that parents should not draw attention to their child's stuttering, the treatment of early stuttering has traditionally been "indirect" in nature.[28, 51, 108] In other words, improvements in fluency are most often accomplished through changes to the child's communication environment rather than through direct suggestions for the child to change his or her own speech. These environmental changes typically attempt to reduce conversational time pressures that may contribute to the child's production of disfluencies and provide a smoother, easier model of communication for the child to emulate. Specific data demonstrating the efficacy of many treatment approaches for childhood stuttering are still lacking, although considerable anecdotal and informal evidence suggests that these treatments are beneficial.[108]

The relative lack of efficacy data has led to the increasing investigation of alternative forms of treatment for young children who stutter. Specifically, more direct techniques have recently gained popularity, including behavioral approaches based on reinforcing fluent speech and correcting disfluent speech.[79] One of the most important contributions of this exploration of direct treatment techniques has been the revelation that it is not necessarily inappropriate for parents to talk with their children about stuttering. To be sure, parents should not criticize children for their communication difficulties, just as they would not criticize them for difficulties learning to color or ride a tricycle. Still, supportive, caring comments acknowledging the child's difficulties can be helpful in minimizing the negative affective and cognitive reactions that often develop in children who stutter.[67]

Not all young children who stutter recover, even if appropriate treatment is available. Because evidence suggests that the chances for complete recovery diminish significantly after age 7 years, the goals of treatment necessarily change as children grow older. For school-aged children, treatment focuses on a combination of improving fluency, diminishing the severity of individual stuttering events, and reducing the negative affective and cognitive reactions that often accompany stuttering in this age group.[29, 52, 86] The ultimate goal of such treatment is to improve children's communication abilities so they can speak freely in real-world situations, even if they still produce some speech disfluencies.

Prognosis

Recent data indicate that approximately 75% of young children who stutter recover completely, either unaided or following treatment.[130] Thus, the overall prognosis for recovery from early stuttering is generally thought to be optimistic. The prognosis is less favorable for children who exhibit concomitant disorders of speech or language development,[133] and the chances for complete recovery diminish significantly as children grow older and as their stuttering persists for a longer period of time.[4] This does not mean that treatment for older children is not effective.[29] Appropriate intervention, focused on improving the child's overall communication abilities, can be successful for most children who stutter at any age and significantly reduces the likelihood that stuttering will develop into the debilitating disorder often experienced by adults who stutter.

It is impossible, however, with the current knowledge about the disorder, to determine with certainty which children will recover and which children will develop a chronic stuttering disorder.[28] Therefore, early intervention for children who appear to be at risk for stuttering is critical. Although recommendations for early intervention may result in the provision of treatment to some children who might have recovered naturally, these false-positive results are preferable to the alternative of missing the opportunity to offer treatment to children at the time when intervention is most likely to result in complete recovery.

Voice Disorders

Definition, Description, and Prevalence

A voice disorder, or dysphonia, can be defined as a significant deviation in pitch, loudness, or vocal quality. Although there are no absolute criteria for distinguishing between a normal and an abnormal voice, speech-language pathologists often describe voice deviations along various perceptual-acoustic dimensions. For example, a child with a voice disorder associated with deviant pitch has a fundamental frequency that is too high or low for the child's chronologic age and gender. Dysphonia associated with abnormal loudness is characterized by a voice that is too soft to be understood or too loud to be tolerated by a listener. Finally, deviations in voice quality are perceived by the listener as being too harsh, breathy, or hoarse.

The incidence of voice disorders in school-aged children (5 to 18 years) ranges from 6% to 23%.[8, 95, 105, 135] Most incidence studies indicate that 6% to 9% of school-aged children display some type of vocal dysfunction.[85, 117] The percentage of children with communicatively handicapping voice disorders has been reported to be less than the overall prevalence: approximately 1% to 3% of children display clinically significant voice problems that require direct intervention.[11, 120, 121, 134]

Causal Factors

Voice disorders in children are often described as existing on a continuum with anatomic or physiologic causes at one end and functional or psychogenic causes at the other.[7, 76, 120] The underlying anatomic and physiologic mechanisms associated with vocal dysfunction, typically referred to as *organic causes*, alter laryngeal structure or function. These mechanisms include a variety of diseases or conditions that can be genetic, neurologic, neoplastic, or inflammatory in origin. Functional or psychogenic voice disorders, on the other hand, are vocal deviations that occur in the absence of structural or physiologic conditions. Functional voice problems are believed to be related to emotional or environmental conditions, although many pediatric voice disorders involve both organic and functional components. For example, structural change to the vocal folds (e.g., vocal nodules) can result from vocal abuse.

Few data are published on the type and frequency of laryngeal pathology in children with vocal dysfunction. In an ongoing study at the Children's Hospital of Pittsburgh, Campbell has examined the endoscopic and direct laryngoscopic findings from 427 patients referred to the Voice and Resonance Clinic between 1989 and 1999 because of abnormal vocal quality (i.e., harshness, breathiness, or hoarseness).[19] In 93% of these children, the abnormal voice quality was associated with laryngeal pathology.

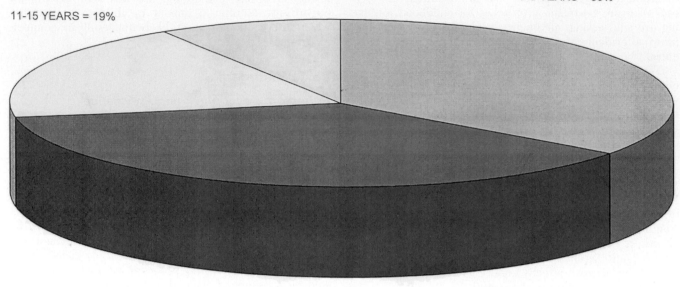

FIGURE 105–1. Percentage of children in each age range who were referred to the Voice and Resonance Clinic at the Children's Hospital of Pittsburgh, 1989–1999 ($N = 427$).

Only 7% of the children exhibited vocal dysfunction despite normal laryngeal structures. As shown in Figure 105–1, the children ranged in age from 1 month to 18 years, the largest percentage (37%) being in the 6- to 10-year-old category. Figure 105–2 illustrates the percentage of children who displayed a specific type of laryngeal or velopharyngeal pathology. The largest percentage (52%) had vocal nodules. This finding is consistent with those of

other studies that have reported that approximately 50% of children with an abnormal voice have vocal nodules.[75]

Referral Indicators

Clinical experience suggests that deviations in vocal quality are often the unique symptom of laryngeal involve-

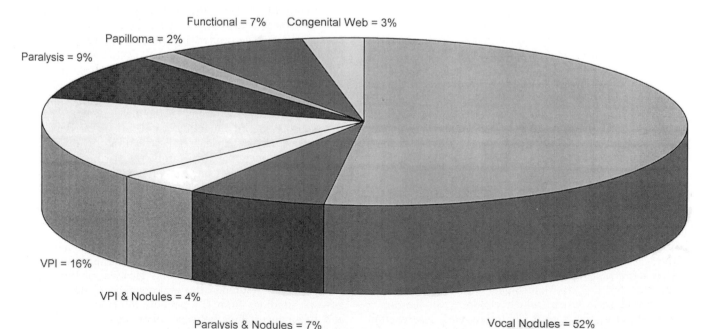

FIGURE 105–2. Percentage of children displaying a specific type of laryngeal or velopharyngeal pathology. VPI, velopharyngeal insufficiency.

ment. Therefore, any child who exhibits a harsh, breathy, or hoarse voice quality for more than 2 to 3 weeks should never be ignored. Referral for a complete voice and laryngeal evaluation should be made if the child has unusual vocal pitch, loudness, or a voice quality that calls attention to itself or if the child has sudden or continual laryngeal pain or discomfort in the absence of a cold or allergies.

Information Expected from a Full Evaluation

After referring a child for a voice evaluation, the physician should expect information on several aspects of voice and laryngeal function. Although there are many ways to approach a pediatric voice evaluation, the assessment framework we propose requires input from a variety of specialists, including a speech-language pathologist, otolaryngologist, pediatrician, and, in some cases, a gastroenterologist, neurologist, psychologist, or social worker. The speech-language pathologist often serves as the team coordinator because this person's responsibilities include obtaining relevant historical information, examining patients, providing treatment, and organizing follow-up. The evaluation should include at least the following components: case history, laryngeal evaluation, voice evaluation, and recommendations and prognosis.

Case History. Information about medical, developmental, and voice history can provide important insights into the child's vocal dysfunction. The case history often informs the eventual diagnosis and recommendations. Historical information is typically collected through a questionnaire that is completed by the parent before the evaluation. The questionnaire should provide information about communicative, developmental, environmental, and medical factors related to the voice disorder. Specific questions should be asked about the child's use of the voice in various speaking situations. The parent interview provides the opportunity for elaboration of specific topics. An example of a complete voice history questionnaire is provided by Maddern et al.[69]

Laryngeal Evaluation. The otolaryngologist should complete a head and neck examination. In addition, the speech-language pathologist should evaluate the structure and function of the oral mechanism to rule out a speech motor disorder. Each child's nasopharynx and larynx should be evaluated by transnasal fiberoptic laryngoscopy. For children who are unable to tolerate endoscopy, direct laryngoscopy can be performed under general anesthesia. A summary of the results should include the type and location of the laryngeal lesion and a description of its structural and physiologic consequences for phonation. It is important to emphasize that no child should be referred for voice or medical intervention without first having the larynx inspected visually.

Voice Evaluation. The speech-language pathologist performs the voice evaluation. As a prerequisite to the voice assessment, an audiologic evaluation should be completed to determine whether an auditory dysfunction is contributing to the voice disorder.

The voice assessment protocol requires the child to perform a variety of speaking tasks that are then submitted to perceptual, acoustic, and aerodynamic analyses. Initially, a 5-minute conversation with the child is audiotaped. Employing a modified version of the Buffalo III Voice Screening Profile,[120] the sample is rated perceptually by trained listeners according to such parameters as voice quality (i.e., harshness, breathiness, hoarseness), pitch (i.e., high or low), and loudness (i.e., loud or soft).

A second task requires the child to count from 1 to 10, 60 to 70, and 90 to 100. Production of these words provides samples of voice in various speech-sound contexts. Each set of numbers is produced (1) at slow and fast speaking rates, (2) at soft, normal, and loud levels, and (3) at low, middle, and high pitch levels. These speaking contexts can reveal deviations in voice quality and resonance that are reported by the parent to be inconsistent in conversation or other spontaneous speech contexts (e.g., home, school, playground). They can also help identify factors that contribute to voice misuse (e.g., loudness, pitch).

For the third speaking task, the child is asked to produce the vowel *a* for approximately 3 seconds. Voice quality (i.e., harshness, breathiness, hoarseness) is rated for this vowel production, and a fundamental frequency is calculated (i.e., number of complete vocal fold vibrations per second). The child's fundamental frequency is compared with published norms to determine whether it is within the range expected for children of the same chronologic age and gender.[12, 55, 93, 120] For some children, additional acoustic and aerodynamic analyses can provide insight into the structure and function of the vocal folds. For example, acoustic measures such as jitter (i.e., variations in the frequency of a vocal fold vibration) and shimmer (i.e., variations in the intensity of a vocal fold vibration) provide additional information on vibratory patterns of the vocal folds. Aerodynamic measurements such as laryngeal airway resistance can be useful in determining the biomechanical integrity of the vocal folds.

In the fourth speaking task, the child's maximum phonation time is obtained. This is accomplished by instructing the child to produce the *a* vowel for as long as possible. By comparing the child's mean phonation time for two trials with the available norms, one can obtain a basic indication of whether there is adequate respiratory drive to maintain continuous voice production.[46, 120]

Finally, the child's articulation and velopharyngeal abilities should be screened. Words and phrases used to screen the child's articulation abilities should include sounds that are especially problematic for persons with inadequate laryngeal and velopharyngeal mechanisms, such as *s, z, sh,* and *ch.*

Recommendations and Prognosis. Performing the laryngeal examination at the time of the voice evaluation affords an opportunity to integrate all diagnostic information and arrive at a consistent diagnosis. In addition to the laryngeal and voice diagnoses, specific recommendations for management of the dysphonia should be provided, with a statement of prognosis. If medical or voice intervention is not appropriate, a plan for follow-up should be specified.

Major Approaches to Treatment

Surgical management is often the first line of treatment for children with organically based voice disorders (e.g., congenital webs, papilloma, and other laryngeal growths). Following surgical intervention, these children usually require voice therapy to change pitch, loudness, and vocal quality.

Whether or not surgical intervention is warranted, a number of treatment techniques are available to modify various parameters of voice in children who have vocal dysfunction. These techniques include laryngeal positioning, posture modification, breathing exercises, stretching exercises, relaxation techniques, and listening training, to name a few. Visual feedback techniques that provide a graphic display to the child (e.g., electromyography tracings, acoustic waveform displays, voice-activated computer software) also can be effective in modifying pitch, intensity, and vocal quality.

For children with vocal nodules or other laryngeal lesions caused by vocal abuse, intervention can present a special challenge. Vocal nodules are typically the result of mechanical trauma caused by one vocal fold making excessive contact with the other. Thus, the primary focus of treatment for these children is to improve vocal hygiene. Achieving this goal, however, is often easier said than done. The basic components of a vocal hygiene program have been discussed by several investigators.[5, 69, 120] These include techniques for providing the child and parent with (1) a clear explanation of the structure and function of the larynx, (2) explicit rules for producing "good" voice, (3) an understanding of the environmental factors related to vocal abuse, and (4) techniques for monitoring appropriate voice production at home, school, and while playing outside. Surgical removal of the nodules typically is not the treatment of choice because the nodules are likely to return if the child continues to employ vocal abuse behaviors. Finally, for the small number of children who display deviant voice in the absence of a known anatomic or physiologic deficit, behavioral training techniques with or without professional counseling may be appropriate.

Prognosis

The prediction for the outcome of voice therapy depends on a number of factors. These include the child's age, specific laryngeal and voice problem, motivation to improve voice, compliance with vocal hygiene guidelines, and amount of treatment provided. Wilson reported that, for school-aged children with deficits in vocal quality, the prognosis is favorable in about 75% of cases, unfavorable in 10%, and guarded in 15%.[119] Children who can be stimulated to improve their voice quality at the time of the assessment (e.g., those children who can alter some aspect of voice quality for even a short time with instruction from the speech-language pathologist) have the most favorable prognosis. For children with anatomic deficits, wherein the primary focus of intervention is to compensate for the structural anomalies, prognosis for achieving normal voice quality is less favorable.

Conclusion

This chapter introduces some of the most common communication disorders seen in preschool children, with the goal of providing physicians with guidelines to help identify children who should be referred to a certified speech-language pathologist. Although this chapter focuses on the more typical pediatric speech, language, fluency, and voice difficulties, children who suffer from a wide range of developmental and medical problems are at risk for communicative disorders. Early identification and treatment of children with communication deficits can significantly improve the quality of their lives, increasing their ability to function effectively in familial, social, and academic contexts.

SELECTED REFERENCES

Paul R. Language Disorders from Infancy through Adolescence. St Louis, Mosby, 2001.

> *This text provides a comprehensive description of procedures for assessing and treating language disorders in children of various ages and includes a review of language disorders in children with other disabilities.*

Bernthal JE, Bankson NW. Articulation and Phonological Disorders, 4th ed. Boston, Allyn & Bacon, 1998.

> *This text provides a description of procedures for assessment and treatment for children with phonologic disorders.*

Curlee RF, Siegel GM. Nature and Treatment of Stuttering, 2nd ed. Boston, Allyn & Bacon, 1997.

> *This edited text contains chapters from many of the leading clinicians and researchers in the field of fluency disorders. Topics include current and historical theories about etiology of stuttering; development of stuttering from early childhood through school age; assessment procedures; clinical management strategies for children, adolescents, and adults; related fluency disorders; and evaluation of treatment outcomes.*

Wilson DK. Voice Problems in Children, 3rd ed. Baltimore, Williams & Wilkins, 1987.

> *This comprehensive textbook on pediatric voice and resonance disorders provides extensive information on organic and functional causes of such disorders. Several chapters are devoted to the clinical management of both organic and functional disorders.*

REFERENCES

1. Adams MR. The young stutterer: diagnosis, treatment and assessment of progress. Semin Speech Lang Hear 1:289, 1980.
2. Ambrose NG, Yairi E. The development of awareness of stuttering in preschool children. J Fluency Disord 19:229, 1994.
3. Ambrose NG, Yairi E. Normative disfluency data for early childhood stuttering. J Speech Lang Hear Res 42:895, 1999.
4. Andrews G, Harris M. The syndrome of stuttering. Clinics in Developmental Medicine 17. London, Spastics Society Medical Education and Information Unit in association with William Heinemann Medical Books, 1964.
5. Andrews ML. Voice Therapy for Children. San Diego, Singular Publishing Group, 1991.
6. Aram D, Ekelman B, Nation J. Preschoolers with language disorders: 10 years later. J Speech Hear Res 27:232, 1984.
7. Aronson AE. Clinical Voice Disorders. New York, Thieme, 1990.
8. Baynes RA. An incident study of chronic hoarseness among children. J Speech Hear Disord 31:172, 1966.
9. Bedore LM, Leonard LB. Specific language impairment and gram-

matical morphology: a discriminant function analysis. J Speech Lang Hear Res 41:1185, 1998.

10. Beitchman JH, Nair R, Clegg M, et al. Prevalence of psychiatric disorders in children with speech and language disorders. J Am Acad Child Psychiatry 25:528, 1986.

11. Beitchman JH, Nair R, Clegg M, Patel PG. Prevalence of speech and language disorders in 5-year-old kindergarten children in the Ottawa-Carleton region. J Speech Hear Disord 51:98, 1986.

12. Bennett S. A 3-year longitudinal study of school-aged children's fundamental frequencies. J Speech Hear Res 26:137, 1983.

13. Bernstein Ratner N. Stuttering: a psycholinguistic perspective. In Curlee RF, Siegel GM (eds). Nature and Treatment of Stuttering: New Directions, 2nd ed. Needham Heights, Mass, Allyn & Bacon, 1997, pp 97–127.

14. Bishop DVM, Bishop SJ, Bright P, et al. Different origin of auditory and phonological processing problems in children with language impairment: evidence from a twin study. J Speech Lang Hear Res 42:155, 1999.

15. Bloodstein O. Stuttering: The Search for a Cause and Cure. Needham Heights, Mass, Allyn & Bacon, 1993.

16. Bloodstein O. A Handbook on Stuttering, 5th ed. San Diego, Singular Publishing Group, 1995.

17. Brand Robertson S, Ellis Weismer S. Effects of treatment on linguistic and social skills in toddlers with delayed language development. J Speech Lang Hear Res 42:1234, 1999.

18. Campbell TF. Functional treatment outcomes in young children with motor speech disorders. In Caruso AJ, Strand EA (eds). Clinical Management of Motor Speech Disorders in Children. New York, Thieme, 1999, pp 385–396.

19. Campbell TF. (Clinical data base: Endoscopic and direct laryngoscopic findings at the Children's Hospital of Pittsburgh, 1989–1999.) Unpublished data.

20. Campbell T, Dollaghan C, Needleman H, Janosky J. Reducing bias in language assessment: processing-dependent measures. J Speech Hear Res 40:519, 1997.

21. Campbell T, Dollaghan C, Paradise JL, et al. Risk factors for speech delay in 3-year-old children. Manuscript in preparation.

22. Cantwell DP, Baker L. Developmental Speech and Language Disorders. New York, Guilford Press, 1987.

23. Catts HW. The relationship between speech-language impairments and reading disabilities. J Speech Hear Res 36:948, 1993.

24. Chapman RS. Comprehension strategies in children. In Kavanagh JF, Strange W (eds). Speech and Language in the Laboratory, School and Clinic. Cambridge, Mass, MIT Press, 1978, pp 308–327.

25. Chapman RS. Exploring children's communicative intents. In Miller JF (ed). Assessing Language Production in Children. Baltimore, University Park Press, 1981, pp 111–136.

26. Cleave P, Fey M. Two approaches to the facilitation of grammar in children with language impairments: rationale and description. Am J Speech Lang Pathol 6:22, 1997.

27. Conture EG. Evaluating childhood stuttering. In Curlee RF, Siegel GM (eds). Nature and Treatment of Stuttering: New Directions, 2nd ed. Needham Heights, Mass, Allyn & Bacon, 1997, pp 239–256.

28. Conture EG. Stuttering: Its Nature, Assessment, and Treatment. Needham Heights, Mass, Allyn & Bacon, in press.

29. Conture EG, Guitar B. Evaluating efficacy of treatment of stuttering: school-age children. J Fluency Disord 18:253, 1993.

30. Coplan J, Gleason JR. Unclear speech: recognition and significance of unintelligible speech in preschool children. Pediatrics 82:447, 1988.

31. Craig A. An investigation into the relationship between anxiety and stuttering. J Speech Hear Disord 55:290, 1990.

32. Crary MA. Developmental Motor Speech Disorders. San Diego, Singular Publishing Group, 1993.

33. Curlee RF. Identification and management of beginning stuttering. In Curlee RF (ed). Stuttering and Related Disorders of Fluency. New York, Thieme, 1993, pp 1–22.

34. Curlee RF, Yairi E. Early intervention with early childhood stuttering: a critical examination of the data. Am J Speech Lang Pathol 6:8, 1997.

35. DeNil LF, Brutten GJ. Speech-associated attitudes of stuttering and nonstuttering children. J Speech Hear Res 34:60, 1991.

36. DeNil LF, Kroll RM, Kapur S, Houle S. A positron emission tomography study of silent and oral single word reading in stuttering and nonstuttering adults. J Speech Lang Hear Res 43:1038, 2000.

37. Dollaghan C, Campbell TF. Nonword repetition and child language impairment. J Speech Lang Hear Res 41:1136, 1998.

38. Dollaghan CA, Campbell TF, Paradise JL, et al. Maternal education and measures of early speech and language. J Speech Lang Hear Res 42:1432, 1999.

39. Elbert M, Gierut JA. Handbook of Clinical Phonology. San Diego, College-Hill Press, 1986.

40. Ellis Weismer S, Murray-Branch J, Miller JF. A prospective longitudinal study of language development in late talkers. J Speech Lang Hear Res 37:852, 1994.

41. Feldman HM, Dollaghan CA, Campbell TF, et al. Measurement properties of the MacArthur Communicative Development Inventories at ages 1 and 2 years. Child Dev 71:310, 2000.

42. Felsenfeld S. Epidemiology and genetics of stuttering. In Curlee RF, Siegel GM (eds). Nature and Treatment of Stuttering: New Directions, 2nd ed. Needham Heights, Mass, Allyn & Bacon, 1997, pp 3–23.

43. Fey ME. Language Intervention with Young Children. San Diego, College-Hill Press, 1986.

44. Fey ME, Cleave PL, Long SH. Two models of grammar facilitation in children with language impairments: phase 2. J Speech Lang Hear Res 40:5, 1997.

45. Fey ME, Cleave PL, Long SH, Hughes DL. Two approaches to the facilitation of grammar in children with language impairment: an experimental evaluation. J Speech Hear Res 36:141, 1993.

46. Finnegan DE. Maximum phonation time for children with normal voices. J Comm Disord 17:309, 1985.

47. Fosnot SM. Research design for examining treatment efficacy in fluency disorders. J Fluency Disord 18:221, 1993.

48. Fox PT, Ingham RJ, Ingham JC, et al. A PET study of the neural systems of stuttering. Nature 382:158, 1996.

49. Gillam RB, Cowan N, Marler JA. Information processing by school-age children with specific language impairment: evidence from a modality effect paradigm. J Speech Lang Hear Res 41:913, 1998.

50. Girolametto L, Steig Pearce P, Weitzman E. Effects of lexical intervention on the phonology of late talkers. J Speech Lang Hear Res 40:338, 1997.

51. Gregory HH, Hill D. Differential evaluation—differential therapy for stuttering children. In Curlee RF (ed). Stuttering and Related Disorders of Fluency, 2nd ed. New York, Thieme, 1999, pp 22–42.

52. Guitar B. Therapy for children's stuttering and emotions. In Curlee RF, Siegel GM (eds). Nature and Treatment of Stuttering: New Directions, 2nd ed. Needham Heights, Mass, Allyn & Bacon, 1997, pp 280–291.

53. Gutierrez JL, Caruso AJ. The variable nature of stuttering: a clinical case study. Natl Student Speech Lang Hear Assoc J 22:29, 1995.

54. Hall P, Tomblin J. A follow-up study of children with articulation and language disorders. J Speech Hear Disord 43:227, 1978.

55. Hasek CS, Singh S, Murray T. Acoustic attributes of preadolescent voices. J Acoust Soc Am 68:1262, 1980.

56. Hillis JW. Ongoing assessment in the management of stuttering: a clinical perspective. Am J Speech Lang Pathol 2:24, 1994.

57. Hodson BW, Paden EP. Phonological processes which characterize unintelligible and intelligible speech in early childhood. J Speech Hear Disord 46:369, 1983.

58. Hodson BW, Paden EP. Targeting Intelligible Speech—A Phonological Approach to Remediation, 2nd ed. Austin, Tex, Pro-Ed, 1991.

59. Hull FM, Mielke PW, Timmons RJ, Willeford JA. The national speech and hearing survey: preliminary results. ASHA 13:501, 1971.

60. Johnson CJ, Beitchman JH, Young A, et al. Fourteen-year follow-up of children with and without speech/language impairments: speech/language stability and outcomes. J Speech Lang Hear Res 42:744, 1999.

61. Johnson W. Stuttering and What You Can Do about It. Minneapolis, University of Minnesota Press, 1961.

62. Johnson W, et al. The Onset of Stuttering. Minneapolis, University of Minnesota Press, 1959.

63. Klee T, Pearce K, Carson DK. Improving the positive predictive value of screening for developmental language disorder. J Speech Lang Hear Res 43:821, 2000.
64. Lahey M. Who shall be called language disordered? Some reflections and one perspective. J Speech Hear Disord 55:612, 1990.
65. Leonard LB. Children with Specific Language Impairment. Cambridge, Mass, MIT Press, 1998.
66. Leonard LB, Miller C, Gerber E. Grammatical morphology and the lexicon in children with specific language impairment. J Speech Lang Hear Res 42:678, 1999.
67. Logan KJ, Yaruss JS. Helping parents address attitudinal and emotional factors with young children who stutter. Contemp Issues Comm Sci Disorders 26:69, 1999.
68. Long SH, Long ST. Language and children with mental retardation. In Reed VA (ed). Children with Language Disorders. New York, Macmillan, 1994, pp 153–191.
69. Maddern BR, Campbell TF, Stool S. Pediatric voice disorders. Otolaryngol Clin North Am 24:1125, 1991.
70. Manning W. Clinical decision making in the diagnosis and treatment of fluency disorders. Albany, NY, Delmar, 1996.
71. Miller JF. Assessing Language Production in Children. Baltimore, University Park Press, 1981.
72. Miller JF, Chapman RS. The relation between age and mean length of utterance in morphemes. J Speech Hear Res 24:154, 1981.
73. Miller JF, Chapman RS, Branston MB, Reichle J. Language comprehension in sensorimotor stages V and VI. J Speech Hear Res 23:284, 1980.
74. Miller JF, Paul R. The Clinical Assessment of Language Comprehension. Baltimore, Brookes, 1995.
75. Miller SA, Madison CL. Public school voice clinics, Part II: Diagnosis and recommendations—a 10-year review. Lang Speech Hear Serv Schools 15:58, 1984.
76. Moore GP. Organic Voice Disorders. Englewood Cliffs, NJ, Prentice-Hall, 1971.
77. Murphy W. A preliminary look at shame, guilt, and stuttering. In Bernstein Ratner N, Healey EC (eds). Stuttering Research and Practice: Bridging the Gap. Mahwah, NJ, Lawrence Erlbaum Associates, 1999, pp 131–144.
78. Nelson KE, Camarata SM, Welsh J, et al. Effects of imitative and conversational recasting treatment on the acquisition of grammar in children with specific language impairment and younger language-normal children. J Speech Hear Res 39:850, 1996.
79. Onslow M, Andrews C, Lincoln M. A control/experimental trial of an operant treatment for early stuttering. J Speech Hear Res 37:1244, 1995.
80. Paul R. Language Disorders from Infancy through Adolescence. St Louis, Mosby, 2001.
81. Paul R, Jennings P. Phonological behavior in toddlers with slow expressive language development. J Speech Hear Res 35:99, 1992.
82. Paul R, Looney S, Dahm PS. Communication and socialization skills at ages 2 and 3 in "late-talking" young children. J Speech Hear Res 34:858, 1991.
83. Paul R, Smith RL. Narrative skills in 4-year-olds with normal, impaired, and late-developing language. J Speech Hear Res 36:592, 1993.
84. Peckham CS. Speech defects in a national sample of children aged seven years. Br J Disord Comm 8:2, 1973.
85. Pont C. Hoarseness in children. West Mich Univ J Speech Ther 2:6, 1965.
86. Ramig PR, Bennett EM. Clinical management of children: direct management strategies. In Curlee RF, Siegel GM (eds). Nature and Treatment of Stuttering: New Directions, 2nd ed. Needham Heights, Mass, Allyn & Bacon, 1997, pp 292–312.
87. Redmond SM, Rice ML. The socio-emotional behaviors of children with SLI: social adaptation or social deviance? J Speech Lang Hear Res 41:688, 1998.
88. Rescorla L. The Language Development Survey: a screening tool for delayed language in toddlers. J Speech Hear Disord 54:587, 1989.
89. Rescorla L. Identifying expressive language delay at age two. Top Lang Disord 11:14, 1991.
90. Rescorla L, Bernstein Ratner N. Phonetic profiles of toddlers with specific expressive language impairment (SLI-E). J Speech Hear Res 39:153, 1996.
91. Rescorla L, Roberts J, Dahlsgaard K. Late talkers at 2: outcome at age 3. J Speech Hear Res 40:556, 1997.
92. Riley G. Stuttering Severity Instrument for Children and Adults, 3rd ed. Austin, Texas, Pro-Ed, 1994.
93. Robb MP, Saxman JH. Developmental trends in vocal frequency of young children. J Speech Hear Res 28:421, 1985.
94. Robbins J, Klee T. Clinical assessment of oropharyngeal motor development in young children. J Speech Hear Disord 52:271, 1987.
95. Senturia BH, Wilson FB. Otorhinolaryngic findings in children with voice deviations. Preliminary report. Ann Otol Rhinol Laryngol 77:1027, 1968.
96. Shelton R, McReynolds L. Functional articulation disorders: preliminaries to treatment. In Lass N (ed). Speech and Language Advances in Basic Research and Practice. New York, Academic Press, 1979, pp 1–111.
97. Shriberg LD. Four new speech and prosody-voice measures for genetics research and other studies in developmental phonological disorders. J Speech Hear Res 36:105, 1993.
98. Shriberg LD, Austin D, Lewis BA, et al. The percentage of consonants correct (PCC) metric: extensions and reliability data. J Speech Lang Hear Res 40:708, 1997.
99. Shriberg LD, Austin D, Lewis BA, et al. The speech disorders classification system (SDCS): extensions and lifespan reference data. J Speech Lang Hear Res 40:723, 1997.
100. Shriberg LD, Kwiatkowski J. Phonological disorders I: a diagnostic classification system. J Speech Hear Disord 47:226, 1982.
101. Shriberg LD, Kwiatkowski J. Phonological disorders III: a procedure for assessing severity of involvement. J Speech Hear Disord 47:256, 1982.
102. Shriberg LD, Kwiatkowski J, Rasmussen C. Prosody-Voice Screening Profile (PVSP): Scoring Forms and Training Materials. Tucson, Ariz, Communication Skill Builders, 1990.
103. Shriberg LD, Tomblin JB, McSweeny JL. Prevalence of speech delay in 6-year-old children and comorbidity with language impairment. J Speech Lang Hear Res 42:1461, 1999.
104. Silva PA, Justin C, McGee R, Williams SM. Some developmental and behavioral characteristics of seven-year-old children with delayed speech development. Br J Disord Comm 19:147, 1980.
105. Silverman EM, Zimmer CH. Incidence of chronic hoarseness among school-age children. J Speech Hear Disord 40:211, 1975.
106. Smith A, Kelly EM. Stuttering: a dynamic, multifactorial model. In Curlee RF, Siegel GM (eds). Nature and Treatment of Stuttering: New Directions, 2nd ed. Needham Heights, Mass, Allyn & Bacon, 1997, pp 204–217.
107. Spitz RV, Tallal P, Flax J, Benasich AA. Look who's talking: a prospective study of familial transmission of language impairments. J Speech Lang Hear Res 40:990, 1997.
108. Starkweather CW. Therapy for younger children. In Curlee RF, Siegel GM (eds). Nature and Treatment of Stuttering: New Directions, 2nd ed. Needham Heights, Mass, Allyn & Bacon, 1997, pp 257–279.
109. Stoel-Gammon C. Normal and disordered phonology in two-year-olds. Topics Lang Disord 11:21, 1991.
110. Stothard SE, Snowling MJ, Bishop DVM, et al. Language-impaired preschoolers: a follow-up into adolescence. J Speech Lang Hear Res 41:407, 1998.
111. Tager-Flusberg H, Cooper J. Present and future possibilities for defining a phenotype for specific language impairment. J Speech Lang Hear Res 42:1275, 1999.
112. Tomblin JB, Buckwalter PR. Heritability of poor language achievement among twins. J Speech Lang Hear Res 41:188, 1998.
113. Tomblin JB, Hardy JC, Hein HA. Predicting poor-communication status in preschool children using risk factors present at birth. J Speech Hear Res 34:1096, 1991.
114. Tomblin JB, Records NL, Buckwalter P, et al. Prevalence of specific language impairment in kindergarten children. J Speech Lang Hear Res 40:1245, 1997.
115. Tomblin JB, Records NL, Zhang X, et al. A system for the diagnosis of specific language impairment in kindergarten children. J Speech Hear Res 39:1284, 1996.
116. Van Riper C. The Nature of Stuttering, 2nd ed. Englewood Cliffs, NJ, Prentice-Hall, 1982.
117. Warr-Leeper GA, McShea RS, Leeper HA. The incidence of voice

and speech deviations in a middle school population. Lang Speech Hear Serv Schools 10:14, 1979.

118. Watkins RV, Kelly DJ, Harbers HM, Hollis W. Measuring children's lexical diversity: differentiating typical and impaired language learners. J Speech Hear Res 38:1349, 1995.

119. Wilson DK. Management of voice disorders in children and adolescents. Semin Speech Lang Hear 4:245, 1983.

120. Wilson DK. Voice Problems of Children. Baltimore, Williams & Wilkins, 1987.

121. Wilson FB. The voice-disordered child: a descriptive approach. Lang Speech Hear Serv Schools 4:14, 1972.

122. Winitz H. Articulatory Acquisition and Behavior. Englewood Cliffs, NJ, Prentice-Hall, 1969.

123. Winitz H, Darley FL. Speech production. In Lassman FM, Fisch RO, Vetter DK, LaBenz ES (eds). Early Correlates of Speech, Language and Hearing. Littleton, Mass, PSG Publishing, 1980, pp 232–265.

124. Wolk L, Conture EG, Edwards ML. Coexistence of stuttering and disordered phonology in young children. The South African J Comm Disord 37:15, 1990.

125. Yairi E. Disfluency rates and patterns of stutterers and nonstutterers. J Comm Disord 5:225, 1972.

126. Yairi E. The onset of stuttering in two- and three-year-old children: a preliminary report. J Speech Hear Disord 48:171, 1983.

127. Yairi E. Disfluency characteristics of childhood stuttering. In Curlee RF, Siegel GM (eds). Nature and Treatment of Stuttering:

New Directions, 2nd ed. Needham Heights, Mass, Allyn & Bacon, 1997, pp 49–78.

128. Yairi E, Ambrose N. A longitudinal study of stuttering in children: a preliminary report. J Speech Hear Res 35:755, 1992.

129. Yairi E, Ambrose N. Onset of stuttering in preschool children: selected factors. J Speech Hear Res 35:782, 1992.

130. Yairi E, Ambrose N. Early childhood stuttering I: persistency and recovery rates. J Speech Lang Hear Res 42:1097, 1999.

131. Yairi E, Ambrose N, Cox N. Genetics of stuttering: a critical review. J Speech Hear Res 39:771, 1996.

132. Yairi E, Ambrose N, Niermann R. The early months of stuttering: a developmental study. J Speech Hear Res 36:521, 1993.

133. Yairi E, Ambrose N, Paden EP, Throneburg RN. Predictive factors of persistence and recovery: pathways of childhood stuttering. J Comm Disord 29:51, 1996.

134. Yairi E, Currin LH, Bulian N, Yairi J. Incidence of hoarseness in school children over a 1-year period. J Comm Disord 7:321, 1974.

135. Yairi E, Lewis B. Disfluencies at the onset of stuttering. J Speech Hear Res 27:154, 1984.

136. Yaruss JS. Clinical implications of situational variability in preschool children who stutter. J Fluency Disord 22:187, 1997.

137. Yaruss JS. Describing the consequences of disorders: stuttering and the International Classification of Impairments, Disabilities, and Handicaps. J Speech Lang Hear Res 49:249, 1998.

138. Yaruss JS, LaSalle LR, Conture EG. Evaluating stuttering in young children: diagnostic data. Am J Speech Lang Pathol 7:62, 1998.

106

Velopharyngeal Insufficiency

J. Paul Willging, M.D., and Robin T. Cotton, M.D.

The Velopharyngeal Sphincter

Speech is a complex motor skill that involves the coordination of diverse muscle groups. Gross motor movements of the muscles responsible for inspiration and expiration must be coupled with intricate muscles of the larynx, soft palate, tongue, and lips to produce sustained intelligible speech. A defect in the structure, position, or motor control of any element involved with the mechanical production of speech alters the quality of the sound produced. Inappropriate tongue placement may cause sibilant distortion. Incomplete closure of the velopharyngeal port may allow audible air escape through the nose during the generation of high–oral pressure consonants or may lead to inappropriate nasal resonance during the production of speech (Fig. 106–1).

Speech production is a task that is taken for granted by those who have mastered the art. Those who have difficulty with the mechanical production of intelligible speech are vulnerable as children to the emotional insults generated by peers and as adults to discrimination in the workplace. Much as first impressions are formulated on the basis of appearance and mannerisms, the vocal qualities of speech carry implications of education and achievement. Generation of speech with normal articulation and resonance is an important developmental task that may have negative ramifications if not achieved.

All otolaryngologists need to understand the mechanics associated with velopharyngeal closure and be able to assess a patient (in collaborative fashion with a speech pathologist) to determine the function of the velopharyngeal sphincter. Velopharyngeal insufficiency (VPI) is the term used in this chapter to reflect hypernasal resonance caused by unsuccessful separation of the nasopharynx from the oropharynx during speech. Other terms in the literature that connote similar problems are *velopharyngeal incompetence*, *velopharyngeal inadequacy*, and *velopharyngeal dysfunction*. This chapter discusses the anatomy of the velopharyngeal sphincter, the multiple causes of VPI, the diagnostic assessment of the malfunctioning sphincter, and the treatment options available for these patients.

Anatomy

The velopharyngeal sphincter is composed of six muscles. Five of these muscles make up the substance of the soft palate: the levator veli palatini, tensor veli palatini, musculus uvulae, palatoglossus, and palatopharyngeus. The sixth muscle is the superior constrictor muscle of the pharynx (Figs. 106–2 and 106–3) (see Chaps. 33 and 50).[17]

The levator veli palatini, the main muscle mass of the soft palate, is the primary velar elevator. Contraction of this muscle moves the midportion of the velum upward and backward.[43] The levator veli palatini originates from the inferior surface of the petrous portion of the temporal bone, anterior to the carotid canal, and from the inferior surface of the adjacent eustachian tube.[58] The origin of this muscle shows little variability, even with overt cleft palate.[42] The muscle inserts into the palatal aponeurosis on the oral surface and into the median raphe of the palate. The levator muscle fibers intermingle with fibers from the other soft palate muscles.[6] The levator veli palatini forms a sling suspended below the skull base that composes approximately 40% of the soft palate.

The tensor veli palatini provides the majority of the fibrous layer of the soft palate, the palatal aponeurosis. Its function is to enhance middle-ear aeration when exerting its effect on the eustachian tube orifice and to tense the soft palate. Involvement of the tensor veli palatini in velopharyngeal closure appears minimal.[40] The origin of the muscle is from the lateral aspect of the medial pterygoid plate, the roof of the pterygoid fossa, and the spine of the sphenoid. Eighty percent of the muscle mass is attached to the lateral hook of the eustachian tube cartilage.[59] The muscle fibers pass vertically down from the skull base and form a broad, flat tendon to pass around the pterygoid hamulus. This 90-degree turn directs the tendon fibers medially, whence they radiate and insert into the palatine aponeurosis.[59]

The musculus uvulae is a paired muscle mass on either side of the midline of the posterior soft palate. The muscle fibers run in an anteroposterior direction, originating from the palatal aponeurosis but not from the posterior edge of the hard palate.[46] They pass over the levator sling to insert into the uvula.[7] Muscle fibers from the palatoglossus and palatopharyngeus insert into the musculus uvulae, further stabilizing this muscle on the free edge of the soft palate.[46] Contraction of the musculus uvulae creates a bulge on the posterior nasal surface of the soft palate. This action is a major contributor to velopharyn-

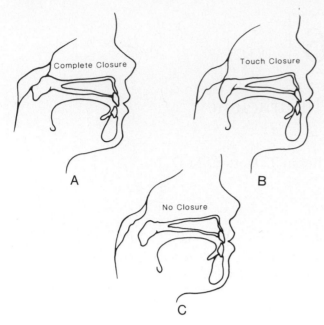

FIGURE 106–1. During non-nasal speech the normal velopharyngeal mechanism produces a complete seal between the nasopharynx and the oropharynx *(A)*. In disturbed velopharyngeal insufficiency closure there may be only touch closure *(B)* or no closure *(C)*, creating hypernasality and nasal escape. In children the adenoid participates in closure (veloadenoidal closure), whereas in adults the velum impacts the posterior pharyngeal wall (velopharyngeal closure).

geal closure.[1] The musculus uvulae also tenses the palate. Hypoplasia of the musculus uvulae may predispose to inadequate separation of the nasopharynx and oropharynx during speech.

The palatoglossus arises from the palatal aponeurosis from the anterior half of the soft palate. It inserts inferior to the posterolateral aspect of the tongue. This muscle makes up the anterior tonsillar pillar and is vulnerable to damage during tonsillectomy. A sheet of elastic fibers extends from the soft palate to the lateral tongue through the palatoglossal arch. Fibers of the palatoglossus insert onto these elastic fibers.[44] The function of the palatoglossus is to depress the soft palate, acting antagonistically to the levator veli palatini.

The palatopharyngeus has vertically and horizontally directed fibers. The origin of the muscle is from the palatal aponeurosis and the posterior border of the hard palate. The vertical fibers of this muscle comprise the posterior tonsillar pillar and insert inferiorly on the thyroid cartilage. The function of these fibers is to depress the soft palate.[30] The horizontal fibers are frequently considered part of the superior pharyngeal constrictors. They insert onto the pharyngobasilar fascia.[79] The superior pharyngeal constrictor muscle arises from the pterygoid hamulus, pterygomandibular raphe, posterior tongue, posterior mandible, and palatine aponeurosis. The wide muscle sheath inserts posteriorly in the median pharyngeal raphe. The function of the superior pharyngeal constrictor is the medial displacement of the lateral pharyngeal walls, to

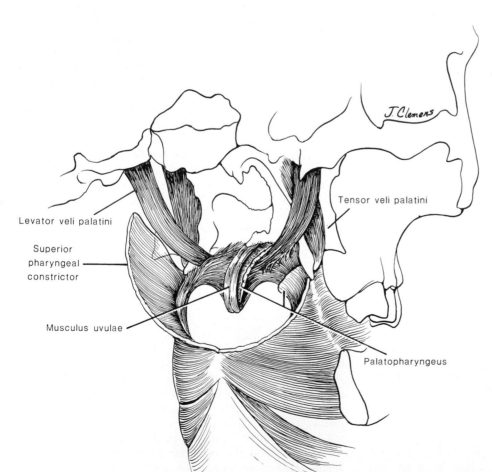

FIGURE 106–2. Muscles of the velopharyngeal sphincter viewed from the posterior aspect.

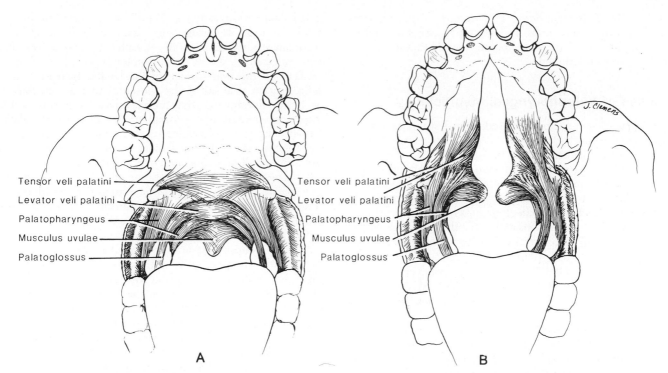

FIGURE 106–3. Muscles of the palate viewed from the anteroinferior aspect. *A,* Normal palate. *B,* Cleft palate.

narrow the velopharyngeal ports.[65] The Passavant ridge, a mucosal bulge located on the posterior pharyngeal wall in 20% of the population, is caused by contraction of a segment of the superior pharyngeal constrictor[17] or the horizontal fibers of the palatopharyngeus.[10, 79] This ridge may, in selected cases, contribute to velopharyngeal closure, but in most normal speakers, the contribution of the Passavant ridge to velopharyngeal closure is minimal.[28] The Passavant ridge is generally found below the level of velopharyngeal closure.

Most muscles that comprise the velopharyngeal sphincter are innervated by the pharyngeal plexus of the vagus nerve. The exception is the tensor veli palatini, which receives innervation from the mandibular division of the trigeminal nerve.[35]

Closure Patterns

Velopharyngeal closure is the combined result of coordinated movements of the pharynx and soft palate. Variations among patients in the contribution to closure from each of these two structures allow identification of discrete patterns of closure. Skolnick and co-workers[69] used the lateral and base projection videofluoroscopic views to illustrate the relative contribution to velopharyngeal closure of the palate and the pharyngeal walls. They observed four basic patterns:

1. Coronal. The posterior surface of the soft palate moves posteriorly, making contact over a broad area against the posterior pharyngeal wall. The major component of velopharyngeal valving is the velum. Little medial movement of the lateral pharyngeal walls is required, and no motion of the posterior

wall is demonstrated. Croft and colleagues[12] demonstrated this closure pattern in 55% of normal patients and in 45% of those with VPI.

2. Circular. Increasing medial movement of the lateral pharyngeal walls obviates a broad area of contact between the posterior pharyngeal wall and the posterior edge of the soft palate. There is no motion of the posterior pharyngeal wall. This pattern is seen in 10% of normal patients and in 20% of patients with VPI.[12]

3. Circular closure with the Passavant ridge. The contribution of the Passavant ridge to velopharyngeal closure, in conjunction with good medial movement of the lateral pharyngeal walls and posterior displacement of the soft palate, creates a true circular sphincter mechanism. It should be noted, however, that the Passavant ridge may not be located at the level where valving occurs. The presence of the Passavant ridge does not, therefore, ensure a circular closure pattern. This pattern is found in 19% of normal patients and 24% of patients with VPI.[12]

4. Sagittal. The lateral pharyngeal walls move medially to make contact in the midline. Posterior motion of the soft palate is minimal. This closure pattern is used in 16% of normal subjects and 11% of VPI patients.[12]

Finkelstein and associates[19] evaluated the location of the Passavant ridge and found it located above the tubercle of the atlas in 55% of patients, at the level of the tubercle in 33%, and below the tubercle in 11%. Because of the variability in the presence of the Passavant ridge and because of the variability in its location in the oropharynx, velopharyngeal closure generally is not at the level of the Passavant ridge. The various valving patterns and levels of closure make it essential to assess accurately the velopharyngeal sphincter before any therapeutic interventions are undertaken.

Causes of Velopharyngeal Insufficiency

Abnormal speech patterns caused by a dysfunctional velopharyngeal sphincter may have a variety of causes (Table 106–1). Available tissue may be insufficient to allow successful velopharyngeal port closure, as in cleft palate patients. Hypertrophic tonsils may interfere with medial displacement of the lateral pharyngeal walls, creating a persistent defect. Adenoidectomy may be the proximate cause of the decompensation of the velopharyngeal sphincter, owing to removal of the tissue mass participating in closure of the sphincter. Acquired and congenital neurologic impairment of the muscles involved with the velopharynx may result in devastating VPI. Mislearning or other behavioral factors may also result in increased nasal resonance or nasal escape.

The incidence of VPI after repair of an overt cleft palate is approximately 50%.[21, 53] On the continuum of palatal defects, the submucosal cleft palate patient may present with severe VPI, but most patients with the triad of bifid uvula, notching of the posterior border of the hard palate with loss of the posterior nasal spine, and diastasis of the soft palate musculature produce normal speech (Fig. 106–4).[71] Submucosal cleft palate patients are at increased risk for VPI following any surgical intervention that affects the velopharyngeal sphincter. Because children normally have veloadenoidal closure, adenoidectomy may precipitate velopharyngeal dysfunction.

Pruzansky and co-workers[57] have divided submucous

TABLE 106–1. Etiology of Velopharyngeal Incompetence

Organic
 Structural
  Acquired
   Palatal scarring
   Palatal resection
   Postadenoidectomy complication
   Post-tonsillectomy complication
   Stress-related condition
  Congenital
   Cleft palate
   Submucous cleft palate
   Occult submucous cleft palate
   Autosomal dominant inheritance
   Short palate
   Large pharynx
   Large tonsils
   Medications during pregnancy
  Associated disorders
   Facioauriculovertebral malformation
   Hearing loss
 Neuromuscular
  Acquired
   Neural diseases
   Muscular diseases
  Congenital
   Encephalopathy
   Möbius syndrome
Functional

cleft palates into two types. Type I has at least one of the visible stigmata of submucous cleft palate. Type II submucous cleft palate, sometimes called the *occult submucous cleft palate*, shows neither notching of the uvula nor diastasis on the oral surface of the palate. Instead, it is a deficiency or absence of the musculus uvulae and diastasis of the levator palatini muscle visible only on endoscopic examination of the nasal surface of the soft palate. The occult submucous cleft palate arises as a result of misdirected mesenchymal fusion of the primordial palate that affects all muscles attaching in the midline of the soft palate.[48] In a study of patients with VPI but no bony cleft palate defects, 55% of the patients were found at endoscopy to have an occult submucous cleft palate, with abnormal muscle orientation in the soft palate.[75]

VPI is associated with other anomalies. The risk of conductive hearing loss and otitis media secondary to eustachian tube dysfunction is well established in cleft palate patients.[33] Patients with submucous cleft palate are similarly at risk. Heller and associates[31] found that 50% of VPI patients without cleft palate had a hearing loss. Seventy-four percent of these patients had a conductive hearing loss, 16% had sensorineural hearing loss, and 10% had mixed loss.

It is estimated that more than 200 recognized syndromes may include palatal clefting as a manifestation. All patients with an obvious cleft should be examined for any structural anomalies (telecanthus, synostosis, maxillary or malar hypoplasia, microtia or atresia, facial nerve paralysis, retrognathia, malocclusion) that may be associated with a syndrome. Similar suspicion should be generated for the submucous cleft palate patient. The anomaly most often associated with VPI is mental retardation.[9] Often, patients with VPI exhibit an identifiable genetic condition. It is imperative that children with VPI have a complete genetic evaluation for proper diagnosis and treatment (Table 106–2).

The incidence of VPI following adenoidectomy ranges from 1 in 1500 to 1 in 10,000.[23, 68] Patients at increased risk for this complication are those with marginal velopharyngeal closure mechanisms, such as those with repaired cleft palate or submucous cleft palate. Because children have veloadenoidal closure, removal of this soft tissue mass in the compromised patient creates a velopharyngeal port that cannot be closed. It is essential to identify children at risk for this complication preoperatively and to discuss the risk of VPI following adenoidectomy with all parents. Approximately 30% of patients with VPI following adenoidectomy had subtle findings suggestive of a compromised velopharyngeal sphincter preoperatively.[23] Specific parameters to explore include the presence of nasal regurgitation, a family history of VPI or palatal clefting, an obvious submucous cleft palate, or preexisting hypernasality.[80] With the use of suction electrocautery, a superior half adenoidectomy may be performed in the patient at risk for development of VPI. This rids the posterior choanae of obstructing tissue while leaving a ridge of tissue inferiorly to approximate the velum. Children with oromotor developmental delays, generalized hypotonia, and mental retardation are also at increased risk for development of VPI following adenoidectomy.[41, 56]

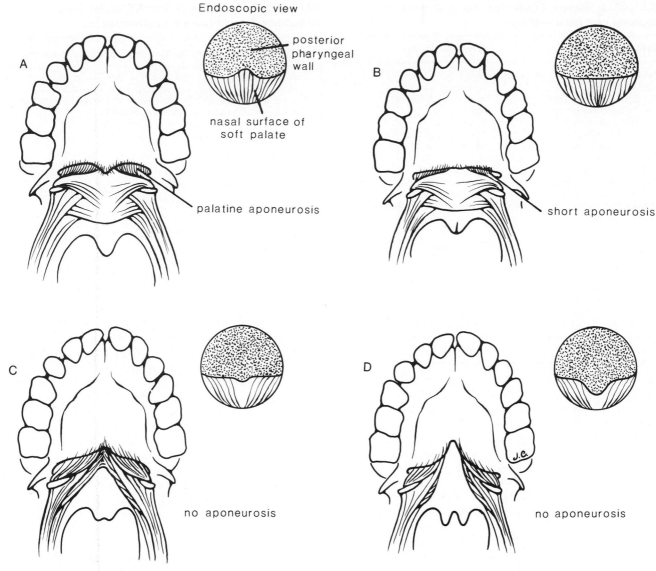

FIGURE 106–4. Oral and endoscopic appearance of the normal palate (*A*), occult submucous cleft palate (*B*), partial submucous cleft palate (*C*), and complete submucous cleft palate (*D*). Note, on the endoscopic view, the obvious bulge of the musculus uvulae in *A*, the bulge in *B*, and the increasing degree of inversion of the bulge due to the diastasis of the muscle (*C* and *D*).

The natural history of adenoid tissue includes atrophy with age. The rate of atrophy is such that continual adjustments in the actions of the velopharyngeal sphincter musculature maintain adequate closure. In the cleft palate patient who has tenuous but adequate velopharyngeal closure, adenoid atrophy may induce VPI. These patients need continual follow-up through this transitional period and speech therapy intervention at the earliest signs of decompensation.

Velocardiofacial syndrome is an under-recognized condition characterized by the presence of VPI, submucous cleft palate, learning disabilities, cardiac anomalies, retrognathia, malar flattening, pharyngeal hypotonia, slender hands and fingers, and small stature.[63] A microdeletion of 22q11.2 has been identified with this condition.[60] There is generally poor velar and little lateral pharyngeal wall movement, which necessitates use of a wide pharyngeal flap for repair of VPI. The surgical treatment of these patients is complicated by excessive tortuosity and medial displacement of the internal carotid arteries in the retropharyngeal area.[50] A pharyngeal flap may be raised in patients with medialized carotid arteries. The plane of dissection of the flap is the prevertebral fascia. The great vessels are deep to this plane. Care must be exercised not to violate this protective tissue layer. Preoperative angiograms (or magnetic resonance angiography) are not necessary. Prosthetic devices may be required for some patients.

Evaluation

The gold standard for the evaluation of speech remains the trained ear. Despite objective findings of mild VPI

TABLE 106–2. Genetic Syndromes Associated with Velopharyngeal Insufficiency

Syndrome	Inheritance Pattern
Syndromes associated with cleft palate	
Stickler syndrome	Autosomal dominant
Velocardiofacial syndrome	Autosomal dominant
Fetal alcohol syndrome	Teratogenic
Fetal hydantoin syndrome	Teratogenic
Kabuki syndrome	Possible autosomal dominant
Van der Woude syndrome	Autosomal dominant
Hemifacial microsomia	Sporadic
CHARGE association	Sporadic
Treacher Collins syndrome	Autosomal dominant
Diabetic embryopathy	Teratogenic
Syndromes associated with cleft lip with or without palatal cleft	
Opitz syndrome	Autosomal dominant, X-link recessive
Trisomy 13	Sporadic chromosomal
Wolf-Hirshhorn syndrome	Sporadic chromosomal
Hemifacial microsomia	Sporadic
Amniotic bands	Sporadic
Diabetic embryopathy	Teratogenic
Fetal alcohol syndrome	Teratogenic
CHARGE association	Sporadic
Van der Woude syndrome	Autosomal dominant
Popliteal pterygium syndrome	Autosomal dominant
Oral-facial-digital syndrome	X-link dominant

TABLE 106–3. Examples of Sound Samples That Accentuate Velopharyngeal Insufficiency

1. Counting from 60 to 70: The sixties contain a combination of sibilants, velar plosives, and alveolar plosives. These sounds require the generation and maintenance of intraoral pressure that may overwhelm an incompetent velopharyngeal sphincter.
2. Sentences loaded with pressure-sensitive phonemes accentuate nasal air emission and compensatory articulation.
   a. Popeye plays baseball.
   b. Take Teddy to town.
   c. Give Kate the cake.
   d. Go get the wagon.
   e. Fred has five fish.
   f. Sally sees the sun in the sky.
   g. She went shopping.
   h. I eat cherries and cheese.
   i. John told a joke to Jim.

and nasal escape, no intervention would be recommended if the impairment in velopharyngeal function causes no disturbance in the overall communication capability of that patient.[14] Sentences that accentuate nasal escape and improve the ability to demonstrate hypernasality are located in Table 106–3.

Several tests are available for objective evaluation of VPI. Pressure flow techniques during speech generate an estimate of the velopharyngeal opening by measuring an airflow and pressure differential between nose and mouth.[73, 78] Aerodynamic tests have not gained widespread acceptance because of the expense involved in obtaining the equipment and the extraordinary amount of training needed to properly interpret the data.

Acoustic output of nasal and oral components of speech can be detected by separate microphones and then expressed as a "nasalance score" (ratio of nasal to nasal-plus-oral output), which permits objective comparison of degrees of hypernasality (Fig. 106–5).[20] Normative data have been collected for this test, but care must be taken in the interpretation of results, because complicating acoustic factors are frequently encountered.

Multiview Fluoroscopy

This investigative technique has largely been replaced by direct examination of the velopharyngeal mechanism by nasopharyngoscopy. There are circumstances, however, when this examination is required. High-density barium is instilled into each nasal cavity and permitted to coat the nasopharynx. Multiple fluoroscopic views are then obtained during active speech to evaluate the velopharyngeal sphincter. The lateral view provides information on the relative length of the soft palate, the depth of the pharynx, palatal mobility (elevation and elongation), and anterior motion of the posterior pharyngeal wall. The frontal view affords visualization of the medial movement of the lateral pharyngeal walls and their vertical symmetry with respect to the level of the hard palate (Fig. 106–6). The base view or the Towne view permits an en face view of the velopharyngeal port (Fig. 106–7). The simultaneous motion of the palate, lateral pharyngeal walls, and posterior pharyngeal wall can be seen on this view, and the sphincteric closure of the aperture can be appreciated.[24, 67, 72] An experienced speech pathologist should be present during the examination to perform a diagnostic speech evaluation during the period of fluoroscopy and maximize velopharyngeal closure attempts.

Videofluoroscopy has disadvantages. The optimal study requires both a speech pathologist and a radiologist to perform the test. The radiation exposure risks are low but are a concern in children when repeat studies may be necessary. Finally, the interpretation of multiple shadows projected when pharyngeal flaps have been placed is often difficult.

FIGURE 106–5. Objective data of nasal emission can be obtained with the use of a nasometer.

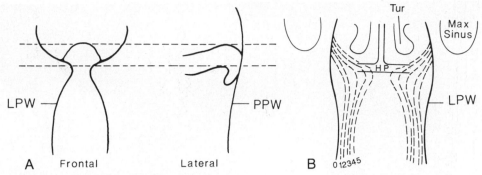

FIGURE 106–6. *A,* Schematic of velopharyngeal closure in frontal and lateral projections. Notice the level of lateral pharyngeal wall (LPW) closure at about the level of the hard palate (HP) and the firm contact of the soft palate against the posterior pharyngeal wall (PPW). *B,* Frontal view schematic showing various degrees of LPW movement rated from 0 (no movement) to 5 (normal movement). Tur, inferior turbinate; Max Sinus, maxillary sinus. (After Kelsey CA, et al. Lateral pharyngeal wall motion as a predictor of surgical success in velopharyngeal insufficiency. N Engl J Med 287:64, 1972. From Cotton RT. Lateral defects in VPI. Arch Otolaryngol Head Neck Surg 103:90, 1977. Copyright 1977, American Medical Association.)

Nasopharyngoscopy

Flexible nasopharyngoscopy for the purpose of evaluating the velopharyngeal apparatus can be performed routinely in children as young as 3 years of age (Fig. 106–8).[15] The nasal cavity is decongested and topically anesthetized. A video camera and appropriate recording equipment should be available to create a permanent record of the examination. A speech pathologist should be in attendance during the endoscopic evaluation to perform a diagnostic speech evaluation. With the endoscope in position in the nasopharynx, observation is made of the adequacy of velopharyngeal closure. The level of closure should be noted. The soft palate is scrutinized for signs of a submucous cleft or deficient musculus uvulae. The degree and symmetry of palatal motion is recorded. The relative motion of the pharyngeal walls is observed to define the predominant pattern of velopharyngeal closure. The larynx should also be examined because 40% of patients with VPI compensate for hypernasality with compensatory

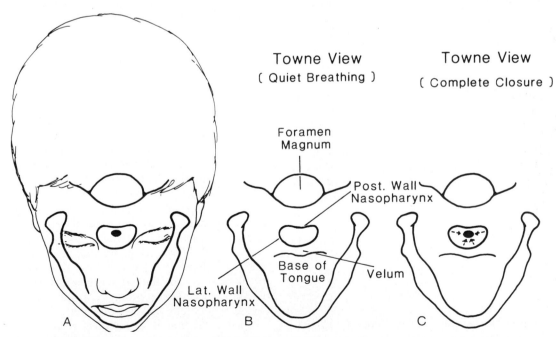

FIGURE 106–7. *A,* Velopharyngeal sphincter in the Towne projection, looking "straight down the barrel" (i.e., at right angles to the plane of velopharyngeal closure). *B,* Landmarks of the velopharyngeal sphincter in quiet breathing. *C,* In complete closure, note the importance of the soft palate and lateral pharyngeal walls, with minimal movement of the posterior pharyngeal wall. (From Cotton RT. Lateral defects in VPI. Arch Otolaryngol Head Neck Surg 103: 90, 1977. Copyright 1977, American Medical Association.)

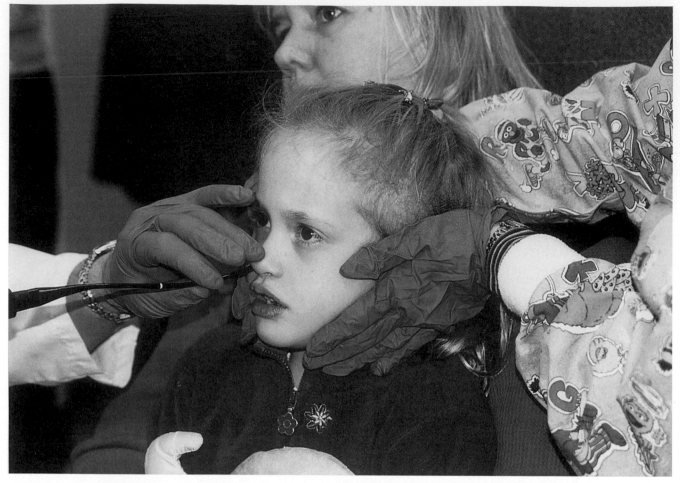

FIGURE 106-8. Flexible nasopharyngoscopy can be performed routinely in children aged 3 years and older. This study should be recorded on videotapes so that the preoperative assessment can be reviewed and surgical result compared.

articulation. Pathologic changes involving the larynx, such as vocal cord nodules, persistent vocal cord edema, or incomplete glottic closure, are common.[16]

Nasopharyngoscopy permits direct observation of the velopharyngeal mechanism during connected speech. It requires a moderate degree of cooperation from the patient to complete the study successfully. It remains a subjective assessment of the degree of velopharyngeal closure, which is minimally invasive and, in general, well tolerated by the patient. Nasopharyngoscopy is superior to radiography if the patient has had a pharyngeal flap procedure.[66] It is difficult to localize unilateral nasal escape fluoroscopically, but it is easily demonstrated endoscopically.

Treatment

Three basic approaches to the management of velopharyngeal dysfunction are possible: speech therapy, prosthetic management, and surgical intervention. Few prospective studies have assessed the outcomes of these strategies. Personal experience remains the basis for the adoption of specific treatment plans.

Speech Therapy

If a patient does not have the basic anatomy necessary to close the velopharyngeal port, speech therapy can have no effect on the disorder. If therapy is instituted in this circumstance, the patient frequently becomes frustrated and loses interest in the treatment program. When the VPI is minimal, and certainly in all postoperative cases, speech therapy does improve velopharyngeal function. Speech therapy is also important in correcting compensatory articulation habits that develop as a result of long-standing VPI. The patient undergoing speech therapy for mild VPI should be given a firm time line, after which the patient is reevaluated for possible surgical intervention in case adequate progress is not observed. The time course is generally 3 to 6 months.

Speech therapy is a nebulous term that encompasses treatments for a wide variety of disorders. It is essential for speech therapists to understand the pathology associated with VPI so that appropriate therapy can be directed at improving articulation, resonance, voice quality, and velopharyngeal closure.[14]

Prosthetic Management

Two basic types of prosthetic devices are used to correct VPI: obturators and palatal lifts. The obturator is used when the closure of the velopharyngeal port is inadequate and the resultant defect can be filled with the device.[3] The palatal lift is generally used in cases of neurologic impairment, when timing and coordination of velopharyngeal closure are poor.[47] These devices have generally been used when there are contraindications to surgical intervention. Fashioning the prosthetic device so that it functions well and is stable despite the continued muscular activity of the pharynx can be tedious. The use of the nasopharyngoscope to visualize the prosthesis and its effects may facilitate construction of these devices.

Another use of the prosthetic device is the object of a resurgence of interest. McGrath and Anderson[51] suggest that gradual reduction in the size of an obturator encourages increased movement of the velum and lateral pharyngeal walls. There is interest in using this technique as a preoperative form of therapy to improve lateral wall motion before pharyngeal flap placement. This may allow a smaller flap to be used, minimizing postoperative nasal airway obstruction. This technique was first described by Blakeley.[3]

Surgical Intervention

The variety of velopharyngeal closure patterns results in a variety of pathologies contributing to VPI. It follows that each pathologic condition requires a unique surgical approach to achieve optimal results. The tenet that one operation will correct all cases of VPI is invalid. A variety of surgical procedures is needed to tailor the correction to the defect.

Posterior Pharyngeal Wall Augmentation

When VPI is caused by an anteroposterior defect of 10 mm or less between the posterior pharyngeal wall and the velum, posterior pharyngeal wall augmentation may be considered. Various materials have been recommended, including paraffin,[18] autogenous cartilage,[2, 76] cadaver cartilage,[29, 45] fascia and fat, silicone,[4] and polytetrafluoroethylene.[5, 26, 49] The implants should be placed at the level of potential contact with the soft palate. This is generally at the level of the atlas promontory.[27, 28] The implants are inserted onto the prevertebral fascia. The materials may be positioned through an external cervical approach, a transoral incision, or a transoral injection. Good results have been obtained with cartilage grafts in the posterior pharynx.[32] The risks of infection and resorption of the graft remain a concern. Silicone was associated with a high extrusion rate, and its use has been forbidden by the United States Food and Drug Administration. Teflon, a 50% suspension of polytetrafluoroethylene particles in glycerin, has a lower rate of extrusion than silicone and has produced the most consistent results.[70] Because the glycerin vehicle is absorbed, overcorrection is essential to maintain the bulk necessary to close the velopharyngeal port.

The U. S. Food and Drug Administration does not approve the use of Teflon in the retropharynx. There have been cases of inadvertent injection into aberrant arteries coursing through the retropharynx. However, Teflon paste remains useful in carefully selected cases. The key to the use of Teflon is depositing it into the plane deep to the muscles so that it lies on the prevertebral fascia. After careful palpation of the posterior pharynx for signs of any aberrant vessels, 1 to 2 mL of paste is injected into two sites adjacent to the midline at the predetermined level of velar closure. A metal tongue blade pushing against the retropharyngeal tissues inferior to the injection site is helpful in preventing inferior spread of the paste upon injection, facilitating the buildup of a transverse ridge across the pharynx. Repeat injections may be required in some cases. Furlow and co-workers report complete elimination of hypernasality in 74% of 36 study patients.[22] Candidates for posterior implantation must be carefully chosen. They must have a velopharyngeal gap smaller than 5 mm and have adequate lateral pharyngeal wall motion and good palatal motion. Teflon is also useful for minor modification of surgical reconstructions. Lateral ports may become ineffectual as scarring thins the area with time. The margins of the port may be plumped by judicious injection of implant material into the area to further narrow the resulting defect.

Teflon has been reported to embolize to the lungs in animal experiments. Because of this potential, the use of Teflon has decreased. In one case, a remote stroke followed Teflon injection used to treat ureteral reflux in a child.[8]

Complications associated with posterior pharyngeal wall implants include infection, extrusion, undercorrection, inappropriate positioning of the implant, and migration of the material after insertion. Perioperative antibiotic coverage is recommended to minimize postoperative infection and extrusion. Accurate preoperative assessment of the level of velopharyngeal closure is essential for successful implantation. Identifying visual landmarks is relatively easy during endoscopic evaluation of the sphincter. Proper positioning of the implant on prevertebral fascia is the most important factor in minimizing postoperative migration of the implant.

Pharyngeal Flap

The *inferiorly based pharyngeal flap* was first described by Schoenborn in 1876.[61] Ten years later, he described the superiorly based pharyngeal flap.[62] The basic tenet of this procedure is that a persistent central defect is surrounded laterally by mobile pharyngeal walls. The flap acts as an obturator against which the lateral pharyngeal walls can be buttressed.[11]

The *superiorly based pharyngeal flap* has become the preferred flap design because there is no tethering of the velum inferiorly to further aggravate an incompetent velopharyngeal port. The posterior soft palate is divided longitudinally or transversely. The superiorly based pharyngeal flap is elevated at the level of the prevertebral fascia. The base of the flap is at the level of the arch of C1. The length and width of the flap are tailored to the degree of velopharyngeal inadequacy. The flap is inserted into the soft palate under minimal tension.[64] Hogan[34] proposed a method of lining the raw surface of the pharyngeal flap to minimize the scar contracture that results from secondary intention healing. The lining of the nasal surface of the soft palate can be "pedicled" on the posterior edge of the palate and used to reline the pharyngeal flap. Creation of appropriately sized lateral ports may be accomplished by the insertion of number 14 French catheters (3.0 to 3.5 endotracheal tube). Creation of lateral ports with no more than 20 mm^2 surface area is thought to ensure adequate velopharyngeal closure.

In a series of 500 pharyngeal flaps, 90% of patients exhibited normalization or improvement in hypernasality, and 74% showed improved speech intelligibility.[33] Overall improvement was related to the width of the flap when healing was complete and to the degree of mobility of the lateral pharyngeal walls. Patients with preoperative muscle dysfunction had more difficulty with persistent VPI postoperatively.

Complications of the pharyngeal flap are generally related to the flap itself. If the flap is too narrow, most commonly a result of scar contracture from secondary intention healing, the lateral velopharyngeal ports are too large and the flap acts as an inappropriately sized obturator. A flap that is set too far inferior may tether the free edge of the soft palate and prevent proper elevation during closure attempts, resulting in velopharyngeal inadequacy. Pharyngeal flaps that are exceptionally wide may obstruct the nasopharynx and lead to hyponasality, and, potentially, obstructive sleep apnea. Continued scar contracture around the lateral ports may cause stenosis of these areas and subsequent airway difficulties. Revision of the lateral ports and occasionally the release of the pharyngeal flap from the posterior pharyngeal wall are required to alleviate excessive nasopharyngeal obstruction.

Patients with tonsillar hypertrophy need to be evaluated for possible tonsillectomy before placement of a posterior pharyngeal flap to minimize postoperative airway obstruction. Patients with retrognathic profiles are at increased risk for postoperative airway obstruction and must be followed up carefully to ensure that an adequate airway is maintained. The prevalence of significant nasal airway obstruction with a tenuous airway has been reported to be as high as 10%.[74] With careful preoperative evaluation of patients at risk for postoperative airway obstruction, severe airway problems should be avoidable. Even so, the incidence of tracheotomy in flap patients is between 0.4% and 3%.[25, 33]

The *rolled pharyngeal flap* is a technique that augments the posterior pharyngeal wall but has a minimal obstructive impact on the airway. The standard pharyngeal flap is elevated. It is then rolled onto itself, creating an area of excess tissue for the velum to oppose. Gray and co-workers describe their experience in 14 children, normalizing the hypernasality listener ratings in 10 of 13 patients, and normalizing the nasometry scores in 6 of 10 patients.[27] The velopharyngeal gap in these patients was small.

Bleeding related to pharyngeal flap surgery may be life threatening. Bronsted and associates[9] reported that 8% of 600 cases had significant bleeding, and Nylen and Wahlin[54] reported 13% of 103 patients had significant bleeding. Each series had one death associated with surgical or anesthesia complications.

Sphincter Pharyngoplasty

When lateral pharyngeal wall motion is poor, a pharyngeal flap would not be expected to correct the VPI. Surgical creation of a dynamic sphincter in which the lateral walls are pulled medially would be better suited to this type of defect.[37] In a sphincter pharyngoplasty, a short, inferiorly based pharyngeal flap is raised, in addition to bilateral superiorly based flaps containing the mucosa of the posterior tonsillar pillar and the underlying palatopharyngeus muscle.[55] The lateral palatopharyngeus muscle flaps are sewn together in the midline and are sewn into the resulting defect of the inferiorly based pharyngeal flap. The result is narrowing of the lateral channels and a dynamic sphincter. The neurovascular supply to the superiorly based palatopharyngeus muscle flaps maintains the viability and innervation of the muscle, allowing it to participate in lateral port closure.[36] Modifications of this technique have used a superiorly based pharyngeal flap to reduce the raw surfaces created during the Orticochea procedure, and thus minimize excessive scarring.[38, 39]

The complications associated with sphincter pharyngoplasty are similar to those of the posterior pharyngeal flap. The prevalence of hyponasality is approximately 2%,[38] and the risk of significant obstructive apnea is significantly less than with pharyngeal flap.

Push-Back Palatoplasty

A patient who has a short palate with adequate lateral pharyngeal wall movement or a submucous cleft palate is well served by the palatal push-back procedure. The procedure can be performed by elevating a mucoperiosteal flap off the hard palate, detaching the soft palate musculature from the posterior edge of the hard palate, and displacing the soft palate posteriorly.[77] Attempts to minimize scarring that develops on the nasal surface of the soft palate have led to the development of mucosal flaps and oropalatal mucoperiosteal flaps to line the raw surfaces, thus minimizing scar contracture.[13, 52] Reconstruction of the levator sling can be combined with the push-back procedure.

SELECTED REFERENCES

D'Antonio LL, Crockett DM. Evaluation and management of velopharyngeal inadequacy. In Smith JD, Bumsted R (eds). Pediatric Facial Plastic and Reconstructive Surgery. New York, Raven Press, 1993, p 173.
   This is an excellent discussion of the semantics associated with VPI. The multidisciplinary approach to the patient with velopharyngeal inadequacy is outlined in terms of the roles of the various specialists.
Kravath RE, Pollak CP, Borowiecki B, Weitzman ED. Obstructive sleep apnea and death associated with surgical correction of velopharyngeal incompetence. J Pediatr 96:645, 1980.
   Three cases of severe obstructive sleep apnea following pharyngeal flap reconstruction of VPI are described. One child was

found dead 4 weeks postoperatively. The possibility of airway compromise is well illustrated.

MacKenzie-Stepner K, Witzel MA, Stinger DA, et al. Abnormal carotid arteries in the velocardiofacial syndrome. A report of three cases. Plast Reconstr Surg 80:347, 1987.

It is essential to recognize velocardiofacial syndrome, because it can put patients at risk for life-threatening complications if they submit to surgical treatment of VPI. This report nicely illustrates the medial displacement and considerable tortuosity of the internal carotid arteries associated with this syndrome.

Witzel MA, Rich RH, Margar-Bacal F, et al. Velopharyngeal insufficiency after adenoidectomy: an 8-year review. Int J Pediatr Otorhinolaryngol 11:15, 1986.

A study of 137 patients with VPI after adenoidectomy is reported, 30% of whose findings suggested, preoperatively, the possibility of postadenoidectomy VPI. Risk factors are described, and the final disposition of the patients is reported.

REFERENCES

1. Azzam NA, Kuehn DP. The morphology of the musculus uvulae. Cleft Palate J 14:78, 1977.
2. Bentley FH, Watkins I. Speech after repair of cleft palate. Lancet 2:862, 1947.
3. Blakeley RW. Temporary speech prosthesis as an aid in speech training. Cleft Palate Bull 10:63, 1960.
4. Blocksma R. Correction of velopharyngeal insufficiency by Silastic pharyngeal implant. Plast Reconstr Surg 31:268, 1963.
5. Bluestone CD, Musgrave RH, McWilliams BJ. Teflon injection pharyngoplasty. Cleft Palate J 5:19, 1968.
6. Boorman JG, Sommerlad BC. Levator palati and palatal dimples: their anatomy, relationship and clinical significance. Br J Plast Surg 38:326, 1985.
7. Boorman JG, Sommerlad BC. Musculus uvulae and levator palatini: theoretical, anatomical and functional relationship in velopharyngeal closure. Br J Plast Surg 38:33, 1985.
8. Borgatti R, Tettamanti A, Piccinelli P. Brain injury in a healthy child one year after periureteral injection of Teflon. Pediatrics 98:290, 1996.
9. Bronsted K, Liisberg WB, Orsted A, et al. Surgical and speech results following palatopharyngoplasty operations in Denmark 1959–1977. Cleft Palate J 21:170, 1984.
10. Cassell MD, Moon JB, Elkadi H. Anatomy and physiology of the velopharynx. In Bardach J, Morris HL (eds). Multidisciplinary Management of Cleft Lip and Palate. Philadelphia, WB Saunders, 1990, p 366.
11. Cotton RT, Quattromani F. Lateral defects in velopharyngeal insufficiency. Arch Otolaryngol 103:90, 1977.
12. Croft CB, Shprintzen RJ, Rakoff SJ. Patterns of velopharyngeal valving in normal and cleft palate subjects: a multiview videofluoroscopic and nasendoscopic study. Laryngoscope 91:265, 1981.
13. Cronin TD. Pushback palatorrhaphy with nasal mucosal flaps. In Grabb WC, Rosenstein SW, Bzoch KR (eds). Cleft Lip and Palate. Boston, Little, Brown, 1977.
14. D'Antonio LL, Crockett DM. Evaluation and management of velopharyngeal inadequacy. In Smith JD, Bumsted R (eds). Pediatric Facial Plastic and Reconstructive Surgery. New York, Raven Press, 1993, p 173.
15. D'Antonio L, Muntz H, Marsh J, et al. Practical application of flexible fiberoptic nasopharyngoscopy for evaluating velopharyngeal function. Plast Reconstr Surg 82:611, 1988.
16. D'Antonio LL, Muntz H, Providence M, Marsh J. Laryngeal/voice findings in patients with velopharyngeal dysfunction. Laryngoscope 98:432, 1988.
17. Dickson DR, Dickson WM. Velopharyngeal anatomy. J Speech Hear Res 15:372, 1972.
18. Eckstein H. Demonstration of paraffin prosthesis in defects of the face and palate [trans]. Dermatologica (Basel) 11:772, 1904.
19. Finkelstein Y, Lerner MA, Ophir D, et al. Nasopharyngeal profile and velopharyngeal valve mechanism. Plast Reconstr Surg 92:603, 1993.
20. Fletcher SG. "Nasalance" vs listener judgements of nasality. Cleft Palate J 13:31, 1976.
21. Furlow LT. Cleft palate repair by double opposing Z-plasty. Plast Reconstr Surg 78:724, 1986.
22. Furlow LT Jr, Williams WN, Eisenbach CR II, et al. A long-term study on treating velopharyngeal insufficiency by Teflon injection. Cleft Palate J 19:47, 1982.
23. Gibb AG. Hypernasality (rhinolalia aperta) following tonsil and adenoid removal. J Laryngol Otol 72:433, 1958.
24. Graber TM, Bzoch KR, Aoba T. A functional study of palatal and pharyngeal structures. Angle Orthodont 29:30, 1959.
25. Graham WP III, Hamilton R, Randall P, et al. Complications following posterior pharyngeal flap surgery. Cleft Palate J 10:176, 1973.
26. Grau HR. Bibliography of foreign substances and implants in reconstructive surgery. Plast Reconstr Surg 29:113, 1962.
27. Gray SD, Pinborough-Zimmerman J, Catten M. Posterior wall augmentation of velopharyngeal insufficiency. Otolaryngol Head Neck Surg 121:107, 1999.
28. Hagerty RF, Hill MJ. Posterior wall and palatal movement in postoperative cleft palates and normal palates. J Speech Hear Res 3:59, 1960.
29. Hagerty RF, Hill MJ. Cartilage pharyngoplasty in cleft palate patients. Surg Gynecol Obstet 112:350, 1961.
30. Harrington R. M. pterygopharyngeus and its relation to m. palatopharyngeus. Laryngoscope 55:499, 1945.
31. Heller JC, Gens GW, Croft CB, et al. Conductive hearing loss in patients with velopharyngeal insufficiency. Cleft Palate J 15:246, 1978.
32. Hess DA, Hagerty RF, Mylin WK. Velar motility, velopharyngeal closure and speech proficiency in cartilage pharyngoplasty: an eight-year study. Cleft Palate J 5:153, 1968.
33. Hirschberg J. Pediatric otolaryngological relations of velopharyngeal insufficiency. Int J Pediatr Otorhinolaryngol 5:199, 1983.
34. Hogan VM. A clarification of the surgical goals in cleft palate speech and the introduction of the lateral port control (L.P.C.) pharyngeal flap. Cleft Palate J 10:331, 1973.
35. Hollinshead WH. Anatomy for Surgeons: The Head and Neck. Philadelphia, Harper and Row, 1982, p 325.
36. Hynes W. Pharyngoplasty by muscle transplantation. Br J Plast Surg 31:128, 1950.
37. Jackson IT. A review of 236 cleft palate patients treated with dynamic muscle sphincter. Plast Reconstr Surg 71:187, 1983.
38. Jackson IT. Pharyngoplasty: Jackson technique. In Bardach J, Morris HC (eds). Multidisciplinary Management of Cleft Lip and Palate. Philadelphia, WB Saunders, 1990, p 386.
39. Jackson IT, Silverton JS. Sphincter pharyngoplasty as a secondary procedure in cleft palate. Plast Reconstr Surg 59:518, 1977.
40. Kamerer DB, Rood SR. The tensor tympani, stapedius and tensor veli palatini muscles—an electromyographic study. Otol Rhinol Laryngol 86:416, 1979.
41. Kavanagh KT, Kahane JC, Kordan B. Risks and benefits of adenotonsillectomy for children with Down syndrome. Am J Ment Defic 91:22, 1986.
42. Kriens OB. Anatomy of the velopharyngeal area in cleft palate. Clin Plast Surg 2:261, 1975.
43. Kuehn DP. Velopharyngeal anatomy and physiology. Ear Nose Throat J 58:316, 1979.
44. Kuehn DP, Azzam NA. Anatomical characteristics of palatoglossus and the anterior faucial pillar. Cleft Palate J 15:349, 1978.
45. Lando RL. Transplant of cadaveric cartilage into the posterior pharyngeal wall in treatment of cleft palate. Stomatologiia (Moskva) 4:38, 1950.
46. Langdon HL, Klueber DM. The longitudinal fibromuscular component of the soft palate in the 15-week human foetus: musculus uvulae and palatine raphe. Cleft Palate J 14:337, 1978.
47. LaVelle W, Hardy J. Palatal left prosthesis for treatment of palatopharyngeal incompetence. J Prosthet Dent 42:308, 1979.
48. Lewin ML, Croft CB, Shprintzen RJ. Velopharyngeal insufficiency due to hypoplasia of the musculus uvulae and occult submucous cleft palate. Plast Reconstr Surg 65:585, 1980.
49. Lewy R, Cole R, Wepman J. Teflon injection in the correction of velopharyngeal insufficiency. Ann Otol 74:3, 1964.
50. MacKenzie-Stepner K, Witzel MA, Stinger DA, et al. Abnormal

.carotid arteries in the velocardiofacial syndrome. A report of three cases. Plast Reconstr Surg 80:347, 1987.

51. McGrath CO, Anderson MW. Prosthetic treatment of velopharyngeal incompetence. In Bardach J, Morris HL (eds). Multidisciplinary Management of Cleft Lip and Palate. Philadelphia, WB Saunders, 1990, p 809.

52. Millard DR Jr. The island flap in cleft surgery. Surg Gynecol Obstet 116:279, 1963.

53. Morris HL. Velopharyngeal competence and primary cleft palate surgery, 1960–1971: a critical review. Cleft Palate J 10:62, 1973.

54. Nylen B, Wahlin A. Postoperative complications in pharyngeal flap surgery. Cleft Palate J 3:347, 1966.

55. Orticochea M. Construction of a dynamic muscle sphincter in cleft palates. Plast Reconstr Surg 41:323, 1968.

56. Pollack MA, Shprintzen RJ, Zimmerman-Manchester KL. Velopharyngeal insufficiency—the neurologic perspective: a report of 32 cases. Dev Med Child Neurol 21:194, 1979.

57. Pruzansky S, Peterson-Falgore S, Laffen J, et al. Hypernasality in the absence of an overt cleft. Commentary on nomenclature, diagnosis, classification and research design. Abstract no. 60. In Third International Congress on Cleft Palate and Related Craniofacial Anomalies, 1977.

58. Rohan RF, Turner L. The levator palati muscle. J Anat 90:153, 1956.

59. Ross MA. Functional anatomy of the tensor palati. Arch Otolaryngol 93:1, 1971.

60. Ryan AK, Goodship JA, Wilson DI, et al. Spectrum of clinical features associated with interstitial chromosome 22q11 deletions: a European collaborative study. J Med Genet 34:798, 1997.

61. Schoenborn D. Ueber eine neue Methode der Staphylorrhapi. Arch Klin Chir 19:527, 1876.

62. Schoenborn D. Vorstellung eines Falles staphyloplastik. Verhandlungen der Deutschen Gesellschaft fur Chirurgie 15:57, 1886.

63. Shprintzen RJ, Goldberg RB, Lewin ML, et al. A new syndrome involving cleft palate, cardiac anomalies, typical facies, and learning disabilities: velocardiofacial syndrome. Cleft Palate J 15:56, 1978.

64. Shprintzen RJ, Lewin ML, Croft CB, et al. A comprehensive study of pharyngeal flap surgery: tailor-made flaps. Cleft Palate J 16:46, 1979.

65. Shprintzen RJ, McCall GN, Skolnick ML, et al. Selective movement of the lateral aspects of the pharyngeal walls during velopharyngeal closure for speech, blowing and whistling in normals. Cleft Palate J 12:51, 1975.

66. Sinclair SW, Davies DM, Bracka A. Comparative reliability of nasal pharyngoscopy and videofluorography in the assessment of velopharyngeal incompetence. Br J Plast Surg 35:113, 1982.

67. Skolnick ML. Videofluoroscopic examination of the velopharyngeal portal during phonation in lateral and base projections—a new technique for studying the mechanics of closure. Cleft Palate J 7: 803, 1970.

68. Skolnick ML. Velopharyngeal function in cleft palate. Clin Plast Surg 2:285, 1975.

69. Skolnick ML, McCall GN, Barnes M. The sphincteric mechanism of velopharyngeal closure. Cleft Palate J 10:286, 1973.

70. Smith JK, McCabe BF. Teflon injection in the nasopharynx to improve velopharyngeal closure. Ann Otol Rhinol Laryngol 86:559, 1977.

71. Stewart JM, Ott JE, Lagare R. Submucous cleft palate: prevalence in a school population. Cleft Palate J 9:246, 1972.

72. Stinger DA, Witzel MA. Velopharyngeal insufficiency on videofluoroscopy: comparison of projections. AJR Am J Roentgenol 146:15, 1986.

73. Thompson AE, Hixon TJ. Nasal air flow during normal speech production. Cleft Palate J 16:412, 1979.

74. Thurston JB, Larsan DL, Shanks JC, et al. Nasal obstruction as a complication of pharyngeal flap surgery. Cleft Palate J 17:148, 1980.

75. Trier WC, Velopharyngeal incompetency in the absence of overt cleft palate: anatomic and surgical considerations. Cleft Palate J 20: 209, 1983.

76. Wardill WEM. Results of operation for cleft palate. Br J Surg 16: 127, 1928.

77. Wardill WEM. Technique of operation for cleft palate. Br J Surg 25:117, 1937.

78. Warren DW. The determination of velopharyngeal incompetence by aerodynamic and acoustical techniques. Clin Plast Surg 2:299, 1975.

79. Whillis J. A note on the muscles of the palate and superior constrictor. J Anat 65:92, 1930.

80. Witzel MA, Rich RH, Margar-Bacal F, et al. Velopharyngeal insufficiency after adenoidectomy: an 8-year review. Int J Pediatr Otorhinolaryngol 11:15, 1986.

107

Amplification Selection for Children with Hearing Impairment

Todd A. Ricketts, Ph.D., Anne Marie Tharpe, Ph.D., Albert R. De Chicchis, Ph.D., Fred H. Bess, Ph.D., and Daniel M. Schwartz, Ph.D.

From the moment infants with normal hearing are born, they are immersed in sound. Among those sounds are those of speech, exposure to which allows infants to lay the foundation for the communication skills of speech and language.[95] Changes in motor, cognitive, and social skills during the first year of life channel the evolution toward language, and at about age 1 year, typical children with normal hearing produce their first word.[96] By the age of 4 years, children have acquired a complex set of grammatical rules that serve as the foundation for adult language. These early years not only constitute the period of most rapid speech and language development but also are critical to the acquisition of normal speech and language skills. However, this innate propensity for speech and language depends on the ability to abstract the acoustic information received from the environment.[97] Thus, the auditory channel must be intact if children are to receive the necessary linguistic input with which to develop the rules of grammar.

On the other hand, the acquisition of speech and language may be delayed or disordered in children with reduced auditory input subsequent to hearing loss. Data have shown a variety of difficulties with communication and academic achievement as well as psychosocial and emotional problems associated with hearing impairment of early onset. These difficulties have long been known to affect children with moderate to profound bilateral hearing loss.[17, 38, 39] More recently, some children with minimal, fluctuating, and unilateral hearing loss have also shown significant difficulties.[19, 150] The impact of hearing loss on the development of oral communication skills varies greatly and depends on a multitude of factors, including (1) the child's age at the onset of the hearing loss, (2) the degree of hearing loss, and (3) when therapeutic intervention is initiated.[23, 98]

The primary objective of early treatment for the child with hearing impairment is the fostering of speech and language development. If the child's potential for acquiring speech and language is to be maximized, exposure to sensory input through the auditory channel must begin during the critical period (birth to 3 years). Because most children with hearing impairment have sufficient residual hearing to benefit from amplification, the hearing aid is the primary source of external environmental input to the auditory modality. According to Ross,[123] "the early and appropriate selection and use of amplification is the single most important habilitative tool available to us."

Fortunately, the age at which hearing loss is being identified in children is younger than ever before.[123] Although subsequent fitting of appropriate amplification has improved significantly,[147] the time between identification and intervention needs to be improved further.[9, 66, 151] Currently, the goal of audiologists, otolaryngologists, and pediatricians should be to identify hearing loss in infants before age 3 months and to intervene by age 6 months.[152] Given the importance of early and appropriate amplification for optimal development of speech and language skills, this chapter reviews the basic characteristics and acoustic properties of personal wearable amplification systems. In addition, the chapter describes available clinical strategies for selecting, verifying, and validating appropriate amplification for children with hearing impairment.

Amplification Candidacy

Children are considered candidates for amplification when a significant bilateral peripheral hearing loss is present, regardless of whether the loss is conductive, mixed, or sensorineural.[152] In addition, some children with fluctuating or unilateral hearing loss, or both, may be considered candidates for hearing aids or other forms of amplification. Auditory thresholds exceeding 25 dB HL are considered sufficient to impede speech perception, thus necessitating consideration of amplification. In certain cases, children with even milder degrees of hearing loss may benefit from some type of amplification. Amplification candidacy should thus not be based on auditory thresholds alone but should be determined in the context of the child's cognitive function, presence of other handicapping conditions, and academic performance.[152]

The first step in determining hearing aid candidacy is defining the type, degree, and configuration of the child's hearing loss. Current technology allows ear-specific and frequency-specific data to be obtained from very young infants. With all children, especially infants and difficult-to-test children, auditory assessment should result in convergence of several audiometric measures. These may include behavioral testing (air and bone conduction), immittance audiometry (tympanometry and acoustic reflexes), evoked otoacoustic emissions (OAEs), and evoked auditory brain stem response (ABR) recordings (click and frequency-specific).

Determination of ABR thresholds and plotting of a latency-intensity function for wave V can provide data on the presence, type, and degree of hearing loss within the frequency region critical to speech recognition. Use of frequency-specific stimuli such as tone pips or tone bursts and bone-conducted signals allows for further definition of the audiometric configuration.[146] The ABR is particularly valuable when testing very young children (i.e., younger than 6 months) or children with developmental disabilities.

For children over a developmental age of 6 months, behavioral testing such as visual reinforcement audiometry, tangible reinforcement operant conditioning audiometry, or conditioned play audiometry is appropriate. The test–retest reliability of such procedures has been demonstrated, and the sensitivity and specificity of these behavioral measures is considered very good.[40] Binaural hearing aid fittings, however, cannot be based on sound-field audiometric thresholds; individual ear data are required. Behavioral responses of children at or under a developmental age of 6 months should always be confirmed with ABR unless neurologic status precludes such.[152]

Other tests contributing to the determination of hearing status of infants and children include the immittance test battery and OAEs. Immittance audiometry includes tympanometry and acoustic reflex thresholds. Tympanometry is a measurement of the mobility of the middle-ear system as air pressure is varied in the external auditory canal. It is a valuable tool for detecting middle-ear fluid and other middle-ear pathology. Measurement of the acoustic reflex can provide information about the functioning of the middle and inner ear as well as the auditory nerve. The acoustic reflex thresholds, viewed in conjunction with the tympanogram and audiogram, can assist in the determination of the type and degree of hearing loss.

OAEs now make it possible to measure responses that are solely the by-product of a healthy cochlea.[111] These echoes of a distorted traveling wave are easily measured clinically from infants and children with normal cochlear and conductive function. Absent or reduced OAEs result from at least moderate conductive or cochlear hearing loss. While not useful for defining degree of hearing loss, OAEs are essential to the differential diagnosis of cochlear and neural dysfunction.[141]

Although it is not appropriate to fit children with amplification when audiometric test data are insufficient, it is equally unacceptable to delay the fitting of amplification while waiting for a child to mature and perhaps become more cooperative for behavioral testing. In the absence of complete audiometric data to quantify the degree, type, and configuration of hearing loss, one can proceed with a hearing aid fitting with a minimum of click and 500-Hz tone ABR thresholds.[3, 60] Amplification can be adjusted as additional audiometric data become available.

General Considerations

The process of selecting and fitting hearing-impaired children with effective amplification depends on a basic knowledge of hearing aid operation, design, and function. Although this chapter does not provide detailed technical information about hearing aid mechanics, the scope of subsequent discussions requires the reader to have a basic understanding of the purpose and function of hearing aids. An understanding of specific hardware advantages and limitations is also necessary in order to make optimal hardware-dependent fitting recommendations.

Devices that are designed to provide a link between the acoustic environment and the person with hearing impairment may conveniently be classified into four types: (1) personalized electroacoustic systems that are wearable, (2) group electroacoustic systems commonly found in classroom settings, (3) systems that use implanted electrodes to stimulate the auditory system directly, and (4) special devices designed to stimulate nonauditory senses. Although all of these instruments are appropriate for children, this chapter discusses primarily the first two categories. The general terms *hearing aid, amplification system,* and *assistive listening device* are used throughout this chapter to denote such devices. Systems that use electrodes to stimulate the auditory system, such as cochlear implants, are not discussed as these devices are addressed in detail in another chapter.

Purpose of Hearing Aids

The fundamental purpose of any amplification system is to assist the communicative ability of persons with hearing impairment. Despite recent advances in microphone design and electronic technology, modern hearing aids cannot restore normal function to an impaired auditory system.[43, 100, 101] Rather, the hearing aid can only assist the communicative process. Therefore, the primary objective in providing children with amplification is not to restore normal auditory function but to select an amplification system that best suits a child's individual auditory needs. The extent to which this goal is realized depends not only on the physical and electroacoustic properties of the hearing aid but on the handicapping effects imposed by the hearing loss. Stated simply, children with the same degree and type of hearing loss frequently present varied patterns of auditory handicap, depending on dissimilarities in the child's age at onset and chronologic age; the age at which language intervention was initiated; the child's mental capacity and emotional adjustment; environmental factors; and numerous other variables. Consequently, the effective use of amplification with children depends on both an appreciation of the physical/electroacoustic properties and an understanding of the relationship between hearing loss and hearing handicap.

Function of Hearing Aids

The main function of all hearing aids is the amplification of environmental sound to improve audibility. In most cases, we are especially concerned with the amplification of speech in an effort to enhance communication. We are also interested in speech understanding in noise. The signal-to-noise ratio (SNR) is the primary factor that affects speech understanding in noise. The SNR quantifies the degree to which the signal of interest is audible above the interfering noise at any given moment. To improve speech intelligibility in noise, the SNR must be improved. Data suggest that hearing-impaired persons require significantly more positive SNRs for equivalent speech recognition performance than listeners with normal hearing.[78, 127] This difficulty may be further exacerbated in children. Specifically, data have shown that children require that speech be received at a more favorable sensation level and SNR for optimal acquisition of speech and language skills than is normally provided to hearing-impaired listeners.[23]

Unfortunately, the input to the hearing aid system consists of environmental sound that may originate from a number of sources. For example, the environmental signal at the input of the hearing aid may consist of a primary message in the form of a speaker's voice and several secondary messages, such as the output from a television set, noise from an air conditioner, and classroom or traffic noise. The acoustic energy from these sources summates to provide a complex input signal to the hearing aid. One difficulty with many hearing aids is that amplification occurs without regard to source, and consequently the aids do not improve the SNR. With the increased use of directional microphones and digital signal processing (DSP), some modern hearing aids can amplify at least somewhat selectively, based on factors such as sound source location and amplitude modulation pattern. Even with these advances, the ability of hearing aids to selectively amplify a speech signal of interest in the presence of background noise that originates from similar direction is quite limited. This difficulty is further exacerbated when the competing noise is of similar frequency and temporal content as the signal of interest. That is, the "noise" is also construed as speech. Regardless of processing, the system must be viewed as changing only the acoustic signal delivered to the user's ear and not as altering the sensitivity of the impaired auditory mechanism. That is, the amplified acoustic signal is always delivered to an impaired system.[100]

Components

The hearing aid is a system composed of mechanical, electric, and acoustic components. Recent advances in microphone and electronic technology have increased the versatility of modern hearing aids. Despite these advances, the basic function of the majority of hearing aids has remained unchanged except for some of the newest digital hearing aids.

Several components are common to any amplification system. These include a microphone, amplifier, power source, volume control, receiver, and coupler. Although it is beyond the scope of this chapter to consider each component in detail, it is important to understand the function of each component and how it interacts with environmental acoustic stimuli.

Figure 107–1 illustrates the basic components of an analog hearing aid. Recall that the input to the hearing aid consists of environmental sound that may originate from any number of sources. This signal is picked up by the hearing aid microphone or telecoils,[91] where it is transformed into an electric analog and is conducted to the amplifier. The electric signal from the microphone is extremely weak; therefore, the amplifier's job is to make the signal more intense by using additional energy derived from the power source, or battery. The amplification process may involve several stages[52]; however, regardless of complexity, the sole purpose of amplification is to make the signal more intense.

A volume control regulates the amount of amplification directed to the receiver. The receiver of the hearing aid in air-conduction systems may be compared to a miniature loudspeaker or, in bone-conduction systems, to a bone vibrator similar to that used with a pure-tone audiometer. The purpose of the receiver is to convert the amplified electric signal into either acoustic energy for air-conduction systems or mechanical energy for bone-conduction systems.[92]

The final component in the hearing aid system is the coupler. The coupler directs the amplified signal transduced by the receiver (output transducer) to the user's ear. Bone-conduction systems use the same mode of coupling that is employed in pure-tone audiometry. That is, the vibrator is placed in contact with the mastoid and the signal is transduced to the user's ear as mechanical vibrations. Theoretically, this mode of transmission essentially bypasses the external and middle ear and stimulates the cochlea directly. In air-conduction systems, the signal is delivered to the user's external auditory canal by the earmold.

The individual components of a hearing aid form a system that amplifies and directs environmental sound by a series of sequential energy transformations. The microphone of the hearing aid system transforms acoustic environmental energy (environmental sound) into mechanical energy represented by the vibration of the microphone's diaphragm. In turn, the mechanical displacement of the diaphragm results in changes in electric resistance in the

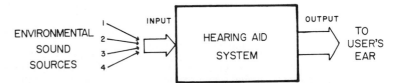

FIGURE 107–1. Block diagram of the common components of an analog hearing aid.

microphone, thus generating electric energy, or voltage. This electric energy is amplified (i.e., voltage is increased) and is used to drive the diaphragm of the receiver. Thus, electric energy is transformed into mechanical energy. Finally, the mechanical energy represented by vibration of the receiver diaphragm either is directed to the mastoid (bone conduction) or is converted into acoustic energy (air conduction) and directed to the user's ear canal.

Amplification Methods

Amplification (gain) in hearing aids can be applied to incoming acoustic signals in either a linear or a nonlinear fashion. In linear amplification systems, a direct relationship is maintained between the signal input and the output. Thus, as the signal input increases, the amplified output increases by an equal amount, and the input/output function reflects a slope of 1.0 over the majority of its operating range (Fig. 107–2). In contrast, nonlinear hearing aids produce an input/output function having a slope other than 1.0 (see Fig. 107–2). That is, nonlinear hearing aids vary gain through amplitude compression (decreasing gain with increasing input intensity levels) or amplitude expansion (decreasing gain with decreasing input intensity levels), or both, so that sound level at the output of the hearing aid remains both audible and comfortable over a broad range of input intensity levels.

Compression is most useful for persons with a reduced dynamic range of hearing compared with those with normal hearing, i.e., a small range between their threshold for hearing and their threshold of discomfort. The dynamic range of hearing is reduced somewhat in nearly all persons with sensorineural hearing loss.[101] Compression can take many forms but generally is categorized by its activation threshold and desired effect. It should be pointed out that all compression hearing aids function as linear devices for sound intensity levels below their specified compression threshold, sometimes called the *kneepoint*. Compression hearing aids with high activation thresholds (often called *compression limiting*) are used to

limit the maximum output level from a hearing aid while providing linear amplification for most speech input levels. In contrast, compression hearing aids with low compression threshold (including wide dynamic range compression) provide nonlinear amplification for most, or sometimes all, speech intensity levels. Wide dynamic range compression is a commonly used type of compression processing in which the compression circuit is active for a broad range of input intensity levels, including those associated with conversational speech. For a more complete discussion of hearing aid compression, the interested reader is referred to the works of Dillon,[43] Kuk,[84] and Plomp.[110]

Some form of compression amplification should be considered the rule rather than the exception in hearing aid selection. The choice of compression parameters depends on the particular needs of the patient, and success with the instrument depends on the success in choosing the appropriate hearing aid characteristics.[43, 77, 158] Nevertheless, in most cases, compression amplification is considered the best way to achieve the primary goals of prescriptive amplification.

In contrast with compression, *expansion*—the other form of nonlinear amplification used in hearing aids—is relatively new. It is currently only available in digital hearing aids and is mainly used to counteract the increased output intensity level of low-intensity microphone noise and annoying environmental sounds that result from certain types of compression.[24]

Signal Processing

Prior to the 1980s, all hearing aids implemented analog signal processing and control over this processing, when available, was relegated to analog potentiometers. Advances in technology have led to hearing aids whose signal processing and control can be generalized into one of three categories: (1) traditional analog, (2) digitally programmable analog, and (3) digital signal processing (DSP). Analog systems provide a constant analysis of the incoming signal and, thereby, constantly modify the input stimulus. Digitally programmable systems use analog processing but, in contrast with the more traditional analog devices, these instruments program the hearing aid response characteristics into digital memory and control the analog circuit digitally.[103, 118]

Programmable hearing aids have at least two potential advantages over their nonprogrammable counterparts for pediatric patients. First, the variety and flexibility of the electroacoustic adjustments available in programmable instruments can be useful, especially when the hearing loss is fluctuating, the hearing loss is of unusual configuration, or—as is often the case in the youngest pediatric patients—precise threshold information is not yet known. Second, access to different signal processing parameters (through multiple user memories) may allow for better aided listening as environmental conditions change.[103] Many programmable systems offer a variety of memories and different channels of signal processing, from which several different hearing aid responses may be selected depending on the listening demands.[145] The use of digitally programmable instruments has grown substantially

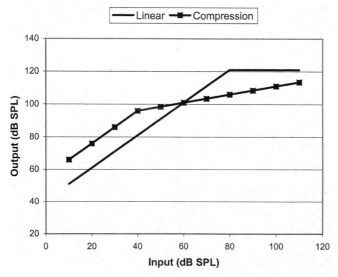

FIGURE 107–2. The input/output function of both linear and nonlinear (compression) amplification schemes.

since their introduction: they accounted for 26.4% of the hearing aid market in 1999.[80] With increased fitting of these devices, cost has declined substantially, making them a viable option for a great many hearing aid candidates, including many in the pediatric population.

The most recent improvements in hearing aid processing technology have centered on DSP. The first two modern digital hearing aids arrived in 1993. Manufacturers quickly embraced this new technology and, as of this writing, there were more than 20 distinct digital devices marketed by 19 different hearing aid companies. DSP differs fundamentally from its analog counterpart in that the incoming acoustic signal is converted to a string of digits so that a DSP scheme (complex mathematical algorithm) can be applied.[130] Figure 107–3 schematically illustrates the processing of a digital hearing aid. As shown in this figure, signal-processing parameters such as gain and compression filtering are arrived at through the application of a mathematical algorithm to a string of numbers. Most current digital hearing aids share the advantages of many of the digitally programmable systems over their traditional analog counterparts. Specifically, the majority of digital hearing aids also incorporate multiple user memories and a flexible frequency response. In fact, the use of digital filters with extremely steep filter slopes affords digital hearing aids a flexibility of frequency response that is unmatched, even among digitally programmable hearing aids.

In addition to these advantages, digital hearing aids also have a few other potential advantages for the pediatric hearing-impaired population over their analog counterparts. As a result of the introduction of DSP in hearing aids, there is currently extensive growth in the number of new sound processing schemes aimed at improved speech recognition, sound quality, and comfort in these devices. For example, DSP has allowed for the application of increasingly complex methods of intensity level specific gain control including the first use of amplitude expansion in hearing aids.[24] Digital hearing aids perform complex signal processing by applying increasingly complex mathematical formulas, rather than requiring the additional physical components necessary in analog systems. Consequently, complex signal processing can be introduced

without the additional circuit noise associated with a greater number of physical components.

Digital noise reduction, spectral enhancement, and digital feedback control have also been implemented into digital hearing aids. Digital noise reduction schemes decrease gain in frequency ranges in which steady state (non-fluctuating) noise signals are detected. These schemes have the potential to reduce listener fatigue in noisy environments by reducing the intensity of sounds when steady state noise is present. In addition, these systems have the potential of improving sound quality and the intensity of the signal of interest relative to the overall intensity of steady-state, band-limited noise.

Spectral enhancement schemes attempt to selectively increase the output intensity for certain segments of speech information based on their spectral or temporal properties, or both. It is assumed that selectively provided small boosts to the gain for low-intensity segments of speech may improve sound quality and potentially speech understanding in noise. Research supporting these methods is scant, although some data show small but consistent improvements in speech intelligibility for certain methods of spectral enhancement.[53]

Children younger than 9 months spend a great majority of their time held against their caregiver's body or lying down. Because of the close proximity of the infant's head to surrounding objects, they are susceptible to problems with acoustic feedback when wearing hearing aids. That is, amplified sound leaves the ear canal through the earmold venting and bounces off nearby objects, such as the caregiver's body or the child's blanket. This previously amplified sound may then again enter the hearing aid microphone, after which it is re-amplified, resulting in a feedback loop.

Slightly older children are also more susceptible to feedback problems than adults, partly because of changes in earmold fit resulting from the changes in ear size and geometry associated with normal growth. Data reveal that ear canal resonance frequency is higher in newborns than in adults, reaching adult values by the second year of life.[83]

One way to limit feedback is to simply reduce gain below the level at which feedback occurs. One potential problem with this method is that it may result in insufficient gain for audibility. This can have an especially negative impact on young children attempting to learn speech and language. Recent advances in digital hearing aids have allowed for the introduction of adaptive feedback reduction (AFR) methods, which have the potential to dynamically reduce feedback that is environmentally specific. AFR methods operate in one of two ways: (1) frequency-specific gain reduction or (2) notch filtering of the frequencies over which feedback is detected. While feedback can be an important cue that warns caregivers of earmolds that are poorly fitting or not properly inserted, the reduction of some environmentally specific feedback through acoustic means may improve a young child's experience with hearing aids. Continued feedback has the potential to distort or mask sounds of interest, such as speech, and may cause a child to reduce the use of or, in extreme cases, outrightly reject amplification.[11] Consequently, the reduction of environmentally specific feed-

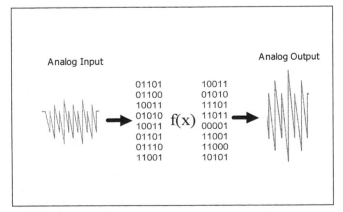

FIGURE 107–3. Schematic diagram of the processing performed by a digital hearing aid. The mathematical processing algorithm used by this system is denoted by the function f(x).

back in children may increase comfort and acceptance of amplification, as well as increase speech reception during situations in which feedback would otherwise be present. Both AFR methods can reduce environmentally specific feedback. However, there are few or no data that support the effectiveness of AFR methods in adults or children.

While still relatively expensive, digital hearing aids could easily rival their analogue counterparts in price if enough of them were dispensed. Accounting for only 13% of the total hearing aids dispensed in 1999, digital devices still constituted a rapidly growing subset.[80] Given the increased flexibility provided by digital hearing aids, they will almost certainly dominate hearing sales in the relatively near future, perhaps completely replacing analog instruments.

Microphone Type

Unfortunately, even the most complex DSP schemes implemented in hearing aids are not very selective for speech, generally amplifying all environmental sounds within specific frequency ranges. Consequently, while many hearing aids can increase the audibility of speech sounds, persons with hearing impairment continue to have particular difficulty with background noise, especially if this "noise" is the speech of other talkers.[109] Data suggest that of persons who own hearing aids but do not wear them, 25% cite poor performance in background noise as the reason for hearing aid rejection.[80]

A large number of hearing aids use omnidirectional microphones. In general, omnidirectional hearing aids do not improve SNR compared with the unaided ear, and SNR is sometimes made worse by amplification.[113] Directional microphone hearing aids incorporate multiple microphones (or microphone ports) to allow for improved SNR based on the spatial location of the signal of interest (front hemisphere) relative to unwanted signals (usually in the rear hemisphere). This can be contrasted with an omnidirectional hearing aid, which shows similar sensitivity to sound arriving from all angles. The improvement in SNR conferred by directional hearing aid fittings can lead to improved speech intelligibility in noisy environments. To date, directional microphones remain one of the only consistently effective tools for improving SNR across a broad range of noisy environments for the hearing aid wearer.[113]

Directional hearing aids take advantage of timing differences between sounds arriving at the front and rear microphone ports.[113] Since these timing differences are crucial for proper operation of a directional microphone, the directional SNR advantage is present only when there is spatial separation between the signal of interest and the competing noise. Any factor that decreases the amount of spatial separation reduces the directional effect. Consequently, the effectiveness of these instruments is reduced with increased levels of reflected (as opposed to direct) sound energy, as occurs in reverberant environments and environments in which the signal of interest is far away.[65, 114, 116] Thus, appropriate classroom acoustics and preferential seating (discussed later in this chapter) remain im-

portant whether or not the child with hearing loss uses directional or omnidirectional amplification.

While a variety of factors affect the performance of directional hearing aids,[104, 115–117] these instruments have been shown to improve speech intelligibility in noise for both adults[79, 116] and children[59] across a number of simulated and real-world listening environments. The SNR improvement provided by the current generation of directional hearing aids ranges from approximately 3 to 5 dB in average real-world environments and can approach 7 to 8 dB in some listening situations.[113] This improved SNR can translate into substantial improvement in speech recognition, particularly when combined with a binaural hearing aid arrangement. Published reports of improved speech intelligibility in noise and improved technology that allows directional microphones to be used in increasingly smaller hearing aid styles have significantly expanded the use of directional microphones in hearing aids in recent years.

While directional microphone hearing aids are recommended for older children, their use with very young children, especially infants, is questionable. Specifically, infants are thought to require acoustic input from all directions since they often cannot or do not orient their heads to face the important sound sources. Consequently, in some listening environments, a directional microphone may act to decrease the intensity of a talker behind infants relative to an unwanted noise in front of them.

The use of more than two microphones for input into hearing aids and other devices such as cochlear implants has also increased.[29, 125] Microphone arrays, sometimes called *beamformers*, use multiple microphones for improved performance in noise over standard directional microphones. Although microphone arrays show significantly more SNR benefit than traditional directional microphones, they are primarily advocated for severe to profound hearing loss because of a few disadvantages. One relates to cosmetics. The use of multiple microphones, each separated in space, results in devices that are usually at least 3 to 4 inches in length. Thus, microphone arrays cannot be used in ear-level devices. Instead, the array is usually fixed to eyeglasses or worn around the neck. This introduces a second problem related to coupling the array to the hearing aid.

Electroacoustic Characteristics

Changes in the spectral characteristics of sound that occur through hearing aid transformation are governed by the electroacoustic properties of the hearing aid circuit—that is, the microphone, amplifier, receiver, and coupler (see Fig. 107–1). The electroacoustic properties of a hearing aid reflect the difference between the spectrum of the signal introduced at the input to the hearing aid microphone (e.g., speech) and the spectrum of that delivered at the output of the amplification system. Of course, knowledge of the electroacoustic properties of any amplification system is critical to the selection of a hearing aid or frequency-modulation (FM) system that is appropriate for compensating a specific hearing loss; such knowledge is also critical to manufacturer's quality control.

In an effort to ensure manufacturer uniformity and the quality of similar hearing aid models, and to permit accurate and comparable measures across clinics and laboratories, the American National Standards Institute (ANSI) has developed specific guidelines on how the physical properties of a hearing aid should be measured and expressed.[2]

To comply with the ANSI standard, every hearing aid manufacturer must measure the output of the hearing aid in a specially constructed anechoic test chamber (hearing aid test box) or room with the hearing aid connected to a device called a 2-cm³ coupler. The 2-cm³ coupler is a ridged walled metal device having a cavity volume (2 mL) thought to represent that of an average adult occluded ear canal. There are two primary types of 2-cm³ couplers: the *HA-2 coupler* is used principally with behind-the-ear (BTE) hearing aids connected by a standard length of polyethylene tubing; the other, the *HA-1 coupler*, connects to the shell of a custom hearing aid or to the button receiver of a body-worn device. Standard electroacoustic measurements are obtained by delivering a known and uniform series of acoustic signals to the inlet port of the hearing aid microphone and measuring the sound-pressure output developed within the 2-cm³ coupler. Hence, the ANSI standard allows coupler-derived hearing aid performance data recorded by one manufacturer or clinical facility to be either the same as or within permissible tolerance limits of those obtained at a different test site or with a similar model of a particular hearing aid.

The most recent standard, updated in 1996, added methods for measuring gain in compression instruments, tests for induction coil sensitivity, equivalent input noise tests, and changes in some terminology.[2] The three most important characteristics associated with the ANSI standard continue to be gain, output sound pressure level for a 90-dB input (OSPL90), and frequency response.

Gain

Perhaps the most fundamental characteristic of the hearing aid is the frequency response, or *gain curve*. *Gain* simply refers to the difference between the decibel sound pressure level (dB SPL) of the input signal and that of the output signal measured at the same frequency. For example, an input sinusoid of 60 dB SPL at 1000 Hz with an output of 90 dB SPL developed in a 2-cm³ coupler represents a gain of 30 dB (90 − 60 = 30 dB). Like the human ear, however, hearing aids are differentially sensitive across frequency. That is, the gain at some frequencies is greater than that at others, depending on the mechanical, electric, and acoustic properties of the system.

The relationship of gain to frequency is called the *frequency response* (Fig. 107–4) and reflects the coupler gain at various frequencies within the spectral range of amplification. According to ANSI S3.22-1996,[2] acoustic gain is commonly reported as the high frequency average across 1000, 1600, and 2500 Hz in response to an input of fixed intensity level (usually 50 or 60 dB SPL). ANSI S3.22-1996 also dictates that gain measurements be made with the volume control of the hearing aid adjusted to a reference test gain position. Reference test gain describes the amount of amplification obtained when the volume control is adjusted such that the average gain at 1000, 1600, and 2500 Hz is 17 dB below the maximum hearing aid output (OSPL90) or full-on gain if the hearing aid has mild gain. Another gain measurement is called *use gain*

FIGURE 107–4. Frequency response (gain as a function of frequency) of a hearing aid system and an example of average gain computation.

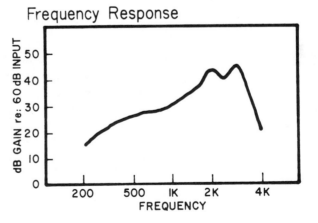

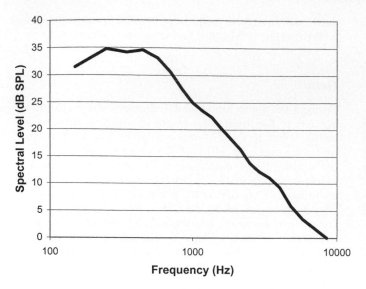

FIGURE 107–5. Example of a long-term average speech spectrum produced with normal vocal effort. (Adapted from American National Standards Institute. Methods for calculation of the speech intelligibility index. ANSI S3.5. New York, Acoustical Society of America, 1997.)

or *as-worn gain*. In this instance, the gain is measured with the volume control adjusted to its normal use position. This output gives a more realistic indication of the amount of gain the aid provides for the patient.

Maximum Hearing Aid Output

The maximum output intensity of a hearing aid in a 2-cm^3 coupler is called the *output sound pressure level for a 90 dB SPL input (OSPL90)*. Unlike with the test of acoustic gain, the volume control is set to the full-on position. This volume control setting, combined with the high input intensity level, is designed to saturate the hearing aid amplifier, thus producing the maximum possible output. The OSPL90 data, like acoustic gain, can be plotted as a curve across test frequency (Fig. 107–5) or can be specified as a high-frequency average value calculated at the frequencies 1000, 1600, and 2500 Hz.

Frequency Response

The frequency response of a hearing aid describes the gain of a hearing aid across a range of frequencies. The range of frequencies for which a hearing aid offers amplification is limited. The aid's frequency response is determined by measuring its reference test gain. From that average, 20 dB is subtracted and a line is drawn parallel to the abscissa until it intersects the low-frequency end of the curve and the high-frequency end. These two cut-off points then represent the aid's frequency response.

Hearing Aid Distortion

In addition to frequency response and OSPL90, ANSI S3.22-1996 requires a determination of harmonic distortion. Harmonic distortion refers to the introduction of signals at the output stage of the amplifier that are integer multiples of the input frequency.

For example, if a 60 dB SPL tone at 800 Hz is introduced to the hearing aid microphone and the output contains not only a strong signal at 800 Hz but weaker

ones at the harmonic frequencies (e.g., 1600, 2400, 3200 Hz), this hearing aid might be malfunctioning. The sound pressure of these harmonics is expressed as a percentage of the output measured at the fundamental input frequency. The lower the intensity of the harmonic relative to the fundamental, the lower the distortion. As with all other measures, ANSI S3.22-1996 provides tolerance limits for hearing aid distortion.[2]

Hearing Aid Selection

Before the adequacy of a hearing aid can be evaluated, and before its actual fitting and final adjustment stages, the audiologist must make a series of key clinical decisions that significantly affect the ultimate success of hearing aid use. Undoubtedly, the primary goal is to match the acoustic and electroacoustic features of the amplification system to the auditory needs of the child. While some hearing aid selection issues related to DSP, the use of compression, and microphone selection have already been discussed, a number of other factors also need to be considered.

Hardware Considerations

In general, depending on how they transduce amplified sound to the user's ear, hearing aids are divided into two distinct classes: air-conduction and bone-conduction devices. Air-conduction instruments constitute by far the greatest number of hearing aid fittings today. These two types of instruments are available in a number of styles, the advantages and disadvantages of which are listed in Table 107–1. Regardless of style, most hearing aids of the same type contain similar, and sometimes identical, internal components.

Hearing Aid Styles

Before the late 1970s, most children were fitted with body-worn hearing aids. The advent of electronic miniaturization and technical advances in earmold and hearing

TABLE 107–1. Advantages, Disadvantages, and Indications for Various Hearing Aid Styles

Type of Hearing Aid	Degree of Hearing Impairment	Advantages	Disadvantages
Body aid	Mild, moderate, severe, profound	Able to reach profound hearing loss because of high level of output. Gain, power output, and frequency response are adjustable. Separation of microphone and receiver reduces feedback problems in severe hearing loss. Volume controls and on/off switches are easier to handle for those with dexterity problems or for bedridden patients.	Not very cosmetically appealing. When worn under clothing, noise is introduced from clothes rubbing against microphone. Increases body baffle. Cords break easily.
Behind the ear (BTE)	Mild, moderate, severe, profound	Range of power sufficient to reach severe and profound hearing loss. More cosmetically appealing. Allows adequate space to accommodate gain, output, and frequency-response controls for adjustment by dispenser. Location of microphone at pinna improves localization of sound source when head is moved. Reduces body baffle. Eliminates noise produced by clothing rubbing against microphone and problems with cords. Allows for the use of a directional microphone.	In severe or profound hearing loss, earmold must fit snugly in ear canal to eliminate feedback problems. May be slightly more difficult to place on ear in cases of manual dexterity problems. For those with small pinnae, particularly small children and infants, accessory devices may be needed to hold the device in place. However, custom instruments are inappropriate for small children and infants because of frequent changes in ear size and geometry.
In the ear (ITE)	Mild, moderate, moderately severe	More cosmetically appealing. Placement of microphone takes advantage of pinna and concha effects, enhancing amplification in the high frequencies. Microphone placement improves sound-source localization as head is moved. May be easier to insert because only one component is involved. Allows for the use of a directional microphone.	Because of close proximity of microphone and receiver, amount of real-ear gain may be limited because of feedback problems, especially in cases of high-frequency hearing loss. Concerns with safety and frequent recasing precludes the recommendation of these devices for small children and infants.
Completely in the canal (CIC)	Mild to moderate	Most cosmetically appealing because it fits entirely in ear canal. Microphone placement takes full advantage of pinna and concha effects, boosting gain in high frequencies. Microphone placement improves localization of sound source as head is moved. Deep insertion reduces problems with the occlusion effect and further increases high-frequency gain.	Amount of gain is sufficient for no more than mild or moderate hearing loss. Because of the small size and small battery, the device may be difficult to handle for persons with manual dexterity problems. Venting options are very limited. Seems to be most fragile of available aid types. Deep placement precludes use of directional microphone. Deep tight fit requires precision and is not possible on all patients because of ear geometry.
Bone-conduction aid	Mild to moderate conductive hearing loss	Provides alternative form of amplification for those with conductive hearing losses that would preclude use of air-conduction hearing aid (e.g., chronic middle-ear drainage, atresia).	Bone conduction requires more energy to drive the cochlea than air conduction. Frequency response is poorer than with air-conduction hearing aids. High-frequency gain is reduced; bone-conduction sensitivity should not be more than mildly impaired for maximum benefit to be achieved.

aid design allowed ear-level hearing aids to achieve equivalent acoustic power. The advantages of the BTE instrument are numerous. Clearly, the elimination of clothing noise, connecting cords or wires (which are easily broken), heavy conspicuous casings, and shoulder or pocket harnesses greatly enhanced appearance and obviated other non-acoustic annoyances associated with body-worn hearing aids. Acoustically, ear-level hearing aids (1) improve sound localization because the microphones are situated close to the ear, (2) eliminate the body baffle effect, which results in a 2- to 6-dB increase of low-frequency (200- to 600-Hz) gain and a 15-dB decrease in high-frequency (1000- to 2500-Hz) gain that is important to consonant recognition, and (3) enable binaural squelch (when worn binaurally). *Binaural squelch,* or free-field binaural release from masking, is the ability to hear better in noisy situations when signals are received binaurally as opposed to monaurally.[10] This phenomenon results from phase differences between the primary signal and the background noise that arrive at the two ears and leads to a small (1- to 3-dB) but significant improvement in effective SNR.

BTE hearing aids are now the most common hearing aid style for young children. Custom hearing aid styles such as the in-the-ear, in-the-canal, and completely-in-the-canal styles, which constituted 80% of total hearing aid sales in 1999,[80] are generally not recommended for infants or young children. One primary reason relates to the cost, inconvenience, and effort associated with repeated refabrication of the hearing aid shell to ensure a proper fit throughout the changes in ear size and geometry that accompany maturational development.[11] A second reason is that it is sometimes difficult to achieve adequate gain with a custom instrument, especially for more severe to profound hearing losses, given the size of an infant's ear. The lack of adequate gain for more severe losses relates both to the physical size constraints placed on the instrument when fitted to a small ear and to the reduced gain before feedback given the close proximity of the microphone and receiver. The use of custom hearing aids in infants and small children also raises safety questions. Custom hearing aids are made of a hard acrylic material, whereas the earmolds of BTE instruments fitted to children are nearly always made of a pliable material. Because of the fragmentary nature of acrylic shells, there is some concern about potential damage to surrounding tissue in the case of shell breakage resulting from a fall or blow to the head. Safety concerns also revolve around the choking and swallowing hazards posed by some small custom instruments for small children and infants.

For older children with mild hearing loss, the use of custom hearing aids can be explored since the location of the input microphone has been shown to improve sound localization and to enhance acoustic gain in the mid to high frequencies. However, concerns about the safety of these devices in an active child's ear remain.[11]

For some people, the use of hearing aids that deliver sound through air conduction is precluded by medical conditions. For example, a hearing aid or earmold placed in the ear may exacerbate an existing ear problem or result in the recurrence of a pathologic condition. Under such circumstances, users must consider an alternative device such as a bone-conduction aid. Bone-conduction systems are used primarily with children who have auricular agenesis, atresia, microtia, or other pathologic conditions that may be exacerbated by using conventional air-conduction type instruments. A bone-conduction receiver is placed on the mastoid and held in position by a headband. A small wire connects the bone oscillator to a BTE hearing aid. With a bone-conduction device, the cochlea is stimulated in the same way as it is during bone-conduction threshold assessments. Bone-conduction instruments present several disadvantages. The first is that they require more energy to stimulate the inner ear and, consequently, are recommended for persons with good cochlear reserve (mild to moderate sensory impairment). A second disadvantage is that traditional BTE instruments provide a better frequency response compared with bone-conduction systems. Other disadvantages include the lack of cosmetic appeal of bone-conduction instruments and frequent complaints of discomfort, a result of the constant pressure applied to the mastoid.

Implantable Hearing Aids

Because of problems with cosmetics, retention, and some physical contraindications for traditional bone-conduction hearing aids, implantable hearing aids have been offered as a viable alternative. In recent years, two different types of surgically implantable hearing aids have been developed: bone-anchored hearing aids (BAHA) and middle-ear implants (MEIs). Huttenbrink[69] described implantable hearing aids as a "technically attractive and clinically promising challenge." However, because of concerns over the mechanical complexity of biotechnical interfaces in the middle ear and technical problems, Huttenbrink urges caution during candidate selection. BAHA devices, like bone-conduction hearing aids, have been developed for persons in whom the specific type of conductive hearing impairment limits the benefit received from air-conduction devices. The Entific Medical Systems BAHA received FDA approval for implantation in adults aged 18 years and older in January 1997, and this device remains the only FDA-approved BAHA still available. In this percutaneous device, the hearing aid transducer is coupled to a titanium screw located in the upper mastoid region of the temporal bone via a titanium abutment screw that protrudes through the skin. Several studies have found the head-worn BAHA to be effective in patients with bone-conduction pure-tone averages (500, 1000, 3000 Hz) up to 45 dB HL.[105, 144, 153] A newer body-worn device is proposed to provide appropriate amplification for those with conductive hearing loss up to 70 dB SPL.[106, 144, 153] Both the body-worn and ear-level units include direct auditory input, a three-position tone switch, and a telecoil. A second implantable bone-conduction system (Xomed Audiant Bone Conductor) has been withdrawn from the market because of power and retention problems associated with a transcutaneous system.

MEIs were also originally developed for those with conductive impairment but have more recently been fitted to persons with pure sensorineural hearing loss.[143, 155] The use of MEIs for listeners with sensorineural hearing loss in lieu of conventional amplification stems from the elimination of feedback and the occlusion effect in listeners fitted with these devices. Because they are implantable, MEIs offer obvious cosmetic appeal (though at the cost of surgery). A final potential benefit of an MEI over conventional amplification is convenience (at least after surgery) related to insertion and removal and to changing batteries. The batteries in current fully implantable MEIs can last as long as 5 years. In addition, some of these devices allow the battery to be easily recharged (rather than requiring surgery for a battery change).

Current MEIs use either piezoelectric (a crystal that bends in response to electrical charge) or electromagnetic principles to drive an output transducer mounted on the ossicular chain. Since the ossicular chain, rather than the mastoid bone, is being vibrated, MEIs require significantly less vibrational and electric power than traditional bone-conduction hearing aids and BAHAs. Maximum output limits are approximately 110 dB SPL for the piezoelectric devices and 140 dB SPL for the electromagnetic devices. This difference is the result of the impedance of the electromagnetic implant being approximately one fifth that of the piezoelectric crystal. Because piezoelectric crystals are so small, some of these devices are entirely implanted,[154] whereas only the output transducer is implanted in the current generation of electromagnetic devices. As of this writing, two MEI devices have received phase I FDA approval (Otologics LLC Implantable Middle Ear Transducer and the SoundTec Directdrive Hearing System), while the Symphonix Vibrant Sound Bridge has received FDA approval.

Binaural Versus Monaural Amplification

Psychoacoustic research generally provides strong support for the value of binaural amplification, unless specifically contraindicated. It is now widely accepted that binaural hearing aids provide a clear advantage over their monaural counterparts relative to such factors as sound localization,[46, 140] binaural summation,[28] and listening in noise.[70] In fact, some commercial digital hearing aids now implement processing that was developed to further enhance the binaural advantage found when listening in noise.[82]

It is well recognized that binaural hearing aids provide a 3-dB improvement in pure-tone threshold, potentially improving audibility for signals near threshold. Although 3 dB appears to be of minimal magnitude, it actually translates into a 10% to 15% improvement in speech recognition. While binaural summation at threshold provides a 3-dB advantage, suprathreshold loudness summation is greater (up to 5 dB), allowing for a lower overall use gain.[45] Thus, the volume adjustment setting can be lowered without consequence, resulting in some reduction in acoustic feedback problems often associated with high-gain hearing aids. These lower gain levels also reduce the risk of hearing aid–induced hearing loss.

Perhaps the most important reason to employ binaural hearing aids as the rule rather than the exception is the impact on head shadow.[65, 117] With monaural hearing aids, the head shadow effect results in up to a 14-dB attenuation of speech and environmental sounds arriving at the hearing aid microphone. The head shadow effect refers to the attenuation of sound by the physical presence of the head on the side is of the sound's origination. Because this phenomenon has its greatest effect above 1500 Hz, the frequency region most critical to consonant recognition, there is an obvious loss of important speech energy when the message originates at the unaided ear of the child and must cross over the head to be amplified by the hearing aid. Binaural hearing aids, on the other hand, eliminate the negative consequence of head shadow because an aided ear is always near the primary sound source.

In addition to the demonstrated psychoacoustic advantages of binaural amplification, several studies also have reported perceived subjective preference for binaural rather than monaural amplified listening.[47, 126] Some of the positive features of binaural hearing aids reported by hearing aid users who alternated between monaural and binaural amplification included (1) improved speech clarity, (2) more balanced hearing, (3) better overall hearing, (4) improved speech clarity in noise, (5) improved sound localization skills, and (6) more natural and less stressful listening.

In any discussion of the potential benefits of binaural amplification, a central issue is the concept of auditory deprivation as described by Silman and colleagues.[138] These authors retrospectively compared word recognition scores in a group of male veterans, some of whom wore monaural and some binaural amplification. The results showed that despite having symmetrical word recognition before the hearing aid fitting, veterans wearing monaural amplification showed a significant decline in word recognition in the unaided ear compared with the aided ear, while a similar decline was absent in veterans wearing binaural amplification. Similar findings are reported for both adults[55, 67] and children.[56, 63, 68] These findings in children are not surprising, considering they have not had the benefit of complete language development or significant exposure to speech, music, and environmental sounds.

According to contemporary evidence, therefore, as well as the recognized need for maximizing auditory stimulation to help foster speech and language development, children with bilateral sensorineural hearing loss should be fitted with binaural hearing aids. Moreover, hearing loss asymmetry should not be considered a limiting factor with regard to binaural amplification. In fact, some research findings reveal that hearing aid wearers may learn to partially compensate for hearing asymmetry.[140] However, in cases of asymmetry, care should be taken to select amplification systems that compensate for the unique deficits of the two distinct auditory systems. This might be in the form of two instruments from different manufacturers or two similar models having electroacoustic characteristics that have been shaped to meet the auditory needs of each impaired ear individually.

Earmold Considerations

The hearing aid earmold is an integral component of any amplification system. The specific choice of earmold style is based on the degree and audiometric contour of the hearing loss, the type and arrangement of hearing aid(s) to be fitted, and other factors such as external-ear anatomy or allergic sensitivity to earmold material. Most professionals who fit hearing aids in children tend to prefer soft hypoallergenic earmolds, which permit a tighter acoustic seal and reduce the possibility of abrasion or injury if the child falls or is struck on the side of the head.

Among the more common pediatric hearing aid problems is acoustic feedback secondary to an improperly fitted earmold (i.e., a poor acoustic seal). As noted previously, changes in the earmold fit normally occur as children grow and age, resulting in concomitant changes in ear size and geometry. Because the child bothered by feedback usually reduces the volume control to eliminate the annoyance of the squeal, the earmold must be examined regularly not only by the parent but also by others involved, including the educator, the pediatrician, and the otolaryngologist. If the earmold is not providing an adequate acoustic seal or is uncomfortable to wear for long periods, or if the condition of the tubing or earmold bore are such that they may be causing the feedback problem, immediate replacement is mandatory. Again, control of feedback by reducing the volume wheel results in suboptimal amplification and may cause the child to use gain levels inadequate for making speech audible.

Modifications to the Hearing Aid Coupling System

Not too long ago, multiple chapters of hearing aid textbooks were sometimes dedicated to hearing aid coupling system modifications that could change acoustic output. This attention to the impact of coupling systems on the acoustic signal resulted from two factors. First, through combinations of changes in venting, shell configuration, earmold tubing, and other physical factors, it is possible to significantly change the frequency response of a hearing aid. Second, hearing aids were fairly limited in terms of frequency response parameters, often resulting in a need for creative modifications to the hearing aid coupling system to obtain the desired frequency response. Although the first factor is still true, the flexibility of modern digitally programmable and true digital hearing aids has greatly improved frequency response. At least two physical modifications affecting acoustic output are still routinely performed by clinicians, however: the use of vents of various sizes and the use of acoustic damping.

Venting

Venting an earmold can be achieved by drilling a hole at the tip of the earmold to create a parallel channel with the main sound bore (parallel vent) or, much less commonly, by drilling at a point inferior and medial to the tip so that it intersects the main sound bore (diagonal vent). In addition to this choice of earmold configuration, the size of the vent can vary considerably in its diameter and length. The combined effects of these variables can alter the acoustic output of the hearing aid significantly, especially in the low frequencies.[148, 149] Generally, increasingly

larger vents result in increasingly more reduction in low-frequency gain. In addition to affecting the frequency response, venting is often used to help alleviate the negative acoustic effects of fully occluding the ear canal. Small vents, on the order of 0.6 mm in diameter, can also provide some relief from the sensation of increased pressure between the tympanic membrane and the tip of the earmold created by a fully occluding earmold. However, these vents have essentially no effect on low-frequency gain.

The most extreme example of acoustic venting is that of an open, or non-occluding, earmold, which is often used to couple a monaural hearing aid to the ear of a patient whose hearing loss is limited to the frequencies above 1500 Hz (ipsilateral routing of signals) or to deliver sound to the aidable ear that is opposite the side of the hearing aid microphone (i.e., contralateral routing of signals). While maximum gain is limited in the ipsilateral configuration, open earmolds have the advantage of providing a direct path for the normal unamplified low-frequency sounds to enter the ear canal while simultaneously delivering amplified high frequencies.

Acoustic Damping

One electroacoustic feature common to almost all hearing aids is the presence of primary and secondary resonance peaks in the output spectrum. While the frequency of these peaks varies with the amplifier/receiver combination used, they can affect the fidelity of amplified sound, potentially creating a more unnatural listening situation. Acoustic dampers or resistors often are added to the transmission line of the hearing aid and smooth these unwanted peaks, which are the by-product of the receiver earmold system. The effects of these damping elements are governed by the value of acoustic resistance (the higher the ohm value, the greater the peak attenuation), the number of dampers used, and their location. Most manufacturers currently offer earhooks already equipped with resistive devices of varying ohm values, depending on the amplification needs of the patient.

Defining Optimal Processing Parameters

The primary purpose of a hearing aid is to provide the child with sufficient acoustic cues from which to maximize speech reception and providing an optimal listening environment for accurate speech perception and recognition. Complete discrete-frequency audiologic data are sometimes limited in infants or difficult to procure in children; therefore, the hearing aid must be flexible in terms of gain, frequency response, maximum output, and other processing characteristics. The goal of amplification is to permit the perception of as many of the phonemic elements of speech as possible and to amplify them within the most comfortable listening range of the child. The importance of selecting a hearing aid with an appropriate gain and frequency-response range for a given hearing loss configuration can be understood best by relating it to the acoustics of speech.

The overall intensity of speech originating at a distance

of 1 m from the speaker's lips is approximately 62 to 70 dB SPL. With each doubling of distance between the sound source and the receiver's ear, the SPL of speech decreases by about 6 dB. The sounds of speech contain acoustic energy between about 100 and 8000 Hz. This frequency range is determined by measuring the long-term average speech spectrum, as shown in Figure 107–5. As illustrated, most of the acoustic energy is below 1000 Hz, with its greatest point at around 500 Hz. Vowels are distributed in the frequency region below 1000 Hz; therefore, they tend to carry more acoustic intensity than the consonants. However, it is these high-frequency speech components that are critical to speech intelligibility. Clearly, the relationship in power among the various frequency components of speech is highly important in providing a shaped frequency response that maximizes speech reception.

Prescriptive Formulas

During the mid-1970s, three events fundamentally changed the way audiologists fitted hearing aids. These events were (1) a growing disenchantment with speech intelligibility measures for comparative hearing aid fittings due to concerns about reliability and time constraints, (2) an increase in the fitting of custom hearing instruments that required preselection of acoustic parameters, and, perhaps most importantly, (3) the publication of research related to prescriptive hearing aid fitting methods.[15, 27] In general, these prescriptive formulas were purported to assist the hearing aid fitter in placing the long-term average speech spectrum at or near the patient's most comfortable level. It is also assumed that these methods generally result in speech that is within the range of audibility between threshold and threshold of discomfort (uncomfortable level of listening). Also common among the majority of these traditional prescriptive hearing aid strategies are the provisions of a smooth frequency response, the extension of high-frequency gain above 3000 Hz, and the attenuation of low-frequency amplification. The majority of traditional hearing aid fitting procedures that are still in widespread use are threshold-based.

The National Acoustic Laboratories (NAL) method was based on the principle that most patients with hearing loss preferred to set the volume controls of their hearing aids to a point where gain equals approximately 50% of their hearing threshold level.[26, 93, 109] Byrne and Tonnison[27] then adjusted the gain requirements accordingly such that the various frequency components of speech would be delivered with approximately equal loudness when the volume control of binaural hearing aids with occluding earmolds was set to the patient's preferred listening level. After 10 years of intensive research and clinical hearing aid fittings using this prescriptive approach, Byrne and Dillon revised this procedure to account for differences in audiometric slope.[25] In recent years, the revised NAL procedure (NAL-R) has become the most popular prescriptive fitting procedure in the United States.

Another popular prescriptive approach is the prescription of gain and output (or *POGO*).[94, 129] Like the NAL procedure, the POGO definition of insertion gain was also initially based on the ½ gain rule—that is, optimal insertion gain is equal to one half the hearing loss at frequencies of 1000 Hz and above, with gain reduction at 250 and 500 Hz to compensate for the differences in loudness of low-frequency speech components. However, based on their research findings, Schwartz et al[129] argued that the ½ gain rule advocated by the majority of prescriptive gain formulas simply was inadequate once the hearing loss exceeded 65 dB at any or all pure-tone test frequencies. For such cases, these authors stated that when the hearing loss exceeds 65 dB, the following gain formula should be applied:

$$\text{Gain} = \tfrac{1}{2}\ \text{hearing loss} + \tfrac{1}{2}\ (\text{hearing loss} - 65)$$

Despite the many hearing aid selection schemes advocated in recent decades, most prescriptive formats have been applied to adults and only a few investigators have examined methods for defining appropriate gain and output for children with sensorineural hearing loss.[128, 133, 134] Currently, the most popular and researched prescriptive method designed for children is the Desired Sensation Level version 4.1 (DSL v 4.1).[30, 136] In developing this method, Seewald and associates[133] developed estimates of the desired sensation levels (DSLs) of amplified speech as a function of degree of sensitivity loss (Fig. 107–6). The DSL procedure is used to calculate the level above threshold that amplified speech should be. As noted in Figure 107–6, the DSL of amplified speech decreases nonlinearly as hearing loss increases. Also, slightly greater emphasis is given to the frequency region between 1500 and 3000 Hz and somewhat less at 500 Hz so as to capitalize on the importance of high-frequency speech sounds for intelligibility and to de-emphasize the lows as a control against upward masking spread. Like the prescriptive schemes developed for adults, the DSL approach[136] focuses on specifying the hearing aid electroacoustic parameters thought to be appropriate for the child's auditory needs, selecting a hearing aid system that best approximates those specifications, and verifying the

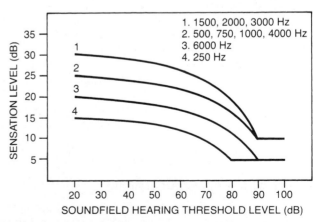

FIGURE 107–6. Desired sensation levels (dB) as a function of hearing threshold level (dB HL) and frequency region. (From Seewald R, Ross M, Spiro M. Selecting amplification characteristics for young hearing impaired children. Ear Hear 6:48, 1985. © Williams and Wilkins, 1985.)

response via real-ear measurements to ensure audibility of the long-term average speech spectrum. Once again, the importance of audibility of speech for development of speech and language skills is well known. In addition, data have shown that young children require higher speech presentation levels than adults for equivalent speech recognition performance.[107] Consequently, the importance of appropriate amplification levels for young children learning language cannot be overemphasized.

With the increased use of nonlinear gain (compression and expansion) in hearing aids, procedures designed to fit a range of amplified speech levels into the residual dynamic range of hearing have been developed.[30, 32, 44, 57, 89] Among the more popular nonlinear fitting methods are nonlinear revisions of existing traditional linear fitting procedures, including the DSL v 4.1 and NAL Nonlinear version 1, as well as other new procedures (e.g., Fig. 6 and the Visual Input-Output Locator Algorithm, or VIOLA). As is the case with linear amplification, the DSL procedure appears to be the most popular nonlinear prescriptive procedure for children. Some of the nonlinear prescriptive methods require only threshold and threshold of discomfort information; others allow for input of other suprathreshold information such as individual loudness growth patterns.[30, 32]

As opposed to the traditional fitting procedures that provide only a single gain target, these nonlinear methods provide multiple frequency- and intensity-specific gain targets for different input levels of speech (e.g., soft, average, and loud speech intensities). Alternatively, a single gain target for a specified input level and specific compression parameters are provided. The individual nonlinear fitting procedures are based on goals ranging from "restoration of normal loudness impression" to "making speech equally loud and comfortable across frequency bands, while attempting to maximize intelligibility."[44, 89] In addition to these fitting methods, several hearing aid manufacturers have developed fitting prescriptions specific to their own products. Usually proprietary, these methods are often based on philosophies similar to those of existing methods. In some cases, the manufacturer's product specific methods are simply modifications of existing fitting schemes.

Regardless of the prescriptive method used, it is essential to understand that these equations serve only as a first-order approximation from which to begin the search for the most appropriate amplification system. Additional verification via probe microphone measurements is necessary to ensure that the output spectrum of the selected hearing aid actually meets the predicted gain requirements of the prescription once it is coupled to the real ear.

Considerations in Output Limiting

The maximum output of a hearing aid, measured as the output sound pressure level with 90 dB input or OSPL90 (ANSI S3.22-1996), is an important electroacoustic characteristic related to user acceptability and safety. The primary purpose of output limiting is to ensure safe and comfortable levels of amplification for a child. Determin-

ing appropriate output with very young and nonverbal children can be difficult since most techniques advocated for adults rely on behavioral measures of the loudness discomfort level (LDL), uncomfortable loudness level, or threshold of discomfort—measurements that require verbal competence and cooperation. The basic premise in selecting OSPL90 is that the hearing aid output does not exceed the patient's LDL range. If a child's LDLs are exceeded, the hearing aid will likely be rejected, the child will lower the volume control to levels that are suboptimal for speech reception, or the child will be placed at risk for additional hearing loss from overamplification.[119]

For young, nonverbal children, the selection of OSPL90 values can be more problematic than with adults and older children. Prescriptive approaches are available for calculating target output-limiting characteristics for children in manual and computerized formats.[99, 137] These recommended output levels are based on real-ear corrections made to adult psychophysical LDL data as a function of hearing loss. In addition, these recommendations are based on guidelines for safe levels of output limiting for children as described by Rintelmann and Bess.[119] Such approaches for selecting output-limiting characteristics should be verified with probe microphone measurements by use of the child's real-ear coupler difference.[152] Real-ear hearing aid performance can be predicted by applying age-average real-ear coupler difference values to coupler measures when probe microphone measures are not possible.

Often those fitting hearing aids in young children use manufacturers' specification data on OSPL90 as a guide to setting output. As discussed previously, measurements made in a 2-cm³ coupler underestimate the actual output of the instrument when fitted to the child's ear by as much as 12 to 15 dB because of the difference in cavity volume between the hard-walled coupler and the child's ear canal.[13, 64] In concert with the underlying philosophy of prescriptive amplification, our goal is to amplify the speech spectrum within the widest dynamic range possible such that the major frequency components of speech are audible without being uncomfortably loud for long-term listening. To accomplish this goal, the clinician first must determine the most appropriate OSPL90 setting and then which form of output limiting will best achieve this goal.

Methods of Output Limiting

Once the OSPL90 has been selected, the audiologist must decide on the type of output limiting. In general, there are two approaches to limiting hearing aid output: (1) peak clipping and (2) compression.

Peak clipping is the most common method for limiting the hearing aid output. The peak-clipping type of hearing aids provides linear amplification (1:1 input/output) up to the limit at which the hearing aid amplifier is incapable of reproducing the characteristics of the input signal without saturation—that is, the point at which further increases in input no longer result in equivalent increases in output. This nonlinearity, which causes the "tops" of the strong input signal to be "clipped," remains the most common and simplest form of output limiting. Its primary disadvantage is increased distortion when the signal is peak clipped. This can be troublesome when the input to the hearing aid microphone plus the use gain is such that it reaches or exceeds the OSPL90 of the instrument that was set to the patient's LDL. Such is often the case when patients fitted with high-gain hearing aids try to monitor their own voices. If we assume that one's voice is about 80 dB SPL at the hearing aid microphone, and if gain and maximum output are 60 and 120 dB SPL, respectively, the user's voice will clearly exceed the OSPL90 (80 + 60 = 140 dB), thereby delivering a distorted clipped signal. Similarly, patients with a severely restricted dynamic range (LDL − hearing threshold level) for whom one would recommend a reduced maximum output (e.g., 100 dB) might also find themselves in the common situation of receiving a highly distorted signal.

As an alternative to peak clipping, many hearing aids today are designed with compression as a means of limiting the signal level delivered to the wearer's ear without distortion. This form of output limiting permits better maintenance of the maximum power output below the user's LDL or within the range of most comfortable level by incorporating a feedback loop either before or after the volume control, which does not allow the output to exceed the capabilities of the amplifier, as occurs with peak-clipping hearing aids.

Verifying the Hearing Aid Selection

The primary purpose of a hearing aid is to provide the child with maximal auditory information, particularly speech, consistent with the hearing loss. The preselection process described previously represents current theory on matching the electroacoustic characteristics of a hearing aid/earmold assembly to the auditory needs of the impaired ear. To reiterate, the goal is to (1) deliver the amplified speech spectrum at an audible yet not uncomfortable level, (2) provide a smooth frequency response without unnecessary resonance peaks, and (3) balance the hearing aid bandwidth so as not to compromise the benefits of low-frequency and high-frequency amplification.

Once the clinician selects a hearing aid and earmold thought to possess the properties necessary to accomplish this goal based on theoretical principles, the next step is to verify that the amplified speech spectrum of the hearing aid is close to the prescription. This verification step allows the clinician to shape the hearing aid response via electroacoustic adjustment or modification of the earmold. Manufacturers are required by law to publish the electroacoustic properties of their particular hearing aids.[51] While this information is certainly useful for ensuring product uniformity and quality control and in troubleshooting hearing aids, it should not be taken to represent the performance characteristics of a hearing aid when it is actually fitted to the real ear.

This is particularly true in the case of a child. Recall that electroacoustic measures are performed with the hearing aid coupled to a standard hard-walled acoustic cavity with a volume of 2 cm^3. However, because of differences in the geometry, impedance, and resonance characteristics of the external ear canal and pinna, coupled with the reflection, diffraction, and baffle characteristics of the human head and torso, the output spectrum of a hearing aid developed in a 2-cm^3 coupler is not the same as that measured directly on the real ear. In fact, the gain developed in a 2-cm^3 cavity significantly overestimates real-ear gain above 2000 Hz. This overestimation reflects the inability of the hard-walled coupler to simulate the loss of concha and ear-canal resonances imposed by an occluding earmold (i.e., insertion loss). These differences, coupled with the fact that the ear-canal volume of a child is markedly less than 2 cm^3, result in hearing outputs generated by a hearing aid in a 2-cm^3 cavity that are up to 15 dB less than those delivered to the ear of an infant or young child.[135] Consequently, hearing aid specification data sheets published by the manufacturer should be used only as an initial guideline in the hearing aid preselection process, not to predict the specific performance in a given individual. Again, considerations of SPL differences between the 2-cm^3 coupler and the real ear are of paramount importance in the selection and verification of appropriate and safe levels of amplification for children.

The discrepancy between 2-cm^3 gain and the gain as measured in the ear of individual children (and adults) encourages most clinicians to verify the gain and output characteristics of hearing aids in terms of data measured in the ear rather than a coupler. Hearing aid gain and output are measured in the real ear using devices that incorporate a thin, soft, flexible probe tube that connects to a measurement microphone on a headset assembly. By inserting the probe tube down the ear canal, it becomes possible to measure and record the spectral characteristics of a uniform or random signal developed within the canal and presumably at the tympanic membrane. Such in situ measurements reflect not only the sound pressure output spectrum of the hearing aid alone but also the interacting influences of the hearing aid earmold or shell plumbing, pinna, concha, ear canal, tympanic membrane, head, and torso. Commonly called *probe microphone procedures,* these measurements allow clinicians to precisely shape the spectral characteristics of the signal delivered to the child to optimize speech reception.

Real-Ear Verification

The existence of commercial probe microphone systems allows for fast and accurate measurement of hearing aid gain and output in the real ear. Consequently, these systems have become invaluable in verifying the hearing aid prescription. Other uses of the probe tube microphone might include assessing the actual effects of earmold modification, such as changing vent size. Even with the speed and convenience of probe microphone hearing aid verification, it is sometimes difficult to get children to tolerate, and remain quiet for, the procedure if multiple measurements are needed for adjustment of frequency response or earmold characteristics. Extended real-ear measurement sessions are especially difficult for active children who are too old to sleep through the procedure but not old enough to sit quietly for any length of time.

Because of difficulties in obtaining repeated real measures in some children, measurement of the real-ear coupler difference (RECD) is advocated as another method of ensuring proper output levels in the real ear. Simply put, the RECD is the difference between hearing aid output measured in the 2-cm³ coupler and that measured in an individual child's ear canal. The RECD requires a single real-ear measurement. Once obtained, all gain and intensity modifications can be assessed in the coupler and converted to real-ear values. Data show that the RECD method provides similar reliability and accuracy to real-ear sound pressure level measures.[131]

Two of the most common ways to express hearing aid characteristics using probe microphone systems are real-ear insertion gain (REIG) and real-ear aided gain (REAG). *REIG* is defined as the difference between the eardrum SPLs measured for an input signal presented to an unaided open ear canal and that developed with the hearing aid and earmold in place (Fig. 107–7). As shown, the gain by frequency response of the unaided condition reflects the principal effects of external ear canal resonance as well as some secondary resonances of the concha and pinna. This measure is called real-ear unaided gain (REUG). In the aided condition, however, these external-ear effects are lost secondary to the insertion of an earmold (insertion loss). Hence, there is a large dip in the hearing aid frequency response in the region or regions responsible for these resonances. In essence, since insertion gain is based on the calculated difference between the unaided and aided sound pressure output spectra, it represents the actual gain of the hearing aid alone without the influence of the external ear, head, or torso since these are subtracted out. The *REAG,* on the other hand, is the difference between the eardrum SPL produced by the hearing aid/earmold combination in the wearer's ear and the SPL of a calibrated, equalized, unoc-

cupied free field. Whether REIG or REAG should be measured when fitting a hearing aid depends in part on the particular prescriptive gain method used. That is, some prescriptive methods provide REIG target while others provide REAG targets. A complete description of probe microphone measurements is beyond the scope of this chapter, and the interested reader is referred to the text of Mueller and coworkers[102] for a more complete description of this topic.

Hearing Aid Validation and Management

After the fitting and verification of amplification, aided auditory function must be validated. The purpose of the validation process is to ensure that the child is receiving optimal speech input from others and that his or her own speech is adequately perceived.[152] This requires that the instrument perform satisfactorily on a continuous basis; anything less compromises the child's educational potential and the acquisition of speech and language.

Unfortunately, studies from recent decades indicate that the majority of children's hearing aids are either grossly inadequate or inoperable.[48, 49, 54, 111, 156] In fact, these studies have estimated that between 27% and 92% of children's hearing aids are malfunctioning at any given time. Such findings are at best discouraging when one considers the amount of time and effort spent to select an optimal amplification system for the child.

Consistent and adequate hearing aid performance can be best ensured by having the parent and the teacher perform a daily hearing aid check. However, at least one study revealed that only 53% of parents queried reported that they conduct daily hearing aid checks.[48] In addition, one third of those parents reported not having the basic equipment needed to assess the battery and sound quality. Education regarding hearing aid care and acceptance of the child's hearing loss have both been cited as factors that result in improved hearing aid maintenance.[41, 91] Children should take responsibility for the use and care of their own hearing aids when it is considered developmentally appropriate.

Further, The Pediatric Working Group[152] recommends audiologic evaluation every 3 months during the first 2 years of using amplification and every 6 months thereafter if there are no concerns. In addition to audiometric evaluation, these evaluations should include electroacoustic evaluation and listening checks of hearing aids, as well as probe microphone measures as appropriate. Continual inquiry by the audiologist, otolaryngologist, and pediatrician to ensure that the child's parents and educators have taken responsibility for managing the hearing aid/earmold assembly is essential.

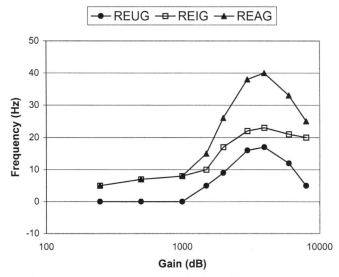

FIGURE 107–7. Examples of real-ear insertion gain (REIG), real-ear aided gain (REAG), and real-ear unaided gain (REUG) in a 9-month-old child. The REUG reflects the unaided open ear-canal response with the characteristic ear-canal resonance peak. The REIG represents the dB difference between the REUG and the REAG.

Functional Assessments

Measures of aided performance in the soundfield environment provide information about the child's auditory abilities at the time of the initial hearing aid fitting. These measures can include a number of speech perception tests designed for use with children.[12, 62, 71, 73, 85] Measures of aided speech perception, however, may not be an adequate predictor of how a child will perform in the real world. Functional assessment tools assist in the monitoring process by evaluating behaviors as they occur in real-world settings. These tools are typically questionnaires designed for administration to parents and teachers. Unlike traditional audiologic measures, functional assessments are less concerned with how much children hear as they are with how well children use their hearing in everyday settings.[122] Functional assessment tools are available for those with mild to profound hearing losses and for young infants, children, and adolescents.[7, 8, 120, 121, 157, 159]

Amplification Systems in Education

The primary nemeses of classroom listening for children with hearing loss include noise, reverberation, and speaker–listener distance. Although classroom acoustic conditions significantly affect the speech perception of all children, children with hearing loss are particularly vulnerable to their effects.

The importance of classroom amplification has been highlighted with the federal mandate of the Education of All Handicapped Children Act (P.L. 94-142)[6] and reauthorized as Individuals with Disabilities Education Act (IDEA) in 1992. This law, which mandates services and funding for children with hearing impairment, addresses several problem areas related to classroom amplification: at no additional cost to the child, the local school system must provide (1) habilitative services such as hearing evaluations, auditory training, and language training, (2) evaluations and fitting for use of personal or group amplification, and (3) appropriate educational placement, including the right to the least-restrictive learning environment.

The law further states that each local educational agency must create a learning environment in which learning can proceed despite aircraft overflights and noise from within the building, such as from adjacent classrooms and hallways, playgrounds, and heating or cooling systems. Noise is also created within the classroom from competing speech, shuffling papers, creaking furniture, and other normal activity caused by the youngsters and teachers. The bottom line is that children with hearing loss have the right to acoustic accessibility to their classrooms. The following paragraphs describe the impact of classroom acoustics on children with hearing loss in more detail.

Classroom Noise Levels

Classrooms are notorious for high noise levels, ranging from about 40 to 67 dB. In addition to the noise originating within a classroom, there are sounds generated outside of the building and sounds generated within the school but outside of the classroom (e.g., street traffic, air traffic, and construction noise). In a traditional classroom setting, noise levels should not exceed 30 to 35 dBA. Unfortunately, as stated earlier, noise levels often far exceed these levels.

These relatively high noise levels typically produce an unfavorable SNR. The American Speech-Hearing-Language Association,[5] among others,[14, 22, 142] has recommended SNRs of at least +15 to +30 dB in educational settings. Unfortunately, most classrooms have SNRs between −6 and +6 dB, thus hampering learning.[18, 35, 36]

Listeners with abnormal hearing find it more difficult to understand speech under noisy conditions than do normal hearers. Numerous investigators have studied this phenomenon in adults. However, far less information is available regarding the effects of noise on children with normal hearing and those with hearing loss. In a classic study, Finitzo-Hieber[50] investigated speech recognition performance under noise conditions in a group of normal-hearing children and a group of children with mild to moderate hearing impairment. The children with hearing loss wore an ear-level hearing aid. The data revealed that as the listening conditions worsened, the disparity between the scores of those with hearing loss and those with normal hearing increased. In quiet conditions, there was a difference of 12% between the two groups. At an SNR of zero, however, the difference in word recognition increased to 30%. In addition, speech understanding in the hearing impaired group decreased from 83% in quiet to 30% at an SNR of zero.

Reverberation

Reverberation is a second variable that interacts in some complicated way with the human auditory system to degrade the speech signal. Reverberation is defined as the amount of time for a sound to decrease by 60 dB after the termination of the signal. The degree of reverberation varies with the environment. When a teacher talks to the child, some of the speech signal reaches the child's amplification system within just a few milliseconds. The remainder of the signal strikes surrounding areas in the form of reflections that reach the child's ear a few milliseconds after the initial sound. The strength and the duration of these reflections are affected by the absorptive quality of the surrounding surfaces. For example, if an area has concrete block walls, tile floors, and a plaster ceiling, the room has a long reverberation time in contrast with a room acoustically treated with carpeting, drapes, and an acoustic tile ceiling. In general, as reverberation time increases, speech understanding decreases. This degradation in speech understanding is more pronounced in children with hearing loss than in those with normal hearing.

An examination of 32 classrooms for children with hearing impairment by Crandell and Smaldino[35] revealed reverberation times of 0.3 to 1.12 seconds. It has been recommended, however, that reverberation times not exceed 0.4 second in educational settings.[5]

Speaker-Listener Distance

The third nemesis of classroom listening for those with hearing loss is the distance between the teacher and the student, or the speaker–listener distance. The SNR deteriorates as the intensity of the speech decreases and the proportion of direct to reflected sound energy decreases. In general, the level of a signal decreases 6 dB for every doubling of distance until a critical distance is reached. The critical distance is defined as the point at which the intensity of the direct sound is equal to the intensity of the reverberated sound. It is not surprising that several studies have documented a decrease in speech recognition ability as a function of increasing distance until the critical distance is reached.[33, 34] Crandell and Smaldino[36] provided a clear example of this phenomenon given a classroom in which the reverberation time was 0.46 second and the SNR at 6 feet was +6 dB (considered a common SNR in the classroom). In this setting, the speech recognition of children with normal hearing deteriorated from 90% at 6 feet to 36% at 24 feet. Of importance is the fact that noise and reverberation combined cause a breakdown in the ability of children to understand speech. In addition to these findings, it has been shown that high but common levels of noise and reverberation can negatively affect not only speech recognition but also behavior, concentration, attention, reading and spelling ability, and academic achievement.[20, 36, 37, 50]

FM Amplification

One popular technology for enhancing the SNR and reducing the effects of reverberation and speaker–listener distance is frequency modulation (FM) systems. About 65% of all classrooms for children with hearing impairment use either self-contained FM systems or an FM system combined with a personal hearing aid.[9] With such systems, the desired signal, usually the teacher's voice, is picked up via an FM wireless microphone that can be positioned near the speaker's mouth (usually around the teacher's neck). This signal is transmitted via an FM signal to a receiver. This signal is then amplified and fed to the listener. FM receivers can be coupled to the listener's ear via hearing aid type housings, "Walkman"-type earphones, or "boots" that slip onto the bottom of a child's own hearing aids (Fig. 107–8). Further, FM systems are now designed to transmit the amplified signal via speakers that are strategically placed around the classroom on stands or shelves or attached to walls or ceilings. This system has the potential advantage of providing needed amplification for children in the classroom with minimal hearing problems as well as for those children who have yet to be identified as having hearing loss. A small receiver/speaker system about the size of a lunchbox can even be placed on a child's desk. These systems can be easily transported from class to class. For an excellent description of this system and other classroom amplification devices, the reader is referred to Berg[14] and to Lewis.[86]

Additional Assistive Listening Devices

While FM systems are the intervention strategy of choice among school systems, a number of other effective amplification options exist for use in and outside of schools. These systems include infrared systems, text telephones, telecaptioning devices, and alerting devices. Many of these devices are available in public theaters, museums, hotels, and other locations where public accessibility is required under the Americans with Disabilities Act.[6]

Infrared group amplification is seldom used in classroom settings but is widely used as an assistive listening device in theaters, churches, and other public facilities. The system employs an infrared light emitter that transmits the speech signal from the input microphone to individually worn infrared receiver audio amplifier units. The advantages of infrared systems include no signal transmission beyond room walls, the relatively low noise of the internal system, and a broad frequency response.

Text telephones (TTs), previously called *telecommunication devices for the deaf* or *teletypewriters*, allow telephone access to persons who would otherwise not be able to communicate by telephone because of significant hearing loss. For this system to work, the party at each end must have a TT system. Communication is achieved by one person's typing a message that is transmitted along telephone lines to be decoded by a receiver on the other end. In addition, the Americans with Disabilities Act

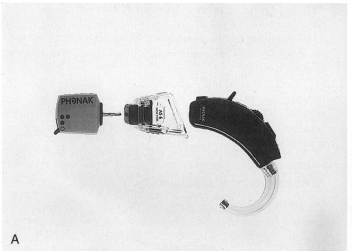

FIGURE 107–8. Example of a "boot" style FM receiver (*A*) and two types of FM transmitters (*B*). (Courtesy of Phonak Hearing Instruments, Naperville, IL.)

(P.L. 101-336) mandated that all telephone companies provide intra- and interstate relay services by 1993. This system allows the user of a voice telephone to communicate with a person using a TT or computer via a TT/computer-using operator. For those with less severe hearing loss, replacement handset amplifiers are available that can be used with or without a hearing aid. Portable amplifiers that couple to the telephone also are available.

Another popular device is the closed-captioned decoder to provide television access to those with hearing loss. These units provide a printed text on the television screen. The value of systems such as these are immense in improving the quality of life for those with hearing loss. The Television De-Coder Circuitry Act of 1990 (P.L. 101-431) requires that all new televisions with screens 13 inches and larger contain decoder circuitry.

A variety of alerting devices exist to assist persons, including children, who want to function independently. This independence becomes especially important to children as they enter adolescence. Alerting devices for common signals such as a doorbell, telephone ring, fire alarm, and wake-up alarm are popular. However, devices are also useful for sounds such as computer prompts, intercom prompts, and oven timers. Alerting devices can be visual (e.g., flashing lights) or vibrational (e.g., vibratory pager or shaking a person awake).

Evaluation Process

One of the major difficulties of amplification systems in education is evaluating the systems electroacoustically or behaviorally. There is no set of standards for assistive listening devices. However, the American Speech-Language-Hearing Association[4] has prepared a set of guidelines for measuring the performance of FM systems, as have others.[87, 102, 132] In addition, Crandell and Smaldino[36] recommend several methods for evaluating soundfield FM systems.

Perhaps the most advantageous way to evaluate such a system is to examine the child's performance for speech recognition in a real classroom environment. This can be accomplished simply by administering a speech recognition test in the classroom and comparing performance between the child's personal hearing aid alone and the FM arrangement. Such a procedure makes it possible to determine how the child actually performs with the system under classroom conditions.

Children with Minimal Hearing Loss

Since the mid-1980s, it has become clear that some children with minimal hearing impairment experience more difficulty in language development and psychoeducational progress than was previously supposed. For the purposes of this discussion, children with minimal hearing loss encompass three unique populations: children with permanent unilateral hearing loss, children with minimal bilateral sensorineural hearing impairment (pure-tone threshold averages between 20 and 40 dB HL) and children with high-frequency sensorineural hearing loss (air-conduction thresholds >25 dB HL at two or more frequencies above

2 kHz) in one or both ears. The prevalence of minimal hearing loss in school-age children has been estimated at 5.4%.[21]

Several studies have reported that children with unilateral hearing loss experience difficulty in educational progress.[11, 19, 20, 150] These studies have led us to the conclusion that children with unilateral sensorineural hearing loss (1) are at greater risk for academic failure than was once thought, (2) experience considerable difficulty in understanding speech in a background of noise, (3) experience trouble with localization, (4) appear to have more behavioral problems in school, and (5) may exhibit a specific profile suggesting greater risk of educational problems. This profile includes early age of onset; perinatal or postnatal complications, or both; severe to profound sensorineural impairment; and right-ear impairment.

Similarly, it appears that children with minimal bilateral sensorineural hearing loss are also experiencing some complications in the school systems. These children are also known to exhibit delays in educational progress, difficulties in understanding speech in a background of noise, delays in receptive vocabulary, and difficulties detected with measures of functional health status.[21]

For many years, the only intervention recommended for those with unilateral or minimal hearing loss was preferential classroom seating. Growing evidence of the academic, communicative, and psychosocial difficulties experienced by these children led to a search for other, more effective intervention strategies. One of the possible management options for children with minimal hearing loss is amplification. One common amplification system for children with unilateral hearing loss, a contralateral routing-of-signal (CROS) hearing aid, is seldom successful. The basic principle of these units is to place the input microphone at the impaired ear and to direct the output signal via a receiver and coupler to the good ear. In a listening situation in which the primary message (speech) originates on the same side as the impaired ear, the signal is picked up by the microphone on that side, is amplified, and is directed to the normal-hearing contralateral ear. When amplification is required for both ears because of hearing loss in the better, as well as the poorer, ear, these instruments are called *BiCROS*. The microphone and receiver may be coupled by a wire that runs around the back of the neck (or through the glasses), or the signal may be transmitted in wirelessly via radio frequencies. Hence, the wearer can use the good ear to hear signals from the impaired side. While the BTE style accounts for the majority of currently available CROS hearing aids, in-the-ear models have been introduced. Of the few eyeglass hearing aids still dispensed, the majority implement CROS amplification.

An alternative to the CROS hearing aid is the FM system. As noted previously, such systems improve the SNR reaching the child's ear. Kenworthy and colleagues[76] examined differences in speech perception across several amplification options in children with one type of minimal hearing loss (unilateral loss). The authors used the unaided condition, an FM system, and a CROS system for both monosyllabic and sentential materials presented under various SNRs similar to those found in typical classrooms. Speech and noise source configurations in-

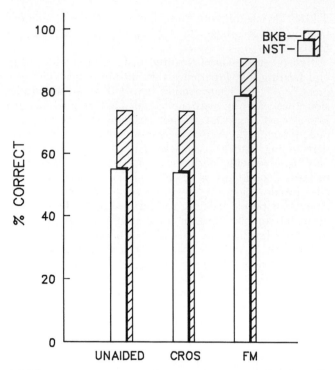

FIGURE 107–9. Mean speech recognition scores of unilaterally hearing-impaired children in an unaided condition and using a CROS hearing aid and FM system for both monosyllabic (Nonsense Syllable Test) and sentence (Bamford-Koval-Bench) materials. For each listening condition, the data reflect average scores collapsed across three different signal-to-noise configurations: monaural direct, monaural indirect, and midline signal–omnidirectional noise.

cluded *monaural direct* (speech to the good ear, noise to the poor ear), *monaural indirect* (speech to the poor ear, noise to the good ear), and *midline signal–omnidirectional noise* (speech immediately in front of and noise sources behind the listener). The speech materials were nonsense syllables and children's sentences. The recorded materials were then presented via headphones to a group of children with unilateral hearing impairment. The findings from this investigation are shown in Figure 107–9. This figure illustrates the performance of the children with unilateral hearing loss collapsed across all three listening conditions. It is clear that the CROS and the unaided conditions varied minimally, whereas the FM system resulted in much improved performance over the CROS or the unaided conditions. It is notable that the unaided condition yielded performance scores equivalent to those of the CROS condition. Hence, for children with minimal hearing loss who experience difficulty, whether it be academic or special listening problems, the FM system may be suitable.

REFERENCES

1. American National Standards Institute. Methods for calculation of the speech intelligibility index. ANSI S3.5. New York, Acoustical Society of America, 1997.
2. American National Standards Institute. Specification for hearing aid characteristics. ANSI S3.22. New York, Acoustical Society of America, 1996.
3. American Speech-Language-Hearing Association. Guidelines for the audiologic assessment of children from birth through 36 months of age. ASHA 33:37, 1991.
4. American Speech-Language-Hearing Association. Guidelines for fitting and monitoring FM systems. ASHA Suppl 36:1, 1994.
5. American Speech-Language-Hearing Association. Position and guidelines for acoustics in educational settings. ASHA Suppl 37:15, 1995.
6. Americans with Disabilities Act of 1990, P.L. 101–336, §2, 104 Stat. 328 (1991).
7. Anderson KL, Matkin ND. Preschool SIFTER. Screening Instrument for Targeting Educational Risk in Preschool Children (age 3–kindergarten). Austin, Pro-Ed, 1989.
8. Anderson KL. Screening Instrument for Targeting Educational Risk (SIFTER). Austin, Pro-Ed, 1989.
9. Arehart KH, Yoshinaga-Itano C, Thomson V, et al. State of the states: the status of universal newborn hearing identification and intervention systems in 16 states. Am J Audiol 7:101, 1998.
10. Arsenault MD, Punch JL. Nonsense syllable recognition in noise using monaural and binaural listening strategies. J Acoust Soc Am 105:1821, 1999.
11. Beauchaine KL, Donaghy KF. Amplification selection considerations in the pediatric population. In Bess F, Gravel J, Tharpe AM (eds). Amplification for Children With Auditory Deficits. Nashville, Bill Wilkerson Center Press, 1996, pp 145–160.
12. Bench J, Koval A, Bamford J. The BKB (Bamford-Koval-Bench) sentence lists for partially-hearing children. Br J Audiol 13:108, 1979.
13. Bentler R, Pavlovic CV. Transfer functions and correction factors used in hearing aid evaluation and research. Ear Hear 10:58, 1989.
14. Berg F. Acoustics and Sound Systems in Schools. San Diego, Singular, 1993.
15. Berger KW. Prescription of hearing aids: a rationale. J Am Audiol Soc 2:71, 1976.
16. Bess FH, Tharpe AM. An introduction to unilateral sensorineural hearing loss in children. Ear Hear 7:3, 1986.
17. Bess FH, McConnell FE. Audiology, Education and the Hearing Impaired Child. St Louis, CV Mosby, 1981.
18. Bess FH, Sinclair JS, Riggs D. Group amplification in schools for the hearing impaired. Ear Hear 5:138, 1984.
19. Bess FH, Tharpe AM. Unilateral hearing impairment in children. Pediatrics 74:206, 1984.
20. Bess FH, Tharpe AM. Case history data on unilaterally hearing impaired children. Ear Hear 7:14, 1986.
21. Bess FH, Dodd-Murphy J, Parker RA. Children with minimal sensorineural hearing loss: prevalence, educational performance, and functional status. Ear Hear 19:339, 1998.
22. Blair J. Front-row seating is not enough for classroom listening. In Flexer C, Wray D, Leavitt R (eds). How the Student with Hearing Loss Can Succeed in College: A Handbook for Students, Families and Professionals. Washington, DC, Alexander Graham Bell Association, 1990, pp 69–82.
23. Boothroyd A, Eran O, Hanin L. Speech perception and production in children with hearing impairment. In Bess F, Gravel J, Tharpe AM (eds). Amplification for Children with Auditory Deficits. Nashville, Bill Wilkerson Center Press, 1996, pp 55–74.
24. Bray V, Ricketts TA. Audio Expansion in DSP Hearing Aids. Adv Audiol 10:27, 2000.
25. Byrne D, Dillon H. The National Acoustic Laboratories' (NAL) new procedure for selecting the gain and frequency response of a hearing aid. Ear Hear 7:257, 1986.
26. Byrne D, Fifield D. Evaluation of hearing aid fittings for infants. Br J Audiol 8:47, 1974.
27. Byrne D, Tonnison W. Selecting the gain of hearing aids for persons with sensorineural hearing impairments. Scand Audiol 5:51, 1976.
28. Byrne D. Binaural hearing aid fitting: research findings and clinical application. In Libby E (ed). Binaural Hearing and Amplification. Chicago, Zenetron, 1980.
29. Clark GM. Research advances for cochlear implants. Auris Nasus Larynx 25:73, 1998.
30. Cornelisse L, Seewald R, Jamieson D. Wide-dynamic-range compression hearing aids: the DSL [i/o] approach. Hear J 47:23, 1994.

31. Cox RM. Acoustic aspects of hearing aid ear canal coupling systems. Monogr Contemp Audiol 1:3, 1979.

32. Cox R. Using loudness data for hearing aid selection: the IHAFF approach. Hear J 48:10, 1995.

33. Crandell C. Classroom acoustics for hearing-impaired children. J Acoust Soc Am 92:2470, 1992.

34. Crandell C, Bess FH. Speech recognition of children in a "typical" classroom setting. ASHA 29:87, 1986.

35. Crandell C, Smaldino J. An update of classroom acoustics for children with hearing impairment. Volta Rev 96:291, 1994.

36. Crandell C, Smaldino J. Classroom acoustics and amplification. In Valente M, Roeser R, Hosford-Dunn H (eds). Audiology, vol II: Treatment. New York, Thieme, 2000.

37. Davis J, Elfenbein J, Schum R, Bentler R. Effects of mild and moderate hearing impairment on language, educational, and psychosocial behavior of children. J Speech Hear Disord 51:53, 1986.

38. Davis JM, Shepherd NT, Stelmachowicz PG, et al. Characteristics of hearing-impaired children in the public schools, part II: psychoeducational data. J Speech Hear Disord 46:130, 1981.

39. de Villiers PA. Educational implications of deafness: Language and literacy. In Eavey RD, Klein JO (eds). Hearing Loss in Childhood: A Primer. Report of the 102nd Ross Conference on Pediatric Research. Columbus, OH, Ross Laboratories, 1992, pp 127–135.

40. Diefendorf AO. Behavioral evaluation of hearing-impaired children. In Bess FH (ed). Hearing Impairment in Children. Nashville, Vanderbilt Bill Wilkerson Center Press, 1988, pp 133–151.

41. Diefendorf AO, Arthur D. Monitoring children's hearing aids: reexamining the problem. Volta Rev 90:17, 1987.

42. Diefendorf AO, Reitz PS, Escobar MW, Wynne MK. Initiating early amplification: TIPS for success. In Bess F, Gravel J, Tharpe AM (eds). Amplification for Children With Auditory Deficits. Nashville, Bill Wilkerson Center Press, 1996, pp 123–144.

43. Dillon H. Compression? Yes, but for low or high frequencies, for low or high intensities, and with what response times. Ear Hear 17:287, 1996.

44. Dillon H. NAL-NL1: a new prescriptive fitting procedure for nonlinear hearing aids. Hear J 52:10, 1999.

45. Domoracki D, Berger K, Millin J. A comparison of monaural and binaural gain settings. Hear Instr 33:18, 1982.

46. Durlach NI, Thompson CL, Colburn HS. Binaural interaction in impaired listeners. Audiology 20:181, 1981.

47. Erdman S, Sedge R. Subjective comparison of binaural versus monaural amplification. Ear Hear 2:225, 1981.

48. Elfenbein JL. Monitoring preschoolers' hearing aids: issues in program design and implementation. Am J Audiol 3:65, 1994.

49. Elfenbein JL, Bentler RA, Davis JM, Niebuhr DP. Status of school children's hearing aids relative to monitoring practices. Ear Hear 9: 212, 1988.

50. Finitzo-Hieber T. Classroom acoustics. In Rosser RJ (ed). Auditory Disorders in School Children, 2nd ed. New York, Thieme, 1988, pp 221–233.

51. Food and Drug Administration. Hearing aid devices—professional and patient labeling and conditions for sale. Fed Reg 42:9286, 1977.

52. Fortune T. Amplifiers and circuit algorithms of contemporary hearing aids. In Valente M (ed). Hearing Aids: Standards, Options, and Limitations. New York, Thieme, 1996, pp 157–209.

53. Franck BAM, van Kreveld-Bos CSGM, Dreschler WA, Verschuure H. Evaluation of spectral enhancement in hearing aids, combined with phonemic compression. J Acoust Soc Am 106:1452, 1999.

54. Gaeth J, Lounsbury E. Hearing aids and children in elementary schools. J Speech Hear Disord 31:283, 1966.

55. Gatehouse S. Apparent auditory deprivation effects of late onset: the role of presentation level. J Acoust Soc Am 86:2103, 1989.

56. Gelfand SA, Silman S. Apparent auditory deprivation in children: implications of monaural versus binaural amplification. J Am Acad Audiol 4:313, 1993.

57. Gitles T, Niquette P. FIG6 in ten. Hear Rev 2:28, 1995.

58. Gorga MP, Neely ST, Ohlrich B, et al. From laboratory to clinic: a large scale study of distortion product otoacoustic emissions in ears with normal hearing and ears with hearing loss. Ear Hear 18:440, 1997.

59. Gravel JS, Fausel N, Liskow C, Chobot J. Children's speech recognition in noise using omni-directional and dual-microphone hearing aid technology. Ear Hear 20:1, 1999.

60. Gravel JS. Auditory assessment of infants. Semin Hear 15:100, 1994.

61. Harford ER. Bilateral CROS: two-sided listening with one hearing aid. Arch Otolaryngol 84:426, 1966.

62. Haskins HA. A Phonetically Balanced Test of Speech Discrimination for Children [Master's thesis]. Evanston, IL, Northwestern University, 1949.

63. Hattori H. Ear dominance for nonsense syllable recognition ability in sensorineural hearing-impaired children: monaural versus binaural amplification. J Am Acad Audiol 4:319, 1993.

64. Hawkins DB, Cooper WA, Thompson DJ. Comparison among SPL's in real ears, 2CM3 and 6CM3 couplers. J Am Acad Audiol 1:154, 1990.

65. Hawkins DB, Yacullo WS. Signal-to-noise ratio advantage of binaural hearing aids and directional microphones under different levels of reverberation. J Speech Hear Disord 49:278, 1984.

66. Hedley-Williams A, Tharpe AM, Bess FH. Fitting hearing aids in the pediatric population: a survey of practice procedures. In Bess F, Gravel J, Tharpe AM (eds). Amplification for Children With Auditory Deficits. Nashville, Bill Wilkerson Center Press, 1996, pp 107–122.

67. Hood JD. Speech discrimination in bilateral and unilateral hearing loss due to Ménière's disease. Br J Audiol 18:173, 1984.

68. Hurley RM. Onset of auditory deprivation. J Am Acad Audiol 10: 529, 1999.

69. Huttenbrink KB. Current status and critical reflections on implantable hearing aids. Am J Otol 20:409, 1999.

70. Jerger J, Darling R, Florin E. Efficacy of the cued-listening task in the evaluation of binaural hearing aids. J Am Acad Audiol 5:279, 1994.

71. Jerger S, Lewis S, Hawkins J, Jerger J. Pediatric speech intelligibility test: I. Generation of test materials. Int J Pediatr Otorhinolaryngol 2:217, 1980.

72. Joint Committee on Infant Hearing. Year 2000 position statement: principles and guidelines for early hearing detection and intervention programs. Am J Audiol 9:9, 2000.

73. Katz DR, Elliott LL. Development of a new children's speech discrimination test. Paper presented at the convention of the American Speech and Hearing Association, Chicago, November 18, 1978.

74. Kemp DT. Stimulated acoustic emissions from within the human auditory system. J Acoust Soc Am 64:1386, 1978.

75. Kemker F, McConnell F, Logan S, Green B. A field study of children's hearing aids in a school environment. Lang Speech Hear Ser Schools 10:47, 1979.

76. Kenworthy OT, Klee T, Tharpe AM. Speech recognition ability of children with unilateral sensorineural hearing loss as a function of amplification, speech stimuli and listening condition. Ear Hear 11: 264, 1990.

77. Killion MC, Staab WJ, Preves DA. Classifying automatic signal processors. Hear Instr 41:24, 1990.

78. Killion MC. SNR loss: I can hear what people say, but I can't understand them. Hear Rev 4:8, 1997.

79. Killion MC, Schulien R, Christensen L, et al. Real world performance of an ITE directional microphone. Hear J 51:24, 1998.

80. Kirkwood D. After a flat 1999, industry leaders suggest strategies to get the market growing again. Hear J 53:21, 2000.

81. Kochkin S, MarkeTrak V. "Why my hearing aids are in the drawer": the consumers' perspective. Hear J 53:34, 2000.

82. Kollmeier B, Peissig J, Hohmann V. Real-time multiband dynamic compression and noise reduction for binaural hearing aids. J Rehabil Res Dev 30:82, 1993.

83. Kruger B. An update on the external ear resonance in infants and young children. Ear Hear 8:333, 1987.

84. Kuk FK. Theoretical and practical considerations in compression hearing aids. Trends Amplif 1:5, 1996.

85. Levitt H, Resnick SB. Speech reception by the hearing impaired: methods of testing and the development of new tests. Scand Audiol Suppl 6:107, 1978.

86. Lewis DA. Classroom acoustics. In Bess FH (ed). Children with Hearing Impairment: Contemporary Trends. Nashville, Vanderbilt Bill Wilkerson Center Press, 1988, pp 277–295.

87. Lewis DA, Kalberer A. Real-ear and 2-cm³ coupler assessment of FM systems. Presented at American Academy of Audiology Convention, Dallas, April, 1995.

88. Lewis DE. Assistive devices for classroom listening. Am J Audiol 3: 58, 1994.

89. Lindley GA, Palmer CV. Fitting wide dynamic range compression hearing aids: DSL [i/o], the IHAFF protocol, and FIG6. AJA 6:19, 1997.

90. Lonsbury-Martin BL, McCoy MJ, Whitehead ML, Martin GK. Clinical testing of distortion product otoacoustic emissions. Ear Hear 1:11, 1993.

91. Luterman DM. Counseling Parents of Hearing-Impaired Children. Boston, Little Brown, 1979.

92. Madaffari PL, Stanely WK. Microphone, receiver and telecoil options: past, present and future. In Valente M (ed). Hearing Aids: Standards, Options, and Limitations. New York, Thieme, 1996, pp 126–156.

93. Martin MC. Hearing aid requirements in sensorineural hearing loss. Br J Audiol 7:21, 1973.

94. McCandless GA, Lyregaard P. Prescription of gain/output (POGO) for hearing aids. Hear Instr 34:16, 1983.

95. McLaughlin S. The beginnings—infant communication. In Introduction to Language Development. San Diego, Singular, 1998, pp 175–218.

96. McLaughlin S. Early language development—toddlers. In Introduction to Language Development. San Diego, Singular, 1998, pp 219–266.

97. McLaughlin S. The structural bases for human communication. In Introduction to Language Development. San Diego, Singular, 1998, pp 43–80.

98. McLaughlin S. The interactive bases for human communication. In Introduction to Language Development. San Diego, Singular, 1998, pp 81–122.

99. Moodie KS, Seewald RC, Sinclair ST. Procedure for predicting real-ear hearing aid performance in young children. Am J Audiol 3: 23, 1994.

100. Moore BC, Vickers DA, Glasberg BR, Baer T. Comparison of real and simulated hearing impairment in subjects with unilateral and bilateral cochlear hearing loss. Br J Audiol 31:227, 1997.

101. Moore BC. Perceptual consequences of cochlear hearing loss and their implications for the design of hearing aids. Ear Hear 17:133, 1996.

102. Mueller HG, Hawkins DB, Northern JL (eds). Probe Microphone Measurements: Hearing Aid Selection and Assessment. San Diego, Singular, 1992.

103. Mueller HG. Update on programmable hearing aids (with an assist from Yogi Berra). Hear Instr 47:13, 1994.

104. Mueller HG, Ricketts TA. Directional microphone hearing aids: an update. Hear J 5:10, 2000.

105. Mylanus EAM, Snik AFM, Cremers CWRJ, et al. Audiological results of the bone-anchored hearing aid HC200: multicenter results. Ann Otol Rhinol Laryngol 103:368, 1994.

106. Mylanus EAM, Snik AFM, Jorritsman FF, Cremers CWRJ. Audiological results for bone-anchored hearing aid HC220. Ear Hear 15:87, 1994.

107. Nozza RJ, Rossman RNF, Bond LC. Infant-adult differences in unmasked thresholds for the discrimination of consonant-vowel syllable pairs. Audiology 30:102, 1991.

108. Pearsons KS, Bennett RL, Fidell S. Speech levels in various environments. Report to the Office of Resources, Development, Environmental Protection Agency, BBN Report No. 3281, 1976.

109. Plomp R. Auditory psychophysics. Annu Rev Psychol 26:207, 1975.

110. Plomp R. Noise, amplification, and compression: considerations of three main issues in hearing aid design. Ear Hear 15:2, 1994.

111. Potts PL, Greenwood J. Hearing aid monitoring: are looking and listening enough? Lang Speech Hear Ser Schools 14:157, 1983.

112. Probst R, Lonsbury-Martin BL, Martin GK. A review of otoacoustic emissions. J Acoust Soc Am 89:2027, 1991.

113. Ricketts TA, Mueller HG. Making sense of directional microphone hearing aids. Am J Audiol 8:117, 1999.

114. Ricketts TA, Dahr S. Aided benefit across directional and omnidirectional hearing aid microphones for behind-the-ear hearing aids. J Am Acad Audiol 10:180, 1999.

115. Ricketts TA. Directivity quantification in hearing aids: fitting and measurement effects. Ear Hear 21:45, 2000.

116. Ricketts TA. Impact of noise source configuration on directional hearing aid benefit and performance. Ear Hear 21:194, 2000.

117. Ricketts TA. The impact of head and body angle on monaural and binaural performance with directional and omnidirectional hearing aids. Ear Hear 21:318, 2000.

118. Ricketts TA, Bentler R. Comparison of two digitally programmable hearing aids. J Am Acad Audiol 3:101, 1992.

119. Rintelmann WF, Bess FH. High-level amplification and potential hearing loss in children. In Bess FH (ed). Hearing Impairment in Children. Parkton, MD, York Press, 1988, pp 278–309.

120. Robbins AM. Mr. Potato Head Task. Indianapolis, Indiana University School of Medicine, 1997.

121. Robbins AM, Renshaw JJ, Berry SW. Evaluating meaningful auditory integration in profoundly hearing impaired children. Am J Otol 12:144, 1991.

122. Robbins AM, Svirsky M, Osberger MJ, Pisoni DB. Beyond the audiogram: the role of functional assessments. In Bess FH (ed). Children with Hearing Impairment: Contemporary Trends. Nashville, Bill Wilkerson Center Press, 1998, pp 105–124.

123. Ross M. Hearing aid selection for children. In Pollack MC (ed). Amplification for the Hearing Impaired. New York, Grune & Stratton, 1975, pp 207–242.

124. Roush J, Harrison M. Age of suspicion, identification and intervention for young children with hearing loss. In Bess FH (ed). Children with Hearing Impairment: Contemporary Trends. Nashville, Vanderbilt Bill Wilkerson Center Press, 1998, pp 25–31.

125. Saunders GH, Kates JM. Speech intelligibility enhancement using hearing-aid array processing. J Acoust Soc Am 102:1827, 1997.

126. Schreurs K, Olsen W. Comparison of monaural and binaural hearing aid use on a trial period basis. Ear Hear 6:198, 1984.

127. Schum D. Speech understanding in background noise. In Valente M (ed). Hearing Aids: Standards, Options, and Limitations. New York, Thieme, 1996, pp 368–406.

128. Schwartz D, Larson V. Hearing aid selection and evaluation procedures in children. In Bess FH (ed). Childhood Deafness: Causation, Assessment, and Management. New York, Grune & Stratton, 1977, p 217.

129. Schwartz DM, Lyregaard PE, Lundh P. Hearing aid selection for severe-to-profound hearing loss. Hear J 51:13, 1988.

130. Schwietzer C. Development of digital hearing aids. Trends Amplif 2:41, 1997.

131. Scollie SD, Seewald RC, Cornelisse LE, Jenstad LM. Validity and repeatability of level-independent HL to SPL transforms. Ear Hear 19:407, 1998.

132. Seewald R, Moodie KS. Electroacoustic considerations. In Ross M (ed). FM Auditory Training Systems: Characteristics, Selection and Use. Timonium, MD, York Press, 1992, pp 75–102.

133. Seewald R, Ross M, Spiro M. Selecting amplification characteristics for young hearing impaired children. Ear Hear 6:48, 1985.

134. Seewald R, Ross M, Stelmachowicz P. Selecting and verifying hearing aid performance characteristics for children. J Acad Rehabil Audiol 20:25, 1987.

135. Seewald RC, Moodie KS, Sinclair ST, Scollie SD. Predictive validity of a procedure for pediatric hearing instrument fitting. Am J Audiol 8:143, 1999.

136. Seewald R, Cornelisse L, Ramji K, et al. DSL v4.0 for Windows. London, Ontario, University of Western Ontario, 1996.

137. Seewald R, Ramji KV, Sinclair ST, et al. Computer-Assisted Implementation of the Desired Sensation Level Method for Electroacoustic Selection and Fitting in Children: User's Manual. London, Ontario, University of Western Ontario, 1993.

138. Silman S, Gelfand SA, Silverman CA. Late onset auditory deprivation: effects of monaural versus binaural hearing aids. J Acoust Soc Am 76:1357, 1984.

139. Silverman CA. Auditory deprivation. Hear Instr 40:26, 1989.

140. Simon HJ, Aleksandrovsky I. Perceived lateral position of narrowband noise in hearing-impaired and normal-hearing listeners under conditions of equal sensation level and sound-pressure level. J Acoust Soc Am 102:1821, 1997.

141. Sininger YS, Abdala C. Otoacoustic emissions for the study of auditory function in infants and children. In Berlin CI (ed). Otoacoustic Emissions: Basic Science and Clinical Applications. San Diego, Singular, 1998, pp 105–125.

142. Smaldino J, Crandell C. Acoustical modifications with schools. In Crandell C, Smaldino J, Flexer C (eds). Sound-Field FM Amplification: Theory and Practical Applications. San Diego, Singular, 1995, pp 83–92.

143. Snik AF, Mylanus EA, Cremers CW. Implantable hearing devices

for sensorineural hearing loss: a review of the audiometric data. Clin Otolaryngol 23:414, 1998.

144. Snik AFM, Mylanus EAM, Cremers CWRJ. Speech recognition with the bone-anchored hearing aid determined objectively and subjectively. Ear Nose Throat 73:115, 1994.

145. Stach BA, Gulya AJ. Hearing aids: I. Conventional hearing devices. Arch Otolaryngol Head Neck Surg 122:227, 1996.

146. Stapells DR. Frequency-specific evoked potential audiometry in infants. In Seewald RC (ed). A Sound Foundation Through Early Amplification: Proceedings of an International Conference. Chicago, Phonak AG, 2000, pp 13–32.

147. Stein LK. On the real age of identification of congenital hearing loss. Audiol Today 7:10, 1995.

148. Studebaker GA, Cox RM. Side branch and parallel vent effects in real ears and in acoustical and electrical models. J Am Audiol Soc 3:108, 1977.

149. Studebaker GA, Zachman TA. Investigation of the acoustics of earmold vents. J Am Audiol Soc 47:110, 1978.

150. Tharpe AM, Bess FH. Minimal, progressive, and fluctuating hearing losses in children: characteristics, identification and management. Pediatr Clin North Am 46:65, 1999.

151. Tharpe AM, Fino-Szumski MS, Bess FH. Hearing aid fitting practices for children with multiple disabilities. Manuscript submitted for publication.

152. The Pediatric Working Group of the Conference on Amplification for Children with Auditory Deficits. Amplification for infants and children with hearing loss. Am J Audiol 5:53, 1996.

153. van der Pouw CT, Snik AF, Cremers CW. The BAHA HC200/300 in comparison with conventional bone conduction hearing aids. Clin Otolaryngol 24:171, 1999.

154. Zenner HP, Leysieffer H, Maassen M, et al. Human studies of a piezoelectric transducer and a microphone for a totally implantable electronic hearing device. Am J Otolaryngol 21:196, 2000.

155. Zenner HP, Leysieffer H. Active electronic hearing implants for middle and inner ear hearing loss—a new era in ear surgery. II: Current state of developments [translation]. HNO 45:758, 1997.

156. Zink G. Hearing aids children wear: a longitudinal study of performance. Volta Rev 74:41, 1972.

157. Zimmerman-Phillips S, Osberger MJ, Robbins AM. Infant toddler: meaningful auditory integration scale (IT-MAIS). 1997.

158. Zorowka PG, Lippert KL. One-channel and multichannel digitally programmable hearing aids in children with hearing impairment. Ann Otol Rhinol Laryngol Suppl 166:159, 1995.

159. Kopun JG, Stelmachowicz PG. Perceived communication difficulties of children with hearing loss. Am J Audiol 7:30, 1998.

108

Behavioral Intervention and Education of Children with Hearing Loss

Sheila Pratt, Ph.D.

The nature of behavioral treatment and education of infants and children with hearing loss is changing rapidly as a result of the implementation of universal newborn hearing screening programs, the push for early intervention of children with handicapping conditions by federal health and education agencies, and advances in auditory prostheses such as hearing aids and cochlear implants. Until recently, the age of identification of hearing loss in the pediatric population in the United States averaged between 12 and 25 months,[23, 35, 56, 85] with at-risk and more severely impaired children being identified earliest. Children with no risk factors for hearing loss and children with mild to moderate losses typically were not identified until about 28 months of age; many hearing losses were left undetected until they were identified at preschool and kindergarten hearing screening programs, or when hearing was tested because of concerns regarding speech, language, and cognitive delays. In areas of the country that have implemented universal newborn hearing screening programs, substantial numbers of infants are being identified and diagnosed with hearing loss shortly after birth (2.1 to 3.3 per 1000 births).[2, 25, 99] As a result, there is opportunity to initiate behavioral intervention and the fitting of sensory aids at increasingly younger ages. The push toward early identification and intervention is consistent with the goals of both the Healthy People 2010 initiative[98] and the Joint Committee of Infant Hearing Year 2000 Position Statement on the Principles and Guidelines for Early Hearing Detection and Intervention Programs.[41] Healthy People 2010 and the Joint Committee of Infant Hearing proposed that all infants born with hearing loss be screened by 1 month of age, diagnosed by 3 months, and enrolled into early intervention by 6 months of age. The Joint Committee of Infant Hearing also recommended that the fitting of hearing aids (given parent permission, appropriateness, and no medical contraindications) occur within 1 month of confirmation of the hearing loss.

Numerous factors, parental, health care, and logistical, over which professionals have little control, interfere with meeting these goals.[25] Despite the roadblocks, many newborn hearing screening programs have been effective at screening and diagnosing hearing loss within the suggested time frame, although quickly fitting sensory aids on newly diagnosed infants has been more difficult. The New York State Universal Newborn Hearing Screening Demonstration Project was able to effectively implement a newborn hearing screen program with timely assessment and enrollment into early intervention programs, but fewer than half of the infants with diagnosed hearing loss were fitted with hearing aids, and, of those, the median age when the fittings occurred was 7.5 months, 4.5 months after diagnosis.[15] With more experience, the lag between diagnosis and fitting likely will decrease. For example, from 1993 to 1996, the Rhode Island Hearing Assessment Program was able to reduce not only the mean age at which hearing loss was confirmed (from 8.7 to 3.5 months) but also the mean age at which hearing aid fittings occurred (from 13.3 to 5.7 months).[99]

The push for early intervention for infants with hearing loss is not without justification, and unlike early intervention for some other types of disabling conditions,[59, 76, 93] the gains tend to be substantive. The data produced by Yoshinaga-Itano and colleagues[60, 61, 105, 107] indicate that infants with hearing loss (regardless of degree of loss) who are enrolled in an early intervention program by 6 months of age maintain language abilities consistent with their cognitive abilities, whereas infants identified and treated after 6 months of age tend to show significant and persistent delay. Development of speech and auditory skills is more normal with early identified infants, and families adjust to the hearing loss more rapidly.[10, 106] The indication is that, soon, many children with hearing loss will exhibit normal or near normal auditory, language, speech, and learning skills by the time they enter school such that a large percentage of them will have the skills to be successful in regular educational settings with only minimal support services. Children identified late will continue to need more extensive special education services, as will children with multiple handicaps, but the number of children needing special placements within or outside of their home school districts should decrease. Correspondingly, the management emphasis likely will shift from the treatment of disabilities and provision of specialized educational services toward prevention or reduction of disability through early intervention. It is likely that some resources and research presently devoted to integrating deaf and hard-of-hearing children into regular school settings will be shifted to preventing the disabilities that segregate children with hearing loss from their normal hearing peers. Moreover, these children will more easily transition into higher education and employment.

Early Intervention

Service Delivery

The management of infants with hearing loss has multiple components and can come in various forms, although it may be constrained for some infants and their families by the state and federal regulations governing the provision of publicly funded early intervention services, as well as by the scope and range of service options and qualified professionals available in a given geographic region. If parents opt for private or supplementary services, the limitations of their insurance coverage also apply.

The nature and scope of early intervention services provided to most infants with hearing loss are fashioned to comply with Part C of Public Law 105-17 (amendment to the Individuals with Disabilities Education Act, IDEA, 1977),[97] which specifies that publicly funded early intervention provided to infants with disabilities or who are at risk for development of disabilities should be family centered. That is, professionals should be sensitive to the needs and concerns of the family and should work as an interdisciplinary group with the family. After hearing loss is diagnosed in infants, families are quickly (within approximately 2 days) referred to the designated lead agency for their area of their state. A service coordinator, assigned by the lead agency, works with the family and diagnosticians from various disciplines to complete a comprehensive interdisciplinary evaluation. The assessment team, which includes the family, medical professionals, developmental specialists, rehabilitation professionals, and learning specialists, determines the strengths, weaknesses, and needs of both the infant and the family. Given the results of the evaluation, an Individualized Family Service Plan is constructed, and the agreed upon goals and services are provided with oversight from the service coordinator (Table 108–1). The parents can reject services even if they and their infant qualify for them, or they can obtain a range of services provided by single or multiple interventionists. In addition, the language in Part C of Public Law 105-17 is explicit that the behavioral management and education of infants and their caregivers should occur in the infant's natural environments where possible, given the goals of the Individualized Family Service Plan. The preferred setting is the home, although community settings frequented by infants and children without disabilities meet the definition of natural environments. It also is acknowledged that the outcome of some services may be compromised if they occur in the home and that other types of services simply are not feasible in the home. For example, if an infant lives in a noisy home environment, auditory training may need to occur in a more sound-controlled location. If a toddler communicates via sign language and the parents have had difficulty

TABLE 108–1. Essential Components of an Individual Family Service Plan

1. A statement of the infant's present level of development.
2. A statement of the family's strengths and needs related to enhancing the infant's development.
3. A statement of major outcomes expected to be achieved for the infant and family and the criteria, procedures, and timelines for determining progress.
4. Statement of specific intervention services necessary to meet the needs of the child, including information about the frequency, intensity, method of delivery, and location of services.
5. The projected dates for the initiation of services and the expected duration.
6. The name of the service coordinator (case manager) responsible for implementing the plan.
7. Procedures for transition from early intervention into the Individualized Educational Program.

learning sign, a preschool with children and adults who are fluent signers may be a more natural environment. It also may be an environment in which the toddler and possibly the parents may learn to sign more easily.

The services provided to infants and their families are determined by the interdisciplinary team as part of the development of the Individualized Family Service Plan. A wide range of services can be included as long as they contribute to the desired outcomes of the intervention. Some of the types of services that families can request include assistive technology services and devices, transportation and related cost of travel, deaf mentors, signing facilitators, family educators, and counselors. They can request health care and rehabilitation services from the areas of medicine, nursing, nutrition, occupational therapy, physical therapy, speech-language pathology, and audiology. They also can request the assistance of early childhood educators, teachers of the deaf and hard of hearing, psychologists, social workers, and vision specialists.

Critical Services

Counseling

Parent counseling and instruction is a critical component to early intervention and should occur from the onset, as well as throughout the intervention process. All professionals working with families of infants and children with hearing loss should contribute to parent counseling and be cognizant that it has far-reaching effects. For example, parents often are more comfortable with audiologic testing, medical interventions, and the fitting of auditory prostheses if they have had counseling before the procedures. Parent counseling and instruction appears to reduce parental stress levels, particularly in parents with restricted social support networks and limited financial means.[31, 80] It facilitates parents moving through the mourning process and promotes positive parent-infant bonding and interaction.[31, 32] Counseling and instruction also help parents make informed decisions about the services that they and their infant receive through their local early intervention agencies and later as the child enters school. Some families ultimately need psychological services to cope with raising a child who has special needs, but most parents prefer to receive counseling from the professionals whom they see on a regular basis such as the early childhood educator, audiologist, or speech-language pathologist. Parents view these professionals as part of their social support network and, as a result, these professionals can significantly reduce the amount of stress that parents experience as part of raising a child with hearing loss.[58] Calderon and Greenberg[9] found that mothers of school-aged children with hearing loss were better adjusted to their children's hearing loss if they perceived themselves as having a good social support network, even in the face of high levels of negative life stress. Some parents may need more concentrated attention than others. Mothers with limited income experience higher levels of stress relative to their children's hearing loss than do mothers from middle or high-income homes.[31, 80] Parents from ethnic minority groups tend to be less satisfied with their children's services than are parents from the majority.[64] In addition, there are special concerns about children with multiple handicaps and children with mild to moderate hearing losses, particularly if they are identified late.[4, 64] Professionals must be mindful that parents need support and periodic counseling and instruction as their children get older and issues, needs, and parental concerns change.

Parents not only benefit from counseling and instruction from professionals but also from participating in parent support groups and from communicating with other parents who have a child with hearing loss. Early in the process most parents appreciate the availability of other parents with whom they can discuss concerns and solicit advice. In addition, some parents find that interactions with deaf and hard of hearing adults provide them with helpful perspectives on deafness and the effects of hearing loss.

Sensory Aids

Another key part of the early intervention process for most infants with hearing loss is the fitting of auditory prostheses or sensory aids. After medical clearance and preliminary determination of the nature and extent of the hearing loss, most infants with hearing loss are fit bilaterally with behind-the-ear hearing aids. Even infants who appear to be eventual candidates for cochlear implants are initially fit with hearing aids and/or tactile aids until there is sufficient documentation and physical maturity to support their candidacy for an implant. The fitting of hearing aids on infants who have unilateral and minimal or fluctuating hearing loss is more controversial, although data from Bess and colleagues[4] and Meadow-Orlans and associates[64] suggest that some type of sensory aids and intervention services may be warranted with these infants as well.

It is essential that the hearing aids be fit as early as possible in order to reduce the effects of prolonged auditory deprivation/privation because there is ample evidence that the early months of life are critical for the development of audition and auditory-dependent skills.[42, 50, 72, 73, 103] Candidates for cochlear implants also should receive implants as soon as possible. There is a negative relationship between the age of implantation and speech perception and production development in children with cochlear implants.[69] Moreover, prelingually deafened children who undergo implantation by 5 years of age tend to have more rapid growth in speech, oral language, and auditory skills subsequent to implantation than children implanted at older ages.[19, 26, 96] Daya and associates[19] also noted that the best predictor of postimplant speech perception skills in children is the duration of deafness before receiving the implant.

The process of securing hearing aids can interfere with the quick implementation of some behavioral interventions. While some parents opt to purchase the hearing aids privately, most parents go through state programs that supply hearing aids to infants and children with hearing loss free of charge regardless of ability to pay. However, the qualification and application process for securing the hearing aids can delay the fitting. In states where the application and the hearing aid securement processes are protracted, many audiologists provide "loaner" hearing aids until the infant's own hearing aids are obtained. Switching between hearing aids may require some adjustments in central auditory processing by infants, and it may create additional anxiety for parents who are insecure about managing their infant's hearing aids, but usually it is preferable to delaying the fitting.

The fitting of hearing aids on infants is a long-term process. Infants initially are fitted from data obtained from physiologic measures such as auditory brain stem evoked potential tests administered with tone bursts or filtered clicks. After the infant has matured and learned to listen to the sounds presented through hearing aids, reliable behavioral hearing thresholds can be obtained. As more complete audiometric data are obtained, the hearing aids are adjusted to best compensate for the hearing loss of the infant. Similar adjustments are made as the infant's ear canals grow and ear molds are replaced because both canal growth and ear mold differences can substantially alter the ear canal acoustics in infants, which, in turn, has an impact on the performance of the hearing aids.

Before and throughout the fitting process, parents benefit from instruction about hearing loss, the function and care of the devices, how to stimulate listening, and what instrumental and behavioral characteristics suggest that the devices are not functioning or fit optimally. After the infant and parents have adjusted to the hearing aids, parents also may benefit from discussions about other types of sensory aids and assistive devices such as personal FM systems, which appear to benefit some young children even outside academic settings.[66] The nature of the counseling and instruction that parents receive about hearing aids may impact the success with which children wear their hearing aids. For example, only one fourth to one half of the hearing aids worn by children are functioning properly at any given time.[43, 70, 77, 78, 109] This lack of hearing aid maintenance and troubleshooting by parents and children implicates the counseling and instruction that occurs relative to the importance of hearing and use of hearing instruments.[21] Moreover, children need to learn how to best use the acoustic information that they receive through sensory aids so that they are acutely aware of when their sensory aids malfunction.

Auditory Training

The process by which infants and children are encouraged to listen to sound and maximize their use of residual hearing is typically referred to as auditory training. Although auditory training is uniformly recommended for children with residual hearing, only a few studies have tested the effectiveness of auditory training with children who have hearing loss, and no studies have been done with infants. Hnath-Chisolm[37] found that school-aged children with severe to profound hearing loss benefited more from auditory training with sentence-level than word-level speech stimuli. Bennett[3] was able to train children with a severe hearing loss to hear voicing differences by first pairing acoustic voicing cognates with a tactile analog.

The auditory training effectiveness literature for adults with hearing impairment also is limited but suggests that benefit is dependent on subject and stimuli. For example, Rubinstein and Boothroyd[82] found only modest benefit with sentence- and syllable-level auditory training with adults who had been successful hearing aid wearers, but they did observe maintenance of the gains that were obtained. In contrast, Walden and associates[100] found that adults newly fit with hearing aids benefited from systematic consonant discrimination training while Kricos and Holmes[47] found that older adults with previous hearing aid experience did not benefit from consonant and vowel discrimination training but they did benefit from active listening training. Although, some adults appear to benefit from auditory training, their perceptual needs may differ substantially from those of infants and young children, which may account for why most clinicians recommend short-term auditory training for adults, whereas children appear to need more long-term, systematic instruction with sound. Some children newly fit with cochlear implants require months of training before showing benefits.[7]

Although well-constructed studies assessing the effectiveness of auditory training with children with hearing loss are few, the perceptual training and phonologic awareness literature has increased substantially in recent years and strongly suggests that normal hearing children and adults benefit from the training of the auditory skills. For example, adults and children have been trained to perceive non-native speech contrasts, although not all speech contrasts can be learned equally well.[6, 92, 103] Children with language and learning problems also have been trained to process speech signals more effectively.[65, 91] Furthermore, Kraus and colleagues[45, 46, 92] argue that such training actually impacts the physiology of the central auditory system and may relate to cortical reorganization. If cortical reorganization is required of infants and children newly fit with sensory aids in order to use auditory information effectively, then it stands to reason that they

would benefit from intensive auditory training during this reorganization period.

Most early intervention programs include auditory training, although the form and emphasis of the training varies across approaches and clinicians. Some approaches include direct listening instruction while others tend to work indirectly through the parents by promoting optimal verbal interactions between the parents and their children. Most auditory-verbal approaches focus on audition alone, whereas multisensory approaches stimulate other modalities along with the auditory system and work to improve perception by promoting integration of all relevant signals. Although research recognizes the importance of integrating sensory information while listening[24, 99] (i.e., we hear speech better when we can see the speaker, especially in adverse listening conditions), there is little evidence to support any one training modality or method over another.

Traditionally, auditory training is integrated into other training activities such as speech and language stimulation. It commonly begins with simple tasks and stimuli such as responding to the presence of sound or localizing a sound source. These tasks are targeted because many newly fitted infants and young children need to become aware that sound exists, that it has a source, and that the location of that source is important information about the environment. With development, the complexity of the response tasks and stimuli is increased, although it may be limited by hearing loss severity as well as developmental delays in cognition and language. Training quickly incorporates speech signals, first working on pattern perception and recognition of words that are relevant in the child's communicative environment. Attempts are made to include listening activities that are linguistically relevant and that stimulate language and literacy development. For children who communicate orally, the stimuli also should promote more normal speech development.

As children become older, their listening activities should be incorporated into academic and communication training activities, although more focused auditory training may be needed when sensory devices are replaced or altered. As part of the auditory training process, children also should become increasingly more responsible for the care and maintenance of their sensory devices. For example, many 2-year-old children can learn to test their hearing aid batteries with supervision and thereby acquire a sense of ownership of their hearing aids. Exploring the independent use of assistive devices also is important in that children mature so that they can perform age-appropriate auditory-based activities, such as using the telephone, answering a doorbell, or using an alarm clock. By increasing auditory skills and the use of assistive devices, children with hearing loss become more independent, and as a consequence less disabled and handicapped.

Communication Training

Language Acquisition

One of the most disabling consequences of prelingual hearing loss is language delay and impairment. Hearing loss can impact linguistic development and, consequently, interfere with children's cognitive, social, and emotional development, their literacy skill acquisition and ability to succeed in school, and ultimately their ability to obtain and maintain gainful employment. Normal hearing infants and children acquire language fairly effortlessly just by being immersed in their native language.[12, 81] However, even infants and children with mild and moderate degrees of hearing loss are at risk for speech and language delay and eventual academic failure.[4, 17, 22] Many children with hearing loss, particularly those identified after 6 months of age, exhibit a slowed but normal sequence of language development until their preteen years, at which time development often plateaus.[14, 16, 18, 67, 68] With this leveling off, many children begin to look increasingly disordered as the mismatches between nonverbal function, world knowledge, and linguistic skill increase. In addition, some children have concomitant language disorders and learning problems that are exacerbated by the hearing loss and are therefore less responsive to training and treatment.[8, 30]

Although children with hearing loss are at substantial risk of language delay, the relationship between hearing loss and language development is less than straightforward. In general, the severity of hearing loss tends to predict the extent of language delay, particularly if children representing the full range of hearing loss severity are considered.[18, 22] The consequence is that language development often arrests at a lower level in children with a profound hearing loss than in children with less severe hearing losses. However, the relationship between severity of hearing loss and language delay is mediated by other factors, such as age of identification, intelligence, language modality, age and means of assessment, method of treatment, and education, all of which have been found to impact language outcome.[10, 60, 61] For example, despite the more normal rate of language development by children who are identified and who receive intervention early, there remains a gap between children with profound hearing loss and children with less severe hearing losses.[60]

Modality

One of the most difficult decisions that parents of infants with hearing loss have to make is deciding the modality with which their infant will communicate. Approximately 93% of infants with hearing loss have parents who are hearing.[64] The natural reaction of these parents is to desire that their child communicate like they do, through oral-aural means. With early amplification and cochlear implantation, there likely will be an increase in the number of children who become successful users of oral-aural communication, although there will continue to be infants and children for whom language is most easily learned and used in a visual-manual form. There are no single predictive factors to help parents decide. The severity and configuration of hearing loss, age of onset, age of intervention, propensity to use speech, cognition, other handicapping conditions, parental socioeconomic status, and parent involvement all contribute to whether a child will be successful with communication via speech and audition.[29, 64, 108]

Speech Acquisition

Audition allows infants and young children exposure to and feedback from the motor act of speaking as well as to the sound system of the ambient language. It therefore stands to reason that hearing loss has an impact on the development and production of speech, particularly in children in whom hearing loss was present at birth or acquired in infancy. Children who have had an extended experience with audition before acquiring their hearing loss may lose some skills with the onset of the loss but usually retain a normal developmental pattern as soon as auditory feedback is restored with sensory aids. In addition, infants who receive intervention services early[10] and are able to benefit from an auditory-verbal training approach tend to acquire more normal speech skills.[108]

Speech delay and disorder is most pronounced in children who have a profound hearing loss,[5, 54, 83, 108] although even children with mild to moderate hearing losses are at risk for speech differences and delays.[22] Children with hearing loss tend to exhibit a slowed developmental pattern with many children showing a plateau in development by 8 to 9 years of age. Recently Obenchain and associates[71] found that the speech sound inventories of infants 16 to 23 months of age was a strong indicator of intelligible speech at 36 months. It also is likely that the size and complexity of earlier (5 to 13 months) sound inventories of deaf and hard of hearing infants are predictive of later speech intelligibility,[101] and that infants having higher speech sound production rates retain both a speech inventory and intelligibility advantages at 5 years of age.[108]

As suggested earlier, the speech sound inventories of infants with severe to profound hearing loss have been found to be highly restricted when compared with normal hearing and less impaired infants.[51, 88, 108] These infants also speak less often (which, in part, may be a function of their reduced language skills) and are frequently described as being quiet babies. The sounds that older children with severe to profound hearing loss produce tend to be less demanding motorically, to be more easily viewed, and to have a low-frequency emphasis.[95] In addition to being delayed in speech sound acquisition, the speech of children with severe to profound hearing loss is more likely to be disordered than the speech of children with less severe hearing loss. Sound omissions are common, as are distortions. Sound production is variable and highly susceptible to perturbation and context. Moreover, basic elements of speech production coordination (e.g., respiratory and vocal control for speech) can be impaired such that the speech production system functions atypically,[36, 79] even when speech is intelligible.[62]

Manual Communication

Success with visual-manual forms of communication also depends on a number of factors. Hearing-impaired infants and children whose parents are motivated to learn and use a visual-manual system, and who have native or fluent signers available to act as normal language models, are most likely to benefit from a manually coded language such as American Sign Language (ASL). However, many infants and children are exposed to non-native, nonfluent signers who use incomplete, inconsistent, or pidgin forms of sign and, as a result, are at substantial risk of language delay and disorder.[53, 57, 90]

A number of visual-manual communication systems are available. Some visual-manual systems code the mainstream oral language, such as Manually Coded English. Others code characteristics of the speech production of the oral language, such as Cued Speech, in order to augment speech reception and production. Other systems consist of the language of the deaf community (e.g., ASL). There are advantages and disadvantages to all of the systems. The role that professionals play in the process of determining which system to use is to provide parents with impartial background about the different methods and letting parents decide what is best for them and their children.

A recent option provided by some early interventionists and educators of the deaf is to provide bilingual intervention and education, with children being exposed to both the mainstream oral language and the manual language of the deaf community (English and ASL in the United States).[40, 55, 75] When bilingual education is coupled with exposure to both the mainstream and deaf cultures, the training approach is referred to as bilingual bicultural (Bi-Bi) education.[86] Proponents argue that children who become oral-aural communicators have an early means of acquiring language and rely less on signing as they become more proficient with speech and oral language. Moreover, with bilingual exposure, these children continue to have access to a visual-manual language that can be used in poor acoustic conditions. It also allows them a means of interacting with friends who sign and gives them greater access to the deaf community. With bilingual exposure, infants who are better suited to signing are exposed to a usable language sooner than if only an oral-aural language is used. If exposed to the language early and by fluent and native signers, the infants are less likely to show the long-term negative effects of language deprivation observed in children who fail to be exposed to a complete and intelligible language early in life. However, with most parents and many professionals not being native or fluent signers, the sign language to which children are frequently exposed is incomplete at best.[104] Even when teachers and parents use a form of Manually Coded English, the signing is less complete than their oral expressions.[44, 88, 90, 104] Another concern is that, in order for ASL signing children to succeed in school, they need to learn the dominant oral language. The bilingual argument is that the oral language is best learned through early literacy instruction as a second language. So, for example, infants learn ASL as their first language and then after their first language has been established, they are taught English as a second language through reading and writing. It should be noted, however, that there is very little effectiveness and efficacy data to support the use of bilingual intervention and instruction. In addition, some parents and interventionists strongly oppose any use of manual instruction with potential users of oral-aural language because of the belief that it will interfere with auditory development and subsequently oral-aural language acquisition.

Language Instruction

With infants and young children, the goal of most interventionists is to optimize the environment so that infants have abundant opportunity to hear or see language, or both. Language training with infants usually consists of working with caregivers and family members to optimize the quality of the language that they use with their infants. There are also indications that infants and young children with hearing loss need greater levels of exposure to good samples of language than infants with normal hearing in order to counter the distorted, incomplete, or poorly formed input that they receive. Along with frequently exposing infants and young children to optimal language models, the models should be associated with a range of world experiences so that language is stimulated across cognitive domains. This type of intervention is indirect but, if substantive language delay or disorder becomes evident, more direct language treatment measures are used. Certain aspects of language are targeted and, with age, the instruction becomes more integrated into the academic activities and needs of the children.

In order to optimize the input to the infants, interventionists (typically speech-language pathologists, early childhood educators, rehabilitation audiologists, or teachers of the deaf and hard of hearing) work with parents to determine the behaviors and situations that optimize communication. They also try to identify which behaviors and situations interfere with language stimulation and contribute to communication breakdowns.[94] For example, hearing parents tend to retain a strong oral bias even when interacting with their infants who are showing indications of being more disposed to manual than oral communication.[53] It also is not unusual for hearing parents to use less than optimal speech when talking with their infants. They may whisper or talk with their backs toward their infants without being cognizant that their infants may not hear them. By working with the parents and other caregivers, the communicative environment of the infant can be optimized, allowing for more normal development.

Speech Instruction

Historically, the speech of infants and young children with hearing loss has been stimulated through auditory training and reinforcement of natural speech attempts and is usually done in conjunction with auditory training and language stimulation activities.[79] Direct treatment typically does not occur until children are of school age, which from linguistic and motor learning perspectives may be too late. It has long been known that children with hearing loss who are unable to produce intelligible speech by 8 years of age are unlikely to show significant improvement even with intensive speech training.[39, 63, 83] The observation that speech sound inventory in infancy can predict intelligibility at 3 years of age and later also implies that speech stimulation and training should occur early for those children who will communicate orally so that by the time they enter school their speech will be largely intelligible in most contexts. There also is reason to believe that children who rely on a signing system to communicate may benefit from early speech treatment as well. It may allow for essential communication in situations where signed or written communication is not possible. In addition, speech instruction may provide a means for learning the sound system of the dominant oral language, which appears to be critical for the development of high-level textual reading.[74]

Educational Options

Educational Models

At least 3 months before a child's third birthday, children with hearing loss begin to transition from early intervention services that are family focused to early education services that are child focused and more classroom- or center-based. The families remain a part of the intervention team and contribute to the development of the Individualized Education Program, but the focus of services begins to shift from what the family needs to promote normal development in their infant to what the team believes the child needs relative to educational outcome (Table 108–2). The child and family remain within this model of service delivery until high school graduation or until they no longer need special educational services. The services provided vary according to the communication modality used by the child and educationally relevant problems that the child may present. In reality, they also may be limited by the availability of qualified personnel and budgetary constraints of the local school district in that most children with hearing loss remain in their local school districts.[64]

The general goal for all children receiving special educational services is that they be academically successful in as normal a setting as possible. For children younger than 5 years of age, the placement can vary from a regular preschool with support services (such as itinerant services from the teacher of the deaf and hard of hearing or the speech-language pathologist) to a self-contained preschool designed specifically for children with hearing loss. As children get older, optimal placements should continue to match the individual needs of the children. For some,

this means placement in a school for the deaf; for others, it means regular classroom placement with an interpreter or a tutor. In response to state and federal mandates, most schools try to mainstream or include children with special needs into regular classrooms as much as possible. However, regular classroom placements should be implemented with care because many children with hearing loss are ill equipped to succeed in regular classrooms even with support services. Inappropriate inclusion of children with hearing loss into regular classrooms often results in academic failure, frustrated parents, and the social and emotional isolation of the children. To avoid the potential negative results that can be associated with premature or inappropriate regular classroom placements, many children with hearing loss begin school in more restrictive learning environments and then transition into less restrictive environments as they acquire the skills to be successful.

The predominant emphasis in the education of deaf and hard of hearing children is the promotion of normal literacy development. If children with hearing loss learn to read and write effectively, their ability to learn other academic materials is facilitated. However, historically, children with severe to profound hearing loss rarely learned to read and write beyond a third to fourth grade level regardless of the mode or method of instruction.[1, 20, 27, 38, 48] Improvement after 10 years of age is minimal,[1, 27] although early intervention and cochlear implantation may alter this typical outcome. Children with more residual hearing and children who have the skills to be in oral-aural and regular classrooms fare better academically than children in manual and self-contained programs.[28] But, as indicated earlier, even children with mild to moderate hearing losses are at risk for academic difficulties. There is some evidence, much of it anecdotal, that deaf children of deaf parents who acquire sign language in a more normal fashion than deaf children of hearing parents also perform well academically.[11] The implication is that the impediment to normal literacy development in individuals with hearing loss is poor linguistic development.

The literature suggests that knowing the grammar and structure of language is important for literacy development, but to become a proficient reader and writer, children also must acquire knowledge of the sound system of the language that they are reading. Moreover, they must be able to relate the sound system to the alphabet.[13, 34, 74, 102] Children who have limited or no residual hearing, for obvious reasons, have more difficulty knowing the sound system and relating it to the written form. They also have difficulty holding the sound-letter correspondence in memory such that comprehension and vocabulary acquisition is impaired. The difficulty in learning the sound system also has implications for learning English as a second language through literacy instruction, with some investigators believing that it may be unrealistic.[74] In rare instances, deaf children who sign in ASL do become proficient readers and writers of English. They learn the grammar of English, but they also acquire the notion (or had some prior notion) of the English sound system from which the text is based. The importance of an auditory image of speech sounds is supported by research that

TABLE 108–2. Essential Components of an Individualized Educational Program

1. A statement of the child's present levels of performance.
2. A statement of measurable annual goals including benchmarks or short-term instructional objectives. Appropriate objective criteria and evaluation procedures and schedules for determining, on at least an annual basis, whether the child will be able to participate in regular educational programs.
3. A statement of specific special education and related services to be provided to the child, and the extent to which the child will be able to participate in regular education.
4. The projected date for initiation of services and anticipated duration of services.
5. A statement of accommodations so that state or district-wide achievement tests can be administered.
6. By age 14 years, inclusion of procedures for transition to special courses of study (e.g., advanced placement or vocational education programs).
7. By age 16 years, inclusion of a transition plan for transition of services from school to work or college or other technical training.

indicates that young children fitted with cochlear implants tend to show more normal literacy development.[84]

Because literacy is dependent on an intact linguistic system and knowledge of the sound system of the oral language from which the text is based, much of early education of children with hearing loss concentrates on promoting language development, relating language and world knowledge to literacy, and promoting early literacy skills. Once in elementary school, most children are taught reading through the same approaches used with normal hearing children. Most programs for children with hearing loss use both a basal readers series and promote literacy and language through whole language experiences.[52] In this manner, both bottom-up and top-down processing skills are stimulated and exploited, although it is not clear whether the two types of approaches augment or interfere with one another. The biggest shift in literacy development is likely to come with the children who are identified, fit with sensory devices, and placed into intervention programs early. With early identified infants showing more normal language, speech, and auditory development, the outlook for breaking the fourth-grade reading barrier is positive. These children also will have greater access to academic content areas such as science and social studies if literacy skills are acquired more normally.

Educational Support Services

Although the primary focus of education for children with hearing loss is normal language and literacy development, the goals are achieved more easily if adequate support services are in place. In order to succeed in regular classrooms, children with hearing loss need audiologists to monitor hearing aid and cochlear implant performance and use. Audiologists also are needed to fit and monitor FM systems and other amplification and assistive devices. Teachers of the deaf and hard of hearing may provide the primary instruction to the children or they may provide itinerant services and act as advisors to the regular classroom teacher. Speech language pathologists often work with the children on improving language, auditory, and speech skills both in and outside the classroom. With about one third of all children with hearing loss having other handicapping conditions, other rehabilitation and medical professionals, such as physical therapists, occupational therapists, learning disability specialists, reading specialists, behavior specialists, nutritionists, and psychologists, are needed to support some children within the educational setting. With age, many children with hearing loss also benefit from tutors, note takers, and interpreters. The active involvement with academic and occupational counselors is critical for children in high school so that the transition to employment or to advanced training or education is smooth. These counselors also may help students with hearing loss obtain reasonable accommodations and support in order for the students to succeed after graduating from high school. Providing accommodations to promote involvement in extracurricular activities is an added issue for children with hearing loss as they become older. When children with hearing loss are provided the opportunity to participate in athletic, social, and recreational activities after school, they tend to become more integrated with their peers. It also provides a platform for children to acquire social and personal skills that can lead to improved self-esteem and academic performance.[33, 87]

Conclusion

To promote normal development in children with hearing loss, behavioral intervention and education should occur as early as possible. It typically begins with a family-focused interdisciplinary approach, but shifts to a more academic focus when children reach 3 years of age. The goal of most intervention and educational programs for preschool-aged children with hearing loss is to prepare the children for successful participation in school. As children enter and progress through school, the priorities for intervention are inclusion and successful learning of educational skills and content. Along with the changes in the delivery models and services, the needs of the children and their families also change with age and development, so that it is important for intervention to be individually tailored.

REFERENCES

1. Allen T. Patterns of academic achievement in hearing impaired students: 1974 and 1983. In Schildroth A, Karchmer M (eds). Deaf Children in America. San Diego, College Hill Press, 1986, pp 161–206.
2. Barsky-Firsker L, Sun S. Universal newborn hearing screenings: a three-year experience. Pediatrics 99:E4, 1997.
3. Bennett CW. Training severely hearing-impaired children in the discrimination of the voiced-voiceless distinction. J Am Aud Soc 2: 213, 1977.
4. Bess FH, Dodd-Murphy J, Parker RA. Children with minimal sensorineural hearing loss: prevalence, education performance and functional status. Ear Hear 19:339, 1988.
5. Boothroyd A. Distribution of Hearing Levels in the Student Population of the Clarke School for the Deaf. Northampton, Mass, Clark School for the Deaf, 1969.
6. Bradlow AR, Pisoni DB, Akahane-Yamada R, Tohkura Y. Training Japanese listeners to identify English /r/ and /l/: IV. Some effects of perceptual learning on speech production. J Acoust Soc Am 101: 2299, 1997.
7. Brookhouser PE, Auslander MC. Aided auditory thresholds in children with postmeningitic deafness. Laryngoscope 99:800, 1989.
8. Bullard CS, Schirmer BR. Understanding questions: hearing-impaired children with learning problems. Volta Rev 93:235, 1991.
9. Calderon R, Greenberg MT. Stress and coping in hearing mothers of children with hearing loss. Am Ann Deaf 144:7, 1999.
10. Calderon R, Naidu S. Further support for the benefits of early identification and intervention for children with hearing loss. Volta Rev 100:53, 2000.
11. Charrow VR, Fletcher JD. English as the second language of deaf children. Dev Psych 10:463, 1974.
12. Clark EV. The Lexicon in Acquisition. Cambridge, Great Britain, Cambridge University Press, 1993.
13. Conrad R. The Deaf School Child. London, Harper & Row, 1979.
14. Conway DF. Semantic relationships in the word meanings of hearing-impaired children. Volta Rev 92:339, 1990.
15. Dalzell L, Orlando M, MacDonald M, et al. The New York State universal newborn hearing screening demonstration project: ages of hearing loss identification, hearing aid fitting, and enrollment in early intervention. Ear Hear 21:118, 2000.

16. Davis JM. Performance of young hearing impaired children on a test of basic concepts. J Speech Hear Res 17:342, 1974.

17. Davis JM, Elfenbein J, Schum R, Bentler RA. Effects of mild and moderate hearing impairments on language, educational, and psychosocial behavior of children. J Speech Hear Disorder 51:53, 1986.

18. Davis JM, Shepard NT, Stelmachowicz PG, Gorga MP. Characteristics of hearing impaired children in the public schools: Part II—psychoeducational data. J Speech Hear Disorder 46:130, 1981.

19. Daya H, Figueirido J, Gordon K, et al. The role of a graded profile analysis in determining candidacy and outcome for cochlear implantation in children. Int J Otorhinolaryngol 49:135, 1999.

20. DiFrancesca S. Academic Achievement Test Results of a National Testing Program for Hearing-Impaired Students—United States, Spring 1971. (Series D, No. 9). Washington, DC: Gallaudet College, Office of Demographic Studies, 1972.

21. Elfenbein JL. Monitoring preschoolers' hearing aids: issues in program design and implementation. Am J Audiol 3:65, 1994.

22. Elfenbein JL, Hardin-Jones MA, Davis JM. Oral communication skills of children who are hard of hearing. J Speech Hear Res 37:216, 1994.

23. Elssmann S, Matkin N, Sabo M. Early identification of congenital sensorineural hearing impairment. Hearing J 40:13, 1987.

24. Erber NP. Auditory-visual perception of speech with reduced optical clarity. J Speech Hear Disorder 22:212, 1978.

25. Finitzo T, Albright K, O'Neal J. The newborn with hearing loss: detection in the nursery. Pediatrics 102:1452, 1998.

26. Fryauf-Bertschy H, Tyler R, Kelsay D, et al. Cochlear implant use by prelingually deafened children: the influences of age at implant and length of device use. J Speech Hear Res 40:183, 1997.

27. Furth HG. A comparison of the reading test norms of deaf and hearing children. Am Ann Deaf 11:461, 1996.

28. Geers AE, Moog JS. Factors predictive of the development of literacy in profoundly hearing-impaired adolescents. Volta Rev 91:69, 1989.

29. Geers AE, Moog JS. Predicting spoken language acquisition of profoundly hearing-impaired children. J Speech Hear Disorder 52:84, 1987.

30. Gilberson M, Kamhi AG. Novel word learning in children with hearing impairment. J Speech Hear Res 38:630, 1995.

31. Greenberg MT. Family stress and child competence: the effects of early intervention for families with deaf infants. Am Ann Deaf 128:407, 1983.

32. Greenberg MT, Calderon R, Kusche C. Early intervention using simultaneous communication with deaf infants: the effects on communication development. Child Dev 55:607, 1984.

33. Griffin S. Students' activities in the middle school: what do they contribute? NASSP Bull 72:87, 1988.

34. Hanson V. Phonology and reading: evidence from profoundly deaf readers. In Shankweiler D, Lieberman I (eds). Phonology and Reading Disability: Solving the Reading Puzzle. Ann Arbor, Mich, University of Michigan Press, 1989, pp 69–89.

35. Harrison M, Roush J. Age of suspicion, identification, and intervention for infants with hearing loss: a national study. Ear Hear 17:55, 1996.

36. Higgins M, Carney A, Schulte L. Physiological assessment of speech and voice production of adults with hearing loss. J Speech Hear Res 37:510, 1994.

37. Hnath-Chisolm T. Context effects in auditory training with children. Scand Audiol Suppl 47:64, 1997.

38. Holt J. Stanford Achievement Test—8th edition: reading comprehension subgroup results. Am Ann Deaf 138:172, 1993.

39. Hudgins C, Numbers F. An investigation of the intelligibility of speech of the deaf. Genet Psychol Monogr 25:289, 1942.

40. Johnson R, Liddell S, Ertin C. Unlocking the Curriculum: Principles for Achieving Access in Deaf Education (Working Paper 89-3). Washington, DC, Gallaudet University, Gallaudet Research Institute, 1989.

41. Joint Committee on Infant Hearing. Year 2000 position statement. Principles and guidelines for early hearing detection and intervention programs. Audiology Today, Special Issue:6, 2000.

42. Jusczyk PW, Aslin RN. Infants' detection of sound patterns of words in fluent speech. Cognit Psychol 29:1, 1995.

43. Kemker FJ, McConnell F, Logan SA, Green BW. A field study of children's hearing aids in a school environment. Language Speech Hearing Services Schools 10:47, 1979.

44. Kluwin T. The grammaticality of manual representations of English in classroom settings. Am Ann Deaf 126:417, 1981.

45. Kraus N, McGee T, Carrell TD, et al. Central auditory system plasticity with speech discrimination training. J Cog Neurosci 7:25, 1995.

46. Kraus N, McGee T, Carrell TD, Sharma T. Neurophysiologic bases of speech discrimination. Ear Hear 16:19, 1995.

47. Kricos PB, Holmes AE. Efficacy of audiologic rehabilitation for older adults. J Am Acad Audiol 7:219, 1996.

48. Krose L, Lotz W, Puffer C, Osberger MJ. Language and learning skills of hearing impaired children. ASHA Monogr 23:66, 1986.

49. Kuhl PK, Meltzoff AN. Speech as an intermodal object of speech. In Yonis A (ed). Perceptual Development in Infancy. The Minnesota Symposia on Child Psychology. Hillsday, NJ, Lawrence Earlbaum & Associates 20:235, 1988.

50. Kuhl P, Williams K, Lacerda F, et al. Linguistic experience alters phonetic perception in infants by 6 months of age. Science 255:606, 1992.

51. Lach R, Ling D, Ling L, Ship N. Early speech development in deaf infants. Am Ann Deaf 115:522, 1970.

52. LaSasso CJ, Mobley RT. National survey of reading instruction for deaf or hard-of-hearing students in the U.S. Volta Rev 99:31, 1999.

53. Lederberg AR, Everhart VS. Communication between deaf children and their hearing mothers: the role of language, gesture, and vocalizations. J Speech Lang Hear Res 41:887, 1998.

54. Levitt H. Interrelationships among the speech and language measures. In Levitt H, McGarr N, Geffner D (eds). Development of language and communication skills of hearing-impaired children. ASHA Monogr 26:123, 1987.

55. Luetke-Stahlman B. Using bilingual instructional models in teaching hearing-impaired students. Am Ann Deaf 128:837, 1983.

56. Mace A, Wallace K, Whan M, Stelmachowicz P. Relevant factors in the identification of hearing loss. Ear Hear 12:287, 1991.

57. MacKay-Soroka S, Trehub SE, Thorpe LA. Reception of mothers' referential messages by deaf and hearing children. Dev Psychol 24:277, 1988.

58. MacTurk RH, Meadow-Orlans KP, Koester LS, Spencer P. Social support, motivation, language, and interaction. Am Ann Deaf 138:19, 1993.

59. Majnemer A. Benefits of early intervention for children with developmental disabilities. Semin Pediatr Neurol 5:62, 1998.

60. Mayne AM, Yoshinaga-Itano C, Sedey AL. Receptive vocabulary development of infants and toddlers who are deaf or hard of hearing. Volta Rev 100:29, 2000.

61. Mayne AM, Yoshinaga-Itano C, Sedey AL, Carey A. Expressive vocabulary development of infants and toddlers who are deaf or hard of hearing. Volta Rev 100:1, 2000.

62. McCaffrey H, Sussman H. An investigation of vowel organization in speakers with severe and profound hearing loss. J Speech Hear Res 37:938, 1994.

63. McGarr N. Communication skills of hearing-impaired children in schools for the deaf. In Levitt H, McGarr N, Geffner D (eds). Development of Language and Communication in Hearing Impaired Children. ASHA Monogr 26: 91–107, 1987.

64. Meadow-Orlans KP, Mertens DM, Sass-Lehrer MA, Scott-Olson K. Support services for parents and their children who are deaf or hard of hearing a national survey. Am Ann Deaf 142:278, 1977.

65. Merzenich MM, Jenkings WM, Johnston P, et al. Temporal processing deficits of language-learning impaired children ameliorated by training. Science 217:77, 1996.

66. Moeller MP, Donaghy KF, Beauchaine KL, et al. Longitudinal study of FM system use in nonacademic settings: effects on language development. Ear Hear 17:28, 1996.

67. Moeller MP, Osberger MJ, Eccarius M. Receptive language skills. In Osberger MJ (ed). Language and learning skills in hearing-impaired children. ASHA Monogr 23:41, 1986.

68. Moeller MP, Osberger MJ, Eccarius M. Expressive language skills. In Osberger MJ (ed). Language and learning skills in hearing-impaired children. ASHA Monogr 23:54, 1986.

69. Nickolopoulous TP, O'Donoghue GM, Archbold S. Age at implantation: its importance in pediatric cochlear implantation. Laryngoscope 109:595, 1999.

70. Northern JL, McChord W, Fischer E, Evans P. Hearing services

in residential schools for the deaf. Maico Audiology Library Series 11:16, 1972.

71. Obenchain P, Menn L, Yoshinaga-Itano C. Can speech development at 36 months in children with hearing loss be predicted from information available in the second year of life? Volta Rev 100:149, 2000.

72. Olsho LW, Koch EG, Carter EA, et al. Pure-tone sensitivity of human infants. J Acoust Soc Am 84:1316, 1988.

73. Olsho LW, Koch EG, Halpin CF. Level and age effects in infant frequency discrimination. J Acoust Soc Am 82:454, 1987.

74. Paul PV. First- and second language English literacy. Volta Rev 98: 5, 1999.

75. Paul PV. Deafness and text-based literacy. Am Ann Deaf 138:72, 1993.

76. Piper MC, Pless IB. Early intervention for infants with Down syndrome: a controlled trial. Pediatrics 65:463, 1980.

77. Porter TA. Hearing aids in a residential school. Am Ann Deaf 118: 31, 1973.

78. Potts PL, Greenwood J. Hearing aid monitoring: are looking and listening enough? Language Speech Hearing Services Schools 14: 157, 1983.

79. Pratt SR, Tye-Murray N. Speech impairment secondary to hearing loss. In McNeil MR (ed). Clinical Management of Sensorimotor Speech Disorders. New York, Thieme, 1997, pp 345–387.

80. Quittner A. Coping with a hearing impaired child: a model of adjustment to chronic stress. In Johnson J, Johnson S (eds). Advances in Child Health Psychology. Gainesville, Fla, University of Florida Press, 1991, pp 206–223.

81. Reznick JS, Goldfield BA. Rapid change in lexical development in comprehension and production. Dev Psychol 28:406, 1992.

82. Rubinstein A, Boothroyd A. Effect of two approaches to auditory training on speech recognition by hearing-impaired adults. J Speech Hear Res 30:153, 1987.

83. Smith C. Residual hearing and speech production in the deaf. J Speech Hear Res 19:795, 1975.

84. Spencer L, Tomblin JB, Gantz BJ. Reading skills in children with multichannel cochlear-implant experience. Volta Rev 99:193, 1999.

85. Stein L, Jabaley T, Spitz R, et al. The hearing-impaired infant: patterns of identification and rehabilitation revisited. Ear Hear 11: 210, 1990.

86. Stewart D. Bi-Bi to MCE? Am Ann Deaf 138:331, 1993.

87. Stewart DA, Stinson MS. The role of sport and extracurricular activities in shaping socialization patterns. In Kluwin TN, Moores DF, Guastad MG (eds). Toward Effective Public School Programs for Deaf Students. New York, Teachers College Press, 1992, pp 129–148.

88. Stole-Gammon C, Otomo K. Babbling development of hearing-impaired and normally hearing subjects. J Speech Hear Disorder 5: 33, 1986.

89. Strong M, Charlson E. Simultaneous communication: are teachers attempting an impossible task? Am Ann Deaf 132:376, 1987.

90. Swisher M. Signed input of hearing mothers to deaf children. Lang Learn 34:69, 1984.

91. Tallal P, Miller SL, Bedi G, et al. Language comprehension in language-learning impaired children improved with acoustically modified speech. Science 271:81, 1986.

92. Tremblay K, Kraus N, Carrell TD, McGee T. Central auditory system plasticity: generalization to novel stimuli following listening training. J Acoust Soc Am 102:3762, 1997.

93. Turnbull JD. Early intervention for children with or at risk of cerebral palsy. Am J Dis Child 147:54, 1993.

94. Tye-Murray N, Kelsay DMR. A communication training program for parents of cochlear implant users. Volta Rev 95:21, 1993.

95. Tye-Murray N, Kirk KI. Vowel and diphthong production by young users of cochlear implants and the relationship between the phonetic level evaluation and spontaneous speech. J Speech Hear Res 36:488, 1993.

96. Tye-Murray N, Spencer L, Woodworth G. Acquisition of speech by children who have prolonged implant experience. J Speech Hear Res 38:327, 1995.

97. United States Department of Education. Assistance to States for the Education of Children with Disabilities and the Early Intervention Program for Infants and Toddlers with Disabilities; Final Regulations. Fed Reg (34 CFR, Parts 300 and 303), March 12, 1999.

98. United States Department of Health and Human Services. Healthy People 2010/U.S. Dept. of Health and Human Services, Conference Edition. Washington, DC, U.S. Department of Health and Human Services, 2000.

99. Vohr BR, Carty LM, Moore PE, Letourneau K. The Rhode Island hearing assessment program: experience with statewide hearing screening (1993–1996). J Pediatr 133:353, 1998.

100. Walden BE, Erdman SA, Montgomery AA, et al. Some effects of training on speech recognition by hearing-impaired adults. J Speech Hear Res 24:207, 1981.

101. Wallace V, Menn L, Yoshinaga-Itano C. Is babble the gateway to speech for all children? A longitudinal study of children who are deaf or hard of hearing. Volta Rev 100:121, 2000.

102. Webster A. Deafness, Development and Literacy. London, Methuen, 1986.

103. Werker JF, Tees RC. Cross-language speech perception: evidence for perceptual reorganization during the first year of life. Infant Behav Dev 7:49, 1984.

104. Woodward J, Allen T. Classroom use of ASL. Sign Lang Studies 54:1, 1987.

105. Yoshinaga-Itano C. Efficacy of intervention strategies used with hearing impaired children. Paper presented at the annual convention of the American Speech, Language, and Hearing Association, San Francisco, Calif, 1999.

106. Yoshinaga-Itano C. Efficacy of early identification and intervention. Semin Hear 16:115, 1995.

107. Yoshinaga-Itano C, Sedey AL, Coulter DK, Mehl AL. The language of early- and later-identified children with hearing loss. Pediatrics 102:1161, 1998.

108. Yoshinaga-Itano C, Sedey A. Early speech development in children who are deaf or hard of hearing: interrelationships with language and hearing. Volta Rev 100:181, 2000.

109. Zink GD. Hearing aids children wear: a longitudinal study of performance. Volta Rev 74:41, 1972.

Pediatric Otolaryngology: A Psychosocial Perspective

Kenny H. Chan, M.D., and Edward Goldson, M.D.

Pediatric Otolaryngology as a Subspecialty

Pediatric otolaryngology has evolved into a distinct entity as the natural maturation process of a specialty.[1] Indeed, it has been a marriage of two specialties, pediatrics and otolaryngology. The uniqueness of this field extends beyond the diseases and surgical procedures encountered in that it rests in the willingness of clinicians to embrace pediatrics. Consequently, the pediatric otolaryngologist needs to be both interested and knowledgeable in the child's growth and development, which entails more than physical dimensions and encompasses areas such as neurodevelopmental maturation, cognitive processes, and psychosocial development. This chapter explores the psychosocial impact of pediatrics on otolaryngologic diseases.

Uniqueness of Pediatrics

Children cannot be viewed as "miniature adults." Therefore, the delivery of pediatric health care is significantly different from that of adult health care. Trad[2] underscored the complexity of pediatric health care with the following observations: (1) psychological aspects of disease assume greater significance in the pediatric population because of a child's immature cognitive and affective responses; (2) children experience a perpetual state of flux as the result of rapid developmental changes; and (3) the physician is challenged to form a relationship not only with the patient but with the caregiver as well. As a result, pediatric health care can be complicated by the child's psychological and developmental state and the unique physician-patient-caregiver triad.

Child Development

When one considers the psychosocial aspects of any pediatric disease, it is essential to have some understanding of child development. How children respond to and cope with both acute and chronic illnesses is strongly influenced not only by their environmental circumstances but also by their developmental level. Children go through a number of developmental stages, including how they conceive of their illness and the world in general, and have a series of developmental and psychological tasks to accomplish. The work of Piaget[3] and Erikson[4] set a framework for conceptualizing these processes.

During the first 12 to 18 months of life, infants are engaged in the process of establishing a trusting relationship with their environment. There is little cognitive representation and awareness of the environment outside of themselves, although there is movement toward simple problem solving and toward a coherent organization of sensorimotor activities. With stability and reliability, the child builds a secure world. The presence of illness, be it acute or chronic, interrupts and perturbs this developmental trajectory. Under conditions of illness, the parental role can be compromised, and the child comes to see the world as an unsafe and unpleasant place.

From the ages of 12 to 30 or 36 months, the child, after establishing trust in his or her environment, engages in the process of developing autonomy and some sense of self-concept. Motor and communication skills are at a level such that children have achieved a degree of competence in their ability to interact with the environment, but they still do not understand causality through logical processes. When a child is ill at this age, restrictions and prohibitions in the forms of medical procedures and prescribed medications are the rule. As a result, rather than becoming independent and assertive, the child continues in the role of dependency, has difficulty separating from familiar persons, may have an emerging poor self-image, and may be fearful of interactions with peers and adults.

When children reach preschool age (3 to 6 years), a much broader repertoire of skills is available to them. There is a major cognitive jump in that the child enters what Piaget calls the preoperational period, during which the child is able to think about things that are not present. Although children still reason about the world from their own viewpoint, they begin to understand that events have causes, but that spatial and temporal contiguity explain these events rather than rules and principles. For the preschool-age child, the presence of an illness limits the ability to achieve motor and social competence. There are physical restrictions with resulting enforced passivity and limitations on many of the child's goal-directed behaviors. This is a time when the child is seeking to achieve mastery over his or her world and is taking the initiative in these activities. Illness often limits the child's success and may result in a child who is passive, fearful, and excessively dependent on adults.

Children in the school-age years (6 to 12 years) are engaged in dealing with industry and mastery versus a sense of inferiority. Peer relationships are developing even further, and sex identity is beginning to crystallize. They now are learning and must respond to both internal and external demands and criteria established in the school and among their peers. From a cognitive viewpoint, they are now capable of concrete operations. That is, they are able to think more abstractly. They are able to consider two aspects of a problem simultaneously. They begin to consider not only their own needs but also those of others. This is in contrast to the more immature, egocentric, and animistic thinking of the preoperational child. The school-age child has an understanding of time and causality, the way the body works, and the meaning of death. Illness in school-age children takes on a new dimension. The sense of being different from peers and the interference of illness with their peer group interactions become an issue, which is not the case for the younger child. The youngster may become embarrassed and uncomfortable in peer relationships and tend to withdraw. On the other hand, children with a chronic illness may be avoided or ostracized by their peers because they are different. Furthermore, psychological factors, such as feelings of inadequacy, poor self-concept, worthlessness, and being different from others, may result in withdrawing from the school environment and not actively engaging in the learning process.

The teen-age years (13 to 18 years) bring into greater focus the issues of the school-age years and present new dimensions. The psychological tasks include the establishment of a personal identity as opposed to identity diffusion. There is a struggle to achieve independence while at the same time needing to rely on parents. The maturation in cognitive processing is characterized by the ability to abstract, to evaluate critically and deductively, to generate and test hypotheses, and to evaluate oneself. The individual can understand the physiologic basis for disease and the multiple causes of disease.

Characteristic of this age is an increasing need to be accepted, liked, included, and valued as the young person stumbles toward adulthood. The presence of an illness, deformity, or disability adds another crisis and more stress to an individual already under stress. It is during this age that the appearance of the condition rather than the severity of disease will influence how the young person adapts. A relatively insignificant anatomic deformity can be more devastating than a major metabolic disorder. On the other hand, the need for cooperation with medical regimens may be compromised as teen-agers battle for acceptance and to establish their autonomy and identity while still being somewhat dependent on their families and medical personnel.

Significance of Psychosocial Issues and Family Function

The developmental level of a child and the influence of a caregiver can have an impact on pediatric health care in many distinct ways. The significance of psychosocial disturbances in pediatrics is illustrated by the finding that

30% of patients in primary care settings have a diagnosable psychiatric disorder, and about 20% have somatic complaints.[5] The most prevalent presentation of somatization overall is recurrent abdominal pain. Although there are numerous contributing biologic factors, psychosocial development is greatly influenced by the family. Basic tasks for a family, such as protection, food, housing, and health care, can be so compromised in a dysfunctional family setting as to affect the immediate welfare of the child or alter the child's future psychosocial maturation. Moreover, outcomes of family dysfunction, aside from inadequate medical care, include nonaccidental trauma, emotional abuse, failure to thrive, medical neglect, and Münchausen by proxy syndrome. Although the prevalence of these issues in otolaryngology has never been studied, their existence in the practice of pediatric otolaryngology is well documented.[6-11]

Biopsychosocial Model of Illness

Traditionally, the interaction of organic disease and psychosocial factors has been viewed dichotomously. Whereas the clinician is interested in the effects of disease, the psychosocial contribution to illness is left to psychosomatic and psychological medicine. This rigid model of illness is contrary to the reality that most diseases are not exclusively organic or psychogenic in origin. The concept of illness has changed since 1980 to accommodate a "multifactorial" approach to its understanding. The term "psychosomatic" in the classic sense is infrequently used today, and psychosomatic disorders are now classified under a group of specific psychiatric diagnostic entities.

Definition

The emergence of the multifactorial model of illness was fostered by Engel.[12] He placed importance on considering the etiology of disease along four continua: disease diagnosis, characteristics of the patient, psychological stressors, and developmental issues. The first two factors are of course central to diagnosis and treatment. However, the last two factors are also of great importance, especially in considering children and adolescents. The biopsychosocial model of illness was further advanced by Molina.[13] He viewed a physiologic disorder as a dynamic process that is an outgrowth of the interaction between biologic, psychological, and sociocultural factors. Vulnerability in each of these factors contributes to the disease process. Therefore, most diseases, including otolaryngologic diseases, should be analyzed taking into consideration this model of illness. The next few sections explore each of these factors and specifically attempt to examine the common childhood illness otitis media from the viewpoint of this model (Fig. 109–1).

Biologic Factors

Biologic factors are primarily concerned with the genetic make-up of an individual and the propensity for development of any given disease. Although some diseases can be

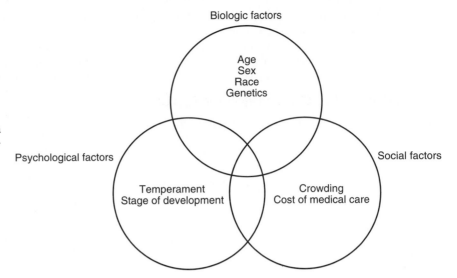

FIGURE 109-1. Pathogenesis of otitis media as viewed in the biopsychosocial model of illness.

defined in terms of specific causes and explained at the molecular level, other diseases and mechanisms, including the inheritance of behavior traits, are more difficult to clearly define.

If one considers otitis media, it becomes obvious that the current understanding of this disease cannot be reduced to the molecular/genetic level. The pathogenesis of otitis media is the result of the interactions of anatomic variations, the individual's response to infectious agents or other antigens, and the individual's capacity to mount a response to these agents. Epidemiologic studies have identified a variety of risk factors that may alert the clinician to a child who is at risk for development of otitis media. These risk factors include age, sex, race, and siblings with significant history of otitis.

Psychological Factors

There is no question that there are psychological factors that contribute to the appearance and persistence of a variety of disease processes. The literature is extensive on the impact of stress on the immune system and on subsequent infectious disease, and on its possible impact on oncologic disorders and perhaps on disorders of the cardiovascular system.[14] Furthermore, there is ample evidence to suggest that stress has an effect on the neuroendocrine system, which can influence biologic function, often leading to disease and even death. Moreover, there are links between the immune and neuroendocrine systems that can influence the emergence of disease.

With respect to pediatric otolaryngology, one could argue that the psychologically stressed child is more vulnerable to disease than is the well-functioning, developmentally and emotionally secure child. At present, there appear to be no specific psychological factors that contribute to otitis media, compared with the biologic factors identified previously. However, there are psychological, temperamental, developmental, and psychosocial factors that influence how the child responds to the illness and treatment and how the child recovers.

How children respond to acute illness is partially influ-

enced by the child's previous experience with illness. Was the child treated in a sensitive, unhurried manner by the health care provider? Was the child supported, comforted, and nurtured by the parents? Were the caretakers and parents honest with the child? Did the caretaker relate to the child in a developmentally age-appropriate manner without being patronizing and condescending? By and large, the child who has been treated in a caring, personal manner will have less difficulty with illness, at least vis-à-vis the health care provider, than the child who was treated cavalierly, impersonally, and in haste.

The child's psychological characteristics and temperamental traits are a second group of factors to be considered. Children who are mild-mannered, are trusting, and have secure and trusting relationships with their parents are at a greater advantage in dealing with illness than are those children who are not so characterized. Lavigne and Faier-Routman[5] reported that the factors contributing most to the psychological adjustment of children to illness included characteristics of the parent/family, characteristics of the child, and, to a lesser degree, disease/disability risk factors. That is, children who are part of disorganized families where there is marital stress and parental disengagement have more difficulty adjusting to illness. Children who are emotionally stable and self-confident do better than those with difficult temperaments, low IQs, increased distractibility, and poor self-concept. In the Lavigne and Faier-Routman study, socioeconomic status and stressors did not play significant roles in how the child adjusted to the illness.

Social Factors

Social factors can have significant influences on how children respond to illness and to treatment. In disorganized families where there is poor compliance and an inadequate commitment to treatment, the child will do poorly. If the parents do not administer the medicine and monitor and support the child, the outcome will be less than optimal. If there is no money to purchase medication or provide other therapies, the outcome will also be less than optimal. When there is parental neglect, maltreatment, and indifference, the child will have difficulty coping with the disease and will probably not respond as promptly to treatment as do children who are in more organized, nurturing environments.

Selected Pediatric Otolaryngology Topics

The premise of a biopsychosocial model of illness as applied to pediatric otolaryngology is to establish a fundamental view that few diseases are solely biologic or psychological in origin but that most diseases are multifactorial, as illustrated in the previous model of otitis media. More important, the psychosocial impact of an illness and the result of psychosocial dysfunction as they relate to pediatric otolaryngology must be addressed. Specifically, the following discussion centers on three topics: chronic illness, sensorineural hearing loss, and child abuse.

Chronic Illness

A chronic illness is defined as a chronic health condition having a severe physiologic impact with restriction of activities and the need for treatment on a regular basis. It is estimated that 1% to 2% of children fall into this category. Chronic illnesses of childhood have an impact on the child's development and behavior as well as on the family. Chronic illness can affect development directly or indirectly through restricting a child's participation in developmentally appropriate activities. Chronic illness affects children of different ages in different ways, and this is related to both the developmental stage of the child and, in turn, the child's understanding of illness. The greatest impact of chronic illness on infants may lie in the direct impact on linear growth and poor weight gain. A more indirect effect of chronic illness is that toddlers and school-age children with such illnesses may be ostracized or teased by peers. Thus, the opportunity to acquire social skills and the chance to practice those skills may be curtailed. Frequent school absences not only interfere with normal socialization but affect school performance and in turn affect self-worth and self-image. As mentioned previously, adolescents are preoccupied with autonomy, self-esteem, and identity. Chronic illnesses during adolescence can result in dependence on others, which may negatively affect the development of appropriate autonomy and individual identity.

At first glance, there are a host of "chronic illnesses" in pediatric otolaryngology (e.g., chronic infections of the ear, pharynx, and paranasal sinuses; voice and speech disorders; and sensorineural hearing loss). However, none of these realistically meets the definition of chronic illness by virtue of either not being a debilitating illness or not requiring regular and periodic treatment. Sensorineural hearing loss is discussed separately in the following section of this chapter as having important psychosocial impact. The most appropriate chronic illness model in pediatric otolaryngology is the tracheotomized child. The underlying pathologic processes for a tracheotomy may be diverse, but the impact on a "normal" functioning child and especially the family is relatively predictable. The most apparent effects of a tracheotomy for a child are in the areas of speech and language development. Tracheotomy in most instances causes aphonia regardless of the age of the child. However, its impact on speech and language has been found to be related to whether a child is prelingual or postlingual at the time of decannulation.[14] Children decannulated during the prelinguistic stage attained speech and language skills commensurate with intellectual functioning. On the contrary, children decannulated in the postlinguistic stage exhibited spoken language delays including phonologic impairment at the time of decannulation. In the majority of these children, both the language and phonologic delays were corrected with appropriate speech/language therapy.

The addition of a chronic illness to a family brings a number of challenges, demands, and sources of anxiety. The impact of a tracheotomized child on the family has been described by Wills,[15] who classified maternal concerns into biologic and psychological. The overwhelming proportion of the biologic concerns expressed by the mothers interviewed were related to maintenance of a patent airway. The psychosocial concerns were (1) need for home, clinical, and group support services; (2) isolation and limitations on time; (3) economic impact; (4) altered family interaction; and (5) provision of medical care.

The role of the pediatric otolaryngologist is to actively assist the child and the family in identifying speech/language delays and to make appropriate referrals. Furthermore, the clinician can help alleviate some of the biologic and psychosocial concerns. Home tracheotomy care could go a long way in resolving some of the issues. See Chapter 93 for an expanded discussion.

Sensorineural Hearing Loss

The psychosocial concerns relating to sensorineural hearing loss lie in its frequency, which is estimated to be 1 to 2 per 1000 children. The impact of hearing loss on development is as complex as the causes and types of hearing loss itself. However, factors that determine developmental outcome have been categorized by Meadow.[16] They include the degree, the etiology, and the age at onset of hearing loss; family climate; and appropriateness of educational interventions. The developmental profile of a deaf child generally shows alterations in the areas of language, cognitive development, and social and emotional development. In terms of language, profoundly deaf children are greatly impeded in the development of spoken language. In prelingual children, auditory memory, imaging, and associations are all compromised. Although it is generally accepted that the intellectual abilities of hearing-impaired children are similar to those of the hearing child except where verbal factors have a part to play, distinct differences in many cognitive skills including memory, temporal processing, semantics, and higher-level thinking exist between these two groups.[17] In the area of social and emotional development, recognizable differences are found between the two groups in terms of peer interaction and aggression, with the hearing-impaired child having significant difficulties (see Chap. 28).

Hearing-impaired children have a profound long-term

impact on their families. This impact begins at the time of diagnosis.[18] The first obstacle for the parents is the grieving process, which is not unlike grieving over a loss or death. A great deal of concern has been expressed in the area of parent-child interaction. Numerous studies have addressed the detrimental effects of a child's hearing handicap on the mother's communication style with her child. The success of habilitation for hearing-impaired children is greatly influenced by parental participation and counseling. A perspective on the influence of parenting and family dynamics on a hearing-impaired child can be gleaned from studies indicating that positive family practices and child-rearing attitudes promote positive academic achievements and are predictors of the development of the child's healthy self-concept.

The first task of the pediatric otolaryngologist is to assist in early detection of sensorineural hearing loss. Once hearing loss is identified, the clinician's role is to assist the child and the family in securing appropriate referrals to speech, language, and educational specialists. See Chapter 108.

Child Abuse

As occurs in most pediatric medical and surgical specialties, the otolaryngologist may become suspicious that child maltreatment has led the parents to bring the child for help. For many practitioners, this is distasteful and unpleasant, and many feel that involvement in such cases is outside of their realm of expertise. However, otolaryngologists are frequently the first to be involved in the child's medical care. Thus, they are in a unique position to recognize when maltreatment has occurred and to initiate the management of the child presenting with an injury to the head and neck that may be the result of nonaccidental trauma or neglect.

Child maltreatment continues to be a major public health issue in the United States and has a profound effect on the child's psychosocial development.[19] The term child maltreatment serves as an umbrella under which are included nonaccidental trauma, neglect (which can also lead to a failure to gain weight), sexual molestation, and emotional abuse. Both nonaccidental trauma and neglect have been reported in the otolaryngology literature.[6–10] Nonaccidental trauma to the head and neck can take many forms that can be confused with accidental injuries unless a comprehensive history is obtained and a complete physical examination is performed. Child maltreatment must always be suspected when the injury does not "match" the history that is provided or when the caretaker claims no knowledge of how the injury occurred. Common presentations include a combination of lip bruising, torn frenulum, and pharyngeal lacerations from forced feeding; petechiae or hematoma of the pinnae can occur in isolation or in association with other, more severe bodily injuries. Not infrequently, one can encounter bloody otorrhea secondary to canal laceration and tympanic membrane perforation. The "tin ear syndrome" is a characteristic triad of ear bruising, hemorrhagic retinopathy, and ipsilateral cerebral edema with obliteration of the basilar cisterns.

Another aspect of maltreatment one needs to consider is neglect. Such cases may involve parents' failing to provide medical treatments suggested by the practitioner. Neglect can occur in common illnesses, such as otitis media, and in life-threatening illnesses, such as neoplasms.

In all of these circumstances, the otolaryngologist plays an important role in differentiating what is abusive from what is not abusive and in initiating appropriate protective interventions and subsequent management of the otolaryngologic problem. It is the practitioner's responsibility to report suspected maltreatment and to work with the team in the management of the child and the family.

Diagnosis of Psychosocial Dysfunction

Clinicians generally find it difficult to work within the biopsychosocial model of illness. Most are uncomfortable with the model itself. Surgeons are particularly influenced by their training to hold on to the binary (surgical versus nonsurgical) approach to medicine. In addition, the biopsychosocial model lacks the "instant gratification" expectation so ingrained in the training of surgeons. In reality, there is not enough time and it is not financially worthwhile to deal with psychosocial problems during a busy surgical practice. Nevertheless, to provide more comprehensive, effective, and long-lasting care, it is important that the practitioner change some approaches and expectations to accept the biopsychosocial model of illness. These include (1) giving up the need to always be in control; (2) being able to tolerate, and letting others tolerate, the unknown; (3) overcoming excessive expectations of oneself and patients; and (4) acknowledging that there may be different, equally acceptable approaches to the management of a given disorder.

After the initial step of accepting the biopsychosocial model of illness, the clinician can then concentrate on recognizing the important psychosocial issues. The diagnosis of psychosocial dysfunction is no different from that of any other clinical disorder. The physician must be a good listener and observer. Effort should be focused on identifying 3 factors: (1) recent important stressful events, (2) dysfunctional family structure, and (3) pathologic parental traits.

Childhood Stressors

Rutter[20] has recognized a variety of childhood stressors that the clinician should take into consideration when evaluating the child (Table 109–1). Obviously, the clini-

TABLE 109–1. Important Childhood Stressors

Disruption of attachment relationship
Persistent rejection, lack of affection, neglect, or abuse
Parental ill health
Chronically disturbed family relationship (e.g., parental divorce)
Major life events (e.g., birth of a sibling, change of school, or hospitalization)
Major trauma (e.g., major illness or injury)

Data from Rutter M. Childhood experiences and adult psychosocial functionings. Ciba Found Symp 156:189, 1991.

TABLE 109–2. Family Functioning Typology

Index	Optimal	Midrange	Dysfunctional
Power	Delineated	Power struggle	Difficult to define
Communication	Candor and flexibility	Intimidation and manipulation	Chronically ineffective
Development	Autonomous	Limited identity	Loss of identity

Data from Beavers WR. Healthy, midrange, and severely dysfunctional families. In Walsh F (ed). Normal Family Processes. New York, Guilford Press, 1982.

cian should use caution when interviewing the parent/caregiver in the presence of a sensitive or stressed child. Sometimes it is beneficial to interview the parent/caregiver separately. In the presence of a dysfunctional family structure, it may become difficult to identify and separate childhood stressors from other dysfunctional family traits.

Family Dysfunction

Parenting has never been an easy task, but changes away from traditional patterns of family organization, as reflected by an increasing prevalence of single-parent and two-wage earner families, has potentiated the risk for dysfunction. Changes in the contemporary family system increase the likelihood that the family will have difficulty coping with stress, including physical illness. Families that have a history of psychiatric disorder, divorce or separation, low socioeconomic status, previous traumatic experience, drug and alcohol abuse, and family turmoil are at greater risk for poor psychological adjustment.[21] Single-parent households, for example, are more likely to have limited financial resources and social supports, and they are often run by adults with little education who are forced to spend time away from the child to support the family. The assessment of an ill child from such an environment requires not only a complete medical evaluation but also an understanding of how psychosocial factors may influence the child's and family's ability to cope with illness.

When a family unit disintegrates and becomes dysfunctional, it occurs along a continuum. Beavers[22] viewed this dysfunctional process using three indices: power, communication, and development (Table 109–2). In an intact and functional family unit, power is well defined, communication is candid and expresses flexibility and respect, and the child is viewed as an autonomous individual with his or her own identity. In contrast, in a dysfunctional family, power is ill defined, communication is truncated, and the child loses his or her identity.

TABLE 109–3. Characteristics of Difficult Parents

Personality Traits	Characteristics
Obsessive	Rigid, perfectionistic, dogmatic
Hysterical	Overemotional, oversensitive, impressionistic
Denying	Inattention to instructions, noncompliant
Dependent	Unending need for contact and support
Demanding	Egocentric and grandiose, litigious
Help-rejecting	Pessimistic, distrusting

Adapted from Beresin EV, Jellinek MS, Herzog DB. The difficult parent: office assessment and management. Curr Probl Pediatr 20:620, 1990.

The diagnostic acumen regarding family dysfunction will be improved if the clinician concentrates on the three indices listed. Therefore, all communication cues between the physician, the caregiver, and the child become important. These include body language, verbalization, and tone of voice, all of which are useful in the evaluation of family structure.

Pathologic Parental Traits

The addition of a caregiver figure to the traditional physician-patient dyad complicates health care delivery, although that person is essential to the child. Under some circumstances, this addition can potentiate the development of psychosocial dysfunction. Factors contributing to dysfunction can involve events covering a child's life span. Early exposure to chronic illness and parents' overconcern with their own body functions are influential factors leading to a child's distorted concept about illness.[23] One may also want to consider the pathologic personality traits of the caregiver and how they may influence the child. During the interview, the clinician should become aware of the presence of difficult parental traits. Beresin et al[24] have identified pathologic parental traits and their associated characteristics (Table 109–3). All too often the clinician becomes offended or disinterested when these parents are encountered. The likely outcome is the termination of communication, potential delay in the diagnosis of psychosocial dysfunction, and compromise of the child's care.

Management of Psychosocial Disorders

Several important steps must be considered in addressing problems of psychosocial dysfunction. The most important step is for the physician to consider the psychosocial causes for illness as an option at the outset rather than as an afterthought. This conveys a firm message to the patient that the caregiver has a comprehensive differential diagnosis and that psychosocial factors can contribute to physical dysfunction. It then sets the stage for the next difficult step, convincing the caretaker of the need for psychosocial evaluation and possible treatment. When therapy is recommended, it is for the purpose of elucidating family conflicts and stresses and helping the family to understand the consequences to the child of the disturbed family environment and the stresses that they have encountered. Through psychosocial interventions, more adaptive methods of coping can be encouraged, more positive patterns of interaction can be developed, and social supports can be explored to help the family become a more adaptive system in its mode of functioning.

The next step is, likewise, crucial to a favorable outcome. A surgeon is not trained in family dynamics and psychiatry, nor does a surgeon have the time to become an expert in these fields. Therefore, at our institution, a team approach to psychosocial dysfunction is used. When a problem is suspected, the surgeon may make a referral to a social worker, who may be able to manage the case or make a referral to a child psychiatrist or psychologist or to a developmental pediatrician. It is helpful to have a social worker who is primarily assigned to the otolaryngology service and thereby is familiar with ear, nose, and throat diseases.

Behavioral science assessment and treatment are also designed to identify those psychosocial factors contributing to the physical disorder and to prevent unnecessary medical assessments and interventions. Furthermore, the behavioral science intervention can often facilitate the process of recovery. Most important, this kind of collaborative approach to the management of disease—behavioral science, medical, and surgical—acknowledges the contributions that all of these factors can have in the etiology and course of the disease. The issue in treatment should not be whether the patient is experiencing purely organic or functional problems, but rather what the relationship is between the two and what kind of strategies can be developed to effectively treat the patient. The approaches and skills of behavioral scientists need to be respected and enlisted. Their participation in the care of the patient is an important key to successful treatment. When the physical disorder is well understood by the staff, a psychopathologic process, when present, should also be clearly recognized.

Moreover, when psychosocial disturbances are apparent in the child, the entire family must be considered in the therapeutic plan. As previously noted, parental and family dysfunction can have significant adverse effects on how the child copes with illness and responds to treatment. It becomes critical, under these complex and stressful circumstances, that the patient not be perceived as a burden or a malingerer. Instead, it should be recognized that the patient and the family have many complex needs, all of which need to be addressed if there is to be a successful resolution of the problem, which is possible if a multidisciplinary, broad-based view of disease is considered.

The treatment plan for a child with disorders that include not only physical disturbances but also psychosocial problems includes coordination of services with the primary care physician, mental health professional, surgeon, and school or other educational institution when appropriate. All of these professionals need to communicate with one another and then with the family. The family also needs to be included in the planning if they are to follow through with the recommendations. All too often plans are made, but they fail because the family has not been included in the process. Parents need to be considered as active and valued participants in the care of their child. This is particularly important when surgical procedures are involved that require some technical skills on the part of the parent. Parents need to know why things are being done and what they can expect with respect to the disease and from their child's caretakers, and what is expected of them, the parents.

Conclusion

An understanding and acceptance of the biopsychosocial model of illness can have far-reaching positive implications for children with otolaryngologic disorders. With the use of this approach, psychosocial disorders can be promptly diagnosed and appropriately managed. To practice pediatric otolaryngology is not only to accept the challenge of becoming conversant in the physical growth and development of a child but also to be willing to address the psychosocial aspects of the child's and family's life. This can be facilitated by accepting and using a more holistic approach to medical and surgical care.

SELECTED REFERENCES

Helfer ME, Kempe RS, Krugman RD, eds. The Battered Child, 5th ed. Chicago and London, The University of Chicago Press, 1997.

Hubbs N, Perrin JM, Ireys HT, eds. Chronically Ill Children and Their Families. San Francisco, Jossey-Bass, 1985.

Hubbs N, Perrin JM, eds. Issues in the Care of Children with Chronic Illness. San Francisco, Jossey-Bass, 1985.

Jessop DJ, Stein PEK. Essential concepts in the care of children with chronic illness. Pediatrician 15:5, 1988.

Goldson E. The behavioral aspects of chronic illness. In Geydamus DE, Wolraich ML (eds). Behavioral Pediatrics. New York, Springer-Verlag, 1992.

REFERENCES

1. Stool SE. Evolution of pediatric otolaryngology. Pediatr Clin North Am 36:1363, 1989.
2. Trad PV. Psychosocial Scenarios for Pediatrics. New York, Springer-Verlag, 1988, pp 28–30.
3. Piaget J, Imhelder B. The Psychology of the Child. New York, Basic Books, 1969.
4. Erikson E. Childhood and Society. New York, Norton, 1964.
5. Lavigne JV, Faier-Routman J. Psychological adjustment to pediatric physical illness: a meta-analytic review. J Pediatr Psychol 17:133, 1992.
6. Grace A, Grace S. Child abuse within the ear, nose and throat. J Otolarynol 16:108, 1987.
7. Manning SC, Casselbrant M, Lammers D. Otolaryngologic manifestations of child abuse. Int J Pediatr Otorhinolaryngol 20:7, 1990.
8. Leavitt EB, Pincus RL, Bukachevsky R. Otolaryngologic manifestations of child abuse. Arch Otolaryngol Head Neck Surg 118:629, 1992.
9. Willner A, Ledereich PS, de Vries EJ. Auricular injury as a presentation of child abuse. Arch Otolaryngol Head Neck Surg 118:634, 1992.
10. Smith ME, Darby KP, Kirchner K, Blager F. Simultaneous functional laryngeal stridor and functional aphonia in an adolescent. Am J Otolaryngol 5:366, 1993.
11. Chan KH, Martini R, Bradley WF, Stool SE. Pediatric otolaryngology: a psychosocial perspective. Int J Pediatr Otorhinolaryngol 32:159, 1995.
12. Engel GL. The need for a new medical model: a challenge for biomedicine. Science 196:129, 1977.
13. Molina JA. Understanding the biopsychosocial model. Int J Psychiatry Med 13:29, 1983.

14. Simon BM, Fowler SM, Handler SD. Communication development in young children with long-term tracheostomies: preliminary report. Int J Pediatr Otorhinolaryngol 13:37, 1983.

15. Wills JM. Concerns and needs of mothers providing home care for children with tracheostomies. Matern Child Nurs J 12:89, 1983.

16. Meadow KP. Deafness and Child Development. Berkeley, CA, University of California Press, 1980.

17. Bench RJ. Communication Skills in Hearing-Impaired Children. San Diego, Singular Publishing Group, 1992.

18. Kricos PB. The counseling process: children and parents. In Alpiner JG, McCarthy PA (eds). Rehabilitative Audiology: Children and Adults. Baltimore, Williams & Wilkins, 1993, pp 211–233.

19. Goldson E. The affective and cognitive sequelae of child maltreatment. Pediatr Clin North Am 38:1481, 1991.

20. Rutter M. Childhood experiences and adult psychosocial functioning. Ciba Found Symp 156:189, 1991.

21. Gortmaker SL, Walker DK, Weitzman M, Sobol AM. Chronic conditions, socioeconomic risks, and behavioral problems in children and adolescents. Pediatrics 85:267, 1990.

22. Beavers WR. Healthy, midrange, and severely dysfunctional families. In Walsh F (ed). Normal Family Processes. New York, Guilford Press, 1982.

23. Engel GL. A reconsideration of the role of conversion in somatic disease. Compr Psychiatry 9:316, 1968.

24. Beresin EV, Jellinek MS, Herzog DB. The difficult parent: office assessment and management. Curr Probl Pediatr 20:620, 1990.

Note: Page numbers followed by b refer to boxes; page numbers followed by f refer to figures; page numbers followed by t refer to tables.

Environmental pollution
  coughing related to, 1397
  incidence of otitis media related to, 494
Enzyme(s)
  hydrolytic, in middle ear infection, 539–540
  oxidative, in middle ear infection, 539–540
Enzyme fluorescence test, for pharyngitis, 1123
Enzyme-linked immunosorbent assay (ELISA)
  for allergic rhinitis, 1072
  in diagnosis of HIV infection, 119
EOAEs. See Evoked otoacoustic emissions
    (EOAEs).
Eosinophil(s), in allergic rhinitis, 1070, 1072
Eosinophilic granuloma, 852
Eosinophilic ulcer, 1245–1246
Epidermoid carcinoma, of mouth, 1275
Epidermoid (cholesteatoma), of middle ear, 392
Epidermoid cyst(s), orbital swelling due to, 944
Epidermolysis bullosa, 1246–1247
    acquisita, 1247
    dystrophica, 1247
    simplex, 1247
Epiglottic vallecula, 1095
Epiglottis
  anatomy of, 1366
  direct examination of, 1383
  high position of, for simultaneous feeding
    and breathing, 1088f, 1089, 1095
  lowering and raising of, muscles in, 1371
  obstruction of, in laryngomalacia, supraglotto-
    plasty for, 1462–1463, 1462f
Epiglottitis
  acute, 1484–1485
    airway obstruction in, in immunocompro-
      mised child, 1604
      intensive care management of, 1599–
        1600, 1623
    clinical features of, 1484, 1485f, 1600
    incidence and etiology of, 1484
    laboratory features of, 1484
    management of, 1484–1485, 1486t
    pharyngitis associated with, 1121
    retropharyngeal abscess vs., 1488
Epignathus, definition of, 1275
Epilepsy
  dysphagia related to, 1351–1352
  hearing impairment associated with, 312t
  myoclonic, with ragged red fibers. See My-
    oclonic epilepsy with ragged red fibers.
Epinephrine
  nebulized, for bronchiolitis, 1489
  racemic, for acute croup, 1486, 1601
    rebound phenomenon in, 1601
Epiphysis, 24, 25f
Epistaxis, 925–930
  etiology of, 925–928, 927t
    dry air in, 925–926
    inflammation in, 925, 927f, 927t
    rare causes in, 926–928, 927t
    trauma in, 926
  management of, 928–930, 928t
  nasal blood supply and, 925, 926f
  nasal packing for, 929
  prevention of, 928–929
  superior and posterior, management of, 929–
    930, 930f
Epithelial tumor(s)
  of mouth, 1272–1273
  of salivary glands, 1262, 1645
Epithelium, pseudostratified columnar, 879,
    879f
Epitympanum
  anatomy of, 509
  development of, 132
Epstein-Barr virus (EBV)
  associated with nasopharyngeal carcinoma,
    1726

Epstein-Barr virus (EBV) (Continued)
  in HIV infection, 125
  in immunodeficient states, 1493t
  in lower respiratory tract infections, 1485t
  in mononucleosis, 1236
    pharyngitis due to, 1120
  in nasopharyngeal tumors, 1063
  in natural killer cell lymphoma, 1057
  mouth ulcers associated with, 1356
  salivary gland involvement by, 1259
Epstein pearls
  of gingiva, 1276
  of palate, 1087
Epulis
  as tumor, confused terminology in, 1275
  congenital (granular cell), 1178, 1179f
    of gingiva, 1276
EquiTest system, 284f, 285–286
Erythema multiforme, 1246, 1246f
Erythromycin
  efficacy of, 594
  for cervical adenopathy, mycoplasmal, 1673
  for chronic bronchitis, 1488
  for diphtheria, 1487
  for lower respiratory tract infection, 1486t
  for pharyngitis, 1125
  for pneumonia
    in immunocompromised child, 1493
    in newborn, 1452
  for rhinitis due to streptococcal infection,
    997
  parenteral administration of, 600
  pharmacology of, 594–595, 594t
  prophylactic, for chronic bronchitis, 1489
  sensorineural hearing loss associated with,
    799
  theophylline interaction with, 602
  toxicity and side effects of, 595
Erythromycin-sulfisoxazole
  for otitis media, with effusion, 614
  for sinusitis, in HIV infection, 120
  resistance to, sinus treatment and, 1006
Escherichia coli
  brain abscess due to, 771
  in pneumonia, 1490t
  meningitis due to, 796
Eskimos. See Inuit people.
Esophageal atresia, 1281–1286
  anomalies associated with, 1281, 1282t
  classification of, 1281, 1282f
  complications of, 1285–1286, 1286f
  diagnosis of, 1477–1478
  dysphagia due to, 1131t, 1133
  embryology of, 1281
  historical background of, 1281
  incidence of, 1477
  long-gap, esophageal replacement in, 1284–
    1285
  presentation and diagnosis of, 1281–1282,
    1283f–1285f
  reflux after, antireflux procedure for, 1285–
    1286, 1286f
  surgical treatment of, 1283–1286
  treatment of
    considerations in, 1284
    risk classification for, 1283–1284
  types of, 1477, 1479f
Esophagitis
  allergic eosinophilic, subglottic stenosis asso-
    ciated with, 1526
  due to corrosive burns, stages of, 1315
  in gastroesophageal reflux disease, 1297
  in immunocompromised host, dysphagia re-
    lated to, 1134
  reflux, dysphagia associated with, 1136

Esophagogastrectomy, in esophageal burns,
    1316
Esophagography, contrast
  double-contrast technique in, 1292
  for esophageal injuries, 1342
  for neck disorders, 1625
  full-column technique in, 1292
  in airway examination, 1385
  mucosal relief technique in, 1292
Esophagoscopy. See also Endoscopy.
  barium, of vascular rings, 1475, 1476f
  direct, for oropharyngeal chemical injuries,
    1347
  esophageal perforation during, 1118
  flexible
    for dysphagia evaluation, 1130
    in physical examination, 1115, 1116, 1117f
  for esophageal disorders, 1294–1295
  for foreign body removal, types of esophago-
    scopes in, 1329
  in esophageal burns, 1317–1318
    management after, 1318
  in laryngotracheal trauma, 1514
  in physical examination, 1115–1116
  rigid, in physical examination, 1115, 1116–
    1118, 1117f–1118f
Esophagus
  anatomy of, 1097–1099, 1099f
    developmental
      in adolescent, 1369–1370
      in child, 1369
      in embryo, 1097, 1097f, 1361–1365,
        1362f–1365f
      in fetus, 1365–1366, 1366f
      in infant, 1366–1369, 1367f–1368f
    functional, 1289, 1290f
  atresia of. See Esophageal atresia.
  Barrett, in gastroesophageal reflux disease,
    1298
  biopsy of
    for gastroesophageal reflux disease, 1302,
      1302t
    for stridor, in laryngomalacia, 1305
    indications for, 1294–1295
  bleeding of, in gastroesophageal reflux dis-
    ease, 1298
  blood supply to, 1098–1099
  burns of
    assessment of social and mental status in,
      1317
    complications of, 1316
    corrosive agents in, 1313–1314
    esophageal replacement for, 1322
    esophagoscopy of, 1317–1318
    incidence of, 1322
    management of
      after esophagoscopy, 1317–1318
      emergent, 1315–1316
      medical, 1316–1317, 1316f
      special nasogastric tube in, 1318
    pathologic stages of, 1314–1315
    strictures due to, management of, 1318–
      1322
  candidiasis of, in HIV infection, 122, 123f
  cerebral palsy and, 1298
  compression of, by vascular rings, 1474–
    1475, 1475f–1476f
  congenital anomaly(ies) of
    atresia as. See Esophageal atresia.
    common types of, 1097, 1098t
    duplications as, 1286–1287
    dysphagia related to, 1131t, 1133
  dilatation of
    for achalasia, 1296, 1409
    for caustic burns, 1319–1322, 1320f–1321f
    prograde, 1319–1321, 1320f

Infant(s) (Continued)
  causes of, 328–330
  characterization of, 328
  confirmation of, 327–328
  evaluation of, 327–330
  illness of, developmental effects of, 1835
  laryngeal development in, 1366–1369,
    1367f–1368f
  positioning of, for otoscopy, 173, 174f
  risk of otitis media in, 489
  screening for hearing loss in
    indicators for, 219–220, 219t
    referral for auditory brain stem response
      testing, 217
  sleep apnea in, 1226
  tracheal development in, 1366–1369, 1367f–
    1368f
  tympanometry in, 202, 203f
Infection(s)
  acute, imaging studies of, 233–237, 234f–
    236f, 238f–239f
  after microtia reconstruction, 432
  bacterial. See Bacterial infection(s).
  dysphagia related to, 1131t, 1133–1134
  facial paralysis due to, 381–382
  fungal. See Fungal infection(s).
  genetic susceptibility to, 75
  in day care centers
    epidemiology of otitis media related to,
      492–493, 493t
    otitis media related to, 694
  in epistaxis, 925, 927f
  in reconstructive surgery, 99
    intracranial, 98
  molecular biologic diagnosis of, 74–75
  opportunistic, associated with AIDS and HIV
    infection, 113, 114t, 121
  orbital swelling due to, 944–945, 944f, 944t
  oropharyngeal manifestation of, 1234–1237,
    1235t
  prenatal, diseases associated with, 405
  susceptibility to, in otitis-prone children,
    487
  tracheal, after tracheotomy, 1591
  upper respiratory tract. See Upper respira-
    tory tract infection(s).
  viral. See Viral infection(s).
Infectious Diseases Society of America, protocols of, for judicious use of antimicrobials,
  607, 607t
Infectious mononucleosis. See Mononucleosis,
  infectious.
Inflammation
  gram-negative sepsis and, 541–542
  in bacterial meningitis, 797
  in epistaxis, 925, 927f, 927t
  in middle ear, 542–543
  in pathogenesis of otitis media, 541–543
  management of, current studies of, 542
  mediators of, in allergic rhinitis, 1069, 1069t,
    1070
  meningitis and, 541–542
Inflammatory disorder(s)
  cervical adenopathy associated with, 1667–
    1674, 1667t
  chronic, computed tomography of, 237,
    244f–245f
  dysphagia related to, 1131t, 1133–1134
  nasal obstruction and rhinorrhea in, 912t,
    914–917
  neck masses due to, 1638, 1639f, 1640
  of larynx, hoarseness associated with, 1416
  of salivary glands, 1256–1262, 1257t
  orbital swelling due to, 944–945, 944f, 944t
  oropharyngeal manifestation of, 1235t, 1238–
    1239

Inflammatory pseudotumor
  bronchial, 1568
  subglottic, 1567
Inflation, of eustachian tube. See Eustachian
  tube, inflation of.
Inflation-deflation tympanometric test
  modified, 528–531, 530f–532f
  nine-step, 528, 529f
Influenza virus
  pharyngitis due to, 1120, 1199
  type A
    identification of, in middle ear and naso-
      pharynx, 553, 554t
    in lower respiratory tract infections, 1485t
    in pneumonia, 1490t
  type B
    in lower respiratory tract infections, 1485t
    in pneumonia, 1490t
Infrabullar cells, development of, 867
Infrahyoid muscles, development of, 1609
Infrared group amplification system, 1818
Infratemporal fossa tumors, otalgia referred
  from, 291
Infundibulum
  anterior, development of, 865
  development of, 864
Inhalant allergen(s), 1067
Inhalation burns, 1345–1347, 1754
Inheritance
  anticipation in, 50, 51f
  autosomal dominant. See Autosomal domi-
    nant inheritance.
  autosomal recessive. See Autosomal recessive
    inheritance.
  dynamic mutations in, 50, 51f, 52t
  imprinting in, 49, 49f, 50t
  in hereditary hearing impairment, 339–340,
    345–346, 346t
  mendelian
    diseases associated with, 42, 396–405
    principles of, 42, 42f
  mitochondrial, 48–49, 49f, 50t
  pedigree construction and analysis of, 43,
    44f–45f, 45
  phenocopy in, 50
  terminology of, 42–43
  uniparental disomy in, 49–50, 49t
  variations and exceptions to traditional men-
    delian inheritance, 48–50
  X-linked. See X-linked inheritance.
  Y-linked, 48, 48f, 49t
Injury(ies). See Trauma.
Inner ear. See also Ear(s); Middle ear.
  anatomy of, developmental, 137–141
  congenital anomaly(ies) of, 441–453
    classification of, 319, 319t
      history of, 441–442, 442f–443f, 443t
    cochlear implantation and, 452–453, 452f
    diagnosis of, 451–452
    enlarged cochlear aqueduct as, 450
    internal auditory canal anomalies in, 450–
      451
    large vestibular aqueduct as. See Vestibular
      aqueduct syndrome, large (LVAS).
    membranous labyrinth malformations in,
      443–446
    middle-ear anomalies associated with, 451,
      451f
    osseous labyrinth malformations in, 444–
      446
    perilymphatic fistula associated with, 458,
      459, 461f
    sensorineural hearing loss associated with,
      784–785, 785f
    structural, 143, 143t

Inner ear (Continued)
  vestibular labyrinth malformations in, 445–
    446
Innominate artery
  aberrant, tracheal compression by, 1473–
    1474, 1475f, 1651
    surgical treatment of, 1651, 1651f–1652f
  erosion of, after tracheotomy, 1590
  injury of
    during tracheotomy, 1589, 1589f
    evaluation and management of, 1750–1751
Insertions, chromosomal, 39
Inspection
  of airways, 1380–1381
  of neck, 1621
  of oropharynx, 1109–1110, 1110f–1111f
  of thorax, 1380
Inspiration, physiology of, 1373, 1373f
Institutions, for pediatric otolaryngology, 64–
  65, 65f
Insurance data, incidence of otitis media indicated by, 486, 486t
Integrin(s), in control of neural crest migration,
  15
Intensity, of sound
  difference limen for, 147
  neural encoding of, 156–157, 157f
Intercom, for monitoring of tracheotomy, 1595
Interferon(s)
  alpha, as antiviral agent, 599
  alpha-2a
    for hemangioma, 967
      of neck, 1643
      of subglottis or trachea, 1471
    for rhinitis prevention, 997
  as antiviral agents, 599
  for recurrent respiratory papillomatosis,
    1561–1562
  for subglottic hemangioma, 1564
  in middle-ear fluids, due to viral or bacterial
    infections, 556
Intergroup Rhabdomyosarcoma Study
  staging system of, 1714, 1714t
  treatment guidelines of, 1714
Interleukin(s), genes encoding, allergy related
  to, 1067
Internal auditory canal (IAC)
  abnormal, hearing loss related to
    radiographic findings in, 322
    size of IAC and, 450–451
  aplasia of, on computed tomography, 241,
    251f
  facial nerve in, 369–370, 370f, 371t
  thin bony plate of, on radiography, 321
  X-linked sensorineural hearing loss associated
    with, 241
International Liaison Committee on Resuscitation, policy statement of, on first aid for
  choking, 1545, 1545b
International Neuroblastoma Staging System
  Committee, 1725, 1725t
International Rhabdomyosarcoma Study classification system, 851
Interstitial lung disease, 1503
Intracranial complications of sinusitis, 1027–
  1029
Intramembranous ossification, 24, 25f
Intratympanic muscle(s)
  congenital anomalies of, 409–410
  tinnitus associated with, 364–365
Intraventricular hemorrhage, in acute respira-
  tory distress syndrome, 1450–1451
Intron, definition of, 79
Intubation. See also Extubation.
  during mandibular distraction procedure, 105
  endotracheal. See Endotracheal intubation.

Stomatitis (Continued)
contact (stomatitis venenata), 1206
gangrenous, 1245
herpetic gingivostomatitis, 1178–1179, 1199–1200
secondary or recurrent, 1200, 1200f–1201f
medicamentosa, 1207–1208, 1208f
Vincent (acute necrotizing ulcerative gingivitis), 1202–1203, 1242, 1243f
viral, treatment of, 1202
Stomeodeum, 1085, 1085f, 1089, 1089f, 1149
Stool, Sylvan, 62–63
Storage disorders, familial, cervical adenopathy associated with, 1666
Storz, Karl, 64
Storz endoscope, with Hopkins rod-lens optical system, 1387, 1387f
Strabismus, after reconstructive surgery, 99
Strangulation, vascular injuries in, 1752
"Strawberry tongue," in streptococcal infection, 1203
Streptococci
alpha-hemolytic, as normal flora, of external ear, 464
group A beta-hemolytic
antimicrobial therapy for, 586
carriers of, treatment of, 1125
in acute glomerulonephritis, 1122–1123
in acute rheumatic fever, 1122–1123
in brain abscess, 771
in cervical adenitis, 1669
in cervical adenopathy, 1638
in head and neck space infections, 1682, 1682t
in immunodeficient states, 1493t
in lower respiratory tract infections, 1485t
in odontogenic cellulitis, 1179
in otitis media, 545, 546t, 546f–547f, 551
with effusion, 557, 557t
in pharyngitis
acute rheumatic fever and glomerulonephritis due to, 1122–1123
complications of, 1120
diagnosis of, 1123–1124
signs and symptoms of, 1123
treatment of, 1124–1125
in pharyngotonsilitis, 1203
in pneumonia, 1490t, 1491
in rhinitis, 997
in scarlet fever, 1203
in toxic shock–like disease, 1122
resistance of, to antimicrobials, 586
group B
antimicrobial therapy for, 586
in otitis media, 551
of newborn, 557
in pneumonia, 1490t, 1491
of newborn, 1451–1452
resistance of, to antimicrobials, 586
Streptococcosis syndrome, 1669
Streptococcus pneumoniae/S. pneumoniae infection
adherence of
in pathogenesis of otitis media, 540
to respiratory mucosa, 549
antimicrobial therapy for, 584–585, 584t
in brain abscess, 771
in immunodeficient states, 1493t
in lower respiratory tract infections, 1485t
in mastoiditis
subacute, 724
with osteitis, acute, 722
with periosteitis, 718, 718t
in meningitis, 768, 798
in nasopharyngeal cultures, 545, 547t
in otitis media

Streptococcus pneumoniae/S. pneumoniae infection (Continued)
failure rate of antimicrobial treatment for, 616
frequency of, 547
in newborn, 557
prevalence of, 543, 546t, 546f–547f
recurrent, 612
serotypes in, 548–549, 548t, 566–567
serum antibody response in, 561–562
with effusion, 557, 557t
in otorrhea, after tympanostomy tube insertion, 645, 646f
in pleural effusions, 1492
in pneumonia, 1490t
in sinusitis, 1004, 1005
in tympanic membrane perforation, 691t, 697
neuraminidase production by, 556
PCR assay in identification of, 553
resistance to antimicrobial agents, 549–550, 584–585
multi-drug resistance in, 549–550
susceptibility of, to antimicrobial agents, 549–550, 584
vaccines for. See Vaccine(s), pneumococcal.
Streptococcus pyogenes
in mastoiditis
with osteitis, acute, 722
with periosteitis, 718, 718t
in otorrhea, after tympanostomy tube insertion, 646f
in tympanic membrane perforation, 691t, 697
Streptococcus viridans
in brain abscess, 771
in sialadenitis, 1257
Streptokinase, for pleural effusions, 1492
Streptomycin
for tuberculosis, 1486t
ototoxicity of, hereditary hearing impairment due to, 309
Stressors, in childhood, 1839–1840, 1839t
Stretch receptor(s), pulmonary
in coughing, 1395
in respiratory rate regulation, 1376–1377
Strictures, esophageal. See Esophagus, strictures of.
Stridor
after foreign body removal, treatment of, 1555
auscultation of, 1382
biphasic, respiratory collapse with, 1438
definition of, 1437
evaluation of, 1439–1446
clinical algorithm for, 1440f
endoscopy in
flexible, 1442–1443
rigid, 1445–1446, 1444f–1445f, 1444t–1445t
history and physical examination in, 1439, 1441–1442, 1439t, 1441f
radiography in, 1443–1444, 1442f–1443f
in dysphagia, 1129
in laryngomalacia
bronchoscopy for, 1305
characteristics of, 1460
esophageal biopsy for, 1305
hoarseness and, 1414
in recurrent respiratory papillomatosis, 1558
in subglottic stenosis, 1467
in vocal cord paralysis, 1465, 1505
induced by gastroesophageal reflux disease, 1305
localization of, 1437–1438, 1438t
pathophysiology of, 1437–1438, 1438f, 1438t
sound of, characteristics of, 1438
Strip craniectomy, for craniosynostosis, 85, 85f

Sturge-Weber syndrome
neurologic manifestation of, 1356
port-wine stain associated with, 969
Stuttering. See also Fluency disorders.
definition of, 1778
Styloglossus muscle, 1091
Styloid process, developmental anatomy of, 134
Stylopharyngeus muscle, 1094, 1349
Subclavian artery(ies)
aberrant, 1476, 1476f
developmental anatomy of, 1605, 1606f
injuries of, evaluation and management of, 1750–1751
right
aberrant, 1605
anomalies of, 1651
Subclavian vein, 1607
Subdural empyema
as complication of otitis media, 769–770
definition of, 483
Subglottic stenosis, 1519–1540
classification of
by endotracheal tube sizing, 1467, 1468t
histopathologic, 1522, 1522t
clinical manifestations of, 1467, 1520–1521
congenital, 1467–1468, 1467f, 1522, 1522t
diagnosis of, 1520–1523
clinical picture in, 1520–1521
endoscopic evaluation in, 1521–1522
radiologic evaluation in, 1521
rigid endoscopy in, 1467, 1468t
differential diagnosis of, 1522–1523, 1522t
etiology and pathophysiology of, 1519–1520, 1520f
grading of
degree of laryngotracheal stenosis in, 1526, 1526t
Myer-Cotton system for, 1445t, 1446, 1522, 1526t
in gastroesophageal reflux disease. See Gastroesophageal reflux disease (GERD), subglottic stenosis associated with.
incidence of, 1540
management of, 1467–1468, 1523–1540
adjunctive procedures in, 1538–1539
anterior laryngotracheal decompression (cricoid split) in, 1468
criteria for performing, 1523, 1523t
procedure for, 1523–1524, 1525f
cricoid cartilage grafting in
anterior, 1530, 1531f–1532f
anteroposterior, 1530, 1532–1533, 1533f, 1535f–1537f
posterior, 1530
cricotracheal resection in, 1534, 1536–1537, 1538f–1539f
endoscopic methods in, 1526–1527, 1526t
graft materials in, 1528
in children, 1524–1540
medical therapy in, 1526
wait-and-See approach in, 1524, 1526
in newborns, 1523–1524
laryngotracheal reconstruction in
complications of, 1539–1540
follow-up for, 1540
revision of, 1537
voice disorders due to, 1431–1432, 1432t
laser surgery in, 1467–1468, 1526–1527, 1526t
open reconstructive surgery in, 1468, 1527
options in, 1467–1468, 1530
pediatric management in, 1524
preoperative evaluation in, 1527
single-stage reconstruction in, 1529–1530
stents in, 1528–1529

Vancomycin (*Continued*)
  for lower respiratory tract infection, 1486t
  for mastoiditis with periosteitis, 719
  for pneumonia, 1491
    in newborn, 1452
  pharmacology of, 596
  sensorineural hearing loss associated with, 799
Varicella-zoster immune globulin (VZIG), 1236
Varicella-zoster virus infection(s)
  associated with HIV infection, 125
  cervical adenopathy associated with, 1668t, 1668–1669
  in epistaxis, 925
  in immunodeficient states, 1493t
  in lower respiratory tract, 1485t
  oropharyngeal manifestation of, 1236
  pneumonitis in, 1493
Vascular disease, of chest, 1501
Vascular injuries, in neck
  arteriography in, 1749
  blunt, 1752
  initial evaluation of, 1748
  penetrating, 1750–1751
Vascular malformation(s). *See also* Arteriovenous malformation(s).
  embolization of, angiography in, 1628
  in neurologic disorders, 1356
  laryngeal, 1469–1471, 1471f
  laser therapy of, 1580–1581
  of neck
    angiography of, 1628
    manifestation of, 1643
    MRI features of, 1634, 1634t
    of major arteries, 1651, 1651f–1652f
    of minor vessels, 1651–1652
    venous malformations in, 1652
  of sinuses, 1060
  plastic surgery of, 967–970
  syndromes associated with, 969–970
  tracheal anomalies related to, 1473–1477, 1475b
Vascular rings, compression of trachea and esophagus by, 1474–1475, 1475f–1476f, 1605
Vascular space, of neck, 1617
Vascular tinnitus, 363–364, 363t
Vasoconstrictor(s), for epistaxis, 928, 929
Vasodilator(s), for diaphragmatic hernia, 1453
Vasomotor reaction
  as host defense, 914
  calcium and magnesium effects on, 919
  due to gastroesophageal reflux, 913
  in nasal obstruction, 908–909
Vasomotor rhinitis, 1073–1074
  allergic rhinitis vs., 1074t
VATER syndrome
  ear anomalies in, 394
  subglottic stenosis associated with, 1528
VDRL (Venereal Disease Research Laboratory) test, for congenital syphilis, 317, 998
Vehicles, motor
  accidents involving, head and neck injuries due to, 1339
  noise-induced hearing loss related to, 803
Veillonella species, in head and neck space infections, 1682, 1682t
Vein(s), of neck, developmental anatomy of, 1606–1608
Velocardiofacial syndrome
  manifestation of, 1793
  subglottic stenosis associated with, 1528
  treatment of, 1793
Velopharyngeal insufficiency, 1789–1798
  after reconstructive surgery, 99, 1792

Velopharyngeal insufficiency (*Continued*)
  as contraindication to tonsillectomy and adenoidectomy, 1218
  causes of, 1792–1793, 1833, 1793f, 1794t
  definition of, 1789
  distraction procedures and, 109
  evaluation of, 1793–1796, 1794f, 1794t
    multiview fluoroscopy in, 1794, 1795f
    nasopharyngoscopy in, 1795–1796, 1796f
  genetic syndromes associated with, 1792, 1794t
  in musculus uvulae absence, 1150
  surgical treatment of, 1797–1798
    pharyngeal flap in, 1797–1798
    posterior pharyngeal wall augmentation in, 1797
    push-back palatoplasty in, 1798
    sphincter pharyngoplasty in, 1798
  treatment of, 1796–1798
    prosthetic management in, 1797
    speech therapy in, 1796
    surgical intervention in, 1797–1798
Velopharyngeal sphincter, 1789–1792
  anatomy of, 1789–1791 2f–3f
  closure patterns of, 1791–1792
  pharyngoplasty of, 1798
Venereal Disease Research Laboratory (VDRL) test, for congenital syphilis, 317, 998
Venous malformation(s). *See also* Arteriovenous malformation(s); Vascular malformation(s).
  of neck, 1652
  treatment of, 968, 1652
Ventilation
  assisted, tracheotomy for, 1585t
  chronic, endotracheal tube vs. tracheotomy for, 1584–1585
  in laryngoscopy, direct, 1385
  mask, in direct laryngoscopy, 1385
  mechanical
    for bronchopulmonary dysplasia, 1457
    for meconium aspiration syndrome, 1455
    for respiratory distress syndrome, 1450
  pulmonary parenchyma in, 1375–1377
  Venturi jet, in direct laryngoscopy, 1385
    "wasted," 1376
Venting, of hearing aid earmold, 660, 1812
Ventricular septal defect
  as multifactorial birth defect, 52t
  recurrence risk associated with, 52t
Venturi jet ventilation, in direct laryngoscopy, 1385
Vermilion
  anatomy of, 1086f, 1088
  burns of, 1343
  repair of, 1340
Vernet's sign de rideau, 1349
Versed (midazolam), for sedation, in computed tomography, 231
Vertebral artery, injuries of, 1750–1751
Vertigo. *See also* Dizziness.
  acute nonrecurring spontaneous, 351–353
    case study of, 352
    causes of, 352t
    in head trauma, 351, 352
    in labyrinthitis, 353
    in perilymphatic fistula, 352–353
    in vestibular neuritis, 353
  after temporal bone fracture, 843–845
    evaluation of, 844–845
  as symptom of middle ear disease, 172
  benign paroxysmal
    of childhood, 354
    positional, 351
  definition of, 273
  evaluation of, 273–286
  recurrent, 353–357

Vertigo (*Continued*)
  associated with seizure disorders, 355
  case study of, 353
  causes of, 352t
  in familial periodic ataxia, 355
  in Meniere's disease, 354
  migraine-related, 354–355, 354t
Vesiculobullous disorder(s), oropharyngeal, 1243t, 1246–1247
Vestibular aqueduct syndrome, large (LVAS), 446–448
  computed tomography of, 241, 252f–253f, 446, 449f
  endolymphatic sac obliteration for, 447
  endolymphatic shunt for, 144
  hearing loss associated with, 144
    radiographic evaluation of, 320–321
    sensorineural, 447
  in acute labyrinthitis, 727, 728f
  measurement of, 446
Vestibular compensation, in vertigo, 351
Vestibular evaluation, 273–286
  audiologic evaluation in, 279–280
  dynamic platform posturography in, 285–286, 284f–285f
  for hearing loss, 318–319
  history in, 276
  in otitis media with effusion, 573–574
  laboratory, 280–285
    caloric testing in, 282–283, 282f
    dynamic platform posturography in, 285–286, 284f–285f
    electronystagmography in, 281
    indications for, 280–281
    ocular motor testing in, 281–282, 280f–281f
    positional testing in, 282
    rotational testing in, 283, 283f, 285
  motor function tests in, 278–279, 278f–279f, 279t
  nystagmus evaluation in, 277–278, 276f–278f
  physical examination in, 276–277
  vestibular laboratory evaluation in, 281–285
Vestibular loss, bilateral peripheral, 355–356
Vestibular nerve, aplasia or hypoplasia of, 450
Vestibular neuritis, vertigo due to, 353
Vestibule
  congenital malformation(s) of
    common cavity as, 445, 448f
    computed tomography of, 241, 252f
    dysplasia as, 445–446
  disturbance of, in otitis media, 695
  dysfunction of, in sensorineural hearing loss, 783
  nasal
    papilloma of, 1055
    physiology of, 876
Vestibulo-ocular reflex, physiology of, 273–274, 274f–275f
Videoendoscopy, of swallowing, 1293
Videofluoroscopy
  in sleep apnea, 1230
  in stridor, 1442f, 1444f
  in velopharyngeal insufficiency, 1794
  of esophagus, 1115
  of foreign body, in airway, 1548
  of nasopharynx, 1111–1112
  of swallowing, 1130, 1292–1293
Videoradiography
  contrast, of esophagus, 1114f, 1115
  of oral cavity, 1111
Vincent stomatitis. *See* Gingivitis, acute necrotizing ulcerative (ANUG).
Vincristine, peripheral neuropathy due to, 1353